NEW • REVISED • EXPANDED
POCKET-SIZE EDITION

WEBSTER'S NEW WORLD DICTIONARY

OF THE AMERICAN LANGUAGE

DAVID B. GURALNIK, Editor in Chief

D0401149

WARNER BOOKS

A Warner Communications Company

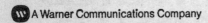

FOREWORD

This latest Paperback Edition of *Webster's New World Dictionary* is an expansion and updating of an earlier revision of the paperback dictionary that has been a best seller since it was first published in 1958. It is based upon and extracted from the materials prepared for *Webster's New World Dictionary*, Second College Edition. The more than 59,000 vocabulary entries in this revised edition include thousands of newer terms and newer senses of established terms not to be found in the first edition.

The selection of vocabulary items has been made largely on the basis of frequency of occurrence within our vast citation file and from various word-count lists. Included in the single alphabetical listing of the dictionary are selected biographical and geographical entries, names from literature and mythology, and common abbreviations. The geographical entries include countries of the world, with area and population, major cities of the world, all cities of the United States with over 100,000 population, and major bodies of water, mountains, and the like.

It has been the intent of the editors of this work to incorporate as much useful information as possible within the available space. As a consequence, in addition to the clear but brief definitions, properly separated and discriminated and, where necessary, identified as to level of usage, there will be found herein illustrative examples of usage to help clarify meanings, a large number of idiomatic expressions, affixes and combining forms, and other features not generally included in a paperback dictionary of this size. Among the unusual features are the etymologies enclosed in boldface brackets following the entry word. These little histories of the origin and development of words often help one to a clearer understanding of the current meanings.

The pronunciations are recorded in a simplified but precise phonemic key, and variant pronunciations, if sufficiently widespread, are given, often in an abbreviated form. The key to pronunciation is printed at the bottom of every right-hand page for the convenience of the user.

Another unusual feature of this paperback dictionary is the inclusion of pictorial illustrations, especially selected and designed to help amplify those definitions that benefit from such illustrations and to brighten the page. The type used is of a modern face in the largest practicable size to facilitate ease of reading.

The members of the dictionary staff involved in preparing this dictionary are: *Managing Editor*, Samuel Solomon; *Supervising Associate Editor*, Clark C. Livensparger; *Associate Editors*, Christopher T. Hoolihan, Ruth K. Kent, Thomas Layman, Paul Murry, Andrew Sparks, Eleanor Rickey Stevens; *Assistant Editors*, Roslyn Block, Jonathan L. Goldman, Judith Clark, *Assistants*, Virginia C. Becker, Dorothy H. Benedict, Cynthia Sadonick, Angie West; *Illustrator*, Anita Rogoff; *Proofreader*, Shirley M. Miller.

David B. Guralnik
Editor in Chief

GUIDE TO THE USE OF THE DICTIONARY

I. THE MAIN ENTRY WORD

A. *Arrangement of Entries*— All main entries, including single words, hyphenated and unhyphenated compounds, proper names, prefixes, suffixes, and abbreviations, are listed in strict alphabetical order and are set in large, boldface type.

a (ə; *stressed*, ā) *adj.* . . .
a- *a prefix meaning:* . . .
a. **1.** about **2.** acre(s) . . .
aard·vark (ärd′värk′) *n.* . . .
Aar·on (er′ən) *Bible* . . .
ab- [L.] *a prefix meaning* . . .
A.B. Bachelor of Arts
a·back (ə bak′) *adv.* [Archaic] backward **—taken aback** startled . . .

Note that in biographical entries only the last, or family, name has been considered in alphabetization, but when two or more persons have the same family name, they have been arranged within the entry block in alphabetical order by first names.

John·son (jän′s'n) **1.** Andrew . . . **2.** Lyn·don Baines . . . **3.** Samuel . . .

Idiomatic phrases listed after a main entry have also been entered alphabetically within each group.

fly¹ (flī) *vi.* **—fly into** . . . **—let fly (at)** . . . **—on the fly** . . .

B. *Variant Spellings & Forms* —When variant spellings of a word are some distance apart alphabetically, the definition appears with the spelling most frequently used, and the other spellings are cross-referred to this entry. If two commonly used variant spellings are alphabetically close to each other, they are entered as a joint boldface entry, but the order of entry does not necessarily indicate that the form entered first is "more correct" or is to be given preference.

the·a·ter, the·a·tre (thē′ə tər) *n.* . . .

If a variant spelling or spellings are alphabetically close to the prevailing spelling, they are given at the end of the entry block in small boldface.

co·or′di·na′tion *n.* . . . Also **co·or′di·na′tion, co·ör′di·na′tion**
par·af·fin . . . *n.* . . . : also **par′af·fine**

C. *Cross-references*— When an entry is cross-referred to another term that has the same meaning but is more frequently used, the entry cross-referred to is usually in small capitals.

an·aes·the·si·a, an·aes·thet·ic, etc. *same as* ANESTHESIA, ANESTHETIC, etc.

D. *Homographs*— Main entries that are spelled alike but are different in meaning and origin, as **bat** (a club), **bat** (the animal), and **bat** (to wink), are given separate entry and are marked by superscript numbers following the boldface spellings.

bat¹ . . . *n.* . . .
bat² . . . *n.* . . .
bat³ . . . *vt.* . . .

E. *Foreign Terms*— Foreign words and phrases encountered with some frequency in English but not completely naturalized are marked with a double dagger (‡). The user of the dictionary is thus signaled that such terms are usually printed in italics or underlined in writing.

‡bon jour (bôn zhōōr′) [Fr.] . . .

F. *Prefixes, Suffixes, & Combining Forms*— Prefixes and initial combining forms are indicated by a hyphen following the entry form.

hemi- . . . *a prefix meaning* half . . .

Suffixes and terminal combining forms are indicated by a hyphen preceding the entry form.

-a·ble . . . *a suffix meaning:* **1.** able to . . .

The abundance of these forms, whose syllabification and pronunciation can be determined from the words containing them, makes it possible for the reader to understand and pronounce countless complex terms not entered in the dictionary but formed with affixes and words that are entered.

G. *Syllabification*— The syllabifications used in this dictionary, indicated by centered dots in the entry words or sometimes by stress marks, are those in general use.

fun·da·men·tal (fun′də men′t'l) *adj.* . . .
coun′ter·rev·o·lu′tion *n.* . . .

II. PRONUNCIATION

A. *Introduction*— The pronunciations recorded in this dictionary are those used by cultivated speakers in normal, relaxed conversation. They are symbolized in as broad a manner as is consistent with accuracy so that speakers of every variety of American English can easily read their own pronunciations into the symbols used here. For some words, variant pronunciations that are dialectal, British, slang, etc. are given along with the standard American pronunciations. Contextual differences in pronunciation also have been indicated wherever practicable, as by showing variants in unstressed or shifted stress form.

iv

Guide to the Dictionary

B. *Key to Pronunciation*—An abbreviated form of this key appears at the bottom of every alternate page of the vocabulary.

Symbol	Key Words	Symbol	Key Words
a	fat	b	bed, dub
ā	ape	d	dip, had
ä	car	f	fall, off
		g	get, dog
e	ten	h	he, ahead
ē	even	j	joy, agile
		k	kill, bake
i	is	l	let, ball
ī	bite	m	met, trim
		n	not, ton
ō	go	p	put, tap
ô	horn	r	red, dear
o͞o	tool	s	sell, pass
oo	look	t	top, hat
yo͞o	use	v	vat, have
yoo	united	w	will, always
oi	oil	y	yet, yard
ou	out	z	zebra, haze
u	up	ch	chin, arch
ur	urn	sh	she, dash
		th	thin, truth
ə	a in ago	t͡h	then, father
	e in agent	zh	azure, leisure
	i in sanity	ŋ	ring, drink
	o in comply	'	[see explanatory note in next column]
	u in focus		
ər	perhaps		

A few explanatory notes on some of the more complex of these symbols follow.

ä This symbol represents essentially the sound of *a* in *car* but may also represent the low central vowel sometimes heard in New England for *bath*.

e This symbol represents the sound of *e* in *ten* and is also used, followed and hence colored by *r*, to represent the vowel sound of *care* (ker).

ē This symbol represents the vowel sound in *meet* and is also used for the vowel in the unstressed final syllable of such words as *lucky* (luk′ē), *pretty* (prit′ē), etc.

i This symbol represents the vowel sound in *hit* and is also used for the vowel in the unstressed syllables of such words as *garbage* (gär′bij), *deny* (di nī′), etc. In such contexts reductions to ə (gär′bəj), (də nī′), etc. are commonly heard and may be assumed as variants. This symbol is also used, followed and hence colored by *r*, to represent the vowel sound of *dear* (dir).

ô This symbol represents essentially the sound of *a* in *all*. When followed by *r*, as in *more* (môr), vowels ranging to ō (mōr *or* mō′ər) are often heard and may be assumed as variants.

ə This symbol, called the schwa, represents the mid central relaxed

vowel of neutral coloration heard in the unstressed syllables of *ago*, *agent*, etc.

ur and **ər** These two clusters of symbols represent respectively the stressed and unstressed r-colored vowels heard successively in the two syllables of *murder* (mur′dər). Where these symbols are shown, some speakers, as in the South and along the Eastern seaboard, will, as a matter of course, pronounce them by "dropping their r's."

ŋ This symbol represents the voiced velar nasal sound of the *-ng* of *sing* and of the *n* before *k* and *g*, as in *drink* (driŋk) and *finger* (fiŋ′gər).

' The apostrophe before an *l*, *m*, or *n* indicates that the following consonant forms the nucleus of a syllable with no appreciable vowel sound, as in *apple* (ap′'l) or *happen* (hap′'n). In some persons' speech, certain syllabic consonants are replaced with syllables containing reduced vowels, as (hap′ən).

C. *Foreign Sounds*—In recording the approximate pronunciation of foreign words, it has been necessary to use the following five symbols in addition to those preceding.

ë This symbol represents the sound made by rounding the lips as for (ô) and pronouncing (e).

ö This symbol represents the sound made by rounding the lips as for (ō) and pronouncing (ā).

ü This symbol represents the sound made by rounding the lips as for (o͞o) and pronouncing (ē).

kh This symbol represents the sound made by arranging the speech organs as for (k) but allowing the breath to escape in a continuous stream, as in pronouncing (h).

n This symbol indicates that the vowel immediately preceding it is given a nasal sound, as in Fr. *mon* (môn).

D. *Styling of Pronunciation*—Pronunciations are given inside parentheses, immediately following the boldface entry. A primary, or strong, stress is indicated by a heavy stroke (′) immediately following the syllable so stressed. A secondary, or weak, stress is indicated by a lighter stroke (′) following the syllable so stressed. Some compound entries formed of words that are separately entered in the dictionary are syllabified and stressed and repronounced only in part or not repronounced at all.

hard·ly (härd′lē) . . .
hard′-nosed′ (-nōzd′) . . .
hard sell . . .
hard′ship . . .

E. *Variants*—Where two or more pronunciations for a single word are given, the order in which they are entered does not necessarily mean that

v

Guide to the Dictionary

the first is preferred to or more correct than another. In most cases the form given first is the most frequent in general cultivated use.

F. *Truncation*—Variant pronunciations for a main entry or a run-in entry are truncated, or shortened, whenever possible. A hyphen after the shortened variant marks it as an initial syllable or syllables; one before the variant, as terminal; and hyphens before and after the variant, as internal.

ab·jure (əb joor′, ab-) . . .
dom·i·cile (däm′ə sīl′, -sil; dō′mə-)
. . .
fu·tu·ri·ty (fyoo toor′ə tē, -tyoor′-)
. . .

Variant pronunciations involving different parts of speech in the same entry block usually appear as follows:
a·buse (ə byōōz′; *for n.* ə byōōs′)
vt. . . .

III. PART-OF-SPEECH LABELS

Part-of-speech labels are given for main entries that are solid or hyphenated forms, except prefixes, suffixes, and abbreviations, and the names of persons, places, etc. When an entry word is used as more than one part of speech in an entry block, long dashes introduce each different part-of-speech label, which appears in boldface italic type.

round . . . *adj.* . . . *—n.* . . . *—vt.*
. . . *—vi.* . . . *—adv.* . . . *—prep.* . . .

Two or more part-of-speech labels are given jointly for an entry when the definition or definitions, or the cross-reference, will suffice for both or all.

des·patch . . . *vt., n. same as* DISPATCH

IV. INFLECTED FORMS

Inflected forms regarded as irregular or offering difficulty in spelling are entered in small boldface immediately following the part-of-speech labels. They are truncated where possible, and syllabified and pronounced where necessary.

hap·py . . . *adj.* **-pi·er, -pi·est** . . .
cit·y . . . *n., pl.* **-ies** . . .
a·moe·ba . . . *n., pl.* **-bas, -bae**
(-bē) . . .

Forms regarded as regular inflections, and hence not normally indicated, include:

a) plurals formed by adding *-s* to the singular (or *-es* after *s, x, z, ch,* and *sh*), as *bats, boxes*
b) present tenses formed by adding *-s* to the infinitive (or *-es* after *s, x, z, ch,* and *sh*), as *waits, searches*
c) past tenses and past participles formed by simply adding *-ed* to the infinitive, as *waited, searched*
d) present participles formed by

simply adding *-ing* to the infinitive, as *waiting, searching*
e) comparatives and superlatives formed by simply adding *-er* and *-est* to the base of an adjective or adverb, as *taller, tallest* or *sooner, soonest*

Where two inflected forms are given for a verb, the first is the form for the past tense and the past participle, and the second is the form for the present participle.

make . . . *vt.* **made, mak′ing** . . .

Where three forms are given, the first represents the past tense, the second the past participle, and the third the present participle.

give . . . *vt.* **gave, giv′en, giv′ing** . . .

Where there are alternative forms for any of the principal parts, these are given and properly indicated.

bid . . . *vt.* **bade** or **bid, bid′den** or **bid, bid′ding;** for *vt.* 2, 4 & for *vi.,* pt. & pp. **bid** . . .

V. ETYMOLOGY

The etymology, or word derivation, appears inside heavy boldface brackets immediately before the definitions proper. The symbols, as < for "derived from," and the abbreviations of language labels, etc. used in the etymologies are dealt with in full in the list immediately preceding page 1 of the vocabulary.

di·shev·el . . . [< OFr. *des-*, dis- + *chevel*, hair] . . .

No etymology is shown where one would be superfluous, as where the elements making up the word are immediately apparent.

VI. THE DEFINITIONS

A. *Order of Senses*—The standard, general senses of a word are given first, and colloquial, slang, etc. senses come next. Technical senses requiring special field labels, as *Astron., Chem.,* etc., follow in order.

B. *Numbering & Grouping of Senses*—Senses are numbered consecutively within any given part of speech in boldface numerals. Where a primary sense of a word can easily be subdivided into several closely related meanings, such meanings are indicated by italicized letters.

time . . . *n.* . . . **1.** every . . . **2.** a system . . . **3.** the period . . . **11.** *Music a)* rhythm . . . *b)* tempo —*vt.* . . . **1.** to arrange . . . **2.** to adjust . . . —*adj.* **1.** having to . . . **2.** set to . . . **3.** having . . . —**in time 1.** eventually **2.** before . . . **3.** keeping . . .

C. *Capitalization*—If a main entry word is capitalized in all its

Guide to the Dictionary

senses, the entry word itself is printed with a capital letter. If a capitalized main entry word has a sense or senses that are uncapitalized, these are marked with the corresponding small-boldface, lower-case letter followed· by a short dash and enclosed in brackets.

Pur·i·tan . . . *n.* . . . **1.** . . . **2.** [p–] . . .

Conversely, capitalized letters are shown, where pertinent, with lower-case main entries. In some instances these designations are qualified by the self-explanatory "*often*," "*occas.*," etc.

left¹ . . . **—*n.*** **1.** . . . **2.** [*often* L-] . . .

D. *Plural Forms*—In a singular noun entry, the designation "[*pl.*]" (or "[*often pl.*]," "[*usually pl.*]," etc.) before a definition indicates that it is (or *often, usually,* etc. is) the plural form of the entry word that has the meaning given in the definition.

look . . . *vi.* . . . **—*n.*** **1.** . . . **2.** . . . **3.** [Colloq.] *a*) [*usually pl.*] appearance *b*) [*pl.*] personal appearance . . .

If a plural noun entry or sense is construed as singular, the designation [*with sing. v.*] is added.

phys·ics . . . *n.pl.* [*with sing. v.*] . . .

E. *Verbs Followed by Prepositions or Objects*—Where certain verbs are, in usage, invariably or usually followed by a specific preposition or prepositions, this has been indicated in either of the following ways: the preposition has been worked into the definition, italicized and enclosed in parentheses, or a note has been added in parentheses indicating that the preposition is so used.

In definitions of transitive verbs, the specific or generalized objects of the verb, where given, are enclosed in parentheses, since such objects are not part of the definition.

VII. USAGE LABELS

The editors of this dictionary decided that the familiarity of the conventional usage designations makes their use advisable if the meaning of these labels is kept clearly in mind. The labels, and what they are intended to indicate, are given below.

Colloquial: The term or sense is generally characteristic of conversation and informal writing. It is not to be regarded as substandard or illiterate.

Slang: The term or sense is not generally regarded as conventional or standard usage, but is used, even by the best speakers, in highly informal contexts. Slang terms either pass into

disuse in time or come to have a more formal status.

Obsolete: The term or sense is no longer used but occurs in earlier writings.

Archaic: The term or sense is rarely used today except in certain restricted contexts, as in church ritual, but occurs in earlier writings.

Poetic: The term or sense is used chiefly in poetry, especially in earlier poetry, or in prose where a poetic quality is desired.

Dialect: The term or sense is used regularly only in some geographical areas or in a certain designated area (*South, West,* etc.) of the United States.

British (or *Canadian, Scottish,* etc.): The term or sense is characteristic of British (or Canadian, etc.) English rather than American English. When preceded by *chiefly,* the label indicates an additional, though less frequent, American usage. *British Dialect* indicates that the term or sense is used regularly only in certain geographical areas of Great Britain, usually in northern England.

In addition to the above usage labels, supplementary information is often given after the definition, indicating whether the term or sense is generally regarded as vulgar, substandard, or derogatory, used with ironic, familiar, or hyperbolic connotations, etc.

pate . . . *n.* . . . . a humorous term

VIII. RUN-IN DERIVED ENTRIES

It is possible in English to form an almost infinite number of derived forms simply by adding certain prefixes or suffixes to the base word. The editors have included as run-in entries in small-boldface type as many of these common derived words as space permitted, but only when the meaning of such words can be immediately understood from the meanings of the base word and the affix. Thus, **greatness** and **liveliness** are run in at the end of the entries for **great** and **lively,** the suffix **-ness** being found as a separate entry meaning "state, quality, or instance of being." Many words formed with common suffixes, as **-able, -er, -less, -like, -ly, -tion,** etc. are similarly treated as run-in entries with the base word from which they are derived. All such entries are syllabified and either accented to show stress in pronunciation or, where necessary, pronounced in full or in part.

When a derived word has a meaning or meanings different from those that can be deduced from the sum of its parts, it has been given separate entry, pronounced, and fully defined (e.g., **folder**).

ABBREVIATIONS USED IN THIS DICTIONARY

abbrev. abbreviated; abbreviation
adj. adjective
adv. adverb
Aeron. Aeronautics
Afr. African
Afrik. Afrikaans
Alb. Albanian
alt. altered; alternative
Am. American
AmInd. American Indian
AmSp. American Spanish
Anat. Anatomy
Ar. Arabic
Aram. Aramaic
Archit. Architecture
art. article
Assyr. Assyrian
Astron. Astronomy
Biochem. Biochemistry
Biol. Biology
Bot. Botany
Braz. Brazilian
Brit. British
Bulg. Bulgarian
C Celsius; Central
c. century; circa
Canad, Canad. Canadian
cap. capital
Celt. Celtic
Chem. Chemistry
Chin. Chinese
cf. compare
Colloq. colloquial
comp. compound
compar. comparative
conj. conjunction
contr. contracted; contraction
Dan. Danish
deriv. derivative
Dial., dial. dialect; dialectal
dim. diminutive
Du. Dutch
E East; eastern
E. East; English (in etym.)
Eccles. Ecclesiastical
Ecol. Ecology
Econ. Economics
Educ. Education
Egypt. Egyptian
Elec. Electricity
Eng. English
equiv. equivalent
Esk. Eskimo
esp. especially
est. estimated
etym. etymology
Ex. example
exc. except
F Fahrenheit
fem. feminine
ff. following
fig. figurative(ly)
Finn. Finnish
Fl. Flemish
fl. flourished
Fr. French
Frank. Frankish
fut. future
G. German (in etym.)
Gael. Gaelic

Geog. Geography
Geol. Geology
Geom. Geometry
Ger. German
Gmc. Germanic
Goth. Gothic
Gr. Greek
Gram. Grammar
Haw. Hawaiian
Heb. Hebrew
Hung. Hungarian
hyp. hypothetical
Ind. Indian
indic. indicative
inf. infinitive
infl. influenced
interj. interjection
Ir. Irish
Iran. Iranian
It. Italian
Jap. Japanese
L Late
L. Latin
Linguis. Linguistics
lit. literally
LL. Late Latin
LowG. Low German
M middle; medieval
masc. masculine
Math. Mathematics
MDu. Middle Dutch
ME. Middle English
Mech. Mechanics
Med. Medicine
Meteorol. Meteorology
Mex. Mexican
MexInd. Mexican Indian
MHG. Middle High German
mi. mile(s)
Mil. Military
Mod, Mod. Modern
Mongol. Mongolic
Myth. Mythology
N North; northern
N. North
n. noun
NAmInd. North American Indian
Naut. nautical usage
NE northeastern
neut. neuter
nom. nominative
Norm, Norm. Norman
Norw. Norwegian
NW northwestern
O Old
Obs., obs. obsolete
occas. occasionally
OE. Old English
OFr. Old French
OHG. Old High German
ON. Old Norse
orig. origin; originally
OS. Old Saxon
P Primitive
p. page
pass. passive
Per. Persian
Peruv. Peruvian
perf. perfect
pers. person

Philos. Philosophy
Phoen. Phoenician
Phonet. Phonetics
Photog. Photography
phr. phrase
Physiol. Physiology
PidE. Pidgin English
pl. plural
Poet., poet. poetic
Pol. Polish
pop. population
Port. Portuguese
poss. possessive
pp. past participle
Pr. Provençal
prec. preceding
prep. preposition
pres. present
prob. probably
pron. pronoun
pronun. pronunciation
prp. present participle
pseud. pseudonym
Psychol. Psychology
pt. past tense
R.C.Ch. Roman Catholic Church
Rom. Roman
Russ. Russian
S South; southern
S. South
SAmInd. South American Indian
Sans. Sanskrit
Scand. Scandinavian
Scot. Scottish
SE southeastern
Sem. Semitic
sing. singular
Slav. Slavic
Sp. Spanish
sp. spelling
specif. specifically
sq. square
subj. subjunctive
superl. superlative
SW southwestern
Sw., Swed. Swedish
t. tense
Tag. Tagalog
Theol. Theology
transl. translation
Turk. Turkish
TV television
ult. ultimately
v. verb
var. variant
v.aux. auxiliary verb
vi. intransitive verb
VL. Vulgar Latin
vt. transitive verb
W West; western
W. Welsh; West
WInd. West Indian
Yid. Yiddish
Zool. Zoology

‡ foreign word or phrase
< derived from; from
? perhaps; uncertain
+ plus
& and

viii

A

A, a (ā) *n., pl.* **A's, a's** the first letter of the English alphabet

A (ā) *n.* **1.** a grade indicating excellence **2.** *Music* the sixth tone in the scale of C major

a (ə; *stressed,* ā) *adj., indefinite article* [< an] **1.** one; one sort of **2.** each; any one **3.** per *[once a day]* A is used before words beginning with a consonant sound *[a child, a union, a history]* See AN

a- *a prefix meaning:* **1.** [< OE.] *a)* in, into, on, at, to *[aboard] b)* in the act or state of *[asleep]* **2.** [< OE.] *a)* up, out *[arise] b)* off, of *[akin]* **3.** [< Gr.] not *[agnostic]*

a. 1. about **2.** acre(s) **3.** adjective **4.** alto **5.** answer

AA, A.A. 1. Alcoholics Anonymous **2.** antiaircraft

A.A. Associate in (or of) Arts

aard·vark (ärd′värk′) *n.* [Du., earth pig] an ant-eating African mammal

Aar·on (er′ən) *Bible* the first high priest of the Hebrews

ab- [L.] *a prefix meaning* away, from, from off, down *[abdicate]*

A.B. Bachelor of Arts

a.b. *Baseball* (times) at bat

a·back (ə bak′) *adv.* [Archaic] backward **—taken aback** startled and confused; surprised

ab·a·cus (ab′ə kəs) *n., pl.* **-cus·es, -ci′** (-sī′) [< Gr. *abax*] a frame with sliding beads for doing arithmetic

ABACUS

a·baft (ə baft′) *adv.* [< OE. *on* + *be,* by + *æftan,* aft] aft **—prep.** *Naut.* behind

ab·a·lo·ne (ab′ə lō′nē) *n.* [AmSp.] a sea mollusk with an oval, somewhat spiral shell

a·ban·don (ə ban′dən) *vt.* [< OFr. *mettre a bandon,* to put under (another's) ban] **1.** to give up completely **2.** to desert **—n.** unrestrained activity; exuberance **—a·ban′don·ment** n.

a·ban·doned *adj.* **1.** deserted **2.** shamefully wicked **3.** unrestrained

a·base (ə bās′) *vt.* **a·based′, a·bas′ing** [< ML. *abassare,* to lower] to humble **—a·base′ment** n.

a·bash (ə bash′) *vt.* [< L. *ex* + *ba,* interj.] to make ashamed and uneasy; disconcert **—a·bash′ed·ly** adv.

a·bate (ə bāt′) *vt., vi.* **a·bat′ed, a·bat′ing** [< OFr. *abattre,* to beat down] **1.** to make or become less **2.** *Law* to end **—a·bate′ment** n.

ab·at·toir (ab′ə twär′, ab′ə twär′) *n.* [Fr.: see prec.] a slaughterhouse

ab·bé (a′bā′) *n.* [Fr.: see ABBOT] a French priest's title

ab·bess (ab′əs) *n.* [see ABBOT] a woman who heads a convent of nuns

ab·bey (ab′ē) *n., pl.* **-beys 1.** a monastery or convent **2.** a church belonging to an abbey

ab·bot (ab′ət) *n.* [< Aram. *abbā,* father] a man who heads a monastery

abbrev., abbr. 1. abbreviated **2.** abbreviation

ab·bre·vi·ate (ə brē′vē āt′) *vt.* **-at·ed, -at′ing** [< L. *ad-,* to + *brevis,* short] to make shorter; esp., to shorten (a word) by omitting letters

ab·bre·vi·a′tion (-ā′shən) *n.* **1.** a shortening **2.** a shortened form of a word or phrase, as *Dr.* for *Doctor*

A B C (ā′ bē′ sē′) *n., pl.* **A B C's 1.** [*usually pl.*] the alphabet **2.** the basic elements (of a subject); rudiments

ab·di·cate (ab′də kāt′) *vt., vi.* **-cat′ed, -cat′ing** [< L. *ab-,* off + *dicare,* to proclaim] **1.** to give up formally (a throne, etc.) **2.** to surrender (a right, responsibility, etc.) **—ab′di·ca′tion** n.

ab·do·men (ab′də mən, ab dō′-) *n.* [L.] the part of the body between the diaphragm and the pelvis; belly **—ab·dom′i·nal** (-däm′ə n'l) adj.

ab·duct (ab dukt′) *vt.* [< L. *ab-,* away + *ducere,* to lead] to kidnap **—ab·duc′tion** n. **—ab·duc′tor** n.

a·beam (ə bēm′) *adv.* at right angles to a ship's length or keel

a·bed (ə bed′) *adv., adj.* in bed

A·bel (ā′b'l) *Bible* the second son of Adam and Eve: see CAIN

ab·er·ra·tion (ab′ər ā′shən) *n.* [< L. *ab-,* from + *errare,* wander] **1.** deviation from what is right, true, normal, etc. **2.** mental derangement **—ab·er·rant** (ə ber′ənt) adj. **—ab′er·ra′tion·al** adj.

a·bet (ə bet′) *vt.* **a·bet′ted, a·bet′ting** [< OFr. *a-,* to + *beter,* to bait] to urge on or help, esp. in crime **—a·bet′tor, a·bet′ter** n.

a·bey·ance (ə bā′əns) n. [< OFr. a-, to, at + bayer, to gape] temporary suspension, as of an activity or ruling

ab·hor (ab hôr′) vt. -horred′, -hor′ring [< L. ab-, from + horrere, to shudder] to shrink from in disgust, hatred, etc. —**ab·hor′rence** n. —**ab·hor′rer** n.

ab·hor·rent (-ənt) adj. causing disgust, etc.; detestable —**ab·hor′rent·ly** adv.

a·bide (ə bīd′) vi. a·bode′ or a·bid′ed, a·bid′ing [OE. abīdan] 1. to remain 2. [Archaic] to reside —vt. to put up with —**abide by** 1. to live up to (a promise, etc.) 2. to submit to and carry out —**a·bid′ance** n.

a·bid·ing adj. enduring; lasting —**a·bid′ing·ly** adv.

a·bil·i·ty (ə bil′ə tē) n., pl. -ties [< L. habilitas] 1. a being able; power to do 2. talent; skill

-a·bil·i·ty (ə bil′ə tē), pl. -ties [L. -abilitas] a suffix used to form nouns from adjectives ending in -ABLE [washability]

ab·ject (ab′jekt, ab jekt′) adj. [< L. ab-, from + jacere, to throw] 1. miserable; wretched 2. degraded —**ab·ject′ly** adv. —**ab·jec′tion** n.

ab·jure (ab joor′, ab-) vt. -jured′, -jur′ing [< L. ab-, away + jurare, swear] to give up (rights, allegiance, etc.) on oath; renounce —**ab·ju·ra·tion** (ab′jə rā′shən) n. —**ab·jur′a·tor′y** (-ə tôr′ē) adj. —**ab·jur′er** n.

ab·late (ab lāt′) vt. -lat′ed, -lat′ing [< L. ablatus, carried away] 1. to remove, as by surgery 2. to wear away, burn away, or vaporize —vi. to be ablated, as a rocket shield in reentry —**ab·la′tion** n.

ab·la·tive (ab′lə tiv) n. [< L. ablatus, carried away] in Latin, etc., the case expressing removal, direction from, cause, agency, etc.

a·blaze (ə blāz′) adv. on fire —adj. 1. flaming 2. greatly excited

a·ble (ā′b'l) adj. a′bler, a′blest [< L. habere, have] 1. having power, skill, etc. (to do something) 2. talented; skilled 3. Law competent —**a′bly** adv.

-a·ble (ə b'l) [< L.] a suffix meaning: 1. able to [durable] 2. capable of being [drinkable] 3. worthy of being [lovable] 4. having qualities of [comfortable] 5. tending to [perishable]

a′ble-bod′ied adj. strong; healthy

able-bodied seaman a trained or skilled seaman: also **able seaman**

a·bloom (ə blōōm′) adj. in bloom

ab·lu·tion (ab lōō′shən) n. [< L. ab-, off + luere, wash] a washing of the body, esp. as a religious ceremony

-a·bly (ə blē) a suffix of adverbs corresponding to adjectives in -ABLE

ABM anti-ballistic missile

ab·ne·gate (ab′nə gāt′) vt. -gat′ed, -gat′ing [< L. ab-, from + negare, deny] to deny and refuse; renounce (a claim, etc.) —**ab·ne·ga′tion** n.

ab·nor·mal (ab nôr′m'l) adj. not normal, average, or typical; irregular —**ab·nor′mal·ly** adv.

ab·nor·mal·i·ty (-mal′ə tē) n. 1. an abnormal condition 2. pl. -ties an abnormal thing; malformation

a·board (ə bôrd′) adv., prep. 1. on or in (a train, ship, etc.) 2. alongside

a·bode (ə bōd′) alt. pt. & pp. of ABIDE —n. a home; residence

a·bol·ish (ə bäl′ish) vt. [< L. abolere, destroy] to do away with; void

ab·o·li·tion (ab′ə lish′ən) n. 1. complete destruction; annulment 2. [occas. A-] the abolishing of slavery in the U.S. —**ab′o·li′tion·ist** n.

A-bomb (ā′bäm′) n. same as ATOMIC BOMB

a·bom·i·na·ble (ə bäm′ə nə b'l) adj. [see ff.] 1. disgusting; vile 2. very bad —**a·bom′i·na·bly** adv.

a·bom′i·nate (-nāt′) vt. -nat′ed, -nat′ing [< L. abominari, regard as an ill omen] 1. to hate; loathe 2. to dislike —**a·bom′i·na′tion** n.

ab·o·rig·i·nal (ab′ə rij′ə n'l) adj. 1. existing (in a region) from the beginning; first 2. of aborigines —n. an aborigine

ab′o·rig′i·ne′ (-ə nē′) n., pl. -nes′ [L. < ab-, from + origine, the beginning] any of the first known inhabitants of a region

a·born·ing (ə bôr′niŋ) adv. while being born or created [the plan died aborning]

a·bort (ə bôrt′) vi. [< L. aboriri, miscarry] to have a miscarriage —vt. 1. to check before fully developed 2. to cut short (a flight, etc.), as because of an equipment failure

a·bor·tion n. premature expulsion of a fetus so that it does not live, esp. if induced on purpose —**a·bor′tion·ist** n.

a·bor′tive adj. 1. unsuccessful; fruitless 2. arrested in development

a·bound (ə bound′) vi. [< L. ab- + undare, to rise in waves] to be plentiful (often with in or with); teem

a·bout (ə bout′) adv. [< OE. onbutan, around] 1. all around 2. near 3. in an opposite direction 4. nearly [about ready] —adj. astir [he is up and about] —prep. 1. on all sides of 2. near to 3. with 4. on the point of 5. concerning

a·bout′-face′ (-fās′, -fās′) n. a reversal of position or opinion —vi. -faced′, -fac′ing to turn or face in the opposite direction

a·bove (ə buv′) adv. [OE. abufan] 1. in a higher place; up 2. earlier (in a book, etc.) 3. higher in rank, etc. —prep. 1. over; on top of 2. better or more than [above average] —adj. mentioned earlier —**above all** most of all; mainly

a·bove′board′ adv., adj. without dishonesty or concealment

ab·rade (ə brād′) vt., vi. -rad′ed, -rad′ing [< L. ab-, away + radere, scrape] to rub off; scrape away

A·bra·ham (ā′brə ham′) Bible the first patriarch of the Hebrews

ab·ra·sion (ə brā′zhən) n. 1. an abrading 2. an abraded spot

ab·ra′sive (-siv) adj. causing abrasion —n. a substance, as sandpaper, used for grinding, polishing, etc.

a·breast (ə brest′) *adv., adj.* **1.** side by side **2.** informed (*of*); aware

a·bridge (ə brij′) *vt.* **a·bridged′, a·bridg′ing** [see ABBREVIATE] **1.** to shorten, lessen, or curtail **2.** to shorten by using fewer words but keeping the substance —**a·bridg′ment, a·bridge′ment** *n.*

a·broad (ə brôd′) *adv.* **1.** far and wide **2.** in circulation; current **3.** outdoors **4.** to or in foreign lands —from abroad from a foreign land

ab·ro·gate (ab′rə gāt′) *vt.* **-gat′ed, -gat′ing** [< L. *ab-*, away + *rogare*, propose] to abolish; repeal; annul —ab′ro·ga′tion *n.* —ab′ro·ga′tor *n.*

a·brupt (ə brupt′) *adj.* [< L. *ab-*, off + *rumpere*, break] **1.** sudden; unexpected **2.** brusque **3.** very steep **4.** disconnected, as some writing —**a·brupt′ly** *adv.* —**a·brupt′ness** *n.*

Ab·sa·lom (ab′sə ləm) *Bible* David's son who rebelled against him

ab·scess (ab′ses) *n.* [< L. *ab(s)-*, from + *cedere*, go] an inflamed area in body tissues, containing pus— *vi.* to form an abscess —**ab′scessed,** *adj.*

ab·scis·sa (ab sis′ə) *n., pl.* **-sas, -sae** (-ē) [L. < *ab-*, from + *scindere*, to cut] *Math.* the horizontal distance of a point from a vertical axis

ab·scond (əb skänd′) *vi.* [< L. *ab(s)-*, from + *condere*, hide] to leave hastily and secretly, esp. to escape the law

ab·sence (ab′s'ns) *n.* **1.** a being absent **2.** the time of this **3.** a lack

ab·sent (ab′s'nt; *for v.* ab sent′) *adj.* [< L. *ab-*, away + *esse*, be] **1.** not present **2.** not existing; lacking **3.** not attentive —*vt.* to keep (oneself) away —**ab′sent·ly** *adv.*

ab·sen·tee (ab′s'n tē′) *n.* one who is absent, as from work —*adj.* of, by, or from one who is absent [*absentee* landlord] —**ab′sen·tee′ism** *n.*

absentee ballot a ballot marked and sent to a board of elections by a voter (**absentee voter**) who cannot be present to vote in an election

ab′sent-mind′ed *adj.* **1.** not attentive; preoccupied **2.** habitually forgetful —**ab′sent-mind′ed·ly** *adv.* —**ab′sent-mind′ed·ness** *n.*

absent without leave *Mil.* absent from duty without official permission

ab·sinthe (ab′sinth) *n.* [Fr., ult. < OPer.] a green, bitter liqueur: also sp. **ab′sinth**

ab·so·lute (ab′sə lōōt′) *adj.* [see ABSOLVE] **1.** perfect; complete **2.** not mixed; pure **3.** not limited [*absolute* power] **4.** positive **5.** not doubted; real [*absolute* truth] **6.** not relat′ve —**ab′so·lute′ly** *adv.*

ab·so·lu′tion (-lōō′shən) *n.* **1.** a freeing (*from* guilt); forgiveness **2.** remission (*of* sin or its penalty)

ab·so·lut·ism (ab′sə lōō′tiz'm) *n.* government by absolute rule; despotism —**ab′so·lut′ist** *n., adj.*

ab·solve (əb zälv′, -sälv′) *vt.* **-solved′, -solv′ing** [< L. *ab-*, from + *solvere*,

to loosen] **1.** to free from guilt, a duty, etc. **2.** to give religious absolution to

ab·sorb (əb zôrb′, -sôrb′) *vt.* [< L. *ab-*, from + *sorbere*, drink in] **1.** to suck up **2.** to assimilate **3.** to interest greatly; engross **4.** to pay for (costs, etc.) **5.** to take in (a shock) without recoil **6.** to take in and not reflect (light or sound) —**ab·sorb′ing** *adj.*

ab·sorb′ent *adj.* capable of absorbing moisture, etc. —*n.* a thing that absorbs —**ab·sorb′en·cy** *n.*

ab·sorp·tion (əb zôrp′shən, -sôrp′-) *n.* **1.** an absorbing or being absorbed **2.** great interest —**ab·sorp′tive** *adj.*

ab·stain (əb stān′) *vi.* [< L. *ab(s)-*, from + *tenere*, hold] to voluntarily do without; refrain (*from*) —**ab·stain′er** *n.* —**ab·sten′tion** (-sten′shən) *n.*

ab·ste·mi·ous (əb stē′mē əs) *adj.* [< L. *ab(s)-*, from + *temetum*, strong drink] moderate in eating and drinking; temperate

ab·sti·nence (ab′stə nəns) *n.* an abstaining from some or all food, liquor, etc. —**ab′sti·nent** *adj.*

ab·stract (ab strakt′, ab′strakt) *adj.* [< L. *ab(s)-*, from + *trahere*, to draw] **1.** thought of apart from material objects **2.** expressing a quality so thought of **3.** theoretical **4.** *Art* not representing things realistically —*n.* (ab′strakt) a summary —*vt.* **1.** (ab strakt′) to take away **2.** (ab′strakt) to summarize —**ab·stract′ly** *adv.*

ab·stract′ed *adj.* absent-minded

ab·strac′tion *n.* **1.** an abstracting; removal **2.** an abstract idea, thing, etc. **3.** mental withdrawal **4.** an abstract painting, etc.

ab·struse (ab strōōs′) *adj.* [< L. *ab(s)-*, away + *trudere*, to thrust] hard to understand —**ab·struse′ly** *adv.* —**ab·struse′ness** *n.*

ab·surd (əb surd′, -zurd′) *adj.* [< L. *absurdus*, not to be heard of] so unreasonable as to be ridiculous —**ab·surd′i·ty** (-sur′də tē) *n., pl.* **-ties** —**ab·surd′ly** *adv.*

a·bun·dance (ə bun′dəns) *n.* [see ABOUND] great plenty; more than enough —**a·bun′dant** *adj.* —**a·bun′dant·ly** *adv.*

a·buse (ə byōōz′; *for n.* ə byōōs′) *vt.* **a·bused′, a·bus′ing** [< L. *abusus*, misused] **1.** to use wrongly **2.** to mistreat **3.** to insult; revile —*n.* **1.** wrong use **2.** mistreatment **3.** a corrupt practice **4.** insulting language —**a·bu·sive** (ə byōōs′iv) *adj.* —**a·bu′sive·ly** *adv.*

a·but (ə but′) *vi.* **a·but′ted, a·but′ting** [< OFr. *a-*, to + *bout*, end] to border (*on* or *upon*)

a·but′ment *n.* **1.** an abutting **2.** a part supporting an arch, bridge, etc.

a·bys·mal (ə biz′m'l) *adj.* **1.** of or like an abyss; not measurable **2.** very bad —**a·bys′mal·ly** *adv.*

a·byss (ə bis′) *n.* [< Gr. *a-*, without + *byssos*, bottom] **1.** a bottomless gulf 2. anything too deep for measurement *[an abyss of shame]*

Ab·ys·sin·i·a (ab'ə sin'ē ə) Ethiopia —**Ab'ys·sin'i·an** *adj.*, *n.*

-ac (ak, ək) [< Gr.] *a suffix meaning:* 1. relating to *[cardiac]* 2. affected by *[maniac]*

Ac *Chem.* actinium

AC, A.C., a.c. alternating current

a·ca·cia (ə kā'shə) *n.* [< Gr. *akakia*, thorny tree] 1. a tree or shrub with yellow or white flower clusters 2. the locust tree

ac·a·dem·ic (ak'ə dem'ik) *adj.* 1. of academies or colleges 2. having to do with liberal arts rather than technical education 3. formal; pedantic 4. merely theoretical —**ac'a·dem'i·cal·ly** *adv.*

a·cad·e·mi·cian (ə kad'ə mish'ən) *n.* a member of an academy (sense 3)

a·cad·e·my (ə kad'ə mē) *n.*, *pl.* -**mies** [< Gr. *akadēmeia*, place where Plato taught] 1. a private secondary school 2. a school for special instruction 3. an association of scholars, writers, etc. for advancing an art or science

a·can·thus (ə kan'thəs) *n.*, *pl.* -**thus·es**, -**thi** (-thī) [< Gr. *acantha*, thorn] 1. a plant with lobed, often spiny leaves 2. *Archit.* a representation of these leaves

a cap·pel·la (ä' kə pel'ə) [It., in chapel style] without instrumental accompaniment: said of choral singing

ac·cede (ak sēd') *vi.* -**ced'ed**, -**ced'ing** [< L. *ad-*, to + *cedere*, go, yield] 1. to enter upon the duties of (an office) 2. to assent; agree (*to*)

ac·cel·er·ate (ək sel'ə rāt', ak-) *vt.* -**at'ed**, -**at'ing** [< L. *ad-*, to + *celerare*, hasten] 1. to increase the speed of 2. to cause to happen sooner —*vi.* to go faster —**ac·cel'er·a'tion** *n.* —**ac·cel'er·a'tor** *n.*

ac·cent (ak'sent; *for v. also* ak sent') *n.* [< L. *ad-*, to + *canere*, sing] 1. emphasis given a spoken syllable or word 2. a mark showing such emphasis or indicating pronunciation 3. a distinguishing manner of pronouncing *[an Irish accent]* 4. special emphasis or attention 5. *Music & Verse* rhythmic stress —*vt.* 1. to emphasize; stress 2. to mark with an accent

ac·cen·tu·ate (ak sen'choo wāt', ək-) *vt.* -**at'ed**, -**at'ing** to accent; emphasize —**ac·cen'tu·a'tion** *n.*

ac·cept (ək sept', ak-) *vt.* [< L. *ad-*, to + *capere*, take] 1. to receive, esp. willingly 2. to approve 3. to agree to 4. to believe in 5. to agree to pay

ac·cept·a·ble *adj.* worth accepting; satisfactory —**ac·cept'a·bil'i·ty**, **ac·cept'a·ble·ness** *n.*

ac·cept'ance *n.* 1. an accepting 2. approval 3. belief in; assent 4. a promise to pay

ac·cept'ed *adj.* generally regarded as true, proper, etc.; approved; conventional

ac·cess (ak'ses) *n.* [see ACCEDE] 1. approach or means of approach 2. the right to enter, use, etc. 3. an outburst; fit *[in an access of rage]*

ac·ces'si·ble *adj.* 1. that can be approached or entered, esp. easily 2. obtainable —**ac·ces'si·bil'i·ty**, **ac·ces'si·ble·ness** *n.* —**ac·ces'si·bly** *adv.*

ac·ces·sion (ak sesh'ən) *n.* 1. the act of attaining (a throne, power, etc.) 2. assent 3. *a)* increase by addition *b)* an addition, as to a collection

ac·ces·so·ry (ək ses'ər ē, ak-) *adj.* [see ACCEDE] 1. additional; extra 2. helping in an unlawful act —*n.*, *pl.* -**ries** 1. something extra or complementary 2. one who, though absent, helps another to break the law

ac·ci·dent (ak'sə dənt) *n.* [< L. *ad-*, to + *cadere*, to fall] 1. an unintended happening 2. a mishap 3. chance

ac'ci·den'tal (-den't'l) *adj.* happening by chance —**ac'ci·den'tal·ly** *adv.*

ac'ci·dent-prone' (-prōn') *adj.* seemingly inclined to become involved in accidents

ac·claim (ə klām') *vt.* [< L. *ad-*, to + *clamare*, to cry out] to greet or announce with loud approval or applause; hail —*n.* loud approval

ac·cla·ma·tion (ak'lə mā'shən) *n.* 1. loud applause or approval 2. an approving vote by voice

ac·cli·mate (ak'lə māt', ə klī'mət) *vt.*, *vi.* -**mat·ed**, -**mat·ing** [see AD- & CLIMATE] to accustom or become accustomed to a new climate or environment: also **ac·cli'ma·tize'** (-tīz') -**tized'**, -**tiz'ing** —**ac'cli·ma·ti·za'tion** (-ti zā'shən) *n.*

ac·cliv·i·ty (ə kliv'ə tē) *n.*, *pl.* -**ties** [< L. *ad-*, up + *clivus*, hill] an upward slope

ac·co·lade (ak'ə lād') *n.* [Fr. < It. *accollare*, to embrace] an approving mention; award

ac·com·mo·date (ə käm'ə dāt') *vt.* -**dat'ed**, -**dat'ing** [< L. *ad-*, to + *commodare*, to fit] 1. to adapt 2. to do a favor for 3. to have space for; lodge

ac·com·mo·dat'ing *adj.* obliging

ac·com·mo·da'tion *n.* 1. adjustment 2. willingness to do favors 3. a help; convenience 4. *[pl.]* *a)* lodgings *b)* traveling space, as in a train

ac·com·pa·ni·ment (ə kump'ni mənt) *n.* anything that accompanies something else, as an instrumental part supporting a solo voice, etc.

ac·com·pa·ny (ə kum'pə nē, ə kump'nē) *vt.* -**nied**, -**ny·ing** [see AD- & COMPANION] 1. to go with 2. to add to 3. to play or sing an accompaniment for or to —**ac·com'pa·nist** *n.*

ac·com·plice (ə käm'plis) *n.* [< *a* (the article) + L. *complex:* see COMPLEX] a partner in crime

ac·com·plish (ə käm'plish) *vt.* [< L. *ad*, intens. + *complere:* see COMPLETE] to succeed in doing; complete

ac·com'plished *adj.* 1. done; completed 2. skilled; expert

ac·com'plish·ment *n.* 1. completion 2. work completed; an achievement 3. a social art or skill

ac·cord (ə kôrd') *vt.* [< L. *ad-*, to + *cor*, heart] 1. to make agree 2. to grant —*vi.* to agree; harmonize (*with*) —*n.* mutual agreement; harmony —

of one's own accord willingly —with one accord all agreeing

ac·cord'ance n. agreement; conformity —**ac·cord'ant** adj.

ac·cord'ing adj. in harmony —adv. accordingly —**according to** 1. in agreement with 2. as stated by

ac·cord'ing·ly adv. 1. in a fitting and proper way 2. therefore

ac·cor·di·on (ə kôr'dē ən) n. [prob. < It. accordare, to be in tune] a keyed musical instrument with a bellows, which is pressed to force air through reeds

ACCORDION

ac·cost (ə kôst') vt. [< L. ad-, to + costa, side] to approach and speak to

ac·count (ə kount') vt. [< L. computare: see COMPUTE] to judge to be —vi. 1. to give a financial reckoning (to) 2. to give reasons (for) —n. 1. a counting 2. [often pl.] a record of business transactions 3. same as a) BANK ACCOUNT b) CHARGE ACCOUNT 4. a credit customer 5. worth; importance 6. an explanation 7. a report —on account as partial payment —on account of because of —on no account under no circumstances —take into account to consider —turn to account to get use or profit from

ac·count'a·ble adj. 1. responsible; liable 2. explainable

ac·count·ant (ə kount'nt) n. one whose work is accounting

ac·count'ing n. the figuring and recording of financial accounts

ac·cou·ter (ə kōōt'ər) vt. [? < L. consuere, to sew] to outfit; equip

ac·cou'ter·ments (-mənts) n.pl. 1. clothes 2. a soldier's equipment

ac·cred·it (ə kred'it) vt. [see CREDIT] 1. to authorize; certify 2. to believe in 3. to attribute —**ac·cred'it·a'tion** (-ə tā'shən) n.

ac·cre·tion (ə krē'shən) n. [< L. ad-, to + crescere, grow] 1. growth in size, esp. by addition 2. accumulated matter 3. a growing together of parts

ac·crue (ə krōō') vi. -crued', -cru'ing [see prec.] to come as a natural growth or periodic increase, as interest on money —**ac·cru'al** n.

acct. account

ac·cul·tu·rate (ə kul'chə rāt') vi., vt. -rat'ed, -rat'ing to undergo, or change by, acculturation

ac·cul·tu·ra·tion (ə kul'chə rā'shən) n. 1. adaptation to a culture, esp. a new or different one 2. mutual influence of different cultures

ac·cu·mu·late (ə kyōōm'yə lāt') vt., vi. -lat'ed, -lat'ing [< L. ad-, to + cumulare, to heap] to pile up or collect —**ac·cu'mu·la'tion** n. —**ac·cu'mu·la'tive** adj.

ac·cu·ra·cy (ak'yər ə sē) n. the state of being accurate; precision

ac'cu·rate (-it) adj. [< L. ad-, to + cura, care] 1. careful and exact 2. free from errors —**ac'cu·rate·ly** adv. —**ac'cu·rate·ness** n.

ac·curs·ed (ə kur'sid, -kurst') adj. 1. under a curse 2. damnable Also **ac·curst'** —**ac·curs'ed·ness** n.

ac·cu·sa·tion (ak'yə zā'shən) n. 1. an accusing 2. what one is accused of —**ac·cu·sa·to·ry** (ə kyōō'zə tôr'ē) adj.

ac·cu·sa·tive (ə kyōō'zə tiv) adj. [see ff.] Gram. designating or in the case of an object of a verb or preposition; objective —n. the accusative case

ac·cuse (ə kyōōz') vt. -cused', -cus'ing [< L. ad-, to + causa, a cause] 1. to blame 2. to bring charges against (of doing wrong) —**ac·cus'er** n.

ac·cus·tom (ə kus'təm) vt. to make familiar by custom, habit, or use

ac·cus'tomed adj. 1. customary; usual 2. wont or used (to)

ace (ās) n. [< L. as, unit] 1. a playing card, etc. with one spot 2. a point, as in tennis, won by a single stroke 3. an expert, esp. in combat flying 4. Golf a hole in one —adj. [Colloq.] first-rate

ace in the hole [Slang] any advantage held in reserve

ac·er·bate (as'ər bāt') vt. -bat'ed, -bat'ing [< L. acerbare] 1. to make sour or bitter 2. to irritate; vex

a·cer·bi·ty (ə sur'bə tē) n., pl. -ties [< L. acerbus, bitter] 1. sourness 2. sharpness of temper, words, etc. —**a·cerb'** adj.

ac·et·an·i·lide (as'ə tan'ə lid') n. [< ACETIC & ANILINE] a drug used to lessen pain and fever

ac·e·tate (as'ə tāt') n. 1. a salt or ester of acetic acid 2. something, esp. a fabric, made of an acetate of cellulose

a·ce·tic (ə sēt'ik) adj. [< L. acetum, vinegar] of the sharp, sour liquid (**acetic acid**) found in vinegar

a·cet·i·fy (ə set'ə fī', -sēt'-) vt., vi. -fied', -fy'ing to change into vinegar or acetic acid

ac·e·tone (as'ə tōn') n. [< prec.] a flammable, colorless liquid used as a solvent for certain oils, etc. —**ac'e·ton'ic** (-tän'ik) adj.

a·cet·y·lene (ə set''l ēn') n. [< ACETIC + -YL + -ENE] a gas used for lighting, and, with oxygen in a blowtorch, for welding, etc.

a·cet·yl·sal·i·cyl·ic acid (ə set''l-sal'ə sil'ik) aspirin

ache (āk) vi. ached, ach'ing [< OE. acan] 1. to have or give dull, steady pain 2. [Colloq.] to yearn —n. a dull, continuous pain —**ach'y** adj.

a·chene (ā kēn', ə-) n. [< Gr. a-, not + chainein, to gape] any small, dry fruit with one seed

a·chieve (ə chēv') vt. a·chieved', a·chiev'ing [< L. ad-, to + caput, head] 1. to do successfully 2. to get by effort —**a·chiev'a·ble** adj.

a·chieve′ment *n.* **1.** an achieving **2.** a thing achieved; feat; exploit

A·chil·les (ə kil′ēz) a Greek hero killed in the Trojan War

Achilles′ heel (one's) vulnerable spot

ach·ro·mat·ic (ak′rə mat′ik) *adj.* [< Gr. *a-*, without + *chrōma*, color] refracting white light without breaking it up into its component colors

ac·id (as′id) *adj.* [< L. *acidus*, sour] **1.** sour; sharp; tart **2.** of an acid —*n.* **1.** a sour substance **2.** [Slang] *same as* LSD **3.** *Chem.* any compound that reacts with a base to form a salt —**a·cid′i·ty** (ə sid′ə tē) *n., pl.* **-ties** —**ac′id·ly** *adv.*

a·cid·i·fy (ə sid′ə fī′) *vt., vi.* **-fied′, -fy′ing 1.** to make or become sour **2.** to change into an acid

ac·i·do·sis (as′ə dō′sis) *n.* a condition in which the alkali reserve of the body is lower than normal

acid rain rain with a high concentration of acids produced by the gases from burning fossil fuels: it is destructive to plants, buildings, etc.

acid test a crucial, final test

a·cid·u·late (ə sij′oo lāt′) *vt.* **-lat′ed, -lat′ing** to make somewhat acid or sour

a·cid·u·lous (ə sij′oo ləs) *adj.* **1.** somewhat acid or sour **2.** sarcastic

-a·cious (ā′shəs) [< L.] a suffix meaning inclined to, full of [*tenacious*]

-ac·i·ty (as′ə tē) a suffix used to form nouns corresponding to adjectives ending in -ACIOUS [*tenacity*]

ac·knowl·edge (ək näl′ij) *vt.* **-edged, -edg·ing** [cf. KNOWLEDGE] **1.** to admit as true **2.** to recognize the authority or claims of **3.** to respond to **4.** to express thanks for **5.** to state that one has received (a letter, etc.) —**ac·knowl′edg·ment, ac·knowl′edge·ment** *n.*

ac·me (ak′mē) *n.* [Gr. *akmē*, a point, top] the highest point; peak

ac·ne (ak′nē) *n.* [? < Gr.: see prec.] a skin disorder usually causing pimples on the face, etc.

ac·o·lyte (ak′ə līt′) *n.* [< Gr. *akolouthos*, follower] **1.** an altar boy **2.** an attendant; helper

ac·o·nite (ak′ə nīt′) *n.* [< Gr.] **1.** a plant with hoodlike flowers **2.** a sedative drug made from its roots

a·corn (ā′kôrn′) *n.* [< OE. *æcern*, nut] the nut of the oak tree

acorn squash a kind of winter squash, acorn-shaped with dark-green skin and yellow flesh

a·cous·tic (ə kōōs′tik) *adj.* [< Gr. *akouein*, to hear] having to do with hearing or acoustics: also **a·cous′ti·cal** —**a·cous′ti·cal·ly** *adv.*

a·cous·tics (-tiks) *n.pl.* **1.** the qualities of a room, etc. that determine how clearly sounds can be heard in it **2.** [*with sing. v.*] the branch of physics dealing with sound

ac·quaint (ə kwānt′) *vt.* [< L. *ad-*, to + *cognoscere*, know] **1.** to inform **2.** to make familiar (*with*)

ac·quaint′ance *n.* **1.** knowledge got from personal experience **2.** a person whom one knows slightly

ac·qui·esce (ak′wē es′) *vi.* **-esced′,**
-esc′ing [< L. *ad-*, to + *quiescere*, to be at rest] to consent without protest (often with *in*) —**ac′qui·es′cence** *n.* —**ac′qui·es′cent** *adj.*

ac·quire (ə kwīr′) *vt.* **-quired′, -quir′ing** [< L. *ad-* + *quaerere*, to seek] **1.** to gain by one's own efforts **2.** to get as one's own —**ac·quir′a·ble** *adj.* —**ac·quire′ment** *n.*

ac·qui·si·tion (ak′wə zish′ən) *n.* **1.** an acquiring **2.** something acquired

ac·quis·i·tive (ə kwiz′ə tiv) *adj.* eager to acquire (money, etc.); grasping —**ac·quis′i·tive·ness** *n.*

ac·quit (ə kwit′) *vt.* **-quit′ted, -quit′ting** [< L. *ad*, to + *quietare*, to quiet] **1.** to release from an obligation, etc. **2.** to clear (a person) of a charge **3.** to conduct (oneself); behave —**ac·quit′tal** *n.*

a·cre (āk′ər) *n.* [OE. *æcer*, field] a measure of land, 43,560 sq. ft.

a′cre·age (-ij) *n.* acres collectively

ac·rid (ak′rid) *adj.* [< L. *acris*, sour] **1.** sharp or bitter to the taste or smell **2.** sharp in speech, etc. —**a·crid·i·ty** (ə krid′ə tē) *n.* —**ac′rid·ly** *adv.*

ac·ri·mo·ny (ak′rə mō′nē) *n., pl.* **-nies** [< L. *acer*, sharp] bitterness or harshness of manner or speech —**ac′ri·mo′ni·ous** *adj.*

ac·ro·bat (ak′rə bat′) *n.* [< Gr. *akrobatos*, walking on tiptoe] a performer on the trapeze, tightrope, etc.; gymnast —**ac′ro·bat′ic** *adj.*

ac′ro·bat′ics (-iks) *n.pl.* [*also with sing. v.*] **1.** an acrobat's tricks **2.** any tricks requiring great skill

ac·ro·nym (ak′rə nim) *n.* [< Gr. *akros*, at the end + *onyma*, name] a word formed from the first (or first few) letters of several words, as *radar*

ac·ro·pho·bi·a (ak′rə fō′bē ə) *n.* [< Gr. *akros*, at the top + -PHOBIA] an abnormal fear of being in high places

A·crop·o·lis (ə kräp′ə ləs) *n.* [< Gr. *akros*, at the top + *polis*, city] the fortified hill in Athens on which the Parthenon was built

a·cross (ə krôs′) *adv.* **1.** crosswise **2.** from one side to the other —*prep.* **1.** from one side to the other of **2.** on the other side of **3.** into contact with by chance (to come *across* a find)

a·cross′-the-board′ *adj.* **1.** combining win, place, and show, as a bet **2.** affecting all classes or groups

a·cros·tic (ə kräs′tik) *n.* [< Gr. *akros*, at the end + *stichos*, line of verse] a poem, etc. in which certain letters in each line, as the first or last, spell out a word, motto, etc.

a·cryl·ic (ə kril′ik) *adj.* **1.** designating any of a group of synthetic fibers used to make fabrics **2.** designating any of a group of clear, synthetic resins

act (akt) *n.* [< L. *agere*, to do] **1.** a thing done **2.** a doing **3.** a law **4.** a main division of a drama or opera **5.** a short performance, as on a variety show **6.** something done merely for show —*vt.* to perform in (a play or part) —*vi.* **1.** to perform on the stage, etc. **2.** to behave **3.** to function **4.** to have an effect (*on*) **5.** to appear to be —**act up** [Colloq.] to misbehave

ACTH [< *a(dreno)c(ortico)t(ropic) h(ormone)*] a pituitary hormone that acts on the adrenal cortex

act·ing (ak′tiŋ) *adj.* temporarily doing the duties of another —*n.* the art of an actor

ac·tin·ic (ak tin′ik) *adj.* [< Gr. *aktis*, ray] designating or of light rays that produce chemical changes

ac·ti·nide series (ak′tə nīd′) a group of radioactive chemical elements from element 89 (actinium) through element 103 (lawrencium)

ac·tin·i·um (ak tin′ē əm) *n.* [< Gr. *aktis*, ray] a radioactive chemical element

ac·tion (ak′shən) *n.* **1.** the doing of something **2.** a thing done **3.** [*pl.*] behavior **4.** the way of working, as of a machine **5.** the moving parts, as of a gun **6.** the sequence of events, as in a story **7.** a lawsuit **8.** military combat **9.** [Slang] activity

ac·ti·vate (ak′tə vāt′) *vt.* **-vat′ed, -vat′ing 1.** to make active **2.** to put (a military unit) on active status **3.** to make radioactive **4.** to purify sewage by aeration —**ac′ti·va′tion** *n.* —**ac′ti·va′tor** *n.*

activated carbon a form of highly porous carbon that can adsorb gases, vapors, and colloidal particles

ac·tive (ak′tiv) *adj.* **1.** acting; working **2.** causing motion or change **3.** lively; agile **4.** indicating the voice of a verb whose subject performs the action —**ac′tive·ly** *adv.*

ac′tiv·ism (-tə viz′m) *n.* a taking direct action to achieve a political or social end —**ac′tiv·ist** *adj., n.*

ac·tiv·i·ty (ak tiv′ə tē) *n., pl.* **-ties 1.** a being active **2.** liveliness **3.** a specific action [student *activities*]

ac·tor (ak′tər) *n.* **1.** one who does a thing **2.** one who acts in plays, movies, etc. —**ac′tress** *n.fem.*

ac·tu·al (ak′chōō wəl) *adj.* [< L. *agere*, to do] **1.** existing in reality **2.** existing at the time —**ac′tu·al·ly** *adv.*

ac′tu·al′i·ty (-wal′ə tē) *n.* **1.** reality **2.** *pl.* -ties an actual thing

ac·tu·al·ize (ak′chōō wə līz′) *vt.* **-ized′, -iz′ing 1.** to make actual or real **2.** to make realistic

ac·tu·ar·y (ak′chōō wer′ē) *n., pl.* -ies [L. *actuarius*, clerk] one who figures insurance risks, premiums, etc. —**ac′tu·ar′i·al** *adj.*

ac·tu·ate (ak′chōō wāt′) *vt.* **-at′ed, -at′ing 1.** to put into action **2.** to impel to action —**ac′tu·a′tor** *n.*

a·cu·i·ty (ə kyōō′ə tē) *n.* [< L. *acus*, needle] keenness of thought or vision

a·cu·men (ə kyōō′mən) *n.* [L. < *acuere*, sharpen] keenness of mind or insight

ac·u·pres·sure (ak′yoo presh′ər) *n.* [ACU(PUNCTURE) + PRESSURE] a practice like acupuncture but applying hand pressure instead of needles to the body

ac·u·punc·ture (ak′yoo puŋk′chər) *n.* [< L. *acus*, needle + PUNCTURE]

the ancient practice, esp. among the Chinese, of piercing parts of the body with needles to treat disease or relieve pain

a·cute (ə kyōōt′) *adj.* [< L. *acuere*, sharpen] **1.** sharp-pointed **2.** keen of mind **3.** sensitive [*acute* hearing] **4.** severe, as pain **5.** severe but not chronic [an *acute* disease] **6.** very serious **7.** less than 90° [*acute* angles] —**a·cute′ly** *adv.* —**a·cute′ness** *n.*

acute accent a mark (′) showing the quality of a vowel, stress, etc.

-a·cy (ə sē) [ult. < Gr.] *a suffix meaning* quality, condition, etc. [*celibacy*]

ad (ad) *n.* [Colloq.] an advertisement

ad- [L.] *a prefix meaning* motion toward, addition to, nearness to: also **a-, ac-, af-, ag-, al-, an-,** etc. before certain consonants

A.D. [L. *Anno Domini*, in the year of the Lord] of the Christian era: used with dates

ad·age (ad′ij) *n.* [< L. *ad-*, to + *aio*, I say] an old saying; proverb

a·da·gio (ə dä′jō, -zhō) *adv.* [It. *ad agio*, at ease] *Music* slowly —*adj.* slow —*n., pl.* **-gios 1.** a slow movement in music **2.** a slow ballet dance

Ad·am (ad′əm) [Heb. < *ādām*, human being] *Bible* the first man

ad·a·mant (ad′ə mant) *n.* [< Gr. *a-*, not + *daman*, subdue] a very hard substance —*adj.* inflexible; unyielding

Ad·ams (ad′əmz) **1. John,** 1735-1826; 2d president of U.S. (1797-1801) **2. John Quin·cy** (kwin′sē), 1767-1848; 6th president of U.S. (1825-29): son of *prec.*

Adam's apple the projection of cartilage in the front of the throat, esp. of a man

a·dapt (ə dapt′) *vt.* [< L. *ad-*, to + *aptare*, to fit] **1.** to make suitable, esp. by changing **2.** to adjust (oneself) to new circumstances —**ad·ap·ta·tion** (ad′əp tā′shən) *n.*

a·dapt′a·ble *adj.* able to adjust or be adjusted —**a·dapt′a·bil′i·ty** *n.*

add (ad) *vt.* [< L. *ad-*, to + *dare*, give] **1.** to join (to) so as to increase **2.** to state further **3.** to combine (numbers) into a sum —*vi.* **1.** to cause an increase (*to*) **2.** to find a sum —**add up** to seem reasonable —**add up to** to mean; signify —**add′a·ble, add′i·ble** *adj.*

ad·den·dum (ə den′dəm) *n., pl.* **-da** (-də) [L.] a thing added, as an appendix

ad·der (ad′ər) *n.* [< OE. *nædre*] a poisonous snake of Europe **2.** any of several harmless snakes of N. America

ad·dict (ə dikt′; *for n.* ad′ikt) *vt.* [< L. *addicere*, give assent] **1.** to give (oneself) up to (a strong habit) **2.** to make become addicted —*n.* one addicted to a habit, as to using drugs —**ad·dic′tion** *n.* —**ad·dic′tive** *adj.*

Ad·dis A·ba·ba (ä′dis ä′bə bə) capital of Ethiopia: pop. 443,000

ad·di·tion (ə dish′ən) *n.* **1.** an adding of numbers to get a sum **2.** a

---

fat, āpe, cär; ten, ēven; is, bīte; gō, hôrn, tōōl, look; oil, out; up, fur; chin; she; thin, then; zh, leisure; ŋ, ring; ə for a in ago; ′, (ā′b'l); ë, Fr. coeur; ö, Fr. feu; Fr. mon; ü, Fr. duc; kh, G. ich, doch; ‡ foreign; < derived from

joining of one thing to another **3.** a part added —**in addition (to)** besides

ad·di·tion·al (-əl) *adj.* added; more; extra —**ad·di'tion·al·ly** *adv.*

ad·di·tive (ad'ə tiv) *n.* something added —*adj.* of addition

ad·dle (ad''l) *vt., vi.* **-dled, -dling** [< OE. *adela*, mud] **1.** to make or become rotten **2.** to make or become confused

ad·dress (ə dres'; *for n., esp. 2 & 3, also* ad'res) *vt.* [< VL. *directiare*, to direct] **1.** to direct (words) *to* **2.** to speak or write *to* **3.** to write the destination on (a letter, etc.) **4.** to apply (oneself) *to* —*n.* **1.** a speech **2.** the place where one lives or receives mail **3.** the destination indicated on an envelope **4.** skill; tact

ad·dress·ee (ad'res ē') *n.* the person to whom mail, etc. is addressed

ad·duce (ə dōōs') *vt.* **-duced', -duc'-ing** [< L. *ad-*, to + *ducere*, to lead] to give as a reason or proof

-ade (ād) [ult. < L.] *a suffix meaning:* **1.** the act of [*blockade*] **2.** participant(s) in an action [*brigade*] **3.** drink made from [*limeade*]

A·den (äd'n, ād'n), Gulf of gulf of the Arabian Sea, south of Arabia

ad·e·noids (ad''n oidz') *n.pl.* [< Gr. *adēn*, gland + -OID] lymphoid growths in the throat behind the nose: they can obstruct nasal breathing

ad·ept (ə dept'; *for n.* ad'ept) *adj.* [< L. *ad-*, to + *apisci*, attain] highly skilled —*n.* an expert —**ad·ept'ly** *adv.* —**ad·ept'ness** *n.*

ad·e·quate (ad'ə kwət) *adj.* [< L. *ad-*, to + *aequare*, make equal] enough for what is required; sufficient; suitable —**ad'e·qua·cy** (-kwə sē) *n.* —**ad'e·quate·ly** *adv.*

ad·here (əd hir') *vi.* **-hered', -her'-ing** [< L. *ad-*, to + *haerere*, to stick] **1.** to stick fast; stay attached **2.** to give allegiance or support (*to*) —**ad·her'ence** *n.*

ad·her'ent *n.* a supporter or follower (*of* a cause, etc.)

ad·he·sion (əd hē'zhən) *n.* **1.** an adhering or a being stuck together **2.** body tissues abnormally joined

ad·he·sive (-hē'siv) *adj.* **1.** sticking **2.** sticky —*n.* an adhesive substance

ad hoc (ad' häk') [L., to this] for a specific purpose [an *ad hoc* committee]

a·dieu (ə dōō', -dyōō'; *Fr.* ä dyō') *interj., n., pl.* **a·dieus'**; *Fr.* **a·dieux'** (-dyō') [Fr.] goodbye

ad in·fi·ni·tum (ad in'fə nīt'əm) [L.] endlessly; without limit

a·di·os (a'dē ōs'; *Sp.* ä dyōs') *interj.* [< Sp.] goodbye

ad·i·pose (ad'ə pōs') *adj.* [< L. *adeps*, fat] of animal fat; fatty

Ad·i·ron·dack Mountains (ad'ə rän'dak) mountain range in NE New York: also **Adirondacks**

adj. 1. adjective **2.** adjutant

ad·ja·cent (ə jās'ənt) *adj.* [< L. *ad-*, to + *jacere*, to lie] near or close (*to*); adjoining —**ad·ja'cen·cy** *n.* —**ad·ja'cent·ly** *adv.*

ad·jec·tive (aj'ik tiv) *n.* [< L. *adjicere*, add to] a word used to limit or qualify a noun or other substantive —**ad·jec·ti·val** (-tī'v'l) *adj.* —**ad'jec·ti'val·ly** *adv.*

ad·join (ə join') *vt.* [< L. *ad-*, to + *jungere*, join] to be next to —*vi.* to be in contact —**ad·join'ing** *adj.*

ad·journ (ə jurn') *vt.* [< OFr. *a*, at + *jorn*, day] to suspend (a meeting, session, etc.) for a time —*vi.* **1.** to suspend a meeting, etc. for a time **2.** [Colloq.] to retire (*to* another room, etc.) —**ad·journ'ment** *n.*

ad·judge (ə juj') *vt.* **-judged', -judg'ing** [< L. *ad-*, to + *judicare*, to judge] **1.** to decide by law **2.** to declare, order, or award by law

ad·ju·di·cate (ə jōō'də kāt') *vt.* **-cat'ed, -cat'ing** *Law* to hear and decide (a case) —*vi.* to serve as judge (*in or on*) —**ad·ju'di·ca'tion** *n.* —**ad·ju'di·ca'tor** *n.* —**ad·ju'di·ca·to·ry** (-kə tôr'ē) *adj.*

ad·junct (aj'uŋkt) *n.* [see ADJOIN] a secondary or nonessential addition

ad·jure (ə joor') *vt.* **-jured', -jur'ing** [< L. *ad-*, to + *jurare*, swear] **1.** to charge solemnly under oath **2.** to ask earnestly —**ad'ju·ra'tion** *n.*

ad·just (ə just') *vt.* [< OFr. *ajoster*, to join] **1.** to change so as to fit **2.** to regulate (a watch, etc.) **3.** to settle rightly **4.** to decide the amount to be paid in settling (an insurance claim) —*vi.* to adapt oneself —**ad·just'a·ble** *adj.* —**ad·just'er, ad·jus'tor** *n.* —**ad·just'ment** *n.*

ad·ju·tant (aj'ə tənt) *n.* [< L. *ad-*, to + *juvare*, to help] **1.** an assistant **2.** a military staff officer who assists the commanding officer **3.** a large stork of India and Africa

ad·lib (ad'lib') *vt., vi.* **-libbed', -lib'bing** [< L. *ad libitum*, at pleasure] [Colloq.] to improvise (words, etc. not in the script) —*n.* [Colloq.] an ad-libbed remark —*adv.* [Colloq.] as one pleases: also **ad lib**

ad·man (ad'man') *n., pl.* **-men'** a man whose work is advertising

ad·min·is·ter (əd min'ə stər) *vt.* [< L. *ad-*, to + *ministrare*, serve] **1.** to manage; direct **2.** to give out, as punishment **3.** to apply (medicine, etc.) **4.** to tender (an oath, etc.)

ad·min·is·trate' (-strāt') *vt.* **-trat'ed, -trat'ing** to administer; manage

ad·min·is·tra·tion (-strā'shən) *n.* **1.** management **2.** [often A-] the executive officials of a government, etc. and their policy **3.** their term of office **4.** the administering (*of* punishment, medicine, etc.) —**ad·min'is·tra'tive** *adj.*

ad·min·is·tra·tor *n.* **1.** one who administers **2.** *Law* one appointed to settle an estate

ad·mi·ra·ble (ad'mər ə b'l) *adj.* deserving admiration; excellent —**ad'mi·ra·bly** *adv.*

ad·mi·ral (ad'mər əl) *n.* [< Ar. *amīr a'ālī*, high leader] **1.** the commanding officer of a fleet **2.** a naval officer of the highest rank

ad·mi·ral·ty (-tē) *n., pl.* **-ties** [often A-] the governmental department in charge of naval affairs, as in England

ad·mi·ra·tion (ad'mə rā'shən) *n.*
1. an admiring 2. pleased approval

ad·mire (əd mīr') *vt.* -mired', -mir'-ing [< L. *ad-*, at + *mirari*, wonder]
1. to regard with wonder and delight
2. to esteem highly —**ad·mir'er** *n.*

ad·mis·si·ble (əd mis'ə b'l) *adj.* that can be accepted or admitted —**ad·mis'si·bil'i·ty** *n.*

ad·mis·sion (əd mish'ən) *n.* 1. an admitting or being admitted 2. an entrance fee 3. a conceding, confessing, etc. 4. a thing conceded, confessed, etc.

ad·mit (əd mit') *vt.* -mit'ted, -mit'ting [< L. *ad-*, to + *mittere*, send]
1. to permit or entitle to enter or use
2. to allow; leave room for 3. to concede or confess —*vi.* to allow (with *of*) —**ad·mit'tance** *n.*

ad·mit'ted·ly *adv.* by admission or general agreement

ad·mix·ture (ad miks'chər) *n.* [< L. *ad-*, to + *miscere*, to mix] 1. a mixture 2. a thing added in mixing —**ad·mix'** *vt.*

ad·mon·ish (əd män'ish) *vt.* [< L. *ad-*, to + *monere*, warn] 1. to warn 2. to reprove mildly 3. to exhort —**ad·mo·ni·tion** (ad'mə nish'ən) *n.* —**ad·mon'i·to'ry** (-ə tôr'ē) *adj.*

ad nau·se·am (ad' nô'zē əm, -shē-) [L.] to the point of disgust

a·do (ə dōō') *n.* fuss; trouble

a·do·be (ə dō'bē) *n.* [Sp.] 1. unburnt, sun-dried brick 2. clay for making this brick 3. a building of adobe

ad·o·les·cence (ad''l es'ns) *n.* the time of life between puberty and maturity; youth

ad'o·les'cent *adj.* [< L. *ad-*, to + *alescere*, grow up] of or in adolescence —*n.* a person during adolescence

A·don·is (ə dän'is, -dō'nis) *Gr. Myth.* a young man loved by Aphrodite —*n.* a handsome young man

a·dopt (ə däpt') *vt.* [< L. *ad-*, to + *optare*, choose] 1. to take legally into one's family and raise as one's own child 2. to take as one's own 3. to choose or accept —**a·dop'tion** *n.*

a·dop·tive (ə däp'tiv) *adj.* that has become so by adoption

a·dor·a·ble (ə dôr'ə b'l) *adj.* 1. [Rare] worthy of adoration 2. [Colloq.] delightful; charming —**a·dor'a·bly** *adv.*

ad·o·ra·tion (ad'ə rā'shən) *n.* 1. a worshiping 2. great love or devotion

a·dore (ə dôr') *vt.* -dored', -dor'ing [< L. *ad-*, to + *orare*, speak] 1. to worship as divine 2. to love greatly 3. [Colloq.] to like very much

a·dorn (ə dôrn') *vt.* [< L. *ad-*, to + *ornare*, deck out] 1. to be an ornament to 2. to put decorations on —**a·dorn'ment** *n.*

ad·re·nal (ə drē'n'l) *adj.* [AD- + RENAL] 1. near the kidneys 2. of two ductless glands (**adrenal glands**), just above the kidneys in mammals

Ad·ren·al·in (ə dren''l in) *a trade-*

mark for a hormone secreted by the adrenal glands or synthesized for use as a drug —*n.* [a-] this hormone

A·dri·at·ic (Sea) (ā'drē at'ik) sea between Italy and Yugoslavia

a·drift (ə drift') *adv., adj.* floating without mooring or direction

a·droit (ə droit') *adj.* [Fr. *à*, to + *droit*, right] skillful and clever —**a·droit'ly** *adv.* —**a·droit'ness** *n.*

ad·sorb (ad sôrb') *vt.* [< AD- + L. *sorbere*, drink in] to collect (a gas, etc.) in condensed form on a surface —**ad·sorp'tion** (-sôrp'shən) *n.*

ad·u·late (aj'ə lāt') *vt.* -lat'ed, -lat'ing [< L. *adulari*, fawn upon] to flatter servilely —**ad·u·la'tion** *n.*

a·dult (ə dult', ad'ult) *adj.* [see ADOLESCENT] grown up; mature —*n.* a mature person, animal, or plant —**a·dult'hood** *n.*

a·dul·ter·ant (ə dul'tər ənt) *n.* a substance that adulterates —*adj.* adulterating

a·dul·ter·ate (ə dul'tə rāt') *vt.* -at'ed, -at'ing [< L. *ad-*, to + *alter*, other] to make inferior, impure, etc. by adding an improper substance —**a·dul'ter·a'tion** *n.*

a·dul·ter·y (ə dul'tər ē) *n., pl.* -ies [see prec.] sexual intercourse between a married person and another not the spouse —**a·dul'ter·er** *n.* —**a·dul'ter·ess** *n.fem.* —**a·dul'ter·ous** *adj.*

ad·um·brate (ad um'brāt) *vt.* -brat'ed, -brat·ing [< L. *ad-* + *umbra*, shade] 1. to outline vaguely 2. to foreshadow —**ad'um·bra'tion** *n.*

adv. 1. adverb 2. advertisement

ad·vance (əd vans') *vt.* -vanced', -vanc'ing [< L. *ab-*, from + *ante*, before] 1. to bring forward 2. to suggest 3. to promote 4. to raise the rate of 5. to lend —*vi.* 1. to go forward 2. to improve; progress 3. to rise in rank, price, etc. —*n.* 1. a moving forward 2. an improvement 3. a rise in value 4. [pl.] approaches to get favor 5. a payment before due —*adj.* 1. in front [advance guard] 2. beforehand —**in advance** 1. in front 2. ahead of time —**ad·vance'ment** *n.*

ad·vanced' *adj.* 1. in front 2. old 3. ahead or higher in progress, price, etc.

advance man a person hired to travel in advance of a theatrical company, political candidate, etc. to arrange for publicity, appearances, etc.

ad·van·tage (əd van'tij) *n.* [< L. *ab ante*, from before] 1. superiority 2. a favorable circumstance, event, etc. 3. gain; benefit —*vt.* -taged, -tag·ing to be a benefit to —**take advantage of** 1. to use for one's own benefit 2. to impose upon —**ad·van·ta·geous** (ad' vən tā'jəs) *adj.*

Ad·vent (ad'vent) *n.* [< L. *ad-*, to + *venire*, come] 1. the period including the four Sundays just before Christmas 2. [a-] a coming

ad·ven·ti·tious (ad'vən tish'əs) *adj.* [see prec.] not inherent; accidental

ad·ven·ture (əd ven′chər) *n.* [see ADVENT] 1. an exciting and dangerous undertaking 2. an unusual, stirring, often romantic experience —*vt., vi.* -tured, -tur·ing to risk; venture — **ad·ven′tur·ous, ad·ven′ture·some** *adj.* —**ad·ven′tur·ous·ly** *adv.*

ad·ven·tur·er *n.* 1. one who has or looks for adventures 2. one who seeks to become rich, etc. by dubious schemes —**ad·ven′tur·ess** *n.fem.*

ad·verb (ad′vurb) *n.* [< L. *ad-*, to + *verbum*, word] a word used to modify a verb, adjective, or another adverb, by expressing time, place, manner, degree, etc. —**ad·ver′bi·al** *adj.* —**ad·ver′bi·al·ly** *adv.*

ad·ver·sar·y (ad′vər ser′ē) *n., pl.* -ies [see ADVERT] an opponent; foe

ad·verse (ad vurs′, ad′vərs) *adj.* [see ADVERT] 1. hostile; opposed 2. unfavorable —**ad·verse′ly** *adv.*

ad·ver·si·ty (ad vur′sə tē) *n.* 1. misfortune; wretched or troubled state 2. *pl.* -ties a calamity; disaster

ad·vert (ad vurt′) *vi.* [< L. *ad-*, to + *vertere*, to turn] to call attention (*to*)

ad·vert′ent (-′nt) *adj.* attentive; heedful —**ad·vert′ence** *n.*

ad·ver·tise (ad′vər tīz′) *vt.* -tised′, -tis′ing [see ADVERT] to describe or praise publicly, usually to promote for sale —*vi.* 1. to call public attention to things for sale 2. to ask (*for*) by public notice Also **advertize** —**ad′ver·tis′er** *n.* —**ad′ver·tis′ing** *n.*

ad·ver·tise·ment (ad′vər tīz′mənt, əd vur′tiz-) *n.* a public notice, usually paid for: also **advertizement**

ad·vice (əd vīs′) *n.* [< L. *ad-*, at + *videre*, to look] opinion given as to what to do; counsel

ad·vis·a·ble (əd vī′zə b′l) *adj.* proper to be advised; wise; sensible — **ad·vis′a·bil′i·ty** *n.*

ad·vise (əd vīz′) *vt.* -vised′, -vis′ing 1. to give advice to; counsel 2. to offer as advice 3. to inform —**ad·vis′er, ad·vi′sor** *n.*

ad·vis′ed·ly (-id lē) *adv.* deliberately

ad·vise·ment *n.* careful consideration —**take under advisement** to consider carefully

ad·vi·so·ry (əd vī′zər ē) *adj.* advising or empowered to advise —*n., pl.* -ries a report, esp. about weather conditions

ad·vo·cate (ad′və kit, -kāt′; *for v.* -kāt′) *n.* [< L. *ad-*, to + *vocare*, to call] one who pleads another's cause or in support of something —*vt.* -cat′ed, -cat′ing to speak or write in support of —**ad′vo·ca·cy** (-kə sē) *n.*

advt. *pl.* **advts.** advertisement

adz, adze (adz) *n.* [OE. *adesa*] an axlike tool for dressing wood, etc.

AEC, A.E.C. Atomic Energy Commission

Ae·ge·an (Sea) (ē jē′ən) sea between Greece and Turkey

ae·gis (ē′jis) *n.* [< Gr. *aigis*, shield of Zeus] 1. protection 2. sponsorship

Ae·ne·as (i nē′əs) *Gr. & Rom. Myth.* a Trojan whose adventures are told in a poem (**the Aeneid**) by Virgil

ae·on (ē′ən, ē′än) *n. same as* EON

aer·ate (er′āt′, ā′ər-) *vt.* -at′ed, -at′ing [AER(O)- + -ATE¹] 1. to expose to air 2. to charge (liquid) with gas, as to make soda water —**aer·a′tion** *n.* —**aer′a′tor** *n.*

aer·i·al (er′ē əl, ā ir′ē-) *adj.* [< Gr. *āēr*, air + -AL] 1. of, in, or by air 2. unreal; imaginary 3. of aircraft or flying —*n.* a radio or TV antenna

aer·i·al·ist (er′ē əl ist) *n.* an acrobat on a trapeze, high wire, etc.

aer·ie (er′ē, ir′ē) *n.* [prob. < L. *ager*, field] the high nest of an eagle or other bird of prey: also **aery**

aero- [< Gr. *āēr*, air] *a combining form meaning:* 1. air; of the air 2. of aircraft 2. of gases

aer·o·bat·ics (er′ə bat′iks) *n.pl.* [prec. + (ACRO)BATICS] stunts done while flying an aircraft

aer·o·bic (er ō′bik) *adj.* [< Gr. *āēr*, air + *bios*, life] 1. able to live or grow only where free oxygen is present 2. of exercise, as running, that conditions the heart and lungs by increasing efficient intake of oxygen by the body —*n., pl.* aerobic exercises

aer·o·dy·nam·ics (er′ō dī nam′iks) *n.pl.* [*with sing. v.*] the branch of mechanics dealing with forces exerted by air or other gases in motion —**aer′o·dy·nam′ic** *adj.*

aer·o·nau·tics (-ə nôt′iks) *n.pl.* [*with sing. v.*] the science of making and flying aircraft —**aer′o·nau′ti·cal** *adj.*

aer·o·plane (-plān′) *n. Brit. var. of* AIRPLANE

aer·o·sol (-sôl′, -säl′) *n.* [AERO- + SOL(UTION)] a suspension of insoluble particles in a gas —*adj.* of a container in which gas under pressure dispenses liquid in a spray or foam

aer·o·space (-ō spās′) *n.* the earth's atmosphere and the space outside it —*adj.* of missiles, etc. for flight in aerospace

Aes·chy·lus (es′kə ləs) 525?-456 B.C.; Gr. writer of tragedies

Ae·sop (ē′säp, ēs′əp) Gr. fable writer: supposedly lived 6th cent. B.C.

aes·thete (es′thēt′) *n.* [Gr. *aisthētēs*, one who perceives] a person who is or pretends to be highly sensitive to art and beauty

aes·thet·ic (es thet′ik) *adj.* 1. of aesthetics 2. of beauty 3. sensitive to art and beauty

aes·thet·ics *n.pl.* [*with sing. v.*] the philosophy of art and beauty

a·far (ə fär′) *adv.* [Poet. or Archaic] at or to a distance

af·fa·ble (af′ə b′l) *adj.* [< L. *ad-*, to + *fari*, speak] pleasant; friendly — **af′fa·bil′i·ty** *n.* —**af′fa·bly** *adv.*

af·fair (ə fer′) *n.* [< L. *ad-*, to + *facere*, do] 1. a thing to do 2. [*pl.*] matters of business 3. any matter, event, etc. 4. an amorous episode

af·fect (ə fekt′) *vt.* [< L. *ad-*, to + *facere*, do] 1. to have an effect on; influence 2. to stir the emotions of 3. to like to use, wear, etc. 4. to make a pretense of being, feeling, etc.

af·fec·ta·tion (af′ek tā′shən) *n.* 1. a pretending to like, have, etc. 2. artificial behavior

af·fect′ed *adj.* 1. afflicted 2. influenced 3. emotionally moved 4. assumed or assuming for effect

af·fect′ing *adj.* emotionally moving

af·fec′tion (ə fek′shən) *n.* 1. fond or tender feeling 2. a disease

af·fec′tion·ate (-it) *adj.* tender and loving —**af·fec′tion·ate·ly** *adv.*

af·fer·ent (af′ər ənt) *adj.* [< L. *ad-*, to + *ferre*, to bear] bringing inward to a central part, as nerves

af·fi·ance (ə fī′əns) *vt.* -anced, -anc·ing [< ML. *ad-*, to + *fidare*, to trust] to betroth

af·fi·da·vit (af′ə dā′vit) *n.* [ML., he has made oath] a written statement made on oath

af·fil·i·ate (ə fil′ē āt′; *for n.* -it) *vt.* -at′ed, -at′ing [< ML. *affiliare*, adopt as a son] 1. to take in as a member 2. to associate (oneself *with*) —*vi.* to join —*n.* an affiliated person, club, etc. —**af·fil′i·a′tion** *n.*

af·fin·i·ty (ə fin′ə tē) *n., pl.* -ties [< L. *affinis*, adjacent] 1. relationship by marriage 2. close relationship 3. a likeness implying common origin 4. a natural liking or sympathy

af·firm (ə furm′) *vt.* [< L. *ad-*, to + *firmare*, make firm] 1. to declare positively; assert 2. to confirm; ratify —*vi. Law* to make a formal statement, but not under oath —**af·fir·ma′tion** (af′ər mā′shən) *n.*

af·firm·a·tive (ə fur′mə tiv) *adj.* affirming; answering "yes" —*n.* 1. an expression of assent 2. the side upholding the proposition in a debate

affirmative action a plan to offset past discrimination in employing or educating women, blacks, etc.

af·fix (ə fiks′; *for n.* af′iks) *vt.* [< L. *ad-*, to + *figere*, fasten] 1. to fasten; attach 2. to add at the end —*n.* 1. a thing affixed 2. a prefix or suffix

af·fla·tus (ə flāt′əs) *n.* [< L. *ad-*, to + *flare*, to blow] inspiration

af·flict (ə flikt′) *vt.* [< L. *ad-*, to + *fligere*, to strike] to cause pain or suffering to; distress greatly

af·flic·tion (ə flik′shən) *n.* 1. pain; suffering 2. any cause of suffering

af·flu·ence (af′loo wəns) *n.* [< L. *ad-*, to + *fluere*, to flow] 1. great plenty; abundance 2. riches; wealth

af′flu·ent *adj.* 1. plentiful 2. rich; wealthy —**af′flu·ent·ly** *adv.*

af·ford (ə fôrd′) *vt.* [< OE. *geforthian*, to advance] 1. to spare (money, time, etc.) without much inconvenience 2. to give; yield [*it affords* pleasure]

af·for·est (ə fôr′əst) *vt.* [see AD- & FOREST] to turn (land) into forest —**af·for′est·a′tion** (-əs tā′shən) *n.*

af·fray (ə frā′) *n.* [< OFr. *esfraer*, frighten] a noisy brawl

af·front (ə frunt′) *vt.* [< ML. *ad-*, to + *frons*, forehead] to insult openly —*n.* an open insult

Af·ghan (af′gan, -gən) *n.* 1. a native of Afghanistan 2. [a-] a crocheted or knitted wool blanket or shawl

Af·ghan·i·stan (af gan′ə stan′) country in SW Asia, east of Iran: c. 250,000 sq. mi.; pop. 15,352,000

a·fi·cio·na·do (ə fish′ə nä′dō) *n.* [Sp.] a devotee of some sport, art, etc.

a·field (ə fēld′) *adv.* 1. in or to the field 2. away (from home); astray

a·fire (ə fīr′) *adv., adj.* on fire

a·flame (ə flām′) *adv., adj.* 1. in flames 2. glowing

AFL-CIO American Federation of Labor and Congress of Industrial Organizations: merged in 1955

a·float (ə flōt′) *adv.* 1. floating 2. at sea 3. flooded, as a ship's deck

a·flut·ter (ə flut′ər) *adv., adj.* in a flutter

a·foot (ə foot′) *adv.* 1. on foot 2. in motion; in progress

a·fore·men·tioned (ə fôr′men′shənd) *adj.* mentioned before

a·fore′said (-sed′) *adj.* spoken of before

a·fore′thought′ *adj.* thought out beforehand; premeditated

a·foul (ə foul′) *adv., adj.* in a collision or tangle —**run** (*or* **fall**) **afoul of** to get into trouble with

a·fraid (ə frād′) *adj.* [see AFFRAY] frightened (*of, that,* or *to*): often merely indicating regret ['m *afraid* I must]

Af·ri·ca (af′ri kə) second largest continent, south of Europe: c. 11,500,000 sq. mi.; pop. c. 310,000,000 —**Af′ri·can** *adj., n.*

African violet a tropical African plant with violet, white, or pinkish flowers and hairy, fleshy leaves, often grown as a house plant

Af·ri·kaans (af′ri känz′) *n.* [Afrik. < *Afrika*, Africa] an official language of South Africa, based on Dutch

Af·ro (af′rō) *adj.* [< ff.] designating or of a full, bouffant hair style, as worn by some blacks —*n.* an Afro hair style

Afro- [< L. *Afer*, an African] a combining form meaning: 1. Africa 2. African

Af·ro-A·mer·i·can (af′rō ə mer′ə kən) *adj.* of Negro Americans, their culture, etc. —*n.* a Negro American

aft (aft) *adv.* [OE. *æftan*] at, near, or toward the stern of a ship or rear of an aircraft

af·ter (af′tər) *adv.* [OE. *æfter*] 1. behind 2. later —*prep.* 1. behind 2. later than 3. in search of 4. as a result of 5. in spite of [*after* all I've said, he's still going] 6. lower in rank or order than 7. in imitation of 8. for [named *after* Lincoln] —*conj.* following the time when —*adj.* 1. next; later 2. nearer the rear

af′ter·birth′ *n.* the placenta and membranes expelled after childbirth

af′ter·burn′er (-bur′nər) *n.* a device attached to some engines for burning or utilizing exhaust gases

af′ter·ef·fect′ *n.* an effect coming later, or as a secondary result

af′ter·life′ *n.* a life after death

af′ter·math′ (-math′) *n.* [< AFTER

+ OE. *mæth*, cutting of grass] a result, esp. an unpleasant one

af·ter·noon′ *n.* the time from noon to evening —*adj.* in the afternoon

af′ter·thought′ *n.* 1. an idea, explanation, part, etc. coming or added later 2. a thought coming too late to be apt

af′ter·ward (-wərd) *adv.* later; subsequently: also **af′ter·wards**

Ag [L. *argentum*] *Chem.* silver

a·gain (ə gen′) *adv.* [< OE. *on-*, up to + *gegn*, direct] 1. back into a former condition 2. once more 3. besides 4. on the other hand —**again and again** often; repeatedly —**as much again** twice as much

a·gainst (ə genst′) *prep.* [see prec.] 1. in opposition to 2. toward so as to strike [thrown *against* the wall] 3. next to 4. in preparation for 5. as a charge on —**over against** 1. opposite to 2. as compared with

Ag·a·mem·non (ag′ə mem′nän) *Gr. Myth.* commander of the Greek army in the Trojan War

a·gape (ə gāp′) *adv., adj.* [A- + GAPE] with the mouth wide open

a·gar-a·gar (ä′gär ä′gär) *n.* [Malay] a gelatinous product made from seaweed, used in bacterial cultures

ag·ate (ag′ət) *n.* [< Gr. *achatēs*] 1. a hard, semiprecious stone with striped or clouded coloring 2. a playing marble made of or like this

a·ga·ve (ə gä′vē) *n.* [< proper name in Gr. myth] a desert plant with thick, fleshy leaves

age (āj) *n.* [< L. *aetas*] 1. the length of time that a person or thing has existed 2. a stage of life 3. old age 4. a historical or geological period 5. [often *pl.*] [Colloq.] a long time —*vi., vt.* **aged, ag′ing** or **age′ing** to grow or make old, ripe, mature, etc. —**of age** having reached the age when one is qualified for full legal rights

-age (ij) [< LL. *-aticum*] a suffix meaning: 1. act, state, or result of [*usage*] 2. amount or number of [*acreage*] 3. place of [*steerage*] 4. cost of [*postage*]

a·ged (ā′jid; *for 2* ājd) *adj.* 1. old 2. of the age of —**the aged** old people

age·ism (āj′iz′m) *n.* [AGE + (RAC)ISM] discrimination against older people

age′less *adj.* 1. seemingly not growing older 2. eternal

a·gen·cy (ā′jən sē) *n., pl.* **-cies** [< L. *agere*, to act] 1. action; power 2. means 3. a firm, etc. empowered to act for another 4. an administrative government division

a·gen·da (ə jen′də) *n., pl.* **-das** [< L. *agere*, to do] a list of things to be dealt with at a meeting, etc.

a·gent (ā′jənt) *n.* [< L. *agere*, to act] 1. an active force or substance producing an effect 2. a person, firm, etc. empowered to act for another 3. a representative of a government agency

Agent Orange [< *orange*-colored containers] *military code name for a* defoliant containing dioxin

age-old (āj′ōld′) *adj.* ancient

ag·er·a·tum (aj′ə rāt′əm) *n.* [< Gr. *agēratos*, not growing old] a plant

of the composite family having small, thick heads of bluish flowers

ag·glom·er·ate (ə gläm′ə rāt′; *for adj. & n.* -ər it) *vt., vi.* **-at′ed, -at′ing** [< L. *ad-*, to + *glomerare*, form into a ball] to gather into a mass or ball —*adj.* gathered into a mass or ball —*n.* a jumbled heap, mass, etc.

ag·glu·ti·nate (ə glōōt′'n it; *for v.* -āt′) *adj.* [< L. *ad-*, to + *gluten*, glue] stuck together —*vt., vi.* **-nat′ed, -nat′ing** to stick together, as with glue —**ag·glu′ti·na′tion** *n.*

ag·gran·dize (ə gran′dīz′, ag′rən-) *vt.* **-dized′, -diz′ing** [< Fr. *a-*, to + *grandir*, to increase] to make greater, more powerful, richer, etc. —**ag·gran′dize·ment** (-diz mənt) *n.*

ag·gra·vate (ag′rə vāt′) *vt.* **-vat′ed, -vat′ing** [< L. *ad-*, to + *gravis*, heavy] 1. to make worse 2. [Colloq.] to annoy; vex —**ag′gra·va′tion** *n.*

ag′gra·vat′ed *adj. Law* designating a grave form of a specified offense

ag·gre·gate (ag′rə gət; *for v.* -gāt′) *adj.* [< L. *ad-*, to + *grex*, a herd] total —*n.* a mass of distinct things gathered into a total or whole —*vt.* **-gat′ed, -gat′ing** 1. to gather into a mass 2. to total —**ag′gre·ga′tion** *n.*

ag·gres·sion (ə gresh′ən) *n.* [< L. *aggredi*, to attack] 1. an unprovoked attack or warlike act 2. a being aggressive —**ag·gres′sor** *n.*

ag·gres·sive (ə gres′iv) *adj.* 1. boldly hostile; quarrelsome 2. bold and active; enterprising —**ag·gres′sive·ly** *adv.* —**ag·gres′sive·ness** *n.*

ag·grieve (ə grēv′) *vt.* **-grieved′, -griev′ing** [see AGGRAVATE] to cause grief or injury to; offend; slight

a·ghast (ə gast′) *adj.* [< OE. *gast*, ghost] feeling great horror or dismay

ag·ile (aj′'l) *adj.* [< L. *agere*, to act] quick and easy of movement —**ag′ile·ly** *adv.* —**a·gil·i·ty** (ə jil′ə tē) *n.*

ag·i·tate (aj′ə tāt′) *vt.* **-tat′ed, -tat′ing** [< L. *agere*, to act] 1. to stir up or shake up 2. to excite the feelings of —*vi.* to stir up people so as to produce changes —**ag′i·ta′tion** *n.* —**ag′i·ta′tor** *n.*

a·gleam (ə glēm′) *adv., adj.* gleaming

a·glit·ter (ə glit′ər) *adv., adj.* glittering

a·glow (ə glō′) *adv., adj.* in a glow of color or emotion

ag·nos·tic (ag näs′tik) *n.* [< Gr. *a-*, not + base of *gignōskein*, know] one who believes it impossible to know if God exists —*adj.* of an agnostic —**ag·nos′ti·cism** (-tə siz′m) *n.*

a·go (ə gō′) *adj.* [< OE. *agan*, pass away] gone by; past [years *ago*] —*adv.* in the past [long *ago*]

a·gog (ə gäg′) *adv., adj.* [< OFr. *a-* + *gogue*, joke] with eager anticipation or excitement

ag·o·nize (ag′ə nīz′) *vi.* **-nized′, -niz′ing** 1. to struggle 2. to be in agony —*vt.* to torture

ag·o·ny (ag′ə nē) *n., pl.* **-nies** [< Gr. *agōn*, a contest] 1. great mental or physical pain 2. death pangs 3. a strong outburst (*of* emotion)

a·grar·i·an (ə grer′ē ən) *adj.* [< L.

ager, field] **1.** of land or the ownership of land **2.** of agriculture

a·gree (ə grē′) *vi.* **-greed′, -gree′ing** [< L. *ad*, to + *gratus*, pleasing] **1.** to consent (*to*) **2.** to be in accord **3.** to be of the same opinion (*with*) **4.** to arrive at an understanding (*about* prices, etc.) **5.** to be suitable, healthful, etc. (*with*) —*vt.* to grant [I agree that it's true]

a·gree′a·ble *adj.* **1.** pleasing or pleasant **2.** willing to consent **3.** conformable —**a·gree′a·bly** *adv.*

a·gree′ment *n.* **1.** an agreeing **2.** an understanding between people, countries, etc. **3.** a contract

ag·ri·busi·ness (ag′rə biz′nis) *n.* [see ff. & BUSINESS] farming and associated businesses and industries

ag·ri·cul·ture (ag′ri kul′chər) *n.* [< L. *ager*, field + *cultura*, cultivation] the work of producing crops and raising livestock; farming —**ag′ri·cul′tur·al** *adj.* —**ag′ri·cul′tur·al·ly** *adv.* —**ag′ri·cul′tur·ist** *n.*

a·gron·o·my (ə grän′ə mē) *n.* [< Gr. *agros*, field + *nemein*, manage] the science and economics of crop production —**a·gron′o·mist** *n.*

a·ground (ə ground′) *adv., adj.* on or onto the shore, a reef, etc.

a·gue (ā′gyōō) *n.* [< ML. (*febris*) *acuta*, violent (fever)] a fever, usually malarial, marked by chills

ah (ä, ô) *interj.* an exclamation of pain, delight, surprise, etc.

a·ha (ä hä′) *interj.* an exclamation of satisfaction, triumph, etc.

a·head (ə hed′) *adv., adj.* **1.** in or to the front **2.** forward; onward **3.** in advance **4.** winning or profiting —**get ahead** to advance financially, etc.

a·hem (ə hem′) *interj.* a cough, etc. made to gain attention, etc.

a·hoy (ə hoi′) *interj. Naut.* a call used in hailing

aid (ād) *vt., vi.* [< L. *ad-*, to + *juvare*, to help] to help; assist —*n.* **1.** help; assistance **2.** a helper

aide (ād) *n.* [Fr.] **1.** an assistant **2.** an aide-de-camp

aide-de-camp, aid-de-camp (ād′ də kamp′) *n., pl.* **aides-, aids-** [Fr.] a military officer serving as an assistant to a superior

AIDS (ādz) *n.* [A(cquired) I(mmune) D(eficiency) S(yndrome)] a condition of deficiency in certain leukocytes, leading to cancer, pneumonia, etc.

ai·grette, ai·gret (ā′gret, ā gret′) *n.* [see EGRET] the long, white, showy plumes of the egret

ail (āl) *vt.* [OE. *eglian*, to trouble] to cause pain and trouble to —*vi.* to be in poor health

ai·le·ron (ā′lə rän′) *n.* [Fr. < L. *ala*, wing] a hinged section at the trailing edge of an airplane wing, used to control its rolling

ail·ment (āl′mənt) *n.* a mild illness

aim (ām) *vi., vt.* [< L. *ad-*, to + *aestimare*, to estimate] **1.** to direct (a

weapon, blow, etc.) so as to hit **2.** to direct (one's efforts) **3.** to intend —*vi.* **1.** an aiming **2.** the direction of a missile, blow, etc. **3.** intention —take aim to aim a weapon, etc.

aim′less *adj.* having no purpose — **aim′less·ly** *adv.* —**aim′less·ness** *n.*

ain′t (ānt) [< *amn't*, contr. of *am not*] [Colloq.] am not: also a dialectal or substandard contraction for *is not, are not, has not,* and *have not*

ai·o·li, ai·o·li (ī ō′lē) *n.* [ult. < L. *allium,* garlic + *oleum,* OIL] a sauce like mayonnaise, containing crushed raw garlic

air (er) *n.* [< Gr. *aēr*] **1.** the invisible mixture of gases surrounding the earth **2.** a breeze; wind **3.** an outward appearance [*air* of dignity] **4.** [*pl.*] affected superior manners **5.** public expression **6.** a tune —*adj.* of aviation —*vt.* **1.** to let air into **2.** to publicize —**in the air** prevalent —**on** (or **off**) **the air** that is (or is not) broadcasting —**up in the air 1.** not settled **2.** [Colloq.] angry, excited, etc.

air bag a bag that inflates automatically inside an automobile in a collision, to protect riders from being thrown forward

air base a base for military aircraft

air′borne′ *adj.* **1.** carried by or through the air **2.** aloft or flying

air brake a brake operated by the action of compressed air on a piston

air′brush′ *n.* an atomizer worked by compressed air and used for spraying on paint, etc.: also **air brush**

air′bus′ *n.* an extremely large passenger airplane, esp. for short trips

air conditioning regulation of air humidity and temperature in buildings, etc. —**air′-con·di′tion** *vt.* —**air′-con·di′tion·er** *n.*

air′-cooled′ *adj.* cooled by having air passed over, into, or through it

air′craft′ *n., pl.* **-craft′** any machine for traveling through air

aircraft carrier a warship with a large flat deck, for carrying aircraft

air curtain (or **door**) a downward forced air current at an open entrance

air′drop′ *n.* the parachuting of supplies or troops from an aircraft in flight —**air′drop′** *vt.*

Aire·dale (er′dāl′) *n.* [< *Airedale*, valley in England] a large terrier with a wiry coat

air′field′ *n.* a field where aircraft can take off and land

air′foil′ *n.* a wing, rudder, etc. of an aircraft

air force the aviation branch of a country's armed forces

AIREDALE

air gun a gun or gunlike device operated by compressed air

air′head′ *n.* [Slang] a stupid or silly person

air lane a route for travel by air; airway

air′lift′ n. a system of transporting troops, supplies, etc. by aircraft —vt. to transport by airlift

air′line′ n. a system or company for transportation by aircraft —adj. of or on an airline

air′lin′er n. a large passenger aircraft operated by an airline

air lock an airtight compartment, with adjustable air pressure, between places of unequal air pressure

air′mail′ n. mail transported by aircraft —vt. to send by airmail

air′man (-mən) n., pl. -men 1. an aviator 2. an enlisted person in the U.S. Air Force

air mass a large body of air keeping uniform temperature as it moves

air′plane′ n. a motor-driven or jet-propelled aircraft kept aloft by the forces of air upon its wings

air′play′ n. the playing of a recording over radio or TV

air′port′ n. a place where aircraft can land and take off, usually with facilities for repair, etc.

air power total capacity of a nation for air war

air pressure the pressure of the atmosphere or of compressed air

air raid an attack by aircraft, esp. bombers

air rifle a rifle operated by compressed air

air′ship′ n. a self-propelled, steerable aircraft that is lighter than air

air′sick′ adj. nauseated because of air travel —**air′sick′ness** n.

air′space′ n. the space above a nation over which it maintains jurisdiction

air′strip′ n. a temporary airfield

air′tight′ adj. 1. too tight for air or gas to enter or escape 2. invulnerable [an airtight alibi]

air′waves′ n.pl. the medium through which radio signals are transmitted

air′way′ n. 1. same as AIR LANE 2. [pl.] airwaves

air′y adj. -i·er, -i·est 1. of air 2. open to the air; breezy 3. unsubstantial as air 4. light as air; graceful 5. lighthearted; gay 6. flippant 7. [Colloq.] putting on airs —**air′i·ly** adv. —**air′i·ness** n.

aisle (īl) n. [< L. ala, wing] a passageway, as between rows of seats

a·jar (ə jär′) adv., adj. [OE. cier, a turn] slightly open, as a door

AK Alaska

a·kim·bo (ə kim′bō) adv., adj. [< ON. keng, bent + bogi, a bow] with hands on hips and elbows bent outward [with arms akimbo]

a·kin (ə kin′) adj. 1. of one kin; related 2. similar

Ak·ron (ak′rən) city in N Ohio: pop. 237,000

-al (əl, 'l) [< L.] a suffix meaning: 1. of, like, or suitable

ARMS AKIMBO

for [comical] 2. the act or process of [avowal]

Al Chem. aluminum

à la, a la (ä′lə, lä) [Fr.] 1. in the style of 2. according to

Al·a·bam·a (al′ə bam′ə) Southern State of SE U.S.: 51,609 sq. mi.; pop. 3,890,000; cap. Montgomery: abbrev. **Ala., AL** —**Al′a·bam′i·an** (-ē ən) adj., n.

al·a·bas·ter (al′ə bas′tər) n. [< Gr. alabastros, perfume vase] a translucent, whitish variety of gypsum: used for statues, etc.

à la carte (ä′ lə kärt′) [Fr.] with a separate price for each item on the menu

a·lac·ri·ty (ə lak′rə tē) n. [< L. alacer, lively] eager willingness, often with quick, lively action

A·lad·din (ə lad′'n) a boy in The Arabian Nights who found a magic lamp

à la king (ä′ lə kiŋ′) in a sauce containing mushrooms, pimentos, etc.

Al·a·mo (al′ə mō′) Franciscan mission at San Antonio, Tex.: scene of a massacre of Texans by Mexican troops (1836)

a la mode (al′ə mōd′) [< Fr.] 1. in fashion 2. served in a certain style, as pie with ice cream Also **à la mode**

a·lar (ā′lər) adj. [< L. ala, wing] 1. of a wing 2. having wings

a·larm (ə lärm′) n. [< It. all'arme, to arms] 1. [Archaic] a sudden call to arms 2. a warning of danger 3. a mechanism that warns of danger, arouses from sleep, etc. 4. fear caused by danger —vt. 1. to warn of danger 2. to frighten

a·larm′ing adj. frightening

a·larm′ist n. 1. one who spreads alarming rumors 2. one who anticipates the worst —adj. of an alarmist

a·las (ə las′) interj. an exclamation of sorrow, pity, etc.

A·las·ka (ə las′kə) State of the U.S. in NW N.America: 586,400 sq. mi.; pop. 400,000; cap. Juneau: abbrev. **Alas., Ak.** —**A·las′kan** adj., n.

alb (alb) n. [< L. albus, white] a white robe worn by a priest at Mass

al·ba·core (al′bə kôr′) n. [< Ar. al, the + bukr, young camel] any of various saltwater fishes of the mackerel family, as the tuna

Al·ba·ni·a (al bā′nē ə) country in the W Balkans: 11,099 sq. mi.; pop. 1,865,000 —**Al·ba′ni·an** adj., n.

Al·ba·ny (ôl′bə nē) capital of N.Y., on the Hudson: pop. 102,000

al·ba·tross (al′bə trôs′) n. [< Sp. < Ar. al qādūs, water container] a large, web-footed sea bird related to the petrel

ALBATROSS

al·be·it (ôl bē′it) conj. [ME. al be it, al(though) it be] although

Al·ber·ta (al bur′tə) province of SW Canada: 255,285 sq. mi.; pop. 1,463,000; cap. Edmonton

al·bi·no (al bī′nō) *n.*, *pl.* **-nos** [< L. *albus*, white] a person, animal, or plant lacking normal coloration: human albinos have white skin, whitish hair, and pink eyes

al·bum (al′bəm) *n.* [< L. *albus*, white] **1.** a book with blank pages for mounting pictures, stamps, etc. **2.** a booklike holder containing phonograph records **3.** a single long-playing record or tape recording

al·bu·men (al byōō′mən) *n.* [L. < *albus*, white] **1.** the white of an egg **2.** protein in germinating cells **3.** *same as* ALBUMIN

al·bu·min (-mən) *n.* [see prec.] a water-soluble protein found in egg, milk, blood, vegetable tissues, etc. —**al·bu′mi·nous** *adj.*

Al·bu·quer·que (al′bə kur′kē) city in C N.Mex.: pop. 332,000

al·che·my (al′kə mē) *n.* [< Ar. < ? Gr. *cheein*, to pour] the chemistry of the Middle Ages, the chief aim of which was to change the baser elements into gold —**al′che·mist** *n.*

al·co·hol (al′kə hôl′) *n.* [< Ar. *al kuhl*, powder of antimony] **1.** a colorless, volatile, pungent liquid, used in various forms as a fuel, an intoxicating ingredient in fermented liquors, etc. **2.** any such intoxicating liquor

al′co·hol′ic *adj.* **1.** of alcohol **2.** suffering from alcoholism —*n.* one who has chronic alcoholism

al′co·hol′ism *n.* the habitual excessive drinking of alcoholic liquor, or a resulting diseased condition

al·cove (al′kōv) *n.* [< Ar. *al*, the + *qubba*, an arch] a recessed section of a room, as a breakfast nook

al·de·hyde (al′də hīd′) *n.* [< ALCOHOL + L. *de*, without + HYDROGEN] a colorless fluid oxidized from alcohol

al·der (ôl′dər) *n.* [OE. *alor*] a small tree or shrub of the birch family

al·der·man (ôl′dər mən) *n.*, *pl.* **-men** [< OE. *eald*, old + *man*] in some cities, a municipal officer representing a certain district or ward

ale (āl) *n.* [OE. *ealu*] a fermented drink made from malt and hops, similar to beer

a·le·a·to·ry (ā′lē ə tôr′ē) *adj.* [< L. *aleatorius*, of gambling < *alea*, chance] depending on chance or luck: also **a′le·a·tor′ic** *adj.*

a·lem·bic (ə lem′bik) *n.* [< Ar. *al anbīq*, the still < Gr. *ambix*, a cup] **1.** an apparatus formerly used for distilling **2.** anything that purifies

a·lert (ə lurt′) *adj.* [< L. *erigere*, to erect] **1.** watchful; vigilantly ready **2.** active; nimble —*n.* **1.** a warning signal; alarm —*vt.* to warn, as to be ready —**on the alert** vigilant —**a·lert′ly** *adv.* —**a·lert′ness** *n.*

A·leu·tian Islands (ə lōō′shən) chain of U.S. islands off the SW tip of Alaska —**A·leu′tian** *adj.*, *n.*

ale·wife (āl′wīf′) *n.*, *pl.* **-wives′** [< ?] a N.American fish resembling the herring, used for food and in fertilizers

Al·ex·an·der the Great (al′ig zan′dər) 356-323 B.C.; military conqueror; king of Macedonia (336-323)

Al′ex·an′dri·a (-drē ə) seaport in N Egypt: pop. 1,513,000

al·fal·fa (al fal′fə) *n.* [Sp. < Ar. *al-fasfaṣah*, the best fodder] a plant of the pea family, used for fodder, pasture, and as a cover crop

Al·fred the Great (al′frid) 849-900? A.D.; king of England (871-900?)

al·fres·co (al fres′kō) *adv.* [It. < *al*, in the + *fresco*, cool] outdoors —*adj.* outdoor Also **al fresco**

al·gae (al′jē) *n.pl.*, *sing.* **al′ga** (-gə) [pl. of L. *alga*, seaweed] a group of primitive plants, one-celled or many-celled, containing chlorophyll and found in water or damp places

al·ge·bra (al′jə brə) *n.* [< Ar. *al*, the + *jabara*, to reunite] a mathematical system used to generalize certain arithmetical operations by using letters or other symbols to stand for numbers —**al′ge·bra′ic** (-brā′ik) *adj.* —**al′ge·bra′ic·al·ly** *adv.*

Al·ge·ri·a (al jir′ē ə) country in N Africa: c.919,000 sq. mi.; pop. 11,290,000 —**Al·ge′ri·an** *adj.*, *n.*

-al·gia (al′jə) [< Gr. *algos*] a suffix meaning pain [*neuralgia*]

Al·giers (al jirz′) seaport and capital of Algeria: pop. 884,000

Al·gon·qui·an (al gän′kē ən, -kwē-) *adj.* designating or of a widespread family of N.American Indian languages —*n.* this family of languages

al·go·rithm (al′gə ri th′m) *n.* [ult. < Ar.] any special way of solving a certain kind of mathematical problem

a·li·as (ā′lē əs) *n.*, *pl.* **-as·es** [L. < *alius*, other] an assumed name —*adv.* otherwise named [Bell *alias* Jones]

A·li Ba·ba (ä′lē bä′bə, al′ē bab′ə) in *The Arabian Nights*, a poor man who finds the treasure of forty thieves

al·i·bi (al′ə bī′) *n.*, *pl.* **-bis′** [L. < *alius ibi*, elsewhere] **1.** *Law* the plea that the accused person was elsewhere than at the scene of the crime **2.** [Colloq.] any excuse —*vi.* **-bied′**, **-bi′ing** [Colloq.] to offer an excuse

al·ien (āl′yən, -ē ən) *adj.* [< L. *alius*, other] **1.** foreign; strange **2.** of aliens —*n.* **1.** a foreigner **2.** a foreign-born resident who is not naturalized **3.** a hypothetical being from outer space

al′ien·a·ble (-ə b′l) *adj.* capable of being transferred to a new owner

al′ien·ate (-āt′) *vt.* **-at′ed**, **-at′ing** **1.** to transfer the ownership of (property) to another **2.** to make unfriendly or withdrawn **3.** to cause a transference of (affection) —**al′ien·a′tion** *n.*

a·light¹ (ə līt′) *vi.* **a·light′ed** or **a·lit′**, **a·light′ing** [ME. *alihtan*] **1.** to get down or off; dismount **2.** to come down after flight

a·light² (ə līt′) *adj.* lighted up; burning

a·lign (ə līn′) *vt.* [< Fr. *a*, to + *ligne*, LINE¹] **1.** to bring into a straight line

2. to bring (components or working parts) into adjustment 3. to bring into agreement, etc. —*vi.* to line up —a·lign′ment *n.*

a·like (ə līk′) *adj.* [OE. *gelic*] like one another —*adv.* 1. similarly 2. equally

al·i·ment (al′ə mənt) *n.* [< L. *alere*, nourish] nourishment; food

al′i·men·ta·ry (-men′tər ē) *adj.* 1. of food or nutrition 2. nourishing

alimentary canal (or tract) the passage in the body (from the mouth to the anus) that food goes through

al·i·mo·ny (al′ə mō′nē) *n.* [< L. *alere*, nourish] money a judge orders paid to a woman by her legally separated or divorced husband

a·line (ə līn′) *vt., vi.* a·lined′, a·lin′ing *same as* ALIGN —a·line′ment *n.*

a·lit (ə lit′) *alt. pt. & pp.* of ALIGHT¹

a·live (ə līv′) *adj.* [< OE. *on*, in + *life*, life] 1. having life; living 2. in existence, operation, etc. 3. lively; alert —alive to aware of —alive with teeming with

a·li·yah, a·li·ya (ä′lē yä′) *n.* [< Heb., lit., ascent] immigration by Jews to Israel

al·ka·li (al′kə lī′) *n., pl.* -lies′, -lis′ [< Ar. *al-qili*, the ashes of a certain plant] 1. any base, as soda, that is soluble in water and gives off ions in solution 2. any mineral salt that can neutralize acids

al′ka·line (-lin, -līn′) *adj.* of, like an alkali —al′ka·lin′i·ty (-lin′ə tē) *n.*

al′ka·lize′ (-līz′) *vt., vi.* -lized′, -liz′ing to make alkaline Also al′ka·lin·ize′ (-lə nīz′), -ized′, -iz′ing —al′ka·li·za′tion *n.*

al′ka·loid′ (-loid′) *n.* a bitter, alkaline organic substance, such as caffeine, morphine, etc., containing nitrogen

al·kyd (al′kid) *n.* [< ALKALI & ACID] a synthetic resin used in paints, varnishes, etc.: also alkyd resin

all (ôl) *adj.* [OE. *eall*] 1. the whole quantity of [*all* the gold] 2. every one of [*all* men] 3. the greatest possible [in *all* sincerity] 4. any [beyond *all* doubt] 5. alone; only [*all* work and no play] —*pron.* 1. [*with pl. v.*] everyone [*all* are going] 2. everything 3. every part or bit —*n.* 1. everything one has [give your *all*] 2. a totality; whole —*adv.* 1. wholly; entirely [*all* worn out] 2. apiece [a score of two *all*] —after all nevertheless —all in [Colloq.] very tired —all in all 1. considering everything 2. as a whole —all the (better, worse, etc.) so much the (better, worse, etc.) —all the same 1. nevertheless 2. unimportant —at all 1. in the least 2. in any way 3. under any considerations —in all altogether

all- *a prefix meaning:* 1. entirely [*all*-American] 2. for every [*all*-purpose] 3. of everything [*all*-inclusive]

Al·lah (al′ə, ä′lə) *n.* [< Ar. *al*, the + *ilāh*, god] *the Moslem name for God*

all′-A·mer′i·can *adj.* chosen as the best in the U.S. —*n.* 1. an imaginary football team, made up of U.S. college players voted best of the year 2. a player on such a team

all′-a·round′ *adj.* having many abilities, talents, or uses; versatile

al·lay (ə lā′) *vt.* -layed′, -lay′ing [< OE. *a-*, down + *lecgan*, lay] 1. to calm; quiet 2. to relieve (pain, etc.)

all′-clear′ *n.* a siren or other signal that an air raid or alert is over

al·le·ga·tion (al′ə gā′shən) *n.* an assertion, esp. one without proof or to be proved

al·lege (ə lej′) *vt.* -leged′, -leg′ing [< L. *ex-*, out of + *litigare*, to dispute] 1. to declare or assert, esp. without proof 2. to offer as an excuse

al·leged (ə lejd′, ə lej′id) *adj.* 1. declared, but without proof 2. not actual; so-called —al·leg′ed·ly *adv.*

Al·le·ghe·ny Mountains (al′ə gā′nē) mountain range in C Pa., Md., W.Va., and Va.: also Alleghenies

al·le·giance (ə lē′jəns) *n.* [< OFr. *liege*, liege] 1. the duty of being loyal to one's ruler, country, etc. 2. loyalty; devotion, as to a cause

al·le·go·ry (al′ə gôr′ē) *n., pl.* -ries [< Gr. *allos*, other + *agoreuein*, speak in assembly] a story in which people, things, and events have a symbolic meaning, often instructive, as in a fable —al′le·gor′i·cal *adj.* —al′le·gor′i·cal·ly *adv.* —al′le·go′rist *n.*

al·le·gret·to (al′ə gret′ō) *adj., adv.* [It., dim. of *allegro*] *Music* moderately fast

al·le·gro (ə leg′rō, -lā′grō) *adj., adv.* [It.] *Music* fast

al·le·lu·ia (al′ə loo′yə) *interj., n.* [L.] *same as* HALLELUJAH

Al·len·town (al′ən toun′) city in E Pa.: pop. 104,000

al·ler·gen (al′ər jən) *n.* [G.] a substance inducing an allergic reaction —al′ler·gen′ic (-jen′ik) *adj.*

al·ler·gic (ə lur′jik) *adj.* 1. of, caused by, or having an allergy 2. averse (*to*)

al·ler·gist (al′ər jist) *n.* a doctor who specializes in treating allergies

al·ler·gy (al′ər jē) *n., pl.* -gies [G. < Gr. *allos*, other + *ergon*, work] 1. a hypersensitivity to a specific substance (as a food, pollen, dust, etc.) or condition (as heat or cold) 2. an aversion

al·le·vi·ate (ə lē′vē āt′) *vt.* -at′ed -at′ing [< L. *ad-*, to + *levis*, light] 1. to lessen or relieve (pain, etc.) 2. to decrease (poverty, etc.) —al·le′vi·a′tion *n.*

al·ley (al′ē) *n., pl.* -leys [< OFr. *aler*, go] 1. a narrow street between or behind buildings 2. a bowling lane

alley cat a homeless, mongrel cat

al′ley·way′ *n.* an alley between buildings

all-fired (ôl′fīrd′) *adv.* [< *hell-fired*] [Slang] completely; extremely

al·li·ance (ə lī′əns) *n.* [see ALLY] 1. an allying or close association, as of nations for a common objective, families by marriage, etc. 2. an agreement for this 3. the countries, groups, etc. in such association

al·lied (ə līd′, al′īd) *adj.* 1. united by kinship, treaty, etc. 2. closely related

al·li·ga·tor (al′ə gāt′ər) *n.* [< Sp.

< L. *lacertus*] a large reptile of the U.S., similar to the crocodile but having a short, blunt snout

alligator pear *same as* AVOCADO

all'-im·por'tant *adj.* highly important; necessary; essential

all'-in·clu'sive *adj.* including everything; comprehensive

al·lit·er·a·tion (ə lit'ə rā'shən) *n.* [< L. *ad-*, to + *littera*, letter] repetition of an initial sound in two or more words of a phrase —**al·lit'er·a'·tive** *adj.*

al·lo·cate (al'ə kāt') *vt.* -cat'ed, -cat'ing [< L. *ad-*, to + *locus*, a place] 1. to set apart for a specific purpose 2. to distribute or allot —**al'lo·ca'tion** *n.*

al·lot (ə lät') *vt.* -lot'ted, -lot'ting [< OFr. *a-*, to + *lot*, lot] 1. to distribute in arbitrary shares; apportion 2. to assign as one's share —**al·lot'ment** *n.*

all'-out' *adj.* complete or wholehearted [an *all-out* effort]

all'o'ver *adj.* over the whole surface

al·low (ə lou') *vt.* [< L. *ad-*, to + *locus*, place] 1. to permit; let [I'm not *allowed* to go] 2. to let have [she *allowed* herself no sweets] 3. to acknowledge as valid 4. to provide (a certain amount), as for shrinkage, waste, etc. —**allow for** to leave room, time, etc. for —**al·low'a·ble** *adj.*

al·low'ance (-əns) *n.* 1. an allowing 2. something allowed 3. an amount of money, food, etc. given regularly to a child, soldier, etc. 4. a reduction in price, as for a trade-in —**make allowance(s) for** to excuse because of mitigating factors

al·loy (al'oi; *also, and for v. usually,* ə loi') *n.* [< L. *ad-*, to + *ligare*, to bind] 1. a substance that is the mixture of two or more metals 2. something that debases another thing when mixed with it —*vt.* to make into an alloy

all'-pur'pose *adj.* useful in many ways

all right 1. satisfactory 2. unhurt 3. correct 4. yes; very well

all'-round' *adj. same as* ALL-AROUND

all'spice (ôl'spīs') *n.* a spice, combining the tastes of several spices, made from the berry of a West Indian tree of the myrtle family

all'-star' *adj.* made up entirely of outstanding or star performers

all'-time' *adj.* unsurpassed until now

al·lude (ə lood') *vi.* -lud'ed, -lud'ing [< L. *ad-*, to + *ludere*, to play] to refer indirectly (to)

al·lure (ə loor') *vt., vi.* -lured', -lur'ing [< OFr. *a-*, to + *lurer*, to lure] to tempt with something desirable; attract —*n.* fascination; charm —**al·lure'ment** *n.* —**al·lur'ing** *adj.*

al·lu·sion (ə loo'zhən) *n.* 1. an alluding 2. indirect or casual reference

al·lu·sive (ə loo'siv) *adj.* 1. containing an allusion 2. full of allusions —**al·lu'sive·ly** *adv.* —**al·lu'sive·ness** *n.*

al·lu·vi·um (ə loo'vē əm) *n., pl.* -vi·ums, -vi·a (-vē ə) [< L. *ad-*, to + *luere*, wash] sand, clay, etc. deposited by moving water —**al·lu'vi·al** *adj.*

al·ly (ə lī'; *also, and for n. usually,* al'ī) *vt., vi.* -lied', -ly'ing [< L. *ad-*, to + *ligare*, to bind] 1. to unite or join for a specific purpose 2. to relate by similarity of structure, etc. —*n., pl.* -lies a country or person joined with another for a common purpose

al·ma ma·ter (al'ma mät'ər, mät'-) [L., fostering mother] 1. the college or school that one attended 2. its anthem

al·ma·nac (ôl'mə nak', al-) *n.* [< LGr. *almenichiaka*, calendar] a calendar with astronomical data, weather forecasts, etc.

al·might·y (ôl mīt'ē) *adj.* all-powerful —**the Almighty** God

al·mond (ä'mənd, am'ənd) *n.* [< Gr. *amygdalē*] 1. the edible, nutlike kernel of a peachlike fruit 2. the tree that it grows on —*adj.* shaped like an almond; oval and pointed at one or both ends

al·most (ôl'mōst, ôl'mōst') *adv.* very nearly; all but

alms (ämz) *n., pl.* **alms** [< Gr. *eleos*, pity] money, food, etc. given to poor people —**alms'giv'er** *n.*

alms'house' *n.* 1. formerly, a poorhouse 2. [Brit.] a privately endowed home for the poor

al·oe (al'ō) *n., pl.* -oes [< Gr. *aloē*] 1. a South African plant of the lily family 2. [*pl., with sing. v.*] a laxative drug made from the juice of certain aloe leaves

a·loft (ə lôft') *adv.* [ME. < *o*, on + *loft*, loft] 1. high up 2. in the air; flying 3. high above the deck of a ship

a·lo·ha (ä lō'ə, ä lō'hä) *n., interj.* [Haw., love] a word used as a greeting or farewell

a·lone (ə lōn') *adj., adv.* [ME. < *al*, all + *one*, one] 1. apart from anything or anyone else 2. without any other person 3. only 4. without equal —**let alone** 1. to refrain from interfering with 2. not to speak of [we hadn't a dime, *let alone* a dollar]

a·long (ə lôŋ') *prep.* [< OE. *and-*, over against + *lang*, long] 1. on or beside the length of 2. in conformity with —*adv.* 1. lengthwise 2. progressively onward or advanced 3. together (*with*) 4. with one [take me *along*] —**all along** from the beginning —**be along** [Colloq.] to come or arrive —**get along** 1. to advance 2. to contrive 3. to succeed 4. to agree

a·long'shore' *adv.* near or beside the shore

a·long'side' *adv.* at or by the side; side by side —*prep.* beside —**alongside of** at the side of

a·loof (ə loof') *adv.* [< a-, on & Du. *loef*, to windward] at a distance but in view —*adj.* cool and reserved [an *aloof* manner] —**a·loof'ness** *n.*

a·loud (ə loud') *adv.* 1. loudly 2. with the normal voice

---

fat, āpe, cär; ten, ēven; is, bīte; gō, hôrn, tōōl, look; oil, out; up, fur; chin, she; thin, then; zh, leisure; ŋ, ring; ə for a in ago; ', (ā'b'l); ē. Fr. coeur; ö, Fr. feu; Fr. mon; ü, Fr. duc; kh, G. ich, doch; ‡ foreign; < derived from

alp (alp) *n.* [< *Alps*] a high mountain

al·pac·a (al pak'ə) *n.* [Sp. < S.AmInd. *allpaca*] **1.** a S.American mammal, related to the llama **2.** its fleecy wool, or cloth woven from it

ALPACA

al·pha (al'fə) *n.* the first letter of the Greek alphabet (A, α)

al'pha·bet' (-bet') *n.* [< Gr. *alpha* + *beta*] the letters used in writing a language, esp. as arranged in their usual order —**al'pha·bet'i·cal** *adj.* —**al'pha·bet'i·cal·ly** *adv.*

al·pha·bet·ize (al'fə bə tīz') *vt.* **-ized'**, **-iz'ing** to arrange in the usual order of the alphabet —**al'pha·bet·i·za'tion** (-bet'i zā'shən) *n.*

al'pha·nu·mer'ic (-noo mer'ik) *adj.* having both alphabetical and numerical symbols

alpha particle a positively charged particle given off by certain radioactive substances

alpha rays rays of alpha particles

Al·pine (al'pīn) *adj.* **1.** of the Alps **2.** [a-] or like high mountains

Alps (alps) mountain system in SC Europe

al·read·y (ôl red'ē) *adv.* **1.** by or before the given or implied time **2.** even now or even then

al·right (ôl rīt') *adv.* all right: a disputed spelling

Al·sace (al säs', al'sas) region and former province of NE France —**Al·sa'tian** (-sā'shən) *adj.*, *n.*

al·so (ôl'sō) *adv.* [< OE. *eal*, all + *swa*, so] likewise; too; in addition

al'so·ran' *n.* [Colloq.] a defeated contestant in a race, election, etc.

alt. 1. alternate **2.** altitude **3.** alto

al·tar (ôl'tər) *n.* [< L. *altus*, high] **1.** a platform where sacrifices are made to a god, etc. **2.** a table, etc. for sacred purposes in a place of worship —**lead to the altar** to marry

altar boy a boy who helps a priest at religious services, esp. at Mass

al·ter (ôl'tər) *vt.*, *vi.* [< L. *alter*, other] to change; make or become different —**al'ter·a'tion** *n.*

al·ter·ca·tion (ôl'tər kā'shən) *n.* [< L. *altercari*, to dispute] an angry or heated argument; quarrel

al·ter·e·go (ôl'tər ē'gō) [L., other I] **1.** one's other self **2.** a constant companion

al·ter·nate (ôl'tər nit; *for v.* -nāt') *adj.* [< L. *alternus*, one after the other] **1.** succeeding each other **2.** every other —*n.* a substitute —*vt.* **-nat'ed**, **-nat'ing** to do or use by turns —*vi.* **1.** to act, happen, etc. by turns **2.** to take turns regularly —**al'ter·nate·ly** *adv.* —**al'ter·na'tion** *n.*

alternating current an electric current reversing direction periodically

al·ter·na·tive (ôl tur'nə tiv) *adj.* providing a choice between things —*n.* **1.** a choice between things **2.** one of the things to be chosen **3.** something left to choose

al·ter·na·tor (ôl'tər nāt'ər) *n.* an electric generator that produces alternating current

al·though (ôl thō') *conj.* in spite of the fact that; though: also **altho**

al·tim·e·ter (al tim'ə tər) *n.* [< L. *altus*, high + -METER] an instrument for measuring altitude

al·ti·tude (al'tə tōōd') *n.* [< L. *altus*, high] **1.** the height of a thing, esp. above sea level **2.** a high place

al·to (al'tō) *n.*, *pl.* **-tos** [It. < L. *altus*, high] **1.** the range of the lowest female voice **2.** a singer with this range —*adj.* of, for, or in the alto

al·to·geth·er (ôl'tə geth'ər) *adv.* **1.** completely **2.** in all **3.** on the whole

al·tru·ism (al'trōō iz'm) *n.* [< L. *alter*, other] unselfish concern for the welfare of others —**al'tru·ist** *n.* —**al'tru·is'tic** (-is'tik) *adj.* —**al'tru·is'ti·cal·ly** *adv.*

al·um (al'əm) *n.* [< L. *alumen*] any of a group of salts of aluminum, etc., used in manufacturing and medicine

al·u·min·ium (al'yoo min'yəm) *n.* Brit. *var.* of ALUMINUM

a·lu·mi·num (ə lōō'mə nəm) *n.* [< L. *alumen*, alum] a silvery, lightweight metallic chemical element

a·lum·nus (ə lum'nəs) *n.*, *pl.* **-ni** (-nī) [L., foster son] a boy or man who has attended or been graduated from a school, college, etc. —**a·lum'na** (-na) *n.fem.*, *pl.* **-nae** (-nē)

al·ways (ôl'wiz, -wāz) *adv.* [OE. *ealne weg*] **1.** at all times **2.** continually **3.** at any time **4.** in every instance

Alz·hei·mer's disease (älts'hī'mərz) [< A. *Alzheimer*, 20th-c. G. doctor] a degenerative brain disease

am (am, əm) [OE. *eom*] *1st pers. sing., pres. indic., of* BE

AM amplitude modulation

Am. 1. America **2.** American

A.M., AM master of arts

A.M., a.m., AM [L. *ante meridiem*] before noon: used to designate the time from midnight to noon

AMA, A.M.A. American Medical Association

a·main (ə mān') *adv.* [A-, on + MAIN] [Archaic] at or with great speed

a·mal·gam (ə mal'gəm) *n.* [< Gr. *malagma*, an emollient] **1.** any alloy of mercury with another metal [a dental filling of silver *amalgam*] **2.** a mixture; blend

a·mal'ga·mate' (-gə māt') *vt.*, *vi.* **-mat'ed**, **-mat'ing** to unite; mix; combine —**a·mal'ga·ma'tion** *n.*

a·man·u·en·sis (ə man'yoo wen'sis) *n.*, *pl.* **-ses** (-sēz) [L. < a-, from + *manus*, hand + -*ensis*, relating to] a secretary: now a jocular usage

am·a·ranth (am'ə ranth') *n.* [< Gr. *amarantos*, unfading] **1.** any of a family of plants, some bearing showy flowers **2.** [Poet.] an imaginary flower that never dies

Am·a·ril·lo (am'ə ril'ō) city in NW Tex.: pop. 149,000

am·a·ryl·lis (am'ə ril'əs) *n.* [< Gr. name for a shepherdess] a bulb plant with white to red lilylike flowers

a·mass (ə mas') *vt.* [< Fr. < L.

massa, a lump] to pile up; accumulate

am·a·teur (am'ə chər, -tər, -toor) *n.* [Fr. < L. *amare,* to love] **1.** one who does something for pleasure, not for pay; nonprofessional **2.** one who is somewhat unskillful —*adj.* of or done by amateurs —**am'a·teur'ish** (-choor'-) *adj.* —**am'a·teur'ish·ly** *adv.* —**am'a·teur·ism** *n.*

am'a·to'ry (-tôr'ē) *adj.* [< L. *amare,* to love] of or showing sexual love

a·maze (ə māz') *vt.* **a·mazed', a·maz'ing** [see MAZE] to fill with great surprise or wonder; astonish —**a·maze'ment** *n.* —**a·maz'ing** *adj.* —**a·maz'ing·ly** *adv.*

Am·a·zon (am'ə zän') river in N S.America: c.3,300 mi. —*n.* [< Gr. *Myth.*] any of a race of female warriors

am·bas·sa·dor (am bas'ə dər) *n.* [< Pr. *ambaissador*] the highest-ranking diplomatic representative of one country to another —**am·bas'sa·do'ri·al** (-dôr'ē əl) *adj.* —**am·bas'sa·dor·ship'** *n.*

am·ber (am'bər) *n.* [< Ar. *'anbar,* ambergris] **1.** a brownish-yellow fossil resin used in jewelry, etc. **2.** its color —*adj.* amberlike or amber-colored

am'ber·gris' (-grēs', -gris') *n.* [< OFr. *ambre gris,* gray amber] a waxy substance secreted by certain whales, used in making perfumes

am·bi- (am'bə) [L.] *a combining form meaning both [ambidextrous]*

am·bi·ance (am'bē əns) *n.* [see AMBIENT] an environment or its distinct atmosphere: also **ambience**

am·bi·dex·trous (am'bə dek'strəs) *adj.* [see AMBI- & DEXTEROUS] using both hands with equal ease —**am'bi·dex·ter'i·ty** (-dek ster'ə tē) *n.*

am'bi·ent (-ənt) *adj.* [L. < *ambi-,* around + *ire,* to go] surrounding

am·bi·gu·i·ty (am'bə gyōō'ə tē) *n.* **1.** a being ambiguous **2.** *pl.* **-ties** an ambiguous expression

am·big·u·ous (am big'yoo wəs) *adj.* [< L. *ambi-,* around + *agere,* to do] **1.** having two or more meanings **2.** not clear; vague —**am·big'u·ous·ly** *adv.*

am·bi·tion (am bish'ən) *n.* [< L. *ambitio,* a going around (to solicit votes)] **1.** strong desire for fame, power, etc. **2.** the thing so desired

am·bi'tious (-shəs) *adj.* **1.** full of or showing ambition **2.** showing great effort —**am·bi'tious·ly** *adv.*

am·biv·a·lence (am biv'ə ləns) *n.* [AMBI- + VALENCE] simultaneous conflicting feelings —**am·biv'a·lent** *adj.* —**am·biv'a·lent·ly** *adv.*

am·ble (am'b'l) *vi.* **-bled, -bling** [< L. *ambulare,* to walk] **1.** to move in an easy gait, as a horse **2.** to walk in a leisurely way —*n.* **1.** a horse's ambling gait **2.** a leisurely walking pace

am·bro·sia (am brō'zhə) *n.* [< Gr. *a-,* not + *brotos,* mortal] **1.** *Gr. & Rom. Myth.* the food of the gods **2.** anything that tastes or smells delicious —**am·bro'sial** *adj.*

am·bu·lance (am'byə ləns) *n.* [< L. *ambulare,* to walk] a vehicle equipped for carrying the sick or wounded

am'bu·late' (-lāt') *vi.* **-lat'ed, -lat'ing** to move about; walk —**am'bu·lant** (-lənt) *adj.* —**am'bu·la'tion** *n.*

am'bu·la·to'ry (-lə tôr'ē) *adj.* **1.** of or for walking **2.** able to walk

am·bus·cade (am'bəs kād') *n., vt., vi.* **-cad'ed, -cad'ing** ambush

am·bush (am'boosh) *n.* [< ML. *in-,* in + *boscus,* woods] **1.** an arrangement of persons in hiding to make a surprise attack **2.** their hiding place —*vt., vi.* to attack from ambush

a·me·ba (ə mē'bə) *n., pl.* **-bas, -bae** (-bē) *same as* AMOEBA —**a·me'bic** *adj.*

a·mel·io·rate (ə mēl'yə rāt') *vt., vi.* **-rat'ed, -rat'ing** [< Fr. < OFr. < L. *melior,* better] to make or become better; improve —**a·mel'io·ra'tion** *n.*

a·men (ā'men', ä'-) *interj.* [< Heb. *āmēn,* truly] may it be so: used after a prayer or to express approval

a·me·na·ble (ə mē'nə b'l, -men'ə-) *adj.* [< OFr. < L. *minare,* to drive (animals)] **1.** responsible; answerable **2.** able to be controlled; submissive —**a·me'na·bil'i·ty** *n.* —**a·me'na·bly** *adv.*

a·mend (ə mend') *vt.* [< L. *emendare*] **1.** to correct; emend **2.** to improve **3.** to change or revise (a law, etc.) —*vi.* to improve one's conduct —**a·mend'a·ble** *adj.*

a·mend'ment *n.* **1.** a correction of errors, faults, etc. **2.** improvement **3.** a revision or change proposed or made in a bill, law, etc.

a·mends (ə mendz') *n.pl.* [*sometimes with sing. v.*] [see AMEND] payment made or satisfaction given for injury, loss, etc.

a·men·i·ty (ə men'ə tē, -mē'nə-) *n., pl.* **-ties** [< L. *amoenus,* pleasant] **1.** pleasantness **2.** an attractive feature or convenience **3.** [*pl.*] courteous acts

am·ent (am'ənt, ā'mənt) *n.* [< L. *amentum,* thong] a tassellike spike of small flowers, as on a willow or birch

a·merce (ə murs') *vt.* **a·merced', a·merc'ing** [< OFr. *a merci,* at the mercy of] to punish, esp. by imposing a fine —**a·merce'ment** *n.*

A·mer·i·ca (ə mer'ə kə) [associated with *Amerigo* VESPUCCI] *same as* **1.** WESTERN HEMISPHERE: also the **Americas 2.** NORTH AMERICA **3.** SOUTH AMERICA **4.** THE UNITED STATES

A·mer'i·can (-kən) *adj.* **1.** of or in America **2.** of the U.S., its people, etc. —*n.* **1.** a native or inhabitant of America **2.** a citizen of the U.S.

A·mer'i·ca'na (-kan'ə) *n.pl.* books, papers, objects, etc. having to do with America, its people, and its history

A·mer'i·can·ism *n.* **1.** a custom or belief of the U.S. **2.** a word or idiom originating in American English **3.** devotion to the U.S., its customs, etc.

A·mer'i·can·ize' (-īz') *vt., vi.* **-ized', -iz'ing** to make or become American

---

in character, manners, etc. —A·mer′·i·can·i·za′tion n.

American plan a system of hotel operation in which the price charged covers room, service, and meals

American Revolution the war (1775–1783) fought by the American colonies to gain independence from England

Am·er·ind (am′ə rind′) n. an American Indian or Eskimo —Am′er·in′di·an adj., n.

am·e·thyst (am′ə thist) n. [< Gr. amethystos, not drunken: the Greeks thought it prevented intoxication] 1. a purple or violet quartz or corundum, used in jewelry 2. purple or violet

a·mi·a·ble (ā′mē ə b'l) adj. [< L. amicus, friend] good-natured; friendly —a′mi·a·bil′i·ty n. —a′mi·a·bly adv.

am·i·ca·ble (am′i kə b'l) adj. [see prec.] friendly; peaceable —am′i·ca·bil′i·ty n. —am′i·ca·bly adv.

a·mid (ə mid′) prep. in the middle of; among: also a·midst (ə midst′)

am·ide (am′īd) n. any of several organic compounds derived from ammonia

a·mid·ships′ adv. in or toward the middle of a ship: also a·mid′ship′

a·mi·go (ə mē′gō) n., pl. -gos (-gōz) [Sp.] a friend

amino acids (ə mē′nō, am′ə nō′) [< AMMONIA] a group of nitrogenous organic compounds found in the proteins and essential to metabolism

Am·ish (ä′mish, am′ish) n.pl. [< Jacob Ammann (or Amen), the founder] Mennonites of a sect founded in the 17th cent. —adj. of this sect

a·miss (ə mis′) adv. [see A- & MISS[1]] in a wrong way; astray —adj. wrong; improper; faulty [what is amiss?]

am·i·ty (am′ə tē) n., pl. -ties [< L. amicus, friend] peaceful relations

am·me·ter (am′mēt′ər) n. [AM(PERE) + -METER] an instrument for measuring an electric current in amperes

am·mo (am′ō) n. [Slang] ammunition

am·mo·ni·a (ə mōn′yə) n. [from a salt found near Libyan shrine of Jupiter Ammon] 1. a colorless, pungent gas, a compound of nitrogen and hydrogen 2. a water solution of this gas: in full, ammonia water

am·mu·ni·tion (am′yə nish′ən) n. [< L. munire, fortify] 1. bullets, gunpowder, bombs, grenades, rockets, etc. 2. any means of attack or defense

am·ne·sia (am ne′zhə, -zhē ə) n. [< Gr. a-, not + mnasthai, to remember] partial or total loss of memory

am·nes·ty (am′nəs tē) n., pl. -ties [< Gr. amnēstia, a forgetting] a general pardon, esp. for political offenses —vt. -tied, -ty·ing to pardon

a·moe·ba (ə mē′bə) n., pl. -bas, -bae (-bē) [< Gr. ameibein, to change] a microscopic, one-celled animal multiplying by fission —a·moe′bic adj.

a·mok (ə muk′) adj., adv. [Malay amoq] in a frenzy to kill

a·mong (ə muŋ′) prep. [< OE. on, in + gemang, a crowd] 1. surrounded by [among friends] 2. in the group of [best among books] 3. to or for each or several of [divide it among the

crowd] 4. by the joint action of Also a·mongst (ə muŋst′)

A·mon-Re (ä′mən rā′) the ancient Egyptian sun god

a·mon·til·la·do (ə män′tə lä′dō) n. [Sp. < Montilla, a town in Spain] a pale, relatively dry sherry

a·mor·al (ā môr′əl) adj. 1. neither moral nor immoral 2. without moral sense —a′mor·al′i·ty n. —a·mor′·al·ly adv.

am·o·rous (am′ər əs) adj. [< L. amor, love] 1. fond of making love 2. full of love 3. of sexual love —am′o·rous·ly adv.

a·mor·phous (ə môr′fəs) adj. [< Gr. a-, without + morphē, form] 1. without definite form 2. vague or indefinite 3. Chem. not crystalline

am·or·tize (am′ər tīz′, ə môr′-) vt. -tized′, -tiz′ing [< ME. < L. ad-, to + mors, death] to put money aside at intervals for gradual payment of (a debt, etc.) —am′or·ti·za′tion n.

a·mount (ə mount′) vi. [< OFr. amont, upward < L. ad, to + mons, mountain] 1. to add up (to) 2. to be equal (to) in value, etc. —n. 1. a sum total 2. the whole value or effect 3. a quantity

a·mour (ə moor′) n. [< L. amor, love] a love affair, esp. an illicit one

†a·mour-pro·pre (ä moor prō′pr') n. [Fr.] self-esteem

amp. 1. amperage 2. ampere; amperes

am·per·age (am′pər ij, am pir′-) n. the strength of an electric current in amperes

am·pere (am′pir) n. [< A. M. Ampère, 19th-c. Fr. physicist] the standard unit for measuring an electric current, equal to one coulomb per second

am·per·sand (am′pər sand′) n. [< and per se and, (the sign) & by itself (is) and] a sign (&) meaning and

am·phet·a·mine (am fet′ə mēn′, -min) n. a drug used esp. as a stimulant and to lessen appetite

am·phib·i·an (am fib′ē ən) n. [see ff.] 1. any animal or plant living both on land and in water 2. an aircraft that can take off from or land on water or land —adj. same as AMPHIBIOUS

am·phib·i·ous adj. [< Gr. amphi-, on both sides + bios, life] that can live or operate on land and in water

am·phi·the·a·ter, am·phi·the·a·tre (am′fə thē′ə tər) n. [< Gr. amphi-, around + theatron, theater] a round or oval building with rising rows of seats around an open space

am·ple (am′p'l) adj. [< L. amplus] 1. large in size, scope, etc. 2. more than enough 3. adequate —am′ply adv.

am·pli·fi·er (am′plə fī′ər) n. one that amplifies; esp., a device for strengthening electrical signals

am′pli·fy′ (-fī′) vt. -fied′, -fy′ing [< L. amplus, large + facere, to make] 1. to make stronger; esp., to strengthen (electrical signals) 2. to develop more fully —am′pli·fi·ca′tion n.

am·pli·tude (am′plə tōōd′) n. [see AMPLE] 1. scope, extent, breadth, etc. 2. abundance 3. range from mean to extreme, as of an alternating current

amplitude modulation the changing of the amplitude of the transmitting radio wave in accordance with the signal being broadcast

am·pul (am′pool) *n.* [< L. *ampulla*, bottle] a small glass container for one dose of a hypodermic medicine: also **am′pule** (-pyool), **am′poule** (-pool)

am·pu·tate (am′pyə tāt′) *vt.* -**tat′ed**, -**tat′ing** [< L. *amb*-, about + *putare*, to prune] to cut off, esp. by surgery —**am′pu·ta′tion** *n.*

am′pu·tee′ (-tē′) *n.* one who has had a limb or limbs amputated

Am·ster·dam (am′stər dam′) constitutional capital of the Netherlands: pop. 866,000

amt. amount

Am·trak (am′trak′) *n.* [*Am(erican) tr(avel) (tr)a(c)k*] a nationwide system of passenger railroad service

a·muck (ə muk′) *adj., adv.* same as AMOK

am·u·let (am′yə lit) *n.* [< L.] something worn to protect against evil

a·muse (ə myōōz′) *vt.* **a·mused′**, **a·mus′ing** [< Fr. < *à*, at + OFr. *muser*, to gaze] 1. to keep pleasantly occupied; entertain 2. to make laugh, etc.

a·muse′ment *n.* 1. a being amused 2. something that amuses

amusement park an outdoor place with devices for entertainment, as a merry-go-round, roller coaster, etc.

am·yl·ase (am′ə lās′) *n.* [< Gr. *amylon*, starch] an enzyme that helps change starch into sugar, found in saliva, etc.

an (ən, 'n; *stressed*, an) *adj., indefinite article* [< OE. *an*, one] 1. one; one sort of 2. each; any one 3. per [*two an hour*] *An* is used before words beginning with a vowel sound [*an eye, an honor*] See also A, *adj.*

-an (ən, in, 'n) [< L. *-anus*] a suffix meaning: 1. of, belonging to [*diocesan*] 2. born in, living in [*Ohioan*] 3. believing in [*Mohammedan*]

a·nach·ro·nism (ə nak′rə niz′m) *n.* [< Gr. *ana*-, against + *chronos*, time] 1. anything out of its proper historical time 2. the representation of this —**a·nach′ro·nis′tic** *adj.*

an·a·con·da (an′ə kän′də) *n.* [< ? Sinhalese] a S.American snake that crushes its prey in its coils

a·nae·mi·a, a·nae·mic, etc. same as ANEMIA, ANEMIC, etc.

an·aer·o·bic (an′er ō′bik) *adj.* [< Gr. *an*-, without + *aēr*, air + *bios*, life] able to live and grow without air or free oxygen, as some bacteria

an·aes·the·si·a, an·aes·thet·ic, etc. same as ANESTHESIA, ANESTHETIC, etc.

an·a·gram (an′ə gram′) *n.* [< Gr. *anagrammatizein*, transpose letters] 1. a word, etc. made by rearranging letters (Ex.: *now—won*) 2. [*pl.*, with *sing. v.*] a word game based on this

An·a·heim (an′ə hīm′) city in SW Calif.: pop. 222,000

a·nal (ā′n'l) *adj.* of or near the anus

an·al·ge·si·a (an′'l jē′zē ə, -sē ə) *n.* [< Gr. *an*-, without + *algēsia*, pain] a state of not feeling pain

an′al·ge′sic (-zik, -sik) *adj.* of or causing analgesia —*n.* a drug that produces analgesia

an·a·log computer (an′ə lôg′) a computer working on the basis of a physical, esp. electrical, analogy of the mathematical problem to be solved

an·a·lo·gize (ə nal′ə jīz′) *vi., vt.* -**gized′**, -**giz′ing** to use, or explain by, analogy

a·nal·o·gous (ə nal′ə gəs) *adj.* [see ANALOGY] similar in some way —**a·nal·o·gous·ly** *adv.*

an·a·logue, an·a·log (an′ə lôg′) something analogous —*adj.* of an analog computer: usually **analog**

a·nal·o·gy (ə nal′ə jē) *n., pl.* -**gies** [< Gr. *ana*-, according to + *logos*, ratio] 1. similarity in some way 2. the inference that certain resemblances imply further similarity

an·al·y·sand (ə sand′) *n.* [see ff.] a person undergoing psychoanalysis

a·nal′y·sis (-sis) *n., pl.* -**ses′** (-sēz′) [< Gr. < *ana*-, up + *lysis*, a loosing] 1. a breaking up of a whole into its parts to find out their nature, etc. 2. a statement of these findings 3. psychoanalysis 4. *Chem.* separation of compounds and mixtures into their constituents to determine their nature or proportion —**an·a·lyt·i·cal** (an′ə lit′i k'l), **an′a·lyt′ic** *adj.* —**an′a·lyt′·i·cal·ly** *adv.*

an·a·lyst (an′ə list) *n.* 1. one who analyzes 2. a psychoanalyst

an′a·lyze′ (-līz′) *vt.* -**lyzed′**, -**lyz′ing** 1. to make an analysis of; examine in detail 2. to psychoanalyze —**an′a·lyz′a·ble** *adj.* —**an′a·lyz′er** *n.*

an·a·pest (an′ə pest′) *n.* [< Gr. *ana*-, back + *paiein*, strike] a metrical foot of two unaccented syllables followed by an accented one

an·ar·chism (an′ər kiz′m) *n.* [see ANARCHY] 1. the theory that all organized government is repressive and undesirable 2. resistance to all government

an′ar·chist (-kist) *n.* 1. one who believes in anarchism 2. a promoter of anarchy —**an′ar·chis′tic** *adj.*

an′ar·chy (-kē) *n., pl.* -**chies** [< Gr. *an*-, without + *archos*, leader] 1. the absence of government 2. political disorder and violence 3. disorder; confusion —**an·ar′chic** (-är′kik), **an·ar′chi·cal** *adj.* —**an·ar′chi·cal·ly** *adv.*

a·nath·e·ma (ə nath′ə mə) *n., pl.* -**mas** [Gr., thing devoted to evil] 1. a person or thing accursed or damned 2. anything greatly detested 3. a formal curse, as in excommunicating a person 4. any strong curse

a·nath′e·ma·tize′ (-tīz′) *vt., vi.* -**tized′**, -**tiz′ing** to utter an anathema (against); curse

a·nat·o·mize (ə nat′ə mīz′) *vt., vi.*

-mized', -miz'ing [see ff.] 1. to dissect (animals, etc.) to study structure 2. to analyze —a·nat'o·mist n.

a·nat·o·my (-mē) n., pl. -mies [< Gr. ana-, up + temnein, to cut] 1. dissection of an organism to study its structure 2. the science of the structure of plants or animals 3. the structure of an organism 4. any analysis — an·a·tom·i·cal (an'ə täm'i k'l), an'a·tom'ic adj.

-ance (əns) [< L.] a suffix meaning: 1. the act of [utterance] 2. the quality or state of being [vigilance] 3. a thing that [conveyance] 4. a thing that is [inheritance]

an·ces·tor (an'ses'tər) n. [< L. ante-, before + cedere, go] 1. a person from whom one is descended; forebear 2. an early kind; forerunner —an·ces'tral adj. —an'ces'tress n.fem.

an·ces·try (-trē) n., pl. -tries 1. family descent 2. all one's ancestors

an·chor (aŋ'kər) n. [< Gr. ankyra, a hook] 1. a heavy object, as a hooked iron weight, lowered from a ship, as by cable, to prevent drifting 2. anything giving stability 3. a newscaster who coordinates the various reports: also an'chor·man' or an'chor·wom'an —vt. 1. to hold secure as with an anchor 2. to be the final contestant on (a relay team, etc.) 3. to be the anchor on (a news broadcast) —vi. 1. to lower an anchor 2. to be or become fixed —at anchor anchored

an'chor·age (-ij) n. 1. an anchoring or being anchored 2. a place to anchor

an·cho·rite (aŋ'kə rīt') n. [< Gr. ana-, back + chōrein, retire] a religious recluse; hermit

an·cho·vy (an'chō'vē, -chə-) n., pl. -vies [< Port. anchova] a tiny, herringlike fish, eaten as a relish

an·cient (ān'shənt) adj. [< L. ante, before] 1. of times long past 2. very old —n. an aged person —the ancients the people of ancient times

an'cient·ly adv. in ancient times

an·cil·lar·y (an'sə ler'ē) adj. [< L. ancilla, maidservant] 1. subordinate (to) 2. auxiliary

-an·cy (ən sē) same as -ANCE

and (ənd, ən; stressed, and) conj. [OE.] 1. also; in addition 2. plus 3. as a result 4. in contrast to; but 5. [Colloq.] to [try and get it]

an·dan·te (än dän'tā) adj., adv. [It. < andare, to walk] Music fairly slow

An·der·sen (an'dər s'n), Hans Christian 1805–75; Dan. writer of fairy stories

An·des (Mountains) (an'dēz) mountain system of W S.America

and·i·ron (and'ī'ərn) n. [< OFr. andier] either of a pair of metal supports for logs in a fireplace

and/or either and or or [personal and/or real property]

An·dor·ra (an dôr'ə) republic in the E Pyrenees: 180 sq. mi.; pop. 11,000

an·dro·gen (an'drə

ANDIRONS

jən) n. [< Gr. andros, of man + -GEN] a male sex hormone that can give rise to masculine characteristics —an'dro·gen'ic (-jen'ik) adj.

an·droid (an'droid) n. [< Gr. andros, of man + -OID] in science fiction, an automaton made to look like a human being

an·ec·dote (an'ik dōt') n. [< Gr. anekdotos, unpublished] a short, entertaining account of some event —an'ec·dot'al adj.

a·ne·mi·a (ə nē'mē ə) n. [< Gr. a-, without + haima, blood] a condition in which the blood is low in red cells or in hemoglobin, resulting in paleness, weakness, etc. —a·ne'mic adj.

an·e·mom·e·ter (an'ə mäm'ə tər) n. [< Gr. anemos, the wind + -METER] a gauge for determining the force or speed of the wind; wind gauge

a·nem·o·ne (ə nem'ə nē') n. [< Gr. anemos, the wind] 1. a plant with cup-shaped flowers of white, pink, red, or purple 2. a sea anemone

a·nent (ə nent') prep. [< OE. on efen, on even (with)] [Now Rare] concerning; about

an·er·oid barometer (an'ər oid) [< Gr. a-, without + nēros, liquid + -OID] a barometer working by the bending of a thin metal plate instead of by the rise or fall of mercury

an·es·the·sia (an'əs thē'zhə) n. [< Gr. an-, without + aisthēsis, feeling] a partial or total loss of the sense of pain, touch, etc.

an·es·the'si·ol'o·gist (-thē'zē äl'ə jist) n. a doctor who specializes in giving anesthetics —an'es·the'si·ol'o·gy n.

an·es·thet'ic (-thet'ik) adj. of or producing anesthesia —n. a drug, gas, etc. used to produce anesthesia, as before surgery

an·es·the·tist (ə nes'thə tist) n. a person trained to give anesthetics

an·es'the·tize' (-tīz') vt. -tized', -tiz'ing to cause anesthesia in —an·es·the·ti·za'tion n.

an·eu·rysm, an·eu·rism (an'yər iz'm) n. [< Gr. ana-, up + eurys, broad] a sac formed by a swelling in a weakened wall of an artery

a·new (ə nōō') adv. 1. once more; again 2. in a new way or form

an·gel (ān'j'l) n. [< Gr. angelos, messenger] 1. Theol. a) a messenger of God b) an immortal spirit 2. an image of a human figure with wings and a halo 3. a person regarded as beautiful, good, etc. 4. [Colloq.] a financial backer, as for a play —an·gel·ic (an jel'ik), an·gel'i·cal adj. —an·gel'i·cal·ly adv.

An·gel·e·no (an'jə lē'nō) n., pl. -nos an inhabitant of Los Angeles

an·gel·fish (ān'j'l fish') n., pl.: see FISH a bright-colored tropical fish with spiny fins

angel (food) cake a light, spongy, white cake made with egg whites

an·ger (aŋ'gər) n. [< ON. angr, distress] hostile feelings because of opposition, a hurt, etc. —vt., vi. to make or become angry

an·gi·na (pec·to·ris) (an jī'nə pek'tər is) [L., distress of the breast] a condition marked by chest pain, caused by a decrease of blood to the heart

an·gle¹ (aŋ'g'l) n. [< Gr. ankylos, bent] 1. the shape or space made by two straight lines or plane surfaces that meet 2. the degrees of difference in direction between them 3. a sharp corner —a point of view; aspect 5. [Colloq.] a tricky scheme or approach, as for personal gain —vt., vi. -gled, -gling 1. to move or bend at an angle 2. [Colloq.] to give a specific aspect to (a story, etc.)

an·gle² (aŋ'g'l) vi. -gled, -gling [< OE. angul, fishhook] 1. to fish with a hook and line 2. to use tricks to get something [to angle for a promotion] —an'gler n.

angle iron a piece of iron or steel bent at a right angle, used for joining or reinforcing two beams, etc.

An·gles (aŋ'g'lz) n.pl. a Germanic people that settled in England in the 5th cent. A.D.

an·gle·worm n. an earthworm

An·gli·can (aŋ'gli kən) adj. [< ML. Anglicus, of the Angles] of or connected with the Church of England —n. an Anglican church member

An·gli·cism (aŋ'glə siz'm) n. a word or trait peculiar to the English

An'gli·cize' (-sīz') vt., vi. -cized', -ciz'ing to change to English idiom, pronunciation, customs, etc. —An'·gli·ci·za'tion (-si zā'shən) n.

Anglo- a combining form meaning English or Anglican

An'glo-A·mer'i·can (aŋ'glō-) adj. English and American —n. an American of English birth or ancestry

An·glo-Sax·on (aŋ'glō sak's'n) n. 1. a member of the Germanic peoples in England before the 12th cent. 2. their language, OLD ENGLISH 3. an Englishman —adj. of the Anglo-Saxons

An·go·la (aŋ gō'lə, an-) country on the SW coast of Africa: 481,351 sq. mi.; pop. 6,761,000

An·go·ra (aŋ gôr'ə) n. [former name of ANKARA] 1. a breed of animal; specif., a cat, rabbit, or goat, with long, silky fur or hair 2. a) yarn of Angora rabbit hair b) mohair

an·gry (aŋ'grē) adj. -gri·er, -gri·est 1. feeling or showing anger 2. wild and stormy —an'gri·ly (-grə lē) adv.

ang·strom (aŋ'strəm) n. [< A. J. Angström, 19th-c. Swed. physicist] one hundred-millionth of a centimeter, a unit used in measuring the length of light waves: also **angstrom unit**

an·guish (aŋ'gwish) n. [< L. angustia, tightness] great mental or physical pain; agony —vt., vi. to feel or make feel anguish —an'guished adj.

an·gu·lar (aŋ'gyə lər) adj. 1. having or forming an angle or angles; sharp-cornered 2. lean; gaunt 3. without ease or grace; stiff —an'gu·lar'i·ty (-ler'ə tē) n., pl. -ties

an·i·line (an'l in) n. [< Ar. al, the + nil, blue + -INE³] a colorless, poisonous, oily derivative of benzene, used in making dyes, varnishes, etc.

an·i·mad·vert (an'ə mad vurt') vi. [< L. animus, mind + advertere, to turn] to comment adversely (on or upon) —an'i·mad·ver'sion (-vur'zhən) n.

an·i·mal (an'ə m'l) n. [< L. anima, breath, soul] 1. any living organism except a plant or bacterium, typically able to move about 2. any such organism other than man; esp., any four-footed creature 3. a brutish or bestial person —adj. 1. of or like an animal 2. gross, bestial, etc. —an'i·mal'i·ty (-mal'ə tē) n.

an·i·mal·cule (an'ə mal'kyool) n. a very small or microscopic animal

an·i·mate (an'ə māt'; for adj. -mit) vt. -mat'ed, -mat'ing [see ANIMAL] 1. to give life or motion to 2. to make gay or spirited 3. to inspire —adj. living —an'i·mat'ed adj. —an'i·ma'tion n. —an'i·ma'tor n.

animated cartoon a motion picture made by filming a series of cartoons

an·i·mism (an'ə miz'm) n. [< L. anima, soul] the belief that all life is produced by a spiritual force, or that all things in nature have souls —an'i·mis'tic adj.

an·i·mos·i·ty (an'ə mäs'ə tē) n., pl. -ties [see ff.] a feeling of strong dislike or hatred; hostility

an·i·mus (an'ə məs) n. [L., passion] animosity; hostility

an·i·on (an'ī'ən) n. [< Gr. ana-, up + ienai, to go] a negatively charged ion: in electrolysis, anions move toward the anode

an·ise (an'is) n. [< Gr. anēson] 1. a plant of the parsley family 2. its fragrant seed, used for flavoring: also **an·i·seed** (an'ə sēd')

an·i·sette (an'ə set', -zet') n. [Fr.] a sweet, anise-flavored liqueur

An·ka·ra (äŋ'kə rə, äŋ'-) capital of Turkey: pop. 650,000

ankh (aŋk) n. [Egypt., life] a cross with a loop at the top, an ancient Egyptian symbol of life

an·kle (aŋ'k'l) n. [OE. ancleow] 1. the joint that connects the foot and the leg 2. the part of the leg between the foot and calf

an'klet (-klit) n. 1. an ornament worn around the ankle 2. a short sock

an·nals (an''lz) n.pl. [< L. annus, year] 1. a written account of events year by year 2. historical records; history —an'nal·ist n.

An·nap·o·lis (ə nap'ə lis) capital of Md.: pop. 32,000

Ann Ar·bor (an är'bər) city in SE Mich.: pop. 107,000

an·neal (ə nēl') vt. [< OE. an-, on + æl, fire] to heat (glass, metals, etc.) and cool slowly to prevent brittleness

an·ne·lid (an''l id) n. [< L. dim. of anulus, a ring] any of various worms with a body made of joined segments or rings, as the earthworm

an·nex (ə neks′; *for n.* an′eks) *vt.* [< L. *ad-*, to + *nectere*, to tie] **1.** to attach, esp. to something larger **2.** to incorporate into a state the territory of (another state) —*n.* something annexed; esp., an addition to a building —**an′nex·a′tion** *n.*

an·ni·hi·late (ə nī′ə lāt′) *vt.* -lated, -lating [< L. *ad*, to + *nihil*, nothing] to destroy entirely —**an·ni′hi·la′tion** *n.* —**an·ni′hi·la′tor** *n.*

an·ni·ver·sa·ry (an′ə vur′sər ē) *n.*, *pl.* -ries [< L. *annus*, year + *vertere*, to turn] the yearly return of the date of some event —*adj.* of an anniversary

an·no·tate (an′ə tāt′) *vt., vi.* -tated, -tating [< L. *ad-*, to + *nota*, a sign] to provide explanatory notes for —**an′no·ta′tion** *n.* —**an′no·ta′tor** *n.*

an·nounce (ə nouns′) *vt.* -nounced′, -nounc′ing [< L. *ad-*, to + *nuntius*, messenger] **1.** to declare publicly **2.** to make known the arrival of **3.** to be an announcer for —*vi.* to serve as announcer —**an·nounce′ment** *n.*

an·nounc·er (ə noun′sər) *n.* one who announces; specif., one who introduces radio or television programs, etc.

an·noy (ə noi′) *vt.* [< VL. *in odio*, in hate] to irritate, bother, etc., as by a repeated action —**an·noy′ance** *n.* —**an·noy′ing** *adj.* —**an·noy′ing·ly** *adv.*

an·nu·al (an′yoo wəl) *adj.* [< L. *annus*, year] **1.** of or measured by a year **2.** yearly **3.** living only one year or season —*n.* **1.** a periodical published once a year **2.** a plant living only one year or season —**an′nu·al·ly** *adv.*

an·nu·i·ty (ə nōō′ə tē) *n.*, *pl.* -ties [see prec.] **1.** an investment yielding fixed payments, esp. yearly **2.** such a payment —**an·nu′i·tant** *n.*

an·nul (ə nul′) *vt.* -nulled′, -nul′-ling [< L. *ad-*, to + *nullum*, nothing] **1.** to do away with **2.** to deprive of legal force; nullify —**an·nul′ment** *n.*

an·nu·lar (an′yoo lər) *adj.* [< L. *annulus*, a ring] like or forming a ring

an·nun·ci·a·tion (ə nun′sē ā′shən) *n.* **1.** an announcing **2.** [A-] *a)* the angel Gabriel's announcement to Mary that she would bear Jesus *b)* the church festival commemorating this

an·ode (an′ōd) *n.* [< Gr. *ana-*, up + *hodos*, way] **1.** the positive electrode in an electrolytic cell **2.** the principal electrode for collecting electrons in an electron tube **3.** the negative electrode in a battery

an·o·dize (an′ə dīz′) *vt.* -dized′, -diz′ing to put a protective oxide film on (a metal) by an electrolytic process in which the metal serves as the anode

an·o·dyne (an′ə dīn′) *n.* [< Gr. *an-*, without + *odynē*, pain] anything that relieves pain or soothes

a·noint (ə noint′) *vt.* [< L. *in-*, on + *ungere*, to smear] to put oil on, as in consecrating —**a·noint′ment** *n.*

a·nom·a·lous (ə näm′ə ləs) *adj.* [< Gr. *an-*, not + *homos*, the same] **1.** abnormal **2.** inconsistent or odd

a·nom′a·ly (-lē) *n.*, *pl.* -lies **1.** abnormality **2.** anything anomalous

an·o·mie, an·o·my (an′ə mē) *n.* [Fr. < Gr. *anomia*, lawlessness] lack of purpose, identity, etc.; rootlessness

a·non (ə nän′) *adv.* [< OE. *on an*, in one] **1.** soon **2.** at another time

anon. anonymous

a·non·y·mous (ə nän′ə məs) *adj.* [< Gr. *an-*, without + *onoma*, name] **1.** with no name known **2.** given, written, etc. by one whose name is withheld or unknown **3.** lacking individuality —**an·o·nym·i·ty** (an′ə nim′ə tē) *n.* —**a·non′y·mous·ly** *adv.*

a·noph·e·les (ə näf′ə lēz′) *n.* [< Gr. *anophelēs*, harmful] the mosquito that can transmit malaria

an·o·rex·i·a (an′ə rek′sē ə) *n.* [< Gr. *an-*, without + *orexis*, desire] a personality disorder characterized by obsession with weight loss: in full, **anorexia ner·vo·sa** (nər vō′sə) —**an′o·rex′ic** (-rek′sik) *adj., n.*

an·oth·er (ə nuth′ər) *adj.* **1.** one more; an additional **2.** a different —*pron.* **1.** one additional **2.** a different one **3.** one of the same kind

an·swer (an′sər) *n.* [< OE. *and-*, against + *swerian*, swear] **1.** a reply to a question, letter, etc. **2.** any retaliation **3.** a solution to a problem —*vi.* **1.** to reply **2.** to be sufficient **3.** to be responsible (*to* a person *for*) **4.** to conform (*to*) [the *answers* to the description] —*vt.* **1.** to reply or respond to **2.** to serve [to *answer* the purpose] **3.** to defend oneself against (a charge) **4.** to conform to [he *answers* the description] —**answer back** [Colloq.] to reply forcefully or insolently —**an′swer·a·ble** *adj.*

ant (ant) *n.* [< OE. *æmete*] any of a family of insects, generally wingless, that live in colonies

ant- *same as* ANTI-

-ant (ənt, 'nt) [ult. < L.] *a suffix meaning:* **1.** that has, shows, or does [*defiant*] **2.** one that [*occupant*]

ant·ac·id (ant′as′id) *adj.* counteracting acidity —*n.* an antacid substance

an·tag·o·nism (an tag′ə niz′m) *n.* [see ANTAGONIZE] **1.** opposition or hostility **2.** an opposing force, principle, etc. —**an·tag′o·nis′tic** *adj.* —**an·tag′o·nis′ti·cal·ly** *adv.*

an·tag′o·nist *n.* adversary; opponent

an·tag′o·nize′ (-nīz′) *vt.* -nized′, -niz′ing [< Gr. *anti-*, against + *agōn*, contest] to incur the dislike of

ant·arc·tic (ant ärk′tik, -ärt′-) *adj.* [see ANTI- & ARCTIC] of or near the South Pole or the region around it —**the Antarctic** *same as* ANTARCTICA

Ant·arc′ti·ca (-ti kə) land area about the South Pole, completely covered by ice: c.5,000,000 sq. mi.

Antarctic Circle [*also* a- c-] an imaginary circle parallel to the equator, 66°33′ south of it

Antarctic Ocean popularly, the oceans surrounding Antarctica

ant bear a large anteater of tropical S. America

an·te (an′tē) *n.* [L., before] *Poker* the stake that each player must put into the pot before receiving cards —*vt.,* *vi.* **-ted** or **-teed, -te-ing** *Poker* to put in (one's stake): also **ante up**

ante- [see prec.] *a prefix meaning* before [*antecedent*]

ant'eat'er *n.* a mammal with a long snout, that feeds mainly on ants

an-te-bel-lum (an'ti bel'əm) *adj.* [L.] before the war; specif., before the American Civil War

an-te-ced-ent (an'tə sēd'nt) *adj.* [< L. *ante-*, before + *cedere*, go] prior; previous —*n.* 1. any thing prior to another 2. [*pl.*] one's ancestry, past life, etc. 3. *Gram.* the word or phrase to which a pronoun refers

an-te-cham-ber (an'ti chām'bər) *n.* a smaller room leading into a larger or main room

an-te-date' (-dāt') *vt.* **-dat'ed, -dat'ing** 1. to put a date on that is earlier than the actual date 2. to come before in time

an-te-di-lu-vi-an (an'ti də lōō'vē ən) *adj.* [< ANTE- + L. *diluvium*, a flood + -AN] 1. of the time before the Biblical Flood 2. very old or old-fashioned

an-te-lope (an'tə lōp') *n.* [< Gr. *antholops*, deer] a swift, cud-chewing, horned animal resembling the deer

ANTELOPE

an-te me-ri-di-em (an'tē mə rid'ē əm) [L.] before noon: abbrev. A.M.

an-ten-na (an ten'ə) *n.* [L., sail yard] 1. *pl.* **-nae** (-ē) either of a pair of feelers on the head of an insect, crab, etc. 2. *pl.* **-nas** *Radio & TV* an arrangement of wires, rods, etc. used in sending and receiving the electromagnetic waves

an-te-ri-or (an tir'ē ər) *adj.* [< L. *ante*, before] 1. at or toward the front 2. earlier; previous

an-te-room (an'ti rōōm') *n.* a room leading to a larger or main room

an-them (an'thəm) *n.* [< Gr. *anti-*, over against + *phōnē*, voice] 1. a religious choral song 2. a song of praise or devotion, as to a nation

an-ther (an'thər) *n.* [< Gr. *anthos*, a flower] the part of a stamen that contains the pollen

ant-hill (ant'hil') *n.* the soil heaped up by ants around their nest opening

an-thol-o-gize (an thäl'ə jīz') *vi.* **-gized', -giz'ing** to make anthologies —*vt.* to include in an anthology

an-thol-o-gy (an thäl'ə jē) *n., pl.* **-gies** [< Gr. *anthos*, flower + *legein*, gather] a collection of poems, stories, etc. —**an-thol'o-gist** *n.*

An-tho-ny (an'thə nē, -tə-), Mark see ANTONY

an-thra-cite (an'thrə sīt') *n.* [< Gr. *anthrax*, coal] hard coal, which gives much heat and little smoke

an-thrax (an'thraks) *n.* [< Gr., coal, carbuncle] an infectious disease of cattle, sheep, etc. which can be transmitted to man

anthropo- [< Gr. *anthrōpos*, man] *a combining form meaning* man, human

an-thro-po-cen-tric (an'thrə pə sen'trik) *adj.* [see prec.] centering one's view of everything around man

an-thro-poid (an'thrə poid') *adj.* [< ANTHROPO- + -OID] 1. manlike; esp., designating or of any of the most highly developed apes, as the chimpanzee 2. apelike —*n.* any anthropoid ape

an-thro-pol-o-gy (an'thrə päl'ə jē) *n.* [ANTHROPO- + -LOGY] the study of the characteristics, customs, etc. of mankind —**an'thro-po-log'i-cal** (-pə läj'i k'l) *adj.* —**an'thro-pol'o-gist** *n.*

an-thro-po-mor-phism (-pə môr'fiz'm) *n.* [< Gr. *anthrōpos*, man + *morphē*, form] the attributing of human characteristics to gods, objects, etc. —**an'thro-po-mor'phic** *adj.* —**an'thro-po-mor'phi-cal-ly** *adv.*

an-ti (an'tī, -tē) *n., pl.* **-tis** [see ff.] [Colloq.] a person opposed to something —*adj.* [Colloq.] opposed

anti- [< Gr. *anti*, against] *a prefix meaning:* 1. against, hostile to 2. that operates against 3. that prevents, cures, or neutralizes 4. opposite, reverse 5. rivaling

an-ti-air-craft (an'tē er'kraft) *adj.* used against hostile aircraft

an-ti-bac-te-ri-al (an'ti bak tir'ē əl) *adj.* that checks the growth or effect of bacteria

an-ti-bal-lis'tic missile (-bə lis'tik) a ballistic missile for intercepting an enemy ballistic missile

an-ti-bi-ot-ic (-bī ät'ik, -bē-) *n.* [< ANTI- + Gr. *bios*, life] any of certain substances, as penicillin or streptomycin, produced by some microorganisms and capable of destroying or weakening bacteria, etc. —*adj.* of antibiotics

an-ti-bod-y (an'ti bäd'ē) *n., pl.* **-ies** a protein produced in the body to neutralize an antigen

an-tic (an'tik) *adj.* [< L.: see ANTIQUE] odd and funny —*n.* a playful or ludicrous act, trick, etc. —*vi.* **-ticked, -tick-ing** to do antics

An-ti-christ (an'ti krīst') *Bible* the great opponent of Christ: I John 2:18

an-tic-i-pate (an tis'ə pāt') *vt.* **-pat'ed, -pat'ing** [< L. *ante-*, before + *capere*, take] 1. to look forward to 2. to forestall 3. to take care of, use, etc. in advance 4. to be ahead of in doing —**an-tic'i-pa'tion** *n.* —**an-tic'i-pa-to'ry** (-pə tôr'ē) *adj.*

an-ti-cli-max (an'ti klī'maks) *n.* 1. a sudden drop from the important to the trivial 2. a descent which is in disappointing contrast to a preceding rise —**an'ti-cli-mac'tic** (-klī mak'tik) *adj.* —**an'ti-cli-mac'ti-cal-ly** *adv.*

an·ti·co·ag·u·lant (-kō ag′yə lənt) *n.* a drug or substance that delays or prevents the clotting of blood

an·ti·de·pres′sant (-də pres′ənt) *adj.* lessening emotional depression —*n.* an antidepressant drug

an·ti·dote (an′tə dōt′) *n.* [< Gr. *anti-*, against + *dotos*, given] 1. a remedy to counteract a poison 2. anything that works against an evil

an·ti·freeze (an′ti frēz′) *n.* a substance used, as in an automobile radiator, to prevent freezing

an·ti·gen (an′tə jən) *n.* [ANTI- + -GEN] a substance to which the body reacts by producing antibodies

an·ti·he·ro (an′ti hir′ō) *n.* the protagonist of a novel, etc. who lacks the stature of a traditional hero

an·ti·his·ta·mine (an′ti his′tə mēn′, -mən) *n.* any of several drugs used in treating such allergic conditions as hay fever, asthma, and hives —**an′ti·his′ta·min′ic** (-min′ik) *adj.*

an·ti·knock′ (-näk′) *n.* a substance added to the fuel of internal-combustion engines to do away with noise resulting from too rapid combustion

An·til·les (an til′ēz) group of islands of the West Indies, including Cuba, Jamaica, etc. **(Greater Antilles)** & the Leeward Islands and Windward Islands **(Lesser Antilles)**

an·ti·log·a·rithm (an′ti lôg′ə rith′m, -läg′-) *n.* the number corresponding to a logarithm *[the antilogarithm* of 1 is 10]

an·ti·ma·cas·sar (an′ti mə kas′ər) *n.* [ANTI- + *macassar*, a hair oil] a small cover on the back or arms of a chair, sofa, etc. to prevent soiling

an′ti·mag·net′ic (-mag net′ik) *adj.* made of metals that resist magnetism

an′ti·mat′ter (-mat′ər) *n.* a form of matter in which the electrical charge or other property of each particle is the reverse of that in the usual matter of our universe

an′ti·mis′sile (-mis′'l) *adj.* designed as a defense against ballistic missiles

an·ti·mo·ny (an′tə mō′nē) *n.* [< ML.] a silvery-white, metallic chemical element used in alloys to harden them

an·ti·neu·tron (an′ti noo̅′trän) *n.* the antiparticle of the neutron

an·ti·par·ti·cle (an′ti pär′tə k'l) *n.* any particle of antimatter

an·ti·pas·to (an′ti pas′tō, -päs′-) *n.* [It. < *anti-*, before + *pasto*, food] an appetizer of salted fish, meat, etc.

an·tip·a·thy (an tip′ə thē) *n., pl.* -thies [< Gr. *anti-*, against + *pathein*, feel] 1. strong dislike; aversion 2. an object of this

an·ti·per·son·nel (an′ti pur′sə nel′) *adj.* intended to destroy people rather than objects *[antipersonnel* mines]

an′ti·per′spir·ant (-pur′spər ənt) *n.* a skin lotion, cream, etc. to reduce perspiration

an·ti·phon (an′tə fän′) *n.* [see ANTHEM] a hymn, psalm, etc. sung in responsive, alternating parts —**an·tiph·o·nal** (an tif′ə n'l) *adj.*

an·tip·o·des (an tip′ə dēz′) *n.pl.* [< Gr. *anti-*, opposite + *pous*, foot] two places directly opposite each other on the earth —**an·tip′o·dal** *adj.*

an·ti·pro·ton (an′ti prō′tän) *n.* the antiparticle of the proton

an·ti·quar·i·an (an′tə kwer′ē ən) *adj.* 1. of antiques or antiquities 2. of antiquaries —*n.* an antiquary

an′ti·quar′y (-ē) *n., pl.* -ies a collector or student of antiquities

an′ti·quate′ (-kwāt′) *vt.* -quat′ed, -quat′ing [see ff.] to make old, obsolete, or out-of-date —**an′ti·quat′ed** *adj.* —**an′ti·qua′tion** *n.*

an·tique (an tēk′) *adj.* [< L. *antiquus*, ancient] 1. of ancient times 2. out-of-date 3. of or in the style of a former period 4. dealing in antiques —*n.* 1. an ancient relic 2. a piece of furniture, etc. of a former period —*vt.* -tiqued′, -tiqu′ing to make look antique —**an·tique′ness** *n.*

an·tiq·ui·ty (an tik′wə tē) *n., pl.* -ties [see prec.] 1. the ancient period of history 2. ancientness 3. [*pl.*] relics, etc. of the distant past

an·ti·scor·bu·tic acid (an′ti skôr·byoo̅′tik) *same as* VITAMIN C

an·ti·Se·mit·ic (an′ti sə mit′ik) *adj.* 1. having prejudice against Jews 2. discriminating against or persecuting Jews —**an′ti·Sem′ite** (-sem′īt) *n.* —**an′ti·Sem′i·tism** (-ə tiz′m) *n.*

an′ti·sep·sis (-sep′sis) *n.* 1. a being antiseptic 2. the use of antiseptics

an′ti·sep′tic (-sep′tik) *adj.* [ANTI- + SEPTIC] 1. preventing infection, decay, etc.; effective against bacteria, etc. 2. using antiseptics 3. sterile —*n.* any antiseptic substance, as alcohol —**an′ti·sep′ti·cal·ly** *adv.*

an′ti·slav′er·y *adj.* against slavery

an′ti·so′cial *adj.* 1. not sociable 2. harmful to the welfare of people

an′ti·tank′ *adj.* for use against tanks in war

an·tith·e·sis (an tith′ə sis) *n., pl.* -ses′ (-sēz′) [< Gr. *anti-*, against + *tithenai*, to place] 1. a contrast or opposition, as of ideas 2. the exact opposite —**an′ti·thet′i·cal** (-ə thet′i k'l) *adj.* —**an′ti·thet′i·cal·ly** *adv.*

an·ti·tox·in (an′ti täk′sin) *n.* 1. a substance formed in the blood to act against a specific toxin 2. a serum containing an antitoxin, injected into a person to prevent a disease

an′ti·trust′ *adj.* opposed to or regulating trusts or business monopolies

an′ti·viv′i·sec′tion·ist (-viv′ə sek′shən ist) *n.* one opposing vivisection

ant·ler (ant′lər) *n.* [< ML. *ante-*, before + *ocularis*, of the eyes] the branched horn of any animal of the deer family —**ant′lered** *adj.*

An·to·ny (an′tə nē), **Mark** or **Marc** 83?–30 B.C.; Rom. general

an·to·nym (an′tə nim′) *n.* [< Gr. *anti-*, opposite + *ōnyma*, name] a word meaning the opposite of another

an·trum (an′trəm) *n., pl.* -tra (-trə), -trums [< Gr. *antron*, cave] *Anat.* a cavity; esp., a sinus in the upper jaw

Ant·werp (an′twərp) seaport in N Belgium; pop. 247,000

a·nus (ā′nəs) *n., pl.* -nus·es, -ni

(-nĭ) [L.] the opening at the lower end of the alimentary canal

an·vil (an'vəl) *n.* [OE. *anfilt*] an iron or steel block on which metal objects are hammered into shape

anx·i·e·ty (aŋ zī'ə tē) *n., pl.* **-ties** 1. worry or uneasiness about what may happen 2. an eager desire [*anxiety* to do well]

anx·ious (aŋk'shəs) *adj.* [< L. *angere*, choke] 1. worried 2. causing anxiety 3. eagerly wishing —**anx'-ious·ly** *adv.*

an·y (en'ē) *adj.* [OE. *ænig*] 1. one (no matter which) of more than two [*any* boy may go] 2. some [has he *any* pain?] 3. even one or the least amount of [he hasn't *any* dogs] 4. every [*any* child can tell] 5. without limit [*any* number can play] —*pron. sing. & pl.* any one or ones —*adv.* to any degree or extent; at all [is he *any* better?]

an'y·bod'y (-bud'ē, -bäd'ē) *pron.* 1. any person 2. an important person

an'y·how' *adv. same as* ANYWAY

an'y·more' *adv.* now; nowadays

an'y·one' *pron.* any person; anybody

any one any single (person or thing)

an'y·place' *adv. same as* ANYWHERE

an'y·thing' *pron.* any object, event, fact, etc. —*n.* a thing, no matter of what kind —*adv.* in any way —**any-thing** but not at all

an'y·way' *adv.* 1. in any manner 2. at any rate 3. haphazardly

an'y·where' *adv.* 1. in, at, or to any place 2. [Colloq.] at all —**get any-where** [Colloq.] to achieve anything

A/o, a/o account of

A-OK (ā'ō kā') *adj.* [A(LL) OK] [Colloq.] excellent, fine, in working order, etc.: also **A'-O·kay'**

A one (ā' wun') [Colloq.] superior; first-class: also **A1, A number 1**

a·or·ta (ā ôr'tə) *n., pl.* **-tas, -tae** (-tē) [< Gr. *aeirein*, to raise] the main artery of the body, carrying blood from the heart

a·pace (ə pās') *adv.* at a fast pace

A·pach·e (ə pach'ē) *n., pl.* **-es, -e** [prob. < Zuni *ápachu*, enemy] a member of a tribe of SW U.S. Indians

a·part (ə pärt') *adv.* [< L. *ad*, to + *pars*, part] 1. aside 2. away in place or time 3. in or to pieces —*adj.* separated —**apart from** other than —**tell apart** to distinguish between

a·part'heid (-hāt, -hīt) *n.* [Afrik., apartness] strict racial segregation as practiced in South Africa

a·part'ment *n.* [< It. *appartare*, to separate] a room or suite of rooms to live in, esp. one of a number in an **apartment house** (or **building**)

ap·a·thy (ap'ə thē) *n., pl.* **-thies** [< Gr. *a-*, without + *pathos*, emotion] 1. lack of emotion 2. indifference; listlessness —**ap'a·thet'ic** (-thet'ik) *adj.* —**ap'a·thet'i·cal·ly** *adv.*

APC aspirin, phenacetin, and caffeine, usually in a tablet (**APC tablet**) used for relieving headaches, etc.

ape (āp) *n.* [< OE. *apa*] 1. a chimpanzee, gorilla, orangutan, or gibbon 2. any monkey 3. a mimic 4. a gross, clumsy man —*vt.* aped, ap'ing to imitate —**ape'like'** *adj.*

Ap·en·nines (ap'ə nīnz') mountain range of C Italy

a·pe·ri·ent (ə pir'ē ənt) *adj., n.* [< L. *aperire*, to open] laxative

a·pe·ri·tif (ä'pā rə tēf') *n.* [Fr.] an alcoholic drink taken before meals

ap·er·ture (ap'ər chər) *n.* [< L. *aperire*, to open] an opening; hole

a·pex (ā'peks) *n., pl.* **a'pex·es, ap·i·ces** (ap'ə sēz') [L.] 1. the highest point 2. pointed end; tip 3. a climax

a·pha·sia (ə fā'zhə) *n.* [Gr. < *a-*, not + *phanai*, speak] loss of the power to use or understand words —**a·pha'-sic** (-zik) *adj., n.*

a·phe·li·on (ə fē'lē ən) *n., pl.* **-li·ons, -li·a** (-ə) [< Gr. *apo-*, from + *hēlios*, sun] the point farthest from the sun in the orbit of a planet or comet or of a man-made satellite

a·phid (ā'fid, af'id) *n.* [< Gr. *apheidēs*, unsparing] an insect that lives on plants by sucking their juices

aph·o·rism (af'ə riz'm) *n.* [< Gr. *apo-*, from + *horizein*, to bound] a concise statement of a truth; adage; maxim —**aph'o·ris'tic** *adj.* —**aph'o·ris'ti·cal·ly** *adv.*

aph·ro·dis·i·ac (af'rə diz'ē ak') *adj.* [< Gr. *Aphroditē*] arousing sexual desire —*n.* an aphrodisiac drug, etc.

Aph·ro·di·te (af'rə dīt'ē) the Greek goddess of love and beauty

a·pi·ar·y (ā'pē er'ē) *n., pl.* **-ies** [< L. *apis*, bee] a place where bees are kept —**a'pi·a·rist** (-ə rist) *n.*

a·piece (ə pēs') *adv.* [ME. *a pece*] for each one; each

a·plen·ty (ə plen'tē) *adj., adv.* [Colloq.] in abundance

a·plomb (ə pläm', -plum') *n.* [Fr.: see PLUMB] self-possession; poise

APO Army Post Office

a·poc·a·lypse (ə päk'ə lips') *n.* [< Gr. *apokalyptein*, disclose] 1. [A-] *Bible* the book of REVELATION 2. any revelation of a violent struggle in which evil will be destroyed —**a·poc'-a·lyp'tic** (-lip'tik) *adj.*

A·poc·ry·pha (ə päk'rə fə) *n.pl.* [< Gr. *apo-*, away + *kryptein*, to hide] fourteen books of the Septuagint rejected in Protestantism and Judaism: eleven are in the Roman Catholic Bible

a·poc'ry·phal *adj.* 1. of doubtful authenticity 2. not genuine; spurious; counterfeit

ap·o·gee (ap'ə jē') *n.* [< Gr. *apo-*, from + *gē*, earth] the point farthest from a heavenly body, as the earth, in the orbit of a satellite around it

a·po·lit·i·cal (ā'pə lit'ə k'l) *adj.* not concerned with political matters —**a'po·lit'i·cal·ly** *adv.*

A·pol·lo (ə päl'ō) the Greek and Roman god of music, poetry, prophecy, and medicine —*n.* any handsome young man

a·pol·o·get·ic (ə päl'ə jet'ik) *adj.* showing apology; expressing regret —**a·pol'o·get·i·cal·ly** *adv.*

a·pol·o·gist (ə päl'ə jist) *n.* one who defends or attempts to justify a doctrine, faith, action, etc.

a·pol'o·gize' (-jīz') *vi.* -**gized'**, -**giz'-ing** to make an apology

a·pol'o·gy (-jē) *n., pl.* -**gies** [< Gr. *apo-*, from + *logos*, speech] **1.** a formal defense of some idea, doctrine, etc.: also **a·pol·o·gi·a** (ap'ə lō'jē ə) **2.** an expressing of regret for a fault, insult, etc. **3.** a poor substitute

ap·o·plex·y (ap'ə plek'sē) *n.* [< Gr. *apo-*, from + *plessein*, to strike] sudden paralysis caused by the breaking or obstruction of a blood vessel in the brain —**ap'o·plec'tic** *adj.*

a·pos·ta·sy (ə päs'tə sē) *n., pl.* -**sies** [< Gr. *apo-*, away + *stasis*, a standing] an abandoning of what one believed in, as a faith, etc.

a·pos'tate' (-tāt') *n.* a person guilty of apostasy

a·pos'ta·tize' (-tə tīz') *vi.* -**tized'**, -**tiz'ing** to become an apostate

a pos·te·ri·o·ri (ā' päs tir'ē ôr'ī) [ML.] **1.** from effect to cause **2.** based on observation or experience

a·pos·tle (ə päs''l) *n.* [< Gr. *apo-*, from + *stellein*, send] **1.** [*usually* A-] any of the disciples of Jesus, esp. the original twelve **2.** the leader of a new movement

ap·os·tol·ic (ap'əs täl'ik) *adj.* **1.** of the Apostles, their teachings, works, etc. **2.** [*often* A-] of the Pope; papal

a·pos·tro·phe (ə päs'trə fē) *n.* [< Gr. *apo-*, from + *strephein*, to turn] the mark (') indicating: **1.** omission of a letter or letters from a word (Ex.: *it's* for *it is*) **2.** the possessive case (Ex.: *Mary's* dress) **3.** certain plural forms (Ex.: five *6's*, dot the *i's*) **4.** an exclamatory address to a person or thing

a·poth·e·car·y (ə päth'ə ker'ē) *n., pl.* -**ies** [< Gr. *apothēkē*, storehouse] a druggist; pharmacist

ap·o·thegm (ap'ə them') *n.* [< Gr. *apo-*, from + *phthengesthai*, to utter] a short, pithy saying

a·poth·e·o·sis (ə päth'ē ō'sis, ap'ə thē'ə sis) *n., pl.* -**ses'** (-sēz') [< Gr. *apo-*, from + *theos*, a god] **1.** the deifying of a person **2.** the glorification of a person or thing **3.** a glorified ideal

Ap·pa·la·chi·a (ap'ə lā'chə, -chē ə) the highland region of the E U.S. extending from N Pa. through N Ala., characterized by poverty

Ap·pa·la·chi·an Mountains (ap' ə lā'chən, -chē ən, -lach'ən) mountain system extending from S Quebec to N Ala.: also **Ap·pa·la'chi·ans**

ap·pall, ap·pal (ə pôl') *vt.* -**palled'**, -**pal'ling** [< L. *ad*, to + *pallidus*, pale] to horrify, dismay, or shock

ap·pa·loo·sa (ap'ə lōō'sə) *n.* [< *Palouse* Indians of NW U.S.] a breed of Western saddle horse with black and white spots on the rump and loins

ap·pa·rat (äp'ə rät', ap'ə rat') *n.* [Russ., apparatus] an organization; esp., a political organization

ap·pa·ra·tus (ap'ə rat'əs, -rāt'-) *n., pl.* -**tus**, -**tus·es** [< L. *ad-*, to + *parare*, prepare] **1.** the materials, tools, etc. for a specific use **2.** any complex machine, device, or system

ap·par·el (ə per'əl) *n.* [ult. < L. *ad-*, to + *parare*, prepare] clothing; attire —*vt.* -**eled** or -**elled**, -**el·ing** or -**el·ling** to clothe; dress

ap·par·ent (ə per'ənt) *adj.* [see APPEAR] **1.** readily seen; visible **2.** evident; obvious **3.** appearing real or true; seeming —**ap·par'ent·ly** *adv.*

ap·pa·ri·tion (ap'ə rish'ən) *n.* [see APPEAR] **1.** anything that appears unexpectedly or strangely **2.** a ghost; phantom **3.** a becoming visible

ap·peal (ə pēl') *vt.* [< L. *ad-*, to + *pellere*, drive] to make an appeal of (a law case) —*vi.* **1.** to make an appeal in a law case **2.** to make an urgent request (*for* help, etc.) **3.** to be attractive or interesting —*n.* **1.** a request for help, etc. **2.** a request for the transference of a law case to a higher court for rehearing **3.** attraction; interest —**ap·peal'ing** *adj.*

ap·pear (ə pir') *vi.* [< L. *ad-*, to + *parere*, become visible] **1.** to come into sight **2.** to become understood or obvious **3.** to seem; look **4.** to present oneself formally in court **5.** to come before the public

ap·pear'ance *n.* **1.** an appearing **2.** the outward aspect of anything; look **3.** a pretense or show —**keep up appearances** to maintain an outward show of being proper, etc. —**put in an appearance** to be present for a short time, as at a party

ap·pease (ə pēz') *vt.* -**peased'**, -**peas'ing** [ult. < L. *ad*, to + *pax*, peace] to pacify, quiet, or satisfy, esp. by giving in to the demands of —**ap·pease'ment** *n.* —**ap·peas'er** *n.*

ap·pel·lant (ə pel'ənt) *n.* a person who appeals, esp. to a higher court

ap·pel'late court (-it) a court that can review appeals and reverse the decisions of lower courts

ap·pel·la·tion (ap'ə lā'shən) *n.* [see APPEAL] a naming or name; title

ap·pend (ə pend') *vt.* [< L. *ad-*, to + *pendere*, suspend] to attach or affix; add as a supplement or appendix

ap·pend'age *n.* anything appended; an external organ or part, as a tail

ap·pen·dec·to·my (ap'ən dek'tə mē) *n., pl.* -**mies** [see -ECTOMY] the surgical removal of the appendix

ap·pen·di·ci·tis (ə pen'də sīt'əs) *n.* [see -ITIS] inflammation of the appendix

ap·pen·dix (ə pen'diks) *n., pl.* -**dix·es**, -**di·ces'** (-də sēz') [see APPEND] **1.** additional material at the end of a book **2.** a small saclike appendage of the large intestine

ap·per·tain (ap'ər tān') *vi.* [< L. *ad-*, to + *pertinere*, to reach] to belong as a function, part, etc.; pertain

ap·pe·ten·cy (ap'ə tən sē) *n., pl.* -**cies** [see ff.] **1.** a craving; appetite **2.**

ap·pe·tite (ap'ə tīt') n. [< L. ad-, to + petere, seek] 1. a desire for food 2. any strong desire; craving

ap'pe·tiz'er (-tī'zər) n. a tasty food that stimulates the appetite

ap'pe·tiz'ing adj. 1. stimulating the appetite 2. savory; delicious

ap·plaud (ə plôd') vt., vi. [< L. ad-, to + plaudere, clap hands] 1. to show approval (of) by clapping the hands, etc. 2. to praise —ap·plaud'er n.

ap·plause (ə plôz') n. approval, esp. as shown by clapping hands

ap·ple (ap''l) n. [< OE. æppel, fruit, apple] 1. a round, firm, fleshy, edible fruit 2. the tree it grows on

apple butter jam made of stewed apples

ap'ple·jack' (-jak') n. a brandy distilled from apple cider

ap'ple·sauce' (-sôs') n. 1. apples cooked to a pulp in water and sweetened 2. [Slang] nonsense

ap·pli·ance (ə plī'əns) n. a device or machine, esp. one for household use

ap·pli·ca·ble (ap'li kə b'l) adj. that can be applied; appropriate —ap'pli·ca·bil'i·ty n.

ap'pli·cant (-kənt) n. one who applies, as for employment, help, etc.

ap·pli·ca·tion (ap'lə kā'shən) n. 1. an applying 2. anything applied, as a remedy 3. a method of being used 4. a request, or a form filled out in making one [an employment application] 5. continued effort; diligence 6. relevance or practicality

ap'pli·ca'tor n. any device for applying medicine or paint, polish, etc.

ap·plied (ə plīd') adj. used in actual practice [applied science]

ap·pli·qué (ap'lə kā') n. [Fr.] decoration made of one material attached to another —vt. -quéd', -qué'ing to decorate with appliqué

ap·ply (ə plī') vt. -plied', -ply'ing [< L. ad-, to + plicare, to fold] 1. to put or spread on [apply glue] 2. to put to practical or specific use [apply your knowledge] 3. to devote (oneself or one's faculties) diligently —vi. 1. to make a request 2. to be suitable or relevant —ap·pli'er n.

ap·point (ə point') vt. [< L. ad-, to + punctum, point] 1. to set (a date, place, etc.) 2. to name for an office, position, etc. 3. to furnish [well-appointed] —ap·point'ee' n.

ap·poin·tive (ə poin'tiv) adj. of or filled by appointment [an appointive office]

ap·point·ment (ə point'mənt) n. 1. an appointing or being appointed 2. a position filled by appointing 3. an engagement to meet someone or be somewhere 4. [pl.] furniture

Ap·po·mat·tox (Court House) (ap'ə mat'əks) former village in C Va., where Lee surrendered to Grant

ap·por·tion (ə pôr'shən) vt. [see AD- & PORTION] to portion out; distribute in shares —ap·por'tion·ment n.

ap·pose (ə pōz') vt. -posed', -pos'ing [< L. ad-, to + ponere, put] to put side by side or opposite —ap·pos'a·ble adj.

ap·po·site (ap'ə zit) adj. [see prec.] appropriate; fitting; apt —ap'po·site·ly adv. —ap'po·site·ness n.

ap·po·si·tion (ap'ə zish'ən) n. 1. an apposing, or the position resulting from this 2. the placing of a word or phrase beside another in explanation, as in Jim, my son, is here —ap·pos·i·tive (ə päz'ə tiv) adj., n.

ap·prais·al (ə prā'z'l) n. 1. an appraising 2. an appraised value

ap·praise (ə prāz') vt. -praised', -prais'ing [< L. ad-, to + pretium, value] 1. to set a price for; estimate the value of 2. to judge the quality or worth of —ap·prais'er n. —ap·prais'ing·ly adv.

ap·pre·ci·a·ble (ə prē'shə b'l, -shē ə b'l) adj. [see prec.] enough to be perceived or estimated; noticeable —ap·pre'ci·a·bly adv.

ap·pre·ci·ate (ə prē'shē āt') vt. -at'ed, -at'ing [see APPRAISE] 1. to think well of; esteem 2. to recognize gratefully 3. to estimate the quality of 4. to be fully or sensitively aware of —vi. to rise in value —ap·pre'ci·a'tor n. —ap·pre'ci·a·to·ry (-shə tôr'ē) adj.

ap·pre'ci·a'tion n. 1. grateful recognition, as of benefits 2. sensitive awareness, as of art

ap·pre'ci·a·tive (-shə tiv, -shē·ə-) adj. feeling or showing appreciation —ap·pre'ci·a·tive·ly adv.

ap·pre·hend (ap'rə hend') vt. [< L. ad-, to + prehendere, seize] 1. to capture or arrest 2. to perceive; understand 3. to fear; dread

ap'pre·hen·sion (-hen'shən) n. 1. capture or arrest 2. perception or understanding 3. fear; anxiety

ap'pre·hen·sive (-siv) adj. anxious; uneasy —ap'pre·hen'sive·ly adv. —ap'pre·hen'sive·ness n.

ap·pren·tice (ə pren'tis) n. [see APPREHEND] 1. a person being taught a craft or trade, now usually as a member of a labor union 2. any beginner —vt. -ticed, -tic·ing to place or accept as an apprentice —ap·pren'tice·ship' n.

ap·prise, ap·prize (ə prīz') vt. -prised' or -prized', -pris'ing or -priz'ing [see APPREHEND] to notify

ap·prize, ap·prise (ə prīz') vt. -prized' or -prised', -priz'ing or -pris'ing same as APPRAISE

ap·proach (ə prōch') vi. [< L. ad, to + propius, nearer] to come closer —vt. 1. to come nearer to 2. to approximate 3. to make a proposal or request to 4. to set about dealing with —n. 1. a coming closer 2. an approximation 3. [pl.] overtures (to someone) 4. means of reaching;

access 5. a preliminary step or movement —**ap·proach′a·ble** *adj.*

ap·pro·ba·tion (ap′rə bā′shən) *n.* [see APPROVE] approval or consent

ap·pro·pri·ate (ə prō′prē āt′; *for adj.* -it) *vt.* **-at′ed, -at′ing** [< L. *ad-*, to + *proprius*, one's own] 1. to take for one's own use, often improperly 2. to set aside (money, etc.) for a specific use —*adj.* suitable; fit; proper —**ap·pro′pri·ate·ly** *adv.* —**ap·pro′pri·ate·ness** *n.* —**ap·pro′pri·a′tor** *n.*

ap·pro·pri·a′tion *n.* 1. an appropriating or being appropriated 2. money, etc. set aside for a specific use

ap·prov·al (ə prōō′v′l) *n.* 1. the act of approving 2. favorable attitude or opinion 3. formal consent —**on approval** for the customer to examine and decide whether to buy or return

ap·prove (ə prōōv′) *vt.* **-proved′, -prov′ing** [< L. *ad-*, to + *probus*, good] 1. to give one's consent to 2. to consider to be good, satisfactory, etc. —*vi.* to have a favorable opinion (*of*) —**ap·prov′ing·ly** *adv.*

ap·prox·i·mate (ə präk′sə mit; *for v.* -māt′) *adj.* [< L. *ad*, to + *proximus*, nearest] 1. much like 2. more or less correct or exact —*vt.* **-mat′ed, -mat′ing** to come near to; be almost the same as —**ap·prox′i·mate·ly** *adv.*

ap·prox′i·ma′tion (-mā′shən) *n.* 1. a close estimate 2. a near likeness

ap·pur·te·nance (ə pur′t′n əns) *n.* [see APPERTAIN] 1. something added to a more important thing 2. [*pl.*] apparatus or equipment 3. *Law.* an additional, subordinate right

a·pri·cot (ap′rə kät′, ā′prə-) *n.* [< L. *praecoquus*, early matured (fruit)] 1. a small, yellowish-orange, peachlike fruit 2. the tree it grows on

A·pril (ā′prəl) *n.* [< L.] the fourth month of the year, having 30 days

a pri·o·ri (ā′ prē ôr′ē, ā′ prī ôr′ī) [L.] 1. from cause to effect 2. based on theory instead of experience

a·pron (ā′prən) *n.* [< L. *mappa*, napkin] 1. a garment worn over the front part of the body to protect one's clothes 2. any extending or protecting part 3. the front part of a stage 4. a paved area, as where a driveway broadens to meet the road —**a′pron-like′** *adj.*

ap·ro·pos (ap′rə pō′) *adv.* [Fr. *à propos*, to the purpose] at the right time; opportunely —*adj.* relevant; apt —**apropos of** in connection with

apse (aps) *n.* [< L. *apsis*, an arch] a semicircular or polygonal projection of a church, usually domed or vaulted

apt (apt) *adj.* [< L. *aptus*] 1. appropriate; fitting 2. tending or inclined; likely 3. quick to learn —**apt′ly** *adv.* —**apt′ness** *n.*

apt. *pl.* **apts.** apartment

ap·ti·tude (ap′tə tōōd′, -tyōōd′) *n.* [see APT] 1. suitability; fitness 2. a natural tendency, ability, or talent 3. quickness to learn

aq·ua (ak′wə, äk′-) *n., pl.* **-uas, -uae** (-wē) [L.] water —*adj.* [< AQUAMARINE] bluish-green

aq·ua·cul·ture (ak′wə kul′chər, äk′-) *n.* [AQUA + CULTURE] the cultivation of water plants and animals for human use

Aq·ua·lung (ak′wə luŋ′, äk′-) *a trademark for* an apparatus for breathing under water —*n.* such an apparatus: usually **aq′ua·lung′**

aq·ua·ma·rine (ak′wə mə rēn′, äk′-) *n.* [L. *aqua marina*, sea water] 1. a transparent, pale bluish-green beryl 2. its color —*adj.* bluish-green

aq·ua·naut (ak′wə nôt′) *n.* [AQUA + (ASTRO)NAUT] one trained to use a watertight underwater chamber as a base for undersea experiments

aq·ua·plane (ak′wə plān′, äk′-) *n.* [AQUA + PLANE¹] a board on which one rides standing up as it is pulled by a motorboat —*vi.* **-planed′, -plan′ing** to ride on such a board as a sport

a·quar·ist (ə kwer′ist) *n.* 1. a hobbyist with an aquarium 2. a person in charge of an aquarium (sense 2)

a·quar′i·um (-ē əm) *n., pl.* **-i·ums, -i·a** (-ə) [< L. *aquarius*, of water] 1. a tank, etc. for keeping live water animals and plants 2. a place where such collections are exhibited

A·quar′i·us (-əs) [L., water carrier] the eleventh sign of the zodiac

a·quat·ic (ə kwät′ik, -kwat′-) *adj.* 1. growing or living in water 2. done in or on the water [*aquatic* sports]

aq·ua·vit (ak′wə vēt′, äk′-) *n.* [< L. *aqua vitae*, water of life] a Scandinavian alcoholic liquor distilled from grain or potatoes and flavored with caraway

aq·ue·duct (ak′wə dukt′) *n.* [< L. *aqua*, water + *ducere*, to lead] 1. a large pipe or conduit for bringing water from a distant source 2. an elevated structure supporting this

a·que·ous (ā′kwē əs, ak′wē-) *adj.* of, like, or formed by water

aqueous humor a watery fluid between the cornea and the lens of the eye

aq·ui·line (ak′wə lin′, -lən) *adj.* [< L. *aquila*, eagle] 1. of or like an eagle 2. like an eagle's beak, as a curved nose

A·qui·nas (ə kwī′nəs), Saint **Thomas** 1225?–74; It. theologian & philosopher

Ar *Chem.* argon

AR Arkansas

Ar·ab (ar′əb, er′-) *n.* 1. a native of Arabia 2. any of a Semitic people in, or orig. from, Arabia; commonly, a Bedouin —*adj.* of the Arabs

ar·a·besque (ar′ə besk′) *n.* [< It. *Arabo*, Arab] an elaborate design of flowers, foliage, etc.

A·ra·bi·a (ə rā′bēə) peninsula in SW Asia —**A·ra′bi·an** *adj., n.*

Arabian Nights, The a collection of ancient tales from Arabia, India, Persia, etc.

ARABESQUE

Arabian Peninsula *same as* ARABIA

Ar·a·bic (ar′ə bik) *adj.* 1. of Arabia 2. of the Arabs —*n.* the Semitic language of the Arabs, spoken in Arabia, Iraq, Syria, N Africa, etc.

Arabic numerals the figures 1, 2, 3, 4, 5, 6, 7, 8, 9, and the 0 (zero)

ar·a·ble (ar'ə b'l) *adj.* [< L. *arare*, to plow] suitable for plowing

a·rach·nid (ə rak'nid) *n.* [< Gr. *arachnē*, spider] any of a group of small animals with eight legs, including spiders and scorpions

Ar·a·ma·ic (ar'ə mā'ik) *n.* a group of Semitic languages of Biblical times

ar·bi·ter (är'bə tər) *n.* [L., a witness] arbitrator; judge; umpire

ar·bi·tra·ment (är bit'rə mənt) *n.* arbitration or an arbitrator's verdict or award

ar·bi·trar·y (är'bə trer'ē) *adj.* [see ARBITER] 1. left to one's judgment 2. based on one's preference or whim; capricious 3. absolute; despotic —**ar'bi·trar'i·ly** *adv.* —**ar'bi·trar'i·ness** *n.*

ar·bi·trate (är'bə trāt') *vt., vi.* -trat'ed, -trat'ing [see ARBITER] 1. to submit (a dispute) to arbitration 2. to decide (a dispute) as an arbitrator —**ar'bi·tra'tion** *n.*

ar'bi·tra'tor (-ər) *n.* a person selected to judge a dispute

ar·bor (är'bər) *n.* [< L. *herba*, herb] a place shaded by trees, shrubs, or vines on a latticework; bower

ar·bo·re·al (är bôr'ē əl) *adj.* [< L. *arbor*, tree] 1. of or like a tree 2. living in trees

ar·bo·re·tum (är'bə rēt'əm) *n., pl.* -tums, -ta (-tə) [L.] a place where many kinds of trees and shrubs are grown for study or display

ar·bor·vi·tae (är'bər vīt'ē) *n.* [L., tree of life] any of various cypress trees having sprays of scalelike leaves

ar·bu·tus (är byōōt'əs) *n.* [L.] 1. a tree or shrub with dark-green leaves and scarlet berries 2. a trailing plant with white or pink flower clusters

arc (ärk) *n.* [< L. *arcus*, a bow, arch] 1. a bowlike curved line or object 2. the band of incandescent light formed when a current leaps a short gap between electrodes 3. any part of a curve, esp. of a circle —*vi.* arced or arcked, arc'ing or arck'ing to move in a curved course or form an arc

ar·cade (är kād') *n.* [see prec.] 1. a covered passageway, esp. one lined with shops 2. a line of arches and their supporting columns

ar·cane (är kān') *adj.* [< L. *arcanus*, hidden] secret or esoteric

arch¹ (ärch) *n.* [see ARC] 1. a curved structure used as a support over an open space, as in a doorway 2. the form of an arch 3. anything shaped like an arch —*vt., vi.* 1. to span with or as an arch 2. to form (into) an arch —**arched** (ärcht) *adj.*

arch² (ärch) *adj.* [< ff.] 1. chief; principal 2. gaily mischievous; pert

arch- [< Gr. *archos*, ruler] *a prefix meaning* chief, principal [*archbishop*]

-arch (ärk) [see prec.] *a suffix meaning* ruler [*matriarch*]

arch. 1. archaic 2. architecture

ar·chae·ol·o·gy (är'kē äl'ə jē) *n.* [< Gr. *archaios*, ancient + -LOGY] the study of the life of ancient peoples, as by excavation of ancient cities, etc.: also sp. **archeology** —**ar'chae·o·log'i·cal** (-ə läj'ə k'l) *adj.* —**ar'chae·o·log'i·cal·ly** *adv.* —**ar'chae·ol'o·gist** *n.*

ar·cha·ic (är kā'ik) *adj.* [< Gr. *archaios*, ancient] 1. ancient 2. old-fashioned 3. no longer used except in poetry, church ritual, etc., as the word *begat* —**ar·cha'i·cal·ly** *adv.*

ar'cha·ism (-kē iz'm) *n.* an archaic word, usage, style, etc. —**ar'cha·ist** *n.*

arch·an·gel (ärk'ān'j'l) *n.* an angel of high rank

arch·bish·op (ärch'bish'əp) *n.* a bishop of the highest rank —**arch'bish'op·ric** (-ə prik) *n.*

arch'dea'con (-dēk'n) *n.* a church official ranking just below a bishop

arch'di'o·cese *n.* the diocese of an archbishop —**arch'di·oc'e·san** (-di-äs'ə sən) *adj.*

arch'duke' (-dōōk') *n.* a prince of the former Austrian royal family —**arch'duch'ess** *n.fem.*

arch'en'e·my *n., pl.* -mies a chief enemy —**the archenemy** Satan

arch·er (är'chər) *n.* [< L. *arcus*, a bow] one who shoots with bow and arrow

arch'er·y *n.* the practice or art of shooting with bow, and arrow

ar·che·type (är'kə tīp') *n.* [< Gr. *archos*, first + *typos*, a mark] an original pattern or model; prototype —**ar'che·typ'al**, **ar'che·typ'i·cal** (-tīp'i k'l) *adj.*

ar·chi·e·pis·co·pal (är'kē ə pis'kə p'l) *adj.* of an archbishop or archbishopric

Ar·chi·me·des (är'kə mē'dēz) 287?–212 B.C.; Gr. physicist & inventor

ar·chi·pel·a·go (är'kə pel'ə gō') *n., pl.* -goes', -gos' [< Gr. *archi-*, chief + *pelagos*, sea] 1. a sea with many islands 2. a group of many islands

ar·chi·tect (är'kə tekt') *n.* [< Gr. *archos*, chief + *tektōn*, carpenter] 1. a person who designs buildings and supervises their construction 2. any builder or planner

ar·chi·tec·ton·ics (är'kə tek tän'iks) *n.pl.* [*with sing. v.*] 1. the science of architecture 2. structural design, as of a symphony —**ar'chi·tec·ton'ic** *adj.*

ar'chi·tec'ture (-tek'chər) *n.* 1. the science or profession of designing and constructing buildings 2. a style of construction 3. design and construction' —**ar'chi·tec'tur·al** *adj.* —**ar'chi·tec'tur·al·ly** *adv.*

ar·chi·trave (är'kə trāv') *n.* [< L. *archi-*, ARCH- + *trabs*, a beam] in a classical building, the beam resting directly on the tops of the columns

ar·chives (är'kīvz) *n.pl.* [< Gr. *archeion*, town hall] 1. a place where public records are kept: also **ar'chive**, *n.sing.* **2.** the public records kept in such a place —**ar·chi·vist** (är'kə vist, -kĭ'-) *n.*

arch·way (ärch'wā') *n.* a passage under an arch, or the arch itself

-ar·chy (är'kē) [< Gr. *archein*, to rule] *a suffix meaning* ruling [*monarchy*]

arc lamp (or **light**) a lamp in which the light is produced by an arc between electrodes

arc·tic (ärk'tik, är'-) *adj.* [< Gr. *arktikos*, northern] **1.** of or near the North Pole **2.** very cold —**the Arctic** the region around the North Pole

Arctic Circle [*also* a- c-] an imaginary circle parallel to the equator, 66°33' north of it

Arctic Ocean ocean surrounding the North Pole

-ard (ərd) [< MHG. *hart*, bold] *a suffix meaning* one who does something to excess [*drunkard*]

ar·dent (är'd'nt) *adj.* [< L. *ardere*, to burn] **1.** passionate **2.** zealous **3.** glowing or burning —**ar'dent·ly** *adv.*

ar·dor (är'dər) *n.* [< L. *ardor*, a flame] **1.** emotional warmth; passion **2.** zeal **3.** intense heat Also, Brit. sp., **ardour**

ar·du·ous (är'joo wəs) *adj.* [L. *arduus*, steep] **1.** difficult to do; laborious **2.** using much energy; strenuous —**ar'du·ous·ly** *adv.*

are (är) [OE. *aron*] *pl. & 2d pers. sing., pres. indic., of* BE

ar·e·a (er'ē ə) *n.* [L., vacant place] **1.** an expanse of land; region **2.** a total outside surface, measured in square units **3.** a part of a house, district, etc. [*play area, slum area*] **4.** scope or extent

area code any of the numbers assigned as a telephone code to the areas into which the U.S. and Canada are divided

a·re·na (ə rē'nə) *n.* [L., sandy place] **1.** the center of an ancient Roman amphitheater, where contests were held **2.** any place or sphere of struggle

arena theater a theater having a central stage surrounded by seats

aren't (ärnt) *are* not

Ar·es (er'ēz) *Gr. Myth.* the god of war

ar·gent (är'jənt) *adj.* [< L. *argentum*, silver] [Poet.] silvery

Ar·gen·ti·na (är'jən tē'nə) country in S S.America: 1,084,120 sq. mi.; pop. 22,691,000 —**Ar'gen·tine'** (-tēn', -tīn') *adj., n.*

ar·gon (är'gän) *n.* [Gr., inert] a chemical element, an inert gas found in the air and used in light bulbs, radio tubes, etc.

Ar·go·naut (är'gə nôt') *n. Gr. Myth.* any of those who sailed with Jason to find the Golden Fleece

ar·go·sy (är'gə sē) *n., pl.* **-sies** [< It. *Ragusea*, ship of Ragusa, a Sicilian city] [Poet.] a large merchant ship or fleet of such ships

ar·got (är'gō, -gət) *n.* [Fr.] the specialized vocabulary of a particular group, as of criminals, tramps, etc.

ar·gue (är'gyōō) *vi.* **-gued, -gu·ing** [< L. *arguere*, prove] **1.** to give reasons (*for* or *against*) **2.** to dispute; quarrel —*vt.* **1.** to dispute about;

debate **2.** to maintain; contend **3.** to persuade by giving reasons —**ar'gu·a·ble** *adj.*

ar'gu·ment (-gyə mənt) *n.* **1.** a reason or reasons offered in arguing **2.** an arguing; debate **3.** a summary

ar'gu·men·ta'tion (-men tā'shən) *n.* the process of arguing; debate

ar'gu·men·ta·tive (-men'tə tiv) *adj.* **1.** controversial **2.** apt to argue; contentious

ar·gyle (är'gīl) *adj.* [< *Argyll*, Scotland] knitted or woven in a diamond-shaped pattern, as socks

a·ri·a (ä'rē ə) *n.* [It. < L. *aer*, air] a song in an opera, etc., for solo voice

-ar·i·an (er'ē ən, ar'-) [< L.] *a suffix variously denoting* age, sect, social belief, or occupation [*octogenarian*]

ar·id (ar'id, er'-) *adj.* [< L. *arere*, be dry] **1.** dry and barren **2.** uninteresting; dull —**a·rid·i·ty** (ə rid'ə tē) *n.*

Ar·i·es (er'ēz, -i ēz') [L., the Ram] the first sign of the zodiac

a·right (ə rīt') *adv.* correctly

a·rise (ə rīz') *vi.* **a·rose'** (-rōz'), **a·ris'en** (-riz'n), **a·ris'ing** [< OE. *a-*, out + *risan*, rise] **1.** to get up, as from bed **2.** to rise; ascend **3.** to come into being **4.** to result (*from*)

ar·is·toc·ra·cy (ar'ə stä'krə sē, er'-) *n., pl.* **-cies** [< Gr. *aristos*, best + *kratein*, to rule] **1.** government by a privileged minority, usually of inherited wealth **2.** a country with such government **3.** a privileged ruling class; upper class

a·ris·to·crat (ə ris'tə krat', ar'is-) *n.* **1.** a member of the aristocracy **2.** one with the tastes, manners, etc. of the upper class —**a·ris'to·crat'ic** *adj.* —**a·ris'to·crat'i·cal·ly** *adv.*

Ar·is·toph·a·nes (ar'ə stäf'ə nēz') 448?–380? B.C.; Gr. writer of comedies

Ar·is·tot·le (ar'is tät'l) 384–322 B.C.; Gr. philosopher —**Ar·is·to·te·li·an** (ar'is tə tēl'yən) *adj., n.*

a·rith·me·tic (ə rith'mə tik) *n.* [< Gr. *arithmos*, number] the science of computing by positive, real numbers —**ar·ith·met·i·cal** (ar'ith met'i k'l, er'-), **ar'ith·met'ic** *adj.* —**a·rith'me·ti'cian** (-mə tish'ən) *n.*

arithmetic mean the average obtained by dividing a sum by the number of quantities added to make the sum

Ar·i·zo·na (ar'ə zō'nə, er'-) State of the SW U.S.: 113,909 sq. mi.; pop. 2,718,000; cap. Phoenix: abbrev. **Ariz.** —**Ar'i·zo'nan** *adj., n.*

ark (ärk) *n.* [< L. *arcere*, enclose] **1.** *Bible* the boat in which Noah, his family, and two of every kind of creature survived the Flood **2.** *same as* ARK OF THE COVENANT **3.** an enclosure in a synagogue for the scrolls of the Torah

Ar·kan·sas (är'k'n sô') State of the SC U.S.: 53,104 sq. mi.; pop. 2,286,000; cap. Little Rock: abbrev. **Ark.** —**Ar·kan'san** (-kan'z'n) *adj.*

ark of the covenant *Bible* the chest containing the two stone tablets inscribed with the Ten Commandments

arm¹ (ärm) *n.* [OE. *earm*] **1.** an upper limb of the human body **2.** anything like this in shape, function, position, etc. —**with open arms** cordially

arm² (ärm) n. [< L. *arma*, weapons] 1. a weapon: *usually used in pl.* 2. any branch of the military forces —vt. to provide with weapons, etc. —vi. to prepare for war or any struggle —**under arms** ready for war —**up in arms** 1. prepared to fight 2. indignant —**armed** adj.

ar·ma·da (är mä′də) n. [Sp. < L. *arma*, weapons] 1. a fleet of warships 2. a fleet of warplanes

ar·ma·dil·lo (är′mə dil′ō) n., pl. **-los** [Sp.: see prec.] a small burrowing mammal of tropical America, covered with bony plates

Ar·ma·ged·don (är′mə ged′'n) n. 1. *Bible* the site of the last decisive battle between the forces of good and evil 2. any great, decisive battle

ar·ma·ment (är′mə mənt) n. 1. [*often pl.*] all the military forces and equipment of a nation 2. all the military equipment of a warship, etc. 3. an arming or being armed for war

ar·ma·ture (är′mə chər) n. [< L. *armare*, to arm] 1. any protective covering 2. the iron core wound with wire, in which electromotive force is produced in a generator or motor

arm′chair′ n. a chair with supports at the sides for one's arms

armed forces all the military, naval, and air forces of a country

Ar·me·ni·a (är mēn′ē ə) former kingdom of SW Asia, now mostly a republic of the U.S.S.R. —**Ar·me′ni·an** adj., n.

arm′ful (-fool′) n., pl. **-fuls′** as much as the arms or an arm can hold

arm′hole′ n. an opening for the arm in a garment

ar·mi·stice (är′mə stis) n. [< L. *arma*, arms + *stare*, stand still] a truce preliminary to a peace treaty

Armistice Day *see* VETERANS DAY

arm′let (-lit) n. an ornamental band worn around the upper arm

ar·mor (är′mər) n. [< L. *armare*, to arm] any defensive or protective covering —vt., vi. to put armor on —**ar′mored** (-mərd) adj.

armored car a vehicle covered with armor plate, as a truck for carrying money to or from a bank

ar·mo·ri·al (är môr′ē əl) adj. of coats of arms; heraldic

ar·mor·y (är′mər ē) n., pl. **-ies** [see ARMOR] 1. an arsenal 2. an armaments factory 3. a military drill hall

arm′pit′ n. the hollow under the arm at the shoulder

arm′rest′ n. a support for the arm as on the inside of a car door

ar·my (är′mē) n., pl. **-mies** [ult. < L. *arma*, weapons] 1. a large, organized body of soldiers for waging war, esp. on land 2. any large number of persons, animals, etc.

Ar·nold (är′nəld), **Benedict** 1741-1801; Am. Revolutionary general who became a traitor

a·ro·ma (ə rō′mə) n. [< Gr. *arōma*, spice] a pleasant odor; fragrance

ar·o·mat·ic (ar′ə mat′ik) adj. of or having an aroma; fragrant or pungent —n. an aromatic plant, chemical, etc. —**ar′o·mat′i·cal·ly** adv.

a·rose (ə rōz′) pt. of ARISE

a·round (ə round′) adv. [ME.] 1. in a circle 2. in every direction 3. in circumference 4. to the opposite direction 5. [Colloq.] nearby [stay *around*] —prep. 1. so as to encircle or envelop 2. on the border of 3. in various places in or on 4. [Colloq.] about [*around* 1890]

a·rouse (ə rouz′) vt. **a·roused′**, **a·rous′ing** 1. to wake from sleep 2. to stir, as to action 3. to evoke [to *arouse* pity] —**a·rous′al** n.

ar·peg·gio (är pej′ō) n., pl. **-gios** [It. < *arpa*, a harp] a chord whose notes are played in quick succession

ar·raign (ə rān′) vt. [< L. *ad*, to + *ratio*, reason] 1. to bring before a law court to answer charges 2. to call to account; accuse —**ar·raign′ment** n.

ar·range (ə rānj′) vt. **-ranged′**, **-rang′ing** [< OFr. *renc*, rank] 1. to put in the correct order 2. to classify 3. to prepare or plan 4. to arrive at an agreement about 5. *Music* to adapt (a work) to particular instruments or voices —vi. *Music* to write arrangements, esp. as a profession —**ar·rang′er** n.

ar·range′ment n. 1. an arranging 2. a result or manner of arranging 3. [*usually pl.*] a plan 4. a settlement 5. *Music a)* an arranging of a composition *b)* the composition as thus arranged

ar·rant (ar′ənt) adj. [var. of ERRANT] out-and-out; notorious

ar·ras (ar′əs) n. [< *Arras*, Fr. city] 1. an elaborate kind of tapestry 2. a wall hanging, esp. of tapestry

ar·ray (ə rā′) vt. [< ML. *arredare*, put in order] 1. to place in order 2. to dress in finery —n. 1. an orderly grouping, esp. of troops 2. an impressive display 3. fine clothes

ar·rears (ə rirz′) n.pl. [< L. *ad*, to + *retro*, behind] overdue debts —**in arrears** behind in paying a debt, doing one's work, etc.

ar·rest (ə rest′) vt. [< L. *ad-*, to + *restare*, to stop] 1. to stop or check 2. to seize by authority of the law 3. to catch and keep (the attention, etc.) —n. an arresting or being arrested —**under arrest** in legal custody

ar·rest′ing adj. attracting attention; interesting

ar·riv·al (ə rī′v′l) n. 1. an arriving 2. a person or thing that arrives

ar·rive (ə rīv′) vi. **-rived′**, **-riv′ing** [< L. *ad-*, to + *ripa*, shore] 1. to reach one's destination 2. to come [the time has *arrived*] 3. to attain fame, etc. —**arrive at** to reach by thinking, etc.

†ar·ri·ve·der·ci (ä rē′ve der′chē) interj. [It.] goodbye

ar·ro·gant (ar′ə gənt) adj. [see ARRO-

fat, āpe, cär; ten, ēven; is, bīte; gō, hôrn, tool, look; oil, out; up, fur; chin; she; thin, then; zh, leisure; ŋ, ring; ə for a in ago; ', (ā′b'l); ë, Fr. coeur; ö, Fr. feu; Fr. mon; ü, Fr. duc; kh, G. ich, doch; ‡ foreign; < derived from

GATE] full of or due to pride; haughty
—**ar′ro·gance** n. —**ar′ro·gant·ly** adv.

ar′ro·gate (-gāt′) vt. **-gat′ed, -gat′·ing** [< L. ad-, for + rogare, ask] to claim or seize without right —**ar′ro·ga′tion** n.

ar·row (ar′ō) n. [OE. arwe] 1. a pointed shaft, shot from a bow 2. a sign (←) used to indicate direction

ar′row·head′ (-hed′) n. the separable, pointed tip of an arrow

ar′row·root′ n. [< use as antidote for poisoned arrows] 1. a tropical American plant with starchy roots 2. a starch made from its roots

ar·roy·o (ə roi′ō) n., pl. **-os** [Sp. < L. arrugia, mine pit] [Southwest] 1. a dry gully 2. a rivulet or stream

ar·se·nal (är′s'n əl) n. [< Ar. dār (ẹ) ṣinā′a, workshop] 1. a place for making or storing weapons, etc. 2. a store or collection

ar·se·nic (är′s'n ik) n. [< L. < Gr.: ult. < Per. zar, gold] a silvery-white, very poisonous chemical element, compounds of which are used in insecticides, etc. —**ar·sen′i·cal** (-sen′ə k'l), **ar′se′ni·ous** (-sē′nē əs) adj.

ar·son (är′s'n) n. [< L. ardere, to burn] the crime of purposely setting fire to a building —**ar′son·ist** n.

art[1] (ärt) n. [< L. ars] 1. human creativity 2. skill 3. any specific skill or its application 4. any craft or its principles 5. a making of things that have form or beauty 6. any branch of this, as painting, sculpture, etc. 7. drawings, paintings, statues, etc. 8. a branch of learning; specif., [pl.] same as LIBERAL ARTS 9. cunning 10. sly trick; wile: usually used in pl.

art[2] (ärt) archaic 2d pers. sing., pres. indic., of BE: used with thou

art. 1. article 2. artificial

art dec·o (dek′ō, dā′kō) a decorative style of the late 1920's and the 1930's, derived from cubism

ar·te·ri·o·scle·ro·sis (är tir′ē ō sklə rō′sis) n. [see ff. & SCLEROSIS] a thickening and hardening of the walls of the arteries, as in old age

ar·ter·y (är′tər ē) n., pl. **-ies** [< Gr. aeirein, to raise] 1. any of the tubes carrying blood from the heart 2. a main route—**ar·te′ri·al** (-tir′ē əl) adj.

ar·te·sian well (är tē′zhən) [< Fr. Artois, former Fr. province] a deep well in which water is forced up by pressure of underground water draining from higher ground

art·ful (ärt′f'l) adj. 1. skillful or clever 2. cunning; crafty —**art′ful·ly** adv. —**art′ful·ness** n.

ar·thri·tis (är thrīt′is) n. [Gr. < arthron, a joint + -ITIS] inflammation of a joint or joints —**ar·thrit′ic** (-thrit′ik) adj.

ar·thro·pod (är′thrə päd′) n. [< Gr. arthron, a joint + -POD] any of a phylum of invertebrate animals with jointed legs and a segmented body

ar′thro·scope′ n. [< Gr. arthron, a joint + -SCOPE] an endoscope used for joints

Ar·thur (är′thər) n. 1. legendary 6th-cent. king of Britain 2. Chester A., 1830–86; 21st president of the U.S. (1881–85) —**Ar·thu′ri·an** (-thoor′ē ən) adj.

ar·ti·choke (är′tə chōk′) n. [ult. < Ar. al-harsūf] 1. a thistlelike plant 2. its flower head, cooked as food

ar·ti·cle (är′ti k'l) n. [< L. artus, a joint] 1. one of the sections of a document 2. a complete piece of writing, as in a newspaper, magazine, etc. 3. a separate item [an article of luggage] 4. Gram. any one of the words a, an, or the, used as adjectives

ar·tic·u·late (är tik′yə lit; for v. -lāt′) adj. [< L. artus, joint] 1. jointed: usually **ar·tic′u·lat′ed** 2. spoken distinctly 3. able to speak 4. expressing oneself clearly —vt. **-lat′ed, -lat′ing** 1. to connect by joints 2. to put together in a connected way 3. to utter distinctly 4. to express clearly —vi. 1. to speak distinctly 2. to be jointed —**ar·tic′u·late·ly** adv. —**ar·tic′u·la′tion** n.

ar·ti·fact (är′tə fakt′) n. any object made by human work

ar·ti·fice (är′tə fis) n. [< L. ars, art + facere, make] 1. skill or ingenuity 2. trickery 3. an artful trick

ar·tif·i·cer (är tif′ə sər) n. 1. a skilled craftsman 2. an inventor

ar·ti·fi·cial (är′tə fish′əl) adj. [see ARTIFICE] 1. made by human work or art; not natural 2. simulated [artificial teeth] 3. affected [an artificial smile] —**ar′ti·fi′ci·al′i·ty** (-ē al′ə tē) n. —**ar′ti·fi′cial·ly** adv.

artificial intelligence in computer science, the development of machines capable of reasoning, learning, etc.

artificial respiration the maintenance of breathing by artificial means, as by forcing breath into the mouth

ar·til·ler·y (är til′ər ē) n. [ult. < L. ars, handicraft] 1. mounted guns, as cannon 2. the science of guns; gunnery —the **artillery** the branch of an army using heavy mounted guns —**ar·til′ler·y·man** (-mən) n., pl. **-men**

ar·ti·san (är′tə z'n) n. [ult. < L. ars, art] a skilled craftsman

art·ist (är′tist) n. 1. one who is skilled in any of the fine arts, esp. in painting, sculpture, etc. 2. one who does anything very well

ar·tis·tic (är tis′tik) adj. 1. of art or artists 2. done skillfully 3. sensitive to beauty —**ar·tis′ti·cal·ly** adv.

art·ist·ry (är′tis trē) n. artistic quality, ability, work, etc.

art·less (ärt′lis) adj. 1. lacking skill or art 2. simple; natural 3. without guile; ingenuous —**art′less·ly** adv. —**art′less·ness** n.

art·y adj. **-i·er, -i·est** [Colloq.] affectedly artistic —**art′i·ness** n.

ar·um (er′əm) n. [L.] any of a family of plants with flowers enveloped within a hoodlike leaf

Ar·y·an (ar′ē ən, er′-) n. [< Sans. ārya, noble] 1. formerly, the hypothetical parent language of the Indo-European family 2. a person supposed to be a descendant of the prehistoric peoples who spoke this language Aryan has no validity as an ethnological term, as in Nazi use

as (az, əz) *adv.* [< ALSO] **1.** equally [*as* happy as a lark] **2.** for instance [certain colors, *as* green and blue] **3.** when related in a specified way [this view *as* contrasted with that] —*conj.* **1.** to the same amount or degree that [straight *as* an arrow] **2.** in the same manner that [do *as* you are told] **3.** while [she wept *as* she spoke] **4.** because [*as* you object, we won't go] **5.** that the consequence is [so clear *as* to be obvious] **6.** though [tall *as* he is, he can't reach it] —*pron.* **1.** a fact that [he is tired, *as* you can see] **2.** that (preceded by *such* or *the same*) [the same color *as* yours] —*prep.* in the role or function of [he poses *as* a friend] —**as for** (or to) concerning —**as if** (or **though**) as it (or one) would if —**as is** [Colloq.] just as it is —**as it were** as if it were so

As *Chem.* arsenic

as·a·fet·i·da, as·a·foet·i·da (as'ə fet'ə də) *n.* [< Per. āzā, gum + L. *fetida*, fetid] a bad-smelling resin formerly used in medicine

as·bes·tos, as·bes·tus (as bes'təs, az-) *n.* [< Gr. *a-*, not + *sbennynai*, extinguish] a fire-resistant, fibrous mineral used in fireproofing, electrical insulation, etc.

as·cend (ə send') *vi., vt.* [< L. *ad-*, to + *scandere*, to climb] **1.** to go up; mount **2.** to succeed to (a throne)

as·cend'an·cy, as·cend'en·cy (-ən sē) *n.* controlling position; domination

as·cend'ant, as·cend'ent (-ənt) *adj.* **1.** rising **2.** in control; dominant —**in the ascendant** at or nearing the height of power, fame, etc.

as·cen·sion (ə sen'shən) *n.* **1.** an ascending **2.** [A-] the fortieth day after Easter, celebrating the Ascension —**the Ascension** *Bible* the bodily ascent of Jesus into heaven

as·cent (ə sent') *n.* **1.** an ascending **2.** an upward slope

as·cer·tain (as'ər tān') *vt.* [see AD- & CERTAIN] to find out with certainty

as·cet·ic (ə set'ik) *adj.* [< Gr. *askein*, to train the body] self-denying; austere —*n.* one who leads a life of strict self-denial, esp. for religious purposes —**as·cet'i·cism** (-ə siz'm) *n.*

a·scor·bic acid (ə skôr'bik) [A- + SCORB(UTIC) + -IC] vitamin C

as·cot (as'kət, -kät') *n.* a necktie with very broad ends hanging from the knot

as·cribe (ə skrīb') *vt.-cribed', -crib'ing* [< L. *ad-*, to + *scribere*, write] **1.** to assign (*to* a supposed cause) **2.** to regard as belonging (*to*) or coming from someone —**as·crib'a·ble** *adj.* —**as·crip·tion** (ə skrip'shən) *n.*

ASCOT

a·sep·tic (ā sep'tik, ə-) *adj.* free from disease-producing germs

a·sex·u·al (ā sek'shoo wəl) *adj.* **1.** having no sex or sexual organs **2.** designating of or reproduction without the union of male and female germ cells —**a·sex'u·al·ly** *adv.*

ash¹ (ash) *n.* [OE. *æsce*] **1.** the grayish powder left after something has burned **2.** fine, volcanic lava **3.** the gray color of wood ash See also ASHES

ash² (ash) *n.* [< OE. *æsc*] **1.** a shade tree of the olive family **2.** its wood

a·shamed (ə shāmd') *adj.* **1.** feeling shame **2.** reluctant because fearing shame beforehand —**a·sham·ed·ly** (ə shā'mid lē) *adv.*

ash·en (ash'ən) *adj.* **1.** of ashes **2.** like ashes, esp. in color; pale

ash·es (ash'iz) *n.pl.* **1.** the substance remaining after a thing has been burned **2.** human remains, esp. the part left after cremation

a·shore (ə shôr') *adv., adj.* **1.** to or on the shore **2.** to or on land

Ash·to·reth (ash'tə reth') same as ASTARTE

ash'tray' *n.* a container for smokers' tobacco ashes: also **ash tray**

Ash Wednesday the first day of Lent: from the putting of ashes on the forehead in penitence

ash'y *adj.* **-i·er, -i·est 1.** of or covered with ashes **2.** ashen; pale

A·sia (ā'zhə) largest continent, in the Eastern Hemisphere: c.16,900,000 sq. mi.; pop. c.1,876,351,000 —**A'sian**, **A·si·at·ic** (ā'zhē at'ik) *adj., n.*

Asia Minor large peninsula in W Asia, between the Black Sea and the Mediterranean

a·side (ə sīd') *adv.* **1.** on or to one side **2.** away; in reserve [put one ticket *aside*] **3.** apart; notwithstanding [joking *aside*] —*n.* words spoken by an actor but supposedly heard only by the audience —**aside from 1.** with the exception of **2.** apart from

as·i·nine (as'ə nīn') *adj.* [< L. *asinus*, ass] like an ass; stupid; silly —**as'i·nine'ly** *adv.* —**as'i·nin'i·ty** (-nin'ə tē) *n.*

ask (ask) *vt.* [OE. *ascian*] **1.** to use words in seeking the answer to (a question) **2.** to inquire of (a person) **3.** to request or demand **4.** to invite —*vi.* **1.** to make a request (*for*) **2.** to inquire (*about* or *after*) —**ask'er** *n.*

a·skance (ə skans') *adv.* **1.** with a sidewise glance **2.** with suspicion, disapproval, etc.

a·skew (ə skyoo') *adv.* to one side; awry —*adj.* on one side; awry

asking price the price asked by a seller, esp. as a basis for bargaining

a·slant (ə slant') *adv.* on a slant —*prep.* slantingly across —*adj.* slanting

a·sleep (ə slēp') *adj.* **1.** sleeping **2.** inactive; dull **3.** numb **4.** dead —*adv.* into a sleeping condition

a·so·cial (ā sō'shəl) *adj.* **1.** avoiding contact with others **2.** selfish

asp (asp) *n.* [< Gr. *aspis*] a small, poisonous snake of Africa and Europe

as·par·a·gus (ə spar'ə gəs, -sper'-) *n.* [< Gr. *asparagos*] **1.** any of a genus of plants with small leaves and edible shoots **2.** these shoots

as·pect (as'pekt) *n.* [< L. *ad-*, to + *specere*, to look] **1.** the way one appears **2.** the appearance of a thing or idea from a specific viewpoint **3.** the side facing a given direction

as·pen (as'pən) *n.* [OE. *æspe*] a poplar tree whose leaves flutter in the least breeze: also **quaking aspen**

as·per·i·ty (as per'ə tē) *n., pl.* **-ties** [< L. *asper*, rough] **1.** roughness or harshness **2.** sharpness of temper

as·perse (ə spurs') *vt.* **-persed'**, **-pers'ing** [< L. *ad-*, to + *spargere*, to sprinkle] to slander

as·per·sion (ə spur'zhən) *n.* a damaging or disparaging remark; slander

as·phalt (as'fôlt) *n.* [< Gr. *asphaltos*] a brown or black tarlike substance mixed with sand or gravel and used for paving, roofing, etc. —*vt.* to pave, roof, etc. with asphalt

as·pho·del (as'fə del') *n.* [< Gr. *asphodelos*] a plant of the lily family having white or yellow flowers

as·phyx·i·ate (as fik'sē āt') *vt., vi.* **-at'ed**, **-at'ing** [< Gr. *a-*, not + *sphyzein*, to throb] **1.** to make or become unconscious from lack of oxygen in the blood **2.** to suffocate —**as·phyx'i·a'tion** *n.*

as·pic (as'pik) *n.* [< OFr. *aspe*] a jelly of meat juice, tomato juice, etc. used as a relish, salad mold, etc.

as·pir·ant (as'pər ənt, ə spīr'ənt) *adj.* aspiring —*n.* one who aspires

as·pi·rate (as'pə rāt'; *for n.* -pər it) *vt.* **-rat'ed**, **-rat'ing** [see ASPIRE] **1.** to begin (a syllable, etc.) with the sound of English *h* **2.** to follow (a consonant) with an audible puff of breath **3.** to suck in or suck up —*n.* an aspirated sound

as·pi·ra·tion (as'pə rā'shən) *n.* **1.** *a)* strong desire or ambition, as for advancement *b)* the thing desired **2.** a drawing in by breathing or suction

as'pi·ra'tor *n.* an apparatus using suction to remove air, fluids, etc.

as·pire (ə spīr') *vi.* **-pired'**, **-pir'ing** [< L. *ad-*, to + *spirare*, breathe] to be ambitious (*to* get or do something); seek (*after*) —**as·pir'ing·ly** *adv.*

as·pi·rin (as'pər in) *n.* [G.] a white, crystalline powder used for reducing fever, relieving pain, etc.

a·squint (ə skwint') *adv., adj.* with a squint; out of the corner of the eye

ass (as) *n.* [< L. *asinus*] **1.** a small animal like the horse but with longer ears **2.** a stupid or silly person

as·sail (ə sāl') *vt.* [< L. *ad-*, to + *salire*, leap] **1.** to attack physically and violently **2.** to attack with arguments, etc. —**as·sail'a·ble** *adj.*

as·sail·ant (-ənt) *n.* an attacker

as·sas·sin (ə sas''n) *n.* [< Ar. *hashshāshīn*, hashish users] a murderer who strikes suddenly, esp. a killer of a politically important person

as·sas'si·nate' (-āt') *vt.* **-nat'ed**, **-nat'ing** to murder as assassins do —**as·sas'si·na'tion** *n.*

as·sault (ə sôlt') *n.* [< L. *ad-*, to + *saltare*, leap] **1.** a violent attack **2.** rape: a euphemism **3.** *Law* an unlawful threat or attempt to harm another physically —*vt., vi.* to make an assault (upon)

assault and battery *Law* the carrying out of threatened physical harm

as·say (as'ā, a sā'; *for v.* a sā') *n.* [< L. *ex-*, out + *agere*, to deal] **1.** a testing **2.** the analysis of an ore, etc. to determine the nature, proportion, etc. of the ingredients —*vt.* to make an assay of; test —*vi.* to be shown by assay to have a specified proportion of something —**as·say'er** *n.*

as·sem·blage (ə sem'blij) *n.* **1.** an assembling **2.** a group of persons or things gathered together **3.** *Art* things assembled in a sculptural collage

as·sem·ble (-b'l) *vt., vi.* **-bled**, **-bling** [< L. *ad-*, to + *simul*, together] **1.** to gather into a group; collect **2.** to fit or put together the parts of —**as·sem'bler** *n.*

as·sem·bly (-blē) *n., pl.* **-blies** **1.** an assembling **2.** a group of persons gathered together **3.** a legislative body, esp. [A-] the lower house of some State legislatures **4.** a fitting together of parts to make a whole

assembly line in many factories, an arrangement by which each worker does a single operation in assembling the work as it is passed along

as·sem'bly·man *n., pl.* **-men** a member of a legislative assembly

as·sent (ə sent') *vi.* [< L. *ad-*, to + *sentire*, feel] to express acceptance or agreement (*to*); concur —*n.* consent or agreement

as·sert (ə surt') *vt.* [< L. *ad-*, to + *serere*, join] **1.** to declare; affirm **2.** to maintain or defend (rights, etc.) —**assert oneself** to insist on one's rights, or on being recognized —**as·sert'er**, **as·sert'or** *n.*

as·ser·tion (ə sur'shən) *n.* **1.** an asserting **2.** a positive statement

as·ser'tive (-tiv) *adj.* persistently positive or confident —**as·ser'tive·ly** *adv.* —**as·ser'tive·ness** *n.*

as·sess (ə ses') *vt.* [< *ad-*, to + *sedere*, sit] **1.** to set an estimated value on (property, etc.) for taxation **2.** to set the amount of (a tax, a fine, etc.) **3.** to impose a fine, tax, etc. on **4.** to judge the worth, importance, etc. of —**as·sess'ment** *n.* —**as·ses'sor** *n.*

as·set (as'et) *n.* [< L. *ad-*, to + *satis*, enough] **1.** anything owned that has value **2.** a desirable thing (charm is an *asset*) **3.** [*pl.*] all the property, accounts receivable, cash, etc. of a person or business **4.** [*pl.*] *Law* property usable to pay debts

as·sev·er·ate (ə sev'ə rāt') *vt.* **-at'ed**, **-at'ing** [< L. *ad-*, to + *severus*, severe] to state positively; assert —**as·sev'er·a'tion** *n.*

as·sid·u·ous (ə sij'oo wəs) *adj.* [< L. *assidere*, to assist] diligent; persevering; careful —**as·si·du·i·ty** (as'ə dyŏŏ′ə tē] n., pl. **-ties** **—as·sid′u- ous·ly** adv. **—as·sid′u·ous·ness** n.

as·sign (ə sīn′) vt. [< L. ad-, to + signare, to sign] 1. to set or mark for a specific purpose; designate 2. to appoint, as to a duty 3. to give out as a task; allot 4. to ascribe; attribute 5. Law to transfer (a right, property, etc.)—**as·sign′a·ble** adj. **—as·sign′- er, as·sign′or** n.

as·sig·na·tion (as′ig nā′shən) n. an appointment to meet, esp. one made secretly by lovers

as·sign·ment (ə sīn′mənt) n. 1. an assigning or being assigned 2. anything assigned

as·sim·i·late (ə sim′ə lāt′) vt. **-lat′- ed, -lat′ing** [< L. ad-, to + similare, make similar to] 1. to absorb and incorporate; digest 2. to make like or alike —vi. 1. to become like 2. to be absorbed and incorporated **—as·sim′- i·la′tion** n.

as·sist (ə sist′) vt., vi. [< L. ad-, to + sistere, make stand] to help; aid —n. an instance or act of helping —**assist** at to be present at; attend

as·sis′tance (-əns) n. help; aid

as·sis′tant (-ənt) adj. assisting; help- ing —n. one who assists; helper; aid

as·siz·es (ə sīz′iz) n.pl. [see ASSESS] 1. court sessions held periodically in each county of England 2. the time or place of these

assn. association

assoc. 1. associated 2. association

as·so·ci·ate (ə sō′shē āt′, -sē-; for n. & adj., usually -it) vt. **-at′ed, -at′ing** [< L. ad-, to + socius, companion] 1. to connect; combine; join 2. to bring into relationship as partner, etc. 3. to connect in the mind —vi. to unite or join (with) as a partner, friend, etc. —n. 1. a partner, col- league, friend, etc. 2. anything joined with another 3. a degree granted by a junior college at the end of a two-year course —adj. 1. united by the same interests, purposes, etc. 2. having secondary status or privileges

as·so′ci·a′tion (-ā′shən) n. 1. an associating or being associated 2. fellowship; partnership 3. an organi- zation; society, etc. 4. a connection between ideas, etc. **—as·so′ci·a′tive** (-ā′tiv) adj.

association football soccer

as·so·nance (as′ə nəns) n. [< L. ad-, to + sonare, to sound] 1. likeness of sound 2. a partial rhyme made by like vowel sounds, as in late and make **—as′so·nant** adj., n.

as·sort (ə sôrt′) vt. [< L. ad-, to + sors, lot] to separate into classes ac- cording to kind; classify

as·sort′ed adj. 1. various; miscella- neous 2. classified

as·sort′ment n. 1. classification 2. a miscellaneous collection; variety

asst. assistant

as·suage (ə swāj′) vt. **-suaged′, -suag′ing** [< L. ad-, to + suavis, sweet] 1. to lessen (pain, etc.) 2. to calm (anger, etc.) 3. to satisfy or slake (thirst, etc.)

as·sume (ə sōōm′) vt. **-sumed′, -sum′ing** [< L. ad-, to + sumere, to take] 1. to take on (the appearance, role, etc. of) 2. to seize; usurp 3. to undertake 4. to take for granted; suppose 5. to pretend to have; feign **—as·sum′ed·ly** adv.

as·sum′ing adj. taking too much for granted; presumptuous

as·sump·tion (ə sump′shən) n. 1. [A-] R.C.Ch. a) the ascent of the Virgin Mary into heaven b) the festi- val celebrating this (Aug. 15) 2. an assuming 3. a supposition **—as·- sump′tive** adj.

as·sur·ance (ə shoor′əns) n. 1. an assuring or being assured 2. sureness; confidence 3. a promise, guarantee, etc. 4. self-confidence 5. [Chiefly Brit.] insurance

as·sure (ə shoor′) vt. **-sured′, -sur′- ing** [< L. ad, to + securus, secure] 1. to make (a person) sure of some- thing 2. to give confidence to; reassure 3. to tell or promise positively 4. to guarantee 5. [Brit.] to insure against loss

as·sured′ adj. 1. made sure; certain 2. self-confident **—as·sur·ed·ly** (ə shoor′id lē) adv.

As·syr·i·a (ə sir′ē ə) ancient empire in SW Asia **—As·syr′i·an** adj., n.

As·tar·te (as tär′tē) ancient Semitic goddess of fertility and sexual love

as·ter (as′tər) n. [< Gr. astēr, star] any of several plants of the composite family with variously colored daisylike flowers

as·ter·isk (as′tər isk) n. [< Gr. dim. of astēr, a star] a starlike sign (*) used in printing to mark footnotes, etc.

a·stern (ə sturn′) adv. 1. behind a ship or aircraft 2. at or toward the rear of a ship, etc. 3. backward

as·ter·oid (as′tə roid′) n. [see ASTER & -OID] any of the small planets be- tween Mars and Jupiter

asth·ma (az′mə) n. [Gr.] a chronic disorder characterized by coughing, difficult breathing, etc. **—asth·mat′ic** (-mat′ik) adj., n.

a·stig·ma·tism (ə stig′mə tiz′m) n. [< Gr. a-, without + stigma, a mark + -ISM] a defect of a lens or the eyes that prevents light rays from meeting in a single focal point **—as·tig·mat′ic** (as′tig mat′ik) adj.

a·stir (ə stur′) adv., adj. 1. in motion 2. out of bed

as·ton·ish (ə stän′ish) vt. [< L. ex- intens. + tonare, to thunder] to fill with sudden surprise; amaze **—as·- ton′ish·ing** adj. **—as·ton′ish·ing·ly** adv. **—as·ton′ish·ment** n.

as·tound (ə stound′) vt. [see prec.] to astonish greatly **—as·tound′ing** adj. **—as·tound′ing·ly** adv.

a·strad·dle (ə strad′'l) adv. in a straddling position

as·tra·khan (as'trə kən) *n.* [< *Astrakhan*, U.S.S.R. city] loosely curled fur from young lamb pelts, or a wool fabric resembling this

as·tral (as'trəl) *adj.* [< Gr. *astron*, star] of, from, or like the stars

a·stray (ə strā') *adv.* [< OFr. *estraier*, STRAY] 1. off the right path 2. into error

a·stride (ə strīd') *adv.* with a leg on either side —*prep.* 1. with a leg on either side of 2. extending over or across

as·trin·gent (ə strin'jənt) *adj.* [< L. *ad-*, to + *stringere*, draw] 1. that contracts body tissues 2. harsh; biting —*n.* an astringent substance —**as·trin'gen·cy** *n.*

as·tro- (as'trō) [< Gr. *astron*, a star] *a combining form meaning* of a star or stars [*astrophysics*]

as·tro·bi·ol·o·gy (as'trō bī äl'ə jē) *n.* the branch of biology that investigates the existence of living organisms on planets other than earth

as·tro·dy·nam·ics (-dī nam'iks) *n.pl.* [*with sing. v.*] the branch of dynamics dealing with the motion and gravitation of objects in space

as·trol·o·gy (ə sträl'ə jē) *n.* [< Gr. *astron*, star + *-logia*, -LOGY] a pseudo-science claiming to foretell the future by the supposed influence of the stars, planets, etc. on human affairs —**as·trol'o·ger** *n.* —**as·tro·log·i·cal** (as'trə läj'i k'l) *adj.*

as·tro·naut (as'trə nôt') *n.* [< Fr. < Gr. *astron*, star + *nautēs*, sailor] one trained to make flights in outer space —**as·tro·nau'tics** *n.*

as·tro·nom·i·cal (as'trə näm'i k'l) *adj.* 1. of astronomy 2. huge, as numbers Also **as'tro·nom'ic** —**as'tro·nom'i·cal·ly** *adv.*

astronomical unit a unit of length equal to the mean radius of the earth's orbit, or about 93 million miles

as·tron·o·my (ə strän'ə mē) *n.* [< Gr. *astron*, star + *nomos*, law] the science of the stars and other heavenly bodies, their motion, position, size, etc. —**as·tron'o·mer** *n.*

as·tro·phys·ics (as'trō fiz'iks) *n.pl.* [*with sing. v.*] the science of the physical properties and phenomena of heavenly bodies —**as'tro·phys'i·cist** (-ə sist) *n.*

as·tute (ə stōōt') *adj.* [< L. *astus*, craft] shrewd; keen; crafty —**as·tute'ly** *adv.* —**as·tute'ness** *n.*

a·sun·der (ə sun'dər) *adv.* [< OE. *on sundran*] 1. into pieces 2. apart in direction or position

a·sy·lum (ə sī'ləm) *n.* [< Gr. *a-*, without + *sylē*, right of seizure] 1. place of safety; refuge 2. an earlier name for an institution for the mentally ill, orphans, the aged, etc.

a·sym·me·try (ā sim'ə trē) *n.* lack of symmetry —**a'sym·met'ri·cal** (-met'ri k'l) *adj.*

at (at, ət) *prep.* [< OE. *æt*] 1. on; in; near; by [*at* the office] 2. to or toward [look *at* her] 3. from [visible *at* one mile] 4. attending [*at* a party] 5. busy with [*at* work] 6. in the state or

manner of [*at* war, *at* a trot] 7. because of [*sad at* his death] 8. with reference to [*good at* tennis] 9. in the amount, etc. of [*at* five cents each] 10. on or near the age or time of [*at* noon]

At·a·brine (at'ə brin) *a trademark for* a synthetic drug used in treating malaria, etc. —*n.* [**a-**] this drug

at·a·vism (at'ə viz'm) *n.* [< L. *atavus*, ancestor] resemblance or reversion to remotely ancestral characteristics —**at'a·vis'tic** *adj.*

ate (āt; *Brit. or U.S. dial.* et) *pt. of* EAT

-ate[1] (āt, it) [< L. *-atus*, pp. ending] *a suffix meaning:* 1. to become, cause to become, form, provide with [*maturate, ulcerate*] 2. of or characteristic of, characterized by, having [*passionate*]

-ate[2] [L. *-atus*, noun ending] *a suffix denoting* a function, official, or agent [*potentate*]

at·el·ier (at'l yā') *n.* [Fr.] a studio or workshop, as of an artist or couturier

Ath·a·pas·can, Ath·a·pas·kan (ath'ə pas'kən) *adj.* designating or of a widespread family of N. American Indian languages —*n.* this family of languages

a·the·ism (ā'thē iz'm) *n.* [< Gr. *a-*, without + *theos*, god] the belief that there is no God —**a'the·ist** *n.* —**a'the·is'tic** *adj.*

A·the·na (ə thē'nə) the Greek goddess of wisdom, skills, and warfare

Ath·ens (ath''nz) capital of Greece, in the SE part: pop. 1,853,000 —**A·the·ni·an** (ə thē'nē ən) *adj., n.*

ath·er·o·scle·ro·sis (ath'ər ō sklə rō'sis) *n.* [< Gr. *athērōma*, grainy tumor + SCLEROSIS] formation of fatty nodules on hardening artery walls

a·thirst (ə thurst') *adj.* 1. [Archaic] thirsty 2. eager; longing (*for*)

ath·lete (ath'lēt') *n.* [< Gr. *athlon*, a prize] a person trained in exercises or games requiring strength, skill, stamina etc.

athlete's foot ringworm of the foot

ath·let·ic (-let'ik) *adj.* 1. of or like athletes or athletics 2. physically strong and active —**ath·let'i·cal·ly** *adv.*

ath·let·ics *n.pl.* [*sometimes with sing. v.*] athletic sports, games, etc.

a·thwart (ə thwôrt') *prep.* 1. across 2. against —*adv.* crosswise

a·tilt (ə tilt') *adj., adv.* tilted

-a·tion (ā'shən) [< Fr. or L.] *a suffix meaning* act, condition, or result of [*alteration*]

-a·tive (ə tiv, āt'iv) [< Fr. or L.] *a suffix meaning* of or relating to, serving to [*demonstrative*]

At·lan·ta (at lan'tə, ət-) capital of Ga.: pop. 425,000

At·lan·tic (ət lan'tik, at-) ocean touching the Americas to the west and Europe and Africa to the east —*adj.* of, in, or near this ocean

Atlantic City ocean resort in SE N.J.: pop. 40,000

At·lan·tis (ət lan'tis) [< Gr.] legendary sunken continent in the Atlantic

At·las (at'ləs) *Gr. Myth.* a giant whose shoulders supported the heavens —*n.* [a-] a book of maps

ATM *n., pl.* **ATMs** [a(*utomated*) t(*eller*) m(*achine*)] a computer terminal that allows a bank customer to deposit, withdraw, or transfer money automatically

at·mos·phere (at'məs fir') *n.* [< Gr. *atmos,* vapor + *sphaira,* sphere] **1.** all the air surrounding the earth **2.** pervading mood or spirit **3.** the general tone or effect **4.** a unit of pressure equal to 14.69 lb. per sq. in. —**at'mos·pher'ic** (-fer'ik) *adj.* — **at'mos·pher'i·cal·ly** *adv.*

at·oll (a'tôl, ā'-) *n.* [< ? Malayalam *adal,* uniting] a ring-shaped coral island surrounding a lagoon

at·om (at'əm) *n.* [< Gr. *atomos,* un-cut] **1.** a tiny particle; jot **2.** *Chem., Physics* any of the smallest particles of an element that form compounds with similar particles of other elements —**the atom** atomic energy

a·tom·ic (ə täm'ik) *adj.* **1.** of an atom or atoms **2.** of or using atomic energy or atomic bombs **3.** tiny —**a·tom'i·cal·ly** *adv.*

atomic bomb, atom bomb a very destructive bomb, whose immense power derives from a chain reaction of nuclear fission

atomic energy the energy released from an atom in nuclear reactions, esp. in nuclear fission or nuclear fusion

at·om·iz·er (at'ə mī'zər) *n.* a device used to shoot out a fine spray, as of medicine or perfume

a·to·nal·i·ty (ā'tō nal'ə tē) *n.* *Music* lack of tonality by intentional disregard of key —**a·ton·al** (ā tōn''l) *adj.*

a·tone (ə tōn') *vi.* **a·toned', a·ton'ing** [< ME. *at one,* in accord] to make amends (*for* wrongdoing, etc.)

a·tone'ment *n.* **1.** an atoning **2.** amends **3.** [A-] *Theol.* the redeeming of mankind through Jesus' death

a·top (ə täp') *adv.* on or at the top —*prep.* on the top of

-a·to·ry (ə tôr'ē) [< L.] *a suffix meaning of, characterized by* [*exclamatory*]

a·tri·um (ā'trē əm) *n., pl.* **a'tri·a** (-ə), **a'tri·ums** [L.] **1.** the main room of an ancient Roman house **2.** an entrance hall **3.** an auricle of the heart

a·tro·cious (ə trō'shəs) *adj.* [< L. *atrox,* fierce + -OUS] **1.** very cruel, evil, etc. **2.** [Colloq.] very bad; offensive —**a·tro'cious·ly** *adv.* — **a·tro'cious·ness** *n.*

a·troc·i·ty (ə träs'ə tē) *n., pl.* **-ties** **1.** atrocious behavior or act **2.** [Colloq.] a very displeasing thing

at·ro·phy (a'trə fē) *n.* [< Gr. *a-,* not

ATOMIZER

+ *trephein,* nourish] a wasting away or failure to grow, esp. of body tissue, an organ, etc. —*vi.* **-phied, -phy·ing** to undergo atrophy —*vt.* to cause atrophy in

at·ro·pine (at'rə pēn', -pin) *n.* [< Gr. *Atropos,* one of the Fates + -INE²] an alkaloid obtained from belladonna, used to relieve spasms

at·tach (ə tach') *vt.* [< OFr. *a-,* to + *tach,* a nail] **1.** to fasten by tying, etc. **2.** to join (often used reflexively) **3.** to connect by ties of affection, etc. **4.** to affix (a signature, etc.) **5.** to ascribe **6.** *Law* to take (property, etc.) by writ —**at·tach'a·ble** *adj.*

at·ta·ché (at'ə shā'; *chiefly Brit.* ə tash'ā) *n.* [Fr.: see prec.] a member of an ambassador's diplomatic staff

attaché case a briefcase

at·tach'ment *n.* **1.** an attaching or being attached **2.** anything that attaches; fastening **3.** devotion **4.** anything attached **5.** an accessory for an electrical appliance, etc. **6.** *Law* a taking of property, etc. into custody

at·tack (ə tak') *vt.* [< OFr. *atachier,* ATTACH] **1.** to use force against in order to harm **2.** to speak or write against **3.** to undertake vigorously **4.** to begin acting upon harmfully —*vi.* to make an assault —*n.* **1.** an attacking **2.** an onset of a disease **3.** a beginning of a task, undertaking, etc. —**at·tack'er** *n.*

at·tain (ə tān') *vt.* [< L. *ad-,* to + *tangere,* to touch] **1.** to gain; accomplish; achieve **2.** to reach; arrive at —**at·tain'a·bil'i·ty** *n.* —**at·tain'-a·ble** *adj.* —**at·tain'ment** *n.*

at·tain'der (-dər) *n.* [see prec.] loss of civil rights and property of one sentenced to death or outlawed

at·taint (ə tānt') *vt.* to punish by attainder

at·tar (at'ər) *n.* [< Ar. *'itr,* perfume] a perfume made from flower petals, esp. of roses (**attar of roses**)

at·tempt (ə tempt') *vt.* [< L. *ad-,* to + *temptare,* to try] to try to do, get, etc. —*n.* **1.** a try; endeavor **2.** an attack, as on a person's life

at·tend (ə tend') *vt.* [< L. *ad-,* to + *tendere,* to stretch] **1.** to take care of **2.** to go with **3.** to accompany as a result **4.** to be present at —*vi.* **1.** to pay attention **2.** to wait (*on* or *upon*) **3.** to apply oneself (*to*) **4.** to give the required care (*to*)

at·tend'ance *n.* **1.** an attending **2.** the number of persons attending

at·tend'ant *adj.* **1.** attending or serving **2.** being present **3.** accompanying —*n.* one who attends or serves

at·ten·tion (ə ten'shən) *n.* [see ATTEND] **1.** mental concentration or readiness **2.** notice or observation **3.** care or consideration **4.** [*usually pl.*] an act of courtesy **5.** the erect posture of soldiers ready for a command

at·ten'tive (-tiv) *adj.* **1.** paying

attention 2. courteous, devoted, etc. —**at·ten'tive·ly** adv.

at·ten·u·ate (ə ten'yoo wāt'; for adj. -wit) vt. -at'ed, -at'ing [< L. ad-, to + tenuis, thin] 1. to make thin 2. to dilute 3. to lessen or weaken —vi. to become thin, weak, etc. —adj. attenuated —**at·ten'u·a'tion** n.

at·test (ə test') vt. [< L. ad-, to + testari, bear witness] 1. to declare to be true or genuine 2. to certify, as by oath 3. to serve as proof of 4. to bear witness (to) —**at·tes·ta'tion** n.

at·tic (at'ik) n. [< Gr. Attikos, of Attica (ancient Gr. region): with reference to architectural style] the room or space just below the roof; garret

At·ti·la (at'l ə, ə til'ə) 406?-453 A.D.; King of the Huns

at·tire (ə tīr') vt. -tired', -tir'ing [< OFr. a-, to + tire, order] to clothe; dress up —n. clothes

at·ti·tude (at'ə tōōd') n. [ult. < L. aptus, APT] 1. a bodily posture showing mood, action, etc. 2. a manner showing one's feelings or thoughts 3. one's disposition, opinion, etc.

at·ti·tu·di·nize (at'ə tōōd'n īz') vi. -nized', -niz'ing to pose for effect

at·tor·ney (ə tur'nē) n., pl. -neys [< OFr. a-, to + torner, to turn] a person legally empowered to act for another; esp., a lawyer

attorney at law a lawyer

attorney general, pl. **attorneys general, attorney generals** the chief law officer of a government

at·tract (ə trakt') vt. [< L. ad-, to + trahere, to draw] 1. to draw to itself or oneself 2. to get the admiration, attention, etc. of; allure —vi. to be attractive —**at·tract'a·ble** adj.

at·trac·tion (ə trak'shən) n. 1. an attracting 2. power of attracting; esp., charm 3. anything that attracts 4. Physics the mutual action by which bodies tend to draw together

at·trac·tive (-tiv) adj. that attracts; esp., pleasing, charming, pretty, etc. —**at·trac'tive·ly** adv. —**at·trac'tive·ness** n.

at·trib·ute (ə trib'yoot; for n. a'trə byōot') vt. -but·ed, -but·ing [< L. ad-, to + tribuere, assign] to think of as belonging to; ascribe (to) —n. a characteristic or quality of a person or thing —**at·trib'ut·a·ble** adj. —**at'tri·bu'tion** n.

at·trib·u·tive (ə trib'yoo tiv) adj. 1. attributing 2. preceding the noun it modifies: said of an adjective —**at·trib'u·tive·ly** adv.

at·tri·tion (ə trish'ən) n. [< L. ad-, to + terere, to rub] a wearing away by or as by friction

at·tune (ə tōōn') vt. -tuned', -tun'ing 1. to tune 2. to bring into harmony

atty. attorney

ATV (ā'tē'vē') n., pl. **ATVs** [A(ll)-T(errain) V(ehicle)] a small motor vehicle for traveling over rough ground, snow, and ice, and in water

a·twit·ter (ə twit'ər) adv., adj. twittering

a·typ·i·cal (ā tip'i k'l) adj. not typical; abnormal —**a·typ'i·cal·ly** adv.

Au [L. aurum] Chem. gold

au·burn (ô'bərn) adj., n. [< L. albus, white: infl. by ME. brun, brown] reddish brown

auc·tion (ôk'shən) n. [< L. augere, to increase] a public sale of items to the highest bidders —vt. to sell at auction —**auction off** to sell at auction —**auc'tion·eer'** n.

au·da·cious (ô dā'shəs) adj. [< L. audax, bold] 1. bold; daring 2. too bold; insolent; brazen —**au·da'cious·ly** adv. —**au·da'cious·ness** n.

au·dac·i·ty (ô das'ə tē) n. 1. bold courage 2. insolence; impudence 3. pl. -ties an audacious act or remark

au·di·ble (ô'də b'l) adj. [< L. audire, hear] loud enough to be heard —**au'di·bil'i·ty** n. —**au'di·bly** adv.

au·di·ence (ô'dē əns) n. [< L. audire, hear] 1. those gathered to hear and see something 2. all those reached by a radio or TV program, book, etc. 3. a hearing, esp. a formal interview

au·di·o (ô'dē ō) adj. [< L. audire, hear] 1. of frequencies corresponding to audible sound waves 2. of the sound phase of television

au'di·ol'o·gy (-äl'ə jē) n. the science of aiding persons with hearing defects —**au'di·ol'o·gist** n.

au'di·om'e·ter (-äm'ə tər) n. an instrument for measuring the sharpness and range of hearing —**au'di·o·met'ric** (-ō met'rik) adj.

au'di·o·phile' (-ə fīl') n. a devotee of high-fidelity sound reproduction, as on record players

au·di·o·vis·u·al (ô'dē ō vizh'oo wəl) adj. involving both hearing and sight

au·dit (ô'dit) n. [< L. audire, hear] a formal checking of financial records —vt., vi. 1. to check (accounts, etc.) 2. to attend (a college class) to listen without credits

au·di·tion (ô dish'ən) n. [< L. audire, hear] a hearing to try out an actor, singer, etc. —vt., vi. to try out in an audition

au·di·tor (ô'də tər) n. 1. a listener 2. one who audits accounts 3. one who audits classes

au·di·to·ri·um (ô'də tôr'ē əm) n. 1. a room where an audience sits 2. a building or hall for speeches, concerts, etc.

au·di·to·ry (ô'də tôr'ē) adj. of hearing or the organs of hearing

†auf Wie·der·se·hen (ouf vē'dər zā'ən) [G.] goodbye

au·ger (ô'gər) n. [< OE. nafogar < nafu, hub (of a wheel) + gar, spear] a tool for boring holes in wood

aught (ôt) n. [< OE. a, one + wiht, crea- ture] 1. any- thing what- ever 2. [<

TYPES OF AUGER
(A, screw auger; B, ship auger; C, lip-ring auger)

(N)AUGHT] a zero —*adv.* in any way

aug·ment (ôg ment′) *vt., vi.* [< L. *augere,* to increase] to make or become greater —**aug′men·ta′tion** *n.* —**aug·ment′er** *n.*

au gra·tin (ō grät′'n) [Fr.] with a crust of crumbs and grated cheese

au·gur (ô′gər) *n.* [L., priest at fertility rites] a prophet; soothsayer —*vt., vi.* 1. to prophesy 2. to be an omen (of) —**augur ill** (or well) to be a bad (or good) omen

au·gu·ry (ô′gyər ē) *n., pl.* -ries 1. the practice of divination 2. an omen

Au·gust (ô′gəst) *n.* [< L. AUGUSTUS] the 8th month of the year, having 31 days: abbrev. Aug.

au·gust (ô gust′) *adj.* [L. *augustus*] inspiring awe; imposing —**au·gust′ly** *adv.* —**au·gust′ness** *n.*

Au·gus·ta (ô gus′tə) capital of Me.: pop. 22,000

Au·gus·tine (ô′gəs tēn′), Saint 354-430 A.D.; Latin church father

Au·gus·tus (ô gus′təs) 63 B.C.-14 A.D.; first emperor of Rome

au jus (ō zhōō′, jōōs′) [Fr.] served in its natural juices: said of meat

auk (ôk) *n.* [< ON. *alka*] a diving bird of northern seas, with webbed feet and short wings used as paddles

auld lang syne (ôld′ lan′ zīn′) [Scot., lit., old long since] the good old days

GREAT AUK

aunt (ant, änt) *n.* [< L. *amita*] 1. a sister of one's mother or father 2. the wife of one's uncle

au·ra (ôr′ə) *n., pl.* -ras, -rae (-ē) [< Gr., akin to *aēr,* air] 1. an invisible emanation 2. a particular quality surrounding a person or thing

au·ral (ôr′əl) *adj.* [< L. *auris,* ear] of the ear or the sense of hearing

au·re·ole (ôr′ē ōl′) *n.* [< L. *aurum,* gold] 1. a halo 2. a sun's corona

Au·re·o·my·cin (ôr′ē ō mīs′'n) [< L. *aureus,* golden + Gr. *mykēs,* fungus] *a trademark for* an antibiotic

au re·voir (ō′ rə vwär′) [Fr.] goodbye

au·ri·cle (ôr′ə k'l) *n.* [< L. dim. of *auris,* ear] 1. the outer part of the ear 2. either of the two upper chambers of the heart 3. an earlike part

au·ric·u·lar (ô rik′yoo lər) *adj.* 1. of the ear or the sense of hearing 2. said privately 3. of or like an auricle

Au·ro·ra (ô rôr′ə) the Rom. goddess of dawn —*n.* 1. [a-] *pl.* -ras, -rae (-ē) the dawn 2. either of the luminous bands sometimes seen in the night sky: in the S Hemisphere, called the **aurora aus·tra·lis** (ô strā′ləs), in the N Hemisphere, the **aurora bo·re·a·lis** (bôr′ē al′is)

aus·cul·ta·tion (ôs′kəl tā′shən) *n.* [< L. *auscultare,* to listen] a listening, often with a stethoscope, to sounds in the chest, abdomen, etc. that indicate heart and lung condition, etc. —**aus′cul·tate′** *vt., vi.*

aus·pice (ôs′pis) *n., pl.* -pi·ces′ (-pə sēz′) [< L. *auspicium,* omen] 1. an omen 2. a favorable omen or sign 3. [*pl.*] sponsorship; patronage

aus·pi·cious (ôs pish′əs) *adj.* 1. favorable; propitious 2. successful —**aus·pi′cious·ly** *adv.*

Aus·sie (ôs′ē) *adj., n.* [Slang] Australian

Aus·ten (ôs′tən), **Jane** 1775-1817; Eng. novelist

aus·tere (ô stir′) *adj.* [< Gr. *austēros,* dry] 1. stern; harsh 2. morally strict 3. unadorned; plain —**aus·tere′ly** *adv.*

aus·ter·i·ty (ô ster′ə tē) *n., pl.* -ties 1. sternness 2. [*pl.*] an austere practice 3. tightened economy

Aus·tin (ôs′tin) capital of Tex., in the C part: pop. 345,000

aus·tral (ôs′trəl) *adj.* [< L. *auster,* the south] southern

Aus·tral·ia (ô strāl′yə) 1. island continent between the S Pacific & Indian oceans 2. country comprising this continent & Tasmania: 2,971,081 sq. mi.; pop. 11,633,000 —**Aus·tral′ian** *adj., n.*

Aus·tri·a (ôs′trē ə) country in C Europe: 32,375 sq. mi.; pop. 7,273,000 —**Aus′tri·an** *adj., n.*

au·then·tic (ô then′tik) *adj.* [< Gr. *authentikos,* genuine] 1. reliable, credible, etc., as a report 2. genuine; real —**au·then′ti·cal·ly** *adv.* —**au·then·tic·i·ty** (ô′thən tis′ə tē) *n.*

au·then′ti·cate′ (-tə kāt′) *vt.* -cat′ed, -cat′ing 1. to make valid 2. to verify 3. to prove to be genuine —**au·then′ti·ca′tion** *n.*

au·thor (ô′thər) *n.* [< L. *augere,* to increase] 1. one who makes or creates something 2. a writer of books, etc. —*vt.* to be the author of —**au′thor·ship′** *n.*

au·thor·i·tar·i·an (ə thôr′ə ter′ēan) *adj.* believing in or characterized by absolute obedience to authority —*n.* an advocate or enforcer of such obedience —**au·thor′i·tar·i·an·ism** *n.*

au·thor′i·ta′tive (-tāt′iv) *adj.* 1. having authority; official 2. based on competent authority; reliable —**au·thor′i·ta′tive·ly** *adv.*

au·thor′i·ty (-tē) *n., pl.* -ties [see AUTHOR] 1. the power or right to command, act, etc. 2. [*pl.*] officials with this power 3. influence resulting from knowledge, prestige, etc. 4. a person, writing, etc. cited to support an opinion 5. an expert

au·thor·ize (ô′thə rīz′) *vt.* -ized′, -iz′ing 1. to give official approval to 2. to give power or authority to 3. to justify —**au′thor·i·za′tion** *n.*

Authorized Version the revised English translation of the Bible, published in 1611, authorized by King James I

au·tism (ô′tiz'm) *n.* [AUT(O)- + -ISM]

Psychol. a mental state marked by disregard of external reality —**au·tis'tic** *adj.*

au·to (ôt'ō) *n., pl.* -**tos** an automobile

auto- [< Gr. *autos,* self] *a prefix meaning:* 1. self 2. by oneself or itself

au·to·bi·og·ra·phy (ôt'ə bī ä'grə fē) *n., pl.* -**phies** the story of one's own life written by oneself —**au'to·bi'og·raph'i·cal** (-ə graf'i k'l) *adj.*

au·toc·ra·cy (ô tä'krə sē) *n., pl.* -**cies** [see ff.] government in which one person has absolute power

au·to·crat (ôt'ə krat') *n.* [< Gr. *autos,* self + *kratos,* power] 1. a ruler with absolute power 2. any domineering person —**au'to·crat'ic** *adj.* —**au'to·crat'i·cal·ly** *adv.*

au·to·di·dact (ôt'ō dī'dakt) *n.* [see AUTO- & DIDACTIC] a person who is self-taught

au·to·graph (ôt'ə graf') *n.* [< Gr. *autos,* self + *graphein,* write] a person's own signature or handwriting —*vt.* to write one's signature on or in

au·to·hyp·no·sis (ôt'ō hip nō'sis) *n.* a hypnotizing of oneself or the state of being so hypnotized

au·to·in·tox·i·ca·tion (ôt'ō in täk' sə kā'shən) *n.* poisoning by toxic substances formed within the body

au·to·mat (ôt'ə mat') *n.* [G.: see AUTOMATIC] a restaurant in which patrons get food from small, coin-operated compartments

au'to·mate' (-māt') *vt.* -**mat'ed,** -**mat'ing** [< AUTOMATION] to convert to or use automation

au'to·mat'ic (-mat'ik) *adj.* [Gr. *automatos,* self-moving] 1. done unthinkingly, as from habit or by reflex 2. working by itself 3. using automatic equipment —*n.* an automatic pistol or rifle —**au'to·mat'i·cal·ly** *adv.*

automatic pilot a gyroscopic instrument that automatically keeps an aircraft, missile, etc. to a predetermined course and attitude

au'to·ma'tion (-mā'shən) *n.* a manufacturing system in which many or all of the processes are automatically performed or controlled, as by electronic devices

au·tom·a·tism (ô täm'ə tiz'm) *n.* automatic quality, condition, or action —**au·tom'a·tize'** (-tīz') *vt.*

au·tom'a·ton' (-tän', -tən) *n., pl.* -**tons',** -**ta** (-tə) [see AUTOMATIC] 1. any automatic device, esp. a robot 2. a person acting like a robot

au·to·mo·bile (ôt'ə mə bēl') *n.* [Fr.: see AUTO- & MOBILE] a four-wheeled passenger car with a built-in engine

au'to·mo'tive (-mōt'iv) *adj.* [AUTO- + -MOTIVE] 1. self-moving 2. having to do with automobiles, trucks, etc.

au'to·nom'ic (-näm'ik) *adj.* of or controlled by that part of the nervous system that regulates the motor functions of the heart, lungs, etc.

au·ton·o·mous (ô tän'ə məs) *adj.* [< Gr. *autos,* self + *nomos,* law] 1. having self-government 2. existing or functioning independently —**au·ton'o·mous·ly** *adv.* —**au·ton'o·my** (-mē) *n.*

au·to·pi·lot (ôt'ō pī'lət) *n. same as* AUTOMATIC PILOT

au·top·sy (ô'täp'sē) *n., pl.* -**sies** [< Gr. *autos,* self + *opsis,* sight] examination of a corpse to find out the cause of death

au·tumn (ôt'əm) *n.* [< L. *autumnus*] the season between summer and winter; fall —**au·tum·nal** (ô tum'n'l) *adj.*

aux·il·ia·ry (ôg zil'yər ē) *adj.* [< L. *augere,* to increase] 1. helping 2. subsidiary 3. supplementary —*n., pl.* -**ries** an auxiliary person or thing

auxiliary verb a verb that helps form tenses, moods, voices, etc. of other verbs, as *have* or *be*

aux·in (ôk'sin) *n.* [< Gr. *auxein,* to increase] a plant hormone that promotes and controls growth

a·vail (ə vāl') *vi., vt.* [< L. *ad,* to + *valere,* be strong] to be of use, help, or worth (to) —*n.* use or help; benefit [to no *avail*] —**avail oneself of** to take advantage of; utilize

a·vail·a·ble (ə vā'lə b'l) *adj.* 1. that can be used 2. that can be got or had; handy —**a·vail'a·bil'i·ty** *n.*

av·a·lanche (av'ə lanch') *n.* [Fr. < L. *labi,* to slip] 1. a large mass of loosened snow, earth, etc. sliding down a mountain 2. an overwhelming amount

a·vant-garde (ä vänt'gärd') *n.* [Fr.] the leaders in new movements, esp. in the arts —*adj.* of such movements

av·a·rice (av'ər is) *n.* [< L. *avere,* desire] greed for money —**av·a·ri·cious** (av'ə rish'əs) *adj.* —**av'a·ri'cious·ly** *adv.*

a·vast (ə vast') *interj.* [< Du. *houd vast,* hold fast] *Naut.* stop! cease!

av·a·tar (av'ə tär') *n.* [Sans. *avatāra,* descent] *Hinduism* a god's coming to earth in bodily form

a·vaunt (ə vônt') *interj.* [< L. *ab,* from + *ante,* before] [Archaic] go away!

avdp. avoirdupois

A·ve Ma·ri·a (ä'vā mə rē'ə) [L.] *R.C.Ch.* 1. "Hail, Mary," the first words of a prayer 2. this prayer

a·venge (ə venj') *vt., vi.* **a·venged',** **a·veng'ing** [< L. *ad,* to + *vindicare,* to claim] 1. to get revenge for (an injury, etc.) 2. to take vengeance on behalf of —**a·veng'er** *n.*

a·ve·nue (av'ə nōō', -nyōō') *n.* [< L. *ad-,* to + *venire,* come] 1. a street, drive, etc., esp. when broad: abbr. **Ave., ave.** 2. a way of approach

a·ver (ə vur') *vt.* **a·verred',** **a·ver'ring** [< L. *ad,* to + *verus,* true] to declare to be true; assert

av·er·age (av'rij) *n.* [< Fr. *avarie,* damage to ship or cargo; hence, idea of shared losses] 1. the result of dividing the sum of two or more quantities by the number of quantities 2. the usual kind, amount, etc. —*adj.* 1. constituting an average 2. usual; normal —*vt.* -**aged,** -**ag·ing** 1. to figure out the average of 2. to do, take, etc. on an average [to *average* six sales a day] —**average out** to arrive at an average eventually —**on the**

average as an average amount, rate, etc.

a·verse (ə vurs′) *adj.* [see AVERT] unwilling; opposed (*to*)

a·ver·sion (ə vur′zhən) *n.* 1. intense dislike 2. the object arousing this

a·vert (ə vurt′) *vt.* [< L. *a-*, from + *vertere*, to turn] 1. to turn (the eyes, etc.) away 2. to ward off; prevent

avg. average

a·vi·ar·y (ā′vē er′ē) *n., pl.* **-ar′ies** [< L. *avis*, bird] a building or large cage for keeping many birds

a·vi·a·tion (ā′vē ā′shən) *n.* [see prec.] 1. the science of flying airplanes 2. the field of airplane design, construction, etc.

a′vi·a·tor *n.* an airplane pilot —**a′vi·a′trix** (-triks) *n.fem.*

av·id (av′id) *adj.* [< L. *avere*, to desire] very eager or greedy —**a·vid·i·ty** (ə vid′ə tē) *n.* —**av′id·ly** *adv.*

a·vi·on·ics (ā′vē än′iks) *n.pl.* [AVI(ATION) + (ELECTR)ONICS] [*with sing. v.*] electronics as applied in aviation and astronautics

av·o·ca·do (av′ə kä′dō, ä′və-) *n., pl.* **-dos** [< MexInd. *ahuacatl*] 1. a thick-skinned, pear-shaped tropical fruit with yellow, buttery flesh 2. the tree it grows on

av·o·ca·tion (av′ə kā′shən) *n.* [< L. *a-*, away + *vocare*, to call] occupation in addition to regular work; hobby —**av′o·ca′tion·al** *adj.*

a·void (ə void′) *vt.* [< ME. < OFr. *esvuidier*, to empty] to keep away from; shun; shirk —**a·void′a·ble** *adj.* —**a·void′a·bly** *adv.* —**a·void′ance** *n.*

av·oir·du·pois (av′ər də poiz′) *n.* [< OFr. *aveir de peis*, goods of weight] 1. a system of weights in which 16 oz. = 1 lb.: also **avoirdupois weight** 2. [Colloq.] weight, esp. of a person

a·vouch (ə vouch′) *vt.* [see ADVOCATE] 1. to vouch for 2. to affirm

a·vow (ə vou′) *vt.* [see ADVOCATE] to declare; acknowledge —**a·vow′al** *n.* —**a·vowed′** *adj.* —**a·vow′ed·ly** *adv.*

a·vun·cu·lar (ə vuŋ′kyə lər) *adj.* [< L. *avunculus*] of an uncle

aw (ô) *interj.* a sound of protest, etc.

a·wait (ə wāt′) *vt., vi.* 1. to wait for 2. to be in store for

a·wake (ə wāk′) *vt., vi.* **a·woke′** or **a·waked′**, **a·waked′**, **a·wak′ing** [< OE.] 1. to rouse from sleep 2. to rouse from inactivity Also **a·wak′en** —*adj.* 1. not asleep 2. active; alert

a·wak′en·ing *n., adj.* 1. (a) waking up 2. (an) arousing or reviving

a·ward (ə wôrd′) *vt.* [< ME. < ONormFr. *eswarder*] 1. to give, as by legal decision 2. to give (a prize, etc.); grant —*n.* 1. a decision, as by a judge 2. a prize

a·ware (ə wer′) *adj.* [< OE. *wær*, cautious] knowing; realizing; conscious —**a·ware′ness** *n.*

a·wash (ə wôsh′) *adv., adj.* 1. at a level where the water washes over the surface 2. flooded 3. afloat

a·way (ə wā′) *adv.* [< OE. *on weg*] 1. from a place [run *away*] 2. in another place or direction [*away* from here] 3. off; aside [turn *away*] 4. far [far *away*] 5. from one's possession [give it *away*] 6. at once [fire *away*] 7. continuously [kept working *away*] —*adj.* 1. absent 2. at a distance [a mile *away*] —*interj.* begone! —**away with** go, come, or take away —**do away with** get rid of or kill

awe (ô) *n.* [< ON. *agi*] a mixed feeling of reverence, fear, and wonder —*vt.* **awed, aw′ing** to fill with awe —**stand (or be) in awe of** to respect and fear

a·weigh (ə wā′) *adj.* being weighed (hoisted): said of an anchor

awe·some (ô′səm) *adj.* inspiring or showing awe —**awe′some·ly** *adv.* —**awe′some·ness** *n.*

awe-struck (ô′struk′) *adj.* filled with awe: also **awe′-strick′en** (-strik′ən)

aw·ful (ô′f'l) *adj.* 1. inspiring awe 2. terrifying 3. [Colloq.] very bad —*adv.* [Colloq.] very —**aw′ful·ness** *n.*

aw·ful·ly (ô′fə lē, -flē) *adv.* 1. in an awful way 2. [Colloq.] very

a·while (ə wīl′, -hwīl′) *adv.* for a short time

awk·ward (ôk′wərd) *adj.* [< ON. *öfugr*, turned backward] 1. clumsy; bungling 2. hard to handle; unwieldy 3. uncomfortable [an *awkward* pose] 4. embarrassed or embarrassing —**awk′ward·ly** *adv.* —**awk′ward·ness** *n.*

awl (ôl) *n.* [< OE. *æl*] a small, pointed tool for making holes in wood, leather, etc.

awn (ôn) *n.* [< ON. *ögn*] the bristly fibers on a head of barley, oats, etc.

awn·ing (ô′niŋ) *n.* [? < MFr. *auvent*, window shade] a structure, as of canvas, extended before a window, door, etc. as a protection from sun or rain

a·woke (ə wōk′) *alt. pp. and occas. Brit. pp.* of AWAKE

A·WOL, a·wol (ā′wôl′) *adj.* absent without leave

a·wry (ə rī′) *adv., adj.* [see A- (on) & WRY] 1. with a twist to a side; askew 2. wrong; amiss [our plans went *awry*]

ax, axe (aks) *n., pl.* **ax′es** [< OE. *æx*] a tool with a long handle and bladed head, for chopping wood, etc. —*vt.* **axed, ax′ing** to trim, split, etc. with an ax —**get the ax** [Colloq.] to be discharged from one's job —**have an ax to grind** [Colloq.] to have an object of one's own to gain or promote

ax·i·al (ak′sē əl) *adj.* 1. of, like, or forming an axis 2. around, on, or along an axis —**ax′i·al·ly** *adv.*

ax·i·om (ak′sē əm) *n.* [< Gr. *axios*, worthy] 1. *a)* a statement universally accepted as true; maxim *b)* a self-evident truth 2. an established principle, scientific law, etc. —**ax′i·o·mat′ic** (-ə mat′ik) *adj.* —**ax′i·o·mat′i·cal·ly** *adv.*

ax·is (ak′sis) *n., pl.* **ax′es** (-sēz) [L.]

1. a real or imaginary straight line on which an object rotates **2.** a central line around which the parts of a thing, system, etc. are evenly arranged —**the Axis** Germany, Italy, and Japan, in World War II

ax·le (ak's'l) *n.* [< ON. *öxull*] **1.** a rod on or with which a wheel turns **2.** *a)* a bar connecting two opposite wheels, as of an automobile *b)* the spindle at either end of such a bar

ax'le·tree' (-trē') *n.* [< prec. + ON. *tre*, beam] an axle of a wagon, carriage, etc.

Ax·min·ster (aks'min'stər) *n.* [< English town where first made] a varicolored, patterned carpet with a cut pile

ax·o·lotl (ak'sə lät''l) *n.* [< MexInd., lit., water toy] a dark salamander of Mexico and the western U.S.

aye¹ (ā) *adv.* [< ON. *ei*][Poet.] always; ever: also **ay**

aye² (ī) *adv.* [? < prec.] yes —*n.* an affirmative vote or voter Also **ay**

AZ Arizona

a·zal·ea (ə zāl'yə) *n.* [< Gr. *azaleos*, dry: it thrives in dry soil] **1.** a shrub of the heath family with flowers of various colors **2.** the flower

az·i·muth (az'ə məth) *n.* [< Ar. *al*, the + *samt*, way] *Astron.*, *Surveying* distance clockwise in degrees from the north point or, in the Southern Hemisphere, south point

A·zores (ā'zôrz, ə zôrz') group of Portuguese islands in the N Atlantic, west of Portugal

Az·tec (az'tek) *n.* **1.** a member of a people who had an advanced civilization in Mexico before the Spanish conquest in 1519 **2.** their language —*adj.* of the Aztecs, their culture, etc.: also **Az'tec·an**

az·ure (azh'ər) *adj.* [< Per. *lāzhuward*, lapis lazuli] sky-blue —*n.* **1.** sky blue or any similar blue color **2.** [Poet.] the blue sky

B

B, b (bē) *n.*, *pl.* **B's, b's** the second letter of the English alphabet

B (bē) *n.* **1.** a grade indicating above-average but not outstanding work **2.** *Chem.* boron **3.** *Music* the 7th tone in the scale of C major —*adj.* inferior to the best [a class *B* motion picture]

B., b. 1. bachelor **2.** *[Baseball a]* base *b)* baseman **3.** *Music* bass **4.** born

Ba *Chem.* barium

B.A. Bachelor of Arts

baa (bä) *n.*, *vi.* [echoic] bleat

Ba·al (bā'əl) *n.* [< Heb.] **1.** an ancient Semitic fertility god **2.** an idol

bab·ble (bab''l) *vi.* -**bled**, -**bling** [echoic] **1.** to talk like a small child; prattle **2.** to talk foolishly or too much **3.** to murmur, as a brook —*vt.* to say incoherently or foolishly —*n.* **1.** incoherent vocal sounds **2.** foolish talk **3.** a murmuring sound — **bab'bler** *n.*

babe (bāb) *n.* **1.** a baby **2.** a naive person: also **babe in the woods 3.** [Slang] a girl or young woman

Ba·bel (bā'b'l, bab''l) *Bible* a city thwarted in building a tower to heaven when God created a confusion of tongues —*n.* [also b-] a confusion of voices, sounds, etc., or the scene of this

ba·boon (ba bōōn') *n.* [< OFr. *babuin*, ape, fool] a large, fierce dog-faced, short-tailed monkey of Africa and Arabia

ba·bush·ka (bə boosh'kə) *n.* [Russ., grandmother] a woman's scarf worn on the head and tied under the chin

BABOON

ba·by (bā'bē) *n.*, *pl.* -**bies** [ME. *babi*] **1.** a very young child; infant **2.** one who acts like an infant **3.** a very young animal **4.** the youngest or smallest in a group **5.** [Slang] *a)* a girl or young woman *b)* any person or thing —*adj.* **1.** of or for an infant **2.** very young **3.** small of its kind **4.** childish —*vt.* -**bied**, -**by·ing** to pamper; coddle —**ba'by·hood'** *n.* —**ba'by·ish** *adj.*

baby beef meat from a prime heifer or steer that is one to two years old

baby boom·er (bōō'mər) a person born during the birthrate increase (the **baby boom**) after World War II

baby carriage a light carriage for wheeling a baby about: also **baby buggy**

baby grand a small grand piano

Bab·y·lon (bab'ə lən, -län') capital of Babylonia, famous for luxury

Bab·y·lo·ni·a (bab'ə lō'nē ə) ancient empire in SW Asia —**Bab'y·lo'ni·an** *adj.*, *n.*

ba·by's breath (bā'bēz) a plant with small, delicate, white or pink flowers

baby sitter a person hired to take care of a child or children, as when the parents are away for the evening —**ba'by-sit'** *vi.* -**sat'**, -**sit'ting**

bac·ca·lau·re·ate (bak'ə lôr'ē it) *n.* [< ML. *baccalaris*, young noble seeking knighthood] **1.** the degree of BACHELOR OF ARTS (or SCIENCE, etc.) **2.** a commencement address

bac·ca·rat, bac·ca·ra (bak'ə rä', bak'ə rä') *n.* [Fr.] a gambling game played with cards

bac·cha·nal (bak'ə nəl, -nal') *n.* **1.** a worshiper of Bacchus **2.** a drunken carouser **3.** a drunken orgy —**bac'cha·na'li·an** (-nä'lē ən) *adj.*, *n.*

Bac·chus (bak'əs) the Greek and Roman god of wine and revelry

Bach (bäkh; *E. also* bäk), **Jo·hann Se·bas·tian** (yō'hän si bäs'tyən),

1685–1750; Ger. organist & composer

bach·e·lor (bach′l ər, bach′lər) *n.* [< ML. *baccalaris:* see BACCALAUREATE] 1. an unmarried man 2. one who is a BACHELOR OF ARTS (or SCIENCE, etc.) —**bach′e·lor·hood′** *n.*

Bachelor of Arts (or **Science,** etc.) 1. a degree given by a college or university to one who has completed a four-year course in the humanities (or in science, etc.) 2. one who has this degree

bachelor's button a plant with showy white, pink, or blue flowers, as the cornflower

ba·cil·lus (bə sil′əs) *n., pl.* **-cil′li** (-I) [< L. *bacillum,* little stick] 1. any of a genus of rod-shaped bacteria 2. loosely, any bacterium —**bac·il·lar·y** (bas′ə ler′ē, bə sil′ər ē) *adj.*

back (bak) *n.* [< OE. *bæk*] 1. the rear part of the body from the nape of the neck to the end of the spine 2. the backbone 3. a part that supports or fits the back 4. the rear part or reverse of anything 5. *Sports* a player or position behind the front line —*adj.* 1. at the rear 2. remote 3. of or for the past [back pay] 4. backward —*adv.* 1. at, to, or toward the rear 2. to or toward a former condition, time, etc. 3. in reserve or concealment 4. in return or requital [pay him *back*] —*vt.* 1. to move backward 2. to support 3. to bet on 4. to provide or be a back for —*vi.* to go backward —**back and forth** backward and forward —**back down** to withdraw from a position or claim —**back off** (or **away,** etc.) to move back (or away, etc.) —**back out** (of) 1. to withdraw from an enterprise 2. to evade keeping a promise, etc. —**back up** 1. to support 2. to move backward 3. to accumulate because of restricted movement [traffic *backed up*] —**go back on** [Colloq.] 1. to be disloyal to; betray 2. to fail to keep (one's word, etc.) —**turn one's back on** 1. to turn away from, as in contempt 2. to abandon

back′ache′ *n.* an ache or pain in the back

back′bite′ (-bīt′) *vt., vi.* **-bit′, -bit′ten** or **-bit′, -bit′ing** to slander (someone absent) —**back′bit′er** *n.*

back′board′ *n.* a board at or forming the back of something; esp., *Basketball* the board behind the basket

back′bone′ *n.* 1. the spine 2. a main support 3. willpower, courage, etc.

back′break′ing *adj.* very tiring

back′drop′ *n.* 1. a curtain, often scenic, at the back of a stage 2. background or setting

back′er *n.* 1. a patron; supporter 2. one who bets on a contestant

back′field′ *n. Football* the players behind the line; esp., the offensive unit

back′fire′ *n.* 1. the burning out of a small area, as in a forest, to check the spread of a big fire 2. premature explosion in an internal-combustion engine 3. reverse explosion in a gun —*vi.* **-fired′, -fir′ing** 1. to explode as a backfire 2. to go wrong or boomerang, as a plan

back′gam′mon (-gam′ən) *n.* [BACK + ME. *gammen,* game] a game for two, with dice governing moves of pieces on a special board

back′ground′ *n.* 1. the distant part of a scene 2. surroundings, sounds, data, etc. behind or subordinate to something 3. one's training and experience 4. events leading up to something

back′hand′ *n.* 1. handwriting that slants up to the left 2. a backhand catch, stroke, etc. —*adj.* 1. done with the back of the hand turned inward, as for a baseball catch, or forward, as for a tennis stroke, and with the arm across the body 2. written in backhand —*adv.* in a backhand way —*vt.* to hit, catch, swing, etc. backhand

back′hand′ed *adj.* 1. *same as* BACKHAND 2. not direct and open; devious —*adv.* in a backhanded way

back′ing *n.* 1. something forming a back for support 2. support given to a person or cause 3. supporters; backers

back′lash′ *n.* sharp reaction; recoil

back′log′ (-lôg′) *n.* an accumulation or reserve —*vi., vt.* **-logged′, -log′-ging** to accumulate as a backlog

back order an order not yet filled

back′pack′ *n.* a knapsack, often on a light frame, worn by campers or hikers —*vi., vt.* to wear, or carry in, a backpack —**back′pack′er** *n.*

back′ped′al *vi.* **-aled** or **-alled, -al·ing** or **-al·ling** 1. to pedal backward, as in braking a bicycle 2. to move backward; retreat; withdraw

back′rest′ *n.* a support for the back

back′side′ *n.* 1. back part 2. rump

back′slap′per (-slap′ər) *n.* [Colloq.] an effusively friendly person

back′slide′ *vi.* **-slid′, -slid′** or **-slid′den, -slid′ing** to slide backward in morals, etc. —**back′slid′er** *n.*

back′space′ *vi.* **-spaced′, -spac′ing** to move a typewriter carriage one or more spaces back along the line

back′spin′ *n.* backward spin in a ball, etc., making it bound backward upon hitting the ground

back′stage′ *adv., adj.* behind and off the stage, as in the wings or dressing rooms

back′stairs′ *adj.* involving intrigue or scandal; secret: also **back′stair′**

back′stop′ *n.* a screen, fence, etc. to keep balls from going too far, as behind the catcher in baseball

back′stretch′ *n.* the part of a race track opposite the homestretch

back′stroke′ *n.* a swimming stroke made while lying face upward

back talk [Colloq.] saucy or insolent retorts

back′-to-back′ *adj.* [Colloq.] one right after another

---

fat, āpe, cär; ten, ēven; is, bīte; gō, hôrn, tōōl, look; oil, out; up, fur; chin; she; thin, *then*; zh, leisure; ŋ, ring; ə for *a* in *ago*; ′, (ä′b'l); ë, Fr. coeur; ö, Fr. feu; Fr. mon; ü, Fr. duc; kh, G. ich, doch; ‡ foreign; < derived from

back′track′ *vi.* **1.** to return by the same path **2.** to retreat or recant

back′up′, back′-up′ *adj.* **1.** standing by as an alternate or auxiliary **2.** supporting —*n.* a backing up; specif., *a)* an accumulation *b)* a support; help

back′ward *adv.* **1.** toward the back **2.** with the back foremost **3.** in reverse order **4.** in a way opposite to usual **5.** into the past Also **back′wards** —*adj.* **1.** turned toward the rear or in the opposite way **2.** shy **3.** slow or retarded —**back′ward·ness** *n.*

back′wash′ *n.* **1.** water or air moved backward by a ship, propeller, etc. **2.** a reaction caused by some event

back′wa′ter *n.* **1.** water moved or held back by a dam, tide, etc. **2.** stagnant water in an inlet, etc. **3.** a backward place or condition

back′woods′ *n.pl.* [*occas. with sing. v.*] **1.** heavily wooded, remote areas **2.** any remote, thinly populated area —*adj.* of or like the backwoods —**back′woods′man** (-mən) *n., pl.* -men

ba·con (bāk′'n) *n.* [< OS. *baco,* side of bacon] salted and smoked meat from the back or sides of a hog —**bring home the bacon** [Colloq.] **1.** to earn a living **2.** to succeed

Ba·con (bāk′'n), Francis, 1561-1626; Eng. philosopher and writer

bac·te·ri·a (bak tir′ē ə) *n.pl., sing.* **-ri·um** (-əm) [< Gr. *baktērion,* small staff] microorganisms which have no chlorophyll and multiply by simple division: some bacteria cause diseases, but others are necessary for fermentation, etc. —**bac·te′ri·al** *adj.*

bac·te′ri·cide′ (-tir′ə sīd′) *n.* an agent that destroys bacteria —**bac·te′ri·cid′al** *adj.*

bac·te·ri·ol·o·gy (-tir′ē äl′ə jē) *n.* the science that deals with bacteria —**bac·te′ri·o·log′i·cal** (-ē ə läj′i k'l) *adj.* —**bac·te′ri·ol′o·gist** *n.*

bad¹ (bad) *adj.* worse, worst [ME.] **1.** not good; not as it should be **2.** inadequate or unfit **3.** unfavorable [*bad news*] **4.** rotten or spoiled **5.** incorrect or faulty **6.** *a)* wicked; immoral *b)* mischievous **7.** harmful **8.** severe **9.** ill **10.** sorry; distressed [he feels *bad* about it] **11.** offensive —*adv.* [Colloq.] badly —*n.* anything bad —**in bad** [Colloq.] in trouble or disfavor —**bad′ness** *n.*

bad² (bad) *archaic pt. of* BID

bad blood (mutual) enmity

bad egg [Slang] a mean or dishonest person: also **bad actor, bad apple, bad hat, bad lot,** etc.

badge (baj) *n.* [ME. *bage*] **1.** an emblem worn to show rank, membership, etc. **2.** any distinctive sign, etc.

badg·er (baj′ər) *n.* [< ?] **1.** a burrowing animal with a broad back and thick, short legs **2.** its fur —*vt.* to nag at; torment

bad·i·nage (bad′ə näzh′, bad′'n ij) *n.* [Fr. < ML. *badare,* to trifle] playful talk —*vt.* **-naged′, -nag′ing** to tease

bad′lands′ *n.pl.* **1.** an area of barren land with dry soil and soft rocks eroded into odd shapes **2.** [B-] any such

W U.S. area: also **Bad Lands**

bad′ly *adv.* **1.** in a bad manner **2.** [Colloq.] very much; greatly

bad′man′ *n., pl.* **-men′** a cattle thief or desperado of the old West

bad·min·ton (bad′min t'n) *n.* [< *Badminton,* Eng. estate] a game in which a feathered cork is batted back and forth with rackets across a net

bad′-mouth′ *vt., vi.* [Slang] to find fault (with)

bad′tem′pered *adj.* irritable

Bae·de·ker (bā′də kər) *n.* **1.** any of a series of guidebooks to foreign countries first published in Germany **2.** loosely, any guidebook

baf·fle (baf′'l) *vt.* **-fled, -fling** [< ?] **1.** to perplex completely; bewilder **2.** to impede; check —*n.* a screen to deflect air, sound, etc. —**baf′fle·ment** *n.* —**baf′fler** *n.* —**baf′fling** *adj.*

bag (bag) *n.* [< ON. *baggi*] **1.** a nonrigid container of paper, plastic, etc., with a top opening that can be closed **2.** a satchel, suitcase, etc. **3.** a purse **4.** game taken in hunting **5.** a baglike shape or part **6.** [Slang] an unattractive woman **7.** [Slang] one's special interest **8.** *Baseball* a base —*vt.* **bagged, bag′ging 1.** to make bulge **2.** to capture **3.** to kill in hunting **4.** [Slang] to get —*vi.* **1.** to swell **2.** to hang loosely —**in the bag** [Slang] certain; assured

bag·a·telle (bag′ə tel′) *n.* [Fr. < L. *baca,* berry] a trifle

ba·gel (bā′g'l) *n.* [Yid.] a hard bread roll shaped like a small doughnut

bag′ful′ *n., pl.* **-fuls′** as much as a bag will hold

bag·gage (bag′ij) *n.* [< ML. *baga,* chest, bag] **1.** the bags, etc. of a traveler; luggage **2.** a lively girl

bag·gy (bag′ē) *adj.* **-gi·er, -gi·est** puffy or hanging loosely, like a bag —**bag′gi·ly** *adv.* —**bag′gi·ness** *n.*

Bagh·dad (bag′dad) capital of Iraq: pop. c.1,000,000: also **Bagdad**

bag lady [Slang] a homeless, poor woman who wanders city streets carrying her belongings in shopping bags

bag′pipe′ *n.* [*often pl.*] a wind instrument, now chiefly Scottish, played by forcing air from a bag into reed pipes and fingering the stops

BAGPIPE

bah (bä, ba) *interj.* an exclamation of contempt, scorn, or disgust

Ba·ha·mas (bə hä′məz) country on a group of islands (**Bahama Islands**) in the West Indies: 4,404 sq. mi., pop. 185,000

bail¹ (bāl) *n.* [< L. *bajulare,* bear a burden] **1.** money deposited with the court to get a prisoner temporarily released **2.** such a release **3.** the person giving bail —*vt.* **1.** to have (a prisoner) set free by giving bail **2.** to help out of financial or other difficulty Often with *out*—**bail′a·ble** *adj.*

bail² (bāl) *n.* [ME. *baille,* bucket] a bucket for dipping water from a boat —*vi.*, *vt.* to dip out (water) from (a boat): usually with *out* —**bail out** to parachute from an aircraft

bail³ (bāl) *n.* [ME. *beil*] a hoop-shaped handle for a bucket, etc.

bail bond a bond deposited as bail for an arrested person as surety that he will appear at his trial

bai·liff (bāˈlif) *n.* [ME. *bailif*] **1.** a deputy sheriff **2.** a court officer who guards the jurors, keeps order in the court, etc. **3.** in England, *a*) a district official *b*) a steward of an estate

bai·li·wick (bāˈlə wik) *n.* [ME. *bailif*, bailiff + *wik*, village] **1.** a bailiff's district **2.** one's particular area of activity, authority, interest, etc.

bails·man (bālzˈmən) *n.*, *pl.* **-men** a person who gives bail for another

bairn (bern) *n.* [Scot.] a child

bait (bāt) *vt.* [< ON. *beita*, make bite] **1.** to set dogs on for sport [*to bait bears*] **2.** to torment or harass, esp. by verbal attacks **3.** to put food on (a hook or trap) as a lure for game **4.** to lure; tempt; entice —*n.* **1.** food, etc. put on a hook or trap as a lure **2.** anything used as a lure; enticement

bait′-and-switch′ *adj.* of or using an unethical sales technique in which a seller lures customers by advertising an often nonexistent bargain item and then tries to switch their attention to more expensive items

baize (bāz) *n.* [< L. *badius*, brown] a coarse, feltlike woolen cloth

bake (bāk) *vt.* **baked**, **bak′ing** [OE. *bacan*] **1.** to cook (food) by dry heat, esp. in an oven **2.** to dry and harden (pottery) by heat; fire —*vi.* **1.** to bake bread, etc. **2.** to become baked —*n.* **1.** a baking **2.** a social affair at which a baked food is served

bak·er (bākˈər) *n.* one whose work or business is baking bread, etc.

baker's dozen thirteen

bak·er·y (bākˈər ē) *n.*, *pl.* **-ies 1.** a place where bread, etc. is baked or sold **2.** baked goods

baking powder a leavening agent containing baking soda and an acid-forming substance

baking soda sodium bicarbonate, used as a leavening agent and as an antacid

bal·a·lai·ka (balˈə līˈkə) *n.* [Russ.] a Russian stringed instrument somewhat like a guitar

bal·ance (balˈəns) *n.* [< LL. *bilanx*, having two scales] **1.** an instrument for weighing, esp. one with two matched hanging scales **2.** a state of equilibrium in weight, value, etc. **3.** bodily or mental stability **4.** harmonious proportion of elements in a design, etc. **5.** a weight, value, etc. that counteracts another **6.** equality of debits and credits, or the difference between them **7.** a remainder **8.** *same as* BALANCE WHEEL —*vt.* **-anced**, **-anc·ing 1.** to weigh in or as in a balance **2.** to compare as to relative value, etc. **3.** to counteract; offset **4.** to bring into proportion, harmony, etc. **5.** to make or be equal to in weight, value, etc. **6.** to find the difference between, or to equalize, the debits and credits of (an account) —*vi.* **1.** to be in equilibrium **2.** to be equal in weight, value, etc. **3.** to have the credits and debits equal —**in the balance** not yet settled

balance sheet a statement showing the financial status of a business

bal·co·ny (balˈkə nē) *n.*, *pl.* **-nies** [< It. *balcone*] **1.** a platform projecting from an upper story and enclosed by a railing **2.** an upper floor of seats in a theater, etc., often projecting over the main floor

bald (bôld) *adj.* [< ME.] **1.** having a head with white fur, etc. growing on it **2.** lacking hair on the head **3.** not covered by natural growth **4.** plain or blunt [*bald truth*] —**bald′ly** *adv.* —**bald′ness** *n.*

bald eagle a large eagle of N. America, with a white-feathered head

bal·der·dash (bôlˈdər dash′) *n.* [orig. (17th c.), an odd mixture] nonsense

bald′-faced′ (-fāst′) *adj.* brazen; shameless [*a baldfaced lie*]

bald′ing *adj.* becoming bald

bal·dric (bôlˈdrik) *n.* [ult. < L. *balteus*, belt] a belt worn over one shoulder to support a sword, etc.

bale (bāl) *n.* [< OHG. *balla*, ball] a large bundle, esp. a standardized quantity of goods, as raw cotton compressed and bound —*vt.* **baled**, **bal′ing** to make into bales —**bal′er** *n.*

ba·leen (bə lēn′) *n.* [ult. < Gr. *phallaina*, whale] *same as* WHALEBONE

bale·ful (bālˈfəl) *adj.* [< OE. *bealu*, evil] deadly; harmful; ominous

Ba·li (bäˈlē) island of Indonesia — **Ba′li·nese′** (-lə nēz′) *adj.*, *n.*

balk (bôk) *n.* [OE. *balca*, ridge] **1.** an obstruction, hindrance, etc. **2.** a blunder; error **3.** *Baseball* an illegal motion by the pitcher entitling base runners to advance one base —*vt.* to obstruct or foil —*vi.* **1.** to stop and refuse to move or act **2.** to hesitate or recoil (*at*)

Bal·kan (bôlˈkən) *adj.* of the Balkans, their people, etc. —**the Balkans** countries of Albania, Bulgaria, Greece, Romania, Yugoslavia, & European Turkey, in SE Europe

Balkan Peninsula peninsula in SE Europe, east of Italy

balk·y (bôkˈē) *adj.* **-i·er**, **-i·est** stubbornly resisting; balking

ball¹ (bôl) *n.* [ME. *bal*] **1.** any round object; sphere; globe **2.** *a*) a round or egg-shaped object used in various games *b*) any of several such games, esp. baseball **3.** a throw or pitch of a ball [*a fast ball*] **4.** a missile for a cannon, rifle, etc. **5.** a rounded part of the body **6.** *Baseball* a pitched ball that is not hit and is not a strike —*vi.*, *vt.* to form into a ball —**ball up**

[Slang] to muddle; confuse —**on the ball** [Slang] alert; efficient

ball[2] (bôl) *n.* [< Fr. < Gr. *ballizein,* to dance] **1.** a formal social dance **2.** [Slang] a good time

bal·lad (bal'əd) *n.* [OFr. *ballade,* dancing song] **1.** a sentimental song with the same melody for each stanza **2.** a narrative song or poem, usually anonymous, with simple words, short stanzas, and a refrain **3.** a slow, sentimental popular song —**bal'lad·eer'** *n.* —**bal'lad·ry** *n.*

ball-and-sock·et joint (bôl'ən säk'it) a joint, as of the hip, formed by a ball in a socket

bal·last (bal'əst) *n.* [< ODan. *bar,* bare + *last,* a load] **1.** anything heavy carried in a ship or vehicle to give stability **2.** crushed rock or gravel, used in railroad beds, etc. —*vt.* to furnish with ballast

ball bearing 1. a bearing in which the parts turn on freely rolling metal balls **2.** one of those balls

bal·le·ri·na (bal'ə rē'nə) *n.* [It.] a woman ballet dancer

bal·let (bal'ā, ba lā') *n.* [Fr.] **1.** an intricate group dance using pantomime and conventionalized movements to tell a story **2.** ballet dancers

bal·let·o·mane (ba let'ə mān') *n.* [Fr.] a person devoted to the ballet

ball game 1. a game played with a ball **2.** [Colloq.] a set of circumstances *[a whole new ball game]*

ballistic missile a long-range guided missile designed to fall free as it approaches its target

bal·lis·tics (bə lis'tiks) *n.pl.* [*with sing. v.*] the science dealing with the motion and impact of projectiles —**bal·lis'tic** *adj.*

bal·loon (bə lōōn') *n.* [< Fr. < It. *palla,* ball] **1.** a large, airtight bag that rises when filled with a gas lighter than air **2.** an airship with such a bag **3.** an inflatable rubber bag, used as a toy —*vt.* to inflate —*vi.* to swell; expand —*adj.* like a balloon —**bal·loon'ist** *n.*

bal·lot (bal'ət) *n.* [< It. *palla,* ball] **1.** a ticket, paper, etc. by which a vote is registered **2.** act or right of voting, as by ballots **3.** the total number of votes cast —*vi.* to vote

ball'park' *n.* a baseball stadium

ball'play'er *n.* a baseball player

ball point pen a fountain pen with a small ball bearing instead of a point: also **ball'-point',** **ball'point'** *n.*

ball'room' *n.* a large hall for dancing

bal·lute (bə lōōt') *n.* [BALL(OON) + (PARACH)UTE] a heat-resistant, balloonlike device inflated by stored gas and used to slow down a spacecraft reentering the atmosphere

bal·ly·hoo (bal'ē hōō') *n.* [< ?] noisy talk, sensational advertising, etc. —*vt., vi.* -**hooed',** -**hoo'ing** [Colloq.] to promote with ballyhoo

balm (bäm) *n.* [< Gr. *balsamon*] **1.** a fragrant, healing ointment or oil **2.** anything healing or soothing

balm'y *adj.* -**i·er, -i·est 1.** soothing, mild, etc. **2.** [Brit. Slang] crazy

ba·lo·ney (bə lō'nē) *n.* [< ? *bologna*] **1.** bologna **2.** [Slang] nonsense

bal·sa (bôl'sə) *n.* [Sp.] **1.** the wood, very light in weight, of a tropical American tree **2.** the tree

bal·sam (bôl'səm) *n.* [see BALM] **1.** an aromatic resin obtained from certain trees **2.** any of various aromatic resinous oils or fluids **3.** balm **4.** any of various trees yielding balsam

Bal·tic Sea (bôl'tik) sea in N Europe, west of the U.S.S.R.

Bal·ti·more (bôl'tə môr') seaport in N Md.: pop. 787,000

bal·us·ter (bal'əs tər) *n.* [< Gr. *balaustion,* wild pomegranate flower: from the shape] any of the small posts of a railing, as on a staircase

bal·us·trade (bal'ə strād') *n.* a railing held up by balusters

Bal·zac (bäl zäk'; *E.* bôl'zak), **Ho·no·ré de** (ô nô rā' də) 1799–1850; Fr. novelist

bam·boo (bam bōō') *n.* [Malay *bambu*] a treelike tropical grass with woody, jointed, often hollow stems used for furniture, canes, etc.

bamboo curtain [*often* B- C-] the political and ideological differences that separate China from the West

bam·boo·zle (bam bōō'z'l) *vt.* -**zled, -zling** [< ?] **1.** to trick; cheat; dupe **2.** to confuse; puzzle

ban (ban) *vt.* **banned, ban'ning** [OE. *bannan,* summon] to prohibit or forbid, esp. officially —*n.* **1.** a condemnation by church authorities **2.** a curse **3.** an official prohibition **4.** strong public condemnation

ba·nal (bā'n'l, bə nal') *adj.* [Fr.: see prec.] trite; hackneyed —**ba·nal'i·ty** *n., pl.* -**ties** —**ba'nal·ly** *adv.*

ba·nan·a (bə nan'ə) *n.* [Sp. & Port.] **1.** a treelike tropical plant with large clusters of edible fruit **2.** the narrow, somewhat curved fruit, having a creamy flesh and a yellow or red skin

band[1] (band) *n.* [ON.] **1.** something that binds, ties, or encircles, as a strip or ring of wood, rubber, metal, etc. **2.** a strip of color or of material **3.** a division of a long-playing phonograph record **4.** a range of wavelengths —*vt.* to put a band on or around

band[2] (band) *n.* [< Fr.; ult. < Goth. *bandwa,* a sign] **1.** a group of people united for some purpose **2.** a group of musicians playing together, esp. upon wind and percussion instruments —*vi., vt.* to unite for some purpose

band·age (ban'dij) *n.* [Fr. < *bande,* a strip] a strip of cloth, etc. used to bind or cover an injury —*vt.* **-aged, -ag·ing** to put a bandage on

Band-Aid (ban'dād') [BAND(AGE) + AID] a *trademark for* a small bandage of gauze and adhesive tape —*n.* [b-] such a bandage: also **band'aid'**

ban·dan·na, ban·dan·a (ban dan'ə) *n.* [Hind. *bāndhnū,* method of dyeing] a large, colored handkerchief

band·box (band'bäks') *n.* a light box, as of pasteboard, for hats, etc.

ban·deau (ban dō') *n., pl.* -**deaux'** (-dōz') [Fr.] **1.** a narrow ribbon **2.** a narrow brassiere

ban·dit (ban′dit) *n.* [< It.] a robber; highwayman —**ban′dit·ry** *n.*

ban·do·leer, ban·do·lier (ban′də lir′) *n.* [< Fr.] a broad belt with pockets for bullets, etc., worn over one shoulder and across the chest

band saw an endless toothed steel belt on pulleys, powered for sawing

bands·man (bandz′mən, banz′-) *n., pl.* **-men** a member of a band of musicians

band′stand′ *n.* a platform for a band, esp. one for outdoor concerts

band′wag′on *n.* a wagon for a band to ride on, as in a parade —**on the bandwagon** [Colloq.] on the popular or apparently winning side

ban·dy¹ (ban′dē) *vt.* **-died, -dy·ing** [Fr. *bander*, bandy at tennis] **1.** to toss or hit back and forth **2.** to pass (rumors, etc.) freely **3.** to exchange (words), esp. angrily

ban·dy² (ban′dē) *adj.* [Fr. *bandé*, bent] curved outward; bowed

ban′dy-leg′ged (-leg′id, -legd′) *adj.* having bandy legs; bowlegged

bane (bān) *n.* [OE. *bana*] **1.** ruin, death, harm, or the cause of this **2.** poison —**bane′ful** *adj.*

bang¹ (baŋ) *vt.* [ON. *banga*, to pound] to hit, shut, etc. hard and noisily —*vi.* **1.** to make a loud noise **2.** to hit noisily or sharply —*n.* **1.** a hard, noisy blow or impact **2.** a loud, sudden noise **3.** [Colloq.] a burst of vigor **4.** [Slang] a thrill —*adv.* **1.** hard and noisily **2.** abruptly —**bang up** to damage

bang² (baŋ) *vt.* [< ?] to cut (hair) short and straight —*n.* [*usually pl.*] banged hair over the forehead

Bang·kok (baŋ′käk) seaport and capital of Thailand: pop. 1,669,000

Ban·gla·desh (baŋ′glə desh′) country in S Asia, on the Bay of Bengal: 55,134 sq. mi.; pop. 50,840,000

ban·gle (baŋ′g'l) *n.* [Hind. *bangrī*] a decorative bracelet or anklet

bang-up (baŋ′up′) *adj.* [Colloq.] very good; excellent

ban·ish (ban′ish) *vt.* [< OFr. *banir*] **1.** to exile **2.** to drive away; get rid of —**ban′ish·ment** *n.*

ban·is·ter (ban′əs tər) *n.* [< BALUSTER] [*often pl.*] a handrail, specif. one with balusters

ban·jo (ban′jō) *n., pl.* **-jos, -joes** [of Afr. origin] a musical instrument with a long neck, circular body, and strings that are plucked —**ban′jo·ist** *n.*

bank¹ (baŋk) *n.* [ult. < OHG. *bank*, bench] **1.** an establishment for receiving or lending money **2.** a reserve supply; pool —*vt., vi.* to put into a bank —**bank on** [Colloq.] to rely on

bank² (baŋk) *n.* [< ON. *bakki*] **1.** a long mound or heap **2.** a steep slope **3.** a rise of land along a river, etc. **4.** a shallow place, as in a sea **5.** the lateral, slanting turn of an aircraft —*vt.* **1.** to cover (a fire) with ashes and fuel so that it will burn slowly **2.** to pile up so as to form a bank **3.** to slope (a curve in a road, etc.) **4.** to make (an aircraft) slant laterally on a turn **5.** to make (a billiard ball) recoil from a cushion

bank³ (baŋk) *n.* [< OFr. *banc*, bench] **1.** a row of oars **2.** a row or tier, as of keys in a keyboard —*vt.* to arrange in a row or tier

bank account money deposited in a bank and credited to the depositor

bank′book′ *n.* a book recording a bank depositor's deposits; passbook

bank′er *n.* a person who owns or manages a bank

bank′ing *n.* the business of a bank

bank note a promissory note issued by a bank: a form of paper money

bank′roll′ *n.* a supply of money —*vt.* [Colloq.] to supply with money; finance

bank·rupt (baŋk′rupt′) *n.* [< It. *banca*, bench + *rotta*, broken] a person legally declared unable to pay his debts —*adj.* **1.** that is a bankrupt; insolvent **2.** lacking in some quality [morally *bankrupt*] —*vt.* to make bankrupt —**bank′rupt·cy** *n.*

ban·ner (ban′ər) *n.* [ME. *banere* < OFr. *baniere*] **1.** a flag **2.** a headline running across a newspaper page —*adj.* foremost

banns (banz) *n.pl.* [see BAN] the proclamation made in church of an intended marriage

ban·quet (baŋ′kwit) *n.* [Fr. < It. *banca*, table] **1.** a feast **2.** a formal dinner —*vt.* to honor with a banquet

ban·quette (baŋ ket′) *n.* [Fr.] **1.** a gunner's platform inside a trench, etc. **2.** an upholstered bench

ban·shee, ban·shie (ban′shē) *n.* [< Ir. *bean*, woman + *sith*, fairy] *Ir. & Scot. Folklore* a female spirit whose wailing warns of impending death

ban·tam (ban′təm) *n.* [< *Bantam*, former province in Java] **1.** [*often* B-] any of several breeds of small fowl **2.** a small, aggressive person —*adj.* like a bantam

ban′tam·weight′ *n.* a boxer or wrestler weighing 113 to 118 lbs.

ban·ter (ban′tər) *vt.* [17th-c. slang] to tease playfully —*vi.* to exchange banter (*with* someone) —*n.* playful teasing —**ban′ter·ing·ly** *adv.*

Ban·tu (ban′tōō) *n., pl.* **-tus, -tu** [Bantu *ba-ntu*, mankind] **1.** any member of a group of Negroid tribes of equatorial and southern Africa **2.** any of the related languages of these people

Ban′tu·stan′ (-stan′) *n.* [prec. + Per. *stān*, a place] any of several territories in South Africa, set aside for native black peoples

ban·yan (ban′yən) *n.* [ult. < Sans.] an East Indian fig tree whose branches take root and become trunks

ba·o·bab (bā′ō bab′, bā′-) *n.* [< native name] a tall tree of Africa and India, with edible gourdlike fruit

bap·tism (bap'tiz'm) *n.* [see BAPTIZE]
1. the rite of admitting a person into
a Christian church by dipping him in
water or sprinkling water on him **2.** an
initiating experience —**bap·tis'mal**
(-tiz'm'l) *adj.*

Bap'tist (-tist) *n.* a member of a
Protestant denomination practicing
baptism of believers by immersion

bap'tis·ter·y (-tis trē) *n., pl.* **-ies** a
place, esp. in a church, used for baptiz-
ing: also **bap'tis·try,** *pl.* **-tries**

bap·tize (bap'tīz, bap tīz') *vt.* **-tized,**
-tiz·ing [< Gr. *baptizein*, to immerse]
1. to administer baptism to **2.** to
initiate **3.** to christen

bar (bär) *n.* [< ML. *barra*] **1.** any
long, narrow piece of wood, metal, etc.,
often used as a barrier, lever, etc. **2.** an
oblong piece, as of soap **3.** anything
that obstructs or hinders **4.** a band or
strip **5.** a law court, esp. that part,
enclosed by a railing, where the lawyers sit **6.** lawyers collectively **7.** the
legal profession **8.** a counter, as for
serving alcoholic drinks **9.** a place
with such a counter **10.** *Music a)* a
vertical line dividing a staff into measures *b)* a measure —*vt.* **barred,**
bar'ring 1. to fasten with a bar **2.** to
obstruct; close, **3.** to oppose **4.** to exclude —*prep.* excluding [the best, *bar*
none*]* —**cross the bar** to die

barb (bärb) *n.* [< L. *barba*, beard] **1.**
a beardlike growth **2.** a sharp point
projecting backward from the main
point of a fishhook, etc. **3.** a cutting
remark —*vt.* to provide with a barb
—**barbed** *adj.*

Bar·ba·dos (bär bā'dōz, -dōs) country on an island in the West Indies:
166 sq. mi.; pop. 245,000

bar·bar·i·an (bär ber'ē ən) *n.* [see
BARBAROUS] **1.** a member of a people
considered primitive, savage, etc. **2.**
a cruel person —*adj.* uncivilized, cruel,
etc. —**bar·bar'i·an·ism** *n.*

bar·bar'ic (-ber'ik) *adj.* **1.** primitive;
uncivilized **2.** wild, crude, etc.

bar·ba·rism (bär'bər iz'm) *n.* **1.** a
word or expression that is not standard
2. the state of being primitive or uncivilized **3.** a barbarous act or custom

bar·bar·i·ty (bär ber'ə tē) *n., pl.*
-ties 1. cruelty; brutality **2.** a bar-
baric taste, manner, etc.

bar·ba·rize (bär'bə rīz') *vt., vi.*
-rized', -riz'ing to make or become
barbarous —**bar'ba·ri·za'tion** *n.*

bar·ba·rous (bär'bər əs) *adj.* [< Gr.
barbaros, foreign] **1.** uncivilized; primitive **2.** crude, coarse, etc. **3.** cruel;
brutal —**bar'ba·rous·ly** *adv.*

bar·be·cue (bär'bə kyōō') *n.* [Sp.
barbacoa] **1.** *a)* a hog, steer, etc.
roasted whole over an open fire *b)* any
meat broiled on a spit **2.** a party,
picnic, or restaurant featuring this
—*vt.* **-cued', -cu'ing** to roast or broil
over an open fire, often with a highly
seasoned sauce (**barbecue sauce**)

barbed wire wire with barbs at close
intervals: also **barb'wire'** *n.*

bar·bel (bär'b'l) *n.* [< L. *barba*,
beard] a threadlike growth from the
lips or jaws of certain fishes

bar·bell (bär'bel') *n.* [BAR + (DUMB)-
BELL] a metal bar
with weights at-
tached at each end,
used for weight-
lifting exercises:
also **bar bell**

BARBELL

bar·ber (bär'bər)
n. [see BARB] one
whose work is cut-
ting hair, shaving
beards, etc. —*vt.,*
vi. to cut the hair
(of), shave, etc.

bar·ber·ry (bär'ber'ē) *n., pl.* **-ries**
[< ML. *barberis*] **1.** a spiny shrub
with sour, red berries **2.** the berry

bar·bi·tu·rate (bär bich'ər it, bär'
bə tyoor'it) *n.* [< G.] a salt or ester of
a crystalline acid (**barbituric acid**),
used as a sedative

bar·ca·role, bar·ca·rolle (bär'kə
rōl') *n.* [< Fr. < It.] a Venetian
gondolier song, or music like this

Bar·ce·lo·na (bär'sə lō'nə) seaport
in NE Spain: pop. 1,696,000

bar code *same as* UNIVERSAL PRODUCT
CODE

bard (bärd) *n.* [Gael. & Ir.] **1.** an
ancient Celtic poet **2.** a poet

bare (ber) *adj.* [OE. *bær*] **1.** not
covered or clothed; naked **2.** without
furnishings; empty **3.** simple; plain **4.**
mere [*bare* needs] —*vt.* **bared, bar'-**
ing to make bare; uncover —**lay bare**
to uncover; expose —**bare'ness** *n.*

bare'back' *adv., adj.* on a horse with
no saddle

bare'faced' *adj.* **1.** with the face
uncovered **2.** open; shameless

bare'foot' *adj., adv.* without shoes
and stockings —**bare'foot'ed** *adj.*

bare'hand'ed *adj., adv.* **1.** with
hands uncovered **2.** without weapons,
etc.

bare'head'ed *adj., adv.* with the
head uncovered

bare'leg'ged (-leg'id, -legd') *adj.,*
adv. with the legs bare

bare'ly *adv.* **1.** plainly **2.** only just;
scarcely **3.** scantily

bar·gain (bär'g'n) *n.* [< OFr. *bar-*
gaignier, haggle] **1.** a mutual agreement or contract **2.** an agreement with
regard to its worth [a bad *bargain*] **3.**
something sold at a price favorable to
the buyer —*vi.* **1.** to haggle **2.** to
make a bargain —**bargain for** (or **on**)
to expect; count on —**into the bar-**
gain besides —**bar'gain·er** *n.*

bargain counter a store counter for
displaying goods at reduced prices

barge (bärj) *n.* [< ML. *barga*] **1.** a
large, flat-bottomed boat for freight
on rivers, etc. **2.** a large pleasure boat
—*vi.* **barged, barg'ing 1.** to move
slowly and clumsily **2.** to enter rudely
or abruptly (*in* or *into*)

bar·i·tone (bar'ə tōn', ber'-) *n.* [<
Gr. *barys*, deep + *tonos*, tone] **1.** the
range of a male voice between tenor
and bass **2.** a singer or instrument
with this range

bar·i·um (ber'ē əm) *n.* [< Gr. *barys*,
heavy] a metallic chemical element

bark¹ (bärk) *n.* [< ON. *börkr*] the out-

side covering of trees and woody
plants —*vt.* 1. to remove bark from (a
tree, etc.) 2. [Colloq.] to scrape; skin
(the knees, etc.)

bark[2] (bärk) *vi.* [OE. *beorcan*] 1. to
make the sharp, abrupt cry of a dog or
a similar sound 2. to speak sharply;
snap —*n.* the characteristic cry of a
dog, or any noise like this —**bark up
the wrong tree** to misdirect one's
attack, energies, etc.

bark[3] (bärk) *n.* [< L. *barca*] 1. [Poet.]
a boat 2. a sailing vessel with two forward square-rigged masts and a rear
mast rigged fore-and-aft: also **barque**

bar'keep'er *n.* 1. an owner of a barroom 2. a bartender Also **bar'keep'**

bark'er *n.* one who talks loud to
attract people to a sideshow, etc.

bar·ley (bär'lē) *n.* [OE. *bærlic*] 1. a
cereal grass 2. its grain, used in making malts, soups, etc.

bar'maid' *n.* a waitress who serves
alcoholic drinks in a bar

bar mitz·vah (bär mits'və) [< Heb.,
son of the commandment] [*also* B- M-]
1. a Jewish boy who has arrived at the
age of religious responsibility, 13 years
2. a ceremony celebrating this —**bat**
(or **bas**) **mitzvah** (bät, bäs) *fem.*

barn (bärn) *n.* [OE. *bern*] a farm
building for sheltering harvested crops,
livestock, etc.

bar·na·cle (bär'nə k'l) *n.* [Fr.
bernicle] a saltwater shellfish that attaches itself to rocks, ship bottoms, etc.

barn·storm (bärn'stôrm') *vi., vt.* to
tour (the country, esp. rural areas),
giving speeches, plays, etc.

Bar·num (bär'nəm), **P(hineas)**
T(aylor) 1810–91; U.S. showman

barn'yard' *n.* the yard near a barn
—*adj.* of, like, or fit for a barnyard

ba·rom·e·ter (bə räm'ə tər) *n.* [<
Gr. *baros*, weight + -METER] 1. an
instrument for measuring atmospheric
pressure and thus forecasting weather
2. anything that marks change —**bar-
o·met·ric** (bar'ə met'rik) *adj.*

bar·on (bar'ən, ber'-) *n.* [ME.] 1. a
member of the lowest rank of British
nobility 2. a magnate —**bar'on·age**
n. —**bar'on·ess** *n.fem.* —**ba·ro·ni·al**
(bə rō'nē əl) *adj.*

bar'on·et (-ə nit, -net') *n.* a man
holding the lowest hereditary British
title, below a baron —**bar'on·et·cy**
n., pl. -**cies**

ba·roque (bə rōk') *adj.* [Fr. < Port.
barroco, imperfect pearl] 1. *a)* very
ornate and full of curved lines, as
much art and architecture of about
1550–1750 *b)* full of highly embellished
melodies, fugues, etc., as much music
of that time 2. fantastically ornate

bar·racks (bar'iks, ber'-) *n.pl.* [*often
with sing. v.*] [< Sp. *barro*, clay] a
building or buildings for housing
soldiers

bar·ra·cu·da (bar'ə kōō'də, ber'-)
n., pl. -**da**, -**das** [Sp.] a fierce, pikelike
fish of tropical seas

bar·rage (bə räzh') *n.* [Fr. < *barrer*,
to stop] 1. a curtain of artillery fire
2. any prolonged attack —*vi., vt.*
-**raged'**, -**rag·ing** to subject to a
barrage

barred (bärd) *adj.* 1. having bars or
stripes 2. closed off with bars 3. not
allowed

bar·rel (bar'əl, ber'-) *n.* [< ML.
barillus] 1. *a)* a large, cylindrical container with slightly bulging sides and
flat ends *b)* its standard capacity
(31 1/2 gal.) 2. any similar container
or cylinder 3. the straight tube of a
gun —*vt.* -**reled** or -**relled**, -**rel·ing**
or -**rel·ling** to put in barrels —*vi.*
[Slang] to go at high speed

barrel organ a mechanical musical
instrument played by turning a crank

bar·ren (bar'ən, ber'-) *adj.* [< OFr.]
1. that cannot bear offspring; sterile
2. without vegetation 3. unproductive
4. boring; dull 5. devoid (*of*) —**bar'-
ren·ness** *n.*

bar·rette (bə ret') *n.* [Fr.] a bar or
clasp for holding a girl's hair in place

bar·ri·cade (bar'ə kād', bar'-; *also,
esp. for v.* bar'ə kād') *n.* [Fr. < It.
barricare, to fortify] a barrier, esp. one
put up hastily for defense —*vt.*
-**cad'ed**, -**cad'ing** to block with a
barricade

bar·ri·er (bar'ē ər, ber'-) *n.* [see BAR]
1. an obstruction, as a fence 2. anything that hinders or blocks

bar·ring (bär'iŋ) *prep.* excepting

bar·ris·ter (bar'is tər, ber'-) *n.* [<
bar (law court)] in England, a lawyer
who pleads cases in court

bar'room' *n.* a room with a bar where
alcoholic drinks are sold

bar·row[1] (bar'ō, ber'-) *n.* [< OE.
beran, to bear] a handbarrow or wheel-
barrow

bar·row[2] (bar'ō, ber'ō) *n.* [< OE.
beorg, hill] a heap of earth or rocks
over a grave

Bart. Baronet

bar'tend'er *n.* a man who serves
alcoholic drinks at a bar

bar·ter (bär'tər) *vi., vt.* [< OFr.
barater] to trade by exchanging
(goods) without money —*n.* a bar-
tering —**bar'ter·er** *n.*

Bar·tók (bär'tôk), **Bé·la** (bā'lä)
1881–1945; Hung. composer

bar·y·on (bar'ē än') *n.* [< Gr. *barys*,
heavy + (ELECTR)ON] any of certain
heavy atomic particles

bas·al (bā's'l) *adj.* 1. of or at the base
2. basic; fundamental

basal metabolism the quantity of
energy used by any organism at rest

ba·salt (bə sôlt', bas'ôlt) *n.* [L.
basaltes] a hard, dark volcanic rock

base[1] (bās) *n.* [see BASIS] 1. the part
of a thing that the thing rests on 2. the
most important element or principal
ingredient 3. the part of a word to
which affixes are attached 4. a basis
5. any of the four goals a baseball
player must reach to score a run 6. a

fat, āpe, cär; ten, ēven; is, bīte; gō, hôrn, tōōl, look; oil, out; up, fur;
chin; she; thin, then; zh, leisure; ŋ, ring; ə for a in ago; ', (ā'b'l); ë, Fr. coeur;
ö, Fr. feu; Fr. mon; ü, Fr. duc; kh, G. ich, doch; ‡ foreign; < derived from

headquarters or a source of supply **7.** *Chem.* a substance that forms a salt when it reacts with an acid —*adj.* forming a base —*vt.* **based, bas'ing** **1.** to make a base for **2.** to establish

base[2] (bās) *adj.* [< VL. *bassus*, low] **1.** ignoble; mean **2.** menial **3.** poor in quality **4.** nonprecious [*base* metal] —**base'ly** *adv.* —**base'ness** *n.*

base'ball' *n.* **1.** a game played with ball and bat by two opposing teams on a field with four bases forming a diamond **2.** the ball used in this game

base'board' *n.* a board or molding at the base of a wall

base hit *Baseball* same as HIT (sense 4)

base'less *adj.* having no basis in fact; unfounded —**base'less·ness** *n.*

base line **1.** a line serving as a base **2.** *Baseball* the lane between any two consecutive bases **3.** the back line at each end of a tennis court

base'man (-mən) *n., pl.* **-men** *Baseball* an infielder stationed at first, second, or third base

base'ment *n.* the story below a main floor and usually below ground

base on balls *Baseball* same as WALK

base pay the basic rate of pay, not counting overtime pay, etc.

base runner *Baseball* a batter who has reached, or is trying to reach, a base

bash (bash) *vt.* [echoic] [Colloq.] to hit hard —*n.* [Slang] a party

bash·ful (bash'fəl) *adj.* [(A)BASH + -FUL] easily embarrassed; shy —**bash'ful·ly** *adv.* —**bash'ful·ness** *n.*

bas·ic (bās'ik) *adj.* **1.** fundamental **2.** *Chem.* alkaline —*n.* a basic principle, factor, etc. —**bas'i·cal·ly** *adv.*

bas·il (baz'l) *n.* [< Gr. *basilikon*] a fragrant herb of the mint family

ba·sil·i·ca (bə sil'i kə) *n.* [< Gr. *basilikē (stoa)*, royal (portico)] **1.** a church with a broad nave, side aisles, and an apse **2.** *R.C.Ch.* a church with special ceremonial rights

bas·i·lisk (bas'ə lisk') *n.* [< Gr. *basileus*, king] a mythical, lizardlike monster whose glance was fatal

ba·sin (bās'n) *n.* [< VL. *bacca*, water vessel] **1.** a wide, shallow container for liquid **2.** its contents **3.** a sink **4.** any large hollow, often with water in it **5.** same as RIVER BASIN

ba·sis (bā'sis) *n., pl.* **-ses** (-sēz) [< Gr., a base] **1.** a base or foundation **2.** a principal constituent **3.** a fundamental principle or theory

bask (bask) *vi.* [ME. *basken*, wallow] to expose oneself pleasantly to warmth, another's favor, etc.

bas·ket (bas'kit) *n.* [ME.] **1.** a container made of interwoven cane, wood strips, etc. **2.** its contents **3.** *Basketball a*) the goal, a round, open, hanging net *b*) a scoring toss of the ball through it

bas'ket·ball' *n.* **1.** a team game played on a floor with a raised basket at either end through which an inflated ball must be tossed **2.** this ball

basket weave a weave of fabrics resembling the weave used in basket making

bas'ket·work' *n.* work that is woven like a basket

Basque (bask) *n.* **1.** a member of a people living in the W Pyrenees **2.** their language —*adj.* of the Basques

bas-re·lief (bä'rə lēf') *n.* [Fr. < It.: see ff. & RELIEF] sculpture with figures projecting only a little from a flat background

bass[1] (bās) *n.* [< VL. *bassus*, low] **1.** the range of the lowest male voice **2.** a singer or instrument with this range; specif., a double bass **3.** a low, deep sound —*adj.* of, for, or in the range of a bass

bass[2] (bas) *n., pl.* **bass, bass'es** [OE. *bærs*] a spiny-finned food and game fish of fresh or salt water

bas·set (bas'it) *n.* [< OFr. *bas*, low] a hunting hound with a long body, short forelegs, and long, drooping ears

bas·si·net (bas'ə net') *n.* [see BASIN] a basketlike bed for an infant, often hooded and on wheels

bas·so (bas'ō, bäs'ō) *n., pl.* **-sos** [It.] a bass voice or singer

bas·soon (ba sōōn', ba-) *n.* [< Fr.] a double-reed bass woodwind instrument

BASSOON

bast (bast) *n.* [OE. *bæst*] plant fiber used in ropes, mats, etc.

bas·tard (bas'tərd) *n.* [< OFr.] an illegitimate child —*adj.* **1.** of illegitimate birth **2.** inferior, sham, etc. —**bas'tard·y** *n., pl.* **-ies**

bas'tard·ize' *vt.* **-ized', -iz'ing** **1.** to make, declare, or show to be a bastard **2.** to make corrupt; debase —**bas'tard·i·za'tion** *n.*

baste[1] (bāst) *vt.* **bast'ed, bast'ing** [< OHG. *bastian*, sew with bast] to sew temporarily with long, loose stitches until properly sewed

baste[2] (bāst) *vt.* **bast'ed, bast'ing** [< OFr. *bassiner*, moisten] to moisten (roasting meat) with drippings, melted butter, etc.

baste[3] (bāst) *vt.* **bast'ed, bast'ing** [ON. *beysta*] **1.** to beat soundly **2.** to attack with words

bas·tille, bas·tile (bas tēl') *n.* [Fr.: see ff.] a prison —**the Bastille** a prison in Paris destroyed (1789) in the French Revolution

bas·tion (bas'chən) *n.* [Fr. < It. *bastire*, build] **1.** a projection from a fortification **2.** any strong defense

bat[1] (bat) *n.* [OE. *batt*] **1.** a stout club **2.** a club to hit the ball in baseball, etc. **3.** a turn at batting [at *bat*] **4.** [Colloq.] a blow —*vt.* **bat'ted, bat'ting** to hit, as with a bat —*vi.* to take a turn at batting

bat[2] (bat) *n.* [< Scand.] a nocturnal, mouselike, flying mammal with a furry body and membranous wings

bat[3] (bat) *vt.* **bat'ted, bat'ting** [see BATTER¹] [Colloq.] to wink —**not bat an eye** not show surprise

batch (bach) *n.* [OE. *bacan*, bake]

1. the amount (of bread, etc.) in one baking 2. one set, lot, group, etc. 3. an amount of work for processing by a computer in a single run

bate (bāt) *vt.* **bat′ed, bat′ing** [ME.] to abate; lessen —**with bated breath** holding the breath, as in fear

bath (bath) *n., pl.* **baths** (ba*thz,* baths) [OE. *bæth*] 1. a washing, esp. of the body, in water 2. water, etc. for bathing or for soaking or treating something 3. a bathtub 4. a bathroom 5. a bathhouse (sense 1)

bathe (bā*th*) *vt.* **bathed, bath′ing** [see prec.] 1. to put into a liquid 2. to give a bath to 3. to cover as with liquid —*vi.* 1. to take a bath 2. to soak oneself in something —**bath′er** *n.*

bath′house′ *n.* 1. a public building for taking baths 2. a building used by bathers for changing clothes

bathing suit a garment worn for swimming

bath′mat′ *n.* a mat used in or next to a bathtub

ba·thos (bā′thäs) *n.* [Gr., depth] 1. anticlimax (sense 1) 2. excessive sentimentality 3. triteness —**ba·thet·ic** (bə thet′ik) *adj.*

bath′robe′ *n.* a loose-fitting robe worn to and from the bath, etc.

bath′room′ *n.* a room with a bathtub, toilet, etc.

bath′tub′ *n.* a tub to bathe in

bath·y·scaph (bath′ə skaf′) *n.* [< Gr. *bathys,* deep + *skaphē,* boat] a deepsea diving apparatus for reaching great depths without a cable: also **bath′y·scaphe′** (-skaf′, -skāf′)

ba·tik (bə tēk′) *n.* [Malay] cloth with a design made by dyeing only the parts not coated with wax

ba·tiste (ba tēst′, bə-) *n.* [Fr.: < supposed original maker, *Baptiste*] a fine, thin cloth of cotton, rayon, etc.

ba·ton (bə tän′) *n.* [Fr.] 1. a staff serving as a symbol of office 2. a slender stick used in directing music 3. a metal rod twirled by a drum major

Bat·on Rouge (bat′'n rōōzh′) capital of La.: pop. 219,000

ba·tra·chi·an (bə trā′kē ən) *n.* [< Gr. *batrachos,* frog] an amphibian without a tail; frog or toad

bat·tal·ion (bə tal′yən) *n.* [see BATTLE] a tactical military unit forming part of a division

bat·ten¹ (bat′'n) *n.* [var. of BATON] 1. a sawed strip of wood 2. a strip of wood put over a seam between boards as a fastening or covering —*vt.* to fasten or supply with battens

bat·ten² (bat′'n) *vi., vt.* [ON. *batna,* improve] to fatten; thrive

bat·ten³ (bat′'n) *n.* [< Fr.: see ff.] in a loom, the frame that is moved to press the woof threads into place

bat·ter¹ (bat′ər) *vt.* [< L. *battuere,* to beat] 1. to strike with blow after blow 2. to injure by pounding, hard wear, or use —*vi.* to pound noisily

bat·ter² (bat′ər) *n.* the baseball or

cricket player whose turn it is to bat: also, in cricket, **bats′man** (-mən) *n.*

bat·ter³ (bat′ər) *n.* [see BATTER¹] a flowing mixture of flour, milk, etc., for making cakes, etc.

battering ram a heavy beam, etc. to batter down walls, etc.

bat·ter·y (bat′ər ē) *n., pl.* **-ies** [see BATTER¹] 1. a battering 2. a set of things used together 3. *Baseball* the pitcher and the catcher 4. *Elec.* a cell or group of cells storing an electrical charge and able to furnish a current 5. *Law* an illegal beating of another person: see ASSAULT AND BATTERY 6. *Mil.* a set of heavy guns

bat·ting (bat′iŋ, -'n) *n.* [see BAT¹] cotton or wool fiber wadded in sheets

bat·tle (bat′'l) *n.* [< L. *battuere,* to beat] 1. a large-scale fight between armed forces 2. armed fighting 3. any fight or conflict —*vt., vi.* **-tled, -tling** to fight —**give** (or **do**) **battle** to fight

bat′tle-ax′, bat′tle-axe′ *n.* 1. a heavy ax formerly used as a weapon 2. [Slang] a harsh, domineering woman

bat·tle·dore (bat′'l dôr′) *n.* [< ? Pr. *batedor,* beater] a racket used to hit a shuttlecock in a game like badminton

bat′tle·field′ *n.* the site of a battle

bat′tle·ment (-mənt) *n.* [< OFr. *batailler,* fortify] a low parapet atop a tower, with spaces to shoot from

battle royal *pl.* **battles royal** 1. a free-for-all 2. a heated dispute

bat′tle·ship′ *n.* a large armored warship with big guns

bat·ty (bat′ē) *adj.* **-ti·er, -ti·est** [< BAT²] [Slang] 1. insane 2. eccentric

bau·ble (bô′b'l) *n.* [< L. *bellus,* pretty] a showy trifle; trinket

baux·ite (bôk′sīt, bō′zīt) *n.* [Fr. < (*Les*) *Baux,* town in S France] a claylike ore, the source of aluminum

Ba·var·i·a (bə ver′ē ə) state of S West Germany —**Ba·var′i·an** *adj., n.*

bawd (bôd) *n.* [ME. *baude*] 1. a woman who keeps a brothel 2. a prostitute

bawd·y (bô′dē) *adj.* **-i·er, -i·est** indecent; obscene —**bawd′i·ness** *n.*

bawl (bôl) *vi., vt.* [< ML. *baulare,* to bark] 1. to shout 2. to weep loudly —*n.* 1. a shout 2. a noisy weeping —**bawl out** [Slang] to reprimand

bay¹ (bā) *n.* [< ML. *baia*] a wide inlet of a sea or lake, along the shore

bay² (bā) *n.* [< VL. *batare,* gape] 1. an alcove or recess 2. a bay window

bay³ (bā) *vi.* [< OFr. *baier,* gape] to bark or howl in long, deep tones —*n.* 1. the sound of baying 2. the situation of a hunted animal forced to turn and fight —**at bay** 1. cornered 2. held off —**bring to bay** to corner

bay⁴ (bā) *n.* [< L. *baca,* berry] 1. the laurel tree 2. [*pl.*] a laurel wreath

bay⁵ (bā) *adj.* [< L. *badius*] reddishbrown —*n.* 1. reddish brown 2. a horse, etc. of this color

bay·ber·ry (bā′ber′ē) *n., pl.* **-ries** 1. a shrub with small, wax-coated berries 2. any of the berries

---

fat, āpe, cär; ten, ēven; is, bīte; gō, hôrn, tōōl, look; oil, out; up, fur; chin; she; thin, *th*en; zh, leisure; ŋ, ring; ə for *a* in *ago;* ′, (ā′b'l); ë, Fr. coeur; ö, Fr. feu; Fr. mon; ü, Fr. duc; kh, G. ich, doch; ‡ foreign; < derived from

bay leaf the aromatic leaf of the laurel, dried and used as a spice in cooking

bay·o·net (bā'ə nit, -net') n. [< Fr. < *Bayonne*, city in France] a detachable blade put on a rifle muzzle, for stabbing —vt., vi. **-net'ed** or **-net'-ted, -net'ing** or **-net'ting** to stab with a bayonet

bay·ou (bī'ōō) n. [< AmInd.] in the southern U.S., a marshy inlet or outlet of a lake, river, etc.

bay window 1. a window or set of windows jutting out from a wall **2.** [Slang] a large, protruding belly

ba·zaar (bə zär') n. [Per. *bāzār*] **1.** in Oriental countries, a marketplace **2.** a benefit sale for a church, etc.

ba·zoo·ka (bə zōōk'ə) n. [< name of a comic horn] a portable weapon for launching armor-piercing rockets

bbl. pl. **bbls.** barrel

BB (shot) [designation of size] a size of shot (diameter, .18 in.) for an air rifle (**BB gun**) or shotgun

B.C. 1. Bachelor of Commerce **2.** before Christ **3.** British Columbia

B cell any of the lymphatic leukocytes not associated with the thymus, that help build antibodies: cf. T CELL

be (bē, bi) vi. **was** or **were, been, being** [< OE. *beon*] **1.** to exist; live **2.** to happen; occur **3.** to remain or continue *Note: be* is used to link its subject to a predicate complement [he *is* handsome] or as an auxiliary: (1) with a past participle: a) to form the passive voice [he will *be* whipped] b) to form the perfect tense [Christ *is* risen] (2) with a present participle to express continuation [the player *is* running] (3) with a present participle or infinitive to express futurity, possibility, obligation, intention, etc. [he *is* going next week, she *is* to scrub the floor] *Be* is conjugated, in the present indicative: (I) *am*, (he, she, it) *is*, (we, you, they) *are*; in the past indicative: (I, he, she, it) *was*, (we, you, they) *were* —**be off** go away

be- [< OE. *be*, by] a *prefix meaning:* **1.** around [*beset*] **2.** completely [*bedeck*] **3.** away [*betake*] **4.** about [*bemoan*] **5.** to make [*besot*] **6.** to furnish with, affect by [*becloud*]

Be *Chem.* beryllium

beach (bēch) n. [E. dial., pebbles] a sandy shore —vt., vi. to ground (a boat) on a beach

beach'comb'er (-kō'mər) n. **1.** a long wave rolling ashore **2.** one who lives on what he finds on beaches, etc.

beach'head' n. a position gained, specif. by invading an enemy shore

bea·con (bēk'n) n. [< OE. *beacen*, a sign] **1.** a light for warning or guiding **2.** a radio transmitter sending guiding signals for aircraft

bead (bēd) n. [< OE. *bed*, prayer bead] **1.** a small ball of glass, etc., pierced for stringing **2.** [pl.] a string of beads **3.** [pl.] a rosary **4.** any small, round object, as the front sight of a rifle **5.** a drop or bubble **6.** the rim edge of a rubber tire —vt. to decorate with beads —**draw a bead on** to take careful aim at —**say** (or **tell** or **count**) one's

beads to say prayers with a rosary —**bead'y** adj. **-i·er, -i·est**

bea·dle (bē'd'l) n. [ME. *bidel*] a minor officer who keeps order in church

bea·gle (bē'g'l) n. [< ? Fr. *bégueule*, wide-throat] a small hound with short legs and drooping ears

beak (bēk) n. [< L. *beccus*] **1.** a bird's bill **2.** the beaklike mouth part of various insects, fishes, etc. —**beak'-less** adj. —**beak'like'** adj.

beak·er (bēk'ər) n. [< L. *bacar*, wine glass] **1.** a goblet **2.** a glass or metal container used by chemists

beam (bēm) n. [ME.] **1.** a long, thick piece of wood, metal, etc. **2.** the crossbar of a balance **3.** a ship's breadth at its widest point **4.** a slender shaft of light, etc. **5.** a radiant look, smile, etc. **6.** a steady radio or radar signal for guiding aircraft or ships —vt. **1.** to give out (shafts of light) **2.** to direct (a radio signal, etc.) —vi. **1.** to shine brightly **2.** to smile warmly

bean (bēn) n. [ME. *ben*] **1.** a plant of the legume family, bearing kidney-shaped seeds **2.** a seed or pod of such a plant **3.** any beanlike seed [coffee *beans*] **4.** [Slang] the head or brain —vt. [Slang] to hit on the head —**spill the beans** [Colloq.] to tell a secret

bear¹ (ber) vt. **bore, borne** or **born, bear'ing** [< OE. *beran*] **1.** to carry **2.** to have or show **3.** to give birth to **4.** to produce or yield **5.** to support or sustain **6.** to withstand or endure **7.** to need [this *bears* watching] **8.** to carry or conduct (oneself) **9.** to give [to *bear* witness] —vi. **1.** to be productive **2.** to lie, point, or move in a given direction **3.** to be relevant to (with *on*) **4.** to put up patiently (with) —**bear down (on) 1.** to exert pressure or effort (on) **2.** to approach —**bear out** to confirm —**bear up** to endure —**bear'a·ble** adj. —**bear'er** n.

bear² (ber) n. [< OE. *bera*] **1.** a large, heavy mammal with shaggy fur and a short tail **2.** [B-] either of two constellations in the Northern Hemisphere (**Great Bear** and **Little Bear**) **3.** one who is clumsy, rude, etc. **4.** one who sells stocks, etc. hoping to buy them back later at a lower price —adj. falling in price —**bear'like'** adj.

beard (bird) n. [OE.] **1.** the hair on the chin and cheeks of a man **2.** any beardlike part **3.** an awn —vt. **1.** to face boldly **2.** to provide with a beard —**beard'ed** adj. —**beard'less** adj.

bear·ing (ber'iŋ) n. **1.** way of carrying and conducting oneself **2.** a supporting part **3.** a producing or ability to produce **4.** endurance **5.** [often pl.] relative direction or position **6.** [pl.] awareness of one's situation **7.** relation; relevance **8.** a part of a machine on which another part revolves, slides, etc.

bear'ish adj. **1.** bearlike; rude, rough, etc. **2.** dropping, or causing a drop, in price on the stock exchange —**bear'ish·ly** adv.

bear'skin' n. **1.** the fur or hide of a bear **2.** a rug, coat, etc. made of this

beast (bēst) *n.* [< L. *bestia*] **1.** any large, four-footed animal **2.** one who is brutal, gross, etc.

beast·ly *adj.* **-li·er, -li·est 1.** of or like a beast; brutal, etc. **2.** [Colloq.] disagreeable; unpleasant —**beast'li·ness** *n.*

beast of burden any animal used for carrying things

beast of prey any animal that hunts and kills other animals for food

beat (bēt) *vt.* **beat, beat'en, beat'ing** [< OE. *beatan*] **1.** to hit repeatedly; pound **2.** to punish by so hitting; whip, spank, etc. **3.** to dash repeatedly against **4.** *a)* to form (a path, way, etc.) by repeated treading or riding *b)* to keep walking on [to *beat* the pavements] **5.** to mix (eggs, etc.) by hard stirring **6.** to move (esp. wings) up and down **7.** to search through (a forest, etc.) **8.** to defeat or outdo **9.** to mark (time or rhythm) by tapping, etc. **10.** [Colloq.] to puzzle **11.** [Colloq.] to cheat **12.** [Slang] to escape the penalties of —*vi.* **1.** to hit, dash, etc. repeatedly **2.** to throb —*n.* **1.** a beating, as of the heart **2.** any of a series of strokes **3.** a throb **4.** a habitual route **5.** the unit of musical rhythm **6.** *same as* BEATNIK —*adj.* **1.** [Slang] tired out **2.** of a group of young persons, esp. of the 1950's, expressing social disillusionment by unconventional dress, actions, etc. —**beat down** to put or force down —**beat it!** [Slang] go away! —**beat off** to drive back —**beat up (on)** [Slang] to give a beating to —**beat'er** *n.* —**beat'nik** *n.*

be·a·tif·ic (bē'ə tif'ik) *adj.* **1.** making blessed **2.** full of bliss

be·at·i·fy (-fī') *vt.* **-fied', -fy'ing** [< L. *beatus*, happy + *facere*, make] **1.** to make blissfully happy **2.** R.C.Ch. to declare one who has died to be among the blessed in heaven —**be·at'i·fi·ca'tion** *n.*

beat'ing *n.* **1.** the act of one that beats **2.** a whipping **3.** a throbbing **4.** a defeat

be·at·i·tude (bē at'ə tōōd') *n.* [< L. *beatus*, happy] perfect blessedness or happiness —**the Beatitudes** the pronouncements in the Sermon on the Mount

beat'-up' *adj.* [Slang] worn-out, battered, dilapidated, etc.

beau (bō) *n., pl.* **beaus, beaux** (bōz) [Fr. < L. *bellus*, pretty] a woman's sweetheart

Beau·mont (bō'mänt) city in SE Tex.: pop. 119,000

beau·te·ous (byōōt'ē əs) *adj.* beautiful —**beau'te·ous·ly** *adv.*

beau·ti·cian (byōō tish'ən) *n.* one who works in a beauty shop

beau·ti·ful (byōō'tə fəl) *adj.* having beauty —**beau'ti·ful·ly** *adv.*

beau·ti·fy (-fī') *vt., vi.* **-fied', -fy'ing** to make or become beautiful —**beau'ti·fi·ca'tion** (-fi kā'shən) *n.* —**beau'ti·fi'er** *n.*

beau·ty (byōōt'ē) *n., pl.* **-ties** [< L. *bellus*, pretty] **1.** the quality of being very pleasing, as in form, color, etc. **2.** a thing with this quality **3.** good looks **4.** a very good-looking woman

beauty shop (or **salon** or **parlor**) a place where women go for hair styling, manicuring, etc.

bea·ver (bē'vər) *n.* [OE. *beofor*] **1.** *a)* a large, amphibious rodent with soft, brown fur, webbed hind feet, and a broad tail *b)* its fur **2.** a man's high silk hat

BEAVER

be·calm (bi käm') *vt.* **1.** to make calm **2.** to make (a ship) motionless from lack of wind

be·cause (bi kôz') *conj.* [ME. *bi*, by + *cause*] for the reason or cause that —**because of** on account of

beck (bek) *n.* a beckoning gesture —**at the beck and call of** obedient to the wishes of

beck·on (bek''n) *vi., vt.* [< OE. *beacen*, a sign] **1.** to summon by a gesture **2.** to lure; entice

be·cloud (bi kloud') *vt.* **1.** to cloud over **2.** to muddle

be·come (bi kum') *vi.* **-came'** (-kām'), **-come', -com'ing** [OE. *becuman*] to come or grow to be —*vt.* to suit; befit —**become of** to happen to

be·com·ing *adj.* **1.** appropriate; seemly **2.** suitable to the wearer

bed (bed) *n.* [OE.] **1.** a piece of furniture for sleeping on **2.** a plot of soil where plants are raised **3.** the bottom of a river, lake, etc. **4.** any flat surface used as a foundation **5.** a stratum —*vt.* **bed'ded, bed'ding 1.** to put to bed **2.** to embed **3.** to plant in a bed of earth **4.** to arrange in layers —*vi.* **1.** to go to bed; rest; sleep **2.** to stratify

be·daz·zle (bi daz''l) *vt.* **-zled, -zling** to dazzle thoroughly; bewilder

bed'bug' *n.* a small, wingless, biting insect that infests beds, etc.

bed'clothes' (-klōz', -klōthz') *n.pl.* sheets, blankets, etc., for a bed

bed'cov'er *n.* a coverlet; bedspread

bed'ding (-iŋ) *n.* **1.** mattresses and bedclothes **2.** a bottom layer; base

be·deck (bi dek') *vt.* to adorn

be·dev·il (bi dev''l) *vt.* **-iled** or **-illed, -il·ing** or **-il·ling** to plague or bewilder —**be·dev'il·ment** *n.*

bed'fast' *adj. same as* BEDRIDDEN

bed'fel'low *n.* **1.** a person who shares one's bed **2.** any associate

be·dim (bi dim') *vt.* **-dimmed', -dim'ming** to make (the eyes or vision) dim

bed jacket a woman's short jacket sometimes worn in bed over a nightgown

bed·lam (bed'ləm) *n.* [< (the old London mental hospital of St. Mary of) *Bethlehem*] any place or situation of noise and confusion

bed of roses [Colloq.] a situation or position of ease and luxury

Bed·ou·in (bed′ōō win) *n., pl.* **-ins, -in** [< Ar. *badāwin*, desert dwellers] [*also* b-] **1.** an Arab of the desert tribes of Arabia, Syria, or North Africa **2.** any wanderer

bed′pan′ *n.* a shallow pan used as a toilet by one who is bedridden

be·drag·gle (bi drag′'l) *vt.* **-gled, -gling** to make wet, limp, and dirty, as by dragging through mire

bed′rid′den (-rid′'n) *adj.* confined to bed by illness, infirmity, etc.

bed′rock′ *n.* **1.** solid rock underlying soil, etc. **2.** the base or bottom

bed′roll′ *n.* a portable roll of bedding, used esp. by campers

bed′room′ *n.* a room for sleeping

bed′side′ *n.* the space beside a bed —*adj.* near a bed

bed′sore′ *n.* a body sore on a bed-ridden person, caused by chafing

bed′spread′ *n.* an ornamental cover spread over the blanket on a bed

bed′stead′ (-sted′) *n.* a framework for the spring and mattress of a bed

bed′time′ *n.* the time when one usually goes to bed

bee[1] (bē) *n.* [OE. *beo*] a broad-bodied, four-winged, hairy insect that gathers pollen and nectar and that can sting

bee[2] (bē) *n.* [< OE. *ben*, service] a meeting of people to work together or to compete

beech (bēch) *n.* [< OE. *bece*] **1.** a tree with smooth, gray bark, hard wood, and edible nuts **2.** its wood

beech′nut′ *n.* the small, three-cornered nut of the beech tree

beef (bēf) *n., pl.* **beeves** (bēvz); also, and for 3 always, **beefs** [< L. *bos*, ox] **1.** *a)* a full-grown ox, cow, bull, or steer, esp. one bred for meat *b)* these animals, collectively *c)* their meat **2.** [Colloq.] brawn **3.** [Slang] a complaint —*vi.* [Slang] to complain —**beef up** to reinforce

beef′cake′ *n.* [BEEF (*n.*2) + (CHEESE)-CAKE] [Slang] photographic display of the figure of a nude, or partly nude, muscular man

beef′eat′er *n.* **1.** a person who eats beef **2.** a guard at the Tower of London **3.** [Slang] an Englishman

beef′steak′ (-stāk′) *n.* a thick cut of beef for broiling or frying

beef′y *adj.* **-i·er, -i·est** brawny —**beef′i·ness** *n.*

bee′hive′ *n.* **1.** a hive for bees **2.** a place of great activity

bee′keep′er *n.* one who keeps bees for producing honey —**bee′keep′ing** *n.*

bee′line′ *n.* a straight line or route from one place to another

Be·el·ze·bub (bē el′zə bub′) *Bible* the chief devil; Satan

been (bin, ben; *Brit.* bēn) *pp.* of BE

beep (bēp) *n.* [echoic] the brief, high-pitched sound of a horn or electronic signal —*vi., vt.* to make or cause to make this sound

beer (bir) *n.* [OE. *beor*] **1.** an alcoholic, fermented drink made from malt and

hops **2.** a soft drink made from extracts of roots, etc. [ginger *beer*]

bees′wax′ *n.* wax secreted by honey-bees, used to make their honeycombs

beet (bēt) *n.* [< L. *beta*] **1.** a plant with a thick, fleshy, red or white root **2.** the edible root, also a source of sugar

Bee·tho·ven (bā′tō vən), **Lud·wig van** (lōōt′vikh vän) 1770–1827; Ger. composer

bee·tle[1] (bēt′'l) *n.* [< OE. *bitan*, to bite] an insect with hard front wings that cover the membranous hind wings when these are folded

bee·tle[2] (bēt′'l) *n.* [OE. *betel*] a heavy mallet or pestle, usually wooden

bee·tle[3] (bēt′'l) *vi.* **-tled, -tling** [prob. < ff.[1] to overhang —*adj.* overhanging: also **bee′tling**

bee·tle-browed′ (-broud′) *adj.* [< ME. < ? *bitel*, sharp + *brouwe*, brow] **1.** having bushy eyebrows **2.** frowning

be·fall (bi fôl′) *vi., vt.* **-fell′, -fall′en, -fall′ing** [< OE. *be-* + *feallan*, fall] to happen or occur (to)

be·fit (bi fit′) *vt.* **-fit′ted, -fit′ting** to be suitable or proper for; be suited to —**be·fit′ting** *adj.*

be·fog (bi fôg′, -fäg′) *vt.* **-fogged′, -fog′ging 1.** to envelop in fog; make foggy **2.** to obscure; confuse

be·fore (bi fôr′) *adv.* [< OE. *be-*, by + *foran*, before] **1.** ahead; in front **2.** previously **3.** earlier; sooner —*prep.* **1.** ahead of **2.** in front of **3.** in or to the sight, presence, notice, etc. of **4.** earlier than **5.** in preference to —*conj.* **1.** earlier than the time that [call *before* you go] **2.** rather than [I'd die *before* I'd tell]

be·fore·hand′ (-hand′) *adv., adj.* ahead of time; in anticipation

be·foul (bi fōul′) *vt.* **1.** to make filthy; soil **2.** to cast aspersions on

be·friend (bi frend′) *vt.* to act as a friend to help

be·fud·dle (bi fud′'l) *vt.* **-dled, -dling** to confuse or stupefy

beg (beg) *vt., vi.* **begged, beg′ging** [ME. *beggen*] **1.** to ask for (alms) **2.** to ask earnestly; entreat —**beg off** to ask to be released from —**go beg-ging** to be available but unwanted

be·gan (bi gan′) *pt.* of BEGIN

be·get (bi get′) *vt.* **-got′** or archaic **-gat′** (-gat′), **-got′ten** or **-got′, -get′ting** [< OE. *begitan*, acquire] **1.** to become the father of **2.** to cause

beg·gar (beg′ər) *n.* **1.** one who begs **2.** a pauper —*vt.* **1.** to impoverish **2.** to make (description, etc.) seem inadequate —**beg′gar·y** *n.*

beg′gar·ly *adj.* very poor, worthless, inadequate, etc. —**beg′gar·li·ness** *n.*

be·gin (bi gin′) *vi., vt.* **-gan′, -gun′, -gin′ning** [< OE. *beginnan*] **1.** to start doing, acting, etc. **2.** to originate

be·gin·ner *n.* one who is just beginning to do or learn something; novice

be·gin·ning *n.* **1.** a starting **2.** the time or place of starting; origin **3.** the first part or [*pl.*] early stages

be·gone (bi gôn′) *interj., vi.* (to be gone; go away; get out

be·gon·ia (bi gōn′yə) *n.* [after M. *Bégon* (1638–1710), Fr. patron of science] a tropical plant with showy flowers and ornamental leaves

be·got (bi gät') *pt. & alt. pp.* of BEGET

be·got·ten (-'n) *alt. pp.* of BEGET

be·grime (bi grīm') *vt.* **-grimed'**, **-grim'ing** to cover with grime; soil

be·grudge (bi gruj') *vt.* **-grudged'**, **-grudg'ing** 1. to resent another's possession of (something) 2. to give with reluctance —**be·grudg'ing·ly** *adv.*

be·guile (bi gīl') *vt.* **-guiled'**, **-guil'ing** 1. to mislead or deprive (*of*) by guile; deceive 2. to pass (time) pleasantly 3. to charm or delight —**be·guile'ment** *n.* —**be·guil'er** *n.*

be·gun (bi gun') *pp.* of BEGIN

be·half (bi haf') *n.* [< OE. *be*, by + *healf*, side] support —**in** (or **on**) **behalf of** in the interest of; for

be·have (bi hāv') *vt.*, *vi.* **-haved'**, **-hav'ing** [see BE- & HAVE] 1. to conduct (oneself) in a specified way 2. to conduct (oneself) properly

be·hav·ior (-yər) *n.* way of behaving; conduct or action —**be·hav'ior·al** *adj.*

behavioral science any of the sciences, as sociology or psychology, that study human behavior

be·head (bi hed') *vt.* to cut off the head of

be·held (-held') *pt. & pp.* of BEHOLD

be·he·moth (bi hē'məth, bē'ə-) *n.* [< Heb.] 1. *Bible* some huge animal 2. any huge or powerful animal or thing

be·hest (bi hest') *n.* [< OE. *behæs*, a vow] a command or earnest request

be·hind (bi hīnd') *adv.* [< OE. *behindan*] 1. in or to the rear 2. in a former time, place, etc. 3. in or into arrears 4. slow; late —*prep.* 1. in or to the rear of 2. inferior to 3. later than [*behind* schedule] 4. beyond [*behind* the hill] 5. advocating [he is *behind* the plan] 6. hidden by [what's *behind* his smile?] —*n.* [Colloq.] the buttocks

be·hind'hand' (-hand') *adv.*, *adj.* late in payment, time, or progress

be·hold (bi hōld') *vt.* **-held'**, **-hold'** or archaic **-hold'en**, **-hold'ing** [< OE. *bihealdan*] to look at; see —*interj.* look! see! —**be·hold'er** *n.*

be·hold·en (-ən) *adj.* indebted

be·hoove (bi hōōv') *vt.* **-hooved'**, **-hoov'ing** [< OE. *behofian*, to need] to be incumbent upon or proper for [it behooves you to go]

beige (bāzh) *n.* [Fr.] grayish tan —*adj.* grayish-tan

be·ing (bē'iŋ) *n.* [see BE] 1. existence; life 2. fundamental nature 3. one that lives or exists —**being as** (or **that**) [Dial. or Colloq.] since; because —**for the time being** for now

Bei·rut (bā rōōt') seaport and capital of Lebanon: pop. c.500,000

be·jew·el (bi jōō'əl) *vt.* **-eled** or **-elled**, **-el·ing** or **-el·ling** to decorate with or as with jewels

be·la·bor (bi lā'bər) *vt.* 1. to beat

severely 2. to attack verbally 3. to labor (a point, etc.): popular usage

be·lat·ed (bi lāt'id) *adj.* tardy —**be·lat'ed·ly** *adv.*

be·lay (bi lā') *vt.*, *vi.* **-layed'**, **-lay'ing** [< OE. *belecgan*, make fast] 1. to make (a rope) secure by winding around a cleat, etc. 2. to secure by a rope 3. [Naut. Colloq.] to hold; stop

bel can·to (bel' kän'tō) [It.] a style of singing with brilliant vocal display and purity of tone

belch (belch) *vi.*, *vt.* [OE. *bealcian*] 1. to expel (gas) through the mouth from the stomach 2. to throw forth violently [the volcano belched flame] —*n.* a belching

be·lea·guer (bi lē'gər) *vt.* [< Du. < *be-*, by + *leger*, a camp] 1. to besiege by encircling 2. to beset or harass

Bel·fast (bel'fast) seaport & capital of Northern Ireland: pop. 410,000

bel·fry (bel'frē) *n.*, *pl.* **-fries** [ult. < OHG.] 1. a bell tower 2. the part of a tower that holds the bell(s)

Belg. 1. Belgian 2. Belgium

Bel·gium (bel'jəm) kingdom in W Europe: 11,779 sq. mi.; pop. 9,499,000 —**Bel'gian** (-jən) *adj.*, *n.*

Bel·grade (bel'grād, -gräd) capital of Yugoslavia: pop. 598,0,00

be·lie (bi lī') *vt.* **-lied'**, **-ly'ing** 1. to disguise or misrepresent 2. to leave unfulfilled 3. to prove false

be·lief (bə lēf') *n.* [< OE. *geleafa*] 1. conviction that certain things are true 2. religious faith 3. trust or confidence 4. creed or doctrine 5. an opinion; expectation; judgment

be·lieve (bə lēv') *vt.* **-lieved'**, **-liev'ing** [< OE. *geliefan*] 1. to take as true, real, etc. 2. to trust a statement or promise of (a person) 3. to suppose or think —*vi.* to have faith (*in*) —**be·liev'a·ble** *adj.* —**be·liev'er** *n.*

be·lit·tle (bi lit''l) *vt.* **-tled**, **-tling** to make seem little, less important, etc. —**be·lit'tle·ment** *n.*

bell (bel) *n.* [OE. *belle*] 1. a hollow, cuplike object, as of metal, which rings when struck 2. the sound of a bell 3. anything shaped like a bell 4. *Naut.* a bell rung to mark the periods of the watch —*vt.* to attach a bell to —*vi.* to become bell-shaped

Bell (bel), **Alexander Gra·ham** (grā'əm) 1847–1922; U.S. inventor of the telephone, born in Scotland

bel·la·don·na (bel'ə dän'ə) *n.* [< It., beautiful lady: from cosmetic use] 1. a poisonous plant of the nightshade family: source of atropine 2. atropine

bell'-bot'tom *adj.* flared at the ankles, as trousers or slacks

bell'boy' *n.* a boy or man employed by a hotel, etc. to carry luggage and do errands: also **bell'hop'**

belle (bel) *n.* [Fr., fem. of BEAU] a pretty woman or girl

belles-let·tres (bel let'rə) *n.pl.* [Fr.] nontechnical literature, as fiction, poetry, drama, etc.

bel·li·cose (bel'ə kōs') *adj.* [< L. *bellicus*, of war] quarrelsome; warlike —**bel'li·cos'i·ty** (-käs'ə tē) *n.*

bel·lig·er·ent (bə lij'ər ənt) *adj.* [< L. *bellum*, war + *gerere*, carry on] 1. at war 2. of war 3. warlike 4. ready to fight or quarrel —*n.* a belligerent person, group, or nation —**bel·lig'er·ence, bel·lig'er·en·cy** *n.* —**bel·lig'er·ent·ly** *adv.*

bell jar (or **glass**) a bell-shaped container made of glass, used to keep air, moisture, etc. in or out

bel·low (bel'ō) *vi* [< OE. *bylgan*] 1. to roar with a reverberating sound, as a bull 2. to cry out loudly, as in anger —*vt.* to utter loudly or powerfully —*n.* a bellowing sound

Bel·low (bel'ō), **Saul** 1915– ; U.S. novelist

bel·lows (bel'ōz) *n. sing. & pl.* [see BELLY] 1. a device that puffs out air by compression of its collapsible sides: used for blowing fires, in pipe organs, etc. 2. anything collapsible like a bellows

bells (belz) *n.pl.* [Colloq.] bell-bottom trousers

bell·weth·er (bel'weth'ər) *n.* 1. a male sheep, usually wearing a bell, that leads the flock 2. a leader

BELLOWS

bel·ly (bel'ē) *n., pl.* -**lies** [< OE. *belg*, leather bag] 1. the part of the body between the chest and thighs; abdomen 2. the stomach 3. the underside of an animal's body 4. the deep interior, as of a ship —*vt., vi.* -**lied, -ly·ing** to swell out

bel'ly·ache' (-āk') *n.* pain in the abdomen —*vi.* -**ached', -ach'ing** [Slang] to complain

bel'ly·but'ton (-but''n) *n.* [Colloq.] the navel: also **belly button**

bel'ly·ful' *n.* 1. more than enough to eat 2. [Slang] all that one can bear

belly laugh [Colloq.] a hearty laugh

be·long (bi lôŋ') *vi.* [< ME.] 1. to have a proper place [it belongs here] 2. to be related (*to*) 3. to be a member (with *to*) 4. to be owned (with *to*)

be·long'ings *n.pl.* possessions

be·lov·ed (bi luv'id, -luvd') *adj.* dearly loved —*n.* a dearly loved person

be·low (bi lō') *adv., adj.* [see BE- & LOW[1]] 1. in or to a lower place; beneath 2. later (in a book, etc.) 3. in or to hell 4. on earth 5. under in rank, amount, etc. —*prep.* 1. lower than 2. unworthy of

Bel·shaz·zar (bel shaz'ər) *Bible* the last king of Babylon

belt (belt) *n.* [< L. *balteus*] 1. a band of leather, etc. worn around the waist 2. any encircling thing like this 3. an endless band, as for transferring motion or conveying 4. a distinctive area [the corn *belt*] 5. [Slang] a hard blow; punch 6. [Slang] *a*) a gulp of liquor *b*) a thrill —*vt.* 1. to encircle or fasten with a belt 2. *a*) to encircle with a belt *b*) [Slang] to hit hard 3. [Colloq.] to sing loudly (usually with *out*) 4. [Slang] to gulp (liquor)

belt'way' *n.* an expressway passing around an urban area

be·mire (bi mīr') *vt.* -**mired', -mir'ing** 1. to make dirty as with mire or mud 2. to cause to bog down in mud

be·moan (bi mōn') *vt., vi.* to lament

be·muse (bi myooz') *vt.* -**mused', -mus'ing** [BE- + MUSE] 1. to muddle 2. to preoccupy

bench (bench) *n.* [OE. *benc*] 1. a long, hard seat 2. *same as* WORKBENCH 3. the place where judges sit in a court 4. [*sometimes* B-] *a*) the status of a judge *b*) judges collectively *c*) a law court —*vt. Sports* to take (a player) out of a game —**on the bench** 1. serving as a judge 2. *Sports* not taking part in the game

bench press a weight-lifting exercise of pushing a barbell up from the chest while lying on a bench with the feet on the floor

bench warrant an order issued by a judge or court for arrest of a person

bend[1] (bend) *vt.* **bent, bend'ing** [< OE. *bendan*, to bind] 1. to make curved or crooked 2. to turn, esp. from a straight line 3. to make submit —*vi.* 1. to turn, esp. from a straight line 2. to yield by curving, as from pressure 3. to curve the body; stoop (*over* or *down*) 4. to give in; yield —*n.* 1. a bending or being bent 2. a bent part —**bend'a·ble** *adj.*

bend[2] (bend) *n.* [ME. < *prec.*] any of various knots for tying rope

be·neath (bi nēth') *adv., adj.* [OE. *beneothan*] in a lower place; underneath —*prep.* 1. below 2. underneath 3. unworthy of [*beneath* scorn]

ben·e·dic·tion (ben'ə dik'shən) *n.* [< L. *bene*, well + *dicere*, speak] 1. a blessing 2. invocation of a blessing, esp. at the end of a church service

ben·e·fac·tion (ben'ə fak'shən) *n.* [< L. *bene*, well + *facere*, do] 1. the act of helping, esp. by charitable gifts 2. the money or help given

ben·e·fac·tor (ben'ə fak'tər) *n.* one who has given help, esp. financially; patron —**ben'e·fac'tress** *n.fem.*

ben·e·fice (ben'ə fis) *n.* [see BENEFACTION] an endowed church office providing a living for a vicar, etc.

be·nef·i·cence (bə nef'ə s'ns) *n.* [see BENEFACTION] 1. a being kind 2. a charitable act or gift

be·nef'i·cent (-s'nt) *adj.* showing beneficence; doing or resulting in good —**be·nef'i·cent·ly** *adv.*

ben·e·fi·cial (ben'ə fish'əl) *adj.* producing benefits; advantageous; favorable —**ben'e·fi'cial·ly** *adv.*

ben'e·fi'ci·ar'y (-fish'ē er'ē, -fish'ər ē) *n., pl.* -**ar'ies** anyone receiving or to receive benefit, as funds from a will, an insurance policy, etc.

ben·e·fit (ben'ə fit) *n.* [see BENEFACTION] 1. anything contributing to improvement; advantage 2. [*often pl.*] payments made by an insurance company, public agency, etc., as during sickness or retirement or for death 3. a public performance, bazaar, etc. the proceeds of which are to help some person or cause —*vt.* -**fit·ed, -fit·ing**

to help; aid —*vi.* to receive advantage; profit

be·nev·o·lence (bə nev′ə ləns) *n.* [< L. *bene*, well + *volere*, to wish] 1. an inclination to do good; kindness 2. a kindly, charitable act —**be·nev′o·lent** *adj.* —**be·nev′o·lent·ly** *adv.*

Ben·gal (ben gôl′), Bay of part of the Indian Ocean, east of India

be·night·ed (bi nīt′id) *adj.* 1. surrounded by darkness 2. ignorant

be·nign (bi nīn′) *adj.* [< L. *bene*, well + *genus*, birth] 1. good-natured; kindly 2. favorable; beneficial 3. *Med.* not malignant —**be·nign′ly** *adv.*

be·nig·nant (bi nig′nənt) *adj.* [< prec.] 1. kindly or gracious 2. favorable; beneficial

be·nig·ni·ty (-nə tē) *n.*, *pl.* -**ties** 1. kindliness 2. a kind act

ben·i·son (ben′ə z′n, -s′n) *n.* [< L.: see BENEDICTION] a blessing

ben·ny (ben′ē) *n.*, *pl.* -**nies** [Slang] an amphetamine pill, esp. Benzedrine

bent (bent) *pt.* and *pp.* of BEND[1] —*adj.* 1. curved or crooked 2. strongly determined (with *on*) —*n.* 1. a tendency 2. a mental leaning; propensity

bent·grass (bent′gras′) *n.* [OE. *beonot*] a low-growing grass that spreads by putting out runners, used for lawns

bent′wood′ *adj.* made of pieces of wood permanently bent [*bentwood* furniture]

be·numb (bi num′) *vt.* 1. to make numb 2. to deaden the mind, will, etc. of

Ben·ze·drine (ben′zə drēn′) *a trademark for* AMPHETAMINE —*n.* [b-] this drug

ben·zene (ben′zēn) *n.* [< BENZOIN] a flammable liquid obtained from coal tar and used as a solvent, in dyes, etc.

ben·zine (ben′zēn) *n.* [< BENZOIN] a flammable liquid obtained from petroleum and used as a motor fuel, in dry cleaning, etc.

ben·zo·ate (ben′zō āt′) *n.* a salt or ester of benzoic acid

ben′zo·caine′ (-kān′) *n.* [< BENZO(IN) + (CO)CAINE] a white powder used in ointments as an anesthetic and to protect against sunburn

ben·zo·ic acid (ben zō′ik) [< ff.] a crystalline acid used as an antiseptic and preservative

ben·zo·in (ben′zō in) *n.* [< Ar. *lubān jāwi*, incense of Java] a resin from certain tropical Asiatic trees, used in medicine, perfumes, etc.

ben·zol (ben′zōl, -zôl) *n.* same as BENZENE

be·queath (bi kwēth′, -kwēth′) *vt.* [< OE. *be-* + *cwethan*, say] 1. to leave (property, etc.) to another by one's will 2. to hand down; pass on

be·quest′ (-kwest′) *n.* 1. a bequeathing 2. anything bequeathed

be·rate (bi rāt′) *vt.* -**rat′ed**, -**rat′ing** [BE- + RATE[2]] to scold severely

Ber·ber (bur′bər) *n.* 1. any of a Moslem people living in N Africa 2.

their language —*adj.* of the Berbers

be·reave (bi rēv′) *vt.* -**reaved′** or -**reft′** (-reft′), -**reav′ing** [< OE. *be-* + *reafian*, rob] 1. to deprive: now usually in the pp. (bereft) [*bereft* of hope] 2. to leave in a sad or lonely state, as by death —**be·reave′ment** *n.*

be·ret (bə rā′) *n.* [< Fr. < L. *birrus*, a hood] a flat, round, soft cap

berg (burg) *n.* same as ICEBERG

ber·i·ber·i (ber′ē ber′ē) *n.* [Sinhalese *beri*, weakness] a disease caused by lack of vitamin B[1] and characterized by nerve disorders, edema, etc.

Ber·ing Sea (ber′iŋ) part of the Pacific, between Siberia & Alaska

Bering Strait strait joining the Bering Sea with the Arctic Ocean

Berke·ley (burk′lē) city in Calif., near San Francisco: pop. 103,000

Ber·lin (bər lin′) city in E Germany: see EAST BERLIN & WEST BERLIN

berm, berme (burm) *n.* [< MDu. *baerm*] a ledge or shoulder, as along the edge of a paved road

Ber·mu·da (bər myōō′də) group of Brit. islands in the W Atlantic

Bermuda onion a large onion with a mild flavor, grown in Tex., Calif., etc.

Bermuda shorts knee-length trousers

Bern, Berne (burn) capital of Switzerland: pop. 167,000

ber·ry (ber′ē) *n.*, *pl.* -**ries** [OE. *berie*] 1. any small, juicy, fleshy fruit, as a strawberry 2. the dry seed of various plants, as a coffee bean —*vi.* -**ried**, -**ry·ing** 1. to bear berries 2. to pick berries —**ber′ry·like′** *adj.*

ber·serk (bər surk′, -zurk′) *adj., adv.* [ON. *berserkr*, warrior] in or into a violent rage or frenzy

berth (burth) *n.* [< base of BEAR[1]] 1. a place where a ship anchors or moors 2. a position, job, etc. 3. a built-in bed, as on a ship or train —*vt.* to put into or furnish with a berth —*vi.* to occupy a berth —**give a wide berth to** to keep well clear of

ber·yl (ber′əl) *n.* [< Gr. *beryllos*] a very hard mineral, of which emerald and aquamarine are two varieties

be·ryl·li·um (bə ril′ē əm) *n.* [ModL. < prec.] a hard, rare, metallic chemical element used in forming alloys

be·seech (bi sēch′) *vt.* -**sought′** or -**seeched′**, -**seech′ing** [< OE. *be-* + *secan*, seek] to ask (for) earnestly; entreat —**be·seech′ing·ly** *adv.*

be·seem (bi sēm′) *vi.* to be suitable or appropriate (to)

be·set (bi set′) *vt.* -**set′**, -**set′ting** [< OE. *be-* + *settan*, set] 1. to attack from all sides; harass 2. to surround or hem in

be·set′ting *adj.* constantly harassing

be·side (bi sīd′) *prep.* [OE. *bi sīdan*] 1. at the side of; near 2. in comparison with [*beside* his share hers seems small] 3. in addition to 4. aside from —**beside oneself** wild or upset, as with fear, rage, etc.

be·sides (-sīdz´) *adv.* **1.** in addition **2.** except for that mentioned **3.** moreover —*prep.* **1.** in addition to **2.** other than

be·siege (bi sēj´) *vt.* **-sieged´, -sieg´ing 1.** to hem in with armed forces **2.** to close in on **3.** to overwhelm, harass, etc. *[besieged* with queries]

be·smear (bi smir´) *vt.* to smear over

be·smirch (bi smurch´) *vt.* to soil

be·som (bē´zəm) *n.* [OE. *besma*] a broom, esp. one made of twigs tied to a handle

be·sot (bi sät´) *vt.* **-sot´ted, -sot´ting** to make a sot of; stupefy, as with liquor —**be·sot´ted** *adj.*

be·sought (bi sôt´) *alt. pt. and pp. of* BESEECH

be·span·gle (bi spaŋ´g'l) *vt.* **-gled, -gling** to cover with or as with spangles

be·spat·ter (bi spat´ər) *vt.* to spatter, as with mud or slander

be·speak (bi spēk´) *vt.* **-spoke´, -spok´en** or **-spoke´, -speak´ing 1.** to speak for in advance; reserve **2.** to be indicative of; show

Bes·se·mer process (bes´ə mər) [< H. *Bessemer,* 19th-c. Eng. inventor] a method of making steel by blasting air through molten iron in a large container (**Bessemer converter**)

best (best) *adj. superl. of* GOOD [OE. *betst*] **1.** most excellent **2.** most suitable, desirable, etc. **3.** largest *[the best* part of a day] —*adv. superl. of* WELL² **1.** in the most excellent manner **2.** in the highest degree —*n.* **1.** the most excellent person, thing, etc. **2.** the utmost —*vt.* to defeat or outdo —**all for the best** ultimately good —**at best** under the most favorable conditions —**get (or have) the best of 1.** to defeat **2.** to outwit —**make the best of** to do as well as one can with

bes·tial (bes´chəl) *adj.* [< L. *bestia,* beast] like a beast; savage, brutal, vile, etc. —**bes´ti·al´i·ty** (-chē al´ə tē) *n., pl.* **-ties**

bes·tial·ize (bes´chə līz´, -tyə-) *vt.* **-ized´, -iz´ing** to make bestial

bes·ti·ar·y (bes´chē er´ē, -tē-) *n., pl.* **-ies** [see BESTIAL] a medieval book with fables about real or mythical animals

be·stir (bi stur´) *vt.* **-stirred´, -stir´ring** to stir to action; busy (oneself)

best man the principal attendant of the bridegroom at a wedding

be·stow (bi stō´) *vt.* [see BE- & STOW] to present as a gift (often with *on* or *upon*) —**be·stow´al** *n.*

be·strew (bi strōō´) *vt.* **-strewed´, -strewed´** or **-strewn´, -strew´ing** to strew or scatter about

be·stride (bi strīd´) *vt.* **-strode´, -strid´den, -strid´ing** to sit, mount, or stand astride

bet (bet) *n.* [prob. < ABET] **1.** *a)* an agreement that the party proved wrong about something will do or pay what is stipulated *b)* the thing or sum thus staked **2.** a person or thing likely to bring about a desired result —*vt., vi.* **bet** or **bet´ted, bet´ting 1.** to declare as in a bet **2.** to stake (money, etc.) in a bet with (someone)

be·ta (bāt´ə) *n.* the second letter of the Greek alphabet (B, β)

be·take (bi tāk´) *vt.* **-took´, -tak´en, -tak´ing** [see BE- & TAKE] to go (used reflexively)

beta particle an electron or positron ejected from the nucleus of an atom during radioactive disintegration

beta ray a stream of beta particles

be·tel (bēt´'l) *n.* [Port. < Malay *veṭṭilai*] a climbing pepper plant of Asia: its leaf, along with lime and the fruit (**betel nut**) of a palm (**betel palm**), is chewed by some Asians

be·think (bi thiŋk´) *vt.* **-thought´, -think´ing** to bring (oneself) to think of, recollect, etc.

Beth·le·hem (beth´lə hem´) ancient town in Palestine: Jesus' birthplace

be·tide (bi tīd´) *vi., vt.* **-tid´ed, -tid´ing** [< ME.: see BE- & TIDE] to happen (to); befall

be·times (bi tīmz´) *adv.* **1.** early or early enough **2.** [Archaic] promptly

be·to·ken (bi tō´k'n) *vt.* **1.** to be a token or sign of; show **2.** to presage

be·tray (bi trā´) *vt.* [ult. < L. *tradere,* deliver] **1.** to help the enemy of (one's country, etc.) **2.** to expose treacherously **3.** to fail to uphold *[to betray* a trust] **4.** to deceive; specif., to seduce and fail to marry **5.** to reveal unknowingly —**be·tray´al** *n.* —**be·tray´er** *n.*

be·troth (bi trōth´, -trôth´) *vt.* [< ME.: see BE- & TRUTH] to promise in marriage —**be·troth´al** *n.*

be·trothed´ (-trōthd´, -trôtht´) *adj.* engaged to be married —*n.* a person engaged to be married

bet·ter (bet´ər) *adj. compar. of* GOOD [OE. *betera*] **1.** more excellent **2.** more suitable, desirable, etc. **3.** larger *[the better* part of a day] **4.** improved in health —*adv. compar. of* WELL² **1.** in a more excellent manner **2.** in a higher degree **3.** more —*n.* **1.** a person superior in position, etc. **2.** a more excellent thing, condition, etc. —*vt.* **1.** to outdo; surpass **2.** to improve —**better off** in better circumstances —**get (or have) the better of 1.** to defeat **2.** to outwit

bet´ter·ment (-mənt) *n.* a bettering; improvement

bet´tor, bet´ter *n.* one who bets

be·tween (bi twēn´) *prep.* [< OE. *be,* by + *tweonum,* by twos] **1.** in the space, time, etc. separating (two things) **2.** involving *[a* struggle *between* powers] **3.** connecting *[a* bond *between* friends] **4.** in the combined possession of **5.** by the joint action of **6.** from one or the other of *[choose between us]* —*adv.* in an intermediate space, time, etc. —**between ourselves (or us or you and me)** as a secret

be·twixt (bi twikst´) *prep., adv.* [OE. *betwix*] between: archaic except in **betwixt and between,** not altogether one nor altogether the other

bev·el (bev´'l) *n.* [< ?] **1.** a tool for measuring or marking angles, etc. **2.** an angle other than a right angle **3.** angled part or surface —*adj.* beveled —*vt.* **-eled** or **-elled, -el·ing** or **-el-**

ling to cut to an angle other than a right angle —*vi.* to slope at an angle

bevel gear a gearwheel meshing with another at an angle

BEVEL GEAR

bev·er·age (bev′rij, -ər ij) *n.* [< L. *bibere,* to drink] any liquid for drinking, esp. one other than water

bev·y (bev′ē) *n., pl.* **-ies** [ME. *bevey*] 1. a group, esp. of girls or women 2. a flock, esp. of quail

be·wail (bi wāl′) *vt.* to wail over; lament; mourn

be·ware (bi wer′) *vi., vt.* **-wared′, -war′ing** [prob. < OE. *bewarian,* to keep watch] to be wary or careful (of)

be·wigged (bi wigd′) *adj.* wearing a wig

be·wil·der (bi wil′dər) *vt.* [ult. < OE. *wilde,* wild] to confuse hopelessly; befuddle —**be·wil′der·ment** *n.*

be·witch (bi wich′) *vt.* [< OE. *wicca:* see WITCH] 1. to cast a spell over 2. to charm and delight greatly

bey (bā) *n.* [Turk.] formerly, 1. the governor of a Turkish district 2. the native ruler of Tunis

be·yond (bi yänd′) *prep.* [< OE. *be- + geond,* yonder] 1. farther on than; past 2. later than 3. outside the reach of *[beyond* help] 4. more than —*adv.* farther away —**the (great) beyond** whatever follows death

bez·el (bez′′l) *n.* [< OFr. *biais,* bias] 1. a sloping cutting edge, as of a chisel 2. the slanting faces of a cut jewel 3. the groove and flange holding a gem or a watch crystal in place

bhang (baŋ) *n.* [< Sans. *bhangā*] 1. the hemp plant 2. its dried leaves and flowers, which have intoxicating properties

Bhu·tan (bōō tän′) monarchy in the Himalayas: c.18,000 sq. mi.; pop. 750,000

bi- [L.] a *prefix meaning:* 1. having two 2. doubly 3. happening every two 4. happening twice during every 5. using two or both 6. joining or involving two

Bi *Chem.* bismuth

bi·an·nu·al (bī an′yōō wəl, -yool) *adj.* coming twice a year; semiannual

bi·as (bī′əs) *n., pl.* **-as·es** [Fr. *biais,* a slant] 1. a slanting or diagonal line, cut or sewn in cloth 2. partiality; prejudice —*adj.* slanting; diagonal —*adv.* diagonally —*vt.* **-ased** or **-assed, -as·ing** or **-as·sing** to prejudice —**on the bias** diagonally

bi·ath·lon (bī ath′län) *n.* [BI- + Gr. *athlon,* contest] an athletic event combining a ski run and marksmanship

bib (bib) *n.* [< L. *bibere,* to drink] 1. a cloth or plastic cover tied under a child's neck at meals 2. the upper part of an apron

Bib. 1. Bible 2. Biblical

bibb lettuce (bib) [after J. *Bibb* (1789–1884), who developed it] a kind of lettuce with loose heads of crisp, dark-green leaves

Bi·ble (bī′b′l) *n.* [< Gr. *biblos,* papyrus < *Byblos,* Phoenician city that exported papyrus] 1. the sacred book of Christianity; Old Testament and New Testament 2. the Holy Scriptures of Judaism; Old Testament 3. [b-] any book regarded as authoritative or official —**Bib·li·cal, bib·li·cal** (bib′li k′l) *adj.*

biblio- [< Gr. *biblion,* book] a *combining form meaning* book, of books

bib·li·og·ra·phy (bib′lē äg′rə fē) *n., pl.* **-phies** a list of writings on a given subject or by a given author —**bib·li·og′ra·pher** *n.* —**bib′li·o·graph′i·cal** (-ə graf′i k′l) *adj.*

bib′li·o·phile′ (-ə fīl′) *n.* one who loves or collects books

bib·u·lous (bib′yoo ləs) *adj.* [< L. *bibere,* to drink] addicted to or fond of alcoholic liquor

bi·cam·er·al (bī kam′ər əl) *adj.* [< BI- + L. *camera,* chamber] having two legislative chambers

bi·car·bon·ate of soda (bī kär′bə nit) *same as* SODIUM BICARBONATE

bi·cen·ten·ni·al (bī′sen ten′ē əl) *adj.* happening once every 200 years —*n.* a 200th anniversary

bi·ceps (bī′seps) *n., pl.* **-ceps** or **-ceps·es** [L. < *bis,* two + *caput,* head] a muscle with two points of origin; esp., the large muscle in the front of the upper arm

bick·er (bik′ər) *vi., n.* [ME. *bikeren*] squabble; quarrel —**bick′er·er** *n.*

bi′con·cave′ (-kän kāv′) *adj.* concave on both surfaces

bi′con·vex′ (-veks′) *adj.* convex on both surfaces

bi·cus·pid (bī kus′pid) *adj.* [< BI- + L. *cuspis,* pointed end] having two points —*n.* any of the eight adult teeth with two-pointed crowns

bi·cy·cle (bī′si k′l) *n.* [Fr.: see BI- & CYCLE] a vehicle consisting of a metal frame on two wheels, and having handlebars and a seat —*vi., vt.* **-cled, -cling** to ride or travel on a bicycle —**bi′cy·clist, bi′cy·cler** *n.*

bid (bid) *vt.* **bade** or **bid, bid′den** or **bid, bid′ding;** for vt. 2, 4 & for vi., pt. & pp. **bid** [< OE. *biddan,* to urge & *beodan,* to command] 1. to command or ask 2. to offer (an amount) as the price one will pay or accept 3. to express [to *bid* farewell] 4. *Card Games* to state (a number of tricks) and declare (trump) —*vi.* to make a bid —*n.* 1. a bidding 2. an amount, etc. bid 3. a chance to bid 4. an attempt or try (*for*) 5. [Colloq.] an invitation —**bid fair** to seem likely —**bid′der** *n.*

bid·dy (bid′ē) *n., pl.* **-dies** [< ?] 1. a hen 2. [Slang] an elderly woman who is gossipy, eccentric, etc.

bide (bīd) *vi.* **bode** or **bid′ed, bid′ed, bid′ing** [OE. *bīdan*] [Archaic or Dial.] 1. to stay; continue 2. to dwell 3. to wait —*vt.* [Archaic or Dial.] to endure

—bide one's time *pt.* **bid'ed** to wait patiently for an opportunity

bi·det (bi dā′) *n.* [Fr.] a low, bowl-shaped bathroom fixture, with running water, for bathing the crotch

bi·en·ni·al (bī en′ē əl) *adj.* [< L. *bis*, twice + *annus*, year] 1. happening every two years 2. lasting for two years —*n.* 1. a biennial event 2. *Bot.* a plant that lives two years —**bi·en′ni·al·ly** *adv.*

bier (bir) *n.* [OE. *bær*] a portable framework on which a coffin is put

biff (bif) *n., v.* [Slang] strike; hit

bi·fo·cals (bī′fō′k′lz) *n.pl.* a pair of glasses with lenses having one part ground for close focus and the other for distant focus

bi·fur·cate (bī′fər kāt′) *vt., vi.* -**cat'ed**, -**cat'ing** [< L. *bi-* + *furca*, a fork] to divide into two parts or branches —**bi′fur·ca′tion** *n.*

big (big) *adj.* **big′ger**, **big′gest** [akin to L. *bucca*, puffed cheek] 1. of great size; large 2. full-grown 3. elder *[his big sister]* 4. noticeably pregnant (*with*) 5. loud 6. important 7. extravagant 8. noble *[a big heart]* —*adv.* [Colloq.] 1. boastfully 2. impressively —**big′ness** *n.*

big·a·my (big′ə mē) *n.* [< L. *bis*, twice + *gamos*, marriage] the crime of marrying a second time when one is already legally married —**big′a·mist** *n.* —**big′a·mous** *adj.*

big game 1. large wild animals hunted for sport, as lions, tigers, etc. 2. the object of any important or dangerous undertaking

big′heart′ed (-härt′id) *adj.* quick to give or forgive; generous

big′horn′ *n.* a Rocky Mountain wild sheep with long, curved horns

bight (bīt) *n.* [ME. *byht*] 1. a bending; corner 2. a slack part in a rope 3. a curve in a coastline 4. a bay

big mouth [Slang] a person who talks too much, esp. in an opinionated way

big·ot (big′ət) *n.* [Fr. < ?] one who holds blindly and intolerantly to a particular creed, opinion, etc. —**big′ot·ed** *adj.* —**big′ot·ry** (-ə trē) *n.*

big shot [Slang] an important or influential person

bike (bīk) *n.* [Colloq.] 1. a bicycle 2. a motorcycle

bi·ki·ni (bi kē′nē) *n.* [< *Bikini*, Pacific atoll] an extremely brief two-piece bathing suit for women

bi·lat·er·al (bī lat′ər əl) *adj.* 1. of, having, or involving two sides 2. affecting both sides equally; reciprocal —**bi·lat′er·al·ly** *adv.*

bile (bīl) *n.* [< L. *bilis*] 1. the bitter, greenish fluid secreted by the liver: it aids digestion 2. bad temper

bilge (bilj) *n.* [var. of BULGE] 1. the rounded, lower part of a ship's hold 2. stagnant water that gathers there: also **bilge water** 3. [Slang] nonsense

bi·lin·gual (bī lin′gwəl) *adj.* [< L. *bis*, two + *lingua*, tongue] of, in, or speaking two languages

bil·ious (bil′yəs) *adj.* 1. of the bile 2. having or resulting from some ailment of the liver 3. bad-tempered

bilk (bilk) *vt.* [? < *balk*] to cheat or swindle; defraud —**bilk′er** *n.*

bill¹ (bil) *n.* [< ML. *bulla*, sealed document] 1. a statement of charges for goods or services 2. a list, as a menu or theater program 3. a poster or handbill 4. a draft of a proposed law 5. *same as* BILL OF EXCHANGE 6. a piece of paper money 7. *Law* a written declaration of charges and complaints filed —*vt.* 1. to make out a bill of (items) 2. to present a statement of charges to 3. *a)* to advertise by bills *b)* to book (a performer) —**fill the bill** [Colloq.] to meet the requirements

bill² (bil) *n.* [OE. *bile*] 1. a bird's beak 2. a beaklike mouth part, as of a turtle —*vi.* to touch bills together —**bill and coo** to kiss, talk softly, etc. in a loving way

bill′board′ *n.* a signboard for advertising posters

bil·let (bil′it) *n.* [see BILL¹] 1. *a)* a written order to provide lodging for military personnel *b)* the lodging 2. a position or job —*vt.* to assign to lodging by billet

bil·let-doux (bil′ē dōō′) *n., pl.* **bil·lets-doux** (bil′ē dōōz′) [Fr.] a love letter

bill′fold′ (-fōld′) *n.* a wallet

bil·liard (bil′yərd) *adj.* of or for billiards

bil·liards (bil′yərdz) *n.* [< Fr. *bil·lard*, orig. a cue] a game played with hard balls driven by a cue on a table with raised, cushioned edges

bill·ing (bil′iŋ) *n.* 1. the order in which actors' names are listed, as on a playbill 2. such a listing

bil·lings·gate (bil′iŋz gāt′) *n.* [< a London fish market] foul, vulgar, abusive talk

bil·lion (bil′yən) *n.* [Fr. < L. *bis*, twice + *million*] 1. a thousand millions (1,000,000,000) 2. formerly, in Great Britain, a million millions (1,000,000,-000,000) —**bil′lionth** *adj., n.*

bil′lion·aire′ (-yə ner′) *n.* a person whose wealth comes to at least a billion dollars, pounds, francs, etc.

bill of exchange a written order to pay a certain sum of money to the person named

bill of fare a menu

bill of lading a receipt issued to a shipper by a carrier, listing the goods received for shipment

Bill of Rights the first ten amendments to the U.S. Constitution, which guarantee civil liberties

bill of sale a written statement transferring ownership by sale

bil·low (bil′ō) *n.* [ON. *bylgja*] 1. a large wave 2. any large, swelling mass or surge, as of smoke —*vi.* to surge or swell in a billow —**bil′low·y** *adj.*

bil·ly (bil′ē) *n., pl.* -**lies** [ult. < OFr. *bille*, tree trunk] a club, esp. a policeman's heavy stick

billy goat [Colloq.] a male goat

bi·met·al·lism (bī met′′l iz′m) *n.* the use of two metals, esp. gold and silver, as the monetary standard, with fixed values in relation to each other

bi·month·ly (bī munth′lē) *adj., adv.*
1. once every two months 2. loosely, twice a month

bin (bin) *n.* [OE., crib] a box, crib, etc. for storing grain, coal, etc.

bi·na·ry (bī′nər ē) *adj.* [< L. *bis*, double] 1. made up of two parts; double 2. designating or of a number system in which the base used is two, each number being expressed by using only two digits, specif. 0 and 1 —*n., pl.* -**ries** a set of two

bind (bīnd) *vt.* **bound, bind′ing** [< OE. *bindan*] 1. to tie together, as with rope 2. to hold or restrain 3. to encircle with a belt, etc. 4. to bandage (often with *up*) 5. to constipate 6. to reinforce or ornament the edges of by a band, as of tape 7. to fasten together the pages of (a book) and protect with a cover 8. to obligate by duty, love, etc. 9. to compel, as by oath or legal restraint —*vi.* 1. to become tight or stiff 2. to stick together 3. to be obligatory —*n.* 1. anything that binds 2. [Colloq.] a difficult situation

bind′er *n.* 1. one who binds 2. a binding substance, as tar 3. a cover for holding sheets of paper together

bind′er·y *n., pl.* -**ies** a place where books are bound

bind′ing *n.* a thing that binds, as a band, tape, the covers and backing of a book, a cohesive substance, etc. —*adj.* that binds, obligates, etc.

binge (binj) *n.* [Colloq.] a spree

bin·go (biŋ′gō) *n.* a gambling game resembling lotto

bin·na·cle (bin′ə k'l) *n.* [ult. < L. *habitaculum*, dwelling place] the case enclosing a ship's compass

bin·oc·u·lar (bi näk′yə lər, bī-) *adj.* [< L. *bini*, double + *oculus*, eye] using, or for, both eyes —*n.* [*pl.*] a binocular instrument, as field glasses

bi·no·mi·al (bī nō′mē əl) *n.* [< L. *bi-*, two + Gr. *nomos*, law] 1. *Math.* an expression consisting of two terms connected by a plus or minus sign 2. a two-word scientific name of a plant or animal

bio- [Gr. < *bios*, life] *a combining form meaning* life, of living things

bi·o·as·tro·nau·tics (bī′ō as′trə nô′tiks) *n.pl.* [*with sing. v.*] the science dealing with the physical responses of living things to space travel

bi·o·a·vail·a·bil′i·ty *n.* the rate at which a drug, etc. enters the blood stream and circulates, as to organs

bi·o·chem·is·try (bī′ō kem′is trē) *n.* the branch of chemistry that deals with the life processes of plants and animals —**bi′o·chem′ist** *n.*

bi·o·cide (bī′ō sīd′) *n.* a poisonous chemical that can kill living organisms

bi′o·clean′ *adj.* as free as possible from microorganisms; esp., aseptic

bi′o·de·grad′a·ble (-di grā′də b'l) *adj.* [BIO- + DEGRAD(E) + -ABLE] readily decomposed by bacterial action,

as some detergents in sewage disposal

bi′o·feed′back *n.* a technique of seeking to control one's emotions by using electronic devices to train oneself to modify involuntary body functions, such as heartbeat

biog. 1. biographical 2. biography

bi·og·ra·phy (bī äg′rə fē) *n., pl.* -**phies** [< Gr.: see BIO- & -GRAPHY] an account of a person's life written by another —**bi·og′ra·pher** *n.* —**bi·o·graph·i·cal** (bī′ə graf′i k'l) *adj.*

biol. 1. biological 2. biology

biological warfare the use of toxic microorganisms, etc. in war

bi·ol·o·gy (bī äl′ə jē) *n.* [BIO- + -LOGY] the science that deals with the origin, history, characteristics, habits, etc. of plants and animals —**bi·o·log·i·cal** (bī′ə läj′i k'l) *adj.* —**bi′o·log′i·cal·ly** *adv.* —**bi·ol′o·gist** *n.*

bi·o·med·i·cine (bī′ō med′ə s'n) *n.* a branch of medicine combined with research in biology —**bi′o·med′i·cal** *adj.*

bi·on·ic (bī än′ ik) *adj.* 1. of bionics 2. having an artificial bodily part or parts, as in science fiction, so as to enhance strength, abilities, etc.

bi·on·ics (bī än′iks) *n.pl.* [*with sing. v.*] [< Gr. *bion*, living + -ICS] the science of designing instruments or systems modeled after living organisms

bi·o·phys·ics (bī′ō fiz′iks) *n.pl.* [*with sing. v.*] the study of biological phenomena in relation to physics —**bi′o·phys′i·cal** *adj.* —**bi′o·phys′i·cist** *n.*

bi·op·sy (bī′äp′sē) *n., pl.* -**sies** [< BIO- + Gr. *opsis*, a sight] *Med.* the removal of bits of living tissue for diagnosis

bi·o·rhythm (bī′ō rith′′m) *n.* any of three hypothetical biological cycles that determine the regular rise and fall of a person's energy levels

bi·o·tin (bī′ə tin) *n.* [< Gr. *bios*, life] a factor of the vitamin B group

bi·par·ti·san (bī pär′tə z′n) *adj.* of, representing, or supported by two parties —**bi·par′ti·san·ship′** *n.*

bi·par·tite (bī pär′tīt) *adj.* [< L. *bi-*, two + *partire*, divide] 1. having two parts 2. involving two

bi·ped (bī′ped) *n.* [< L. *bi-*, two + *pes*, foot] any two-footed animal

bi·plane (bī′plān′) *n.* an airplane with one set of wings over another set

bi·ra·cial (bī rā′shəl) *adj.* consisting of or involving two races

birch (burch) *n.* [< OE. *beorc*] 1. a tree having smooth bark in thin layers, and hard, closegrained wood 2. its wood 3. a bunch of birch twigs used for whipping —*vt.* to flog

bird (burd) *n.* [< OE. *bridd*, young bird] any of a class of warm-blooded vertebrates with feathers and wings —**birds of a feather** people with the same traits or tastes —**for the birds** [Slang] ridiculous, worthless, etc.

bird·ie (bur′dē) *n. Golf* a score of one stroke under par for a hole

bird's-eye (burdz′ī′) *adj.* 1. seen from high above; overall [a *bird's-eye* view*]* **2.** having marks resembling birds' eyes *[bird's-eye maple]*

bi·ret·ta (bə ret*'*ə) *n.* [< LL. *birrettum*, small cloak] a square cap with three projections, worn by Roman Catholic clergy

Bir·ming·ham (bur*'*miŋ əm *for 1;* -ham*' for 2*) **1.** city in C England: pop. 1,116,000 **2.** city in NC Ala.: pop. 284,000

birth (burth) *n.* [< OE. *beran*, to bear] **1.** the act of bringing forth offspring **2.** a being born **3.** origin or descent **4.** the beginning of anything **5.** natural inclination *[an actor by birth]* —**give birth to 1.** to bring forth (offspring) **2.** to create

birth*'*day*'* n. the anniversary of the day of a person's birth —**in one's birthday suit** [Colloq.] naked

birth*'*mark*'* n. a skin blemish present at birth

birth*'*place*'* n. the place of one's birth or of a thing's origin

birth*'*rate*'* n. the number of births per year per thousand people in a given area, group, etc.

birth*'*right*'* n. any right that a person has by birth

birth*'*stone*'* n. a gem symbolizing the month of one's birth

bis·cuit (bis*'*kit) *n., pl.* **-cuits, -cuit** [< L. *bis*, twice + *coquere*, to cook] **1.** [Chiefly Brit.] a cracker or cookie **2.** a quick bread baked in small pieces

bi·sect (bī*'*sekt*'*) *vt.* [< L. *bi-* + *secare*, to cut] **1.** to cut in two **2.** *Geom.* to divide into two equal parts —*vi.* to divide; fork —**bi*'*sec*'*tor** *n.*

bi·sex·u·al (bī sek*'*shoo wəl) *adj.* of, or sexually attracted by, both sexes —*n.* one who is bisexual

bish·op (bish*'*əp) *n.* [< Gr. *episkopos*, overseer] **1.** a high-ranking Christian clergyman governing a diocese or church district **2.** a chessman that can move in a diagonal direction

bish*'*op·ric (-ə prik) *n.* the district, position, rank, etc. of a bishop

Bis·marck (biz*'*märk) capital of N.Dak.: pop. 44,000

Bis·marck (biz*'*märk), **Prince Otto von** 1815–98; Prussian chancellor (1871–90) who unified Germany

bis·muth (biz*'*məth) *n.* [< G.] a brittle, grayish-white metallic element used in alloys of low melting point

bi·son (bīs*'*n) *n., pl.* **bi*'*son** [Fr. < L., wild ox] a four-legged bovine mammal with a shaggy mane and a humped back, as the American buffalo

bisque (bisk) *n.* [Fr.] a thick creamy soup made as from shellfish

bis·tro (bis*'*trō) *n.* [Fr.] a small café

bit¹ (bit) *n.* [< OE. *bite*, a bite] **1.** a metal mouthpiece on a bridle, used as a control **2.** anything that curbs or controls **3.** a drilling or boring tool for use in a brace, drill press, etc.

bit² (bit) *n.* [< OE. *bita*, piece] **1.** *a)* a small piece or quantity *b)* small extent *[a bit bored]* *c)* a short time **2.** [Colloq.] 12 1/2 cents: now chiefly in *two bits* —*adj.* very small *[a bit role]* —**bit by bit** gradually —**do one's bit** to do one's share

bitch (bich) *n.* [< OE. *bicce*] the female of the dog, fox, etc. —*vi.* [Slang] to complain —**bitch*'*y** *adj.*

bite (bīt) *vt.* **bit** (bit), **bit*'*ten** (bit*'*n) or **bit, bit*'*ing** [< OE. *bītan*] **1.** to seize or pierce with or as with the teeth **2.** to cut into, as with a sharp weapon **3.** to sting, as an insect **4.** to cause to smart **5.** to eat into; corrode —*vi.* **1.** to press or snap the teeth (*into, at,* etc.) **2.** to cause a biting sensation **3.** to grip **4.** to seize a bait **5.** to be caught, as by a trick —*n.* **1.** a biting **2.** biting quality; sting **3.** a wound or sting from biting **4.** a mouthful **5.** a snack **6.** [Colloq.] a sum deducted, as by a tax —**bite the bullet** to confront a painful situation bravely: from the patient's biting a bullet during battlefield surgery without anesthetic

bit·ing (bīt*'*iŋ) *adj.* **1.** cutting; sharp **2.** sarcastic —**bit*'*ing·ly** *adv.*

bit·ter (bit*'*ər) *adj.* [OE. < base of *bitan*, to bite] **1.** having a sharp, often unpleasant taste **2.** causing or showing sorrow, pain, etc. **3.** sharp and disagreeable; harsh *[a bitter wind]* **4.** resentful; cynical —**bit*'*ter·ly** *adv.* —**bit*'*ter·ness** *n.*

bit·tern (bit*'*ərn) *n.* [< OFr. *butor*] a heronlike bird with a thumping cry

bit*'*ters *n.pl.* a liquor containing bitter herbs, etc., used in some cocktails

bit*'*ter·sweet*'* n. **1.** a woody vine bearing small orange fruits which open to expose bright-red seeds **2.** a poisonous vine with purple flowers and red berries **3.** pleasure mixed with sadness —*adj.* both bitter and sweet; pleasant and sad

BITTERN

bi·tu·men (bī too*'*mən, bī-) *n.* [L. < Celt.] any of several substances obtained as residue in the distillation of coal tar, petroleum, etc., or occurring as natural asphalt —**bi·tu*'*mi·nous** (-mə nəs) *adj.*

bituminous coal coal that yields pitch or tar when it burns; soft coal

bi·valve (bī*'*valv*'*) *n.* any mollusk having two valves or shells hinged together, as a clam

biv·ou·ac (biv*'*wak, -oo wak*'*) *n.* [Fr. < OHG. *bi-,* by + *wacht,* a guard] a temporary encampment (esp. of soldiers) in the open —*vi.* **-acked, -ack·ing** to encamp in the open

bi·week·ly (bī wēk*'*lē) *adj., adv.* **1.** once every two weeks **2.** semiweekly

bi·zarre (bi zär*'*) *adj.* [Fr. < Basque *bizar,* beard] **1.** odd; grotesque; eccentric **2.** unexpected; fantastic

bk. *pl.* **bks. 1.** bank **2.** book

bl. 1. bale(s) **2.** barrel(s)

B/L *pl.* **BS/L** bill of lading

blab (blab) *vt., vi.* **blabbed, blab*'*bing** [< dial. *blabber,* babble] **1.** to reveal (a secret) **2.** to gossip —*n.* gossip

black (blak) *adj.* [OE. *blæc*] **1.** opposite to white; of the color of coal **2.** having dark-colored skin and hair; esp., Negro **3.** without light; dark **4.** dirty **5.** evil; wicked **6.** sad; dismal

7. sullen —*n.* **1.** black color or pigment **2.** black clothes, esp. when worn in mourning **3.** a Negro: *black* is now generally preferred **4.** darkness—*vt.,* *vi.* to blacken —**black out** to lose consciousness —**in the black** operating at a profit —**black'ish** *adj.*— **black'ly** *adv.*—**black'ness** *n.*

black'-and-blue' *adj.* discolored, as by a bruise

black'ball' *n.* a vote against —*vt.* **1.** to vote against **2.** to ostracize

black belt a black belt awarded to an expert of the highest skill in judo or karate

black'ber'ry *n., pl.* -**ries** **1.** the fleshy, edible, purple or black fruit of various brambles of the rose family **2.** the plant it grows on

black'bird' *n.* any of various birds the male of which is almost all black

black'board' *n.* a smooth surface on which to write with chalk

black'en (-'n) *vi.* to become black or dark —*vt.* **1.** to make black; darken **2.** to slander; defame

black eye a discoloration of the skin around an eye, resulting from a blow or contusion

black'-eyed' Su'san (-īd' sōō'z'n) a yellow, daisylike wildflower with a dark center

black'guard (blag'ərd) *n.* a scoundrel; villain

black'head' *n.* a dark plug of dried fatty matter in a pore of the skin

black'jack' (-jak') *n.* **1.** a small, leather-covered bludgeon with a flexible handle **2.** the card game TWENTY-ONE —*vt.* to hit with a blackjack

black light ultraviolet or infrared radiation used for fluorescent effects

black'list' (-list') *n.* a list of those censured, refused employment, etc. —*vt.* to put on a blacklist

black lung (disease) a disease of the lungs caused by the continual inhalation of coal dust

black magic sorcery

black'mail' (-māl') *n.* [lit., black rent < ME. *male,* rent] payment extorted to prevent disclosure of information that would bring disgrace —*vt.* to get or try to get blackmail from —**black'mail'er** *n.*

black mark a mark indicating something unfavorable in one's record

black market a system for selling goods illegally —**black mar'ket·eer'**

Black Muslim a member of a militant Islamic sect of American blacks

black'out' (-out') *n.* **1.** an extinguishing of stage lights to end a scene **2.** a concealing of lights that might be visible to enemy aircraft **3.** lack of lights due to a power failure **4.** momentary unconsciousness

black power political and economic power sought by American blacks in the struggle for civil rights

Black Sea sea surrounded by the U.S.S.R., Asia Minor, & the Balkans

black sheep a person regarded as not respectable by his family or group

black'smith' *n.* a smith who works in iron and makes and fits horseshoes

black'thorn' *n.* a thorny shrub with purple or black, plumlike fruit; sloe

black'top' *n.* a bituminous mixture, usually asphalt, used as a surface for roads, etc. —*vt.* -**topped', -top'ping** to cover with blacktop

black widow a black spider with red underneath: the female has a poisonous bite and eats its mate

blad·der (blad'ər) *n.* [OE. *blæddre*] **1.** a sac that fills with fluid, esp. one that holds urine flowing from the kidneys **2.** a thing resembling this [a football *bladder*]

blade (blād) *n.* [OE. *blæd*] **1.** *a)* the leaf of a plant, esp. grass *b)* the flat part of a leaf **2.** a broad, flat surface, as of an oar **3.** the cutting part of a tool, knife, etc. **4.** a sword or swordsman **5.** a gay, dashing young man

blam·a·ble, blame·a·ble (blām'ə-b'l) *adj.* that deserves blame — **blam'a·bly** *adv.*

blame (blām) *vt.* **blamed, blam'ing** [see BLASPHEME] **1.** to accuse of being at fault; condemn *(for)* **2.** to put the responsibility of (an error, etc.) *on* —*n.* **1.** a blaming **2.** responsibility for a fault —**be to blame** to deserve blame —**blame'less** *adj.*—**blame'less·ly** *adv.*—**blame'less·ness** *n.*

blame'wor'thy (-wur'thē) *adj.* deserving to be blamed

blanch (blanch) *vt.* [see BLANK] **1.** to whiten or bleach **2.** to make pale **3.** to scald (vegetables, almonds, etc.) —*vi.* to turn pale

bland (bland) *adj.* [L. *blandus*] **1.** gently agreeable **2.** *a)* mild and soothing *b)* insipid —**bland'ly** *adv.*— **bland'ness** *n.*

blan·dish (blan'dish) *vt., vi.* [see prec.] to flatter; coax; cajole — **blan'dish·ment** *n.*

blank (blank) *adj.* [< OFr. *blanc,* white] **1.** not written on **2.** empty; vacant **3.** empty of thought [a *blank* mind] **4.** utter; complete [a *blank* denial] —*n.* **1.** an empty space, esp. one to be filled out in a printed form **2.** such a printed form **3.** an empty place or time **4.** a powder-filled cartridge without a bullet —*vt.* to hold (an opponent) scoreless —**blank out** to conceal by covering over —**draw a blank** [Colloq.] **1.** to be unsuccessful **2.** to be unable to remember a particular thing —**blank'ly** *adv.*—**blank'ness** *n.*

blan·ket (blan'kit) *n.* [see prec.] **1.** a large, soft piece of cloth used for warmth, esp. as a bed cover **2.** anything like this [a *blanket* of leaves] —*adj.* including many or all items [*blanket* insurance] —*vt.* **1.** to cover; overlie **2.** to obscure

blank verse unrhymed verse with five iambic feet per line

blare (bler) *vt., vi.* **blared, blar'ing** [ME. *bleren*, wail] to sound or exclaim loudly —*n.* a loud, harsh sound

blar·ney (blär'nē) *n.* [< *Blarney* stone in Ireland, traditionally kissed to gain skill in flattery] flattery —*vt., vi.* **-neyed, -ney·ing** to flatter or coax

bla·sé (blä zā') *adj.* [Fr.] satiated and bored

blas·pheme (blas fēm') *vt.* **-phemed', -phem'ing** [< Gr. *blasphēmein*, speak evil of] 1. to speak profanely of or to (God or sacred things) 2. to curse —*vi.* to utter blasphemy — **blas·phem'er** *n.*

blas'phe·my (-fə mē) *n., pl.* **-mies** profane abuse of God or sacred things —**blas'phe·mous** *adj.*

blast (blast) *n.* [< OE. *blæst*] 1. a strong rush of air 2. the sound of a sudden rush of air, as through a horn 3. a blight 4. an explosion, as of dynamite 5. an outburst of criticism —*vi.* 1. to make a loud, harsh sound 2. to set off explosives, etc. —*vt.* 1. to wither; ruin 2. to blow up; explode 3. to criticize sharply —**blast off** to take off: said of a rocket or missile —(at) **full blast** at full speed

blast furnace a smelting furnace in which a blast of air produces the intense heat

blast'off', blast'-off' *n.* the launching of a rocket, space vehicle, etc.

bla·tant (blāt'nt) *adj.* [prob. < L. *blaterare*, to babble] 1. disagreeably loud; noisy 2. boldly conspicuous or obtrusive —**bla'tan·cy** *n., pl.* **-cies**

blaze¹ (blāz) *n.* [OE. *blæse*] 1. a bright burst of flame; fire 2. a bright light 3. a spectacular outburst or display —*vi.* **blazed, blaz'ing** 1. to burn rapidly or shine brightly 2. to be excited, as with anger

blaze² (blāz) *n.* [< ON. *blesi*] 1. a white spot on an animal's face 2. a mark made on a tree by cutting off bark —*vt.* **blazed, blaz'ing** to mark (a tree or trail) with blazes

blaze³ (blāz) *vt.* **blazed, blaz'ing** [< OE. or ON.] to proclaim

blaz·er (blā'zər) *n.* a light sports jacket in a solid, often bright color

bla·zon (blā'z'n) *n.* [OFr. *blason*, a shield] 1. a coat of arms 2. showy display —*vt.* 1. to proclaim 2. to adorn

bldg. building

bleach (blēch) *vt., vi.* [< OE. *blac*, pale] to make or become white or colorless —*n.* a substance for bleaching

bleach'ers *n.pl.* seats, usually roofless, for spectators at sporting events

bleak (blēk) *adj.* [see BLEACH] 1. exposed to wind and cold; bare 2. cold; harsh 3. gloomy 4. not hopeful —**bleak'ly** *adv.* —**bleak'ness** *n.*

blear·y (blir'ē) *adj.* **-i·er, -i·est** [< ME. *blere*] dim or blurred, as the eyes by tears, fatigue, etc.: also **blear**

bleat (blēt) *vi.* [OE. *blætan*] to make the cry of a sheep, goat, or calf —*n.* a bleating cry or sound

bleed (blēd) *vi.* **bled** (bled), **bleed'ing** [< OE. *blod*, blood] 1. to emit or lose

blood 2. to feel pain, grief, or sympathy 3. to ooze sap, juice, etc. —*vt.* 1. to draw blood from 2. to ooze (sap, juice, etc.) 3. [Colloq.] to extort money from —**bleed'er** *n.*

bleep (blēp) *n., vi. same as* BEEP

blem·ish (blem'ish) *vt.* [< OFr. *blesmir*, injure] to mar; spoil —*n.* a flaw, defect, etc., as a spot

blench¹ (blench) *vt., vi. same as* BLANCH

blench² (blench) *vi.* [< OE. *blencan*, deceive] to shrink back; flinch

blend (blend) *vt.* **blend'ed** or **blent, blend'ing** [OE. *blendan*] 1. to mix or mingle (varieties of tea, etc.) 2. to mix thoroughly —*vi.* 1. to mix; merge 2. to shade gradually into each other, as colors 3. to harmonize —*n.* 1. a blending 2. a mixture of varieties

blend'er *n.* 1. a person or thing that blends 2. an electrical appliance that can chop, whip, mix, or liquefy foods

bless (bles) *vt.* **blessed** or **blest, bless'ing** [< OE. *bletsian*, consecrate with blood] 1. to make holy 2. to ask divine favor for 3. to endow (*with*) 4. to make happy 5. to praise 6. to make the sign of the cross over

bless·ed (bles'id, blest) *adj.* 1. holy; sacred 2. fortunate; blissful 3. beatified —**bless'ed·ly** *adv.* —**bless'-ed·ness** *n.*

bless'ing *n.* 1. invocation or benediction 2. a grace said before or after eating 3. good wishes or approval 4. anything that gives happiness

blew (blōō) *pt. of* BLOW

blight (blīt) *n.* [? < ME. *bliknen*, to lose color] 1. any insect, disease, etc. that destroys plants 2. anything that destroys, frustrates, etc. —*vt.* 1. to wither 2. to destroy

blimp (blimp) *n.* [Colloq.] a small nonrigid or semirigid airship

blind (blīnd) *adj.* [OE.] 1. without the power of sight 2. of or for sightless persons 3. lacking insight 4. hard to see; hidden 5. closed at one end [a *blind* alley] 6. not controlled by reason [*blind* fate] 7. Aeron. by the use of instruments only [*blind* flying] —*vt.* 1. to make sightless 2. to dazzle 3. to deprive of insight —*n.* 1. anything that obscures sight or keeps out light, as a window shade 2. a place of concealment 3. a decoy —**blind'ly** *adv.* —**blind'ness** *n.*

blind date [Colloq.] 1. a date with a stranger, arranged by a third person 2. either person involved

blind'fold' (-fōld') *vt.* [< ME. *blindfeld*, struck blind] to cover the eyes of, as with a cloth —*n.* a cloth used to cover the eyes —*adj.* 1. with the eyes covered 2. reckless

blink (blink) *vi.* [< ME. *blenchen*] 1. to wink one or more times 2. to flash on and off 3. to ignore (with *at*) —*vt.* 1. to cause (eyes, light, etc.) to blink 2. to evade or avoid —*n.* 1. a blinking 2. a glimmer —**on the blink** [Slang] out of order

blink'er *n.* a flashing warning light

blintz (blints) *n.* [Yid. *blintse* < Russ. *blin*, pancake] a thin pancake rolled with a filling of cottage cheese, fruit, etc.

blip (blip) *n.* [echoic] a luminous image on an oscilloscope

bliss (blis) *n.* [< OE. *blithe*, blithe] 1. great happiness 2. spiritual joy — **bliss'ful** *adj.* —**bliss'ful·ly** *adv.* — **bliss'ful·ness** *n.*

blis·ter (blis'tər) *n.* [< ON. *blastr*] 1. a raised patch of skin, filled with watery matter and caused as by burning 2. anything like a blister —*vt.* 1. to raise blisters on 2. to lash with words —*vi.* to form blisters

blithe (blīth, blīth) *adj.* [OE.] gay; joyful: also **blithe'some** (-səm) — **blithe'ly** *adv.* —**blithe'ness** *n.*

blitz (blits) *n.* [< G. *blitz*, lightning] a sudden, destructive or overwhelming attack —*vt.* to subject to a blitz

bliz·zard (bliz'ərd) *n.* [< dial. *bliz*, violent blow + -ARD] a violent snowstorm with very cold winds

bloat (blōt) *vt.*, *vi.* [< ON. *blautr*, soft] 1. to swell, as with water or air 2. to puff up, as with pride

blob (bläb) *n.* [echoic] a small drop or spot —*vt.* blobbed, blob'bing to splash, as with blobs

bloc (bläk) *n.* [Fr. < LowG. *block*, log] a group of persons, nations, etc. combined for a common purpose

block (bläk) *n.* [see prec.] 1. a solid piece of wood, stone, metal, etc. 2. a heavy stand on which chopping, etc. is done 3. an auctioneer's platform 4. an obstruction or hindrance 5. a pulley in a frame 6. a city square 7. a group or row of buildings 8. a number of things regarded as a unit 9. *Printing* a piece of engraved wood, etc. with a design —*vt.* 1. to obstruct; hinder 2. to mount or mold on a block 3. to sketch roughly (often with *out*) —block'er *n.*

block·ade (blä kād') *n.* [prec. + -ADE] 1. a shutting off of a place by troops or ships to prevent passage 2. any strategic barrier —*vt.* -ad'ed, -ad'ing to subject to a blockade

block and tackle pulley blocks and ropes, used for lifting heavy objects

block'bust'ing *n.* [Colloq.] the inducing of owners to sell their homes out of fear that a minority group may move into their neighborhood

block grant a grant of Federal funds to a State or local government to fund a block of programs

block'head' *n.* a stupid person

block'house' *n.* 1. formerly, a wooden fort 2. a reinforced structure for observers, as of missile launchings

blond (bländ) *adj.* [Fr. < ? Gmc.] 1. having light-colored hair and skin 2. light-colored Also **blonde** —*n.* a blond person —**blonde** *n.fem.* — **blond'ness** *n.*

blood (blud) *n.* [OE. *blod*] 1. the red fluid circulating in the arteries and veins of animals 2. bloodshed 3. the essence of life; life 4. the sap of a

plant 5. passion, temperament, etc. 6. parental heritage; lineage 7. kinship 8. people, esp. youthful people —**bad blood** anger; hatred —**in cold blood** 1. with cruelty 2. deliberately

blood bank a supply of blood stored for future use in transfusion

blood count the number of red and white cells in a given unit of blood

blood'cur'dling (-kurd'liŋ) *adj.* very frightening; causing terror

blood'ed (-id) *adj.* 1. having (a specific kind of) blood [hot-*blooded*] 2. of fine breed

blood'hound' *n.* any of a breed of large, keen-scented tracking dogs

blood'less (-ləs) *adj.* 1. without bloodshed 2. anemic or pale 3. having little energy —**blood'less·ly** *adv.* — **blood'less·ness** *n.*

blood'mo·bile' (-mō bēl') *n.* a mobile unit for collecting blood from donors for blood banks

blood poisoning any of various diseases in which the blood contains infectious microorganisms

blood pressure the pressure of the blood against the blood-vessel walls

blood relation (or **relative**) a person related by birth

blood'shed' *n.* killing; slaughter

blood'shot' *adj.* tinged with red because small blood vessels are broken: said of the eyes

blood'suck'er *n.* an animal that sucks blood, esp. a leech

blood'thirst'y *adj.* murderous; cruel —**blood'thirst'i·ness** *n.*

blood vessel an artery, vein, or capillary

blood'y *adj.* -i·er, -i·est 1. of, containing, or covered with blood 2. involving bloodshed 3. bloodthirsty 4. [Brit. Slang] cursed; damned —*adv.* [Brit. Slang] very —*vt.* -ied, -y·ing to stain with blood —**blood'i·ly** *adv.* —**blood'i·ness** *n.*

bloom (blōōm) *n.* [< ON. *blomi*, flowers] 1. a flower; blossom 2. the state or time of flowering 3. a period of most health, vigor, etc. 4. a youthful, healthy glow 5. the powdery coating on some fruits and leaves —*vi.* 1. to blossom 2. to be at one's prime 3. to glow with health, etc.

bloom·ers (blōō'mərz) *n.pl.* [< Amelia *Bloomer*, U.S. feminist] a woman's underpants gathered above the knee

bloom'ing *adj.* 1. blossoming 2. flourishing 3. [Colloq.] complete

bloop·er (blōōp'ər) *n.* [< imitation of a vulgar noise] [Slang] 1. a stupid mistake 2. *Baseball* a fly that falls just beyond the infield for a hit

blos·som (bläs'əm) *n.* [OE. *blostma*] 1. a flower, esp. of a fruit-bearing plant 2. a state or time of flowering —*vi.* 1. to have or open into blossoms 2. to begin to flourish

blot (blät) *n.* [ME. < ?] 1. a spot or stain, esp. of ink 2. anything that spoils or mars 3. a moral stain —*vt.*

blot'ted, blot'ting 1. to spot; stain 2. to disgrace 3. to erase, obscure, or get rid of (with *out*) 4. to dry, as with blotting paper —*vi*. 1. to make blots 2. to become blotted 3. to be absorbent

blotch (bläch) *n*. [? < *prec*.] 1. a discoloration on the skin 2. any large blot or stain —*vt*. to mark with blotches —**blotch'y** *adj*. **-i·er**, **-i·est**

blot'ter *n*. 1. a piece of blotting paper 2. a book for recording events as they occur [a police *blotter*]

blotting paper a soft, absorbent paper used to dry a surface freshly written on in ink

blouse (blous) *n*. [Fr., workman's smock] 1. a shirtlike garment worn by women and children 2. a uniform coat worn by soldiers, etc. —*vi*., *vt*. **bloused, blous'ing** to gather in and drape at the waistline

blow¹ (blō) *vi*. **blew, blown** (blōn), **blow'ing** [OE. *blawan*] 1. to move with some force, as the wind 2. to send forth air, as with the mouth 3. to pant 4. to give sound by blowing 5. to spout water and air, as whales do 6. to be carried by the wind 7. to be stormy 8. to burst suddenly (often with *out*) 9. [Colloq.] to brag 10. [Slang] to leave —*vt*. 1. to force air from, into, onto, or through 2. to drive by blowing 3. to sound by blowing 4. to burst by an explosion (often with *up*) 5. to melt (a fuse, etc.) 6. [Colloq.] to spend (money) freely 7. [Slang] to leave 8. [Slang] to bungle —*n*. 1. a blowing 2. a blast or gale —**blow off** [Colloq.] to release emotions, as by shouting —**blow over** to pass over or by —**blow up** [Colloq.] to lose one's temper —**blow'er** *n*.

blow² (blō) *n*. [ME. *blowe*] 1. a hard hit, as with the fist 2. a sudden attack 3. a sudden calamity; shock —**come to blows** to begin fighting

blow³ (blō) *vi*. **blew, blown** (blōn), **blow'ing** [OE. *blowan*] to bloom

blow'-by-'blow *adj*. detailed; full

blow'-dry' *vt*. **-dried', -dry'ing** to dry (wet hair) with hot air blown from an electric device (**blow'-dry'er**)

blow'fly' *n*., *pl*. **-flies'** a fly that lays its eggs on meat, etc.

blow'gun' *n*. a long tube through which darts, etc. are blown

blow'out' *n*. 1. the bursting of a tire 2. [Slang] a party, banquet, etc.

blow'torch' *n*. a small gasoline torch that shoots out a hot flame

blow'up' *n*. 1. an explosion 2. an enlarged photograph 3. [Colloq.] an angry outburst

blow'y *adj*. **-i·er, -i·est** windy

blowz·y (blou'zē) *adj*. **-i·er, -i·est** < obs. *blouse* wench] slovenly: also **blows'y**

blub·ber (blub'ər) *n* [ME. *blober*, a bubble] the fat of the whale —*vi*. to weep loudly —**blub'ber·y** *adj*

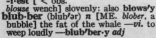

BLOWTORCH

blu·cher (bloo'chər, -kər) *n*. [< *von Blücher*, Prussian general (1742–1819)] a kind of shoe in which the vamp is of one piece with the tongue

bludg·eon (bluj'n) *n*. [? < MFr. *bouge*, club] a short club with a heavy end —*vt*., *vi*. 1. to strike with a bludgeon 2. to bully or coerce

blue (bloo) *adj*. [< Frank. *blao*] 1. of the color of the clear sky 2. livid: said of the skin 3. gloomy 4. puritanical [*blue* laws] 5. [Colloq.] indecent —*n*. 1. the color of the clear sky 2. any blue pigment 3. [*pl*.] [Colloq.] a depressed feeling (with *the*) 4. [*pl*.] Negro folk music having, usually, slow tempo, melancholy words, etc. (often with *the*) —**out of the blue** unexpectedly —**the blue** 1. the sky 2. the sea

blue baby a baby born with bluish skin, esp. because of a heart defect

blue'bell' *n*. any of various plants with blue, bell-shaped flowers

blue'ber'ry *n*., *pl*. **-ries** 1. a shrub bearing small, edible, blue-black berries 2. any of the berries

blue'bird' *n*. a small N.American songbird with a bluish back

blue blood an aristocrat: also **blue'-blood'** *n*. —**blue'-blood'ed** *adj*.

blue cheese a cheese like Roquefort

blue'-col'lar *adj*. designating or of industrial workers

blue'fish' *n*., *pl*.: see FISH a bluish food fish of the Atlantic coast

blue flu [from bluish police uniforms] a sickout, esp. by police officers

blue'gill' (-gil') *n*. a freshwater sunfish of a bluish color

blue'grass' *n*. a type of grass with bluish-green stems

blue'jack'et *n*. an enlisted man in the U.S. or British navy

blue jay a noisy, crested bird with a bluish upper part: also **blue'jay'** *n*.

blue law a puritanical law, esp. one prohibiting certain activities on Sunday

blue'nose' *n*. [Colloq.] a puritanical person

blue'-pen'cil *vt*. **-ciled** or **-cilled**, **-cil·ing** or **-cil·ling** to edit or correct with or as with a blue pencil

blue'-plate' special an inexpensive restaurant meal served at a fixed price

blue'point' *n*. [< *Blue Point*, Long Island] a small oyster, usually eaten raw

blue'print' *n*. 1. a photographic reproduction in white on a blue background, as of architectural plans 2. any detailed plan or outline —*vt*. to make a blueprint of

blue'stock'ing *n*. a bookish woman

blu·et (bloo'it) *n*. [< Fr. dim. of *bleu*, blue] a small plant with little, pale-blue flowers

bluff¹ (bluf) *vt*., *vi*. [prob. < Du. *bluffen*, to baffle] to mislead or frighten by a false, bold front —*n*. 1. a bluffing 2. one who bluffs: also **bluff'er** *n*.

bluff² (bluf) *adj*. [< Du. *blaf*, flat] 1. ascending steeply with a flat front 2. having a rough, frank manner —*n*. a high, steep bank or cliff

blu·ing (blōō′iŋ) *n.* a blue rinse used on white fabrics to prevent yellowing: also **blue′ing**

blu′ish (-ish) *adj.* somewhat blue: also **blue′ish**

blun·der (blun′dər) *vi.* [< ON. *blunda*, shut the eyes] **1.** to move clumsily **2.** to make a foolish mistake —*vt.* to do poorly —*n.* a foolish mistake —**blun′der·er** *n.*

blun′der·buss′ (-bus′) *n.* [Du. *donderbus*, thunder box] an obsolete short gun with a broad muzzle

blunt (blunt) *adj.* [< ?] **1.** having a dull edge, etc. **2.** plain-spoken —*vt.*, *vi.* to make or become dull —**blunt′ly** *adv.* —**blunt′ness** *n.*

blur (blur) *vt.*, *vi.* blurred, blur′ring [? akin to BLEAR(Y)] **1.** to smear; blot **2.** to make or become indistinct in shape, etc. **3.** to dim —*n.* **1.** an obscuring stain **2.** anything indistinct —**blur′ry** *adj.* —**blur′ri·ness** *n.*

blurb (blurb) *n.* [a coinage] [Colloq.] an exaggerated advertisement

blurt (blurt) *vt.* [prob. echoic] to say impulsively (with *out*)

blush (blush) *vi.* [< OE. *blyscan*, to shine] **1.** to become red in the face, as from embarrassment **2.** to be ashamed (*at* or *for*) **3.** to become rosy —*n.* **1.** a reddening of the face, as from shame **2.** a rosy color —*adj.* rosy —**at first blush** at first sight

blush′er *n.* **1.** a person who blushes readily **2.** a cosmetic cream, powder, etc. that gives color to the face

blus·ter (blus′tər) *vi.* [< LowG. *blüstern*] **1.** to blow stormily: said of wind **2.** to speak in a noisy or swaggering manner —*n.* **1.** noisy commotion **2.** noisy or swaggering talk —**blus′ter·er** *n.* —**blus′ter·y** *adj.*

blvd. boulevard

BM [Colloq.] bowel movement

BO, B.O. body odor

bo·a (bō′ə) *n.* [L.] **1.** a tropical snake that crushes its prey in its coils, as the python **2.** a woman's long scarf of fur or feathers

boar (bôr) *n.* [OE. *bar*] **1.** an uncastrated male pig **2.** a wild hog

board (bôrd) *n.* [OE. *bord*, plank] **1.** a long, flat piece of sawed wood **2.** a flat piece of wood, etc. for some special use *[a bulletin board]* **3.** pasteboard **4.** *a)* a table for meals *b)* meals, esp. as provided regularly for pay **5.** a group of administrators; council **6.** the side of a ship *[overboard]* —*vt.* **1.** to provide with meals, or room and meals, regularly for pay **2.** to come onto the deck of (a ship) **3.** to get on (a train, bus, etc.) —*vi.* to receive meals, or room and meals, regularly for pay —**board up** to cover with boards —**on board** on a ship, aircraft, etc. —**the boards** the stage (of a theater) —**board′er** *n.*

board′ing·house′ *n.* a house where meals, or room and meals, can be had for pay: also **boarding house**

board′walk′ *n.* a walk made of thick boards, esp. one along a beach

boast (bōst) *vi.* [< Anglo-Fr.] to talk, esp. about oneself, with too much pride; brag —*vt.* to brag about or glory in —*n.* **1.** a boasting **2.** anything boasted of —**boast′er** *n.* —**boast′ful** *adj.* —**boast′ful·ly** *adv.*

boat (bōt) *n.* [OE. *bat*] **1.** a small, open watercraft **2.** loosely, a ship **3.** a boat-shaped dish —**in the same boat** in the same unfavorable situation —**rock the boat** [Colloq.] to disturb the status quo —**boat′man** (-mən) *n., pl.* **-men**

boat′er *n.* a stiff straw hat with a flat crown and brim

boat′ing *n.* rowing, sailing, etc.

boat·swain (bōs′n) *n.* a ship's petty officer in charge of the deck crew, the rigging, anchors, etc.

bob (bäb) *n.* [ME. *bobbe*, hanging cluster; 3 & 4 < *the v.*] **1.** any knoblike hanging weight **2.** a woman's or girl's short haircut **3.** a quick, jerky motion **4.** a float on a fishing line —*vt.* bobbed, bob′bing [ME. *bobben*, knock against] **1.** to make move with a jerky motion **2.** to cut (hair, etc.) short —*vi.* to move with a jerky motion —**bob up** to appear suddenly

bob·bin (bäb′in) *n.* [< Fr. *bobiner*, to wind] a spool for thread, etc. used in spinning, machine sewing, etc.

bob·ble (bäb″l) *n.* [Colloq.] *Sports* an awkward juggling of the ball —*vt.* **-bled, -bling** [Colloq.] to make a bobble with

bob·by (bäb′ē) *n., pl.* **-bies** [after Sir Robert (*Bobby*) Peel (1788–1850), who reorganized the London police force] [Brit. Colloq.] a policeman

bobby pin [from use with *bobbed* hair] a small metal hairpin with the sides pressing close together

bobby socks (or **sox**) [< BOB (*vt.* 2)] [Colloq.] girls' ankle-length socks

bob′by-sox′er, bob′by·sox′er (-säk′sər) *n.* [Colloq.] a girl in her teens

bob′cat′ *n.* a wildcat of the E U.S.

bob·o·link (bäb′ə liŋk′) *n.* [echoic] a migratory songbird of N.America

bob′sled′ *n.* a long racing sled —*vi.* **-sled′ded, -sled′ding** to ride or race on a bobsled

bob·white (bäb′hwīt′) *n.* [echoic] a small N.American quail

Boc·cac·cio (bō kä′chē ō′), **Gio·van·ni** (jô vän′nē) 1313–75; It. writer

boc·cie, boc·ce, boc·ci (bäch′ē) *n.* [It. *bocce*, (wooden) balls] an Italian game like bowls

bock (beer) (bäk) [< *Einbeck*, Ger. city where first brewed] a dark beer

bode[1] (bōd) *vt.* bod′ed, bod′ing [< OE. *boda*, messenger] to be an omen of —**bode ill** (or **well**) to be a bad (or good) omen

bode[2] (bōd) *alt. pt.* of BIDE

bod·ice (bäd′is) *n.* [alt. < *bodies*, pl. of BODY] the upper part of a dress

bod·i·ly (bäd′'l ē) *adj.* **1.** physical

2. of, in, or to the body —*adv.* 1. in person 2. as a single group

bod·kin (bäd′k'n) *n.* [ME. *bodekin* < ?] 1. a pointed instrument for making holes in cloth 2. a thick, blunt needle 3. [Obs.] a dagger

bod·y (bäd′ē) *n.*, *pl.* -ies [OE. *bodig*, cask] 1. the whole physical substance of a man, animal, or plant 2. the trunk of a man or animal 3. a corpse 4. [Colloq.] a person 5. a distinct mass [a *body* of water] 6. a distinct group of people or things 7. the main part 8. substance or consistency, as of liquid 9. richness of flavor

bod·y·guard *n.* a person or persons assigned to guard someone

body language gestures, unconscious bodily movements, etc. which function as a means of communication

body stocking a tightfitting garment, usually of one piece, that covers the torso and, sometimes, the legs

bod·y·suit *n.* a one-piece, tightfitting garment that covers the torso, usually worn with slacks, a skirt, etc.

Boer (bôr, boor) *n.* [Du. *boer*, peasant] a South African of Dutch descent

bog (bäg, bôg) *n.* [< Gael. & Ir. *bog*, soft, moist] wet, spongy ground; a small marsh —*vt.*, *vi.* bogged, bog′ging to sink in or as in a bog (often with *down*) —bog′gy *adj.*

bo·gey (bō′gē) *n.*, *pl.* -geys 1. same as BOGY 2. [after an imaginary Colonel *Bogey*] *Golf* one stroke more than par on a hole: also bo′gie

bog·gle (bäg″'l) *vi.* -gled, -gling [< Scot. *bogle*, specter] 1. to be startled (*at*) 2. to hesitate (*at*) —*vt.* to confuse (the mind, imagination, etc.)

Bo·go·tá (bō′gə tä′) capital of Colombia: pop. 1,697,000

bo·gus (bō′gəs) *adj.* [< ?] not genuine; spurious; counterfeit

bo·gy (bō′gē, boog′ē) *n.*, *pl.* -gies [< Scot. *bogle*, specter] an imaginary evil spirit; goblin: also bo′gie

bo·gy·man, bo·gey·man (bō′gē man′, boog′ē-) *n.*, *pl.* -men′ an imaginary frightful being

Bo·he·mi·a (bō hē′mē ə) region of W Czechoslovakia: a former kingdom

Bo·he·mi·an *n.* 1. a native of Bohemia 2. same as CZECH (*n.* 2) 3. [*often* b-] one who lives unconventionally —*adj.* 1. of Bohemia, its people, etc. 2. [*often* b-] like a Bohemian (*n.* 3) —Bo·he′mi·an·ism *n.*

boil[1] (boil) *vi.* [< L. *bulla*, a bubble] 1. to bubble up and vaporize by being heated 2. to seethe like boiling liquids 3. to be agitated, as with rage 4. to cook in boiling liquid —*vt.* 1. to heat to the boiling point 2. to cook in boiling liquid —*n.* the act or state of boiling —boil down 1. to lessen in quantity by boiling 2. to condense

boil[2] (boil) *n.* [OE. *byle*] an inflamed, painful, pus-filled swelling on the skin

boil′er *n.* 1. a container in which to boil things 2. a tank in which water is turned to steam 3. a tank for heating water and storing it

Boi·se (boi′sē, -zē) capital of Idaho: pop. 102,000

bois·ter·ous (bois′tər əs) *adj.* [ME. *boistrous*, crude] 1. rough and stormy; turbulent 2. loud and exuberant; rowdy —bois′ter·ous·ly *adv.*

bok choy (bäk choi) [Chin.] a cabbagelike plant with long, narrow leaves

bold (bōld) *adj.* [OE. *beald*] 1. daring; fearless 2. too free in manner; impudent 3. steep 4. prominent and clear —bold′ly *adv.* —bold′ness *n.*

bold′faced′ (-fāst′) *adj.* impudent

bole (bōl) *n.* [ON. *bolr*] a tree trunk

bo·le·ro (bə ler′ō) *n.*, *pl.* -ros [Sp.: see BOIL[1]] 1. a lively Spanish dance, or music for it 2. a short, open vest

Bol·í·var (bäl′ə vər), **Si·món** (sī′mən) 1783-1830; S.American revolutionary

Bo·liv·i·a (bə liv′ē ə) country in WC S.America: 424,000 sq. mi.; pop. 3,748,000 —Bo·liv′i·an *adj.*, *n.*

boll (bōl) *n.* [ME. *bolle*, bowl] the pod of a plant, esp. of cotton or flax

boll weevil a small weevil whose larvae destroy cotton bolls

bo·lo·gna (bə lō′nē) *n.* [< *Bologna*, It. city] a large, smoked sausage of beef, pork, or veal

Bol·she·vik (bäl′shə vik′, bäl′-) *n.*, *pl.* -viks′, -vi′ki (-vē′kē) [Russ. < *bolshe*, the majority] [*also* b-] 1. a member of a majority faction that came into power in Russia in 1917 2. a Communist, esp. of the Soviet Union —Bol′she·vism *n.* —Bol′she·vist *n.*, *adj.*

bol·ster (bōl′stər) *n.* [OE.] 1. a long, narrow pillow 2. any bolsterlike object or support —*vt.* to prop up as with a bolster (often with *up*)

bolt[1] (bōlt) *n.* [OE.] 1. a short, blunt arrow used with a crossbow 2. a flash of lightning 3. a sudden dash 4. a sliding bar for locking a door, etc. 5. a threaded metal rod used with a nut to hold parts together 6. a roll (of cloth, paper, etc.) —*vt.* 1. to say suddenly; blurt (*out*) 2. to swallow (food) hurriedly 3. to fasten as with a bolt 4. to abandon (a party, group, etc.) —*vi.* 1. to start suddenly; spring away 2. to withdraw support from one's party, etc. —*adv.* erectly [to sit *bolt* upright]

bolt[2] (bōlt) *vt.* [< OFr. *buleter*] to sift (flour, grain, etc.)

bo·lus (bō′ləs) *n.* [< Gr. *bōlos*] 1. a small, round lump 2. a large pill

bomb (bäm) *n.* [< Gr. *bombos*, hollow sound] 1. an explosive, incendiary, or chemical-filled container for dropping, hurling, etc. 2. a small container with compressed gas in it 3. [Slang] a complete failure —*vt.* to attack with bombs —*vi.* [Slang] to have a failure

bom·bard (bäm bärd′) *vt.* [< Fr. *bombarde*, mortar] 1. to attack with artillery or bombs 2. to attack with questions, etc. 3. to direct particles against the atomic nuclei of (an element) —bom·bard′ment *n.*

bom·bar·dier (bäm′bə dir′) *n.* one who releases the bombs in a bomber

bom·bast (bäm′bast) *n.* [< Per. *pambak*, cotton] high-sounding, pom-

pous language —**bom·bas′tic** *adj.* —
bom·bas′ti·cal·ly *adv.*

Bom·bay (bäm′bā′) seaport in W
India: pop. 2,772,000

bomb·er (bäm′ər) *n.* **1.** an airplane
for dropping bombs **2.** one who bombs

bomb′shell′ *n.* **1.** a bomb **2.** any
sudden, shocking surprise

bo·na fi·de (bō′nə fīd′ *or* fī′dē) [L.]
in good faith; without fraud

bo·nan·za (bə nan′zə) *n.* [Sp., pros-
perity] **1.** a rich vein of ore **2.** any
source of wealth

Bo·na·parte (bō′nə pärt′) *see* NA-
POLEON I

bon·bon (bän′bän′) *n.* [< Fr. *bon*,
good] a small piece of candy

bond (bänd) *n.* [ult. < Gothic *bindan*,
bind] **1.** anything that binds, fastens,
or unites **2.** [*pl.*] shackles **3.** a binding
agreement **4.** an obligation imposed
by a contract, promise, etc. **5.** the
status of goods kept in a warehouse
until taxes are paid **6.** an interest-
bearing certificate issued by a government or business, redeemable on a
specified date **7.** *a)* surety against
theft, absconding, etc. *b)* an amount
paid as surety or bail —*vt.* **1.** to join;
bind **2.** to furnish a bond (*n.* 7 *a*) for
3. to place or hold (goods) in bond

bond·age (bän′dij) *n.* [ult. < ON.
bua, inhabit] serfdom or slavery

bond′man (-mən) *n., pl.* -**men 1.**
a serf **2.** a slave —**bond′wom′an**
n.fem., pl. -**wom′en**

bonds·man (bändz′mən) *n., pl.*
-**men 1.** *same as* BONDMAN **2.** one
who furnishes bond (*n.* 7)

bone (bōn) *n.* [OE. *ban*] **1.** any of the
parts of hard tissue forming the skeleton of most vertebrates **2.** this hard
tissue **3.** a bonelike substance or thing
—*vt.* **boned, bon′ing** to remove the
bones from —*vi.* [Slang] to study hard
(usually with *up*) —**have a bone to
pick** to have cause to quarrel —**make
no bones about** [Colloq.] to admit
freely —**bone′less** *adj.*

bone china translucent china made
of white clay to which the ash of
burned bones has been added

bone′-dry′ *adj.* very dry

bone meal crushed or ground bones,
used as feed or fertilizer

bon·er (bōn′ər) *n.* [Slang] a blunder

bon·fire (bän′fīr′) *n.* [ME. *banefyre*,
bone fire, pyre] an outdoor fire

bong (bôŋ, bäŋ) *n.* [echoic] a deep
ringing sound, as of a large bell
—*vi.* to make this sound

bon·go (bäŋ′gō) *n., pl.* -**gos** [AmSp.
< ?] either of a pair
of small drums of dif-
ferent pitch struck
with the fingers: in
full **bongo drum**

bo·ni·to (bə nēt′ō)
n., pl. -**tos, -toes**
[Sp.] any of several
saltwater food fishes
related to the tuna

BONGO DRUM

‡**bon·jour** (bôn zhōōr′) *interj., n.*
[Fr.] good day; hello

bon mot (bän′ mō′) *pl.* **bons mots**
(bōn′ mōz′) [Fr., lit., good word] a
clever or witty remark

Bonn (bän) capital of West Germany,
on the Rhine: pop. 142,000

bon·net (bän′it) *n.* [< OFr. *bonet*]
a hat with a chin ribbon, worn by
children and women

bon·ny, bon·nie (bän′ē) *adj.* -**ni·er,
-ni·est** [< L. *bonus*, good] [Chiefly
Scot.] **1.** handsome or pretty, with a
healthy glow **2.** pleasant

bon·sai (bän sī′) *n., pl.* -**sai′** [Jap.]
a tree or shrub grown in a pot and
dwarfed by pruning, etc.

bo·nus (bō′nəs) *n., pl.* -**nus·es** [L.,
good] anything given in addition to
the customary or required amount

bon voy·age (bän′ voi äzh′) [Fr.]
pleasant journey

bon·y (bō′nē) *adj.* -**i·er, -i·est 1.** of,
like, or having bones **2.** thin; emaciated —**bon′i·ness** *n.*

boo (bōō) *interj., n.* **boos** a sound
made to express disapproval, etc., or
to startle —*vi., vt.* **booed, boo′ing** to
shout "boo" (at)

boo-boo, boo·boo (bōō′bōō′) *n., pl.*
-**boos′** [Slang] a stupid mistake

boob tube [Slang] TV or a TV set

boo·by (bōō′bē) *n., pl.* -**bies** [prob. <
Sp. *bobo*] a fool; nitwit: also **boob**
(bōōb)

booby trap any scheme or device for
tricking a person unawares

boo·dle (bōō′d'l) *n.* [? < Du. *boedel*,
property] [Slang] **1.** something given
as a bribe; graft **2.** loot

book (book) *n.* [OE. *boc*] **1.** a printed
work on sheets of paper bound to-
gether, usually between hard covers
2. a main division of a literary work
3. a record or account **4.** a libretto
5. a booklike package, as of matches
—*vt.* **1.** to record in a book· list
2. to engage (rooms, etc.) ahead of
time —**by the book** according to the
rules —**the (Good) Book** the Bible

book′bind′ing *n.* the art or work of
binding books —**book′bind′er** *n.* —
book′bind′er·y *n., pl.* -**ies**

book′case′ (-kās′) *n.* a set of shelves
for holding books

book′end′ *n.* a weight or bracket that
keeps a row of books upright

book·ie (-ē) *n.* [Slang] a bookmaker

book′ing *n.* an engagement, as for a
lecture, performance, etc.

book′ish (-ish) *adj.* **1.** inclined to
read and study **2.** pedantic

book′keep′ing *n.* the work of keeping a systematic record of business
transactions —**book′keep′er** *n.*

book′let (-lit) *n.* a small book

book′mak′er *n.* a person in the business of taking bets, as on horses

book′mark′ *n.* a thing put between
the pages of a book to mark the place

book matches safety matches of
paper fastened in a cardboard holder

book'mo·bile' (-mō bēl') n. a lending library traveling in a truck, etc.

book'shelf' n., pl. **-shelves'** a shelf on which books are kept

book'store' n. a store where books are sold: also **book'shop'**

book'worm' n. 1. an insect larva that feeds on the binding, paste, etc. of books 2. one who reads much

boom[1] (bōōm) vi., vt. [echoic] to make, or say with, a deep hollow sound —n. this sound

boom[2] (bōōm) n. [Du., a beam] 1. a spar extending from a mast to hold the bottom of a sail outstretched 2. a long beam extending as from an upright·for supporting and guiding anything lifted 3. a barrier, as of logs, to prevent floating logs from dispersing —vi. to sail at top speed

boom[3] (bōōm) vi. [< ? prec. vi.] to increase or grow rapidly —vt. to cause to flourish; support —n. 1. swift growth 2. a period of prosperity

boom·er·ang (bōōm'ə raŋ') n. [< Australian native name] 1. a flat, curved stick that can be thrown so that it returns to the thrower 2. a scheme gone awry, to the schemer's harm —vi. to act as a boomerang

boon[1] (bōōn) n. [ON. bon, petition] a welcome benefit; blessing

boon[2] (bōōn) adj. [< L. bonus, good] merry; convivial: in **boon companion**

boon·docks, the (bōōn'däks) n.pl. [< native Philippine name] [Colloq.] 1. a jungle or wilderness 2. any remote rural region

boon·dog·gle (bōōn'dôg''l, -däg'-) vi. **-gled, -gling** [Colloq.] to do trifling, pointless work —n. trifling, pointless work —**boon'dog'gler** n.

boor (boor) n. [Du. boer, a peasant] a rude, awkward, ill-mannered person —**boor'ish** adj. —**boor'ish·ly** adv.

boost (bōōst) vt. [< ?] 1. to raise as by a push from below 2. to urge others to support 3. to increase —n. 1. a push upward or forward 2. an increase —**boost'er** n.

booster shot a later injection of a vaccine, for maintaining immunity

boot[1] (bōōt) n. [OFr. bote] 1. a covering of leather, rubber, etc. for the foot and part of the leg 2. a patch for the inside of a tire casing 3. a kick —vt. 1. to put boots on 2. to kick 3. [Slang] to dismiss 4. to bring a computer program from a disc into computer memory —**the boot** [Slang] dismissal

boot[2] (bōōt) n., vt., vi. [OE. bot, advantage] [Poet.] profit —**to boot** besides; in addition

boot'black' n. one whose work is shining shoes or boots

boot·ee, boot·ie (bōō tē'; for 2 bōōt'ē) n. 1. a short boot for women or children 2. a baby's knitted shoe

booth (bōōth) n., pl. **booths** (bōō thz) [< ON. bua, dwell] 1. a stall for selling goods 2. a small enclosure for voting at elections 3. a small structure to house a public telephone, etc.

boot'leg' vt., vi. **-legged', -leg'ging** [< hiding liquor in a boot] to make or sell (esp. liquor) illegally —adj. bootlegged; illegal —n. bootlegged liquor —**boot'leg'ger** n.

boot'less adj. [< BOOT[2]] useless

boo·ty (bōōt'ē) n., pl. **-ties** [MLowG. bute] 1. spoils of war 2. plunder

booze (bōōz) vi. **boozed, booz'ing** [Du. buisen] [Colloq.] to drink too much liquor —n. [Colloq.] liquor

bop (bäp) vt. **bopped, bop'ping** [Slang] to hit; punch

bo·rax (bôr'aks) n. [< Per. būrah] a white, crystalline salt used in glass, soaps, etc.

Bor·deaux (bôr dō') seaport in SW France: pop. 250,000

bor·der (bôr'dər) n. [< OHG. bord, margin] 1. an edge or part near an edge; margin 2. a dividing line between two countries, etc. 3. a narrow strip along an edge —vt. 1. to provide with a border 2. to extend along the edge of —adj. of or near a border —**border on** (or **upon**) to be next to

bor'der·land' n. 1. land near a border 2. a vague condition

bor'der·line' n. a boundary —adj. 1. on a boundary 2. indefinite

bore[1] (bôr) vt. **bored, bor'ing** [< OE. bor, auger] 1. to make a hole in with a drill, etc. 2. to make (a well, etc.) as by drilling 3. to weary by being dull —vi. to bore a hole or passage —n. 1. a hole made as by boring 2. a) the hollow part of a tube or gun barrel b) its inside diameter 3. a tiresome, dull person or thing —**bor'er** n.

bore[2] (bôr) pt. of BEAR[1]

bore·dom (bôr'dəm) n. the condition of being bored or uninterested

bo·ric acid (bôr'ik) a white crystalline compound, used as an antiseptic

born (bôrn) alt. pp. of BEAR[1] —adj. 1. brought into life 2. natural, as if from birth [a born athlete]

born'-a·gain' adj. professing a new or renewed faith or enthusiasm [a born-again Christian]

borne (bôrn) alt. pp. of BEAR[1]

Bor·ne·o (bôr'nē ō) large island in the Malay Archipelago

bo·ron (bôr'än) n. [< BORAX] a nonmetallic chemical element

bor·ough (bur'ō, bur'-) n. [OE. burg, town] 1. a self-governing, incorporated town 2. any of the five administrative units of New York City

bor·row (bär'ō, bôr'-) vt., vi. [OE. borgian] 1. to take or receive (something) intending to return it 2. to adopt (an idea, etc.) as one's own —**bor'row·er** n.

borsch (bôrsh) n. [Russ. borshch] beet soup, served usually with sour cream: also **borsht** (bôrsht)

bor·zoi (bôr'zoi) n. [Russ., swift] a large dog with a narrow head, long legs, and silky coat

bosh (bäsh) n., interj. [Turk., empty] [Colloq.] nonsense

bos·om (booz'əm, bōō'zəm) n. [OE. bosm] 1. the human breast 2. the breast regarded as the source of feelings 3. the interior; midst [the bosom of one's family] 4. the part of a garment that covers the breast —adj. close; intimate [a bosom friend]

bos'om·y (-ē) *adj.* having large breasts

boss¹ (bôs) *n.* [Du. *baas*, a master] 1. an employer or manager 2. one who controls a political organization —*vt.* 1. to act as boss of 2. [Colloq.] to order (a person) about —*adj.* [Slang] excellent

boss² (bôs, bäs) *n.* [OFr. *boce*, a swelling] a protruding ornament or projecting knob —*vt.* to stud

boss'ism *n.* control by bosses, esp. of a political machine or party

boss'y *adj.* -i·er, -i·est [Colloq.] domineering —**boss'i·ly** *adv.*

Bos·ton (bôs't'n, bäs'-) seaport and capital of Mass.: pop. 563,000 — **Bos·to'ni·an** (-tō'nē ən) *adj., n.*

bo·sun (bōs'n) *n.* *same as* BOATSWAIN

bot·a·ny (bät'n ē) *n.* [< Gr. *botanē*, a plant] the science that deals with plants and plant life —**bo·tan·i·cal** (bə tan'i k'l), **bo·tan'ic** *adj.* —**bot'a·nist** *n.*

botch (bäch) *vt.* [< ? Du. *botsen*, to patch] 1. to patch clumsily 2. to bungle —*n.* a bungled or unskilled piece of work

both (bōth) *adj., pron.* [OE. *ba tha*, both these] the two [*both* birds sang loudly] —*conj., adv.* together; equally [*both* tired and hungry]

both·er (bäth'ər) *vt., vi.* [prob. < *pother*] 1. to worry; harass 2. to concern (oneself) —*n.* 1. worry; trouble 2. one who gives trouble —**both'er·some** (-səm) *adj.*

Bot·swa·na (bät swä'nə) country in S Africa: 222,000 sq. mi.; pop. 576,000

Bot·ti·cel·li (bät'i chel'ē), **San·dro** (sän'drō) 1445?-1510; It. painter

bot·tle (bät''l) *n.* [< LL. *buttis*, a cask] 1. a narrow-necked container for liquids, usually of glass 2. its contents —*vt.* -tled, -tling to put into a bottle —**bottle up** to restrain —**hit the bottle** [Slang] to drink much alcoholic liquor —**bot'tler** *n.*

bot'tle·neck' *n.* 1. a narrow passage or road 2. any hindrance to movement or progress

bot·tom (bät'əm) *n.* [OE. *botm*, ground] 1. the lowest part or place 2. the part on which something rests 3. the side underneath 4. the seat of a chair 5. the ground beneath a body of water 6. basis; cause; source 7. [Colloq.] the buttocks —*adj.* lowest; last; basic —**at bottom** fundamentally —**bot'tom·less** *adj.*

bot·u·lism (bäch'ə liz'm) *n.* [< L. *botulus*, sausage] poisoning from the toxin produced by a bacillus sometimes found in improperly preserved foods

bou·doir (bōōd'wär) *n.* [< Fr., pouting room] a woman's private room

bouf·fant (bōō fänt') *adj.* [< Fr. *bouffer*, puff out] puffed out; full

bou·gain·vil·le·a, bou·gain·vil·lae·a (bōō'gən vil'ē ə) *n.* [ModL.] a woody tropical vine having large purple or red bracts

bough (bou) *n.* [OE. *bog*, shoulder] a main branch of a tree

bought (bôt) *pt. & pp.* of BUY

bouil·lon (bool'yän, -yən) *n.* [< Fr. *bouillir*, to boil] a clear broth

boul·der (bōl'dər) *n.* [< ME. *bulderstan*, noisy stone] a large rock worn by weather and water

boul·e·vard (bool'ə värd') *n.* [Fr. < MDu. *bolwerc*, bulwark] a broad street, often lined with trees

bounce (bouns) *vi.* **bounced, bounc·ing** [ME. *bounsen*, to thump] 1. to spring back, as upon impact; rebound 2. to spring; leap 3. [Slang] to be returned: said of a worthless check —*vt.* 1. to cause (a ball, etc.) to bounce 2. [Slang] to put (a person) out by force 3. [Slang] to fire from a job —*n.* 1. a bouncing; rebound 2. a leap or jump 3. capacity for bouncing 4. [Colloq.] energy, dash, etc. —**the bounce** [Slang] dismissal —**bounc'y** *adj.*

bounc·er (boun'sər) *n.* [Slang] a man hired to remove disorderly people from nightclubs, etc.

bounc'ing *adj.* big, healthy, etc.

bound¹ (bound) *vi.* [Fr. *bondir*, to leap] 1. to move with a leap or leaps 2. to bounce; rebound —*vt.* to cause to bound or bounce —*n.* 1. a jump; leap 2. a bounce; rebound

bound² (bound) *pt. & pp.* of BIND —*adj.* 1. tied 2. closely connected 3. certain [*bound* to win] 4. obliged 5. having a binding, as a book 6. [Colloq.] determined; resolved

bound³ (bound) *adj.* [< ON. *bua*, prepare] going; headed [*bound* east]

bound⁴ (bound) *n.* [< ML. *butina*] 1. a boundary 2. [*pl.*] an area near a boundary —*vt.* 1. to limit 2. to be a limit or boundary to 3. to name the boundaries of —**out of bounds** 1. beyond the boundaries 2. forbidden —**bound'less** *adj.* —**bound'less·ly** *adv.*

bound·a·ry (boun'drē, -dər ē) *n., pl.* -ries anything marking a limit; bound

bound'en (-dən) *adj.* [old pp. of BIND] 1. obligated 2. obligatory [one's *bounden* duty]

bound'er (-dər) *n.* [< BOUND¹] [Chiefly Brit. Colloq.] a cad

boun·te·ous (boun'tē əs) *adj.* [see ff.] 1. generous 2. abundant Also **boun'ti·ful** (-tə f'l)

boun'ty (-tē) *n., pl.* -ties [< L. *bonus*, good] 1. generosity 2. a generous gift 3. a reward or premium

bou·quet (bō kā', bōō-) *n.* [Fr.] 1. a bunch of flowers 2. aroma, as of wine

bour·bon (bur'bən, bōōr'-) *n.* [< *Bourbon* County, Ky.] [*sometimes* B-] a whiskey distilled from corn mash

bour·geois (boor zhwä') *n., pl.* -geois [Fr. < LL. *burgus*, castle] a member of the bourgeoisie —*adj.* of the bourgeoisie: used variously to mean commonplace, respectable, smug, etc.

bour·geoi·sie (boor'zhwä'zē') *n.* [with sing. or pl. v.] the social class between the very wealthy and the working class; middle class

bourn, bourne (bôrn, boorn) n. [OFr. *bunne*] [Archaic] 1. a limit; boundary 2. a goal

bout (bout) n. [ME. *bught*] 1. a struggle or contest 2. a period spent in some activity; spell

bou·tique (boo tēk′) n. [Fr. < Gr. *apothēkē*, storehouse] a small shop which sells fashionable articles

bou·ton·niere, bou·ton·nière (boot′′n ir′, -er′) n. [Fr., buttonhole] a flower worn in a buttonhole

bo·vine (bō′vīn, -vin) adj. [< L. *bos, ox*] 1. of an ox or cow 2. slow, stupid, etc. —n. an ox, cow, etc.

bow[1] (bou) vi. [< OE. *bugan*, to bend] 1. to bend the head or body in respect, agreement, etc. 2. to submit; yield —vt. 1. to bend (the head or body) in agreement, etc. 2. to weigh (*down*) —n. a bending of the head or body, as in greeting —**take a bow** to acknowledge applause, etc.

bow[2] (bō) n. [OE. *boga*] 1. anything curved [a *rainbow*] 2. a curve; bend 3. a flexible, curved strip of wood with a cord connecting the ends, for shooting arrows 4. a slender stick strung with horsehairs, for playing a violin, etc. 5. same as BOWKNOT —adj. curved —vt., vi. 1. to bend; curve 2. to play (a violin, etc.) with a bow

bow[3] (bou) n. [< LowG. *būg*] the front part of a ship, etc. —adj. of or near the bow

bowd·ler·ize (boud′lə rīz′) vt. -ized′, -iz′ing [< T. *Bowdler* (1754-1825), Eng. editor] to expurgate —bowd′-ler·ism n. —bowd′ler·i·za′tion n.

bow·el (bou′əl) n. [< L. *botulus*, sausage] 1. an intestine, esp. of a human being 2. [pl.] the inner part —**move one's bowels** to defecate

bow·er (bou′ər) n. [< OE. *bur*, dwelling] a place enclosed by boughs or vines; arbor

bow·ie knife (bōō′ē, bō′-) [< Col. J. *Bowie* (1799?-1836)] a long single-edged hunting knife

bow·knot (bō′nät′) n. a knot usually with two loops and two ends

bowl[1] (bōl) n. [OE. *bolla*] 1. a deep, rounded dish 2. a large drinking cup 3. a bowl-like thing or part 4. an amphitheater 5. the contents of a bowl

bowl[2] (bōl) n. [< L. *bulla*, a bubble] 1. a heavy ball used in the game of bowls 2. a roll of the ball in bowling —vi., vt. 1. to roll (a ball) or participate in bowling 2. to move swiftly and smoothly —**bowl over** 1. to knock over 2. [Colloq.] to astonish —**bowl′er** n.

bowl·der (bōl′dər) n. same as BOULDER

bow·leg (bō′leg′) n. a leg with outward curvature —**bow′leg′ged** (-leg′-id, -legd′) adj.

bowl·ing n. a game in which a heavy ball is bowled along a wooden lane (**bowling alley**) at ten wooden pins

bowls (bōlz) n. a bowling game played on a smooth lawn (**bowling green**)

bow·man (bō′mən) n., pl. -men an archer

bow·sprit (bou′sprit, bō′-) n. [prob. < Du.] a tapered spar extending forward from the bow of a sailing ship

bow tie (bō) a necktie tied in a bow

box[1] (bäks) n. [< Gr. *pyxos*, BOX[3]] 1. a container, usually rectangular and lidded; case 2. the contents of a box 3. a boxlike thing or space [a jury *box*] 4. a small, enclosed group of seats, as in a theater 5. a booth 6. *Baseball* an area designated for the batter, pitcher, etc. —vt. to put into a box —**box in** (or **up**) to shut in or keep in; surround or confine —**in a box** [Colloq.] in difficulty —**box′like′** adj.

box[2] (bäks) n. [< ?] a blow struck with the hand —vt. 1. to strike such a blow 2. to fight by boxing with —vi. to fight with the fists

box[3] (bäks) n. [< Gr. *pyxos*] an evergreen shrub with small leathery leaves: also **box′wood′**

box′car′ n. a fully enclosed railroad freight car

box′er n. 1. a man who boxes; prizefighter 2. a medium-sized dog with a sturdy body and a smooth coat

box′ing n. the skill or sport of fighting with the fists, esp. in padded leather mittens (**boxing gloves**)

box office 1. a place where admission tickets are sold, as in a theater 2. [Colloq.] the power, as of a performer, to attract a paying audience

boy (boi) n. [ME. *boie*] 1. a male child 2. any man: familiar term 3. a male servant: patronizing term —*interj.* [Slang] an exclamation of pleasure, surprise, awe, etc.: often **oh, boy!** —**boy′hood′** n. —**boy′ish** adj.

boy·cott (boi′kät) vt. [< Capt. *Boycott*, Irish land agent so treated] to join together in refusing to deal with, buy, etc. so as to punish or coerce —n. a boycotting

boy′friend′ n. [Colloq.] 1. a sweetheart or escort of a girl or woman 2. a boy who is one's friend

boy scout a member of the **Boy Scouts**, a boys' club that stresses outdoor life and service to others

boy·sen·ber·ry (boi′z'n ber′ē) n., pl. -ries [< R. *Boysen*, U.S. horticulturist] a berry that is a cross of the raspberry, loganberry, and blackberry

Br *Chem.* bromine

Br. 1. Britain 2. British

bra (brä) n. [< BRASSIERE] a brassiere

brace (brās) vt. braced, brac′ing [< Gr. *brachiōn*, arm] 1. to bind 2. to strengthen by supporting the weight of, etc. 3. to make ready for an impact, shock, etc. 4. to stimulate —n. 1. a couple; pair 2. a thing that clamps or connects 3. [pl.] [Brit.] suspenders 4. a device for setting up or maintaining tension 5. either of the signs { }, used to connect words, lines, etc. 6. any propping device 7. a) a device for supporting a weak part of the body b) [often pl.] a device worn for straightening the teeth 8. a tool for holding a

BOWIE KNIFE

drilling bit —**brace up** [Colloq.] to call forth one's courage, etc.

brace and bit a boring tool consisting of a removable drill (*bit*) in a rotating handle (*brace*)

brace·let (brās'lit) *n.* [< Gr. *brachiōn*, arm] an ornamental band or chain worn about the wrist or arm

brack·en (brak'ʼn) *n.* [ME. *braken*] a large, coarse, weedy fern found in meadows, woods, and wastelands

brack·et (brak'it) *n.* [< Fr. *brague*, knee pants] **1.** a support projecting from a wall, etc. **2.** any angle-shaped support **3.** either of the signs [ ], used to enclose a word, etc. **4.** a classification [high income *bracket*] —*vt.* **1.** to support with brackets **2.** to enclose within brackets **3.** to classify together

brack·ish (brak'ish) *adj.* [< MDu. *brak*] **1.** salty **2.** nauseating

bract (brakt) *n.* [L. *bractea*, thin metal plate] a modified leaf growing at the base of a flower or on its stalk

brad (brad) *n.* [ON. *broddr*, a spike] a thin wire nail with a small head

brae (brā) *n.* [ON. *bra*, brow] [Scot.] a sloping bank; hillside

brag (brag) *vt., vi.* **bragged, brag'ging** [prob. < OFr. *braguer*] to boast —*n.* boastful talk —**brag'ger** *n.*

brag'gart (-ərt) *n.* an offensively boastful person —*adj.* boastful

Brah·ma (brä'mə) the chief member of the Hindu trinity (Brahma, Vishnu, and Siva), regarded as the creator of the universe

Brah·man (brä'mən) *n., pl.* -mans [Hind. < Sans., worship] **1.** a member of the priestly Hindu caste **2.** a breed of domestic cattle related to the zebu of India

Brahms (brämz), **Jo·han·nes** (yō hän'əs) 1833–97; Ger. composer

braid (brād) *vt.* [< OE. *bregdan*, move quickly] **1.** to interweave three or more strands of (hair, straw, etc.) **2.** to make by such interweaving —*n.* **1.** a strip, as of hair, formed by braiding **2.** a woven band of cloth, etc., used to bind or decorate clothing

Braille (brāl) *n.* [< Louis *Braille*, its 19th-c. Fr. inventor] [*also* b-] a system of printing for the blind, using raised dots felt with the fingers

brain (brān) *n.* [OE. *brægen*] **1.** the mass of nerve tissue in the cranium of vertebrates **2.** [*often pl.*] intelligence —*vt.* to dash out the brains of

brain'child' *n.* [Colloq.] an idea, plan, etc. produced by one's mental labor

brain drain [Colloq.] an exhausting of the intellectual or professional resources of a country or region, esp. through emigration

brain'less *adj.* foolish or stupid

brain'storm' *n.* [Colloq.] a sudden inspiration or idea

brain'storm'ing *n.* the unrestrained offering of ideas by all members of a group to seek solutions to problems

brain'wash' *vt.* [Colloq.] to indoctri-

nate so thoroughly as to effect a radical change of beliefs

brain wave 1. rhythmic electric impulses from the nerve centers in the brain **2.** [Colloq.] a brainstorm

brain'y *adj.* -i·er, -i·est [Colloq.] having a good mind; intelligent

braise (brāz) *vt.* **braised, brais'ing** [< Fr. *braise*, live coals] to brown (meat) and then simmer slowly

brake (brāk) *n.* [< MLowG. *breken*, to break] any device for slowing or stopping a vehicle or machine, as by pressing a block or band against a moving part —*vt., vi.* **braked, brak'ing** to slow down or stop as with a brake —**brake'less** *adj.*

brake'man (-mən) *n., pl.* -men formerly, an operator of brakes on a railroad train, now, assistant to the conductor

bram·ble (bram'b'l) *n.* [< OE. *brom*, broom] a prickly shrub of the rose family, as the raspberry, blackberry, etc. —**bram'bly** *adj.*

bran (bran) *n.* [OFr. *bren*] the husk of grains of wheat, rye, etc. separated from the flour, as by sifting

branch (branch) *n.* [< LL. *branca*, a claw] **1.** any woody extension from a tree or shrub; limb **2.** a tributary stream **3.** any part or extension of a main body or system, as a division of a family or a separately located unit of a business —*vt.* **1.** to put forth branches **2.** to come out (*from* the main part) as a branch —**branch off 1.** to separate into branches **2.** to diverge —**branch out** to extend one's interests, activities, etc. —**branched** *adj.* —**branch'like'** *adj.*

brand (brand) *n.* [OE. < *biernan*, to burn] **1.** a burning or partially burned stick **2.** a mark burned on the skin, formerly used to punish criminals, now used on cattle to show ownership **3.** the iron used in branding **4.** a stigma **5.** *a*) an identifying mark or label *b*) the make of a commodity [a *brand* of tea] *c*) a special kind —*vt.* **1.** to mark with a brand **2.** to put a stigma on —**brand'er** *n.*

bran·dish (bran'dish) *vt.* [< Gmc. *brand*, sword] to wave menacingly or as a challenge; to flourish

brand name the name by which a certain brand or make of commodity is known —**brand'-name'** *adj.*

brand'-new' *adj.* [orig., fresh from the fire: see BRAND] entirely new

bran·dy (bran'dē) *n., pl.* -dies [< Du. *brandewijn*, distilled wine] an alcoholic liquor distilled from wine or from fermented fruit juice —*vt.* -died, -dy·ing to flavor or preserve with brandy

brash (brash) *adj.* [orig. Scot. < ?] **1.** hasty and reckless **2.** insolent; impudent —**brash'ness** *n.*

brass (bras) *n.* [OE. *bræs*] **1.** a yellowish metal, an alloy of copper and zinc **2.** [*often pl.*] brass-wind musical instru-

---

ments **3.** [Colloq.] bold impudence **4.** [Slang] officers or officials of high rank —*adj.* of brass —**brass′y** *adj.* **-i·er, -i·est**

bras·siere, bras·sière (brə zir′) *n.* [Fr. < *bras,* an arm] an undergarment worn by women to support the breasts

brass tacks [Colloq.] basic facts

brass winds musical instruments made of coiled metal tubes and having a cup-shaped mouthpiece, as the trumpet and tuba —**brass′-wind′** *adj.*

brat (brat) *n.* [< Gael. *bratt,* cloth, rag] a child, esp. an impudent, unruly child: scornful or playful term

brat·wurst (brat′wərst) *n.* [G. < OHG. *brato,* lean meat + *wurst,* sausage] highly spiced, fresh sausage of veal and pork

braun·schwei·ger (broun′shwī′gər) *n.* [< *Braunschweig,* Germany, where orig. made] smoked liver sausage

bra·va·do (brə vä′dō) *n.* [< Sp. < *bravo,* BRAVE] pretended courage or feigned confidence

brave (brāv) *adj.* [Fr. < It. *bravo*] **1.** not afraid; having courage **2.** having a fine appearance —*n.* **1.** any brave man **2.** a N. American Indian warrior —*vt.* **braved, brav′ing 1.** to face with courage **2.** to defy; dare —**brave′ly** *adv.* —**brave′ness** *n.*

brav·er·y (brā′vər ē) *n.* courage; valor

bra·vo (brä′vō) *interj.* [It.] well done! excellent! —*n.* a shout of "bravo"

bra·vu·ra (brə voor′ə) *n.* [It. < *bravo,* brave] **1.** bold daring; dash **2.** a brilliant musical passage or technique

brawl (brôl) *vi.* [< Du. *brallen,* to boast] to quarrel or fight noisily —*n.* a noisy quarrel or fight

brawn (brôn) *n.* [< OFr. *braon,* muscle] **1.** strong, well-developed muscles **2.** muscular strength —**brawn′i·ness** *n.* —**brawn′y** *adj.* **-i·er, -i·est**

bray (brā) *vi.* [< VL. *bragire,* cry out] to make the loud, harsh cry of a donkey —*n.* the harsh cry of a donkey, or a sound like this

braze (brāz) *vt.* **brazed, braz′ing** [Fr. *braser*] to solder with a metal having a high melting point

bra·zen (brā′z′n) *adj.* [< OE. *bræs,* brass] **1.** of brass **2.** like brass in color, etc. **3.** shameless; bold **4.** harsh and piercing —**brazen it out** to act in a bold, unashamed way —**bra′zen·ly** *adv.* —**bra′zen·ness** *n.*

bra·zier¹ (brā′zhər) *n.* [see BRAISE] a metal container to hold burning coals

bra·zier² (brā′zhər) *n.* [see BRASS] a person who works in brass

Bra·zil (brə zil′) country in C & NE S.America: c.3,287,000 sq. mi.; pop. 84,829,000 —**Bra·zil′ian** *adj., n.*

Brazil nut the edible, three-sided seed of a tree of S. America

breach (brēch) *n.* [< OE. *brecan,* to break] **1.** a failure to observe a law, promise, etc. **2.** an opening made by a breakthrough **3.** a break in friendship —*vt.* to make a breach in — **breach of promise** a breaking of a promise to marry

bread (bred) *n.* [OE., crumb] **1.** a

baked food made of flour or meal mixed with water, etc. **2.** livelihood / to earn one's *bread*] —*vt.* to coat with bread crumbs before cooking —**break bread** to eat

breadth (bredth) *n.* [< OE. *brad,* broad] **1.** width **2.** scope; extent

bread′win′ner *n.* one who supports dependents by his earnings

break (brāk) *vt.* **broke, bro′ken, break′ing** [OE. *brecan*] **1.** to split or crack into pieces; smash **2.** to cut open the surface of (soil, the skin, etc.) **3.** to make unusable by cracking, disrupting, etc. **4.** to tame as with force **5.** to get rid of (a habit) **6.** to demote **7.** to make poor, ill, bankrupt, etc. **8.** to surpass (a record) **9.** to violate (a promise, etc.) **10.** to disrupt the order of [to *break* ranks] **11.** to interrupt (a journey, electric circuit, etc.) **12.** to reduce the force of by interrupting (a fall, etc.) **13.** to bring to an end suddenly or by force **14.** to penetrate (silence, darkness, etc.) **15.** to disclose **16.** to decipher or solve [*break* a code] —*vi.* **1.** to 'split' into pieces; come apart **2.** to force one's way (*through* obstacles, etc.) **3.** to stop associating (*with*) **4.** to become unusable **5.** to change suddenly [his voice *broke*] **6.** to begin suddenly [to *break* into song] **7.** to come into being, notice, etc. [the story *broke*] **8.** to stop activity temporarily **9.** to suffer a collapse, as of spirit —*n.* **1.** a breaking **2.** a broken place **3.** a beginning or appearance [the *break* of day] **4.** an interruption of regularity **5.** an interval, gap, or rest **6.** a sudden change **7.** an escape **8.** [Slang] a chance piece of luck —**break down 1.** to go out of working order **2.** to have a physical or emotional collapse **3.** to analyze —**break in 1.** to enter forcibly **2.** to interrupt **3.** to train (a beginner) **4.** to work the stiffness out of —**break off** to stop abruptly — **break out 1.** to become covered with pimples, etc. **2.** to escape suddenly —**break up 1.** to separate; disperse **2.** to stop **3.** [Colloq.] to make laugh —**break′a·ble** *adj.*

break′age (-ij) *n.* **1.** a breaking **2.** things broken **3.** loss due to breaking **4.** the sum allowed for such loss

break′down′ *n.* **1.** a breaking down **2.** a failure of health **3.** an analysis

break′er *n.* **1.** a thing that breaks **2.** a wave that breaks into foam

break·fast (brek′fəst) *n.* the first meal of the day —*vi.* to eat breakfast

break·front (brāk′frunt′) *adj.* having a projecting center section in front —*n.* a breakfront cabinet

break′-in′ *n.* the act of forcibly entering a building, esp. in order to rob

break·neck (brāk′nek′) *adj.* highly dangerous [*breakneck* speed]

break′through′ *n.* **1.** the act of forcing a way through against resistance, as in warfare **2.** a very important advance or discovery

break′up′ *n.* **1.** a dispersion **2.** a disintegration **3.** a collapse

break′wa′ter *n.* a barrier to break

the impact of waves, as before a harbor

breast (brest) *n.* [OE. *breost*] **1.** either of two milk-secreting glands in a woman's body **2.** the upper, front part of the body **3.** the part of a garment, etc. over the breast **4.** the breast regarded as the center of emotions —*vt.* to face firmly; oppose

breast'bone' *n.* same as STERNUM

breast'-feed' *vt.* -fed', -feed'ing to feed (a baby) milk from the breast

breast'plate' *n.* a piece of armor for the breast

breast stroke a swimming stroke in which both arms are brought out sideways from the chest

breast'work' *n.* a low wall put up quickly as a defense in battle

breath (breth) *n.* [OE. *bræth*, odor] **1.** air taken into the lungs and then let out **2.** respiration **3.** the power to breathe easily **4.** life; spirit **5.** a fragrant odor **6.** a slight breeze **7.** a whisper; murmur —**below** (or **under**) **one's breath** in a whisper —**catch one's breath 1.** to gasp or pant **2.** to pause or rest —**out of breath** breathless, as from exertion —**take one's breath away** to thrill

breathe (brēth) *vi., vt.* breathed, **breath'ing 1.** to take (air) into the lungs and let it out again; inhale and exhale **2.** to live **3.** to speak or sing softly; whisper **4.** to rest —**breathe again** (or **freely**) to have a feeling of relief —**breath'a·ble** *adj.*

breath·er (brē'thər) *n.* **1.** one who breathes **2.** [Colloq.] a pause for rest

breath·less (breth'lis) *adj.* **1.** without breath **2.** panting; gasping **3.** unable to breathe easily because of emotion —**breath'less·ly** *adv.*

breath'tak'ing *adj.* very exciting

breath·y (breth'ē) *adj.* marked by an audible emission of breath

bred (bred) *pt. & pp. of* BREED

breech (brēch) *n.* [OE. *brec*] **1.** the buttocks **2.** the part of a gun behind the barrel

breech'cloth' *n.* same as LOINCLOTH

breech·es (brich'iz) *n.pl.* **1.** trousers reaching to the knees **2.** [Colloq.] any trousers

breed (brēd) *vt.* bred, breed'ing [< OE. *brod*, fetus] **1.** to bring forth (offspring) **2.** to be the source of; produce **3.** to raise (animals) **4.** to rear; train —*vi.* **1.** to be produced; originate **2.** to reproduce —*n.* **1.** a stock; strain **2.** a sort; type — **breed'er** *n.*

breed'ing *n.* **1.** the producing of young **2.** good upbringing **3.** the producing of plants and animals, esp. for improving the stock

breeze (brēz) *n.* [< Fr. *brise*] **1.** a gentle wind **2.** [Colloq.] a thing easy to do —*vi.* breezed, breez'ing [Slang] to move or go briskly

breeze'way' *n.* a covered passageway, as between a house and garage

breez·y (brēz'ē) *adj.* -i·er, -i·est **1.** having a breeze **2.** light and gay — **breez'i·ly** *adv.* —**breez'i·ness** *n.*

Bre·men (brem'ən; *G.* brā'mən) seaport in N West Germany: pop. 588,000

breth·ren (breth'rən) *n.pl.* [ME. *bretheren*] brothers: chiefly religious

bre·vet (brə vet') *n.* [< L. *brevis*, brief] *Mil.* a commission giving higher honorary rank without extra pay —*vt.* -vet'ted or -vet'ed, -vet'ting or -vet'ing to give a brevet to

bre·vi·ar·y (brē'vē er'ē) *n., pl.* -ies [< L. *brevis*, brief] a book of prayers, hymns, etc. to be recited daily by priests, nuns, etc.

brev·i·ty (brev'ə tē) *n.* [< L. *brevis*, brief] briefness

brew (brōō) *vt.* [OE. *breowan*] **1.** to make (beer, ale, etc.) from malt and hops by boiling and fermenting **2.** to steep (tea, etc.) **3.** to plot; scheme —*vi.* to begin to form —*n.* a beverage brewed —**brew'er** *n.*

brew·er·y (brōō'ər ē) *n., pl.* -ies a place where beer, etc. is brewed

Brezh·nev (brezh'nef), **Le·o·nid** (lā'ō nēt') 1906-82; general secretary of the Communist Party of the U.S.S.R. (1964-82)

bri·ar (brī'ər) *n.* same as BRIER

bribe (brīb) *n.* [< OFr. *briber*, beg] anything given or promised as an inducement, esp. to do something illegal or wrong —*vt.* bribed, brib'ing to offer or give a bribe to —**brib'er·y** *n.*

bric-a-brac (brik'ə brak') *n.* [< Fr. *à bric et à brac*, by hook or crook] **1.** small artistic objects used to ornament a room **2.** knickknacks

brick (brik) *n.* [< MDu. *breken*, piece of baked clay] **1.** an oblong block of baked clay, used in building, etc. **2.** anything shaped like a brick —*adj.* built or paved with brick —*vt.* to build or cover with brick

brick'bat' *n.* **1.** a piece of brick used as a missile **2.** an unfavorable remark

brick'lay'ing *n.* the work of building with bricks —**brick'lay'er** *n.*

brid·al (brīd''l) *n.* [< OE. *bryd ealo*, bride feast] a wedding —*adj.* **1.** of a bride **2.** of a wedding

bride (brīd) *n.* [OE. *bryd*] a woman just married or about to be married

bride'groom' *n.* [< OE. *bryd*, bride + *guma*, man] a man just married or about to be married

brides·maid (brīdz'mād') *n.* a young woman attending the bride during a wedding

bridge[1] (brij) *n.* [OE. *brycge*] **1.** a structure built over a river, etc. to provide a way across **2.** a thing that provides connection, contact, etc. **3.** the bony part of the nose **4.** a raised platform on a ship **5.** a mounting for false teeth —*vt.* bridged, bridg'ing to build or to make a bridge over —**burn one's bridges (behind one)** to follow a course from which there is no retreat —**bridge'a·ble** *adj.*

bridge² (brij) *n.* [< ? Russ.] a card game for two pairs of players in which they bid for the right to name the trump suit or declare no-trump

bridge′head′ *n.* a fortified position established by an attacking force in enemy territory

Bridge·port (brij′pôrt′) seaport in SW Conn.: pop. 143,000

bridge′work′ *n.* a dental bridge or bridges

bri·dle (brīd′'l) *n.* [< OE. *bregdan*, to pull] 1. a head harness for guiding a horse 2. anything that controls or restrains —*vt.* -dled, -dling 1. to put a bridle on 2. to curb or control —*vi.* to draw one's head back as an expression of anger, scorn, etc.

BRIDLE

bridle path a path for horseback riding

brief (brēf) *adj.* [< L. *brevis*] 1. short 2. concise —*n.* 1. a summary, specif. of the main points of a law case 2. [*pl.*] legless undershorts —*vt.* 1. to summarize 2. to supply with all pertinent information —**brief′ing** *n.* —**brief′ly** *adv.* —**brief′ness** *n.*

brief′case′ *n.* a flat, flexible case for carrying papers, books, etc.

bri·er¹ (brī′ər) *n.* [OE. *brer*] any thorny bush, as a bramble

bri·er² (brī′ər) *n.* [Fr. *bruyère*] a variety of heath, whose root is used for making tobacco pipes

brig (brig) *n.* 1. [< *brigantine*] a two-masted ship with square sails 2. [< ?] a prison on a warship

bri·gade (bri gād′) *n.* [< It. *briga*, strife] 1. a military unit composed of two or more battalions with service and administrative units 2. a group of people organized to function as a unit in some work [a fire *brigade*]

brig·a·dier general (brig′ə dir′) a military officer ranking just above a colonel

brig·and (brig′ənd) *n.* [see BRIGADE] a bandit, esp. one of a roving band

brig′and·age (-ən dij) *n.* 1. plundering by brigands 2. brigands collectively

brig·an·tine (brig′ən tēn′) *n.* [< It. *brigantino*, pirate vessel] a ship with the foremast square-rigged and a fore-and-aft mainsail

bright (brīt) *adj.* [OE. *bryht*] 1. shining with light 2. brilliant in color or sound; vivid 3. lively; cheerful 4. mentally quick; clever 5. favorable or hopeful 6. illustrious —**bright′ly** *adv.* —**bright′ness** *n.*

bright′en (-'n) *vt., vi.* to make or become bright or brighter

Brigh·ton (brīt′'n) resort city in S England: pop. 163,000

bril·liant (bril′yənt) *adj.* [< Fr. < It. *brillare*, to sparkle] 1. shining brightly 2. vivid 3. very splendid 4. very intelligent, talented, etc. —**bril′liance, bril′lian·cy** *n.* —**bril′liant·ly** *adv.*

bril·lian·tine (bril′yən tēn′) *n.* [< Fr.] an oily dressing for the hair

brim (brim) *n.* [OE., sea] 1. the topmost edge of a cup, glass, etc. 2. a projecting rim, as of a hat —*vt., vi.* **brimmed, brim′ming** to fill or be full to the brim —**brim′less** *adj.*

brim′ful′ *adj.* full to the brim

brim′stone′ *n.* [< OE. *biernan*, burn + *stan*, stone] sulfur

brin·dle (brin′d'l) *adj.* same as BRINDLED —*n.* a brindled color

brin′dled (-d'ld) *adj.* [prob. < ME. *brennen*, to burn] having a gray or tawny coat marked with darker streaks

brine (brīn) *n.* [OE.] 1. water full of salt 2. the ocean —**brin′y** *adj.*

bring (brin) *vt.* **brought, bring′ing** [OE. *bringan*] 1. to carry or lead "here" or to the place where the speaker will be 2. to cause to happen 3. to lead to an action or belief 4. to sell for —**bring about** to cause —**bring forth** to give birth to; produce —**bring off** to accomplish —**bring out** 1. to reveal 2. to offer (a play, book, etc.) to the public —**bring to** to revive (an unconscious person) —**bring up** 1. to rear (children) 2. to introduce, as into discussion 3. to cough or vomit up

brink (brink) *n.* [< MLowG. or Dan., shore] the edge, esp. at the top of a steep place; verge

brink′man·ship′ (-mən ship′) *n.* the policy of pursuing a risky course of action to the brink of disaster: also **brinks′man·ship′**

bri·oche (brē ōsh′) *n.* [Fr.] a light, rich roll made with flour, eggs, etc.

bri·quette, bri·quet (bri ket′) *n.* [Fr. < *brique*, brick] a brick of compressed coal dust, etc.

Bris·bane (briz′bān) seaport in E Australia: pop. 664,000

brisk (brisk) *adj.* [< ? Fr. *brusque*, brusque] 1. quick in manner; energetic 2. keen, bracing, etc. —**brisk′ly** *adv.* —**brisk′ness** *n.*

bris·ket (bris′kit) *n.* [ME. *brusket*] meat from the breast of an animal

bris·ling (bris′lin, briz′-) *n.* [Norw.] a small sprat canned as a sardine

bris·tle (bris′'l) *n.* [OE. *byrst*] any short, stiff hair —*vi.* -tled, -tling 1. to be stiff and erect 2. to have the bristles become erect 3. to become tense with fear, anger, etc. 4. to be thickly covered (*with*) —**bris′tly** (-lē) *adj.* -tli·er, -tli·est

Bris·tol (bris′t'l) seaport in SW England: pop. 434,000

Brit. 1. Britain 2. British

Brit·ain (brit′'n) same as GREAT BRITAIN

britch·es (brich′iz) *n.pl.* [Colloq.] same as BREECHES (sense 2)

Brit·i·cism (brit′ə siz′m) *n.* a word or idiom peculiar to the British

Brit·ish (brit′ish) *adj.* 1. of Great Britain or its people 2. of the British Commonwealth —*n.* English as spoken and written in England —**the British** the people of Great Britain

British Columbia province of SW Canada: 366,255 sq. mi.; pop. 1,629,000; cap. Victoria

British Commonwealth (of Nations) confederation of nations, including the United Kingdom, united under the British crown

British Isles group of islands including Great Britain, Ireland, etc.

British thermal unit a unit of heat equal to about 252 calories

Brit·on (brit′'n) n. 1. a member of an early Celtic people of S Britain 2. a native or inhabitant of Great Britain; esp., an Englishman

brit·tle (brit′'l) adj. [< OE. breotan, to break] easily broken or shattered —n. a brittle, crunchy candy with nuts in it —**brit′tle·ness** n.

bro. pl. **bros.** brother

broach (brōch) n. [< ML. brocca, spike] a tapered bit for boring holes —vt. 1. to make a hole in so as to let out liquid 2. to ream with a broach 3. to start a discussion of

broad (brôd) adj. [OE. brad] 1. of large extent from side to side; wide 2. extending across; full [broad daylight] 3. obvious [a broad hint] 4. tolerant; liberal [a broad view] 5. wide in range [a broad variety] 6. not detailed; general [in a broad sense] —**broad′ly** adv. —**broad′ness** n.

broad′cast′ (-kast′) vt., vi. -cast′ or -cast′ing, in radio, occas. -cast′ed, -cast′ing 1. to scatter or spread widely 2. to transmit by radio or television —vi. 1. widely scattered 2. of or for radio or television broadcasting —n. 1. a sowing by broadcasting 2. a radio or television program —adv. far and wide —**broad′cast′er** n.

broad′cloth′ n. a fine, smooth woolen, cotton, or silk cloth

broad′en (-'n) vt., vi. to widen

broad jump same as LONG JUMP

broad′loom′ adj. woven on a wide loom [broadloom carpeting]

broad′-mind′ed adj. tolerant of unconventional behavior, etc.; liberal —**broad′-mind′ed·ly** adv. —**broad′-mind′ed·ness** n.

broad′side′ n. 1. the side of a ship above the waterline 2. the firing of all guns on one side of a ship 3. a vigorous critical attack —adv. with the side facing

broad′-spec′trum adj. effective against a wide range of germs

broad′sword′ n. a broad-bladed sword for slashing

Broad′way′ (-wā′) street in New York City with many theaters, etc.

bro·cade (brō kād′) n. [< Sp. < It. broccare, embroider] a rich cloth with a raised design woven into it —vt. -cad′ed, -cad′ing to weave a raised design into (cloth)

broc·co·li (bräk′ə lē) n. [It. < ML. brocca, a spike] a kind of cauliflower with loose heads of tiny green buds

bro·chette (brō shet′) n. [Fr.] a skewer for broiling chunks of meat

bro·chure (brō shoor′) n. [Fr. < brocher, to stitch] a pamphlet

bro·gan (brō′g'n) n. [Ir.] a heavy work shoe, fitting high on the ankle

brogue¹ (brōg) n. [prob. < Ir. barróg, a grip] a dialectal pronunciation, esp. that of English by the Irish

brogue² (brōg) n. [< Ir. brōg, a shoe] a man's heavy oxford shoe

broil (broil) vt., vi. [< OFr. bruillir] to cook by exposure to direct heat —n. a broiling

broil′er n. 1. a pan, grill, etc. for broiling 2. a chicken fit for broiling

broke (brōk) pt. of BREAK —adj. [Colloq.] without money; bankrupt

bro·ken (brō′k'n) pp. of BREAK —adj. 1. splintered, fractured, etc. 2. not in working order 3. violated [a broken vow] 4. ruined 5. interrupted; discontinuous 6. imperfectly spoken 7. tamed —**bro′ken·ly** adv. —**bro′ken·ness** n.

bro′ken-down′ adj. 1. sick or worn out 2. out of order; useless

bro′ken·heart′ed adj. crushed by sorrow, grief, etc.

bro·ker (brō′kər) n. [< OFr. brokier, to tap; orig. sense "wine dealer"] a person hired as an agent in making contracts, selling stocks, etc.

bro′ker·age (-ij) n. 1. the business of a broker 2. a broker's fee

bro·mide (brō′mīd) n. 1. a compound of bromine with another element or a radical 2. potassium bromide, used as a sedative 3. a trite saying

bro·mid′ic (-mid′ik) adj. trite; dull

bro·mine (brō′mēn) n. [< Gr. brōmos, stench] a chemical element, a reddish-brown, corrosive liquid

bron·chi (bräŋ′kī) n.pl., sing. **-chus** (-kəs) [< Gr. bronchos, windpipe] the two main branches of the windpipe —**bron′chi·al** (-kē əl) adj.

bron·chi′tis (-kīt′is) n. inflammation of the bronchial tubes

bron·co (bräŋ′kō) n., pl. **-cos** [Sp., rough] a wild or only partly tamed horse or pony of the western U.S.: also **bron′cho**, pl. **-chos**

bron′co·bust′er n. [Colloq.] a tamer of broncos —**bron′co·bust′ing** n.

Bron·të (brän′tē) 1. **Charlotte**, 1816–55; Eng. novelist 2. **Emily**, 1818–48; Eng. novelist: sister of prec.

bron·to·sau·rus (brän′tə sôr′əs) n., pl. **-sau′rus·es**, **-sau′ri** (-ī) [< Gr. brontē, thunder + sauros, lizard] an extinct American dinosaur

Bronx (bräŋks) borough of New York City; pop. 1,169,000

bronze (bränz) n. [Fr., prob. ult. < Per. birinj, copper] 1. an alloy of copper and tin 2. a reddish-brown color —adj. of or like bronze —vt. **bronzed**, **bronz′ing** to make bronze in color

brooch (brōch) n. [see BROACH] a large ornamental pin with a clasp

brood (brood) n. [OE. brod] 1. a group of birds hatched at one time 2. the children in a family —vi. 1. to sit on and hatch eggs 2. to worry (often with on, over, or about)

brood'er n. 1. one that broods 2. a heated shelter for raising fowl

brook¹ (brook) n. [OE. *broc*] a small stream

brook² (brook) vt. [OE. *brucan*, to use] to put up with; endure

Brook·lyn (brook'lən) borough of New York City: pop. 2,231,000

brook trout a mottled stream trout of NE N. America

broom (broom, broom) n. [OE. *brom*, brushwood] 1. a flowering shrub of the legume family 2. a bundle of fibers or straws attached to a long handle (**broom'stick'**), used for sweeping

bros. brothers

broth (brôth) n. [OE.] a thin soup made by boiling meat, etc. in water

broth·el (brôth'əl) n. [< OE. *broethan*, go to ruin] a house of prostitution

broth·er (bruth'ər) n., pl. **-ers;** chiefly religious **breth'ren** [OE. *brothor*] 1. a male related to one by having the same parents 2. a friend who is like a brother 3. a fellow member of the same race, creed, profession, etc. 4. a lay member of a men's religious order

broth'er·hood' n. 1. the bond between brothers 2. an association of men united in some interest, work, etc.

broth'er-in-law' n., pl. **broth'ers-in-law'** 1. the brother of one's spouse 2. the husband of one's sister 3. the husband of the sister of one's spouse

broth'er·ly adj. 1. of or like a brother 2. friendly, kind, loyal, etc. —**broth'er·li·ness** n.

brougham (broom, broo'əm) n. [< Lord *Brougham* (1778–1868)] a closed carriage (or automobile) with the driver's seat outside

brought (brôt) pt. & pp. of BRING

brou·ha·ha (broo'hä hä') n. [Fr.] an uproar or commotion

brow (brou) n. [OE. *bru*] 1. the eyebrow 2. the forehead 3. the edge of a cliff

brow'beat' (-bēt')vt. **-beat', -beat'en, -beat'ing** to intimidate with harsh looks and talk; bully

brown (broun) adj. [OE. *brun*] 1. having the color of chocolate, a mixture of red, black, and yellow 2. tanned; dark-skinned —n. brown color —vt., vi. to make or become brown —**brown'ish** adj.

Brown (broun), **John** 1800–59; U.S. abolitionist: hanged for treason

brown'-bag' vt. **-bagged', -bag'-ging** to carry one's lunch to work or school, as in a brown paper bag

brown·ie (broun'ē) n. 1. a small, helpful elf in stories 2. a small bar cut from a flat chocolate cake

Brown·ing (broun'iŋ), **Robert** 1812–89; Eng. poet

brown'out' n. a turning off of some lights in a city, as during an electric power shortage

brown rice unpolished rice

brown'stone' n. a reddish-brown sandstone, used for building

brown study deep thought; reverie

brown sugar sugar whose crystals retain a brown coating of syrup

browse (brouz) n. [< OS. *brustian*, to sprout] leaves, shoots, etc. which animals feed on —vt., vi. **browsed, brows'ing** 1. to nibble at (leaves, shoots, etc.) 2. to examine (a book, articles for sale, etc.) in a casual way —**brows'er** n.

bru·in (broo'ən) n. [Du., brown] a bear

bruise (brooz) vt. **bruised, bruis'ing** [< OE. *brysan*, crush] 1. to injure and discolor (body tissue) without breaking the skin 2. to injure the surface of, causing spoilage, denting, etc. 3. to hurt (the feelings, spirit, etc.) —vi. 1. to bruise tissue, etc. 2. to be or become bruised —n. a bruised area, as of tissue

bruis'er n. a strong, pugnacious man

bruit (broot) vt. [< OFr., noise, rumor] to spread (*about*) by rumor

brunch (brunch) n. [Colloq.] a combined breakfast and lunch

bru·net (broo net') adj. [< OFr., dim. of *brun*, brown] having black or dark-brown hair, often with dark eyes and complexion —n. a brunet person

bru·nette' (-net') adj. same as BRUNET —n. a brunette woman or girl

Bruns·wick (brunz'wik) city in NC West Germany: pop. 239,000

brunt (brunt) n. [ME. *bront*] 1. the shock (of an attack) or impact (of a blow) 2. the hardest part

brush¹ (brush) n. [< OFr. *broce*, bush] 1. brushwood 2. sparsely settled country 3. a device for cleaning, painting, etc., having bristles, wires, etc. fastened into a back 4. a brushing 5. a light, grazing stroke 6. a bushy tail, as of a fox —vt. 1. to clean, paint, etc. as with a brush 2. to apply, remove, etc. as with a brush 3. to touch or graze in passing —vi. to graze past something —**brush up** to refresh one's memory

brush² (brush) vi. [ME. *bruschen*] to rush; hurry —n. a short, quick fight

brush'off' n. [Slang] curt dismissal: esp. in the phrase **give** (or **get**) **the brushoff**

brush'wood' n. 1. chopped-off tree branches 2. underbrush

brusque (brusk) adj. [< Fr. < ML. *bruscus*, brushwood] rough and abrupt in manner or speech; curt: also **brusk** —**brusque'ly** adv. —**brusque'ness** n.

Brus·sels (brus'lz) capital of Belgium: pop. (with suburbs) 1,058,000

Brussels sprouts 1. a plant that bears small cabbagelike heads on an erect stem 2. its edible heads

bru·tal (broot'l) adj. 1. like a brute; very savage, cruel, etc. 2. very harsh —**bru'tal·ly** adv.

bru·tal·i·ty (broo tal'ə tē) n. 1. a being brutal 2. pl. **-ties** a brutal act

BRUSSELS SPROUTS

bru·tal·ize (broot'l īz') vt. **-ized', -iz'ing** 1. to make brutal 2. to treat brutally —**bru′·tal·i·za′tion** n.

brute (broot) adj. [< L. brutus, irrational] 1. lacking the ability to reason [a brute beast.] 2. of or like an animal; specif., savage, stupid, etc. —n. 1. an animal 2. a brutal person —**brut′ish** adj. —**brut′ish·ly** adv.

B.S., B.Sc. Bachelor of Science

b.s. bill of sale

B.t.u. British thermal unit(s)

bu. bushel(s)

bub·ble (bub′'l) n. [echoic] 1. a film of liquid forming a ball around air or gas 2. a tiny ball of air or gas in a liquid or solid 3. a transparent dome 4. a plausible scheme that proves worthless —vi. **-bled, -bling** 1. to rise in bubbles; boil 2. to make a gurgling sound —**bub′bly** adj.

bubble gum a kind of chewing gum that can be blown into large bubbles

bubble memory a solid-state computer memory device that stores bits of data by means of magnetized, microscopic areas in sheets

bub′ble-top′ n. a bulletproof, transparent dome, as over an automobile

bu·bo (byoo′bo) n., pl. **-boes** [< Gr. boubon, groin] an inflamed swelling of a lymph gland, esp. in the groin

bu·bon′ic plague (-bän′ik) a contagious disease characterized by buboes, fever, and delirium

buc·ca·neer (buk′ə nir′) n. [< Fr. boucanier] a pirate

Bu·chan·an (byoo kan′ən), **James** 1791–1868; 15th president of the U.S. (1857–61)

Bu·cha·rest (boo′kə rest′) capital of Romania: pop. 1,511,000

buck¹ (buk) n. [OE. bucca, male goat] 1. a male deer, goat, etc. 2. the act of bucking 3. [Colloq.] a bold, vigorous young man —vi. 1. to rear upward quickly, as to throw off a rider: said of a horse 2. [Colloq.] to resist something as if plunging against it —vt. 1. to charge against, as in football 2. to throw by bucking 3. [Colloq.] to resist stubbornly —**buck for** [Slang] to work eagerly for (a promotion, raise, etc.) —**buck up** [Colloq.] to cheer up

buck² (buk) n. [Du. zaagbok] 1. a sawbuck; sawhorse 2. a gymnastic apparatus for vaulting over

buck³ (buk) n. [< ?] [Slang] a dollar —**pass the buck** [Colloq.] to throw the responsibility on another

buck′board′ n. [< ?] an open carriage whose floorboards rest directly on the axles

buck·et (buk′it) n. [< OE. buc, pitcher] 1. a cylindrical container with a curved handle, for carrying water, etc.; pail 2. the amount held by a bucket: also **buck′et·ful′**, pl. **-fuls′** 3. a thing like a bucket, as a scoop on a steam shovel —**kick the bucket** [Slang] to die

bucket seat a single contoured seat with a movable back, as in sports cars

buck·eye (buk′i′) n. [BUCK¹ + EYE¹: the appearance of the seed] 1. a horse chestnut with large burs enclosing shiny brown seeds 2. the seed

buck·le¹ (buk′'l) n. [< L. buccula, cheek strap of a helmet] a clasp for fastening a strap, belt, etc. —vt., vi. **-led, -ling** to fasten with a buckle —**buckle down** to apply oneself

buck·le² (buk′'l) vt., vi. **-led, -ling** [prob. < Du. bukken, to bend] to bend or crumple —n. a bend, bulge, etc.

buck·ler (buk′lər) n. [OFr. bocler] a small, round shield

buck′-pass′er n. [Colloq.] one who regularly shifts blame or responsibility to someone else —**buck′-pass′ing** n.

buck·ram (buk′rəm) n. [? < Bokhara, in Asia Minor] a coarse, stiff cloth used in bookbinding, etc.

buck·saw (buk′sô′) n. a wood-cutting saw set in a frame

buck′shot′ n. a large lead shot for shooting deer and other large game

buck′skin′ n. 1. a soft leather made from the skins of deer or sheep 2. [pl.] clothes made of buckskin

buck′tooth′ n., pl. **-teeth′** a projecting front tooth —**buck′toothed′** adj.

buck′wheat′ n. [< OE. boc-, BEECH + WHEAT] 1. a plant with beechnut-shaped seeds 2. a dark flour made from the seeds

bu·col·ic (byoo käl′ik) adj. [< Gr. boukolos, herdsman] 1. of shepherds; pastoral 2. rural; rustic —n. a pastoral poem —**bu·col′i·cal·ly** adv.

bud (bud) n. [ME. budde] 1. a small swelling on a plant, from which a shoot, leaf, or flower develops 2. an early stage of development —vi. **bud′ded, bud′ding** 1. to put forth buds 2. to begin to develop —**in (the) bud** 1. in a budding condition 2. in an early stage —**bud′like′** adj.

Bu·da·pest (boo′də pest′) capital of Hungary: pop. 1,900,000

Bud·dha (bood′ə) a religious leader who lived in India 563?–483? B.C.: founder of Buddhism

Bud·dhism (bood′iz'm) n. a religion of Asia teaching that by right living and right thinking one achieves Nirvana —**Bud′dhist** n., adj.

bud·dy (bud′ē) n., pl. **-dies** [< ? Brit. dial.] [Colloq.] a comrade

budge (buj) vt., vi. **budged, budg′ing** [Fr. bouger, to move] to move even a little

budg·er·i·gar (buj′ə ri gär′) n. [native name] a greenish-yellow Australian parakeet: also [Colloq.] **budg′ie**

budg·et (buj′it) n. [< L. bulga, bag] 1. a stock of items 2. a plan adjusting expenses to income 3. estimated cost of living, operating, etc. —vt. 1. to put on a budget 2. to plan [budget your time] —**budg′et·ar′y** adj.

Bue·nos Ai·res (bwā′nəs er′ēz) capital of Argentina: pop. 3,876,000

buff (buf) *n.* [< It. *bufalo*, buffalo]
1. a heavy, soft, brownish-yellow
leather 2. a military coat made of this
3. a dull brownish yellow 4. [Colloq.]
a devotee; fan —*adj.* 1. made of buff
2. of the color buff —*vt.* to clean or
shine with leather or a leather-covered
wheel —**in the buff** naked —**buff′er** *n.*

Buf·fa·lo (buf′ə lō′) city in W N.Y.,
on Lake Erie: pop. 358,000

buf·fa·lo (buf′ə lō′) *n., pl.* -**loes′**,
-**los′** [< It. → Gr. *bous*, ox] 1. any of
various wild oxen, as the water buffalo
of India 2. popularly, the American
bison —*vt.* -**loed′**, -**lo′ing** [Slang] to
baffle, bluff, etc.

buff·er (buf′ər) *n.* [< OFr. *buffe*, a
blow] 1. anything that lessens shock,
as of collision 2. a temporary storage
area in a computer, for data being
transferred to another device

buf·fet[1] (buf′it) *n.* [OFr. < *buffe*, a
blow] a blow or shock —*vt.* 1. to
punch; fight 2. to thrust about

buf·fet[2] (bə fā′, boo-) *n.* [Fr.] 1. a
sideboard 2. a sideboard or table at
which guests serve themselves food
3. a meal served thus

buf·foon (bə fōōn′) *n.* [< Fr. < It.
buffare, to jest] one who is always
trying to be funny; clown —**buf-
foon′er·y** *n.* —**buf·foon′ish** *adj.*

bug (bug) *n.* [? < ME. *bugge*] 1. an
insect with sucking mouth parts 2.
any insect 3. [Colloq.] a germ or virus
4. [Slang] a defect, as in a machine
5. [Slang] a hidden microphone —*vt.*
bugged, bug′ging [Slang] 1. to
annoy, anger, etc. 2. to hide a microphone in (a room, etc.)

bug′bear′ *n.* [< W. *bwg* + BEAR[2]] 1.
a bogy 2. a cause of needless fear Also
bug′a·boo′ (-ə bōō′) *n., pl.* -**boos′**

bug′-eyed′ *adj.* [Slang] with bulging
eyes

bug·gy (bug′ē) *n., pl.* -**gies** [< ?] 1.
a light, one-horse carriage with one
seat 2. a small carriage for a baby

bu·gle (byōō′g'l) *n.* [< L. *buculus*,
young ox] a brass-wind instrument like
a small trumpet, usually without
valves —*vi., vt.* -**gled, -gling** to
signal by blowing a bugle —**bu′gler** *n.*

build (bild) *vt.* **built** (bilt), **build′ing**
[< OE. *bold*, house] 1. to make by
putting together materials, parts, etc.;
construct 2. to establish; base [*build* a
theory on facts] 3. to create or
develop (often with *up*) —*vi.* 1. to
put up buildings 2. to grow or intensify (often with *up*) —*n.* the way
a thing is built or shaped [a stocky
build] —**build up** to make more attractive, healthy, etc. —**build′er** *n.*

build′ing *n.* 1. anything that is built;
structure 2. the work or business of
making houses, etc.

build·up′, build′-up′ *n.* [Colloq.]
1. favorable publicity or praise 2. a
gradual increase or expansion

built′-in′ *adj.* 1. made as part of
the structure 2. inherent

built′-up′ *adj.* 1. made higher,
stronger, etc. with added parts [*built-up*
heels] 2. having many buildings on it

bulb (bulb) *n.* [< Gr. *bolbos*] 1. an
underground bud with roots and a
short, scaly stem, as in a lily or onion
2. a tuber or tuberous root resembling
a bulb, as in a crocus 3. anything
shaped like a bulb [an electric light
bulb] —**bul′bous** *adj.*

Bul·gar·i·a (bul ger′ē ə) country in
SE Europe: 42,796 sq. mi.; pop.
8,230,000 —**Bul·gar′i·an** *adj., n.*

bulge (bulj) *n.* [< L. *bulga*, leather
bag] an outward swelling; protuberance —*vi., vt.* **bulged, bulg′ing** to
swell or bend outward —**bulg′y** *adj.*

bulk (bulk) *n.* [ON. *bulki*, a heap] 1.
size, mass, or volume, esp. if great
2. the main mass; largest part —*vi.* to
have, or to increase in, size or importance —*adj.* 1. total; aggregate 2. not
packaged —**bulk′y** *adj.* -**i·er**, -**i·est**

bulk·head (bulk′hed′) *n.* [< ON.
balkr, partition + HEAD] 1. an upright
partition, as in a ship, that is watertight, fireproof, etc. 2. a retaining wall
3. a boxlike structure over an opening

bull[1] (bool) *n.* [< OE. *bula*, a steer]
1. the adult male of any bovine animal,
as the ox, or of certain other large
animals, as the elephant, whale, etc.
2. a speculator who buys stocks expecting their prices to rise, or seeks
to bring about such a rise 3. [Slang]
insincere talk; nonsense —*adj.* 1. male
2. rising in price —**bull′ish** *adj.*

bull[2] (bool) *n.* [< LL. *bulla*, a seal]
an official document from the Pope

bull′dog′ *n.* a short-haired, square-
jawed, heavily built dog; like a
bulldog; stubborn —*vt.* -**dogged′**,
-**dog′ging** to throw (a steer) by holding its horns and twisting its neck

bull′doze′ (-dōz′) *vt.* -**dozed′**, -**doz′-
ing** [< *bull*, a flogging + DOSE] 1.
[Colloq.] to force or frighten by threatening; bully 2. to move, make level,
etc. with a bulldozer

bull′doz′er *n.* a tractor with a large
shovellike blade in front for pushing
earth, debris, etc.

bul·let (bool′it) *n.* [< L. *bulla*, a
knob] a small, shaped piece of lead,
steel, etc. to be shot from a firearm

bul·le·tin (bool′ət 'n) *n.* [< L. *bulla*,
a seal] 1. a brief statement of late
news 2. a regular publication, as of
an organization, etc.

bulletin board a board or wall on
which bulletins, notices, etc. are put up

bul′let·proof′ *adj.* that bullets cannot pierce —*vt.* to make bulletproof

bull′fight′ (-fīt′) *n.* a spectacle in
which a bull is provoked in various
ways and then killed with a sword by
the matador —**bull′fight′er** *n.*

bull′finch′ (-finch′) *n.* a small European songbird

bull′frog′ *n.* a large N.American frog
with a deep, loud croak

bull′head′ed (-hed′id) *adj.* stubborn; headstrong

bull′horn′ *n.* a portable electronic
voice amplifier

bul·lion (bool′yən) *n.* [< OFr. *billon*,
small coin] ingots of gold or silver

bull′ish *adj.* 1. of or like a bull
2. rising, or causing a rise, in price on
the stock exchange 3. optimistic

bull'ock (-ək) *n.* [< OE. dim. of *bula*, steer] a castrated bull; steer

bull'pen' (-pen') *n.* **1.** [Colloq.] a temporary detention room in a jail **2.** *Baseball* a practice area for relief pitchers

bull's-eye (boolz'ī') *n.* **1.** the central mark of a target **2.** a direct hit

bul·ly (bool'ē) *n., pl.* **-lies** [< MHG. *buole*, lover; infl. by BULL[1]] one who hurts or browbeats those who are weaker —*vt., vi.* **-lied, -ly·ing** to act the bully (toward) —*adj., interj.* [Colloq.] fine; good

bul·rush (bool'rush') *n.* [< OE. *bol*, tree trunk + *risc*, a rush] a tall plant of the sedge family, found in wet places

bul·wark (bool'wərk) *n.* [MDu. *bolwerc*] **1.** a defensive wall; rampart **2.** a defense; protection

bum (bum) *n.* [prob. < G. *bummeln*, go slowly] [Colloq.] **1.** a vagrant; loafer **2.** a devotee, as of golf or skiing —*vi.* **bummed, bum'ming** [Colloq.] to live as a bum or by begging —*vt.* [Slang] to get by begging [to *bum* a cigar] —*adj.* **bum'mer, bum'mest** [Slang] **1.** poor in quality **2.** false **3.** lame —**on the bum** [Colloq.] **1.** living as a vagrant **2.** out of repair

bum·ble·bee (bum'b'l bē') *n.* [< ME. *bomblen*, buzz] a large, hairy, yellow-and-black bee

bum'bling *adj.* [< obs. *bumble*, buzz] self-important in a blundering way

bum·mer (bum'ər) *n.* [Slang] an unpleasant experience, esp. with drugs

bump (bump) *vt., vi.* [echoic] **1.** to collide (with); hit against **2.** to move with jolts —*n.* **1.** a knock; light jolt **2.** a swelling, esp. one caused by a blow —**bump into** [Colloq.] to meet unexpectedly —**bump off** [Slang] to murder —**bump'y** *adj.*

bump'er[1] *n.* a device to absorb the shock of a collision; esp., a bar at the front or back of an automobile

bump'er[2] *n.* [prob. < *bombard*, liquor jug] a cup or glass filled to the brim —*adj.* unusually abundant [a *bumper* crop]

bumper sticker a slogan, witticism, etc. printed on gummed paper for sticking on an automobile bumper

bump·kin (bump'k'n) *n.* [prob. < MDu. *bommekijn*, small cask] an awkward or simple person from the country

bump'tious (-shəs) *adj.* [prob. < BUMP] disagreeably conceited or forward —**bump'tious·ly** *adv.*

bun (bun) *n.* [prob. < OFr. *buigne*, a swelling] **1.** a small roll, usually somewhat sweetened **2.** hair worn in a roll or knot

bunch (bunch) *n.* [< Fl. *boudje*, little bundle] **1.** a cluster of similar things growing or grouped together **2.** [Colloq.] a group of people —*vt., vi.* to collect into a bunch —**bunch'y** *adj.*

bun·combe (bun'kəm) *n.* [< *Buncombe* County, N.C., loquaciously represented in 16th Congress] [Colloq.] empty insincere talk: also **bunkum**

bun·dle (bun'd'l) *n.* [MDu. *bondel*] **1.** a number of things bound together **2.** a package **3.** a bunch; collection —*vt.* **-dled, -dling** **1.** to make into a bundle **2.** to hustle (*away, off, out,* or *into*) —**bundle up** to dress warmly

bung (bun) *n.* [< MDu. *bonge*] a stopper for a bunghole

bun·ga·low (bun'gə lō') *n.* [< Hind. *bānglā*, thatched house] a small, one-storied house or cottage

bung·hole (bun'hōl') *n.* a hole in a barrel or keg for pouring in or drawing out liquid

bun·gle (bun'g'l) *vt., vi.* **-gled, -gling** [< ?] to do clumsily; spoil; botch —*n.* **1.** a bungling **2.** a bungled piece of work —**bun'gler** *n.*

bun·ion (bun'yən) *n.* [prob. < OFr.: see BUN] an inflamed swelling at the base of the big toe

bunk[1] (bunk) *n.* [prob. < Scand. cognate of BENCH] **1.** a shelflike bed built against a wall, as in a ship **2.** [Colloq.] any sleeping place —*vi.* to sleep in a bunk —*vt.* to provide sleeping place for

bunk[2] (bunk) *n.* [Slang] buncombe

bunk'er *n.* [Scot. < ?] **1.** a large bin, as for a ship's fuel **2.** an underground fortification **3.** a mound serving as an obstacle on a golf course

bunk'house' *n.* a barracks for ranch hands, etc.

bun·ny (bun'ē) *n., pl.* **-nies** [dim. of dial. *bun*] a rabbit: a child's term

Bun·sen burner (bun's'n) [< R. W. *Bunsen*, 19th-c. G. chemist] a small tubular gas burner that produces a hot, blue flame

bunt (bunt) *vt., vi.* [< ? Bret. *bounta*, to butt] *Baseball* to bat (a pitch) lightly so that it does not go beyond the infield —*n.* a bunted ball

bun·ting[1] (bun'tin) *n.* [< ? ME. *bonten*, sift] **1.** a thin cloth for making flags, etc. **2.** decorative flags

bun·ting[2] (bun'tin) *n.* [ME.] a small, brightly colored, short-billed bird

buoy (boo'ē, boi) *n.* [< L. *boia*, fetter] **1.** a floating object anchored in water to warn of rocks, etc. or to mark a channel **2.** same as LIFE PRESERVER —*vt.* [< Sp. *boyar*, to float] **1.** to mark with a buoy **2.** to keep afloat **3.** to lift up in spirits

buoy·ant (boi'ənt, boo'yənt) *adj.* [< ? Sp. *boyar*, to float] **1.** having the ability or tendency to float **2.** cheerful —**buoy'an·cy** *n.*

bur (bur) *n.* [< Scand.] **1.** a rough prickly seed capsule of certain plants **2.** a plant with burs **3.** same as BURR

bur·den[1] (burd'n) *n.* [< OE. *beran*, to bear] **1.** anything that is carried; load **2.** heavy load, as of work, care, etc. **3.** the carrying capacity of a ship —*vt.* to put a burden on; oppress —**bur'den·some** *adj.*

bur·den[2] *n.* [< OFr. *bourdon*, a humming] **1.** a chorus or refrain of a song **2.** a repeated, central idea; theme

bur·dock (bur'däk') *n.* [BUR +

DOCK³] a plant with large leaves and purple-flowered heads with prickles

bu·reau (byoor'ō) n., pl. **-reaus, -reaux** (-rōz) [Fr., desk] 1. a chest of drawers for clothing, etc. 2. an agency 3. a government department

bu·reau·cra·cy (byoo rä'krə sē) n., pl. **-cies** 1. government by departmental officials following an inflexible routine 2. the officials collectively 3. governmental officialism 4. the concentration of authority in administrative bureaus —**bu·reau·crat** (byoor'ə krat') n. —**bu'reau·crat'ic** adj. —**bu'reau·crat'i·cal·ly** adv.

bu·reau·cra·tize' (-tīz') vt., vi. **-tized', -tiz'ing** to develop into a bureaucracy —**bu·reau'cra·ti·za'tion** n.

burg (burg) n. [var. of BOROUGH] [Colloq.] a quiet or dull town

bur·geon (bur'jən) vi. [< OFr. burjon, a bud] 1. to put forth buds, etc. 2. to grow or develop rapidly

-bur·ger (bur'gər) [< (HAM)BURGER] a combining form meaning: 1. sandwich of ground meat, etc. [turkeyburger] 2. hamburger and [cheeseburger]

burgh (burg; Scot. bu'rə) n. [Scot. var. of BOROUGH] 1. [Brit.] a borough 2. in Scotland, a chartered town

burgh'er n. a citizen of a town

bur·glar (bur'glər) n. [< OFr. burgeor] one who commits burglary

bur'glar·ize' vt. **-ized', -iz'ing** [Colloq.] to commit burglary in

bur'gla·ry n., pl. **-ries** the act of breaking into a building to commit a felony, as theft, or a misdemeanor

bur·gle (bur'g'l) vt., vi. **-gled, -gling** [Colloq.] to burglarize or commit burglary

bur·go·mas·ter (bur'gə mas'tər) n. [< MDu. burg, town + meester, MASTER] the mayor of a town in the Netherlands, Flanders, Austria, or Germany

Bur·gun·dy (bur'gən dē) n. [occas. b-] pl. **-dies** a red or white wine, orig. made in Burgundy, a region in SE France —**Bur·gun'di·an** adj., n.

bur·i·al (ber'ē əl) n. the burying of a dead body in a grave, tomb, etc.

Bur·ki·na Fa·so (boor kē'nə fä'sō) country in W Africa: 108,880 sq. mi; pop. 5,330,000

burl (burl) n. [< VL. burrula, wool tuft] 1. a knot in thread or yarn that makes cloth look nubby 2. a knot on some tree trunks 3. veneer from wood with burls —**burled** adj.

bur·lap (bur'lap) n. [< ? ME. borel] a coarse cloth of jute or hemp

bur·lesque (bər lesk') n. [Fr. < It. burla, a jest] 1. any broadly comic or satirical imitation; parody 2. a sort of vaudeville, with low comedy, striptease acts, etc. —vt., vi. **-lesqued', -lesqu'ing** to imitate comically

bur·ly (bur'lē) adj. **-li·er, -li·est** [ME. borlich, excellent] 1. big and strong 2. hearty in manner; bluff

Bur·ma (bur'mə) country in SE Asia: 261,789 sq. mi.; pop. 24,732,000 —**Bur·mese'** (-mēz') adj., n.

burn (burn) vt. **burned** or **burnt,**

burn'ing [OE. biernan] 1. to set on fire, as in order to produce heat, light, or power 2. to destroy by fire 3. to injure or damage by fire, acid, etc. 4. to consume as fuel 5. to sunburn 6. to cause (a hole, etc.) as by fire 7. to cause a sensation of heat in —vi. 1. to be on fire 2. to give out light or heat 3. to be destroyed or injured by fire or heat 4. to feel hot 5. to be excited —n. 1. an injury or damage caused by fire, heat, etc. 2. the process or result of burning —**burn down** to burn to the ground —**burn up** [Slang] to make or become angry —**burn'a·ble** adj., n.

burn'er n. the part of a stove, lamp, etc. from which the flame comes

bur·nish (bur'nish) vt., vi. [< OFr. brunir, make brown] to make or become shiny by rubbing —n. gloss; polish —**bur'nish·er** n.

bur·noose (bər nōōs') n. [< Ar. burnus] a hooded cloak worn by Arabs

burn·out (burn'out') n. 1. the point at which missile fuel is burned up and the missile enters free flight 2. emotional exhaustion from mental stress

Burns (burnz), **Robert** 1759–96; Scot. poet

burnt (burnt) alt. pt. & pp. of BURN

burp (burp) n., vi. [echoic] [Slang] belch —vt. to cause (a baby) to belch

burp gun [Mil. Slang] a type of automatic pistol or small submachine gun

burr¹ (bur) n. 1. a bur 2. a rough edge left on metal, etc. by cutting or drilling —vt. to form a rough edge on

burr² (bur) n. [prob. echoic] 1. the trilling of r, as in Scottish speech 2. a whir

bur·ro (bur'ō) n., pl. **-ros** [Sp. < LL. burricus, small horse] a donkey

bur·row (bur'ō) n. [see BOROUGH] 1. a hole dug in the ground by an animal 2. any similar hole —vi. 1. to make a burrow 2. to live or hide in a burrow 3. to search, as if by digging —vt. 1. to make burrows in 2. to make by burrowing

bur·sa (bur'sə) n., pl. **-sae** (-sē) **-sas** [< Gr. byrsa, a hide] Anat. a sac or cavity with a lubricating fluid, as between a tendon and bone

bur·sar (bur'sər) n. [< ML. bursa, a purse] a college treasurer

bur·si·tis (bər sīt'is) n. [< BURSA + -ITIS] inflammation of a bursa

burst (burst) vi. **burst, burst'ing** [OE. berstan] 1. to come apart suddenly and violently; explode 2. to give sudden vent; break (into tears, etc.) 3. to appear, start, etc. suddenly 4. to be as full or crowded as possible —vt. to cause to burst —n. 1. a bursting 2. a break or rupture 3. a sudden action or effort; spurt 4. a volley of shots

Bu·run·di (boo roon'dē) country in EC Africa: 10,745 sq. mi.; pop. 2,800,000

bur·y (ber'ē) vt. **-ied, -y·ing** [OE. byrgan] 1. to put (a dead body) into the earth, a tomb, etc. 2. to hide or cover 3. to put away 4. to immerse

bus (bus) n., pl. **bus'es, bus'ses** (OMNI)BUS] a large motor coach for many passengers, usually following a regular route —*vt.* **bused** or **bussed**, **bus′ing** or **bus′sing** to transport by bus —*vi.* **1.** to go by bus **2.** to do the work of a busboy

bus′boy′ *n.* a waiter's assistant who clears tables, brings water, etc.

bus·by (buz′bē) *n., pl.* **-bies** [prob. < name *Busby*] a tall fur hat worn with a full-dress uniform, as by guardsmen

bush (boosh) *n.* [OE. *busc*] **1.** a low woody plant with spreading branches; shrub **2.** anything like a bush **3.** uncleared land —*vi.* to grow thickly —**beat around the bush** to talk around a subject without getting to the point —**bush′y** *adj.* **-i·er**, **-i·est**

bushed (boosht) *adj.* [Colloq.] very tired; exhausted

bush·el (boosh′'l) *n.* [< OFr. *boisse*, grain measure] a dry measure equal to 4 pecks, or 32 quarts

bush·ing (boosh′iŋ) *n.* [< MDu. *busse*, box] a removable metal lining, for reducing friction on moving parts

bush league [Slang] *Baseball* a small or second-rate minor league —**bush′-league′** *adj.* —**bush leaguer**

bush′man (-mən) *n., pl.* **-men** one who lives in the Australian bush

bush′mas′ter (-mas′tər) *n.* a large poisonous snake of C and S.America

bush′whack′er (-hwak′ər) *n.* a guerrilla fighter

bus·i·ly (biz′ə lē) *adv.* in a busy manner

busi·ness (biz′nis) *n.* [OE. *bisignes:* see BUSY] **1.** one's work; occupation **2.** a special task, duty, etc. **3.** rightful concern; a matter or affair **5.** commerce; trade **6.** a commercial or industrial establishment —*adj.* of or for business —**mean business** [Colloq.] to be in earnest

business college (or **school**) a school of typing, bookkeeping, etc.

busi′ness·like′ *adj.* efficient, methodical, systematic, etc.

busi′ness·man′ *n., pl.* **-men′** a man in business, esp. as an owner —**busi′ness·wom′an** *n.fem., pl.* **-wom′en**

bus·ing, bus·sing (bus′iŋ) *n.* the transporting of children by bus to a school outside of their neighborhood, esp. so as to desegregate the schools

bus·kin (bus′kin) *n.* [? < MDu. *brosekin*, small boot] **1.** a high, laced boot worn in ancient tragedy **2.** a tragedy

buss (bus) *n., vt., vi.* [< ?] [Archaic or Dial.] kiss

bust¹ (bust) *n.* [< It. *busto*] **1.** a sculpture of a person's head and shoulders **2.** a woman's bosom

bust² (bust) *vt., vi.* [< BURST] [Slang] **1.** to burst or break **2.** to make or become bankrupt or demoted **3.** to hit **4.** to arrest —*n.* [Slang] **1.** a failure **2.** financial collapse **3.** a punch **4.** a spree **5.** an arrest

bus·tle¹ (bus′'l) *vi., vt.* **-tled, -tling** [< ME. *busken*, prepare] to hurry busily —*n.* busy and noisy activity

bus·tle² (bus′'l) *n.* [< ? G. *buschel*, pad] a padding worn to fill out the upper back of a woman's skirt

bus·y (biz′ē) *adj.* **-i·er**, **-i·est** [OE. *bisig*] **1.** active; at work **2.** full of activity **3.** in use, as a telephone **4.** too detailed —*vt.* **-ied**, **-y·ing** to make or keep busy —**bus′y·ness** *n.*

bus′y·bod′y (-bäd′ē) *n., pl.* **-ies** a meddler in the affairs of others

but (but) *prep.* [OE. *butan*, BUSTLE without] except; save [nobody went *but* me] —*conj.* **1.** yet; still [it's good, *but* not great] **2.** on the contrary [I am old, *but* he is young] **3.** unless [it never rains *but* it pours] **4.** that [I don't doubt *but* he's right] **5.** that . . . not [I never gamble *but* I lose] —*adv.* **1.** only [if I had *but* known] **2.** merely [he is *but* a child] **3.** just [I heard it *but* now] —*pron.* who . . . not; which . . . not [not a man *but* felt it] —**but for** if it were not for

bu·tane (byoō′tān) *n.* [ult. < *butyrum*, butter] a hydrocarbon used as a fuel, in organic synthesis, etc.

butch (booch) *adj.* [< ? BUTCHER] [Slang] **1.** designating a man's closely cropped haircut **2.** masculine: said of a lesbian

butch·er (booch′ər) *n.* [< OFr. *bouc*, he-goat] **1.** one whose work is killing and dressing animals for meat **2.** one who cuts meat for sale **3.** a brutal killer —*vt.* **1.** to kill or dress (animals) for meat **2.** to kill brutally or senselessly **3.** to botch —**butch′er·y** *n., pl.* **-ies**

but·ler (but′lər) *n.* [< OFr. *bouteille*, bottle] a manservant, usually the head servant of a household

butt¹ (but) *n.* [< ?] **1.** the thick end of anything **2.** a stub or stump, as of a cigar **3.** a target **4.** an object of ridicule **5.** [Slang] a cigarette —*vt., vi.* to join end to end

butt² (but) *vt., vi.* [< OFr. *buter*, to thrust against] **1.** to ram with the head **2.** to project —*n.* a butting —**butt in(to)** [Slang] to mix into (another's business, etc.)

butt³ (but) *n.* [< LL. *bottis*, cask] a large cask for wine or beer

butte (byoōt) *n.* [Fr., mound] a steep hill standing alone in a plain

but·ter (but′ər) *n.* [< Gr. *bous*, cow + *tyros*, cheese] **1.** the thick, yellowish product that results from churning cream **2.** any substance somewhat like butter —*vt.* **1.** to spread with butter **2.** [Colloq.] to flatter (with *up*) —**but′ter·y** *adj.*

butter bean *same as:* **1.** LIMA BEAN **2.** WAX BEAN

but′ter·cup′ *n.* a plant with yellow, cup-shaped flowers

but′ter·fat′ *n.* the fatty part of milk, from which butter is made

but·ter·fin′gers *n.* one who often fumbles and drops things

but′ter·fly′ *n., pl.* **-flies′** [OE. *buttorfleoge*] an insect with a slender body and four broad, usually brightly colored wings

but′ter·milk′ *n.* the sour liquid left after churning butter from milk

but′ter·nut′ *n.* **1.** a walnut tree of E N.America **2.** its edible, oily nut

but′ter·scotch′ (-skäch′) *n.* **1.** a hard, sticky candy made with brown sugar, butter, etc. **2.** a syrup with the flavor of this

but·tocks (but′əks) *n.pl.* [< OE. *buttuc,* end] the fleshy, rounded parts of the hips; rump

but·ton (but′'n) *n.* [< OFr. *boton*] **1.** any small disk or knob used as a fastening, ornament, etc., as on a garment **2.** anything small and shaped like a button —*vt., vi.* to fasten with a button or buttons

but′ton-down′ *adj.* **1.** designating a collar, as on a shirt, fastened down by small buttons **2.** conservative, unimaginative, etc. [*a button-down* mind]

but′ton·hole′ *n.* a slit or loop through which a button is inserted —*vt.* **-holed′, -hol′ing 1.** to make buttonholes in **2.** to detain and talk to

but·tress (but′ris) *n.* [see BUTT²] **1.** a structure built against a wall to support or reinforce it **2.** a support or prop —*vt.* to prop up; bolster

bux·om (buk′səm) *adj.* [ME., humble] healthy, comely, plump, etc.: specif. said of a full-bosomed woman

buy (bī) *vt.* **bought, buy′ing** [OE. *bycgan*] **1.** to get by paying money; purchase **2.** to get by an exchange [*to buy* time by negotiating] **3.** to bribe **4.** [Slang] to accept as true [I can't *buy* his excuse] —*n.* **1.** anything bought **2.** [Colloq.] something worth its price —**buy off** to bribe —**buy out** to buy all the stock, rights, etc. of —**buy up** to buy all that is available of

buy′er *n.* **1.** one who buys; consumer **2.** one whose work is to buy merchandise for a retail store

buzz (buz) *vi.* [echoic] **1.** to hum like a bee **2.** to gossip **3.** to be filled with noisy activity or talk —*vt.* to fly an airplane low over —*n.* a sound like a bee's hum

buz·zard (buz′ərd) *n.* [< L. *buteo,* kind of hawk] **1.** a kind of hawk that is slow and heavy in flight **2.** *same as* TURKEY BUZZARD

buzz′er *n.* an electrical device that makes a buzzing sound as a signal

buzz saw a circular saw rotated by machinery

bx. box

by (bī) *prep.* [OE. *be, bi*] **1.** near; at [*sit by* the fire] **2.** *a)* in or during [*travel by* day] *b)* for a fixed time [to

work *by* the hour] *c)* not later than [*be back by* noon] **3.** *a)* through; via [*to* Boston *by* Route 6] *b)* past; beyond [*he* walked right *by* me] **4.** in behalf of [*he* did well *by* me] **5.** through the agency of [gained *by* fraud] **6.** *a)* according to [*to* go *by* the book] *b)* in [*to* die *by* degrees] *c)* following in series [marching two *by* two] **7.** *a)* in or to the amount of [*apples by* the peck] *b)* and in another dimension [two *by* four] *c)* using (the given number) as multiplier or divisor —*adv.* **1.** close at hand [stand *by*] **2.** away; aside [*to* put money *by*] **3.** past [*he* sped *by*] **4.** at the place specified [*stop by* on your way] —**by and by** soon or eventually —**by and large** considering everything —**by the by** incidentally

by- *a prefix meaning:* **1.** near **2.** secondary [*byproduct*]

by-and-by (bī′'n bī) *n.* a future time

bye (bī) *n.* [see BY] the advantage obtained by an unpaired contestant in a tournament, who advances to the next round without playing

bye-bye (bī′bī′) *n., interj.* goodbye

Bye·lo·rus·sian Soviet Socialist Republic (bye′lō rush′ən) republic of the U.S.S.R., in W European Russia: 80,154 sq. mi.; pop. 8,633,000: also **Bye′lo·rus′sia**

by·gone (bī′gôn′, -gän′) *adj.* past; former —*n.* anything gone or past

by·law (bī′lô′) *n.* [< ME. *bi,* village + *laue,* law] a law or rule adopted by an organization or assembly for its own meetings or affairs

by′line′ *n.* a line above a newspaper article, etc., telling who wrote it

by′pass′ *n.* **1.** a way, pipe, channel, etc. between two points that avoids or is auxiliary to the main way **2.** a surgical operation to allow fluid to pass around a diseased or blocked part or organ —*vt.* **1.** to detour **2.** to furnish with a bypass **3.** to ignore

by′path′, by′-path′ *n.* a secluded, little-used path; byway

by′play′ *n.* action, gestures, etc. going on aside from the main action or conversation

by′prod′uct, by′-prod′uct *n.* anything produced, as from residues, in the course of making another thing

by′road′ *n.* a road that is not a main road

By·ron (bī′rən), **George Gordon** 1788–1824; Eng. poet

by′stand′er *n.* a person who stands near but does not participate

by′way′ *n.* a side road or path

by′word′ *n.* **1.** a proverb **2.** an object of scorn, ridicule, etc. to many

By·zan·tine Empire (biz′'n tēn′) empire (395–1453 A.D.) in SE Europe & SW Asia

C

C, c (sē) *n.*, *pl.* **C's, c's** the third letter of the English alphabet

C (sē) *n.* **1.** a Roman numeral for 100 **2.** a grade for average work **3.** *Chem.* carbon **4.** *Music* the first tone in the scale of C major

C, C. Celsius or centigrade

C., c. 1. carat **2.** catcher **3.** Catholic **4.** cent **5.** center **6.** centimeter **7.** century **8.** circa **9.** college **10.** copyright **11.** cycle

Ca *Chem.* calcium

CA California

cab (kab) *n.* [< CABRIOLET] **1.** a carriage, esp. one for public hire **2.** a taxicab **3.** the place in a truck, crane, etc. where the operator sits

ca·bal (kə bal') *n.* [Fr., intrigue] **1.** a small group joined in a secret intrigue **2.** the intrigue itself

cab·a·la (kab'ə lə, kə bäl'ə) *n.* [< Heb. *qabbālāh*, tradition] **1.** a medieval occult Jewish philosophy **2.** occultism

ca·bal·le·ro (kab'ə ler'ō, -əl yer'ō) *n.*, *pl.* **-ros** [Sp.] **1.** a Spanish gentleman **2.** [Southwest] *a*) a horseman *b*) a lady's escort

ca·ba·na (kə bän'ə, -ban'ə) *n.* [Sp. < LL. *capanna*] **1.** a cabin or hut **2.** a small shelter used as a bathhouse

cab·a·ret (kab'ə rā') *n.* [Fr.] a café providing musical entertainment

cab·bage (kab'ij) *n.* [< L. *caput*, head] a vegetable with thick leaves formed into a round compact head

cab·by, cab·bie (kab'ē) *n.*, *pl.* **-bies** [Colloq.] one who drives a cab

cab·in (kab'n) *n.* [< LL. *capanna*, hut] **1.** a small, crudely or simply built house; hut **2.** a room on a ship or boat **3.** the space for passengers, crew, or cargo in an aircraft

cab·i·net (kab'ə nit) *n.* [Fr. < ?] **1.** a case with drawers or shelves **2.** a case holding a TV, radio, etc. **3.** [*often* C-] a body of official advisers to a chief executive

cab'i·net·mak'er *n.* a maker of fine furniture —**cab'i·net·work'** *n.*

ca·ble (kā'b'l) *n.* [< L. *capere*, to take hold] **1.** a thick, heavy rope, often of wire strands **2.** a bundle of insulated wires to carry an electric current **3.** a cablegram —*vt.* **-bled, -bling 1.** to fasten with a cable **2.** to send a cablegram to —*vi.* to send a cablegram

cable car a car drawn by a moving cable, as up a steep incline

ca'ble·gram' (-gram') *n.* a message sent by undersea cable

cable television a TV system in which various antennas receive local and distant signals and transmit them by cable to subscribers' receivers

ca·bo·chon (kab'ə shän') *n.* [Fr. < *caboche*, the head] any precious stone cut in convex shape

ca·boo·dle (kə bōōd'l) *n.* [< BOODLE] [Colloq.] lot; group [the whole *caboodle*]

ca·boose (kə bōōs') *n.* [MDu. *kambuis*, cabin house] the trainmen's car at the rear of a freight train

cab·ri·o·let (kab'rē ə lā') *n.* [< Fr. *cabriole*, a leap] **1.** a light, two-wheeled, one-horse carriage **2.** a former style of convertible coupe

ca·ca·o (kə kā'ō, -kā'ō) *n.*, *pl.* **-os** [Sp. < MexInd. *cacauatl*] **1.** the seed of a tropical American tree from which cocoa and chocolate are made: also **cacao bean 2.** this tree

cache (kash) *n.* [Fr. < VL. *coacticare*, store up] **1.** a place in which stores of food, supplies, etc. are hidden **2.** anything so hidden —*vt.*, *vi.* **cached, cach'ing** to place in a cache

cache·pot (kash'pät, -pō) *n.* [Fr. < *cacher*, to hide] a decorative jar for holding potted plants: also **cache pot**

ca·chet (ka shā') *n.* [Fr.] **1.** a stamp or official seal, as on a document **2.** any sign of official approval, or of quality, prestige, etc. **3.** a design, slogan, advertisement, etc. stamped or printed on mail

cack·le (kak'l) *vi.* **-led, -ling** [echoic] **1.** to make the shrill, broken sounds of a hen **2.** to laugh or chatter with similar sounds —*n.* a cackling

ca·coph·o·ny (kə käf'ə nē) *n.*, *pl.* **-nies** [< Gr. *kakos*, bad + *phōnē*, voice] harsh, jarring sound; discord —**ca·coph'o·nous** *adj.*

cac·tus (kak'təs) *n.*, *pl.* **-tus·es, -ti** (-tī) [< Gr. *kaktos*, a kind of thistle] any of a family of desert plants with fleshy stems and spinelike leaves

cad (kad) *n.* [< CADET] a man whose behavior is not gentlemanly —**cad'dish** *adj.* —**cad'dish·ly** *adv.* —**cad'dish·ness** *n.*

ca·dav·er (kə dav'ər) *n.* [L., prob. < *cadere*, to fall] a corpse, as for dissection

ca·dav·er·ous (-əs) *adj.* [< L.] of or like a cadaver; pale; ghastly

cad·die, cad·dy¹ (kad'ē) *n.* [Scot. form of Fr. *cadet*: see CADET] one who attends a golf player, carrying his clubs, etc. —*vi.* **-died, -dy·ing** to act as a caddie

cad·dy² (kad'ē) *n.*, *pl.* **-dies** [< Malay *kati*, unit of weight] a small container, specif. one used for tea

-cade (kād) [< (CAVAL)CADE] *a suffix meaning* procession, parade [*motorcade*]

ca·dence (kād'ns) n. [< L. *cadere*, to fall] 1. fall of the voice in speaking 2. flow of rhythm 3. measured movements, as in marching

ca·den·za (kə den'zə) n. [It.: see prec.] an elaborate passage for the solo instrument in a concerto

ca·det (kə det') n. [Fr. < L. dim. of *caput*, head] 1. a student in training at an armed forces academy 2. any trainee, as a practice teacher

cadge (kaj) vt., vi. cadged, cadg'ing [ME. *caggen*, to tie] to beg or get by begging —cadg'er n.

cad·mi·um (kad'mē əm) n. [< L. *cadmia*, zinc ore (with which it occurs)] a metallic chemical element used in alloys, pigment, etc.

ca·dre (kad'rē) n. [< Fr. < L. *quadrum*, a square] a nucleus around which an expanded organization, as a military unit, can be built

ca·du·ce·us (kə dōō'sē əs) n., pl. -ce·i (-sē ī') [L.] the winged staff of Mercury: now a symbol of the medical profession

cae·cum (sē'kəm) n., pl. -ca (-kə) same as CECUM

Cae·sar (sē'zər), **Julius** 100?–44 B.C.; Rom. general & dictator

Cae·sar·e·an section (si zer'ē ən) the delivery of a baby by cutting through the mother's abdominal and uterine walls: Caesar was supposedly born thus

cae·su·ra (si zhoor'ə, -zyoor'ə) n., pl. -ras, -rae (-ē) [L. < *caedere*, to cut] a break or pause in a line of verse, usually in the middle

ca·fé, ca·fe (ka fā', kə-) n. [Fr., coffeehouse] a small restaurant or a barroom, nightclub, etc.

caf·e·te·ri·a (kaf'ə tir'ē ə) n. [AmSp., coffee store] a self-service restaurant

caf·feine, caf·fein (kaf'ēn) n. [G. *kaffein*] the alkaloid present in coffee, tea, and kola: it is a stimulant

caf·tan (kaf'tən) n. [Turk. *qaftān*] a long-sleeved robe, worn in eastern Mediterranean countries

cage (kāj) n. [< L. *cavea*, hollow place] 1. a structure of wires, bars, etc. for confining animals 2. any openwork frame or structure —vt. caged, cag'ing to put or confine, as in a cage

cag·er (kā'jər) n. [Slang] a basketball player

ca·gey, ca·gy (kā'jē) adj. -gi·er, -gi·est [< ?] [Colloq.] 1. sly; tricky; cunning 2. cautious —ca'gi·ly adv. —ca'gi·ness n.

ca·hoots (kə hōōts') n.pl. [< ?] [Slang] partnership: implying scheming in phr. **in cahoots**

Cain (kān) Bible oldest son of Adam and Eve: he killed his brother Abel —**raise Cain** [Slang] to create a great commotion

cairn (kern) n. [Scot.] a conical heap of stones built as a monument

Cai·ro (kī'rō) capital of Egypt: pop. 3,346,000

cais·son (kā'sän) n. [Fr. < L. *capsa*, box] 1. a two-wheeled wagon with a chest for ammunition 2. a watertight box for underwater construction work

cai·tiff (kāt'if) n. [< L. *captivus*, CAPTIVE] a mean, evil, or cowardly person —adj. evil, mean, or cowardly

ca·jole (kə jōl') vt., vi. -joled', -jol'ing [< Fr.] to coax with flattery and insincere talk —ca·jol'er n. —ca·jol'er·y n.

Ca·jun, Ca·jan (kā'jən) n. 1. a native of Louisiana of Canadian French ancestry 2. the dialect of Cajuns

cake (kāk) n. [< ON.] 1. a small, flat mass of baked or fried dough, batter, hashed food, etc. 2. a mixture of flour, eggs, sugar, etc. baked as in a loaf and often covered with icing 3. a shaped, solid mass, as of soap —vt., vi. caked, cak'ing to form into a hard mass or crust —**take the cake** [Slang] to win the prize —cak'y adj.

cal. 1. caliber 2. calorie

cal·a·bash (kal'ə bash') n. [< Sp. *calabaza* < ?] 1. the gourdlike fruit of a tropical American tree 2. a gourd; specif., the bottle gourd or a smoking pipe made from it

cal·a·boose (kal'ə bōōs') n. [Sp. *calabozo*] [Slang] a jail

cal·a·mine (kal'ə mīn') n. [Fr. < L. *cadmia*, zinc ore] a zinc oxide powder used in skin lotions, etc.

ca·lam·i·ty (kə lam'ə tē) n., pl. -ties [< L. *calamitas*] a great misfortune; disaster —ca·lam'i·tous adj. —ca·lam'i·tous·ly adv. —ca·lam'i·tous·ness n.

cal·car·e·ous (kal ker'ē əs) adj. [< L. *calx*, lime] of or like limestone, calcium, or lime

cal·ci·fy (kal'sə fī') vt., vi. -fied', -fy'ing [< L. *calx*, lime + -FY] to change into a hard, stony substance by the deposit of lime or calcium salts —cal'ci·fi·ca'tion n.

cal·ci·mine (-mīn') n. [< L. *calx*, lime] a white or colored liquid used as a wash for plastered surfaces —vt. -mined', -min'ing to cover with calcimine

cal·cine (kal'sīn) vt., vi. -cined, -cin·ing [< ML. *calcinare*] to change to an ashy powder by heat

cal·cite (kal'sīt) n. calcium carbonate, a mineral found as limestone, chalk, and marble

cal·ci·um (kal'sē əm) n. [< L. *calx*, lime] a soft, silver-white metallic chemical element found combined in limestone, chalk, etc.

calcium carbonate a white powder or crystalline compound found in limestone, chalk, bones, shells, etc.

cal·cu·late (kal'kyə lāt') vt. -lat'ed, -lat'ing [< L. *calculare*, reckon] 1. to determine by using mathematics; compute 2. to determine by reasoning; estimate 3. to plan or intend for a purpose —vi. 1. to reckon 2. to rely (on) —cal'cu·la·ble (-lə b'l) adj.

cal'cu·lat'ed adj. deliberately planned or carefully considered

cal'cu·lat'ing adj. shrewd or cunning; scheming

cal'cu·la'tion n. 1. a calculating 2. something deduced by calculating 3. careful planning or forethought —cal'cu·la'tive adj.

cal·cu·la·tor *n.* **1.** one who calculates **2.** a machine for doing arithmetic rapidly: also **calculating machine**

cal·cu·lus (kal'kyə ləs) *n., pl.* **-li'** (-lī'), **-lus·es** [L., pebble used in counting] **1.** an abnormal stony mass in the body **2.** a method of calculation or analysis in higher mathematics

Cal·cut·ta (kal kut'ə) seaport in NE India: pop. 2,927,000

cal·dron (kôl'drən) *n.* [< L. *calidus*, warm] **1.** a large kettle or boiler **2.** a state of violent agitation

cal·en·dar (kal'ən dər) *n.* [< L. *kalendarium*, account book] **1.** a system of determining the length and divisions of a year **2.** a table that shows the days, weeks, and months of a given year **3.** a schedule, as of pending court cases

cal·en·der (kal'ən dər) *n.* [< Gr. *kylindros*, cylinder] a machine with rollers for giving paper, cloth, etc. a smooth or glossy finish —*vt.* to process (paper, etc.) in a calender

calf[1] (kaf) *n., pl.* **calves**; esp. for 3, **calfs** [OE. *cealf*] **1.** a young cow or bull **2.** the young of some other large animals, as the elephant, seal, etc. **3.** leather from a calf's hide

calf[2] (kaf) *n., pl.* **calves** [ON. *kalfr*] the fleshy back part of the leg below the knee

calf·skin' *n.* **1.** the skin of a calf **2.** a soft leather made from this

Cal·ga·ry (kal'gər ē) city in S Alberta, Canada: pop. 331,000

cal·i·ber, cal·i·bre (kal'ə bər) *n.* [Fr. & Sp. < Ar. *gālib*, a mold] **1.** the diameter of a cylindrical body, esp. of a bullet or shell **2.** the diameter of the bore of a gun **3.** quality; ability

cal·i·brate (kal'ə brāt') *vt.* **-brat'ed, -brat'ing** **1.** to determine the caliber of **2.** to fix or correct the graduations of (a measuring instrument) —**cal'i·bra'tion** *n.* —**cal'i·bra'tor** *n.*

cal·i·co (kal'ə kō') *n., pl.* **-coes', -cos'** [< *Calicut*, city in India] a kind of coarse, printed, cotton fabric —*adj.* spotted like calico [a *calico* cat]

Cal·i·for·ni·a (kal'ə fôr'nyə, -nē ə) State of the SW U.S., on the Pacific: 158,693 sq. mi.; pop. 23,669,000; cap. Sacramento: abbrev. **Calif.** —**Cal'i·for'ni·an** *adj., n.*

cal·i·per (kal'ə pər) *n.* [var. of CALIBER] [*usually pl.*] an instrument consisting of a pair of hinged legs, for measuring thickness or diameter —*vt., vi.* to measure with calipers   **CALIPERS**

ca·liph, ca·lif (kā'lif, kal'if) *n.* [Ar. *khalīfa*] supreme ruler: the title taken by Mohammed's successors as heads of Islam —**cal'iph·ate** *n.*

cal·is·then·ics (kal'əs then'iks) *n. pl.* [< Gr. *kallos*, beauty + *sthenos*, strength] athletic exercises

calk (kôk) *vt. same as* CAULK

call (kôl) *vt.* [< ON. *kalla*] **1.** to say in a loud tone; shout **2.** to summon **3.** to give or apply a name to **4.** to describe as specified **5.** to awaken **6.** to telephone **7.** to give orders for **8.** to stop (a game, etc.) **9.** to demand payment of (a loan, etc.) **10.** *Poker* to require (a player) to show his hand by equaling his bet —*vi.* **1.** to shout **2.** to visit for a while (often with *on*) **3.** to telephone —*n.* **1.** a calling **2.** a loud utterance **3.** the distinctive cry of an animal or bird **4.** a summons; invitation **5.** an economic demand, as for a product **6.** need [no *call* for tears] **7.** a demand for payment **8.** a brief visit —**call down** [Colloq.] to scold —**call for 1.** to demand **2.** to come and get —**call off** to cancel (a scheduled event) —**call up 1.** to recall **2.** to summon for duty **3.** to telephone —**on call** available when summoned —**call'er** *n.*

cal·la (kal'ə) *n.* [< L., a plant (of unc. kind)] a plant with a large, white leaf surrounding a yellow flower spike: also **calla lily**

call girl a prostitute who is called by telephone to assignations

cal·lig·ra·phy (kə lig'rə fē) *n.* [< Gr. *kallos*, beauty + *graphein*, write] handwriting, esp. when attractive —**cal·lig'ra·pher** *n.* —**cal·li·graph·ic** (kal'ə graf'ik) *adj.*

call·ing *n.* **1.** act of one that calls **2.** one's work or profession **3.** an inner urging toward some vocation

cal·li·o·pe (kə lī'ə pē', kal'ē ōp') *n.* [< Gr. *kallos*, beauty + *ops*, voice] a keyboard instrument like an organ, having a series of steam whistles

call letters the letters, and sometimes numbers, that identify a radio station

cal·los·i·ty (ka läs'ə tē) *n.* **1.** the state of being callous **2.** a callus

cal·lous (kal'əs) *adj.* [< L. *callum*, hard skin] **1.** hardened **2.** unfeeling —**cal'lous·ly** *adv.* —**cal'lous·ness** *n.*

cal·low (kal'ō) *adj.* [OE. *calu*, bare, bald] immature; inexperienced —**cal'low·ness** *n.*

cal·lus (kal'əs) *n., pl.* **-lus·es** [L., var. of *callum*, hard skin] a hardened, thickened place on the skin

calm (käm) *n.* [< Gr. *kauma*, heat] stillness; tranquillity —*adj.* still; quiet; tranquil —*vt., vi.* to make or become calm (often with *down*) —**calm'ly** *adv.* —**calm'ness** *n.*

cal·o·mel (kal'ə mel', -məl) *n.* [Fr. < Gr. *kalos*, beautiful + *melas*, black] a white, tasteless powder, formerly used as a cathartic, etc.

ca·lor·ic (kə lôr'ik, lär'-) *adj.* **1.** of heat **2.** of calories

cal·o·rie (kal'ə rē) *n.* [Fr. < L. *calor*, heat] a unit for measuring heat, esp. for measuring the energy produced by food when oxidized in the body

cal·o·rif·ic (kal'ə rif'ik) *adj.* [< L. *calor*, heat + *facere*, make] producing heat

cal·u·met (kal′yə met′) *n.* [Fr. < L. *calamus*, reed] a long-stemmed ceremonial pipe smoked by N.American Indians as a token of peace

ca·lum·ni·ate (kə lum′nē āt′) *vt.*, *vi.* -at′ed, -at′ing [see ff.] to slander —ca·lum′ni·a′tion *n.* —ca·lum′ni·a′tor *n.*

cal·um·ny (kal′əm nē) *n.*, *pl.* -nies [< L. *calumnia*, slander] a false and malicious statement; slander

Cal·va·ry (kal′vər ē) *Bible* the place where Jesus was crucified

calve (kav) *vi.*, *vt.* calved, calv′ing to give birth to (a calf)

calves (kavz) *n.* *pl.* of CALF

Cal·vin (kal′vin), **John** 1509–64; Fr. Protestant reformer

Cal′vin·ism (-iz′m) *n.* the theological system of John Calvin and his followers, stressing predestination —Cal′vin·ist *n.*, *adj.* —Cal′vin·is′tic *adj.*

cal·vi·ti·es (kal vish′i ēz′) *n.* [L.] baldness

ca·lyp·so (kə lip′sō) *n.* [< ?] a lively, topical folk song, orig. of Trinidad

ca·lyx (kā′liks, kal′iks) *n.*, *pl.* -lyx·es, -ly·ces (-lə sēz′) [L., pod] the outer whorl of protective leaves, or sepals, of a flower

cam (kam) *n.* [Du. *cam*, orig., a comb] a wheel, projection on a wheel, etc. which gives an irregular motion as to a wheel or shaft, or receives such motion from it

ca·ma·ra·de·rie (käm′ə räd′ər ē) *n.* [Fr.] good fellowship; comradeship

cam·ber (kam′bər) *n.* [OFr. < L. *camur*, arched] a slight convex curve of a surface, as of a road —*vt.*, *vi.* to arch slightly

cam·bi·um (kam′bē əm) *n.* [LL., change] a layer of cells between the wood and bark in woody plants, from which new wood and bark grow

Cam·bo·di·a (kam bō′dē ə) country in S Indochina: 69,884 sq. mi.; pop. 6,250,000: official name **Kam·pu·che·a** (kam′poo chē′ə) —**Cam·bo′di·an** *adj.*, *n.*

cam·bric (kām′brik) *n.* [< *Cambrai*, Fr. city] a fine linen or cotton cloth

Cam·bridge (kām′brij) **1.** city in EC England: pop. 100,000 **2.** city in E Mass.: pop. 95,000

Cam·den (kam′dən) city in SW N.J.: pop. 85,000

came (kām) *pt.* of COME

cam·el (kam′'l) *n.* [ult. < Heb. *gāmāl*] a large, domesticated mammal with a humped back and long neck: because it can store water in its body, it is used in Asian and African deserts

ca·mel·lia (kə mēl′yə) *n.* [after G. J. *Kamel*, 17th-c. missionary to the Far East] **1.** an Asiatic evergreen tree or shrub with dark-green leaves and roselike flowers **2.** the flower

cam·el·o·pard (kə mel′ə pärd′) *n.* [< Gr. *kamēlos*, camel + *pardalis*, leopard: from its neck and spots] *early name for the* GIRAFFE

Cam·em·bert (cheese) (kam′əm ber′) [< *Camembert*, Fr. village] a soft, creamy, rich cheese

cam·e·o (kam′ē ō′, kam′yō) *n.*, *pl.* -os [< It. < ML. *camaeus*] **1.** a gem carved with a figure raised in relief **2.** *a)* an outstanding bit role *b)* a bit of fine writing

cam·er·a (kam′ər ə) *n.* [L., a vault] **1.** the private office of a judge **2.** a device for taking photographs, a closed box containing a sensitized plate or film on which an image is formed when light enters through a lens **3.** *TV* the device that receives the image and transforms it into a flow of electrical impulses for transmission —**in camera** in privacy or secrecy

cam′er·a·man′ *n.*, *pl.* -men′ an operator of a motion-picture or television camera

Cam·e·roon (kam′ə rōōn′) country in WC Africa: c.183,000 sq. mi.; pop. 5,229,000 —**Cam′e·roon′i·an** *adj.*, *n.*

cam·i·sole (kam′ə sōl′) *n.* [Fr. < VL. *camisia*, shirt] a woman's lacetrimmed underwaist

cam·o·mile (kam′ə mīl′, -mēl′) *n.* *same as* CHAMOMILE

cam·ou·flage (kam′ə fläzh′, -fläj′) *n.* [Fr. < *camoufler*, to disguise] **1.** a disguising, as of ships or guns, to conceal them from the enemy **2.** a disguise; deception —*vt.*, *vi.* -flaged′, -flag′ing to disguise in order to conceal —**cam′ou·flag′er** *n.*

camp (kamp) *n.* [< L. *campus*, field] **1.** *a)* a place where temporary tents, huts, etc. are put up, as for soldiers *b)* a group of such tents, etc. **2.** the supporters of a particular cause **3.** a recreational place in the country for vacationers, esp. children **4.** the people living in a camp **5.** [Slang] banality, artifice, etc. so extreme as to amuse or have a perversely sophisticated appeal —*vi.* **1.** to set up a camp **2.** to live or stay in a camp (often with *out*) —**break camp** to dismantle a camp and depart

cam·paign (kam pān′) *n.* [Fr. < L. *campus*, field] **1.** a series of military operations with a particular objective **2.** a series of planned actions, as for electing a candidate —*vi.* to participate in a campaign —**cam·paign′er** *n.*

cam·pa·ni·le (kam′pə nē′lē) *n.*, *pl.* -les, -li (-lē) [It. < LL. *campana*, a bell] a bell tower

camp·er (kamp′ər) *n.* **1.** a vacationer at a camp **2.** a motor vehicle or trailer equipped for camping out

camp′fire′ *n.* **1.** an outdoor fire at a camp **2.** a social gathering around such a fire

cam·phor (kam′fər) *n.* [< Sans. *karpūrah*, camphor tree] a crystalline substance with a strong odor, derived chiefly from an Oriental evergreen tree (**camphor tree**): used to repel moths, in medicine as a stimulant, etc. —**cam′phor·at′ed** *adj.*

camp meeting a religious meeting held outdoors or in a tent, etc.

camp′site′ *n.* **1.** any site for a camp **2.** an area in a park set aside for camping

cam·pus (kam′pəs) *n.*, *pl.* -pus·es [L., a field] the grounds, and sometimes buildings, of a school or college

—*adj.* of a school or college [*campus* politics]

camp'y *adj.* **-i·er, -i·est** [Slang] characterized by camp (n. 5)

cam'shaft' *n.* a shaft having a cam, or to which a cam is fastened

can¹ (kan, kən) *vi. pt.* **could** [< OE. *cunnan,* know] 1. to know how to 2. to be able to 3. to be likely to [*can* that be true?] 4. to have the right to 5. [Colloq.] to be permitted to; may —**can but** can only

can² (kan) *n.* [OE. *canne,* cup] 1. a container, usually metal, with a separate cover [a garbage *can*] 2. a tinned metal container in which foods, etc. are sealed for preservation 3. the contents of a can —*vt.* **canned, can'ning** 1. to put up in cans or jars for preservation 2. [Slang] to dismiss

Ca·naan (kā'nən) Promised Land of the Israelites, a region between the Jordan and the Mediterranean

Can·a·da (kan'ə də) country in N N.America: 3,852,000 sq. mi.; pop. 20,015,000; cap. Ottawa: abbrev. Can. —**Ca·na'di·an** (kə nā'dē ən) *adj., n.*

Ca·na'di·an·ism *n.* 1. a custom or belief of Canada 2. a word or idiom originating in Canadian English

ca·nal (kə nal') *n.* [< L. *canalis,* channel] 1. an artificial waterway for transportation or irrigation 2. *Anat.* a tubular passage or duct

Canal Zone *former name of* a strip of land on either side of the Panama Canal: leased by the U.S. (1904–79)

ca·na·pé (kan'ə pē, -pā') *n.* [Fr.] a cracker, etc. spread with spiced meat, cheese, etc., served as an appetizer

ca·nard (kə närd') *n.* [Fr., a duck] a false, esp. malicious report

ca·nar·y (kə ner'ē) *n., pl.* **-ies** [< *Canary* Islands] 1. a yellow songbird of the finch family 2. a light yellow

Canary Islands group of Sp. islands off NW Africa

ca·nas·ta (kə nas'tə) *n.* [Sp., basket] a double-deck card game

Can·ber·ra (kan'bər ə) capital of Australia: pop. 67,000

can·can (kan'kan') *n.* [Fr.] a gay dance with much high kicking

can·cel (kan's'l) *vt.* **-celed** or **-celled, -cel·ing** or **-cel·ling** [< L. *cancellus,* lattice] 1. to mark over with lines, etc., as in deleting written matter or marking a postage stamp, check, etc. as used 2. to make invalid 3. to do away with; abolish 4. to neutralize or balance (often with *out*) 5. *Math.* to remove (a common factor, equivalents, etc.) —**can'cel·la'tion** *n.*

can·cer (kan'sər) *n.* [< L., a crab] [C-] the fourth sign of the zodiac —*n.* 1. a malignant tumor that can spread. 2. any spreading evil —**can'cer·ous** *adj.*

can·de·la·brum (kan'də lä'brəm, -lab'rəm) *n., pl.* **-bra** (-brə), **-brums** [L.: see CHANDELIER] a large branched candlestick: also **can'de·la'bra,** *pl.* **-bras**

can·did (kan'did) *adj.* [< L. *candidus,* white, sincere] 1. honest; frank 2. unposed and informal [a *candid* photo] —**can'did·ly** *adv.* —**can'did·ness** *n.*

can·di·date (kan'də dāt', -dit) *n.* [L. *candidatus,* white-robed, as office seekers] one seeking an office, award, etc. —**can'di·da·cy** (-də də sē) *n.*

can·died (kan'dēd) *adj.* 1. cooked in sugar. 2. sugary

can·dle (kan'd'l) *n.* [< L. *candela*] a cylinder of tallow or wax with a wick through it, which gives light when burned —*vt.* **-dled, -dling** to examine (eggs) for freshness by holding in front of a light —**can'dler** *n.*

can·dle·stick' *n.* a cupped or spiked holder for a candle or candles

can·dor (kan'dər) *n.* [L., sincerity] honesty or frankness in expressing oneself: Brit. sp., **candour**

can·dy (kan'dē) *n., pl.* **-dies** [< Per. *qand,* cane sugar] a solid confection of sugar or syrup with flavoring, fruit, nuts, etc. —*vt.* **-died, -dy·ing** 1. to cook in sugar, esp. to preserve 2. to crystallize into sugar

cane (kān) *n.* [< Gr. *kanna*] 1. the slender, jointed stem of certain plants, as bamboo 2. a plant with such a stem, as sugar cane 3. a walking stick 4. split rattan —*vt.* **caned, can'ing** 1. to flog with a cane 2. to make (chair seats, etc.) with cane —**can'er** *n.*

cane·brake (kān'brāk') *n.* a dense growth of cane plants

ca·nine (kā'nīn) *adj.* [< L. *canis,* dog] 1. of or like a dog 2. of the family of animals that includes dogs, wolves, and foxes —*n.* 1. a dog or other canine animal 2. any of the four sharp-pointed teeth next to the incisors: in full **canine tooth**

can·is·ter (kan'is tər) *n.* [< Gr. *kanistron,* wicker basket] a small box or can for coffee, tea, etc.

can·ker (kan'kər) *n.* [< L.: see CANCER] a spreading sore, esp. in the mouth —**can'ker·ous** *adj.*

can·na·bis (kan'ə bis) *n.* [L., hemp] 1. *same as* HEMP 2. the female flowering tops of the hemp

canned (kand) *adj.* 1. preserved, as in cans 2. [Slang] recorded for reproduction as on radio or TV

can·nel (coal) (kan'l) [< ? *candle coal*] a tough bituminous coal that burns with a bright flame

can·ner·y (kan'ər ē) *n., pl.* **-ies** a factory where foods are canned

can·ni·bal (kan'ə b'l) *n.* [Sp. *canibal*] 1. a person who eats human flesh 2. an animal that eats its own kind —*adj.* of or like cannibals —**can'ni·bal·ism** *n.* —**can'ni·bal·is'tic** *adj.*

can'ni·bal·ize' (-īz') *vt., vi.* **-ized', -iz'ing** to strip (old equipment) of parts for use in other units

can·non (kan'ən) *n., pl.* **-nons, -non** [< L. *canna,* cane] 1. a large, mounted piece of artillery 2. an automatic gun on an aircraft

can'non·ade' (-ād') n. a continuous firing of artillery —vt., vi. **-ad'ed, -ad'ing** to fire artillery (at)

can·not (kan'ät, kə nät') can not —**cannot but** have no choice but to

can·ny (kan'ē) adj. **-ni·er, -ni·est** [< CAN[1]] 1. cautious and shrewd 2. wise and well-informed —**can'ni·ly** adv. —**can'ni·ness** n.

ca·noe (kə nōō') n. [Sp. canoa < AmInd.] a narrow, light boat moved by paddles —vi. **-noed', -noe'ing** to paddle, or go in, a canoe —**ca·noe'ist** n.

can·on (kan'ən) n. [OE., a rule < L.] 1. a law or body of laws of a church 2. a) a basic law or principle b) a criterion 3. an official list, as of books of the Bible 4. a clergyman serving in a cathedral 5. Music a round

ca·ñon (kan'yən) n. same as CANYON

ca·non·i·cal (kə nän'i k'l) adj. 1. of or according to church law 2. of or belonging to a canon

can·on·ize (kan'ə nīz') vt. **-ized', -iz'ing** 1. to declare (a dead person) a saint 2. to glorify —**can'on·i·za'tion** n.

can·o·py (kan'ə pē) n., pl. **-pies** [< Gr. kōnōpeion, couch with mosquito nets] 1. a drapery, etc. fastened above a bed, throne, etc., or held over a person 2. a rooflike projection —vt. **-pied, -py·ing** to place or form a canopy over

cant[1] (kant) n. [< L. canere, sing] 1. the secret slang of beggars, thieves, etc.; argot 2. the special vocabulary of those in a certain occupation; jargon 3. insincere talk, esp. when pious —vi. to use cant

cant[2] (kant) n. [< L. cant(h)us, tire of a wheel] 1. an outside angle 2. a beveled edge 3. a tilt, slant, turn, etc. —vt., vi. to slant; tilt

can't (kant, känt) cannot

can·ta·loupe, can·ta·loup (kan'tə lōp') n. [Fr. < It. Cantalupo, estate near Rome, where first grown in Europe] a muskmelon, esp. one with a rough rind and juicy orange flesh

can·tan·ker·ous (kan taŋ'kər əs) adj. [prob. < ME. contakour, troublemaker] bad-tempered; quarrelsome —**can·tan'ker·ous·ly** adv. —**can·tan'ker·ous·ness** n.

can·ta·ta (kən tät'ə) n. [It. < cantare, sing] a choral composition for a story to be sung but not acted

can·teen (kan tēn') n. [< Fr. < It. cantina, wine cellar] 1. a recreation center for servicemen, teen-agers, etc. 2. a small flask for carrying water

can·ter (kan'tər) n. [< Canterbury gallop, a riding pace] a moderate gallop —vt., vi. to ride at this pace

can·ti·cle (kan'ti k'l) n. [< L. canere, sing] a song or chant, esp. a hymn with words from the Bible

can·ti·le·ver (kan't'l ē'vər, -ev'ər) n. [< ?] a bracket or block projecting as a support; esp., a projecting structure anchored at one end to a pier or wall —vt. to support by means of cantilevers —**can'ti·le'vered** adj.

can·to (kan'tō) n., pl. **-tos** [It. < L.

canere, sing] any of the main divisions of certain long poems

Can·ton (kan tän'; for 2 kan'tən) 1. former name of KWANGCHOW. 2. city in EC Ohio: pop. 95,000

can·ton (kan'tən, kan tän') n. [Fr. < LL. cantus, corner] any of the states in the Swiss Republic

Can·ton·ese (kan'tə nēz') adj. of Canton, China, its people, or language

can·ton·ment (kan tän'mənt,-tōn'-) n. [< Fr.: see CANTON] temporary quarters for troops

can·tor (kan'tər) n. [L., singer] a singer of liturgical solos in a synagogue

can·vas (kan'vəs) n. [< L. cannabis, hemp] 1. a coarse cloth of hemp, cotton, etc., used for tents, sails, etc. 2. a sail, tent, etc. 3. an oil painting on canvas

can'vas·back' n. a N. American wild duck with a grayish back

can·vass (kan'vəs) vt., vi. [< canvas (?) used for sifting)] to go through (places) or among (people) asking for votes, opinions, orders, etc. —n. a canvassing —**can'vass·er** n.

can·yon (kan'yən) n. [Sp. cañón, tube < L. canna, reed] a long, narrow valley between high cliffs

cap (kap) n. [< LL. cappa, hooded cloak] 1. any closefitting head covering, visored or brimless 2. a caplike thing; cover or top —vt. **capped, cap'ping** 1. to put a cap on 2. to cover (the end of) 3. to equal or excel

cap. 1. capacity 2. pl. **caps.** capital

ca·pa·ble (kā'pə b'l) adj. [< L. capere, take] having ability; skilled; competent —**capable of** 1. having the qualities necessary for 2. able or ready to —**ca'pa·bil'i·ty** (-bil'ə tē) n., pl. **-ties** —**ca'pa·bly** adv.

ca·pa·cious (kə pā'shəs) adj. [< L. capere, take] roomy; spacious —**ca·pa'cious·ly** adv. —**ca·pa'cious·ness** n.

ca·pac·i·tor (kə pas'ə tər) n. a device for storing an electrical charge

ca·pac·i·ty (-tē) n., pl. **-ties** [< L. capere, take] 1. the ability to contain, absorb, or receive 2. all that can be contained; volume 3. ability 4. maximum output 5. position; function

ca·par·i·son (kə par'ə s'n) n. [< LL. cappa, cloak] trappings for a horse —vt. to cover (a horse) with trappings

cape[1] (kāp) n. [see prec.] a sleeveless garment fastened at the neck and hanging over the back and shoulders

cape[2] (kāp) n. [< L. caput, head] a piece of land projecting into water

ca·per[1] (kā'pər) vi. [< Fr. capriole, a leap] to skip about in a playful manner —n. 1. a gay, playful leap 2. a prank —**cut a caper (or capers)** 1. to caper 2. to play silly tricks

ca·per[2] (kā'pər) n. [< Gr. kapparis] the green flower bud of a Mediterranean bush, pickled and used as a seasoning

cape'skin' n. fine leather made from goatskin or sheepskin, orig. from the Cape of Good Hope

Cape Town seaport in South Africa; seat of the legislature: pop. 807,000

cap·il·lar·y (kap'ə ler'ē) adj. [< L.

capillus, hair] very slender —*n.*, *pl.* **-ies** 1. a tube with a very small bore: also **capillary tube** 2. any of the tiny blood vessels connecting arteries with veins

capillary attraction (or **action**) the action by which liquids in contact with solids, as in a capillary tube, rise or fall: also **cap'il·lar'i·ty** (-ə tē) *n.*

cap·i·tal (kap'ə t'l) *adj.* [< L. *caput*, head] 1. punishable by death 2. principal; chief 3. of, or being, the seat of government 4. of capital, or wealth 5. excellent —*n.* 1. a capital letter 2. a city that is the seat of government of a state or nation 3. money or property owned or used in business 4. [*often* C-] capitalists collectively 5. the top part of a column

CAPITAL

capital gain profit made from the sale of capital investments, as stocks

cap'i·tal·ism (-iz'm) *n.* the economic system in which the means of production and distribution are privately owned and operated for profit

cap'i·tal·ist *n.* 1. an owner of wealth used in business 2. an upholder of capitalism 3. a wealthy person —**cap'i·tal·is'tic** *adj.*

cap'i·tal·ize (-iz') *vt.* -ized', -iz'ing 1. to use as or convert into capital 2. to use to one's advantage (with *on*) 3. to supply capital to or for 4. to begin (a word) with a capital letter —**cap'i·tal·i·za'tion** *n.*

capital letter the form of an alphabetical letter used to begin a sentence or proper name, as A, B, C, etc.

cap'i·tal·ly *adv.* very well

capital punishment penalty of death for a crime

capital stock the capital of a corporation, divided into shares

Cap·i·tol (kap'ə t'l) [< L. *Capitolium*, temple of Jupiter] the building in which the U.S. Congress meets, at Washington, D.C. —*n.* [*usually* c-] the building in which a state legislature meets

ca·pit·u·late (kə pich'ə lāt') *vi.* -lat'ed, -lat'ing [< L. *capitulare*, arrange conditions] 1. to give up (*to* an enemy) on prearranged conditions 2. to stop resisting —**ca·pit'u·la'tion** *n.*

ca·pon (kā'pän) *n.* [< L. *capo*] a castrated rooster fattened for eating

ca·price (kə prēs') *n.* [Fr. < It.] 1. a sudden, impulsive change in thinking or acting 2. a capricious quality

ca·pri·cious (kə prish'əs) *adj.* subject to caprices; erratic —**ca·pri'cious·ly** *adv.* —**ca·pri'cious·ness** *n.*

Cap·ri·corn (kap'rə kôrn') [< L. *caper*, goat + *cornu*, horn] the tenth sign of the zodiac

cap·size (kap'sīz) *vt.*, *vi.* -sized, -siz·ing [< ?] to overturn or upset: said esp. of a boat

cap·stan (kap'stən) *n.* [< L. *capere*, take] an upright drum, as on ships,

around which cables are wound so as to haul them in

cap·sule (kap's'l, -syool) *n.* [Fr. < L. *capsa*, chest] 1. a soluble gelatin container enclosing a dose of medicine 2. a detachable compartment to hold men, instruments, etc. in a rocket 3. *Bot.* a seedcase —*adj.* in a concise form —**cap'su·lar** *adj.*

cap'sul·ize (-iz') *vt.* -ized, -iz'ing 1. to enclose in a capsule 2. to condense

cap·tain (kap'tən) *n.* [< L. *caput*, head] 1. a chief; leader 2. *U.S. Mil.* an officer ranking just above lieutenant 3. a navy officer ranking just above commander 4. the master of a ship 5. the leader of a team, as in sports Abbrev. **Capt.** —*vt.* to be captain of —**cap'tain·cy** *n.*, *pl.* -cies

cap·tion (kap'shən) *n.* [< L. *capere*, take] 1. a heading or title, as of a newspaper article or an illustration 2. *Motion Pictures* a subtitle —*vt.* to supply a caption for

cap'tious (-shəs) *adj.* [see prec.] 1. made for the sake of argument, as a remark 2. quick to find fault —**cap'tious·ly** *adv.* —**cap'tious·ness** *n.*

cap·ti·vate (kap'tə vāt') *vt.* -vat'ed, -vat'ing to capture the attention or affection of —**cap'ti·va'tion** *n.*

cap·tive (kap'tiv) *n.* [< L. *capere*, take] a prisoner —*adj.* 1. taken or held prisoner 2. obliged to listen —**cap·tiv'i·ty** *n.*

cap·tor (-tər) *n.* one who captures

cap·ture (-chər) *vt.* -tured, -tur·ing [< L. *capere*, take] 1. to take or seize by force, surprise, etc. 2. to represent in a more permanent form [a picture *capturing* her charm] —*n.* a capturing or being captured

car (kär) *n.* [< L. *carrus*, chariot] 1. any vehicle on wheels 2. a vehicle that moves on rails 3. an automobile 4. an elevator cage

Ca·ra·cas (kə räk'əs, -rak'-) capital of Venezuela: pop. 787,000

car·a·cul (kar'ə kəl) *n.* same as KARAKUL

ca·rafe (kə raf') *n.* [Fr.] a glass or metal bottle for water, coffee, etc.

car·a·mel (kar'ə m'l, kär'm'l) *n.* [Fr.] 1. burnt sugar used to color or flavor food 2. chewy candy made from sugar, milk, etc.

car'a·mel·ize' (-mə līz') *vt.*, *vi.* -ized', -iz'ing to turn into caramel

car·a·pace (kar'ə pās') *n.* [Fr. < Sp.] an upper shell, as of the turtle

car·at (kar'ət) *n.* [Fr. < Gr. *keration*] 1. a unit of weight for precious stones, equal to 200 milligrams 2. same as KARAT

car·a·van (kar'ə van') *n.* [< Per. *kārwān*] 1. a company of people traveling together for safety, as through a desert 2. same as VAN²

car·a·van·sa·ry (kar'ə van'sə rē) *n.*, *pl.* -ries [< Per. *kārwān*, caravan + *sarāi*, palace] in the Orient, an inn for caravans

car·a·way (kar'ə wā') n. [< Ar. *karawiyā'*] the spicy seeds of a plant, used to flavor bread, etc.

car·bide (kär'bīd) n. a compound of a metal with carbon

car·bine (kär'bīn, -bēn) n. [< Fr. *scarabée*, beetle] **1.** a short-barreled rifle **2.** U.S. Armed Forces a light, semiautomatic or automatic .30-caliber rifle

carbo- a *combining form meaning* carbon: also **carb-**

car·bo·hy·drate (kär'bə hī'drāt) n. [CARBO- + HYDRATE] an organic compound composed of carbon, hydrogen, and oxygen, as a sugar or starch

car·bol·ic acid (kär bäl'ik) *same as* PHENOL

car·bon (kär'bən) n. [< L. *carbo*, coal] **1.** a nonmetallic chemical element found esp. in all organic compounds: diamond and graphite are pure carbon: a radioactive isotope of carbon (**carbon 14**) is used in dating fossils, etc. **2.** carbon paper **3.** a copy made with carbon paper: in full **carbon copy** **4.** a copy or like carbon

car·bon·ate (-bə nit, -nāt') n. a salt or ester of carbonic acid —vt. (-nāt') -at'ed, -at'ing to charge with carbon dioxide —**car'bon·a'tion** n.

carbon black finely divided carbon produced by the incomplete burning of oil or gas

car'bon-date' vt. -dat'ed, -dat'ing to establish the approximate age of (fossils, etc.) by measuring the carbon 14 content

carbon dioxide a heavy, colorless, odorless gas: it passes out of the lungs in respiration

car·bon·ic acid (kär bän'ik) a weak acid formed by carbon dioxide in water

car·bon·if·er·ous (kär'bə nif'ər əs) adj. containing carbon or coal

carbon monoxide a colorless, odorless, highly poisonous gas

carbon paper thin paper coated on one side, as with a carbon preparation, used to make copies of letters, etc.

carbon tet·ra·chlo·ride (tet'rə klôr'īd) a nonflammable liquid used in cleaning mixtures, etc.

Car·bo·run·dum (kär'bə run'dəm) [CARB(ON) + (c)orundum] a trademark for a hard abrasive, esp. of carbon and silicon —n. [c-] such a substance

car·boy (kär'boi) n. [< Per.] a large bottle to hold corrosive liquids, enclosed in a protective container

car·bun·cle (kär'buŋ k'l) n. [< L. dim. of *carbo*, coal] a painful, pus-bearing inflammation of the tissue beneath the skin —**car·bun'cu·lar** (-kyoo lər) adj.

car·bu·ret·or (kär'bə rāt'er) n. a device for mixing air with gasoline spray to make an explosive mixture in an internal-combustion engine

car·cass (kär'kəs) n. [< Fr. *carcasse*] **1.** the dead body of an animal **2.** a framework or frame

car·cin·o·gen (kär sin'ə jən) n. [< ff. + -GEN] any substance that produces cancer —**car·ci·no·gen·ic** (kär'sə nō jen'ik) adj.

car·ci·no·ma (kär'sə nō'mə) n., pl. -mas, -ma·ta (-mə tə) [L. < Gr. *karkinos*, a crab] any of several kinds of epithelial cancer

car coat a short overcoat

card[1] (kärd) n. [< Gr. *chartēs*, leaf of paper] **1.** a flat, stiff piece of paper or pasteboard; specif., a) any of a pack of playing cards b) a card identifying a person, esp. as a member, agent, etc. c) a post card d) a card bearing a greeting e) any of a series of cards on which information is recorded **2.** an attraction [drawing card] **3.** [Colloq.] a witty or clowning person —**put** (or **lay**) **one's cards on the table** to reveal something frankly

card[2] (kärd) n. [< L. *carere*, to card] a metal comb or a machine with wire teeth for combing fibers of wool, cotton, etc. —vt. to use a card on

card'board' n. stiff, thick paper or pasteboard, for cards, boxes, etc.

car·di·ac (kär'dē ak') adj. [< Gr. *kardia*, heart] of or near the heart

car·di·gan (kär'də gən) n. [< 7th Earl of *Cardigan*] a sweater or jacket that opens down the front

car·di·nal (kärd'ʼn əl) adj. [< L. *cardo*, pivot] **1.** principal; chief **2.** bright-red —n. **1.** an official appointed by the Pope to his council **2.** bright red **3.** a bright-red American songbird **4.** a cardinal number

cardinal number any number used in counting or showing how many (e.g., two, forty, 627, etc.)

cardio- [< Gr. *kardia*, heart] a combining form meaning of the heart

car·di·o·gram (kär'dē ə gram') n. same as ELECTROCARDIOGRAM —**car'di·o·graph'** n.

car·di·ol·o·gy (-äl'ə jē) n. the branch of medicine dealing with the heart

car·di·o·vas·cu·lar (-ō vas'kyoo lər) adj. of the heart and the blood vessels as a unified system

cards (kärdz) n.pl. any game played with a deck of playing cards, as poker

card'sharp' n. [Colloq.] a professional cheater at cards: also **card shark**

care (ker) n. [< OE. *caru*, sorrow] **1.** a) a troubled state of mind; worry b) a cause of such a mental state **2.** close attention; heed **3.** a liking or regard (for) **4.** charge; protection **5.** a responsibility —vi. **cared, car'ing 1.** to feel concern **2.** to feel love or liking (for) **3.** to look after; provide (for) **4.** to wish (for); want —vt. **1.** to feel concern about or interest in **2.** to wish —**care of** at the address of —**take care of 1.** to attend to **2.** to provide for

ca·reen (kə rēn') vt., vi. [< L. *carina*, keel] to lean or cause to lean sideways; tip; lurch

ca·reer (kə rir') n. [< Fr. < It. *carro*, car] **1.** a swift course **2.** one's progress through life **3.** a profession or occupation —vi. to rush wildly

care'free' adj. without care

care'ful adj. **1.** cautious; wary **2.** accurately or thoroughly done —**care'ful·ly** adv. —**care'ful·ness** n.

care'less adj. **1.** carefree; untroubled **2.** not paying enough heed; neglectful

3. done or made without enough attention, precision, etc. —**care′less·ly** adv. —**care′less·ness** n.

ca·ress (kə res′) vt. [ult. < L. carus, dear] to touch lovingly or gently —n. an affectionate touch, kiss, etc.

car·et (kar′it, ker′-) n. [L., there is lacking] a mark (∧) used to show where something is to be added in a written or printed line

care′tak′er n. **1.** a person hired to take care of something or someone **2.** one acting as temporary replacement

care′worn′ adj. haggard or worn out by troubles and worry

car·fare (kär′fer′) n. the price of a ride on a streetcar, bus, etc.

car·go (kär′gō) n., pl. -goes, -gos [< Sp. cargar, to load] the load carried by a ship, truck, etc.; freight

car′hop′ n. [CAR + (BELL)HOP] one who serves food at a drive-in restaurant

Car·ib·be·an (Sea) (ker′ə bē′ən, kə rib′ē ən) sea bounded by the West Indies, Central America, & S.America

car·i·bou (kar′ə bōō′) n. [CanadFr.] a large N. American deer

car·i·ca·ture (kar′ə kə chər) n. [Fr. < It. caricare, exaggerate] **1.** the exaggerated imitation of a person, literary style, etc. for satirical effect **2.** a picture, etc. in which this is done —vt. -tured, -tur·ing to depict as in a caricature —**car′i·ca·tur·ist** n.

car·ies (ker′ēz) n. [L., decay] decay of bones or, esp., of teeth

car·il·lon (kar′ə län′) n. [Fr., chime of four bells < L. quattuor, four] a set of bells tuned to the chromatic scale

car′il·lon·neur′ (-lə nur′) n. [Fr.] a carillon player

car′load′ n. a load that fills a car

car·min·a·tive (kär min′ə tiv) adj. [< L. carminare, cleanse] expelling gas from the stomach and intestines —n. a carminative medicine

car·mine (kär′min, -mīn) n. [ult. < Ar. qirmiz, crimson] a red or purplish-red color —adj. red or purplish-red

car·nage (kär′nij) n. [Fr. < L. caro, flesh] extensive slaughter; massacre

car′nal (-n'l) adj. [< L. caro, flesh] **1.** of the flesh; material; worldly **2.** sensual —**car·nal′i·ty** (-nal′ə tē) n. —**car′nal·ly** adv.

car·na·tion (kär nā′shən) n. [< L. caro, flesh] **1.** a variety of the pink **2.** its pink, white, or red flower

Car·ne·gie (kär′nə gē′, kär nā′gē), Andrew 1835–1919; U.S. industrialist

car·nel·ian (kär nēl′yən) n. [< L. carnis, of flesh (color)] a red kind of chalcedony, used as a gem

car·ni·val (kär′nə vəl) n. [< Fr. or It.] **1.** the period of feasting and revelry just before Lent **2.** a reveling; festivity **3.** an entertainment with sideshows, rides, etc.

car·ni·vore (kär′nə vôr′) n. a carnivorous animal or plant

car·niv·o·rous (kär niv′ə rəs) adj.

[< L. caro, flesh + vorare, devour, eat] **1.** flesh-eating **2.** insect-eating, as certain plants **3.** of the carnivores —**car·niv′o·rous·ness** n.

car·ol (kar′əl) n. [< OFr. carole, kind of dance] a song of joy or praise; esp., a Christmas song —vi., vt. -oled or -olled, -ol·ing or -ol·ling to sing; warble —**car′ol·er, car′ol·ler** n.

car·om (kar′əm) n. [< Sp. carambola] **1.** Billiards a shot in which the cue ball successively hits two balls **2.** a hitting and rebounding —vi. **1.** to make a carom **2.** to hit and rebound

ca·rot·id (kə rät′id) adj. [Gr. karōtis] designating or of either of the two main arteries, one on each side of the neck, which convey blood to the head —n. a carotid artery

ca·rous·al (kə rou′zəl) n. a carouse

ca·rouse (kə rouz′) vi. -roused′, -rous′ing [< G. gar austrinken, to drink] to engage in a noisy drinking party —n. a noisy drinking party

carp¹ (kärp) n., pl. carp, carps [< Gmc. carpa] an edible freshwater fish living in tranquil waters

carp² (kärp) vi. [< ON. karpa, to brag] to find fault pettily or unfairly

car·pel (kär′pəl) n. [< Gr. karpos, fruit] a simple pistil, regarded as a modified leaflike structure

car·pen·ter (kär′pən tər) n. [< L. carpentum, a cart] one who builds and repairs wooden things, esp. buildings, ships, etc. —vi. to do a carpenter's work —**car′pen·try** (-trē) n.

carpenter ant any of the large, black ants that build nests by gnawing the wood in buildings, tree trunks, etc.

car·pet (kär′pit) n. [< L. carpere, to card] **1.** a heavy fabric for covering a floor **2.** anything that covers like a carpet —vt. to cover as with a carpet —**on the carpet** being reprimanded

car′pet·bag′ n. an old-fashioned traveling bag, made of carpeting —vi. -bagged′, -bag′ging to act as a carpetbagger

car′pet·bag′ger n. a Northerner who went South to profit from unsettled conditions after the Civil War

car′pet·ing n. carpets; carpet fabric

car pool a plan by a group to use their cars in rotation, to and from work

car·port (kär′pôrt′) n. an automobile shelter built as a roof at the side of a building

car·rel, car·rell (kar′əl) n. [< ML. carula] a small enclosure in a library, for privacy in studying

car·riage (kar′ij) n. [ult. < L. carrus, car] **1.** a carrying; transportation **2.** manner of carrying oneself; bearing **3.** a) a four-wheeled, horse-drawn passenger vehicle b) a baby buggy **4.** a moving part, as on a typewriter, that supports and shifts something

car·ri·er (kar′ē ər) n. **1.** one that carries **2.** one in the business of transporting **3.** one that transmits disease germs **4.** an aircraft carrier

carrier pigeon a homing pigeon

car·ri·on (kar'ē ən) n. [< L. *caro*, flesh] decaying flesh of a dead body

Car·roll (kar'əl), **Lewis** (pseud. of *C. L. Dodgson*) 1832–98; Eng. writer

car·rot (kar'ət) n. [< Gr. *karōton*] 1. a plant with an edible, fleshy, orange-red root 2. the root —**car'rot·y** adj.

car·rou·sel (kar'ə sel', -zel') n. [Fr.; < It. dial. *carusiello*, kind of tournament] a merry-go-round: also **carousel**

car·ry (kar'ē) vt. **-ried, -ry·ing** [< L. *carrus*, car] 1. to hold or support 2. to take from one place to another 3. to lead or impel 4. to transmit [air *carries* sounds] 5. to transfer or extend 6. to involve; imply 7. to bear (oneself) in a specified way 8. a) to gain support for b) to win (an election, debate, etc.) 9. a) to keep in stock b) to keep on one's account books, etc. —vi. 1. to act as a bearer, conductor, etc. 2. to cover a range, as a voice —n., pl. **car'ries** 1. the distance covered by a gun, ball, etc. 2. a portage —be (or get) **carried away** to become very emotional or enthusiastic —**carry on** 1. to engage in 2. to continue 3. [Colloq.] to behave wildly or childishly —**carry out** (or **through**) 1. to put (plans, etc.) into practice 2. to accomplish —**carry over** to postpone; continue

carrying charge interest paid on the balance owed in installment buying

car'ry-on' adj. small enough to fit under an airplane seat —n. a piece of carry-on luggage

car'ry-out' adj. designating or of prepared food or beverages sold as by a restaurant to be consumed elsewhere

car'ry-o'ver n. something carried over, as a remainder of crops or goods

car seat a portable automobile seat used to secure a small child

car'sick' adj. nauseated from riding in an automobile, bus, etc.

Car·son City (kär'sən) capital of Nev., in the W part: pop. 32,000

cart (kärt) n. [< ON. *kartr*] a small wagon —vt., vi. to carry in a cart, truck, etc.; transport —**cart'er** n.

cart·age (kär'tij) n. 1. the work of carting 2. the charge for this

carte blanche (kärt' blänsh') [Fr., blank card] full authority

car·tel (kär tel') n. [<G. < Fr.] an association of businesses in an international monopoly; trust

Car·ter (kär'tər), **James E.** 1924– ; 39th president of the U.S. (1977–81)

car·ti·lage (kärt'l ij) n. [< L. *cartilago*] a tough, elastic tissue forming parts of the skeleton; gristle — **car'ti·lag'i·nous** (-aj'ə nəs) adj.

car·tog·ra·phy (kär tä'grə fē) n. [see CARD[1] & -GRAPHY] the art of making maps or charts —**car·tog'ra·pher** n.

car·ton (kärt'n) n. [Fr. < It. *carta*, card] a cardboard box or container

car·toon (kär toon') n. [< Fr.: see prec.] 1. a drawing caricaturing a person or event 2. *same as* a) COMIC STRIP b) ANIMATED CARTOON —vi., vt. to draw a cartoon (of) —**car·toon'ist** n.

car·tridge (kär'trij) n. [< Fr. < It.

carta, card] 1. a cylindrical case of cardboard, metal, etc. containing the charge and primer, and usually the projectile, for a firearm 2. a small container, as for camera film, a phonograph needle, etc.

cart'wheel' n. 1. a handspring performed sidewise 2. [Slang] a large coin

carve (kärv) vt. **carved, carv'ing** [OE. *ceorfan*] 1. to make or shape by or as by cutting 2. to decorate the surface of with cut designs 3. to divide by cutting; slice —vi. 1. to carve statues or designs 2. to carve meat —**carv'er** n. —**carv'ing** n.

CARTWHEEL

car'wash' n. an establishment at which automobiles are washed

car·y·at·id (kar'ē at'id) n., pl. **-ids, -id·es'** (-ə dēz') [< Gr. *karyatides*, priestesses at Karyai, in ancient Greece] a supporting column having the form of a draped female figure

ca·sa·ba (kə sä'bə) n. [< *Kassaba*, town in Asia Minor] a kind of muskmelon with a yellow rind

Ca·sa·blan·ca (kas'ə blaŋ'kə, kä'sə bläŋ'-) seaport in NW Morocco: pop. 1,177,000

Ca·sa·no·va (kas'ə nō'və, kaz'-), **Gio·van·ni** (jō vän'nē) 1725–98; It. adventurer and writer

cas·cade (kas kād') n. [Fr. < L. *cadere*, to fall] 1. a small, steep waterfall 2. a shower, as of sparks, etc. —vt., vi. **-cad'ed, -cad'ing** to fall or drop in a cascade

cas·car·a (kas ker'ə) n. [< Sp., bark] 1. a thorny tree growing on the Pacific coast of the U.S. 2. a laxative made from its bark

case[1] (kās) n. [< L. *casus*, event < *cadere*, to fall] 1. an example or instance [a *case* of flu] 2. a person being helped by a doctor, etc. 3. any matter requiring study 4. a statement of the facts, as in a law court 5. convincing arguments [he has no *case*] 6. a lawsuit 7. a form taken by a noun, pronoun, or adjective to show its relation to neighboring words —vt. **cased, cas'ing** [Slang] to look over carefully —**in any case** in case in the event that; if —**in case of** in the event of —**in no case** by no means

case[2] (kās) n. [< L. *capsa*, box] 1. a container, as a box 2. a protective cover [a watch *case*] 3. a frame, as for a window —vt. **cased, cas'ing** 1. to put in a container 2. to enclose

ca·se·in (kā'sē in, -sēn) n. [< L. *caseus*, cheese] a protein that is one of the chief constituents of milk

case'load' n. the number of cases handled by a court, caseworker, etc.

case·ment (kās'mənt) n. [< OFr. *encassement*, a frame] a window frame that opens on hinges along the side

case'work' n. social work in which guidance is given in cases of personal and family maladjustment —**case'work'er** n.

cash (kash) n. [Fr. *caisse*, money box] 1. money that one actually has; esp., ready money 2. money, a check, etc. paid at the time of purchase —*vt.* to give or get cash for —*adj.* of or for cash —**cash in** to turn into cash

cash·ew (kash'ōō, kə shōō') n. [< SAmInd. *acajú*] 1. a tropical tree bearing kidney-shaped nuts 2. the nut

cash·ier[1] (ka shir') n. [Fr. *caissier*] a person in charge of the cash transactions of a bank or store

cash·ier[2] (ka'shir') vt. [< LL. *cassare*, destroy] to dismiss in dishonor

cash·mere (kazh'mir) n. [< *Kashmir*, region in India] 1. a fine carded wool from goats of N India and Tibet 2. a soft, twilled cloth as of this wool

cash register a device, usually with a money drawer, used for registering visibly the amount of a sale

cas·ing (kās'iŋ) n. 1. the skin of a sausage 2. the outer covering of a pneumatic tire 3. a frame, as for a door

ca·si·no (kə sē'nō) n., *pl.* -**nos** [It. < L. *casa*, cottage] 1. a room or building for dancing, gambling, etc. 2. *same as* CASSINO

cask (kask) n. [< Sp. < L. *quassare*, shatter] 1. a barrel of any size, esp. one for liquids 2. its contents

cas·ket (kas'kit) n. [prob. < OFr. *casse*, box] 1. a small box or chest, as for valuables 2. a coffin

Cas·pi·an Sea (kas'pē ən) inland sea between Caucasia and Asiatic U.S.S.R.

Cas·san·dra (kə san'drə) *Gr. Myth.* a Trojan prophetess of doom whose prophecies were never believed

cas·sa·va (kə sä'və) n. [< Fr. < WInd. *casávi*] 1. a tropical plant with starchy roots 2. a starch made from these roots, used in tapioca

cas·se·role (kas'ə rōl') n. [Fr. < Gr. *kyathos*, a bowl] 1. a dish in which food can be baked and served 2. food baked in such a dish

cas·sette (ka set', kə-) n. [Fr. < L. *capere*, contain] a case with magnetic tape or film in it, for loading a tape recorder or movie projector quickly

cas·sia (kash'ə) n. [ult. < Heb. *qeṣi'āh*] 1. *a)* the bark of a tree of SE Asia: used as a source of cinnamon *b)* the tree 2. any of various tropical plants whose leaves yield senna

cas·si·no (kə sē'nō) n. [see CASINO] a card game for two to four players

cas·sock (kas'ək) n. [< Fr. < Per. *kazh*, raw silk] a long, closefitting vestment worn by clergymen

cast (kast) vt. cast, cast'ing [< ON. *kasta*] 1. to throw with force; fling; hurl 2. to deposit (a ballot or vote) 3. to direct [to *cast* one's eyes] 4. to project [to *cast* light] 5. to throw off or shed (a skin) 6. to shape (molten metal, etc.) by pouring into a mold 7. to select (an actor) for (a role or play) —*vi.* to throw; hurl —*n.* 1. a casting; throw 2. something formed in a mold 3. a plaster form for immobilizing a

limb 4. the set of actors in a play or movie 5. an appearance, as of features 6. kind; quality 7. a tinge; shade —**cast about** to search; look (*for*) —**cast aside** (or **away**) to discard; abandon —**cast off** 1. to discard 2. to free a ship from a dock, etc. —**cast up** 1. to turn upward 2. to add up

cas·ta·nets (kas'tə nets') n.pl. [< Sp. < L. *castanea*, chestnut: from the shape] a pair of small, hollowed pieces of hard wood or ivory, clicked together in the hand in time to music

cast'a·way n. 1. a person or thing cast off 2. a shipwrecked person —*adj.* 1. discarded 2. shipwrecked

caste (kast) n. [Fr. < L. *castus*, pure] 1. any of the hereditary Hindu social classes of a formerly segregated system of India 2. any exclusive group 3. class distinction based on birth, wealth, etc. —**lose caste** to lose social status

cast'er n. 1. a container for vinegar, oil, etc. at the table 2. any of a set of small wheels for supporting and moving furniture: also **cas'tor**

cas·ti·gate (kas'tə gāt') vt. -gat'ed, -gat'ing [< L. *castigare*] to rebuke severely, esp. by public criticism — **cas'ti·ga'tion** n. —**cas'ti·ga'tor** n.

cast'ing n. a thing, esp. of metal, cast in a mold

cast iron a hard, brittle alloy of iron made by casting —**cast'-i'ron** adj.

cas·tle (kas'l) n. [< L. *castrum*, fort] 1. a large fortified building or group of buildings 2. any massive dwelling like this 3. *same as* ROOK[2]

cast'off' adj. discarded; abandoned —*n.* a person or thing cast off

cas·tor-oil plant (kas'tər oil') [< Gr. *kastōr*, beaver] a tropical plant with large seeds which yield an oil (castor oil) used as a cathartic

cas·trate (kas'trāt) vt. -trat·ed, -trat·ing [< L. *castrare*] to remove the testicles of; emasculate —**cas·tra'tion** n.

cas·u·al (kazh'ōō wəl) adj. [< L. *casus*, chance] 1. happening by chance; not planned; incidental 2. occasional 3. careless or cursory 4. nonchalant 5. for informal use — **cas'u·al·ly** adv. —**cas'u·al·ness** n.

cas·u·al·ty (-əl tē, -ōō wəl-) n., *pl.* -ties 1. an accident, esp. a fatal one 2. a member of the armed forces killed, wounded, captured, etc. 3. anyone hurt or killed in an accident

cas·u·ist·ry (kazh'ōō wis trē) n., *pl.* -ries [< L. *casus*, CASE[1]] subtle but false reasoning, esp. about moral issues; sophistry —**cas'u·ist** n.

cat (kat) n. [OE.] 1. a small, soft-furred animal, often kept as a pet or for killing mice 2. any flesh-eating mammal related to this, as the lion, tiger, leopard, etc. 3. a spiteful woman —**let the cat out of the bag** to let a secret be found out

cat·a·clysm (kat'ə kliz'm) n. [< Gr. *kata-*, down + *klyzein*, wash] any

sudden, violent change, as in war —
cat'a·clys'mic (-kliz'mik) *adj.*

cat·a·comb (kat'ə kōm') *n.* [< ?
L. *cata*, by + *tumba*, tomb] a gallery
in an underground burial place

cat'a·falque' (-falk', -fôlk') *n.* [Fr.
< It. *catafalco*, funeral canopy] a
wooden framework on which a body
in a coffin lies in state

cat·a·lep·sy (kat'l ep'sē) *n.* [< Gr.
katalēpsis, a seizing] a condition of
muscle rigidity and sudden, temporary
loss of consciousness, as in epilepsy
—**cat'a·lep'tic** *adj., n.*

cat·a·log, cat·a·logue (kat'l ôg')
n. [< Gr. *kata-*, down + *legein*, to
count] a complete list, as an alphabetical card file of the books in a
library, a list of articles for sale, etc.
—*vt., vi.* -**loged'** or -**logued'**, -**log'ing**
or -**logu'ing** to arrange in a catalog
—**cat'a·log'er** or **cat'a·logu'er** *n.*

ca·tal·pa (kə tal'pə) *n.* [< AmInd.]
a tree with large, heart-shaped leaves
and slender, beanlike pods

ca·tal·y·sis (kə tal'ə sis) *n., pl.* -**ses'**
(-sēz') [< Gr. *katalysis*, dissolution]
the speeding up or, sometimes, slowing
down of a chemical reaction by adding
a substance which itself is not changed
thereby —**cat·a·lyt·ic** (kat'l it'ik)
adj.

cat·a·lyst (kat'l ist) *n.* a substance
serving as the agent in catalysis

cat·a·ma·ran (kat'ə mə ran') *n.*
[Tamil *kaṭṭumaram*] 1. a narrow log
raft propelled by sails or paddles 2. a
boat like this with two parallel hulls

cat·a·mount (kat'ə mount') *n.* [CAT
+ *a*, of + MOUNT¹] 1. a puma 2. a
lynx

cat·a·pult (kat'ə pult') *n.* [< Gr.
kata-, down + *pallein*, hurl] 1. an
ancient military device for throwing
stones, etc. 2. a device for launching
an airplane, rocket missile, etc. as from
a deck or ramp —*vt.* to shoot as from
a catapult —*vi.* to leap

cat·a·ract (kat'ə rakt') *n.* [< Gr.
kata-, down + *rhēgnynai*, to break] 1.
a large waterfall 2. *a)* an eye disease
in which the lens becomes opaque,
causing partial or total blindness *b)*
the opaque area

ca·tarrh (kə tär') *n.* [< Gr. *kata-*,
down + *rhein*, to flow] inflammation
of the mucous membrane of the nose
or throat: old-fashioned term

ca·tas·tro·phe (kə tas'trə fē) *n.* [<
Gr. *kata-*, down + *strephein*, to turn]
any sudden, great disaster —**cat·a·
stroph·ic** (kat'ə sträf'ik) *adj.*

cat·a·ton·ic (kat'ə tän'ik) *adj.* [<
Gr. *kata-*, down + *tonos*, tension] designating or of a state of stupor or
catalepsy, as in schizophrenia

cat'bird' *n.* a slate-gray N.American
songbird with a call like a cat's

cat'boat' *n.* a sailboat with a single
sail and mast set well forward

cat'call' *n.* a shrill noise or whistle
expressing derision, etc. —*vt., vi.* to
make catcalls (at)

catch (kach) *vt.* **caught, catch'ing**
[< L. *capere*, take] 1. to seize and
hold; capture 2. to take by a trap 3.

to deceive 4. to surprise 5. to get to in
time *[to catch a bus]* 6. to lay hold of;
grab *[catch a ball]* 7. to become infected with *[he caught a cold]* 8. to
understand 9. to get entangled 10.
[Colloq.] to see, hear, etc. —*vi.* 1. to
become held, fastened, etc. 2. to take
hold, as fire 3. to keep hold, as a lock
—*n.* 1. a catching 2. a thing that
catches 3. something caught 4. one
worth catching as a spouse 5. a snatch
or fragment 6. a break in the voice
7. [Colloq.] a tricky qualification —
catch at to seize desperately —**catch
on** 1. to understand 2. to become
popular —**catch up** 1. to snatch 2.
to overtake

catch'all' (-ôl') *n.* a container for
holding all sorts of things

catch'er *n. Baseball* the player behind
home plate, who catches pitched balls

catch'ing *adj.* 1. contagious 2.
attractive

catch·up (kech'əp, kach'-) *n. same as*
KETCHUP

catch'y *adj.* -**i·er**, -**i·est** 1. easily
caught up and remembered 2. tricky

cat·e·chism (kat'ə kiz'm) *n.* [< Gr.
kata-, thoroughly + *ēchein*, to sound]
1. a handbook of questions and
answers for teaching the tenets of a
religion 2. a close questioning

cat'e·chize' (-kīz') *vt.* -**chized'**,
-**chiz'ing** [see prec.] to question
searchingly: also **catechise**

cat·e·gor·i·cal (kat'ə gôr'ə k'l) *adj.*
1. positive; explicit: said of a statement, etc. 2. of, as, or in a category
—**cat'e·gor'i·cal·ly** *adv.*

cat·e·go·rize (kat'ə gə rīz') *vt.*
-**rized'**, -**riz'ing** to place in a category; classify

cat·e·go·ry (-gôr'ē) *n., pl.* -**ries** [<
Gr. *katēgorein*, assert] a class or division in a scheme of classification

ca·ter (kā'tər) *vi.* [< L. *ad-*, to +
capere, take] 1. to provide food and
service, as for parties 2. to seek to
gratify another's desires (with *to*)
—**ca'ter·er** *n.*

cat·er·cor·nered (kat'ē kôr'nərd)
adj. [< OFr. *catre*, four + CORNERED]
diagonal —*adv.* diagonally Also
cat'er·cor'ner

cat·er·pil·lar (kat'ər pil'ər) *n.* [<
L. *catta pilosus*, hairy cat] the wormlike larva of a butterfly, moth, etc.

cat·er·waul (kat'ər wôl') *vi.* [prob.
echoic] to make a shrill sound like that
of a cat; wail —*n.* such a sound

cat'fish' *n., pl.:* see FISH a scaleless
fish with long, whiskerlike feelers about
the mouth

cat'gut' *n.* a tough thread made from
dried intestines, as of sheep, and used
for surgical sutures, etc.

ca·thar·sis (kə thär'sis) *n.* [< Gr.
katharos, pure] 1. a purging, esp. of
the bowels 2. a relieving of the emotions, as through the arts or psychotherapy

ca·thar'tic *adj.* purging —*n.* a
medicine for purging the bowels;
laxative

ca·the·dral (kə thē'drəl) *n.* [< Gr.
kata-, down + *hedra*, a seat] 1. the

main church of a bishop's see **2.** any large, imposing church

cath·e·ter (kath′ə tər) *n.* [< Gr. *kata-*, down + *hienai*, to send] a slender tube inserted into a body passage, as into the bladder for drawing off urine —**cath′e·ter·ize′** (-īz′) *vt.* **-ized′, -iz′ing**

cath·ode (kath′ōd) *n.* [< Gr. *kata-*, down + *hodos*, way] **1.** the negative electrode in an electrolytic cell **2.** the electron emitter in a vacuum tube **3.** the positive terminal in a battery

cathode rays streams of electrons projected from a cathode: they produce X-rays when they strike solids

cath·o·lic (kath′ə lik, kath′lik) *adj.* [< Gr. *kata-*, completely + *holos*, whole] **1.** universal; all-inclusive **2.** broad in sympathies, tastes, etc. **3.** [C-] *same as* ROMAN CATHOLIC —*n.* [C-] *same as* ROMAN CATHOLIC — **Ca·thol·i·cism** (kə thäl′ə siz′m) *n.* —**cath·o·lic′i·ty** (kath′ə lis′ə tē) *n.*

cat·i·on (kat′ī′ən) *n.* [< Gr. *kata*, downward + *ienai*, to go] a positively charged ion: in electrolysis, cations move toward the cathode

cat·kin (kat′kin) *n.* [< Du. *katte*, cat] a drooping, scaly spike of small flowers without petals, as on a willow

cat′nap′ *n.* a short nap —*vi.* **-napped′, -nap′ping** to doze briefly

cat′nip *n.* [< CAT + dial. *nep*, catnip] a plant of the mint family: cats are fond of its odor

CATKIN

cat-o′-nine-tails (kat′ə nīn′tālz′) *n., pl.* **-tails′** a whip made of nine knotted cords attached to a handle

CAT scan (kat) [*c*(omputerized) *a*(*xial*) *t*(omography), an X-ray technique] **1.** a diagnostic X-raying of soft tissues, using many single-plane X-rays (*tomograms*) to form the image **2.** such an image

cat′s cradle a game in which a piece of string is looped back and forth over the fingers to make various designs

Cats·kill Mountains (kat′skil′) mountain range in SE N.Y.: also **Cats′kills′**

cat′s-paw (kats′pô′) *n.* a person used to do distasteful or unlawful work

cat·sup (kech′əp, kat′səp) *n.* *same as* KETCHUP

cat·tail (kat′tāl′) *n.* a tall marsh plant with long, brown, fuzzy spikes

cat·tle (kat′'l) *n.* [ult. < L. *caput*, the head] **1.** [Archaic] livestock **2.** cows, bulls, steers, or oxen —**cat′tle·man** (-mən) *n., pl.* **-men**

cat·ty (kat′ē) *adj.* **-ti·er, -ti·est 1.** of or like a cat **2.** spiteful, mean, malicious, etc. —**cat′ti·ness** *n.*

cat′ty-cor′nered *adj., adv.* *same as* CATER-CORNERED: also **cat′ty-cor′ner**

cat′walk′ *n.* a narrow, elevated walk

Cau·ca·sian (kô kā′zhən) *adj.* **1.** of the Caucasus, its people, etc. **2.** *same as* CAUCASOID —*n.* **1.** a native of the Caucasus **2.** *same as* CAUCASOID

Cau·ca·soid (kôk′ə soid′) *adj.* designating or of one of the major groups of mankind, loosely called the *white race* —*n.* a member of the Caucasoid group

Cau·ca·sus (kô′kə səs) **1.** region in SE European U.S.S.R., between the Black Sea and the Caspian **2.** mountain range in this region

cau·cus (kôk′əs) *n.* [< ?] a meeting of a party or faction to decide policy, pick candidates, etc. —*vi.* **-cused** or **-cussed, -cus·ing** or **-cus·sing** to hold a caucus

cau·dal (kôd′'l) *adj.* [< L. *cauda*, tail + -AL] of, like, at, or near the tail

caught (kôt) *pt. & pp.* of CATCH

caul (kôl) *n.* [< OE. *cawl*, basket] the membrane enclosing a fetus, esp. the part sometimes covering the head at birth

caul·dron (kôl′drən) *n.* *same as* CALDRON

cau·li·flow·er (kôl′ə flou′ər) *n.* [< It. *cavolo*, cabbage + *fiore*, flower] **1.** a variety of cabbage with a dense white head of fleshy flower stalks **2.** this head, eaten as a vegetable

caulk (kôk) *vt.* [< L. *calx*, a heel] **1.** to make (a boat, etc.) watertight by filling the seams with oakum, tar, etc. **2.** to stop up (cracks) with a filler —**caulk′er** *n.*

caus·al (kôz′'l) *adj.* **1.** of, being, or expressing a cause **2.** relating to cause and effect —**cau·sal·i·ty** (kô zal′ə tē) *n.* —**caus′al·ly** *adv.*

cau·sa·tion (kô zā′shən) *n.* **1.** a causing **2.** a causal agency; anything producing an effect

cause (kôz) *n.* [< L. *causa*] **1.** anything producing an effect or result **2.** a reason or motive for producing an effect **3.** any objective or movement that people are interested in and support **4.** a case to be decided by a court —*vt.* **caused, caus′ing** to be the cause of; bring about —**caus′a·tive** *adj.* —**cause′less** *adj.* —**caus′er** *n.*

cau·se·rie (kō′zə rē′) *n.* [Fr.] **1.** a chat **2.** a short, chatty composition

cause·way (kôz′wā′) *n.* [ult. < L. *calx*, lime + WAY] a raised path or road, as across wet ground

caus·tic (kôs′tik) *adj.* [< Gr. *kaiein*, to burn] **1.** that can burn tissue by chemical action; corrosive **2.** sarcastic; biting —*n.* a caustic substance —**caus′ti·cal·ly** *adv.* —**caus·tic′i·ty** (-tis′ə tē) *n.*

cau·ter·ize (kôt′ər īz′) *vt.* **-ized′, -iz′ing** [see prec.] to burn with a hot iron, or with a caustic substance, so as to destroy dead tissue, etc. —**cau′ter·i·za′tion** *n.*

cau·tion (kô′shən) *n.* [< L. *cautio*] **1.** a warning **2.** wariness; prudence —*vt.* to warn —**cau′tion·ar′y** *adj.*

cau·tious (kô/shəs) *adj.* full of caution; careful to avoid danger —**cau/tious·ly** *adv.* —**cau/tious·ness** *n.*

cav·al·cade (kav/'l kād/) *n.* [Fr. < L. *caballus*, horse] a procession, as of horsemen, carriages, etc.

cav·a·lier (kav/ə lir/) *n.* [Fr.: see prec.] 1. an armed horseman; knight 2. a gallant gentleman, esp. a lady's escort —*adj.* 1. casual 2. arrogant —**cav/a·lier/ly** *adv.*

cav·al·ry (kav/'l rē) *n., pl.* **-ries** [< Fr.: see CAVALCADE] combat troops mounted originally on horses but now often on motorized armored vehicles —**cav/al·ry·man** (-mən) *n., pl.* **-men**

cave (kāv) *n.* [< L. *cavus*, hollow] a hollow place inside the earth; cavern —*vt., vi.* caved, cav/ing to collapse or make collapse (with *in*)

ca·ve·at emp·tor (kā/vē at/ emp/tôr) [L.] let the buyer beware

cave-in/ *n.* 1. a caving in 2. a place where the ground, etc. has caved in

cave man a prehistoric human being of the Stone Age who lived in caves

cav·ern (kav/ərn) *n.* a cave, esp. a large cave —**cav/ern·ous** *adj.*

cav·i·ar, cav·i·are (kav/ē är/) *n.* [Fr. < Per. *khāya*, egg + *-dār*, bearing] the salted eggs of sturgeon, etc. eaten as an appetizer

cav·il (kav/'l) *vi.* **-iled** or **-illed, -il-ing** or **-il·ling** [< L. *cavilla*, quibbling] to object unnecessarily; carp —*n.* a trivial objection; quibble —**cav/il·er, cav/il·ler** *n.*

cav·i·ty (kav/ə tē) *n., pl.* **-ties** [see CAVE] a hollow place, as in a tooth

ca·vort (kə vôrt/) *vi.* [< ?] 1. to prance or caper 2. to romp; frolic

caw (kô) *n.* [echoic] the harsh cry of a crow —*vi.* to make this sound

cay·enne (pepper) (kī en/, kā-) [< native Braz. *kynnha*] very hot red pepper made from the dried fruit of a pepper plant

cay·use (kī/ōōs, kī ōōs/) *n., pl.* **-us·es** [< AmInd. tribal name] a small Western horse used by cowboys

CB (sē/bē/) *adj.* [citizens' band] designating or of shortwave radio frequencies set aside by the FCC for local use by private persons

CBW chemical and biological warfare

cc., c.c. cubic centimeter(s)

Cd *Chem.* cadmium

cease (sēs) *vt., vi.* ceased, ceas/ing [see CEDE] to end; stop

cease-fire/ *n.* a temporary cessation of warfare; truce

cease/less (-lis) *adj.* unceasing; continual —**cease/less·ly** *adv.*

ce·cro·pi·a moth (si krō/pē ə) [after *Cecrops*, legendary Gr. king] the largest moth of the U.S., with a white spot on each wing

ce·cum (sē/kəm) *n., pl.* **-ca** (-kə) [< L. *caecus*, blind] the pouch at the beginning of the large intestine

ce·dar (sē/dər) *n.* [< Gr. *kedros*] 1. a pine tree having fragrant, durable wood 2. its wood —*adj.* of cedar

cede (sēd) *vt.* ced/ed, ced/ing [< L. *cedere*, to yield] 1. to surrender formally 2. to transfer the title of

ce·dil·la (si dil/ə) *n.* [Sp. dim. of *zeda*, ZETA] a mark put under *c* in some French words (Ex.: *façade*) to show that it has an *s* sound

ceil·ing (sēl/iŋ) *n.* [< L. *caelum*, heaven] 1. the inside top part of a room, opposite the floor 2. an upper limit [a price *ceiling*] 3. the upper limit of visibility —**hit the ceiling** [Slang] to lose one's temper

cel·an·dine (sel/ən dīn/, -dēn/) *n.* [< Gr. *chelidōn*, a swallow] 1. a variety of poppy with yellow flowers 2. a variety of buttercup

cel·e·brate (sel/ə brāt/) *vt.* **-brat/ed, -brat/ing** [< L. *celebrare*, to honor] 1. to perform (a ritual, etc.) 2. to commemorate (an anniversary, holiday, etc.) with festivity 3. to honor publicly —*vi.* [Colloq.] to have a good time —**cel/e·brant** (-brənt) *n.* —**cel/e·bra/tion** *n.* —**cel/e·bra/tor** *n.*

cel/e·brat/ed *adj.* famous; renowned

ce·leb·ri·ty (sə leb/rə tē) *n.* 1. fame 2. *pl.* **-ties** a famous person

ce·ler·i·ty (sə ler/ə tē) *n.* [< L. *celer*, swift] swiftness; speed

cel·er·y (sel/ər ē) *n.* [< Gr. *selinon*, parsley] a plant whose crisp leaf stalks are eaten as a vegetable

ce·les·tial (sə les/chəl) *adj.* [< L. *caelum*, heaven] 1. of the heavens or sky 2. heavenly; divine 3. perfect

cel·i·ba·cy (sel/ə bə sē) *n.* 1. the state of being unmarried 2. complete sexual abstinence

cel·i·bate (sel/ə bət, -bāt/) *n.* [< L. *caelebs*] an unmarried person —*adj.* of or in a state of celibacy

cell (sel) *n.* [< L. *cella*] 1. a small room, as in a prison 2. a small hollow, as in a honeycomb 3. a small unit of protoplasm: all plants and animals are made up of one or more cells 4. a receptacle for generating electricity by chemical reactions 5. a small unit of an organization —**celled** (seld) *adj.*

cel·lar (sel/ər) *n.* [see prec.] a room or rooms below ground and usually under a building

cel·lo, 'cel·lo (chel/ō) *n., pl.* **-los, -li** (-ē) [< VIOLONCELLO] an instrument of the violin family, between the viola and double bass in pitch —**cel/list, 'cel/list** *n.*

CELLO

cel·lo·phane (sel/ə fān/) *n.* a thin, transparent material made from cellulose, used as a wrapping

cel·lu·lar (sel/yoo lər) *adj.* of, like, or containing a cell or cells

Cel·lu·loid (sel/yoo loid/) [CELLUL(OSE) + -OID] *a trademark for* a flammable plastic substance made from nitrocellulose and camphor —*n.* [c-] this substance

cel·lu·lose (sel/yoo lōs/) *n.* [Fr. < L. *cella*, cell + -OSE¹] the chief substance in the cell walls of plants, used in making paper, textiles, etc.

cellulose acetate a cellulose resin used in making plastics, lacquers, etc.

cellulose nitrate *same as* NITROCEL-LULOSE

Cel·si·us (sel'sē əs) *adj.* [< A. *Celsius* (1701–44), Swed. inventor] designating, of, or according to a thermometer on which 0° is the freezing point and 100° is the boiling point of water

Celt (selt, kelt) *n.* [< L.] a Celtic-speaking person

Celt·ic (sel'tik, kel'-) *adj.* of the Celts, their languages, etc. —*n.* a subfamily of languages including Gaelic and Welsh

ce·ment (si ment') *n.* [< L. *caementum*, rough stone] 1. a powdered substance of lime and clay, mixed with water, etc. to make mortar or concrete: it hardens upon drying 2. any adhesive substance —*vt.* 1. to unite as with cement 2. to cover with cement —*vi.* to be cemented —**ce·ment'er** *n.*

cem·e·ter·y (sem'ə ter'ē) *n., pl.* **-ies** [< Gr. *koiman*, put to sleep] a place for the burial of the dead

cen·o·bite (sen'ə bīt') *n.* [< LGr. *koinos*, common + *bios*, life] a member of a religious order in a monastery or convent

cen·o·taph (sen'ə taf') *n.* [Fr. < Gr. *kenos*, empty + *taphos*, tomb] a monument honoring a dead person buried elsewhere

Ce·no·zo·ic (sē'nə zō'ik, sen'ə-) *adj.* [< Gr. *kainos*, recent + zo(o)- + -IC] designating the geologic era that includes the present, during which the various mammals have developed

cen·ser (sen'sər) *n.* a container in which incense is burned

cen·sor (sen'sər) *n.* [L. < *censere*, to judge] an official with the power to examine literature, mail, etc. and remove or prohibit anything considered obscene, objectionable, etc. —*vt.* to act as a censor of (a book, etc.) —**cen'sor·ship'** *n.*

cen·so·ri·ous (sen sôr'ē əs) *adj.* inclined to find fault; harshly critical

cen·sure (sen'shər) *n.* [see CENSOR] strong disapproval; condemnation —*vt.* **-sured, -sur·ing** to condemn as wrong —**cen'sur·a·ble** *adj.*

cen·sus (sen'səs) *n.* [L. < *censere*, enroll] an official count of population and recording of age, sex, etc.

cent (sent) *n.* [< L. *centum*, hundred] a 100th part of a dollar, or a coin of this value; penny

cent. 1. centigrade 2. century

cen·taur (sen'tôr) *n.* [< Gr. *Kentauros*] *Gr. Myth.* a monster with a man's head and trunk and a horse's body

cen·ta·vo (sen tä'vō) *n., pl.* **-vos** [Sp.: see CENT] a small coin of the Philippines, Mexico, and some S.American countries; one 100th of a peso

cen·te·nar·i·an (sen'tə ner'ē ən) *n.* [< ff.] a person at least 100 years old

cen·te·nar·y (sen ten'ər ē; sen'tə ner'ē) *adj.* [< L. *centum*, hundred] 1. of a century 2. of a centennial —*n., pl.* **-ies** 1. a century 2. a centennial

cen·ten·ni·al (sen ten'ē əl) *adj.* [< L. *centum*, hundred + *annus*, year] of or lasting 100 years —*n.* a 100th anniversary or its celebration

cen·ter (sen'tər) *n.* [< Gr. *kentron*, a point] 1. a point equally distant from all points on the circumference of a circle or surface of a sphere 2. a pivot 3. the approximate middle point or part of anything 4. a focal point of activity 5. [*often* C-] a political party between left (liberals) and right (conservatives) 6. *Sports* a player at the center of a line, floor, etc. —*vt.* 1. to place in or near the center 2. to gather to one place —*vi.* to be centered

cen'ter·board' *n.* a movable keellike board in a shallow sailboat

cen'ter·fold' *n.* the center facing pages of a magazine, often with an extra fold or folds, showing a photograph, as of a nude woman or man

center of gravity that point in a body around which its weight is evenly balanced

cen·ter·piece (sen'tər pēs') *n.* an ornament for the center of a table

centi- [L.] *a combining form meaning:* 1. hundred 2. a 100th part of

cen·ti·grade (sen'tə grād') *adj.* [Fr.: see CENTI- & GRADE] *same as* CELSIUS

cen'ti·gram', cen'ti·gramme' (-gram') *n.* [Fr.: see CENTI- & GRAM] a unit of weight, 1/100 gram

cen·time (sän'tēm) *n.* [Fr.] the 100th part of a franc

cen·ti·me·ter, cen·ti·me·tre (sen'tə mēt'ər) *n.* [Fr.: see CENTI- & -METER] a unit of measure, 1/100 meter

cen·ti·pede (sen'tə pēd') *n.* [Fr. < L. *centum*, hundred + *pes*, foot] a wormlike animal with a pair of legs for each body segment

cen·tral (sen'trəl) *adj.* 1. in, near, or of the center 2. equally accessible from various points 3. basic; chief 4. of a controlling source in a system —**cen'tral·ly** *adv.*

Central African Republic country in C Africa: 238,224 sq. mi.; pop. 1,352,000

Central America part of N.America between Mexico and S.America —**Central American**

central city the crowded, industrial central area of a large city

cen'tral·ize' (-īz') *vt.* **-ized', -iz'ing** 1. to make central; bring to a center 2. to organize under one control —*vi.* to become centralized —**cen'tral·i·za'tion** *n.* —**cen'tral·iz'er** *n.*

cen·tre (sen'tər) *n., vt., vi.* **-tred, -tring** *Brit. sp. of* CENTER

centri- *same as* CENTRO-

cen·trif·u·gal (sen trif'yə gəl, -ə gəl) *adj.* [< CENTRI- + L. *fugere*, flee] using or acted upon by a force (**centrifugal force**) that tends to make rotating bodies move away from the center of rotation

cen·tri·fuge (sen'trə fyōōj') *n.* a machine using centrifugal force to separate particles of varying density

cen·trip·e·tal (sen trip′ət ′l) *adj.* [< CENTRI- + L. *petere,* seek] using or acted upon by a force (**centripetal force**) that tends to make rotating bodies move toward the center of rotation

cen·trist (sen′trist) *n.* a member of a political party of the center

centro- [< L. *centrum,* CENTER] *a combining form meaning* center

cen·tu·ri·on (sen tyoor′ē ən) *n.* [see ff.] the commanding officer of an ancient Roman military unit, originally of 100 men

cen·tu·ry (sen′chər ē) *n., pl.* **-ries** [< L. *centum,* hundred] a period of 100 years, esp. as reckoned from 1 A.D.

ce·phal·ic (sə fal′ik) *adj.* [< Gr. *kephalē,* head] 1. of the head or skull 2. in, on, or near the head

ce·ram·ic (sə ram′ik) *adj.* [< Gr. *keramos,* clay] 1. of pottery, porcelain, etc. 2. of ceramics —*n.* 1. [*pl.,* with *sing. v.*] the art or work of making pottery, porcelain, etc. 2. an object made of such materials

ce·ram·ist (sə ram′ist) *n.* an expert in ceramics; ceramic artist: also **ce·ram′i·cist** (-ə sist)

ce·re·al (sir′ē əl) *adj.* [< L. *Cerealis,* of Ceres, Rom. goddess of agriculture] of grain —*n.* 1. any grain used for food, as wheat, oats, etc. 2. any grass producing such grain 3. food made from grain, as oatmeal

cer·e·bel·lum (ser′ə bel′əm) *n., pl.* **-lums, -la** [L., dim. of *cerebrum*] the section of the brain behind and below the cerebrum

cer·e·bral (ser′ə brəl, sə rē′-) *adj.* of the brain or the cerebrum

cerebral palsy spastic paralysis due to brain damage

cer·e·brate (ser′ə brāt′) *vi.* **-brat′ed, -brat′ing** [< L. *cerebrum,* the brain] to think —**cer′e·bra′tion** *n.*

cer·e·brum (ser′ə brəm, sə rē′-) *n., pl.* **-brums, -bra** [L.] the upper, main part of the brain

cere·ment (ser′ə mənt, sir′mənt) *n.* [< Gr. *kēros,* wax] 1. a shroud for a dead person 2. [*usually pl.*] any burial clothes

cer·e·mo·ni·al (ser′ə mō′nē əl) *adj.* of or consisting of ceremony; formal —*n.* 1. a set system of forms or rites 2. a rite —**cer′e·mo′ni·al·ly** *adv.*

cer′e·mo′ni·ous (-nē əs) *adj.* 1. full of ceremony 2. very polite or formal —**cer′e·mo′ni·ous·ly** *adv.*

cer·e·mo·ny (ser′ə mō′nē) *n., pl.* **-nies** [L. *caerimonia*] 1. a set of formal acts proper to a special occasion, as a religious rite 2. behavior that follows rigid etiquette 3. *a*) formality *b*) empty formality —**stand on ceremony** to insist on formality

ce·rise (sə rēs′, -rēz′) *n., adj.* [Fr., a cherry] bright red

cer·tain (surt′′n) *adj.* [< L. *cernere,* decide] 1. fixed; settled 2. inevitable 3. reliable; dependable 4. sure; positive 5. definite, but unnamed [a *certain* person] 6. some [to a *certain* extent] —**for certain** without doubt

cer′tain·ly *adv.* undoubtedly; surely

cer′tain·ty (-tē) *n.* 1. the state or fact of being certain 2. *pl.* **-ties** anything certain

cer·tif·i·cate (sur tif′ə kit) *n.* [see ff.] a document attesting to a fact, qualification, etc. —*vt.* (-kāt′) **-cat′ed, -cat′ing** to issue a certificate to

certificate of deposit a bank certificate issued for a specified large deposit of money drawing a higher rate of interest if not withdrawn during a specified period

certified public accountant a public accountant certified as passing a State examination

cer·ti·fy (sur′tə fī′) *vt.* **-fied′, -fy′ing** [< L. *certus,* certain + *facere,* to make] 1. to declare (a thing) true, accurate, etc. by formal statement 2. to guarantee (a check, document, etc.) 3. to grant a certificate to —**cer′ti·fi′a·ble** *adj.* —**cer′ti·fi·ca′tion** *n.*

cer·ti·tude (sur′tə tōōd′, -tyōōd′) *n.* sureness; inevitability

ce·ru·le·an (sə rōō′lē ən) *adj.* [< L. *caelum,* heaven] sky-blue; azure

Cer·van·tes (sər van′tēz), **Mi·guel** (mē gel′) **de** 1547–1616; Sp. writer

cer·vix (sur′viks) *n., pl.* **-vi·ces′** (-və sēz′), **-vix·es** [L., neck] a necklike part, as of the uterus —**cer′vi·cal** (-vi kəl) *adj.*

ces·sa·tion (se sā′shən) *n.* [< L. *cessare,* to cease] a ceasing or stopping

ces·sion (sesh′ən) *n.* [< L. *cedere,* to yield] a ceding or giving up (of rights, etc.) to another

cess·pool (ses′pōōl′) *n.* [< It. *cesso,* privy] a deep hole in the ground to receive drainage or sewage from sinks, toilets, etc.

ce·ta·cean (si tā′shən) *adj.* [< L. *cetus,* whale] of water mammals such as whales and dolphins —*n.* any of these

Cey·lon (sə län′) country on an island off the SE tip of India: 25,332 sq. mi.; pop. 11,500,000: official name *Sri Lanka* —**Cey·lo·nese** (sel′ə nēz′) *adj., n.*

cf. [L. *confer*] compare

cg, cg., cgm, cgm. centigram(s)

Ch., ch. 1. chapter 2. church

Cha·blis (shab′lē) *n.* a dry, white Burgundy wine, orig. from Chablis, France

Chad (chad) country in NC Africa: c.495,000 sq. mi.; pop. 3,361,000

chafe (chāf) *vt.* **chafed, chaf′ing** [< L. *calefacere,* make warm] 1. to rub so as to make warm 2. to wear away or make sore by rubbing 3. to annoy; irritate —*vi.* 1. to rub (on or against) 2. to be vexed

chaff (chaf) *n.* [OE. *ceaf*] 1. threshed or winnowed husks of grain 2. anything worthless 3. teasing; banter —*vt., vi.* to tease

chaf·ing dish (chāf′iŋ) a pan with a heating device beneath it, to cook food at the table or to keep food hot

cha·grin (shə grin′) *n.* [Fr.] embarrassment due to disappointment, failure, etc. —*vt.* **-grined′, -grin′ing** to make feel chagrin

chain (chān) *n.* [< L. *catena*] 1. a flexible series of joined links 2. [*pl.*] *a)* bonds; fetters *b)* captivity 3. a chainlike measuring instrument, as for surveying 4. a series of related things or events 5. a group of stores, etc. owned by a company —*vt.* 1. to fasten with chains 2. to restrain, etc.

chain gang a gang of prisoners chained together, as when working

chain'-re·act' *vi.* to be involved in or subjected to a chain reaction

chain reaction 1. a self-sustaining series of chemical or nuclear reactions in which reaction products keep the process going 2. a series of events each of which results in the following

chain saw a portable power saw with an endless chain carrying cutting teeth

chair (cher) *n.* [< L. *cathedra*: see CATHEDRAL] 1. a piece of furniture with a back, for one person to sit on 2. an important or official position 3. a chairman —*vt.* 1. to seat 2. to preside over as chairman

chair'lift' *n.* a line of seats suspended from a power-driven endless cable, used to carry skiers up a slope

chair'man (-mən) *n.*, *pl.* -men a person in charge of a meeting, committee, etc.: also **chair'per'son** — **chair'man·ship'** *n.*

chaise (shāz) *n.* [Fr.] a lightweight carriage, having two or four wheels

chaise longue (lôŋ') *pl.* **chaise longues** (lôŋz') [Fr., long chair] a couchlike chair with a long seat: also **chaise lounge** (lounj)

chal·ced·o·ny (kal sed'n ē, kal'sə dō'nē) *n.*, *pl.* -nies [< Gr.] a kind of colored quartz with the luster of wax

cha·let (sha lā', shal'ē) *n.* [Swiss-Fr.] 1. a Swiss house with overhanging eaves 2. any similar building

chal·ice (chal'is) *n.* [< L. *calix*] 1. a cup 2. the cup for Communion wine

chalk (chôk) *n.* [< L. *calx*, limestone] 1. a soft, whitish limestone 2. a piece of chalk or chalklike substance used for writing on a blackboard —*adj.* made with chalk —*vt.* to mark or rub with chalk —**chalk up** 1. to score, get, or achieve 2. to charge or credit — **chalk'i·ness** *n.* —**chalk'y** *adj.*

chalk'board' *n.* same as BLACKBOARD

chal·lenge (chal'ənj) *n.* [< L. *calumnia*, false accusation] 1. a demand for identification 2. a calling into question 3. a call to a duel, contest, etc. 4. anything that calls for special effort —*vt.* -lenged, -leng'ing to subject to a challenge —*vi.* to make a challenge —**chal'leng·er** *n.*

chal·lis, chal·lie (shal'ē) *n.* [< ?] a lightweight fabric of wool, etc.

cham·ber (chām'bər) *n.* [< L. *camera*, a vault] 1. a room; esp., a bedroom 2. [*pl.*] a judge's office near the courtroom 3. an assembly hall 4. a legislative or judicial body 5. a council [*chamber* of commerce] 6. an enclosed

space 7. the part of a gun holding the charge or of a revolver holding the cartridge —**cham'bered** *adj.*

cham·ber·lain (chām'bər lin) *n.* [< OHG. *chamarlinc*] 1. an officer in charge of the household of a ruler or lord 2. a high official in certain royal courts 3. [Brit.] a treasurer

cham'ber·maid' *n.* a woman whose work is taking care of bedrooms

chamber music music for performance by a small group, as a string quartet

chamber of commerce an association established to further the business interests of its community

cham·bray (sham'brā) *n.* [< *Cambrai*, Fr. city] a smooth cotton fabric of white threads woven across a colored warp

cha·me·le·on (kə mēl'yən, -mē'lē ən) *n.* [< Gr. *chamai*, on the ground + *leōn*, lion] any of various lizards that can change the color of their skin

cham·ois (sham'ē) *n.*, *pl.* **cham'ois** [Fr.] 1. a small, goatlike antelope of the mountains of Europe and the Caucasus 2. a soft leather made from the skin of chamois, sheep, etc.: also **cham'my** (sham'ē)

cham·o·mile (kam'ə mīl', -mēl') *n.* [< Gr. *chamai*, on the ground + *melon*, apple] a plant with dried flower heads used in a medicinal tea

champ[1] (champ) *vt.*, *vi.* [prob. echoic] to chew or bite hard and noisily

champ[2] (champ) *n.* [Slang] a champion

cham·pagne (sham pān') *n.* an effervescent white wine, orig. from Champagne, region in NE France

cham·paign (sham pān') *n.* [< L. *campus*, field] flat, open country

cham·pi·on (cham'pē ən) *n.* [< LL. *campio*, gladiator] 1. one who fights for another or for a cause; defender 2. a winner of first place in a competition —*adj.* excelling all others —*vt.* to fight for; defend; support —**cham'pi·on·ship'** *n.*

chance (chans) *n.* [< L. *cadere*, to fall] 1. the way things happen without apparent cause; luck 2. an unpredictable event 3. a risk or gamble 4. a ticket in a lottery 5. an opportunity 6. a possibility or probability —*adj.* accidental —*vi.* chanced, chanc'ing to have the luck or occasion (*to*) —*vt.* to risk —**by chance** accidentally — **chance on** (or **upon**) to find or meet by chance —**on the** (off) **chance** —(the) **chances are** the likelihood of relying on the (remote) possibility

chan·cel (chan's'l) *n.* [< L. *cancelli*, lattices] the part of a church around the altar, for the clergy and the choir

chan'cel·ler·y (-sə lə rē) *n.*, *pl.* -ies the position or office of a chancellor

chan'cel·lor (-lər) *n.* [< LL. *cancellarius*, secretary] 1. a high government official, as, in certain countries, a prime minister 2. in some universities, the president or other executive officer

3. a chief judge of a court of chancery or equity in some States 4. any of several church officials —**chan'cel·lor·ship'** n.

chance'-med'ley n. 1. accidental homicide 2. haphazard action

chan·cer·y (chan'sər ē) n., pl. **-ies** [< ML. cancellaria] 1. a court of equity 2. an office of public archives 3. a chancellery

chan·cre (shaŋ'kər) n. [Fr.: see CANCER] a sore or ulcer of syphilis

chan·cy (chan'sē) adj. **-i·er**, **-i·est** risky; uncertain

chan·de·lier (shan'də lir') n. [Fr. < L. candela, candle] a lighting fixture hung from a ceiling, with branches for candles, electric bulbs, etc.

chan·dler (chan'dlər) n. [< L. candela, candle] 1. a maker of candles 2. a retailer of supplies, as for ships —**chan'dler·y** n.

change (chānj) vt. **changed**, **chang'ing** [< L. cambire, to barter] 1. to put or take (a thing) in place of something else [change jobs] 2. to exchange [change seats] 3. to make different; alter —vi. 1. to alter; vary 2. to leave one train, bus, etc. and board another 3. to put on other clothes 4. to make an exchange —n. 1. a substitution, alteration, or variation 2. variety 3. another set of clothes 4. a) money returned as the difference between the price and the greater sum presented b) coins or bills that together equal the larger value of a single coin or bill c) loose coins —**change off** to take turns —**ring the changes** 1. to ring a set of bells with all possible variations 2. to do or say a thing in many ways —**change'a·ble** adj. —**change'less** adj.

change·ling n. a child secretly put in the place of another

change of life menopause

change'o'ver n. a complete change, as in goods produced

chan·nel (chan'l) n. [see CANAL] 1. the bed or deeper part of a river, harbor, etc. 2. a body of water joining two larger ones 3. any means of passage 4. [pl.] the official course of transmission of communications 5. a groove or furrow 6. a frequency band assigned to a radio or television station —vt. **-neled** or **-nelled**, **-nel·ing** or **-nel·ling** 1. to make a channel in 2. to send through a channel

Channel Islands group of Brit. islands in the English Channel

chan'nel·ize (-īz') vt. **-ized'**, **-iz'ing** to provide a channel for

†chan·son (shän sōn') n., pl. **-sons'** (-sōn') [Fr.] a song

chant (chant) n. [< L. cantare, sing] 1. a song; esp., a liturgical song with a series of words sung to each tone 2. a singsong way of speaking —vi., vt. 1. to sing or say in a chant 2. to celebrate in song —**chant'er** n.

chan·teuse (shän tooz') n. [Fr.] a woman singer, esp. of popular ballads

chan·tey (shan'tē, chan'-) n., pl. **-teys** a song that sailors sing in rhythm with their motions while working: also **chan'ty**, pl. **-ties**

chan·ti·cleer (chan'tə klir') n. [see CHANT & CLEAR] a rooster

Cha·nu·kah (khä'noo kä') same as HANUKA

cha·os (kā'äs) n. [< Gr., space] extreme confusion or disorder —**cha·ot'ic** (-ät'ik) adj.

chap¹ (chäp, chap) n. [< ?] same as CHOP²

chap² (chap) n. [< Brit. chapman, peddler] [Colloq.] a man; fellow

chap³ (chap) vt., vi. **chapped** or **chapt**, **chap'ping** [ME. chappen, cut] to crack open; split; roughen, as skin —n. a chapped place in the skin

chap. 1. chaplain 2. chapter

chap·ar·ral (chap'ə ral', shap'-) n. [Sp. < chaparro, evergreen oak] [Southwest] a dense thicket of shrubs, etc.

cha·peau (sha pō') n., pl. **-peaus'**, **-peaux'** (-pōz') [Fr.] a hat

chap·el (chap'l) n. [< VL. cappa, cape] 1. a small church 2. a private place of worship, as in a school

chap·er·on, chap·er·one (shap'ə rōn') n. [Fr., hood] a person, esp. an older woman, who accompanies young unmarried people for propriety —vt., vi. **-oned'**, **-on'ing** to act as chaperon (to) —**chap'er·on·age** n.

chap·lain (chap'lən) n. [see CHAPEL] 1. a clergyman attached to a chapel 2. a clergyman serving in a religious capacity with the armed forces, or in a prison, hospital, etc.

chap·let (chap'lit) n. [< LL. cappa, hood] 1. a garland for the head 2. a string of beads, esp. prayer beads

chaps (chaps, shaps) n.pl. [< MexSp. chaparreras] leather trousers without a seat, worn over ordinary trousers by cowboys to protect their legs

CHAPS

chap·ter (chap'tər) n. [< L. caput, head] 1. a main division, as of a book 2. a local branch of an organization

char¹ (chär) vt., vi. **charred**, **char'ring** [< CHARCOAL] 1. to reduce to charcoal 2. to burn partly; scorch

char² (chär) n. [< Gael. ceara, red] a kind of red-bellied trout

char·ac·ter (kar'ik tər) n. [< Gr. charattein, engrave] 1. any letter, figure, or symbol used in writing and printing 2. a distinctive trait 3. kind or sort 4. behavior typical of a person or group 5. moral strength 6. reputation 7. status; position 8. a person in a play, novel, etc. 9. [Colloq.] an eccentric person

char·ac·ter·is·tic (-tə ris'tic) adj. typical; distinctive —n. a distinguishing trait or quality —**char'ac·ter·is'ti·cal·ly** adv.

char·ac·ter·ize (-tə rīz') vt. **-ized'**, **-iz'ing** 1. to describe the particular traits of 2. to be a characteristic of —**char'ac·ter·i·za'tion** n.

cha·rade (shə rād') n. [Fr. < Pr. charrar, to gossip] [often pl.] a game in

which words to be guessed are panto-
mimed, often syllable by syllable

char·broil, char-broil (chär'-
broil') vt. to broil over a charcoal fire

char·coal (chär'kōl') n. [ME. char
cole] a black form of carbon made by
partially burning wood, etc. in an
airless kiln or retort

chard (chärd) n. [< L. carduus,
thistle] a kind of beet with large,
edible leaves and stalks

charge (chärj) vt. charged, charg'-
ing [ult. < L. carrus, car] 1. to load
or fill (with something) 2. to add an
electrical charge to (a battery, etc.)
3. to give as a duty, command, etc. to
4. to accuse 5. to make liable for (an
error, etc.) 6. to ask as a price 7. to
record as a debt 8. to attack vigorously —vi. 1. to ask payment (for)
2. to attack vigorously —n. 1. a
load or burden 2. the necessary
quantity, as of fuel, for a container
or device 3. the amount of chemical
energy stored in a battery 4. responsibility or care (of) 5. a person
or thing entrusted to one's care 6.
instruction; command 7. accusation;
indictment 8. cost 9. a debt, debit,
or expense 10. an onslaught 11.
[Slang] a thrill —in charge (of)
in control (of) —charge'a·ble adj.

charge account an arrangement by
which a customer may pay for purchases within a specified future period

charge plate a metal or plastic plate
embossed with the owner's name, used
as a stamp on bills in making purchases
on credit: also **charge'-a·plate'** n.

charg'er n. 1. a person or thing that
charges 2. a horse ridden in battle

char·i·ot (char'ē ət) n. [see CAR] a
horse-drawn, two-wheeled cart used in
ancient times for war, racing, etc.
—char'i·o·teer' (-ə tir') n.

cha·ris·ma (kə riz'mə) n., pl. -ma·ta
(-mə tə) [< Gr., favor, grace] a
special, inspiring quality of leadership

char·is·mat·ic (kar'iz mat'ik) adj.
1. of or having charisma 2. designating
or of a religious group seemingly inspired by God, as in healing powers
—n. a member of a charismatic group

char·i·ta·ble (char'i tə b'l) adj. 1.
generous to the needy 2. of or for
charity 3. kind and forgiving —
char'i·ta·bly adv.

char'i·ty (-ə tē) n., pl. -ties [< L.
caritas, affection] 1. Christian Theol.
love for one's fellow men 2. leniency
in judging others 3. a) generosity
toward the needy b) the help given
4. a welfare institution, fund, etc.

char·la·tan (shär'lə t'n) n. [ult. <
LL. cerretanus, seller of papal indul-
gences] a fraud; quack; impostor

Char·le·magne (shär'lə mān') 742-
814 A.D.; emperor of the Western
Roman Empire (800–814)

Charles·ton (chärlz'stən) capital of
W.Va., in the W part: pop. 64,000 —n.
a lively dance of the 1920's in 4/4 time

char·ley horse (chär'lē) [Colloq.] a
cramp in the leg or arm muscles

Char·lotte (shär'lət) city in S N.C.:
pop. 314,000

charm (chärm) n. [< L. carmen] 1.
an action, object, or words assumed to
have magic power 2. a trinket worn on
a bracelet, etc. 3. a quality that
attracts or delights —vt., vi. 1. to
act on as if by magic 2. to fascinate;
delight —charm'er n. —charm'-
ing adj. —charm'ing·ly adv.

char·nel (house) (chär'n'l) [< LL.
carnale, graveyard] a building, etc.
used for dead bodies and bones

Cha·ron (ker'ən) Gr. Myth. the
ferryman on the river Styx

chart (chärt) n. [< Gr. chartēs, leaf
of paper] 1. a map, esp. for use in
navigation 2. an information sheet
with tables, graphs, etc. 3. a table,
graph, etc. —vt. 1. to make a chart of
2. to plan (a course of action)

char·ter (chär'tər) n. [see prec.] 1.
a franchise given by a government 2.
a written statement of basic laws
or principles; constitution 3. written
permission to form a local chapter of a
society —vt. 1. to grant a charter to
2. to hire (a bus, plane, etc.) for
private use —char'ter·er n.

charter member a founding member

char·treuse (shär trōz') n. [Fr.]
pale, yellowish green

char'wom'an (chär'-) n., pl. -wom'-
en [see CHORE] a cleaning woman

char·y (cher'ē) adj. -i·er, -i·est [<
OE. cearu, care] 1. not taking
chances; cautious 2. sparing —char'-
i·ly adv. —char'i·ness n.

chase[1] (chās) vt. chased, chas'ing
[ult. < L. capere, take] 1. to follow
so as to catch 2. to run after 3. to
drive away 4. to hunt —vi. 1. to go
in pursuit 2. [Colloq.] to rush —n.
1. a chasing; pursuit 2. the hunting
of game for sport 3. anything hunted;
quarry —give chase to pursue

chase[2] (chās) vt. chased, chas'ing
[< Fr. enchâsser, enshrine] to ornament (metal) as by engraving

chas'er n. [Colloq.] a mild drink, as
water, taken after whiskey, etc.

chasm (kaz'm) n. [< Gr. chasma]
1. a deep crack in the earth's surface;
abyss 2. any break or gap; rift

chas·sis (chas'ē, shas'ē) n., pl. -sis
(-ēz) [Fr. < L. capsa, a box] 1. the
frame, wheels, etc. of a motor vehicle,
but not the body or engine 2. a) a
frame, as for the parts of a TV set
b) the assembled frame and parts

chaste (chāst) adj. [< L. castus,
pure] 1. not indulging in unlawful
sexual activity 2. decent; modest 3.
simple in style —chaste'ly adv. —
chaste'ness n.

chas·ten (chās'n) vt. [< L. castigare, punish] 1. to punish so as to
correct 2. to restrain or subdue

chas·tise (chas tīz') vt. -tised',
-tis'ing [see prec.] 1. to punish, esp.

fat, āpe, cär; ten, ēven; is, bīte; gō, hôrn, tōōl, look; oil, out; up, fur;
chin; she; thin, then, zh, leisure, ŋ, ring, ə for a in ago; ', (ā'b'l); ë, Fr. coeur;
ö, Fr. feu; Fr. mon; ü, Fr. duc; kh, G. ich, doch; ‡ foreign; < derived from

by beating **2.** to scold sharply —
chas·tise·ment *n.* —**chas·tis·er** *n.*

chas·ti·ty (chas'tə tē) *n.* **1.** abstention from unlawful sexual activity **2.** celibacy or virginity **3.** decency; modesty **4.** simplicity of style

chas·u·ble (chaz'yoo b'l, chas'-) *n.* [< ML. *casula*] a sleeveless outer vestment worn by priests at Mass

chat (chat) *vi.* chat'ted, chat'ting [< CHATTER] to talk in a light, informal manner —*n.* light, informal talk

châ·teau (sha tō') *n.*, *pl.* -teaux' (-tōz', -tō'), -teaus' [Fr. < L. *castellum*, castle] **1.** a French feudal castle **2.** a large country house and estate, esp. in France Also **cha·teau'**

chat·e·laine (shat'l ān') *n.* [Fr.] **1.** the mistress of a château **2.** an ornamental clasp or chain

Chat·ta·noo·ga (chat'ə nōō'gə) city in SE Tenn.: pop. 170,000

chat·tel (chat'l) *n.* [see CATTLE] a movable item of personal property

chat·ter (chat'ər) *vi.* [echoic] **1.** to make short, rapid, indistinct sounds, as apes do **2.** to talk much and foolishly **3.** to click together rapidly as teeth do from cold —*n.* **1.** a chattering **2.** foolish talk —**chat'ter·er** *n.*

chat'ter·box' *n.* an incessant talker

chat·ty (chat'ē) *adj.* -ti·er, -ti·est fond of chatting —**chat'ti·ness** *n.*

Chau·cer (chô'sər), Geoffrey 1340?-1400; Eng. poet

chauf·feur (shō'fər, shō fur') *n.* [Fr., lit., stoker] one hired to drive a private automobile for someone else —*vt.* to act as chauffeur to

chau·vin·ism (shō'və niz'm) *n.* [< N. *Chauvin*, fanatical Fr. patriot] **1.** militant and fanatical patriotism **2.** unreasoning devotion to one's race, sex, etc. —**chau'vin·ist** *n.*, *adj.* —**chau'vin·is'tic** *adj.* —**chau'vin·is'ti·cal·ly** *adv.*

cheap (chēp) *adj.* [ult. < L. *caupo*, tradesman] **1.** low in price **2.** worth more than the price **3.** easily got **4.** of little value **5.** contemptible **6.** [Colloq.] stingy —*adv.* at a low cost —**cheap'ly** *adv.* —**cheap'ness** *n.*

cheap'en *vt.*, *vi.* to make or become cheap or cheaper —**cheap'en·er** *n.*

cheap shot [Slang] an uncalled-for, rough or mean act or remark

cheap'skate' *n.* [Slang] a stingy person

cheat (chēt) *n.* [< L. *ex-*, out + *cadere*, fall] **1.** a fraud; swindle **2.** a swindler —*vt.* **1.** to defraud; swindle **2.** to foil or elude *[to cheat death]* —*vi.* **1.** to be dishonest or deceitful **2.** [Slang] to be sexually unfaithful (often with *on*) —**cheat'er** *n.*

check (chek) *n.* [< OFr. *eschec*, a check at chess] **1.** a sudden stop **2.** any restraint **3.** one that restrains **4.** a supervision or test of accuracy, etc. **5.** a mark (√) to show verification **6.** an identification ticket, token, etc. *[a hat check]* **7.** one's bill at a restaurant or bar **8.** a written order to a bank to pay a sum of money **9.** a pattern of squares, or one of the squares **10.** *Chess* the state of a

king that is in danger —*interj.* [Colloq.] agreed! right! —*vt.* **1.** to stop suddenly **2.** to restrain; curb; block **3.** to test, verify, etc. by examination or comparison (often with *out*) **4.** to mark with a check (√) (often with *off*) **5.** to mark with a pattern of squares **6.** to deposit temporarily **7.** to clear (esp. luggage) for shipment **8.** *Chess* to place (the opponent's king) in check —*vi.* **1.** to agree with one another, item for item (often with *out*) **2.** to investigate or verify (often with *on*, *up on*) —**check in 1.** to register at a hotel, etc. **2.** [Colloq.] to present oneself, as at work —**check out 1.** to pay and leave a hotel, etc. **2.** to add up the prices of (items selected) for payment **3.** to prove to be accurate, etc. —**in check** under control —**check'er** *n.*

check'book' *n.* a book of forms for writing checks (sense 8)

checked (chekt) *adj.* having a pattern of squares

check'er·board' *n.* a board with 64 squares of two alternating colors, used in checkers and chess

check'ered (-ərd) *adj.* **1.** having a pattern of squares **2.** varied

check'ers (-ərz) *n.pl.* **1.** *[with sing. v.]* a game for two played with flat disks on a checkerboard **2.** the disks

checking account a bank account against which the depositor can draw checks

check'list' *n.* a list of things, names, etc. to be referred to: also **check list**

check'mate' (-māt') *n.* [ult. < Per. *shāh māt*, the king is dead] **1.** *Chess a)* the winning move that puts the opponent's king in a position where it cannot be saved *b)* this position **2.** total defeat, frustration, etc. —*vt.* -mat'ed, -mat'ing **1.** to place in checkmate **2.** to defeat completely

check'off' *n.* the withholding of dues for the union by the employer

check'out' *n.* **1.** the act or place of checking out purchases **2.** the time by which one must check out of a hotel, etc.

check'point' *n.* a place on a road, etc. where traffic is inspected

check'room' *n.* a room for checking hats, coats, etc.

check'up' *n.* a medical examination

Ched·dar (cheese) (ched'ər) [< *Cheddar*, England] a hard, smooth cheese

cheek (chēk) *n.* [OE. *ceoke*, jaw] **1.** either side of the face below the eye **2.** [Colloq.] sauciness; impudence —**tongue in cheek** jestingly

cheek'bone' *n.* the bone of the upper cheek, just below the eye

cheek'y *adj.* -i·er, -i·est [Colloq.] saucy; impudent —**cheek'i·ness** *n.*

cheep (chēp) *n.* [echoic] the short, shrill sound made by a young bird —*vt.*, *vi.* to make, or utter with, this sound —**cheep'er** *n.*

cheer (chir) *n.* [ult. < Gr. *kara*, the head] **1.** a state of mind or of feeling; spirit *[be of good cheer]* **2.** gladness; joy **3.** festive food or entertainment

4. encouragement **5.** *a)* a glad, excited shout to urge on, greet, etc. *b)* a rallying cry —*vt.* **1.** to comfort or gladden (often with *up*) **2.** to urge on, greet, etc. with cheers —*vi.* **1.** to become cheerful (usually with *up*) **2.** to shout cheers

cheer′ful *adj.* **1.** full of cheer; gay **2.** bright and attractive **3.** willing *[a cheerful* helper*]* —**cheer′ful·ly** *adv.* —**cheer′ful·ness** *n.*

cheer′i·o′ (-ē ō′) *interj., n., pl.* -os′ [Brit. Colloq.] **1.** goodbye **2.** good health: used as a toast

cheer′lead′er (-lē′dər) *n.* a leader of cheers, as at a football game

cheer′less *adj.* not cheerful; dismal; dreary —**cheer′less·ly** *adv.* —**cheer′less·ness** *n.*

cheers (chirz) *interj.* [Chiefly Brit.] good health: used as a toast

cheer′y *adj.* -i·er, -i·est cheerful; gay; bright —**cheer′i·ly** *adv.* —**cheer′i·ness** *n.*

cheese (chēz) *n.* [OE. *cyse*] a solid food made from milk curds

cheese′burg′er (-bur′gər) *n.* a hamburger topped with melted cheese

cheese′cake′ *n.* **1.** a cake made with cottage cheese or cream cheese **2.** [Slang] photographic display of the figure, esp. the legs, of a pretty girl

cheese′cloth′ *n.* [from its use for wrapping cheese] a thin, cotton cloth with a very loose weave

chees·y (chēz′ē) *adj.* -i·er, -i·est **1.** like cheese **2.** [Slang] inferior; poor

chee·tah (chēt′ə) *n.* [< Hind. < Sans. *citra*, spotted] a swift, leopard-like animal of Africa and S Asia

chef (shef) *n.* [Fr., head, chief] **1.** a head cook **2.** any cook

Che·khov (chek′ôf), **An·ton** (än tōn′) 1860–1904; Russ. writer

che·la (kē′lə) *n.* [< Gr. *chēlē*, claw] a pincerlike claw, as of a crab

chem. 1. chemical **2.** chemistry

chem·i·cal (kem′i k'l) *adj.* **1.** of, made by, or used in chemistry **2.** made with or operated by chemicals —*n.* any substance used in or obtained by a chemical process —**chem′i·cal·ly** *adv.*

chemical engineering the science or profession of applying chemistry to industrial uses

chemical warfare warfare using poisonous gases, napalm, etc.

che·mise (shə mēz′) *n.* [< VL. *camisia*, tunic] a woman's loose, short slip **2.** a straight, loose dress

chem·ist (kem′ist) *n.* [< ALCHEMIST] **1.** a specialist in chemistry **2.** [Brit.] a pharmacist, or druggist

chem·is·try (kem′is trē) *n.* [< CHEMIST] the science dealing with the composition and properties of substances, and with the reactions by which substances are produced from or converted into other substances

chem·o·sur·ger·y (kem′ō sur′jər ē, kē′mō-) *n.* the removal of diseased tissue, etc. with chemicals

chem′o·ther′a·py (-ther′ə pē) *n.* the use of chemical drugs in medicine

chem·ur·gy (kem′ər jē) *n.* chemistry dealing with the use of organic, esp. farm, products in industrial manufacture

che·nille (shi nēl′) *n.* [Fr., caterpillar] **1.** a tufted, velvety yarn **2.** a fabric woven with this

cheque (chek) *n. Brit. sp.* of CHECK (*n.* 8)

cher·ish (cher′ish) *vt.* [< L. *carus*, dear] **1.** to hold dear **2.** to cling to; hold to; nurture

Cher·o·kee (cher′ə kē′) *n., pl.* -kees′, -kee′ a member of a tribe of N.American Indians now chiefly of SW U.S.

che·root (shə rōōt′) *n.* [< Tamil] a cigar with both ends cut square

cher·ry (cher′ē) *n., pl.* -ries [< Gr. *kerasion*] **1.** a small, fleshy fruit with a smooth, hard pit **2.** the tree that it grows on **3.** the wood of this tree **4.** a bright red

cher′ry·stone′ (**clam**) a small quahog, a variety of clam

cher·ub (cher′əb) *n., pl.* -ubs; for 1 usually -u·bim (-ə bim, -yoo bim) [< Heb. *kerūbh*] **1.** any of a kind of angel, often represented as a chubby, rosy-faced child with wings **2.** an innocent or lovely child —**che·ru·bic** (chə rōō′bik) *adj.* —**che·ru′bi·cal·ly** *adv.*

cher·vil (chur′vəl) *n.* [< Gr. *chairephyllon*] a plant like parsley, with leaves used to flavor salads, soups, etc.

Ches·a·peake Bay (ches′ə pēk′) arm of the Atlantic, extending into Va. & Md.

chess (ches) *n.* [< OFr. *eschec*, a check at chess] a game played on a checkerboard by two players, using a variety of pieces (**chessmen**)

chess′board′ *n.* a checkerboard used for playing chess

chest (chest) *n.* [< Gr. *kistē*, a box] **1.** a box with a lid **2.** a cabinet with drawers, as for clothes **3.** a cabinet with shelves, as for medicines **4.** the part of the body enclosed by the ribs and breastbone

ches·ter·field (ches′tər fēld′) [< a 19th-c. Earl of *Chesterfield*] a single-breasted topcoat, usually with a velvet collar

chest·nut (ches′nut′) *n.* [< Gr. *kastaneia*] **1.** the edible nut of a tree of the beech family **2.** this tree, or its wood **3.** reddish brown **4.** [Colloq.] an old, stale joke, story, etc.

che·val glass (shə val′) [Fr. *cheval*, horse] a full-length mirror mounted on swivels in a frame

chev·i·ot (shev′ē ət) *n.* [< *Cheviot* Hills, on the Scottish-English border] a rough, twilled wool fabric

chev·ron (shev′rən) *n.* [OFr., rafter] a V-shaped bar on the sleeves of a uniform, showing rank

chew (chōō) *vt., vi.* [OE. *ceowan*] to bite and crush with the teeth —*n.* **1.**

a chewing **2.** something chewed or for chewing —**chew'a·ble** adj.— **chew'er** n. —**chew'y** adj. **-i·er, -i·est**

chewing gum a sweet, flavored substance, as chicle, used for chewing

Chey·enne (shī an', -en') capital of Wyo., in the SE part: pop. 47,000

chg. pl. **chgs.** charge

chi (kī) n. the 22d letter of the Greek alphabet (X, χ)

Chi·an·ti (kē än'tē, -an'-) n. [It.] a dry, red wine

chi·a·ro·scu·ro (kē är'ə skyoor'ō) n., pl. **-ros** [It. < L. clarus, clear + obscurus, dark] **1.** treatment of light and shade in a painting, etc., esp. when emphasized **2.** a painting, drawing, etc. notable for this

chic (shēk) n. [Fr. < MLowG. schick, skill] smart elegance —adj. **chic'quer, chic'quest** smartly stylish

Chi·ca·go (shə kä'gō, -kô'-) city and port in NE Ill.: pop. 3,005,000

chi·can·er·y (shə kān'ər ē) n., pl. **-ies** [< Fr.] **1.** trickery **2.** a trick

Chi·ca·no (chi kä'nō) n., pl. **-nos** [< AmSp.] [also c-] a U.S. citizen or inhabitant of Mexican descent

chi·chi, chi-chi (shē'shē, chē'chē) adj. [Fr.] extremely chic, in an affected or showy way

chick (chik) n. [ME. chike] **1.** a young chicken or bird **2.** a child **3.** [Slang] a young woman

chick·a·dee (chik'ə dē') n. [echoic] a small bird related to the titmouse

chick·en (chik'ən) n. [< OE. cycen, little cock] **1.** a common farm bird raised for its edible eggs and flesh; hen or rooster, esp. a young one **2.** its flesh —adj. [Slang] cowardly —**chicken (out)** [Slang] to quit from fear

chicken feed [Slang] a paltry sum

chick'en-fried' adj. coated with seasoned flour or batter and fried

chick·en-heart'ed adj. cowardly; timid: also **chick·en-liv'ered**

chicken pox an acute, contagious virus disease, esp. of children, characterized by skin eruptions

chicken wire light, pliable, wire fencing

chick'pea' n. [< L. cicer, pea] **1.** a bushy annual plant with short, hairy pods **2.** the edible seeds

chick'weed' n. a low-growing plant often found as a lawn weed

chic·le (chik''l) n. [< MexInd.] gumlike substance from a tropical American tree, used in chewing gum

chic·o·ry (chik'ə rē) n., pl. **-ries** [< Gr. kichora] **1.** a plant with blue flowers and with leaves used for salad **2.** its root, ground for mixing with coffee or as a coffee substitute

chide (chīd) vt., vi. **chid'ed** or **chid** (chid), **chid'ed** or **chid** or **chid·den** (chid''n), **chid'ing** [OE. cidan] to rebuke mildly —**chid'ing·ly** adv.

chief (chēf) n. [< L. caput, head] a leader; head —adj. main; principal

chief'ly adv. **1.** most of all **2.** mainly —adj. of or like a chief

chief'tain (-tən) n. [< L. caput, head] a chief, esp. of a clan or tribe

chif·fon (shi fän') n. [Fr.] a sheer, silky cloth —adj. **1.** of chiffon **2.** made fluffy as with beaten egg whites

chif·fo·nier, chif·fon·nier (shif'ə nir') n. [Fr.] a high bureau or chest of drawers, often with a mirror

chig·ger (chig'ər) n. [of Afr. origin] the tiny, red larva of certain mites, whose bite causes itching

chi·gnon (shēn'yän) n. [Fr. < L. catena, chain] a coil of hair worn at the back of the neck by women

Chi·hua·hua (chi wä'wä) n. [< Chihuahua, a Mex. state] a breed of tiny dog with large, pointed ears

CHIHUAHUA

chil·blain (chil'blān') n. [CHIL(L) + blain < OE. blegen, a sore] a painful swelling or sore on the foot or hand, caused by exposure to cold

child (chīld) n., pl. **chil'dren** [OE. cild] **1.** an infant **2.** a boy or girl before puberty **3.** a son or daughter —**with child** pregnant —**child'hood'** n. —**child'less** adj.

child'birth' n. the act of giving birth to a child

child'ish adj. of or like a child; specif., immature, foolish, etc. —**child'ish·ly** adv. —**child'ish·ness** n.

child'like' adj. of or like a child; specif., innocent, trusting, etc.

chil·dren (chil'drən) n. pl. of CHILD

child's play any very simple task

Chil·e (chil'ē) country on the SW coast of S.America: 286,397 sq. mi.; pop. 8,690,000 —**Chil'e·an** adj., n.

chil·i (chil'ē) n., pl. **-ies** [MexSp.] **1.** the very hot dried pod of red pepper, often ground **2.** a highly seasoned dish of beef, chilies or chili powder, beans, and often tomatoes: in full **chili con car·ne** (kən kär'nē) Also **chile**

chili sauce a spiced sauce of chopped tomatoes, sweet peppers, onions, etc.

chill (chil) n. [OE. ciele] **1.** coldness or coolness causing shivers **2.** a moderate coldness **3.** a sudden fear, etc. **4.** unfriendliness —adj. same as CHILLY —vi., vt. **1.** to make or become cold **2.** to cause a chill (in)

chill factor the combined effect of low temperatures and high winds on exposed skin

chill·y adj. **-i·er, -i·est 1.** moderately cold **2.** chilling **3.** unfriendly —**chill'i·ness** n.

chime (chīm) n. [< Gr. kymbalon, cymbal] **1.** [usually pl.] a) a set of tuned bells or metal tubes b) the musical sounds made by these **2.** a single bell, as in a clock —vi. **chimed, chim'ing 1.** to sound as a chime or chimes **2.** to agree —vt. to give (the time) by chiming —**chime in 1.** to join in **2.** to agree —**chim'er** n.

Chi·me·ra, Chi·mae·ra (kə mir'ə, kī-) [< Gr. chimaira, orig., goat] Gr. Myth. a monster with a lion's head, goat's body, and serpent's tail —n. [c-] an impossible fancy

chi·mer·i·cal (-mir′i k'l, -mer′-) *adj.*
1. imaginary; unreal 2. visionary

chim·ney (chim′nē) *n., pl.* -neys
[ult. < Gr. *kaminos*, oven] 1. the
passage or structure through which
smoke escapes from a fire, often extending above the roof 2. a glass tube
around the flame of a lamp

chim·pan·zee (chim′pan zē′, chim
pan′zē) *n.* [< Afr. native name] a
medium-sized anthropoid ape of
Africa: also [Colloq.] **chimp** (chimp)

chin (chin) *n.* [OE. *cin*] the part of
the face below the lower lip —*vt.*
chinned, chin′ning to pull (oneself)
up, while hanging by the hands from
a bar, until the chin is just above
the bar

Chin. 1. China 2. Chinese

Chi·na (chī′nə) country in E Asia:
3,691,000 sq. mi.; pop. 646,530,000

chi·na *n.* 1. *a)* porcelain, orig. made
in China *b)* vitrified ceramic ware
c) any earthenware 2. dishes, etc.
made of china Also **chi′na·ware′**

chinch (bug) (chinch) [< Sp. < L.
cimex, bug] a small, white-winged,
black bug that damages grain plants

chin·chil·la (chin chil′ə) *n.* [prob.
dim. of Sp. *chinche*, chinch] 1. *a)* a
small rodent of S.America *b)* its
gray fur 2. a heavy wool cloth

chine (chīn) *n.* [OFr. *eschine*] 1. the
backbone 2. a cut of meat from the
backbone 3. a ridge

Chi·nese (chī nēz′, -nēs′) *n.* 1. *pl.*
-nese′ a native of China 2. the language of the Chinese —*adj.* of China,
its people, language, etc.

Chinese checkers a game like
checkers, using marbles on a board
with holes in a star-shaped pattern

Chinese lantern a paper lantern
that can be folded up

chink[1] (chingk) *n.* [OE. *cine*] a crack
—*vt.* to close up the chinks in

chink[2] (chingk) *n.* [echoic] a sharp,
clinking sound —*vi., vt.* to make or
cause to make this sound

chi·no (chē′nō, shē′-) *n.* [< ?] 1. a
strong, twilled cotton cloth 2. [*pl.*]
men's pants of chino for casual wear

Chi·nook (chi nook′, -nook′) *n., pl.* -nooks′,
-nook′ [< AmInd. name] a member
of a tribe of American Indians of
Wash. and Oreg.

chintz (chints) *n.* [< Hind. *chhint*] a
cotton cloth printed in colored designs
and usually glazed

chintz′y *adj.* -i·er, -i·est 1. like
chintz 2. [Colloq.] cheap, stingy, etc.

chip (chip) *vt.* **chipped, chip′ping**
[< OE.] to break or cut off small
pieces from —*vi.* to break off in small
pieces —*n.* 1. a small piece of wood,
etc. cut or broken off 2. a place where
a small piece has been chipped off
3. a small disk used in gambling
games as a counter 4. a thin slice of
food [a potato *chip*] 5. *same as* INTE-
GRATED CIRCUIT —**chip in** [Colloq.]
to contribute (money, etc.) —**chip on**
one's shoulder [Colloq.] an inclination to fight —**in the chips** [Slang]
wealthy

chip′munk′ (-muŋk′) *n.* [<
AmInd.] a small, striped N. American
squirrel

chipped beef dried or smoked beef
sliced into shavings

chip·per (chip′ər) *adj.* [< Brit. dial.]
[Colloq.] in good spirits; lively; spry

chiro- [< Gr. *cheir*, hand] a combining form meaning hand

chi·rog·ra·phy (kī räg′rə fē) *n.* [CHIRO-
+ -GRAPHY] handwriting

chi·rop·o·dy (kə räp′ə dē, kī-) *n.*
[CHIRO- + -POD + -y³] *same as*
PODIATRY —**chi·rop′o·dist** *n.*

chi·ro·prac·tic (kī′rə prak′tik) *n.*
[< CHIRO- + Gr. *praktikos*, practical]
a method of treating disease by
manipulation of the body joints, esp.
of the spine —**chi′ro·prac′tor** *n.*

chirp (churp) *vi., vt.* [echoic] to
make, or utter in, short, shrill tones, as
some birds do —*n.* this sound

chir·rup (chur′əp) *vi.* [< prec.] to
chirp repeatedly —*n.* this sound

chis·el (chiz′'l) *n.* [< L. *caedere*, to
cut] a sharp-edged tool for cutting
or shaping wood, stone, etc. —*vi., vt.*
-eled or -elled, -el·ing or -el·ling
1. to cut or shape with a chisel 2.
[Colloq.] to swindle or get by swindling
—**chis′el·er, chis′el·ler** *n.*

chit (chit) *n.* [< Hind.] a voucher of
a sum owed for drink, food, etc.

chit·chat (chit′chat′) *n.* [< CHAT]
1. light, informal talk 2. gossip

chi·tin (kīt′'n) *n.* [< Gr. *chitōn*,
tunic] the tough, horny outer covering of insects, crustaceans, etc.

**chit·ter·lings, chit·lins, chit·
lings** (chit′lənz) *n.pl.* [< Gmc. base]
small intestines of pigs, used for food

chiv·al·rous (shiv′'l rəs) *adj.* 1.
gallant, courteous, etc. like an ideal
knight 2. of chivalry Also **chiv·al·ric**
(shi val′rik, shiv′'l-) —**chiv′al·rous·
ly** *adv.* —**chiv′al·rous·ness** *n.*

chiv·al·ry *n.* [< OFr. *chevaler*, knight]
1. medieval knighthood 2. the qualities of an ideal knight, as courage,
courtesy, etc.

chives (chīvz) *n.pl.* [< L. *cepa*,
onion] [*often with sing. v.*] a plant with
slender, hollow leaves and a mild
onion odor, used for flavoring

chlo·ral (klôr′əl) *n.* 1. a thin, oily,
pungent liquid made from chlorine
and alcohol 2. chloral hydrate

chloral hydrate a colorless, crystalline compound used as a sedative

chlor′dane (-dān) *n.* a chlorinated,
poisonous, volatile oil used as an
insecticide: also **chlor′dan** (-dan)

chlo·ride (-īd) *n.* a compound of
chlorine and another element or radical

chlo·ri·nate (klôr′ə nāt′) *vt.* -nat·
ed, -nat′ing to combine (a substance)
with chlorine; esp., to treat (water or
sewage) with chlorine for purification
—**chlo′ri·na′tion** *n.*

fat, āpe, cär; ten, ēven; is, bīte; gō, hôrn, tōōl, look; oil, out; up, fur;
chin; she; thin, then; zh, leisure; ŋ, ring; ə for a in ago; ', (ā′b'l); ë, Fr. coeur;
ö, Fr. feu; Fr. mon; ü, Fr. duc; kh, G. ich, doch; ‡ foreign; < derived from

chlo·rine (klôr′ēn, -in) *n.* [< Gr. *chlōros*, pale green] a greenish-yellow, poisonous, gaseous chemical element with a disagreeable odor, used in bleaching, water purification, etc.

chlo·ro·form (klôr′ə fôrm′) *n.* [< Fr.: see prec. & FORMIC] a colorless, volatile liquid used as an anesthetic and solvent —*vt.* to anesthetize or kill with chloroform

chlo′ro·phyll′, chlo′ro·phyl′ (-fil′) *n.* [< Gr. *chlōros*, green + *phyllon*, leaf] the green pigment in plant cells, a factor in photosynthesis

chock (chäk) *n.* [ONormFr. *choque*, a block] a block or wedge placed under a wheel, etc. to prevent motion —*vt.* to wedge fast as with chocks —*adv.* as close or tight as can be

chock′-full′ *adj.* as full as possible

choc·o·late (chôk′lət, chäk′-; -ə lət) *n.* [< MexInd. *chocolatl*] 1. a substance made from roasted and ground cacao seeds 2. a drink or candy made with chocolate 3. reddish brown —*adj.* 1. made of or flavored with chocolate 2. reddish-brown —**choc′o·lat·y, choc′o·lat·ey** *adj.*

choice (chois) *n.* [< OFr. < Gothic *kausjan*, to test] 1. a choosing; selection 2. the right or power to choose 3. a person or thing chosen 4. the best part 5. a variety from which to choose 6. an alternative —*adj.* **choic′er, choic′est** 1. of special excellence 2. carefully chosen

choir (kwīr) *n.* [< L. < Gr. *choros*] 1. a group of singers, esp. in a church 2. the part of a church they occupy

choke (chōk) *vt.* **choked, chok′ing** [< OE. *aceocian*] 1. to prevent from breathing by blocking the windpipe; strangle; suffocate 2. to obstruct by clogging 3. to hinder the growth or action of 4. to cut off some air from the carburetor of (a gasoline engine) so as to make a richer gasoline mixture —*vi.* 1. to be suffocated 2. to be obstructed —*n.* 1. a choking 2. a sound of choking 3. the valve that chokes a carburetor —**choke back** to hold back (feelings, sobs, etc.) —**choke down** to swallow with difficulty —**choke off** to bring to an end

choke collar a training collar for a dog, that tightens when the dog strains at the leash

chok′er *n.* a close-fitting necklace

chol·er (käl′ər) *n.* [< Gr. *cholē*, bile] [Now Rare] anger or ill humor

chol·er·a (käl′ər ə) *n.* [see prec.] any of several severe, infectious intestinal diseases

chol′er·ic *adj.* easily angered

cho·les·ter·ol (kə les′tə rōl′, -rôl′) *n.* [< Gr. *cholē*, bile + *stereos*, solid] a crystalline alcohol found esp. in animal fats, blood, and bile

chomp (chämp) *vt., vi. same as* CHAMP¹

choose (chōōz) *vt., vi.* **chose, cho′sen, choos′ing** [OE. *ceosan*] 1. to take as a choice; select 2. to decide or prefer *[I choose to go]* —**cannot choose but** cannot do otherwise —**choos′er** *n.*

choos′y, choos′ey *adj.* **-i·er, -i·est** [Colloq.] fussy in choosing

chop¹ (chäp) *vt.* **chopped, chop′ping** [ME. *choppen*] 1. to cut by blows with a sharp tool 2. to cut into small bits —*vi.* to make quick, cutting strokes —*n.* 1. a short, sharp stroke 2. a cut of meat and bone from the rib, loin, or shoulder 3. a short, broken movement of waves

chop² (chäp) *n.* [< ?] 1. a jaw 2. [*pl.*] the mouth and lower cheeks

chop′house′ *n.* a restaurant that specializes in chops and steaks

Cho·pin (shō′pan; *Fr.* shô pan′), **Fré·dé·ric** (frā dā rēk′) 1810–49; Pol. composer in France after 1831

chop′per *n.* 1. one that chops 2. [*pl.*] [Slang] teeth 3. [Colloq.] a helicopter

chop·py (chäp′ē) *adj.* **-pi·er, -pi·est** 1. rough with short, broken waves, as the sea 2. making abrupt starts and stops —**chop′pi·ness** *n.*

chop′sticks′ *n.pl.* [PidE.] two small sticks held together in one hand and used in some Asian countries in eating

chop su·ey (chäp′ sōō′ē) [< Chin. *tsa-sui*, various pieces] a Chinese-American dish of meat, bean sprouts, etc., served with rice

CHOPSTICKS

cho·ral (kôr′əl) *adj.* of, for, or sung by a choir or chorus —**cho′ral·ly** *adv.*

cho·rale, cho·ral (kə ral′) *n.* 1. a hymn tune 2. a choir or chorus

chord¹ (kôrd) *n.* [alt. (after L. *chorda*) < CORD] 1. [Poet.] the string of a musical instrument 2. a straight line joining any two points on an arc

chord² (kôrd) *n.* [< ACCORD] *Music* a combination of three or more tones sounded together in harmony

chore (chôr) *n.* [< OE. *cierr*, job] 1. a routine task 2. a hard task

chor·e·o·graph (kôr′ē ə graf′) *vt., vi.* [see ff.] to design or plan the movements of (a dance) —**chor′e·o·graph′ic** *adj.*

chor·e·og·ra·phy (kôr′ē äg′rə fē) *n.* [< Gr. *choreia*, dance + -GRAPHY] 1. dancing, esp. ballet dancing 2. the art of devising dances or ballets —**chor′e·og′ra·pher** *n.*

chor·is·ter (kôr′is tər) *n.* [see CHORUS] a member of a choir

chor·tle (chôr′t'l) *vi., vt.* **-tled, -tling** [prob. < CHUCKLE + SNORT] to make, or utter with, a gleeful chuckling or snorting sound —*n.* such a sound

cho·rus (kôr′əs) *n.* [< Gr. *choros*] 1. a group of dancers and singers performing together 2. the part of a drama, song, etc. performed by a chorus 3. a group singing or speaking something together 4. music written for group singing 5. the refrain of a song —*vt., vi.* to sing, speak, or say in unison —**in chorus** in unison

chose (chōz) *pt. of* CHOOSE

cho·sen (chō′z'n) *pp. of* CHOOSE —*adj.* selected; choice

Chou En-lai (jō′ en lī′) 1898–1976; Chin. prime minister (1949–76)

chow (chou) *n.* [< Chin.] **1.** any of a breed of medium-sized dog, originally from China **2.** [Slang] food

chow·der (chou′dǝr) *n.* [< Fr. *chaudière*, pot] a thick soup usually of onions and potatoes and, often, clams and milk

chow mein (chou mān′) [Chin. *ch'ao*, fry + *mien*, flour] a Chinese-American dish of meat, bean sprouts, etc., served with fried noodles

chrism (kriz′m) *n.* [< Gr. *chrisma*, oil] holy oil used in baptism

Christ (krīst) [< Gr. *christos*, the anointed] Jesus of Nazareth, regarded by Christians as the Messiah

chris·ten (kris′'n) *vt.* **1.** to take into a Christian church by baptism; baptize **2.** to give a name to, esp. at baptism —**chris′ten·ing** *n.*

Chris′ten·dom (-dǝm) *n.* **1.** Christians collectively **2.** those parts of the world where most of the inhabitants profess Christianity

Chris·tian (kris′chǝn) *n.* a believer in Jesus as the Christ, or in the religion based on the teachings of Jesus —*adj.* **1.** of Jesus Christ **2.** of or professing the religion based on his teachings **3.** having the qualities taught by Jesus, as love, kindness, etc. **4.** of Christians or Christianity

Chris·ti·an·i·ty (kris′chē an′ǝ tē) *n.* **1.** Christians collectively **2.** the Christian religion **3.** the state of being a Christian

Chris·tian·ize (kris′chǝ nīz′) *vt.* **-ized′, -iz′ing 1.** to convert to Christianity **2.** to cause to conform with Christian character or precepts

Christian name the baptismal name or given name, as distinguished from the surname or family name

Christian Science a religion and system of healing: official name **Church of Christ, Scientist**

chris·tie, chris·ty (kris′tē) *n., pl.* **-ties** [< *Christiania*, former name of Oslo] a high-speed turn in skiing with the skis parallel

Christ·mas (kris′mǝs) *n.* [see CHRIST & MASS] a holiday on Dec. 25 celebrating the birth of Jesus Christ

chro·mat·ic (krō mat′ik) *adj.* [< Gr. *chrōma*, color] **1.** of or having color or colors **2.** *Music* progressing by half tones —**chro·mat′i·cal·ly** *adv.*

chrome (krōm) *n.* [Fr. < Gr. *chrōma*, color] chromium or chromium alloy —*adj.* designating any of various pigments (**chrome red, chrome yellow,** etc.) made from chromium compounds —*vt.* **chromed, chrom′ing** to plate with chromium

-chrome (krōm) [< Gr. *chrōma*, color] *a suffix meaning:* **1.** color or coloring agent **2.** chromosome

chro·mi·um (krō′mē ǝm) *n.* [see CHROME] a hard metallic chemical element resistant to corrosion

chromo- [< Gr. *chrōma*] *a combining form meaning* color or pigment [*chromosome*]: also **chrom-**

chro·mo·some (krō′mǝ sōm′) *n.* [prec. + -SOME²] any of the microscopic rod-shaped bodies bearing genes

chron·ic (krän′ik) *adj.* [< Gr. *chronos*, time] **1.** lasting a long time or recurring: said of a disease **2.** having had an ailment for a long time **3.** habitual —**chron′i·cal·ly** *adv.*

chron·i·cle (krän′i k'l) *n.* [< Gr. *chronika*, annals] a historical record of events in the order in which they happened —*vt.* **-cled, -cling** to tell the history of; recount; record —**chron′i·cler** *n.*

chrono- [< Gr. *chronos*] *a combining form meaning* time: also **chron-**

chro·nol·o·gy (krǝ näl′ǝ jē) *n., pl.* **-gies** [CHRONO- + -LOGY] **1.** the science of measuring time and of dating events **2.** the arrangement of events in the order of occurrence —**chron·o·log·i·cal** (krän′ǝ läj′i k'l) *adj.* —**chron′o·log′i·cal·ly** *adv.*

chro·nom·e·ter (krǝ näm′ǝ tǝr) *n.* [CHRONO- + -METER] a highly accurate kind of clock or watch

chrys·a·lis (kris′'l ǝs) *n.* [< Gr. *chrysallis*] **1.** the pupa of a butterfly, encased in a cocoon **2.** the cocoon

chrys·an·the·mum (kri san′thǝ mǝm) *n.* [< Gr. *chrysos*, gold + *anthemon*, flower] **1.** a late-blooming plant of the composite family, with showy flowers **2.** the flower

chub (chub) *n.* [ME. *chubbe*] a freshwater fish related to the carp

chub·by *adj.* **-bi·er, -bi·est** [< prec.] round and plump —**chub′bi·ness** *n.*

chuck¹ (chuk) *vt.* [< ? Fr. *choquer*, strike against] **1.** to tap playfully, esp. under the chin **2.** to throw; toss **3.** [Slang] to get rid of —*n.* a chucking

chuck² (chuk) *n.* [? var. of CHOCK] **1.** a cut of beef from around the neck and shoulder blade **2.** a clamplike holding device, as on a lathe

chuck′-full′ *adj. same as* CHOCK-FULL

chuck′hole′ *n.* [see CHOCK & HOLE] a rough hole in pavement

chuck·le (chuk′'l) *vi.* **-led, -ling** [? var. of CLUCK] to laugh softly in a low tone —*n.* a soft, low-toned laugh

chuck wagon a wagon equipped as a kitchen for feeding cowboys, etc.

chug (chug) *n.* [echoic] a puffing or explosive sound, as of a locomotive —*vi.* **chugged, chug′ging** to make, or move with, such sounds

chuk·ka boot (chuk′ǝ) [ult. < Sans. *cakra*, wheel] a man's ankle-high shoe

chum (chum) *n.* [prob. < *chamber (mate)*] [Colloq.] a close friend —*vi.* **chummed, chum′ming** [Colloq.] to be close friends —**chum′mi·ness** *n.* —**chum′my** *adj.* **-mi·er, -mi·est**

chump (chump) *n.* [< ?] [Colloq.] a stupid person; fool

Chung·king (choon′kin′, chun′-) city in SC China: pop. 4,070,000

chunk (chunk) *n.* [< ? CHUCK²] a short, thick piece

chunk·y *adj.* **-i·er, -i·est** 1. short and thick 2. stocky —**chunk′i·ness** *n.*

church (church) *n.* [< Gr. *kyriakē (oikia)*, Lord's (house)] 1. a building for public worship, esp. Christian worship 2. religious service 3. [*usually* C-] *a)* all Christians *b)* a particular Christian denomination 4. ecclesiastical, as opposed to secular, government

church′go′er (-gō′ər) *n.* a person who attends church regularly —**church′go′ing** *n., adj.*

Church·ill (chur′chil), **Win·ston** (win′stən) 1874–1965; Brit. prime minister (1940–45; 1951–55)

church·man (-mən) *n., pl.* **-men** 1. a clergyman 2. a church member

Church of England the episcopal church of England: it is an established church headed by the sovereign

church′ward′en (-wôr′d'n) *n.* a lay officer handling certain secular affairs of a church

church′yard′ *n.* the yard adjoining a church, often used as a cemetery

churl (churl) *n.* [OE. *ceorl*, peasant] 1. a peasant 2. a surly, ill-bred person; boor —**churl′ish** *adj.* —**churl′ish·ness** *n.*

churn (churn) *n.* [OE. *cyrne*] a container in which milk or cream is stirred and shaken to form butter —*vt., vi.* 1. to stir and shake (milk or cream) in a churn 2. to make (butter) thus 3. to stir up or move vigorously

chute[1] (shōōt) *n.* [Fr., a fall] an inclined or vertical trough or passage down which things slide or drop

chute[2] (shōōt) *n.* [Colloq.] a parachute

chut·ney (chut′nē) *n., pl.* **-neys** [Hindi *chatnī*] a relish of fruits, spices, and herbs: also **chutnee**

chutz·pah, chutz·pa (khoots′pə) *n.* [Heb. via Yid.] [Colloq.] impudence; brass

CIA, C.I.A. Central Intelligence Agency

ci·ca·da (si kā′də) *n., pl.* **-das, -dae** (-dē) [L.] a large, flylike insect with transparent wings: the male makes a loud, shrill sound

cic·a·trix (sik′ə triks) *n., pl.* **ci·ca·tri·ces** (si kat′rə sēz′) [L.] fibrous tissue that forms at a healing wound; scar

Cic·er·o (sis′ə rō′) 106–43 B.C.; Rom. statesman and orator

-cide (sīd) [< L. *caedere*, kill] *a suffix meaning:* 1. killer 2. killing

ci·der (sī′dər) *n.* [< Gr. *sikera*, intoxicant] juice pressed from apples, used as a drink or for making vinegar

ci·gar (si gär′) *n.* [< Sp.] a compact roll of tobacco leaves for smoking

cig·a·rette (sig′ə ret′) *n.* [Fr.] a small roll of finely cut tobacco wrapped in thin paper for smoking

cig′a·ril′lo (-ril′ō) *n., pl.* **-los** [Sp.] a small, thin cigar

cil·i·a (sil′ē ə) *n.pl., sing.* **-i·um** (-ē əm) [L.] 1. the eyelashes 2. *Biol.* small, hairlike processes

cinch (sinch) *n.* [< Sp. < L. *cingulum*, girdle] 1. a saddle or pack girth 2. [Slang] a thing easy to do or sure to happen —*vt.* 1. to tighten a girth on 2. [Slang] to make sure of

cin·cho·na (sin kō′nə) *n.* [< 17th-c. Peruv. Countess del *Chinchón*] 1. a tropical tree with a bitter bark 2. the bark, from which quinine is made

Cin·cin·nat·i (sin′sə nat′ē, -ə) city in SW Ohio: pop. 385,000

cinc·ture (siŋk′chər) *n.* [L. *cinctura*] a belt or girdle —*vt.* **-tured, -tur·ing** to encircle with a cincture

cin·der (sin′dər) *n.* [OE. *sinder*] 1. a tiny piece of partly burned wood, etc. 2. [*pl.*] ashes from coal or wood

Cin·der·el·la (sin′də rel′ə) in a fairy tale, a household drudge who eventually marries a prince

cin·e·ma (sin′ə mə) *n.* [< Gr. *kinēma*, motion] [Chiefly Brit.] 1. a motion picture 2. a motion-picture theater —**the cinema** motion pictures collectively —**cin′e·mat′ic** *adj.*

cin·e·ma·tog·ra·phy (sin′ə mə tägʹrə fē) *n.* the art of photography in making motion pictures —**cin′e·ma·togʹra·pher** *n.* —**cin′e·mat′o·graphʹic** (-mat′ə chər′ik) *adj.*

cin·na·bar (sin′ə bär′) *n.* [ult. < Per.] mercuric sulfide, a heavy, bright-red mineral

cin·na·mon (sin′ə mən) *n.* [< Heb. *qinnāmōn*] 1. the light-brown spice made from the inner bark of a laurel tree of the East Indies 2. this bark

ci·pher (sī′fər) *n.* [< Ar. *ṣifr*] 1. the symbol 0; zero 2. a nonentity 3. secret writing based on a key; code 4. the key to such a code —*vi.* [Now Rare] to solve arithmetical problems

cir·ca (sur′kə) *prep.* [L.] about: used to indicate an approximate date

cir·ca·di·an (sər kā′dē ən) *adj.* [< L. *circa*, about + *dies*, day] of the physiological rhythms associated with the 24-hour cycle of the earth's rotation

Cir·ce (sur′sē) in the *Odyssey*, an enchantress who turned men to swine

cir·cle (sur′k'l) *n.* [< Gr. *kirkos*] 1. a plane figure bounded by a single curved line every point of which is equally distant from the center 2. this curved line 3. anything like a circle, as a ring 4. a complete or recurring series; cycle 5. a group of people with common interests 6. extent; scope, as of influence —*vt.* **-cled, -cling** 1. to form a circle around 2. to move around, as in a circle —*vi.* to go around in a circle —**cir′cler** *n.*

cir′clet (-klit) *n.* 1. a small circle 2. a circular band for the finger, etc.

cir·cuit (sur′kit) *n.* [< L. *circum-*, around + *ire*, go] 1. a boundary line or its length 2. a going around something 3. the regular journey through a district of a person in his work 4. a chain or association, as of theaters or resorts 5. the path or line of an electric current —*vi.* to go in a circuit —*vt.* to make a circuit about —**cir′cuit·al** *adj.*

circuit breaker a device that automatically interrupts the flow of an electric current

cir·cu·i·tous (sər kyōō′ə təs) *adj.* roundabout; indirect —**cir·cu′i·tous·ly** *adv.* —**cir·cu′i·ty** *n.*

cir·cuit·ry (sur′kə trē) *n.* the system or the elements of an electric circuit

cir·cu·lar (sur′kyə lər) *adj.* 1. in the shape of a circle; round 2. moving in a circle 3. circuitous —*n.* an advertisement, etc. intended for many —**cir′cu·lar′i·ty** (-ler′ə tē) *n.*

cir·cu·lar·ize (-lə rīz′) *vt.* -ized′, -iz′ing 1. to make circular 2. to send circulars to 3. to canvass —**cir·cu·lar·i·za′tion** *n.* —**cir′cu·lar·iz′er** *n.*

cir·cu·late (sur′kyə lāt′) *vi.* -lat′ed, -lat′ing [< L. *circulari*, form a circle] 1. to move in a circle or circuit and return, as the blood 2. to go from person to person or from place to place —*vt.* to make circulate —**cir′cu·la′tor** *n.* —**cir′cu·la·to′ry** (-lə tôr′ē) *adj.*

cir·cu·la′tion *n.* 1. a circulating 2. the movement of the blood through veins and arteries 3. distribution of newspapers, magazines, etc.

circum- [< L. *circum*] a prefix meaning around, about, surrounding

cir·cum·cise (sur′kəm sīz′) *vt.* -cised′, -cis′ing [< L. *circum-*, around + *caedere*, to cut] to cut off all or part of the foreskin of —**cir′cum·ci′sion** (-sizh′ən) *n.*

cir·cum·fer·ence (sər kum′fər əns) *n.* [< L. *circum-*, around + *ferre*, carry] 1. the line bounding a circle, ball, etc. 2. length of this line

cir·cum·flex (sur′kəm fleks′) *n.* [< L. *circum-*, around + *flectere*, to bend] a mark (^, ˆ, ˜) used over a vowel to indicate pronunciation

cir·cum·lo·cu·tion (-lō kyōō′shən) *n.* [< L.: see CIRCUM- & LOCUTION] a roundabout way of saying something

cir·cum·nav·i·gate (-nav′ə gāt′) *vt.* -gat′ed, -gat′ing [< L.: see CIRCUM- & NAVIGATE] to sail or fly around (the earth, etc.) —**cir′cum·nav′i·ga′tion** *n.*

cir·cum·scribe (-skrīb′) *vt.* -scribed′, -scrib′ing [< L.: see CIRCUM- & SCRIBE] 1. to trace a line around; encircle 2. to limit; confine —**cir′cum·scrip′tion** (-skrip′shən) *n.*

cir·cum·spect (-spekt′) *adj.* [< L. *circum-*, around + *specere*, look] cautious —**cir′cum·spec′tion** *n.*

cir·cum·stance (-stans′) *n.* [< L. *circum-*, around + *stare*, stand] 1. a fact or event accompanying another 2. [*pl.*] conditions affecting one, esp. financial conditions 3. mere chance 4. much ceremony —**under no circumstances** never —**cir′cum·stanced′** *adj.*

cir·cum·stan′tial (-stan′shəl) *adj.* 1. having to do with or depending on circumstances 2. incidental 3. complete in detail

circumstantial evidence *Law* indirect evidence of a fact at issue, based on attendant circumstances

cir·cum·stan′ti·ate (-stan′shē āt′) *vt.* -at′ed, -at′ing to give detailed proof or support of —**cir′cum·stan′ti·a′tion** *n.*

cir·cum·vent (-vent′) *vt.* [< L. *circum-*, around + *venire*, come] to get the better of or prevent by craft or ingenuity —**cir′cum·ven′tion** *n.*

cir·cus (sur′kəs) *n.* [L., a circle] 1. in ancient Rome, an amphitheater 2. a traveling show of clowns, acrobats, trained animals, etc. 3. [Colloq.] a source of much fun

ci·ré (sə rā′) *adj.* [< Fr. *cire*, wax] having a smooth, glossy finish

cirque (surk) *n.* [see CIRCUS] a natural amphitheater in a mountainside

cir·rho·sis (sə rō′sis) *n.* [< Gr. *kirrhos*, tawny + -OSIS] a degenerative disease, esp. of the liver, marked by excess formation of connective tissue

cir·rus (sir′əs) *n.* [L., a curl] a formation of clouds in wispy filaments or feathery tufts

cis·tern (sis′tərn) *n.* [< L. *cista*, chest] a large tank for storing water

cit·a·del (sit′ə d'l, -del′) *n.* [< L. *civitas*, city] a fortress

cite (sīt) *vt.* cit′ed, cit′ing [< L. *citare*, summon] 1. to summon before a court of law 2. to quote 3. to mention by way of example, proof, etc. 4. to mention in an official report as meritorious —**ci·ta′tion** *n.*

cit·i·fied (sit′i fīd′) *adj.* having the ways, dress, etc. of city people

cit·i·zen (sit′ə zən) *n.* [< L. *civis*] a member of a state or nation who owes allegiance to it by birth or naturalization and is entitled to full civil rights —**cit′i·zen·ship′** *n.*

cit′i·zen·ry (-rē) *n.* all citizens as a group

cit·ric (si′trik) *adj.* designating or of an acid obtained from citrus fruits

cit·ron (-trən) *n.* [Fr. < L.: see CITRUS] 1. a yellow, thick-skinned, lemonlike fruit 2. its rind candied

cit·ron·el·la (si′trə nel′ə) *n.* [ModL.] a sharp-smelling oil used in perfume, soap, insect repellents, etc.

cit·rus (si′trəs) *n.* [L.] 1. any of the trees bearing oranges, lemons, limes, etc. 2. any such fruit —*adj.* of these trees: also **citrous**

cit·y (sit′ē) *n., pl.* -ies [< L. *civis*, citizen] 1. a population center larger or more important than a town 2. in the U.S., an incorporated municipality with boundaries, powers, etc. defined by State charter 3. the people of a city —*adj.* of a city

city hall a building housing a municipal government

civ·et (siv′it) *n.* [< Ar. *zabād*] 1. the musky secretion of a catlike, flesh-eating animal (**civet cat**) of Africa and S Asia: used in some perfumes 2. the animal, or its fur

civ·ic (siv′ik) *adj.* [< L. *civis*, citizen] of a city, citizens, or citizenship

civ·ics (-iks) *n.pl.* [*with sing. v.*] the study of civic affairs and the duties and rights of citizenship

civ·il (siv′l) *adj.* [see CIVIC] 1. of a

citizen or citizens **2.** civilized **3.** polite **4.** of citizens in matters not military or religious —**civ′il·ly** *adv.*

civil disobedience nonviolent opposition to a law by refusing to comply with it, on the grounds of conscience

civil engineering engineering dealing with the construction of bridges, roads, etc. —**civil engineer**

ci·vil·ian (sə vil′yən) *n.* [see CIVIC] a person not in military or naval service —*adj.* of civilians; nonmilitary

ci·vil·i·ty (-ə tē) *n., pl.* **-ties** **1.** politeness **2.** a civil, or polite, act

civ·i·li·za·tion (siv′ə lə zā′shən) *n.* **1.** a civilizing or being civilized **2.** the total culture of a people, period, etc. **3.** the peoples considered to have reached a high social development

civ·i·lize (siv′ə līz′) *vt., vi.* **-lized′, -liz′ing** [see CIVIC] **1.** to bring out of a condition of savagery or barbarism to a higher level of social organization, esp. in the arts and sciences **2.** to refine —**civ′i·lized′** *adj.*

civil law the body of law having to do with private rights

civil liberties liberties guaranteed to the individual by law; rights of thinking, speaking, and acting as one likes without hindrance except in the interests of public welfare

civil rights those rights guaranteed to the individual, esp. by the 13th, 14th, 15th, and 19th Amendments to the U.S. Constitution

civil servant a civil service employee

civil service those employed in government service, esp. through public competitive examination

civil war war between different factions of the same nation —**the Civil War** the war between the North and the South in the U.S. (1861–1865)

civ·vies (siv′ēz) *n.pl.* [Colloq.] civilian clothes: also sp. **civ′ies**

ck. *pl.* **cks. 1.** cask **2.** check

Cl *Chem.* chlorine

clack (klak) *vi., vt.* [prob. echoic < ON.] to make or cause to make a sudden, sharp sound —*n.* this sound

clad (klad) *alt. pt. & pp. of* CLOTHE —*adj.* clothed; dressed

claim (klām) *vt.* [< L. *clamare,* cry out] **1.** to demand as rightfully belonging to one **2.** to require; deserve *[to* claim *attention]* **3.** to assert —*n.* **1.** a claiming **2.** a right to something **3.** something claimed —**claim′a·ble** *adj.* —**claim′ant, claim′er** *n.*

clair·voy·ance (kler voi′əns) *n.* [Fr. < *clair,* clear + *voyant,* seeing] the supposed ability to perceive things not in sight —**clair·voy′ant** *n., adj.*

clam (klam) *n.* [< earlier *clam,* a clamp] a hard-shelled bivalve mollusk —*vi.* **clammed, clam′ming** to dig for clams —**clam up** [Colloq.] to keep silent

clam′bake′ *n.* **1.** a picnic at which steamed or baked clams are served **2.** [Colloq.] any large, noisy party

clam·ber (klam′bər) *vi., vt.* [ME. *clambren*] to climb clumsily, esp. by using both hands and feet

clam·my (klam′ē) *adj.* **-mi·er, -mi-**

est [ME. < *clam,* mud] moist, cold, and sticky —**clam′mi·ness** *n.*

clam·or (klam′ər) *n.* [< L. *clamare,* cry out] **1.** a loud outcry; uproar **2.** a loud demand or complaint —*vi.* to make a clamor —**clam′or·ous** *adj.*

clamp (klamp) *n.* [< MDu. *klampe*] a device for clasping or fastening things together —*vt.* to fasten or brace, as with a clamp —**clamp down (on)** to become more strict (with)

clan (klan) *n.* [< Gael. < L. *planta,* offshoot] **1.** a group of families claiming descent from a common ancestor **2.** a group of people with interests in common —**clan′nish** *adj.* —**clans·man** (klanz′mən) *n., pl.* **-men**

clan·des·tine (klan das′t'n) *adj.* [< L. *clam,* secret] secret or hidden; furtive —**clan·des′tine·ly** *adv.*

clang (klaŋ) *vi., vt.* [echoic] to make or cause to make a loud, ringing sound, as by striking metal —*n.* this sound

clan′gor (-ər) *n.* [L. < *clangere,* to sound] a continuous clanging sound

clank (klaŋk) *n.* [echoic] a sharp metallic sound —*vi., vt.* to make or cause to make this sound

clap (klap) *vi.* **clapped, clap′ping** [OE. *clæppan,* to beat] **1.** to make the explosive sound of two flat surfaces struck together **2.** to strike the hands together, as in applause —*vt.* **1.** to strike together briskly **2.** to strike with an open hand **3.** to put, move, etc. abruptly *[clapped* into jail] —*n.* **1.** the sound or act of clapping **2.** a sharp slap

clap·board (klab′ərd, klap′bôrd′) *n.* [transl. of MDu. *klapholt* < *klappen,* to fit + *holt,* wood] a thin board with one thicker edge, used as siding —*vt.* to cover with clapboards

clap′per *n.* a thing that makes a clapping sound, as the tongue of a bell

clap′trap′ *n.* [CLAP + TRAP¹] insincere, empty talk intended to get applause —*adj.* showy and cheap

claque (klak) *n.* [Fr. < *claquer,* to clap] a group of people paid to applaud at a play, opera, etc.

clar·et (klar′it) *n.* [< L. *clarus,* clear] a dry red wine

clar·i·fy (klar′ə fī′) *vt., vi.* **-fied′, -fy′ing** [< L. *clarus,* clear + *facere,* make] to make or become clear —**clar′i·fi·ca′tion** *n.*

clar·i·net (klar′ə net′) *n.* [< Fr. < L. *clarus,* clear] a single-reed, woodwind instrument played by means of holes and keys —**clar′i·net′ist, clar′i·net′tist** *n.*

clar·i·on (klar′ē ən) *adj.* [< L. *clarus,* clear] clear, sharp, and ringing *[a* clarion *call]*

clar·i·ty (klar′ə tē) *n.* [< L. *clarus,* clear] clear quality; clearness

CLARINET

clash (klash) *vi.* [echoic] **1.** to collide with a loud, harsh, metallic noise **2.** to conflict; disagree —*vt.* to strike with a clashing noise —*n.* **1.** the sound of clashing **2.** conflict

clasp (klasp) *n.* [ME. *claspe*] **1.** a fastening, as a hook, to hold things together **2.** a grasping; embrace **3.** a grip of the hand —*vt.* **1.** to fasten with a clasp **2.** to hold or embrace tightly **3.** to grip with the hand

class (klas) *n.* [< L. *classis*] **1.** a number of people or things grouped together because of likenesses; kind; sort **2.** social or economic rank *[* the working *class]* **3.** *a)* a group of students taught together *b)* a group graduating together **4.** grade or quality **5.** [Slang] excellence, as of style —*vt.* to classify —*vi.* to be classified —**class′less** *adj.*

class action (suit) a legal action brought by one or more persons on behalf of themselves and a much larger group

clas·sic (klas′ik) *adj.* [< L. *classis,* class] **1.** being an excellent model of its kind **2.** of the art, literature, etc. of the ancient Greeks and Romans **3.** balanced, formal, simple, etc. **4.** famous as traditional or typical —*n.* **1.** a literary or artistic work of the highest excellence **2.** a creator of such a work **3.** a famous traditional or typical event —**the classics** ancient Greek and Roman literature

clas·si·cal (-i k′l) *adj.* **1.** *same as* CLASSIC (senses 1, 2, 3) **2.** versed in Greek and Roman literature, etc. **3.** designating or of music conforming to certain standards of form, complexity, etc. **4.** standard and traditional *[classical economics]* —**clas′si·cal·ly** *adv.*

clas·si·cism (-ə siz′m) *n.* **1.** the aesthetic principles of ancient Greece and Rome **2.** adherence to these principles **3.** knowledge of classical art and literature —**clas′si·cist** *n.*

classified advertising advertising under such listings as *help wanted*

clas·si·fy (klas′ə fī′) *vt.* -**fied′**, -**fy′ing 1.** to arrange in classes according to a system **2.** to designate (government documents) to be secret or restricted —**clas′si·fi·ca′tion** *n.*—**clas′si·fi′er** *n.*

class′mate′ *n.* a member of the same class at a school or college

class′room′ *n.* a room where a class is taught at a school or college

class′y *adj.* -**i·er, -i·est** [Slang] first-class, esp. in style; elegant

clat·ter (klat′ər) *vi., vt.* [ME. *clateren*] to make or cause to make a clatter —*n.* **1.** a rapid succession of loud, sharp noises **2.** a tumult; hubbub

clause (klôz) *n.* [< L. *claudere,* to close] **1.** a group of words containing a subject and verb: an independent (principal) clause can stand alone as a sentence; a dependent (subordinate) clause functions as a noun, adjective, or adverb **2.** a particular article or provision in a document

claus·tro·pho·bi·a (klôs′trə fō′bēə) *n.* [< L. *claustrum,* enclosure + -PHOBIA] a fear of enclosed places —**claus′tro·pho′bic** *adj.*

clav·i·chord (klav′ə kôrd′) *n.* [< L. *clavis,* key + *chorda,* a string] a stringed musical instrument with a keyboard: predecessor of the piano

clav·i·cle (klav′i k′l) *n.* [< L. *clavis,* key] a bone connecting the breastbone with the shoulder blade

cla·vi·er (klə vir′; *for 1, also* klav′ē ər) *n.* [Fr. < L. *clavis,* key] **1.** the keyboard of an organ, piano, etc. **2.** any stringed keyboard instrument

claw (klô) *n.* [OE. *clawu*] **1.** a sharp, hooked nail on an animal's or bird's foot **2.** the pincers of a lobster, etc. —*vt., vi.* to scratch, clutch, etc. as with claws

clay (klā) *n.* [OE. *clæg*] **1.** a firm, plastic earth, used in making bricks, etc. **2.** *a)* earth *b)* the human body —**clay′ey** *adj.* **clay′i·er, clay′i·est**

clean (klēn) *adj.* [OE. *clæne*] **1.** free from dirt and impurities; unsoiled **2.** morally pure **3.** fair; sportsmanlike **4.** neat and tidy **5.** free from flaws; **6.** thorough —*adv.* completely —*vt., vi.* to make or be made clean —**clean up 1.** to make neat **2.** [Colloq.] to finish **3.** [Slang] to make much profit —**come clean** [Slang] to confess —**clean′ly** *adv.* —**clean′ness** *n.*

clean′-cut′ *adj.* **1.** clearly outlined **2.** well-formed **3.** trim, neat, etc.

clean′er *n.* a person or thing that cleans; esp., one who dry-cleans

clean·ly (klen′lē) *adj.* -**li·er, -li·est 1.** having clean habits **2.** always kept clean —**clean′li·ness** *n.*

clean room a room, as in a computer center, designed to be nearly 100% free of dust, pollen, etc.

cleanse (klenz) *vt.* **cleansed, cleans′ing** [OE. *clænsian*] to make clean, pure, etc. —**cleans′er** *n.*

clean′up′ *n.* **1.** a cleaning up **2.** elimination of crime **3.** [Slang] profit; gain

clear (klir) *adj.* [< L. *clarus*] **1.** bright; free from clouds **2.** transparent **3.** easily seen or heard; distinct **4.** keen or logical *[a clear mind]* **5.** not obscure; obvious **6.** certain; positive **7.** free from guilt **8.** free from deductions; net **9.** free from debt **10.** free from obstruction; open —*adv.* **1.** in a clear manner **2.** all the way; completely —*vt.* **1.** to make clear **2.** to free from impurities, blemishes, etc. **3.** to make lucid **4.** to open *[clear a path]* **5.** to get rid of **6.** to prove the innocence of **7.** to pass or leap over, by, etc., esp. without touching **8.** to be passed or approved by **9.** to make as profit —*vi.* to become clear —**clear away** (or **off) 1.** to remove so as to leave a cleared space **2.** to go away —**clear out** [Colloq.] to depart —**clear up** to make or become clear —**in the clear 1.** free from obstruction **2.** [Colloq.] guiltless —**clear′ly** *adv.* —**clear′ness** *n.*

clear′ance (-əns) *n.* **1.** the clear space between an object and that which is passing **2.** the adjustment of accounts in a clearinghouse

---

clear'-cut' *adj.* 1. clearly outlined 2. distinct; definite

clear'ing *n.* an area of land cleared of trees

clear'ing·house' *n.* an office maintained by several banks for exchanging checks, balancing accounts, etc.

cleat (klēt) *n.* [< ME.] a piece of wood or metal fastened to something to strengthen it or give secure footing

cleav·age (klē'vij) *n.* 1. a cleaving; dividing 2. a cleft; fissure; division

cleave[1] (klēv) *vt., vi.* **cleaved** or **cleft** or **clove, cleaved** or **cleft** or **clo'ven, cleav'ing** [OE. *cleofan*] to divide by a blow; split; sever —**cleav'a·ble** *adj.*

cleave[2] (klēv) *vi.* **cleaved, cleav'ing** [OE. *cleofian*] 1. to adhere; cling (*to*) 2. to be faithful (*to*)

cleav'er *n.* a heavy cutting tool with a broad blade, used by butchers

clef (klef) *n.* [Fr. < L. *clavis*, key] a symbol used in music to indicate the pitch of the notes on the staff

cleft (kleft) *alt. pt. & pp. of* CLEAVE[1] —*adj.* split; divided —*n.* an opening made by cleaving; crack; crevice

clem·a·tis (klem'ə tis) *n.* [< Gr. *klēma*, vine] a vine of the buttercup family, with bright-colored flowers

Clem·ens (klem'ənz), **Samuel L.** (pseud. *Mark Twain*) 1835–1910; U.S. writer

clem·ent (klem'ənt) *adj.* [L. *clemens*] 1. lenient; merciful 2. mild, as weather —**clem'en·cy** (-ən sē) *n.*

clench (klench) *vt.* [< OE. (*be*)-*clencan*, make cling] 1. to close (the teeth or fist) firmly 2. to grip tightly —*n.* a firm grip

Cle·o·pa·tra (klē'ə pat'rə, -pā'trə) 69?–30 B.C.; queen of Egypt (51–30)

clere·sto·ry (klir'stôr'ē) *n., pl.* -ries [< ME. *cler*, CLEAR + *storie*, STORY[2]] an outside wall with windows that rises above a roofed section of a building

cler·gy (klur'jē) *n., pl.* -gies [see CLERK] ministers, priests, rabbis, etc., collectively

cler'gy·man (-mən) *n., pl.* -men a minister, priest, rabbi, etc.

cler·ic (kler'ik) *n.* a clergyman

cler'i·cal (-i k'l) *adj.* 1. of a clergyman or the clergy 2. of an office clerk or clerks; of office work

cler'i·cal·ism (-iz'm) *n.* political power of the clergy —**cler'i·cal·ist** *n.*

clerk (klurk) *n.* [< L. *klēros*, clergy] 1. a layman with minor duties in a church 2. an office worker who types, files, etc. 3. a public official who keeps the records of a court, town, etc. 4. a salesclerk —*vi.* to work as a salesclerk

Cleve·land (klēv'lənd) city and port in NE Ohio: pop. 574,000

Cleveland, (Stephen) Gro·ver (grō'vər) 1837–1908; 22d and 24th president of the U.S. (1885–89; 1893–97)

clev·er (klev'ər) *adj.* [? < Norw. *klōver*] 1. skillful; adroit 2. intelligent; ingenious; smart —**clev'er·ly** *adv.* —**clev'er·ness** *n.*

clev·is (klev'is) *n.* [see CLEAVE[2]] a U-shaped piece of iron with holes for a pin for attaching one thing to another

clew (kloo) *n.* [OE. *cliwen*] 1. a ball of thread or yarn 2. *same as* CLUE 3. a metal loop in the corner of a sail

cli·ché (klē shā') *n.* [Fr. < *clicher*, to stereotype] a trite expression

click (klik) *n.* [echoic] a slight, sharp sound like that of a door latch snapping into place —*vi., vt.* to make or cause to make a click

cli·ent (klī'ənt) *n.* [< L. *cliens*, follower] 1. a person or company for whom a lawyer, accountant, etc. is acting 2. a customer

cli·en·tele (klī'ən tel') *n.* [< Fr. < L. *clientela*, patronage] all one's clients or customers, collectively

cliff (klif) *n.* [OE. *clif*] a high, steep face of rock, esp. on a coast

cliff'hang'er (-haŋ'ər) *n.* a suspenseful movie, story, situation, etc.

cli·mac·ter·ic (klī mak'tər ik, klī'mak ter'ik) *n.* [< Gr. *klimax*, ladder] a crucial period in life, esp. the menopause —*adj.* crucial

cli·mate (klī'mət) *n.* [< Gr. *klima*, region] 1. the prevailing weather conditions of a place 2. a region with reference to its prevailing weather —**cli·mat'ic** (-mat'ik) *adj.*

cli·max (klī'maks) *n.* [L. < Gr. *klimax*, ladder] 1. the final, culminating element in a series; highest point of interest, excitement, etc. 2. the turning point of action in a drama, etc. —*vi., vt.* to reach, or bring to, a climax —**cli·mac'tic** (-mak'tik) *adj.*

climb (klīm) *vi., vt.* **climbed, climb'-ing** [OE. *climban*] 1. to move up by using the feet and often the hands 2. to move (*down, over, along*, etc.) using the hands and feet 3. to ascend gradually 4. to grow upward —*n.* 1. a climbing 2. a place to be climbed —**climb'er** *n.*

clime (klīm) *n.* [see CLIMATE] [Poet.] a region, esp. with regard to climate

clinch (klinch) *vt.* [var. of CLENCH] 1. to fasten (a driven nail, etc.) by bending the projecting end 2. to settle (an argument, bargain, etc.) definitely —*vi.* 1. *Boxing* to grip the opponent with the arms so as to hinder his punching 2. [Slang] to embrace —*n.* a clinching

clinch'er *n.* 1. one that clinches 2. a decisive point, argument, etc.

cling (kliŋ) *vi.* **clung, cling'ing** [OE. *clingan*] 1. to adhere; hold fast, as by embracing 2. to be or stay near 3. to be emotionally attached

clin·ic (klin'ik) *n.* [< Gr. *klinē*, bed] 1. the teaching of medicine by treating patients in the presence of students 2. a place where medical specialists practice as a group 3. an outpatient department, as of a hospital

clin·i·cal (-i k'l) *adj.* 1. of or connected with a clinic or sickbed 2. having to do with the treatment and observation of patients, as distinguished from theoretical study 3. purely scientific; impersonal —**clin'i·cal·ly** *adv.*

cli·ni·cian (klī nish'ən) *n.* one who practices clinical medicine, psychology, etc.

clink (kliŋk) *vi., vt.* [echoic] to make or cause to make a slight, sharp sound, as of glass struck —*n.* 1. such a sound 2. [Colloq.] a jail

clink′er *n.* [Du. *klinker*] 1. [Archaic] a hard brick 2. a hard mass of fused matter, formed as from burned coal 3. [Slang] a mistake

clip¹ (klip) *vt.* **clipped, clip′ping** [< ON. *klippa*] 1. to cut as with shears 2. to cut short 3. to cut the hair of 4. [Colloq.] to hit sharply 5. [Slang] to swindle —*vi.* to move rapidly —*n.* 1. a clipping 2. a thing clipped 3. a rapid pace 4. [Colloq.] a quick, sharp punch 5. *same as* CLIPPED FORM

clip² (klip) *vi., vt.* **clipped, clip′ping** [OE. *clyppan,* to embrace] to grip tightly; fasten —*n.* anything that clips or fastens *[a paper clip]*

clip′board′ *n.* a writing board with a clip at the top to hold papers

clip joint [Slang] a nightclub, store, etc. that charges excessive prices

clipped form (or **word**) a shortened form of a word, as *pike* (for *turnpike*)

clip·per (klip′ər) *n.* 1. [*usually pl.*] a tool for cutting or trimming 2. a sailing ship built for great speed

clip′ping *n.* a piece cut out or off, as an item clipped from a newspaper

CLIPPER SHIP

clique (klēk) *n.* [Fr. < *cliquer,* make a noise] a small, exclusive circle of people; coterie —**cliqu′ish** *adj.* —**cliqu′ish·ly** *adv.* —**cliqu′ish·ness** *n.*

cli·to·ris (klit′ər əs) *n.* [< Gr.] a small, sensitive organ of the vulva

cloak (klōk) *n.* [< ML. *clocca,* bell: from its shape] 1. a loose, usually sleeveless outer garment 2. something that covers or conceals; disguise —*vt.* 1. to cover with a cloak 2. to conceal

clob·ber (kläb′ər) *vt.* [< ?] [Slang] 1. to beat or hit repeatedly 2. to defeat decisively

cloche (klōsh) *n.* [Fr., a bell] a women's closefitting, bell-shaped hat

clock¹ (kläk) *n.* [ME. *clokke,* orig., clock with bells < ML. *clocca,* bell] a device for measuring and indicating time, usually by means of pointers moving over a dial —*vt.* to record the time of (a race, etc.) with a stopwatch

clock² (kläk) *n.* [< ? prec., because of orig. bell shape] a woven or embroidered ornament on a sock, going up from the ankle

clock radio a radio with a built-in clock that can turn it on or off

clock′wise′ (-wīz′) *adv., adj.* in the direction that hands of a clock rotate

clock′work′ (-wurk′) *n.* 1. the mechanism of a clock 2. any similar mechanism, with springs and gears — **like clockwork** very regularly

clod (kläd) *n.* [OE.] 1. a lump, esp. of earth or clay 2. a dull, stupid fellow —**clod′dish** *adj.* —**clod′dy** *adj.*

clod′hop′per (-häp′ər) *n.* [prec. + HOPPER] 1. a plowman 2. a clumsy, stupid fellow 3. a coarse, heavy shoe

clog (kläg) *n.* [ME. *clogge,* lump of wood] 1. anything that hinders or obstructs 2. a shoe with a thick, usually wooden, sole —*vt.* **clogged, clog′ging** 1. to hinder 2. to obstruct (a passage); stop up; jam —*vi.* to become stopped up —**clog′gy** *adj.*

cloi·son·né (kloi′zə nā′) *adj.* [Fr., lit., partitioned] denoting enamel work in which the surface decoration is set in hollows formed by thin strips of wire

clois·ter (klois′tər) *n.* [< L. *claudere,* to close] 1. a monastery or convent 2. monastic life 3. a covered walk along a courtyard wall with an open colonnade —*vt.* to confine as in a cloister

clomp (klämp) *vi.* to walk heavily or noisily

clone (klōn) *n.* [< Gr. *klōn,* a twig] an identical duplicate of an organism produced by replacing the nucleus of an unfertilized ovum with the nucleus of a body cell from the organism —*vt.* **cloned, clon′ing** to produce as a clone

clop (kläp) *n.* a clapping sound as of a hoofbeat —*vi.* **clopped, clop′ping** to make, or move with, such sounds

close¹ (klōs) *adj.* **clos′er, clos′est** [see ff.] 1. confined or confining *[close quarters]* 2. hidden; secluded 3. secretive; reserved 4. miserly; stingy 5. warm and stuffy, as stale air 6. with little space between; near together 7. compact; dense *[a close weave]* 8. near to the surface *[a close shave]* 9. intimate; familiar *[a close friend]* 10. strict; careful *[close attention]* 11. nearly alike *[a close resemblance]* 12. nearly equal or even *[a close contest]* 13. hard to get *[credit is close]* —*adv.* in a close manner — **close′ly** *adv.* —**close′ness** *n.*

close² (klōz) *vt.* **closed, clos′ing** [< L. *claudere,* to close] 1. to shut 2. to stop up (an opening) 3. to finish; conclude —*vi.* 1. to undergo shutting 2. to come to an end 3. to come close or together —*n.* an end or conclusion — **close down** (or **up**) to shut or stop entirely —**close in** to draw near from all directions; surround —**close out** to dispose of (a stock of goods) by sale

close call (klōs) [Colloq.] a narrow escape from danger: also **close shave**

closed circuit a system for telecasting by cable only to receivers connected in the circuit —**closed′-cir′cuit** *adj.*

close-fist′ed (klōs′fis′tid) *adj.* stingy

close′fit′ting *adj.* fitting tightly

close′-knit′ *adj.* closely united

close′mouthed′ (-mou*th*d′, -moutht′) *adj.* not talking much; taciturn

clos·et (kläz′it) *n.* [< L. *claudere,* to close] 1. a small room or cupboard for clothes, supplies, etc. 2. a small room for privacy —*vt.* to shut up in a private room for confidential talk

close-up (klōs′up′) *n.* a photograph, etc. taken at very close range

clo·sure (klō′zhər) *n.* [< L. *claudere*, to close] 1. a closing or being closed 2. a finish; end 3. anything that closes 4. *same as* CLOTURE

clot (klät) *n.* [OE.] a soft lump or thickened mass [a blood *clot*] —*vt.*, *vi.* **clot′ted, clot′ting** to form into a clot or clots; coagulate

cloth (klôth) *n., pl.* **cloths** (klôthz, klôths) [OE. *clath*] 1. a woven, knitted, or pressed fabric of fibrous material, as cotton, wool, silk, synthetic fibers, etc. 2. a tablecloth, washcloth, dustcloth, etc. —*adj.* made of cloth —**the cloth** the clergy

clothe (klōth) *vt.* **clothed** or **clad, cloth′ing** [see prec.] 1. to provide with or dress in clothes 2. to cover

clothes (klōz, klōthz) *n.pl.* [OE. *clathas*] clothing; wearing apparel

clothes′pin′ *n.* a small clip for fastening clothes on a line

cloth·ier (klōth′yər) *n.* a dealer in clothes or cloth

cloth·ing (klō′thiŋ) *n.* 1. wearing apparel; clothes 2. a covering

clo·ture (klō′chər) *n.* [see CLOSURE] the ending of legislative debate by having the bill put to immediate vote

cloud (kloud) *n.* [OE. *clud*, mass of rock] 1. a visible mass of vapor in the sky 2. a mass of smoke, dust, steam, etc. 3. a crowd; swarm [a *cloud* of locusts] 4. anything that darkens, obscures, etc. —*vt.* 1. to darken or obscure as with clouds 2. to make gloomy 3. to sully —*vi.* to become cloudy, gloomy, etc. —**in the clouds** 1. impractical 2. in a daydream —**under a cloud** under suspicion —**cloud′less** *adj.* —**cloud′y** *adj.* **-i·er, -i·est**

cloud′burst′ *n.* a sudden, heavy rain

clout (klout) *n.* [< OE. *clut*, a patch] a blow, as with the hand —*vt.* 1. [Colloq.] to strike, as with the hand 2. [Slang] to hit (a ball) a far distance

clove¹ (klōv) *n.* [< L. *clavus*, nail: from its shape] 1. the dried flower bud of a tropical evergreen tree, used as a spice 2. the tree

clove² (klōv) *n.* [OE. *clufu*] a segment of a bulb, as of garlic

clove³ (klōv) *alt. pt.* of CLEAVE¹

clo·ven (klō′v'n) *alt. pp.* of CLEAVE¹ —*adj.* divided; split

clo·ver (klō′vər) *n.* [OE. *clafre*] any of various herbs with leaves of three leaflets and small flowers in dense heads: some are used for forage

clo′ver·leaf′ (-lēf′) *n., pl.* **-leafs′** a highway interchange with overpass and curving ramps, letting traffic move unhindered in any of four directions

clown (kloun) *n.* [< ? Fr. *colon*, farmer] 1. a clumsy or boorish person 2. one who entertains, as in a circus, by antics, jokes, etc. —*vi.* to act the clown —**clown′ish** *adj.*

cloy (kloi) *vt., vi.* [< OFr. *encloyer*, nail up < L. *clavus*, nail] to surfeit with too much that is sweet, rich, etc.

club (klub) *n.* [< ON. *klumba*, mass] 1. a heavy stick used as a weapon 2. any stick used in a game, as golf 3. *a)* a group of people associated for a common purpose *b)* its meeting place 4. *a)* any of a suit of playing cards marked with a black trefoil (♣) *b)* [*pl.*] this suit —*vt.* **clubbed, club′bing** to strike as with a club —*vi.* to unite for a common purpose

club′foot′ *n., pl.* **-feet′** a congenitally misshapen, often clublike, foot

club′house′ (-hous′) *n.* 1. the building used by a club 2. a locker room used by an athletic team

club soda *same as* SODA WATER

cluck (kluk) *vi.* [echoic] to make a low, clicking sound, as of a hen calling her chicks —*n.* a clucking sound

clue (klōō) *n.* a fact, object, etc. that helps to solve a mystery or problem —*vt.* **clued, clu′ing** to provide with clues or needed facts

clump (klump) *n.* [< LowG. *klump*] 1. a lump; mass 2. a cluster, as of trees 3. the sound of heavy footsteps —*vi.* 1. to tramp heavily 2. to form clumps —**clump′y** *adj.* **-i·er, -i·est**

clum·sy (klum′zē) *adj.* **-si·er, -si·est** [ME. *clumsid*, numb with cold] 1. lacking grace or skill; awkward 2. awkwardly shaped or made —**clum′si·ly** *adv.* —**clum′si·ness** *n.*

clung (kluŋ) *pt. & pp.* of CLING

clunk·er (kluŋk′ər) *n.* [echoic of its noisiness] [Slang] an old machine or automobile in poor repair

clus·ter (klus′tər) *n.* [OE. *clyster*] a number of persons or things grouped together —*vi., vt.* to gather or grow in a cluster

clutch¹ (kluch) *vt.* [OE. *clyccan*, clench] to grasp or hold eagerly or tightly —*vi.* to snatch or seize (*at*) —*n.* 1. [*usually pl.*] power; control 2. a grasp; grip 3. a device for engaging and disengaging a motor or engine

clutch² (kluch) *n.* [< ON. *klekja*, hatch] 1. a nest of eggs 2. a brood of chicks 3. a cluster

clut·ter (klut′ər) *n.* [< CLOT] a number of things scattered in disorder; jumble —*vt.* to put into disorder; jumble (often with *up*)

cm. centimeter(s)

co- (kō) *a prefix shortened from* COM-, *meaning:* 1. together with [*cooperation*] 2. joint [*co-owner*] 3. equally [*coextensive*]

Co *Chem.* cobalt

CO Colorado

Co., co. *pl.* **Cos., cos.** 1. company 2. county

C/O, c.o. care of

C.O., CO Commanding Officer

coach (kōch) *n.* [< *Kócs*, village in Hungary] 1. a large, covered, four-wheeled carriage 2. a railroad passenger car 3. a bus 4. the lowest-priced class of airline accommodations 5. an instructor or trainer, as of athletes, actors, singers, etc. —*vt., vi.* to instruct and train (students, etc.)

coach′man (-mən) *n., pl.* **-men** the driver of a coach, or carriage

co·ad·ju·tor (kō aj′ə tər, kō′ə jōō′-)

n. [< L. *co-*, together + *adjuvare*, help] an assistant, esp. to a bishop

co·ag·u·late (kō ag'yoo lāt') *vt.* **-lat'ed, -lat'ing** [< L. *co-*, together + *agere*, drive] to cause (a liquid) to become semisolid; clot —*vi.* to become coagulated —**co·ag'u·lant** (-lənt) *n.* —**co·ag'u·la'tion** *n.* —**co·ag'u·la'tive** *adj.* —**co·ag'u·la'tor** *n.*

coal (kōl) *n.* [OE. *col*] **1.** a black, combustible mineral used as fuel **2.** a piece of coal **3.** an ember —*vt., vi.* to supply or be supplied with coal —**haul (or rake, drag, call) over the coals** to criticize sharply

co·a·lesce (kō'ə les') *vi.* **-lesced', -lesc'ing** [< L. *co-*, together + *alescere*, grow up] to unite into a single body or group —**co'a·les'cence** *n.*

co'a·li'tion (-lish'ən) *n.* [see prec.] a combination or union, esp. a temporary one

coal oil kerosene

coal tar a black, thick liquid obtained by the distillation of coal: used in dyes, medicines, etc.

coarse (kôrs) *adj.* [< COURSE in sense of "usual"] **1.** of poor quality; common **2.** consisting of rather large particles [*coarse* sand] **3.** rough; harsh **4.** unrefined; vulgar; crude —**coarse'ly** *adv.* —**coarse'ness** *n.*

coars'en (-'n) *vt., vi.* to make or become coarse

coast (kōst) *n.* [< L. *costa*, rib, side] **1.** land alongside the sea; seashore **2.** a slide down an incline, as on a sled —*vi.* **1.** to sail near or along a coast **2.** to go down an incline, as on a sled **3.** to continue in motion on momentum —**coast'al** *adj.*

coast'er *n.* **1.** a person or thing that coasts **2.** a small mat, etc. placed under a glass to protect a table

coaster brake a brake on a bicycle operated by reverse pressure on the pedals

coast guard a governmental force employed to defend a nation's coast, aid vessels in distress, etc.; specif. [C- G-], such a branch in the U.S. armed forces

coast'line' *n.* the outline of a coast

coat (kōt) *n.* [< ML. *cota*, tunic] **1.** a sleeved outer garment opening down the front **2.** the natural covering of a plant or animal **3.** a layer of a substance, as paint, over a surface —*vt.* to cover with a coat or layer

coat'ing *n.* a surface coat or layer

coat of arms heraldic insignia, as on a family escutcheon

coat'tail' (-tāl') *n.* either half of the divided lower back part of a coat

co·au·thor (kō ô'thər) *n.* a joint author; collaborator

coax (kōks) *vt., vi.* [< obs. slang *cokes*, a fool] to urge or get with soft words, flattery, etc. —**coax'er** *n.* —**coax'ing·ly** *adv.*

co·ax·i·al (kō ak'sē əl) *adj.* **1.** having a common axis **2.** designating a double-conductor high-frequency transmission line, as for television

cob (käb) *n.* [prob. < LowG.] **1.** a corncob **2.** a male swan **3.** a short, thickset horse

co·balt (kō'bôlt) *n.* [< G. *kobold*, demon of the mines] a hard, steel-gray metallic chemical element

cob·ble (käb''l) *vt.* **-bled, -bling** [< ?] **1.** to mend (shoes, etc.) **2.** to mend or put together clumsily

cob·bler (käb'lər) *n.* **1.** one who mends shoes **2.** a deep-dish fruit pie

cob'ble·stone' *n.* a rounded stone formerly much used for paving streets

co·bra (kō'brə) *n.* [Port.] a very poisonous snake of Asia and Africa

cob·web (käb'web') *n.* [< ME. *coppe*, spider + WEB] **1.** a web spun by a spider **2.** anything flimsy, gauzy, or ensnaring like this

co·caine, co·cain (kō kān') *n.* [< *coca*, tropical shrub from whose leaves it is extracted] an alkaloid drug used as a narcotic and local anesthetic

coc·cus (käk'əs) *n., pl.* **coc'ci** (-sī) [< Gr. *kokkos*, kernel] a spherically shaped bacterium

coc·cyx (käk'siks) *n., pl.* **coc·cy·ges** (käk sī'jēz) [< Gr. *kokkyx*, cuckoo: it is shaped like a cuckoo's beak] a small, triangular bone at the base of the spine

coch·i·neal (käch'ə nēl') *n.* [ult. < L. *coccum*, a (red) berry] a red dye made from a dried Mexican insect

coch·le·a (käk'lē ə) *n., pl.* **-ae'** (-ē'), **-as** [< Gr. *kochlias*, snail] the spiral-shaped part of the internal ear

cock¹ (käk) *n.* [OE. *coc*] **1.** a rooster or other male bird **2.** a faucet or valve **3.** *a)* the hammer of a gun *b)* its firing position **4.** a jaunty tilt, as of a hat —*vt.* **1.** to tilt jauntily **2.** to raise or turn alertly **3.** to set (a gun hammer) in firing position

cock² (käk) *n.* [ME. *cokke*] a small, cone-shaped pile, as of hay

cock·ade (kä kād') *n.* [< Fr. *coq*, a cock] a rosette, knot of ribbon, etc., worn on the hat as a badge

cock·a·ma·mie (käk'ə mā'mē) *adj.* [< DECALCOMANIA] [Slang] poor; inferior

cock-and-bull story (käk''n bool') an absurd, improbable story

cock·a·too (käk'ə tōō') *n., pl.* **-toos'** [< Malay *kakatua*] a large, crested parrot of Australia & the East Indies

cock·a·trice (käk'ə tris') *n.* [< L. *calcare*, to tread] a fabulous serpent supposedly able to kill by a look

cock·crow (käk'krō') *n.* dawn

cocked hat a three-cornered hat

cock·er·el (käk'ər əl) *n.* a young rooster, less than a year old

cock·er (spaniel) (käk'ər) [< use in hunting woodcock] a small spaniel with long, silky hair and drooping ears

cock'eyed' (-īd') *adj.* [< COCK¹, *v.* + EYE] **1.** cross-eyed **2.** [Slang] *a)* crooked; awry *b)* silly; foolish *c)* drunk

---

fat, āpe, cär; ten, ēven; is, bīte; gō, hôrn, tōōl, look; oil, out; up, fur; chin; she; thin, *th*en; zh, leisure; ŋ, ring; ə for *a* in *ago*; ', (ā'b'l); ë, Fr. coeur; ö, Fr. feu; Fr. mon; ü, Fr. duc; kh, G. ich, doch; ‡ foreign; < derived from

cock'fight' *n.* a fight between game-cocks, usually wearing metal spurs
cock·le[1] (käk'l) *n.* [< Gr. *konchē*, mussel] an edible shellfish with two heart-shaped shells —**cockles of one's heart** one's deepest emotions
cock·le[2] (käk'l) *n.* [OE. *coccel*] any of various weeds in grainfields
cock'ney (käk'nē) *n., pl.* **-neys** [ME. *cokenei*, spoiled child, milksop] [*often* C-] 1. a native of the East End of London, England, speaking a characteristic dialect 2. this dialect
cock'pit' *n.* 1. a pit for cockfighting 2. the space in a small airplane for the pilot and passengers or in a large airplane for the pilot and crew
cock'roach' (-rōch') *n.* [Sp. *cucaracha*] an insect with long feelers and a flat body: a common household pest
cocks·comb (käks'kōm') *n.* 1. the red, fleshy growth on a rooster's head 2. a plant with flowers like this
cock·sure (käk'shoor') *adj.* [< COCK[1] + SURE] absolutely sure or self-confident, esp. in an arrogant way
cock'tail' (-tāl') *n.* [< ?] 1. a mixed alcoholic drink, usually iced 2. an appetizer, as of shrimp or juice
cock·y (käk'ē) *adj.* **-i·er, -i·est** [< COCK[1] + -Y[2]] [Colloq.] jauntily conceited —**cock'i·ly** *adv.* —**cock'i·ness** *n.*
co·co (kō'kō) *n., pl.* **-cos** [< Gr. *kokkos*, berry] 1. the coconut palm 2. its fruit; coconut
co·coa (kō'kō) *n.* [see CACAO] 1. powder made from roasted cacao seeds 2. a drink made of this and hot milk, etc. 3. a reddish-yellow brown
cocoa butter a yellowish-white fat made from cacao seeds
co·co·nut, co·coa·nut (kō'kə nut') *n.* the fruit of a tropical tree (**coconut palm**), a thick, brown, oval husk with edible white meat and a sweet, milky fluid (**coconut milk**) inside
co·coon (kə kōōn') *n.* [< ML. *coco*, shell] the silky case which the larvae of some insects spin about themselves as a shelter during the pupa stage
cod (käd) *n., pl.* **cod, cods** [ME.] a food fish of northern seas
C.O.D., c.o.d. collect on delivery
Cod (käd), **Cape** hook-shaped peninsula in E Mass.: 65 mi. long
co·da (kō'də) *n.* [It. < L. *cauda*, tail] *Music* a final passage
cod·dle (käd'l) *vt.* **-dled, -dling** [< ?] 1. to cook (esp. eggs) in water not quite boiling 2. to pamper
code (kōd) *n.* [< L. *codex*, wooden tablet] 1. a systematized body of laws 2. a set of principles, as of ethics 3. a set of signals for sending messages 4. a system of symbols for secret writing, etc. —*vt.* **cod'ed, cod'ing** to put into code
co·deine (kō'dēn) *n.* [< Gr. *kōdeia*, poppy head] an alkaloid derived from opium: used for pain relief and in cough medicines: also **co'dein**
co·dex (kō'deks) *n., pl.* **-di·ces** (-də sēz') [see CODE] a manuscript volume, esp. of the Scriptures or a classic text

cod'fish' *n., pl.:* see FISH *same as* COD
codg·er (käj'ər) *n.* [< ?] [Colloq.] an eccentric fellow, esp. an older one
cod·i·cil (käd'i s'l) *n.* [< L. dim.: see CODE] an addition to a will
cod·i·fy (käd'ə fī', kō'də-) *vt.* **-fied', -fy'ing** to arrange (laws, etc.) systematically —**cod'i·fi·ca'tion** *n.* —**cod'i·fi'er** *n.*
co·ed, co-ed (kō'ed') *n.* [Colloq.] a girl attending a coeducational college —*adj.* [Colloq.] 1. coeducational 2. of a coed
co·ed·u·ca·tion (kō'ej ə kā'shən) *n.* the educational system in which students of both sexes attend classes together —**co'ed·u·ca'tion·al** *adj.*
co·ef·fi·cient (kō'ə fish'ənt) *n.* [CO- + EFFICIENT] 1. a factor contributing to a result or measuring some physical property 2. a multiplier of a variable or unknown quantity (as 6 in 6x)
co·e·qual (kō ē'kwəl) *adj., n.* equal —**co'e·qual'i·ty** (-i kwäl'ə tē) *n.* —**co·e'qual·ly** *adv.*
co·erce (kō urs') *vt.* **-erced', -erc'ing** [< L. *co-*, together + *arcere*, confine] 1. to restrain by force 2. to compel 3. to enforce —**co·er'cion** (-ur'shən) *n.* —**co·er'cive** (-siv) *adj.*
co·e·val (kō ē'v'l) *adj., n.* [< L. *co-*, together + *aevum*, age] contemporary
co'ex·ist' (-ig zist') *vi.* 1. to exist together at the same time or in the same place 2. to live together peacefully, despite differences —**co'ex·ist'·ence** *n.* —**co'ex·ist'ent** *adj.*
co'ex·ten·sive (-ik sten'siv) *adj.* extending equally in time or space
cof·fee (kôf'ē) *n.* [< Ar. *qahwa*] 1. a drink made from the roasted, ground, beanlike seeds of a tropical shrub of the madder family 2. the seeds, whole or ground, or the shrub 3. milky brown
coffee break a brief respite from work when coffee, etc. is taken
cof'fee·cake' *n.* a kind of cake or roll to be eaten with coffee, etc.
cof'fee·house' *n.* a place where coffee is served and people gather for talk, entertainment, etc.
cof'fee·pot' *n.* a pot with a spout, for brewing or serving coffee
coffee shop a small restaurant serving coffee and light refreshments or meals
coffee table a small, low table for serving refreshments
cof·fer (kôf'ər) *n.* [see ff.] 1. a chest for holding money or valuables 2. [*pl.*] a treasury; funds
cof·fin (kôf'in) *n.* [< Gr. *kophinos*, basket] the case or box in which a corpse is buried
cog (käg) *n.* [< Scand.] 1. one of the teeth on the rim of a cogwheel 2. a cogwheel
co·gent (kō'jənt) *adj.* [< L. *co-*, together + *agere*, drive] convincingly to the point —**co'gen·cy** *n.*
cog·i·tate (käj'ə tāt') *vi., vt.* **-tat'ed, -tat'ing** [< L.] to think deeply (about); ponder —**cog'i·ta'tion** *n.* —**cog'i·ta'tive** *adj.* —**cog'i·ta'tor** *n.*
co·gnac (kōn'yak) *n.* [Fr.] brandy; specif., a brandy from Cognac, France
cog·nate (käg'nāt) *adj.* [< L. *co-*,

together + (g)nasci, be born] 1. related by family 2. from a common original form, as two words 3. related; similar —n. a cognate person or thing

cog·ni·tion (käg nish'ən) n. [< L. co-, together + gnoscere, know] 1. the process of knowing, perceiving, etc. 2. an idea, perception, etc.

cog·ni·za·ble (käg'ni zə b'l) adj. 1. that can be known or perceived 2. Law within the jurisdiction of a court

cog·ni·zance (käg'nə zəns) n. 1. perception or knowledge 2. notice; heed —cog'ni·zant adj.

cog·no·men (käg nō'mən) n. [< L. co-, with + nomen, name] 1. surname 2. any name; esp., a nickname

cog'wheel' n. a wheel rimmed with teeth that mesh with those of another wheel, etc., to transmit or receive motion

COGWHEELS

co·hab·it (kō hab'it) vi. [< L. co-, together + habitare, dwell] to live together as husband and wife, esp. when not legally married —co·hab'i·ta'tion n.

co·heir (kō'er') n. one who inherits jointly with another or others

co·here (kō hir') vi. -hered', -her'ing [< L. co-, together + haerere, to stick] 1. to stick together 2. to be connected naturally or logically

co·her·ent (-ənt) adj. 1. sticking together; cohering 2. logically connected and intelligible —co·her'ence n. —co·her'ent·ly adv.

co·he·sion (kō hē'zhən) n. a cohering; tendency to stick together —co·he'sive (-hēs'iv) adj.

co·ho (kō'hō) n., pl. -ho, -hos [< ?] a small salmon of the North Pacific, introduced into fresh waters of N U.S.

co·hort (kō'hôrt) n. [< L. cohors, enclosure] 1. a band of soldiers 2. a group 3. an associate

coif (koif; for 2, usually kwäf) n. 1. [< LL. cofea, cap] a closefitting cap 2. [< ff.] a hair style

coif·fure (kwä fyoor') n. [Fr.] 1. a headdress 2. a hair style

coil (koil) vt., vi. [< L. com-, together + legere, gather] to wind into circular or spiral form —n. 1. a series of rings or a spiral, or anything in this form 2. a single turn of a coil 3. Elec. a spiral of wire

coin (koin) n. [< L. cuneus, a wedge] 1. a piece of stamped metal, issued by a government as money 2. such pieces collectively —vt. 1. to stamp (metal) into (coins) 2. to invent (a new word, phrase, etc.) —coin'age n.

co·in·cide (kō'in sīd') vi. -cid'ed, -cid'ing [< L. co-, together + incidere, fall upon] 1. to take up the same place in space 2. to occur at the same time 3. to agree exactly

co·in·ci·dence (kō in'sə dəns) n. 1. a coinciding 2. an accidental occurrence of related or identical events, ideas, etc. at the same time —co·in'ci·dent, co·in'ci·den'tal adj. —co·in'ci·den'tal·ly adv.

co·i·tus (kō'it əs) n. [< L. < co-, together + ire, go] sexual intercourse: also co·i·tion (kō ish'ən)

coke (kōk) n. [ME. colke, a core] coal from which most of the gases have been removed by heating: used as an industrial fuel

col- (käl) same as COM-: used before l

Col. Colonel

col. 1. color(ed) 2. column

co·la (kō'lə) n. [< WAfr. name] 1. an African tree with nuts that yield an extract used in soft drinks and medicine 2. a carbonated soft drink flavored with this extract

col·an·der (kul'ən dər, käl'-) n. [prob. < L. colum, strainer] a perforated pan for draining off liquids

cold (kōld) adj. [OE. cald] 1. of a temperature much lower than that of the human body 2. too cool; chilly 3. unfriendly, indifferent, or depressing 4. devoid of feeling; emotionless 5. a) not fresh: said of a hunting scent b) off the track 6. [Colloq.] unprepared [to enter a game cold] 7. [Slang] perfectly memorized 8. [Slang] unconscious [knocked cold] —n. 1. lack of heat or warmth 2. cold weather 3. a virus infection of the respiratory tract, causing sneezing, coughing, etc. —catch (or take) cold to become ill with a cold —have (or get) cold feet [Colloq.] to be (or become) timid —in the cold neglected —cold'ly adv. —cold'ness n.

cold'blood'ed adj. 1. having a body temperature that varies with the surrounding air, water, etc., as fish and reptiles 2. cruel or callous

cold cream a creamy preparation for softening and cleansing the skin

cold cuts a variety of sliced cold meats and, usually, cheeses

cold duck a drink that is a mixture of burgundy and champagne

cold front the forward edge of a cold air mass advancing into a warmer mass

cold shoulder [Colloq.] a slight; snub; rebuff —cold'-shoul'der vt.

cold sore little blisters about the mouth during a cold or fever

cold turkey [Slang] 1. the abrupt and total withdrawal of drugs from an addict 2. without preparation

cold war hostility and conflict without actual warfare

cole (kōl) n. [< L. caulis, cabbage] any of various plants of the mustard family; esp., rape

cole·slaw' (-slô') n. [< Du.: see prec. & SLAW] a salad of shredded raw cabbage: also cole slaw

col·ic (käl'ik) n. [< Gr. kōlon, colon] acute abdominal pain —col'ick·y adj.

col·i·se·um (käl'ə sē'əm) n. [< L. colosseum] a large stadium

co·li·tis (kō lī'tis) n. [< COLON² + -ITIS] inflammation of the colon

coll. 1. collect 2. college

col·lab·o·rate (kə lab'ə rāt') vi. -rat'ed, -rat'ing [< L. com-, with + laborare, to work] 1. to work together, esp. in literary or scientific work 2. to cooperate with the enemy —col·lab'o·ra'tion n. —col·lab'o·ra'tor n.

col·lage (kə läzh') n. [Fr., a pasting] an art form in which bits of objects are pasted on a surface

col·lapse (kə laps') vi. -lapsed', -laps'ing [< L. com-, together + labi, to fall] 1. to fall down or cave in 2. to break down suddenly 3. to fail suddenly in health 4. to fold together compactly —vt. to make collapse —n. a collapsing —col·laps'i·ble adj.

col·lar (käl'ər) n. [< L. collum, neck] 1. the part of a garment encircling the neck 2. a band of leather, etc., for an animal's neck 3. anything like a collar —vt. 1. to put a collar on 2. to seize, as by the collar

col'lar·bone' n. the clavicle

col·lard (käl'ərd) n. [< ME.] a kind of kale, with coarse leaves

col·late (kä lāt') vt. -lat'ed, -lat'ing [< L. com-, together + latus, brought] 1. to compare (texts) carefully 2. to put (pages) in proper order —col·la'tor n.

col·lat·er·al (kə lat'ər əl) adj. [< L. com-, together + latus, a side] 1. parallel or corresponding 2. accompanying or supporting [collateral evidence] 3. having the same ancestors but in a different line 4. designating or of security given as a pledge for the repayment of a loan, etc. —n. 1. a collateral relative 2. collateral security

col·la·tion (kä lā'shən) n. 1. act or result of collating 2. a light meal

col·league (käl'ēg) n. [< Fr. < L. com-, with + legare, appoint as deputy] a fellow worker; associate in office

col·lect (kə lekt') vt. [< L. com-, together + legere, gather] 1. to gather together 2. to gather (stamps, etc.) as a hobby 3. to call for and receive (money) for (bills, etc.) 4. to regain control of (oneself) —vi. to assemble or accumulate —adj., adv. with payment to be made by the receiver [to telephone collect] —n. (käl'ekt) [also C-] a short prayer used in certain services —col·lect'a·ble, col·lect'i·ble adj. —col·lec'tor n.

col·lect'ed adj. 1. gathered together 2. in control of oneself; calm

col·lec'tion n. 1. a collecting 2. things collected 3. a mass or pile; accumulation 4. money collected

col·lec'tive adj. 1. formed by collecting 2. of or as a group [collective effort] 3. designating a singular noun, as tribe, denoting a collection of individuals —n. 1. a) any collective enterprise; specif., a collective farm b) the people who work together in it 2. a collective noun —col·lec'tive·ly adv.

collective bargaining negotiation between organized workers and their employer concerning wages, hours, etc.

col·lec'tiv·ism n. collective ownership and control, esp. under socialism —col·lec'tiv·ist n., adj. —col·lec'tiv·ize' vt. -ized', -iz'ing

col·leen (käl'ēn, kə lēn') n. [< Ir. caile, girl] [Ir.] a girl

col·lege (käl'ij) n. [see COLLEAGUE] 1. a group of individuals with certain powers and duties [the electoral college] 2. an institution of higher education that grants degrees 3. any of the schools of a university 4. a school offering specialized instruction [a business college]

col·le·gian (kə lē'jən) n. a college student

col·le'giate (-jət, -jē ət) adj. of or like a college or college students

col·lide (kə līd') vi. -lid'ed, -lid'ing [< L. com-, together + laedere, to strike] 1. to come into violent contact; crash 2. to conflict; clash

col·lie (käl'ē) n. [< ?] a large, long-haired dog, orig. bred in Scotland

col·lier (käl'yər) n. [ME. < col, charcoal] [Chiefly Brit.] 1. a coal miner 2. a coal freighter

col'lier·y n., pl. -ies [Chiefly Brit.] a coal mine and its buildings, etc.

col·li·sion (kə lizh'ən) n. 1. a colliding 2. a clash or conflict

col·lo·cate (käl'ə kāt') vt. -cat'ed, -cat'ing [< L. com-, together + locare, to place] to arrange together, esp. side by side —col'lo·ca'tion n.

col·lo·di·on (kə lō'dē ən) n. [< Gr. kolla, glue + eidos, form] a nitrocellulose solution that dries into a tough, elastic film: used to protect wounds, in photographic films, etc.

col·loid (käl'oid) n. [< Gr. kolla, glue + -OID] a substance made up of tiny, insoluble, nondiffusible particles that remain suspended in a medium of different matter —col·loid'al adj.

colloq. colloquial

col·lo·qui·al (kə lō'kwē əl) adj. [see ff.] designating or of the words, phrases, etc. characteristic of informal speech and writing; conversational —col·lo'qui·al·ism n. —col·lo'qui·al·ly adv.

col·lo·qui·um n., pl. -qui·a, -qui·ums [L.: see ff.] an organized conference or seminar on some subject

col·lo·quy (käl'ə kwē) n., pl. -quies [< L. com-, together + loqui, speak] a conversation or conference

col·lu·sion (kə lōō'zhən) n. [< L. com-, with + ludere, to play] a secret agreement for fraudulent or illegal purpose; conspiracy —col·lu'sive (-siv) adj.

Colo. Colorado

Co·logne (kə lōn') city in W West Germany, on the Rhine: pop. 857,000

co·logne (kə lōn') n. [< Fr. eau de Cologne, lit., water of Cologne] a perfumed toilet water made of alcohol and aromatic oils

Co·lom·bi·a (kə lum'bē ə) country in NW S.America: 455,335 sq. mi.; pop. 18,068,000 —Co·lom'bi·an adj., n.

co·lon¹ (kō'lən) n. [< Gr. kōlon, verse part] a mark of punctuation (:) used before a long quotation, explanation, example, series, etc. and after the salutation of a formal letter

co·lon² (kō'lən) n., pl. -lons, -la (-lə) [< Gr. kolon] that part of the large intestine extending from the cecum to the rectum

colo·nel (kur'n'l) *n.* [< It. *colonna*, (military) column] a military officer ranking just above a lieutenant colonel —**colo'nel·cy** *n., pl.* **-cies**

co·lo·ni·al (kə lō'nē əl) *adj.* 1. of, in, or having a colony 2. [*often* C-] of or in the thirteen British colonies that became the U.S. —*n.* an inhabitant of a colony —**co·lo'ni·al·ly** *adv.*

co·lo'ni·al·ism (-iz'm) *n.* the system by which a country maintains foreign colonies, esp. for economic exploitation —**co·lo'ni·al·ist** *n., adj.*

col·o·nist (käl'ə nist) *n.* a settler or inhabitant of a colony

col'o·nize' (-nīz') *vt., vi.* **-nized', -niz'ing** 1. to found a colony (in) 2. to settle in a colony —**col'o·ni·za'tion** *n.* —**col'o·niz'er** *n.*

col·on·nade (käl'ə nād') *n.* [< L. *columna*, column] *Archit.* a row of columns, as along a side of a building

col·o·ny (käl'ə nē) *n., pl.* **-nies** [< L. *colere*, to cultivate] 1. *a)* a group of settlers in a distant land, under the jurisdiction of their native land *b)* the region settled 2. any territory ruled over by a distant state 3. a community of the same nationality or pursuits, as within a city 4. *Biol.* a group living or growing together

col·o·phon (käl'ə fän') *n.* [LL. < Gr. *kolophon*, top] a publisher's emblem

col·or (kul'ər) *n.* [L.] 1. the property of reflecting light of a particular visible wavelength: the *colors* of the spectrum are red, orange, yellow, green, blue, indigo, and violet 2. any coloring matter; pigment; dye; paint 3. color of the face or skin 4. [*pl.*] a colored badge, etc. to identify the wearer 5. [*pl.*] a flag 6. outward appearance 7. vivid quality —*vt.* 1. to give color to; paint, dye, etc. 2. to change the color of 3. to alter, as by distorting [to *color* a story] —*vi.* 1. to become colored 2. to change color 3. to blush or flush —**show one's colors** to show one's true self

Col·o·rad·o (käl'ə rad'ō) Western State of the U.S., in the Rockies: 104,247 sq. mi.; pop. 2,889,000; cap. Denver —**Col'o·rad'an** *adj., n.*

col·or·ant (kul'ər ənt) *n.* a dye or other coloring agent

col'or·a'tion (-ə rā'shən) *n.* coloring

col'or·a·tu·ra (soprano) (kul'ər ə toor'ə, -tyoor'-) [It.] a soprano skilled at singing brilliant trills, etc.

color bar *same as* COLOR LINE

col'or·blind' *adj.* 1. unable to distinguish certain colors or any colors 2. not influenced by considerations of race —**col'or·blind'ness** *n.*

col'or·cast' *n.* a color television broadcast —*vt., vi.* **-cast'** or **-cast'ed, -cast'ing** to televise in color

col'ored (-ərd) *adj.* 1. having color 2. non-Caucasoid; specif., Negro

col'or·fast' (-fast') *adj.* with color not subject to fading or running

col'or·ful *adj.* 1. full of color 2. picturesque, vivid, etc. —**col'or·ful·ly** *adv.* —**col'or·ful·ness** *n.*

col'or·ing *n.* 1. anything applied to impart color; pigment, etc. 2. the way a thing is colored 3. false appearance

col'or·less *adj.* 1. without color 2. lacking variety or interest; dull —**col'or·less·ly** *adv.* —**col'or·less·ness** *n.*

color line any barrier of social, political, or economic restrictions imposed on Negroes or other nonwhites

co·los·sal (kə läs'l) *adj.* 1. like a colossus, in size; huge 2. [Colloq.] extraordinary —**co·los'sal·ly** *adv.*

co·los·sus (kə läs'əs) *n., pl.* **-si** (-ī), **-sus·es** [< Gr.] 1. a gigantic statue 2. anything huge or important

col·our (kul'ər) *n., vt., vi. Brit. sp.* of COLOR

colt (kōlt) *n.* [OE.] a young horse, zebra, etc.; esp., a young male horse

colt'ish *adj.* of or like a colt; esp., frisky, frolicsome, etc.

Co·lum·bi·a (kə lum'bē ə) 1. capital of S.C.; pop. 99,000 2. river flowing from Canada, through Wash., & along the Wash.-Oreg. border into the Pacific

col·um·bine (käl'əm bīn') *n.* [< L. *columbinus*, dovelike] a plant of the buttercup family, with showy, spurred flowers

Co·lum·bus (kə lum'bəs) 1. capital of Ohio, in the C part: pop. 565,000 2. city in W Ga.: pop. 169,000

Columbus, Christopher 1451?-1506; It. discoverer of America (1492)

col·umn (käl'əm) *n.* [< L. *columna*] 1. a slender upright structure, usually a supporting member in a building 2. anything like a column [the spinal *column*] 3. a file formation of troops, etc. 4. any of the vertical sections of printed matter on a page 5. a feature article appearing regularly in a newspaper, etc. —**col·um·nar** (kə lum'nər) *adj.*

COLUMN

col·um·nist (käl'əm nist) *n.* a writer of a column (sense 5)

com- [L. < *cum*, with] a *prefix* meaning with or together: also an intensive

Com. 1. Commission(er) 2. Committee

com. 1. commerce 2. common

co·ma (kō'mə) *n.* [< Gr. *kōma*, deep sleep] deep, prolonged unconsciousness caused by injury or disease

co·ma·tose (kō'mə tōs', käm'ə-) *adj.* 1. of, like, or in a coma 2. lethargic

comb (kōm) *n.* [< OE. *camb*] 1. a thin strip of hard rubber, plastic, etc., with teeth, used to arrange or clean the hair 2. any similar tool, as for cleaning and straightening wool, flax, etc. 3. a red, fleshy outgrowth on the head, as of a rooster 4. a honeycomb —*vt.* 1. to arrange, etc. with a comb 2. to search thoroughly

---

com·bat (*for v.* kəm bat′, käm′bat; *for n.* käm′bat) *vt., vi.* **-bat′ed** *or* **-bat′ted, -bat′ing** *or* **-bat′ting** [< Fr. < L. *com-,* with + *battuere,* to fight] to fight or actively oppose —*n.* 1. armed fighting; battle 2. any struggle or conflict —**com·bat·ant** (käm′bə tənt, kəm bat′ənt) *adj., n.*

combat fatigue a psychoneurosis with anxiety, depression, etc., as after prolonged combat in warfare

com·bat·ive (kəm bat′iv; käm′bə tiv) *adj.* ready or eager to fight

comb·er (kō′mər) *n.* 1. one that combs 2. a wave, curling at the top

com·bi·na·tion (käm bə nā′shən) *n.* 1. a combining or being combined 2. a thing formed by combining 3. an association formed for a common purpose 4. the series of numbers to which a dial is turned on a lock (**combination lock**) to open it

com·bine (kəm bīn′; *for n.* käm′bīn) *vt., vi.* **-bined′, -bin′ing** [< L. *com-,* together + *bini,* two by two] to join into one, as by blending; unite —*n.* 1. a machine for harvesting and threshing grain 2. an association formed for commercial or political, often unethical, purposes —**com·bin′er** *n.*

comb·ings (kō′miŋz) *n.pl.* loose hair, wool, etc. removed in combing

combining form a word form occurring only in compounds and derivatives (Ex.: *cardio-* in *cardiograph*)

com·bo (käm′bō) *n., pl.* **-bos** [Colloq.] a combination; specif., a small jazz ensemble

com·bus·ti·ble (kəm bus′tə b'l) *adj.* that can burn; flammable —**com·bus′ti·bil′i·ty** *n.* —**com·bus′ti·bly** *adv.*

com·bus′tion (-chən) *n.* [< L. *com-,* intens. + *urere,* to burn] the act or process of burning

Comdr. Commander

come (kum) *vi.* **came, come, com′ing** [< OE. *cuman*] 1. to move from "there" to "here" 2. to arrive or appear 3. to extend; reach 4. to happen 5. to occur in a certain order [after 8 *comes* 9] 6. to be derived or descended 7. to be caused; result 8. to become [to *come* loose] 9. to be available [it *comes* in four sizes] 10. to amount (*to*) —*interj.* see here!: used to express impatience, etc. —**come about** 1. to happen 2. to turn about —**come across** (or **upon**) to find or meet by chance —**come along** 1. to appear or arrive 2. to proceed or succeed —**come around** (or **round**) 1. to recover 2. to yield —**come by** to get; gain —**come into** 1. to enter into 2. to inherit —**come off** 1. to become detached 2. to end up 3. [Colloq.] to prove effective, etc. —**come out** 1. to be disclosed 2. to make a debut 3. to end up —**come out for** to announce endorsement of —**come through** 1. to complete something successfully 2. [Slang] to do or give what is wanted —**come to** to recover consciousness —**come up** to arise, as a point in a discussion —**how come?** [Colloq.] why?

come′back′ *n.* [Colloq.] 1. a return to a previous position, as of power 2. a witty answer; retort

co·me·di·an (kə mē′dē ən) *n.* an actor who plays comic parts —**co·me′di·enne′** (-en′) *n.fem.*

co·me·dic (kə mē′dik, -med′ik) *adj.* of or having to do with comedy

come′down′ *n.* a loss of status

com·e·dy (käm′ə dē) *n., pl.* **-dies** [< Gr. *kōmos,* festival + *aeidein,* sing] 1. a humorous play, etc. with a nontragic ending 2. an amusing event

come·ly (kum′lē) *adj.* **-li·er, -li·est** [< OE. *cymlic*] attractive; fair —**come′li·ness** *n.*

come′-on′ *n.* [Slang] an inducement

co·mes·ti·ble (kə mes′tə b'l) *n.* [< L. *com-,* intens. + *edere,* to eat] [*usually pl.*] food

com·et (käm′ət) *n.* [< Gr. *komē,* hair] a heavenly body with a starlike nucleus and, usually, a long, luminous tail: comets move in orbits around the sun

come·up·pance (kum′up′ns) *n.* [Colloq.] deserved punishment

com·fit (kum′fit) *n.* [< L. *com-,* with + *facere,* do] a candy; sweetmeat

com·fort (kum′fərt) *vt.* [< L. *com-,* intens. + *fortis,* strong] to soothe in distress or sorrow; console —*n.* 1. relief from distress, etc. 2. one that comforts 3. a state of, or thing that provides, ease and quiet enjoyment —**com′fort·ing** *adj.* —**com′fort·less** *adj.*

com·fort·a·ble (kumf′tər b'l, kum′fər tə b'l) *adj.* 1. providing comfort 2. at ease in body or mind 3. [Colloq.] sufficient to satisfy [a *comfortable* salary] —**com′fort·a·bly** *adv.*

com′fort·er *n.* 1. one that comforts 2. a quilted bed covering

comfort station a public toilet or restroom

com·fy (kum′fē) *adj.* **-fi·er, -fi·est** [Colloq.] comfortable

com·ic (käm′ik) *adj.* 1. of comedy 2. amusing; funny —*n.* 1. a comedian 2. the humorous part of art or life 3. *a) same as* COMIC STRIP *b)* [*pl.*] a section of comic strips

com′i·cal (-i k'l) *adj.* causing amusement; humorous; funny —**com′i·cal·i·ty** (-kal′ə tē) *n.* —**com′i·cal·ly** *adv.*

comic strip a series of cartoons telling a humorous or adventurous story, as in a newspaper or in a booklet (**comic book**)

com·ing (kum′iŋ) *adj.* 1. approaching; next 2. showing promise of being successful, etc. —*n.* arrival; approach

com·i·ty (käm′ə tē) *n., pl.* **-ties** [< L. *comis,* polite] courtesy

comm. 1. commission 2. committee

com·ma (käm′ə) *n.* [< Gr. *komma,* clause] a mark of punctuation (,) used to indicate a slight separation of sentence elements

com·mand (kə mand′) *vt.* [< L. *com-,* intens. + *mandare,* entrust] 1. to give an order to; direct 2. to have authority over; control 3. to have for use [to *command* a fortune] 4. to deserve and get [to *command* respect]

&, to control (a position); overlook —*vi.* to have authority —*n.* 1. order; direction 2. controlling power or position 3. mastery 4. a military or naval force, or district, under a specified authority

com·man·dant (käm'ən dant') *n.* a commanding officer, as of a fort

com·man·deer (käm'ən dir') *vt.* [see COMMAND] to seize (property) for military or governmental use

com·mand·er *n.* 1. one who commands 2. *U.S. Navy* an officer ranking just above a lieutenant commander

commander in chief *pl.* **commanders in chief** the supreme commander of the armed forces of a nation

com·mand·ment *n.* 1. a command 2. any of the Ten Commandments

com·man·do (kə man'dō) *n., pl.* **-dos, -does** [Afrik. < Port.] a member of a small force trained to raid enemy territory

command post the field headquarters of a military unit, from which operations are directed

com·mem·o·rate (kə mem'ə rāt') *vt.* **-rat'ed, -rat'ing** [< L. *com-*, intens. + *memorare*, remind] 1. to honor the memory of, as by a ceremony 2. to serve as a memorial to —**com·mem'o·ra'tion** *n.* —**com·mem'o·ra'tive** *adj.* —**com·mem'o·ra'tor** *n.*

com·mence (kə mens') *vi., vt.* **-menced', -menc'ing** [< L. *com-*, together + *initiare*, begin] to begin

com·mence'ment *n.* 1. a beginning 2. the ceremony of conferring degrees or diplomas at a school

com·mend (kə mend') *vt.* [see COMMAND] 1. to put in the care of another; entrust 2. to recommend 3. to praise —**com·mend'a·ble** *adj.* —**com·mend'a·bly** *adv.* —**com·men·da·tion** (käm'ən dā'shən) *n.*

com·mend·a·to·ry (kə men'də tôr'ē) *adj.* praising or recommending

com·men·su·ra·ble (kə men'shər ə b'l) *adj.* [< L. *com-*, together + *mensura*, measurement] measurable by the same standard or measure

com·men·su·rate (-shər it) *adj.* [see prec.] 1. equal in measure or size 2. proportionate 3. commensurable

com·ment (käm'ent) *n.* [< L. *com-*, intens. + *meminisse*, remember] 1. an explanatory or critical note 2. a remark or observation 3. talk; gossip —*vi.* to make a comment or comments

com·men·tar·y (käm'ən ter'ē) *n., pl.* **-ies** a series of explanatory notes or remarks

com·men·tate' (-tāt') *vi.* **-tat'ed, -tat'ing** to perform as a commentator

com·men·ta'tor (-tāt'ər) *n.* one who reports and analyzes events, trends, etc., as on television

com·merce (käm'ərs) *n.* [< L. *com-*, together + *merx*, merchandise] trade on a large scale, as between countries

com·mer·cial (kə mur'shəl) *adj.* 1.

of commerce or business 2. made or done for profit —*n. Radio & TV* a paid advertisement —**com·mer'cial·ism** *n.* —**com·mer'cial·ly** *adv.*

com·mer·cial·ize (-iz') *vt.* **-ized', -iz'ing** to put on a business basis, esp. so as to make profit —**com·mer'cial·i·za'tion** *n.*

com·min·gle (kə miŋ'g'l) *vt., vi.* **-gled, -gling** to mingle together

com·mis·er·ate (kə miz'ə rāt') *vt.* **-at'ed, -at'ing** [< L. *com-*, intens. + *miserari*, to pity] to feel or show pity for —*vi.* to condole (*with*) —**com·mis'er·a'tion** *n.* —**com·mis'er·a'tive** *adj.*

com·mis·sar (käm'ə sär') *n.* [Russ. *komissar*] the head of any former U.S.S.R. commissariat (sense 2): now called *minister*

com·mis·sar·i·at (-ser'ē ət) *n.* [Fr. < L.: see COMMIT] 1. an army branch providing food and supplies 2. formerly, a government department in the U.S.S.R.: now called *ministry*

com·mis·sar·y (käm'ə ser'ē) *n., pl.* **-ies** [see COMMIT] 1. formerly, an army officer in charge of supplies 2. a store, as in an army camp, where food and supplies are sold 3. a restaurant in a movie or TV studio

com·mis·sion (kə mish'ən) *n.* [see COMMIT] 1. a document authorizing certain duties and powers 2. authority to act for another, or that which one is authorized to do 3. a group of people chosen to do something 4. a committing; doing 5. a percentage of money from sales, allotted to the agent 6. *Mil. a)* an official certificate conferring rank *b)* the rank conferred —*vt.* 1. to give a commission to 2. to authorize 3. *Naut.* to put (a vessel) into service —**in** (or **out of**) **commission** in (or not in) working order

commissioned officer an officer in the armed forces holding a commission

com·mis·sion·er *n.* 1. a member of a commission 2. an official in charge of a governmental department 3. a man selected to regulate and control a professional sport

com·mit (kə mit') *vt.* **-mit'ted, -mit'ting** [< L. *com-*, together + *mittere*, to send] 1. to give in charge; consign 2. to put in custody or confinement [*committed* to prison] 3. to do or perpetrate (a crime) 4. to bind, as by a promise; pledge —**com·mit'ment** *n.* —**com·mit'ta·ble** *adj.* —**com·mit'tal** *n.*

com·mit·tee (kə mit'ē) *n.* [see prec.] a group of people chosen to report or act upon a certain matter —**com·mit'tee·man** (-mən) *n., pl.* **-men** —**com·mit'tee·wom'an** *n.fem., pl.* **-wom'en**

com·mode (kə mōd') *n.* [Fr. < L.: see COM- & MODE] 1. a chest of drawers 2. a movable washstand 3. a toilet

com·mo·di·ous (kə mō'dē əs) *adj.* [see prec.] spacious; roomy

com·mod·i·ty (kə mäd'ə tē) *n.*, *pl.* **-ties** [see COMMODE] 1. any useful thing 2. anything bought and sold

com·mo·dore (käm'ə dôr') *n.* [< Fr.: see COMMAND] *U.S. Navy* formerly, an officer ranking just above a captain

com·mon (käm'ən) *adj.* [< L. *communis*] 1. belonging to or shared by each or all 2. of an entire community; public 3. general; widespread 4. familiar; usual 5. below ordinary 6. vulgar; coarse 7. designating a noun (as book) that refers to any of a group —*n.* [*sometimes pl.*] land owned or used by all the inhabitants of a place —**in common** shared by each or all —**com'mon·ly** *adv.*

com'mon·al·ty (-əl tē) *n.*, *pl.* **-ties** the common people; public

common carrier a person or company in the business of transporting people or goods for a fee

common denominator 1. a common multiple of the denominators of two or more fractions 2. a characteristic in common

common divisor (or **factor**) a factor common to two or more numbers

com'mon·er *n.* a person not of the nobility; one of the common people

common law law based on custom, usage, and judicial decisions

common market an association of countries for closer economic union

common multiple *Math.* a multiple of each of two or more quantities

com'mon·place' *n.* 1. a trite remark; platitude 2. anything common or ordinary —*adj.* trite or ordinary

common pleas *Law* in some States, a court having jurisdiction over civil and criminal trials

com·mons (käm'ənz) *n.pl.* 1. the common people 2. [C-] *same as* HOUSE OF COMMONS 3. a dining room, as at college

common sense good sense or practical judgment —**com'mon-sense'** *adj.*

com'mon·weal' (-wēl') *n.* the public good; general welfare

com'mon·wealth' (-welth') *n.* 1. the people of a nation or state 2. a democracy or republic 3. a federation of states

com·mo·tion (kə mō'shən) *n.* [< L. *com-*, together + *movere*, move] 1. violent motion 2. confusion; bustle

com·mu·nal (käm'yoon 'l, kə myōōn' 'l) *adj.* 1. of a commune 2. of the community; public 3. marked by common ownership of property —**com'mu·nal·ize'** *vt.* -**ized'**, -**iz'ing** —**com·mu'nal·ly** *adv.*

com·mune[1] (kə myōōn') *vi.* -**muned'**, -**mun'ing** [< OFr. *comuner*, share] to talk together intimately

com·mune[2] (käm'yōōn) *n.* [< L. *communis*, common] 1. the smallest administrative district of local government in some European countries, esp. France 2. a small group of people living communally

com·mu·ni·ca·ble (kə myōō'ni kə b'l) *adj.* that can be communicated, as an idea, or transmitted, as a disease —**com·mu'ni·ca·bil'i·ty** *n.*

com·mu·ni·cant (-kənt) *n.* one who receives Holy Communion

com·mu·ni·cate (kə myōō'nə kāt') *vt.* -**cat'ed**, -**cat'ing** [< L. *communicare*] 1. to impart; transmit 2. to give (information, etc.) —*vi.* 1. to receive Holy Communion 2. to give or exchange information 3. to have a meaningful relationship 4. to be connected, as rooms —**com·mu'ni·ca'tor** *n.*

com·mu·ni·ca·tion *n.* 1. a transmitting 2. *a)* a giving or exchanging of information, messages, etc. *b)* a message, letter, etc. 3. [*often pl.*] a means of communicating —**com·mu'ni·ca'tive** *adj.*

com·mun·ion (kə myōōn'yən) *n.* [see COMMON] 1. possession in common 2. a communing 3. a Christian denomination 4. [C-] *same as* HOLY COMMUNION

com·mu·ni·qué (kə myōō'nə kā') *n.* [Fr.] an official communication

com·mu·nism (käm'yə niz'm) *n.* [see COMMON] 1. any theory or system of common ownership of property 2. [*often* C-] *a)* socialism as formulated by Marx, Lenin, etc. *b)* any government or political movement supporting this

com'mu·nist (-nist) *n.* 1. an advocate or supporter of communism 2. [C-] a member of a Communist Party —*adj.* of, like, or supporting communism or communists —**com'mu·nis'tic** *adj.*

com·mu·ni·ty (kə myōō'nə tē) *n.*, *pl.* **-ties** [see COMMON] 1. *a)* any group living in the same area or having interests, work, etc. in common *b)* such an area 2. the general public 3. a sharing in common

community antenna television a system by which telecasts from distant stations are received by a single, high antenna and sent to subscribers by direct cable

community college a junior college serving a certain community

com·mute (kə myōōt') *vt.* -**mut'ed**, -**mut'ing** [< L. *com-*, intens. + *mutare*, to change] 1. to exchange; substitute 2. to change (an obligation, punishment, etc.) to a less severe one —*vi.* to travel regularly, esp. by train, etc., between two points at some distance —**com·mu·ta·tion** (käm'yə tā'shən) *n.* —**com·mut'er** *n.*

comp. 1. comparative 2. compound

com·pact (kəm pakt', käm'pakt; *for n.* käm'pakt) *adj.* [< L. *com-*, with + *pangere*, fix] 1. closely and firmly packed 2. taking little space 3. terse —*vt.* 1. to pack or join firmly together 2. to make by putting together —*n.* 1. a small cosmetic case, usually containing face powder and a mirror 2. a smaller model of car 3. an agreement; covenant —**com·pact'ly** *adv.* —**com·pact'ness** *n.*

com·pac'tor (-pak'tər) *n.* a device that compresses trash into small bundles

com·pan·ion (kəm pan′yən) *n.* [< L. *com-*, with + *panis*, bread] 1. an associate; comrade 2. a person paid to live or travel with another 3. one of a pair or set —**com·pan′ion·a·ble** *adj.* —**com·pan′ion·ship** *n.*

com·pan·ion·way *n.* a stairway from a ship's deck to the space below

com·pa·ny (kum′pə nē) *n., pl.* -**nies** 1. companionship; society 2. a group of people gathered or associated for some purpose 3. a guest or guests 4. companions 5. a body of troops 6. a ship's crew —**keep company** 1. to associate (*with*) 2. to go together, as a couple intending to marry —**part company** to stop associating (*with*)

com·pa·ra·ble (käm′pər ə b'l) *adj.* 1. that can be compared 2. worthy of comparison —**com′pa·ra·bly** *adv.*

com·par·a·tive (kəm par′ə tiv) *adj.* 1. involving comparison 2. not absolute; relative 3. *Gram.* designating the second degree of comparison of adjectives and adverbs —*n. Gram.* the comparative degree [*finer* is the *comparative of fine*] —**com·par′a·tive·ly** *adv.*

com·pare (kəm per′) *vt.* -**pared′**, -**par′ing** [< L. *com-*, with + *par*, equal] 1. to liken (*to*) 2. to examine for similarities or differences 3. *Gram.* to form the degrees of comparison of —*vi.* 1. to be worth comparing (*with*) 2. to make comparisons —**beyond** (or **past** or **without**) **compare** without equal

com·par·i·son (kəm par′ə s'n) *n.* 1. a comparing or being compared 2. likeness; similarity 3. *Gram.* change in an adjective or adverb to show the positive, comparative, and superlative degrees —**in comparison with** compared with

com·part·ment (kəm pärt′mənt) *n.* [< L. *com-*, intens. + *partire*, divide] 1. any of the divisions into which a space is partitioned off 2. a separate section or category —**com·part′men·tal·ize′** (-men′t'n līz′) *vt.* -**ized′**, -**iz′ing**

com·pass (kum′pəs) *vt.* [< L. *com-*, together + *passus*, a step] 1. to go round 2. to surround 3. to understand 4. to achieve or contrive —*n.* 1. [*often pl.*] an instrument with two pivoted legs, for drawing circles, measuring, etc. 2. a boundary 3. an enclosed area 4. range; scope 5. an instrument for showing direction, esp. one with a swinging magnetic needle pointing north

DRAWING COMPASS

com·pas·sion (kəm pash′ən) *n.* [< L. *com-*, together + *pati*, suffer] deep sympathy; pity —**com·pas′sion·ate** *adj.* —**com·pas′sion·ate·ly** *adv.*

com·pat·i·ble (kəm pat′ə b'l) *adj.* [see prec.] getting along or going well together —**com·pat′i·bil′i·ty** *n.*

com·pa·tri·ot (kəm pā′trē ət) *n.* [see COM- & PATRIOT] a countryman —*adj.* of the same country

com·peer (käm′pir) *n.* [see COMPARE] 1. an equal; peer 2. a comrade

com·pel (kəm pel′) *vt.* -**pelled′**, -**pel′ling** [< L. *com-*, together + *pellere*, drive] to force or get by force

com·pen·di·um (kəm pen′dē əm) *n., pl.* -**ums, -a** (-ə) [< L. *com-*, together + *pendere*, weigh] a concise but comprehensive summary

com·pen·sate (käm′pən sāt′) *vt.* -**sat′ed, -sat′ing** [< L. *com-*, with + *pendere*, weigh] 1. to make up for; counterbalance 2. to pay —*vi.* to make amends (*for*) —**com′pen·sa′tion** *n.* —**com·pen·sa·to·ry** (kəm pen′sə·tôr′ē) *adj.*

com·pete (kəm pēt′) *vi.* -**pet′ed, -pet′ing** [< L. *com-*, together + *petere*, seek] to be in rivalry; contend; vie (*in* a contest, etc.)

com·pe·tence (käm′pə təns) *n.* 1. sufficient means for one's needs 2. ability; fitness 3. legal jurisdiction, power, etc. Also **com′pe·ten·cy**

com·pe·tent (-tənt) *adj.* [see COMPETE] 1. capable; fit 2. sufficient; adequate 3. having legal competence —**com′pe·tent·ly** *adv.*

com·pe·ti·tion (käm′pə tish′ən) *n.* 1. a competing; rivalry, esp. in business 2. a contest; match —**com·pet·i·tive** (kəm pet′ə tiv) *adj.*

com·pet·i·tor (kəm pet′ə tər) *n.* one who competes, as a business rival

com·pile (kəm pīl′) *vt.* -**piled′, -pil′ing** [< L. *com-*, together + *pilare*, to compress] 1. to collect and assemble (data, writings, etc.) 2. to compose (a book, etc.) of materials from various sources —**com·pi·la·tion** (käm′pə lā′shən) *n.*

com·pla·cen·cy (kəm plās′'n sē) *n., pl.* -**cies** [< L. *com-*, intens. + *placere*, please] contentment; often, specif., self-satisfaction, or smugness: also **com·pla′cence** —**com·pla′cent** *adj.*

com·plain (kəm plān′) *vi.* [< L. *com-*, intens. + *plangere*, strike (the breast)] 1. to express pain, displeasure, etc. 2. to find fault 3. to make an accusation —**com·plain′er** *n.*

com·plain·ant (-ənt) *n.* a plaintiff

com·plaint (-plānt′) *n.* 1. a complaining 2. a cause for complaining 3. an ailment 4. *Law* a formal charge

com·plai·sant (kəm plā′z'nt, -s'nt) *adj.* [see COMPLACENCY] willing to please; obliging —**com·plai′sance** *n.*

com·plect·ed (kəm plek′tid) *adj.* [*Colloq.*] same as COMPLEXIONED

com·ple·ment (käm′plə mənt; *for v.* -ment′) *n.* [see ff.] 1. that which completes or perfects 2. the amount needed to fill or complete 3. an entirety —*vt.* to make complete —**com′ple·men′ta·ry** (-men′tər ē) *adj.*

com·plete (kəm plēt′) *adj.* [< L. *com-*, intens. + *plere*, fill] 1. whole;

entire 2. finished 3. thorough —*vt.* -plet'ed, -plet'ing 1. to finish 2. to make whole or perfect —com·plete'· ly *adv.* —com·plete'ness *n.* —com· ple'tion (-plē'shən) *n.*

com·plex (kəm pleks'; *also, and for n. always,* kăm'pleks) *adj.* [< L. *com-,* with + *plectere,* to weave] 1. consisting of two or more related parts 2. complicated —*n.* 1. a complex whole 2. a unified grouping, as of buildings 3. *Psychoanalysis a)* a group of mostly unconscious impulses, etc. strongly influencing behavior *b)* loosely, an obsession —com·plex'i·ty *n.*

com·plex·ion (kəm plek'shən) *n.* [see prec.] 1. the color, texture, etc. of the skin, esp. of the face 2. nature; character; aspect

com·plex'ioned *adj.* having a (specified) complexion [light-*complexioned*]

complex sentence a sentence consisting of a main clause and one or more subordinate clauses

com·pli·ance (kəm plī'əns) *n.* 1. a complying; acquiescence 2. a tendency to give in to others Also com·pli'an· cy —com·pli'ant *adj.*

com·pli·cate (kăm'plə kāt') *vt., vi.* -cat'ed, -cat'ing [< L. *com-,* together + *plicare,* to fold] to make or become intricate, difficult, or involved —com'pli·ca'tion *n.*

com'pli·cat'ed *adj.* intricately involved; hard to solve, analyze, etc.

com·plic·i·ty (kəm plis'ə tē) *n., pl.* -ties [see COMPLEX] partnership in wrongdoing

com·pli·ment (kăm'plə mənt; *for v.* -ment') *n.* [Fr. < L.: see COMPLETE] 1. a formal act of courtesy; esp., something said in praise 2. [*pl.*] respects —*vt.* to pay a compliment to

com'pli·men'ta·ry (-men'tər ē) *adj.* 1. paying or containing a compliment 2. given free as a courtesy

com·ply (kəm plī') *vi.* -plied', -ply'· ing [see COMPLETE] to act in accordance (*with* a request, order, etc.)

com·po·nent (kəm pō'nənt) *adj.* [< L. *com-,* together + *ponere,* put] serving as one of the parts of a whole —*n.* a part, element, or ingredient

com·port (kəm pôrt') *vt.* [< L. *com-,* together + *portare,* bring] to behave (oneself) in a specified way —*vi.* to accord (*with*) —com·port'ment *n.*

com·pose (kəm pōz') *vt.* -posed', -pos'ing [< OFr. *com-,* with + *poser,* to place] 1. to make up; constitute 2. to put into proper form 3. to create (a musical or literary work) 4. to make calm 5. to set (type) —*vi.* to create musical works, etc. —com·pos'er *n.*

com·posed' *adj.* calm; self-possessed

com·pos·ite (kəm păz'it) *adj.* [< L. *com-,* together + *ponere,* put] 1. compound 2. *Bot.* of a family of plants, as the daisy, with flower heads composed of clusters of small flowers —*n.* a composite thing —com·pos'ite·ly *adv.*

com·po·si·tion (kăm'pə zish'ən) *n.* 1. a composing, esp. of literary or musical works 2. the makeup of a thing or person 3. something composed

com·pos·i·tor (kəm păz'ə tər) *n.* a person who sets type; typesetter

com·post (kăm'pōst) *n.* [see COM-POSITE] a mixture of decomposing vegetation for fertilizing soil

com·po·sure (kəm pō'zhər) *n.* [see COMPOSE] calmness; self-possession

com·pote (kăm'pōt) *n.* [Fr.: see COMPOSITE] 1. a dish of stewed fruits 2. a long-stemmed dish, as for candy

com·pound[1] (kăm pound'. kəm-; *for adj. usually, and for n. always,* kăm'pound) *vt.* [see COMPOSITE] 1. to mix or combine 2. to make by combining parts 3. to compute (compound interest) 4. to intensify by adding new elements —*adj.* made up of two or more parts —*n.* 1. a thing formed by combining parts 2. a substance containing two or more elements chemically combined —compound a felony (or crime) to agree, for payment, not to prosecute a felony (or crime)

com·pound[2] (kăm'pound) *n.* [Malay *kampong*] an area enclosing a building or buildings, esp. in the Orient

compound fracture a fracture in which the broken bone pierces the skin

compound interest interest paid on both the principal and the accumulated unpaid interest

compound sentence a sentence consisting of two or more independent, coordinate clauses

com·pre·hend (kăm'prə hend') *vt.* [< L. *com-,* with + *prehendere,* seize] 1. to grasp mentally; understand 2. to include; take in; comprise — com·pre·hen·si·ble (kăm'prə hen'-sə b'l) *adj.* —com'pre·hen'sion *n.*

com'pre·hen'sive *adj.* wide in scope; inclusive —com'pre·hen'·sive·ly *adv.* —com'pre·hen'sive·ness *n.*

com·press (kəm pres'; *for n.* kăm'pres) *vt.* [< L. *com-,* together + *premere,* press] 1. to press together and make more compact 2. to put (air) under pressure —*n.* a pad of folded cloth, often wet or medicated, applied to the skin —com·pressed' *adj.* —com·pres'sion *n.*

com·pres'sor (-ər) *n.* a machine for compressing air, gas, etc.

com·prise (-prīz') *vt.* -prised', -pris'ing [see COMPREHEND] 1. to include; contain 2. to consist of 3. to make up; form: a loose usage

com·pro·mise (kăm'prə mīz') *n.* [< L. *com-,* together + *promittere,* to promise] 1. a settlement in which each side makes concessions 2. something midway —*vt., vi.* -mised', -mis'ing 1. to adjust by compromise 2. to lay open to suspicion, disrepute, etc.

comp·trol·ler (kən trōl'ər) *n.* [altered (after Fr. *compte,* account) < CONTROLLER] *same as* CONTROLLER (sense 1)

com·pul·sion (kəm pul'shən) *n.* a compelling or being compelled; force —com·pul'sive (-siv) *adj.* —com·pul'sive·ly *adv.* —com·pul'sive·ness *n.*

com·pul·so·ry (-sər ē) *adj.* 1. obligatory; required 2. compelling

com·punc·tion (kəm puŋk'shən) n. [< L. com-, intens. + pungere, to prick] an uneasy feeling prompted by guilt

com·pute (kəm pyōōt') vt., vi. -put'ed, -put'ing [< L. com-, with + putare, reckon] to determine (an amount, etc.) by reckoning —com·pu·ta·tion (käm'pyoo tā'shən) n.

com·put·er n. an electronic machine that performs rapid, complex calculations or compiles and correlates data —com·put'er·ize' vt. -ized' -iz'ing

com·rade (käm'rad) n. [< Sp. camarada, chamber mate < L. camera, room] 1. a friend; close companion 2. an associate —com'rade·ship' n.

com·sat (käm'sat) n. a communications satellite for relaying microwave transmissions, as of television

con¹ (kän) adv. [< L. contra] against —n. an opposing reason, vote, etc.

con² (kän) vt. conned, con'ning [< OE. cunnan, know] to study carefully

con³ (kän) adj. [Slang] confidence [con game/ —vt. conned, con'ning [Slang] to swindle or trick

con⁴ (kän) n. [Slang] a convict

con- (kän) same as COM-: used before c, d, g, j, n, q, s, t, and v

con·cat·e·na·tion (kän kat''n ā'shən) n. [< L. com-, together + catena, chain] a connected series, as of events

con·cave (kän kāv', kän'kāv) adj. [< L. com-, intens. + cavus, hollow] hollow and curved like the inside half of a hollow ball —con·cav'i·ty (-kav'ə tē) n., pl. -ties

con·ceal (kən sēl') vt. [< L. com-, together + celare, hide] 1. to hide 2. to keep secret —con·ceal'ment n.

con·cede (kən sēd') vt. -ced'ed, -ced'ing [< L. com-, with + cedere, cede] 1. to admit as true, valid, certain, etc. 2. to grant as a right

con·ceit (kən sēt') n. [see CONCEIVE] 1. an exaggerated opinion of oneself, one's merits, etc.; vanity 2. a fanciful expression or notion

con·ceit'ed adj. vain

con·ceiv·a·ble (kən sē'və b'l) adj. that can be understood or believed —con·ceiv'a·bil'i·ty n. —con·ceiv'a·bly adv.

con·ceive (kən sēv') vt. -ceived', -ceiv'ing [< L. com-, together + capere, take] 1. to become pregnant with 2. to form in the mind; imagine 3. to understand —vi. 1. to become pregnant 2. to form an idea (of)

con·cel·e·brate (kän sel'ə brāt') vt. -brat'ed, -brat'ing [< L. com-, together + celebrare, to honor] to celebrate (the Eucharistic liturgy) jointly, two or more priests officiating —con'cel·e·bra'tion n.

con·cen·trate (kän'sən trāt') vt. -trat'ed, -trat'ing [< L. com-, together + centrum, a center + -ATE¹] 1. to focus (one's thoughts, efforts, etc.) 2. to increase the strength, den-

sity, etc. of —vt. to fix one's attention (on or upon) —n. a concentrated substance —con'cen·tra'tion n.

concentration camp a place of confinement for political foes, members of minority ethnic groups, etc.

con·cen·tric (kən sen'trik) adj. [< L. com-, together + centrum, center] having a common center, as circles —con·cen'tri·cal·ly adv.

con·cept (kän'sept) n. [see CONCEIVE] an idea; general notion

con·cep·tion (kən sep'shən) n. 1. a conceiving or being conceived in the womb 2. the beginning, as of a process 3. the formulation of ideas 4. a concept 5. an original idea or design

con·cep'tu·al (-choo wəl) adj. of conception or concepts —con·cep'tu·al·ly adv.

con·cep'tu·al·ize' (-choo wəl iz') vt. -ized', -iz'ing to form a concept of —con·cep'tu·al·i·za'tion n.

con·cern (kən surn') vt. [< L. com-, with + cernere, sift] 1. to have a relation to 2. to engage or involve —n. 1. a matter; affair 2. interest in or regard for a person or thing 3. reference 4. worry 5. a business firm —as concerns in regard to —concern oneself 1. to busy oneself 2. to be worried

con·cerned' adj. 1. involved or interested (in) 2. uneasy or anxious

con·cern'ing prep. relating to

con·cert (kän'sərt) n. [< L. com-, with + certare, strive] 1. mutual agreement; concord 2. a performance of music —in concert in unison

con·cert·ed (kən sur'tid) adj. mutually arranged or agreed upon; combined —con·cert'ed·ly adv.

con·cer·ti·na (kän'sər tē'nə) n. [< CONCERT] a small accordion

con·cert·ize (kän'sər tiz') vi. -ized', -iz'ing to perform as a soloist in concerts, esp. on a tour

con'cert·mas'ter n. the leader of the first violin section of a symphony orchestra, and often the assistant to the conductor

con·cer·to (kən cher'tō) n., pl. -tos, -ti (-tē) [It.] a musical composition for one or more solo instruments and an orchestra

con·ces·sion (kən sesh'ən) n. 1. a conceding 2. a thing conceded; acknowledgment 3. a privilege granted by a government, company, etc., as the right to sell food at a park

con·ces'sion·aire' (-ə ner') n. [< Fr.] the holder of a concession (sense 3)

conch (käŋk, känch) n., pl. conchs (käŋks), conch·es (kän'chəz) [< Gr. konchē] 1. the spiral, one-piece shell of various sea mollusks 2. the mollusk

con·ci·erge (kän'sē urzh'; Fr. kôn syerzh') n. [Fr. < L. conservus, fellow slave] an attendant, custodian, etc. guarding an apartment house, etc.

con·cil·i·ar (kən sil'ē ər) adj. of, from, or by means of a council

con·cil·i·ate' (-āt') vt. -at'ed,

-at'ing [see COUNCIL] to win over; make friendly; placate —con·cil'i·a'tion n. —con·cil'i·a'tor n. —con·cil'i·a·to'ry (-ə tôr'ē) adj.

con·cise (kən sīs') adj. [< L. com-, intens. + caedere, to cut] brief and to the point; terse —con·cise'ly adv. —con·cise'ness, con·ci'sion (-sizh'-ən) n.

con·clave (kän'klāv, käŋ'-) n. [< L. com-, with + clavis, key] a private meeting; specif., one held by cardinals to elect a pope

con·clude (kən klōōd') vt., vi. -clud'ed, -clud'ing [< L. com-, together + claudere, to shut] 1. to end; finish 2. to deduce 3. to decide; determine 4. to arrange (a treaty, etc.)

con·clu·sion (-klōō'zhən) n. 1. the end 2. a judgment or opinion formed after thought 3. an outcome 4. a concluding (of a treaty, etc.) —in conclusion lastly; in closing

con·clu·sive (-siv) adj. decisive; final —con·clu'sive·ly adv. —con·clu'sive·ness n.

con·coct (kən käkt', kän-) vt. [< L. com-, together + coquere, to cook] 1. to make by combining ingredients 2. to devise; plan —con·coc'tion n.

con·com·i·tant (-käm'ə tənt) adj. [< L. com-, together + comes, companion] accompanying; attendant —n. a concomitant thing —con·com'i·tant·ly adv.

Con·cord (käŋ'kərd) capital of N.H.; pop. 30,000 —n. a large, dark-blue grape: also Concord grape

con·cord (kän'kôrd, käŋ'-) n. [< L. com-, together + cor, heart] 1. agreement; harmony 2. peaceful relations, as between nations

con·cord·ance (kən kôr'd'ns, kän-) n. 1. agreement 2. an alphabetical list of the words in a book, with references to the passages where they occur

con·cord'ant adj. agreeing

con·cor·dat (kən kôr'dat, kän-) n. [see CONCORD] a formal agreement

con·course (kän'kôrs, käŋ'-) n. [see CONCUR] 1. a crowd; throng 2. an open space for crowds, as in a park 3. a broad boulevard

con·crete (kän krēt'; also, and for n. & vt. 2 usually, kän'krēt) adj. [< L. com-, together + crescere, grow] 1. having a material existence; real; actual 2. specific, not general 3. made of concrete —n. 1. anything concrete 2. a hard building material made of sand and gravel, bonded together with cement —vt., vi. -cret'ed, -cret'ing 1. to solidify 2. to cover with concrete —con·crete'ly adv. —con·crete'ness n.

con·cre'tion (-krē'shən) n. 1. a solidifying 2. a solidified mass

con·cu·bine (käŋ'kyə bīn', kän'-) n. [< L. com-, with + cubare, to lie down] in some societies, a secondary wife having inferior status

con·cu·pis·cence (kän kyōō'pə s'ns) n. [< L. com-, intens. + cupiscere, to desire] strong desire, esp. sexual desire; lust —con·cu'pis·cent adj.

con·cur (kən kur') vi. -curred', -cur'ring [< L. com-, together + currere, to run] 1. to occur at the same time 2. to act together 3. to agree —con·cur'rence n.

con·cur·rent adj. 1. occurring at the same time 2. acting together 3. Law having equal authority —con·cur'rent·ly adv.

con·cus·sion (kən kush'ən) n. [< L. com-, together + quatere, to shake] 1. a violent shaking; shock, as from impact 2. impaired functioning, esp. of the brain, caused by a violent blow

con·demn (kən dem') vt. [< L. com-, intens. + damnare, to harm] 1. to disapprove of strongly 2. to declare guilty 3. to inflict a penalty upon 4. to doom 5. to appropriate (property) for public use 6. to declare unfit for use —con·dem·na·tion (kän'dem nā'shən) n. —con·dem'na·to'ry (-nə tôr'ē) adj. —con·demn'er n.

con·dense (kən dens') vt. -densed', -dens'ing [< L. com-, intens. + densus, dense] 1. to make more dense or compact 2. to express in fewer words 3. to change to a denser form, as from gas to liquid —vi. 1. to become condensed —con·den·sa·tion (kän'dən sā'shən) n.

condensed milk a thick milk made by evaporating part of the water from cow's milk and adding sugar

con·dens'er n. one that condenses; specif., a) an apparatus for liquefying gases b) a lens for concentrating light rays 2) Elec. same as CAPACITOR

con·de·scend (kän'də send') vi. [< L. com-, together + descendere, descend] 1. to be gracious about doing a thing considered beneath one's dignity 2. to deal with others patronizingly —con'de·scend'ing·ly adv. —con'de·scen'sion n.

con·dign (kən dīn') adj. [< L. com-, intens. + dignus, worthy] deserved; suitable: said esp. of punishment

con·di·ment (kän'də mənt) n. [< L. condire, to pickle] a seasoning or relish, as pepper, mustard, sauces, etc.

con·di·tion (kən dish'ən) n. [< L. com-, together + dicere, speak] 1. anything required for the performance, completion, or existence of something else; provision or prerequisite 2. a) state of being b) [Colloq.] an illness c) a healthy state 3. social position; rank —vt. 1. to stipulate 2. to impose a condition on 3. to bring into fit condition 4. to make accustomed (to) —on condition that provided that —con·di'tion·er n.

con·di'tion·al adj. containing, expressing, or dependent on a condition; qualified —con·di'tion·al·ly adv.

con·di'tioned (-ənd) adj. 1. subject to conditions 2. in a desired condition 3. affected by conditioning 4. accustomed (to)

con·do (kän'dō) n., pl. -dos, -does short for CONDOMINIUM (sense 2)

con·dole (kən dōl') vi. -doled', -dol'ing [< L. com-, with + dolere, grieve] to express sympathy; commiserate —con·do'lence n.

con·dom (kun'dəm, kän'-) n. [? after a 17th-c. Brit. colonel] a thin, rubber sheath for the penis, used as a prophylactic or contraceptive

con·do·min·i·um (kän'də min'ē əm) n. [ModL. < com-, with + dominium, ownership] 1. joint rule by two or more states 2. the territory ruled 3. one of the units in a multi-unit dwelling, each separately owned

con·done (kən dōn') vt. -doned', -don'ing [< L. com-, intens. + donare, give] to forgive or overlook (an offense) —con·don'a·ble adj.

con·dor (kän'dər) n. [< Sp. < Peruv-Ind.] 1. a large vulture of the S. American Andes, with a bare head 2. a similar vulture of S Calif.

con·duce (kən dōōs') vi. -duced', -duc'ing [< L. com-, together + ducere, to lead] to tend or lead (to an effect) —con·du'cive adj.

con·duct (kän'dukt'; for v. kən dukt') n. [see prec.] 1. management 2. behavior —vt., vi. 1. to lead 2. to manage 3. to direct (an orchestra, etc.) 4. to behave (oneself) 5. to transmit or convey —con·duc'tion n. —con·duc'tive adj. —con'duc·tiv'i·ty (-tiv'ə tē) n.

con·duct·ance (kən duk'təns) n. the ability to conduct electricity

con·duc·tor n. 1. the leader of an orchestra, etc. 2. one in charge of passengers on a train, etc. 3. a thing that conducts electricity, heat, etc.

con·duit (kän'dit, -doo wit) n. [see CONDUCE] 1. a channel for conveying fluids 2. a tube for electric wires

con·dyle (kän'dil) n. [< Gr. kondylos, hard knob] a rounded process at the end of a bone

cone (kōn) n. [< Gr. kōnos] 1. a solid with a circle for its base and a curved surface tapering evenly to a point 2. any cone-shaped object 3. the scaly fruit of evergreen trees

co·ney (kō'nē) n., pl. -neys [< L. cuniculus] a rabbit or its fur

EVERGREEN CONES

Co·ney Island (kō'nē) beach and amusement park in Brooklyn, N.Y.

con·fab (kän'fab') n. [ult. < L. com-, together + fabulari, to converse] [Colloq.] an informal talk; chat

con·fec·tion (kən fek'shən) n. [< L. com-, with + facere, make] a candy, ice cream, preserves, etc.

con·fec·tion·er n. one who makes or sells candy and other confections

con·fec·tion·er·y (-er'ē) n., pl. -ies a confectioner's shop; candy store

con·fed·er·a·cy (kən fed'ər ə sē) n., pl. -cies a league or alliance —the **Confederacy** the eleven Southern States that seceded from the U.S. in 1860 & 1861

con·fed·er·ate (kən fed'ər it; for v. -ə rāt') adj. [< L. com-, together +

foedus, a league] 1. united in an alliance 2. [C-] of the Confederacy —n. 1. an ally; associate 2. an accomplice 3. [C-] a Southern supporter of the Confederacy —vt., vi. -at'ed, -at'ing to unite in a confederacy; ally

con·fed·er·a'tion n. an alliance; federation —the **Confederation** the United States from 1781 to 1789

con·fer (kən fur') vt. -ferred', -fer'ring [< L. com-, together + ferre, bring] to give; bestow —vi. to have a conference —con·fer·ee (kän'fə rē') n. —con·fer'ment n. —con·fer'rer n.

con·fer·ence (kän'fər əns) n. 1. a formal meeting for discussion 2. an association of schools, churches, etc.

con·fess (kən fes') vt., vi. [< L. com-, together + fateri, acknowledge] 1. to admit or acknowledge (a fault, crime, belief, etc.) 2. a) to tell (one's sins) to a priest b) to hear the confession of (a person) —**confess to** to acknowledge

con·fess'ed·ly (-id lē) adv. admittedly

con·fes·sion (kən fesh'ən) n. 1. a confessing 2. something confessed 3. a creed 4. a sect; denomination

con·fes'sion·al n. an enclosure in a church where a priest hears confessions

con·fes'sor n. 1. one who confesses 2. a priest who hears confessions

con·fet·ti (kən fet'ē) n.pl. [with sing. v.] [< It.] bits of colored paper scattered about at celebrations, etc.

con·fi·dant (kän'fə dant') n. a close, trusted friend —con'fi·dante' n.fem.

con·fide (kən fīd') vi. -fid'ed, -fid'ing [< L. com-, intens. + fidere, to trust] to trust (in someone), esp. by sharing secrets —vt. 1. to tell about as a secret 2. to entrust (to)

con·fi·dence (kän'fə dəns) n. 1. trust; reliance 2. assurance 3. belief in one's own abilities 4. the belief that another will keep a secret 5. something told as a secret —adj. swindling or used to swindle

confidence game a swindle effected by one (**confidence man**) who first gains the confidence of his victim

con·fi·dent (-dənt) adj. full of confidence; specif., a) certain b) sure of oneself —con'fi·dent·ly adv.

con'fi·den'tial (-den'shəl) adj. 1. secret 2. of or showing confidence 3. entrusted with private matters —con'fi·den'ti·al'i·ty (-shē al'ə tē) n. —con'fi·den'tial·ly adv.

con·fig·u·ra·tion (kən fig'yə rā'shən) n. [< L. com-, together + figurare, to form] contour; outline

con·fine (kən fīn'; for n. kän'fīn') n. [< L. com-, with + finis, an end] [usually pl.] a boundary or bounded region —vt. -fined', -fin'ing 1. to keep within limits; restrict 2. to keep shut up, as in prison, a sickbed, etc. —con·fine'ment n.

con·firm (kən furm') vt. [< L. com-, intens. + firmare, strengthen] 1. to make firm 2. to give formal approval to 3. to prove the truth of 4. to admit to full church membership

con·fir·ma·tion (kän'fər mā'shən) n. 1. a confirming 2. something that confirms 3. a ceremony admitting a person to full membership in a church

con·firmed' adj. 1. firmly established; habitual 2. corroborated

con·fis·cate (kän'fə skāt') vt. -cat'-ed, -cat'ing [< L. com-, together + fiscus, treasury] 1. to seize (private property) for the public treasury 2. to seize as by authority; appropriate — **con'fis·ca'tion** n.

con·fis·ca·to·ry (kən fis'kə tôr'ē) adj. of or effecting confiscation

con·fla·gra·tion (kän'flə grā'shən) n. [< L. com-, intens. + flagrare, to burn] a big, destructive fire

con·flict (kən flikt'; for n. kän'flikt) vi. [< L. com-, together + fligere, to strike] to be antagonistic, incompatible, etc. —n. 1. a fight or war 2. sharp disagreement, as of interests or ideas 3. emotional disturbance

conflict of interest a conflict between the obligation to the public and the self-interest of a public office-holder, etc.

con·flu·ence (kän'floo əns) n. [< L. com-, together + fluere, flow] 1. a flowing together, esp. of streams 2. the place of this 3. a coming together; crowd —**con'flu·ent** adj.

con·form (kən fôrm') vt. [< L. com-, together + formare, to form] 1. to make similar 2. to bring into agreement —vi. 1. to be or become similar 2. to be in agreement 3. to act in accordance with rules, customs, etc. —**con·form'ism** n. —**con·form'ist** n.

con·for·ma·tion (kän'fôr mā'shən) n. 1. a symmetrical arrangement of the parts of a thing 2. the shape or outline, as of an animal

con·form·i·ty (kən fôr'mə tē) n., pl. -ties 1. agreement; correspondence; similarity 2. conventional behavior

con·found (kən found', kän-) vt. [< L. com-, together + fundere, pour] 1. to confuse; bewilder 2. to damn: a mild oath —**con·found'ed** adj.

con·fra·ter·ni·ty (kän'frə tur'nə tē) n., pl. -ties [see COM- & FRATERNAL] 1. brotherhood 2. a religious society, usually of laymen

con·frere (kän'frer, kôn'-) n. [OFr.] a colleague; associate

con·front (kən frunt') vt. [< L. com-, together + frons, front] 1. to face, esp. boldly or defiantly 2. to bring face to face (with) —**con·fron·ta·tion** (kän'frən tā'shən) n.

Con·fu·cius (kən fyōō'shəs) 551?-479? B.C.; Chin. philosopher & teacher —**Con·fu'cian** adj., n.

con·fuse (kən fyōōz') vt. -fused', -fus'ing [see CONFOUND] 1. to mix up; put into disorder 2. to bewilder or embarrass 3. to mistake the identity of —**con·fus'ed·ly** adv.

con·fu·sion (-fyōō'zhən) n. a confusing or being confused; specif., disorder, bewilderment, etc.

con·fute (kən fyōōt') vt. -fut'ed,

-fut'ing [< L. confutare] to prove to be in error or false —**con·fu·ta·tion** (kän'fyoo tā'shən) n.

Cong. 1. Congregational 2. Congress

con·geal (kən jēl') vt., vi. [< L. com-, together + gelare, freeze] 1. to freeze 2. to thicken; coagulate; jell —**con·geal'a·ble** adj. —**con·geal'ment** n.

con·gen·ial (kən jēn'yəl) adj. [see COM- & GENIAL] 1. kindred; compatible 2. of the same temperament; friendly 3. suited to one's needs; agreeable —**con·ge'ni·al'i·ty** (-jēn'ē al'ə tē) n. —**con·gen'ial·ly** adv.

con·gen·i·tal (kən jen'ə t'l) adj. [< L. congenitus, born with] existing as such at birth —**con·gen'i·tal·ly** adv.

con·ger (eel) (käŋ'gər) [< Gr. gongros] a large, edible, saltwater eel

con·ge·ries (kän'jə rēz') n., pl. -ries [L.: see ff.] a heap or pile of things

con·gest (kən jest') vt. [< L. com-, together + gerere, carry] 1. to cause too much blood to accumulate in (a part of the body) 2. to fill to excess; overcrowd —**con·ges'tion** n.

con·glom·er·ate (kən gläm'ə rāt'; for adj. & n. -ər it) vt., vi. -at'ed, -at'ing [< L. com-, together + glomus, ball] to form into a rounded mass —adj. 1. formed into a rounded mass 2. formed of substances collected into a single mass, esp. of rock fragments or pebbles cemented together by clay, silica, etc. —n. 1. a conglomerate mass 2. a large corporation formed by merging many diverse companies 3. a conglomerate rock —**con·glom'er·a'tion** n.

Con·go (käŋ'gō) 1. river in C Africa, flowing into the Atlantic 2. country mostly west of Zaire: 132,046 sq. mi.; pop. 826,000 3. former name of ZAIRE —**Con'go·lese'** (-gə lēz') adj., n.

con·grat·u·late (kən grach'ə lāt') vt. -lat'ed, -lat'ing [< L. com-, together + gratulari, wish joy] to express to (a person) one's pleasure at his good fortune, etc.; felicitate —**con·grat'u·la·to·ry** (-lə tôr'ē) adj.

con·grat·u·la·tion n. 1. a congratulating 2. [pl.] expressions of pleasure over another's good fortune

con·gre·gate (käŋ'grə gāt') vt., vi. -gat'ed, -gat'ing [< L. com-, together + grex, a flock] to gather into a crowd; assemble

con'gre·ga'tion n. 1. a gathering; assemblage 2. an assembly of people for religious worship —**con'gre·gant** n.

con'gre·ga'tion·al adj. 1. of or like a congregation 2. [C-] of a Protestant denomination in which each member church is self-governing

con·gress (käŋ'grəs) n. [< L. com-, together + gradi, to walk] 1. an association or society 2. an assembly or conference 3. a legislature, esp. of a republic 4. [C-] the legislature of the U.S.; the Senate and the House of Representatives —**con·gres·sion·al** (kən gresh'ən 'l) adj. —**con·gres'·sion·al·ly** adv.

con'gress·man (-mən) n., pl. -men a member of Congress, esp. of the House of Representatives

con·gru·ent (käŋ'groo wənt) *adj.* [<
L. *congruere*, agree] corresponding;
harmonious —**con'gru·ence** *n.*

con·gru·ous (käŋ'groo wəs) *adj.* 1.
congruent 2. fitting; suitable; appropriate —**con·gru·i·ty** (kən grōō'ə tē)
n., pl. -**ties** —**con'gru·ous·ly** *adv.*

con·i·cal (kän'i k'l) *adj.* 1. of a cone
2. resembling or shaped like a cone
Also **con'ic** —**con'i·cal·ly** *adv.*

co·ni·fer (kän'ə fər, kō'nə-) *n.* [L.
< *conus*, cone + *ferre*, to bear] any
of an order of cone-bearing trees and
shrubs, mostly evergreens —**con·if-
er·ous** (kə nif'ər əs) *adj.*

conj. 1. conjugation 2. conjunction

con·jec·ture (kən jek'chər) *n.* [< L.
com-, together + *jacere*, throw] 1. an
inferring, theorizing, or predicting
from incomplete evidence; guesswork
2. a guess —*vt., vi.* -**tured, -tur·ing**
to guess —**con·jec'tur·al** *adj.*

con·join (kən join') *vt., vi.* [< L.
com-, together + *jungere*, join] to join
together; unite —**con·joint'** *adj.*

con·ju·gal (kän'jə gəl) *adj.* [< L.
conjunx, spouse] of marriage or the
relation between husband and wife

con·ju·gate (kän'jə gāt, -gət') *adj.*
[< L. *com*-, together + *jugare*, join]
joined together, esp. in a pair —*vt.*
(-gāt') -**gat'ed, -gat'ing** 1. [Archaic]
to join together; couple 2. *Gram.* to
give in order the inflectional forms of
(a verb) —**con'ju·ga'tion** *n.*

con·junc·tion (kən junk'shən) *n.*
[see CONJOIN] 1. a joining together;
union; combination 2. coincidence 3.
a word used to connect words, phrases,
or clauses (Ex.: *and, but, if,* etc.) —
con·junc'tive *adj.*

con·junc·ti·va (kän'jəŋk tī'və) *n.,
pl.* -**vas, -vae** (-vē) [see CONJOIN] the
mucous membrane covering the inner
eyelid and the front of the eyeball

con·junc·ti·vi·tis (kən juŋk'tə vīt'-
is) *n.* inflammation of the conjunctiva

con·junc·ture (kən junk'chər) *n.*
[see CONJOIN] a combination of events
creating a crisis

con·jure (kän'jər, kun'-; for *vt. 1*
kən joor') *vi.* -**jured, -jur·ing** [< L.
com-, together + *jurare*, swear] 1. to
summon a demon, spirit, etc. by magic
2. to practice magic —*vt.* 1. to adjure
2. to cause to appear, come (*up*), etc.
by or as by magic —**con'ju·ra'tion**
n. —**con'jur·er, con'jur·or** *n.*

conk (käŋk) *n., vt.* [< CONCH] [Slang]
hit on the head —**conk out** [Slang] 1.
to fail suddenly, as a motor 2. to fall
asleep from fatigue; pass out

con man [Slang] *same as* CONFIDENCE
MAN

con·nect (kə nekt') *vt.* [< L. *com*-,
together + *nectere*, fasten] 1. to join
(two things together, or one thing *with*
or *to* another) 2. to show or think of
as related —*vi.* to join —**con·nec'tor,
con·nect'er** *n.*

Con·nect·i·cut (kə net'ə kət) New
England State of the U.S.: 5,009 sq.

mi.; pop. 3,108,000; cap. Hartford:
abbrev. **Conn.**

con·nec·tion (kə nek'shən) *n.* 1. a
connecting or being connected 2. a
thing that connects 3. a relation;
association 4. *a*) a relative, esp. by
marriage *b*) an associate, etc.: *usually
used in pl.* 5. [*usually pl.*] a transferring
from one bus, plane, etc. to another
Brit. sp., **con·nex'ion**

con·nec'tive (-tiv) *adj.* connecting
—*n.* that which connects, esp. a
connecting word, as a conjunction

con·nip·tion (fit) (kə nip'shən)
[pseudo-L.] [Colloq.] a fit of anger,
hysteria, etc.: also **con·nip'tions**

con·nive (kə nīv') *vi.* -**nived',
-niv'ing** [< L. *conivere*, to wink, con-
nive] 1. to pretend not to look (*at*
crime, etc.), thus giving tacit consent
2. to cooperate secretly (*with* someone), esp. in wrongdoing; scheme —
con·niv'ance *n.* —**con·niv'er** *n.*

con·nois·seur (kän'ə sur') *n.* [<
Fr. < L. *cognoscere*, know] one who
has expert knowledge and keen discrimination, esp. in the fine arts

con·note (kə nōt') *vt.* -**not'ed,
-not'ing** [< L. *com*-, together +
notare, to mark] to suggest or convey
(associations, etc.) in addition to the
explicit, or denoted, meaning —**con-
no·ta·tion** (kän'ə tā'shən) *n.* —
con'no·ta'tive *adj.*

con·nu·bi·al (kə nōō'bē əl) *adj.* [<
L. *com*-, together + *nubere*, marry] of
marriage; conjugal

con·quer (käŋ'kər) *vt.* [< L. *com*-,
intens. + *quaerere*, seek] 1. to get
control of as by winning a war 2. to
overcome; defeat —**con'quer·or** *n.*

con·quest (kän'kwest, kän'-) *n.* 1. a
conquering 2. something conquered
3. a winning of someone's affection or
favor

con·quis·ta·dor (kän kwis'tə dôr',
-kēs'-) *n., pl.* -**dors, -dores** [Sp.,
conqueror] any of the 16th-c. Spanish
conquerors of Mexico, Peru, etc.

con·san·guin·e·ous (kän'saŋ gwin'-
ē əs) *adj.* [see COM- & SANGUINE] related by blood —**con·san·guin'i·ty** *n.*

con·science (kän'shəns) *n.* [< L.
com-, with + *scire*, know] an awareness of right and wrong, with a compulsion to do right —**con'science-
less** *adj.*

con·sci·en·tious (kän'shē en'shəs)
adj. 1. governed by one's conscience;
scrupulous 2. painstaking —**con'sci-
en'tious·ly** *adv.* —**con'sci·en'tious-
ness** *n.*

conscientious objector one who
refuses to take part in warfare because
his conscience prohibits killing

con·scious (kän'shəs) *adj.* [< L.: see
CONSCIENCE] 1. having an awareness
(*of* or *that*) 2. able to feel and think;
awake 3. aware of oneself as a thinking being 4. intentional [*conscious*
humor] —**con'scious·ly** *adv.*

con'scious·ness *n.* 1. the state of

fat, āpe, cär; ten, ēven; is, bīte; gō, hôrn, tōōl, look; oil, out; up, fur;
chin; she; thin, then; zh, leisure; ŋ, ring; ə for a in ago; ', (ā'b'l); ë, Fr. coeur;
ö, Fr. feu; Fr. mon; ü, Fr. duc; kh, G. ich, doch; ‡ foreign; < derived from

being conscious; awareness **2.** the totality of one's thoughts and feelings

con·script (kən skript'; *for n.* kän' skript) *vt.* [< L. *com*-, with + *scribere*, write] to enroll for compulsory service in the armed forces; draft —*n.* a draftee —**con·scrip'tion** *n.*

con·se·crate (kän'sə krāt') *vt.* **-crat·ed, -crat·ing** [< L. *com*-, together + *sacrare*, make holy] to set apart as holy; devote to sacred or serious use —**con'se·cra'tion** *n.*

con·sec·u·tive (kən sek'yə tiv) *adj.* [see CONSEQUENCE] following in order, without interruption; successive —**con·sec'u·tive·ly** *adv.*

con·sen·sus (kən sen'səs) *n.* [see ff.] **1.** an opinion held by all or most **2.** general agreement, esp. in opinion

con·sent (kən sent') *vi.* [< L. *com*-, with + *sentire*, feel] to agree, permit, or assent —*n.* **1.** permission; approval **2.** agreement [by common *consent*]

con·se·quence (kän'sə kwens') *n.* [< L. *com*-, with + *sequi*, follow] **1.** a result; effect **2.** importance —**take the consequences** to accept the results of one's actions

con'se·quent (-kwent', -kwənt) *adj.* following as a result; resulting —**con'se·quent'ly** *adv.*

con'se·quen'tial (-kwen'shəl) *adj.* **1.** consequent **2.** important

con·ser·va·tion (kän'sər vā'shən) *n.* **1.** a conserving **2.** the official care and protection of natural resources —**con'ser·va'tion·ist** *n.*

con·ser·va·tive (kən sur'və tiv) *adj.* **1.** tending to conserve **2.** tending to preserve established institutions, etc.; opposed to change **3.** moderate; cautious —*n.* a conservative person —**con·ser'va·tism** *n.* —**con·ser'va·tive·ly** *adv.*

con·ser·va·to·ry (kən sur'və tôr'ē) *n., pl.* **-ries 1.** a greenhouse **2.** a school, or academy of music, art, etc.

con·serve (kən surv') *vt.* **-served', -serv'ing** [< L. *com*-, with + *servare*, keep] to keep from being damaged, lost, or wasted; save —*n. (usually* kän'sərv) *[often pl.]* a jam of two or more fruits

con·sid·er (kən sid'ər) *vt.* [< L. *considerare*, observe] **1.** to think about in order to understand or decide **2.** to keep in mind **3.** to be thoughtful of (others) **4.** to regard as; believe

con·sid'er·a·ble *adj.* **1.** worth considering; important **2.** much or large —**con·sid'er·a·bly** *adv.*

con·sid'er·ate (-it) *adj.* having regard for others and their feelings —**con·sid'er·ate·ly** *adv.*

con·sid'er·a'tion (-ə rā'shən) *n.* **1.** the act of considering; deliberation **2.** thoughtful regard for others **3.** something considered in making a decision **4.** a recompense; fee —**take into consideration** to keep in mind —**under consideration** being thought over

con·sid'ered (-ərd) *adj.* arrived at after careful thought

con·sid'er·ing *prep.* in view of; taking into account

con·sign (kən sīn') *vt.* [< L. *consignare*, to seal] **1.** to hand over; deliver **2.** to entrust **3.** to assign **4.** to send or deliver (goods)

con·sign'ment (-mənt) *n.* **1.** a consigning or being consigned **2.** a shipment of goods sent to an agent for sale, etc. —**on consignment** with payment due after sale of the consignment

con·sist (kən sist') *vi.* [< L. *com*-, together + *sistere*, stand] **1.** to be formed or composed (*of*) **2.** to be contained or inherent (*in*)

con·sis·ten·cy (-ən sē) *n., pl.* **-cies 1.** firmness or thickness, as of a liquid **2.** agreement; harmony **3.** conformity with previous practice

con·sis·tent (-ənt) *adj.* **1.** in harmony or agreement; compatible **2.** holding to the same principles or practice —**con·sis'tent·ly** *adv.*

con·sis·to·ry (kən sis'tər ē) *n., pl.* **-ries** [see CONSIST] **1.** a church council or court, as the papal senate **2.** a session of such a body

con·so·la·tion (kän'sə lā'shən) *n.* **1.** comfort; solace **2.** one that consoles

con·sole¹ (kən sōl') *vt.* **-soled', -sol'ing** [< L. *com*-, with + *solari*, to solace] to make feel less sad or disappointed; comfort —**con·sol'a·to'ry** *adj.* —**con·sol'ing·ly** *adv.*

con·sole² (kän'sōl) *n.* [Fr.] **1.** the desklike frame containing the keys, stops, etc. of an organ **2.** a radio, television, or phonograph cabinet designed to stand on the floor **3.** a control panel for operating aircraft, computers, electronic systems, etc.

con·sol·i·date (kən säl'ə dāt') *vt., vi.* **-dat·ed, -dat·ing** [< L. *com*-, together + *solidus*, solid] **1.** to combine into one; unite **2.** to make or become strong or stable —**con·sol'i·da'tion** *n.* —**con·sol'i·da'tor** *n.*

con·som·mé (kän'sə mā') *n.* [Fr.] a clear, strained meat soup

con·so·nance (kän'sə nəns) *n.* [< L. *com*-, with + *sonus*, sound] harmony, esp. of musical tones; agreement: also **con'so·nan·cy**

con'so·nant (-nənt) *adj.* in harmony or accord —*n.* a letter representing a speech sound made by obstructing the air stream, as *p, t, l, f,* etc. —**con'so·nan'tal** (-nant'l) *adj.*

con·sort (kän'sôrt; *for v.* kən sôrt') *n.* [< L. *com*-, with + *sors*, a share] a wife or husband, esp. of a reigning king or queen —*vt., vi.* to associate

con·sor·ti·um (kən sôr'shē əm) *n., pl.* **-ti·a** [see prec.] an international alliance, as of business firms or banks

con·spec·tus (kən spek'təs) *n.* [L.: see ff.] **1.** a general view **2.** a summary; digest

con·spic·u·ous (kən spik'yoo wəs) *adj.* [< L. *com*-, intens. + *specere*, see] **1.** easy to see **2.** outstanding; striking —**con·spic'u·ous·ly** *adv.*

con·spir·a·cy (kən spir'ə sē) *n., pl.* **-cies 1.** a conspiring **2.** an unlawful plot **3.** a conspiring group

con·spire' (-spīr') *vi.* **-spired', -spir'ing** [< L. *com*-, together + *spirare*, to breathe] **1.** to plan together

constable

135

contact lens

secretly, as to commit a crime 2. to work together toward a single end —**con·spir'a·tor** (-spir'ə tər) *n.* —**con·spir'a·to'ri·al** (-spir'ə tôr'ē əl) *adj.*

con·sta·ble (kän'stə b'l, kun'-) *n.* [< LL. *comes stabuli,* lit., count of the stable] [Chiefly Brit.] a policeman

con·stab·u·lar·y (kən stab'yə ler'ē) *n., pl.* -ies 1. constables, collectively 2. a militarized police force

con·stant (kän'stənt) *adj.* [< L. *com-,* together + *stare,* to stand] 1. not changing; regular; faithful 2. continual; persistent —*n.* anything that does not change or vary —*con'*stan·cy *n.* —con'stant·ly *adv.*

Con·stan·tine (kän'stən tēn', -tīn') 280?–337 A.D.; first Christian emperor of Rome (306–337 A.D.)

Con·stan·ti·no·ple (kän'stan tə nō'p'l) *former name of* ISTANBUL

con·stel·la·tion (kän'stə lā'shən) *n.* [< L. *com-,* with + *stella,* star] a group of fixed stars

con·ster·na·tion (kän'stər nā'shən) *n.* [< L. *consternare,* terrify] great fear or shock

con·sti·pate (kän'stə pāt') *vt.*-pat·ed, -pat'ing [< L. *com-,* together + *stipare,* cram] to cause constipation in **con'sti·pa'tion** *n.* infrequent and difficult movement of the bowels

con·stit·u·en·cy (kən stich'oo wən sē) *n., pl.* -cies the voters in a district

con·stit·u·ent (-wənt) *adj.* [see ff.] 1. necessary to the whole; component 2. that elects 3. authorized to make or revise a constitution —*n.* 1. a voter in a district 2. a component

con·sti·tute (kän'stə tōōt', -tyōōt') *vt.* -tut'ed, -tut'ing [< L. *com-,* together + *statuere,* to set] 1. to establish (a law, government, etc.) 2. to set up (an assembly, etc.) in a legal form 3. to appoint 4. to form; compose —con'sti·tu'tive *adj.*

con·sti·tu·tion (-tōō'shən, -tyōō'-) *n.* 1. a constituting 2. structure; organization 3. *a)* the system of basic laws and principles of a government, society, etc. *b)* a document stating these; specif., [C-] the Constitution of the U.S.

con·sti·tu·tion·al *adj.* 1. of or in one's constitution or structure; basic 2. of or in accordance with the constitution of a government, society, etc. —*n.* a walk taken for one's health —con'sti·tu'tion·al'i·ty (-al'ə tē) *n.* —con'sti·tu'tion·al·ly *adv.*

con·strain (kən strān') *vt.* [< L. *com-,* together + *stringere,* draw tight] 1. to confine 2. to restrain 3. to compel

con·straint' *n.* 1. confinement; restriction 2. force; compulsion 3. forced, unnatural manner

con·strict (kən strikt') *vt.* [see CONSTRAIN] to make smaller or narrower by squeezing, etc. —con·stric'tion *n.*

con·struct (kən strukt') *vt.* [< L. *com-,* together + *struere,* pile up] to build, devise, etc. —con·struc'tor *n.*

con·struc·tion (-struk'shən) *n.* 1. a constructing or manner of being constructed 2. a structure 3. an interpretation, as of a statement 4. the arrangement of words in a sentence

con·struc·tion·ist *n.* a person who interprets a law, document, etc. in a specified way

con·struc·tive *adj.* helping to construct; leading to improvement

con·strue (kən strōō') *vt., vi.* -strued', -stru'ing [see CONSTRUCT] 1. to analyze the grammatical construction of (a sentence) 2. to translate 3. to explain; interpret

con·sul (kän's'l) *n.* [< L. *consulere,* to deliberate] 1. a chief magistrate of ancient Rome 2. a government official appointed to live in a foreign city and look after his country's citizens and business there —con'su·lar *adj.*

con·sul·ate (-it) *n.* 1. the position, powers, etc. of a consul 2. the office or residence of a consul

con·sult (kən sult') *vi.* [< L. *consulere,* consider] to talk things over; confer —*vt.* 1. to seek information or instruction from 2. to consider —con·sul·ta·tion (kän's'l tā'shən) *n.*

con·sult'ant *n.* 1. a person who consults another 2. one who gives professional or technical advice

con·sume (kən sōōm') *vt.* -sumed', -sum'ing [< L. *com-,* together + *sumere,* to take] 1. to destroy, as by fire 2. to use up or waste (time, money, etc.) 3. to eat or drink up

con·sum'er *n.* a person or thing that consumes; specif., one who uses goods or services for his own needs rather than to produce other goods

con·sum'er·ism (-iz'm) *n.* a movement for protecting the consumer against defective products, misleading business practices, etc.

con·sum·mate (kən sum'it; *for v.* kän'sə māt') *adj.* [< L. *com-,* together + *summa,* a sum] complete; perfect —*vt.* -mat'ed, -mat'ing 1. to complete 2. to complete (marriage) by sexual intercourse —con·sum'mate·ly *adv.* —con'sum·ma'tion *n.*

con·sump·tion (kən sump'shən) *n.* 1. a consuming or being consumed 2. the using up of goods or services 3. the amount consumed 4. a wasting disease, esp. tuberculosis of the lungs

con·sump·tive (-tiv) *adj.* 1. consuming or tending to consume 2. of or having tuberculosis of the lungs —*n.* one who has tuberculosis of the lungs

cont., contd. continued

con·tact (kän'takt) *n.* [< L. *com-,* together + *tangere,* to touch] 1. a touching or meeting 2. the state of being in association (*with*) 3. a connection —*vt.* 1. to place in contact 2. to get in touch with —*vi.* to come into contact

contact flying piloting an airplane by observing objects on the ground

contact lens a tiny, thin correctional

fat, āpe, cär; ten, ēven; is, bīte; gō, hôrn, tōōl, look; oil, out; up, fur; chin; she; thin, then; zh, leisure; ŋ, ring; ə for *a* in ago; ', (ā'b'l); ë, Fr. coeur; ö, Fr. feu; Fr. mon; ü, Fr. duc; kh, G. ich, doch; ‡ foreign; < derived from

lens placed in the fluid over the cornea of the eye

con·ta·gion (kən tā′jən) n. [see prec.] 1. the spreading of disease by contact 2. a contagious disease 3. the spreading of an emotion, idea, etc.

con·ta′gious (-jəs) adj. 1. spread by contact: said of diseases 2. carrying the causative agent of a contagious disease 3. spreading from person to person —con·ta′gious·ness n.

con·tain (kən tān′) vt. [< L. com-, together + tenere, to hold] 1. to have in it; hold 2. to have the capacity for holding 3. to hold back or restrain within fixed limits —con·tain′ment n.

con·tain′er n. a thing for containing something; box, can, etc.

con·tain′er·ize′ vt. -ized′, -iz′ing to pack (cargo) into huge, standardized containers for shipment

con·tam·i·nant (kən tam′ə nənt) n. a contaminating substance

con·tam′i·nate′ (-nāt′) vt. -nat′ed, -nat′ing [< L. com-, together + tangere, to touch] to make impure, corrupt, etc. by contact; pollute; taint —con·tam′i·na′tion n.

con·temn (kən tem′) vt. [< L. com-, intens. + temnere, to scorn] to treat with contempt; scorn

con·tem·plate (kän′təm plāt′) vt. -plat′ed, -plat′ing [< L. contemplari, observe] 1. to gaze at or think about intently 2. to expect or intend —vi. to muse —con′tem·pla′tion n. —con·tem·pla·tive (kən tem′plə tiv, kän′təm plāt′iv) adj., n.

con·tem·po·rar·y (kən tem′pə rer′ē) adj. [< L. com-, with + tempus, time] 1. living or occurring in the same period 2. of about the same age 3. modern Also con·tem′po·ra′ne·ous (-rā′nē əs) —n., pl. -ies one existing in the same period as another or others

con·tempt (kən tempt′) n. [see CONTEMN] 1. the feeling one has toward someone or something he considers low, worthless, etc. 2. the condition of being despised 3. Law a showing disrespect for the dignity of a court (or legislature)

con·tempt′i·ble adj. deserving contempt or scorn; despicable —con·tempt′i·bly adv.

con·temp·tu·ous (kən temp′choo wəs) adj. full of contempt; scornful —con·temp′tu·ous·ly adv.

con·tend (kən tend′) vi. [< L. com-, together + tendere, extend] 1. to fight or argue 2. to compete —vt. to assert —con·tend′er n.

con·tent¹ (kən tent′) adj. [see CONTAIN] 1. satisfied 2. willing; assenting —vt. to satisfy —n. contentment

con·tent² (kän′tent) n. [see CONTAIN] 1. [usually pl.] a) what is in a container b) what is in a book, etc. 2. what is dealt with in a talk, etc. 3. substance or meaning 4. amount contained

con·tent′ed adj. satisfied —con·tent′ed·ly adv. —con·tent′ed·ness n.

con·ten·tion (kən ten′shən) n. [see CONTEND] 1. dispute; strife 2. a point argued for —con·ten′tious adj. —

con·ten′tious·ly adv. —con·ten′tious·ness n.

con·tent′ment n. the state or fact of being contented

con·ter·mi·nous (kən tur′mə nəs) adj. [< L. com-, together + terminus, end] 1. having a common boundary 2. contained within the same boundaries —con·ter′mi·nous·ly adv.

con·test (kən test′; for n. kän′test) vt. [< L. com-, together + testis, witness] 1. to dispute (a point, etc.) 2. to fight for (a position, etc.) —vi. to struggle (with or against) —n. 1. a fight; struggle 2. a competitive game, race, etc. —con·test′a·ble adj.

con·test′ant n. [Fr.] 1. a competitor in a game, etc. 2. one who contests

con·text (kän′tekst) n. [< L. com-, together + texere, weave] the parts just before and after a word or passage, that determine its meaning —con·tex·tu·al (kən teks′choo wəl) adj.

con·tig·u·ous (kən tig′yoo wəs) adj. [see CONTACT] 1. in contact; touching 2. near; next —con·ti·gu·i·ty (kän′tə gyōō′ə tē) n., pl. -ties

con·ti·nence (känt′n əns) n. [see CONTAIN] 1. self-restraint 2. self-restraint in sexual activity, esp. total abstinence —con′ti·nent adj.

con′ti·nent (-ənt) n. [see CONTAIN] any of the main large land areas of the earth —the Continent the mainland of Europe

con′ti·nen′tal (-en′t′l) adj. 1. of a continent 2. [sometimes C-] European 3. [C-] of the American colonies at the time of the American Revolution

con·tin·gen·cy (kən tin′jən sē) n., pl. -cies 1. dependence on chance 2. a possible or chance event

con·tin′gent adj. [see CONTACT] 1. possible 2. accidental 3. dependent (on or upon an uncertainty) —n. 1. a chance happening 2. a quota, as of troops 3. a part of a large group

con·tin·u·al (kən tin′yoo wəl) adj. 1. repeated often 2. continuous —con·tin′u·al·ly adv.

con·tin′u·ance n. 1. a continuing 2. duration 3. an unbroken succession 4. Law postponement or adjournment

con·tin′u·a′tion (-wā′shən) n. 1. a continuing 2. a beginning again; resumption 3. a part added; sequel

con·tin·ue (kən tin′yōō) vi. -ued, -u·ing [< L. continuare, join] 1. to last; endure 2. to go on in a specified action or condition 3. to stay 4. to extend 5. to go on again after an interruption —vt. 1. to go on with 2. to extend 3. to cause to remain, as in office 4. Law to postpone

con·ti·nu·i·ty (kän′tə nōō′ə tē, -nyōō′-) n., pl. -ties 1. a continuous state or quality 2. an unbroken, coherent whole 3. the script for a motion picture, radio program, etc.

con·tin·u·ous (kən tin′yoo wəs) adj. going on without interruption; unbroken —con·tin′u·ous·ly adv.

con·tin·u·um (-yoo wəm) n., pl. -u·a, -u·ums [L.] a continuous whole, quantity, or series

con·tort (kən tôrt′) vt., vi. [< L.

com-, together + *torquere*, to twist] to twist or wrench out of shape; distort —con·tor′tion n.

con·tor·tion·ist n. one who can twist his body into unnatural positions

con·tour (kän′toor) n. [Fr. < L. com-, intens. + *tornare*, to turn] the outline of a figure, land, etc. —vt. to shape to the contour of —adj. conforming to or following the shape or contour of something

con·tra (kän′trə, kōn′-) n. [AmSp.] one of a rebel group trying to overthrow the Nicaraguan government established in 1979

contra- [< L. *contra*] a prefix meaning against, opposite, opposed to

con·tra·band (kän′trə band′) n. [< Sp. < It.] smuggled goods —adj. illegal to import or export

con·tra·cep·tion (kän′trə sep′shən) n. [CONTRA- + (CON)CEPTION] prevention of the fertilization of the human ovum —con′tra·cep′tive adj., n.

con·tract (kän′trakt for n. & usually for vt. 1 & vi. 1; kən trakt′ for vi. generally) n. [< L. com-, together + *trahere*, draw] an agreement, esp. a written one enforceable by law, between two or more people —vt. 1. to undertake by contract 2. to get or incur (a debt, disease, etc.) 3. to reduce in size; shrink 4. to shorten (a word or phrase) —vi. 1. to make a contract 2. to become smaller

con·trac·tile (kən trak′t'l) adj. having the power of contracting

con·trac·tion (kən trak′shən) n. 1. a contracting or being contracted 2. the shortened form of a word or phrase [Ex.: *don't* for *do not*]

con·trac·tor (kän′trak tər, kən trak′-) n. a builder, etc. who contracts to supply materials or do work

con·trac·tu·al (kən trak′choo wəl) adj. of or constituting a contract

con·tra·dict (kän′trə dikt′) vt. [< L. *contra-*, against + *dicere*, speak] 1. to assert the opposite of or deny 2. to deny the statement of (a person) 3. to be contrary to —con′tra·dic′tion n. —con′tra·dic′to·ry adj.

con·tra·dis·tinc·tion (-dis tiŋk′shən) n. distinction by contrast

con·trail (kän′trāl′) n. a white trail of water vapor in an airplane's wake

con′tra·in′di·cate vt. -cat′ed, -cat′ing Med. to make (the indicated drug or treatment) inadvisable

con·tral·to (kən tral′tō) n., pl. -tos, -ti (-tē) [It.: see CONTRA- & ALTO] 1. a female voice of the lowest range 2. a woman with such a voice

con·trap·tion (kən trap′shən) n. [< ?] [Colloq.] a contrivance; gadget

con′tra·pun′tal (kän′trə pun′t'l) adj. [< It. *contrapunto*, counterpoint] of or characterized by counterpoint

con·tra·ri·wise (kän′trer ē wīz′) adv. 1. on the contrary 2. in the opposite way, order, etc.

con·tra·ry (kän′trer ē; for adj. 4,

often kən trer′ē) adj. [< L. *contra*, against] 1. opposed 2. opposite in nature, order, etc.; quite different 3. unfavorable 4. always resisting; perverse —n., pl. -ries the opposite —on the contrary as opposed to what has been said —to the contrary to the opposite effect —con′tra·ri′e·ty (-tra rī′ə tē) n. —con′trar·i·ly adv. —con′trar·i·ness n.

con·trast (kən trast′; for n. kän′trast) vt. [< L. *contra*, against + *stare*, to stand] to compare so as to point out the differences —vi. to show differences when compared —n. 1. a contrasting or being contrasted 2. a striking difference between things being compared 3. a person or thing showing differences when compared with another —con·trast′a·ble adj.

con·tra·vene (kän′trə vēn′) vt. -vened′, -ven′ing [< L. *contra*, against + *venire*, come] 1. to go against; violate 2. to contradict

con·tre·temps (kōn trə tän′) n., pl. -temps′ (-tän′) [Fr.] a confusing, embarrassing, or awkward occurrence

con·trib·ute (kən trib′yoot) vt., vi. -ut·ed, -ut·ing [< L.: see COM- & TRIBUTE] 1. to give together with others 2. to write (an article, etc.) as for a magazine 3. to furnish (ideas, etc.) —contribute to to share in bringing about —con·trib′u·tor n. —con·trib′u·to·ry adj.

con·tri·bu·tion (kän′trə byoo′shən) n. 1. a contributing 2. something contributed, as money

con·trite (kən trīt′) adj. [< L. com-, together + *terere*, to rub] deeply sorry for having done wrong; penitent —con·trite′ly adv. —con·trite′ness n. —con·tri′tion (-trish′ən) n.

con·triv·ance (kən trī′vəns) n. 1. the act, way, or power of contriving 2. something contrived; device, etc.

con·trive (kən trīv′) vt. -trived′, -triv′ing [ult. < VL. *contropare*, compare] 1. to think up, devise, design, etc. 2. to make inventively 3. to bring about; manage —con·triv′er n.

con·trol (kən trōl′) vt. -trolled′, -trol′ling [< ML. *contrarotulus*, a register] 1. to regulate or direct 2. to verify (an experiment) by comparison 3. to exercise authority over; direct 4. to restrain —n. 1. power to direct or regulate 2. a means of controlling; check 3. an apparatus to regulate a mechanism: *usually used in pl.* —con·trol′la·ble adj.

con·trol′ler n. 1. a person in charge of finances, as in a business 2. a person or device that controls

con·tro·ver·sial (kän′trə vur′shəl) adj. subject to controversy; debatable

con′tro·ver·sy (-sē) n., pl. -sies [< L. *contra*, against + *vertere*, to turn] a conflict of opinion; dispute

con′tro·vert′ (-vurt′) vt. 1. to argue against; dispute 2. to argue about; debate —con′tro·vert′i·ble adj.

con·tu·ma·cy (kän'too mə sē) *n.*, *pl.* **-cies** [< L. *contumax*, stubborn] stubborn resistance to authority — **con'tu·ma'cious** (-mā'shəs) *adj.*

con·tu·me·ly (kän'too mə lē) *n.*, *pl.* **-lies** [< L. *contumelia*, abuse] humiliating treatment or scornful insult — **con'tu·me'li·ous** (-mē'lē əs) *adj.*

con·tuse (kən tooz') *vt.* **-tused', -tus'ing** [see ff.] to bruise

con·tu·sion (kən too'zhən) *n.* [< L. *com-*, intens. + *tundere*, to beat] a bruise

co·nun·drum (kə nun'drəm) *n.* [pseudo-L.] 1. a riddle whose answer is a pun 2. any puzzling problem

con·ur·ba·tion (kän'ər bā'shən) *n.* a vast urban area around and including a large city

con·va·lesce (kän'və les') *vi.* **-lesced', -lesc'ing** [< L. *com-*, intens. + *valere*, be strong] to regain health and strength; get better — **con'va·les'cence** *n.* — **con'va·les'cent** *adj., n.*

con·vec·tion (kən vek'shən) *n.* [< L. *com-*, together + *vehere*, carry] 1. a transmitting 2. a) movement of parts of a fluid within the fluid because of differences in heat, etc. b) heat transference by such movement — **con·vec'tion·al** *adj.* — **con·vec'tive** *adj.*

con·vene (kən vēn') *vi., vt.* **-vened', -ven'ing** [< L. *com-*, together + *venire*, come] to assemble for a meeting — **con·ven'er** *n.*

con·ven·ience (kən vēn'yəns) *n.* [see prec.] 1. the quality of being convenient 2. comfort 3. anything that adds to one's comfort or saves work —at **one's convenience** at a time or place suitable to one

con·ven·ient (-yənt) *adj.* easy to do, use, or get to; handy — **con·ven'ient·ly** *adv.*

con·vent (kän'vənt, -vent) *n.* [see CONVENE] 1. a community of nuns 2. the place where they live

con·ven·ti·cle (kən ven'ti k'l) *n.* [see CONVENE] an assembly, esp. a religious assembly, held secretly

con·ven·tion (kən ven'shən) *n.* 1. an assembly, often periodical, or its members 2. an agreement, as between nations 3. custom; usage

con·ven·tion·al (-'l) *adj.* 1. having to do with a convention 2. sanctioned by or following custom or usage; customary 3. formal — **con·ven'tion·al'i·ty** (-al'ə tē) *n.*, *pl.* **-ties** — **con·ven'tion·al·ly** *adv.*

con·ven·tion·al·ize' (-īz') *vt.* **-ized', -iz'ing** to make conventional

con·verge (kən vurj') *vi., vt.* **-verged', -verg'ing** [< L. *com-*, together + *vergere*, to turn] to come or bring together at a point — **con·ver'gence** *n.* — **con·ver'gent** *adj.*

con·ver·sant (kən vur's'nt, kän'vər-) *adj.* familiar or acquainted (*with*)

con·ver·sa·tion (kän'vər sā'shən) *n.* a talking together; informal talk — **con'ver·sa'tion·al** *adj.* — **con'ver·sa'tion·al·ist** *n.* — **con'ver·sa'tion·al·ly** *adv.*

conversation piece something, as an unusual article of furniture, that attracts attention or invites comment

con·verse¹ (kən vurs'; *for n.* kän'vərs) *vi.* **-versed', -vers'ing** [< L. *con-versari*, to live with] to hold a conversation; talk — *n.* conversation

con·verse² (kän'vərs; *also for adj.* kən vurs') *adj.* [see CONVERT] reversed in position, order, etc.; opposite; contrary — *n.* a converse thing; the opposite — **con·verse'ly** *adv.*

con·ver·sion (kən vur'zhən) *n.* a converting or being converted

con·vert (kən vurt'; *for n.* kän'vərt) *vt.* [< L. *com-*, together + *vertere*, to turn] 1. to change; transform 2. to change from one religion, doctrine, etc. to another 3. to exchange for something equal in value 4. to misappropriate — *vi.* to be converted — *n.* a person converted, as to a religion — **con·vert'er, con·ver'tor** *n.*

con·vert·i·ble (kən vur'tə b'l) *adj.* that can be converted — *n.* an automobile with a folding top

con·vex (kän veks', kän'veks) *adj.* [< L. *com-*, together + *vehere*, bring] curving outward like the surface of a sphere — **con·vex'i·ty** *n.*, *pl.* **-ties**

con·vey (kən vā') *vt.* [< L. *com-*, together + *via*, way] 1. to take from one place to another; transport; carry 2. to transmit — **con·vey'a·ble** *adj.* — **con·vey'or, con·vey'er** *n.*

con·vey·ance *n.* 1. a conveying 2. a means of conveying, esp. a vehicle

con·vict (kən vikt'; *for n.* kän'vikt) *vt.* [see CONVINCE] to prove or find (a person) guilty — *n.* a convicted person serving a prison sentence

con·vic·tion (kən vik'shən) *n.* 1. a convicting or being convicted 2. a being convinced; strong belief

con·vince (kən vins') *vt.* **-vinced', -vinc'ing** [< L. *com-*, intens. + *vincere*, conquer] to persuade by argument or evidence; make feel sure — **con·vinc'er** *n.* — **con·vinc'ing** *adj.* — **con·vinc'ing·ly** *adv.*

con·viv·i·al (kən viv'ē əl) *adj.* [< L. *com-*, together + *vivere*, to live] 1. festive 2. fond of eating, drinking, and good company; sociable — **con·viv'i·al'i·ty** (-al'ə tē) *n.*

con·vo·ca·tion (kän'və kā'shən) *n.* 1. a convoking 2. an assembly

con·voke (kən vōk') *vt.* **-voked', -vok'ing** [< L. *com-*, together + *vocare*, to call] to call together; convene

con·vo·lut·ed (kän'və loot'id) *adj.* 1. coiled 2. complicated; involved

con·vo·lu·tion (-loo'shən) *n.* [< L. *com-*, together + *vol-vere*, to roll] 1. a twisting, coiling, or winding together 2. a fold, twist, or coil

CONVOLUTIONS OF BRAIN

con·voy (kän'voi; *also for v.* kən voi') *vt.* [see CONVEY] to escort in order to protect — *n.* 1. a convoying 2. a protecting escort 3. ships, vehicles, etc. being convoyed

con·vulse (kən vuls') *vt.* **-vulsed', -vuls'ing** [< L. *com-*, together +

vellere, to pluck] 1. to shake violently; agitate   2. to cause to shake with laughter, rage, etc.

con·vul·sion (-vul'shən) *n.* 1. a violent, involuntary spasm of the muscles: *often in pl.* 2. a fit of laughter 3. a violent disturbance —**con·vul'sive** *adj.* —**con·vul'sive·ly** *adv.*

co·ny (kō'nē) *n., pl.* -nies *same as* CONEY

coo (kōō) *vi.* [echoic] to make the soft, murmuring sound of pigeons or doves —*n.* this sound

cook (kook) *vt.* [< L. *coquere*] to prepare (food) by boiling, baking, frying, etc. —*vi.* 1. to be a cook 2. to undergo cooking —*n.* one who prepares food —**cook up** [Colloq.] to devise; invent —**cook'er** *n.*

cook'book' *n.* a book with recipes and other information for preparing food

cook'er·y *n.* [Chiefly Brit.] the art or practice of cooking

cook'ie (-ē) *n.* [prob. < Du. *koek*, cake] a small, sweet, flat cake: also **cook'y**, *pl.* -ies

cook'out' *n.* a meal cooked and eaten outdoors

cool (kōōl) *adj.* [OE. *col*] 1. moderately cold 2. tending to reduce the effects of heat [*cool* clothes] 3. not excited; composed 4. showing dislike or indifference 5. calmly bold 6. [Colloq.] without exaggeration [a *cool* $1,000] 7. [Slang] very good —*n.* 1. a cool place, time, etc. [the *cool* of the night] 2. [Slang] cool, dispassionate manner —*vt.*, *vi.* to make or become cool —**cool'ly** *adv.* —**cool'ness** *n.*

cool'ant (-ənt) *n.* a fluid or other substance for cooling engines, etc.

cool'er *n.* 1. a place for keeping things cool 2. [Slang] jail

Coo·lidge (kōō'lij), (John) **Calvin** 1872–1933; 30th president of the U.S. (1923–29)

coo·lie (kōō'lē) *n.* [Hind. *qūlī*, servant] an unskilled native laborer, esp. formerly, in India, China, etc.

coon (kōōn) *n. short for* RACCOON

coon'skin' *n.* the skin of a raccoon, used as a fur

coop (kōōp) *n.* [< L. *cupa*, cask] 1. a small pen for poultry, etc. 2. [Slang] jail —*vt.* to confine as in a coop

co-op (kō'äp) *n.* a cooperative

coop'er *n.* [see COOP] one whose work is making or repairing barrels and casks —**coop'er·age** (-ij) *n.*

co·op·er·ate (kō äp'ə rāt') *vi.* -at'ed, -at'ing [< L. *co-*, with + *opus*, work] to act or work together with another or others Also **co-op'er·ate'**, **co·öp'er·ate'** —**co·op'er·a'tion** *n.*

co·op'er·a·tive (-ər ə tiv, -ə rāt'iv) *adj.* 1. cooperating 2. owned collectively by members who share in its benefits —*n.* a cooperative store, etc. Also **co·op'er·a·tive**, **co·öp'er·a·tive**

co-opt (kō äpt') *vt.* [< L. < *co-*, with + *optare*, choose] 1. to elect or appoint as an associate 2. to get (an opponent) to join one's side

co·or·di·nate (kō ôr'd'n it; *also, and for v. always,* -də nāt') *adj.* [< L. *co-*, with + *ordo*, order] 1. of equal order, rank, or importance [*coordinate* clauses in a sentence] 2. of coordination or coordinates —*n.* a coordinate person or thing —*vt.* -nat'ed, -nat'ing 1. to make coordinate 2. to bring into proper order or relation; adjust Also **co·or'di·nate**, **co·ör'di·nate** —**co·or'di·na'tor** *n.*

coordinating conjunction a conjunction connecting coordinate words, clauses, etc. (Ex.: *and, but*)

co·or'di·na'tion *n.* 1. a coordinating or being coordinated 2. harmonious action, as of muscles Also **co·or'di·na'tion**, **co·ör'di·na'tion**

coot (kōōt) *n.* [ME. *cote*] 1. a ducklike water bird 2. [Colloq.] a fool

coot·ie (kōōt'ē) *n.* [Slang] a louse

cop (käp) *vt.* copped, cop'ping [< ? L. *capere*, take] [Slang] to seize; steal —*n.* [Slang] a policeman —**cop out** [Slang] 1. to confess to police 2. to renege 3. to give up; quit

co·part·ner (kō pärt'nər) *n.* a partner

cope¹ (kōp) *vi.* coped, cop'ing [< OFr. *couper*, to strike] to fight or contend (*with*) successfully

cope² (kōp) *n.* [< LL. *cappa*] 1. a large capelike vestment worn by priests 2. any cover like this

Co·pen·hag·en (kō'pən hā'gən, -hā'-) capital of Denmark: pop. 874,000

Co·per·ni·cus (kō pur'ni kəs), **Nic·o·la·us** (nik'ə lā'əs) 1473–1543; Pol. astronomer —**Co·per'ni·can** *adj.*, *n.*

cop·i·er (käp'ē ər) *n.* 1. one who copies 2. a duplicating machine

co·pi·lot (kō'pī'lət) *n.* the assistant pilot of an airplane

cop·ing (kōp'iŋ) *n.* [< COPE²] the top layer of a masonry wall

co·pi·ous (kō'pē əs) *adj.* [< L. *copia*, abundance] plentiful; abundant —**co'pi·ous·ly** *adv.* —**co'pi·ous·ness** *n.*

cop'-out' *n.* [Slang] a copping out, as by confessing, reneging, or quitting

cop·per (käp'ər) *n.* [< L. *cuprum*] 1. a reddish-brown, ductile, metallic element 2. [Chiefly Brit.] a penny 3. a reddish brown —*adj.* 1. of copper 2. reddish-brown —**cop'per·y** *adj.*

cop·per·as (käp'ər əs) *n.* [< ML. (*aqua*) *cuprosa*, copper (water)] a green sulfate of iron used in making dyes, inks, etc.

cop'per·head' *n.* a poisonous N. American snake

co·pra (kō'prə, käp'rə) *n.* [Port. < Hindi *khoprā*] dried coconut meat, the source of coconut oil

copse (käps) *n.* [< OFr. *couper*, to cut] a thicket of small trees or shrubs: also **cop·pice** (käp'is)

cop·ter (käp'tər) *n. shortened form of* HELICOPTER

cop·u·la (käp'yə lə) *n., pl.* -las [L..

a link] a verb form, as of *be, seem, appear,* etc., that links a subject with a predicate —**cop'u·la·tive** (-lāt'iv) *adj.*

cop·u·late (käp'yə lāt') *vi.* **-lat'ed, -lat'ing** [< L. *co-*, together + *apere*, to join] to have sexual intercourse —**cop'u·la'tion** *n.*

cop·y (käp'ē) *n., pl.* **-ies** [< L. *copia*, plenty] **1.** a thing made just like another **2.** any of a number of books, magazines, etc. having the same contents **3.** matter to be set in type **4.** the words of an advertisement —*vt., vi.* **cop'ied, cop'y·ing 1.** to make a copy of **2.** to imitate —**cop'y·ist** *n.*

cop'y·cat' (-kat') *n.* an imitator

cop'y·right' *n.* the exclusive legal right to the publication, sale, etc. of a literary or artistic work —*vt.* to protect (a book, etc.) by copyright

cop'y·writ'er *n.* a writer of copy, esp. for advertisements

co·quette (kō ket') *n.* [Fr.] a girl or woman flirt —*vi.* **-quet'ted, -quet'ting** to flirt —**co·quet'tish** *adj.* — **co·quet'tish·ly** *adv.*

cor- same as COM-: used before *r*

cor·al (kôr'əl) *n.* [< Gr. *korallion*] **1.** the hard skeleton secreted by certain marine polyps: reefs and atolls of coral occur in tropical seas **2.** a yellowish red —*adj.* of coral

cor·bel (kôr'bəl) *n.* [< L. *corvus*, raven] a piece of stone, wood, etc. projecting from a wall, to support a cornice, arch, etc.

cord (kôrd) *n.* [< Gr. *chordē*] **1.** thick string **2.** a measure of wood cut for fuel (128 cu. ft.) **3.** a rib on the surface of a fabric **4.** ribbed fabric **5.** *Anat.* any part like a cord **6.** *Elec.* a slender cable —*vt.* to fasten with a cord

cord'age (-ij) *n.* cords and ropes

cor·dial (kôr'jəl) *adj.* [< L. *cor*, heart] warm; hearty; sincere —*n.* a liqueur —**cor'di·al'i·ty** (-jē al'ə tē) *n., pl.* **-ties** —**cor'dial·ly** *adv.*

cor·dil·le·ra (kôr'dil yer'ə, kôr dil'ər ə) *n.* [Sp. < L. *chorda*, a cord] a system or chain of mountains

cord·ite (kôr'dīt) *n.* [< CORD: it is stringy] a smokeless explosive made of nitroglycerin, guncotton, etc.

cord·less (kôrd'lis) *adj.* operated by batteries, as an electric shaver

cor·don (kôr'd'n) *n.* [see CORD] **1.** a line or circle of police, troops, etc. guarding an area **2.** a cord or braid worn as a decoration —*vt.* to encircle with a cordon

cor·do·van (kôr'də vən) *n.* [< *Córdoba,* Spain] a soft, colored leather

cor·du·roy (kôr'də roi') *n.* [prob. < CORD + obs. *duroy*, coarse fabric] a heavy, ribbed cotton fabric

core (kôr) *n.* [prob. < L. *cor*, heart] **1.** the central part of an apple, pear, etc. **2.** the central part of anything **3.** the most important part —*vt.* **cored, cor'ing** to remove the core of

co·re·spond·ent (kō'ri spän'dənt) *n.* [CO- + RESPONDENT] *Law* a person charged with having committed adultery with the husband or wife from whom a divorce is sought

co·ri·an·der (kôr'ē an'dər) *n.* [< Gr. *koriandron*] **1.** an annual herb of the parsley family **2.** its strong-smelling seedlike fruit, used as a flavoring

cork (kôrk) *n.* [ult. < L. *quercus*, oak] **1.** the light, thick, elastic outer bark of an oak tree (**cork oak**) **2.** a piece of cork; esp., a stopper for a bottle, etc. **3.** any stopper —*adj.* of cork —*vt.* to stop with a cork

cork'screw' *n.* a spiral-shaped device for pulling corks out of bottles —*adj.* spiral —*vi., vt.* to twist

corm (kôrm) *n.* [< Gr. *kormos*, log] the fleshy, underground stem of certain plants, as the gladiolus

cor·mo·rant (kôr'mə rənt) *n.* [< L. *corvus*, raven + *marinus*, marine] a large, voracious sea bird

corn[1] (kôrn) *n.* [OE.] **1.** a small, hard seed, esp. of a cereal grass **2.** *a*) an American cereal plant with kernels growing in rows along a woody, husk-enclosed core (**corncob**); maize *b*) the kernels **3.** [Brit.] grain, esp. wheat **4.** in Scotland and Ireland, oats **5.** [Slang] ideas, humor, etc. regarded as old-fashioned, trite, etc. —*vt.* to pickle (meat, etc.) in brine

corn[2] (kôrn) *n.* [< L. *cornu*, horn] a hard, thick, painful growth of skin, esp. on a toe

corn'ball' (-bôl') *adj.* [CORN[1], *n.* 5 + (SCREW)BALL] [Slang] corny

cor·ne·a (kôr'nē ə) *n.* [< L. *cornu*, horn] the transparent outer coat of the eyeball —**cor'ne·al** *adj.*

cor·ner (kôr'nər) *n.* [< L. *cornu*, horn] **1.** the point or place where lines or surfaces join and form an angle **2.** the angle formed **3.** any of the angles formed at a street intersection **4.** a remote, secluded place **5.** a region; quarter **6.** a position hard to escape from **7.** a monopoly acquired on a stock or commodity so as to raise the price —*vt.* **1.** to force into a corner (sense 6) **2.** to get a monopoly on (a stock, etc.) —*adj.* at, on, or for a corner —**cut corners** to cut down expenses, time, etc. —**cor'nered** *adj.*

cor'ner·back' *n.* *Football* either of two defensive backs stationed between the line of scrimmage and the safety men

cor'ner·stone' *n.* **1.** a stone at the corner of a building, often laid at a ceremony **2.** the basic or main part; foundation

cor·net (kôr net') *n.* [< L. *cornu*, a horn] a brass-wind musical instrument of the trumpet class

corn'flow'er *n.* an annual plant of the composite family with showy flowers

cor·nice (kôr'nis) *n.* [< Gr. *korōnis*, wreath] a horizontal molding projecting along the top of a wall, etc.

corn'meal' *n.* **1.** meal made from corn (maize) **2.** meal made from other grain

corn snow coarse granules of snow formed by partial melting then freezing

corn'starch' *n.* a starch made from corn (maize), used in cooking

corn syrup a sweet syrup made from cornstarch

cor·nu·co·pi·a (kôr′nə kō′pē ə, -nyoo-) *n.* [L. *cornu copiae*, horn of plenty] **1.** a horn-shaped container overflowing with fruits, flowers, etc. **2.** an abundance

corn·y (kôr′nē) *adj.* -i·er, -i·est [Colloq.] hackneyed, trite, etc.

co·rol·la (kə rôl′ə) *n.* [< L. *corona*, crown] the petals of a flower

CORNUCOPIA

cor·ol·lar·y (kôr′ə ler′ē) *n.*, *pl.* -ies [see prec.] **1.** a proposition following from one already proved **2.** a normal result

co·ro·na (kə rō′nə) *n.*, *pl.* -nas, -nae (-nē) [L.] **1.** a crown or crownlike part **2.** a circle of light around the sun or moon; esp., the halo seen around the sun during a total eclipse

cor·o·nar·y (kôr′ə ner′ē) *adj.* **1.** of or like a crown **2.** of the arteries supplying blood to the heart muscle —*n.* -ies a thrombosis in a coronary artery: in full **coronary thrombosis**

cor·o·na·tion (kôr′ə nā′shən) *n.* the crowning of a sovereign

cor·o·ner (kôr′ə nər) *n.* [ME., officer of the crown] a public officer who must determine the cause of any death not obviously due to natural causes

cor·o·net (kôr′ə net′) *n.* [< OFr. *corone*, crown] **1.** a small crown worn by nobility **2.** a band of jewels, flowers, etc. for the head

corp., corpn. corporation

cor·po·ral¹ (kôr′pər əl) *n.* [< L. *caput*, head] the lowest-ranking noncommissioned officer, just below a sergeant: abbrev. **Corp., Cpl**

cor·po·ral² (kôr′pər əl) *adj.* [< L. *corpus*, body] of the body; bodily

corporal punishment bodily punishment, as flogging

cor·po·rate (kôr′pər it) *adj.* [< L. *corpus*, body] **1.** of, like, or being a corporation **2.** shared; joint

cor·po·ra·tion (kôr′pə rā′shən) *n.* a group of people organized, as to operate a business, under a charter granting them as a body some of the legal rights, etc. of an individual

cor·po·re·al (kôr pôr′ē əl) *adj.* [< L. *corpus*, body] **1.** of or for the body **2.** of a material nature; physical

corps (kôr) *n.*, *pl.* **corps** (kôrz) [< L. *corpus*, body] **1.** a body of people associated under common direction **2.** *a)* a specialized branch of the armed forces *[the Marine Corps] b)* a tactical subdivision of an army

corpse (kôrps) *n.* [var. of prec.] a dead body, esp. of a person

cor·pu·lence (kôr′pyoo ləns) *n.* [< L. *corpus*, body] fatness; obesity — **cor′pu·lent** *adj.*

cor·pus (kôr′pəs) *n.*, *pl.* **cor′po·ra** (-pər ə) [L.] **1.** a body, esp. a dead one **2.** a body of laws, writings, etc.

Cor·pus Christ·i (kôr′pəs kris′tē) city in SE Tex.: pop. 232,000

cor·pus·cle (kôr′pəs ′l, -pus′ l) *n.* [< L. *corpus*, body] **1.** a very small particle **2.** any of the cells in the blood, lymph, etc. of vertebrates

corpus de·lic·ti (di lik′tī) [ModL., lit., body of the crime] **1.** the facts constituting a crime **2.** loosely, the body of a murder victim

cor·ral (kə ral′) *n.* [Sp. < L. *currere*, to run] an enclosure for horses, cattle, etc.; pen —*vt.* -ralled′, -ral′ling **1.** to drive into or confine in a corral **2.** to surround or capture

cor·rect (kə rekt′) *vt.* [< L. *com-*, together + *regere*, to direct] **1.** to make right **2.** to mark the errors of **3.** to punish or discipline **4.** to remove or counteract (a defect) —*adj.* **1.** conforming to an established standard **2.** true; accurate; right —**cor·rec′tive** *adj.*, *n.* —**cor·rect′ly** *adv.* —**cor·rect′ness** *n.*

cor·rec·tion (kə rek′shən) *n.* **1.** a correcting or being corrected **2.** a change that corrects a mistake **3.** punishment to correct faults —**cor·rec′tion·al** *adj.*

cor·re·late (kôr′ə lāt′) *vi.*, *vt.* -lat′ed, -lat′ing [COR- + RELATE] to be in or bring into mutual relation —**cor′re·la′tion** *n.*

cor·rel·a·tive (kə rel′ə tiv) *adj.* **1.** having a mutual relationship **2.** *Gram.* expressing mutual relation and used in pairs, as the conjunctions *neither* . . . *nor* —*n.* a correlative word, etc.

cor·re·spond (kôr′ə spänd′) *vi.* [< L. *com-*, together + *respondere*, to answer] **1.** to be in agreement (*with* something); tally **2.** to be similar or equal (*to*) **3.** to communicate by letters —**cor′re·spond′ing·ly** *adv.*

cor′re·spond′ence *n.* **1.** agreement **2.** similarity **3.** *a)* communication by letters *b)* the letters

cor′re·spond′ent *adj.* corresponding —*n.* **1.** a thing that corresponds **2.** one who exchanges letters with another **3.** a journalist supplying news from a place away from the home office

cor·ri·dor (kôr′ə dər, -dôr′) *n.* [< L. *currere*, to run] a long hall

cor·rob·o·rate (kə räb′ə rāt′) *vt.* -rat′ed, -rat′ing [< L. *com-*, intens. + *robur*, strength] to confirm; support —**cor·rob′o·ra′tion** *n.* —**cor·rob′o·ra′tive** *adj.*

cor·rode (kə rōd′) *vt.*, *vi.* -rod′ed, -rod′ing [< L. *com-*, intens. + *rodere*, gnaw] to eat into or wear away gradually, as by chemical action —**cor·ro′sion** (-rō′zhən) *n.* —**cor·ro′sive** (-siv) *adj.*, *n.* —**cor·ro′sive·ly** *adv.*

cor·ru·gate (kôr′ə gāt′) *vt.*, *vi.* -gat′ed, -gat′ing [< L. *com-*, intens + *rugare*, to wrinkle] to form into parallel ridges and grooves —**cor′ru·ga′tion** *n.*

cor·rupt (kə rupt′) *adj.* [< L. *com-*, together + *rumpere*, to break] **1.** evil;

---

fat, āpe, cär; ten, ēven; is, bīte; gō, hôrn, tōōl, look; oil, out; up, fur; chin; she; thin, then; zh, leisure; ŋ, ring; ə for a in ago; ', (ä′b'l); ē, Fr. coeur; ö, Fr. feu; Fr. mon; ü, Fr. duc; kh, G. ich, doch; ‡ foreign; < derived from

depraved; debased **2.** taking bribes; dishonest —*vt., vi.* to make or become corrupt —**cor·rupt'i·ble** *adj.* —**cor·rup'tion** *n.* —**cor·rupt'ly** *adv.*

cor·sage (kôr säzh') *n.* [see CORPS + -AGE] a small bouquet for a woman to wear, as at the waist or shoulder

cor·sair (kôr'ser) *n.* [< Fr. < L. *cursus*, course] a pirate or pirate ship

cor·set (kôr'sit) *n.* [see CORPS] [*sometimes pl.*] a closefitting undergarment worn, chiefly by women, to give support to or shape the torso

cor·tege, cor·tège (kôr tezh', -tāzh') *n.* [< Fr. < L. *cohors*, retinue] **1.** a retinue **2.** a ceremonial procession

cor·tex (kôr'teks) *n., pl.* **-ti·ces** (-tə sēz') [L., bark of a tree] **1.** the outer part of an internal organ; esp., the layer of gray matter over most of the brain **2.** an outer layer of plant tissue —**cor'ti·cal** (-ti k'l) *adj.*

cor·ti·sone (kôrt'ə sōn', -zōn') *n.* [< CORTEX (of adrenals)] a hormone used in adrenal insufficiency and for inflammatory diseases, etc.

co·run·dum (kə run'dəm) *n.* [< Sans. *kuruvinda*, ruby] a very hard mineral used for grinding and polishing

cor·us·cate (kôr'əs kāt') *vi.* **-cat'ed, -cat'ing** [< L. *coruscus*, vibrating] to glitter; sparkle —**cor'us·ca'tion** *n.*

cor·vette (kôr vet') *n.* [Fr.] a small, fast, British warship for convoy duty

co·ry·za (kə rī'zə) *n.* [< Gr.] a cold in the head

co·sign (kō'sīn') *vt., vi.* **1.** to sign (a promissory note) along with the maker, thus becoming responsible if the maker defaults **2.** to sign jointly —**co'sign'er** *n.*

co·sig·na·to·ry (kō sig'nə tôr'ē) *n., pl.* **-ries** one of two or more joint signers, as of a treaty

cos·met·ic (käz met'ik) *adj.* [< Gr. *kosmos*, order] beautifying, or correcting faults in, the face, hair, etc. —*n.* a cosmetic preparation, as lipstick —**cos·met'i·cal·ly** *adv.*

cos·me·tol·o·gy (käz'mə täl'ə jē) *n.* the work of a beautician —**cos'me·tol'o·gist** *n.*

cos·mic (käz'mik) *adj.* [< Gr. *kosmos*, universe] **1.** of the cosmos **2.** vast

cosmic rays streams of highly penetrating charged particles bombarding the earth from outer space

cos·mog·o·ny (käz mäg'ə nē) *n.* [< Gr. *kosmos*, universe + *gignesthai*, produce] **1.** the origin of the universe **2.** *pl.* **-nies** a theory of this

cos·mol'o·gy (-mäl'ə jē) *n.* [< ML.] the study of the physical nature, form, etc. of the universe as a whole —**cos'mo·log'i·cal** (-mə läj'ə k'l) *adj.*

cos·mo·naut (käz'mə nôt') *n.* [< Russ.] *same as* ASTRONAUT

cos·mo·pol·i·tan (käz'mə päl'ə t'n) *adj.* [< Gr. *kosmos*, world + *polis*, city] **1.** common to or representative of all or many parts of the world **2.** not narrow in outlook, habits, etc.; at home anywhere in the world —*n.* a cosmopolitan person or thing: also **cos·mop'o·lite'** (-mäp'ə līt')

cos·mos (käz'məs, -mōs) *n.* [< Gr.

kosmos, universe] **1.** the universe considered as an orderly system **2.** any complete and orderly system

co·spon·sor (kō'spän'sər) *n.* a joint sponsor, as of a proposed piece of legislation —*vt.* to be a cosponsor of —**co'spon'sor·ship'** *n.*

Cos·sack (käs'ak, -ək) *n.* any of a people of S Russia famous as horsemen

cost (kôst) *vt.* **cost, cost'ing** [< L. *com-*, together + *stare*, to stand] **1.** to be obtained for (a certain price) **2.** to require the expenditure, loss, etc. of —*n.* **1.** the amount of money, effort, etc. asked or paid for a thing; price **2.** loss; sacrifice —**at all costs** by any means required

co·star (kō'stär'; *for v., usually* kō'stär') *n.* any of the leading actors or actresses given equal prominence in a movie or play —*vt., vi.* **-starred', -star'ring** to make or be a costar

Cos·ta Ri·ca (käs'tə rē'kə, kōs'-) country in Central America: 19,575 sq. mi.; pop. 1,502,000 —**Cos'ta Ri'can**

cos·tive (käs'tiv, kôs'-) *adj.* [see CONSTIPATE] constipated or constipating

cost'ly *adj.* **-li·er, -li·est 1.** costing much; dear **2.** magnificent; sumptuous —**cost'li·ness** *n.*

cost of living the average cost of the necessities of life, as food, shelter, and clothes

cos·tume (käs'tōōm) *n.* [Fr. < L. *consuetudo*, custom] **1.** *a)* style of clothes typical of a certain country, period, etc. *b)* a set of such clothes **2.** a set of outer clothes —*vt.* **-tumed, -tum·ing** to provide with a costume

co·sy (kō'zē) *adj.* **-si·er, -si·est** & *n., pl.* **-sies** *same as* COZY —**co'si·ly** *adv.* —**co'si·ness** *n.*

cot¹ (kät) *n.* [< Hind. *khāt*] a narrow, collapsible bed, as one made of canvas on a folding frame

cot² (kät) *n.* [ME.] **1.** a small shelter **2.** a sheath, as for a hurt finger

cote (kōt) *n.* [ME.] a small shelter for fowl, sheep, etc.

co·te·rie (kōt'ər ē) *n.* [Fr.] a close circle of friends or colleagues; clique

co·ter·mi·nous (kō tur'mə nəs) *adj.* *same as* CONTERMINOUS

co·til·lion (kō til'yən) *n.* [< Fr.] **1.** an intricate, formal group dance **2.** a formal ball Also **co·til'lon**

cot·tage (kät'ij) *n.* [ME.] **1.** a small house **2.** a house used for vacations —**cot'tag·er** *n.*

cottage cheese a soft, white cheese made from the curds of sour milk

cot·ter, cot·tar (kät'ər) *n.* [Scot.] a tenant farmer

cot·ter pin (kät'ər) [ME.] a split pin fastened in place by spreading apart its ends after insertion

cot·ton (kät''n) *n.* [< Ar. *qutun*] **1.** the soft, white, fibrous substance around the seeds of certain mallow plants

COTTER PIN

2. such a plant or plants **3.** thread or cloth made of cotton —**cotton to** [Colloq.] **1.** to take a liking to **2.** to become aware of (a situation) —**cot′ton·y** *adj.*

cotton gin [see GIN²] a machine for separating cotton from the seeds

cot′ton·mouth′ *n.* same as WATER MOCCASIN

cot′ton·seed′ *n.* the seed of the cotton plant, yielding an oil used in margarine, cooking oil, soap, etc.

cot′ton·tail′ *n.* a common American rabbit with a fluffy tail

cot′ton·wood′ *n.* a poplar that has seeds thickly covered with cottony or silky hairs

cot·y·le·don (kät″l ēd″n) *n.* [< Gr. *kotylē*, cavity] the first leaf or a leaf of the first pair produced by the embryo of a flowering plant

couch (kouch) *n.* [< OFr. *couchier*, lie down] an article of furniture on which one may lie down; sofa —*vt., vi.* 1. to recline as on a couch 2. to put in words; express

cou·gar (kōō′gər) *n.* [< Fr. < S. Am. Ind.] a large, tawny-brown wild cat

cough (kôf) *vi.* [ME. *coughen*] to expel air suddenly and noisily from the lungs —*vt.* to expel by coughing —*n.* 1. a coughing 2. a condition of coughing frequently

could (kood) 1. *pt.* of CAN¹ 2. an auxiliary generally equivalent to *can,* expressing esp. a shade of doubt [it *could* be so]

could·n′t (-′nt) could not

cou·lomb (kōō läm′) *n.* [after C. A. de *Coulomb* (1736-1806), Fr. physicist] a unit of electric charge equal to 6.25 x 10¹⁸ electrons passing a point in one second

coun·cil (koun′s'l) *n.* [< L. *com-,* together + *calere,* to call] 1. a group of people called together for discussion, advice, etc. 2. an administrative or legislative body [a city *council*] — **coun′cil·man** (-mən) *n., pl.* -men

coun·ci·lor, coun′cil·lor (-ər) *n.* a member of a council

coun·sel (koun′s'l) *n.* [< L. *consilium*] 1. mutual exchange of ideas, etc.; discussion 2. advice 3. a lawyer or group of lawyers 4. a consultant —*vt.* -seled or -selled, -sel·ing or -sel·ling 1. to give advice to 2. to recommend (an action, etc.) —*vi.* to give or take advice

coun′se·lor, coun′sel·lor (-ər) *n.* 1. an adviser 2. a lawyer

count¹ (kount) *vt.* [< L. *computare,* compute] 1. to name or add up, unit by unit, to reach a total 2. to take account of; include 3. to believe to be; consider —*vi.* 1. to name numbers or add up items in order 2. to be taken into account; have importance 3. to have a specified value (often with *for*) 4. to rely or depend (*on* or *upon*) —*n.* 1. a counting 2. the total number 3. a reckoning 4. *Law* any of the charges in an indictment

count² (kount) *n.* [< L. *comes,* companion] a European nobleman with a

rank equal to that of an English earl

count′down′ *n.* 1. the schedule of operations just before firing a rocket, etc. 2. the counting off, in reverse order, of time units in this schedule

coun·te·nance (koun′tə nəns) *n.* [< L. *continentia,* bearing] 1. facial expression 2. the face; visage 3. approval; support —*vt.* -nanced, -nanc·ing to approve or tolerate

count·er¹ (koun′tər) *n.* 1. a person, device, etc. that counts something 2. a small disk for keeping count in games 3. an imitation coin, or token 4. a long table, board, etc. for serving customers, displaying goods, etc.

coun·ter² (koun′tər) *adv.* [< L. *contra,* against] in opposition; contrary —*adj.* opposed; contrary —*n.* the opposite or contrary —*vt., vi.* to act, do, etc. in opposition to; oppose

counter- [< L. *contra-,* against] *a combining form meaning:* 1. contrary to [*counterclockwise*] 2. in retaliation [*counterattack*] 3. complementary [*counterpart*]

coun′ter·act′ *vt.* to act against; neutralize —**coun′ter·ac′tion** *n.*

coun′ter·at·tack′ *n.* an attack made in opposition to another attack —*vt., vi.* to attack in opposition

coun′ter·bal′ance *n.* a weight, force, etc. that balances another —*vt., vi.* -anced, -anc·ing to be a counterbalance (to); offset

coun′ter·claim′ *n.* an opposing claim to offset another —*vt., vi.* (koun′tər klām′) to make a counterclaim (of)

coun′ter·clock′wise (-wīz) *adj., adv.* in a direction opposite to that in which the hands of a clock move

coun′ter·cul′ture *n.* the culture of those young people whose life style is opposed to the prevailing culture

coun′ter·es′pi·on·age′ *n.* actions to prevent or thwart enemy espionage

coun·ter·feit (koun′tər fit) *adj.* [< OFr. *contre-,* counter- + *faire,* make] 1. made in imitation of the genuine so as to defraud; forged 2. pretended; sham —*n.* an imitation made to deceive —*vt., vi.* 1. to make an imitation of (money, etc.) so as to defraud 2. to pretend —**coun′ter·feit′er** *n.*

count′er·man′ *n., pl.* -men a man who serves customers at the counter of a lunchroom or cafeteria

coun·ter·mand (koun′tər mand′) *vt.* [< L. *contra,* against + *mandare,* to command] to revoke or call back by a contrary order

coun′ter·pane′ (-pān′) *n.* [ult. < L. *culcita puncta,* embroidered quilt] a bedspread

coun′ter·part′ *n.* 1. a person or thing that closely resembles another 2. a copy or duplicate

coun′ter·point′ *n.* [< It.: see COUNTER- & POINT] 1. the art of adding related, independent melodies to a basic melody 2. such a composition

coun′ter·poise′ *n.* [see COUNTER² &

POISE] 1. a counterbalance 2. equilibrium —*vt.* **-poised', -pois'ing** to counterbalance

coun'ter·pro·duc'tive *adj.* having results contrary to those intended

coun'ter·rev'o·lu'tion *n.* a political movement to restore the system overthrown by a revolution —**coun'ter·rev'o·lu'tion·ar'y** *adj., n.*

coun'ter·sign' *n.* 1. a signature added to a previously signed document to confirm it 2. a secret signal given to identify oneself as to a sentry —*vt.* to confirm with one's own signature

coun'ter·sink' *vt.* **-sunk', -sink'ing** 1. to enlarge the top part of (a hole) for receiving the head of a bolt, screw, etc. 2. to sink (a bolt, etc.) into such a hole

coun'ter·ten'or (-ten'ər) *n.* 1. range of the highest male voice, above tenor 2. a singer with this range

coun'ter·weight' *n.* a counterbalance

count·ess (koun'tis) *n.* the wife or widow of a count or earl

count·less (kount'lis) *adj.* too many to count; innumerable; myriad

coun·try (kun'trē) *n., pl.* **-tries** [< VL. *contrata*, region] 1. an area; region 2. the whole territory, or the people, of a nation 3. the land of one's birth or citizenship 4. land with farms and small towns

country club a social club in or near a city, with a golf course, etc.

coun'try·man (-mən) *n., pl.* **-men** a man of one's own country

country music rural folk music, esp. of the Southern U.S.

coun'try·side' *n.* a rural region

coun·ty (koun'tē) *n., pl.* **-ties** [< ML. *comitatus*, jurisdiction of a count] an administrative district of a country or State, or its people

coup (kōō) *n., pl.* **coups** (kōōz) [Fr. < L. *colaphus*, a blow] a sudden, brilliantly successful move

‡**coup de grâce** (kōō də gräs') [Fr., lit., stroke of mercy] the blow, shot, etc. that brings death to a sufferer

‡**coup d'é·tat** (kōō dā tä') [Fr., lit., stroke of state] the sudden, forcible overthrow of a government

coupe (kōōp; *now rarely* kōō pā') *n.* [< Fr. *couper*, to cut] a closed, two-door automobile: also **coupé**

cou·ple (kup''l) *n.* [< L. *copula*, a link] 1. anything joining two things together; link 2. a pair of persons or things; esp., a man and woman who are engaged, married, or partners in a dance, game, etc. 3. [Colloq.] a few —*vt., vi.* **-pled, -pling** to link or unite

cou·plet (kup'lit) *n.* two successive rhyming lines of poetry

cou·pling (kup'liŋ) *n.* 1. a joining together 2. a mechanical device for joining parts or things together

cou·pon (kōō'pän, kyōō'-) *n.* [Fr. < *couper*, to cut] 1. a detachable certificate on a bond, presented for payment of interest 2. a certificate entitling one to a discount, gift, etc., or for use in ordering goods

cour·age (kur'ij) *n.* [< L. *cor*, heart] the quality of being brave; valor

cou·ra·geous (kə rā'jəs) *adj.* brave; valorous —**cou·ra'geous·ly** *adv.*

cou·ri·er (koor'ē ər, kur'-) *n.* [< L. *currere*, to run] 1. a messenger 2. a person hired to take care of hotel accommodations, etc. for a traveler

course (kôrs) *n.* [< L. *currere*, to run] 1. an onward movement; progress 2. a way, path, or channel 3. the direction taken 4. a regular mode of procedure or conduct [our wisest *course*] 5. a series of like things in order 6. a part of a meal served at one time 7. *Educ.* a) a complete series of studies b) any of the studies —*vi.* **coursed, cours'ing** 1. to run or race 2. to hunt with hounds —**in due course** in the usual sequence (of events) —**in the course of** during —**of course** 1. naturally 2. certainly

cours·er (kôr'sər) *n.* [Poet.] a graceful, spirited or swift horse

court (kôrt) *n.* [< L. *cohors*, enclosure] 1. an uncovered space surrounded by buildings or walls 2. a short street 3. a playing space, as for tennis 4. a) the palace, or the family, attendants, etc., of a sovereign b) a sovereign and his councilors, etc. as a governing body c) a formal assembly held by a sovereign 5. courtship; wooing 6. a) a judge or judges b) a place where trials, etc. are held c) a judicial assembly —*vt.* 1. to pay attention to (a person) so as to get something 2. to seek as a mate; woo 3. to try to get [to *court* favor] —*vi.* to carry on a courtship —**pay court to** to court, as for favor or love —**court'er** *n.*

cour·te·ous (kur'tē əs) *adj.* [see prec. & -EOUS] polite and gracious —**cour'te·ous·ly** *adv.*

cour·te·san, cour·te·zan (kôr'tə z'n) *n.* [see COURT] a prostitute

cour·te·sy (kur'tə sē) *n., pl.* **-sies** 1. courteous behavior 2. a polite or considerate act or remark

court'house' *n.* 1. a building housing law courts 2. a building housing offices of a county government

cour·ti·er (kôr'tē ər, -tyər) *n.* an attendant at a royal court

court'ly *adj.* **-li·er, -li·est** suitable for a king's court; dignified; elegant —**court'li·ness** *n.*

court'-mar'tial (-mär'shəl) *n., pl.* **courts'-mar'tial** 1. a military or naval court to try offenses against military law 2. a trial by such a court —*vt.* **-tialed** or **-tialled, -tial·ing** or **-tial·ling** to try by such a court

court'room' *n.* a room in which a law court is held

court'ship' *n.* the act, process, or period of courting, or wooing

court'yard' *n.* a space enclosed by walls, adjoining or in a large building

cous·in (kuz''n) *n.* [ult. < L. *com-* with + *soror*, sister] the son or daughter of one's uncle or aunt

‡**cou·tu·rier** (kōō tü ryā'; *E.* -toor'ē ā') *n.* [Fr.] a male designer of women's fashions —**cou·tu·riere'** (-ryer'; *E.* -ē er') *n.fem.*

cove (kōv) *n.* [< OE. *cofa*, cave] a small bay or inlet

cov·en (kuv′ən) *n.* [see CONVENE] a gathering or meeting of witches

cov·e·nant (kuv′ə nənt) *n.* [see CONVENE] an agreement; compact —*vt.* to promise by a covenant —*vi.* to make a covenant

cov·er (kuv′ər) *vt.* [< L. *co-*, intens. + *operire*, to hide] 1. to place something on or over 2. to extend over 3. to clothe 4. to conceal; hide 5. to shield 6. to include or deal with [to *cover* a subject] 7. to protect financially [to *cover* a loss] 8. to travel over 9. to point a firearm at 10. *Journalism* to get news, pictures, etc. of —*vi.* 1. to spread over, as a liquid does 2. to provide an excuse (*for*) —*n.* 1. anything that covers, as a lid, top, etc. 2. a shelter for protection 3. a tablecloth and setting 4. something used to hide one's real actions, etc. —**take cover** to seek shelter —**under cover** in secrecy or concealment

cov′er·age (-ij) *n.* the amount, extent, etc. covered by something

cov′er·all′ *n.* [usually *pl.*] a one-piece protective outer garment, often worn over regular clothing, as by mechanics

cover charge a fixed charge, as at a nightclub, besides food and drink cost

cover crop a crop, as clover, grown to keep soil fertile and uneroded

covered wagon a large wagon with an arched cover of canvas

cov′er·ing *n.* anything that covers

cov·er·let (kuv′ər lit) *n.* [< OFr. *covrir*, cover + *lit*, bed] a bedspread

cover story the article in a magazine that deals with the subject shown on the cover

cov·ert (kuv′ərt) *adj.* [see COVER] hidden or disguised —*n.* a protective shelter, as for game —**cov′ert·ly** *adv.*

cov·er-up′ *n.* something used for hiding one's real activities, etc.

cov·et (kuv′it) *vt., vi.* [< L. *cupiditas*, cupidity] to want ardently (something that another person has)

cov′et·ous (-əs) *adj.* tending to covet; greedy —**cov′et·ous·ness** *n.*

cov·ey (kuv′ē) *n., pl.* **-eys** [< OFr. *cover*, to hatch] a small flock of birds, esp. partridges or quail

cow¹ (kou) *n.* [< OE. *cu*] 1. the mature female of domestic cattle, valued for its milk 2. the mature female of certain other animals, as the elephant

cow² (kou) *vt.* [< ON. *kuga*, subdue] to make timid; intimidate

cow·ard (kou′ərd) *n.* [ult. < L. *cauda*, tail] one who lacks courage or is shamefully afraid —*adj.* cowardly

cow′ard·ice (-is) *n.* lack of courage

cow′ard·ly *adj.* of or like a coward —*adv.* in the manner of a coward —**cow′ard·li·ness** *n.*

cow′boy′ *n.* a ranch worker who herds cattle: also **cow′hand′**

cow·er (kou′ər) *vi.* [ME.] to crouch or huddle up, as from fear or cold; shrink; cringe

cow′hide′ *n.* 1. the hide of a cow 2. leather from it 3. a whip of this

cowl (koul) *n.* [< L. *cucullus*, hood] 1. *a*) a monk's hood *b*) a monk's cloak with a hood 2. the top part at the front of a car body, to which the windshield and dashboard are attached

cow′lick *n.* [< its looking as if licked by a cow] a tuft of hair that cannot easily be combed flat

cowl·ing (kou′liŋ) *n.* [see COWL] a metal covering for an airplane engine

co′-work′er *n.* a fellow worker

cow′poke′ *n.* [Colloq.] *same as* COWBOY

cow pony a pony used in herding cattle

cow·pox (kou′päks′) *n.* a disease of cows: vaccination with its virus gives temporary immunity to smallpox

cox·comb (käks′kōm′) *n.* [for *cock's comb*] a silly, vain, foppish fellow

cox·swain (käk′s'n, -swān′) *n.* [< *cock* (small boat) + SWAIN] one who steers a boat or racing shell

coy (koi) *adj.* [ME., quiet] 1. bashful; shy 2. pretending to be shy —**coy′ly** *adv.* —**coy′ness** *n.*

coy·o·te (kī ōt′ē, kī′ōt) *n.* [< Mex.-Ind.] a small wolf of W N.America

coz·en (kuz′'n) *vt., vi.* [ME.] to cheat; deceive —**coz′en·age** *n.*

co·zy (kō′zē) *adj.* **-zi·er, -zi·est** [Scot. < ?] warm and comfortable; snug —*n., pl.* **-zies** a padded cover for a teapot, to keep the tea hot —**co′zi·ly** *adv.* —**co′zi·ness** *n.*

CPA Certified Public Accountant

Cpl, Cpl. Corporal

CPO, C.P.O. Chief Petty Officer

cps, c.p.s. cycles per second

Cr *Chem.* chromium

crab (krab) *n.* [OE. *crabba*] 1. a crustacean with four pairs of legs and a pair of pincers 2. a peevish person —*vi.* **crabbed, crab′bing** [Colloq.] to complain

crab apple 1. a small, very sour apple 2. a tree bearing such apples

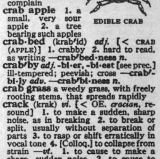
EDIBLE CRAB

crab·bed (krab′id) *adj.* [< CRAB (APPLE)] 1. crabby 2. hard to read, as writing —**crab′bed·ness** *n.*

crab′by *adj.* **-bi·er, -bi·est** [see prec.] ill-tempered; peevish; cross —**crab′bi·ly** *adv.* —**crab′bi·ness** *n.*

crab grass a weedy grass, with freely rooting stems, that spreads rapidly

crack (krak) *vi.* [< OE. *cracian*, re-sound] 1. to make a sudden, sharp noise, as in breaking 2. to break or split, usually without separation of parts 3. to rasp or shift erratically in vocal tone 4. [Colloq.] to collapse from strain —*vt.* 1. to cause to make a sharp, sudden noise 2. to cause to break or split 3. to break down (petroleum hydrocarbons) into the lighter hydrocarbons of gasoline, etc.

4. [Colloq.] to hit hard **5.** to solve **6.** [Colloq.] to break into or force open **7.** [Slang] to make (a joke) —*n.* **1.** a sudden, sharp noise **2.** a partial break; fracture **3.** a chink; crevice **4.** a cracking of the voice **5.** [Colloq.] a sudden, sharp blow **6.** [Colloq.] an attempt or try **7.** [Slang] a joke or gibe —*adj.* [Colloq.] excelling; first-rate —**crack down (on)** to become strict (with) —**cracked up to be** [Colloq.] believed to be —**crack up 1.** to crash **2.** [Colloq.] to break down physically or mentally —**get cracking** to start moving fast

crack'down' *n.* a resorting to strict or stricter discipline or punishment

cracked (krakt) *adj.* **1.** having a crack or cracks **2.** sounding harsh or strident **3.** [Colloq.] insane

crack'er *n.* **1.** a firecracker **2.** a thin, crisp wafer or biscuit

crack'er-jack' *adj.* [Slang] first-rate; excellent —*n.* [Slang] a first-rate person or thing

crack-le (krak''l) *vi.* **-led, -ling** [ME.] to make a series of slight, sharp, popping sounds —*n.* **1.** a series of such sounds **2.** a finely cracked surface, as on some pottery

crack'pot' *n.* [Colloq.] an eccentric person —*adj.* [Colloq.] eccentric

crack'up' *n.* **1.** a crash **2.** [Colloq.] a mental or physical breakdown

-cra·cy (krə sē) [< Gr. *kratos*, rule] a combining form meaning a (specified) type of government, rule by [*autocracy*]

cra·dle (krā'd'l) *n.* [OE. *cradol*] **1.** a baby's small bed, usually on rockers **2.** infancy **3.** the place of a thing's beginning **4.** anything like a cradle —*vt.* **-dled, -dling 1.** to place or rock in or as in a cradle **2.** to take care of in infancy

cra'dle-song' *n.* a lullaby

craft (kraft) *n.* [OE. *cræft*, power] **1.** a special skill or art **2.** an occupation requiring special manual skill **3.** the members of a skilled trade **4.** guile; slyness **5.** *pl.* **craft** a boat, ship, or aircraft

crafts-man (krafts'mən) *n., pl.* **-men** a skilled worker; artisan —**crafts'-man·ship'** *n.*

craft'y *adj.* **-i-er, -i-est** subtly deceitful; sly; cunning —**craft'i-ly** *adv.* —**craft'i-ness** *n.*

crag (krag) *n.* [< Celt.] a steep, rugged rock rising from a rock mass —**crag'gy** *adj.* **-gi-er, -gi-est**

cram (kram) *vt.* **crammed, cram'-ming** [OE. *crammian*] **1.** to pack full or too full **2.** to stuff; force **3.** to feed to excess —*vi.* **1.** to eat too much or too quickly **2.** [Colloq.] to prepare for an examination in a hurried, intensive way

cramp (kramp) *n.* [< OFr. *crampe*, bent] **1.** a sudden, painful contraction of muscles from chill, strain, etc. **2.** [*usually pl.*] abdominal spasms and pain —*vt.* **1.** to cause a cramp or cramps in **2.** to hamper; restrain

cramped (krampt) *adj.* **1.** confined or restricted **2.** irregular and crowded, as some handwriting

cran·ber·ry (kran'ber'ē, -bər i) *n., pl.* **-ries** [< Du. *kranebere*] **1.** a firm, sour, edible, red berry, the fruit of an evergreen shrub **2.** the shrub

crane (krān) *n.* [OE. *cran*] **1.** a large wading bird with very long legs and neck **2.** a machine for lifting and moving heavy weights, using a movable projecting arm or a horizontal traveling beam —*vt., vi.* craned, cran'ing to stretch (the neck)

cra·ni·um (krā'nē əm) *n., pl.* **-ni-ums, -ni·a** (-ə) [Gr. *kranion*] the skull, esp. the part containing the brain —**cra'ni·al** *adj.*

crank (krank) *n.* [ME.] **1.** a handle, etc. bent at right angles and connected to a machine shaft to transmit motion **2.** [Colloq.] an eccentric or peevish person —*vt.* to start or operate by a crank

crank'case' *n.* the metal casing that encloses the crankshaft of an engine

crank'shaft' *n.* a shaft with one or more cranks for transmitting motion

crank'y *adj.* **-i-er, -i-est 1.** peevish **2.** eccentric —**crank'i·ly** *adv.*

cran·ny (kran'ē) *n., pl.* **-nies** [< LL. *crena*, notch] a crevice; crack

crap (krap) *n.* [< OFr. *crape*, ordure] [Vulgar Slang] **1.** nonsense **2.** junk; trash —**crap'py** *adj.* **-pi-er, -pi-est**

crape (krāp) *n.* crepe; esp., black crepe as a sign of mourning

crap·pie (krap'ē) *n.* a small N.American sunfish

craps (kraps) *n.pl.* [with sing. v.] a gambling game played with two dice

crap-shoot-er (krap'shoot'ər) *n.* a gambler at craps

crash[1] (krash) *vi.* [ME.] **1.** to fall, collide, break, etc. with a loud noise; smash **2.** to collapse; fail —*vt.* **1.** to cause (a car, airplane, etc.) to crash **2.** to force with a crashing noise (*in, out, through,* etc.) **3.** [Colloq.] to get into (a party, etc.) without an invitation —*n.* **1.** a loud, sudden noise **2.** a crashing **3.** a sudden collapse, as of business —*adj.* [Colloq.] using all possible resources, effort, and speed [*a crash* program to build roads]

crash[2] (krash) *n.* [? < Russ. *krashenina*] a coarse linen cloth

crash'-land' *vt., vi.* to bring (an airplane) down in a forced landing, esp. without use of the landing gear —**crash landing**

crash pad [Slang] a temporary sleeping place or quarters

crass (kras) *adj.* [L. *crassus*] grossly stupid or dull —**crass'ly** *adv.*

-crat (krat) [see **-CRACY**] a combining form meaning member or supporter of (a specified kind of) government

crate (krāt) *n.* [L. *cratis*] a packing case made of slats of wood —*vt.* **crat'ed, crat'ing** to pack in a crate

cra·ter (krāt'ər) *n.* [< Gr. *kratēr*, bowl] **1.** a bowl-shaped cavity, as at the mouth of a volcano **2.** a pit made by an explosion, as of a bomb

cra·vat (krə vat') *n.* [Fr. < *Cravate*, Croatian: from scarves worn by Croatian soldiers] a necktie

crave (krāv) *vt.* **craved, crav'ing**

[OE. *crafian*] 1. to ask for earnestly; beg 2. to long for eagerly

cra·ven (krā'vən) *adj.* [< L. *crepare*, to creak] cowardly —*n.* a coward —**cra'ven·ly** *adv.* —**cra'ven·ness** *n.*

crav·ing (krā'viŋ) *n.* an intense and prolonged desire, as for food

craw (krô) *n.* [ME. *craue*] 1. the crop of a bird 2. the stomach

craw·fish (krô'fish') *n., pl.:* see FISH *same as* CRAYFISH

crawl (krôl) *vi.* [< ON. *krafla*] 1. to move slowly by dragging the body along the ground 2. to go on hands and knees; creep 3. to move slowly 4. to swarm (*with* crawling things) 5. to feel as if insects were crawling on the skin —*n.* 1. a slow movement 2. an overarm swimming stroke

crawl space a narrow space, as under a floor, allowing access to wiring, plumbing, etc.

crawl·y *adj.* -i·er, -i·est *same as* CREEPY

cray·fish (krā'fish') *n., pl.:* see FISH [< OHG.] 1. a freshwater crustacean somewhat like a little lobster 2. *same as* SPINY LOBSTER

CRAYFISH

cray·on (krā'ən, -än') *n.* [Fr., pencil < L. *creta*, chalk] 1. a small stick of white or colored chalk, waxy material, etc. used for drawing or writing 2. a drawing made with crayons —*vt.* to draw or color with crayons —**cray'on·ist** *n.*

craze (krāz) *vt., vi.* crazed, craz'ing [ME. *crasen*, to crack] to make or become insane —*n.* a fad

cra·zy (krā'zē) *adj.* -zi·er, -zi·est [< prec.] 1. unsound of mind; insane 2. [Colloq.] foolish; not sensible 3. [Colloq.] very enthusiastic or eager —*n., pl.* -zies [Slang] a crazy person **cra'zi·ly** *adv.* —**cra'zi·ness** *n.*

crazy bone *same as* FUNNY BONE

crazy quilt a patchwork quilt with no regular design

creak (krēk) *vi.* [echoic] to make, or move with, a harsh, squeaking sound —*n.* such a sound —**creak'y** *adj.* -i·er, -i·est —**creak'i·ly** *adv.* —**creak'i·ness** *n.*

cream (krēm) *n.* [< Gr. *chrisma*, ointment] 1. the oily, yellowish part of milk 2. a creamlike cosmetic ointment 3. the finest part 4. a yellowish white —*adj.* made of or with cream —*vt.* 1. to add cream to 2. to beat into a soft, smooth consistency —cream of creamed purée of —**cream'y** *adj.* -i·er, -i·est —**cream'i·ness** *n.*

cream cheese a soft, white cheese made of cream or of milk and cream **cream'er** *n.* a pitcher for cream **cream'er·y** (-ər ē) *n., pl.* -ies a place where dairy products are processed or sold

crease (krēs) *n.* [< ME. *creste*, ridge] 1. a line made by folding and pressing 2. a fold or wrinkle —*vt.* creased, creas'ing 1. to make a crease in 2. to wrinkle —*vi.* to become creased

cre·ate (krē āt') *vt.* -at'ed, -at'ing [< L. *creare*] 1. to cause to come into existence; make; originate 2. to bring about; give rise to; cause

cre·a·tion (krē ā'shən) *n.* 1. a creating or being created 2. the universe 3. anything created —**the Creation** God's creating of the world

cre·a·tive (krē āt'iv) *adj.* 1. creating or able to create 2. inventive 3. stimulating the inventive powers —**cre'a·tiv'i·ty** *n.*

cre·a·tor (krē āt'ər) *n.* [L.] 1. one who creates 2. [C-] God

crea·ture (krē'chər) *n.* [< L. *creatura*] a living being, animal or human

crèche (kresh) *n.* [Fr.] a display of the stable scene of Jesus' birth

cre·dence (krēd'ns) *n.* [< L. *credere*, believe] belief, esp. in the reports or testimony of another

cre·den·tial (kri den'shəl) *n.* [see prec.] [*usually pl.*] a letter or certificate showing one's right to a certain position or authority

cre·den·za (kri den'zə) *n.* [It.] a type of buffet, or sideboard

credibility gap 1. a disparity between a statement and the true facts 2. inability to have one's truthfulness or honesty accepted

cred·i·ble (kred'ə b'l) *adj.* [< L. *credere*, believe] that can be believed; reliable —**cred'i·bil'i·ty** *n.*

cred·it (kred'it) *n.* [< L. *credere*, believe] 1. belief; confidence 2. favorable reputation 3. praise or approval 4. a person or thing bringing approval or honor 5. [*pl.*] a list of acknowledgments of work done, as on a motion picture 6. a sum available to one, as in a bank account 7. the entry in an account of payment on a debt 8. trust in one's ability to meet payments 9. the time allowed for payment 10. a completed unit of study in a school —*vt.* 1. to believe; trust 2. to give credit to or commendation for 3. to give credit in a bank account, etc. —**credit one with** to ascribe to one —**do credit to** to bring honor to —**on credit** agreeing to pay later

cred'it·a·ble *adj.* deserving some credit or praise —**cred'it·a·bly** *adv.*

credit card a card entitling one to charge bills at certain places

cred·i·tor (kred'it ər) *n.* one to whom money is owed

credit union a cooperative association for pooling savings of members and making low-interest loans to them

cre·do (krē'dō, krā'-) *n., pl.* -dos [L., I believe] a creed

cred·u·lous (krej'oo ləs) *adj.* [< L. *credere*, believe] tending to believe too readily —**cre·du·li·ty** (krə dōō'lə tē) *n.* —**cred'u·lous·ly** *adv.*

creed (krēd) *n.* [< L. *credo*, lit., I believe] 1. a brief statement of religious belief, esp. one accepted as authoritative by a church 2. any statement of belief, principles, etc.

creek (krēk, krik) *n.* [< ON. *-kriki*, a winding] a small stream —**up the creek** [Slang] in trouble

creel (krēl) *n.* [< L. *cratis*, wickerwork] a wicker basket for holding fish

creep (krēp) *vi.* crept, creep'ing [OE. *creopan*] 1. to move with the body close to the ground, as on hands and knees 2. to move slowly or stealthily 3. to grow along the ground or a wall, as ivy —*n.* [Slang] an annoying or disgusting person —**make one's flesh creep** to make one feel fear, disgust, etc. —**the creeps** [Colloq.] a feeling of fear, repugnance, etc. —**creep'er** *n.*

creep'y *adj.* -i-er, -i-est having or causing a feeling of fear or disgust —**creep'i·ly** *adv.* —**creep'i·ness** *n.*

cre·mate (krē'māt) *vt.* -mat·ed, -mat·ing [< L. *cremare*] to burn (a dead body) to ashes —**cre·ma'tion** *n.*

cre·ma·to·ry (krē'mə tôr'ē) *n., pl.* -ries a furnace for cremating: also **cre'ma·to'ri·um** (-ē əm), *pl.* -ums, -a (-ə) —*adj.* of or for cremation

crème de menthe (krem' də mänt') [Fr.] a green, mint-flavored liqueur

crème fraîche (fresh') [Fr.] slightly fermented high-fat cream used on desserts and in sauces

cren·el·ate, cren·el·late (kren''l āt') *vt.* -el·at'ed or el·lat'ed, -el·at'ing or -el·lat'ing [< VL. *crena*, a notch] to furnish with battlements or with squared notches

Cre·ole (krē'ōl) *n.* [< Fr. < Port. *crioulo*, native] 1. a person descended from the original French settlers of Louisiana 2. a person of mixed Creole and Negro descent —*adj.* [*usually* c-] prepared with sautéed tomatoes, green peppers, onions, etc. [*creole* sauce]

cre·o·sote (krē'ə sōt') *n.* [< Gr. *kreas*, flesh + *sōzein*, save] an oily liquid with a pungent odor, distilled from wood tar or coal tar: used as an antiseptic and as a wood preservative

crepe, crêpe (krāp; *for 5, also* krep) *n.* [< Fr. < L. *crispus*, curly] 1. a thin, crinkled cloth of silk, rayon, wool, etc. 2. *same as* CRAPE 3. thin paper like crepe: also **crepe paper** 4. wrinkled soft rubber: also **crepe rubber** 5. a thin pancake, rolled and filled

crêpes su·zette (krāp' sooō zet'; *Fr.* krep') [Fr.] thin pancakes folded in orange sauce and served in flaming brandy

crept (krept) *pt. & pp.* of CREEP

cre·scen·do (krə shen'dō) *adj., adv.* [It. < L. *crescere*, grow] *Music* gradually increasing in loudness —*n., pl.* -dos a gradual increase in loudness

cres·cent (kres''nt) *n.* [< L. *crescere*, grow] 1. the shape of the moon in its first or last quarter 2. anything shaped like this —*adj.* shaped like a crescent

cress (kres) *n.* [OE. *cressa*] a plant of the mustard family, as water cress, whose leaves are used in salads

crest (krest) *n.* [< L. *crista*] 1. a

comb, tuft, etc. on the head of an animal or bird 2. a heraldic device, as on note paper, etc. 3. the top line or surface; summit 4. the highest point, level, degree, etc. —*vi.* to form or reach a crest —**crest'ed** *adj.*

crest'fall'en (-fôl'ən) *adj.* dejected, disheartened, or humbled

Crete (krēt) Gr. island in the E Mediterranean

cre·tin (krēt'n) *n.* [< Fr. *chrétien*, Christian, hence human being] a person suffering from cretinism

cre'tin·ism *n.* a congenital deficiency of thyroid secretion with resulting deformity and idiocy

cre·tonne (krē'tän, kri tän') *n.* [Fr. < *Creton*, village in Normandy] a heavy, printed cotton or linen cloth, used for curtains, slipcovers, etc.

cre·vasse (krə vas') *n.* [Fr., *crevice*] a deep crack, esp. in a glacier

crev·ice (krev'is) *n.* [< L. *crepare*, to rattle] a narrow opening caused by a crack or split; fissure

crew[1] (krōō) *n.* [< L. *crescere*, grow] a group of people working together [a road *crew*, a ship's *crew*] —**crew'man** (-mən) *n., pl.* -men

crew[2] (krōō) *alt. pt.* of CROW[2]

crew cut a man's cropped haircut

crew·el (krōō'əl) *n.* [< ?] a loosely twisted, worsted yarn used in embroidery —**crew'el·work'** *n.*

crib (krib) *n.* [OE., ox stall] 1. a rack or box for fodder 2. a small bed with high sides, for a baby 3. an enclosure for storing grain 4. an underwater structure serving as a pier, water intake, etc. 5. [Colloq.] a translation or other aid used dishonestly in doing schoolwork —*vt.* cribbed, crib'bing 1. to confine 2. to furnish with a crib 3. [Colloq.] to plagiarize —*vi.* [Colloq.] to use a crib for schoolwork

crib·bage (krib'ij) *n.* [< prec. + -AGE] a card game in which the object is to form combinations for points

crick (krik) *n.* [< ? ON.] a painful cramp in the neck or back

crick·et[1] (krik'it) *n.* [< OFr. *criquer*, to creak] a leaping insect related to the grasshoppers

crick·et[2] (krik'it) *n.* [prob. < MDu. *cricke*, a stick] an outdoor game played by two teams of eleven men each, using a ball, bats, and wickets

cried (krīd) *pt. & pp.* of CRY

cri·er (krī'ər) *n.* one who shouts out news, announcements, etc.

crime (krīm) *n.* [< L. *crimen*, offense] 1. an act committed or omitted in violation of a law 2. a sin

Cri·me·a (krī mē'ə) peninsula in SW U.S.S.R., extending into the Black Sea

crim·i·nal (krim'ə n'l) *adj.* 1. being a crime 2. relating to or guilty of crime —*n.* a person guilty of a crime —**crim'i·nal'i·ty** (-nal'ə tē) *n.* —**crim'i·nal·ly** *adv.*

crim·i·nol·o·gy (krim'ə näl'ə jē) *n.* the scientific study of crime and criminals —**crim'i·nol'o·gist** *n.*

crimp (krimp) *vt.* [< MDu. *crimpen*, to wrinkle] 1. to press into narrow folds; pleat 2. to curl (hair) —*n.* 1. a crimping 2. anything crimped —**put a crimp in** [Colloq.] to hinder

crim·son (krim′z'n) n. [< Sans. *kṛmi*, insect] deep red —*adj.* deep-red —*vt.*, *vi.* to make or become crimson

cringe (krinj) *vi.* cringed, cring′ing [< OE. *cringan*, fall (in battle)] 1. to draw back, crouch, etc., as when afraid; cower 2. to fawn

crin·kle (kriŋ′k'l) *vt.*, *vi.* -kled, -kling [see prec.] 1. to wrinkle; ripple 2. to rustle, as crushed paper —**crin′kly** *adj.* -kli·er, -kli·est

crin·o·line (krin′'l in) n. [Fr. < It. < *crino*, horsehair + *lino*, linen] 1. a coarse, stiff cloth used as a lining in garments 2. *same as* HOOP SKIRT

crip·ple (krip′'l) n. [< OE. *creopan*, to creep] one who is lame or otherwise disabled —*vt.* -pled, -pling 1. to lame 2. to disable; impair

cri·sis (krī′sis) n., *pl.* -ses (-sēz) [L. < Gr. *krinein*, to separate] 1. the turning point in a disease, when it becomes clear whether the patient will recover 2. any crucial situation

crisp (krisp) *adj.* [< L. *crispus*, curly] 1. brittle; easily crumbled 2. sharp and clear 3. fresh and firm 4. bracing 5. curly and wiry Also **crisp′y** —**crisp′ly** *adv.* —**crisp′ness** n.

criss·cross (kris′krôs′) n. [ME. *Christcros*, Christ's cross] a mark or pattern made of crossed lines —*adj.* marked by crossing lines —*vt.* to mark with crossing lines —*vi.* to move crosswise —*adv.* 1. crosswise 2. awry

cri·ter·i·on (krī tir′ē ən) n., *pl.* -i·a (-ē ə), -i·ons [< Gr. *kritēs*, judge] a standard, rule, or test by which something can be judged

crit·ic (krit′ik) n. [< Gr. *krinein*, discern] 1. one who writes judgments of books, plays, music, etc. professionally 2. one who finds fault

crit′i·cal (-i k'l) *adj.* 1. tending to find fault 2. of critics or criticism 3. of or forming a crisis; crucial —**crit′i·cal·ly** *adv.*

crit′i·cism (-ə siz'm) n. 1. the act of making judgments, esp. of literary or artistic work 2. a review, article, etc. expressing such judgment 3. a finding fault 4. the art, principles, or methods of critics

crit′i·cize′ (-ə sīz′) *vi.*, *vt.* -cized′, -ciz′ing 1. to analyze and judge as a critic 2. to find fault (with) Brit. sp. **criticise** —**crit′i·ciz′a·ble** *adj.* —**crit′i·ciz′er** n.

cri·tique (kri tēk′) n. [Fr.] a critical analysis or review

crit·ter (krit′ər) n. [Dial.] a creature

croak (krōk) *vi.* [echoic] 1. to make a deep, hoarse sound [frogs *croak*] 2. [Slang] to die —*vt.* to utter in deep, hoarse tones —n. a croaking sound

Cro·a·tia (krō ā′shə) n. a republic of Yugoslavia —**Cro·a′tian** *adj.*, n.

cro·chet (krō shā′) n. [Fr., a small hook] needlework done with one hooked needle —*vt.*, *vi.* -cheted′

(-shād′), -chet′ing to do, or make by, crochet —**cro·chet′er** n.

crock (kräk) n. [OE. *crocca*] an earthenware pot or jar —**crock′er·y** n.

crocked (kräkt) *adj.* [< *crock*, to disable] [Slang] drunk

croc·o·dile (kräk′ə dīl′) n. [< Gr. *krokodilos*, lizard] a large, lizardlike reptile of tropical streams, having a long, narrow head with massive jaws

cro·cus (krō′kəs) n., *pl.* -cus·es, -ci (-sī) [< Gr. *krokos*, saffron] a spring-blooming plant of the iris family, with grasslike leaves and a yellow, purple, or white flower

Croe·sus (krē′səs) a wealthy king of ancient times —n. a very rich man

crois·sant (krə sänt′; Fr. krwä sän′) n. [Fr.] a crescent-shaped roll

Cro-Mag·non (krō mag′nən) *adj.* [< *Cro-Magnon* cave in France] of a prehistoric type of tall man on the European continent in the Stone Age

Crom·well (kräm′wel), **Oliver** 1599-1658; Eng. revolutionary leader and head of England (1653-1658)

crone (krōn) n. [< MDu. *kronje*, old ewe] an ugly, withered old woman

cro·ny (krō′nē) n., *pl.* -nies [< Gr. *chronios*, long-time] a close friend

crook (krook) n. [< ON. *krōkr*, hook] 1. a hook; hooked or curved staff, etc. 2. a bend or curve 3. [Colloq.] a swindler —*vt.*, *vi.* crooked (krookt). **crook′ing** to bend or curve

crook·ed (krookt; for 2 & 3 krook′id) *adj.* 1. having a crook 2. not straight; bent 3. dishonest —**crook′ed·ly** *adv.* —**crook′ed·ness** n.

crook′neck′ n. a squash with a long, curved neck

croon (krōōn) *vi.*, *vt.* [ME.] to sing or hum in a low, gentle tone —n. a low, gentle singing or humming —**croon′er** n.

crop (kräp) n. [OE. *croppa*, cluster] 1. a saclike part of a bird's gullet, in which food is stored before digestion 2. any agricultural product, growing or harvested 3. the yield of any product in one season or place 4. a group 5. the handle of a whip 6. a riding whip 7. hair cut close to the head —*vt.* cropped, crop′ping 1. to cut or bite off the tops or ends of 2. to reap 3. to cut short —**crop out** (or **up**) to appear unexpectedly

crop′-dust′ing n. the spraying of crops with pesticides from an airplane —**crop′-dust′** *vi.*, *vt.*

crop′per n. 1. one that crops 2. a sharecropper —**come a cropper** [Colloq.] to come to ruin; fail

cro·quet (krō kā′) n. [Fr.: see CROTCHET] an outdoor game in which the players use mallets to drive a ball through hoops in the ground

cro·quette (krō ket′) n. [Fr. < *croquer*, to crunch] a small mass of meat, fish, etc. fried in deep fat

cro·sier (krō′zhər) n. [< OFr. *croce*] the staff of a bishop or abbot

---

fat, āpe, cär; ten, ēven; is, bīte; gō, hôrn, tōōl, look; oil, out; up, fur; chin; she; thin, then; zh, leisure; ŋ, ring; ə for *a* in *ago;* ′, (ā′b'l); ē, Fr. coeur; ö, Fr. feu; Fr. mon; ü, Fr. duc; kh, G. ich, doch; ‡ foreign; < derived from

cross (krôs) *n.* [< L. *crux*] 1. an upright post with another across it, on which the ancient Romans executed people 2. [*often* C-] a representation of this as a symbol of the crucifixion of Jesus, and hence of Christianity 3. any trouble or affliction 4. any mark or design made by intersecting lines, bars, etc. 5. a crossing of varieties or breeds —*vt., vi.* 1. to make the sign of the cross upon 2. to place or lie across or crosswise 3. to intersect 4. to draw a line or lines across 5. to go or extend across 6. to meet and pass (each other) 7. to thwart; oppose 8. to interbreed (animals or plants) — *adj.* 1. lying or passing across 2. contrary; opposed 3. cranky; irritable 4. of mixed variety or breed —**cross off** (or **out**) to cancel as by drawing lines across —**cross one's mind** to come to mind briefly —**cross one's path** to meet one —**cross'ly** *adv.*

cross'bar' *n.* a bar, line, or stripe placed crosswise

cross'beam' *n.* a beam placed across another or from one wall to another

cross'bones' *n.* a representation of two bones placed across each other, under a skull, used to symbolize death

cross'bow' (-bō') *n.* a medieval weapon consisting of a bow set transversely on a wooden stock —**cross'bow'man** (-mən) *n., pl.* -men

cross'breed' *vt., vi.* -bred', -breed'ing to hybridize —*n.* a hybrid

cross'-coun'try *adj.* across open country or fields, as a race

cross'cut' *adj.* 1. used for cutting across [a crosscut saw] 2. cut across —*n.* a cut across —*vt., vi.* -cut', -cut'ting to cut across

cross'-ex·am'ine *vt., vi.* *Law* to question (a witness already questioned by the opposing side) to determine the validity of his testimony —**cross'-ex·am'i·na'tion** *n.*

cross'-eye' *n.* an abnormal condition in which the eyes are turned toward each other —**cross'-eyed'** *adj.*

cross'hatch' (-hach') *vt., vi.* to shade (a drawing) with two sets of parallel lines that cross each other

cross'ing *n.* 1. the act of passing across, thwarting, etc. 2. an intersection, as of streets 3. a place where a street, etc. may be crossed

cross'piece' *n.* a piece lying across another

cross'-pol'li·nate' *vt., vi.* -nat'ed, -nat'ing to transfer pollen from the anther of (one flower) to the stigma of (another) —**cross'-pol'li·na'tion** *n.*

cross'-pur'pose *n.* a contrary purpose —**at cross-purposes** having a misunderstanding as to each other's purposes

cross'-ref'er·ence *n.* a reference from one part of a book, etc. to another —**cross'-re·fer'** *vt., vi.*

cross'road' *n.* 1. a road that crosses another 2. [*usually pl.*] the place where roads intersect

cross section 1. *a*) a cutting through something *b*) a piece so cut off, or a representation of this 2. a representative part of a whole

cross'-town' *adj.* going across the main avenues of a city

cross'walk' *n.* a lane marked off for pedestrians to use crossing a street

cross'wise' *adv.* so as to cross; across: also **cross'ways'** (-wāz')

cross'word' puzzle an arrangement of numbered squares to be filled in with words whose definitions are given

crotch (kräch) *n.* [see CRUTCH] 1. a place where two branches fork from a tree 2. the place where the legs fork from the human body

crotch·et (kräch'it) *n.* [< OFr. *croc*, a hook] a peculiar whim or stubborn notion —**crotch'et·y** (-ē) *adj.*

crouch (krouch) *vi.* [< OFr. *croc*, a hook] 1. to stoop or bend low 2. to cringe —*n.* a stooping position

croup (krōōp) *n.* [< obs. *croup*, speak hoarsely] an inflammation of the respiratory passages, with labored breathing and hoarse coughing

crou·pi·er (krōō'pē ā') *n.* [Fr.] a person in charge of a gambling table

crou·ton (krōō'tän, krōō tän') *n.* [< Fr.: see CRUST] a small piece of toasted bread served in soup

crow[1] (krō) *n.* [OE. *crawa*] a large, glossy-black bird with a harsh call — **as the crow flies** in a straight, direct line —**eat crow** [Colloq.] to admit an error, recant, etc.

crow[2] (krō) *vi.* crowed, or for 1 **crew**, crowed, crow'ing [OE. *crawan*] 1. to make the shrill cry of a rooster 2. to boast in triumph 3. to make a sound of pleasure —*n.* a crowing sound

crow'bar' (krō'bär') *n.* a long, metal bar used as a lever for prying, etc.

crowd (kroud) *vi.* [OE. *crudan*] 1. to push one's way (*into*) 2. to throng —*vt.* 1. to press or push 2. to fill too full; cram —*n.* 1. a large number of people or things grouped closely 2. [Colloq.] a set; clique —**crowd'ed** *adj.*

crow'foot' *n., pl.* -foots' a plant of the buttercup family, with leaves resembling a crow's foot

crown (kroun) *n.* [< Gr. *korōnē*, wreath] 1. a wreath worn on the head in victory 2. a reward; honor 3. the head covering of a monarch 4. [*often* C-] *a*) the power of a monarch *b*) the monarch 5. the top part, as of the head, a hat, etc. 6. a British coin equal to five shillings 7. the highest quality, point, state, etc. of anything 8. the part of a tooth projecting beyond the gum line —*vt.* 1. to put a crown on 2. to cause to be a monarch 3. to honor 4. to be the highest part of 5. to put the finishing touch on

crown prince the male heir apparent to a throne

crow's-foot (krōz'foot') *n., pl.* -feet' any of the wrinkles that often develop at the outer corners of the eyes

crow's-nest (-nest') *n.* a lookout platform high on a ship's mast

cro·zier (krō'zhər) *n. same as* CROSIER

cru·cial (krōō'shəl) *adj.* [< L. *crux*, a cross] 1. decisive; critical 2. severe; trying —**cru'cial·ly** *adv.*

cru·ci·ble (krōō'sə b'l) *n.* [< ML. *crucibulum*, lamp, crucible] 1. a heat-resistant container for melting ores, metals, etc. 2. a severe trial

cru·ci·fix (kr$\overline{oo}$′sə fiks′) *n.* [< L. *crux*, a cross + *figere*, fasten] a representation of a cross with Jesus crucified on it: a Christian symbol

cru·ci·fix′ion (-fik′shən) *n.* 1. a crucifying 2. [C-] the crucifying of Jesus, or a representation of this

cru′ci·form′ *adj.* formed in a cross

cru′ci·fy′ (-fī′) *vt.* -**fied′**, -**fy′ing** [see CRUCIFIX] 1. to execute by nailing to a cross and leaving to die 2. to be very cruel to; torment

crude (kr$\overline{oo}$d) *adj.* [< L. *crudus*, raw] 1. in a raw or natural condition 2. lacking grace, taste, etc. 3. roughly made —**crude′ly** *adv.* —**cru·di·ty** (kr$\overline{oo}$′də tē), **crude′ness** *n.*

cru·el (kr$\overline{oo}$′əl) *adj.* [see prec.] causing pain and suffering; pitiless —**cru′el·ly** *adv.* —**cru′el·ty** *n.*, *pl.* -**ties**

cru·et (kr$\overline{oo}$′it) *n.* [< OFr. *crue*, earthen pot] a small glass bottle to hold vinegar, oil, etc. for the table

cruise (kr$\overline{oo}$z) *vi.* **cruised, cruis′ing** [< Du. *kruisen*, to cross] 1. to sail or drive about from place to place, as for pleasure or in search of something 2. to move at the most efficient speed for sustained travel —*vt.* to sail or journey over or about —*n.* a cruising voyage

cruise missile a long-range, jet-propelled winged bomb, launched from an airplane, submarine, or ship and guided by remote control

cruis′er *n.* 1. anything that cruises, as a police car 2. a fast warship smaller than a battleship

crul·ler (krul′ər) *n.* [Du. < *krullen*, to curl] a kind of twisted doughnut

crumb (krum) *n.* [< OE. *cruma*] 1. a small piece broken off, as of bread 2. any bit or scrap [*crumbs* of knowledge] —*vt.* Cooking to cover with crumbs —**crum·by** (krum′ē) *adj.*

crum·ble (krum′b'l) *vt.* -**bled, -bling** [freq. of prec.] to break into crumbs —*vi.* to fall to pieces —**crum′bly** *adj.* -**bli·er, -bli·est**

crum·my (krum′ē) *adj.* -**mi·er, -mi·est** [Slang] shabby, mean, etc.

crum·pet (krum′pit) *n.* [OE. *crompeht*] a batter cake baked on a griddle

crum·ple (krum′p'l) *vt., vi.* -**pled, -pling** [ME. *crumplen*] to crush together into wrinkles

crunch (krunch) *vt.* [echoic] to chew, press, grind, etc. with a noisy, crackling or crushing sound —*n.* 1. the act or sound of crunching 2. [Slang] a showdown or tight situation — **crunch′y** *adj.* -**i·er, -i·est**

crup·per (krup′ər, kr$\overline{oo}$p′-) *n.* [< OFr. *crope*, rump] a leather strap attached to a saddle or harness and passed under a horse's tail

cru·sade (kr$\overline{oo}$ sād′) *n.* [ult. < L. *crux*, a cross] 1. [*often* C-] any of the Christian military expeditions (11th-13th cent.) to recover the Holy Land from the Moslems 2. vigorous, concerted action for some cause, or against some abuse —*vi.* -**sad′ed, -sad′ing** to engage in a crusade —**cru·sad′er** *n.*

cruse (kr$\overline{oo}$z, kr$\overline{oo}$s) *n.* [OE.] a small container for water, oil, etc.

crush (krush) *vt.* [< OFr. *croisir*] 1. to press with force so as to break or put out of shape 2. to grind or pound into small bits 3. to subdue; overwhelm 4. to extract by squeezing —*vi.* to become crushed —*n.* 1. a crushing 2. a crowded mass of people 3. [Colloq.] an infatuation —**crush′er** *n.*

crust (krust) *n.* [< L. *crusta*] 1. the hard, outer part of bread 2. any dry, hard piece of bread 3. the pastry shell of a pie 4. any hard surface layer, as of snow 5. [Slang] insolence —*vt., vi.* to cover or become covered with a crust —**crust′y** *adj.* -**i·er, -i·est**

crus·ta·cean (krus tā′shən) *n.* [see prec.] any of a class of arthropods, including shrimps, crabs, lobsters, etc., that have a hard outer shell

crutch (kruch) *n.* [OE. *crycce*] 1. a staff with a top crosspiece that fits under the armpit, used to aid the lame in walking 2. any prop or support

crux (kruks) *n.* [L., a cross] 1. a difficult problem 2. the essential or deciding point

cry (krī) *vi.* **cried, cry′ing** [< L. *quiritare*, to wail] 1. to utter a loud sound, as in pain, fright, etc. 2. to sob and shed tears; weep 3. to plead or clamor (*for*) 4. to utter its characteristic call: said of an animal —*vt.* 1. to utter loudly; shout 2. to call out (wares for sale, etc.) —*n., pl.* **cries** 1. a loud vocal sound; call; shout 2. a plea; appeal 3. a fit of weeping 4. the characteristic call of an animal —**a far cry** a great distance or difference

cry′ba′by *n., pl.* -**bies** one who complains constantly, in a childish way

cry·o·gen·ics (krī′ə jen′iks) *n.* [< Gr. *kryos*, cold + -GEN + -ICS] the science that deals with the production of very low temperatures and their effect on the properties of matter

cry·o·sur·ger·y (krī′ə sur′jə rē) *n.* [< Gr. *kryos*, cold + SURGERY] surgery that destroys tissues by freezing

crypt (kript) *n.* [< Gr. *kryptein*, hide] an underground vault, esp. one under a church, used for burial

cryp·tic (krip′tik) *adj.* 1. hidden or mysterious; baffling 2. obscure and curt —**cryp′ti·cal·ly** *adv.*

cryp·to·gram (krip′tə gram′) *n.* [see ff.] a message in code or cipher

cryp·tog·ra·phy (krip täg′rə fē) *n.* [< Gr. *kryptos*, hidden + -GRAPHY] the art of writing or deciphering messages in code —**cryp·tog′ra·pher** *n.*

crys·tal (kris′t'l) *n.* [< Gr. *kryos*, frost] 1. a clear, transparent quartz 2. *a*) a very clear, brilliant glass *b*) articles of such glass, as goblets 3. anything clear like crystal, as the covering over a watch face 4. a solidified form of a substance having plane faces arranged in a symmetrical, three-dimensional pattern —*adj.* 1. of crystal 2. like crystal; clear

crys·tal·line (-tə lin) *adj.* 1. made of crystals 2. like crystal in clearness, structure, etc.

crys·tal·lize (-līz') *vi., vt.* -lized', -liz'ing 1. to become or cause to become crystalline 2. to take on or cause to take on a definite form —**crys'tal·li·za'tion** *n.*

cs., case(s)

CST, C.S.T. Central Standard Time

CT Connecticut

ct. 1. *pl.* **cts.** cent 2. court

Cu [L. *cuprum*] *Chem.* copper

cu., cubic

cub (kub) *n.* [< ? OIr. *cuib*, whelp] 1. a young fox, bear, lion, whale, etc. 2. a youth or novice

Cu·ba (kyōō'bə) island country in the West Indies, south of Fla.: 44,218 sq. mi.; pop. 7,833,000 —**Cu'ban** *adj., n.*

cub·by·hole (kub'ē hōl') *n.* [< Brit. dial. *cub*, little shed + HOLE] a small, enclosed space: also *cub'by*

cube (kyōōb) *n.* [< Gr. *kybos*] 1. a solid with six equal, square sides 2. the product obtained by multiplying a given number by its square [the *cube* of 3 is 27] —*vt.* cubed, cub'ing 1. to obtain the cube of (a number) 2. to cut or shape into cubes —**cub'er** *n.*

cube root the quantity of which a given quantity is the cube [the *cube root* of 8 is 2]

cu·bic (kyōō'bik) *adj.* 1. having the shape of a cube: also **cu'bi·cal** 2. having three dimensions: a cubic foot is the volume of a cube one foot in length, width, and breadth

cu·bi·cle (kyōō'bi k'l) *n.* [< L. *cubare*, lie down] a small compartment

cub·ism (kyōō'biz'm) *n.* a school of modern art characterized by the use of cubes and other geometric forms —**cub'ist** *adj., n.* —**cu·bis'tic** *adj.*

cu·bit (kyōō'bit) *n.* [< L. *cubitum*] an ancient measure of length, about 18 to 22 inches

cuck·old (kuk'ld) *n.* [see ff.] a man whose wife has committed adultery —*vt.* to make a cuckold of —**cuck'old·ry** (-rē) *n.*

cuck·oo (kōō'kōō', kook'ōō) *n.* [< OFr. *cucu*, echoic] 1. a gray-brown bird with a long, slender body: one species lays eggs in the nests of other birds 2. its call —*adj.* [Slang] crazy

cu·cum·ber (kyōō'kum bər) *n.* [< L. *cucumis*] a long, green-skinned fruit with firm, white flesh, used in salads or preserved as pickles

cud (kud) *n.* [OE. *cudu*] a mouthful of swallowed food regurgitated from the first stomach of cattle and other ruminants and chewed again

cud·dle (kud''l) *vt.* -dled, -dling [< ?] to embrace and fondle —*vi.* to lie close and snug

cud·dly (-lē) *adj.* -dli·er, -dli·est that invites cuddling; lovable: also **cud'dle·some** (-səm)

cudg·el (kuj'əl) *n.* [OE. *cycgel*] a short, thick stick or club —*vt.* -eled

or -elled, -el·ing or -el·ling to beat with a cudgel

cue¹ (kyōō) *n.* [< *q* (? for L. *quando*, when) found in 16th-c. plays] 1. a signal in dialogue, etc. for an actor's entrance or speech 2. any signal to do something 3. a hint —*vt.* cued, cu'ing or cue'ing to give a cue to

cue² (kyōō) *n.* [var. of QUEUE] a long, tapering rod used in billiards and pool to strike the ball (cue ball)

cuff (kuf) *n.* [ME. *cuffe*, glove] 1. a band at the wrist end of a sleeve 2. a turned-up fold at the bottom of a trouser leg 3. a slap —*vt.* to slap — **off the cuff** [Slang] offhandedly — **on the cuff** [Slang] on credit

cuff link a pair of linked buttons, etc. for fastening a shirt cuff

cui·sine (kwi zēn') *n.* [Fr. < L. *coquere*, to cook] 1. a style of cooking or preparing food 2. the food prepared, as at a restaurant

cul-de-sac (kul'də sak') *n., pl.* -sacs' [Fr., lit., bottom of a sack] a blind alley

cu·li·nar·y (kyōō'lə ner'ē) *adj.* [< L. *culina*, kitchen] of cooking

cull (kul) *vt.* [< L. *colligere*, collect] to pick out; select and gather —*n.* something picked out for rejection as not being up to standard

cul·len·der (kul'ən dər) *n.* same as COLANDER

cul·mi·nate (kul'mə nāt') *vi.* -nat'ed, -nat'ing [< L. *culmen*, peak] to reach its highest point or climax — **cul'mi·na'tion** *n.*

cu·lotte (koo lät', kyoo-) *n.* [Fr. < L. *culus*, posterior] [often *pl.*] a women's garment consisting of trousers made to resemble a skirt

cul·pa·ble (kul'pə b'l) *adj.* [< L. *culpa*, fault] deserving blame —**cul'pa·bil'i·ty** *n.* —**cul'pa·bly** *adv.*

cul·prit (kul'prit) *n.* [< early law Fr. *culpable*, guilty + *prit*, ready (to prove)] a person accused, or found guilty, of a crime

cult (kult) *n.* [< L. *cultus*, care] 1. a system of religious worship 2. devoted attachment to a person, principle, etc. 3. a sect —**cult'ism** *n.* —**cult'ist** *n.*

cul·ti·vate (kul'tə vāt') *vt.* -vat'ed, -vat'ing [see prec.] 1. to prepare (land) for growing crops; till 2. to grow (plants) 3. to loosen the soil and kill weeds around (plants) 4. to develop or improve [cultivate your mind] 5. to seek to become familiar with —**cul'ti·va·ble** (-və b'l), **cul'ti·vat'a·ble** *adj.* —**cul'ti·va'tor** *n.*

cul·ti·va'tion *n.* 1. the act of cultivating 2. refinement, or culture

cul·ture (kul'chər) *n.* [see CULT] 1. cultivation of the soil 2. a growth of bacteria, etc. in a prepared substance 3. improvement of the mind, manners, etc. 4. development by special training or care 5. the skills, arts, etc. of a given people in a given period; civilization —*vt.* -tured, -tur·ing to cultivate —**cul'tur·al** *adj.* —**cul'tur·al·ly** *adv.*

cul·vert (kul'vərt) *n.* [< ?] a drain or conduit under a road or embankment

cum·ber (kum′bər) *vt.* [< OFr. *combre*, barrier] to hinder; hamper

cum′ber·some (-səm) *adj.* burden-some; unwieldy: also **cum′brous** (-brəs)

cum·in (kum′in) *n.* [< Gr. *kyminon*] 1. a plant of the parsley family 2. its aromatic fruits, used for flavoring

cum·mer·bund (kum′ər bund′) *n.* [< Ar.-Per. *kamar*, loins + Per. *band*, band] a wide sash worn as a waist-band, esp. with men's formal dress

cu·mu·la·tive (kyōōm′yə lāt′iv, -lə tiv) *adj.* [< L. *cumulus*, a heap] in-creasing in effect, size, etc. by succes-sive additions

cu·mu·lus (kyōōm′yə ləs) *n., pl.* -li′ (-li′) [L., a heap] a thick cloud type with upper parts resembling domes

cu·ne·i·form (kyōō nē′ə fôrm′) *adj.* [< L. *cuneus*, a wedge + -FORM] wedge-shaped, as the characters used in ancient Assyrian and Babylonian inscriptions —*n.* cuneiform characters

cun·ning (kun′iŋ) *adj.* [< ME. *cunnen*, know] 1. sly; crafty 2. made with skill 3. pretty; cute —*n.* slyness; craftiness —**cun′ning·ly** *adv.*

cup (kup) *n.* [< L. *cupa*, tub] 1. a small, bowl-shaped container for beverages, usually with a handle 2. a cup and its contents 3. a cupful 4. anything shaped like a cup —*vt.* **cupped, cup′ping** to shape like a cup

cup·board (kub′ərd) *n.* a closet or cabinet with shelves for cups, plates, food, etc.

cup′cake′ *n.* a small cake

cup′ful′ *n., pl.* -fuls′ as much as a cup will hold; specif., eight ounces

Cu·pid (kyōō′pid) *Rom. Myth.* the god of love —*n.* [c-] a representation of Cupid as a winged boy with bow and arrow

cu·pid·i·ty (kyōō pid′ə tē) *n.* [< L. *cupere*, to desire] strong desire for wealth; avarice

cu·po·la (kyōō′pə lə) *n.* [It. < L. *cupa*, a tub] a small dome, etc. on a roof —**cu′po·laed** (-ləd) *adj.*

cu·pro·nick·el (kyōō′prō nik′'l) *n.* [< L. *cuprum*, copper + NICKEL] an alloy of copper and nickel, used in coins

cur (kur) *n.* [prob. < ON. *kurra*, to growl] 1. a dog of mixed breed; mongrel 2. a contemptible person

cu·rate (kyoor′it) *n.* [< L. *cura*, care] a clergyman who assists a vicar or rector —**cu′ra·cy** (-ə sē) *n., pl.* -cies

cur·a·tive (kyoor′ə tiv) *adj.* having the power to cure —*n.* a remedy

cu·ra·tor (kyoo rāt′ər) *n.* [< L. *curare*, take care of] a person in charge of a museum, library, etc. —**cu·ra·to·ri·al** (kyoor′ə tôr′ē əl) *adj.*

curb (kurb) *n.* [< L. *curvus*, bent] 1. a chain or strap attached to a horse's bit, used to check the horse 2. any-thing that checks or restrains 3. a stone or concrete edging along a street 4. a market dealing in stocks and bonds not listed on the exchange —*vt.* to restrain; control

curb service service offered to cus-tomers who wish to remain in their cars

curb′stone′ *n.* the stone or stones making up a curb: also **curb′ing**

curd (kurd) *n.* [< ME. *crud*, coagu-lated substance] the coagulated part of soured milk from which cheese is made

cur·dle (kur′d'l) *vt., vi.* -dled, -dling to form into curd; coagulate

cure (kyoor) *n.* [< L. *cura*, care] 1. a healing or being healed 2. a remedy 3. a method of medical treatment —*vt.* **cured, cur′ing** 1. to restore to health 2. to get rid of (an ailment, evil, etc.) 3. *a)* to preserve (meat), as by salting or smoking *b)* to process (tobacco, leather, etc.), as by drying or aging —**cur′a·ble** *adj.* —**cur′er** *n.*

cu·ré (kyoo rā′) *n.* [Fr. < L. *cura*, care] in France, a parish priest

cure′-all′ *n.* something supposed to cure all ailments or evils

cu·ret·tage (kyoor′ə täzh′) *n.* [Fr.] the process of cleaning or scraping the walls of a body cavity with a spoonlike instrument

cur·few (kur′fyōō) *n.* [< OFr. *covrefeu*, lit., cover fire: orig. a nightly signal to cover fires and retire] a time in the evening beyond which children, etc. may not appear on the streets

Cu·ri·a (kyoor′ē ə) *n., pl.* -ri·ae′ (-ē′) [L.] the official body governing the Roman Catholic Church under the authority of the Pope

Cu·rie (kyoo rē′, kyoor′ē), **Marie** 1867–1934; Pol. chemist in France

cu·ri·o (kyoor′ē ō′) *n., pl.* -os′ [contr. of ff.] an unusual or rare article

cu·ri·os·i·ty (kyoor′ē äs′ə tē) *n., pl.* -ties 1. a desire to learn 2. inquisi-tiveness 3. anything curious or rare

cu·ri·ous (kyoor′ē əs) *adj.* [< L. *curiosus*, careful] 1. eager to learn or know 2. prying or inquisitive 3. unusual; strange —**cu′ri·ous·ly** *adv.*

curl (kurl) *vt.* [< ME. *crul*, curly] 1. to twist (esp. hair) into ringlets 2. to cause to bend around —*vi.* to become curled —*n.* 1. a ringlet of hair 2. any-thing with a curled shape —**curl′er** *n.* —**curl′y** *adj.* -i·er, -i·est

cur·lew (kur′lōō) *n.* [echoic] a large, brownish wading bird with long legs

curl·i·cue (kur′li kyōō′) *n.* [< CURLY + CUE²] a fancy curve, flourish, etc.

curl·ing (kur′liŋ) *n.* a game played on ice by sliding a flat stone at a mark

CURLEW

cur·rant (kur′ənt) *n.* [ult. < *Corinth*, an-cient Gr. city] 1. a small, seedless raisin from the Mediterranean region 2. *a)* the sour berry of several species of hardy shrubs *b)* the shrub

cur·ren·cy (kur'ən sē) n., pl. **-cies** [see ff.] 1. circulation 2. the money in circulation in any country 3. general use or acceptance

cur·rent (kur'ənt) adj. [< L. currere, to run] 1. now going on; of the present time 2. circulating 3. commonly accepted; prevalent —n. 1. a flow of water or air in a definite direction 2. a general tendency 3. the flow or rate of flow of electricity in a conductor —**cur'rent·ly** adv.

cur·ric·u·lum (kə rik'yə ləm) n., pl. **-la** (-lə), **-lums** [L., course for racing] a course of study in a school —**cur·ric'u·lar** adj.

cur·ry¹ (kur'ē) vt. **-ried**, **-ry·ing** [< OFr. correier, put in order] 1. to rub down and clean the coat of (a horse, etc.) with a comb or brush 2. to prepare (tanned leather) 3. to try to win (favor) by flattery, etc.

cur·ry² (kur'ē) n., pl. **-ries** [Tamil kari] 1. a powder prepared from various spices, or a sauce made with this 2. a stew made with curry —vt. **-ried**, **-ry·ing** to prepare with curry

cur'ry·comb' n. a comb with teeth or ridges, for currying a horse —vt. to use a currycomb on

curse (kurs) n. [OE. curs] 1. a calling on God or the gods to bring evil on some person or thing 2. a profane or obscene oath 3. evil coming as if in answer to a curse —vt. **cursed** or **curst**, **curs'ing** 1. to call evil down on 2. to swear at 3. to afflict —vi. to swear; blaspheme —**be cursed with** to suffer from

curs·ed (kur'sid, kurst) adj. 1. under a curse 2. deserving to be cursed; evil; hateful

cur·sive (kur'siv) adj. [ult. < L. currere, to run] designating writing in which the letters are joined

cur·so·ry (kur'sər ē) adj. [< L. cursor, runner] hastily, often superficially, done —**cur'so·ri·ly** adv.

curt (kurt) adj. [L. curtus, short] brief, esp. to the point of rudeness —**curt'ly** adv. —**curt'ness** n.

cur·tail (kər tāl') vt. [< L. curtus, short] to cut short; reduce —**cur·tail'ment** n.

cur·tain (kur't'n) n. [< L. cors, a court] a piece of cloth, etc. hung at a window, in front of a stage, etc. to decorate or conceal —vt. to provide or shut off as with a curtain

curtain call 1. a call, usually by applause, for performers to return to the stage 2. such a return

curt·sy (kurt'sē) n., pl. **-sies** [var. of COURTESY] a woman's bow of greeting, respect, etc. made by bending the knees and dipping the body slightly —vi. **-sied**, **-sy·ing** to make a curtsy Also **curtsey**

cur·va·ceous (kər vā'shəs) adj. [< CURVE] [Colloq.] having a full, shapely figure: said of a woman

cur·va·ture (kur'və chər) n. 1. a curving or being curved 2. a curve

curve (kurv) n. [L. curvus, bent] 1. a line having no straight part; bend with no angles 2. something shaped like.

or moving in, a curve —vt., vi. **curved**, **curv'ing** 1. to form a curve by bending 2. to move in a curve —**curv'y** adj. **-i·er**, **-i·est**

cush·ion (koosh'ən) n. [< ML. coxinum] 1. a pillow or pad 2. a thing like this in shape or use 3. anything that absorbs shock —vt. to provide with a cushion

cush·y (koosh'ē) adj. **-i·er**, **-i·est** [< Per. khūsh, pleasant] [Slang] easy; comfortable

cusp (kusp) n. [L. cuspis] a point, as on the chewing surface of a tooth

cus·pi·dor (kus'pə dôr') n. [< Port. cuspir, to spit] a spittoon

cuss (kus) n., vt., vi. [Colloq.] same as CURSE

cus·tard (kus'tərd) n. [< L. crusta, crust] 1. a mixture of eggs, milk, sugar, etc., boiled or baked 2. a somewhat similar frozen mixture: in full **frozen custard**

cus·to·di·an (kus tō'dē ən) n. 1. one who has the custody or care of something; caretaker 2. a janitor

cus·to·dy (kus'tə dē) n. [< L. custos, a guard] a guarding or keeping safe; care —**in custody** under arrest —**cus·to·di·al** (kəs tō'dē əl) adj.

cus·tom (kus'təm) n. [< L. com-, intens. + suere, be accustomed] 1. a usual practice; habit 2. social conventions carried on by tradition 3. [pl.] duties or taxes imposed on imported goods 4. the regular patronage of a business —adj. 1. made to order 2. making things to order

cus'tom·ar'y (-tə mer'ē) adj. in keeping with custom; usual; habitual —**cus'tom·ar'i·ly** adv.

cus'tom-built' adj. built to order, to the customer's specifications

cus'tom·er n. a person who buys, esp. one who buys regularly

cus'tom-house' n. an office where customs or duties are paid

cus'tom·ize (-īz') vt., vi. **-ized'**, **-iz'ing** to make according to individual specifications

cus'tom-made' adj. made to order, to the customer's specifications

cut (kut) vt. **cut**, **cut'ting** [ME. cutten] 1. to make an opening in with a sharp-edged instrument; gash 2. to pierce sharply so as to hurt 3. to have (a new tooth) grow through the gum 4. to divide into parts with a sharp-edged instrument; sever 5. to hew 6. to reap 7. to reduce; curtail 8. to trim; pare 9. to divide (a pack of cards) 10. to make or do as by cutting 11. to hit (a ball) so that it spins 12. [Colloq.] to pretend not to recognize (a person) 13. [Colloq.] to be absent from (a school class, etc.) 14. [Slang] to stop —vi. 1. to pierce, sever, gash, etc. 2. to take cutting (pine cuts easily) 3. to go (across or through) 4. to swing a bat, etc. (at a ball) 5. to change direction suddenly —adj. 1. that has been cut 2. made or formed by cutting —n. 1. a cutting or being cut 2. a stroke or opening made by a sharp-edged instrument 3. a piece cut off, as of meat 4. a reduction 5. a passage or channel cut out 6. the style in which a thing is cut 7. an act, remark, etc. that hurts one's feelings 8. a block or plate engraved for printing, or the impression from this 9. [Colloq.] an unauthorized absence from school, etc. 10. [Slang] a share, as of profits —**cut and dried** 1. arranged beforehand 2. lifeless; dull —**cut down** (on) to reduce; lessen —**cut it out** [Colloq.] to stop what one is doing —**cut off** 1. to sever 2. to stop abruptly; shut off —**cut out for** suited for —**cut up** 1. to cut into pieces 2. [Slang] to clown, joke, etc.

cu·ta·ne·ous (kyōō tā′nē əs) *adj.* [< L. *cutis*, skin] of or on the skin

cut′a·way′ *n.* a man's formal coat cut so as to curve back to the tails

cut′back′ *n.* a reduction or discontinuance, as of production

cute (kyōōt) *adj.* cut′er, cut′est [< ACUTE] [Colloq.] 1. clever; shrewd 2. pretty or attractive, esp. in a dainty way —**cute′ly** *adv.* —**cute′ness** *n.*

cut·i·cle (kyōōt′i k'l) *n.* [L. *cuticula*, skin] 1. the outer layer of the skin 2. hardened skin as at the base and sides of a fingernail

cut·lass (kut′ləs) *n.* [< L. *culter*, knife] a short, thick, curved sword

cut·ler·y (kut′lər ē) *n.* [< L. *culter*, knife] cutting implements, as knives; often, specif., eating implements

cut·let (kut′lit) *n.* [< L. *costa*, a rib] 1. a small slice of meat from the ribs or leg 2. a small, flat croquette of chopped meat or fish

cut′off′ *n.* 1. a road, etc. that is a shortcut 2. any device for shutting off the flow of a fluid, a connection, etc.

cut′-rate′ *adj.* selling or on sale at a lower price

cut·ter (kut′ər) *n.* 1. a person or thing that cuts 2. a small, swift vessel 3. a small, light sleigh

cut′throat′ *n.* a murderer —*adj.* 1. murderous 2. merciless; ruthless

cut·ting (kut′iŋ) *n.* a shoot cut away from a plant for rooting or grafting —*adj.* 1. that cuts; sharp 2. chilling or piercing 3. sarcastic; wounding

cut·tle·fish (kut′'l fish′) *n.*, *pl.*: see FISH [OE. *cudele*] a sea mollusk with ten sucker-bearing arms and a hard internal shell (cuttlebone)

cwt. hundredweight

-cy (sē) [< Gr. *-kia*] a suffix meaning: 1. quality, condition, or fact of being [*hesitancy*] 2. position, rank, or office of [*captaincy*]

cy·a·nide (sī′ə nīd′) *n.* a highly poisonous, white, crystalline compound

cy·ber·na·tion (sī′bər nā′shən) *n.* [CYBERN(ETICS) + -ATION] the use of computers coupled to automatic machinery to do routine, repetitive tasks, etc.

cy·ber·net·ics (sī′bər net′iks) *n.pl.* [*with sing. v.*] [< Gr. *kybernētēs*, helmsman] the comparative study of electronic computers and the human nervous system —**cy′ber·net′ic** *adj.*

cy·cla·mate (sik′lə māt′, sī′klə-) *n.* a salt of an organic acid, esp. sodium or calcium salt with a sweet taste

cy·cla·men (sī′klə mən) *n.* [< Gr. *kyklaminos*] a plant of the primrose family with heart-shaped leaves

cy·cla·zo·cine (sī′klə zō′sēn) *n.* a pain-killing drug that blocks the effects of heroin or morphine

cy·cle (sī′k'l) *n.* [< Gr. *kyklos*, a circle] 1. *a)* a period of time within which a round of regularly recurring events is completed *b)* a complete set of such events 2. a series of poems or songs on one theme 3. a bicycle, motorcycle, etc. —*vi.* -cled, -cling to ride a bicycle, etc. —**cy·clic** (sī′klik) *adj.*

cy·clist (sī′klist) *n.* a cycle rider

cyclo- [< *kyklos*, circle] a combining form meaning of a circle or wheel

cy·clom·e·ter (sī kläm′ə tər) *n.* [prec. + -METER] an instrument that records the revolutions of a wheel for measuring distance traveled

cy·clone (sī′klōn) *n.* [< Gr. *kyklos*, circle] a storm with strong winds rotating about a center of low pressure

cy·clo·pe·di·a, **cy·clo·pae·di·a** (sī′klə pē′dē ə) *n.* same as ENCYCLOPEDIA

Cy·clops (sī′kläps) *n.*, *pl.* **Cy·clo·pes** (sī klō′pēz) *Gr. Myth.* any of a race of one-eyed giants

cy·clo·tron (sī′klə trän′) *n.* [CYCLO- + (ELEC)TRON] an apparatus for giving high energy to particles, as protons, etc.: used in atomic research

cyg·net (sig′nət) *n.* [< Gr. *kyknos*, swan] a young swan

cyl·in·der (sil′ən dər) *n.* [< Gr. *kylindein*, to roll] 1. a solid figure described by the edge of a rectangle rotated around the parallel edge as axis 2. anything with this shape; specif., *a)* the turning part of a revolver *b)* the piston chamber of an engine —**cy·lin·dri·cal** (sə lin′dri k'l) *adj.*

cym·bal (sim′b'l) *n.* [< Gr. *kymbē*, hollow of a vessel] *Music* a circular brass plate that makes a sharp, ringing sound when hit —**cym′bal·ist** *n.*

cyn·ic (sin′ik) *n.* a cynical person

cyn·i·cal (-i k'l) *adj.* [< Gr. *kyōn*, dog] 1. denying the sincerity of people's motives and actions 2. sarcastic, sneering, etc. —**cyn′i·cal·ly** *adv.*

cyn′i·cism (-ə siz′m) *n.* the attitude or beliefs of a cynic

cy·no·sure (sī′nə shoor′, sin′ə-) *n.* [< Gr. *kynosoura*, dog's tail] a center of attention or interest

cy·pher (sī′fər) *n.*, *vi.* Brit. var. of CIPHER

cy·press (sī′prəs) *n.* [< Gr. *kyparissos*] 1. an evergreen tree with cones and dark foliage 2. its wood

Cy·prus (sī′prəs) country on an island at the E end of the Mediter-

ranean: 3,572 sq. mi.; pop. 607,000
—**Cyp·ri·ot** (sip′rē ət) *adj., n.*
cyst (sist) *n.* [< Gr. *kystis*, sac] a sac-like structure in plants or animals, esp. one filled with diseased matter — **cyst·ic** (sis′tik) *adj.*
cystic fibrosis a children's disease in which there is fibrosis of the pancreas and respiratory infections
cy·tol·o·gy (sī täl′ə jē) *n.* [< Gr. *kytos*, a hollow + -LOGY] the branch of biology dealing with cells
C.Z., CZ Canal Zone
czar (zär) *n.* [< Russ. < L. *Caesar*] 1.

the title of any of the former emperors of Russia 2. an autocrat —**cza·ri·na** (zä rē′nə) *n.fem.*
Czech (chek) *n.* 1. a member of a Slavic people of central Europe 2. the West Slavic language of the Czechs 3. loosely, a native or inhabitant of Czechoslovakia —*adj.* of Czechoslo-vakia, its people, or their language: also **Czech′ish**
Czech·o·slo·va·ki·a (chek′ə slō vä′kē ə) country in C Europe: 49,367 sq. mi.; pop. 14,274,000 —**Czech′o·slo′-vak, Czech′o·slo·va′ki·an** *adj., n.*

D

D, d (dē) *n., pl.* **D's, d's** the fourth letter of the English alphabet
D (dē) *n.* 1. a Roman numeral for 500 2. a grade for below-average work 3. *Music* the second tone in the scale of C major
d. 1. day(s) 2. degree 3. diameter 4. died 5. [L. *denarii*] pence
D.A. District Attorney
dab (dab) *vt., vi.* **dabbed, dab′bing** [ME. *dabben*, to strike] 1. to touch lightly and quickly; pat 2. to put on (paint, etc.) with light, quick strokes —*n.* 1. a tap; pat 2. a soft or moist bit of something
dab·ble (dab′'l) *vi.* **-bled, -bling** [< Du. *dabben*, to strike] 1. to play in water, as with the hands 2. to do something superficially (with *in* or *at*)
Dac·ca (dak′ə) capital of Bangladesh: pop. 557,000
dace (dās) *n., pl.* **dace, dac′es** [< VL. *darsus*] a small freshwater fish of the carp family
dachs·hund (däks′hoond) *n.* [G. < *dachs*, badger + *hund*, dog] a small dog with a long body, short legs, and drooping ears
Da·cron (dā′krän, dak′rän) *a trade-mark for* a synthetic wrinkle-resistant fabric —*n.* [*also* d-] this fabric
dac·tyl (dak′t'l) *n.* [< Gr. *daktylos*, finger] a metrical foot of three syl-lables, one accented and two unac-cented —**dac·tyl′ic** (-til′ik) *adj.*
dad (dad) *n.* [< child's cry *dada*] [Colloq.] father: also **dad′dy, -dies**
dad·dy-long·legs′ *n., pl.* **-long′-legs′** an arachnid with long legs
da·do (dā′dō) *n., pl.* **-does** [It. < L. *datum*, a die] 1. the part of a pedestal between the cap and the base 2. the lower part of a wall if decorated differently from the upper part
dae·mon (dē′mən) *n.* [< Gr. *daimōn*] 1. *Gr. Myth.* a secondary deity 2. a guardian spirit 3. *same as* DEMON —**dae·mon·ic** (di män′ik) *adj.*
daf·fo·dil (daf′ə dil′) *n.* [< Gr. *asphodelos*] a narcissus with long leaves and yellow flowers
daf·fy (daf′ē) *adj.* **-fi·er, -fi·est** [< ME. *dafte*, daft] [Colloq.] crazy; silly —**daf′fi·ness** *n.*

daft (daft) *adj.* [< OE. (*ge*)*dæfte*, mild] 1. silly 2. insane
dag·ger (dag′ər) *n.* [< ML. *daggar-ius*] 1. a weapon with a short, pointed blade, used for stabbing 2. *Printing* a reference mark (†)
da·guerre·o·type (də ger′ə tīp′) *n.* [< L.J.M. *Daguerre*, 19th-c. Fr. in-ventor] an early kind of photograph made on a chemically treated plate—*vt.* -typed′, -typ′ing to photograph by this method
dahl·ia (dal′yə, däl′-) *n.* [< A. *Dahl*, 18th-c. Swed. botanist] a perennial plant with large, showy flowers
dai·ly (dā′lē) *adj.* done, happening, or published every (week)day —*n., pl.* **-lies** a daily newspaper —*adv.* every day
daily double a bet or betting pro-cedure in which a bettor wins by choosing both winners in two specified races on the same program
dain·ty (dān′tē) *n., pl.* **-ties** [< L. *dignitas*, worth] a delicacy —*adj.* **-ti·er, -ti·est** 1. delicious and choice 2. delicately pretty 3. *a)* of refined taste; fastidious *b)* squeamish — **dain′ti·ly** *adv.* —**dain′ti·ness** *n.*
dai·qui·ri (dak′ər ē) *n.* [after *Dai-quiri*, Cuban village] a cocktail made of rum, sugar, and lime or lemon juice
dair·y (der′ē) *n., pl.* **-ies** [ME. *daie*, dairymaid] 1. a place where milk and cream are made into butter, cheese, etc. 2. a farm that produces, or a store that sells, milk and milk products — **dair′y·man** (-mən) *n., pl.* **-men**
dair′y·ing *n.* the business of produc-ing or selling dairy products
da·is (dā′is) *n., pl.* **da′is·es** [< ML. *discus*, table] a raised platform
dai·sy (dā′zē) *n., pl.* **-sies** [OE. *dæges eage*, day's eye] a plant of the composite family, bearing flowers with white rays around a yellow disk
dale (dāl) *n.* [OE. *dæl*] a valley
Dal·las (dal′əs) city in NE Tex.: pop. 904,000
dal·ly (dal′ē) *vi.* **-lied, -ly·ing** [< OFr. *dalier*, to trifle] 1. to make love in a playful way 2. to deal carelessly (*with*); trifle 3. to waste time; loiter —**dal′li·ance** (-ē əns) *n.*

Dalmatian · 157 · dare

Dal·ma·tian (dal mā'shən) *n.* a large, short-haired dog with dark spots on a white coat

DALMATIAN

dam¹ (dam) *n.* [ME.] a barrier built to hold back flowing water —*vt.* **dammed, dam'ming 1.** to build a dam in **2.** to keep back or confine

dam² (dam) *n.* [see DAME] the female parent of any four-legged animal

dam·age (dam'ij) *n.* [< L. *damnum*] **1.** injury or harm resulting in a loss **2.** [*pl.*] *Law* money compensating for injury, loss, etc. —*vt.* **-aged, -ag·ing** to do damage to —**dam'age·a·ble** *adj.*

Da·mas·cus (də mas'kəs) capital of Syria: pop. 530,000

dam·ask (dam'əsk) *n.* [< It. < prec.] **1.** a reversible fabric in figured weave, used for table linen, etc. **2.** steel decorated with wavy lines **3.** deep pink or rose —*adj.* **1.** of or like damask **2.** deep-pink or rose

dame (dām) *n.* [< L. *domina*, lady] **1.** [D-] in Great Britain, a woman's title of honor **2.** [Slang] any woman

damn (dam) *vt.* **damned, damn'ing** [< L. *damnare*, condemn] **1.** to condemn to an unhappy fate or, *Theol.*, to hell **2.** to condemn as bad, inferior, etc. **3.** to swear at by saying "damn" —*n.* the saying of "damn" as a curse —*adj., adv.* [Colloq.] *clipped form of* DAMNED —*interj.* an expression of anger, etc.

dam·na·ble (dam'nə b'l) *adj.* **1.** deserving damnation **2.** deserving to be sworn at —**dam'na·bly** *adv.*

dam·na'tion (-nā'shən) *n.* a damning or being damned —*interj.* an expression of anger, etc.

damned (damd) *adj.* **1.** condemned, as to hell **2.** [Colloq.] deserving cursing; outrageous —*adv.* [Colloq.] very

Dam·o·cles (dam'ə klēz') *Gr. Legend* a man whose king seated him under a sword hanging by a hair to show him the perils of a ruler's life

Da·mon and Pyth·i·as (dā'mən ən pith'ē əs) *Classical Legend* two very devoted friends

damp (damp) *n.* [MDu., vapor] **1.** a slight wetness **2.** a harmful gas sometimes found in mines —*adj.* somewhat moist or wet —*vt.* **1.** to bank (a fire) **2.** to check or reduce —**damp'ness** *n.*

damp'-dry' *vt.* **-dried', -dry'ing** to dry (laundry) so that some moisture is retained —*adj.* designating or of laundry so treated

damp·en (dam'pən) *vt.* **1.** to make damp; moisten **2.** to deaden, depress, or reduce —*vi.* to become damp —**damp'en·er** *n.*

damp'er (-pər) *n.* **1.** anything that deadens or depresses **2.** a valve in a flue to control the draft **3.** a device to check vibration in piano strings

dam·sel (dam'z'l) *n.* [see DAME] [Archaic] a girl; maiden

dam·son (dam'z'n) *n.* [< DAMASCUS] a variety of small, purple plum

Dan. Danish

dance (dans) *vi.* **danced, danc'ing** [< OFr. *danser*] **1.** to move the body and the feet in rhythm, ordinarily to music **2.** to move lightly, rapidly, gaily, etc. —*vt.* **1.** to perform (a dance) **2.** to cause to dance —*n.* **1.** rhythmic movement, ordinarily to music **2.** a particular kind of dance **3.** the art of dancing **4.** a party for dancing **5.** a piece of music for dancing **6.** rapid movement —**danc'er** *n.*

dan·de·li·on (dan'də lī'ən) *n.* [< OFr. *dent*, tooth + *de*, of + *lion*, lion] a common weed with yellow flowers

dan·der (dan'dər) *n.* [< ?] [Colloq.] anger or temper

dan·dle (dan'd'l) *vt.* **-dled, -dling** [< ?] to dance (a child) up and down on the knee or in the arms

dan·druff (dan'drəf) *n.* [< earlier *dandro* + dial. *hurf*, scab] little scales of dead skin on the scalp

dan·dy (dan'dē) *n., pl.* **-dies** [< ?] **1.** a man overly attentive to his clothes and appearance **2.** [Colloq.] something very good —*adj.* **-di·er, -di·est** [Colloq.] very good; fine

Dane (dān) *n.* a native or inhabitant of Denmark

dan·ger (dān'jər) *n.* [ult. < L. *dominus*, a master] **1.** liability to injury, damage, loss, etc.; peril **2.** a thing that may cause injury, pain, etc.

dan'ger·ous *adj.* full of danger; unsafe —**dan'ger·ous·ly** *adv.*

dan·gle (dan'g'l) *vi.* **-gled, -gling** [< Scand.] to hang swinging loosely —*vt.* to cause to dangle —**dan'gler** *n.*

Dan·iel (dan'yəl) *Bible* a Hebrew prophet whose faith saved him in the lions' den

Dan·ish (dā'nish) *adj.* of Denmark, the Danes, or their language —*n.* **1.** the language of the Danes **2.** [*also* d-] rich, flaky pastry filled with fruit, cheese, etc.: in full **Danish pastry**

dank (dank) *adj.* [ME.] disagreeably damp —**dank'ly** *adv.* —**dank'ness** *n.*

dan·seuse (dän sooz') *n.* [Fr.] a woman dancer, esp. a ballet dancer

Dan·te (Alighieri) (dän'tā, dän'tē) 1265-1321; It. poet

Dan·ube (dan'yoob) river flowing from SW Germany into the Black Sea

dap·per (dap'ər) *adj.* [< ? MDu.] **1.** small and active **2.** trim; neat

dap·ple (dap''l) *adj.* [< ON. *depill*, a spot] marked with spots; mottled: also **dap'pled** —*vt.* **-pled, -pling** to cover with spots

Dar·da·nelles (där'də nelz') **W** strait separating the Balkan Peninsula from Asia Minor

dare (der) *vt., vi.* **dared** or archaic **durst, dared, dar'ing** [OE. *durran*] **1.** to have enough courage for (some act) **2.** to face (something) bravely **3.**

fat, āpe, cär; ten, ēven; is, bīte; gō, hôrn, tōōl, look; oil, out; up, fer; chin; she; thin, then; zh, leisure; ŋ, ring; ə for *a* in *ago;* ', (ā'b'l); ë, Fr. coeur; ö, Fr. feu; Fr. mon; ü, Fr. duc; kh, G. ich, doch; ‡ foreign; < derived from

to challenge (someone) to do something —n. a challenge —**dare** say to think probable —**dar′er** n.

dare′dev′il (-dev′′l) adj. bold and reckless —n. a bold, reckless person

dar′ing adj. fearless; bold —n. bold courage —**dar′ing·ly** adv.

dark (därk) adj. [OE. deorc] 1. entirely or partly without light 2. a) almost black b) not light in color 3. hidden 4. gloomy 5. evil 6. ignorant —n. 1. the state of being dark 2. night —**dark′ly** adv. —**dark′ness** n.

Dark Ages [< prec., adj. 6] the Middle Ages, esp. the earlier part

dark′en (-′n), vi. to make or become dark or darker —**dark′en·er** n.

dark horse [Colloq.] a little-known contestant thought unlikely to win

dark′room′ n. a darkened room for developing photographs

dar·ling (där′liŋ) n. [OE. deorling] a person much loved by another —adj. 1. very dear; beloved 2. [Colloq.] cute

darn¹ (därn) vt., vi. [< MFr. dial. darner] to mend (cloth, etc.) by sewing a network of stitches across the gap —n. a darned place in fabric

darn² (därn) vt., n., adj., adv., interj. [Colloq.] damn: a euphemism —**darned** adj., adv.

dar·nel (där′n′l) n. [< Fr. dial. darnelle] a weedy rye grass

dart (därt) n. [< OFr.] 1. a small, pointed missile for throwing or shooting 2. a sudden movement 3. a short, tapered seam —vt., vi. to send out or move suddenly and fast

Dar·von (där′vän) a trademark for a pain-killing drug containing an analgesic related to methadone

Dar·win (där′win), **Charles Robert** 1809–82; Eng. naturalist and propounder of theory of evolution

dash (dash) vt. [< Scand.] 1. to smash; destroy 2. to strike violently (against) 3. to throw or thrust (away, down, etc.) 4. to splash —vi. 1. to strike violently (against) 2. to rush —n. 1. a splash 2. a bit of something added 3. a rush 4. a short, fast race 5. spirit; vigor 6. the mark of punctuation (—) used to indicate a break, omission, etc. —**dash off** to do, write, etc. hastily —**dash′er** n.

dash′board′ n. a panel with instruments and gauges, as in an automobile

da·shi·ki (dä shē′kē) n. a loose-fitting, brightly colored robe modeled after an African tribal garment

dash′ing adj. 1. full of dash or spirit; lively 2. showy; striking —**dash′ing·ly** adv.

das·tard (das′tərd) n. [ME., a craven] a sneaky, cowardly evildoer

das′tard·ly adj. mean, cowardly, etc.

dat. dative

da·ta (dāt′ə, dat′ə) n.pl. [often with sing. v.] [see DATUM] facts or figures from which conclusions can be drawn

data base (or **bank**) a mass of data in a computer, arranged for rapid expansion, updating, and retrieval: also **da′ta·base′, da′ta·bank′** n.

data processing the handling of information esp. by a computer

date¹ (dāt) n. [< L. dare, give] 1. the time at which a thing happens, was made, etc. 2. the day of the month 3. a) an appointment b) a social engagement with a person of the opposite sex c) this person —vt. dat′ed, dat′ing 1. to mark (a letter, etc.) with a date 2. to find out or give the date of 3. to make seem old-fashioned 4. to have social engagements with —vi. 1. to belong to a definite period in the past 2. to date persons of the opposite sex —**out of date** old-fashioned —**up to date** modern —**dat′er** n.

date² (dāt) n. [< Gr. daktylos, lit., a finger] the sweet, fleshy fruit of a tall palm tree (**date palm**)

date′line′ n. the date and place of writing or issue, as given in a line in a newspaper story, etc.

dating bar a bar frequented by persons seeking casual acquaintances, as for sexual purposes

da·tive (dāt′iv) n. [see DATE¹] the case expressing an indirect object

da·tum (dāt′əm, dat′əm) n. [L., what is given] sing. of DATA

daub (dôb) vt., vi. [< L. de-, intens. + albus, white] 1. to cover or smear with sticky, soft matter 2. to paint badly —n. 1. anything daubed on 2. a daubing stroke 3. a poorly painted picture —**daub′er** n.

daugh·ter (dôt′ər) n. [OE. dohtor] 1. a girl or woman as she is related to either or both parents 2. a female descendant —**daugh′ter·ly** adj.

daugh′ter-in-law′ n., pl. **daugh′ters-in-law′** the wife of one's son

Dau·mier (dō myā′), **Ho·no·ré** (ô nô rā′) 1809–79; Fr. painter

daunt (dônt) vt. [< L. domare, tame] to frighten or dishearten

daunt′less adj. that cannot be daunted, intimidated, etc.; fearless —**daunt′less·ly** adv. —**daunt′less·ness** n.

dau·phin (dô′fin) n. [Fr., dolphin] the eldest son of the king of France: a title used from 1349 to 1830

dav·en·port (dav′ən pôrt′) n. [< ?] a large couch or sofa

Da·vid (dā′vid) Bible the second king of Israel and Judah

Da·vis (dā′vis), **Jefferson** 1808–89; president of the Confederacy (1861–65)

dav·it (dav′it) n. [< OFr. dim. of David] either of a pair of curved uprights on a ship for suspending and for lowering a small boat

daw·dle (dôd′′l) vi., vt. -**dled,** -**dling** [< ?] to waste (time) in trifling; loiter —**daw′dler** n.

dawn (dôn) vi. [OE. dagian] 1. to begin to be day 2. to begin to appear, develop, etc. 3. to begin to be understood or felt —n. 1. daybreak 2. the beginning (of something)

day (dā) n. [OE. dæg] 1. the period of light between sunrise and sunset 2. the time (24 hours) that it takes the earth to revolve once on its axis 3. [also pl.] a period; era 4. a time of power, glory, etc. 5. daily work period [an 8-hour day] —**day after day** every day: also **day in, day out**

day'bed' *n.* a couch that can also be used as a bed

day'break' *n.* the time in the morning when light first appears

day care daytime care, as at a day nursery, or for the elderly as at a social agency

day'dream' *n.* **1.** a pleasant, dreamy series of thoughts **2.** a visionary scheme —*vi.* to have daydreams

day'light' *n.* **1.** the light of day **2.** dawn **3.** daytime **4.** understanding

day'light'-sav'ing time time that is one hour later than standard time

day nursery a place for daytime care of preschool children, as of working mothers: also **day-care center**

Day of Atonement Yom Kippur

day'time' *n.* the time between dawn and sunset

day'-to-day' *adj.* daily; routine

Day·ton (dāt''n) city in SW Ohio: pop. 204,000

daze (dāz) *vt.* **dazed, daz'ing** [< ON. *dasi,* tired] to stun or bewilder —*n.* a dazed condition —**daz'ed·ly** *adv.*

daz·zle (daz''l) *vt., vi.* **-zled, -zling** [< prec.] **1.** to overpower or be overpowered by the glare of bright light **2.** to surprise or arouse admiration with brilliant qualities, display, etc. —*n.* a dazzling —**daz'zler** *n.*

db decibel(s)

DC, D.C., d.c. direct current

D.C., DC District of Columbia

D.D. Doctor of Divinity

D.D.S. Doctor of Dental Surgery

DDT [< its chemical name] a powerful insecticide

de- [< Fr. *dé* or L. *de*] a *prefix meaning:* **1.** away from, off [*derail*] **2.** down [*decline*] **3.** entirely [*defunct*] **4.** reverse the action of [*decode*]

DE Delaware

de·ac·ces·sion (dē'ak sesh'ən) *vt.* to remove (a work of art) from a museum collection preparatory to selling it

dea·con (dēk''n) *n.* [< Gr. *diakonos,* servant] **1.** a cleric ranking just below a priest **2.** a church officer who helps the minister —**dea'con·ess** *n.fem.*

de·ac·ti·vate (dē ak'tə vāt') *vt.* **-vat'ed, -vat'ing** **1.** to make (an explosive, chemical, etc.) inactive **2.** *Mil.* to demobilize

dead (ded) *adj.* [OE.] **1.** no longer living **2.** without life **3.** deathlike **4.** lacking warmth, interest, brightness, etc. **5.** without feeling, motion, or power **6.** extinguished; extinct **7.** no longer used; obsolete **8.** unerring [a *dead shot*] **9.** complete [a *dead stop*] **10.** [Colloq.] very tired —*n.* the time of most cold, most darkness, etc. [the *dead of night*] —*adv.* **1.** completely **2.** directly —**the dead** those who have died

dead·beat' (ded'bēt') *n.* [Slang] one who tries to evade paying for things

dead·en (ded''n) *vt.* **1.** to lessen the vigor or intensity of; dull **2.** to make numb **3.** to make soundproof

dead end a street, alley, etc. closed at one end —**dead'-end'** *adj.*

dead heat a race in which two or more contestants finish even

dead letter **1.** a rule, law, etc. no longer enforced **2.** an unclaimed letter

dead'line' (-līn') *n.* the latest time by which something must be done

dead'lock' (-läk') *n.* a standstill resulting from the action of equal and opposed forces —*vt., vi.* to bring or come to a deadlock

dead'ly *adj.* **-li·er, -li·est** **1.** causing or likely to cause death **2.** implacable **3.** typical of death [*deadly pallor*] **4.** extreme **5.** very boring **6.** very accurate —*adv.* extremely —**dead'li·ness** *n.*

dead'pan' (-pan') *adj., adv.* [Slang] without expression; blank(ly)

Dead Sea inland body of salt water between Israel and Jordan

dead'wood' (-wood') *n.* anything useless or burdensome

deaf (def) *adj.* [OE.] **1.** unable to hear **2.** unwilling to respond, as to a plea —**deaf'ness** *n.*

deaf'en (-'n) *vt.* **1.** to make deaf **2.** to overwhelm with noise

deaf'-mute' (-myoot') *n.* a person who is deaf and has not learned to speak

deal¹ (dēl) *vt.* **dealt** (delt), **deal'ing** [OE. *dælen*] **1.** to portion out or distribute **2.** to give; administer (a blow, etc.) —*vi.* **1.** to have to do (*with*) [*science deals* with facts] **2.** to conduct oneself [*deal* fairly with others] **3.** to do business; trade (*with* or *in*) —*n.* **1.** the distributing of playing cards **2.** a business transaction **3.** an agreement, esp. when secret **4.** [Colloq.] treatment [a fair *deal*] —**deal'er** *n.*

deal² (dēl) *n.* [OE. *dæl,* a part] an indefinite amount —**a good** (or **great**) **deal 1.** a large amount **2.** very much

deal'er·ship' (-ship') *n.* a franchise to sell a product in a specified area

deal'ing *n.* **1.** way of acting **2.** [*usually pl.*] transactions or relations

dean (dēn) *n.* [< LL. *decanus,* chief of ten (monks, etc.)] **1.** the presiding official of a cathedral **2.** a college official in charge of students or faculty **3.** the senior member of a group

dean's list a list of the students at a college getting high grades

dear (dir) *adj.* [OE. *deore*] **1.** much loved **2.** esteemed: a polite form of address [*Dear Sir*] **3.** high-priced; costly **4.** earnest [our *dearest* wish] —*n.* a loved one; darling —**dear'ly** *adv.* —**dear'ness** *n.*

Dear John (letter) [Colloq.] a letter, as to a fiancé, breaking off a close relationship

dearth (durth) *n.* [< ME. *dere,* dear] scarcity or lack

death (deth) *n.* [OE.] **1.** the act or fact of dying **2.** the state of being dead **3.** end or destruction **4.** the cause of death —**death'like'** *adj.*

death′bed′ n. 1. the bed on which a person dies 2. a person's last hours

death′blow′ n. 1. a blow that kills 2. a thing fatal (to something)

death′less adj. that cannot die; immortal —**death′less·ly** adv.

death′ly adj. 1. causing death; deadly 2. like or characteristic of death —adv. extremely [deathly ill]

death′trap′ n. any unsafe structure

Death Valley dry, hot desert basin in E Calif. & S Nev.

deb (deb) n. [Colloq.] a debutante

de·ba·cle (di bäk″l, -bak′-) n. [< Fr. débâcler, break up] 1. a crushing defeat 2. a ruinous collapse

de·bar (dē bär′) vt. -barred′, -bar′ring [< Fr.: see DE- & BAR] 1. to keep (from) some right, etc. 2. to prevent or prohibit —de·bar′ment n.

de·bark (di bärk′) vt., vi. [< Fr.: see DE- & BARK²] to unload from or leave a ship or aircraft —de·bar·ka·tion (dē′bär kā′shən) n.

de·base (di bās′) vt. -based′, -bas′ing [DE- + BASE²] to make lower in value, dignity, etc. —de·base′ment n.

de·bate (di bāt′) vi., vt. -bat′ed, -bat′ing [< OFr.: see DE- & BATTER¹] 1. to discuss reasons for and against (something) 2. to take part in a debate with (a person) or about (a question) —n. 1. a discussion of opposing reasons 2. a formal contest of skill in reasoned argument —de·bat′a·ble adj. —de·bat′er n.

de·bauch (di bôch′) vt. [< OFr. desbaucher, seduce] to lead astray morally; corrupt —n. an orgy —de·bauch′er·y n., pl. -ies

deb·au·chee (di bôch′ee′; deb′ô chē′, -shē′) n. a dissipated person

de·ben·ture (di ben′chər) n. [< L.: see DEBT] 1. a voucher acknowledging a debt 2. an interest-bearing bond, often issued without security

de·bil·i·tate (di bil′ə tāt′) vt. -tat′ed, -tat′ing [< L. debilis, weak] to make weak; enervate

de·bil·i·ty (-tē) n., pl. -ties [see prec.] weakness; feebleness

deb·it (deb′it) n. [< L. debere, owe] 1. an entry in an account of money owed 2. the total of such entries —vt. to enter as a debit

deb·o·nair, deb·o·naire (deb′ə ner′) adj. [< OFr. de bon aire, lit., of good breed] 1. genial; affable 2. carefree; jaunty —deb′o·nair′ly adv.

de·brief (dē brēf′) vt. [DE- + BRIEF] to receive information from (a pilot, etc.) about a recent mission

de·bris, dé·bris (də brē′) n. [Fr. < OFr. desbrisier, break apart] bits and pieces of stone, rubbish, etc.

debt (det) n. [< L. debere, owe] 1. something owed to another 2. the condition of owing [to be in debt]

debt′or (-ər) n. one who owes a debt

de·bug (dē bug′) vt. -bugged′, -bug′ging [Slang] 1. to correct defects in 2. to find and remove hidden electronic listening devices from

de·bunk (di buŋk′) vt. [DE- + BUNK²] [Colloq.] to expose the false or exaggerated claims, etc. of

De·bus·sy (də bü sē′; E. deb′yoo sē′), **Claude** 1862–1918; Fr. composer

de·but, dé·but (di byōō′, dā′byōō) n. [Fr. < débuter, to lead off] 1. a first public appearance 2. the formal introduction of a girl into society

deb·u·tante (deb′yoo tänt′, deb′yoo tänt′) n. [Fr.] a girl making a debut into society

Dec. December

deca- [< Gr. deka, ten] a combining form meaning ten: also **dec-**

dec·ade (dek′ād) n. [< Gr. deka, ten] a period of ten years

dec·a·dence (dek′ə dəns, di kād′ns) n. [< L. de-, from + cadere, to fall] a decline; as in morals, art, etc.; deterioration —dec′a·dent adj., n.

de·caf·fein·at·ed (dē kaf′ə nāt′id) adj. with caffeine removed

de·cal·co·ma·ni·a (di kal′kə mā′ nē ə) n. [< Fr. < L. calcare, to tread + Gr. mania, madness] a picture or design transferred from prepared paper to glass, wood, etc.: also **de·cal**

Dec·a·logue, Dec·a·log (dek′ə lôg′) n. [see DECA- & -LOGUE] [sometimes d-] same as TEN COMMANDMENTS

de·camp (di kamp′) vi. [< Fr.: see DE- & CAMP] 1. to break camp 2. to go away suddenly and secretly

de·cant (di kant′) vt. [< Fr. < L. de-, from + canthus, tire of a wheel] to pour off (a liquid) gently without stirring up the sediment

de·cant·er n. a decorative glass bottle for serving wine, etc.

de·cap·i·tate (di kap′ə tāt′) vt. -tat′ed, -tat′ing [< L. de-, off + caput, head] to behead —de·cap′i·ta′tion n.

DECANTER

de·cath·lon (di kath′län) n. [DEC- + Gr. athlon, contest] an athletic contest in which each contestant takes part in ten track and field events

de·cay (di kā′) vi. [see DECADENCE] 1. to lose strength, prosperity, etc. gradually; deteriorate 2. to rot 3. to undergo radioactive disintegration —vt. to cause to decay —n. 1. deterioration 2. a rotting or rottenness

de·cease (di sēs′) n. [< L. de-, from + cedere, go] death —vi. -ceased′, -ceas′ing to die

de·ceased′ adj. dead —the deceased the dead person or persons

de·ceit (di sēt′) n. 1. a deceiving or lying 2. a lie 3. deceitful quality

de·ceit′ful adj. 1. apt to lie or cheat 2. deceptive —de·ceit′ful·ly adv.

de·ceive (di sēv′) vt., vi. -ceived′, -ceiv′ing [< L. de-, from + capere, take] to make (a person) believe what is not true; mislead —de·ceiv′er n. —de·ceiv′ing·ly adv.

de·cel·er·ate (dē sel′ə rāt′) vt., vi. -at′ed, -at′ing [DE- + (AC)CELERATE] to reduce the speed (of); slow down —de·cel′er·a′tion n.

De·cem·ber (di sem′bər) n. [< L. decem, ten: tenth month in Rom. calendar] the twelfth and last month of the year, having 31 days

de·cen·cy (dē′s'n sē) *n.*, *pl.* **-cies** a being decent; propriety, courtesy, etc.

de·cen·ni·al (di sen′ē əl) *adj.* [< L. *decem*, ten + *annus*, year] 1. of or for ten years 2. occurring every ten years

de·cent (dē′s'nt) *adj.* [< L. *decere*, befit] 1. proper and fitting 2. not obscene 3. respectable 4. adequate [*decent* wages] 5. fair and kind —**de′cent·ly** *adv.*

de·cen·tral·ize (dē sen′trə līz′) *vt.* **-ized′, -iz′ing** to break up a concentration of (governmental authority, industry, etc.) and distribute more widely —**de·cen′tral·i·za′tion** *n.*

de·cep·tion (di sep′shən) *n.* 1. a deceiving or being deceived 2. an illusion or fraud —**de·cep′tive** *adj.*

dec·i·bel (des′ə bel′) *n.* [< L. *decem*, ten + A.G. BELL] a unit for measuring relative loudness of sound

de·cide (di sīd′) *vt.* **-cid′ed, -cid′ing** [< L. *de-*, off + *caedere*, to cut] 1. to end (a contest, dispute, etc.) by giving one side the victory 2. to reach a decision about; resolve —*vi.* to reach a decision —**de·cid′a·ble** *adj.*

de·cid′ed *adj.* 1. definite; clear-cut 2. determined —**de·cid′ed·ly** *adv.*

de·cid·u·ous (di sij′oo wəs) *adj.* [< L. *de-*, off + *cadere*, to fall] 1. falling off at a certain season, as some leaves or antlers 2. shedding leaves annually

dec·i·mal (des′ə m'l) *adj.* [< L. *decem*, ten] of or based on the number 10 —*n.* a fraction with a denominator of ten or some power of ten, shown by a point (**decimal point**) before the numerator (Ex.: .5 = 5/10)

dec·i·mate (des′ə māt′) *vt.* **-mat′ed, -mat′ing** [< L. *decem*, ten] to destroy or kill a large part of (lit., a tenth part of) —**dec′i·ma′tion** *n.*

de·ci·pher (di sī′fər) *vt.* [DE- + CIPHER] 1. *same as* DECODE 2. to make out the meaning of (a scrawl, etc.)

de·ci·sion (di sizh′ən) *n.* 1. the act of deciding or settling a dispute or question 2. the act of making up one's mind 3. a judgment or conclusion 4. determination; firmness of mind

de·ci·sive (di sī′siv) *adj.* 1. that settles a dispute, question, etc. 2. showing decision —**de·ci′sive·ly** *adv.*

deck¹ (dek) *n.* [prob. < MLowG. *verdeck*] 1. a floor of a ship 2. a pack of playing cards

deck² (dek) *vt.* [MDu. *decken*, to cover] to array or adorn

de·claim (di klām′) *vi.*, *vt.* [< L. *de-*, intens. + *clamare*, to cry] to recite or speak in a studied, dramatic, or impassioned way —**dec·la·ma·tion** (dek′lə mā′shən) *n.* —**de·clam·a·to·ry** (di klam′ə tôr′ē) *adj.*

dec·la·ra·tion (dek′lə rā′shən) *n.* 1. a declaring; announcement 2. a formal statement

de·clar·a·tive (di klar′ə tiv) *adj.* making a statement or assertion

de·clare (di kler′) *vt.* **-clared′, -clar′ing** [< L. *de-*, intens. + *clarus*,

clear] 1. to announce openly or formally 2. to show or reveal 3. to say emphatically 4. *Card Games* to establish by a successful bid —**de·clar′er** *n.*

de·clas·si·fy (dē klas′ə fī′) *vt.* **-fied′, -fy′ing** to make (secret documents) available to the public

de·clen·sion (di klen′shən) *n.* [see ff.] 1. a descent 2. a decline 3. *Gram.* the inflection of nouns, pronouns, or adjectives

de·cline (di klīn′) *vi.* **-clined′, -clin′ing** [< L. *de-*, from + *clinare*, to bend] 1. to bend or slope downward 2. to deteriorate 3. to refuse something —*vt.* 1. to cause to bend or slope downward 2. to refuse politely 3. *Gram.* to give the inflected forms of (a noun, pronoun, or adjective) —*n.* 1. a declining; a dropping, falling, decay, etc. 2. a period of decline 3. a downward slope —**dec·li·na·tion** (dek′lə nā′shən) *n.* —**de·clin′er** *n.*

de·cliv·i·ty (di kliv′ə tē) *n.*, *pl.* **-ties** [< L. *de-*, down + *clivus*, a slope] a downward slope

de·code (dē kōd′) *vt.* **-cod′ed, -cod′ing** to decipher (a coded message)

dé·col·le·té (dā kä l′ə tā′) *adj.* [Fr. < L. *de*, from + *collum*, neck] cut low so as to bare the neck and shoulders

de·col·o·ni·za·tion (dē kä l′ə nə zā′shən) *n.* a freeing or being freed from colonial status —**de·col′o·nize′** (-ə nīz′) *vt.*, *vi.* **-nized′, -niz′ing**

de·com·pose (dē′kəm pōz′) *vt.*, *vi.* **-posed′, -pos′ing** [< Fr.: see DE- & COMPOSE] 1. to break up into basic parts 2. to rot —**de′com·po·si′tion** (-käm pə zish′ən) *n.*

de·com·press (dē′kəm pres′) *vt.* to free from pressure, esp. from air pressure —**de′com·pres′sion** *n.*

de·con·gest·ant *n.* a medication that relieves congestion, as in the nose

de·con·struc·tion *n.* [< Fr.] a 20th-c. literary theory in which the text has no fixed meaning

de·con·tam·i·nate (-tam′ə nāt′) *vt.* **-nat′ed, -nat′ing** to rid of a harmful substance, as radioactive products

dé·cor, de·cor (dā kôr′) *n.* [Fr.] a decorative scheme, as of a room

dec·o·rate (dek′ə rāt′) *vt.* **-at′ed, -at′ing** [< L. *decus*, an ornament] 1. to adorn; ornament 2. to paint or wallpaper 3. to give a medal or similar honor to —**dec′o·ra·tive** (-ər ə tiv, -ə rāt′iv) *adj.* —**dec′o·ra′tor** *n.*

dec′o·ra′tion *n.* 1. a decorating 2. an ornament 3. a medal, etc.

Decoration Day Memorial Day

dec·o·rous (dek′ər əs, di kôr′əs) *adj.* having or showing decorum, good taste, etc. —**dec′o·rous·ly** *adv.*

de·co·rum (di kôr′əm) *n.* [< L. *decorus*, proper] 1. whatever is suitable or proper 2. propriety in behavior, speech, etc.

de·cou·page, dé·cou·page (dā′-kŏŏ pä zh′) *n.* [Fr.] the art of decorating a surface with paper cutouts

de·coy (di koi'; *for n. also* dē'koi) *n.* [< Du. *de kooi*, the cage] **1.** an artificial or trained bird, etc. used to lure game within gun range **2.** a thing or person used to lure into danger —*vt.* to lure into a trap

de·crease (di krēs'; *esp. for n.* dē'krēs) *vi., vt.* -creased', -creas'ing [< L. *de-*, from + *crescere*, grow] to become or make gradually less, smaller, etc.; diminish —*n.* **1.** a decreasing **2.** amount of decreasing

de·cree (di krē') *n.* [< L. *de-*, from + *cernere*, see] an official order or decision —*vt.* -creed', -cree'ing to order or decide by decree

de·crep·it (di krep'it) *adj.* [< L. *de-*, intens. + *crepare*, to creak] broken down or worn out by old age or long use —de·crep'i·tude' (-ə tōōd') *n.*

de·crim·i·nal·ize (dē krim'ə n'l īz') *vt.* -ized', -iz'ing to eliminate or reduce the penalties for (a crime)

de·cry (di krī') *vt.* -cried', -cry'ing [< Fr.: see DE- & CRY] to speak out against openly; denounce

ded·i·cate (ded'ə kāt') *vt.* -cat'ed, -cat'ing [< L. *de-*, intens. + *dicare*, proclaim] **1.** to set apart for, or devote to, a special purpose **2.** to address (a book, etc.) to someone as a sign of honor —ded'i·ca'tion *n.*

de·duce (di dōōs', -dyōōs') *vt.* -duced', -duc'ing [< L. *de-*, down + *ducere*, to lead] to infer or decide by reasoning —de·duc'i·ble *adj.*

de·duct (di dukt') *vt.* [see prec.] to take away or subtract (a quantity) —de·duct'i·ble *adj.*

de·duc'tion (-duk'shən) *n.* **1.** a deducting **2.** an amount deducted **3.** *a)* reasoning from the general to the specific *b)* a conclusion reached by such reasoning —de·duc'tive *adj.*

deed (dēd) *n.* [< OE. *dēd*] **1.** a thing done; act **2.** a feat of courage, skill, etc. **3.** a legal document which transfers a property —*vt.* to transfer (property) by deed —in deed in fact

deem (dēm) *vt., vi.* [OE. *deman*, to judge] to think, believe, or judge

de·em·pha·size (dē em'fə sīz') *vt.* -sized', -siz'ing to lessen the importance of —de·em'pha·sis (-sis) *n.*

deep (dēp) *adj.* [OE. *dēop*] **1.** extending far downward, inward, or backward **2.** hard to understand; abstruse **3.** serious; profound **4.** dark and rich [a *deep* red] **5.** absorbed by (with *in*) [*deep* in thought] **6.** great in degree; intense **7.** of low pitch [a *deep* voice] —*n.* a deep place —*adv.* far down, far back, etc. —the deep [Poet.] the ocean —deep'ly *adv.* —deep'ness *n.*

deep'en (-'n) *vt., vi.* to make or become deep or deeper

deep'freeze' *vt.* -froze' or -freezed', -fro'zen or -freezed', -freez'ing *same as* QUICK-FREEZE

deep'-fry' *vt.* -fried', -fry'ing to fry in a deep pan of boiling fat

deep'-root'ed *adj.* **1.** having deep roots **2.** firmly fixed

deep'-seat'ed *adj.* **1.** buried deep **2.** firmly fixed

deep'-six' *vt.* [< six fathoms] [Slang] to get rid of, as by throwing into water

deep space *same as* OUTER SPACE

deer (dir) *n., pl.* deer, deers [OE. *deor*, wild animal] a hoofed, cud-chewing animal, the male of which bears antlers that are shed annually

de·es·ca·late (dē es'kə lāt') *vi., vt.* -lat'ed, -lat'ing to reduce in scope, magnitude, etc. —de·es'ca·la'tion *n.*

de·face (di fās') *vt.* -faced', -fac'ing [see DE- & FACE] to spoil the look of; mar —de·face'ment *n.*

de fac·to (di fak'tō) [L.] actually existing but not officially approved

de·fal·cate (di fal'kāt) *vi.* -cat·ed, -cat·ing [< L. *de-*, from + *falx*, a sickle] to steal or misuse funds entrusted to one; embezzle —de·fal·ca·tion (dē'fal kā'shən) *n.*

de·fame (di fām') *vt.* -famed', -fam'ing [< L. *dis-*, from + *fama*, fame] to attack the reputation of; slander or libel —def·a·ma·tion (def'ə mā'shən) *n.* —de·fam·a·to·ry (di fam'ə tôr'ē) *adj.* —de·fam'er *n.*

de·fault (di fôlt') *n.* [< L. *de-*, away + *fallere*, fail] failure to do or appear as required; specif., failure to pay money due —*vi., vt.* **1.** to fail to do or pay when required **2.** to lose (a contest) by default —de·fault'er *n.*

de·feat (di fēt') *vt.* [< L. *dis-*, from + *facere*, do] **1.** to win victory over **2.** to bring to nothing; frustrate —*n.* a defeating or being defeated

de·feat'ist *n.* one who too readily accepts defeat —de·feat'ism *n.*

def·e·cate (def'ə kāt') *vi.* -cat'ed, -cat'ing [< L. *de-*, from + *faex*, dregs] to excrete waste matter from the bowels —def'e·ca'tion *n.*

de·fect (dē'fekt; *also, and for v. always,* di fekt') *n.* [< L. *de-*, from + *facere*, do] **1.** lack of something necessary for completeness **2.** an imperfection; fault —*vi.* to forsake a party, cause, etc., esp. so as to join the opposition —de·fec'tion *n.* —de·fec'tor *n.*

de·fec·tive (di fek'tiv) *adj.* having defects; imperfect; faulty

de·fend (di fend') *vt.* [< L. *de-*, away + *fendere*, to strike] **1.** to guard from attack; protect **2.** to support or justify **3.** *Law a)* to oppose (an action, etc.) *b)* to act as lawyer for (an accused) —de·fend'er *n.*

de·fend·ant (di fen'dənt) *n. Law* the person sued or accused

de·fense (di fens', dē'fens) *n.* **1.** a defending against attack **2.** something that defends **3.** justification by speech or writing **4.** *a)* the arguments of a defendant *b)* the defendant and his counsel Brit. sp. defence —de·fense'less *adj.* —de·fen'si·ble *adj.*

defense mechanism any thought process used unconsciously to protect oneself against painful feelings

de·fen·sive *adj.* **1.** defending **2.** of or for defense —*n.* a position of defense —de·fen'sive·ly *adv.*

de·fer¹ (di fur') *vt., vi.* -ferred', -fer'ring [see DIFFER] **1.** to postpone; delay **2.** to postpone the induction of

(a person) into the armed forces —
de·fer′ment n.

de·fer (di fur′) vi. **-ferred′, -fer′ring**
[< L. de-, down + ferre, to bear] to
yield with courtesy (to)

def·er·ence (def′ər əns) n. 1. a
yielding in opinion, judgment, etc.
2. courteous respect

def·er·en′tial (-ə ren′shəl) adj. showing deference; very respectful

de·fi·ance (di fi′əns) n. a defying;
open, bold resistance to authority —
de·fi′ant adj. —**de·fi′ant·ly** adv.

de·fi·cien·cy (di fish′ən sē) n. [< L.
de-, from + facere, do] 1. a being
deficient 2. pl. **-cies** a shortage

deficiency disease a disease due to
a lack of vitamins, minerals, etc. in
the diet

de·fi′cient (-ənt) adj. [see prec.] 1.
lacking in some essential; incomplete
2. inadequate in amount

def·i·cit (def′ə sit) n. [L. < deficere,
to lack] the amount by which a sum
of money is less than the required
amount

de·file¹ (di fil′) vt. **-filed′, -fil′ing** [<
OFr. defouler, tread underfoot] 1. to
make filthy 2. to profane; sully —
de·file′ment n. —**de·fil′er** n.

de·file² (di fil′, dē′fil) vi. **-filed′, -fil′-
ing** [< Fr. dé-, from + fil, a thread]
to march in single file —n. a narrow
passage, valley, etc.

de·fine (di fin′) vt. **-fined′, -fin′ing**
[< L. de-, from + finis, boundary] 1.
to determine the limits or nature of;
describe exactly 2. to state the meaning of (a word, etc.) —**de·fin′er** n.

def·i·nite (def′ə nit) adj. [see prec.]
1. having exact limits 2. precise in
meaning; explicit 3. certain; positive
4. Gram. limiting or specifying /"the"
is the definite article] —**def′i·nite·ly**
adv. —**def′i·nite·ness** n.

def·i·ni′tion (-nish′ən) n. 1. a
defining or being defined 2. a statement of the meaning of a word 3.
clarity of outline, sound, etc.

de·fin·i·tive (di fin′ə tiv) adj 1.
conclusive; final 2. most nearly complete 3. serving to define

de·flate (di flāt′) vt., vi. **-flat′ed,
-flat′ing** [DE- + (IN)FLATE] 1. to
collapse by letting out air or gas 2. to
lessen in size, importance, etc. 3. to
cause deflation (of currency)

de·fla·tion n. 1. a deflating 2. a
lessening of the amount of money in
circulation, making it rise in value

de·flect (di flekt′) vt., vi. [< L. de-,
from + flectere, to bend] to turn or
make go to one side —**de·flec′tion** n.
—**de·flec′tive** adj. —**de·flec′tor** n.

De·foe (di fō′), **Daniel** 1660?-1731;
Eng. writer

de·fo·li·ant (dē fō′lē ənt) n. [< L.
de-, from + folium, leaf] a chemical
spray that strips growing plants of
their leaves —**de·fo′li·ate′** (-āt′)
vt. **-at′ed, -at′ing**

de·form (di fôrm′) vt. [< L. de-,

from + forma, form] 1. to impair the
form of 2. to make ugly —**de·for-
ma·tion** (dē′fôr mā′shən, def′ər-) n.

de·formed′ adj. misshapen

de·form·i·ty (di fôr′mə tē) n., pl.
-ties 1. a deformed part, as of the
body 2. ugliness or depravity

de·fraud (di frôd′) vt. to take
property, rights, etc. from by fraud;
cheat —**de·fraud′er** n.

de·fray (di frā′) vt. [Fr. défrayer] to
pay (the cost or expenses) —**de·fray′-
a·ble** adj. —**de·fray′al** n.

de·frost (di frôst′) vt., vi. to rid or
get rid of frost or ice —**de·frost′er** n.

deft (deft) adj. [see DAFT] skillful;
dexterous —**deft′ly** adv.

de·funct (di funkt′) adj. [< L.
defungi, to finish] no longer existing;
dead or extinct

de·fy (di fi′) vt. **-fied′, -fy′ing** [<
LL. dis-, from + fidus, faithful] 1. to
resist boldly or openly 2. to dare to
do or prove something

de·gen·er·ate (di jen′ər it; for v.
-ə rāt′) adj. [< L. de-, from + genus,
race] 1. having sunk below a former
or normal condition, etc.; deteriorated
2. depraved —n. a degenerate person
—vi. **-at′ed, -at′ing** to lose former,
normal, or higher qualities —**de-
gen′er·a·cy** (-ə sē) n. —**de·gen′-
er·a′tion** n. —**de·gen′er·a·tive** adj.

de·grade (di grād′) vt. **-grad′ed,
-grad′ing** [< L. de-, down + gradus,
a step] 1. to demote 2. to lower in
quality, moral character, dignity, etc.;
debase, dishonor, etc. —**deg·ra·da-
tion** (deg′rə dā′shən) n.

de·gree (di grē′) n. [see prec.] 1. any
of the successive steps in a process 2.
social or official rank 3. extent,
amount, or intensity 4. a rank given
by a college or university to one who
has completed a course of study, or to
a distinguished person as an honor 5.
a grade of comparison of adjectives
and adverbs [the superlative degree]
6. Law the seriousness of a crime
[murder in the first degree] 7. a unit
of measure for angles or arcs, 1/360
of the circumference of a circle 8. a
unit of measure for temperature —**to
a degree** somewhat

de·hu·man·ize (dē hyōō′mə niz′)
vt. **-ized′, -iz′ing** to deprive of
human qualities; make machinelike
—**de·hu′man·i·za′tion** n.

de·hu·mid·i·fy (dē′hyōō mid′ə fi′)
vt. **-fied′, -fy′ing** to remove moisture
from (air, etc.) —**de·hu·mid′i-
fi′er** n.

de·hy·drate (dē hi′drāt) vt. **-drat-
ed, -drat·ing** to remove water from;
dry —vi. to lose water —**de·hy·dra′-
tion** n. —**de·hy′dra·tor** n.

de·ice (dē is′) vt. **-iced′, -ic′ing** to
melt ice from —**de·ic′er** n.

de·i·fy (dē′ə fi′) vt. **-fied′, -fy′ing**
[< L. deus, god + facere, make] 1. to
make a god of 2. to look upon as a god
—**de·i·fi·ca′tion** (-fi kā′shən) n.

fat, āpe, cär; ten, ēven; is, bīte; gō, hôrn, tōōl, look; oil, out; up, fur;
chin; she; thin, then; zh, leisure; ŋ, ring; ə for a in ago; ′, (ā′b'l); ë, Fr. coeur;
ö, Fr. feu; Fr. mon; ü, Fr. duc; kh, G. ich, doch; ‡ foreign; < derived from

deign (dān) *vi.*, *vt.* [< L. *dignus*, worthy] to condescend (to do or give)

de·ism (dē′iz′m) *n.* [< L. *deus*, god] the belief that God exists and created the world but thereafter assumed no control over it —**de′ist** *n.*

de·i·ty (dē′ə tē) *n.*, *pl.* -ties [< L. *deus*, god] 1. the state of being a god 2. a god or goddess —**the Deity** God

de·ject (di jekt′) *vt.* [< L. *de*-, down + *jacere*, throw] to dishearten; depress —**de·ject′ed** *adj.* —**de·jec′-tion** *n.*

Del·a·ware (del′ə wer′) Eastern State of the U.S.: 2,057 sq. mi.; pop. 595,000; cap. Dover: abbrev. **Del.** —**Del′a·war′e·an** *adj.*, *n.*

de·lay (di lā′) *vt.* [< OFr. *de*-, intens. + *laier*, to leave] 1. to put off; postpone 2. to make late; detain —*vi.* to linger —*n.* a delaying or being delayed

de·lec·ta·ble (di lek′tə b′l) *adj.* [see DELIGHT] delightful or delicious

de·lec·ta·tion (dē′lek tā′shən) *n.* [see DELIGHT] delight; enjoyment

del·e·gate (del′ə gāt′; *also for n.* -git) *n.* [< L. *de*-, from + *legare*, send] a person authorized to act for others; representative —*vt.* -gat′ed, -gat′-ing 1. to appoint as a delegate 2. to entrust (authority, etc.) to another

del′e·ga′tion *n.* 1. a delegating or being delegated 2. a body of delegates

de·lete (di lēt′) *vt.* -let′ed, -let′ing [< L. *delere*, destroy] to take out (a word, etc.); cross out —**de·le′tion** *n.*

del·e·te·ri·ous (del′ə tir′ē əs) *adj.* [< Gr. *dēleisthai*, injure] harmful to health, well-being, etc.; injurious

delft·ware (delft′wer′) *n.* [< *Delft*, city in Holland] glazed earthenware, usually blue and white: also **delft**

Del·hi (del′ē) city in N India: pop. 2,062,000

del·i (del′ē) *n.* clipped form of DELICATESSEN

de·lib·er·ate (di lib′ər it; *for v.* -āt′) *adj.* [< L. *de*-, intens. + *librare*, weigh] 1. carefully thought out; premeditated 2. not rash or hasty 3. unhurried —*vi.*, *vt.* -at′ed, -at′ing to consider carefully —**de·lib′er·ate·ly** *adv.* —**de·lib′er·a′tive** *adj.*

de·lib·er·a′tion *n.* 1. a deliberating 2. [*often pl.*] consideration of alternatives 3. carefulness; slowness

del·i·ca·cy (del′i kə sē) *n.*, *pl.* -cies 1. the quality or state of being delicate; fineness, weakness, sensitivity, etc. 2. a choice food

del·i·cate (-kit) *adj.* [< L. *delicatus*, delightful] 1. pleasing in its lightness, mildness, etc. 2. beautifully fine in texture, workmanship, etc. 3. slight and subtle 4. easily damaged 5. frail in health 6. *a)* needing careful handling *b)* showing tact, consideration, etc. 7. finely sensitive —**del′i-cate·ly** *adv.* —**del′i·cate·ness** *n.*

del·i·ca·tes·sen (del′i kə tes′′n) *n.* [< G. *pl.* < Fr. *délicatesse*, delicacy] 1. prepared cooked meats, fish, cheeses, salads, etc. 2. a shop where such foods are sold

de·li·cious (di lish′əs) *adj.* [see ff.] 1. delightful 2. very pleasing to taste or smell —**de·li′cious·ly** *adv.* —**de·li′cious·ness** *n.*

de·light (di līt′) *vt.* [< L. *de*-, from + *lacere*, entice] to give great pleasure to —*vi.* 1. to give great pleasure 2. to be highly pleased; rejoice —*n.* 1. great pleasure 2. something giving great pleasure —**de·light′ed** *adj.*

de·light′ful *adj.* giving delight; very pleasing —**de·light′ful·ly** *adv.*

De·li·lah (di lī′lə) *Bible* the mistress and betrayer of Samson

de·lim·it (di lim′it) *vt.* to fix the limits of —**de·lim′i·ta′tion** *n.*

de·lin·e·ate (di lin′ē āt′) *vt.* -at′ed, -at′ing [< L. *de*-, from + *linea*, a line] 1. to draw; sketch 2. to depict in words —**de·lin·e·a′tion** *n.*

de·lin·quent (di liŋ′kwənt) *adj.* [< L. *de*-, from + *linquere*, leave] 1. failing to do what duty or law requires 2. overdue, as taxes —*n.* a delinquent person; esp., *same as* JUVENILE DELINQUENT —**de·lin′quen·cy** *n.*, *pl.* -cies —**de·lin′quent·ly** *adv.*

de·li·quesce (del′ə kwes′) *vi.* -quesced′, -quesc′ing [< L. *de*-, from + *liquere*, be liquid] to become liquid by absorbing moisture from the air —**del′i·ques′cent** *adj.*

de·lir·i·ous (di lir′ē əs) *adj.* 1. in a state of delirium 2. of or caused by delirium 3. wildly excited —**de·lir′i·ous·ly** *adv.* —**de·lir′i·ous·ness** *n.*

de·lir′i·um (-əm) *n.* [< L. *de*-, from + *lira*, a line] 1. a temporary mental disturbance, as during a fever, marked by confused speech and hallucinations 2. uncontrollably wild excitement

de·liv·er (di liv′ər) *vt.* [< L. *de*-, from + *liber*, free] 1. to set free or rescue 2. to assist at the birth of 3. to make (a speech, etc.) 4. to hand over 5. to distribute (mail, etc.) 6. to strike (a blow) 7. to throw (a ball)

de·liv′er·ance *n.* a freeing or being freed; rescue

de·liv·er·y *n.*, *pl.* -ies 1. a handing over 2. a distributing, as of mail 3. a giving birth 4. any giving forth 5. the act or manner of delivering a speech, ball, etc. 6. something delivered

dell (del) *n.* [OE. *del*] a small, secluded valley or glen, usually wooded

del·phin·i·um (del fin′ē əm) *n.* [< Gr. *delphin*, dolphin] a tall plant bearing spikes of flowers, usually blue

del·ta (del′tə) *n.* 1. the fourth letter of the Greek alphabet (Δ, δ) 2. a deposit of soil, usually triangular, formed at the mouth of some rivers

DELTA

de·lude (di lōōd′) *vt.* -lud′ed, -lud′-ing [< L. *de*-, from + *ludere*, to play] to mislead; deceive

del·uge (del′yōōj) *n.* [< L. *dis*-, off + *lavere*, to wash] 1. a great flood 2. a heavy rainfall —*vt.* -uged, -ug-ing 1. to flood 2. to overwhelm

de·lu·sion (di lōō′zhən) *n.* 1. a deluding or being deluded 2. a false belief, specif. one that persists psychotically —de·lu'sive *adj.*

de·luxe (di luks', -looks') *adj.* [Fr., of luxury] of extra fine quality —*adv.* in a deluxe manner

delve (delv) *vi.* delved, delv'ing [OE. *delfan*] 1. [Archaic or Brit. Dial.] to dig 2. to search (*into*) —delv'er n.

Dem. 1. Democrat 2. Democratic

de·mag·net·ize (dē mag'nə tīz') *vt.* -ized', -iz'ing to deprive of magnetic properties —de·mag'net·i·za'tion n.

dem·a·gogue, dem·a·gog (dem'ə gäg', -gôg') n. [< Gr. *dēmos*, the people + *agōgos*, leader] one who tries to stir up people's emotions so as to further his own interests —dem'a·gog'y (-gō'jē, -gäg'ē), dem'a·gog'uer·y (-gäg'ər ē) n.

de·mand (di mand') *vt.* [< L. *de-*, from + *mandare*, entrust] 1. to ask for boldly or urgently 2. to ask for as a right 3. to require; need —*vi.* to make a demand —n. 1. a demanding 2. a thing demanded 3. a strong request 4. an urgent requirement 5. *Econ.* the desire for a commodity together with ability to pay for it; also, the amount people are ready to buy —in demand wanted or sought —on demand when presented for payment

de·mand'ing *adj.* making difficult demands on one's patience, energy, etc. —de·mand'ing·ly *adv.*

de·mar·ca·tion (dē'mär kā'shən) n. [< Sp. *de-*, from + *marcar*, to mark] 1. the act of setting and marking boundaries 2. a limit or boundary

de·mean¹ (di mēn') *vt.* [DE- + MEAN²] to degrade; humble

de·mean² (di mēn') *vt.* [see ff.] to behave or conduct (oneself)

de·mean·or (di mēn'ər) n. [< OFr. *demener*, to lead] outward behavior; conduct; deportment: Brit. sp. de·meanour

de·ment·ed (di ment'id) *adj.* [see ff.] mentally deranged; insane

de·men·tia (di men'shə) n. [< L. *de-*, out from + *mens*, the mind] loss or impairment of mental powers

de·mer·it (di mer'it) n. [< L. *de-*, intens. + *merere*, deserve, with de- taken as negative] 1. a fault; defect 2. a mark recorded against a student, etc. for poor conduct or work

de·mesne (di mān', -mēn') n. [see DOMAIN] a region or domain

De·me·ter (di mēt'ər) Gr. *Myth.* the goddess of agriculture

demi- [< L. *dimidius*, half] a *prefix meaning:* 1. half 2. less than usual in size, power, etc. [*demigod*]

dem·i·god (dem'ē gäd') n. 1. a minor deity 2. a godlike person

dem'i·john' (-jän') n. [Fr. *dame-jeanne*] a large bottle of glass or earthenware in a wicker casing

de·mil·i·ta·rize (dē mil'ə tə rīz') *vt.* -rized', -riz'ing to free from organized military control

dem·i·monde (dem'ē mänd') n. [Fr. < *demi-* + *monde*, world] the class of women who have lost social standing because of sexual promiscuity

de·mise (di mīz') n. [< L. *de-*, down + *mittere*, send] 1. *Law* transfer of an estate by lease 2. death —*vt.* -mised', -mis'ing to transfer (an estate) by lease

dem·i·tasse (dem'ē tas', -täs') n. [Fr. < *demi-*, DEMI- + *tasse*, cup] a small cup of or for after-dinner coffee

dem·o (dem'ō) n. [Colloq.] a phonograph or tape recording made to demonstrate a performer's talent, etc.

de·mo·bi·lize (dē mō'bə līz') *vt.* -lized', -liz'ing to disband (troops) —de·mo'bi·li·za'tion n.

de·moc·ra·cy (di mäk'rə sē) n., *pl.* -cies [< Gr. *dēmos*, the people + *kratein*, to rule] 1. government by the people, directly or through representatives 2. a country, etc. with such government 3. equality of rights, opportunity, and treatment

dem·o·crat (dem'ə krat') n. 1. one who supports or practices democracy 2. [D-] a Democratic Party member

dem'o·crat'ic *adj.* 1. of or for democracy 2. of or for all the people 3. not snobbish 4. [D-] of the Democratic Party —dem'o·crat'i·cal·ly *adv.*

Democratic Party one of the two major political parties in the U.S.

de·mod·u·la·tion (dē mäj'oo lā'shən) n. *Radio* the recovery, at the receiver, of a signal that has been modulated on a carrier wave

de·mog·ra·phy (di mäg'rə fē) n. [< Gr. *dēmos*, people + -GRAPHY] the statistical study of populations —de·mog'ra·pher n. —de'mo·graph'ic *adj.* —de'mo·graph'i·cal·ly *adv.*

de·mol·ish (di mäl'ish) *vt.* [< L. *de-*, down + *moliri*, build] to wreck —dem·o·li·tion (dem'ə lish'ən) n.

de·mon (dē'mən) n. [< L. *daemon*] 1. a devil; evil spirit 2. a person or thing regarded as evil, cruel, etc. —de·mon·ic (di män'ik) *adj.*

de·mon·e·tize (dē män'ə tīz') *vt.* -tized', -tiz'ing to deprive (currency) of its standard value

de·mo·ni·ac (di mō'nē ak') *adj.* of or like a demon; fiendish; frenzied: also de·mo·ni·a·cal (dē'mə nī'ə k'l)

de·mon·stra·ble (di män'strə b'l) *adj.* that can be demonstrated, or proved —de·mon'stra·bly *adv.*

dem·on·strate (dem'ən strāt') *vt.* -strat'ed, -strat'ing [< L. *de-*, from + *monstrare*, to show] 1. to show by reasoning; prove 2. to explain by using examples, etc. 3. to show how something works —*vi.* to show feelings or views publicly by meetings, etc. —dem'on·stra'tion n. —dem'on·stra'tor n.

de·mon·stra·tive (di män'strə tiv) *adj.* 1. illustrative 2. giving proof (*of*) 3. showing feelings openly 4. *Gram.*

pointing out ["this" is a *demonstrative pronoun*] —*n.* a demonstrative pronoun or adjective

de·mor·al·ize (di môr'ə līz') *vt.* **-ized', -iz'ing** 1. to lower the morale of 2. to throw into confusion —**de·mor'al·i·za'tion** *n.*

De·mos·the·nes (di mäs'thə nēz') 384?–322 B.C.; Athenian orator

de·mote (di mōt') *vt.* **-mot'ed, -mot'ing** [DE- + (PRO)MOTE] to reduce to a lower rank —**de·mo'tion** *n.*

de·mul·cent (di mul's'nt) *adj.* [< L. *de-*, down + *mulcere*, to stroke] soothing —*n.* a soothing ointment

de·mur (di mur') *vi.* **-murred', -mur'ring** [< L. *de-*, from + *mora*, a delay] to hesitate, as because of doubts; have scruples; object —*n.* a demurring: also **de·mur'ral**

de·mure (di myoor') *adj.* [< *de-* (prob. intens.) + OFr. *mëur*, mature] 1. decorous; modest 2. affectedly modest; coy —**de·mure'ly** *adv.*

de·mur·rage (di mur'ij) *n.* 1. the delaying of a ship, freight car, etc., as by failure to load, unload, etc. 2. the compensation paid for this

de·mur·rer (di mur'ər) *n.* [see DE-MUR] 1. a plea that a lawsuit be dismissed because statements supporting a claim are defective 2. an objection

den (den) *n.* [OE. *denn*] 1. the lair of a wild animal 2. a haunt, as of thieves 3. a small, cozy room where one can be alone to read, work, etc.

de·na·ture (dē nā'chər) *vt.* **-tured, -tur·ing** 1. to change the nature of 2. to make (alcohol) unfit to drink

de·ni·al (di nī'əl) *n.* 1. a denying; saying "no" (to a request, etc.) 2. a contradiction 3. a refusal to believe or accept (a doctrine, etc.) 4. *same as* SELF-DENIAL —**de·ni'er** *n.*

de·nier (den'yər) *n.* [< L. *deni*, by tens] a unit of weight for measuring fineness of threads of silk, nylon, etc.

den·i·grate (den'ə grāt') *vt.* **-grat'ed, -grat'ing** [< L. *de-*, entirely + *nigrare*, blacken] to belittle the character of; defame —**den'i·gra'tion** *n.*

den·im (den'əm) *n.* [< Fr. (*serge*) *de Nîmes*, serge of Nîmes, town in France] a coarse, twilled cotton cloth

den·i·zen (den'i zən) *n.* [< L. *de intus*, from within] an inhabitant or frequenter of a particular place

Den·mark (den'märk) country in Europe, on a peninsula & several islands in the North & Baltic seas: 16,615 sq. mi.; pop. 4,797,000

de·nom·i·nate (di näm'ə nāt') *vt.* **-nat'ed, -nat'ing** [< L. *de-*, intens. + *nominare*, to name] to name; call

de·nom·i·na·tion (-nā'shən) *n.* 1. the act of naming 2. a name 3. a class or kind, as of coins, having a specific name or value 4. a religious sect

de·nom·i·na·tion·al *adj.* of, or under the control of, a religious sect

de·nom·i·na·tor (-nāt'ər) *n.* 1. a shared characteristic 2. *Math.* the term below the line in a fraction

de·note (di nōt') *vt.* **-not'ed, -not'ing** [< L. *de-*, down + *notare*, to

mark] to indicate or signify —**de·no·ta·tion** (dē'nō tā'shən) *n.*

dé·noue·ment, de·noue·ment (dā noo'män) *n.* [Fr.] the outcome or unraveling of a plot in a drama, etc.

de·nounce (di nouns') *vt.* **-nounced', -nounc'ing** [see DENUNCIATION] 1. to accuse publicly; inform against 2. to condemn strongly 3. to give formal notice of the ending of (a treaty, etc.) —**de·nounce'ment** *n.*

dense (dens) *adj.* [< L. *densus*, compact] 1. packed tightly together 2. difficult to get through 3. stupid —**dense'ly** *adv.* —**dense'ness** *n.*

den·si·ty (den'sə tē) *n.*, *pl.* **-ties** 1. a dense condition 2. stupidity 3. number per unit, as of area 4. ratio of the mass of an object to its volume

dent (dent) *n.* [ME., var. of DINT] 1. a slight hollow made in a surface by a blow 2. a slight impression —*vt., vi.* to make or receive a dent (in)

den·tal (den't'l) *adj.* [< L. *dens*, tooth] of or for the teeth or dentistry

dental floss thread for removing food particles between the teeth

den·ti·frice (den'tə fris') *n.* [< L. *dens*, tooth + *fricare*, rub] any preparation for cleaning teeth

den·tin (den'tin) *n.* [see DENTAL] the hard tissue under the enamel of a tooth: also **den'tine** (-tēn, -tin)

den·tist (den'tist) *n.* one whose profession is the care and repair of teeth —**den'tist·ry** *n.*

den·ture (den'chər) *n.* [see DENTAL] a set of artificial teeth

de·nu·cle·ar·ize (dē nōō'klē ə rīz') *vt.* **-ized', -iz'ing** to prohibit the possession of nuclear weapons in

de·nude (di nood', -nyood') *vt.* **-nud'ed, -nud'ing** [< L. *de-*, off + *nudare*, to strip] to make bare or naked; strip

de·nun·ci·a·tion (di nun'sē ā'shən) *n.* [< L. *de-*, intens. + *nuntiare*, announce] the act of denouncing

Den·ver (den'vər) capital of Colo.: pop. 491,000

de·ny (di nī') *vt.* **-nied', -ny'ing** [< L. *de-*, intens. + *negare*, to deny] 1. to declare (a statement) untrue 2. to refuse to accept as true or right 3. to repudiate 4. to refuse to grant or give 5. to refuse the request of —**deny oneself** to do without desired things

de·o·dor·ant (dē ō'dər ənt) *adj.* that can counteract undesired odors —*n.* any deodorant preparation

de·o·dor·ize' (-də rīz') *vt.* **-ized', -iz'ing** to counteract the odor of —**de·o'dor·iz'er** *n.*

de·part (di pärt') *vi.* [< L. *dis-*, apart + *partire*, divide] 1. to go away; leave 2. to die 3. to deviate (*from*)

de·part·ed *adj.* 1. gone away 2. dead —**the departed** the dead

de·part·ee (di pär'tē') *n.* one who has departed, as from a job, country, etc.

de·part·ment (-mənt) *n.* 1. a separate part or division, as of a business 2. a field of activity, etc. —**de·part'men·tal** (-men't'l) *adj.*

de·part·men·tal·ize' (-men'tə līz') *vt.* **-ized', -iz'ing** to organize into departments —de·part′men′tal·i·za′tion n.

department store a large retail store for the sale of many kinds of goods arranged in departments

de·par·ture (di pär′chər) n. 1. a departing 2. a starting out, as on a trip 3. a deviation (from something)

de·pend (di pend′) vi. [< L. de-, down + pendere, to hang] 1. to be determined by something else; be contingent (on) 2. to rely (on) 3. to rely (on) for support or aid

de·pend′a·ble adj. trustworthy; reliable —de·pend′a·bil′i·ty n.

de·pend′ence n. 1. a being dependent 2. reliance (on) for support or aid 3. reliance; trust

de·pend′en·cy n., pl. -cies 1. dependence 2. something dependent 3. a territory, as a possession, subordinate to its governing country

de·pend′ent adj. 1. hanging down 2. determined by something else 3. relying (on) for support, etc. 4. subordinate —n. one relying on another for support, etc. Also de·pend′ant —de·pend′ent·ly adv.

de·pict (di pikt′) vt. [< L. de-, intens. + pingere, to paint] 1. to represent by drawing, painting, etc. 2. to describe —de·pic′tion n.

de·pil·a·to·ry (di pil′ə tôr′ē) adj. [< L. de-, from + pilus, hair] serving to remove unwanted hair —n., pl. -ries a depilatory substance or device

de·plane (dē plān′) vi. -planed′, -plan′ing to leave an airplane after it lands

de·plete (di plēt′) vt. -plet′ed, -plet′ing [< L. de-, from + plere, fill] 1. to use up (funds, etc.) 2. to use up the resources, etc. of —de·ple′-tion n.

de·plor·a·ble (di plôr′ə b'l) adj. regrettable or wretched

de·plore (di plôr′) vt. -plored′, -plor′ing [< L. de-, intens. + plorare, weep] to regret deeply

de·ploy (di ploi′) vt., vi. [< L. dis-, apart + plicare, to fold] Mil. to spread out so as to form a wider front —de·ploy′ment n.

de·po·lar·ize (dē pō′lə rīz′) vt. -ized′, -iz′ing to destroy or counteract the polarization of —de·po′lar·i·za′tion n.

de·po·lit·i·cize (dē′pə lit′ə sīz′) vt. -cized′, -ciz′ing to remove from political influence

de·po·nent (di pō′nənt) adj. [< L. de-, down + ponere, put] Law one who gives written testimony under oath

de·pop·u·late (dē päp′yə lāt′) vt. -lat′ed, -lat′ing to reduce the population of —de·pop′u·la′tion n.

de·port (di pôrt′) vt. [< L. de-, from + portare, carry] 1. to behave (oneself) 2. to expel (an alien) —de·por·ta·tion (dē′pôr tā′shən) n.

de·port′ment n. conduct; behavior

de·pose (di pōz′) vt. -posed′, -pos′-

ing [< OFr. de-, from + poser, cease] 1. to remove from office 2. to testify

de·pos·it (di päz′it) vt. [< L. de-, down + ponere, put] 1. to place (money, etc.) for safekeeping, as in a bank 2. to give as a pledge or partial payment 3. to set down 4. to leave (sediment, etc.) lying —n. 1. something placed for safekeeping, as money in a bank 2. a pledge or part payment 3. something deposited or left lying —de·pos′i·tor n.

dep·o·si·tion (dep′ə zish′ən) n. 1. a deposing or being deposed 2. testimony 3. something deposited

de·pos·i·to·ry (di päz′ə tôr′ē) n., pl. -ries a place where things are put for safekeeping

de·pot (dē′pō; military & Brit. dep′ō) n. [< Fr.: see DEPOSIT] 1. a warehouse 2. a railroad or bus station 3. a storage place for military supplies

de·prave (di prāv′) vt. -praved′, -prav′ing [< L. de-, intens. + pravus, crooked] to make morally bad; corrupt —de·praved′ adj. —de·prav′i·ty (-prav′ə tē) n., pl. -ties

dep·re·cate (dep′rə kāt′) vt. -cat′-ed, -cat′ing [< L. de-, off + precari, pray] 1. to express disapproval of 2. to belittle —dep′re·ca′tion n. —dep′re·ca·to′ry (-kə tôr′ē) adj.

de·pre·ci·ate (di prē′shē āt′) vt., vi. -at′ed, -at′ing [< L. de-, from + pretium, price] 1. to lessen in value 2. to belittle —de·pre′ci·a′tion n.

dep·re·da·tion (dep′rə dā′shən) n. [< L. de-, intens. + praedari, to plunder] a robbing or plundering

de·press (di pres′) vt. [< L. de-, down + premere, to press] 1. to press down 2. to sadden; deject 3. to make less active 4. to lower in value, price, etc. —de·pressed′ adj. —de·press′ant n.

de·pres·sion (di presh′ən) n. 1. a depressing or being depressed 2. a hollow or low place 3. low spirits; dejection 4. a decrease in force, activity, etc. 5. a period of reduced business, much unemployment, etc.

de·prive (di prīv′) vt. -prived′, -priv′ing [< L. de-, intens. + privare, to separate] 1. to take away from forcibly 2. to keep from having, etc. —dep·ri·va·tion (dep′rə vā′shən) n.

dept. 1. department 2. deputy

depth (depth) n. [< ME. dep, deep + -TH¹] 1. the distance from the top downward, or from front to back 2. deepness 3. intensity 4. [usually pl.] the deepest or inmost part —in depth comprehensively

dep·u·ta·tion (dep′yoo tā′shən) n. 1. a deputing 2. a delegation

de·pute (di pyoot′) vt. -put′ed, -put′ing [< L. de-, from + putare, cleanse] 1. to give (authority, etc.) to a deputy 2. to appoint as one's substitute

dep·u·tize (dep′yə tīz′) vt. -tized′, -tiz′ing to appoint as deputy

dep·u·ty (dep′yə tē) n., pl. -ties a person appointed to act for another

de·rail (di rāl′) *vt.*, *vi.* to run off the rails, as a train —**de·rail′ment** *n.*

de·rail·leur (di rā′lər) *n.* [Fr.] a gearshifting mechanism on a bicycle for shifting the sprocket chain from one size of sprocket wheel to another

de·range (di rānj′) *vt.* -ranged′, -rang′ing [< OFr. *des-*, apart + *rengier*, to range] 1. to upset the arrangement or working of 2. to make insane —**de·range′ment** *n.*

Der·by (dur′bē; *Brit.* där′-) *n.*, *pl.* -bies 1. any of certain famous horse races; orig., one founded (1780) by an Earl of Derby 2. [d-] a stiff felt hat with a round crown

de·reg·u·late (dē reg′yə lāt′) *vt.* -lat′ed, -lat′ing to remove regulations governing —**de·reg′u·la′tion** *n.*

DERBY

der·e·lict (der′ə likt′) *adj.* [< L. *de-*, intens. + *relinquere*: see RELINQUISH] 1. deserted by the owner; abandoned 2. negligent —*n.* 1. a ship deserted at sea 2. a destitute and rejected person

der′e·lic′tion (-lik′shən) *n.* 1. a forsaking or being forsaken 2. a neglect of, or failure in, duty

de·ride (di rīd′) *vt.* -rid′ed, -rid′ing [< L. *de-*, down + *ridere*, to laugh] to laugh at in scorn; ridicule —**de·ri′sion** (-rizh′ən) *n.* —**de·ri′sive** (-rī′siv) *adj.* —**de·ri′sive·ly** *adv.*

der·i·va·tion (der′ə vā′shən) *n.* 1. a deriving or being derived 2. the source or origin of something 3. the origin and development of a word

de·riv·a·tive (də riv′ə tiv) *adj.* derived —*n.* something derived

de·rive (di rīv′) *vt.* -rived′, -riv′ing [< L. *de-*, from + *rivus*, a stream] 1. to get or receive (*from* a source) 2. to deduce or infer 3. to trace from or to a source —*vi.* to be derived

der·ma·ti·tis (dur′mə tīt′is) *n.* [< Gr. *derma*, skin + -ITIS] inflammation of the skin

der·ma·tol·o·gy (dur′mə täl′ə jē) *n.* [< Gr. *derma*, skin + -LOGY] the branch of medicine dealing with the skin —**der′ma·tol′o·gist** *n.*

der·o·gate (der′ə gāt′) *vi.*, *vt.* -gat′ed, -gat′ing [< L. *de-*, from + *rogare*, ask] to detract or disparage —**der′o·ga′tion** *n.*

de·rog·a·to·ry (di räg′ə tôr′ē) *adj.* [see prec.] 1. detracting 2. disparaging; belittling

der·rick (der′ik) *n.* [after *Derrick*, 17th-c. London hangman: orig. applied to a gallows] 1. a pivoted beam for lifting and moving heavy objects 2. a tall framework, as over an oil well, to support drilling machinery, etc.

der·ri·ère (der′ē er′) *n.* [Fr., back part] the buttocks

der·vish (dur′vish) *n.* [< Per. *darvēsh*, beggar] a member of any of various Moslem ascetic orders

de·sal·i·na·tion (dē sal′ə nā′shən) *n.* [DE- + SALIN(E) + -ATION] the removal of salt, esp. from sea water to make it drinkable —**de·sal′i·nate′** *vt.* -nat′ed, -nat′ing

des·cant (des′kant, des kant′) *vi.* [< L. *dis-*, apart + *cantus*, song] 1. to discourse (*on* or *upon*) 2. to sing

Des·cartes (dā kärt′), **Re·né** (rə nā′) 1596-1650; Fr. philosopher

de·scend (di send′) *vi.* [< L. *de-*, down + *scandere*, climb] 1. to move down to a lower place 2. to pass from an earlier to a later time, from greater to less, etc. 3. to slope downward 4. to come down (*from* a source) 5. to stoop (*to*) 6. to make a sudden attack or visit (*on*) —*vt.* to move down along

de·scend′ant *n.* an offspring of a certain ancestor, family, group, etc.

de·scent (di sent′) *n.* 1. a coming or going down 2. ancestry 3. a downward slope 4. a way down 5. a sudden attack 6. a decline

de·scribe (di skrīb′) *vt.* -scribed′, -scrib′ing [< L. *de-*, from + *scribere*, write] 1. to tell or write about 2. to trace the outline of —**de·scrib′er** *n.*

de·scrip·tion (di skrip′shən) *n.* 1. the act or technique of describing 2. a statement or passage that describes 3. sort; kind 4. a tracing or outlining —**de·scrip′tive** (-tiv) *adj.*

de·scry (di skrī′) *vt.* -scried′, -scry′ing [< OFr. *descrier*, proclaim] 1. to catch sight of; discern 2. to detect

des·e·crate (des′ə krāt′) *vt.* -crat′ed, -crat′ing [< DE- + (CON)SECRATE] to violate the sacredness of; profane —**des′e·cra′tion** *n.*

de·seg·re·gate (dē seg′rə gāt′) *vt.*, *vi.* -gat′ed, -gat′ing to abolish racial segregation in (public schools, etc.) —**de·seg′re·ga′tion** *n.*

de·sen·si·tize (dē sen′sə tīz′) *vt.* -tized′, -tiz′ing to make less sensitive, as to an allergen

de·sert¹ (di zurt′) *vt.*, *vi.* [< L. *de-*, from + *serere*, join] 1. to abandon; forsake 2. to leave (one's military post, etc.) without permission and with no intent to return —**de·sert′er** *n.* —**de·ser′tion** (-zur′shən) *n.*

des·ert² (dez′ərt) *n.* [see prec.] 1. an uninhabited region; wilderness 2. a dry, barren, sandy region

de·sert³ (di zurt′) *n.* [see ff.] [*often pl.*] deserved reward or punishment

de·serve (di zurv′) *vi.*, *vt.* -served′, -serv′ing [< L. *de-*, intens. + *servire*, serve] to be worthy (of); merit —**de·serv′ed·ly** *adv.* —**de·serv′ing** *adj.*, *n.*

des·ic·cate (des′i kāt′) *vt.*, *vi.* -cat′ed, -cat′ing [< L. *de-*, intens. + *siccus*, dry] to dry out completely —**des′ic·ca′tion** *n.* —**des′ic·ca′tor** *n.*

de·sid·er·a·tum (di sid′ə rät′əm) *n.*, *pl.* -ta (-ə) [see DESIRE] something needed and wanted

de·sign (di zīn′) *vt.* [< L. *de-*, out + *signum*, a mark] 1. to sketch an outline for; plan 2. to contrive 3. to plan to do; intend —*vi.* to make original plans, etc. —*n.* 1. a plan; scheme 2. purpose; aim 3. a working plan; pattern 4. arrangement of parts, form, color, etc.; artistic invention —by design purposely —**de·sign′er** *n.*

des·ig·nate (dez′ig nāt′) *vt.* -nat′-

ed, -nat'ing [see prec.] 1. to point out; specify 2. to name 3. to appoint —des'ig·na'tion n.

de·sign'ing adj. scheming; artful — n. the art of creating designs, etc.

de·sir·a·ble (di zīr'ə b'l) adj. worth having; pleasing —de·sir'a·bil'i·ty n. —de·sir'a·bly adv.

de·sire (di zīr') vt. -sired', -sir'ing [< L. desiderare] 1. to long for; crave 2. to ask for —vi. to have a desire —n. 1. a wish; craving 2. sexual appetite 3. a request 4. thing desired

de·sir'ous (-əs) adj. desiring

de·sist (di zist') vi. [< L. de-, from + sistere, to stand] to cease; stop

desk (desk) n. [< ML. desca, table] a table for writing, drawing, or reading

Des Moines (də moin') capital of Iowa: pop. 191,000

des·o·late (des'ə lit; for v. -lāt') adj. [< L. de-, intens. + solus, alone] 1. lonely; solitary 2. uninhabited 3. laid waste 4. forlorn —vt. -lat'ed, -lat'ing 1. to rid of inhabitants 2. to lay waste 3. to make forlorn —des'o·late·ly adv. —des'o·late·ness n.

des·o·la'tion n. 1. a making desolate 2. a desolate condition or place 3. misery 4. loneliness

de·spair (di sper') vi. [< L. de-, without + sperare, to hope] to lose hope —n. 1. loss of hope 2. a person or thing causing despair

des·patch (di spach') vt., n. same as DISPATCH —des·patch'er n.

des·per·a·do (des'pə rä'dō, -rä'-) n., pl. -does, -dos [< OSp.: see DESPAIR] a dangerous criminal; bold outlaw

des·per·ate (des'pər it) adj. 1. rash or violent because of despair 2. having a very great need 3. very serious 4. drastic —des'per·ate·ly adv.

des·per·a·tion (des'pə rā'shən) n. 1. the state of being desperate 2. recklessness resulting from despair

des·pi·ca·ble (des'pik ə b'l, di spik'-) adj. deserving scorn; contemptible

de·spise (di spīz') vt. -spised', -spis'ing [< L. de, down + specere, look at] 1. to scorn 2. to loathe

de·spite (di spīt') prep. [see prec.] in spite of; notwithstanding

de·spoil (di spoil') vt. [< L. de-, intens. + spoliare, to strip] to rob; plunder —de·spoil'ment n.

de·spond·en·cy (di spän'dən sē) n. [< L. de-, from + spondere, to promise] loss of hope; dejection: also de·spond'ence —de·spond'ent adj.

des·pot (des'pat) n. [< Gr. despotēs, a master] 1. an absolute ruler 2. a tyrant —des·pot·ic (di spät'ik) adj. —des'pot·ism (-pə tiz'm) n.

des·sert (di zurt') n. [< L. de-, from + servire, serve] the final course of a meal, typically cake, fruit, etc.

des·ti·na·tion (des'tə nā'shən) n. 1. the purpose for which something or someone is destined 2. the place toward which one is going or sent

des·tine (des'tin) vt. -tined, -tin-

ing [< L. de-, intens. + stare, to stand] 1. to predetermine, as by fate 2. to intend —destined for 1. bound for 2. intended for

des·tin·y (des'tə nē) n., pl. -ies 1. the seemingly inevitable succession of events 2. (one's) fate

des·ti·tute (des'tə tōōt') adj. [< L. de, down + statuere, to set] 1. lacking (with of) 2. totally impoverished — des'ti·tu'tion n.

de·stroy (di stroi') vt. [< L. de-, down + struere, to build] 1. to tear down; demolish 2. to wreck; ruin 3. to do away with 4. to kill

de·stroy'er n. 1. one that destroys 2. a small, fast warship

de·struct (di strukt', dē'strukt') n. [< DESTRUCTION] deliberate destruction of a rocket, etc. after its launch —vi. to be automatically destroyed

de·struc·tion (di struk'shən) n. 1. a destroying or being destroyed 2. a cause or means of destroying —de·struc'tive adj. —de·struc'tive·ly adv. —de·struc'tive·ness n.

des·ue·tude (des'wi tōōd') n. [< L. de-, from + suescere, be accustomed] disuse

des·ul·to·ry (des''l tôr'ē) adj. [< L. de-, from + salire, to leap] 1. aimless; disconnected 2. random

de·tach (di tach') vt. [< Fr.: see DE- & ATTACH] 1. to unfasten and remove; disconnect; disengage 2. to send (troops, etc.) on a special mission —de·tach'a·ble adj.

de·tached' adj. 1. not connected 2. aloof; disinterested; impartial

de·tach'ment n. 1. a detaching 2. a unit of troops, etc. on a special mission 3. impartiality or aloofness

de·tail (di tāl', dē'tāl) n. [< Fr. < dé-, from + tailler, to cut] 1. a dealing with things item by item 2. a minute account 3. a small part; item 4. a) one or more soldiers, etc. on special duty b) the duty —vt. 1. to tell, item by item 2. to assign to special duty — in detail with particulars

de·tain (di tān') vt. [< L. de-, off + tenere, to hold] 1. to keep in custody; confine 2. to keep from going on —de·tain'ment n.

de·tect (di tekt') vt. [< L. de-, from + tegere, to cover] to discover (something hidden, not clear, etc.) —de·tect'a·ble, de·tect'i·ble adj. —de·tec'tion n. —de·tec'tor n.

de·tec'tive n. one whose work is solving crimes, tracking people, etc.

dé·tente (dā tänt') n. [Fr.] a lessening of tension, esp. between nations

de·ten·tion (di ten'shən) n. a detaining or being detained

detention home a place where juvenile offenders are held in custody

de·ter (di tur') vt. -terred', -ter'ring [< L. de-, from + terrere, frighten] to keep or discourage (a person) from doing something through fear, doubt, etc. —de·ter'ment n.

de·ter·gent (di tur'jənt) *adj.* [< L. *de-*, off + *tergere*, wipe] cleansing —*n.* a soaplike cleansing substance

de·te·ri·o·rate (di tir'ē ə rāt') *vt.*, *vi.* -rat·ed, -rat·ing [< L. *deterior*, worse] to make or become worse —**de·te·ri·o·ra'tion** *n.*

de·ter·mi·nant (di tur'mi nənt) *n.* a thing or factor that determines

de·ter'mi·nate (-nit) *adj.* clearly determined; fixed; settled

de·ter·mi·na·tion (di tur'mə nā' shən) *n.* 1. a determining or being determined 2. a firm intention 3. firmness of purpose

de·ter·mine (di tur'mən) *vt.* -mined, -min·ing [< L. *de-*, from + *terminus*, a limit] 1. to set limits to 2. to settle conclusively 3. to decide or decide upon 4. to be the deciding factor in; direct 5. to find out exactly —*vi.* to decide —**de·ter'mi·na·ble** *adj.*

de·ter'mined *adj.* 1. having one's mind made up 2. resolute; firm

de·ter·rent (di tur'ənt) *adj.* deterring —*n.* something that deters

de·test (di test') *vt.* [< L. *detestari*, to curse by the gods] to dislike intensely; hate —**de·test'a·ble** *adj.* —**de·tes·ta·tion** (dē'tes tā'shən) *n.*

de·throne (dē thrōn') *vt.* -throned', -thron'ing to depose (a monarch)

det·o·nate (det''n āt') *vi.*, *vt.* -nat·ed, -nat·ing [< L. *de-*, intens. + *tonare*, to thunder] to explode violently —**det'o·na'tion** *n.* —**det'o·na'tor** *n.*

de·tour (dē'toor, di toor') *n.* [< Fr.: see DE- & TURN] 1. a roundabout way 2. a substitute route —*vi.*, *vt.* to go or route on a detour

de·tox·i·fy (dē täk'sə fī') *vt.* -fied', -fy'ing [DE- + TOXI(N) + -FY] to remove a poison or poisonous effect from: also [Colloq.] **de·tox'** (-täks')

de·tract (di trakt') *vt.* [< L. *de-*, from + *trahere*, to draw] to take away —*vi.* to take something desirable (*from*) —**de·trac'tion** *n.* —**de·trac'tor** *n.*

det·ri·ment (det'rə mənt) *n.* [< L. *de-*, off + *terere*, to rub] 1. damage; injury 2. anything that causes this —**det'ri·men'tal** *adj.*

de·tri·tus (di trīt'əs) *n.* [L., a rubbing away: see prec.] rock fragments, etc. from disintegration

De·troit (di troit') city & port in SE Mich.: pop. 1,203,000

deuce (doos) *n.* [< L. *duo*, two] 1. a playing card or side of a die with two spots 2. *Tennis* a tie score after which one side must score twice in a row to win 3. the devil: a mild oath

deu·te·ri·um (doo tir'ē əm) *n.* [ModL.] a heavy isotope of hydrogen

Deu·ter·on·o·my (doot'ər än'ə mē) [< Gr. *deuteros*, second + *nomos*, law] the fifth book of the Pentateuch

de·val·ue (dē val'yoo) *vt.* -ued, -u·ing 1. to lessen the value of 2. to lower the exchange value of (a currency) —**de·val'u·a'tion** *n.*

dev·as·tate (dev'ə stāt') *vt.* -tat·ed, -tat·ing [< L. *de-*, intens. + *vastus*, empty] 1. to lay waste; ravage; destroy 2. to overwhelm —**dev'as·ta'tion** *n.* —**dev'as·ta'tor** *n.*

de·vel·op (di vel'əp) *vt.* [< Fr. *dé-*, apart + OFr. *voloper*, to wrap] 1. to make fuller, bigger, better, etc. 2. to show or work out by degrees; disclose 3. *Photog.* to put (a film, etc.) into chemicals to make the pictures visible —*vi.* 1. to come into being or activity; occur 2. to become developed —**de·vel'op·er** *n.* —**de·vel'op·ment** *n.*

de·vi·ant (dē'vē ənt) *adj.* deviating, esp. from what is considered normal —*n.* one whose behavior is deviant

de·vi·ate (dē'vē āt'; *for adj. & n.* -it) *vi.* -at·ed, -at·ing [< L. *de-*, from + *via*, road] to turn aside (*from* a course, standard, etc.); diverge —*adj.* deviant —*n.* a deviant, esp. in sexual behavior —**de'vi·a'tion** *n.* —**de'vi·a'tor** *n.*

de·vice (di vīs') *n.* [see DEVISE] 1. a thing devised; plan, scheme, or trick 2. a mechanical contrivance 3. an ornamental design, esp. on a coat of arms —**leave to one's own devices** to allow to do as one wishes

dev·il (dev''l) *n.* [ult. < Gr. *diabolos*, slanderer] 1. [*often* D-] *Theol.* a) the chief evil spirit; Satan (with *the*) b) any demon of hell 2. a very wicked person 3. a person who is mischievous, reckless, unlucky, etc. 4. anything hard to operate, control, etc. 5. a printer's apprentice —*vt.* -iled or -illed, -il·ing or -il·ling 1. to prepare (food) with hot seasoning 2. to annoy; tease —**dev'il·ish** *adj.*

dev'il-may-care' *adj.* reckless

dev'il·ment *n.* mischievous action

devil's advocate a person upholding the wrong side for argument's sake

dev'il's-food' cake a rich chocolate cake

dev'il·try (-trē) *n.*, *pl.* -tries reckless mischief, fun, etc.: also **dev'il·ry**

de·vi·ous (dē'vē əs) *adj.* [< L. *de-*, off + *via*, road] 1. not direct; roundabout or deviating 2. not straightforward —**de'vi·ous·ness** *n.*

de·vise (di vīz') *vt.*, *vi.* -vised', -vis'ing [< L. *dividere*, to divide] 1. to work out or create (a plan, device, etc.) 2. to bequeath (real property) by will —*n.* a bequest of property

de·vi·tal·ize (dē vīt''l īz') *vt.* -ized', -iz'ing to deprive of vitality

de·void (di void') *adj.* [see DE- & VOID] completely without; empty (*of*)

de·voir (də vwär') *n.* [< L. *debere*, to owe] 1. duty 2. [*pl.*] courteous acts

de·volve (di välv') *vt.*, *vi.* -volved', -volv·ing [< L. *de-*, down + *volvere*, to roll] to pass (*on*) to another: said of duties, responsibilities, etc.

de·vote (di vōt') *vt.* -vot·ed, -vot'ing [< L. *de-*, from + *vovere*, to vow] to set apart for or give up to some purpose, activity, or person; dedicate

de·vot'ed *adj.* very loving, loyal, or faithful —**de·vot'ed·ly** *adv.*

dev·o·tee (dev'ə tē', -tā') *n.* one strongly devoted to something

de·vo·tion *n.* 1. a devoting or being devoted 2. piety 3. religious worship 4. [*pl.*] prayers 5. loyalty or deep affection —**de·vo'tion·al** *adj.*

de·vour (di vour´) *vt.* [< L. *de-*, intens. + *vorare*, swallow whole] 1. to eat hungrily 2. to swallow up 3. to take in greedily, as with the eyes

de·vout (di vout´) *adj.* [see DEVOTE] 1. very religious; pious 2. earnest; sincere —**de·vout´ly** *adv.*

dew (dōō) *n.* [OE. *deaw*] 1. atmospheric moisture that condenses in drops on cool surfaces at night 2. anything refreshing, pure, etc., like dew —**dew´y** *adj.* **-i·er, -i·est**

dew´ber´ry *n., pl. -ries* 1. a trailing blackberry plant 2. its berry

dew´claw´ *n.* a functionless digit as on the inner side of a dog's leg

dew´drop´ *n.* a drop of dew

dew´lap´ *n.* [see LAP + LAP¹] loose skin under the throat of cattle, etc.

dex·ter·i·ty (dek ster´ə tē) *n.* [see ff.] skill in using one's hands, body, or mind

dex·ter·ous (dek´strəs, -stər əs) *adj.* [< L. *dexter*, right] having or showing dexterity: also **dex´trous**

dex·trose (dek´strōs) *n.* a glucose in plants and animals

Dha·ka (dä´kə) *the official sp. of* DACCA

dho·ti (dō´tē) *n.* [Hind. *dhotī*] a loincloth worn by Hindu men

dhur·rie (dur´ē, dur´-) *n.* [Hind.] a coarse rug woven in India

di-¹ [Gr. *di-* < *dis*, twice] a prefix meaning twice, double, twofold

di-² *same as* DIS-

di·a·be·tes (dī´ə bēt´is, -ēz) *n.* [< Gr. *dia-*, through + *bainein*, to go] a disease characterized by excess sugar in the blood and urine, hunger, thirst, etc.: also **sugar diabetes** —**dī´a·bet´ic** (-bet´ik) *adj., n.*

di·a·bol·ic (dī´ə bäl´ik) *adj.* [see DEVIL] very wicked or cruel; fiendish: also **dī´a·bol´i·cal**

di·a·crit·ic (dī´ə krit´ik) *adj.* [< Gr. *dia-*, across + *krinein*, to separate] distinguishing: also **dī´a·crit´i·cal** —*n.* a mark, as a macron, added to a letter or symbol to show pronunciation, etc.: in full **diacritical mark**

di·a·dem (dī´ə dem´) *n.* [< Gr. *dia-*, through + *dein*, to bind] 1. a crown 2. an ornamental headband

di·ag·nose (dī´əgnōs´) *vt., vi.* **-nosed´, -nos´ing** to make a diagnosis (of)

di·ag·no·sis (-nō´sis) *n., pl. -ses** (-sēz) [< Gr. *dia-*, through + *gignōskein*, know] 1. the act of deciding the nature of a disease, situation, problem, etc. by examination and analysis 2. the resulting decision —**dī´ag·nos´tic** (-näs´tik) *adj.* —**dī´ag·nos·ti´cian** (-tish´ən) *n.*

di·ag·o·nal (dī ag´ə n'l) *adj.* [< Gr. *dia-*, through + *gōnia*, an angle] 1. extending slantingly between opposite corners 2. slanting; oblique —*n.* a diagonal line, plane, course, part, etc. —**di·ag´o·nal·ly** *adv.*

di·a·gram (dī´ə gram´) *n.* [< Gr. *dia-*, across + *graphein*, write] a sketch, plan, graph, etc. that explains something, as by outlining its parts —*vt.* **-gramed´** or **-grammed´, -gram´ing** or **-gram´ming** to make a diagram of

di·al (dī´əl, dīl) *n.* [< L. *dies*, day] 1. the face of a clock, etc. 2. the face of a meter, etc. for indicating, as by a pointer, an amount, direction, etc. 3. a graduated disk on a radio, etc., esp. for tuning in stations 4. a rotating disk on a telephone, to make automatic connections —*vt., vi.* **-aled** or **-alled, -al·ing** or **-al·ling** 1. to show on or measure with a dial 2. to tune in (a radio station, etc.) 3. to call by using a telephone dial

dial. 1. dialect(al) 2. dialectic(al)

di·a·lect (dī´ə lekt´) *n.* [< Gr. *dia-*, between + *legein*, to talk] the form of a spoken language peculiar to a region, social group, etc. —**dī´a·lec´tal** *adj.*

di·a·lec·tic (-lek´tik) *n.* [*often pl.*] 1. a logical test of ideas for validity 2. logical debate —*adj.* dialectical

di·a·lec·ti·cal *adj.* 1. of or using dialectics 2. of a dialect

di·a·logue, di·a·log (dī´ə lôg´) *n.* [see DIALECT] 1. interchange of ideas by open discussion 2. the passages of talk in a play, story, etc.

Dialogue Mass *R.C.Ch.* a Mass at which the congregation responds aloud

di·am·e·ter (dī am´ət ər) *n.* [< Gr. *dia-*, through + *metron*, a measure] 1. a straight line passing through the center of a circle, sphere, etc. from one side to the other 2. its measure

di·a·met·ri·cal (dī´ə met´ri k'l) *adj.* 1. of or along a diameter 2. designating an opposite altogether such

di·a·mond (dī´mənd, -ə mənd) *n.* [< Gr. *adamas*, adamant] 1. a nearly pure, brilliant, crystalline carbon, the hardest mineral known 2. a gem, etc. cut from it 3. *a)* the plane figure ◊ *b)* a playing card so marked 4. *Baseball* the infield or the whole field

di·a·mond·back´ *n.* a large, poisonous rattlesnake of the S U.S.

Di·an·a (dī an´ə) *Rom. Myth.* the goddess of the moon and of hunting

di·a·pa·son (dī´ə pāz´'n) *n.* [< Gr. *dia*, through + *pas*, all] an organ stop covering the instrument's entire range

di·a·per (dī´pər, dī´ə pər) *n.* [< ML. *diasprum*, flowered cloth] a soft, absorbent cloth folded around a baby's loins —*vt.* to put a diaper on (a baby)

di·aph·a·nous (dī af´ə nəs) *adj.* [< Gr. *dia-*, through + *phainein*, to show] letting much light through

di·a·phragm (dī´ə fram´) *n.* [< Gr. *dia-*, through + *phragma*, fence] 1. the muscular partition between the chest and abdominal cavities 2. a vibrating disk producing sound waves 3. a vaginal contraceptive device —**dī´a·phrag·mat´ic** (-frag mat´ik) *adj.*

di·ar·rhe·a (dī´ə rē´ə) *n.* [< Gr. *dia-*,

through + *rhein*, to flow] too frequent and loose bowel movements

di·a·ry (dī′ə rē) *n., pl.* **-ries** [< L. *dies*, day] a daily written record of one's experiences, etc. —**di′a·rist** *n.*

di·as·to·le (dī as′tə lē′) *n.* [< Gr. *dia-*, apart + *stellein*, put] the usual rhythmic expansion of the heart — **di·a·stol·ic** (dī′ə stäl′ik) *adj.*

di·a·ther·my (dī′ə thur′mē) *n.* [< Gr. *dia-*, through + *thermē*, heat] *Med.* high-frequency electrical induction of heat into tissues below the skin

di·a·tom (dī′ə täm′, -ət əm) *n.* [< Gr. *diatomos*, cut in two] any of various microscopic algae that are an important source of food for marine life

di·a·ton·ic (dī′ə tän′ik) *adj.* [< Gr. *dia-*, through + *teinein*, to stretch] designating or of any standard major or minor scale of eight tones

di·a·tribe (dī′ə trīb′) *n.* [< Gr. *dia-*, through + *tribein*, to rub] a bitter, abusive denunciation

dib·ble (dib′'l) *n.* [ME. *dibbel*] a pointed tool for making holes in the soil for seeds, bulbs, etc.

dice (dīs) *n.pl., sing.* **die** or **dice** [see DIE²] small cubes marked on each side with from one to six dots, used in games of chance —*vi.* **diced, dic′ing** to play or gamble with dice —*vt.* to cut (vegetables, etc.) into small cubes —**no dice** [Colloq.] **1.** no: used in refusing a request **2.** no luck

di·chot·o·my (dī kät′ə mē) *n., pl.* **-mies** [< Gr. *dicha*, in two + *temnein*, to cut] division into two parts

dick (dik) *n.* [Slang] a detective

Dick·ens (dik′'nz), **Charles** (pseud. *Boz*) 1812–70; Eng. novelist

dick·er (dik′ər) *vi., vt.* [ult. < L. *decem*, ten] to bargain or haggle

dick·ey (dik′ē) *n., pl.* **-eys** [< nickname *Dick*] **1.** a detachable collar or shirt front **2.** a small bird: also **dickey bird** **3.** a back seat in a carriage Also **dick′y**, *pl.* **-ies**

di·cot·y·le·don (dī′kät 'l ēd′'n) *n.* a plant with two seed leaves (cotyledons) —**di′cot·y·le′don·ous** *adj.*

dict. 1. dictator **2.** dictionary

Dic·ta·phone (dik′tə fōn′) [DICTA-(TE) + -PHONE] *a trademark for a* machine that records and plays back speech for typed transcripts, etc. —*n.* this machine

dic·tate (dik′tāt; also for *v.* dik tāt′) *vt., vi.* **-tat·ed, -tat·ing** [< L. *dicere*, speak] **1.** to speak (something) aloud for someone else to write down **2.** to command expressly **3.** to give (orders) with authority —*n.* an authoritative order —**dic·ta′tion** *n.*

dic′ta·tor *n.* one who dictates; esp., a ruler or tyrant with absolute power —**dic′ta·to′ri·al** (-tə tôr′ē əl) *adj.* —**dic·ta′tor·ship′** *n.*

dic·tion (dik′shən) *n.* [< L. *dicere*, say] **1.** manner of expression in words; choice of words **2.** enunciation

dic′tion·ar′y (-er′ē) *n., pl.* **-ies** [see prec.] a book of alphabetically listed words in a language, with definitions, pronunciations, etc.

dic·tum (dik′təm) *n., pl.* **-tums, -ta**

(-tə) [L. < *dicere*, speak] a formal statement of opinion; pronouncement

did (did) *pt. of* DO¹

di·dac·tic (dī dak′tik) *adj.* [< Gr. *didaskein*, teach] **1.** intended for instruction **2.** morally instructive

did·dle (did′'l) *vt., vi.* **-died, -dling** [< ?] [Colloq.] **1.** to cheat **2.** to waste (time) in trifling

did·n't (did′'nt) did not

di·do (dī′dō) *n., pl.* **-does, -dos** [< ?] [Colloq.] a mischievous trick; prank

die¹ (dī) *vi.* **died, dy′ing** [< ON. *deyja*] **1.** to stop living **2.** to stop functioning; end **3.** to lose force or activity **4.** [Colloq.] to wish very much [I'm *dying* to go] —**die away** (or **down**) to cease gradually —**die off** to die one by one until all are gone —**die out** to stop existing

die² (dī) *n., pl.,* for 2, **dies** (dīz) [< L. *dare*, give] **1.** *sing.* of DICE **2.** a tool for shaping, punching, etc. metal or other material

die′hard′ *n.* a person stubbornly resistant to new ideas, reform, etc.

diel·drin (dēl′drin) *n.* [*Diel*(s-Al)*d*-(e)*r reaction* + -IN¹] a highly toxic insecticide

di·e·lec·tric (dī′ə lek′trik) *n.* [< *dia-*, across + ELECTRIC] a material that does not conduct electricity

di·er·e·sis (dī er′ə sis) *n., pl.* **-ses′** (-sēz′) [< Gr. *dia-*, apart + *hairein*, to take] a mark (¨) placed over the second of two consecutive vowels to show that it is pronounced separately

die·sel (dē′z'l, -s'l) *n.* [< R. *Diesel*, Ger. inventor] [*often* D-] an internal-combustion engine that burns oil ignited by the heat from air compression: also **diesel engine (or motor)**

di·et¹ (dī′ət) *n.* [< Gr. *diaita*, way of life] **1.** what a person or animal usually eats or drinks **2.** a regimen of special or limited food and drink, as to lose weight —*vi., vt.* to adhere to or place on a diet —**di′e·tar′y** (-ə ter′ē) *adj.* —**di′et·er** *n.*

di·et² (dī′ət) *n.* [< ML. *dieta*] a formal assembly

di′e·tet′ic (-ə tet′ik) *adj.* of or for a particular diet of food and drink

di′e·tet′ics (-ə tet′iks) *n.pl.* [*with sing. v.*] the study of the kinds and quantities of food needed for health

di′e·ti′tian, di′e·ti′cian (-tish′ən) *n.* a specialist in dietetics

dif- (dif) *same as* DIS-: used before *f*

dif·fer (dif′ər) *vi.* [< L. *dis-*, apart + *ferre*, carry] **1.** to be different **2.** to be of a different opinion; disagree

dif·fer·ence (dif′ər əns, dif′rəns) *n.* **1.** a being different **2.** the way in which people or things are different **3.** a differing in opinion; disagreement **4.** a quarrel **5.** the amount by which one quantity is less than another

dif′fer·ent *adj.* **1.** not alike **2.** not the same **3.** various **4.** unusual — **dif′fer·ent·ly** *adv.*

dif′fer·en′tial (-ə ren′shəl) *adj.* of, showing, or constituting a difference —*n.* **1.** a differentiating amount, degree, etc. **2.** a differential gear **3.** *Math.* an infinitesimal difference between values of a variable quantity

dif·fer·en·tial gear (or **gearing**) a gear arrangement allowing one axle to turn faster than the other

dif·fer·en·ti·ate' (-ren'shē āt') *vt.* **-at'ed, -at'ing 1.** to constitute a difference in or between **2.** to make unlike **3.** to distinguish between —*vi.* **1.** to become different or differentiated **2.** to note a difference —**dif'fer·en'·ti·a'tion** *n.*

dif·fi·cult (dif'i kəlt, -kult') *adj.* **1.** hard to do, understand, etc. **2.** hard to satisfy, deal with, etc.

dif'fi·cul·ty *n., pl.* **-ties** [< L. *dis-*, not + *facilis*, easy] **1.** a being difficult **2.** something difficult; problem, obstacle, or objection **3.** trouble

dif·fi·dent (dif'ə dənt) *adj.* [< L. *dis-*, not + *fidere*, to trust] lacking self-confidence; shy —**dif'fi·dence** *n.*

dif·frac·tion (di frak'shən) *n.* [< L. *dis-*, apart + *frangere*, to break] **1.** the breaking up of a ray of light into dark and light bands or into the colors of the spectrum **2.** a similar breaking up of other waves, as of sound

dif·fuse (di fyoos'; *for v.* -fyooz') *adj.* [< L. *dis-*, apart + *fundere*, pour] **1.** spread out; not concentrated **2.** using more words than are needed —*vt., vi.* **-fused', -fus'ing** to pour in every direction; spread widely —**dif·fuse'·ly** *adv.* —**dif·fuse'ness** *n.* —**dif·fu'·sion** *n.* —**dif·fu'sive** *adj.*

dig (dig) *vt.* **dug, dig'ging** [< OFr. < Du. *dijk*, dike] **1.** to turn up or remove (ground, etc.) as with a spade, the hands, etc. **2.** to make (a hole, etc.) by digging **3.** to get out by digging **4.** to find out, as by careful study **5.** to jab **6.** [Slang] *a)* to understand *b)* to like —*vi.* to excavate —*n.* **1.** *a)* [Colloq.] a poke, nudge, etc. *b)* a taunt **2.** an archaeological excavation —**dig'ger** *n.*

di·gest (dī'jest; *for v.* di jest', dī-) *n.* [< L. *dis-*, apart + *gerere*, to bear] a collection of condensed, systematic information; summary —*vt.* **1.** to summarize **2.** to change (food taken into the body) into an absorbable form **3.** to absorb mentally —*vi.* to undergo digestion —**di·gest'i·ble** *adj.*

di·ges'tion *n.* **1.** a digesting or being digested **2.** the ability to digest —**di·ges'tive** *adj.*

dig·it (dij'it) *n.* [< L. *digitus*] **1.** a finger or toe **2.** any number from 0 to 9 —**dig'it·al** *adj.*

digital clock (or **watch**) a timepiece that shows the time in a row of digits

digital computer a computer using numbers to perform calculations

dig·i·tal·is (dij'ə tal'is) *n.* [ModL., foxglove: see DIGIT] **1.** a plant with long spikes of thimblelike flowers; foxglove **2.** a medicine made from the leaves of the purple foxglove, used as a heart stimulant

dig·ni·fied (dig'nə fīd') *adj.* having or showing dignity

dig·ni·fy (dig'nə fī') *vt.* **-fied', -fy'ing** [< L. *dignus*, worthy + *facere*, to make] to give dignity to; exalt

dig·ni·tar·y (-ter'ē) *n., pl.* **-ies** [< L. *dignitas*, dignity + -ARY] a person holding a high position

dig·ni·ty (-tē) *n., pl.* **-ties** [< L. *dignus*, worthy] **1.** honorable quality; worthiness **2.** high repute or honor, or the degree of this **3.** a high position, rank, or title **4.** stately appearance or manner. **5.** self-respect

di·graph (dī'graf) *n.* a combination of two letters to express a simple sound, as *sh* in *show*

di·gress (di gres', dī-) *vi.* [< L. *dis-*, apart + *gradi*, to go] to turn aside, esp. from the main subject, in talking or writing —**di·gres'sion** (-gresh'ən) *n.* —**di·gres'sive** *adj.*

Di·jon mustard (dē zhōn') [after *Dijon*, city in France] a mild mustard paste blended with white wine

dike (dīk) *n.* [OE. *dic*, ditch] an embankment or dam made to prevent flooding by the sea or by a stream

di·lap·i·dat·ed (di lap'ə dāt'id) *adj.* [< L. *dis-*, apart + *lapidare*, throw stones at] falling to pieces; broken down —**di·lap'i·da'tion** *n.*

di·late (dī lāt', di-) *vt., vi.* **-lat'ed, -lat'ing** [< L. *dis-*, apart + *latus*, wide] **1.** to make or become wider or larger **2.** to speak or write at length (*on* or *upon* a subject) —**di·la'tion, dil·a·ta·tion** (dil'ə tā'shən) *n.*

di·la·to·ry (dil'ə tôr'ē) *adj.* [see prec.] **1.** causing delay **2.** inclined to delay; slow; tardy

di·lem·ma (di lem'ə) *n.* [< LGr. *di-*, two + *lēmma*, proposition] any situation requiring a choice between unpleasant alternatives

dil·et·tante (dil'ə tänt', -tän'tē, -tan'tē) *n., pl.* **-tantes', -tan'ti** (-tän'tē) [It. < L. *delectare*, to delight] one who dabbles in art, literature, etc. in a superficial way —**dil'et·tant'ish** *adj.* —**dil'et·tant'ism** *n.*

dil·i·gent (dil'ə jent) *adj.* [< L. *di-*, apart + *legere*, choose] **1.** persevering and careful in work; hard-working **2.** done carefully —**dil'i·gence** *n.* —**dil'i·gent·ly** *adv.*

dill (dil) *n.* [OE. *dile*] a plant of the parsley family, with aromatic leaves and seeds, used to flavor pickles, etc.

dil·ly (dil'ē) *n.* [? < DRL(IGHTFUL) + -y¹] [Slang] a remarkable person or thing

dil·ly·dal·ly (dil'ē dal'ē) *vi.* **-lied, -ly·ing** [redupl. form of DALLY] to waste time by hesitating; loiter or dawdle

di·lute (di loot', dī-) *vt.* **-lut'ed, -lut'ing** [< L. *dis-*, off + *lavere*, to wash] to thin down or weaken as by mixing with water —*adj.* diluted —**di·lu'tion** *n.*

dim (dim) *adj.* **dim'mer, dim'mest** [OE.] **1.** not bright, clear, or distinct; dull, obscure, etc. **2.** not clearly seeing, hearing, or understanding —*vt., vi.*

dimmed, dim′ming to make or grow dim —**dim′ly** adv. —**dim′ness** n.

dim. 1. diminuendo **2.** diminutive

dime (dīm) n. [< L. decem, ten] a U.S. and Canadian 10-cent coin

di·men·sion (də men′shən) n. [< L. dis-, off + metiri, to measure] **1.** any measurable extent, as length, width, etc. **2.** [pl.] measurements in length, width, and often depth **3.** [often pl.] extent; scope —**di·men′sion·al** adj.

dime store same as FIVE-AND-TEN-CENT STORE

di·min·ish (də min′ish) vt., vi. [< L. deminuere, reduce] to make or become smaller in size, degree, importance, etc.; lessen —**dim·i·nu·tion** (dim′ə ny<del>oo</del>′shən, -n<del>oo</del>′-) n.

di·min·u·en·do (də min′yoo wen′dō) adj., adv. [It.: see prec.] Music with gradually diminishing volume

di·min·u·tive (də min′yoo tiv) adj. [see DIMINISH] very small; tiny —n. a word having a suffix that expresses smallness, endearment, etc.

dim·i·ty (dim′ə tē) n., pl. -ties [< Gr. dis-, two + mitos, a thread] a thin, strong, corded cotton cloth

dim′mer n. a device for dimming electric lights

dim·ple (dim′p'l) n. [ME. dimpel] a small, natural hollow, as on the cheek or chin —vi., vt. -pled, -pling to form dimples (in) —**dim′ply** (-plē) adj.

dim sum (dim soom) [Chin.] Chinese dumplings filled with meat, etc.

dim′wit′ n. [Slang] a stupid person; simpleton —**dim′wit′ted** adj.

din (din) n. [OE. dyne] a loud, continuous noise; confused uproar —vt. **dinned, din′ning 1.** to beset with a din **2.** to repeat insistently or noisily

din·din (din′din′) n. [Colloq.] dinner

dine (dīn) vi. **dined, din′ing** [ult. < L. dis-, away + jejunus, fasting] to eat dinner —vt. to provide dinner for

din·er (dī′nər) n. **1.** a person eating dinner **2.** a railroad car equipped to serve meals **3.** a small restaurant built to look like such a car

di·nette (dī net′) n. an alcove or small space used as a dining room

ding (diŋ) n. [< Scand.] the sound of a bell: also **ding′-dong′** (-dôŋ′)

din·ghy (diŋ′gē, diŋ′ē) n., pl. -ghies [Hind. dīṅgī] any of various small boats, as a ship's tender

din·gle (diŋ′g'l) n. [ME. dingel, abyss] a small, deep, wooded valley

din·go (diŋ′gō) n., pl. -goes [native name] the Australian wild dog, usually tawny in color

ding·us (diŋ′əs) n. [< Du. ding, thing] [Colloq.] any device; gadget

din·gy (din′jē) adj. -gi·er, -gi·est [orig. dial. var. < DUNG] **1.** not clean or bright; grimy **2.** dismal; shabby —**din′gi·ness** n.

din·ky (diŋ′kē) adj. -ki·er, -ki·est [< Scot. dink, trim] [Colloq.] small

din·ner (din′ər) n. [see DINE] **1.** the chief meal of the day **2.** a banquet honoring a person or event

din′ner·ware′ (-wer′) n. **1.** plates,

cups, saucers, etc., collectively **2.** a set of such dishes

di·no·saur (dī′nə sôr′) n. [< Gr. deinos, terrible + sauros, lizard] a prehistoric, extinct reptile, often huge

DINOSAUR

dint (dint) n. [OE. dynt] **1.** force; exertion **2.** a dent

di·o·cese (dī′ə sis, -sēs′) n. [< Gr. dioikein, keep house] the district under a bishop's jurisdiction —**di·oc′e·san** (-äs′ə s'n) adj.

di·ode (dī′ōd) n. [DI- + -ODE] an electron tube used esp. as a rectifier

Di·og·e·nes (dī äj′ə nēz′) 412?-323? B.C.; Gr. philosopher

Di·o·ny·sus, Di·o·ny·sos (dī′ə nī′səs) Gr. Myth. the god of wine

di·o·ra·ma (dī′ə ram′ə) n. [< Gr. dia-, through + horama, a view] a scenic display, as of three-dimensional figures against a painted background

di·ox·ide (dī äk′sīd) n. an oxide with two atoms of oxygen per molecule

di·ox·in (-sin) n. a highly toxic chemical contaminant

dip (dip) vt. **dipped, dip′ping** [OE. dyppan] **1.** to immerse briefly **2.** to scoop (liquid) up or out **3.** to lower (a flag, etc.) and immediately raise again —vi. **1.** to plunge into a liquid and quickly come out **2.** to sink suddenly **3.** to decline slightly **4.** to slope down **5.** to lower a container, the hand, etc. as into water **6.** to read or inquire superficially (with into) —n. **1.** a dipping or being dipped **2.** a brief plunge into water, etc. **3.** a liquid, sauce, etc. into which something is dipped **4.** whatever is removed by dipping **5.** a downward slope or plunge

diph·the·ri·a (dif thir′ē ə, dip-) n. [< Gr. diphthera, leather] an acute infectious disease marked by high fever and difficult breathing

diph·thong (dif′thôŋ, dip′-) n. [< Gr. di-, two + phthongos, sound] a sound made by gliding from one vowel to another in one syllable, as in oil

di·plo·ma (di plō′mə) n. [< Gr. diplōma, folded letter] a certificate issued by a school, college, etc. indicating graduation or conferring a degree

di·plo·ma·cy (-sē) n., pl. -cies [see ff.] **1.** the conducting of relations between nations **2.** tact

dip·lo·mat (dip′lə mat′) n. **1.** a representative of a government who conducts relations with another government **2.** a tactful person

dip′lo·mat′ic adj. **1.** of diplomacy **2.** tactful —**dip′lo·mat′i·cal·ly** adv.

dip·per (dip′ər) n. **1.** a long-handled cup, etc. for dipping **2.** [D-] either of two groups of stars in the shape of a dipper (**Big Dipper, Little Dipper**)

dip·so·ma·ni·a (dip′sō mā′nē ə) n. [< Gr. dipsa, thirst + mania, madness] an abnormal craving for alcoholic drink —**dip′so·ma′ni·ac′** (-ak′) n.

dip′stick′ n. a graduated rod for measuring quantity or depth

dire (dīr) *adj.* **dir′er**, **dir′est** [L. *dirus*] 1. dreadful; terrible: also **dire′-ful** 2. urgent *[dire* need*]*.

di·rect (di rekt′, dī-) *adj.* [< L. *di-*, apart + *regere*, to rule] 1. not round-about or interrupted; straight 2. honest; frank 3. with nothing be-tween; immediate 4. in unbroken line of descent; lineal 5. exact; complete *[the direct* opposite*]* 6. in the exact words *[a direct* quote*]* —*vt.* 1. to manage; guide 2. to order; command 3. to turn or point; aim; head 4. to tell (a person) the way to a place 5. to address (a letter, etc.) 6. to supervise the action and effects of (a play, etc.) —*adv.* directly —**di·rect′ness** *n.*

direct current an electric current flowing in one direction

di·rec·tion (də rek′shən, dī-) *n.* 1. a directing 2. *[usually pl.]* instructions for doing, using, etc. 3. a command 4. the point toward which something faces or the line along which it moves or lies —**di·rec′tion·al** *adj.*

di·rec′tive (-tiv) *adj.* directing —*n.* a general order issued authoritatively

di·rect′ly *adv.* 1. in a direct way or line; straight 2. with nothing coming between 3. exactly *[directly* opposite*]* 4. instantly; right away

direct object the word or words that denote the receiver of the action of a verb (Ex.: *me* in he hit me)

di·rec′tor *n.* one who directs a school, corporation, etc. or a play, choir, etc. —**di·rec′tor·ship′** *n.*

di·rec·to·ry (-tə rē) *n., pl.* **-ries** a book listing the names, addresses, etc. of a specific group of pesrson

dirge (durj) *n.* [< L. *dirige* (direct), first word of a prayer] a song, poem, etc. of grief or mourning

dir·i·gi·ble (dir′i jə b'l) *n.* [see DIRECT & -IBLE] *same as* AIRSHIP

dirk (durk) *n.* [< ?] a short dagger

dirn·dl (durn′d'l) *n.* [< G. *dirne*, girl] a full skirt gathered at the waist

dirt (durt) *n.* [< ON. *drit*, excre-ment] 1. any unclean matter, as mud, trash, etc.; filth 2. earth; soil 3. dirtiness, corruption, etc. 4. obscenity 5. malicious gossip

dirt′-cheap′ *adj., adv.* [Colloq.] very inexpensive

dirt′y *adj.* **-i·er**, **-i·est** 1. not clean 2. obscene 3. contemptible or nasty 4. unfair; dishonest 5. rough, as weather —*vt., vi.* **-ied**, **-y·ing** to make or become dirty —**dirt′i·ness** *n.*

dis- [< L.] a *prefix meaning* separa-tion, negation, reversal *[disjoint, dis-honest, disown]*

dis·a·bil·i·ty (dis′ə bil′ə tē) *n., pl.* **-ties** 1. a disabled condition 2. that which disables or disqualifies

dis·a′ble (-ā′b'l) *vt.* **-bled**, **-bling** to make unable, unfit, or disqualified

dis·a·buse (dis′ə byōoz′) *vt.* **-bused′**, **-bus′ing** to rid of false ideas

dis·ad·van·tage (dis′əd van′tij) *n.* 1. an unfavorable situation or circum-stance 2. detriment —**dis·ad′van-ta′geous** (-ad′vən tā′jəs) *adj.*

dis′ad·van′taged *adj.* underprivi-leged

dis·af·fect (dis′ə fekt′) *vt.* to make unfriendly, discontented, or disloyal —**dis′af·fec′tion** *n.*

dis·af·fil·i·ate′ (-ə fil′ē āt′) *vt., vi.* **-at′ed**, **-at′ing** to end an affiliation (with) —**dis′af·fil′i·a′tion** *n.*

dis·a·gree′ (-ə grē′) *vi.* **-greed′**, **-gree′ing** 1. to fail to agree; differ 2. to differ in opinion; quarrel 3. to give distress (with *with*) —**dis′a-gree′ment** *n.*

dis′a·gree′a·ble *adj.* 1. unpleasant; offensive 2. quarrelsome —**dis′a-gree′a·bly** *adv.*

dis·al·low (dis′ə lou′) *vt.* to refuse to allow (a claim, etc.); reject

dis·ap·pear′ (-ə pir′) *vi.* 1. to cease to be seen; vanish 2. to cease existing —**dis′ap·pear′ance** *n.*

dis·ap·point′ (-ə point′) *vt.* to fail to satisfy the hopes or expectations of —**dis′ap·point′ment** *n.*

dis·ap·pro·ba·tion (dis ap′rə bā′shən) *n.* a disapproving; disapproval

dis·ap·prove (dis′ə prōōv′) *vt., vi.* **-proved′**, **-prov′ing** 1. to have or express an unfavorable opinion (of) 2. to refuse to approve —**dis′ap-prov′al** *n.* —**dis′ap·prov′ing·ly** *adv.*

dis·arm (dis ärm′) *vt.* 1. to take away weapons from 2. to make harm-less 3. to make friendly —*vi.* to reduce armed forces and armaments —**dis-ar′ma·ment** (-är′mə mənt) *n.*

dis·ar·range (dis′ə rānj′) *vt.* **-ranged′**, **-rang′ing** to undo the order of —**dis′ar·range′ment** *n.*

dis·ar·ray′ (-ə rā′) *vt.* to throw into disorder —*n.* disorder

dis·as·sem·ble (-ə sem′b'l) *vt.* **-bled**, **-bling** to take apart

dis′as·so′ci·ate′ (-ə sō′shē āt′, -sē-) *vt.* **-at′ed**, **-at′ing** to sever associa-tion with; dissociate

dis·as·ter (di zas′tər) *n.* [< L. *dis-* + *astrum*, a star] any happening that causes great harm or damage; calamity —**dis·as′trous** (-trəs) *adj.*

dis·a·vow (dis′ə vou′) *vt.* to deny any knowledge of or responsibility for; disclaim —**dis′a·vow′al** *n.*

dis·band (dis band′) *vi., vt.* to break up, as an organization

dis·bar (-bär′) *vt.* **-barred′**, **-bar′-ring** to deprive (a lawyer) of the right to practice law —**dis·bar′ment** *n.*

dis·be·lieve (dis′bə lēv′) *vt., vi.* **-lieved′**, **-liev′ing** to refuse to believe —**dis′be·lief′** (-lēf′) *n.*

dis·burse (dis burs′) *vt.* **-bursed′**, **-burs′ing** [< OFr. *desbourser*] to pay out; expend —**dis·burse′ment** *n.*

disc (disk) *n.* 1. *same as* DISK 2. a phonograph record

dis·card (dis kärd′; *for n.* dis′kärd) *vt.* [< OFr.: see DIS- & CARD] 1. *Card Games* to throw away (undesired cards) 2. to get rid of as no longer useful —*n.* **1.** a discarding or being discarded **2.** something discarded

disc brake a brake, as on an auto, with two friction pads that press on a disc rotating along with the wheel

dis·cern (di surn′, -zurn′) *vt.* [< L. *dis-*, apart + *cernere*, to separate] to perceive or recognize clearly —**dis·cern′i·ble** *adj.* —**dis·cern′ment** *n.*

dis·cern′ing *adj.* having good judgment; astute —**dis·cern′ing·ly** *adv.*

dis·charge (dis chärj′; *for n., usually* dis′chärj) *vt.* -**charged′**, -**charg′ing** [< L. *dis-*, from + *carrus*, wagon] **1.** to release or dismiss **2.** to unload (a cargo) **3.** to shoot (a gun or projectile) **4.** to emit [to *discharge* pus] **5.** to pay (a debt) or perform (a duty) **6.** *Elec.* to remove stored energy from (a battery, etc.) —*vi.* **1.** to get rid of a load, etc. **2.** to go off, as a gun —*n.* **1.** a discharging or being discharged **2.** that which discharges or is discharged

dis·ci·ple (di sī′p'l) *n.* [< L. *dis-*, apart + *capere*, to hold] **1.** a pupil or follower of any teacher or school **2.** an early follower of Jesus; esp., one of the Apostles —**dis·ci′ple·ship′** *n.*

dis·ci·pli·nar·i·an (dis′ə pli ner′ē ən) *n.* one who believes in or enforces strict discipline

dis·ci·pline (dis′ə plin) *n.* [see DISCIPLE] **1.** training that develops self-control, efficiency, etc. **2.** strict control to enforce obedience **3.** orderly conduct **4.** a system of rules, as for a monastic order **5.** treatment that corrects or punishes —*vt.* -**plined**, -**plin·ing 1.** to train; control **2.** to punish —**dis′ci·pli·nar′y** (-pli ner′ē) *adj.*

disc jockey one who conducts a radio program of recorded music

dis·claim (dis klām′) *vt.* **1.** to give up any claim to **2.** to repudiate

dis·claim′er *n.* a denial or renunciation, as of responsibility

dis·close (dis klōz′) *vt.* -**closed′**, -**clos′ing** to uncover; reveal —**dis·clo′sure** (-klō′zhər) *n.*

dis·co (dis′kō) *n.,* **1.** *pl.* -**cos** *clipped form of* DISCOTHÈQUE **2.** a kind of popular dance music with a strong beat

dis·col·or *vt., vi.* to change in color by streaking, staining, etc.: Brit. sp. **discolour** —**dis·col′or·a′tion** *n.*

dis·com·fit (dis kum′fit) *vt.* [< L. *dis-*, away + *conficere*, prepare] **1.** to frustrate the plans of **2.** to disconcert —**dis·com′fi·ture** (-fi chər) *n.*

dis·com·fort *n.* **1.** lack of comfort; uneasiness **2.** anything causing this —*vt.* to cause discomfort to

dis·com·mode (dis′kə mōd′) *vt.* -**mod′ed**, -**mod′ing** [< DIS- + L. *commodare*, make suitable] to cause bother to; inconvenience

dis·com·pose (-kəm pōz′) *vt.* -**posed′**, -**pos′ing** to disturb; fluster —**dis·com·po′sure** (-pō′zhər) *n.*

dis·con·cert (-kən surt′) *vt.* to upset; embarrass; confuse

dis·con·nect′ (-kə nekt′) *vt.* to break the connection of; separate —**dis·con·nec′tion** *n.*

dis·con·nect′ed *adj.* **1.** separated **2.** incoherent

dis·con·so·late (dis kän′sə lit) *adj.* [see DIS- & CONSOLE¹] inconsolable; dejected —**dis·con′so·late·ly** *adv.*

dis·con·tent (dis′kən tent′) *adj. same as* DISCONTENTED —*n.* dissatisfaction with one's situation: also **dis′con·tent′ment** —*vt.* to make discontented

dis′con·tent′ed *adj.* not contented; wanting something more or different

dis·con·tin·ue (dis′kən tin′yōō) *vt., vi.* -**ued**, -**u·ing** to stop; cease; give up —**dis′con·tin′u·ance**, **dis′con·tin′u·a′tion** *n.*

dis′con·tin′u·ous *adj.* not continuous; having interruptions or gaps

dis·cord (dis′kôrd) *n.* [< L. *dis-*, apart + *cor*, heart] **1.** disagreement **2.** a harsh noise **3.** a lack of musical harmony —**dis·cord′ant** *adj.*

dis·co·thèque (dis′kə tek) *n.* [Fr.] a place for dancing to recorded music

dis·count (dis′kount; *for v. also* dis kount′) *n.* [see DIS- & COMPUTE] **1.** a reduction from the usual or list price **2.** the rate of interest charged on a discounted bill —*vt.* **1.** to pay or receive the value of (a bill, promissory note, etc.) minus a deduction for interest **2.** to deduct an amount from (a bill, price, etc.) **3.** to sell at less than the regular price **4.** *a)* to allow for exaggeration, bias, etc. in (a story, etc.) *b)* to disregard **5.** to lessen the effect of by anticipating

dis·coun·te·nance (dis koun′tə nəns) *vt.* -**nanced**, -**nanc·ing 1.** to make ashamed or embarrassed; disconcert **2.** to refuse approval or support to

discount house (or **store**) a retail store that sells goods for less than regular prices

dis·cour·age (dis kur′ij) *vt.* -**aged**, -**ag·ing 1.** to deprive of courage or confidence **2.** to persuade (a person) to refrain **3.** to try to prevent by disapproving —**dis·cour′age·ment** *n.*

dis·course (dis′kôrs; *for v., usually* dis kôrs′) *n.* [< L. *dis-*, from + *currere*, to run] **1.** talk; conversation **2.** a formal treatment of a subject, spoken or written —*vi.* -**coursed′**, -**cours′ing** to talk

dis·cour·te·ous (dis kur′tē əs) *adj.* impolite; ill-mannered

dis·cour·te·sy (-tə sē) *n.* **1.** lack of courtesy; rudeness **2.** *pl.* -**sies** a rude or impolite act or remark

dis·cov·er (dis kuv′ər) *vt.* [see DIS- & COVER] **1.** to be the first to find out, see, etc. **2.** to learn the existence of —**dis·cov′er·er** *n.*

dis·cov′er·y *n., pl.* -**ies 1.** a discovering **2.** anything discovered

dis·cred·it (dis kred′it) *vt.* **1.** to disbelieve **2.** to cast doubt on **3.** to disgrace —*n.* **1.** loss of belief; doubt **2.** disgrace —**dis·cred′it·a·ble** *adj.*

dis·creet (dis krēt′) *adj.* [see DISCERN] careful about what one says or does; prudent —**dis·creet′ly** *adv.*

dis·crep·an·cy (dis krep′ən sē) *n., pl.* -**cies** [< L. *dis-*, from + *crepare*, to rattle] disagreement; inconsistency

dis·crete (dis krēt′) *adj.* [see DISCERN] separate and distinct; unrelated

dis·cre·tion (dis kresh'ən) n. 1. the freedom to make decisions 2. the quality of being discreet; prudence —**dis·cre'tion·ar'y** (-er'ē) adj.

dis·crim·i·nate (dis krim'ə nāt') vi. -nat'ed, -nat'ing [see DISCERN] 1. to distinguish 2. to make distinctions in treatment; show partiality or prejudice —**dis·crim'i·nat'ing** adj. —**dis·crim'i·na'tion** n.

dis·crim·i·na·to·ry (-nə tôr'ē) adj. showing discrimination or bias

dis·cur·sive (dis kur'siv) adj. [see DISCOURSE] wandering from one topic to another; rambling

dis·cus (dis'kəs) n. [< Gr. diskos] a disk, as of metal and wood, thrown in a contest of strength and skill

dis·cuss (dis kus') vt. [< L. dis-, apart + quatere, to shake] to talk or write about; consider the pros and cons of —**dis·cus'sion** (-kush'ən) n.

dis·cus·sant (-ənt) n. a participant in an organized discussion

dis·dain (dis dān') vt. [< L. dis-, not + dignari, deign] to regard as beneath one's dignity; scorn —n. aloof contempt —**dis·dain'ful** adj.

dis·ease (di zēz') n. [< OE. des- + aise, ease] 1. illness in general 2. a particular destructive process in an organism; specif., an illness —**dis·eased'** adj.

dis·em·bark (dis'im bärk') vi., vt. to leave, or unload from, a ship, aircraft, etc. —**dis'em·bar·ka'tion** n.

dis·em·bod·y (-im bäd'ē) vt. -ied, -y·ing to free from bodily existence —**dis'em·bod'i·ment** n.

dis·em·bow·el (-im bou'əl) vt. -eled or -elled, -el·ing or -el·ling to take out the entrails of

dis·em·ployed (dis'im ploid') adj. out of work, esp. because of lack of training or education

dis·en·chant (-in chant') vt. to free from an enchantment; disillusion —**dis'en·chant'ment** n.

dis·en·cum·ber (-in kum'bər) vt. to relieve of a burden

dis·en·gage vt., vi. -gaged', -gag'ing to release or get loose from something that engages, holds, entangles, etc.; unfasten —**dis'en·gage'ment** n.

dis·en·tan·gle vt. -gled, -gling to free from something that entangles, confuses, etc.; extricate; untangle

dis·es·teem n. lack of esteem

dis·fa·vor (dis fā'vər) n. 1. an unfavorable opinion; dislike; disapproval 2. the state of being disliked, etc.

dis·fig·ure (dis fig'yər) vt. -ured, -ur·ing to hurt the appearance of; mar —**dis·fig'ure·ment** n.

dis·fran·chise (dis fran'chīz) vt. -chised, -chis·ing to deprive of a right, privilege, etc., esp. the right to vote: also **dis·en·fran'chise**

dis·gorge (-gôrj') vt., vi. -gorged', -gorg'ing [< OFr.: see DIS- & GORGE] 1. to vomit 2. to pour forth (its contents); empty (itself)

dis·grace (-grās') n. [< It. dis-, not + grazia, favor] 1. loss of favor or respect; shame; disrepute 2. a person or thing bringing shame —vt. -graced', -grac'ing to bring shame or dishonor upon —**dis·grace'ful** adj.

dis·grun·tle (-grun't'l) vt. -tled, -tling [ult. < DIS- + GRUNT] to make peevishly discontented; make sulky

dis·guise (-gīz') vt. -guised', -guis·ing [< OFr.: see DIS- & GUISE] 1. to make appear, sound, etc. so different as to be unrecognizable 2. to hide the real nature of —n. 1. anything that disguises 2. a being disguised —**dis·guise'ment** n.

dis·gust (-gust') n. [< DIS- + L. gustus, taste] a sickening dislike —vt. to make feel disgust —**dis·gust'ed** adj. —**dis·gust'ing** adj.

dish (dish) n. [see DISCUS] 1. a container, generally shallow and concave, for holding food 2. as much as a dish holds 3. a particular kind of food —vt. to serve in a dish (with up or out)

dis·ha·bille (dis'ə bēl') n. [< Fr. dés-, dis- + habiller, to dress] the state of being dressed only partially or in night clothes

dish antenna a radio antenna with a dish-shaped reflector

dis·har·mo·ny (dis här'mə nē) n. lack of harmony; discord —**dis'har·mo'ni·ous** (-mō'nē əs) adj.

dish'cloth' n. a cloth for washing dishes; also **dish'rag'**

dis·heart·en (dis härt''n) vt. to discourage; depress

di·shev·el (di shev'l) vt. -eled or -elled, -el·ing or -el·ling [< OFr. des-, dis- + chevel, hair] to cause (hair, clothes, etc.) to become disarranged; rumple —**di·shev'el·ment** n.

dis·hon·est adj. not honest; not to be trusted —**dis·hon'est·ly** adv.

dis·hon·es·ty n. 1. a being dishonest 2. pl. -ties a dishonest act

dis·hon·or n. 1. loss of honor or respect; shame; disgrace 2. a cause of dishonor —vt. to insult or disgrace —**dis·hon'or·a·ble** adj.

dish'wash'er n. a person or machine that washes dishes, etc.

dis·il·lu·sion (-'l) vt. 1. to free from illusion 2. to take away the idealism of and make bitter, etc. —**dis'il·lu'sion·ment** n.

dis·in·cline (dis'in klīn') vt. -clined', -clin'ing to make unwilling

dis·in·fect (dis'in fekt') vt. to destroy the harmful bacteria, viruses, etc. in; sterilize —**dis'in·fect'ant** n.

dis·in·gen·u·ous (dis'in jen'yoo·wəs) adj. not candid or frank

dis·in·her·it (dis'in her'it) vt. to deprive of an inheritance

dis·in·te·grate (dis in'tə grāt') vt., vi. -grat'ed, -grat'ing to separate into parts or fragments; break up —**dis·in'te·gra'tion** n.

dis·in·ter (dis'in tur') vt. -terred', -ter'ring to remove from a grave, etc.

dis·in·ter·est·ed (dis in'trist id, -tər ist id) *adj.* 1. impartial; unbiased 2. uninterested; indifferent

dis·in·ter·me·di·a'tion (-tər mē'-dē ā'shən) *n.* the withdrawal of funds from banks to invest them at higher interest, as in government securities

dis·joint' *vt.* 1. to put out of joint; dislocate 2. to dismember 3. to destroy the unity, connections, etc. of —**dis·joint'ed** *adj.*

disk *n.* [see DISCUS] 1. any thin, flat, circular thing 2. *same as* DISC

dis·like' *vt.* -liked', -lik'ing to have a feeling of not liking —*n.* a feeling of not liking; distaste

dis·lo·cate (dis'lō kāt') *vt.* -cat'ed, -cat'ing 1. to displace (a bone) from its proper position 2. to disarrange; disrupt —**dis'lo·ca'tion** *n.*

dis·lodge' *vt., vi.* -lodged', -lodg'-ing to force from or leave a place where lodged, hiding, etc.

dis·loy'al *adj.* not loyal or faithful —**dis·loy'al·ty** *n., pl.* -ties

dis·mal (diz'm'l) *adj.* [< ML. *dies mali*, evil days] 1. causing gloom or misery 2. dark and gloomy; dreary

dis·man·tle (dis man't'l) *vt.* -tled, -tling [see DIS- & MANTLE] 1. to strip (a house, etc.) as of furniture 2. to take apart —**dis·man'tle·ment** *n.*

dis·may' (-mā') *vt.* [< Anglo-Fr.] to make afraid at the prospect of trouble; daunt —*n.* consternation

dis·mem'ber (-mem'bər) *vt.* [see DIS- & MEMBER] 1. to cut or tear the limbs from 2. to pull or cut to pieces —**dis·mem'ber·ment** *n.*

dis·miss' (-mis') *vt.* [< L. *dis-*, from + *mittere*, send] 1. to cause or allow to leave 2. to discharge from an office, employment, etc. 3. to put aside mentally —**dis·miss'al** *n.*

dis·mount' *vi.* to get off, as from a horse —*vt.* 1. to remove (a thing) from its mounting 2. to take apart

dis·o·be·di·ence (dis'ə bē'dē əns) *n.* refusal to obey; insubordination —**dis'o·be'di·ent** *adj.*

dis'o·bey' *vt., vi.* to refuse to obey

dis'o·blige' *vt.* -bliged', -blig'ing 1. to refuse to oblige 2. to offend

dis·or'der *n.* 1. a lack of order; confusion 2. a breach of public peace; riot 3. an upset of normal function; ailment —*vt.* 1. to throw into disorder 2. to upset the normal functions of

dis·or'der·ly *adj.* 1. untidy 2. unruly 3. violating public peace, safety, etc. —**dis·or'der·li·ness** *n.*

dis·or'gan·ize (dis ôr'gə nīz') *vt.* -ized', -iz'ing to break up the order or system of; throw into confusion —**dis·or'gan·i·za'tion** *n.*

dis·o'ri·ent' (-ôr'ē ent') *vt.* [see DIS- & ORIENT, *v.*] 1. to cause to lose one's bearings 2. to confuse mentally

dis·own' *vt.* to refuse to acknowledge as one's own; repudiate

dis·par·age (dis par'ij) *vt.* -aged, -ag·ing [< OFr. *des-* (see DIS-) + *parage*, rank] 1. to discredit 2. to belittle —**dis·par'age·ment** *n.*

dis·pa·rate (dis'pər it) *adj.* [< L. *dis-*, not + *par*, equal] distinct or

different in kind; unequal —**dis·par'-i·ty** (-par'ə tē) *n., pl.* -ties

dis·pas·sion·ate *adj.* free from passion or bias; calm; impartial —**dis·pas'sion·ate·ly** *adv.*

dis·patch (dis pach') *vt.* [< L. *dis-*, away + *pes*, foot] 1. to send promptly, as on an errand 2. to kill 3. to finish quickly —*n.* 1. a sending off 2. a killing 3. speed; promptness 4. a message 5. a news story sent by a reporter —**dis·patch'er** *n.*

dis·pel' (dis pel') *vt.* -pelled', -pel'-ling [< L. *dis-*, apart + *pellere*, to drive] to scatter and drive away

dis·pen·sa·ble (dis pen'sə b'l) *adj.* 1. that can be dealt out 2. that can be dispensed with; not important

dis·pen·sa·ry (-sə rē) *n., pl.* -ries a room or place where medicines and first-aid treatment are available

dis·pen·sa·tion (dis'pən sā'shən) *n.* 1. a dispensing 2. anything distributed 3. an administrative system 4. a release from an obligation 5. *Theol. a)* the ordering of events under divine authority *b)* any religious system

dis·pense (dis pens') *vt.* -pensed', -pens'ing [< L. *dis-*, out + *pendere*, weigh] 1. to give out; distribute 2. to prepare and give out (medicines) 3. to administer (the law or justice) —**dispense with** 1. to get rid of 2. to do without —**dis·pens'er** *n.*

dis·perse' (-purs') *vt.* -persed', -pers'ing [< L. *dis-*, out + *spargere*, strew] 1. to break up and scatter 2. to dispel (mist, etc.) —*vi.* to scatter —**dis·per'sal** *n.* —**dis·per'sion** *n.*

dis·pir·it (di spir'it) *vt.* to depress; discourage —**dis·pir'it·ed** *adj.*

dis·place' *vt.* -placed', -plac'ing 1. to move from its usual place 2. to remove from office 3. to replace

displaced person one forced from his country, esp. as a result of war

dis·place'ment *n.* 1. a displacing or being displaced 2. the weight or volume of air, water, or other fluid displaced by a floating object

dis·play (dis plā') *vt.* [< L. *dis-*, apart + *plicare*, to fold] 1. to unfold; spread out 2. to exhibit —*n.* 1. an exhibition 2. anything displayed

dis·please' *vt., vi.* -pleased', -pleas'ing to fail to please; offend

dis·pleas'ure (-plezh'ər) *n.* a being displeased; dissatisfaction

dis·port (dis pôrt') *vi.* [< OFr. *des-* (see DIS-) + *porter*, carry] to play; frolic —*vt.* to amuse (oneself)

dis·pose (dis pōz') *vt.* -posed', -pos'ing [see DIS- & POSITION] 1. to arrange 2. to settle (affairs) 3. to make willing —**dispose of** 1. to settle 2. to give away or sell 3. to get rid of —**dis·pos'a·ble** *adj.* —**dis·pos'al** *n.*

dis·pos'er *n.* 1. one that disposes 2. a device in the drain of a kitchen sink for grinding up garbage

dis·po·si·tion (dis'pə zish'ən) *n.* 1. arrangement 2. management of affairs 3. a selling or giving away 4. the authority to settle, etc.; control 5. a tendency 6. one's temperament

dis'pos·sess' *vt.* to deprive of the

possession of land, a house, etc.; oust

dis·praise (dis prāz′) *vt.* -praised′, -prais′ing [< OFr. *despreisier*] to blame; censure —*n.* blame

dis′pro·por′tion *n.* a lack of proportion —**dis′pro·por′tion·ate** *adj.*

dis·prove′ *vt.* -proved′, -prov′ing to prove to be false —**dis·proof′** *n.*

dis·pu·ta·tion (dis′pyoo tā′shən) *n.* 1. a disputing 2. debate

dis′pu·ta′tious (-pyoo tā′shəs) *adj.* inclined to dispute; contentious — **dis′pu·ta′tious·ly** *adv.*

dis·pute (dis pyōōt′) *vi.* -put′ed, -put′ing [< L. *dis-*, apart + *putare*, think] 1. to argue; debate 2. to quarrel —*vt.* 1. to argue (a question) 2. to doubt 3. to oppose in any way —*n.* 1. a disputing; debate 2. a quarrel —**in dispute** not settled — **dis·pu′ta·ble** *adj.* —**dis·pu′tant** *adj., n.*

dis·qual·i·fy *vt.* -fied′, -fy′ing to make or declare unqualified, unfit, or ineligible —**dis·qual′i·fi·ca′tion** *n.*

dis·qui·et (dis kwī′ət) *vt.* to make uneasy; disturb —*n.* restlessness: also **dis·qui′e·tude′** (-ə tōōd′)

dis·qui·si·tion (dis′kwə zish′ən) *n.* [< L. *dis-*, apart + *quaerere*, seek] a formal discussion; treatise

dis·re·gard (dis′ri gärd′) *vt.* 1. to pay little or no attention to 2. to treat without due respect —*n.* 1. lack of attention 2. lack of due regard or respect —**dis′re·gard′ful** *adj.*

dis·re·pair′ *n.* the condition of needing repairs; state of neglect

dis·rep′u·ta·ble *adj.* 1. not reputable 2. not fit to be seen

dis′re·pute′ *n.* lack or loss of repute; bad reputation; disgrace

dis′re·spect′ *n.* lack of respect; discourtesy —**dis′re·spect′ful** *adj.*

dis·robe (dis rōb′) *vt., vi.* -robed′, -rob′ing to undress

dis·rupt (dis rupt′) *vt., vi.* [< L. *dis-*, apart + *rumpere*, to break] 1. to break apart 2. to disturb or interrupt —**dis·rup′tion** *n.* —**dis·rup′tive** *adj.*

dis·sat·is·fy *vt.* -fied′, -fy′ing to fail to satisfy; displease —**dis·sat′is·fac′tion** *n.*

dis·sect (di sekt′) *vt.* [< L. *dis-*, apart + *secare*, to cut] 1. to cut apart piece by piece, as a body for purposes of study 2. to analyze closely —**dis·sec′tion** *n.* —**dis·sec′tor** *n.*

dis·sem·ble (di sem′b'l) *vt., vi.* -bled, -bling [< OFr. *dessembler*] to conceal (the truth, one's feelings, etc.) under a false appearance —**dis·sem′blance** *n.* —**dis·sem′bler** *n.*

dis·sem·i·nate (di sem′ə nāt′) *vt.* -nat′ed, -nat′ing [< L. *dis-*, apart + *seminare*, to sow] to scatter about; spread widely —**dis·sem′i·na′tion** *n.*

dis·sen·sion (di sen′shən) *n.* a dissenting; disagreement or quarreling

dis·sent (di sent′) *vi.* [< L. *dis-*, apart + *sentire*, feel] 1. to disagree 2. to reject the doctrines of an estab-

lished church —*n.* a dissenting —**dis·sent′er** *n.*

dis·ser·ta·tion (dis′ər tā′shən) *n.* [< L. *dis-*, apart + *serere*, join] a formal discourse or treatise; thesis

dis·serv·ice (dis sur′vis) *n.* harm

dis·sev·er (di sev′ər) *vt.* 1. to sever 2. to divide into parts —*vi.* to separate; disunite

dis·si·dence (dis′ə dəns) *n.* [< L. *dis-*, apart + *sidere*, sit] disagreement —**dis′si·dent** (-dənt) *adj., n.*

dis·sim·i·lar (di sim′ə lər) *adj.* not similar; different —**dis·sim′i·lar′i·ty** (-lar′ə tē) *n., pl.* -ties

dis·si·mil·i·tude (dis′si mil′ə tōōd′) *n.* dissimilarity; difference

dis·sim·u·late (di sim′yə lāt′) *vt., vi.* -lat′ed, -lat′ing [see DIS- & SIMULATE] to dissemble —**dis·sim′u·la′tion** *n.* —**dis·sim′u·la′tor** *n.*

dis·si·pate (dis′ə pāt′) *vt.* -pat′ed, -pat′ing [< L. *dis-*, apart + *supare*, to throw] 1. to scatter; disperse 2. to make disappear 3. to waste or squander —*vi.* 1. to vanish 2. to indulge in pleasure to the point of harming oneself —**dis′si·pa′tion** *n.*

dis·so·ci·ate (di sō′shē āt′) *vt.* -at′ed, -at′ing [< L. *dis-*, apart + *sociare*, join] to break the connection between; disunite —**dis·so′ci·a′tion** *n.*

dis·so·lute (dis′ə lōōt′) *adj.* [see DISSOLVE] dissipated and immoral —**dis′so·lute′ly** *adv.* —**dis′so·lute′ness** *n.*

dis·so·lu·tion (dis′ə lōō′shən) *n.* a dissolving or being dissolved; specif., *a*) a breaking up or into parts *b*) termination *c*) death

dis·solve (di zälv′, -zôlv′) *vt., vi.* -solved′, -solv′ing [< L. *dis-*, apart + *solvere*, loosen] 1. to make or become liquid; melt 2. to pass or make pass into solution 3. to break up 4. to end as by breaking up 5. to disappear or make disappear

dis·so·nance (dis′ə nəns) *n.* [< L. *dis-*, apart + *sonus*, a sound] 1. an inharmonious combination of sounds; discord 2. any lack of harmony or agreement —**dis′so·nant** *adj.*

dis·suade (di swād′) *vt.* -suad′ed, -suad′ing [< L. *dis-*, away + *suadere*, persuade] to turn (a person) aside (*from* a course, etc.) by persuasion or advice —**dis·sua′sion** *n.*

dis·taff (dis′taf) *n.* [< OE. *dis-*, flax + *stæf*, staff] a staff on which flax, wool, etc. is wound for use in spinning —*adj.* female

dis·tal (dis′t'l) *adj.* [DIST(ANT) + -AL] *Anat.* farthest from the point of attachment or origin —**dis′tal·ly** *adv.*

dis·tance (dis′təns) *n.* [< L. *dis-*, apart + *stare*, to stand] 1. a being separated in space or time; remoteness 2. an interval between two points in space or time 3. a remoteness in behavior; reserve 4. a faraway place

dis′tant (-tənt) *adj.* 1. far away in space or time 2. away [100 miles *distant]* 3. far apart in relationship 4. aloof; reserved 5. from or at a distance —**dis·tant·ly** adv.

dis·taste (dis tāst′) n. dislike —**dis·taste′ful** adj.

dis·tem·per (dis tem′pər) n. [< ML. *distemperare*, to disorder] an infectious virus disease of young dogs

dis·tend (dis tend′) vt., vi. [< L. *dis-*, apart + *tendere*, to stretch] 1. to stretch out 2. to make or become swollen —**dis·ten′tion** n.

dis·till, dis·til (dis til′) vi., vt. -tilled′, -till′ing [< L. *de-*, down + *stillare*, to drop] 1. to fall or let fall in drops 2. to undergo, subject to, or produce by distillation —**dis·till′er** n.

dis·til·late (dis′tə lāt′, -t′l it) n. a liquid obtained by distilling

dis·til·la·tion (dis′tə lā′shən) n. 1. the process of heating a mixture and condensing the resulting vapor to produce a more nearly pure substance 2. anything distilled

dis·till′er·y n., pl. -ies a place where alcoholic liquors are distilled

dis·tinct (dis tiŋkt′) adj. [see DISTINGUISH] 1. not alike 2. separate 3. clearly marked off; plain 4. unmistakable —**dis·tinct′ly** adv.

dis·tinc′tion (-tiŋk′shən) n. 1. the act of making or keeping distinct 2. difference 3. a quality or feature that differentiates 4. fame; eminence 5. the quality that makes one seem superior 6. a mark of honor

dis·tinc′tive adj. making distinct; characteristic —**dis·tinc′tive·ly** adv. —**dis·tinc′tive·ness** n.

dis·tin·guish (dis tiŋ′gwish) vt. [< L. *dis-*, apart + *stinguere*, to prick] 1. to perceive or show the difference in 2. to characterize 3. to perceive clearly 4. to classify 5. to make famous —vi. to make a distinction (*between* or *among*) —**dis·tin′guish·a·ble** adj.

dis·tin′guished adj. celebrated; famous

dis·tort (dis tôrt′) vt. [< L. *dis-*, intens. + *torquere*, to twist] 1. to twist out of shape 2. to misrepresent (facts, etc.) —**dis·tor′tion** n.

dis·tract (dis trakt′) vt. [< L. *dis-*, apart + *trahere*, draw] 1. to draw the mind, etc.) away in another direction; divert 2. to confuse; bewilder —**dis·tract′ed** adj. —**dis·tract′ing** adj.

dis·trac′tion n. 1. a distracting or being distracted 2. anything that distracts confusingly or amusingly; diversion 3. great mental distress

dis·trait (dis trā′) adj. [see DISTRACT] absent-minded; inattentive

dis·traught (-trôt′) adj. [var. of prec.] 1. distracted; confused 2. driven mad; crazed

dis·tress (dis tres′) vt. [ult. < L. *dis-*, apart + *stringere*, to stretch] to cause misery or suffering to —n. 1. pain, suffering, etc. 2. an affliction 3. a state of danger or trouble

dis·trib·ute (dis trib′yoot) vt. -uted, -ut·ing [< L. *dis-*, apart + *tribuere*, allot] 1. to give out in shares 2. to spread out 3. to classify 4. to put (things) in various distinct places —**dis·tri·bu′tion** n.

dis·trib·u·tor n. one that distributes; specif., a) a dealer who distributes goods to consumers b) a device for distributing electric current to the spark plugs of a gasoline engine

dis·trict (dis′trikt) n. [< L. *dis-*, apart + *stringere*, to stretch] 1. a division of a state, city, etc. made for a specific purpose 2. any region

district attorney the prosecuting attorney for the State or the Federal government in a specified district

District of Columbia federal district of the U.S., on the Potomac: coextensive with city of Washington

dis·trust n. a lack of trust; doubt —vt. to have no trust in; doubt —**dis·trust′ful** adj.

dis·turb (dis turb′) vt. [< L. *dis-*, intens. + *turbare*, to disorder] 1. to break up the quiet or settled order of 2. to make uneasy; upset 3. to interrupt —**dis·turb′er** n.

dis·turb′ance n. 1. a disturbing or being disturbed 2. anything that disturbs 3. commotion; disorder

dis·u·nite (dis′yoo nīt′) vt., vi. -nit·ed, -nit·ing to divide or separate into parts, factions, etc. —**dis·u′ni·ty** n.

dis·use (dis yōōs′) n. lack of use

ditch (dich) n. [OE. *dic*] a long, narrow channel dug into the earth, as for drainage —vt. 1. to make a ditch in 2. [Slang] to get rid of

dith·er (dith′ər) n. [ME. *dideren*] a nervously excited or confused state

dit·to (dit′ō) n., pl. -tos [It. < L. *dicere*, speak] 1. the same (as above or before) 2. *same as* DITTO MARK

ditto mark a mark (″) used in lists or tables to show that the item above is to be repeated

dit·ty (dit′ē) n., pl. -ties [< L. *dicere*, speak] a short, simple song

di·u·ret·ic (dī′yoo ret′ik) adj. [< Gr. *dia-*, through + *ourein*, urinate] increasing the flow of urine —n. a diuretic drug or substance

di·ur·nal (dī ur′n'l) adj. [< L. *dies*, day] 1. daily 2. of the daytime —**di·ur′nal·ly** adv.

div. 1. dividend 2. division

di·va (dē′və) n., pl. -vas; It. -ve (-ve) [It. < L., goddess] *same as* PRIMA DONNA

di·van (dī′van, di van′) n. [< Per. *diwan*] a large, low couch or sofa

dive (dīv) vi. dived or dove, dived, div′ing [OE. *dyfan*] 1. to plunge headfirst into water 2. to submerge 3. to plunge suddenly into something 4. to make a steep descent, as an airplane —n. 1. a diving 2. any sudden plunge 3. a sharp descent 4. [Colloq.] a cheap, disreputable saloon, etc. —**div′er** n.

di·verge (də vurj′, dī-) vi. -verged′, -verg′ing [< L. *dis-*, apart + *vergere*, to turn] 1. to go or move in different directions; branch off 2. to differ, as in opinion —**di·ver′gence** n. —**di·ver′gent** adj.

di·vers (dī′vərz) adj. [see ff.] various

di·verse (dī vurs′, də-) adj. [< L.

dis-, apart + *vertere*, to turn] 1. different 2. varied —**di·verse'ly** *adv.*

di·ver·si·fy (də vur'sə fī') *vt.* **-fied', -fy'ing** to make diverse; vary —**di·ver'si·fi·ca'tion** *n.*

di·ver·sion (də vur'zhən, dī-) *n.* 1. a diverting or turning aside 2. distraction of attention 3. a pastime

di·ver·sion·ar'y *adj.* serving to divert or distract [*diversionary tactics*]

di·ver·si·ty (də vur'sə tē, dī-) *n., pl.* **-ties** 1. difference 2. variety

di·vert' (-vurt') *vt.* [see DIVERSE] 1. to turn aside (*from* a course) 2. to amuse

di·ver·tic·u·li·tis (dī'vər tik'yoo līt'əs) *n.* [< L. *de-*, from + *vertere*, to turn + *-ITIS*] inflammation of a sac (**diverticulum**) opening out from a tubular organ or main cavity

di·vest' (-vest') *vt.* [< L. *dis-*, from + *vestire*, to dress] 1. to strip (of clothing, etc.) 2. to deprive (of rank, rights, etc.) 3. to rid (of something unwanted)

di·vide (də vīd') *vt.* **-vid'ed, -vid'ing** [< L. *dividere*] 1. to separate into parts; sever 2. to classify 3. to make or keep separate 4. to apportion 5. to cause to disagree 6. *Math.* to separate into equal parts by a divisor —*vi.* 1. to be or become separate 2. to disagree 3. to share 4. *Math.* to do division —*n.* a ridge that divides two drainage areas —**di·vid'er** *n.*

div·i·dend (div'ə dend) *n.* 1. the number or quantity to be divided 2. *a)* a sum to be divided among stockholders, etc. *b)* a single share of this 3. a bonus

di·vid'ers *n.pl.* an instrument for dividing lines, etc.; compasses

div·i·na·tion (div'ə nā'shən) *n.* [see ff.] the practice of trying to foretell the future or the unknown

di·vine (də vīn') *adj.* [< L. *divus*, a god] 1. of, like, or from God or a god; holy 2. devoted to God; religious 3. supremely great, good, etc. —*n.* a clergyman —*vt.* **-vined', -vin'ing** 1. to prophesy 2. to guess 3. to find out by intuition —**di·vine'ly** *adv.*

divining rod a forked stick alleged to dip downward when held over an underground supply of water, etc.

di·vin·i·ty (də vin'ə tē) *n., pl.* **-ties** 1. a being divine 2. a god 3. theology —**the Divinity God**

di·vis·i·ble (də viz'ə b'l) *adj.* that can be divided. esp. without leaving a remainder —**di·vis'i·bil'i·ty** *n.*

di·vi·sion (də vizh'ən) *n.* 1. a dividing or being divided 2. a sharing 3. a difference of opinion 4. anything that divides 5. a segment, section, department, class, etc. 6. the process of finding how many times a number (the *divisor*) is contained in another (the *dividend*) 7. a major military unit

di·vi·sive (də vī'siv) *adj.* causing disagreement or dissension —**di·vi'sive·ly** *adv.* —**di·vi'sive·ness** *n.*

di·vi·sor (də vī'zər) *n.* the number by which the dividend is divided

di·vorce (də vôrs') *n.* [< L. *dis-*, apart + *vertere*, to turn] 1. legal dissolution of a marriage 2. complete separation —*vt.* **-vorced', -vorc'ing** 1. to dissolve legally a marriage between 2. to separate from (one's spouse) by divorce 3. to separate —**di·vorce'ment** *n.*

di·vor·cée, di·vor·cee (də vôr'sā'. -sē') *n.* [Fr.] a divorced woman

div·ot (div'ət) *n.* [Scot.] *Golf* a lump of turf dislodged in hitting a ball

di·vulge (də vulj') *vt.* **-vulged', -vulg'ing** [< L. *dis-*, apart + *vulgare*, make public] to make known; reveal

div·vy (div'ē) *vt., vi.* **-vied, -vy·ing** [Slang] to share; divide (*up*)

Dix·ie (dik'sē) [< *Dixie*, the minstrel song] the Southern States of the U.S.

Dix'ie·land *adj.* in, of, or like a style of jazz with a ragtime tempo

diz·zy (diz'ē) *adj.* **-zi·er, -zi·est** [OE. *dysig*, foolish] 1. feeling giddy or unsteady 2. causing giddiness 3. confused 4. [Colloq.] silly —**diz'zi·ly** *adv.* —**diz'zi·ness** *n.*

D.J., DJ disc jockey

DNA [< *d(eoxyribo)n(ucleic) a(cid)*] an essential component of all living matter and the basic chromosomal material transmitting the hereditary pattern

Dne·pr (ně'pər) river in W U.S.S.R.. flowing into the Black Sea

do[1] (dōō) *vt.* **did, done, do'ing** [OE. *don*] 1. to perform (an action, etc.) 2. to finish; complete 3. to cause (*it does no harm*) 4. to exert (*do your best*) 5. to deal with as required (*do the ironing*) 6. to have as one's occupation; work at 7. [Colloq.] to cheat 8. [Colloq.] to serve (a jail term) —*vi.* 1. to behave (*do as you please*) 2. to be active (*up and doing*) 3. to get along; fare (*how is he doing?*) 4. to be adequate (*the red hat will do*) 5. to take place (*anything doing tonight?*) Auxiliary uses of *do*: 1. to give emphasis (*please do stay*) 2. to ask a question (*did you go?*) 3. to serve as a substitute verb (*act as I do* (act)) —**do in** [Slang] to kill —**do over** [Colloq.] to redecorate —**do up** [Colloq.] to wrap up —**do with** to make use of —**do without** to get along without —have to **do with** to be related to —**make do** to get along with what is available

do[2] (dō) *n.* [It.] *Music* the first or last tone of the diatonic scale

do·a·ble (dōō'ə b'l) *adj.* that can be done

Do·ber·man pin·scher (dō'bər mən pin'shər) [< *Dobermann*, 19th-c. Ger. breeder + G. *pinscher*, terrier] a large dog with short, dark hair

doc (däk) *n.* [Slang] doctor

do·cent (dō's'nt) *n.* [< L. *docere*, to teach] in some American universities, a teacher not on the regular faculty

doc·ile (däs′'l) *adj.* [< L. *docere*, teach] easy to discipline; tractable —**do·cil·i·ty** (dä sil′ə tē, dō-) *n.*

dock¹ (däk) *n.* [< It. *doccia*, canal] 1. an excavated basin for receiving ships between voyages 2. a wharf; pier 3. the water between two piers 4. a platform for loading and unloading trucks, etc. —*vt.* to pilot (a ship) to a dock —*vi.* to come into a dock

dock² (däk) *n.* [< Fl. *dok*, a cage] the place where the accused stands or sits in court

dock³ (däk) *n.* [OE. *docce*] a coarse weed of the buckwheat family

dock⁴ (däk) *n.* [ME. *dok*] the solid part of an animal's tail —*vt.* 1. to cut off the end of (a tail, etc.); bob 2. to deduct from (wages, etc.)

dock·et (däk′it) *n.* [< ?] 1. a list of cases to be tried by a law court 2. an agenda —*vt.* to enter in a docket

dock′yard′ *n.* a place with docks, etc. for repairing or building ships

doc·tor (däk′tər) *n.* [< L., teacher] 1. a person on whom a university has conferred a high degree, as a Ph.D. 2. a physician or surgeon 3. a person licensed to practice any of the healing arts —*vt.* [Colloq.] 1. to try to heal 2. to mend 3. to tamper with —**doc′tor·al** *adj.*

doc′tor·ate (-it) *n.* the degree of doctor conferred by a university

doc·tri·naire (däk′trə ner′) *adj.* [Fr.] adhering to a doctrine dogmatically —**doc′tri·nair′ism** *n.*

doc·trine (däk′trən) *n.* [see DOCTOR] something taught, esp. as the principles of a religion, political party, etc.; tenet or tenets; dogma —**doc′tri·nal** (-trə nəl) *adj.*

doc·u·ment (däk′yə mənt; *for v.* -ment′) *n.* [< L. *documentum*, proof] anything printed, written, etc., relied upon to record or prove something —*vt.* to provide with or support by documents —**doc′u·men·ta′tion** *n.*

doc′u·men·ta·ry (-men′tə rē) *adj.* 1. of or supported by documents 2. showing or analyzing news events, social conditions, etc. in nonfictional but dramatic form —*n.*, *pl.* -ries a documentary film, TV show, etc.

dod·der (däd′ər) *vi.* [ME. *daderen*] 1. to shake or tremble, as from old age 2. to totter —**dod′der·ing** *adj.*

dodge (däj) *vi., vt.* dodged, dodg′ing [< ?] 1. to move quickly aside, or avoid by so moving 2. to use tricks or evasions, or evade by so doing —*n.* 1. a dodging 2. a trick used in evading or cheating —**dodg′er** *n.*

do·do (dō′dō) *n., pl.* -dos, -does [Port. *doudo*, lit., stupid] a large, flightless bird, now extinct

doe (dō) *n.* [OE. *da*] the female of the deer, antelope, rabbit, etc.

do·er (dō′ər) *n.* 1. one who does something 2. one who gets things done

does (duz) *3d pers. sing., pres. indic., of* DO¹

DODO

doe′skin′ *n.* 1. leather from the skin of a female deer 2. a soft wool cloth

does·n't (duz′'nt) does not

doff (däf, dôf) *vt.* [see DO¹ & OFF] to take off (one's hat, etc.)

dog (dôg) *n.* [OE. *docga*] 1. a domesticated animal related to the fox, wolf, and jackal 2. a mean, contemptible fellow 3. a mechanical device for holding or grappling 4. [pl.] [Slang] feet 5. [Slang] an unsatisfactory person or thing —*vt.* dogged, dog′ging to follow or hunt like a dog —go to the dogs [Colloq.] to deteriorate

doge (dōj) *n.* [It. < L. *dux*, leader] the chief magistrate in the former republics of Venice and Genoa

dog′ear′ *n.* a turned-down corner of the leaf of a book —**dog′eared′** *adj.*

dog′fish′ *n., pl.:* see FISH any of various small sharks

dog·ged (dôg′id) *adj.* persistent; stubborn —**dog′ged·ly** *adv.*

dog·ger·el (dôg′ər əl) *n.* [prob. < It. *doga*, barrel stave] trivial verse, poorly constructed and usually comic

dog′gie bag (-ē) a bag supplied to a restaurant patron, in which he may place leftovers, as for his dog

dog′gone′ *interj.* damn! darn! —*vt.* -goned′, -gon′ing [Colloq.] to damn

dog′house′ *n.* a dog's shelter —in the doghouse [Slang] in disfavor

do·gie, do·gy (dō′gē) *n., pl.* -gies [< ?] in the western U.S., a stray calf

dog·ma (dôg′mə) *n.* [< Gr., opinion] a doctrine; belief; esp., a body of theological doctrines strictly adhered to

dog·mat·ic (-mat′ik) *adj.* 1. of or like dogma 2. asserted without proof 3. positive or arrogant in stating opinion —**dog·mat′i·cal·ly** *adv.*

dog·ma·tism (-tiz′m) *n.* dogmatic assertion of opinion —**dog′ma·tist** *n.*

do′-good′er *n.* [Colloq.] an idealistic, but impractical person who seeks to correct social ills

dog′-tired′ *adj.* [Colloq.] very tired

dog′tooth′ *n., pl.* -teeth′ a canine tooth; eyetooth

dog′trot′ *n.* a slow, easy trot

dog′wood′ *n.* a small tree bearing pink or white flowers in early spring

doi·ly (doi′lē) *n., pl.* -lies [after a 17th-c. London draper] a small mat, as of lace, put under a plate, etc. as a decoration or to protect a surface

do·ings (dōō′iŋz) *n.pl.* things done; actions

do′-it-your·self′ *n.* the practice of making or repairing things oneself, not hiring it done

dol·drums (dāl′drəmz, dōl′-) *n.pl.* [< ? DULL] 1. *a)* low spirits *b)* sluggishness 2. equatorial ocean regions noted for dead calms

dole (dōl) *n.* [OE. *dal*, a share] 1. money or food given in charity 2. money paid by a government to the unemployed —*vt.* doled, dol′ing to give sparingly or as a dole

dole′ful (-fəl) *adj.* [< L. *dolere*, suffer] sad; mournful —**dole′ful·ly** *adv.*

doll (däl) *n.* [< nickname for *Dorothy*] 1. a child's toy made to resemble a human being 2. [Slang] any attractive or lovable person —*vt.*, *vi.* [Colloq.] to dress stylishly or showily (with *up*)

dol·lar (däl'ər) *n.* [< G. *thaler*] 1. the monetary unit of the U.S., equal to 100 cents 2. the monetary unit of certain other countries, as Canada 3. a coin or paper bill of the value of a dollar

dol·lop (däl'əp) *n.* [< ?] 1. a soft mass 2. a quantity, often a small one

dol·ly (däl'ē) *n.*, *pl.* -lies 1. a doll: child's word 2. a low, flat, wheeled frame for moving heavy objects

dol·men (däl'mən, dōl'-) *n.* [Fr.] a prehistoric monument consisting of a large, flat stone laid across upright stones

do·lor·ous (dō'lər əs, däl'ər-) *adj.* [< L. *dolere*, suffer] 1. sorrowful; sad 2. painful —**do'lor·ous·ly** *adv.*

dol·phin (däl'fən, dôl'-) *n.* [< Gr. *delphis*] a water-dwelling mammal, often with a beaklike snout

dolt (dōlt) *n.* [prob. < ME. *dolte*] a stupid person —**dolt'ish** *adj.*

-dom (dəm) [OE. *dom*, state] *a suffix meaning:* 1. rank or domain of [*kingdom*] 2. fact or state of being [*martyrdom*] 3. a body of [*officialdom*]

do·main (dō mān') *n.* [< L. *dominus*, a lord] 1. territory under one government or ruler 2. field of activity or influence

dome (dōm) *n.* [< Gr. *dōma*, housetop] 1. a rounded roof or ceiling 2. any dome-shaped object

do·mes·tic (də mes'tik) *adj.* [< L. *domus*, house] 1. of the home or family 2. of or made in one's country 3. tame: said of animals 4. homeloving —*n.* a maid, cook, etc. —**do·mes'ti·cal·ly** *adv.*

do·mes'ti·cate' (-tə kāt') *vt.* -cat'ed, -cat'ing 1. to accustom to home life 2. to tame for man's use —**do·mes'ti·ca'tion** *n.*

do·mes·tic·i·ty (dō'mes tis'ə tē) *n.* home life, or devotion to it

dom·i·cile (däm'ə sīl', -sil; dō'mə-) *n.* [see DOMESTIC] a home; residence —*vt.* -ciled', -cil'ing to establish in a domicile

dom·i·nant (däm'ə nənt) *adj.* dominating; ruling; prevailing —**dom'i·nance** *n.* —**dom'i·nant·ly** *adv.*

dom·i·nate' (-nāt') *vt.*, *vi.* -nat'ed, -nat'ing [< L. *dominus*, a master] 1. to rule or control by superior power 2. to rise above (the surroundings) —**dom'i·na'tion** *n.*

dom·i·neer (däm'ə nir') *vi.*, *vt.* [< Du.: see prec.] to rule (*over*) in a harsh or arrogant way; tyrannize —**dom'i·neer'ing** *adj.* overbearing

Do·min·i·can Republic (də min'i kən) country in the E part of Hispaniola: 18,816 sq. mi.; pop. 3,889,000

do·min·ion (də min'yən) *n.* [see DOMINATE] 1. rule or power to rule 2. a governed territory, or, sometimes, a self-governing nation

dom·i·no (däm'ə nō') *n.*, *pl.* -noes', -nos' [Fr. & It.] 1. a loose cloak with a hood and mask, worn at masquerades 2. a mask for the eyes 3. a small, oblong tile marked with dots 4. [*pl.*, *with sing. v.*] a game played with such tiles

domino theory a theory that if one country should become Communistic its neighbors would quickly follow, like a row of dominoes falling down

Don (dän) river in C European U.S.S.R., flowing into the Black Sea

don[1] (dän) *n.* [Sp. < L. *dominus*, master] 1. [D-] Sir; Mr.: a Spanish title of respect 2. a Spanish gentleman 3. [Colloq.] a tutor at a British college

don[2] (dän) *vt.* donned, don'ning (contr. of *do on*) to put on (clothes)

‡**Do·ña** (dō'nyä) *n.* [Sp.] Lady; Madam: a Spanish title of respect

do·nate (dō'nāt) *vt.*, *vi.* -nat'ed, -nat'ing [< L. *donum*, gift] to give or contribute —**do·na'tion** *n.*

done (dun) *pp.* of DO[1] —*adj.* 1. completed 2. cooked —**done in** [Colloq.] exhausted —**done (for)** [Colloq.] dead, ruined, finished, etc.

Don Juan (dän' jōō'ən, dän' wän') *Sp. Legend* a dissolute nobleman and seducer of women

don·key (däŋ'kē, dôŋ'-, duŋ'-) *n.*, *pl.* -keys [< ?] 1. the domesticated ass 2. a stupid or foolish person

don·ny·brook (dän'ē brook') *n.* [< a fair formerly held near Dublin, Ireland] a rowdy fight or free-for-all

do·nor (dō'nər) *n.* one who donates

Don Qui·xo·te (dän' kē hōt'ē, kwik' sət) 1. a satirical romance by Cervantes 2. its chivalrous, unrealistic hero

don't (dōnt) do not

do·nut (dō'nut') *n. same as* DOUGHNUT

doo·dle (dōōd''l) *vi.* -dled, -dling [G. *dudeln*, to trifle] to scribble aimlessly —*n.* a mark made in doodling —**doo'dler** *n.*

doom (dōōm) *n.* [OE. *dom*] 1. a judgment; sentence 2. fate 3. ruin or death —*vt.* 1. to pass judgment on; condemn 2. to destine to a tragic fate

dooms'day' *n.* Judgment Day

door (dôr) *n.* [OE. *duru*] 1. a movable structure for opening or closing an entrance 2. a doorway 3. a means of access —**out of doors** outdoors

door'bell' *n.* a bell rung by one who wishes to enter a building or room

door'man' (-man', -mən) *n.*, *pl.* -men' (-men', -mən) a man whose work is opening the door of a building, hailing taxicabs, etc.

door'mat' *n.* a mat to wipe the shoes on before entering a house, etc.

door'step' *n.* a step leading from an outer door to a path, lawn, etc.

door'way' *n.* 1. an opening in a wall that can be closed by a door 2. any means of access

door'yard' *n.* a yard onto which a door of a house opens

do·pa (dō′pə) *n.* [< chemical name] an amino acid converted into an essential amine in the bloodstream: one isomer (L-dopa) is used in treating Parkinson's disease

dope (dōp) *n.* [Du. *doop,* sauce] 1. any thick liquid used as a lubricant, varnish, filler, etc. 2. [Slang] a drug or narcotic 3. a stupid person 4. [Slang] information —*vt.* doped, dop′ing to drug —**dope out** [Colloq.] to solve

dop·ey, dop·y (dō′pē) *adj.* dop′l·er, dop′l·est [Slang] 1. under the influence of a narcotic 2. lethargic or stupid

Dor·ic (dôr′ik) *adj.* designating or of a Greek style of architecture marked by fluted columns with plain capitals

dorm (dôrm) *n.* [Colloq.] a dormitory

dor·mant (dôr′mənt) *adj.* [< L. *dormire,* to sleep] 1. inactive 2. Biol. in a resting or torpid state —**dor′man·cy** *n.*

dor·mer (dôr′mər) *n.* [see prec.] a window set upright in a structure projecting from a sloping roof: also **dormer window**

dor·mi·to·ry (dôr′mə tôr′ē) *n., pl.* -ries [see DORMANT] 1. a room with beds for a number of people 2. a building, as at a college, with many rooms for sleeping and living in

DORMER

dor·mouse (dôr′mous′) *n., pl.* -mice (-mīs′) [ME. *dormous*] a small European rodent resembling a squirrel

dor·sal (dôr′s′l) *adj.* [< L. *dorsum,* the back] of, on, or near the back

do·ry (dôr′ē) *n., pl.* -ries [Central Amind. *dori,* dugout] a small, flat-bottomed fishing boat with high sides

dose (dōs) *n.* [< Gr. *dosis,* a giving] an amount of medicine to be taken at one time —*vt.* dosed, dos′ing to give doses to —**dos′age** *n.*

do·sim·e·ter (dō sim′ə tər) *n.* a device for measuring the roentgens absorbed in a single exposure to radiation

dos·si·er (däs′ē ā′) *n.* [Fr.] a collection of documents about some person or matter

dost (dust) *archaic 2d pers. sing. pres. indic.,* of DO[1]: used with thou

Dos·to·ev·ski (dôs′tô yef′skē), Feodor (fyô′dôr) 1821–81; Russ. novelist: also **Dos′to·yev′sky**

dot (dät) *n.* [OE. *dott,* head of boil] 1. a tiny speck or mark 2. a small, round spot —*vt.* dot′ted, dot′ting to mark as with a dot or dots —**on the dot** [Colloq.] at the exact time

DOT Department of Transportation

dot·age (dōt′ij) *n.* [ME. < *doten,* DOTE] childish state due to old age

dot′ard (-ərd) *n.* one in his dotage

dote (dōt) *vi.* dot′ed, dot′ing [ME. *doten*] 1. to be weak-minded, esp. because of old age 2. to be excessively fond (with *on* or *upon*) —**dot′ing** *adj.*

doth (duth) *archaic 3d pers. sing. pres. indic.,* of DO[1] (in auxiliary uses)

Dou·ay Bible (dōō ā′) [< *Douai,*

France, where one part was first published] an English version of the Bible for the use of Roman Catholics

dou·ble (dub′'l) *adj.* [< L. *duplus*] 1. twofold 2. having two layers 3. having two of one kind 4. being of two kinds [a *double* standard] 5. twice as much, as many, etc. 6. made for two —*adv.* 1. twofold or twice 2. in a pair —*n.* 1. anything twice as much, as many, etc. as normal 2. a duplicate; counterpart 3. a fold 4. [*pl.*] a game of tennis, etc. with two players on each side 5. *Baseball* a hit on which the batter reaches second base 6. *Bridge* the doubling of an opponent's bid —*vt.* -bled, -bling 1. to make twice as much or many 2. to fold 3. to repeat or duplicate 4. *Bridge* to increase the point value or penalty of (an opponent's bid) —*vi.* 1. to become double 2. to turn sharply backward [to *double* on one's tracks] 3. to serve as a double 4. to serve an additional purpose 5. *Baseball* to hit a double —**double up** 1. to clench (one's fist) 2. to bend over, as in pain 3. to share a room, etc. with someone

double agent a spy who infiltrates an enemy espionage organization

dou′ble-bar′reled *adj.* 1. having two barrels, as a kind of shotgun 2. having a double purpose or meaning

double bass (bās) the largest, deepest-toned instrument of the violin family

double boiler a cooking utensil with an upper pan for food, fitting into a lower one in which water is boiled

dou′ble-breast′ed *adj.* overlapping across the breast, as a coat

dou′ble-cross′ *vt.* [Colloq.] to betray —**dou′ble-cross′er** *n.*

double date [Colloq.] a social engagement shared by two couples —**dou′ble-date′** *vi., vt.* -dat′ed, -dat′ing

dou′ble-deal′ing *n.* duplicity

dou′ble-deck′er *n.* 1. any structure or vehicle with an upper deck 2. [Colloq.] a two-layer sandwich made with three slices of bread

dou·ble-en·ten·dre (dōō′blän tän′drə, dub″l än-) *n.* [Fr. (now obs.), double meaning] a term with two meanings, esp. when one is risqué

dou′ble-head′er *n.* two games played in succession on the same day

dou′ble-joint′ed *adj.* having joints that permit limbs, fingers, etc. to bend at other than the usual angles

dou′ble-knit′ *adj.* knit with a double stitch that makes the fabric extra thick

double play *Baseball* a play in which two players are put out

dou′ble-reed′ *adj.* designating or of a woodwind instrument, as the oboe, having two reeds separated by a narrow opening

double standard a system, code, etc. applied unequally; specif., a moral code stricter for women than for men

dou·blet (dub′lit) *n.* [< OFr. *double,* orig., something folded] 1. a man's closefitting jacket of the 14th-16th cent. 2. a pair, or one of a pair

double take a delayed reaction following unthinking acceptance

double talk 1. ambiguous and deceptive talk 2. meaningless syllables made to sound like talk

dou·bloon (du blōōn′) *n.* [< Fr. < Sp. < L. *duplus*, double] an obsolete Spanish gold coin

dou·bly (dub′lē) *adv.* 1. twice 2. two at a time

doubt (dout) *vi.* [< L. *dubitare*] to be uncertain or undecided —*vt.* 1. to be uncertain about 2. to tend to disbelieve —*n.* 1. *a*) a wavering of opinion or belief *b*) lack of trust 2. a condition of uncertainty 3. an unsettled point or matter —**beyond (or without) doubt** certainly —**no doubt** 1. certainly 2. probably —**doubt′er** *n.* —**doubt′ing·ly** *adv.*

doubt′ful *adj.* 1. uncertain 2. causing doubt or suspicion 3. feeling doubt —**doubt′ful·ly** *adv.*

doubt′less *adv.* 1. certainly 2. probably —**doubt′less·ly** *adv.*

douche (dōōsh) *n.* [Fr. < It. *doccia*] 1. a jet of liquid applied externally or internally to the body 2. a device for douching —*vt.*, *vi.* douched, douch′ing to apply a douche (to)

dough (dō) *n.* [OE. *dag*] 1. a mixture of flour, liquid, etc. worked into a soft mass for baking 2. [Slang] money

dough′nut′ *n.* a small, usually ring-shaped cake, fried in deep fat

dough·ty (dout′ē) *adj.* -ti·er, -ti·est [OE. *dohtig*] valiant; brave: now humorous and somewhat archaic

dough′y *adj.* -i·er, -i·est of or like dough; soft, pasty, etc.

dour (door, dōōr, dour) *adj.* [< L. *durus*, hard] 1. [Scot.] stern; severe 2. sullen; gloomy —**dour′ness** *n.*

douse (dous) *vt.* doused, dous′ing [< ?] 1. to thrust suddenly into liquid 2. to drench 3. [Colloq.] to extinguish, as a light

dove¹ (duv) *n.* [ME. *douve*] 1. a bird of the pigeon family, with a cooing cry: a symbol of peace 2. an advocate of peaceful international relationships

dove² (dōv) *alt. pt. of* DIVE

Do·ver (dō′vər) capital of Del.: pop. 24,000

dove·tail (duv′tāl′) *n.* a projecting part that fits into a corresponding indentation to form a joint —*vt.*, *vi.* to join or fit together closely or by means of dovetails

dow·a·ger (dou′ə jər) *n.* [< L. *dotare*, endow] 1. a widow with title or property derived from her dead husband 2. an elderly, wealthy woman

DOVETAIL

dow·dy (dou′dē) *adj.* -di·er, -di·est [< ME. *doude*, plain woman] not neat or smart in dress —**dow′di·ness** *n.*

dow·el (dou′əl) *n.* [ME. *doule*] a peg of wood, etc., usually fitted into corresponding holes in two pieces to fasten them together —*vt.* -eled or -elled, -el·ing or -el·ling to fasten with dowels

dow·er (dou′ər) *n.* [< L. *dare*, give] 1. that part of a man's property which his widow inherits for life 2. a dowry —*vt.* to endow (*with*)

down¹ (doun) *adv.* [OE. *adune*, from the hill] 1. to, in, or on a lower place or level 2. in or to a low or lower condition, amount, etc. 3. from an earlier to a later period 4. out of one's hands [put it *down*] 5. in a serious manner [get *down* to work] 6. completely [loaded *down*] 7. in cash [$5 down and $5 a week] 8. in writing [take *down* notes] —*adj.* 1. descending 2. in a lower place 3. gone, brought, etc. down 4. dejected; discouraged 5. ill 6. finished [four *down*, six to go] 7. in cash [a *down* payment] —*prep.* down toward, along, through, into, or upon —*vt.* to put or throw down —*n.* 1. a misfortune [ups and *downs*] 2. *Football* one of a series of plays in which a team tries to advance the ball —**down and out** penniless, ill, etc. —**down on** [Colloq.] angry or annoyed with —**down with!** away with!

down² (doun) *n.* [< ON. *dūnn*] 1. soft, fine feathers 2. soft, fine hair

down³ (doun) *n.* [OE. *dun*, hill] open, high, grassy land: *usually used in pl.*

down′beat′ *n. Music* the downward stroke of the conductor's hand indicating the first beat of each measure

down′cast′ *adj.* 1. directed downward 2. unhappy; dejected

Down East [Colloq.] New England, esp. Maine: also **down east**

down′er *n.* [Slang] any depressant or sedative

down′fall′ *n.* 1. *a*) a sudden fall, as from power *b*) the cause of this 2. a heavy fall, as of snow

down′fall′en *adj.* fallen; ruined

down′grade′ *n.* a downward slope —*adv.*, *adj.* downward —*vt.* -grad′ed, -grad′ing 1. to demote 2. to belittle

down′heart′ed *adj.* discouraged

down′hill′ *adv.*, *adj.* toward the bottom of a hill; downward

Down′ing Street a street in London containing British government offices

down′pour′ *n.* a heavy rain

down′right′ *adv.* utterly —*adj.* 1. absolute; utter 2. plain; frank

down′scale′ *adj.* of or for people who are unstylish, not affluent, etc.

Down's syndrome (dounz) [after J. Down, 19th-c. Eng. physician] a congenital disease characterized by mental deficiency, a broad face, etc.

down′stage′ *adj.*, *adv.* of or toward the front of the stage

down′stairs′ *adv.* 1. down the stairs 2. on or to a lower floor —*adj.* on a lower floor —*n.* a lower floor

down′state′ *adj.*, *adv.* in, to, or from the southerly part of a State

down′stream′ *adv.*, *adj.* in the direction of the current of a stream

down'swing' n. 1. a downward swing, as of a golf club 2. a downward trend: also **down'turn'**

down'-to-earth' adj. realistic or practical

down'town' adj., adv. in or toward the main business section of a city —n. the downtown section of a city

down'trod'den adj. oppressed

down'ward (-wərd) adv., adj. toward a lower place, position, etc.: also **down'wards** adv.

down·y (doun'ē) adj. -i·er, -i·est 1. covered with soft, fine feathers or hair 2. soft and fluffy, like down

dow·ry (dou'rē) n., pl. -ries [see DOWER] the property that a woman brings to her husband at marriage

dowse (douz) vi. dowsed, dows'ing [< ?] to use a divining rod

dox·ol·o·gy (däk säl'ə jē) n., pl. -gies [< Gr. doxa, praise + -logia, -LOGY] a hymn of praise to God

doz. dozen(s)

doze (dōz) vi. dozed, doz'ing [prob. < Scand.] to sleep lightly; nap —n. a light sleep —doz'er n.

doz·en (duz''n) n., pl. -ens or esp. after a number, -en [< L. duo, two + decem, ten] a set of twelve —doz'enth adj.

dpt. 1. department 2. deponent

Dr. 1. Doctor 2. Drive

drab (drab) n. [< VL. drappus, cloth] a dull yellowish brown —adj. drab'-ber, drab'best 1. dull yellowish-brown 2. dull —drab'ness n.

drach·ma (drak'mə) n. [see DRAM] a Greek coin and monetary unit

draft (draft) n. [OE. dragan, to draw] 1. a drawing or pulling, as of a vehicle or load 2. a) a drawing in of a fish net b) the amount of fish caught in one draw 3. a) a drinking or the amount taken at one drink b) [Colloq.] a portion of beer, etc. drawn from a cask 4. an inhalation 5. a preliminary or tentative piece of writing 6. a plan or drawing of a work to be done 7. a current of air 8. a device for regulating the current of air in a heating system 9. a written order for payment of money; check 10. a) the choosing or taking of persons, esp. for compulsory military service b) those so taken 11. the depth of water that a ship displaces —vt. 1. to take, as for military service, by drawing from a group 2. to make a sketch of or plans for —adj. 1. used for pulling loads 2. drawn from a cask [draft beer] —draft'er n.

draft·ee (draf tē') n. a person drafted, esp. for military service

drafts·man (drafts'mən) n., pl. -men one who draws plans of structures or machinery —drafts'man·ship' n.

draft·y adj. -i·er, -i·est full of or exposed to drafts of air

drag (drag) vt., vi. dragged, drag'-ging [see DRAW] 1. to pull or be pulled with effort, esp. along the ground 2. to search (a lake bottom, etc.) with a dragnet or the like 3. to draw (something) out over a period of time; move or pass too slowly (often

with on or out) —n. 1. something dragged along the ground, as a harrow 2. a dragnet, grapnel, etc. 3. anything that hinders 4. a dragging 5. [Slang] influence 6. [Slang] a puff of a cigarette, etc. 7. [Slang] street [the main drag] 8. [Slang] same as DRAG RACE 9. [Slang] a dull person, situation, etc.

drag·gy (drag'ē) adj. -gi·er, -gi·est dragging; slow-moving, dull, etc.

drag'net' n. 1. a net dragged along a lake bottom, etc., as for catching fish 2. an organized system or network for catching criminals, etc.

drag·on (drag'ən) n. [< Gr. drakōn] a mythical monster, typically a large, winged reptile breathing out fire

drag'on·fly' n., pl. -flies' a large, long-bodied insect with narrow, transparent wings

dra·goon (drə gōōn') n. [see DRAGON] a heavily armed cavalryman —vt. to force (into) doing something; coerce

drag race [Slang] a race between hot-rod cars accelerating from a standstill on a short, straight course (**drag strip**) —**drag'-race'** vi. -raced', -rac'ing

drain (drān) vt. [< OE. dryge, dry] 1. to draw off (liquid) gradually 2. to draw liquid from gradually 3. to exhaust (strength, resources, etc.) gradually —vi. 1. to flow off or trickle through gradually 2. to become dry by draining —n. 1. a channel or pipe for draining 2. a draining —drain'er n.

drain·age (-ij) n. 1. a draining 2. a system of drains 3. that which is drained off 4. an area drained

drain'pipe' n. a large pipe used to carry off water, sewage, etc.

drake (drāk) n. [ME.] a male duck

dram (dram) n. [< Gr. drachmē, handful] 1. Apothecaries' Weight a unit equal to 1/8 oz. 2. Avoirdupois Weight a unit equal to 1/16 oz. 3. a small drink of alcoholic liquor

dra·ma (drä'mə, dram'ə) n. [< Gr.] 1. a literary composition to be performed by actors; play 2. the art of writing, acting, or producing plays 3. a series of events suggestive of those of a play 4. dramatic quality

Dram·a·mine (dram'ə mēn') a trademark for a drug to relieve motion sickness —n. [d-] a tablet of this drug

dra·mat·ic (drə mat'ik) adj. 1. of drama 2. like a play 3. vivid, striking, etc. —dra·mat'i·cal·ly adv.

dra·mat·ics n.pl. 1. [usually with sing. v.] the performing or producing of plays 2. exaggerated emotionalism

dram·a·tist (dram'ə tist) n. a playwright

dram·a·tize' (-tīz') vt. -tized', -tiz'-ing 1. to make into a drama 2. to regard or show in a dramatic manner —dram'a·ti·za'tion n.

drank (draŋk) pt. of DRINK

drape (drāp) vt. draped, drap'ing [< VL. drappus, cloth] 1. to cover or hang as with cloth in loose folds 2. to arrange (a garment, etc.) in folds or hangings —n. cloth hanging in loose folds; drapery: usually used in pl.

drap·er (drā'pər) n. [Brit.] a dealer in cloth and dry goods

dra·per·y n., pl. **-ies** 1. [Brit.] same as DRY GOODS 2. hangings or clothing arranged in loose folds 3. [pl.] curtains of heavy material

dras·tic (dras'tik) adj. [< Gr. drastikos, active] having a violent effect; severe; harsh —**dras'ti·cal·ly** adv.

draught (draft) n., vt., adj. now chiefly Brit. sp. of DRAFT

draughts (drafts) n.pl. [Brit.] the game of checkers

draw (drô) vt. **drew, drawn, draw'ing** [OE. dragan] 1. to make move toward one; pull 2. to pull up, down, back, in, or out 3. to need (a specified depth of water) to float in: said of a ship 4. to attract 5. to breathe in 6. to elicit (a reply, etc.) 7. to bring on; provoke 8. to receive [draw a salary] 9. to withdraw (money) held in an account 10. to write (a check or draft) 11. to deduce 12. to take or get (cards, etc.) 13. to stretch 14. to make (lines, pictures, etc.), as with a pencil 15. to make (comparisons, etc.) —vi. 1. to draw something 2. to be drawn 3. to come; move 4. to shrink 5. to allow a draft, as of smoke, to move through 6. to make a demand (on) —n. 1. a drawing or being drawn 2. the result of drawing 3. a thing drawn 4. a tie; stalemate 5. a thing that attracts —**draw out** 1. to extend 2. to take out 3. to get (a person) to talk —**draw up** 1. to arrange in order 2. to draft (a document) 3. to stop

draw'back' n. anything that prevents or lessens satisfaction; shortcoming

draw'bridge' n. a bridge that can be raised, lowered, or drawn aside

draw·er (drô'ər; for 2 drôr) n. 1. a person or thing that draws 2. a sliding box in a table, chest, etc.

draw·ers (drôrz) n.pl. an undergarment for the lower part of the body

draw'ing n. 1. the act of one that draws; specif., the art of making pictures, etc. as with a pencil 2. a picture, etc. thus made 3. a lottery

drawing card an entertainer, show, etc. that draws a large audience

drawing room [< withdrawing room: guests withdrew there after dinner] a room where guests are received or entertained

drawl (drôl) vt., vi. [prob. < DRAW, v.] to speak slowly, prolonging the vowels —n. a manner of speaking thus

drawn (drôn) pp. of DRAW —adj. 1. disemboweled 2. tense; haggard

drawn butter melted butter

draw'string' n. a string drawn through a hem, as to tighten a garment

dray (drā) n. [< OE. dragan, to draw] a wagon for carrying heavy loads

dread (dred) vt. [< OE. ondraedan] to anticipate with fear or distaste —n. 1. intense fear 2. fear mixed with awe —adj. inspiring dread

dread'ful adj. 1. inspiring dread; awesome; terrible 2. [Colloq.] very bad.

offensive, etc. —**dread'ful·ly** adv.

dread'nought', **dread'naught'** (-nôt') n. a large battleship with big guns

dream (drēm) n. [< OE., joy, music] 1. a sequence of images, etc. passing through a sleeping person's mind 2. a daydream; reverie 3. a fond hope 4. anything dreamlike —vi., vt. **dreamed** or **dreamt** (dremt), **dream'ing** to have a dream or remote idea (of) — **dream up** [Colloq.] to devise (a fanciful plan, etc.) —**dream'er** n. — **dream'less** adj. —**dream'like'** adj.

dream'land' n. 1. any lovely but imaginary place 2. sleep

dream world 1. same as DREAMLAND 2. the realm of fantasy

dream'y adj. **-i·er, -i·est** 1. of or like a dream 2. filled with dreams 3. visionary 4. soothing 5. [Slang] wonderful —**dream'i·ly** adv.

drear·y (drir'ē) adj. **-i·er, -i·est** [OE. dreorig, sad] dismal: also [Poet.] **drear** —**drear'i·ly** adv. —**drear'i·ness** n.

dredge¹ (drej) n. [? < MDu.] an apparatus for scooping up mud, etc., as in deepening channels —vt., vi. **dredged, dredg'ing** 1. to search (for) or gather (up) as with a dredge 2. to enlarge or clean out with a dredge

dredge² (drej) vt. **dredged, dredg'ing** [ME. dragge, sweetmeat] to coat (food) with flour or the like

dregs (dregz) n.pl. [< ON. dregg] 1. particles settling at the bottom in a liquid 2. the most worthless part

Drei·ser (drī'sər, -zər), **Theodore (Herman Albert)** 1871–1945; U.S. novelist

drench (drench) vt. [OE. drincan, to make drink] to make wet all over; soak

Dres·den (drez'dən) city in SC East Germany: pop. 508,000

dress (dres) vt. **dressed** or **drest, dress'ing** [< L. dirigere, lay straight] 1. to put clothes on; clothe 2. to trim; adorn 3. to arrange (the hair) in a certain way 4. to align (troops, etc.) 5. to apply medicines and bandages to (a wound, etc.) 6. to prepare for use, esp. for cooking [to dress a fowl] 7. to smooth or finish (leather, stone, etc.) —vi. 1. to clothe oneself 2. to dress formally 3. to line up in rank —n. 1. clothing 2. the usual outer garment of women, generally of one piece with a skirt —adj. 1. of or for dresses 2. for formal wear —**dress down** to scold —**dress up** to dress formally, elegantly, etc.

dres·sage (drə säzh') n. [< Fr. dresser, to train] horsemanship using slight movements to control the horse

dress circle a semicircle of seats in a theater, etc., usually behind and above the orchestra seats

dress'er n. 1. one who dresses (in various senses) 2. a chest of drawers for clothes, usually with a mirror

dress'ing n. 1. the act of one that dresses 2. bandages, etc. applied to wounds 3. a sauce for salads, etc. 4. a stuffing for roast fowl

dress'ing-down' *n.* a sound scolding

dressing gown a loose robe for one not fully clothed, as when lounging

dress'mak'er *n.* one who makes dresses, etc. —**dress'mak'ing** *n.*

dress rehearsal a final rehearsal, as of a play, with costumes, etc.

dress'y *adj.* -i·er, -i·est 1. showy or elaborate in dress or appearance 2. elegant; smart —**dress'i·ness** *n.*

drew (drōō) *pt. of* DRAW

drib·ble (drib''l) *vt., vi.* -bled, -bling [< DRIP] 1. to flow, or let flow, in drops 2. to drool 3. *Sports* to move (a ball or puck) along by repeated bouncing, kicking, or tapping —*n.* 1. a dribbling 2. a tiny amount: also **drib'let** (-lit) —**drib'bler** *n.*

dried (drīd) *pt. & pp. of* DRY

dri·er (drī'ər) *n.* 1. a substance added to paint, etc. to make it dry fast 2. *same as* DRYER —*adj. compar. of* DRY

dri'est (-ist) *adj. superl. of* DRY

drift (drift) *n.* [OE. *drifan*, to drive] 1. *a)* a being carried along, as by a current *b)* the course of this 2. a tendency; trend 3. general meaning 4. a heap of snow, etc. piled up by wind 5. gravel, etc. deposited by a glacier —*vi.* 1. to be carried along, as by a current 2. to go along aimlessly 3. to pile up in drifts —*vt.* to make drift —**drift'er** *n.*

drift'wood' *n.* wood drifting in the water or washed ashore

drill[1] (dril) *n.* [Du. *drillen*, to bore] 1. a tool for boring holes 2. *a)* systematic military or physical training *b)* the method or practice of teaching by repeated exercises —*vt., vi.* 1. to bore with a drill 2. to train in, or teach by means of, drill (sense 2) —**drill'er** *n.*

drill[2] (dril) *n.* [< ? *prec.*] a planting machine for making holes or furrows and dropping seeds into them

drill[3] (dril) *n.* [< L. *trilix*, three-threaded] a coarse, twilled cotton cloth, used for uniforms, etc.

drill'mas'ter *n.* 1. an instructor in military drill 2. one who teaches by drilling

drill press a power-driven machine for drilling holes in metal, etc.

dri·ly (drī'lē) *adv. same as* DRYLY

drink (driŋk) *vt.* **drank, drunk, drink'ing** [OE. *drincan*] 1. to swallow (liquid) 2. to absorb (liquid) 3. to swallow the contents of —*vi.* 1. to swallow liquid 2. to drink alcoholic liquor, esp. to excess —*n.* 1. any liquid for drinking 2. alcoholic liquor —**drink in** to take in eagerly with the senses or mind —**drink to** to drink a toast to —**drink'a·ble** *adj.* —**drink'er** *n.*

drip (drip) *vi., vt.* **dripped** or **dript, drip'ping** [OE. *dryppan*] to fall, or let fall, in drops —*n.* 1. a dripping 2. [Slang] a person regarded as unpleasant —**drip'per** *n.*

drip'-dry' *adj.* designating garments that dry quickly when hung wet and need little or no ironing

drip grind a fine grind of coffee

drive (drīv) *vt.* **drove, driv'en** (driv''n), **driv'ing** [OE. *drifan*] 1. to force to go 2. to force into or from a state or act 3. to force to work, esp. to excess 4. to hit (a ball, etc.) hard 5. to make penetrate 6. *a)* to control the movement of; operate (a car, bus, etc.) *b)* to transport in a car, etc. 7. to push (a bargain, etc.) through —*vi.* 1. to advance violently 2. to try hard, as to reach a goal 3. to drive a ball, blow, etc. 4. to be driven: said of a car, bus, etc. 5. to operate, or go in, a car, etc. —*n.* 1. a driving 2. a trip in a car, etc. 3. *a)* a road for cars, etc. *b)* a driveway 4. a rounding up of animals 5. a campaign 6. energy and initiative 7. a strong impulse or urge 8. the propelling mechanism of a machine, etc. —**drive at** to mean; intend —**drive in** 1. to force in, as by a blow 2. *Baseball* to cause (a runner) to score or (a run) to be scored

drive'-in' *n.* a restaurant, movie theater, bank, etc. designed to serve people seated in their cars

driv·el (driv''l) *vi., vt.* -eled or -elled, -el·ing or -el·ling [OE. *dreflian*] 1. to let (saliva) drool 2. to speak or say in a silly, stupid way —*n.* silly, stupid talk —**driv'el·er, driv'el·ler** *n.*

driv'er *n.* a person or thing that drives, as *a)* one who drives a car, etc. *b)* one who herds cattle *c)* the golf club for hitting the ball from the tee

drive shaft a shaft that transmits motion, as to the rear axle of a car

drive'way' *n.* a path for cars, from a street to a garage, house, etc.

driz·zle (driz''l) *vi., vt.* -zled, -zling [prob. < ME.] to rain in fine, misty drops —*n.* such rain —**driz'zly** *adj.*

drogue (drōg) *n.* [prob. < Scot. *drug*, drag] a funnel-shaped device towed behind an aircraft for drag effect, use as a target, etc.

droll (drōl) *adj.* [< Fr. < MDu. *drol*, stout fellow] amusing in an odd way —**droll'er·y** (-ər ē) *n., pl.* -ies —**droll'ness** *n.* —**drol'ly** *adv.*

drom·e·dar·y (dräm'ə der'ē) *n., pl.* -ies [< LL. *dromedarius (camelus)*, running (camel)] the one-humped or Arabian camel

drone[1] (drōn) *n.* [OE. *dran*] 1. a male honeybee, which does no work 2. an idler; loafer

drone[2] (drōn) *vi.* **droned, dron'ing** [< prec.] 1. to make a continuous humming sound 2. to talk in a monotonous way —*vt.* to utter in a monotonous tone —*n.* a droning sound

drool (drōōl) *vi.* [< DRIVEL] 1. to let saliva flow from one's mouth 2. to flow from the mouth, as saliva

droop (drōōp) *vi.* [< ON. *drūpa*] 1. to sink, hang, or bend down 2. to lose vitality 3. to become dejected —*vt.* to let sink or hang down —*n.* a drooping —**droop'y** *adj.* -i·er, -i·est —**droop'i·ness** *n.*

drop (dräp) *n.* [OE. *dropa*] 1. a bit of liquid rounded in shape by falling, etc. 2. anything like this in shape, etc. 3. a very small quantity 4. a sudden fall, slump, descent, etc. 5. something that drops, as a curtain or trapdoor 6. the distance between a higher and lower level —*vi.* **dropped, drop'ping** 1. to fall in drops 2. *a)* to fall suddenly down *b)* to fall exhausted, wounded, or dead 3. to pass into a specified state [to *drop* off to sleep] 4. to come to an end [let the matter *drop*] —*vt.* 1. to let or make fall 2. to utter (a hint, etc.) casually 3. to send (a letter) 4. to stop, end, or dismiss 5. to lower 6. [Colloq.] to deposit at a specified place —**drop in** (or over, by, etc.) to pay a casual visit —**drop out** to stop participating —**drop'let** *n.*

drop kick *Football* a kick of the ball made just as it rebounds from the ground after being dropped —**drop'-kick'** *vt.*, *vi.* —**drop'-kick'er** *n.*

drop'off' *n.* 1. a very steep drop 2. a decline, as in sales or prices

drop'out' *n.* a student who withdraws from school before graduating

drop'per *n.* a small tube with a hollow rubber bulb at one end, used to measure out a liquid in drops

drop·sy (dräp'sē) *n.* [< Gr. *hydrōps* < *hydōr*, water] an earlier term for EDEMA —**drop'si·cal** (-si k'l) *adj.*

DROPPER

dross (drôs) *n.* [OE. *dros*] 1. scum on molten metal 2. refuse; rubbish

drought (drout, drouth) *n.* [< OE. *drugoth*, dryness] prolonged dry weather: also **drouth** (drouth, drout)

drove[1] (drōv) *n.* [OE. *draf*] 1. a number of cattle, sheep, etc. driven or moving along as a group; flock; herd 2. a moving crowd of people

drove[2] (drōv) *pt.* of DRIVE

dro·ver (drō'vər) *n.* one who herds animals, esp. to market

drown (droun) *vi.* [ME. *drounen*] to die by suffocation in water —*vt.* 1. to kill by such suffocation 2. to flood 3. to be so loud as to overcome (another sound): usually with *out*

drowse (drouz) *vi.* **drowsed, drows'ing** [< OE. *drusian*, become sluggish] to be half asleep; doze —*n.* a doze

drow'sy *adj.* **-si·er, -si·est** being or making sleepy or half asleep —**drow'si·ly** *adv.* —**drow'si·ness** *n.*

drub (drub) *vt.* **drubbed, drub'bing** [< Ar. *daraba*, to cudgel] 1. to beat as with a stick 2. to defeat soundly —**drub'ber** *n.* —**drub'bing** *n.*

drudge (druj) *n.* [ME. *druggen*] a person who does hard, menial, or tedious work —*vi.* **drudged, drudg'ing** to do such work —**drudg'er·y** *n.*, *pl.* **-ies**

drug (drug) *n.* [< OFr. *drogue*] 1. any substance used as or in a medicine 2. a narcotic, hallucinogen, etc. —*vt.* **drugged, drug'ging** 1. to put a narcotic, etc. in (a drink, etc.) 2. to stupefy as with a drug —**a drug on the market** a thing in much greater supply than demand

drug'gist (-ist) *n.* 1. a dealer in drugs, medical supplies, etc. 2. a pharmacist 3. a drugstore owner or manager

drug'store' *n.* a store where drugs, medical supplies, and various items are sold and prescriptions are filled

dru·id (drōō'id) *n.* [< Celt.] [often D-] a member of a Celtic religious order in ancient Britain, Ireland, and France —**dru'id·ism** *n.*

drum (drum) *n.* [< Du. *trom*] 1. a percussion instrument consisting of a hollow cylinder with a membrane stretched over the end or ends. 2. the sound produced by beating a drum 3. any drumlike cylindrical object 4. the eardrum —*vi.* **drummed, drum'ming** 1. to beat a drum 2. to tap continually —*vt.* 1. to play (a rhythm, etc.) as on a drum 2. to instill (ideas, facts, etc. *into*) by continued repetition —**drum out of** to expel from in disgrace —**drum up** to get (business, etc.) by soliciting

drum·lin (drum'lin) *n.* [< Ir.] a long ridge formed of glacial drift

drum major a person who twirls a baton at the head of a marching band —**drum ma'jor·ette'** (-et') *fem.*

drum'mer *n.* 1. a drum player 2. [Colloq.] a traveling salesman

drum'stick' *n.* 1. a stick for beating a drum 2. the lower half of the leg of a cooked fowl

drunk (drunk) *pp.* of DRINK —*adj.* 1. overcome by alcoholic liquor; intoxicated 2. [Colloq.] *same as* DRUNKEN (sense 2) —*n.* [Slang] 1. a drunken person 2. a drinking spree

drunk·ard (drun'kərd) *n.* a person who often gets drunk

drunk·en (-kən) *adj.* [used before the noun] 1. intoxicated 2. caused by or occurring during intoxication —**drunk'en·ly** *adv.* —**drunk'en·ness** *n.*

drupe (drōōp) *n.* any fleshy fruit with an inner stone, as a peach

dry (drī) *adj.* **dri'er, dri'est** [OE. *dryge*] 1. not under water [dry land] 2. not wet or damp 3. lacking rain or water; arid 4. thirsty 5. not yielding milk 6. solid; not liquid 7. not sweet [dry wine] 8. prohibiting alcoholic liquors [a dry town] 9. funny in a quiet but sharp way [dry wit] 10. unproductive 11. boring; dull —*n.*, *pl.* **drys** [Colloq.] a prohibitionist —*vt.*, *vi.* **dried, dry'ing** to make or become dry —**dry up** 1. to make or become thoroughly dry 2. to make or become unproductive 3. [Slang] to stop talking —**dry'ly** *adv.* —**dry'ness** *n.*

dry·ad (drī'əd) *n.* [< Gr. *drys*, tree] *Classical Myth.* [also D-] a tree nymph

dry cell a voltaic cell containing an absorbent so that its contents cannot spill

dry'-clean' *vt.* to clean (garments, etc.) with a solvent other than water, as naphtha —**dry cleaner**

Dry·den (drīd'n), **John** 1631-1700; Eng. poet, critic, & playwright

dry dock a dock from which the water can be emptied, used for building and repairing ships

dry'er n. 1. a person or thing that dries: specif., an appliance for drying clothes with heat 2. *same as* DRIER

dry farming farming without irrigation, by conserving the soil's moisture

dry goods cloth, cloth products, etc.

dry ice a refrigerant consisting of solidified carbon dioxide

dry run [Slang] a simulated or practice performance; rehearsal

dry wall a wall made of wallboard, etc., without using wet plaster

D.S.C. Distinguished Service Cross

D.S.T., DST Daylight Saving Time

Du. 1. Duke 2. Dutch

du·al (dōō'əl) adj. [< L. *duo*, two] 1. of two 2. double; twofold —**du'al·ism** n. —**du·al'i·ty** (-al'ə tē) n.

dub[1] (dub) vt. **dubbed, dub'bing** [< OE. *dubbian*, to strike] 1. a) to confer a title or rank upon b) to name or nickname 2. to smooth by hammering, scraping, etc. 3. [Slang] to bungle (a golf stroke, etc.) —**dub'ber** n.

dub[2] (dub) vt. **dubbed, dub'bing** [< DOUBLE] to insert (dialogue, etc.) in a sound track of a movie, etc. —**dub'ber** n.

dub·bin (dub'n) n. [< DUB[1]] a greasy substance for waterproofing leather

du·bi·e·ty (dōō bī'ə tē) n. 1. a being dubious 2. pl. **-ties** a doubtful thing

du·bi·ous (dōō'bē əs) adj. [< L. *dubius*, uncertain] 1. causing doubt 2. feeling doubt; skeptical 3. questionable —**du'bi·ous·ly** adv.

Dub·lin (dub'lən) capital of Ireland: pop. 568,000

Du Bois (dōō bois'), **W(illiam) E. B.** 1868-1963; U.S. historian & educator

du·cal (dōō'k'l) adj. [< LL. *ducalis*, of a leader] of a duke or dukedom

duc·at (duk'ət) n. [see DUCHY] any of several former European coins

duch·ess (duch'is) n. 1. a duke's wife or widow 2. a woman ruling a duchy

duch'y (-ē) n., pl. **-ies** [< L. *dux*, leader] the territory ruled by a duke or duchess

duck[1] (duk) n. [< OE. *duce*, lit., diver] 1. a swimming fowl with a flat bill, short neck, and webbed feet 2. the flesh of a duck as food

duck[2] (duk) vt., vi. [ME. *douken*] 1. to plunge or dip under water for a moment 2. to lower or bend (the head, body, etc.) suddenly, as to avoid a blow 3. [Colloq.] to avoid (a task, person, etc.) —n. a ducking

duck[3] (duk) n. [Du. *doek*] a cotton or linen cloth like canvas but finer and lighter in weight

duck'bill' n. *same as* PLATYPUS

duck'ling n. a young duck

duck'pins' n.pl. [with sing. v.] a game like bowling, played with smaller pins and balls

duck'y adj. **-i·er, -i·est** [Slang] pleasing, delightful, etc.

duct (dukt) n. [< L. *ducere*, to lead] a tube, channel, or pipe, as for passage of a liquid —**duct'less** adj.

duc·tile (duk't'l) adj. [see prec.] 1. that can be drawn or hammered thin without breaking: said of metals 2. easily led; tractable —**duc·til·i·ty** (duk til'ə tē) n.

ductless gland an endocrine gland

dud (dud) n. [prob. < Du. *dood*, dead] [Colloq.] 1. a bomb or shell that fails to explode 2. a failure

dude (dōōd) n. [< ?] 1. a dandy; fop 2. [Western Slang] a city fellow or tourist 3. [Slang] any man or boy

dude ranch a vacation resort on a ranch, with riding horses, etc.

due (dōō, dyōō) adj. [< L. *debere*, owe] 1. owed or owing as a debt; payable 2. suitable; proper 3. enough [due care] 4. expected or scheduled to arrive —adv. exactly; directly [due west] —n. anything due; specif., [pl.] fees or other charges [membership dues] —**due to** 1. caused by 2. [Colloq.] because of —**pay one's dues** [Slang] to earn certain rights as by having suffered in struggle

du·el (dōō'əl) n. [< OL. *dvellum*, war] 1. a prearranged fight between two persons armed with deadly weapons 2. any contest like this —vi., vt. **-eled** or **-elled, -el·ing** or **-el·ling** to fight a duel with —**du'el·ist** or **du'el·list, du'el·er** or **du'el·ler** n.

due process (of law) legal proceedings established to protect individual rights and liberties

du·et (dōō et') n. [< L. *duo*, two] 1. a composition for two voices or instruments 2. the two performers of this

duf·fel (or **duf·fle**) **bag** (duf''l) [< *Duffel*, town in Belgium] a large cloth bag for carrying clothing, etc.

duf·fer (duf'ər) n. [< thieves' slang *duff*, to fake] [Slang] an awkward or incompetent person

dug (dug) pt. & pp. of DIG

dug'out' n. 1. a boat hollowed out of a log 2. a shelter, as in warfare, dug in the ground 3. *Baseball* a covered shelter for the players

duke (dōōk) n. [< L. *dux*, leader] 1. a prince ruling an independent duchy 2. a nobleman next in rank to a prince —**duke'dom** n.

dul·cet (dul'sit) adj. [< L. *dulcis*, sweet] soothing or pleasant to hear

dul·ci·mer (dul'sə mər) n. [< L. *dulce*, sweet + *melos*, song] a musical instrument with metal strings, struck with two small hammers or plucked with a plectrum or quill

dull (dul) adj. [< OE. *dol*, stupid] 1. mentally slow; stupid 2. physically slow; sluggish 3. boring; tedious 4. not sharp; blunt 5. not feeling or felt keenly 6. not vivid or bright [a dull color] —vt., vi. to make or become dull —**dull'ness** n. —**dul'ly** adv.

dull'ard (-ərd) n. a stupid person

Du·luth (də lōōth') city in NE Minn., on Lake Superior: pop. 93,000

du·ly (dōō'lē) adv. in due manner; in the proper way, time, etc.

Du·mas (dōō'mä), **Alexandre** 1802-70; Fr. writer

dumb (dum) *adj.* [OE.] 1. lacking the power of speech; mute 2. silent 3. [G. *dumm*] [Colloq.] stupid —**dumb′ly** *adv.* —**dumb′ness** *n.*

dumb·bell (dum′bel′) *n.* 1. a device consisting of round weights joined by a short bar, used for muscular exercise 2. [Slang] a stupid person

dumb·found, dum·found (dum′found′) *vt.* [DUMB + (CON)FOUND] to make speechless by shocking; amaze

dumb′wait′er *n.* a small elevator for sending food, etc. between floors

dum·dum (bullet) (dum′dum′) [< *Dumdum*, arsenal in India] a soft-nosed bullet that expands when it hits

dum·my (dum′ē) *n., pl.* -mies 1. a figure made in human form, as for displaying clothing 2. an imitation; sham 3. [Slang] a stupid person 4. *Bridge,* etc. the declarer's partner, whose hand is exposed on the board and played by the declarer —*adj.* sham

dump (dump) *vt.* [prob. < ON.] 1. to unload in a heap or mass 2. to throw away (rubbish, etc.) —*n.* 1. a place for dumping rubbish, etc. 2. *Mil.* a temporary storage center in the field 3. [Slang] an ugly, run-down place —**(down) in the dumps** in low spirits

dump·ling (dump′liŋ) *n.* [< ?] 1. a small piece of steamed or boiled dough served with meat or soup 2. a crust of baked dough filled with fruit

Dump·ster (dump′stər) *a trademark for* a large, metal trash bin, often one emptied by a special truck —*n.* [d-] such a trash bin

dump·y (dum′pē) *adj.* -i·er, -i·est 1. short and thick; squat 2. [Slang] ugly, run-down, etc.

dun¹ (dun) *adj., n.* [OE.] dull grayish brown

dun² (dun) *vt., vi.* **dunned, dun′ning** [? dial. var. of DIN] to ask (a debtor) repeatedly for payment —*n.* an insistent demand for payment

dunce (duns) *n.* [< *Dunsman,* follower of *Duns* Scotus, 13th-c. Scot. scholar] a dull, ignorant person

dune (dōōn) *n.* [< ODu. *duna*] a rounded hill or ridge of drifted sand

dune buggy [orig. used on sand dunes] a small, light automobile generally made from a standard, compact chassis and a prefabricated body

dung (duŋ) *n.* [OE.] animal excrement; manure

dun·ga·ree (duŋ′gə rē′) *n.* [Hind. *dungrī*] 1. a coarse cotton cloth 2. [*pl.*] work pants or overalls of this

dun·geon (dun′jən) *n.* [< OFr. *donjon*] a dark underground cell or prison

dung′hill′ *n.* a heap of dung

dunk (duŋk) *vt.* [G. *tunken*] 1. to dip (bread, etc.) into coffee, etc. before eating it 2. to immerse briefly

Dun·kirk (dun′kərk) seaport in N France: scene of evacuation of Allied troops under fire (May, 1940)

du·o (dōō′ō) *n., pl.* -os [It.] *same as* DUET (esp. sense 2)

du·o·de·num (dōō′ə dē′nəm) *n., pl.* -na (-nə). -nums [< L. *duodeni,* twelve each: it is about 12 fingers'-breadth long] the first section of the small intestine, below the stomach —**du′o·de′nal** *adj.*

dup. duplicate

dupe (dōōp) *n.* [< L. *upupa,* bird easily tricked] a person easily tricked —*vt.* duped, dup′ing to deceive; fool; trick —**dup′er** *n.*

du·plex (dōō′pleks) *adj.* [L.] double —*n.* 1. an apartment with rooms on two floors 2. a house consisting of two separate family units

du·pli·cate (dōō′plə kit; *for v.* -kāt′) *adj.* [< L. *duplicare,* to double] 1. double 2. corresponding exactly —*n.* an exact copy —*vt.* -cat′ed, -cat′ing 1. to make an exact copy of 2. to do or make again —**du′pli·ca′tion** *n.*

duplicating machine a machine for making copies of a letter, drawing, etc.: also du′pli·ca′tor (-kāt′ər) *n.*

du·plic·i·ty (dōō plis′ə tē) *n., pl.* -ties [< LL. *duplicitas*] hypocritical cunning or deception

du·ra·ble (door′ə b'l) *adj.* [< L. *durare,* to last] 1. lasting in spite of hard wear or frequent use 2. stable —**du′ra·bil′i·ty** *n.* —**du′ra·bly** *adv.*

dur·ance (door′əns) *n.* [see prec.] imprisonment: esp. in in durance vile

du·ra·tion (dōō rā′shən) *n.* [see DURABLE] the time that a thing continues or lasts

du·ress (doo res′) *n.* [< L. *durus,* hard] 1. imprisonment 2. coercion

dur·ing (door′iŋ) *prep.* [see DURABLE] 1. throughout the entire time of 2. in the course of

durst (durst) *archaic pt. of* DARE

du·rum (door′əm) *n.* [< L. *durus,* hard] a hard wheat that yields flour used for macaroni, spaghetti, etc.

dusk (dusk) *n.* [< OE. *dox,* dark-colored] 1. the dim part of twilight 2. gloom —**dusk′y** *adj.* -i·er, -i·est

dust (dust) *n.* [OE.] 1. powdery earth or any finely powdered matter 2. earth 3. disintegrated mortal remains 4. anything worthless —*vt.* 1. to sprinkle with dust, powder, etc. 2. to rid of dust, as by wiping —*vi.* to remove dust, as from furniture —**bite the dust** to be killed, esp. in battle —**dust′less** *adj.*

dust bowl an arid region with eroded topsoil easily blown off by winds

dust′er *n.* 1. a person or thing that dusts 2. a lightweight housecoat

dust′pan′ *n.* a shovellike receptacle into which floor dust is swept

dust′y *adj.* -i·er, -i·est 1. covered with or full of dust 2. powdery 3. dust-colored —**dust′i·ness** *n.*

Dutch (duch) *adj.* 1. of the Netherlands, its people, language, etc. 2. [Slang] German —*n.* the language of the Netherlands —**go Dutch** [Colloq.] to have each pay his own expenses —**in Dutch** [Colloq.] in trouble or disfavor —**the Dutch** Dutch people

Dutch door a door with upper and lower halves opening separately

Dutch oven a heavy pot with an arched lid, for pot roasts, etc.

Dutch treat [Colloq.] any entertainment, etc. at which each pays his own expenses

Dutch uncle [Colloq.] one who bluntly and sternly lectures another

du·te·ous (dōōt′ē əs) *adj.* dutiful; obedient —**du′te·ous·ly** *adv.*

du·ti·a·ble (dōōt′ē ə b'l) *adj.* necessitating payment of a duty

du·ti·ful (dōōt′ə fəl) *adj.* showing, or resulting from, a sense of duty; obedient —**du′ti·ful·ly** *adv.*

du·ty (dōōt′ē) *n., pl.* -**ties** [see DUE & -TY] **1.** obedience or respect to be shown to one's parents, elders, etc. **2.** any action required by one's position or by moral or legal considerations, etc. **3.** service, esp. military service [overseas *duty*] **4.** a tax, as on imports —**on** (or **off**) **duty** at (or temporarily relieved from) one's work

du·vet (dōō vā′, dyōō-) *n.* [Fr.] a comforter, often filled with down

dwarf (dwôrf) *n., pl.* **dwarfs, dwarves** (dwôrvz) [OE. *dweorg*] any abnormally small person, animal, or plant —*vt.* **1.** to stunt the growth of **2.** to make seem small in comparison —*vi.* to become dwarfed —*adj.* abnormally small —**dwarf′ish** *adj.* —**dwarf′ism** *n.*

dwell (dwel) *vi.* **dwelt** or **dwelled, dwell′ing** [OE. *dwellan*, to hinder] to make one's home; live —**dwell on** (or **upon**) to linger over —**dwell′er** *n.*

dwell′ing (**place**) an abode; residence

DWI, D.W.I. driving while intoxicated

dwin·dle (dwin′d'l) *vi., vt.* -**dled, -dling** [< OE. *dwinan*, waste away] to keep on becoming or making smaller or less; diminish; shrink

dyb·buk (dib′ək) *n.* [Heb. *dibbūq*] *Jewish Folklore* a spirit of one deceased

that enters the body of a person

dye (dī) *n.* [OE. *deag*] a substance or solution for coloring fabric, hair, etc.; also, the color produced —*vt., vi.* **dyed, dye′ing** to color with dye —**dy′er** *n.*

dyed′-in-the-wool′ *adj.* thoroughgoing; unchanging

dye′stuff′ *n.* any substance constituting or yielding a dye

dy·ing (dī′iŋ) *prp.* of DIE[1] —*adj.* **1.** about to die or end **2.** at death

dy·nam·ic (dī nam′ik) *adj.* [< Gr. *dynasthai*, be able] **1.** of energy or physical force in motion **2.** energetic; forceful —**dy·nam′i·cal·ly** *adv.*

dy·nam′ics *n.pl.* [*with sing. v. for 1*] **1.** the science dealing with motions produced by given forces **2.** the forces operative in any field

dy·na·mism (dī′nə miz'm) *n.* dynamic quality; forcefulness

dy·na·mite (dī′nə mīt′) *n.* [see DYNAMIC] a powerful explosive made with nitroglycerin —*vt.* -**mit′ed, -mit′ing** to blow up with dynamite

dy·na·mo (dī′nə mō′) *n., pl.* -**mos′** [see DYNAMIC] **1.** *earlier term for* GENERATOR **2.** a dynamic person

dy·nas·ty (dī′nəs tē) *n., pl.* -**ties** [< Gr. *dynasthai*, be strong] a succession of rulers, members of the same family —**dy·nas′tic** (-nas′tik) *adj.*

dys- [Gr.] *a prefix meaning* bad, ill, difficult, etc.

dys·en·ter·y (dis′'n ter′ē) *n.* [< Gr. *dys-*, bad + *entera*, bowels] an intestinal inflammation characterized by bloody diarrhea and abdominal pain

dys·func·tion (dis fuŋk′shən) *n.* abnormal or impaired functioning

dys·lex·i·a (dis lek′sē ə) *n.* [< Gr. *dys-*, bad + *lexis*, speech] impairment of reading ability

dys·pep·si·a (dis pep′shə, -sē ə) *n.* [< Gr. *dys-*, bad + *peptein*, to digest] indigestion —**dys·pep′tic** *adj., n.*

dz. dozen(s)

E

E, e (ē) *n., pl.* **E's, e's** the fifth letter of the English alphabet

E (ē) *n.* **1.** *Music* the third tone in the scale of C major **2.** *symbol for* energy

e- *a prefix meaning* out, out of, from, without: see EX-

E, E-, e, e 1. east **2.** eastern

E. 1. Earl **2.** Easter **3.** English

each (ēch) *adj., pron.* [OE. *ælc*] every one of two or more considered separately —*adv.* apiece Abbrev. **ea.**

ea·ger (ē′gər) *adj.* [< L. *acer*, keen] keenly desiring; impatient or anxious —**ea′ger·ly** *adv.* —**ea′ger·ness** *n.*

ea·gle (ē′g'l) *n.* [< L. *aquila*] **1.** a large bird of prey, with sharp vision and powerful wings **2.** a representation of an eagle, as the U.S. emblem **3.** a former U.S. $10 gold coin **4.** *Golf* a score of two under par on a hole

ea′gle-eyed′ *adj.* having keen vision

ea·glet (ē′glit) *n.* a young eagle

ear[1] (ir) *n.* [OE. *eare*] **1.** the part of the body that perceives sound **2.** the outer part of the ear **3.** one's sense of hearing or hearing ability **4.** anything like an ear —**be all ears** to listen attentively —**give** (or **lend**) **ear** to give attention; heed —**play by ear** to play (music) without using notation —**play it by ear** [Colloq.] to improvise

ear[2] (ir) *n.* [OE. *ær*] the grain-bearing spike of a cereal plant, as of corn —*vi.* to sprout ears

ear′ache′ *n.* an ache in an ear

ear′drum′ *n.* the tympanic membrane

earl (url) *n.* [OE. *eorl*, warrior] a British nobleman ranking just above a viscount —**earl′dom** *n.*

ear·ly (ur′lē) *adv., adj.* -**li·er, -li·est** [< OE. *ær*, before + *-lice*, -ly] **1.**

near the beginning 2. before the expected or usual time 3. in the distant past 4. in the near future — **early on** at an early stage

ear′mark′ *n.* 1. a brand put on the ear of livestock 2. an identifying mark or feature —*vt.* 1. to set such a brand or mark on 2. to reserve for a special purpose

ear′muffs′ (-mufs′) *n.pl.* coverings for the ears, worn in cold weather

earn (urn) *vt.* [OE. *earnian*] 1. to receive (wages, etc.) for one's work 2. to get as deserved 3. to gain (interest, etc.) as profit

ear·nest¹ (ur′nist) *adj.* [OE. *eornost*] 1. serious and intense; not joking 2. important —**in earnest** 1. serious 2. with determination —**ear′nest·ly** *adv.* —**ear′nest·ness** *n.*

ear·nest² (ur′nist) *n.* [ult. < Heb. *'ērābōn*] money, etc. given as a pledge in binding a bargain

earn′ings *n.pl.* 1. wages or other recompense 2. profits, interest, etc.

ear′phone′ *n.* a receiver for radio, etc., held to, or put into, the ear

ear′ring′ *n.* a ring or other small ornament for the lobe of the ear

ear′shot′ (-shät′) *n.* the distance within which a sound can be heard

ear′split′ting *adj.* so loud as to hurt the ears; very loud

earth (urth) *n.* [OE. *eorthe*] 1. the planet we live on, the fifth largest of the solar system: see PLANET 2. this world, as distinguished from heaven and hell 3. land, as distinguished from sea or sky 4. soil; ground —**down to earth** practical; realistic

earth′en *adj.* made of earth or clay

earth′en·ware′ *n.* clay pottery

earth′ling *n.* a person who lives on the earth; human being

earth′ly *adj.* 1. *a)* terrestrial *b)* worldly *c)* temporal 2. conceivable

earth mother a buxom, sensuous woman who is inclined to mother others

earth′quake′ *n.* a shaking of the earth's crust, caused by underground volcanic forces or shifting of rock

earth station a device for sending or receiving signals to or from communications satellites

earth′ward (-wərd) *adv., adj.* toward the earth: also **earth′wards** *adv.*

earth′work′ *n.* an embankment or fortification made by piling up earth

earth′worm′ *n.* a round, segmented worm that burrows in the soil

earth·y (ur′thē) *adj.* -i·er, -i·est 1. of or like earth 2. coarse; unrefined

ease (ēz) *n.* [< L. *adjacens*, lying nearby] 1. freedom from pain or trouble; comfort 2. natural manner; poise 3. freedom from difficulty; facility 4. affluence —*vt.* eased, eas′ing 1. to free from pain or trouble; comfort 2. to lessen (pain, anxiety, etc.) 3. to facilitate 4. to reduce the strain or pressure of 5. to move by careful shifting, etc. —*vi.* to become

less tense, severe, etc. —**ease′ful** *adj.*

ea·sel (ē′z'l) *n.* [ult. < L. *asinus*, ass] an upright frame to hold an artist's canvas, etc.

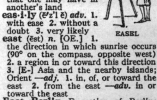

ease·ment (ēz′mənt) *n.* 1. an easing or being eased 2. *Law* a right that one may have in another's land

eas·i·ly (ē′z'l ē) *adv.* 1. with ease 2. without a doubt 3. very likely

EASEL

east (ēst) *n.* [OE.] 1. the direction in which sunrise occurs (90° on the compass, opposite west) 2. a region in or toward this direction 3. [E-] Asia and the nearby islands; Orient —*adj.* 1. in, of, or toward the east 2. from the east —*adv.* in or toward the east

East Berlin E section of Berlin; capital of East Germany: pop. 1,077,000

East China Sea part of the Pacific Ocean, between China & Japan

East·er (ēs′tər) *n.* [< OE. *Eastre*, dawn goddess] an annual Christian festival in the spring celebrating the resurrection of Jesus

east′er·ly *adj., adv.* 1. toward the east 2. from the east

east′ern *adj.* 1. in, of, or toward the east 2. from the east 3. [E-] of the East

east′ern·er *n.* a native or inhabitant of the east

Eastern Hemisphere that half of the earth which includes Europe, Africa, Asia, and Australia

East Germany E section of Germany; country in NC Europe: c. 41,800 sq. mi.; pop. 17,067,000

East In·dies (in′dēz) the Malay Archipelago —**East Indian**

east′ward (-wərd) *adv., adj.* toward the east: also **east′wards** *adv.*

eas·y (ē′zē) *adj.* -i·er, -i·est [see EASE] 1. not difficult 2. free from anxiety, pain, etc. 3. comfortable; restful 4. free from constraint; not stiff 5. not strict or severe 6. *a)* unhurried *b)* gradual —*adv.* [Colloq.] easily —**take it easy** [Colloq.] 1. to refrain from anger, haste, etc. 2. to relax; rest —**eas′i·ness** *n.*

easy chair a stuffed armchair

eas′y·go′ing *adj.* dealing with things in a relaxed or carefree way

eat (ēt) *vt.* ate, eat′en, eat′ing [OE. *etan*] 1. to chew and swallow (food) 2. to consume or ravage (with *away* or *up*) 3. to destroy, as acid does; corrode 4. to make by eating [acid *eats* holes in cloth] 5. [Slang] to worry or bother —*vi.* to eat food; have a meal —**eat′er** *n.*

eat′a·ble *adj.* fit to be eaten —*n.* a thing fit to be eaten: *usually in pl.*

eat′er·y *n., pl.* -ies [Colloq.] a restaurant

eats (ēts) *n.pl.* [Colloq.] food

eaves (ēvz) *n.pl.* [< OE. *efes*] the projecting lower edge or edges of a roof

eaves'drop' (-dräp') *vi.* -dropped', -drop'ping [prob. < *eavesdropper*, one standing under eaves to overhear] to listen secretly to a private conversation —**eaves'drop'per** *n.*

ebb (eb) *n.* [OE. *ebba*] 1. the flow of the tide back toward the sea 2. a lessening; decline —*vi.* 1. to recede, as the tide 2. to lessen; decline

eb·on·ite (eb'ən it') *n. same as* VULCANITE

eb·on·y (eb'ən ē) *n., pl.* -ies [< Gr. *ebenos*] the hard, heavy, dark wood of certain tropical trees —*adj.* 1. of ebony 2. like ebony; black

e·bul·lient (i bool'yənt, -bul'-) *adj.* [< L. *e-*, out + *bullire*, to boil] 1. boiling or bubbling up 2. enthusiastic; exuberant —**e·bul'lience** *n.*

e·bul·li·tion (eb'ə lish'ən) *n.* [see prec.] 1. a boiling or bubbling up 2. a sudden outburst, as of emotion

ec·cen·tric (ik sen'trik) *adj.* [< Gr. *ek-*, out of + *kentron*, center] 1. not having the same center, as two circles 2. having the axis off center 3. not exactly circular 4. odd, as in conduct; unconventional —*n.* 1. a disk set off center on a shaft, for converting circular motion into back-and-forth motion 2. an eccentric person —**ec·cen'tri·cal·ly** *adv.* —**ec·cen·tric·i·ty** (ek'sen tris'ə tē, -sən-) *n., pl.* -ties

Ec·cle·si·as·tes (i klē'zē as'tēz) [< Gr. *ek-*, out + *kalein*, to call] a book of the Old Testament: abbrev. **Eccles.**, **Eccl.**

ec·cle·si·as·tic (-tik) *adj.* [see prec.] ecclesiastical —*n.* a clergyman

ec·cle·si·as·ti·cal *adj.* of the church or the clergy

ECG electrocardiogram

ech·e·lon (esh'ə län') *n.* [< Fr. < L. *scala*, ladder] 1. a steplike formation of ships, troops, or aircraft 2. a subdivision of a military force 3. any of the levels of responsibility in an organization

ech·o (ek'ō) *n., pl.* -oes [< Gr. *ēchō*] 1. the repetition of a sound by reflection of the sound waves from a surface 2. a sound so produced —*vi.* -oed, -o·ing 1. to reverberate 2. to make an echo —*vt.* to repeat (another's words, etc.)

e·cho·ic (e kō'ik) *adj.* imitative in sound, as the word *tinkle*

é·clair (ā kler', ē-) *n.* [Fr., lit., lightning] an oblong frosted pastry shell filled with custard, etc.

é·clat (ā klä') *n.* [Fr. < *éclater*, to burst (out)] 1. brilliant success 2. striking effect 3. acclaim; fame

ec·lec·tic (i klek'tik, e-) *adj.* [< Gr. *ek-*, out + *legein*, to pick] selecting or selected from various sources —*n.* one who uses eclectic methods —**ec·lec'ti·cal·ly** *adv.* —**ec·lec'ti·cism** *n.*

e·clipse (i klips') *n.* [< Gr. *ek-*, out + *leipein*, to leave] 1. the obscuring of the sun when the moon comes between it and the earth (**solar eclipse**), or of the moon when the earth's shadow is cast upon it (**lunar eclipse**) 2. any obscuring of light, or of fame, glory, etc. —*vt.* **e·clipsed'**, **e·clips'ing** 1. to cause an eclipse of 2. to surpass

e·clip·tic (i klip'tik) *n.* the sun's apparent annual path; great circle of the celestial sphere

ec·logue (ek'lôg) *n.* [see ECLECTIC] a short pastoral poem

e·co·cide (ē'kō sīd') *n.* [< Gr. *oikos*, house + -CIDE] the destruction of the environment, as by pollutants

e·col·o·gy (ē käl'ə jē) *n.* [< Gr. *oikos*, house + -*logia*, -LOGY] the branch of biology that deals with the relations between living organisms and their environment —**e'co·log'i·cal** *adj.* —**e'co·log'i·cal·ly** *adv.* —**e·col·o·gist** *n.*

econ. 1. economic(s) 2. economy

e·co·nom·ic (ē'kə näm'ik, ek'ə-) *adj.* 1. of the management of income, expenditures, etc. 2. of economics 3. of the satisfaction of the material needs of people

e'co·nom'i·cal *adj.* 1. not wasting money, time, etc.; thrifty 2. of economics —**e'co·nom'i·cal·ly** *adv.*

e'co·nom'ics *n.pl.* [with sing. v.] 1. the science that deals with the production, distribution, and consumption of wealth 2. economic factors

e·con·o·mist (i kän'ə mist) *n.* a specialist in economics

e·con'o·mize' (-mīz') *vi.* -mized', -miz'ing to reduce waste or expenses —*vt.* to manage or use with thrift —**e·con'o·miz'er** *n.*

e·con'o·my (-mē) *n., pl.* -mies [< Gr. *oikos*, house + *nomos*, managing] 1. the management of the income, expenditures, etc. of a household, government, etc. 2. careful management of wealth, etc.; thrift 3. an instance of thrift 4. a system of producing and distributing wealth

e·co·sys·tem (ē'kō sis'təm) *n.* [< Gr. *oikos*, house + SYSTEM] a community of animals and plants and the environment with which it is interrelated

e·cru (ek'rōō) *adj., n.* [< Fr. < L. *ex-*, intens. + *crudus*, raw] light tan

ec·sta·sy (ek'stə sē) *n., pl.* -sies [< Gr. *ek-*, out + *histanai*, to place] a state or feeling of overpowering joy; rapture —**ec·stat·ic** (ik stat'ik) *adj.* —**ec·stat'i·cal·ly** *adv.*

-ec·to·my (ek'tə mē) [< Gr. *ek-*, out + *temnein*, to cut] *a combining form meaning* a surgical excision of [*appendectomy*]

Ec·ua·dor (ek'wə dôr') country on the NW coast of S. America: 104,506 sq. mi.; pop. 5,508,000

ec·u·men·i·cal (ek'yoo men'i k'l) *adj.* [< Gr. *oikoumenē* (*gē*), the inhabited (world)] 1. general or universal; esp., of the Christian Church as a whole 2. furthering religious unity, esp. among Christian churches —**ec'u·men'i·cal·ism** *n.* —**ec'u·men'i·cal·ly** *adv.*

ec'u·men·ism (-mə niz'm, e kyōō'-) *n.* the ecumenical movement, esp. among Christian churches: also **ec·u·men·i·cism** (ek'yoo men'i siz'm)

ec·ze·ma (ek'sə mə, eg'zə-; ig zē'mə) *n.* [< Gr. *ek-*, out + *zein*, to boil] a skin disease characterized by inflammation, itching, and scaliness

-ed [OE.] a suffix used: a) to form the past tense and past participle of many verbs b) to form adjectives from nouns or verbs [cultured]

ed. 1. edited 2. pl. **eds.** a) edition b) editor

E·dam (cheese) (ē'dəm) [< Edam, Netherlands] a mild yellow cheese

ed·dy (ed'ē) n., pl. **-dies** [prob. < ON. itha] a little whirlpool or whirlwind —vi. **-died, -dy·ing** to whirl

e·del·weiss (ā'd'l vīs') n. [G. < edel, noble + weiss, white] a small, flowering plant, esp. of the Alps, with white, woolly leaves

e·de·ma (i dē'mə) n. [< Gr. oidēma, swelling] an abnormal accumulation of fluid in body tissues or cavities

E·den (ē'd'n) Bible the garden where Adam and Eve first lived; Paradise — n. any delightful place

edge (ej) n. [OE. ecg] 1. the sharp, cutting part of a blade 2. sharpness; keenness 3. the projecting ledge of a cliff, etc.; brink 4. the part farthest from the middle; border or margin 5. [Colloq.] advantage [he has the edge on me] —vt., vi. **edged, edg'ing** 1. to form an edge (on) 2. to make (one's way) sideways 3. to move gradually —**on edge** 1. very tense; irritable 2. impatient —**take the edge off** to dull the intensity, force, or pleasure of —**edg'er** n.

edge'ways' (-wāz') adv. with the edge foremost: also **edge'wise** (-wīz')

edg'ing n. trimming along an edge

edg·y (ej'ē) adj. **-i·er, -i·est** irritable; on edge —**edg'i·ness** n.

ed·i·ble (ed'ə b'l) adj. [< L. edere, eat] fit to be eaten —n. [usually pl.] food —**ed'i·bil'i·ty** n.

e·dict (ē'dikt) n. [< L. e-, out + dicere, speak] a public order; decree

ed·i·fice (ed'ə fis) n. [see ff.] a building, esp. a large, imposing one

ed·i·fy (ed'ə fī') vt. **-fied', -fy'ing** [< L. aedificare, build] to instruct; esp., to instruct or improve morally —**ed'i·fi·ca'tion** n. —**ed'i·fi'er** n.

Ed·in·burgh (ed''n bur'ə, -ō) capital of Scotland: pop. 469,000

Ed·i·son (ed'ə s'n), Thomas A. 1847-1931; U.S. inventor

ed·it (ed'it) vt. [< EDITOR] 1. to prepare (a manuscript, etc.) for publication by arranging, revising, etc. 2. to control the policy and contents of (a newspaper, etc.) 3. to prepare (a film, tape, etc.) for presentation by cutting, dubbing, etc.

edit. 1. edited 2. edition 3. editor

e·di·tion (i dish'ən) n. [see ff.] 1. the size or form in which a book is published 2. the total number of copies of a book, etc. published at one time 3. any particular issue of a newspaper

ed·i·tor (ed'i tər) n. [L. < e-, out + dare, give] 1. one that edits 2. a writer of editorials

ed·i·to·ri·al (ed'ə tôr'ē əl) adj. of or by an editor —n. an article in a newspaper, etc., explicitly stating opinions of the editor or publisher —**ed'i·to'ri·al·ly** adv.

ed'i·to'ri·al·ize' (-īz') vi. **-ized', -iz'ing** to express editorial opinions

editor in chief pl. **editors in chief** the editor who heads the editorial staff of a publication

Ed·mon·ton (ed'mən tən) capital of Alberta, Canada: pop. 377,000

educ. 1. education 2. educational

ed·u·ca·ble (ej'ə kə b'l) adj. that can be educated or trained —**ed'u·ca·bil'i·ty** n.

ed·u·cate (ej'ə kāt') vt. **-cat'ed, -cat'ing** [< L. e-, out + ducere, to lead] 1. to develop the knowledge, skill, or character of, esp. by formal schooling; teach 2. to pay for the schooling of —**ed'u·ca'tor** n.

ed·u·ca·tion n. 1. the process of educating; teaching 2. knowledge, etc. thus developed 3. formal schooling —**ed'u·ca'tion·al** adj.

e·duce (i dōōs', ē-) vt. **-duced', -duc'ing** [see EDUCATE] 1. to draw out; elicit 2. to deduce

-ee (ē) [< Anglo-Fr. pp. ending] a suffix designating: 1. the recipient of an action [appointee] 2. one in a specified condition [absentee]

EEG electroencephalogram

eel (ēl) n. [OE. ǣl] a long, slippery, snakelike fish —**eel'y** (-ē) adj.

e'er (er, ar) adv. [Poet.] ever

-eer (ir) [L. -arius] a suffix denoting a person involved with or an action involving [auctioneer]

ee·rie, ee·ry (ir'ē) adj. **-ri·er, -ri·est** [< OE. earg, timid] mysterious, uncanny, or weird —**ee'ri·ly** adv.

ef- same as EX-: used before f

ef·face (i fās', e-) vt. **-faced', -fac'ing** [< L. ex-, out + facies, face] 1. to rub out; erase 2. to make (oneself) inconspicuous —**ef·face'ment** n.

ef·fect (ə fekt', i-) n. [< L. ex-, out + facere, do] 1. anything brought about by a cause; result 2. the power to cause results 3. influence 4. meaning [spoke to this effect] 5. an impression made on the mind, or its cause 6. a being operative or in force 7. [pl.] belongings; property —vt. to bring about; accomplish —**in effect** 1. actually 2. virtually 3. in operation —**take effect** to become operative

ef·fec·tive adj. 1. producing a desired effect; efficient 2. in effect; operative 3. impressive —**ef·fec'tive·ly** adv. —**ef·fec'tive·ness** n.

ef·fec·tu·al (ə fek'choo wəl, i-) adj. 1. producing, or able to produce, the desired effect 2. having legal force; valid —**ef·fec'tu·al·ly** adv.

ef·fec'tu·ate' (-wāt') vt. **-at'ed, -at'ing** to bring about; effect

ef·fem·i·nate (i fem'ə nit) adj. [< L. ex-, out + femina, woman] showing qualities attributed to women, as

weakness, delicacy, etc.; unmanly —
ef·fem'i·na·cy (-nə sē) n.

ef·fer·ent (ef'ər ənt) adj. [< L. ex-,
out + ferre, BEAR¹] carrying away
from a central part, as nerves

ef·fer·vesce (ef'ər ves') vi. -vesced',
-vesc'ing [< L. ex-, out + fervere, to
boil] 1. to give off gas bubbles; bubble
2. to be lively —**ef'fer·ves'cence** n.
—**ef'fer·ves'cent** adj.

ef·fete (e fēt', i-) adj. [< L. ex-, out
+ fetus, productive] 1. no longer able
to produce; sterile 2. decadent —
ef·fete'ly adv. —**ef·fete'ness** n.

ef·fi·ca·cious (ef'ə kā'shəs) adj. [see
EFFECT] that produces the desired
effect —**ef'fi·ca'cious·ly** adv. —
ef'fi·ca·cy (-kə sē) n.

ef·fi·cient (ə fish'ənt, i-) adj. [see
EFFECT] producing the desired result
with a minimum of effort, expense, or
waste —**ef·fi'cien·cy** n. —**ef·fi'·
cient·ly** adv.

ef·fi·gy (ef'ə jē) n., pl. -gies [< L.
ex-, out + fingere, to form] a statue or
other image; esp., a crude representation (for hanging or burning) of a
despised person

ef·flu·ent (ef'loo wənt) adj. [< L.
effluere, to flow out] flowing out —n.
the outflow of a sewer, septic tank,
etc. —**ef'flu·ence** n.

ef·flu·vi·um (e floo've əm) n., pl.
-vi·a (-ə), -vi·ums [see prec.] a
disagreeable vapor or odor

ef·fort (ef'ərt) n. [< L. ex-, intens. +
fortis, strong] 1. the use of energy to
do something 2. a try; attempt 3. a
result of working or trying —**ef'fort·
less** adj. —**ef'fort·less·ly** adv.

ef·fron·ter·y (e frun'tər ē, i-) n., pl.
-ies [< L. ex-, from + frons, fore-
head] impudence; audacity

ef·ful·gence (e ful'jəns, i-) n. [< L.
ex-, forth + fulgere, shine] radiance;
brilliance —**ef·ful'gent** adj.

ef·fuse (e fyooz', i-) vt., vi. -fused',
-fus'ing [< L. ex-, out + fundere,
pour] 1. to pour out or forth 2. to
spread; diffuse

ef·fu·sion (-fyoo'zhən) n. 1. a pouring forth 2. unrestrained expression in
speaking or writing —**ef·fu'sive** adj.
—**ef·fu'sive·ly** adv. —**ef·fu'sive·
ness** n.

e.g. [L. exempli gratia] for example

e·gad (i gad', ē-) interj. [prob. < oh
God] a softened oath

e·gal·i·tar·i·an (i gal'ə ter'ē ən) adj.
[< Fr. égalité, equality] advocating
full political and social equality for all
people —n. one advocating this

egg¹ (eg) n. [ON.] 1. the oval body
laid by a female bird, fish, etc., containing the germ of a new individual
2. a female reproductive cell; ovum 3.
a hen's egg, raw or cooked

egg² (eg) vt. [< ON. eggja, give edge
to] to urge or incite (with on)

egg'beat'er n. a kitchen utensil for
beating eggs, cream, etc.

egg foo yong (or **young**) (eg' foo
yuŋ') a Chinese-American dish of eggs
beaten and cooked with bean sprouts,
onions, minced pork, etc.

egg'head' n. [Slang] an intellectual

egg'nog' (-näg', -nôg') n. [EGG¹ +
nog, strong ale] a drink made of eggs,
milk, sugar, and, often, whiskey

egg'plant' n. a plant with a large
purple-skinned fruit, eaten
as a vegetable

e·gis (ē'jis) n. same as
AEGIS

eg·lan·tine (eg'lən tīn',
-tēn') n. [< L. aculeus, a
sting] a European pink
rose with sweet-scented
leaves

EGGPLANT

e·go (ē'gō) n., pl. -gos [L.,
I] 1. the individual as aware of himself; the self 2. conceit 3. Psychoanalysis the part of the psyche which
governs action rationally

e'go·cen'tric (-sen'trik) adj. viewing
everything in relation to oneself —n.
an egocentric person

e'go·ism n. 1. selfishness; self-interest
2. conceit —**e'go·ist** n. —**e'go·is'tic,
e'go·is'ti·cal** adj.

e·go·tism (ē'gə tiz'm) n. 1. excessive
reference to oneself in speaking or
writing 2. conceit —**e'go·tist** n. —
e'go·tis'tic, e'go·tis'ti·cal adj.

ego trip an experience, activity, etc.
that is self-fulfilling or increases one's
vanity

e·gre·gious (i grē'jəs) adj. [< L. e-,
out + grex, a herd] outstandingly bad;
flagrant —**e·gre'gious·ly** adv.

e·gress (ē'gres) n. [< L. e-, out +
gradi, go] a way out; exit

e·gret (ē'grit, eg'rit) n. [OFr. aigrette]
1. a heronlike bird with long white
plumes 2. such a plume

E·gypt (ē'jipt) country in NE Africa,
on the Mediterranean: 386,000 sq. mi.;
pop. 34,383,000; cap. Cairo

E·gyp·tian (i jip'shən, ē-) adj. of
Egypt, its people, etc. —n. 1. a native
or inhabitant of Egypt 2. the language
of the ancient Egyptians

eh (ā, e) interj. a sound expressing: 1.
surprise 2. doubt or inquiry

EHF extremely high frequency

ei·der (ī'dər) n. [ult. < ON. æthr] 1.
a large sea duck of northern regions
2. eiderdown

ei'der·down' n. the soft, fine down of
the eider duck, used as a stuffing for
quilts, pillows, etc.

eight (āt) adj., n. [OE. eahta] one
more than seven; 8; VIII —**eighth**
(ātth, āth) adj., n.

eight ball a black ball with the number eight on it, used in playing pool —
behind the eight ball [Slang] in a
very unfavorable position

eight·een (ā'tēn') adj., n. eight more
than ten; 18; XVIII —**eight'eenth'**
(-tēnth') adj., n.

eight·y (āt'ē) adj., n., pl. -ies eight
times ten; 80; LXXX —**the eighties**
the numbers or years, as of a century,
from 80 through 89 —**eight'i·eth**
(-ith) adj., n.

Ein·stein (īn'stīn), **Albert** 1879–
1955; U.S. physicist born in Germany;
formulated theory of relativity

Eir·e (er'ə) Gaelic name of IRELAND
(sense 2)

Ei·sen·how·er (ī'z'n hou'ər), **Dwight**

David 1890–1969; U.S. general & 34th president of the U.S. (1953–1961)

ei·ther (ē'thər, ī'-) *adj.* [OE. ǣgh-wæther] **1.** one or the other (of two) **2.** each (of two) —*pron.* one or the other —*conj.* a correlative used with *or* to denote a choice of alternatives [*either* go or stay] —*adv.* any more than the other; also [if you don't go, I won't *either*]

e·jac·u·late (i jak'yə lāt') *vt., vi.* -lat'ed, -lat'ing [see ff.] **1.** to eject (esp. semen) **2.** to utter suddenly; exclaim —e·jac'u·la'tion *n.*

e·ject (i jekt') *vt.* [< L. *e-*, out + *jacere*, throw] to throw or force out; expel; discharge —e·jec'tion *n.*

eke (ēk) *vt.* eked, ek'ing [< OE. *eacan*, to increase] to manage to make (a living) with difficulty: with *out*

EKG electrocardiogram

e·kis·tics (i kis'tiks) *n.pl.* [*with sing. v.*] [< Gr. *oikos*, house + -ICS] the science of city and area planning to meet both individual and community needs

e·lab·o·rate (i lab'ər it; *for v.* -ə rāt') *adj.* [< L. *e-*, out + *labor*, work] developed in great detail; complicated —*vt.* -rat'ed, -rat'ing to work out in great detail —*vi.* to add more details (usually with *on* or *upon*) —e·lab'o·rate·ly *adv.* —e·lab'o·rate·ness *n.* —e·lab'o·ra'tion *n.*

é·lan (ā län') *n.* [Fr. < *élancer*, to dart] spirited self-assurance; dash

e·lapse (i laps') *vi.* e·lapsed', e·laps'ing [< L. *e-*, out + *labi*, to glide] to slip by; pass: said of time

e·las·tic (i las'tik) *adj.* [< Gr. *elaunein*, set in motion] **1.** able to return immediately to its original size, shape, etc. after being stretched, squeezed, etc.; flexible **2.** able to recover easily, as from dejection; buoyant **3.** adaptable —*n.* an elastic band or fabric —e·las'tic'i·ty (-tis'ə tē) *n.*

e·las'ti·cize' (-tə sīz') *vt.* -cized', -ciz'ing to make (fabric) elastic

e·late (i lāt', ē-) *vt.* -lat'ed, -lat'ing [< L. *ex-*, out + *ferre*, BEAR] to raise the spirits of; make very proud, happy, etc. —e·la'tion *n.*

el·bow (el'bō) *n.* [see ELL² & BOW¹] **1.** the joint between the upper and lower arm; esp., the outer angle made by a bent arm **2.** anything bent like an elbow —*vt., vi.* to shove as with the elbows —out at (the) elbows shabby

elbow grease [Colloq.] hard work

el'bow·room' *n.* ample space or room

eld·er¹ (el'dər) *adj.* [< OE. *ald*, old] **1.** older **2.** of superior rank, position, etc. **3.** earlier; former —*n.* **1.** an older or aged person **2.** an older person with some authority, as in a tribe **3.** any of certain church officers

el·der² (el'dər) *n.* [OE. *ellern*] a shrub or tree of the honeysuckle family, with red or purple berries

el'der·ber'ry *n., pl.* -ries **1.** same as

ELDER² **2.** its berry, used for making wines, jelly, etc.

eld'er·ly *adj.* somewhat old

eld·est (el'dist) *adj.* oldest

El Do·ra·do, El·do·ra·do (el'də rä'dō) *pl.* -dos [Sp., the gilded] any place supposed to be rich in gold, opportunity, etc.

e·lect (i lekt') *adj.* [< L. *e-*, out + *legere*, choose] **1.** chosen **2.** elected but not yet installed in office [mayor-*elect*] —*vt., vi.* **1.** to select for an office by voting **2.** to choose

e·lec·tion (i lek'shən) *n.* **1.** a choosing or choice **2.** a choosing by vote

e·lec'tion·eer' (-shə nir') *vi.* to canvass votes in an election

e·lec'tive (-tiv) *adj.* **1.** *a)* filled by election [an *elective* office] *b)* chosen by election **2.** having the power to choose **3.** optional —*n.* an optional course or subject in a school curriculum

e·lec'tor (-tər) *n.* **1.** one who elects; specif., a qualified voter **2.** a member of the electoral college —e·lec'tor·al *adj.*

electoral college an assembly elected by the voters to perform the formal duty of electing the president and vice-president of the U.S.

e·lec'tor·ate (-it) *n.* all those qualified to vote in an election

E·lec·tra (i lek'trə) *Gr. Myth.* a daughter of Agamemnon: she plotted the death of her mother

e·lec·tric (i lek'trik) *adj.* [< Gr. *ēlektron*, amber: from the effect of friction upon amber] **1.** of or charged with electricity **2.** producing, or produced by, electricity **3.** operated by electricity **4.** thrilling; exciting Also e·lec'tri·cal —e·lec'tri·cal·ly *adv.*

electric chair a chair used in electrocuting those sentenced to death

e·lec·tri·cian (i lek'trish'ən, ē'lek-) *n.* a person whose work is the construction and repair of electric apparatus

e·lec'tric'i·ty (-tris'ə tē) *n.* **1.** a property of certain fundamental particles of all matter, as electrons (negative charges) and protons or positrons (positive charges): electric charge is generated by friction, induction, or chemical change **2.** an electric current **3.** electric current as a public utility for lighting, etc.

e·lec·tri·fy (i lek'trə fī') *vt.* -fied', -fy'ing **1.** to charge with electricity **2.** to excite; thrill **3.** to equip for the use of electricity —e·lec'tri·fi·ca'tion *n.* —e·lec'tri·fi'er *n.*

electro- *a combining form meaning* electric, electricity

e·lec·tro·car·di·o·gram (i lek'trō kär'dē ə gram') *n.* [prec. + CARDIO- + -GRAM] a tracing showing the changes in electric potential produced by contractions of the heart

e·lec'tro·car'di·o·graph' (-graf') *n.* an instrument for making electrocardiograms

e·lec'tro·chem'is·try *n.* the science dealing with chemical changes produced by electrical energy

e·lec·tro·cute (i lek'trə kyōōt') *vt.* -cut'ed, -cut'ing [ELECTRO- + (EXE)CUTE] to kill or execute with electricity —**e·lec'tro·cu'tion** *n.*

e·lec·trode (i lek'trōd) *n.* [ELECTR(O)- + -ODE] any terminal by which electricity enters or leaves a battery, etc.

e·lec'tro·en·ceph'a·lo·gram' (-trō en sef'ə lə gram') *n.* [see ENCEPHALITIS & -GRAM] a tracing showing the changes in electric potential produced by the brain

e·lec'tro·en·ceph'a·lo·graph' (-graf') *n.* an instrument for making electroencephalograms

e·lec·trol·o·gist (i lek·träl'ə jist) *n.* a practitioner of electrolysis (sense 2)

e·lec·trol·y·sis (i lek·träl'ə sis) *n.* [ELECTRO- + -LYSIS] 1. the decomposition of an electrolyte by the action of an electric current passing through it 2. the eradication of unwanted hair with an electrified needle

e·lec·tro·lyte (i lek'trə līt') *n.* [ELECTRO- + -LYTE] any substance which in solution is capable of conducting an electric current by the movement of its dissociated ions —**e·lec'tro·lyt'ic** (-lit'ik) *adj.*

e·lec·tro·mag·net (i lek'trō mag'nit) *n.* a soft iron core that becomes a magnet when an electric current flows through a coil surrounding it —**e·lec'·tro·mag·net'ic** (-net'ik) *adj.*

electromagnetic wave a wave generated by an oscillating electric charge

e·lec·tro·mo·tive (i lek'trə mōt'iv) *adj.* producing an electric current through differences in potential

e·lec·tron (i lek'trän) *n.* [see ELECTRIC] any of the negatively charged particles that form a part of all atoms

e·lec·tron·ic (i lek·trän'ik, ē'lek-) *adj.* 1. of electrons 2. operating, produced, or done by the action of electrons —**e·lec'tron'i·cal·ly** *adv.*

electronic music music in which the sounds are originated by electronic devices and recorded on tape

e·lec'tron'ics *n.pl.* [*with sing. v.*] the science that deals with electronic action and the use of electron tubes, transistors, etc.

electron microscope a device that focuses a beam of electrons to form a greatly enlarged image of an object, as on a fluorescent screen

electron tube a sealed glass or metal tube with a gas or a vacuum inside, used to control the flow of electrons

e·lec·tro·plate (i lek'trə plāt') *vt.* -plat'ed, -plat'ing to deposit a coating of metal on by electrolysis —*n.* anything so plated

e·lec'tro·shock' therapy shock therapy using electricity

e·lec'tro·ther'a·py (-ther'ə pē) *n.* the treatment of disease by means of electricity, as by diathermy

e·lec'tro·type' (-tīp') *n.* Printing a facsimile plate made by electroplating a wax or plastic impression of the surface to be reproduced

el·ee·mos·y·nar·y (el'i mäs'ə ner'ē, el'ē ə-) *adj.* [< Gr. *eleēmosynē*, pity] of, for, or supported by charity

el·e·gant (el'ə gənt) *adj.* [< L. *e-*, out + *legere*, choose] 1. having dignified richness and grace, as of manner, design, dress, etc.; tastefully luxurious 2. cleverly apt and simple [an *elegant* solution] 3. [Colloq.] excellent —**el'·e·gance** *n.* —**el'e·gant·ly** *adv.*

el·e·gi·ac (el'ə jī'ək, i lē'jē ak') *adj.* 1. of, like, or fit for an elegy 2. sad; mournful Also **el'e·gi'a·cal**

el·e·gy (el'ə jē) *n., pl.* -gies [< Gr. *elegos*, a lament] a mournful poem, esp. of lament and praise for the dead

el·e·ment (el'ə mənt) *n.* [< L. *elementum*] 1. the natural or suitable environment for a person or thing 2. a component part or quality, often one that is basic or essential 3. *Chem.* any substance that cannot be separated into different substances except by radioactive decay or by nuclear reactions: all matter is composed of such substances —**the elements** 1. the first principles; rudiments 2. wind, rain, etc.; forces of the atmosphere

el·e·men·tal (el'ə men't'l) *adj.* 1. of or like basic, natural forces; primal 2. *same as* ELEMENTARY (sense 2) 3. being an essential part or power

el'e·men·ta·ry (-tər ē, -trē) *adj.* 1. *same as* ELEMENTAL 2. of first principles or fundamentals; basic; simple

elementary particle a subatomic particle, as a neutron, electron, etc.

elementary school a school of the first six (or eight) grades, where basic subjects are taught

el·e·phant (el'ə fənt) *n.* [< Gr. *elephas*] a huge, thick-skinned mammal with a long flexible snout, or trunk, and, usually, two ivory tusks

el·e·phan·ti·a·sis (el'ə fən tī'ə sis) *n.* a chronic disease of the skin causing enlargement of certain bodily parts

el·e·phan·tine (el'ə fan'tēn, -tīn) *adj.* like an elephant; clumsy, etc.

el·e·vate (el'ə vāt') *vt.* -vat'ed, -vat'ing [< L. *e-*, out + *levare*, to lift] 1. to lift up; raise 2. to raise in rank 3. to raise to a higher moral or intellectual level 4. to elate; exhilarate

el'e·va'tion *n.* 1. an elevating or being elevated 2. a high place or position 3. height above the surface of the earth or above sea level

el'e·va'tor *n.* 1. one that elevates, or lifts up 2. a suspended cage for hoisting or lowering people or things 3. a warehouse for storing and discharging grain 4. a device like a horizontal rudder, for making an aircraft go up or down

e·lev·en (i lev'ən) *adj., n.* [OE. *endleofan*] one more than ten; 11; XI —**e·lev'enth** (-ənth) *adj., n.*

elf (elf) *n., pl.* **elves** (elvz) [OE. *ælf*] Folklore a tiny, often mischievous fairy —**elf'in**, **elf'ish** *adj.*

El Gre·co (el grek'ō) 1541?-1614?; painter in Spain, born in Crete

e·lic·it (i lis'it) *vt.* [< L. *e-*, out + *lacere*, entice] to draw forth; evoke (a response, etc.) —e·lic′i·ta′tion n.

e·lide (i līd′) vt. e·lid′ed, e·lid′ing [< L. e-, out + laedere, to strike] to leave out; esp., to slur over (a letter, etc.) in pronunciation —e·li·sion (i lizh′ən) n.

el·i·gi·ble (el′i jə b'l) adj. [see ELECT] fit to be chosen; qualified —an eligible person —el′i·gi·bil′i·ty n.

E·li·jah (i lī′jə) Bible a prophet of Israel in the 9th c. B.C.

e·lim·i·nate (i lim′ə nāt′) vt. -nat′ed, -nat′ing [< L. e-, out + limen, threshold] 1. to get rid of; remove 2. to leave out of consideration; omit 3. to excrete —e·lim′i·na′tion n.

El·i·ot (el′ē ət) 1. George (pseud. of Mary Ann Evans) 1819–80; Eng. novelist 2. T(homas) S(tearns), 1888–1965; Brit. poet, born in the U.S.

e·lite, é·lite (i lēt′, ā-) n. [Fr. < L.: see ELECT] [also used with pl. v.] the group or part of a group regarded as the best, most powerful, etc.

e·lit·ism n. government or control by an elite —e·lit′ist adj., n.

e·lix·ir (i lik′sər) n. [Ar. al-iksīr] 1. a hypothetical substance sought for by medieval alchemists to prolong life indefinitely; in full elixir of life 2. a medicine in alcoholic solution

E·liz·a·beth (i liz′ə bəth) city in NE N.J.: pop. 106,000

E·liz·a·beth I 1533–1603; queen of England (1558–1603)

E·liz′a·be′than (-bē′thən, -beth′ən) adj. of or characteristic of the time of Elizabeth I —n. an English person, esp. a writer, of that time

elk (elk) n., pl. elk, elks [OE. eolh] 1. a large, mooselike deer of N Europe and Asia 2. the wapiti

ell¹ (el) n. 1. an extension or wing at right angles to the main structure 2. an L-shaped joint, as of pipes

ell² (el) n. [OE. eln] a former measure of length (in England, 45 in.)

ELK

e·lipse (i lips′) n., pl. -lip′ses (-lip′siz) [< Gr. elleipein, to fall short] a closed curve in the form of a symmetrical oval

e·lip·sis (i lip′sis) n., pl. -ses (-sēz) [see prec.] 1. the omission of a word or words understood in the context, as in "if (it is) possible" 2. a mark (. . .) indicating an omission of words

e·lip·ti·cal (i lip′ti k'l) adj. 1. of, or having the form of, an ellipse 2. of or characterized by ellipsis Also e·lip′tic —e·lip′ti·cal·ly adv.

elm (elm) n. [OE.] 1. a tall, hardy shade tree 2. its hard, heavy wood

e·lo·cu·tion (el′ə kyōō′shən) n. [see ELOQUENT] the art of public speaking —el′o·cu′tion·ist n.

e·lon·gate (i lôn′gāt) vt., vi. -gat·ed, -gat·ing [< L. e-, out + longus, long] to make or become longer; lengthen —e·lon′ga′tion n.

e·lope (i lōp′) vi. e·loped′, e·lop′ing [prob. < OE. a-, away + hleapan, to run] to run away secretly, esp. in order to get married —e·lope′ment n.

el·o·quent (el′ə kwənt) adj. [< L. e-, out + loqui, speak] vivid, forceful, fluent, etc. in speech or writing —el′o·quence n. —el′o·quent·ly adv.

El Pas·o (el pas′ō) city in westernmost Tex.: pop. 425,000

El Sal·va·dor (el sal′və dôr′) country in Central America, on the Pacific: 8,260 sq. mi.; pop. 3,037,000

else (els) adj. [OE. elles] 1. different; other [somebody else] 2. in addition [is there anything else?] —adv. 1. differently; otherwise [where else can I go?] 2. if not [study, (or) else you will fail]

else′where′ (-hwer′, -wer′) adv. in or to some other place

e·lu·ci·date (i lōō′sə dāt′) vt., vi. -dat′ed, -dat′ing [< L. e-, out + lucidus, clear] to make (something) clear; explain —e·lu′ci·da′tion n.

e·lude (i lōōd′) vt. e·lud′ed, e·lud′ing [< L. e-, out + ludere, to play] 1. to avoid or escape from by quickness, cunning, etc.; evade 2. to escape the mental grasp of —e·lud′er n.

e·lu·sive (i lōō′siv) adj. tending to elude —e·lu′sive·ness n.

elves (elvz) n. pl. of ELF

E·ly·si·um (i lizh′ē əm, -liz′-) Gr. Myth. the place where virtuous people dwell after death —n. any state of ideal bliss; paradise —E·ly′sian (-lizh′ən, -ē ən) adj.

em (em) n. [< the letter M] Printing a unit of measure, as of column width

'em (əm, 'm) pron. [Colloq.] them

em- same as EN-: used before p, b, or m

e·ma·ci·ate (i mā′shē āt′, -sē-) vt. -at′ed, -at′ing [< L. e-, out + macies, leanness] to cause to become abnormally lean —e·ma′ci·a′tion n.

em·a·nate (em′ə nāt′) vi. -nat′ed, -nat′ing [< L. e-, out + manare, to flow] to come forth; issue, as from a source —em′a·na′tion n.

e·man·ci·pate (i man′sə pāt′) vt. -pat′ed, -pat′ing [< L. e-, out + manus, the hand + capere, to take] 1. to set free (a slave, etc.) 2. to free from restraint —e·man′ci·pa′tion n. —e·man′ci·pa′tor n.

e·mas·cu·late (i mas′kyə lāt′) vt. -lat′ed, -lat′ing [< L. e-, out + masculus, male] 1. to castrate 2. to weaken —e·mas′cu·la′tion n.

em·balm (im bäm′) vt. [see EN- & BALM] to preserve (a dead body) with various chemicals —em·balm′er n.

em·bank (im baŋk′) vt. to protect, support, or enclose with a bank of earth, etc. —em·bank′ment n.

em·bar·go (im bär′gō) n., pl. -goes

[Sp. < L. *in-*, in + ML. *barra*, a bar]
1. a government order prohibiting the entry or departure of commercial ships at its ports 2. any legal restriction of commerce —*vt.* -**goed**, -**go·ing** to put an embargo upon

em·bark (-bärk′) *vt.* [< L. *in-*, in + *barca*, small boat] to put or take aboard a ship, airplane, etc. —*vi.* 1. to go aboard a ship, airplane, etc. 2. to begin a journey 3. to engage in an enterprise —**em′bar·ka′tion** *n.*

em·bar·rass (im ber′əs) *vt.* [< It. *in-*, in + *barra*, a bar] 1. to cause to feel self-conscious 2. to hinder 3. to cause to be in debt —**em·bar′rass·ing** *adj.* —**em·bar′rass·ment** *n.*

em·bas·sy (em′bə sē) *n.*, *pl.* -**sies** [see AMBASSADOR] 1. the residence or offices of an ambassador 2. an ambassador and his staff 3. a group sent on an official mission

em·bat·tled (im bat′'ld) *adj.* [< OFr.] ready for battle

em·bed (im bed′) *vt.* -**bed′ded**, -**bed′ding** to set or fix firmly in a surrounding mass —**em·bed′ment** *n.*

em·bel·lish (im bel′ish) *vt.* [< OFr. *em-*, in + *bel*, beautiful] 1. to decorate; adorn 2. to improve (a story, etc.) by adding details, often fictitious —**em·bel′lish·ment** *n.*

em·ber (em′bər) *n.* [OE. *æmerge*] 1. a glowing piece of coal, wood, etc. 2. [*pl.*] the smoldering remains of a fire

em·bez·zle (im bez′'l) *vt.* -**zled**, -**zling** [< OFr. *en-*, in + *bessillier*, destroy] to steal (money, etc. entrusted to one) —**em·bez′zle·ment** *n.* —**em·bez′zler** *n.*

em·bit·ter (-bit′ər) *vt.* to make bitter

em·bla·zon (im blā′z'n) *vt.* [see BLAZON] 1. to decorate (*with* coats of arms, etc.) 2. to display brilliantly 3. to extol —**em·bla′zon·ment** *n.*

em·blem (em′bləm) *n.* [< Gr. *en-*, in + *ballein*, to throw] a visible symbol of a thing, idea, etc.; sign; badge —**em′blem·at′ic** (-blə mat′ik) *adj.*

em·bod·y (im bäd′ē) *vt.* -**ied**, -**y·ing** 1. to give bodily form to 2. to give definite form to 3. to form into, or make part of, an organized whole; incorporate —**em·bod′i·ment** *n.*

em·bold·en (im bōl′d'n) *vt.* to give courage to; cause to be bold

em·bo·lism (em′bə liz′m) *n.* [< Gr. *en-*, in + *ballein*, to throw] the obstruction of a blood vessel as by a blood clot or air bubble

em·boss (im bôs′) *vt.* [see EN- & BOSS²] 1. to decorate with raised designs, patterns, etc. 2. to raise (a design, etc.) in relief —**em·boss′ment** *n.*

em·bou·chure (äm′boo shoor′) *n.* [Fr. < L. *in*, in + *bucca*, cheek] the method of applying the lips to the mouthpiece of a wind instrument

em·brace (im brās′) *vt.* -**braced′**, -**brac′ing** [< L. *im-*, in + *brachium*, an arm] 1. to clasp in the arms lovingly; hug 2. to accept readily 3. to take up (a profession, etc.) 4. to encircle 5. to include —*vi.* to clasp each other in the arms —*n.* an embracing; hug —**em·brace′a·ble** *adj.*

em·bra·sure (im brā′zhər) *n.* [Fr. < *embraser*, widen an opening] 1. an opening (for a door or window) wider on the inside than on the outside 2. an opening in a wall for a gun, with the sides slanting outward

em·bro·cate (em′brō kāt′, -brə-) *vt.* -**cat′ed**, -**cat′ing** [< Gr. *en-*, in + *brechein*, to wet] to moisten and rub (a part of the body) with an oil, liniment, etc. —**em′bro·ca′tion** *n.*

em·broi·der (im broi′dər) *vt.*, *vi.* [< OFr. *en-*, on + *brosder*, embroider] 1. to make (a design, etc.) on (fabric) with needlework 2. to embellish (a story); exaggerate

em·broi′der·y *n.*, *pl.* -**ies** 1. the art of embroidering 2. embroidered work or fabric 3. embellishment

em·broil (im broil′) *vt.* [< OFr. *en-*, in + *brouillier*, to dirty] 1. to confuse; muddle 2. to involve in conflict or trouble —**em·broil′ment** *n.*

em·bry·o (em′brē ō′) *n.*, *pl.* -**os′** [< Gr. *en-*, in + *bryein*, to swell] 1. an animal in the earliest stages of its development in the uterus 2. the rudimentary plant contained in a seed 3. an early stage of something —**em′bry·on′ic** (-än′ik) *adj.*

em′bry·ol′o·gy (-äl′ə jē) *n.* [EMBRYO + -LOGY] the branch of biology dealing with the formation and development of embryos —**em′bry·ol′o·gist** *n.*

em·cee (em′sē′) *vt.*, *vi.* -**ceed′**, -**cee′ing** [< M.C.] [Colloq.] to act as master of ceremonies (for) —*n.* [Colloq.] a master of ceremonies

e·mend (i mend′) *vt.* [< L. *emendare*, to correct] to make scholarly corrections in (a text) —**e·men·da·tion** (ē′mən dā′shən, em′ən-) *n.*

em·er·ald (em′ər əld) *n.* [< Gr. *smaragdos*] 1. a bright-green, transparent precious stone 2. bright green

e·merge (i murj′) *vi.* **e·merged′**, **e·merg′ing** [< L. *e-*, out + *mergere*, to dip] 1. to rise as from a fluid 2. to become visible or apparent 3. to evolve —**e·mer′gence** *n.* —**e·mer′gent** *adj.*

e·mer·gen·cy (i mur′jən sē) *n.*, *pl.* -**cies** [orig. sense, an emerging] a sudden, generally unexpected occurrence demanding immediate action

e·mer·i·tus (i mer′ə təs) *adj.* [L. < *e-*, out + *mereri*, to serve] retired from active service, usually for age, but retaining one's title [professor *emeritus*]

Em·er·son (em′ər sən), **Ralph Waldo** (wôl′dō) 1803–82; U.S. writer

em·er·y (em′ər ē) *n.* [< Gr. *smyris*] a dark, hard variety of corundum used for grinding, etc.

e·met·ic (i met′ik) *adj.* [< Gr. *emein*, to vomit] causing vomiting —*n.* an emetic substance

-e·mi·a (ēm′ē ə) [< Gr. *haima*, blood] *a suffix meaning* a (specified) condition of the blood [*leukemia*]

em·i·grate (em′ə grāt′) *vi.* -**grat′ed**, -**grat′ing** [< L. *e-*, out + *migrare*, to move] to leave a country or region to settle in another —**em′i·grant** (-grənt) *adj.*, *n.* —**em′i·gra′tion** *n.*

é·mi·gré, e·mi·gré (em'ə grā', ā'mə grā') *n*. [Fr.] a person forced to flee his country for political reasons

em·i·nence (em'ə nəns) *n*. [< L. *eminere*, stand out] 1. a high place, thing, etc. 2. superiority in rank, position, etc. 3. [E-] a title of honor of a cardinal, preceded by *His* or *Your*

em'i·nent *adj*. [see prec.] 1. high; lofty 2. projecting; prominent 3. renowned; distinguished 4. outstanding —**em'i·nent·ly** *adv*.

eminent domain the right of a government to take (usually by purchase) private property for public use

e·mir (i mir') *n*. [< Ar. *amara*, to command] a Moslem ruler

em·is·sar·y (em'ə ser'ē) *n*., *pl*. **-ies** [see EMIT] a person, esp. a secret agent, sent on a specific mission

e·mis·sion (i mish'ən) *n*. 1. an emitting 2. something emitted; discharge

e·mit (i mit') *vt*. **e·mit'ted, e·mit'ting** [< L. *e-*, out + *mittere*, send] 1. to send out; give forth; discharge 2. to utter (sounds, etc.) —**e·mit'ter** *n*.

e·mol·li·ent (i mäl'yənt) *adj*. [< L. *e-*, out + *mollire*, soften] softening, soothing —*n*. a medicine that softens or soothes surface tissues

e·mol·u·ment (-yoo mənt) *n*. [< L. *e-*, out + *molere*, grind] gain from employment or position; salary, fees, etc.

e·mote (i mōt') *vi*. **e·mot'ed, e·mot'ing** [Colloq.] to display one's emotions dramatically

e·mo·tion (i mō'shən) *n*. [< L. *e-*, out + *movere*, to move] 1. strong feeling 2. any specific feeling, as love, hate, fear, anger, etc.

e·mo·tion·al *adj*. 1. of or showing emotion 2. easily aroused to emotion 3. appealing to the emotions —**e·mo'tion·al·ism** *n*. —**e·mo'tion·al·ly** *adv*.

e·mo·tion·al·ize' *vt*. **-ized', -iz'ing** to deal with in an emotional way

em·pa·thize (em'pə thīz') *vi*. **-thized', -thiz'ing** to feel empathy (*with*)

em'pa·thy (-thē) *n*. [< Gr. *en-*, in + *pathos*, feeling] intellectual or emotional identification with another

em·pen·nage (em'pə näzh') *n*. [Fr. < *em*, in + *penne*, a feather] the tail assembly of an airplane, including the fin, rudder, elevators, etc.

em·per·or (em'pər ər) *n*. [< L. *imperare*, to command] the supreme ruler of an empire

em·pha·sis (em'fə sis) *n*., *pl*. **-ses'** (-sēz') [< Gr. *en-*, in + *phainein*, to show] 1. force of expression, action, etc. 2. special stress given to a syllable, word, etc. in speaking 3. importance; stress

em'pha·size' (-sīz') *vt*. **-sized', -siz'ing** to give emphasis to; stress

em·phat·ic (im fat'ik) *adj*. 1. felt or done with emphasis 2. using emphasis in speaking, etc. 3. forcible; striking —**em·phat'i·cal·ly** *adv*.

em·phy·se·ma (em'fə sē'mə) *n*. [< Gr. *en-*, in + *physaein*, to blow] a disease of the lungs in which the air sacs become distended and lose elasticity

em·pire (em'pīr) *n*. [see EMPEROR] 1. supreme rule 2. government by an emperor or empress 3. a group of states or territories under one ruler

em·pir·i·cal (em pir'i k'l) *adj*. [< Gr. *en-*, in + *peira*, trial] relying or based on experiment or experience —**em·pir'i·cism** (-ə siz'm) *n*.

em·place·ment (im plās'mənt) *n*. the prepared position from which a heavy gun or guns are fired

em·ploy (im ploi') *vt*. [< L. *in-*, in + *plicare*, to fold] 1. to use 2. to keep busy or occupied 3. to engage the services of; hire —*n*. employment

em·ploy'a·ble —*adj*. physically and mentally fit to be hired for work

em·ploy·ee, em·ploy·e (im ploi'ē, em'ploi ē') *n*. a person employed by another for wages or salary

em·ploy'er *n*. one who employs others for wages or salary

em·ploy'ment *n*. 1. an employing or being employed 2. work; occupation 3. the number or percentage of persons gainfully employed

em·po·ri·um (em pôr'ē əm) *n*., *pl*. **-ri·ums, -ri·a** (-ə) [< Gr. *en-*, in + *poros*, way] a large store with a wide variety of things for sale

em·pow·er (im pou'ər) *vt*. 1. to give power to; authorize 2. to enable

em·press (em'pris) *n*. 1. an emperor's wife 2. a woman ruler of an empire

emp·ty (emp'tē) *adj*. **-ti·er, -ti·est** [OE. *æmettig*] 1. having nothing or no one in it; unoccupied 2. worthless [*empty* pleasure] 3. insincere [*empty* promises] —*vt*. **-tied, -ty·ing** 1. to make empty 2. to remove (the contents) of something —*vi*. 1. to become empty 2. to pour out; discharge —*n*., *pl*. **-ties** an empty truck, bottle, etc. —**emp'ti·ly** *adv*. —**emp'ti·ness** *n*.

emp·ty-hand'ed *adj*. bringing or carrying away nothing

em·py·re·an (em'pi rē'ən) *n*. [< Gr. *en-*, in + *pyr*, fire] 1. the highest heaven 2. the sky; firmament

e·mu (ē'myōō) *n*. [prob. < Port. *ema*, a crane] a large, nonflying Australian bird, like the ostrich but smaller

em·u·late (em'yə lāt') *vt*. **-lat'ed, -lat'ing** [< L. *aemulus*, trying to equal or excel] 1. to try to equal or surpass 2. to rival successfully —**em'u·la'tion** *n*. —**em'u·la'tive** *adj*. —**em'u·la'tor** *n*. —**em'u·lous** *adj*.

e·mul·si·fy (i mul'sə fī') *vt*., *vi*. **-fied', -fy'ing** to form into an emulsion —**e·mul'si·fi·ca'tion** *n*.

e·mul·sion (i mul'shən) *n*. [< L. *e-*, out + *mulgere*, to milk] a fluid formed by the suspension of one liquid in another; specif., *Pharmacy* a preparation of an oily substance suspended in a watery liquid

en- [< L. *in-*], in] *a prefix meaning:* 1. to put or get into or on [*enthrone*] 2. to make, cause to be [*endanger, enfeeble*] 3. in or into [*enclose*]

-en (ən, 'n) [OE.] *a suffix used:* 1. to form plurals [*children*] 2. to form diminutives [*chicken*] 3. to mean: *a*) to become or cause to be [*weaken*] *b*) to cause to have [*heighten*] *c*) made of [*woolen*]

en·a·ble (in ā'b'l) *vt.* **-bled, -bling** to make able; provide with means, power, etc. (*to do* something)

en·act (in akt') *vt.* 1. to pass (a bill, law, etc.) 2. to represent as in a play —**en·act′ment** *n.* —**en·ac′tor** *n.*

en·am·el (i nam'l) *n.* [< OFr. *esmail*] 1. a glassy, opaque substance fused to metal, pottery, etc. as an ornamental or protective coating 2. the hard, white coating of teeth 3. paint or varnish producing a hard, glossy surface —*vt.* **-eled** or **-elled, -el·ing** or **-el·ling** to coat or coat with enamel —**en·am′el·er, en·am′el·ier** *n.*

en·am′el·ware′ (-wer') *n.* kitchen utensils, etc. made of enameled metal

en·am·or (in am'ər) *vt.* [ult. < L. *in-*, in + *amor*, love] to fill with love; charm: mainly in the passive voice, with *of* [*enamored* of her]

en bloc (en bläk) [Fr., lit., in a block] all together; as a whole

†en bro·chette (än brô shet') [Fr.] broiled on small skewers

en·camp (in kamp') *vi., vt.* to set up, or put in, a camp —**en·camp′ment** *n.*

en·cap·su·late (in kap'sə lāt') *vt.* **-lat′ed, -lat′ing** 1. to enclose in a capsule 2. to make concise; condense Also **en·cap′sule** (-s'l, -syool), **-suled, -sul·ing** —**en·cap′su·la′tion** *n.*

en·case (in kās') *vt.* **-cased′, -cas′ing** to enclose, as in a case

en cas·se·role (en kas'ə rōl') [Fr.] (baked and served) in a casserole

-ence (əns, 'ns) [< L.] *a suffix meaning* act, state, or result [*conference*]

en·ceph·a·li·tis (en sef'ə līt'is) *n.* [< Gr. *en-*, in + *kephalē*, the head + *-ITIS*] inflammation of the brain

en·chain (in chān') *vt.* to bind with or as with chains; fetter

en·chant (in chant') *vt.* [< L. *in-*, in + *cantare*, sing] 1. to cast a spell over 2. to charm greatly; delight —**en·chant′er** *n.* —**en·chant′ing** *adj.* —**en·chant′ment** *n.*

en·chi·la·da (en'chə lä'də) *n.* [Am-Sp.] a tortilla rolled with meat inside, served with a chili-flavored sauce

en·cir·cle (in sur'k'l) *vt.* **-cled, -cling** 1. to surround 2. to move in a circle around —**en·cir′cle·ment** *n.*

en·clave (en'klāv) *n.* [< L. *in-*, in + *clavis*, a key] a territory surrounded by another country's territory

en·close (in klōz') *vt.* **-closed′, -clos′ing** 1. to shut in all around; surround 2. to insert in an envelope, etc., often along with a letter, etc.

en·clo·sure (-klō'zhər) *n.* 1. an en-

closing or being enclosed 2. something that encloses 3. something enclosed, as in an envelope or by a wall

en·code (in kōd') *vt.* **-cod′ed, -cod′ing** to put (a message) into code

en·co·mi·um (en kō'mē əm) *n., pl.* **-ums, -a** (-ə) [< Gr. *en-*, in + *kōmos*, a revel] high praise; eulogy

en·com·pass (in kum'pəs) *vt.* 1. to surround 2. to contain; include

en·core (äŋ'kôr) *interj.* [Fr.] again; once more —*n.* a further performance in response to an audience's applause

en·coun·ter (in koun'tər) *vt., vi.* [< L. *in*, in + *contra*, against] 1. to meet unexpectedly 2. to meet in conflict —*n.* 1. a battle; fight 2. an unexpected meeting

encounter group a small group that meets for therapy in personal interrelationship, with open exchange of feelings, etc.

en·cour·age (in kur'ij) *vt.* **-aged, -ag·ing** 1. to give courage, hope, or confidence to 2. to give support to; help —**en·cour′age·ment** *n.*

en·croach (in krōch') *vi.* [< OFr. *en-*, in + *croc*, a hook] to trespass or intrude (*on* or *upon*) —**en·croach′ment** *n.*

en croûte (än kr oot') [Fr.] wrapped in pastry and baked, esp. meats

en·crust (in krust') *vt., vi.* same as INCRUST —**en′crus·ta′tion** *n.*

en·cum·ber (in kum'bər) *vt.* [see EN- & CUMBER] 1. to hold back the motion or action of; hinder 2. to burden —**en·cum′brance** *n.*

-en·cy (ən sē) [L. *-entia*] *a suffix meaning* act, state, or result [*efficiency*]

en·cyc·li·cal (in sik'li k'l) *n.* [< Gr. *en-*, in + *kyklos*, a circle] a letter from the Pope to the bishops

en·cy·clo·pe·di·a (in sī'klə pē'dē ə) *n.* [< Gr. *enkyklios*, general + *paideia*, education] a book or set of books with alphabetically arranged articles on all branches, or on one field, of knowledge: also **en·cy′clo·pae′di·a** —**en·cy′clo·pe′dic** *adj.*

en·cyst (en sist') *vt., vi.* to enclose or become enclosed in a cyst, capsule, or sac —**en·cyst′ment** *n.*

end (end) *n.* [OE. *ende*] 1. a boundary; limit 2. the last part of anything; finish; conclusion 3. a ceasing to exist; death or destruction 4. the part at or near an extremity; tip 5. an aim; purpose 6. an outcome; result 7. *Football* a player at either end of the line —*vt., vi.* to bring or come to an end; finish; stop —*adj.* at the end; final —**make** (both) **ends meet** to manage to keep one's expenses within one's income —**put an end to** 1. to stop 2. to do away with

en·dan·ger (in dān'jər) *vt.* to expose to danger, harm, etc.; imperil

en·dear (in dir') *vt.* to make dear or beloved —**en·dear′ing** *adj.*

en·dear′ment *n.* 1. an endearing 2. a word or act expressing affection

en·deav·or (in dev'ər) *vt.* [< EN- + OFr. *deveir*, duty] to try (*to do* something) —*n.* an earnest attempt or effort Brit. sp. **en·deav′our**

en·dem·ic (en dem′ik) *adj.* [< Gr. *en-*, in + *dēmos*, people] prevalent in or restricted to a particular locality, as a disease —**en·dem′i·cal·ly** *adv.*

end·ing (en′diŋ) *n.* 1. the last part; finish 2. death

en·dive (en′dīv, än′dēv) *n.* [< Gr. *entybon*] a cultivated plant with curled, narrow leaves used in salads

end′less *adj.* 1. having no end; eternal; infinite 2. lasting too long [an endless speech] 3. with the ends joined to form a closed ring [an endless chain] —**end′less·ly** *adv.* —**end′less·ness** *n.*

end′most′ *adj.* at the end; farthest

endo- [< Gr. *endon*] a combining form meaning within, inner

en·do·crine (en′də krin, -krīn′) *adj.* [ENDO- + Gr. *krinein*, to separate] designating or of any gland producing an internal secretion carried by the blood to some body part whose functions it regulates

end organ a structure at the end of nerve fibers having either sensory or motor functions

en·dorse (in dôrs′) *vt.* -**dorsed′**, -**dors′ing** [< L. *in*, on + *dorsum*, back] 1. to write on the back of (a document); specif., to sign (one's name) as payee on the back of (a check, etc.) 2. to sanction, approve, or support 3. to recommend (an advertised product) for a fee —**en·dorse′ment** *n.* —**en·dors′er** *n.*

en·do·scope (en′də skōp′) *n.* an instrument for examining visually the inside of a hollow organ, as the rectum

en·dow (in dou′) *vt.* [ult. < L. *in*, in + *dotare*, endow] 1. to provide with some talent, quality, etc. [endowed with courage] 2. to give money to (a college, etc.) —**en·dow′ment** *n.*

end product the final result of a series of changes, processes, etc.

end table a small table placed at the end of a sofa, etc.

en·due (in dōō′) *vt.* -**dued′**, -**du′ing** [< L. *in-*, in + *ducere*, to lead] to provide (with qualities)

en·dur·ance (in door′əns) *n.* the ability to last, stand pain, etc.

en·dure (in door′) *vt.* -**dured′**, -**dur′ing** [< L. *in-*, in + *durus*, hard] 1. to stand (pain, fatigue, etc.) 2. to tolerate —*vi.* 1. to last; continue 2. to bear pain, etc. without flinching —**en·dur′a·ble** *adj.*

end′ways′ (-wāz′) *adv.* 1. on end; upright 2. with the end foremost 3. lengthwise Also **end′wise′** (-wīz′)

-ene (ēn) [after Gr. *-enos*, adj. suffix] a suffix used to form names for certain hydrocarbons [benzene]

en·e·ma (en′ə mə) *n.* [< Gr. *en-*, in + *hienai*, send] the injection of a liquid, as a purgative, medicine, etc., into the colon through the anus

en·e·my (en′ə mē) *n.*, *pl.* -**mies** [< L. *in-*, not + *amicus*, friend] 1. a person who hates another and wishes

to injure him 2. *a)* a nation hostile to another *b)* a soldier, citizen, etc. of a hostile nation 3. one hostile to a cause, idea, etc. 4. anything injurious

en·er·get·ic (en′ər jet′ik) *adj.* having or showing energy; vigorous —**en′er·get′i·cal·ly** *adv.*

en·er·gize (en′ər jīz′) *vt.* -**gized′**, -**giz′ing** to give energy to; activate —**en′er·giz′er** *n.*

en·er·gy (en′ər jē) *n.*, *pl.* -**gies** [< Gr. *en-*, in + *ergon*, work] 1. force of expression 2. *a)* inherent power; capacity for action *b)* [often *pl.*] such power, esp. in action 3. *Physics* the capacity for doing work

en·er·vate (en′ər vāt′) *vt.* -**vat′ed**, -**vat′ing** [< L. *enervis*, weak] to deprive of strength, force, vigor, etc.; devitalize —**en′er·va′tion** *n.*

en·fee·ble (in fē′b'l) *vt.* -**bled**, -**bling** to make feeble; weaken

en·fi·lade (en′fə lād′) *n.* [Fr.] gunfire directed along a line of troops

en·fold (in fōld′) *vt.* 1. to wrap in folds; wrap up 2. to embrace

en·force (in fôrs′) *vt.* -**forced′**, -**forc′ing** 1. to impose by force [to enforce one's will] 2. to compel observance of (a law, etc.) —**en·force′a·ble** *adj.* —**en·force′ment** *n.*

en·fran·chise (in fran′chīz) *vt.* -**chised**, -**chis·ing** 1. to free from slavery 2. to give the right to vote —**en·fran′chise·ment** (-chiz mənt, -chīz-) *n.*

Eng. 1. England 2. English

en·gage (in gāj′) *vt.* -**gaged′**, -**gag′ing** [see EN- & GAGE¹] 1. to pledge (oneself) 2. to bind by a promise of marriage 3. to hire 4. to involve or occupy 5. to attract and hold (the attention, etc.) 6. to enter into conflict with (the enemy) 7. to mesh together (gears, etc.) —*vi.* 1. to pledge oneself 2. to involve or occupy oneself [to engage in dramatics] 3. to enter into conflict 4. to mesh

en·gaged′ *adj.* 1. betrothed 2. occupied; employed 3. involved in combat, as troops 4. meshed

en·gage′ment *n.* an engaging or being engaged; specif., *a)* a betrothal *b)* an appointment *c)* employment *d)* a conflict; battle

en·gag′ing *adj.* attractive; charming —**en·gag′ing·ly** *adv.*

en·gen·der (in jen′dər) *vt.* [< L. *in-*, in + *generare*, to beget] to bring into being; cause; produce

en·gine (en′jən) *n.* [< L. *in-*, in + base of *gignere*, to produce] 1. any machine that uses energy to develop mechanical power 2. a railroad locomotive 3. any machine

en·gi·neer (en′jə nir′) *n.* 1. one skilled in some branch of engineering 2. one who operates or supervises the operation of engines or technical equipment [a locomotive *engineer*] —*vt.* 1. to plan, construct, etc. as an engineer 2. to manage skillfully

en·gi·neer·ing *n.* 1. the putting of scientific knowledge in various branches to practical uses 2. the planning, designing, construction, etc. of machinery, roads, bridges, etc.

Eng·land (iŋ′glənd) division of the United Kingdom, in S Great Britain: 50,331 sq. mi.; pop. 43,461,000

Eng·lish (iŋ′glish) *adj.* 1. of England, its people, etc. 2. of their language —*n.* 1. the language of the people of England, the official language of the British Commonwealth, the U.S., etc. 2. [*sometimes* e-] a spinning motion given to a ball —**the English** the people of England

English Channel arm of the Atlantic, between England & France

English horn a double-reed instrument of the woodwind family

Eng′lish·man (-mən) *n.*, *pl.* -**men** a native or inhabitant of England —**Eng′lish·wom′an** *n.fem.*, *pl.* -**wom′en**

en·graft (in graft′) *vt.* to graft (a shoot, etc.) from one plant onto another

en·grave (in grāv′) *vt.* -**graved′**, -**grav′ing** [< Fr. *en-*, in + *graver*, to incise] 1. to cut or etch (letters, designs, etc.) in or on (a metal plate, wooden block, etc.) 2. to print from such a plate, etc. 3. to impress deeply —**en·grav′er** *n.*

ENGLISH HORN

en·grav·ing *n.* 1. the act or art of one who engraves 2. an engraved plate, design, etc. 3. a printed impression made from an engraved surface

en·gross (in grōs′) *vt.* [< OFr. *en-groissier*, become thick] to take the entire attention of; occupy wholly —**en·gross′ing** *adj.* —**en·gross′ment** *n.*

en·gulf (in gulf′) *vt.* to swallow up

en·hance (in hans′) *vt.* -**hanced′**, -**hanc′ing** [ult. < L. *in*, in + *altus*, high] to make better, greater, etc.; heighten —**en·hance′ment** *n.*

e·nig·ma (ə nig′mə) *n.*, *pl.* -**mas** [< Gr. *ainigma*] 1. a riddle 2. a perplexing or baffling matter, person, etc. —**e·nig·mat·ic** (en′ig mat′ik, ē′nig-), **e′nig·mat′i·cal** *adj.*

en·jamb·ment, **en·jambe·ment** (in jam′mənt) *n.* [< Fr. *enjamber*, to encroach] the running on of a phrase from one line to the next of a poem

en·join (in join′) *vt.* [< L. *in-*, in + *jungere*, join] 1. to command; order 2. to prohibit, esp. by legal injunction

en·joy (in joi′) *vt.* [< OFr. *en-*, in + *joir*, rejoice] 1. to get joy or pleasure from; relish 2. to have the use or benefit of —**enjoy oneself** to have a good time —**en·joy′a·ble** *adj.* —**en·joy′ment** *n.*

en·large (in lärj′) *vt.* -**larged′**, -**larg′ing** to make larger; expand —*vi.* 1. to become larger; expand 2. to discuss at greater length (with *on* or *upon*) —**en·large′ment** *n.*

en·light·en (in līt′'n) *vt.* 1. to free from ignorance, prejudice, etc. 2. to inform —**en·light′en·ment** *n.*

en·list (in list′) *vt.*, *vi.* 1. to enroll in some branch of the armed forces 2. to engage in support of a cause or movement —**en·list′ment** *n.*

enlisted man any man in the armed forces who is not a commissioned officer or warrant officer

en·liv·en (in līv′'n) *vt.* to make active, cheerful, etc.; liven up

en masse (en mas′) [Fr., lit., in mass] in a group; as a whole

en·mesh (en mesh′) *vt.* to catch as in the meshes of a net; entangle

en·mi·ty (en′mə tē) *n.*, *pl.* -**ties** [see ENEMY] the attitude or feelings of an enemy or enemies; hostility

en·no·ble (i nō′b'l) *vt.* -**bled**, -**bling** to give a noble quality to; dignify —**en·no′ble·ment** *n.*

en·nui (än′wē) *n.* [Fr.: see ANNOY] a feeling of boredom and weariness

e·nor·mi·ty (i nôr′mə tē) *n.*, *pl.* -**ties** [< L. *enormis*, immense] 1. great wickedness 2. an outrageous act 3. loosely, enormous size or extent

e·nor·mous (i nôr′məs) *adj.* [see prec.] of great size, number, etc.; huge; vast —**e·nor′mous·ly** *adv.*

e·nough (i nuf′) *adj.* [OE. *genoh*] as much or as many as necessary; sufficient —*n.* the amount needed —*adv.* 1. sufficiently 2. fully; quite [*oddly enough*] 3. tolerably

e·now (i nou′) *adj.*, *n.*, *adv.* [Archaic] enough

en·plane (en plān′) *vi.* -**planed′**, -**plan′ing** to board an airplane

en·quire (in kwīr′) *vt.*, *vi.* -**quired′**, -**quir′ing** *same as* INQUIRE —**en·quir′y** (-ē) *n.*, *pl.* -**ies**

en·rage (in rāj′) *vt.* -**raged′**, -**rag′ing** to put into a rage; infuriate

en·rap·ture (in rap′chər) *vt.* -**tured**, -**tur·ing** to fill with delight

en·rich (in rich′) *vt.* to make rich or richer; give greater value, better quality, etc. to —**en·rich′ment** *n.*

en·roll, **en·rol** (in rōl′) *vt.*, *vi.* -**rolled′**, -**roll′ing** 1. to record or be recorded in a roll or list 2. to enlist 3. to make or become a member —**en·roll′ment**, **en·rol′ment** *n.*

en route (än root′) [Fr.] on the way

en·sconce (in skäns′) *vt.* -**sconced′**, -**sconc′ing** [< Du. *schans*, small fort] to place or settle snugly or securely

en·sem·ble (än säm′b'l) *n.* [Fr. < L. *in-*, in + *simul*, at the same time] 1. total effect 2. a whole costume of matching parts 3. *a)* a small group of musicians playing or singing together *b)* the performance of such a group, or of an orchestra, chorus, etc.

en·shrine (in shrīn′) *vt.* -**shrined′**, -**shrin′ing** 1. to enclose in a shrine 2. to hold as sacred; cherish

en·shroud (in shroud′) *vt.* to cover as with a shroud; hide; obscure

en·sign (en′sīn; *also, and for 2 always,* -s'n) *n.* [see INSIGNIA] 1. a flag or banner 2. *U.S. Navy* a commissioned officer of the lowest rank

en·si·lage (en′s'l ij) *n.* [Fr.] green fodder preserved in a silo

en·sile (en sīl′) *vt.* -**siled′**, -**sil′ing** [Fr.] to store (green fodder) in a silo

en·slave (in slāv′) *vt.* -slaved′, -slav′ing 1. to make a slave of 2. to subjugate —en·slave′ment *n.*

en·snare (in sner′) *vt.* -snared′, -snar′ing to catch as in a snare

en·sue (in sōō′) *vi.* -sued′, -su′ing [< L. *in-*, in + *sequi*, follow] 1. to come afterward 2. to result

en·sure (in shoor′) *vt.* -sured′, -sur′ing 1. to make sure 2. to protect

-ent (ənt) [< Fr. *-ent*, L. *-ens*, prp. ending] *a suffix meaning:* 1. that has, shows, or does [*insistent*] 2. a person or thing that does [*superintendent, solvent*]

en·tail (in tāl′) *vt.* [< OFr. *taillier*, to cut] 1. *Law* to limit the inheritance of (property) to a specific line of heirs 2. to make necessary; require

en·tan·gle *vt.* -gled, -gling 1. to involve in a tangle 2. to involve in difficulty 3. to confuse 4. to complicate —en·tan′gle·ment *n.*

en·tente (än tänt′) *n.* [Fr. < OFr. *entendre*, to understand] 1. an understanding or agreement, as between nations 2. the parties to this

en·ter (en′tər) *vt.* [< L. *intra*, within] 1. to come or go into 2. to penetrate 3. to insert 4. to write down in a list, etc. 5. to become a member of or participant in 6. to get (someone) admitted 7. to begin 8. to put on record, formally or before a law court —vi. 1. to come or go into some place 2. to penetrate —enter into 1. to take part in 2. to form a part of —enter on (or upon) to begin; start

en·ter·i·tis (en′tə rīt′is) *n.* [< Gr. *enteron*, intestine + -ITIS] inflammation of the intestine

en·ter·prise (en′tər prīz′) *n.* [ult. < L. *inter-*, in + *prehendere*, take] 1. an undertaking, esp. a big, bold, or difficult one 2. energy and initiative

en′ter·pris′ing *adj.* showing enterprise; full of energy and initiative

en·ter·tain (en′tər tān′) *vt.* [ult. < L. *inter*, between + *tenere*, to hold] 1. to amuse; divert 2. to have as a guest 3. to have in mind; consider —vi. to give hospitality to guests

en′ter·tain′er *n.* one who entertains; esp., a popular singer, comedian, etc.

en′ter·tain′ing *adj.* interesting and pleasurable; amusing

en′ter·tain′ment *n.* 1. an entertaining or being entertained 2. something that entertains; esp., a show

en·thrall, en·thral (in thrôl′) *vt.* -thralled′, -thrall′ing [see EN- & THRALL] to fascinate; captivate

en·throne *vt.* -throned′, -thron′ing 1. to place on a throne 2. to exalt

en·thuse (in thōōz′) *vi.* -thused′, -thus′ing [Colloq.] to express enthusiasm —vt. [Colloq.] to make enthusiastic

en·thu·si·asm (in thōō′zē az′m) *n.* [< Gr. *enthous*, inspired] intense or eager interest; zeal —en·thu′si·ast′ (-ast′) *n.* —en·thu′si·as′tic *adj.* —en·thu′si·as′ti·cal·ly *adv.*

en·tice (in tīs′) *vt.* -ticed′, -tic′ing [< L. *in*, in + *titio*, a burning brand] to tempt with hope of reward or pleasure —en·tice′ment *n.*

en·tire (in tīr′) *adj.* [< L. *integer*, whole] not lacking any parts; complete; whole; intact —en·tire′ly *adv.*

en·tire′ty (-tē) *n., pl.* -ties 1. the state or fact of being entire; wholeness 2. an entire thing; whole

en·ti·tle (in tīt′'l) *vt.* -tled, -tling 1. to give a title or name to 2. to give a right or claim to

en·ti·ty (en′tə tē) *n., pl.* -ties [ult. < L. *esse*, to be] 1. existence 2. a thing that has real existence

en·tomb (in tōōm′) *vt.* to place in a tomb; bury —en·tomb′ment *n.*

en·to·mol·o·gy (en′tə mäl′ə jē) *n.* [< Gr. *entomon*, insect + -LOGY] the branch of zoology that deals with insects —en′to·mo·log′i·cal (-mə läj′i k'l) *adj.* —en′to·mol′o·gist *n.*

en·tou·rage (än′too räzh′) *n.* [Fr. < *entourer*, surround] a group of associates or attendants; retinue

en·trails (en′trālz, -trəlz) *n.pl.* [< L. *interaneus*, internal] the inner organs; specif., the intestines; viscera

en·train (in trān′) *vt., vi.* to put or go aboard a train

en·trance¹ (en′trəns) *n.* 1. the act of entering 2. a place for entering; door, etc. 3. permission or right to enter; admission

en·trance² (in trans′) *vt.* -tranced′, -tranc′ing [see EN- & TRANCE] to fill with delight; enchant

en·trant (en′trənt) *n.* one who enters

en·trap (in trap′) *vt.* -trapped′, -trap′ping to catch as in a trap

en·treat (in trēt′) *vt., vi.* [< OFr. *en-*, in + *traiter*: see TREAT] to ask earnestly; beseech; implore —en·treat′ing·ly *adv.* —en·treat′ment *n.*

en·treat′y *n., pl.* -ies an earnest request; prayer

en·tree, en·trée (än′trā) *n.* [Fr. < OFr. *entrer*: see ENTER] 1. right to enter 2. the main course of a meal

en·trench (in trench′) *vt.* 1. to surround with trenches 2. to establish securely —en·trench′ment *n.*

en·tre·pre·neur (än′trə prə nur′) *n.* [Fr.: see ENTERPRISE] one who organizes a business undertaking, assuming the risk for the sake of the profit

en·tro·py (en′trə pē) *n.* [< Gr. *entropē*, a turning toward] 1. a measure of the energy unavailable for useful work in a system 2. the tendency of an energy system to run down

en·trust (in trust′) *vt.* 1. to charge with a trust or duty 2. to turn over for safekeeping

en·try (en′trē) *n., pl.* -tries [< OFr.: see ENTER] 1. an entering; entrance 2. a way by which to enter 3. an item or note entered in a list, journal, etc. 4. one entered in a race, etc.

en·twine (in twīn′) *vt., vi.* -twined′, -twin′ing to twine together or around

e·nu·mer·ate (i nōō'mə rāt') *vt.* -at'ed, -at'ing [< L. *e-*, out + *numerare*, to count] 1. to count 2. to name one by one —**e·nu'mer·a'tion** *n.*

e·nun·ci·ate (i nun'sē āt') *vt., vi.* -at'ed, -at'ing [< L. *e-*, out + *nuntiare*, announce] 1. to state definitely 2. to announce 3. to pronounce (words) —**e·nun'ci·a'tion** *n.*

en·u·re·sis (en'yoo rē'sis) *n.* [< Gr. *enourein*, to urinate in] inability to control urination, esp. during sleep

en·vel·op (in vel'əp) *vt.* [< OFr.: see EN- & DEVELOP] 1. to wrap up; cover completely 2. to surround 3. to conceal; hide —**en·vel'op·ment** *n.*

en·ve·lope (en'və lōp', än'-) *n.* 1. a thing that envelops; covering 2. a folded paper container for letters, etc., usually with a gummed flap

en·ven·om (in ven'əm) *vt.* 1. to put venom into 2. to fill with hate

en·vi·a·ble (en'vē ə b'l) *adj.* good enough to be envied or desired —**en'vi·a·bly** *adv.*

en·vi·ous (en'vē əs) *adj.* feeling or showing envy —**en'vi·ous·ly** *adv.*

en·vi·ron·ment (in vī'rən mənt) *n.* [see ENVIRONS] 1. surroundings 2. all the conditions, etc. surrounding, and affecting the development of, an organism —**en·vi'ron·men'tal** *adj.*

en·vi'ron·men'tal·ist *n.* a person working to solve environmental problems, as air and water pollution

en·vi·rons (in vī'rəns) *n.pl.* [< OFr. *en-*, in + *viron*, a circuit] 1. the districts surrounding a city; suburbs 2. surrounding area; vicinity

en·vis·age (en viz'ij) *vt.* -aged, -ag·ing [see EN- & VISAGE] to form an image of in the mind; visualize

en·vi·sion (en vizh'ən) *vt.* [EN- + VISION] to imagine (something not yet in existence)

en·voy (en'voi, än'-) *n.* [< Fr. < L. *in*, in + *via*, way] 1. a messenger 2. a diplomatic agent ranking just below an ambassador

en·vy (en'vē) *n.,* *pl.* -vies [< L. *invidia*] 1. discontent and ill will over another's advantages, possessions, etc. 2. desire for something that another has 3. an object of such feeling —*vt.* -vied, -vy·ing to feel envy toward or because of —**en'vy·ing·ly** *adv.*

en·zyme (en'zīm) *n.* [< Gr. *en-*, in + *zymē*, leaven] a proteinlike substance, formed in plant and animal cells, acting as a catalyst in chemical reactions

e·on (ē'ən, ē'än) *n.* [< Gr. *aiōn*, an age] an extremely long, indefinite period of time

-e·ous (ē əs) [< L. *-eus*] a suffix meaning having the nature of, like [*beauteous*]

EPA Environmental Protection Agency

ep·au·let, ep·au·lette (ep'ə let') *n.* [< Fr.: see SPATULA] a shoulder ornament, as on military uniforms

e·pee, é·pée (e pā') *n.* [Fr.] a fencing sword like a foil, but more rigid

e·pergne (i purn') *n.* an ornamental dish or stand with several compartments for candy, flowers, etc.

e·phed·rine (i fed'rin) *n.* [< L. *ephedra*, the plant horsetail] an alkaloid used to relieve nasal congestion and asthma

e·phem·er·al (i fem'ər əl) *adj.* [< Gr. *epi-*, upon + *hēmera*, day] 1. lasting one day 2. short-lived; transitory

epi- [< Gr. *epi*, at, on] a prefix meaning on, upon, over, among [*epiglottis*]

ep·ic (ep'ik) *n.* [< Gr. *epos*, a word, song, epic] a long narrative poem in a dignified style about the deeds of a hero or heroes —*adj.* of or like an epic; heroic; grand

ep·i·cen·ter (ep'ə sen'tər) *n.* 1. the area of the earth's surface directly above the place of origin of an earthquake 2. a focal or central point

ep·i·cure (ep'i kyoor') *n.* [< *Epicurus*, ancient Gr. philosopher] one who enjoys and has a discriminating taste for fine foods and drinks

ep·i·cu·re·an (ep'i kyoo rē'ən) *adj.* 1. fond of sensuous pleasure 2. having to do with an epicure —*n.* same as EPICURE

ep·i·dem·ic (ep'ə dem'ik) *adj.* [< Fr. < Gr. *epi-*, among + *dēmos*, people] spreading rapidly among many people in a community, as a disease —*n.* 1. an epidemic disease 2. the spreading of such a disease —**ep'i·dem'i·cal·ly** *adv.*

ep·i·der·mis (-dur'mis) *n.* [< Gr. *epi-*, upon + *derma*, the skin] the outermost layer of the skin —**ep'i·der'mal, ep'i·der'mic** *adj.*

ep·i·glot·tis (-glät'is) *n.* [see EPI- & GLOTTIS] the thin cartilage lid that covers the windpipe during swallowing

ep·i·gram (ep'ə gram') *n.* [< Gr. *epi-*, upon + *graphein*, write] a terse, witty, pointed statement —**ep·i·gram·mat·ic** (ep'i grə mat'ik) *adj.*

e·pig·ra·phy (i pig'rə fē) *n.* the study of inscriptions, esp. ancient ones

ep·i·lep·sy (ep'ə lep'sē) *n.* [< Gr. *epi-*, upon + *lambanein*, seize] a chronic nervous disease, characterized by convulsions and unconsciousness

ep·i·lep·tic (-tik) *adj.* of or having epilepsy —*n.* one who has epilepsy

ep·i·logue (ep'ə lôg') *n.* [< Gr. *epi-*, upon + *legein*, speak] a closing section added to a novel, play, etc. providing further comment; specif., a speech to the audience by an actor

E·piph·a·ny (i pif'ə nē) *n.* [< Gr. *epiphainein*, show forth] a Christian festival (Jan. 6) commemorating the revealing of Jesus as the Christ to the Gentiles

e·pis·co·pa·cy (i pis'kə pə sē) *n.,* *pl.* -cies [< Gr. *epi-*, upon + *skopein*, to look] 1. church government by bishops 2. same as EPISCOPATE

e·pis·co·pal (-p'l) *adj.* 1. of or governed by bishops 2. [E-] designating or of any of various churches governed by bishops

E·pis·co·pa'li·an (-pāl'yən, -pā'lē ən) *adj.* same as EPISCOPAL —*n.* a member of the Protestant Episcopal Church

e·pis·co·pate (i pis'kə pit, -pāt') *n.*

1. the position, rank, etc. of a bishop
2. bishops collectively

ep·i·sode (ep'ə sōd') *n.* [< Gr. *epi-*, upon + *eisodos*, entrance] 1. any part of a novel, poem, etc. that is complete in itself 2. an event or series of events complete in itself —**ep'i·sod'ic** (-säd'ik) *adj.* —**ep·i·sod'i·cal·ly** *adv.*

e·pis·tle (i pis'l) *n.* [< Gr. *epi-*, to + *stellein*, send] 1. a letter 2. [E-] any of the letters in the New Testament —**e·pis'to·lar'y** (-tə ler'ē) *adj.*

ep·i·taph (ep'ə taf') *n.* [< Gr. *epi-*, upon + *taphos*, tomb] an inscription, as for a tomb, in memory of a dead person

ep·i·the·li·um (ep'ə thē'lē əm) *n.* [< Gr. *epi-*, upon + *thēlē*, nipple] membranelike tissue that covers body surfaces and lines body cavities —**ep'i·the'li·al** (-əl) *adj.*

ep·i·thet (ep'ə thet') *n.* [< Gr. *epi-*, on + *tithenai*, put] a word or phrase characterizing some person or thing

e·pit·o·me (i pit'ə mē) *n., pl.* -**mes** [< Gr. *epi-*, upon + *temnein*, to cut] 1. an abstract; summary 2. a person or thing that typifies a whole class

e·pit'o·mize' (-mīz') *vt.* -**mized'**, -**miz'ing** to make or be an epitome of

‡e plu·ri·bus u·num (ē' ploor'ə bəs yōō'nəm) [L.] out of many, one: a motto of the U.S.

ep·och (ep'ək) *n.* [< Gr. *epi-*, upon + *echein*, hold] 1. the start of a new period of something [radio marked an *epoch* in communication] 2. a period of time in terms of noteworthy events, persons, etc. —**ep'och·al** *adj.*

ep·ox·y (e päk'sē) *adj.* [EP(I)- + OXY(GEN)] designating a resin used in strong, resistant glues, enamels, etc. —*n., pl.* -**ies** an epoxy resin

ep·si·lon (ep'sə län') *n.* the fifth letter of the Greek alphabet (E, ε)

Ep·som salts (or **salt**) (ep'səm) [< *Epsom*, town in England] a white, crystalline salt, magnesium sulfate, used as a cathartic

eq·ua·ble (ek'wə b'l) *adj.* [see ff.] steady; uniform; even; tranquil —**eq'ua·bil'i·ty** *n.* —**eq'ua·bly** *adv.*

e·qual (ē'kwəl) *adj.* [< L. *aequus*, even] 1. of the same quantity, size, value, etc. 2. having the same rights, ability, rank, etc. 3. evenly proportioned 4. having the necessary ability, strength, etc. (with *to*) —*n.* any person or thing that is equal —*vt.* e'qualed or e'qualled, e'qual·ing or e'qual·ling 1. to be equal to 2. to do or make something equal to —**e·qual·i·ty** (i kwäl'ə tē, -kwôl'-) *n., pl.* -**ties** —**e'qual·ly** *adv.*

e·qual·ize (ē'kwə līz') *vt.* -**ized'**, -**iz'ing** to make equal or uniform —**e'qual·i·za'tion** *n.* —**e'qual·iz'er** *n.*

equal sign (or **mark**) the arithmetical sign (=), indicating that the terms on either side of it are equal

e·qua·nim·i·ty (ek'wə nim'ə tē, ē'kwə-) *n.* [< L. *aequus*, even +

animus, mind] calmness of mind; composure

e·quate (i kwāt') *vt.* e·quat'ed, e·quat'ing 1. to make equal 2. to treat, regard, or express as equal —**e·quat'a·ble** *adj.*

e·qua·tion (i kwā'zhən) *n.* 1. an equating or being equated 2. a statement of equality between two quantities, as shown by the equal sign (=)

e·qua·tor (i kwāt'ər) *n.* an imaginary circle around the earth, equally distant from both the North Pole and the South Pole —**e·qua·to·ri·al** (ē'kwə tôr'ē əl, ek'wə-) *adj.*

Equatorial Guinea country in C Africa: 10,832 sq. mi.; pop. 246,000

eq·uer·ry (ek'wər ē, i kwer'ē) *n., pl.* -**ries** [< Fr.] 1. formerly, an officer in charge of royal horses 2. an officer who attends a person of royalty

e·ques·tri·an (i kwes'trē ən) *adj.* [< L. *equus*, horse] 1. of horses or horsemanship 2. on horseback —*n.* a rider or circus performer on horseback —**e·ques'tri·enne'** (-trē en') *n.fem.*

equi- *a combining form meaning* equal, equally [*equidistant*]

e·qui·an·gu·lar (ē'kwə aŋ'gyə lər) *adj.* having all angles equal

e·qui·dis·tant (ē'kwə dis'tənt) *adj.* equally distant

e·qui·lat·er·al (-lat'ər əl) *adj.* [< L. *aequus*, equal + *latus*, side] having all sides equal

e·qui·lib·ri·um (-lib'rē əm) *n., pl.* -**ri·ums**, -**ri·a** (-ə) [< L. *aequus*, equal + *libra*, a balance] a state of balance between opposing forces

e·quine (ē'kwīn, ek'wīn) *adj.* [< L. *equus*, horse] of or like a horse

e·qui·nox (ē'kwə näks') *n.* [< L. *aequus*, equal + *nox*, night] the time when the sun crosses the equator, making night and day of equal length in all parts of the earth —**e'qui·noc'·tial** (-näk'shəl) *adj.*

e·quip (i kwip') *vt.* e·quipped', e·quip'ping [< OFr. *esquiper*, embark] to provide with what is needed

eq·ui·page (ek'wə pij) *n.* a carriage with horses and liveried servants

e·quip·ment (i kwip'mənt) *n.* 1. an equipping or being equipped 2. whatever one is equipped with; supplies, furnishings, etc.

e·qui·poise (ek'wə poiz') *n.* [EQUI- + POISE] 1. state of equilibrium 2. counterbalance

eq'ui·ta·ble (-wit ə b'l) *adj.* [see EQUITY] fair; just —**eq'ui·ta·bly** *adv.*

eq·ui·ta·tion (ek'wə tā'shən) *n.* [< L. *equitare*, to ride] horsemanship

eq·ui·ty (ek'wə tē) *n., pl.* -**ties** [< L. *aequus*, equal] 1. fairness; impartiality; justice 2. the value of property beyond the amount owed on it 3. *Law* a system of doctrines supplementing common and statute law

e·quiv·a·lent (i kwiv'ə lənt) *adj.* [< L. *aequus*, equal + *valere*, be strong] equal in quantity, value, force, meaning, etc. —*n.* an equivalent thing — **e·quiv′a·lence** *n.*

e·quiv·o·cal (i kwiv′ə k'l) *adj.* [< L. *aequus*, equal + *vox*, voice] 1. having two or more meanings; purposely ambiguous 2. uncertain; doubtful 3. suspicious —**e·quiv′o·cal·ly** *adv.* —**e·quiv′o·cal·ness** *n.*

e·quiv·o·cate′ (-kāt′) *vi.* -**cat′ed**, -**cat′ing** to use equivocal terms in order to deceive or mislead —**e·quiv′o·ca′tion** *n.* —**e·quiv′o·ca′tor** *n.*

-**er** (-ər) [< OE.] 1. *a suffix meaning: a)* a person or thing having to do with [*hatter*] *b)* a person living in [*New Yorker*] *c)* a person or thing that [*sprayer*] *d)* repeatedly [*flicker*] 2. *a suffix forming the comparative degree* [*greater*]

e·ra (ir′ə, er′ə) *n.* [LL. *aera*] 1. a period of time measured from some important event 2. a period of history having some special characteristic

ERA 1. *Baseball* earned run average 2. Equal Rights Amendment

e·rad·i·cate (i rad′ə kāt′) *vt.* -**cat′ed**, -**cat′ing** [< L. *e-*, out + *radix*, root] to uproot; wipe out; destroy — **e·rad′i·ca′tion** *n.* —**e·rad′i·ca′tor** *n.*

e·rase (i rās′) *vt.* **e·rased′**, **e·ras′ing** [< L. *e-*, out + *radere*, scrape] 1. to rub, scrape, or wipe out (esp. writing) 2. to obliterate, as from the mind —**e·ras′a·ble** *adj.*

e·ras′er *n.* a thing that erases; specif., a rubber device for erasing ink or pencil marks, or a pad for removing chalk marks from a blackboard

E·ras·mus (i raz′məs), **Des·i·der·i·us** (des′ə dir′ē əs) 1466?-1536; Du. humanist and writer

e·ra·sure (i rā′shər) *n.* 1. an erasing 2. an erased word, mark, etc.

ere (er) *prep.* [OE. *ær*] [Archaic] before (in time) —*conj.* [Archaic] 1. before 2. rather than

e·rect (i rekt′) *adj.* [< L. *e-*, up + *regere*, make straight] upright —*vt.* 1. to construct (a building, etc.) 2. to set in an upright position 3. to set up; assemble —**e·rec′tion** *n.* —**e·rect′ly** *adv.* —**e·rect′ness** *n.* —**e·rec′tor** *n.*

e·rec·tile (i rek′t'l) *adj.* that can become erect, as tissue that becomes rigid when filled with blood

erg (urg) *n.* [< Gr. *ergon*, work] *Physics* a unit of work or energy

† **er·go** (ur′gō) *adv.* [L.] therefore

er·gos·ter·ol (ər gäs′tə rōl′) *n.* a steroid alcohol prepared from yeast, that produces vitamin D when exposed to ultraviolet rays

Er·ie (ir′ē) 1. city in NW Pa.: pop. 119,000 2. **Lake**, one of the Great Lakes, between Lake Huron & Lake Ontario

Er·in (er′in) *poet.* name for IRELAND

er·mine (ur′mən) *n.* [prob. < OHG. *harmo*, weasel] 1. a weasel whose fur is white in winter 2. its white fur

e·rode (i rōd′) *vt.* **e·rod′ed**, **e·rod′ing** [< L. *e-*, out + *rodere*, gnaw] 1. to

wear away 2. to form by wearing away gradually [the stream *eroded* a gully] —*vi.* to become eroded

e·rog·e·nous (i räj′ə nəs) *adj.* [< Gr. *erōs*, love + -GEN + -OUS] sensitive to sexual stimulation: also **e·ro·to·gen·ic** (i rät′ə jen′ik)

e·ro·sion (i rō′zhən) *n.* an eroding or being eroded —**e·ro′sive** (-siv) *adj.*

e·rot·ic (i rät′ik) *adj.* [< Gr. *erōs*, love] of or arousing sexual feelings or desires; amatory —**e·rot′i·cal·ly** *adv.*

e·rot′i·ca (-i kə) *n.pl.* [*often with sing. v.*] erotic books, pictures, etc.

err (ur, er) *vi.* [< L. *errare*, wander] 1. to be wrong or mistaken 2. to deviate from the established moral code

er·rand (er′ənd) *n.* [< OE. *ærende*, mission] 1. a trip to do a thing, as for someone else 2. the thing to be done

er·rant (er′ənt) *adj.* [see ERR] 1. roving or wandering, esp. in search of adventure 2. erring 3. shifting about

er·rat·ic (i rat′ik) *adj.* [see ERR] 1. irregular; random 2. eccentric; queer —**er·rat′i·cal·ly** *adv.*

er·ra·tum (e rāt′əm, -rät′-) *n., pl.* -**ta** [see ERR] an error in printing or writing

er·ro·ne·ous (ə rō′nē əs) *adj.* containing error; mistaken; wrong —**er·ro·ne·ous·ly** *adv.*

er·ror (er′ər) *n.* [see ERR] 1. the state of believing what is untrue 2. a wrong belief 3. something incorrectly done; mistake 4. a transgression 5. *Baseball* any misplay in fielding

er·satz (ur′zäts, er′-) *adj.* [G.] substitute or synthetic and inferior

Erse (urs) *adj., n.* [< ME. var. of *Irisc*, IRISH] *same as* GAELIC

erst (urst) *adv.* [< OE. *ær*, ere] [Archaic] formerly

erst′while′ (-hwīl′) *adv.* [Archaic] formerly —*adj.* former

e·ruct (i rukt′) *vt., vi.* [< L. < *e-*, out + *ructare*, belch] to belch — **e·ruc′ta′tion** *n.*

er·u·dite (er′yoo dīt′, -oo-) *adj.* [< L. *e-*, out + *rudis*, rude] learned; scholarly —**er′u·dite′ly** *adv.*

er′u·di′tion (-dish′ən) *n.* learning acquired by reading and study

e·rupt (i rupt′) *vi.* [< L. *e-*, out + *rumpere*, to break] 1. to burst forth or out [*erupting* lava] 2. to throw forth lava, water, etc. 3. to break out in a rash —*vt.* to cause to burst forth

e·rup·tion (i rup′shən) *n.* 1. a bursting forth or out 2. *a)* a breaking out in a rash *b)* a rash

-**er·y** (ər ē) [< LL. -*aria*] *a suffix meaning:* 1. a place to [*tannery*] 2. a place for [*nunnery*] 3. the practice or act of [*robbery*] 4. the product of [*pottery*] 5. a collection of [*crockery*] 6. the condition of [*drudgery*]

er·y·sip·e·las (er′ə sip′'l əs, ir′-) *n.* [< Gr. *erythros*, red + -*pelas*, skin] an acute, infectious skin disease with local inflammation and fever

e·ryth·ro·cyte (i rith′rə sīt′) *n.* [< Gr. *erythros*, red + *kytos*, a hollow] a red corpuscle in the blood: it contains hemoglobin, which carries oxygen to the body tissues

ERMINE

-es (iz, əz) [< OE.] a suffix used to form: 1. certain plurals *(fishes)* 2. the third person singular, present indicative, of verbs *(he) kisses)*

E·sau (ē′sô) *Bible* Isaac's son, who sold his birthright to his brother, Jacob

es·ca·late (es′kə lāt′) *vi.* -lat′ed, -lat′ing 1. to rise as on an escalator 2. to expand step by step 3. to increase rapidly —**es′ca·la′tion** *n.*

es·ca·la·tor (es′kə lāt′ər) *n.* [ult. < L. *scala*, ladder] a moving stairway on an endless belt

es·cal·lop, es·cal·op (e skal′əp, -skäl′-) *n., vt. same as* SCALLOP

es·ca·pade (es′kə pād′) *n.* [Fr.: see ff.] a reckless adventure or prank

es·cape (ə skāp′, e-) *vi.* -caped′, -cap′ing [< L. *ex-*, out of + *cappa*, a cloak] 1. to get free 2. to avoid harm, injury, etc. 3. to leak away —*vt.* 1. to get away from 2. to avoid *(he escaped death)* 3. to come from involuntarily 4. to be forgotten or not noticed by —*n.* 1. an escaping 2. a means of escape 3. a leakage 4. a temporary mental release from reality —*adj.* providing an escape

es·cap·ee (ə skā′pē′, e-) *n.* a person who has escaped, as from prison

es·cape′ment *n.* a notched wheel with a detaining catch that controls the action of a clock or watch

escape velocity the minimum speed required for a space vehicle, etc. to escape permanently from the gravitational field of a planet, star, etc.

es·cap·ism (-iz′m) *n.* a tendency to escape from reality, responsibilities, etc. through the imagination —**es·cap′ist** *adj., n.*

es·ca·role (es′kə rōl′) *n.* [Fr. < L. *esca*, food] a kind of endive with wide leaves

es·carp·ment (e skärp′mənt) *n.* [< Fr.] a steep slope or cliff

-es·cence (es′ns) a noun suffix corresponding to the suffix -ESCENT

-es·cent (es′nt) [< L. *-escens*] an adjective suffix meaning: 1. starting to be, being, or becoming *(putrescent)* 2. giving off light *(incandescent)*

es·chew (es chōō′) *vt.* [< OHG. *sciuhan*, to fear] to shun; avoid

es·cort (es′kôrt; *for v.* i skôrt′) *n.* [< L. *ex-*, out + *corrigere*, set right] 1. one or more persons, cars, etc. accompanying another to protect it or show honor 2. a man accompanying a woman —*vt.* to go with as an escort

es·cri·toire (es′krə twär′) *n.* [< L. *scribere*, to write] a writing desk

es·crow (es′krō) *n.* [see SCROLL] the state of a deed, etc. put in the care of a third party until certain conditions are fulfilled

es·cutch·eon (i skuch′ən) *n.* [< L. *scutum*, shield] a shield on which a coat of arms is displayed

-ese (ēz, ēs) [< L. *-ensis)* a suffix meaning: 1. (an inhabitant) of *(Japanese)* 2. (in) the language of *(Cantonese)*

Es·ki·mo (es′kə mō′) *n.* [< Fr. < Algonquian] 1. *pl.* -mos, -mo a member of a people living in Greenland, arctic N. America, etc. 2. either of their two languages —*adj.* of the Eskimos, their language, etc.

Eskimo dog a strong breed of dog used by the Eskimos to pull sleds

ESKIMO DOG

e·soph·a·gus (i säf′ə gəs) *n., pl.* -gi′ (-jī′) [< Gr. *oisophagos*] the passage for food from the pharynx to the stomach

es·o·ter·ic (es′ə ter′ik) *adj.* [< Gr. *esōteros*, inner] meant for or understood by only a chosen few

ESP extrasensory perception

esp., espec., especially

es·pa·drille (es′pə dril′) *n.* [Fr. < Sp. *esparto*, coarse grass] a casual shoe with a canvas upper and a rope or rubber sole

es·pal·ier (es pal′yər) *n.* [Fr. < L. *spalla*, shoulder] 1. a lattice on which trees or shrubs are trained to grow flat 2. such a tree or shrub

es·pe·cial (ə spesh′əl) *adj.* special; particular —**es·pe′cial·ly** *adv.*

Es·pe·ran·to (es′pə rän′tō, -ran′-) *n.* an artificial international language based on European word roots

es·pi·o·nage (es′pē ə näzh′, -nij′) *n.* [< Fr. < It. *spia*, spy] the act or practice of spying

es·pla·nade (es′plə nād′, -näd′) *n.* [< Fr. < It. < L. *explanare*, to level] a level stretch of ground, esp. a public walk

es·pous·al (i spou′z'l) *n.* 1. *[often pl.]* a wedding 2. an espousing (of some cause, idea, etc.); advocacy

es·pouse (i spouz′) *vt.* -poused′, -pous′ing [see SPOUSE] 1. to marry 2. to advocate (some cause, idea, etc.)

es·pres·so (es pres′ō) *n., pl.* -sos [It.] coffee made by forcing steam through finely ground coffee beans

es·prit de corps (es prē′ də kôr′) [Fr.] group spirit; pride, etc. shared by those in the same group

es·py (ə spī′) *vt.* -pied′, -py′ing [see SPY] to catch sight of; make out

-esque (esk) [Fr.] *a suffix meaning:* 1. in the manner or style of *(Romanesque)* 2. like *(picturesque)*

es·quire (es′kwir, ə skwir′) *n.* [< LL. *scutarius*, shield-bearer] 1. formerly, an attendant on a knight 2. in England, a member of the gentry ranking just below a knight 3. [E-] a title of courtesy, usually abbrev. **Esq.**, **Esqr.**, placed after a man's surname

es·say (e sā′) *vt.* [< L. *exagium*, a weighing] to try; attempt —*n.* 1. (es′ā, e sā′) an attempt; trial 2. (es′ā) a short, personal literary composition dealing with a single subject —**es·say′er** *n.* —**es·say·ist** (es′ā ist) *n.*

es·sence (es′ns) *n.* [< L. *esse*, to be] 1. the basic nature (of something) 2.

a) a concentrated substance that keeps the flavor, etc. of that from which it is extracted *b*) perfume

Es·sene (es'ēn, ə sēn') *n.* a member of an ancient Jewish ascetic sect (2d cent. B.C. to 2d cent. A.D.)

es·sen·tial (ə sen'shəl) *adj.* 1. of or constituting the essence of something; basic 2. absolutely necessary; indispensable —*n.* something necessary or fundamental —**es·sen'tial·ly** *adv.*

-est (ist, əst) a suffix forming the superlative degree [*greatest*]

EST, E.S.T. Eastern Standard Time

est. 1. established 2. estimate 3. estimated

es·tab·lish (ə stab'lish) *vt.* [< L. *stabilis*, stable] 1. to ordain or appoint (a law, official, etc.) permanently 2. to found (a nation, business, etc.) 3. to cause to be; bring about 4. to set up in a business, etc. 5. to cause to be accepted 6. to prove; demonstrate

es·tab·lish·ment *n.* 1. an establishing or being established 2. a thing established, as a business —**the Establishment** an inner circle thought of as holding decisive power in a nation, institution, etc.

es·tate (ə stāt') *n.* [ME. *estat*] 1. a condition or stage of life 2. property; possessions 3. a large, individually owned piece of land containing a large residence

es·teem (ə stēm') *vt.* [< L. *aestimare*, to value] 1. to value highly; respect 2. to consider —*n.* favorable opinion

es·ter (es'tər) *n.* [G. < *essig*, vinegar + *äther*, ether] an organic compound formed by the reaction of an acid and an alcohol

Es·ther (es'tər) *Bible* the Jewish wife of a Persian king: she saved her people from slaughter

es·thete, es·thet·ics, etc. *same as* AESTHETE, AESTHETICS, etc.

es·ti·ma·ble (es'tə mə b'l) *adj.* worthy of esteem; fine

es·ti·mate (es'tə māt'; *for n.* -mit) *vt.* -mat'ed, -mat'ing [see ESTEEM] 1. to form an opinion about 2. to calculate approximately (size, cost, etc.) —*n.* 1. a general calculation; esp., an approximate computation of probable cost 2. an opinion or judgment —**es'ti·ma'tor** *n.*

es'ti·ma'tion *n.* 1. an opinion or judgment 2. esteem; regard

Es·to·ni·a (es tō'nē ə) republic of the U.S.S.R., in NE Europe —**Es·to'ni·an** *adj., n.*

es·trange (ə strānj') *vt.* -tranged', -trang'ing [< L. *extraneus*, strange] to turn (a person) from an affectionate attitude to an indifferent or unfriendly one —**es·trange'ment** *n.*

es·tro·gen (es'trə jən) *n.* [< Gr. *oistros*, frenzy] any of several female sex hormones

es·tu·ar·y (es'choo wer'ē) *n., pl.* -ies [< L. *aestus*, tide] the wide mouth of a river into which the tide flows

-et (it, ət) [< LL. *-itus*] a suffix meaning little [*islet*]

e·ta (āt'ə, ēt'ə) *n.* the seventh letter of the Greek alphabet (H, η)

‡**é·ta·gère** (ā tä zher') *n.* [Fr.] a stand with open shelves, for displaying art objects, ornaments, etc.

et al. [L. *et alii*] and others

et cet·er·a (et set'ər ə, set'rə) [L.] and others; and so forth: abbrev. etc.

etch (ech) *vt.* [< MHG. *ezzen*, eat] to make (a drawing, design, etc.) on (metal plate, glass, etc.) by the action of an acid —**etch'er** *n.*

etch'ing *n.* 1. the art of an etcher 2. a print made from an etched plate

e·ter·nal (i tur'n'l) *adj.* [< L. *aeternus*] 1. without beginning or end; everlasting 2. always the same 3. seeming never to stop —**e·ter'nal·ly** *adv.* —**e·ter'nal·ness** *n.*

e·ter·ni·ty (i tur'nə tē) *n., pl.* -ties 1. the state or fact of being eternal 2. infinite or endless time 3. a long period of time that seems endless 4. the endless time after death

eth·ane (eth'ān) *n.* [see ETHYL] an odorless, colorless, gaseous hydrocarbon, found in natural gas and used as a fuel

e·ther (ē'thər) *n.* [< Gr. *aithein*, to burn] 1. the upper regions of space 2. a volatile, colorless, highly flammable liquid, used as an anesthetic and solvent 3. an invisible substance once thought to pervade space

e·the·re·al (i thir'ē əl) *adj.* 1. very light; airy; delicate 2. not earthly; heavenly —**e·the're·al·ly** *adv.*

eth·ic (eth'ik) *n.* [see ff.] ethics or a system of ethics

eth·i·cal (eth'i k'l) *adj.* [< Gr. *ēthos*, character] 1. having to do with ethics; of or conforming to moral standards 2. conforming to professional standards of conduct —**eth'i·cal·ly** *adv.*

eth·ics (eth'iks) *n.pl.* 1. [*with sing. v.*] the study of standards of conduct and moral judgment 2. the system of morals of a particular person, religion, group, etc.

E·thi·o·pi·a (ē'thē ō'pē ə) country in E Africa, on the Red Sea: 457,000 sq. mi.; pop. 23,000,000 —**E'thi·o'pi·an** *adj., n.*

eth·nic (eth'nik) *adj.* [< Gr. *ethnos*, nation] of any of the basic divisions of mankind, as distinguished by customs, language, etc. —*n.* a member of a minority or nationality group that is part of a larger community —**eth'ni·cal·ly** *adv.*

eth·nic·i·ty (eth nis'ə tē) *n.* ethnic classification or affiliation

eth·nol·o·gy (eth näl'ə jē) *n.* [< Gr. *ethnos*, nation + -LOGY] the branch of anthropology that deals with the distribution, culture, etc. of various peoples —**eth'no·log'i·cal** (-nə läj'i k'l) *adj.* —**eth·nol'o·gist** *n.*

e·thos (ē'thäs) *n.* [Gr. *ēthos*, character] the characteristic attitudes, habits, etc. of an individual or group

eth·yl (eth'l) *n.* [< ETHER] the hydrocarbon radical which forms the base of common alcohol, ether, etc.

ethyl alcohol *same as* ALCOHOL (n. 1)

eth·yl·ene (eth'ə lēn') *n.* [ETHYL + -ENE] a colorless, flammable, gaseous hydrocarbon with a disagreeable odor

e·ti·ol·o·gy (ēt'ē äl'ə jē) *n., pl.* **-gies** [< Gr. *aitia*, cause + *logia*, description] 1. the cause assigned, as for a disease 2. the science of causes or origins —**e'ti·o·log'ic** (-ə läj'ik) *adj.*

et·i·quette (et'i kət, -ket') *n.* [Fr. *étiquette*, a ticket] the forms, manners, etc. conventionally acceptable or required in society, a profession, etc.

Et·na (et'nə) volcanic mountain in E Sicily

E·trus·can (i trus'kən) *adj.* of an ancient country (*Etruria*) in WC Italy

et seq. [L. *et sequens*] and the following

-ette (et) [Fr.] *a suffix meaning:* 1. little [*statuette*] 2. female [*majorette*]

é·tude (ā'tōōd) *n.* [Fr., study] a musical composition for a solo instrument, designed to give practice in some point of technique

ETV educational television

et·y·mol·o·gy (et'ə mäl'ə jē) *n., pl.* **-gies** [< Gr. *etymos*, true + *logos*, word] 1. the origin and development of a word 2. the scientific study of word origins Abbrev. **etym.** —**et'y·mo·log'i·cal** (-mə läj'ə k'l) *adj.* —**et'y·mol'o·gist** *n.*

eu- [Fr. < Gr.] *a prefix meaning* good, well [*eulogy, euphony*]

eu·ca·lyp·tus (yōō'kə lip'təs) *n.* [< Gr. *eu-*, well + *kalyptos*, covered] a tall, aromatic, chiefly Australian evergreen of the myrtle family

Eu·cha·rist (yōō'kə rist) *n.* [< Gr. *eucharistia*, gratitude] 1. *same as* HOLY COMMUNION 2. the consecrated bread and wine used in this —**Eu'cha·ris'tic** *adj.*

eu·chre (yōō'kər) *n.* [< ?] a card game played with thirty-two cards

Eu·clid (yōō'klid) fl. 300 B.C.; Gr. mathematician: author of a basic work in geometry —**Eu·clid'e·an, Eu·clid'i·an** (-ē ən) *adj.*

eu·gen·ics (yoo jen'iks) *n.pl.* [*with sing. v.*] [see EU- & GENESIS] the movement devoted to improving the human species by controlling heredity —**eu·gen'ic** *adj.* —**eu·gen'i·cal·ly** *adv.* —**eu·gen'i·cist** (-ə sist) *n.*

eu·lo·gize (yōō'lə jīz') *vt.* **-gized', -giz'ing** [see ff.] to praise highly —**eu'lo·gist, eu'lo·giz'er** *n.*

eu'lo·gy (-jē) *n., pl.* **-gies** [< Gr. *eulogein*, speak well of] 1. speech or writing praising a person or thing; esp., a funeral oration 2. high praise —**eu'lo·gis'tic** (-jis'tik) *adj.*

eu·nuch (yōō'nək) *n.* [< Gr. *eunē*, bed + *echein*, have] a castrated man

eu·phe·mism (yōō'fə miz'm) *n.* [< Gr. *eu-*, good + *phēmē*, voice] 1. the use of a less direct word or phrase for one considered offensive 2. a word or phrase so substituted —**eu'phe·mis'tic** *adj.* —**eu'phe·mis'ti·cal·ly** *adv.*

eu·pho·ni·ous (yoo fō'nē əs) *adj.* having a pleasant sound; harmonious

eu·pho·ny (yōō'fə nē) *n., pl.* **-nies** [< Gr. *eu-*, well + *phōnē*, voice] a

pleasant combination of agreeable sounds, as in speech

eu·pho·ri·a (yoo fôr'ē ə) *n.* [< Gr. *eu-*, well + *pherein*, to bear] a feeling of well-being —**eu·phor'ic** *adj.*

Eu·phra·tes (yoo frāt'ēz) river flowing from EC Turkey through Syria & Iraq into the Persian Gulf: cf. TIGRIS

Eur·a·sia (yoo rā'zhə) land mass of Europe & Asia

Eur·a'sian *adj.* 1. of Eurasia 2. of mixed European and Asian descent —*n.* a person of Eurasian descent

eu·re·ka (yoo rē'kə) *interj.* [< Gr. *heurēka*, I have found (it)] an exclamation of triumphant achievement

Eu·rip·i·des (yoo rip'ə dēz') 479?-406? B.C.; Gr. writer of tragedies

Eu·rope (yoor'əp) continent between Asia & the Atlantic: c.3,750,000 sq. mi.; pop. c.628,000,000 —**Eu'ro·pe'an** (-ə pē'ən) *adj., n.*

European plan a system of hotel operation in which guests are charged for rooms, and pay for meals separately

eu·ryth·mics (yoo ri th'miks) *n.pl.* [*with sing. v.*] [< Gr. *eu-*, well + *rhythmos*, rhythm] the art of performing bodily movements in rhythm, usually to music

Eu·sta·chi·an tube (yoo stā'shən, -kē ən) [after B. *Eustachio*, 16th-c. It. anatomist] a slender tube between the middle ear and the pharynx

eu·tha·na·si·a (yōō'thə nā'zhə) *n.* [< Gr. *eu-*, well + *thanatos*, death] act of causing death painlessly, so as to end suffering

eu·then·ics (yoo then'iks) *n.pl.* [*with sing. v.*] [< Gr. *euthēnein*, flourish] a movement to improve the human species by controlling the environment

e·vac·u·ate (i vak'yoo wāt') *vt.* **-at'ed, -at'ing** [< L. *e-*, out + *vacuus*, empty] 1. to make empty 2. to discharge (bodily waste, esp. feces) 3. to withdraw from; remove —*vi.* to withdraw —**e·vac'u·a'tion** *n.* —**e·vac'u·ee'** (-wē') *n.*

e·vade (i vād') *vi., vt.* **e·vad'ed, e·vad'ing** [< L. *e-*, out + *vadere*, go] 1. to avoid or escape (from) by deceit or cleverness 2. to avoid doing or answering directly —**e·vad'er** *n.*

e·val·u·ate (i val'yoo wāt') *vt.* **-at'ed, -at'ing** [ult. < L. *ex-*, out + *valere*, be worth] 1. to find the value or amount of 2. to judge the worth of —**e·val'u·a'tion** *n.*

ev·a·nes·cent (ev'ə nes''nt) *adj.* [< L. *e-*, out + *vanescere*, vanish] tending to fade from sight; fleeting; ephemeral —**ev'a·nes'cence** *n.*

e·van·gel·i·cal (ē'van jel'i k'l, ev'ən-) *adj.* [< Gr. *euangelos*, bringing good news] 1. of or according to the Gospels or the New Testament 2. of those Protestant churches that emphasize salvation by faith in Jesus

e·van·gel·ist (i van'jə list) *n.* 1. [E-] any of the four writers of the Gospels 2. a preacher of the gospel;

esp., a traveling preacher; revivalist —e·van'gel·ism n. —e·van'gel·is'-tic adj. —e·van'gel·is'ti·cal·ly adv.

e·van'gel·ize' (-līz') vt. -ized', -iz'-ing to convert to Christianity —vi. to preach the gospel

Ev·ans·ville (ev'ənz vil') city in SW Ind.: pop. 139,000

e·vap·o·rate (i vap'ə rāt') vt. -rat'-ed, -rat'ing [< L. e-, out + vaporare, emit vapor] 1. to change (a liquid or solid) into vapor 2. to remove moisture from (milk, etc.), as by heating, so as to get a concentrated product —vi. 1. to become vapor 2. to give off vapor 3. to vanish —e·vap'o·ra'tion n. —e·vap'o·ra'tor n.

e·va·sion (i vā'zhən) n. 1. an evading; specif., an avoiding of a duty, question, etc. by deceit or cleverness 2. a way of doing this; subterfuge

e·va'sive (-siv) adj. 1. tending or seeking to evade; tricky 2. elusive — e·va'sive·ly adv. —e·va'sive·ness n.

Eve (ēv) Bible Adam's wife, the first woman

eve (ēv) n. [< OE. æfen, evening] 1. [Poet.] evening 2. [often E-] the evening or day before a holiday 3. the period just prior to some event

e·ven (ē'vən) adj. [OE. efne] 1. flat; level; smooth 2. not varying; constant [an even tempo] 3. calm; tranquil [an even temper] 4. in the same plane or line [even with the rim] 5. owing and being owed nothing 6. equal in number, quantity, etc. 7. exactly divisible by two 8. exact [an even mile] —adv. 1. however improbable; indeed 2. exactly; just [it happened even as I expected] 3. still; yet [he's even better] —vt., vi. to make or become even — break even [Colloq.] to finish as neither a winner nor a loser —even if though —e'ven·ly adv. —e'ven·ness n.

e'ven·hand'ed adj. impartial; fair

eve·ning (ēv'niŋ) n. [< OE. æfnung] 1. the last part of the day and early part of night 2. [Dial.] afternoon

even money equal stakes in betting, with no odds

e·vent (i vent') n. [< L. e-, out + venire, come] 1. an occurrence, esp. when important 2. an outcome 3. a particular contest in a program of sports —in any event anyhow —in the event of in case of —in the event that if it should happen that

e'ven-tem'pered adj. not quickly angered; calm

e·vent'ful adj. 1. full of outstanding events 2. having an important outcome —e·vent'ful·ly adv. —e·vent'-ful·ness n.

e·ven·tide (ē'vən tīd') n. [Archaic] evening

e·ven·tu·al (i ven'choo wəl) adj. ultimate; final —e·ven'tu·al·ly adv.

e·ven·tu·al·i·ty (-wal'ə tē) n., pl. -ties a possible event or outcome

e·ven'tu·ate' (-wāt') vi. -at·ed, -at'ing to happen in the end; result

ev·er (ev'ər) adv. [< OE. æfre] 1. always [ever the same] 2. at any time [do you ever see her?] 3. at all; by any

chance [how can I ever repay you?] —ever so [Colloq.] very

Ev·er·est (ev'ər ist), Mount peak of the Himalayas: highest known mountain in the world: 29,028 ft.

ev'er·glade' (-glād') n. swampy land

ev'er·green' adj. having green leaves all year long, as most conifers —n. an evergreen plant or tree

ev'er·last'ing adj. lasting forever; eternal —n. eternity

ev'er·more' adv. forever; constantly

ev·er·y (ev'rē, ev'ər ē) adj. [OE. æfre ælc, lit., ever each] 1. each, individually and separately 2. the greatest possible [to make every effort] 3. each interval of [a dose every two hours] —every other each alternate, as the first, third, fifth, etc. —every so often [Colloq.] occasionally —every which way [Colloq.] in complete disorder

ev'er·y·bod'y (-bäd'ē, -bud'ē) pron. every person; everyone

ev'er·y·day' adj. 1. daily 2. suitable for ordinary days [everyday shoes] 3. usual; common

ev'er·y·one' pron. every person

every one every person or thing of those named [every one of the boys]

ev'er·y·thing' pron. every thing; all

ev'er·y·where' adv. in or to every place

e·vict (i vikt') vt. [< L. e-, intens. + vincere, conquer] to remove (a tenant) by legal procedure —e·vic'tion n.

ev·i·dence (ev'ə dəns) n. 1. the state of being evident 2. something that makes another thing evident; sign 3. a statement of a witness, an object, etc. bearing on or establishing the point in question in a court of law —vt. -denced, -denc·ing to make evident —in evidence plainly seen

ev'i·dent (-dənt) adj. [< L. e-, from + videre, see] easy to see or perceive; clear —ev'i·dent·ly adv.

e·vil (ē'v'l) adj. [OE. yfel] 1. morally bad or wrong; wicked 2. harmful; injurious 3. unlucky; disastrous —n. 1. wickedness; sin 2. anything causing harm, pain, etc. —e'vil·ly adv.

e'vil·do'er (-doo'ər) n. one who does evil —e'vil·do'ing n.

e·vince (i vins') vt. e·vinced', e·vinc'ing [< L. e-, intens. + vincere, conquer] to show plainly; make clear

e·vis·cer·ate (i vis'ə rāt') vt. -at·ed, -at'ing [< L. e-, out + viscera, VISCERA] 1. to remove the entrails from 2. to deprive of an essential part —e·vis'cer·a'tion n.

e·voke (i vōk') vt. e·voked', e·vok'-ing [< L. e-, out + vox, voice] 1. to call forth 2. to elicit (a reaction, etc.) —ev·o·ca·tion (ev'ə kā'shən) n.

ev·o·lu·tion (ev'ə loo'shən) n. [see ff.] 1. an unfolding; process of development or change 2. a thing evolved 3. a movement that is part of a series 4. Biol. a) the development of a species, organism, etc. from its original to its present state b) the theory that all species developed from earlier forms —ev'o·lu'tion·ar'y adj. — ev'o·lu'tion·ist n.

e·volve (i välv′) *vt.*, *vi.* **e·volved′**, **e·volv′ing** [< L. *e-*, out + *volvere*, to roll] 1. to develop gradually; unfold 2. to develop by evolution

ewe (yōō) *n.* [OE. *eowu*] a female sheep

ew·er (yōō′ər) *n.* [< L. *aqua*, water] a large, wide-mouthed water pitcher

ex- [< OFr. or L.] *a prefix meaning:* 1. from, out [*expel*] 2. beyond [*excess*] 3. thoroughly [*exterminate*] 4. upward [*exalt*] 5. former [*ex*-president]

EWER

Ex. Exodus

ex. 1. example 2. except(ed)

ex·ac·er·bate (ig zas′ər bāt′) *vt.* **-bat′ed**, **-bat′ing** [< L. *ex-*, intens. + *acerbus*, sour] 1. to aggravate (pain, annoyance, etc.) 2. to exasperate; irritate —**ex·ac′er·ba′tion** *n.*

ex·act (ig zakt′) *adj.* [< L. *ex-*, out + *agere*, do] 1. characterized by or requiring accuracy; methodical; correct 2. without variation; precise —*vt.* 1. to extort 2. to demand; require —**ex·act′ly** *adv.* —**ex·act′ness** *n.*

ex·act′ing *adj.* 1. making severe demands; strict 2. demanding great care, effort, etc.; arduous —**ex·act′ing·ly** *adv.* —**ex·act′ing·ness** *n.*

ex·ac′tion *n.* 1. an exacting 2. an extortion 3. something exacted

ex·ac′ti·tude (-tə tōōd′) *n.* the quality of being exact; accuracy

ex·ag·ger·ate (ig zaj′ə rāt′) *vt.*, *vi.* **-at′ed**, **-at′ing** [< L. *ex-*, out + *agger*, a heap] to think or tell of (something) as greater than it is; overstate —**ex·ag·ger·a′tion** *n.* —**ex·ag′ger·a′tive** *adj.* —**ex·ag′ger·a′tor** *n.*

ex·alt (ig zôlt′) *vt.* [< L. *ex-*, up + *altus*, high] 1. to raise in status, dignity, etc. 2. to praise; glorify 3. to fill with joy, pride, etc.; elate —**ex·al·ta·tion** (eg′zôl tā′shən) *n.*

ex·am·i·na·tion (ig zam′ə nā′shən) *n.* 1. an examining or being examined 2. a set of questions asked in testing: also [Colloq.] ex·am′

ex·am·ine (ig zam′ən) *vt.* **-ined**, **-in·ing** [< L. *examinare*, weigh] 1. to look at critically or methodically; investigate; inspect 2. to test by questioning —**ex·am′in·er** *n.*

ex·am·ple (ig zam′p'l) *n.* [< L. *eximere*, take out] 1. something selected to show the character of the rest; sample 2. a case that serves as a warning 3. a model; pattern 4. an instance that illustrates a principle

ex·as·per·ate (ig zas′pə rāt′) *vt.* **-at′ed**, **-at′ing** [< L. *ex-*, out + *asper*, rough] to irritate; anger; vex —**ex·as′per·a′tion** *n.*

ex·ca·vate (eks′kə vāt′) *vt.* **-vat′ed**, **-vat′ing** [< L. *ex-*, out + *cavus*, hollow] 1. to make a hole or cavity in 2. to form (a tunnel, etc.) by hollowing out 3. to unearth 4. to dig out (earth, etc.) —**ex′ca·va′tion** *n.* —**ex′ca·va′tor** *n.*

ex·ceed (ik sēd′) *vt.*, *vi.* [< L. *ex-*, out + *cedere*, go] 1. to go or be beyond (a limit, etc.) 2. to surpass

ex·ceed′ing (-iŋ) *adj.* surpassing; extreme —**ex·ceed′ing·ly** *adv.*

ex·cel (ik sel′) *vi.*, *vt.* **-celled′**, **-cel′ling** [< L. *ex-*, out of + *-cellere*, to rise] to be better or greater than (another or others)

ex·cel·lence (ek′s'l əns) *n.* 1. the fact or state of excelling; superiority 2. a particular virtue

ex′cel·len·cy (-ən sē) *n.*, *pl.* **-cies** 1. [E-] a title of honor for certain dignitaries 2. *same as* EXCELLENCE

ex′cel·lent *adj.* [see EXCEL] outstandingly good of its kind; of exceptional merit —**ex′cel·lent·ly** *adv.*

ex·cel·si·or (ek sel′sē ôr′; *for n.* ik sel′sē ər) *adj.*, *interj.* [see EXCEL] always upward —*n.* long, thin wood shavings used for packing

ex·cept (ik sept′) *vt.* [< L. *ex-*, out + *capere*, take] to leave out or take out; exclude —*prep.* leaving out; but —*conj.* [Colloq.] were it not that; only —**except for** if it were not for

ex·cept′ing *prep. same as* EXCEPT

ex·cep′tion *n.* 1. an excepting 2. a person or thing different from others of the same class; case to which a rule does not apply 3. an objection —**take exception** to object

ex·cep′tion·a·ble *adj.* liable to exception; open to objection

ex·cep′tion·al *adj.* 1. unusual; esp., unusually good 2. requiring special education, as because mentally handicapped —**ex·cep′tion·al·ly** *adv.*

ex·cerpt (ik surpt′; *for n.* ek′surpt′) *vt.* [< L. *ex-*, out + *carpere*, to pick] to select or quote (passages from a book, etc.); extract —*n.* a passage selected or quoted; extract

ex·cess (ik ses′; *also & for adj. usually* ek′ses′) *n.* [see EXCEED] 1. action that goes beyond a reasonable limit 2. an amount greater than is necessary 3. the amount by which one thing exceeds another; surplus —*adj.* extra; surplus —**in excess of** more than

ex·ces′sive *adj.* being too much; immoderate —**ex·ces′sive·ly** *adv.*

ex·change (iks chānj′) *vt.*, *vi.* **-changed′**, **-chang′ing** [see EX- & CHANGE] 1. to give or receive (something) *for* another thing; barter; trade 2. to interchange (similar things) —*n.* 1. an exchanging; interchange 2. a thing exchanged 3. a place for exchanging [a stock *exchange*] 4. a central office providing telephone service 5. the value of one currency in terms of another —**ex·change′a·ble** *adj.*

exchange rate the ratio of the value of one currency in relation to the value of another

ex·cheq·uer (iks chek′ər, eks′chek-) *n.* [< ML. *scaccarium*, chessboard: accounts of revenue were kept on a squared board] 1. a national treasury 2. funds; finances

ex·cise[1] (ek'sīz, -sīs) *n.* [ult. < L. *assidere*, assist (in office)] a tax on various commodities, as tobacco, within a country: also **excise tax**

ex·cise[2] (ik sīz') *vt.* -cised', -cis'ing [< L. *ex-*, out + *caedere*, to cut] to remove by cutting out —**ex·cis'a·ble** *adj.* —**ex·ci'sion** (-sizh'ən) *n.*

ex·cit·a·ble (ik sīt'ə b'l) *adj.* easily excited —**ex·cit'a·bil'i·ty** *n.*

ex·cite (ik sīt') *vt.* -cit'ed, -cit'ing [< L. *ex-*, out + *ciere*, to call] 1. to make active; stimulate 2. to arouse; provoke 3. to arouse the feelings of —**ex·ci·ta·tion** (ek'sī tā'shən) *n.* —**ex·cit'ed·ly** *adv.* —**ex·cit'er** *n.*

ex·cite'ment *n.* 1. an exciting or being excited 2. that which excites

ex·cit'ing *adj.* causing excitement; stirring, thrilling, etc.

ex·claim (iks klām') *vi., vt.* [< L. *ex-*, out + *clamare*, to shout] to cry out; say suddenly and vehemently

ex·cla·ma·tion (eks'klə mā'shən) *n.* 1. an exclaiming 2. something exclaimed; interjection —**ex·clam·a·to·ry** (iks klam'ə tôr'ē) *adj.*

exclamation mark (or **point**) a mark (!) used in punctuating to show surprise, strong emotion, etc.

ex·clude (iks klōōd') *vt.* -clud'ed, -clud'ing [< L. *ex-*, out + *claudere*, shut] 1. to refuse to admit, consider, etc.; reject 2. to put or force out; expel —**ex·clu'sion** (-klōō'zhən) *n.*

ex·clu·sive (-klōō'siv) *adj.* 1. excluding all others 2. not shared or divided; sole [an *exclusive* right] 3. excluding certain people, as for social or economic reasons —**exclusive of** not including —**ex·clu'sive·ly** *adv.* —**ex·clu'sive·ness** *n.*

ex·com·mu·ni·cate (eks'kə myōō'nə kāt') *vt.* -cat'ed, -cat'ing to exclude from communion with a church —**ex'com·mu'ni·ca'tion** *n.*

ex·co·ri·ate (ik skôr'ē āt') *vt.* -at'ed, -at'ing [< L. *ex-*, off + *corium*, the skin] to denounce harshly —**ex·co'ri·a'tion** *n.*

ex·cre·ment (eks'krə mənt) *n.* waste matter excreted from the bowels

ex·cres·cence (iks kres''ns) *n.* [< L. *ex-*, out + *crescere*, grow] an abnormal outgrowth, as a bunion

ex·cre·ta (eks krēt'ə) *n.pl.* waste matter excreted from the body

ex·crete (iks krēt') *vt., vi.* -cret'ed, -cret'ing [< L. *ex-*, out of + *cernere*, sift] to eliminate (waste matter) from the body —**ex·cre'tion** *n.* —**ex·cre·to·ry** (eks'krə tôr'ē) *adj.*

ex·cru·ci·at·ing (iks krōō'shē āt'iŋ) *adj.* [< L. *ex-*, intens. + *cruciare*, crucify] 1. intensely painful; agonizing 2. intense; extreme [*excruciating* care]

ex·cul·pate (eks'kəl pāt') *vt.* -pat'ed, -pat'ing [< L. *ex-*, out + *culpa*, fault] to free from blame; prove guiltless —**ex·cul·pa'tion** *n.*

ex·cur·sion (ik skur'zhən) *n.* [< L. *ex-*, out + *currere*, to run] 1. a short trip, as for pleasure 2. a round trip at reduced rates 3. a digression —*adj.* for an excursion —**ex·cur'sion·ist** *n.*

ex·cur·sive (-siv) *adj.* rambling; digressive —**ex·cur'sive·ly** *adv.* —**ex·cur'sive·ness** *n.*

ex·cuse (ik skyōōz'; *for n.* -skyōōs') *vt.* -cused', -cus'ing [< L. *ex-*, from + *causa*, a charge] 1. to apologize or give reasons for 2. to overlook (an offense or fault) 3. to release from an obligation, etc. 4. to permit to leave 5. to justify —*n.* 1. a defense of some action; apology 2. something that excuses 3. a pretext —**excuse oneself** 1. to apologize 2. to ask for permission to leave —**ex·cus'a·ble** *adj.*

ex·e·cra·ble (ek'sī krə b'l) *adj.* [see ff.] 1. detestable 2. very inferior

ex'e·crate' (-krāt') *vt.* -crat'ed, -crat'ing [< L. *execrare*, to curse] 1. to denounce scathingly 2. to loathe; abhor —**ex'e·cra'tion** *n.*

ex·e·cute (ek'sə kyōōt') *vt.* -cut'ed, -cut'ing [see EXECUTOR] 1. to carry out; do 2. to administer (laws, etc.) 3. to put to death by a legal sentence 4. to create in accordance with a plan, etc. 5. to make valid (a deed, will, etc.)

ex'e·cu'tion *n.* 1. an executing; specif., *a)* a carrying out, performing, etc. *b)* a putting to death by a legal sentence 2. the manner of performing

ex'e·cu'tion·er *n.* one who carries out a court-imposed death penalty

ex·ec·u·tive (ig zek'yə tiv) *adj.* [see ff.] 1. of or capable of carrying out duties, functions, etc. 2. empowered to administer (laws, government affairs, etc.) —*n.* 1. the branch of government administering the laws and affairs of a nation 2. one who administers or manages affairs

ex·ec·u·tor (ig zek'yə tər) *n.* [< L. *ex-*, intens. + *sequi*, follow] a person appointed to carry out the provisions of another's will

ex·e·ge·sis (ek'sə jē'sis) *n., pl.* -ses (-sēz) [< Gr. *ex-*, out + *hēgeisthai*, to guide] interpretation of a word, passage, etc., esp. in the Bible

ex·em·plar (ig zem'plär) *n.* [< L. *exemplum*, a pattern] 1. a model; pattern 2. a typical specimen

ex·em·pla·ry (ig zem'plə rē) *adj.* [< L. *exemplum*, a pattern] serving as a model or example [an *exemplary* life]

ex·em·pli·fy (ig zem'plə fī') *vt.* -fied', -fy'ing [< L. *exemplum*, example + *facere*, make] to show by example —**ex·em'pli·fi·ca'tion** *n.*

ex·empt (ig zempt') *vt.* [< L. *ex-*, out + *emere*, take] to free from a rule or obligation which applies to others —*adj.* freed from a usual rule, duty, etc. —**ex·emp'tion** *n.*

ex·er·cise (ek'sər sīz') *n.* [< L. *exercere*, put to work] 1. active use or operation 2. performance (of duties, etc.) 3. activity for developing the body or mind 4. a task to be practiced for developing some skill 5. [*pl.*] a program of speeches, etc. —*vt.* -cised', -cis'ing 1. to put into action; use 2. to put into use so as to develop or train 3. to exert (influence, etc.) 4. to worry; disturb —*vi.* to do exercises

ex·ert (ig zurt') *vt.* [< L. *exserere*, stretch out] 1. to put into action 2.

to apply (oneself) with great effort

ex·er′tion *n.* 1. the act, fact, or process of exerting 2. effort

ex·hale (eks hāl′) *vt., vi.* -haled′, -hal′ing [< L. *ex-*, out + *halare*, breathe] 1. to breathe forth (air) 2. to give off (vapor, etc.) —**ex·ha·la·tion** (eks′hə lā′shən) *n.*

ex·haust (ig zôst′) *vt.* [< L. *ex-*, out + *haurire*, to draw] 1. to use up 2. to empty completely; drain 3. to tire out 4. to deal with thoroughly —*n.* 1. *a*) the discharge of used steam, gas, etc. from an engine *b*) the pipe through which it is released 2. fumes, etc. given off —**ex·haust′i·ble** *adj.*

ex·haus·tion (ig zôs′chən) *n.* 1. an exhausting 2. great fatigue

ex·haus′tive *adj.* leaving nothing out

ex·hib·it (ig zib′it) *vt.* [< L. *ex-*, out + *habere*, to hold] 1. to show; display 2. to present to public view —*vi.* to put art objects, etc. on public display —*n.* 1. a display 2. a thing exhibited 3. *Law* an object produced as evidence in a court —**ex·hib′i·tor** *n.*

ex·hi·bi·tion (ek′sə bish′ən) *n.* 1. an exhibiting 2. that which is exhibited 3. a public showing

ex′hi·bi′tion·ism *n.* 1. a tendency to call attention to oneself or show off 2. a tendency to expose oneself sexually —**ex′hi·bi′tion·ist** *n.*

ex·hil·a·rate (ig zil′ə rāt′) *vt.* -rat′ed, -rat′ing [< L. *ex-*, intens. + *hilaris*, glad] 1. to make lively and gay 2. to stimulate —**ex·hil′a·ra′tion** *n.* —**ex·hil′a·ra′tive** *adj.*

ex·hort (ig zôrt′) *vt., vi.* [< L. *ex-*, out + *hortari*, to urge] to urge earnestly; advise strongly —**ex·hor·ta·tion** (eg′zôr tā′shən, ek′sər-) *n.*

ex·hume (ig zyoom′, iks hyoom′) *vt.* -humed′, -hum′ing [< L. *ex*, out + *humus*, the ground] to dig out of the earth; disinter —**ex·hu·ma·tion** (eks′hyoo mā′shən) *n.*

ex·i·gen·cy (ek′sə jən sē) *n., pl.* -cies [< L. *ex-*, out + *agere*, to do] 1. urgency 2. a situation calling for immediate attention 3. [*pl.*] pressing needs —**ex′i·gent** *adj.*

ex·ig·u·ous (eg zig′yoo wəs) *adj.* [< L.: see prec.] scanty; meager

ex·ile (eg′zīl, ek′sīl) *n.* [< L. *exul*, an exile] 1. a prolonged living away from one's country, usually enforced 2. a person in exile —*vt.* -iled, -il·ing to force (one) into exile; banish

ex·ist (ig zist′) *vi.* [< L. *ex-*, out + *sistere*, to set, place] 1. to have reality or being; be 2. to occur or be present 3. to continue being; live

ex·ist′ence *n.* 1. the state or fact of being 2. life; living 3. occurrence —**ex·ist′ent** *adj.*

ex·is·ten·tial (eg′zis ten′shəl) *adj.* 1. of existence 2. of existentialism

ex·is·ten·tial·ism (eg′zis ten′shəl iz′m) *n.* a philosophical movement stressing individual existence and holding that man is totally free and

responsible for his acts —**ex′is·ten′tial·ist** *adj., n.*

ex·it (eg′zit, ek′sit) *n.* [< L. *ex-*, out + *ire*, go] 1. an actor's departure from the stage 2. a going out; departure 3. a way out —*vi.* to leave a place

exo- [< Gr. *exō*] *a prefix meaning* outside, outer, outer part

ex′o·bi·ol′o·gy *n.* the branch of biology studying the possible existence of living organisms elsewhere in the universe than on earth

ex·o·dus (ek′sə dəs) *n.* [< Gr. *ex-*, out + *hodos*, way] a going out or forth —[E-] 1. the departure of the Israelites from Egypt (with *the*) 2. the second book of the Bible, describing this

ex of·fi·ci·o (eks′ ə fish′ē ō′) [L., lit., from office] because of one's position

ex·on·er·ate (ig zän′ə rāt′) *vt.* -at′ed, -at′ing [< L. *ex-*, out + *onerare*, to load] to declare or prove blameless —**ex·on′er·a′tion** *n.*

ex·or·bi·tant (ig zôr′bə tənt) *adj.* [< L. *ex-*, out + *orbita*, a track] going beyond what is reasonable, just, etc.; excessive —**ex·or′bi·tance** *n.*

ex·or·cise, ex·or·cize (ek′sôr sīz′) *vt.* -cised′ or -cized′, -cis′ing or -ciz′ing [< Gr. *ex-*, out + *horkos*, oath] 1. to expel (an evil spirit) by incantations, etc. 2. to free from such a spirit —**ex′or·cism** (-siz′m) *n.* —**ex′or·cist** *n.*

ex·ot·ic (ig zät′ik) *adj.* [< Gr. *exō*, outside] 1. foreign 2. strangely beautiful, enticing, etc.

ex·pand (ik spand′) *vt., vi.* [< L. *ex-*, out + *pandere*, to spread] 1. to spread out; unfold 2. to increase in size, scope, etc.; enlarge; develop

ex·panse (ik spans′) *n.* a large area or unbroken surface; wide extent

ex·pan·si·ble (ik span′sə b'l) *adj.* that can be expanded: also **ex·pand′a·ble**

ex·pan′sion *n.* 1. an expanding or being expanded; enlargement 2. an expanded thing or part 3. the degree or extent of expansion

expansion bolt a bolt with an attachment that expands in use to act as a wedge

ex·pan′sive *adj.* 1. that can expand 2. broad; extensive 3. effusive; demonstrative —**ex·pan′sive·ly** *adv.*

ex·pa·ti·ate (ik spā′shē āt′) *vi.* -at′ed, -at′ing [< L. *ex(s)patiari*, wander] to speak or write at length (*on* or *upon*) —**ex·pa′ti·a′tion** *n.*

ex·pa·tri·ate (eks pā′trē āt′; *for n.* -it) *vt., vi.* -at′ed, -at′ing [< L. *ex*, out of + *patria*, fatherland] to exile (a person or oneself) —*n.* an expatriated person —**ex·pa′tri·a′tion** *n.*

ex·pect (ik spekt′) *vt.* [< L. *ex-*, out + *spectare*, to look] 1. to look for as likely to occur or appear 2. to look for as proper or necessary 3. [Colloq.] to suppose; guess —**be expecting** [Colloq.] to be pregnant

ex·pect·an·cy *n., pl.* -cies 1. *same as* EXPECTATION 2. that which is expected, esp. on a statistical basis

ex·pect'ant *adj.* that expects; expecting —**ex·pect'ant·ly** *adv.*

ex·pec·ta·tion (ek'spek tā'shən) *n.* 1. an expecting; anticipation 2. a thing looked forward to 3. [*also pl.*] a reason for expecting something

ex·pec·to·rant (ik spek'tər ənt) *n.* [see ff.] a medicine that helps to bring up phlegm

ex·pec'to·rate' (-tə rāt') *vt.*, *vi.* -rat'ed, -rat'ing [< L. *ex-*, out + *pectus*, breast] to spit —**ex·pec'to·ra'tion** *n.*

ex·pe·di·en·cy (ik spē'dē ən sē) *n.*, *pl.* -cies 1. a being expedient; suitability for a given purpose 2. the doing of what is selfish rather than of what is right or just; self-interest 3. an expedient Also **ex·pe'di·ence**

ex·pe'di·ent *adj.* [see ff.] 1. useful for effecting a desired result; convenient 2. based on or guided by self-interest —*n.* an expedient thing; means to an end

ex·pe·dite (ek'spə dīt') *vt.* -dit'ed, -dit'ing [< L. *expedire*, lit., to free the foot] 1. to speed up the progress of; facilitate 2. to do quickly

ex'pe·dit'er *n.* one employed to expedite urgent or involved projects

ex'pe·di'tion (-dish'ən) *n.* [see EXPEDITE] 1. *a*) a voyage, march, etc., as for exploration or battle *b*) those on such a journey 2. efficient speed — **ex'pe·di'tion·ar'y** *adj.*

ex'pe·di'tious (-dish'əs) *adj.* efficient and speedy; prompt —**ex·pe·di'tious·ly** *adv.*

ex·pel (ik spel') *vt.* -pelled', -pel'ling [< L. *ex-*, out + *pellere*, to thrust] 1. to drive out by force 2. to dismiss by authority [*expelled* from college] —**ex·pel'la·ble** *adj.* —**ex·pel'ler** *n.*

ex·pend (ik spend') *vt.* [< L. *ex-*, out + *pendere*, weigh] 1. to spend 2. to use up

ex·pend'a·ble *adj.* 1. that can be expended 2. *Mil.* designating equipment (or men) expected to be used up (or sacrificed) in service

ex·pend'i·ture (-spen'də chər) *n.* 1. an expending of money, time, etc. 2. the amount of money, etc. expended

ex·pense (ik spens') *n.* [see EXPEND] 1. financial cost; charge 2. any cost or sacrifice 3. [*pl.*] charges met with in one's work, etc.

ex·pen'sive *adj.* costly; high-priced

ex·pe·ri·ence (ik spir'ē əns) *n.* [< L. *experiri*, to try] 1. the act of living through an event 2. anything or everything observed or lived through 3. *a*) training and personal participation *b*) knowledge, skill, etc. resulting from this —*vt.* -enced, -enc·ing to have experience of; undergo

ex·pe'ri·enced *adj.* having had or having learned from experience

ex·per·i·ment (ik sper'ə mənt) *n.* [see EXPERIENCE] a test or trial undertaken to discover or demonstrate something —*vi.* to make an experiment —**ex·per'i·men·ta'tion** (-mən tā'shən) *n.* —**ex·per'i·ment'er** *n.*

ex·per'i·men'tal *adj.* 1. based on or used for experiments 2. testing; trial —**ex·per'i·men'tal·ly** *adv.*

ex·pert (ek'spərt) *adj.* [see EXPERIENCE] very skillful —*n.* one who is very skillful or well-informed in some special field —**ex'pert·ly** *adv.* —**ex'pert·ness** *n.*

ex·per·tise (ek'spər tēz') *n.* [Fr.] the skill or knowledge of an expert

ex·pi·ate (ek'spē āt') *vt.* -at'ed, -at'ing [< L. *ex-*, out + *piare*, appease] to make amends for (wrongdoing or guilt); atone for —**ex'pi·a'tion** *n.* —**ex'pi·a·to'ry** (-ə tôr'ē) *adj.*

ex·pire (ik spīr') *vi.* -pired', -pir'ing [< L. *ex-*, out + *spirare*, breathe] 1. to exhale 2. to die 3. to come to an end —**ex·pi·ra·tion** (ek'spə rā'shən) *n.*

ex·plain (ik splān') *vt.* [< L. *ex-*, out + *planus*, level] 1. to make plain or understandable 2. to give the meaning of; expound 3. to account for —*vi.* to give an explanation —**ex·plain'a·ble** *adj.*

ex·pla·na·tion (eks'plə nā'shən) *n.* 1. an explaining 2. something that explains; interpretation, meaning, etc.

ex·plan·a·to·ry (ik splan'ə tôr'ē) *adj.* explaining or intended to explain

ex·ple·tive (eks'plə tiv) *n.* [< L. *ex-*, out + *plere*, to fill] an oath or exclamation

ex·pli·ca·ble (eks'pli kə b'l) *adj.* [see ff.] that can be explained

ex'pli·cate' (-kāt') *vt.* -cat'ed, -cat'ing [< L. *ex-*, out + *plicare*, to fold] to make clear; explain fully

ex·plic·it (ik splis'it) *adj.* [see prec.] 1. clearly stated or shown; definite 2. outspoken —**ex·plic'it·ly** *adv.*

ex·plode (ik splōd') *vt.* -plod'ed, -plod'ing [orig., to drive off the stage < L. *ex-*, off + *plaudere*, applaud] 1. to expose as false 2. to make burst with a loud noise 3. to cause to change suddenly or violently, as from a solid to an expanding gas —*vi.* to burst forth noisily —**ex·plod'a·ble** *adj.*

ex·ploit (eks'ploit; *for v., usually* ik sploit') *n.* [see EXPLICATE] a daring act; bold deed —*vt.* 1. to make use of 2. to make unethical use of for one's own profit —**ex'ploi·ta'tion** *n.* —**ex·ploit'a·tive** *adj.* —**ex·ploit'er** *n.*

ex·plore (ik splôr') *vt.*, *vi.* -plored', -plor'ing [< L. *ex-*, out + *plorare*, cry out] 1. to examine (something) carefully; investigate 2. to travel in (a little-known region) for discovery —**ex·plo·ra·tion** (eks'plə rā'shən) *n.* —**ex·plor'a·to'ry** (-ə tôr'ē) *adj.* —**ex·plor'er** *n.*

ex·plo·sion (ik splō'zhən) *n.* 1. an exploding 2. the noise made by exploding 3. a noisy outburst 4. a sudden, widespread increase

ex·plo·sive (-siv) *adj.* 1. of, causing, or like an explosion 2. tending to explode —*n.* a substance that can explode, as gunpowder —**ex·plo'sive·ly** *adv.* —**ex·plo'sive·ness** *n.*

ex·po·nent (ik spō'nənt; *for n. 3, usually* ek'spō'nənt) *n.* [see EXPOUND] 1. one who expounds or promotes (principles, etc.) 2. a person or thing that is an example or symbol (*of* something) 3. *Math.* a symbol placed at the upper right of another to show how many times the latter is to be used as a factor (Ex.: $b^2 = b \times b$) —**ex·po·nen·tial** (eks'pō nen'shəl) *adj.*

ex·port (ik spōrt'; *also, and for n. always,* eks'pōrt) *vt.* [< L. *ex-*, out + *portare*, carry] to send (goods, etc.) to another country, esp. for sale —*n.* 1. something exported 2. an exporting Also **ex'por·ta'tion** —**ex·port'er** *n.*

ex·pose (ik spōz') *vt.* -**posed'**, -**pos'- ing** [see EXPOUND] 1. to lay open (to danger, attack, etc.) 2. to reveal; exhibit; make known 3. *Photography* to subject (a sensitized film or plate) to actinic rays

ex·po·sé (eks'pō zā') *n.* [Fr.] a public disclosure of a scandal, crime, etc.

ex·po·si·tion (eks'pə zish'ən) *n.* [see EXPOUND] 1. a detailed explanation 2. writing or speaking that explains 3. a large public exhibition

ex·pos·i·tor (ik späz'ə tər) *n.* one who expounds or explains

ex·pos'i·to'ry (-ə tôr'ē) *adj.* of or containing exposition; explanatory

ex post fac·to (eks pōst fak'tō) [L., from (the thing) done afterward] done afterward, but retroactive

ex·pos·tu·late (ik späs'chə lāt') *vi.* -**lat'ed**, -**lat'ing** [< L. *ex-*, intens. + *postulare*, to demand] to reason with a person earnestly, objecting to his actions —**ex·pos'tu·la'tion** *n.*

ex·po·sure (ik spō'zhər) *n.* 1. an exposing or being exposed 2. facing position of a house, etc. [a *southern exposure*] 3. frequent appearance before the public 4. the time during which photographic film is exposed 5. a section of film for one picture

ex·pound (ik spound') *vt.* [< L. *ex-*, out + *ponere*, put] 1. to set forth; state in detail 2. to explain

ex·press (ik spres') *vt.* [< L. *ex-*, out + *premere*, to press] 1. to squeeze out (juice, etc.) 2. to put into words; state 3. to reveal; show 4. to signify or symbolize 5. to send by express —*adj.* 1. expressed; stated; explicit 2. exact 3. specific 4. fast and direct [an *express* bus, highway, etc.] 5. related to express —*adv.* by express —*n.* 1. an express train, bus, etc. 2. *a*) a service for transporting things rapidly *b*) the things sent by express

ex·pres·sion (-spresh'ən) *n.* 1. a putting into words; stating 2. a manner of expressing, esp. with eloquence 3. a particular word or phrase 4. a showing of feeling, character, etc. 5. a look, intonation, etc. that conveys meaning 6. a mathematical symbol or symbols —**ex·pres'sion·less** *adj.*

ex·pres·sion·ism *n.* a movement in art, literature, etc. seeking to give symbolic, objective expression to inner experience —**ex·pres'sion·ist** *adj., n.* —**ex·pres'sion·is'tic** *adj.*

ex·pres·sive *adj.* 1. that expresses 2. full of meaning or feeling —**ex·pres'- sive·ly** *adv.* —**ex·pres'sive·ness** *n.*

ex·press·ly *adv.* 1. plainly; definitely 2. especially; particularly

ex·press·way *n.* a divided highway for high-speed, through traffic, with grade separations at intersections

ex·pro·pri·ate (eks prō'prē āt') *vt.* -**at'ed**, -**at'ing** [< L. *ex*, out + *proprius*, one's own] to take (land, etc.) from its owner, esp. for public use —**ex·pro'pri·a'tion** *n.*

ex·pul·sion (ik spul'shən) *n.* an expelling or being expelled

ex·punge (ik spunj') *vt.* -**punged'**, -**pung'ing** [< L. *ex-*, out + *pungere*, to prick] to blot or strike out; erase

ex·pur·gate (eks'pər gāt') *vt.* -**gat'- ed**, -**gat'ing** [< L. *ex-*, out + *purgare*, cleanse] to remove passages considered obscene, etc. from (a book, etc.) —**ex'pur·ga'tion** *n.*

ex·qui·site (eks'kwi zit, ik skwiz'it) *adj.* [< L. *ex-*, out + *quaerere*, ask] 1. carefully or elaborately done 2. very beautiful, delicate, etc. 3. of highest quality 4. very intense; keen

ex·tant (ek'stənt, ik stant') *adj.* [< L. *ex-*, out + *stare*, stand] still existing

ex·tem·po·ra·ne·ous (ik stem'pə rā'nē əs) *adj.* [see ff.] done or spoken with little preparation; offhand —**ex·tem'po·ra'ne·ous·ly** *adv.*

ex·tem·po·re (ik stem'pə rē) *adv., adj.* [L. < *ex*, out of + *tempus*, time] with little preparation; offhand

ex·tem·po·rize (-rīz') *vi., vt.* -**rized'**, -**riz'ing** to speak, perform, etc. extempore; improvise

ex·tend (ik stend') *vt.* [< L. *ex-*, out + *tendere*, to stretch] 1. to make longer; stretch out; prolong 2. to enlarge in area, scope, etc.; expand 3. to stretch forth 4. to offer; grant 5. to make (oneself) work very hard —*vi.* to be extended —**ex·tend'ed** *adj.* —**ex·tend'er** *n.* —**ex·ten'si·ble** (-sten'sə-b'l), **ex·tend'i·ble** *adj.*

extended care nursing care in a facility for convalescents, the disabled, etc.

extended family a social unit consisting of parents and their relatives, living as one family

ex·ten·sion (-sten'shən) *n.* 1. an extending or being extended 2. range; extent 3. a part forming a continuation or addition

ex·ten·sive (-siv) *adj.* having great extent; vast; comprehensive; far-reaching —**ex·ten'sive·ly** *adv.* —**ex·ten'sive·ness** *n.*

ex·tent (ik stent') *n.* 1. the space, amount, or degree to which a thing extends; size 2. scope; limits 3. an extended space; vast area

ex·ten·u·ate (ik sten'yoo wāt') *vt.* -**at'ed**, -**at'ing** [< L. *ex-*, out + *tenuis*, thin] to make (an offense, etc.) seem less serious —**ex·ten'u·a'tion** *n.*

---

făt, āpe, cär; ten, ēven; is, bīte; gō, hôrn, tōōl, look; oil, out; up, fŭr; chin; she; thin, then; zh, leisure; ŋ, ring; ə for *a* in *ago*; ', (ā'b'l); ë, Fr. coeur; ö, Fr. feu; Fr. mon; ü, Fr. duc; kh, G. ich, doch; ‡ foreign; < derived from

ex·te·ri·or (ik stir'ē ər) *adj.* [see EXTERNAL] 1. on the outside; outer 2. for use on the outside 3. coming from without —*n.* an outside or outside surface —**ex·te'ri·or·ly** *adv.*

ex·ter·mi·nate (ik stur'mə nāt') *vt.* -nat'ed, -nat'ing [< L. *ex-*, out + *terminus*, boundary] to destroy entirely; wipe out —**ex·ter'mi·na'tion** *n.* —**ex·ter'mi·na'tor** *n.*

ex·tern (ek'stərn) *n.* [see ff.] a doctor, etc. connected with an institution, as a hospital, but not living in it

ex·ter·nal (ik stur'n'l) *adj.* [< L. *externus*] 1. on the outside; outer 2. material; existing apart from the mind 3. coming from without 4. superficial 5. foreign —*n.* an outside surface or part —**ex·ter'nal·ly** *adv.*

ex·tinct (ik stiŋkt') *adj.* [see EXTINGUISH] 1. having died down; extinguished 2. no longer in existence

ex·tinc·tion *n.* 1. an extinguishing 2. a destroying or being destroyed 3. a dying out, as a species

ex·tin·guish (ik stiŋ'gwish) *vt.* [< L. *ex-*, out + *stinguere*, extinguish] 1. to put out (a fire, etc.) 2. to destroy —**ex·tin'guish·er** *n.*

ex·tir·pate (ek'stər pāt') *vt.* -pat'ed, -pat'ing [< L. *ex-*, out + *stirps*, root] 1. to pull up by the roots 2. to destroy completely —**ex'tir·pa'tion** *n.*

ex·tol, ex·toll (ik stōl') *vt.* -tolled', -tol'ling [< L. *ex-*, up + *tollere*, raise] to praise highly; laud

ex·tort (ik stôrt') *vt.* [< L. *ex-*, out + *torquere*, twist] to get (money, etc.) from someone by force or threats

ex·tor·tion (-stôr'shən) *n.* 1. an extorting 2. something extorted —**ex·tor'tion·ate** *adj.* —**ex·tor'tion·er** *n.* —**ex·tor'tion·ist** *n.*

ex·tra (eks'trə) *adj.* [< L. *extra*, more than] more or better than normal, expected, etc.; additional —*n.* an extra person or thing; specif., *a)* a special edition of a newspaper *b)* an extra benefit *c)* an actor hired by the day for a minor part —*adv.* more than usually; esp., exceptionally

extra- [see EXTERNAL] *a prefix meaning* outside, beyond, besides

ex·tract (ik strakt'; *for n.* eks'trakt) *vt.* [< L. *ex-*, out + *trahere*, draw] 1. to draw out by effort 2. to obtain by pressing, distilling, etc. 3. to deduce; derive 4. to select or quote (a passage, etc.) —*n.* something extracted; specif., *a)* a concentrate [beef *extract*] *b)* an excerpt

ex·trac·tion *n.* 1. the act or process of extracting 2. origin; descent

ex·tra·cur·ric·u·lar (eks'trə kə rik'yə lər) *adj.* not part of the required curriculum

ex·tra·dite (eks'trə dīt') *vt.* -dit'ed, -dit'ing [< L. *ex*, out + *traditio*, a surrender] to turn over (an alleged criminal, etc.) to the jurisdiction of another country, State, etc. —**ex'tra·di'tion** (-dish'ən) *n.*

ex'tra·le'gal *adj.* outside law

ex·tra·ne·ous (ik strā'nē əs) *adj.* [L. *extraneus*, foreign] 1. coming from outside; foreign 2. not pertinent;

irrelevant —**ex·tra'ne·ous·ly** *adv.*

ex·traor·di·nar·y (ik strôr'd'n er'ē) *adj.* [< L. *extra ordinem*, out of order] 1. not ordinary 2. going far beyond the ordinary; unusual; remarkable

ex·trap·o·late (ik strap'ə lāt') *vt.*, *vi.* -lat'ed, -lat'ing [see EXTRA- & INTERPOLATE] to estimate (something unknown) on the basis of known facts —**ex·trap'o·la'tion** *n.*

ex·tra·sen·so·ry (eks'trə sen'sər ē) *adj.* apart from, or in addition to, normal sense perception

ex'tra·ter·res'tri·al *adj.* being, of, or from outside the earth's limits —*n.* an extraterrestrial being, as in science fiction

ex·trav·a·gant (ik strav'ə gənt) *adj.* [< L. *extra*, beyond + *vagari*, wander] 1. going beyond reasonable limits; excessive 2. costing or spending too much; wasteful —**ex·trav'a·gance** *n.*

ex·trav·a·gan·za (ik strav'ə gan'zə) *n.* [< It. *estravaganza*, extravagance] a spectacular theatrical production

ex·tra·ve·hic·u·lar (eks'trə vē hik'yoo lər) *adj.* designating activity by an astronaut outside a vehicle in space

ex·treme (ik strēm') *adj.* [< L. *exterus*, outer] 1. farthest away; utmost 2. very great; excessive 3. unconventional or radical, as in politics 4. harsh; drastic —*n.* 1. either of two things that are at different or far as possible from each other 2. an extreme act, state, etc. —**ex·treme'ly** *adv.* —**ex·treme'ness** *n.*

ex·trem·ism (-iz'm) *n.* a going to extremes, esp. in politics —**ex·trem'ist** *adj.*, *n.*

ex·trem·i·ty (ik strem'ə tē) *n.*, *pl.* -ties 1. the outermost part; end 2. the greatest degree 3. great need, danger, etc. 4. an extreme measure 5. [*pl.*] the hands and feet

ex·tri·cate (eks'trə kāt') *vt.* -cat'ed, -cat'ing [< L. *ex-*, out + *tricae*, vexations] to set free (*from* a net, difficulty, etc.) —**ex'tri·ca'tion** *n.*

ex·trin·sic (ek strin'sik) *adj.* [< L. *exter*, without + *secus*, otherwise] not essential —**ex·trin'si·cal·ly** *adv.*

ex·tro·vert (eks'trə vurt') *n.* [< L. *extra-*, outside + *vertere*, to turn] one whose interest is more in his environment and in other people than in himself —**ex'tro·ver'sion** (-vur'zhən) *n.* —**ex'tro·vert'ed** *adj.*

ex·trude (ik strōōd') *vt.* -trud'ed, -trud'ing [< L. *ex-*, out + *trudere*, to thrust] to force out, as through a small opening —*vi.* to be extruded; esp., to protrude —**ex·tru'sion** (-strōō'zhən) *n.* —**ex·tru'sive** *adj.*

ex·u·ber·ant (ig zōō'bər ənt) *adj.* [< L. *ex-*, intens. + *uberare*, bear abundantly] 1. growing profusely; luxuriant 2. characterized by good health and high spirits —**ex·u'ber·ance** *n.* —**ex·u'ber·ant·ly** *adv.*

ex·ude (ig zōōd') *vt.*, *vi.* -ud'ed, -ud'ing [< L. *ex-*, out + *sudare*, to sweat] 1. to ooze 2. to seem to radiate [*to exude* joy] —**ex·u·da·tion** (eks'yə dā'shən) *n.*

ex·ult (ig zult') *vi.* [< L. *ex-*, intens.

+ *saltare*, to leap] to rejoice greatly; glory —**ex·ult′ant** *adj.* —**ex·ul·ta·tion** (eg′zəl tā′shən, ek′səl-) *n.*

ex·ur·bi·a (eks ur′bē ə) *n.* [EX- + (SUB)URBIA] the semirural communities beyond the suburbs, lived in by upper-income families —**ex·ur′ban** *adj.* —**ex·ur·ban·ite′** *n., adj.*

eye (ī) *n.* [OE. *eage*] 1. the organ of sight in man and animals 2. *a*) the eyeball *b*) the iris [blue *eyes*] 3. the area around the eye [a black *eye*] 4. [*often pl.*] sight; vision 5. a look; glance 6. attention; observation 7. the power of judging, etc. by eyesight [an *eye* for distances] 8. [*often pl.*] judgment; opinion [in the *eyes* of the law] 9. a thing like an eye in appearance or function —*vt.* eyed, eye′ing or ey′ing to look at; observe —**have an eye for** to have a keen appreciation of —**keep an eye on** to look after —**lay (or set or clap) eyes on** to look at —**make eyes at** to look at amorously —**see eye to eye** to agree completely —**with an eye to** paying attention to; considering

eye′ball′ *n.* the ball-shaped part of the eye

eye′brow′ *n.* the bony arch over each eye, or the hair growing on this

eye′-catch′er *n.* something that espe-cially attracts one's attention —**eye′-catch′ing** *adj.*

eye′ful (-fool′) *n.* [Slang] a person or thing that looks striking

eye′glass′ *n.* 1. a lens to help faulty vision 2. [*pl.*] a pair of such lenses in a frame; glasses

eye′lash′ *n.* any of the hairs on the edge of the eyelid

eye′let (-lit) *n.* 1. a small hole for receiving a cord, hook, etc. 2. a metal ring, etc. for lining It 3. a small hole edged by stitching in embroidery

eye′lid′ *n.* either of two folds of flesh that cover and uncover the eyeball

eye′-o′pen·er (-ō′p′n ər) *n.* a sur-prising piece of news, sudden realiza-tion, etc.

eye′piece′ *n.* in a telescope, micro-scope, etc., the lens or lenses nearest the viewer's eye

eye′sight′ *n.* 1. the power of seeing; sight 2. the range of vision

eye′sore′ *n.* an unpleasant sight

eye′strain′ *n.* a tired or strained condition of the eye muscles

eye′tooth′ *n., pl.* **-teeth′** a canine tooth of the upper jaw

eye′wit′ness *n.* one who has himself seen a specific thing happen

ey·rie, ey·ry (er′ē, ir′ē) *n., pl.* **-ries** same as AERIE

F

F, f (ef) *n., pl.* **F's, f's** the sixth letter of the English alphabet

F (ef) *n.* 1. *Chem.* fluorine 2. *Educ.* a grade for failing work or, sometimes, fair or average work 3. *Music* the fourth tone in the scale of C major

F, F. 1. Fahrenheit 2. Friday

F., f. 1. feminine 2. folio(s) 3. follow-ing 4. *Music* forte 5. franc(s)

fa (fä) *n.* [< ML.] *Music* the fourth tone of the diatonic scale

fa·ble (fā′b'l) *n.* [< L. *fabula*, a story] 1. a fictitious story, usually about animals, meant to teach a moral lesson 2. a myth or legend 3. a falsehood

fa′bled *adj.* 1. legendary; mythical 2. unreal; fictitious

fab·ric (fab′rik) *n.* [< L. *fabrica*, workshop] 1. a framework; structure 2. a material made from fibers, etc. by weaving, felting, etc., as cloth

fab·ri·cate (fab′rə kāt′) *vt.* **-cat′ed, -cat′ing** [see prec.] 1. to make, con-struct, etc.; manufacture 2. to make up (a story, lie, etc.); invent —**fab′ri·ca′tion** *n.* —**fab′ri·ca′tor** *n.*

fab·u·lous (fab′yoo ləs) *adj.* [see FABLE] 1. of or like a fable; fictitious 2. incredible 3. [Colloq.] wonderful —**fab′u·lous·ly** *adv.*

fa·çade, fa·cade (fə säd′) *n.* [Fr.: see ff.] 1. the front or main face of a building 2. an imposing appearance concealing something inferior

face (fās) *n.* [< L. *facies*] 1. the front of the head 2. the expression of the countenance 3. the main or front surface 4. the surface that is marked, as of a clock, fabric, etc. 5. appear-ance; outward aspect 6. dignity; self-respect: usually in **to lose** (or **save**) **face** —*vt.* faced, fac′ing 1. to turn, or have the face turned, toward 2. to confront with boldness, etc. 3. to cover with a new surface —*vi.* to turn, or have the face turned, in a specified direction —**face to face** 1. confront-ing one another 2. very close (with *with*) —**face up to** to face with courage —**in the face of** 1. in the presence of 2. in spite of —**make a face** to grimace —**on the face of it** apparently

face′less *adj.* lacking a distinct char-acter; anonymous

face lifting 1. plastic surgery to re-move wrinkles, etc. from the face 2. an altering, repairing, etc., as of a building's exterior Also **face lift** —**face′-lift′** *vt.*

face′-off′ *n. Hockey* the start or re-sumption of play when the referee drops the puck between two opposing players

face′-sav′ing adj. preserving one's dignity or self-respect

fac·et (fas′it) n. [see FACE] 1. any of the polished plane surfaces of a cut gem 2. any of a number of sides or aspects, as of a personality —vt. -et·ed or -et·ted, -et·ing or -et·ting to cut or make facets on

fa·ce·tious (fə sē′shəs) adj. [< L. facetus, witty] joking, esp. at an inappropriate time —fa·ce′tious·ly adv.

face value 1. the value written on a bill, bond, etc. 2. the seeming value

fa·cial (fā′shəl) adj. of or for the face —n. a cosmetic treatment, massage, etc. for the skin of the face

facial tissue a sheet of soft tissue paper used as a handkerchief, etc.

fac·ile (fas′'l) adj. [Fr. < L. facere, do] 1. not hard to do or done easily; fluent 3. superficial

fa·cil·i·tate (fə sil′ə tāt′) vt. -tat′ed, -tat′ing [see prec.] to make easy or easier —fa·cil′i·ta′tion n.

fa·cil·i·ty (-tē) n., pl. -ties 1. absence of difficulty 2. skill; dexterity 3. [usually pl.] the means by which something can be done 4. a building, etc. that facilitates some activity

fac·ing (fās′iŋ) n. 1. a lining on the edge of a garment 2. a covering of contrasting material on a building

fac·sim·i·le (fak sim′ə lē) n. [< L. facere, make + simile, like] (an) exact reproduction or copy

fact (fakt) n. [< L. facere, do] 1. a deed, esp. a criminal deed [an accessory before (or after) the fact] 2. a thing that has actually happened or is true 3. reality; truth 4. something stated as being true —as a matter of fact really: also in fact

fac·tion (fak′shən) n. [see prec.] 1. a group of people in an organization working in a common cause against the main body 2. dissension —fac′tion·al adj. —fac′tion·al·ism n.

fac′tious (-shəs) adj. of, produced by, or tending to produce faction

fac·ti·tious (fak tish′əs) adj. [see FACT] forced or artificial

fac·tor (fak′tər) n. [< L. facere, do] 1. one who transacts business for another 2. any of the conditions, etc. that bring about a result 3. Math. any of the quantities which form a product when multiplied together —vt. Math. to resolve into factors

fac·to·ry (fak′tə rē) n., pl. -ries [see prec.] a building or buildings in which things are manufactured

fac·to·tum (fak tōt′əm) n. [< L. facere, do + totum, all] a handyman

fac·tu·al (fak′choo wəl) adj. of or containing facts; real; actual

fac·ul·ty (fak′'l tē) n., pl. -ties [see FACILE] 1. any natural or specialized power of a living organism 2. special aptitude 3. all the teachers of a school or of one of its departments

fad (fad) n. [< Brit. dial.] a style, etc. that interests many people for a short time; passing fashion —fad′dish adj.

fade (fād) vi. fad′ed, fad′ing [< OFr. fade, pale] 1. to lose color, brilliance, etc. 2. to lose freshness or

strength 3. to disappear slowly; die out —vt. to cause to fade —**fade in** (or **out**) Motion Pictures & TV to appear (or disappear) gradually

faer·ie, faer·y (fer′ē) n. [Archaic] 1. fairyland 2. pl. -ies a fairy

fag (fag) vt., vi. fagged, fag′ging [< ?] to make or become very tired by hard work —n. [Slang] a male homosexual

fag·ot, fag·got (fag′ət) n. [ult. < Gr. phakelos, a bundle] a bundle of sticks or twigs, esp. for use as fuel

fag′ot·ing, fag′got·ing n. 1. a hemstitch with wide spaces 2. openwork with crisscross or barlike stitches across the open seam

Fahr·en·heit (fer′ən hīt′) adj. [< G. D. Fahrenheit, 18th-c. G. physicist] designating or of a thermometer on which 32° is the freezing point and 212° is the boiling point of water —n. this thermometer or its scale

fail (fāl) vi. [< L. fallere, deceive] 1. to be insufficient; fall short 2. to weaken; die away 3. to stop operating 4. to be negligent in a duty, expectation, etc. 5. to be unsuccessful 6. to become bankrupt 7. Educ. to get a grade of failure —vt. 1. to be of no help to; disappoint 2. to leave; abandon 3. to neglect [to fail to go] 4. Educ. to give a grade of failure or get such a grade in —**without fail** without failing (to do, occur, etc.)

fail′ing n. 1. a failure 2. a fault —prep. without; lacking

faille (fīl, fāl) n. [Fr.] a ribbed, soft fabric of silk or rayon

fail′-safe′ adj. of an intricate procedure for preventing accidental operation, as of nuclear weapons

fail·ure (fāl′yər) n. 1. a) a falling short b) a weakening c) a breakdown in operation d) neglect e) a not succeeding f) a becoming bankrupt 2. one that does not succeed 3. Educ. a failing to pass, or a grade showing this

fain (fān) adj., adv. [< OE. fægen, glad] [Archaic] glad(ly); willing(ly)

faint (fānt) adj. [see FEIGN] 1. weak; feeble 2. timid 3. feeling weak and dizzy 4. dim; indistinct —n. a state of temporary unconsciousness —vi. to fall into a faint —**faint′ly** adv. —**faint′ness** n.

fair¹ (fer) adj. [OE. fæger] 1. attractive; beautiful 2. unblemished; clean 3. blond [fair hair] 4. clear and sunny 5. easy to read [a fair hand] 6. just and honest 7. according to the rules 8. moderately large 9. average [in fair condition] 10. that may be hunted [fair game] 11. Baseball that is not foul —adv. 1. in a fair manner 2. squarely —**fair′ness** n.

fair² (fer) n. [< L. feriae, festivals] 1. a regular gathering for barter and sale of goods 2. a carnival or bazaar, often for charity 3. a competitive exhibition of farm, household, and manufactured products, with various amusements and educational displays

fair′-haired′ adj. 1. having blond hair 2. [Colloq.] favorite

fair′ly *adv.* 1. justly; honestly 2. somewhat; moderately 3. completely or really

fair shake [Colloq.] fair or just treatment

fair′-trade′ *adj.* designating or of an agreement whereby a seller of a product charges no less than the minimum price set by the producer

fair′way′ *n.* the mowed part of a golf course between a tee and a green

fair·y (fer′ē) *n., pl.* **-ies** [< OFr. *feie*] 1. a tiny, graceful imaginary being in human form, with magic powers. 2. [Slang] a male homosexual —*adj.* 1. of fairies 2. fairylike

fair′y·land′ *n.* 1. the imaginary land where the fairies live 2. a lovely, enchanting place

fairy tale 1. a story about fairies 2. an unbelievable or untrue story

†**fait ac·com·pli** (fe tä kōn plē′) [Fr.] a thing done that cannot be changed

faith (fāth) *n.* [< L. *fidere*, to trust] 1. unquestioning belief, specif. in God, religion, etc. 2. a particular religion 3. complete trust or confidence 4. loyalty —**good** (or **bad**) **faith** (in)sincerity; (dis)honesty

faith′ful (-fəl) *adj.* 1. loyal 2. conscientious 3. accurate; reliable —**faith′ful·ly** *adv.* —**faith′ful·ness** *n.*

faith′less (-lis) *adj.* untrue, dishonest, or disloyal —**faith′less·ly** *adv.* —**faith′less·ness** *n.*

fake (fāk) *vt., vi.* **faked, fak′ing** [< ?] to make (something) seem real, etc. by deception —*n.* a fraud; counterfeit —*adj.* sham; false —**fak′er** *n.*

fa·kir (fə kir′) *n.* [Ar. *faqir,* lit., poor] 1. one of a Moslem holy sect of beggars 2. a Hindu ascetic

fa·la·fel (fə läf′l) *n.* [< Ar.] a deep-fried patty of ground chickpeas

fal·con (fal′kən, fôl′-, fô′-) *n.* [ult. < L. *falx,* sickle] a hawk trained to hunt small game —**fal′con·er** *n.* —**fal′con·ry** *n.*

fall (fôl) *vi.* **fell, fall′en, fall′ing** [OE. *feallan*] 1. to come down by gravity; drop; descend 2. to come down suddenly from an upright position; tumble or collapse 3. to be wounded or killed in battle 4. to take a downward direction 5. to become lower, less, weaker, etc. 6. to lose power, status, etc. 7. to do wrong; sin 8. to be captured 9. to take on a sad look *[his face fell]* 10. to pass into a specified condition *[to fall ill]* 11. to take place; occur 12. to be directed by chance 13. to come by inheritance, lot, etc. 14. to be divided (*into*) —*n.* 1. a dropping; descending 2. a coming down suddenly from an upright position 3. a downward direction or slope 4. a becoming lower or less 5. a capture 6. a loss of status, reputation, etc. 7. a yielding to temptation 8. autumn 9. the amount of what has fallen *[a six-inch fall of snow]* 10. the distance something

falls 11. [*pl.*, *often with sing. v.*] water falling over a cliff, etc. 12. a long tress of hair, added to a woman's hairdo —*adj.* of, for, or in the autumn —**fall back** to withdraw; retreat —**fall flat** to fail completely —**fall for** [Colloq.] 1. to fall in love with 2. to be tricked by —**fall in** to line up in formation —**fall off** to become smaller, worse, etc. —**fall on** (or **upon**) to attack —**fall out** 1. to quarrel 2. to leave one's place in a formation —**fall through** to fail —**fall to** 1. to begin 2. to start eating

fal·la·cious (fə lā′shəs) *adj.* [see ff.] 1. erroneous 2. misleading or deceptive —**fal·la′cious·ly** *adv.*

fal·la·cy (fal′ə sē) *n., pl.* **-cies** [< L. *fallere,* deceive] 1. a mistaken idea; error 2. a flaw in reasoning

fall·en (fôl′ən) *adj.* that fell; dropped; prostrate, ruined, dead, etc.

fal·li·ble (fal′ə b'l) *adj.* [< L. *fallere,* deceive] liable to be mistaken, deceived, or erroneous —**fal′li·bil′i·ty, fal′li·ble·ness** *n.* —**fal′li·bly** *adv.*

fall′ing-out′ *n.* a quarrel

falling star *same as* METEOR (sense 1)

fall′off′ *n.* a decline

Fal·lo·pi·an tube (fə lō′pē ən) [< G. *Fallopius,* 16th-c. It. anatomist] either of two tubes that carry ova to the uterus

fall′out′ *n.* 1. the descent to earth of radioactive particles, as after a nuclear explosion 2. these particles

fal·low (fal′ō) *adj.* [< OE. *fealh*] 1. left unplanted 2. inactive

false (fôls) *adj.* **fals′er, fals′est** [< L. *fallere,* deceive] 1. not true; incorrect; wrong 2. untruthful; lying 3. unfaithful 4. misleading 5. not real; artificial —*adv.* in a false manner —**false′ly** *adv.* —**false′ness** *n.*

false′hood′ *n.* 1. falsity 2. a lie

fal·set·to (fôl set′ō) *n., pl.* **-tos** [It., dim. of *falso,* false] an artificial way of singing in which the voice is much higher-pitched than normal

fal·si·fy (fôl′sə fī′) *vt.* **-fied′, -fy′ing** 1. to misrepresent 2. to alter (a record, etc.) fraudulently —**fal′si·fi·ca′tion** *n.* —**fal′si·fi′er** *n.*

fal·si·ty (-tē) *n., pl.* **-ties** 1. the quality of being false 2. a lie

Fal·staff, Sir John (fôl′staf) a character in Shakespeare's plays, a fat, blustering, witty knight

fal·ter (fôl′tər) *vi.* [prob. < ON.] 1. to move unsteadily; stumble 2. to stammer 3. to act hesitantly; waver —**fal′ter·ing·ly** *adv.*

fame (fām) *n.* [< L. *fama*] 1. reputation, esp. for good 2. the state of being well known —**famed** *adj.*

fa·mil·ial (fə mil′yəl) *adj.* of or common to a family

fa·mil·iar (fə mil′yər) *adj.* [see FAMILY] 1. friendly; intimate 2. too friendly; unduly intimate 3. closely acquainted (*with*) 4. common; ordinary —**fa·mil′iar·ly** *adv.*

fa·mil·i·ar·i·ty (-yar'ə tē) *n.*, *pl.* **-ties** 1. intimacy 2. free and intimate behavior 3. undue intimacy 4. close acquaintance (*with* something)

fa·mil·iar·ize (-yə rīz') *vt.* -**ized'**, -**iz'ing** 1. to make commonly known 2. to make (another or oneself) fully acquainted —**fa·mil'iar·i·za'tion** *n.*

fam·i·ly (fam'ə lē, fam'lē) *n.*, *pl.* -**lies** [< L. *famulus*, servant] 1. a household 2. parents and their children 3. relatives 4. all those descended from a common ancestor; lineage 5. a group of similar or related things

family room a room in a home set apart for relaxation and recreation

fam·ine (fam'ən) *n.* [< L. *fames*, hunger] 1. an acute and general shortage of food 2. any acute shortage

fam·ish (-ish) *vt.*, *vi.* [see prec.] to make or be very hungry

fa·mous (fā'məs) *adj.* 1. having fame; renowned 2. [Colloq.] excellent; very good —**fa'mous·ly** *adv.*

fan¹ (fan) *n.* [< L. *vannus*, basket for winnowing grain] any device used to set up a current of air for ventilating or cooling —*vt.*, *vi.* **fanned, fan'ning** 1. to move (air) as with a fan 2. to direct air toward as with a fan 3. to stir up; excite 4. *Baseball* to strike out —**fan out** to spread out

fan² (fan) *n.* [< FAN(ATIC)] [Colloq.] a person enthusiastic about a specified sport, performer, etc.

fa·nat·ic (fə nat'ik) *adj.* [< L. *fanum*, temple] unreasonably enthusiastic; overly zealous: also **fa·nat'i·cal** —*n.* a fanatic person —**fa·nat'i·cal·ly** *adv.* —**fa·nat'i·cism** *n.*

fan·ci·er (fan'sē ər) *n.* a person with a special interest in something, esp. plant or animal breeding

fan·ci·ful (fan'si fəl) *adj.* 1. full of fancy; imaginative 2. imaginary; not real —**fan'ci·ful·ly** *adv.*

fan·cy (fan'sē) *n.*, *pl.* -**cies** [contr. < ME. *fantasie*, FANTASY] 1. imagination when light, playful, etc. 2. a mental image 3. a notion; caprice; whim 4. an inclination or fondness —*adj.* -**ci·er**, -**ci·est** 1. capricious; whimsical 2. extravagant [a *fancy* price] 3. ornamental; elaborate [a *fancy* necktie] 4. of superior skill or quality —*vt.* -**cied**, -**cy·ing** 1. to imagine 2. to be fond of 3. to suppose —**fan'ci·ly** *adv.* —**fan'ci·ness** *n.*

fan'cy-free' *adj.* 1. not married, engaged, etc. 2. carefree

fan'cy·work' *n.* embroidery, crocheting, and other ornamental needlework

fan·dom (fan'dəm) *n.* fans, collectively, as of a sport or entertainer

fan·fare (fan'fer') *n.* [Fr., prob. < *fanfaron*, braggart] 1. a loud flourish of trumpets 2. noisy or showy display

fang (fang) *n.* [OE. < *fon*, seize] 1. one of the long, pointed teeth of meat-eating mammals 2. one of the long, hollow teeth through which poisonous snakes inject venom

fan·ta·size (fan'tə

sīz') *vt.*, *vi.* -**sized'**, -**siz'ing** to indulge in fantasies or have daydreams (about) —**fan'ta·sist** (-sist) *n.*

fan·tas·tic (fan tas'tik) *adj.* [see ff.] 1. imaginary; unreal 2. grotesque; odd 3. extravagant —**fan·tas'ti·cal·ly** *adv.* —**fan·tas'ti·cal·ness** *n.*

fan·ta·sy (fan'tə sē) *n.*, *pl.* -**sies** [< Gr. *phainein*, to show] 1. imagination or fancy 2. an illusion or reverie 3. an imaginative poem, play, etc.

FAO Food and Agriculture Organization (of the UN)

far (fär) *adj.* **far'ther, far'thest** [OE. *feorr*] 1. distant in space or time 2. more distant [the *far* side] —*adv.* 1. very distant in space, time, or degree 2. to or from a distance in time or position 3. very much [*far* better] —**as far as** to the distance or degree that —**by far** very much; considerably: also **far and away** —(in) **so far as** to the extent that —**so far** up to this place, time, or degree

far'a·way' *adj.* 1. distant in time or place 2. dreamy

farce (färs) *n.* [Fr. < L. *farcire*, to stuff] 1. (an) exaggerated comedy based on broadly humorous situations 2. an absurd or ridiculous action, pretense, etc. —**far·ci·cal** (fär'si k'l) *adj.*

fare (fer) *vi.* **fared, far'ing** [< OE. *faran*, go] 1. to happen; result 2. to be in a specified condition [to fare well] 3. to eat —*n.* 1. money paid for transportation 2. a passenger who pays a fare 3. food

Far East E Asia; China, Japan, etc.

fare·well (fer'wel'; *for adj.* -wel') *interj.* goodbye —*n.* good wishes at parting —*adj.* parting; final [a *fare-well* gesture]

far·fetched (fär'fecht') *adj.* forced; strained; unlikely

far'flung' (-fluŋ') *adj.* extending over a wide area

fa·ri·na (fə rē'nə) *n.* [< L., meal] flour or meal made from cereal grains, potatoes, etc., eaten as a cooked cereal

far·i·na·ceous (far'ə nā'shəs) *adj.* [see prec.] 1. consisting of or made from flour or meal 2. like meal

farm (färm) *n.* [< ML. *firma*, fixed payment] a piece of land (with house, barns, etc.) on which crops or animals are raised; orig., such land let out to tenants —*vt.* 1. to cultivate (land) 2. to turn over to another for a fee —*vi.* to work on or operate a farm

farm'er *n.* a person who manages or operates a farm

farm'hand' *n.* a hired farm worker

farm'house' *n.* a house on a farm

farm'ing *n.* the business of operating a farm; agriculture

farm'yard' *n.* the yard surrounding or enclosed by farm buildings

far·o (fer'ō) *n.* [< ? PHARAOH] a gambling game played with cards

far-off (fär'ôf') *adj.* distant; remote

far'-out' *adj.* [Colloq.] nonconformist; esp., avant-garde

far·ra·go (fə rā'gō, -rā'-) *n.*, *pl.* -**goes** [< L. *far*, kind of grain] a jumble

far'-reach'ing *adj.* having a wide range, extent, influence, or effect

far·ri·er (far'ē ər) n. [< L. *ferrum*, iron] [Brit.] a blacksmith

far·row (far'ō) n. [< OE. *fearh*, young pig] a litter of pigs —vt., vi. to give birth to (a litter of pigs)

far·sight'ed adj. 1. planning ahead; provident: also **far·see'ing** 2. seeing distant objects more clearly than near ones —**far'sight'ed·ness** n.

far·ther (fär'thər) compar. of FAR —adj. 1. more distant 2. additional; more —adv. 1. at or to a greater distance 2. to a greater degree 3. in addition Cf. FURTHER

far·thest (fär'thist) superl. of FAR —adj. most distant —adv. at or to the greatest distance or degree

far·thing (fär'thiŋ) n. [OE. *feorthing*] a former British coin worth 1/4 penny

fas·ci·nate (fas'ə nāt') vt. -nat·ed, -nat·ing [< L. *fascinum*, an enchanting] 1. to hold motionless, as by inspiring terror 2. to charm; captivate —**fas'ci·na'tion** n.

fas·cism (fash'iz'm) n. [< It. < L. *fasces*, rods bound about an ax, ancient Roman symbol of authority] [occas. F-] a system of government characterized by dictatorship, belligerent nationalism and racism, militarism, etc.: first instituted in Italy (1922–43) —**fas'cist** n., adj.

fash·ion (fash'ən) n. [< L. *factio*, a making] 1. the form or shape of a thing 2. way; manner 3. the current style of dress, conduct, etc. —vt. 1. to make; form 2. to fit; accommodate (to) —after (or in) a fashion to some extent —**fash'ion·er** n.

fash·ion·a·ble adj. 1. stylish 2. of or used by people who follow fashion —**fash'ion·a·bly** adv.

fast¹ (fast) adj. [OE. *fæst*] 1. firm; firmly fastened 2. loyal; devoted 3. nonfading [fast colors] 4. swift; quick 5. ahead of time [a fast watch] 6. wild, promiscuous, or dissipated 7. [Colloq.] glib —adv. 1. firmly; fixedly 2. thoroughly [fast asleep] 3. rapidly —**fast'ness** n.

fast² (fast) vi. [OE. *fæstan*] to abstain from all or certain foods —n. 1. a fasting 2. a period of fasting

fast'back' n. an automobile body whose roof forms an unbroken curve from windshield to rear bumper

fas·ten (fas''n) vt. [see FAST¹] 1. to attach; connect 2. to make secure, as by locking, buttoning, etc. 3. to fix (the attention, etc. on) —vi. to become fastened —**fas'ten·er** n.

fas'ten·ing n. anything used to fasten; bolt, clasp, hook, etc.

fast'-food' adj. designating a business, as a hamburger stand, that offers food prepared and served quickly

fas·tid·i·ous (fas tid'ē əs) adj. [< L. *fastus*, disdain] 1. not easy to please 2. daintily refined; oversensitive —**fas·tid'i·ous·ly** adv. —**fas·tid'i·ous·ness** n.

fast'-talk' vt. [Colloq.] to persuade

with smooth, but often deceitful talk

fast time same as DAYLIGHT-SAVING TIME

fat (fat) adj. **fat'ter, fat'test** [OE. *fætt*] 1. containing fat; oily 2. a) fleshy; plump b) too plump 3. thick; broad 4. fertile [fat land] 5. profitable [a fat job] 6. plentiful —n. 1. an oily or greasy material found in animal tissue and plant seeds 2. the richest part of anything 3. superfluous part —chew the fat [Slang] to chat —**fat'ly** adv. —**fat'ness** n.

fa·tal (fāt''l) adj. 1. fateful; decisive 2. resulting in death 3. destructive; disastrous —**fa'tal·ly** adv.

fa'tal·ism n. the belief that all events are determined by fate and are hence inevitable —**fa'tal·ist** n. —**fa'tal·is'tic** adj. —**fa'tal·is'ti·cal·ly** adv.

fa·tal·i·ty (fə tal'ə tē, fā-) n., pl. -ties 1. a deadly effect; deadliness 2. a death caused by a disaster or accident

fat'back' n. fat from a hog's back, usually dried and salted in strips

fat cat [Slang] a wealthy, influential donor, esp. to a political campaign

fate (fāt) n. [< L. *fatum*, oracle] 1. the power supposed to determine the outcome of events; destiny 2. one's lot or fortune 3. final outcome 4. death; destruction —the Fates Gr. & Rom. Myth. the three goddesses who control human destiny and life

fat·ed (fāt'id) adj. 1. destined 2. doomed

fate'ful (-fəl) adj. 1. prophetic 2. significant; decisive 3. controlled as if by fate 4. bringing death or destruction —**fate'ful·ly** adv.

fa·ther (fä'thər) n. [OE. *fæder*] 1. a male parent 2. [F-] God 3. an ancestor 4. an originator, founder, or inventor 5. a Christian priest: used esp. as a title —vt. to be the father of —**fa'ther·hood'** n. —**fa'ther·less** adj.

fa'ther-in-law' n., pl. **fa'thers-in-law'** the father of one's spouse

fa'ther·land' n. one's native land

fa'ther·ly adj. of or like a father; kindly —**fa'ther·li·ness** n.

fath·om (fath'əm) n. [OE. *fæthm*, the two arms outstretched] a nautical unit of depth or length, equal to 6 feet —vt. 1. to measure the depth of 2. to understand thoroughly —**fath'om·a·ble** adj. —**fath'om·less** adj.

fa·tigue (fə tēg') n. [Fr. < L. *fatigare*, to weary] 1. exhaustion; weariness 2. [pl.] soldiers' work clothing —vt., vi. -tigued', -tigu'ing to tire out

fat·ten (fat''n) vt., vi. to make or become fat (in various senses)

fat'ty adj. -ti·er, -ti·est 1. of or containing fat 2. like fat; greasy

fat·u·ous (fach'oo wəs) adj. [L. *fatuus*] complacently stupid; foolish —**fa·tu·i·ty** (fə tōō'ə tē) n. —**fat'u·ous·ly** adv. —**fat'u·ous·ness** n.

fau·cet (fô'sit) n. [prob. < OFr. *faulser*, to breach] a device with a

fat, āpe, cär; ten, ēven; is, bīte; gō, hôrn, tōōl, look; oil, out; up, fur; chin; she; thin, then; zh, leisure; ŋ, ring; ə for a in ago; ', (ā'b'l); ë, Fr. coeur; ö, Fr. feu; Fr. mon; ü, Fr. duc; kh, G. ich, doch; ‡ foreign; < derived from

valve for regulating the flow of a liquid from a pipe, etc.; tap

Faulk·ner (fôk′nər), **William** 1897-1962; U.S. novelist

fault (fôlt) *n.* [< L. *fallere*, deceive] 1. something that mars; flaw; defect 2. a misdeed or mistake 3. blame for something wrong 4. a fracture in rock strata —**at fault** deserving blame —**find fault (with)** to criticize

fault′find′ing *n., adj.* criticizing

fault′less *adj.* perfect

fault′y *adj.* **-i·er, -i·est** having a fault or faults; defective —**fault′i·ly** *adv.* —**fault′i·ness** *n.*

faun (fôn) *n.* [< L. *faunus*] any of a class of minor Roman deities, half man and half goat

fau·na (fô′nə) *n.* [< LL. *Fauna*, Rom. goddess] the animals of a specified region or time

Faust (foust) a man in legend and literature who sells his soul to the devil for knowledge and power

faux pas (fō′pä′) *pl.* **faux pas** (fō′päz′) [Fr., lit., false step] a social blunder

fa·vor (fā′vər) *n.* [< L. *favere*, to favor] 1. friendly regard; approval 2. partiality 3. a kind or obliging act 4. a small gift or token —*vt.* 1. to approve or like 2. to be partial to 3. to support; advocate 4. to help 5. to do a kindness for 6. to resemble [to *favor* one's mother] Brit. sp. **favour** —**in favor of** 1. approving 2. to the advantage of —**fa′vor·er** *n.*

fa′vor·a·ble *adj.* 1. approving 2. helpful 3. pleasing —**fa′vor·a·bly** *adv.*

fa·vor·ite (fā′vər it) *n.* 1. a person or thing regarded with special liking 2. a contestant regarded as most likely to win —*adj.* highly regarded; preferred

fa′vor·it·ism *n.* partiality; bias

fawn¹ (fôn) *vi.* [< OE. *fægen*, glad] 1. to show friendliness by licking hands, etc.: said of a dog 2. to cringe and flatter —**fawn′er** *n.*

fawn² (fôn) *n.* [< L. *fetus*, FETUS] 1. a deer less than one year old 2. a pale, yellowish brown —*adj.* of this color

fay (fā) *n.* [see FATE] a fairy

faze (fāz) *vt.* **fazed, faz′ing** [< OE. *fesan*, to drive] [Colloq.] to disturb

FBI, F.B.I. Federal Bureau of Investigation

FCC, F.C.C. Federal Communications Commission

FDA, F.D.A. Food and Drug Administration

FDIC, F.D.I.C. Federal Deposit Insurance Corporation

Fe [L. *ferrum*] *Chem.* iron

fe·al·ty (fē′əl tē) *n., pl.* **-ties** [< L. *fidelitas*, fidelity] loyalty, esp. as owed to a feudal lord

fear (fir) *n.* [< OE. *fær*, danger] 1. anxiety caused by real or possible danger, pain, etc.; fright 2. awe; reverence 3. apprehension; concern 4. a cause for fear —*vt., vi.* 1. to be afraid (of) 2. to be in awe (of) 3. to expect with misgiving —**fear′less** *adj.* —**fear′less·ly** *adv.*

fear′ful *adj.* 1. causing, feeling, or showing fear 2. [Colloq.] very bad, great, etc. —**fear′ful·ly** *adv.* —**fear′ful·ness** *n.*

fear′some *adj.* 1. causing fear; frightful 2. frightened; timid

fea·si·ble (fē′zə b'l) *adj.* [< OFr. *faire*, to do] 1. capable of being done; possible 2. likely; probable 3. suitable —**fea′si·bil′i·ty** *n.* —**fea′si·bly** *adv.*

feast (fēst) *n.* [< L. *festus*, festal] 1. a religious festival 2. a rich and elaborate meal —*vi.* to have a feast —*vt.* 1. to entertain at a feast 2. to delight [to *feast* one's eyes on a sight]

feat (fēt) *n.* [< L. *factum*, a deed] a deed of unusual daring or skill

feath·er (feth′ər) *n.* [OE. *fether*] 1. any of the soft, light growths covering the body of a bird 2. [*pl.*] *a*) plumage *b*) attire 3. class; kind [birds of a *feather*] —*vt.* 1. to provide or adorn with feathers 2. to turn (an oar or propeller blade) so that the edge is foremost —**feather in one's cap** a distinctive achievement —**feath′er·y** *adj.*

feath′er·bed′ding (-bed′iŋ) *n.* the employment of extra, standby workers

feath′er·weight′ *n.* 1. a boxer weighing from 119 to 126 lbs. 2. a wrestler weighing from 124 to 134 lbs.

fea·ture (fē′chər) *n.* [< L. *facere*, make] 1. *a*) [*pl.*] facial form or appearance *b*) any of the parts of the face 2. a distinct or outstanding part or quality of something 3. a special attraction, sale item, newspaper article, etc. 4. a full-length motion picture —*vt., vi.* **-tured, -tur·ing** to make or be a feature of (something)

fe·brile (fē′brəl, -brïl) *adj.* [< L. *febris*, fever] feverish

Feb·ru·ar·y (feb′rə wer′ē, feb′yoo-) *n.* [< L. *Februarius* (*mensis*), orig. month of expiation] the second month of the year, having 28 days (or 29 days in leap years): abbrev. **Feb., F.**

fe·ces (fē′sēz) *n.pl.* [< L. *faeces*, dregs] excrement —**fe′cal** (-kəl) *adj.*

feck·less (fek′lis) *adj.* [Scot. < *feck*, effect + -LESS] 1. weak; ineffective 2. irresponsible —**feck′less·ly** *adv.*

fe·cund (fē′kənd, fek′ənd) *adj.* [< L. *fecundus*] fertile; productive —**fe·cun·di·ty** (fi kun′də tē) *n.*

fe·cun·date (fē′kən dāt′, fek′ən-) *vt.* **-dat′ed, -dat′ing** 1. to make fecund 2. to fertilize

fed (fed) *pt. & pp.* of FEED —**fed up** [Colloq.] having had enough to become disgusted, bored, etc.

Fed. 1. Federal 2. Federation

fed·a·yeen (fed′ä yēn′) *n.pl.* [Ar., lit., the sacrificers] Arab guerrillas

fed·er·al (fed′ər əl) *adj.* [< L. *foedus*, a league] 1. designating of or of a union of states, etc. in which each member subordinates its power to a central authority 2. designating or of a central government of this sort; specif., [*usually* F-] the central government of the U.S. 3. [F-] of or supporting a former U.S. political party (**Federalist Party**) which favored a strong centralized government 4. [F-] of or supporting the Union in the Civil War —*n.* [F-] a supporter or soldier of the Union in the Civil War —**fed′er·al·ism** *n.* —**fed′er·al·ist** *adj., n.* —**fed′er·al·ly** *adv.*

fed′er·al·ize′ (-ə liz′) *vt.* -ized′, -iz′ing 1. to unite (states, etc.) in a federal union 2. to put under federal authority —**fed′er·al·i·za′tion** *n.*

fed·er·ate (fed′ə rāt′) *vt., vi.* -at′ed, -at′ing to unite in a federation

fed·er·a·tion (fed′ə rā′shən) *n.* [see FEDERAL] 1. a union of states, groups, etc. in which each subordinates its power to that of the central authority 2. a federated organization

fe·do·ra (fə dôr′ə) *n.* [Fr.] a soft felt hat worn by men

fee (fē) *n.* [ult. < Gmc.] 1. a charge for professional services, licenses, etc. 2. *Law* an inheritance in land

fee·ble (fē′b'l) *adj.* -bler, -blest [< L. *flere*, weep] 1. weak; infirm [a *feeble* old man] 2. without force or effectiveness [a *feeble* attempt] —**fee′ble·ness** *n.* —**fee′bly** *adv.*

fee′ble·mind′ed (-mīn′did) *adj.* mentally retarded

feed (fēd) *vt.* fed, feed′ing [< OE. *foda*, food] 1. to give food to 2. to provide something necessary for the growth, operation, etc. of 3. to gratify [to *feed* one's vanity] —*vi.* to eat: said esp. of animals —*n.* 1. food for animals 2. *a)* the material fed into a machine *b)* the part of a machine supplying this material —**feed′er** *n.*

feed′back′ *n.* the transfer of part of the output back to the input, as of electricity or of information

feel (fēl) *vt.* felt, feel′ing [OE. *felan*] 1. to touch; examine by handling 2. to be aware of through physical sensation 3. to experience (an emotion or condition); be affected by 4. to be aware of 5. to think or believe —*vi.* 1. to have physical sensation 2. to appear to be to the senses [it *feels* warm] 3. to grope 4. to be aware of being [I *feel* sad] 5. to be moved to sympathy, pity, etc. (*for*) —*n.* 1. the act of feeling 2. the sense of touch 3. the nature of a thing perceived through touch —**feel (a person) out** to find out the opinions of (a person) cautiously —**feel like** [Colloq.] to have a desire for —**feel one's way** to advance cautiously —**feel up to** [Colloq.] to feel capable of

feel′er *n.* 1. a specialized organ of touch in an animal or insect, as an antenna 2. a remark, offer, etc. made to feel another out

feel′ing *n.* 1. the sense of touch 2. the ability to experience physical sensation 3. an awareness; sensation 4. an emotion 5. [pl.] sensitivities [hurt *feelings*] 6. sympathy; pity 7. an opinion or sentiment

feet (fēt) *n., pl.* of FOOT

feign (fān) *vt., vi.* [< L. *fingere*, to

shape] 1. to make up (an excuse, etc.) 2. to pretend; dissemble

feint (fānt) *n.* [see prec.] a pretended attack intended to take the opponent off his guard, as in boxing —*vi., vt.* to deliver (such an attack)

feld·spar (feld′spär′) *n.* [< G. *feld*, field + *spath*, a mineral] any of several hard, crystalline minerals

fe·lic·i·tate (fə lis′ə tāt′) *vt.* -tat′ed, -tat′ing [< L. *felix*, happy] to wish happiness to; congratulate —**fe·lic′i·ta′tion** *n.* —**fe·lic′i·ta′tor** *n.*

fe·lic′i·tous (-təs) *adj.* [< ff.] used or expressed in a way suitable to the occasion; appropriate

fe·lic′i·ty *n., pl.* -ties [< L. *felix*, happy] 1. happiness; bliss 2. anything producing happiness 3. apt and pleasing expression in writing, etc.

fe·line (fē′līn) *adj.* [< L. *feles*, cat] 1. of a cat or the cat family 2. catlike; sly —*n.* any animal of the cat family

fell[1] (fel) *pt.* of FALL

fell[2] (fel) *vt.* [OE. *fellan*] 1. to knock down 2. to cut down (a tree)

fell[3] (fel) *adj.* [< ML. *fello*] fierce; cruel

fell[4] (fel) *n.* [OE.] an animal's hide

fel·low (fel′ō, -ə) *n.* [Late OE. *feolaga*, partner] 1. an associate 2. one of the same rank; equal 3. one of a pair; mate 4. one holding a fellowship in a college, etc. 5. a member of a learned society 6. [Colloq.] a man or boy —*adj.* having the same position, work, etc. [*fellow* workers]

fel′low·ship′ *n.* 1. companionship 2. a mutual sharing 3. a group of people with the same interests 4. an endowment for the support of a student or scholar doing advanced work

fellow traveler a nonmember who supports the cause of a party

fel·on[1] (fel′ən) *n.* [< ML. *fello*] a person guilty of a felony; criminal

fel·on[2] (fel′ən) *n.* [ME.] a painful, pus-producing infection at the end of a finger or toe, near the nail

fel·o·ny (fel′ə nē) *n., pl.* -nies [< ML.] a major crime, as murder, arson, etc. —**fe·lo·ni·ous** (fə lō′nē əs) *adj.*

felt[1] (felt) *n.* [OE.] a fabric of wool, often mixed with fur or hair, worked together by pressure, etc. —*adj.* made of felt —*vt.* to make into felt

felt[2] (felt) *pt. & pp.* of FEEL

fe·male (fē′māl) *adj.* [< L. *femina*, woman] 1. designating or of the sex that bears offspring 2. of, like, or suitable to women or girls; feminine 3. having a hollow part (as a pipe fitting) for receiving an inserted part —*n.* a female person, animal, or plant

fem·i·nine (fem′ə nin) *adj.* [< L. *femina*, woman] 1. of women or girls 2. having qualities characteristic of or suitable to women; gentle, delicate, etc. 3. *Gram.* designating or of the gender of words referring to females or things orig. regarded as female —**fem′i·nin′i·ty** *n.*

fem·i·nism n. the movement to win political, economic, and social equality for women —**fem'i·nist** n., adj.

fe·mur (fē'mər) n., pl. **fe'murs, fem·o·ra** (fem'ər ə) [< L., thigh] the thighbone —**fem'o·ral** adj.

fen (fen) n. [OE.] an area of low, flat, marshy land; swamp; bog

fence (fens) n. [< ME. *defens*, defense] 1. a protective or confining barrier of posts, wire mesh, etc. 2. one who deals in stolen goods —vt. **fenced, fenc'ing** 1. to enclose as with a fence (with *in, off*, etc.) 2. to keep (*out*) as by a fence —vi. 1. to practice the art of fencing 2. to avoid giving a direct reply —**fenc'er** n.

fenc'ing n. 1. the art of fighting with a foil or other sword 2. material for making fences 3. a system of fences

fend (fend) vi. [ME. *fenden*, defend] to resist —**fend for oneself** to manage by oneself —**fend off** to ward off

fend'er n. anything that fends off or protects something else, as the part of an automobile body over the wheel

fen·nel (fen'l) n. [< L. *faenum*, hay] a tall herb of the parsley family, with aromatic seeds used in cooking

fe·ral (fir'əl) adj. [< L. *ferus*, wild] 1. untamed; wild 2. savage

fer·ment (fur'ment; *for v.* fər ment') n. [< L. *fervere*, to boil] 1. a substance causing fermentation, as yeast 2. excitement or agitation —vt. 1. to cause fermentation in 2. to excite; agitate —vi. 1. to be in the process of fermentation 2. to be excited or agitated; seethe

fer·men·ta·tion (fur'mən tā'shən, -men-) n. 1. the breakdown of complex molecules in organic compounds, caused by the influence of a ferment [*bacteria* cause milk to curdle by *fermentation*] 2. excitement; agitation

fern (furn) n. [OE. *fearn*] any of a large class of nonflowering plants having roots, stems, and fronds, and reproducing by spores

fe·ro·cious (fə rō'shəs) adj. [< L. *ferus*, wild] 1. fierce; savage; violently cruel 2. [Colloq.] very great [a *ferocious* appetite] —**fe·ro'cious·ly** adv. —**fe·roc·i·ty** (fə räs'ə tē) n.

FERN

-fer·ous (fər əs) [< L. *ferre*, to bear] a *suffix meaning* bearing, yielding

fer·ret (fer'it) n. [< L. *fur*, thief] a weasellike animal, tamed for hunting rats, etc. —vt. 1. to force out of hiding with a ferret 2. to search (*out*)

Fer·ris wheel (fer'is) [after G. *Ferris*, 1859–96, U.S. engineer] a large, upright wheel revolving on a fixed axle and having suspended seats: used as an amusement ride

ferro- [< L. *ferrum*, iron] *a combining form meaning:* 1. iron 2. iron and

fer·rous (fer'əs) adj. [< L. *ferrum*, iron] of, containing, or derived from iron: also **fer'ric** (-ik)

fer·rule (fer'əl, -ool) n. [< L. *viriae*, bracelets] a metal ring or cap put around the end of a cane, tool handle, etc. to give added strength

fer·ry (fer'ē) vt., vi. **-ried, -ry·ing** [OE. *ferian*] 1. to take across or cross (a river, etc.) in a boat 2. to deliver (airplanes) by flying them 3. to transport by airplane —n., pl. **-ries** 1. a system for carrying people, goods, etc. across a river, etc. by boat 2. a boat (also **ferryboat**) used for this —**fer'ry·man** (-mən) n., pl. **-men**

fer·tile (furt'l) adj. [< L. *ferre*, to bear] 1. producing abundantly; fruitful 2. able to produce young, seeds, fruit, pollen, spores, etc. 3. fertilized —**fer·til·i·ty** (fər til'ə tē) n.

fer'til·ize' (-īz') vt. **-ized', -iz'ing** 1. to make fertile 2. to spread fertilizer on 3. to make (the female cell or female) fruitful by introducing the male germ cell; impregnate —**fer'til·iz'a·ble** adj. —**fer'til·i·za'tion** n.

fer'til·iz'er n. manure, chemicals, etc. used to enrich the soil

fer·ule (fer'əl, -ool) n. [< L. *ferula*, a whip, rod] a flat stick or ruler used for punishing children

fer·vent (fur'vənt) adj. [< L. *fervere*, to glow] showing great warmth of feeling; intensely devoted or earnest —**fer'ven·cy** n. —**fer'vent·ly** adv.

fer·vid (fur'vəd) adj. [see prec.] impassioned; fervent —**fer'vid·ly** adv.

fer·vor (fur'vər) n. [see FERVENT] great warmth of emotion; ardor; zeal

-fest (fest) [< G. *fest*, a feast] *a combining form meaning* an occasion of much [*gabfest*]

fes·tal (fes't'l) adj. [< L. *festum*, feast] of or like a joyous celebration; gay

fes·ter (fes'tər) n. [< L. *fistula*, ulcer] a small sore filled with pus —vi. 1. to form pus 2. to rankle

fes·ti·val (fes'tə v'l) n. [see ff.] 1. a time or day of feasting or celebration 2. a celebration or series of performances 3. merrymaking

fes·tive (fes'tiv) adj. [< L. *festum*, feast] of or for a feast or festival; merry; joyous —**fes'tive·ly** adv. —**fes'tive·ness** n.

fes·tiv·i·ty (fes tiv'ə tē) n., pl. **-ties** 1. merrymaking; gaiety 2. a festival 3. [*pl.*] things done in celebration

fes·toon (fes tōōn') n. [< It. *festa*, feast] a curved garland of flowers, etc. —vt. to adorn with festoons

fet·a (cheese) (fet'ə) [< ModGr. < It. *fetta*, a slice] a white, soft cheese made in Greece

fe·tal (fēt'l) adj. of a fetus

fetch (fech) vt. [OE. *feccan*] 1. to go after and bring back; get 2. to cause to come 3. to sell for

fetch'ing adj. attractive; charming

fete, fête (fāt) n. [Fr. *fête*: see FEAST] a festival; entertainment, esp. outdoors —vt. **fet'ed** or **fêt'ed, fet'ing** or **fêt'ing** to honor with a fete

fet·id (fet'id, fēt'-) adj. [< L. *foetere*, to stink] having a bad smell; stinking; putrid —**fet'id·ness** n.

fet·ish (fet'ish, fēt'-) n. [< Port. *feitiço*] 1. any object believed to have magical power 2. anything to which one is irrationally devoted 3. any non-sexual object that abnormally excites erotic feelings Also **fetich** —**fet'ish·ism** n. —**fet'ish·ist** n.

fet·lock (fet'läk') n. [< ME. *fet*, feet + *lok*, LOCK[2]] 1. a tuft of hair on the back of a horse's leg above the hoof 2. the joint bearing this tuft

fet·ter (fet'ər) n. [< OE. *fot*, foot] 1. a shackle or chain for the feet 2. any check or restraint —vt. 1. to bind with fetters 2. to restrain

fet·tle (fet'l) n. [ME. *fetlen*, make ready] condition; state [in fine *fettle*]

fe·tus (fēt'əs) n., pl. -**tus·es** [L., a bringing forth] 1. the unborn young of an animal, esp. in its later stages 2. in man, the offspring in the womb from the fourth month until birth

feud (fyood) n. [< OFr.] a deadly quarrel, esp. between clans or families —vi. to carry on a feud; quarrel

feu·dal (fyood''l) adj. [< OHG. *feho*, property] of or like feudalism

feu·dal·ism n. the economic and social system in medieval Europe, in which land, worked by serfs, was held by vassals in exchange for military and other services to overlords

fe·ver (fē'vər) n. [< L. *febris*] 1. an abnormally increased body temperature 2. any disease marked by a high fever 3. a restless excitement —**fe'ver·ish** adj. —**fe'ver·ish·ly** adv.

fever blister (or **sore**) same as COLD SORE

few (fyoo) adj. [OE. *feawe*, pl.] not many —pron., n. a small number —**quite a few** [Colloq.] a rather large number —**the few** the minority

fey (fā) adj. [OE. *fæge*] 1. [Archaic] fated 2. strange or unusual

fez (fez) n., pl. **fez'zes** [< *Fez*, city in Morocco] a red, tapering felt hat, worn, esp. formerly, by Turkish men

ff. 1. folios 2. following (pages, etc.)

FHA Federal Housing Administration

fi·an·cé (fē'än sā') n. [Fr. < OFr. *fiance*, a promise] the man to whom a woman is engaged to be married

fi·an·cée (fē'än sā') n. [Fr.: see prec.] the woman to whom a man is engaged to be married

fi·as·co (fē as'kō) n., pl. -**coes**, -**cos** [Fr. < It.] a complete, ridiculous failure

fi·at (fī'at, -ət) n. [L., let it be done] 1. a decree; order 2. a sanction

fib (fib) n. [< ? FABLE] a lie about something unimportant —vi. **fibbed**, **fib'bing** to tell a fib —**fib'ber** n.

fi·ber, **fi·bre** (fī'bər) n. [< L. *fibra*] 1. a threadlike structure that combines with others to form animal or vegetable tissue 2. any substance that can be separated into threadlike parts for weaving, etc. 3. texture 4. character or nature —**fi'brous** (-brəs) adj.

fi'ber·board' n. a boardlike material made from pressed fibers of wood, etc.

Fi'ber·glas' (-glas') a trademark for finespun filaments of glass made into

textiles or insulating material —n. [f-] this substance: also **fiberglass**

fi·bril·la·tion (fib'rə lā'shən) n. [< L. *fibra*, fiber + -ATION] a rapid series of contractions of the heart, causing weak, irregular heartbeats

fi·brin (fī'brən) n. a threadlike, elastic protein formed in blood clots

fi·brin·o·gen (fī brin'ə jən) n. [prec. + -GEN] a protein in the blood from which fibrin is formed

fi·broid (fī'broid) adj. like or composed of fibrous tissue, as a tumor

fi·bro·sis (fī brō'sis) n. an abnormal increase in the amount of fibrous connective tissue in an organ, part, etc.

fib·u·la (fib'yoo lə) n., pl. -**lae** (-lē'), -**las** [L., a clasp] the long, thin outer bone of the lower leg —**fib'u·lar** adj.

-fic (fik) [< L. *facere*, make] a suffix meaning making [terrific]

FICA Federal Insurance Contributions Act

-fi·ca·tion (fi kā'shən) [see -FIC] a suffix meaning a making [glorification]

fich·u (fish'oo) n. [Fr.] a triangular lace or muslin cape for women, worn with the ends fastened in front

fick·le (fik''l) adj. [< OE. *ficol*, tricky] changeable or unstable; capricious

fic·tion (fik'shən) n. [< L. *fingere*, to form] 1. an imaginary statement, story, etc. 2. a) any literary work with imaginary characters and events, as a novel, play, etc. b) such works collectively —**fic'tion·al** adj.

fic'tion·al·ize' (-'l īz') vt. -**ized'**, -**iz'ing** to deal with (historical events) as fiction

fic·ti·tious (fik tish'əs) adj. 1. of or like fiction; imaginary 2. false 3. assumed for disguise [a *fictitious* name]

fic·tive (fik'tiv) adj. 1. of fiction 2. imaginary —**fic'tive·ly** adv.

fid·dle (fid''l) n. [OE. *fithele*] [Colloq.] a violin —vi. -**dled**, -**dling** 1. [Colloq.] to play on a violin 2. to tinker (with) nervously —**fid'dler** n.

fid'dle·sticks' interj. nonsense!

fi·del·i·ty (fə del'ə tē, fī-) n., pl. -**ties** [< L. *fides*, faith] 1. faithful devotion to duty; loyalty 2. accuracy of description, sound reproduction, etc.

fidg·et (fij'it) n. [< ME. < ?] a restless or nervous state, esp. in phr. **the fidgets** —vi. to make restless or nervous movements —**fidg'et·y** adj.

fi·du·ci·ar·y (fi doo'shē er'ē) adj. [< L. *fiducia*, trust] holding or held in trust —n., pl. -**ies** a trustee

fie (fī) interj. for shame!

fief (fēf) n. [Fr.: see FEE] in feudalism, heritable land held by a vassal

field (fēld) n. [OE. *feld*] 1. a stretch of open land 2. a piece of cleared land for crops or pasture 3. a piece of land used for a particular purpose [a landing *field*] 4. any wide unbroken expanse [a *field* of ice] 5. a) a battlefield b) a battle 6. a realm of knowledge or work 7. the background, as on a flag 8. all the entrants in a contest 9. *Physics* a space within which magnetic or electrical lines of force are active —*vt.* 1. to stop or catch and return (a baseball, etc.) 2. to put (a player or a team) into active play —**play the field** to expand one's activities to a broad area —**field′er** *n.*

field glass(es) a small, portable, binocular telescope

field goal 1. *Basketball* a basket toss made from play, scoring two points 2. *Football* a goal kicked from the field, scoring three points

field hand a hired farm laborer

field hockey *same as* HOCKEY (sense 2)

field marshal in some armies, an officer of the highest rank

field′-test′ *vt.* to test (a device, method, etc.) under operating conditions

fiend (fēnd) *n.* [OE. *feond*] 1. an evil spirit; devil 2. an inhumanly wicked person 3. [Colloq.] an addict [a dope *fiend,* fresh-air *fiend*] —**fiend′ish** *adj.*

fierce (firs) *adj.* **fierc′er, fierc′est** [< L. *ferus,* wild] 1. savage 2. violent 3. intense [a *fierce* effort] 4. [Colloq.] very distasteful —**fierce′ly** *adv.* —**fierce′ness** *n.*

fi·er·y (fī′ər ē) *adj.* **-i·er, -i·est** 1. like fire; glaring, hot, etc. 2. ardent; spirited 3. excitable 4. inflamed

fi·es·ta (fē es′tə) *n.* [Sp. < L. *festus, festal*] 1. a religious festival 2. any gala celebration; holiday

fife (fīf) *n.* [G. *pfeife*] a small, shrill musical instrument like a flute

fif·teen (fif′tēn′) *adj., n.* [OE. *fiftene*] five more than ten; 15; XV —**fif′-teenth′** (-tēnth′) *adj., n.*

fifth (fifth) *adj.* [< OE. *fif,* five] preceded by four others in a series; 5th —*n.* 1. the one following the fourth 2. any of the five equal parts of something; 1/5 3. a fifth of a gallon

Fifth Amendment an amendment to the U.S. Constitution assuring certain legal safeguards, as that no person shall be compelled in any criminal case to be a witness against himself

fif·ty (fif′tē) *adj., n., pl.* **-ties** [OE. *fiftig*] five times ten; 50; L —**the fifties** the numbers or years, as of a century, from 50 through 59 —**fif′ti-eth** (-ith) *adj., n.*

fif′ty-fif′ty *adj.* [Colloq.] equal; even —*adv.* [Colloq.] equally

fig (fig) *n.* [< L. *ficus*] 1. *a)* a small, sweet, pear-shaped fruit that grows on a tree related to the mulberry *b)* the tree 2. a trifle [not worth a *fig*]

fig. 1. figurative(ly) 2. figure(s)

fight (fīt) *vi.* **fought, fight′ing** [OE. *feohtan*] to take part in a struggle, contest, etc. esp. against a foe or for a cause —*vt.* 1. to oppose physically or in battle 2. to struggle against 3. to engage in (a war, etc.) 4. to gain (one's way) by struggle —*n.* 1. any struggle, contest, or quarrel 2. power or readiness to fight

fight′er *n.* 1. one that fights; esp., a prizefighter 2. a fast, highly maneuverable combat airplane

fig·ment (fig′mənt) *n.* [< L. *fingere,*

to make] something merely imagined

fig·u·ra·tion (fig′yə rā′shən) *n.* [see FIGURE] 1. a forming; shaping 2. form; appearance

fig·u·ra·tive (fig′yər ə tiv) *adj.* 1. representing by means of a figure or symbol 2. not in its usual or exact sense; metaphorical 3. using figures of speech —**fig′u·ra·tive·ly** *adv.*

fig·ure (fig′yər) *n.* [< L. *fingere,* to form] 1. an outline or shape; form 2. the human form 3. a person thought of in a specified way [a historical *figure*] 4. a likeness of a person or thing 5. an illustration; diagram 6. a design; pattern 7. the symbol for a number 8. [*pl.*] arithmetic 9. a sum of money 10. *Geom.* a surface or space bounded by lines or planes —*vt.* **-ured, -ur·ing** 1. to represent in definite form 2. to imagine 3. to ornament with a design 4. to compute with figures 5. [Colloq.] to believe; consider —*vi.* 1. to appear prominently 2. to do arithmetic —**figure in** to include —**figure on** to rely on —**figure out** 1. to solve 2. to understand —**figure up** to add; total

fig′ure·head′ *n.* 1. a carved figure on the bow of a ship 2. one put in a position of leadership, but having no real power or authority

figure of speech an expression, as a metaphor or simile, using words in a nonliteral or unusual sense

fig·u·rine (fig′yə rēn′) *n.* [Fr.] a small sculptured or molded figure

Fi·ji (fē′jē) country on a group of islands (**Fiji Islands**) in the SW Pacific, north of New Zealand: 7,000 sq. mi.; pop. 535,000

fil·a·ment (fil′ə mənt) *n.* [< L. *filum,* thread] a very slender thread or threadlike part; specif., the fine wire in a light bulb or electron tube

fil·bert (fil′bərt) *n.* [ME. *filberde*] *same as* HAZELNUT

filch (filch) *vt.* [ME. *filchen*] to steal (usually something small or petty)

file¹ (fīl) *vt.* **filed, fil′ing** [< L. *filum,* thread] 1. to put (papers, etc.) in order for future reference 2. to dispatch or register (a news story, application, etc.) 3. to put on public record —*vi.* 1. to move in a line 2. to make application (*for* divorce, etc.) —*n.* 1. a container for keeping papers, etc. in order 2. an orderly arrangement of papers, etc. 3. a line of persons or things —**file′a·ble** *adj.* —**fil′er** *n.*

file² (fīl) *n.* [OE. *feol*] a steel tool with a rough, ridged surface for smoothing or grinding —*vt.* **filed, fil′ing** to smooth or grind, as with a file

fi·let mi·gnon (fi lā′ min yōn′) [Fr., lit., tiny fillet] a thick, round cut of lean beef tenderloin broiled

fil·i·al (fil′ē əl, fil′yəl) *adj.* [< L. *filius,* son] of, suitable to, or due from a son or daughter

fil·i·bus·ter (fil′ə bus′tər) *n.* [< Sp. < MDu. *vrijbuiter,* freebooter] 1. a member of a legislature who obstructs a bill by making long speeches 2. such obstruction of a bill —*vt., vi.* to obstruct (a bill) by such methods

fil·i·gree (fil′ə grē′) *n.* [< L. *filum,*

thread + *granum*, grain] lacelike ornamental work of intertwined wire of gold, silver, etc. —*vt.* -greed´, -gree´ing to ornament with filigree

fil·ing (fīl´iŋ) *n.* a small piece scraped off with a file: *usually in pl.*

Fil·i·pi·no (fil´ə pē´nō) *n., pl.* -nos [Sp.] a native of the Philippines —*adj.* Philippine

fill (fil) *vt.* [OE. *fyllan*] 1. to put as much as possible into 2. to occupy wholly 3. to put a person into or to occupy (a position, etc.) 4. to supply the things called for in (an order, etc.) 5. to close or plug (holes, etc.) —*vi.* to become full —*n.* 1. enough to make full or to satisfy 2. anything that fills —**fill in** 1. to complete by supplying something 2. to supply for completion 3. to be a substitute —**fill out** 1. to make or become larger, etc. 2. to make (a document, etc.) complete with data —**fill up** to make or become completely full —**fill´er** *n.*

fil·let (fil´it; *for n. 2 & v. usually* fil´ā, fi lā´) *n.* [< L. *filum*, thread] 1. a thin strip or band 2. a boneless, lean piece of fish or meat —*vt.* to bone and slice (fish or meat)

fill´-in´ *n.* 1. one that fills a vacancy or gap 2. [Colloq.] a brief summary of the pertinent facts

fill´ing *n.* a substance used to fill something, as gold in a tooth cavity

filling station *same as* SERVICE STATION

fil·lip (fil´əp) *n.* [< FLIP¹] 1. an outward snap of a finger from the thumb 2. something stimulating —*vt.* to strike or toss with a fillip

Fill·more (fil´mōr), **Mill·ard** (mil´ərd) 1800–74; 13th president of the U.S. (1850–53)

fil·ly (fil´ē) *n., pl.* -lies [< ON. *fylja*] a young female horse

film (film) *n.* [OE. *filmen*] 1. a fine, thin skin, coating, etc. 2. a flexible cellulose material covered with a substance sensitive to light and used in photography 3. a haze or blur 4. a motion picture —*vt., vi.* 1. to cover or be covered as with a film 2. to photograph or make a motion picture (of)

film´strip´ *n.* a strip of film for projection, with stills of pictures, charts, etc. on some subject

film´y *adj.* -i·er, -i·est 1. gauzy; sheer; thin 2. blurred; hazy

fil·ter (fil´tər) *n.* [< ML. *filtrum*, FELT¹] 1. a device or substance for straining out solid particles, impurities, etc. from a liquid or gas 2. a device or substance for screening out electric oscillations, light waves, etc. of certain frequencies —*vt., vi.* 1. to pass through or as through a filter 2. to remove with a filter —**fil´ter·a·ble**, **fil´tra·ble** (-trə b'l) *adj.*

filter tip 1. a cigarette with a tip of cellulose, cotton, etc. for filtering the smoke 2. such a tip

filth (filth) *n.* [OE. *fylthe*] 1. foul dirt

2. obscenity —**filth´i·ness** *n.* —**filth´y** *adj.* -i·er, -i·est

fil·trate (fil´trāt) *vt.* -trat·ed, -trat·ing to filter —*n.* a filtered liquid —**fil·tra´tion** *n.*

fin (fin) *n.* [OE. *finn*] 1. any of several winglike organs on the body of a fish, dolphin, etc., used in swimming 2. anything like this in shape or use

fi·na·gle (fə nā´g'l) *vt., vi.* -gled, -gling [< ?] [Colloq.] to use, or get by, craftiness or trickery —**fi·na´gler** *n.*

fi·nal (fī´n'l) *adj.* [< L. *finis*, end] 1. of or coming at the end; last 2. deciding; conclusive —*n.* 1. anything final 2. [*pl.*] the last of a series of contests 3. a final examination —**fi·nal´i·ty** (-nal´ə tē) *n.* —**fi´nal·ly** *adv.*

fi·na·le (fə nä´lē) *n.* [It.] the concluding part of a musical work, etc.

fi´nal·ist *n.* a contestant in the final, deciding contest of a series

fi´nal·ize *vt.* -ized´, -iz´ing to make final; complete —**fi´nal·i·za´tion** *n.*

fi·nance (fə nans´, fī´nans) *n.* [< L. *finis*, end] 1. [*pl.*] money resources, income, etc. 2. the science of managing money —*vt.* -nanced´, -nanc´ing to supply or get money for —**fi·nan´cial** (-nan´shəl) *adj.* —**fi·nan´cial·ly** *adv.*

fin·an·cier (fin´ən sir´, fī´nan-) *n.* [Fr.] one skilled in finance

finch (finch) *n.* [OE. *finc*] any of a group of small songbirds, including the canary, cardinal, etc.

find (fīnd) *vt.* found, find´ing [OE. *findan*] 1. to discover by chance; come upon 2. to get by searching 3. to perceive; learn 4. to recover (something lost) 5. to reach; attain 6. to decide and declare to be —*vi.* to reach a decision [the jury *found* for the accused] —*n.* a finding 2. something found —**find out** to discover; learn

find´er *n.* 1. one that finds 2. a camera device for sighting the field of view

find´ing *n.* 1. discovery 2. something found 3. [*often pl.*] the verdict of a judge, scholar, etc.

fine¹ (fīn) *adj.* fin´er, fin´est [< L. *finis*, end] 1. very good; excellent 2. with no impurities; refined 3. clear and bright [*fine* weather] 4. not heavy or coarse [*fine* sand] 5. very thin or small [*fine* print] 6. sharp [a *fine* edge] 7. subtle; delicate [a *fine* distinction] 8. elegant —*adv.* 1. in a fine manner 2. [Colloq.] very well —**fine´ly** *adv.* —**fine´ness** *n.*

fine² (fīn) *n.* [see prec.] a sum of money paid as a penalty —*vt.* fined, fin´ing to order to pay a fine

fine arts any of certain art forms, esp. drawing, painting, sculpture, etc.

fin·er·y (fīn´ər ē) *n., pl.* -ies elaborate clothes, jewelry, etc.

fi·nesse (fi nes´) *n.* [Fr.: see FINE¹] 1. adroitness; skill 2. the ability to handle delicate situations diplomatically 3. cunning; artfulness

fin·ger (fiŋ'gər) n. [OE.] 1. any of the five jointed parts extending from the palm of the hand, esp. one other than the thumb 2. anything like a finger in shape or use —vt. 1. to touch with the fingers; handle 2. *Music* to use the fingers in a certain way in playing —**have** (or **keep**) **one's fingers crossed** to hope for something —**put one's finger on** to ascertain exactly

fin'ger·board' n. the part of a stringed instrument against which the strings are pressed to produce the desired tones

fin'ger·ling (-liŋ) n. a small fish

fin'ger·nail' n. the horny substance at the upper end of a finger

finger painting a painting done by using the fingers, hand, or arm to spread paints made of starch, glycerine, and pigments (**finger paints**) on wet paper —**fin'ger-paint'** vi., vt.

fin'ger·print' n. an impression of the lines and whorls on a finger tip, used to identify a person —vt. to take the fingerprints of

finger tip the tip of a finger —**have at one's finger tips** to have available for instant use

fin·i·al (fin'ē əl) n. [ult. < L. *finis*, end] a decorative terminal part at the tip of a spire, lamp, etc.

fin·ick·y (fin'i kē) adj. [< FINE¹] too particular; fussy: also **fin'i·cal** (-k'l), **fin'ick·ing**

fi·nis (fin'is, fē nē') n., pl. **-nis·es** [L.] the end; finish

FINIAL

fin·ish (fin'ish) vt. [< L. *finis*, end] 1. a) to bring to an end b) to come to the end of 2. to consume all of 3. to give final touches to; perfect 4. to give a desired surface effect to —vi. to come to an end —n. 1. the last part; end 2. a) anything used to finish a surface b) the finished effect 3. means or manner of completing or perfecting 4. polished manners, speech, etc. —**finish off** 1. to end 2. to kill or ruin —**finish with** to bring to an end —**fin'ished** adj. —**fin'ish·er** n.

fi·nite (fi'nit) adj. [< L. *finis*, end] having definable limits; not infinite

fink (fiŋk) n. [< ?] [Slang] an informer or strikebreaker

Fin·land (fin'lənd) country in N Europe: 130,119 sq. mi.; pop. 4,664,000

Finn (fin) n. a native or inhabitant of Finland

fin·nan had·die (fin'ən had'ē) [prob. < *Findhorn* (Scotland) *haddock*] smoked haddock

Finn·ish (fin'ish) adj. of Finland, its people, their language, etc. —n. the language of the Finns: abbrev. **Finn.**

fin·ny (fin'ē) adj. 1. having fins 2. like a fin 3. of, full of, or being fish

fiord (fyôrd) n. [Norw. < ON. *fjörthr*] a narrow inlet of the sea bordered by steep cliffs

fir (fur) n. [OE. *fyrh*] 1. a cone-bearing evergreen tree of the pine family 2. its wood

fire (fir) n. [OE. *fyr*] 1. the flame, heat, and light of combustion 2. something burning 3. a destructive burning [a forest *fire*] 4. strong feeling 5. a discharge of firearms —vt., vi. **fired, fir'ing** 1. to start burning; ignite 2. to supply with fuel 3. to bake (bricks, etc.) in a kiln 4. to excite or become excited 5. to shoot (a gun, bullet, etc.) 6. to hurl or direct with force 7. to dismiss from a position; discharge —**catch** (**on**) **fire** to ignite —**on fire** 1. burning 2. greatly excited —**under fire** under attack —**fir'er** n.

fire'arm' n. any hand weapon from which a shot is fired by explosive force, as a rifle or pistol

fire'base' n. a military base in a combat zone, from which artillery, rockets, etc. are fired

fire'bomb' n. an incendiary bomb —vt. to attack or damage with a firebomb

fire'brand' n. 1. a piece of burning wood 2. one who stirs up others to revolt or strife

fire'break' (-brāk') n. a strip of forest or prairie land cleared or plowed to stop the spread of fire

fire'brick' n. a highly heat-resistant brick for lining fireplaces or furnaces

fire'bug' n. [Colloq.] one who compulsively starts destructive fires

fire'crack'er n. a roll of paper containing an explosive, set off as a noise-maker at celebrations, etc.

fire'damp' n. *same as* DAMP (sense 2)

fire'dog' (-dôg') n. *same as* ANDIRON

fire engine a motor truck with equipment for fighting fires

fire escape an outside stairway, etc. for escape from a burning building

fire'fight'er n. a person who helps fight fires —**fire'fight'ing** n.

fire'fly' n., pl. **-flies'** a winged beetle whose abdomen glows with a luminescent light

fire'man (-mən) n., pl. **-men** 1. a man whose work is fighting fires 2. a man who tends a fire in a furnace, etc.

fire'place' n. a place for a fire, esp. an open place built in a wall

fire'plug' n. a street hydrant supplying water for fighting fires

fire'proof' adj. not easily destroyed by fire —vt. to make fireproof

fire'side' n. 1. the space around a fireplace 2. home or home life

fire'storm' n. an intense fire over a wide area, as one caused by an atomic explosion with its high winds

fire tower a tower used as a lookout for forest fires

fire'trap' n. a building easily set afire or hard to get out of if afire

fire'wa'ter n. [Colloq.] alcoholic liquor

fire'wood' n. wood used as fuel

fire'works' n. pl. firecrackers, rockets, etc., for noisy effects or brilliant displays: *sometimes used in sing.*

firing line 1. the line from which gunfire is directed at the enemy 2. any vulnerable front position

firm¹ (furm) adj. [< L. *firmus*] 1. solid; hard 2. not moved easily; fixed 3. unchanging; steady 4. resolute; constant 5. showing determination;

strong 6. definite *[a firm contract]* —*vt.*, *vi.* to make or become firm — **firm′ly** *adv.* —**firm′ness** *n.*

firm² (fʉrm) *n.* [< It. < L. *firmus*, firm] a business company

fir·ma·ment (fʉr′mə mənt) *n.* [< L. *firmus*, firm] the sky, viewed poetically as a solid arch or vault

first (fʉrst) *adj.* [OE. *fyrst*] 1. before all others in a series; 1st 2. earliest 3. foremost, as in rank, quality, etc. — *adv.* 1. before anyone or anything else 2. for the first time 3. sooner; preferably —*n.* 1. any person or thing that is first 2. the beginning 3. the winning place, as in a race 4. low gear

first aid emergency treatment for injury, etc. before regular medical aid is available —**first′-aid′** *adj.*

first′born′ *adj.* born first in a family; oldest —*n.* the firstborn child

first′-class′ *adj.* 1. of the highest class, quality, etc. 2. of the most expensive regular class of sealed mail —*adv.* 1. with first-class accommodations 2. by first-class mail

first′hand′ *adj.*, *adv.* from the original producer or source; direct

first lady *[often* F- L-] the wife of the U.S. president

first lieutenant a military officer ranking just above a second lieutenant

first′ly *adv.* in the first place; first

first person that form of a pronoun or verb which refers to the speaker

first′-rate′ *adj.* highest in quality, rank, etc. —*adv.* [Colloq.] very well

first′-string′ *adj.* [Colloq.] *Sports* that is the first choice for regular play at the specified position

firth (fʉrth) *n.* [< ON. *fjörthr*] a narrow inlet or arm of the sea

fis·cal (fis′kəl) *adj.* [< L. *fiscus*, public chest] 1. relating to the public treasury or revenues 2. financial —**fis′cal·ly** *adv.*

fish (fish) *n.*, *pl.* **fish**; in referring to different species, **fish′es** [OE. *fisc*] 1. any of a large group of coldblooded animals living in water and having backbones, gills for breathing, and fins 2. the flesh of a fish used as food —*vi.* 1. to catch or try to catch fish 2. to try to get something indirectly (often with *for*) —*vt.* to grope for, find, and bring to view (often with *out*)

fish′er (-ər) *n.* 1. an animal related to the marten, with dark fur 2. this fur

fish′er·man (-ər mən) *n.*, *pl.* **-men** 1. a person who fishes for sport or for a living 2. a ship used in fishing

fish′er·y *n.*, *pl.* **-ies** 1. the business of catching fish 2. a place where fish are caught or bred

fish′eye′ lens a camera lens designed for a full 180° field of vision

fish′hook′ *n.* a hook, usually barbed, for catching fish

fish′ing *n.* the catching of fish for sport or for a living

fish′wife′ *n.*, *pl.* **-wives′** a coarse, scolding woman

fish′y *adj.* **-i·er**, **-i·est** 1. like a fish in odor, taste, etc. 2. dull; without expression *[a fishy stare]* 3. [Colloq.] questionable; odd —**fish′i·ness** *n.*

fis·sion (fish′ən) *n.* [< L. *findere*, to split] 1. a splitting apart; cleavage 2. *same as* NUCLEAR FISSION —**fis′sion·a·ble** *adj.*

fis·sure (fish′ər) *n.* [see prec.] a cleft or crack

fist (fist) *n.* [OE. *fyst*] a hand with the fingers closed tightly into the palm

fis·ti·cuffs (fis′ti kufs′) *n.pl.* 1. a fight with the fists 2. *same as* BOXING

fis·tu·la (fis′choo lə) *n.*, *pl.* **-las**, **-lae′** (-lē′) [L.] an abnormal passage, as from an abscess to the skin

fit¹ (fit) *vt.* **fit′ted** or **fit**, **fit′ted**, **fit′ting** [ME. *fitten*] 1. to be suitable to 2. to be the proper size, shape, etc. for 3. to adjust so as to fit 4. to equip; outfit —*vi.* 1. to be suitable or proper 2. to have the proper size or shape —*adj.* **fit′ter**, **fit′test** 1. suited to some purpose, function, etc. 2. proper; right 3. healthy 4. [Colloq.] inclined; ready —*n.* the manner of fitting *[a tight fit]* —**fit′ly** *adv.* — **fit′ness** *n.* —**fit′ter** *n.*

fit² (fit) *n.* [OE. *fitt*, conflict] 1. any sudden, uncontrollable attack, as of coughing 2. an outburst, as of anger 3. a seizure involving convulsions or loss of consciousness —**by fits (and starts)** in an irregular way —**have (or throw) a fit** [Colloq.] to become very angry or upset

fit′ful (-fəl) *adj.* characterized by intermittent activity; spasmodic — **fit′ful·ly** *adv.* —**fit′ful·ness** *n.*

fit′ting *adj.* suitable; proper —*n.* 1. an adjustment or trying on of clothes, etc. 2. a small part used to join or adapt other parts 3. *[pl.]* fixtures

five (fīv) *adj.*, *n.* [OE. *fīf*] one more than four; 5; V

five′-and-ten′-cent′ store a store that sells a wide variety of inexpensive merchandise: also **five′-and-ten′** *n.*

fix (fiks) *vt.* **fixed**, **fix′ing** [< L. *figere*, fasten] 1. to fasten firmly 2. to set firmly in the mind 3. to direct (one's eyes) steadily at something 4. to make rigid 5. to make permanent 6. to establish (a date, etc.) definitely 7. to set in order; adjust 8. to repair 9. to prepare (food or meals) 10. [Colloq.] to influence the result or action of (a race, jury, etc.) as by bribery 11. [Colloq.] to punish —*vi.* 1. to become fixed 2. [Dial.] to prepare or intend —*n.* 1. the position of a ship, etc. determined from the bearings of two known positions 2. [Colloq.] a predicament 3. [Slang] a situation that has been fixed (sense 10) 4. [Slang] an injection of a narcotic by an addict —**fix up** [Colloq.] 1. to repair 2. to arrange; set in order —**fix′a·ble** *adj.* —**fix′er** *n.*

fix·a·tion (fik sā′shən) *n.* 1. a fixing or being fixed 2. an obsession 3. a remaining at an early stage of psycho-sexual development

fix·a·tive (fik′sə tiv) *adj.* that can, or tends to, make permanent, prevent fading, etc. —*n.* a fixative substance

fixed (fikst) *adj.* 1. firmly in place 2. clearly established 3. resolute; unchanging 4. persistent [a *fixed* idea] —**fix′ed·ly** (fik′sid lē) *adv.*

fix·ings (fik′siŋz) *n.pl.* [Colloq.] accessories or trimmings

fix·i·ty (fik′sə tē) *n.* the quality or state of being fixed or steady

fix·ture (fiks′chər) *n.* [see FIX] 1. anything firmly in place 2. any attached piece of equipment in a house, etc. 3. a person long-established in a job, etc.

fizz (fiz) *n.* [echoic] 1. a hissing, bubbling sound 2. an effervescent drink —*vi.* fizzed, fizz′ing 1. to make a bubbling sound 2. to effervesce

fiz·zle (fiz′'l) *vi.* -zled, -zling [< ME.] 1. *same as* FIZZ 2. [Colloq.] to fail, esp. after a good start —*n.* 1. a hissing sound 2. [Colloq.] a failure

fjord (fyôrd) *n. same as* FIORD

fl. 1. floor 2. [L. *floruit*] (he or she) flourished 3. fluid

Fla., **FL** Florida

flab (flab) *n.* [back-formation < FLABBY] [Colloq.] sagging flesh

flab·ber·gast (flab′ər gast′) *vt.* [18th-c. slang < ?] to dumbfound

flab·by (flab′ē) *adj.* -bi·er, -bi·est [< FLAP] 1. limp and soft 2. weak —**flab′bi·ly** *adv.* —**flab′bi·ness** *n.*

flac·cid (flak′sid, flas′id) *adj.* [< L. *flaccus*] soft and limp; flabby

flack (flak) *n.* [< ?] [Slang] *same as* PRESS AGENT

‡fla·con (flä kōn′) *n.* [Fr.] a small flask with a stopper, for perfume, etc.

flag¹ (flag) *n.* [< ? FLAG⁴, to flutter] a cloth with colors, patterns, etc. used as a symbol, as of a nation, or as a signal —*vt.* flagged, flag′ging to signal as with a flag; esp., to signal to stop (often with *down*)

flag² (flag) *n.* [< ON. *flaga*, slab of stone] a flagstone —*vt.* flagged, flag′ging to pave with flagstones

flag³ (flag) *n.* [ME. *flagge*] any of various irises, or a flower or leaf of one

flag⁴ (flag) *vi.* flagged, flag′ging [< ? ON. *flakka*, flutter] 1. to become limp 2. to grow weak or tired

flag·el·late (flaj′ə lāt′) *vt.* -lat′ed, -lat′ing [< L. *flagellum*, a whip] to whip —**flag′el·la′tion** *n.*

flag·on (flag′ən) *n.* [< LL. *flasca*] a container for liquids, with a handle, narrow neck, spout, and, often, a lid

flag′pole′ *n.* a pole on which a flag is raised and flown: also **flag′staff′**

fla·grant (flā′grənt) *adj.* [< L. *flagrare*, to blaze] glaringly bad; outrageous —**fla′gran·cy** (-grən sē), **fla′grance** *n.* —**fla′grant·ly** *adv.*

flag′ship′ *n.* the ship that carries the commander of a fleet or squadron

flag′stone′ *n.* a flat paving stone

flail (flāl) *n.* [< L. *flagellum*, a whip] a farm tool for threshing grain by hand —*vt., vi.* 1. to thresh with a flail 2. to beat 3. to move (one's arms) like flails

flair (fler) *n.* [< L. *fragrare*, to smell] 1. a natural talent; aptitude 2. [Colloq.] a sense of style; dash

flak (flak) *n.* [G. acronym] 1. the fire of antiaircraft guns 2. strong criticism: also **flack**

flake (flāk) *n.* [< Scand.] 1. a small, thin mass 2. a piece split off; chip —*vt., vi.* flaked, flak′ing 1. to form into flakes 2. to peel off in flakes —**flak′y** *adj.* -i·er, -i·est

‡flam·bé (flän bā′) *adj.* [Fr.] served with a brandy or rum sauce set afire to flame —*n.* a dessert so served

flam·boy·ant (flam boi′ənt) *adj.* [< Fr. < L. *flamma*, a flame] 1. flamelike or brilliant 2. ornate; too showy —**flam·boy′ance** *n.* —**flam·boy′ant·ly** *adv.*

flame (flām) *n.* [< L. *flamma*] 1. the burning gas of a fire, appearing as a tongue of light 2. the state of burning with a blaze 3. a thing like a flame 4. an intense emotion 5. a sweetheart: now humorous —*vi.* flamed, flam′ing 1. to burst into flame 2. to grow red or hot 3. to become excited

fla·men·co (flä meŋ′kō) *n.* [Sp.] Spanish gypsy style of music or dancing

flame′out′ *n.* a failure of combustion in a jet engine during flight

flame thrower a military weapon that shoots flaming gasoline, oil, etc.

fla·min·go (flä miŋ′gō) *n., pl.* -gos, -goes [Port.] a tropical wading bird with long legs and pink or red feathers

flam·ma·ble (flam′ə b'l) *adj.* easily set on fire; that will burn readily —**flam′ma·bil′i·ty** *n.*

Flan·ders (flan′dərz) region in NW Europe, in France, Belgium, & the Netherlands

flange (flanj) *n.* [< ? ME.] a projecting rim on a wheel, etc., as to hold it in place or give it strength

flank (flaŋk) *n.* [< OFr. *flanc*] 1. the side of an animal between the ribs and the hip 2. the side of anything 3. Mil. the right or left side of a formation —*vt.* 1. to be at the side of 2. to attack, or pass around, the side of (enemy troops)

flank·en (flaŋ′kən, flän′-) *n.* [Yid. < G. *flanke*, flank] a thin cut of beef from the forequarter, usually boiled

flan·nel (flan′'l) *n.* [prob. < W. *gwlan*, wool] 1. a loosely woven cloth of wool or cotton 2. [*pl.*] trousers, etc. made of this

flan·nel·ette, **flan·nel·et** (flan′ə let′) *n.* a soft, fleecy, cotton cloth

flap (flap) *n.* [ME. *flappe*] 1. anything flat and broad hanging loose at one end 2. the motion or sound of a swinging flap 3. a slap 4. [Slang] a commotion; stir —*vt., vi.* flapped, flap′ping 1. to slap 2. to move back and forth or up and down, as wings

flap′jack′ *n.* a pancake

flap·per (flap′ər) *n.* 1. one that flaps 2. [Colloq.] in the 1920's, a bold, unconventional young woman

flare (fler) *vi.* flared, flar′ing [ME. *fleare* < ?] **1.** *a)* to blaze brightly *b)* to burn unsteadily **2.** to blaze brightly **3.** to burst out suddenly, as in anger (often with *up* or *out*) **3.** to curve outward, as a bell lip —*n.* **1.** a bright, unsteady blaze **2.** a brightly flaming light for signaling, etc. **3.** an outburst, as of emotion **4.** a curving outward

flare′-up′ *n.* a sudden outburst of flame or of anger, trouble, etc.

flash (flash) *vi.* [ME. *flashen*, to splash] **1.** to send out a sudden, brief light **2.** to sparkle **3.** to come or pass suddenly —*vt.* **1.** to cause to flash **2.** to send (news, etc.) swiftly —*n.* **1.** a sudden, brief light **2.** a brief moment **3.** a sudden, brief display **4.** a brief news item sent by radio, etc. **5.** a gaudy display —*adj.* happening swiftly or suddenly —flash′er *n.*

flash′back′ *n.* an interruption in the continuity of a story, etc. by telling or showing an earlier episode

flash′bulb′ *n.* a bulb giving a brief, dazzling light, for taking photographs

flash′cube′ *n.* a rotating cube containing flashbulbs in four sides

flash′-for′ward *n.* an interruption in the continuity of a story, etc. by telling or showing a future episode

flash′ing *n.* sheets of metal used to weatherproof roof joints or edges

flash′light′ *n.* **1.** a portable electric light **2.** a brief, dazzling light for taking photographs, esp. indoors

flash point the lowest temperature at which vapor, as of an oil, will ignite with a flash

flash′y *adj.* -i·er, -i·est **1.** dazzling **2.** gaudy; showy —flash′i·ness *n.*

flask (flask) *n.* [< LL. *flasco*, bottle] **1.** any of various bottles used in laboratories, etc. **2.** a small, flat pocket container for liquor, etc.

flat¹ (flat) *adj.* flat′ter, flat′test [< ON. *flatr*] **1.** having a smooth, level surface **2.** lying spread out **3.** broad, even, and thin **4.** absolute [a *flat* denial] **5.** not fluctuating [a *flat* rate] **6.** tasteless; insipid **7.** not interesting **8.** emptied of air [a *flat* tire] **9.** without gloss [*flat* paint] **10.** *Music* below true pitch —*adv.* **1.** in a flat manner or position **2.** exactly **3.** *Music* below true pitch —*n.* **1.** anything flat, esp. a surface, part, or expanse **2.** a deflated tire **3.** *Music a)* a note one half step below another *b)* the symbol (♭) for this —*vt.*, *vi.* flat′ted, flat′ting to make or become flat —flat′ly *adv.* —flat′ness *n.* —flat′tish *adj.*

flat² (flat) *n.* [< Scot. dial. *flet*, floor] an apartment or suite of rooms

flat′bed′, **flat′-bed′** *n.* a truck, trailer, etc. having a platform without sides or stakes

flat′boat′ *n.* a flat-bottomed boat for carrying freight on rivers, etc.

flat′car′ *n.* a railroad freight car without sides or a roof

flat′fish′ *n.*, *pl.*: see FISH a flat-bodied

fish with both eyes on the upper side, as the flounder

flat′foot′ *n.* **1.** a condition of the foot in which the instep arch is flattened **2.** *pl.* **-foots′** [Slang] a policeman —flat′-foot′ed *adj.*

flat′i′ron *n.* same as IRON (sense 2)

flat′ten (-'n) *vt.*, *vi.* to make or become flat or flatter

flat·ter (flat′ər) *vt.* [< OFr. *flater*, to smooth] **1.** to praise insincerely **2.** to try to please, as by praise **3.** to make seem more attractive than is so **4.** to gratify the vanity of —flat′ter·er *n.* —flat′ter·ing·ly *adv.* —flat′ter·y *n.*

flat′top′ *n.* [Slang] an aircraft carrier

flat·u·lent (flach′ə lənt) *adj.* [ult. < L. *flare*, to blow] **1.** having or producing gas in the stomach or intestines **2.** pompous —flat′u·lence *n.*

flat′ware′ *n.* flat tableware

flaunt (flônt) *vi.*, *vt.* [< ? dial. *flant*, to strut] to show off proudly or defiantly —flaunt′ing·ly *adv.*

flau·tist (flôt′ist, flout′-) *n.* [< It.] one who plays the flute; flutist

fla·vor (flā′vər) *n.* [ult. < L. *flare*, to blow] **1.** that quality of a substance that is a mixing of its characteristic taste and smell **2.** flavoring **3.** characteristic quality —*vt.* to give flavor to Brit. sp. flavour —fla′vor·ful *adj.* —fla′vor·less *adj.*

fla′vor·ing *n.* an essence, extract, etc. that adds flavor to food or drink

flaw (flô) *n.* [prob. < Scand.] **1.** a crack, as in a gem **2.** a defect; fault —flaw′less *adj.* —flaw′less·ly *adv.* —flaw′less·ness *n.*

flax (flaks) *n.* [OE. *fleax*] **1.** a slender, erect plant with delicate, blue flowers: its seed (flaxseed) is used to make linseed oil **2.** the threadlike fibers of this plant, spun into linen thread

flax′en (-'n) *adj.* **1.** of or made of flax **2.** pale-yellow

flay (flā) *vt.* [OE. *flean*] **1.** to strip off the skin of **2.** to criticize harshly

flea (flē) *n.* [OE. *fleah*] a small, wingless, jumping insect that is a bloodsucking parasite as an adult

flea market an outdoor bazaar dealing mainly in cheap, secondhand goods

fleck (flek) *n.* [ON. *flekkr*] a spot, speck, or flake —*vt.* to spot; speckle

fled (fled) *pt.* & *pp.* of FLEE

fledg·ling (flej′liŋ) *n.* [< ME. *flegge*, fit to fly] **1.** a young bird just able to fly **2.** a young, inexperienced person Also, chiefly Brit., fledgeling

flee (flē) *vi.*, *vt.* fled, flee′ing [OE. *fleon*] **1.** to go swiftly or escape, as from danger, etc. **2.** to vanish

fleece (flēs) *n.* [OE. *fleos*] **1.** the wool covering a sheep or similar animal **2.** a soft, napped fabric —*vt.* fleeced, fleec′ing **1.** to shear the fleece from **2.** to swindle —fleec′er *n.*

fleec′y *adj.* -i·er, -i·est of or like fleece; soft and light —fleec′i·ness *n.*

fleet¹ (flēt) *n.* [OE. *fleot*] **1.** a number of warships under one command **2.** any group of ships, trucks, etc. under one control

fleet² (flēt) *adj.* [< OE. *fleotan*, to float] swift; rapid —**fleet′ness** *n.*

fleet′ing *adj.* passing swiftly —**fleet′ing·ly** *adv.* —**fleet′ing·ness** *n.*

Flem·ish (flem′ish) *adj.* of Flanders, its people, or their language —*n.* the West Germanic language of Flanders

flesh (flesh) *n.* [OE. *flæsc*] 1. the soft substance of the body; esp., the muscular tissue 2. the pulpy part of fruits and vegetables 3. meat 4. the body as distinct from the soul 5. all mankind 6. yellowish pink —**in the flesh** 1. alive 2. in person —**one's (own) flesh and blood** one's close relatives —**flesh′y** *adj.* **-i·er, -i·est**

flesh′ly *adj.* **-li·er, -li·est** 1. of the body; corporeal 2. sensual 3. fleshy

fleur-de-lis (flur′də lē′) *n., pl.* **fleurs′-de-lis′** (-lēz′) [< OFr. *fleur de lis*, lit., flower of the lily] a lilylike emblem: the coat of arms of the former French royal family

flew (flo͞o) *pt. of* FLY¹

flex (fleks) *vt., vi.* [< L. *flectere*, to bend] 1. to bend (an arm, etc.) 2. to contract (a muscle)

flex·i·ble (flek′sə b'l) *adj.* 1. able to bend without breaking; pliant 2. easily influenced 3. adjustable to change —**flex′i·bil′i·ty** *n.*

flib·ber·ti·gib·bet (flib′ər tē jib′it) *n.* [< ?] a frivolous, flighty person

flick¹ (flik) *n.* [echoic] a light, quick stroke —*vt.* to strike, throw, etc. with a light, quick stroke

flick² (flik) *n.* [< ff.] [Slang] a movie —**the flicks** a showing of a movie

flick′er *vi.* [OE. *flicorian*] 1. to move with a quick, light, wavering motion 2. to burn or shine unsteadily —*n.* 1. a flickering 2. a dart of flame or light

fli·er (flī′ər) *n.* 1. a thing that flies 2. an aviator 3. a bus, train, etc. with a fast schedule 4. a widely distributed handbill 5. [Colloq.] a reckless gamble

flight¹ (flīt) *n.* [OE. *flyht*] 1. the act, manner, or power of flying 2. the distance flown 3. a group of things flying together 4. an airplane scheduled to fly a certain trip 5. a trip by airplane 6. a soaring above the ordinary [a *flight* of fancy] 7. a set of stairs, as between landings

flight² (flīt) *n.* [< OE. *fleon*, flee] a fleeing, as from danger

flight attendant an attendant on an airplane who sees to passenger comfort

flight′less *adj.* not able to fly

flight strip an emergency runway

flight′y *adj.* **-i·er, -i·est** 1. given to sudden whims; frivolous 2. slightly demented or silly —**flight′i·ness** *n.*

flim·sy (flim′zē) *adj.* **-si·er, -si·est** [< ?] 1. easily broken or damaged; frail 2. ineffectual [a *flimsy* excuse] —**flim′si·ly** *adv.* —**flim′si·ness** *n.*

flinch (flinch) *vi.* [< OFr. *flenchir*] to draw back from a blow or anything difficult or painful —*n.* a flinching

fling (fliŋ) *vt.* **flung, fling′ing** [< ON. *flengja*, to whip] 1. to throw, esp. with force; hurl 2. to put abruptly or violently 3. to move (one's arms,

legs, etc.) suddenly —*n.* 1. a flinging 2. a brief time of wild pleasures 3. a spirited dance 4. [Colloq.] a try

Flint (flint) city in SE Mich.: pop. 160,000

flint (flint) *n.* [OE.] a very hard, siliceous rock, usually gray, that produces sparks when struck against steel —**flint′y** *adj.* **-i·er, -i·est**

flip¹ (flip) *vt.* **flipped, flip′ping** [echoic] 1. to toss with a quick jerk; flick 2. to snap (a coin) into the air, with the thumb 3. to turn or turn over —*vi.* 1. to move jerkily 2. [Slang] to lose self-control —*n.* a flipping —**flip one's lid** [Slang] to go berserk

flip² (flip) *adj.* **flip′per, flip′pest** *colloq. var. of* FLIPPANT

flip′pant (-ənt) *adj.* [prob. < FLIP¹] frivolous and disrespectful; saucy —**flip′pan·cy** *n., pl.* **-cies** —**flip′pant·ly** *adv.*

flip′per (-ər) *n.* [< FLIP¹] 1. a broad, flat limb adapted for swimming, as in seals 2. a paddlelike rubber device worn on each foot by swimmers

flip side [Colloq.] the reverse side (of a phonograph record), esp. the less popular side

flirt (flurt) *vt.* [< ?] to move jerkily [the bird *flirted* its tail] —*vi.* 1. to make love without serious intentions 2. to trifle or toy [to *flirt* with an idea] —*n.* 1. a quick, jerky movement 2. one who plays at love

fir·ta·tion (flər tā′shən) *n.* a frivolous love affair —**flir·ta′tious** *adj.*

flit (flit) *vi.* **flit′ted, flit′ting** [< ON. *flytja*] to move lightly and rapidly

flitch (flich) *n.* [OE. *flicce*] the cured and salted side of a hog; side of bacon

float (flōt) *n.* [< OE. *flota*, a ship] 1. anything that stays on the surface of a liquid, as a raft, a cork on a fishing line, etc. 2. a low, flat vehicle decorated for exhibit in a parade —*vi.* 1. to stay on the surface of a liquid 2. to drift easily on water, in air, etc. 3. to move about aimlessly —*vt.* 1. to cause to float 2. to put into circulation [to *float* a bond issue] 3. to arrange for (a loan) —**float′er** *n.*

flock¹ (fläk) *n.* [OE. *flocc*] 1. a group of certain animals, as birds, sheep, etc., living or feeding together 2. a group of people or things —*vi.* to assemble or travel in a flock or crowd

flock·ing (fläk′iŋ) *n.* [< L. *floccus*, tuft of wool] 1. tiny fibers of wool, cotton, etc. applied to a fabric, wallpaper, etc. as a velvetlike surface: also **flock** 2. such a fabric, etc.

floe (flō) *n.* [< ON. *flo*, layer] *same as* ICE FLOE

flog (fläg, flôg) *vt.* **flogged, flog′ging** [< ? L. *flagellare*] to beat with a stick, whip, etc. —**flog′ger** *n.*

flood (flud) *n.* [OE. *flod*] 1. an overflowing of water on an area normally dry 2. the rising of the tide 3. a great outpouring, as of words —*vt.* 1. to cover or fill, as with a flood 2. to put too much water, fuel, etc. on or in —*vi.* 1. to gush out in a flood 2. to become flooded —**the Flood** *Bible* the great flood in Noah's time

flood′light′ *n.* 1. a lamp that casts a broad beam of bright light 2. such a beam of light —*vt.* -light′ed or -lit′, -light′ing to illuminate by a floodlight

flood tide the rising tide

floor (flôr) *n.* [OE. *flor*] 1. the inside bottom surface of a room 2. the bottom surface of anything [the ocean *floor*] 3. a story in a building 4. the right to speak in an assembly —*vt.* 1. to furnish with a floor 2. to knock down 3. [Colloq.] *a)* to defeat *b)* to shock, confuse, etc.

floor′board′ *n.* 1. a board in a floor 2. the floor of an automobile, etc.

floor exercise any gymnastic exercise done without apparatus

floor′ing *n.* 1. a floor or floors 2. material for making a floor

floor show a show presenting singers, dancers, etc., as in a nightclub

floor′walk′er *n.* formerly, a person employed by a department store to direct customers, supervise sales, etc.: now usually floor (or sales) manager

flop (fläp) *vt.* flopped, flop′ping [var. of FLAP] to flap or throw noisily and clumsily —*vi.* 1. to move, drop, or flap -around loosely or clumsily 2. [Colloq.] to fail —*n.* 1. the act or sound of flopping 2. [Colloq.] a failure —flop′py *adj.* -pi-er, -pi-est

flop′house′ *n.* [Colloq.] a cheap hotel

flop′o′ver *n.* TV faulty reception when the picture seems to move repeatedly up or down the screen

floppy disk a small, flexible disk for storing computer data

flo·ra (flôr′ə) *n.* [L. < *flos*, a flower] the plants of a specified region or time

flo′ral (-əl) *adj.* of or like flowers

Flor·ence (flôr′əns) city in C Italy: pop. 454,000 —Flor′en·tine′ (-ən tēn′) *adj., n.*

flo·res·cence (flô res′ns) *n.* [< L. *flos*, a flower] a blooming or flowering —flo·res′cent *adj.*

flor·id (flôr′id) *adj.* [< L. *flos*, a flower] 1. ruddy: said of the complexion 2. ornate; showy; gaudy

Flor·i·da (flôr′ə də) SE State of the U.S.: 58,560 sq. mi.; pop. 9,740,000; cap. Tallahassee —Flo·rid·i·an (flô rid′ē ən) *adj., n.*

flor·in (flôr′in) *n.* [< L. *flos*, a flower] any of various European or S. African silver or gold coins

flo·rist (flôr′ist) *n.* [< L. *flos*, a flower] one who grows or sells flowers

floss (flôs, fläs) *n.* [ult. < L. *floccus*, tuft of wool] 1. the short, downy waste fibers of silk 2. a soft, loosely twisted thread or yarn, as of silk, used in embroidery 3. a substance like this —floss′y *adj.* -i-er, -i-est

flo·ta·tion (flō tā′shən) *n.* the act or condition of floating

flo·til·la (flō til′ə) *n.* [Sp., dim. of *flota*, a fleet] 1. a small fleet 2. a fleet of boats or small ships

flot·sam (flät′səm) *n.* [< MDu. *vloten*, to float] the wreckage of a ship or its cargo found floating on the sea: chiefly in flotsam and jetsam

flounce¹ (flouns) *vi.* flounced, flounc′ing [prob. < Scand.] to move with quick, flinging motions of the body, as in anger —*n.* a flouncing

flounce² (flouns) *n.* [< OFr. *froncir*, to wrinkle] a wide ruffle sewed to a skirt, sleeve, etc. —flounc′y *adj.*

floun·der¹ (floun′dər) *vi.* [< ? FOUN-DER] 1. to struggle awkwardly, as in deep snow 2. to speak or act in an awkward, confused manner

floun·der² (floun′dər) *n.* [< Scand.] any of various flatfishes caught for food, as the halibut

flour (flour) *n.* [orig. flower (i.e., best) of meal] 1. a fine, powdery substance produced by grinding and sifting grain, esp. wheat 2. any finely powdered substance —flour′y *adj.*

flour·ish (flur′ish) *vi.* [< L. *flos*, a flower] 1. to grow vigorously; thrive 2. to be at the peak of development, etc. —*vt.* to brandish (a sword, etc.) —*n.* 1. anything done in a showy way 2. a brandishing 3. decorative lines in writing 4. a musical fanfare

flout (flout) *vt., vi.* [< ? ME. *flouten*, play the flute] to mock or scorn —*n.* a scornful act or remark —flout′er *n.*

flow (flō) *vi.* [OE. *flowan*] 1. to move as a liquid does 2. to pour out 3. to move gently and smoothly 4. to proceed; issue 5. to be plentiful 6. to hang loose [flowing hair] —*n.* 1. a flowing 2. the rate of flow 3. anything that flows 4. the rising of the tide

flow chart a diagram showing the progress of work in a series of operations

flow·er (flou′ər, flour) *n.* [< L. *flos*] 1. the seed-producing structure of a flowering plant; blossom 2. a plant cultivated for its blossoms 3. the best or finest part —*vi.* 1. to produce blossoms 2. to reach the best stage —in flower flowering

flow′er·pot′ *n.* a container to hold earth for a plant to grow in

flow′er·y *adj.* -i·er, -i·est 1. covered or decorated with flowers 2. full of ornate expressions and fine words —flow′er·i·ness *n.*

flown (flōn) *pp.* of FLY¹

flu (flōō) *n.* 1. short for INFLUENZA 2. popularly, a respiratory or intestinal infection caused by a virus

flub (flub) *vt., vi.* flubbed, flub′bing [< ? FL(OP) + (D)UB¹] [Colloq.] to bungle (a job, stroke, etc.) —*n.* [Colloq.] a blunder

fluc·tu·ate (fluk′choo wāt′) *vi.* -at′ed, -at′ing [< L. *fluctus*, a wave] to be continually varying in an irregular way —fluc′tu·a′tion *n.*

flue (flōō) *n.* [< ? OFr. *fluie*, a flowing] a shaft for the passage of smoke, hot air, etc., as in a chimney

flu·ent (flōō′ənt) *adj.* [< L. *fluere*, to flow] 1. flowing smoothly 2. able to write or speak easily, expressively, etc. —flu′en·cy *n.* —flu′ent·ly *adv.*

fluff (fluf) *n.* [? blend of *flue*, soft mass + PUFF] **1.** soft, light down **2.** a loose, soft mass, as of hair —*vt.* **1.** to shake or pat until loose or fluffy **2.** to bungle (one's lines), as in acting

fluff'y (-ē) *adj.* **-i·er, -i·est** like fluff; soft and light; feathery

flu·id (flŏŏ'id) *adj.* [< L. *fluere*, to flow] **1.** that can flow as a liquid or gas does **2.** that can change rapidly or easily **3.** available for investment or as cash —*n.* a liquid or gas —**flu·id'i·ty** *n.* —**flu'id·ly** *adv.*

fluke (flŏŏk) *n.* [< ?] **1.** either of the pointed ends of an anchor, which catch in the ground **2.** a barb of a harpoon, etc. **3.** a lobe of a whale's tail **4.** [Colloq.] a stroke of luck

flume (flŏŏm) *n.* [< L. *flumen*, river] an inclined chute for carrying water, as to transport logs, furnish power, etc.

FLUKES OF
A WHALE

flung (fluŋ) *pt. & pp.* of FLING

flunk (fluŋk) *vt., vi.* [< ?] [Colloq.] to fail, as in schoolwork

flun·ky (fluŋ'kē) *n., pl.* **-kies** [orig. Scot.] **1.** orig., a liveried manservant **2.** a toady **3.** a person with menial tasks Also **flunkey**

flu·o·resce (flŏŏ'ə res', floo res') *vi.* **-resced', -resc'ing** to show or undergo fluorescence

flu·o·res·cence (flŏŏ'ə res'ns; floo res'-) *n.* [ult. < L. *fluor*, flux] **1.** the property of producing light when acted upon by radiant energy **2.** light so produced —**flu'o·res'cent** *adj.*

fluorescent lamp (or **tube**) a glass tube coated on the inside with a fluorescent substance that gives off light (**fluorescent light**) when mercury vapor in the tube is acted upon by a stream of electrons

fluor·i·date (flôr'ə dāt', floor'-) *vt.* **-dat'ed, -dat'ing** to add fluorides to (a water supply) in order to reduce tooth decay —**fluor'i·da'tion** *n.*

flu·o·ride (floor'īd, flŏŏ'ə rīd') *n.* any of various compounds of fluorine

flu·o·rine (floor'ēn; flŏŏ'ə rēn', -rin) *n.* [< L. *fluor*, flux] a greenish-yellow gaseous chemical element

fluor·o·scope (floor'ə skōp') *n.* a machine for examining internal structures by viewing the shadows cast on a fluorescent screen by objects through which X-rays are directed

flur·ry (flur'ē) *n., pl.* **-ries** [< ?] **1.** a sudden gust of wind, rain, or snow **2.** a sudden commotion —*vt.* **-ried, -ry·ing** to confuse; agitate

flush¹ (flush) *vi.* [blend of FLASH & ME. *flusshen*, fly up suddenly] **1.** to flow rapidly **2.** to blush or glow **3.** to be washed out with a sudden flow of water **4.** to start up from cover: said of birds —*vt.* **1.** to wash out with a sudden flow of water **2.** to make blush or glow **3.** to excite **4.** to drive (birds) from cover —*n.* **1.** a rapid flow, as of water **2.** a sudden, vigorous growth **3.** sudden excitement **4.** a blush; glow

5. a sudden feeling of heat, as in a fever —*adj.* **1.** well supplied; esp. with money **2.** abundant **3.** level or even (*with*) **4.** direct; full (*a blow flush in the face*) —*adv.* **1.** so as to be level **2.** directly

flush² (flush) *n.* [< L. *fluere*, to flow] a hand of cards all in the same suit

flus·ter (flus'tər) *vt., vi.* [prob. < Scand.] to make or become confused —*n.* a being flustered

flute (flŏŏt) *n.* [< Pr. *flaüt*] **1.** a high-pitched wind instrument consisting of a long, slender tube with finger holes and keys **2.** a groove in the shaft of a column, etc. —**flut'ed** *adj.* —**flut'ing** *n.* —**flut'ist** *n.*

flut·ter (flut'ər) *vi.* [< OE. *fleotan*, to float] **1.** to flap the wings rapidly, without flying **2.** to wave, move, or beat rapidly and irregularly —*vt.* to cause to flutter —*n.* **1.** a fluttering movement **2.** an excited or confused state —**flut'ter·y** *adj.*

flux (fluks) *n.* [< L. *fluere*, to flow] **1.** a flowing **2.** a continual change **3.** any abnormal discharge from the body **4.** a substance used to help metals fuse together, as in soldering

fly¹ (flī) *vi.* **flew, flown, fly'ing** [OE. *fleogan*] **1.** to move through the air by using wings, as a bird, or in an aircraft **2.** to wave or float in the air **3.** to move or pass swiftly **4.** to flee **5.** flied, fly'ing *Baseball* to hit a fly —*vt.* **1.** to cause to float in the air **2.** to operate (an aircraft) **3.** to flee from —*n., pl.* **flies 1.** a flap that conceals the zipper, etc. in a garment **2.** a flap serving as the door of a tent **3.** *Baseball* a ball batted high in the air **4.** *Theater* [*pl.*] the space above a stage —**fly into** to have a violent outburst of —**let fly (at) 1.** to hurl (at) **2.** to direct a verbal attack (at) —**on the fly** [Colloq.] while in a hurry

fly² (flī) *n., pl.* **flies** [OE. *fleoge*] **1.** any of a large group of insects with two transparent wings; esp., the housefly **2.** an artificial fly used as a fish lure

fly'a·ble *adj.* suitable for flying

fly'by', **fly'-by'** *n., pl.* **-bys'** a flight past a designated point or place by an aircraft or spacecraft

fly'-by-night' *adj.* financially irresponsible —*n.* an absconding debtor

fly'-by-wire' *adj.* of a system for controlling an airplane or spacecraft electronically, as from a computer

fly'-cast' *vi.* to fish by casting artificial flies

fly'catch'er *n.* a small bird, as the phoebe, that catches insects in flight

fly'er *n. same as* FLIER

flying buttress a buttress connected with a wall by an arch, serving to resist outward pressure

flying colors notable success

flying fish a fish with winglike fins used in gliding through the air

flying saucer *same as* UFO

fly'leaf' *n., pl.* **-leaves'** a blank leaf at the beginning or end of a book

fly'pa'per *n.* a sticky or poisonous paper set out to catch flies

fly'speck' *n.* **1.** a speck of fly excrement **2.** any tiny spot or petty flaw

fly'way' *n.* a route flown by birds migrating to and from breeding grounds

fly'weight' *n.* a boxer who weighs 112 pounds or less

fly'wheel' *n.* a heavy wheel on a machine, for regulating its speed

FM frequency modulation

foal (fōl) *n.* [OE. *fola*] a young horse, mule, etc.; colt or filly —*vt., vi.* to give birth to (a foal)

foam (fōm) *n.* [OE. *fam*] **1.** the froth formed on liquids by shaking, etc. **2.** something like foam, as frothy saliva **3.** a rigid or spongy cellular mass, made from liquid rubber, plastic, etc. —*vi.* to froth —**foam'y** *adj.*

fob (fäb) *n.* [prob. < dial. G. *fuppe*, a pocket] **1.** a short ribbon or chain attached to a watch **2.** any ornament worn on such a chain, etc.

F.O.B., f.o.b. free on board

fo·cal (fō'k'l) *adj.* of or at a focus

focal length the distance from the optical center of a lens to the point where the light rays converge

fo'c's'le (fōk's'l) *n.* *phonetic spelling* of FORECASTLE

fo·cus (fō'kəs) *n., pl.* **-cus·es, -ci** (-sī) [L., hearth] **1.** the point where rays of light, heat, etc. come together; specif., the point where rays of reflected or refracted light meet **2.** *same as* FOCAL LENGTH **3.** an adjustment of this length to make a clear image [move the lens into *focus*] **4.** any center of activity, attention, etc. —*vt.* **-cused** or **-cussed, -cus·ing** or **-cus·sing 1.** to bring into focus **2.** to adjust the focal length of (the eye, a lens, etc.) so as to produce a clear image **3.** to concentrate —**in focus** clear —**out of focus** blurred

fod·der (fäd'ər) *n.* [OE. *fodor*] coarse food for cattle, horses, etc., as hay

foe (fō) *n.* [OE. *fah*, hostile] an enemy; opponent

foe·tus (fēt'əs) *n.* *same as* FETUS

fog (fôg, fäg) *n.* [prob. < Scand.] **1.** a large mass of water vapor condensed to fine particles, just above the earth's surface **2.** a state of mental confusion —*vt., vi.* **fogged, fog'ging** to make or become foggy

fog bank a dense mass of fog

fog'gy *adj.* **-gi·er, -gi·est 1.** full of fog **2.** dim; blurred **3.** confused

fog'horn' *n.* a horn blown to give warning to ships in a fog

fo·gy (fō'gē) *n., pl.* **-gies** [< ?] one who is old-fashioned in ideas and actions: also **fo'gey**, *pl.* **-geys**

foi·ble (foi'b'l) *n.* [< Fr. *faible*, feeble] a small weakness in character

foil¹ (foil) *vt.* [< OFr. *fuler*, trample] to keep from success; thwart

foil² (foil) *n.* [< L. *folium*, leaf] **1.** a very thin sheet of metal **2.** a person or thing that sets off or enhances another by contrast **3.** [etym. unc.] a long, thin, blunted fencing sword

foist (foist) *vt.* [prob. < dial. Du.

vuisten, to hide in the hand] to get (a thing) accepted, sold, etc. by fraud, deception, etc.; palm off (on or upon)

fold¹ (fōld) *vt.* [OE. *faldan*] **1.** to double (material) up on itself **2.** to draw together and intertwine [fold your arms] **3.** to embrace **4.** to wrap up; envelop —*vi.* **1.** to be or become folded **2.** [Colloq.] *a)* to fail, as a play, business, etc. *b)* to collapse —*n.* a folded part

fold² (fōld) *n.* [OE. *fald*] **1.** a pen for sheep **2.** a flock of sheep **3.** a group of people, esp. in a church

-fold (fōld) [< OE. *-feald*] a suffix meaning: **1.** having (a specified number of) parts **2.** (a specified number of) times as many or as much

fold'a·way' *adj.* that can be folded together for easy storage

fold'er *n.* **1.** a sheet of heavy paper folded for holding papers **2.** a booklet of folded, unstitched sheets

fo·li·age (fō'lē ij) *n.* [< L. *folia*] leaves, as of a plant or tree

fo·li·o (fō'lē ō') *n., pl.* **-os'** [< L. *folium*, leaf] **1.** a large sheet of paper folded once **2.** the largest regular size of book, made of sheets so folded **3.** the number of a page in a book

folk (fōk) *n., pl.* **folk, folks** [OE. *folc*] **1.** *a)* a people; nation *b)* the common people of a nation **2.** [*pl.*] people; persons —*adj.* of or originating among the common people —**(one's) folks** [Colloq.] (one's) family

folk'lore' *n.* the traditional beliefs, legends, etc. of a people

folk'-rock' *n.* rock-and-roll music using lyrics like those of a folk song

folk song a song made and handed down among the common people, or one like it of known authorship —**folk singer**

folk'sy (-sē) *adj.* **-si·er, -si·est** [Colloq.] friendly or sociable

fol·li·cle (fäl'i k'l) *n.* [< L. *follis*, bellows] any small sac, cavity, or gland [a hair *follicle*]

fol·low (fäl'ō) *vt.* [< OE. *folgian*] **1.** to come or go after **2.** to pursue **3.** to go along [follow the road] **4.** to take up (a trade, etc.) **5.** to result from **6.** to take as a model; imitate **7.** to obey **8.** to watch or listen to closely **9.** to understand —*vi.* **1.** to come or go after something else in place, time, etc. **2.** to result —**follow out** (or **up**) to carry out fully —**follow through** to continue and finish a stroke or action

fol'low·er *n.* one that follows; specif., *a)* one who follows another's teachings; disciple *b)* an attendant

fol'low·ing *adj.* that follows; next after —*n.* a group of followers —*prep.* after [following dinner he left]

fol'low-up' *n.* a letter, visit, etc. that follows as a review or addition

fol·ly (fäl'ē) *n., pl.* **-lies** [see FOOL] **1.** a lack of sense; foolishness **2.** a foolish action or belief

fo·ment (fō ment′) *vt.* [< L. *fovere*, keep warm] to stir up (trouble); incite —**fo′men·ta′tion** *n.*

fond (fänd) *adj.* [< ME. *fonnen*, be foolish] 1. tender and affectionate; loving or doting 2. cherished [a fond hope] —**fond** of having a liking for —**fond′ly** *adv.* —**fond′ness** *n.*

fon·dle (fän′d'l) *vt.* -**dled**, -**dling** [< FOND] to caress or handle lovingly

fon·due, fon·du (fän′dōō′) *n.* [Fr. < *fondre*, melt] melted cheese, etc. used for dipping cubes of bread

font[1] (fänt) *n.* [< L. *fons*, spring] 1. a bowl to hold baptismal water 2. a basin for holy water 3. a source

font[2] (fänt) *n.* [see FOUND[2]] *Printing* a complete assortment of type in one size and style

food (fōōd) *n.* [OE. *foda*] 1. any substance, esp. a solid, taken in by a plant or animal to enable it to live and grow. 2. anything that nourishes

food chain *Ecol.* a sequence (as fox, rabbit, grass) of organisms in a community in which each feeds on the member below it

food cycle (or **web**) *Ecol.* all the individual food chains in a community

food poisoning sickness caused by contaminants, as bacteria, in food

food proc′es·sor an electrical appliance that can blend, purée, slice, grate, chop, etc. foods rapidly

food stamp any of the Federal stamps sold at less than face value to persons with low income for use in buying food

food′stuff′ *n.* any material made into or used as food

fool (fōōl) *n.* [< L. *follis*, windbag] 1. a silly person; simpleton 2. a jester 3. a dupe —*vi.* 1. to act like a fool 2. to joke 3. [Colloq.] to meddle (*with*) —*vt.* to trick; deceive —**fool around** [Colloq.] to trifle —**fool′er·y** *n.*

fool′har′dy *adj.* -**di·er**, -**di·est** foolishly daring; reckless —**fool′har′di·ly** *adv.* —**fool′har′di·ness** *n.*

fool′ish *adj.* silly; unwise; absurd —**fool′ish·ly** *adv.* —**fool′ish·ness** *n.*

fool′proof′ *adj.* so harmless, simple, etc. as not to be mishandled, damaged, etc. even by a fool

fools·cap (fōōlz′kap′) *n.* [from a watermark of a jester's cap] a size of writing paper, 13 by 16 in. in the U.S.

foot (foot) *n.*, *pl.* **feet** [OE. *fot*] 1. the end part of the leg, on which one stands 2. the base or bottom [the foot of a page] 3. a measure of length, equal to 12 inches: symbol ′ 4. [Brit.] infantry 5. a group of syllables serving as a unit of meter in verse —*vt.* 1. to add (a column of figures) (often with *up*) 2. [Colloq.] to pay (costs, etc.) —**foot it** [Colloq.] to dance or walk —**on foot** walking —**under foot** in the way

foot′age (-ij) *n.* measurement in feet

foot′ball′ *n.* 1. a field game played with an inflated leather ball by two teams 2. the ball used

foot′bridge′ *n.* a narrow bridge for pedestrians

foot′ed *adj.* having feet of a specified number or kind [four-footed]

foot′fall′ *n.* the sound of a footstep

foot′hill′ *n.* a low hill at the foot of a mountain or mountain range

foot′hold′ *n.* 1. a place for the feet, as in climbing 2. a secure position

foot′ing *n.* 1. a secure placing of the feet 2. a foothold 3. a secure position 4. a basis for relationship

foot′less *adj.* 1. without feet 2. without basis 3. [Colloq.] clumsy; inept

foot′lights′ *n.pl.* a row of lights along the front of a stage floor —**the footlights** the theater or acting

foot′lock′er *n.* a small trunk, usually kept at the foot of a bed

foot′loose′ *adj.* free to go about

foot′man (-mən) *n.*, *pl.* -**men** a male servant who assists the butler

foot′note′ *n.* a note of comment or reference at the bottom of a page —*vt.* -**not′ed**, -**not′ing** to add a footnote or footnotes to

foot′path′ *n.* a narrow path for use by pedestrians only

foot′print′ *n.* a mark left by a foot

foot′sore′ *adj.* having sore or tender feet, as from much walking

foot′step′ *n.* 1. the distance covered in a step 2. the sound of a step 3. a footprint

foot′stool′ *n.* a low stool for supporting the feet of a seated person

foot′wear′ *n.* shoes, boots, etc.

foot′work′ *n.* the manner of using the feet, as in boxing, dancing, etc.

fop (fäp) *n.* [ME. *foppe*, a fool] same as DANDY (*n.* 1) —**fop′per·y** *n.*, *pl.* -**ies** —**fop′pish** *adj.*

for (fôr, fər) *prep.* [OE.] 1. in place of [use a rope for a belt] 2. in the interest of [acting for another] 3. in favor of [vote for the levy] 4. in honor of [a party for him] 5. in order to have, get, keep, find, reach, etc. [walk for exercise, start for home] 6. meant to be received by [flowers for a girl] 7. suitable to [a room for sleeping] 8. with regard to; concerning [an ear for music] 9. as being [to know for a fact] 10. considering the nature of [cool for July] 11. because of [to cry for pain] 12. to the length, amount, or duration of 13. at the price of [two for a dollar] —*conj.* because

for- (fôr, fər) [OE.] *a prefix meaning* away, apart, off [forbid, forgo]

for·age (fôr′ij, fär′-) *n.* [< Frank. *fodr*, food] 1. food for domestic animals 2. a search for food —*vi.* -**aged**, -**ag·ing** to search for food —*vt.* to get or take food from; raid —**for′ag·er** *n.*

fo·ra·men (fō rā′mən) *n.*, *pl.* -**ram′i·na** (-ram′ə nə), -**ra′mens** [L., a hole] a small opening, as in a bone

for·ay (fôr′ā) *vt.*, *vi.* [< OFr. *forrer*, to forage] to plunder —*n.* a raid in order to seize things

for·bear′[1] (fôr ber′) *vt.*-**bore′**, -**borne′**, -**bear′ing** [see FOR- & BEAR[1]] to refrain from (doing, saying, etc.) —*vi.* 1. to refrain 2. to control oneself

for·bear′[2] *n.* same as FOREBEAR

for·bear·ance (-əns) *n.* 1. the act of forbearing 2. self-restraint

for·bid (fər bid′, fôr-) *vt.* -**bade′** (-bad′) or -**bad′**, -**bid′den**, -**bid′ding**

[see FOR- & BID] 1. to order (a person) not to do (something); prohibit 2. to prevent

for·bid'ding *adj.* looking dangerous or disagreeable; repellent —**for·bid'ding·ly** *adv.*

force (fôrs) *n.* [< L. *fortis*, strong] 1. strength; power 2. physical coercion against a person or thing 3. the power to control, persuade, etc.; effectiveness 4. military power 5. any group of people organized for some activity [a sales *force*] 6. energy that causes or alters motion —*vt.* **forced, forc'ing** 1. to make do something by force; compel 2. to break open, into, or through by force 3. to take by force; extort 4. to impose as by force (with *on* or *upon*) 5. to produce as by force [she *forced* a smile] 6. to cause (plants, etc.) to develop faster by artificial means —**in force** 1. in full strength 2. in effect; valid —**force'less** *adj.*

forced (fôrst) *adj.* 1. compulsory [*forced* labor] 2. not natural; strained [a *forced* smile]

force'-feed' *vt.* **-fed', -feed'ing** to feed as by a tube through the throat to the stomach

force'ful (-fəl) *adj.* full of force; powerful, vigorous, effective, etc. —**force'ful·ly** *adv.* —**force'ful·ness** *n.*

for·ceps (fôr'səps) *n., pl.* **-ceps** [L. < *formus*, warm + *capere*, to take] small pincers for grasping, pulling, etc.

for·ci·ble (fôr'sə b'l) *adj.* 1. done by force 2. having force —**for'ci·bly** *adv.*

ford (fôrd) *n.* [OE.] a shallow place in a stream, etc. that can be crossed by wading —*vt.* to cross at a ford

Ford (fôrd) 1. Gerald R., 1913– ; 38th president of the U.S. (1974–77) 2. Henry, 1863–1947; U.S. automobile manufacturer

fore (fôr) *adv., adj.* [OE.] at, in, or toward the front part, as of a ship —*n.* the front —*interj.* Golf a shout warning that one is about to hit the ball

fore- (fôr) [OE.] *a prefix meaning:* 1. before in time, place, etc. [*forenoon*] 2. the front part of [*forearm*]

fore'-and-aft' *adj.* from the bow to the stern; set lengthwise, as a rig

fore·arm'[1] *n.* the part of the arm between the elbow and the wrist

fore·arm'[2] *vt.* to arm in advance

fore'bear' (-ber') *n.* [< FORE + BE + -ER] an ancestor

fore·bode' (-bōd') *vt., vi.* **-bod'ed, -bod'ing** [< OE.] 1. to foretell; predict 2. to have a presentiment of (something evil) —**fore·bod'ing** *n.*

fore·cast' *vt.* **-cast'** or **-cast'ed, -cast'ing** 1. to predict 2. to serve as a prediction of —*n.* a prediction —**fore'cast'er** *n.*

fore·cas·tle (fōk's'l) *n.* 1. the upper deck of a ship in front of the foremast 2. the front part of a merchant ship, where the sailors' quarters are located

fore·close' (fôr klōz') *vt., vi.* **-closed', -clos'ing** [< OFr. *fors*, outside +

clore, CLOSE[2]] to take away the right to redeem (a mortgage, etc.) —**fore·clo'sure** (-klō'zhər) *n.*

fore·doom' *vt.* to doom in advance

fore'fa'ther *n.* an ancestor

fore'fin'ger *n.* the finger nearest the thumb

fore'foot' *n., pl.* **-feet'** either of the front feet of an animal

fore'front' *n.* 1. the extreme front 2. the position of most importance

fore·go'[1] *vt., vi.* **-went', -gone', -go'ing** to precede

fore·go'[2] *vt. same as* FORGO

fore'go'ing *adj.* previously said, written, etc.; preceding

fore·gone' *adj.* 1. previous 2. previously determined; inevitable

fore'ground' *n.* the part of a scene, etc. nearest the viewer

fore'hand' *n.* a stroke, as in tennis, made with the palm of the hand turned forward —*adj.* done as with a forehand

fore·head (fôr'id, -hed'; fär'-) *n.* the part of the face between the eyebrows and the hairline

for·eign (fôr'in, fär'-) *adj.* [< L. *foras*, out-of-doors] 1. situated outside one's own country, locality, etc. 2. of, from, or having to do with other countries 3. not characteristic or belonging

for'eign-born' *adj.* born in some other country; not native

for'eign·er *n.* a person from another country; alien

foreign minister a member of a governmental cabinet in charge of foreign affairs for his country

fore·know' *vt.* **-knew', -known', -know'ing** to know beforehand —**fore'knowl'edge** (-näl'ij) *n.*

fore'leg' *n.* either of the front legs of an animal

fore'lock' *n.* a lock of hair growing just above the forehead

fore'man (-mən) *n., pl.* **-men** 1. the chairman of a jury 2. the head of a group of workers —**fore'la'dy** *n.fem.*

fore'mast' *n.* the mast nearest the bow of a ship

fore'most' (-mōst') *adj.* first in place, time, rank, etc. —*adv.* first

fore'noon' *n.* the time from sunrise to noon; morning

fo·ren·sic (fə ren'sik) *adj.* [< L. *forum*, marketplace] of or suitable for public debate —**fo·ren'si·cal·ly** *adv.*

fore·or·dain' *vt.* to ordain beforehand; predestine —**fore'or·di·na'tion** (-d'n ā'shən) *n.*

fore'quar'ter *n.* the front half of a side of beef or the like

fore·run'ner *n.* 1. a herald 2. a sign that tells or warns of something to follow 3. a predecessor; ancestor

fore'sail' (-sāl', -səl) *n.* the main sail on the foremast of a schooner

fore·see' *vt.* **-saw', -seen', -see'ing** to see or know beforehand —**fore·see'a·ble** *adj.* —**fore·se'er** *n.*

fore·shad'ow *vt.* to indicate or suggest beforehand; presage

fore·short·en *vt.* in drawing, etc. to shorten some lines of (an object) to give the illusion of proper relative size

fore·sight *n.* 1. a) a foreseeing b) the power to foresee 2. prudent regard or provision for the future

fore·skin *n.* the fold of skin that covers the end of the penis

for·est (fôr'ist) *n.* [< L. *foris*, out-of-doors] a thick growth of trees, etc. covering a large tract of land —*vt.* to plant with trees

FORE-SHORTENED ARM

fore·stall (fôr stôl') *vt.* [< OE. *fore-steall*, ambush] 1. to prevent by doing something ahead of time 2. to act in advance of; anticipate

for·est·a·tion (fôr'is tā'shən) *n.* the planting or care of forests

for·est·er *n.* one trained in forestry

for·est·ry *n.* the science of planting and taking care of forests

fore·taste *n.* a taste or sample of what can be expected

fore·tell *vt.* -told', -tell'ing to tell or indicate beforehand; predict

fore·thought *n.* 1. a thinking or planning beforehand 2. foresight

for·ev·er (fər ev'ər, fôr-) *adv.* 1. for always; endlessly 2. always; at all times Also **for·ev'er·more'**

fore·warn *vt.* to warn beforehand

fore·word *n.* an introductory remark or preface

for·feit (fôr'fit) *n.* [< OFr. *forfaire*, transgress] 1. a fine or penalty for some crime, fault, or neglect 2. the act of forfeiting —*adj.* lost or taken away as a forfeit —*vt.* to lose or be deprived of as a forfeit

for·fei·ture (-fə chər) *n.* 1. the act of forfeiting 2. anything forfeited

for·gath·er (fôr gaᵗʰ'ər) *vi.* to come together; assemble; meet

for·gave (fər gāv', fôr-) *pt. of* FORGIVE

forge¹ (fôrj) *n.* [< L. *faber*, workman] 1. a furnace for heating metal to be wrought 2. a place where metal is heated and wrought; smithy —*vt., vi.* forged, forg'ing 1. to shape (metal) by heating and hammering 2. to form; shape 3. to imitate (a signature, etc.) fraudulently; counterfeit (a check, etc.) —**forg'er** *n.*

forge² (fôrj) *vt., vi.* forged, forg'ing [prob. alt. < FORCE] to move forward steadily: often with *ahead*

for·ger·y *n., pl.* -ies 1. the act or crime of forging documents, signatures, etc., to deceive 2. anything forged

for·get (fər get', fôr-) *vt., vi.* -got', -got'ten or -got', -get'ting [OE. *forgitan*] 1. to be unable to remember 2. to overlook or neglect —**forget oneself** to act in an improper manner —**for·get'a·ble** *adj.*

for·get'ful *adj.* 1. apt to forget 2. heedless or negligent —**for·get'ful·ly** *adv.* —**for·get'ful·ness** *n.*

for·get'-me-not' *n.* a marsh plant

with small blue, white, or pink flowers

for·give (fər giv', fôr-) *vt., vi.* -gave', -giv'en, -giv'ing [OE. *forgiefan*] to give up resentment against or the desire to punish; pardon (an offense or offender) —**for·giv'a·ble** *adj.* —**for·give'ness** *n.* —**for·giv'er** *n.*

for·giv·ing *adj.* inclined to forgive —**for·giv'ing·ly** *adv.*

for·go (fôr gō') *vt.* -went', -gone', -go'ing [OE. *forgan*] to do without; abstain from; give up —**for·go'er** *n.*

for·got (fər gät', fôr-) *pt. & alt. pp. of* FORGET

for·got·ten (-'n) *pp. of* FORGET

fork (fôrk) *n.* [< L. *furca*] 1. an instrument of varying size with prongs at one end, as for eating food, pitching hay, etc. 2. something like a fork in shape, etc. 3. the place where a road, etc. divides into branches 4. any of these branches —*vi.* to divide into branches —*vt.* to pick up or pitch with a fork —**fork over** (or **out, up**) [Colloq.] to pay out; hand over —**fork'ful** *n., pl.* **-fuls'**

fork'lift' *n.* a device for lifting heavy objects by means of projecting prongs slid under the load

for·lorn (fər lôrn', fôr-) *adj.* [< OE. *forleosan*, lose utterly] 1. abandoned 2. wretched; miserable 3. without hope —**for·lorn'ly** *adv.*

form (fôrm) *n.* [< L. *forma*] 1. shape; general structure 2. the figure of a person or animal 3. a mold 4. a particular mode, kind, type, etc. [ice is a *form* of water, the *forms* of poetry] 5. arrangement; style 6. a way of doing something requiring skill 7. a customary or conventional procedure; formality; ceremony 8. a printed document with blanks to be filled in 9. condition of mind or body 10. a chart giving information about horses in a race 11. a changed appearance of a word to show inflection, etc. 12. type, etc. locked in a frame for printing —*vt.* 1. to shape; fashion 2. to train; instruct 3. to develop (habits) 4. to make up; constitute —*vi.* to be formed

-form (fôrm) [< L.] *a suffix meaning* having the form of [*cuneiform*]

for·mal (fôr'məl) *adj.* [< L. *formalis*] 1. according to fixed customs, rules, etc. 2. stiff in manner 3. a) designed for wear at ceremonies, etc. b) requiring clothes of this kind 4. done or made in explicit, definite form [a *formal* contract] —*n.* 1. a formal dance 2. a woman's evening dress —**for'mal·ly** *adv.*

form·al·de·hyde (fôr mal'də hīd') *n.* [FORM(IC) + ALDEHYDE] a colorless, pungent gas used in solution as a disinfectant and preservative

for'mal·ism *n.* strict attention to outward forms and customs

for·mal·i·ty (fôr mal'ə tē) *n., pl.* -ties 1. a) an observing of customs, rules, etc.; propriety b) excessive attention to convention; stiffness 2. a formal act; ceremony

for·mal·ize (fôr'mə līz') *vt.* -ized', -iz'ing 1. to shape 2. to make formal —**for'mal·i·za'tion** *n.*

for·mat (fôr′mat) *n.* [< L. *formatus*, formed] 1. the shape, size, and arrangement of a book, etc. 2. the arrangement or plan of a presentation

for·ma·tion (fôr mā′shən) *n.* 1. a forming or being formed 2. a thing formed 3. the way in which something is formed; structure 4. an arrangement or positioning, as of troops

form·a·tive (fôr′mə tiv) *adj.* helping or involving formation or development

for·mer (fôr′mər) *adj.* [ME. *formere*] 1. previous; past 2. being the first mentioned of two

for·mer·ly *adv.* in the past

for·mic (fôr′mik) *adj.* [< L. *formica*, ant] designating a colorless acid found in ants, spiders, etc.

For·mi·ca (fôr mīk′ə) *a trademark for* a laminated, heat-resistant plastic used for table and sink tops, etc.

for·mi·da·ble (fôr′mə də b'l) *adj.* [< L. *formidare*, to dread] 1. causing dread, fear, or awe 2. hard to handle

form′less *adj.* shapeless; amorphous

form letter a standardized letter, usually one of many, with the date, address, etc. added separately

For·mo·sa (fôr mō′sə) *former (Portuguese) name of* TAIWAN

for·mu·la (fôr′myə lə) *n., pl.* -las, -lae′ (-lē′) [L. < *forma*, form] 1. a fixed form of words, esp. a conventional expression 2. any conventional rule for doing something 3. a prescription or recipe 4. fortified milk for a baby 5. a set of symbols expressing a mathematical rule 6. *Chem.* an expression of the composition, as of a compound, using symbols and figures

for·mu·late′ (-lāt′) *vt.* -lat′ed, -lat′ing 1. to express in a formula 2. to express in a definite way —**for′mu·la′tion** *n.* —**for′mu·la′tor** *n.*

for·ni·cate (fôr′nə kāt′) *vi.* -cat′ed, -cat′ing [< L. *fornix*, brothel] to commit fornication —**for′ni·ca′tor** *n.*

for·ni·ca′tion *n.* sexual intercourse between unmarried persons

for·sake (fər sāk′, fôr-) *vt.* -sook′ (-sook′), -sak′en, -sak′ing [< OE. *for-* + *sacan*, strive] 1. to give up (a habit, etc.) 2. to leave; abandon

for·sooth (fər sooth′, fôr-) *adv.* [ME. *forsoth*] [Archaic] indeed

for·swear (fôr swer′) *vt.* -swore′, -sworn′, -swear′ing to deny or renounce on oath —*vi.* to commit perjury

for·syth·i·a (fər sith′ē ə, fôr-) *n.* [< W. *Forsyth*, 18th-c. Eng. botanist] a shrub with yellow, bell-shaped flowers in early spring

fort (fôrt) *n.* [< L. *fortis*, strong] 1. a fortified place for military defense 2. a permanent army post

forte[1] (fôrt) *n.* [< OFr.: see prec.] that which one does particularly well

for·te[2] (fôr′tā, -tē) *adj., adv.* [It. < L. *fortis*, strong] *Music* loud

forth (fôrth) *adv.* [OE.] 1. forward; onward 2. out into view

Forth (fôrth), **Firth of** estuary of the Forth River in SE Scotland

forth′com′ing *adj.* 1. approaching; about to appear 2. ready when needed

forth′right′ *adj.* direct and frank

forth′with′ *adv.* without delay

for·ti·fy (fôr′tə fī′) *vt.* -fied′, -fy′ing [< L. *fortis*, strong + *facere*, make] 1. to strengthen physically, emotionally, etc. 2. to strengthen against attack, as with forts 3. to support 4. to add alcohol to (wine, etc.) 5. to add vitamins, etc. to (milk, etc.) —**for′ti·fi·ca′tion** *n.* —**for′ti·fi′er** *n.*

for·tis·si·mo (fôr tis′ə mō′) *adj., adv.* [It., superl. of *forte*, strong] *Music* very loud

for·ti·tude (fôr′tə tood′) *n.* [< L. *fortis*, strong] courage; patient endurance of trouble, pain, etc.

Fort Knox (näks) military reservation in N Ky.: U.S. gold depository

Fort Lau·der·dale (lô′dər dāl′) city on the SE coast of Fla.: pop. 153,000

fort·night (fôrt′nīt′) *n.* [ME. *fourte(n) niht*] [Chiefly Brit.] two weeks —**fort′night′ly** *adv., adj.*

for·tress (fôr′trəs) *n.* [< L. *fortis*, strong] a fortified place; fort

for·tu·i·tous (fôr too′ə təs) *adj.* [< L. *fors*, luck] 1. happening by chance 2. lucky —**for·tu′i·tous·ly** *adv.*

for·tu·nate (fôr′chə nit) *adj.* 1. having good luck 2. coming by good luck; favorable —**for′tu·nate·ly** *adv.*

for·tune (fôr′chən) *n.* [< L. *fors*, chance] 1. luck; chance; fate 2. one's future lot, good or bad 3. good luck; success 4. wealth; riches

for′tune-tell′er *n.* one who professes to foretell the future of others —**for′tune-tell′ing** *n., adj.*

Fort Wayne (wān) city in NE Ind.: pop. 172,000

Fort Worth (wurth) city in N Tex.: pop. 385,000

for·ty (fôr′tē) *adj., n., pl.* -ties [OE. *feowertig*] four times ten; 40; XL — **the forties** the numbers or years, as of a century, from 40 through 49 — **for′ti·eth** (-ith) *adj., n.*

fo·rum (fôr′əm) *n.* [L.] 1. the public square of an ancient Roman city 2. an assembly, program, etc. for the discussion of public matters

for·ward (fôr′wərd) *adj.* [OE. *foreweard*] 1. at, toward, or of the front 2. advanced 3. onward 4. prompt; ready 5. bold; presumptuous 6. of or for the future —*adv.* toward the front; ahead —*n. Basketball, Hockey,* etc. a player in a front position —*vt.* 1. to promote 2. to send on

for′wards *adv. same as* FORWARD

fos·sil (fäs′'l) *n.* [< L. *fossilis*, dug up] 1. any hardened remains of a plant or animal of a previous geological age, preserved in the earth's crust 2. a person with outmoded ideas or ways —*adj.* 1. of or like a fossil 2. dug from the earth [coal is a *fossil* fuel] 3. antiquated

fos·sil·ize′ (-īz′) *vt., vi.* **-ized′, -iz′-ing** 1. to change into a fossil 2. to make or become outdated, rigid, etc. —**fos′sil·i·za′tion** *n.*

fos·ter (fôs′tər) *vt.* [OE. *fostrian*, nourish] 1. to bring up; rear 2. to help to develop; promote —*adj.* having a specified standing in a family but not by birth [a foster brother]

fought (fôt) *pt. & pp.* of FIGHT

foul (foul) *adj.* [OE. *ful*] 1. stinking; loathsome 2. extremely dirty 3. indecent; profane 4. wicked; abominable 5. stormy [foul weather] 6. tangled [a foul rope] 7. not within the limits or rules set 8. designating lines setting limits on a playing area 9. dishonest 10. [Colloq.] unpleasant, disagreeable, etc. —*adv.* in a foul manner —*n. Sports* a hit, blow, move, etc. that is foul (sense 7) —*vt.* 1. to make filthy 2. to dishonor 3. to obstruct [grease fouls drains] 4. to entangle (a rope, etc.) 5. to make a foul against, as in a game 6. *Baseball* to bat (the ball) foul —*vi.* to be or become fouled —foul up [Colloq.] to bungle —**foul′ly** *adv.* —**foul′ness** *n.*

fou·lard (foō lärd′) *n.* [Fr.] a lightweight printed fabric of silk, etc.

foul′-up′ *n.* [Colloq.] a mix-up

found¹ (found) *vt.* [< L. *fundus*, bottom] 1. to set for support; base 2. to bring into being; set up; establish —**found′er** *n.*

found² (found) *vt.* [< L. *fundere*, pour] 1. to melt and pour (metal) into a mold 2. to make by founding metal

found³ (found) *pt. & pp.* of FIND

foun·da·tion (foun dā′shən) *n.* 1. a founding or being founded; establishment 2. *a)* an endowment for an institution *b)* such an institution 3. basis 4. the base of a wall, house, etc.

foun·der (foun′dər) *vi.* [< L. *fundus*, bottom] 1. to stumble, fall, or go lame 2. to fill with water and sink: said of a ship 3. to break down

found·ling (found′liŋ) *n.* an infant of unknown parents, found abandoned

found·ry (foun′drē) *n., pl.* **-ries** a place where metal is cast

fount (fount) *n.* [< L. *fons*] 1. [Poet.] a fountain; spring 2. a source

foun·tain (foun′t'n) *n.* [< L. *fons*] 1. a natural spring of water 2. a source 3. *a)* an artificial jet or flow of water [a drinking fountain] *b)* the basin where this flows 4. a reservoir, as for ink

foun′tain·head′ *n.* the source, as of a stream

fountain pen a pen which is fed ink from its own reservoir

four (fôr) *adj., n.* [OE. *feower*] one more than three; 4; IV

four′flush′er (-flush′ər) *n.* [< FLUSH²] [Colloq.] one who bluffs

four′-in-hand′ *n.* a necktie tied in a slipknot with the ends left hanging

four′score′ *adj., n.* four times twenty; eighty

four·some (-səm) *n.* four people

four′square′ *adj.* 1. square 2. unyielding; firm 3. frank; forthright —*adv.* in a square form or manner

four·teen′ (-tēn′) *adj., n.* [OE. *feowertyne*] four more than ten; 14; XIV —**four′teenth′** *adj., n.*

fourth (fôrth) *adj.* [OE. *feortha*] preceded by three others in a series; 4th —*n.* 1. the one following the third 2. any of the four equal parts of something; 1/4 3. the fourth forward gear

fourth′-class′ *adj., adv.* of or in a class of mail including parcels over 1 lb. in weight and books, films, etc.

fourth dimension in the theory of relativity, time added as a dimension to those of length, width, and depth

fourth estate [often F- E-] journalism or journalists

Fourth of July *see* INDEPENDENCE DAY

fourth world [often F- W-] the poorest countries of the third world

fowl (foul) *n.* [OE. *fugol*] 1. any bird 2. any of the domestic birds used as food, as the chicken, duck, etc. 3. the flesh of these birds used for food

fox (fäks) *n.* [OE.] 1. a small, wild animal of the dog family, considered sly and crafty 2. its fur 3. a sly, crafty person —*vt.* to trick by slyness

fox′glove′ *n.* common name for DIGITALIS (sense 1)

fox′hole′ *n.* a hole dug in the ground as a protection against enemy gunfire

fox′hound′ *n.* a hound with a keen scent, bred and trained to hunt foxes

fox terrier a small, active terrier with a smooth or wiry coat, formerly trained to drive foxes out of hiding

fox trot a dance for couples in 4/4 time, or music for it —**fox′-trot′** *vi.* **-trot′ted, -trot′ting**

fox·y (fäk′sē) *adj.* **-i·er, -i·est** 1. foxlike; crafty; sly 2. [Slang] attractive or sexy: used esp. of women

foy·er (foi′ər, foi yā′) *n.* [Fr. < L. *focus*, hearth] an entrance hall or lobby, as in a theater or hotel

FPO Fleet Post Office

Fr. 1. Father 2. French 3. Friday

frab·jous (frab′jəs) *adj.* [coined by Lewis Carroll] [Colloq.] splendid; fine

fra·cas (frā′kəs) *n.* [Fr. < It. *fracassare*, smash] a noisy fight; brawl

frac·tal (frak′t'l) *n.* [< L. *fractus*] *Geom.* an irregular line or plane formed of an infinite number of irregular sections, and having fractional dimensions

frac·tion (frak′shən) *n.* [< L. *frangere*, break] 1. a small part, amount, etc. 2. *Math. a)* a quantity less than a whole, expressed as a decimal *b)* a quantity with a numerator and denominator —**frac′tion·al** *adj.*

frac·tious (frak′shəs) *adj.* [< ?] 1. unruly; rebellious 2. irritable; cross

frac·ture (frak′chər) *n.* [< L. *frangere*, to break] a breaking or break, esp. of a bone —*vt., vi.* **-tured, -tur·ing** to break, crack, or split

frag·ile (fraj′'l) *adj.* [< L. *frangere*, to break] easily broken or damaged; delicate —**fra·gil·i·ty** (frə jil′ə tē) *n.*

frag·ment (frag′mənt) *n.* [< L. *frangere*, to break] 1. a part broken away 2. an incomplete part, as of a novel —*vt., vi.* to break up —**frag′men·ta′tion** (-mən tā′shən) *n.*

frag·men·tar·y (-mən ter′ē) *adj.* consisting of fragments; not complete

fra·grant (frā′grənt) *adj.* [< L. *fragrare*, emit a (sweet) smell] having a pleasant odor —**fra′grance** *n.*

frail (frāl) *adj.* [see FRAGILE] 1. easily broken 2. not robust; weak 3. easily tempted; morally weak —**frail′ly** *adv.*

frail′ty (-tē) *n.* 1. *a* being frail; esp., moral weakness 2. *pl.* **-ties** a fault arising from such weakness

frame (frām) *vt.* **framed, fram′ing** [prob. < ON. *frami*, profit] 1. to form according to a pattern; design [to *frame* laws] 2. to construct 3. to put into words [to *frame* an excuse] 4. to enclose (a picture, etc.) in a border 5. [Colloq.] to falsify evidence in order to make appear guilty —*n.* 1. body structure 2. the framework, as of a house 3. the structural case enclosing a window, door, etc. 4. an ornamental border, as around a picture 5. the way that anything is put together; form 6. mood; temper [good *frame* of mind] 7. one exposure in a filmstrip or movie film 8. Bowling, etc. a division of a game —*adj.* having a wooden framework [a *frame* house] —**fram′er** *n.*

frame′-up′ *n.* [Colloq.] a secret, deceitful scheme, as a falsifying of evidence to make a person seem guilty

frame′work′ *n.* 1. a structure to hold together or to support something 2. a basic structure, system, etc.

franc (fraŋk) *n.* [Fr. < L. *Francorum rex*, king of the French, on the coin in 1360] the monetary unit and a coin of France, Belgium, Switzerland, etc.

France (frans, fräns) country in W Europe: 212,821 sq. mi.; pop. 49,750,000

fran·chise (fran′chīz) *n.* [< OFr. *franc*, free] 1. any special right or privilege granted by a government 2. the right to vote; suffrage 3. the right to sell a product or service —*vt.* **-chised, -chis·ing** to grant a franchise to

Franco- *a combining form meaning:* 1. of France or the French 2. France and

fran·gi·ble (fran′jə b'l) *adj.* [< L. *frangere*, to break] breakable; fragile

Frank (fraŋk) *n.* a member of the Germanic tribes whose 9th-cent. empire extended over what is now France, Germany, and Italy

frank (fraŋk) *adj.* [< OFr. *franc*, free] free in expressing oneself; candid —*vt.* to send (mail) free of postage —*n.* 1. the right to send mail free 2. a mark indicating this right —**frank′ly** *adv.* —**frank′ness** *n.*

Frank·en·stein (fraŋ′kən stīn′) the title character in a novel (1818), creator of a monster that destroys him —*n.* popularly, the monster

Frank·fort (fraŋk′fərt) capital of Ky.: pop. 26,000

frank·furt·er (fraŋk′fər tər) *n.* [G. < *Frankfurt*, city in Germany] a smoked sausage of beef, beef and pork, etc.; wiener: also [Colloq.] **frank**

frank·in·cense (fraŋ′kən sens′) *n.* [see FRANK & INCENSE[1]] a gum resin burned as incense

Frank·ish (fraŋ′kish) *n.* the West Germanic language of the Franks

Frank·lin (fraŋk′lin), **Benjamin** 1706–90; Am. statesman, scientist, inventor, & writer

fran·tic (fran′tik) *adj.* [< Gr. *phrenitis*, madness] wild with anger, pain, worry, etc. —**fran′ti·cal·ly** *adv.*

frap·pé (fra pā′) *n.* [Fr. < *frapper*, to strike] 1. a dessert made of partly frozen fruit juices, etc. 2. a beverage poured over shaved ice 3. [Eastern] a milk shake Also **frappe** (frap)

fra·ter·nal (frə tur′n'l) *adj.* [< L. *frater*, brother] 1. of brothers; brotherly 2. designating or of a society organized for fellowship

fra·ter·ni·ty (frə tur′nə tē) *n., pl.* **-ties** 1. brotherliness 2. a group of men joined together for fellowship, etc., as in college 3. a group of people with the same beliefs, work, etc.

frat·er·nize (frat′ər nīz′) *vi.* **-nized′, -niz′ing** to associate in a friendly way —**frat·er·ni·za′tion** *n.*

‡**Frau** (frou) *n., pl.* **Frau′en** (-ən) [G.] a wife: a title corresponding to *Mrs.*

fraud (frôd) *n.* [< L. *fraus*] 1. deceit; trickery 2. Law intentional deception 3. a trick 4. an impostor

fraud·u·lent (frô′jə lənt) *adj.* 1. based on or using fraud 2. done or obtained by fraud —**fraud′u·lence** *n.* —**fraud′u·lent·ly** *adv.*

fraught (frôt) *adj.* [< MDu. *vracht*, a load] filled or loaded (*with*) [a situation *fraught* with danger]

‡**Fräu·lein** (froi′līn) *n., pl.* **-lein,** E. **-leins** [G.] an unmarried woman: a title corresponding to *Miss*

fray[1] (frā) *n.* [< AFFRAY] a noisy quarrel or fight; brawl

fray[2] (frā) *vt., vi.* [< L. *fricare*, rub] 1. to make or become worn or ragged 2. to make or become weak

fraz·zle (fraz′'l) *vt., vi.* **-zled, -zling** [< dial. *fasle*] [Colloq.] 1. to wear to tatters 2. to tire out —*n.* [Colloq.] a being frazzled

freak (frēk) *n.* [< ?] 1. an odd notion; whim 2. an unusual happening 3. any abnormal animal, person, or plant 4. [Slang] *a*) a drug user *b*) a devotee; buff [a chess *freak*] —**freak** (**out**) [Slang] 1. to have hallucinations, etc., as from a psychedelic drug 2. to become a hippie —**freak′ish** *adj.*

freak′out′ *n.* [Slang] the act of freaking out

freck·le (frek′'l) *n.* [< Scand.] a small, brownish spot on the skin —*vt., vi.* **-led, -ling** to make or become spotted with freckles

Fred·er·ick the Great (fred′ər ik) 1712–86; king of Prussia (1740–86)

free (frē) *adj.* **fre′er, fre′est** [OE. *freo*] 1. not under the control or power

of another; having liberty; independent
2. having civil and political liberty
3. able to move in any direction; loose
4. not burdened by obligations, debts, discomforts, etc. 5. not confined to the usual rules *[free* verse] 6. not exact *[a free* translation] 7. generous; profuse *[a free* spender] 8. frank 9. with no cost or charge 10. exempt from taxes, duties, etc. 11. clear of obstructions *[a free* road] 12. not fastened *[a* rope's *free* end] —*adv.* 1. without cost 2. in a free manner —*vt.* **freed, free′ing** to make free; specif., *a)* to release from bondage or arbitrary power, obligation, etc. *b)* to clear of obstruction, etc. —**free from** (or **of**) without —**make free with** to use freely —**free′ly** *adv.* —**free′ness** *n.*

free·bie, free·by (frē′bē) *n., pl.* **-bies** [Slang] something given free of charge, as a theater ticket

free′boot′er (-bōōt′ər) *n.* [< Du. *frij,* free + *buit,* plunder] a pirate

freed·man (frēd′mən) *n., pl.* **-men** a man legally freed from slavery

free·dom (frē′dəm) *n.* 1. a being free; esp., *a)* independence *b)* civil or political liberty *c)* exemption from an obligation, discomfort, etc. *d)* a being able to act, use, etc. freely *e)* ease of movement *f)* frankness 2. a right or privilege

free fall unchecked fall, as of a parachutist before the parachute opens

free flight the flight of a rocket after the fuel supply has been used up or shut off —**free′-flight′** *adj.*

free′-for-all′ *n.* a disorganized, general fight; brawl —*adj.* open to all

free′hand′ *adj.* drawn by hand without the use of instruments, etc.

free′hold′ *n.* an estate held for life or with the right to pass it on through inheritance —**free′hold′er** *n.*

free lance a writer, actor, etc. who sells his services to individual buyers —**free′-lance′** (-lans′) *adj., vi.* **-lanced′, -lanc′ing**

free′load′er (-lō′dər) *n.* [Colloq.] one who habitually imposes on others for free food, etc. —**free′load′** *vi.*

free′man (-mən) *n., pl.* **-men** 1. a person not in slavery 2. a citizen

Free·ma·son (frē′mās′'n) *n.* a member of an international secret society based on brotherliness and mutual aid —**Free′ma′son·ry** *n.*

free on board delivered (by the seller) aboard the train, ship, etc. at no extra charge

free′stone′ *n.* a peach, etc. in which the pit does not cling to the pulp

free′think′er *n.* one who forms his opinions about religion independently

free trade trade conducted without protective tariffs, quotas, etc.

free university a loosely organized forum for studying subjects not normally offered at universities

free′way′ *n.* a multiple-lane divided highway with fully controlled access

free′will′ *adj.* voluntary

freeze (frēz) *vi.* **froze, fro′zen, freez′ing** [OE. *freosan*] 1. to be formed into, or become covered with, ice 2. to

become very cold 3. to be damaged or killed by cold 4. to become motionless 5. to be made speechless by strong emotion 6. to become formal or unfriendly —*vt.* 1. to form into, or cover with, ice 2. to make very cold 3. to preserve (food) by rapid refrigeration 4. to kill or damage by cold 5. to make motionless 6. to make formal or unfriendly 7. *a)* to fix (prices, etc.) at a given level by authority *b)* to make (funds, etc.) unavailable to the owners —*n.* 1. a freezing or being frozen 2. a period of freezing weather —**freeze out** 1. to die out through freezing, as plants 2. [Colloq.] to keep out by a cold manner, competition, etc. —**freeze over** to become covered with ice —**freez′a·ble** *adj.*

freeze′-dry′ *vt.* **-dried′, -dry′ing** to quick-freeze (food, etc.) and then dry under high vacuum

freez′er *n.* 1. a refrigerator, compartment, etc. for freezing and storing perishable food 2. a machine for making ice cream

freight (frāt) *n.* [< MDu. *vracht,* a load] 1. the transporting of goods by water, land, or air 2. the cost for this 3. the goods transported 4. a railroad train for transporting goods: in full **freight train** —*vt.* 1. to load with freight 2. to send by freight

freight′er *n.* a ship for carrying freight

Fre·mont (frē′mänt) city in W Calif. on San Francisco Bay: pop., 132,000

French (french) *adj.* of France, its people, language, etc. —*n.* the language of France —**the French** the French people —**French′man** (-mən) *n., pl.* **-men**

French cuff a shirt-sleeve cuff turned back and fastened with a link

French doors a pair of doors hinged at the sides to open in the middle

French dressing a salad dressing made of vinegar, oil, and seasonings

French fried fried in hot, deep fat

French fries [Colloq.] potatoes cut into strips and then French fried

French Guiana Fr. overseas department in NE S. America

French horn a brass-wind instrument: its coiled tube ends in a flaring bell

French leave an unauthorized departure

French toast sliced bread dipped in a batter of egg and milk and fried

fre·net·ic (frə net′ik) *adj.* [see PHRENETIC] frantic; frenzied —**fre·net′i·cal·ly** *adv.*

fren·zy (fren′zē) *n., pl.* **-zies** [< Gr. *phrenitis,* madness] wild excitement; delirium

FRENCH HORN

fre·quen·cy (frē′kwən sē) *n., pl.* **-cies** 1. frequent occurrence 2. the number of times any event recurs in a given period 3. *Physics* the number of oscillations or cycles per unit of time

frequency modulation the variation of the frequency of the transmitting radio wave in accordance with the signal transmitted

fre·quent (frē′kwənt; *for v. usually* frē kwent′) *adj.* [< L. *frequens*, crowded] **1.** occurring often **2.** constant; habitual —*vt.* to go to or be at or in habitually —**fre′quent·ly** *adv.*

fres·co (fres′kō) *n., pl.* **-coes, -cos** [It., fresh] a painting with water colors on wet plaster

fresh¹ (fresh) *adj.* [OE. *fersc*] **1.** recently made, grown, etc. *[fresh coffee]* **2.** not salted, pickled, etc. **3.** not spoiled **4.** not tired; lively **5.** not worn, soiled, faded, etc. **6.** new; recent **7.** inexperienced **8.** cool and refreshing *[a fresh spring day]* **9.** brisk: said of wind **10.** not salt: said of water —**fresh′ly** *adv.* —**fresh′ness** *n.*

fresh² (fresh) *adj.* [< G. *frech*, bold] [Slang] bold; impertinent; impudent

fresh′en (-ən) *vt., vi.* to make or become fresh —**freshen up** to bathe, put on fresh clothes, etc.

fresh·et (fresh′it) *n.* a flooding of a stream, as because of melting snow

fresh′man (-mən) *n., pl.* **-men** 1. a beginner **2.** a person in his first year in college, Congress, etc.

fresh′wa′ter *adj.* **1.** of or living in water that is not salty **2.** sailing only on inland waters

Fres·no (frez′nō) city in C Calif.: pop. 218,000

fret¹ (fret) *vt., vi.* **fret′ted, fret′ting** [OE. *fretan*, devour] **1.** to gnaw, wear away, rub, etc. **2.** to ripple or ruffle **3.** to irritate or be irritated; worry —*n.* irritation; worry —**fret′ter** *n.*

fret² (fret) *n.* [< OFr. *frette*, a band] any of the ridges on the fingerboard of a banjo, guitar, etc.

fret³ (fret) *n.* [ME. *frette*] a running design of interlacing small bars —*vt.* **fret′ted, fret′ting** to furnish with frets

FRETS

fret′ful *adj.* irritable; peevish — **fret′ful·ly** *adv.* —**fret′ful·ness** *n.*

fret′work′ *n.* decorative carving or openwork, as of interlacing lines

Freud (froid), **Sigmund** 1856–1939; Austrian psychiatrist: founder of psychoanalysis —**Freud′i·an** *adj., n.*

fri·a·ble (frī′ə b'l) *adj.* [Fr. < L. *friare*, to rub] easily crumbled

fri·ar (frī′ər) *n.* [< L. *frater*, brother] R.C.Ch. a member of certain religious orders

fric·as·see (frik′ə sē′, frik′ə sē′) *n.* [< Fr. *fricasser*, cut up and fry] meat cut into pieces and stewed —*vt.* **-seed′, -see′ing** to prepare in this way

fric·tion (frik′shən) *n.* [< L. *fricare*, to rub] **1.** a rubbing of one object against another **2.** conflict, as because of differing opinions **3.** the resistance to motion of surfaces that touch —**fric′tion·al** *adj.*

Fri·day (frī′dē, -dā) *n.* [< *Frig*, Germanic goddess] **1.** the sixth day of the week **2.** [< the devoted servant of ROBINSON CRUSOE] a faithful helper: usually **man** (or **girl**) **Friday**

fried (frīd) *pt. & pp.* of FRY¹

fried′cake′ *n.* a small cake fried in deep fat; doughnut or cruller

friend (frend) *n.* [ME. *freond*] **1.** a person whom one knows well and is fond of **2.** an ally, supporter, or sympathizer **3.** [F-] a member of the Society of Friends; Quaker —**make** (or **be**) **friends with** to become (or be) a friend of —**friend′less** *adj.*

friend′ly *adj.* **-li·er, -li·est 1.** of or like a friend; kindly **2.** not hostile; amicable **3.** supporting; helping — **friend′li·ly** *adv.* —**friend′li·ness** *n.*

friend′ship′ *n.* **1.** the state of being friends **2.** friendly feeling

frieze (frēz) *n.* [< ML. *frisium*] a horizontal band with designs or carvings along a wall or around a room

frig·ate (frig′it) *n.* [< It. *fregata*] a fast, medium-sized sailing warship of the 18th and early 19th cent.

fright (frīt) *n.* [OE. *fyrhto*] **1.** sudden fear; alarm **2.** something unsightly

fright′en *vt.* **1.** to make suddenly afraid; scare **2.** to force (*away, off,* etc.) by scaring —**fright′en·ing·ly** *adv.*

fright′ful *adj.* **1.** causing fright; alarming **2.** shocking; terrible **3.** [Colloq.] *a)* unpleasant *b)* great —**fright′ful·ly** *adv.*

frig·id (frij′id) *adj.* [< L. *frigus*, coldness] **1.** extremely cold **2.** not warm or friendly **3.** sexually unresponsive: said of a woman —**fri·gid′i·ty** *n.* —**frig′id·ly** *adv.*

Frigid Zone either of two zones (**North** or **South Frigid Zone**) between the polar circles and the poles

frill (fril) *n.* [< ?] **1.** any unnecessary ornament **2.** a ruffle —**frill′y** *adj.*

fringe (frinj) *n.* [< L. *fimbria*] **1.** a border of threads, etc. hanging loose, often tied in bunches **2.** an outer edge; border **3.** a marginal or minor part —*vt.* **fringed, fring′ing** to be or make a fringe for —*adj.* **1.** at the outer edge **2.** additional **3.** minor

fringe benefit payment other than wages, as in pension, insurance, etc.

frip·per·y (frip′ər ē) *n., pl.* **-ies** [< OFr. *frepe*, rag] **1.** cheap, gaudy clothes **2.** showy display in dress, etc.

Fris·bee (friz′bē) [after "Mother Frisbie's" cookie jar lids] *a trademark for* a plastic, saucer-shaped disk tossed back and forth in a game —*n.* [f-] such a disk

fri·sé (fri zā′) *n.* [Fr. < *friser*, to curl] an upholstery fabric with a thick pile of loops

Fri·sian (frizh′ən) *n.* the West Germanic language of an island chain (**Frisian Islands**) along the coast of the Netherlands, West Germany, & Denmark

frisk (frisk) *vi.* [< OHG. *frisc*, lively] to frolic —*vt.* [Slang] to search (a person) for weapons, etc. by passing the hands quickly over his clothing

frisk'y adj. -i·er, -i·est lively; frolicsome —**frisk'i·ly** adv. —**frisk'i·ness** n.

frit·ter[1] (frit'ər) vt. [< L. frangere, to break] to waste (money, time, etc.) bit by bit (usually with away)

frit·ter[2] (frit'ər) n. [< VL. frigere, to fry] a small cake of fried batter, usually containing corn, fruit, etc.

friv·o·lous (friv'ə ləs) adj. [< L. frivolus] 1. of little value; trivial 2. silly and light-minded; flighty —**fri·vol·i·ty** (fri val'ə tē) n., pl. -ties —**friv'o·lous·ly** adv.

frizz, friz (friz) vt., vi. **frizzed, friz'zing** [Fr. friser] to form into small, tight curls in hair, etc. that is frizzed —**friz'zi·ly, friz'zy** adj.

friz·zle[1] (friz'ʼl) vt., vi. -zled, -zling [< FRY[1]] to sizzle, as in frying

friz·zle[2] (friz'ʼl) n., vt., vi. -zled, -zling same as FRIZZ

fro (frō) adv. [< ON. frā] backward; back: now only in to and fro: see under TO

frock (fräk) n. [< OFr. froc] 1. a robe worn by friars, monks, etc. 2. a dress

frog (frôg, fräg) n. [OE. frogga] 1. a tailless, leaping amphibian with long hind legs and webbed feet 2. a fancy braided loop used to fasten clothing —**frog in the throat** hoarseness

frog'man' (-'man') n., pl. -men (-mən) one trained and equipped for underwater demolition, exploration, etc.

frol·ic (fräl'ik) n. [< MDu. vrō, merry] 1. a lively party or game 2. merriment; fun —vi. -icked, -icking 1. to make merry; have fun 2. to romp about; gambol —**frol'ick·er** n.

frol'ic·some (-səm) adj. playful; gay

from (frum, främ) prep. [OE.] 1. beginning at; starting with [from noon to midnight] 2. out of [from her purse] 3. originating with [a letter from me] 4. out of the possibility or use of [kept from going] 5. as not being like [to know good from evil] 6. because of [to tremble from fear]

frond (fränd) n. [L. frons, leafy branch] the leaf of a fern or palm

front (frunt) n. [< L. frons, forehead] 1. a) outward behavior [a bold front] b) [Colloq.] an appearance of social standing, wealth, etc. 2. the part facing forward 3. the first part; beginning 4. a forward or leading position 5. the land bordering a lake, street, etc. 6. the advanced battle area in warfare 7. an area of activity [the home front] 8. a person or group used to hide another's activity 9. Meteorology the boundary between two differing air masses —adj. at, to, in, on, or of the front —vt., vi. 1. to face 2. to serve as a front (for) —**in front of** before —**front'al** adj.

front'age (-ij) n. 1. the front part of a building 2. the front boundary line of a lot or the length of this line 3. land bordering a street, etc.

fron·tier (frun tir') n. [see FRONT] 1. the border between two countries

2. the part of a country which borders an unexplored region 3. any new field of learning, etc. —adj. of or on the frontier —**fron·tiers'man** (-tirz'mən) n., pl. -men

fron·tis·piece (frun'tis pēs') n. [< L. frons, front + specere, to look] an illustration facing the title page of a book

front office the management or administration, as of a company

front'-run'ner n. a leading contestant

frost (frôst, fräst) n. [OE. < freosan, freeze] 1. a temperature low enough to cause freezing 2. frozen dew or vapor —vt. 1. to cover with frost 2. to cover with frosting 3. to give a frostlike, opaque surface to (glass) —**frost'y** adj. -i·er, -i·est

Frost (frôst, fräst), **Robert (Lee)** 1874–1963; U.S. poet

frost'bite' vt. -bit', -bit'ten, -bit'ing to injure the tissues of (a body part) by exposure to intense cold —n. injury caused by such exposure

frost'ing n. 1. a mixture of sugar, butter, etc. for covering a cake; icing 2. a dull finish on glass, metal, etc.

froth (frôth, fräth) n. [< ON. frotha] 1. foam 2. foaming saliva 3. light, trifling talk, ideas, etc. —vi. to foam —**froth'y** adj. -i·er, -i·est

frou-frou (frōō'frōō') n. [Fr.] [Colloq.] excessive ornateness

fro·ward (frō'ərd, -wərd) adj. [see FRO- & -WARD] not easily controlled; willful; contrary —**fro'ward·ness** n.

frown (froun) vi. [< OFr. froigne, sullen face] 1. to contract the brows, as in displeasure 2. to show disapproval (with on or upon) —n. a frowning

frow·zy (frou'zē) adj. -zi·er, -zi·est [< ?] dirty and untidy; slovenly —**frow'zi·ly** adv. —**frow'zi·ness** n.

froze (frōz) pt. of FREEZE

fro·zen (-'n) pp. of FREEZE —adj. 1. turned into or covered with ice 2. damaged or killed by freezing 3. preserved by freezing 4. made motionless 5. kept at a fixed level 6. not readily convertible into cash

fruc·ti·fy (fruk'tə fī') vi., vt. -fied', -fy'ing [< L. fructificare] to bear or cause to bear fruit

fruc·tose (fruk'tōs, frook'-) n. [< L. fructus, fruit + -OSE[1]] a sugar found in sweet fruit, honey, etc.

fru·gal (frōō'g'l) adj. [< L. frugi, fit for food] 1. not wasteful; thrifty 2. inexpensive or meager —**fru·gal'i·ty** (-gal'ə tē) n. —**fru'gal·ly** adv.

fruit (frōōt) n. [< L. fructus] 1. any plant product, as grain, vegetables, etc.: usually used in pl. 2. a) a sweet, edible plant structure, containing the seeds inside a juicy pulp b) Bot. the seed-bearing part of any plant 3. the result or product of any action

fruit'cake' n. a rich cake containing nuts, preserved fruit, citron, etc.

fruit'ful adj. 1. bearing much fruit 2. productive; prolific 3. profitable

fru·i·tion (frōō ish'ən) n. 1. the bearing of fruit 2. a coming to fulfillment; realization

fruit′less *adj.* 1. without results; unsuccessful 2. bearing no fruit; sterile; barren —**fruit′less·ly** *adv.*

trump (trump) *n.* [prob. < Du. *rompelen,* rumple] a dowdy woman —**frump′ish, frump′y** *adj.*

frus·trate (frus′trāt) *vt.* -trat·ed, -trat·ing [< L. *frustra,* in vain] 1. to cause to have no effect 2. to prevent from achieving a goal or gratifying a desire —**frus·tra′tion** *n.*

fry¹ (frī) *vt., vi.* fried, fry′ing [< L. *frigere*] to cook over direct heat, usually in hot fat —*n., pl.* fries 1. [*pl.*] fried potatoes 2. a social gathering at which food is fried and eaten

fry² (frī) *n., pl.* fry [< OFr. *freier,* to spawn] young fish —**small fry** 1. children 2. insignificant people

fry′er (-ər) *n.* 1. a utensil for deep-frying 2. a chicken for frying

ft. foot; feet

FTC Federal Trade Commission

fuch·sia (fyōō′shə) *n.* [< L. *Fuchs* (1501–66), G. botanist] 1. a shrubby plant with pink, red, or purple flowers 2. purplish red

fud·dle (fud′'l) *vt.* -dled, -dling [< ?] to confuse or stupefy as with alcoholic liquor —*n.* a fuddled state

fud·dy-dud·dy (fud′ē dud′ē) *n., pl.* -dies [Slang] a fussy, critical, or old-fashioned person

fudge (fuj) *n.* [< ?] a soft candy made of butter, milk, sugar, flavoring, etc. —*vi.* 1. to refuse to commit oneself; hedge 2. to be dishonest; cheat

fu·el (fyōō′əl) *n.* [ult. < L. *focus,* fireplace] 1. coal, oil, gas, wood, etc., burned to supply heat or power 2. material from which atomic energy can be obtained 3. anything that intensifies strong feeling —*vt., vi.* -eled or -elled, -el·ing or -el·ling to supply with or get fuel

fuel cell a device that converts chemical energy into electrical energy

fuel injection a system for forcing fuel into combustion chambers of an internal-combustion engine

fu·gi·tive (fyōō′jə tiv) *adj.* [< L. *fugere,* flee] 1. fleeing, as from danger or justice 2. fleeting —*n.* one who is fleeing from justice, etc.

fugue (fyōōg) *n.* [< L. *fugere,* flee] a musical work in which a theme is taken up successively and developed by the various parts in counterpoint

-ful (fəl, f'l; *for 3* fool) [< FULL¹] *a suffix meaning:* 1. full of, having [*joyful*] 2. having the qualities of or tendency to [*helpful*] 3. *pl.* -fuls the quantity that will fill [*handful*]

ful·crum (fool′krəm, ful′-) *n.* [L., a support] the support on which a lever turns in raising something

FULCRUM

ful·fill, ful·fil (fool fil′) *vt.* -filled′, -fill′ing [OE. *fullfyllan*]

1. to carry out (a promise, etc.) 2. to do (a duty, etc.) 3. to satisfy (a condition) 4. to bring to an end; complete —**ful·fill′ment, ful·fil′ment** *n.*

full¹ (fool) *adj.* [OE.] 1. having in it all there is space for; filled 2. having eaten all that one wants 3. having a great deal or number (*of*) 4. complete [*a full dozen*] 5. having reached the greatest size, extent, etc. 6. plump; round 7. with wide folds; flowing [*a full skirt*] —*n.* the greatest amount, extent, etc. —*adv.* 1. to the greatest degree; completely 2. directly; exactly —**full′ness, ful′ness** *n.*

full² (fool) *vt., vi.* [< L. *fullo,* cloth fuller] to shrink and thicken (wool cloth) —**full′er** *n.*

full′back′ *n. Football* a member of the offensive backfield, stationed behind the quarterback

full′-blood′ed *adj.* 1. of unmixed breed or race 2. vigorous

full′-blown′ *adj.* 1. in full bloom 2. fully developed; matured

full′-fledged′ *adj.* completely developed or trained; of full status

full moon the moon when it reflects light as a full disk

full′-scale′ *adj.* 1. according to the original or standard scale 2. to the utmost degree; all-out

full′-time′ *adj.* of or engaged in work, study, etc. that takes all of one's regular working hours

full′y *adv.* 1. completely; thoroughly 2. at least

ful·mi·nate (ful′mə nāt′) *vi., vt.* -nat′ed, -nat′ing [< L. *fulmen,* lightning] 1. to explode 2. to shout forth —**ful′mi·na′tion** *n.*

ful·some (fool′səm) *adj.* [see FULL¹ & -SOME¹, but infl. by ME. *ful,* foul] disgusting, esp. because excessive

fum·ble (fum′b'l) *vi., vt.* -bled, -bling [prob. < ON. *famla*] 1. to grope (*for*) or handle (a thing) clumsily 2. to lose one's grasp on (a football, etc.) —*n.* a fumbling —**fum′bler** *n.*

fume (fyōōm) *n.* [< L. *fumus*] a gas, smoke, or vapor, esp. if offensive or suffocating —*vi.* fumed, fum′ing 1. to give off fumes 2. to show anger

fu·mi·gate (fyōō′mə gāt′) *vt.* -gat′ed, -gat′ing [< L. *fumus,* smoke + *agere,* do] to expose to fumes, esp. to disinfect or kill the vermin in —**fu′mi·ga′tion** *n.* —**fu′mi·ga′tor** *n.*

fum·y (fyōō′mē) *adj.* -i·er, -i·est full of or producing fumes; vaporous

fun (fun) *n.* [< ME. *fonne,* foolish] 1. *a)* lively, gay play or playfulness *b)* pleasure 2. a source of merriment —**make fun of** to ridicule

func·tion (funk′shən) *n.* [< L. *fungi,* perform] 1. the normal or characteristic action of anything 2. a special duty required in work 3. a formal ceremony or social occasion 4. a thing that depends on and varies with something else —*vi.* to act in a required manner; work; be used —**func′tion·less** *adj.*

func·tion·al *adj.* **1.** of a function **2.** performing a function **3.** *Med.* affecting a function of some organ without apparent organic changes

func·tion·ar·y (-er'ē) *n., pl.* **-ies** an official performing some function

function word a word, as an article or conjunction, serving mainly to show grammatical relationship

fund (fund) *n.* [L. *fundus*, bottom] **1.** a supply that can be drawn upon; stock **2.** *a*) a sum of money set aside for a purpose *b*) [*pl.*] ready money —*vt.* to put or convert into a long-term debt that bears interest

fun·da·men·tal (fun'də men't'l) *adj.* [see prec.] of or forming a foundation or basis; basic; essential —*n.* a principle, theory, law, etc. serving as a basis —**fun'da·men'tal·ly** *adv.*

fun'da·men'tal·ism *n.* [*sometimes* F-] religious beliefs based on a literal interpretation of the Bible —**fun'da·men'tal·ist** *n., adj.*

fu·ner·al (fyōō'nər əl) *n.* [< L. *funus*] the ceremonies connected with burial or cremation of the dead

funeral director the manager of an establishment (**funeral home** or **parlor**) where funeral services can be held

fu·ne·re·al (fyoo nir'ē əl) *adj.* suitable for a funeral; sad and solemn; dismal —**fu·ne·re·al·ly** *adv.*

fun·gi·cide (fun'jə sīd') *n.* [see -CIDE] any substance that kills fungi

fun·gus (fuŋ'gəs) *n., pl.* **-gi** (fun'jī), **-gus·es** [< Gr. *spongos*, sponge] any of various plants, as molds, mildews, mushrooms, etc., that lack chlorophyll, stems, and leaves and reproduce by spores —**fun'gous** *adj.*

fu·nic·u·lar (fyoo nik'yoo lər) *adj.* [< L. *funiculus*, little rope] worked by a rope or cable —*n.* a mountain railway with counterbalanced cable cars on parallel sets of rails

funk (fuŋk) *n.* [< ? Fl. *fonck*, dismay] [Colloq.] **1.** a cowering through fear; panic **2.** a depressed mood

fun·ky (fuŋ'kē) *adj.* **-ki·er, -ki·est** [*orig.*, earthy] *Jazz* of an earthy style derived from early blues

fun·nel (fun''l) *n.* [ult. < L. *fundere*, pour] **1.** a tapering tube with a cone-shaped mouth, for pouring things into small-mouthed containers **2.** the smokestack of a steamship —*vi., vt.* **-neled** or **-nelled, -nel·ing** or **-nel·ling** to move or pour as through a funnel

fun·ny (fun'ē) *adj.* **-ni·er, -ni·est** **1.** causing laughter; humorous **2.** [Colloq.] *a*) strange; queer *b*) tricky —*n., pl.* **-nies** [Colloq.] *same as* COMIC STRIP: *usually in pl.* —**fun'ni·ly** *adv.* —**fun'ni·ness** *n.*

funny bone a place on the elbow where a sharp impact on a nerve causes a strange, tingling sensation

fur (fur) *n.* [< OFr. *fuerre*, sheath] **1.** the soft, thick hair covering certain animals **2.** a processed skin bearing such hair —*adj.* of fur —**furred** *adj.*

fur·be·low (fur'bə lō') *n.* [ult. < Fr. *falbala*] **1.** a flounce or ruffle **2.** [*usually pl.*] showy, useless trimming

fur·bish (fur'bish) *vt.* [< OFr. *forbir*] **1.** to polish; brighten **2.** to renovate

Fu·ries (fyoor'ēz) *n.pl. Gr. & Rom. Myth.* the three terrible female spirits who punished unavenged crimes

fu·ri·ous (fyoor'ē əs) *adj.* **1.** full of fury; very angry **2.** very great, intense, wild, etc. —**fu·ri·ous·ly** *adv.*

furl (furl) *vt.* [< L. *firmus*, FIRM[1] + *ligare*, to tie] to roll up (a sail, flag, etc.) tightly and make secure

fur·long (fur'lôŋ) *n.* [< OE. *furh*, a furrow + *lang*, LONG[1]] a measure of distance equal to 1/8 of a mile

fur·lough (fur'lō) *n.* [< Du. *verlof*] a leave of absence, esp. for military personnel —*vt.* to grant a furlough

fur·nace (fur'nəs) *n.* [< L. *fornus*, oven] an enclosed structure in which heat is produced, as by burning fuel

fur·nish (fur'nish) *vt.* [< OFr. *furnir*] **1.** to supply with furniture, etc.; equip **2.** to supply; provide

fur·nish·ings *n.pl.* **1.** the furniture, carpets, etc. as for a house **2.** things to wear [men's *furnishings*]

fur·ni·ture (fur'ni chər) *n.* [Fr. *fourniture*] **1.** the things in a room, etc. which equip it for living, as chairs, beds, etc. **2.** necessary equipment

fu·ror (fyoor'ôr) *n.* [< L.] **1.** fury; frenzy **2.** *a*) a widespread enthusiasm; craze *b*) a commotion or uproar Also for 2. [*Chiefly Brit.*] **fu'rore** (-ôr)

fur·ri·er (fur'ē ər) *n.* one who processes furs or deals in fur garments

fur·ring (fur'iŋ) *n.* thin strips of wood fixed on a wall, floor, etc. before adding boards or plaster

fur·row (fur'ō) *n.* [OE. *furh*] **1.** a narrow groove made in the ground by a plow **2.** anything like this, as a deep wrinkle —*vt.* to make furrows in —*vi.* to become wrinkled

fur·ry (fur'ē) *adj.* **-ri·er, -ri·est** **1.** of or like fur **2.** covered with fur —**fur'ri·ness** *n.*

fur·ther (fur'thər) *adj.* [OE. *furthra*] **1.** additional **2.** more distant; farther —*adv.* **1.** to a greater degree or extent **2.** in addition **3.** at or to a greater distance; farther In sense 2 of the *adj.* and sense 3 of the *adv.*, FARTHER is more commonly used —*vt.* to give aid to; promote —**fur'ther·ance** *n.*

fur·ther·more' *adv.* in addition; besides; moreover

fur·thest (fur'thist) *adj.* most distant; farthest: also **fur'ther·most'** —*adv.* at or to the greatest distance or degree

fur·tive (fur'tiv) *adj.* [< L. *fur*, thief] done or acting in a stealthy manner; sneaky —**fur'tive·ly** *adv.* —**fur'tive·ness** *n.*

fu·ry (fyoor'ē) *n., pl.* **-ries** [< L. *furere*, to rage] **1.** violent anger; wild rage **2.** violence; vehemence

furze (furz) *n.* [OE. *fyrs*] a prickly evergreen shrub native to Europe

fuse[1] (fyōōz) *vt., vi.* fused, fus'ing [< L. *fundere*, to shed] **1.** to melt **2.** to unite as if by melting together

fuse[2] (fyōōz) *n.* [< L. *fusus*, spindle] **1.** a tube or wick filled with combustible material, for setting off an explosive charge 2. *Elec.* a strip of easily melted metal placed in a circuit: it melts and breaks the circuit if the current becomes too strong

fu·see (fyōō zē') *n.* [Fr. *fusée*, a rocket] a colored flare used as a signal, as by truck drivers

fu·se·lage (fyōō'sə läzh') *n.* [Fr.] the body of an airplane, exclusive of the wings, tail assembly, and engines

fu·si·ble (fyōō'zə b'l) *adj.* that can be fused or easily melted

fu·sil·ier, fu·sil·eer (fyōō'zə lir') *n.* [Fr.] formerly, a soldier armed with a flintlock musket

fu·sil·lade (fyōō'sə läd') *n.* [Fr. < *fusiller*, to shoot] a simultaneous or rapid discharge of many firearms

fu·sion (fyōō'zhən) *n.* 1. a fusing or melting together 2. a blending; coalition 3. *same as* NUCLEAR FUSION

fuss (fus) *n.* [prob. echoic] 1. nervous, excited activity; bustle 2. a nervous state 3. [Colloq.] a quarrel 4. [Colloq.] a showy display of approval, etc. —*vi.* 1. to bustle about or worry over trifles 2. to whine, as a baby

fuss'budg'et (-buj'it) *n.* [FUSS + BUDGET] [Colloq.] a fussy person: also **fuss'pot'** (-pät')

fuss'y *adj.* -i·er, -i·est 1. a) worrying over trifles b) hard to please c) whining, as a baby 2. full of needless, showy details —**fuss'i·ness** *n.*

fus·tian (fus'chən) *n.* [< L. *fustis*, wooden stick] pompous, pretentious talk or writing; bombast

fus·ty (fus'tē) *adj.* -ti·er, -ti·est [< OFr. *fust*, cask] 1. musty; moldy

2. old-fashioned —**fus'ti·ly** *adv.* —**fus'ti·ness** *n.*

fut. future

fu·tile (fyōōt''l) *adj.* [< L. *futilis*, that easily pours out] useless; vain —**fu·til·i·ty** (fyōō til'ə tē) *n.*

fu·ton (fōō'tän) *n.* [Jap.] a thin mattress, placed on the floor for use as a bed

fu·ture (fyōō'chər) *adj.* [< L. *futurus*, about to be] 1. that is to be or come 2. indicating time to come [the *future* tense] —*n.* 1. the time that is to come 2. what is going to be 3. the chance to succeed —**fu'tur·is'tic** *adj.*

future shock [after A. Toffler's book *Future Shock* (1970)] an inability to cope with rapid social changes that have not been properly anticipated

fu·tu·ri·ty (fyōō toor'ə tē, -tyoor'-) *n., pl.* -ties 1. the future 2. a future condition or event

fu·tur·ol·o·gy (fyōō'chər äl'ə jē) *n.* [FUTUR(E) + -OLOGY] a method of stating the probable form of future conditions by making assumptions based on known facts —**fu'tur·ol'o·gist** *n.*

futz (futs) *vi.* [< Yid.] [Slang] to trifle or fool (*around*)

fuze (fyōōz) *n., vt., vi.* fuzed, fuz'ing *same as* FUSE

fuzz (fuz) *n.* [< ?] loose, light particles of down, wool, etc.; fine hairs or fibers —**the fuzz** [Slang] a policeman or the police —**fuzz'y** *adj.* -i·er, -i·est

-fy (fī) [< L. *facere*, do] *a suffix meaning:* 1. to make [*liquefy*] 2. to cause to have [*glorify*] 3. to become [*putrefy*]

G

G, g (jē) *n., pl.* **G's, g's** 1. the 7th letter of the English alphabet 2. *Physics* gravity

G (jē) *n. Music* the fifth tone in the scale of C major

G a motion-picture rating for a film considered suitable for general audiences, with no age restriction

G. German

G., g. 1. gauge 2. gram(s) 3. gulf

Ga., GA Georgia

gab (gab) *n., vi.* gabbed, gab'bing [ON. *gabba*, mock] [Colloq.] chatter

gab·ar·dine (gab'ər dēn') *n.* [< OFr. *gaverdine*, kind of cloak] a twilled cloth of wool, cotton, etc., with a fine, diagonal weave Also [Brit.] **gab'er·dine**

gab·ble (gab''l) *vi., vt.* -bled, -bling [< GAB] to talk or utter rapidly or incoherently —*n.* such talk

gab·by (gab'ē) *adj.* -bi·er, -bi·est [Colloq.] talkative —**gab'bi·ness** *n.*

gab'fest' (-fest') *n.* [Colloq.] an informal gathering to talk or gab

ga·ble (gā'b'l) *n.* [< Gmc.] the triangular wall enclosed by the sloping ends of a ridged roof —**ga'bled** *adj.*

Ga·bon (gä bōn') country on the W coast of Africa: 103,089 sq. mi.; pop. 473,000

Ga·bri·el (gā'brē əl) *Bible* an archangel, the herald of good news

gad (gad) *vi.* gad'ded, gad'ding [LME. *gadden*, to hurry] to wander about idly or restlessly —**gad'der** *n.*

gad'a·bout' *n.* [Colloq.] one who gads about, looking for fun, etc.

gad'fly' *n., pl.* -flies' [see GOAD & FLY] 1. a large fly that bites livestock 2. one who annoys others

gadg·et (gaj'it) *n.* [< ?] any small mechanical contrivance or device

Gael·ic (gāl'ik) *adj.* of the Celtic people of Ireland, Scotland, or the Isle of Man —*n.* any Celtic language spoken by these people Abbrev. **Gael.**

gaff (gaf) *n.* [< Pr. *gaf* or Sp. *gafa*] 1. a large hook on a pole for landing fish 2. a spar supporting a fore-and-aft sail —**stand the gaff** [Slang] to bear up well under punishment, ridicule, etc.

gaffe (gaf) *n.* [Fr.] a blunder

gag (gag) *vt.* **gagged, gag'ging** [echoic] 1. to cause to retch 2. to keep from speaking, as by stopping the mouth of —*vi.* to retch —*n.* 1. something put into or over the mouth to prevent talking, etc. 2. any restraint of free speech 3. a joke

gage¹ (gāj) *n.* [< OFr., a pledge] 1. something pledged; security 2. a glove, etc. thrown down as a challenge to fight 3. a challenge

gage² (gāj) *n., vt.* **gaged, gag'ing** *same as* GAUGE (esp. in technical use)

gag.gle (gag'′l) *n.* [echoic] 1. a flock of geese 2. any group

gai.e.ty (gā'ə tē) *n., pl.* **-ties** 1. the quality of being gay; cheerfulness 2. merrymaking 3. showy brightness

gai.ly (gā'lē) *adv.* in a gay manner; specif., *a*) merrily *b*) brightly

gain (gān) *n.* [< OFr. *gaaigne*] 1. an increase; specif., *a*) [*often pl.*] profit *b*) an increase in advantage 2. acquisition —*vt.* 1. to earn 2. to win 3. to attract 4. to get as an addition, profit, or advantage 5. to make an increase in 6. to get to; reach —*vi.* 1. to make progress 2. to increase in weight —**gain on** to draw nearer to (an opponent in a race, etc.)

gain'er *n.* 1. a person or thing that gains 2. a fancy dive forward, but with a backward somersault

gain'ful *adj.* producing gain; profitable —**gain'ful.ly** *adv.*

gain.say (gān'sā') *vt.* **-said'** (-sed', -sād'), **-say'ing** [< OE. *gegn*, against + *seggen*, say] 1. to deny 2. to contradict —**gain'say'er** *n.*

gait (gāt) *n.* [< ON. *gata*, path] 1. manner of walking or running 2. any of the various foot movements of a horse, as a trot, pace, canter, etc.

gai.ter (gāt'ər) *n.* [< Fr. *guêtre*] a cloth or leather covering for the instep, ankle, and lower leg

gal (gal) *n.* [Colloq.] a girl

gal. gallon(s)

ga.la (gā'lə, gal'ə) *n.* [It. < OFr. *gale*, pleasure] a celebration —*adj.* festive

gal.a.bi.a, gal.a.bi.ya (gal'ə bē'ə) *n.* [< Ar.] a long, loose cotton gown, worn in Arabic countries

Gal.a.had (gal'ə had') *Arthurian Legend* the knight who, because of his purity, found the Holy Grail

gal.ax.y (gal'ək sē) [< Gr. *gala*, milk] [*often* G-] *same as* MILKY WAY —*n., pl.* **-ies** 1. any similar group of stars 2. a group of illustrious people —**ga.lac.tic** (gə lak'tik) *adj.*

gale (gāl) *n.* [< ?] 1. a strong wind 2. an outburst [a *gale* of laughter]

ga.le.na (gə lē'nə) *n.* [L., lead ore] native lead sulfide, a lead-gray mineral with metallic luster

Gal.i.lee (gal'ə lē'), **Sea of** lake in NE Israel

Gal.i.le.o (gal'ə lē'ō, -lā'-) 1564-1642; It. astronomer & physicist

gall¹ (gôl) *n.* [OE. *galla*] 1. bile, the bitter, greenish fluid secreted by the liver 2. something bitter or distasteful 3. bitter feeling 4. [Colloq.] impudence

gall² (gôl) *n.* [see ff.] a sore on the skin caused by chafing —*vt.* 1. to make sore by rubbing 2. to annoy

gall³ (gôl) *n.* [< L. *galla*] a tumor on plant tissue caused by irritation due to fungi, insects, or bacteria

gal.lant (gal'ənt; *for adj. 3 & n. usually* gə lant' *or* -länt') *adj.* [< OFr. *gale*, pleasure] 1. stately; imposing 2. brave and noble 3. polite and attentive to women —*n.* [Rare] 1. a high-spirited, stylish man 2. a man attentive and polite to women

gal.lant.ry (gal'ən trē) *n., pl.* **-ries** 1. heroic courage 2. the behavior of a gallant 3. a courteous act or remark

gall.blad.der (gôl'blad'ər) *n.* a membranous sac attached to the liver, in which excess gall or bile is stored

gal.le.on (gal'ē ən) *n.* [ult. < MGr. *galaia*, kind of ship] a large Spanish ship of the 15th and 16th cent.

gal.ler.y (gal'ə rē) *n., pl.* **-ies** [< ML. *galeria*] 1. a covered walk or porch open at one side 2. a long, narrow, outside balcony 3. *a*) a balcony in a theater, etc.; esp., the highest balcony with the cheapest seats *b*) the people in these seats 4. the spectators at a sports event, etc. 5. an establishment for exhibitions, etc.

gal.ley (gal'ē) *n., pl.* **-leys** [< MGr. *galaia*, kind of ship] 1. a long, low ship of ancient times, propelled by oars and sails 2. a ship's kitchen 3. *Printing a*) a shallow tray for holding composed type *b*) proof printed from such type: in full, **gal.ley proof**

GALLEY

Gal.lic (gal'ik) *adj.* 1. of ancient Gaul or its people 2. French

Gal'li.cism (-ə siz'm) *n.* [< prec.] [*also* g-] a French idiom, custom, etc.

gal.li.vant (gal'ə vant') *vi.* [arbitrary elaboration of GALLANT] to go about in search of amusement

gal.lon (gal'ən) *n.* [< ML. *galo*, jug] a liquid measure, equal to 4 quarts

gal.lop (gal'əp) *vi., vt.* [< OFr. *galoper*] to go, or cause to go, at a gallop —*n.* the fastest gait of a horse, etc., a succession of leaping strides

gal.lows (gal'ōz) *n., pl.* **-lows.es, -lows** [OE. *galga*] an upright frame with a crossbeam and a rope, for hanging condemned persons

gall.stone (gôl'stōn') *n.* a small solid mass sometimes formed in the gallbladder or bile duct

ga.lore (gə lôr') *adv.* [Ir. *go leór*, enough] in abundance; plentifully

ga.losh, ga.loshe (gə läsh') *n.* [OFr. *galoche*] a high, warmly lined overshoe of rubber and fabric

gal.van.ic (gal van'ik) *adj.* [< L. *Galvani*, 18th-c. It. physicist] 1. of or producing an electric current, esp. from a battery 2. startling

gal'va.nism (-və niz'm) *n.* electricity produced by chemical action

gal·va·nize (gal′və nīz′) *vt.* **-nized′, -niz′ing** 1. to apply an electric current to 2. to startle; excite 3. to plate (metal) with zinc

Gam·bi·a (gam′bē ə) country on the W coast of Africa: c.4,000 sq. mi.; pop. 343,000

gam·bit (gam′bit) *n.* [< Sp. *gambito,* a tripping] 1. *Chess* an opening in which a pawn, etc. is sacrificed to get an advantage in position 2. an action intended to gain an advantage

gam·ble (gam′b'l) *vi.* **-bled, -bling** [OE. *gamenian,* to play] 1. to play games of chance for money, etc. 2. to take a risk for some advantage —*vt.* to risk in gambling; bet —*n.* an undertaking involving risk —**gam′bler** *n.*

gam·bol (gam′b'l) *n.* [< It. *gamba,* leg] a gamboling; frolic —*vi.* **-boled** or **-bolled, -bol·ing** or **-bol·ling** to jump and skip about in play; frolic

gam·brel (roof) (gam′brəl) [< ML. *gamba,* leg] a roof with two slopes on each side

game[1] (gām) *n.* [OE. *gamen*] 1. any form of play; amusement 2. *a*) amusement or sport involving competition under rules *b*) a single contest in such a competition 3. the number of points required for winning 4. a scheme; plan 5. wild birds or animals hunted for sport or food 6. [Colloq.] a business or job, esp. one involving risk —*vi.* **gamed, gam′ing** to play cards, etc. for stakes; gamble —*adj.* 1. designating or of wild birds or animals hunted for sport or food 2. *a*) plucky; courageous *b*) enthusiastic; ready (*for*) —**the game is up** failure is certain —**game′ly** *adv.* —**game′ness** *n.*

game[2] (gām) *adj.* [< ?] [Colloq.] lame or injured (*a game* leg)

game′cock′ *n.* a specially bred rooster trained for cockfighting

game′keep′er *n.* a person who takes care of game birds and animals, as on an estate

game plan 1. the strategy planned before a game 2. any long-range strategy

game point 1. the situation when the next point scored could win a game 2. the winning point

games·man·ship (gāmz′mən ship′) *n.* skill in using ploys to gain an advantage

game·ster (gām′stər) *n.* a gambler

gam·ete (gam′ēt, ga mēt′) *n.* [< Gr. *gamos,* marriage] a reproductive cell that unites with another to form the cell that develops into a new individual

game theory a mathematical method of selecting the best strategy for a game, war, competition, etc. so as to minimize one's maximum losses

gam·in (gam′ən) *n.* [Fr.] 1. a homeless child who roams the streets 2. a girl with a roguish, saucy charm: also **ga·mine** (ga mēn′)

gam·ma (gam′ə) *n.* the third letter of the Greek alphabet (Γ, γ)

gamma glob·u·lin (gläb′yə lin) that fraction of blood serum which contains most antibodies

gamma rays strong electromagnetic radiation from a radioactive substance

gam·ut (gam′ət) *n.* [< Gr. letter *gamma,* for the lowest note of the medieval scale] 1. any complete musical scale 2. the entire range or extent

gam·y (gā′mē) *adj.* **-i·er, -i·est** 1. having the strong flavor of cooked game 2. slightly tainted 3. plucky 4. risqué —**gam′i·ness** *n.*

gan·der (gan′dər) *n.* [OE. *gan(d)ra*] 1. a male goose 2. [Slang] a look

Gan·dhi (gän′dē), **Mo·han·das K.** (mō hän′dəs) 1869–1948; Hindu nationalist leader: called *Mahatma Gandhi*

gang (gaŋ) *n.* [< OE. *gang,* a going] a group of people working or acting together (a school *gang*) —**gang up on** [Colloq.] to attack as a group

Gan·ges (gan′jēz) river in N India & Bangladesh

gan·gling (gaŋ′gliŋ) *adj.* [< ?] thin, tall, and awkward; lanky: also **gan′gly**

gan·gli·on (gaŋ′glē ən) *n., pl.* **-gli·a** (-ə), **-gli·ons** [ult. < Gr., tumor] a mass of nerve cells from which nerve impulses are transmitted

gang′plank′ *n.* a movable ramp by which to board or leave a ship

gan·grene (gaŋ′grēn, gaŋ grēn′) *n.* [< Gr. *gran, gnaw*] decay of body tissue when the blood supply is obstructed —**gan′gre·nous** (-grə nəs) *adj.*

gang·ster (gaŋ′stər) *n.* a member of a gang of criminals —**gang′ster·ism** *n.*

gang′way′ *n.* [OE. *gangweg*] a passageway; specif., *a*) an opening in a ship's side for loading, etc. *b*) a gangplank —*interj.* clear the way!

gan·net (gan′it) *n.* [OE. *ganot*] a large, web-footed sea bird

gant·let (gônt′lit, gant′-) *n.* [< Sw. *gata,* lane + *lopp,* a run] 1. a former punishment in which the offender ran between two rows of men who struck him 2. a series of troubles, etc. Now equally sp. **gaunt′let**

gan·try (gan′trē) *n., pl.* **-tries** [< L. *canterius,* beast of burden] 1. a framework, often on wheels, for a traveling crane 2. a wheeled framework with a crane, platforms, etc., for readying a rocket to be launched

gaol (jāl) *n. Brit. sp. of* JAIL

gap (gap) *n.* [< ON. *gapa,* to gape] 1. an opening made by breaking or parting 2. a mountain pass or ravine 3. a blank space 4. a lag; disparity

gape (gāp) *vi.* **gaped, gap′ing** [< ON. *gapa*] 1. to open the mouth wide, as in yawning 2. to stare with the mouth open 3. to open wide —*n.* 1. a gaping 2. a wide opening

gar (gär) *n., pl.* **gar, gars** [< OE. *gar,* a spear] a long fish with a beaklike snout: also **gar′fish′**

ga·rage (gə räzh′, -räj′) *n.* [Fr. < *garer,* protect] 1. a shelter for automotive vehicles **2.** a business place where such vehicles are repaired, stored, serviced, etc.

garb (gärb) *n.* [< It. *garbo,* elegance] **1.** clothing; style of dress **2.** external appearance —*vt.* to clothe

gar·bage (gär'bij) *n.* [ME., entrails of fowls] waste parts of food

gar·ban·zo (gär ban'zō, -bän'-) *n., pl.* -**zos** [Sp.] *same as* CHICKPEA

gar·ble (gär'b'l) *vt.* -**bled,** -**bling** [< Ar. *ghirbāl,* a sieve] to distort or confuse (a story, etc.) so as to mislead

‡**gar·çon** (gär sōn') *n.* [Fr.] a waiter

gar·den (gär'd'n) *n.* [< Frank.] **1.** a piece of ground for growing flowers, vegetables, etc. **2.** an area of fertile land **3.** [*often pl.*] a public parklike place, often having displays of animals or plants —*vi.* to make, or work in, a garden —*adj.* of, for, or grown in a garden —**gar'den·er** *n.*

Garden Grove city in SW Calif.: pop. 123,000

gar·de·nia (gär dēn'yə) *n.* [< A. *Garden* (1730–91), U.S. botanist] a fragrant flower with waxy, white petals

Gar·field (gär'fēld), **James Abram** 1831–81; 20th president of the U.S. (1881); assassinated

Gar·gan·tu·a (gär gan'choo wə) a giant king in a satire by Rabelais —**Gar·gan'tu·an, gar·gan'tu·an** *adj.*

gar·gle (gär'g'l) *vt., vi.* -**gled,** -**gling** [< Fr. *gargouille,* throat] to rinse (the throat) with a liquid kept in motion by the expulsion of air from the lungs —*n.* a liquid for gargling

gar·goyle (gär'goil) *n.* [see prec.] a waterspout formed like a fantastic creature, projecting from a building

Gar·i·bal·di (gar'ə bôl'dē), **Giu·sep·pe** (jōō zep'pe) 1807–82; It. patriot

gar·ish (ger'ish) *adj.* [prob. < ME. *gauren,* to stare] too gaudy; showy —**gar'ish·ly** *adv.* —**gar'ish·ness** *n.*

gar·land (gär'lənd) *n.* [< OFr. *garlande*] a wreath of flowers, leaves, etc. —*vt.* to decorate with garlands

gar·lic (gär'lik) *n.* [< OE. *gar,* a spear + *leac,* a leek] **1.** a plant of the lily family **2.** its strong-smelling bulb, used as seasoning —**gar'lick·y** *adj.*

gar·ment (gär'mənt) *n.* [see GARNISH] any article of clothing

gar·ner (gär'nər) *vt.* [< L. *granum,* grain] to gather up and store

gar·net (gär'nit) *n.* [< ML. *granatum*] a hard, glasslike mineral: deep-red varieties are often used as gems

gar·nish (gär'nish) *vt.* [< OFr. *garnir,* furnish] **1.** to decorate; trim **2.** to add color or flavor to food **3.** to garnishee —*n.* **1.** a decoration **2.** something used to garnish food, as parsley

gar·nish·ee (gär'nə shē') *vt.* -**eed',** -**ee'ing** [< prec.] *Law* to attach (a debtor's property, wages, etc.) so that it can be used to pay the debt

gar·ret (gar'it) *n.* [< OFr. *garite,* watchtower] an attic

gar·ri·son (gar'ə s'n) *n.* [< OFr. *garir,* to watch] **1.** troops stationed in a fort **2.** a fortified place with troops, etc. —*vt.* to station (troops)

in (a fortified place) for its defense

gar·rote (gə rät', -rōt') *n.* [Sp.] **1.** a cord, thong, etc. used in strangling a person **2.** strangulation with a cord, thong, etc. —*vt.* -**rot'ed** or -**rot'ted,** -**rot'ing** or -**rot'ting** to execute or attack by such strangling Also **ga·rotte', gar·rotte'** —**gar·rot'er** *n.*

gar·ru·lous (gar'ə ləs, -yoo-) *adj.* [< L. *garrire,* to chatter] talking much, esp. about unimportant things —**gar·ru·li·ty** (gə rōō'lə tē) *n.*

gar·ter (gär'tər) *n.* [< OFr. *garet,* the back of the knee] an elastic band or strap for holding a stocking in place —*vt.* to fasten with a garter

garter snake a small, harmless snake, common in N. America

Gar·y (ger'ē) city in NW Ind.: pop. 152,000

gas (gas) *n.* [coined < Gr. *chaos,* chaos] **1.** the fluid form of a substance in which it can expand indefinitely; vapor **2.** any mixture of flammable gases used for lighting or heating **3.** any gas used as an anesthetic **4.** any poisonous substance dispersed in the air, as in war **5.** [Colloq.] *a*) gasoline *b*) the accelerator in an automobile, etc. —*vt.* **gassed, gas'sing** to attack or kill by gas —**gas'e·ous** (-ē əs) *adj.*

gas chamber a room in which people are put to be killed with poison gas

gash (gash) *vt.* [< OFr. *garser*] to make a long, deep cut in; slash —*n.* a long, deep cut

gas·ket (gas'kit) *n.* [prob. < OFr. *garcette,* small cord] a piece or ring of rubber, metal, etc. used to make a piston or joint leakproof

gas mask a filtering mask to protect against breathing in poisonous gases

gas·o·hol (gas'ə hôl') *n.* a mixture of gasoline and alcohol: a motor fuel

gas·o·line, gas·o·lene (gas'ə lēn', gas'ə lēn') *n.* [< *gas* + L. *oleum,* oil] a volatile, flammable liquid distilled from petroleum and used chiefly as a fuel in internal-combustion engines

gasp (gasp) *vi.* [< ON. *geispa,* to yawn] to catch the breath with effort —*vt.* to say with gasps —*n.* a gasping

gas station *same as* SERVICE STATION

gas·sy (gas'ē) *adj.* -**si·er,** -**si·est** **1.** full of gas; esp., flatulent **2.** like gas

gas·tric (gas'trik) *adj.* [GASTR(O)- + -IC] of, in, or near the stomach

gastric juice the thin, acid digestive fluid produced by glands in the stomach lining

gas·tri·tis (gas trīt'is) *n.* [GASTR(O)- + -ITIS] inflammation of the stomach

gastro- [< Gr. *gastēr*] a combining form meaning the stomach (and)

gas·tron·o·my (gas trän'ə mē) *n.* [< Gr. *gastēr,* stomach + *nomos,* a rule] the art of good eating —**gas'tro·nom'i·cal** (-trə näm'i k'l) *adj.*

gas·tro·pod (gas'trə päd') *n.* [GASTRO- + -POD] a mollusk of the class including snails, slugs, etc.

gate (gāt) *n.* [OE. *geat*] **1.** a movable structure controlling passage through an opening in a fence or wall **2.** a gateway **3.** a movable barrier **4.** a structure controlling the flow of water, as in a canal 5. the total amount or number of paid admissions to a performance —**give (someone) the gate** [Slang] to get rid of

gate′-crash′er *n.* [Colloq.] one who attends an affair without an invitation or a performance without paying

gate′fold′ *n.* an oversize page in a magazine or book, bound so that it can be folded out

gate′way′ *n.* 1. an entrance in a wall, etc. fitted with a gate 2. a means of entrance or access

gath·er (gath′ər) *vt.* [OE. *gad(e)rian*] 1. to bring together in one place or group 2. to get gradually; accumulate 3. to collect by picking; harvest 4. to infer; conclude 5. to draw into folds or pleats —*vi.* 1. to assemble 2. to increase —*n.* a pleat

gath′er·ing *n.* 1. a meeting; crowd 2. a series of folds in cloth

gauche (gōsh) *adj.* [Fr. < MFr. *gauchir*, become warped] lacking social grace; awkward; tactless

gau·che·rie (gō′shə rē′) *n.* gauche behavior or a gauche act

gau·cho (gou′chō) *n., pl.* -**chos** [AmSp.] a S. American cowboy

gaud·y (gôd′ē) *adj.* -**i·er, -i·est** [ME. *gaude*] bright and showy, but in bad taste —**gaud′i·ly** *adv.* —**gaud′i·ness** *n.*

gauge (gāj) *n.* [ONormFr.] 1. a standard measure or criterion 2. any device for measuring 3. the distance between rails of a railway 4. the size of the bore of a shotgun 5. the thickness of sheet metal, wire, etc. —*vt.* **gauged, gaug′ing** 1. to measure the size, amount, etc. of 2. to judge

Gaul (gôl) ancient division of the Roman Empire, in W Europe —*n.* any of the people of Gaul

Gaul′ish *n.* the Celtic language spoken in ancient Gaul

gaunt (gônt) *adj.* [ME. *gawnte*] 1. thin and bony; haggard, as from great hunger or age 2. looking grim or forbidding —**gaunt′ness** *n.*

gaunt·let¹ (gônt′lit, gänt′-) *n.* [< OFr. *gant*, glove] 1. a knight's armored glove 2. a long glove with a flaring cuff —**throw down the gauntlet** to challenge, as to combat

gaunt′let² *n.* same as GANTLET

gauze (gôz) *n.* [Fr. *gaze*] any very thin, transparent, loosely woven material, as of cotton or silk —**gauz′y** *adj.*

ga·vage (gə väzh′) *n.* [Fr.] forced feeding of liquids through a stomach tube

gave (gāv) *pt. of* GIVE

gav·el (gav′′l) *n.* [< Scot. *gable,* fork] a small mallet used, as by a presiding officer, to call for attention, etc.

ga·votte (gə vät′) *n.* [Fr.] a 17th-c. dance like the minuet, but livelier

gawk (gôk) *vi.* [prob. < *gowk,* stupid person] to stare stupidly

gawk·y (gô′kē) *adj.* -**i·er, -i·est** clumsy; ungainly —**gawk′i·ness** *n.*

gay (gā) *adj.* [OFr. *gai*] 1. joyous and lively; merry 2. bright; brilliant [*gay colors*] 3. homosexual —*n.* a homosexual, esp., a male homosexual

gay·e·ty (gā′ə tē) *n. same as* GAIETY

gay·ly (gā′lē) *adv. same as* GAILY

gaze (gāz) *vi.* **gazed, gaz′ing** [< Scand.] to look steadily; stare —*n.* a steady look —**gaz′er** *n.*

ga·ze·bo (gə zē′bō, -zā′-) *n., pl.* -**bos, -boes** [< ? prec.] a windowed balcony, summerhouse, etc. for gazing at scenery

ga·zelle (gə zel′) *n.* [< Ar. *ghazāl*] a small, swift antelope of Africa and Asia, with large, lustrous eyes

ga·zette (gə zet′) *n.* [Fr. < It. dial. *gazeta,* a small coin, price of the paper] 1. a newspaper: now mainly in newspaper titles 2. in England, an official publication —*vt.* -**zet′ted, -zet′ting** [Chiefly Brit.] to list in a gazette

gaz·et·teer (gaz′ə tir′) *n.* a dictionary or index of geographical names

gaz·pa·cho (gäz pä′chō) *n.* [Sp.] a cold Spanish soup of tomatoes, chopped cucumbers, peppers, onions, oil, vinegar, etc.

G.B. Great Britain

Ge *Chem.* germanium

gear (gir) *n.* [< ON. *gervi,* preparation] 1. clothing 2. equipment, esp. for some task 3. *a)* a toothed wheel designed to mesh with another *b)* [often *pl.*] a system of such gears meshed together to pass motion along *c)* a specific adjustment of such a system [high *gear*] *d)* a part of a mechanism with a specific function [steering *gear*] —*vt.* 1. to connect by or furnish with gears 2. to adapt (one thing) to conform with another [to *gear* supply to demand] —**in (or out of) gear** 1. (not) connected to the motor 2. (not) in proper working order

gear′shift′ *n.* a device for connecting or disconnecting any of several sets of transmission gears to a motor, etc.

gear′wheel′ *n.* a toothed wheel in a system of gears; cogwheel

gee (jē) *interj.* [< JE(SUS)] [Slang] an exclamation of surprise, etc.

geese (gēs) *n. pl. of* GOOSE

gee·zer (gē′zər) *n.* [< GUISE] [Slang] an eccentric old man

ge·fil·te fish (gə fil′tə) [Yid.] chopped, seasoned fish, boiled and served in balls or cakes

Gei·ger counter (gī′gər) [< H. *Geiger* (1882-1945), G. physicist] an instrument for detecting and counting ionizing particles, as from radioactive ores

gei·sha (gā′shə) *n., pl.* -**sha, -shas** [Jap.] a Japanese girl trained as an entertainer to serve as a hired companion to men

gel (jel) *n.* [< ff.] a jellylike substance formed by a colloidal solution —*vi.* **gelled, gel′ling** to form a gel

gel·a·tin, gel·a·tine (jel′ət′n) *n.* [< L. *gelare,* freeze] a tasteless, odorless substance extracted by boiling bones, hoofs, etc., or a similar vegetable substance: dissolved and cooled, it forms a jellylike substance used in foods, photographic film, etc. —**ge·lat·i·nous** (jə lat'n əs) *adj.*

geld (geld) *vt.* **geld'ed** or **gelt, geld'ing** [< ON. *geldr,* barren] to castrate (esp. a horse)

geld'ing *n.* a castrated horse

gel·id (jel'id) *adj.* [< L. *gelu,* frost] extremely cold; frozen

gem (jem) *n.* [< L. *gemma*] 1. a precious stone, cut for use as a jewel 2. something very precious or valuable

Gem·i·ni (jem'ə nī', -nē') [L., twins] the third sign of the zodiac

gem'stone' *n.* any mineral that can be used as a gem when cut and polished

‡**ge·müt·lich** (gə müt'likh) *adj.* [G.] agreeable, cheerful, cozy, etc.

-gen (jən, jen) [< Gr. *-genēs,* born] *a suffix meaning:* 1. something that produces [*oxygen*] 2. something produced (in a specified way)

Gen. 1. General 2. Genesis

gen·darme (zhän'därm) *n.* [Fr. < *gens d'armes,* men-at-arms] an armed policeman in France, etc.

gen·der (jen'dər) *n.* [< L. *genus,* origin] *Gram.* the classification by which words are grouped as masculine, feminine, or neuter

gene (jēn) *n.* [see -GEN] any of the units in the chromosomes by which hereditary characters are transmitted

ge·ne·al·o·gy (jē'nē äl'ə jē, -al'-) *n., pl.* **-gies** [< Gr. *genea,* race + *-logia,* -LOGY] 1. a recorded history of one's ancestry 2. the study of family descent 3. lineage —**ge'ne·a·log'i·cal** (-ə läj'i k'l) *adj.* —**ge'ne·al'o·gist** *n.*

gen·er·a (jen'ər ə) *n. pl. of* GENUS

gen·er·al (jen'ər əl) *adj.* [< L. *genus,* class] 1. of, for, or from all; not local, special, or specialized 2. of or for a whole genus, kind, etc. 3. widespread [*general* unrest] 4. most common; usual 5. not specific or precise [in *general* terms] 6. highest in rank [attorney *general*] —*n.* 1. a military officer ranking just above a lieutenant general: also **full general** 2. a military officer ranking above a colonel —**in general** 1. usually 2. without specific details —**gen'er·al·ship'** *n.*

general assembly 1. the legislative assembly in some States 2. [G- A-] the legislative assembly of the UN

general delivery delivery of mail at the post office to addressees who call for it

gen·er·al·is·si·mo' (-ə lis'ə mō') *n., pl.* **-mos'** [It.] in some countries, the commander in chief of the armed forces

gen·er·al·i·ty (jen'ə ral'ə tē) *n., pl.* **-ties** 1. the quality of being general 2. a nonspecific or vague statement, idea, etc. 3. the bulk; main body

gen·er·al·ize (jen'ər ə līz') *vt.* **-ized', -iz'ing** 1. to state in terms of a general law 2. to infer or derive (a general law) from (particular instances) —*vi.* 1. to formulate general principles 2. to talk in generalities —**gen'er·al·i·za'tion** *n.*

gen'er·al·ly *adv.* 1. widely; popularly

2. usually 3. not specifically

general practitioner a practicing physician who does not specialize in a particular field of medicine

gen·er·ate (jen'ə rāt') *vt.* **-at'ed, -at'ing** [< L. *genus,* race] 1. to produce (offspring); beget 2. to bring into being —**gen'er·a·tive** *adj.*

gen·er·a'tion *n.* 1. the producing of offspring 2. production 3. a single stage in the succession of descent 3. the average time (c.30 years) between human generations 4. all the people born and living at about the same time —**gen'er·a'tion·al** *adj.*

gen'er·a'tor *n.* a machine for changing mechanical energy into electrical energy; dynamo

ge·ner·ic (jə ner'ik) *adj.* [< L. *genus,* race, kind] 1. of a whole class, kind, or group; inclusive 2. that is not a trademark 3. of or characteristic of a genus—*n.* a product without a brand name: *often used in pl.* —**ge·ner'i·cal·ly** *adv.*

gen·er·ous (jen'ər əs) *adj.* [< L. *generosus,* noble] 1. noble-minded; magnanimous 2. willing to give or share; unselfish 3. large; ample —**gen·er·os·i·ty** (jen'ə räs'ə tē) *n., pl.* **-ties** —**gen'er·ous·ly** *adv.*

gen·e·sis (jen'ə sis) *n., pl.* **-ses'** (-sēz') [Gr.] the beginning; origin —[G-] the first book of the Bible

genetic code the order in which four chemical constituents are arranged in huge molecules of DNA

ge·net·ics (jə net'iks) *n.pl.* [with sing. v.] [< prec.] the branch of biology dealing with heredity and variation in animal and plant species—**ge·net'ic** *adj.*—**ge·net'i·cal·ly** *adv.*—**ge·net'i·cist** (-ə sist) *n.*

Ge·ne·va (jə nē'və) city in SW Switzerland: pop. 175,000

Gen·ghis Khan (geŋ'gis kän', jeŋ'-) 1162?-1227; Mongol conqueror

ge·nial (jēn'yəl) *adj.* [see GENIUS] 1. good for life and growth [a *genial* climate] 2. cordial and kindly; amiable —**ge·ni·al·i·ty** (jē'nē al'ə tē) *n.* —**ge'nial·ly** *adv.*

ge·nie (jē'nē) *n.* [< Fr. < Ar. *jinni*] *same as* JINNI

gen·i·tal (jen'ə t'l) *adj.* [< L. *genere,* to beget] of reproduction or the sexual organs

gen'i·tals *n.pl.* [see prec.] the reproductive organs; esp., the external sex organs: also **gen'i·ta'li·a** (-tāl'yə)

gen·i·tive (jen'ə tiv) *adj.* [< Gr. *gēnos,* genus] designating or of the grammatical case expressing possession, source, etc. —*n.* the genitive case

gen·i·to·u·ri·nar·y (jen'ə tō yoor'ə ner'ē) *adj.* of the genital and urinary organs

gen·ius (jēn'yəs) *n.* [L., guardian spirit] 1. particular spirit of a nation, place, age, etc. 2. natural ability; strong inclination (*for*) 3. great mental capacity and inventive ability 4. one having such capacity or ability

Gen·o·a (jen'ə wə) seaport in NW Italy: pop. 848,000

gen·o·cide (jen'ə sīd') *n.* [< Gr.

gēnos, race + -CIDE] the systematic killing of a whole people or nation

gen·re (zhän′rə) n. [Fr. < L. *genus*, a kind] 1. a kind or type 2. painting in which subjects from everyday life are treated realistically

gent (jent) n. [Colloq.] a gentleman: humorous or vulgar term

gen·teel (jen tēl′) adj. [< Fr. *gentil*] polite or well-bred; now, esp., affectedly refined, polite, etc.

gen·tian (jen′shən) n. [< L. *gentiana*] a plant typically with blue, fringed flowers

gen·tile (jen′tīl) n. [*also* G-] [< L. *gentilis*, of the same clan] any person not a Jew —*adj.* not Jewish

gen·til·i·ty (jen til′ə tē) n., pl. -ties [see ff.] 1. the gentry (sense 1) or their status 2. the quality of being genteel

gen·tle (jent′l) adj. -tler, -tlest [< L. *gentilis*, of the same clan] 1. of the upper classes 2. refined; courteous 3. generous; kind 4. tame [a *gentle* dog] 5. kindly; patient 6. not harsh or rough; mild [a *gentle* tap] 7. gradual [a *gentle* slope] —**gen′tle·ness** n. —**gen′tly** adv.

gen′tle·folk′ n.pl. people of good social standing: also **gen′tle·folks′**

gen·tle·man (-mən) n., pl. -men 1. a man of good family and social standing 2. a courteous, gracious, and honorable man 3. any man: polite term, as (chiefly in pl.) of address —**gen′tle·man·ly** adj. —**gen′tle·wom′an** n.fem., pl. -wom′en

gen·tri·fy (jen′trə fī′) vt. -fied′, -fy′ing [< ff. + -FY] to convert (an aging neighborhood) into a more affluent one, as by remodeling homes

gen·try (jen′trē) n. [see GENTLE] 1. people of high social standing 2. people of a particular class or group

gen·u·flect (jen′yə flekt′) vi. [< L. *genu*, knee + *flectere*, bend] to bend the knee, as in worship —**gen′u·flec′tion** n.

gen·u·ine (jen′yōō wən) adj. [L. *genuinus*, inborn] 1. not fake or artificial; real; true 2. sincere —**gen′u·ine·ly** adv. —**gen′u·ine·ness** n.

ge·nus (jē′nəs) n., pl. gen·er·a (jen′ər ə), ge′nus·es [L., race, kind] 1. a class; kind; sort 2. a classification of related plants or animals

geo- [< Gr. *gē*] a combining form meaning earth, of the earth [*geology*]

ge·o·cen·tric (jē′ō sen′trik) adj. 1. viewed as from the center of the earth 2. having the earth as a center Also **ge′o·cen′tri·cal**

ge·o·des·ic (jē′ə des′ik) adj. 1. same as GEODETIC (sense 1) 2. a) designating the shortest line between two points on a curved surface b) of the geometry of such lines 3. having a surface formed of straight bars in a grid of polygons [*geodesic* dome]

ge′o·det′ic (-det′ik) adj. [< Gr. *gē*, earth + *daiein*, divide] 1. of or concerned with the measurement of the

earth and its surface 2. same as GEODESIC (sense 2)

ge·og·ra·phy (jē äg′rə fē) n., pl. -phies [< Gr. *gē*, earth + *graphein*, write] 1. the science dealing with the earth's surface, continents, climates, plants, animals, resources, etc. 2. the physical features of a region —**ge·og′ra·pher** n. —**ge′o·graph′i·cal** (-ə graf′i k'l), **ge′o·graph′ic** adj.

ge·ol·o·gy (jē äl′ə jē) n. [see GEO- & -LOGY] the science dealing with the development of the earth's crust, its rocks and fossils, etc. —**ge′o·log′ic** (-ə läj′ik), **ge′o·log′i·cal** adj. —**ge·ol′o·gist** n.

ge·o·mag·net·ic (jē′ō mag net′ik) adj. of the magnetic properties of the earth —**ge′o·mag′ne·tism** n.

ge·om·e·try (jē äm′ə trē) n., pl. -tries [< Gr. *gē*, earth + *metrein*, measure] the branch of mathematics dealing with the properties, measurement, and relationships of points, lines, planes, and solids —**ge′o·met′ric** (-ə met′rik), **ge′o·met′ri·cal** adj. —**ge′o·met′ri·cal·ly** adv.

ge·o·phys·ics (jē′ō fiz′iks) n.pl. [with sing. v.] the science dealing with the effects of weather, winds, tides, etc. on the earth —**ge′o·phys′i·cal** adj.

George III (jôrj) 1738–1820; king of England (1760–1820)

Geor·gia (jôr′jə) 1. SE State of the U.S.: 58,876 sq. mi.; pop. 5,464,000; cap. Atlanta 2. republic of the U.S.S.R., on the Black Sea —**Geor′gian** adj., n.

ge·o·syn·chro·nous (jē′ō siŋ′krə·nəs) adj. designating of or a satellite in orbit above the equator at the same speed that the earth rotates, so as to seem to hover over the same point: also **ge′o·sta′tion·ar′y**

ge·o·ther·mic (jē′ō thur′mik) adj. [< GEO- + Gr. *thermē*, heat] of the heat inside the earth: also **ge′o·ther′mal**

ge·ra·ni·um (jə rā′nē əm) n. [< Gr. *geranos*, a crane] 1. a common garden plant with showy red, pink, or white flowers 2. a related wildflower

ger·bil (jur′b'l) n. [ult. < Ar.] a small rodent with long hind legs

ger·i·at·rics (jer′ē at′riks) n.pl. [with sing. v.] [< Gr. *gēras*, old age + -IATRICS] the branch of medicine dealing with the diseases of old age —**ger′i·at′ric** adj.

germ (jurm) n. [< L. *germen*] 1. the rudimentary form from which a new organism is developed; seed, bud, etc. 2. any microscopic, disease-causing organism, esp. one of the bacteria 3. an origin [the *germ* of an idea]

Ger·man (jur′mən) adj. of Germany, its people, language, etc. —n. 1. a native or inhabitant of Germany 2. the language of Germany, Austria, etc.

ger·mane (jər mān′) adj. [see GERM] 1. truly relevant; pertinent 2. akin

Ger·man·ic (jər man′ik) adj. 1. German 2. designating or of the original language of the German peoples or the languages descended from it —*n.* the Germanic branch of languages including English, Dutch, Danish, etc.

ger·ma·ni·um (jər mā′nē əm) *n.* [< L. *Germania*, Germany] a rare, metallic chemical element used in transistors

German measles *same as* RUBELLA

Ger·ma·ny (jur′mə nē) former country in NE Europe: divided (1945) into EAST GERMANY & WEST GERMANY

germ cell an ovum or sperm cell

ger·mi·cide (jur′mə sīd′) *n.* [< GERM + -CIDE] any antiseptic, etc. used to destroy germs —**ger′mi·ci′dal** *adj.*

ger·mi·nal (jur′mə n′l) *adj.* 1. of or like germ cells 2. in the first stage of growth or development

ger·mi·nate (jur′mə nāt′) *vi., vt.* -nat′ed, -nat′ing [< L. *germen*, a sprout] to start developing; sprout, as from a seed —**ger′mi·na′tion** *n.*

ger·on·tol·o·gy (jer′ən tāl′ə jē) *n.* [< Gr. *gerōn*, old man + -LOGY] the study of aging and the problems of the aged —**ger′on·tol′o·gist** *n.*

ger·ry·man·der (jer′i man′dər, ger′-) *vt., vi.* [< E. *Gerry*, governor of Mass. (1812) + SALAMANDER, from shape of the county redistricted then] to divide (a voting area) so as to give unfair advantage to one political party

ger·und (jer′ənd) *n.* [< L. *gerere*, carry out] a verbal noun ending in -*ing*

Ge·sta·po (gə stä′pō) *n.* [< G. *Ge(heime) Sta(ats)po(lizei)*, secret state police] the terrorist secret state police force of Nazi Germany

ges·ta·tion (jes tā′shən) *n.* [< L. *gerere*, to bear] the act or period of carrying young in the uterus; pregnancy —**ges′tate** *vt.* -tat·ed, -tat·ing

ges·tic·u·late (jes tik′yə lāt′) *vi.* -lat′ed, -lat′ing [see ff.] to make gestures —**ges·tic′u·la′tion** *n.*

ges·ture (jes′chər) *n.* [< L. *gerere*, to bear] 1. movement of part of the body to express or emphasize ideas, emotions, etc. 2. any act or remark conveying a state of mind, intention, etc., often made merely for effect —*vi.* -tured, -tur·ing to make gestures

get (get) *vt.* got, got or got′ten, get′ting [< ON. *geta*] 1. to come into the state of having; receive; obtain; acquire 2. to arrive at [get home early] 3. to go and bring [get your books] 4. to catch 5. to persuade [get him to go] 6. to cause to be [get the jar open] 7. to prepare [to get lunch] 8. [Colloq.] *a*) to be obliged to (with have or has) [he's got to pass] *b*) to possess (with have or has) [he's got red hair] *c*) to strike, kill, baffle, defeat, etc. *d*) to understand 9. [Slang] to cause an emotional response in [her singing gets me] —*vi.* 1. to come, go, or arrive 2. to come to be [to get caught] 3. to manage or contrive [to get to do something] *Get* is used as an auxiliary for emphasis in passive construction [to get praised] —*n.* the young of an animal —**get around** 1. to move from place to place; circulate: also **get about** 2. to circumvent 3. to influ-

ence as by flattery —**get away** 1. to go away 2. to escape —**get away with** [Slang] to do something without being discovered or punished —**get by** [Colloq.] to survive; manage —**get it** [Colloq.] 1. to understand 2. to be punished —**get off** 1. to come off, down, or out of 2. to leave or start 3. to escape or help to escape —**get on** 1. to go on or into 2. to put on 3. to proceed 4. to grow older 5. to succeed —**get out** 1. to go out or away 2. to take out 3. to be disclosed 4. to publish —**get over** 1. to recover from 2. to forget —**get through** 1. to finish 2. to manage to survive —**get together** 1. to assemble 2. [Colloq.] to reach an agreement —**get up** 1. to rise (from sleep, etc.) 2. to organize

get′a·way′ *n.* 1. the act of starting, as in a race 2. the act of escaping

get′-to·geth′er *n.* an informal social gathering or meeting

Get·tys·burg (get′iz burg′) town in S Pa.: site of crucial Civil War battle

get′-up′ *n.* [Colloq.] costume; dress

gew·gaw (gyoo′gô) *n.* [ME.] a trinket

gey·ser (gī′zər, -sər) *n.* [< ON. *gjosa*, to gush] a spring from which columns of boiling water and steam gush into the air at intervals

Gha·na (gä′nə) country in W Africa: 91,843 sq. mi.; pop. 8,143,000

ghast·ly (gast′lē) *adj.* -li·er, -li·est [< OE. *gast*, spirit] 1. horrible; frightful 2. ghostlike; pale 3. [Colloq.] very bad or unpleasant —**ghast′li·ness** *n.*

ghat, ghaut (gôt, gät) *n.* [Hindi *ghāt*] in India, a flight of steps at a river landing for ritual bathers

gher·kin (gur′kin) *n.* [< Per. *angārah*, watermelon] a small pickled cucumber

ghet·to (get′ō) *n., pl.* -tos, -toes [It.] 1. a section of some European cities to which Jews were restricted 2. any section of a city in which many members of a minority group live

ghet′to·ize′ (-īz′) *vt.* -ized′, -iz′ing 1. to keep in a ghetto 2. to make into a ghetto

ghost (gōst) *n.* [< OE. *gast*] 1. the supposed disembodied spirit of a dead person, appearing as a pale, shadowy apparition 2. a slight trace; shadow [not a ghost of a chance] —**give up the ghost** to die —**ghost′ly** *adj.*

ghost′writ′er *n.* one who writes speeches, articles, etc. for another who professes to be the author —**ghost′write′** *vt., vi.*

ghoul (gōōl) *n.* [< Ar. *ghāla*, seize] *Oriental Folklore* an evil spirit that robs graves and feeds on the dead —**ghoul′ish** *adj.* —**ghoul′ish·ly** *adv.*

GHQ, G.H.Q. General Headquarters

GI (jē′ī′) *adj.* 1. government issue: designating clothing, etc. issued to military personnel 2. [Colloq.] of or characteristic of the U.S. armed forces [a GI haircut] —*n., pl.* GI's, GIs [Colloq.] a U.S. enlisted soldier

gi·ant (jī′ənt) *n.* [< Gr. *gigas*] 1. an imaginary being of superhuman size 2. a person or thing of great size, strength, intellect, etc. —*adj.* like a giant —**gi′ant·ess** *n.fem.*

gib·ber (jib′ər, gib′-) *vi., vt.* [echoic] to speak rapidly and incoherently

gib′ber·ish *n.* unintelligible chatter

gib·bet (jib′it) *n.* [< Frank. *gibb,* forked stick] 1. a gallows 2. a structure from which bodies of executed criminals were hung and exposed to public scorn —*vt.* to hang on a gibbet

gib·bon (gib′ən) *n.* [Fr.] a small, slender, long-armed ape of India, S China, and the East Indies

gibe (jīb) *vi., vt.* **gibed, gib′ing** [< ? OFr. *giber,* to handle roughly] to jeer or taunt —*n.* a jeer or taunt

gib·let (jib′lit) *n.* [< OFr. *gibelet,* stew made of game] any of the edible internal parts of a fowl, as the gizzard

Gi·bral·tar (ji brôl′tər) Brit. colony occupying a peninsula consisting mostly of a rocky hill (**Rock of Gibraltar**) at the S tip of Spain

gid·dy (gid′ē) *adj.* **-di·er, -di·est** [< OE. *gydig,* insane] 1. having or causing a whirling, dazed sensation; dizzy 2. frivolous —**gid′di·ness** *n.*

Gid·e·on (gid′ē ən) *Bible* a judge of Israel and victorious leader in battle

gift (gift) *n.* [< OE. *giefan,* give] 1. something given; present 2. the act of giving 3. a natural ability —*vt.* to present with or as a gift

gift′ed *adj.* 1. having a natural ability; talented 2. of superior intelligence

gig (gig) *n.* [ME. *gigge,* whirligig] 1. a light, two-wheeled, open carriage 2. a long, light ship's boat

gi·gan·tic (jī gan′tik) *adj.* [see GIANT] huge; enormous; immense

gig·gle (gig′'l) *vi.* **-gled, -gling** [< Du. *giggelen*] to laugh with high, quick sounds in a silly or nervous way —*n.* such a laugh —**gig′gly** *adj.*

gig·o·lo (jig′ə lō) *n., pl.* **-los** [Fr.] a man paid to be a woman's escort

Gi·la monster (hē′lə) [< the *Gila* River, Ariz.] a poisonous, black-and-orange lizard of the SW U.S. deserts

gild (gild) *vt.* **gild′ed** or **gilt, gild′ing** [< OE. *gyldan*] 1. to coat with gold leaf or a gold color 2. to make seem more attractive or valuable than is so —**gild′er** *n.* —**gild′ing** *n.*

gill¹ (gil) *n.* [ME. *gile*] the breathing organ of most water animals, as fish

gill² (jil) *n.* [< LL. *gillo,* cooling vessel] a liquid measure, equal to 1/4 pint

gilt (gilt) *alt. pt. & pp. of* GILD —*n.* gold leaf or color —*adj.* coated with gilt

gilt′-edged′ *adj.* of the highest quality or value [*gilt-edged* securities]: also **gilt′-edge′**

gim·bals (gim′b'lz, jim′-) *n.pl.* [*with sing. v.*] [< L. *gemellus,* twin] a pair of rings so pivoted that one swings freely within the other: used to keep a ship's compass level

gim·crack (jim′krak′) *adj.* [< ME. *gibbecrak,* an ornament] showy but cheap and useless —*n.* a gimcrack thing —**gim′crack′er·y** *n.*

gim·let (gim′lit) *n.* [< MDu. *wimpel*] a small boring tool with a spiral cutting edge

gim·mick (gim′ik) *n.* [< ?] 1. [Colloq.] a tricky device 2. [Slang] an attention-getting feature or device, as for promoting a product, etc.

gimp (gimp) *n.* [< ?] [Colloq.] 1. a lame person 2. a limp —**gimp′y** *adj.*

gin¹ (jin) *n.* [< L. *juniperus,* juniper] a distilled alcoholic liquor flavored typically with juniper berries

GIMLET

gin² (jin) *n.* [< OFr. *engin,* ENGINE] 1. a snare, as for game 2. a cotton gin —*vt.* ginned, gin′ning to remove seeds from (cotton) with a gin

gin·ger (jin′jər) *n.* [< Gr. *zingiberi*] 1. a tropical plant with rhizomes used esp. as a spice 2. this spice 3. [Colloq.] vigor; spirit —**gin′ger·y** *adj.*

ginger ale a carbonated soft drink flavored with ginger

gin′ger·bread′ *n.* 1. a cake flavored with ginger 2. showy ornamentation

gin′ger·ly *adv.* very carefully —*adj.* very careful; cautious

gin′ger·snap′ *n.* a crisp cookie flavored with ginger and molasses

ging·ham (giŋ′əm) *n.* [< Malay *ginggang*] a cotton cloth, usually woven in stripes, checks, or plaids

gin·gi·vi·tis (jin′jə vīt′əs) *n.* [< L. *gingiva,* the gum + -ITIS] inflammation of the gums

gink·go (giŋk′gō) *n., pl.* **gink′goes** [Jap. *ginkyo*] an Asian tree with fan-shaped leaves: also **ging′ko**

gin rummy a variety of the card game rummy: also **gin**

gip (jip) *n., vi., vt. same as* GYP

Gip·sy (jip′sē) *n., adj., vi. same as* GYPSY

gi·raffe (jə raf′) *n.* [< Ar. *zarāfa*] a large cud-chewing animal of Africa, with a very long neck and legs

gird (gurd) *vt.* **gird′ed** or **girt, gird′ing** [OE. *gyrdan*] 1. to encircle or fasten with a belt 2. to surround 3. to prepare (oneself) for action

gird·er (gur′dər) *n.* a large wooden or steel beam for supporting joists, the framework of a building, etc.

gir·dle (gur′d'l) *n.* [OE. *gyrdel*] 1. a belt for the waist 2. anything that encircles 3. a woman's elasticized undergarment supporting the waist and hips —*vt.* **-dled, -dling** to encircle or bind, as with a girdle

girl (gurl) *n.* [ME. *girle,* youngster] 1. a female child 2. a young, unmarried woman 3. a female servant 4. [Colloq.] a sweetheart —**girl′hood′** *n.* —**girl′ish** *adj.*

girl scout a member of the **Girl Scouts,** a girls' club providing healthful, character-building activities

girt[1] (gurt) *alt. pt. & pp. of* GIRD

girt[2] (gurt) *vt.* 1. *same as* GIRD 2. to fasten with a girth

girth (gurth) *n.* [< ON. *gyrtha*, encircle] 1. a band put around the belly of a horse, etc. to hold a saddle or pack 2. the circumference, as of a tree trunk

gist (jist) *n.* [< OFr. *giste*, point at issue] the essence or main point, as of an article or argument

give (giv) *vt.* **gave, giv'en, giv'ing** [OE. *giefan*] 1. to hand over as a present 2. to hand over [*to give* the porter a bag] 3. to hand over in or for payment 4. to pass (regards, etc.) along 5. to cause to have [*to give* pleasure] 6. to act as host or sponsor of 7. to produce; supply [*cows give* milk] 8. to concede; yield 9. to offer [*give* advice] 10. to perform [*to give* a concert] 11. to utter [*give* a reply] 12. to inflict (punishment, etc.) 13. to devote or sacrifice —*vi.* to bend, move, etc. from force or pressure —*n.* a bending, moving, etc. under pressure —**give away** 1. to make a gift of 2. to give (the bride) to the bridegroom 3. [Colloq.] to reveal or betray —**give forth** (or **off**) to emit —**give in** to yield —**give it to** [Colloq.] to beat or scold —**give or take** plus or minus —**give out** 1. to make public 2. to distribute 3. to become worn out, etc. —**give up** 1. to hand over 2. to cease 3. to stop trying 4. to despair of 5. to devote wholly —**giv'er** *n.*

give'-and-take' *n.* 1. mutual concession 2. banter or repartee

give'a·way' *n.* [Colloq.] 1. an unintentional revelation 2. something given free or sold cheap 3. a radio or television program giving prizes

give'back' *n.* a workers' benefit, relinquished to management, usually in exchange for some concession

giv·en (giv'n) *pp. of* GIVE —*adj.* 1. accustomed (*to*) by habit, etc. 2. specified 3. assumed; granted

given name a person's first name

giz·mo, gis·mo (giz'mō) *n.* [< ?] [Slang] a gadget or gimmick

giz·zard (giz'ərd) *n.* [< L. *gigeria*, cooked entrails of poultry] the muscular second stomach of a bird

Gk. Greek

gla·cé (gla sā') *adj.* [Fr.] 1. glossy, as silk 2. candied, as fruits —*vt.* **-céed', -cé'ing** to glaze (fruits, etc.)

gla·cial (glā'shəl) *adj.* of or like ice, glaciers, or a glacial epoch —**gla'cial·ly** *adv.*

glacial epoch any period when much of the earth was covered with glaciers

gla·cier (glā'shər) *n.* [< L. *glacies*, ice] a large mass of ice and snow moving slowly down a mountain or valley

glad (glad) *adj.* **glad'der, glad'dest** [OE. *glæd*] 1. happy 2. causing joy 3. very willing 4. bright —**glad'ly** *adv.* —**glad'ness** *n.*

glad·den (glad'n) *vt., vi.* to make or become glad

glade (glād) *n.* [ME.] 1. an open space in a forest 2. an everglade

glad hand [Slang] a cordial or effusive welcome —**glad'-hand'** *vt., vi.*

glad·i·a·tor (glad'ē āt'ər) *n.* [L. < *gladius*, sword] 1. in ancient Rome, a man, often a slave, who fought in an arena as a public show 2. any person involved in a fight —**glad'i·a·to'ri·al** (-ə tôr'ē əl) *adj.*

glad·i·o·lus (glad'ē ō'ləs) *n., pl.* **-lus·es, -li** (-lī) [L., small sword] a plant of the iris family with swordlike leaves and tall spikes of funnel-shaped flowers: also **glad'i·o'la** (-lə)

glad·some (glad'səm) *adj.* joyful or cheerful —**glad'some·ly** *adv.*

Glad·stone (bag) (glad'stōn) [after W. *Gladstone*, 19th-c. Brit. statesman] a traveling bag hinged to open flat

glam·or·ize (glam'ə rīz') *vt.* **-ized', -iz'ing** to make glamorous —**glam'or·i·za'tion** *n.*

glam·our, glam·or (glam'ər) *n.* [Scot. var. of *grammar*, magic] seemingly mysterious allure; bewitching charm —**glam'or·ous, glam'our·ous** *adj.*

glance (glans) *vi.* **glanced, glanc'ing** [ME. *glansen*] 1. to strike obliquely and go off at an angle 2. to flash 3. to look quickly —*n.* 1. a glancing off 2. a flash 3. a quick look

gland (gland) *n.* [< L. *glans*, acorn] any organ that separates certain elements from the blood and secretes them for the body to use or throw off —**glan·du·lar** (glan'jə lər) *adj.*

glans (glanz) *n., pl.* **glan·des** (glan'dēz) [L., lit., acorn] 1. the head of the penis 2. the tip of the clitoris

glare (gler) *vi.* **glared, glar'ing** [ME. *glaren*] 1. to shine with a steady, dazzling light 2. to stare fiercely —*vt.* to express with a glare —*n.* 1. a steady, dazzling light 2. a fierce stare 3. a bright, glassy surface, as of ice

glar·ing *adj.* 1. dazzlingly bright 2. too showy 3. staring fiercely 4. flagrant [a *glaring* mistake] —**glar'ing·ly** *adv.*

Glas·gow (glas'kō, glaz'gō) seaport in SC Scotland: pop. 980,000

glass (glas) *n.* [OE. *glæs*] 1. a hard, brittle substance, usually transparent, made by fusing silicates with soda, lime, etc. 2. glassware 3. *a)* a glass article, as a drinking container *b)* [*pl.*] eyeglasses or binoculars 4. the amount held by a drinking glass —*vt.* to equip with glass panes —*adj.* of or made of glass —**glass'ful** *n., pl.* **-fuls**

glass'ware' *n.* articles made of glass

glass'y *adj.* **-i·er, -i·est** 1. like glass, as in smoothness 2. expressionless [a *glassy* stare] —**glass'i·ly** *adv.*

glau·co·ma (glô kō'mə) *n.* [< Gr. *glaukos*, gleaming] a disease of the eye, with hardening of the eyeball

glaze (glāz) *vt.* **glazed, glaz'ing** [ME. *glasen*] 1. to provide (windows, etc.) with glass 2. to give a hard, glossy finish to (pottery, etc.) 3. to cover (foods) with a coating of sugar syrup, etc. —*vi.* to become glassy or glossy —*n.* a glassy finish or coating

gla·zier (glā'zhər) *n.* one whose work is fitting glass in windows

gleam (glēm) *n.* [OE. *glæm*] 1. a flash or beam of light 2. a faint light 3. a

faint manifestation, as of hope —vi.
1. to shine with a gleam 2. to appear
suddenly —gleam′y adj.

glean (glēn) vt., vi. [< Celt.] 1. to
collect (grain left by reapers) 2. to
collect (facts, etc.) gradually

glee (glē) n. [OE. gleo] lively joy;
merriment —glee′ful adj.

glee club a group singing part songs

glen (glen) n. [Late MScot.] a narrow,
secluded valley

Glen·dale (glen′dāl) city in SW Calif.:
pop. 139,000

glen plaid [also G-] a plaid pattern
with thin crossbarred stripes

glib (glib) adj. glib′ber, glib′best [<
or akin to Du. glibberig, slippery]
speaking or spoken smoothly, often
too smoothly to be convincing —
glib′ly adv. —glib′ness n.

glide (glīd) vi. glid′ed, glid′ing [OE.
glidan] 1. to move smoothly and easily
2. Aeron. to descend with little or no
engine power —vt. to make glide
—n. 1. a gliding 2. a disk or ball, as
of nylon, under a furniture leg to
allow easy sliding

glid·er n. 1. one that glides 2. an
engineless aircraft carried along by
air currents 3. a porch swing suspended in a frame

glim·mer (glim′ər) vi. [< OE. glæm,
gleam] 1. to give a faint, flickering
light 2. to appear faintly —n. 1. a
faint, flickering light 2. a faint manifestation —glim′mer·ing n.

glimpse (glimps) vt. glimpsed,
glimps′ing [OE. glæm, gleam] to
catch a brief, quick view of —vi. to
look quickly —n. a brief, quick view

glint (glint) vi. [ME. glenten] to
gleam or glitter —n. a glinting

glis·san·do (gli sän′dō) n., pl. -di
(-dē), -dos [as if It. < Fr. glisser, to
slide] Music a sliding effect, with tones
sounded in rapid succession

glis·ten (glis′'n) vi. [OE. glisian] to
shine with reflected light, as a wet
surface —n. a glistening

glitch (glich) n. [< G. glitsche, a
slip] [Slang] a mishap; error

glit·ter (glit′ər) vi. [prob. < ON.
glitra] 1. to shine brightly; sparkle
2. to be showy and bright —n. 1.
bright, sparkling light 2. showiness or
brightness 3. bits of glittering material
—glit′ter·y adj.

glitz·y (glit′sē) adj. -i·er, -i·est [< G.
glitzern, to glitter] [Slang] 1. glittery;
sparkling 2. showy

gloam·ing (glōm′ing) n. [< OE. glom]
evening dusk; twilight

gloat (glōt) vi. [prob. < ON. glotta,
grin scornfully] to gaze or think with
malicious pleasure

glob (gläb) n. [prob. < GLOBULE] a
rounded mass or lump, as of mud

glob·al (glō′b'l) adj. worldwide —
glob′al·ly adv.

glob·al·ism (-iz′m) n. a policy, outlook, etc. that is worldwide in scope

globe (glōb) n. [< L. globus] 1. any-

thing spherical or somewhat spherical
2. the earth, or a model of the earth

globe′-trot′ter n. one who travels
widely about the world

glob·u·lar (gläb′yə lər) adj. 1.
spherical 2. made up of globules

glob′ule (-yool) n. [< L. globus, ball]
a tiny ball; very small drop

glock·en·spiel (gläk′ən spēl′) n. [G.
< glocke, bell + spiel, play] a percus-
sion instrument with tuned metal bars
in a frame, played with hammers

gloom (gloom) n. [< Scand.] 1. darkness; dimness 2. deep sadness; dejection —gloom′y adj. -i·er, -i·est

glop (gläp) n. [< ? GL(UE) + (SL)OP]
[Slang] any soft, gluey substance

glo·ri·fy (glôr′ə fī′) vt. -fied′, -fy′ing
[< L. gloria, glory + facere, make]
1. to give glory to 2. to exalt (God),
as in worship 3. to honor; extol 4. to
make seem better, greater, etc. than
is so —glo′ri·fi·ca′tion n.

glo·ri·ous (-ē əs) adj. 1. full of,
receiving, or deserving glory 2. splendid —glo′ri·ous·ly adv.

glo·ry (glôr′ē) n., pl. -ries [< L.
gloria] 1. great honor or fame, or its
source 2. adoration 3. great splendor,
prosperity, etc. 4. heavenly bliss
—vi. -ried, -ry·ing to exult (in)

gloss[1] (glôs) n. [< ? Scand.] 1. the
shine of a polished surface 2. a deceptive outward show —vt. 1. to give
a shiny surface to 2. to hide (an error,
etc.) or make seem right or trivial
—gloss′y adj. -i·er, -i·est

gloss[2] (glôs) n. [< Gr. glōssa, tongue]
a note of comment or explanation, as
in a footnote —vt. to annotate

glos·sa·ry (gläs′ə rē, glôs′-) n., pl.
-ries [see prec.] a list of difficult terms
with explanations, as for a book

glos·so·la·li·a (gläs′ə lā′lē ə, glôs′-)
n. [< Gr. glōssa, tongue + lalein, to
speak] an uttering of unintelligible
sounds, as in a religious ecstasy

glot·tis (glät′is) n. [< Gr. glōssa,
tongue] the opening between the vocal
cords in the larynx —glot′tal adj.

glove (gluv) n. [OE. glof] 1. a covering
for the hand, with separate sheaths
for the fingers and thumb 2. a baseball
player's mitt 3. a boxing glove —vt.
gloved, glov′ing to cover with a glove

glow (glō) vi. [OE. glowan] 1. to give
off a bright light due to great heat
2. to give out a steady light 3. to
give out heat 4. to be elated 5. to be
bright with color —n. 1. light given
off, due to great heat 2. steady, even
light 3. brightness, warmth, etc.

glow·er (glou′ər) vi. [prob. < ON.]
to stare with sullen anger; scowl —n. a
sullen, angry stare; scowl

glow′worm′ (glō′-) n. a luminescent,
wingless insect or insect larva

glu·cose (glōō′kōs) n. [Fr. < Gr.
gleúkos, sweetness] 1. a crystalline
sugar occurring naturally in fruits,
honey, etc. 2. a sweet syrup prepared
by the hydrolysis of starch

fat, āpe, cär; ten, ēven; is, bīte; gō, hôrn, tōōl, look; oil, out; up, fur;
chin; she; thin, then; zh, leisure; ŋ, ring; ə for a in ago; ', (ā′b'l); ë, Fr. coeur;
ö, Fr. feu; Fr. mon; ü, Fr. duc; kh, G. ich, doch; ‡ foreign; < derived from

glue (gloo) *n.* [< LL. *glus*] **1.** a sticky, viscous liquid made from animal gelatin, used as an adhesive **2.** any similar substance —*vt.* **glued,** **glu′ing** to make stick as with glue —**glue′y** *adj.* **glu′i·er, glu′i·est**

glum (glum) *adj.* **glum′mer, glum′-mest** [prob. < ME. *glomen,* look morose] gloomy; sullen —**glum′ly** *adv.* —**glum′ness** *n.*

glut (glut) *vi.* **glut′ted, glut′ting** [< L. *gluttire,* to swallow] to eat to excess —*vt.* **1.** to feed, fill, etc. to excess **2.** to supply (the market) beyond demand —*n.* **1.** a glutting or being glutted **2.** a supply beyond demand

glu·ten (gloot′'n) *n.* [L., glue] a gray, sticky, nutritious protein substance found in wheat, etc. —**glu′ten·ous** *adj.*

glu′ti·nous (-əs) *adj.* [see prec.] gluey; sticky —**glu′ti·nous·ly** *adv.*

glut·ton (glut′'n) *n.* [see GLUT] **1.** one who eats to excess **2.** one with a great capacity for something —**glut′ton·ous** *adj.* —**glut′ton·ous·ly** *adv.*

glut′ton·y *n., pl.* **-ies** the habit or act of eating too much

glyc·er·in, glyc·er·ine (glis′ər in) *n.* [< Gr. *glykeros,* sweet] *popular and commercial name for* GLYCEROL

glyc·er·ol (glis′ər ōl′, -ôl′) *n.* [< prec.] a colorless, syrupy liquid made from fats and oils: used in skin lotions, in making explosives, etc.

gly·co·gen (glī′kə jən) *n.* [see prec.] a substance in animal tissues that is changed into a simple sugar as the body needs it

gm. gram(s)

Gmc. Germanic

gnarl (närl) *n.* [< ME. *knorre*] a knot on a tree trunk or branch —*vt.* to make knotted; twist —**gnarled** *adj.*

gnash (nash) *vt., vi.* [prob. < ON.] to grind (the teeth) together, as in anger —*n.* a gnashing

gnat (nat) *n.* [OE. *gnæt*] any of various small, two-winged insects that bite or sting

gnaw (nô) *vt., vi.* [OE. *gnagen*] **1.** to bite away bit by bit; consume **2.** to torment, as by constant pain

gneiss (nīs) *n.* [< OHG. *gneisto,* a spark] a granitelike rock formed of layers of quartz, mica, etc.

gnome (nōm) *n.* [LL. < Gr. *gnōmē,* thought] *Folklore* a dwarf who dwells in the earth and guards its treasures —**gnom′ish** *adj.*

GNP gross national product

gnu (noo) *n.* [< the native name] a large African antelope with an oxlike head and a horse-like tail

GNU

go (gō) *vi.* **went, gone, go′ing** [OE. *gan*] **1.** to move along; travel; proceed **2.** to work properly; operate [the motor won't *go*] **3.** to act, sound, etc. as specified [the balloon *went* "pop"] **4.** to result; turn out [the game *went* badly] **5.** to pass: said of time **6.** to become [to *go* mad] **7.** to be expressed, sung, etc. [as the saying *goes*] **8.** to harmonize; agree [blue *goes* with gold] **9.** to be accepted, valid, etc. **10.** to leave; depart **11.** to come to an end; fail [his eyesight is *going*] **12.** to be allotted or sold **13.** to reach, extend, etc. **14.** to be able to pass (*through*), fit (*into*), etc. **15.** to be capable of being divided (*into*) [5 *goes* into 10 twice] **16.** to belong [socks *go* in this drawer] —*vt.* **1.** to travel along [to *go* the wrong way] **2.** [Colloq.] *a)* to put up with *b)* to furnish (bail) for an arrested person —*n., pl.* **goes 1.** a success [make a *go* of marriage] **2.** [Colloq.] energy; animation **3.** [Colloq.] a try; attempt —**go back on** [Colloq.] **1.** to betray **2.** to break (a promise, etc.) —**go for 1.** to try to get **2.** [Colloq.] to attack **3.** [Colloq.] to be attracted by —**go in for 1.** to engage or indulge in —**go off 1.** to depart **2.** to explode —**go on 1.** to proceed; continue **2.** to happen —**go out 1.** to be extinguished, become outdated, etc. **2.** to attend social affairs, etc. —**go over 1.** to examine thoroughly **2.** to do again **3.** [Colloq.] to be successful —**go through 1.** to endure; experience **2.** to look through —**go through with** to pursue to the end —**go together 1.** to match; harmonize **2.** [Colloq.] to be sweethearts —**go under** to fail, as in business —**let go 1.** to let escape **2.** to release one's hold —**let oneself go** to be unrestrained —**on the go** [Colloq.] in constant motion or action —**to go** [Colloq.] **1.** to be taken out: said of food in a restaurant **2.** still to be done, etc.

goad (gōd) *n.* [OE. *gad*] **1.** a sharp-pointed stick used in driving oxen **2.** any driving impulse; spur —*vt.* to drive as with a goad; urge on

go′-a·head′ *n.* permission or a signal to proceed: usually with *the*

goal (gōl) *n.* [ME. *gol,* boundary] **1.** the place at which a race, trip, etc. is ended **2.** an end that one strives to attain **3.** in some games, *a)* the place over or into which the ball or puck must go to score *b)* the score made

goal′keep′er *n.* in some games, a player stationed at a goal to prevent the ball or puck from crossing it: also **goal′ie** (-ē), **goal′tend′er**

goat (gōt) *n.* [OE. *gat*] **1.** a cud-chewing mammal with hollow horns, related to the sheep **2.** a lecherous man **3.** [Colloq.] a scapegoat —**get one's goat** [Colloq.] to irritate one

goat·ee (gō tē′) *n.* a small, pointed beard on a man's chin

goat′herd′ *n.* one who herds goats

goat′skin′ *n.* the skin of a goat, or leather made from this skin

gob¹ (gäb) *n.* [< OFr. *gobe,* mouthful] **1.** a soft lump or mass **2.** [*pl.*] [Colloq.] a large quantity

gob² (gäb) *n.* [< ?] [Slang] a sailor in the U.S. Navy

gob·ble¹ (gäb′'l) *n.* [echoic] the

throaty sound made by a male turkey
—*vi.* **-bled, -bling** to make this sound

gob·ble (gäb′l) *vt., vi.* **-bled, -bling**
[prob. < OFr. *gobe*, mouthful] 1. to
eat quickly and greedily 2. to seize
eagerly; snatch (*up*)

gob′ble·dy·gook′ (-dē gook′) *n.* [?
echoic] [Slang] pompous, wordy, usually meaningless talk or writing

gob′bler (gäb′lər) *n.* a male turkey

go-be·tween (gō′bi twēn′) *n.* one
who makes arrangements between
each of two sides; intermediary

Go·bi (gō′bē) large desert plateau in
E Asia, chiefly in Mongolia

gob·let (gäb′lit) *n.* [< OFr. *gobel*] a
drinking glass with a base and stem

gob·lin (gäb′lin) *n.* [< ML. *gobelinus*]
Folklore an evil or mischievous sprite

go-by (gō′bī′) *n.* [Colloq.] an intentional disregard or slight

god (gäd) *n.* [OE.] 1. any of various
beings conceived of as supernatural
and immortal; esp., a male deity
2. an idol 3. a person or thing deified
—[G-] in monotheistic religions, the
creator and ruler of the universe;
Supreme Being —**god′like′** *adj.*

god′child′ *n., pl.* **-chil′dren** the
person a godparent sponsors

god′daugh′ter *n.* a female godchild

god·dess (gäd′is) *n.* 1. a female god
2. a woman of great beauty, charm, etc.

god′fa′ther *n.* a male godparent

god′head′ (-hed′) *n.* 1. *same as* GOD-
HOOD 2. [G-] God (usually with *the*)

god′hood (-hood) *n.* the state of being
a god

Go·di·va (gə dī′və) *Eng. Legend* an
11th-cent. noblewoman who rode
naked through the streets on condition
that her husband would abolish a
heavy tax

god′less *adj.* 1. irreligious 2. wicked
—**god′less·ness** *n.*

god′ly *adj.* **-li·er, -li·est** devoted to
God; devout —**god′li·ness** *n.*

god′moth′er *n.* a female godparent

god′par′ent *n.* a person who sponsors
a child, as at baptism, taking responsibility for its faith

god′send′ *n.* anything that comes
unexpectedly and when needed or
desired, as if sent by God

god′son′ *n.* a male godchild

God′win Austen (gäd′win) mountain in N India: 2d highest in the
world; 28,250 ft.

Goe·the (gō′tə; *Eng.* gur′tə), Jo-
hann Wolf·gang von (yō′hän völf′
gäŋ fôn) 1749–1832; Ger. poet

go-get·ter (gō′get′ər) *n.* [Colloq.] an
enterprising and aggressive person
who usually gets what he wants

gog·gle (gäg′'l) *vi.* **-gled, -gling** [ME.
gogelen] to stare with bulging eyes
—*n.* [*pl.*] large spectacles with flexible
the eyes against dust, wind, sparks,
etc. —*adj.* bulging or staring: said of
the eyes

go-go (gō′gō′) *adj.* [< Fr. *à gogo*, in
plenty] of rock-and-roll dancing per-

formed in cafés, often in topless costumes

go·ing (gō′iŋ) *n.* 1. a departure 2. the
condition of the ground or land as it
affects traveling, walking, etc. —*adj.*
1. moving; working 2. commonly accepted —**be going to** will or shall

go′ing-o′ver *n.* [Colloq.] 1. a thorough inspection 2. a severe scolding
or beating

go′ings-on′ *n.pl.* [Colloq.] actions or
events, esp. when disapproved of

goi·ter, goi·tre (goit′ər) *n.* [< L.
guttur, throat] an enlargement of the
thyroid gland, often seen as a swelling
in the front of the neck

gold (gōld) *n.* [OE.] 1. a heavy, yellow, metallic, highly malleable chemical element: it is a precious metal
2. money; wealth 3. bright yellow

gold′brick′ (-brik′) *n.* 1. [Colloq.]
anything worthless passed off as
valuable 2. [Mil. Slang] one who
avoids work: also **gold′brick′er** —*vi.*
[Mil. Slang] to avoid work

gold′en *adj.* 1. made of or containing
gold 2. bright-yellow 3. very valuable; excellent 4. flourishing

golden ag·er (āj′ər) [Colloq.] [*also*
G- A-] an elderly person, esp. one 65
or older and retired

Golden Fleece *Gr. Myth.* the fleece
of gold captured by Jason

Golden Gate strait between San
Francisco Bay & the Pacific

gold′en·rod′ *n.* a N.American plant
with long, branching stalks bearing
clusters of small, yellow flowers

golden rule the precept that one
should act toward others as he would
want them to act toward him

gold′-filled′ *adj.* made of a base
metal overlaid with gold

gold′finch′ *n.* [OE. *goldfinc*] a small
American finch, the male of which
has a yellow body

gold′fish′ *n., pl.:* see FISH a small,
golden-yellow or orange fish, often
kept in ponds or fishbowls

gold leaf gold beaten into very thin
sheets, used for gilding

gold′smith′ *n.* a skilled worker who
makes articles of gold

gold standard a monetary standard
in which the basic currency unit equals
a specified quantity of gold

golf (golf, gälf) *n.* [< ? Du. *kolf*, club]
an outdoor game played with a small,
hard ball and a set of clubs, the object
being to hit the ball into each of a
series of 9 or 18 holes with the fewest
possible strokes —*vi.* to play golf
—**golf′er** *n.*

golf course (or **links**) a tract of land
for playing golf

Go·li·ath (gə lī′əth) *Bible* the Philistine giant killed by David

gol·ly (gäl′ē) *interj.* an exclamation
of surprise, etc.

-gon (gän) [< Gr. *gōnia*, an angle] *a
combining form meaning* a figure having (a specified number of) angles

---

fat, āpe, cär; ten, ēven; is, bīte; gō, hôrn, tōōl, look; oil, out; up, fur;
chin; she; thin, then; zh, leisure; ŋ, ring; ə for *a* in *ago*; ʼ, (ā′b′l); ë, Fr. coeur;
ö, Fr. feu; Fr. mon; ü, Fr. duc; kh, G. ich, doch; ‡ foreign; < derived from

go·nad (gō′nad) *n.* [< Gr. *gonē*, seed] an animal organ that produces reproductive cells; ovary or testis

gon·do·la (gän′də lə) *n.* [It.] 1. a long, narrow boat used on the canals of Venice 2. a railroad freight car with low sides and no top: also **gondola car** 3. a cabin suspended under a dirigible or balloon

gon·do·lier′ (-lir′) *n.* a man who rows or poles a gondola

gone (gôn, gän) *pp.* of GO —*adj.* 1. departed 2. ruined 3. lost 4. dead 5. consumed 6. ago; past

gon′er *n.* [Colloq.] a person or thing certain to die, be ruined, etc.

gong (gôn, gän) *n.* [Malay *guṅ*] a slightly convex metallic disk that gives a loud, resonant tone when struck

gon·or·rhe·a, gon·or·rhoe·a (gän′ə rē′ə) *n.* [< Gr. *gonos*, semen + *rhein*, to flow] a venereal disease with inflammation of the genital organs

goo (gōō) *n.* [Slang] 1. anything sticky, or sticky and sweet 2. sentimentality —**goo′ey** *adj.* **-i·er, -i·est**

goo·ber (gōō′bər) *n.* [< Afr. *nguba*] [Chiefly South] a peanut

good (good) *adj.* **bet′ter, best** [OE. *god*] 1. having the proper qualities 2. beneficial 3. valid; real [*good money*] 4. healthy or sound [*good eyesight*] 5. honorable [*one's good name*] 6. enjoyable, pleasant, etc. 7. thorough 8. virtuous, devout, kind, dutiful, etc. 9. skilled 10. considerable [*a good many*] —*n.* something good; worth, benefit, etc. —*adv.* [Dial. or Colloq.] well; fully —**as good as** virtually; nearly —**for good (and all)** permanently —**good and** [Colloq.] very or altogether —**good for** 1. able to endure or be used for (a period of time) 2. worth 3. able to pay or give —**make good** 1. to repay or replace 2. to fulfill 3. to succeed —**no good** useless; worthless

good′bye′, good′-bye′ (-bī′) *interj., n.* [contr. of *God be with ye*] farewell: also **good′by′, good′-by′**

Good Friday the Friday before Easter, commemorating the Crucifixion

good′-heart′ed *adj.* kind; generous —**good′-heart′ed·ly** *adv.* —**good′-heart′ed·ness** *n.*

Good Hope, Cape of cape at the SW tip of Africa

good humor a cheerful, agreeable mood —**good′-hu′mored** *adj.* — **good′-hu′mored·ly** *adv.*

good′-look′ing *adj.* handsome

good′ly *adj.* **-li·er, -li·est** 1. of good appearance or quality 2. ample

good·na′tured *adj.* agreeable; affable —**good′-na′tured·ly** *adv.*

good′ness *n.* the state or quality of being good; virtue, kindness, etc. —*interj.* an exclamation of surprise

goods (goodz) *n.pl.* 1. movable personal property 2. merchandise; wares 3. fabric; cloth —**get (or have) the goods on** [Slang] to discover (or know) something incriminating about

good Sa·mar·i·tan (sə mer′ə t′n) anyone who helps others unselfishly: see Luke 10:30-37

good′-sized′ *adj.* ample; fairly big

good′-tem′pered *adj.* amiable

good turn a friendly, helpful act

good will 1. benevolence 2. willingness 3. the value of a business in patronage, reputation, etc., beyond its tangible assets Also **good′will′** *n.*

good′y *n., pl.* **-ies** [Colloq.] something good to eat, as a candy —*interj.* a child's exclamation of delight

good′y-good′y [Colloq.] affectedly moral or pious —*n.* [Colloq.] a goody-goody person

goof (gōōf) *n.* [Slang] 1. a stupid person 2. a mistake; blunder —*vi.* [Slang] 1. to err or blunder 2. to waste time, shirk duties, etc. (with *off* or *around*) —**goof′y** *adj.*

gook (gook, gōōk) *n.* [GOO + (GUN)K] [Slang] any sticky or slimy substance

goon (gōōn) *n.* [Slang] 1. a ruffian or thug 2. a stupid person

goop (gōōp) *n.* [Slang] any sticky, semiliquid substance

goose (gōōs) *n., pl.* **geese** [OE. *gos*] 1. a long-necked, web-footed bird like a duck but larger 2. its flesh as food 3. a silly person —**cook one's goose** [Colloq.] to spoil one's chances

goose′ber′ry *n., pl.* **-ries** 1. a small, sour berry 2. the shrub it grows on

goose flesh (or bumps or pimples) a roughened condition of the skin

GOP, G.O.P. Grand Old Party (Republican Party)

go·pher (gō′fər) *n.* [< ? Fr. *gaufre*, honeycomb: from its burrowing] 1. a burrowing rodent with wide cheek pouches 2. a striped ground squirrel of the prairies

Gor·ba·chev (gôr′bə chev′, -chôf′), **Mi·kha·il** (mē′khäēl′) 1931– ; general secretary of the Communist Party of the U.S.S.R. (1985–)

gore¹ (gôr) *n.* [OE. *gor*, filth] blood from a wound, esp. clotted blood

gore² (gôr) *vt.* **gored, gor′ing** [OE. *gar*, a spear] 1. to pierce as with a horn or tusk 2. to insert gores in —*n.* a tapering piece of cloth inserted in a skirt, sail, etc. to give it fullness

gorge (gôrj) *n.* [< L. *gurges*, whirlpool] 1. the gullet 2. what has been swallowed 3. resentment, disgust, etc. 4. a deep, narrow pass between steep heights —*vi., vt.* **gorged, gorg′ing** to eat greedily or glut (oneself)

gor·geous (gôr′jəs) *adj.* [< OFr. *gorgias*] 1. brilliantly colored; magnificent 2. [Slang] beautiful, delightful, etc. —**gor′geous·ly** *adv.*

go·ril·la (gə ril′ə) *n.* [< WAfr.] the largest and most powerful ape native to Africa

Gor·ki (gôr′kē) city in W U.S.S.R.: pop. 1,100,000

gor·mand·ize (gôr′mən dīz′) *vi., vt.* **-ized′, -iz′ing** [< Fr. *gourmandise*, gluttony] to eat like a glutton

GORILLA

gorp (gôrp) *n.* a mix of raisins, nuts, etc. eaten for energy

gorse (gôrs) *n.* [OE. *gorst*] *same as* FURZE

gor·y (gôr′ē) *adj.* -i·er, -i·est 1. covered with gore; bloody 2. with much bloodshed —**gor′i·ness** *n.*

gosh (gäsh) *interj.* an exclamation of surprise, etc.: a euphemism for *God*

gos·ling (gäz′liŋ) *n.* a young goose

gos·pel (gäs′p'l) *n.* [OE. *gŏdspel*, good news] 1. [*often* G-] the teachings of Jesus and the Apostles 2. [G-] any of the first four books of the New Testament 3. anything proclaimed or accepted as the absolute truth: also **gospel truth**

gos·sa·mer (gäs′ə mər) *n.* [ME. *gosesomer*, lit., goose summer] 1. a filmy cobweb 2. a very thin, filmy cloth —*adj.* light, thin, and filmy

gos·sip (gäs′əp) *n.* [< Late OE. *godsibbe*, godparent] 1. one who chatters idly about others 2. such talk —*vi.* to be a gossip —**gos′sip·y** *adj.*

got (gät) *pt. & alt. pp. of* GET

Goth (gäth) *n.* any member of a Germanic people that conquered most of the Roman Empire in the 3d, 4th, and 5th c. A.D.

Goth′ic *adj.* 1. of the Goths or their language 2. designating or of a style of architecture developed in W Europe between the 12th & 16th c., with pointed arches, steep roofs, etc. 3. [*sometimes* g-] uncivilized —*n.* 1. the East Germanic language of the Goths 2. Gothic architecture

got·ten (gät′'n) *alt. pp. of* GET

Gou·da (**cheese**) (gou′də, gōō′-) [< *Gouda*, Netherlands] a mild cheese made from curds, usually coated with red wax

gouge (gouj) *n.* [< LL. *gulbia*] 1. a chisel for cutting grooves or holes in wood 2. such a groove or hole —*vt.* gouged, goug′ing 1. to scoop out as with a gouge 2. [Colloq.] to defraud or overcharge —**goug′er** *n.*

gou·lash (gōō′läsh, -lash) *n.* [< Hung. *gulyás*] a beef or veal stew seasoned with paprika

gou·ra·mi (goor′ə mē, goo rä′mē) *n.*, *pl.* **-mis, -mi** [Malay *gurami*] 1. a food fish of SE Asia 2. a related fish, brightly colored, often kept in aquariums

gourd (gôrd, goord) *n.* [< L. *cucurbita*] 1. any trailing or climbing plant of a family that includes the squash, melon, etc. 2. the fruit of one species or its dried, hollowed-out shell, used as a cup, dipper, etc.

gour·mand (goor′mənd, goor mänd′) *n.* [OFr.] one who likes good food and drink, often to excess

gour·met (goor′mā) *n.* [Fr. < OFr., wine taster] one who likes and is an excellent judge of fine foods and drinks

gout (gout) *n.* [< L. *gutta*, a drop] a disease characterized by painful swelling of the joints, esp. in the big toe —**gout′y** *adj.* -i·er, -i·est

gov., Gov. 1. government 2. governor

gov·ern (guv′ərn) *vt., vi.* [< Gr. *kybernan*, to steer] 1. to exercise authority over; rule, control, etc. 2. to influence the action of; guide 3. to determine —**gov′ern·a·ble** *adj.*

gov′ern·ance (-ər nəns) *n.* the action, function, or power of government

gov′ern·ess (-ər nəs) *n.* a woman employed in a private home to train and teach the children

gov·ern·ment (guv′ər mənt, -ərn mənt) *n.* 1. the exercise of authority over a state, organization, etc.; control; rule 2. a system of ruling, political administration, etc. 3. those who direct the affairs of a state, etc.; administration —**gov′ern·men′tal** *adj.*

gov·er·nor (guv′ə nər, -ər nər) *n.* 1. one who governs; esp., *a*) one appointed to govern a province, etc. *b*) the elected head of any State of the U.S. 2. a mechanical device for automatically controlling the speed of an engine —**gov′er·nor·ship′** *n.*

governor general *pl.* **governors general, governor generals** a governor who has deputy governors under him

govt., Govt. government

gown (goun) *n.* [< LL. *gunna*] a long, loose outer garment; specif., *a*) a woman's formal dress *b*) a nightgown *c*) a long, flowing robe worn by judges, clergymen, scholars, etc.

Gr. Greek

gr. 1. grain(s) 2. gram(s) 3. gross

grab (grab) *vt.* grabbed, grab′bing [prob. < MDu. *grabben*] 1. to snatch suddenly 2. to get by unscrupulous methods 3. [Slang] to affect; impress —*n.* a grabbing —**grab′ber** *n.*

grab·by (grab′ē) *adj.* -bi·er, -bi·est grasping; avaricious

grace (grās) *n.* [< L. *gratus*, pleasing] 1. beauty or charm of form, movement, or expression 2. good will; favor 3. a delay granted for payment of an obligation 4. a short prayer of thanks for a meal 5. [G-] a title of an archbishop, duke, or duchess 6. the love and favor of God toward man —*vt.* graced, grac′ing 1. to decorate 2. to dignify —**in the good (or bad) graces of** in favor (or disfavor) with

grace′ful *adj.* having beauty of form, movement, or expression —**grace′ful·ly** *adv.* —**grace′ful·ness** *n.*

grace′less *adj.* 1. lacking any sense of what is proper 2. clumsy —**grace′less·ly** *adv.* —**grace′less·ness** *n.*

gra·cious (grā′shəs) *adj.* 1. having or showing kindness, charm, courtesy, etc. 2. compassionate 3. polite to supposed inferiors 4. marked by luxury, ease, etc. [*gracious living*] —**gra′cious·ly** *adv.* —**gra′cious·ness** *n.*

grack·le (grak′'l) *n.* [< L. *graculus*, jackdaw] any of various blackbirds somewhat smaller than a crow

grad (grad) *n.* [Colloq.] a graduate

gra·da·tion (grā dā′shən) *n.* 1. an arranging in grades, or stages 2. a gradual change by stages **3.** a step or degree in a graded series

grade (grād) *n.* [< L. *gradus*] **1.** a stage or step in a progression **2.** *a)* a degree in a scale of quality, rank, etc. *b)* a group of people of the same rank, merit, etc. **3.** *a)* the degree of slope *b)* a sloping part **4.** any of the divisions of a school course, by years **5.** a mark or rating in an examination, etc. —*vt.* grad′ed, grad′ing **1.** to classify by grades; sort **2.** to give a grade (sense 5) to **3.** to make (ground) level or evenly sloped, as for a road —**make the grade** to succeed

grade crossing the place where a railroad intersects another railroad or a roadway on the same level

grade school *same as* ELEMENTARY SCHOOL

grade separation a crossing with an overpass or underpass

gra·di·ent (grā′dē ənt) *n.* [< L. *gradi*, to step] **1.** a slope, as of a road **2.** the degree of slope

grad·u·al (graj′ᵒᵒ wəl) *adj.* [< L. *gradus*, a step] taking place by degrees; little by little —**grad′u·al·ly** *adv.*

grad·u·al·ism *n.* the principle of promoting gradual rather than rapid change

grad·u·ate (graj′ᵒᵒ wit; *for n.* -wāt′) *n.* [< L. *gradus*, a step] one who has completed a course of study at a school or college —*vt.* -at′ed, -at′ing **1.** to give a degree or diploma to upon completion of a course of study **2.** to mark with degrees for measuring **3.** to classify into grades according to size, quality, etc. —*vi.* to become a graduate of a school, etc. —*adj.* **1.** being a graduate of a school, etc. **2.** of or for graduates —**grad′u·a′tor** *n.*

grad·u·a′tion *n.* **1.** a graduating from a school or college **2.** the ceremony connected with this

graf·fi·to (grə fēt′ō) *n., pl.* -ti (-ē) [It. < L.: see ff.] a crude inscription or drawing on a wall or other public surface

graft (graft) *n.* [< Gr. *grapheion*, stylus] **1.** *a)* a shoot or bud of one plant or tree inserted into another, where it grows permanently *b)* the inserting of such a shoot **2.** the transplanting of skin, bone, etc. **3.** *a)* the dishonest use of one's position to gain money, etc., as in politics *b)* anything so gained —*vt., vi.* **1.** to insert (a graft) **2.** to obtain (money, etc.) by graft —**graft′er** *n.*

gra·ham (grā′əm) *adj.* [< S. *Graham*, 19th-c. U.S. dietary reformer] designating or made of finely ground, wholewheat flour [*graham* crackers]

Grail (grāl) [< ML. *gradalis*, cup] *Medieval Legend* the cup used by Jesus at the Last Supper

grain (grān) *n.* [< L. *granum*] **1.** the small, hard seed of any cereal plant, as wheat, corn, etc. **2.** cereal plants **3.** a tiny, solid particle, as of salt or sand **4.** a tiny bit **5.** the smallest unit of weight **6.** *a)* the arrangement of fibers, layers, etc. of wood, leather, etc. *b)* the markings or texture due to this **7.** disposition; nature

grain′y *adj.* -i·er, -i·est **1.** having a clearly defined grain, as wood **2.** coarsely textured; granular —**grain′i·ness** *n.*

gram (gram) *n.* [< Gr. *gramma*, small weight] the basic unit of weight in the metric system, equal to about 1/28 of an ounce: also **gramme**

-gram (gram) [< Gr. *gramma*, writing] *a combining form meaning:* **1.** something written [*telegram*] **2.** a specified number of grams [*kilogram*]

gram·mar (gram′ər) *n.* [< Gr. *gramma*, writing] **1.** language study dealing with the forms of words and with their arrangement in sentences **2.** a system of rules for speaking and writing a given language **3.** one's manner of speaking or writing as judged by such rules —**gram·mar·i·an** (grə mer′ē ən) *n.* —**gram·mat·i·cal** (grə mat′i k'l) *adj.*

grammar school [Now Rare] *same as* ELEMENTARY SCHOOL

gran·a·ry (gran′ər ē, grā′nər ē) *n., pl.* -ries [< L. *granum*, grain] a building for storing grain

grand (grand) *adj.* [< L. *grandis*, large] **1.** higher in rank than others [a *grand* duke] **2.** most important; main [the *grand* ballroom] **3.** imposing in size, beauty, extent, etc. **4.** distinguished; illustrious **5.** overall; comprehensive [the *grand* total] **6.** [Colloq.] very good; delightful —*n.* [Slang] a thousand dollars —**grand′ly** *adv.*

grand- *a combining form meaning* of the generation older (or younger) than [*grandfather, grandson*]

gran·dam (gran′dam, -dəm) *n.* [see *prec.* & DAME] [Archaic or Rare] **1.** a grandmother **2.** an old woman

grand′child′ *n., pl.* -chil′dren a child of one's son or daughter

grand′daugh′ter *n.* a daughter of one's son or daughter

grande dame (gränd däm) [Fr.] a woman, esp. an older one, of great dignity

gran·dee (gran dē′) *n.* [< Sp. & Port.: see GRAND] a man of high rank

gran·deur (gran′jər, -joor) *n.* [see GRAND] **1.** splendor; magnificence **2.** nobility; dignity

grand′fa′ther *n.* **1.** the father of one's father or mother **2.** a forefather

grandfather (or **grandfather′s**) **clock** a large clock with a pendulum, in a tall, upright case

gran·dil·o·quent (gran dil′ə kwənt) *adj.* [< L. *grandis*; grand + *loqui*, speak] using pompous, bombastic words —**gran·dil′o·quence** *n.*

gran·di·ose (gran′dē ōs′) *adj.* [< L. *grandis*, great] **1.** having grandeur; imposing **2.** pompous and showy —**gran′di·os′i·ty** (-äs′ə tē) *n.*

grand jury a jury that investigates accusations and indicts persons for trial if there is sufficient evidence

grand′ma (gran′mä) *n.* [Colloq.] grandmother

grand′mas′ter *n.* any highly skilled chess player: also **grand master**

grand′moth′er *n.* the mother of one's father or mother

grand opera opera in which the whole text is set to music

grand·pa (gran'pä) *n.* [Colloq.] grandfather

grand'par'ent *n.* a grandfather or grandmother

grand piano a large piano with a horizontal, harp-shaped case

Grand Rapids city in SW Mich.: pop. 182,000

grand slam 1. *Baseball* a home run hit when there is a runner on each base 2. *Bridge* the winning of all the tricks in a deal

grand'son' *n.* a son of one's son or daughter

grand'stand' *n.* the main structure for spectators at a sporting event

grange (grānj) *n.* [< L. *granum*, grain] 1. a farm 2. [G-] an association of farmers or a local lodge of this

gran·ite (gran'it) *n.* [< L. *granum*, grain] a hard, igneous rock consisting chiefly of feldspar and quartz

gran·ny, gran·nie (gran'ē) *n.*, *pl.* **-nies** [Colloq.] 1. a grandmother 2. an old woman 3. any fussy person —*adj.* of an old-fashioned style [*granny* glasses]

gran·o·la (grə nō'lə) *n.* [? < L. *granum*, grain] a breakfast cereal of rolled oats, wheat germ, sesame seeds, brown sugar or honey, nuts or dried fruit, etc.

grant (grant) *vt.* [< L. *credere*, believe] 1. to give (what is requested, as permission, etc.) 2. to give or transfer by legal procedure 3. to admit as true; concede —*n.* 1. a granting 2. something granted, as property, a right, etc. —**take for granted** to consider as true, already settled, etc.

Grant (grant), **Ulysses S.** 1822–85; 18th president of the U.S. (1869–77); Union commander in Civil War

grant'-in-aid' *n.*, *pl.* **grants'-in-aid'** a grant of funds, as by a foundation to a scientist, artist, etc., to support a specific project

grants'man·ship' (-mən ship') *n.* the skill of getting grants-in-aid

gran·u·lar (gran'yə lər) *adj.* 1. containing or consisting of grains 2. like grains or granules —**gran'u·lar·ly** *adv.*

gran'u·late' (-lāt') *vt.*, *vi.* **-lat'ed**, **-lat'ing** to form into grains or granules —**gran'u·la'tion** *n.*

gran·ule (gran'yool) *n.* [< L. *granum*, a grain] a small grain or particle

grape (grāp) *n.* [< OFr. *graper*, gather with a hook] 1. a small, round, juicy berry, growing in clusters on a vine 2. a grapevine 3. a dark purplish red

grape'fruit' *n.* a large, round, sour citrus fruit with a yellow rind

grape hyacinth a small plant of the lily family, with spikes of blue or white, small, bell-shaped flowers

grape'vine' *n.* 1. a woody vine bearing grapes 2. a secret means of spreading information 3. a rumor

graph (graf) *n.* [short for *graphic formula*] a diagram representing the successive changes in the value of a variable quantity or quantities —*vt.* to represent by a graph

-graph (graf) [< Gr. *graphein*, write] *a combining form meaning:* 1. something that writes or records [*telegraph*] 2. something written [*autograph*]

graph·ic (graf'ik) *adj.* [< Gr. *graphein*, write] 1. described in realistic detail 2. of those arts (**graphic arts**) that include any form of visual artistic representation, esp. painting, drawing, etching, etc. Also **graph'i·cal** — **graph'i·cal·ly** *adv.*

graph·ics (-iks) *n.pl.* [*with sing. v.*] 1. the graphic arts 2. design as used in the graphic arts

graph·ite (graf'īt) *n.* [< Gr. *graphein*, write] a soft, black form of carbon used in pencils, for lubricants, etc.

graph·ol·o·gy (gra fäl'ə jē) *n.* [< Fr.: see GRAPHIC & -LOGY] the study of handwriting, esp. as a clue to character —**graph·ol'o·gist** *n.*

-graph·y (grə fē) [< Gr. *graphein*, write] *a combining form meaning:* 1. a process or method of writing, or graphically representing [*lithography*] 2. a descriptive science [*geography*]

grap·nel (grap'n'l) *n.* [< Pr. *grapa*, a hook] 1. a small anchor with several flukes 2. an iron bar with claws at one end for grasping things

grap·ple (grap''l) *n.* [OFr. *grappil*] 1. *same as* GRAPNEL (sense 2) 2. a hand-to-hand fight —*vt.* **-pled**, **-pling** to grip and hold —*vi.* 1. to use a grapnel (sense 2) 2. to wrestle 3. to try to cope (*with*)

GRAPNEL

grappling iron (or **hook**) *same as* GRAPNEL (sense 2)

grasp (grasp) *vt.* [ME. *graspen*] 1. to grip, as with the hand 2. to take hold of eagerly; seize 3. to comprehend —*vi.* 1. to try to seize (with *at*) 2. to accept eagerly (with *at*) —*n.* 1. a grasping; grip 2. control; possession 3. the power to hold or seize 4. comprehension —**grasp'a·ble** *adj.*

grasp'ing *adj.* avaricious; greedy

grass (gras) *n.* [OE. *græs*] 1. a plant with narrow leaves, jointed stems, and seedlike fruit, as wheat, rye, etc. 2. any of various green plants with narrow leaves, growing densely in meadows, lawns, etc. 3. pasture or lawn 4. [Slang] marijuana —**grass'y** *adj.*

grass'hop'per *n.* any of a group of plant-eating, winged insects with powerful hind legs for jumping

grass roots [Colloq.] 1. the common people 2. the basic source or support, as of a movement —**grass'-roots'** *adj.*

grass widow a woman divorced or separated from her husband

grate¹ (grāt) *vt.* **grat'ed**, **grat'ing** [< OFr. *grater*] 1. to grind into particles by scraping 2. to rub against (an object) or grind (the teeth) together

with a harsh sound 3. to irritate —*vi.*
1. to rub with or make a rasping sound
2. to be irritating —**grat'er** *n.*

grate² (grāt) *n.* [< L. *cratis*, a hurdle]
1. *same as* GRATING¹ 2. a frame of
metal bars for holding fuel in a fireplace, etc. 3. a fireplace

grate·ful (grāt'fəl) *adj.* [obs. *grate*
(< L. *gratus*), pleasing] 1. thankful
2. welcome —**grate'ful·ly** *adv.* —
grate'ful·ness *n.*

grat·i·fy (grat'ə fī') *vt.* -**fied'**, -**fy'ing**
[< L. *gratus*, pleasing + *facere*, make]
1. to please or satisfy 2. to indulge;
humor —**grat'i·fi·ca'tion** *n.*

grat·ing¹ (grāt'iŋ) *n.* a framework of
bars set in a window, door, etc.

grat·ing² *adj.* 1. rasping 2. irritating

gra·tis (grat'is, grāt'-) *adv., adj.* [L.
< *gratia*, a favor] free of charge

grat·i·tude (grat'ə tōōd') *n.* [< L.
gratus, pleasing] thankful appreciation
for favors received

gra·tu·i·tous (grə tōō'ə təs, -tyōō'-)
adj. [< L. *gratus*, pleasing] 1. given
free of charge 2. uncalled-for —**gra·
tu'i·tous·ly** *adv.*

gra·tu'i·ty (-tē) *n., pl.* -**ties** a gift
as of money, esp. for a service; tip

grave¹ (grāv) *adj.* [< L. *gravis*, heavy]
1. important 2. serious [a *grave*
illness] 3. solemn 4. somber; dull
—**grave'ly** *adv.* —**grave'ness** *n.*

grave² (grāv) *n.* [< OE. *grafan*, dig]
1. *a)* a hole in the ground in which to
bury a dead body *b)* any burial place;
tomb 2. death —*vt.* **graved, grav'en**
or **graved, grav'ing** 1. to sculpture
2. to impress sharply

grave accent a mark (`) showing the
quality of a vowel, stress, etc.

grav·el (grav'l) *n.* [< OFr. *grave*,
coarse sand] a loose mixture of pebbles
and rock fragments coarser than sand

grav'el·ly (-ē) *adj.* 1. full of or like
gravel 2. harsh or rasping

grav·en (grāv'n) *alt. pp.* of GRAVE²

grave'stone' *n.* a tombstone

grave'yard' *n.* a cemetery

graveyard shift [Colloq.] a night work
shift, esp. one starting at midnight

grav·id (grav'id) *adj.* [< L. *gravis*,
heavy] pregnant

gra·vim·e·ter (grə vim'ə tər) *n.* [<
L. *gravis*, heavy + Fr. *-mètre*, -METER]
1. a device for determining specific
gravity 2. an instrument for measuring the earth's gravitational pull

grav·i·tate (grav'ə tāt') *vi.* -**tat'ed**,
-**tat'ing** 1. to move or tend to move
in accordance with the force of gravity
2. to be attracted (*toward*)

grav'i·ta'tion *n.* 1. a gravitating
2. *Physics* the force by which every
mass attracts and is attracted by every
other mass —**grav'i·ta'tion·al** *adj.*

grav·i·ty (grav'ə tē) *n., pl.* -**ties** [<
L. *gravis*, heavy] 1. graveness; seriousness 2. weight [*specific gravity*]
3. *Physics* gravitation; esp., the pull
on all bodies in the earth's sphere
toward the earth's center

gra·vy (grā'vē) *n., pl.* -**vies** [< ?]
1. the juice given off by meat in
cooking 2. a sauce made from this
juice 3. [Slang] money easily obtained

gray (grā) *n.* [< OE. *græg*] a color
made by mixing black and white —
adj. 1. of this color 2. having hair this
color 3. *a)* darkish *b)* dreary 4. designating a vague, intermediate area
—*vt., vi.* to make or become gray
—**gray'ish** *adj.* —**gray'ness** *n.*

gray'beard' (-bird') *n.* an old man

gray'ling (-liŋ) *n., pl.* -**ling, -lings**
a freshwater salmonlike game fish

gray matter 1. grayish nerve tissue
of the brain and spinal cord 2. [Col-
loq.] intelligence

graze¹ (grāz) *vt.* **grazed, graz'ing** [<
OE. *græs*, grass] 1. to put livestock
to graze on (growing grass, etc.)
2. to tend (grazing livestock) —*vi.* to
feed on growing grass, etc.

graze² (grāz) *vt., vi.* **grazed, graz'ing**
[prob. < prec.] to scrape or rub
lightly in passing —*n.* a grazing

Gr. Brit., Gr. Br. Great Britain

grease (grēs; *for v., also* grēz) *n.* [<
L. *crassus*, fat] 1. melted animal fat
2. any thick, oily substance or lubricant —*vt.* **greased, greas'ing** to
smear or lubricate with grease

grease'paint' *n.* greasy coloring matter used in making up for the stage

greas·y (grē'sē, -zē) *adj.* -**i·er**, -**i·est**
1. soiled with grease 2. containing or
like grease; oily —**greas'i·ness** *n.*

great (grāt) *adj.* [OE.] 1. of much
more than ordinary size, extent, etc.
2. much above the average; esp., *a)* intense [*great pain*] *b)* eminent [a *great*
writer] 3. most important; main
4. designating a relationship one generation removed [*great*-grandparent]
5. [Colloq.] skillful (often with *at*)
6. [Colloq.] excellent; fine —*n.* a
distinguished person —**great'ly** *adv.*
—**great'ness** *n.*

Great Britain England, Scotland, &
Wales

Great Dane a large, powerful dog
with short, smooth hair

great'-grand'child' *n.* a child of
any of one's grandchildren

great'-grand'par'ent *n.* a parent
of any of one's grandparents

great'heart'ed *adj.* 1. brave; fearless 2. generous; unselfish

Great Lakes chain of five freshwater
lakes in EC N. America

Great Salt Lake shallow saltwater
lake in NW Utah

grebe (grēb) *n.* [Fr. *grèbe*] a diving
and swimming bird related to the loons

Gre·cian (grē'shən) *adj., n.* Greek

Gre·co- (grē'kō) *a combining form
meaning* Greek or Greek and

Greece (grēs) country in the S Balkan
peninsula, on the Mediterranean:
50,534 sq. mi.; pop. 8,614,000

greed (grēd) *n.* [< ff.] excessive desire,
esp. for wealth; avarice

greed·y *adj.* -**i·er**, -**i·est** [OE. *grædig*]
1. wanting more than one needs or
deserves 2. having too strong a desire
for food and drink; gluttonous —
greed'i·ly *adv.* —**greed'i·ness** *n.*

Greek (grēk) *n.* 1. a native or inhabitant of Greece 2. the language, ancient
or modern, of Greece —*adj.* of Greece,
its people, language, etc.

green (grēn) *adj.* [OE. *grene*] 1. of the color of growing grass 2. covered with plants or foliage 3. sickly or bilious 4. unripe 5. inexperienced or naive 6. not dried or seasoned 7. [Colloq.] jealous —*n.* 1. the color of growing grass 2. [*pl.*] green leafy vegetables, as spinach, etc. 3. an area of smooth turf [a putting *green*] —green'ish *adj.* —green'ness *n.*

green'back' *n.* any U.S. paper money printed in green on the back

green bean the edible, immature green pod of the kidney bean

green'belt' *n.* a beltlike area around a city, reserved for park land or farms

green'er·y *n., pl.* -ies green vegetation; verdure

green'-eyed' *adj.* very jealous

green'gro'cer (-grō'sər) *n.* [Brit.] a retail dealer in fruit and vegetables

green'horn' *n.* 1. an inexperienced person 2. a person easily duped

green'house' *n.* a heated building, mainly of glass, for growing plants

Green·land (grēn'lənd) Danish island northeast of N. America

green manure a crop, as of clover, plowed under to fertilize the soil

green onion an immature onion with green leaves, eaten raw; scallion

green pepper the green, immature fruit of the sweet red pepper

green power money, as the source of power

Greens·bor·o (grēnz'bur'ō) city in NC N.C.; pop. 156,000

green'sward' (-swôrd') *n.* green turf

green thumb a knack for growing plants

Green·wich (gren'ich, grin'ij) borough of London, on the prime meridian

Green·wich Village (gren'ich) section of New York City, a center for artists, writers, etc.

green'wood' *n.* a forest in leaf

greet (grēt) *vt.* [OE. *gretan*] 1. to address with friendliness 2. to meet or receive (a person, event, etc.) in a specified way 3. to present itself to

greet'ing *n.* 1. the act or words of one who greets 2. [*often pl.*] a message of regards

gre·gar·i·ous (grə ger'ē əs) *adj.* [< L. *grex*, herd] 1. living in herds 2. fond of the company of others; sociable

Gre·go·ri·an calendar (grə gôr'ē ən) the calendar now widely used, introduced by Pope Gregory XIII in 1582

grem·lin (grem'lən) *n.* [< ?] an imaginary small creature humorously blamed for disruption of any procedure

gre·nade (grə nād') *n.* [Fr. < OFr., pomegranate] a small bomb detonated by a fuse and usually thrown by hand

gren·a·dier (gren'ə dir') *n.* 1. orig., a soldier who threw grenades 2. a member of a special regiment

gren·a·dine (gren'ə dēn') *n.* [Fr.] a syrup made from pomegranate juice

grew (grōō) *pt.* of GROW

grey (grā) *adj., n., v.* Brit. *sp.* of GRAY

grey'hound' *n.* a tall, slender, swift hound with a narrow head

grid (grid) *n.* [< GRIDIRON] 1. a gridiron or grating 2. a metallic plate in a storage battery 3. an electrode, as of wire mesh, for controlling the flow of electrons in an electron tube

grid·dle (grid'l) *n.* [< L. *craticula*, gridiron] a heavy, flat metal pan for cooking pancakes, etc.

grid'dle·cake' *n.* a pancake

grid·i·ron (grid'ī'ərn) *n.* [see GRIDDLE] 1. a framework of metal bars or wires for broiling 2. anything resembling this, as a football field

grid'lock' *n.* a traffic jam in which no vehicle can move in any direction

grief (grēf) *n.* [see GRIEVE] 1. intense emotional suffering caused as by a loss 2. a cause of such suffering —**come to grief** to fail or be ruined

griev·ance (grē'vəns) *n.* 1. a circumstance thought to be unjust and ground for complaint 2. complaint against a real or imagined wrong

grieve (grēv) *vi., vt.* grieved, griev'ing [< L. *gravis*, heavy] to feel or cause to feel grief —**griev'er** *n.*

griev·ous (grē'vəs) *adj.* 1. causing grief 2. showing or full of grief 3. severe 4. deplorable; atrocious

grif·fin (grif'ən) *n.* [< Gr.] a mythical animal, part eagle and part lion

grill (gril) *n.* [see GRIDDLE] 1. a gridiron 2. grilled food 3. a restaurant that specializes in grilled foods —*vt.* 1. to broil 2. to question relentlessly

grille (gril) *n.* [see GRIDDLE] an open grating forming a screen

grim (grim) *adj.* grim'mer, grim'mest [OE. *grimm*] 1. hard and unyielding; stern 2. appearing forbidding, harsh, etc. 3. repellent; ghastly —**grim'ly** *adv.* —**grim'ness** *n.*

gri·mace (gri mās', grim'əs) *n.* [Fr.] a distortion of the face, as in expressing pain, disgust, etc. —*vi.* -maced', -mac'ing to make grimaces

grime (grīm) *n.* [prob. < Fl. *grijm*] sooty dirt rubbed into a surface, as of the skin —**grim'y** *adj.* -i·er, -i·est

Grimm (grim), **Ja·kob** (yä'kôp) 1785-1863; Ger. philologist and collector (with his brother **Wilhelm**) of fairy tales

grin (grin) *vi.* grinned, grin'ning [< OE. *grennian*, bare the teeth] 1. to smile broadly as in amusement 2. to show the teeth in pain, scorn, etc. —*n.* the act or look of grinning

grind (grīnd) *vt.* ground, grind'ing [OE. *grindan*] 1. to crush into fine particles; pulverize 2. to oppress 3. to sharpen or smooth by friction 4. to rub (the teeth, etc.) together gratingly 5. to operate by turning the crank of —*n.* 1. a grinding 2. long, difficult work or study 3. [Colloq.] a student who studies hard

grind·er (grīn'dər) *n.* 1. a person or thing that grinds 2. [*pl.*] [Colloq.] the teeth 3. *same as* HERO SANDWICH

grindstone

268

grind**grindstone** n. a revolving stone disk for sharpening tools or polishing things —**keep one's nose to the grindstone** to work steadily

grip (grip) n. [< OE. *gripan*, seize] 1. a secure grasp; firm hold 2. the manner of holding a bat, club, etc. 3. the power of grasping firmly 4. mental grasp 5. firm control; mastery 6. a handle 7. a small traveling bag —vt. **gripped** or **gript**, **grip'ping** 1. to take firmly and hold fast 2. to get and hold the attention of —vi. to get a grip —**come to grips** to struggle (*with*) —**grip'per** n.

gripe (grip) vt. **griped**, **grip'ing** [OE. *gripan*, seize] 1. formerly, to distress 2. to cause sharp pain in the bowels of 3. [Slang] to annoy —vi. [Slang] to complain —n. 1. a sharp pain in the bowels: *usually in pl.* 2. [Slang] a complaint —**grip'er** n.

grippe (grip) n. [Fr.] *earlier term for* INFLUENZA: also **grip**

gris-gris (grē'grē) n., pl. **gris'-gris** [of Afr. origin] an amulet, charm, or spell associated with voodoo

gris-ly (griz'lē) adj. **-li-er**, **-li-est** [OE. *grislic*] terrifying; ghastly

grist (grist) n. [OE.] grain that is to be or has been ground

gris-tle (gris'l) n. [OE.] cartilage —**gris'tly** (-lē) adj.

grist-mill (grist'mil') n. a mill for grinding grain

grit (grit) n. [< OE. *greot*] 1. rough particles as of sand 2. coarse sandstone 3. stubborn courage; pluck —vt. **grit'ted**, **grit'ting** to grind (the teeth) as in determination —vi. to grate —**grit'ty** adj. **-ti-er**, **-ti-est**

grits (grits) n.pl. [OE. *grytte*] coarsely ground grain

griz-zled (griz''ld) adj. [< OFr. *gris*, gray] 1. gray or streaked with gray 2. having gray hair

griz-zly (-lē) adj. **-zli-er**, **-zli-est** grayish; grizzled

grizzly (**bear**) a large, ferocious brown or grayish bear of W N. America

groan (grōn) vi., vt. [< OE. *granian*] to utter (with) a deep sound expressing pain, distress, etc. —n. such a sound

gro-cer (grō'sər) n. [< OFr. *grossier*] a dealer in food and household supplies

gro-cer-y n., pl. **-ies** 1. a grocer's store 2. [pl.] the goods a grocer sells

grog (gräg) n. [after Old *Grog*, nickname of an 18th-c. Brit. admiral] 1. orig., rum diluted with water 2. any alcoholic liquor

grog-gy adj. **-gi-er**, **-gi-est** [< prec.] 1. orig., intoxicated 2. dizzy; dazed

groin (groin) n. [< ? OE. *grynde*, abyss] 1. the fold where the abdomen joins either thigh 2. *Archit.* the sharp, curved edge at the intersection of two vaults

GROIN

grom-met (gräm'it, grum'-) n. [< obs. Fr. *gormette*, a curb] 1. a ring of rope 2. a metal eyelet in cloth, etc.

groom (grōōm) n. [ME. *grom*, boy] 1. one whose work is tending horses 2. a bridegroom —vt. 1. to clean and curry (a horse, etc.) 2. to make neat and tidy 3. to train (a person) for a particular purpose

groove (grōōv) n. [< ON. *grof*, a pit] 1. a long, narrow furrow cut with a tool 2. any channel or rut 3. a settled routine —vt. **grooved**, **groov'ing** to make a groove in —vi. [Slang] to react with empathy to persons, situations, etc. around one (often with *on*)

groov-y adj. **-i-er**, **-i-est** [Slang] very pleasing or attractive

grope (grōp) vi. **groped**, **grop'ing** [< OE. *grapian*, to touch] to feel or search about blindly or uncertainly —vt. to seek or find by groping

gros-beak (grōs'bēk') n. [< Fr.: see GROSS & BEAK] a finchlike bird with a thick, conical bill

gros-grain (grō'grān') n. [Fr., lit., coarse grain] a ribbed silk or rayon fabric for ribbons, etc.

gross (grōs) adj. [< LL. *grossus*, thick] 1. fat and coarse-looking; burly 2. flagrant; very bad 3. dense; thick 4. lacking in refinement 5. coarse; vulgar 6. total; with no deductions —n. 1. overall total 2. pl. **gross** twelve dozen —vt., vi. [Colloq.] to earn (a specified total amount) before expenses are deducted —**gross'ly** adv.

gross national product the total value of a nation's annual output of goods and services

gro-tesque (grō tesk') adj. [< It. *grotta*, grotto: from designs found in grottoes] 1. distorted or fantastic in appearance, shape, etc. 2. ridiculous; absurd —**gro-tesque'ly** adv.

grot-to (grät'ō) n., pl. **-toes**, **-tos** [< It. < L. *crypta*, crypt] 1. a cave 2. a cavelike shrine, summerhouse, etc.

grouch (grouch) vi. [< ME. *grucchen*] to grumble or complain sulkily —n. 1. one who grouches 2. a sulky mood —**grouch'y** adj. **-i-er**, **-i-est**

ground[1] (ground) n. [OE. *grund*, bottom] 1. the solid surface of the earth 2. soil; earth 3. [*often pl.*] a tract of land [*grounds* of an estate] 4. area, as of discussion 5. [*often pl.*] a) basis; foundation b) valid reason or motive c the background, as in a design 7. [pl.] sediment [coffee *grounds*] 8. the connection of an electrical conductor with the ground —adj. of, on, or near the ground —vt. 1. to set on the ground 2. to cause to run aground 3. to base; found; establish 4. to instruct in the first principles of 5. to keep (an aircraft or pilot) from flying 6. *Elec.* to connect (a conductor) with the ground —vi. 1. to run ashore 2. *Baseball* to be put out on a grounder (usually with *out*) —**gain** (or **lose**) **ground** to gain (or lose) in achievement, popularity, etc. —**give ground** to retreat; yield —**hold** (or **stand**) **one's ground** to remain firm, not yielding —**run into the ground** [Colloq.] to overdo

ground[2] (ground) pt. & pp. of GRIND

ground cover low, dense-growing

plants used for covering bare ground

ground crew a group of workers who repair and maintain aircraft

ground′er n. *Baseball* a batted ball that travels along the ground

ground floor the floor of a building more or less level with the ground; first floor —**in on the ground floor** in at the start (of a business, etc.)

ground glass non-transparent glass, whose surface has been ground to diffuse light

ground′hog′ n. same as WOODCHUCK

ground′less adj. without reason

ground rule 1. *Baseball* a rule adapted to playing conditions in a specific ballpark 2. any basic rule

ground′swell′ n. 1. a large, rolling wave 2. a wave of popular feeling

ground′work′ n. a foundation; basis

group (grōōp) n. [< It. *gruppo*] a number of persons or things gathered or classified together —*vt.*, *vi.* to form into a group or groups

group·er (grōōp′ər) n. [Port. *garoupa*] a large fish found in warm seas

group·ie (grōōp′ē) n. [Colloq.] a girl fan of rock groups or other popular personalities, who follows them about

group therapy (or **psychotherapy**) a form of treatment for a group of patients with similar emotional problems, as by mutual criticism

grouse[1] (grous) n., pl. **grouse** [< ?] a game bird with a round, plump body, feathered legs, and mottled feathers

grouse[2] (grous) vi. **groused**, **grous′ing** [< ?] [Colloq.] to complain

grout (grout) n. [ME.] a thin mortar used as between tiles

grove (grōv) n. [OE. *graf*] a group of trees, often without undergrowth

grov·el (gruv′'l, gräv′-) vi. **-eled** or **-elled**, **-el·ing** or **-el·ling** [< ME. *grufelinge*, down on one's face] 1. to lie or crawl in a prostrate position, esp. abjectly 2. to behave abjectly

grow (grō) vi. **grew**, **grown**, **grow′ing** [< OE. *growan*] 1. to come into being or be produced naturally 2. to develop or thrive, as a living thing 3. to increase in size, quantity, etc. 4. to become [to grow weary] —*vt.* to cause to or let grow; raise; cultivate —**grow on** to have an increasing effect on —**grow up** to mature —**grow′er** n.

growl (groul) n. [ME. *groulen*] a rumbling, menacing sound such as an angry dog makes —*vi.*, *vt.* to make, or express by, such a sound

grown (grōn) pp. of GROW —adj. having completed its growth; mature

grown′-up′ adj., n. adult: also, for n., **grown′up′**

growth (grōth) n. 1. a growing or developing 2. *a)* increase in size, etc. *b)* the full extent of this 3. something that grows or has grown 4. an abnormal mass of tissue, as a tumor

growth stock a stock that is expected to grow in value and that pays relatively low dividends

grub (grub) vi. **grubbed**, **grub′bing** [ME. *grubben*] 1. to dig in the ground 2. to work hard —*vt.* 1. to clear (ground) of roots 2. to uproot —n. 1. a wormlike larva, esp. of a beetle 2. a drudge 3. [Slang] food

grub′by adj. **-bi·er**, **-bi·est** dirty; untidy —**grub′bi·ness** n.

grub′stake′ (-stāk′) n. [GRUB, n. 3 + STAKE] [Colloq.] money or supplies advanced as to a prospector

grudge (gruj) vt. **grudged**, **grudg′ing** [< OFr. *grouchier*] 1. same as BEGRUDGE 2. to give with reluctance —n. resentment or ill will over some grievance —**grudg′ing·ly** adv.

gru·el (grōō′əl) n. [< ML. *grutum*, meal] a thin broth of meal cooked in water or milk

gru·el·ing, **gru·el·ling** adj. [prp. of obs. v. *gruel*, punish] very trying; exhausting

grue·some (grōō′səm) adj. [< dial. *grue*, to shudder + -SOME[1]] causing horror or loathing; grisly

gruff (gruf) adj. [Du. *grof*] 1. rough or surly 2. harsh and throaty; hoarse —**gruff′ly** adv. —**gruff′ness** n.

grum·ble (grum′b'l) vi. **-bled**, **-bling** [prob. < Du. *grommelen*] 1. to growl 2. to mutter in discontent 3. to rumble —*vt.* to express by grumbling —n. a grumbling —**grum′bler** n.

grump·y (grum′pē) adj. **-i·er**, **-i·est** [prob. echoic] peevish; grouchy

grun·gy (grun′jē) adj. **-gi·er**, **-gi·est** [Slang] dirty, messy, slovenly, etc.

grunt (grunt) vi., vt. [< OE. *grunian*] to utter (with) the deep, throaty sound of a hog —n. this sound

GSA, G.S.A. General Services Administration

G-suit (jē′sōōt′) n. [G for *gravity*] an astronaut's or pilot's garment, pressurized to counteract the effects as of rapid acceleration

Guam (gwäm) island in the W Pacific: a possession of the U.S.

gua·no (gwä′nō) n., pl. **-nos** [Sp. < SAmInd.] manure of sea birds, used as fertilizer

guar·an·tee (gar′ən tē′) n. 1. same as GUARANTY (sense 1) 2. *a)* a pledge to replace something if it is not as represented *b)* assurance that something will be done as specified 3. a guarantor —*vt.* **-teed′**, **-tee′ing** 1. to give a guarantee for 2. to promise

guar·an·tor (gar′ən tôr′, -tər) n. one who gives a guaranty or guarantee

guar′an·ty (-tē) n., pl. **-ties** [< OFr. *garant*, a warrant] 1. a pledge or security for another's debt or obligation 2. an agreement that secures the existence or maintenance of something

guard (gärd) vt. [< OFr. *garder*] 1. to watch over and protect; defend 2. to keep from escape or trouble —*vi.* 1. to keep watch (against) 2. to act as a guard —n. 1. defense; protection 2. a posture of readiness for defense 3. any device to protect against injury or loss **4.** a person or group that guards **5.** a defensive basketball player or offensive football lineman —**on (one's) guard** vigilant

guard′ed *adj.* **1.** kept safe **2.** cautious [a *guarded* reply] —**guard′ed·ly** *adv.*

guard′house′ *n. Mil.* **1.** a building used by a guard when not walking a post **2.** a jail for temporary confinement

guard′i·an (-ē ən) *n.* **1.** one who guards or protects; custodian **2.** a person legally in charge of a minor or of someone incapable of taking care of his own affairs —*adj.* protecting —**guard′i·an·ship′** *n.*

guard′rail′ *n.* a protective railing, as along a highway

Gua·te·ma·la (gwä′tə mä′lə) country in Central America: 42,042 sq. mi.; pop. 4,717,000

gua·va (gwä′və) *n.* [< native name] a yellow, pear-shaped tropical fruit

gu·ber·na·to·ri·al (gōō′bər nə tôr′ē əl) *adj.* [L. *gubernator*, governor] of a governor or his office

Guern·sey (gurn′zē) *n., pl.* **-seys** [< *Guernsey*, one of the Channel Islands] a breed of dairy cattle, usually fawn-colored with white markings

guer·ril·la, gue·ril·la (gə ril′ə) *n.* [Sp., dim. of *guerra*, war] a member of a small defensive force of irregular soldiers, making surprise raids

guess (ges) *vt., vi.* [ME. *gessen*] **1.** to form a judgment or estimate of without actual knowledge; surmise **2.** to judge correctly by doing this **3.** to think or suppose —*n.* **1.** a guessing **2.** something guessed; conjecture

guess′work′ *n.* **1.** a guessing **2.** a judgment, result, etc. arrived at by guessing

guest (gest) *n.* [< ON. *gestr*] **1.** a person entertained at the home, club, etc. of another **2.** any paying customer of a hotel, restaurant, etc. —*adj.* **1.** for guests **2.** performing by special invitation [a *guest* artist]

guff (guf) *n.* [echoic] [Slang] **1.** nonsense **2.** brash or insolent talk

guf·faw (gə fô′) *n., vi.* [echoic] laugh in a loud, coarse burst

guid·ance (gīd′ns) *n.* **1.** a guiding; leadership **2.** advice or counsel

guide (gīd) *vt.* **guid′ed, guid′ing** [< OFr. *guier*] **1.** to point out the way for; lead **2.** to direct the course of; control —*n.* **1.** one whose work is conducting tours, etc. **2.** a controlling device **3.** a book of basic instruction

guide′book′ *n.* a book containing directions and information for tourists

guided missile a military missile whose course is controlled by radar, etc.

guide′line′ *n.* a principle by which to determine a course of action

guild (gild) *n.* [< OE. *gieldan*, to pay] an association for mutual aid and the promotion of common interests

guil·der (gil′dər) *n.* [< MDu. *gulden*, golden] the monetary unit and a coin of the Netherlands

guile (gīl) *n.* [< OFr.] slyness and cunning in dealing with others —**guile′ful** *adj.* —**guile′less** *adj.*

guil·lo·tine (gil′ə tēn′; *for v., usually* gil′ə tēn′) *n.* [Fr. < J. *Guillotin*, who advocated its use in 18th c.] an instrument for beheading, having a heavy blade dropped between two grooved uprights —*vt.* **-tined′, -tin′ing** to behead with a guillotine

guilt (gilt) *n.* [OE. *gylt*, a sin] **1.** the fact of having done a wrong or committed an offense **2.** a feeling of self-reproach from believing that one has done a wrong —**guilt′less** *adj.*

guilt′y *adj.* **-i·er, -i·est 1.** having guilt **2.** legally judged an offender **3.** of or showing guilt [a *guilty* look] —**guilt′i·ly** *adv.* —**guilt′i·ness** *n.*

Guin·ea (gin′ē) country on the W coast of Africa: 94,925 sq. mi.; pop. 3,702,000

guin·ea (gin′ē) *n.* [first coined of gold from Guinea] a former English gold coin equal to 21 shillings

guinea fowl (or **hen**) [orig. imported from Guinea] a domestic fowl with a rounded body and speckled feathers

guinea pig [prob. orig. brought to England by ships plying between England, Guinea, and S. America] **1.** a small, fat rodent used in biological experiments **2.** any subject used in an experiment

guise (gīz) *n.* [< OHG. *wisa*, manner] **1.** manner of dress; garb **2.** semblance **3.** a false appearance; pretense

gui·tar (gi tär′) *n.* [< Sp. < Gr. *kithara*, lyre] a musical instrument with usually six strings plucked with the fingers or a plectrum —**gui·tar′ist** *n.*

gulch (gulch) *n.* [prob. < dial. *gulch*, swallow greedily] a deep, narrow ravine

gulf (gulf) *n.* [ult. < Gr. *kolpos*, bosom] **1.** a large area of ocean reaching into land **2.** a wide, deep chasm **3.** a vast separation

Gulf Stream warm ocean current flowing from the Gulf of Mexico northward toward Europe

gull¹ (gul) *n.* [< Celt.] a gray and white water bird with webbed feet

gull² (gul) *n.* [< ?] a person easily tricked; dupe —*vt.* to cheat or trick

gul·let (gul′ət) *n.* [< L. *gula*, throat] **1.** the esophagus **2.** the throat

gul·li·ble (gul′ə b'l) *adj.* easily gulled; credulous —**gul′li·bil′i·ty** *n.*

gul·ly (gul′ē) *n., pl.* **-lies** [see GULLET] a small, narrow ravine

gulp (gulp) *vt., vi.* [prob. < Du. *gulpen*] **1.** to swallow hastily or greedily **2.** to choke back as if swallowing —*n.* a gulping or swallowing

gum¹ (gum) *n.* [< L. *gumma*] **1.** a sticky substance found in certain trees and plants **2.** an adhesive **3.** *same as* CHEWING GUM —*vt.* gummed, gum′ming to coat or unite with gum —*vi.* to become sticky or clogged —**gum up** [Slang] to cause to go awry —**gum′my** *adj.* **-mi·er, -mi·est**

gum² (gum) *n.* [OE. *goma*] [*often pl.*] the firm flesh surrounding the teeth —*vt.* gummed, gum′ming to chew with toothless gums

gum arabic a gum from certain acacia trees, used in medicine, candy, etc.

gum·bo (gum′bō) *n.* [< Bantu name for okra] a soup thickened with okra

gum′drop′ *n.* a small, firm candy made of sweetened gelatin, etc.

gump·tion (gump′shən) *n.* [< Scot.] [Colloq.] initiative; enterprise

gun (gun) *n.* [< ME. *gonnilde,* cannon < ON.] 1. a weapon with a metal tube from which a projectile is discharged by the force of an explosive 2. any similar device not discharged by an explosive [an air *gun*] 3. anything like a gun —*vi.* **gunned, gun′ning** to shoot or hunt with a gun —*vt.* 1. [Colloq.] to shoot (a person) 2. [Slang] to advance the throttle of (an engine) —**gun for** [Slang] to try to get —**jump the gun** [Slang] to begin before the proper time —**stick to one's guns** to stand fast; be firm —**under the gun** [Colloq.] in a tense situation, often involving a deadline

gun′boat′ *n.* a small armed ship

gun′fight′ *n.* a fight between persons using pistols or revolvers

gun′fire′ *n.* the firing of guns

gung-ho (guŋ′hō′) *adj.* [Chin., lit., work together] enthusiastic

gunk (guŋk) *n.* [Slang] a viscous or thick, messy substance

gun′man (-mən) *n., pl.* **-men** an armed gangster or hired killer

gun′met′al *n.* 1. bronze with a dark tarnish 2. its dark-gray color

gun′ner *n.* 1. a soldier, etc. who helps fire artillery 2. a naval warrant officer in charge of a ship's guns

gun′ner·y *n.* the science of making and using heavy guns and projectiles

gun·ny (gun′ē) *n.* [< Sans. *gōnī,* sack] a coarse fabric of jute or hemp

gun′ny·sack′ *n.* a sack made of gunny

gun′play′ *n.* an exchange of gunshots, as between gunmen and police

gun′pow′der *n.* an explosive powder used in guns, for blasting, etc.

gun′ship′ *n.* a heavily armed helicopter used to assault enemy ground forces

gun′shot′ *n.* shot fired from a gun

gun′-shy′ *adj.* easily frightened at the firing of a gun [a *gun-shy* dog]

gun′smith′ *n.* one who makes or repairs small guns

gun·wale (gun′'l) *n.* [< supporting a ship's guns] the upper edge of the side of a ship or boat

gup·py (gup′ē) *n., pl.* **-pies** [< R. *Guppy,* of Trinidad] a tiny freshwater fish of the West Indies, etc.

gur·gle (gur′g'l) *vi.* **-gled, -gling** [< L. *gurgulio,* gullet] to make a bubbling sound —*n.* such a sound

gu·ru (goor′o͞o, go͝o ro͞o′) *n.* [< Sans. *guru-ḥ,* venerable] in Hinduism, one's personal spiritual adviser or teacher

gush (gush) *vi.* [ME. *guschen*] 1. to flow out plentifully 2. to have a sudden flow 3. to talk or write effusively —*vt.* to cause to gush —*n.* a gushing —**gush′y** *adj.* **-i·er, -i·est**

gush′er *n.* 1. one who gushes 2. an oil well from which oil spouts forth

gus·set (gus′it) *n.* [< OFr. *gousset*] a triangular piece inserted to strengthen or enlarge a garment

gus·sie, gus·sy (gus′ē) *vt., vi.* **-sied, -sy·ing** [Slang] to dress (*up*) in a showy way

gust (gust) *n.* [< ON. *gjosa,* gush] 1. a sudden, strong rush of air 2. a sudden outburst of rain, laughter, etc. —**gust′y** *adj.* **-i·er, -i·est**

gus·ta·to·ry (gus′tə tôr′ē) *adj.* [< L. *gustus,* taste] of the sense of taste

gus·to (gus′tō) *n.* [see prec.] 1. zest; relish 2. great vigor or liveliness

gut (gut) *n.* [< OE. *geotan,* pour] 1. [*pl.*] the bowels or the stomach 2. the intestine 3. tough cord made from animal intestines 4. [*pl.*] [Slang] daring; courage —*vt.* **gut′ted, gut′ting** 1. to remove the intestines from 2. to destroy the interior of —*adj.* [Slang] 1. basic 2. not hard; easy

gut′less *adj.* [Slang] lacking courage

guts·y (gut′sē) *adj.* **-i·er, -i·est** [Slang] courageous, forceful, etc.

gut·ter (gut′ər) *n.* [< L. *gutta,* a drop] a channel to carry off water, as along the eaves of a roof or the side of a street —*vi.* to flow in a stream

gut·tur·al (gut′ər əl) *adj.* [L. *guttur,* throat] 1. of the throat 2. produced in the throat; rasping

guy¹ (gī) *n.* [< OFr. *guier,* to guide] a wire, rope, etc. used to steady or guide something —*vt.* to guide or steady with a guy

guy² (gī) *n.* [< *Guy* Fawkes, Eng. conspirator] [Slang] a man or boy —*vt.* to tease

Guy·a·na (gī an′ə) country in NE S. America: 83,000 sq.mi.; pop. 662,000

guz·zle (guz′'l) *vi., vt.* **-zled, -zling** [< ? OFr. *gosier,* throat] to drink greedily or immoderately

gym (jim) *n.* [Colloq.] *same as:* 1. GYMNASIUM 2. PHYSICAL EDUCATION

gym·na·si·um (jim nā′zē əm) *n., pl.* **-si·ums, -si·a** (-ə) [< Gr. *gymnos,* naked] a room or building equipped for physical training and sports

gym·nas·tics (jim nas′tiks) *n.pl.* exercises to develop and train the muscles —**gym′nast** *n.* —**gym·nas′tic** *adj.* —**gym·nas′ti·cal·ly** *adv.*

gyn·e·col·o·gy (gī′nə käl′ə jē, jin′ə-, jī′nə-) *n.* [< Gr. *gynē,* woman + -LOGY] the branch of medicine dealing with women's diseases, etc. —**gyn′e·col′o·gist** *n.*

gyp (jip) *n.* [prob. < GYPSY] [Colloq.] 1. a swindle 2. a swindler: also **gyp′per, gyp′ster** —*vt., vi.* **gypped, gyp′ping** [Colloq.] to swindle; cheat

gyp·sum (jip′səm) *n.* [< Gr. *gypsos*] a sulfate of calcium used for making plaster of Paris, in treating soil, etc.

Gyp·sy (jip′sē) *n., pl.* **-sies** [< *Egipcien,* Egyptian: orig. thought to be from Egypt] 1. [*also* g-] a member of a wandering Caucasoid people, perhaps orig. from India, with dark skin and black hair 2. their language 3.

[g-] one who looks or lives like a Gypsy

gypsy moth a moth in E U.S.: its larvae feed on leaves, damaging trees

gy·rate (jī'rāt) *vi.* -rat·ed, -rat·ing [< Gr. *gyros*, a circle] to move in a circular or spiral path; whirl — **gy·ra'tion** *n.* —**gy'ra'tor** *n.*

gy·ro (yir'ō, jī'rō) *n., pl.* -ros [see prec.] 1. layers of lamb and beef, roasted and sliced 2. a sandwich of this Also **gy·ros** (yir'ōs)

gyro- [see GYRATE] *a combining form meaning gyrating* [*gyroscope*]

gy·ro·scope (jī'rə skōp') *n.* [GYRO- + -SCOPE] a wheel mounted in a ring so that its axis is free to turn in any direction: when the wheel is spun rapidly, it will keep its original plane of rotation

gyve (jīv) *n., vt.* **gyved, gyv'ing** [ME. *give*] [Archaic] fetter; shackle

GYROSCOPE

H

H, h (āch) *n., pl.* **H's, h's** the eighth letter of the English alphabet

H *Chem.* hydrogen

H., h. 1. height 2. high 3. *Baseball* hits 4. hour(s)

ha (hä) *interj.* an exclamation of wonder, surprise, anger, triumph, etc.

‡ha·be·as cor·pus (hā'bē əs kôr'pəs) [L., (that) you have the body] *Law* a writ requiring that a prisoner be brought before a court to decide the legality of his detention

hab·er·dash·er (hab'ər dash'ər) *n.* [< ME.] a dealer in men's hats, shirts, neckties, etc. —**hab'er·dash'er·y** *n.*

ha·bil·i·ment (hə bil'ə mənt) *n.* [< MFr. *habiller*, clothe] 1. [*usually pl.*] clothing; attire 2. [*pl.*] trappings

hab·it (hab'it) *n.* [< L. *habere*, have] 1. a distinctive costume, as of a nun, etc. 2. a thing done often and, hence, easily 3. a usual way of doing 4. an addiction, esp. to narcotics

hab'it·a·ble *adj.* fit to be lived in

hab·i·tat (hab'ə tat') *n.* [L., it inhabits] 1. the region where a plant or animal naturally lives 2. the place where a person is ordinarily found

hab·i·ta'tion (-tā'shən) *n.* 1. an inhabiting 2. a dwelling; home

hab'it-form'ing *adj.* leading to the formation of a habit or addiction

ha·bit·u·al (hə bich'oo wəl) *adj.* 1. done or acquired by habit 2. steady; inveterate [*a habitual* smoker] 3. much seen, done, or used; usual —**ha·bit'u·al·ly** *adv.* —**ha·bit'u·al·ness** *n.*

ha·bit·u·ate' (-wāt') *vt.* **-at·ed, -at'ing** to accustom (*to*)

ha·bit·u·é (hə bich'oo wā') *n.* [Fr.] one who frequents a certain place

ha·ci·en·da (hä'sē en'də) *n.* [Sp. < L. *facere*, do] in Spanish America, a large estate, ranch, or its main house

hack¹ (hak) *vt.* [OE. *haccian*] to chop or cut roughly —*vi.* 1. to make rough cuts 2. to give harsh, dry coughs —*n.* 1. a tool for hacking 2. a gash or notch 3. a harsh, dry cough —**hack'er** *n.*

hack² (hak) *n.* [< HACKNEY] 1. a horse for hire 2. an old, worn-out horse 3. a literary drudge 4. a coach for hire 5. [Colloq.] a taxicab —*adj.* 1. employed as, or done by, a hack [*hack*

writer] 2. trite; hackneyed

hack'er (-ər) *n.* a talented amateur user of computers

hack·le (hak'l) *n.* [ME. *hechele*] 1. the neck feathers of a rooster, pigeon, etc., collectively 2. [*pl.*] the hairs on a dog's neck and back that bristle

hack·ney (hak'nē) *n., pl.* -neys [< *Hackney*, England] 1. a horse for driving or riding 2. a carriage for hire

hack'neyed' (-nēd') *adj.* made trite by overuse

hack'saw' *n.* a fine-toothed saw for cutting metal: also **hack saw**

had (had) *pt. & pp.* of HAVE

had·dock (had'ək) *n., pl.* -dock, -docks [ME. *hadok*] an Atlantic food fish, related to the cod

HACKSAW

Ha·des (hā'dēz) *Gr. Myth.* the home of the dead —*n.* [*often* h-] [Colloq.] hell

had·n't (had'nt) had not

haft (haft) *n.* [OE. *hæft*] the handle or hilt of a knife, ax, etc.

hag (hag) *n.* [< OE. *hægtes*] 1. a witch 2. an ugly, often vicious old woman —**hag'gish** *adj.*

hag·gard (hag'ərd) *adj.* [MFr. *hagard*, untamed (hawk)] having a wild, wasted, worn look; gaunt

hag·gle (hag'l) *vi.* **-gled, -gling** [< Scot. *hag*, to hack] to argue about terms, price, etc. —*n.* a haggling —**hag'gler** *n.*

Hague (hāg), **The** the political capital of the Netherlands: pop. 593,000

hah (hä) *interj. same as* HA

hai·ku (hī'kōō) *n.* [Jap.] 1. a Japanese verse form of three unrhymed lines of 5, 7, and 5 syllables respectively 2. *pl.* -ku a poem in this form

hail¹ (hāl) *vt.* [< ON. *heill*, whole, sound] 1. to greet with cheers; acclaim 2. to call out to —*n.* a greeting —*interj.* an exclamation of tribute, greeting, etc. —**hail from** to be from

hail² (hāl) *n.* [OE. *hægel*] 1. frozen raindrops falling during thunderstorms 2. a shower of or like hail —*vt., vi.* to pour down like hail

hail'stone' *n.* a pellet of hail

hail'storm' n. a storm with hail

hair (her) n. [OE. hær] 1. any of the threadlike outgrowths from the skin 2. a growth of these, as on the human head 3. a very small space, degree, etc. 4. a threadlike growth on a plant —**get in one's hair** [Slang] to annoy one —**split hairs** to quibble —**hair'less** adj. —**hair'like'** adj.

hair'ball' n. a ball of hair often found in the stomach of a cow, cat, or other animal that licks its coat

hair'breadth' (-bredth') n. a very small space or amount —adj. very narrow; close Also **hairs'breadth'**

hair'cut' n. the act of, or a style of, cutting the hair

hair'do' n., pl. -**dos** the style in which (a woman's) hair is arranged

hair'dress'er n. one whose work is dressing (women's) hair

hair'line' n. 1. a very thin line 2. the outline of the hair on the head

hair'piece' n. a toupee or wig

hair'pin' n. a small, bent piece of wire, etc. for keeping the hair in place —adj. U-shaped [a hairpin turn]

hair'-rais'ing adj. [Colloq.] terrifying or shocking

hair'split'ting adj., n. making petty distinctions; quibbling

hair'spring' n. a slender, hairlike coil spring, as in a watch

hair'y adj. -**i·er**, -**i·est** covered with hair —**hair'i·ness** n.

Hai·ti (hāt'ē) country occupying the W portion of Hispaniola: 10,714 sq. mi.; pop. 4,485,000 —**Hai·tian** (hā'shən, hāt'ē ən) adj., n.

hake (hāk) n., pl. **hake**, **hakes** [prob. < ON.] a marine food fish related to the cod

hal·berd (hal'bərd) n. [< MHG. helmbarte] a combination spear and battle-ax of the 15th and 16th c.

hal·cy·on (hal'sē ən) adj. [< Gr. alkyōn, kingfisher (fabled calmer of the sea)] tranquil, happy, idyllic, etc.

hale[1] (hāl) adj. [OE. hal] vigorous and healthy

hale[2] (hāl) vt. **haled**, **hal'ing** [< OFr. haler] to force (a person) to go

half (haf) n., pl. **halves** [OE. healf] 1. either of the two equal parts of something 2. either of the two equal periods of some games —adj. 1. being a half 2. incomplete; partial —adv. 1. to the extent of a half 2. [Colloq.] partly [half done] 3. [Colloq.] at all: used with not [not half bad]

half'-and-half' n. something half one thing and half another, as a mixture of milk and cream —adj. partly one thing and partly another —adv. in two equal parts

half'back' n. Football either of two backs, in addition to the fullback and the quarterback

half'-breed' n. one whose parents are of different races: also **half'-caste'**

half brother a brother through one parent only

half dollar a coin of the U.S. and Canada, worth 50 cents

half'heart'ed adj. with little enthusiasm, determination, interest, etc. —**half'heart'ed·ly** adv.

half'-mast' n. the position of a flag halfway down its staff, as a sign of mourning or a distress signal

half note Music a note (♩) having one half the duration of a whole note

half·pen·ny (hā'pə nē, hāf'pen'ē) n., pl. -**pence** (hā'pəns), -**pen·nies** a British coin equal to half a penny

half sister a sister through one parent only

half sole a sole (of a shoe or boot) from the arch to the toe

half'track' n. an army truck, armored vehicle, etc. with a continuous tread instead of rear wheels

half'way' adj. 1. midway between two points, etc. 2. partial [halfway measures] —adv. 1. to the midway point 2. partially —**meet halfway** to be willing to compromise with

halfway house a place for helping people adjust to society after being imprisoned, hospitalized, etc.

half'-wit' n. a stupid, silly, or imbecilic person —**half'-wit'ted** adj.

hal·i·but (hal'ə bət) n., pl. -**but**, -**buts** [ME. hali, holy + butt, a flounder: eaten on holidays] a large, edible flatfish found in northern seas

Hal·i·fax (hal'ə faks') capital of Nova Scotia: pop. 87,000

hal·ite (hal'īt, hā'līt) n. [< Gr. hals, salt + -ITE] same as ROCK SALT

hal·i·to·sis (hal'ə tō'sis) n. [< L. halitus, breath] bad-smelling breath

hall (hôl) n. [OE. heall] 1. the main dwelling on an estate 2. a public building with offices, etc. 3. a large room for gatherings, exhibits, etc. 4. a college building 5. a vestibule at the entrance of a building 6. a hallway

hal·le·lu·jah, **hal·le·lu·iah** (hal'ə lōō'yə) interj. [< Heb. hallelū, praise + yāh, Jehovah] praise (ye) the Lord! —n. a hymn of praise to God

hall·mark (hôl'märk') n. [< the mark stamped on gold and silver articles at Goldsmith's Hall in London] a mark or symbol of genuineness or high quality

hal·loo (hə lōō') interj., n. a shout to attract attention —vi., vt. -**looed'**, -**loo'ing** to shout or call

hal·low (hal'ō) vt. [OE. halgian] to make or regard as holy

hal·lowed (hal'ōd; in liturgy, often hal'ə wid) adj. holy or sacred

Hal·low·een, **Hal·low·e'en** (hal'ə wēn') n. [contr. < all hallow even] the evening of October 31, followed by All Saints' Day

hal·lu·ci·nate (hə lōō'sə nāt') vi., vt. -**nat'ed**, -**nat'ing** [see ff.] to have or cause to have hallucinations

hal·lu·ci·na·tion (hə lōō'sə nā'shən) n. [< L. hallucinari, to wander mentally] the apparent perception of sights, sounds, etc. that are not actually present —**hal·lu'ci·na·to'ry** (-nə tôr'ē) *adj.*

hal·lu·ci·no·gen (-nə jen, hal'yoo sin'ə jen) *n.* a drug or other substance that produces hallucinations

hall'way' *n.* a passageway; corridor

ha·lo (hā'lō) *n., pl.* **-los, -loes** [< Gr. *halōs,* circular threshing floor] **1.** a ring of light, as around the sun **2.** a symbolic ring of light around the head of a saint in pictures

hal·o·gen (hal'ə jən) *n.* [< Gr. *hals,* salt] any of the very active chemical elements, fluorine, chlorine, bromine, astatine, and iodine

halt¹ (hôlt) *n., vi., vt.* [< Fr. *faire halte* and G. *halt machen*] stop

halt² (hôlt) *vi.* [< OE. *healt*] **1.** [Archaic] to limp **2.** to hesitate —*adj.* lame —**the halt** those who are lame

hal·ter (hôl'tər) *n.* [OE. *hælftre*] **1.** a rope or strap for tying or leading an animal **2.** a hangman's noose **3.** a woman's upper garment, held up by a loop around the neck

halve (hav) *vt.* **halved, halv'ing 1.** to divide into two equal parts **2.** to reduce to half

halves (havz) *n. pl. of* HALF —**by halves** halfway; imperfectly —**go halves** to share expenses equally

hal·yard (hal'yərd) *n.* [< ME. *halier* (see HALE²)] a rope or tackle for raising or lowering a flag, sail, etc.

ham (ham) *n.* [OE. *hamm*] **1.** the back of the thigh **2.** the upper part of a hog's hind leg, salted, smoked, etc. **3.** [Colloq.] an amateur radio operator **4.** [Slang] an actor who overacts —*ham'my adj.* **-mi·er, -mi·est**

Ham·burg (ham'bərg) seaport in N West Germany: pop. 1,854,000

ham·burg·er (ham'bur'gər) *n.* [< prec.] **1.** ground beef **2.** a cooked patty of such meat, often in a sandwich Also **ham'burg**

Ham·il·ton (ham'əl t'n) city & port in SE Ontario: pop. 298,000

Ham·let (ham'lit) the title hero of a tragedy by Shakespeare

ham·let (ham'lit) *n.* [< LowG. *hamm,* enclosed area] a very small village

ham·mer (ham'ər) *n.* [OE. *hamor*] **1.** a tool for pounding, having a metal head and a handle **2.** a thing like this in shape or use, as the part of a gun that strikes the firing pin **3.** a bone of the middle ear —*vt., vi.* **1.** to strike repeatedly, as with a hammer **2.** to drive, force, or shape, as with hammer blows —**hammer (away) at** to keep emphasizing —**ham'mer·er** *n.*

ham'mer·head' *n.* **1.** the head of a hammer **2.** a shark with a mallet-shaped head having an eye at each end

ham'mer·toe' *n.* a toe that is deformed, with its first joint bent downward

ham·mock (ham'ək) *n.* [Sp. *hamaca,* of WInd. origin] a bed of canvas, etc. swung from ropes at both ends

Ham·mond (ham'ənd) city in NW Ind., near Chicago: pop. 94,000

ham·per¹ (ham'pər) *vt.* [ME. *hampren*] to hinder; impede; encumber

ham·per² (ham'pər) *n.* [< OFr. *hanap,* a cup] a large basket, usually covered

Hamp·ton (hamp'tən) seaport in SE Va.: pop. 123,000

ham·ster (ham'stər) *n.* [< OHG. *hamustro*] a ratlike animal of Europe and Asia used in scientific experiments

ham·string (ham'striŋ') *n.* a tendon at the back of the knee —*vt.* **-strung', -string'ing** to disable, as by cutting a hamstring

hand (hand) *n.* [OE.] **1.** the part of the arm below the wrist, used for grasping **2.** a side or direction [at my right *hand*] **3.** possession or care [the land is in my *hands*] **4.** control [to strengthen one's *hand*] **5.** an active part [take a *hand* in the work] **6.** a promise to marry **7.** skill **8.** one having a special skill **9.** manner of doing something **10.** handwriting **11.** applause **12.** help [to lend a *hand*] **13.** a hired worker [a farm *hand*] **14.** a source [to get news at first *hand*] **15.** anything like a hand, as a pointer on a clock **16.** the breadth of a hand **17.** *Card Games a)* the cards held by a player at one time *b)* a round of play —*adj.* of, for, or controlled by the hand —*vt.* **1.** to give as with the hand **2.** to help or conduct with the hand —**at hand** near —**hand in hand** together —**hand it to** [Slang] to give credit to —**hand over fist** [Colloq.] easily and in large amounts —**hands down** easily —**on hand 1.** near **2.** available **3.** present —**on the one (or other) hand** from one (or the opposed) point of view

hand'bag' *n.* a woman's purse

hand'ball' *n.* a game in which players bat a small rubber ball against a wall or walls with the hand

hand'bar'row *n.* a frame carried by two people by handles at the ends

hand'bill' *n.* a small printed notice to be passed out by hand

hand'book' *n.* a compact reference book; manual

hand'breadth' *n.* the breadth of the human palm, about 4 inches

hand'cart' *n.* a small cart pulled or pushed by hand

hand'clasp' *n. same as* HANDSHAKE

hand'craft' *n. same as* HANDICRAFT —*vt.* to make skillfully by hand

hand'cuff' *n.* either of a pair of connected rings for shackling the wrists of a prisoner: *usually used in pl.* —*vt.* to put handcuffs on; manacle

hand'ed *adj.* having or involving (a specified kind or number of) hands [right-*handed,* two-*handed*]

Han·del (han'd'l), **George Frederick** 1685-1759; Eng. composer, born in Germany

hand'ful' *n., pl.* **-fuls' 1.** as much or as many as the hand will hold **2.** a few; not many **3.** [Colloq.] someone or something hard to manage

hand'gun' *n.* any firearm that is held and fired with one hand, as a pistol

hand·i·cap (han'dē kap') *n.* [< *hand in cap,* former kind of lottery] **1.** a competition in which difficulties are imposed on, or advantages given to, the various contestants to equalize their chances 2. such a difficulty or advantage 3. any hindrance —vt. -capped', -cap'ping 1. to give a handicap to 2. to hinder —the handicapped those who are physically disabled or mentally retarded

hand'i·cap'per n. a person, as a sports writer, who tries to predict the winners in horse races

hand·i·craft (han'dē kraft') n. skill with the hands, or work calling for it

hand'i·work' n. 1. same as HAND-WORK 2. work done by a person himself

hand·ker·chief (haŋ'kər chif) n. [HAND + KERCHIEF] a small cloth for wiping the nose, face, etc.

han·dle (han'd'l) n. [OE. < hand] that part of a tool, etc. by which it is held or lifted —vt. -dled, -dling 1. to touch, lift, operate, etc. with the hand 2. to manage; control 3. to deal with; treat 4. to sell or deal in —vi. to respond to control [the car handles well] —han'dler n.

han'dle·bar' n. [often pl.] a curved metal bar with handles on the ends, for steering a bicycle, etc.

hand'made' adj. made by hand, not by machine

hand'maid'en n. [Archaic] a woman or girl servant: also **hand'maid'**

hand'-me-down' n. [Colloq.] a used garment, etc. passed on to one

hand'out' n. 1. a gift of food, clothing, etc., as to a beggar 2. a leaflet handed out 3. an official news release

hand'pick' vt. 1. to pick by hand 2. to choose with care or for a purpose

hand'rail' n. a rail serving as a support or guard, as along a stairway

hand'set' n. a telephone mouthpiece and receiver in a single unit

hand'shake' n. a gripping of each other's hand in greeting, promise, etc.

hands'-off' adj. designating or of a policy of not interfering

hand·some (han'səm) adj. [orig., easily handled] 1. considerable 2. generous; gracious 3. good-looking, esp. in a manly or impressive way

hand'spring' n. a spring in which one turns over in midair with one or both hands touching the ground

hand'-to-hand' adj. at close quarters: said of fighting

hand'-to-mouth' adj. consuming all that is obtained

hand'work' n. handmade work

hand'writ'ing n. 1. writing done by hand, as with a pen 2. a style of such writing —**hand'writ'ten** adj.

hand'y adj. -i·er, -i·est 1. close at hand; easily reached 2. easily used; convenient 3. clever with the hands —**hand'i·ly** adv. —**hand'i·ness** n.

han'dy·man' n., pl. -men' a man who does odd jobs

hang (haŋ) vt. hung, hang'ing; for vt. 3 & vi. 5 hanged is preferred pt. & pp. [OE. hangian] 1. to attach from above with no support from below;

suspend 2. to attach (a door, etc.) so as to move freely 3. to kill by suspending from a rope about the neck 4. to attach (wallpaper, etc.) to walls 5. to let (one's head) droop downward 6. to deadlock (a jury) —vi. 1. to be attached above with no support from below 2. to hover in the air 3. to swing freely 4. to fall or drape, as cloth 5. to die by hanging 6. to droop; bend —n. the way a thing hangs —get (or have) the hang of 1. to learn (or have) the knack of 2. to understand the meaning or idea of —hang around (or about) [Colloq.] to loiter around —hang back (or off) to be reluctant, as from shyness —hang on 1. to go on; persevere 2. to depend on 3. to listen attentively to —hang out [Slang] to spend much time —hang up 1. to put on a hanger, hook, etc. 2. to end a telephone call by replacing the receiver 3. to delay

hang·ar (haŋ'ər) n. [Fr.] a repair shed or shelter for aircraft

hang'dog' adj. abject or ashamed

hang'er n. 1. one who hangs things 2. that on which something is hung

hang gliding the sport of gliding through the air while hanging by a harness from a large type of kite (hang glider)

hang'ing adj. that hangs —n. 1. a killing by hanging 2. something hung on a wall, etc., as a drapery

hang'man (-mən) n., pl. -men a man who hangs convicted criminals

hang'nail' n. [< OE. angnægl, a corn (on the toe)] a bit of torn skin hanging next to a fingernail

hang'o'ver n. 1. a survival 2. nausea, headache, etc. from drinking much alcoholic liquor

hang'-up' n. [Slang] an unresolvable personal or emotional problem

hank (haŋk) n. [prob. < Scand.] a skein of yarn or thread

hank·er (haŋ'kər) vi. [prob. < Du. or LowG.] to long or yearn (for) —hank'er·ing n.

Ha·noi (hä noi', ha-) capital of Vietnam: pop. 1,378,000

han·som (cab) (han'səm) [< J. A. Hansom, 19th-c. Eng. inventor] a two-wheeled covered carriage, pulled by one horse, with the driver's seat behind

HANSOM

Ha·nu·ka (khä'noo kä', -kə; hä'-) n. [< Heb. dedication] an 8-day Jewish festival commemorating the rededication of the Temple: also **Ha'nuk·kah'**

hap (hap) n. [< ON. happ] luck

hap·haz·ard (hap'haz'ərd) adj. not planned; random —adv. by chance

hap·less (hap'lis) adj. unlucky

hap'ly adv. [Archaic] by chance

hap·pen (hap'n) vi. [ME. *happenen*] 1. to take place; occur 2. to be, occur, or come by chance 3. to have the luck or occasion [I *happened* to see it] —**happen on** (or **upon**) to meet or find by chance

hap'pen·ing n. an occurrence; event

hap'pen·stance (-stans') n. [Colloq.] chance or accidental happening

hap·pi coat (hap'ē) [< Jap.] a short, light Japanese coat worn with a sash

hap·py (hap'ē) adj. -**pi·er**, -**pi·est** [< HAP] 1. lucky; fortunate 2. having, showing, or causing great pleasure or joy 3. suitable and clever; apt —**hap'pi·ly** adv. —**hap'pi·ness** n.

hap'py-go-luck'y adj. easygoing

ha·ra·ki·ri (hä'rə kir'ē) n. [Jap. *hara*, belly + *kiri*, a cutting] ritual suicide by ripping out the bowels

ha·rangue (hə raŋ') n. [< OIt. *aringo*, site for public assemblies] a long, blustering speech; tirade —vi., vt. -**rangued'**, -**rangu'ing** to speak or address in a harangue

har·ass (hə ras', har'əs) vt. [< OFr. *harer*, set a dog on] 1. to worry or torment 2. to trouble by constant raids or attacks —**har·ass'ment** n.

Har·bin (här'bin) city in NE China: pop. 1,800,000

har·bin·ger (här'bin jər) n. [< OFr. *herberge*, a shelter] a forerunner; herald

har·bor (här'bər) n. [< OE. *here*, army + *beorg*, shelter] 1. a shelter 2. a protected inlet for anchoring ships; port —vt. 1. to shelter or house 2. to hold in the mind [to *harbor* envy] —vi. to take shelter Brit. sp. **harbour**

hard (härd) adj. [OE. *heard*] 1. firm and unyielding to the touch; solid and compact 2. powerful [a *hard* blow] 3. difficult to do, understand, or deal with 4. a) unfeeling [a *hard* heart] b) unfriendly [*hard* feelings] 5. harsh; severe 6. having mineral salts that interfere with lathering 7. energetic [a *hard* worker] 8. containing much alcohol [*hard* liquor] 9. addictive and harmful [*heroin* is a *hard* drug] —adv. 1. energetically [*work hard*] 2. with strength [*hit hard*] 3. with difficulty [*hard*-earned] 4. close; near [we live *hard* by] 5. so as to be solid [*frozen hard*] 6. sharply [*turn hard* right] —**hard and fast** invariable; strict —**hard of hearing** partially deaf —**hard up** [Colloq.] in great need of money —**hard'ness** n.

hard'back' n. a hard-cover book

hard'ball' n. same as BASEBALL

hard'-bit'ten adj. tough; dogged

hard'-boiled' adj. 1. boiled until solid: said of eggs 2. [Colloq.] unfeeling; tough; callous

hard'-core' adj. absolute; unqualified

hard'-cov'er adj. designating any book bound in a stiff cover

hard·en (här'd'n) vt., vi. to make or become hard —**hard'en·er** n.

hard hat 1. a protective helmet worn by construction workers, miners, etc. 2. [Slang] such a worker

hard'head'ed adj. 1. shrewd and unsentimental; practical 2. stubborn

hard'heart'ed adj. unfeeling; cruel

har·di·hood (här'dē hood') n. boldness

Har·ding (här'diŋ), **Warren G.** 1865-1923; 29th president of the U.S. (1921-23)

hard'-line' adj. aggressive; unyielding

hard·ly (härd'lē) adv. 1. only just; scarcely 2. probably not; not likely

hard'-nosed' (-nōzd') adj. [Slang] tough and stubborn or shrewd

hard sell high-pressure salesmanship

hard'ship' n. a thing hard to bear, as poverty, pain, etc.

hard'stand' n. a paved area for parking aircraft or other vehicles

hard'tack' (-tak') n. unleavened bread made in hard, large wafers

hard'top' n. an automobile like a convertible but having a fixed metal top

hard'ware' (-wer') n. 1. articles made of metal, as tools, nails, fittings, etc. 2. the mechanical, magnetic, and electronic devices of a computer

hard'wood' n. 1. any tough, heavy timber with a compact texture 2. the wood of any tree with broad, flat leaves, as the oak, maple, etc.

har·dy (här'dē) adj. -**di·er**, -**di·est** [< OFr. *hardir*, make bold] 1. bold and resolute 2. robust; vigorous—**har'di·ly** adv. —**har'di·ness** n.

hare (her) n. [OE. *hara*] a mammal related to and resembling the rabbit

hare'brained' adj. giddy, rash, etc.

hare'lip' n. a congenital deformity consisting of a cleft of the upper lip

ha·rem (her'əm) n. [Ar. *harim*, prohibited (place)] 1. that part of a Moslem's house in which the women live 2. the women in a harem

hark (härk) vi. [ME. *herkien*] to listen carefully: usually in the imperative —**hark back** to go back in thought or speech

hark·en (här'k'n) vi., vt. same as HEARKEN

Har·le·quin (här'lə kwin, -kin) a comic character in pantomime, who wears a mask and gay, spangled tights —n. [h-] a clown; buffoon

har·lot (här'lət) n. [< OFr., rogue] a prostitute —**har'lot·ry** (-rē) n.

harm (härm) n. [OE. *hearm*] hurt; injury; damage —vt. to do harm to

harm'ful adj. causing harm; hurtful —**harm'ful·ly** adv.

harm'less adj. causing no harm —**harm'less·ly** adv.

har·mon·ic (här män'ik) adj. Music of or in harmony —n. an overtone —**har·mon'i·cal·ly** adv.

har·mon·i·ca (-i kə) n. a small wind instrument with a series of metal reeds that produce tones when air is blown or sucked across them

har·mon·ics n.pl. [with sing. v.] the science of musical sounds

har·mo·ni·ous (här mō'nē əs) adj. 1. having parts arranged in an orderly or pleasing way 2. having similar ideas, interests, etc. 3. having musical tones combined to give a pleasing effect —**har·mo'ni·ous·ly** adv.

har·mo·ni·um (här mō'nē əm) n. [Fr.] a small kind of reed organ

har·mo·nize (här'mə nīz') *vi.* **-nized', -niz'ing** 1. to be in harmony 2. to sing in harmony —*vt.* to make harmonious —**har'mo·ni·za'tion** *n.* —**har'mo·niz'er** *n.*

har·mo·ny (här'mə nē) *n.,* *pl.* **-nies** [< Gr. *harmos,* a fitting] 1. pleasing agreement of parts in color, size, etc. 2. agreement in action, ideas, etc.; friendly relations 3. the pleasing combination of tones in a chord

har·ness (här'nis) *n.* [< OFr. *harneis,* armor] the leather straps and metal pieces by which a horse, mule, etc. is fastened to a vehicle, plow, etc. —*vt.* 1. to put a harness on 2. to control so as to use the power of

harp (härp) *n.* [OE. *hearpe*] a musical instrument with strings stretched across a triangular frame, played by plucking —*vi.* 1. to play a harp 2. to persist in talking or writing tediously (*on* or *upon* something) —**harp'ist** *n.*

har·poon (här pōōn') *n.* [< ON. *harpa,* to squeeze] a barbed spear with an attached line, for spearing whales, etc. —*vt.* to strike with a harpoon

harp·si·chord (härp'si körd') *n.* [< It. *arpa,* harp + *corda,* CORD] a pianolike keyboard instrument whose strings are plucked rather than struck

Har·py (här'pē) *n.,* *pl.* **-pies** [< Gr. *harpazein,* snatch] 1. Gr. *Myth.* any of several monsters, part woman and part bird 2. [h-] a greedy person

har·ri·dan (har'i d'n) *n.* [< Fr. *haridelle,* worn-out horse] a disreputable, shrewish old woman

har·ri·er (har'ē ər) *n.* [< HARE + -IER] 1. a small dog used for hunting hares 2. a cross-country runner

Har·ris·burg (har'is burg') capital of Pa.: pop. 53,000

Har·ri·son (har'ə s'n) 1. Benjamin, 1833–1901; 23d president of the U.S. (1889–93) 2. William Henry, 1773–1841; 9th president of the U.S. (1841); grandfather of *prec.*

har·row (har'ō) *n.* [prob. < ON.] a heavy frame with spikes or disks, used for breaking up and leveling plowed ground, etc. —*vt.* 1. to draw a harrow over (land) 2. to cause mental distress to —**har'row·ing** *adj.*

har·ry (har'ē) *vt.* **-ried, -ry·ing** [< OE. *here,* army] 1. to raid and ravage or rob 2. to torment or worry

harsh (härsh) *adj.* [ME. *harsk*] 1. unpleasantly rough to the eye, ear, taste, or touch 2. offensive to the mind or feelings 3. cruel or severe —**harsh'ly** *adv.* —**harsh'ness** *n.*

hart (härt) *n.* [OE. *heorot*] a full-grown, male European red deer

Hart·ford (härt'fərd) capital of Conn.: pop. 136,000

har·um-scar·um (her'əm sker'əm) *adj.* [< ?] reckless or irresponsible —*adv.* in a harum-scarum way

har·vest (här'vist) *n.* [OE. *hærfest*] 1. the time of the year when grain, fruit, etc. are gathered in 2. a season's crop 3. the gathering in of a crop 4. the outcome of any effort —*vt., vi.* to gather in (a crop) —**har'vest·er** *n.*

has (haz; *before* "to" has) 3d *pers. sing., pres. indic.,* of HAVE

has'-been' *n.* [Colloq.] a person or thing whose popularity is past

hash (hash) *vt.* [< Fr. *hacher,* to chop] to chop up (meat or vegetables) for cooking —*n.* 1. a chopped mixture of cooked meat and vegetables, usually baked 2. a mixture 3. a muddle; mess 4. [Slang] hashish —**hash out** [Colloq.] to settle by long discussion —**hash over** [Colloq.] to discuss at length

hash·ish (hash'ēsh, -ish) *n.* [Ar. *hashish,* dried hemp] a narcotic and intoxicant made from Indian hemp

has·n't (haz'nt) has not

hasp (hasp) *n.* [OE. *hæsp*] a hinged fastening for a door, etc.; esp., a metal piece fitted over a staple and fastened as by a bolt or padlock

has·sle (has'l) *n.* [< ?] [Colloq.] a heated argument; squabble —*vi.* **-sled, -sling** [Colloq.] to argue heatedly —*vt.* [Slang] to annoy or harass

HASP

has·sock (has'ək) *n.* [OE. *hassuc,* (clump of) coarse grass] a firm cushion used as a footstool or seat

hast (hast) *archaic* 2d *pers. sing., pres. indic.,* of HAVE: *used with* thou

haste (hāst) *n.* [OFr.] quickness of motion; rapidity —*vt., vi.* [Rare] *same as* HASTEN —**make haste** to hurry

has·ten (hās'n) *vt.* to make be or come faster; speed up —*vi.* to move or act swiftly; hurry

hast·y (hās'tē) *adj.* **-i·er, -i·est** 1. done with haste; hurried 2. done, made, or acting too quickly or rashly —**hast'i·ly** *adv.* —**hast'i·ness** *n.*

hat (hat) *n.* [OE. *hæt*] a head covering, usually with a brim and a crown —**pass the hat** to take up a collection —**talk through one's hat** to talk nonsense —**throw one's hat into the ring** to enter a contest, esp. for political office —**under one's hat** [Colloq.] confidential

hatch¹ (hach) *vt.* [ME. *hacchen*] 1. to bring forth (young) from (an egg or eggs) 2. to contrive (a plan, plot, etc.) —*vi.* 1. to bring forth young: said of eggs 2. to emerge from the egg

hatch² (hach) *n.* [OE. *hæcc,* grating] 1. a hatchway 2. a lid for a hatchway

hatch'back' *n.* [HATCH² + BACK] an automobile with a rear that swings up, giving wide entry to a storage area

hat'check' *adj.* of or working in a checkroom for hats, coats, etc.

hatch'er·y *n.,* *pl.* **-ies** a place for

hatching eggs, esp. of fish or poultry

hatch·et (hach′it) *n.* [< OFr. *hache*, *ax*] a small ax with a short handle —**bury the hatchet** to make peace

hatchet job [Colloq.] a biased, malicious attack on another's character

hatch′way′ *n.* an opening in a ship's deck, or in a floor or roof

hate (hāt) *vt.* hat′ed, hat′ing [OE. *hatian*] 1. to have strong dislike or ill will for 2. to wish to avoid [to *hate* fights] —*vi.* to feel hatred —*n.* 1. a strong feeling of dislike or ill will 2. a person or thing hated

hate′ful *adj.* deserving hate —**hate′-ful·ly** *adv.* —**hate′ful·ness** *n.*

hath (hath) *archaic 3d pers. sing., pres. indic.,* of HAVE

ha·tred (hā′trid) *n.* strong dislike or ill will; hate

hat·ter (hat′ər) *n.* a person who makes or sells men's hats

hau·berk (hô′bərk) *n.* [< Frank. *hals*, neck + *bergan*, protect] a medieval coat of armor, usually of chain mail

haugh·ty (hôt′ē) *adj.* -ti·er, -ti·est [< OFr. *haut*, high] having or showing great pride in oneself and contempt for others; arrogant —**haugh′ti·ly** *adv.* —**haugh′ti·ness** *n.*

haul (hôl) *vt., vi.* [< OFr. *haler*] 1. to move by pulling; drag 2. to transport by wagon, truck, etc. —*n.* 1. the act of hauling; pull 2. the amount gained, caught, etc. at one time 3. the distance over which something is transported —**haul off** [Colloq.] to draw the arm back before hitting —**in** (or **over**) **the long haul** over a long period of time

haunch (hônch) *n.* [< OFr. *hanche* < Gmc.] 1. the hip, buttock, and upper thigh together 2. an animal's loin and leg together

haunt (hônt) *vt.* [< OFr. *hanter*, to frequent] 1. to visit often or continually 2. to recur repeatedly to [*haunted* by memories] —*n.* a place often visited

haunt′ed *adj.* supposedly frequented by ghosts [a *haunted* house]

haunt′ing *adj.* recurring often to the mind; not easily forgotten

hau·teur (hō tur′) *n.* [Fr. < *haut*, high] disdainful pride; haughtiness

Ha·van·a (hə van′ə) capital of Cuba: pop. 788,000 —*n.* a cigar made of Cuban tobacco

have (hav; *before "to"* haf) *vt.* had, hav′ing [OE. *habban*] 1. to hold; own; possess [to *have* money, a week has 7 days] 2. to experience [*have* a good time] 3. to hold mentally [to *have* an idea] 4. to state [so rumor *has* it] 5. to get, take, consume, etc. [*have* a drink] 6. to bear or beget (offspring) 7. to engage in [to *have* a fight] 8. to cause to; cause to be [*have* her leave] 9. to permit; tolerate [I won't *have* this noise!] 10. [Colloq.] *a*) to hold at a disadvantage *b*) to deceive; cheat *Have* is used as an auxiliary to express completed action (Ex.: I had left), and with infinitives to express obligation or necessity (Ex.:

we *have* to go). *Have got* often replaces *have. Have* is conjugated in the present indicative: (I) *have*, (he, she, it) *has*, (we, you, they) *have* —*n.* a wealthy person or nation —**have it out** to settle an issue by fighting or discussion —**have on** to be wearing

ha·ven (hā′vən) *n.* [OE. *hæfen*] 1. a port 2. any sheltered place; refuge

have-not (hav′nät′) *n.* a person or nation with little or no wealth

have·n′t (hav′nt) have not

hav·er·sack (hav′ər sak′) *n.* [< G. *habersack,* lit., sack of oats] a canvas bag for rations, worn over one shoulder, as by soldiers or hikers

hav·oc (hav′ək) *n.* [< OFr. *havot*] great destruction and devastation —**play havoc with** to devastate; ruin

haw¹ (hô) *n.* [OE. *haga*] 1. the berry of the hawthorn 2. the hawthorn

haw² (hô) *vi.* [echoic] to grope for words: in HEM AND HAW (see HEM²)

Ha·wai·i (hə wä′ē, -yē) 1. State of the U.S., consisting of a group of islands (**Hawaiian Islands**) in the N Pacific: 6,424 sq. mi.; pop. 965,000; cap. Honolulu 2. largest of these islands —**Ha·wai′ian** (-yən) *adj., n.*

hawk¹ (hôk) *n.* [OE. *hafoc*] 1. a bird of prey with short, rounded wings, a long tail, and a hooked beak and claws 2. an advocate of war

hawk² (hôk) *vt., vi.* [< HAWKER] to advertise or peddle (goods) in the streets by shouting

hawk³ (hôk) *vi., vt.* [echoic] to clear the throat (of) audibly

hawk·er (hôk′ər) *n.* [< MLowG. *hoker*] one who hawks goods; huckster

hawk′-eyed′ (-īd′) *adj.* keen-sighted

haw·ser (hô′zər) *n.* [< OFr. *haucier* < L. *altus,* high] a rope or cable by which a ship is anchored, towed, etc.

haw·thorn (hô′thôrn′) *n.* [< OE. *haga,* hedge + THORN] a thorny shrub or small tree of the rose family, with flowers and small, red fruits

Haw·thorne (hô′thôrn′), **Nathaniel** 1804–64; U.S. writer

hay (hā) *n.* [< OE. *hieg*] grass, clover, etc. cut and dried for fodder —*vi.* to mow and dry grass, etc. for hay —**hit the hay** [Slang] to go to sleep

hay′cock′ (-käk′) *n.* a small, conical heap of hay drying in a field

Hay·dn (hīd′'n), **Franz Jo·seph** (fränts yō′zef) 1732–1809; Austrian composer

Hayes (hāz), **Ruth·er·ford B.** (ruth′ər fərd) 1822–93; 19th president of the U.S. (1877–81)

hay fever an acute inflammation of the eyes and respiratory tract: an allergic reaction to some kinds of pollen

hay′loft′ *n.* a loft, or upper story, in a barn or stable, for storing hay

hay′mow′ (-mou′) *n.* 1. a pile of hay in a barn 2. *same as* HAYLOFT

hay′stack′ *n.* a large heap of hay piled up outdoors

hay′wire′ *adj.* [Slang] 1. out of order; disorganized 2. crazy: usually in **go haywire,** to become crazy

haz·ard (haz′ərd) *n.* [< OFr. *hasard,*

game of dice] 1. risk; danger 2. an obstacle to a golf course —*vt.* to risk

haz′ard·ous *adj.* risky; dangerous

haze¹ (hāz) *n.* [prob. < HAZY] 1. a thin vapor of fog, smoke, etc. in the air 2. slight vagueness of mind —*vi., vt.* hazed, haz′ing to make or become hazy (often with *over*)

haze² (hāz) *vt.* hazed, haz′ing [< ?] to force to do ridiculous or painful things, as in initiation

ha·zel (hā′z'l) *n.* [OE. *hæsel*] 1. a shrub or tree of the birch family, with edible nuts 2. a reddish brown —*adj.* light reddish-brown

ha′zel·nut′ *n.* the small, edible, roundish nut of the hazel; filbert

ha·zy (hā′zē) *adj.* -zi·er, -zi·est [prob. < OE. *hasu*, dusky] 1. somewhat foggy or smoky 2. somewhat vague —ha′zi·ly *adv.* —ha′zi·ness *n.*

H-bomb (āch′bäm′) *n.* same as HYDROGEN BOMB

he (hē) *pron., for pl. see* THEY [OE.] 1. the man, boy, or male animal previously mentioned 2. anyone *[he* who laughs last laughs best] —*n.* a male

He *Chem.* helium

head (hed) *n.* [OE. *heafod*] 1. the part of the body containing the brain, and the jaws, eyes, ears, nose, and mouth 2. the mind; intelligence 3. *pl.* head a unit of counting *[ten head* of cattle] 4. the main side of a coin 5. the uppermost part or thing; top 6. the topic or title of a section, chapter, etc. 7. the foremost or projecting part; front 8. the part designed for holding, striking, etc. *[the head* of a nail] 9. the membrane across the end of a drum, etc. 10. the source of a river, etc. 11. froth, as on beer 12. the pressure in an enclosed fluid, as steam 13. a position of leadership or honor 14. a leader, ruler, etc. —*adj.* 1. most important; principal 2. at the top or front 3. striking against the front *[head* current] —*vt.* 1. to be the chief of; command 2. to lead; precede 3. to cause to go in a specified direction —*vi.* to set out; travel *[to head* eastward] —**come to a head** 1. to be about to suppurate, as a boil 2. to culminate, or reach a crisis —**go to one's head** 1. to confuse or intoxicate one 2. to make one vain —**head off** to get ahead of and intercept —**head over heels** deeply; completely —**heads up!** [Colloq.] look out! —**keep (or lose) one's head** to keep (or lose) one's poise, self-control, etc. —**on (or upon) one's head** as one's responsibility or misfortune —**over one's head** 1. too difficult for one to understand 2. to a higher authority —**turn one's head** to make one vain —head′less *adj.*

head′ache′ (-āk′) *n.* 1. a continuous pain in the head 2. [Colloq.] a cause of worry, annoyance, or trouble

head′board′ (-bôrd′) *n.* a board that forms the head of a bed, etc.

head cold a common cold with congestion of the nasal passages

head′dress′ *n.* 1. a decorative covering for the head 2. a hairdo; coiffure

-head·ed (hed′id) *a combining form meaning* having a head or heads *[clearheaded, two-headed]*

head′first′ *adv.* 1. with the head in front; headlong 2. recklessly; rashly

head′gear′ *n.* a hat, cap, etc.

head′ing *n.* 1. something forming the head, top, or front 2. the title, topic, etc., as of a chapter 3. the direction in which a ship, plane, etc. is moving

head′land′ *n.* a point of land reaching out into the water; promontory

head′light′ *n.* a light with a reflector and lens, at the front of a vehicle

head′line′ *n.* printed lines at the top of a newspaper article, giving the topic —*vt.* -lined′, -lin′ing to give featured billing or publicity to

head′long′ (-lông′) *adv., adj.* [ME. *hedelinge(s)*] 1. with the head first 2. with uncontrolled speed and force 3. reckless(ly); rash(ly)

head′mas′ter *n.* the principal of a private school —head′mis′tress *n.fem.*

head′-on′ *adj., adv.* with the head or front foremost *[hit head-on]*

head′phone′ *n.* a telephone or radio receiver held to the head by a band

head′quar′ters (-kwôr′tərz) *n.pl.* *[often with sing. v.]* 1. the main office, or center of operations, of one in command, as in an army 2. the main office in any organization

head′rest′ *n.* a support for the head

head′room′ *n.* space overhead, as in a doorway or tunnel

head start an early start or other competitive advantage

head′stone′ *n.* a stone marker placed at the head of a grave

head′strong′ *adj.* determined to do as one pleases

head′wa′ters *n.pl.* the small streams that are the sources of a river

head′way′ *n.* 1. forward motion 2. progress or success

head·y (hed′ē) *adj.* -i·er, -i·est 1. impetuous; rash 2. intoxicating

heal (hēl) *vt., vi.* [OE. *hælan*] 1. to make or become well or healthy again 2. to cure (a disease) or mend, as a wound —heal′er *n.*

health (helth) *n.* [OE. *hælth*] 1. physical and mental well-being; freedom from disease, etc. 2. condition of body or mind *[poor health]* 3. a wish for one's health and happiness, as in a toast 4. soundness, as of a society

health food food thought to be very healthful, as food grown with natural fertilizers and free of additives

health′ful *adj.* helping to produce or maintain health; wholesome

health·y (hel′thē) *adj.* -i·er, -i·est 1. having good health 2. showing or resulting from good health *[a healthy*

appetite] 3. *same as* HEALTHFUL
—**health'i·ness** *n.*

heap (hēp) *n.* [< OE. *heap*, a troop]
1. a pile or mass of jumbled things
2. [Colloq.] a large amount —*vt.* 1. to
make a heap of 2. to give in large
amounts 3. to fill (a plate, etc.) full or
to overflowing —*vi.* to rise in a heap

hear (hir) *vt.* **heard** (hurd), **hear'ing**
[OE. *hieran*] 1. to be aware of
(sounds) by the ear 2. to listen to
3. to conduct a hearing of (a law
case, etc.) 4. to be informed of;
learn —*vi.* 1. to be able to hear
sounds 2. to be told (*of* or *about*)
—**hear from** to get a letter, etc. from
—**not hear of** to refuse to consider
—**hear'er** *n.*

hear'ing *n.* 1. the act or process of
perceiving sounds 2. the ability to
hear 3. opportunity to be heard 4.
an appearance before a judge, inves-
tigative committee, etc. 5. the distance a sound will carry [within
hearing]

heark·en (här'kən) *vi.* [OE. *heorc-
nean*] to listen carefully; pay heed

hear·say (hir'sā') *n.* rumor; gossip

hearse (hurs) *n.* [< L. *hirpex*, a
harrow] a vehicle used in a funeral
for carrying the corpse

heart (härt) *n.* [OE. *heorte*] 1. the
hollow, muscular organ that circulates
the blood by alternate dilation and
contraction 2. the central, vital, or
main part; core 3. the human heart
considered as the center of emotions,
personality attributes, etc.; specif.,
a) inmost thought and feeling *b)* love,
sympathy, etc. *c)* spirit or courage
4. a conventionalized design of a
heart (♥) 5. any of a suit of playing
cards marked with such symbols in
red —**after one's own heart** that
pleases one perfectly —**at heart** in
one's innermost nature —**by heart** by
or from memorization —**set one's
heart on** to have a fixed desire for
—**take to heart** 1. to consider
seriously 2. to be troubled by

heart'ache (-āk') *n.* sorrow or grief

heart attack any sudden instance of
heart failure; esp., a CORONARY
THROMBOSIS

heart'beat *n.* one full contraction
and dilation of the heart

heart'break *n.* overwhelming sorrow or grief —**heart'bro'ken** *adj.*

heart'burn *n.* a burning, acid sensation beneath the breastbone

heart·en (härt'n) *vt.* to encourage

heart failure the inability of the
heart to pump enough blood to supply
the body tissues adequately

heart'felt' *adj.* sincere; genuine

hearth (härth) *n.* [OE. *heorth*] 1. the
stone or brick floor of a fireplace 2. *a)*
the fireside *b)* family life; home

heart'less *adj.* unkind; unfeeling —
heart'less·ly *adv.* —**heart'less·ness** *n.*

heart'-rend'ing *adj.* causing much
grief or mental anguish

heart'sick' *adj.* sick at heart;
extremely unhappy or despondent

heart'strings' *n.pl.* deepest feelings
or affections

heart'-to-heart' *adj.* intimate and
candid

heart'warm'ing *adj.* such as to
cause genial feelings

heart'y *adj.* **-i·er**, **-i·est** 1. warm
and friendly; cordial 2. strongly felt;
unrestrained [*hearty* laughter] 3.
strong and healthy 4. nourishing and
plentiful [a *hearty* meal] —*n.*, *pl.*
-ies [Archaic] a fellow sailor —**heart'-
i·ly** *adv.* —**heart'i·ness** *n.*

heat (hēt) *n.* [OE. *hætu*] 1. the quality
of being hot; hotness, or the perception of this 2. much hotness 3. hot
weather or climate 4. the warming of
a house, etc. 5. *a)* strong feeling;
ardor, anger, etc. *b)* the period of this
6. a single bout, round, or trial 7. the
period of sexual excitement in animals,
esp. females 8. [Slang] coercion —*vt.*,
vi. 1. to make or become warm or hot
2. to make or become excited

heat'ed *adj.* 1. hot 2. vehement or
angry —**heat'ed·ly** *adv.*

heat'er *n.* an apparatus for giving
heat; stove, furnace, radiator, etc.

heath (hēth) *n.* [OE. *hæth*] 1. a tract
of open wasteland, esp. in the British
Isles 2. any of various shrubs that
grow on heaths, as heather

hea·then (hē'thən) *n.*, *pl.* **-thens**,
-then [OE. *hæthen*] 1. anyone not a
Jew, Christian, or Moslem 2. a person
regarded as irreligious, uncivilized,
etc. —*adj.* 1. pagan 2. irreligious,
uncivilized, etc. —**hea'then·ish** *adj.*

heath·er (heth'ər) *n.* [ME. *haddyr*]
a plant of the heath family, esp. common in the British Isles, with small,
bell-shaped, purplish flowers

heating pad a pad with a fabric
cover containing an electric heating
element, for applying heat to the body

heat lightning lightning without
thunder, seen on hot evenings

heat'stroke' *n.* a condition of high
fever, collapse, etc., resulting from
exposure to intense heat

heave (hēv) *vt.* **heaved** or (esp.
Naut.) **hove**, **heav'ing** [OE. *hebban*]
1. to lift, esp. with effort 2. to lift in
this way and throw 3. to utter (a
sigh, etc.) with effort 4. *Naut.* to
raise, haul, etc. by pulling as with a
rope —*vi.* 1. to swell up 2. to rise
and fall rhythmically 3. *a)* to vomit
b) to pant; gasp 4. *Naut.* to haul
(*on* or *at* a rope, etc.) —*n.* the act or
effort of heaving —**heave to** *Naut.* to
stop —**heav'er** *n.*

heave'-ho' (-hō') *n.* [Colloq.] dismissal, as from a job: chiefly in **give**
(or **get**) **the** (**old**) **heave-ho**

heav·en (hev'n) *n.* [OE. *heofon*] 1.
[*usually pl.*] the visible sky; firmament
2. *Theol.* [H-] *a)* the dwelling place
of God and his angels, where the
blessed go after death *b)* God 3. any
place or state of great happiness
—**heav'en·ly** *adj.*

heav'en·ward (-wərd) *adv.*, *adj.* toward heaven: also **heav'en·wards** *adv.*

heav·y (hev'ē) *adj.* **-i·er**, **-i·est** [OE.
hefig] 1. hard to lift because of great
weight 2. of more than the usual,
expected, or defined weight 3. larger,

greater, or more intense than usual [a heavy blow, a heavy vote, heavy applause] 4. to an unusual extent [a heavy drinker] 5. hard to do [heavy work] 6. sorrowful [a heavy heart] 7. burdened with sleep [heavy eyelids] 8. hard to digest [a heavy meal] 9. clinging; penetrating [a heavy odor] 10. cloudy; gloomy [a heavy sky] 11. using massive machinery to produce basic materials, as steel —adv. in a heavy manner —n., pl. -ies Theater a villain —heav'i·ly adv. —heav'i·ness n.

heav'y-du'ty adj. made to withstand great strain, bad weather, etc.

heav'y-hand'ed adj. 1. clumsy or tactless 2. oppressive or tyrannical

heav'y-heart'ed adj. sad; unhappy

heavy hydrogen same as DEUTERIUM

heav'y-set' (-set') adj. having a stout or stocky build

heav'y·weight' n. a boxer or wrestler who weighs over 175 pounds

Heb. 1. Hebrew 2. Hebrews

He·bra·ic (hi brā'ik) adj. of or characteristic of the Hebrews, their language, culture, etc.; Hebrew

He·brew (hē'brōō) n. 1. a) member of an ancient Semitic people; Israelite b) a Jew 2. a) the ancient Semitic language of the Israelites b) its modern form, the language of Israel —adj. of Hebrew or the Hebrews

Heb·ri·des (heb'rə dēz') group of Scottish islands off NW Scotland

heck (hek) interj., n. [Colloq.] a euphemism for HELL

heck·le (hek'l) vt. -led, -ling [ME. hekelin] to harass (a speaker) with questions or taunts —heck'ler n.

hec·tare (hek'ter) n. [Fr.] a metric measure of area, 10,000 square meters

hec·tic (hek'tik) adj. [< Gr. hektikos, habitual] 1. feverish; flushed 2. confused, rushed, excited, etc.—hec'ti·cal·ly adv.

Hec·tor (hek'tər) in Homer's Iliad, a Trojan hero killed by Achilles —vt. [h-] to browbeat; bully

he'd (hēd) 1. he had 2. he would

hedge (hej) n. [OE. hecg] 1. a dense row of shrubs, etc. forming a boundary 2. any fence or barrier 3. a hedging —vt. hedged, hedg'ing 1. to put a hedge around 2. to hinder or guard as with a barrier 3. to try to avoid loss in (a bet, etc.) as by making counterbalancing bets —vi. to refuse to commit oneself or give direct answers

hedge'hog' n. 1. a small, insect-eating mammal of the Old World, with sharp spines on the back 2. the American porcupine

he·don·ism (hēd'n iz'm) n. [< Gr. hēdonē, pleasure] the doctrine that pleasure

HEDGEHOG

is the principal good —he'don·ist n. —he'do·nis'tic adj.

-he·dron (hē'drən) [< Gr.] a combining form meaning a figure or crystal with (a specified number of) surfaces

heed (hēd) vt., vi. [OE. hedan] to pay close attention (to) —n. close attention —heed'ful adj. —heed'less adj. —heed'less·ly adv. —heed'less·ness n.

hee·haw (hē'hô') n., vi. [echoic] bray

heel[1] (hēl) n. [OE. hela] 1. the back part of the foot, under the ankle 2. that part of a stocking or shoe at the heel 3. anything like a heel in location, shape, crushing power, etc. 4. [Colloq.] a despicable person —vt. 1. to furnish with a heel 2. to follow closely 3. [Colloq.] to provide with money, etc. —vi. to follow along at the heels of someone —down at the heel(s) shabby; seedy —kick up one's heels to have fun —on (or upon) the heels of close behind

heel[2] (hēl) vi. [OE. hieldan] to lean to one side; list: said esp. of a ship —vt. to make (a ship) list

heft (heft) n. [< base of HEAVE] [Colloq.] 1. weight; heaviness 2. importance; influence —vt. [Colloq.] to try to judge the weight of by lifting

heft·y (hef'tē) adj. -i·er, -i·est [Colloq.] 1. heavy 2. large and strong 3. big —heft'i·ness n.

he·gem·o·ny (hi jem'ə nē) n., pl. -nies [< Gr. hēgemōn, leader] leadership or dominance, esp. that of one nation over others

he·gi·ra (hi ji'rə) n. [< Ar. hijrah, flight] 1. [often H-] the flight of Mohammed from Mecca in 622 A.D. 2. any journey for safety or escape

Hei·del·berg (hid'l burg') city in SW West Germany: pop. 125,000

heif·er (hef'ər) n. [OE. heahfore] a young cow that has not borne a calf

height (hit) n. [< OE. heah, high] 1. the topmost point 2. the highest limit; extreme 3. the distance from the bottom to the top 4. elevation above a given level; altitude 5. a relatively great distance above a given level 6. [often pl.] an eminence; hill

height'en (-'n) vt., vi. 1. to bring or come to a higher position 2. to make or become larger, greater, etc.

hei·nous (hā'nəs) adj. [< OFr. haine, hatred] outrageously evil —hei'nous·ly adv. —hei'nous·ness n.

heir (er) n. [< L. heres] one who inherits or is entitled to inherit another's property, title, etc.

heir apparent the heir whose right to inherit cannot be denied if he outlives the ancestor

heir'ess (-is) n. a woman or girl who is an heir, esp. to great wealth

heir'loom' (-lōōm') n. [see HEIR & LOOM[1]] any possession handed down from generation to generation

heist (hist) n. [< HOIST] [Slang] a robbery —vt. [Slang] to rob or steal

held (held) *pt. & pp. of* HOLD[1]

Hel·e·na (hel'i nə) capital of Mont.: pop. 23,000

Helen of Troy *Gr. Legend* the beautiful wife of the king of Sparta: the Trojan War was started by her elopement with Paris to Troy

hel·i·cal (hel'i kəl) *adj.* [see HELIX] shaped like a helix; spiral

hel·i·cop·ter (hel'ə käp'tər, hē'lə-) *n.* [< Gr. *helix*, spiral + *pteron*, wing] a kind of aircraft lifted and moved, or kept hovering, by large rotary blades mounted horizontally

he·li·o·cen·tric (hē'lē ō sen'trik) *adj.* [< Gr. *hēlios*, the sun + *kentron*, a point] having or regarding the sun as the center

he·li·o·trope (hē'lē ə trōp') *n.* [< Gr. *hēlios*, the sun + *trepein*, to turn] 1. a plant with fragrant clusters of small, white or reddish-purple flowers 2. reddish purple —*adj.* reddish-purple

hel·i·port (hel'ə pôrt') *n.* a flat area where helicopters land and take off

he·li·um (hē'lē əm) *n.* [Gr. *hēlios*, sun] a chemical element, a very light, inert gas having the lowest known boiling and melting points: used for inflating balloons, etc.: symbol, He

he·lix (hē'liks) *n., pl.* -**lix·es**, -**li·ces** (hel'ə sēz') [L. & Gr.] a spiral

hell (hel) *n.* [< OE. *helan*, to hide] 1. [*often* H-] *Christianity* the place to which sinners and unbelievers go to eternal punishment after death 2. any place or state of misery, cruelty, etc. —**catch** (or **get**) **hell** [Slang] to be severely scolded, punished, etc.

he'll (hēl) 1. he will 2. he shall

hell'bent' *adj.* [Slang] 1. recklessly determined 2. moving fast

hell'cat' *n.* an evil, spiteful woman

hel·le·bore (hel'ə bôr') *n.* [< Gr. *helleboros*] a plant of the buttercup family whose rhizomes were used in medicine

Hel·len·ic (hə len'ik) *adj.* 1. Greek 2. of the history, language, or culture of the ancient Greeks —**Hel·len·ism** (hel'ən iz'm) *n.* —**Hel·len·is·tic** *adj.*

hell·gram·mite (hel'grə mīt') *n.* [< ?] the dark-brown aquatic larva of a fly, used as fish bait

hel·lion (hel'yən) *n.* [< Scot. dial. *hallion*, a low fellow] [Colloq.] a person fond of deviltry; troublemaker

hell'ish *adj.* 1. devilish; fiendish 2. [Colloq.] very unpleasant —**hell'ish·ly** *adv.* —**hell'ish·ness** *n.*

hel·lo (he lō', hel'ō) *interj.* an exclamation of greeting

helm (helm) *n.* [OE. *helma*] 1. the wheel or tiller by which a ship is steered 2. the control or leadership of an organization, government, etc.

hel·met (hel'mət) *n.* [< OFr. *helme*] a protective, rigid head covering for use in combat, certain sports, etc.

helms·man (helmz'mən) *n., pl.* -**men** the man who steers a ship

he·lot (hel'ət, hē'lət) *n.* [? < *Helos*, ancient Greek town] a serf or slave

help (help) *vt.* [OE. *helpan*] 1. to make things easier or better for; aid; assist 2. to remedy [to *help* a cough] 3. to

keep from; avoid [can't *help* crying] 4. to serve or wait on (a customer, etc.) —*vi.* to give aid; be useful —*n.* 1. a helping; aid; assistance 2. a remedy 3. one that helps; esp., a hired person or persons; servant(s), farm hand(s), etc. —**help oneself** to to take without asking —**help out** to help in getting or doing something —**help'er** *n.*

help·ful (help'fəl) *adj.* giving help; useful —**help'ful·ly** *adv.* —**help'ful·ness** *n.*

help·ing (-iŋ) *n.* a portion of food served to one person

help·less *adj.* 1. not able to help oneself; weak 2. lacking help or protection 3. incompetent —**help'less·ly** *adv.* —**help'less·ness** *n.*

help·mate *n.* [< ff.] a helpful companion; specif., a wife or husband

help·meet *n.* [misreading of "an *help meet* for him" (Gen. 2:18)] *same as* HELPMATE

Hel·sin·ki (hel'siŋ kē) capital of Finland: pop. 519,000

hel·ter·skel·ter (hel'tər skel'tər) *adv., adj.* in or showing haste or confusion

helve (helv) *n.* [OE. *helfe*] the handle of an ax, hatchet, etc.

Hel·ve·tian (hel vē'shən) *adj., n.* Swiss

hem[1] (hem) *n.* [OE.] the border on a garment, etc. made by folding and sewing down the edge —*vt.* **hemmed**, **hem'ming** to fold back the edge of and sew down —**hem in** (or **around** or **about**) 1. to surround 2. to confine

hem[2] (hem) *interj., n.* the sound made in clearing the throat —*vi.* **hemmed**, **hem'ming** 1. to make this sound, as for attracting attention 2. to grope about in speech for the right words: usually used in the phrase **to hem and haw**

he'·man' *n.* [Colloq.] a strong, virile man

hem·a·tite (hem'ə tīt', hē'mə-) *n.* [< Gr. *haimatitēs*, bloodlike] native ferric oxide, an important iron ore

he·ma·tol·o·gy (hē'mə täl'ə jē) *n.* [< Gr. *haima*, blood + -LOGY] the study of blood and its diseases —**he'·ma·tol'o·gist** *n.*

heme (hēm) *n.* [< Gr. *haima*, blood] the iron-containing pigment in hemoglobin

hemi- [Gr. *hēmi-*] *a prefix meaning* half [*hemi*sphere]

hem·i·sphere (hem'ə sfir') *n.* 1. half of a sphere or globe 2. any of the halves (northern, southern, eastern, or western) of the earth —**hem'i·spher'i·cal** (-sfer'i kəl) *adj.*

hem·line (hem'līn') *n.* the bottom edge of a dress, skirt, coat, etc.

hem·lock (hem'läk) *n.* [OE. *hemlic*] 1. *a*) a poisonous plant of the parsley family *b*) a poison made from this plant 2. *a*) an evergreen tree of the pine family *b*) the wood of this tree

hemo- [< Gr. *haima*] *a combining form meaning* blood

he·mo·glo·bin (hē'mə glō'bin) *n.* [< prec. + GLOBULE] the red coloring matter of the red blood corpuscles

he·mo·phil·i·a (hē'mə fil'ē ə) *n.*
[see HEMO- & -PHILE] a hereditary
condition in which the blood fails to
clot normally, causing prolonged
bleeding from even minor injuries —
he'mo·phil'i·ac (-ak) *n.*

hem·or·rhage (hem'ər ij, hem'rij)
n. [< Gr. *haima*, blood + *rhēgnynai*,
to break] the escape of blood from a
blood vessel; heavy bleeding —*vi.*
-rhaged, -rhag·ing to have a
hemorrhage —**hem'or·rhag'ic** (-ə
raj'ik) *adj.*

hem·or·rhoid (hem'ə roid', hem'
roid) *n.* [< Gr. *haima*, blood +
rhein, to flow] a painful swelling of a
vein in the region of the anus, often
with bleeding: *usually used in pl.*

hemp (hemp) *n.* [OE. *hænep*] 1. a
tall Asiatic plant having tough fiber
2. its fiber, used to make rope, sail-
cloth, etc. 3. a substance, as hashish,
made from its leaves and flowers

hemp·en (hem'pən) *adj.* of or like
hemp

hem·stitch (hem'stich') *n.* an ornamental stitch, used esp. at a hem,
made by pulling out several parallel
threads and tying the cross threads
into small bunches —*vt.* to put hem-
stitches on

hen (hen) *n.* [OE. *henn*] 1. the female
of the chicken (the domestic fowl)
2. the female of various other birds

hence (hens) *adv.* [< OE. *heonan*,
from here] 1. from this place; away
[*go hence*] 2. from this time [a year
hence] 3. as a result; therefore 4.
[Archaic] from this origin or source

hence·forth' *adv.* from this time
on: also **hence'for'ward**

hench·man (hench'mən) *n.,* *pl.*
-men [< OE. *hengest*, stallion +
-man] a trusted helper or follower

hen·na (hen'ə) *n.* [Ar. *hinnā'*] 1. an
old-world plant with minute flowers
2. a dye extracted from its leaves,
used to tint the hair auburn 3. reddish brown —*adj.* reddish-brown
—*vt.* **-naed, -na·ing** to tint with
henna

hen·peck (hen'pek') *vt.* to nag and
domineer over (one's husband)

Hen·ry VIII (hen'rē) 1491-1547;
king of England (1509-47)

hep (hep) *adj.* [Slang] *same as* HIP²

hep·a·rin (hep'ər in) *n.* [Gr. *hēpar*,
the liver + -IN¹] a substance in body
tissues, esp. in the liver, that prevents
the clotting of blood

he·pat·ic (hi pat'ik) *adj.* [< Gr.
hēpar, liver] of or like the liver

hep·a·ti·tis (hep'ə tīt'is) *n.* [< Gr.
hēpar, liver + -ITIS] inflammation of
the liver

her (hur) *pron.* [OE. *hire*] *objective
case of* SHE —*poss. pronominal adj.*
of, belonging to, or made by her

He·ra (hir'ə) Gr. *Myth.* the wife of
Zeus and queen of the gods

her·ald (her'əld) *n.* [< OFr. *heralt*]
1. formerly, an official who made

proclamations, carried state messages, etc. 2. one who announces
significant news, etc. 3. a forerunner;
harbinger —*vt.* to announce, foretell,
etc.

he·ral·dic (he ral'dik) *adj.* of
heraldry or heralds

her'ald·ry *n.* 1. the science dealing
with coats of arms, genealogies, etc.
2. ceremony or pomp

herb (urb, hurb) *n.* [< L. *herba*] 1.
any seed plant whose stem withers
away annually 2. any plant used as
a medicine, seasoning, etc. —**her·ba·
ceous** (hər bā'shəs, ər-) *adj.* —
herb'al *adj.*

herb·age (ur'bij, hur'-) *n.* herbs collectively; esp., pasturage; grass

herb·al·ist (hur'b'l ist, ur'-) *n.* one
who grows or deals in herbs

her·bi·cide (hur'bə sīd', ur'-) *n.* any
chemical substance used to destroy
plants, esp. weeds —**her'bi·ci'dal** *adj.*

her·biv·o·rous (hər biv'ər əs) *adj.*
[< L. *herba*, herb + *vorare*, devour]
feeding chiefly on grass or plants

her·cu·le·an (hur'kyə lē'ən, hər
kyōō'lē ən) *adj.* [*sometimes* H-] 1.
having the great size or strength of
Hercules 2. calling for great strength,
size, or courage

Her·cu·les (hur'kyə lēz') Gr. &
Rom. *Myth.* a hero famous for feats of
strength —*n.* [h-] a very strong man

herd (hurd) *n.* [OE. *heord*] 1. a
number of cattle or other large animals feeding or living together 2. *a)*
a crowd *b)* the common people;
masses: contemptuous term —*vt., vi.*
to gather or move as a herd

herds·man (hurdz'mən) *n.,* *pl.* -men
one who keeps or tends a herd

here (hir) *adv.* [OE. *her*] 1. at or in
this place: often used as an intensive
[*John here* is an actor] 2. to or into
this place [*come here*] 3. at this
point; now 4. on earth —*n.* this place
—**neither here nor there** irrelevant

here'a·bout' *adv.* in this general
vicinity: also **here'a·bouts'**

here·af'ter *adv.* 1. from now on; in
the future 2. following this —*n.* 1.
the future 2. the state after death

here'by' *adv.* by this means

he·red·i·tar·y (hə red'ə ter'ē) *adj.*
1. *a)* of, or passed down by, inheritance from an ancestor *b)* having
title, etc. by inheritance 2. of or
passed down by heredity

he·red·i·ty (hə red'ə tē) *n., pl.* -ties
[< L. *heres*, heir] the transmission
of characteristics from parent to offspring by means of genes

here·in (hir in') *adv.* 1. in here
2. in this writing, container, etc.

here·of' *adv.* of or concerning this

her·e·sy (her'ə sē) *n., pl.* -sies [<
Gr. *hairesis*, selection, sect] 1. a
religious belief opposed to the orthodox
doctrines of a church 2. any opinion
opposed to established views

her'e·tic (-tik) *n.* one who professes

fat, āpe, cär; ten, ēven; is, bīte; gō, hôrn, tōol, look; oil, out; up, fur;
chin; she; thin, then; zh, leisure; ŋ, ring; ə for *a* in *ago*; ' (ā'b'l); ɵ, Fr. coeur;
ö, Fr. feu; ü, Fr. mon; u, Fr. duc; kh, G. ich, doch; ‡ foreign; < derived from

a heresy; esp., a church member who holds beliefs opposed to church dogma —he·ret·i·cal (hə ret'i k'l) *adj.*

here'to·fore' *adv.* up to now

here'up·on' *adv.* 1. at once; following this 2. concerning this point

here·with' *adv.* 1. along with this 2. by this method or means

her·it·a·ble (her'it ə b'l) *adj.* that can be inherited

her·it·age (her'ət ij) *n.* 1. property that is or can be inherited 2. a tradition, etc. handed down from one's ancestors or the past

her·maph·ro·dite (hər maf'rə dīt') *n.* [< Gr. *Hermaphroditos*, son of Hermes and Aphrodite, united in a single body with a nymph] a person, animal, or plant with the sexual organs of both the male and the female — her·maph'ro·dit'ic (-dit'ik) *adj.*

Her·mes (hur'mēz) *Gr. Myth.* a god who was messenger of the other gods

her·met·ic (hər met'ik) *adj.* [< prec. (reputed founder of alchemy)] airtight: also her·met'i·cal —her·met'i·cal·ly *adv.*

her·mit (hur'mit) *n.* [< Gr. *erēmos*, desolate] one who lives by himself in a lonely or secluded spot; recluse

her'mit·age (-ij) *n.* a secluded retreat, as the place where a hermit lives

her·ni·a (hur'nē ə) *n., pl.* -as, -ae (-ē') [L.] the protrusion of an organ, esp. a part of the intestine, through a tear in the wall of the surrounding structure; rupture —her'ni·al *adj.*

her'ni·ate' (-āt') *vi.* -at'ed, -at'ing to protrude so as to form a hernia —her'ni·a'tion *n.*

he·ro (hir'ō, hē'rō) *n., pl.* -roes [< Gr. *hērōs*] 1. a man of great courage, nobility, etc. or one admired for his exploits 2. the central male character in a novel, play, etc.

He·rod·o·tus (hə räd'ə təs) 485?-425? B.C.; Gr. historian

he·ro·ic (hi rō'ik) *adj.* 1. of or like a hero 2. of or about heroes and their deeds 3. daring and risky —n. [pl.] extravagant talk or action —he·ro'i·cal·ly *adv.*

her·o·in (her'ə win) *n.* [G., orig. a trademark] a habit-forming narcotic derived from morphine

her·o·ine (her'ə win) *n.* a girl or woman hero in life or literature

her'o·ism (-wiz'm) *n.* the qualities and actions of a hero or heroine

her·on (her'ən) *n.* [< OFr. *hairon*] a wading bird with a long neck, long legs, and a long bill

hero sandwich a large roll sliced lengthwise and filled with cold meats, cheeses, etc.

her·pes (hur'pēz) *n.* [L. < Gr. *herpein*, to creep] a virus disease causing small blisters on the skin

herpes zos·ter (zäs'tər) [< prec. + Gr. *zōstēr*, a girdle] *same as* SHINGLES

‡Herr (her) *n., pl.* Her'ren (-ən) [G.] 1. a man; gentleman 2. Mr.; Sir

her·ring (her'iŋ) *n.* [OE. *hæring*] a small food fish of the N Atlantic

her'ring·bone' *n.* 1. the spine of a herring with the ribs extending in rows

of parallel, slanting lines 2. anything having such a pattern

hers (hurz) *pron.* that or those belonging to her [*hers* are better]

her·self (hər self') *pron.* 1. *the intensive form of* SHE [she went *herself*] 2. *the reflexive form of* SHE [she hurt *herself*] 3. her true self [she's not *herself* today]

hertz (hurts) *n., pl.* hertz [after H. R. *Hertz*, 19th-c. G. physicist] the international unit of frequency, equal to one cycle per second

Hertz·i·an waves (hurt'sē ən) [see prec.] [*sometimes* h-] electromagnetic radiation resulting from the oscillations of electricity in a conductor

he's (hēz) 1. he is 2. he has

hes·i·tant (hez'ə tənt) *adj.* hesitating or undecided; doubtful —hes'i·tan·cy *n.* —hes'i·tant·ly *adv.*

hes'i·tate' (-tāt') *vi.* -tat'ed, -tat'ing [< L. *haerere*, to stick] 1. to stop in indecision; waver 2. to pause 3. to be reluctant [I *hesitate* to ask] 4. to pause continually in speaking —hes'i·tat'ing·ly *adv.* —hes'i·ta'tion *n.*

hetero- [Gr. *hetero-*] *a combining form meaning* other, another, different

het·er·o·dox (het'ər ə däks') *adj.* [< prec. + Gr. *doxa*, opinion] opposed to the usual beliefs, esp. in religion; unorthodox —het'er·o·dox'y *n.*

het·er·o·ge·ne·ous (het'ər ə jē'nē əs) *adj.* [< HETERO- + Gr. *genos*, a kind] 1. differing in structure, quality, etc.; dissimilar 2. composed of unlike parts

het'er·o·sex'u·al (-sek'shoo wəl) *adj.* 1. of or having sexual desire for those of the opposite sex 2. of different sexes —n. a heterosexual individual

heu·ris·tic (hyoo ris'tik) *adj.* [< Gr. *heuriskein*, invent] helping to learn, as by a method of self-teaching

hew (hyoo) *vt.* hewed or hewn, hew'ing [OE. *heawan*] 1. to chop or cut with an ax, knife, etc. 2. to make or shape thus —vi. to conform (*to* a rule, principle, etc.)

HEW (Department of) Health, Education, and Welfare

hex (heks) *n.* [< G. *hexe*, witch] something supposed to bring bad luck —vt. to cause to have bad luck

hexa- [< Gr. *hex*, six] *a combining form meaning* six

hex·a·gon (hek'sə gän') *n.* [< Gr. *hex*, six + *gōnia*, an angle] a plane figure with six angles and six sides —hex·ag'o·nal (-sag'ə n'l) *adj.*

hex·am·e·ter (hek sam'ə tər) *n.* [see HEXA- & METER[1]] 1. a line of verse containing six metrical feet 2. verse consisting of hexameters

hey (hā) *interj.* an exclamation used to attract attention, etc.

hey·day (hā'dā') *n.* the time of greatest vigor, prosperity, etc.; prime

Hg [L. *hydrargyrum*] *Chem.* mercury

hi (hī) *interj.* an exclamation of greeting

HI Hawaii

hi·a·tus (hī āt'əs) *n., pl.* -tus·es, -tus [L. < *hiare*, to gape] a gap or break, as where a part is missing

hi·ba·chi (hi bä′chē) *n.*, *pl.* -chis [Jap. < *hi*, fire + *bachi*, bowl] a charcoal-burning brazier and grill

hi·ber·nate (hī′bər nāt′) *vi.* -nat′ed, -nat′ing [< L. *hibernus*, wintry] to spend the winter in a dormant state —hi′ber·na′tion *n.*

hi·bis·cus (hī bis′kəs, hi-) *n.* [< L.] a plant of the mallow family, with large, colorful flowers

hic·cup (hik′əp) *n.* [echoic] an involuntary contraction of the diaphragm that closes the glottis at the moment of breathing in so that a sharp sound is produced —*vi.* -cuped or -cupped, -cup·ing or -cup·ping to make a hiccup Also **hic·cough** (hik′əp)

hick (hik) *n.* [< *Richard*] [Colloq.] an awkward, unsophisticated person, esp. from a rural area

hick·ey (hik′ē) *n.*, *pl.* -eys, -ies [Colloq.] any device or gadget

hick·o·ry (hik′ər ē) *n.*, *pl.* -ries [< AmInd. *pawcohiccora*] 1. a N. American tree of the walnut family 2. its hard, tough wood 3. its smooth-shelled, edible nut: also **hickory nut**

hide¹ (hīd) *vt.* **hid** (hid), **hid′den** (hid′'n) or **hid**, **hid′ing** [OE. *hydan*] 1. to put or keep out of sight; conceal 2. to keep secret 3. to keep from sight by obscuring, etc. —*vi.* 1. to be concealed 2. to conceal oneself

hide² (hīd) *n.* [OE. *hid*] an animal skin or pelt, either raw or tanned

hide′a·way′ (-ə wā′) *n.* [Colloq.] a place where one can hide, be secluded, etc.

hide′bound′ *adj.* obstinately conservative and narrow-minded

hid·e·ous (hid′ē əs) *adj.* [< OFr. *hide*, fright] horrible; very ugly —**hid′e·ous·ly** *adv.* —**hid′e·ous·ness** *n.*

hide′-out′ *n.* [Colloq.] a hiding place, as for gangsters

hie (hī) *vi.*, *vt.* **hied**, **hie′ing** or **hy′ing** [< OE. *higian*] to hasten

hi·er·ar·chy (hī′ə rär′kē) *n.*, *pl.* -chies [< Gr. *hieros*, sacred + *archos*, ruler] 1. church government by clergy in graded ranks 2. the highest officials in such a system 3. a group of persons or things arranged in order of rank, grade, etc. —**hi·er·ar′chi·cal** *adj.*

hi·er·o·glyph·ic (hī′ər ə glif′ik, hī′rə-) *n.* [< Gr. *hieros*, sacred + *glyphein*, carve] 1. a picture or symbol representing a word, sound, etc., in a system used by ancient Egyptians and others 2. a symbol, etc. hard to understand —*adj.* of or like hieroglyphics

hi·er·o·phant (hī′ər ə fant′) *n.* [< Gr. *hieros*, sacred + *phainein*, to show] a priest in ancient Greece who presided at sacred mysteries

hi-fi (hī′fī′) *n.* a phonograph, etc. having high fidelity —*adj.* of or having high fidelity of sound reproduction

high (hī) *adj.* [OE. *heah*] 1. lofty; tall 2. extending upward a (specified) distance 3. reaching to, situated at, or done from a height 4. above others in rank, position, etc.; superior 5. grave [*high* treason] 6. greater in size, amount, cost, etc. than usual [*high* prices] 7. luxurious [*high* living] 8. raised or acute in pitch; shrill 9. slightly tainted, as meat 10. elated [*high* spirits] 11. [Slang] *a*) drunk *b*) under the influence of a drug —*adv.* in or to a high level, degree, rank, etc. —*n.* 1. a high level, place, etc. 2. that gear of a motor vehicle, etc. producing the greatest speed 3. [Slang] a euphoric condition induced as by drugs —**high and low** everywhere —**on high** in heaven

high′ball′ *n.* whiskey or brandy mixed with soda water, ginger ale, etc.

high′born′ *adj.* of noble birth

high′boy′ *n.* a high chest of drawers mounted on legs

high′brow′ *n.* [Colloq.] one having or affecting highly cultivated tastes; intellectual —*adj.* [Colloq.] of or for highbrows

HIGHBOY

high′er-up′ *n.* [Colloq.] a person of higher rank or position

high′fa·lu′tin(g) (-fə lōōt′'n) *adj.* [Colloq.] pretentious or pompous

high fidelity in radio, sound recording, etc., nearly exact reproduction of a wide range of sound waves

high′-flown′ (-flōn′) *adj.* 1. extravagantly ambitious 2. bombastic

high frequency any radio frequency between 3 and 30 megahertz

High German the West Germanic dialects spoken in C and S Germany

high′hand′ed *adj.* overbearing —**high′hand′ed·ly** *adv.* —**high′hand′ed·ness** *n.*

high′-hat′ *adj.* [Slang] snobbish —*vt.* -hat′ted, -hat′ting [Slang] to snub

high′land (-lənd) *n.* a region with many hills or mountains —**the Highlands** mountainous region occupying most of N Scotland —**High′land·er** *n.*

high′-lev′el *adj.* 1. of or by persons of high office 2. in a high office

high′light′ *n.* 1. the part on which light is brightest: also **high light** 2. the most important or interesting part, scene, etc. —*vt.* 1. to give highlights to 2. to give prominence to

high′ly *adv.* 1. very much 2. favorably 3. at a high level, wage, rank, etc.

high′-mind′ed *adj.* having high ideals, principles, etc.

high′ness *n.* 1. height 2. [H-] a title used in speaking to or of royalty

high′-pres′sure *adj.* 1. having or withstanding high pressure 2. using forcefully persuasive or insistent methods —*vt.* -sured, -sur·ing [Colloq.] to urge with such methods

high′-rise′ *n.* an apartment house, office building, etc. of many stories

high'road' *n.* **1.** [Chiefly Brit.] a highway **2.** an easy or direct way

high school a secondary school for students in grades 10, 11, and 12, and sometimes grade 9

high seas open ocean waters outside the territorial limits of any nation

high sign a secret warning signal

high'-spir'it·ed *adj.* **1.** courageous **2.** lively; spirited

high'-strung' *adj.* highly sensitive or nervous and tense; excitable

high'-tech' (-tek′) *adj.* **1.** of specialized, complex technology: in full **high'-tech·nol'o·gy 2.** of furniture, fashions, etc. utilitarian in design

high'-ten'sion *adj.* having or carrying a high voltage

high tide the highest level to which the tide rises

high time time beyond the proper time but before it is too late

high'way' *n.* **1.** a public road **2.** a main road; thoroughfare

high'way·man (-mən) *n., pl.* -men one who robs travelers on a highway

high wire a wire stretched high above the ground, used by aerialists

hi·jack (hī′jak′) *vt.* [Colloq.] **1.** to steal (goods in transit, etc.) by force **2.** to force (an aircraft) to make a nonscheduled flight —**hi'jack'er** *n.*

hike (hīk) *vi.* **hiked, hik'ing** [< dial. *heik*] to take a long walk; tramp —*vt.* [Colloq.] **1.** to pull up; hoist **2.** to raise (prices, etc.) —*n.* **1.** a long walk **2.** [Colloq.] a rise —**hik'er** *n.*

hi·lar·i·ous (hi ler′ē əs, hī-) *adj.* [< Gr. *hilaros*, cheerful] noisily merry; very gay —**hi·lar'i·ty** (-ə tē) *n.*

hill (hil) *n.* [OE. *hyll*] **1.** a natural raised part of the earth's surface, smaller than a mountain **2.** a small pile, as of soil heaped around plants

hill'bil'ly *n., pl.* -lies [< nickname *Billy*] [Colloq.] one who lives in or comes from the mountains or backwoods, esp. of the South

hill'ock (-ək) *n.* a small hill

hill'side *n.* the side of a hill

hill'top' *n.* the top of a hill

hill'y *adj.* -i·er, -i·est **1.** full of hills **2.** like a hill; steep —**hill'i·ness** *n.*

hilt (hilt) *n.* [OE.] the handle of a sword, dagger, tool, etc.

him (him) *pron. objective case of* HE

Hi·ma·la·yas (him′ə lā′əz, hi mäl′yəz) mountain system of SC Asia, mostly in India —**Hi'ma·la'yan** *adj.*

him·self' *pron.* **1.** *the intensive form of* HE *[he went himself]* **2.** *the reflexive form of* HE *[he hurt himself]* **3.** his true self *[he is not himself today]*

hind¹ (hīnd) *adj.* **hind'er, hind'most'** or **hind'er·most'** [prob. < HINDER] back; rear; posterior

hind² (hīnd) *n.* [OE.] the female of the red deer

Hind. 1. Hindi **2.** Hindu

hin·der¹ (hin′dər) *vt.* [OE. *hindrian*] **1.** to keep back; stop **2.** to thwart

hind·er² (hīn′dər) *adj.* [OE.] rear

Hin·di (hin′dē) *n.* the main (and official) language of India

hind'most' *adj.* farthest back; last

hind'quar'ter *n.* the hind half of a side of veal, beef, lamb, etc.

hin·drance (hin′drəns) *n.* **1.** the act of hindering **2.** an obstacle

hind'sight' *n.* ability to see, after the event, what should have been done

Hin·du (hin′dōō) *n.* **1.** any of several peoples of India **2.** a follower of Hinduism —*adj.* **1.** of the Hindus, their language, etc. **2.** of Hinduism

Hin'du·ism *n.* the religion and social system of the Hindus

Hin·du·stan (hin′doo stan′) **1.** region in N India **2.** the Indian peninsula **3.** the republic of India

hinge (hinj) *n.* [< ME. *hengen*, hang] **1.** a joint on which a door, lid, etc. swings **2.** a natural joint, as of the shell of a clam —*vt.* **hinged, hing'ing** to attach by a hinge —*vi.* to hang as on a hinge; depend

hint (hint) *n.* [prob. < OE. *hentan*, to grasp] a slight indication; indirect allusion —*vt., vi.* to give a hint (of)

hin·ter·land (hin′tər land′) *n.* [G.] **1.** the land behind that bordering a coast or river **2.** a remote area

hip¹ (hip) *n.* [OE. *hype*] the part of the body around the joint formed by each thigh bone and the pelvis

hip² (hip) *adj.* **hip'per, hip'pest** [< ? *hep*] [Slang] **1.** sophisticated; aware; fashionable **2.** of hippies —**get** (or **be**) **hip to** [Slang] to become (or be) informed about

hip'pie *n.* [Slang] a young person who, in his alienation from conventional society, has turned to mysticism, psychedelic drugs, communal living, etc.: also **hippy**, *pl.* -**pies**

hip·po (hip′ō) *n., pl.* -**pos** [Colloq.] *same as* HIPPOPOTAMUS

Hip·poc·ra·tes (hi päk′rə tēz′) 460?–370? B.C.; Gr. physician

Hip·po·crat·ic oath (hip′ə krat′ik) the oath, attributed to Hippocrates, generally taken by medical graduates: it sets forth their ethical code

hip·po·drome (hip′ə drōm′) *n.* [< Gr. *hippos*, horse + *dromos*, course] an arena for a circus, games, etc.

hip·po·pot·a·mus (hip′ə pät′ə məs) *n., pl.* -**mus·es, -a·mi** (-mī′) [< Gr. *hippos*, horse + *potamus*, river] a large, plant-eating mammal with a heavy, thick-skinned body: it lives in or near rivers in Africa

hire (hīr) *vt.* **hired, hir'ing** [< OE. *hyr*, wages] to pay for the services of (a person) or the use of (a thing) —*n.* **1.** a hiring **2.** the amount paid in hiring —**hire out** to work for pay

hire'ling *n.* one who will follow anyone's orders for pay; mercenary

Hi·ro·shi·ma (hir′ə shē′mə) seaport in SW Honshu, Japan: largely destroyed (Aug. 6, 1945) by a U.S. atomic bomb, the first ever used in warfare: pop. 504,000

hir·sute (hur′sōōt, hir′-; hər sōōt′) *adj.* [L. *hirsutus*] hairy; shaggy

his (hiz) *pron.* [OE.] that or those belonging to him *[his* are better*]* — *poss. pronominal adj.* of, belonging to, or done by him

His·pan·io·la (his′pən yō′lə) island in the West Indies

hiss (his) *vi.* [echoic] 1. to make a sound like that of a prolonged *s* 2. to show disapproval by hissing —*vt.* to say or indicate by hissing —*n.* the act or sound of hissing

hist (st, hist) *interj.* be quiet!

his·ta·mine (his′tə mēn′) *n.* [< Gr. *histos*, tissue + AMMONIA] an ammonia derivative released by the tissues in allergic reactions

his·tol·o·gy (his täl′ə jē) *n.* [< Gr. *histos*, tissue + -LOGY] *Biol.* the microscopic study of tissue structure —**his·tol′o·gist** *n.*

his·to·ri·an (his tôr′ē ən) *n.* a writer of, or authority on, history

his·tor′ic (-ik) *adj.* 1. same as HISTORICAL 2. famous in history

his·tor′i·cal (-i k′l) *adj.* 1. of or concerned with history 2. based on people or events of the past 3. established by history; factual —**his·tor′i·cal·ly** *adv.*

his·to·ric·i·ty (his′tə ris′ə tē) *n.* historical authenticity

his·to·ri·og·ra·phy (his tôr′ē äg′rə fē) *n.* the study of the techniques of historical research

his·to·ry (his′tə rē, -trē) *n., pl.* **-ries** [< Gr. *histōr*, learned] 1. an account of what has happened, esp. in the life of a people, country, etc. 2. all recorded past events 3. the branch of knowledge that deals with the recording, analysis, etc. of past events 4. a known past [my coat has a *history*]

his·tri·on·ic (his′trē än′ik) *adj.* [< L. *histrio*, actor] 1. of acting or actors 2. overacted or overacting

his′tri·on′ics *n.pl.* [sometimes with sing. v.] 1. dramatics 2. an artificial or affected manner or outburst

hit (hit) *vt., vi.* **hit, hit′ting** [< ON. *hitta*, meet with] 1. to come against (something) with force; knock; bump 2. to give a blow (to); strike 3. to strike with a missile 4. to affect strongly [a town hard *hit* by floods] 5. to come (upon) by accident or after search 6. to arrive at [stocks *hit* a new high] 7. *Baseball* to get (a hit) —*n.* 1. a blow that strikes its mark 2. a collision 3. a successful and popular song, book, etc. 4. [Slang] a murder 5. [Slang] a dose of a drug, a drink of liquor, etc. 6. *Baseball* a ball struck fairly by which a batter gets on base —**hit it off** to get along well together —**hit′ter** *n.*

hit′-and-run′ *adj.* hitting with a vehicle, usually an automobile, and then escaping: also **hit′-skip′**

hitch (hich) *vi.* [ME. *hicchen*] 1. to move jerkily 2. to become fastened or caught —*vt.* 1. to move, pull, etc. with jerks 2. to fasten with a hook, knot, etc. 3. [Slang] to get (a ride) in hitchhiking —*n.* 1. a tug; jerk 2. a limp 3. a hindrance; obstacle 4. a catching or fastening 5. a kind of knot 6. [Slang] a period of time served

hitch′hike′ (-hīk′) *vi.* **-hiked′,**

-hik′ing to travel by asking for rides from motorists along the way —**hitch′hik′er** *n.*

hith·er (hith′ər) *adv.* [< OE.] to this place —*adj.* nearer

hith′er·to′ *adv.* until this time

Hit·ler (hit′lər), **Adolf** 1889–1945; Nazi dictator of Germany (1933–45)

hit man [Slang] a hired murderer

hit′-or-miss′ *adj.* haphazard; random

hive (hīv) *n.* [< OE.] 1. a shelter for a colony of bees; beehive 2. the bees of a hive 3. a crowd of busy people 4. a place of great activity —*vt.* **hived, hiv′ing** to gather (bees) into a hive —*vi.* to enter a hive

hives (hīvz) *n.* [orig. Scot. dial.] same as URTICARIA

HMO health maintenance organization

H.M.S. 1. His (or Her) Majesty's Service 2. His (or Her) Majesty's Ship

hoa·gy, hoa·gie (hō′gē) *n., pl.* **-gies** [< ?] same as HERO SANDWICH

hoard (hôrd) *n.* [OE. *hord*] a supply stored up and hidden —*vi., vt.* to accumulate and store away (money, goods, etc.) —**hoard′er** *n.*

hoar·frost (hôr′frôst′) *n.* white, frozen dew on the ground, leaves, etc.

hoarse (hôrs) *adj.* [OE. *has*] 1. harsh and grating in sound 2. having a rough, husky voice —**hoarse′ness** *n.*

hoar·y (hôr′ē) *adj.* **-i·er, -i·est** [< OE. *har*] 1. white or gray 2. having white or gray hair from old age 3. very old Also **hoar** —**hoar′i·ness** *n.*

hoax (hōks) *n.* [< ? HOCUS-POCUS] a trick or fraud; esp., a practical joke —*vt.* to deceive with a hoax

hob (häb) *n.* [< *Robin* or *Robert*] [Eng. Dial.] an elf or goblin —**play (or raise) hob with** to make trouble for

hob·ble (häb′'l) *vi.* **-bled, -bling** [ME. *hobelen*] to go haltingly; limp —*vt.* 1. to cause to limp 2. to hamper (a horse, etc.) by tying two feet together 3. to hinder —*n.* 1. a limp 2. a rope, etc. used to hobble a horse

hob·by (häb′ē) *n., pl.* **-bies** [ME. *hoby*] 1. same as HOBBYHORSE 2. something that a person likes to do in his spare time —**hob′by·ist** *n.*

hob′by·horse′ *n.* 1. a child's toy consisting of a stick with a horse's head 2. same as ROCKING HORSE

hob·gob·lin (häb′gäb′lin) *n.* [HOB + GOBLIN] 1. an elf 2. a bugbear

hob′nail′ *n.* [*hob*, a peg + NAIL] a broad-headed nail put on the soles of heavy shoes to prevent wear, etc. —*vt.* to put hobnails on

hob′nob′ (-näb′) *vi.* **-nobbed′, -nob′bing** [< ME. *habben*, have + *nabben*, not have] to be on close terms

ho·bo (hō′bō) *n., pl.* **-bos, -boes** 1. a migratory worker 2. a tramp

hock¹ (häk) *n.* [< OE. *hoh*, heel] the joint bending backward in the hind leg of a horse, ox, etc.

hock² (häk) *vt., n.* [< Du. *hok*, prison, debt] [Slang] same as PAWN¹

hock·ey (häk′ē) *n.* [prob. < OFr. *hoquet,* bent stick] **1.** a team game played on ice skates, with curved sticks and a rubber disk (*puck*) **2.** a similar game played on foot on a field, with a small ball

hock′shop′ *n.* [Slang] a pawnshop

ho·cus-po·cus (hō′kəs pō′kəs) *n.* [imitation L.] **1.** meaningless words used as a formula by conjurers **2.** *same as* SLEIGHT OF HAND **3.** trickery

hod (häd) *n.* [prob. < MDu. *hodde*] **1.** a long-handled wooden trough used for carrying bricks, mortar, etc. on the shoulder **2.** a coal scuttle

hodge·podge (häj′päj′) *n.* [< OFr. *hochepot,* a stew] a jumbled mixture

hoe (hō) *n.* [< OHG. *houwan,* hew] a tool with a thin blade set across the end of a long handle, for weeding, loosening soil, etc. —*vt., vi.* **hoed, hoe′ing** to cultivate with a hoe

hoe′cake′ (-kāk′) *n.* a thin bread made of cornmeal

hoe′down′ *n.* **1.** a lively, rollicking dance **2.** a party with such dances

hog (hôg, häg) *n.* [OE. *hogg*] **1.** a pig; esp., a full-grown pig raised for its meat **2.** [Colloq.] a selfish, greedy, or filthy person —*vt.* **hogged, hog′ging** [Slang] to take all of or an unfair share of —**go** (the) **whole hog** [Slang] to go all the way —**high on** (or **off**) **the hog** [Colloq.] in a luxurious or costly way —**hog′gish** *adj.* —**hog′gish·ly** *adv.*

ho·gan (hō′gôn, -gən) *n.* [< AmInd.] a Navaho Indian dwelling, built of earth walls supported by timbers

hogs·head (hôgz′hed′, hägz′-) *n.* **1.** a large barrel or cask holding from 63 to 140 gallons **2.** a liquid measure, esp. one equal to 63 gallons

hog′tie′ *vt.* **-tied′, -ty′ing** or **-tie′-ing 1.** to tie the four feet or the hands and feet of **2.** [Colloq.] to make incapable of effective action

hog′wash′ *n.* **1.** refuse fed to hogs; swill **2.** insincere talk, writing, etc.

hoi pol·loi (hoi′ pə loi′) [Gr., the many] the common people; the masses

hoist (hoist) *vt.* [< Du. *hijschen*] to raise aloft; lift, esp. with a pulley, crane, etc. —*n.* **1.** a hoisting **2.** an apparatus for lifting; elevator or tackle

hoke (hōk) *vt.* **hoked, hok′ing** [< ff.] [Slang] to treat in a too sentimental or crudely comic way: usually with *up* —**hok′ey** *adj.*

ho·kum (hōk′əm) *n.* [< HOCUS-POCUS] [Slang] **1.** mawkish sentiment in a play, story, etc. **2.** nonsense; humbug

hold¹ (hōld) *vt.* **held, hold′ing** [OE. *haldan*] **1.** to keep in the hands, arms, etc.; grasp **2.** to keep in a certain position or condition **3.** to restrain or control; keep back **4.** to possess; occupy [to *hold* an office] **5.** to guard; defend [*hold* the fort] **6.** to carry on (a meeting, etc.) **7.** to contain [the jar *holds* a pint] **8.** to regard; consider [I *hold* the story to be true] —*vi.* **1.** to go on being firm, loyal, etc. **2.** to remain unbroken or unyielding [the rope *held*] **3.** to be true or valid [this rule *holds* for most cases] **4.** to con-

tinue [the wind *held* steady] —*n.* **1.** a grasping or seizing; grip **2.** a thing to hold on by **3.** a thing for holding something else **4.** a dominating force [she has a *hold* over him] **5.** a prison —**get** (**catch, lay,** or **take**) **hold of** to take, seize, acquire, etc. —**hold forth 1.** to preach; lecture **2.** to offer —**hold out 1.** to last; endure **2.** to stand firm **3.** to offer **4.** [Colloq.] to refuse to hand over something —**hold over 1.** to postpone **2.** to stay for an additional period —**hold up 1.** to prop up **2.** to show **3.** to last; endure **4.** to stop; delay **5.** to stop forcibly and rob —**hold′er** *n.*

hold² (hōld) *n.* [< HOLE or MDu. *hol*] **1.** the interior of a ship below decks, in which the cargo is carried **2.** the compartment for cargo in an aircraft

hold′ing *n.* **1.** land, esp. a farm, rented from another **2.** [*usually pl.*] property owned, esp. stocks or bonds

hold′o′ver *n.* [Colloq.] one staying on from a previous period

hold′up′ *n.* **1.** a delay **2.** the act of stopping forcibly and robbing

hole (hōl) *n.* [OE. *hol*] **1.** a hollow place; cavity **2.** an animal's burrow **3.** a small, dingy, squalid place **4.** an opening in anything; gap; tear; rent **5.** *Golf a)* a small cavity into which the ball is to be hit *b)* the tee, fairway, etc. leading to this —**hole up** [Colloq.] to hibernate, as in a hole —**in the hole** [Colloq.] financially embarrassed or behind

hol·i·day (häl′ə dā′) *n.* **1.** a religious festival; holy day **2.** a day of freedom from labor, often one set aside by law to celebrate some event **3.** [often *pl.*] [Chiefly Brit.] a vacation —*adj.* of or for a holiday; joyous; gay

ho·li·er-than-thou (hō′lē ər *th*ən *th*ou′) *adj.* annoyingly self-righteous

ho·li·ness (hō′lē nis) *n.* **1.** a being holy **2.** [H-] a title of the Pope (with *His* or *Your*)

Hol·land (häl′ənd) *same as* NETHERLANDS —**Hol′land·er** *n.*

hol·lan·daise sauce (häl′ən dāz′) [Fr., of Holland] a creamy sauce made of butter, egg yolks, lemon juice, etc.

hol·ler (häl′ər) *vi., vt., n.* [Colloq.] shout; yell

hol·low (häl′ō) *adj.* [OE. *holh*] **1.** having a cavity inside; not solid **2.** shaped like a bowl; concave **3.** sunken [hollow cheeks] **4.** empty or worthless [hollow praise] **5.** hungry **6.** deep-toned and dull —*n.* **1.** a hollow place; cavity **2.** a valley —*vt., vi.* to make or become hollow —**hol′low·ness** *n.*

hol·ly (häl′ē) *n., pl.* **-lies** [OE. *holegn*] an evergreen shrub with glossy leaves and red berries

hol·ly·hock (häl′ē häk′) *n.* [< OE. *halig,* holy + *hoc,* mallow] a tall plant of the mallow family, with large, showy flowers

Hol·ly·wood (häl′ē wood′) **1.** section of Los Angeles: once the site of many U.S. motion-picture studios **2.** city on the SE coast of Fla.: pop. 117,000

Holmes (hōmz), **Oliver Wendell**

1841–1935; associate justice, U.S. Supreme Court (1902–32)

hol·o·caust (häl′ə kôst′, hō′lə-) *n.* [< Gr. *holos*, whole + *kaustos*, burnt] great destruction of life, esp. by fire — **the Holocaust** the destruction of millions of Jews by the Nazis

hol·o·graph (häl′ə graf′) *n.* [< Gr. *holos*, whole + *graphein*, to write] a document, letter, etc. in the handwriting of the person under whose name it appears —**hol′o·graph′ic** *adj.*

Hol·stein (hōl′stēn, -stīn) *n.* [< Schleswig-*Holstein*, Germany] a breed of large, black-and-white dairy cattle

hol·ster (hōl′stər) *n.* [Du.] a pistol case attached to a belt

ho·ly (hō′lē) *adj.* -li·er, -li·est [OE. *halig*] 1. dedicated to religious use; sacred 2. spiritually pure; sinless 3. deserving reverence or adoration

Holy Communion a Christian rite in which bread and wine are consecrated and received as (symbols of) the body and blood of Jesus

Holy Land *same as* PALESTINE

Holy Roman Empire empire of WC Europe, from 962 A.D. until 1806

Holy Spirit (or **Ghost**) the third person of the Trinity; spirit of God

hom·age (häm′ij, äm′-) *n.* [< L. *homo*, man] anything given or done to show reverence, honor, etc.

hom·burg (häm′bərg) *n.* [after *Homburg*, Prussia] a man's felt hat with a crown indented front to back and a stiff, curved brim

home (hōm) *n.* [OE. *ham*] 1. the place where one lives 2. the city, state, etc. where one was born or reared 3. a place thought of as home or as a place of origin 4. a household and its affairs 5. an institution for orphans, the aged, etc. 6. the natural environment of an animal, plant, etc. 7. *same as* HOME PLATE —*adj.* 1. of one's home or country; domestic 2. central [*home office*] —*adv.* 1. at, to, or in the direction of home 2. to the point aimed at [*to drive a nail home*] —**at home** 1. in one's home 2. at ease —**bring home to** to impress upon — **home′less** *adj.* —**home′like′** *adj.*

home economics the science and art of homemaking, nutrition, etc.

home′land′ *n.* the country in which one was born or makes one's home

home′ly *adj.* -li·er, -li·est 1. suitable for home life; everyday 2. crude 3. not good-looking —**home′li·ness** *n.*

home′made′ *adj.* made, or as if made, at home

home′mak′er *n.* a housewife or one who manages a home

home plate *Baseball* the slab that the batter stands beside: it is the last base touched in scoring a run

score a run: also [Colloq.] **hom′er** *n.*

home′sick′ *adj.* longing for home —**home′sick′ness** *n.*

home′spun *n.* 1. cloth made of yarn spun at home 2. coarse cloth like this —*adj.* 1. spun at home 2. made of homespun 3. plain; homely

home′stead′ (-sted′) *n.* 1. a place for a family's home, including the land and buildings 2. a 160-acre tract of U.S. public land, granted as a farm —**home′stead′er** *n.*

home′stretch′ *n.* 1. the part of a race track between the last turn and the finish line 2. the final part

home′ward (-wərd) *adv., adj.* toward home: also **home′wards** *adv.*

home′work′ *n.* 1. work, esp. piecework, done at home 2. schoolwork to be done outside the classroom 3. preliminary study for a project: usually in **do one's homework**

home′y (-ē) *adj.* **hom′i·er, hom′i·est** cozy, familiar, etc. —**home′y·ness** *n.*

hom·i·cide (häm′ə sīd′, hō′mə-) *n.* [< L. *homo*, man + *caedere*, kill] 1. the killing of one person by another 2. a person who kills another —**hom′i·ci′dal** *adj.*

hom·i·let·ics (häm′ə let′iks) *n.pl.* [*with sing. v.*] [see ff.] the art of writing and preaching sermons

hom·i·ly (häm′ə lē) *n., pl.* **-lies** [< Gr. *homilos*, assembly] 1. a sermon 2. a solemn moral talk or writing

homing pigeon a pigeon trained to find its way home from distant places

hom·i·ny (häm′ə nē) *n.* [< AmInd.] dry corn hulled and coarsely ground (**hominy grits**): it is boiled for food

homo- [< Gr. *homos*] *a combining form meaning* same, equal, like

ho·mo·ge·ne·ous (hō′mə jē′nē əs, häm′ə-; -jēn′yəs) *adj.* [see prec. & GENUS] 1. the same in structure, quality, etc.; similar 2. composed of similar parts —**ho′mo·ge·ne′i·ty** (-jə nē′ə tē) *n.*

ho·mog·e·nize (hə mäj′ə nīz′) *vt.* -nized′, -niz′ing to make homogeneous, or more uniform throughout; specif., to process (milk) so that fat particles are so finely emulsified that the cream does not separate

hom·o·graph (häm′ə graf′, hō′mə-) *n.* [HOMO- + -GRAPH] a word with the same spelling as another but different in meaning and origin

ho·mol·o·gous (hō mäl′ə gəs) *adj.* [Gr. *homologos*, agreeing] matching in structure, position, origin, etc.

hom·o·nym (häm′ə nim) *n.* [< Gr. *homos*, same + *onyma*, name] a word with the same pronunciation as another but with a different meaning, origin, and, usually, spelling

ho·mo·pho·bi·a (hō′mə fō′bē ə) *n.* [HOMO (SEXUAL) + -PHOBIA] hatred or fear of homosexuals or homosexuality —**ho′mo·pho′bic** (-fō′bik) *adj.*

Ho·mo sa·pi·ens (hō′mō sā′pē enz′)

[ModL. *homo*, man + *sapiens*, prp. of *sapere*, know] man; human being

ho'mo·sex'u·al (-mə sek'shoo wəl) *adj.* of or having sexual desire for those of the same sex —*n.* a homosexual person —**ho'mo·sex'u·al'i·ty** *n.*

Hon., hon. honorable

Hon·du·ras (hän door'əs, -dyoor'-) country in Central America: 43,227 sq. mi.; pop. 2,445,000

hone (hōn) *n.* [OE. *han*, a stone] a hard stone used to sharpen cutting tools, esp. razors —*vt.* **honed, hon'ing** to sharpen, as with a hone

hon·est (än'əst) *adj.* [< L. *honor*, honor] 1. truthful; trustworthy 2. *a)* sincere or genuine [*honest* effort] *b)* gained by fair means [*honest* living] 3. frank and open [*honest* face] —**hon'est·ly** *adv.* —**hon'es·ty** *n.*

hon·ey (hun'ē) *n., pl.* **-eys** [OE. *hunig*] 1. a sweet, syrupy substance that bees make as food from the nectar of flowers 2. sweetness 3. darling

hon'ey·comb' (-kōm') *n.* 1. the structure of six-sided wax cells made by bees to hold their honey, eggs, etc. 2. anything like this —*vt.* to fill with holes like a honeycomb —*adj.* of or like a honeycomb

hon'ey·dew' melon (-dōō') a variety of melon with a smooth, whitish rind and sweet, green flesh

HONEYCOMB

hon'ey·moon' *n.* the vacation spent together by a newly married couple —*vi.* to have or spend a honeymoon

hon'ey·suck'le (-suk''l) *n.* any of a genus of plants with small, fragrant flowers of red, yellow, or white

Hong Kong (häŋ' käŋ', hôŋ' kôŋ') Brit. colony in SE China

honk (hôŋk, häŋk) *n.* [echoic] 1. the call of a wild goose 2. a similar sound, as of an automobile horn —*vi., vt.* to make or cause to make such a sound

hon·ky-tonk (hôŋ'kē tôŋk') *n.* [Slang] a cheap, noisy nightclub —*adj.* designating music played on a piano with a tinkling sound

Hon·o·lu·lu (hän'ə lōō'lōō) capital of Hawaii, on Oahu: pop. 365,000

hon·or (än'ər) *n.* [L.] 1. high regard or respect; esp., *a)* glory; fame *b)* good reputation 2. adherence to principles considered right; integrity 3. chastity 4. high rank; distinction 5. [H-] a title of certain officials, as judges (with *His, Her,* or *Your*) 6. something done or given as a token of respect 7. a source of respect and fame —*vt.* 1. to respect greatly 2. to show high regard for 3. to do or give something in honor of 4. to accept and pay [to *honor* a check] —**do the honors** to act as host Brit. sp. **honour**

hon'or·a·ble *adj.* 1. worthy of being honored 2. honest; upright 3. bringing honor [*honorable* mention] —**hon'or·a·bly** *adv.*

hon·o·rar·i·um (än'ə rer'ē əm) *n., pl.* **-ri·ums, -ri·a** (-ə) [L.] a payment

as to a professional person for services on which no fee is set

hon'or·ar'y (-rer'ē) *adj.* 1. given as an honor 2. designating or in an office held as an honor, without service or pay —**hon'or·ar'i·ly** *adv.*

hon·or·if·ic (än'ə rif'ik) *adj.* conferring honor [an *honorific* title]

Hon·shu (hän'shōō') largest of the islands forming Japan

hood (hood) *n.* [OE. *hod*] 1. a covering for the head and neck, often part of a cloak 2. anything like a hood, as the metal cover over an automobile engine —*vt.* to cover as with a hood —**hood'ed** *adj.*

-hood (hood) [OE. *had*] a *suffix meaning:* 1. state or quality [*childhood*] 2. the whole group of [*priesthood*]

hood·lum (hōōd'ləm) *n.* [prob. < G. dial. *hudilump*, wretch] a member of a lawless gang

hoo·doo (hōō'dōō) *n., pl.* **-doos** [var. of VOODOO] 1. *same as* VOODOO 2. [Colloq.] bad luck or a person or thing that causes it

hood·wink (hood'wiŋk') *vt.* [HOOD + WINK] to mislead by trickery; dupe

hoo·ey (hōō'ē) *interj., n.* [echoic] [Slang] nonsense; bunk

hoof (hoof, hōōf) *n., pl.* **hoofs** or **hooves** [OE. *hof*] the horny covering on the feet of cattle, horses, etc., or the entire foot —*vt., vi.* [Colloq.] to walk —**hoofed** *adj.*

hook (hook) *n.* [OE. *hoc*] 1. a bent piece of metal, etc. used to catch, hold, or pull something 2. a fishhook 3. something shaped like a hook 4. a strike, blow, etc. in which a curving motion is involved —*vt.* 1. to catch, fasten, throw, hit, etc. with a hook 2. [Colloq.] to steal —*vi.* 1. to curve as a hook does 2. to be fastened or caught by a hook —**by hook or by crook** by any means, honest or dishonest —**hook up** to connect (a radio, etc.) —**off the hook** [Colloq.] out of trouble

hook·ah, hook·a (hook'ə) *n.* [Ar. *huqqah*] an Oriental tobacco pipe with a long tube for drawing smoke through water to cool it

hooked (hookt) *adj.* 1. like a hook 2. made with a hook [*hooked* rug] 3. [Slang] *a)* obsessed with or addicted to (often with *on*) *b)* married

hook'er *n.* [Slang] a prostitute

hook'up' *n.* the arrangement and connection of parts, circuits, etc., as in (a) radio

hook'worm' *n.* a small, parasitic roundworm with hooks around the mouth, infesting the small intestine

hoo·li·gan (hōō'li gən) *n.* [< ? *Hooligan*, a family name] a hoodlum

hoop (hōōp) *n.* [OE. *hop*] 1. a circular band for holding together the staves of a barrel 2. anything like this, as a ring in a hoop skirt —*vt.* to bind or fasten as with a hoop

hoop·la (hōōp'lä) *n.* [< ?] [Colloq.] 1. great excitement 2. showy publicity

hoop skirt a woman's skirt worn spread over a framework of hoops

hoo·ray (hoo rā', hə-, hōō-) *interj., n., vi. same as* HURRAH

hoose·gow (hoos'gou) *n.* [< Sp. *juzgado,* court of justice] [Slang] a jail
Hoo·sier (hoo'zhər) *n.* [Colloq.] a native or inhabitant of Indiana
hoot (hoot) *n.* [echoic] 1. the sound that an owl makes 2. any sound like this, as a shout of scorn —*vi.* to utter a hoot —*vt.* to express (scorn) of (someone) by hooting —**hoot'er** *n.*
hoot·en·an·ny (hoot'n an'ē) *n., pl.* -nies a gathering or performance of folk singers
Hoo·ver (hoo'vər), **Herbert C.** 1874-1964; 31st president of the U.S. (1929-33)
hop[1] (häp) *vi.* **hopped, hop'ping** [OE. *hoppian*] 1. to make a short leap or leaps on one foot 2. to leap with all feet at once, as a frog, etc. 3. [Colloq.] to go briskly —*vt.* 1. to jump over 2. to get aboard —*n.* 1. a hopping 2. [Colloq.] *a)* a dance *b)* a short flight in an airplane
hop[2] (häp) *n.* [< MDu. *hoppe*] 1. a twining vine with small, cone-shaped flowers 2. [*pl.*] the dried ripe cones, used for flavoring beer, ale, etc. —**hop up** [Slang] 1. to stimulate, as by a drug 2. to supercharge (an automobile engine, etc.)
hope (hōp) *n.* [OE. *hopa*] 1. a feeling that what is wanted will happen 2. the object of this 3. a person or thing on which one may base some hope —*vt.* **hoped, hop'ing** to want and expect —*vi.* to have hope (*for*) —**hope'ful** *adj.* —**hope'ful·ly** *adv.* —**hope'less** *adj.* —**hope'less·ly** *adv.*
hop'head' *n.* [Slang] a drug addict
hop·per (häp'ər) *n.* 1. one that hops 2. a hopping insect 3. a container from which the contents can be emptied slowly and evenly
hop·sack·ing (häp'sak'iŋ) *n.* a sturdy fabric somewhat like a coarse material for bags, used for suits, coats, etc.: also **hopsack**
hop'scotch' *n.* [HOP[1] + *scotch,* line] a game in which children hop about in figures drawn on the ground
Hor·ace (hôr'is, här'-) 65-8 B.C.; Rom. poet
horde (hôrd) *n.* [ult. < Tatar *urdu,* a camp] a crowd or throng; swarm —*vi.* **hord'ed, hord'ing** to form or gather in a horde
hore·hound (hôr'hound') *n.* [OE. *harhune*] 1. a bitter mint plant 2. medicine or candy made from its juice
ho·ri·zon (hə rī'z'n) *n.* [< Gr. *horos,* boundary] 1. the line where the sky seems to meet the earth 2. the limit of one's experience, interest, etc.
hor·i·zon·tal (hôr'ə zän't'l, här'-) *adj.* 1. parallel to the plane of the horizon; not vertical 2. flat and even; level —**hor'i·zon'tal·ly** *adv.*
hor·mone (hôr'mōn) *n.* [< Gr. *hormē,* impulse] a substance formed in some organ of the body and carried to another part, where it takes effect — **hor·mo'nal** *adj.*

horn (hôrn) *n.* [OE.] 1. a hard, bonelike projection growing on the head of a cow, goat, etc. 2. the substance horns are made of 3. anything like a horn in position, shape, etc. 4. any brass-wind instrument 5. a device sounded to give a warning —*adj.* made of horn —**horn in (on)** [Colloq.] to intrude or meddle (in) —**horned** *adj.* —**horn'less** *adj.* —**horn'like** *adj.*
Horn, Cape southernmost point of S. America, on an island of Chile
horned toad a small, scaly, insect-eating lizard with hornlike spines
hor·net (hôr'nit) *n.* [OE. *hyrnet*] a large, yellow and black wasp
horn of plenty same as CORNUCOPIA
horn'pipe' *n.* a lively dance formerly popular with sailors
horn'y *adj.* **-i·er, -i·est** 1. made of horn 2. having horns 3. toughened and calloused [*horny* hands] 4. [Slang] sexually aroused
ho·rol·o·gy (hō räl'ə jē) *n.* [< Gr. *hōra,* hour + -LOGY] the science of measuring time or making timepieces
hor·o·scope (hôr'ə skōp', här'-) *n.* [< Gr. *hōra,* hour + *skopos,* watcher] a chart of the zodiacal signs and positions of planets, etc., by which astrologers profess to tell fortunes
hor·ren·dous (hō ren'dəs) *adj.* [see HORROR] horrible; dreadful
hor·ri·ble (hôr'ə b'l, här'-) *adj.* [see HORROR] 1. causing horror; terrible; dreadful 2. [Colloq.] very bad, ugly, unpleasant, etc. —**hor'ri·bly** *adv.*
hor'rid (-id) *adj.* 1. causing horror; terrible 2. very bad, ugly, unpleasant, etc. —**hor'rid·ly** *adv.*
hor·ri·fy (hôr'ə fī', här'-) *vt.* **-fied', -fy'ing** 1. to cause to feel horror 2. [Colloq.] to shock or disgust
hor·ror (hôr'ər, här'-) *n.* [< L. *horrere,* to bristle] 1. the strong feeling caused by something frightful or shocking 2. strong dislike 3. something that causes horror, disgust, etc.
hors de com·bat (ôr' də kôn bä') [Fr., lit., out of combat] disabled
hors d'oeuvre (ôr' durv') *pl.* **d'oeuvres** (durvz') [Fr., lit., outside of work] an appetizer, as olives, canapés, etc., served before a meal
horse (hôrs) *n.* [OE. *hors*] 1. a large, four-legged, solid-hoofed animal with flowing mane and tail, domesticated for drawing loads, carrying riders, etc. 2. a frame with legs to support something —*vt.* **horsed, hors'ing** to supply with a horse or horses; put on horseback —*adj.* of or on horses —**hold one's horses** [Slang] to curb one's impatience —**horse around** [Slang] to engage in horseplay
horse'back' *n.* the back of a horse —*adv.* on horseback
horse chestnut 1. a flowering tree with large leaves and glossy brown seeds 2. its seed
horse'feath'ers *n., interj.* [Slang] nonsense; bunk

---

horse′fly′ *n.*, *pl.* **-flies′** a large fly that sucks the blood of horses, etc.

horse′hair′ *n.* **1.** hair from the mane or tail of a horse **2.** a stiff fabric made from this hair

horse′hide′ *n.* **1.** the hide of a horse **2.** leather made from this

horse′laugh′ *n.* a boisterous, usually derisive laugh; guffaw

horse′man (-mən) *n.*, *pl.* **-men** a man skilled in the riding or care of horses **—horse′man·ship′** *n.* **—horse′wom′an** *n.*, *pl.* **-wom′en**

horse opera [Slang] a cowboy movie

horse′play′ *n.* rough, boisterous fun

horse′pow′er *n.* a unit for measuring the power of engines, etc., equal to 746 watts or 33,000 foot-pounds per minute

horse′rad′ish *n.* **1.** a plant of the mustard family, with a pungent root **2.** a relish made by grating this root

horse sense [Colloq.] common sense

horse′shoe′ *n.* **1.** a flat, U-shaped, protective metal plate nailed to a horse's hoof **2.** anything shaped like this **3.** [*pl.*] a game in which the players toss horseshoes at a stake

horse′whip′ *n.* a whip for driving horses **—vt. -whipped′, -whip′ping** to lash with a horsewhip

hors·y (hôr′sē) *adj.* **-i·er, -i·est 1.** of, like, or suggesting a horse **2.** of or like people who are fond of horses, fox hunting, or horse racing Also **horsey**

hor·ta·to·ry (hôr′tə tôr′ē) *adj.* [< L. *hortari*, incite] exhorting; advising

hor·ti·cul·ture (hôr′tə kul′chər) *n.* [< L. *hortus*, garden + *cultura*, culture] the art or science of growing flowers, fruits, and vegetables **—hor′ti·cul′tur·al** *adj.*

ho·san·na (hō zan′ə) *n., interj.* [< Heb. *hōshī′ăh nnā*, lit., save, we pray] an exclamation of praise to God

hose (hōz) *n., pl.* **hose;** for **2**, usually **hos′es** [OE. *hosa*] **1.** [*pl.*] *a*) stockings *b*) socks **2.** a flexible tube, used to convey fluids **—vt. hosed, hos′ing** to water with a hose

ho·sier·y (hō′zhər ē) *n.* stockings

hos·pice (häs′pis) *n.* [< L. *hospes*, host, guest] **1.** a shelter for travelers **2.** a homelike facility for the care of terminally ill patients

hos·pi·ta·ble (häs′pi tə b'l, häs pit′ə-) *adj.* [see prec.] friendly and solicitous toward guests, new arrivals, etc. **—hos′pi·ta·bly** *adv.*

hos·pi·tal (häs′pi t'l) *n.* [< L. *hospes*, host, guest] an institution where the ill or injured may receive medical treatment, nursing, etc.

hos·pi·tal·i·ty (häs′pə tal′ə tē) *n., pl.* **-ties** the act, practice, or quality of being hospitable

hos·pi·tal·ize (häs′pi t'l īz′) *vt.* **-ized′, -iz′ing** to put in, or admit to, a hospital **—hos′pi·tal·i·za′tion** *n.*

host[1] (hōst) *n.* [< L. *hospes*, host, guest] **1.** a man who entertains guests, esp. in his own home **2.** a man who keeps an inn or hotel **3.** an organism on or in which another lives **—vt., vi.** to act as host (to)

host[2] (hōst) *n.* [< ML. *hostis*, army] **1.** an army **2.** a great number

host[3] (hōst) *n.* [< ML. *hostia*] a wafer of bread used in the Eucharist

hos·tage (häs′tij) *n.* [< OFr.] a person kept or given as a pledge until certain conditions are met

hos·tel (häs′t'l) *n.* [see HOSPITAL] a lodging place; inn: also **hos′tel·ry** (-rē), *pl.* **-ries —hos′tel·er** *n.*

host·ess (hōs′tis) *n.* **1.** a woman who entertains guests, esp. in her home; often, the host's wife **2.** a woman employed in a restaurant to supervise the waitresses, seating, etc.

hos·tile (häs′t'l) *adj.* [< L. *hostis*, enemy] **1.** of or characteristic of an enemy **2.** unfriendly; antagonistic **—hos′tile·ly** *adv.*

hos·til·i·ty (häs til′ə tē) *n., pl.* **-ties 1.** a feeling of enmity, ill will, etc. **2.** *a*) a hostile act *b*) [*pl.*] warfare

hos·tler (häs′lər, äs′-) *n.* [contr. of HOSTELER] one who takes care of horses at an inn, stable, etc.

hot (hät) *adj.* **hot′ter, hot′test** [OE. *hat*] **1.** *a*) having a temperature higher than that of the human body *b*) having a relatively high temperature **2.** producing a burning sensation [*hot* pepper] **3.** full of intense feeling, as, *a*) impetuous [a *hot* temper] *b*) violent [a *hot* battle] *c*) lustful *d*) very controversial **4.** following closely [in *hot* pursuit] **5.** electrically charged [a *hot* wire] **6.** [Colloq.] recent; fresh [*hot* news] **7.** [Slang] *a*) recently stolen or smuggled *b*) [Slang] excellent; good **—make it hot for** [Colloq.] to make things uncomfortable for **—hot′ly** *adv.* **—hot′ness** *n.*

hot air [Slang] empty talk

hot′bed′ *n.* **1.** a bed of earth covered with glass and heated by manure, for forcing plants **2.** any place that fosters rapid growth or extensive activity

hot′-blood′ed *adj.* easily excited; passionate, reckless, etc.

hot′box′ *n.* an overheated bearing on an axle or shaft

hot cake a griddlecake **—sell like hot cakes** [Colloq.] to be sold rapidly and in large quantities

hot dog [Colloq.] a wiener, esp. one served in a long, soft roll

ho·tel (hō tel′) *n.* [see HOSPITAL] an establishment providing lodging, and often food, for travelers, etc.

ho·tel·ier (hō′tel yā′, -tə lir′) *n.* [Fr.] an owner or manager of a hotel

hot′head′ed *adj.* **1.** quick-tempered **2.** impetuous **—hot′head′** *n.*

hot′house′ *n.* same as GREENHOUSE

hot line a telephone or telegraph line for immediate communication, as between heads of state in a crisis

hot plate a small stove for cooking

hot potato [Colloq.] a troubling problem that no one wants to handle

hot rod [Slang] an automobile, often an old one, whose engine has been supercharged **—hot rod′der**

hot seat [Slang] **1.** same as ELECTRIC CHAIR **2.** a difficult situation

hot′shot′ *n.* [Slang] one who is expert at something in an aggressive way

hot′-tem′pered *adj.* having a fiery temper

Hot·ten·tot (hät′'n tät′) *n.* 1. a member of a nomadic people of SW Africa 2. their language

hot tub a large wooden tub in which several people can soak in hot water

hound (hound) *n.* [OE. *hund*, dog] 1. any of several breeds of hunting dog 2. any dog —*vt.* 1. to hunt or chase with or as with hounds 2. to urge on

hounds·tooth check (houndz′ tooth′) a pattern of irregular broken checks, used in woven material

hour (our) *n.* [< Gr. *hōra*] 1. one of the twenty-four parts of a day; sixty minutes 2. the time for a particular activity [lunch *hour*] 3. [*pl.*] a period fixed for work, etc. [office *hours*] 4. the time of day [the *hour* is 2:30] 5. *Educ.* a credit, equal to each hour spent in class per week —**after hours** after the regular hours for business, school, etc. —**hour after hour** every hour

hour·glass′ *n.* an instrument for measuring time by the trickling of sand, etc. from one part to another

hou·ri (hoor′ē, hou′rē) *n.*, *pl.* **-ris** [< Ar. *ḥūriyah*, black-eyed woman] a beautiful nymph of the Moslem paradise

hour·ly *adj.* 1. happening every hour 2. done during an hour 3. frequent —*adv.* 1. at every hour 2. often

HOURGLASS

house (hous; *for v.* houz) *n.*, *pl.* **hous·es** (hou′ziz) [OE. *hus*] 1. a building to live in; specif., a building occupied by one family or person 2. the people who live in a house; household 3. a family as including kin, ancestors, and descendants 4. shelter, living or storage space, etc. 5. *a*) a theater *b*) the audience in a theater 6. a business firm 7. a legislative assembly —*vt.* housed, hous′ing 1. to provide a house or lodgings for 2. to cover, shelter, etc. —**keep house** to take care of a home —**on the house** at the expense of the establishment

house′boat′ *n.* a large, flat-bottomed boat used as a residence

house′break′ing *n.* the breaking into and entering another's house to commit theft or some other felony

house′bro′ken *adj.* trained to live in a house (i.e., to void in a special place): said of a dog, cat, etc.

house′fly′ *n.*, *pl.* **-flies′** a two-winged fly found in and around houses

house′hold′ *n.* 1. all those living in one house 2. the home and its affairs —**house′ hold′er** *n.*

household word a common saying or thing, familiar to nearly everyone

house′hus′band *n.* a married man whose job is keeping house and doing the work usually done by a housewife

house′keep′er *n.* a woman who runs a home, esp. one hired to do so

house′maid′ *n.* a maid for housework

House of Commons the lower branch of the legislature of Great Britain or Canada

House of Lords the upper branch of the legislature of Great Britain

House of Representatives the lower branch of the legislature of the U.S., or of most States of the U.S.

house′wares′ (-werz′) *n.pl.* articles for household use, esp. in the kitchen

house′warm′ing *n.* a party to celebrate moving into a new home

house′wife′ (*n.*; *pl.* **-wives′**) a woman in charge of her own household

house′work′ *n.* the work involved in housekeeping; cleaning, cooking, etc.

hous·ing (hou′ziŋ) *n.* 1. the providing of shelter or lodging 2. shelter or lodging 3. houses collectively 4. an enclosing frame, box, etc.

Hous·ton (hyōōs′tən) city & port in SE Tex.: pop. 1,594,000

hove (hōv) *alt. pt. & pp. of* HEAVE

hov·el (huv′'l, häv′-) *n.* [ME.] any small, miserable dwelling; hut

hov·er (huv′ər, häv′-) *vi.* [< ME. *hoven*, to stay (suspended)] 1. to flutter in the air near one place 2. to linger close by 3. to waver (*between*)

how (hou) *adv.* [OE. *hu*] 1. in what manner or way 2. in what state or condition 3. for what reason 4. to what extent, degree, etc. *How* is also used as an intensive —**how about** what is your thought concerning?

how·be·it (hou bē′it) *adv.* [Archaic] however it may be; nevertheless

how·dah (hou′də) *n.* [Hind. *hauda*] a seat for riding on the back of an elephant or camel

how·ev′er *adv.* 1. in whatever manner 2. to whatever degree 3. nevertheless Also [Poet.] **how·e′er′** (-er′)

how·itz·er (hou′it sər) *n.* [< Czech *haufnice*, orig., a sling] a short cannon, firing shells in a high trajectory

howl (houl) *vi.* [ME. *hulen*] 1. to utter the long, wailing cry of wolves, dogs, etc. 2. to utter a similar cry of pain, anger, etc. 3. to shout or laugh in scorn, mirth, etc. —*vt.* 1. to utter with a howl 2. to drive by howling —*n.* 1. the wailing cry of a wolf, dog, etc. 2. any similar sound 3. [Colloq.] a joke

howl′er *n.* 1. one who howls 2. [Colloq.] a ludicrous blunder

how·so·ev·er (hou′sō ev′ər) *adv.* 1. to whatever degree or extent 2. by whatever means

hoy·den (hoid′'n) *n.* [< ? Du.] a bold, boisterous girl; tomboy

Hoyle (hoil) *n.* a book of rules for card games, orig. compiled by E. Hoyle (1672-1769) —**according to Hoyle** according to the rules

HP, H.P., hp, h.p. horsepower

HQ, H.Q. headquarters

hr. *pl.* **hrs.** hour(s)

H.R. House of Representatives

H.R.H. His (or Her) Royal Highness

H.S., h.s. high school

ht. 1. heat 2. *pl.* **hts.** height

hua·ra·ches (hə rä'chēz, wə-) *n.pl.* [MexSp.] flat sandals with uppers made of straps or woven leather strips

hub (hub) *n.* [< ?] 1. the center part of a wheel 2. a center of activity

hub·bub (hub'ub) *n.* [prob. < Irish exclamation] an uproar; tumult

hu·bris (hyōō'bris) *n.* [Gr. *hybris*] arrogance caused by too great pride

huck·le·ber·ry (huk'l ber'ē) *n., pl.* **-ries** [prob. < ME. *hurtilberye*] 1. a shrub with blue berries 2. this berry

huck·ster (huk'stər) *n.* [< MDu. *hoeken*, peddle] a peddler, esp. of fruits, vegetables, etc. —*vt.* to peddle

HUD (Department of) Housing and Urban Development

hud·dle (hud'l) *vi., vt.* **-dled, -dling** [prob. < ME. *hoderen*, cover up] 1. to crowd close together 2. to draw (oneself) up —*n.* 1. a confused crowd or heap 2. [Slang] a private conference 3. *Football* a grouping of a team to get signals before a play

Hud·son (hud's'n) river in E N.Y.

Hudson Bay inland sea in NE Canada; arm of the Atlantic

hue[1] (hyōō) *n.* [OE. *heow*] 1. color 2. a particular shade or tint of a color

hue[2] (hyōō) *n.* [< OFr. *hu*, outcry] a shouting: now only in **hue and cry**

huff (huf) *vi.* to blow; puff —*n.* state of smoldering anger or resentment —**huff'y** *adj.* **-i·er, -i·est**

hug (hug) *vt.* **hugged, hug'ging** [prob. < ON. *hugga*, to comfort] 1. to clasp closely and fondly in the arms; embrace 2. to cling to (a belief, etc.) 3. to keep close to —*vi.* to embrace one another —*n.* a close embrace

huge (hyōōj) *adj.* [< OFr. *ahuge*] very large; gigantic; immense —**huge'ly** *adv.* —**huge'ness** *n.*

Hu·go (hyōō'gō), **Victor Marie** 1802-85; Fr. poet, novelist, & playwright

Hu·gue·not (hyōō'gə nät') *n.* a 16th or 17th-c. French Protestant

huh (hu, hun) *interj.* an exclamation used to express contempt, surprise, etc., or to ask a question

hu·la (hōō'lə) *n.* [Haw.] a native Hawaiian dance: also **hu'la-hu'la**

hulk (hulk) *n.* [< Gr. *holkas*, towed ship] 1. the body of a ship, esp. if old and dismantled 2. a big, clumsy person or thing

hulk'ing *adj.* bulky and clumsy

hull (hul) *n.* [OE. *hulu*] 1. the outer covering of a seed or fruit, as the husk of grain, shell of nuts, etc. 2. the frame or main body of a ship, airship, etc. 3. any outer covering —*vt.* to take the hulls off (nuts, etc.) —**hull'er** *n.*

hul·la·ba·loo (hul'ə bə lōō') *n.* [echoic] clamor; hubbub

hum (hum) *vi.* **hummed, hum'ming** [echoic] 1. to make a low, continuous, murmuring sound 2. to sing with closed lips 3. [Colloq.] to be full of activity —*vt.* to sing (a tune) with closed lips —*n.* a continuous murmur

hu·man (hyōō'mən) *adj.* [< L. *humanus*] of, characteristic of, or having the qualities typical of mankind —*n.* a person: also **human being** —**hu'man·ness** *n.*

hu·mane (hyōō mān') *adj.* [var. of prec.] 1. kind, tender, merciful, etc. 2. civilizing; refining —**hu·mane'ly** *adv.* —**hu·mane'ness** *n.*

hu·man·ism (hyōō'mə niz'm) *n.* 1. any system of thought based on the interests and ideals of man 2. [H-] the intellectual movement that stemmed from the study of Greek and Latin classics during the Middle Ages —**hu'man·ist** *n., adj.* —**hu'man·is'tic** *adj.* —**hu'man·is'ti·cal·ly** *adv.*

hu·man·i·tar·i·an (hyōō man'ə ter'ē ən) *n.* a person devoted to promoting the welfare of humanity; philanthropist —*adj.* helping humanity —**hu·man'i·tar'i·an·ism** *n.*

hu·man·i·ty (hyōō man'ə tē) *n., pl.* **-ties** 1. the fact or quality of being human or humane 2. mankind; people —**the humanities** literature, philosophy, the fine arts, etc. as distinguished from the sciences

hu·man·ize (hyōō'mə nīz') *vt., vi.* **-ized', -iz'ing** to make or become human or humane —**hu'man·i·za'tion** *n.* —**hu'man·iz'er** *n.*

hu'man·kind' *n.* mankind; people

hu'man·ly *adv.* 1. in a human manner 2. by human means

hu'man·oid' (-oid') *adj.* nearly human —*n.* a nearly human creature

hum·ble (hum'b'l, um'-) *adj.* **-bler, -blest** [< L. *humilis*, low] 1. having or showing a consciousness of one's defects; modest 2. lowly; unpretentious —*vt.* **-bled, -bling** 1. to lower in condition or rank 2. to lower in pride; make modest —**hum'ble·ness** *n.* —**hum'bly** *adv.*

hum·bug (hum'bug') *n.* [< ?] 1. fraud; sham; hoax 2. an impostor —*vt.* **-bugged', -bug'ging** to dupe; deceive —*interj.* nonsense!

hum·drum (hum'drum') *adj.* [echoic] dull; monotonous

hu·mer·us (hyōō'mər əs) *n., pl.* **-mer·i'** (-ī') [L.] the bone of the upper arm or forelimb —**hu'mer·al** *adj.*

hu·mid (hyōō'mid) *adj.* [< L. *umere*, be moist] damp; moist

hu·mid·i·fy (hyōō mid'ə fī') *vt.* **-fied', -fy'ing** to make humid —**hu·mid'i·fi'er** *n.*

hu·mid·i·ty *n.* 1. moistness; dampness 2. amount of moisture in the air

hu·mi·dor (hyōō'mə dôr') *n.* a case or jar for keeping tobacco moist

hu·mil·i·ate (hyōō mil'ē āt') *vt.* **-at'ed, -at'ing** [< L. *humilis*, humble] to hurt the pride or dignity of; mortify —**hu·mil'i·a'tion** *n.*

hu·mil·i·ty (-ə tē) *n.* the state or quality of being humble

hum·ming·bird (hum'iŋ burd') *n.* a very small, brightly colored bird with narrow wings that vibrate rapidly, making a humming sound

hum·mock (hum'ək) *n.* [< ?] a low, rounded hill; knoll

hu·mon·gous (hyōō mäŋ'gəs, hyōō muŋ'-) *adj.* [? a blend of *huge, monstrous.* etc.] [Slang] enormous

hu·mor (hyōō'mər, yōō'-) *n.* [< L. *humor*, fluid: after former belief in four body fluids (humors) held responsible for one's disposition] 1. mood; state of mind 2. whim; caprice 3. a comical quality 4. *a)* the ability to appreciate or express what is funny, amusing, etc. *b)* the expression of this —*vt.* to comply with the mood or whim of; indulge —**out of humor** not in a good mood; disagreeable Brit. *sp.* **humour** — **hu′mor·ist** *n.*

hu·mor·ous *adj.* funny; amusing; comical —**hu′mor·ous·ly** *adv.*

hump (hump) *n.* [< ?] a rounded, protruding lump, as on a camel's back —*vt.* to hunch; arch —**over the hump** [Colloq.] past the difficult point

hump′back′ *n.* 1. a humped, deformed back 2. a person having this —**hump′backed′** *adj.*

hu·mus (hyōō′məs) *n.* [L., earth] the dark part of the soil, resulting from the partial decay of leaves, etc.

Hun (hun) *n.* a member of a warlike Asiatic people who invaded Europe in the 4th and 5th centuries A.D.

hunch (hunch) *vt.* [< ?] to arch into a hump —*vi.* to move forward jerkily —*n.* 1. a hump 2. [Colloq.] a feeling that something is going to happen

hunch′back′ *n.* same as HUMPBACK

hun·dred (hun′drid) *n., adj.* [OE.] ten times ten; 100; C —**hun′dredth** (-dridth) *adj., n.*

hun′dred·fold′ *adj., adv.* a hundred times as much or as many

hun′dred·weight′ *n.* a unit of weight, equal to 100 pounds in the U.S. and 112 pounds in England

hung (huŋ) *pt. & pp.* of HANG — **hung over** [Slang] having a hangover —**hung up (on)** [Slang] emotionally disturbed, frustrated, or obsessed (by)

Hung. 1. Hungarian 2. Hungary

Hun·gar·i·an (huŋ ger′ē ən) *adj.* of Hungary, its people, etc. —*n.* 1. a native or inhabitant of Hungary 2. the language of the Hungarians

Hun·ga·ry (huŋ′gər ē) country in SC Europe: 35,919 sq. mi.; pop. 10,231,000

hun·ger (huŋ′gər) *n.* [OE. *hungor*] 1. discomfort caused by a need for food 2. starvation 3. a desire for food 4. any strong desire —*vi.* 1. to be hungry 2. to desire —**hun′gri·ly** *adv.* —**hun′gry** *adj.* **-gri·er, -gri·est**

hunger strike a refusal of a prisoner, protester, etc. to eat until certain demands are granted

hunk (huŋk) *n.* [Fl. *hunke*] [Colloq.] a large piece, lump, etc.

hun·ker (huŋ′kər) *vi.* [< dial.] to squat —*n.* [*pl.*] haunches or buttocks

hunt (hunt) *vt., vi.* [OE. *huntian*] 1. to kill or catch (game) for food or sport 2. to try to find; search; seek 3. to chase; harry —*n.* 1. a hunting 2. a group of people who hunt together 3. a search —**hunt′er, hunts′man** *n., pl.* **-men** —**hunt′ress** *n.fem.*

Hun·ting·ton Beach (hun′tiŋ tən) city in SW Calif.: pop. 171,000

Hunts·ville (hunts′vil′) city in N Ala.: pop. 143,000

hur·dle (hur′d'l) *n.* [OE. *hyrdel*] 1. a framelike barrier which horses or runners must leap in a race 2. an obstacle —*vt.* **-dled, -dling** 1. to jump over 2. to overcome (an obstacle) —**hur′dler** *n.*

HURDLES

hur·dy-gur·dy (hur′dē gur′dē) *n., pl.* **-dies** [? echoic] same as BARREL ORGAN

hurl (hurl) *vt.* [prob. < ON.] 1. to throw with force or violence 2. to cast down 3. to utter vehemently —*vi.* [Colloq.] *Baseball* to pitch —**hurl′er** *n.*

hurl·y-burl·y (hur′lē bur′lē) *n., pl.* **-burl′ies** a turmoil; uproar

Hu·ron (hyoor′ən), **Lake** one of the Great Lakes, between Mich.& Canada

hur·rah (hə rô′, -rä′) *interj., n.* [echoic] a shout of joy, approval, etc. —*vi.* to shout "hurrah"; cheer Also **hur·ray′** (-rā′)

hur·ri·cane (hur′ə kān′) *n.* [< WInd. *huracan*] a violent tropical cyclone

hurricane lamp 1. an oil lamp or candlestick with a glass chimney to protect the flame 2. an electric lamp like this

hur·ry (hur′ē) *vt.* **-ried, -ry·ing** [prob. akin to HURL] 1. to move or send with haste 2. to cause to occur or be done more rapidly or too rapidly 3. to urge to act soon or too soon —*vi.* to move or act with haste —*n.* 1. rush; urgency 2. eagerness to do, go, etc. quickly —**hur′ried·ly** *adv.*

hurt (hurt) *vt.* **hurt, hurt′ing** [< OFr. *hurier*, to hit] 1. to cause pain or injury to 2. to harm 3. to offend —*vi.* 1. to cause pain, injury, etc. 2. to have pain; be sore —*n.* 1. a pain or injury 2. harm; damage

hurt′ful *adj.* causing hurt; harmful

hur·tle (hurt′'l) *vi., vt.* **-tled, -tling** [ME. *hurtlen*] to move or throw with great speed or much force

hus·band (huz′bənd) *n.* [< ON. *hús*, house + *bondi*, freeholder] a married man —*vt.* to manage economically; conserve

hus′band·man (-mən) *n., pl.* **-men** [Archaic] a farmer

hus′band·ry *n.* 1. careful, thrifty management 2. farming

hush (hush) *vt., vi.* [< ME. *huscht*, quiet] 1. to make or become quiet or silent 2. to soothe; lull —*n.* quiet; silence —*interj.* an exclamation calling for silence

hush′-hush′ *adj.* [Colloq.] very secret

hush puppy [South] a cornmeal fritter

husk (husk) *n.* [prob. < MDu. *huus*, house] 1. the dry outer covering of various fruits or seeds, as of corn 2. any dry, rough, or useless covering —*vt.* to remove the husk from

hus·ky¹ (hus′kē) n., pl. **-kies** [< ? ESKIMO] [also H-] same as ESKIMO DOG

husk·y² (hus′kē) adj. **-i·er, -i·est** 1. dry in the throat; hoarse 2. [< toughness of a HUSK] big and strong

hus·sar (hoo zär′) n. [< Serb. husar] a European light-armed cavalryman, usually with a brilliant dress uniform

hus·sy (huz′ē, hus′ē) n., pl. **-sies** [< ME. huswife, housewife] 1. a woman of low morals 2. a bold, saucy girl

hus·tings (hus′tiŋz) n.pl. [usually with sing. v.] [OE. hūsthing, house council] the process of, or a place for, political campaigning

hus·tle (hus′'l) vt. **-tled, -tling** [Du. husselen, shake up] 1. to push about; jostle 2. to force in a rough, hurried manner —vi. 1. to move hurriedly 2. [Colloq.] to work energetically 3. [Slang] to obtain money aggressively or immorally —n. 1. a hustling 2. [Colloq.] energetic action; drive —hus′tler n.

hut (hut) n. [< OHG. hutta] a very plain or crude little house or cabin

hutch (huch) n. [< ML. hutica, chest] 1. a chest or cupboard 2. a pen or coop for small animals 3. a hut

hutz·pah (hoots′pə) n. same as CHUTZPAH

huz·zah, huz·za (hə zä′) interj., n., vi. former var. of HURRAH

Hwang Ho (hwäŋ′ hō′) river in N China, flowing into the Yellow Sea

hwy. highway

hy·a·cinth (hī′ə sinth′) n. [< Gr. hyakinthos] a plant of the lily family, with spikes of bell-shaped flowers

hy·brid (hī′brid) n. [L. hybrida] 1. the offspring of two animals or plants of different species, varieties, etc. 2. anything of mixed origin —adj. of or like a hybrid —hy′brid·ism n.

hy·brid·ize (hī′brə dīz′) vt., vi. **-ized′, -iz′ing** to produce or cause to produce hybrids; crossbreed

Hy·der·a·bad (hī′dər ə bad′) city in SC India: pop. 1,119,000

hy·dra (hī′drə) n., pl. **-dras, -drae** (-drē) [< Gr. water serpent] a small, freshwater polyp with a soft, tubelike body

hy·dran·ge·a (hī drān′jə, -dran′-jē ə) n. [< HYDRO- + Gr. angeion, vessel] a shrub with large, showy clusters of white, blue, or pink flowers

hy·drant (hī′drənt) n. [< Gr. hydōr, water] a large pipe with a valve for drawing water from a water main

hy·drate (hī′drāt) n. [HYDRO(O)- + -ATE²] a chemical compound of water and some other substance

hy·drau·lic (hī drô′lik) adj. [ult. < Gr. hydōr, water + aulos, tube] 1. of hydraulics 2. operated by the movement and force of liquid [hydraulic brakes] —hy·drau′li·cal·ly adv.

hy·drau·lics n.pl. [with sing. v.] the science dealing with the mechanical properties of liquids, as water, and their application in engineering

hydro- [< Gr. hydōr, water] a combining form meaning: 1. water [hydrometer] 2. hydrogen [hydrocarbon]

hy·dro·car·bon (hī′drə kär′bən) n. any compound containing only hydrogen and carbon

hy·dro·chlo·ric acid (hī′drə klôr′ik) a strong, highly corrosive acid, that is a solution of the gas hydrogen chloride in water

hy·dro·e·lec·tric (hī′drō i lek′trik) adj. producing, or relating to the production, of electricity by water power —hy′dro·e·lec′tric′i·ty n.

hy·dro·fluor·ic acid (hī′drə flôr′ik, -floor′-) a colorless, corrosive acid, used in etching glass

hy·dro·foil (hī′drə foil′) n. [HYDRO- + (AIR)FOIL] 1. a winglike structure that lifts and carries a watercraft just above the water at high speed 2. such a watercraft

hy·dro·gen (hī′drə jən) n. [see HYDRO- & -GEN] a flammable, colorless, odorless, gaseous chemical element: the lightest known substance

hy·dro·gen·ate (hī′drə jə nāt′, hī-dräj′ə-) vt. **-at′ed, -at′ing** to combine with or treat with hydrogen [oil is hydrogenated to make a solid fat]

hydrogen bomb an extremely destructive atom bomb in which atoms of hydrogen are fused by explosion of a nuclear-fission unit in the bomb

hydrogen peroxide an unstable liquid used as a bleach or disinfectant

hy·drol·y·sis (hī dräl′ə sis) n., pl. **-ses** (-sēz′) [HYDRO- + -LYSIS] a chemical reaction in which a compound reacts with the ions of water to produce a weak acid, a weak base, or both

hy·drom·e·ter (hī dräm′ə tər) n. [HYDRO- + -METER] an instrument for determining the specific gravity of liquids

hy·dro·pho·bi·a (hī′drə fō′bē ə) n. [see HYDRO- & -PHOBIA] 1. an abnormal fear of water 2. [from the symptomatic inability to swallow liquids] same as RABIES

hy·dro·plane (hī′drə plān′) n. [HYDRO- + PLANE¹] 1. a small, high-speed motorboat with hydrofoils or a flat bottom 2. same as SEAPLANE

hy·dro·pon·ics (hī′drə pän′iks) n.pl. [with sing. v.] [< HYDRO- & Gr. ponos, labor] the science of growing plants in liquid mineral solutions

hy′dro·ther′a·py (-ther′ə pē) n. the treatment of disease, etc. by the use of water

hy·drous (hī′drəs) adj. [HYDR(O)- + -OUS] containing water, esp. in chemical combination

hy·drox·ide (hī dräk′sīd) n. [HYDR(O)- + OXIDE] a compound consisting of an element or radical combined with the radical OH

hy·e·na (hī ē′nə) n. [< Gr. hyaina] a wolflike, flesh-eating animal of Africa and Asia, with a shrill cry

hy·giene (hī′jēn) n. [Gr. hygiēs, healthy] 1. a system of principles for preserving health 2. cleanliness

hy·gi·en·ic (hī′jē en′ik, -jē′nik, -jen′ik) adj. 1. of hygiene or health 2. sanitary —hy′gi·en′i·cal·ly adv.

hy·grom·e·ter (hī gräm′ə tər) n. [< Gr. hygros, wet + -METER] an instrument for measuring humidity

hy·men (hī′mən) *n.* [Gr. *hymēn,* membrane] the thin mucous membrane that usually closes part of the opening of the vagina in a virgin

hy·me·ne·al (hī′mə nē′əl) *adj.* [< *Hymen,* Gr. god of marriage] of a wedding or marriage

hymn (him) *n.* [< Gr. *hymnos*] a song of praise, esp. in honor of God

hym·nal (him′nəl) *n.* a collection of hymns: also **hymn′book′**

hype (hīp) *n.* [Slang] 1. *same as* HYPODERMIC 2. a drug addict 3. deception, esp. exaggerated promotion —*vt.* **hyped, hyp′ing** [Slang] 1. to stimulate, excite, etc. as by a drug injection: usually with *up* 2. to promote in a sensational way

hyper- [Gr. < *hyper*] *a prefix meaning* over, above, excessive

hy·per·bo·le (hī pur′bə lē) *n.* [L. < Gr. < *hyper-,* above + *ballein,* throw] exaggeration for effect, not meant to be taken literally —**hy·per·bol·ic** (hī′pər bäl′ik) *adj.*

hy·per·crit·i·cal (hī′pər krit′i k'l) *adj.* too critical

hy·per·sen·si·tive (hī′pər sen′sə tiv) *adj.* excessively sensitive —**hy′per·sen′si·tiv′i·ty** *n.*

hy·per·ten·sion (hī′pər ten′shən) *n.* abnormally high blood pressure

hy′per·thy′roid·ism (-thī′roid iz′m) *n.* excessive activity of the thyroid gland, causing nervousness, rapid pulse, etc. —**hy′per·thy′roid** *adj., n.*

hy·per·tro·phy (hī pur′trə fē) *n.* [< HYPER- + Gr. *trephein,* to nourish] abnormal increase in the size of an organ or tissue —*vi., vt.* **-phied, -phy·ing** to increase abnormally in size

hy·phen (hī′f'n) *n.* [< Gr. *hypo-,* under + *hen,* one] a mark (-) used between the parts of a compound word or the syllables of a divided word, as at the end of a line —*vt.* to hyphenate

hy′phen·ate′ (-āt′) *vt.* **-at′ed, -at′ing** to join or write with a hyphen —**hy′phen·a′tion** *n.*

hyp·no·sis (hip nō′sis) *n., pl.* **-ses** (-sēz) [< Gr. *hypnos,* sleep + -OSIS] a sleeplike condition psychically induced, in which the subject responds to the suggestions of the hypnotist

hyp·not·ic (hip nät′ik) *adj.* 1. causing sleep; soporific 2. of, like, or inducing hypnosis —*n.* any agent causing hypnosis —**hyp·not′i·cal·ly** *adv.*

hyp·no·tism (hip′nə tiz′m) *n.* the act or practice of inducing hypnosis —**hyp′no·tist** *n.*

hyp′no·tize′ (-tīz′) *vt.* **-tized′, -tiz′ing** to induce hypnosis in

hy·po (hī′pō) *n., pl.* **-pos** *short for* HYPODERMIC

hypo- [Gr. < *hypo,* less than] *a prefix meaning:* 1. under, beneath [*hypodermic*] 2. less than [*hypothyroid*]

hy·po·chon·dri·a (hī′pə kän′drē ə) *n.* [LL., pl.: abdomen (supposed seat of this condition)] abnormal anxiety over one's health, often with imaginary illnesses —**hy′po·chon′dri·ac′** (-ak′) *n., adj.*

hy·poc·ri·sy (hi päk′rə sē) *n., pl.* **-sies** [< Gr. *hypokrisis,* acting a part] a pretending to be what one is not, or to feel what one does not; esp., a pretense of virtue, piety, etc.

hyp·o·crite (hip′ə krit) *n.* [see prec.] one who pretends to be pious, virtuous, etc. without really being so —**hyp′o·crit′i·cal** *adj.*

hy·po·der·mic (hī′pə dur′mik) *adj.* [< HYPO- + Gr. *derma,* skin] injected under the skin —*n.* a hypodermic syringe, needle, or injection

hypodermic syringe a syringe attached to a hollow needle (**hypodermic needle**) used for the injection of a medicine or drug under the skin

hy·pot·e·nuse (hī pät′'n ōōs′) *n.* [< Gr. *hypoteinein,* under + *teinein,* stretch] the side of a right-angled triangle opposite the right angle

hy·poth·e·sis (hī päth′ə sis, hi-) *n., pl.* **-ses′** (-sēz′) [< Gr. *hypo,* under + *tithenai,* to place] an unproved theory, etc. tentatively accepted to explain certain facts —**hy·poth′e·size′** (-sīz′) *vt., vi.* **-sized′, -siz′ing**

hy·po·thet·i·cal (hī′pə thet′i k'l) *adj.* based on a hypothesis; assumed; supposed —**hy′po·thet′i·cal·ly** *adv.*

hy·po·thy′roid·ism (hī′pō thī′roid iz′m) *n.* deficient activity of the thyroid gland, causing sluggishness, goiter, etc. —**hy′po·thy′roid** *adj., n.*

hys·sop (his′əp) *n.* [< Heb. *ēzōbh*] a fragrant, blue-flowered plant of the mint family

hys·ter·ec·to·my (his′tə rek′tə mē) *n., pl.* **-mies** [< Gr. *hystera,* uterus + -ECTOMY] surgical removal of the uterus

hys·te·ri·a (his tir′ē ə, -ter′-) *n.* [< Gr. *hystera,* uterus: orig. attributed to disturbances of the uterus] 1. a psychiatric condition characterized by excitability, anxiety, the simulation of organic disorders, etc. 2. any outbreak of wild, uncontrolled feeling: also **hys·ter′ics** (-ter′iks) —**hys·ter′i·cal** (-ter′-), **hys·ter′ic** *adj.* —**hys·ter′i·cal·ly** *adv.*

Hz, hz hertz

I

I, i (I) *n., pl.* **I's, i's** the ninth letter of the English alphabet

I¹ (I) *n.* **1.** a Roman numeral for 1 **2.** *Chem.* iodine

I² (I) *pron., for pl. see* WE [OE. *ic*] the person speaking or writing

i., i. **1.** island(s) **2.** isle(s)

Ia., IA Iowa

-i·al (ē əl, yəl) [L. *-ialis*] *same as* -AL

i·am·bic (ī am′bik) *n.* [< Gr. *iambos*] a metrical foot of two syllables, the first unaccented and the other accented —*adj.* in iambics

-i·at·rics (ē at′riks) [< Gr. *iatros*, physician] *a combining form meaning* treatment of disease [*pediatrics*]

-i·a·try (ī′ə trē) [< Gr. *iatreia*, healing] *a combining form meaning* medical treatment [*psychiatry*]

I·be·ri·a (ī bir′ē ə) the Spanish-Portuguese peninsula: also **Iberian Peninsula** —**I·be′ri·an** *adj., n.*

i·bex (ī′beks) *n., pl.* **i′bex·es, i·bi·ces** (ib′ə sēz′) [L.] a wild goat of Europe, Asia, or Africa, with large, backward-curved horns

ibid. [L. *ibidem*] in the same place, i.e., the book, page, etc. just cited

i·bis (ī′bis) *n.* [< Egypt. *hīb*] a large wading bird related to the herons

-i·ble (i b'l, ə b'l) [L. *-ibilis*] *same as* -ABLE —**-i·bil·i·ty** (ə bil′ə tē)

Ib·sen (ib′s'n), **Hen·rik** (hen′rik) 1828-1906; Norw. playwright

-ic (ik) [< Gr. *-ikos*] *a suffix meaning:* **1.** *a)* of, having to do with [*volcanic*] *b)* like [*angelic*] *c)* produced by [*photographic*] *d)* consisting of, containing [*alcoholic*] **2.** a person or thing *a)* having [*paraplegic*] *b)* supporting [*Socratic*] *c)* producing [*hypnotic*] Also **-i·cal** (i k'l, ə k'l)

ICBM intercontinental ballistic missile

ICC, I.C.C. Interstate Commerce Commission

ice (īs) *n.* [OE. *is*] **1.** water frozen solid by cold **2.** a frozen dessert of fruit juice, sugar, etc. **3.** [Slang] diamonds —*vt.* **iced, ic′ing 1.** to change into ice; freeze **2.** to cool with ice **3.** to cover with icing —*vi.* to freeze (often with *up* or *over*) —**break the ice** to make a start, as in getting acquainted —**cut no ice** [Colloq.] to have no influence —**on thin ice** [Colloq.] in danger

Ice. 1. Iceland **2.** Icelandic

ice age *same as* GLACIAL EPOCH

ice′berg′ (-burg′) *n.* [prob. < Du. *ijsberg*, lit., ice mountain] a great mass of ice broken off from a glacier and floating in the sea

ice′bound′ (-bound′) *adj.* held fast or shut in by ice

ice′box′ (-bäks′) *n.* a refrigerator, esp. one in which ice is used

ice′break′er *n.* a sturdy boat for breaking a channel through ice

ice′cap′ *n.* a mass of glacial ice spreading slowly from a center

ice cream a sweet, frozen food made from flavored cream or milk —**ice′-cream′** *adj.*

ice floe a piece of floating sea ice

ice hockey *same as* HOCKEY (sense 1)

Ice·land (īs′lənd) island country in the N. Atlantic, southeast of Greenland: 39,768 sq. mi.; pop. 192,000 —**Ice′land·er** *n.*

Ice·lan·dic (īs lan′dik) *adj.* of Iceland, its people, etc. —*n.* the Germanic language of the Icelanders

ice′man′ (-man′, -mən) *n., pl.* **-men′** one who sells or delivers ice

ice milk a frozen dessert like ice cream, but with less butterfat

ice skate *see* SKATE¹ (sense 1) —**ice′-skate′** *vi.*

ich·thy·ol·o·gy (ik′thē äl′ə jē) *n.* [< Gr. *ichthys*, a fish + -LOGY] the branch of zoology dealing with fishes —**ich′thy·ol′o·gist** *n.*

i·ci·cle (ī′si k'l) *n.* [< OE. *is*, ice + *gicel*, piece of ice] a hanging piece of ice, formed by the freezing of dripping water

ic·ing (ī′siŋ) *n.* a mixture of sugar, flavoring, egg whites, etc. for covering a cake; frosting

ick·y (ik′ē) *adj.* **-i·er, -i·est** [< STICKY] [Slang] **1.** unpleasantly sticky or sweet **2.** very distasteful

i·con (ī′kän) *n.* [< Gr. *eikōn*, image] **1.** an image; figure **2.** *Orthodox Eastern Ch.,* a sacred image or picture of Jesus, Mary, etc.

i·con·o·clast (ī kän′ə klast′) *n.* [< LGr. *eikōn*, image + *klaein*, to break] one who attacks venerated institutions or ideas —**i·con′o·clas′tic** *adj.*

-ics (iks) [see -IC] *a suffix meaning* art, science, study [*physics*]

i·cy (ī′sē) *adj.* **i′ci·er, i′ci·est 1.** full of or covered with ice **2.** of ice **3.** like ice; slippery or very cold **4.** cold in manner; unfriendly —**i′ci·ly** *adv.* —**i′ci·ness** *n.*

id (id) *n.* [L., it] *Psychoanalysis* that part of the psyche which is the source of psychic energy

I'd (īd) **1.** I had **2.** I would **3.** I should

ID, I.D. identification

I·da·ho (ī′də hō′) Northwestern State of the U.S.: 83,557 sq. mi.; pop. 944,000; cap. Boise: abbrev. **Ida., ID**

i·de·a (ī dē′ə) *n.* [< Gr. *idea*, appearance of a thing] **1.** a thought; mental conception or image **2.** an opinion or belief **3.** a plan; scheme **4.** meaning or significance

i·de·al (ī dē′əl) *adj.* [see prec.] **1.** existing as an idea, model, etc. **2.** thought of as perfect **3.** existing only in the mind; imaginary —*n.* **1.** a conception of something in its most excellent form 2. a perfect model 3. a goal or principle

i·de·al·ism *n.* 1. behavior or thought based on a conception of things as one thinks they should be 2. a striving to achieve one's ideals —**i·de′al·ist** *n.* —**i′de·al·is′tic** *adj.*

i·de·al·ize (ī dē′ə līz′) *vt.* -ized′, -iz′ing to regard or show as perfect or more nearly perfect than is true —**i·de′al·i·za′tion** *n.*

i·de′al·ly *adv.* 1. in an ideal manner; perfectly 2. in theory

i·den·ti·cal (ī den′ti k'l) *adj.* [< L. *idem*, the same] 1. the very same 2. exactly alike —**i·den′ti·cal·ly** *adv.*

i·den·ti·fi·ca·tion (ī den′tə fi kā′shən, i-) *n.* 1. an identifying or being identified 2. anything by which one can be identified

i·den·ti·fy (ī den′tə fī′, i-) *vt.* -fied′, -fy′ing 1. to make identical; treat as the same 2. to fix the identity of 3. to connect or associate closely

i·den·ti·ty (ī den′tə tē, i-) *n., pl.* -ties 1. the state or fact of being the same 2. *a)* the state or fact of being some specific person or thing; individuality *b)* the state of being as described

identity crisis the state of being uncertain about oneself, one's character, goals, etc., esp. in adolescence

id·e·o·gram (id′ē ə gram′, ī′dē-) *n.* [see IDEA & -GRAM] a symbol representing an object or idea without expressing the word for it: also **id′e·o·graph′**

i·de·ol·o·gy (ī′dē äl′ə jē, id′ē-) *n., pl.* -gies [< Gr. *idea*, idea + *logos*, word] the doctrines, opinions, etc. of an individual, class, etc. —**i′de·o·log′i·cal** (-ə läj′i k'l) *adj.*

ides (īdz) *n.pl.* [< L. *idus*] in the ancient Roman calendar, the 15th day of March, May, July, or October, or the 13th of the other months

id·i·o·cy (id′ē ə sē) *n., pl.* -cies 1. great foolishness or stupidity 2. an idiotic act or remark

id·i·om (id′ē əm) *n.* [< Gr. *idios*, one's own] 1. the dialect of a people, region, etc. 2. the usual way in which words of a language are joined together to express thought 3. an accepted phrase or expression having a meaning different from the literal 4. a characteristic style, as in art or music —**id′i·o·mat′ic** (-ə mat′ik) *adj.*

id·i·o·path·ic (id′ē ə path′ik) *adj.* [< Gr. *idios*, one's own + -PATHIC] of a disease whose cause is unknown

id·i·o·syn·cra·sy (id′ē ə sin′krə sē) *n., pl.* -sies [< Gr. *idio-*, one's own + *synkrasis*, a mixture] any personal peculiarity, mannerism, etc.

id·i·ot (id′ē ət) *n.* [< Gr. *idiōtēs*, ignorant person] 1. an adult mentally inferior to a child of three: an obsolescent term 2. a very foolish or stupid person —**id′i·ot′ic** (-ät′ik) *adj.* —**id′i·ot′i·cal·ly** *adv.*

i·dle (ī′d'l) *adj.* **i′dler, i′dlest** [OE. *idel*, empty] 1. useless; futile 2. un-

founded [*idle rumors*] 3. *a)* unemployed; not busy *b)* inactive; not in use 4. lazy —*vi.* **i′dled, i′dling** 1. to move slowly or aimlessly 2. to be unemployed or inactive 3. to operate without transmitting power [the motor *idled*] —*vt.* 1. to waste 2. to cause (a motor, etc.) to idle —**i′dle·ness** *n.* —**i′dler** *n.* —**i′dly** *adv.*

i·dol (ī′d'l) *n.* [< Gr. *eidōlon*, image] 1. an image of a god, used as an object of worship 2. any object of ardent or excessive devotion

i·dol·a·try (ī däl′ə trē) *n., pl.* -tries 1. worship of idols 2. excessive devotion to or reverence for some person or thing —**i·dol′a·ter** *n.* —**i·dol′a·trous** *adj.*

i·dol·ize (ī′d'l īz′) *vt.* -ized′, -iz′ing 1. to make an idol of 2. to love or admire excessively

i·dyll, i·dyl (ī′d'l) *n.* [< Gr. *eidos*, a form] 1. a short poem or prose work describing a simple, pleasant scene of rural or pastoral life 2. a scene or incident suitable for such a work —**i·dyl·lic** (ī dil′ik) *adj.*

-ie (ē) (earlier form of -Y¹) a suffix meaning: 1. small, little [*lassie*] 2. one that is as specified [*a softie*]

IE. Indo-European

i.e. [L. *id est*] that is (to say)

-i·er (ir, ər, ē′ər) [< L. *-arius*] a suffix meaning a person concerned with (a specified action or thing) [*bombardier*]

if (if) *conj.* [OE. *gif*] 1. on condition that; in case that [*if* I were you, I'd quit] 2. allowing that [*if* he was there, I didn't see him] 3. whether [ask him *if* he knows her] —**as if** as it would be if

if·fy (if′ē) *adj.* [Colloq.] containing doubtful elements; not definite

ig·loo (ig′loo) *n., pl.* -loos [Esk. *igdlu*] an Eskimo hut, usually dome-shaped and built of blocks of packed snow

IGLOO

ig·ne·ous (ig′nē əs) *adj.* [< L. *ignis*, a fire] 1. of fire 2. produced by volcanic action or intense heat [*igneous* rock]

ig·nite (ig nīt′) *vt.* -nit′ed, -nit′ing [see prec.] to set fire to —*vi.* to catch fire; start burning —**ig·nit′a·ble, ig·nit′i·ble** *adj.*

ig·ni·tion (ig nish′ən) *n.* 1. an igniting or being ignited 2. the system for igniting the explosive mixture in the cylinder of an internal-combustion engine

ig·no·ble (ig nō′b'l) *adj.* [< L. *in-*, not + (g)*nobilis*, known] not noble; base; mean —**ig·no′bly** *adv.*

ig·no·min·y (ig′nə min′ē) *n., pl.* -ies [< L. *in-*, without + *nomen*, name] loss of reputation; shame; disgrace —**ig′no·min′i·ous** *adj.* —**ig′no·min′i·ous·ly** *adv.*

---

fat, āpe, cär; ten, ēven; is, bīte; gō, hôrn, tōōl, look; oil, out; up, fur; chin; she; thin, then; zh, leisure; ŋ, ring; ə for a in ago; ′, (ā′b'l); ä, Fr. coeur; ö, Fr. feu; Fr. mon; ü, Fr. duc; kh, G. ich, doch; ‡ foreign; < derived from

ig·no·ra·mus (ig′nə rā′məs) *n., pl.* **-mus·es** an ignorant person

ig′no·rant *adj.* [see ff.] **1.** lacking knowledge or experience **2.** caused by or showing lack of knowledge **3.** unaware (*of*) —**ig′no·rance** *n.* —**ig′no·rant·ly** *adv.*

ig·nore (ig nôr′) *vt.* -nored′, -nor′ing [< L. *in-*, not + *gnarus*, knowing] to disregard; pay no attention to

i·gua·na (i gwä′nə) *n.* [< SAmInd.] a large tropical American lizard

il- *same as:* **1.** IN-¹ **2.** IN-² Used before *l-*

Il·i·ad (il′ē əd) [< Gr. *Ilios*, Troy] a Greek epic poem, ascribed to Homer, about the Trojan War

ilk (ilk) *n.* [< OE. *ilca*, same] kind; sort; class: only in *that* (or *his, her, etc.*) *ilk*

ill (il) *adj.* worse, worst [< ON. *illr*] **1.** bad [*ill* repute, *ill* will, an *ill* omen] **2.** not well; sick —*n.* an evil or disease —*adv.* worse, worst **1.** badly **2.** scarcely [*I can ill afford it*] —**ill at ease** uncomfortable

I'll (īl) **1.** I shall **2.** I will

Ill., IL Illinois

ill′-ad·vised′ *adj.* showing or resulting from poor advice; unwise

ill′-bred′ *adj.* rude; impolite

il·le·gal (i lē′gəl) *adj.* prohibited by law; against the law —**il·le·gal·i·ty** (il′ē gal′ə tē) *n.* —**il·le′gal·ly** *adv.*

il·leg·i·ble (i lej′ə b'l) *adj.* hard or impossible to read because badly written or printed —**il·leg′i·bly** *adv.*

il·le·git·i·mate (il′ə jit′ə mit) *adj.* **1.** born of parents not married to each other **2.** contrary to law, rules, or logic —**il′le·git′i·ma·cy** (-mə sē) *n.*

ill′-fat′ed *adj.* **1.** certain to have an evil fate or unlucky end **2.** unlucky

ill′-fa′vored *adj.* ugly or unpleasant

ill′-got′ten *adj.* obtained by evil, unlawful, or dishonest means

il·lib·er·al (i lib′ər əl) *adj.* **1.** narrow-minded **2.** not generous

il·lic·it (i lis′it) *adj.* [< L. *illicitus*, not allowed] unlawful; improper —**il·lic′it·ly** *adv.* —**il·lic′it·ness** *n.*

il·lim·it·a·ble (i lim′it ə b'l) *adj.* without limit; immeasurable

Il·li·nois (il′ə noi′) Middle Western State of the U.S.: 56,400 sq. mi.; pop. 11,418,000; cap. Springfield —**Il′li·nois′an** *adj., n.*

il·lit·er·ate (i lit′ər it) *adj.* uneducated; esp., not knowing how to read or write —*n.* an illiterate person —**il·lit′er·a·cy** (-ə sē) *n.*

ill′-man′nered *adj.* having bad manners; rude; impolite

ill nature a disagreeable or mean disposition —**ill′-na′tured** *adj.*

ill′ness *n.* the condition of being in poor health; sickness; disease

il·log·i·cal (i läj′i k'l) *adj.* not logical or reasonable —**il·log′i·cal·ly** *adv.*

ill-starred (il′stärd′) *adj.* unlucky

ill′-suit′ed *adj.* not suited or appropriate

ill′-tem′pered *adj.* sullen; irritable

ill′-timed′ *adj.* inopportune

ill′-treat′ *vt.* to treat unkindly, unfairly, etc. —**ill′-treat′ment** *n.*

il·lu·mi·nate (i lōō′mə nāt′) *vt.* -nat′ed, -nat′ing [< L. *in-*, in + *luminare*, to light] **1.** to give light to; light up **2.** *a)* to make clear; explain *b)* to inform **3.** to decorate as with lights —**il·lu′mi·na·ble** *adj.*

il·lu′mi·na′tion *n.* **1.** an illuminating **2.** the intensity of light

il·lu′mine (-min) *vt.* -mined, -min·ing to light up

illus. illustration

ill-us·age (il′yōō′sij, -zij) *n.* unkind or cruel treatment: also **ill usage**

ill′-use′ (-yōōz′; *for n.* -yōōs′) *vt.* -used′, -us′ing to abuse —*n.* same as **ILL-USAGE**

il·lu·sion (i lōō′zhən) *n.* [< L. *illudere*, to mock] **1.** a false idea or conception **2.** an unreal or misleading appearance or image —**il·lu′so·ry** (-sər ē), **il·lu′sive** (-siv) *adj.*

il·lus·trate (il′ə strāt′) *vt.* -trat′ed, -trat′ing [< L. *in-*, in + *lustrare*, illuminate] **1.** to explain; make clear, as by examples **2.** to furnish (books, etc.) with explanatory or decorative pictures, etc. —**il′lus·tra′tor** *n.*

il′lus·tra′tion *n.* **1.** an illustrating **2.** an example, etc. used to help explain **3.** a picture, diagram, etc. used to decorate or explain

il·lus·tra·tive (i lus′trə tiv) *adj.* serving as an illustration or example

il·lus·tri·ous (i lus′trē əs) *adj.* [< L. *illustris*, clear] distinguished; famous; outstanding —**il·lus′tri·ous·ly** *adv.* —**il·lus′tri·ous·ness** *n.*

ill will hostility; hate; dislike

I'm (īm) I am

im- *same as:* **1.** IN-¹ **2.** IN-² Used before *b, m,* and *p*

im·age (im′ij) *n.* [< L. *imago*] **1.** a representation of a person or thing; esp., a statue **2.** the visual impression of something in a lens, mirror, etc. **3.** a copy; likeness **4.** *a)* a mental picture; idea *b)* the concept of a person, product, etc. held by the general public **5.** a metaphor or simile —*vt.* -aged, -ag·ing **1.** to make a representation of **2.** to reflect **3.** to imagine

im·age·ry (im′ij rē) *n.* **1.** mental images **2.** figurative language

i·mag·i·na·ble (i maj′ə nə b'l) *adj.* that can be imagined

i·mag′i·nar′y (-ner′ē) *adj.* existing only in the imagination; unreal

i·mag′i·na′tion (-nā′shən) *n.* **1.** *a)* the act or power of forming mental images of what is not present *b)* the act or power of creating new ideas by combining previous experiences **2.** the ability to understand the imaginative creations of others **3.** resourcefulness

i·mag′i·na·tive (-nə tiv) *adj.* **1.** having, using, or showing imagination **2.** of or resulting from imagination —**i·mag′i·na·tive·ly** *adv.*

i·mag·ine (i maj′in) *vt., vi.* -ined, -in·ing [< L. *imago*, image] **1.** to make a mental image (of); conceive in the mind **2.** to suppose; think

im·bal·ance (im bal′əns) *n.* lack of balance, as in proportion or force

im·be·cile (im′bə s'l) *n.* [< L.

imbecilis, feeble] 1. an adult mentally equal to a child between three and eight: an obsolescent term 2. a foolish or stupid person —*adj.* foolish or stupid: also **im'be·cil'ic** (-sil'ik) —**im'be·cil'i·ty** *n.*

im·bed (im bed') *vt. same as* EMBED

im·bibe (im bīb') *vt.* -**bibed'**, -**bib'ing** [< L. *in-*, in + *bibere*, to drink] 1. to drink (esp. alcoholic liquor) 2. to absorb into the mind —*vi.* to drink, esp. alcoholic liquor

im·bro·glio (im brōl'yō) *n., pl.* -**glios** [It. < *imbrogliare*, embroil] 1. an involved, confusing situation 2. a confused misunderstanding

im·bue (im byōō') *vt.* -**bued'**, -**bu'ing** [< L. *imbuere*, to wet] 1. to dye 2. to permeate (*with* ideas, feelings, etc.)

im·i·tate (im'ə tāt') *vt.* -**tat'ed**, -**tat'ing** [< L. *imitari*] 1. to seek to follow the example of 2. to mimic 3. to reproduce in form, color, etc. 4. to resemble —**im'i·ta'tor** *n.*

im'i·ta'tion *n.* 1. an imitating 2. the result of imitating; copy —*adj.* not real; sham [*imitation* leather] —**im'i·ta'tive** *adj.*

im·mac·u·late (i mak'yə lit) *adj.* [< L. *in-*, not + *macula*, a spot] 1. perfectly clean 2. without a flaw or error 3. pure; innocent; sinless —**im·mac'u·late·ly** *adv.* —**im·mac'u·late·ness** *n.*

im·ma·nent (im'ə nənt) *adj.* [< L. *in-*, in + *manere*, remain] 1. operating within; inherent 2. present throughout the universe: said of God —**im'ma·nence** *n.* —**im'ma·nent·ly** *adv.*

im·ma·te·ri·al (im'ə tir'ē əl) *adj.* 1. spiritual 2. unimportant

im·ma·ture (im'ə toor', -tyoor', -choor') *adj.* 1. not mature; not completely developed 2. not finished or perfected —**im'ma·tu'ri·ty** *n.*

im·meas·ur·a·ble (i mezh'ər ə b'l) *adj.* that cannot be measured; boundless; vast —**im·meas'ur·a·bly** *adv.*

im·me·di·a·cy (i mē'dē ə sē) *n.* a being immediate; esp., direct relevance to the present time or purpose

im·me'di·ate (-it) *adj.* [see IN-2 & MEDIATE] 1. not separated in space; closest 2. without delay; instant 3. next in order or relation 4. direct; first-hand —**im·me'di·ate·ly** *adv.*

im·me·mo·ri·al (im'ə môr'ē əl) *adj.* extending back beyond memory or record; ancient

im·mense (i mens') *adj.* [< L. *in-*, not + *metiri*, to measure] very large; vast; huge —**im·mense'ly** *adv.* —**im·men'si·ty** *n.*

im·merse (i murs') *vt.* -**mersed'**, -**mers'ing** [< L. *immergere*] 1. to plunge into or as if into a liquid 2. to baptize by dipping under water 3. to absorb deeply; engross [*immersed* in study] —**im·mer'sion** *n.*

immersion heater an electric coil or rod immersed in water to heat it

im·mi·grant (im'ə grənt) *n.* one who immigrates —*adj.* immigrating

im'mi·grate' (-grāt') *vi.* -**grat'ed**, -**grat'ing** [see IN-1 & MIGRATE] to come into a new country, etc., esp. to settle there —**im'mi·gra'tion** *n.*

im·mi·nent (im'ə nənt) *adj.* [< L. *in-*, on + *minere*, to project] likely to happen without delay; impending —**im'mi·nence** *n.* —**im'mi·nent·ly** *adv.*

im·mo·bile (i mō'b'l) *adj.* 1. firmly placed; stable 2. motionless —**im'mo·bil'i·ty** *n.*, —**im·mo'bi·lize'** (-līz') *vt.* -**lized'**, -**liz'ing**

im·mod·er·ate (i mäd'ər it) *adj.* without restraint; excessive

im·mod·est (i mäd'ist) *adj.* 1. indecent 2. not shy; forward —**im·mod'est·ly** *adv.* —**im·mod'es·ty** *n.*

im·mo·late (im'ə lāt') *vt.* -**lat'ed**, -**lat'ing** [< L. *immolare*, sprinkle with sacrificial meal] to kill as a sacrifice —**im'mo·la'tion** *n.*

im·mor·al (i môr'əl, i mär'-) *adj.* 1. not moral 2. lewd —**im·mor'al·ly** *adv.*

im·mo·ral·i·ty (im'ə ral'ə tē, im'ô-) *n.* 1. a being immoral 2. *pl.* -**ties** an immoral act or practice; vice

im·mor·tal (i môr't'l) *adj.* 1. not mortal; living forever 2. enduring 3. having lasting fame —*n.* an immortal being —**im'mor·tal'i·ty** (-tal'ə tē) *n.*

im·mor'tal·ize' (-tə līz') *vt.* -**ized'**, -**iz'ing** to make immortal, as in fame

im·mov·a·ble (i mōov'ə b'l) *adj.* 1. firmly fixed 2. unyielding; steadfast

im·mune (i myōon') *adj.* [< L. *in-*, without + *munia*, duties] 1. exempt from or protected against something disagreeable or harmful 2. not susceptible to some specified disease

im·mu·ni·ty (i myōon'ə tē) *n., pl.* -**ties** 1. exemption from something burdensome, as a legal obligation 2. resistance to a specified disease

im·mu·nize (im'yə nīz') *vt.* -**nized'**, -**niz'ing** to make immune, as by inoculation —**im'mu·ni·za'tion** *n.*

im·mu·nol·o·gy (im'yoo näl'ə jē) *n.* the branch of medicine dealing with immunity to disease or with allergic reactions —**im'mu·nol'o·gist** *n.*

im·mure (i myoor') *vt.* -**mured'**, -**mur'ing** [< L. *in-*, in + *murus*, wall] to shut up within walls; confine

im·mu·ta·ble (i myōōt'ə b'l) *adj.* unchangeable —**im·mu'ta·bly** *adv.*

imp (imp) *n.* [< Gr. *em-*, in + *phyton*, growth] 1. a young demon 2. a mischievous child —**imp'ish** *adj.*

im·pact (im pakt'; *for n.* im'pakt) *vt.* [< L. *impingere*, press firmly together] 1. to force tightly together 2. [Colloq.] to have an effect on —*vi.* 1. to hit with force 2. [Colloq.] to have an effect (*on*) —*n.* 1. violent contact 2. a shocking effect

im·pact'ed (-pak'tid) *adj.* abnormally lodged in the jaw: said of a tooth

im·pair (im per') *vt.* [< L. *in-*, intens. + *pejor*, worse] to make worse, less, etc. —**im·pair'ment** *n.*

im·pa·la (im pä'lə) *n., pl.* -**la**, -**las**

a reddish antelope of C and S Africa

im·pale (im pāl′) *vt.* **-paled′, -pal′ing** [< L. *in-*, on + *palus*, a pole] to pierce through with, or fix on, something pointed —**im·pale′ment** *n.*

im·pal·pa·ble (im pal′pə b'l) *adj.* 1. not perceptible to the touch 2. too subtle to be easily understood

im·pan·el (im pan′'l) *vt.* **-eled** or **-elled, -el·ing** or **-el·ling** 1. to enter the name(s) of on a jury list 2. to choose (a jury) from such a list

im·part (im pärt′) *vt.* [see IN-[1] & PART] 1. to give a share of; give 2. to make known; reveal

im·par·tial (im pär′shəl) *adj.* without bias; fair —**im·par′ti·al′i·ty** (-shē al′ə tē) *n.* —**im·par′tial·ly** *adv.*

im·pass·a·ble (im pas′ə b'l) *adj.* that cannot be passed or traveled over

im·passe (im′pas, im pas′) *n.* [Fr.] a situation offering no escape; deadlock

im·pas·sioned (im pash′ənd) *adj.* passionate; fiery; ardent

im·pas·sive (im pas′iv) *adj.* not feeling or showing emotion; calm —**im·pas·siv·i·ty** (im′pə siv′ə tē) *n.*

im·pas·to (im päs′tō) *n.* [It.] 1. painting in which the paint is laid thickly on the canvas 2. such paint

im·pa·tient (im pā′shənt) *adj.* lacking patience; specif., *a)* annoyed because of delay, opposition, etc. *b)* restlessly eager to do something, etc. —**im·pa′tience** *n.*

im·peach (im pēch′) *vt.* [< L. *in-*, in + *pedica*, a fetter] 1. to discredit (a person's honor, etc.) 2. to try (a public official) on a charge of wrongdoing —**im·peach′ment** *n.*

im·pec·ca·ble (im pek′ə b'l) *adj.* [< L. *in-*, not + *peccare*, to sin] without defect or error; flawless —**im·pec′ca·bil′i·ty** *n.* —**im·pec′ca·bly** *adv.*

im·pe·cu·ni·ous (im′pi kyoō′nē əs) *adj.* [< L. *in-*, not + *pecunia*, money] having no money; poor

im·ped·ance (im pēd′'ns) *n.* [< ff. + -ANCE] the total resistance in an electric circuit to the flow of an alternating current of a single frequency

im·pede (im pēd′) *vt.* **-ped′ed, -ped′ing** [< L. *in-*, in + *pes*, foot] to hinder the progress of; obstruct

im·ped·i·ment (im ped′ə mənt) *n.* anything that impedes; specif., a speech defect

im·ped′i·men′ta (-men′tə) *n.pl.* encumbrances, as baggage or supplies

im·pel (im pel′) *vt.* **-pelled′, -pel′ling** [< L. *in-*, in + *pellere*, to drive] 1. to drive or move forward 2. to force, compel, or urge

im·pend (im pend′) *vi.* [< L. *in-*, in + *pendere*, hang] to be about to happen; be imminent [*impending* disaster]

im·pen·e·tra·ble (im pen′i trə b'l) *adj.* 1. that cannot be penetrated 2. that cannot be solved or understood

im·pen·i·tent (im pen′ə tənt) *adj.* not penitent; without regret or shame

im·per·a·tive (im per′ə tiv) *adj.* [< L. *imperare*, to command] 1. indicating authority or command 2. necessary; urgent 3. designating or of the mood of a verb that expresses a command, etc. —*n.* a command

im·per·cep·ti·ble (im′pər sep′tə b'l) *adj.* not easily perceived by the senses or the mind; very slight, subtle, etc. —**im′per·cep′ti·bly** *adv.*

im′per·cep′tive (-tiv) *adj.* not perceiving —**im′per·cep′tive·ness** *n.*

im·per·fect (im pur′fikt) *adj.* 1. not complete 2. not perfect 3. designating a verb tense that indicates a past action or state as incomplete or continuous —**im·per′fect·ly** *adv.*

im·per·fec·tion (im′pər fek′shən) *n.* 1. a being imperfect 2. a defect; fault

im·pe·ri·al (im pir′ē əl) *adj.* [< L. *imperium*, empire] 1. of an empire, emperor, or empress 2. having supreme authority 3. majestic; august 4. of great size or superior quality —*n.* a small, pointed chin beard

imperial gallon the standard British gallon, equal to c. 1 1/5 U.S. gallons

im·pe·ri·al·ism *n.* 1. imperial state or authority 2. the policy of forming and maintaining an empire, as by subjugating territories, establishing colonies, etc. 3. the policy of seeking to dominate the affairs of weaker countries —**im·pe′ri·al·ist** *n., adj.* —**im·pe′ri·al·is′tic** *adj.*

im·per·il (im per′əl) *vt.* **-iled** or **-illed, -il·ing** or **-il·ling** to put in peril; endanger

im·pe·ri·ous (im pir′ē əs) *adj.* [< L. *imperium*, empire] 1. overbearing, arrogant, etc. 2. urgent; imperative —**im·pe′ri·ous·ly** *adv.*

im·per·ish·a·ble (im per′ish ə b'l) *adj.* not perishable; indestructible

im·per·ma·nent (im pur′mə nənt) *adj.* not permanent; temporary —**im·per′ma·nent·ly** *adv.*

im·per·son·al (im pur′s'n əl) *adj.* 1. without reference to any particular person 2. not existing as a person [*an impersonal force*] 3. designating or of a verb occurring only in the third person singular, usually with *it* as subject —**im·per′son·al·ly** *adv.*

im·per·son·ate (im pur′sə nāt′) *vt.* **-at′ed, -at′ing** to assume the role of, for purposes of entertainment or fraud —**im·per′son·a′tion** *n.* —**im·per′son·a′tor** *n.*

im·per·ti·nent (im pur′t'n ənt) *adj.* 1. not pertinent 2. impudent; insolent —**im·per′ti·nence** *n.*

im·per·turb·a·ble (im′pər tur′bə b'l) *adj.* that cannot be perturbed; calm; impassive

im·per·vi·ous (im pur′vē əs) *adj.* 1. incapable of being penetrated, as by moisture 2. not affected by (with *to*)

im·pe·ti·go (im′pə tī′gō) *n.* [see IMPETUS] a contagious skin disease with eruption of pustules

im·pet·u·ous (im pech′oo wəs) *adj.* [see ff.] acting or done suddenly with little thought; rash —**im·pet′u·os′i·ty** (-wäs′ə tē) *n.* —**im·pet′u·ous·ly** *adv.*

im·pe·tus (im′pə təs) *n.* [< L. *in-*, in + *petere*, rush at] 1. the force with which a body moves against resistance 2. driving force or motive

im·pi·e·ty (im pī′ə tē) *n.* 1. lack of reverence for God 2. disrespect

im·pinge (im pinj′) *vi.* -pinged′, -ping′ing [< L. *in-*, in + *pangere*, to strike] 1. to strike, hit, etc. (*on* or *upon*) 2. to encroach (*on* or *upon*) —im·pinge′ment *n.*

im·pi·ous (im′pē əs) *adj.* not pious; specif., lacking reverence for God

im·plac·a·ble (im plak′ə b'l, -plā′kə-) *adj.* not to be placated or appeased; relentless —im·pla′ca·bly *adv.*

im·plant (im plant′) *vt.* 1. to plant firmly 2. to fix firmly in the mind

im·plau·si·ble (im plô′zə b'l) *adj.* not plausible —im·plau′si·bly *adv.*

im·ple·ment (im′plə mənt; *for v.* -ment′) *n.* [< L. *in-*, in + *plere*, to fill] something used in a given activity; tool, instrument, etc. —*vt.* to carry into effect; accomplish —im′ple·men·ta′tion *n.*

im·pli·cate (im′plə kāt′) *vt.* -cat′ed, -cat′ing [< L. *in-*, in + *plicare*, to fold] to show to be a party to a crime, etc. —im′pli·ca′tive *adj.*

im′pli·ca′tion *n.* 1. an implicating or being implicated 2. an implying or being implied 3. something implied

im·plic·it (im plis′it) *adj.* [see IMPLICATE] 1. suggested though not plainly expressed; implied 2. necessarily involved though not apparent; inherent 3. without reservation; absolute —im·plic′it·ly *adv.*

im·plode (im plōd′) *vt., vi.* -plod′ed, -plod′ing [< IN-¹ + (EX)PLODE] to burst inward —im·plo′sion (-plō′zhən) *n.* —im·plo′sive *adj.*

im·plore (im plôr′) *vt.* -plored′, -plor′ing [< L. *in-*, intens. + *plorare*, cry out] 1. to ask earnestly for 2. to beg (a person) to do something —im·plor′ing·ly *adv.*

im·ply (im plī′) *vt.* -plied′, -ply′ing [< L. *implicare*, involve] 1. to have as a necessary part, condition, etc. 2. to indicate indirectly; hint; suggest

im·po·lite (im′pə līt′) *adj.* not polite; discourteous —im′po·lite′ly *adv.*

im·pol·i·tic (im päl′ə tik) *adj.* unwise; not politic

im·pon·der·a·ble (im pän′dər ə b'l) *adj.* that cannot be weighed or measured —*n.* anything imponderable

im·port (im pôrt′; *also, and for n.* *always,* im′pôrt) *vt.* [< L. *in-*, in + *portare*, carry] 1. to bring (goods) into one country from another in commerce 2. to mean; signify —*vi.* to be of importance; matter —*n.* 1. something imported 2. meaning; signification 3. importance —im′por·ta′tion *n.* —im·port′er *n.*

im·por·tant (im pôr′t'nt) *adj.* [see prec.] 1. meaning a great deal; having much significance or value 2. having, or acting as if having, power, authority, etc. —im·por′tance *n.* —im·por′tant·ly *adv.*

im·por·tu·nate (im pôr′chə nit) *adj.* persistent in asking or demanding

im·por·tune (im′pôr tōōn′) *vt., vi.* -tuned′, -tun′ing [< L. *importunus,* troublesome] to urge or entreat persistently or repeatedly —im′por·tu′ni·ty *n., pl.* -ties

im·pose (im pōz′) *vt.* -posed′, -pos′ing [< L. *in-*, on + *ponere*, to place] 1. to place (a burden, tax, etc. *on* or *upon*) 2. to force (oneself) on others —impose on (or upon) 1. to take advantage of 2. to cheat or defraud —im′po·si′tion (-pə zish′ən) *n.*

im·pos·ing *adj.* impressive because of great size, strength, dignity, etc. —im·pos′ing·ly *adv.*

im·pos·si·ble (im päs′ə b'l) *adj.* 1. not capable of being, being done, or happening 2. not capable of being endured, used, etc. because disagreeable or unsuitable —im·pos′si·bil′i·ty *n., pl.* -ties —im·pos′si·bly *adv.*

im·post (im′pōst) *n.* [see IMPOSE] a tax; esp., a duty on imported goods

im·pos·tor (im päs′tər) *n.* [see IMPOSE] one who deceives or cheats others by pretending to be what he is not

im·pos′ture (-chər) *n.* the act or practice of an impostor; fraud

im·po·tent (im′pə tənt) *adj.* 1. lacking physical strength 2. ineffective; powerless 3. unable to engage in sexual intercourse: said of males —im′po·tence, im′po·ten·cy *n.* —im′po·tent·ly *adv.*

im·pound (im pound′) *vt.* 1. to shut up (an animal) in a pound 2. to take and hold in legal custody 3. to gather and enclose (water), as for irrigation

im·pov·er·ish (im päv′ər ish) *vt.* [< L. *in-*, in + *pauper*, poor] 1. to make poor 2. to deprive of strength, resources, etc. —im·pov′er·ish·ment *n.*

im·prac·ti·ca·ble (im prak′ti kə b'l) *adj.* not capable of being carried out in practice

im·prac·ti·cal (im prak′tə k'l) *adj.* not practical

im·pre·cate (im′prə kāt′) *vt.* -cat′ed, -cat′ing [< L. *in-*, on + *precari*, pray] to invoke (evil, a curse, etc.) —im′pre·ca′tion *n.*

im·pre·cise (im′pri sīs′) *adj.* not precise; vague —im′pre·cise′ly *adv.* —im′pre·ci′sion (-sizh′ən) *n.*

im·preg·na·ble (im preg′nə b'l) *adj.* 1. that cannot be overcome or entered by force 2. unyielding —im·preg′na·bil′i·ty *n.* —im·preg′na·bly *adv.*

im·preg·nate (im preg′nāt) *vt.* -nat·ed, -nat·ing 1. to make pregnant; fertilize 2. to saturate 3. to imbue (*with* ideas, etc.) —im·preg′na·ble *adj.* —im′preg·na′tion *n.*

im·pre·sa·ri·o (im′prə sär′ē ō) *n., pl.* -os [It.] the manager of an opera, concert series, etc.

im·press¹ (im pres′) *vt.* [< IN-¹ + PRESS²] 1. to force into military service 2. to seize for public use

im·press² (im pres′; *for n.* im′pres) *vt.* [see IN-¹ + PRESS¹] 1. to stamp; imprint 2. to affect strongly the mind or emotions of 3. to fix in the memory —n. 1. an impressing 2. an imprint

im·press'i·ble (-ə b'l) *adj.* that can be impressed —**im·press'i·bil'i·ty** *n.*

im·pres·sion (im presh'ən) *n.* 1. an impressing 2. *a)* a mark, imprint, etc. *b)* an effect produced on the mind 3. a vague notion 4. an amusing impersonation; mimicking

im·pres'sion·a·ble *adj.* easily impressed or influenced; sensitive

im·pres'sion·ism *n.* a theory of art, music, etc., whose aim is to reproduce the immediate, overall impression —**im·pres'sion·ist** *adj., n.* —**im·pres'sion·is'tic** *adj.*

im·pres'sive (im pres'iv) *adj.* tending to impress the mind or emotions; eliciting wonder or admiration —**im·pres'sive·ly** *adv.*

im·pri·ma·tur (im'pri mät'ər, -māt'-) *n.* [ModL., lit., let it be printed] permission or license, esp. to publish

im·print (im print'; *for n.* im'print) *vt.* [< L. *in-*, on + *premere*, to press] to mark or fix as by pressing or stamping —*n.* 1. a mark made by imprinting 2. a lasting effect 3. a note in a book giving facts of its publication

im·pris·on (im priz''n) *vt.* to put in or as in prison —**im·pris'on·ment** *n.*

im·prob·a·ble (im präb'ə b'l) *adj.* not probable; unlikely —**im'prob·a·bil'i·ty** *n.* —**im·prob'a·bly** *adv.*

im·promp·tu (im prämp'tōō) *adj., adv.* [< L. *in promptu*, in readiness] without preparation; offhand

im·prop·er (im präp'ər) *adj.* 1. not suitable; unfit 2. incorrect 3. not in good taste —**im·prop'er·ly** *adv.*

im·pro·pri·e·ty (im'prə prī'ə tē) *n., pl.* **-ties** 1. a being improper 2. an improper act, usage, etc.

im·prove (im prōōv') *vt.* **-proved'**, **-prov'ing** [ult. < L. *in-*, in + *prodesse*, to be of profit] 1. to use (time) well 2. to make better 3. to make (land or structures) more valuable by cultivation, construction, etc. —*vi.* to become better —**improve on** (or **upon**) to do or make better than —**im·prov'a·ble** *adj.*

im·prove'ment *n.* 1. an improving or being improved 2. a change that improves or adds value to something

im·prov·i·dent (im präv'ə dənt) *adj.* lacking foresight or thrift —**im·prov'i·dence** *n.* —**im·prov'i·dent·ly** *adv.*

im·pro·vise (im'prə vīz') *vt., vi.* **-vised'**, **-vis'ing** [< L. *in-*, not + *providere*, foresee] 1. to compose and perform without preparation 2. to make or do with whatever is at hand —**im·prov'i·sa'tion** (-präv'ə zā'shən) *n.* —**im·prov'i·sa'tion·al** *adj.*

im·pru·dent (im prōōd'nt) *adj.* not prudent; rash —**im·pru'dence** *n.*

im·pu·dent (im'pyōō dənt) *adj.* [< L. *in-*, not + *pudere*, feel shame] shamelessly bold; insolent —**im'pu·dence** *n.* —**im'pu·dent·ly** *adv.*

im·pugn (im pyōōn') *vt.* [< L. *in-*, against + *pugnare*, to fight] to oppose or challenge as false

im·pulse (im'puls) *n.* [see IMPEL] 1. *a)* a driving forward *b)* an impelling

force; impetus *c)* the motion or effect caused by such a force 2. *a)* incitement to action by a stimulus *b)* a sudden inclination to act

im·pul·sion (im pul'shən) *n.* 1. an impelling or being impelled 2. an impelling force 3. impetus 4. *same as* IMPULSE (sense 2)

im·pul·sive (im pul'siv) *adj.* 1. driving forward 2. given to acting on impulse —**im·pul'sive·ly** *adv.*

im·pu·ni·ty (im pyōō'nə tē) *n.* [< L. *in-*, without + *poena*, punishment] freedom from punishment, harm, etc.

im·pure (im pyoor') *adj.* 1. unclean; dirty 2. immoral; obscene 3. mixed with foreign matter; adulterated —**im·pure'ly** *adv.* —**im·pure'ness** *n.*

im·pu·ri·ty *n.* 1. a being impure 2. *pl.* **-ties** an impure thing or part

im·pute (im pyōōt') *vt.* **-put'ed**, **-put'ing** [< L. *in-*, to + *putare*, to think] to attribute (esp. a fault or misconduct) to another —**im'pu·ta'tion** (-pyoo tā'shən) *n.*

in (in) *prep.* [OE.] 1. contained by [in the room] 2. wearing [in formal dress] 3. during [done in a day] 4. at the end of [due in an hour] 5. not beyond [in sight] 6. employed at [a man in business] 7. out of a group of [one in ten] 8. amidst [in a storm] 9. affected by [in trouble] 10. with regard to [to vary in size] 11. using [speak in English] 12. because of; for [he cried in pain] 13. into [come in the house] —*adv.* 1. to the inside [he went in] 2. to or at a certain place 3. so as to be contained by a certain space, condition, etc. —*adj.* 1. that is in power [the in group] 2. inner; inside 3. gathered, counted, etc. 4. [Colloq.] currently smart, popular, etc. —*n.* 1. one that is in power: *usually used in pl.* 2. [Colloq.] special influence or favor —**have it in for** [Colloq.] to hold a grudge against —**ins and outs** all the details and intricacies —**in that** because; since —**in with** associated with

in-¹ [< the prep. IN or L. *in*, in] *a prefix meaning* in, into, within, on, toward [inbreed, infer]

in-² [L.] *a prefix meaning* no, not, without, non-. The following list includes some common compounds formed with *in-*, with no special meanings; they will be understood if *not* or *lack of* is used with the meaning of the base word:

inability	incautious
inaccessible	incivility
inaccuracy	incombustible
inaccurate	incommensurate
inaction	incommunicable
inactive	incomprehensible
inadequacy	inconceivable
inadequate	inconclusive
inadmissible	inconsistency
inadvisable	inconsistent
inanimate	incorrect
inapplicable	incurable
inappropriate	indecorous
inapt	indefinable
inartistic	indiscernible
inaudible	indisputable
inauspicious	indistinct
incapable	indistinguishable

indivisible	inharmonious
inedible	inhospitable
ineffective	inhumane
ineffectual	injudicious
inefficacy	inoperable
inelastic	inopportune
ineligible	inseparable
inequality	insignificance
inequitable	insignificant
inequity	insolvable
inexact	insufficient
inexcusable	insurmountable
inexpensive	insusceptible
infertile	invariable

-in (in) *a combining form used in forming words analogous to* SIT-IN *to describe similar demonstrations* [*teach-in, be-in,*]

IN Indiana

in. inch(es)

in ab·sen·ti·a (in əb sen′shə, -shē ə) [L.] although not present [*to receive a college degree in absentia*]

in·ac·ti·vate (in ak′tə vāt′) *vt.* **-vat′ed, -vat′ing** to make no longer active —**in·ac′ti·va′tion** *n.*

in·ad·vert·ent (in′əd vur′tənt) *adj.* 1. not attentive or observant 2. due to oversight —**in′ad·vert′ence** *n.* —**in′ad·vert′ent·ly** *adv.*

in·al·ien·a·ble (in āl′yən ə b'l) *adj.* [see ALIEN] that cannot be taken away or transferred —**in·al′ien·a·bly** *adv.*

in·am·o·ra·ta (in am′ə rät′ə) *n.* [It.] one's sweetheart or mistress

in·ane (in ān′) *adj.* [L. *inanis*] 1. empty 2. lacking sense; silly —**in·an·i·ty** (in an′ə tē) *n.*

in·ar·tic·u·late (in′är tik′yə lit) *adj.* 1. without the articulation of normal speech [*an inarticulate cry*] 2. mute 3. unable to speak clearly or coherently 4. unexpressed or inexpressible

in·as·much as (in′əz much′ əz) 1. since; because 2. to the extent that

in·at·ten·tion (in′ə ten′shən) *n.* failure to pay attention; negligence —**in′at·ten′tive** *adj.*

in·au·gu·ral (in ôg′yə rəl) *adj.* [Fr.] 1. of an inauguration 2. first in a series —*n.* 1. a speech made at an inauguration 2. an inauguration

in·au·gu·rate′ (-rāt′) *vt.* **-rat′ed, -rat′ing** [< L. *inaugurare*, to practice augury] 1. to induct into office with a formal ceremony 2. to make a formal beginning of 3. to dedicate formally —**in·au′gu·ra′tion** *n.*

in·board (in′bôrd′) *adv., adj.* 1. inside the hull of a ship or boat 2. close to the fuselage of an aircraft —*n.* a marine motor mounted inboard

in·born (in′bôrn′) *adj.* present in the organism at birth; innate; natural

in′bound′ (-bound′) *adj.* traveling or going inward

in·bred (in′bred′) *adj.* 1. inborn; natural 2. resulting from inbreeding

in·breed (in′brēd′) *vt., vi.* **-bred′, -breed′ing** 1. to breed by continual mating of individuals of the same or closely related stocks 2. to make or become too refined, effete, etc.

inc. 1. incorporated 2. increase

In·ca (iŋ′kə) *n.* a member of the highly civilized Indian people that dominated ancient Peru until the Spanish conquest

in·cal·cu·la·ble (in kal′kyə lə b'l) *adj.* 1. that cannot be calculated; too great or too many to be counted 2. unpredictable —**in·cal′cu·la·bly** *adv.*

in·can·des·cent (in′kən des′'nt) *adj.* [< L. *in-*, in + *candere*, to shine] 1. glowing with intense heat 2. very bright —**in′can·des′cence** *n.*

incandescent lamp a lamp with a filament in a vacuum heated to incandescence by an electric current

in·can·ta·tion (in′kan tā′shən) *n.* [< L. *in-*, in + *cantare*, to chant] words chanted in magic spells or rites

in·ca·pac·i·tate (in′kə pas′ə tāt′) *vt.* **-tat′ed, -tat′ing** 1. to make unable or unfit 2. *Law* to disqualify

in′ca·pac′i·ty *n., pl.* **-ties** 1. lack of capacity, power, or fitness 2. legal ineligibility

in·car·cer·ate (in kär′sə rāt′) *vt.* **-at′ed, -at′ing** [< L. *in*, in + *carcer*, prison] to imprison —**in·car′cer·a′tion** *n.*

in·car·na·dine (in kär′nə dīn′) *vt.* **-dined′, -din′ing** to make red

in·car·nate (in kär′nit; *for v.* -nāt) *adj.* [< L. *in-*, in + *caro*, flesh] endowed with a human body; personified —*vt.* **-nat·ed, -nat·ing** 1. to give bodily form to 2. to be the type or embodiment of —**in′car·na′tion** *n.*

in·cen·di·ar·y (in sen′dē er′ē) *adj.* [< L. *incendium*, a fire] 1. having to do with the willful destruction of property by fire 2. designed to cause fires, as certain bombs 3. willfully stirring up strife, riot, etc. —*n., pl.* **-ies** one who willfully stirs up strife, riot, etc.

in·cense[1] (in′sens) *n.* [< L. *in-*, in + *candere*, to burn] 1. any substance burned to produce a pleasant odor 2. the fragrance from this 3. any pleasant odor

in·cense[2] (in sens′) *vt.* **-censed′, -cens′ing** [see prec.] to make very angry; enrage —**in·cense′ment** *n.*

in·cen·tive (in sen′tiv) *n.* [< L. *in-*, on + *canere*, sing] a stimulus; motive

in·cep·tion (in sep′shən) *n.* [see INCIPIENT] the act of beginning; start

in·cer·ti·tude (in sur′tə tōōd′, -tyōōd′) *n.* 1. doubt 2. insecurity

in·ces·sant (in ses′'nt) *adj.* [< L. *in-*, not + *cessare*, cease] never ceasing; continuing without stopping; constant —**in·ces′sant·ly** *adv.*

in·cest (in′sest) *n.* [< L. *in-*, not + *castus*, chaste] sexual intercourse between persons too closely related to marry legally —**in·ces·tu·ous** (in ses′choo wəs) *adj.* —**in·ces′tu·ous·ly** *adv.* —**in·ces′tu·ous·ness** *n.*

inch (inch) *n.* [< L. *uncia*, twelfth part] a measure of length, equal to 1/12 foot; symbol, ″ —*vt., vi.* to move very slowly, or by degrees —**every**

inch in all respects —**inch by inch** gradually: also **by inches** —**within an inch of** very close to

in·cho·ate (in kō′it) *adj.* [< L. *inchoare*, begin] 1. just begun; rudimentary 2. not yet clearly formed

in·ci·dence (in′si dəns) *n.* the degree or range of occurrence or effect

in′ci·dent (-dənt) *adj.* [< L. *in-*, on + *cadere*, to fall] 1. likely to happen as a result 2. falling upon or affecting —*n.* 1. something that happens; an event, esp. a minor one 2. a minor conflict

in·ci·den′tal (-den′t'l) *adj.* 1. happening in connection with something more important; casual 2. secondary or minor —*n.* 1. something incidental 2. [*pl.*] miscellaneous items

in′ci·den′tal·ly *adv.* 1. in an incidental manner 2. by the way

in·cin·er·ate (in sin′ə rāt′) *vt.*, *vi.* -at′ed, -at′ing [< L. *in*, in + *cinis*, ashes] to burn to ashes; burn up —**in·cin′er·a′tion** *n.*

in·cin′er·a′tor *n.* a furnace for burning trash

in·cip·i·ent (in sip′ē ənt) *adj.* [< L. *in-*, on + *capere*, take] just beginning to exist or appear —**in·cip′i·ence** *n.*

in·cise (in sīz′) *vt.* -cised′, -cis′ing [< L. *in-*, into + *caedere*, to cut] to cut into with a sharp tool; specif., to engrave or carve

in·ci·sion (in sizh′ən) *n.* 1. an incising 2. cut; gash 3. incisive quality

in·ci·sive (in sī′siv) *adj.* 1. cutting into 2. sharp; penetrating; acute —**in·ci′sive·ly** *adv.* —**in·ci′sive·ness** *n.*

in·ci·sor (in sī′zər) *n.* any of the front cutting teeth between the canines

in·cite (in sīt′) *vt.* -cit′ed, -cit′ing [< L. *in-*, on + *citare*, urge] to urge to action; rouse —**in·cite′ment** *n.*

incl. 1. including 2. inclusive

in·clem·ent (in klem′ənt) *adj.* [< L. *in-*, not + *clemens*, lenient] 1. rough; stormy 2. lacking mercy; harsh —**in·clem′en·cy** *n.*

in·cli·na·tion (in′klə nā′shən) *n.* 1. a bending, leaning, or sloping 2. an inclined surface; slope 3. *a)* a bias; tendency *b)* a preference

in·cline (in klīn′; *for n. usually* in′klīn) *vi.* -clined′, -clin′ing [< L. *in-*, on + *clinare*, lean] 1. to lean; slope 2. to have a tendency 3. to have a preference or liking —*vt.* 1. to cause to lean, slant, etc. 2. to make willing; influence —*n.* a slope; grade

in·close (in klōz′) *vt.* -closed′, -clos′ing *same as* ENCLOSE —**in·clo′sure** (-klō′zhər) *n.*

in·clude (in klōōd′) *vt.* -clud′ed, -clud′ing [< L. *in-*, in + *claudere*, to close] 1. to enclose or contain 2. to have as part of a whole; contain; comprise 3. to take into account —**in·clu′sion** (-klōō′zhən) *n.*

in·clu·sive (-klōō′siv) *adj.* 1. taking everything into account 2. including the terms or limits mentioned (the first to the tenth *inclusive*) —**inclusive of** including —**in·clu′sive·ly** *adv.* —**in·clu′sive·ness** *n.*

in·cog·ni·to (in′käg nēt′ō, in käg′-

ni tō′) *adv.*, *adj.* [It. < L. *in-*, not + *cognitus*, known] disguised under an assumed name, rank, etc.

in·co·her·ent (in′kō hir′ənt) *adj.* 1. not logically connected; disjointed 2. characterized by incoherent speech, etc. —**in′co·her·ence** *n.* —**in′co·her′ent·ly** *adv.*

in·come (in′kum′) *n.* the money, etc. received for labor or services, or from property, investments, etc.

in·com·mu·ni·ca·do (in′kə myōō′nə kä′dō) *adj.* [Sp.] not allowed to communicate with others

in·com·pa·ra·ble (in käm′pər ə b'l) *adj.* 1. having no basis of comparison 2. beyond comparison; matchless

in·com·pat·i·ble (in′kəm pat′ə b'l) *adj.* not compatible; specif., unable to live together harmoniously —**in′com·pat′i·bil′i·ty** *n.*

in·com·pe·tent (in käm′pə tənt) *adj.* without adequate ability, knowledge, fitness, etc. —*n.* an incompetent person —**in·com′pe·tence** *n.* —**in·com′pe·tent·ly** *adv.*

in·com·plete (in′kəm plēt′) *adj.* 1. lacking a part or parts 2. unfinished; not concluded 3. not perfect

in·con·gru·ous (in käŋ′grōō wəs) *adj.* 1. lacking harmony or agreement of parts, etc. 2. unsuitable; inappropriate —**in′con·gru′i·ty** (-kən grōō′ə tē) *n.*

in·con·se·quen·tial (in kän′sə kwen′shəl) *adj.* of no consequence

in·con·sid·er·a·ble (in′kən sid′ər ə b'l) *adj.* trivial; small

in′con·sid·er·ate (-it) *adj.* without thought or consideration for others; thoughtless —**in′con·sid′er·ate·ly** *adv.* —**in′con·sid′er·ate·ness**, **in′con·sid′er·a′tion** (-ə rā′shən) *n.*

in·con·sol·a·ble (in′kən sōl′ə b'l) *adj.* that cannot be consoled

in·con·spic·u·ous (in′kən spik′yoo wəs) *adj.* attracting little attention

in·con·stant (in kän′stənt) *adj.* not constant; changeable, fickle, irregular, etc. —**in·con′stan·cy** *n.*

in·con·test·a·ble (in′kən tes′tə b'l) *adj.* unquestionable; indisputable —**in′con·test′a·bil′i·ty** *n.* —**in′con·test′a·bly** *adv.*

in·con·ti·nent (in känt′'n ənt) *adj.* 1. without self-restraint, esp. in sexual activity 2. unable to restrain a natural discharge, as of urine —**in·con′ti·nence** *n.*

in·con·ven·ience (in′kən vēn′yəns) *n.* 1. lack of comfort, ease, etc. 2. anything inconvenient —*vt.* -ienced, -ienc·ing to cause inconvenience to

in′con·ven′ient *adj.* not favorable to one's comfort; causing bother, etc.

in·cor·po·rate (in kôr′pə rāt′) *vt.* -rat′ed, -rat′ing [see IN-[1] & CORPORATE] 1. to combine; include; embody 2. to bring together into a single whole; merge 3. to form into a corporation —*vi.* to unite into one group or substance; form a corporation —**in·cor′po·ra′tion** *n.*

in·cor·ri·gi·ble (in kôr′i jə b'l, -kär′-) *adj.* [see IN-[2] & CORRECT] that cannot be corrected or reformed, esp.

in·cor·ri·gi·bil·i·ty *n.* —**in·cor′ri·gi·bly** *adv.* morally

in·cor·rupt·i·ble (in′kə rup′tə b'l) *adj.* that cannot be corrupted, esp. morally

in·crease (in krēs′; *for n.* in′krēs) *vi.* -creased′, -creas′ing [< L. *in-,* in + *crescere,* grow] to become greater in size, amount, number, etc. —*vt.* to make greater in size, etc. —*n.* 1. an increasing or becoming increased 2. the result or amount of an increasing —**on the increase** increasing

in·creas′ing·ly *adv.* more and more

in·cred·i·ble (in kred′ə b'l) *adj.* not credible; seeming too unusual to be possible —**in·cred′i·bly** *adv.*

in·cred·u·lous (in krej′oo ləs) *adj.* 1. unwilling to believe 2. showing doubt or disbelief —**in·cre·du·li·ty** (in′krə dōō′lə tē) *n.*

in·cre·ment (in′krə mənt, iŋ′-) *n.* [< L. *incrementum*] 1. an increase 2. amount of increase

in·crim·i·nate (in krim′ə nāt′) *vt.* -nat′ed, -nat′ing [< L. *in-,* in + *crimen,* offense] 1. to accuse of a crime 2. to involve in, or make appear guilty of, a crime or fault —**in·crim′·i·na′tion** *n.*

in·crust (in krust′) *vt.* to cover as with a crust —*vi.* to form a crust —**in′crus·ta′tion** *n.*

in·cu·bate (iŋ′kyə bāt′) *vt., vi.* -bat′ed, -bat′ing [< L. *in-,* on + *cubare,* to lie] 1. to sit on and hatch (eggs) 2. to keep (eggs, embryos, etc.) in a favorable environment for hatching or developing 3. to develop, as by planning —**in′cu·ba′tion** *n.*

in′cu·ba′tor *n.* 1. a heated container for hatching eggs 2. a similar apparatus in which premature babies are kept for a period

in·cu·bus (iŋ′kyə bəs) *n.* [LL.] 1. a nightmare 2. an oppressive burden

in·cul·cate (in kul′kāt, in′kul kāt′) *vt.* -cat′ed, -cat′ing [< L. *in-,* in + *calcare,* trample underfoot] to impress upon the mind, as by insistent urging —**in′cul·ca′tion** *n.*

in·cul·pate (in kul′pāt, in′kul pāt′) *vt.* -pat′ed, -pat′ing [< L. *in,* on + *culpa,* blame] *same as* INCRIMINATE

in·cum·ben·cy (in kum′bən sē) *n., pl.* -cies 1. a duty or obligation 2. a term of office

in·cum·bent (-bənt) *adj.* [< L. *in-,* on + *cubare,* lie down] 1. resting (*on* or *upon* one) as a duty or obligation 2. currently in office —*n.* the holder of an office, etc.

in·cum·ber (in kum′bər) *vt. same as* ENCUMBER —**in·cum′brance** *n.*

in·cu·nab·u·la (in′kyoo nab′yə lə) *n.pl., sing.* -u·lum [L., pl., swaddling clothes] 1. infancy; beginnings 2. books printed before 1500

in·cur (in kur′) *vt.* -curred′, -cur′ring [< L. *in-,* in + *currere,* to run] to meet with or bring upon oneself (something undesirable)

in·cu·ri·ous (in kyoor′ē əs) *adj.* not curious; uninterested

in·cur·sion (in kur′zhən) *n.* [see prec.] an invasion or raid

in·cus (iŋ′kəs) *n., pl.* **in·cu·des** (in·kyōō′dēz) [< L., anvil] the central one of the three small bones in the middle ear

Ind. 1. India 2. Indian 3. Indiana

ind. 1. independent 2. index

in·debt·ed (in det′id) *adj.* 1. in debt 2. obliged; owing gratitude

in·debt′ed·ness *n.* 1. a being indebted 2. the amount owed

in·de·cent (in dē′s'nt) *adj.* not decent; specif., *a)* improper *b)* morally offensive; obscene —**in·de′cen·cy** *n.* —**in·de′cent·ly** *adv.*

in·de·ci·pher·a·ble (in′di sī′fər ə b'l) *adj.* that cannot be deciphered

in·de·ci·sion (in′di sizh′ən) *n.* inability to decide; vacillation

in·de·ci·sive (-sī′siv) *adj.* 1. not decisive 2. showing indecision —**in′·de·ci′sive·ly** *adv.* —**in′de·ci′sive·ness** *n.*

in·deed (in dēd′) *adv.* certainly; truly —*interj.* an exclamation of surprise, doubt, sarcasm, etc.

in·de·fat·i·ga·ble (in′di fat′i gə b'l) *adj.* [< L. *in-,* not + *defatigare,* tire out] not tiring; tireless

in·de·fen·si·ble (in′di fen′sə b'l) *adj.* 1. that cannot be defended 2. that cannot be justified

in·def·i·nite (in def′ə nit) *adj.* 1. having no exact limits 2. not precise in meaning; vague 3. not certain; unsure 4. *Gram.* not limiting or specifying [*a* and *an* are **indefinite** articles] —**in·def′i·nite·ly** *adv.*

in·del·i·ble (in del′ə b'l) *adj.* [< L. *in-,* not + *delere,* destroy] 1. that cannot be erased, blotted out, etc. 2. leaving an indelible mark

in·del·i·cate (in del′i kit) *adj.* lacking propriety or modesty; coarse —**in·del′i·ca·cy** *n., pl.* -cies

in·dem·ni·fy (in dem′nə fī′) *vt.* -fied′, -fy′ing [< L. *indemnis,* unhurt + -FY] 1. to insure against loss, damage, etc. 2. to repay for (loss or damage) —**in·dem′ni·fi·ca′tion** *n.*

in·dem·ni·ty *n., pl.* -ties 1. insurance against loss, damage, etc. 2. repayment for loss, damage, etc.

in·dent¹ (in dent′) *vt., vi.* [< L. *in,* in + *dens,* tooth] 1. to notch 2. to space (the beginning of a paragraph, etc.) in from the regular margin

in·dent² (in dent′) *vt.* [IN-¹ + DENT] to make a dent in

in′den·ta′tion (-den tā′shən) *n.* 1. a being indented 2. a notch, cut, inlet, etc. 3. a dent 4. a spacing in from the margin, or a blank space so made: in this sense, usually, **in·den′tion**

in·den·ture (in den′chər) *n.* 1. a written contract [*often pl.*] a contract binding one person to work for another —*vt.* -tured, -tur·ing to bind by indenture

---

fat, āpe, cär; ten, ēven; is, bīte; gō, hôrn, tōōl, look; oil, out; up, fur; chin; she; thin, then; zh, leisure; ŋ, ring; ə for *a* in *ago;* ', (ā′b'l); ë, Fr. coeur; ö, Fr. feu; Fr. mon; ü, Fr. duc; kh, G. ich, doch; ‡ foreign; < derived from

In·de·pend·ence (in'di pen'dəns) city in W Mo.: pop. 112,000

in·de·pend·ence (in'di pen'dəns) *n.* a being independent; freedom from the control of another

Independence Day the anniversary of the adoption of the American Declaration of Independence on July 4, 1776

in'de·pend'ent (-dənt) *adj.* 1. free from the influence or control of others; specif., *a)* self-governing *b)* self-determined, self-reliant, etc. *c)* not adhering to any political party *d)* not connected with others [an *independent* grocer] 2. not depending on another for financial support —*n.* one who is independent in thinking, action, etc. —**in'de·pend'ent·ly** *adv.*

independent clause *same as* MAIN CLAUSE

in'-depth' *adj.* profound; thorough

in·de·scrib·a·ble (in'di skrī'bə b'l) *adj.* beyond the power of description —**in'de·scrib'a·bly** *adv.*

in·de·struct·i·ble (in'di struk'tə b'l) *adj.* that cannot be destroyed

in·de·ter·mi·nate (in'di tur'mi nit) *adj.* 1. indefinite; vague 2. unsettled; inconclusive

in·dex (in'deks) *n., pl.* **-dex·es, -di·ces'** (-də sēz') [L.: see INDICATE] 1. the forefinger: also **index finger** 2. a pointer, as the needle on a dial 3. an indication [an *index* of ability] 4. an alphabetical list of names, subjects, etc. indicating pages where found, as in a book 5. a figure showing ratio or relative change 6. [I-] *R.C.Ch.* formerly, a list of books forbidden to be read —*vt.* to make an index of or for

In·di·a (in'dē ə) 1. region in S Asia, south of the Himalayas 2. republic in the Brit. Commonwealth, in C & S India: 1,177,000 sq. mi.; pop. 507,386,000

India ink a black liquid ink

In'di·an *n.* 1. a native of India or the East Indies 2. a member of any of the aboriginal peoples of the Americas: also **American Indian** 3. any of the languages spoken by the American Indians —*adj.* 1. of India or the East Indies, their people, etc. 2. of the American Indians or their culture

In·di·an·a (in'dē an'ə) Middle Western State of the U.S.: 36,291 sq. mi.; pop. 5,490,000; cap. Indianapolis —**In'di·an'i·an** *adj., n.*

In·di·an·ap·o·lis (in'dē ə nap'ə lis) capital of Indiana: pop. 701,000

Indian corn *same as* CORN[1] (sense 2)

Indian file *same as* SINGLE FILE

Indian Ocean ocean south of Asia, between Africa & Australia

Indian summer mild, warm weather after the first frosts of late autumn

India paper 1. a thin, absorbent paper used in taking proofs from engraved plates 2. a thin, strong, opaque printing paper, as for Bibles

indic. indicative

in·di·cate (in'də kāt') *vt.* -cat'ed, -cat'ing [< L. *in-*, in + *dicare*, declare] 1. to direct attention to;

point out 2. to be a sign of; signify 3. to show the need for 4. to express briefly or generally —**in'di·ca'tion** *n.*

in·dic·a·tive (in dik'ə tiv) *adj.* 1. giving an indication 2. designating that mood of a verb used to express an act, state, etc. as actual, or to ask a question —*n.* the indicative mood

in'di·ca'tor *n.* a person or thing that indicates; specif., a gauge, dial, etc. that measures something

in·dict (in dīt') *vt.* [ult. < L. *in*, against + *dicere*, speak] to charge with a crime —**in·dict'ment** *n.*

in·dif·fer·ent (in dif'ər ənt) *adj.* 1. showing no bias; neutral 2. unconcerned; apathetic 3. of no importance 4. fair; average —**in·dif'fer·ence** *n.* —**in·dif'fer·ent·ly** *adv.*

in·dig·e·nous (in dij'ə nəs) *adj.* [< OL. *indu*, in + L. *gignere*, be born] existing or growing naturally in a region or country; native

in·di·gent (in'di jənt) *adj.* [< OL. *indu*, in + *egere*, to need] poor; needy —*n.* an indigent person —**in'di·gence** *n.* —**in'di·gent·ly** *adv.*

in·di·gest·i·ble (in'di jes'tə b'l) *adj.* not easily digested

in'di·ges'tion (-jes'chən) *n.* difficulty in digesting food

in·dig·nant (in dig'nənt) *adj.* [< L. *in-*, not + *dignus*, worthy] feeling or expressing anger, esp. at unjust or mean action —**in·dig'nant·ly** *adv.*

in·dig·na·tion (in'dig nā'shən) *n.* righteous anger

in·dig·ni·ty (in dig'nə tē) *n., pl.* **-ties** an insult or affront to one's dignity or self-respect

in·di·go (in'di gō') *n., pl.* **-gos', -goes'** [Sp. < Gr. *Indikos*, Indian] 1. a blue dye obtained from certain plants or made synthetically 2. a deep violet blue —*adj.* of this color

in·di·rect (in'di rekt', -dī-) *adj.* 1. not straight 2. not straight to the point 3. dishonest [*indirect* dealing] 4. not immediate; secondary [an *indirect* result] —**in'di·rect'ly** *adv.* —**in'di·rect'ness** *n.*

indirect object the word or words denoting the person or thing indirectly affected by the action of the verb (Ex.: *us* in *give us time*)

in·dis·creet (in'dis krēt') *adj.* lacking prudence; unwise

in·dis·cre·tion (in'dis kresh'ən) *n.* 1. lack of discretion 2. an indiscreet act or remark

in·dis·crim·i·nate (in'dis krim'ə nit) *adj.* 1. confused; random 2. making no distinctions —**in'dis·crim'i·nate·ly** *adv.*

in·dis·pen·sa·ble (in'dis pen'sə b'l) *adj.* absolutely necessary

in·dis·posed (in'dis pōzd') *adj.* 1. slightly ill 2. unwilling; disinclined —**in'dis·po·si'tion** (-pə zish'ən) *n.*

in·dis·sol·u·ble (in'di säl'yoo b'l) *adj.* that cannot be dissolved or destroyed; lasting

in·dite (in dīt') *vt.* -dit'ed, -dit'ing [see INDICT] to compose and write

in·di·vid·u·al (in'də vij'oo wəl) *adj.* [< L. < *in-*, not + *dividere*, to divide]

1. existing as a separate thing or being; single 2. of, for, by, or relating to a single person or thing —*n.* 1. a single thing or being 2. a person

in′di·vid′u·al·ism *n.* 1. individuality 2. the doctrine that the state exists for the individual 3. the leading of one's life in one's own way —**in′di·vid′u·al·ist** *n.* —**in′di·vid′u·al·is′tic** *adj.*

in′di·vid′u·al′i·ty (-wal′ə tē) *n., pl.* -ties 1. the sum of the characteristics that set one person or thing apart 2. existence as an individual

in′di·vid′u·al·ize′ (-wə liz′) *vt.* -ized′, -iz′ing 1. to make individual 2. to treat as an individual —**in′di·vid′u·al·i·za′tion** *n.*

in′di·vid′u·al·ly *adv.* 1. as individuals; separately 2. distinctively

In·do·chi·na (in′dō chī′nə) 1. large peninsula south of China 2. E part of this peninsula, consisting of Laos, Cambodia, & Vietnam

in·doc·tri·nate (in däk′trə nāt′) *vt.* -nat′ed, -nat′ing to instruct in doctrines, theories, beliefs, etc. —**in·doc′tri·na′tion** *n.*

In·do-Eu·ro·pe·an (in′dō yoor′ə pē′ən) *adj.* designating a family of languages including most of those of Europe and some of those of Asia

in·do·lent (in′də lənt) *adj.* [< L. *in-*, not + *dolere*, feel pain] idle; lazy —**In′do·lence** *n.* —**in′do·lent·ly** *adv.*

in·dom·i·ta·ble (in däm′it ə b'l) *adj.* [< L. *in-*, not + *domare*, to tame] not easily discouraged or defeated

In·do·ne·si·a (in′də nē′zhə, -shə) republic in the Malay Archipelago, including Java, Sumatra, & most of Borneo: 736,510 sq. mi.; pop. 100,795,000 —**In′do·ne′sian** *adj., n.*

in·door (in′dôr′) *adj.* living, belonging, etc. in a building

in·doors (in′dôrz′) *adv.* in or into a building

in·dorse (in dôrs′) *vt.* -dorsed′, -dors′ing *same as* ENDORSE

in·du·bi·ta·ble (in dōō′bi tə b'l) *adj.* that cannot be doubted —**in·du′bi·ta·bly** *adv.*

in·duce (in dōōs′) *vt.* -duced′, -duc′ing [< L. *in-*, in + *ducere*, to lead] 1. to persuade 2. to bring on /sleep *induced* by drugs/ 3. to draw (a conclusion) from particular facts 4. to bring about (an electric or magnetic effect) in a body by placing it within a field of force —**in·duc′er** *n.*

in·duce·ment *n.* 1. an inducing or being induced 2. a motive; incentive

in·duct (in dukt′) *vt.* [see INDUCE] 1. to place formally in an office, a society, etc. 2. to enroll (esp. a draftee) in the armed forces

in·duct·ance (in duk′təns) *n.* the property of an electric circuit by which a varying current in it produces a magnetic field that induces voltages in the same or a nearby circuit

in·duct·ee (in duk′tē′) *n.* a person

inducted, esp. into the armed forces

in·duc·tion (in duk′shən) *n.* 1. an inducting or being inducted 2. reasoning from particular facts to a general conclusion 3. the inducing of an electric or magnetic effect by a field of force —**in·duc′tive** *adj.*

in·due (in dōō′) *vt.* -dued′, -du′ing *same as* ENDUE

in·dulge (in dulj′) *vt.* -dulged′, -dulg′ing [L. *indulgere*, be kind to] 1. to satisfy (a desire) 2. to gratify the wishes of; humor —*vi.* to give way to one's desires —**in·dulg′er** *n.*

in·dul·gence (in dul′jəns) *n.* 1. an indulging or being indulgent 2. a thing indulged in 3. a favor or privilege 4. *R.C.Ch.* a remission of punishment still due for a sin after the guilt has been forgiven

in·dul·gent *adj.* indulging or inclined to indulge; kind or lenient, often to excess —**in·dul′gent·ly** *adv.*

in·dus·tri·al (in dus′trē əl) *adj.* having to do with industries or with the people working in industries —**in·dus′tri·al·ly** *adv.*

industrial arts the mechanical and technical skills used in industry

in·dus′tri·al·ism *n.* social and economic organization characterized by large industries, machine production, urban workers, etc.

in·dus′tri·al·ist *n.* one who owns or manages an industrial enterprise

in·dus′tri·al·ize′ (-ə līz′) *vt.* -ized′, -iz′ing 1. to establish or develop industrialism in 2. to organize as an industry —**in·dus′tri·al·i·za′tion** *n.*

industrial park an area zoned for industrial and business use, usually on the outskirts of a city

in·dus·tri·ous (in dus′trē əs) *adj.* hard-working; diligent —**in·dus′tri·ous·ly** *adv.* —**in·dus′tri·ous·ness** *n.*

in·dus·try (in′dəs trē) *n., pl.* -tries [< L. *industrius*, active] 1. earnest, steady effort 2. any branch of productive, manufacturing enterprise, or all of these collectively 3. any large-scale business activity 4. the owners and managers of industry

-ine¹ (*variously* īn, in, ēn, ən) [< L. *-inus*] a suffix meaning of, having the nature of, like /*divine, crystalline*/

-ine² (in, ən) [< L. *-ina*] a suffix used to form certain abstract nouns /*medicine, doctrine*/

-ine³ (*variously* ēn, in, īn, ən) [< L. *-inus*] a suffix used to form the chemical names of: 1. halogens /*iodine*/ 2. alkaloids or nitrogen bases /*morphine*/ Often used to form commercial names /*Vaseline*/

in·e·bri·ate (in ē′brē āt′; *for n., usually* -it) *vt.* -at′ed, -at′ing [ult. < L. *in-*, intens. + *ebrius*, drunk] to make drunk; intoxicate —*n.* a drunkard —**in·e′bri·a′tion** *n.*

in·ed·u·ca·ble (in ej′ə kə b'l) *adj.* thought to be incapable of being educated

---

fat, āpe, cär; ten, ēven; is, bīte; gō, hôrn, tōōl, look; oil, out; up, fur; chin; she; thin, then; zh, leisure; ŋ, ring; ə for *a* in *ago*; ΄, (ā′b'l); ë, Fr. coeur; ö, Fr. feu; Fr. mon; ü, Fr. duc; kh, G. ich, doch; ‡ foreign; < derived from

in·ef·fa·ble (in ef'ə b'l) *adj.* [< L. *in-*, not + *effabilis*, utterable] 1. inexpressible 2. too sacred to be spoken

in·ef·fi·cient (in'ə fish'ənt) *adj.* 1. not producing the desired effect with a minimum of energy, time, etc. 2. incapable —**in'ef·fi'cien·cy** *n.* —**in'ef·fi'cient·ly** *adv.*

in·el·e·gant (in el'ə gənt) *adj.* not elegant; crude —**in·el'e·gant·ly** *adv.*

in·e·luc·ta·ble (in'i luk'tə b'l) *adj.* [< L. *in-*, not + *eluctari*, to struggle] not to be avoided or escaped —**in'e·luc'ta·bly** *adv.*

in·ept (in ept') *adj.* [< L. *in-*, not + *aptus*, apt] 1. unsuitable; unfit 2. foolish 3. awkward; clumsy —**in·ept'·i·tude** (-ep'tə tōōd'), **in·ept'ness** *n.*

in·ert (in urt') *adj.* [< L. *in-*, not + *ars*, skill] 1. without power to move or to resist 2. inactive; dull; slow 3. with few or no active properties

in·er·tia (in ur'shə) *n.* [see prec.] 1. *Physics* the tendency of matter to remain at rest (or continue in a fixed direction) unless affected by an outside force 2. disinclination to act —**in·er'tial** *adj.*

in·es·cap·a·ble (in'ə skāp'ə b'l) *adj.* that cannot be escaped or avoided

in·es·ti·ma·ble (in es'tə mə b'l) *adj.* too great to be properly estimated

in·ev·i·ta·ble (in ev'ə tə b'l) *adj.* [< L. *in-*, not + *evitabilis*, avoidable] that must happen; unavoidable —**in·ev'i·ta·bil'i·ty** *n.* —**in·ev'i·ta·bly** *adv.*

in·ex·haust·i·ble (in'ig zôs'tə b'l) *adj.* 1. that cannot be used up or emptied 2. tireless

in·ex·o·ra·ble (in ek'sər ə b'l) *adj.* [< L. *in-*, not + *exorare*, move by entreaty] 1. that cannot be influenced by persuasion or entreaty; unrelenting 2. that cannot be altered, checked, etc. —**in·ex'o·ra·bly** *adv.*

in·ex·pe·ri·ence (in'ik spir'ē əns) *n.* lack of experience or of the knowledge or skill resulting from experience —**in'ex·pe'ri·enced** *adj.*

in·ex·pert (in ek'spərt, in'ik spurt') *adj.* not expert; unskillful

in·ex·pi·a·ble (in ek'spē ə b'l) *adj.* that cannot be explated or atoned for

in·ex·pli·ca·ble (in eks'pli kə b'l) *adj.* that cannot be explained

in·ex·press·i·ble (in'ik spres'ə b'l) *adj.* that cannot be expressed

in·ex·tin·guish·a·ble (in'ik stiŋ'gwish ə b'l) *adj.* that cannot be put out or stopped

†**in ex·tre·mis** (in' ik strē'mis) [L., in extremity] at the point of death

in·ex·tri·ca·ble (in eks'tri kə b'l) *adj.* 1. that one cannot extricate himself from 2. that cannot be disentangled or untied 3. insolvable

inf. 1. infantry 2. infinitive

in·fal·li·ble (in fal'ə b'l) *adj.* [see IN-² & FALLIBLE] 1. incapable of error 2. dependable; reliable —**in·fal'li·bil'i·ty** *n.* —**in·fal'li·bly** *adv.*

in·fa·mous (in'fə məs) *adj.* 1. having a bad reputation; notorious 2. causing a bad reputation; scandalous

in·fa·my (-mē) *n., pl.* **-mies** 1. very

bad reputation; disgrace 2. great wickedness 3. an infamous act

in·fan·cy (in'fən sē) *n., pl.* **-cies** 1. the state or period of being an infant 2. the earliest stage of anything

in·fant (in'fənt) *n.* [< L. *in-*, not + *fari*, speak] a very young child; baby —*adj.* 1. of or for infants 2. in a very early stage

in·fan·ti·cide (in fan'tə sīd') *n.* 1. the murder of a baby 2. a person guilty of this

in·fan·tile (in'fən tīl', -til) *adj.* 1. of infants 2. like an infant; babyish

infantile paralysis poliomyelitis

in·fan·try (in'fən trē) *n., pl.* **-tries** [< It. *infante*, a youth] that branch of an army consisting of soldiers trained to fight on foot —**in'fan·try·man** (-mən) *n., pl.* **-men**

in·farct (in färkt') *n.* [< L. *in-*, in + *farcire*, to stuff] an area of dying or dead tissue caused by obstruction of blood vessels: also **in·farc'tion** (-färk'shən)

in·fat·u·ate (in faoh'ŏō wāt') *vt.* **-at'ed, -at'ing** [< L. *in-*, intens. + *fatuus*, foolish] to inspire with foolish love or affection —**in·fat'u·a'tion** *n.*

in·fect (in fekt') *vt.* [< L. *inficere*, to stain] 1. to contaminate, or cause to become diseased, with a germ or virus 2. to imbue with one's feelings or beliefs, esp. so as to harm

in·fec·tion (in fek'shən) *n.* 1. an infecting or being infected 2. an infectious disease

in·fec·tious (-shəs) *adj.* 1. likely to cause infection 2. designating a disease caused by the presence in the body of certain microorganisms 3. tending to spread to others —**in·fec'tious·ly** *adv.* —**in·fec'tious·ness** *n.*

in·fe·lic·i·tous (in'fə lis'ə təs) *adj.* not felicitous; unsuitable; not apt —**in'fe·lic'i·ty** *n., pl.* **-ties**

in·fer (in fur') *vt.* **-ferred', -fer'ring** [< L. *in-*, in + *ferre*, bring] 1. to conclude by reasoning from something known or assumed 2. to imply: still sometimes regarded as a loose usage —**in'fer·ence** *n.*

in·fer·en·tial (in'fə ren'shəl) *adj.* based on or relating to inference

in·fe·ri·or (in fir'ē ər) *adj.* [< L. *inferus*, low] 1. lower in space 2. lower in order, status, quality, etc. (with *to*) 3. poor in quality; below average —*n.* an inferior person or thing —**in·fe'ri·or'i·ty** (-ôr'ə tē) *n.*

in·fer·nal (in fur'n'l) *adj.* [< L. *inferus*, below] 1. of hell or Hades 2. hellish; fiendish

in·fer·no (in fur'nō) *n., pl.* **-nos** [It. < L.: see prec.] *same as* HELL

in·fest (in fest') *vt.* [< L. *infestus*, hostile] 1. to overrun in large numbers, usually so as to be harmful 2. to be parasitic in or on —**in'fes·ta'tion** *n.* —**in·fest'er** *n.*

in·fi·del (in'fə d'l) *n.* [< L. *in-*, not + *fidelis*, faithful] 1. one who does not believe in a certain religion 2. one who has no religion

in·fi·del·i·ty (in'fə del'ə tē) *n.* unfaithfulness, esp. in marriage

in·field (in'fēld') *n.* 1. the area of a baseball field enclosed by the base lines 2. the players (**infielders**) whose field positions are there

in'fight·ing *n.* 1. fighting, esp. boxing, at close range 2. personal conflict within a group —**in'fight'er** *n.*

in·fil·trate (in fil'trāt, in'fil trāt') *vi., vt.* -**trat·ed**, -**trat·ing** 1. to filter or pass gradually through or into 2. to penetrate (enemy lines, a region, etc.) gradually or stealthily, so as to attack or seize control from within —**in'fil·tra'tion** *n.* —**in'fil·tra'tor** *n.*

in·fi·nite (in'fə nit) *adj.* [see IN-² & FINITE] 1. lacking limits; endless 2. very great; vast —*n.* something infinite —**in'fi·nite·ly** *adv.*

in·fin·i·tes·i·mal (in'fin ə tes'ə məl) *adj.* [< L. *infinitus*, infinite] too small to be measured; very minute —**in'fin·i·tes'i·mal·ly** *adv.*

in·fin·i·tive (in fin'ə tiv) *n.* [see INFINITE] the form of a verb without reference to person, number, or tense: usually with *to*, as in "I want *to go*"

in·fin'i·tude (-tood') *n.* 1. a being infinite 2. an infinite quantity

in·fin·i·ty (-tē) *n., pl.* -**ties** [< L. *infinitas*] 1. the quality of being infinite 2. unlimited space, time, etc. 3. an indefinitely large quantity

in·firm (in furm') *adj.* 1. weak; feeble 2. not firm; unstable; frail; shaky —**in·firm'ly** *adv.* —**in·firm'ness** *n.*

in·fir·ma·ry (in fur'mə rē) *n., pl.* -**ries** a place for the care of the sick, injured, or infirm; hospital

in·fir'mi·ty (-mə tē) *n., pl.* -**ties** physical weakness or defect

in·flame (in flām') *vt., vi.* -**flamed'**, -**flam'ing** [see IN-¹ & FLAME] 1. to arouse, excite, etc. or become aroused, excited, etc. 2. to undergo or cause to undergo inflammation

in·flam·ma·ble (in flam'ə b'l) *adj.* 1. same as FLAMMABLE 2. easily excited —**in·flam'ma·bil'i·ty** *n.*

in·flam·ma·tion (in'flə mā'shən) *n.* 1. an inflaming or being inflamed 2. redness, pain, heat, and swelling in the body, due to injury or disease

in·flam·ma·to·ry (in flam'ə tôr'ē) *adj.* 1. rousing excitement, anger, etc. 2. of or caused by inflammation

in·flate (in flāt') *vt.* -**flat'ed**, -**flat'ing** [< L. *in-*, in + *flare*, blow] 1. to blow full with air or gas 2. to puff up with pride 3. to increase beyond what is normal; specif., to cause inflation of (money, credit, etc.) —*vi.* to become inflated —**in·flat'a·ble** *adj.*

in·fla'tion *n.* 1. an inflating or being inflated 2. an increase in the currency in circulation or a marked expansion of credit, resulting in a fall in currency value and a sharp rise in prices —**in·fla'tion·ar'y** *adj.*

in·flect (in flekt') *vt.* [< L. *in-*, in + *flectere*, to bend] 1. to vary the tone of (the voice) 2. to change the form of (a word) by inflection

in·flec·tion (in flek'shən) *n.* 1. a change in the tone of the voice 2. the change of form in a word to indicate number, case, tense, etc. Brit. sp. **inflexion** —**in·flec'tion·al** *adj.*

in·flex·i·ble (in flek'sə b'l) *adj.* not flexible; stiff, rigid, fixed, unyielding, etc. —**in·flex'i·bil'i·ty** *n.*

in·flict (in flikt') *vt.* [< L. *in-*, on + *fligere*, to strike] 1. to cause (wounds, pain, etc.) as by striking 2. to impose (a punishment, etc. *on* or *upon*) —**in·flic'tion** *n.* —**in·flic'tive** *adj.*

in·flight (in'flīt') *adj.* done, shown, etc. while an aircraft is in flight

in·flo·res·cence (in'flô res''ns) *n.* 1. the producing of blossoms 2. the arrangement of flowers on a stem 3. a flower cluster 4. flowers collectively

in·flu·ence (in'floo wəns) *n.* [< L. *in-*, in + *fluere*, to flow] 1. power to affect others 2. power to produce effects because of wealth, position, ability, etc. 3. one that has influence —*vt.* -**enced**, -**enc·ing** to have influence or effect on

in'flu·en'tial (-wen'shəl) *adj.* exerting influence, esp. great influence

in·flu·en·za (in'floo wen'zə) *n.* [It., an influence] an acute, contagious virus infection, characterized by inflammation of the respiratory tract, fever, muscular pain, etc.

in·flux (in'fluks') *n.* [see INFLUENCE] a flowing in or streaming in

in·fold (in fōld') *vt. same as* ENFOLD

in·form (in fôrm') *vt.* [see IN-¹ & FORM] to give knowledge of something to —*vi.* to give information, esp. in accusing another —**in·form'er** *n.*

in·for·mal (in fôr'məl) *adj.* not formal; specif., *a)* not according to fixed customs, rules, etc. *b)* casual, relaxed, etc. *c)* not requiring formal dress *d)* colloquial —**in'for·mal'i·ty** (-mal'ə tē) *n., pl.* -**ties** —**in·for'mal·ly** *adv.*

in·form·ant (in fôr'mənt) *n.* a person who gives information

in·for·ma·tion (in'fər mā'shən) *n.* 1. an informing or being informed 2. something told or facts learned; news or knowledge 3. data stored in or retrieved from a computer

in·for·ma·tive (in fôr'mə tiv) *adj.* giving information; instructive

infra- [< L.] *a prefix meaning* below

in·frac·tion (in frak'shən) *n.* [see INFRINGE] a violation of a law, pact, etc.

in·fran·gi·ble (in fran'jə b'l) *adj.* [see IN-² & FRANGIBLE] unbreakable or inviolable —**in·fran'gi·bly** *adv.*

in·fra·red (in'frə red') *adj.* designating or of those invisible rays just beyond the red of the visible spectrum: they have a penetrating heating effect

in'fra·son'ic (-sän'ik) *adj.* of a frequency of sound below that audible to the human ear

in·fra·struc·ture (-struk'chər) *n.* basic installations and facilities, as roads, power plants, transportation and communication systems, etc.

in·fre·quent (in frē'kwənt) *adj.* not frequent; happening seldom; rare — **in·fre'quen·cy**, **in·fre'quence** *n.* —**in·fre'quent·ly** *adv.*

in·fringe (in frinj') *vt.* **-fringed'**, **-fring'ing** [< L. *in-*, in + *frangere*, to break] to break (a law or pact) —**infringe on** (or **upon**) to encroach on (the rights, etc. of others) —**in·fringe'ment** *n.*

in·fu·ri·ate (in fyoor'ē āt') *vt.* **-at'ed**, **-at'ing** [< L. *in-*, in + *furia*, rage] to make very angry; enrage

in·fuse (in fyōoz') *vt.* **-fused'**, **-fus'ing** [< L. *in-*, in + *fundere*, pour] 1. to instill or impart (qualities, etc.) 2. to fill; inspire 3. to steep (tea leaves, etc.) to extract the essence —**in·fus'er** *n.* —**in·fu'sion** *n.*

-ing (iŋ) [< OE.] a suffix used to form the present participle or verbal nouns [*talking*, *painting*]

in·gen·ious (in jēn'yəs) *adj.* [< L. *in-*, in + *gignere*, to produce] 1. clever, resourceful, etc. 2. made or done in a clever or original way —**in·gen'ious·ly** *adv.*

in·gé·nue (an'zh₂ nōo', -jə-) *n.* [Fr., ingenuous] *Theater* the role of an inexperienced young woman, or an actress in this role

in·ge·nu·i·ty (in'jə nōo'ə tē) *n.* ingenious quality; cleverness

in·gen·u·ous (in jen'yoo wəs) *adj.* [< L. *in-*, in + *gignere*, to produce] 1. frank; open 2. simple; naive — **in·gen'u·ous·ly** *adv.* —**in·gen'u·ous·ness** *n.*

in·gest (in jest') *vt.* [< L. *in-*, into + *gerere*, carry] to take (food, etc.) into the body —**in·ges'tion** *n.*

in·glo·ri·ous (in glôr'ē əs) *adj.* shameful; disgraceful

in·got (iŋ'gət) *n.* [prob. < OFr. *lingo*, tongue] a mass of metal cast into a bar or other convenient shape

in·grained (in grānd') *adj.* 1. firmly established, as habits 2. inveterate [*an ingrained liar*]

in·grate (in'grāt) *n.* [< L. *in-*, not + *gratus*, grateful] an ungrateful person

in·gra·ti·ate (in grā'shē āt') *vt.* **-at'ed**, **-at'ing** [< L. *in*, in + *gratia*, favor] to bring (oneself) into another's favor —**in·gra'ti·a'tion** *n.*

in·grat·i·tude (in grat'ə tōod') *n.* lack of gratitude; ungratefulness

in·gre·di·ent (in grē'dē ənt) *n.* [see ff.] any of the things that make up a mixture; component

in·gress (in'gres) *n.* [< L. *in-*, into + *gradi*, to go] entrance

in·grown (in'grōn') *adj.* grown inward, esp. into the flesh, as a toenail

in·gui·nal (iŋ'gwə n'l) *adj.* [< L. *inguen*, groin] of or near the groin

in·hab·it (in hab'it) *vt.* [< L. *in-*, in + *habitare*, dwell] to live in —**in·hab'it·a·ble** *adj.*

in·hab·it·ant (-i tənt) *n.* a person or animal inhabiting a specified place

in·hal·ant (in hāl'ənt) *n.* a medicine, etc. to be inhaled

in·ha·la·tor (in'hə lāt'ər) *n.* an

apparatus used in inhaling medicinal vapors 2. *same as* RESPIRATOR (sense 2)

in·hale (in hāl') *vt.*, *vi.* **-haled'**, **-hal'ing** [< L. *in-*, in + *halare*, breathe] to breathe in (air or smoke) —**in·ha·la·tion** (in'hə lā'shən) *n.*

in·hal·er (-ər) *n.* 1. one who inhales 2. *same as* RESPIRATOR (sense 1) 3. *same as* INHALATOR (sense 1)

in·here (in hir') *vi.* **-hered'**, **-her'ing** [< L. *in-*, in + *haerere*, to stick] to be inherent

in·her·ent (in hir'ənt, -her'-) *adj.* existing in someone or something as a natural and inseparable quality

in·her·it (in her'it) *vt.*, *vi.* [< L. *in*, in + *heres*, heir] 1. to receive (property, etc.) as an heir 2. to have (certain characteristics) by heredity

in·her'it·ance *n.* 1. the action of inheriting 2. something inherited

in·hib·it (in hib'it) *vt.* [< L. *in-*, in + *habere*, to hold] to check or repress

in·hi·bi·tion (in'hi bish'ən, in'ə-) *n.* 1. an inhibiting or being inhibited 2. a mental process that restrains an action, emotion, or thought

in·hu·man (in hyōo'mən) *adj.* not having worthy human characteristics; heartless, cruel, brutal, etc. —**in'hu·man'i·ty** (-man'ə tē) *n.*

in·im·i·cal (in im'i k'l) *adj.* [< L. *in-*, not + *amicus*, friend] 1. hostile; unfriendly 2. in opposition; adverse

in·im·i·ta·ble (in im'ə tə b'l) *adj.* that cannot be imitated; matchless

in·iq·ui·ty (in ik'wə tē) *n.* [< L. *in-*, not + *aequus*, equal] 1. wickedness 2. *pl.* **-ties** a wicked or unjust act —**in·iq'ui·tous** *adj.*

in·i·tial (i nish'əl) *adj.* [< L. *in-*, in + *ire*, go] of or at the beginning; first —*n.* the first letter of a name —*vt.* **-tialed** or **-tialled**, **-tial·ing** or **-tial·ling** to mark with initials —**in·i'tial·ly** *adv.*

in·i·ti·ate (i nish'ē āt') *vt.* **-at'ed**, **-at'ing** [see prec.] 1. to bring into practice or use 2. to teach the fundamentals of a subject to 3. to admit as a member into a fraternity, club, etc., esp. with a special or secret ceremony —**in·i'ti·a'tion** *n.* —**in·i'ti·a·to'ry** (-ə tôr'ē) *adj.*

in·i·ti·a·tive (i nish'ē ə tiv, -nish'ə-) *n.* 1. the action of taking the first step or move 2. ability in originating new ideas or methods 3. the introduction of proposed legislation, as to popular vote, by voters' petitions

in·ject (in jekt') *vt.* [< L. *in-*, in + *jacere*, to throw] 1. to force (a fluid) into a vein, tissue, etc. with a syringe or the like 2. to introduce (a remark, quality, etc.) —**in·jec'tion** *n.* —**in·jec'tor** *n.*

in·junc·tion (in juŋk'shən) *n.* [< L. *in-*, in + *jungere*, join] 1. a command; order 2. a court order prohibiting or ordering a given action

in·jure (in'jər) *vt.* **-jured**, **-jur·ing** [see INJURY] 1. to do harm or damage to; hurt 2. to wrong or offend

in·ju·ri·ous (in joor'ē əs) *adj.* injuring or likely to injure; harmful

in·ju·ry (in'jər ē) *n.*, *pl.* **-ries** [< L.

in- not + *jus,* right] 1. harm or damage 2. an injurious act

in·jus·tice (in jus'tis) *n.* 1. a being unjust 2. an unjust act; wrong

ink (iŋk) *n.* [< Gr. *en-,* in + *kaiein,* to burn] a colored liquid used for writing, printing, etc. —*vt.* to cover, mark, or color with ink

ink'blot' *n.* any of the patterns made by blots of ink that are used in the RORSCHACH TEST

ink·ling (iŋk'liŋ) *n.* [ME. *ingkiling*] 1. a hint 2. a vague notion

ink'well' *n.* a container for ink

ink'y *adj.* **-i·er, -i·est** 1. like very dark ink in color; black 2. covered with ink —**ink'i·ness** *n.*

in·laid (in'lād', in lād') *adj.* set into a surface or formed, decorated, etc. by inlaying

in·land (in'lənd; *for n. & adv. usually* -land') *adj.* of or in the interior of a country —*n.* inland region —*adv.* into or toward this region

INLAID WOOD

in-law (in'lô') *n.* [< (MOTHER)-IN-LAW, etc.] [Colloq.] a relative by marriage

in·lay (in'lā'; *for v., also in* lā') *vt.* **-laid', -lay'ing** 1. to set (pieces of wood, etc.) into a surface, specif. for decoration 2. to decorate thus —*n., pl.* **-lays'** 1. inlaid decoration or material 2. a shaped filling, as of gold, cemented into the cavity of a tooth

in·let (in'let) *n.* a narrow strip of water extending into a body of land

in·mate (in'māt') *n.* a person confined with others in a prison or institution

in·most (in'mōst') *adj.* 1. farthest within 2. most secret

inn (in) *n.* [OE.] 1. a small hotel 2. a restaurant or tavern Now usually only in the names of such places

in·nards (in'ərdz) *n.pl.* [< INWARDS] [Colloq.] inner organs or parts

in·nate (i nāt', in'āt) *adj.* [< L. *in-,* in + *nasci,* be born] inborn; natural

in·ner (in'ər) *adj.* 1. farther within 2. more secret

inner circle the small, exclusive, most influential part of a group

inner city the crowded or blighted central sections of a large city

in'ner·most' *adj. same as* INMOST

in'ner·sole' *n. same as* INSOLE

in'ner·spring' mattress a mattress with built-in coil springs

in·ner·vate (i nur'vāt, in'ər vāt') *vt.* **-vat·ed, -vat·ing** 1. to supply (a part) with nerves 2. to stimulate (a muscle, etc.) —**in'ner·va'tion** *n.*

in·ning (in'iŋ) *n.* [< OE. *innung,* getting in] *Baseball &* (*pl.*) *Cricket* 1. a team's turn at bat 2. a numbered round of play in which both teams have a turn at bat

inn'keep'er *n.* the owner of an inn

in·no·cent (in'ə sənt) *adj.* [< L. *in-,* not + *nocere,* to harm] 1. free from sin, evil, etc.; specif., not guilty of a specific crime 2. harmless 3. knowing no evil 4. without guile — an innocent person, as a child —**in'no·cence** *n.* —**in'no·cent·ly** *adv.*

in·noc·u·ous (i näk'yoo wəs) *adj.* [see prec.] harmless —**in·noc'u·ous·ly** *adv.* —**in·noc'u·ous·ness** *n.*

in·no·va·tion (in'ə vā'shən) *n.* [< L. *in-,* in + *novus,* new] 1. the process of making changes 2. a new method, custom, device, etc. —**in'no·vate'** *vi., vt.* **-vat'ed, -vat'ing** —**in'no·va'tor** *n.*

in·nu·en·do (in'yoo wen'dō) *n., pl.* **-does, -dos** [L. < *in-,* in + *-nuere,* to nod] a hint or sly remark, usually derogatory; insinuation

in·nu·mer·a·ble (i nōō'mər ə b'l) *adj.* too numerous to be counted

in·oc·u·late (i näk'yoo lāt') *vt.* **-lat·ed, -lat'ing** [< L. *in-,* in + *oculus,* eye] to inject a serum or vaccine into, esp. in order to create immunity —**in·oc'u·la'tion** *n.*

in·of·fen·sive (in'ə fen'siv) *adj.* causing no harm or annoyance; unobjectionable —**in'of·fen'sive·ly** *adv.*

in·op·er·a·tive (in äp'ər ə tiv, -ə rāt'iv) *adj.* not working or functioning

in·or·di·nate (in ôr'd'n it) *adj.* [< L. *in-,* not + *ordo,* an order] excessive; immoderate —**in·or'di·nate·ly** *adv.*

in·or·gan·ic (in'ôr gan'ik) *adj.* not organic; specif., designating or of matter not animal or vegetable; not living

in·put (in'poot') *n.* what is put in, as power into a machine, data into a computer, etc. —*vt.* **-put', -put'ting** to feed (data) into a computer

in·quest (in'kwest) *n.* [see INQUIRE] a judicial inquiry, esp. before a jury, as a coroner's inquiry of a death

in·qui·e·tude (in kwī'ə tōōd', -tyōōd') *n.* restlessness; uneasiness

in·quire (in kwīr') *vi.* **-quired', -quir'ing** [< L. *in-,* into + *quaerere,* seek] 1. to ask a question or questions 2. to investigate (usually with *into*) —*vt.* to seek information about

in·quir·y (in'kwə rē, in kwīr'ē) *n., pl.* **-ies** 1. an inquiring; investigation 2. a question

in·qui·si·tion (in'kwə zish'ən) *n.* 1. an investigation or inquest 2. [I-] *R.C.Ch.* formerly, the tribunal for suppressing heresy and heretics 3. any relentless questioning or harsh suppression —**in·quis'i·tor** *n.*

in·quis·i·tive (in kwiz'ə tiv) *adj.* 1. inclined to ask many questions 2. unnecessarily curious; prying —**in·quis'i·tive·ness** *n.*

in re (in rē, rā) [L.] in the matter (of)

in·res·i·dence *adj.* having specific duties, often as a teacher, but given time to work at one's profession

in·road (in'rōd') *n.* 1. a raid 2. [usually *pl.*] any injurious encroachment

in·sane (in sān′) *adj.* 1. not sane; mentally ill or deranged 2. of or for insane people 3. very foolish —**in·sane′ly** *adv.* —**in·san′i·ty** (-san′ə tē) *n.*

in·sa·ti·a·ble (in sā′shə b'l, -shē ə-) *adj.* [see IN-² & SATIATE] that cannot be satisfied —**in·sa′ti·a·bly** *adv.*

in·scribe (in skrīb′) *vt.* -**scribed′**, -**scrib′ing** [< L. *in-*, in + *scribere*, write] 1. to mark or engrave (words, etc.) on (a surface) 2. to add (a person's name) to a list 3. *a)* to dedicate (a book, etc.) to someone *b)* to autograph 4. to fix in the mind —**in·scrip′tion** (-skrip′shən) *n.*

in·scru·ta·ble (in skrōōt′ə b'l) *adj.* [< L. *in-*, not + *scrutari*, examine] not easily understood; enigmatic —**in·scru′ta·bly** *adv.*

in·seam (in′sēm′) *n.* an inner seam; specif., the seam from the crotch to the bottom of a trouser leg

in·sect (in′sekt) *n.* [< L. *insectum*, lit., notched] any of a large class of small, usually winged, invertebrates, as beetles, flies, wasps, etc., having three pairs of legs

in·sec·ti·cide (in sek′tə sīd′) *n.* any substance used to kill insects —**in·sec′ti·cid′al** *adj.*

in·sec·tiv·o·rous (-tiv′ər əs) *adj.* [< INSECT + L. *vorare*, devour] feeding chiefly on insects

in·se·cure (in′si kyoor′) *adj.* 1. not safe 2. feeling anxiety 3. not firm or dependable —**in′se·cure′ly** *adv.* —**in′se·cu′ri·ty** *n.*

in·sem·i·nate (in sem′ə nāt′) *vt.* -**nat′ed**, -**nat′ing** [< L. *in-*, in + *semen*, seed] 1. to fertilize; impregnate 2. to imbue (with ideas, etc.) —**in·sem′i·na′tion** *n.*

in·sen·sate (in sen′sāt, -sit) *adj.* 1. not feeling sensation 2. stupid 3. without regard or feeling; cold

in·sen·si·ble (in sen′sə b'l) *adj.* 1. unable to perceive with the senses 2. unconscious 3. unaware; indifferent 4. so slight as to be virtually imperceptible —**in·sen′si·bil′i·ty** *n.*

in·sen′si·tive (-sə tiv) *adj.* not sensitive; not responsive —**in·sen′si·tive·ly** *adv.* —**in·sen′si·tiv′i·ty** *n.*

in·sen·ti·ent (in sen′shē ənt, -shənt) *adj.* not sentient; without life or consciousness —**in·sen′ti·ence** *n.*

in·sert (in surt′; *for n.* in′sərt) *vt.* [< L. *in-*, in + *serere*, join] to put or fit (something) into something else —*n.* anything inserted or to be inserted —**in·ser′tion** *n.*

in·set (in set′; *for n.* in′set) *vt.* -**set′**, -**set′ting** to set in; insert —*n.* something inserted

in·shore (in′shôr′, in shôr′) *adv., adj.* near or in toward the shore

in·side (in′sīd′, -sīd′; *for prep. & adv. usually* in sīd′) *n.* 1. the inner side, surface, or part 2. [*pl.*] [Colloq.] the viscera —*adj.* 1. internal 2. known only to insiders; secret —*adv.* 1. on or in the inside; within 2. indoors —*prep.* in or within —**inside of** within the space or time of —**inside out** 1. reversed 2. [Colloq.] thoroughly

in·sid·er *n.* 1. a person inside a given place or group 2. one having secret or confidential information

in·sid·i·ous (in sid′ē əs) *adj.* [< L. *insidiae*, an ambush] 1. characterized by treachery or slyness 2. more dangerous than seems evident

in·sight (in′sīt′) *n.* 1. the ability to see and understand clearly the inner nature of things, esp. by intuition 2. an instance of such understanding

in·sig·ni·a (in sig′nē ə) *n.pl., sing.* -**sig′ni·a**, -**sig′ne** (-nē) [ult. < L. *in-*, in + *signum*, a mark] distinguishing marks, as emblems of rank, membership, etc.

in·sin·cere (in′sin sir′) *adj.* not sincere; deceptive or hypocritical —**in′sin·cer′i·ty** (-ser′ə tē) *n.*

in·sin·u·ate (in sin′yōo wāt′) *vt.* -**at′ed**, -**at′ing** [< L. *in-*, in + *sinus*, a curve] 1. to work in or introduce slowly, indirectly, etc. 2. to hint or suggest indirectly; imply —**in·sin′u·a′tion** *n.* —**in·sin′u·a′tor** *n.*

in·sip·id (in sip′id) *adj.* [< L. *in-*, not + *sapidus*, savory] 1. without flavor; tasteless 2. not exciting; dull

in·sist (in sist′) *vi.* [< L. *in-*, on + *sistere*, to stand] to take and maintain a stand (often with *on* or *upon*) —*vt.* 1. to demand strongly 2. to declare firmly —**in·sist′ing·ly** *adv.*

in·sist′ent *adj.* insisting or demanding —**in·sist′ence** *n.*

†**in si·tu** (in sīt′ōō) [L.] in position; in its original place

in·so·far (in′sə fär′) *adv.* to such a degree or extent (usually with *as*)

in·sole (in′sōl′) *n.* 1. the inside sole of a shoe 2. a removable sole put inside a shoe for comfort

INSOLE

in·so·lent (in′sə lənt) *adj.* [< L. *in-*, not + *solere*, be accustomed] boldly disrespectful; impudent —**in′so·lence** *n.*

in·sol·u·ble (in säl′yōo b'l) *adj.* 1. that cannot be solved 2. that cannot be dissolved —**in·sol′u·bil′i·ty** *n.*

in·sol·vent (in säl′vənt) *adj.* not solvent; unable to pay debts; bankrupt —**in·sol′ven·cy** *n.*

in·som·ni·a (in säm′nē ə) *n.* [< L. *in-*, without + *somnus*, sleep] abnormal inability to sleep —**in·som′ni·ac′** (-ak′) *n.*

in·so·much (in′sō much′) *adv.* 1. to such an extent (*that*) 2. inasmuch (*as*)

in·sou·ci·ant (in sōō′sē ənt) *adj.* [Fr. < *in-*, not + *soucier*, to care] calm and unbothered; carefree

in·spect (in spekt′) *vt.* [< L. *in-*, at + *specere*, look at] 1. to look at carefully 2. to examine or review officially —**in·spec′tion** *n.*

in·spec′tor *n.* 1. one who inspects 2. an officer on a police force, ranking next below a superintendent

in·spi·ra·tion (in′spə rā′shən) *n.* 1. an inhaling 2. an inspiring or being

,inspired mentally or emotionally 3. *a)* any stimulus to creative thought *(or action b)* an inspired idea, action, 'etc. —**in′spi·ra′tion·al** *adj.*

in·spire (in spīr′) *vt.* **-spired′, -spir′-ing** [< L. *in-*, in + *spirare*, breathe] 1. to inhale 2. to stimulate or impel, as to some creative effort 3. to motivate by divine influence 4. to arouse (a thought or feeling) in (someone) 5. to occasion or cause —*vi.* 1. to inhale 2. to give inspiration

in·spir·it (in spir′it) *vt.* to put spirit into; cheer; hearten

Inst. 1. Institute 2. Institution

in·sta·bil·i·ty (in′stə bil′ə tē) *n.* lack of firmness, determination, etc.

in·stall, in·stal (in stôl′) *vt.* **-stalled′, -stall′ing** [< ML. *in-*, in + *stallum*, a place] 1. to place in an office, rank, etc. with formality 2. to establish in a place 3. to fix in position for use *[to install* new fixtures*]* —**in·stal·la·tion** (in′stə lā′shən) *n.* —**in·stall′er** *n.*

in·stall·ment, in·stal′ment *n.* 1. an installing or being installed 2. any of the parts of a sum of money to be paid at regular specified times 3. any of several parts, as of a serial

installment plan a system by which debts, as for purchased articles, are paid in installments

in·stance (in′stəns) *n.* [see ff.] 1. an example; case 2. a step in proceeding; occasion *[in the first instance]* —*vt.* **-stanced, -stanc·ing** to give as an example; cite —**at the instance of** at the suggestion or instigation of

in·stant (in′stənt) *adj.* [< L. *in-*, upon + *stare*, to stand] 1. urgent; pressing 2. of the current month: an old usage *[your letter of the 8th instant]* 3. imminent 4. immediate 5. concentrated or precooked for quick preparation, as a food or beverage —*n.* 1. a moment 2. a particular moment —**the instant** as soon as

in·stan·ta·ne·ous (in′stən tā′nē əs) *adj.* done or happening in an instant —**in′stan·ta′ne·ous·ly** *adv.*

in·stan·ter (in stan′tər) *adv.* [L.] immediately

in′stant·ly *adv.* immediately

in·state (in stāt′) *vt.* **-stat′ed, -stat′-ing** [IN-¹ + STATE] to put in a particular rank, etc.; install

in·stead (in sted′) *adv.* [IN + STEAD] in place of the one mentioned —**instead of** in place of

in·step (in′step′) *n.* the upper part of the arch of the foot, between the ankle and the toes

in·sti·gate (in′stə gāt′) *vt.* **-gat′ed, -gat′ing** [< L. *in-*, on + *stigare*, to prick] 1. to urge on to some action 2. to foment (rebellion, etc.) —**in′sti·ga′tion** *n.* —**in′sti·ga′tor** *n.*

in·still, in·stil (in stil′) *vt.* **-stilled′, -still′ing** [< L. *in-*, in + *stilla*, a drop] 1. to put in drop by drop 2. to

put (an idea, etc.) in or into gradually

in·stinct (in′stiŋkt) *n.* [< L. *instinguere*, impel] 1. (an) inborn tendency to behave in a way characteristic of a species 2. a natural or acquired tendency; knack —**instinc′tive** *adj.* —**in·stinc′tu·al** *adj.*

in·sti·tute (in′stə tōōt′) *vt.* **-tut′ed, -tut′ing** [< L. *in-*, in + *statuere*, set up] 1. to set up; establish 2. to start; initiate —*n.* something instituted; specif., *a)* an organization for the promotion of art, science, etc. *b)* a school or college specializing in some field —**in′sti·tut′er, in′sti·tut′or** *n.*

in·sti·tu·tion (-tōō′shən) *n.* 1. an instituting or being instituted 2. an established law, custom, etc. 3. *a)* an organization having a social, educational, or religious purpose *b)* the building housing it 4. [Colloq.] a person or thing long established in a place —**in′sti·tu′tion·al** *adj.*

in·sti·tu·tion·al·ize (-iz′) *vt.* **-ized′, -iz′ing** 1. to make into an institution 2. to make institutional 3. to place in an institution, as for treatment —**in′sti·tu′tion·al·i·za′tion** *n.*

in·struct (in strukt′) *vt.* [< L. *in-*, in + *struere*, pile up] 1. to teach; educate 2. to inform 3. to order or direct

in·struc′tion (-struk′shən) *n.* 1. an instructing; education 2. something taught 3. [*pl.*] orders or directions

in·struc′tive *adj.* giving knowledge

in·struc′tor *n.* 1. a teacher 2. a college teacher of the lowest rank

in·stru·ment (in′strə mənt) *n.* [see INSTRUCT] 1. a thing by means of which something is done; means 2. a tool or implement 3. any of various devices for indicating, measuring, controlling, etc. 4. any of various devices for producing musical sound 5. *Law* a formal document

in·stru·men·tal (-men′t′l) *adj.* 1. serving as a means; helpful 2. of, performed on, or written for a musical instrument or instruments

in·stru·men′tal·ist *n.* a person who performs on musical instruments

in·stru·men·tal′i·ty (-tal′ə tē) *n.*, *pl.* **-ties** a means; agency

in·stru·men·ta′tion (-tā′shən) *n.* 1. the writing or scoring of music for instruments 2. use of or equipment with instruments

instrument flying the flying of an aircraft by instruments only

in·sub·or·di·nate (in′sə bôr′d′n it) *adj.* not submitting to authority; disobedient —**in′sub·or′di·na′tion** *n.*

in·sub·stan·tial (in′səb stan′shəl) *adj.* not substantial; specif., *a)* unreal; imaginary *b)* weak or flimsy

in·suf·fer·a·ble (in suf′ər ə b′l) *adj.* not sufferable; intolerable; unbearable

in·su·lar (in′sə lər) *adj.* [< L. *insula*, island] 1. of or like an island or islanders 2. narrow-minded; illiberal

in·su·late (-lāt′) *vt.* **-lat′ed, -lat′ing**

[< L. *insula*, island] 1. to set apart; isolate 2. to cover with a nonconducting material in order to prevent the escape of electricity, heat, sound, etc. —**in′su·la′tor** n.

in·su·la′tion n. 1. an insulating or being insulated 2. material for this

in·su·lin (in′sə lin) n. [< L. *insula*, island] 1. a hormone vital to carbohydrate metabolism, secreted by islets of tissue in the pancreas 2. an extract from the pancreas of sheep, oxen, etc., used in the treatment of diabetes

in·sult (in sult′; *for* n. in′sult) vt. [< L. *in-*, on + *salire*, to leap] to subject to an act, remark, etc. meant to hurt the feelings or pride —n. an insulting act, remark, etc.

in·su·per·a·ble (in sōō′pər ə b'l) adj. [< L. *in-*, not + *superare*, overcome] that cannot be overcome

in·sup·port·a·ble (in′sə pôrt′ə b'l) adj. not supportable; incapable of being borne, upheld, proved, etc.

in·sur·ance (in shoor′əns) n. 1. an insuring or being insured 2. a contract (**insurance policy**) purchased to guarantee compensation for a specified loss by fire, death, etc. 3. the amount for which something is insured 4. the business of insuring against loss

in·sure (in shoor′) vt. -sured′, -sur′ing [see IN-1 & SURE] 1. to take out or issue insurance on 2. *same as* ENSURE —**in·sur′a·ble** adj.

in·sured′ n. a person whose life, property, etc. is insured against loss

in·sur′er n. a person or company that insures others against loss

in·sur·gent (in sur′jənt) adj. [< L. *in-*, upon + *surgere*, rise] rising up against established authority —n. an insurgent person —**in·sur′gence** n.

in·sur·rec·tion (in′sə rek′shən) n. [see prec.] a rising up against established authority; rebellion —**in′sur·rec′tion·ist** n.

int. 1. interest 2. international

in·tact (in takt′) adj. [< L. *in-*, not + *tactus*, touched] unimpaired or uninjured; kept or left whole

in·tagl·io (in tal′yō) n., pl. -ios [It. < *in-*, in + *tagliare*, to cut] a design carved or engraved below the surface

in·take (in′tāk′) n. 1. a taking in 2. amount taken in 3. the place in a pipe, etc. where a fluid is taken in

in·tan·gi·ble (in tan′jə b'l) adj. 1. that cannot be touched; incorporeal 2. representing value, but either without material being or without intrinsic value, as good will or stocks 3. that cannot be easily defined; vague —n. something intangible

in·te·ger (in′tə jər) n. [L., whole] a whole number (e.g., 5, −10) or zero

in′te·gral (-grəl) adj. [see prec.] 1. necessary for completeness; essential 2. whole or complete 3. made up of parts forming a whole

in′te·grate′ (-grāt′) vt., vi. -grat′ed, -grat′ing [< L. *integer*, whole] 1. to make or become whole or complete 2. to bring (parts) together into a whole 3. *a)* to remove barriers imposing segregation upon (racial groups)

b) to abolish segregation in —**in′te·gra′tion** n. —**in′te·gra′tive** adj.

integrated circuit an electronic circuit with many interconnected circuit elements formed on a single body of semiconductor material

in·teg·ri·ty (in teg′rə tē) n. [see INTEGER] 1. completeness; wholeness 2. unimpaired condition; soundness 3. honesty, sincerity, etc.

in·teg·u·ment (in teg′yoo mənt) n. [< L. *in-*, upon + *tegere*, to cover] an outer covering; skin, shell, etc.

in·tel·lect (in′t'l ekt′) n. [< L. *inter-*, between + *legere*, choose] 1. the ability to reason or understand 2. high intelligence 3. a very intelligent person

in·tel·lec·tu·al (in′t'l ek′choo wəl) adj. 1. of, involving, or appealing to the intellect 2. requiring intelligence 3. showing high intelligence —n. one with intellectual interests or tastes —**in′tel·lec′tu·al·ly** adv.

in′tel·lec′tu·al·ize′ (-īz′) vt. -ized′, -iz′ing to examine rationally, often without proper regard for emotional considerations

in·tel·li·gence (in tel′ə jəns) n. [see INTELLECT] 1. *a)* the ability to learn or understand *b)* the ability to cope with a new situation 2. news or information 3. those engaged in gathering secret, esp. military, information

intelligence quotient *see* IQ

in·tel′li·gent (-jənt) adj. having or showing intelligence; clever, wise, etc. —**in·tel′li·gent·ly** adv.

in·tel′li·gent′si·a (-jənt′sē ə) n. [< Russ.] intellectuals collectively

in·tel·li·gi·ble (in tel′i jə b'l) adj. that can be understood; clear —**in·tel′li·gi·bly** adv.

in·tem·per·ate (in tem′pər it) adj. 1. not temperate or moderate; excessive 2. drinking too much alcoholic liquor —**in·tem′per·ance** n.

in·tend (in tend′) vt. [< L. *in-*, at + *tendere*, to stretch] 1. to plan; purpose 2. to mean (something) to be or be used (*for*) 3. to mean; signify

in·tend′ed n. [Colloq.] one's prospective wife or husband; fiancé(e)

in·tense (in tens′) adj. [see INTEND] 1. very strong *[an intense light]* 2. strained to the utmost; strenuous *[intense thought]* 3. characterized by much action, strong emotion, etc. —**in·tense′ly** adv.

in·ten·si·fy (in ten′sə fī′) vt., vi. -fied′, -fy′ing to make or become more intense —**in·ten′si·fi·ca′tion** n.

in·ten·si·ty n., pl. -ties 1. a being intense 2. great energy or vehemence, as of emotion 3. the amount of force or energy of heat, light, sound, etc.

in·ten·sive adj. 1. of or characterized by intensity; thorough 2. designating very attentive care given to patients right after surgery, etc. 3. *Gram.* giving force or emphasis *["very" is an intensive adverb]* —n. *Gram.* an intensive word, prefix, etc. —**in·ten′sive·ly** adv. —**in·ten′sive·ness** n.

in·tent (in tent′) adj. [see INTEND] 1. firmly directed; earnest 2. having one's attention or purpose firmly fixed *[intent* on going] —*n.* 1. an intending 2. something intended; purpose or meaning —**to all intents and purposes** in almost every respect —**in·tent′ly** *adv.* —**in·tent′ness** *n.*

in·ten·tion (in ten′shən) *n.* 1. a determination to act in a specified way 2. anything intended; purpose

in·ten′tion·al *adj.* done purposely

in·ter (in tur′) *vt.* -terred′, -ter′ing [< L. *in*, in + *terra*, earth] to put (a dead body) into a grave or tomb

inter- [L.] *a combining form meaning:* 1. between, among, or involving individual elements named in the base adjective or singular noun

| intercultural | interfaith |
| interdepartmental | intergroup |

2. with or on each other (or one another)

| interact | interaction |

in·ter·breed (in′tər brēd′) *vt., vi.* -bred′, -breed′ing *same as* HYBRIDIZE

in′ter·cede (-sēd′) *vi.* -ced′ed, -ced′ing [< L. *inter-*, between + *cedere*, go] 1. to plead in behalf of another 2. to mediate

in′ter·cept′ (-sept′) *vt.* [< L. *inter-*, between + *capere*, take] 1. to stop or seize in its course *[to intercept* a message] 2. *Math.* to cut off or mark off between two points, lines, etc. —**in′ter·cep′tion** *n.*

in′ter·ces·sion (-sesh′ən) *n.* an interceding; mediation or prayer in behalf of another —**in′ter·ces′sor** (-ses′ər) *n.* —**in′ter·ces′so·ry** *adj.*

in·ter·change (in′tər chānj′; *for n.* in′tər chānj′) *vt.* -changed′, -chang′ing 1. to give and take mutually; exchange 2. to put (each of two things) in the other's place 3. to alternate —*n.* 1. an interchanging 2. a place on a freeway where traffic can enter or depart —**in′ter·change′·a·ble** *adj.*

in′ter·col·le′gi·ate *adj.* between or among colleges and universities

in·ter·com (in′tər käm′) *n.* a radio or telephone intercommunication system, as between rooms

in′ter·com·mu′ni·cate *vt., vi.* -cat′ed, -cat′ing to communicate with or to each other or one another —**in′ter·com·mu′ni·ca′tion** *n.*

in′ter·con·nect′ (-kə nekt′) *vt., vi.* to connect with one another —**in′ter·con·nec′tion** *n.*

in′ter·con′ti·nen′tal *adj.* 1. between or among continents 2. able to travel from one continent to another, as a missile, etc.

in·ter·course (in′tər kôrs′) *n.* [see INTER- & COURSE] 1. communication or dealings between people, countries, etc. 2. the sexual joining of two individuals: in full, **sexual intercourse**

in′ter·de·nom′i·na′tion·al *adj.* between or among religious denominations

in′ter·de·pend′ence *n.* mutual dependence —**in′ter·de·pend′ent** *adj.*

in·ter·dict (in′tər dikt′; *for n.* in′tər dikt′) *vt.* [< L. *inter-*, between + *dicere*, say] 1. to prohibit (an action) 2. to restrain from doing or using something —*n.* an official prohibition —**in′ter·dic′tion** *n.*

in′ter·dis′ci·pli·nar′y *adj.* involving two or more disciplines, or branches of learning

in·ter·est (in′trist, in′tər ist) *n.* [< L. *inter-*, between + *esse*, be] 1. a right to, or share in, something 2. anything in which one has a share 3. *[often pl.]* advantage; benefit 4. *[usually pl.]* those having a common concern or power in some industry, cause, etc. *[the steel interests]* 5. *a)* a feeling of concern, curiosity, etc. about something *b)* the power of causing this feeling *c)* something causing this feeling 6. *a)* money paid for the use of money *b)* the rate of such payment —*vt.* 1. to involve or excite the interest or attention of 2. to cause to have an interest, or share, in —**in the interest(s)** of for the sake of

in′ter·est·ed *adj.* 1. having an interest or share 2. influenced by personal interest; biased 3. feeling or showing interest

in′ter·est·ing *adj.* exciting curiosity or attention; of interest

in·ter·face (in′tər fās′) *n.* a surface that forms the common boundary between two parts of matter or space

in·ter·fere (in′tər fir′) *vi.* -fered′, -fer′ing [ult. < L. *inter-*, between + *ferire*, to strike] 1. to clash; collide 2. *a)* to come between; intervene *b)* to meddle 3. *Sports* to hinder an opposing player in any of various illegal ways —**interfere with** to hinder —**in′ter·fer′ence** *n.*

in·ter·im (in′tər im) *n.* [L. < *inter*, between] the period of time between; meantime —*adj.* temporary

in·te·ri·or (in tir′ē ər) *adj.* [< L. *inter*, between] 1. situated within; inner 2. inland 3. private —*n.* 1. the interior part, as of a room, country, etc. 2. the internal, or domestic, affairs of a country

interior decoration the art or business of decorating and furnishing interiors of homes, offices, etc. —**interior decorator**

in·te′ri·or·ize′ (-īz′) *vt.* -ized′, -iz′ing to make (a concept, value, etc.) part of one's inner nature

interj. interjection

in·ter·ject (in′tər jekt′) *vt.* [< L. *inter-*, between + *jacere*, to throw] to throw in between; interrupt with

in′ter·jec′tion (-jek′shən) *n.* 1. an interjecting 2. something interjected 3. *Gram.* an exclamation

in′ter·lace′ *vt., vi.* -laced′, -lac′ing to lace or weave together

in′ter·lard′ (-lärd′) *vt.* [see INTER- & LARD] to intersperse; diversify *[to interlard* a talk with quotations]

fat, āpe, cär; ten, ēven; is, bīte; gō, hôrn, tool, look; oil, out; up, fur; chin; she; thin, *th*en; zh, leisure; ŋ, ring; ə for *a* in ago; ', (ā'b'l); ĕ, Fr. coeur; ö, Fr. feu; Fr. mon; ü, Fr. duc; kh, G. ich, doch; ‡ foreign; < derived from

in·ter·line[1] *vt.* **-lined′, -lin′ing** to write (something) between the lines of (a text, etc.)

in·ter·line[2] *vt.* **-lined′, -lin′ing** to put an inner lining under the ordinary lining of (a garment)

in·ter·lock *vt., vi.* to lock together; join with one another

in·ter·loc·u·to·ry (in′tər läk′yə tôr′ē) *adj.* [< L. *inter-*, between + *loqui*, speak] *Law* not final, as a decree

in·ter·lop·er (in′tər lō′pər) *n.* [prob. < INTER- + LOPE] one who meddles

in·ter·lude (in′tər lōōd′) *n.* [< L. *inter*, between + *ludus*, play] anything that fills time between two events, as music between acts of a play

in·ter·mar·ry *vi.* **-ried, -ry·ing** 1. to become connected by marriage: said of different clans, races, etc. 2. to marry: said of closely related persons —**in′ter·mar′riage** *n.*

in·ter·me·di·ar·y (-mē′dē er′ē) *adj.* 1. acting as a go-between or mediator 2. intermediate —*n., pl.* **-ies** a go-between; mediator

in·ter·me·di·ate (-mē′dē it) *adj.* [< L. *inter-*, between + *medius*, middle] in the middle; in between

in·ter·ment (in tur′mənt) *n.* the act of interring; burial

in·ter·mez·zo (in′tər met′sō) *n., pl.* **-zos, -zi** [It. < L.: see INTER-MEDIATE] a short piece of music, as between parts of a composition

in·ter·mi·na·ble (in tur′mi nə b′l) *adj.* lasting, or seeming to last, forever; endless —**in·ter′mi·na·bly** *adv.*

in·ter·min·gle *vt., vi.* **-gled, -gling** to mix together; mingle

in·ter·mis·sion (in′tər mish′ən) *n.* [< L. *inter-*, between + *mittere*, send] an interval of time between periods of activity, as between acts of a play

in′ter·mit′tent (-mit′′nt) *adj.* [see prec.] stopping and starting again at intervals; periodic

in·tern (in′tərn; *for vt. usually in* turn′) *n.* [< L. *internus*, inward] 1. a doctor serving as assistant resident in a hospital, usually just after graduation from medical school 2. an apprentice teacher, journalist, etc. Also **interne** —*vi.* to serve as an intern —*vt.* to detain and confine within an area [to *intern* aliens in wartime] —**in·tern′ment** *n.*

in·ter·nal (in tur′n′l) *adj.* [< L. *internus*] 1. of or on the inside; inner 2. to be taken inside the body [*internal* remedies] 3. intrinsic [*internal* evidence] 4. domestic [*internal* revenue] —**in·ter′nal·ly** *adv.*

in·ter′nal-com·bus′tion engine an engine, as in an automobile, powered by the explosion of a fuel-and-air mixture within the cylinders

in·ter′nal·ize′ (-īz′) *vt.* **-ized′, -iz′ing** to make (others′ ideas, etc.) a part of one′s own way of thinking

internal medicine the branch of medicine dealing with the diagnosis and nonsurgical treatment of diseases

internal revenue governmental income from taxes on income, profits, etc.

in·ter·na·tion·al (in′tər nash′ə n′l) *adj.* 1. between or among nations 2. concerned with the relations between nations 3. for the use of all nations 4. of or for people in various nations —**in′ter·na′tion·al·ize′** *vt.* **-ized′, -iz′ing** —**in′ter·na′tion·al·ly** *adv.*

in·ter·ne·cine (in′tər nē′sin) *adj.* [< L. *inter-*, between + *necare*, kill] extremely destructive to both sides

in·ter·nist (in′tər nist, in tur′nist) *n.* a doctor who specializes in the nonsurgical treatment of diseases

in·ter·of·fice (in′tər ôf′is) *adj.* between the offices of an organization

in′ter·per′son·al (-pur′sə n′l) *adj.* between persons

in′ter·plan′e·tar′y (-plan′ə ter′ē) *adj.* between planets

in′ter·play′ *n.* action, effect, or influence on each other

in·ter·po·late (in tur′pə lāt′) *vt.* **-lat′ed, -lat′ing** [< L. *inter-*, between + *polire*, to polish] 1. to change (a text, etc.) by inserting new material 2. to insert between or among others —**in·ter′po·la′tion** *n.*

in·ter·pose (in′tər pōz′) *vt., vi.* **-posed′, -pos′ing** 1. to place or come between 2. to intervene (with) 3. to interrupt (with) —**in′ter·po·si′tion** (-pə zish′ən) *n.*

in·ter·pret (in tur′prit) *vt.* [< L. *interpres*, negotiator] 1. to explain or translate 2. to construe [to *interpret* a silence as contempt] 3. to give one′s own conception of, as a role in a play —*vi.* to translate —**in·ter′pre·ta′tion** *n.* —**in·ter′pret·er** *n.*

in·ter·pre·tive (in tur′prə tiv) *adj.* that interprets: also **in·ter′pre·ta′tive** (-tāt′iv)

in·ter·ra·cial (in′tər rā′shəl) *adj.* between, among, or for persons of different races: also **in′ter·race′**

in′ter·re·late′ (-ri lāt′) *vt., vi.* **-lat′ed, -lat′ing** to make or be mutually related —**in′ter·re·lat′ed** *adj.*

in·ter·ro·gate (in ter′ə gāt′) *vt., vi.* **-gat′ed, -gat′ing** [< L. *inter-*, between + *rogare*, ask] to question, esp. formally —**in·ter′ro·ga′tion** *n.* —**in·ter′ro·ga′tor** *n.*

in·ter·rog·a·tive (in′tə räg′ə tiv) *adj.* asking a question: also **in′ter·rog′a·to′ry** (-ə tôr′ē)

in·ter·rupt (in′tə rupt′) *vt.* [< L. *inter-*, between + *rumpere*, to break] 1. to break into (a discussion, etc.) or break in upon (a speaker, worker, etc.) 2. to make a break in the continuity of —*vi.* to interrupt an action, talk, etc. —**in′ter·rup′tion** *n.*

in·ter·scho·las·tic (in′tər skə las′tik) *adj.* between or among schools

in·ter·sect (in′tər sekt′) *vt.* [< L. *inter-*, between + *secare*, to cut] to divide into two parts by passing through —*vi.* to cross each other

in′ter·sec′tion (-sek′shən) *n.* 1. an intersecting 2. the place where two lines, roads, etc. meet or cross

in′ter·serv′ice *adj.* between or among branches of the armed forces

in′ter·ses′sion *n.* a short session between regular college sessions, for concentration on specialized projects

in·ter·sperse (in'tər spurs') *vt.* -spersed', -spers'ing [< L. *inter-*, among + *spargere*, scatter] 1. to put here and there; scatter 2. to vary with things scattered here and there

in'ter·state' *adj.* between or among states of a federal government

in'ter·stel'lar (-stel'ər) *adj.* between or among the stars

in·ter·stice (in·tur'stis) *n.*, *pl.* -stic·es [< L. *inter-*, between + *sistere*, to set] a crack; crevice

in'ter·twine' *vt.*, *vi.* -twined', -twin'ing to twine together

in'ter·ur'ban (-ur'bən) *adj.* between cities or towns

in·ter·val (in'tər v'l) *n.* [< L. *inter-*, between + *vallum*, wall] 1. a space between things 2. the time between events 3. the difference in pitch between two tones —**at intervals** 1. now and then 2. here and there

in·ter·vene (in'tər vēn') *vi.* -vened', -ven'ing [< L. *inter-*, between + *venire*, come] 1. to come or be between 2. to occur between two events, etc. 3. to come in to modify, settle, or hinder some action, etc.

in'ter·ven'tion (-ven'shən) *n.* 1. an intervening 2. interference, esp. of one state in the affairs of another

in'ter·view' (-vyoo') *n.* 1. a meeting of people face to face to confer 2. *a)* a meeting in which a person is asked about his views, etc., as by a reporter *b)* a published account of this —*vt.* to have an interview with —**in'ter·view·ee'** *n.* —**in'ter·view'er** *n.*

in'ter·weave' *vt.*, *vi.* -wove', -wov'en, -weav'ing 1. to weave together 2. to connect closely

in·tes·tate (in tes'tāt, -tit) *adj.* [< L. *in-*, not + *testari*, make a will] having made no will

in·tes·tine (in tes'tin) *n.* [< L. *intus*, within] [*usually pl.*] the lower part of the alimentary canal, extending from the stomach to the anus and consisting of a long, winding upper part (**small intestine**) and a shorter, thicker lower part (**large intestine**); bowel(s) —**in·tes'·tin·al** *adj.*

INTESTINES

in·ti·mate (in'tə mit; *for v.* -māt') *adj.* [< L. *intus*, within] 1. most private or personal 2. very close or familiar 3. deep and thorough —*n.* an intimate friend —*vt.* -mat'ed, -mat'ing to hint or imply —**in'ti·ma·cy** (-mə sē) *n.*, *pl.* -cies —**in'ti·mate·ly** *adv.* —**in'ti·ma'tion** *n.*

in·tim·i·date (in tim'ə dāt') *vt.* -dat'ed, -dat'ing [< L. *in-*, in + *timidus*, afraid] to make afraid, as with threats —**in·tim'i·da'tion** *n.*

in·to (in'tōō, -too) *prep.* [OE.] 1. toward and within [*into* a room] 2. continuing to the midst of [to talk *into* the night] 3. to the form, substance, or condition of [divided *into* parts] 4. so as to strike [to run *into* a wall] 5. [Colloq.] involved in [she's *into* jazz now]

in·tol·er·a·ble (in tält'ər ə b'l) *adj.* unbearable; too severe, painful, etc. to be endured —**in·tol'er·a·bly** *adv.*

in·tol'er·ant (-ənt) *adj.* unwilling to tolerate others' beliefs, etc. —**intolerant** of not able or willing to tolerate —**in·tol'er·ance** *n.*

in·to·na·tion (in'tə nā'shən) *n.* 1. an intoning 2. the manner of producing tones with regard to accurate pitch 3. variations in pitch within an utterance

in·tone (in tōn') *vt.*, *vi.* -toned', -ton'ing to speak or recite in a singing tone; chant —**in·ton'er** *n.*

in to·to (in tō'tō) [L.] as a whole

in·tox·i·cate (in täk'sə kāt') *vt.* -cat'ed, -cat'ing [< L. *in-*, in + *toxicum*, poison] 1. to make drunk 2. to excite greatly —**in·tox'i·cant** *n.* —**in·tox'i·ca'tion** *n.*

intra- [L., within] *a combining form meaning* within, inside of

in·tra·cit·y (in'trə sit'ē) *adj.* of or within a large municipality, often specif. the inner city

in·trac·ta·ble (in trak'tə b'l) *adj.* hard to manage; unruly or stubborn

in·tra·mu·ral (in'trə myoor'əl) *adj.* [INTRA- + MURAL] between or among members of the same school, college, etc.

in·tran·si·gent (in tran'sə jənt) *adj.* [< L. *in-*, not + *transigere*, to settle] refusing to compromise —**in·tran'si·gence** *n.*

in·tran·si·tive (in tran'sə tiv) *adj.* not transitive; designating a verb that does not take a direct object —**in·tran'si·tive·ly** *adv.*

in·tra·u·ter·ine device (in'trə yōōt'ər in) a device, as a plastic loop, inserted in the uterus as a contraceptive

in·tra·ve·nous (-vē'nəs) *adj.* [INTRA- + VENOUS] directly into a vein —**in'tra·ve'nous·ly** *adv.*

in·trench (in trench') *vt.*, *vi.* same as ENTRENCH

in·trep·id (in trep'id) *adj.* [< L. *in-*, not + *trepidus*, alarmed] bold; fearless; brave —**in·trep'id·ly** *adv.*

in·tri·cate (in'tri kit) *adj.* [< L. *in-*, in + *tricae*, vexations] 1. hard to follow or understand because full of puzzling parts, details, etc. 2. full of elaborate detail —**in·tri·ca·cy** (-kə sē) *n.* —**in'tri·cate·ly** *adv.*

in·trigue (in trēg') *vi.* -trigued', -trigu'ing [see prec.] to plot secretly or underhandedly —*vt.* to excite the interest or curiosity of —*n.* 1. secret or underhand plotting 2. a secret or underhand plot or scheme 3. a

secret love affair —**in·trigu'er** *n.*
—**in·trigu'ing·ly** *adv.*

in·trin·sic (in trin'sik) *adj.* [< L. *intra-*, within + *secus*, close] belonging to the real nature of a thing; inherent —**in·trin'si·cal·ly** *adv.*

in·tro·duce (in'trə dōōs') *vt.* -**duced'**, -**duc'ing** [< L. *intro-*, in + *ducere*, to lead] 1. to put in; insert 2. to bring in as a new feature 3. to bring into use or fashion 4. *a)* to make acquainted; present [*introduce* me to her] *b)* to give experience of [they *introduced* him to music] 5. to bring forward 6. to start; begin [to *introduce* a talk with a joke]

in·tro·duc·tion (-duk'shən) *n.* 1. an introducing or being introduced 2. the preliminary section of a book, speech, etc.; preface

in·tro·duc·to·ry (-duk'tər ē) *adj.* serving to introduce; preliminary

in·tro·it (in trō'it, in'troit) *n.* [< L. *intro-*, in + *ire*, to go] 1. a psalm or hymn at the opening of a Christian worship service 2. [I-] R.C.Ch. the first variable part of the Mass

in·tro·spec·tion (in'trə spek'shən) *n.* [< L. *intro-*, within + *specere*, to look] a looking into one's own mind, feelings, etc. —**in'tro·spec'tive** *adj.*

in·tro·vert (in'trə vʉrt') *n.* [< L. *intro-*, within + *vertere*, to turn] one who is more interested in his own thoughts, feelings, etc. than in external objects or events —**in'tro·ver'sion** (-vʉr'zhən) *n.* —**in'tro·vert'ed** *adj.*

in·trude (in trōōd') *vt.*, *vi.* -**trud'ed**, -**trud'ing** [< L. *in-*, in + *trudere*, to push] to force (oneself) upon others unasked —**in·trud'er** *n.*

in·tru·sion (in trōō'zhən) *n.* an intruding —**in·tru'sive** (-siv) *adj.* —**in·tru'sive·ly** *adv.* —**in·tru'sive·ness** *n.*

in·trust (in trust') *vt.* same as ENTRUST

in·tu·i·tion (in'tōō wish'ən) *n.* [< L. *in-*, in + *tueri*, look at] the immediate knowing of something without the conscious use of reasoning —**in·tu·i·tive** (in tōō'i tiv) *adj.*

In·u·it (in'ōō wit) *n.*, *adj.* [Esk.] same as ESKIMO: now the preferred term

in·un·date (in'ən dāt') *vt.* -**dat'ed**, -**dat'ing** [< L. *in-*, in + *unda*, a wave] to cover with or as with a flood; deluge —**in'un·da'tion** *n.*

in·ure (in yoor') *vt.* -**ured'**, -**ur'ing** [< ME. *in ure*, in practice] to accustom to pain, trouble, etc.

in·vade (in vād') *vt.* -**vad'ed**, -**vad'ing** [< L. *in-*, in + *vadere*, go] 1. to enter forcibly or hostilely 2. to intrude upon; violate —**in·vad'er** *n.*

in·va·lid (in'və lid) *adj.* [< L. *in-*, not + *validus*, strong] 1. weak and sickly 2. of or for invalids —*n.* one who is ill or disabled

in·val·id (in val'id) *adj.* not valid

in·val'i·date' (-ə dāt') *vt.* -**dat'ed**, -**dat'ing** to make invalid; deprive of legal force —**in·val'i·da'tion** *n.*

in·val·u·a·ble (in val'yōō wə b'l, -yə b'l) *adj.* too valuable to be meas-ured; priceless —**in·val'u·a·bly** *adv.*

in·va·sion (in vā'zhən) *n.* an invading or being invaded, as by an army

in·vec·tive (in vek'tiv) *n.* [see ff.] a violent verbal attack; vituperation

in·veigh (in vā') *vi.* [< L. *in-*, in + *vehere*, carry] to make a violent verbal attack; rail (*against*)

in·vei·gle (in vē'g'l, -vā'-) *vt.* -**gled**, -**gling** [< MFr. *aveugler*, to blind] to entice or trick into doing something —**in·vei'gler** *n.*

in·vent (in vent') *vt.* [< L. *in-*, on + *venire*, come] 1. to think up [*invent* excuses] 2. to think out or produce (a new device, process, etc.); originate —**in·ven'tor** *n.*

in·ven'tion (-ven'shən) *n.* 1. an inventing 2. the power of inventing 3. something invented

in·ven'tive (-tiv) *adj.* 1. of invention 2. skilled in inventing —**in·ven'tive·ly** *adv.* —**in·ven'tive·ness** *n.*

in·ven·to·ry (in'vən tôr'ē) *n.*, *pl.* -**ries** [see INVENT] 1. an itemized list of goods, property, etc., as of a business 2. the store of goods, etc. for such listing; stock —*vt.* -**ried**, -**ry·ing** to make an inventory of

in·verse (in vʉrs'; also in'vʉrs') *adj.* inverted; directly opposite —*n.* any inverse thing —**in·verse'ly** *adv.*

in·ver·sion (in vʉr'zhən) *n.* 1. an inverting or being inverted 2. something inverted; reversal

in·vert (in vʉrt') *vt.* [< L. *in-*, to + *vertere*, to turn] 1. to turn upside down 2. to reverse the order, position, direction, etc. of

in·ver·te·brate (in vʉr'tə brit, -brāt') *adj.* not vertebrate; having no backbone —*n.* any invertebrate animal

in·vest (in vest') *vt.* [< L. *in-*, in + *vestis*, clothing] 1. to clothe 2. to install in office with ceremony 3. to furnish with power, authority, etc. 4. to put (money) into business, bonds, etc., in order to get a profit —*vi.* to invest money —**in·ves'tor** *n.*

in·ves·ti·gate (in ves'tə gāt') *vt.*, *vi.* -**gat'ed**, -**gat'ing** [< L. *in-*, in + *vestigare*, to track] to search (into); inquire —**in·ves'ti·ga'tor** *n.*

in·ves'ti·ga'tion *n.* an investigating; careful search; systematic inquiry

in·ves·ti·ture (in ves'tə chər) *n.* a formal investing, as with an office

in·vest·ment (in vest'mənt) *n.* 1. an investing or being invested 2. *a)* money invested *b)* anything in which money is or may be invested

in·vet·er·ate (in vet'ər it) *adj.* [< L. *inveterare*, to age] firmly established; habitual —**in·vet'er·a·cy** *n.*

in·vid·i·ous (in vid'ē əs) *adj.* [< L. *invidia*, envy] such as to excite ill will; giving offense, as by discriminating unfairly —**in·vid'i·ous·ly** *adv.* —**in·vid'i·ous·ness** *n.*

in·vig·or·ate (in vig'ə rāt') *vt.* -**at'ed**, -**at'ing** to give vigor to; fill with energy —**in·vig'or·a'tion** *n.*

in·vin·ci·ble (in vin'sə b'l) *adj.* [< L. *in-*, not + *vincere*, overcome] that cannot be overcome; unconquerable —**in·vin'ci·bil'i·ty** *n.*

in·vi·o·la·ble (in vī'ə lə b'l) *adj.* **1.** not to be violated; not to be profaned or injured; sacred **2.** indestructible —**in·vi'o·la·bil'i·ty** *n.*

in·vi'o·late (-lit) *adj.* not violated; kept sacred or unbroken

in·vis·i·ble (in viz'ə b'l) *adj.* **1.** not visible; that cannot be seen **2.** out of sight **3.** imperceptible —**in·vis'i·bil'i·ty** *n.* —**in·vis'i·bly** *adv.*

in·vi·ta·tion (in'və tā'shən) *n.* **1.** an inviting **2.** a message used in inviting

in'vi·ta'tion·al *adj.* only for those invited to take part, as an art show

in·vite (in vīt') *vt.* -**vit'ed**, -**vit'ing** [< L. *invitare*] **1.** to ask to come somewhere or do something **2.** to ask for **3.** to give occasion for [*his conduct invites gossip*] **4.** to tempt; entice —*n.* [Colloq.] an invitation

in·vit'ing *adj.* tempting; enticing

in·vo·ca·tion (in'və kā'shən) *n.* an invoking of God, the Muses, etc.

in·voice (in'vois) *n.* [prob. < ME. *envoie*, message] a list of goods shipped to a buyer, stating prices, etc. —*vt.* -**voiced**, -**voic·ing** to present an invoice for or to

in·voke (in vōk') *vt.* -**voked'**, -**vok'ing** [< L. *in-*, on + *vocare*, to call] **1.** to call on (God, the Muses, etc.) for blessing, help, etc. **2.** to resort to (a law, ruling, etc.) as pertinent **3.** to conjure **4.** to beg for; implore

in·vol·un·tar·y (in väl'ən ter'ē) *adj.* **1.** not done by choice **2.** not consciously controlled —**in·vol'un·tar'i·ly** *adv.* —**in·vol'un·tar'i·ness** *n.*

in·vo·lu·tion (in'və lōō'shən) *n.* **1.** an involving or being involved; entanglement **2.** a complication; intricacy

in·volve (in välv') *vt.* -**volved'**, -**volv'ing** [< L. *in-*, in + *volvere*, to roll] **1.** to make intricate; complicate **2.** to entangle in difficulty, danger, etc.; implicate **3.** to affect or include [*the riot involved thousands*] **4.** to require [*saving involves thrift*] **5.** to make busy; occupy [*involved in study*] —**in·volved'** —**in·volve'ment** *n.*

in·vul·ner·a·ble (in vul'nər ə b'l) *adj.* **1.** that cannot be wounded or injured **2.** proof against attack

in·ward (in'wərd) *adj.* **1.** situated within; internal **2.** mental or spiritual **3.** directed toward the inside —*adv.* **1.** toward the inside **2.** into the mind or soul Also **in'wards,** *adv.*

in'ward·ly *adv.* **1.** in or on the inside **2.** in the mind or spirit **3.** toward the inside or center

i·o·dine (ī'ə dīn', -din) *n.* [< Gr. *iōdēs*, violetlike] **1.** a nonmetallic chemical element used in medicine, etc. **2.** tincture of iodine, used as an antiseptic

i'o·dize' (-dīz') *vt.* -**dized'**, -**diz'ing** to treat with iodine

i·on (ī'ən, -än) *n.* [< Gr. *ienai*, to go] an electrically charged atom or group of atoms

-ion [< L. *-io*] a suffix meaning: **1.** the act or condition of [*translation*] **2.** the result of [*correction*]

I·on·ic (ī än'ik) *adj.* designating or of a Greek style of architecture characterized by ornamental scrolls on the capitals

i·on·ize (ī'ə nīz') *vt.*, *vi.* -**ized'**, -**iz'·ing** to dissociate into ions, as a salt dissolved in water, or become electrically charged, as a gas under radiation —**i'on·i·za'tion** *n.* —**i'on·iz'er** *n.*

IONIC CAPITAL

i·on·o·sphere (ī än'ə sfir') *n.* the outer layers of the earth's atmosphere, with some electron and ion content

i·o·ta (ī ōt'ə, ē-) *n.* **1.** the ninth letter of the Greek alphabet (I, ι) **2.** a very small quantity; jot

IOU, I.O.U. (ī'ō'yōō') **1.** I owe you **2.** a signed note bearing these letters, acknowledging a specified debt

-ious (ē əs, yəs, əs) [see -OUS] *a suffix meaning* characterized by [*furious*]

I·o·wa (ī'ə wə) Middle Western State of the U.S.: 56,290 sq. mi.; pop. 2,913,000; cap. Des Moines —**I'o·wan** *adj.*, *n.*

ip·e·cac (ip'ə kak') *n.* [< SAmInd. name] an emetic made from the dried roots of a S. American plant

ip·so fac·to (ip'sō fak'tō) [L.] by the fact (or act) itself

IQ, I.Q. [intelligence quotient] a number indicating a person's level of intelligence, based on a test

ir- *same as:* **1.** IN-1 **2.** IN-2 Used before *r*

Ir. **1.** Ireland: also **Ire.** **2.** Irish

IRA individual retirement account

I·ran (i ran', I-; ē rän') country in SW Asia: formerly called *Persia*: 636,000 sq. mi.; pop. 26,015,000 —**I·ra·ni·an** (i rā'nē ən, I-) *adj.*, *n.*

I·raq (i räk', -rak'; ē-) country in SW Asia, west of Iran: 171,599 sq. mi.; pop. 8,338,000 —**I·ra·qi** (i rä'kē, -rak'ē) *adj.*, *n.*

i·ras·ci·ble (i ras'ə b'l) *adj.* [see ff.] easily angered; hot-tempered

i·rate (ī rāt', ī'rāt) *adj.* [< L. *ira*, anger] angry; wrathful; incensed —**i·rate'ly** *adv.* —**i·rate'ness** *n.*

ire (īr) *n.* [< L. *ira*] anger; wrath

Ire·land (īr'lənd) **1.** one of the British Isles, west of Great Britain **2.** republic comprising most of this island: 27,136 sq. mi.; pop. 2,884,000

i·ren·ic (ī ren'ik) *adj.* [< Gr. *eirēnē*, peace] promoting peace

ir·i·des·cent (ir'ə des'nt) *adj.* [< Gr. *iris*, rainbow] having or showing an interplay of rainbowlike colors —**ir'i·des'cence** *n.*

i·rid·i·um (i rid'ē əm) *n.* [see ff.] a white, metallic chemical element: symbol, Ir

i·ris (ī'ris) *n.*, *pl.* **i'ris·es** [Gr., rainbow] **1.** the round, pigmented membrane surrounding the pupil of the eye

2. a plant with sword-shaped leaves and a showy flower

I·rish (ī'rish) *adj.* of Ireland, its people, language, etc. —*n.* **1.** the Celtic language of Ireland **2.** the English dialect of Ireland —**the Irish** the people of Ireland —**I'rish·man** *n., pl.* -men —**I'rish·wom'an** *n.fem., pl.* -wom'en

Irish coffee brewed coffee with Irish whiskey, topped with whipped cream

Irish Sea arm of the Atlantic between Ireland & Great Britain

irk (urk) *vt.* [ME. *irken*, be weary of] to annoy, irritate, tire out, etc.

irk·some (-səm) *adj.* that tends to irk; annoying or tiresome

i·ron (ī'ərn) *n.* [OE. *īren*] **1.** a metallic chemical element, the most common of all the metals **2.** any device of iron; esp., such a device with a flat undersurface, heated for pressing cloth **3.** [*pl.*] shackles of iron **4.** firm strength; power **5.** any of certain golf clubs with angled metal heads —*adj.* **1.** of iron **2.** like iron; strong; firm —*vt., vi.* to press with a hot iron —**iron out** to smooth out; eliminate

i'ron·clad' (-klad') *adj.* **1.** covered or protected with iron **2.** difficult to change or break [*an* ironclad *lease*]

iron curtain a barrier of secrecy and censorship, esp. around the U.S.S.R.

i·ron·i·cal (ī rän'i k'l) *adj.* **1.** meaning the contrary of what is expressed **2.** using irony **3.** opposite to what might be expected Also **i·ron'ic** —**i·ron'i·cal·ly** *adv.*

iron lung a large respirator enclosing all of the body but the head

i'ron·stone' *n.* **1.** any rock rich in iron **2.** a hard, white ceramic ware

i'ron·ware' *n.* things made of iron

i·ro·ny (ī'rən ē, ī'ər nē) *n., pl.* -nies [< Gr. *eirōn*, dissembler in speech] **1.** expression in which the intended meaning of the words is the opposite of their usual sense **2.** an event or result that is the opposite of what is expected

Ir·o·quois (ir'ə kwoi') *n., pl.* -quois' (-kwoi', -kwoiz') a member of a tribe of N. American Indians that lived in and near W and N New York —*adj.* of the Iroquois —**Ir'o·quoi'an** *adj., n.*

ir·ra·di·ate (i rā'dē āt') *vt.* -at'ed, -at'ing **1.** to shine upon; light up **2.** to enlighten **3.** to radiate **4.** to expose to X-rays or other radiant energy —*vi.* to emit rays; shine —**ir·ra'di·a'tion** *n.*

ir·ra·tion·al (i rash'ə n'l) *adj.* **1.** lacking the power to reason **2.** senseless; unreasonable; absurd —**ir·ra'tion·al'i·ty** (-ə nal'ə tē) *n., pl.* -ties —**ir·ra'tion·al·ly** *adv.*

ir·re·claim·a·ble (ir'i klā'mə b'l) *adj.* that cannot be reclaimed

ir·rec·on·cil·a·ble (i rek'ən sīl'ə b'l) *adj.* that cannot be brought into agreement; incompatible

ir·re·cov·er·a·ble (ir'i kuv'ər ə b'l) *adj.* that cannot be recovered, rectified, or remedied

ir·re·deem·a·ble (ir'i dēm'ə b'l) *adj.* **1.** that cannot be bought back **2.** that

cannot be converted into coin, as certain paper money **3.** that cannot be changed or reformed

ir·ref·u·ta·ble (i ref'yoo tə b'l, ir'i fyōot'ə b'l) *adj.* indisputable

ir·re·gard·less (ir'i gärd'lis) *adj., adv. a substandard or humorous redundancy for* REGARDLESS

ir·reg·u·lar (i reg'yə lər) *adj.* **1.** not conforming to established rule, standard, etc. **2.** not straight, even, or uniform **3.** *Gram.* not inflected in the usual way —**ir·reg'u·lar'i·ty** *n.*

ir·rel·e·vant (i rel'ə vənt) *adj.* not pertinent; not to the point —**ir·rel'e·vance** *n.* —**ir·rel'e·vant·ly** *adv.*

ir·re·li·gious (ir'i lij'əs) *adj.* **1.** not religious; indifferent or hostile to religion **2.** profane; impious

ir·re·me·di·a·ble (ir'i mē'dē ə b'l) *adj.* that cannot be remedied or corrected —**ir're·me'di·a·bly** *adv.*

ir·rep·a·ra·ble (i rep'ər ə b'l) *adj.* that cannot be repaired, mended, etc.

ir·re·place·a·ble (ir'i plās'ə b'l) *adj.* that cannot be replaced

ir·re·press·i·ble (ir'i pres'ə b'l) *adj.* that cannot be repressed

ir·re·proach·a·ble (ir'i prō'chə b'l) *adj.* blameless; faultless

ir·re·sist·i·ble (ir'i zis'tə b'l) *adj.* that cannot be resisted; too strong, fascinating, etc. to be withstood

ir·res·o·lute (i rez'ə lōot') *adj.* not resolute; wavering; indecisive —**ir·res'o·lu'tion** *n.*

ir·re·spec·tive (ir'i spek'tiv) *adj.* regardless (*of*)

ir·re·spon·si·ble (ir'i spän'sə b'l) *adj.* **1.** not responsible for actions **2.** lacking a sense of responsibility —**ir're·spon'si·bil'i·ty** *n.*

ir·re·triev·a·ble (ir'i trēv'ə b'l) *adj.* that cannot be retrieved

ir·rev·er·ent (i rev'ər ənt) *adj.* not reverent; showing disrespect —**ir·rev'er·ence** *n.*

ir·re·vers·i·ble (ir'i vur'sə b'l) *adj.* that cannot be reversed; esp., that cannot be annulled or turned back

ir·rev·o·ca·ble (i rev'ə kə b'l) *adj.* that cannot be revoked or undone —**ir·rev'o·ca·bly** *adv.*

ir·ri·ga·ble (ir'i gə b'l) *adj.* that can be irrigated

ir·ri·gate (ir'ə gāt') *vt.* -gat'ed, -gat'ing [< L. *in-*, in + *rigare*, to water] **1.** to supply (land) with water as by means of artificial ditches **2.** *Med.* to wash out (a cavity, wound, etc.) —**ir'ri·ga'tion** *n.*

ir·ri·ta·ble (ir'i tə b'l) *adj.* **1.** easily irritated or provoked **2.** *Med.* excessively sensitive to a stimulus —**ir'ri·ta·bil'i·ty** *n.* —**ir'ri·ta·bly** *adv.*

ir·ri·tant (-tənt) *adj.* causing irritation —*n.* a thing that irritates

ir·ri·tate (-tāt') *vt.* -tat'ed, -tat'ing [< L. *irritare*, excite] **1.** to provoke to anger; annoy **2.** to make inflamed or sore —**ir'ri·ta'tion** *n.*

ir·rupt (i rupt') *vi.* [< L. *in-*, in + *rumpere*, to break] **1.** to burst suddenly or violently (*into*) **2.** *Ecology* to increase abruptly in size of population —**ir·rup'tion** *n.* —**ir·rup'tive** *adj.*

IRS, I.R.S. Internal Revenue Service

is (iz) [OE.] *3d pers. sing., pres. indic., of* BE

is. 1. island(s) 2. isle(s)

I·saac (ī'zək) *Bible* one of the patriarchs, son of Abraham, and father of Jacob and Esau

I·sa·iah (ī zā'ə) *Bible* 1. a Hebrew prophet of the 8th cent. B.C. 2. the book containing his teachings: abbrev. **Isa.**

-ise (īz) *chiefly Brit. var. of* -IZE

-ish (ish) [OE. *-isc*] *a suffix meaning: a)* of (a specified people) *[Irish] b)* like *[boyish] c)* somewhat *[tallish] d)* [Colloq.] approximately *[thirtyish]*

Ish·tar (ish'tär) the Babylonian and Assyrian goddess of fertility

i·sin·glass (ī'z'n glas', -zin-) *n.* [< MDu. *huizen*, sturgeon + *blas*, bladder] 1. a gelatin prepared from fish bladders 2. mica, esp. in thin sheets

I·sis (ī'sis) the Egyptian goddess of fertility

isl. *pl.* **isls.** 1. island 2. isle

Is·lam (is'läm, iz'-; is läm') *n.* [Ar. *islām*, lit., submission (to God's will)] 1. the Moslem religion, a monotheistic religion founded by Mohammed 2. Moslems collectively or the lands in which they predominate

is·land (ī'lənd) *n.* [< OE. *igland*, lit., island land: sp. after *isle*] 1. a land mass smaller than a continent and surrounded by water 2. anything like this in position or isolation

is'land·er *n.* a native or inhabitant of an island

isle (īl) *n.* [< L. *insula*] an island, esp. a small one

is·let (ī'lit) *n.* a very small island

ism (iz'm) *n.* any doctrine, theory, system, etc. whose name ends in *-ism*

-ism (iz'm) [< Gr. *-ismos*] *a suffix meaning:* 1. act or result of *[terrorism]* 2. condition, conduct, or qualities of *[patriotism]* 3. theory of *[socialism]* 4. devotion to *[nationalism]* 5. an instance of *[witticism]*

is·n't (iz'nt) is not

iso- [< Gr. *isos*] *a combining form meaning* equal, similar, identical

i·so·bar (ī'sə bär') *n.* [< prec. + Gr. *baros*, weight] a line on a map connecting points of equal barometric pressure

i·so·late (ī'sə lāt') *vt.* -lat'ed, -lat'ing [< It. *isola* (< L. *insula*), island] to set apart from others; place alone —*n.* a person or thing that is isolated —i'so·la'tion *n.* —i'so·la'tor *n.*

i'so·la'tion·ist *n.* one who believes his country should not take part in international alliances, etc. —*adj.* of isolationists —i'so·la'tion·ism *n.*

i·so·mer (ī'sə mər) *n.* [< Gr. *isos*, equal + *meros*, a part] any of two or more chemical compounds whose molecules contain the same atoms but in different arrangements —i'so·mer'ic (-mer'ik) *adj.*

i'so·met'ric (-met'rik) *adj.* [< Gr. *isos*, equal + Gr. *metron*, measure] 1. equal in measure 2. of isometrics —*n.* [pl.] exercise in which muscles are briefly tensed in opposition to other muscles or to an immovable object —i'so·met'ri·cal·ly *adv.*

i·sos·ce·les (ī säs'ə lēz') *adj.* [< Gr. *isos*, equal + *skelos*, leg] designating a triangle with two equal sides

i·so·tope (ī'sə tōp') *n.* [< iso- + Gr. *topos*, place] any of two or more forms of an element having the same atomic number but different atomic weights

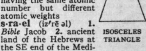

ISOSCELES TRIANGLE

Is·ra·el (iz'rē əl) 1. *Bible* Jacob 2. ancient land of the Hebrews at the SE end of the Mediterranean 3. kingdom in the N part of this land 4. country between the Mediterranean & the country of Jordan: 7,992 sq. mi.; pop. 2,813,000 5. the Jewish people

Is·rae·li (iz rā'lē) *adj.* of modern Israel or its people —*n., pl.* -lis, -li a native or inhabitant of modern Israel

Is·ra·el·ite (iz'rē ə līt', -rā-) *n.* any of the people of ancient Israel

is·su·ance (ish'oo wəns) *n.* an issuing; issue

is·sue (ish'oo) *n.* [< L. *ex-*, out + *ire*, go] 1. an outgoing; outflow 2. an outlet; exit 3. a result; consequence 4. offspring 5. a point under dispute 6. a sending or giving out 7. all that is put forth at one time *[an issue of bonds, a periodical, etc.]* 8. *Med.* a discharge of blood, etc. —*vi.* -sued, -su·ing 1. to go or flow out; emerge 2. to result (*from*) or end (*in*) 3. to be published —*vt.* 1. to let out; discharge 2. to give or deal out, as supplies 3. to publish —at issue in dispute —take issue to disagree

-ist (ist, əst) [< Gr. *-istēs*] *a suffix meaning:* 1. one who does, makes, or practices *[satirist]* 2. one skilled in or occupied with *[druggist, violinist]* 3. an adherent of *[anarchist]*

Is·tan·bul (is'tan bool', -tän-) seaport in NW Turkey: pop. 1,467,000

isth·mus (is'məs) *n., pl.* -mus·es, -mi (-mī) [< Gr. *isthmos*, a neck] a narrow strip of land having water at each side and connecting two larger bodies of land

it (it) *pron.* [for *pl.* see THEY] [< OE. *hit*] the animal or thing previously mentioned It is also used as: *a)* the subject of an impersonal verb *[it is snowing] b)* a subject or object of indefinite sense in various idiomatic constructions *[it's all right, he lords it over us]* —*n.* the player, as in tag, who must try to catch another —with it [Slang] alert, informed, or hip

It., Ital. 1. Italian 2. Italy

I·tal·ian (i tal'yən) *adj.* of Italy, its people, language, etc. —*n.* **1.** a native or inhabitant of Italy **2.** the Romance language of Italy

i·tal·ic (i tal'ik) *adj.* [< its early use in *Italy*] designating a type in which the letters slant upward to the right *[this is italic type]* —*n.* [*usually pl.*, *sometimes with sing. v.*] italic type or print: abbrev. *ital.*

i·tal·i·cize (i tal'ə sīz') *vt.* **-cized'**, **-ciz'ing** to print in italics

It·a·ly (it'l ē) country in S Europe: 116,304 sq. mi.; pop. 51,945,000

itch (ich) *vi.* [OE. *giccan*] **1.** to feel a tingling of the skin, with the desire to scratch **2.** to have a restless desire —*n.* **1.** an itching **2.** a restless desire —**the itch** an itching skin disorder —**itch'y** *adj.* **-i·er**, **-i·est**

-ite (īt) [< Gr. *-itēs*] a suffix meaning: **1.** an inhabitant of *[Akronite]* **2.** an adherent of *[laborite]* **3.** a manufactured product *[dynamite]*

i·tem (īt'əm) *n.* [< L. *ita*, so, thus] **1.** an article; unit; separate thing **2.** a bit of news or information

i'tem·ize (-īz') *vt.* **-ized'**, **-iz'ing** to specify the items of; set down by items —**i'tem·i·za'tion** *n.*

it·er·ate (it'ə rāt') *vt.* **-at'ed**, **-at'ing** [< L. *iterum*, again] to utter or do again; repeat —**it'er·a'tion** *n.*

i·tin·er·ant (ī tin'ər ənt) *adj.* [< L. *iter*, a walk] traveling from place to place —*n.* a traveler

i·tin·er·ar'y (-ə rer'ē) *n., pl.* **-ies 1.** a route **2.** a record of a journey **3.** a detailed plan of a journey

-i·tis (īt'əs) [< Gr. *-itis*] a suffix meaning inflammation of (a specified part or organ) *[neuritis]*

it'll (it''l) **1.** it will **2.** it shall

its (its) *pron.* that or those belonging

to it —*possessive pronominal adj.* of, belonging to, or done by it

it's (its) **1.** it is **2.** it has

it·self (it self') *pron.* **1.** *the intensive form of* IT *[the work itself is easy]* **2.** *the reflexive form of* IT *[the dog bit itself]* **3.** its true self *[the cat is not itself today]*

it·ty-bit·ty (it'ē bit'ē) *adj.* [baby talk < *little bit*] [Colloq.] very small; tiny Also **it·sy-bit·sy** (it'sē bit'sē)

-i·ty (ə tē, i-) [< L. *-itas*] a suffix meaning state, quality, or instance *[chastity]*

IUD intrauterine device

i.v. intravenous(ly)

I've (īv) I have

-ive (iv) [L. *-ivus*] a suffix meaning: **1.** of or having the nature of *[substantive]* **2.** tending to *[creative]*

i·vied (ī'vēd) *adj.* covered or overgrown with ivy

i·vo·ry (ī'vər ē, īv'rē) *n., pl.* **-ries** [ult. < Egypt. *ābu*] **1.** the hard, white substance forming the tusks of elephants, walruses, etc. **2.** any substance like ivory **3.** creamy white **4.** [*pl.*] [Slang] *a*) piano keys *b*) dice —*adj.* **1.** of or like ivory **2.** creamy-white

Ivory Coast country in WC Africa: 124,500 sq. mi.; pop. 3,750,000

ivory tower a retreat away from reality or action

i·vy (ī'vē) *n., pl.* **i'vies** [OE. *ifig*] **1.** a climbing vine with a woody stem and evergreen leaves **2.** any of various similar climbing plants

-ize (īz) [< Gr. *-izein*] a suffix meaning: **1.** to cause to be *[sterilize]* **2.** to become (like) *[crystallize]* **3.** to combine with *[oxidize]* **4.** to engage in *[soliloquize]* —**-i·za·tion** (ə zā'shən, ī-)

J

J, j (jā) *n., pl.* **J's**, **j's** the tenth letter of the English alphabet

jab (jab) *vt., vi.* **jabbed**, **jab'bing** [< ME. *jobben*, to peck] **1.** to poke, as with a sharp instrument **2.** to punch with short, straight blows —*n.* a quick thrust or blow

jab·ber (jab'ər) *vi., vt.* [prob. echoic] to talk quickly, incoherently, or foolishly; chatter —*n.* chatter —**jab'ber·er** *n.*

ja·bot (zha bō', ja-) *n.* [Fr., bird's crop] a ruffle or frill down the front of a blouse, etc.

jack (jak) *n.* [< the name *Jack*] **1.** [*often* J-] a man or boy **2.** any of various machines used to lift something heavy a short distance *[an automobile jack]* **3.** a playing card with a page boy's picture on it **4.** a small flag flown on a ship's bow as a signal or to show nationality **5.** any of the small 6-pronged metal pieces tossed and picked up in the game of jacks

6. a plug-in receptacle used to make electric contact **7.** [Slang] money —*vt.* to raise by means of a jack —**jack up** [Colloq.] to raise (prices, wages, etc.)

jack- [see prec.] *a combining form meaning:* **1.** male *[jack-ass]* **2.** large or strong *[jack-knife]* **3.** boy, fellow *[jack-in-the-box]*

JACK (sense 2)

jack·al (jak'əl, -ôl) *n.* [< Sans.] a wild dog of Asia and N Africa

jack·ass (jak'as') *n.* [*jack-* + *ass*] **1.** a male donkey **2.** a fool

jack·daw (jak'dô') *n.* [< *jack* +

ME. *dawe*, jackdaw] a European black bird like the crow, but smaller

jack·et (jak′it) *n.* [< Ar. *shakk*] 1. a short coat 2. an outer covering, as the removable paper cover on a book, the cardboard holder of a phonograph record, the skin of a potato, etc.

Jack Frost frost or cold weather personified

jack′-in-the-box′ *n., pl.* -box′es a toy consisting of a box from which a figure on a spring jumps up when the lid is lifted: also **jack′-in-a-box′**

jack′-in-the-pul′pit (-pool′pit) *n., pl.* -pits a plant with a flower spike partly arched over by a hoodlike covering

jack′knife′ *n., pl.* -knives′ 1. a large pocketknife 2. a dive in which the diver touches his feet with knees unbent and then straightens out —*vi., vt.* -knifed′, -knif′ing to bend or fold at the middle or at a connection

jack′-of-all′-trades′ *n., pl.* jacks′- [see JACK.] [*often* J-] one who can do many kinds of work acceptably

jack-o′-lan·tern (jak′ə lan′tərn) *n., pl.* -terns a hollow pumpkin cut to look like a face and used as a lantern

jack′pot′ *n.* [*jack*, playing card + *pot*] cumulative stakes, as in poker

jack rabbit a large hare of W N. America, with strong hind legs

Jack·son (jak′s′n) capital of Miss.: pop. 203,000

Jack·son (jak′s′n), **Andrew** 1767–1845; 7th U.S. president (1829–1837)

Jack·son·ville (jak′s′n vil′) port in NE Fla.: pop. 541,000

Ja·cob (jā′kəb) *Bible* a son of Isaac

Jac·quard (jə kärd′) *n.* [< J. M. *Jacquard* (1752–1834), Fr. inventor] a fabric with a figured weave

Ja·cuz·zi (jə kōō′zē) [< *Jacuzzi*, U.S. developers] *a trademark for* a kind of whirlpool bath

jade¹ (jād) *n.* [< Sp. *piedra de ijada*, stone of the side: supposed to cure pains in the side] 1. a hard, ornamental stone 2. its green color

jade² (jād) *n.* [< ON. *jalda*, mare] 1. a worn-out, worthless horse 2. a disreputable woman —*vt.* jad′ed, jad′ing 1. to tire 2. to satiate — jad′ed·ly *adv.* —jad′ed·ness *n.*

jade·ite (jā′dīt) *n.* a hard, translucent variety of jade

jade plant a plant with thick, green leaves, native to S Africa and Asia

jag (jag) *n.* [ME. *jagge*] a sharp, toothlike projection

jag·ged (jag′id) *adj.* having sharp projecting points; notched or ragged —jag′ged·ly *adv.* —jag′ged·ness *n.*

jag·uar (jag′wär) *n.* [Port. < SAmInd.] a large leopardlike cat found from SW U.S. to Argentina

jai a·lai (hī′ lī′, ə lī′) [< Basque *jai*, celebration + *alai*, merry] a game like handball, played with a basketlike racket

jail (jāl) *n.* [ult. < L. *cavea*, cage] a prison, esp. for minor offenders or persons awaiting trial —*vt.* to put or keep in jail

jail′break′ (-brāk′) *n.* a breaking out of jail

jail′er, jail′or *n.* a person in charge of a jail or of prisoners

Ja·kar·ta (jə kär′tə) capital of Indonesia: pop. c.3,500,000

ja·lop·y (jə läp′ē) *n., pl.* -ies [< ?] [Slang] an old, ramshackle car

jal·ou·sie (jal′ə sē) *n.* [Fr.: see JEALOUS] a window, shade, door, etc. formed of adjustable horizontal slats of wood, metal, or glass

jam¹ (jam) *vt.* jammed, jam′ming [< ?] 1. to squeeze into a confined space 2. to crush 3. to crowd 4. to crowd into or block (a passageway, etc.) 5. to cause to be stuck tight and unworkable 6. to make (radio broadcasts, etc.) unintelligible, as by sending out other signals on the same wavelength —*vi.* 1. *a)* to become stuck fast *b)* to become unworkable because of jammed parts 2. to become squeezed into a confined space 3. [Slang] *Jazz* to improvise —*n.* 1. a jamming or being jammed [a traffic *jam*] 2. [Colloq.] a difficult situation

jam² (jam) *n.* [< ? prec.] fruit boiled with sugar to a thick mixture

Ja·mai·ca (jə mā′kə) country on an island in the West Indies, south of Cuba: 4,411 sq. mi.; pop. 1,876,000 —**Ja·mai′can** *adj., n.*

jamb (jam) *n.* [< LL. *gamba*, leg] a side post of a doorway, etc.

jam·bo·ree (jam′bə rē′) *n.* [< ?] 1. [Colloq.] a noisy revel 2. a large assembly of boy scouts from many places

James·town (jāmz′toun′) former village in Va.: 1st Eng. colonial settlement in America (1607)

jam-packed (jam′pakt′) *adj.* tightly packed

jan·gle (jaŋ′g′l) *vi.* -gled, -gling [< OFr. *jangler*] to make a harsh, usually metallic sound —*vt.* 1. to cause to jangle 2. to irritate [jangled nerves] —*n.* a jangling —jan′gler *n.*

jan·i·tor (jan′i tər) *n.* [L., doorkeeper] one who takes care of a building, doing routine repairs, etc. —jan′i·to′ri·al (-ə tôr′ē əl) *adj.*

Jan·u·ar·y (jan′yoo wer′ē) *n., pl.* -ies [< L. < *Janus*, Roman god who was patron of beginnings and endings] the first month of the year, having 31 days: abbrev. **Jan.**

Ja·pan (jə pan′) 1. island country in the Pacific, off the E coast of Asia: 142,726 sq. mi.; pop. 100,020,000 2. **Sea of,** arm of the Pacific, between Japan & Asia

ja·pan (jə pan′) *n.* [< *Japan*] a hard lacquer giving a glossy finish —*vt.* -panned′, -pan′ning to lacquer with japan

Jap·a·nese (jap′ə nēz′) *adj.* of Japan, its people, language, etc. —*n.*

1. *pl.* **-nese′** a native of Japan **2.** the language of Japan

Jap′anese beetle′ a shiny, green-and-brown beetle, orig. from Japan, damaging to crops

jape (jāp) *vi.*, *vt.*, *n.* **japed, jap′ing** [ME. *japen*] joke; trick

jar¹ (jär) *vi.* **jarred, jar′ring** [ult. echoic] **1.** to make a harsh sound; grate **2.** to have an irritating effect (on one) **3.** to vibrate from an impact **4.** to clash; conflict —*vt.* to jolt —*n.* **1.** a grating sound **2.** a vibration due to impact **3.** a jolt

jar² (jär) *n.* [< Ar. *jarrah*, earthen container] **1.** a container made of glass, earthenware, etc., with a large opening **2.** as much as a jar will hold: also **jar′ful′**

jar·di·niere (jär′d'n ir′) *n.* [< Fr. < *jardin*, a garden] an ornamental pot or stand for flowers or plants

jar·gon (jär′gən) *n.* [< MFr., a chattering] **1.** unintelligible talk **2.** the specialized vocabulary of those in the same work, way of life, etc.

jas·mine (jaz′min; *chiefly Brit.* jas′-) *n.* [< Per. *yāsamin*] any of certain plants of warm regions, with fragrant flowers of yellow, red, or white

Ja·son (jās′n) *Gr.Myth.* the leader of the Argonauts: cf. ARGONAUT

jas·per (jas′pər) *n.* [< Gr. *iaspis*] an opaque variety of colored quartz

ja·to, JA·TO (jā′tō) *n.* [*j(et)-a(ssist-ed) t(ake)o(ff)*] an airplane takeoff assisted by a jet-producing unit or units

jaun·dice (jôn′dis) *n.* [ult. < L. *galbus*, yellow] a diseased condition in which the eyeballs, skin, and urine become abnormally yellow as a result of bile in the blood —*vt.* **-diced, -dic·ing 1.** to cause to have jaundice **2.** to make prejudiced through envy, etc.

jaunt (jônt) *vi.* [< ?] to take a short pleasure trip —*n.* such a trip

jaun·ty (jôn′tē) *adj.* **-ti·er, -ti·est** [< Fr. *gentil*, genteel] showing an easy confidence; perky or sprightly — **jaun′ti·ly** *adv.* —**jaun′ti·ness** *n.*

Ja·va (jä′və, jav′ə) large island of Indonesia —*n.* **1.** a coffee grown there **2.** [*often* **j-**] [Slang] any coffee —**Jav′-a·nese′** (-nēz′) *adj.*, *n.*, *pl.* **-nese′**

jav·e·lin (jav′lin, -ə lin) *n.* [MFr. *javeline*] a light spear, esp. one thrown for distance in a contest

jaw (jô) *n.* [< ? OFr. *joue*, cheek] **1.** either of the two bony parts that hold the teeth and frame the mouth **2.** either of two movable parts that grasp or crush something, as in a vise —*vi.* [Slang] to talk

jaw′bone′ *n.* a bone of a jaw, esp. of the lower jaw —*vt.*, *vi.* **-boned′, -bon′ing** to try to persuade by using the influence of one's office

jaw′break′er (-brā′kər) *n.* **1.** a machine for crushing rocks, ore, etc. **2.** a hard, usually round candy **3.** [Slang] a word hard to pronounce

jay (jā) *n.* [< LL. *gaius*, jay] **1.** any of several birds of the crow family **2.** *same as* BLUE JAY

jay′walk′ *vi.* [Colloq.] to walk across a street carelessly without obeying traffic rules or signals —**jay′walk′er** *n.*

jazz (jaz) *n.* [< ?] **1.** a kind of syncopated, highly rhythmic music originated by New Orleans musicians, esp. Negroes **2.** [Slang] talk, acts, etc. regarded disparagingly —*vt.* **1.** to play as jazz **2.** [Slang] to enliven or embellish (with *up*)

jazz′y *adj.* **-i·er, -i·est 1.** of or like jazz **2.** [Slang] lively, flashy, etc.

jeal·ous (jel′əs) *adj.* [see ZEAL] **1.** watchful in guarding [*jealous* of his rights] **2.** *a*) resentfully suspicious of rivalry [a *jealous* lover] *b*) resentfully envious *c*) resulting from such feelings [a *jealous* rage] —**jeal′ous·ly** *adv.*

jeal′ous·y *n.*, *pl.* **-ies** the quality, condition, or feeling of being jealous

jean (jēn) *n.* [< L. *Genua*, Genoa] **1.** a durable, twilled cotton cloth **2.** [*pl.*] trousers of this or of denim

jeep (jēp) *n.* [< creature in a comic strip by E. C. Segar] a small, rugged, military automobile of World War II

jeer (jir) *vi.*, *vt.* [? < *cheer*] to make fun of in a rude, sarcastic manner; scoff (at) —*n.* a jeering cry or remark

Jef·fer·son (jef′ər s'n), **Thomas** 1743–1826; 3d U.S. president (1801–09)

Jefferson City capital of Mo.: pop. 34,000

Je·ho·vah (ji hō′və) [< Heb.] God

je·june (ji jōōn′) *adj.* [L. *jejunus*, empty] **1.** not satisfying or interesting **2.** not mature; childish

je·ju·num (ji jōō′nəm) *n.*, *pl.* **-na** (-nə) [< L. *jejunus*, empty] the middle part of the small intestine

jell (jel) *vi.*, *vt.* [< ff.] **1.** to become, or make into, jelly **2.** to crystallize, as a plan

jel·ly (jel′ē) *n.*, *pl.* **-lies** [< L. *gelare*, freeze] **1.** a soft, gelatinous food made from cooked fruit syrup or meat juice **2.** any substance like this —*vi.*, *vt.* **-lied, -ly·ing** to jell (sense 1)

jel′ly·bean′ *n.* a small, bean-shaped, gelatinous candy

jel′ly·fish′ *n.*, *pl.* see FISH **1.** a sea animal with an umbrella-shaped, jelly-like body and long tentacles **2.** [Colloq.] a weak-willed person

jel′ly·roll′ *n.* a thin sheet of sponge cake spread with jelly and rolled up

jeop·ard·ize (jep′ər dīz′) *vt.* **-ized′, -iz′ing** to put in jeopardy

jeop·ard·y (-dē) *n.*, *pl.* **-ies** [< OFr. *jeu parti*, lit., a game with even chances] great danger or risk

jer·e·mi·ad (jer′ə mī′əd, -ad) *n.* a tale of woe; in allusion to the *Lamentations of Jeremiah*

Jer·e·mi·ah (jer′ə mī′ə) *Bible* a Hebrew prophet of the 7th and 6th cent. B.C.

Jer·i·cho (jer′ə kō′) city in W Jordan: site of an ancient city in Canaan

jerk (jurk) *n.* [< ?] **1.** a sharp, abrupt pull, twist, etc. **2.** a sudden muscular contraction or reflex **3.** [Slang] a person regarded as stupid, foolish, etc. —*vi.*, *vt.* **1.** to move with a jerk; pull sharply **2.** to twitch

jer·kin (jur'kin) *n.* [< ?] a short, closefitting jacket, often sleeveless

jerk'wa·ter *adj.* [Colloq.] small, unimportant, etc. *[jerkwater town]*

jerk·y¹ (jurk'ē) *adj.* **-i·er, -i·est** 1. moving by jerks; spasmodic 2. [Slang] stupid, foolish, etc. **—jerk'i·ly** *adv.*

jer·ky² (jur'kē) *n.* [< Sp. *charqui*] meat preserved by being sliced into strips and dried in the sun

jer·ry-built (jer'ē bilt) *adj.* built poorly, of cheap materials

jer·sey (jur'zē) *n., pl.* **-seys** [< *Jersey*, Brit. island in the English Channel] 1. [J-] a breed of reddish-brown dairy cattle originally from Jersey 2. a soft knitted cloth 3. a closefitting, knitted upper garment

Jersey City city in N.J., across the Hudson from New York: pop. 224,000

Je·ru·sa·lem (jə roo'sə ləm) capital of Israel (sense 4): pop. 250,000

jest (jest) *n.* [< L. *gerere*, perform] 1. a mocking remark; taunt 2. a joke 3. fun; joking 4. a thing to be laughed at *—vi.* 1. to jeer 2. to joke

jest'er *n.* one who jests; esp., a man kept by a medieval ruler to amuse him by joking and clowning

Jes·u·it (jezh'oo wit, jez'-) *n.* a member of the Society of Jesus, a R.C. religious order, founded 1534

Je·sus (jē'zəs) the founder of the Christian religion: also **Jesus Christ**

jet¹ (jet) *vt., vi.* **jet'ted, jet'ting** [< L. *jacere*, to throw] 1. to gush out in a stream 2. to travel or convey by jet airplane *—n.* 1. a stream of liquid or gas suddenly emitted 2. a spout for emitting a jet 3. a jet-propelled airplane: in full, **jet (air)plane** *—adj.* driven by jet propulsion

jet² (jet) *n.* [< Gr. *Gagas*, town in Asia Minor] 1. a hard, black mineral like coal, polished and used in jewelry 2. a lustrous black *—adj.* black

jet lag a disruption of the daily body rhythms, associated with high-speed travel by jet airplane

jet'lin'er *n.* a commercial jet aircraft for carrying passengers

jet'port' *n.* an airport with long runways, for use by jet airplanes

jet propulsion propulsion of airplanes, boats, etc. by the discharge of gases under pressure from a rear vent **—jet'-pro·pelled'** (-prə peld') *adj.*

jet·sam (jet'səm) *n.* [var. of JETTISON] cargo thrown overboard to lighten a ship in danger

jet set fashionable people who travel widely for pleasure, esp. in jets

jet·ti·son (jet'ə s'n) *vt.* [< L. *jactare*, to throw] 1. to throw (goods) overboard so as to lighten a ship in danger 2. to discard

jet·ty (jet'ē) *n., pl.* **-ties** [see JET¹] 1. a wall built out into the water to restrain currents, protect a harbor, etc. 2. a landing pier

Jew (joo) *n.* [< Heb. *yehūdī*, citizen of Judah] 1. a person descended, or regarded as descended, from the ancient Hebrews 2. a person whose religion is Judaism

jew·el (joo'əl) *n.* [ult. < L. *jocus*, a joke] 1. a precious stone; gem 2. any person or thing very dear to one 3. a small gem used as a bearing in a watch *—vt.* **-eled** or **-elled, -el·ing** or **-el·ling** to decorate or set with jewels

jew'el·er, jew'el·ler (-ər) *n.* one who makes or deals in jewelry

jew'el·ry *n.* jewels collectively

Jew·ish (joo'ish) *adj.* of or having to do with Jews or Judaism *—n.* [Colloq.] *same as* YIDDISH **—Jew'ish·ness** *n.*

Jew·ry (joo'rē) *n.* the Jewish people

jew's-harp (jooz'härp') *n.* [< Du. *jeugd-tromp*, child's trumpet] a small, metal musical instrument held between the teeth and plucked to produce twanging tones: also **jews'-harp**

Jez·e·bel (jez'ə bel') *Bible* a wicked queen of Israel

jg, j.g. junior grade

jib (jib) *n.* [Dan. *gib*] a triangular sail projecting ahead of the foremast

jibe¹ (jib) *vi.* **jibed, jib'ing** [< Du. *gijpen*] 1. to shift from one side of a ship to the other, as a fore-and-aft sail 2. to change the course of a ship so that the sails jibe 3. [Colloq.] to be in agreement or accord

jibe² (jib) *n., vi., vt. same as* GIBE

jif·fy (jif'ē) *n., pl.* **-fies** [< ?] [Colloq.] a very short time: also **jiff**

jig (jig) *n.* [prob. < MFr. *giguer*, to dance] 1. a fast, springy dance in triple time, or music for this 2. a device used to guide a tool *—vi., vt.* **jigged, jig'ging** to dance (a jig) **—in jig time** [Colloq.] very quickly **—the jig is up** [Slang] no chance is left

jig·ger (jig'ər) *n.* 1. a small glass, usually of 1 1/2 ozs., used to measure liquor 2. the contents of a jigger

jig·gle (jig''l) *vi., vt.* **-gled, -gling** [< JIG] to move in quick, slight jerks *—n.* a jiggling

jig·saw (jig'sô') *n.* a saw consisting of a narrow blade set in a frame, used for cutting along irregular lines

jigsaw puzzle a puzzle consisting of disarranged, irregularly cut pieces of a picture that are to be fitted together

jilt (jilt) *vt.* [< *Jill*, sweetheart] to reject or cast off (a lover or sweetheart) after encouraging him

Jim Crow [name of an early Negro minstrel song] [*also* **j- c-**] [Colloq.] discrimination against or segregation of Negroes **—Jim'Crow'** *vt., adj.*

jim·my (jim'ē) *n., pl.* **-mies** [< *James*] a short crowbar, used by burglars to pry open windows, etc. *—vt.* **-mied, -my·ing** to pry open with or as with a jimmy

jim·son weed (jim's'n) [< *Jamestown weed*] a poisonous weed with white or purplish, trumpet-shaped flowers

jin·gle (jiŋ'g'l) *vi.* **-gled, -gling** [echoic] to make light, ringing sounds, as small bells —*vt.* to cause to jingle —*n.* 1. a jingling sound 2. a catchy verse or song with easy rhythm, simple rhymes, etc.

jin·go·ism (jiŋ′gō iz′m) *n.* [< phr. *by jingo* in a patriotic Brit. song] chauvinistic advocacy of an aggressive, warlike foreign policy —**jin′go·ist** *n.* —**jin′go·is′tic** *adj.*

jin·ni (ji ne′, jin′ē) *n.*, *pl.* **jinn** [Ar.] *Moslem Legend* a supernatural being that can influence human affairs

jin·rik·i·sha (jin rik′shô) *n.* [Jap. < *jin*, a man + *riki*, power + *sha*, carriage] a small, two-wheeled carriage pulled by a man, esp. formerly in the Orient: also **jin·rick′sha, jin·rik′sha**

jinx (jiŋks) *n.* [< Gr. *iynx*, the wryneck (bird used in black magic)] [Colloq.] a person or thing supposed to bring bad luck —*vt.* [Colloq.] to be a jinx to

jit·ney (jit′nē) *n.*, *pl.* -**neys** [< ? Fr. *jeton*, a token] 1. [Old Slang] a five-cent coin 2. a bus or car carrying passengers for a small fare

jit′ter·bug′ *n.* a fast, acrobatic dance for couples, esp. in the 1940's —*vi.* -**bugged′**, -**bug′ging** to do this dance

jit·ters (jit′ərz) *n.pl.* [Colloq.] an uneasy, nervous feeling; fidgets (with *the*) —**jit′ter·y** *adj.*

jive (jīv) *n.* [< JIBE²] [Slang] foolish, exaggerated, or insincere talk

Joan of Arc (jōn′ əv ärk′), Saint 1412–31; Fr. military heroine: burned at the stake

Job (jōb) *Bible* a man who suffered much but kept his faith in God

job (jäb) *n.* [< ?] 1. a piece of work done for pay 2. task; duty 3. the thing or material being worked on 4. employment; work —*adj.* hired or done by the job —*vt.*, *vi.* **jobbed**, **job′bing** 1. to deal in (goods) as a jobber 2. to sublet (work, etc.) —**job′hold′er** *n.* —**job′less** *adj.*

job action a refusal by a group of employees to perform their duties, in order to win certain demands, esp. by a group forbidden by law to strike

job·ber (jäb′ər) *n.* 1. one who buys goods in quantity and sells them to dealers 2. one who does piecework

job lot an assortment of goods for sale as one quantity

jock (jäk) *n.* [Slang] *short for* DISC JOCKEY

jock·ey (jäk′ē) *n.*, *pl.* -**eys** [< Scot. dim. of *Jack*] one whose job is riding horses in races —*vt.*, *vi.* -**eyed**, -**ey·ing** 1. to cheat; swindle 2. to maneuver for position or advantage

jock·strap (jäk′strap′) *n.* [*jock*, penis + STRAP] 1. an elastic belt with a pouch for supporting the genitals, worn by male athletes 2. [Slang] an athlete Also **jock**

jo·cose (jō kōs′) *adj.* [< L. *jocus*, a joke] joking or playful —**jo·cose′ly** *adv.* —**jo·cos′i·ty** (-käs′ə tē) *pl.* -**ties**, **jo·cose′ness** *n.*

joc·u·lar (jäk′yə lər) *adj.* [< L. *jocus*, a joke] joking; full of fun —**joc′u·lar′i·ty** (-lar′ə tē) *n.*, *pl.* -**ties**

joc·und (jäk′ənd) *adj.* [< L. *ju-cundus*, pleasant] cheerful; genial; gay —**joc′und·ly** *adv.*

jodh·purs (jäd′pərz) *n.pl.* [< *Jodhpur*, former state in India] riding breeches made loose and full above the knees and closefitting below

jog¹ (jäg) *vt.* **jogged, jog′ging** [ME. *joggen*, to spur (a horse)] 1. to give a little shake to; nudge 2. to rouse (the memory) —*vi.* to move along at a slow, steady, jolting pace —*n.* 1. a little shake or nudge 2. a slow, steady, jolting motion —**jog′ger** *n.*

jog² (jäg) *n.* [var. of JAG¹] 1. a projecting or notched part in a surface or line 2. a sharp change of direction

jog′ging *n.* trotting slowly and steadily as a form of exercise

jog·gle (jäg′'l) *vt.*, *vi.* -**gled**, -**gling** [< JOG¹] to shake or jolt slightly —*n.* a slight jolt

Jo·han·nes·burg (jō han′is burg′, yō hän′is-) city in NE South Africa: pop. 1,153,000

John (jän) *Bible* 1. a Christian apostle, the reputed author of the fourth Gospel 2. this book

john (jän) *n.* [Slang] 1. a toilet 2. [*also* J-] a prostitute's customer

John Bull (bool) England, or an Englishman, personified

John Doe (dō) a fictitious name used in legal papers for an unknown person

John·son (jän′s'n) 1. Andrew, 1808–75; 17th president of the U.S. (1865–69) 2. Lyn·don Baines (lin′dən bānz), 1908–73; 36th president of the U.S. (1963–69) 3. Samuel, 1709–84; Eng. lexicographer & writer

John the Baptist *Bible* the forerunner and baptizer of Jesus

join (join) *vt.*, *vi.* [< L. *jungere*] 1. to bring or come together (with); connect; unite 2. to become a part or member of (a club, etc.) 3. to participate (*in* a conversation, etc.)

join′er *n.* 1. a carpenter who finishes interior woodwork 2. [Colloq.] one who joins many organizations

joint (joint) *n.* [< L. *jungere*, join] 1. a place where, or way in which, two things are joined 2. any of the parts of a jointed whole 3. a large cut of meat with the bone still in it 4. [Slang] a cheap bar, restaurant, etc., or any house, building, etc. 5. [Slang] a marijuana cigarette —*adj.* 1. common to two or more [*joint* property] 2. sharing with another [a *joint* owner] —*vt.* 1. to fasten together by or provide with a joint or joints 2. to cut (meat) into joints —**out of joint** 1. dislocated 2. disordered

joint′ly *adv.* in common

joist (joist) *n.* [< OFr. *giste*, a bed] any of the parallel beams that hold up the planks of a floor or the laths of a ceiling

JOISTS

joke (jōk) *n.* [L. *jocus*] 1. anything said or done to arouse laughter, as a funny anecdote 2. a thing done or said merely in fun 3. a person or thing to be laughed at

—*vi.* **joked, jok′ing** to make jokes
—**jok′ing·ly** *adv.*

jok′er *n.* 1. one who jokes 2. a hidden provision, as in a legal document, that makes it different from what it seems to be 3. an extra playing card

jol·li·ty (jäl′ə tē) *n.* a being jolly

jol·ly (jäl′ē) *adj.* -**li·er**, -**li·est** [OFr. *joli*] 1. full of high spirits and good humor; merry 2. [Colloq.] enjoyable —*vt., vi.* -**lied**, -**ly·ing** [Colloq.] 1. to try to make (a person) feel good, as by coaxing (often with *along*) 2. to make fun of (someone) —**jol′li·ly** *adv.* —**jol′li·ness** *n.*

jolt (jōlt) *vt.* [< earlier *jot*] 1. to shake up, as with a bumpy ride 2. to shock or surprise —*vi.* to move along in a bumpy manner —*n.* 1. a sudden jerk, bump, etc. 2. a shock or surprise

Jo·nah (jō′nə) 1. *Bible* a Hebrew prophet: cast overboard and swallowed by a big fish, he was later cast up unharmed 2. one who brings bad luck

Jones (jōnz), **John Paul** 1747–92; Am. naval officer in the Revolutionary War, born in Scotland

jon·quil (jäŋ′kwəl, jän′-) *n.* [< L. *juncus*, a rush] a species of narcissus with small yellow flowers

Jon·son (jän′s'n), **Ben** 1572?–1637; Eng. dramatist & poet

Jor·dan (jôr′d'n) 1. river in the Near East, flowing into the Dead Sea 2. country east of Israel: 37,300 sq. mi.; pop. 2,101,000

Jo·seph (jō′zəf) *Bible* 1. one of Jacob's sons, who became a high official in Egypt 2. the husband of Mary, mother of Jesus

josh (jäsh) *vt., vi.* [< ?] [Colloq.] to tease; banter —**josh′er** *n.*

Josh·u·a (jäsh′ōo wə) *Bible* Moses' successor, and leader of the Israelites into the Promised Land

jos·tle (jäs′'l) *vt., vi.* -**tled**, -**tling** [see JOUST] to push, as in a crowd; shove roughly —*n.* a jostling

jot (jät) *n.* [< Gr. *iōta*, the smallest letter] a very small amount —*vt.* **jot′ted, jot′ting** to make a brief note of (usually with *down*) —**jot′ter** *n.*

jounce (jouns) *vt., vi.* **jounced, jounc′ing** [< ?] to jolt or bounce —*n.* a jolt —**jounc′y** *adj.*

jour·nal (jur′n'l) *n.* [< L. *diurnalis*, daily] 1. a daily record of happenings, as a diary 2. a newspaper or periodical 3. *Bookkeeping* a book of original entry for recording transactions 4. [orig. Scot.] the part of an axle or shaft that turns in a bearing

jour·nal·ese (jur′n'l ēz′) *n.* a facile style of writing found in many newspapers, magazines, etc.

jour·nal·ism (-iz′m) *n.* the work of gathering news for, or producing, a newspaper, etc. —**jour′nal·ist** *n.* —**jour′nal·is′tic** *adj.*

jour·ney (jur′nē) *n., pl.* -**neys** [< OFr. *journee*; ult. < L. *dies*, day] a traveling from one place to another;

trip —*vi.* -**neyed**, -**ney·ing** to travel —**jour′ney·er** *n.*

jour′ney·man (-mən) *n., pl.* -**men** [ME. < *journee*, day's work + *man*] 1. a worker who has learned his trade 2. an average or mediocre performer

joust (joust, just) *n.* [ult. < L. *juxta*, close to] a combat with lances between two knights on horseback —*vi.* to engage in a joust

jo·vi·al (jō′vē əl) *adj.* [< LL. *Jovialis*, of Jupiter: from astrological notion of planet's influence] full of playful good humor —**jo′vi·al′i·ty** (-al′ə tē) *n.* —**jo′vi·al·ly** *adv.*

jowl¹ (joul) *n.* [OE. *ceafl*, jaw] 1. the lower jaw 2. the cheek, esp. of a hog

jowl² (joul) *n.* [OE. *ceole*, throat] [often *pl.*] the fleshy, hanging part under the jaw —**jowl′y** *adj.*

joy (joi) *n.* [ult. < L. *gaudium*, joy] 1. a very glad feeling; happiness; delight 2. anything causing this

Joyce (jois), **James** 1882–1941; Ir. novelist & poet

joy′ful *adj.* feeling, expressing, or causing joy; glad —**joy′ful·ly** *adv.*

joy′ous (-əs) *adj.* joyful; gay —**joy′ous·ly** *adv.* —**joy′ous·ness** *n.*

joy ride [Colloq.] an automobile ride, often at reckless speed, just for pleasure —**joy rider** —**joy riding**

joy′ stick′ *n.* [Colloq.] 1. the control stick of an airplane 2. a manual device with a control lever for positioning a lighted indicator, as on a video screen

J.P. justice of the peace

Jpn. 1. Japan 2. Japanese

Jr., jr. junior

ju·bi·lant (jōo′b'l ənt) *adj.* [< L. *jubilum*, wild shout] joyful and triumphant; rejoicing; elated

ju·bi·la·tion (jōo′bə lā′shən) *n.* 1. a rejoicing 2. a happy celebration

ju·bi·lee (jōo′bə lē′) *n.* [< Heb. *yōbēl*, a ram's horn (trumpet)] 1. a 50th or 25th anniversary 2. a time of rejoicing 3. jubilation

Ju·dah (jōo′də) 1. *Bible* one of Jacob's sons 2. kingdom in the S part of ancient Palestine

Ju·da·ism (jōo′də iz′m) *n.* the Jewish religion —**Ju·da′ic** (-dā′ik) *adj.*

Ju·das (Is·car·i·ot) (jōo′dəs is ker′ē ət) the disciple who betrayed Jesus for money —*n.* a traitor; betrayer

judge (juj) *n.* [< L. *jus*, law + *dicere*, say] 1. a public official with authority to hear and decide cases in a court of law 2. a person designated to determine the winner, settle a controversy, etc. 3. a person qualified to decide on the relative worth of anything —*vt., vi.* **judged, judg′ing** 1. to hear and pass judgment (on) in a court of law 2. to determine the winner of (a contest) or settle (a controversy) 3. to form an opinion about 4. to criticize or censure 5. to think; suppose —**judge′ship′** *n.*

judg′ment *n.* 1. a judging; deciding 2. a legal decision; order given by a judge, etc. **3.** an opinion **4.** the ability to come to an opinion **5.** [J-] *short for* LAST JUDGMENT *Also* **judgement** —**judg·men'tal** (-men't'l) *adj.*

Judgment Day *Theol.* the time of God's final judgment of all people

ju·di·ca·to·ry (jōō'di kə tôr'ē) *adj.* [see JUDGE] having to do with administering justice —*n., pl.* **-ries** a law court, or law courts collectively

ju'di·ca·ture (-chər) *n.* **1.** the administering of justice **2.** jurisdiction **3.** judges or courts collectively

ju·di·cial (jōō dish'əl) *adj.* **1.** of judges, courts, or their functions **2.** allowed, enforced, etc. by a court **3.** befitting a judge **4.** fair; impartial

ju·di·ci·ar·y (jōō dish'ē er'ē) *adj.* of judges or courts —*n., pl.* **-ies 1.** the part of government that administers justice **2.** judges collectively

ju·di'cious (-dish'əs) *adj.* having or showing sound judgment —**ju·di'· cious·ly** *adv.*

ju·do (jōō'dō) *n.* [Jap. < *jū,* soft + *dō,* art] a form of jujitsu

jug (jug) *n.* [a pet form of *Judith* or *Joan*] **1.** a container for liquids, with a small opening and a handle **2.** [Slang] a jail

jug·ger·naut (jug'ər nôt') *n.* [< Sans. *Jagannātha,* lord of the world] a terrible, irresistible force

jug·gle (jug'l) *vt.* **-gled, -gling** [< L. *jocus,* a joke] **1.** to perform skillful tricks of sleight of hand with (balls, etc.) **2.** to manipulate so as to deceive —*vi.* to toss up balls, etc. and keep them in the air —**jug'gler** *n.* —**jug'· gler·y** *n.*

jug·u·lar (jug'yoo lər) *adj.* [< L. *jugum,* a yoke] of the neck or throat —*n.* either of two large veins in the neck carrying blood from the head: in full, **jugular vein**

juice (jōōs) *n.* [< L. *jus,* broth] **1.** the liquid part of a plant, fruit, etc. **2.** a liquid in or from animal tissue **3.** [Colloq.] vitality **4.** [Slang] *a)* electricity *b)* alcoholic liquor —*vt.* **juiced, juic'ing** to extract juice from

juic·er (jōō'sər) *n.* a device for extracting juice from fruit

juic·y (jōō'sē) *adj.* **-i·er, -i·est 1.** full of juice **2.** [Colloq.] *a)* very interesting *b)* highly profitable — **juic'i·ness** *n.*

ju·jit·su, ju·jut·su (jōō jit'sōō) *n.* [< Jap. *jū,* pliant + *jutsu,* art] a Japanese system of wrestling in which the strength and weight of an opponent are used against him

ju·ju·be (jōō'jōō bē') *n.* [< Gr.] a gelatinous fruit-flavored candy

juke·box (jōōk'bäks') *n.* [< Am. Negro *juke,* wicked] a coin-operated electric phonograph

ju·lep (jōō'ləp) *n.* [< Per. *gul,* rose + *āb,* water] *same as* MINT JULEP

ju·li·enne (jōō'lē en') *adj.* [Fr.] cut into strips: said of vegetables

Ju·li·et (jōōl'yət, jōō'lē et') the heroine of Shakespeare's tragedy *Romeo and Juliet*

Ju·ly (joo lī', jōō-) *n.* [< L. < *Julius* Caesar] the seventh month of the

year, having 31 days: abbrev. **Jul.**

jum·ble (jum'b'l) *vt., vi.* **-bled, -bling** [? blend of JUMP + TUMBLE] to mix or be mixed in a confused heap —*n.* a confused mixture or heap

jum·bo (jum'bō) *n., pl.* **-bos** [< Am. Negro *jamba,* elephant] a large person, animal, or thing —*adj.* very large

jump (jump) *vi.* [< ?] **1.** to spring or leap from the ground, a height, etc. **2.** to jerk; bob **3.** to move or act eagerly (often with *at*) **4.** to pass suddenly, as to a new topic **5.** to rise suddenly, as prices **6.** [Slang] to be lively —*vt.* **1.** *a)* to leap over *b)* to pass over **2.** to cause to leap **3.** to leap upon **4.** to cause (prices, etc.) to rise **5.** [Colloq.] *a)* to attack suddenly *b)* to react to prematurely **6.** [Slang] to leave suddenly *(to jump town)* —*n.* **1.** a jumping **2.** a distance jumped **3.** a sudden transition **4.** a sudden rise, as in prices **5.** a sudden, nervous start —**get** (or **have**) **the jump on** [Slang] to get (or have) an advantage over —**jump bail** to forfeit bail by running away —**jump'er** *n.*

jump·er (jum'pər) *n.* [< dial. *jump,* short coat] **1.** a loose jacket **2.** a sleeveless dress for wearing over a blouse, etc. **3.** [*pl.*] *same as* ROMPERS

jump suit 1. a coverall worn by paratroops, etc. **2.** any one-piece garment like this

jump'y *adj.* **-i·er, -i·est 1.** moving in jumps, etc. **2.** easily startled —**jump'i·ly** *adv.* —**jump'i·ness** *n.*

jun·co (juŋ'kō) *n., pl.* **-cos** [< Sp.] a small bird with a gray or black head

junc·tion (juŋk'shən) *n.* [< L. *jungere,* join] **1.** a joining or being joined **2.** a place of joining, as of roads —**junc'tion·al** *adj.*

junc·ture (juŋk'chər) *n.* **1.** a junction **2.** a point of time **3.** a crisis

June (jōōn) *n.* [< L. *Junius,* of Juno] the sixth month of the year, having 30 days

Ju·neau (jōō'nō) capital of Alas., on the SE coast: pop. 20,000

jun·gle (juŋ'g'l) *n.* [< Sans. *jaṅgala,* wasteland] **1.** land densely covered with trees, vines, etc., as in the tropics **2.** [Slang] a situation in which people struggle fiercely to survive

jun·ior (jōōn'yər) *adj.* [L. < *juvenis,* young] **1.** the younger: written *Jr.* after a son's name if it is the same as his father's **2.** of more recent position or lower status *(a junior partner)* **3.** of juniors —*n.* **1.** one who is younger, of lower rank, etc. **2.** a student in the next-to-last year, as of a college

junior college a school offering courses two years beyond high school

junior high school a school usually including 7th, 8th, and 9th grades

ju·ni·per (jōō'nə pər) *n.* [L. *juniperus*] a small evergreen shrub or tree with berrylike cones

junk[1] (juŋk) *n.* [< ?] **1.** old metal, paper, rags, etc. **2.** [Colloq.] trash **3.** [Slang] heroin —*vt.* [Colloq.] to scrap

junk[2] (juŋk) *n.* [< Javanese *joṅ*] a Chinese flat-bottomed ship

Jun·ker (yooŋ'kər) *n.* [G.] a Prussian

of the land-owning, militaristic class

junk·er (juŋ′kər) *n.* [Slang] an old, dilapidated car or truck

jun·ket (juŋ′kit) *n.* [ME. *joncate*, cream cheese] 1. milk sweetened, flavored, and thickened into curd 2. a picnic 3. an excursion, esp. one by an official at public expense —*vi.* to go on a junket —**jun′ket·eer′** (-kə-tir′), **jun′ket·er** *n.*

junk food snack food with chemical additives and little food value

junk·ie, junk·y (juŋ′kē) *n., pl.* **-ies** [Slang] a narcotics addict

Ju·no (jōō′nō) *Rom. Myth.* the wife of Jupiter and queen of the gods

jun·ta (hoon′tə, jun′-) *n.* [Sp. < L. *jungere*, join] a group of political intriguers, esp. military men, in power after a coup d'état: also **jun·to** (jun′tō), *pl.* **-tos**

Ju·pi·ter (jōō′pə tər) 1. the chief Rom. god 2. the largest planet of the solar system: see PLANET

ju·rid·i·cal (joo rid′i k'l) *adj.* [< L. *jus*, law + *dicere*, declare] of judicial proceedings or law

ju·ris·dic·tion (joor′is dik′shən) *n.* [see prec.] 1. the administering of justice 2. authority or its range — **ju′ris·dic′tion·al** *adj.*

ju·ris·pru·dence (joor′is prōō′d'ns) *n.* [< L. *jus*, law + *prudentia*, a foreseeing] 1. the science or philosophy of law 2. a division of law

ju·rist (joor′ist) *n.* [< L. *jus*, law] an expert in law or writer on law

ju·ror (joor′ər) *n.* a member of a jury: also **ju′ry·man** (-mən), *pl.* **-men**

ju·ry (joor′ē) *n., pl.* **-ries** [< L. *jurare*, swear] 1. a group of people sworn to hear evidence in a law case and to give a decision 2. a committee that decides winners in a contest

just (just) *adj.* [< L. *jus*, law] 1. right or fair [a *just* decision] 2. righteous [a *just* man] 3. deserved [*just* praise] 4. lawful 5. proper 6.

correct or true 7. accurate; exact —*adv.* 1. exactly [*just* one o'clock] 2. nearly - 3. only [*just* a taste] 4. barely [*just* missed him] 5. a very short time ago [she's *just* left] 6. immediately [*just* east of here] 7. [Colloq.] really [*just* beautiful] —**just the same** [Colloq.] nevertheless —**just′ly** *adv.* —**just′ness** *n.*

jus·tice (jus′tis) *n.* 1. a being righteous 2. fairness 3. rightfulness 4. reward or penalty as deserved 5. the use of authority to uphold what is just 6. the administration of law 7. *same as: a)* JUDGE (sense 1) *b)* JUSTICE OF THE PEACE —**do justice to** to treat fairly

justice of the peace a local magistrate who decides minor cases, performs marriages, etc.

jus·ti·fy (jus′tə fi′) *vt.* **-fied′, -fy′ing** [< L. *justus*, just + *facere*, to do] 1. to show to be just, right, etc. 2. *Theol.* to free from blame or guilt 3. to supply grounds for —**jus′ti·fi′a·ble** *adj.* —**jus′ti·fi·ca′tion** *n.*

Jus·tin·i·an I (jəs tin′ē ən) 483–565 A.D.; Eastern Roman emperor (527–565): codified Roman law

jut (jut) *vi., vt.* **jut′ted, jut′ting** [prob. var. of JET[1]] to stick out; project —*n.* a part that juts

jute (jōōt) *n.* [< Sans. *jūta*, matted hair] 1. a strong fiber used for making burlap, rope, etc. 2. an Indian plant having this fiber

ju·ve·nile (jōō′və n'l, -nīl′) *adj.* [< L. *juvenis*, young] 1. young; immature 2. of or for young persons —*n.* 1. a young person 2. an actor who plays youthful roles 3. a book for children

juvenile delinquency antisocial or illegal behavior by minors, usually 18 or younger —**juvenile delinquent**

jux·ta·pose (juks′stə pōz′) *vt.* **-posed′, -pos′ing** [< L. *juxta*, beside + POSE] to put side by side —**jux′-ta·po·si′tion** *n.*

K

K, k (kā) *n., pl.* **K's, k's** the eleventh letter of the English alphabet

K[1] 1. [ModL. *kalium*] *Chem.* potassium 2. *Baseball* strikeout

K[2] *Electronics* 1. the number 1,024 or 2[10] 2. kindergarten

K., k. 1. karat (carat) 2. kilo 3. king

kad·dish (käd′ish) *n.* [Aram. *qaddish*, holy] *Judaism* a hymn in praise of God, recited at the daily service or as a mourner's prayer

kaf·fee·klatsch (kä′fā kläch′, kô′fē klach′) *n.* [G. < *kaffee*, coffee + *klatsch*, gossip] [*also* K-] an informal gathering to drink coffee and chat

kai·ser (kī′zər) *n.* [< L. *Caesar*]

emperor: the title [K-] of the former rulers of Austria and Germany

kale, kail (kāl) *n.* [var. of COLE] a hardy cabbage with spreading leaves

ka·lei·do·scope (kə lī′də skōp′) *n.* [< Gr. *kalos*, beautiful + *eidos*, form + -SCOPE] 1. a small tube containing bits of colored glass reflected by mirrors to form symmetrical patterns as the tube is rotated 2. anything that constantly changes —**ka·lei′do·scop′ic** (-skäp′ik) *adj.*

kan·ga·roo (kaŋ′gə rōō′) *n.* [< ?] a leaping, marsupial mammal of Australia and nearby islands, with short forelegs and strong, large hind legs

fat, āpe, cär; ten, ēven; is, bīte; gō, hôrn, tōōl, look; oil, out; up, fur; chin; she; thin, then; zh, leisure; ŋ, ring; ə for a in *ago*; ', (ā′b'l); ë, Fr. coeur; ö, Fr. feu; Fr. mon; ü, Fr. duc; kh, G. ich, doch; ‡ foreign; < derived from

kangaroo court [Colloq.] a mock court illegally passing and executing judgment, as among frontiersmen

Kan·sas (kan′zəs) Middle Western State of the U.S.: 82,264 sq. mi.; pop. 2,363,000; cap. Topeka: abbrev. **Kans.**

Kansas City 1. city in W Mo., on the Missouri River: pop. 448,000 2. city opposite this, in NE Kansas: pop. 168,000

Kant (kant), **Im·man·u·el** (i man′ yoo wəl) 1724–1804; Ger. philosopher

ka·o·lin (kā′ə lin) n. [Fr. < Chin. name of hill where found] a white clay used in porcelain, etc.

ka·pok (kā′päk) n. [Malay kapoq] the silky fibers around the seeds of certain tropical trees, used for stuffing mattresses, etc.

kap·pa (kap′ə) n. the tenth letter of the Greek alphabet (K, κ)

ka·put (kə poot′) adj. [G. kaputt] [Slang] ruined, destroyed, etc.

Ka·ra·chi (kə rä′chē) seaport in SW Pakistan: pop. 1,913,000

kar·a·kul (kar′ə kəl) n. [< Kara Kul, lake in the U.S.S.R.] 1. a sheep of C Asia 2. the curly black fur from the fleece of its lambs: usually sp. caracul

kar·at (kar′ət) n. [var. of CARAT] one 24th part (of pure gold)

ka·ra·te (kə rät′ē) n. [Jap.] a Japanese system of self-defense by sharp, quick blows with the hands and feet

kar·ma (kär′mə) n. [Sans., act] 1. Buddhism & Hinduism the totality of one's acts in each state of one's existence 2. loosely, fate

kart (kärt) n. [< CART] a small, flat motorized vehicle, used in racing

ka·ty·did (kāt′ē did′) n. [echoic of its shrill sound] a large, green, tree insect resembling the grasshopper

kay·ak (kī′ak) n. [Esk.] an Eskimo canoe made of skins on a wooden frame

kay·o (kā′ō′) vt. -oed′, -o′ing [< KO] [Slang] Boxing to knock out —n. [Slang] Boxing a knockout

ka·zoo (kə zoo′) n. [echoic] a toy musical instrument, a small tube with a paper-covered hole that makes buzzing tones when hummed into

KAYAK

kc, kc. kilocycle(s)

Keats (kēts), **John** 1795–1821; Eng. poet

ke·bab (kə bäb′) n. [Ar. kabāb] [often pl.] a dish of small pieces of marinated meat stuck on a skewer, often with vegetables, and broiled

keel (kēl) n. [< ON. kjölr] the chief timber or piece extending along the length of the bottom of a boat or ship —**keel over** [Colloq.] 1. to capsize 2. to fall over suddenly —**on an even keel** in an upright, level position

keen (kēn) adj. [OE. cene, wise] 1. having a sharp edge or point [a keen knife] 2. cutting; piercing [a keen wind] 3. very perceptive [keen eyes] 4. shrewd 5. eager 6. strongly felt; in-tense —**keen′ly** adv. —**keen′ness** n.

keep (kēp) vt. kept, keep′ing [OE. cepan, behold] 1. to celebrate; observe [keep the Sabbath] 2. to fulfill (a promise, etc.) 3. to protect; guard; take care of; tend 4. to preserve 5. to provide for; support 6. to make regular entries in [to keep books] 7. to maintain in a specified state, position, etc. [keep prices down] 8. to hold for the future; retain 9. to hold and not let go; detain, withhold, restrain, etc. 10. to stay in or on (a course, place, etc.) —vi. 1. to stay in a specified state, position, etc. 2. to continue; go on 3. to refrain [to keep from eating] 4. to stay fresh; not spoil —n. 1. care or custody 2. food and shelter; support 3. the inner stronghold of a castle —**for keeps** [Colloq.] 1. with the winner keeping what he wins 2. permanently —**keep to oneself** 1. to avoid others 2. to refrain from telling —**keep up** 1. to maintain in good condition 2. to continue 3. to maintain the pace 4. to remain informed (with on or with)

keep′er n. one that keeps; specif., a) a guard b) a guardian c) a custodian

keep′ing n. 1. observance of a rule, etc. 2. care; charge —**in keeping** with in conformity or accord with

keep′sake′ n. something kept, or to be kept, in memory of the giver

keg (keg) n. [< ON. kaggi] 1. a small barrel 2. a unit of weight for nails, equal to 100 lb.

kelp (kelp) n. [ME. culp] large, coarse, brown seaweed, rich in iodine

Kelt (kelt) n. same as CELT

ken (ken) vt. kenned, ken′ning [OE. cennan, cause to know] [Scot.] to know —n. range of knowledge

Ken·ne·dy (ken′ə dē), **John F.** 1917–63; 35th president of the U.S. (1961–63)

ken·nel (ken′'l) n. [< L. canis, dog] 1. a doghouse 2. [often pl.] a place where dogs are bred or kept —vt. -neled or -nelled, -nel·ing or -nel-ling to keep in a kennel

Ken·tuck·y (kən tuk′ē) EC State of the U.S.: 40,395 sq. mi.; pop. 3,661,000; cap. Frankfort

Ken·ya (ken′yə, kēn′-) country in EC Africa: 224,960 sq. mi.; pop. 9,948,000

kept (kept) pt. & pp. of KEEP —adj. maintained as a mistress [a kept woman]

ker·a·tin (ker′ət 'n) n. [< Gr. keras, horn + -IN] a tough, fibrous protein, the basic substance of hair, nails, etc.

kerb (kurb) n. Brit. sp. of CURB (n. 3)

ker·chief (kur′chif) n. [< OFr. covrir, to cover + chef, head] 1. a piece of cloth worn over the head or around the neck 2. a handkerchief

ker·nel (kur′n'l) n. [OE. cyrnel] 1. a grain or seed, as of corn 2. the inner, softer part of a nut, etc. 3. the central, most important part; essence

ker·o·sene (ker′ə sēn′) n. [< Gr. kēros, wax] a thin oil distilled from petroleum, used as a fuel, solvent, etc.: also **kerosine**

kes·trel (kes′trəl) n. [echoic] a small European falcon

ketch (kech) *n.* [ME. *cache*] a fore-and-aft rigged sailing vessel

ketch·up (kech'əp) *n.* [Malay *kēchap*, sauce] a sauce for meat, fish, etc.; esp., a thick sauce (**tomato ketchup**) of tomatoes, onions, spices, etc.

ket·tle (ket''l) *n.* [< L. *catinus*, bowl] 1. a metal container for boiling or cooking things 2. a teakettle

ket'tle·drum' *n.* a hemispheric percussion instrument of copper with a parchment top that can be tightened or loosened to change the pitch

Kev·lar (kev'lär) *a trademark for* a tough, light, synthetic fiber used in bulletproof vests, boat hulls, etc.

key¹ (kē) *n., pl.* **keys** [OE. *cæge*] 1. a device for moving the bolt of a lock and thus locking or unlocking something 2. any somewhat similar device, as a lever pressed in operating a piano, typewriter, etc. 3. a thing that explains or solves, as a code, the legend of a map, etc. 4. a controlling person or thing 5. style or mood of expression 6. *Music* a system of related tones based on a keynote and forming a given scale —*adj.* controlling; important —*vt.* keyed, key'ing 1. to furnish with a key 2. to regulate the tone or pitch of 3. to bring into harmony —**key up** to make nervous

key² (kē) *n., pl.* **keys** [Sp. *cayo*] a reef or low island

key'board' *n.* 1. the row or rows of keys of a piano, typewriter, etc. 2. an instrument with a keyboard

key club a private nightclub, etc., to which each member has a key

key'hole' *n.* an opening (in a lock) into which a key is inserted

key'note' *n.* 1. the lowest, basic note or tone of a musical scale 2. the basic idea or ruling principle —*vt.* -not'ed, -not'ing 1. to give the keynote of 2. to give the keynote speech at —**key'not'er** *n.*

keynote speech (or **address**) a speech, as at a convention, setting forth the main line of policy

key punch a machine with a keyboard for recording data by punching holes in cards for use in data processing

key'stone' *n.* 1. the central, topmost stone of an arch 2. essential part

Key West westernmost island of the Florida Keys

kg, kg. kilogram(s)

kha·ki (kak'ē, kä'kē) *adj.* [< Per. *khāk*, dust] 1. dull yellowish-brown 2. made of khaki (cloth) —*n., pl.* -kis 1. a dull yellowish brown 2. strong, twilled cloth of this color 3. [*often pl.*] a khaki uniform or trousers

khan (kän, kan) *n.* [Turki *khān*, lord] 1. a title of Tatar or Mongol rulers in the Middle Ages 2. a title of various dignitaries in India, Iran, etc.

Khar·kov (kär'kôf) city in NE Ukrainian S.S.R.: pop. 1,092,000

Khar·toum (kär tōōm') capital of Sudan: pop. 135,000

kHz kilohertz

kib·butz (ki bōōts', -boots') *n., pl.* -but·zim (kē'bōō tsēm') [ModHeb.] an Israeli collective settlement, esp. a collective farm

kib·itz·er (kib'its ər) *n.* [Yid. < G. *kiebitz*] [Colloq.] an onlooker at a card game, etc., esp. one who volunteers advice —**kib'itz** *vi.*

ki·bosh (kī'bäsh) *n.* [< ?] [Slang] end: usually in **put the kibosh on**, to check, squelch, etc.

kick (kik) *vi.* [ME. *kiken*] 1. to strike out with the foot 2. to recoil, as a gun 3. [Colloq.] to complain 4. *Football* to kick the ball —*vt.* 1. to strike with the foot 2. to drive, force, etc. as by kicking 3. to score (a goal, etc.) by kicking 4. [Slang] to get rid of (a habit) —*n.* 1. an act or method of kicking 2. a sudden recoil 3. [Colloq.] a complaint 4. [Colloq.] an intoxicating effect 5. [Colloq.] [*often pl.*] pleasure —**kick in** [Slang] to pay (one's share) —**kick over** to start working, as an automobile engine —**kick'er** *n.*

kick'back' *n.* [Slang] 1. a giving back of part of money received as payment 2. the money so returned

kick'off' *n.* 1. *Football* a kick that puts the ball into play 2. a beginning, as of a campaign

kick'stand' *n.* a pivoted metal bar that can be kicked down to support a bicycle, etc. in an upright position

kick·y (kik'ē) *adj.* -i·er, -i·est [Slang] 1. fashionable 2. exciting

kid (kid) *n.* [ME. *kide*] 1. a young goat 2. leather from the skin of young goats: also **kid'skin'** 3. [Colloq.] a child —*vt., vi.* kid'ded, kid'ding [Colloq.] to tease or fool playfully

kid'dy, kid'die (-ē) *n., pl.* -dies [dim. of KID, *n.* 3] [Colloq.] a child

kid'nap' (-nap') *vt.* -napped' or -naped', -nap'ping or -nap'ing [KID, *n.* 3 + dial. *nap*, to snatch] to seize and hold (a person) by force or fraud, as for ransom —**kid'nap'per, kid'nap'er** *n.*

kid·ney (kid'nē) *n., pl.* -neys [< ?] 1. either of a pair of glandular organs that separate waste products from the blood and excrete them as urine 2. an animal's kidney used as food 3. *a)* disposition *b)* class; kind

kidney bean the kidney-shaped seed of the common garden bean

kidney stone a hard, mineral deposit sometimes formed in the kidney

kiel·ba·sa (kēl bä'sə) *n., pl.* -si (-sē), -sas [Pol.] a smoked Polish sausage

Ki·ev (kē'ef) capital of the Ukrainian S.S.R.: pop. 1,371,000

kill (kil) *vt.* [< ? OE. *cwellan*] 1. to cause the death of; slay 2. to destroy; put an end to 3. to defeat or veto (legislation) 4. to spend (time) on trivial matters 5. to turn off (an engine, etc.) 6. to stop publication of —*n.* 1. the act of killing 2. an animal or animals killed —**kill'er** *n.*

kill'ing *adj.* **1.** causing death; deadly **2.** exhausting; fatiguing —*n.* **1.** slaughter; murder **2.** [Colloq.] a sudden great profit

kill'-joy' *n.* one who destroys or lessens other people's enjoyment

kiln (kil, kiln) *n.* [< L. *culina*, cookstove] a furnace or oven for drying, burning, or baking bricks, pottery, etc.

ki·lo (kē′lō, kil′ō) *n., pl.* **-los** [Fr.] *short for* **1.** KILOGRAM **2.** KILOMETER

kilo- [< Gr. *chilioi*] *a combining form meaning* a thousand

kil·o·cy·cle (kil′ə sī′k'l) *n.* former name for KILOHERTZ

kil'o·gram' (-gram′) *n.* a unit of weight and mass, equal to 1,000 grams (2.2046 lb.): also, chiefly Brit., **kil'o·gramme'**

kil'o·hertz' (-hurts′) *n., pl.* **-hertz** one thousand hertz

ki·lo·me·ter (ki läm′ə tər, kil′ə mēt′ər) *n.* a unit of length, equal to 1,000 meters (3,280.8 ft.): also, chiefly Brit., **ki·lo′me·tre**

kil·o·watt (kil′ə wät′) *n.* a unit of electrical power, equal to 1,000 watts

kilt (kilt) *n.* [prob. < ON.] a knee-length, pleated tartan skirt worn sometimes by men of the Scottish Highlands

kil·ter (kil′tər) *n.* [< ?] [Colloq.] good condition; proper order: now chiefly in **out of kilter**

ki·mo·no (kə mō′nə) *n., pl.* **-nos** [Jap.] **1.** a loose outer garment with a sash, part of the traditional Japanese costume **2.** a woman's dressing gown

kin (kin) *n.* [OE. *cynn*] relatives; family —*adj.* related, as by blood

-kin (kin) [< MDu. *-ken*] *a suffix meaning* little [*lambkin*]

kind (kīnd) *n.* [OE. *cynd*] **1.** a natural group or division **2.** essential character **3.** sort; variety; class —*adj.* sympathetic, gentle, benevolent, etc. —**in kind** in the same way —**kind-of** [Colloq.] somewhat; rather —**of a kind** alike

kin·der·gar·ten (kin′dər gär′t'n) *n.* [G. < *kinder*, children + *garten*, garden] a school or class of young children, usually four to six years old, that develops basic skills and social behavior by games, handicraft, etc. — **kin′der·gart′ner, kin′der·gar′ten·er** *n.*

kind'heart'ed *adj.* kind

kin·dle (kin′d'l) *vt.* **-dled, -dling** [< ON. *kynda*] **1.** to set on fire; ignite **2.** to excite (interest, feelings, etc.) —*vi.* **1.** to catch fire **2.** to become aroused or excited

kin·dling (kin′dliŋ) *n.* material, as bits of dry wood, for starting a fire

kind'ly *adj.* **-li·er, -li·est 1.** kind; gracious **2.** agreeable; pleasant —*adv.* **1.** in a kind, gracious manner **2.** agreeably; favorably **3.** please [*kindly* shut the door] —**kind'li·ness** *n.*

kind'ness *n.* **1.** the state, quality, or habit of being kind **2.** a kind act

kin·dred (kin′drid) *n.* [< OE. *cynn*, kin + *ræden*, condition] relatives or family —*adj.* similar [*kindred* spirits]

kine (kīn) *n.pl.* [< OE. *cy*, cows] [Archaic] cows; cattle

ki·net·ic (ki net′ik) *adj.* [< Gr. *kinein*, to move] of or resulting from motion

kin·folk (kin′fōk′) *n.pl.* family; relatives: also **kin'folks'**

king (kiŋ) *n.* [< OE. *cyning*] **1.** a male ruler of a state **2.** a man who is supreme in some field **3.** something supreme in its class **4.** a playing card with a picture of a king on it **5.** *Chess* the chief piece —*adj.* chief (in size, importance, etc.) —**king'ly** *adj.*

King, Martin Luther, Jr., 1929–68; U.S. clergyman; civil rights leader

king'dom (-dəm) *n.* **1.** a country headed by a king or queen; monarchy **2.** a realm; domain [the *kingdom* of poetry] **3.** any of three divisions into which all natural objects have been classified (the animal, vegetable, and mineral kingdoms)

king'fish'er *n.* a short-tailed diving bird that feeds chiefly on fish

King James Version *same as* AUTHORIZED VERSION

King Lear (lir) the title character of a tragedy by Shakespeare

king'-size' (-sīz′) *adj.* [Colloq.] larger than the usual size: also **king'-sized'**

kink (kiŋk) *n.* [< Scand.] **1.** a short twist or curl in a rope, hair, etc. **2.** a painful cramp in the neck, back, etc. **3.** a mental twist; queer notion; whim —*vt., vi.* to form or cause to form a kink or kinks —**kink'y** *adj.*

kin·ship (kin′ship′) *n.* **1.** family relationship **2.** close connection

kins·man (kinz′mən) *n., pl.* **-men** a relative; esp., a male relative — **kins'wom'an** *n.fem., pl.* **-wom'en**

ki·osk (kē′äsk, kē äsk′) *n.* [< Per. *kũshk*, palace] a small, open structure, used as a newsstand, etc.

kip·per (kip′ər) *vt.* [< ?] to cure (herring, salmon, etc.) by salting and drying or smoking —*n.* a kippered herring, etc.

kirk (kurk, kirk) *n.* [Scot. & North Eng.] a church

kis·met (kiz′met) *n.* [< Ar. *qasama*, to divide] fate; destiny

kiss (kis) *vt., vi.* [< OE. *cyssan*] **1.** to touch or caress with the lips as an act of affection, greeting, etc. **2.** to touch lightly or gently —*n.* **1.** an act of kissing **2.** a light, gentle touch **3.** any of various candies —**kiss'a·ble** *adj.*

kit (kit) *n.* [ME. *kyt*, tub] **1.** *a)* personal equipment, esp. as packed for travel *b)* a set of tools *c)* equipment for some particular activity, etc. *d)* a set of parts to be put together **2.** a box, bag, etc. for carrying such parts, tools, or equipment —**the whole kit and caboodle** [Colloq.] the whole lot

kitch·en (kich′ən) *n.* [ult. < L. *coquere*, to cook] a room or place for the preparation and cooking of food

kitch'en·ette', kitch·en·et' (-et′) *n.* a small, compact kitchen

kitch'en·ware' (-wer′) *n.* kitchen utensils

kite (kīt) *n.* [< OE. *cyta*] **1.** any of several long-winged birds of the hawk family **2.** a light, wooden frame covered with paper or cloth, to be flown in the wind at the end of a string

kith (kith) *n.* [< OE. *cyth*] friends: now only in **kith and kin**, friends and relatives; also, relatives, or kin

kitsch (kich) *n.* [G., gaudy trash] pretentious but worthless art or writing —**kitsch′y** *adj.*

kit·ten (kit′'n) *n.* [< OFr. dim. of *chat*, cat] a young cat —**kit′ten·ish** *adj.*

kit·ty¹ (kit′ē) *n., pl.* **-ties** 1. a kitten 2. *a pet name for* a cat

kit·ty² (kit′ē) *n., pl.* **-ties** [prob. < KIT] 1. the stakes in a poker game 2. money pooled for some purpose

kit′ty-cor′nered (-kôr′nərd) *adj., adv. same as* CATER-CORNERED: also **kit′ty-cor′ner**

ki·wi (kē′wē) *n., pl.* **-wis** [of echoic origin] a flightless bird of New Zealand

K.K.K., KKK Ku Klux Klan

klep·to·ma·ni·a (klep′tə mā′nē ə) *n.* [< Gr. *kleptēs*, thief + MANIA] an abnormal, persistent impulse to steal —**klep′to·ma′ni·ac′** *n., adj.*

Klon·dike (klän′dīk) gold-mining region in W Yukon Territory, Canada

klutz (kluts) *n.* [< Yid. *klots*, a block] [Slang] a clumsy or stupid person

km, km. kilometer(s)

knack (nak) *n.* [ME. *knak*, sharp blow] 1. a clever expedient 2. ability to do something easily

knack·wurst (näk′wurst′) *n.* [G. < *knacken*, to split + *wurst*, sausage] a thick, highly seasoned sausage

knap·sack (nap′sak′) *n.* [< Du. *knappen*, eat + *zak*, a sack] a leather or canvas bag for carrying equipment or supplies on the back

knave (nāv) *n.* [< OE. *cnafa*, boy] 1. a dishonest, deceitful person; rogue 2. a jack (playing card) —**knav′ish** *adj.*

knav·er·y (nāv′ər ē) *n., pl.* **-ies** rascality; dishonesty

knead (nēd) *vt.* [< OE. *cnedan*] 1. to work (dough, clay, etc.) into a plastic mass by pressing and squeezing 2. to massage —**knead′er** *n.*

knee (nē) *n.* [< OE. *cneow*] 1. the joint between the thigh and the lower leg 2. anything shaped like a bent knee —*vt.* **kneed, knee′ing** to hit or touch with the knee

knee′cap′ *n.* a movable bone at the front of the human knee

knee′-deep′ *adj.* 1. up to the knees 2. very much involved

knee′-jerk′ *adj.* [< the reflex when the kneecap is tapped] designating, or reacting with, an automatic response

kneel (nēl) *vi.* **knelt** or **kneeled, kneel′ing** [< OE. *cneow*, knee] to bend or rest on one's knee or knees

knell (nel) *vi.* [< OE. *cnyllan*] 1. to ring slowly; toll 2. to sound ominously —*vt.* to call or announce as by a knell —*n.* 1. the sound of a bell rung slowly, as at a funeral 2. an omen of death, failure, etc.

knelt (nelt) *alt. pt. and pp. of* KNEEL

knew (nōō, nyōō) *pt. of* KNOW

knick·ers (nik′ərz) *n.pl.* [< D. *Knickerbocker*, fictitious Du. author of W. Irving's *History of New York*] loose breeches gathered just below the knees: also **knick′er·bock′ers** (-bäk′ərz)

knick·knack (nik′nak′) *n.* [< KNACK] a small ornamental article

knife (nīf) *n., pl.* **knives** (nīvz) [< OE. *cnif*] 1. a cutting instrument with a sharp-edged blade set in a handle 2. a cutting blade, as in a machine —*vt.* **knifed, knif′ing** 1. to cut or stab with a knife 2. [Colloq.] to injure or defeat by treachery —**under the knife** [Colloq.] undergoing surgery

knight (nīt) *n.* [< OE. *cniht*, boy] 1. in medieval times, a man formally raised to honorable military rank and pledged to chivalrous conduct 2. in Britain, a man who for some achievement is given honorary rank entitling him to use *Sir* before his given name 3. a chessman shaped like a horse's head —*vt.* to make (a man) a knight

knight′-er′rant (-er′ənt) *n., pl.* **knights′-er′rant** 1. a medieval knight wandering in search of adventure 2. a chivalrous or quixotic person

knight′hood′ (-hood′) *n.* 1. the rank, status, or vocation of a knight 2. chivalry 3. knights collectively

knight′ly *adj.* of or like a knight; chivalrous, brave, etc.

knit (nit) *vt., vi.* **knit′ted** or **knit, knit′ting** [< OE. *cnotta*, a knot] 1. to make (a fabric) by looping yarn or thread together with special needles 2. to join or grow together closely and firmly, as a broken bone 3. to draw or become drawn together in wrinkles, as the brows —**knit′ter** *n.*

knit′wear′ (-wer′) *n.* knitted clothing

knob (näb) *n.* [prob. < MLowG. *knobbe*, a knot] 1. a rounded lump or protuberance 2. a handle, usually round, of a door, drawer, etc.

knob′by *adj.* **-bi·er, -bi·est** 1. covered with knobs 2. like a knob

knock (näk) *vi.* [< OE. *cnocian*] 1. to strike a blow 2. to rap on a door 3. to bump; collide 4. to make a thumping noise: said of an engine, etc. —*vt.* 1. to hit; strike 2. to hit so as to cause to fall (with *down* or *off*) 3. to make by hitting [to knock a hole in the wall] 4. [Colloq.] to find fault with —*n.* 1. a knocking 2. a hit; rap 3. a thumping noise in an engine, etc. 4. [Colloq.] an adverse criticism —**knock about (or around)** [Colloq.] to wander about —**knock down** 1. to take apart 2. to indicate the sale of (an article) at an auction —**knock off** 1. [Colloq.] to stop working 2. [Colloq.] to deduct 3. [Slang] to kill, overcome, etc. —**knock out** to make unconscious or exhausted —**knock together** [Colloq.] to make or compose hastily

knock′er *n.* one that knocks; esp., a small ring, knob, etc. on a door for use in knocking

knock′-kneed′ (-nēd′) *adj.* having legs that bend inward at the knees

knock'out' *n.* 1. a knocking out or being knocked out 2. [Slang] a very attractive person or thing 3. *Boxing* a victory won when an opponent is unable to continue to fight, as by being knocked unconscious

knock·wurst (näk'wurst') *n.* same *as* KNACKWURST

knoll (nōl) *n.* [< OE. *cnoll*] a little rounded hill; mound

knot (nät) *n.* [< OE. *cnotta*] 1. a lump in a thread, etc. formed by a tightened loop or tangle 2. a fastening made by tying together pieces of string, rope, etc. 3. an ornamental bow of ribbon, etc. 4. a small group or cluster 5. something that ties closely; esp., the bond of marriage 6. a problem; difficulty 7. a hard lump on a tree where a branch grows out, or a cross section of such a lump in a board 8. *Naut.* a unit of speed of one nautical mile (6,076.12 feet) an hour —*vt., vi.* **knot'ted, knot'ting** 1. to make or form a knot (in) 2. to entangle or become entangled —**tie the knot** [Colloq.] to get married

knot'hole' *n.* a hole in a board, etc. where a knot has fallen out

knot'ty *adj.* **-ti·er, -ti·est** 1. full of knots [*knotty* pine] 2. hard to solve; puzzling [a *knotty* problem]

know (nō) *vt.* **knew, known, know'ing** [< OE. *cnawan*] 1. to be well-informed about 2. to be aware of [he *knew* why we left] 3. to be acquainted with 4. to recognize or distinguish [to *know* right from wrong] —*vi.* 1. to have knowledge 2. to be sure or aware —**in the know** [Colloq.] having confidential information

know'-how' *n.* [Colloq.] technical skill

know'ing *adj.* 1. having knowledge 2. shrewd; clever 3. implying shrewd or secret understanding [a *knowing* look] —**know'ing·ly** *adv.*

know'-it-all' *n.* [Colloq.] one who acts as if he knows much about nearly everything: also **know'-all'**

knowl·edge (näl'ij) *n.* 1. the fact or state of knowing 2. range of information or understanding 3. what is known; learning 4. the body of facts, etc. accumulated by mankind —**to (the best of) one's knowledge** as far as one knows

knowl'edge·a·ble (-ə b'l) *adj.* having knowledge or intelligence —**knowl'edge·a·bly** *adv.*

known (nōn) *pp.* of KNOW

Knox·ville (näks'vil) city in E Tenn.: pop. 183,000

knuck·le (nuk''l) *n.* [< or akin to MDu. & MLowG. *knokel*, dim. of *knoke*, bone] 1. a joint of the finger; esp., the joint connecting a finger to the rest of the hand 2. the knee or hock joint of an animal, used as food —**knuckle down** to work hard —**knuckle under** to yield; give in

knuck'le·head' (-hed') *n.* [Colloq.] a stupid person

KO (kā'ō') *vt.* **KO'd, KO'ing** [Slang] *Boxing* to knock out —*n., pl.* **KO's** [Slang] *Boxing* a knockout Also **K.O., k.o.**

ko·a·la (kō ä'lə) *n.* [< native name] an Australian tree-dwelling marsupial with thick, gray fur

KOALA

kohl·ra·bi (kōl'rä'bē) *n., pl.* **-bies** [< It. *cavolo rapa*] a kind of cabbage with an edible, turnip-like stem

ko·la (kō'lə) *n. same as* COLA

kook (kook) *n.* [prob. < CUCKOO] [Slang] a person regarded as silly, eccentric, etc. —**kook'y, kook'ie** *adj.*

kook·a·bur·ra (kook'ə bur'ə) *n.* [< native name] an Australian kingfisher with a harsh cry like loud laughter

ko·peck, ko·pek (kō'pek) *n.* [Russ. < *kopye*, a lance] a coin equal to 1/100 of a Russian ruble

Ko·ran (kō ran', kô rän') *n.* [< Ar. *qur'ān*, book] the sacred book of the Moslems

Ko·re·a (kō rē'ə) peninsula northeast of China, divided into *a)* **North Korea**, 47,255 sq. mi.; pop. 11,568,000 *b)* **South Korea**, 38,030 sq. mi.; pop. 30,010,000 —**Ko·re'an** *adj., n.*

ko·sher (kō'shər) *adj.* [Heb. *kāshēr*, proper] *Judaism* clean or fit to eat according to the dietary laws

Kos·suth (käs'ōōth), **Louis** 1802–94; Hung. patriot & statesman

kow·tow (kou'tou', kō'-) *vi.* [Chin. *k'o-t'ou*, lit., knock head] to show great deference, respect, etc. *(to)*

KP, K.P. kitchen police, a detail to assist the cooks in an army kitchen

kraal (kräl) *n.* [Afrik.] 1. a village of South African natives 2. an enclosure for cattle or sheep in S Africa

Krem·lin (krem'lin) [< Russ. *kreml'*] 1. the citadel of Moscow, formerly housing many Soviet government offices 2. the Soviet government

Krem'lin·ol'o·gy (-äl'ə jē) *n.* the study of the policies, etc. of the Soviet Union —**Krem'lin·ol'o·gist** *n.*

Krish·na (krish'nə) a Hindu god, an incarnation of Vishnu

kro·na (krō'nə) *n., pl.* **-nor** (-nôr) [ult. < L. *corona*, crown] 1. the monetary unit and a coin of Sweden 2. *pl.* **-nur** (-nər) the monetary unit and a coin of Iceland

kro·ne (krō'nə) *n., pl.* **-ner** (-nər) [see prec.] the monetary unit and a coin of Denmark or Norway

Kru·ger·rand (krōō'gə rand') *n.* a gold coin of South Africa

KS Kansas

ku·chen (kōō'kən) *n.* [G., cake] a kind of cake made of yeast dough, often filled with raisins, nuts, etc.

ku·dos (kōō'däs) *n.* [Gr. *kydos*] [Colloq.] credit for an achievement; glory; fame

Ku Klux Klan (kōō' kluks' klan', kyōō') [< Gr. *kyklos*, circle] a U.S. secret society that is anti-Negro, anti-Semitic, anti-Catholic, etc. and uses terrorist methods

kum·quat (kum'kwät) *n.* [< Chin.

chin-chŭ, lit., golden orange] a small, orange-colored, oval citrus fruit, with a sour pulp and a sweet rind
kung fu (koon/ foo/, goon/) [< Chin.] a Chinese system of self-defense, like karate but with circular movements
Ku·wait (kōō wāt/, -wĭt/) independent

Arab state in E Arabia: 6,000 sq. mi.; pop. 491,000
kw. kilowatt(s)
Kwang·chow (kwäŋ/chō/) port in SE China: pop. 2,200,000
Ky., KY Kentucky
Kyo·to (kyō/tō/) city in S Honshu, Japan: pop. 1,365,000

L

L, l (el) *pl.* **L's, l's** the twelfth letter of the English alphabet
L (el) *n.* **1.** a Roman numeral for 50 **2.** an extension forming an L with the main structure
L. Latin
L., l. 1. lake **2.** latitude **3.** left **4.** length **5.** *pl.* **LL., ll.** line **6.** liter **7.** [L. *libra*, pl. *librae*] pound(s)
la (lä) *n.* [< L.] *Music* the sixth tone of the diatonic scale
La., LA Louisiana
L.A. [Colloq.] Los Angeles
lab (lab) *n.* [Colloq.] a laboratory
la·bel (lā/b'l) *n.* [< OFr., a rag] **1.** a card, paper, etc. marked and attached to an object to indicate its contents, destination, owner, producer, etc. **2.** a term of generalized classification —*vt.* **-beled** or **-belled, -bel·ing** or **-bel·ling 1.** to attach a label to **2.** to classify as; call
la·bi·al (lā/bē əl) *adj.* [< L. *labium*, lip] **1.** of the lips **2.** *Phonetics* formed mainly with the lips, as *b, m,* and *p*
la/bi·um (-əm) *n., pl.* **-bi·a** (-ə) [L., lip] any one of two pairs of liplike folds of the vulva
la·bor (lā/bər) *n.* [< L.] **1.** physical or mental exertion; work **2.** a specific task **3.** all wage-earning workers **4.** labor unions collectively **5.** the process of childbirth —*vi.* **1.** to work **2.** to work hard **3.** to move slowly and with difficulty **4.** to suffer (*under* a false idea, etc.) **5.** to be in childbirth —*vt.* to develop in too great detail [*to labor* a point]
lab·o·ra·to·ry (lab/rə tôr/ē, lab/ər ə-) *n., pl.* **-ries** [see prec.] a room or building for scientific work or research
Labor Day the first Monday in September, a legal holiday honoring labor
la·bored (lā/bərd) *adj.* made or done with great effort; strained
la/bor·er *n.* one who labors; esp., a wage-earning worker whose work is characterized by physical exertion
la·bo·ri·ous (lə bôr/ē əs) *adj.* **1.** involving much hard work; difficult **2.** hard-working —**la·bo/ri·ous·ly** *adv.*
labor union an association of workers to promote and protect the welfare, rights, etc. of its members
la·bour (lā/bər) *n., vi., vt. Brit. sp.* of LABOR

Lab·ra·dor (lab/rə dôr/) **1.** large peninsula in NE Canada, between the Atlantic & Hudson Bay **2.** its E section, the mainland of Newfoundland
la·bur·num (lə bur/nəm) *n.* [< L.] a small tree or shrub of the legume family, with drooping yellow flowers
lab·y·rinth (lab/ə rinth/) *n.* [< Gr. *labyrinthos*] a structure containing winding passages hard to follow without losing one's way; maze
lac (lak) *n.* [< Sans. *lākṣā*] a resinous substance secreted on certain Asiatic trees by a scale insect: source of shellac
lace (lās) *n.* [< L. *laqueus*, noose] **1.** a string, etc. used to draw together and fasten the parts of a shoe, corset, etc. **2.** an openwork fabric of linen, silk, etc., woven in ornamental designs —*vt.* **laced, lac/ing 1.** to fasten with a lace **2.** to weave together; intertwine **3.** to thrash; whip
lac·er·ate (las/ə rāt/) *vt.* **-at/ed, -at/ing** [< L. *lacer*, mangled] to tear jaggedly; mangle —**lac/er·a/tion** *n.*
lace·work (lās/wurk/) *n.* lace, or any openwork decoration like lace
lach·ry·mal (lak/rə məl) *adj.* [< L. *lacrima*, TEAR²] **1.** of or producing tears **2.** *same as* LACRIMAL (sense 1)
lach/ry·mose/ (-mōs/) *adj.* [see prec.] shedding, or causing to shed, tears; tearful or sad
lack (lak) *n.* [< or akin to MLowG. *lak*] **1.** the fact or state of not having enough or of not having any **2.** the thing that is needed —*vi., vt.* to be deficient in or entirely without
lack·a·dai·si·cal (lak/ə dā/zi k'l) *adj.* [< archaic *lackaday*, an exclamation of regret, etc.] showing lack of interest or spirit; listless
lack·ey (lak/ē) *n., pl.* **-eys** [< Sp. *lacayo*] **1.** a male servant of low rank **2.** a servile follower; toady
lack·lus·ter (lak/lus/tər) *adj.* lacking brightness; dull: also, chiefly Brit., **lack/lus/tre**
la·con·ic (lə kän/ik) *adj.* [< Gr. *Lakōn*, a Spartan] terse in expression; using few words; concise —**la·con/i·cal·ly** *adv.*
lac·quer (lak/ər) *n.* [< Fr. < Port. *laca*, lac] **1.** a coating substance made of shellac, gum resins, etc. dissolved in ethyl alcohol or other solvent that

evaporates quickly   2. a resinous varnish obtained from certain Oriental trees   3. a wooden article coated with this —*vt.* to coat with lacquer

lac·ri·mal (lak'rə məl) *adj.* 1. of or near the glands that secrete tears 2. *same as* LACHRYMAL (sense 1)

la·crosse (lə krôs') *n.* [CanadFr. < Fr. *la,* the + *crosse,* crutch] a ball game played by two teams using long-handled, pouched rackets

lac·te·al (lak'tē əl) *adj.* [< L. *lac,* milk] of or like milk; milky

lac·tic (lak'tik) *adj.* [< L. *lac,* milk] of or obtained from milk

lactic acid a clear, syrupy acid formed when milk sours

LACROSSE

lac·tose (lak'tōs) *n.* [< L. *lac,* milk] a sugar found in milk: used in foods

la·cu·na (lə kyōō'nə) *n., pl.* **-nas, -nae** (-nē) [L., a ditch] a blank space; esp., a missing portion in a text, etc.

lac·y (lā'sē) *adj.* **-i·er, -i·est** of or like lace —**lac'i·ness** *n.*

lad (lad) *n.* [ME. *ladde*] a boy; youth

lad·der (lad'ər) *n.* [OE. *hlæder*] 1. a framework of two sidepieces connected by a series of rungs, for use in climbing up or down   2. any means of climbing

lad·die (lad'ē) *n.* [Chiefly Scot.] a lad

lade (lād) *vt., vi.* **lad'ed, lad'ed** *or* **lad'en, lad'ing** [OE. *hladan*] 1. to load   2. to bail; ladle

lad·en *alt. pp. of* LADE —*adj.* 1. loaded 2. burdened; afflicted

la-di-da, la-de-da (lä'dē dä') *adj.* [imitative] [Colloq.] affectedly refined

lad'ing *n.* a load; cargo; freight

la·dle (lā'd'l) *n.* [OE. *hlædel*] a long-handled, cuplike spoon —*vt.* **-dled, -dling** to dip out with a ladle

la·dy (lā'dē) *n., pl.* **-dies** [< OE. *hlaf,* loaf + base of *dæge,* kneader] 1. *a*) a woman of high social position   *b*) a woman who is polite, refined, etc.   2. any woman: used to address a group 3. [L-] a British title given to women of certain ranks —*adj.* female

la'dy·bug' *n.* a small, roundish beetle with a spotted back: also **la'dy·bird'**

la'dy·fin'ger *n.* a small spongecake shaped somewhat like a finger

la'dy-in-wait'ing *n., pl.* **la'dies-in-wait'ing** a woman waiting upon a queen or princess

la'dy·like' *adj.* like or suitable for a lady; refined; well-bred

la'dy·love' *n.* a sweetheart

la'dy·ship' *n.* 1. the rank or position of a lady 2. a title used in speaking to or of a titled Lady: with *your* or *her*

la'dy-slip'per *n.* an orchid with flowers somewhat like slippers: also **la'dy's-slip'per**

la·e·trile (lā'ə tril') *n.* any of several compounds got from certain substances, as almond seeds, and claimed to be effective in treating cancer

La·fa·yette (lä'fi yet'), marquis de 1757–1834; Fr. general; served in the American Revolutionary army

lag (lag) *vi.* **lagged, lag'ging** [< ?] 1. to fall behind or move slowly; loiter 2. to become less intense —*n.* 1. a falling behind   2. the amount of this

la·ger (*beer*) (lä'gər) [G. *lager bier,* storehouse beer] a beer that has been aged for several months

lag·gard (lag'ərd) *n.* [< LAG + -ARD] a slow person, esp. one who falls behind —*adj.* slow; falling behind

la·gniappe, la·gnappe (lan yap') *n.* [Creole < Fr. & Sp.] 1. [Chiefly South] a present given to a customer with a purchase 2. a gratuity

la·goon (lə gōōn') *n.* [< L. *lacuna,* pool] 1. a shallow lake or pond, esp. one connected with a larger body of water   2. the water enclosed by a circular coral reef   3. shallow water separated from the sea by sand dunes

La·hore (lə hôr') city in NE Pakistan: pop. 1,296,000

laid (lād) *pt. & pp. of* LAY[1]

laid'back' *adj.* [Slang] relaxed, easygoing, etc.; not hurried

lain (lān) *pp. of* LIE[1]

lair (ler) *n.* [OE. *leger*] a resting place of a wild animal; den

lais·sez faire (les'ā fer', lez'-) [Fr., allow to do] noninterference; specif., absence of governmental control over industry and business

la·i·ty (lā'ət ē) *n., pl.* **-ties** [< LAY[1]] laymen collectively

lake (lāk) *n.* [< L. *lacus*] 1. a large inland body of usually fresh water   2. a pool of oil or other liquid

lal·ly·gag (läl'ē gag') *vi.* **-gagged', -gag'ging** [Colloq.] *same as* LOLLYGAG

lam (lam) *n.* [< ?] [Slang] headlong flight —*vi.* **lammed, lam'ming** [Slang] to flee; escape —**on the lam** [Slang] in flight, as from the police

la·ma (lä'mə) *n.* [Tibetan *blama*] a priest or monk in Lamaism

La·ma·ism (lä'mə iz'm) *n.* a form of Buddhism in Tibet and Mongolia

la·ma·ser·y (lä'mə ser'ē) *n., pl.* **-ies** a monastery of lamas

La·maze (lə mäz') *n.* [< F. *Lamaze,* 20th-c. Fr. physician] a training program in natural childbirth, involving the help of the father

lamb (lam) *n.* [OE.] 1. a young sheep 2. its flesh used as food   3. a gentle, innocent, or gullible person

lam·baste (lam bāst', -bast') *vt.* **-bast'ed, -bast'ing** [< *lam,* to beat + *baste,* to flog] [Colloq.] 1. to beat soundly 2. to scold severely

lamb·da (lam'də) *n.* the eleventh letter of the Greek alphabet (Λ, λ)

lam·bent (lam'bənt) *adj.* [< L. *lambere,* to lick] 1. playing lightly over a surface: said of a flame 2. giving off a soft glow   3. light and graceful *[lambent wit]* —**lam'ben·cy** *n.*

lamb'kin *n.* a little lamb

lame (lām) *adj.* [OE. *lama*] 1. crippled; esp., having an injury that makes one limp   2. stiff and painful 3. poor; ineffectual *[a lame excuse]* —*vt.* lamed, lam'ing to make lame —**lame'ly** *adv.* —**lame'ness** *n.*

la·mé (la mā') *n.* [< Fr. *lame,* metal plate] a cloth interwoven with metal threads, especially of gold or silver

lame duck an elected official whose term extends beyond the time of his defeat for reelection

la·mel·la (lə mel'ə) *n., pl.* **-lae** (-ē), **-las** [L.] a thin plate, scale, or layer

la·ment (lə ment') *vi., vt.* [< L. *lamentum*, a wailing] to feel or express deep sorrow (for); mourn —*n.* 1. a lamenting 2. an elegy, dirge, etc. mourning some loss or death —**lam·en·ta·ble** (lam'ən tə b'l, lə men'-) *adj.* —**lam'en·ta'tion** *n.*

lam·i·na (lam'ə nə) *n., pl.* **-nae'** (-nē'), **-nas** [L.] a thin scale or layer, as of metal, tissue, etc.

lam'i·nate (-nāt'; *for adj. usually* -nit) *vt.* **-nat'ed, -nat'ing** 1. to cover with one or more thin layers 2. to make by building up in layers —*adj.* built in thin sheets or layers: also **lam'i·nat'ed** —**lam'i·na'tion** *n.*

lamp (lamp) *n.* [< Gr. *lampein*, to shine] 1. a container with a wick for burning oil, etc. to produce light or heat 2. any device for producing light or therapeutic rays 3. a holder or base for such a device

lamp'black' *n.* fine soot used as a black pigment

lam·poon (lam pōōn') *n.* [< Fr. *lampons*, let us drink: used as a refrain] a satirical writing attacking someone —*vt.* to attack in a lampoon

lamp·post (lamp'pōst', lamp'-) *n.* a post supporting a street lamp

lam·prey (lam'prē) *n., pl.* **-preys** [< ML. *lampreda*] an eellike water animal with a jawless, sucking mouth

la·nai (lä nī', la-) *n.* [Haw.] a veranda or open-sided living room

lance (lans) *n.* [< L. *lancea*] 1. a long wooden spear with a sharp metal head 2. *same as:* a) LANCER b) LANCET 3. any instrument like a lance —*vt.* **lanced, lanc'ing** 1. to pierce with a lance 2. to cut open with a lancet

Lan·ce·lot (lan'sə lät') the bravest of the Knights of the Round Table

lan·cer (lan'sər) *n.* a cavalry soldier armed with a lance

lan·cet (lan'sit) *n.* [< OFr. dim. of *lance*, LANCE] a small, pointed surgical knife, usually two-edged

land (land) *n.* [OE.] 1. the solid part of the earth's surface 2. a country or nation 3. ground or soil 4. real estate —*vt.* 1. to put on shore from a ship 2. to bring to a particular place [it *landed* him in jail] 3. to set (an aircraft) down on land or water 4. to catch [to *land* a fish] 5. [Colloq.] to get or secure [to *land* a job] 6. [Colloq.] to deliver (a blow) —*vi.* 1. to leave a ship and go on shore 2. to come to a port, etc.: said of a ship 3. to arrive at a specified place 4. to come to rest

land contract a contract in which the seller of real estate transfers his interest to the buyer only after the purchase price is fully paid in regular payments over a specified period

land·ed (lan'did) *adj.* owning land [*landed* gentry]

land'fall' *n.* 1. a sighting of land from a ship at sea 2. the land sighted

land'fill' *n.* disposal of garbage or rubbish by burying it in the ground

land grant a grant of land by the government for a college, railroad, etc.

land'hold'er *n.* an owner of land —**land'hold'ing** *adj., n.*

land·ing (lan'diŋ) *n.* 1. the act of coming to shore 2. the place where a ship is loaded or unloaded 3. a platform at the end of a flight of stairs 4. the act of alighting

landing gear the undercarriage of an aircraft, including wheels, etc.

land'locked' *adj.* 1. surrounded by land, as a bay 2. cut off from the sea and confined to fresh water [*landlocked* salmon]

land'lord' *n.* 1. a man who leases land, houses, etc. to others 2. a man who keeps a rooming house, inn, etc. —**land'la'dy** *n.fem., pl.* **-dies**

land'lub·ber (-lub'ər) *n.* one who has had little experience at sea

land'mark' *n.* 1. an object that marks the boundary of a piece of land 2. any prominent feature of the landscape, distinguishing a locality 3. an important event or turning point

land'mass' *n.* a very large area of land; esp., a continent

land office a government office that handles the sales of public lands

land'-of'fice business [Colloq.] a booming business

land'scape' (-skāp') *n.* [< Du. *land*, land + *-schap*, -ship] 1. a picture of natural, inland scenery 2. an expanse of natural scenery seen in one view —*vt.* **-scaped', -scap'ing** to make (a plot of ground) more attractive, as by adding lawns, bushes, etc. —**land'scap'er** *n.*

land'slide' *n.* 1. the sliding of a mass of earth or rocks down a slope 2. the mass sliding down 3. an overwhelming victory, esp. in an election

land'ward (-wərd) *adv., adj.* toward the land: also **land'wards** *adv.*

lane (lān) *n.* [OE. *lanu*] 1. a narrow way, path, road, etc. 2. a path or strip designated, for reasons of safety, for ships, aircraft, automobiles, etc.

lan·guage (laŋ'gwij) *n.* [< L. *lingua*, tongue] 1. human speech or the written symbols for speech 2. *a)* any means of communicating *b)* a special set of symbols used in a computer 3. the speech of a particular nation, etc. [the French *language*] 4. the particular style of verbal expression characteristic of a person, group, profession, etc.

lan·guid (laŋ'gwid) *adj.* [< L. *languere*, be faint] 1. without vigor or vitality; weak 2. listless; indifferent 3. slow; dull —**lan'guid·ly** *adv.*

lan'guish (-gwish) *vi.* [see prec.] 1. to become weak; droop 2. to long; pine 3. to put on a wistful air

lan·guor (laŋ′gər) *n.* [see LANGUID] lack of vigor or vitality; weakness; listlessness —**lan′guor·ous** *adj.*

lank (laŋk) *adj.* [OE. *hlanc*] 1. long and slender; lean 2. straight and limp: said of hair —**lank′ness** *n.*

lank·y (laŋ′kē) *adj.* **-i·er, -i·est** awkwardly tall and lean

lan·o·lin (lan′′l in) *n.* [< L. *lana*, wool + *oleum*, oil] a fatty substance obtained from wool and used in ointments, cosmetics, etc.

Lan·sing (lan′siŋ) capital of Mich., in the SC part: pop. 132,000

lan·tern (lan′tərn) *n.* [ult. < Gr. *lampein*, to shine] a transparent case for holding and shielding a light

lan′tern-jawed′ *adj.* having long, thin jaws and sunken cheeks

lan·yard (lan′yərd) *n.* [< OFr. *lasne*, noose] a short rope used on board ship for holding or fastening something

La·os (lä′ōs) kingdom in NW Indochina: 91,429 sq. mi.; pop. 2,635,000 —**La·o·tian** (lā ō′shən) *adj.,* *n.*

lap¹ (lap) *n.* [OE. *læppa*] 1. the front part from the waist to the knees of a sitting person 2. the part of the clothing covering this 3. that in which a person or thing is cared for 4. *a)* an overlapping *b)* a part that overlaps 5. one complete circuit of a race track —*vt.* **lapped, lap′ping** 1. to fold (*over* or *on*) 2. to wrap; enfold 3. to overlap 4. to get a lap ahead of (an opponent) in a race —*vi.* 1. to overlap 2. to extend beyond something in space or time (with *over*)

lap² (lap) *vi.,* *vt.* **lapped, lap′ping** [OE. *lapian*] 1. to drink (a liquid) by dipping it up with the tongue as a dog does 2. to strike gently with a light splash: said of waves —*n.* 1. a lapping 2. the sound of lapping —**lap up** [Colloq.] to accept eagerly

La Paz (lä päs′) city & seat of government of Bolivia: pop. 461,000

lap′board′ *n.* a board placed on the lap for use as a table or desk

lap dog any pet dog small enough to be held in the lap

la·pel (lə pel′) *n.* [dim. of LAP¹] the front part of a coat folded back and forming a continuation of the collar

lap·i·dar·y (lap′ə der′ē) *n.,* *pl.* **-ies** [< L. *lapis*, a stone] a workman who cuts and polishes precious stones

lap·in (lap′in) *n.* [Fr., rabbit] rabbit fur, often dyed to resemble other fur

lap·is laz·u·li (lap′is laz′yoo lī′, lazh′-; -lē′) [< L. *lapis*, a stone + ML. *lazulus*, azure] an azure, opaque, semiprecious stone

Lap·land (lap′land′) region of N Europe, including the N parts of Norway, Sweden, & Finland

Lapp (lap) *n.* a member of a Mongoloid people living in Lapland

lap·pet (lap′it) *n.* [dim. of LAP¹] a small, loose flap or fold of a garment or head covering

lap robe a heavy blanket, fur covering, etc. laid over the lap for warmth

lapse (laps) *n.* [< L. *labi*, to slip] 1. a small error 2. *a)* a moral slip *b)* a falling into a lower condition 3. a passing, as of time 4. the termination as of a privilege through failure to meet requirements —*vi.* **lapsed, laps′ing** 1. to fall into a specified state *[he lapsed into silence]* 2. to backslide 3. to elapse 4. to come to an end; stop 5. to become void because of failure to meet requirements

lar·board (lär′bərd) *n.,* *adj.* [< OE. *hladan*, lade + *bord*, side] port; left

lar·ce·ny (lär′sə nē) *n.,* *pl.* **-nies** [ult. < L. *latro*, robber] the unlawful taking of another's property; theft —**lar′ce·nist** *n.* —**lar′ce·nous** *adj.*

larch (lärch) *n.* [< L. *larix*] 1. a tree of the pine family, that sheds its needles annually 2. its tough wood

lard (lärd) *n.* [< L. *lardum*] the fat of hogs, melted and clarified —*vt.* 1. to put strips of bacon or fat pork on (meat, etc.) before cooking 2. to embellish *[a talk larded with jokes]*

lard′er *n.* 1. a place where food supplies are kept 2. food supplies

la·res and pe·na·tes (ler′ēz ənd pi nät′ēz) the household gods of the ancient Romans

large (lärj) *adj.* **larg′er, larg′est** [< L. *largus*] 1. of great extent or amount; big, bulky, spacious, etc. 2. bigger than others of its kind 3. operating on a big scale *[a large producer]* —*adv.* in a large way *[write large]* —**at large** 1. free; not confined 2. fully; in detail 3. representing no particular district *[a congressman at large]* —**large′ness** *n.* —**larg′ish** *adj.*

large′heart′ed *adj.* generous; kindly

large·ly *adv.* 1. much; in great amounts 2. for the most part; mainly

large′-scale′ *adj.* 1. drawn to a large scale 2. of wide scope; extensive

lar·gess, lar·gesse (lär jes′, lär′jis) *n.* [see LARGE] 1. generous giving 2. a gift generously given

lar·go (lär′gō) *adj.,* *adv.* [It., slow] *Music* slow and stately

lar·i·at (lar′ē it) *n.* [Sp. *la reata*, the rope] 1. a rope used for tethering grazing horses, etc. 2. *same as* LASSO

lark¹ (lärk) *n.* [< OE. *læwerce*] any of a large family of chiefly old-world songbirds; esp., the skylark

lark² (lärk) *vi.* [< ? ON. *leika*] to play or frolic —*n.* a frolic or spree

lark·spur (lärk′spur′) *n.* a common name for DELPHINIUM

lar·va (lär′və) *n.,* *pl.* **-vae** (-vē), **-vas** [L., ghost] the early form of any animal that changes structurally when it becomes an adult *[the tadpole is the larva of the frog]* —**lar′val** *adj.*

lar·yn·gi·tis (lar′ən jīt′əs) *n.* an inflammation of the larynx, often with a temporary loss of voice

lar·ynx (lar′iŋks) *n.,* *pl.* **lar′ynx·es,** **la·ryn·ges** (lə rin′jēz) [< Gr.] the structure at the upper end of the trachea, containing the vocal cords

la·sa·gna (lə zän′yə) *n.* [It., the noodle] a dish of wide noodles baked in layers with cheese, tomato sauce, and ground meat

las·civ·i·ous (lə siv′ē əs) *adj.* [< L. *lascivus*, wanton] 1. characterized by or expressing lust 2. exciting lust

la·ser (lā′zər) n. [l(ight) a(mplification by) s(timulated) e(mission of) r(adiation)] a device that amplifies light waves and concentrates them in an intense, penetrating beam

laser disc a videodisc for recording audio and video data to be read by a laser beam

lash¹ (lash) n. [< ?] 1. the flexible striking part of a whip 2. a stroke as with a whip 3. an eyelash —vt. 1. to strike or drive as with a lash 2. to switch energetically [the cat lashed her tail] 3. to censure or rebuke —vi. to make strokes as with a whip —lash out 1. to strike out violently 2. to speak angrily

lash² (lash) vt. [see LACE] to fasten or tie with a rope, etc.

lass (las) n. [prob. < ON. lǫskr, weak] a young woman

Las·sa fever (läs′ə) [< Lassa, Nigerian village] an acute virus disease endemic to western Africa

las·sie (las′ē) n. [Scot.] a young girl

las·si·tude (las′ə tōōd′) n. [< L. lassus, faint] weariness; languor

las·so (las′ō) n., pl. -sos, -soes [< Sp. < L. laqueus, noose] a rope with a sliding noose used in catching cattle, etc. —vt. to catch with a lasso

last¹ (last) alt. superl. of LATE —adj. 1. being or coming after all others in place or time; final 2. only remaining 3. most recent [last month] 4. least likely [the last person to suspect] 5. conclusive [the last word] —adv. 1. after all others 2. most recently 3. finally —n. the one coming last —at (long) last finally

last² (last) vi. [OE. læstan] to remain in existence, use, etc.; endure —vt. 1. to continue during 2. to be enough for

last³ (last) n. [< OE. last, footstep] a form shaped like a foot, used in making or repairing shoes

last hurrah a final attempt or appearance, as in politics

last′ing adj. that lasts a long time

Last Judgment Theol. the final judgment at the end of the world

last′ly adv. in conclusion; finally

last straw [< the straw that broke the camel's back] a final trouble that results in a defeat, loss of patience, etc.

Las Ve·gas (läs vā′gəs) city in SE Nev.: pop. 165,000

lat. latitude

latch (lach) n. [< OE. læccan] a fastening for a door, gate, or window; esp., a bar, etc. that fits into a notch —vt., vi. to fasten with a latch —latch onto [Colloq.] to get or obtain

late (lāt) adj. lat′er or lat′ter, lat′est or last [OE. læt] 1. happening, coming, etc. after the usual or expected time, or at a time far advanced in a period [late to class, late Victorian] 2. a) recent b) having recently died

LATCH

—adv. lat′er, lat′est or last 1. after the expected time 2. at or until an advanced time of the day, year, etc. 3. toward the end of a period 4. recently —of late recently —late′ness n. —lat′ish adj., adv.

late′ly adv. not long ago; recently

la·tent (lāt′nt) adj. [< L. latere, lurk] lying hidden and undeveloped in a person or thing —la′ten·cy n.

lat·er·al (lat′ər əl) adj. [< L. latus, a side] of, at, from, or toward the side; sideways —lat′er·al·ly adv.

la·tex (lā′teks) n. [L., a fluid] a milky liquid in certain plants and trees: a latex is the basis of rubber

lath (lath) n., pl. **laths** (la thz, laths) [< OE. læti] 1. any of the thin, narrow strips of wood used as a groundwork for plastering, etc. 2. any framework for plastering

lathe (lā th) n. [prob. < MDu. lade] a machine for shaping wood, metal, etc. by holding and turning it rapidly against a cutting tool —vt. lathed, lath′ing to shape on a lathe

lath·er (la th′ər) n. [OE. leathor, soap] 1. the foam formed by soap and water 2. foamy sweat 3. [Slang] an excited state —vt., vi. to cover with or form lather —lath′er·y adj.

Lat·in (lat′n) adj. [< Latium, ancient country in C Italy] 1. of ancient Rome, its people, their language, etc. 2. designating or of the languages derived from Latin, the peoples who speak them, their countries, etc. —n. 1. a native or inhabitant of ancient Rome 2. the language of ancient Rome 3. a person, as a Spaniard or Italian, whose language is derived from Latin

Latin America that part of the Western Hemisphere south of the U.S. in which Spanish, Portuguese, and French are the official languages

lat·i·tude (lat′ə tōōd′) n. [< L. latus, wide] 1. extent; scope 2. freedom from narrow restrictions 3. a) distance north or south from the equator, measured in degrees b) a region with reference to this distance

la·trine (lə trēn′) n. [< L. lavare, to wash] a toilet for the use of many people, as in an army camp

lat·ter (lat′ər) adj. alt. compar. of LATE 1. a) later; more recent b) nearer the end or close 2. being the last mentioned of two—lat′ter·ly adv.

lat·tice (lat′is) n. [< MHG. latte, lath] an openwork structure of crossed strips of wood, metal, etc. used as a screen, support, etc.

lat′tice·work′ (-wurk′) n. 1. a lattice 2. lattices collectively

Lat·vi·a (lat′vē ə) republic of the U.S.S.R., in NE Europe —Lat′vi·an adj., n.

laud (lôd) n. [< L. laus] praise —vt. to praise; extol

laud′a·ble praiseworthy; commendable

laud·a·num (lôd′n əm) *n.* [< L. *ladanum*, a dark resin] 1. formerly, any of various opium preparations 2. a solution of opium in alcohol

laud·a·to·ry (lôd′ə tôr′ē) *adj.* expressing praise; commendatory

laugh (laf) *vi.* [< OE. *hleahhan*] to make the sounds and facial movements that express mirth, ridicule, etc. —*n.* 1. the act or sound of laughing 2. a cause of laughter —**laugh at** 1. to be amused by 2. to make fun of

laugh′a·ble *adj.* amusing or ridiculous —**laugh′a·bly** *adv.*

laughing gas nitrous oxide used as an anesthetic: inhaling it may cause a reaction of laughter

laugh′ing·stock′ (-stäk′) *n.* an object of ridicule

laugh′ter (-tər) *n.* the action or sound of laughing

launch[1] (lônch) *vt.* [< L. *lancea*, lance] 1. to hurl or send forth with some force [to *launch* a rocket] 2. to slide (a vessel) into the water 3. to set in operation or on some course; start [to *launch* an attack] —*vi.* 1. a) to put to sea b) to start something new With *out* or *forth* 2. to plunge (*into*) —*n.* a launching —*adj.* designating or of facilities, sites, etc. used in launching spacecraft or missiles

launch[2] (lônch) *n.* [Sp. or Port. *lancha*] an open, or partly enclosed, motorboat

launch pad the platform from which a rocket, guided missile, etc. is launched: also **launching pad**

launch window a favorable time period for launching a spacecraft

laun·der (lôn′dər) *vt., vi.* [< L. *lavare*, to wash] to wash, or wash and iron, (clothes, etc.) —**laun′der·er** *n.* —**laun′dress** (-dris) *n.fem.*

Laun·dro·mat (lôn′drə mat′) *a service mark for* a self-service laundry —*n.* [l-] such a laundry

laun·dry (lôn′drē) *n., pl.* -**dries** 1. a place for laundering 2. clothes, etc. laundered or to be laundered

laun′dry·man (-mən) *n., pl.* -**men** a man who collects and delivers laundry

lau·re·ate (lôr′ē it) *adj.* [< L. *laurus*, laurel] honored, as with a crown of laurel —*n. same as* POET LAUREATE

lau·rel (lôr′əl) *n.* [< L. *laurus*] 1. an evergreen tree or shrub of S Europe, with large, glossy leaves 2. its foliage, esp. as woven into crowns 3. [*pl.*] fame; honor 4. any of various trees and shrubs resembling the true laurel

la·va (lä′və, lav′ə) *n.* [It. < L. *labi*, to slide] 1. melted rock issuing from a volcano 2. such rock when solidified by cooling

la·va·bo (lə vä′bō, -vä′-) *n., pl.* -**boes** [L., I shall wash] 1. a washbasin and water tank hung on a wall 2. a wall planter resembling this

lav·a·liere (lav′ə lir′, lä′və-) *n.* [< Fr.] an ornament on a chain, worn around the neck

lav·a·to·ry (lav′ə tôr′ē) *n., pl.* -**ries** [< L. *lavare*, to wash] 1. a washbowl with faucets and drain 2. a room with a washbowl and a toilet

lave (lāv) *vt., vi.* laved, lav′ing [< L. *lavare*] [Poet.] to wash; bathe

lav·en·der (lav′ən dər) *n.* [< ML. *lavandria*] 1. a fragrant European mint, with spikes of pale-purplish flowers 2. its dried flowers and leaves, used to perfume clothes, etc. 3. a pale purple —*adj.* pale-purple

lav·ish (lav′ish) *adj.* [< OFr. *lavasse*, downpour] 1. very generous; prodigal 2. very abundant —*vt.* to give or spend liberally —**lav′ish·ly** *adv.*

law (lô) *n.* [OE. *lagu*] 1. a) all the rules of conduct established by the authority or custom of a nation, etc. b) any one of such rules 2. obedience to such rules 3. the study of such rules; jurisprudence 4. the seeking of justice in courts under such rules 5. the profession of lawyers, judges, etc. 6. a) a sequence of natural events occurring with unvarying uniformity under the same conditions b) the stating of such a sequence 7. any rule expected to be observed [the *laws* of health] —**the Law** 1. the Mosaic law, or the part of the Bible containing it 2. [l-] [Colloq.] a policeman or the police

law′-a·bid′ing *adj.* obeying the law

law′break′er *n.* one who violates the law —**law′break′ing** *adj., n.*

law′ful *adj.* 1. in conformity with the law 2. recognized by law [*lawful* debts] —**law′ful·ly** *adv.*

law′giv′er *n.* a lawmaker; legislator

law′less *adj.* 1. not regulated by the authority of law 2. not in conformity with law; illegal 3. not obeying the law; unruly —**law′less·ness** *n.*

law′mak′er *n.* one who makes or helps to make laws; esp., a legislator

lawn[1] (lôn) *n.* [< OFr. *launde*, heath] land covered with grass kept closely mowed, esp. around a house

lawn[2] (lôn) *n.* [< *Laon*, city in France] a fine, sheer cloth of linen or cotton

lawn mower a hand-propelled or power-driven machine to cut lawn grass

law·ren·ci·um (lô ren′sē əm) *n.* [after E. O. *Lawrence* (1901-58), U.S. physicist] a radioactive chemical element produced by nuclear bombardment

law′suit′ (-sōōt′) *n.* a suit between private parties in a law court

law·yer (lô′yər) *n.* one whose profession is advising others in matters of law or representing them in lawsuits

lax (laks) *adj.* [< L. *laxus*] 1. loose; slack; not tight 2. not strict or exact

lax·a·tive (lak′sə tiv) *adj.* [see prec.] making the bowels loose and relieving constipation —*n.* any laxative medicine

lax′i·ty *n.* lax quality or condition

lay[1] (lā) *vt.* laid, lay′ing [< OE. *lecgan*] 1. to cause to fall with force; knock down 2. to place or put in a resting position (often with *on* or *in*) 3. to put down (bricks, carpeting, etc.) in the correct position or way 4. to place; put; set [to *lay* emphasis on accuracy] 5. to produce (an egg) 6. to allay, suppress, etc. 7. to bet (a specified sum, etc.) 8. to devise [to *lay* plans] 9. to present or assert [to *lay* claim to property] —*n.* the way or position in which something is situated

lay   343   lean

[the lay of the land] —**lay aside** to put away for future use; save: also **lay away, lay by** —**lay in** to get and store away —**lay off 1.** to discharge (an employee), esp. temporarily **2.** [Slang] to cease —**lay open 1.** to cut open **2.** to expose —**lay out 1.** to spend **2.** to arrange according to a plan **3.** to spread out (clothes, etc.) ready for wear, etc. —**lay over** to stop a while in a place before going on —**lay up 1.** to store for future use **2.** to confine to a sickbed

lay² (lā) *pt.* of LIE¹

lay³ (lā) *adj.* [< Gr. *laos,* the people] **1.** of a layman **2.** not belonging to a given profession

lay⁴ (lā) *n.* [ME. & OFr. *lai*] **1.** a short poem, esp. a narrative poem, for singing **2.** [Archaic] a song

lay analyst a psychoanalyst who is not a medical doctor

lay′a·way′ plan a method of buying by making a deposit on something which is delivered only after full payment

lay′er *n.* **1.** a person or thing that lays **2.** a single thickness, fold, etc.

lay·ette (lā et′) *n.* [< MDu. *lade,* chest] a complete outfit of clothes, bedding, etc. for a newborn baby

lay·man (lā′mən) *n., pl.* **-men** a person not a clergyman or one not belonging to a given profession

lay·off (lā′ôf′) *n.* a putting out of work temporarily, or the period of this

lay′out′ *n.* **1.** the manner in which anything is laid out; specif., the makeup of a newspaper, advertisement, etc. **2.** the thing laid out

lay′o′ver *n.* a stop in a journey

Laz·a·rus (laz′ə rəs) *Bible* a man raised from the dead by Jesus

laze (lāz) *vi., vt.* **lazed, laz′ing** to idle or loaf

la·zy (lā′zē) *adj.* **-zi·er, -zi·est** [prob. < MLowG. or MDu.] **1.** not eager or willing to work or exert oneself **2.** sluggish —*vi., vt.* **-zied, -zy·ing** to laze —**la′zi·ly** *adv.* —**la′zi·ness** *n.*

la′zy·bones′ *n.* [Colloq.] a lazy person

Lazy Su·san (sōō′z′n) a revolving tray for food

lb. [L. *libra,* pl. *librae*] **1.** pound **2.** pounds: also **lbs.**

l.c. [L. *loco citato*] in the place cited

LCD [*l(iquid)-c(rystal) d(isplay)*] a device for alphanumeric displays, as on digital watches, using a crystalline liquid

lea (lē) *n.* [OE. *leah*] [Poet.] a meadow

leach (lēch) *vt.* [prob. < OE. *leccan,* to water] **1.** to wash (wood ashes, etc.) with a filtering liquid **2.** to extract (a soluble substance) from some material —*vi.* to lose soluble matter through a filtering liquid

lead¹ (lēd) *vt.* **led, lead′ing** [OE. *lædan*] **1.** to direct, as by going before or along with, by physical contact, pulling a rope, etc.; guide **2.** to direct by influence **3.** to be the head of (an expedition, orchestra, etc.) **4.** to be

at the head of *[to lead one's class]* **5.** to be ahead of in a contest **6.** to live; spend *[to lead a full life]* —*vi.* **1.** to show the way, as by going before **2.** to tend in a certain direction (with *to, from,* etc.) **3.** to bring as a result (with *to) [hate led to war]* **4.** to be or go first —*n.* **1.** the role or example of a leader **2.** first or front place **3.** the amount or distance ahead *[to hold a safe lead]* **4.** anything that leads, as a clue. **5.** the leading role in a play, etc. **6.** the right of playing first in cards or the card played —**lead off** to begin —**lead on** to lure —**lead up to** to prepare the way for

lead² (led) *n.* [OE.] **1.** a heavy, soft, bluish-gray metallic chemical element, used for pipes **2.** a weight for sounding depths at sea, etc. **3.** bullets **4.** a stick of graphite, used in pencils —*adj.* of or containing lead —*vt.* to cover, line, or weight with lead

lead·en (led′'n) *adj.* **1.** of lead **2.** heavy **3.** sluggish **4.** gloomy **5.** gray

lead·er (lē′dər) *n.* one that leads; guiding head —**lead′er·ship′** *n.*

lead·ing (lē′diŋ) *adj.* **1.** that leads; guiding *[a leading question]* **2.** principal; chief

lead poisoning (led) poisoning due to absorbing lead into the body

lead time (lēd) the period of time needed from the decision to make a product to the start of production

leaf (lēf) *n., pl.* **leaves** (lēvz) [OE.] **1.** any of the flat, thin parts, usually green, growing from the stem of a plant **2.** a petal **3.** a sheet of paper **4.** a very thin sheet of metal **5.** a hinged or removable part of a table top —*vi.* **1.** to bear leaves **2.** to turn the pages of (with *through)* —**leaf′less** *adj.*

leaf′let (-lit) *n.* **1.** a small or young leaf **2.** a separate sheet of printed matter, often folded

leaf′y *adj.* **-i·er, -i·est** having many or broad leaves *[a leafy vegetable]*

league¹ (lēg) *n.* [< L. *ligare,* bind] **1.** an association of nations, groups, etc. for promoting common interests **2.** *Sports* a group of teams formed to play one another —*vt., vi.* **leagued, leagu′ing** to form into a league

league² (lēg) *n.* [ult. < Celt.] a measure of distance, about 3 miles

League of Nations an association of nations (1920-46) succeeded by UN

leak (lēk) *vi.* [< ON. *leka,* to drip] **1.** to let a fluid out or in accidentally **2.** to enter or escape in this way, as a fluid **3.** to become known gradually, accidentally, etc. *[news leaked out]* —*vt.* to allow to leak —*n.* **1.** an accidental crack, etc. that lets something out or in **2.** any accidental means of escape **3.** leakage —**leak′y** *adj.*

leak′age (-ij) *n.* **1.** a leaking **2.** that which or the amount that leaks

lean¹ (lēn) *vi.* **leaned** or **leant** (lent), **lean′ing** [OE. *hlinian*] **1.** to bend or slant from an upright position **2.** to

---

fat, āpe, cär; ten, ēven; is, bīte; gō, hôrn, tōōl, look; oil, out; up, fur; chin; she; thin, then; zh, leisure; ŋ, ring; ə for a in ago; ', (ā'b'l); ë, Fr. coeur; ö, Fr. feu; Fr. mon; ü, Fr. duc; kh, G. ich, doch; ‡ foreign; < derived from

bend the body and rest part of one's weight on something **3.** to rely (on or upon) **4.** to tend (toward or to) —vt. to cause to lean —**lean'er** n.

lean² (lēn) adj. [OE. hlæne] **1.** with little flesh or fat; thin; spare **2.** meager —n. meat containing little or no fat —**lean'ness** n.

lean'ing n. tendency; inclination

lean'-to' n., pl. **-tos'** a structure whose sloping roof abuts a wall, etc.

leap (lēp) vi. **leaped** or **leapt** (lept, lēpt), **leap'ing** [OE. hléapan] **1.** to jump; spring; bound **2.** to accept eagerly something offered (with at) —vt. **1.** to pass over by a jump **2.** to cause to leap —n. **1.** a jump; spring **2.** the distance covered in a jump **3.** a sudden transition —**leap'er** n.

leap'frog' n. a game in which each player in turn leaps over the bent backs of the others —vt., vi. **-frogged'**, **-frog'ging** to leap or jump in or as in this way; skip (over)

leap year every fourth year, containing an extra day in February

learn (lurn) vt., vi. **learned** (lurnd) or **learnt** (lurnt), **learn'ing** [OE. leornian] **1.** to get knowledge of or skill in (an art, trade, etc.) by study, experience, etc. **2.** to come to know; hear (of or about) **3.** to memorize —**learn'er** n.

learn·ed (lur'nid; for 2 lurnd) adj. **1.** having or showing much learning **2.** acquired by study, experience, etc.

learn'ing n. **1.** the acquiring of knowledge or skill **2.** acquired knowledge or skill

lease (lēs) n. [< L. laxus, loose] a contract by which a landlord rents lands, buildings, etc. to a tenant for a specified time —vt. **leased**, **leas'ing** to give or get by a lease —**leas'er** n.

lease'hold' (-hōld') n. **1.** the act of holding by lease **2.** land, buildings, etc. held by lease —**lease'hold'er** n.

leash (lēsh) n. [< L. laxus, loose] a cord, strap, etc. by which a dog or the like is held in check —vt. to check or control as by a leash

least (lēst) alt. superl. of LITTLE—adj. [OE. læst] smallest in size, degree, etc.; slightest —adv. in the smallest degree —n. the smallest in amount, importance, etc. —**at (the) least 1.** at the lowest **2.** at any rate —**not in the least** not at all

least'wise' adv. [Colloq.] at least; anyway: also **least'ways'**

leath·er (leth'ər) n. [< OE. lether-] animal skin prepared for use by removing the hair and tanning —adj. of leather

leath'er·neck' n. [< former leather-lined collar] [Slang] a U.S. Marine

leath'er·y adj. like leather; tough and flexible —**leath'er·i·ness** n.

leave¹ (lēv) vt. **left**, **leav'ing** [OE. læfan, let remain] **1.** to allow to remain [leave a sip for me, leave it open] **2.** to have remaining behind or after one **3.** to bequeath **4.** to go away from **5.** to abandon **6.** [Dial. or Slang] to let [leave us go] —vi. to go away or set out —**leave off** to stop —**leave out** to omit —**leav'er** n.

leave² (lēv) n. [OE. leaf] **1.** permission **2.** a) permission to be absent from duty b) the period for which this is granted —**take leave of** to say goodbye to —**take one's leave** to depart

leave³ (lēv) vi. **leaved**, **leav'ing** to put forth, or bear, leaves; leaf

leav·en (lev'n) n. [< L. levare, raise] **1.** a substance, as fermenting dough from a previous baking, yeast, etc., used to make dough rise **2.** a tempering or modifying quality or thing —vt. **1.** to make (dough) rise **2.** to spread through, causing gradual change

leav'en·ing n. **1.** same as LEAVEN **2.** a causing to be leavened

leave of absence leave from work or duty, esp. for a long time; also, the period of time

leaves (lēvz) n. pl. of LEAF

leave'-tak'ing n. a parting; farewell

leav·ings (lēv'iŋz) n.pl. leftovers, remnants, refuse, etc.

Leb·a·non (leb'ə nən) country in SW Asia, on the Mediterranean: 4,000 sq. mi.; pop. 2,367,000 —**Leb'a·nese'** (-nēz') adj., n., pl. **-nese'**

lech (lech) vi., n. [see ff.] [Slang] lust

lech·er (lech'ər) n. [OFr. lechier, live debauchedly] a lustful, grossly sensual man —**lech'er·ous** adj. —**lech'er·y** n.

lec·i·thin (les'ə thin) n. [< Gr. lekithos, egg yolk] a nitrogenous, fatty compound found in animal and plant cells: used in medicine, foods, etc.

lec·tern (lek'tərn) n. [< L. legere, read] a reading stand

lec·ture (lek'chər) n. [< L. legere, read] **1.** an informative talk to a class, etc. **2.** a lengthy scolding —vt., vi. **-tured**, **-tur·ing** **1.** to give a lecture (to) **2.** to scold —**lec'tur·er** n.

LECTERN

led (led) pt. & pp. of LEAD¹

ledge (lej) n. [ME. legge] **1.** a shelf **2.** a projecting ridge of rocks

ledg·er (lej'ər) n. [ME. legger] a book of final entry, in which a record of debits, credits, etc. is kept

lee (lē) n. [OE. hleo, shelter] **1.** shelter **2.** Naut. the side or part away from the wind —adj. of or on the lee

Lee (lē), **Robert E.** 1807-70; commander of the Confederate army

leech (lēch) n. [OE. læce] **1.** a blood-sucking worm living in water and used, esp. formerly, to bleed patients **2.** one who clings to another to get what he can from him —vi. to cling (onto) thus

leek (lēk) n. [OE. leac] a vegetable that resembles a thick green onion

leer (lir) n. [OE. hleor] a sly, sidelong look showing lust, malicious triumph, etc. —vi. to look with a leer

leer·y (lir'ē) adj. **-i·er**, **-i·est** wary; suspicious

lees (lēz) n.pl. [< ML. lia] dregs or sediment, as of wine

lee·ward (lē'wərd; naut. lōō'ərd) adj. away from the wind —n. the lee side —adv. toward the lee

Lee·ward Islands (lē'wərd) group of islands in the E West Indies

lee·way (lē'wā') n. **1.** leeward drift

of a ship or aircraft from its course 2. [Colloq.] *a)* margin of time, money, etc. *b)* room for freedom of action

left[1] (left) *adj.* [< OE. *lyft*, weak] 1. of or on the side that is toward the west when one faces north 2. closer to the left side of one facing the thing mentioned—*n.* 1. the left side 2. *[often* L-] *Politics* a radical or liberal position, party, etc. (often with *the*) —*adv.* on or toward the left hand or side

left[2] (left) *pt. & pp. of* LEAVE[1]

left'-hand' *adj.* 1. on the left 2. of, for, or with the left hand

left'-hand'ed *adj.* 1. using the left hand more skillfully than the right 2. done with or made for use with the left hand 3. ambiguous or backhanded *[a left-handed compliment]* —*adv.* with the left hand *[to write left-handed]*

left'ist *n., adj.* radical or liberal

left'o'ver *n.* something left over

left wing the more radical or liberal section of a political party, group, etc. —**left'-wing'** *adj.* —**left'-wing'er** *n.*

left'y *n., pl.* **-ies** [Slang] a left-handed person: often a nickname

leg (leg) *n.* [ON. *leggr*] 1. one of the parts of the body by means of which men and animals stand and walk 2. the part of a garment covering the leg 3. anything like a leg in shape or use 4. a stage, as of a trip —*vi.* **legged**, **leg'ging** [Colloq.] to walk or run (usually with *it*)

leg·a·cy (leg'ə sē) *n., pl.* **-cies** [ult. < L. *lex*, law] 1. money or property left to one by a will 2. anything handed down as from an ancestor

le·gal (lē'gəl) *adj.* [< L. *lex*, law] 1. of or based on law 2. permitted by law 3. of or for lawyers —**le'gal·ly** *adv.*

le·gal·ese (lē'gə lēz') *n.* the special vocabulary and formulations of legal forms, documents, etc.

legal holiday a holiday set by law

le'gal·ism *n.* strict or too strict adherence to the law —**le'gal·is'tic** *adj.*

le·gal·i·ty (li gal'ə tē) *n., pl.* **-ties** quality, condition, or instance of being legal or lawful

le·gal·ize (lē'gə līz') *vt.* **-ized'**, **-iz'-ing** to make legal or lawful

legal tender money acceptable by law in payment of an obligation

leg·ate (leg'it) *n.* [< L. *lex*, law] an envoy, esp. of the Pope

leg·a·tee (leg'ə tē') *n.* one to whom a legacy is bequeathed

le·ga·tion (li gā'shən) *n.* a diplomatic minister and his staff and headquarters

le·ga·to (li gät'ō) *adj., adv.* [< It. *legare*, to tie] *Music* in a smooth, even style, with no breaks between notes

leg·end (lej'ənd) *n.* [< L. *legere*, read] 1. a story or body of stories handed down for generations and popularly believed to have a historical basis 2. a notable person or the stories of his exploits 3. an inscription on a coin, etc. 4. a title, key, etc. accompanying an illustration or map

leg·end·ar·y (lej'ən der'ē) *adj.* of, based on, or presented in legends

leg·er·de·main (lej'ər di mān') *n.* [< MFr. *leger de main*, light of hand] 1. sleight of hand 2. trickery

leg·ged (leg'id, legd) *adj.* having (a specified number or kind of) legs *[long-legged]*

leg·ging (leg'iŋ) *n.* a covering for the leg: *usually used in pl.*

leg·horn (leg'hôrn, -ərn) *n.* [< *Leghorn*, It. seaport] *[often* L-] any of a breed of small chicken

leg·i·ble (lej'ə b'l) *adj.* [< L. *legere*, read] that can be read, esp. easily —**leg'i·bil'i·ty** *n.* —**leg'i·bly** *adv.*

le·gion (lē'jən) *n.* [< L. *legere*, to select] 1. a large group of soldiers; army 2. a large number; multitude —**le'gion·ar'y** *adj., n.* —**le'gion·naire'** (-jə ner') *n.*

Legionnaires' disease [after an outbreak at an American Legion convention in July, 1976] [Colloq.] a severe bacterial disease occurring sporadically

leg·is·late (lej'is lāt') *vi.* **-lat'ed**, **-lat'ing** [see ff.] to make or pass laws —*vt.* to cause to be, go, etc. by making laws —**leg'is·la'tor** *n.*

leg·is·la·tion *n.* [< L. *lex*, law + *latio*, a bringing] 1. the making of laws 2. the laws made

leg·is·la·tive *adj.* 1. of legislation or a legislature 2. having the power to make laws —**leg'is·la'tive·ly** *adv.*

leg·is·la·ture (-lā'chər) *n.* a body of persons given the power to make laws

le·git·i·mate (lə jit'ə mit ; *for v.* -māt') *adj.* [< L. *lex*, law] 1. born of parents married to each other 2. lawful 3. *a)* reasonable *b)* justifiable 4. conforming to accepted rules, standards, etc. 5. of stage plays, as distinguished from burlesque, etc. —**le·git'i·ma·cy** (-mə sē) *n.* —**le·git'i·mate·ly** *adv.*

le·git·i·mize (-mīz') *vt.* **-mized'**, **-miz'ing** to make or declare legitimate : also **le·git'i·ma·tize'**

leg·man (leg'man') *n., pl.* **-men'** 1. a reporter who turns in news from on the scene 2. an assistant who does routine tasks outside the office

leg'room' *n.* adequate space for the legs while seated, as in a car

leg·ume (leg'yoom, li gyoom') *n.* [< L. *legere*, gather] 1. any of a large family of plants having seeds growing in pods, including peas, beans, etc. 2. the pod or seed of such a plant —**le·gu·mi·nous** (li gyoo'min əs) *adj.*

leg'work' *n.* [Colloq.] necessary routine travel as part of a job

lei (lā, lā'ē) *n., pl.* **leis** [Haw.] a garland of flowers

Leip·zig (līp'sig) city in SC East Germany: pop. 596,000

lei·sure (lē'zhər, lezh'ər) *n.* [< L. *licere*, be permitted] free time during which one may indulge in rest, recreation, etc. —*adj.* free and unoccupied

lei·sure·ly *adj.* without haste; slow —*adv.* in an unhurried manner

---

fat, āpe, cär; ten, ēven; is, bīte; gō, hôrn, tōōl, look; oil, out; up, fur; chin; she; thin, *then*; zh, leisure; ŋ, ring; ə for *a* in ago; ', (ā'b'l); ë, Fr. coeur; ö, Fr. feu; Fr. mon; ü, Fr. duc; kh, G. ich; doch. ‡foreign; < derived from

leit·mo·tif, leit·mo·tiv (līt′mō-tēf′) n. [G. *leitmotiv* < *leiten*, to LEAD[1] + *motiv*, motive] a dominant theme

lem·ming (lem′iŋ) n. [< ON. *læmingi*] a small arctic rodent with a short tail

lem·on (lem′ən) n. [< Per. *līmūn*] 1. a small, sour, pale-yellow citrus fruit 2. the spiny, semitropical tree that it grows on 3. [Slang] something that is defective —adj. pale-yellow

lem′on·ade′ (-ə nād′) n. a drink made of lemon juice, sugar, and water

le·mur (lē′mər) n. [< L. *lemures*, ghosts] a small primate related to the monkey

lend (lend) vt. lent, lend′ing [< OE. *læn*, a loan] 1. to let another use or have (a thing) temporarily 2. to let out (money) at interest 3. to give; impart —vi. to make loans —lend itself (or oneself) to be useful to or open to —lend′er n.

lend′-lease′ n. in World War II, material aid granted countries whose defense the U.S. deemed vital

length (leŋkth) n. [< OE. *lang*, long] 1. the distance from end to end of a thing 2. extent in space or time 3. a long stretch or extent 4. a piece of a certain length —at length 1. finally 2. in full

length′en vt., vi. to make or become longer

length′wise′ (-wīz′) adv., adj. in the direction of the length: also **length′ways′** (-wāz′)

length′y adj. -i·er, -i·est long; esp., too long —**length′i·ly** adv.

le·ni·ent (lē′ni ənt, lēn′yənt) adj. [< L. *lenis*, soft] not harsh or severe; merciful —**le′ni·en·cy, le′ni·ence** n.

Len·in (len′in), V. I. 1870-1924; leader of the Soviet revolution

Len·in·grad (len′in grad′) seaport in NW R.S.F.S.R.: pop. 3,665,000

len·i·tive (len′ə tiv) adj. [< L. *lenire*, to soften] lessening pain or distress

lens (lenz) n. [L., lentil: < its shape] 1. a curved piece of glass, plastic, etc. for bringing together or spreading rays of light passing through it: used in optical instruments to form an image 2. any device used to focus electromagnetic waves, sound waves, etc. 3. a similar transparent part of the eye: it focuses light rays upon the retina

Lent (lent) n. [OE. *lengten*, the spring] *Christianity* the forty weekdays of fasting and penitence, from Ash Wednesday to Easter —**Lent′en, lent′en** adj.

lent (lent) pt. & pp. of LEND

len·til (lent′'l) n. [< L. *lens*] 1. a kind of legume, with small, edible seeds 2. this seed

Le·o (lē′ō) [L., lion] the fifth sign of the zodiac

le·o·nine (lē′ə nīn′) adj. [< L. *leo*, lion] of or like a lion

leop·ard (lep′ərd) n. [< Gr. *leōn*, lion + *pardos*, panther] 1. a large, wild animal of the cat family, with a black-spotted tawny coat, found in Africa and Asia 2. same as JAGUAR

le·o·tard (lē′ə tärd′) n. [< J. *Léotard*, 19th-c. Fr. aerial performer] a tight-fitting garment for an acrobat or dancer

lep·er (lep′ər) n. [< Gr. *lepros*, scaly] a person having leprosy

lep·re·chaun (lep′rə kôn′) n. [< OIr. *lu*, little + *corp*, body] Ir. Folklore a fairy who can reveal hidden treasure

lep·ro·sy (lep′rə sē) n. [see LEPER] a chronic infectious disease of the skin, flesh, nerves, etc., characterized by ulcers, white scaly scabs, deformities, etc. —**lep′rous** adj.

les·bi·an (lez′bē ən) n. [< *Lesbos*, Gr. island home of the poetess Sappho] a homosexual woman —**les′bi·an·ism** n.

lese maj·es·ty (lēz′ maj′is tē) [< Fr. < L. *laesa majestas*, injured majesty] 1. a crime against the sovereign 2. any lack of proper respect as toward one in authority

le·sion (lē′zhən) n. [< L. *laedere*, to harm] an injury of an organ or tissue resulting in impairment of function

Le·so·tho (le suth′ō, le sō′thō) country in SE Africa: 11,716 sq. mi.; pop. 975,000

less (les) alt. compar. of LITTLE —adj. [OE. *læs(sa)*] not so much, so great, etc.; smaller; fewer —adv. to a smaller extent —n. a smaller amount —prep. minus —**less and less** decreasingly

-less (lis, ləs) [OE. *leas*, free] a suffix meaning: 1. without [*valueless*] 2. that does not [*tireless*] 3. that cannot be [*dauntless*]

les·see (les ē′) n. [see LEASE] one to whom a lease is given; tenant

less·en (les′'n) vt., vi. to make or become less; decrease, diminish, etc.

less·er (les′ər) alt. compar. of LITTLE —adj. smaller, less, or less important

les·son (les′'n) n. [< L. *legere*, to read] 1. an exercise for a student to learn 2. something learned for one's safety, etc. 3. [pl.] course of instruction 4. a selection read from the Bible

les·sor (les′ôr) n. [see LEASE] one who gives a lease; landlord

lest (lest) conj. [< OE. *thy læs the*, by the less that] for fear that

let[1] (let) vt. let, let′ting [OE. *lætan*, leave behind] 1. to leave; now only in **let alone**, **let be** 2. a) to rent b) to assign (a contract) 3. to cause to escape [*let* blood] 4. to allow; permit Also used as an auxiliary in commands or suggestions [*let* us go] —vi. to be rented —**let down** 1. to lower 2. to slow up 3. to disappoint —**let off** 1. to give forth 2. to deal leniently with —**let on** [Colloq.] 1. to pretend 2. to indicate one's awareness —**let out** 1. to release 2. to rent out 3. to make a garment larger —**let up** 1. to relax 2. to cease

let[2] (let) n. [< OE. *lettan*, make late] an obstacle: in **without let or hindrance**

-let (lit, lət) [MFr. -el + -et: dim. suffixes] a suffix meaning small [*ringlet*]

let′down′ n. 1. a slowing up 2. the descent of an airplane about to land 3. a disappointment

le·thal (lē′thəl) adj. [< L. *letum*, death] causing death; fatal

leth·ar·gy (leth′ər jē) n., pl. -gies

[< Gr. *lēthē*, oblivion + *argos*, idle] 1. an abnormal drowsiness 2. sluggishness; apathy —le·thar·gic (li thär'jik) *adj.* —le·thar'gi·cal·ly *adv.*

let's (lets) let us

let·ter (let'ər) *n.* [< L. *littera*] 1. any character of the alphabet 2. a written or printed message, usually sent by mail 3. [*pl.*] *a)* literature *b)* learning; knowledge 4. literal meaning —*vt.* to mark with letters —let'ter·er *n.*

letter bomb a small explosive device, mailed in an envelope

letter carrier a postman; mailman

let'tered *adj.* 1. literate 2. highly educated 3. marked with letters

let'ter·head' *n.* the name, address, etc. as a heading on stationery

let'ter·ing *n.* the act of making or inscribing letters, or such letters

let'ter-per'fect *adj.* entirely correct

letters patent a document granting a patent

let·tuce (let'is) *n.* [< L. *lac*, milk] 1. a plant with crisp, green leaves 2. the leaves, much used for salads

let-up (let'up') *n.* [Colloq.] 1. a slackening 2. a stop; pause

leu·ke·mi·a (loo kē'mē ə) *n.* [see ff. & -EMIA] a disease characterized by abnormal increase in the number of leukocytes: also leu·kae'mi·a

leu·ko·cyte (loo'kə sīt') *n.* [< Gr. *leukos*, white + *kytos*, hollow] a white corpuscle in the blood: it destroys disease-causing organisms

lev·ee (lev'ē) *n.* [ult. < L. *levare*, raise] an embankment to prevent a river from flooding bordering land

lev·el (lev'l) *n.* [< L. *libra*, a balance] 1. an instrument for determining the horizontal 2. a horizontal plane or line [*sea level*] 3. a horizontal area 4. normal position with reference to height [*water seeks its level*] 5. position in a scale of values [*income level*] —*adj.* 1. perfectly flat and even 2. not sloping 3. even in height (*with*) 4. equal in importance, advancement, quality, etc. 5. calm or steady —*vt.*, *vi.* -eled or -elled, -el·ing or -el·ling 1. to make or become level 2. to demolish 3. to raise and aim (a gun, etc.) —level with [Slang] to be honest with —lev'el·er, lev'el·ler *n.*

lev·el-head'ed *adj.* having an even temper and sound judgment

lev·er (lev'ər, lē'vər) *n.* [< L. *levare*, raise] 1. a bar used as a pry 2. a means to an end 3. a device consisting of a bar turning about a fixed point, using force at a second point to lift a weight at a third

LEVERS

lev'er·age (-ij) *n.* the action or mechanical power of a lever

le·vi·a·than (lə vī'ə thən) *n.* [< Heb. *liwyāthān*] 1. Bible a sea monster 2. any huge thing

Le·vi's (lē'vīz) [< *Levi* Strauss, U.S. manufacturer] *a trademark for* closefitting trousers of heavy denim

lev·i·ta·tion (lev'ə tā'shən) *n.* [< L. *levis*, light] the illusion of raising a body in the air with no support — lev'i·tate' *vt.*, *vi.* -tat'ed, -tat'ing

Le·vit·i·cus (lə vit'i kəs) the third book of the Pentateuch

lev·i·ty (lev'ə tē) *n.*, *pl.* -ties [< L. *levis*, light] frivolity; improper gaiety

lev·y (lev'ē) *n.*, *pl.* -ies [< L. *levare*, to raise] 1. an imposing and collecting of a tax, fine, etc. 2. the amount collected 3. compulsory enlistment for military service 4. a group so enlisted —*vt.* -ied, -y·ing 1. to impose (a tax, fine, etc.) 2. to enlist (troops) 3. to wage (war)

lewd (lood) *adj.* [OE. *lǣwede*, unlearned] indecent; lustful; obscene —lewd'ly *adv.* —lewd'ness *n.*

lex·i·cog·ra·phy (lek'sə käg'rə fē) *n.* [see ff. & -GRAPHY] the act, art, or work of writing a dictionary —lex'i·cog'ra·pher *n.*

lex·i·con (lek'si kən) *n.* [< Gr. *lexis*, word] 1. a dictionary 2. a special vocabulary

Lex·ing·ton (lek'siŋ tən) city in NC Ky.: with the county in which it is located, pop. 204,000

Li *Chem.* lithium

li·a·bil·i·ty (lī'ə bil'ə tē) *n.*, *pl.* -ties 1. the state of being liable 2. anything for which a person is liable 3. [*pl.*] the debts of a person or business 4. something that works to one's disadvantage

li·a·ble (lī'ə b'l) *adj.* [< L. *ligare*, bind] 1. legally bound or responsible 2. subject to [*liable to suspicion*] 3. likely (*to*) [*liable to die*]

li·ai·son (lē'ə zän', -zōn') *n.* [< L. *ligare*, bind] 1. intercommunication as between units of a military force 2. an illicit love affair

li·ar (lī'ər) *n.* one who tells lies

lib (lib) *n. short for* LIBERATION

li·ba·tion (lī bā'shən) *n.* [< L. *libare*, pour out] 1. the ritual of pouring out wine or oil in honor of a god 2. this liquid 3. an alcoholic drink

li·bel (lī'b'l) *n.* [< L. *liber*, book] 1. any written or printed matter tending to injure a person's reputation unjustly 2. the act or crime of publishing such a thing —*vt.* -beled or -belled, -bel·ing or -bel·ling to make a libel against —li'bel·er, li'bel·ler *n.* — li'bel·ous, li'bel·lous *adj.*

lib·er·al (lib'ər əl) *adj.* [< L. *liber*, free] 1. generous 2. ample; abundant 3. not literal or strict 4. tolerant; broad-minded 5. favoring reform or progress —*n.* one who favors reform or progress —lib'er·al·ism *n.* —lib'er·al·ly *adv.* —lib'er·al·ness *n.*

liberal arts literature, languages, history, etc. as courses of study

lib·er·al·i·ty (-ə ral'ə tē) *n.*, *pl.* -ties 1. generosity 2. broad-mindedness

lib'er·al·ize' (-ə līz') *vt.*, *vi.* -ized',

-iz'ing to make or become liberal —
lib'er·al·i·za'tion n.

lib·er·ate (lib'ə rāt') vt. -at'ed,
-at'ing [< L. liber, free] 1. to release
from slavery, enemy occupation, etc.
2. to secure equal rights for (women,
etc.) —lib'er·a'tion n. —lib'er·a'-
tor n.

Li·ber·i·a (lī bir'ē ə) country on the
W coast of Africa, founded by freed
U.S. slaves: 43,000 sq. mi.; pop.
1,090,000 —Li·ber'i·an adj., n.

lib·er·tar·i·an (lib'ər ter'ē ən) n. 1.
a believer in free will 2. an advocate
of full civil liberties

lib·er·tine (lib'ər tēn') n. [< L.
liber, free] a man who is sexually
promiscuous —adj. licentious

lib·er·ty (lib'ər tē) n., pl. -ties [< L.
liber, free] 1. freedom from slavery,
captivity, etc. 2. a particular right,
freedom, etc. 3. an impertinent attitude 4. leave given to a sailor to go
ashore See also CIVIL LIBERTIES —at
liberty 1. not confined 2. permitted
(to) 3. not busy or in use —take
liberties 1. to be impertinent or too
familiar 2. to deal inaccurately (with
facts, data, etc.)

Liberty Bell the bell of Independence
Hall, Philadelphia, rung July 4, 1776,
to proclaim U.S. independence

li·bid·i·nize (li bid'n iz') vt. -nized',
-niz'ing to regard as a source of
sexual gratification

li·bid·i·nous (li bid'n əs) adj. [see
ff.] lustful; lascivious

li·bi·do (li bē'dō, -bī'-) n. [< L.,
desire] 1. the sexual urge 2. Psychoanalysis psychic energy generally;
specif., that comprising the positive,
loving instincts

Li·bra (lī'brə, lē'-) [L., a balance] the
seventh sign of the zodiac

li·brar·i·an (lī brer'ē ən) n. one in
charge of a library or trained in
library science

li·brar·y (lī'brer'ē) n., pl. -ies [< L.
liber, book] 1. a collection of books,
etc. 2. a room or building for, or an
institution in charge of, such a collection

li·bret·to (li bret'ō) n., pl. -tos, -ti
(-ē) [It. < L. liber, book] the words,
or text, of an opera, oratorio, etc.
—li·bret'tist n.

Lib·y·a (lib'ē ə) country in N Africa,
on the Mediterranean: 679,359 sq. mi.;
pop. 1,738,000 —Lib'y·an adj., n.

lice (līs) n. pl. of LOUSE

li·cense (līs'ns) n. [< L. licere, be
permitted] 1. formal or legal permission to do something specified 2. a
document indicating such permission
3. freedom to deviate from rule, practice, etc. [poetic license] 4. excessive
freedom, constituting an abuse of liberty Brit. sp. licence —vt. -censed,
-cens·ing to permit formally

li·cen·see' (-'n sē') n. a person to
whom a license is granted

li·cen·ti·ate (lī sen'shē it, -āt') n. a
person having a professional license

li·cen·tious (lī sen'shəs) adj. [see
LICENSE] morally unrestrained; lascivious —li·cen'tious·ness n.

li·chen (lī'kən) n. [< Gr. leichein, to
lick] a mosslike plant growing in
patches on rock, wood, soil, etc.

lic·it (lis'it) adj. [< L. licitus, per-
mitted] lawful —lic'it·ly adv.

lick (lik) vt. [OE. liccian] 1. to pass
the tongue over 2. to pass lightly over
like a tongue 3. [Colloq.] a) to whip
b) to vanquish —n. 1. a licking with
the tongue 2. a small quantity 3.
short for SALT LICK 4. [Colloq.] a) a
sharp blow b) a short, rapid burst of
activity: also lick and a promise
—lick up to consume as by licking

lic·o·rice (lik'ər ish, -is) n. [< Gr.
glykys, sweet + rhiza, root] 1. a black
flavoring extract made from the root
of a European plant 2. candy flavored
with this extract

lid (lid) n. [OE. hlid] 1. a movable
cover, as for a box, etc. 2. an eyelid
3. [Colloq.] a restraint —lid'ded adj.

li·dar (lī'där) n. [LI(GHT) + (RA)DAR]
an instrument using laser light to detect pollutants in the atmosphere

lie[1] (lī) vi. lay, lain, ly'ing [OE.
licgan] 1. to be or put oneself in a
reclining or horizontal position 2. to
rest on a support in a horizontal
position 3. to be in a specified condition 4. to be situated [Canada lies to
the north] 5. to exist [love lies in her
eyes] —n. the way in which something is situated; lay

lie[2] (lī) vi. lied, ly'ing [OE. leogan] to
make a statement that one knows is
false —vt. to bring, put, accomplish,
etc. by lying —n. a false statement
made with intent to deceive

Liech·ten·stein (lēkh'tən shtīn')
country between Switzerland &
Austria: 61 sq. mi.; pop. 19,000

lie detector same as POLYGRAPH

lief (lēf) adv. [< OE. leof, dear]
[Archaic] willingly; gladly: only in
would (or had) as lief, etc.

liege (lēj) adj. [< OFr.] loyal; faithful
—n. Feudal Law 1. a lord or sovereign
2. a subject or vassal

li·en (lēn, lē'ən) n. [Fr. < L. ligare, to
bind] a legal claim on another's
property as security for the payment
of a just debt

lieu (lōō) n. [< L. locus] place: in
phrase in lieu of, instead of

lieu·ten·ant (lōō ten'ənt) n. [<
MFr. lieu, place + tenant, holding] 1.
one who acts for a superior 2. U.S.
Mil. an officer ranking below a captain:
see FIRST LIEUTENANT, SECOND LIEU-
TENANT 3. U.S. Navy an officer ranking just above a lieutenant junior
grade Abbrev. Lieut., Lt. —lieu·
ten'an·cy n.

lieutenant colonel U.S. Mil. an
officer ranking just above a major

lieutenant commander U.S. Navy
an officer ranking just above a lieutenant

lieutenant general U.S. Mil. an
officer ranking just above a major
general

lieutenant governor an elected
official of a State who ranks below and
substitutes for the governor

lieutenant junior grade U.S.

Navy an officer ranking just above an ensign

life (līf) *n., pl.* **lives** [OE. *līf*] 1. that property of plants and animals (ending at death) which makes it possible for them to take in food, get energy from it, grow, etc. 2. the state of having this property 3. a human being *{100 lives were lost}* 4. living things collectively *{plant life}* 5. the time a person or thing is alive or exists 6. one's manner of living *{a life of ease}* 7. the people and activities of a given time, place, etc. *{military life}* 8. *a)* one's animate existence *b)* a biography 9. the source of liveliness *{the life of the party}* 10. vigor; liveliness

life belt a life preserver in belt form

life'blood' *n.* 1. the blood necessary to life 2. a vital element

life'boat' *n.* one of the small rescue boats carried by a ship

life'guard' *n.* a swimmer employed at beaches, etc. to prevent drownings

life insurance insurance in which a stipulated sum is paid at the death of the insured

life jacket (or **vest**) a life preserver like a sleeveless jacket or vest

life'less *adj.* 1. without life; specif., *a)* inanimate *b)* dead 2. dull

life'like' *adj.* resembling real life or a real person or thing

life'line' *n.* 1. the rope for raising or lowering a diver 2. a very important commercial route

life'long' *adj.* lasting or not changing during one's whole life

life net a strong net used by firemen, etc. as to catch people jumping from a burning building

life preserver a buoyant device for saving a person from drowning by keeping his body afloat

lif'fer *n.* [Slang] a person sentenced to prison for life

life raft a small, inflatable raft or boat for emergency use at sea

life'sav'er *n.* 1. a lifeguard 2. [Colloq.] a help in time of need

LIFE PRESERVER

life'-size' *adj.* as big as the person or thing represented: said of a statue, picture, etc.: also **life'-sized'**

life style an individual's whole way of living

life'time' *n.* the length of time that one lives or that a thing lasts

life'work' *n.* the work to which a person devotes his life

lift (lift) *vt.* [< ON. *lopt*, air] 1. to bring up to a higher position; raise 2. to raise in rank, condition, etc.; exalt 3. to pay off (a mortgage, debt, etc.) 4. to end (a blockade, etc.) 5. [Slang] to steal —*vi.* 1. to exert strength in raising something 2. to rise; go up —*n.* 1. a lifting or rising 2. the amount lifted 3. the distance something is lifted 4. lifting power or influence 5. elevation of mood, etc. 6. elevated position or carriage 7. a ride in the direction one is going 8. help of any kind 9. [Brit.] an elevator —**lift up one's voice** to speak out loudly

lift'off' *n.* 1. the vertical thrust of a spacecraft, missile, etc. at launching 2. the time of this

lig·a·ment (lig'ə mənt) *n.* [< L. *ligare*, bind] a band of tissue connecting bones or holding organs in place

lig·a·ture (lig'ə chər) *n.* [< L. *ligare*, bind] 1. a tying or binding together 2. a tie, bond, etc. 3. two or more letters united, as æ, th 4. *Surgery* a thread used to tie up an artery, etc.

li·ger (lī'gər) *n.* [LI(ON) + (TI)GER] the offspring of a male lion and a female tiger

light¹ (līt) *n.* [OE. *leoht*] 1. *a)* the form of radiant energy acting on the retina of the eye to make sight possible *b)* ultraviolet or infrared radiation 2. brightness; illumination 3. a source of light, as the sun, a lamp, etc. 4. daylight 5. a thing used to ignite something 6. a window or windowpane 7. knowledge; enlightenment 8. public view *{to bring new facts to light}* 9. aspect *{viewed in another light}* 10. an outstanding person —*adj.* 1. having light; bright 2. pale in color; fair —*adv.* palely *{a light blue color}* —*vt.* **light'ed** or **lit, light'ing** 1. to ignite *{to light a bonfire}* 2. to cause to give off light 3. to furnish with light 4. to brighten; animate —*vi.* 1. to catch fire 2. to be lighted (usually with *up*) —**in the light of** considering —**see the light (of day)** 1. to come into being 2. to come into public view 3. to understand

light² (līt) *adj.* [OE. *leoht*] 1. having little weight; not heavy, esp. for its size 2. less than usual in weight, amount, force, etc. *{a light blow}* 3. of little importance 4. easy to bear *{a light tax}* 5. easy to do *{light work}* 6. gay; happy 7. dizzy; giddy 8. not serious *{light reading}* 9. moderate *{a light meal}* 10. moving with ease *{light on her feet}* 11. producing small products *{light industry}* —*adv.* same as LIGHTLY —*vi.* **light'ed** or **lit, light'ing** 1. to come to rest after traveling through the air 2. to come or happen (*on* or *upon*) 3. to strike suddenly, as a blow —**light out** [Colloq.] to depart suddenly —**make light of** to treat as unimportant

light'en¹ *vt., vi.* 1. to make or become light or brighter 2. to shine; flash

light'en² *vt., vi.* 1. to make or become lighter in weight 2. to make or become more cheerful

light'er¹ *n.* a person or thing that starts something burning

light'er² *n.* [< MDu. *licht*, LIGHT²] a large barge used in loading or unloading larger ships lying offshore

---

fat, āpe, cär; ten, ēven; is, bīte; gō, hôrn, tōōl, look; oil, out; up, fur; chin; she; thin, then; zh, leisure; ŋ, ring; ə for a in *ago*; ', (ā'b'l); ĕ, Fr. coeur; ö, Fr. feu; Fr. mon; ü, Fr. duc; kh, G. ich, doch; ‡ foreign; < derived from

light′-fin′gered *adj.* skillful at stealing, esp. by picking pockets

light′-foot′ed *adj.* stepping lightly and gracefully

light′head′ed *adj.* 1. giddy; dizzy 2. flighty; frivolous

light′heart′ed *adj.* gay; cheerful —**light′heart′ed·ly** *adv.* —**light′-heart′ed·ness** *n.*

light heavyweight a boxer or wrestler weighing 161 to 175 lb.

light′house′ *n.* a tower with a bright light to guide ships at night

light′ing *n.* the act or manner of giving light, or illuminating

light′ly *adv.* 1. with little weight or pressure; gently 2. to a small degree or amount 3. nimbly; deftly 4. cheerfully 5. with indifference

light′-mind′ed *adj.* silly; frivolous

light′ness¹ *n.* 1. the amount of light; brightness 2. paleness in color

light′ness² *n.* 1. a being light, not heavy 2. mildness, carefreeness, etc.

light′ning (-niŋ) *n.* a flash of light in the sky caused by the discharge of atmospheric electricity

lightning bug *same as* FIREFLY

lightning rod a metal rod placed high on a building and grounded to divert lightning from the structure

light opera *same as* OPERETTA

light′weight′ *adj.* light in weight —*n.* a boxer or wrestler weighing 127 to 135 lb.

light′-year′ *n.* the distance that light travels in one year, c. 6 trillion miles

lig·nite (lig′nīt) *n.* [< L. *lignum,* wood] a soft, brownish-black coal with the texture of the original wood

lik·a·ble (līk′a b′l) *adj.* attractive, pleasant, genial, etc.: also **likeable** —**lik′a·ble·ness, lik′a·bil′i·ty** *n.*

like¹ (līk) *adj.* [OE. *gelic*] having the same characteristics; similar; equal —*adv.* [Colloq.] likely [like as not, he'll go] —*prep.* 1. similar to 2. similarly to [to sing *like* a bird] 3. characteristic of [not *like* him to cry] 4. in the mood for [to feel *like* eating] 5. indicative of [it looks *like* rain] 6. as for example [fruit, *like* pears and plums] —*conj.* [Colloq.] 1. as [it's just *like* he said] 2. as if [it looks *like* he's late] —*n.* an equal; counterpart [the *like* of it] —**and the like** and others of the same kind —**like blazes** (or **crazy, the devil, mad,** etc.) [Colloq.] with furious energy, speed, etc. —**the like** (or **likes**) **of** [Colloq.] any person or thing like

like² (līk) *vi.* **liked, lik′ing** [OE. *lician*] to be so inclined [do as you *like*] —*vt.* 1. to be pleased with; enjoy 2. to wish [I'd *like* to go] —*n.* [pl.] preferences; tastes —**lik′er** *n.*

-like (līk) *a suffix meaning* like, characteristic of [ball-like, homelike]

like·li·hood (līk′lē hood′) *n.* a being likely to happen; probability

like′ly *adj.* **-li·er, -li·est** [OE. *geliclic*] 1. credible [a likely story] 2. reasonably to be expected [*likely* to rain] 3. suitable [a *likely* place to swim] —*adv.* probably [*likely* he'll win]

like′-mind′ed *adj.* having the same ideas, plans, tastes, etc. —**like′-mind′ed·ness** *n.*

lik·en (līk′'n) *vt.* to compare

like′ness *n.* 1. a being like 2. (the same) form 3. a copy, portrait, etc.

like′wise′ *adv.* [< *in like wise*] 1. in the same manner 2. also; too

lik·ing (līk′iŋ) *n.* 1. fondness; affection 2. preference; taste; pleasure

li·lac (lī′lək, -läk) *n.* [ult. < Per. *lilak,* bluish] 1. a shrub with large clusters of tiny, fragrant flowers 2. a pale purple —*adj.* pale-purple

Lil·li·pu·tian (lil′i pyōō′shən) *adj.* [< *Lilliput,* place in J. Swift's *Gulliver's Travels*] 1. tiny 2. petty

lilt (lilt) *n.* [ME. *lilten,* to sound] a light, swingy rhythm or tune

lil·y (lil′ē) *n., pl.* **-ies** [< L. *lilium*] 1. a plant grown from a bulb and having typically trumpet-shaped flowers 2. its flower 3. any similar plant, as the water lily —*adj.* like a lily, as in whiteness, purity, etc.

lil′y-liv′ered (-liv′ərd) *adj.* cowardly; timid

lily of the valley *pl.* **lilies of the valley** a low plant with a spike of fragrant, white, bell-shaped flowers

Li·ma (lē′mə) capital of Peru: pop. 1,716,000

li·ma bean (lī′mə) [< *Lima,* Peru] [also L- b-] 1. a bean with broad pods 2. its broad, flat, edible seed

limb (lim) *n.* [OE. *lim*] 1. an arm, leg, or wing 2. a large branch of a tree —**out on a limb** [Colloq.] in a precarious position —**limb′less** *adj.*

lim·ber (lim′bər) *adj.* [< ? prec.] 1. easily bent; flexible 2. able to bend the body easily —*vt., vi.* to make or become limber

lim·bo (lim′bō) *n.* [< L. (*in*) *limbo,* (on) the border] 1. [*often* L-] in some Christian theologies, the abode after death of unbaptized children, etc. 2. a place of oblivion 3. a vague condition

Lim·bur·ger (cheese) (lim′bər gər) [< *Limburg,* Belgian province] a semisoft cheese with a strong odor

lime¹ (līm) *n.* [OE. *lim*] a white substance, calcium oxide, obtained from limestone, etc. and used in mortar and cement and to neutralize acid soil —*vt.* **limed, lim′ing** to treat with lime

lime² (līm) *n.* [< Ar. *līma*] a small, lemon-shaped, greenish-yellow citrus fruit with a juicy, sour pulp

lime′ade′ (-ād′) *n.* a drink made of lime juice and water, usually sweetened

lime′light′ *n.* 1. a brilliant light created by the incandescence of lime: formerly used in theaters 2. a prominent position before the public

lim·er·ick (lim′ər ik) *n.* [prob. < *Limerick,* Ir. county] a rhymed nonsense poem of five lines

lime′stone′ *n.* rock consisting mainly of calcium carbonate

lim·it (lim′it) *n.* [< L. *limes*] 1. the point, line, etc. where something ends; boundary 2. [pl.] bounds 3. the greatest amount allowed —*vt.* to set a limit to; restrict —**lim′i·ta′tion** *n.* —**lim′it·er** *n.* —**lim′it·less** *adj.*

lim′it·ed *adj.* 1. confined within

bounds 2. making a restricted number of stops: said of a train, bus, etc.

limn (lim) *vt.* [< L. *illuminare,* make light] 1. to paint or draw 2. to describe

lim·o (lim′ō) *n., pl.* **-os** [Colloq.] *same as* LIMOUSINE

lim·ou·sine (lim′ə zēn′) *n.* [Fr., lit., a hood] a large, luxury automobile, esp. one driven by a chauffeur

limp (limp) *vi.* [< OE. *limpan*] to walk with or as with a lame leg —*n.* a halt or lameness in walking —*adj.* lacking firmness; wilted, flexible, etc. —**limp′ly** *adv.* —**limp′ness** *n.*

limp·et (lim′pit) *n.* [< ML. *lempreda*] a mollusk that clings to rocks, etc.

lim·pid (lim′pid) *adj.* [< L. *limpidus*] perfectly clear; transparent —**lim·pid′i·ty** *n.* —**lim′pid·ly** *adv.*

lim·y (li′mē) *adj.* **-i·er, -i·est** of, like, or containing lime

lin·age (li′nij) *n.* the number of written or printed lines, as on a page

linch·pin (linch′pin′) *n.* [OE. *lynis,* linchpin] a pin in an axle to keep the wheel from coming off

Lin·coln (liŋ′kən) capital of Nebr.: pop. 172,000

Lincoln, Abraham 1809–65; 16th president of the U.S. (1861–65)

lin·den (lin′dən) *n.* [OE.] a tree with dense, heart-shaped leaves

line¹ (lin) *n.* [< L. *linea,* lit., llnen thread] 1. a cord, rope, wire, etc. 2. any wire, pipe, etc., or system of these, conducting fluid, electricity, etc. 3. a thin, threadlike mark 4. a border or boundary 5. a limit 6. outline; contour 7. a row of persons or things, as of printed letters across a page 8. a succession of persons or things 9. lineage 10. a transportation system of buses, ships, etc. 11. the course a moving thing takes 12. a course of conduct, action, explanation, etc. 13. a person's trade or occupation 14. a stock of goods 15. a piece of information 16. a short letter, note, etc. 17. a verse of poetry 18. [*pl.*] all the speeches of a character in a play 19. the forward combat position in warfare 20. *Football* the players in the forward row 21. *Math.* the path of a moving point —*vt.* lined, lin′ing 1. to mark with lines 2. to form a line along —**bring** (or **come**) **into line** to bring or come into alignment or conformity —**draw the** (or **a**) **line** to set a limit —**hold the line** to stand firm —**in line** for being considered for —**line up** to form, or bring into, a line

line² (lin) *vt.* **lined, lin′ing** [< L. *linum,* flax] to put, or serve as, a lining in

lin·e·age (lin′ē ij) *n.* [see LINE¹] 1. direct descent from an ancestor 2. ancestry; family

lin·e·al (lin′ē əl) *adj.* 1. in the direct line of descent from an ancestor 2. hereditary 3. of lines; linear

lin·e·a·ment (lin′ē ə mənt) *n.* [< L. *linea,* LINE¹] a distinctive feature, esp. of the face: *usually used in pl.*

lin·e·ar (lin′ē ər) *adj.* 1. of, made of, or using a line or lines 2. narrow and long 3. in relation to length only

line·back·er (lin′bak′ər) *n. Football* a defensive player directly behind the line

line drive a baseball hit in a straight line parallel to the ground

line·man (-mən) *n., pl.* **-men** 1. a man who sets up and repairs telephone or electric power lines 2. *Football* a player in the line

lin·en (lin′ən) *n.* [< OE. *lin,* flax: see LINE²] 1. thread or cloth made of flax 2. [*often pl.*] sheets, cloths, etc. of linen, or of cotton, etc.

lin·er (li′nər) *n.* 1. a steamship, airplane, etc. in regular service for some line 2. a cosmetic applied in a fine line, as along the eyelid

lines·man (linz′mən) *n., pl.* **-men** 1. *Football* an official who marks the gains or losses in ground 2. *Tennis* an official who determines if the balls land outside the foul lines

line′up′ *n.* an arrangement of persons or things in or as in a line

-ling (liŋ) [OE.] *a suffix meaning:* 1. small [*duckling*] 2. contemptible; unimportant [*princeling*]

lin·ger (liŋ′gər) *vi.* [OE. *lengan,* to delay] 1. to continue to stay, as through reluctance to leave 2. to loiter —**lin′ger·er** *n.* —**lin′ger·ing** *adj.*

lin·ge·rie (län′zhə rā′, -rē′; -jə-) *n.* [Fr.] women's underwear

lin·go (liŋ′gō) *n., pl.* **-goes** [< L. *lingua,* tongue] a dialect, jargon, etc. that one is not familiar with

lin·gua fran·ca (liŋ′gwə fraŋ′kə) a hybrid language used for communication by speakers of different languages

lin·gual (liŋ′gwəl) *adj.* [see ff.] of, or pronounced with, the tongue

lin′guist (-gwist) *n.* [< L. *lingua,* tongue] 1. a specialist in linguistics 2. *same as* POLYGLOT (sense 1)

lin·guis′tics (-gwis′tiks) *n.pl.* [*with sing. v.*] 1. the science of language 2. the study of a particular language —**lin·guis′tic** *adj.*

lin·i·ment (lin′ə mənt) *n.* [< L. *linere,* to smear] a soothing medicated liquid to be rubbed on the skin

lin·ing (li′niŋ) *n.* the material covering an inner surface

link (liŋk) *n.* [< Scand.] 1. any of the loops forming a chain 2. *a)* a section of something like a chain [*a link of sausage*] *b)* an element in a series [*a weak link in evidence*] 3. anything that connects [*a link with the past*] —*vt., vi.* to join; connect

link·age (liŋ′kij) *n.* 1. a linking 2. a series or system of links

links (liŋks) *n.pl.* [OE. *hlinc,* a slope] a golf course

link′up′ *n.* a linking together

Lin·nae·us (li nē′əs), **Car·o·lus** (kar′ə ləs) 1707–78; Swed. botanist

lin·net (lin′it) *n.* [< L. *linum*, flax: it feeds on flaxseed] a small finch of Europe, Asia, and Africa

li·no·le·um (li nō′lē əm) *n.* [< L. *linum*, flax + *oleum*, oil] a hard floor covering made of ground cork and linseed oil on a backing, as of canvas

lin·seed (lin′sēd′) *n.* [OE. *linsæd*] the seed of flax

linseed oil a yellowish oil extracted from flaxseed, used in oil paints, etc.

lint (lint) *n.* [< L. *linum*, flax] 1. scraped and softened linen 2. bits of thread, fluff, etc. from cloth or yarn —lint′y *adj.* -i·er, -i·est

lin·tel (lin′t'l) *n.* [ult. < L. *limen*, threshold] the horizontal crosspiece over a door, window, etc.

lin·y (lī′nē) *adj.* -i·er, -i·est 1. linelike 2. marked with lines

li·on (lī′ən) *n.* [< Gr. *leōn*] 1. a large, powerful mammal of the cat family, found in Africa and SW Asia 2. a person of great courage or strength 3. a celebrity —li′on·ess *n.fem.*

li′on·heart′ed *adj.* very brave

li·on·ize (lī′ə nīz′) *vt.* -ized′, -iz′ing to treat as a celebrity

lip (lip) *n.* [OE. *lippa*] 1. either of the two fleshy folds forming the edges of the mouth 2. anything like a lip, as the rim of a pitcher 3. [Slang] insolent talk —*adj.* spoken, but insincere [*lip* service] —**keep a stiff upper lip** [Colloq.] to bear pain or distress bravely

lip′py *adj.* -pi·er, -pi·est [Slang] impudent; insolent —lip′pi·ness *n.*

lip reading recognition of a speaker's words, as by the deaf, by watching the movement of his lips —lip′-read′ *vt., vi.* —lip reader

lip′stick′ *n.* a small stick of cosmetic paste for coloring the lips

lip′-sync′, lip′-synch′ (-siŋk′) *vt., vi.* [< *lip synchronization*] to move the lips silently so as to seem to be speaking or singing (something recorded) —*n.* a lip-syncing

liq·ue·fy (lik′wə fī′) *vt., vi.* -fied′, -fy′ing [< L. *liquere*, be liquid + *facere*, make] to change to a liquid —liq′ue·fac′tion (-fak′shən) *n.*

li·queur (li kur′) *n.* [Fr.] a sweet, syrupy, flavored alcoholic liquor

liq·uid (lik′wid) *adj.* [< L. *liquidus*] 1. readily flowing; fluid 2. clear; limpid 3. flowing smoothly and musically, as verse 4. readily convertible into cash —*n.* a substance that, unlike a solid, flows readily but, unlike a gas, does not expand indefinitely —liq·uid′i·ty *n.*

liq·ui·date (lik′wə dāt′) *vt.* -dat′ed, -dat′ing [see prec.] 1. to settle the accounts of (a business) by apportioning assets and debts 2. to pay (a debt) 3. to convert into cash 4. to get rid of, as by killing —liq′ui·da′tion *n.* —liq′ui·da′tor *n.*

liq′uid·ize′ (-dīz′) *vt.* -ized′, -iz′ing to make of liquid quality

liq·uor (lik′ər) *n.* [L.] 1. any liquid 2. an alcoholic drink, esp. a distilled drink, as whiskey or rum

li·ra (lir′ə) *n., pl.* li′re (-ā), li′ras [< L. *libra*, pound] the monetary unit of Italy

Lis·bon (liz′bən) capital of Portugal: pop. 802,000

lisle (līl) *n.* [< *Lisle* (now *Lille*), in France] 1. a fine, hard, extra-strong cotton thread 2. a fabric, or stockings, gloves, etc., woven of this

lisp (lisp) *vi.* [< OE. *wlisp*, a lisping] 1. to substitute the sounds (th) and (*th*) for the sounds of *s* and *z* 2. to speak imperfectly —*vt.* to utter with a lisp —*n.* the act or sound of lisping

lis·some (lis′əm) *adj.* [< *lithesome*] lithe, supple, agile, etc.

list¹ (list) *n.* [< OE. *liste*, border] a series of names, words, etc. set forth in order —*vt.* to set forth or enter in a list, directory, etc.

list² *vt., vi.* [prob. ult. < OE. *lust*, desire] to tilt to one side, as a ship —*n.* such a tilting

lis·ten (lis′n) *vi.* [OE. *hlysnan*] 1. to make a conscious effort to hear 2. to give heed; take advice —lis′ten·er *n.*

list·ing (lis′tiŋ) *n.* 1. the making of a list 2. an entry in a list

list·less (list′lis) *adj.* [< OE. *lust*, desire + -LESS] indifferent because of illness, dejection, etc.; languid —list′less·ly *adv.* —list′less·ness *n.*

list price retail price as given in a list or catalog

lists (lists) *n.pl.* [< ME. *liste*, border] a fenced area in which knights jousted

Liszt (list), **Franz** (fränts) 1811-86; Hung. composer & pianist

lit (lit) *alt. pt. & pp.* of LIGHT

lit. 1. liter(s) 2. literal(ly) 3. literature

lit·a·ny (lit′n ē) *n., pl.* -nies [< Gr. *litē*, a request] prayer in which the congregation recites responses

li·tchi (lē′chē′) *n.* [< Chin.] the raisinlike fruit of a Chinese evergreen tree, enclosed in a papery shell

li·ter (lēt′ər) *n.* [< Gr. *litra*, a pound] the basic unit of capacity in the metric system, equal to 1.0567 liquid quarts or .908 dry quart: Brit. sp. li′tre

lit·er·a·cy (lit′ər ə sē) *n.* the ability to read and write

lit·er·al (lit′ər əl) *adj.* [< L. *littera*, a letter] 1. following the exact words of the original [a *literal* translation] 2. in a basic or strict sense [the *literal* meaning] 3. prosaic; matter-of-fact [a *literal* mind] 4. real [the *literal* truth] —lit′er·al·ly *adv.*

lit·er·ar·y (lit′ə rer′ē) *adj.* 1. of or dealing with literature 2. familiar with or versed in literature

lit·er·ate (lit′ər it) *adj.* [< L. *littera*, a letter] 1. able to read and write 2. well-educated —*n.* a literate person

lit·e·ra·ti (lit′ə rät′ē) *n.pl.* [It. < L. *litterati*: see prec.] scholarly people

lit·er·a·ture (lit′ər ə chər) *n.* [< L. *littera*, a letter] 1. *a)* all writings in prose or verse of an imaginative character *b)* all such writings having permanent value, excellence of form, etc. *c)* all the writings of a particular time, country, etc. *d)* all the writings on a particular subject 2. [Colloq.] any printed matter

lithe (lī*th*) *adj.* [OE. *lithe*, soft] bending easily; flexible; supple

lith·i·um (lith'ē əm) *n.* [< Gr. *lithos*, stone] a soft, silver-white chemical element

lithium carbonate a white, powdery salt, used in making glass, dyes, etc. and in treating manic-depressive disorders

lith·o·graph (lith'ə graf') *n.* a print made by lithography —*vi.*, *vt.* to make (prints or copies) by this process —**li·thog·ra·pher** (li thäg'rə fər) *n.*

li·thog·ra·phy (li thäg'rə fē) *n.* [< Gr. *lithos*, stone + -GRAPHY] printing from a flat stone or metal plate, parts of which have been treated to repel ink —**lith·o·graph·ic** (lith'ə graf'ik) *adj.*

Lith·u·a·ni·a (lith'ōō wā'nē ə) republic of the U.S.S.R., in NE Europe —**Lith·u·a′ni·an** *adj.*, *n.*

lit·i·gant (lit'ə gənt) *n.* [see ff.] a party to a lawsuit

lit′i·gate′ (-gāt') *vt.*, *vi.* **-gat′ed, -gat′ing** [< L. *lis*, dispute + *agere*, do] to contest in a lawsuit —**lit′i·ga′tion** *n.* —**lit′i·ga′tor** *n.*

lit·mus (lit'məs) *n.* [< ON. *litr*, color + *mosi*, moss] a purple coloring matter obtained from lichens: paper treated with it (**litmus paper**) turns blue in bases and red in acids

Litt.D. Doctor of Letters

lit·ter (lit'ər) *n.* [< L. *lectus*, a couch] **1.** a framework enclosing a couch on which a person can be carried **2.** a stretcher for carrying the sick or wounded **3.** straw, hay, etc. used as bedding for animals **4.** the young borne at one time by a dog, cat, etc. **5.** things lying about in disorder, esp. bits of rubbish —*vt.* **1.** to make untidy **2.** to scatter about carelessly

lit′ter·bug′ (-bug') *n.* one who litters public places with rubbish, etc.

lit·tle (lit'l) *adj.* **lit′tler** or **less** or **less′er, lit′tlest** or **least** [OE. *lytel*] **1.** small in size, amount, degree, etc. **2.** short in duration; brief **3.** small in importance or power [the *little* man] **4.** narrow-minded [a *little* mind] —*adv.* **less, least 1.** slightly; not much **2.** not in the least —*n.* a small amount, degree, etc. —**little by little** gradually —**make** (or **think**) **little of** to consider as not very important —**lit′tle·ness** *n.*

Little Rock capital of Ark.: pop. 158,000

little slam *Bridge* the winning of all but one trick in a deal

lit·to·ral (lit'ər əl) *adj.* [< L. *litus*, seashore] of or along the shore

lit·ur·gy (lit'ər jē) *n.*, *pl.* **-gies** [ult. < Gr. *leōs*, people + *ergon*, work] prescribed ritual for public worship —**li·tur·gi·cal** (li tur'ji k'l) *adj.* —**lit′ur·gist** *n.*

liv·a·ble (liv'ə b'l) *adj.* **1.** fit or pleasant to live in [a *livable* house] **2.** endurable Also **liveable**

live¹ (liv) *vi.* **lived, liv′ing** [OE. *libban*] **1.** to have life **2.** *a*) to remain alive *b*) to endure **3.** to pass life in a specified

manner **4.** to enjoy a full life **5.** to feed [to *live* on fruit] **6.** to reside —*vt.* **1.** to carry out in one's life [*live* one's faith] **2.** to spend; pass [to *live* a useful life] —**live down** to live so as to wipe out the shame of (a misdeed, etc.) —**live up to** to act in accordance with (one's ideals, etc.)

live² (līv) *adj.* [< ALIVE] **1.** having life **2.** of the living state or living beings **3.** of present interest [a *live* issue] **4.** still burning [a *live* spark] **5.** unexploded [a *live* shell] **6.** carrying electrical current [a *live* wire] **7.** *a*) in person *b*) broadcast, recorded, etc. during the actual performance **8.** *Sports* in play [a *live* ball]

-lived (līvd; *occas.* livd) *a combining form meaning* having (a specified kind of) life [short-*lived*]

live·li·hood (līv'lē hood') *n.* [< OE. *lif*, life + *-lad*, course] means of living or of supporting life

live·long (liv'lôŋ') *adj.* [ME. *lefe longe*, lief long: *lief* is merely intens.] long in passing; whole; entire

live·ly (līv'lē) *adj.* **-li·er, -li·est** [OE. *liflic*] **1.** full of life; vigorous **2.** full of spirit; exciting **3.** gay; cheerful **4.** vivid; keen **5.** bounding back with great resilience [a *lively* ball] —**live′li·ness** *n.*

liv·en (līv'vən) *vt.*, *vi.* to make or become lively or gay; cheer (*up*)

liv·er (liv'ər) *n.* [OE. *lifer*] **1.** the largest glandular organ in vertebrate animals: it secretes bile and is important in metabolism **2.** this organ of an animal used as food

Liv·er·pool (liv'ər pōōl') seaport in NW England: pop. 740,000

liv·er·wurst (liv'ər wurst') *n.* [< G. *leber*, liver + *wurst*, sausage] a sausage containing ground liver

liv·er·y (liv'ər ē) *n.*, *pl.* **-ies** [ME., gift of clothes to a servant] **1.** an identifying uniform as of a servant **2.** *a*) the care and feeding of horses for a fee *b*) the keeping of horses or vehicles for hire —**liv′er·ied** *adj.*

lives (līvz) *n. pl.* of LIFE

live·stock (līv'stäk') *n.* domestic animals raised for use or sale

liv·id (liv'id) *adj.* [< L. *lividus*] **1.** discolored by a bruise; black-and-blue **2.** grayish-blue or pale [*livid* with rage]

liv·ing (liv'iŋ) *adj.* **1.** alive; having life **2.** in active operation or use [a *living* language] **3.** of persons alive [within *living* memory] **4.** true; lifelike **5.** of life [*living* conditions] —*n.* **1.** a being alive **2.** livelihood **3.** manner of existence —**the living** those that are still alive

living room a room in a home, with sofas, chairs, etc., for social activities, entertaining guests, etc.

living wage a wage sufficient to maintain a reasonable level of comfort

living will a document directing that the signer's life not be artificially supported during a terminal illness

liz·ard (liz′ərd) *n.* [< L. *lacerta*] any of a group of slender, scaly reptiles with four legs and a tail

LL. Late Latin

ll., ll lines

lla·ma (lä′mə) *n.* [Sp. < Peruv. native name] a S.American beast of burden related to the camel but smaller

lla·no (lä′nō) *n., pl.* **-nos** [Sp. < L. *planus*, plain] any of the level, grassy plains of Spanish America

LL.B. Bachelor of Laws

LL.D. Doctor of Laws

lo (lō) *interj.* [OE. *la*] look! see!

load (lōd) *n.* [< OE. *lad*, a course] 1. an amount carried at one time 2. something borne with difficulty; burden 3. [*often pl.*] [Colloq.] a great amount —*vt.* 1. to put a (load) into or upon (a carrier) 2. to burden; oppress 3. to supply in large quantities 4. to put a charge of ammunition into (a firearm) —*vi.* to take on a load —**load′er** *n.* —**load′ing** *n.*

load′star′ *n. same as* LODESTAR

load′stone′ *n. same as* LODESTONE

loaf¹ (lōf) *n., pl.* **loaves** [OE. *hlaf*] 1. a portion of bread baked in one piece 2. any food baked in this shape

loaf² (lōf) *vi.* [prob. < ff.] to spend time idly; idle, dawdle, etc.

loaf′er *n.* [prob. < G. *landläufer*, vagabond] one who loafs; idler

loam (lōm) *n.* [OE. *lam*] a rich soil, esp. one composed of clay, sand, and some organic matter —**loam′y** *adj.*

loan (lōn) *n.* [< ON. *lān*] 1. the act of lending 2. something lent, esp. money at interest —*vt., vi.* to lend

loan′word′ (-wurd′) *n.* a word of one language taken and used in another

loath (lōth) *adj.* [< OE. *lath*, hostile] reluctant (to be *loath* to depart)

loathe (lōth) *vt.* **loathed, loath′ing** [< OE. *lathian*, be hateful] to feel intense dislike or disgust for; abhor

loath·ing (lōth′iŋ) *n.* intense dislike, disgust, or hatred

loath′some (-səm) *adj.* causing loathing; disgusting

loaves (lōvz) *n. pl. of* LOAF¹

lob (läb) *vt., vi.* **lobbed, lob′bing** [ME. *lobbe-*, heavy] to toss or hit (a ball) in a high curve —**lob′ber** *n.*

lob·by (läb′ē) *n., pl.* **-bies** [LL. *lobia*] 1. an entrance hall, as of a hotel, theater, etc. 2. a group of lobbyists representing the same interest —*vi.* **-bied, -by·ing** to act as a lobbyist

lob′by·ist *n.* one who tries to get legislators to support certain measures

lobe (lōb) *n.* [< Gr. *lobos*] a rounded projection, as the lower end of the ear or any of the divisions of the lung

lob·ster (läb′stər) *n.* [< OE. *loppe*, spider + *-estre*, *-ster*] an edible sea crustacean with four pairs of legs and a pair of large pincers

lobster tail the edible tail of any of various crayfish

lo·cal (lō′k'l) *adj.* [< L. *locus*, a place] 1. of, characteristic

LOBSTER

of, or confined to a particular place 2. of or for a particular part of the body 3. making all stops along its run (a *local* bus) —*n.* 1. a local train, bus, etc. 2. a branch, as of a labor union —**lo′cal·ly** *adv.*

lo·cale (lō kal′) *n.* [Fr. *local*] a locality, esp. with reference to events, etc. associated with it

lo·cal·i·ty (lō kal′ə tē) *n., pl.* **-ties** 1. position with regard to surrounding objects, etc. 2. a place or district

lo·cal·ize (lō′kə līz′) *vt.* **-ized′, -iz′ing** to limit, confine, or trace to a particular place —**lo′cal·i·za′tion** *n.*

lo·cate (lō′kāt) *vt.* **-cat·ed, -cat·ing** [< L. *locus*, a place] 1. to establish in a certain place (offices *located* downtown) 2. to discover the position of 3. to show the position of (*locate* Guam on this map) —*vi.* [Colloq.] to settle (he *located* in Ohio)

lo·ca′tion *n.* 1. a locating or being located 2. position; place —**on location** *Movies* away from the studio

loc. cit. [L. *loco citato*] in the place cited

loch (läk, läkh) *n.* [< Gael. & OIr.] [Scot.] 1. a lake 2. an arm of the sea

lock¹ (läk) *n.* [< OE. *loc*, a bolt] 1. a mechanical device for fastening a door, strongbox, etc. as with a key or combination 2. an enclosed part of a canal, etc. equipped with gates for raising or lowering the level of the water 3. the mechanism of a firearm that explodes the charge —*vt.* 1. to fasten with a lock 2. to shut (*up, in,* or *out*); confine 3. to fit; link (to *lock* arms) 4. to jam together so as to make immovable —*vi.* 1. to become locked 2. to interlock

lock² (läk) *n.* [OE. *loc*] 1. a curl of hair 2. a tuft of wool, etc.

lock′er *n.* 1. a chest, closet, etc. which can be locked 2. a large compartment for freezing and storing foods

lock·et (läk′it) *n.* [< OFr. *loc*, a lock] a small, hinged case for holding a picture, lock of hair, etc.: usually worn on a necklace

lock′jaw′ *n.* a form of tetanus, in which the jaws become firmly closed

lock′out′ *n.* the shutdown of a plant to bring the workers to terms

lock′smith′ *n.* one whose work is making or repairing locks and keys

lock′up′ (läk′up′) *n.* a jail

lo·co (lō′kō) *adj.* [Sp., mad] [Slang] crazy; demented

lo·co·mo·tion (lō′kə mō′shən) *n.* [< L. *locus*, a place + MOTION] motion, or the power of moving, from one place to another

lo′co·mo′tive (-mōt′iv) *adj.* of locomotion —*n.* an electric, steam, or diesel engine on wheels, designed to push or pull a railroad train

lo·co·weed (lō′kō wēd′) *n.* a plant of W N.America that causes a nervous disease in horses, cattle, etc.

lo·cus (lō′kəs) *n., pl.* **lo′ci** (-sī) [L.] 1. a place 2. *Math.* a line, plane, etc. every point of which satisfies a given condition

lo·cust (lō′kəst) *n.* [< L. *locusta*] 1.

a large grasshopper often traveling in swarms and destroying crops **2.** *same as* SEVENTEEN-YEAR LOCUST **3.** a tree of the S U.S., with clusters of fragrant white flowers

lo·cu·tion (lō kyōō′shən) *n.* [< L. *loqui*, speak] a word, phrase, etc.

lode (lōd) *n.* [< OE. *lad*, course] a vein, stratum, etc. of metallic ore

lode′star′ *n.* a star by which one directs his course; esp., the North Star

lode′stone′ *n.* a strongly magnetic iron ore

lodge (läj) *n.* [< OFr. *loge*, arbor] **1.** *a)* a small house for some special use [a hunting *lodge*] *b)* a resort hotel or motel **2.** the local chapter or hall of a fraternal society —*vt.* **lodged, lodg′ing 1.** to house temporarily **2.** to shoot, thrust, etc. firmly (*in*) **3.** to bring (a complaint, etc.) before legal authorities **4.** to confer (powers) upon (with *in*) —*vi.* **1.** to live in a place for a time **2.** to live (*with* or *in*) as a paying guest **3.** to come to rest and stick firmly (*in*)

lodg′er *n.* one who lives in a rented room in another's home

lodg′ing *n.* **1.** a place to live in, esp. temporarily **2.** [*pl.*] a room or rooms rented in a private home

loft (lôft, läft) *n.* [< ON. *lopt*, upper room, air] **1.** the space just below the roof of a house, barn, etc. **2.** an upper story of a warehouse or factory **3.** a gallery [a choir *loft*] **4.** height given to a ball hit or thrown —*vt.* to send (a ball) into a high curve

loft′y *adj.* **-i·er, -i·est 1.** very high **2.** elevated; noble **3.** haughty; arrogant —**loft′i·ness** *n.*

log¹ (lôg, läg) *n.* [ME. *logge*] **1.** a section of the trunk or of a large limb of a felled tree **2.** a device for measuring the speed of a ship **3.** a record of progress, speed, etc.; specif. one kept on a ship's voyage or aircraft's flight —*vt.* **logged, log′ging 1.** to saw (trees) into logs **2.** to record in a log **3.** to sail or fly (a specified distance) —*vi.* to cut down trees and remove the logs —**log′ger** *n.*

log² (lôg, läg) *n.* *short for* LOGARITHM

-log (lôg, läg) *same as* -LOGUE

lo·gan·ber·ry (lō′gən ber′ē) *n., pl.* **-ries** [< J. H. *Logan*, who developed it (1881)] **1.** a hybrid developed from the blackberry and the red raspberry **2.** its purplish-red fruit

log·a·rithm (lôg′ə ri*th*′m, läg′-) [< Gr. *logos*, ratio + *arithmos*, number] the exponent expressing the power to which a fixed number must be raised to produce a given number —**log′a·rith′mic** *adj.*

loge (lōzh) *n.* [Fr.: see LODGE] a theater box or mezzanine section

log·ger·head (lôg′ər hed′, läg′-) *n.* [dial. *logger*, block of wood + HEAD] a blockhead —**at loggerheads** in sharp disagreement

log·ic (läj′ik) *n.* [ult. < Gr. *logos*, word] **1.** correct reasoning, or the science of this **2.** way of reasoning [bad *logic*] **3.** what is expected by the working of cause and effect —**lo·gi·cian** (lō jish′ən) *n.*

log′i·cal (-i k'l) *adj.* **1.** based on or using logic **2.** expected because of what has gone before —**log′i·cal·ly** *adv.*

lo·gis·tics (lō jis′tiks) *n.pl.* [*with sing. v.*] [< Fr. *loger*, to quarter] the military science of procuring, maintaining, and transporting materiel and personnel —**lo·gis′tic, lo·gis′ti·cal** *adj.* —**lo·gis′ti·cal·ly** *adv.*

log′jam′ *n.* **1.** an obstacle of logs jamming together in a stream **2.** piled-up work, etc. that obstructs progress

log·o·type (lôg′ə tīp′, läg′-) *n.* [< Gr. *logos*, a word + -TYPE] a distinctive company signature, trademark, etc.: also **log·o** (lôg′ō, läg′ō, lō′gō)

log′roll′ing *n.* **1.** mutual exchange of favors, esp. among legislators **2.** the sport of balancing oneself while revolving a floating log with one's feet

-logue (lôg) [see LOGIC] *a combining form meaning* a (specified kind of) speaking or writing [monologue]

lo·gy (lō′gē) *adj.* **-gi·er, -gi·est** [< ? Du. *log*, dull] [Colloq.] dull or sluggish

-lo·gy (lə jē) [see LOGIC] *a combining form meaning:* **1.** a (specified kind of) speaking [eulogy] **2.** science, doctrine, or theory of [biology]

loin (loin) *n.* [< L. *lumbus*] **1.** [*usually pl.*] the lower part of the back between the hipbones and the ribs **2.** the front part of the hindquarters of beef, lamb, etc. **3.** [*pl.*] the hips and the lower abdomen regarded as the region of strength, etc.

loin′cloth′ *n.* a cloth worn about the loins, as by some tropical tribes

loi·ter (loit′ər) *vi.* [< MDu. *loteren*] **1.** to spend time idly; linger **2.** to move slowly and idly —**loi′ter·er** *n.*

loll (läl) *vi.* [< MDu. *lollen*] **1.** to lean or lounge about lazily **2.** to hang loosely; droop, as the head on the shoulders —*vt.* to let hang loosely

lol·li·pop, lol·ly·pop (läl′ē päp′) *n.* [prob. < dial. *lolly*, tongue + *pop*] a piece of candy on the end of a stick

lol·ly·gag (läl′ē gag′) *vi.* **-gagged′, -gag′ging** [var. of *lallygag* < ?] [Colloq.] to waste time in aimless activity

Lon·don (lun′dən) **1.** capital of England, the United Kingdom, & the Brit. Commonwealth, in SE England: pop. (incl. suburbs) 8,183,000 **2.** city in SE Ontario, Canada: pop. 194,000

lone (lōn) *adj.* [< *alone*] **1.** by oneself; solitary **2.** isolated

lone′ly *adj.* **-li·er, -li·est 1.** solitary or isolated **2.** unhappy at being alone —**lone′li·ness** *n.*

lon·er (lō′nər) *n.* [Colloq.] one who avoids the company, counsel, etc. of others

lone′some *adj.* **1.** having or causing a lonely feeling **2.** unfrequented

long¹ (lôn) *adj.* [< OE.] **1.** measuring much in space or time **2.** in length [*six feet long*] **3.** of greater than usual length, quantity, etc. [*a long list*] **4.** tedious; slow **5.** far-reaching [*a long view of the matter*] **6.** well-supplied [*long on excuses*] —*adv.* **1.** for a long time **2.** from start to finish [*all day long*] **3.** at a remote time [*long ago*] —**as** (or **so**) **long as 1.** during the time that **2.** since **3.** provided that —**before long** soon

long² (lôn) *vi.* [< OE. *langian*] to feel a strong yearning; wish earnestly

long. longitude

Long Beach seaport in SW Calif., on the Pacific: pop. 361,000

long distance a telephone exchange for calls to and from distant places —**long'-dis'tance** *adj., adv.*

lon·gev·i·ty (län jev'ə tē) *n.* [< L. *longus,* long + *aevum,* age] long life

long'-faced' *adj.* glum

long'hair' *adj.* [Colloq.] of intellectuals or intellectual tastes

long'hand' *n.* ordinary handwriting, as distinguished from shorthand

long'ing *n.* strong desire; yearning —*adj.* feeling or showing a yearning

Long Island island in SE N.Y., in the Atlantic south of Conn.

lon·gi·tude (län'jə tōōd') *n.* [< L. *longus,* long] distance east or west of the prime meridian, expressed in degrees or time

lon'gi·tu'di·nal (-tōōd'n əl) *adj.* **1.** of or in length **2.** running or placed lengthwise **3.** of longitude

long jump *Sports* a jump for distance, made either from a stationary position or with a running start

long'-lived' (-līvd', -livd') *adj.* having or tending to have a long life span

long play a long-playing record

long'-play'ing *adj.* designating or of a phonograph record having microgrooves and playing at 33⅓ revolutions per minute

long'-range' *adj.* reaching over a long distance or period of time

long·shore·man (lôn'shôr'mən) *n.,* *pl.* **-men** [< *alongshore* + MAN] a person who works on a waterfront loading and unloading ships

long shot [Colloq.] in betting, a choice that is little favored and, hence, carries great odds

long'-stand'ing *adj.* having continued for a long time

long'-suf'fer·ing *adj.* bearing trouble, etc. patiently for a long time

long'-term' *adj.* for or extending over a long time

long ton 2,240 pounds: see TON

long'-wind'ed (-win'did) *adj.* **1.** speaking or writing at great length **2.** tiresomely long

look (look) *vi.* [< OE. *locian*] **1.** to direct one's eyes in order to see **2.** to search **3.** to appear; seem **4.** to be facing in a specified direction —*vt.* **1.** to direct one's eyes on **2.** to have an appearance befitting [*to look the part*] —*n.* **1.** a looking; glance **2.** appearance; aspect **3.** [Colloq.] *a)* [*usually pl.*] appearance *b)* [*pl.*] personal appearance —*interj.* **1.** see! **2.** pay attention! —**look after** to take care of —**look down on** (or upon) to regard with contempt —**look for 1.** to expect **2.** to search for —**look forward to** to anticipate —**look in** (on) to pay a brief visit (to) —**look into** to investigate —**look out** to be careful —**look over** to examine —**look to 1.** to take care of **2.** to rely on —**look up 1.** to search for as in a reference book **2.** [Colloq.] to call on —**look up to** to admire —**look'er on**

look'er-on' *n., pl.* **look'ers-on'** an observer or spectator; onlooker

looking glass a (glass) mirror

look'out' *n.* **1.** a careful watching **2.** a place for keeping watch **3.** a person detailed to watch **4.** [Colloq.] concern

look'-see' *n.* [Slang] a quick look

loom¹ (lōōm) *n.* [< OE. *(ge)loma,* tool] a machine for weaving thread or yarn into cloth —*vt.* to weave on a loom

loom² (lōōm) *vi.* [< ?] **1.** to come into sight indistinctly, esp. threateningly **2.** to appear large and impending

loon¹ (lōōn) *n.* [< ON. *lomr*] a fish-eating, diving bird, similar to a duck

loon² (lōōn) *n.* [< ?] **1.** a clumsy, stupid person **2.** a crazy person

loon·y (lōō'nē) *adj.* **-i·er, -i·est** [< LUNATIC] [Slang] crazy; demented

loop (lōōp) *n.* [ME. *loup*] **1.** the figure made by a line, thread, etc. that curves back to cross itself **2.** anything forming this figure **3.** an intrauterine contraceptive device **4.** a segment of movie film or magnetic tape —*vt.* **1.** to make a loop of **2.** to fasten with a loop —*vi.* to form a loop or loops

loop'hole' *n.* [prob. < MDu. *lupen,* to peer + HOLE] **1.** a hole in a wall for looking or shooting through **2.** a means of evading an obligation, etc.

loose (lōōs) *adj.* [< ON. *lauss*] **1.** not confined or restrained; free **2.** not firmly fastened **3.** not tight or compact **4.** not precise; inexact **5.** sexually immoral **6.** [Colloq.] relaxed —*adv.* loosely —*vt.* **loosed, loos'ing 1.** to set free; unbind **2.** to make less tight, compact, etc. **3.** to relax **4.** to release (an arrow, etc.) —*vi.* to become loose —**on the loose** not confined; free —**loose'ly** *adv.* —**loose'ness** *n.*

loose ends unsettled details —**at loose ends** unsettled, idle, etc.

loose'-leaf' *adj.* having leaves, or sheets, that can easily be removed or replaced

loos·en (lōōs'n) *vt., vi.* to make or become loose or looser

loot (lōōt) *n.* [Hind. *lūt*] **1.** goods stolen or taken by force; plunder **2.** [Slang] money, presents, etc. —*vt., vi.* to plunder

lop¹ (läp) *vt.* **lopped, lop'ping** [< OE. *loppian*] **1.** to trim (a tree, etc.) by cutting off branches, etc. **2.** to remove as by cutting off —**lop'per** *n.*

lop² (läp) *vi.* **lopped, lop'ping** [prob. akin to LOB] to hang down loosely

lope (lōp) *vi.* **loped, lop'ing** [< ON. *hlaupa,* to leap] to move with a long, swinging stride —*n.* such a stride

lop·sid·ed (läp'sīd'id) *adj.* noticeably heavier, bigger, or lower on one side

lo·qua·cious (lō kwā'shəs) *adj.* [<

L. *loqui*, speak] very talkative —**lo-quac'i·ty** (-kwas'ə tē) *n.*

lord (lôrd) *n.* [< OE. *hlaf*, loaf + *weard*, keeper] 1. a ruler; master 2. the head of a feudal estate 3. [L-] *a)* God *b)* Jesus Christ 4. in Great Britain, a titled nobleman —**lord** it (over) to be overbearing (toward)

lord'ly *adj.* -**li·er**, -**li·est** 1. noble; magnificent 2. haughty —*adv.* in the manner of a lord

Lord's day Sunday

lord'ship' *n.* 1. the rank or authority of a lord 2. rule; dominion 3. a title used in speaking of or to a lord: with *his* or *your*

Lord's Prayer the prayer beginning *Our Father*: Matt. 6:9–13

lore (lôr) *n.* [< OE. *lar*] knowledge; learning, esp. of a traditional nature

lor·gnette (lôr nyet′) *n.* [Fr. < OFr. *lorgne*, squinting] eyeglasses, or opera glasses, attached to a handle

lorn (lôrn) *adj.* [ME. < *losen*, lose] [Archaic] forsaken, forlorn, etc.

lor·ry (lôr′ē, lär′-) *n.*, *pl.* -**ries** [prob. < dial. *lurry*, to pull] [Brit.] a motor truck

Los An·gel·es (lôs an′jə ləs, läs ang′gə ləs) seaport on the SW coast of Calif.: pop. 2,967,000

lose (lōōz) *vt.* **lost**, **los'ing** [< OE. *losian*] 1. to become unable to find [to lose one's keys] 2. to have taken from one by accident, death, removal, etc. 3. to fail to keep [to lose one's temper] 4. to fail to see, hear, or understand 5. to fail to have, get, etc. [to lose one's chance] 6. to fail to win 7. to cause the loss of 8. to wander from (one's way, etc.) 9. to squander —*vi.* to suffer (a) loss —**lose oneself** to become absorbed —**los'er** *n.*

loss (lôs) *n.* [< ? OE. *los*, ruin] 1. a losing or being lost 2. the damage, trouble, etc. caused by losing 3. the person, thing, or amount lost —**at a loss** (to) uncertain (how to)

lost (lôst) *pt. & pp.* of LOSE —*adj.* 1. ruined; destroyed 2. not to be found; missing 3. no longer held, seen, heard, etc. 4. not gained or won 5. having wandered astray 6. wasted

lot (lät) *n.* [< OE. *hlot*] 1. the deciding of a matter by chance, as by drawing counters 2. the decision thus arrived at 3. one's share by lot 4. fortune [his unhappy *lot*] 5. a plot of ground 6. a group of persons or things 7. [often *pl.*] [Colloq.] a great amount 8. [Colloq.] sort [he's a bad *lot*] —*adv.* very much: also **lots** —**draw** (or **cast**) **lots** to decide by lot

Lo·thar·i·o (lō ther′ē ō′) *n.*, *pl.* -**i·os** [< the rake in the play *The Fair Penitent*] a gay seducer of women

lo·tion (lō′shən) *n.* [< L. *lavare*, to wash] a liquid preparation used, as on the skin, for washing, healing, etc.

lot·ter·y (lät′ər ē) *n.*, *pl.* -**ies** [< MDu. *lot*, lot] 1. a game of chance in which people buy numbered tickets on

prizes, winners being chosen by lot 2. a drawing, event, etc. based on chance

lot·to (lät′ō) *n.* [It. < MDu. *lot*, lot] a game of chance played on cards with numbered squares: counters are placed on numbers chosen by lot

lo·tus (lōt′əs) *n.* [< Gr. *lōtos*] 1. *Gr. Legend* a plant whose fruit induced forgetfulness 2. any of several tropical waterlilies

lotus position an erect sitting posture in yoga, with the legs crossed close to the body

loud (loud) *adj.* [< OE. *hlud*] 1. strongly audible: said of sound 2. sounding with great intensity 3. noisy 4. emphatic [loud denials] 5. [Colloq.] *a)* flashy *b)* vulgar —*adv.* in a loud manner —**loud'ly** *adv.* —**loud'ness** *n.*

loud'mouthed' (-moutht′, -mouthd′) *adj.* talking in a loud, irritating voice

loud'speak'er *n.* a device for converting electrical energy to sound and amplifying it

Lou·is (lōō′ē) 1. XIV 1638–1715; king of France (1643–1715) 2. XV 1710–74; king of France (1715–74) 3. XVI 1754–93; king of France (1774–92): guillotined

Lou·i·si·an·a (loo wē′zē an′ə, lōō′ə zē-) Southern State of the U.S.: 48,523 sq. mi.; pop. 4,204,000; cap. Baton Rouge

Lou·is·ville (lōō′ē vil) city in N Ky.: pop. 298,000

lounge (lounj) *vi.* **lounged**, **loung'ing** [Scot. dial. < ? *lungis*, a laggard] 1. to move, sit, lie, etc. in a relaxed way 2. to spend time in idleness —*n.* 1. a room with comfortable furniture for lounging 2. a couch or sofa

louse (lous) *n.*, *pl.* **lice** [< OE. *lus*] 1. a small, wingless insect parasitic on man and other animals 2. any similar insect parasitic on plants 3. [Slang] a mean, contemptible person —**louse up** [Slang] to spoil; ruin

lous·y (lou′zē) *adj.* -**i·er**, -**i·est** 1. infested with lice 2. [Slang] *a)* disgusting *b)* poor; inferior *c)* well supplied (*with*) —**lous'i·ness** *n.*

lout (lout) *n.* [prob. < or akin to ME. *lutien*, lurk] a clumsy, stupid fellow —**lout'ish** *adj.*

lou·ver (lōō′vər) *n.* [< MDu. *love*, gallery] 1. an opening, window, etc. fitted with a series of sloping slats arranged so as to admit light and air but shed rain 2. any of these slats

Lou·vre (lōō′vrə, lōōv) national art museum in Paris

love (luv) *n.* [< OE. *lufu*] 1. strong affection or liking for someone or something 2. a passionate affection for one of the opposite sex 3. the object of such affection; sweetheart 4. *Tennis* a score of zero —*vt.*, *vi.* **loved**, **lov'ing** to feel love (for) —**in love** feeling love —**make love** 1. to woo, embrace, etc. 2. to have sexual intercourse —**lov'a·ble**, **love'a·ble** *adj.* —**love'less** *adj.*

---

love'lorn' *adj.* pining from love

love'ly *adj.* -li·er, -li·est 1. beautiful 2. [Colloq.] highly enjoyable —**love'-li·ness** *n.*

lov·er (luv'ər) *n.* one who loves; specif., *a*) sweetheart *b*) a paramour *c*) [*pl.*] a couple in love with each other *d*) a devotee, as of music

love seat a small sofa for two people

lov'ing *adj.* feeling or expressing love —**lov'ing·ly** *adv.*

loving cup a large drinking cup with two handles, often given as a prize

low¹ (lō) *adj.* [< ON. *lagr*] 1. not high or tall 2. below the normal level [*low ground*] 3. shallow 4. less in size, degree, etc. than usual [*low speed*] 5. deep in pitch 6. depressed in spirits 7. not of high rank; humble 8. vulgar; coarse 9. poor; inferior 10. not loud —*adv.* in or to a low level, degree, etc. —*n.* 1. a low level, degree, etc. 2. an arrangement of gears giving the lowest speed and greatest power —**lay low to** overcome or kill —**lie low to** keep oneself hidden —**low'ness** *n.*

low² (lō) *vi., n.* [< OE. *hlowan*] same as MOO

low'born' *adj.* of humble birth

low'boy' *n.* a chest of drawers mounted on short legs

low'brow' *n.* [Colloq.] one considered to lack cultivated tastes

Low Countries the Netherlands, Belgium, & Luxembourg

low-down (lō'doun'; *for adj.* -doun') *n.* [Slang] the true, pertinent facts (with *the*) —*adj.* [Colloq.] mean; contemptible

low·er¹ (lō'ər) *adj. compar.* of LOW 1. below in place, rank, etc. 2. less in amount, degree, etc. —*vt.* 1. to let or put down [to *lower* a window] 2. to reduce in height, amount, etc. 3. to bring down in respect, etc. —*vi.* to become lower

low·er² (lou'ər) *vi.* [ME. *louren*] 1. to scowl or frown 2. to appear black and threatening, as the sky —**low'er·ing** *adj.* —**low'er·ing·ly** *adv.*

lower case small-letter type used in printing, as distinguished from capital letters —**low'er-case'** *adj.*

low frequency any radio frequency between 30 and 300 kilohertz

Low German 1. the vernacular dialects of N Germany 2. the branch of Germanic languages including English, Dutch, Flemish, etc.

low'-grade' *adj.* of low quality, degree, etc.

low'-key' *adj.* of low intensity, tone, etc.; subdued: also **low'-keyed'**

low'land' *n.* land below the level of the surrounding land —**the Lowlands** lowlands of SC Scotland

low'ly *adj.* -li·er, -li·est 1. of low position or rank 2. humble; meek —*adv.* humbly —**low'li·ness** *n.*

low'-mind'ed *adj.* having or showing a coarse, vulgar mind

low profile a barely noticeable presence or concealed activity

low'-spir'it·ed *adj.* sad; melancholy

low tide the lowest level reached by the ebbing tide

lox¹ (läks) *n.* [< Yid. < G. *lachs*, salmon] a kind of smoked salmon

lox² (läks) *n.* liquid oxygen, used in a fuel mixture for rockets

loy·al (loi'əl) *adj.* [see LEGAL] 1. faithful to one's country, friends, ideals, etc. 2. showing such faithfulness —**loy'al·ly** *adv.* —**loy'al·ty** *n.*, *pl.* -ties

loy'al·ist *n.* one who supports the government during a revolt

loz·enge (läz'ənj) *n.* [< OFr. *losenge*] a cough drop, candy, etc., orig. diamond-shaped

LP [*L(ong) P(laying)*] *a trademark for* a long-playing record

LPN, L.P.N. Licensed Practical Nurse

Lr *Chem.* lawrencium

LSD [*l(y)s(ergic acid) d(iethylamide)*] a chemical compound used in the study of mental disorders and as a psychedelic drug

Lt. Lieutenant

Ltd., ltd. limited

lu·au (lōō ou') *n.* a Hawaiian feast

lub·ber (lub'ər) *n.* [< ME. *lobbe*, heavy] 1. a big, slow, clumsy person 2. an inexperienced, clumsy sailor

Lub·bock (lub'ək) city in NW Tex.; pop. 174,000

lube (lōōb) *n.* 1. a lubricating oil for machinery: also **lube oil** 2. [Colloq.] a lubrication

lu·bri·cant (lōō'brə kənt) *adj.* reducing friction by providing a smooth surface film over parts coming into contact —*n.* a lubricant oil, etc.

lu'bri·cate' (-kāt') *vt.* -cat'ed, -cat'ing [< L. *lubricus*, smooth] 1. to make slippery or smooth 2. to apply a lubricant to (machinery, etc.) —**lu'bri·ca'tion** *n.* —**lu'bri·ca'tor** *n.*

lu·cid (lōō'sid) *adj.* [< L. *lucere*, shine] 1. shining 2. transparent 3. sane 4. clear; readily understood —**lu·cid'i·ty** *n.* —**lu'cid·ly** *adv.*

Lu·ci·fer (lōō'sə fər) Satan

luck (luk) *n.* [prob. < MDu. *gelucke*] 1. the seemingly chance happening of events which affect one; fortune; lot 2. good fortune —**luck out** [Colloq.] to be lucky —**luck'less** *adj.*

luck'y *adj.* -i·er, -i·est 1. having good luck 2. resulting fortunately 3. believed to bring good luck —**luck'i·ly** *adv.* —**luck'i·ness** *n.*

lu·cra·tive (lōō'krə tiv) *adj.* [< L. *lucrum*, riches] producing wealth or profit; profitable

lu·cre (lōō'kər) *n.* [< L. *lucrum*] riches; money: chiefly derogatory

lu·cu·brate (lōō'kyoo brāt') *vi.* -brat'ed, -brat'ing [< L. *lucubrare*, work by candlelight] to work, study, or write laboriously, esp. late at night —**lu'cu·bra'tion** *n.*

lu·dic (lōō'dik) *adj.* [see ff.] of or with playful behavior

lu·di·crous (lōō'di krəs) *adj.* [< L. *ludus*, a game] causing laughter because absurd or ridiculous —**lu'di·crous·ly** *adv.* —**lu'di·crous·ness** *n.*

luff (luf) *vi.* [< ODu. *loef*, windward side (of a ship)] to turn the bow of a ship toward the wind

lug (lug) *vt.* **lugged, lug′ging** [prob. < Scand.] to carry or drag with effort —*n.* **1.** an earlike projection by which a thing is held or supported **2.** a heavy nut for securing a wheel to an axle

lug·gage (lug′ij) *n.* [< prec.] suitcases, trunks, etc.: baggage

lu·gu·bri·ous (loo goo′brē əs) *adj.* [< L. *lugere*, mourn] very sad or mournful, esp. in an exaggerated way —lu·gu′bri·ous·ly *adv.* —lu·gu′bri·ous·ness *n.*

Luke (look) *Bible* **1.** an early Christian, the reputed author of the third Gospel **2.** this book

luke·warm (look′wôrm′) *adj.* [< ME. *luke*, tepid + *warm*, warm] **1.** barely warm; tepid **2.** lacking enthusiasm —luke′warm′ly *adv.* —luke′warm′ness *n.*

lull (lul) *vt.* [ME. *lullen*] **1.** to calm by gentle sound or motion **2.** to bring into a specified condition by soothing and reassuring —*vi.* to become calm —*n.* a short period of calm

lull′a·by′ (-ə bī′) *n., pl.* **-bies′** a song for lulling a baby to sleep

lum·ba·go (lum bā′gō) *n.* [L. < *lumbus*, loin] pain in the lower back

lum·bar (lum′bər, -bär) *adj.* [< L. *lumbus*, loin] of or near the loins

lum·ber¹ (lum′bər) *n.* [< ? pawnbrokers of *Lombardy*, Italy; hence, stored articles] **1.** discarded household articles, furniture, etc. **2.** timber sawed into boards, etc. —*vi.* to cut down timber and saw it into lumber —lum′ber·ing *n.*

lum·ber² (lum′bər) *vi.* [< ? Scand.] to move heavily and noisily —lum′ber·ing *adj.*

lum·ber·jack (lum′bər jak′) *n.* a man whose work is cutting down timber and preparing it for the sawmill

lum′ber·man (-mən) *n., pl.* **-men** one who deals in lumber

lu·mi·nar·y (loo′mə ner′ē) *n., pl.* **-ies** [< L. *lumen*, light] **1.** a body that gives off light, such as the sun **2.** a famous or notable person

lu·mi·nes·cence (loo′mə nes′'ns) *n.* [< L. *lumen*, LIGHT¹ + -ESCENCE] the giving off of light without heat, as in fluorescence or phosphorescence — lu′mi·nes′cent *adj.*

lu·mi·nous (loo′mə nəs) *adj.* [< L. *lumen*, light] **1.** giving off light; bright **2.** clear; readily understood —lu′mi·nos′i·ty (-näs′ə tē) *n.*

lum·mox (lum′əks) *n.* [< ?] [Colloq.] a clumsy, stupid person

lump¹ (lump) *n.* [ME. *lompe*] **1.** an indefinitely shaped mass of something **2.** a swelling **3.** [*pl.*] [Colloq.] hard blows, criticism, etc. —*adj.* in a lump or lumps —*vt.* **1.** to put together in a lump or lumps **2.** to treat or deal with in a mass —*vi.* to become lumpy —lump′i·ness *n.* —lump′y *adj.*

lump² (lump) *vt.* [Early ModE., look sour] [Colloq.] to have to put up with (something disagreeable)

lump sum a gross, or total, sum paid at one time

lu·na·cy (loo′nə sē) *n., pl.* **-cies** [< LUNATIC] **1.** insanity **2.** utter folly

lu·nar (loo′nər) *adj.* [< L. *luna*, moon] of or like the moon

lu·na·tic (loo′nə tik) *adj.* [< L. *luna*, the moon] **1.** insane or for the insane **2.** utterly foolish —*n.* an insane person

lunch (lunch) *n.* [< ? Sp. *lonja*, slice of ham] a light meal; esp., the midday meal between breakfast and dinner —*vi.* to eat lunch

lunch·eon (lun′chən) *n.* a lunch; esp., a formal lunch

lunch′eon·ette′ (-chə net′) *n.* a small restaurant serving light lunches

luncheon meat meat processed in loaves, sausages, etc. and ready to eat

lung (lung) *n.* [OE. *lungen*] either of the two spongelike breathing organs in the thorax of vertebrates

lunge (lunj) *n.* [< Fr. *allonger*, lengthen] **1.** a sudden thrust as with a sword **2.** a sudden plunge forward —*vi., vt.* **lunged, lung′ing** to move, or cause to move, with a lunge

lung·fish (lung′fish′) *n., pl.:* see FISH any of various fishes having lungs as well as gills

lunk·head (lunk′hed′) *n.* [prob. echoic alt. of LUMP¹ + HEAD] [Colloq.] a stupid person: also **lunk**

lu·pine (loo′pin) *adj.* [< L. *lupus*, wolf] of or like a wolf —*n.* a plant with long spikes of white, rose, or blue flowers

lu·pus (loo′pəs) *n.* [< L. wolf] any of various diseases with skin lesions

lurch¹ (lurch) *vi.* [< ?] **1.** to pitch or sway suddenly to one side **2.** to stagger —*n.* a lurching movement

lurch² (lurch) *n.* [prob. < OFr. *lourche*, duped] a difficult situation: only in **leave in the lurch**

lure (loor) *n.* [< OFr. *loirre*] **1.** anything that tempts or entices **2.** a bait used in fishing —*vt.* **lured, lur′ing** to attract; tempt; entice

lu·rid (loor′id) *adj.* [L. *luridus*, ghastly] **1.** glowing through a haze, as flames enveloped by smoke **2.** shocking; sensational —lu′rid·ness *n.*

lurk (lurk) *vi.* [ME. *lurken*] **1.** to stay hidden, ready to attack, etc. **2.** to move furtively

lus·cious (lush′əs) *adj.* [ME. *lucius*] **1.** highly gratifying to taste or smell; delicious **2.** delighting any of the senses —lus′cious·ness *n.*

lush¹ (lush) *adj.* [< ? OFr. *lasche*, lax] **1.** of or showing luxuriant growth **2.** rich, abundant, extravagant, etc.

lush² (lush) *n.* [Slang] an alcoholic

lust (lust) *n.* [OE., pleasure] **1.** bodily appetite; esp., excessive sexual desire **2.** overmastering desire *[a lust for power]* —*vi.* to feel an intense desire —lust′ful *adj.* —lust′ful·ly *adv.*

lus·ter (lus′tər) *n.* [< L. *lustrare*, illumine] **1.** gloss; sheen **2.** brightness; radiance **3.** brilliant beauty or

fame; glory Also, chiefly Brit., **lustre**
lus′trous *adj.* having luster; shiny
lust·y (lus′tē) *adj.* **-i·er, -i·est** full of vigor; robust —**lust′i·ly** *adv.* — **lust′i·ness** *n.*
lute (lōōt) *n.* [ult. < Ar. *al′ūd*, the wood] an old stringed instrument like the guitar, with a rounded body

LUTE

Lu·ther (lōō′thər), **Martin** 1483-1546; Ger. Reformation leader
Lu′ther·an *adj.* of the Protestant denomination founded by Luther —*n.* a member of a Lutheran Church
lut·ist (lōōt′ist) *n.* a lute player: also **lu·ta·nist** (lōōt′'n ist)
Lux·em·bourg (luk′səm bʉrg′) grand duchy in W Europe, north of France: 998 sq. mi.; pop. 335,000
lux·u·ri·ant (lug zhoor′ē ənt) *adj.* [see LUXURY] **1.** growing with vigor and in abundance **2.** having rich ornamentation, etc.—**lux·u′ri·ance** *n.*
lux·u′ri·ate′ (-āt′) *vi.* **-at′ed, -at′ing 1.** to live in great luxury **2.** to revel (*in*) —**lux·u′ri·a′tion** *n.*
lux·u′ri·ous *adj.* **1.** fond of or indulging in luxury **2.** constituting luxury; rich, comfortable, etc. —**lux·ur′i·ous·ly** *adv.*
lux·u·ry (luk′shə rē, lug′zhə-) *n.,* *pl.* **-ries** [< L. *luxus*] **1.** the enjoyment of the best and most costly things **2.** anything contributing to such enjoyment, usually not necessary
Lu·zon (lōō zän′) main island of the Philippines
-ly (lē) [< OE. *-lic*] *a suffix meaning:* **1.** like or characteristic of [*manly*] **2.** in a (specified) manner, to a (specified) extent or direction, in or at a (specified) time or place [*harshly, outwardly, hourly*] **3.** in sequence [*thirdly*] **4.** happening (once) every (specified period) [*monthly*]
ly·ce·um (lī sē′əm, lī′sē-) *n.* [< Gr. *Lykeion,* grove at Athens where Aristotle taught] **1.** a lecture hall **2.** an organization providing lectures, etc.

lye (lī) *n.* [OE. *leag*] any strongly alkaline substance, used in cleaning and in making soap·
ly·ing¹ (lī′iŋ) *prp.* of LIE¹·
ly·ing² (lī′iŋ) *prp.* of LIE² —*adj.* false; not truthful —*n.* the telling of a lie or lies
ly′ing-in′ *n.* confinement in childbirth —*adj.* of or for childbirth
lymph (limf) *n.* [L. *lympha,* spring water] a clear, yellowish body fluid resembling blood plasma, found in intercellular spaces and in the lymphatic vessels
lym·phat·ic (lim fat′ik) *adj.* **1.** of or containing lymph **2.** sluggish
lymph node any of the compact structures lying in groups along the course of the lymphatic vessels
lymph·oid (lim′foid) *adj.* of or like lymph or tissue of the lymph nodes
lynch (linch) *vt.* [< W. *Lynch,* vigilante in Va. in 1780] to murder (an accused person) by mob action, without lawful trial, as by hanging
lynx (liŋks) *n.* [< Gr. *lynx*] a wildcat found throughout the N Hemisphere, having a short tail and tufted ears·
lynx′-eyed′ (-īd′) *adj.* keen-sighted
Lyon (lyōn) city in EC France: pop. 529,000
ly·on·naise (lī′ə nāz′) *adj.* [Fr.] prepared with sliced, fried onions
lyre (līr) *n.* [< Gr. *lyra*] a small stringed instrument of the harp family, used by the ancient Greeks
lyr·ic (lir′ik) *adj.* [< Gr. *lyrikos*] **1.** suitable for singing; specif., designating or of poetry expressing the poet's personal emotion **2.** of or having a high voice with a light, flexible quality [*a lyric tenor*] —*n.* **1.** a lyric poem **2.** [*usually pl.*] the words of a song
lyr′i·cal *adj.* **1.** lyric **2.** expressing rapture or enthusiasm
lyr·i·cist (lir′ə sist) *n.* a writer of lyrics, esp. for popular songs
ly·ser·gic acid (lī sʉr′jik) *see* LSD
-ly·sis (lə sis) [< Gr. *lysis,* a loosening] *a combining form meaning* a loosing, dissolution, dissolving, destruction [*electrolysis, paralysis*]
-lyte (līt) [see prec.] *a combining form meaning* a substance undergoing decomposition [*electrolyte*]

M

M, m (em) *n.,* *pl.* **M's, m's** the 13th letter of the English alphabet
M (em) *n.* **1.** a Roman numeral for 1,000 **2.** *symbol for* mass
M. 1. Medieval **2.** Monday **3.** *pl.* **MM.** Monsieur
M., m. 1. male **2.** married **3.** masculine **4.** mile(s) **5.** minute(s) **6.** month **7.** [L. *meridies*] noon
m., m meter(s)
ma (mä) *n.* [Colloq.] mother
MA Massachusetts
MA, M.A. Master of Arts

ma'am (mam, mäm, məm) *n.* [Colloq.] madam; used in direct address
ma·ca·bre (mə käb′rə, mə käb′) *adj.* [< OFr. (*danse*) *Macabré,* (dance) of death] gruesome; grim and horrible
mac·ad·am (mə kad′əm) *n.* [< J. L. *McAdam* (1756-1836), Scot. engineer] small broken stones, or a road made by rolling successive layers of these, often with tar or asphalt —**mac·ad′am·ize′** *vt.* **-ized′, -iz′ing**
Ma·cao (mə kou′) Port. territory in SE China, near Hong Kong

mac·a·ro·ni (mak′ə rō′nē) *n.* [It. *maccaroni*, ult. < Gr. *makar*, blessed] pasta in the form of tubes, etc.

mac·a·roon (mak′ə rōōn′) *n.* [see prec.] a small, sweet cookie made with crushed almonds or coconut

ma·caw (mə kô′) *n.* [prob. < Braz. native name] a large, bright-colored parrot of Central and South America

Mac·beth (mək beth′) the title hero of a tragedy by Shakespeare.

Mac·ca·bees (mak′ə bēz′) a family of Jewish patriots who headed a successful revolt against Syria (175–164 B.C.)

Mace (mās) [< ff.] a trademark for a combined tear gas and nerve gas

mace¹ (mās) *n.* [OFr. *masse*] 1. a heavy, spiked war club, used in the Middle Ages 2. a staff used as a symbol of authority by certain officials

mace² (mās) *n.* [< ML. *macis*] a spice made from the husk of the nutmeg

Mac·e·do·ni·a (mas′ə dō′nē ə) ancient kingdom in SE Europe —**Mac′-e·do′ni·an** *adj., n.*

mac·er·ate (mas′ə rāt′) *vt.* -at′ed, -at′ing [< L. *macerare*, soften] 1. to soften or separate the parts of by soaking in liquid 2. loosely, to tear, chop, etc. into bits —**mac′er·a′tion** *n.*

mach. 1. machine 2. machinery

ma·che·te (mə shet′ē, -chet′ē) *n.* [Sp. < L. *marcus*, hammer] a large knife used for cutting sugar cane, underbrush, etc., esp. in S. America

Mach·i·a·vel·li·an (mak′ē ə vel′ē ən) *adj.* [< N. *Machiavelli*, (1469–1527), It. statesman] crafty; deceitful

mach·i·na·tion (mak′ə nā′shən) *n.* [< L. *machinari*, to plot] a plot or scheme, esp. an evil one

ma·chine (mə shēn′) *n.* [< Gr. *mēchos*, contrivance] 1. a vehicle, as an automobile: an old term 2. a structure consisting of a framework with various moving parts, for doing some kind of work 3. an organization functioning like a machine 4. the controlling group in a political party 5. a device, as the lever, etc., that transmits, or changes the application of, energy —*adj.* 1. of machines 2. done by machinery —*vt.* -chined′, -chin′-ing to shape, etc. by machinery

machine gun an automatic gun, firing a rapid stream of bullets

machine language the system of signs, symbols, etc. used by a computer

ma·chin·er·y (mə shēn′ər ē, -shēn′rē) *n., pl.* -ies 1. machines collectively 2. the working parts of a machine 3. the means for keeping something going

ma·chin′ist *n.* one who makes, repairs, or operates machinery

‡**ma·chis·mo** (mä chēz′mō) *n.* [Sp. < *macho*, masculine] strong or assertive masculinity; virility

Mach (number) (mäk) [< E. *Mach* (1838–1916), Austrian physicist] a number indicating the ratio of an object's speed to the speed of sound

ma·cho (mä′chō) *adj.* [Sp., masculine] masculine, virile, courageous, etc.

mack·er·el (mak′ər əl) *n., pl.* -el, -els [< OFr. *makerel*] an edible fish of the North Atlantic

Mack·i·naw coat (mak′ə nô′) [< *Mackinac* Is. in N Lake Huron] a short, heavy, double-breasted coat, usually plaid: also **mackinaw** *n.*

mack·in·tosh (mak′in täsh′) *n.* [< C. *Macintosh*, 19th-c. Scot. inventor] a raincoat of rubberized cloth

Ma·con (mā′kən) city in C Ga.: pop. 122,000

mac·ra·mé (mak′rə mā′) *n.* [Fr., ult. < Ar. *miqramah*, a veil] coarse string or lace knotted in designs

macro- [< Gr. *makros*, long] a combining form meaning long, large

mac·ro·bi·ot·ics (mak′rō bī ät′iks) *n.pl.* [with sing. v.] [< prec. & Gr. *bios*, life] the art of prolonging life, as by diet —**mac′ro·bi·ot′ic** *adj.*

mac·ro·cosm (mak′rə käz′m) *n.* [see MACRO- & COSMOS] 1. the universe 2. any large, complex entity

ma·cron (mā′krən) *n.* [< Gr. *makros*, long] a mark (¯) placed over a vowel to indicate its pronunciation

mad (mad) *adj.* **mad′der, mad′dest** [< OE. (ge)*mædan*, make mad] 1. mentally ill; insane 2. frantic [mad with fear] 3. foolish and rash 4. infatuated [she's mad about him] 5. wildly gay 6. having rabies [a mad dog] 7. angry —*n.* an angry mood —**mad′ly** *adv.* —**mad′ness** *n.*

Mad·a·gas·car (mad′ə gas′kar) an island country off the SE coast of Africa: 229,000 sq. mi.; pop. 6,750,000.

mad·am (mad′əm) *n., pl.* **-ams**; for 1, usually **mes·dames** (mā däm′) [< Fr., orig. *ma dame*, my lady] 1. a woman; lady: a polite term of address 2. a woman in charge of a brothel

mad·ame (mad′əm; Fr. mä däm′) *n., pl.* **mes·dames** (mā däm′) [Fr.] a married woman: equivalent to *Mrs.*

mad′cap′ *n.* [MAD + CAP, fig. for head] a reckless, impulsive person —*adj.* reckless and impulsive

mad·den (mad′n) *vt., vi.* to make or become insane, angry, or wildly excited —**mad′den·ing** *adj.*

mad·der (mad′ər) *n.* [OE. *mædere*] 1. any of various plants; esp., a vine with yellow flowers and a red root 2. a red dye made from the root

made (mād) *pt. & pp.* of MAKE

ma·de·moi·selle (mad′ə mə zel′; Fr. mäd mwä zel′) *n., pl.* **mesde·moi·selles** (mäd mwä zel′) [Fr. < *ma*, my + *demoiselle*, young lady] an unmarried woman or girl: title equivalent to *Miss*

made′-to-or′der *adj.* made to conform to the customer's specifications

made′-up′ *adj.* 1. put together 2. invented; false [a made-up story] 3. with cosmetics applied

mad′house′ *n.* 1. an insane asylum 2. any place of turmoil, noise, etc.

Mad·i·son (mad′i s'n) capital of Wis.: pop. 173,000

Madison, James 1751-1836; 4th president of the U.S. (1809-17)

mad′man′ n., pl. **-men**′ an insane person; lunatic —**mad′wom**′an n.fem., pl. **-wom**′en

Ma·don·na (mə dän′ə) [It. < ma, my + donna, lady] Mary, mother of Jesus —n. a picture or statue of Mary

Ma·dras (mə dras′, -dräs′) seaport on SE coast of India: pop. 1,729,000

ma·dras (mad′rəs, mə dras′) n. [< prec.] a fine, firm cotton cloth, usually striped or plaid

Ma·drid (mə drid′) capital of Spain, in the C part: pop. 2,559,000

mad·ri·gal (mad′ri gəl) n. [< It.] a part song, without accompaniment, popular in the 15th to 17th c.

mael·strom (māl′strəm) n. [< Du. malen, grind + stroom, a stream] 1. a large or violent whirlpool 2. an agitated state of mind, affairs, etc.

ma·es·tro (mīs′trō, mä es′-) n., pl. **-tros, -tri** (-trē) [It. < L. magister, master] a master in any art; esp., a great composer or conductor of music

Ma·fi·a, Maf·fi·a (mä′fē ə) n. [It.] an alleged secret society of criminals

mag. 1. magazine 2. magnetism

mag·a·zine (mag′ə zēn′) n. [< Ar. makhzan, granary] 1. a warehouse or military supply depot 2. a space in which explosives are stored, as in a fort 3. a supply chamber, as in a rifle, camera, etc. 4. a periodical publication containing stories, articles, etc.

Ma·gel·lan (mə jel′ən), **Ferdinand** 1480?-1521; Port. navigator

ma·gen·ta (mə jen′tə) n. [< Magenta, town in Italy] 1. a purplish-red dye 2. purplish red —adj. purplish-red

mag·got (mag′ət) n. [ME. magotte] a wormlike larva, as of the housefly —**mag′got·y** adj.

Ma·gi (mā′jī) n.pl., sing. **-gus** (-gəs) [< OPer. magus, magician] Douay Bible the wise men who came bearing gifts to the infant Jesus

mag·ic (maj′ik) n. [< Gr. magikos, of the Magi] 1. the use of charms, spells, etc. in seeking or pretending to control events 2. any mysterious power [the magic of love] 3. the art of producing illusions by sleight of hand, etc. —adj. 1. of, produced by, or using magic 2. producing extraordinary results, as if by magic —**mag′i·cal** adj. —**mag′i·cal·ly** adv.

ma·gi·cian (mə jish′ən) n. [< OFr. magicien] an expert in magic

mag·is·te·ri·al (maj′is tir′ē əl) adj. 1. of or suitable for a magistrate 2. authoritative

mag·is·trate (maj′is trāt) n. [< L. magister, master] 1. a civil officer empowered to administer the law 2. a minor official, as a justice of the peace

Mag·na Char·ta (or **Car·ta**) (mag′nə kär′tə) [ML., great charter] the charter, granted in 1215, that guaranteed certain civil and political liberties to the English people

mag·nan·i·mous (mag nan′ə məs, adj. [< L. magnus, great + animus)

soul] generous in overlooking injury or insult; rising above pettiness; noble —**mag′na·nim′i·ty** (-nə nim′ə tē) n. —**mag·nan′i·mous·ly** adv.

mag·nate (mag′nāt) n. [< L. magnus, great] a very influential person

mag·ne·sia (mag nē′zhə, -shə) n. [< LGr. Magnèsia, district in ancient Greece] a white powder, an oxide of magnesium, used as a laxative

mag·ne·si·um (-zē əm, -zhē-) n. [< prec.] a light metallic chemical element

mag·net (mag′nit) n. [see MAGNESIA] 1. any piece of iron, steel, or lodestone that has the property of attracting iron or steel 2. anything that attracts

mag·net·ic (mag net′ik) adj. 1. having the properties of a magnet 2. of, producing, or caused by magnetism 3. of the earth's magnetism 4. that can be magnetized 5. powerfully attractive —**mag·net′i·cal·ly** adv.

magnetic field any space in which there is an appreciable magnetic force

magnetic tape a thin plastic ribbon with a magnetized coating for recording sound, digital computer data, etc.

mag·net·ism (mag′nə tiz′m) n. 1. the property, quality, or condition of being magnetic 2. the force to which this is due 3. personal charm

mag′net·ite′ (-tīt′) n. [< G.] a black iron oxide, an important iron ore

mag′net·ize′ (-tīz′) vt. **-ized′, -iz′ing** 1. to give magnetic properties to (steel, iron, etc.) 2. to charm (a person) —**mag′net·i·za′tion** n.

mag·ne·to (mag nēt′ō) n., pl. **-tos** a small generator in which one or more permanent magnets produce the magnetic field

mag·ne·tom·e·ter (mag′nə täm′ə tər) n. an instrument for measuring magnetic forces: one form is used to check airline passengers for concealed metal weapons

magnet school a public school offering new and special courses to attract students from a broad urban area so as to promote desegregation

mag·nif·i·cent (mag nif′ə s'nt) adj. [< L. magnus, great + facere, do] 1. splendid, stately, or sumptuous, as in form 2. exalted: said of ideas, etc. 3. [Colloq.] excellent —**mag·nif′i·cence** n. —**mag·nif′i·cent·ly** adv.

mag·ni·fy (mag′nə fī′) vt., vi. **-fied′, -fy′ing** [see prec.] 1. to exaggerate 2. to increase the apparent size of (an object), as (with) a lens 3. [Archaic] to praise —**mag′ni·fi·ca′tion** n. —**mag′ni·fi′er** n.

mag·ni·tude (mag′nə tōōd′) n. [< L. magnus, great] 1. greatness of size, extent, etc. 2. a) size b) loudness (of sound) c) importance 3. the degree of brightness of a fixed star

mag·no·li·a (mag nōl′ē ə, -nōl′yə) n. [< P. Magnol (1638-1715), Fr. botanist] a tree with large, fragrant flowers of white, pink, or purple

mag·num (mag′nəm) n. [< L. magnus, great] a wine bottle holding about 2/5 of a gallon

†**mag·num o·pus** (mag′nəm ō′pəs) [L.] a great work; masterpiece

mag·pie (mag′pī′) *n.* [< *Mag*, dim. of *Margaret* + *pie*, magpie] **1.** a noisy, black-and-white bird of the crow family **2.** one who chatters

Mag·yar (mag′yär) *n.* **1.** a member of the main ethnic group in Hungary **2.** the Hungarian language

ma·ha·ra·jah, ma·ha·ra·ja (mä′hə rä′jə) *n.* [< Sans. *mahā*, great + *rājā*, king] in India, a prince; formerly the ruler of a native state —**ma′ha·ra′ni, ma′ha·ra′nee** (-nē) *n.fem.*

ma·ha·ri·shi (mä′hä rish′ē) *n.* [Hindi < *mahā*, great + *ṛshi*, sage] a Hindu teacher of mysticism and meditation

ma·hat·ma (mə hat′mə, -hät′-) *n.* [< Sans. *mahā*, great + *ātman*, soul] *Buddhism* any of a class of wise and holy persons held in special regard

mah-jongg, mah·jong (mä′jôṅ′) *n.* [< Chin. *ma-ch'iao*, sparrow (a figure on one of the tiles)] a game of Chinese origin, played with small tiles

ma·hog·a·ny (mə häg′ə nē, -hôg′-) *n., pl.* **-nies** [< ?] **1.** *a*) the reddish-brown wood of a tropical American tree *b*) this tree **2.** reddish brown

Ma·hom·et (mə häm′it) *same as* MOHAMMED

ma·hout (mə hout′) *n.* [Hind. < Sans.] in India, an elephant driver

maid (mād) *n.* **1.** *same as* MAIDEN **2.** a girl or woman servant

maid·en (-'n) *n.* [OE. *mægden*] a girl or young unmarried woman —*adj.* **1.** of or for a maiden **2.** unmarried or virgin **3.** untried **4.** first [a *maiden* voyage] —**maid′en·hood′** *n.* —**maid′en·ly** *adj., adv.*

maid′en·hair′ *n.* a delicate fern

maid′en·head′ *n.* the hymen

maiden name the surname that a woman had when not yet married

maid of honor an unmarried woman acting as chief attendant to a bride

maid′ser′vant *n.* a female servant

mail[1] (māl) *n.* [< OHG. *malaha*, wallet] **1.** letters, packages, etc. transported and delivered by the post office **2.** a postal system —*adj.* of mail —*vt.* to send by mail —**mail′er** *n.*

mail[2] (māl) *n.* [< L. *macula*, mesh of a net] a body armor made of small metal rings, scales, etc. —**mailed** *adj.*

mail′box′ *n.* a box into which mail is delivered or a box for depositing outgoing mail   Also **mail box**

mail′man′ *n., pl.* **-men′** a man who carries and delivers mail

mail order an order for goods to be sent by mail —**mail′-or′der** *adj.*

maim (mām) *vt.* [OFr. *mahaigner*] to cripple; mutilate

main (mān) *n.* [OE. *mægen*, strength] **1.** a principal pipe in a distributing system for water, gas, etc. **2.** [Poet.] the ocean —*adj.* chief in size, importance, etc.; principal —**by main**

COAT OF MAIL

force (or **strength**) by sheer force (or strength) —**in the main** mostly; chiefly —**with might and main** with all one's strength

main clause a clause that can function as a complete sentence

main drag [Slang] the principal street of a city or town

Maine (mān) New England State of the U.S.: 33,215 sq. mi.; pop. 1,125,000; cap. Augusta

main·land (mān′land′, -lənd) *n.* the principal land mass of a continent, as distinguished from nearby islands

main′line′ *n.* the principal road, course, etc. —*vt.* **-lined′, -lin′ing** [Slang] to inject (a narcotic drug) directly into a large vein

main′ly *adv.* chiefly; principally

main′mast (-məst, -mast′) *n.* the principal mast of a vessel

main′sail (-s'l, -sāl′) *n.* the principal sail of a vessel, set from the mainmast

main′spring′ *n.* **1.** the principal spring in a clock, watch, etc. **2.** the chief motive, incentive, etc.

main′stay′ (-stā′) *n.* **1.** the supporting line extending forward from the mainmast **2.** a chief support

main′stream′ (-strēm′) *n.* a major trend or line of thought, action, etc. —*vt.* to cause to undergo mainstreaming

main′stream′ing *n.* the placement of disabled people into regular school classes, work places, etc.

main·tain (mān tān′) *vt.* [< L. *manu tenere*, hold in the hand] **1.** to keep or keep up; carry on **2.** to keep in continuance or in a certain state, as of repair **3.** to defend **4.** to affirm or assert **5.** to support by supplying what is needed —**main·tain′a·ble** *adj.*

main·te·nance (mān′t'n əns) *n.* a maintaining or being maintained

mai tai (mī′ tī′) [Tahitian] a cocktail of rum, fruit juices, etc.

maî·tre d'hô·tel (me′tr' dô tel′) [Fr.] a headwaiter or steward: also [Colloq.] **mai·tre d'** (māt′ər dē′)

maize (māz) *n.* [< WInd. *mahiz*] **1.** *same as* CORN[1] (*n.* 2) **2.** yellow

Maj, Major

ma·jes·tic (mə jes′tik) *adj.* grand; stately —**ma·jes′ti·cal·ly** *adv.*

maj·es·ty (maj′is tē) *n., pl.* **-ties** [< L. *magnus*, great] **1.** [M-] a title used in speaking to or of a sovereign: with *His, Her,* or *Your* **2.** grandeur

ma·jol·i·ca (mə jäl′i kə) *n.* [It.] Italian glazed pottery

ma·jor (mā′jər) *adj.* [L., compar. of *magnus*, great] **1.** greater in size, importance, amount, etc. **2.** *Music* higher than the corresponding minor by a half tone —*vi. Educ.* to specialize (*in* a field of study) —*n.* **1.** *U.S. Mil.* an officer ranking just above a captain **2.** *Educ.* a principal field of study

ma′jor-do′mo (-dō′mō) *n., pl.* **-mos** [< L. *major*, greater + *domus*, house] a man in charge of a great household

major general *pl.* **major generals**

U.S. Mil. an officer ranking just above a brigadier general

ma·jor·i·ty (mə jôr'ə tē) *n., pl.* **-ties** [see MAJOR] **1.** the greater number; more than half of a total **2.** the excess of the larger number of votes cast for one candidate, etc. over all the rest of the votes **3.** full legal age **4.** the military rank of a major

major scale a musical scale with half steps between the third and fourth and the seventh and eighth tones

make (māk) *vt.* **made, mak'ing** [OE. *macian*] **1.** to bring into being; build, create, produce, etc. **2.** to cause to be or become [*made king, made sad*] **3.** to prepare for use [*make the beds*] **4.** to amount to [*two pints make a quart*] **5.** to have the qualities of [*to make a fine leader*] **6.** to acquire; earn **7.** to cause the success of [*that venture made him*] **8.** to understand [*what do you make of that?*] **9.** to execute, do, etc. [*to make a speech*] **10.** to cause or force [*make him go*] **11.** to arrive at; reach [*the ship made port*] **12.** [Colloq.] to get on or in [*to make the team*] —*vi.* **1.** to start (to do something) **2.** to behave as specified [*make bold*] **3.** to cause something to be as specified [*make ready*] —*n.* **1.** the way in which something is made; style **2.** type; brand —**make away with 1.** to steal **2.** to kill —**make believe** to pretend —**make for 1.** to go toward **2.** to help effect —**make it** [Colloq.] to achieve a certain thing —**make off with** to steal —**make out 1.** to see with difficulty **2.** to understand **3.** to fill out (a blank form, etc.) **4.** to (try to) show or prove to be **5.** to succeed; get along **6.** [Slang] to make love: see phr. under LOVE —**make over 1.** to change; renovate **2.** to transfer the ownership of —**make up 1.** to put together **2.** to form; constitute **3.** to invent **4.** to provide (what is lacking) **5.** to compensate (*for*) **6.** to become friends again after a quarrel **7.** to put on cosmetics, etc. **8.** to decide (one's mind) —**make up to** to try to win over, as by flattering —**mak'er** *n.*

make-be·lieve *n.* pretense; feigning —*adj.* pretended; feigned

make'shift' (-shift') *n.* a temporary substitute or expedient —*adj.* that will do as a temporary substitute

make'up', make'-up' *n.* **1.** the way something is put together; composition **2.** nature; disposition **3.** the cosmetics, etc. used by an actor **4.** cosmetics generally

make'-work' *adj.* that serves no other purpose than to give an idle or unemployed person something to do [a *make-work* project]

mal- [< L. *malus*, bad] *a prefix meaning* bad or badly, wrong, ill

mal·ad·just·ed (mal'ə jus'tid) *adj.* poorly adjusted, esp. to the environment —**mal'ad·just'ment** *n.*

mal·a·droit (mal'ə droit') *adj.* [Fr.: see MAL- & ADROIT] awkward; clumsy; bungling —**mal'a·droit'ly** *adv.*

mal·a·dy (mal'ə dē) *n., pl.* **-dies** [< VL. *male habitus*, badly kept] the

fact of being sick; disease; illness

ma·laise (ma lāz') *n.* [Fr. < *mal*, bad + *aise*, ease] a vague feeling of physical discomfort or of uneasiness

mal·a·mute (mal'ə myōōt') *n.* [< *Malemute*, an Eskimo tribe] a strong dog developed as a sled dog by Eskimos

mal·a·prop·ism (mal'ə präp iz'm) *n.* [< Mrs. *Malaprop* in Sheridan's *The Rivals* (1775)] a ludicrous misuse of words that sound alike

ma·lar·i·a (mə ler'ē ə) *n.* [It. < *mala aria*, bad air] an infectious disease transmitted by the anopheles mosquito, characterized by intermittent chills and fever —**ma·lar'i·al** *adj.*

ma·lar·key, ma·lar·ky (mə lär'kē) *n.* [< ?] [Slang] nonsensical talk

mal·a·thi·on (mal'ə thī'ən) *n.* [< chem. names] an organic insecticide

Ma·la·wi (mä'lä wē) country in SE Africa, in the Brit. Commonwealth: 46,066 sq. mi.; pop. 4,042,000

Ma·lay (mā'lā, mə lā') *n.* **1.** a member of a group of brown-skinned peoples living chiefly in the Malay Peninsula and the Malay Archipelago **2.** their language —*adj.* of the Malays, their language, etc. Also **Ma·lay'an**

Mal·a·ya·lam (mal'ə yä'ləm) *n.* a language of the SW coast of India

Malay Archipelago large group of islands between SE Asia & Australia

Malay Peninsula peninsula in SE Asia

Ma·lay·sia (mə lā'zhə) country in SE Asia, mostly on the Malay Peninsula, in the Brit. Commonwealth: 128,654 sq. mi.; pop. 10,223,000 —**Ma·lay'sian** *adj., n.*

mal·con·tent (mal'kən tent') *adj.* [see MAL- & CONTENT¹] dissatisfied; rebellious —*n.* a malcontent person

Mal·dive Islands (mal'dīv) sultanate on a group of islands in the Indian Ocean: 115 sq. mi.; pop. 93,000

male (māl) *adj.* [< L. *mas*, a male] **1.** designating or of the sex that fertilizes the ovum **2.** of, like, or suitable for men or boys; masculine **3.** *Mechanics* having a part shaped to fit into a corresponding hollow part —*n.* a male person, animal, or plant

mal·e·dic·tion (mal'ə dik'shən) *n.* [see MAL- & DICTION] a curse

mal·e·fac·tor (mal'ə fak'tər) *n.* [< L. *male*, evil + *facere*, do] an evildoer or criminal —**mal'e·fac'tion** *n.*

ma·lef·i·cent (mə lef'ə s'nt) *adj.* [< L.: see MALEFACTOR] harmful; evil —**ma·lef'i·cence** *n.*

ma·lev·o·lent (mə lev'ə lənt) *adj.* [< L. *male*, evil + *velle*, to wish] wishing evil or harm to others; malicious —**ma·lev'o·lence** *n.*

mal·fea·sance (mal fē'z'ns) *n.* [< Fr. *mal*, evil + *faire*, do] wrongdoing, esp. by a public official

mal·for·ma·tion (mal'fôr mā'shən) *n.* faulty or abnormal formation of a body or part —**mal·formed'** *adj.*

mal·func·tion (mal fuŋk'shən) *vi.* to fail to function as it should —*n.* an instance of malfunctioning

Ma·li (mä'lē) country in W Africa: 464,873 sq. mi.; pop. 4,305,000

mal·ice (mal'is) *n.* [< L. *malus*, bad]
1. active ill will; desire to harm
another 2. *Law* evil intent

ma·li·cious (mə lish'əs) *adj.* having,
showing, or caused by malice; spiteful
—**ma·li'cious·ly** *adv.*

ma·lign (mə lin') *vt.* [< L. *male*, ill
+ *genus*, born] to speak evil of;
slander —*adj.* 1. malicious 2. evil;
baleful 3. very harmful

ma·lig·nant (mə lig'nənt) *adj.* [see
prec.] 1. having an evil influence 2.
wishing evil 3. very harmful 4. causing or likely to cause death [a *malignant* tumor] —**ma·lig'nan·cy** *n.* —
ma·lig'ni·ty (-nə tē) *n.*

ma·lin·ger (mə lin'gər) *vi.* [< Fr.
malingre, sickly] to feign illness so as
to escape duty —**ma·lin'ger·er** *n.*

mall (môl) *n.* [< *maul*, mallet: from
use in a game on outdoor lanes] 1. a
shaded walk or public promenade 2.
a) a shop-lined street for pedestrians
only *b)* an enclosed shopping center

mal·lard (mal'ərd) *n.* [< OFr.
malart] the common wild duck

mal·le·a·ble (mal'ē ə b'l) *adj.* [<
L. *malleus*, a hammer] 1. that can be
hammered, pounded, or pressed into
various shapes without breaking 2.
adaptable —**mal'le·a·bil'i·ty** *n.*

mal·let (mal'it) *n.* [see prec.] 1. a
short-handled hammer
with a wooden head,
for driving a chisel, etc.
2. any similar long-
handled hammer, as for
use in croquet or polo
3. a small hammer for
playing a xylophone,
etc.

MALLET

mal·low (mal'ō) *n.* [<
L. *malva*] any of a family of plants,
including the hollyhock, cotton, and
okra, with large, showy flowers

mal·nour·ished (mal nur'isht) *adj.*
improperly nourished

mal·nu·tri·tion (mal'nōō trish'ən)
n. faulty or inadequate nutrition; poor
nourishment

mal·oc·clu·sion (-ə klōō'zhən) *n.* a
faulty position of the teeth so that
they do not meet properly

mal·o·dor·ous (mal ō'dər əs) *adj.*
having a bad odor; stinking

mal·prac·tice (mal prak'tis) *n.* professional misconduct or improper practice, esp. by a physician

malt (môlt) *n.* [OE. *mealt*] 1. barley
or other grain soaked and then kiln-
dried: used in brewing and distilling
2. beer, ale, etc. —*adj.* made with malt
—**malt'y** *adj.* **-i·er**, **-i·est**

Mal·ta (môl'tə) country on a group of
islands in the Mediterranean, south
of Sicily, in the Brit. Commonwealth:
122 sq. mi.; pop. 328,000 —**Mal'tese'**
(-tēz') *adj., n.*

malted milk powdered malt and dried
milk, used in a drink with milk, etc.

malt liquor beer, ale, or the like
made from malt by fermentation

mal·treat (mal trēt') *vt.* [see MAL- &
TREAT] to treat roughly or brutally;
abuse —**mal·treat'ment** *n.*

mam·ma, ma·ma (mä'mə; *occas.*
mə mä') *n.* mother: a child's word

mam·mal (mam'əl) *n.* [< L. *mamma*,
breast] any of a group of vertebrates
the females of which have milk-secreting glands (**mam'ma·ry glands**)
for feeding their offspring —**mam·
ma·li·an** (mə mā'lē ən) *adj., n.*

mam·mog·ra·phy (mə mäg'rə fē)
n. [< L. *mamma*, breast + -GRAPHY]
an X-ray technique for detecting breast
tumors before they can be seen or felt

mam·mon (mam'ən) *n.* [< Aram.]
[often M-] riches regarded as an object
of worship and greedy pursuit

mam·moth (mam'əth) *n.* [Russ.
mamont] an extinct elephant with long
tusks —*adj.* very big; huge

man (man) *n., pl.* **men** (men) [OE.
mann] 1. a human being; person 2.
the human race; mankind 3. an adult
male person 4. an adult male servant,
employee, etc. 5. a husband 6. any of
the pieces used in chess, checkers, etc.
—*vt.* **manned, man'ning** 1. to
furnish with men for work, defense,
etc. 2. to strengthen; brace [to man
oneself for an ordeal] —**as a** (or **one**)
man in unison; unanimously —**to a
man** with no exception

-man (mən, man) *a combining form
meaning* man or person of a specified
kind, in a specified activity, etc.
[*Frenchman, sportsman*]

Man. Manitoba

Man, Isle of one of the Brit. Isles,
between Northern Ireland & England

man·a·cle (man'ə k'l) *n.* [< L.
manus, hand] a handcuff: *usually used
in pl.* —*vt.* **-cled, -cling** 1. to put
handcuffs on 2. to restrain

man·age (man'ij) *vt.* **-aged, -ag·ing**
[< L. *manus*, hand] 1. to control the
movement or behavior of 2. to have
charge of; direct [to *manage* a hotel]
3. to succeed in accomplishing —*vi.* 1.
to carry on business 2. to contrive to
get along —**man'age·a·ble** *adj.*

man'age·ment *n.* 1. a managing or
being managed; control, direction, etc.
2. the persons managing a business,
institution, etc.

man'ag·er *n.* one who manages; esp.,
one who manages a business, etc.

man·a·ge·ri·al (man'ə jir'ē əl) *adj.*
of a manager or management

†ma·ña·na (mä nyä'nä) *n., adv.* [Sp.]
tomorrow or an indefinite future time

man·a·tee (man'ə tē') *n.* [< WInd.
native name] a large, plant-eating
aquatic mammal of tropical waters

Man·ches·ter (man'ches'tər) seaport in NW England: pop. 661,000

Man·chu (man chōō') *n.* 1. *pl.*
-chus', -chu' a member of a Mongolian people of Manchuria who ruled
China from 1644 to 1912 2. their
language

Man·chu·ri·a (man choor'ē ə) re-

fat, āpe, cär; ten, ēven; is, bīte; gō, hôrn, tōōl, look; oil, out; up, fur;
chin; she; thin, then; zh, leisure; ŋ, ring; ə for a in ago; ', (ā'b'l); ē, Fr. coeur;
ö, Fr. feu; Fr. mon; ü, Fr. duc; kh, G. ich, doch; ‡ foreign; < derived from

gion in NE China —**Man·chu'ri·an** adj., n.

man·da·rin (man'də rin) n. [< Sans. *mantra*, counsel] 1. a high official of the former Chinese Empire 2. [M-] the main dialect of Chinese

man·date (man'dāt) n. [< L. *mandare*, to command] 1. an order or command 2. a) formerly, a League of Nations' commission to a country to administer some region b) this region 3. the will of constituents expressed to their representative, legislature, etc.

man·da·to·ry (man'də tôr'ē) adj. 1. of or containing a mandate 2. authoritatively commanded; obligatory

man·di·ble (man'də b'l) n. [< L. *mandere*, chew] the jaw; specif., a) the lower jaw of a vertebrate b) either jaw of a beaked animal —**man·dib'u·lar** (-dib'yoo lər) adj.

man·do·lin (man'd'l in', man'də lin') n. [< LGr. *pandoura*, kind of lute] a musical instrument with four or five pairs of strings

man·drake (man'drāk) n. [< Gr. *mandragoras*] a poisonous plant of the nightshade family, with a thick, forked root suggesting the human form

man·drel, man·dril (man'drəl) n. [prob. < Fr. *mandrin*] a spindle inserted into a lathe center to support work while it is being machined

man·drill (man'dril) n. [MAN + *drill*, W Afr. monkey] a large, strong baboon of W Africa: the male has blue and scarlet patches on the face and rump

mane (mān) n. [OE. *manu*] the long hair growing on the neck of the horse, lion, etc. —**maned** adj.

man'-eat'er n. an animal that eats human flesh —**man'-eat'ing** adj.

ma·nège, ma·nege (ma nezh') n. [Fr. < It. *maneggiare*, MANAGE] the art of riding and training horses

ma·neu·ver (mə noō'vər) n. [< L. *manu operare*, to work by hand] 1. a planned and controlled movement of troops, warships, etc. 2. a skillful or shrewd move; stratagem —vi., vt. 1. to perform or cause to perform maneuvers 2. to manage or plan skillfully 3. to move, get, make, etc. by some scheme —**ma·neu'ver·a·ble** adj.

man·ful (man'fəl) adj. manly; brave, resolute, etc. —**man'ful·ly** adv.

man·ga·nese (maŋ'gə nēs', -nēz') n. [ult. < ML. *magnesia*] a grayish, metallic chemical element, used in alloys

mange (mānj) n. [< OFr. *mangeue*, an itch] a skin disease of mammals, causing itching, loss of hair, etc.

man·ger (mān'jər) n. [< L. *mandere*, to chew] a box or trough to hold hay, etc. for horses or cattle to eat

man·gle¹ (maŋ'g'l) vt. -gled, -gling [< OFr. *mehaigner*, maim] 1. to mutilate by roughly cutting, tearing, crushing, etc. 2. to spoil; botch; mar

man·gle² (maŋ'g'l) n. [< Gr. *manganon*, war machine] a machine for ironing sheets, etc. between rollers

man·go (maŋ'gō) n., pl. -goes, -gos [< Tamil *mān-kāy*] 1. the yellow-red, somewhat acid fruit of a tropical tree 2. the tree

man·grove (maŋ'grōv) n. [< WInd. name] a tropical tree with branches that spread and send down roots, thus forming more trunks

man·gy (mān'jē) adj. -gi·er, -gi·est 1. having the mange 2. filthy, low, etc. —**man'gi·ly** adv. —**man'gi·ness** n.

man'han'dle vt. -dled, -dling to handle roughly

Man·hat·tan (man hat'n) island borough of New York City: pop. 1,428,000 —n. [often m-] a cocktail made of whiskey and sweet vermouth

man'hole' n. a hole through which one can enter a sewer, conduit, etc.

man'hood' n. 1. the state or time of being a man 2. virility, courage, etc. 3. men collectively

man'-hour' n. a time unit equal to one hour of work done by one person

man'hunt' n. a hunt for a fugitive

ma·ni·a (mā'nē ə) n. [Gr.] 1. wild or violent mental disorder 2. an excessive enthusiasm; obsession; craze

-ma·ni·a (mā'nē ə) [see prec.] a combining form meaning a (specified) type of mental disorder [*kleptomania*]

ma·ni·ac (mā'nē ak') adj. wildly insane —n. a violently insane person —**ma·ni·a·cal** (mə nī'ə k'l) adj.

man·ic (man'ik) adj. having, characterized by, or like mania

man'ic-de·pres'sive adj. characterized by alternating periods of mania and mental depression

man·i·cure (man'ə kyoor') n. [< L. *manus*, a hand + *cura*, care] a trimming, polishing, etc. of fingernails —vt. -cured', -cur'ing to trim, polish, etc. (fingernails) —**man'i·cur'ist** n.

man·i·fest (man'ə fest') adj. [< L. *manifestus*, lit., struck by the hand] apparent to the senses or the mind; obvious —vt. to show plainly; reveal —n. an itemized list of a craft's cargo or passengers —**man'i·fest'ly** adv.

man·i·fes·ta·tion (-fes tā'shən) n. 1. a manifesting or being manifested 2. something that manifests

man·i·fes·to (man'ə fes'tō) n., pl. -toes [It. < L.: see MANIFEST] a public declaration of intention by an important person or group

man·i·fold (man'ə fōld') adj. [see MANY & -FOLD] 1. having many forms, parts, etc. 2. of many sorts 3. being such in many ways [a *manifold* villain] 4. operating several parts of one kind —n. a pipe with several outlets, as for conducting cylinder exhaust from an engine —vt. to make copies of, as with carbon paper

man·i·kin, man·ni·kin (man'ə k'n) n. [< Du. *manneken*, little man] same as MANNEQUIN

Ma·ni·la (mə nil'ə) capital of the Philippines, on Luzon: pop. 1,438,000

Manila hemp a strong fiber from the leafstalk of a Philippine plant, used for making rope, paper, etc.

Manila paper a strong, buff-colored paper, orig. made of Manila hemp

man in the street the average person

man·i·ple (man'ə p'l) n. [ult. < L. *manus*, a hand] a silk band worn over the left forearm by priests at Mass

ma·nip·u·late (mə nip′yə lāt′) *vt.*
-lat′ed, -lat′ing [ult. < L. *manus*, a hand + *plere*, to fill] 1. to work or handle skillfully 2. to manage artfully or shrewdly, often in an unfair way 3. to alter (figures, etc.) for one's own purposes —**ma·nip′u·la′tion** *n.*

Man·i·to·ba (man′ə tō′bə) province of SC Canada: 251,000 sq. mi.; pop. 963,000; cap. Winnipeg

man·kind *n.* 1. (man′kīnd′) the human race 2. (-kīnd′) all human males

man′ly *adj.* -li·er, -li·est having the qualities regarded as suitable for a man; virile, brave, etc. —*adv.* in a manly way —**man′li·ness** *n.*

man′-made′ *adj.* artificial; synthetic

Mann (män), **Thomas** 1875-1955; Ger. novelist in the U.S., etc.

man·na (man′ə) *n.* [< Heb. *mān*] 1. *Bible* food miraculously provided for the Israelites in the wilderness 2. any help that comes unexpectedly

man·ne·quin (man′ə kin) *n.* [see MANIKIN] 1. a model of the human body, used by tailors, etc. 2. a woman who models clothes in stores, etc.

man·ner (man′ər) *n.* [< L. *manus*, a hand] 1. a way of doing something; mode of procedure 2. a way, esp. a usual way, of acting; habit 3. [*pl.*] *a)* ways of social behavior [bad *manners*] *b)* polite ways of social behavior [to learn *manners*] 4. kind; sort

man′nered (-ərd) *adj.* 1. having manners of a specified kind [well-*mannered*] 2. artificial, stylized, etc.

man′ner·ism *n.* 1. excessive use of some distinctive manner in art, literature, etc. 2. a peculiarity of manner in behavior, speech, etc.

man′ner·ly *adj.* polite

man·nish (man′ish) *adj.* like a man or man's [her *mannish* stride]

ma·noeu·vre (mə nōō′vər) *n.*, *vi.*, *vt.* -vred, -vring *chiefly Brit. sp. of* MANEUVER

man of letters a writer, scholar, etc., esp. in the field of literature

man′-of-war′ *n.*, *pl.* **men′-of-war′** an armed naval vessel; warship

man·or (man′ər) *n.* [< L. *manere*, dwell] 1. in England, a landed estate 2. the main incuse on an estate — **ma·no·ri·al** (mə nôr′ē əl) *adj.*

man′pow′er *n.* 1. power furnished by human strength 2. the collective strength or availability for work of the people in a given area, nation, etc.

‡**man·qué** (män kā′) *adj.* [Fr.] unfulfilled; would-be [a poet *manqué*]

man·sard (roof) (man′särd) [< F. *Mansard*, 17th-c. Fr. architect] a roof with two slopes on each of four sides, the lower steeper than the upper

MANSARD ROOF

manse (mans) *n.* [see MANSION] the residence of a minister; parsonage

man′ser′vant *n.*, *pl.* **men′ser′vants** a male servant: also **man servant**

-man·ship (mən ship) *a combining form meaning* talent or skill (esp. in gaining advantage) in [gamesmanship]

man·sion (man′shən) *n.* [< L. *manere*, dwell] a large, imposing house

man′-sized′ *adj.* [Colloq.] of a size fit for a man; big: also **man′-size′**

man′slaugh′ter (-slôt′ər) *n.* the killing of a human being by another, esp. when unlawful but without malice

man·tel (man′t'l) *n.* [see MANTLE] 1. the facing about a fireplace, including a projecting shelf 2. this shelf: also **man′tel·piece′**

man·til·la (man til′ə, -tē′ə) *n.* [Sp. < L.: see MANTLE] a woman's scarf, as of lace, worn over the hair and shoulders

man·tis (man′tis) *n.*, *pl.* **-tis·es, -tes** (-tēz) [< Gr. *mantis*, prophet] an insect with forelegs held as if praying

man·tis·sa (man tis′ə) *n.* [L. (useless) addition] the decimal part of a logarithm

man·tle (man′t'l) *n.* [< L. *mantellum*] 1. a loose, sleeveless cloak 2. anything that envelops or conceals 3. a small hood which when placed over a flame becomes white-hot and gives off light —*vt.* -tled, -tling to cover as with a mantle —*vi.* 1. to be or become covered 2. to blush or flush

man·tra (mun′trə, man′-) *n.* [Sans.] a chant of a Vedic hymn, text, etc.

man·u·al (man′yoo wəl) *adj.* [< L. *manus*, a hand] 1. of the hands 2. made, done, or worked by hand 3. involving skill or hard work with the hands —*n.* 1. a handy book for use as a guide, reference, etc. 2. prescribed drill in the handling of a weapon —**man′u·al·ly** *adv.*

manual training training in practical arts and crafts, as woodworking

man·u·fac·ture (man′yə fak′chər) *n.* [< L. *manus*, a hand + *facere*, make] 1. the making of goods, esp. by machinery and on a large scale 2. the making of any product, as of bile by the liver —*vt.* -tured, -tur·ing 1. to make, esp. by machinery 2. to make up (excuses, etc.); invent —**man′u·fac′tur·er** *n.*

man·u·mit (man′yə mit′) *vt.* -mit′ted, -mit′ting [< L. *manus*, a hand + *mittere*, send] to free from slavery —**man′u·mis′sion** *n.*

ma·nure (mə noor′, -nyoor′) *vt.* -nured′, -nur′ing [< OFr. *manouvrer*, work with the hands] to put manure on or into —*n.* animal excrement, etc. used to fertilize soil

man·u·script (man′yə skript′) *adj.* [< L. *manus*, hand + *scriptus*, written] 1. written by hand or typewritten 2. written with printlike letters —*n.* 1. a written or typewritten document, book, etc., as submitted to a publisher 2. writing as opposed to print

Manx (maŋks) *adj.* of the Isle of Man, its people, etc. —*n.* the language spoken on the Isle of Man

man·y (men′ē) *adj.* **more, most** [OE. *manig*] numerous —*n.* a large number (of persons or things) —*pron.* many persons or things

Mao·ri (mou′rē) *n.* **1.** *pl.* **-ris, -ri** any of the Polynesians native to New Zealand **2.** their language —*adj.* of the Maoris, their language, etc.

Mao Tse-tung (mou′ dzu′dŏōŋ′) 1893–1976; Chin. communist leader —**Mao′ism** *n.* —**Mao′ist** *n.*

map (map) *n.* [< L. *mappa*, napkin, cloth] **1.** a representation of all or part of the earth's surface, showing countries, bodies of water, etc. **2.** a representation of the sky, showing the stars, etc. —*vt.* **mapped, map′ping 1.** to make a map of **2.** to plan

ma·ple (mā′p'l) *n.* [OE. *mapel*] **1.** any of a large group of trees with two-winged fruits, grown for wood, sap, or shade **2.** the hard, light-colored wood **3.** the flavor of the syrup or sugar made from the sap

mar (mär) *vt.* **marred, mar′ring** [OE. *mierran*, hinder] to injure so as to make imperfect, etc.; spoil

mar·a·bou (mar′ə bōō′) *n.* [Fr. < Ar. *murābit*, hermit] **1.** a large stork of Africa or India **2.** its plumes

ma·ra·ca (mə rä′kə) *n.* [< the Braz. native name] a percussion instrument made of a dried gourd or gourd-shaped rattle with pebbles in it

mar·a·schi·no (mar′ə skē′nō, -shē′-) *n.* [It. < *marasca*, cherry] a liqueur made from the black wild cherry

maraschino cherries cherries in a syrup flavored with maraschino

mar·a·thon (mar′ə thän′) *n.* [< *Marathon*, in ancient Greece] **1.** a foot race of 26 miles, 385 yards **2.** any endurance contest

ma·raud (mə rôd′) *vi.*, *vt.* [< Fr. *maraud*, vagabond] to raid and plunder —**ma·raud′er** *n.*

mar·ble (mär′b'l) *n.* [< Gr. *marmaros*, white stone] **1.** a hard limestone, white or colored, which takes a high polish **2.** a piece of this stone, used in sculpture, etc. **3.** anything like marble in hardness, coldness, etc. **4.** *a)* a little ball of stone, glass, etc. *b)* [*pl.*, *with sing. v.*] a children's game played with such balls **5.** [*pl.*] [Slang] brains: good sense —*adj.* of or like marble —*vt.* **-bled, -bling 1.** to make (book edges) look mottled like marble **2.** to cause (meat) to be streaked with fat

mar·ble·ize′ *vt.* **-ized′, -iz′ing** to make look like marble

March (märch) *n.* [< L. *Mars*, Mars] the third month of the year, having 31 days; abbrev. Mar.

march¹ (märch) *vi.* [Fr. *marcher*] **1.** to walk with regular steps, as in military formation **2.** to advance steadily —*vt.* to cause to march —*n.* **1.** a marching **2.** a steady advance; progress **3.** a regular, steady step **4.** the distance covered in marching **5.** a piece of music for marching —**on the march** marching —**steal a march on**

to get an advantage over secretly —**march′er** *n.*

march² (märch) *n.* [< OFr.] a boundary, border, or frontier

March hare a hare in breeding time, proverbially an example of madness

marching orders orders to march, go, or leave

mar·chion·ess (mär′shə nis) *n.* **1.** the wife or widow of a marquess **2.** a lady of the rank of a marquess

Mar·co·ni (mär kō′nē), **Gu·gliel·mo** (gōō lyel′mō) 1874–1937; It. physicist: developed wireless telegraphy

Mar·di gras (mär′di grä′) [Fr., fat Tuesday] the last day before Lent: a day of carnival in New Orleans, etc.

mare¹ (mer) *n.* [< OE. *mere*] a mature female horse, mule, donkey, etc.

ma·re² (mer′ē) *n.*, *pl.* **-ri·a** [L., sea] a large, dark area on the moon

mare's-nest (merz′nest′) *n.* **1.** a hoax **2.** a jumble; mess

mar·ga·rine (mär′jə rin) *n.* [Fr.] a spread or cooking fat of vegetable oils processed, often with skim milk, to the consistency of butter

mar·gin (mär′jən) *n.* [< L. *margo*] **1.** a border; edge **2.** the blank border of a printed or written page **3.** an amount beyond what is needed **4.** provision for increase, error, etc. **5.** the difference between the cost and selling price of goods —**mar′gin·al** *adj.*

mar·gi·na·li·a (mär′jə nā′lē ə) *n.pl.* notes in the margins, as of a book

ma·ri·a·chi (mär′ē ä′chē) *n.*, *pl.* **-chis** [Mex. Sp. < ?] **1.** one of a strolling band of musicians in Mexico **2.** such a band **3.** its music

Mar·i·an (mer′ē ən, mar′-) *adj.* of the Virgin Mary

Ma·rie An·toi·nette (mə rē′ an′ twə net′) 1755–93; wife of Louis XVI: guillotined

mar·i·gold (mar′ə gōld′) *n.* [< Virgin *Mary* + *gold*] a plant of the composite family, with yellow or orange flowers

ma·ri·jua·na, ma·ri·hua·na (mar′ə wä′nə) *n.* [AmSp.] **1.** *same as* HEMP (*n.* 1) **2.** its dried leaves and flowers, smoked, esp. as cigarettes, for the psychological and euphoric effects

ma·rim·ba (mə rim′bə) *n.* [< native Afr. name] a kind of xylophone with a resonant tube beneath each bar

ma·ri·na (mə rē′nə) *n.* [< L. *mare*, sea] a small harbor with docks, services, etc. for pleasure craft

mar·i·nade (mar′ə nād′) *n.* [Fr. < Sp. *marinar*, to pickle] **1.** a spiced pickling solution for steeping meat, fish, etc., often before cooking **2.** meat or fish thus steeped —*vt.* **-nad′ed, -nad′ing** *same as* MARINATE

mar·i·nate (mar′ə nāt′) *vt.* **-nat′ed, -nat′ing** [< It. *marinare*, to pickle] to steep (meat or fish) in a marinade

ma·rine (mə rēn′) *adj.* [< L. *mare*, sea] **1.** of or found in the sea **2.** *a)* maritime; nautical *b)* naval —*n.* **1.** a soldier trained or service at sea **2.** [*often* M-] a member of the MARINE CORPS **3.** naval or merchant ships

Marine Corps a branch of the U.S.

armed forces trained for land, sea, and aerial combat

mar·i·ner (mar'ə nər) *n.* a sailor

mar·i·o·nette (mar'ē ə net') *n.* [Fr. < *Marie*, Mary] a little jointed doll moved by strings or wires

mar·i·tal (mar'ə t'l) *adj.* [< L. *maritus*, a husband] of marriage; matrimonial —**mar'i·tal·ly** *adv.*

mar·i·time (mar'ə tīm') *adj.* [< L. *mare*, sea] 1. on, near, or living near the sea 2. of navigation, shipping, etc.

mar·jo·ram (mär'jər əm) *n.* [? ult. < Gr. *amarakos*] a fragrant plant of the mint family, used in cooking

Mark (märk) *Bible* 1. a Christian apostle, the reputed author of the second Gospel 2. this book

mark¹ (märk) *n.* [OE. *mearc*, boundary] 1. a spot, scratch, etc. on a surface 2. a printed or written symbol [*punctuation marks*] 3. a brand or label on an article showing the maker, etc. 4. an indication of some quality, character, etc. 5. a grade [a *mark* of B in Latin] 6. a standard of quality 7. impression, influence, etc. 8. an object of known position, serving as a guide 9. a line, dot, etc. indicating position, as on a graduated scale 10. a target; goal —*vt.* 1. to put or make a mark or marks on 2. to identify as by a mark 3. to indicate by a mark 4. to show plainly [*her smile marked her joy*] 5. to set off; characterize 6. to take notice of; heed [*mark my words*] 7. to grade; rate —**make one's mark** to achieve fame —**mark down** (or up) to mark for sale at a reduced (or an increased) price —**mark time** 1. to keep time while at a halt by lifting the feet as if marching 2. to suspend progress for a time —**mark'er** *n.*

mark² (märk) *n.* [< ON. *mork*] the monetary unit of Germany

mark'down' *n.* 1. a selling at a reduced price 2. the amount of reduction

marked (märkt) *adj.* 1. having a mark or marks 2. noticeable; obvious —**mark·ed·ly** (märk'id lē) *adv.*

mar·ket (mär'kit) *n.* [ult. < L. *merx*, merchandise] 1. a gathering of people for buying and selling things 2. an open space or building where goods are shown for sale: also **mar'ket·place'** 3. a shop for the sale of provisions [a meat *market*] 4. a region in which goods can be bought and sold [the European *market*] 5. trade; buying and selling 6. demand for (goods, etc.) [a good *market* for tea] —*vt.* 1. to offer for sale 2. to sell —*vi.* to buy provisions —**mar'ket·a·ble** *adj.* —**mar'ket·er, mar'ket·eer'** (-kə tir') *n.*

mark'ing *n.* 1. a mark or marks 2. the characteristic arrangement of marks, as on fur or feathers

marks·man (märks'mən) *n., pl.* -**men** one who shoots, esp. one who shoots well —**marks'man·ship'** *n.*

mark'up' *n.* 1. a selling at an increased price 2. the amount of increase

mar·lin (mär'lin) *n., pl.* -**lin**, -**lins** [< ff.] a large, slender deep-sea fish

mar·line·spike (mär'lin spīk') *n.* [< Du. *marlijn*, small cord & SPIKE¹] a pointed iron tool for splicing rope

mar·ma·lade (mär'mə lād') *n.* [ult. < Gr. *meli*, honey + *mēlon*, apple] a jamlike preserve of oranges, etc.

mar·mo·set (mär'mə zet') *n.* [< OFr. *marmouset*, grotesque figure] a small monkey of S. and C.America

mar·mot (mär'mət) *n.* [prob. < L. *mus montanus*, mountain mouse] any of a group of thick-bodied rodents, as the woodchuck or prairie dog

ma·roon¹ (mə rōōn') *n., adj.* [Fr. *marron*, chestnut] dark brownish red

ma·roon² (mə rōōn') *vt.* [< AmSp. *cimarrón*, wild] 1. to put (a person) ashore in a lonely place and leave him 2. to leave helpless and alone

marque (märk) *n.* [Fr., a sign] a distinctive emblem on an automobile

mar·quee (mär kē') *n.* [< Fr. *marquise*, awning] a rooflike projection over an entrance, as to a theater

mar·quess (mär'kwis) *n.* [see MARQUIS] 1. a British nobleman ranking above an earl 2. *same as* MARQUIS

mar·que·try (mär'kə trē) *n.* [see MARQUE] decorative inlaid work, as in furniture

mar·quis (mär'kwis; *Fr.* mär kē') *n.* [< ML. *marchisus*, a prefect] in some European countries, a nobleman ranking above an earl or count

mar·quise' (-kēz') *n.* 1. the wife or widow of a marquis 2. a lady of the rank of a marquis

mar·qui·sette (mär'ki zet', -kwi-) *n.* [see MARQUEE] a thin, meshlike fabric used for curtains

mar·riage (mar'ij) *n.* 1. the state of being married 2. a wedding 3. a close union —**mar'riage·a·ble** *adj.*

mar·ried *adj.* 1. being husband and wife 2. having a husband or wife 3. of marriage —*n.* a married person

mar·row (mar'ō) *n.* [OE. *mearg*] the soft, fatty tissue that fills the cavities of most bones

mar·ry (mar'ē) *vt.* -**ried**, -**ry·ing** [< L. *maritus*, husband] 1. to join as husband and wife 2. to take as husband or wife 3. to unite —*vi.* to get married —**marry off** to give in marriage

Mars (märz) 1. the Roman god of war 2. a planet of the solar system: see PLANET

Mar·seille (mär sā') seaport in SE France: pop. 778,000 *Eng. sp.* Marseilles

marsh (märsh) *n.* [OE. *merisc*] a tract of low, wet, soft land; swamp —**marsh'y** *adj.* -**i·er**, -**i·est**

mar·shal (mär'shəl) *n.* [< OHG. *marah*, horse + *scalh*, servant] 1. in various foreign armies, a general officer

---

of the highest rank 2. an official in charge of ceremonies, parades, etc. 3. in the U.S., a) a Federal officer appointed to a judicial district with duties like those of a sheriff b) the head of some police or fire departments —vt. -shaled or -shalled, -shal·ing or -shal·ling 1. to arrange (troops, ideas, etc.) in order 2. to guide

Mar·shall (mär'shəl), **John** 1755–1835; U.S. chief justice (1801–35)

marsh·mal·low (märsh'mel'ō, -mal'ō) n. [orig. made of the root of a mallow found in marshes] a soft, spongy confection of sugar, gelatin, etc.

mar·su·pi·al (mär sōō'pē əl) adj. [< Gr. marsypos, pouch] of a group of mammals that carry their incompletely developed young in an external abdominal pouch on the mother —n. an animal of this kind, as a kangaroo

mart (märt) n. [MDu. markt] a market

mar·ten (mär't'n) n. [< OFr. martre] 1. a small mammal like a weasel, with soft, thick fur 2. the fur

mar·tial (mär'shəl) adj. [< L. martialis, of Mars] 1. of or suitable for war 2. warlike; bold 3. military —mar'tial·ly adv.

martial arts Asian systems of self-defense, such as karate or kung fu

martial law rule by military authorities over civilians, as during a war

Mar·tian (mär'shən) adj. of Mars —n. an imagined inhabitant of Mars

mar·tin (mär't'n) n. [Fr.] any of several birds of the swallow family

mar·ti·net (mär't'n et') n. [< Martinet, 17th-c. Fr. general] a very strict disciplinarian

mar·ti·ni (mär tē'nē) n., pl. -nis [< ?] a cocktail made of gin (or vodka) and dry vermouth

mar·tyr (mär'tər) n. [< Gr. martyr, a witness] 1. one who chooses to suffer or die for his faith or principles 2. one who suffers misery for a long time —vt. to kill or persecute for a belief —mar'tyr·dom n.

mar·vel (mär'v'l) n. [< L. mirari, admire] a wonderful or astonishing thing —vt., vi. -veled or -velled, -vel·ing or -vel·ling to become full of wonder (often followed by a clause)

mar·vel·ous (mär'v'l əs) adj. 1. causing wonder; extraordinary, etc. 2. improbable; incredible 3. [Colloq.] fine; splendid Also, chiefly Brit. **mar'vel·lous** —**mar'vel·ous·ly** adv.

Marx (märks), **Karl** 1818–83; Ger. founder of modern socialism

Marx·ism (märk'siz'm) n. the system of thought developed by Karl Marx and Friedrich Engels, serving as a basis for socialism and communism —**Marx'ist, Marx'i·an** adj., n.

Mar·y (mer'ē) Bible mother of Jesus

Mar·y·land (mer'ə lənd) E State of the U.S.: 10,577 sq. mi.; pop. 4,216,000; cap. Annapolis

Mary Mag·da·le·ne (mag'də lēn) Bible a woman out of whom Jesus cast devils

mar·zi·pan (mär'zi pan') n. [G. < It. marzapane] a pasty confection of

ground almonds, sugar, and egg white

masc., mas. masculine

mas·ca·ra (mas kar'ə) n. [< Ar. maskhara, a clown] a cosmetic for coloring the eyelashes and eyebrows —vt. -ca'raed, -ca'ra·ing to put mascara on

mas·con (mas'kän') n. [mas(s) con(centration)] dense material beneath the moon's surface

mas·cot (mas'kät) n. [< Fr. masco, sorcerer] any person, animal, or thing supposed to bring good luck

mas·cu·line (mas'kyə lin) adj. [< L. mas, male] 1. male; of men or boys 2. suitable to or characteristic of men; strong, vigorous, manly, etc. 3. mannish: said of women 4. Gram. designating or of the gender of words referring to males or things originally regarded as male —**mas'cu·lin'i·ty** n.

ma·ser (mā'zər) n. [m(icrowave) a(mplification by) s(timulated) e(mission of) r(adiation)] a device that stimulates atoms, as in a gas, to emit radiation in a narrow beam

mash (mash) n. [< OE. mascwyrt] 1. crushed malt or meal soaked in hot water for making wort 2. a mixture of watered bran, meal, etc. for feeding horses, etc. 3. any soft mass —vt. 1. to change into a soft mass by beating, crushing, etc. 2. to crush or injure —**mash'er** n.

mask (mask) n. [ult. < Ar. maskhara, a clown] 1. a covering to conceal or protect the face 2. anything that conceals or disguises 3. a masquerade 4. a) a molded likeness of the face b) a grotesque representation of the face, worn to amuse or frighten —vt. to cover or conceal as with a mask —**masked** adj.

mas·och·ism (mas'ə kiz'm) n. [< L. von Sacher-Masoch, 19th-c. Austrian writer] the getting of pleasure, often sexual, from being hurt or humiliated —**mas'och·ist** n. —**mas'och·is'tic** adj. —**mas'och·is'ti·cal·ly** adv.

ma·son (mā's'n) n. [< ML. matio] 1. one whose work is building with stone, brick, etc. 2. [M-] same as FREEMASON

Ma·son-Dix·on line (mā's'n dik's'n) [< C. Mason & J. Dixon, who surveyed it, 1763–67] boundary line between Pa. & Md., regarded as separating the North from the South

Ma·son·ic (mə sän'ik) adj. [also m-] of Freemasons or Freemasonry

ma·son·ry (mā's'n rē) n., pl. -ries 1. a mason's trade 2. something built by a mason; brickwork or stonework 3. [also M-] same as FREEMASONRY

masque (mask) n. [see MASK] 1. same as MASQUERADE (sense 1) 2. a former kind of dramatic entertainment, with a mythical or allegorical theme

mas·quer·ade (mas'kə rād') n. [see MASK] 1. a ball or party at which masks and fancy costumes are worn 2. a) a disguise b) an acting under false pretenses —vi. -ad'ed, -ad'ing 1. to take part in a masquerade 2. to act under false pretenses

Mass (mas) n. [< L. missa in the

words said by the priest *ite, missa est, go, (you) are dismissed* [*also* m-] R.C.Ch. the service of the Eucharist

mass (mas) *n.* [< Gr. *maza*, barley cake] **1.** a quantity of matter of indefinite shape and size; lump **2.** a large quantity or number [*a mass* of bruises] **3.** bulk; size **4.** the main part **5.** *Physics* the quantity of matter in a body as measured in its relation to inertia —*adj.* of or for the masses or for a large number —*vt., vi.* to gather or form into a mass —**the masses** the common people; specif., the lower social classes

Mas·sa·chu·setts (mas'ə chōō'sits) New England State of the U.S.: 8,257 sq. mi.; pop. 5,737,000; cap. Boston: abbrev. **Mass.**

mas·sa·cre (mas'ə kər) *n.* [< OFr. *maçacre*, shambles] the indiscriminate, cruel killing of many people or animals —*vt.* **-cred, -cring** to kill in large numbers

mas·sage (mə säzh') *n.* [Fr. < Ar. *massa*, to touch] a rubbing, kneading, etc. of part of the body, as to stimulate circulation —*vt.* **-saged', -sag'ing** to give a massage to

mass·cult (mas'kult') *n.* [MASS + CULT(URE)] [Colloq.] a commercialized culture popularized through the mass media

mas·seur (ma sur', mə-) *n.* [Fr.] a man whose work is giving massages — **mas·seuse'** (-sooz', -sōōz') *n.fem.*

mas·sive (mas'iv) *adj.* **1.** forming or consisting of a large mass; big and solid **2.** large and imposing —**mas'sive·ly** *adv.* —**mas'sive·ness** *n.*

mass media newspapers, magazines, radio, and television as the means of reaching the mass of people

mass number the number of neutrons and protons in the nucleus of an atom

mass production quantity production of goods, esp. by machinery and division of labor

mast (mast) *n.* [OE. *mæst*] **1.** a tall vertical spar used to support the sails, yards, etc. on a ship **2.** a vertical pole

mas·tec·to·my (mas tek'tə mē) *n., pl.* **-mies** surgical removal of a breast

mas·ter (mas'tər) *n.* [< L. *magister*] **1.** a man who rules others or has control over something; specif., *a)* one who is head of a household *b)* an employer *c)* an owner of an animal or slave *d)* the captain of a merchant ship *e)* [Chiefly Brit.] a male teacher **2.** an expert; specif., *a)* a workman skilled in his trade *b)* an artist regarded as great **3.** [M-] a title applied to: *a)* a boy too young to be addressed as *Mr. b)* one holding an advanced academic degree [*Master* of Arts] —*adj.* **1.** being a master **2.** of a master **3.** chief; main; controlling —*vt.* **1.** to be or become master of **2.** to become an expert in (art, etc.)

mas·ter·ful *adj.* **1.** acting the part of

a master; domineering **2.** expert; skillful —**mas'ter·ful·ly** *adv.*

master key a key that will open up every one of a set of locks

mas'ter·ly *adj.* expert; skillful —*adv.* in a masterly manner

mas'ter·mind' *n.* a very clever person, esp. one who plans or directs a project —*vt.* to be the mastermind of

master of ceremonies a person who presides over an entertainment

mas'ter·piece' *n.* **1.** a thing made or done with masterly skill **2.** the greatest work of a person or group

master sergeant *U.S. Mil.* a non-commissioned officer of high rank

mas'ter·stroke' *n.* a masterly action, move, or achievement

mas'ter·work' *n. same as* MASTER-PIECE

mas'ter·y *n., pl.* **-ies 1.** control as by a master **2.** ascendancy or victory **3.** expert skill or knowledge

mast'head' *n.* **1.** the top part of a ship's mast **2.** a newspaper or magazine listing of owner, address, etc.

mas·ti·cate (mas'tə kāt') *vt.* **-cat'ed, -cat'ing** [ult. < Gr. *mastax*, mouth] to chew up —**mas'ti·ca'tion** *n.*

mas·tiff (mas'tif) *n.* [< L. *mansuetus*, tame] a large, smooth-coated dog with powerful jaws

mas·to·don (mas'tə dän') *n.* [< Gr. *mastos*, breast + *odous*, tooth: from the nipplelike processes on its molars] a large, extinct animal resembling the elephant but larger

mas·toid (mas'toid) *adj.* [< Gr. *mastos*, breast + *eidos*, form] designating, of, or near a projection of the temporal bone behind the ear —*n.* the mastoid projection

mas·tur·bate (mas'tər bāt') *vi.* **-bat'ed, -bat'ing** [< L. *masturbari*] to manipulate the genitals for sexual gratification —**mas'tur·ba'tion** *n.*

mat¹ (mat) *n.* [< LL. *matta*] **1.** a flat piece of cloth, woven straw, rubber, etc., variously used for protection, as under a vase, etc. or on the floor **2.** a thickly padded floor covering used for wrestling, etc. **3.** anything interwoven or tangled into a thick mass —*vt., vi.* **mat'ted, mat'ting 1.** to cover as with a mat **2.** to interweave or tangle into a thick mass —**go to the mat** [Colloq.] to engage in a struggle or dispute

mat² (mat) *n.* [< OFr.] **1.** *same as* MATTE **2.** a border, as of cardboard, put around a picture —*vt.* **mat'ted, mat'ting 1.** to put a dull finish on **2.** to frame with a mat

mat³ (mat) *n.* [Colloq.] *Printing* a matrix

mat·a·dor (mat'ə dôr') *n.* [< Sp. *matar*, to kill] the bullfighter who kills the bull with a sword

match¹ (mach) *n.* [< ? L. *myxa*, candlewick] a slender piece of wood, cardboard, etc. tipped with a composition that catches fire by friction

match² (mach) *n.* [OE. *(ge)mæcca*, *mate*] **1.** any person or thing equal or similar to another **2.** two persons or things that go well together **3.** a contest or game **4.** a marriage or mating —*vt.* **1.** to join in marriage; mate **2.** to put in opposition (*with, against*) **3.** to be equal or similar to **4.** to make or get a counterpart or equivalent to **5.** to suit (one thing) to another —*vi.* to be equal, similar, suitable, etc.

match′book′ *n.* a folder of paper matches

match′less *adj.* having no equal

match′mak′er *n.* one who arranges marriages for others

mate (māt) *n.* [< MDu.] **1.** a companion or fellow worker **2.** one of a matched pair **3.** *a)* a husband or wife *b)* the male or female of paired animals **4.** an officer of a merchant ship, ranking below the captain —*vt., vi.* **mat′ed, mat′ing 1.** to join as a pair **2.** to couple in marriage or sexual union

ma·te·ri·al (mə tir′ē əl) *adj.* [< L. *materia*, matter] **1.** of matter; physical [a *material* object] **2.** of the body or bodily needs, comfort, etc.; not spiritual **3.** important, essential, etc. —*n.* **1.** what a thing is, or may be made of; elements or parts **2.** cloth; fabric **3.** [*pl.*] tools, etc. needed to make or do something

ma·te′ri·al·ism (-iz′m) *n.* **1.** the doctrine that everything in the world, including thought, can be explained only in terms of matter **2.** the tendency to be more concerned with material than with spiritual or intellectual values —**ma·te′ri·al·ist** *adj., n.* —**ma·te′ri·al·is′tic** *adj.*

ma·te′ri·al·ize′ (-ə līz′) *vt.* **-ized′, -iz′ing** to give material form to —*vi.* **1.** to become fact; be realized **2.** to take on bodily form: said of spirits, etc. —**ma·te′ri·al·i·za′tion** *n.*

ma·te′ri·al·ly *adv.* **1.** physically **2.** to a great extent; substantially

ma·te·ri·el, ma·té·ri·el (mə tir′ē el′) *n.* [Fr.: see MATERIAL] the necessary materials and tools; specif., military weapons, supplies, etc.

ma·ter·nal (mə tur′n'l) *adj.* [< L. *mater*, mother] **1.** of, like, or from a mother **2.** related through the mother's side of the family —**ma·ter′nal·ly** *adv.*

ma·ter′ni·ty (-nə tē) *n.* the state of being a mother; motherhood —*adj.* **1.** for pregnant women **2.** for the care of mothers and their newborn babies

math·e·mat·i·cal (math′ə mat′i k'l) *adj.* **1.** of, like, or concerned with mathematics **2.** very precise, accurate, etc. —**math′e·mat′i·cal·ly** *adv.*

math·e·mat·ics (math′ə mat′iks) *n.pl.* [*with sing. v.*] [< Gr. *manthanein*, learn] the science dealing with quantities, forms, etc. and their relationships by the use of numbers and symbols: also **math** —**math′e·ma·ti′cian** (-mə tish′ən) *n.*

mat·i·nee, mat·i·née (mat′'n ā′) *n.* [< Fr. *matin*, morning] an afternoon performance of a play, etc.

mat·ins (mat′'nz) *n.pl.* [< L. *matutinus*, of the morning] [*often* M-] a church service of the morning prayer

Ma·tisse (mä tēs′), **Hen·ri** (än rē′) 1869–1954; Fr. painter

matri- [< L. *mater*] *a combining form meaning* mother

ma·tri·arch (mā′trē ärk′) *n.* [prec. + -ARCH] a woman who rules a family, tribe, etc. —**ma′tri·ar′chal** *adj.* —**ma′tri·ar′chy** *n., pl.* **-chies**

ma·tric·u·late (mə trik′yoo lāt′) *vt., vi.* **-lat′ed, -lat′ing** [see MATRIX] to enroll, esp. as a student in a college —**ma·tric′u·la′tion** *n.*

mat·ri·mo·ny (mat′rə mō′nē) *n., pl.* **-nies** [< L. *mater*, mother] **1.** the act or rite of marriage **2.** the married state —**mat′ri·mo′ni·al** *adj.*

ma·trix (mā′triks) *n., pl.* **-tri·ces** (mā′trə sēz′, mat′rə-), **-trix·es** [LL., womb < L. *mater*, mother] that within which something originates, takes form, etc.; specif., a mold for the face of a type or for a printing plate

ma·tron (mā′trən) *n.* [< L. *mater*, mother] **1.** a wife or widow, esp. one who has a mature appearance and manner **2.** a woman manager of the domestic arrangements of a hospital, prison, etc. —**ma′tron·ly** *adj.*

matron of honor a married woman acting as chief attendant to a bride

matte (mat) *n.* [va.: of MAT²] a dull surface or finish —*adj.* not glossy

mat·ted (mat′id) *adj.* closely tangled in a dense mass

mat·ter (mat′ər) *n.* [< L. *materia*] **1.** what a thing is made of; material **2.** whatever occupies space and is perceptible to the senses **3.** any specified substance [coloring *matter*] **4.** content of thought or expression **5.** an amount or quantity **6.** *a)* a thing or affair *b)* cause or occasion [no laughing *matter*] **7.** importance; significance [it's of no *matter*] **8.** trouble; difficulty [what's the *matter*?] **9.** pus **10.** mail —*vi.* **1.** to be of importance **2.** to form pus —**as a matter of fact** in fact; really —**no matter 1.** it is not important **2.** in spite of

mat′ter-of-fact′ *adj.* sticking to facts; literal, practical, etc.

Mat·thew (math′yōō) *Bible* **1.** a Christian apostle, reputed author of the first Gospel **2.** this book: abbrev. Matt.

mat·ting (mat′iŋ) *n.* **1.** a fabric of straw, hemp, etc. for mats, floor covering, etc. **2.** mats collectively

mat·tock (mat′ək) *n.* [OE. *mattuc*] a tool like a pickax, for loosening the soil, digging roots, etc.

mat·tress (mat′ris) *n.* [< Ar. *matrah*, cushion] a casing of strong cloth filled with cotton, foam rubber, coiled springs, etc., used on a bed

MATTOCK

ma·ture (mə toor′, -choor′, -tyoor′) *adj.* [< L. *maturus*, ripe] **1.** full-grown; ripe **2.** fully developed, perfected, etc. **3.** due: said of a note, bond, etc. —*vt., vi.* **-tured′, -tur′ing** to make or become mature —**mat·u·ra·tion** (mach′ŏŏ rā′shən) *n.* —**ma·tu′ri·ty** *n.*

mat·zo (mät′sə, -sô) *n., pl.* **mat′zot, mat′zoth** (-sōt), **mat′zos** [Heb. *matstsāh,* unleavened] flat, thin unleavened bread eaten during the Passover, or a piece of this

maud·lin (môd′lin) *adj.* [< ME. *Maudeleyne,* (Mary) Magdalene (often represented as weeping)] foolishly, often tearfully, sentimental

maul (môl) *n.* [< L. *malleus,* a hammer] a heavy hammer for driving stakes, etc. —*vt.* **1.** to bruise or lacerate **2.** to handle roughly; manhandle —**maul′er** *n.*

maun·der (môn′dər) *vi.* [prob. < obs. *maund,* to beg] to talk or move in a confused or aimless way

Mau·pas·sant (mō′pə sänt′), **Guy de** (gē də) 1850–93; Fr. writer

Mau·ri·ta·ni·a (môr′ə tā′nē ə) country in W Africa: 419,230 sq. mi.; pop. 1,100,000

Mau·ri·ti·us (mô rish′ē əs) island country in the Indian Ocean, in the Brit. Commonwealth: 809 sq. mi.; pop. 780,000

mau·so·le·um (mô′sə lē′əm, -zə-) *n., pl.* **-le′ums, -le′a** (-ə) [< the tomb of King *Mausolus,* in ancient Asia Minor] a large, imposing tomb

mauve (mōv, môv) *n.* [Fr. < L. *malva,* mallow] any of several shades of pale purple —*adj.* of this color

mav·er·ick (mav′ər ik) *n.* [after S. *Maverick,* 19th-c. Texan whose cattle had no brand] **1.** an unbranded animal, esp. a lost calf **2.** [Colloq.] a person who acts independently of any organization, political party, etc.

maw (mô) *n.* [OE. *maga*] **1.** orig., the stomach **2.** the throat, gullet, jaws, or oral cavity of a voracious animal

mawk·ish (mô′kish) *adj.* [< ON. *mathkr,* maggot] sentimental in a weak, insipid way —**mawk′ish·ly** *adv.*

maxi- [< MAXI(MUM)] *a combining form meaning* maximum, very large, very long

max·il·la (mak sil′ə) *n., pl.* **-lae** (-ē) [L.] the upper jawbone —**max·il·lar·y** (mak′sə ler′ē) *adj.*

max·im (mak′sim) *n.* [< LL. *maxima* (*propositio*), the greatest (premise)] a concise rule of conduct; precept

max·i·mize (mak′sə mīz′) *vt.* **-mized′, -miz′ing** to increase to a maximum

max·i·mum (mak′sə məm) *n., pl.* **-mums, -ma** (-mə) [< L. superl. of *magnus,* great] **1.** the greatest quantity, number, etc. possible **2.** the highest degree or point reached —*adj.* greatest possible, permissible, or reached —**max′i·mal** (-m'l) *adj.*

May (mā) *n.* [< L. *Maius*] the fifth month of the year, having 31 days

may (mā) *v. pt.* **might** [OE. *mæg*] an auxiliary expressing: **1.** possibility /it *may* rain/ **2.** permission /you *may* go/: see also CAN¹ **3.** contingency /be quiet so that we *may* hear/ **4.** wish or hope /*may* he live!/

Ma·ya (mä′yə) *n.* **1.** a member of a tribe of Indians of C. America, who had a highly developed civilization **2.** their language —**Ma′yan** *adj., n.*

may·be (mā′bē) *adv.* [ME. (for it *may be*)] perhaps

May Day May 1: celebrated as a traditional spring festival: observed in many countries as a labor holiday

may·flow·er (mā′flou′ər) *n.* an early spring flower; esp., the trailing arbutus —[M-] the ship on which the Pilgrims came to America (1620)

may·hem (mā′hem, -əm) *n.* [see MAIM] **1.** *Law* the offense of maiming a person **2.** any violent destruction

may·n't (mā′ənt, mānt) may not

may·o (mā′ō) *n.* [Colloq.] *clipped form of* MAYONNAISE

may·on·naise (mā′ə nāz′) *n.* [< *Mahón,* port on a Sp. island] a creamy salad dressing made with egg yolks

may·or (mā′ər, mer) *n.* [< L. *major,* greater] the chief administrative officer of a municipality —**may′or·al·ty** (-əl tē) *n., pl.* **-ties** the office or term of office of a mayor

maze (māz) *n.* [< OE. *amasian,* amaze] **1.** a confusing, intricate network of pathways **2.** a confused state

‡maz·el tov (mä′z'l tôv′) [Heb.] good luck: also **maz′el·tov′**

ma·zur·ka (mə zur′kə) *n.* [Pol.] a lively Polish dance in 3/4 or 3/8 time

M.C. 1. master of ceremonies **2.** Member of Congress

Mc·Kin·ley (mə kin′lē), **Mount** mountain in Alas.: highest peak in N.America

McKinley, William 1843–1901; 25th president of the U.S. (1897–1901)

Md., MD Maryland

M.D. Doctor of Medicine

me (mē) *pron.* [OE.] *objective case of* I

Me., ME Maine

mead¹ (mēd) *n.* [OE. *meodu*] an alcoholic liquor made from fermented honey

mead² (mēd) *n. poet. var. of* MEADOW

mead·ow (med′ō) *n.* [< OE. *mæd*] **1.** a piece of land where grass is grown for hay **2.** low, level, moist grassland

mea·ger (mē′gər) *adj.* [< L. *macer,* lean] **1.** thin; lean **2.** poor; not full or rich; inadequate Brit. sp. **mea′gre** —**mea′ger·ly** *adv.* —**mea′ger·ness** *n.*

meal¹ (mēl) *n.* [OE. *mæl*] **1.** any of the times for eating, as lunch, dinner, etc. **2.** the food served at such a time

meal² (mēl) *n.* [OE. *melu*] **1.** any edible grain, coarsely ground [*cornmeal*] **2.** any substance similarly ground —**meal′y** *adj.* **-i·er, -i·est**

meal′y-mouthed′ (-ē mou′thd′) *adj.* not outspoken or blunt; euphemistic

mean¹ (mēn) *vt.* **meant** (ment),

mean'ing [OE. *mænan*] 1. to have in mind; intend *[he means to go]* 2. to intend to express *[say what you mean]* 3. to signify; denote *["oui" means "yes"]* —*vi.* 1. to have a (specified) degree of importance, effect, etc. *[honors mean little to him]* —**mean well** to have good intentions

mean² (mēn) *adj.* [OE. *(ge)mǣne*] 1. low in quality or value; paltry; inferior 2. poor in appearance; shabby 3. ignoble; petty 4. stingy 5. contemptibly selfish, bad-tempered, etc. 6. [Slang] *a)* difficult *b)* expert —**mean'ly** *adv.* —**mean'ness** *n.*

mean³ (mēn) *adj.* [< L. *medius*, middle] 1. halfway between extremes 2. average —*n.* 1. what is between extremes 2. *Math.* a number between the smallest and largest values of a set of quantities; esp., an average

me·an·der (mē an'dər) *vi.* [< Gr. *Maiandros*, a winding river in Asia Minor] 1. to take a winding course: said of a stream 2. to wander idly

mean'ie, mean'y *n., pl.* **-ies** [Colloq.] one who is mean, selfish, etc.

mean'ing *n.* what is meant; what is intended to be signified, understood, etc.; import *[a look full of meaning]* —**mean'ing·ful** *adj.* —**mean'ing·less** *adj.*

means (mēnz) *n.pl.* [< MEAN³, *n.*] 1. *[with sing. or pl. v.]* that by which something is done or obtained; agency *[a means to an end]* 2. resources; wealth —**by all means** 1. without fail 2. certainly —**by means of** by using —**by no means** not at all

meant (ment) *pt. & pp. of* MEAN¹

mean'time' *adv.* 1. in or during the intervening time 2. at the same time —*n.* the intervening time Also **mean'while'**

mea·sles (mē'z'lz) *n.pl.* [*with sing. v.*] [ME. *maseles*] 1. an acute, infectious, communicable virus disease, usually of children, characterized by small red spots on the skin, high fever, etc. 2. a similar but milder disease: in full **German measles**

mea·sly (mēz'lē) *adj.* **-sli·er, -sli·est** 1. infected with measles 2. [Colloq.] contemptibly slight or worthless

meas·ure (mezh'ər) *n.* [< L. *metiri*, to measure] 1. the extent, dimensions, capacity, etc. of anything 2. a determining of this; measurement 3. *a)* a unit of measurement *b)* any standard of valuation 4. a system of measurement 5. an instrument for measuring 6. a definite quantity measured out 7. a course of action *[reform measures]* 8. a statute; law 9. a rhythmical pattern or unit; specif., the notes and rests between two bars on a musical staff —*vt.* **-ured, -ur·ing** 1. to find out or estimate the extent, dimensions, etc. of, esp. by a standard 2. to mark off by measuring 3. to be a measure of —*vi.* 1. to take measurements 2. to be of specified measurements —**beyond measure** exceedingly —**for good measure** as something extra —**in a measure to** some extent —**measure up** to prove

to be competent —**meas'ur·a·ble** *adj.* —**meas'ur·a·bly** *adv.* —**meas'ur·e·less** *adj.*

meas'ured *adj.* 1. set or marked off by a standard *[a measured mile]* 2. regular or steady *[measured steps]* 3. planned with care *[measured words]*

meas'ure·ment *n.* 1. a measuring or being measured 2. extent or quantity determined by measuring 3. a system of measuring or of measures

meat (mēt) *n.* [OE. *mete*] 1. food: now archaic except in **meat and drink** 2. the flesh of animals, esp. of mammals, used as food 3. the edible part *[a nut meat]* 4. the substance or essence —**meat'y** *adj.* **-i·er, -i·est**

meat'pack'ing *n.* the industry of preparing the meat of animals for market

Mec·ca (mek'ə) one of the two capitals of Saudi Arabia: birthplace of Mohammed, hence Moslem pilgrimage center: pop. 200,000 —*n.* [*often* **m-**] any place that one yearns to go to

me·chan·ic (mə kan'ik) *n.* [< Gr. *mēchanē*, machine] a worker skilled in using tools or repairing machines

me·chan·i·cal *adj.* 1. having to do with machinery or tools 2. produced or operated by machinery 3. of the science of mechanics 4. machinelike; spiritless —**me·chan'i·cal·ly** *adv.*

me·chan·ics *n.pl.* [*with sing. v.*] 1. the science of motion and the action of forces on bodies 2. knowledge of machinery 3. the technical aspect *[the mechanics of poetry]*

mech·a·nism (mek'ə niz'm) *n.* [see MECHANIC] 1. the working parts of a machine 2. any system of interrelated parts 3. any physical or mental process by which a result is produced —**mech'a·nis'tic** *adj.*

mech'a·nize' (-nīz') *vt.* **-nized', -niz'ing** 1. to make mechanical 2. to equip (an industry) with machinery or (an army, etc.) with motor vehicles, tanks, etc. —**mech'a·ni·za'tion** *n.*

mech'an·o·ther'a·py *n.* the treatment of disease by mechanical means, as massage —**mech'an·o·ther'a·pist** *n.*

med·al (med'l) *n.* [< LL. *medialis*, medial] 1. a small, flat piece of inscribed metal, commemorating some event or awarded for some distinguished action, merit, etc. 2. a disk bearing a religious symbol

med'al·ist *n.* one awarded a medal

me·dal·lion (mə dal'yən) *n.* [< Fr.] 1. a large medal 2. a design, portrait, etc. shaped like a medal

med·dle (med'l) *vi.* **-dled, -dling** [< L. *miscere*, mix] to interfere in another's affairs —**med'dler** *n.* —**med'dle·some** (-səm) *adj.*

me·di·a (mē'dē ə) *n. alt. pl. of* MEDIUM: see MEDIUM (*n.* 3)

me·di·al (mē'dē əl) *adj.* [< L. *medius*] 1. middle 2. ordinary

me·di·an (mē'dē ən) *n.* 1. middle; intermediate 2. designating the middle number in a series —*n.* a median number, point, line, etc.

me·di·ate (mē'dē āt') *vi.* **-at'ed,**

-at′ing 1. to be in an intermediate position 2. to be an intermediary — vt. to settle (differences) between persons, nations, etc. by intervention —me′di·a′tion n. —me′di·a′tor n.

med·ic (med′ik) n. [Colloq.] 1. a physician or surgeon 2. a member of a military medical corps

Med′i·caid′(-ā′) n. [also m-] a State and Federal health program for paying certain medical expenses of persons having a low income

med·i·cal (med′i k'l) adj. of or connected with the practice or study of medicine —med′i·cal·ly adv.

Med′i·care′ (-ker′) n. [also m-] a Federal health program for paying certain medical expenses of the aged

med′i·cate′ (-kāt′) vt.-cat′ed, -cat′ing [< L. medicari, heal] to treat with medicine —med′i·ca′tion n.

me·dic·i·nal (mə dis′n'l) adj. of, or having the properties of, medicine

med·i·cine (med′ə s'n) n. [< L. medicus, physician] 1. the science of treating and preventing disease 2. any substance, as a drug, used in treating disease, relieving pain, etc.

medicine man among N.American Indians, etc., a man supposed to have supernatural powers to heal the sick

me·di·e·val (mē′dē ē′v'l) adj. [< L. medius, middle + aevum, age] of or characteristic of the Middle Ages

me·di·o·cre (mē′dē ō′kər) adj. [< L. medius, middle + ocris, peak] 1. ordinary; average 2. inferior —me′di·oc′ri·ty (-äk′rə tē) n., pl. -ties

med·i·tate (med′ə tāt′) vt.-tat′ed, -tat′ing [< L. meditari] to plan or intend —vi. to think deeply —med′i·ta′tion n. —med′i·ta′tive adj.

Med·i·ter·ra·ne·an (med′i tə rā′nē ən) adj. 1. of the large sea (Mediterranean Sea) surrounded by Europe, Africa, & Asia 2. designating furniture made to simulate heavy, ornately carved Renaissance furniture

me·di·um (mē′dē əm) n., pl. -di·ums, -di·a (-ə) [L. < medius, middle] 1. a) something intermediate b) a middle state or degree; mean 2. an intervening thing through which a force acts 3. any means, agency, etc.; specif., a means of communication that reaches the general public: a singular form media (pl. medias) is sometimes heard 4. any surrounding substance or environment 5. pl. -di·ums one through whom messages are supposedly sent from the dead —adj. intermediate in size, quality, etc.

med·ley (med′lē) n., pl. -leys [ult. < L. miscere, mix] 1. a mixture of dissimilar things 2. a musical piece made up of various tunes or passages

me·dul·la (mi dul′ə) n., pl. -las, -lae (-ē) [L.. the marrow] Anat. 1. a widening of the spinal cord forming the lowest part of the brain: in full medulla ob·lon·ga·ta (äb′lŏŋ gät′ə) 2. the inner substance of an organ

meek (mēk) adj. [< ON. miukr, gentle] 1. patient and mild 2. too submissive; spiritless —meek′ly adv. —meek′ness n.

meer·schaum (mir′shəm) n. [G. < meer, sea + schaum, foam] 1. a white, claylike mineral used for tobacco pipes 2. a pipe made of this

meet¹ (mēt) vt. met, meet′ing [OE. metan] 1. to come upon; encounter 2. to be present at the arrival of [to meet a bus] 3. to come into contact with 4. to be introduced to 5. to contend with; deal with 6. to experience [to meet disaster] 7. to be perceived by (the eye, etc.) 8. a) to satisfy (a demand, etc.) b) to pay (a bill, etc.) —vi. 1. to come together 2. to come into contact, etc. 3. to be introduced 4. to assemble —n. a meeting [a track meet] —meet with 1. to experience 2. to receive

meet² (mēt) adj. [< OE. (ge)mæte, fitting] [Now Rare] suitable; proper

meet′ing n. 1. a coming together 2. a gathering of people 3. a junction

meg·a- [Gr. < megas, great] a combining form meaning: 1. large, great, powerful 2. a million of

meg·a·hertz (meg′ə hurts′) n., pl. -hertz′ [MEGA- + HERTZ] one million hertz: formerly meg′a·cy′cle (-sī′k'l)

meg·a·lo·ma·ni·a (meg′ə lō mā′nē ə) n. [< Gr. megas, large + -MANIA] a mental disorder characterized by delusions of grandeur, power, etc.

meg·a·lop·o·lis (meg′ə läp′ə ləs) n. [Gr., great city] a vast urban area

meg·a·phone (meg′ə fōn′) n. [MEGA- + -PHONE] a funnel-shaped device for increasing the volume of the voice

meg′a·ton′ (-tun′) n. the explosive force of a million tons of TNT

Me·kong (mā′käŋ′, -kôŋ′) river in SE Asia, flowing into the South China Sea

mel·a·mine (mel′ə mēn′) n. [G. melamin] a white crystalline compound used in making synthetic resins

mel·an·cho·li·a (mel′ən kō′lē ə) n. a mental disorder, often psychotic, characterized by extreme depression

mel·an·chol·y (mel′ən käl′ē) n. [< Gr. melas, black + cholē, bile] sadness and depression of spirits —adj. 1. sad and depressed 2. causing sadness

Mel·a·ne·sia (mel′ə nē′zhə) a group of islands in the South Pacific — Mel′a·ne′sian adj., n.

mé·lange (mā länzh′, -länj′) n. [Fr. < mêler, to mix] a mixture; medley

mel·a·nin (mel′ə nin) n. [< Gr. melas, black] a brownish-black pigment found in skin, hair, etc.

mel·a·no·ma (mel′ə nō′mə) n., pl. -mas, -ma·ta (-mə tə) a tumor containing melanin

Mel·ba toast (mel′bə) [< N. Melba (1861-1931), Australian soprano] very crisp, thinly sliced toast

Mel·bourne (mel′bərn) seaport in SE Australia: pop. 2,108,000

meld (meld) vt., vi. [G. melden, announce] *Card Games* to expose and declare (certain cards) for a score —*n.* the cards melded

me·lee, mê·lée (mā′lā, mā lā′) *n.* [Fr.] a confused fight or hand-to-hand struggle among a number of people

mel·io·rate (mēl′yə rāt′) *vt.*, *vi.* -rat′ed, -rat′ing [< L. *melior*, better] to make or become better

mel·lif·lu·ous (mə lif′loo wəs) *adj.* [< L. *mel*, honey + *fluere*, to flow] sounding sweet and smooth: also **mel·lif′lu·ent** —**mel·lif′lu·ence** *n.*

mel·low (mel′ō) *adj.* [prob. < OE. *melu*, MEAL²] 1. soft, sweet, etc. because ripe: said of fruit 2. full-flavored: said of wine, etc. 3. full, rich, soft, etc.: said of sound, light, etc. 4. grown gentle and understanding —*vt.*, *vi.* to make or become mellow

me·lo·di·ous (mə lō′dē əs) *adj.* 1. producing melody 2. pleasing to hear; tuneful —**me·lo′di·ous·ly** *adv.*

mei·o·dra·ma (mel′ə drä′mə, -dram′ə) *n.* [< Fr. < Gr. *melos*, song + LL. *drama*, drama] a drama with sensational action, extravagant emotions, stereotyped characters, etc. — **mel′o·dra·mat′ic** (-drə mat′ik) *adj.* **mel′o·dra·mat′ics** (-drə mat′iks) *n.pl.* melodramatic behavior

mel·o·dy (mel′ə dē) *n.*, *pl.* -dies [< Gr. *melos*, song + *aeidein*, sing] 1. pleasing sounds in sequence 2. *Music a)* a tune, song, etc. *b)* the leading part in a harmonic composition — **me·lod·ic** (mə läd′ik) *adj.* —**me·lod′i·cal·ly** *adv.*

mel·on (mel′ən) *n.* [< Gr. *mēlon*, apple] the large, juicy many-seeded fruit of certain trailing plants, as the watermelon, cantaloupe, etc.

melt (melt) *vt.*, *vi.* [OE. *m(i)eltan*] 1. to change from a solid to a liquid state, generally by heat 2. to dissolve 3. to disappear or cause to disappear gradually 4. to soften in feeling

melting pot a country, etc. in which people of various nationalities and races are assimilated

Mel·ville (mel′vil), **Herman** 1819-91; U.S. novelist

mem·ber (mem′bər) *n.* [< L. *membrum*] 1. a limb or other part of a person, animal, or plant 2. a distinct part of a whole 3. any of the persons constituting an organization or group

mem′ber·ship′ *n.* 1. the state of being a member 2. all the members of a group or organization 3. the number of members

mem·brane (mem′brān) *n.* [< L. *membrum*, member] a thin, soft layer of animal or plant tissue that covers or lines an organ or part —**mem′bra·nous** (-brə nəs) *adj.*

me·men·to (mi men′tō, mə-) *n.*, *pl.* -tos, -toes [< L. *meminisse*, remember] a reminder; esp., a souvenir

mem·o (mem′ō) *n.*, *pl.* -os *clipped form of* MEMORANDUM

mem·oirs (mem′wärz) *n.pl.* [< L. *memoria*, memory] 1. an autobiography 2. a record of events based on the writer's personal observation and knowledge

mem·o·ra·bil·i·a (mem′ər ə bil′ē ə) *n.pl.* [L.] things worth remembering

mem·o·ra·ble (mem′ər ə b'l) *adj.* worth remembering; notable; remarkable —**mem′o·ra·bly** *adv.*

mem·o·ran·dum (mem′ə ran′dəm) *n.*, *pl.* -dums, -da (-də) [L.] 1. a short note written to remind oneself of something 2. an informal written communication, as within an office

me·mo·ri·al (mə môr′ē əl) *adj.* [see MEMORY] serving as a remembrance —*n.* anything meant to help people remember a person, event, etc., as a monument, holiday, etc. — **mo′ri·al·ize′** (-īz′) *vt.* -ized′, -iz′ing

Memorial Day a legal holiday in the U.S. (the last Monday in May in most States) in memory of dead servicemen of all wars

mem·o·rize (mem′ə rīz′) *vt.* -rized′, -riz′ing to commit to memory

mem·o·ry (mem′ər ē) *n.*, *pl.* -ries [< L. *memor*, mindful] 1. the power or act of remembering 2. all that one remembers 3. something remembered 4. the period of remembrance [not within my *memory*] 5. commemoration

Mem·phis (mem′fis) city in SW Tenn.: pop. 646,000

men (men) *n.*, *pl. of* MAN

men·ace (men′is) *n.* [< L. *minari*, threaten] a threat or danger —*vt.*, *vi.* -aced, -ac·ing to threaten —**men′ac·ing·ly** *adv.*

mé·nage, me·nage (mā näzh′, mə-) *n.* [Fr. < L. *mansio*, a dwelling] a household

me·nag·er·ie (mə naj′ər ē) *n.* [see prec.] a collection of wild animals kept in cages, etc. for exhibition

mend (mend) *vt.* [see AMEND] 1. to repair 2. to make better; reform [mend your manners] —*vi.* 1. to improve, esp. in health 2. to heal, as a fracture —*n.* 1. a mending 2. a mended place —**on the mend** improving, esp. in health —**mend′er** *n.*

men·da·cious (men dā′shəs) *adj.* [< L. *mendax*] not truthful; lying —**men·dac′i·ty** (-das′ə tē) *n.*

Men·del (men′d'l), **Gre·gor** (grā′gôr) 1822-84; Austrian geneticist

Men·dels·sohn (men′d'l sən), **Felix** (fā′liks) 1809-47; Ger. composer

men·di·cant (men′di kənt) *adj.* [< L. *mendicus*, needy] begging —*n.* 1. a beggar 2. a mendicant friar

men′folk′ *n.pl.* [Dial. or Colloq.] men

me·ni·al (mē′nē əl) *adj.* [< L. *mansio*, house] 1. of or fit for servants; 2. servile; low —*n.* 1. a domestic servant 2. a servile, low person — **me′ni·al·ly** *adv.*

men·in·gi·tis (men′in jīt′is) *n.* [< Gr. *mēninx*, membrane] inflammation of the membranes enveloping the brain and spinal cord

me·nis·cus (mi nis′kəs) *n.*, *pl.* -nis′cus·es, -nis′ci (-nis′ī, -kī) [< Gr. dim. of *mēnē*, the moon] 1. a crescent 2. the convex or concave upper surface of a column of liquid

Men·non·ite (men′ə nīt′) *n.* [< *Menno* Simons, 16th-c. Du. reformer] a member of an evangelical Christian sect living and dressing plainly and rejecting military service, oaths, etc.

men·o·pause (men′ə pôz′) *n.* [< Gr. *mēn*, month + *pauein*, to end] the permanent cessation of menstruation

men·o·rah (mə nô′rə, -nôr′ə) *n.* [Heb., lamp stand] *Judaism* a candelabrum with seven (or nine) branches

men·ses (men′sēz) *n.pl.* [L., pl. of *mensis*, month] the periodic flow, usually monthly, of blood from the uterus

men·stru·ate (men′strōo wāt′, -strāt) *vi.* -at′ed, -at′ing [< L. *mensis*, month] to have a discharge of the menses —**men′stru·al** *adj.* —**men′stru·a′tion** *n.*

men·su·ra·tion (men′shə rā′shən) *n.* [< L. *mensura*, measure] a measuring —**men′sur·a·ble** (-shər ə b′l) *adj.*

-ment (mənt, mint) [< L. *-mentum*] *a suffix meaning:* 1. a result [*improvement*] 2. a means [*adornment*] 3. an act [*movement*] 4. a state [*bereavement*]

men·tal (men′t′l) *adj.* [< L. *mens*, the mind] 1. of, for, by, or in the mind 2. ill in mind [*mental* patients] 3. for the ill in mind [*mental* hospital] —**men′tal·ly** *adv.*

men′tal·ist *n. same as* MIND READER

men·tal·i·ty (men tal′ə tē) *n., pl.* -ties mental capacity or power

mental reservation qualification of (a statement) that one makes to oneself but does not express

mental retardation congenital lowness of intelligence

men·ta·tion (men tā′shən) *n.* the act or process of using the mind

men·thol (men′thôl, -thōl) *n.* [G. < L. *mentha*, MINT²] a white, crystalline alcohol obtained from oil of peppermint and used in medicine, cosmetics, etc. —**men′tho·lat′ed** (-thə lāt′id) *adj.*

men·tion (men′shən) *n.* [< L. *mens*, the mind] 1. a brief reference 2. a citing for honor —*vt.* to refer to briefly or incidentally —**make mention** to mention —**not to mention** without even mentioning

men·tor (men′tər, -tôr) *n.* [< *Mentor*, friend of Odysseus] 1. a wise adviser 2. a teacher or coach

men·u (men′yōō) *n., pl.* -us [Fr. < L. *minutus*, small] a detailed list of the foods served at a meal

me·ow, me·ou (mē ou′) *n.* [echoic] the characteristic vocal sound made by a cat —*vi.* to make this sound

mer·can·tile (mur′kən til) *adj.* of or characteristic of merchants or trade

mer·ce·nar·y (mur′sə ner′ē) *adj.* [< L. *merces*, wages] working or done for payment only —*n., pl.* -ies a soldier hired to serve in a foreign army

mer·cer (mur′sər) *n.* [< L. *merx*, wares] [Brit.] a dealer in textiles

mer·cer·ize (mur′sə rīz′) *vt.* -ized′, -iz′ing [< J. *Mercer*, 19th-c. Eng. calico dealer] to treat (cotton thread or fabric) with an alkali solution to strengthen it, give it a gloss, etc.

mer·chan·dise (mur′chən dīz′; *for n. also* -dīs′) *n.* [see ff.] things bought and sold; wares —*vt., vi.* -dised′, -dis′ing 1. to buy and sell 2. to promote the sale of (a product) Also, for v.. **mer′chan·dize** —**mer′chan·dis′er, mer′chan·diz′er** *n.*

mer·chant (mur′chənt) *n.* [ult. < L. *merx*, wares] 1. one whose business is buying and selling goods 2. a dealer at retail; storekeeper —*adj.* mercantile

mer′chant·man (-mən) *n., pl.* -men a ship used in commerce

merchant marine all the ships of a nation that are used in commerce

mer·ci (mer sē′) *interj.* [Fr.] thanks

mer·ci·ful (mur′si fəl) *adj.* having or showing mercy —**mer′ci·ful·ly** *adv.*

mer′ci·less *adj.* without mercy; pitiless —**mer′ci·less·ly** *adv.*

mer·cu·ri·al (mər kyoor′ē əl) *adj.* having qualities suggestive of mercury; quick, changeable, fickle, etc.

Mer·cu·ro·chrome (mər kyoor′ə krōm′) [see ff.. *n.* & -CHROME] a *trademark for* a red solution of a compound of mercury, used as an antiseptic

Mer·cu·ry (mur′kyoo rē) 1. a Roman god who was the messenger of the other gods 2. the smallest planet in the solar system: see PLANET —*n.* [m-] a heavy, silver-white metallic chemical element, liquid at ordinary temperatures, used in thermometers, etc. —**mer·cu·ric** (mər kyoor′ik) *adj.* —**mer′cu·rous** *adj.*

mer·cy (mur′sē) *n., pl.* -cies [< L. *merces*, payment] 1. a refraining from harming offenders, enemies, etc. 2. imprisonment rather than death for a capital crime 3. a disposition to forgive or be kind 4. the power to forgive 5. a lucky thing; blessing —**at the mercy of** in the power of

mercy killing *same as* EUTHANASIA

mere (mir) *adj. superl.* **mer′est** [< L. *merus*, pure] nothing more or other than; bare [a *mere* trifle]

mere′ly *adv.* only; simply

mer·e·tri·cious (mer′ə trish′əs) *adj.* [< L. *meretrix*, a prostitute] 1. alluring but tawdry 2. specious

mer·gan·ser (mər gan′sər) *n.* [< L. *mergus*, diver (bird) + *anser*, goose] a large, fish-eating, diving duck

merge (murj) *vi., vt.* merged, merg′ing [L. *mergere*, to dip] 1. to lose or cause to lose identity by being absorbed or combined 2. to unite

merg′er *n.* a merging; specif.. a combining of several companies in one

me·rid·i·an (mə rid′ē ən) *n.* [< L. *meridies*, noon] 1. the highest point of power, etc. 2. *a)* a circle on the earth's surface passing through the geographical poles and any given point *b)* any of the lines of longitude

me·ringue (mə raŋ′) *n.* [Fr. < ?] egg whites beaten stiff and mixed with sugar: used as a pie covering, etc.

me·ri·no (mə rē′nō) *n., pl.* -nos [Sp.] 1. one of a hardy breed of sheep with long, fine, silky wool 2. the wool 3. yarn or cloth made of it

mer·it (mer'it) *n.* [< L. *merere,* deserve] 1. worth; value; excellence 2. something deserving reward, praise, etc. 3. [*pl.*] intrinsic rightness or wrongness —*vt.* to deserve

mer·i·to·ri·ous (mer'ə tôr'ē əs) *adj.* having merit; deserving reward, praise, etc. —**mer'i·to'ri·ous·ly** *adv.* —**mer'i·to'ri·ous·ness** *n.*

Mer·lin (mur'lin) *Arthurian Legend* a magician, helper of King Arthur

mer·maid (mur'mād') *n.* [< OE. *mere,* sea + MAID] an imaginary sea creature with the head and upper body of a woman and the tail of a fish —**mer'man'** *n.masc., pl.* -**men'**

mer·ri·ment (mer'i mənt) *n.* merrymaking; gaiety and fun; mirth

mer·ry (mer'ē) *adj.* -**ri·er,** -**ri·est** [< OE. *myrge,* pleasing] 1. full of fun; gay 2. festive —**make merry** to be gay or festive —**mer'ri·ly** *adv.* —**mer'ri·ness** *n.*

MERMAID

mer·ry-go-round' *n.* 1. a circular, revolving platform with wooden animals and seats on it, used as an amusement ride 2. a whirl, as of work

mer·ry·mak·ing *n.* a having fun; festivity —**mer'ry·mak'er** *n.*

me·sa (mā'sə) *n.* [Sp. < L. *mensa,* table] a high plateau with steep sides

mes·ca·line (mes'kə lēn', -lin) *n.* [< MexInd. *mexcalli,* a spineless cactus] a psychedelic drug obtained from a cactus plant (**mescal**)

mes·dames (mā däm') *n. pl. of* MADAME, MADAM (sense 1), *or* MRS.

mes·de·moi·selles (mā'də mə zel') *n. pl. of* MADEMOISELLE

mesh (mesh) *n.* [prob. < MDu. *mæsche*] 1. any of the open spaces of a net, screen, etc. 2. a net or network 3. a netlike material, as for stockings 4. the engagement of the teeth of gears —*vt., vi.* 1. to entangle or become entangled 2. to engage or become engaged: said of gears 3. to interlock

mes·mer·ize (mez'mər īz', mes'-) *vt.* -**ized',** -**iz'ing** [< F. A. *Mesmer,* 18th-c. G. physician] to hypnotize —**mes'mer·ism** *n.* —**mes'mer·ist** *n.*

Mes·o·po·ta·mi·a (mes'ə pə tā'mē ə) ancient country in SW Asia, between the Tigris & Euphrates rivers

Mes·o·zo·ic (mes'ə zō'ik, mez'-) *adj.* [< Gr. *mesos,* middle + ZO(O)- + -IC] designating the geologic era (c.230–65 million years ago) characterized by dinosaurs, the appearance of birds, etc.

mes·quite, mes·quit (mes kēt') *n.* [< MexInd. *mizquitl*] a thorny shrub of the SW U.S. and Mexico

mess (mes) *n.* [< L. *missus,* course (as at a meal)] 1. a serving, as of porridge 2. a group of people who regularly eat together, as in the army 3. the meal they eat 4. a jumble 5. a state of trouble, disorder, untidiness, etc. —*vt.* 1. to make dirty or untidy 2. to bungle; botch (*up*) —*vi.* 1. to eat as one of a mess 2. to make a mess 3. to putter or meddle (*in, with, around,* etc.) —**mess'y** *adj.* -**i·er,** -**i·est** —**mess'i·ly** *adv.* —**mess'i·ness** *n.*

mes·sage (mes'ij) *n.* [< L. *mittere,* send] 1. a communication sent between persons 2. the chief idea that a writer, artist, etc. seeks to communicate in a work —**get the message** [Colloq.] to understand a hint

mes·sen·ger (mes''n jər) *n.* one who carries messages, or does errands

mess hall a room or building where soldiers, etc., regularly have meals

Mes·si·ah (mə sī'ə) [< Heb. *māshīah,* anointed] 1. *Judaism* the expected deliverer of the Jews 2. *Christianity* Jesus —**Mes·si·an·ic** (mes'ē an'ik) *adj.*

mes·sieurs (mes'ərz; Fr. mā syö') *n. pl. of* MONSIEUR

Messrs. (mes'ərz) *Messieurs:* now used chiefly as the pl. of MR.

mes·ti·zo (mes tē'zō) *n., pl.* -**zos,** -**zoes** [Sp. < L. *miscere,* mix] a person of mixed parentage, esp. Spanish and American Indian

met (met) *pt. & pp. of* MEET[1]

met. metropolitan

meta- [< Gr. *meta,* after] *a prefix meaning:* 1. changed [*metamorphosis*] 2. after, beyond, higher [*metaphysics*]

me·tab·o·lism (mə tab'ə liz'm) *n.* [< Gr. *meta,* beyond + *ballein,* throw] the process in organisms by which protoplasm is formed from food and broken down into waste matter, with release of energy —**met·a·bol·ic** (met'ə bäl'ik) *adj.* —**me·tab'o·lize'** (-līz') *vt., vi.* -**lized',** -**liz'ing**

met·a·car·pus (met'ə kär'pəs) *n., pl.* -**pi** (-pī) [ModL. < Gr. *meta-,* over + *karpos,* wrist] the part of the hand between the wrist and the fingers —**met'a·car'pal** *adj., n.*

met·al (met''l) *n.* [< Gr. *metallon,* a mine] 1. *a)* any of a class of chemical elements, as iron, gold, copper, etc., that have luster, can conduct heat and electricity, etc. *b)* an alloy of such elements, as brass, bronze, etc. 2. anything consisting of metal —**me·tal·lic** (mə tal'ik) *adj.* —**me·tal'li·cal·ly** *adv.*

met·al·lur·gy (met''l ur'jē) *n.* [< Gr. *metallon,* metal + *ergon,* work] the science of separating metals from their ores and preparing them for use by smelting, refining, etc. —**met'al·lur'gi·cal** *adj.* —**met'al·lur'gist** *n.*

met·a·mor·phose (met'ə môr'fōz, -fōs) *vt., vi.* -**phosed,** -**phos·ing** to change in form; transform

met·a·mor·pho·sis (met'ə môr'fə sis, -môr fō'-) *n., pl.* -**ses** (-sēz) [< Gr. *meta,* over + *morphē,* form] 1. a change in form, structure, or function; specif., the physical change undergone by some animals, as of the tadpole to the frog 2. any marked change, as in character, appearance, or condition —**met'a·mor'phic** *adj.*

met·a·phor (met'ə fôr') *n.* [< Gr. *meta,* over + *pherein,* to bear] a figure of speech in which one thing is spoken of as if it were another (Ex.: "all the world's a stage") —**met'a·phor'i·cal** *adj.* —**met'a·phor'i·cal·ly** *adv.*

met·a·phys·i·cal (met'ə fiz'i k'l) *adj.* 1. of, or having the nature of, metaphysics 2. very abstract or subtle 3. supernatural

met'a·phys'ics (-iks) *n.pl. [with sing. v.]* [< Gr. *meta* (ta) *physika*, after (the) *Physics* (of Aristotle)] 1. the branch of philosophy that seeks to explain the nature of being and reality 2. speculative philosophy in general

me·tas·ta·sis (mə tas'tə sis) *n., pl.* -ses' (-sēz') [< Gr. *meta*, after + *histanai*, to place] the transfer, as of malignant cells, from one part of the body to another through the bloodstream —**me·tas'ta·size'** (-sīz') *vi.* -sized', -siz'ing

met·a·tar·sus (met'ə tär'səs) *n., pl.* -si (-sī) [ModL. < Gr. *meta-*, over + *tarsos*, flat of the foot] the part of the foot between the ankle and toes —**met'a·tar'sal** *adj., n.*

me·tath·e·sis (mə tath'ə sis) *n., pl.* -ses' (-sēz') [LL. < Gr. < *meta*, over + *tithenai*, to place] transposition, specif. of letters or sounds in a word

mete (mēt) *vt.* met'ed, met'ing [OE. *metan*] to allot; portion (*out*)

met·em·psy·cho·sis (mi temp'si kō'sis, met'əm sī-) *n., pl.* -ses (-sēz) [LL. < Gr. < *meta*, over + *en*, in + *psychē*, soul] transmigration of souls

me·te·or (mēt'ē ər) *n.* [< Gr. *meta*, beyond + *eōra*, a hovering] 1. the streak of light, etc. occurring when a meteoroid enters the earth's atmosphere 2. a meteoroid or meteorite

me·te·or·ic (mēt'ē ôr'ik) *adj.* 1. of a meteor. 2. like a meteor; swift, momentarily brilliant, etc.

me·te·or·ite (mēt'ē ə rīt') *n.* a stone or metal mass remaining from a meteoroid fallen to earth

me'te·or·oid' (-roid') *n.* a small, solid body traveling through outer space, seen as a streak of light when falling to earth

me·te·or·ol·o·gy (mēt'ē ə räl'ə jē) *n.* [see METEOR & -LOGY] the science of the atmosphere and its phenomena; study of weather and climate —**me'te·or·o·log'i·cal** (-ər ə läj'i k'l) *adj.* —**me'te·or·ol'o·gist** *n.*

me·ter¹ (mēt'ər) *n.* [< Gr. *metron*, measure] 1. rhythmic pattern in verse; measured arrangement of syllables according to stress 2. rhythmic pattern in music 3. the basic unit of length in the metric system, equal to 39.37 in.

me·ter² (mēt'ər) *n.* [< METE] 1. an apparatus for measuring and recording the quantity of gas, water, etc. passing through it 2. *same as* PARKING METER

-me·ter (mēt'ər, mi tər) [see METER¹] *a suffix meaning:* 1. a device for measuring [*barometer*] 2. meter(s) in length [*kilometer, centimeter*]

meter maid a woman employed by a police department to issue summonses for illegal parking, jaywalking, etc.

meth·a·done (meth'ə dōn') *n.* [< its chemical name] a synthetic narcotic drug used in medicine, more potent than morphine and not so habit-forming

meth·ane (meth'ān) *n.* [< METHYL] a colorless, odorless, flammable gas formed by the decomposition of vegetable matter, as in marshes

meth·a·nol (meth'ə nôl') *n.* [< METHAN(E) + (ALCOH)OL] a poisonous liquid used as a fuel, solvent, antifreeze, etc.: also called **methyl alcohol**

me·thinks (mi thinks') *v.impersonal* *pt.* -thought' [< OE. *me*, to me + *thyncth*, it seems] [Archaic] it seems to me

meth·od (meth'əd) *n.* [< Fr. < Gr. *meta*, after + *hodos*, a way] 1. a way of doing anything; process 2. system in doing things or handling ideas

me·thod·i·cal (mə thäd'i k'l) *adj.* characterized by method; orderly; systematic —**me·thod'i·cal·ly** *adv.*

Meth·od·ist (meth'ə dist) *n.* a member of a Protestant Christian denomination that developed from the teachings of John Wesley —**Meth'od·ism** *n.*

meth·od·ol·o·gy (meth'ə däl'ə jē) *n.* a system of methods, as in a science

Me·thu·se·lah (mə thōō'zə lə) *Bible* a patriarch who lived 969 years

meth·yl (meth'əl) *n.* [< Gr. *methy*, wine + *hylē*, wood] a hydrocarbon radical found in methanol

me·tic·u·lous (mə tik'yoo ləs) *adj.* [< L. *metus*, fear] very careful or too careful about details; scrupulous or finicky —**me·tic'u·lous·ly** *adv.*

mé·tier (mā tyā') *n.* [Fr., trade] work that one is particularly suited for

me·tre (mēt'ər) *n. Brit. sp.* of METER

met·ric (met'rik) *adj.* 1. *same as* METRICAL 2. *a)* of the meter (unit of length) *b)* of the metric system

met'ri·cal *adj.* 1. of or composed in meter or verse 2. of or used in measurement —**met'ri·cal·ly** *adv.*

met·ri·ca·tion (met'rə kā'shən) *n.* [METRIC + -ATION] a changing over to the metric system of weights and measures —**met'ri·cate'** *vt.* -cat'ed, -cat'ing

met'ri·cize' (-sīz') *vt.* -cized', -ciz'ing to change to the metric system

metric system a decimal system of weights and measures whose basic units are the gram (.0022046 pound), the meter (39.37 inches), and the liter (61.025 cubic inches)

met·ro·nome (met'rə nōm') *n.* [< Gr. *metron*, measure + *nomos*, law] a device that beats time at a desired rate, as for piano practice

me·trop·o·lis (mə träp'′l is) *n., pl.* -lis·es [< Gr. *mētēr*, mother + *polis*, city] 1. the main city, often the capital, of a country, state, etc. 2. any large or important city —**met·ro·pol·i·tan** (met'rə päl'ɪ t'n) *adj.*

met·tle (met'l) *n.* [var. of METAL] spirit; courage; ardor —**on one's mettle** prepared to do one's best

met'tle·some (-səm) *adj.* full of mettle; spirited, ardent, brave, etc.

mew[1] (myoō) *vt.* [ult. < L. *mutare*, to change] to confine: see also MEWS

mew[2] (myoō) *n.* [echoic] the characteristic vocal sound made by a cat —*vi.* to make this sound

mewl (myoōl) *vi.* [< MEW[2]] to cry weakly, like a baby; whimper

mews (myoōz) *n.pl.* [*usually with sing. v.*] [< MEW[1]] [Chiefly Brit.] stables or carriage houses in a court or alley

Mex. 1. Mexican 2. Mexico

Mex·i·co (mek'si kō') 1. country in N.America, south of the U.S.: 760,373 sq. mi.; pop. 45,671,000 2. Gulf of, arm of the Atlantic, east of Mexico —**Mex'i·can** (-kən) *adj., n.*

Mexico City capital of Mexico: pop. 3,353,000

mez·za·nine (mez'ə nēn') *n.* [< It. *mezzano*, middle] 1. a low-ceilinged story between two main stories, often a balcony over the main floor 2. the lowest balcony section of a theater

mez'zo-so·pra'no (met'sō-, mez'ō-) *n., pl.* **-nos, -ni** (-nē) [It. < *mezzo*, medium + SOPRANO] a voice or singer between soprano and contralto

mfg. manufacturing

mfr. *pl.* **mfrs.** manufacturer

Mg *Chem.* magnesium

mg, mg. milligram(s)

Mgr. Manager

MHz, Mhz megahertz

mi (mē) *n.* [ML.] *Music* the third tone of the diatonic scale

MI Michigan

mi. 1. mile(s) 2. mill(s)

Mi·am·i (mī am'ē) city on the SE coast of Fla.: pop. 347,000

mi·as·ma (mī az'mə) *n.* [< Gr., pollution] a vapor as from marshes, formerly supposed to poison the air

mi·ca (mī'kə) *n.* [L., a crumb] a mineral that crystallizes in thin, flexible layers, resistant to heat

mice (mīs) *n., pl. of* MOUSE

Mi·chel·an·ge·lo (mī'k'l an'jə lō') 1475–1564; It. painter & sculptor

Mich·i·gan (mish'ə gən) 1. Middle Western State of the U.S.: 58,216 sq. mi.; pop. 9,258,000; cap. Lansing: abbrev. **Mich.** 2. Lake, one of the Great Lakes, between Mich. & Wis.

micro- [< Gr. *mikros*, small] *a combining form meaning:* 1. little, small [*microfilm*] 2. enlarging [*microscope*] 3. microscopic [*microbiology*] 4. one millionth [*microgram*]

mi·crobe (mī'krōb) *n.* [< Gr. *mikros*, small + *bios*, life] a microorganism, esp. one causing disease

mi·cro·chip (mī'krō chip') *n.* same as INTEGRATED CIRCUIT

mi·cro·cosm (mī'krə käz'm) *n.* [see MICRO- & COSMOS] something regarded as a world in miniature

mi·cro·fiche (-fēsh') *n.* [Fr. < *micro-* + *fiche*, small card] a film card on which many pages of greatly reduced microfilm copy are recorded

mi·cro·film' *n.* film on which documents, etc. are photographed in a reduced size for convenience —*vt., vi.* to photograph on microfilm

mi·cro·groove' *n.* a very narrow needle groove, as for an LP record

mi·crom·e·ter (mī kräm'ə tər) *n.* [< Fr.: see MICRO- & -METER] an instrument for measuring very small distances, angles, etc.

mi·cron (mī'krän) *n.* [< Gr. *mikros*, small] one millionth of a meter

Mi·cro·ne·sia (mī'krə nē'zhə) the groups of islands in the Pacific east of Philippines —**Mi'cro·ne'sian** *adj., n.*

mi·cro·or·gan·ism (mī'krō ôr'gə niz'm) *n.* any microscopic animal or vegetable organism; esp., any of the bacteria, protozoans, viruses, etc.

mi·cro·phone (mī'krə fōn') *n.* [MICRO- + -PHONE] an instrument for transforming sound waves into corresponding electrical signals

mi·cro·scope' (-skōp') *n.* [see MICRO- & -SCOPE] an instrument consisting of a combination of lenses, for making very small objects, as microorganisms, look larger

mi·cro·scop'ic (-skäp'ik) *adj.* 1. so small as to be invisible or obscure except through a microscope; minute 2. of, with, or like a microscope —**mi'cro·scop'i·cal·ly** *adv.*

mi·cro·wave' *n.* an electromagnetic wave between 300,000 megahertz and 300 megahertz in frequency —*adj.* of or with an oven using microwaves to penetrate food and cook it fast

mid[1] (mid) *adj.* [OE. *midd*] middle

mid[2] (mid) *prep.* [Poet.] amid: also **'mid**

mid- *a combining form meaning* middle or middle part of

mid'air' *n.* any point not in contact with the ground or other surface

Mi·das (mī'dəs) *Gr. Myth.* a king granted the power of turning everything that he touched into gold

mid·day (mid'dā') *n., adj.* noon

mid·dle (mid'l) *adj.* [OE. *middel*] 1. halfway between two given points, times, etc. 2. intermediate 3. [M-] designating a stage in language development intermediate between *Old* and *Modern* [*Middle* English] —*n.* 1. a point or part halfway between extremes; middle point, time, etc. 2. something intermediate 3. the middle part of the body; waist

middle age the time between youth and old age —**mid'dle-aged'** *adj.*

Middle Ages the period of European history between ancient and modern times, 476 A.D.–c.1450 A.D.

Middle America the conventional or conservative American middle class

mid'dle·brow' (-brou') *n.* [Colloq.] one regarded as having conventional, middle-class tastes or opinions

middle class the social class between the aristocracy or very wealthy and the lower working class

middle ear the part of the ear including the eardrum and a cavity containing three small bones; tympanum

Middle East 1. area from Afghanistan to Egypt, including the Arabian

Peninsula & Asiatic Turkey 2. the Near East, excluding the Balkans

Middle English the English language between c.1100 and c.1500

mid′dle·man′ n., pl. **-men′** 1. a trader who buys from a producer and sells at wholesale or retail 2. a go-between

mid′dle·most′ adj. same as MIDMOST

mid′dle-of-the-road′ adj. avoiding extremes, esp. political extremes

middle school in some school systems, a school with usually grades 5 to 8

mid′dle-weight′ n. a boxer or wrestler between a welterweight and a light heavyweight (in boxing, 148-160 lb.)

Middle West region of the NC U.S., between the Rocky Mountains & the E border of Ohio —**Middle Western**

mid·dling (mid′liŋ) adj. of middle size, quality, state, etc.; medium —adv. [Colloq.] fairly; moderately —**fair to middling** [Colloq.] moderately good or well

mid·dy (mid′ē) n., pl. **-dies** 1. [Colloq.] a midshipman 2. a loose blouse with a sailor collar, worn by women and children

midge (mij) n. [OE. mycg] a small, gnatlike insect

midg·et (mij′it) n. 1. a very small person 2. anything very small of its kind —adj. miniature

mid·land (mid′lənd) n. the middle region of a country; interior —adj. in or of the midland; inland

mid′most′ adj. exactly in the middle, or nearest the middle

mid′night′ (-nīt′) n. twelve o'clock at night —adj. 1. of or at midnight 2. like midnight; very dark

mid′point′ n. a point at or close to the middle or center

mid·riff (mid′rif) n. [< OE. midd, MID¹ + hrif, belly] 1. same as DIAPHRAGM (sense 1) 2. the middle part of the torso, between the abdomen and the chest

mid′ship′man (-ship′mən) n., pl. **-men** a student in training to be a naval officer

midst¹ (midst) n. the middle; central part —**in the midst of** 1. in the middle of 2. during

midst² (midst) prep. [Poet.] in the midst of; amidst: also ′**midst**

mid·stream (mid′strēm′) n. the middle of a stream

mid′sum′mer n. 1. the middle of summer 2. the time of the summer solstice, about June 21

mid′term′ adj. in the middle of the term —n. [Colloq.] a midterm examination

mid′way′ (-wā′) n. that part of a fair where sideshows, etc. are located —adj., adv. in the middle of the way or distance; halfway

Mid′west′ n. same as MIDDLE WEST

mid′wife′ (-wīf′) n., pl. **-wives′** [< ME. mid, with + wif, woman] a

woman who helps women in childbirth —**mid′wife′ry** (-wī′fə rē, -wīf′rē) n.

mid′win′ter n. 1. the middle of winter 2. the time of the winter solstice, about Dec. 22

mid′year′ adj. in the middle of the year —n. [Colloq.] a midyear examination

mien (mēn) n. [short for DEMEAN²] one's appearance, bearing, or manner

miff (mif) vt. [prob. orig. cry of disgust] [Colloq.] to offend

MIG (mig) n. [< Mikoyan & Gurevich, its Soviet designers] a small, fast, highly maneuverable jet military aircraft: also **MiG**

might¹ (mīt) v. [OE. mihte] 1. pt. of MAY 2. an auxiliary generally equivalent to MAY [it might rain]

might² (mīt) n. [OE. miht] strength, power, or vigor

might·y (-ē) adj. **-i·er, -i·est** 1. powerful; strong 2. remarkably large, etc.; great —adv. [Colloq.] very —**might′i·ly** adv. —**might′i·ness** n.

mi·gnon·ette (min′yə net′) n. [< Fr. mignon, small] a plant with spikes of small, fragrant flowers

mi·graine (mī′grān) n. [< Gr. hēmi-, half + kranion, skull] an intense, periodic headache, usually limited to one side of the head

mi·grant (mī′grənt) adj. migrating —n. one that migrates; specif., a farm laborer who moves from place to place to harvest seasonal crops

mi·grate (mī′grāt) vi. **-grat·ed, -grat·ing** [< L. migrare] 1. to settle in another country or region 2. to move to another region with the change in season, as many birds —**mi·gra·to·ry** (mī′grə tôr′ē) adj.

mi·gra·tion (mī grā′shən) n. 1. a migrating 2. a group of people, birds, etc. migrating together

mi·ka·do (mi kä′dō) n., pl. **-dos** [< Jap. mi, exalted + kado, gate] [Obs.] an emperor of Japan

mike (mīk) n. [Colloq.] a microphone

mil (mil) n. [L. mille, thousand] a unit of length, .001 of an inch

mil. military

mi·la·dy, mi·la·di (mi lā′dē) n. [Fr. < Eng. my lady] 1. a noblewoman 2. a woman of fashion: advertisers' term

Mi·lan (mi lan′) city in NW Italy: pop. 1,673,000

milch (milch) adj. [ME. milche] kept for milking [milch cows]

mild (mīld) adj. [OE. milde] 1. gentle or kind; not severe 2. having a soft, pleasant flavor [a mild cheese] —**mild′ly** adv. —**mild′ness** n.

mil·dew (mil′dōō′) n. [OE. meledeaw, lit., honeydew] a fungus that attacks some plants or appears on damp cloth, etc. as a whitish coating —vt., vi. to affect or be affected with mildew

mile (mīl) n. [< L. milia (passuum), thousand (paces)] a unit of linear measure, equal to 5,280 ft.: the **nautical mile** is 6,076.12 feet

---

mile'age (-ij) *n.* **1.** an allowance per mile for traveling expenses **2.** total miles traveled **3.** the average number of miles that can be traveled, as per gallon of fuel

mile'post' *n.* a signpost showing the number of miles to or from a place

mil'er (-ər) *n.* one who competes in mile races

mile'stone' *n.* **1.** a stone set up to show the distance in miles from some place **2.** a significant event

mi·lieu (mēl yoo') *n.* [Fr. < L. *medius*, middle + *locus*, a place] environment; esp., social setting

mil·i·tant (mil'i tənt) *adj.* [< L. *miles*, soldier] **1.** fighting **2.** ready to fight, esp. for some cause —*n.* a militant person —**mil'i·tan·cy** *n.* — **mil'i·tant·ly** *adv.*

mil'i·ta·rism (-tər iz'm) *n.* **1.** military spirit **2.** a policy of aggressive military preparedness —**mil'i·ta·rist** *n.* —**mil'i·ta·ris'tic** *adj.*

mil'i·ta·rize' (-tə rīz') *vt.* -rized', -riz'ing to equip and prepare for war

mil'i·tar'y (-ter'ē) *adj.* [< L. *miles*, soldier] **1.** of, for, or done by soldiers **2.** of, for, or fit for war **3.** of the army —the military the army

military police soldiers assigned to carry on police duties for the army

mil·i·tate (mil'ə tāt') *vi.* -tat'ed, -tat'ing [< L. *militare*, be a soldier] to operate or work (*against*)

mi·li·tia (mə lish'ə) *n.* [< L. *miles*, soldier] an army composed of citizens called out in time of emergency — **mi·li'tia·man** (-mən) *n., pl.* -men

milk (milk) *n.* [OE. *meolc*] **1.** a white liquid secreted by special glands of female mammals for suckling their young; esp., cow's milk **2.** any liquid like this (coconut *milk*) —*vt.* **1.** to squeeze milk from (a cow, goat, etc.) **2.** to extract money, ideas, etc. from as if by milking —**milk'er** *n.*

milk glass a nearly opaque whitish glass

milk'maid' *n.* a girl or woman who milks cows or works in a dairy

milk'man' *n., pl.* -men' a man who sells or delivers milk for a dairy

milk of magnesia a milky-white suspension of magnesium hydroxide in water, used as a laxative and antacid

milk'shake' *n.* a drink of milk, flavoring, and ice cream, shaken until frothy

milk'sop' (-säp') *n.* a sissy

milk tooth any of the temporary, first teeth of a child or animal

milk'weed' *n.* any of a group of plants with a milky juice

milk'y (-ē) *adj.* -i·er, -i·est **1.** like milk; esp., white as milk **2.** of or containing milk —**milk'i·ness** *n.*

Milky Way a broad, faintly luminous band of very distant stars and clouds of gas, seen across the sky at night

mill¹ (mil) *n.* [< L. *mola*, millstone] **1.** a building with machinery for grinding grain into flour or meal **2.** any of various machines for grinding, crushing, cutting, etc. **3.** a factory (a textile *mill*) —*vt.* to grind, form, etc.

by or in a mill —*vi.* to move (*around* or *about*) confusedly, as a crowd —**in the mill** in preparation —**through the mill** [Colloq.] through a hard, painful, instructive experience

mill² (mil) *n.* [< L. *mille*, thousand] 1/10 of a cent: unit used in calculating

mil·lage (mil'ij) *n.* taxation in mills per dollar of valuation

mil·len·ni·um (mi len'ē əm) *n., pl.* -**ni·ums**, -**ni·a** (-ə) [< L. *mille*, thousand + *annus*, year] **1.** a thousand years **2.** *Theol.* the period of a thousand years during which Christ will reign on earth (with *the*) **3.** any period of great happiness, peace, etc.

mill·er (mil'ər) *n.* one who owns or operates a mill, esp. a flour mill

mil·let (mil'it) *n.* [< L. *milium*] **1.** a cereal grass whose grain is used for food in Europe and Asia **2.** any of several similar grasses used for forage

milli- [< L. *mille*, thousand] *a combining form meaning a 1000th part of* [*millimeter*]

mil·li·gram (mil'ə gram') *n.* one thousandth of a gram: chiefly Brit. sp. **mil'li·gramme'**

mil'li·me'ter (-mēt'ər) *n.* one thousandth of a meter (.03937 inch): chiefly Brit. sp. **mil'li·me'tre**

mil·li·ner (mil'ə nər) *n.* [< *Milaner*, importer of dress wares from Milan] one who makes or sells women's hats

mil·li·ner·y (mil'ə ner'ē) *n.* **1.** women's hats, headdresses, etc. **2.** the work or business of a milliner

mil·lion (mil'yən) *n.* [< L. *mille*, thousand] a thousand thousands; 1,000,000 —**mil'lionth** *adj., n.*

mil'lion·aire' (-yə ner') *n.* a person whose wealth comes to at least a million dollars, pounds, francs, etc.

mill'race' *n.* the channel in which the water driving a mill wheel runs

mill'stone' *n.* **1.** either of a pair of flat, round stones used for grinding grain, etc. **2.** a heavy burden

mill'stream' *n.* water flowing in a millrace

mill'wright' (-rīt') *n.* a worker who builds, installs, or repairs the machinery in a mill

milt (milt) *n.* [prob. < Scand.] the sex glands or sperm of male fishes

Mil·ton (mil't'n), **John** 1608-74; Eng. poet

Mil·wau·kee (mil wô'kē) city in SE Wis.: pop. 636,000

mime (mīm) *n.* [< Gr. *mimos*] **1.** the representation of an action, mood, etc. by gestures, not words **2.** a mimic or pantomimist —*vt.* mimed, mim'-ing to mimic or pantomime

mim·e·o·graph (mim'ē ə graf') *n.* [< Gr. *mimeomai*, I imitate] a machine for making copies of graphic matter by means of an inked stencil —*vt.* to make (such copies) of

mi·met·ic (mi met'ik, mī-) *adj.* [< Gr. *mimeisthai*, to imitate] **1.** imitative **2.** characterized by mimicry

mim·ic (mim'ik) *adj.* [< Gr. *mimos*, a mime] **1.** imitative **2.** make-believe —*n.* an imitator; esp., an actor skilled in mimicry —*vt.* -icked, -ick·ing **1.**

to imitate, often so as to ridicule 2.
to copy or resemble closely

mim·ic·ry (-rē) *n., pl.* **-ries** the
practice, art, or way of mimicking

mi·mo·sa (mi mō′sə) *n.* [see MIME] a
tree, shrub, or herb growing in warm
regions and usually having spikes of
white or pink flowers

min. 1. minimum 2. minute(s)

min·a·ret (min′ə ret′) *n.* [< Ar.
manārah, lighthouse] a
high, slender tower at-
tached to a Moslem
mosque

min·a·to·ry (min′ə
tôr′ē) *adj.* [< L. *min-
ari*, threaten] menac-
ing

mince (mins) *vt.*
minced, minc′ing
[< L. *minutus*, small]
1. to cut up (meat,
etc.) into small pieces
2. to express or do
with affected dainti-
ness 3. to lessen the force of [to mince
no words] —*vi.* to speak or act with
affected daintiness —**minc′ing** *adj.*

mince′meat′ *n.* a mixture of chopped
apples, spices, raisins, etc., and sometimes meat, used as a filling for a pie

mind (mīnd) *n.* [OE. (ge)*mynd*] 1.
memory [to bring to *mind* a story]
2. opinion [to speak one's *mind*] 3. the
seat of consciousness, in which thinking, feeling, etc. take place 4. intellect
5. *same as* PSYCHE (sense 2) 6. reason;
sanity —*vt.* 1. to pay attention to;
heed 2. to obey 3. to take care of
[*mind* the baby] 4. to be careful about
[*mind* the stairs] 5. to care about;
object to [don't *mind* the noise] —*vi.*
1. to pay attention 2. to be obedient
3. to be careful 4. to care; object
—**bear (or keep) in mind** to remember —**blow one's mind** [Slang] to
undergo hallucinations, etc. as from
psychedelic drugs —**change one's
mind** to change one's opinion, purpose, etc. —**have in mind** to intend
—**make up one's mind** to reach a
decision —**on one's mind** 1. filling
one's thoughts 2. worrying one —**out
of one's mind** frantic

mind′ed *adj.* having a specified kind
of mind [high-*minded*]

mind′ful *adj.* having in mind; aware
or careful (*of*) —**mind′ful·ly** *adv.*
—**mind′ful·ness** *n.*

mind reader one who professes ability
to perceive another's thoughts

mind's eye the imagination

mine¹ (mīn) *pron.* [OE. *min*] that or
those belonging to me [this is *mine*]

mine² (mīn) *n.* [MFr.] 1. a large
excavation made in the earth, from
which to extract ores, coal, etc. 2. a
deposit of ore, coal, etc. 3. any great
source of supply 4. *Mil. a*) a tunnel
dug under an enemy's fort, etc., in
which an explosive is placed *b*) an
explosive charge hidden underground

MINARET

or in the sea, for destroying enemy
vehicles, ships, etc. —*vt., vi.* **mined,
min′ing** 1. to dig (ores, etc.) from
(the earth) 2. to dig or lay military
mines in or under 3. to undermine

min′er *n.* one whose work is digging
coal, ore, etc. in a mine

min·er·al (min′ər əl) *n.* [< ML.
minera, a mine] 1. an inorganic
substance found naturally in the earth,
as metallic ore 2. any substance
neither vegetable nor animal —*adj.*
of or containing minerals

mineral jelly *same as* PETROLATUM

min·er·al·o·gy (min′ə räl′ə jē, -ral′-)
n. the scientific study of minerals
—**min′er·al·o·gist** *n.*

mineral oil a colorless, tasteless oil
from petroleum, used as a laxative

mineral water water impregnated
with mineral salts or gases

Mi·ner·va (mi nur′və) the Roman
goddess of wisdom and invention

mi·ne·stro·ne (min′ə strō′nē) *n.* [It.:
ult. < L. *ministrare*, serve] a thick
vegetable soup in a meat broth

min·gle (min′g'l) *vt.* **-gled, -gling**
[< OE. *mengan*, mix] to mix together;
blend —*vi.* 1. to become mixed or
blended 2. to join or unite with others

mini- [< MINI(ATURE)] *a combining
form meaning* miniature, very small,
very short [*miniskirt*]

min·i·a·ture (min′ē ə chər, min′i
chər) *n.* [< L. *miniare*, paint red] 1.
a small painting, esp. a portrait 2. a
copy or model on a very small scale
—*adj.* done on a very small scale

min′i·a·tur·ize′ (-īz′) *vt.* **-ized′,
-iz′ing** to make in a small and compact form —**min′i·a·tur′i·za′tion** *n.*

min·i·cam (min′ē kam′) *n.* a portable TV camera for telecasting or
videotaping news events, sports, etc.

min·im (min′im) *n.* [< L. *minimus*,
least] 1. the smallest liquid measure,
about a drop 2. *Music* a half note

min·i·mize (min′ə mīz′) *vt.* **-mized′,
-miz′ing** to reduce to or estimate at a
minimum

min·i·mum (-məm) *n., pl.* **-mums,
-ma** (-mə) [L., least] 1. the smallest
quantity, number, etc. possible 2. the
lowest degree or point reached —*adj.*
smallest possible, permissible, or
reached: also **min′i·mal**

min·ion (min′yən) *n.* [Fr. *mignon*,
darling] 1. a favorite, esp. one who is
a servile follower: term of contempt
2. a subordinate official

min·is·cule (min′ə skyōōl′) *adj.*
erroneous sp. of MINUSCULE

min·i·se·ries (min′ē sir′ēz) *n., pl.*
-ries a TV drama broadcast serially
in a limited number of episodes

min·i·skirt (min′ē skurt′) *n.* a very
short skirt ending well above the knee

min·is·ter (min′is tər) *n.* [L., a
servant] 1. a person appointed to
head a governmental department 2. a
diplomat representing his government
in a foreign nation 3. one authorized

fat, āpe, cär; ten, ēven; is, bīte; gō, hôrn, tōōl, look; oil, out; up, fur;
chin; she; thin, then; zh, leisure; ŋ, ring; ə for a in ago; ′, (ā′b'l); ē, Fr. coeur;
ö, Fr. feu; Fr. mon; ü, Fr. duc; kh, G. ich, doch; ‡ foreign; < derived from

to conduct religious services in a church; pastor —*vi.* 1. to serve as a minister in a church 2. to give help (*to*) —min'is·te'ri·al (-tir'ē əl) *adj.* —min'is·trant (-trənt) *adj., n.*

min'is·tra'tion (-trā'shən) *n.* the act of giving help or care; service

min'is·try (-trē) *n., pl.* -tries 1. the act of ministering, or serving 2. *a)* the office or function of a clergyman *b)* the clergy 3. *a)* the department under a minister of government *b)* his term of office *c)* the ministers of a particular government as a group

mink (miŋk) *n.* [< Scand.] 1. a weasellike mammal living on land and in water 2. its valuable fur

Min·ne·ap·o·lis (min'ē ap' 'l is) city in E Minn.: pop. 371,000

Min·ne·so·ta (min'ə sōt'ə) Middle Western State of the U.S.: 84,068 sq. mi.; pop. 4,077,000; cap. St. Paul: abbrev. Minn. —Min'ne·so'tan *adj., n.*

min·now (min'ō) *n.* [< OE. *myne*] any of a number of usually small freshwater fishes, commonly used as bait

Mi·no·an (mi nō'ən) *adj.* [< *Minos*, mythical king of Crete] of an advanced prehistoric culture in Crete (c.2800–c.1100 B.C.)

mi·nor (mī'nər) *adj.* [L.] 1. lesser in size, amount, importance, etc. 2. *Music* lower than the corresponding major by a half tone —*vi. Educ.* to have a secondary field of study (*in*) —*n.* 1. a person under full legal age 2. *Educ.* a secondary field of study

mi·nor·i·ty (mə nôr'ə tē, mī-) *n., pl.* -ties 1. the lesser part or smaller number; less than half 2. a racial, religious, or political group that differs from the larger, controlling group 3. the state of being under full legal age

min·strel (min'strəl) *n.* [see MINISTER] 1. a traveling singer of the Middle Ages 2. a member of a comic variety show (**minstrel show**) in which the performers blacken their faces —min'strel·sy (-sē) *n., pl.* -sies

mint¹ (mint) *n.* [< L. < *Juno Moneta*, whose temple was the mint] 1. a place where money is coined by the government 2. a large amount —*adj.* new, as if freshly minted —*vt.* to coin (money) —mint'age *n.*

mint² (mint) *n.* [< Gr. *mintha*] 1. an aromatic plant whose leaves are used for flavoring 2. a mint-flavored candy

mint julep an iced drink of whiskey or brandy, sugar, and mint leaves

min·u·end (min'yoo wend') *n.* [< L. *minuere*, lessen] the number from which another is to be subtracted

min·u·et (min'yoo wet') *n.* [< Fr. < OFr. *menu*, small] 1. a slow, stately dance 2. the music for this

mi·nus (mī'nəs) *prep.* [< L. *minor*, less] 1. less (*four minus two*) 2. [Colloq.] without [*minus a toe*] —*adj.* 1. involving subtraction [*a minus sign*] 2. negative 3. less than [*a grade of* A *minus*] —*n.* a sign (−), indicating subtraction or negative quantity: in full **minus sign**

mi·nus·cule (mi nus'kyool, min'ə skyool') *adj.* [L. *minusculus*] tiny

min·ute¹ (min'it) *n.* [see ff.] 1. the sixtieth part of an hour or of a degree of an arc 2. a moment 3. a specific point in time 4. [*pl.*] an official record of a meeting, etc. —**the minute (that)** just as soon as

mi·nute² (mī nōōt') *adj.* [< L. *minor*, less] 1. very small 2. of little importance 3. of or attentive to tiny details; precise —mi·nute'ly *adv.*

min'ute·man' *n., pl.* -men' [*also* M-] a member of the American citizen army at the time of the Revolution

min·ute steak (min'it) a small, thin steak that can be cooked quickly

mi·nu·ti·ae (mi nōō'shi ē') *n.pl., sing.* -ti·a (-shē ə) [see MINUTE²] small or unimportant details

minx (miŋks) *n.* [< ?] a pert girl

mir·a·cle (mir'ə k'l) *n.* [< L. *mirus*, wonderful] 1. an event or action that apparently contradicts known scientific laws 2. a remarkable thing

mi·rac·u·lous (mi rak'yoo ləs) *adj.* 1. having the nature of, or like, a miracle 2. able to work miracles —mi·rac'u·lous·ly *adv.*

mi·rage (mi räzh') *n.* [< VL. *mirare*, look at] an optical illusion, caused by the refraction of light, in which a distant object appears to be nearby

mire (mīr) *n.* [< ON. *myrr*] 1. an area of wet, soggy ground 2. deep mud; slush —*vt.* mired, mir'ing 1. to cause to get stuck, as in mire 2. to soil with mud, etc. —*vi.* to sink in mud —mir'y *adj.* -i·er, -i·est

mir·ror (mir'ər) *n.* [< ML. *mirare*, look at] 1. a smooth, reflecting surface; esp., a glass coated as with silver 2. anything giving a true representation —*vt.* to reflect, as in a mirror

mirth (murth) *n.* [< OE. *myrig*, pleasant] joyfulness or gaiety, esp. with laughter —mirth'ful *adj.*

MIRV (murv) *n., pl.* MIRV's [*m(ultiple) i(ndependently targeted) r(eentry) v(ehicle)*] an intercontinental ballistic missile whose several warheads can be scattered

mis- [< OE. *mis-* or OFr. *mes-*] *a prefix meaning:* 1. wrong(ly), bad(ly) 2. no, not

mis·ad·ven·ture (mis'əd ven'chər) *n.* a mishap; bad luck

mis·an·thrope (mis'ən thrōp') *n.* [< Gr. *misein*, to hate + *anthrōpos*, man] one who hates or distrusts all people: also **mis·an'thro·pist** (-an'thrə pist) —mis'an·throp'ic (-thräp'ik) *adj.* —mis·an'thro·py *n.*

mis'ap·ply' *vt.* -plied', -ply'ing to apply badly or improperly

mis·ap·pre·hend (mis'ap rə hend') *vt.* to misunderstand —mis'ap·pre·hen'sion *n.*

mis'ap·pro'pri·ate' *vt.* -at'ed, -at'ing to appropriate to a wrong or dishonest use —mis'ap·pro'pri·a'tion *n.*

mis'be·got'ten *adj.* wrongly or unlawfully begotten; illegitimate

mis'be·have' *vt., vi.* -haved', -hav'ing to behave (oneself) wrongly —mis'be·hav'ior (-yər) *n.*

misc. 1. miscellaneous 2. miscellany

mis·cal·cu·late' *vt., vi.* -lat'ed,

-lat'ing to calculate incorrectly; mis-judge —mis'cal·cu·la'tion n.

mis·call' vt. to call by a wrong name

mis·car·ry (mis kar'ē) vi. -ried, -ry·ing 1. to fail; go wrong / the plan *miscarried* / 2. to fail to arrive: said of mail, etc. 3. to give birth to a fetus before it has developed enough to live —mis·car'riage (-ij) n.

mis·cast' vt. -cast', -cast'ing to cast (an actor or a play) unsuitably

mis·ce·ge·na·tion (mis'i jə nā'shən, mi sej'ə-) n. [< L. *miscere*, mix + *genus*, race] marriage or sexual relations between a man and woman of different races

mis·cel·la·ne·ous (mis'ə lā'nē əs) adj. [< L. *miscere*, mix] consisting of various kinds or qualities

mis·cel·la·ny (mis'ə lā'nē) n., pl. -nies a miscellaneous collection, esp. of literary works

mis·chance' n. bad luck

mis·chief (mis'chif) n. [< OFr. *mes-*, MIS- + *chief*, end] 1. harm or damage 2. a cause of harm or annoyance 3. *a*) a prank *b*) gay teasing

mis·chie·vous (mis'chi vəs) adj. 1. causing mischief; specif., *a*) harmful *b*) prankish 2. inclined to annoy with playful tricks —mis'chie·vous·ly adv.

mis·ci·ble (mis'ə b'l) adj. [< L. *miscere*, to mix] that can be mixed

mis·con·ceive (mis'kən sēv') vt., vi. -ceived', -ceiv'ing to misunderstand —mis'con·cep'tion (-sep'shən) n.

mis·con·duct n. 1. bad or dishonest management 2. improper behavior

mis·con·strue (mis'kən strōō') vt. -strued', -stru'ing to misinterpret —mis'con·struc'tion n.

mis·count' vt., vi. to count incorrectly —n. an incorrect count

mis·cre·ant (mis'krē ənt) adj. [< OFr. *mes-*, MIS- + *croire*, believe] villainous; evil —n. a villain

mis·deal' vt., vi. -dealt', -deal'ing to deal (playing cards) wrongly —n. a wrong deal

mis·deed' (mis dēd') n. a wrong or wicked act; crime, sin, etc.

mis·de·mean·or (mis'di mēn'ər) n. *Law* any minor offense bringing a lesser punishment than a felony

mis'di·rect' vt. to direct wrongly or badly —mis'di·rec'tion n.

mis·do·ing n. wrongdoing

mi·ser (mī'zər) n. [L. wretched] a greedy, stingy person who hoards money for its own sake —mi'ser·ly adj. —mi'ser·li·ness n.

mis·er·a·ble (miz'ər ə b'l) adj. 1. in misery 2. causing misery, discomfort, etc. 3. bad; inadequate 4. pitiable —mis'er·a·bly adv.

mis·er·y (miz'ər ē) n., pl. -ies [see MISER] 1. a condition of great suffering; distress 2. a cause of such suffering; pain, poverty, etc.

mis·file' vt. -filed', -fil'ing to file (papers, etc.) in the wrong place

mis·fire' vi. -fired', -fir'ing 1. to fail to go off or ignite properly 2. to fail to achieve a desired effect —n. a misfiring

mis·fit' vt., vi. -fit'ted, -fit'ting to fit badly —n. 1. an improper fit 2. a maladjusted person

mis·for·tune n. 1. ill fortune; trouble 2. a mishap, calamity, etc.

mis·giv·ing (-giv'iŋ) n. [*often pl.*] a disturbed feeling of fear, doubt, etc.

mis·gov·ern vt. to govern badly —mis·gov'ern·ment n.

mis·guide (-gīd') vt. -guid'ed, -guid'ing to lead into error or misconduct; mislead —mis·guid'ance n.

mis·han·dle vt. -dled, -dling to handle badly or roughly; abuse

mis·hap (mis'hap) n. an unlucky or unfortunate accident

mis·hear' vt., vi. -heard', -hear'ing to hear wrongly

mish·mash (mish'mash') n. a jumble

mis'in·form' vt. to supply with false or misleading information —mis'in·for·ma'tion n.

mis'in·ter'pret vt. to interpret wrongly; understand or explain incorrectly —mis'in·ter'pre·ta'tion n.

mis·judge' vt., vi. -judged', -judg'ing to judge wrongly or unfairly

mis·la·bel vt., vi. -beled or -belled, -bel·ing or -bel·ling to label incorrectly or improperly

mis·lay' (-lā') vt. -laid', -lay'ing 1. to put in a place afterward forgotten 2. to put down or install improperly

mis·lead' (-lēd') vt. -led', -lead'ing 1. to lead in a wrong direction 2. to deceive or delude 3. to lead into wrongdoing

mis·man·age vt., vi. -aged, -ag·ing to manage badly or dishonestly —mis·man'age·ment n.

mis·match' vt. to match badly or unsuitably —n. a bad match

mis·mate' vt., vi. -mat'ed, -mat'ing to mate badly or unsuitably

mis·name' vt. -named', -nam'ing to give an inappropriate name to

mis·no·mer (mis nō'mər) n. [< MIS- + L. *nomen*, name] a wrong name

mi·sog·y·ny (mi säj'ə nē) n. [< Gr. *misein*, to hate + *gynē*, woman] hatred of women —mi·sog'y·nist n.

mis·place' vt. -placed', -plac'ing 1. to put in a wrong place 2. to bestow (one's trust, etc.) unwisely 3. same as MISLAY (sense 1)

mis·play' vt., vi. to play wrongly or badly, as in games or sports —n. a wrong or bad play

mis·print' vt. to print incorrectly —n. a printing error

mis·pri·sion (-prizh'ən) n. [< OFr. *mesprendre*, take wrongly] misconduct or neglect of duty by a public official

mis'pro·nounce' vt., vi. -nounced', -nounc'ing to pronounce differently from the accepted pronunciations —mis'pro·nun'ci·a'tion n.

mis·quote' vt., vi. -quot'ed, -quot'-

ing to quote incorrectly —**mis′quo-ta′tion** (-kwō tā′shən) n.

mis·read′ (-rēd′) vt., vi. **-read′** (-red′), **-read′ing** to read wrongly, esp. so as to misunderstand

mis′rep·re·sent′ vt. to represent falsely; give an untrue idea of —**mis′-rep·re·sen·ta′tion** n.

mis·rule′ vt. **-ruled′, -rul′ing** to rule badly; misgovern —n. misgovernment

miss¹ (mis) vt. [OE. missan] 1. to fail to hit, meet, catch, do, attend, see, hear, etc. 2. to let (a chance, etc.) go by 3. to avoid (he missed being hit) 4. to notice or feel the absence or loss of —vi. 1. to fail to hit 2. to fail to be successful 3. to misfire, as an engine —n. a failure to hit, obtain, etc.

miss² (mis) n., pl. **miss′es** [< MISTRESS] 1. [M-] a title used before the name of an unmarried woman or girl 2. a young unmarried woman or girl

mis·sal (mis′l) n. [< LL. missa, Mass] R.C.Ch. the official, liturgical book containing the prayers used in celebrating Mass throughout the year

mis·shape′ vt. **-shaped′, -shap′ing** to shape badly; deform —**mis·shap′-en** adj.

mis·sile (mis′l) n. [< L. mittere, send] an object, as a bullet, spear, rocket, etc., to be thrown, fired, or launched toward a target

mis′sile·ry, mis′sil·ry (-rē) n. 1. the science of building and launching guided missiles 2. such missiles

miss·ing (mis′iŋ) adj. absent; lost

mis·sion (mish′ən) n. [< L. mittere, send] 1. a sending out or being sent out to perform a special duty 2. a) a group of missionaries b) its headquarters 3. a diplomatic delegation 4. a group of technicians, specialists, etc. sent to a foreign country 5. the special duty for which one is sent 6. a special task to which one devotes his life; calling

mis′sion·ar′y (-er′ē) adj. of religious missions —n., pl. **-ies** a person sent out by his church to preach and make converts in a foreign country

Mis·sis·sip·pi (mis′ə sip′ē) 1. river in C U.S., flowing from N Minn. to the Gulf of Mexico 2. Southern State of the U.S.: 47,716 sq. mi.; pop. 2,521,000; cap. Jackson: abbrev. **Miss.** —**Mis′sis·sip′pi·an** adj., n.

mis·sive (mis′iv) n. [< L. mittere, send] a letter or written message

Mis·sour·i (mi zoor′ē) 1. river in WC U.S., flowing from NW Mont. to the Mississippi 2. Middle Western State of the U.S.: 69,686 sq. mi.; pop. 4,917,000; cap. Jefferson City — **Mis·sour′i·an** adj., n.

mis·spell′ vt., vi. **-spelled′** or **-spelt′, -spell′ing** to spell incorrectly

mis·spend′ vt. **-spent′, -spend′ing** to spend improperly or wastefully

mis·state′ vt. **-stat′ed, -stat′ing** to state incorrectly or falsely —**mis-state′ment** n.

mis·step′ n. 1. a wrong or awkward step 2. a mistake in conduct

mist (mist) n. [OE.] 1. a large mass of water vapor, less dense than a fog 2. anything that dims or obscures —vt., vi. to make or become misty

mis·take (mi stāk′) vt. **-took′, -tak′-en, -tak′ing** [< ON. mistaka, take wrongly] to understand or perceive wrongly —vi. to make a mistake —n. an idea, answer, act, etc. that is wrong; error or blunder —**mis·tak′a·ble** adj.

mis·tak′en adj. 1. wrong; having an incorrect understanding 2. incorrect: said of ideas, etc.

mis·ter (mis′tər) n. [< MASTER] 1. [M-] a title used before the name of a man or his office and usually written Mr. 2. [Colloq.] sir

mis·time (mis tīm′) vt. **-timed′, -tim′ing** to do or say at the wrong time

mis·tle·toe (mis′′l tō′) n. [< OE. mistel, mistletoe + tan, a twig] a parasitic evergreen plant with yellowish flowers and waxy white, poisonous berries

mis·took (mi stook′) pt. of MISTAKE

mis·treat′ vt. to treat wrongly or badly —**mis·treat′ment** n.

mis·tress (mis′tris) n. [< OFr., fem. of maistre, master] 1. a woman who is head of a household or institution 2. a woman, nation, etc. that has control or power 3. a woman with whom a man is having a prolonged affair 4. [Chiefly Brit.] a woman schoolteacher 5. [M-] formerly, a title used before the name of a woman: now replaced by Mrs. or Miss

mis·tri·al (mis trī′əl) n. Law a trial made void as because of an error in proceedings or the inability of the jury to reach a verdict

mis·trust′ n. lack of trust or confidence —vt., vi. to have no trust in; doubt —**mis·trust′ful** adj.

mist·y (mis′tē) adj. **-i·er, -i·est** 1. of, like, or covered with mist 2. blurred, as by mist; vague —**mist′i·ly** adv.

mis′un·der·stand′ vt. **-stood′, -stand′ing** to fail to understand correctly; misinterpret

mis′un·der·stand′ing n. 1. a failure to understand; mistake of meaning, etc. 2. a quarrel or disagreement

mis·use (mis yōōz′; for n. -yōōs′) vt. **-used′, -us′ing** 1. to use improperly 2. to treat badly or harshly; abuse —n. incorrect or improper use

mite (mīt) n. [OE.] 1. a tiny arachnid, often parasitic upon animals or plants 2. a very small sum of money 3. a very small creature or object

mi·ter (mīt′ər) n. [< Gr. mitra, headband] 1. a tall, ornamented cap worn by bishops and abbots 2. Carpentry a joint formed by fitting together two pieces beveled to form a corner: also **miter joint**

mit·i·gate (mit′ə gāt′) vt., vi. **-gat′ed, -gat′-ing** [< L. mitis, mild] to make or become less severe, less painful, etc. —**mit′i·ga′tion** n.

MITER JOINT

mi·to·sis (mī tō′sis) *n.* [< Gr. *mitos*, thread] the process by which a cell divides into two so that the nucleus of each new cell has the full number of chromosomes —**mi·tot′ic** (-tät′ik) *adj.*

mitt (mit) *n.* [< ff.] 1. a glove covering the hand and forearm, but only part of the fingers 2. [Slang] a hand 3. *a*) *Baseball* a padded glove, worn for protection *b*) a boxing glove

mit·ten (mit′ⁿ) *n.* [< OFr. *mitaine*] a glove with a thumb but no separately divided fingers

mix (miks) *vt.* mixed or mixt, mix′ing [< L. *miscere*] 1. to blend together in a single mass 2. to make by blending ingredients [to mix a cake] 3. to combine [mix work and play] —*vi.* 1. to be mixed or blended 2. to get along together —*n.* 1. a mixture 2. a beverage for mixing with alcoholic liquor —**mix up** 1. to mix thoroughly 2. to confuse 3. to involve or implicate (*in*) —**mix′a·ble** *adj.* —**mix′er** *n.*

mixed (mikst) *adj.* 1. blended 2. made up of different parts, classes, races, sexes, etc. 3. confused

mixed number a number made up of a whole number and a fraction, as 8⅔

mix·ture (miks′chər) *n.* 1. a mixing or being mixed 2. something mixed

mix′-up′ *n.* confusion; tangle

miz·zen·mast (miz′ⁿ məst, -mast′) *n.* [< L. *medius*, middle] the mast closest to the stern of a ship

Mlle. *pl.* **Mlles.** Mademoiselle

mm, mm. millimeter; millimeters

MM. Messieurs

Mme. *pl.* **Mmes.** Madame

Mn *Chem.* manganese

MN Minnesota

mne·mon·ic (nē män′ik) *adj.* [< Gr. *mnēmōn*, mindful] of or helping the memory

Mo., MO Missouri

mo. *pl.* **mos.** month

moan (mōn) *n.* [prob. < OE. *mænan*, complain] a low, mournful sound as of sorrow or pain —*vi., vt.* 1. to say with or utter a moan 2. to complain

moat (mōt) *n.* [< OFr. *mote*, mound] a deep, broad ditch, often filled with water, around a fortress or castle

mob (mäb) *n.* [< L. *mobile* (*vulgus*), movable (crowd)] 1. a disorderly, lawless crowd 2. any crowd 3. the masses: contemptuous term 4. [Slang] a gang of criminals —*vt.* mobbed, mob′bing 1. to crowd around and attack, annoy, etc. 2. to throng

Mo·bile (mō bēl′) seaport in SW Ala.: pop. 200,000

mo·bile (mō′b'l, -bēl) *adj.* [< L. *movere*, to move] 1. moving or movable 2. movable by means of a motor vehicle [a mobile X-ray unit] 3. that can change rapidly or easily; adaptable 4. characterized by ease in change of social status —*n.* (-bēl) a piece of abstract sculpture which aims to depict movement, as by an arrangement of thin forms, rings, etc. suspended and set in motion by air currents —**mo·bil′i·ty** (-bil′ə tē) *n.*

mobile home a large trailer outfitted as a home

mo′bi·lize′ (-bə līz′) *vt., vi.* -lized′, -liz′ing to make or become organized and ready, as for war —**mo′bi·li·za′tion** *n.*

mob·ster (mäb′stər) *n.* [Slang] a gangster

moc·ca·sin (mäk′ə s'n) *n.* [< Am-Ind.] 1. a heelless slipper of soft, flexible leather 2. any similar heeled slipper 3. *same as* WATER MOCCASIN

mo·cha (mō′kə) *n.* a choice grade of coffee grown orig. in Arabia —*adj.* flavored with coffee and, often, chocolate

mock (mäk) *vt.* [< OFr. *mocquer*] 1. to ridicule 2. to mimic, as in fun or derision 3. to defy and make futile —*vi.* to express scorn, ridicule, etc. —*adj.* sham; imitation

mock′er·y *n., pl.* -ies 1. a mocking 2. one receiving or deserving ridicule 3. a false or derisive imitation

mock′ing·bird′ *n.* an American bird that imitates the calls of other birds

mock′-up′ *n.* [< Fr. *maquette*] a model built to scale, often full-sized, for teaching, testing, etc.

mod (mäd) *adj.* [< MODERN] ultra-stylish in the mode of the 1960's

mode (mōd) *n.* [< L. *modus*] 1. a manner or way of acting, doing, or being 2. customary usage, or current fashion 3. *Gram. same as* MOOD²

mod·el (mäd′'l) *n.* [< L. *modus*, a measure] 1. a small representation of a planned or existing object 2. a person or thing regarded as a standard of excellence to be imitated 3. a style or design 4. *a*) one who poses for an artist or photographer *b*) one employed to display clothes by wearing them —*adj.* 1. serving as a model 2. representative of others of the same style, etc. [a model home] —*vt.* -eled or -elled, -el·ing or -el·ling 1. *a*) to make a model of *b*) to plan or form after a model 2. to display (clothes) by wearing —*vi.* to serve as a model (sense 4)

mod·er·ate (mäd′ər it; *for v.* -ə rāt′) *adj.* [< L. *moderare*, restrain] 1. within reasonable limits; avoiding extremes 2. mild; calm 3. of medium quality, amount, etc. —*n.* one holding moderate opinions —*vt., vi.* -at′ed, -at′ing 1. to make or become moderate 2. to preside over (a meeting, etc.) —**mod′er·ate·ly** *adv.*

mod′er·a′tion *n.* 1. a moderating 2. avoidance of extremes 3. calmness

mod′er·a′tor *n.* one who presides at an assembly, debate, etc.

mod·ern (mäd′ərn) *adj.* [< L. *modo*, just now] 1. of the present or recent times; specif., up-to-date 2. [often M-] designating the most recent form of a language —*n.* a person living in modern times, with modern ideas, etc.

Modern English the English language since about the mid-15th cent.

mod·ern·ism n. (a) modern usage, practice, thought, etc. —**mod′ern·ist** n., adj. —**mod′ern·is′tic** adj.

mod·ern·ize vt., vi. -ized′, -iz′ing to make or become modern —**mod′ern·i·za′tion** n.

mod·est (mäd′ist) adj. [< L. modus, measure] 1. not vain or boastful; unassuming 2. shy or reserved 3. decorous; decent 4. not extreme; unpretentious —**mod′est·ly** adv. —**mod′es·ty** n.

mod·i·cum (mäd′i kəm) n. [L., moderate] a small amount; bit

mod·i·fy (mäd′ə fī′) vt. -fied′, -fy′ing [< L. modificare, to limit] 1. to change partially in character, form, etc. 2. to limit slightly 3. Gram. to limit in meaning; qualify —**mod′i·fi·ca′tion** n. —**mod′i·fi′er** n.

mod·ish (mōd′ish) adj. fashionable; stylish —**mod′ish·ness** n.

mod·u·lar (mäj′ə lər) adj. of modules

mod·u·late (-lāt′) vt. -lat′ed, -lat′ing [< L. modus, measure] 1. to regulate or adjust 2. to vary the pitch, intensity, etc. of (the voice) 3. to vary the frequency of (radio waves, etc.) —**mod′u·la′tion** n. —**mod′u·la′tor** n.

mod·ule (mäj′ool) n. [Fr. < L. modus, measure] 1. a standard or unit of measurement, as of building materials 2. any of a set of units to be variously fitted together 3. a detachable unit with a specific function, as in a spacecraft

mo·gul (mō′gul) n. [Per. Mughul, Mongol] a powerful or important person

mo·hair (mō′her) n. [< Ar. mukhayyar] 1. the hair of the Angora goat 2. yarn or fabric made of this

Mo·ham·med (mō ham′id) 570?-632 A.D.; Arabian prophet; founder of the Moslem religion

Mo·ham′med·an adj., n. same as MOSLEM —**Mo·ham′med·an·ism** n.

moi·e·ty (moi′ə tē) n., pl. -ties [< L. medius, middle] 1. a half 2. an indefinite part

moire (mwär, môr) n. [Fr.] a fabric, esp. silk, etc., having a wavy pattern: also **moi·ré** (mwä rā′, mô-)

moist (moist) adj. [< L. mucus, mucus] slightly wet; damp —**moist′ly** adv. —**moist′ness** n.

mois·ten (mois′'n) vt., vi. to make or become moist

mois′ture (-chər) n. water or other liquid causing a slight wetness

mois′tur·ize′ (-īz′) vt., vi. -ized′, -iz′ing to make (the skin, air, etc.) moist —**mois′tur·iz′er** n.

Mo·ja·ve Desert (mō hä′vē) desert in SE Calif.: also **Mohave Desert**

mo·lar (mō′lər) adj. [< L. mola, millstone] designating a tooth or teeth adapted for grinding —n. a molar tooth

mo·las·ses (mə las′iz) n. [< L. mel, honey] a thick, dark syrup produced during the refining of sugar

mold¹ (mōld) n. [< L. modus, meas-

ure] 1. a hollow form for giving a certain shape to something plastic or molten 2. a frame on which something is modeled 3. a pattern; model 4. something formed in or on a mold 5. distinctive character —vt. 1. to make in or on a mold 2. to form; shape

mold² (mōld) n. [ME. moul] 1. a fungus producing a furry growth on the surface of organic matter 2. this growth —vi. to become moldy

mold³ (mōld) n. [OE. molde] loose, soft soil rich in decayed organic matter

mold′board′ n. a curved plate on a plowshare, for turning over the soil

mold·er (mōl′dər) vi. [< OE. molde, dust] to crumble into dust

mold·ing (mōl′diŋ) n. 1. the act of one that molds 2. something molded 3. a shaped strip of wood, etc., as around the upper walls of a room

mold·y (mōl′dē) adj. -i·er, -i·est 1. covered or overgrown with mold 2. musty or stale —**mold′i·ness** n.

mole¹ (mōl) n. [OE. mal] a small, congenital spot on the human skin, usually dark-colored and raised

mole² (mōl) n. [ME. molle] a small, burrowing mammal with soft fur

mole³ (mōl) n. [< L. moles, dam] a breakwater

MOLE

mol·e·cule (mäl′ə kyōōl′) n. [< L. dim. of moles, a mass] 1. the smallest particle of an element or compound that can exist in the free state and still retain the characteristics of the substance 2. a small particle —**mo·lec·u·lar** (mə lek′yə lər) adj.

mole′hill′ n. a small ridge of earth formed by a burrowing mole

mole·skin (mōl′skin′) n. 1. the fur of the mole 2. a napped cotton fabric

mo·lest (mə lest′) vt. [< L. moles, a burden] 1. to annoy or to meddle with so as to trouble or harm 2. to make improper sexual advances to —**mo·les·ta·tion** (mō′les tā′shən) n.

Mo·lière (mōl yer′) 1622-73; Fr. dramatist

moll (mäl) n. [Slang] a gangster's mistress

mol·li·fy (mäl′ə fī′) vt. -fied′, -fy′ing [< L. mollis, soft + facere, make] 1. to soothe; appease 2. to make less severe or violent

mol·lusk, mol·lusc (mäl′əsk) n. [< L. mollis, soft] any of a group of invertebrates, as oysters, snails, squids, etc., characterized by a soft body often enclosed in a shell

mol·ly·cod·dle (mäl′ē käd′'l) n. [< Molly, dim. of Mary + CODDLE] a man or boy used to being coddled —vt. -dled, -dling to pamper; coddle

molt (mōlt) vi. [< L. mutare, to change] to shed hair, skin, horns, etc. prior to replacement by a new growth, as reptiles, birds, etc.

mol·ten (mōl′t'n) adj. [archaic pp. of MELT] 1. melted by heat 2. made by being melted and cast in a mold

mo·lyb·de·num (mə lib′də nəm) *n.* [< Gr. *molybdos*, lead] a silvery metallic chemical element, used in alloys

mom (mäm) *n.* [Colloq.] mother

mo·ment (mō′mənt) *n.* [< L. *momentum*, movement] 1. an indefinitely brief period of time; instant 2. a definite point in time 3. a brief time of importance 4. importance

mo·men·tar·i·ly (mō′mən ter′ə lē) *adv.* 1. for a short time 2. in an instant 3. at any moment

mo·men·tar·y (mō′mən ter′ē) *adj.* lasting only for a moment; passing

mo·men·tous (mō men′təs) *adj.* of great moment; very important

mo·men·tum (mō men′təm) *n., pl.* -tums, -ta (-tə) [L.: see MOMENT] the impetus of a moving object, equal to the product of its mass and its velocity

mom·my (mäm′ē) *n., pl.* -mies mother: a child's word

Mon·a·co (män′ə kō′) principality on the Mediterranean; enclave in SE France; 1/2 sq. mi.; pop. 25,000

mon·arch (män′ərk) *n.* [< Gr. *monos*, alone + *archein*, to rule] a hereditary ruler; king, queen, etc. —**mo·nar·chi·cal** (mə när′ki k′l) *adj.*

mon′ar·chist (-ər kist) *n.* one who favors monarchical government

mon′ar·chy (-kē) *n., pl.* -ies a government or state headed by a monarch

mon·as·ter·y (män′ə ster′ē) *n., pl.* -ies [< Gr. *monos*, alone] the residence of a group of monks or nuns

mo·nas·tic (mə nas′tik) *adj.* of or characteristic of monks or nuns; ascetic: also **mo·nas′ti·cal** —**mo·nas′ti·cism** (-tə siz′m) *n.*

mon·au·ral (män ôr′əl) *adj.* of sound reproduction using a single channel to carry and reproduce sound

Mon·day (mun′dē, -dā) *n.* [OE. *monandæg*, moon's day] the second day of the week: abbrev. **Mon.**

mon·e·tar·y (män′ə ter′ē, mun′-) *adj.* [< L. *moneta*, a MINT¹] 1. of the coinage or currency of a country 2. of money; pecuniary

mon·ey (mun′ē) *n., pl.* -eys, -ies [< L. *moneta*, a MINT¹] 1. stamped pieces of metal, or any paper notes, authorized by a government as a medium of exchange 2. property; wealth —**in the money** [Slang] 1. among the winners in a race, etc. 2. wealthy —**make money** to gain profits —**put money into** to invest money in

mon′ey·bag′ *n.* 1. a bag for money 2. [*pl., with sing. v.*] [Colloq.] a rich person

mon·eyed (mun′ēd) *adj.* rich; wealthy

mon′ey·mak′er *n.* 1. one good at acquiring money 2. something profitable —**mon′ey·mak′ing** *adj., n.*

money market any short-term system for providing loanable funds, usually for six to thirty months

money of account a monetary denomination not issued as currency or a coin but used in keeping accounts

money order an order for payment of a specified sum of money, issued for a fee at one post office, bank, etc. and payable at another

mon·ger (muŋ′gər) *n.* [< OE. *mangere*] [Chiefly Brit.] a dealer; trader

Mon·gol (mäŋ′gəl, -gōl) *adj., n. same as* MONGOLIAN

Mon·go·li·a (mäŋ gō′lē ə) region in EC Asia, consisting of a country (**Mongolian People's Republic**, 592,600 sq. mi.; pop. 1,121,000) and a region in China (**Inner Mongolia**)

Mon·go′li·an *adj.* 1. of Mongolia, its people, or their culture 2. *same as:* a) MONGOLOID b) MONGOLIC —*n.* 1. a native of Mongolia 2. *same as:* a) MONGOLOID b) MONGOLIC

Mon·go·lic (mäŋ gäl′ik) *adj.* designating or of a subfamily of languages spoken in Mongolia —*n.* any of these languages

Mon·gol·oid (mäŋ′gə loid′) *adj.* 1. of the Mongolians 2. designating or of one of the major groups of mankind, including most of the peoples of Asia —*n.* a member of the Mongoloid group

mon·goose (mäŋ′gōōs) *n., pl.* -goos·es [< native Indian name] a ferret-like, flesh-eating mammal of the Old World, that kills snakes, etc.

mon·grel (muŋ′grəl, mäŋ′-) *n.* [< OE. *gemong*, mixture] an animal or plant, esp. a dog, of mixed breed —*adj.* of mixed breed, origin, character, etc.

mon·ied (mun′ēd) *adj. same as* MONEYED

mon·i·ker, mon·ick·er (män′i kər) *n.* [< ?] [Slang] a person's name

mo·ni·tion (mō nish′ən) *n.* [< L. *monere*, warn] admonition; warning

mon·i·tor (män′ə tər) *n.* [< L. *monere*, warn] 1. a student chosen to help the teacher 2. any device for regulating the performance of a machine, aircraft, etc. 3. *Radio & TV* a receiver for checking the quality of transmission —*vt., vi.* to watch or check on (a person or thing)

monk (muŋk) *n.* [< Gr. *monos*, alone] a man who joins a religious order living in retirement —**monk′ish** *adj.*

mon·key (muŋ′kē) *n., pl.* -keys [< ? Fr. or Sp. *mona*, ape + LowG. *-ke*, -KIN] any of the primates except man and the lemurs; specif., any of the smaller, long-tailed primates —*vi.* [Colloq.] to play, trifle, or meddle

monkey business [Colloq.] foolishness, mischief, or deceit

mon′key·shines′ (-shīnz′) *n.pl.* playful tricks or pranks

monkey wrench a wrench with an adjustable jaw —**throw a monkey wrench into** [Colloq.] to disrupt the orderly functioning of

monk's cloth a heavy cloth with a basket weave, used for drapes, etc.

mon·o (män′ō) *n. short for* MONONUCLEOSIS

mono- [< Gr. *monos*, single] *a prefix meaning* one, alone, single

mon·o·cle (män'ə k'l) *n.* [ult. < Gr. *monos*, single + L. *oculus*, eye] an eyeglass for one eye only

mon'o·clon'al (-klō'n'l) *adj.* of or cloned from one cell

mo·nog·a·my (mə näg'ə mē) *n.* [ult. < Gr. *monos*, single + *gamos*, marriage] the practice or state of being married to only one person at a time —**mo·nog'a·mous** *adj.*

mon·o·gram (män'ə gram') *n.* [< Gr. *monos*, single + *gramma*, letter] the initials of a name, combined in a single design —*vt.* **-grammed'**, **-gram'ming** to put a monogram on

mon·o·graph (män'ə graf') *n.* [MONO- + -GRAPH] a book or paper, esp. a scholarly one, on a single subject

mon·o·lin·gual (män'ə liŋ'gwəl) *adj.* using or knowing one language

mon·o·lith (-lith') *n.* [< Gr. *monos*, single + *lithos*, stone] 1. a single large block of stone, as one made into an obelisk, etc. 2. any massive, unyielding structure —**mon'o·lith'ic** *adj.*

mon·o·logue', mon·o·log' (-lôg') *n.* [< Gr. *monos*, single + *legein*, speak] 1. a long speech 2. a soliloquy 3. a skit, etc. for one actor only

mon·o·ma·ni·a (män'ə mā'nē ə) *n.* an excessive interest in or enthusiasm for some one thing; craze —**mon'o·ma'ni·ac'** (-ak') *n.* —**mon'o·ma·ni'a·cal** (-mə nī'ə k'l) *adj.*

mon'o·nu'cle·o'sis (-nōō'klē ō'sis) *n.* [MONO- + NUCLE(US) + -OSIS] an acute disease, esp. of young people, with fever, swollen lymph nodes, etc.

mon'o·phon'ic (-fän'ik) *adj.* of sound reproduction using a single channel to carry and reproduce sounds

mo·nop·o·list (mə näp'ə list) *n.* one who has a monopoly or favors monopoly —**mo·nop'o·lis'tic** *adj.*

mo·nop'o·lize' (-līz') *vt.* **-lized'**, **-liz'ing** 1. to get, have, or exploit a monopoly of 2. to get full control of

mo·nop'o·ly (-lē) *n., pl.* **-lies** [< Gr. *monos*, single + *pōlein*, sell] 1. exclusive control of a commodity or service in a given market 2. such control granted by a government 3. something held as a monopoly 4. a company that has a monopoly

mon·o·rail (män'ə rāl') *n.* a single rail that is a track for cars suspended from it or balanced on it

mon'o·syl'la·ble (-sil'ə b'l) *n.* a word of one syllable —**mon'o·syl·lab'ic** (-si lab'ik) *adj.*

mon'o·the·ism (-thē iz'm) *n.* [MONO- + THEISM] the belief that there is only one God —**mon'o·the·ist** *n.* —**mon'o·the·is'tic** *adj.*

mon'o·tone' (-tōn') *n.* [see MONO- & TONE] 1. utterance of successive words without change of pitch or key 2. tiresome sameness of style, color, etc. 3. a single, unchanging tone

mo·not·o·nous (mə nät'n əs) *adj.* 1. going on in the same tone 2. having no variety 3. tiresome because unvarying —**mo·not'o·ny** *n.*

mon·ox·ide (mə näk'sīd) *n.* an oxide

with one atom of oxygen per molecule

Mon·roe (mən rō'), **James** 1758-1831; 5th president of the U.S. (1817-25)

mon·sieur (mə syur'; *Fr.* mə syø') *n., pl.* **mes·sieurs** (mes'ərz; *Fr.* mā syø') [Fr., lit., my lord] a man; gentleman: French title [M-] equivalent to *Mr.* or *Sir*

Mon·si·gnor (män sēn'yər) *n.* [It., lit., my lord] a title given to certain Roman Catholic prelates

mon·soon (män sōōn') *n.* [< Ar. *mausim*, a season] 1. a seasonal wind of the Indian Ocean and S Asia 2. the rainy season during which this wind blows from the southwest

mon·ster (män'stər) *n.* [< L. *monere*, warn] 1. any greatly malformed plant or animal 2. any grotesque imaginary creature 3. a very wicked person 4. any huge animal or thing —*adj.* huge

mon·strance (män'strəns) *n.* [ult. < L. *monstrare*, to show] R.C.Ch. a receptacle for displaying the consecrated host

mon·strous (män'strəs) *adj.* 1. greatly malformed 2. huge 3. horrible; hideous 4. hideously evil —**mon·stros'i·ty** (-sträs'ə tē) *n.*

mon·tage (män tänzh') *n.* [Fr. < *monter*, to mount] 1. a composite picture 2. a rapid sequence of movie scenes, often superimposed

Mon·tan·a (män tan'ə) Northwestern State of the U.S.: 147,138 sq. mi.; pop. 787,000; cap. Helena: abbrev. *Mont.* —**Mon·tan'an** *adj., n.*

Mon·te Car·lo (män'ti kär'lō) town in Monaco: gambling resort

Mon·tes·so·ri method (män'tə sôr'ē) a method of teaching young children, emphasizing training of the senses

Mon·te·vid·e·o (män'tə vi dā'ō) capital of Uruguay: pop. 1,204,000

Mont·gom·er·y (mənt gum'ər ē, mänt-) capital of Ala.: pop. 178,000

month (munth) *n.* [OE. *monath*] 1. any of the twelve divisions of the calendar year 2. a period of four weeks or 30 days 3. one twelfth of the solar year

month'ly *adj.* 1. continuing for a month 2. done, happening, payable, etc. every month —*n., pl.* **-lies** a periodical published once a month —*adv.* once a month; every month

Mont·pel·ier (mänt pēl'yər) capital of Vt.: pop. 8,000

Mont·re·al (män'trē ôl') seaport in SW Quebec, on an island in the St. Lawrence River: pop. 1,222,000

mon·u·ment (män'yə mənt) *n.* [< L. *monere*, remind] 1. something set up to keep alive the memory of a person or event, as a tablet, statue, etc. 2. a work of enduring significance

mon'u·men'tal (-men't'l) *adj.* 1. of or serving as a monument 2. like a monument: massive, enduring, etc.

moo (mōō) *n., pl.* **moos** [echoic] the vocal sound made by a cow —*vi.* **mooed**, **moo'ing** to make this sound

mooch (mōōch) *vt., vi.* [ult. < OFr. *muchier*, to hide] [Slang] to get (food, money, etc.) by begging, imposition, etc. —**mooch'er** n.

mood[1] (mōōd) n. [< OE. mod, mind] 1. a particular state of mind or feeling 2. a predominant feeling or spirit

mood[2] (mōōd) n. [< MODE] Gram. that aspect of verbs which indicates whether the action or state expressed is a fact, supposition, or command

mood'y adj. -i·er, -i·est characterized by gloomy or changing moods —**mood'i·ly** adv. —**mood'i·ness** n.

moon (mōōn) n. [OE. mona] 1. the satellite of the earth, that revolves around it once about every 29 1/2 days and shines by reflected sunlight 2. anything shaped like the moon (i.e., an orb or crescent) 3. any satellite of a planet —vi. to behave in an idle or abstracted way

moon'beam' n. a ray of moonlight

moon'light' n. the light of the moon

moon'light'ing n. the holding of a second job along with one's main job

moon'lit' adj. lighted by the moon

moon'quake' n. a trembling of the moon's surface, as because of internal rock shifting or meteorite impact

moon'scape' (-skāp') n. [MOON + (LAND)SCAPE] the surface of the moon or a representation of it

moon'shine' n. 1. same as MOON-LIGHT 2. [Colloq.] whiskey unlawfully distilled —**moon'shin'er** n.

moon'shot' n. the launching of a spacecraft to the moon

moon'stone' n. a feldspar with a pearly luster, used as a gem

moon'struck' adj. 1. crazed; lunatic 2. romantically dreamy

moon'walk' n. a walking about by an astronaut on the surface of the moon

Moor (moor) n. any of a Moslem people of NW Africa —**Moor'ish** adj.

moor[1] (moor) n. [OE. mor] [Brit.] a tract of open wasteland, usually covered with heather and often marshy

moor[2] (moor) vt. [< ? MDu. maren, to tie] 1. to hold (a ship, etc.) in place by cables to the shore, or by anchors 2. to secure —vi. to moor a ship, etc.

moor'ings n.pl. 1. the lines, cables, etc. by which a ship is moored 2. a place where a ship is moored

moose (mōōs) n., pl. **moose** [< AmInd.] the largest animal of the deer family, native to N U.S. and Canada

moot (mōōt) adj. [OE. mot, a meeting] 1. debatable 2. hypothetical

mop (mäp) n. [earlier mappe] 1. a bundle of rags, a sponge, etc. at the end of a stick, as for washing floors 2. anything suggesting this, as a thick head of hair —vt. mopped, mop'ping to wash or wipe with a mop —mop up 1. to clear of remnants of beaten enemy forces 2. [Colloq.] to finish

mope (mōp) vi. moped, mop'ing [< ?] to be gloomy and apathetic —mop'ey, mop'y, mop'ish adj.

mop·pet (mäp'it) n. [< ME. moppe, rag doll] [Colloq.] a little child

mo·raine (mə rān') n. [Fr.] a mass of rocks, sand, etc. left by a glacier

mor·al (môr'əl, mär'-) adj. [< L. mos, pl. mores, morals] 1. dealing with, or capable of distinguishing between, right and wrong 2. of, teaching, or in accordance with the principles of right and wrong 3. good in conduct or character; specif., sexually virtuous 4. involving sympathy without action [moral support] 5. virtually such because of effects on thoughts or attitudes [a moral victory] 6. based on probability [a moral certainty] —n. 1. a moral lesson taught by a fable, event, etc. 2. [pl.] principles or standards with respect to right and wrong in conduct —**mor'al·ly** adv.

mo·rale (mə ral', mô-) n. moral or mental condition with respect to courage, discipline, confidence, etc.

mo·ral·i·ty (mə ral'ə tē) n., pl. -ties 1. rightness or wrongness, as of an action 2. right or moral conduct 3. moral principles

mor·al·ize (môr'ə līz', mär'-) vi. -ized', -iz'ing to consider or discuss moral questions, often in a self-righteous or tedious way —**mor'al·ist** n. —**mor'al·is'tic** adj.

mo·rass (mə ras', mô-) n. [< Frank.] a bog; marsh; swamp

mor·a·to·ri·um (môr'ə tôr'ē əm) n., pl. -ri·ums, -ri·a (-ə) [< L. mora, a delay] 1. a legally authorized delay in the payment of money due 2. an authorized delay of any activity

mo·ray (eel) (môr'ā) [< Gr. myraina] a voracious, brilliantly colored eel

mor·bid (môr'bid) adj. [< L. morbus, disease] 1. of or caused by disease; diseased 2. resulting as from a diseased state of mind 3. gruesome [the morbid details] —**mor·bid'i·ty** n. —**mor'bid·ly** adv.

mor·dant (môr'd'nt) adj. [< L. mordere, to bite] caustic; sarcastic —n. a substance that fixes colors in dyeing —**mor'dan·cy** n. —**mor'dant·ly** adv.

more (môr) adj. superl. MOST [OE. mara] 1. greater in amount or degree: compar. of MUCH 2. greater in number: compar. of MANY 3. additional [more news later] —n. 1. a greater amount or degree 2. [with pl. v.] a greater number (of) 3. something additional —adv. superl. MOST 1. in or to a greater degree or extent 2. in addition

more·o·ver (-ō'vər) adv. in addition to what has been said; besides

mo·res (môr'ēz, -āz) n.pl. [L., customs] folkways so basic as to develop the force of law

morgue (môrg) n. [Fr.] 1. a place where the bodies of unknown dead or those dead of unknown causes are temporarily kept 2. a newspaper office's file of back copies, etc.

mor·i·bund (môr'ə bund') adj. [< L. mori, to die] dying

Mor·mon (môr'mən) n. a member of the Church of Jesus Christ of Latter-

---

fat, āpe, cär; ten, ēven; is, bīte; gō, hôrn, tōōl, look; oil, out; up, far; chin; she; thin, then; zh, leisure; ŋ, ring; ə for a in ago; ', (ā'b'l); ë, Fr. coeur; ö, Fr. feu; Fr. mon; ü, Fr. duc; kh, G. ich, doch; ‡ foreign; < derived from

day Saints, founded (1830) in the U.S.

morn (môrn) n. [Poet.] morning

morn·ing (môr′niŋ) n. [OE. morgen] the first or early part of the day, from midnight, or esp. dawn, to noon

morning glory a twining vine with trumpet-shaped flowers

Mo·roc·co (mə rä′kō) kingdom on the NW coast of Africa: 171,300 sq. mi.; pop. 14,140,000 —n. [m-] a fine, soft leather made from goatskins —**Mo·roc′can** adj., n.

mo·ron (môr′än) n. [< Gr. mōros, foolish] an adult mentally equal to a child between eight and twelve: an obsolescent term —**mo·ron′ic** adj.

mo·rose (mə rōs′) adj. [< L. mos, manner] gloomy, sullen, surly, etc. —**mo·rose′ly** adv. —**mo·rose′ness** n.

mor·pheme (môr′fēm) n. [< Gr. morphē, form] the smallest meaningful language unit, as a base or affix

mor·phine (môr′fēn) n. [< Morpheus, Gr. god of dreams] an alkaloid derived from opium and used in medicine to relieve pain

mor·phol·o·gy (môr fäl′ə jē) n. [G. < Gr. morphē, form + logie, -LOGY] form and structure, as in biology

mor·row (mär′ō, môr′-) n. [< OE. morgen, morning] [Archaic or Poet.] 1. morning 2. the following day

Morse (môrs) adj. [after ff.] [often m-] designating or of a code, or alphabet, consisting of a system of dots and dashes, used in telegraphy, etc.

Morse (môrs), **Samuel F. B.** 1791-1872; U.S. inventor of the telegraph

mor·sel (môr′s'l) n. [< L. morsum, a bite] 1. a small bite or portion of food 2. a small piece or amount

mor·tal (môr′t'l) adj. [< L. mors, death] 1. that must eventually die 2. of man as a being who must die 3. of death 4. causing or liable to cause death of the body or (Theol.) the soul 5. very intense [mortal terror] —n. a human being —**mor′tal·ly** adv.

mor·tal·i·ty (môr tal′ə tē) n. 1. the mortal nature of man 2. death on a large scale, as from war 3. the ratio of deaths to population; death rate

mor·tar (môr′tər) n. [< L. mortarium] 1. a bowl in which substances are pulverized with a pestle 2. a short-barreled cannon which hurls shells in a high trajectory 3. a mixture of cement or lime with sand and water, used between bricks or stones

mor·tar·board′ (-bôrd′) n. 1. a square board for carrying mortar 2. an academic cap with a square, flat top

mort·gage (môr′gij) n. [< OFr. mort, dead + gage, pledge] 1. the pledging of property to a creditor as security for the payment of a debt 2. the deed by which this is done —vt. -gaged, -gag·ing 1. to pledge (property) by a mortgage 2. to put an advance claim on [to mortgage one's future] —**mort′ga·gor, mort′gage·or** n.

mort·ga·gee (môr′gə jē′) n. one to whom property is mortgaged

mor·ti·cian (môr tish′ən) n. [< L. mors, death] a funeral director

mor·ti·fy (môr′tə fī′) vt. -fied′, -fy′ing [< L. mors, death + facere, make] 1. to subdue (physical desires) by self-denial, fasting, etc. 2. to humiliate —**mor′ti·fi·ca′tion** n.

mor·tise (môr′tis) n. [< Ar. murtazza, joined] a notch or hole cut in a piece of wood to receive a projecting part (tenon) shaped to fit

mor·tu·ar·y (môr′choo wer′ē) n., pl. -ies [< L. mortuus, dead] same as FUNERAL HOME

Mo·sa·ic (mō zā′ik) adj. of Moses or the laws, etc. attributed to him

mo·sa·ic (mō zā′ik) n. [< L. musivus, artistic] 1. the making of pictures or designs by inlaying small bits of colored stone, etc. in mortar 2. a picture or design so made

Mos·cow (mäs′kou, -kō) capital of the U.S.S.R. in the WC European part: pop. 6,464,000

Mo·ses (mō′ziz) Bible the leader and lawgiver who brought the Israelites out of slavery in Egypt

mo·sey (mō′zē) vi. [< VAMOOSE] [Slang] to amble along

Mos·lem (mäz′ləm, muz′-) n. [ult. < Ar. aslama, resign oneself (to God)] an adherent of Islam —adj. of Islam or the Moslems

mosque (mäsk) n. [ult. < Ar. sajada, pray] a Moslem place of worship

mos·qui·to (mə skēt′ō) n., pl. -toes, -tos [Sp. < L. musca, a fly] a two-winged insect, the female of which bites animals and sucks blood

moss (môs, mäs) n. [OE. mos, a swamp] a very small green plant that grows in velvety clusters on rocks, moist ground, etc. —**moss′y** adj.

moss′back′ (-bak′) n. 1. an old turtle or shellfish with a back overgrown with algae 2. [Colloq.] an old-fashioned or very conservative person

most (mōst) adj. compar. MORE [OE. mast] 1. greatest in amount or degree: superl. of MUCH 2. greatest in number: superl. of MANY 3. in the greatest number of instances —n. 1. the greatest amount or degree 2. [with pl. v.] the greatest number (of) —adv. compar. MORE in or to the greatest degree or extent

most′ly adv. 1. for the most part 2. chiefly 3. usually

mote (mōt) n. [OE. mot] a speck, as of dust

mo·tel (mō tel′) n. [MO(TORIST) + (HO)TEL] a hotel for motorists

moth (môth) n., pl. moths (môthz, môths) [OE. moththe] a four-winged, chiefly night-flying insect related to the butterfly: the larvae of one kind eat holes in woolens, furs, etc.

moth′ball′ n. a small ball of naphthalene or camphor, the fumes of which repel clothes moths —**in mothballs** put into storage or reserve

moth·er (muth′ər) n. [OE. modor] 1. a female parent 2. an origin or source 3. a woman who is the head (mother superior) of a religious establishment —adj. 1. of or like a mother 2. native *[mother tongue]* —*vt.* to be the mother of or a mother to —**moth'er·hood'** *n.* —**moth'er·less** *adj.*

Mother Goose the imaginary creator of a collection of nursery rhymes

moth·er-in-law' *n., pl.* **moth'ers-in-law'** the mother of one's husband or wife

moth'er·land' *n.* one's native land

moth'er·ly *adj.* of or like a mother; maternal —**moth'er·li·ness** *n.*

moth'er-of-pearl' *n.* the hard internal layer of the shell of the pearl oyster, etc., used to make buttons, etc.

mother tongue one's native language

mo·tif (mō tēf') *n.* [Fr.: see MOTIVE] Art, Literature, & Music a main theme or subject for development

mo·tile (mōt'l) *adj.* [< L. *movere,* to move] *Biol.* capable of or exhibiting spontaneous motion —**mo·til'i·ty** *n.*

mo·tion (mō'shən) *n.* [< L. *movere,* to move] 1. a moving from one place to another; movement 2. a moving of a part of the body; specif., a gesture 3. a proposal formally made in an assembly —*vi.* to make a meaningful movement of the hand, etc. —*vt.* to direct by a meaningful gesture —**go through the motions** to do something mechanically, without real meaning —**in motion** moving —**mo'tion·less** *adj.*

motion picture 1. a series of still pictures on film projected on a screen in such rapid succession as to create the illusion of moving persons and objects 2. a play, etc. in this form

mo·ti·vate (mōt'ə vāt') *vt.* -**vat'ed,** -**vat'ing** to provide with, or affect as, a motive; incite —**mo'ti·va'tion** *n.*

mo·tive (mōt'iv) *n.* [< L. *movere,* to move] 1. an inner drive, impulse, etc. that causes one to act; incentive 2. a motif —*adj.* of or causing motion

-motive (mōt'iv) *a suffix meaning* moving, of motion [*automotive*]

mot·ley (mät'lē) *adj.* [< ?] 1. of many colors 2. of many different or clashing elements [*a motley group*]

mo·to·cross (mō'tō krôs') *n.* [Fr.] a cross-country race for lightweight motorcycles

mo·tor (mōt'ər) *n.* [L. < *movere,* to move] 1. anything that produces motion 2. an engine; esp., an internal-combustion engine 3. a machine for converting electrical energy into mechanical energy —*adj.* 1. producing motion 2. of or powered by a motor 3. of, by, or for motor vehicles 4. of or involving muscular movements —*vi.* to travel by automobile

mo'tor·bike' *n.* [Colloq.] 1. a motor-driven bicycle 2. a light motorcycle

mo'tor·boat' *n.* a boat propelled by a motor or gasoline engine

mo'tor·cade' (-kād') *n.* [MOTOR + (CAVAL)CADE] an automobile procession

mo'tor·car' *n.* an automobile

mo'tor·cy'cle (-sī'k'l) *n.* a two-wheeled vehicle propelled by an internal-combustion engine

motor home an automotive vehicle with a truck chassis, outfitted as a traveling home

mo'tor·ist *n.* one who drives an automobile or travels by automobile

mo'tor·ize' (-ə rīz') *vt.* -**ized',** -**iz'-ing** to equip with a motor or with motor-driven vehicles

mo'tor·man (-mən) *n., pl.* -**men** one who drives an electric railway car

motor vehicle an automotive vehicle, esp. an automobile, truck, or bus

mot·tle (mät''l) *vt.* -**tled, -tling** [< MOTLEY] to mark with blotches, etc. of different colors —**mot'tled** *adj.*

mot·to (mät'ō) *n., pl.* -**toes, -tos** [It., a word] a word or saying that expresses one's aims, ideals, or guiding rule

mould, mould'er, mould'ing, mould'y, moult (mōld, *etc.*) *chiefly Brit. sp.* of MOLD, MOLDER, MOLDING, MOLDY, MOLT

mound (mound) *n.* [< ? MDu. *mond,* protection] a heap or bank of earth, sand, etc. —*vt.* to heap up

mount¹ (mount) *n.* [< L. *mons*] a mountain

mount² (mount) *vi.* [< L. *mons,* mountain] 1. to climb; ascend 2. to climb up on something, as a horse 3. to increase in amount —*vt.* 1. to go up; ascend [*to mount stairs*] 2. to get up on (a horse, platform, etc.) 3. to provide with horses [*mounted police*] 4. to fix (a jewel, picture, etc.) on or in the proper support, backing, setting, etc. 5. to arrange (a dead animal, etc.) for exhibition 6. to place (a gun) into position ready for use —*n.* 1. the act of mounting 2. a horse, etc. for riding 3. the support, setting, etc. on or in which a thing is mounted

moun·tain (moun't'n) *n.* [ult. < L. *mons*] 1. a natural raised part of the earth, larger than a hill 2. a big pile, amount, etc. —*adj.* of or in mountains

moun'tain·eer' (-ir') *n.* 1. one who lives in a mountainous region 2. a mountain climber

mountain goat a long-haired, goat-like antelope of the Rocky Mountains

mountain lion *same as* COUGAR

moun'tain·ous *adj.* 1. full of mountains 2. like a mountain; huge

moun·te·bank (moun'tə baŋk') *n.* [< It. *montare,* to mount + *in,* on + *banco,* bench] a charlatan; quack

mount'ing *n.* something serving as a backing, support, setting, etc.

mourn (môrn) *vi., vt.* [OE. *murnan*] 1. to feel or express sorrow for (something regrettable) 2. to grieve for (someone dead) —**mourn'er** *n.*

mourn'ful *adj.* 1. feeling or expressing grief or sorrow 2. causing sorrow

mourn'ing *n.* 1. a sorrowing; specif., the expression of grief at someone's death 2. black clothes, etc., worn as a sign of grief for the dead

---

fat, āpe, cär; ten, ēven; is, bīte; gō, hôrn, tōōl, look; oil, out; up, fur; chin; she; thin, *then*; zh, leisure; ŋ, ring; ə *for a in ago*; ', (ā'b'l); ë, Fr. coeur; ö, Fr. feu; Fr. mon; ü, Fr. duc; kh, G. ich, doch; ‡ foreign; < derived from

mouse (mous; *for v.* mouz) *n., pl.* **mice** [OE. *mus*] **1.** any of many small rodents, esp. the **house mouse** that infests human dwellings **2.** a timid person **3.** a hand-held device moved in front of a terminal screen to position the lighted indicator **4.** [Slang] a black eye —*vi.* moused, mous'ing to hunt mice

mousse (mōōs) *n.* [Fr., foam] a light, chilled dessert made with egg white, gelatin, whipped cream, etc.

mous·tache (mə stash', mus'tash) *n. var. of* MUSTACHE

mous·y, mous·ey (mou'sē, -zē) *adj.* -i·er, -i·est or like a mouse; specif., quiet, timid, drab, etc. — mous'i·ness *n.*

mouth (mouth) *n., pl.* mouths (mouthz) [OE. *muth*] **1.** an opening in the head through which food is taken in and sounds are made **2.** any opening regarded as like this [the *mouth* of a jar, river, etc.] —*vt.* (mouth) **1.** to say, esp. insincerely **2.** to rub with the mouth —**down in** (or at) **the mouth** [Colloq.] unhappy

mouth'ful *n., pl.* -fuls' **1.** all the mouth can hold **2.** the usual amount taken into the mouth **3.** a small amount **4.** [Slang] a pertinent remark: chiefly in **say a mouthful**

mouth organ *same as* HARMONICA

mouth'piece *n.* **1.** a part, as of a musical instrument, held to or in the mouth **2.** a person, periodical, etc. serving as a spokesman for others

mouth'wash *n.* a flavored, often antiseptic liquid for rinsing the mouth

mouth'wa·ter·ing (-wôt'ər iŋ, -wät'-) *adj.* appetizing; tasty

mouth'y *adj.* -i·er, -i·est talkative esp. in a rude or bombastic way

mou·ton (mōō'tän) *n.* [Fr., sheep] lamb fur made to resemble seal, beaver, etc.

mov·a·ble, move·a·ble (mōō'və b'l) *adj.* that can be moved from one place to another —*n.* **1.** something movable **2.** *Law* personal property, esp. furniture: *usually used in pl.*

move (mōōv) *vt.* moved, mov'ing [< L. *movere*] **1.** to change the place or position of **2.** to set or keep in motion **3.** to cause (*to do, say,* etc.) **4.** to arouse the emotions, etc. of **5.** to propose formally, as in a meeting —*vi.* **1.** to change place or position **2.** to change one's residence **3.** to be active **4.** to make progress **5.** to take action **6.** to be, or be set, in motion **7.** to make a formal application (*for*) **8.** to evacuate: said of the bowels **9.** *Commerce* to be sold: said of goods —*n.* **1.** act of moving **2.** an action toward some goal **3.** *Chess, Checkers,* etc. the act of moving a piece, or one's turn to move —**move up** to promote or be promoted —**on the move** [Colloq.] moving about or active

move'ment *n.* **1.** a moving or manner of moving **2.** an evacuation (of the bowels) **3.** a change in the location of troops, etc. **4.** organized action by people working toward a goal **5.** the moving parts of a mechanism, as of a clock **6.** *Music a)* a principal division of a symphony, etc. *b)* rhythm

mov'er *n.* one that moves; specif., one whose work is moving furniture, etc. for those changing residence

mov·ie (mōō'vē) *n.* [< *moving picture*] a motion picture —**the movies 1.** the motion-picture industry **2.** the showing of a motion picture

mow¹ (mō) *vt., vi.* mowed, mowed or mown (mōn), mow'ing [OE. *mawan*] to cut down (grass, etc.) from (a lawn, etc.) with a sickle or lawn mower —**mow down** to cause to fall like cut grass —**mow'er** *n.*

mow² (mou) *n.* [OE. *muga*] **1.** a heap of hay, etc., esp. in a barn **2.** the part of a barn where hay, etc. is stored

Mo·zam·bique (mō'zəm bēk') country in SE Africa: c. 302,300 sq. mi.; pop. 8,519,000

Mo·zart (mō'tsärt), **Wolf·gang A·ma·de·us** (vôlf'gäŋk' ä'mä dā'ōos) 1756–91; Austrian composer

MP, M.P. Military Police

M.P. Member of Parliament

mph, m.p.h. miles per hour

Mr. (mis'tər) *pl.* **Messrs.** (mes'ərz) mister: before a man's name or title

Mrs. (mis'iz) *pl.* **Mmes.** (mā däm') mistress: before a married woman's name

MS Mississippi

MS., ms., ms *pl.* **MSS., mss., mss** manuscript

Ms. (miz, em'es') a title, free of reference to marital status, used in place of either *Miss* or *Mrs.*

M.S., M.Sc. Master of Science

Msgr. Monsignor

MSgt, M/Sgt Master Sergeant

MST, M.S.T. Mountain Standard Time

MT Montana

Mt., mt. *pl.* **Mts., mts. 1.** mount **2.** mountain

mu (myōō) *n.* the twelfth letter of the Greek alphabet (M, μ)

much (much) *adj.* more, most [< OE. *mycel*] great in quantity, degree, etc. —*adv.* more, most **1.** to a great degree or extent [*much* happier] **2.** nearly [*much* the same] —*n.* **1.** a great amount **2.** anything great or outstanding [not much to look at] —**mu·ci·lage** (myōō'sʼl ij) *n.* [< L. *mucus,* mucus] **1.** a thick, sticky substance in some plants **2.** any watery solution of gum, glue, etc. used as an adhesive

muck (muk) *n.* [< ON. *myki*] **1.** moist manure **2.** black earth with decaying matter, used as manure **3.** mud; dirt; filth —**muck'y** *adj.*

muck'rake' *vi.* -raked', -rak'ing [see prec. & RAKE¹] to search for and publicize real or alleged corruption in politics, etc. —**muck'rak'er** *n.*

mu·cous (myōō'kəs) *adj.* **1.** of, containing, or secreting mucus **2.** slimy **mucous membrane** a mucus-secreting lining of body cavities

mu·cus (myōō'kəs) *n.* [L.] the slimy secretion of mucous membranes

mud (mud) *n.* [prob. < a LowG. source] wet, soft, sticky earth

mud·dle (mud′'l) *vt.* -dled, -dling [< prec.] 1. to mix up; bungle 2. to confuse mentally; befuddle —*vi.* to act or think confusedly —*n.* 1. a mess, jumble, etc. 2. mental confusion

mud′dle-head′ed *adj.* confused

mud′dy (mud′ē) *adj.* -di·er, -di·est 1. full of or spattered with mud 2. not clear; cloudy *[muddy coffee]* 3. confused, obscure, etc. *[muddy thinking]* —*vt.*, *vi.* -died, -dy·ing to make or become muddy —**mud′di·ness** *n.*

mud′sling′ing *n.* the practice of making unscrupulous verbal attacks, as against a political opponent —**mud′sling′er** *n.*

mu·ez·zin (myōō ez′in) *n.* [< Ar. *mu′adhdhin*, proclaiming] a Moslem crier who calls the people to prayer

muff (muf) *n.* [< Fr. *moufle*, mitten] 1. a cylindrical covering of fur, etc. to warm the hands 2. *a)* a failure to hold the ball when catching it *b)* any bungle —*vt.*, *vi.* 1. to miss (a catch, etc.) 2. to bungle

muf·fin (muf′'n) *n.* [< ?] a quick bread baked in a cup-shaped mold

muf·fle (muf′'l) *vt.* -fled, -fling [prob. < OFr. *moufle*, mitten] 1. to wrap or cover closely so as to keep warm, etc. 2. to cover so as to deaden sound 3. to deaden (a sound)

muf·fler (muf′lər) *n.* 1. a scarf worn around the throat, as for warmth 2. a device for deadening noise

muf·ti (muf′tē) *n.*, *pl.* -tis [< Ar.] ordinary clothes, not a uniform

mug (mug) *n.* [prob. < Scand.] 1. a cup of earthenware or metal, with a handle 2. as much as a mug will hold 3. [Slang] the face —*vt.* mugged, mug′ging to assault, usually with intent to rob —*vi.* [Slang] to grimace, esp. in overacting —**mug′ger** *n.*

mug·gy (mug′ē) *adj.* -gi·er, -gi·est [< dial. *mug*, mist] hot, damp, and close —**mug′gi·ness** *n.*

Mu·ham·mad (moo ham′əd) *same as* MOHAMMED

muk·luk (muk′luk′) *n.* [Esk. *muklok*, a seal] 1. an Eskimo boot of sealskin or reindeer skin 2. any similar boot

mu·lat·to (mə lat′ō) *n.*, *pl.* -toes [Sp. & Port. *mulato*, of mixed breed] a person who has one Negro parent and one white parent

mul·ber·ry (mul′ber′ē, -bər ē) *n.*, *pl.* -ries [OE. *morberie*] 1. a tree with purplish-red, edible, berrylike fruit 2. the fruit 3. purplish red

mulch (mulch) *n.* [ME. *molsh*, soft] leaves, straw, etc., spread around plants to prevent freezing of roots, etc. —*vt.* to apply mulch to

mulct (mulkt) *vt.* [< L. *mul(c)ta*, a fine] 1. to fine 2. to take (money, etc.) from by fraud —*n.* a fine; penalty

mule[1] (myōōl) *n.* [< L. *mulus*] 1. the (usually sterile) offspring of a male donkey and a female horse 2. a machine that spins cotton fibers into yarn 3. [Colloq.] a stubborn person

mule[2] (myōōl) *n.* [< L. *mulleus*, red shoe] a lounging slipper that does not cover the heel

mu·le·teer (myōō′lə tir′) *n.* [< OFr.] a driver of mules: also [Colloq.] **mule skin′ner**

mul′ish *adj.* stubborn; obstinate

mull[1] (mul) *vt.*, *vi.* [ME. *mullen*, to grind] [Colloq.] to ponder (*over*)

mull[2] (mul) *vt.* [< ?] to heat, sweeten, and spice (ale, wine, etc.)

mul·lein (mul′in) *n.* [< OFr. *moleine*] a tall plant with spikes of variously colored flowers

mul·let (mul′it) *n.* [< L. *mullus*] any of a family of edible, spiny-finned fishes of fresh and salt waters

mul·li·gan (stew) (mul′i g′n) [prob. < name *Mulligan*] [Slang] a kind of meat stew

mul·li·ga·taw·ny (mul′i gə tô′nē) *n.* [Tamil *milagutannir*, lit., pepper water] an East Indian soup of meat, etc., flavored with curry

mul·lion (mul′yən) *n.* [ult. < L. *medianus*, middle] a vertical dividing bar, as between windowpanes

Mul·ro·ney (mul rōō′nē), (**Martin**) **Brian** 1939– ; prime minister of Canada (1984–)

multi- [L. < *multus*, much] *a combining form meaning:* 1. having many 2. more than two 3. many times

mul·ti·far·i·ous (mul′tə far′ē əs) *adj.* [< L.] having many kinds of parts or elements; diverse

mul·ti·mil′lion·aire′ *n.* a person whose wealth amounts to many millions of dollars, pounds, etc.

mul′ti·na′tion·al *adj.* 1. of many nations 2. designating or of a corporation with branches in many countries —*n.* a multinational corporation

mul·ti·ple (mul′tə p'l) *adj.* [< L. *multus*, many + *plicare*, fold] having many parts, elements, etc. —*n.* a number that is a product of some specified number and another number

mul′ti·ple-choice′ *adj.* listing several answers from which the correct one is to be chosen

multiple sclerosis a disease of the central nervous system, with loss of muscular coordination, etc.

mul·ti·plex (mul′tə pleks′) *adj.* [L., multiple] designating a system for sending two or more signals simultaneously over a single circuit, etc.

mul′ti·pli·cand′ (-pli kand′) *n.* a number to be multiplied by another

mul′ti·pli·ca′tion (-pli kā′shən) *n.* a multiplying or being multiplied; specif., the process of finding the quantity obtained by repeating a specified quantity a specified number of times

mul′ti·plic′i·ty (-plis′ə tē) *n.* a great number or variety (*of*)

mul′ti·pli′er (-plī′ər) *n.* one that multiplies; specif., the number by which another is to be multiplied

mul·ti·ply (mul′tə plī′) *vt.*, *vi.*

-piled', -ply'ing [see MULTIPLE] 1. to increase in number, degree, etc. 2. to find the product (of) by multiplication

mul'ti·stage' adj. having, or operating in, more than one stage; specif., having several propulsion systems, as a rocket or missile

mul·ti·tude (mul'tə tōōd') n. [< L. multus, many] a large number; host

mul'ti·tu'di·nous (-tōōd'n əs) adj. very numerous; many

mum[1] (mum) n. [Colloq.] a chrysanthemum

mum[2] (mum) adj. [ME. momme] silent; not speaking

mum·ble (mum'b'l) vt., vi. -bled, -bling [ME. momelen] to speak or say indistinctly; mutter —n. a mumbled utterance —**mum'bler** n.

mum·bo jum·bo (ˌum'bō jum'bō) [of Afr. origin] 1. an idol or fetish 2. meaningless ritual, talk, etc.

mum·mer (mum'ər) n. [< OFr. momo, grimace] one who wears a mask or costume, esp. in a pantomime

mum'mer·y n., pl. -ies 1. performance by mummers 2. a hypocritical display or ceremony

mum·mi·fy (mum'ə fī') vt., vi. -fied', -fy'ing to make into or become a mummy

mum·my (mum'ē) n., pl. -mies [ult. < Per. mum, wax] a carefully preserved dead body; esp., an embalmed corpse of ancient Egypt

mumps (mumps) n.pl. [with sing. v.] [< obs. mump, a grimace] an acute communicable disease characterized by swelling of the salivary glands

mun. municipal

munch (munch) vt., vi. [ME. monchen] to chew steadily, often with a crunching sound

mun·dane (mun dān', mun'dān) adj. [< L. mundus, world] 1. of the world; worldly 2. commonplace; ordinary

Mu·nich (myōō'nik) city in SE West Germany: pop. 1,215,000

mu·nic·i·pal (myoo nis'ə p'l) adj. [< L. municeps, inhabitant of a free town] of or concerning a city, town, etc., or its local government

mu·nic'i·pal'i·ty (-pal'ə tē) n., pl. -ties a city, town, etc. having its own incorporated government

mu·nif·i·cent (myoo nif'ə s'nt) adj. [< L. munus, gift + facere, make] very generous in giving; lavish —**mu·nif'i·cence** n.

mu·ni·tions (myōō nish'ənz) n.pl. [< L. munire, fortify] war supplies; esp., weapons and ammunition

mu·ral (myoor'əl) adj. [< L. murus, wall] of, on, or for a wall —n. a picture, esp. a large one, painted directly on a wall —**mu'ral·ist** n.

mur·der (mur'dər) n. [OE. morthor] 1. the unlawful and malicious or premeditated killing of a person 2. [Colloq.] something very hard, unsafe, etc. to do or deal with —vt. 1. to kill (a person) unlawfully and with malice 2. to spoil, as in performance [to murder a song] —**mur'der·er** n. —**mur'der·ess** n.fem.

mur'der·ous adj. 1. of or characteristic of murder; brutal 2. capable of, or intending, murder —**mur'der·ous·ly** adv.

murk (murk) n. [< ON. myrkr, dark] darkness; gloom

murk·y (mur'kē) adj. -i·er, -i·est dark or gloomy —**murk'i·ness** n.

mur·mur (mur'mər) n. [< L.] 1. a low, indistinct, continuous sound 2. a mumbled complaint 3. Med. an abnormal sound in the body, esp. in the region of the heart —vi. to make a murmur —vt. to say in a murmur

mur·rain (mur'in) n. [< L. mori, die] a plague, specif. of cattle

mus·cat (mus'kət) n. [Fr. < LL. muscus, musk] a sweet European grape

mus·ca·tel (mus'kə tel') n. a rich, sweet wine made from the muscat

mus·cle (mus''l) n. [< L. < dim. of mus, mouse] 1. any body organ consisting of fibrous tissue that can be contracted and expanded to produce bodily movements 2. this tissue 3. muscular strength —vi. -cled, -cling [Colloq.] to force one's way (in)

mus'cle-bound' adj. having some of the muscles enlarged and less elastic, as from too much exercise

mus·cu·lar (mus'kyə lər) adj. 1. of or done by muscles 2. having well-developed muscles; strong —**mus'cu·lar'i·ty** (-lar'ə tē) n.

muscular dys·tro·phy (dis'trə fē) [prec. + dystrophy, faulty nutrition] a disease characterized by a progressive wasting of the muscles

mus'cu·la·ture (-lə chər) n. [Fr.] the arrangement of the muscles of a body, limb, etc.; muscular system

Muse (myōōz) n. [< Gr. mousa] 1. Gr. Myth. any of the nine goddesses who presided over literature and the arts and sciences 2. [m-] the spirit regarded as inspiring a poet

muse (myōōz) vi. mused, mus'ing [< OFr. muser, ponder] to meditate —vt. to think or say meditatively

mu·sette (bag) (myoo zet') [< OFr., bagpipe] a bag with a shoulder strap, worn as by soldiers to carry supplies

mu·se·um (myōō zē'əm) n. [< Gr. mousa, Muse] a building, room, etc. for exhibiting artistic, historical, or scientific objects

mush[1] (mush) n. [prob. var. of MASH] 1. a thick porridge of boiled meal 2. any thick, soft mass 3. [Colloq.] maudlin sentimentality —**mush'y** adj. -i·er, -i·est

mush[2] (mush) interj. [< ? Fr. marcher, go] a shout to urge on sled dogs —vi. to travel on foot over snow, usually with a dog sled

mush'room' (-rōōm') n. [< LL. mussirio] any of various fleshy fungi, typically with a stalk capped by an umbrellalike top; esp., any edible variety —adj. of or like a mushroom —vi. to grow or spread rapidly

mu·sic (myōō'zik) n. [< Gr. mousikē (technē), art of the Muses] 1. the art of combining tones to form expressive compositions **2.** such compositions **3.** any rhythmic sequence of pleasing sounds —**face the music** [Colloq.] to accept the consequences

mu·si·cal (myōō'zi kǝl) *adj.* **1.** of or for music **2.** melodious or harmonious **3.** fond of or skilled in music **4.** set to music —*n.* a light play or movie with dialogue, songs, and dances: often, **musical comedy, musical play** —**mu'si·cal·ly** *adv.*

mu·si·cale (myōō'zǝ kal') *n.* [Fr.] a social affair featuring music

mu·si·cian (myōō zish'ǝn) *n.* one skilled in music; esp., a performer

mu·si·col·o·gy (myōō'zi käl'ǝ jē) *n.* the study of the history, forms, etc. of music —**mu'si·col'o·gist** *n.*

musk (musk) *n.* [< Sans. *mus*, mouse] an animal secretion having a strong odor: used in making perfumes —**musk'y** *adj.* —**musk'i·ness** *n.*

mus·kel·lunge (mus'kǝ lunj') *n., pl.* **-lunge'** [< AmInd.] a very large, edible pike of N.America: also **mus'kie** (-kē)

mus·ket (mus'kit) *n.* [< L. *musca*, a fly] a former kind of firearm with a long barrel and smooth bore

mus·ket·eer (mus'kǝ tir') *n.* a soldier armed with a musket

musk'mel·on *n.* any of various sweet, juicy melons, as the cantaloupe

musk·rat (musk'rat') *n.* **1.** a N.American water rodent with brown fur and a musky odor **2.** its fur

MUSKRAT

Mus·lim (muz'lǝm) *n. same as* MOSLEM

mus·lin (muz'lin) *n.* [< *Mosul*, city in Iraq] a strong cotton cloth; esp., a heavy kind used for sheets, etc.

muss (mus) *vt.* [prob. var. of MESS] to make messy or disordered; disarrange —*n.* a mess; disorder —**muss'y** *adj.* **-i·er, -i·est**

mus·sel (mus'l) *n.* [< OE. *muscle*] any of various saltwater or freshwater bivalve mollusks

must (must) *v.aux. pt.* **must** [< OE. *moste*] an auxiliary expressing: **1.** necessity [I *must* go] **2.** probability [it *must* be Joe] **3.** certainty [all *must* die] —*n.* [Colloq.] something that must be done, had, etc.

mus·tache (mǝ stash', mus'tash) *n.* [ult. < Gr. *mastax*, mouth] the hair on the upper lip of men

mus·tang (mus'taŋ) *n.* [< L. *mixtus*, a mingling] a small wild horse of the SW plains

mus·tard (mus'tǝrd) *n.* [< OFr.] **1.** a plant with yellow flowers and slender pods **2.** the yellow powder made from its ground seeds, often used in paste form as a condiment

mustard gas [< its mustardlike odor] an oily liquid used in warfare for its blistering, disabling effects

mus·ter (mus'tǝr) *vt.* [< L. *monere*, warn] **1.** to assemble (troops, etc.) **2.** to collect; summon [to *muster* up strength] —*vi.* to assemble, as troops —*n.* **1.** a gathering or assembling, as of troops for inspection **2.** the persons or things assembled —**muster in** (or **out**) to enlist in (or discharge from) military service

must·n't (mus'nt) must not

mus·ty (mus'tē) *adj.* **-ti·er, -ti·est** [< ? MOIST] **1.** having a stale, moldy smell or taste **2.** stale or trite; antiquated —**mus'ti·ly** *adv.* —**mus'ti·ness** *n.*

mu·ta·ble (myōōt'ǝ b'l) *adj.* [< L. *mutare*, to change] **1.** that can be changed **2.** inconstant; fickle —**mu·ta·bil'i·ty** *n.* —**mu'ta·bly** *adv.*

mu'tant (-'nt) *adj.* of mutation —*n.* an animal or plant with inheritable characteristics that differ from those of the parents; sport

mu·ta·tion (myōō tā'shǝn) *n.* **1.** a change, as in form, nature, etc. **2.** a sudden variation in some inheritable characteristic of a plant or animal —**mu'tate** *vi., vt.* **-tat·ed, -tat·ing**

mute (myōōt) *adj.* [< L. *mutus*] **1.** not speaking; silent **2.** unable to speak —*n.* **1.** a deaf-mute **2.** a device that softens the sound of a musical instrument —*vt.* **mut'ed, mut'ing** to soften the sound of (an instrument) —**mute'ly** *adv.* —**mute'ness** *n.*

mu·ti·late (myōōt'l āt') *vt.* **-lat'ed, -lat'ing** [< L. *mutilus*, maimed] to cut off, damage, or spoil an important part of —**mu'ti·la'tion** *n.* —**mu'ti·la'tor** *n.*

mu·ti·ny (myōōt'n ē) *n., pl.* **-nies** [< L. *movere*, to move] revolt against constituted authority; esp., rebellion of soldiers or sailors against their officers —*vi.* **-nied, -ny·ing** to revolt in this way —**mu'ti·neer'** *n.* —**mu'ti·nous** *adj.*

mutt (mut) *n.* [Slang] a mongrel dog

mut·ter (mut'ǝr) *vi., vt.* [ME. *moteren*] **1.** to speak or say in low, indistinct tones **2.** to grumble —*n.* **1.** a muttering **2.** something muttered

mut·ton (mut'n) *n.* [< ML. *multo*, sheep] the flesh of a sheep, esp. a grown sheep, used as food

mu·tu·al (myōō'choo wǝl) *adj.* [< L. *mutare*, to change] **1.** *a)* done, felt, etc. by each of two or more for or toward the other or others *b)* of each other **2.** shared in common [our *mutual* friend] —**mu'tu·al·ly** *adv.*

mutual fund a corporation that invests its shareholders' funds in diversified securities

muu·muu (mōō'mōō) *n.* [Haw.] a long, loose dress of Hawaiian style

muz·zle (muz'l) *n.* [< ML. *musum*] **1.** the nose and jaws of a dog, horse, etc. **2.** a device put over the mouth of an animal to prevent its biting or eating **3.** the front end of the barrel of a firearm —*vt.* **-zled, -zling** **1.** to put a muzzle on (an animal) **2.** to prevent from talking

MX missile [< *m(issile)*, (*e*)*x(peri-mental)*] a projected U.S. ICBM designed to be highly destructive and mobile and concealable underground

my (mī) *possessive pronominal adj.* [< OE. *min*] of, belonging to, or done by me

my·e·li·tis (mī′ə līt′is) *n.* [< Gr. *myelos*, marrow + -ITIS] inflammation of the spinal cord or the bone marrow

My·lar (mī′lär) *a trademark for* a strong, thin polyester used for recording tapes, fabrics, etc. —*n.* [m-] this substance

my·na, my·nah (mī′nə) *n.* [Hindi *mainā*] any of certain tropical birds of SE Asia: some can mimic speech

my·o·pi·a (mī ō′pē ə) *n.* [< Gr. *myein*, to close + *ōps*, eye] nearsightedness —**my·op′ic** (-äp′ik) *adj.*

myr·i·ad (mir′ē əd) *n.* [< Gr. *myrios*, countless] a great number of persons or things —*adj.* very many

myr·mi·don (mur′mə dän′, -dən) *n.* [after name of a Gr. tribe led by Achilles] an unquestioning follower

myrrh (mur) *n.* [< Ar. *murr*] a fragrant gum resin of Arabia and E Africa, used in incense, perfume, etc.

myr·tle (mur′t'l) *n.* [< Gr. *myrtos*] **1.** an evergreen shrub with white or pink flowers and dark berries **2.** any of various other plants, as the periwinkle

my·self (mī self′) *pron.* **1.** *the intensive or reflexive form of* I [I myself went,

I hurt *myself*] **2.** my true self [I am not *myself* today]

mys·te·ri·ous (mis tir′ē əs) *adj.* of, containing, implying, or characterized by mystery —**mys·te′ri·ous·ly** *adv.* —**mys·te′ri·ous·ness** *n.*

mys·ter·y (mis′tə rē) *n., pl.* -ies [< Gr. *mystērion*, secret rite] **1.** something unexplained or secret **2.** a story about a secret crime, etc. [a murder *mystery*] **3.** secrecy

mys·tic (mis′tik) *adj.* **1.** of esoteric rites or doctrines **2.** *same as* MYSTICAL **3.** mysterious —*n.* one professing to undergo profound spiritual experiences

mys′ti·cal *adj.* **1.** spiritually significant or symbolic **2.** of mystics or mysticism **3.** occult —**mys′ti·cal·ly** *adv.*

mys·ti·cism (mis′tə siz′m) *n.* **1.** belief in direct or intuitive attainment of communion with God or of spiritual truths **2.** obscure thinking or belief

mys′ti·fy′ (-fī′) *vt.* -fied′, -fy′ing **1.** to puzzle or perplex **2.** to involve in mystery —**mys′ti·fi·ca′tion** *n.*

mys·tique (mis tēk′) *n.* [Fr., mystic] a complex of quasi-mystical attitudes and feelings surrounding something

myth (mith) *n.* [< Gr. *mythos*] **1.** a traditional story serving to explain some phenomenon, custom, etc. **2.** mythology **3.** any fictitious story, person, or thing —**myth′i·cal** *adj.*

my·thol·o·gy (mi thäl′ə jē) *n., pl.* -gies **1.** the study of myths **2.** myths collectively, as of a specific people —**myth·o·log·i·cal** (mith′ə läj′i k'l) *adj.*

N

N, n (en) *n., pl.* **N's, n's** the 14th letter of the English alphabet

N *Chem.* nitrogen

N, N., n, n. 1. north **2.** northern

N. Norse

N., n. 1. name **2.** navy **3.** neuter **4.** no **5.** nominative **6.** noun

Na [L. *natrium*] *Chem.* sodium

N.A. North America

nab (nab) *vt.* **nabbed, nab′bing** [prob. < dial. *nap*, snatch] [Colloq.] **1.** to snatch or seize **2.** to arrest or catch (a felon or wrongdoer)

na·bob (nā′bäb) *n.* [< Hindi < Ar. *na′ib*, deputy] a very rich or important man

na·cre (nā′kər) *n.* [Fr. < Ar.] *same as* MOTHER-OF-PEARL

na·dir (nā′dər, -dir) *n.* [< Ar. *nazīr*, opposite] **1.** the point opposite the zenith and directly below the observer **2.** the lowest point

nae (nā) *adv.* [Scot.] no; not —*adj.* no

nag¹ (nag) *vt., vi.* **nagged, nag′ging** [< Scand.] **1.** to annoy by continual scolding, faultfinding, etc. **2.** to keep troubling [nagged by doubts] —*n.* one who nags: also **nag′ger**

nag² (nag) *n.* [ME. *nagge*] an inferior horse, esp. an old one

Na·ga·sa·ki (nä′gə sä′kē) seaport in SW Japan: U.S. atomic-bomb target (1945): pop. 405,000

Na·go·ya (nä′gō yä′) seaport in S Honshu, Japan: pop. 1,935,000

nai·ad (nā′ad, nī′-) *n.* [< Gr. *naein*, flow] [*also* N-] *Gr. & Rom. Myth.* any nymph living in springs, rivers, etc.

nail (nāl) *n.* [< OE. *nægl*] **1.** the thin, horny growth at the ends of fingers and toes **2.** a slender, pointed piece of metal driven with a hammer to hold pieces of wood together —*vt.* **1.** to fasten, secure, etc. with or as with nails **2.** [Colloq.] to catch or hit

Nai·ro·bi (nī rō′bē) capital of Kenya: pop., 297,000

na·ive, na·ïve (nä ēv′) *adj.* [Fr. < L. *nativus*, natural] unaffectedly simple; artless; unsophisticated —**na·ive′ly, na·ïve′ly** *adv.* —**na·ive·té′, na·ïve·té′** (-tā′) *n.*

na·ked (nā′kid) *adj.* [OE. *nacod*] **1.** completely unclothed; nude **2.** without covering [a naked sword] **3.** without additions, disguises, etc.; plain [the naked truth] —**na′ked·ly** *adv.* —**na′ked·ness** *n.*

nam·by-pam·by (nam′bē pam′bē) *adj.* [18th-c. play on name *Ambrose*] weak, insipid, indecisive, etc. —*n., pl.* -bies a namby-pamby person

name (nām) n. [OE. *nama*] 1. a word or phrase by which a person, thing, or class is known; title 2. a word or words considered descriptive; epithet, often an abusive one 3. fame or reputation 4. appearance only, not reality *[chief in name only]* —*adj.* well-known —*vt.* **named, nam'ing** 1. to give a name to 2. to mention by name 3. to identify by the right name *[name the States]* 4. to appoint to an office, etc. 5. to specify (a date, price, etc.) —**in the name of** 1. in appeal to 2. by the authority of

name'less *adj.* 1. not having a name 2. left unnamed 3. indescribable

name'ly *adv.* that is to say; to wit

name'sake' (-sāk') n. a person with the same name as another, esp. if named after the other

Nan·king (nan'kiŋ') city in E China, on the Yangtze; pop. 2,700,000

nan·ny goat (nan'ē) [< fem. name *Nan*] [Colloq.] a female goat

nap¹ (nap) *vi.* **napped, nap'ping** [OE. *hnappian*] to sleep lightly for a short time —n. a brief, light sleep

nap² (nap) n. [ME. *noppe*] the downy or hairy surface of cloth or suede formed by short hairs or fibers — **nap'less** *adj.* —**napped** *adj.*

na·palm (nā'päm) n. [< constituents *na(phthene)* & *palm(itate)*] 1. a substance added to gasoline to form a jelly-like compound used in flame throwers and fire bombs 2. this compound —*vt.* to attack or burn with napalm

nape (nāp) n. [ME.] the back of the neck

naph·tha (naf'thə, nap'-) n. [< Per. *neft*, pitch] a flammable liquid distilled from petroleum, coal tar, etc.: it is used as a fuel, solvent, etc.

naph'tha·lene' (-lēn') n. [< prec.] a white, crystalline hydrocarbon produced from coal tar: it is used in moth repellents, in certain dyes, etc.

nap·kin (nap'kin) n. [< L. *mappa*] 1. a small piece of cloth or paper used while eating to protect the clothes and wipe the lips, etc. 2. any small cloth or towel

Na·ples (nā'p'lz) seaport in S Italy; pop. 1,236,000

Na·po·le·on I (nə pō'lē ən) (*Napoléon Bonaparte*) 1769–1821; Fr. general and emperor (1804–15) —**Na·po'le·on'ic** (-än'ik) *adj.*

narc, nark (närk) n. [Slang] a police agent who enforces laws dealing with narcotics

nar·cis·sism (när'sə siz'm) n. [< ff.] self-love —**nar'cis·sist** n. —**nar'cis·sis'tic** *adj.*

Nar·cis·sus (när sis'əs) *Gr. Myth.* a youth who fell in love with his reflection in a pool and was changed into the narcissus —n. [n-] *pl.* **-sus, -sus·es, -si** (-ī) a bulb plant with white, yellow, or orange flowers

nar·co·sis (när kō'sis) n. unconsciousness caused by a narcotic

nar·cot·ic (när kät'ik) n. [< Gr. *narkē*, numbness] a drug, as morphine, used to relieve pain and induce sleep: narcotics are often addictive —*adj.* of or having to do with narcotics

nar·co·tize (när'kə tīz') *vt.* **-tized', -tiz'ing** to subject to a narcotic —**nar'co·ti·za'tion** n.

nar·rate (nar'āt, na rāt') *vt., vi.* **-rat·ed, -rat·ing** [< L. *narrare*, tell] to tell (a story), relate (events), etc. —**nar'ra·tor** n.

nar·ra·tion (na rā'shən) n. 1. a narrating 2. a narrative

nar·ra·tive (nar'ə tiv) *adj.* in story form —n. 1. a story; account 2. the art or practice of narrating

nar·row (nar'ō) *adj.* [OE. *nearu*] 1. small in width; not wide 2. limited in meaning, size, amount, etc. *[a narrow majority]* 3. limited in outlook; not liberal 4. with limited margin *[a narrow escape]* —*vi., vt.* to decrease or limit in width, extent, etc. —n. *[usually pl.]* a narrow passage; strait —**nar'row·ly** *adv.* —**nar'row·ness** n.

nar'row-mind'ed *adj.* limited in outlook; bigoted; prejudiced —**nar'row-mind'ed·ness** n.

nar·whal (när'wəl) n. [< ON. *nahvalr*, lit. corpse whale: from its white coloring] a small arctic whale: the male has a long tusk

nar·y (ner'ē) *adj.* [< *ne'er a*, never a] [Dial.] not any; no (with *a* or *an*)

NASA (nas'ə) National Aeronautics and Space Administration

na·sal (nā'z'l) *adj.* [< L. *nasus*, nose] 1. of the nose 2. uttered with the breath passing through the nose —**na'sal·ize'** *vt., vi.* **-ized', -iz'ing** to pronounce or speak with a nasal sound —**na'sal·i·za'tion** n.

nas·cent (nas'nt, nās'nt) *adj.* [< L. *nasci*, be born] 1. coming into being 2. beginning to form or develop

Nash·ville (nash'vil) capital of Tenn.: with the county in which it is located, pop. 456,000

na·stur·tium (nə stur'shəm) n. [< L. *nasus*, nose + *torquere*, to twist] a plant with red, yellow, or orange flowers and a pungent odor

nas·ty (nas'tē) *adj.* **-ti·er, -ti·est** [< ?] 1. filthy 2. morally offensive; indecent 3. very unpleasant *[nasty weather]* 4. mean; malicious —**nas'ti·ly** *adv.* —**nas'ti·ness** n.

na·tal (nāt'l) *adj.* [< L. *nasci*, be born] of or relating to one's birth

na·tes (nā'tēz) *n.pl.* [L.] the buttocks

na·tion (nā'shən) n. [< L. *natus*, born] 1. a stable community of people with a territory, history, culture, and language in common 2. people united under a single government; country

na·tion·al (nash'ə n'l) *adj.* of or affecting a nation as a whole —n. a citizen or subject —**na'tion·al·ly** *adv.*

National Guard in the U.S., the organized militia in each State: it can be activated into the U.S. Army

na·tion·al·ism n. 1. devotion to one's nation, its interests, etc.; patriotism or chauvinism 2. the advocacy of national independence —**na'tion·al·ist** n., adj. —**na'tion·al·is'tic** adj.

na·tion·al·i·ty (nash'ə nal'ə tē) n., pl. -ties 1. the status of belonging to a nation by birth or naturalization 2. a nation or national group

na·tion·al·ize (-ə līz') vt. -ized', -iz'ing 1. to make national 2. to transfer ownership or control of (land, industries, etc.) to the nation —**na'tion·al·i·za'tion** n.

na·tion·wide adj. by or throughout the whole nation; national

na·tive (nāt'iv) adj. [< L. natus, born] 1. inborn 2. belonging to a locality or country by birth, production, or growth 3. being, or associated with, the place of one's birth [one's native land or language] 4. as found in nature; natural 5. of or characteristic of the original inhabitants of a place —n. 1. a person born in the place indicated 2. an original inhabitant 3. an indigenous plant or animal

Native American same as INDIAN (n. 2): now often the preferred term

na·tive-born' adj. born in a specified place or country

na·tiv·i·ty (nə tiv'ə tē) n., pl. -ties [see NATIVE] birth —**the Nativity** the birth of Jesus

nati. national

NATO (nā'tō) North Atlantic Treaty Organization

nat·ty (nat'ē) adj. -ti·er, -ti·est [< ? NEAT] trim and stylish —**nat'ti·ly** adv.

nat·u·ral (nach'ər əl) adj. [< L. naturalis, by birth] 1. of or dealing with nature 2. produced or existing in nature; not artificial 3. innate; not acquired 4. true to nature; lifelike 5. normal [a natural result] 6. free from affectation; at ease 7. Music neither sharped nor flatted —n. [Colloq.] a person or thing sure to be successful —**nat'u·ral·ness** n.

natural childbirth childbirth without anesthesia through prior training

natural history the study of the animal, vegetable, and mineral world

nat·u·ral·ism n. 1. action or thought based on natural desires 2. Literature, Art, etc. the portrayal of people and things as they really are

nat·u·ral·ist n. 1. one who studies animals and plants 2. an advocate of naturalism —**nat'u·ral·is'tic** adj.

nat·u·ral·ize (-ə līz') vt. -ized', -iz'ing to confer citizenship upon (an alien) —**nat'u·ral·i·za'tion** n.

nat'u·ral·ly adv. 1. in a natural manner 2. by nature 3. of course

natural resources those forms of wealth supplied by nature, as coal, oil, water power, etc.

natural science the systematized knowledge of nature, including biology, chemistry, physics, etc.

na·ture (nā'chər) n. [< L. nasci, be born] 1. the essential quality of a thing; essence 2. inherent tendencies of a person 3. kind; type 4. a) the entire physical universe b) [sometimes

N-] the power, force, etc. that seems to regulate this 5. the primitive state of man 6. natural scenery —**by nature** inherently

Naug·a·hyde (nôg'ə hīd') [arbitrary coinage] a trademark for an imitation leather, used for upholstery —n. [n-] this material

naught (nôt) n. [< OE. na wiht, no person] 1. nothing 2. a zero (0)

naugh·ty (nôt'ē) adj. -ti·er, -ti·est [< obs. naught, wicked] 1. mischievous or disobedient 2. indelicate —**naugh'ti·ly** adv. —**naugh'ti·ness** n.

nau·se·a (nô'shə, -sē ə) n. [< Gr. nausia, seasickness] 1. a feeling of sickness at the stomach, with an impulse to vomit 2. disgust; loathing

nau'se·ate' (-shē āt', -sē-, -zē-) vt. -at'ed, -at'ing to cause to feel nausea

nau·seous (nô'shəs, -zē əs) adj. 1. causing nausea 2. [Colloq.] nauseated

nau·ti·cal (nôt'i k'l) adj. [< Gr. naus, ship] of sailors, ships, or navigation —**nau'ti·cal·ly** adv.

nau·ti·lus (nôt''l əs) n., pl. -lus·es, -li' (-ī') [< Gr. naus, ship] a tropical mollusk with a spiral shell

NAUTILUS

Nav·a·ho, Nav·a·jo (nav'ə hō') n., pl. -hos', -ho', -hoes' a member of a tribe of SW U.S. Indians

na·val (nā'v'l) adj. [< L. navis, ship] of, having, characteristic of, or for a navy, its ships, etc.

nave (nāv) n. [< L. navis, ship] the main part of a church, from the chancel to the principal entrance

na·vel (nā'v'l) n. [OE. nafela] the small scar in the abdomen, marking the place where the umbilical cord was attached to the fetus

navel orange a seedless orange with a navellike hollow at its apex

nav·i·ga·ble (nav'i gə b'l) adj. 1. wide or deep enough to be traveled on by ships 2. that can be steered —**nav'i·ga·bil'i·ty** n.

nav·i·gate (nav'ə gāt') vt., vi. -gat'ed, -gat'ing [< L. navis, ship + agere, to lead] 1. to steer or direct (a ship or aircraft) 2. to travel through or over (water, air, etc.) in a ship or aircraft 3. [Colloq.] to walk

nav·i·ga·tion (-gā'shən) n. a navigating; esp., the science of locating the position and plotting the course of ships and aircraft

nav·i·ga·tor n. one skilled in the navigation of a ship or aircraft

na·vy (nā'vē) n., pl. -vies [< L. navis, ship] 1. all the warships of a nation 2. [often N-] a nation's entire sea force, including ships, men, stores, etc. 3. very dark blue: also **navy blue**

navy bean [from use in U.S. Navy] a small, white variety of bean

navy blue very dark, purplish blue

nay (nā) adv. [< ON. ne, not + ei, ever] not only that, but beyond that [he's well-off, nay rich] —n. 1. a denial 2. a negative vote or voter

Na·zi (nät'sē) *adj.* [G. contr. of the party name] designating or of the German fascist political party which ruled Germany under Hitler (1933-1945) —*n.* a member of this party

NB Nebraska

N.B. New Brunswick

N.B., n.b. [L. *nota bene*] note well

N.C., NC North Carolina

NCO, N.C.O. noncommissioned officer

N.Dak., ND North Dakota

Ne *Chem.* neon

NE, N.E., n.e. 1. northeast 2. northeastern

Ne·an·der·thal (nē an'dər thôl') *adj.* [< a G. valley] designating or of a form of early man of the Stone Age

neap (nēp) *adj.* [OE. in *nepflod*, neap tide] designating either of the two lowest high tides in the month —*n.* neap tide

Ne·a·pol·i·tan (nē'ə päl'ə t'n) *adj.* of Naples —*n.* a native or inhabitant of Naples

Neapolitan ice cream brick ice cream in layers of different flavors

near (nir) *adv.* [OE. compar. of *neah*, nigh] 1. at a short distance in space or time 2. almost [*near* right] 3. closely; intimately —*adj.* 1. close in distance or time 2. close in relationship; akin 3. close in friendship; intimate 4. close in degree [a *near* escape] 5. short or direct [the *near* way] —*prep.* close to —*vt., vi.* to draw near (to); approach —*near'ness n.*

near'by' *adj., adv.* near; close at hand

Near East countries near the E end of the Mediterranean, including those of Arabia, &, sometimes, the Balkans

near'ly *adv.* almost; not quite

near miss a result that is nearly but not quite successful

near'sight'ed *adj.* having better vision for near objects than for distant ones; myopic —**near'sight'ed·ness** *n.*

neat (nēt) *adj.* [< L. *nitere*, to shine] 1. unmixed; undiluted [whiskey *neat*] 2. clean and tidy 3. skillful and precise 4. well-proportioned 5. cleverly done or said 6. [Slang] nice, pleasing, etc. —*neat'ly adv.* —*neat'ness n.*

'neath, neath (nēth) *prep. poet. var. of* BENEATH

Ne·bras·ka (nə bras'kə) Middle Western State of the U.S.: 77,227 sq. mi.; pop. 1,570,000; cap. Lincoln: abbrev. Nebr. —**Ne·bras'kan** *adj., n.*

neb·u·la (neb'yə lə) *n., pl.* **-lae'** (-lē'), **-las** [L., mist] any of the cloud-like patches in the sky consisting of gaseous matter, far distant stars, or external galaxies —**neb'u·lar** *adj.*

neb'u·lous (-ləs) *adj.* unclear; vague

nec·es·sar·i·ly (nes'ə ser'ə lē) *adv.* 1. because of necessity 2. as a necessary result

nec'es·sar'y (-ser'ē) *adj.* [< L. *ne-, not + cedere,* give way] 1. essential; indispensable 2. inevitable 3. required —*n., pl.* **-ies** something necessary

ne·ces·si·tate (nə ses'ə tāt') *vt.* **-tat'ed, -tat'ing** to make necessary or unavoidable

ne·ces'si·ty (-tē) *n., pl.* **-ties** [see NECESSARY] 1. natural causation; fate 2. great need 3. something that cannot be done without 4. want; poverty —**of necessity** necessarily

neck (nek) *n.* [OE. *hnecca*] 1. that part of man or animal joining the head to the body 2. that part of a garment nearest the neck 3. a necklike part; specif., *a)* a narrow strip of land *b)* the narrowest part of a bottle, etc. *c)* a strait —*vt., vi.* [Slang] to kiss and caress in making love —**neck and neck** very close, as in a contest —**stick one's neck out** to act boldly, risking possible failure

neck·er·chief (nek'ər chif, -chēf') *n.* [see NECK & KERCHIEF] a handkerchief or scarf worn around the neck

neck'lace (-lis) *n.* [NECK + LACE, *n.* 1] an ornamental chain of gold, beads, etc., worn around the neck

neck'tie' *n.* a band worn around the neck under a collar and tied in front

neck'wear' *n.* articles worn about the neck, as neckties, scarfs, etc.

ne·crol·o·gy (ne kräl'ə jē) *n., pl.* **-gies** [< Gr. *nekros*, dead body + -LOGY] a list of people who have died

nec·ro·man·cy (nek'rə man'sē) *n.* [< Gr. *nekros,* corpse + *manteia,* divination] 1. divination by alleged communication with the dead 2. sorcery

ne·cro·sis (ne krō'sis) *n.* [< Gr. *nekros,* dead body] the death or decay of tissue in a part of the body

nec·tar (nek'tər) *n.* [< Gr. *nektar*] 1. *Gr. Myth.* the drink of the gods 2. any very delicious beverage 3. the sweetish liquid in many flowers, used by bees to make honey

nec·tar·ine (nek'tə rēn') *n.* [< prec.] a kind of smooth-skinned peach

nee, née (nā; *now often* nē) *adj.* [Fr.] born [Mrs. Helen Jones, *nee* Smith]

need (nēd) *n.* [OE. *nied*] 1. necessity 2. lack of something required or desired [the *need* of a rest] 3. something required or desired that is lacking [my daily *needs*] 4. *a)* a time or condition when help is required [a friend in *need*] *b)* poverty —*vt.* 1. to have need of; require 2. to be obliged [I *need* to be careful] —**have need to** to be required to —**if need be** if it is required

need'ful *adj.* necessary; required

nee·dle (nēd''l) *n.* [OE. *nædl*] 1. a slender, pointed piece of steel with a hole for thread, used for sewing 2. a slender rod of steel, bone, etc. used for crocheting or knitting 3. the short, pointed piece that moves in the groove of a phonograph record and transmits vibrations 4. the pointer of a compass, gauge, etc. 5. the thin, short leaf of the pine, spruce, etc. 6. the sharp, slender metal tube at the end of a hypodermic syringe —*vt.* **-dled,**

---

fat, āpe, cär; ten, ēven; is, bīte; gō, hôrn, tōōl, look; oil, out; up, fur; chin; she; thin, then; zh, leisure; ŋ, ring; ə for *a* in ago; ', (ā'b'l); ë, Fr. coeur; ö, Fr. feu; Fr. mon; ü, Fr. duc; kh, G. ich, doch; ‡ foreign; < derived from

-dling [Colloq.] 1. to goad; prod 2. to tease

nee'dle·point' n. 1. embroidery of woolen threads upon canvas 2. lace made on a paper pattern with a needle: in full **needlepoint lace**

need'less adj. not needed; unnecessary —need'less·ly adv.

nee'dle·work' n. work done with a needle; embroidery, needlepoint, etc.

need'n't (nēd'nt) need not

needs (nēdz) adv. [OE. nedes] of necessity [I must needs go]

need'y adj. -i·er, -i·est in need; very poor; destitute —need'i·ness n.

ne'er (ner) adv. [Poet.] never

ne'er-do-well' n. a shiftless, irresponsible person

ne·far·i·ous (ni fer'ē əs) adj. [< L. ne-, not + fas, lawful] very wicked —ne·far'i·ous·ly adv. —ne·far'i·ous·ness n.

ne·gate (ni gāt') vt. -gat'ed, -gat'ing [< L. negare, deny] 1. to deny 2. to make ineffective; nullify

ne·ga·tion (ni gā'shən) n. 1. act or instance of denying 2. the lack or opposite of something positive

neg·a·tive (neg'ə tiv) adj. 1. expressing denial or refusal; saying "no" 2. opposite to or lacking in that which is positive [a negative force] 3. Math. designating a quantity less than zero, or one to be subtracted 4. Photography reversing the light and shade of the original subject 5. Elec. a) of electricity predominating in a body of resin that has been rubbed with wool b) charged with negative electricity c) having an excess of electrons —n. 1. a negative word, reply, etc. 2. the point of view that opposes the positive 3. the plate in a voltaic battery where the lower potential is 4. an exposed and developed photographic plate or film on which light and shadow are reversed —vt. -tived, -tiv·ing to reject or deny —in the negative in refusal or denial of a plan, etc. —neg'a·tive·ly adv.

neg·lect (ni glekt') vt. [< L. neg-, not + legere, gather] 1. to ignore or disregard 2. to fail to attend to properly 3. to leave undone —n. 1. a neglecting 2. lack of proper care 3. a being neglected —neg·lect'ful adj.

neg·li·gee (neg'lə zhā') n. [< Fr. négliger, to neglect] a woman's loosely fitting dressing gown

neg·li·gent (neg'li jənt) adj. 1. habitually failing to do the required thing; neglectful 2. careless, inattentive, etc. —neg'li·gence n.

neg·li·gi·ble (-jə b'l) adj. that can be neglected or disregarded; trifling

ne·go·ti·ate (ni gō'shē āt') vi. -at'ed, -at'ing [< L. negotium, business] to discuss with a view to reaching agreement —vt. 1. to settle (a transaction, treaty, etc.) 2. to transfer or sell (bonds, stocks, etc.) 3. to succeed in crossing, passing, etc. —ne·go'ti·a·ble (-shē ə b'l, -shə b'l) adj. — ne·go'ti·a'tion n. —ne·go'ti·a'tor n.

ne·gri·tude (neg'rə tood', nē'grə-) n. [Fr. négritude] an awareness and

affirmation by blacks of their distinctive cultural heritage

Ne·gro (nē'grō) n., pl. -groes [Sp. & Port. negro, black] 1. a member of the dominant group of mankind in Africa, characterized generally by a dark skin 2. a member of the Negroid group 3. any person with some Negro ancestors —adj. of or for Negroes

Ne'groid (-groid) adj. designating or of one of the major groups of mankind, including most of the peoples of Africa south of the Sahara

Neh·ru (nā'rōō), Ja·wa·har·lal (jə wä'hər läl') 1889-1964; prime minister of India (1947-64)

neigh (nā) vi. [OE. hnægan] to utter the characteristic cry of a horse —n. this cry; whinny

neigh·bor (nā'bər) n. [OE. neah, nigh + hyp. gebur, freeholder] 1. one who lives or is situated near another 2. a fellow man —adj. nearby —vt., vi. to live or be situated nearby Brit. sp. neighbour —neigh'bor·ing adj.

neigh'bor·hood' n. 1. a particular community, district, or area 2. the people living near one another —in the neighborhood of [Colloq.] 1. near 2. about; approximately

neigh'bor·ly adj. like or appropriate to neighbors; friendly, helpful, etc. —neigh'bor·li·ness n.

nei·ther (nē'thər, nī'-) adj., pron. [OE. na-hwæther, lit., not whether] not one or the other (of two); not either [neither boy went, neither of them was invited] —conj. not either [I can neither go nor stay]

nem·e·sis (nem'ə sis) n., pl. -ses' (-sēz') [Gr. < nemein, deal out] 1. a) just punishment b) one who imposes it 2. anyone or anything that seems inevitably to defeat or frustrate one

neo- [< Gr. neos] [often N-] a combining form meaning: 1. new; recent 2. in a new or different way

ne·o·clas·sic (nē'ō klas'ik) adj. designating or of a revival of classic style and form in art, literature, etc.

ne'o·co·lo'ni·al·ism n. the exploiting of a supposedly independent region, as by imposing a puppet government

ne·ol·o·gism (nē äl'ə jiz'm) n. [see NEO-, -LOGY, & -ISM] a new word or a new meaning for an established word

ne·on (nē'än) n. [< Gr. neos, new] a rare, inert gaseous chemical element found in the earth's atmosphere

neon lamp a glass tube containing neon, which glows red when an electric current is sent through it

ne·o·phyte (nē'ə fīt') n. [< Gr. neos, new + phyein, to produce] 1. a new convert 2. a beginner; novice

ne'o·plasm (-plaz'm) n. [< NEO- + Gr. plassein, to mold] an abnormal growth of tissue, as a tumor

ne'o·prene' (-prēn') n. a synthetic rubber resistant to oil, heat, etc.

Ne·pal (ni pôl') country in the Himalayas: 54,362 sq. mi.; pop. 10,294,000 —Nep·a·lese (nep'ə lēz') adj., n., pl. -lese'

ne·pen·the (ni pen'thē) n. [< Gr.

ne-, not + *penthos*, sorrow] anything that causes forgetfulness of sorrow

neph·ew (nef′yōō) n. [< L. *nepos*] the son of one's brother or sister, or of one's brother-in-law or sister-in-law

ne·phri·tis (ne frīt′əs) n. [< Gr. *nephros*, kidney + -ITIS] disease of the kidneys, accompanied by inflammation

ne plus ul·tra (nē plus ul′trə) [L., no more beyond] the utmost limit

nep·o·tism (nep′ə tiz'm) n. [< L. *nepos*, nephew] favoritism shown to relatives, esp. in securing jobs

Nep·tune (nep′tōōn) 1. the Roman god of the sea 2. the planet eighth in distance from the sun: see PLANET

nep·tu·ni·um (nep tōō′nē əm) n. a radioactive chemical element produced from uranium

nerd (nurd) n. [Slang] a person scorned as dull, ineffective, etc.

Ne·ro (nir′ō) 37–68 A.D.; emperor of Rome (54–68)

nerve (nurv) n. [< L. *nervus*] 1. any of the cordlike fibers carrying impulses between body organs and the central nervous system 2. coolness in danger; courage 3. [pl.] nervousness 4. [Colloq.] impudent boldness —vt. **nerved, nerv′ing** to give strength or courage to —**get on one's nerves** [Colloq.] to make one irritable — **nerve oneself** to collect one's energies or courage for an effort

nerve center 1. any group of nerve cells that work together in controlling a specific sense or bodily activity 2. a control center; headquarters

nerve gas a poisonous gas causing respiratory and nerve paralysis

nerve′less adj. 1. without strength, vigor, etc.; weak 2. not nervous; cool; controlled —**nerve′less·ly** adv.

nerve′-rack′ing, nerve′-wrack′ing (-rak′iŋ) adj. very trying to one's patience or equanimity

nerv·ous (nur′vəs) adj. 1. animated 2. of or made up of nerves 3. emotionally tense, restless, etc. 4. fearful — **nerv′ous·ly** adv. —**nerv′ous·ness** n.

nervous system all the nerve cells and nervous tissues in an organism, including, in the vertebrates, the brain, spinal cord, nerves, etc.

nerv′y adj. -i·er, -i·est 1. bold 2. [Colloq.] brazen; impudent

-ness (nis, nəs) [OE. -*nes(s)*] a suffix meaning state, quality, or instance of being [*sadness*]

nest (nest) n. [OE.] 1. the structure or place where a bird lays its eggs and shelters its young 2. the place used by insects, fish, etc. for spawning or breeding 3. a cozy place; retreat 4. a resort or its frequenters [a *nest* of criminals] 5. a set of things, each fitting within the one next larger —vi., vt. 1. to build or settle in (a nest) 2. to fit (an object) closely within another

nest egg money, etc. put aside as a reserve or to establish a fund

nes·tle (nes′'l) vi. -tled, -tling [OE.

nestlian] 1. to settle down comfortably 2. to press close for comfort or in affection 3. to lie sheltered, as a house among trees —vt. to rest snugly

nest·ling (nest′liŋ, nes′-) n. a young bird not yet ready to leave the nest

net¹ (net) n. [OE. *net*] 1. an openwork fabric, as of string, used to snare birds, fish, etc. 2. a trap; snare 3. a meshed fabric, esp. one used to hold, protect, etc. [a *hairnet*] —vt. **net′ted, net′ting** to snare or enclose as with a net

net² (net) adj. [Fr., clear] left over after deductions or allowances have been made —n. a net amount, profit, weight, price, etc. —vt. **net′ted, net′ting** to clear as profit, etc.

neth·er (neth′ər) adj. [OE. *neothera*] lower or under [the *nether* world]

Neth·er·lands (neth′ər ləndz) country in W Europe: 12,978 sq. mi.; pop. 12,597,000

neth′er·most′ adj. lowest

net′ting n. netted material

net·tle (net′'l) n. [OE. *netele*] a weed with stinging hairs —vt. -tled, -tling to irritate; annoy; vex

net′tle·some adj. annoying; vexing

net′work′ (-wurk′) n. 1. an arrangement of parallel wires, etc. crossed at intervals by others so as to leave open spaces 2. anything like this, as a system of interconnected roads, individuals, etc. 3. *Radio & TV* a chain of transmitting stations —adj. broadcast over the stations of a network

net′work·ing n. 1. the making of contacts and trading of information, as for career advancement 2. the interconnection of computer systems

neu·ral (noor′əl) adj. [NEUR(O)- + -AL] of a nerve or the nervous system

neu·ral·gia (noo ral′jə) n. [see NEURO- & -ALGIA] severe pain along a nerve —**neu·ral′gic** (-jik) adj.

neu·ras·the·ni·a (noor′əs thē′nē ə) n. [< NEUR(O)- + Gr. *asthenia*, weakness] a type of neurosis characterized by fatigue, anxiety, etc. —**neu′ras·then′ic** (-then′ik) adj., n.

neu·ri·tis (noo rīt′əs) n. [NEUR(O)- + -ITIS] inflammation of a nerve or nerves —**neu·rit′ic** (-rit′ik) adj.

neuro- [< Gr. *neuron*, nerve] a combining form meaning of a nerve or the nervous system: also **neur-**

neu·rol·o·gy (noo räl′ə jē) n. [prec. + -LOGY] the branch of medicine dealing with the nervous system and its diseases —**neu·ro·log·i·cal** (noor′ə läj′i k'l) adj. —**neu·rol′o·gist** n.

neu·ron (noor′än) n. the nerve cell body and all its processes

neu·ro·sis (noo rō′sis) n., pl. -ses (-sēz) [NEUR(O)- + -OSIS] a mental disorder characterized by anxieties, compulsions, obsessions, phobias, etc.

neu·rot·ic (-rät′ik) adj. of, characteristic of, or having a neurosis —n. a neurotic person —**neu·rot′i·cal·ly** adv.

neu·ter (nōōt′ər) adj. [< L. *ne-*, not + *uter*, either] 1. *Biol.* a) having no sexual organ b) having undeveloped sexual organs in the adult **2.** *Gram.* designating or of the gender of words neither masculine nor feminine —*vt.* to castrate or spay (an animal)

neu·tral (nōō'trəl) *adj.* [see prec.] **1.** supporting neither side in a quarrel or war **2.** of neither extreme in type, kind, etc.; indifferent **3.** having little or no decided color **4.** *Chem.* neither acid nor alkaline —*n.* **1.** a neutral person or nation **2.** a neutral color **3.** *Mechanics* a disengaged position of gears —**neu'tral·ly** *adv.*

neu'tral·ism (-iz'm) *n.* a policy of remaining neutral, esp. in international conflicts —**neu'tral·ist** *adj., n.*

neu·tral'i·ty (-tral'ə tē) *n.* **1.** a being neutral **2.** the status or policy of a neutral nation

neu·tral·ize (nōō'trə līz') *vt.* **-ized', -iz'ing** **1.** to declare (a nation, etc.) neutral in war **2.** to destroy or counteract the effectiveness, force, etc. of —**neu'tral·i·za'tion** *n.*

neutral spirits ethyl alcohol of 190 proof or over, used in blended whiskeys, liqueurs, etc.

neu·tri·no (nōō trē'nō) *n., pl.* **-nos** [It., little neutron] *Physics* an uncharged particle with almost no mass

neu·tron (nōō'trän) *n.* [< NEUTRAL] one of the elementary, uncharged particles of an atom

neutron bomb a small thermonuclear bomb, that would release radioactive neutrons that could kill people without destroying buildings, etc.

Ne·vad·a (nə vad'ə, -vä'də) Western State of the U.S.: 110,540 sq. mi.; pop. 799,000; cap. Carson City: abbrev. Nev. —**Ne·vad'an** *adj., n.*

nev·er (nev'ər) *adv.* [< OE. *ne,* not + *æfre,* ever] **1.** not ever; at no time **2.** not at all; in no case

nev'er·more' *adv.* never again

never-never land an unreal or imaginary place or situation

nev'er·the·less' (-ƚhə les') *adv.* in spite of that; however

ne·vus (nē'vəs) *n., pl.* **ne'vi** (-vī) [L. *naevus*] a birthmark or mole

new (nōō) *adj.* [OE. *niwe*] **1.** appearing, thought of, discovered, made, etc. for the first time **2.** different from (the) one in the past *[a new hairdo]* **3.** strange; unfamiliar **4.** recently grown; fresh *[new potatoes]* **5.** unused **6.** modern; recent **7.** more; additional **8.** starting as a repetition of a cycle, series, etc. *[the new moon]* **9.** having just reached a position, rank, place, etc. *[a new arrival]* —*adv.* **1.** again **2.** newly; recently —**new'ness** *n.*

New·ark (nōō'ərk) city in NE N.J.: pop. 329,000

New Bed·ford (bed'fərd) seaport in SE Mass.: pop. 98,000

new blood new people as a possible source of new ideas, vigor, etc.

new'born' *adj.* **1.** just born **2.** reborn

New Bruns·wick (brunz'wik) province of SE Canada: 28,354 sq. mi.; pop. 617,000

new'com'er *n.* a recent arrival

New Deal the principles and policies adopted by President F. D. Roosevelt in the 1930's to advance economic recovery and social welfare

New Delhi capital of India, adjacent to Delhi: pop. 261,000

new·el (nōō'əl) *n.* [ult. < L. *nux,* nut] **1.** the pillar around which the steps of a winding staircase turn **2.** the post that supports the handrail of a flight of stairs: also **newel post**

New England the six NE States of the U.S.: Me., Vt., N.H., Mass., R.I., & Conn. —**New Englander**

new'fan'gled (-faŋ'g'ld) *adj.* [ME. < *newe,* new + *-fangel* < OE. *fon,* to take] new; novel: contemptuous term

new'-fash'ioned *adj.* **1.** recently come into fashion **2.** new in form

New·found·land (nōō'fənd land', -lənd) province of Canada, including an island off the E coast & Labrador: 156,185 sq. mi.; pop. 494,000

New Guinea large island in the East Indies, north of Australia

New Hamp·shire (hamp'shir) New England State of the U.S.: 9,304 sq. mi.; pop. 921,000; cap. Concord

New Ha·ven (hā'vən) city in S Conn.: pop. 126,000

New Jersey Eastern State of the U.S.: 7,836 sq. mi.; pop. 7,364,000; cap. Trenton

new'ly *adv.* recently; lately

new'ly·wed' *n.* a recently married person

New Mexico Southwestern State of the U.S.: 121,666 sq. mi.; pop. 1,300,000; cap. Santa Fe

new moon the moon when it is between the earth and the sun, with its dark side toward the earth: in a few days it reappears as a thin crescent

New Or·le·ans (ôr'lē ənz, ôr lēnz') city & port in SE La.: pop. 557,000

New·port News (nōō'pôrt') seaport in SE Va.: pop. 145,000

news (nōōz) *n.pl.* [with sing. v.] **1.** new information; information previously unknown **2.** *a)* recent happenings *b)* reports of these **3.** a newscast —**make news** to do something reported as news

news'boy' *n.* a paperboy

news'cast' *n.* a radio or television news broadcast —**news'cast'er** *n.*

news'deal'er *n.* a retailer of newspapers, magazines, etc.

news'let'ter *n.* a bulletin issued regularly, containing news, often of interest to a special group

news'man' (-man', -mən) *n., pl.* **-men** (-men', -mən) **1.** *same as* NEWSDEALER **2.** one who gathers and reports news for a newspaper, TV station, etc.

news'pa'per *n.* a regular publication, usually daily or weekly, containing news, opinions, advertising, etc.

news'pa'per·man' *n., pl.* **-men'** **1.** a man working for a newspaper, esp. a reporter, editor, etc. **2.** a newspaper owner or publisher —**news'pa'per·wom'an** *n.fem., pl.* **-wom'en**

news'print' *n.* a cheap paper used chiefly for newspapers

news'stand' *n.* a stand at which

newspapers, magazines, etc. are sold

news/wor/thy (-wur/*th*ē) *adj.* timely and important or interesting

news/y *adj.* -i·er, -i·est [Colloq.] containing much news

newt (nōōt, nyōōt) *n.* [by merging of ME. *an eute*, a newt] any of various small amphibious salamanders

New Testament the part of the Bible that contains the life and teachings of Jesus and his followers

New·ton (nōōt'n), **Sir Isaac** 1642-1727; Eng. mathematician

NEWT

New World the Western Hemisphere —**new/-world/**, **New/-World/** *adj.*

New Year's (Day) January 1

New Year's Eve the evening before New Year's Day

New York (yôrk) 1. State of the NE U.S.: 49,576 sq. mi.; pop. 17,557,000; cap. Albany 2. city & port in SE N.Y.: often **New York City**: pop. 7,071,000 —**New York/er**

New Zea·land (zē/lənd) country in the Brit. Commonwealth, including two large islands in the S Pacific: 103,736 sq. mi.; pop. 2,726,000 — **New Zea/land·er**

next (nekst) *adj.* [OE. *neahst*, superl. of *neah*, nigh] nearest; immediately preceding or following —*adv.* 1. in the nearest time, place, rank, etc. 2. on the first subsequent occasion —*prep.* nearest to [sit *next* the tree]

next/-door/ *adj.* in or at the next house, building, etc.

nex·us (nek/səs) *n., pl.* -us·es, nex/us [L.] a link or connection

Nfld., Nfd. Newfoundland

N.H., NH New Hampshire

ni·a·cin (nī/ə sin) *n.* [NI(COTINIC) AC(ID) + -*in*] *same as* NICOTINIC ACID

Ni·ag·a·ra Falls (nī ag/rə, -ag/ər ə) 1. large waterfall on a river (**Niagara River**) flowing from Lake Erie into Lake Ontario 2. city in W N.Y.: pop. 71,000

nib (nib) *n.* [< ME. *nebb*] 1. a bird's beak 2. a point, esp. a pen point

nib·ble (nib/'l) *vt., vi.* -bled, -bling [LME. *nebyllen*] 1. to eat (food) with quick, small bites 2. to bite (*at*) lightly and intermittently —*n.* a small bite —**nib/bler** *n.*

nibs (nibz) *n.* [< ?] [Colloq.] a self-important person (with *his*)

Nic·a·ra·gua (nik/ə rä/gwə) country in C America: 54,342 sq. mi.; pop. 1,715,000 —**Nic/a·ra/guan** *adj. n.*

nice (nīs) *adj.* nic/er, nic/est [< L. *nescius*, ignorant] 1. fastidious; refined 2. delicate; precise; subtle [a *nice* distinction] 3. calling for care, tact, etc. 4. finely discriminating or minutely accurate 5. pleasant, attractive, kind, good, etc.: a generalized term of approval —**nice/ly** *adv.*

ni·ce·ty (nī/sə tē) *n., pl.* -ties 1. precision; accuracy 2. fastidiousness; refinement 3. a subtle or minute detail, distinction, etc. 4. something choice or dainty

niche (nich) *n.* [Fr. < L. *nidus*, a nest] 1. a recess in a wall, for a statue, vase, etc. 2. an especially suitable place or position

‡**nicht wahr?** (nikht vär/) [G., not true?] isn't that so?

nick (nik) *n.* [LME. *nyke*] a small cut, chip, etc. made on a surface —*vt.* 1. to make a nick or nicks in 2. to wound superficially —**in the nick of time** exactly when needed

nick·el (nik/'l) *n.* [< G. *kupfernickel*, copper demon: the copperlike ore contained no copper] 1. a hard, silver-white, metallic chemical element, much used in alloys 2. a U.S. or Canadian coin of nickel and copper, equal to five cents

nick·el·o·de·on (nik/ə lō/dē ən) *n.* [NICKEL + (*mel*)odeon, a small keyboard organ] a coin-operated player piano or early type of jukebox

nick·er (nik/ər) *vi., n. same as* NEIGH

nick·name (nik/nām/) *n.* [by merging of ME. *an ekename*, a surname] 1. a substitute, often descriptive name given in fun, etc., as "Shorty" 2. a familiar form of a proper name, as "Jim" for "James" —*vt.* -named/, -nam/ing to give a nickname to

ni·çoise (nē swäz/) *adj.* [Fr.] designating a salad of tuna, tomatoes, black olives, etc. in vinegar and oil

nic·o·tine (nik/ə tēn/) *n.* [Fr. < J. *Nicot*, 16th-c. Fr. diplomat who took tobacco into France] a poisonous, oily liquid from tobacco leaves

nic·o·tin/ic acid (-tin/ik, -tē/nik) a member of the vitamin B complex

niece (nēs) *n.* [< L. *neptis*] the daughter of one's brother or sister or of one's brother-in-law or sister-in-law

Nie·tzsche (nē/chə), **Frie·drich** (frē/drikh) 1844-1900; Ger. philosopher

nif·ty (nif/tē) *adj.* -ti·er, -ti·est [prob. < MAGNIFICENT] [Slang] attractive, smart, stylish, etc.

Ni·ger (nī/jər) country in WC Africa: 458,500 sq. mi.; pop. 3,546,000

Ni·ger·i·a (nī jir/ē ə) country in WC Africa, in the Brit. Commonwealth: 327,186 sq. mi.; pop. 43,265,000 — **Ni·ger/i·an** *adj., n.*

nig·gard (nig/ərd) *n.* [prob. < Scand.] a stingy person; miser —*adj.* stingy —**nig/gard·li·ness** *n.* —**nig/gard·ly** *adj., adv.*

nig·gle (nig/'l) *vi.* -gled, -gling [prob. akin to Norw. *nigla*] to work fussily; be finicky —**nig/gler** *n.* —**nig/gling** *adj.*

nigh (nī) *adj., adv., prep.* [OE. *neah*] [Chiefly Archaic or Dial.] near

night (nīt) *n.* [OE. *niht*] 1. the period of darkness from sunset to sunrise 2. any period or condition of darkness or gloom

night blindness poor vision in near darkness or dim light

night'cap' *n.* 1. a cap worn in bed 2. [Colloq.] an alcoholic drink taken just before going to bed

night clothes clothes to be worn in bed, as pajamas

night'club' *n.* a place of entertainment for drinking, dancing, etc. at night

night crawl'er a large earthworm that comes to the surface at night

night'dress' *n. same as* NIGHTGOWN

night'fall' *n.* the close of the day

night'gown' *n.* a loose gown worn in bed by women or girls

night'hawk' *n.* 1. any of a group of night birds related to the whippoorwill 2. *same as* NIGHT OWL

night'ie (-ē) *n.* [Colloq.] a nightgown

night-in-gale (nīt'n gāl') *n.* [< OE. *niht*, night + *galan*, sing] a small European thrush, the male of which sings melodiously, esp. at night

Night-in-gale (nīt'n gāl'), **Florence** 1820–1910; Eng. pioneer in modern nursing

night life pleasure-seeking activity at night, as in nightclubs

night'ly *adj.* 1. of or like the night 2. done or occurring every night —*adv.* 1. at night 2. every night

night'mare' (-mer') *n.* [< ME. < *niht*, night + *mare*, demon] 1. a frightening dream 2. any frightening experience

night owl a person who works at night or otherwise stays up late

night'shade' (-shād') *n.* any of various flowering plants related to the potato and tomato; esp., a poisonous variety, as the belladonna

night'shirt' *n.* a kind of nightgown worn, esp. formerly, by men or boys

night'spot' *n.* [Colloq.] a nightclub

night stand a small bedside table

night stick a long, heavy club carried by a policeman

night'time' *n.* the period of darkness from sunset to sunrise

night'wear' *n. same as* NIGHT CLOTHES

ni-hil-ism (nī'ə liz'm) *n.* [< L. *nihil*, nothing] the general rejection of customary beliefs in morality, religion, etc. —**ni'hil-ist** *n.* —**ni'hil-is'tic** *adj.*

nil (nil) *n.* [L. < *nihil*] nothing

Nile (nīl) river in NE Africa, flowing through Egypt into the Mediterranean

nim-ble (nim'b'l) *adj.* **-bler, -blest** [< OE. *niman*, to take] 1. quickwitted; alert 2. moving or acting quickly and lightly —**nim'bly** *adv.*

nim-bus (nim'bəs) *n., pl.* **-bi** (-bī), **-bus-es** [L.] 1. any rain-producing cloud 2. a halo around the head of a saint, etc., as on a picture

Nim-rod (nim'räd) *Bible* a mighty hunter

nin-com-poop (nin'kəm pōōp') *n.* [< ?] a stupid, silly person; fool

nine (nīn) *adj., n.* [OE. *nigon*] one more than eight; 9; IX —**ninth** (nīnth) *adj., n.*

nine'pins' *n.pl.* [with sing. v.] a British version of the game of tenpins, played with nine wooden pins

nine'teen' (-tēn') *adj., n.* nine more than ten; 19; XIX —**nine'teenth'** (-tēnth') *adj., n.*

nine'ty (-tē) *adj., n., pl.* **-ties** nine times ten; 90; XC (or LXXXX) —**the nineties** the numbers or years, as of a century, from 90 through 99 —**nine'ti-eth** (-ith) *adj., n.*

nin-ny (nin'ē) *n., pl.* **-nies** [prob. contr. of *an innocent*] a fool; dolt

nip¹ (nip) *vt.* **nipped, nip'ping** [prob. < MLowG. *nippen*] 1. to pinch or bite 2. to sever (shoots, etc.) as by clipping 3. to check the growth of 4. to have a painful or injurious effect on because of cold —*n.* 1. a nipping; pinch; bite 2. a stinging, as in cold air 3. stinging cold; frost —**nip and tuck** so close as to leave the outcome in doubt

nip² (nip) *n.* [prob. < Du. *nippen*, to sip] a small drink of liquor —*vt., vi.* **nipped, nip'ping** to drink in nips

nip-per (nip'ər) *n.* 1. anything that nips 2. [pl.] pliers, pincers, etc. 3. the claw of a crab or lobster

nip-ple (nip''l) *n.* [prob. < *neb*, a beak] 1. the small protuberance on a breast or udder, through which the milk passes; teat 2. a teatlike, rubber part in the cap of a baby's bottle

Nip-pon (nip'än, ni pän') *Jap. name for* JAPAN —**Nip'pon-ese'** (-ə nēz') *adj., n., pl.* **-ese'**

nip-py (nip'ē) *adj.* **-pi-er, -pi-est** 1. sharp; biting 2. cold in a stinging way

nir-va-na (nir vä'nə, nər-, -van'ə) *n.* [< Sans.] [also N-] 1. *Buddhism* the state of perfect blessedness achieved by the absorption of the soul into the supreme spirit 2. great bliss

nit (nit) *n.* [OE. *hnitu*] 1. the egg of a louse or similar insect 2. a young louse, etc.

ni-ter (nīt'ər) *n.* [< Gr. *nitron*] potassium nitrate or sodium nitrate, used in making explosives, fertilizers, etc.; saltpeter: also, *esp. Brit.,* **ni'tre**

nit-pick-ing (nit'pik'iŋ) *adj., n.* paying too much attention to petty details; niggling —**nit'-pick'er** *n.*

ni-trate (nī'trāt) *n.* a salt of nitric acid, as sodium nitrate —*vt.* **-trat-ed, -trat-ing** to combine with nitric acid or, esp., to make into a nitrate

ni-tric acid (nī'trik) a colorless, corrosive acid containing nitrogen

ni-tro-cel-lu-lose (nī'trō sel'yoo lōs') *n.* a substance obtained by treating cellulose with nitric acid, used in making explosives, lacquers, etc.

ni-tro-gen (nī'trə jən) *n.* [< Fr.: see NITER & -GEN] a colorless, odorless, gaseous chemical element forming nearly four fifths of the atmosphere —**ni-trog'e-nous** (-träj'ə nəs) *adj.*

ni-tro-glyc-er-in, ni-tro-glyc-er-ine (nī'trə glis'ər in) *n.* a thick, explosive oil, prepared by treating glycerin with nitric and sulfuric acids; used in dynamite

ni-trous oxide (nī'trəs) a colorless gas containing nitrogen, used as an anesthetic and in aerosols

nit-ty-grit-ty (nit'ē grit'ē) *n.* [Slang] the actual basic facts, issues, etc.

nit′wit′ *n.* [? NIT + WIT¹] a stupid person

nix (niks) *adv.* [G. *nichts*] [Slang] 1. no 2. not at all —*interj.* [Slang] 1. stop! 2. I forbid, disagree, etc. —*vt.* [Slang] to disapprove of or stop

Nix·on (nik′s′n), Richard M. (1913–   ); 37th president of the U.S. (1969–74): resigned

N.J., **NJ** New Jersey

N.Mex. New Mexico: also N.M., NM

no (nō) *adv.* [< OE. *ne a*, not ever] 1. not at all *[no worse]* 2. nay; not so: used to deny, refuse, or disagree —*adj.* not a; not one *[no errors]* —*n.*, *pl.* **noes**, **nos** 1. a refusal or denial 2. a negative vote or voter

No., **no.** number

No·ah (nō′ə) *Bible* the patriarch commanded by God to build the ark: see ARK (sense 1)

No·bel′ist, **No·bel′list** *n.* a person who has won a Nobel prize

No·bel prizes (nō bel′) [after A. B. *Nobel*, 19th-c. Swed. inventor who established them] annual international prizes given for distinction in physics, chemistry, medicine, and literature, and for the promotion of peace

no·bil·i·ty (nō bil′ə tē) *n.*, *pl.* **-ties** 1. a being noble 2. high rank in society 3. the class of people of noble rank

no·ble (nō′b′l) *adj.* **-bler**, **-blest** [< L. *nobilis*, well-known] 1. famous or renowned 2. having high moral qualities 3. excellent 4. grand; stately 5. of high hereditary rank —*n.* one having hereditary rank or title —*no′-ble·ness n.* —*no′bly adv.*

no·ble·man (-mən) *n.*, *pl.* **-men** a member of the nobility; peer

no·blesse o·blige (nō bles′ ō blēzh′) [Fr., nobility obliges] the inferred obligation of people of high rank to behave nobly toward others

no·bod·y (nō′bud′ē, -bäd′ē; -bə dē) *pron.* not anybody; no one —*n.*, *pl.* **-ies** a person of no importance

noc·tur·nal (näk tur′n′l) *adj.* [< L. *nox*, night] 1. of the night 2. functioning, done, or active during the night —*noc·tur′nal·ly adv.*

noc·turne (näk′tərn) *n.* [Fr.] a romantic or dreamy musical composition thought appropriate to night

nod (näd) *vi.* **nod′ded**, **nod′ding** [ME. *nodden*] 1. to bend the head forward quickly, as in agreement, greeting, etc. 2. to let the head fall forward because of drowsiness —*vt.* 1. to bend (the head) forward quickly 2. to signify (assent, etc.) by doing this —*n.* a nodding

node (nōd) *n.* [L. *nodus*] 1. a knot; knob; swelling 2. that part of a stem from which a leaf starts to grow —*nod·al* (nōd′′l) *adj.*

nod·ule (näj′ool) *n.* [L. *nodulus*] a small knot or rounded lump

No·el, **No·ël** (nō el′) *n.* [Fr. < L. *natalis*, natal] *same as* CHRISTMAS

no′-fault′ *adj.* 1. being a form of automobile insurance in which the insured collects damages without blame being fixed 2. being a form of divorce granted without blame being charged

nog·gin (näg′in) *n.* [prob. < nog, strong ale] 1. a small cup or mug 2. [Colloq.] the head

no′-good′ *adj.* [Slang] contemptible

noise (noiz) *n.* [< OFr.] 1. clamor; din 2. sound; esp., any loud disagreeable sound —*vt.* noised, nois′ing to spread (a rumor, report, etc.)

noise′less *adj.* with little or no noise; silent —*noise′less·ly adv.*

noi·some (noi′səm) *adj.* [see ANNOY & -SOME¹] 1. injurious to health; harmful 2. foul-smelling; offensive

nois·y (noi′zē) *adj.* **-i·er**, **-i·est** 1. making noise 2. full of noise —*nois′i·ly adv.* —*nois′i·ness n.*

no-knock (nō′näk′) *adj.* [Colloq.] letting police with search warrants enter private dwellings by force without announcing or identifying themselves *[a no-knock law]*

no·mad (nō′mad) *n.* [< Gr. *nemein*, to pasture] 1. any of a people having no permanent home, but moving about constantly, as in search of pasture 2. a wanderer —*no·mad′ic adj.*

no man's land the area on a battlefield separating the combatants

nom de plume (näm′ də plōōm′) [Fr.] a pen name

no·men·cla·ture (nō′mən klā′chər) *n.* [< L. *nomen*, name + *calare*, call] the system of names used in a science, etc. or for parts of a device, etc.

nom·i·nal (näm′i n′l) *adj.* [< L. *nomen*, a name] 1. of or like a name 2. in name only, not in fact *[a nominal leader]* 3. relatively very small *[a nominal fee]* —*nom′i·nal·ly adv.*

nom·i·nate (näm′ə nāt′) *vt.* **-nat′ed**, **-nat′ing** 1. to appoint to an office or position 2. to name as a candidate for election —*nom′i·na′tion n.*

nom·i·na·tive (näm′ə nə tiv) *adj. Gram.* designating or of the case of the subject of a verb and the words that agree with it —*n.* 1. this case 2. a word in this case

nom·i·nee (näm′ə nē′) *n.* a person who is nominated

non- [< L. *non*] a *prefix* meaning not: less emphatic than *in-* and *un-*, which often give a word an opposite meaning The terms in the following list will be understood if *not* is used before the meaning of the base word

nonabrasive	nonbeliever
nonabsorbent	nonbelligerent
nonactive	nonbreakable
nonadministrative	nonburnable
nonaggression	non-Catholic
nonalcoholic	nonchargeable
nonallergenic	nonclerical
nonassignable	nonclinical
nonattendance	noncollectable
nonbasic	noncombustible

noncommercial
noncommunicable
non-Communist
noncompeting
noncompetitive
noncompliance
noncomplying
nonconducting
nonconforming
nonconsecutive
nonconstructive
noncontagious
noncontributory
noncontroversial
nonconvertible
noncorroding
noncritical
noncrystalline
noncumulative
nondeductible
nondelivery
nondepartmental
nondepreciating
nondestructive
nondetachable
nondisciplinary
nondiscrimination
nondramatic
nondrinker
nondrying
noneducational
noneffective
nonenforceable
non-English
nonessential
nonexchangeable
nonexclusive
nonexempt
nonexistence
nonexistent
nonexplosive
nonfactual
nonfading
nonfat
nonfatal
nonfiction
nonfictional
nonflammable
nonflowering
nonfluctuating
nonflying
nonfreezing
nonfunctional
nongovernmental
nongranular
nonhazardous
nonhereditary
nonhuman
nonidentical
noninclusive
nonindependent
noninductive
nonindustrial
noninfected
noninflammatory
noninflationary
nonintellectual
noninterchangeable
noninterference
nonintoxicating
nonirritating
nonjudicial
nonlegal
nonliterary
nonmagnetic
nonmalignant

nonmigratory
nonmilitant
nonmilitary
nonnegotiable
nonobjective
nonobligatory
nonobservance
nonoccupational
nonofficial
nonoperational
nonoperative
nonpaying
nonpayment
nonperishable
nonphysical
nonpoisonous
nonpolitical
nonporous
nonprejudicial
nonproductive
nonprofessional
nonprofitable
nonpunishable
nonracial
nonreciprocal
nonreciprocating
nonrecoverable
nonrecurring
nonredeemable
nonrefillable
nonreligious
nonrepresentational
nonresidential
nonresidual
nonresistant
nonreturnable
nonrhythmic
nonrigid
nonsalaried
nonscientific
nonscoring
nonseasonal
nonsecular
nonsensitive
nonsmoker
nonsocial
nonspeaking
nonspecializing
nonspiritual
nonstaining
nonstandard
nonstrategic
nonstriking
nonstructural
nonsuccessive
nonsupporting
nonsustaining
nonsympathizer
nontarnishable
nontaxable
nontechnical
nontheatrical
nonthinking
nontoxic
nontransferable
nontransparent
nontropical
nonuser
nonvenomous
nonvirulent
nonvocal
nonvocational
nonvoter
nonvoting
nonwhite
nonyielding

non·age (nän'ij, nō'nij) n. [see NON- & AGE] the state of being under full legal age (usually 21)

non·a·ge·nar·i·an (nän'ə jə ner'ē ən, nō'nə-) n. [< L. nonaginta, ninety] a person between the ages of 90 and 100

non'a·ligned' adj. not aligned with either side in a conflict of power, esp. power politics —**non'a·lign'ment** n.

nonce (näns) n. [by merging of ME. (for then) ones, lit., (for the) once] the present use, occasion, or time: chiefly in for the nonce

non·cha·lant (nän'shə länt') adj. [Fr., ult. < L. non, not + calere, be warm] 1. without warmth or enthusiasm 2. casually indifferent —non'cha·lance' n. —non'cha·lant'ly adv.

non-com (nän'käm') n. colloq. clipped form of NONCOMMISSIONED OFFICER

non·com·bat·ant (nän käm'bə tənt, nän'kəm bat'ənt) n. 1. a member of the armed forces not engaged in actual combat 2. any civilian in wartime

non'com·mis'sioned officer an enlisted person of any of various grades in the armed forces: in the U.S. Army, from corporal to sergeant major inclusive

non·com·mit·tal (nän'kə mit'l) adj. not committing one to a definite point of view or course of action

non com·pos men·tis (nän' käm'pəs men'tis) [L.] not of sound mind

non'con·duc'tor n. a substance that does not readily transmit sound, heat, and, esp., electricity

non'con·form'ist n. one who does not conform to prevailing attitudes, behavior, etc.; esp., [N-] in England, a Protestant who is not an Anglican —non'con·form'i·ty n.

non·de·script (nän'di skript') adj. [< L. non, not + describere, describe] belonging to no definite class or type; hard to classify or describe

none (nun) pron. [< OE. ne, not + an, one] 1. no one; not anyone 2. [usually with pl. v.] not any [none are his] —n. not any; no part [I want none of it] —adv. not at all [none too soon]

non·en·ti·ty (nän en'tə tē) n., pl. -ties a person or thing of little or no importance

none-such (nun'such') n. a person or thing unrivaled or unequaled

none-the-less (nun'thə les') adv. nevertheless; also none the less

non-fer·rous (nän fer'əs) adj. 1. not containing iron 2. designating or of metals other than iron

non-he'ro n. same as ANTIHERO

non'in·ter·ven'tion n. refusal to intervene; esp., a refusal by one nation to interfere in another's affairs

non-met'al n. an element lacking the characteristics of a metal, as oxygen, carbon, nitrogen, fluorine, etc. —non'me·tal'lic adj.

non·pa·reil (nän'pə rel') adj. [Fr. < non, not + pareil, equal] unequaled; unrivaled; peerless

non-par'ti·san adj. not partisan; esp., not connected with any single political party: also non-par'ti·zan

non·plus (nän′plus′) vt. **-plused′** or **-plussed′, -plus′ing** or **-plus′sing** [L. *non*, not + *plus*, more] to cause to be so perplexed that one cannot go, speak, or act further

non·prof′it adj. not intending or intended to earn a profit

non·res′i·dent adj. not residing in the locality where one works, attends school, etc. —n. a nonresident person

non·re·stric′tive (-ri strik′tiv) adj. Gram. designating a clause, phrase, or word felt as not essential to the sense, usually set off by commas (Ex.: John, *who is tall*, is Bill′s brother)

non·sched′uled adj. licensed for commercial air flights as demand warrants rather than on a schedule

non·sec·tar′i·an (-sek ter′ē ən) adj. not confined to any specific religion

non·sense (nän′sens, -səns) n. words, actions, etc. that are absurd or meaningless —**non·sen′si·cal** adj.

non se·qui·tur (nän sek′wi tər) [L., it does not follow] 1. a conclusion that does not follow from the premises 2. a remark having no bearing on what has just been said

non′stop′ adj., adv. without a stop

non′sup·port′ n. failure to provide for a legal dependent

non·un′ion adj. 1. not belonging to a labor union 2. not made or serviced under labor-union conditions 3. refusing to recognize a labor union

non·vi′o·lence n. an abstaining from violence, as in the struggle for civil rights —**non·vi′o·lent** adj.

noo·dle¹ (nōō′d′l) n. [< ?] [Slang] the head

noo·dle² (nōō′d′l) n. [G. *nudel*] a flat, narrow strip of dry dough, usually made with egg and served in soups, etc.

nook (nook) n. [ME. *nok*] 1. a corner, esp. of a room 2. a small, secluded spot

noon (nōōn) n. [< L. *nona* (*hora*), ninth (hour)] twelve o′clock in the daytime; midday —adj. of or at noon Also **noon′day′, noon′time′**

no one not anybody; nobody

noose (nōōs) n. [< L. *nodus*, a knot] a loop formed in a rope, etc. by means of a slipknot so that the loop tightens as the rope is pulled

nor (nôr) conj. [ME., contr. of *nother*, neither] and not; and not either/I can neither go nor stay]

Nor·dic (nôr′dik) adj. [OE. *north*] of a Caucasoid physical type exemplified by the tall, blond Scandinavians

Nor·folk (nôr′fək) seaport in SE Va.; pop. 267,000

norm (nôrm) n. [< L. *norma*, rule] a standard or model; esp., the standard of achievement of a large group

nor·mal (nôr′m′l) adj. 1. conforming with an accepted standard or norm; natural; usual 2. average in intelligence, etc. —n. 1. anything normal 2.

NOOSE

the usual state, amount, etc. —**nor′mal·cy, nor·mal′i·ty** (-mal′ə tē) n. —**nor′mal·ize′** vt., vi. **-ized′, -iz′ing** —**nor′mal·i·za′tion** n.

nor′mal·ly adv. 1. in a normal manner 2. under normal circumstances

Nor·man (nôr′mən) n. [< OFr.] 1. any of the people of Normandy who conquered England in 1066 2. a native of Normandy —adj. of Normandy, the Normans, their language, etc.

Nor·man·dy (nôr′mən dē) region in NW France, on the English Channel

norm·a·tive (nôr′mə tiv) adj. of or establishing a norm

Norse (nôrs) adj., n. [prob. < Du. *noord*, north] 1. Scandinavian 2. (of) the languages of W Scandinavia

Norse′man (-mən) n., pl. **-men** any of the ancient Scandinavian people

north (nôrth) n. [OE.] 1. the direction to the right of one facing the sunset (0° or 360° on the compass) 2. a region in or toward this direction 3. [often N-] the northern part of the earth —adj. 1. in, of, or toward the north 2. from the north —adv. in or toward the north —**the North** that part of the U.S. north of Maryland, the Ohio River, and Missouri

North America N continent in the Western Hemisphere: c.9,330,000 sq. mi.; pop. 312,000,000 —**North American**

North Car·o·li·na (kar′ə lī′nə) Southern State of the U.S.: 52,712 sq. mi.; pop. 5,874,000; cap. Raleigh —**North Car′o·lin′i·an** (-lin′ē ən)

North Da·ko·ta (də kō′tə) Middle Western State of the U.S.: 70,665 sq. mi.; pop. 653,000; cap. Bismarck —**North Da·ko′tan**

north′east′ n. 1. the direction halfway between north and east 2. a region in or toward this direction —adj. in, of, or toward the northeast 2. from the northeast —adv. in, toward, or from the northeast —**north′east′er·ly** adj., adv. —**north′east′ern** adj. —**north′east′ward** (-wərd) adv., adj. —**north′east′wards** adv.

north·er (nôr′thər) n. a storm or strong wind from the north

north·er·ly (nôr′thər lē) adj., adv. 1. toward the north 2. from the north

north·ern (nôr′thərn) adj. 1. in, of, or toward the north 2. from the north 3. [N-] of the North

north′ern·er n. a native or inhabitant of the north

Northern Hemisphere that half of the earth north of the equator

Northern Ireland division of the United Kingdom, in NE Ireland: 5,462 sq. mi.; pop. 1,487,000

northern lights aurora borealis

North Pole the northern end of the earth′s axis

North Sea arm of the Atlantic, between Great Britain & the European mainland

North Star Polaris, the bright star

almost directly above the North Pole

north'ward (-wərd) *adj.* toward the north: also **north'wards** *adv.*

north'west' *n.* 1. the direction halfway between north and west 2. a region in or toward this direction — *adj.* 1. in, of, or toward the northwest 2. from the northwest —*adv.* in, toward, or from the northwest —the **Northwest** the northwestern U.S., esp. Wash., Oreg., and Ida. —**north'-west'er·ly** *adj., adv.* —**north'west'-ern** *adj.* —**north'west'ward** *adv., adj.* —**north'west'wards** *adv.*

Northwest Territories division of N Canada: 1,304,903 sq. mi.

Norw. 1. Norway 2. Norwegian

Nor·way (nôr'wā') country in N Europe: 125,064 sq. mi.; pop. 3,769,000

Nor·we·gian (nôr wē'jən) *adj.* of Norway, its people, language, etc. —*n.* 1. a native or inhabitant of Norway 2. the language of Norway

nose (nōz) *n.* [OE. *nosu*] 1. the part of the face above the mouth, having two openings for breathing and smelling; in animals, the snout, muzzle, etc. 2. the sense of smell 3. anything like a nose in shape or position —*vt.* **nosed, nos'ing** 1. to discover as by smell 2. to nuzzle 3. to push (a way, etc.) with the front forward —*vi.* 1. to pry inquisitively 2. to move forward — **nose out** to defeat by a very small margin —**on the nose** [Slang] precisely; exactly —**pay through the nose** to pay more for something than it is worth —**turn up one's nose at** to sneer at; scorn —**under one's (very) nose** in plain view

nose'bleed' *n.* a bleeding from the nose

nose cone the cone-shaped foremost part of a rocket or missile

nose dive 1. a swift downward plunge of an airplane, nose first 2. any sudden, sharp drop, as in prices — **nose'-dive'** *vi.* **-dived', -div'ing**

nose drops medication administered through the nose with a dropper

nose'gay' *n.* [NOSE + GAY (obs. "gay object")] a small bunch of flowers

nos·tal·gia (näs tal'jə) *n.* [< Gr. *nostos*, a return + -ALGIA] a longing for something far away or long ago —**nos·tal'gic** (-jik) *adj.*

nos·tril (näs'trəl) *n.* [< OE. *nosu*, the nose + *thyrel*, hole] either of the external openings of the nose

nos·trum (näs'trəm) *n.* [L., ours] 1. a quack medicine 2. a panacea

nos·y, nos·ey (nō'zē) *adj.* **-i·er, -i·est** [Colloq.] prying; inquisitive

not (nät) *adv.* [< ME. *nought*] in no manner, degree, etc.: a word expressing negation or the idea of *no*

no·ta·ble (nōt'ə b'l) *adj.* [< L. *notare*, to note] worthy of notice; remarkable; outstanding —*n.* a person of distinction —**no'ta·bly** *adv.*

no·ta·rize (nōt'ə rīz') *vt.* **-rized', -riz'ing** to certify or attest (a document) as a notary

no·ta·ry (nōt'ər ē) *n., pl.* **-ries** [< L. *notare*, to note] an official authorized to certify or attest documents, take affidavits, etc.: in full **notary public**

no·ta·tion (nō tā'shən) *n.* 1. the use of signs or symbols to represent words, quantities, etc. 2. any such system of signs or symbols, as in mathematics, music, etc. 3. a brief note or noting

notch (näch) *n.* [by merging of ME. *an oche*, a notch] 1. a V-shaped cut in an edge or surface 2. a narrow pass with steep sides 3. [Colloq.] a step; degree —*vt.* to cut notches in

note (nōt) *n.* [< L. *nota*, a mark] 1. a distinguishing feature [a *note* of sadness] 2. importance, distinction, etc. [a man of *note*] 3. a brief writing to aid the memory; memorandum 4. a comment or explanation; annotation 5. notice; heed [worthy of *note*] 6. a short letter 7. a written acknowledgment of a debt 8. a cry or call, as of a bird 9. *Music a)* a tone of definite pitch *b)* a symbol for a tone, indicating its duration and pitch —*vt.* **not'ed, not'ing** 1. to heed; observe 2. to set down in writing 3. to mention particularly —**compare notes** to exchange views

note'book' *n.* a book in which notes, or memorandums, are kept

not·ed (nōt'id) *adj.* distinguished; renowned; eminent

note'wor'thy *adj.* worthy of note; outstanding; remarkable

noth·ing (nuth'iŋ) *n.* [OE. *na thing*] 1. no thing; not anything 2. nothingness 3. a thing that does not exist 4. a person or thing considered of little or no importance 5. a zero —*adv.* not at all; in no way —**for nothing** 1. free 2. in vain 3. without reason —**think nothing of** 1. to attach no importance to 2. to regard as easy to do

noth'ing·ness *n.* 1. nonexistence 2. insignificance 3. unconsciousness

no·tice (nōt'is) *n.* [see NOTE] 1. an announcement or warning 2. a short article about a book, play, etc. 3. a sign giving some public information, warning, etc. 4. attention; heed 5. a formal warning of intention to end an agreement or contract at a certain time —*vt.* **-ticed, -tic·ing** 1. to mention; refer to 2. to observe; pay attention to —**take notice** to observe

no'tice·a·ble *adj.* readily noticed; conspicuous —**no'tice·a·bly** *adv.*

no·ti·fy (nōt'ə fī') *vt.* **-fied', -fy'ing** [< L. *notus*, known + *facere*, make] to give notice to; inform —**no'ti·fi·ca'-tion** (-fi kā'shən) *n.*

no·tion (nō'shən) *n.* [see NOTE] 1. a general idea 2. a belief; opinion 3. an inclination; whim 4. [*pl.*] small, useful articles, as needles, thread, etc., sold in a store —**no'tion·al** *adj.*

no·to·ri·e·ty (nōt'ə rī'ə tē) *n.* a being notorious

no·to·ri·ous (nō tôr'ē əs) *adj.* [see NOTE] widely known, esp. unfavorably —**no·to'ri·ous·ly** *adv.*

no'-trump' *n. Bridge* a bid to play with no suit being trumps

not·with·stand·ing (nät'with stan'diŋ, -with-) *prep.* in spite of — *adv.* nevertheless —*conj.* although

nou·gat (nōō'gət) *n.* [< Pr. *noga,*

nut] a confection of sugar paste with nuts

nought (nôt) *n.* [< OE. *ne*, not + *awiht*, aught] 1. nothing 2. the figure zero

noun (noun) *n.* [< L. *nomen*, a name] *Gram.* a word that names or denotes a person, thing, action, etc.

nour·ish (nur'ish) *vt.* [< L. *nutrire*] 1. to provide with substances necessary to life and growth 2. to foster; promote —**nour'ish·ing** *adj.*

nour'ish·ment (-mənt) *n.* 1. a nourishing or being nourished 2. food

nou·veau riche (nōō'vō rēsh') *pl.* **-veaux riches** (-vō rēsh') [Fr.] a newly rich person, esp. one lacking cultural taste or social grace

Nov. November

no·va (nō'və) *n., pl.* **-vae, -vae** (-vē) [< L., new] a star that brightens intensely and then gradually dims

No·va Sco·tia (nō'və skō'shə) province of SE Canada: 21,425 sq. mi.; pop. 756,000; cap. Halifax

nov·el (näv'l) *adj.* [< L. dim. of *novus*, new] new and unusual —*n.* a relatively long fictional prose narrative

nov·el·ette (-ə let') *n.* a short novel

nov·el·ist *n.* one who writes novels

nov·el·ty (-tē) *n., pl.* **-ties** 1. the quality of being novel; newness 2. something new, fresh, or unusual 3. a small, often cheap, cleverly made article: *usually used in pl.*

No·vem·ber (nō vem'bər) *n.* [< L. *novem*, nine: 9th month in Roman year] the eleventh month of the year, having 30 days

no·ve·na (nō vē'nə) *n.* [< L. *novem*, nine] *R.C.Ch.* special prayers for nine days

nov·ice (näv'is) *n.* [< L. *novus*, new] 1. a person on probation in a religious order before taking final vows 2. a person new to something; beginner

no·vi·ti·ate (nō vish'ē it) *n.* the period or state of being a novice

No·vo·cain (nō'və kān') [L. *nov(us)*, new + (c)OCAIN(E)] a trademark for PROCAINE: also sp. **Novocaine**

now (nou) *adv.* [OE. *nu*] 1. *a*) at the present time *b*) at once 2. at that time; then 3. with things as they are [*now* we'll never know] —*conj.* since; seeing that —*n.* the present time [*that's* all for *now*] —*adj.* of the present time —**just now** recently —**now and then** (or **again**) occasionally

now'a·days' (-ə dāz') *adv.* in these days; at the present time

no·where (nō'hwer', -wer') *adv.* not in, at, or to any place —**nowhere near** not by a wide margin

no'wise' (-wīz') *adv.* in no way: also **no'way', no'ways'**

nox·ious (näk'shəs) *adj.* [< L. *nocere*, to hurt] harmful to health or morals; injurious or unwholesome

noz·zle (näz'l) *n.* [dim. of *nose*] the spout at the end of a hose, pipe, etc.

N.S. Nova Scotia

NT., NT, N.T. New Testament

nth (enth) *adj.* of an indefinitely great number, amount, or degree

nt. wt. net weight

nu (nōō, nyōō) *n.* the 13th letter of the Greek alphabet (N, ν)

nu·ance (nōō'äns) *n.* [Fr. < *nuer*, to shade] a slight variation in tone, color, meaning, etc. —**nu'anced** *adj.*

nub (nub) *n.* [var. of *knub*, knob] 1. a lump or small piece 2. [Colloq.] the main point; gist

nub·bin (nub'in) *n.* [dim. of prec.] 1. a small ear of corn 2. a small piece

nub·by (nub'ē) *adj.* **-bi·er, -bi·est** having a rough, knotted surface [a *nubby* fabric]

nu·bile (nōō'b'l, -bīl) *adj.* [< L. *nubere*, marry] ready for marriage: said of a girl

nu·cle·ar (nōō'klē ər) *adj.* 1. of, like, or forming a nucleus 2. of, involving, or using atomic nuclei or atomic energy, bombs, power, etc.

nuclear family a family unit consisting of parents and their children living in one household

nuclear fission the splitting of the nuclei of atoms, accompanied by conversion of part of the mass into energy: the principle of the atomic bomb

nuclear fusion the fusion of lightweight atomic nuclei into a nucleus of heavier mass, with a resultant loss in the combined mass converted into energy, as in the hydrogen bomb

nuclear physics the branch of physics dealing with the structure of atomic nuclei, nuclear forces, etc.

nuclear reactor a device for creating a controlled nuclear chain reaction in a fissionable fuel, as for the production of energy

nu·cle·ate (nōō'klē it; *for v.* -āt') *adj.* having a nucleus —*vt., vi.* **-at'ed, -at'ing** to form into a nucleus —**nu'cle·a'tion** *n.*

nu·cle·us (nōō'klē əs) *n., pl.* **-cle·i'** (-ī') [L., kernel] 1. a central thing or part around which others are grouped; core 2. any center of growth or development 3. the central part of an atom 4. the central mass of protoplasm in a cell

nude (nōōd) *adj.* [L. *nudus*] naked; bare —*n.* 1. a nude human figure, esp. in a work of art 2. the state of being nude [in the *nude*] —**nu'di·ty** *n.*

nudge (nuj) *vt.* **nudged, nudg'ing** [< ?] to push gently, esp. with the elbow, in order to get attention, hint slyly, etc. —*n.* a gentle push

nud'ism *n.* the practice or cult of going nude —**nud'ist** *n., adj.*

nu·ga·to·ry (nōō'gə tôr'ē) *adj.* [< L. *nugari*, to trifle] 1. trifling; worthless 2. not operative; invalid

nug·get (nug'it) *n.* [prob. < dial. *nug*, lump] a lump, esp. of native gold

nui·sance (nōō's'ns) *n.* [< L. *nocere*, annoy] an act, thing, or person causing trouble, annoyance, etc.

null (nul) *adj.* [< L. *nullus*, none] 1. without legal force; invalid: usually in phrase **null and void** 2. amounting to nought 3. of no value, effect, etc.

nul·li·fy (nul'ə fī') *vt.* -fied', -fy'ing [< L. *nullus*, none + *facere*, make] 1. to make legally null or valueless 2. to cancel out —**nul'li·fi·ca'tion** *n.*

numb (num) *adj.* [< ME. *nimen*, take] deadened; insensible [*numb* with grief] —*vt.* to make numb —**numb'ly** *adv.* —**numb'ness** *n.*

num·ber (num'bər) *n.* [< L. *numerus*] 1. a symbol or word showing how many or which one in a series (Ex.: 2, 27, four, sixth) 2. [*pl.*] arithmetic 3. the sum of persons or things; total 4. *a*) [*often pl.*] many *b*) [*pl.*] numerical superiority 5. quantity 6. *a*) a single issue of a periodical *b*) a single song, dance, etc. in a program of entertainment 7. [Colloq.] a person or thing singled out [a smart *number*] 8. Gram. the form of a word as indicating either singular or plural —*vt.* 1. to count; enumerate 2. to give a number to 3. to include as one of a group 4. to limit the number of 5. to have or comprise; total —*vi.* to be included —**a number of** several or many; some —**beyond** (or **without**) **number** too numerous to be counted —**the numbers** an illegal lottery based on certain numbers published in newspapers: also **numbers pool** (or **racket**)

num'ber·less *adj. same as* COUNTLESS

Num·bers (num'bərz) the 4th book of the Pentateuch in the Bible: abbrev. **Num.**

nu·mer·al (nōō'mər əl) *adj.* [< L. *numerus*, number] of or denoting a number or numbers —*n.* a figure, letter, or word expressing a number

nu'mer·ate (-mə rāt') *vt.* -at'ed, -at'ing to count one by one; enumerate

nu·mer·a'tor (-mə rāt'ər) *n.* the part of a fraction above the line

nu·mer·i·cal (noo mer'i k'l) *adj.* 1. of, or having the nature of, number 2. in or by numbers 3. expressed by numbers —**nu·mer'i·cal·ly** *adv.*

nu·mer·ol·o·gy (nōō'mə räl'ə jē) *n.* the attributing of occult meaning to numbers, as in birth dates

nu·mer·ous (nōō'mər əs) *adj.* 1. of great number 2. very many

nu·mis·mat·ics (nōō'miz mat'iks, -mis-) *n.pl.* [*with sing. v.*] [< L. *numisma*, a coin] the study or collection of coins, medals, paper money, etc. —**nu·mis'ma·tist** (-mə tist) *n.*

num·skull, numb·skull (num' skul') *n.* [NUM(B) + SKULL.] a dunce

nun (nun) *n.* [< LL. *nonna*] a woman devoted to a religious life. esp. one living in a convent under vows

nun·ci·o (nun'shē ō', -sē-) *n.*, *pl.* -os' [< It. < L. *nuntius*, messenger] a papal ambassador to a foreign state

nun·ner·y (nun'ər ē) *n.*, *pl.* -ies a *former name for* CONVENT

nup·tial (nup'shəl, -chəl) *adj.* [< L. *nubere*, marry] of marriage or a wedding —*n.* [*pl.*] a wedding

nurse (nurs) *n.* [< L. *nutrire*, nourish]

1. a woman hired to care for another's children 2. a person trained to care for the sick, assist surgeons, etc. —*vt.* nursed, nurs'ing 1. to suckle (an infant) 2. to take care of (a child, invalid, etc.) 3. to nourish, foster, etc. 4. to try to cure [to *nurse* a cold] 5. to use or handle so as to protect or conserve —*vi.* 1. to feed at the breast; suckle 2. to serve as a nurse

nurse'maid' *n.* a woman hired to care for a child or children

nurs·er·y (nur'sə rē) *n.*, *pl.* -ies 1. a room set aside for children 2. a place where parents may temporarily leave children to be cared for 3. a place where young trees or plants are raised for transplanting, etc.

nurs'er·y·man (-mən) *n.*, *pl.* -men one who owns or works in a tree nursery

nursery rhyme a poem for children

nursery school a prekindergarten school for young children

nursing home a residence providing care for the infirm, chronically ill, disabled, etc.

nur·ture (nur'chər) *n.* [< L. *nutrire*, nourish] 1. food 2. training; rearing —*vt.* -tured, -tur·ing 1. to feed or nourish 2. to train, educate, rear, etc. —**nur'tur·er** *n.*

nut (nut) *n.* [OE. *hnutu*] 1. a dry, one-seeded fruit, consisting of a kernel, often edible, in a woody shell, as the walnut 2. the kernel itself 3. loosely, any hard-shelled, relatively non-perishable fruit, as the peanut 4. a small metal block with a threaded hole, for screwing onto a bolt, etc. 5. [Slang] *a*) a crazy or eccentric person *b*) a devotee; fan

NUT ON A BOLT

nut'crack'er *n.* 1. an instrument for cracking nutshells 2. a bird of the crow family that feeds on nuts

nut'hatch' (-hach') *n.* a small, nut-eating bird with a sharp beak

nut'meat' *n.* the kernel of a nut

nut'meg' (-meg') *n.* [< L. *nux*, nut + LL. *muscus*, musk] the aromatic seed of an East Indian tree, grated and used as a spice

nut'pick' *n.* a small, sharp instrument for digging out the kernels of cracked nuts

nu·tri·a (nōō'trē ə) *n.* [Sp. < L. *lutra*, otter] the soft, brown fur of a S.American rodent

nu·tri·ent (nōō'trē ənt) *adj.* [< L. *nutrire*, nourish] nourishing —*n.* anything nutritious

nu'tri·ment (-trə mənt) *n.* anything that nourishes; food

nu·tri·tion (nōō trish'ən) *n.* [see NUTRIENT] 1. the process by which an organism takes in and assimilates food 2. anything that nourishes; food 3. the study of diet and health —**nu·tri'tion·al** *adj.* —**nu·tri'tion·al·ly** *adv.* —**nu·tri'tive** (-trə tiv) *adj.*

nu·tri'tious (-shəs) *adj.* nourishing

nuts *adj.* [Slang] crazy; foolish —*interj.* [Slang] an exclamation of disgust, scorn, etc.: often in the phrase **nuts to (someone or something)** —**be nuts about** [Slang] 1. to be very enthusiastic about 2. to be greatly in love with

nut'shell' n. the shell enclosing the kernel of a nut —**in a nutshell** in concise form; in a few words

nut'ty adj. -ti·er, -ti·est 1. containing or producing nuts 2. having a nutlike flavor 3. [Slang] a) very enthusiastic b) queer, crazy, etc. — **nut'ti·ness** n.

nuz·zle (nuz'l) vt., vi. -zled, -zling [< NOSE] 1. to push (against) or rub with the nose or snout 2. to nestle; snuggle —**nuz'zler** n.

NV Nevada

NW, N.W., n.w. 1. northwest 2. northwestern

N.Y., NY New York

N.Y.C. New York City

ny·lon (nī'län) n. [arbitrary coinage] 1. an elastic, very strong, synthetic material made into fiber, bristles, etc. 2. [pl.] stockings made of this

nymph (nimf) n. [< Gr. nymphē] 1. Gr. & Rom. Myth. any of a group of minor nature goddesses, living in rivers, trees, etc. 2. a lovely young woman 3. the young of an insect with incomplete metamorphosis

nym·pho·ma·ni·a (nim'fə mā'nē ə) n. uncontrollable desire by a woman for sexual intercourse —**nym'pho·ma'ni·ac'** (-ak') n., adj.

O

O, o (ō) n., pl. **O's, o's** 1. the fifteenth letter of the English alphabet 2. the numeral zero 3. Physics ohm

O (ō) interj. 1. an exclamation in direct address [O Lord!] 2. oh

O 1. Old 2. Chem. oxygen

O. 1. Ocean 2. October 3. Ohio

oaf (ōf) n. [< ON. alfr, elf] a stupid, clumsy fellow —**oaf'ish** adj.

O·a·hu (ō ä'hōō) chief island of Hawaii

oak (ōk) n. [OE. ac] 1. a large hardwood tree with nuts called acorns 2. its wood —adj. of oak —**oak'en** adj.

Oak·land (ōk'lənd) seaport in W Calif.: pop. 339,000

Oak Ridge city in E Tenn.: a center for atomic research: pop. 28,000

oa·kum (ō'kəm) n. [< OE. a-, out + camb, a comb] hemp fiber got by taking apart old ropes, for caulking boat seams

oar (ôr) n. [OE. ar] a long pole with a broad blade at one end, used in rowing —**rest on one's oars** to stop to rest —**oars·man** (ôrz'mən) n., pl. **-men**

oar'lock' n. a device, often U-shaped, for holding an oar in place in rowing

OAS, O.A.S. Organization of American States

o·a·sis (ō ā'sis) n., pl. **-ses** (-sēz) [< Gr. oasis] a fertile place in a desert, due to the presence of water

oat (ōt) n. [OE. ate] [usually pl.] 1. a hardy cereal grass 2. its edible grain —**oat'en** adj.

oat'cake' n. a thin, flat cake of oatmeal

oath (ōth) n., pl. **oaths** (ō‑ths, ōths) [OE. ath] 1. a declaration based on an appeal to God that one will speak the truth, keep a promise, etc. 2. the profane use of God's name, as in anger 3. a swearword; curse

oat'meal' n. 1. oats crushed into meal or flakes 2. a porridge of this

ob- [< L. ob] a prefix meaning: 1. to, toward, before [object] 2. against [obnoxious] 3. upon, over [obfuscate] 4. completely [obsolete]

OB, O.B. 1. obstetrician 2. obstetrics

ob. [L. obiit] he (or she) died

ob·bli·ga·to (äb'lə gät'ō) n., pl. **-tos, -ti** (-ē) [see OBLIGE] an elaborate musical accompaniment, orig. thought necessary to the performance of a piece

ob·du·rate (äb'door ət) adj. [< L. ob-, intens. + durus, hard] 1. hardhearted 2. stubborn; obstinate —**ob'du·ra·cy** (-ə sē) n. —**ob'du·rate·ly** adv.

o·be·di·ent (ō bē'dē ənt) adj. obeying or willing to obey —**o·be'di·ence** n. —**o·be'di·ent·ly** adv.

o·bei·sance (ō bā's'ns, -bē'‑) n. [< OFr. obeir, obey] 1. a gesture of respect, as a bow 2. homage; deference —**o·bei'sant** adj.

ob·e·lisk (äb'ə lisk, ō'bə‑) n. [< Gr. obelos, needle] a tall, four-sided stone pillar tapering to its pyramidal top

o·bese (ō bēs') adj. [< L. ob- (see OB-) + edere, eat] very fat; stout —**o·be'si·ty** (-ə tē) n.

o·bey (ō bā') vt. [< L. ob- (see OB-) + audire, hear] 1. to carry out the orders of 2. to carry out (an order, etc.) 3. to be guided by [to obey one's conscience] —vi. to be obedient

ob·fus·cate (äb'fəs kāt', äb fus'kāt) vt. **-cat'ed, -cat'ing** [< L. ob- (see OB-) + fuscus, dark] to obscure; confuse; bewilder —**ob'fus·ca'tion** n.

o·bit·u·ar·y (ō bich'ōō wer'ē) n., pl. **-ies** [< L. obire, die] a notice of someone's death, usually with a brief biography: also **o·bit** (ō'bit)

obj. 1. object 2. objective

ob·ject (äb'jikt; for v. əb jekt', äb‑) n. [< ML. objectum, thing thrown in the way < L. ob- (see OB-) + jacere, to throw] **1.** a thing that can be seen or touched **2.** a person or thing to which action, feeling, etc. is directed **3.** purpose; goal **4.** *Gram.* a noun or substantive that receives the action of a verb or is governed by a preposition —*vt.* to feel or express disapproval or opposition —**ob·jec'tor** *n.*

ob·jec·tion (əb jek'shən) *n.* **1.** a feeling or expression of opposition or disapproval **2.** a reason for objecting

ob·jec'tion·a·ble *adj.* **1.** open to objection **2.** disagreeable; offensive

ob·jec'tive *adj.* **1.** existing as an object or fact, independent of the mind; real **2.** concerned with the realities of the thing dealt with rather than the thoughts of the artist, writer, etc. **3.** without bias or prejudice **4.** *Gram.* designating or of the case of an object of a preposition or verb —*n.* something aimed at —**ob·jec'tive·ly** *adv.* —**ob·jec·tiv·i·ty** (äb'jek tiv'ə tē), **ob·jec'tive·ness** *n.*

object lesson an actual or practical demonstration or exemplification of some principle

ob·jet d'art (äb'zhä där') *pl.* **ob·jets d'art** (äb'zhä) [Fr.] a small object of artistic value

ob·jur·gate (äb'jər gāt') *vt.* **-gat'ed,** **-gat'ing** [< L. *ob*- (see OB-) + *jurgare,* chide] to upbraid sharply; rebuke

ob·late (äb'lāt) *adj.* [< ModL. *oblatus,* thrust forward] *Geom.* flattened at the poles [*an oblate* spheroid]

ob·la·tion (ä blā'shən) *n.* [< L. *oblatus,* offered] an offering or sacrifice to God or a god

ob·li·gate (äb'lə gāt') *vt.* **-gat'ed,** **-gat'ing** [see OBLIGE] to bind by a contract, promise, sense of d', etc.

ob·li·ga·tion *n.* **1.** an obli .ing or being obligated **2.** a binding contract, promise, responsibility, etc. **3.** the binding power of a contract, etc. **4.** a being indebted for a favor, etc.

ob·lig·a·to·ry (ə blig'ə tôr'ē, äb'lig ə-) *adj.* legally or morally binding

o·blige (ə blīj', ō-) *vt.* **o·bliged',** **o·blig'ing** [< L. *ob*- (see OB-) + *ligare,* bind] **1.** to compel by moral, legal, or physical force **2.** to make indebted for a favor; do a favor for

o·blig'ing *adj.* ready to do favors; helpful —**o·blig'ing·ly** *adv.*

ob·lique (ə blēk', ō-; *also, esp. in mil. use,* -blīk') *adj.* [< L. *ob*- (see OB-) + *liquis,* awry] **1.** slanting **2.** indirect or evasive —**ob·lique'ly** *adv.* —**ob·liq·ui·ty** (ə blik'wə tē), **ob·lique'ness** *n.*

ob·lit·er·ate (ə blit'ə rāt') *vt.* **-at'ed,** **-at'ing** [< L. *ob*- (see OB-) + *litera,* a letter] **1.** to blot out; efface **2.** to destroy —**ob·lit·er·a'tion** *n.*

ob·liv·i·on (ə bliv'ē ən) *n.* [< L. *oblivisci,* forget] **1.** forgetfulness **2.** the condition of being forgotten

ob·liv'i·ous *adj.* forgetful or unmindful (usually with *of* or *to*)

ob·long (äb'lôŋ) *adj.* [< L. *ob*- (see OB-) + *longus,* long] longer than broad; specif., rectangular and longer in one direction —*n.* an oblong figure

ob·lo·quy (äb'lə kwē) *n., pl.* **-quies** [< L. *ob*- (see OB-) + *loqui,* speak] **1.** widespread censure or abuse **2.** disgrace or infamy resulting from this

ob·nox·ious (əb näk'shəs) *adj.* [< L. *ob*- (see OB-) + *noxa,* harm] very unpleasant; offensive —**ob·nox'ious·ly** *adv.* —**ob·nox'ious·ness** *n.*

o·boe (ō'bō) *n.* [< Fr. *haut,* high (pitch) + *bois,* wood] a double-reed woodwind instrument having a high, penetrating tone —**o'bo·ist** *n.*

Obs., obs. obsolete

OBOE

ob·scene (äb sēn') *adj.* [< L. *obscenus,* filthy] **1.** offensive to modesty or decency; lewd **2.** repulsive —**ob·scen'i·ty** (-sen'ə tē) *n., pl.* **-ties**

ob·scure (əb skyoor') *adj.* [< L. *obscurus,* covered over] **1.** dim; dark **2.** not easily seen; faint **3.** vague; ambiguous [*an obscure* answer] **4.** inconspicuous; hidden **5.** not well-known [*an obscure* actor] —*vt.* **-scured',** **-scur'ing** to make obscure —**ob·scure'ly** *adv.* —**ob·scu'ri·ty** *n.*

ob·se·quies (äb'sə kwēz) *n.pl.* [< L. *obsequium,* compliance, substituted for L. *exsequiae,* funeral] funeral rites

ob·se·qui·ous (əb sē'kwē əs) *adj.* [< L. *obsequis,* comply with] much too willing to serve or obey; fawning

ob·serv·ance (əb zur'vəns) *n.* **1.** the observing of a law, duty, custom, etc. **2.** a customary act, rite, etc.

ob·serv'ant *adj.* **1.** strict in observing a law, custom, etc. **2.** paying careful attention **3.** perceptive or alert

ob·ser·va·tion (äb'zər vā'shən) *n.* **1.** *a)* the act or power of noticing *b)* something noticed **2.** a being seen **3.** a noting and recording of facts, as for research **4.** a comment or remark

ob·serv·a·to·ry (əb zur'və tôr'ē) *n., pl.* **-ries** a building equipped for astronomical research, esp. one with a large telescope

ob·serve (əb zurv') *vt.* **-served',** **-serv'ing** [< L. *ob*- (see OB-) + *servare,* keep] **1.** to adhere to (a law, custom, etc.) **2.** to celebrate (a holiday, etc.) **3.** *a)* to notice (something) *b)* to pay special attention to **4.** to arrive at as a conclusion **5.** to say casually; remark **6.** to examine scientifically —**ob·serv'a·ble** *adj.* —**ob·serv'er** *n.*

ob·sess (əb ses') *vt.* [< L. *ob*- (see OB-) + *sedere,* sit] to haunt or trouble in mind; preoccupy —**ob·ses'sive** *adj.* —**ob·ses'sive·ly** *adv.*

ob·ses·sion (-) *n.* **1.** a being obsessed **2.** an idea, desire, etc. that obsesses one

ob·sid·i·an (əb sid'ē ən) *n.* [after one *Obsius,* its alleged discoverer] a hard, dark, volcanic glass

ob·so·lesce (äb'sə les') *vi.* **-lesced',** **-lesc'ing** to be obsolescent

ob·so·les·cent (äb′sə les′nt) *adj.* becoming obsolete —**ob′so·les′cence** *n.*

ob·so·lete (äb′sə lēt′) *adj.* [< L. *ob-* (see OB-) + *solere*, become accustomed] 1. no longer in use 2. out-of-date

ob·sta·cle (äb′sti k'l) *n.* [< L. *ob-* (see OB-) + *stare*, to stand] anything that stands in the way; obstruction

ob·stet·rics (əb stet′riks) *n.pl.* [*with sing. v.*] [< L. *obstetrix*, midwife] the branch of medicine concerned with the care and treatment of women during pregnancy and childbirth —**ob·stet′ric, ob·stet′ri·cal** *adj.* —**ob·ste·tri·cian** (äb′stə trish′ən) *n.*

ob·sti·nate (äb′stə nit) *adj.* [< L. *obstinare*, resolve on] 1. determined to have one's own way; stubborn 2. resisting treatment [an *obstinate* fever] —**ob′sti·na·cy** (-nə sē) *n.* —**ob′sti·nate·ly** *adv.*

ob·strep·er·ous (əb strep′ər əs) *adj.* [< L. *ob-* (see OB-) + *strepere*, to roar] noisy or unruly, esp. in resisting —**ob·strep′er·ous·ly** *adv.* —**ob·strep′er·ous·ness** *n.*

ob·struct (əb strukt′) *vt.* [< L. *ob-* (see OB-) + *struere*, pile up] 1. to block or stop up (a passage) 2. to hinder (progress, etc.) 3. to cut off from view —**ob·struc′tive** *adj.* —**ob·struc′tive·ly** *adv.* —**ob·struc′tive·ness** *n.*

ob·struc′tion *n.* 1. an obstructing 2. anything that obstructs; hindrance

ob·struc′tion·ist *n.* one who obstructs progress —*adj.* that obstructs —**ob′vi·a′tion** *n.*

ob·tain (əb tān′) *vt.* [< L. *ob-* (see OB-) + *tenere*, to hold] to get possession of by trying; procure —*vi.* to prevail [peace will *obtain*] —**ob·tain′a·ble** *adj.* —**ob·tain′ment** *n.*

ob·trude (əb trood′) *vt.* **-trud′ed, -trud′ing** [< L. *ob-* (see OB-) + *trudere*, to thrust] 1. to push out; eject 2. to force (oneself, etc.) upon others unasked or unwanted —*vi.* to obtrude oneself —**ob·tru′sion** (-troo′zhən) *n.* —**ob·tru′sive** (-troo′siv) *adj.* —**ob·tru′sive·ly** *adv.* —**ob·tru′sive·ness** *n.*

ob·tuse (äb toos′, əb-) *adj.* [< L. *obtundere*, to strike upon, blunt] 1. not sharp; blunt 2. greater than 90° and less than 180° [an *obtuse* angle] 3. slow to understand or perceive —**ob·tuse′ly** *adv.* —**ob·tuse′ness** *n.*

ob·verse (äb vurs′; *for n.* äb′vərs) *adj.* [< L. *ob-* (see OB-) + *vertere*, to turn] 1. turned toward the observer 2. forming a counterpart —*n.* 1. the side, as of a coin or medal, bearing the main design 2. a counterpart

ob·vi·ate (äb′vē āt′) *vt.* **-at′ed, -at′ing** [see ff.] to do away with or prevent by effective measures; make unnecessary —**ob′vi·a′tion** *n.*

ob·vi·ous (äb′vē əs) *adj.* [L. *obvius*, in the way] easy to see or understand; evident —**ob′vi·ous·ly** *adv.* —**ob′vi·ous·ness** *n.*

oc- *same as* OB-: used before *c*

oc·a·ri·na (äk′ə rē′nə) *n.* [It. < LL. *auca*, goose: from its shape] a small wind instrument with finger holes and a mouthpiece

occas. occasional(ly)

oc·ca·sion (ə kā′zhən) *n.* [< L. *ob-* (see OB-) + *cadere*, to fall] 1. a favorable time; opportunity 2. an event, etc. that makes something else possible 3. *a*) a happening *b*) a particular time 4. a special time or event 5. need arising from circumstances —*vt.* to cause —**on occasion** sometimes

oc·ca′sion·al *adj.* 1. of or for special occasions 2. happening now and then; infrequent —**oc·ca′sion·al·ly** *adv.*

oc·ci·dent (äk′sə dənt) *n.* [< L. *occidere*, to fall: with reference to the setting sun] [Poet.], the west —[O-] Europe and the Americas —**oc′ci·den′tal, Oc′ci·den′tal** *adj., n.*

Oc′ci·den′tal·ize (-den′t'l īz′) *vt., vi.* **-ized′, -iz′ing** to turn to the ways of the Occident

oc·clude (ə klood′) *vt.* **-clud′ed, -clud′ing** [< L. *ob-* (see OB-) + *claudere*, shut] 1. to close or block (a passage) 2. to shut in or out —*vi.* Dentistry to meet with the cusps fitting closely —**oc·clu′sion** (-kloo′zhən) *n.* —**oc·clu′sive** *adj.*

oc·cult (ə kult′, äˈkult) *adj.* [< L. *occulere*, conceal] 1. hidden 2. secret 3. mysterious 4. of mystic arts, such as magic, astrology, etc.

oc·cu·pan·cy (äk′yə pən sē) *n.*, *pl.* **-cies** an occupying; a taking or keeping in possession

oc′cu·pant *n.* one who occupies

oc·cu·pa·tion (äk′yə pā′shən) *n.* 1. an occupying or being occupied 2. that which occupies one's time; work; profession —**oc′cu·pa′tion·al** *adj.*

occupational therapy therapy by means of work in the arts and crafts, as for hospital patients

oc·cu·py (äk′yə pī′) *vt.* **-pied′, -py′ing** [< L. *ob-* (see OB-) + *capere*, seize] 1. to take possession of by settlement or seizure 2. to hold possession of; specif., *a*) to dwell in *b*) to hold (a position or office) 3. to take up (space, time, etc.) 4. to employ (oneself, one's mind, etc.)

oc·cur (ə kur′) *vi.* **-curred′, -cur′ring** [< L. *ob-* (see OB-) + *currere*, to run] 1. to be or be met with; exist 2. to come to mind 3. to take place; happen

oc·cur′rence *n.* 1. the act or fact of occurring 2. an event; incident

o·cean (ō′shən) *n.* [< Gr. *Ōkeanos*] 1. the body of salt water that covers about 71% of the earth's surface 2. any of its five principal divisions: the Atlantic, Pacific, Indian, Arctic, or Antarctic Ocean 3. a great quantity —**o·ce·an·ic** (ō′shē an′ik) *adj.*

o′cean·aut′ (-ôt′) *n.* [< OCEAN + Gr. *nautēs*, sailor] *same as* AQUANAUT

o′cean·go′ing *adj.* of or for ocean travel

O·ce·an·i·a (ō′shē an′ē ə) islands in

the Pacific, including Melanesia, Micronesia, & Polynesia

o·cean·og·ra·phy (ō'shə·nǎg'rə·fē) *n.* the study of the environment in the ocean, its plants and animals, etc. — **o'cean·o·graph'ic** (-nə·grăf'ik) *adj.*

o·cel·lus (ō·sel'əs) *n., pl.* **-li** (-ī) [L. < *oculus*, eye] the simple eye of certain invertebrates

o·ce·lot (ǒs'ə·lǎt', ō'sə-) *n.* [Fr. < Mex. *ocelotl*, jaguar] a medium-sized, spotted wildcat of N. and S. America

o·cher, o·chre (ō'kər) *n.* [< Gr. *ōchros*, pale-yellow] 1. a yellow or reddish-brown clay containing iron, used as a pigment 2. its color

o'clock (ə·klǎk', ō-) *adv.* of or according to the clock

octa- [< Gr. *oktō*, eight] *a combining form meaning* eight: also **octo-**, **oct-**

oc·ta·gon (ǎk'tə·gǎn') *n.* [< Gr.: see prec. & -GON] a plane figure with eight angles and eight sides — **oc·tag'o·nal** (-tǎg'ə·n'l) *adj.*

oc·tane number (or **rating**) (ǎk'tān) a number representing the antiknock properties of a gasoline, etc.

oc·tave (ǎk'tiv, -tāv) *n.* [< L. *octavus*, eighth] 1. any group of eight 2. *Music a)* the eighth full tone above or below a given tone *b)* the interval of eight degrees between a tone and either of its octaves *c)* the series of tones within this interval, or the keys of an instrument producing such a series

oc·ta·vo (ǎk·tā'vō, -tǎ'-) *n., pl.* **-vos** [< L. (*in*) *octavo*, (in) eight] 1. the page size (about 6 by 9 in.) of a book made up of printer's sheets folded into eight leaves 2. a book of such pages

oc·tet, oc·tette (ǎk·tet') *n.* [OCT(A)- + (DU)ET] *Music* 1. a composition for eight voices or instruments 2. the eight performers of this

Oc·to·ber (ǎk·tō'bər) *n.* [< L. *octo*, eight: eighth month in Rom. calendar] the tenth month of the year, having 31 days: abbrev. **Oct., O.**

oc·to·ge·nar·i·an (ǎk'tə·ji·ner'ē·ən) *adj.* [< L. *octoginta*, eighty] between the ages of eighty and ninety — *n.* a person of this age

oc·to·pus (ǎk'tə·pəs) *n., pl.* **-pus·es**, **-pi** (-pī') [< Gr. *oktō*, eight + *pous*, foot] a mollusk with a soft body and eight arms covered with suckers

oc·u·lar (ǎk'yə·lər) *adj.* [< L. *oculus*, eye] 1. of, for, or like the eye 2. by eyesight

oc'u·list (-list) *n.* earlier term for OPHTHALMOLOGIST

OD (ō'dē') *n., pl.* **ODs, OD's** [Slang] an overdose, esp. of a narcotic — *vi.* **OD'd, ODed, OD'ing, ODing** [Slang] to take an overdose, esp. a fatal dose of a narcotic

OD, O.D. 1. Officer of the Day 2. overdraft 3. overdrawn

o·da·lisque, o·da·lisk (ōd'l·isk) *n.* [Fr. < Turk. *ōdalik*, chambermaid] a female slave or concubine in an Oriental harem

odd (ǎd) *adj.* [< ON. *oddi*] 1. with the other of the pair missing [an odd glove] 2. having a remainder of one

when divided by two 3. left over after taking a round number 4. with a few more [sixty odd years ago] 5. occasional [odd jobs] 6. a) peculiar b) queer; eccentric —**odd'ly** *adv.* — **odd'ness** *n.*

odd'ball *adj.* [Slang] strange or eccentric —*n.* [Slang] one who is oddball

odd'i·ty (-ə·tē) *n.* 1. strangeness 2. *pl.* **-ties** an odd person or thing

odds (ǎdz) *n.pl.* 1. difference in favor of one side over the other; advantage 2. advantage given by a bettor or competitor in proportion to the assumed chances in his favor —**at odds** quarreling —**by (all) odds** by far

odds and ends scraps; remnants

odds'-on *adj.* having a very good chance of winning [an odds-on favorite]

ode (ōd) *n.* [< Gr. *ōidē*, song] a lyric poem characterized by lofty feeling and dignified style

-ode (ōd) [< Gr. *hodos*] *a suffix meaning* way, path [anode, cathode]

O·des·sa (ō·des'ə) seaport in S Ukrainian S.S.R.: pop. 753,000

O·din (ō'din) *Norse Myth.* the chief god

o·di·ous (ō'dē·əs) *adj.* [< L. *odium*, hatred] disgusting; offensive —**o'di·ous·ly** *adv.* —**o'di·ous·ness** *n.*

o·di·um (ō'dē·əm) *n.* [< L. *odi*, I hate] 1. hatred 2. the disgrace brought on by hateful action

o·dom·e·ter (ō·dǎm'ə·tər) *n.* [< Gr. *hodos*, way + *metron*, a measure] an instrument for measuring the distance traveled by a vehicle

o·dor (ō'dər) *n.* [L.] a smell; scent; aroma: Brit. sp. **odour** —**be in bad** (or **ill**) **odor** to be in ill repute —**o'dor·less** *adj.* —**o'dor·ous** *adj.*

o·dor·if·er·ous (ō'də·rif'ər·əs) *adj.* [< L. *odor*, odor + *ferre*, to bear] giving off an odor, esp. a fragrant one

O·dys·se·us (ō·dis'yoōs, -ē·əs) the hero of the *Odyssey*, one of the Greek leaders in the Trojan War

Od·ys·sey (ǎd'ə·sē) an ancient Greek epic poem, ascribed to Homer, about the wanderings of Odysseus after the fall of Troy —*n.* [sometimes o-] *pl.* **-seys** any extended journey

OE, OE., O.E. Old English

Oed·i·pus (ed'ə·pəs, ē'də-) *Gr. Myth.* a king who unwittingly killed his father and married his mother

o'er (ōr) *prep., adv.* [Poet.] over

of (uv, ǎv, əv) *prep.* [OE.] 1. from; specif., a) coming from [men of Ohio] b) resulting from [to die of fever] c) at a distance from [east of the city] d) by [the poems of Poe] e) separated from [robbed of his money] f) from the whole constituting [one of her hats] g) made from [a sheet of paper] 2. belonging to 3. a) possessing [a man of wealth] b) containing [a bag of nuts] 4. specified as [a height of six feet] 5. characterized by [a man of honor] 6. concerning; about 7. during [of recent years]

of- same as OB-: used before *f*

off (ôf) *adv.* [LME. var. of *of*] 1. so as to be away, at a distance, etc. 2. so as to be no longer on, attached, etc.

[take off your hat] **3.** (a specified distance) away in space or time *[20 yards off]* **4.** so as to be no longer in operation, etc. *[turn the motor off]* **5.** so as to be less, etc. *[5% off for cash]* **6.** away from one's work —*prep.* **1.** (so as to be) no longer (or not) on, attached, etc. *[off the road]* **2.** from the substance of *[live off the land]* **3.** away from *[a mile off shore]* **4.** branching out from *[an alley off Main Street]* **5.** relieved from *[off duty]* **6.** not up to the usual standard, etc. of *[off one's game]* —*adj.* **1.** not on or attached **2.** not in operation **3.** on the way *[off to bed]* **4.** away from work *[we are off today]* **5.** not up to the usual standard, etc. **6.** more remote *[on the off chance]* **7.** in (specified) circumstances *[to be well off]* **8.** wrong *[his figures are off]* —*vt.* [Slang] to kill; murder —*interj.* go away! —**off and on** now and then

of·fal (ôf′l, äf′-) *n.* [ME. *ofall*, lit., off-fall] **1.** *[with sing. or pl. v.]* the entrails, etc. of a butchered animal **2.** refuse; garbage

off′beat′ *n. Music* a beat having a weak accent —*adj.* [Colloq.] unconventional, unusual, strange, etc.

off′-col′or *adj.* **1.** varying from the standard color **2.** improper; risqué

of·fend (ə fend′) *vi.* [< L. *ob-* (see OB-) + *-fendere*, to hit] **1.** to commit a sin or crime **2.** to create resentment, anger, etc. —*vt.* **1.** to hurt the feelings of; insult **2.** to be displeasing to (the taste, sense, etc.) —**of·fend′er** *n.*

of·fense (ə fens′, ôf′ens) *n.* **1.** a sin or crime **2.** a creating of resentment, displeasure, etc. **3.** a feeling hurt, angry, etc. **4.** something that causes anger, etc. **5.** the act of attacking **6.** the side that is attacking or seeking to score in a contest Brit. sp. **offence** —**take offense** to be offended

of·fen·sive *adj.* **1.** attacking or for attack **2.** unpleasant; disgusting **3.** insulting —*n.* attitude or position of attack (often with *the*) —**of·fen′sive·ly** *adv.* —**of·fen′sive·ness** *n.*

of·fer (ôf′ər, äf′-) *vt.* [< L. *ob-* (see OB-) + *ferre*, bring] **1.** to present in worship *[to offer prayers]* **2.** to present for acceptance *[to offer help]* **3.** to suggest; propose **4.** to show or give signs of *[to offer resistance]* **5.** to bid (a price, etc.) —*vi.* to present itself —*n.* the act of offering or thing offered

offer·ing *n.* **1.** the act of making an offer **2.** something offered; specif., *a)* a gift *b)* presentation in worship

offer·to·ry (-tôr′ē) *n., pl.* **-ries** [often O-] **1.** the offering of the bread and wine to God in the Eucharist **2.** money collected at a church service, or the prayers or music during the collection

off′hand′ *adv.* without preparation —*adj.* **1.** said or done offhand **2.** casual, curt, etc. Also **off′hand′ed**

of·fice (ôf′is, äf′-) *n.* [< L. *officium*] **1.** a service done for another **2.** a duty, esp. as a part of one's work **3.** a position of authority or trust, as in government **4.** *a)* the place where the affairs of a business, etc. are carried on *b)* the people working there **5.** a religious ceremony or rite

of′fice-hold′er *n.* a government official

of·fi·cer (ôf′ə sər, äf′-) *n.* **1.** anyone holding an office, or position of authority, in a government, business, club, etc. **2.** a policeman **3.** one holding a position of authority, esp. by commission, in the armed forces

officer of the day *Mil.* the officer in charge of the interior guard and security of his garrison for the day

of·fi·cial (ə fish′əl) *adj.* **1.** of or holding an office, or position of authority **2.** authorized or authoritative **3.** formal —*n.* a person holding office —**of·fi′cial·dom** (-dəm), **of·fi′cial·ism** *n.* —**of·fi′cial·ly** *adv.*

of·fi·ci·ant (ə fish′ē ənt) *n.* an officiating priest, minister, etc.

of·fi·ci·ate (ə fish′ē āt′) *vi.* **-at′ed, -at′ing** **1.** to perform the duties of an office **2.** to perform the functions of a priest, minister, rabbi, etc.

of·fi·cious (ə fish′əs) *adj.* [see OFFICE] offering unwanted advice or services; meddlesome, esp. highhandedly so — **of·fi′cious·ly** *adv.* —**of·fi′cious·ness** *n.*

off·ing (ôf′iŋ) *n.* [< OFF] the distant part of the sea visible from the shore —**in the offing** **1.** far but in sight **2.** at some vague future time

off′-key′ (-kē′) *adj.* **1.** *Music* flat or sharp **2.** not harmonious

off′-lim′its *adj.* ruled a place not to be gone to by a specified group

off′-put′ting *adj.* [Chiefly Brit.] distracting, annoying, etc.

off′-sea′son (-sē′z'n) *n.* a time of the year when the usual activity is reduced or not carried on

off·set (ôf set′; *for n.* ôf′set′) *vt.* **-set′, -set′ting** to balance, compensate for, etc. —*n.* **1.** a thing that offsets another **2.** offset printing

offset printing a printing process in which the inked impression is first made on a rubber-covered roller, then transferred to paper

off′shoot′ *n.* anything that derives from a main source; specif., a shoot growing from the main stem of a plant

off′shore′ *adj.* **1.** moving away from the shore **2.** at some distance from the shore —*adv.* away from the shore

off′side′ *adj. Sports* not in proper position for play

off′spring′ *n., pl.* **-spring′, -springs′** a child or children; progeny; young

off′stage′ *n.* the part of the stage not seen by the audience —*adj.* in or from this —*adv.* to the offstage

off′-track′ *adj.* designating or of legalized betting on horse races, carried on away from the race track

off′-white′ *adj.* grayish-white or yellowish-white

off year 1. a year in which a major election does not take place **2.** a year of little production

oft (ôft) *adv.* [OE.] [Poet.] often

of·ten (ôf′'n) *adv.* [ME. var. of prec.] many times; frequently: also **often-times′**

o·gle (ō′g'l) *vi., vt.* **o′gled, o′gling** [prob. < LowG. *oog*, an eye] to keep looking (at) flirtatiously —*n.* an ogling look —**o′gler** *n.*

o·gre (ō′gər) *n.* [Fr.] **1.** in fairy tales and folklore, a man-eating giant **2.** a hideous, cruel man

oh (ō) *interj., n., pl.* **oh's, ohs** an exclamation of surprise, fear, pain, etc.

OH Ohio

O·hi·o (ō hī′ō) **1.** Middle Western State of the U.S.: 41,222 sq. mi.; pop. 10,797,000; cap. Columbus **2.** river flowing from W Pa. into the Mississippi —**O·hi′o·an** *adj., n.*

ohm (ōm) *n.* [< G.S. *Ohm*, 19th-c. G. physicist] unit of electrical resistance

o·ho (ō hō′) *interj.* an exclamation of surprise, taunting, triumph, etc.

-oid (oid) [< Gr. *eidos*, form] *a suffix meaning* like, resembling [*spheroid*]

oil (oil) *n.* [< L. *oleum*] **1.** any of various greasy, combustible, liquid substances obtained from animal, vegetable, and mineral matter **2.** *same as* PETROLEUM **3.** *same as:* a) OIL COLOR b) OIL PAINTING —*vt.* to lubricate or supply with oil —*adj.* of, from, or like oil

oil′cloth′ *n.* cloth made waterproof by being treated with oil or paint

oil color paint made by grinding a pigment in oil

oil painting 1. a picture painted in oil colors **2.** painting in oil colors

oil shale shale from which oil can be extracted by distillation

oil′skin′ *n.* **1.** cloth made waterproof by treatment with oil **2.** [*often pl.*] a garment or outfit made of this

oil well a well bored through layers of rock, etc. to a supply of petroleum

oil′y *adj.* **-i·er, -i·est 1.** of, like, or containing oil **2.** greasy **3.** too suave or smooth; unctuous —**oil′i·ness** *n.*

oink (oink) *n.* [echoic] the grunt of a pig —*vi.* to make this sound

oint·ment (oint′mant) *n.* [< L. *unguentum*, a salve] a fatty substance used on the skin for healing or cosmetic purposes; salve

OK, O.K. (ō′kā′, ō′kā′) *adj., adv., interj.* [< "oll korrect," facetious misspelling of *all correct*] all right; correct —*n., pl.* **OK's, O.K.'s** approval —*vt.* **OK'd, O.K.'d, OK′ing, O.K.′ing** to put an OK on; approve Also [Colloq.] **o′kay′**

o·key-doke (ō′kē dōk′) *adj., interj. slang var. of* OK also **o′key-do′key** (-ē)

O·kla·ho·ma (ō′klə hō′mə) State of the SC U.S.: 69,919 sq. mi.; pop. 3,025,000; cap. Oklahoma City: abbrev. Okla., OK —**O′kla·ho′man** *adj., n.*

Oklahoma City capital of Okla.: pop. 403,000

o·kra (ō′krə) *n.* [< WAfr. name] **1.** a plant with sticky green pods **2.** the pods, used in soups, etc.

OKRA

old (ōld) *adj.* **old·er or eld′er, old′est or eld′est** [OE. *ald*] **1.** having lived or existed for a long time **2.** of aged people **3.** of a certain age [two years *old*] **4.** not new **5.** worn out by age or use **6.** former **7.** experienced [an *old* hand] **8.** ancient **9.** of long standing **10.** designating the earlier or earliest of two or more [the *Old* World] —*n.* **1.** time long past [days of *old*] **2.** something old (with *the*) —**old′ness** *n.*

old country the country, esp. in Europe, from which an immigrant came

old·en (ōl′d'n) *adj.* [Poet.] (of) old

Old English the Germanic language of the Anglo-Saxons, spoken in England from c.400 to c.1100 A.D.

old′-fash′ioned *adj.* suited to or favoring the methods, ideas, etc. of past times —*n.* a cocktail made with whiskey, bitters, soda, and bits of fruit

old fogy, old fogey *see* FOGY

Old French the French language from c.800 to c.1550 A.D.

Old Glory the flag of the U.S.

Old Guard [transl. < Fr.] the conservative faction, as of a party

old hat [Slang] old-fashioned or stale

Old High German the High German language before the 12th c.

old·ie, old′y (-ē) *n., pl.* **-ies** [Colloq.] an old joke, movie, etc.

old lady [Slang] **1.** one's mother **2.** one's wife

old′-line′ *adj.* long-established, traditional, conservative, etc.

Old Low German the Low German language before the 12th c.

old maid 1. a woman, esp. an older woman, who has never married **2.** a prim, prudish, fussy person

old man [Slang] **1.** one's father **2.** one's husband **3.** [*usually* O- M-] a man in authority: with *the*

old master 1. any of the great European painters before the 18th century **2.** a painting by any of these

Old Norse the Germanic language of the Scandinavians before the 14th c.

Old Saxon the Low German dialect of the Saxons before the 10th c.

old school a group of people who cling to traditional or conservative ideas —**old′-school′** *adj.*

old·ster (-stər) *n.* [Colloq.] an old or elderly person

Old Testament *Christian designation for* the Holy Scriptures of Judaism, the first of the two general divisions of the Christian Bible

old′-time′ *adj.* **1.** of past times **2.** of long standing

old′-tim′er *n.* [Colloq.] a long-time resident, employee, member, etc.

Old World Europe, Asia, and Africa: often with reference to European culture, customs, etc. —**old'-world', Old'-World'** *adj.*

ţo·lé (ō lā') *interj., n.* [Sp.] a shout of approval, triumph, etc.

o·le·ag·i·nous (ō'lē aj'i nəs) *adj.* [< L. *olea*, olive tree] oily; unctuous

o·le·an·der (ō'lē an'dər) *n.* [ML.] a poisonous evergreen shrub with fragrant white or red flowers and narrow, leathery leaves

o·le·o·mar·ga·rine (ō'lē ō mär'jə rin) *n.* [< L. *oleum*, oil + MARGARINE] *same as* MARGARINE: also **o'le·o'**

ol·fac·to·ry (äl fak'tər ē, ōl–) *adj.* [< L. *olere*, have a smell + *facere*, make] of the sense of smell

ol·i·gar·chy (äl'ə gär'kē) *n., pl.* **-ies** [< Gr. *oligos*, few + -ARCHY] **1.** (a) government in which a few persons have the ruling power **2.** the ruling persons —**ol'i·gar'chic** *adj.*

ol·ive (äl'iv) *n.* [< L. *oliva*] **1.** *a)* an evergreen tree of S Europe and the Near East *b)* its small oval fruit, eaten as a relish or pressed, when ripe, to extract its light-yellow oil (**olive oil**) **2.** the yellowish-green color of the unripe fruit

olive branch the branch of the olive tree, a symbol of peace

O·lym·pi·a (ō lim'pē ə) capital of Wash.: pop. 23,000

O·lym·pic games (ō lim'pik) [< *Olympia*, plain in Greece, site of ancient games] an international athletic competition generally held every four years: also the **O·lym'pics** (-piks)

O·lym'pus (-pəs) mountain in N Greece: *Gr. Myth.* the home of the gods —**O·lym'pi·an** (-pē ən) *adj.*

om (ōm, ōŋ) *n.* [Sans.] *Hinduism* a word intoned as during meditation

O·ma·ha (ō'mə hô) city in E Nebr.: pop. 312,000

om·buds·man (äm'bədz mən) *n., pl.* **-men** [Sw. < *ombud*, deputy] a public official appointed to investigate citizens' complaints

o·me·ga (ō mā'gə, -mē'gə) *n.* the 24th & last letter of the Greek alphabet (Ω, ω)

om·e·let, om·e·lette (äm'lit, äm'ə let) *n.* [< L. *lamella*, small plate] eggs beaten and cooked flat in a pan

o·men (ō'mən) *n.* [L.] a thing or happening supposed to foretell a future event, either good or evil

om·i·cron (äm'ə krän', ō'mə-) *n.* the 15th letter of the Greek alphabet (O, o)

om·i·nous (äm'ə nəs) *adj.* of or serving as an evil omen; threatening —**om'i·nous·ly** *adv.*

o·mis·sion (ō mish'ən) *n.* **1.** an omitting **2.** anything omitted

o·mit (ō mit') *vt.* **o·mit'ted, o·mit'ting** [< L. *ob-* (see OB-) + *mittere*, send] **1.** to leave out; fail to include **2.** to neglect; fail to do

omni- [L. < *omnis*, all] *a combining form meaning* all, everywhere

om·ni·bus (äm'nə bəs) *n., pl.* **-bus·es** [< L., for all] *same as* BUS —*adj.* dealing with many things at once

om·nip·o·tent (äm nip'ə tənt) *adj.* [< L. *omnis*, all + *potens*, able] having unlimited power or authority; all-powerful —**om·nip'o·tence** *n.*

om·ni·pres·ent (äm'ni prez'nt) *adj.* present in all places at the same time —**om'ni·pres'ence** *n.*

om·nis·cient (äm nish'ənt) *adj.* [< L. *omnis*, all + *sciens*, knowing] knowing all things —**om·nis'cience** *n.*

om·niv·o·rous (äm niv'ər əs) *adj.* [< L. *omnis*, all + *vorare*, devour] **1.** eating any sort of food, esp. both animal and vegetable food **2.** taking in everything indiscriminately [an *omnivorous* reader] —**om·niv'o·rous·ly** *adv.* —**om·niv'o·rous·ness** *n.*

on (än, ôn) *prep.* [OE.] **1.** in contact with, supported by, or covering **2.** in the surface of [scars *on* it] **3.** near to [*on* my left] **4.** at the time of [*on* Monday] **5.** connected with [*on* the team] **6.** engaged in [*on* a trip] **7.** in a state of [*on* parole] **8.** as a result of [a profit *on* the sale] **9.** in the direction of [light shone *on* us] **10.** through the use of [live *on* bread] **11.** concerning [an essay *on* war] **12.** [Colloq.] at the expense of [a drink *on* the house] **13.** [Slang] using; addicted to [*on* drugs] —*adv.* **1.** in a situation of contacting, being supported by, or covering **2.** in a direction toward [he looked *on*] **3.** forward [move *on*] **4.** without stopping [she sang *on*] **5.** into action or operation [turn *on* the light] —*adj.* in action or operation [the play is *on*] —**and so on** and more like the preceding —**on and off** intermittently —**on and on** for a long time; continuously —**on to** [Slang] aware of the real nature or meaning of

once (wuns) *adv.* [ME. *ones*] **1.** one time only **2.** at any time; ever **3.** formerly **4.** by one degree [cousin *once* removed] —*conj.* as soon as [*once* he hears, he'll tell] —*n.* one time [go this *once*] —**at once 1.** immediately **2.** at the same time —**once (and) for all** conclusively —**once in a while** now and then

once'-o'ver *n.* [Colloq.] a quick look

on·col·o·gy (äŋ käl'ə jē, än–) *n.* [Gr. *onkos*, a mass + -LOGY] the branch of medicine dealing with tumors

on·com·ing (än'kum'iŋ) *adj.* coming nearer in position or time

one (wun) *adj.* [OE. *an*] **1.** being a single thing **2.** united [with *one* accord] **3.** a certain but not named; some [take *one* path or the other, *one* day last week] **4.** the same **5.** being uniquely such [the *one* solution] —*n.* **1.** the first and lowest cardinal number; 1; I **2.** a single person or thing —*pron.* **1.** a certain person or thing **2.** any person or thing —**at one in** accord —**one by one** individually in succession

O'Neill (ō nēl′), **Eugene** 1888–1953; U.S. playwright

one′ness (-nis) *n.* 1. singleness; unity 2. unity of mind, feeling, etc.

on·er·ous (än′ər əs) *adj.* [< L. *onus*, a load] burdensome; oppressive

one·self (wun′self′) *pron.* a person's own self: also **one's self —be oneself** 1. to function normally 2. to be natural —**by oneself** alone

one′-sid′ed (-sīd′id) *adj.* 1. on, having, or involving only one side 2. unfair 3. unequal [a *one-sided* race]

one′-time′ *adj.* former

one′-track′ *adj.* [Colloq.] limited in scope [a *one-track* mind]

one′-up′ *adj.* [Colloq.] having superiority or an advantage (over another)

one′-way′ *adj.* moving, or allowing movement, in one direction only

on′go·ing *adj.* going on; progressing

on·ion (un′yən) *n.* [< L. *unus*, one] 1. a plant of the lily family with an edible bulb 2. this bulb, having a sharp smell and taste

on′ion-skin′ *n.* a tough, thin, translucent, glossy paper

on′look′er *n.* a spectator

on·ly (ōn′lē) *adj.* [< OE. *an*, one + *-lic*, -ly] 1. alone of its or their kind; sole 2. alone in superiority; best —*adv.* 1. and no other; and no more; solely 2. (but) in the end 3. as recently as —*conj.* [Colloq.] except that; but —**only too** very

on·o·mat·o·poe·ia (än′ə mat′ə pē′ə, -māt′-) *n.* [< Gr. *onoma*, a name + *poiein*, make] the formation of words by imitating sounds (Ex.: *buzz*)

on′rush′ *n.* a headlong rush forward

on′set′ *n.* 1. an attack 2. a start

on·slaught (än′slôt′) *n.* [< Du. *slagen*, to strike] a violent attack

On·tar·i·o (än ter′ē ō) 1. province of SE Canada: 412,582 sq. mi.; pop. 6,961,000; cap. Toronto: abbrev. **Ont.** 2. **Lake,** smallest of the Great Lakes, between N.Y. and Ontario

on·to (än′tōo) *prep.* 1. to a position on 2. [Slang] aware of Also **on to**

on·tog·e·ny (än täj′ə nē) *n.* [ult. < Gr. *einei*, be + *-genēs*, born] the life cycle of a single organism

o·nus (ō′nəs) *n.* [L.] 1. a burden, unpleasant duty, etc. 2. blame

on·ward (än′wərd) *adv.* toward or at a position ahead; forward: also **onwards** —*adj.* advancing

on·yx (än′iks) *n.* [< Gr. *onyx*, fingernail] a type of agate with alternate colored layers

oo·dles (ōo′d'lz) *n.pl.* [< ?] [Colloq.] a great amount; very many

ooze[1] (ōoz) *n.* [OE. *wos*, sap] something that oozes —*vi.* oozed, ooz′ing to flow or leak out slowly —*vt.* to exude

ooze[2] (ōoz) *n.* [OE. *wase*] soft mud or slime, as at the bottom of a lake

op- same as OB-: used before *p*

o·pal (ō′p'l) *n.* [< Sans. *upala*, gem] an iridescent silica of various colors: some varieties are semiprecious — **o·pal·es·cent** (ō′pə les′'nt) *adj.*

o·paque (ō pāk′) *adj.* [< L. *opacus*, shady] 1. not transparent 2. not reflecting light; dull 3. hard to under-

stand —**o·pac·i·ty** (ō pas′ə tē), **o·paque′ness** *n.* —**o·paque′ly** *adv.*

op (ärt) (äp) a style of abstract painting creating optical illusions

op. cit. [L. *opere citato*] in the work cited

OPEC Organization of Petroleum Exporting Countries

Op′-Ed′ *adj.* [*Op(posite)* *Ed(itorial page)*] designating or on a page in a newspaper, featuring a wide variety of columns, articles, letters, etc.

o·pen (ō′p'n) *adj.* [OE.] 1. not closed, covered, clogged, or shut 2. not enclosed [*open* fields] 3. spread out; unfolded [an *open* book] 4. having gaps, holes, etc. 5. free to be entered, used, etc. [an *open* meeting] 6. not decided [an *open* question] 7. not closed to new ideas, etc. [an *open* mind] 8. generous 9. free from legal or discriminatory restrictions [*open* season, *open* housing] 10. not conventional [*open* marriage] 11. not already taken [the job is *open*] 12. not secret; public 13. frank; candid [an *open* manner] —*vt., vi.* 1. to cause to be, or to become, open 2. to spread out; expand; unfold 3. to make or become available for use, etc. without restriction 4. to begin; start 5. to start operating —**open to** 1. willing to receive, discuss, etc. 2. available to —**the open** 1. the outdoors 2. public knowledge —**o′pen·er** *n.* —**o′pen·ly** *adv.* —**o′pen·ness** *n.*

o′pen-air′ *adj.* outdoor

o′pen-and-shut′ *adj.* easily decided

o′pen-end′ed *adj.* unlimited

o′pen-eyed′ *adj.* with the eyes wide open, as in surprise or watchfulness

o′pen-faced′ *adj.* 1. having a frank, honest face 2. designating a sandwich without a top slice of bread: also **o′pen-face′**

o′pen-hand′ed *adj.* generous

o′pen-hearth′ *adj.* designating or using a furnace with a wide hearth and low roof, for making steel

open-heart′ surgery surgery on the heart during which the blood is circulated by a mechanical apparatus

open house 1. an informal reception at one's home 2. a time when an institution is open to visitors

o′pen·ing *n.* 1. an open place; gap; hole 2. a clearing 3. a beginning 4. start of operations 5. a favorable chance 6. an unfilled job

o′pen-mind′ed *adj.* having a mind open to new ideas; unprejudiced

o′pen·work′ *n.* ornamental work, as in cloth, with openings in it

op·er·a[1] (äp′ər ə) *n.* [< L., a work] a play having its text set to music and sung to orchestral accompaniment — **op′er·at′ic** (-ə rat′ik) *adj.*

op·er·a[2] (äp′ər ə) *n. pl.* of OPUS

op·er·a·ble (äp′ər ə b'l) *adj.* [see OPERATE + -ABLE] 1. feasible 2. that can be treated by a surgical operation

opera glasses a small binocular telescope used in theaters, etc.

op·er·ate (äp′ə rāt′) *vi.* -at′ed, -at′ing [< L. *operari*, to work] 1. to be in action; act; work 2. to bring about a certain effect **3.** to perform a surgical operation —*vt.* **1.** to put or keep in action **2.** to direct; manage

op·er·a'tion *n.* **1.** the act or method of operating **2.** a being in action or at work **3.** any of a series of procedures in some work or plan, as in industry, warfare, etc. **4.** any surgical procedure to remedy a physical ailment

op·er·a'tion·al (-'l) *adj.* **1.** of, or having to do with, the operation of a device, system, etc. **2.** *a)* that can be used or operated *b)* in use; operating

op·er·a·tive (äp'ə rā'tiv, äp'ər ə-) *adj.* **1.** in operation; active **2.** effective **3.** connected with physical work or mechanical action

op·er·a'tor (-rāt'ər) *n.* **1.** a person who operates a machine [a telephone *operator*] **2.** a person engaged in business or industrial operations

op·er·et·ta (äp'ə ret'ə) *n.* [It. < *opera*] a short, amusing musical play

oph·thal·mic (äf thal'mik) *adj.* [< Gr. *ophthalmos*, the eye] of or connected with the eyes

oph·thal·mol·o·gy (äf'thal mäl'ə jē, äp'-; -thə-) *n.* the branch of medicine dealing with the eye and its diseases —**oph'thal·mol'o·gist** *n.*

o·pi·ate (ō'pē it) *n.* **1.** a narcotic drug containing opium or any of its derivatives **2.** anything quieting

o·pine (ō pīn') *vt.*, *vi.* **o·pined'**, **o·pin'ing** [< L. *opinari*, think] to think; suppose: usually humorous

o·pin·ion (ə pin'yən) *n.* [< L. *opinari*, think] **1.** a belief not based on certainty but on what seems true or probable **2.** an evaluation, estimation, etc. **3.** formal expert judgment

o·pin'ion·at'ed (-āt'id) *adj.* holding obstinately to one's opinions

o·pi·um (ō'pē əm) *n.* [< Gr. *opos*, vegetable juice] a narcotic drug prepared from the seed of a certain poppy

o·pos·sum (ə päs'əm) *n.* [< AmInd.] a small, tree-dwelling mammal that carries its young in a pouch

op·po·nent (ə pō'nənt) *n.* [< L. *ob-* (see OB-) + *ponere*, to place] one who opposes, as in a fight, game, etc.; adversary

op·por·tune (äp'ər tōōn') *adj.* [< L. *opportunus*, lit., before the port] **1.** suitable: said of time **2.** well-timed

OPOSSUM

op·por·tun'ism *n.* the adapting of one's actions, thoughts, etc. to circumstances, as in politics, without regard for principles —**op'por·tun'ist** *n.* —**op'por·tun·is'tic** *adj.*

op·por·tu·ni·ty (äp'ər tōō'nə tē) *n.*, *pl.* **-ties** **1.** a combination of circumstances favorable for the purpose **2.** a good chance

op·pose (ə pōz') *vt.* **-posed'**, **-pos'ing** [see OB- & POSITION] **1.** to place

opposite, in balance or contrast **2.** to contend with; resist

op·po·site (äp'ə zit) *adj.* [see OB- & POSITION] **1.** set against; in a contrary direction (often with *to*) **2.** entirely different; exactly contrary —*n.* anything opposed —*prep.* across from —**op'po·site·ly** *adv.*

opposite number a person whose position, rank, etc. parallels another's in a different place or organization

op·po·si·tion (-zish'ən) *n.* **1.** an opposing **2.** resistance, contrast, hostility, etc. **3.** one that opposes; specif., [often O-] a political party opposing the party in power

op·press (ə pres') *vt.* [< L. *ob-* (see OB-) + *premere*, to press] **1.** to weigh heavily on the mind of; worry **2.** to keep down by the cruel or unjust use of authority —**op·pres'sor** *n.*

op·pres·sion (ə presh'ən) *n.* **1.** an oppressing or being oppressed **2.** a thing that oppresses **3.** physical or mental distress

op·pres·sive (ə pres'iv) *adj.* **1.** causing discomfort **2.** tyrannical **3.** distressing —**op·pres'sive·ly** *adv.*

op·pro·bri·ous (ə prō'brē əs) *adj.* expressing opprobrium; abusive

op·pro·bri·um (-əm) *n.* [< L. *opprobrare*, to reproach] **1.** the disgrace attached to shameful conduct **2.** anything bringing shame

opt (äpt) *vi.* [see OPTION] to make a choice (often with *for*) —**opt out (of)** to choose not to be or continue in (some activity, organization, etc.)

op·ta·tive (äp'tə tiv) *adj.* [see OPTION] designating or of that mood of a verb expressing wish or desire

op·tic (äp'tik) *adj.* [< Gr. *optikos*] of the eye or sense of sight

op'ti·cal (-'l) *adj.* **1.** of the sense of sight; visual **2.** of optics **3.** for aiding vision —**op'ti·cal·ly** *adv.*

op·ti·cian (äp tish'ən) *n.* one who makes or sells eyeglasses, etc.

op·tics (äp'tiks) *n.pl.* [with sing. v.] the branch of physics dealing with light and vision

op·ti·mism (äp'tə miz'm) *n.* [< L. *optimus*, best] **1.** the belief that good ultimately prevails over evil **2.** the tendency to take the most hopeful view of matters —**op'ti·mist** (-mist) *n.* —**op'ti·mis'tic** (-mis'tik) *adj.*

op'ti·mum (-məm) *n.* [see prec.] the best or most favorable degree, condition, etc. —*adj.* most favorable; best: also **op'ti·mal** (-məl)

op·tion (äp'shən) *n.* [< L. *optare*, to wish] **1.** a choosing; choice **2.** the right of choosing **3.** something that is or can be chosen **4.** the right to buy, sell, or lease at a fixed price within a specified time —**op'tion·al** *adj.*

op·tom·e·try (äp täm'ə trē) *n.* [< Gr. *optikos*, optic + *metron*, a measure] the profession of testing the vision and prescribing glasses to correct eye defects —**op·tom'e·trist** *n.*

op·u·lent (äp'yə lənt) *adj.* [< L. *ops*, riches] 1. having much wealth; rich 2. abundant —**op'u·lence** *n.*

o·pus (ō'pəs) *n., pl.* **op·er·a** (äp'ər ə), **o'pus·es** [L., a work] a work; composition; esp., any of the numbered musical works of a composer

or (ôr) *conj.* [< OE. *oththe*] a coordinating conjunction introducing: *a*) an alternative [red or blue] or the last in a series of choices *b*) a synonymous word or phrase [oral, or spoken]

-or (ər) [< L.] *a suffix meaning:* 1. a person or thing that [inventor] 2. quality or condition [error]

OR Oregon

or·a·cle (ôr'ə k'l, är'-) *n.* [< L. *orare*, pray] 1. *a*) in ancient Greece and Rome, the place where, or medium by which, deities were consulted *b*) the revelation of a medium or priest 2. *a*) a person of great knowledge *b*) statements of such a person —**o·rac·u·lar** (ō rak'yoo lər) *adj.*

o·ral (ôr'əl) *adj.* [< L. *os*, mouth] 1. uttered; spoken 2. of or near the mouth —**o'ral·ly** *adv.*

or·ange (ôr'inj, är'-) *n.* [ult. < Sans. *naranga*] 1. a reddish-yellow, round citrus fruit with a sweet, juicy pulp 2. the evergreen tree it grows on 3. reddish yellow

or'ange·ade' (-ād') *n.* a drink made of orange juice, water, and sugar

orange stick a pointed stick of wood of the orange tree, for manicuring

o·rang·u·tan (ô raŋ'oo tan', -taŋ') *n.* [< Malay *oraŋ*, man + *utan*, forest] a manlike ape with reddish-brown hair, found only in Borneo and Sumatra

o·rate (ô rāt', ôr'āt) *vi.* **-rat'ed, -rat'ing** to make an oration; speak in a pompous or bombastic way

o·ra·tion (ô rā'shən) *n.* [< L. *orare*, speak] a formal speech, esp. one given at a ceremony

or·a·tor (ôr'ət ər, är'-) *n.* an eloquent public speaker; expert in oratory

or·a·to·ri·o (ôr'ə tôr'ē ō', är'-) *n., pl.* **-os'** [It., small chapel] a long, dramatic musical work, usually on a religious theme, but not acted out

or·a·to·ry (ôr'ə tôr'ē, är'-) *n., pl.* **-ries** [< L. *oratoria*] skill in public speaking —**or'a·tor'i·cal** *adj.*

orb (ôrb) *n.* [< L. *orbis*, a circle] 1. a sphere, or globe 2. any heavenly sphere, as the sun or moon

or·bit (ôr'bit) *n.* [< L. *orbis*, a circle] 1. the path of a heavenly body in its revolution around another 2. the path of an artificial satellite or spacecraft around a heavenly body —*vi., vt.* to move in, or put into, an orbit —**or'bit·al** *adj.*

or·chard (ôr'chərd) *n.* [OE. *ortgeard*] 1. an area for growing fruit trees 2. the trees

or·ches·tra (ôr'kis trə) *n.* [< Gr. *orcheisthai*, to dance] 1. the space in front of a theater stage, where the musicians sit: in full **orchestra pit** 2. the seats on the main floor of a theater 3. *a*) a group of musicians playing together *b*) their instruments —**or·ches'tral** (-kes'trəl) *adj.*

or·ches·trate' (-trāt') *vt., vi.* **-trat'ed, -trat'ing** to arrange (music) for an orchestra —**or'ches·tra'tion** *n.*

or·chid (ôr'kid) *n.* [< Gr. *orchis*, testicle: from the shape of the roots] 1. any of certain plants having flowers with three petals, one of which is lip-shaped 2. this flower 3. pale purple

or·dain (ôr dān') *vt.* [< L. *ordo*, an order] 1. to decree; establish; enact 2. to invest with the office of minister, priest, or rabbi —*vi.* to command —**or·dain'ment** *n.*

or·deal (ôr dēl') *n.* [OE. *ordal*] any difficult or painful experience

or·der (ôr'dər) *n.* [< L. *ordo*, straight row] 1. social position 2. a state of peace; orderly conduct 3. arrangement of things or events; series 4. a definite plan; system 5. a military, monastic, or social brotherhood 6. a condition in which everything is in its place and functioning properly 7. condition in general [in good order] 8. an authoritative command, instruction, etc. 9. a class; kind 10. an established method, as of conduct in meetings, etc. 11. *a*) a request to supply something [an order for books] *b*) the goods supplied 12. [*pl.*] the position of ordained minister [to take holy orders] —*vt., vi.* 1. to put or keep (things) in order; arrange 2. to command 3. to request (something to be supplied) —**in** (or **out of**) **order** 1. in (or out of) proper position 2. in (or not in) working condition 3. in (or not in) accordance with the rules —**in order that** so that —**in order to** for the purpose of —**in short order** quickly —**on the order of** similar to —**to order** in accordance with the buyer's specifications

or'der·ly *adj.* 1. neat or tidy 2. well-behaved; law-abiding —*adv.* methodically —*n., pl.* **-lies** 1. an enlisted man assigned to render personal services to an officer 2. a male hospital attendant —**or'der·li·ness** *n.*

or·di·nal (ôr'd'n əl) *adj.* [< L. *ordo*, order] expressing order in a series —*n.* any number showing order in a series (e.g., first, third): in full **ordinal number**

or·di·nance (ôr'd'n əns) *n.* [< L. *ordo*, an order] a statute or regulation, esp. a municipal one

or·di·nar·i·ly (ôr'd'n er'ə lē) *adv.* usually; as a rule

or·di·nar·y (ôr'd'n er'ē) *adj.* [< L. *ordo*, an order] 1. customary; usual 2. familiar; unexceptional; common —**out of the ordinary** unusual

or·di·na·tion (ôr'd'n ā'shən) *n.* an ordaining or being ordained to the clergy

ord·nance (ôrd'nəns) *n.* [< ORDI-NANCE] 1. artillery 2. all military weapons, ammunition, vehicles, etc.

or·do (ôr'dō) *n., pl.* **-dos, -di·nes'** (-də nēz') [L., order] *R.C.Ch.* an annual calendar giving directions for each day's Mass and Office

or·dure (ôr'jər) *n.* [ult. < L. *horridus*, horrid] dung; excrement

ore (ôr) *n.* [OE. *ar*, brass] a natural combination of minerals, esp. one from which a metal or metals can be profitably extracted

o·reg·a·no (ō reg′ə nō) *n.* [< Sp. < Gr. *origanon*] any of certain plants of the mint family, with fragrant leaves used for seasoning

Or·e·gon (ôr′i gən, -gän′) Northwestern State of the U.S.: 96,981 sq. mi.; pop. 2,633,000; cap. Salem: abbrev. Oreg. —**Or′e·go′ni·an** (-gō′nē ən) *adj., n.*

or·gan (ôr′gən) *n.* [< Gr. *organon*, implement] 1. a keyboard musical instrument with sets of graduated pipes through which compressed air is passed, causing sound by vibration 2. in animals and plants, a part adapted to perform a specific function 3. a means for performing some action 4. a means of communicating ideas or opinions, as a periodical

or·gan·dy, or·gan·die (ôr′gən dē) *n., pl.* **-dies** [Fr. *organdi*] a very sheer, crisp cotton fabric

or·gan·ic (ôr gan′ik) *adj.* 1. of or having to do with a bodily organ 2. inherent; inborn 3. systematically arranged 4. designating or of any chemical compound containing carbon 5. of, like, or derived from living organisms —**or·gan′i·cal·ly** *adv.*

or·gan·ism (ôr′gə niz′m) *n.* any living thing —**or′gan·is′mic** *adj.*

or′gan·ist *n.* a player of the organ

or·gan·i·za·tion (ôr′gə ni zā′shən) *n.* 1. an organizing or being organized 2. any organized group, as a club — **or′gan·i·za′tion·al** *adj.*

or·gan·ize (ôr′gə nīz′) *vt.* **-ized′, -iz′ing** 1. to provide with an organic structure 2. to arrange for 3. to establish; institute 4. to persuade to join a cause, group, etc. —*vi.* to become organized —**or′gan·iz′er** *n.*

or·gan·za (ôr gan′zə) *n.* [< ?] a thin, stiff fabric of rayon, silk, etc.

or·gasm (ôr′gaz′m) *n.* [< Gr. *organ*, to swell] the climax of a sexual act

or·gy (ôr′jē) *n., pl.* **-gies** [< Gr. *orgia*, secret rites] 1. a wild merrymaking in a group, esp. with sexual activity 2. an overindulgence in any activity

o·ri·el (ôr′i əl) *n.* [< ? ML. *oriolum*, gallery] a bay window resting on a bracket or a corbel

o·ri·ent (ôr′ē ənt; *also, esp. for v.* -ent′) *n.* [< L. *oriri*, arise: used of the rising sun] [O-] the East, or Asia; esp., the Far East —*vt., vi.* to adjust (oneself) to a particular situation —**o′ri·en·ta′tion** *n.*

O′ri·en′tal (-en′t'l) *adj.* of the Orient, its people, etc. —*n.* a member of a people native to the Orient

or·i·fice (ôr′ə fis, är′-) *n.* [< L. *os*, mouth + *facere*, make] a mouth of a tube, cavity, etc.; opening

orig. 1. origin 2. original(ly)

o·ri·ga·mi (ôr′ə gä′mē) *n.* [Jap.] a Japanese art of folding paper to form flowers, animal figures, etc.

or·i·gin (ôr′ə jin, är′-) *n.* [< L. *oriri*,

to rise] 1. a coming into existence or use; beginning 2. parentage; birth 3. source; root; cause

o·rig·i·nal (ə rij′ə n'l) *adj.* 1. first; earliest 2. never having been before; new; novel 3. capable of creating something new; inventive 4. being that from which copies are made —*n.* 1. a primary type that has given rise to varieties 2. an original work, as of art or literature —**o·rig′i·nal′i·ty** (-nal′ə tē) *n.* —**o·rig′i·nal·ly** *adv.*

o·rig·i·nate (-nāt′) *vt.* **-nat′ed, -nat′ing** to bring into being; esp., to invent —*vi.* to begin; start —**o·rig′i·na′tion** *n.* —**o·rig′i·na′tor** *n.*

o·ri·ole (ôr′ē ōl′) *n.* [ult. < L. *aurum*, gold] any of a genus of American birds with bright-orange and black plumage: they build hanging nests

O·ri·on (ō rī′ən, ô-) a very bright equatorial constellation

Or·lon (ôr′län) *a trademark for* a synthetic fiber similar to nylon

or·mo·lu (ôr′mə loo′) *n.* [Fr. *or moulu*, ground gold] an imitation gold made of a copper and tin alloy, used in ornaments, gilding, etc.

or·na·ment (ôr′nə mənt; *for v.* -ment′) *n.* [< L. *ornare*, adorn] 1. anything that adorns; decoration 2. one whose character or talent adds luster to his surroundings, etc. —*vt.* to decorate —**or′na·men′tal** *adj.* — **or′na·men·ta′tion** *n.*

or·nate (ôr nāt′) *adj.* [< L. *ornare*, adorn] heavily ornamented; showy — **or·nate′ly** *adv.* —**or·nate′ness** *n.*

or·ner·y (ôr′nər ē) *adj.* [< ORDINARY] [Chiefly Dial.] 1. mean; nasty 2. obstinate —**or′ner·i·ness** *n.*

or·ni·thol·o·gy (ôr′nə thäl′ə jē) *n.* [< Gr. *ornis*, bird + -LOGY] the branch of zoology dealing with birds —**or′ni·thol′o·gist** *n.*

o·ro·tund (ôr′ə tund′) *adj.* [< L. *os*, mouth + *rotundus*, round] 1. resonant: said of the voice 2. bombastic

or·phan (ôr′fən) *n.* [< Gr.] a child whose parents are dead —*adj.* 1. being an orphan 2. of or for orphans —*vt.* to cause to become an orphan

or′phan·age (-ij) *n.* an institution that is a home for orphans

Or·phe·us (ôr′fē əs) *Gr. Myth.* a poet-musician with magic musical powers

or·ris (ôr′is, är′-) *n.* [prob. < L. *iris*, iris] any of several European irises. esp. the one yielding a root (**or′ris-root′**) pulverized for perfumery, etc.

ortho- [< Gr. *orthos*, straight] a combining form meaning: 1. straight [*orthodontics*] 2. proper; correct [*orthography*] Also **orth-**

or·tho·don·tics (ôr′thə dän′tiks) *n.pl.* [*with sing. v.*] [< ORTH(O)- + Gr. *odōn*, tooth + -ICS] the branch of dentistry concerned with correcting tooth irregularities —**or′tho·don′tist** *n.*

or·tho·dox (ôr′thə däks′) *adj.* [< Gr. *orthos*, straight + *doxa*, opinion]

conforming to the usual beliefs or
established doctrines, as in religion;
conventional —or′tho·dox′y n.

Or·tho·dox (Eastern) Church the
Christian church dominant in E
Europe, W Asia, and N Africa

or·thog·ra·phy (ôr thäg′rə fē) n., pl.
-phies [< Gr.: see ORTHO- & -GRAPHY]
1. correct spelling 2. spelling as a
subject for study —or·tho·graph·ic
(ôr′thə graf′ik) adj.

or·tho·pe·dics (ôr′thə pē′diks) n.pl.
[with sing. v.] [< Gr. orthos, straight +
pais, child] the branch of surgery dealing with deformities, diseases, and
injuries of the bones and joints —or′-
tho·pe′dic adj. —or′tho·pe′dist n.

-o·ry (ôr′ē, ər ē) [< L. -orius] a suffix
meaning: 1. of, having the nature of
[commendatory] 2. a place or thing for
[laboratory]

OS., OS, O.S. Old Saxon

O·sa·ka (ō sä′kə) seaport in S Honshu, Japan: pop. 3,156,000

os·cil·late (äs′ə lāt′) vi. **-lat′ed,**
-lat′ing [< L. oscillare, to swing] 1.
to swing to and fro 2. to vacillate 3.
Physics to vary regularly between
high and low values, as an electric
current —os′cil·la′tion n. —os′-
cil·la′tor n.

os·cil·lo·scope (ä sil′ə skōp′) n. [<
L. oscillare, swing + -SCOPE] an instrument that visually displays an
electrical wave on a fluorescent screen

os·cu·late (äs′kyə lāt′) vt., vi. **-lat′-**
ed, -lat′ing [< L. osculum, a kiss] to
kiss —os′cu·la′tion n.

-ose¹ (ōs) [Fr. < (gluc)ose] a suffix
designating: 1. a carbohydrate [cellu-
lose] 2. the product of a protein
hydrolysis

-ose² (ōs) [L. -osus] a suffix meaning
full of, like [bellicose, verbose]

o·sier (ō′zhər) n. [< ML. ausaria,
bed of willows] a willow with lithe
branches used for baskets and furniture

-o·sis (ō′sis) [< Gr.] a suffix meaning:
1. condition, action [osmosis] 2. an
abnormal or diseased condition
[neurosis]

Os·lo (äs′lō, äz′-) capital of Norway:
pop. 483,000

os·mi·um (äz′mē əm) n. [< Gr.
osmē, odor] a hard, bluish-white,
metallic chemical element, occurring
as an alloy with platinum

os·mo·sis (äs mō′sis, äz-) n. [< Gr.
ōsmos, impulse] the tendency of fluids
to pass through a membrane and so
equalize concentrations on both sides
—os·mot′ic (-mät′ik) adj.

os·prey (äs′prē) n., pl. **-preys** [< L.
os, a bone + frangere, to break] a large
hawk that feeds solely on fish

os·si·fy (äs′ə fī′) vt., vi. **-fied′, -fy′-**
ing [< L. os, a bone + -FY] 1. to
change into bone 2. to fix rigidly in a
custom, etc. —os′si·fi·ca′tion n.

os·ten·si·ble (äs ten′sə b'l) adj. [<
L. ostendere, to show] apparent;
seeming —os·ten′si·bly adv.

os·ten·ta·tion (äs′tən tā′shən) n.
[see prec.] showy display; pretentiousness —os′ten·ta′tious adj.

os·te·op·a·thy (äs′tē äp′ə thē) n. [<
Gr. osteon, a bone + -PATHY] a school
of medicine and surgery that emphasizes the interrelationship of the
muscles and bones to all other body
systems —os′te·o·path′ (-ə path′) n.

os·tra·cize (äs′trə sīz′) vt. **-cized′,**
-ciz′ing [< Gr. ostrakon, a shell (cast
as a ballot)] to banish from a group,
society, etc. —os′tra·cism n.

os·trich (ôs′trich, äs′-) n. [< L. avis,
bird + struthio, ostrich] a large, swift-
running, nonflying bird of Africa and
the Near East

OT., OT, O.T. Old Testament

O·thel·lo (ə thel′ō) a tragedy by
Shakespeare in which the title character, madly jealous, kills his wife

oth·er (uth′ər) adj. [OE.] 1. being
the remaining one or ones [Bill and
the other boy(s)] 2. different or distinct from that or those implied [use
your other foot] 3. additional [he has
no other coat] —pron. 1. the other one
2. some other one [to do as others do]
—adv. otherwise [he can't do other
than go] —the other day (or night,
etc.) not long ago; recently

oth·er·wise (-wīz′) adv. 1. in
another manner; differently [I believe
otherwise] 2. in all other respects [he
is otherwise intelligent] 3. in other
circumstances —adj. different

oth·er·world·ly (-wurld′lē) adj. being apart from earthly interests

o·ti·ose (ō′shē ōs′) adj. [< L. otium,
leisure] 1. idle 2. futile 3. useless

Ot·ta·wa (ät′ə wə, -wä′) capital of
Canada, in SE Ontario: pop. 291,000

ot·ter (ät′ər) n. [OE. oter] 1. a furry,
swimming mammal related to the
weasel and mink 2. its fur

ot·to·man (ät′ə mən) n. [< Fr.] a
low, cushioned seat or footstool

ouch (ouch) interj. an exclamation of
sudden pain

ought (ôt) v.aux. [OE. agan, owe] an
auxiliary used to express: 1. obligation, duty, or desirability [she ought
to stay home] 2. probability [it ought
to be over soon]

oui (wē) adv. [Fr.] yes

Oui·ja (wē′jə, -jē) [< prec. + G. ja,
yes] a trademark for a supposedly
spiritualistic device consisting of a
board with the alphabet, and a sliding,
three-legged pointer

ounce (ouns) n. [< L. uncia, a twelfth]
1. a unit of weight, 1/16 pound
avoirdupois or 1/12 pound troy 2. a
fluid ounce, 1/16 pint

our (our) poss. pronominal adj. [OE.
ure] of, belonging to, or done by us

ours (ourz) pron. that or those belonging to us [a friend of ours]

our·selves (our selvz′) pron. 1. the
intensive form of WE [we went our-
selves] 2. the reflexive form of WE [we
hurt ourselves] 3. our true selves [we
are not ourselves when sick]

-ous [< L. -osus] a suffix meaning
having, full of, characterized by
[hazardous, dangerous]

oust (oust) vt. [< L. ostare, obstruct]
to force out; expel; dispossess

oust·er n. an ousting or being ousted

out (out) *adv.* [< OE. *ūt*] 1. away or forth from a place, position, etc. 2. into the open air 3. into existence or activity *[disease broke out]* 4. *a)* to a conclusion *[argue it out]* *b)* completely *[tired out]* 5. into sight or notice *[the moon came out]* 6. from existence or activity *[fade out]* 7. aloud *[sing out]* 8. beyond a regular surface, condition, etc. *[stand out]* 9. into disuse *[long skirts went out]* 10. from a group or stock *[pick out]* 11. [Slang] into unconsciousness 12. *Baseball* in a manner producing an out *[to fly out]* —*adj.* 1. external: usually in combination *[outpost]* 2. beyond regular limits 3. away from work, etc. 4. in error *[out in my estimates]* 5. not in operation, use, etc. 6. [Colloq.] having suffered a financial loss *[out five dollars]* 7. [Colloq.] outmoded 8. *Baseball* having failed to get on base —*prep.* 1. out of 2. along the way of —*n.* 1. something that is out 2. [Slang] a way out; excuse 3. *Baseball* the failure of a player to reach base safely —*vi.* to become known *[the truth will out]* —all out wholeheartedly —on the outs [Colloq.] on unfriendly terms —out for trying to get or do —out of 1. from inside of 2. beyond 3. from (material, etc.) *[made out of stone]* 4. because of *[out of spite]* 5. having no *[out of gas]* 6. so as to deprive —out to trying to

out- *a combining form meaning:* 1. at or from a point away; outside *[outpatient]* 2. going away or forth; outward *[outbound]* 3. better or more than *[outdo, outplay]*

out'age (-ij) *n.* an accidental suspension of operation, as of electric power

out'-and-out' *adj.* thorough

out'back' *n.* any remote, sparsely settled region viewed as uncivilized

out'bal'ance *vt.* -anced, -anc·ing to be greater than in weight, value, etc.

out'bid' *vt.* -bid', -bid'ding to bid or offer more than (someone else)

out'board' *adj.* outside the hull of a ship, boat, etc. *[an outboard motor]*

out'bound' *adj.* outward bound

out'break' *n.* a breaking out; sudden occurrence, as of disease, rioting, etc.

out'build'ing *n.* a structure, as a barn, separate from the main building

out'burst' *n.* a sudden release, as of feeling, energy, etc.

out'cast' *adj.* driven out; rejected —*n.* a person rejected, as by society

out'class' *vt.* to surpass

out'come' *n.* result; consequence

out'crop' *n.* 1. the emergence of a mineral at the earth's surface 2. the mineral thus exposed

out'cry' *n., pl.* -cries' 1. a crying out 2. a strong protest

out'dat'ed *adj.* no longer current

out'dis'tance *vt.* -tanced, -tanc-ing to get ahead of, as in a race

out'do' *vt.* -did', -done', -do'ing to exceed or surpass —outdo oneself to do better than one expected to do

out'door' (-dôr') *adj.* 1. being or occurring outdoors 2. of or fond of the outdoors

out'doors' *adv.* in or into the open; outside —*n.* the outdoor world

out'er *adj.* farther out or away

out'er·most' *adj.* farthest out

outer space space beyond the earth's atmosphere or beyond the solar system

out'er·wear' *n.* garments, as overcoats, worn over the usual clothing

out'field' *n. Baseball* 1. the playing area beyond the infield 2. the players (**outfielders**) positioned there

out'fit' *n.* 1. the equipment used in an activity 2. clothes worn together; ensemble 3. a group of people associated in an activity —*vt.* -fit'ted, -fit'ting to furnish with an outfit —out'fit'ter *n.*

out'flank' *vt.* to go around and beyond the flank of (enemy troops)

out'fox' (-fäks') *vt.* to outwit

out'go' *n., pl.* -goes' that which is paid out; expenditure

out'go'ing *adj.* 1. *a)* leaving *b)* retiring from office 2. sociable

out'grow' *vt.* -grew', -grown', -grow'ing 1. to grow faster or larger than 2. to lose in becoming mature *[he outgrew his credulity]* 3. to grow too large for

out'growth' *n.* 1. a growing out or that which grows out 2. a consequence, result, or development

out'guess' *vt.* to outwit

out'house' *n.* a boothlike shelter outdoors, used as a toilet

out'ing *n.* 1. a pleasure trip 2. an outdoor walk, ride, picnic, etc.

out·land'ish (-lan'dish) *adj.* very odd or strange; fantastic; bizarre

out'last' *vt.* to endure longer than

out'law' (-lô') *n.* 1. orig., a person deprived of legal rights and protection 2. a habitual or notorious criminal —*vt.* 1. orig., to declare to be an outlaw 2. to declare illegal

out'lay' (-lā') *n.* 1. a spending (of money, etc.) 2. money, etc. spent

out'let' *n.* 1. a passage for letting something out 2. a means of expression *[an outlet for anger]* 3. a market for goods

out'line' *n.* 1. a line bounding the limits of an object 2. a sketch showing only contours 3. a general plan 4. a systematic summary —*vt.* -lined', -lin'ing 1. to draw in outline 2. to make an outline of

out'live' *vt.* -lived', -liv'ing to live or endure longer than; outlast

out'look' *n.* 1. the view from a place 2. viewpoint 3. expectation or prospect

out'ly'ing (-lī'ip) *adj.* relatively far out from a central point; remote

out·ma·neu'ver, out'ma·noeu'vre *vt.* -vered or -vred, -ver-ing or -vring to outwit by maneuvering

out'mod'ed (-mōd'id) *adj.* no longer in fashion or accepted; obsolete

out'num'ber vt. to exceed in number

out'-of-date' adj. no longer in style or use; old-fashioned

out'-of-door' adj. outdoor

out'-of-doors' adv., n. outdoors

out'-of-the-way' adj. 1. secluded 2. not common; unusual

out'-of-town'er n. a visitor from another town or city

out'pa'tient n. a patient, not an inmate, being treated at a hospital

out'play' vt. to play better than

out'post' n. 1. Mil. a) a small group stationed at a distance from the main force b) the station so occupied c) a foreign base 2. a frontier settlement

out'put' n. 1. the work done or amount produced, esp. over a given period 2. information delivered by a computer 3. Elec. the useful voltage, current, or power delivered

out·rage (out'rāj') n. [ult. < L. ultra, beyond] 1. an extremely vicious or violent act 2. a grave insult or offense 3. great anger, etc. aroused by this —vt. -raged', -rag'ing 1. to commit an outrage upon or against 2. to cause outrage in

out·ra'geous (-rā'jəs) adj. 1. involving or doing great injury or wrong 2. very offensive or shocking — **out·ra'geous·ly** adv.

out'rank' vt. to exceed in rank

†out·ré (ōō trā') adj. [Fr.] 1. exaggerated 2. outlandish; bizarre

out'reach' vt., vi. 1. to reach beyond; surpass 2. to reach out; extend —n. a reaching out —adj. designating or of a branch away from the main office of a social agency, etc.

out'rid'er n. 1. a rider on horseback who accompanies a stagecoach, etc. 2. a cowboy riding a range to keep cattle from straying 3. a forerunner

out'rig'ger (-rig'ər) n. a timber rigged out from the side of a canoe to prevent tipping; also, a canoe of this type

out'right' (-rīt') adj. 1. utter; downright 2. complete —adv. 1. entirely 2. openly 3. at once

OUTRIGGER

out'run' vt. -ran', -run', -run'ning 1. to run faster than 2. to exceed

out'sell' vt. -sold', -sell'ing to sell in greater amounts than

out'set' n. a setting out; beginning

out'shine' vt. -shone' or -shined', -shin'ing 1. to shine brighter or longer than 2. to surpass; excel

out'side' n. 1. the outer side or part; exterior 2. outward appearance 3. any area not inside —adj. 1. of, on, or from the outside; outer 2. extreme [an outside estimate] 3. slight [an outside chance] —adv. 1. on or to the outside 2. outdoors —prep. 1. on or to the outer side of 2. beyond the limits of —**outside of** 1. outside 2. [Colloq.] other than

out'sid'er n. one who is not included in a given group

out'size' n. an odd size, esp. an unusually large one

out'skirts' (-skurts') n.pl. districts remote from the center, as of a city

out'smart' vt. [Colloq.] to overcome by cunning or cleverness; outwit — **outsmart oneself** to have one's efforts at cunning or cleverness result in one's own disadvantage

out'spo'ken adj. 1. unrestrained in speech 2. spoken boldly or candidly

out'spread' adj. spread out; extended

out'stand'ing adj. 1. projecting 2. prominent; distinguished 3. unpaid; uncollected 4. issued and sold: said of stocks and bonds

out'sta'tion n. a post or station in a remote or unsettled area

out'stretch' vt. 1. to stretch out; extend 2. to stretch beyond

out'strip' vt. -stripped', -strip'ping 1. to go at a faster pace than 2. to excel; surpass

out'vote' vt. -vot'ed, -vot'ing to defeat or surpass in voting

out'ward (-wərd) adj. 1. having to do with the outside; outer 2. clearly apparent 3. away from the interior —adv. toward the outside: also **out'wards** —**out'ward·ly** adv.

out'wear' vt. -wore', -worn', -wear'ing 1. to wear out 2. to outlast

out'weigh' vt. 1. to weigh more than 2. to be more important than

out'wit' vt. -wit'ted, -wit'ting to get the better of by cleverness

o·va (ō'və) n. pl. of OVUM

o·val (ō'v'l) adj. [< L. ovum, egg] shaped like an egg in longitudinal cross section —n. anything oval

o·va·ry (ō'vər ē) n., pl. -ries [< L. ovum, egg] 1. either of two female reproductive glands producing eggs 2. Botany the enlarged hollow part of the pistil, containing ovules —**o·var·i·an** (ō ver'ē ən) adj.

o·vate (ō'vāt) adj. egg-shaped; oval

o·va·tion (ō vā'shən) n. [< L. ovare, celebrate a triumph] an enthusiastic burst of applause or public welcome

ov·en (uv'ən) n. [OE. ofen] a receptacle or compartment for baking, drying, or heating

o·ver (ō'vər) prep. [OE. ofer] 1. a) in, at, or to a position above b) across and down from [to fall over a cliff] 2. so as to cover [a board over the well] 3. upon, as an effect [to cast a spell over someone] 4. above in authority, power, etc. 5. on or to the other side of [fly over the lake] 6. throughout [over the whole city] 7. during [over the year] 8. more than [over ten cents] 9. in preference to 10. concerning —adv. 1. a) above or across b) across the brim or edge 2. more [three hours or over] 3. from start to finish [talk it over] 4. a) from an upright position [to fall over] b) upside down [turn the cup over] 5. again [do it over] 6. at, on, to, or in a specified place [over in Spain] 7. from one belief, etc. to another [win him over] —adj. 1. upper, outer, superior, excessive, or extra 2. finished; past 3. having reached the other side 4. [Colloq.] as a surplus

o·ver- a combining form meaning: 1. above in position, rank, etc. [overlord]

2. passing across or beyond [*overrun*]
3. excessive(ly) [*overrate*] : the list below includes some common compounds formed with *over-* that can be understood if *too much* or *excessively* is added to the meaning of the base word

overabundance	overheat
overactive	overindulge
overambitious	overload
overanxious	overpay
overbid	overpopulate
overburden	overprice
overcautious	overproduce
overconfident	overproduction
overcook	overrefined
overcritical	overripe
overcrowd	oversell
overdevelop	oversensitive
overeager	overspecialize
overeat	overspend
overemphasize	overstimulate
overenthusiastic	overstock
overexercise	overstrict
overexert	oversupply
overexpose	overtire

o·ver·act′ *vt.*, *vi.* to act with exaggeration
o·ver·age¹ (ō′vər āj′) *adj.* over the age fixed as a standard
o·ver·age² (ō′vər ij) *n.* [OVER- + -AGE] a surplus or excess
o′ver·all′ *adj.* 1. from end to end 2. including everything; total —*adv.* 1. from end to end 2. in general
o·ver·alls (-ôlz′) *n.pl.* loose trousers, often with an attached bib, worn over other clothes as a protection
o′ver·awe′ *vt.* -awed′, -aw′ing to overcome or subdue by inspiring awe
o′ver·bal′ance *vt.* -anced, -anc·ing 1. *same as* OUTWEIGH 2. to throw off balance
o′ver·bear′ing (-ber′iŋ) *adj.* arrogant; domineering
o′ver·board′ *adv.* from a ship into the water —**go overboard** [Colloq.] to go to extremes
o′ver·cast′ (-kast′) *adj.* cloudy; dark: said of the sky
o′ver·charge′ *vt.*, *vi.* -charged′, -charg′ing 1. to charge too much 2. to overload —*n.* (ō′vər chärj′) 1. an excessive charge 2. too full a load
o′ver·clothes′ *n.pl. same as* OUTERWEAR
o′ver·cloud′ *vt.*, *vi.* to make or become cloudy, gloomy, etc.
o′ver·coat′ *n.* a heavy coat worn over the usual clothing for warmth
o′ver·come′ *vt.* -came′, -come′, -com′ing 1. to get the better of in competition, etc. 2. to master, surmount, overwhelm, etc. —*vi.* to win
o′ver·do′ *vt.* -did′, -done′, -do′ing 1. to do too much 2. to exaggerate 3. to overcook —*vi.* to exhaust oneself by doing too much
o′ver·dose′ *n.* too large a dose
o′ver·draw′ *vt.* -drew′, -drawn′, -draw′ing to draw on in excess of the amount credited to the drawer —
o′ver·draft′ *n.*

o′ver·dress′ *vt.*, *vi.* to dress too warmly, too showily, or too formally
o′ver·due′ *adj.* past the time set for payment, arrival, etc.
o′ver·es′ti·mate′ (-es′tə māt′) *vt.* to set too high an estimate on or for
o′ver·flight′ *n.* the flight of an aircraft over a foreign territory, as in reconnaissance
o′ver·flow′ *vt.* 1. to flow across; flood 2. to flow over the brim of —*vi.* 1. to run over 2. to be superabundant —*n.* (ō′vər flō′) 1. an overflowing 2. the amount that overflows 3. an outlet for overflowing liquids
o′ver·grow′ *vt.* -grew′, -grown′, -grow′ing to overspread, as with foliage, so as to cover —*vi.* to grow too fast or beyond normal —**o′ver·grown′** *adj.* —**o′ver·growth′** *n.*
o′ver·hand′ *adj.*, *adv.* with the hand raised above the elbow or the arm above the shoulder
o′ver·hang′ *vt.*, *vi.* -hung′, -hang′ing to hang over or project beyond (something) —*n.* (ō′vər haŋ′) the projection of one thing over another
o′ver·haul′ (-hôl′) *vt.* 1. *a)* to check thoroughly as for needed repairs *b)* to make such repairs, etc., as on a motor 2. to catch up with —*n.* (ō′vər hôl′) an overhauling
o′ver·head′ *adj.* 1. above the head 2. in the sky 3. on a higher level, with reference to related objects —*n.* the general, continuing costs of a business, as of rent, taxes, etc. —*adv.* (ō′vər hed′) above the head; aloft
o′ver·hear′ *vt.* -heard′, -hear′ing to hear (something spoken or a speaker) without the speaker's knowledge
o′ver·joy′ *vt.* to give great joy to; delight —**o′ver·joyed′** *adj.*
o′ver·kill′ *n.* the capacity of a nuclear stockpile to kill more than the total population of a given nation
o′ver·land′ *adv.*, *adj.* by, on, or across land
o′ver·lap′ *vt.*, *vi.* -lapped′, -lap′ping to lap over; extend over (a thing or each other) so as to coincide in part
o′ver·lay′ *vt.* -laid′, -lay′ing 1. to lay or spread over 2. to cover, as with a decorative layer
o′ver·lie′ *vt.* -lay′, -lain′, -ly′ing to lie on or over
o′ver·look′ *vt.* 1. to look at from above 2. to give a view of from above 3. *a)* to fail to notice *b)* to ignore; neglect 4. to excuse 5. to supervise
o′ver·lord′ *n.* a lord ranking above other lords
o′ver·ly (-lē) *adv.* too or too much
o′ver·mas′ter *vt.* to overcome
o′ver·much′ *adj.*, *adv.*, *n.* too much
o′ver·night′ *adv.* 1. during the night 2. suddenly —*adj.* (ō′vər nīt′) 1. done or going on during the night 2. for one night [an *overnight* guest] 3. of or for a brief trip [an *overnight* bag]
o′ver·pass′ *n.* a bridge, etc. over a road, railway, etc.

o′ver·play′ *vt.* 1. to overact, overdo, or overemphasize 2. to overestimate the strength of (one's card hand)

o′ver·pow′er *vt.* to get the better of; subdue or overwhelm

o′ver·rate′ *vt.* **-rat′ed, -rat′ing** to rate or estimate too highly

o′ver·reach′ *vt.* to reach beyond or above —**overreach oneself** to fail because of trying to do too much

o′ver·re·act′ *vi.* to react in an excessively emotional way

o′ver·ride′ *vt.* **-rode′, -rid′den, -rid′ing** 1. to ride over 2. to prevail over 3. to disregard or nullify

o′ver·rule′ *vt.* **-ruled′, -rul′ing** 1. to rule out or set aside, as by higher authority 2. to prevail over

o′ver·run′ *vt.* **-ran′, -run′, -run′ning** 1. to spread out over so as to cover 2. to swarm over, as vermin 3. to extend beyond (certain limits)

o′ver·seas′ *adv.* over or beyond the sea —*adj.* 1. foreign 2. over or across the sea Also **o′ver·sea′**

o′ver·see′ *vt.* **-saw′, -seen′, -see′ing** to supervise; superintend —**o′ver·se′er** *n.*

o′ver·sexed′ *adj.* having exceptional sexual drive or interest

o′ver·shad′ow *vt.* 1. *a*) to cast a shadow over *b*) to darken 2. to be more important than by comparison

o′ver·shoe′ *n.* a boot of rubber or fabric, worn over the regular shoe to protect from cold or dampness

o′ver·shoot′ *vt.* **-shot′, -shoot′ing** 1. to shoot or pass over or beyond (a target, mark, etc.) 2. to exceed

o′ver·sight′ (-sīt ′) *n.* a careless mistake or omission

o′ver·sim′pli·fy′ *vt., vi.* **-fied′, -fy′ing** to simplify to the point of distortion —**o′ver·sim′pli·fi·ca′tion** *n.*

o′ver·size′ *adj.* 1. too large 2. larger than the usual Also **o′ver·sized′**

o′ver·sleep′ *vi.* **-slept′, -sleep′ing** to sleep longer than intended

o′ver·spread′ *vt.* **-spread′, -spread′ing** to spread or cover over

o′ver·state′ *vt.* **-stat′ed, -stat′ing** to exaggerate —**o′ver·state′ment** *n.*

o′ver·stay′ *vt.* to stay beyond the time or limit of

o′ver·step′ *vt.* **-stepped′, -step′ping** to go beyond the limits of

o′ver·stuff′ *vt.* 1. to stuff with too much of something 2. to upholster (furniture) with deep stuffing

o·vert′ (ō vurt′, ō′vurt) *adj.* [< L. *aperire*, to open] 1. not hidden; manifest 2. *Law* done openly, with evident intent —**o·vert′ly** *adv.*

o′ver·take′ *vt.* **-took′, -tak′en, -tak′ing** 1. to catch up with 2. to come upon suddenly

o′ver·tax′ *vt.* 1. to tax too heavily 2. to make excessive demands on

o′ver·throw′ *vt.* **-threw′, -thrown′, -throw′ing** 1. to throw or turn over 2. to conquer 3. to throw beyond —*n.* (ō′vər thrō′) 1. an overthrowing or being overthrown 2. destruction; end

o′ver·time′ *n.* 1. time beyond the established limit, as of working hours 2. pay for work done in such time —*adj., adv.* of, for, or during overtime

o′ver·tone′ *n.* 1. a faint, higher tone accompanying a fundamental tone produced by a musical instrument 2. an implication; nuance

o·ver·ture (ō′vər chər) *n.* [< L. *apertura*, aperture] 1. an introductory proposal or offer 2. a musical introduction to an opera, etc.

o′ver·turn′ *vt.* 1. to turn over 2. to conquer —*vi.* to tip over; capsize

o′ver·ween′ing (-wē′niŋ) *adj.* [< OE. *ofer*, over + *wenan*, to hope] 1. arrogant 2. excessive

o′ver·weight′ *adj.* above the normal or allowed weight

o′ver·whelm′ (-hwelm′) *vt.* [see OVER & WHELM] 1. to pour down on and bury beneath 2. to crush; overpower —**o′ver·whelm′ing** *adj.*

o′ver·work′ *vt.* to work or use to excess —*vi.* to work too hard or too long —*n.* (ō′vər wurk′) severe or burdensome work

o′ver·wrought′ (-rôt′) *adj.* 1. very nervous or excited 2. too elaborate

Ov·id (äv′id) 43 B.C.–17? A.D.; Rom. poet

ov·i·duct (ō′vi dukt′) *n.* [< L. *ovum*, egg + DUCT] a tube through which the ova pass from an ovary to the uterus

o·vip·a·rous (ō vip′ər əs) *adj.* [< L. *ovum*, egg + *parere*, to bear] producing eggs which hatch after leaving the body

o·void (ō′void) *adj.* [< L. *ovum*, egg] egg-shaped —*n.* anything ovoid

o·vu·late (ō′vyə lāt′, äv′yə-) *vi.* **-lat′ed, -lat′ing** [< L. *ovum*, egg] to produce and discharge ova from the ovary —**o′vu·la′tion** *n.*

o·vule (ō′vyōōl) *n.* [< L. *ovum*, egg] 1. *Bot.* the part of a plant which develops into a seed 2. *Zool.* the immature ovum —**o′vu·lar** *adj.*

o·vum (ō′vəm) *n., pl.* **o·va** (ō′və) [L., egg] a female germ cell

ow (ou) *interj.* a cry of pain

owe (ō) *vt.* **owed, ow′ing** [OE. *agan*, to own] 1. to be indebted to the amount of 2. to have the need to give, do, etc., as because of gratitude 3. to be indebted (*to*) for

ow·ing (ō′iŋ) *adj.* 1. that owes 2. due; unpaid —**owing to** because of

owl (oul) *n.* [OE. *ule*] 1. a night bird of prey having a large head, large eyes, and a short, hooked beak 2. a person of nocturnal habits, solemn appearance, etc. —**owl′ish** *adj.*

owl′et (-it) *n.* a young or small owl

own (ōn) *adj.* [< OE. *agan*, possess] belonging or relating to oneself or itself [*his own car*] —*n.* that which belongs to oneself [*that is his own*] —*vt.* 1. to possess; have 2. to admit; acknowledge —*vi.* to confess (*to*) —**on one's own** [Colloq.] by one's own efforts —**own′er** *n.* —**own′er·ship′** *n.*

ox (äks) *n., pl.* **ox′en** [OE. *oxa*] 1. any of various cud-chewing mammals of the cattle family, as the buffalo, yak, etc. 2. a castrated bull

ox′blood′ *n.* a deep red color

ox′bow′ (-bō′) *n.* the U-shaped part of an ox yoke which passes under and around the animal's neck

Ox·ford (äks'fərd) city in SC England: pop. 110,000

ox·ford (äks'fərd) *n.* [after prec.] [*sometimes* O-] **1.** a low shoe laced over the instep: also **oxford shoe 2.** a cotton or rayon fabric with a basket-like weave: also **oxford cloth**

ox·i·dant (äk'sə dənt) *n.* an oxidizing agent

ox·i·da·tion (äk'sə dā'shən) *n.* an oxidizing or being oxidized

ox·ide (äk'sīd) *n.* [< Gr. *oxys*, sour + Fr. *(ac)ide*, acid] a compound of oxygen with another element or a radical

ox·i·dize (äk'sə dīz') *vt.* **-dized', -diz'ing** to unite with oxygen, as in burning or rusting —*vi.* to become oxidized —**ox'i·diz'er** *n.*

ox·y·acet·y·lene (äk'sē ə set''l ēn') *adj.* of or using a mixture of oxygen and acetylene, as for producing a hot flame used in welding

ox·y·gen (äk'si jən) *n.* [< Fr. < Gr.

oxys, acid + Fr. *-gène*, -GEN] a colorless, odorless, gaseous chemical element, the most abundant of all elements: it is essential to life processes and to combustion

ox'y·gen·ate' (-jə nāt') *vt.* **-at'ed, -at'ing** to combine or treat with oxygen —**ox'y·gen·a'tion** *n.*

oxygen tent a transparent enclosure supplied with oxygen, fitted around a bed patient to facilitate breathing

oys·ter (oi'stər) *n.* [< Gr. *ostreon*] an edible marine mollusk with an irregular, hinged shell

oyster cracker a very small, round, salted soda cracker

oz. *pl.* **oz., ozs.** ounce

o·zone (ō'zōn) *n.* [Fr. < Gr. *ozein*, to smell] **1.** a form of oxygen with a strong odor, formed by an electrical discharge in air and used as a bleaching agent, water purifier, etc. **2.** [Slang] pure, fresh air

P

P, p (pē) *n.,* *pl.* **P's, p's** the 16th letter of the English alphabet —**mind one's p's and q's** to be careful of what one says and does

P *Chem.* phosphorus

p. 1. *pl.* **pp.** page **2.** participle **3.** past **4.** per **5.** pint

pa (pä) *n.* [Colloq.] father

Pa., PA Pennsylvania

P.A. public address (system)

pace (pās) *n.* [< L. *passus*, a step] **1.** a step in walking, etc. **2.** the length of a step or stride **3.** the rate of speed in walking, etc. **4.** rate of progress, etc. **5.** a gait **6.** the gait of a horse in which both legs on the same side are raised together —*vt.* **paced, pac'ing 1.** to walk back and forth across **2.** to measure by paces **3.** to set the pace for (a runner, etc.) —*vi.* **1.** to walk with regular steps **2.** to move at a pace: said of a horse —**put through one's paces** to test one's abilities or skills —**pac'er** *n.*

pace'mak'er *n.* **1.** a person, horse, automobile, etc. that leads the way: also **pace'set'ter 2.** an electronic device placed in the body to regulate the heartbeat

pach·y·derm (pak'ə durm') *n.* [< Gr. *pachys*, thick + *derma*, skin] a large, thick-skinned, hoofed animal, as the elephant, rhinoceros, etc.

pach·y·san·dra (pak'ə san'drə) *n.* [< ModL. name of genus] a low, hardy evergreen plant often grown as ground cover

Pa·cif·ic (pə sif'ik) largest of the earth's oceans, between Asia & the American continents —*adj.* of, in, on, or near this ocean

pa·cif·ic (pə sif'ik) *adj.* [see PACIFY] **1.** making peace **2.** of a peaceful nature; tranquil; calm

pac·i·fi·er (pas'ə fī'ər) *n.* **1.** a person or thing that pacifies **2.** a nipple or teething ring for babies

pac'i·fism (-fiz'm) *n.* opposition to the use of force under any circumstances; specif., refusal to participate in war —**pac'i·fist** *n., adj.*

pac·i·fy (pas'ə fī') *vt.* **-fied', -fy'ing** [< L. *pax*, peace + *facere*, make] to make peaceful, calm, nonhostile, etc. —**pac'i·fi·ca'tion** *n.*

pack[1] (pak) *n.* [< MDu. *pak*] **1.** a bundle of things tied up for carrying **2.** a group or mass [a *pack* of lies] **3.** a package of a standard number [a *pack* of cigarettes or of playing cards] **4.** a number of wild animals living together —*vt.* **1.** to make a pack of **2.** *a)* to put together in a box, trunk, etc. *b)* to fill (a box, etc.) **3.** to crowd; cram [the hall was *packed*] **4.** to fill in tight'y, as for prevention of leaks **5.** to carry in a pack **6.** to send (*off*) [to *pack* him off to school] **7.** [Slang] *a)* to carry (a gun, etc.) *b)* to deliver (a punch, etc.) with force —*vi.* **1.** to make up packs **2.** to put one's clothes, etc. into luggage for a trip **3.** to crowd together **4.** to settle into a compact mass —*adj.* used for carrying packs, loads, etc. [a *pack* animal] —**send packing** to dismiss abruptly

pack[2] (pak) *vt.* to choose (a jury, etc.) dishonestly so as to get desired results

pack·age (pak'ij) *n.* **1.** a wrapped or boxed thing or group of things; parcel **2.** a number of items, plans, etc. offered as a unit —*vt.* **-aged, -ag·ing** to make a package of —**pack'ag·er** *n.*

package store a store where alcoholic liquor is sold by the bottle

pack'er *n.* one who packs; specif., one who operates a packing house

pack'et (-it) *n.* **1.** a small package **2.** a boat that travels a regular route carrying passengers, freight, and mail: in full **packet boat**

pack'ing house a plant where meats, etc. are processed and packed for sale

pack rat a N.American rat that often hides small articles in its nest

pack'sad'dle *n.* a saddle with fastenings to secure the load carried by a pack animal

pact (pakt) *n.* [< L. *pax*, peace] a compact or agreement

pad¹ (pad) *n.* [echoic] the dull sound of a footstep —*vi.* **pad'ded, pad'ding** to walk, esp. with a soft step

pad² (pad) *n.* [? var. of POD] **1.** anything soft used to protect against friction, blows, etc.; cushion **2.** the cushionlike sole of an animal's paw **3.** the floating leaf of a water lily **4.** a number of sheets of paper glued along one edge; tablet **5.** [Slang] the place where one lives —*vt.* **pad'ded, pad'ding 1.** to stuff or cover with soft material **2.** to expand (a speech, etc.) with superfluous matter or (an expense account, etc.) with fraudulent entries

pad'ding *n.* any material used to pad

pad·dle¹ (pad''l) *n.* [ME. *padell*, small spade] **1.** a short oar with a wide blade at one or both ends, used without an oarlock **2.** an implement shaped like this, used to beat someone, hit a ball, etc. —*vt., vi.* **-dled, -dling 1.** to propel (a canoe, etc.) by a paddle **2.** to beat as with a paddle; spank

pad·dle² (pad''l) *vi.* **-dled, -dling** [prob. < PAD¹] to move the hands or feet about in the water, as in playing

paddle wheel a wheel with boards around it for propelling a steamboat

pad·dock (pad'ək) *n.* [< OE. *pearruc*, enclosure] **1.** a small enclosure near a stable, where horses are exercised **2.** an enclosure at a race track, where horses are saddled before a race

PADDLE WHEEL

pad·dy (pad'ē) *n., pl.* **-dies** [Malay *padi*] a rice field

pad·lock (pad'läk') *n.* a removable lock with a hinged link to be passed through a staple, chain, or eye —*vt.* to fasten or close up as with a padlock

pa·dre (pä'drā) *n.* [< L. *pater*, father] **1.** father: the title of a priest in Italy, Spain, etc. **2.** [Slang] a priest or chaplain

pae·an (pē'ən) *n.* [< Gr. *paian*, hymn] a song of joy, triumph, etc.

pa·gan (pā'gən) *n.* [< L. *paganus*, peasant] **1.** *same as* HEATHEN (sense 1) **2.** one who has no religion —*adj.* of pagans —**pa'gan·ism** *n.*

page¹ (pāj) *n.* [< L. *pangere*, fasten] **1.** *a)* one side of a leaf of a book, etc. *b)* an entire leaf **2.** [*often pl.*] a record of events —*vt.* **paged, pag'ing** to number the pages of a

page² (pāj) *n.* [< It. *paggio*] a boy attendant, esp. now one who runs errands, etc., as in a hotel —*vt.* **paged, pag'ing** to try to find (a person) by calling his name, as a hotel page does

pag·eant (paj'ənt) *n.* [< ME. *pagent*, stage scene] **1.** a spectacular exhibition, parade, etc. **2.** an outdoor drama celebrating historical events

pag'eant·ry (-ən trē) *n., pl.* **-ries 1.** grand spectacle; gorgeous display **2.** empty show or display

pag·i·na·tion (paj'ə nā'shən) *n.* **1.** the numbering of pages **2.** the arrangement and number of pages

pa·go·da (pə gō'də) *n.* [prob. < Per. *but*, idol + *kadah*, house] in India and the Far East, a several-storied temple in the form of a pyramidal tower

paid (pād) *pt. & pp.* of PAY

pail (pāl) *n.* [< OE. *pægel*, wine vessel] **1.** a cylindrical container, usually with a handle, for holding liquids, etc.; bucket **2.** the amount held by a pail: also **pail'ful'** (-fool) *n.*

pain (pān) *n.* [< Gr. *poinē*, penalty] **1.** physical or mental suffering caused by injury, disease, anxiety, grief, etc. **2.** [*pl.*] great care [take *pains* with the work] —*vt.* to cause pain to; hurt —**on** (or **under) pain of** at the risk of a penalty —**pain'ful** *adj.* —**pain'fully** *adv.* —**pain'less** *adj.*

Paine (pān), **Thomas** 1737–1809; Am. Revolutionary patriot & writer

pain'kill'er (-kil'ər) *n.* [Colloq.] a medicine that relieves pain

pains·tak·ing (pānz'tā'kiŋ) *adj.* requiring or showing great care; very careful —**pains'tak'ing·ly** *adv.*

paint (pānt) *vt.* [< L. *pingere*] **1.** *a)* to make (a picture) using oil pigments, etc. *b)* to depict with paints **2.** to describe vividly **3.** to cover or decorate with paint —*vi.* to paint pictures —*n.* **1.** a mixture of pigment with oil, water, etc. used as a covering or coloring **2.** a dried coat of paint

paint'er *n.* **1.** an artist who paints pictures **2.** one whose work is covering surfaces, as walls, with paint

paint'ing *n.* a painted picture

pair (per) *n., pl.* **pairs;** occas. after a number **pair** [< L. *par*, equal] **1.** two corresponding things associated or used together [a *pair* of shoes] **2.** a single unit of two corresponding parts [a *pair* of pants] **3.** any two persons or animals regarded as a unit —*vi., vt.* **1.** to form a pair (of) **2.** to mate

pais·ley (pāz'lē) *adj.* [< *Paisley*, Scotland] [*also* P-] having an elaborate, colorful pattern of swirls, etc.

pa·ja·mas (pə jam'əz, -jä'məz) *n.pl.* [< Per. *pāi*, leg + *jāma*, garment] a loosely fitting sleeping or lounging suit consisting of jacket and trousers

Pa·ki·stan (pä'ki stän', pak'i stan') country in S Asia, at the head of the Arabian Sea: 310,403 sq. mi.; pop. 66,749,000 —**Pa'ki·stan'i** (-ē) *adj., n.*

pal (pal) *n.* [Eng. Gypsy, brother, ult. < Sans.] [Colloq.] a close friend

pal·ace (pal'is) *n.* [< L. *Palatium*, one of the seven hills of Rome] 1. the official residence of a king, etc. 2. any large, magnificent building

pal·at·a·ble (pal'it ə b'l) *adj.* pleasant or acceptable to the taste or mind

pal·ate (pal'it) *n.* [< L. *palatum*] 1. the roof of the mouth 2. taste — **pal'a·tal** (-'l) *adj.*

pa·la·tial (pə lā'shəl) *adj.* [see PALACE] 1. of, suitable for, or like a palace 2. magnificent; stately

pal·a·tine (pal'ə tīn', -tin) *adj.* [see PALACE] designating or of a count or earl who ruled in his own territory

pa·lav·er (pə lav'ər) *n.* [Port. *palavra*, a word] talk, esp. profuse or idle talk —*vi.* to talk idly or profusely

pale¹ (pāl) *adj.* [< L. *pallere*, be pale] 1. of a whitish or colorless complexion 2. lacking intensity, as color, light, etc. —*vi., vt.* paled, pal'ing to become or make pale —**pale'ness** *n.*

pale² (pāl) *n.* [< L. *palus*, a stake] 1. a pointed stake used in fences 2. a boundary: now chiefly figurative

pa·le·on·tol·o·gy (pā'lē än täl'ə jē) *n.* [< Gr. *palaios*, ancient + *ōn*, a being + -LOGY] the branch of geology studying prehistoric life by means of fossils —**pa'le·on·tol'o·gist** *n.*

Pa'le·o·zo'ic (-ə zō'ik) *adj.* [< Gr. *palaios*, ancient + ZO(O)- + -IC] designating the geologic era (c.600–230 million years ago) characterized by the first fishes, reptiles, etc.

Pal·es·tine (pal'əs tīn') region on the E coast of the Mediterranean, including modern Israel —**Pal'es·tin'i·an** (-tin'ē ən) *adj., n.*

pal·ette (pal'it) *n.* [Fr. < L. *pala*, a shovel] a thin board on which an artist mixes his paints

pal·frey (pôl'frē) *n., pl.* -freys [ult. < Gr. *para*, beside + L. *veredus*, post horse] [Archaic] a saddle horse, esp. a gentle one for a woman

pal·i·mo·ny (pal'ə mō'nē) *n.* [PAL + (AL)IMONY] [Slang] an allowance claimed by one member of a couple who separate after living together unmarried

pal·imp·sest (pal'imp sest') *n.* [< Gr. *palimpsēstos*, lit., rubbed again] a parchment previously written upon that bears traces of the erased texts

pal·in·drome (pal'in drōm') *n.* [< Gr. *palindromos*, running back] a word, phrase, or sentence that reads the same backward and forward (Ex.: name no one man)

pal·ing (pāl'iŋ) *n.* a fence of pales

pal·i·sade (pal'ə sād') *n.* [< Fr. < L. *palus*, a stake] 1. any of a row of large pointed stakes forming a fence as for fortification 2. such a fence 3. [*pl.*] a line of steep cliffs

pall¹ (pôl) *vi.* palled, pall'ing [ME. *pallen*, appall] 1. to become cloying, insipid, etc. 2. to become satiated

pall² (pôl) *n.* [< L. *pallium*, a cover] 1. a piece of velvet, etc. used to cover a coffin 2. a dark or gloomy covering

pall·bear·er (pôl'ber'ər) *n.* [PALL² + BEARER] one of the persons who attend or carry the coffin at a funeral

pal·let¹ (pal'it) *n.* [see PALETTE] a low, portable platform used for stacking materials, as in a warehouse

pal·let² (pal'it) *n.* [< L. *palea*, chaff] a simple bed, esp. a straw-filled pad or mattress on the floor

pal·li·ate (pal'ē āt') *vt.* -at'ed, -at'ing [< L. *pallium*, a cloak] 1. to lessen the severity of without curing; alleviate 2. to make (an offense) appear less serious; excuse —**pal'li·a'tion** *n.* —**pal'li·a'tive** *adj., n.*

pal·lid (pal'id) *adj.* [L. *pallidus*, pale] faint in color; pale

pal·lor (pal'ər) *n.* [L. < *pallere*, be pale] unnatural paleness

palm¹ (päm; *occas.* pälm) *n.* [< L. *palma*: from its handlike leaf] 1. any of numerous tropical or subtropical trees or shrubs with a branchless trunk and a bunch of huge leaves at the top 2. a leaf of this tree carried as a symbol of victory

palm² (päm; *occas.* pälm) *n.* [< L. *palma*] the inner surface of the hand between the fingers and wrist —*vt.* to hide (something) in the palm, as in a sleight-of-hand trick —**palm off** to pass off by fraud

pal·met·to (pal met'ō) *n., pl.* -tos, -toes any of certain palms with fan-shaped leaves

palm·is·try (päm'is trē, pälm'is-) *n.* [prob. < ME. *paume*, PALM² + *maistrie*, mastery] fortunetelling by means of the lines, etc. on the palm of a person's hand —**palm'ist** *n.*

Palm Sunday the Sunday before Easter, commemorating Jesus' entry into Jerusalem, when palm branches were strewn before him

palm'y *adj.* -i·er, -i·est 1. of, like, or full of palm trees 2. prosperous

pal·o·mi·no (pal'ə mē'nō) *n., pl.* -nos [AmSp. < Sp., dove-colored] a pale-yellow horse with a white mane

pal·pa·ble (pal'pə b'l) *adj.* [< L. *palpare*, to touch] 1. that can be touched, felt, etc. 2. easily perceived by the senses; perceptible 3. obvious; plain —**pal'pa·bly** *adv.*

pal·pi·tate (pal'pə tāt') *vi.* -tat'ed, -tat'ing [< L. *palpare*, to feel] 1. to beat rapidly, as the heart 2. to throb —**pal'pi·ta'tion** *n.*

pal·sy (pôl'zē) *n., pl.* -sies [see PARALYSIS] paralysis of any muscle, sometimes with involuntary tremors —*vt.* -sied, -sy·ing to paralyze

pal·try (pôl'trē) *adj.* -tri·er, -tri·est [prob. < LowG. *palte*, rag] almost worthless; trifling —**pal'tri·ness** *n.*

pam·pas (pam'pəz) *n.pl.* [< SAm. Ind. *pampa*, plain, field] the extensive treeless plains of Argentina

pam·per (pam'pər) *vt.* [< LowG.] to

be overindulgent with; coddle; humor

pam·phlet (pam'flit) *n.* [< OFr. *Pamphilet*, shortened name of a ML. poem] a thin, unbound booklet, often on some topic of current interest —**pam'phlet·eer'** (-flə tir')' *n.*

Pan (pan) *Gr. Myth.* a god of fields, forests, flocks, and shepherds, represented with the legs of a goat

pan¹ (pan) *n.* [OE. *panne*] **1.** any broad, shallow container used in cooking, etc. **2.** a pan-shaped part or object —*vt., vi.* **panned, pan'ning 1.** [Colloq.] to criticize unfavorably **2.** *Mining* to wash (gravel) in a pan in order to separate (gold, etc.) —**pan out** [Colloq.] to turn out; esp., to turn out well; succeed

pan² (pan) *vt., vi.* **panned, pan'ning** [< PAN(ORAMA)] to move a movie or television camera so as to get a panoramic effect —*n.* the act of panning

pan- [< Gr. *pan*, all] *a combining form meaning:* **1.** all [*pantheism*] **2.** [P-] of, comprising, or uniting every [*Pan-American*]

pan·a·ce·a (pan'ə sē'ə) *n.* [< Gr. *pan*, all + *akeisthai*, to cure] a supposed remedy for all ills

pa·nache (pə nash', -näsh') *n.* [Fr., ult. < L. *penna*, a feather] **1.** a plume, esp. on a helmet **2.** dashing elegance of manner or style

Pan·a·ma (pan'ə mä', -mô') Central American country on a strip of land connecting Central & South America: 29,201 sq. mi.; pop. 1,329,000 — **Pan'a·ma'ni·an** (-mä'nē ən) *adj., n.*

Panama Canal ship canal across Panama, joining the Atlantic & Pacific

Panama (hat) [*also* p-] a handwoven hat made with strawlike strips of the leaves of a tropical plant

Pan'-A·mer'i·can *adj.* of the Americas

pan'cake' *n.* a flat cake of batter fried on a griddle or in a pan

pan·chro·mat·ic (pan'krō mat'ik) *adj.* sensitive to light of all colors [*panchromatic* film]

pan·cre·as (pan'krē əs, paŋ'-) *n.* [< Gr. *pan*, all + *kreas*, flesh] a large gland that secretes a digestive juice into the intestine and also produces insulin —**pan'cre·at'ic** (-at'ik) *adj.*

pan·da (pan'də) *n.* [< native name] **1.** a black-and-white, bearlike mammal of China: also **giant panda 2.** a reddish, raccoonlike animal of the Himalayas: also **lesser panda**

pan·dem·ic (pan dem'ik) *adj.* [< Gr. *pan*, all + *dēmos*, people] epidemic over a large region

pan·de·mo·ni·um (pan'də mō'nē əm) *n.* [< name of demons' abode in Milton's *Paradise Lost* < PAN- + Gr. *daimōn*, demon] wild disorder or noise

pan·der (pan'dər) *n.* [< L. *Pandarus*, lovers' go-between in Chaucer, etc.] **1.** a procurer; pimp **2.** one who helps others to satisfy their vices, etc. Also **pan'der·er** —*vi.* to act as a pander (*to*)

Pan·do·ra (pan dôr'ə) [< Gr. *pan*, all + *dōron*, gift] *Gr. Myth.* the first mortal woman: she opened a box letting all human ills into the world

pane (pān) *n.* [< L. *pannus*, piece of cloth] a sheet of glass in a frame of a window, door, etc.

pan·e·gyr·ic (pan'ə jir'ik) *n.* [< Gr. *panēgyris*, public meeting] **1.** a formal speech or writing praising a person or event **2.** high praise

pan·el (pan'l) *n.* [see PANE] **1.** a) a section or division, usually rectangular, forming a part of a wall, door, etc. b) a board for instruments or controls **2.** a lengthwise strip in a skirt, etc. **3.** a list of persons summoned for jury duty **4.** a group of people selected for judging, discussing, etc. —*vt.* **-eled** or **-elled, -el·ing** or **-el·ling** to provide with panels

pan'el·ing, pan'el·ling *n.* **1.** panels collectively **2.** sheets of plastic, wood, etc. used for panels

pan'el·ist *n.* a member of a panel (*n.* 4)

panel truck an enclosed pickup truck

pang (paŋ) *n.* [< ?] a sudden, sharp pain or feeling, as of hunger or regret

pan·han·dle¹ (pan'han'd'l) *n.* [*often* P-] a strip of land projecting like the handle of a pan

pan·han·dle² (pan'han'd'l) *vt., vi.* **-dled, -dling** [Colloq.] to beg (from) on the streets —**pan'han'dler** *n.*

pan·ic (pan'ik) *n.* [< Gr. *panikos*, of Pan, as inspirer of sudden fear] a sudden, unreasoning fear, often spreading quickly —*vt.* **-icked, -ick·ing 1.** to affect with panic **2.** [Slang] to convulse (an audience, etc.) with delight —*vi.* to show panic —**pan'ick·y** *adj.*

pan'ic-strick'en *adj.* badly frightened: also **pan'ic-struck'**

pan·nier, pan·ier (pan'yər, -ē ər) *n.* [< L. *panis*, bread] a large basket for carrying loads on the back

pa·no·cha (pə nō'chə) *n.* [AmSp., ult. < L. *panis*, bread] **1.** a coarse Mexican sugar **2.** *var. of* PENUCHE

pan·o·ply (pan'ə plē) *n., pl.* **-plies** [< Gr. *pan*, all + *hopla*, arms] **1.** a complete suit of armor **2.** any magnificent covering or array

pan·o·ra·ma (pan'ə ram'ə) *n.* [< PAN- + Gr. *horama*, a view] **1.** a wide view in all directions **2.** a constantly changing scene —**pan'o·ram'ic** *adj.*

pan·sy (pan'zē) *n., pl.* **-sies** [< Fr. *penser*, think] a small plant of the violet family, with velvety petals

pant (pant) *vi.* [ult. < L. *phantasia*, nightmare] **1.** to breathe rapidly and heavily, as from running fast **2.** to yearn eagerly (with *for* or *after*) —*vt.* to gasp out —*n.* any of a series of rapid, heavy breaths; gasp

pan·ta·loons (pan't'l ōōnz') *n.pl.* [< It.: ult. after St. *Pantalone*] formerly, a kind of tight trousers

pan·the·ism (pan'thē iz'm) *n.* [PAN- + THEISM] the doctrine that all forces, manifestations, etc. of the universe are God —**pan'the·ist** *n.*

pan·the·on (pan'thē än') *n.* [< Gr. *pan*, all + *theos*, a god] **1.** a temple for all the gods **2.** [*often* P-] a building in which the famous dead of a nation are entombed or commemorated

pan·ther (pan'thər) *n.* [< Gr.

panthēr] 1. a leopard, specif. one that is black 2. a cougar or a jaguar

pan·ties (pan'tēz) *n.pl.* women's or children's short underpants: also **pan'tie, pan'ty**

pan·to·mime (pan'tə mīm') *n.* [< Gr.: see PAN- & MIME] 1. a drama without words, using only action and gestures 2. action or gestures without words —*vt., vi.* -mimed', -mim'ing to express or act in pantomime — **pan'to·mim'ic** (-mim'ik) *adj.* — **pan'to·mim'ist** (-mī'mist, -mim'-ist) *n.*

pan·try (pan'trē) *n., pl.* -tries [< L. *panis*, bread] a small room off the kitchen, where cooking ingredients and utensils, china, etc. are kept

pants (pants) *n.pl.* [< PANTALOONS] 1. trousers 2. drawers or panties

pant'suit' *n.* matched jacket and pants for women: also **pants suit**

panty hose a woman's undergarment combining panties and hose

pap (pap) *n.* [ME.] 1. any soft food for babies or invalids 2. any oversimplified or insipid writing, ideas, etc.

pa·pa (pä'pə) *n.* father: a child's word

pa·pa·cy (pā'pə sē) *n., pl.* -cies [< LL. *papa*, pope] 1. the position or authority of the Pope 2. the period during which a pope rules 3. [*also* P-] the government of the Roman Catholic Church, headed by the Pope

pa·pal (pā'pəl) *adj.* 1. of the Pope or the papacy 2. of the Roman Catholic Church

pa·paw (pô'pô) *n.* [prob. < ff.] 1. *same as* PAPAYA 2. *a)* a tree of the C and S U.S. with an oblong, yellowish, edible fruit *b)* its fruit

pa·pa·ya (pə pä'yə) *n.* [< SAmInd.] 1. a tropical American tree with a large yellowish-orange fruit 2. its fruit

pa·per (pā'pər) *n.* [see PAPYRUS] 1. a thin, flexible material in sheets, made from rags, wood, etc. and used to write or print on, wrap, etc. 2. a single sheet of this 3. an official document 4. an essay, dissertation, etc. 5. a newspaper 6. wallpaper 7. [*pl.*] credentials —*adj.* 1. of, or made of, paper 2. like paper; thin —*vt.* to cover with wallpaper —**pa'per·y** *adj.*

pa'per·back' *n.* a book bound in paper

pa'per·boy' *n.* a boy who sells or delivers newspapers

paper clip a flexible clasp for holding loose sheets of paper together

pa'per·hang'er *n.* a person whose work is covering walls with wallpaper

paper tiger a person, nation, etc. that seems to pose a threat but is really powerless

pa'per·weight' (-wāt') *n.* any small, heavy object set on papers to keep them from being scattered

paper work the keeping of records, etc. incidental to some task

pa·pier-mâ·ché (pā'pər mə shā') *n.*

[Fr. < *papier*, paper + *mâcher*, to chew] a material made of paper pulp mixed with size, glue, etc. and molded into various objects when moist

pa·pil·la (pə pil'ə) *n., pl.* -lae (-ē) [L. < *papula*, pimple] any small, nipplelike projection of tissue, as on the tongue —**pap·il·lar·y** (pap'ə ler'ē) *adj.*

pa·poose (pa pōōs') *n.* [< AmInd.] a N.American Indian baby

pap·ri·ka (pa prē'kə, pap'ri-) *n.* [ult. < Gr. *peperi*, a pepper] a mild red condiment ground from the fruit of certain peppers

Pap test (pap) [< G. *Papanicolaou*, 20th-c. U.S. anatomist who developed it] a test for uterine cancer

pa·py·rus (pə pī'rəs) *n., pl.* -ri (-rī), -rus·es [< Gr. *papyros*] 1. a tall water plant of Egypt 2. a writing material made from the pith of this plant by the ancients

par (pär) *n.* [L., an equal] 1. the established value of a currency in foreign-exchange rates 2. an equal status, level, etc.: usually in phrase **on a par (with)** 3. the average state, condition, etc. [his work is above *par*] 4. the face value of stocks, etc. 5. *Golf* the number of strokes established as a skillful score for a hole or course —*adj.* 1. of or at par 2. average

par. 1. paragraph 2. parish

par·a- *a prefix meaning:* 1. beside, beyond [*parapsychology*] 2. helping in a secondary way, accessory [*paramedical*]

par·a·ble (par'ə b'l) *n.* [< Gr. *para-*, beside + *ballein*, to throw] a short, simple story teaching a moral lesson

pa·rab·o·la (pə rab'ə lə) *n.* [see prec.] *Math.* a curve formed by the intersection of a cone with a plane parallel to its side —**par·a·bol·ic** (par'ə bäl'ik) *adj.*

par·a·chute (par'ə shōōt') *n.* [Fr. < *para-*, protecting + *chute*, a fall] a large cloth contrivance, umbrella-shaped when unfolded, used to retard the speed of one dropping from an airplane, etc. —*vt., vi.* -chut'ed, -chut'ing to drop by parachute —**par'a·chut'ist** *n.*

pa·rade (pə rād') *n.* [< L. *parare*, prepare] 1. ostentatious display 2. a review of troops 3. any organized procession or march, as for display —*vt.* -rad'ed, -rad'ing 1. to march or walk through, as for display 2. to show off [to *parade* one's knowledge] —*vi.* 1. to march in a parade 2. to walk about ostentatiously

par·a·digm (par'ə dim, -dīm') *n.* [< Gr. *para-*, beside + *deigma*, example] 1. an example or model 2. *Gram.* an example of a declension or conjugation, giving all the inflections of a word

par·a·dise (par'ə dīs') *n.* [< Gr. *paradeisos*, garden] 1. [P-] the garden of Eden 2. heaven 3. any place or state of great happiness

---

fat, āpe, cär; ten, ēven; is, bīte; gō, hôrn, tōōl, look; oil, out; up, fur; chin; she; thin, *then*; zh, leisure; ŋ, ring; ə for *a* in ago; ', (ā'b'l); ë, Fr. coeur; ö, Fr. feu; Fr. mon; ü, Fr. duc; kh, G. ich, doch; ‡ foreign; < derived from

par·a·dox (par'ə däks') *n.* [< Gr. *para-*, beyond + *doxa*, opinion] 1. a statement that seems contradictory, etc. but may be true in fact 2. a statement that is self-contradictory and, hence, false —**par'a·dox'i·cal** *adj.*

par·af·fin (par'ə fin) *n.* [G. < L. *parum*, too little + *affinis*, akin: from its inertness] a white, waxy substance used for making candles, sealing jars, etc.: also **par'af·fine** (-fin, -fēn')

par·a·gon (par'ə gän', -gən) *n.* [< It. *paragone*, touchstone] a model of perfection or excellence

par·a·graph (par'ə graf') *n.* [< Gr. *para-*, beside + *graphein*, write] 1. a distinct section of a writing, begun on a new line and often indented 2. a brief item in a newspaper, etc. —*vt.* to arrange in paragraphs

Par·a·guay (par'ə gwā', -gwī') country in SC S.America: 157,042 sq. mi.; pop. 2,161,000 —**Par'a·guay'an** *adj., n.*

par·a·keet (par'ə kēt') *n.* [see PARROT] a small, slender parrot with a long, tapering tail

par·a·le·gal (par'ə lē'gəl) *adj.* designating or of persons trained to aid lawyers but not licensed to practice law —*n.* such a person

par·al·lax (par'ə laks') *n.* [< Gr. *para-*, beyond + *allassein*, to change] the apparent change in the position of an object resulting from a change in the viewer's position

par·al·lel (par'ə lel') *adj.* [< Gr. *para-*, side by side + *allēlos*, one another] 1. extending in the same direction and at a constant distance apart, so as never to meet 2. similar or corresponding —*n.* 1. a parallel line, surface, etc. 2. any person or thing similar to another; counterpart 3. any comparison showing likeness 4. any of the imaginary lines parallel to the equator and representing degrees of latitude —*vt.* -leled' or -lelled', -lel'ing or -lel'ling 1. to be parallel with [the road *parallels* the river] 2. to compare 3. to match; equal —**par'al·lel·ism** (-iz'm) *n.*

par·al·lel·o·gram' (-ə gram') *n.* a four-sided plane figure having the opposite sides parallel and equal

pa·ral·y·sis (pə ral'ə sis) *n., pl.* -ses' (-sēz') [< Gr. *para-*, beside + *lyein*, to loose] 1. partial or complete loss of voluntary motion or of sensation in part or all of the body 2. a condition of helpless inactivity —**par·a·lyt·ic** (par'ə lit'ik) *adj., n.*

par·a·lyze (par'ə līz') *vt.* -lyzed', -lyz'ing 1. to cause paralysis in 2. to make ineffective or powerless

par·a·me·ci·um (par'ə mē'shē əm, -sē-) *n., pl.* -ci·a (-ə) [< Gr. *paramēkēs*, oval] an oval freshwater protozoan that moves by means of cilia

par·a·med·i·cal (par'ə med'i k'l) *adj.* [PARA- + MEDICAL] of auxiliary medical personnel, as midwives, aidmen, nurses' aides, etc.

pa·ram·e·ter (pə ram'ə tər) *n.* [< Gr. *para-*, beside + *metron*, a measure] a constant with variable values

par·a·mil·i·tar·y (par'ə mil'ə ter'ē) *adj.* [PARA- + MILITARY] of a private quasimilitary organization

par·a·mount (par'ə mount') *adj.* [< OFr. *par*, by + *amont*, uphill] ranking higher than any other; chief

par·a·mour (par'ə moor') *n.* [< OFr. *par amour*, with love] a lover or mistress in an illicit relation

par·a·noi·a (par'ə noi'ə) *n.* [< Gr. *para-*, beside + *nous*, the mind] a mental disorder characterized by delusions, as of grandeur or, esp., persecution —**par'a·noid'** *adj., n.*

par·a·pet (par'ə pit, -pet') *n.* [< It. *parare*, to guard + *petto*, breast] 1. a wall or bank for screening troops from enemy fire 2. a low wall or railing

par·a·pher·na·lia (par'ə fər nāl'yə) *n.pl.* [often with sing. *v.*] [< Gr. *para-*, beyond + *phernē*, dowry] 1. personal belongings 2. equipment

par·a·phrase (par'ə frāz') *n.* [< Gr. *para-*, beyond + *phrazein*, say] a rewording of the meaning of something spoken or written —*vt., vi.* -phrased', -phras'ing to express in a paraphrase

par·a·ple·gi·a (par'ə plē'jē ə) *n.* [< Gr. *para-*, beside + *plēgē*, a stroke] paralysis of the lower half of the body —**par'a·pleg'ic** (-plē'jik) *adj., n.*

par'a·pro·fes'sion·al *n.* [see PARA-] a trained assistant to licensed professionals, as in medicine or education

par'a·psy·chol'o·gy (-sī käl'ə jē) *n.* [see PARA-] psychology dealing with psychic phenomena such as telepathy

par·a·site (par'ə sīt') *n.* [< Gr. *para-*, beside + *sitos*, food] 1. one who lives at others' expense without making any useful return 2. a plant or animal that lives on or within another —**par'a·sit'ic** (-sit'ik) *adj.*

par·a·sol (par'ə sôl') *n.* [< It. *parare*, ward off + *sole*, sun] a lightweight umbrella used as a sunshade

par·a·thi·on (par'ə thī'än) *n.* [< PARA- + *theion*, sulfur] a highly poisonous insecticide

par'a·thy'roid (-thī'roid) *adj.* [see PARA-] designating or of the small glands near the thyroid that regulate calcium and phosphorus metabolism

par·a·troops (par'ə trōōps') *n.pl.* [PARA(CHUTE) + TROOP] troops trained and equipped to parachute into a combat area —**par'a·troop'er** *n.*

par·boil (pär'boil') *vt.* [< L. *per*, through + *bullire*, to boil: infl. by *part*] to boil until partly cooked

par·cel (pär's'l) *n.* [see PARTICLE] 1. a small bundle; package 2. a piece (of land) —*vt.* -celed or -celled, -cel·ing or -cel·ling to divide into parts and distribute (with *out*)

parcel post a mail service for parcels of a specified weight and size

parch (pärch) *vt.* [< ?] 1. to expose to great heat so as to dry or roast 2. to make very thirsty —*vi.* to become very dry and hot

parch·ment (pärch'mənt) *n.* [< L. (*charta*) *Pergamenum*, (paper) of Pergamum, city in Asia Minor] 1. the skin of a sheep, goat, etc. prepared as a surface for writing 2. paper like parchment 3. a manuscript on this

par·don (pär′d'n) *vt.* [< L. *per-*, through + *donare*, give] 1. to release from further punishment 2. to forgive (an offense) 3. to excuse (a person) for a fault, etc. —*n.* 1. forgiveness 2. an official document granting a pardon — **par′don·a·ble** *adj.* —**par′don·er** *n.*

pare (per) *vt.* pared, par′ing [< L. *parare*, prepare] 1. to cut or trim away (the rind, skin, etc.) of; peel 2. to reduce gradually (often with *down*)

par·e·gor·ic (par′ə gôr′ik) *n.* [< Gr. *parēgoros*, soothing] a tincture of opium, used to relieve diarrhea

par·ent (per′ənt) *n.* [< L. *parere*, beget] 1. a father or mother 2. any organism in relation to its offspring 3. a source; origin —**pa·ren·tal** (pə ren′t'l) *adj.* —**par′ent·hood′** *n.*

par′ent·age (-ij) *n.* descent from parents or ancestors; lineage

pa·ren·the·sis (pə ren′thə sis) *n., pl.* -**ses′** (-sēz′) [< Gr. *para-*, beside + *entithenai*, insert] 1. a word, clause, etc. added as an explanation or comment within a sentence 2. either of the curved lines ( ) used to set this off — **par·en·thet·i·cal** (par′ən thet′i k'l), **par′en·thet′ic** *adj.*

par′ent·ing (-iŋ) *n.* the work of a parent in raising a child or children

pa·re·sis (pə rē′sis) *n.* [Gr. < *parienai*, relax] 1. partial paralysis 2. a brain disease caused by syphilis of the central nervous system

par·fait (pär fā′) *n.* [Fr., perfect] a frozen dessert of rich cream and eggs, or ice cream, syrup, fruit, etc.

pa·ri·ah (pə rī′ə) *n.* [Tamil *paṟaiyan*] 1. a member of one of the lowest social castes in India 2. any outcast

par·i·mu·tu·el (par′ə myo͞o′cho͞o wəl) *n.* [Fr., lit., a mutual bet] a system of betting on races in which the winning bettors share the net of each pool in proportion to their wagers

par·ing (per′iŋ) *n.* a piece pared off

Par·is¹ (par′is) *Gr. Legend* a prince of Troy: see HELEN OF TROY

Par·is² (par′is; *Fr.* pä′rē′) capital of France: pop. 2,790,000 —**Pa·ri·sian** (pə rizh′ən, -rē′zhən) *adj., n.*

par·ish (par′ish) *n.* [< LGr. *paroikia*, diocese] 1. a part of a diocese, under the charge of a priest or minister 2. the congregation of a church 3. a civil division in Louisiana, like a county

pa·rish·ion·er (pə rish′ə nər) *n.* a member of a parish

par·i·ty (par′ə tē) *n.* [< L. *par*, equal] 1. equality in power, value, etc. 2. equality of value at a given ratio between different kinds of money, etc.

park (pärk) *n.* [< ML. *parricus*] 1. wooded land held as part of an estate or preserve 2. an area of public land, with playgrounds, etc. for recreation —*vt., vi.* 1. to leave (a vehicle) in a certain place temporarily 2. to maneu-

ver (a vehicle) into a parking space

par·ka (pär′kə) *n.* [Aleutian < Russ., fur coat] a heavy, hooded jacket

parking meter a coin-operated device for indicating the amount of time a parking space may be occupied

Par·kin·son's disease (pär′kin sənz) [< J. *Parkinson* (1755-1824), Eng. physician] a degenerative disease of later life, causing rhythmic tremor and muscular rigidity

Parkinson's Law [stated by C. *Parkinson* (1909-), Brit. economist] a parody of economic laws, such as that work expands to fill the allotted time

park′way′ *n.* a broad roadway landscaped with trees, bushes, etc.

par·lance (pär′ləns) *n.* [< OFr. *parler*, speak] language or idiom

par·lay (pär′lā, -lē; *for v. also* pär lā′) *vt., vi.* [< It. *paro*, a pair] to bet (an original wager plus its winnings) on another race, etc. —*n.* a parlayed bet

par·ley (pär′lē) *vi.* [< Fr. *parler*, speak] to confer, esp. with an enemy —*n., pl.* -**leys** a conference, as to settle a dispute or discuss terms

par·lia·ment (pär′lə mənt) *n.* [< OFr. *parler*, speak] 1. an official government council 2. [P-] the national legislative body of certain countries, esp. Great Britain

par·lia·men·tar·i·an (-men ter′ē ən) *n.* one skilled in parliamentary rules

par·lia·men·ta·ry (-men′tər ē) *adj.* 1. of or by a parliament 2. conforming to the rules of a parliament

par·lor (pär′lər) *n.* [< OFr. *parler*, speak] 1. a living room 2. any of certain business establishments [a beauty *parlor*] Brit. sp. **par·lour**

Par·me·san (cheese) (pär′mə zän′) [< *Parma*, an It. city] a very hard, dry Italian cheese, usually grated

pa·ro·chi·al (pə rō′kē əl) *adj.* [see PARISH] 1. of or in a parish or parishes 2. narrow in scope; provincial

parochial school a school supported and controlled by a church

par·o·dy (par′ə dē) *n., pl.* -**dies** [< Gr. *para-*, beside + *ōidē*, song] a farcical imitation of a literary or musical work or style —*vt.* -**died**, -**dy·ing** to make a parody of

pa·role (pə rōl′) *n.* [< LL. *parabola*, a speech] the release of a prisoner before his sentence has expired, on condition of future good behavior —*vt.* -**roled′**, -**rol′ing** to release on parole

par·ox·ysm (par′ək siz′m) *n.* [< Gr. *para-*, beyond + *oxynein*, sharpen] 1. a sudden attack of a disease 2. a sudden outburst, as of laughter

par·quet (pär kā′) *n.* [Fr. < MFr. *parc*, a park] 1. the main floor of a theater: usually called *orchestra* 2. a flooring of parquetry —*vt.* -**queted′** (-kād′), -**quet′ing** (-kā′iŋ) to make of parquetry

parquet circle the part of a theater below the balcony and behind the parquet

---

par·quet·ry (pär′kə trē) *n.* inlaid flooring in geometric forms

par·ri·cide (par′ə sīd′) *n.* [< L. *paricida*: see -CIDE] 1. one who murders his parent, close relative, etc. 2. the act of a parricide

par·rot (par′ət) *n.* [Fr. *perrot*] 1. a bird with a hooked bill and brightly colored feathers: some parrots can learn to imitate speech 2. one who parrots what others say —*vt.* to repeat without understanding

par·ry (par′ē) *vt.* -ried, -ry·ing [< L. *parare*, prepare] 1. to ward off (a blow, etc.) 2. to evade (a question, etc.) —*n.*, *pl.* -ries a parrying

parse (pärs) *vt.* parsed, pars′ing [< L. *pars* (*orationis*), part (of speech)] to break (a sentence) down, giving the form and function of each part

par·si·mo·ny (pär′sə mō′nē) *n.* [< L. *parcere*, to spare] stinginess; extreme frugality —**par′si·mo′ni·ous** *adj.*

pars·ley (pärs′lē) *n.* [< Gr. *petros*, a rock + *selinon*, celery] a plant with aromatic, often curled leaves used to flavor or garnish some foods

pars·nip (pärs′nip) *n.* [< L. *pastinare*, dig up] 1. a plant with a long, white root used as a vegetable 2. this root

par·son (pär′s'n) *n.* [see PERSON] a clergyman, esp. one having a parish

par′son·age (-ij) *n.* the dwelling provided for a parson by his church

part (pärt) *n.* [< L. *pars*] 1. a portion, segment, or a whole [a *part* of a book] 2. an essential, separable element [automobile *parts*] 3. a portion or share; specif., *a)* duty [to do one's *part*] *b)* [*usually pl.*] talent; ability [a man of *parts*] *c)* a role in a play *d)* any of the voices or instruments in a musical ensemble, or the score for this 4. a region; esp., [*usually pl.*], a district 5. one of the sides in a conflict, etc. 6. a dividing line formed in combing the hair —*vt.* 1. to break or divide into parts 2. to comb (the hair) so as to leave a part 3. to break or hold apart —*vi.* 1. to break or divide into parts 2. to separate and go different ways 3. to cease associating 4. to go away; leave (with *from*) —*adj.* partial —**for one's part** so far as one is concerned —**for the most part** mostly —**in part** partly —**part with** to relinquish —**take part** to participate

par·take (pär tāk′) *vi.* -took′, -tak′-en, -tak′ing [< *part taker*] 1. to participate (*in* an activity) 2. to eat or drink something, esp. with others (usually with *of*)

part·ed (pär′tid) *adj.* separated

par·terre (pär ter′) *n.* [Fr. < *par*, on + *terre*, earth] 1. a garden with beds and path in a pattern 2. same as PARQUET CIRCLE

par·the·no·gen·e·sis (pär′thə nō jen′ə sis) *n.* [see ff. & GENESIS] reproduction from an unfertilized ovum, seed, or spore

Par′the·non′ (-nän′) [< Gr. *parthenos*, a virgin (i.e., Athena)] the Doric temple of Athena on the Acropolis

par·tial (pär′shəl) *adj.* [< L. *pars*, a part] 1. favoring one person, faction,

etc. more than another; biased 2. not complete —**partial to** fond of —**par′ti·al′i·ty** (-shē al′ə tē) *n.* —**par′tial·ly** *adv.*

par·tic·i·pate (pär tis′ə pāt′) *vi.* -pat′ed, -pat′ing [< L. *pars*, a part + *capere*, take] to have or take a share with others (in some activity) —**par·tic′i·pant** *adj.*, *n.* —**par·tic′i·pa·tion** *n.* —**par·tic′i·pa·tor** *n.* —**par·tic′i·pa·to′ry** (-pə tôr′ē) *adj.*

par·ti·ci·ple (pär′tə sip′'l) *n.* [see prec.] a verbal form having the qualities of both verb and adjective —**par′ti·cip′i·al** (-sip′ē əl) *adj.*

par·ti·cle (pär′ti k'l) *n.* [< L. *pars*, part] 1. a tiny fragment or trace 2. a short, invariable part of speech, as an article, preposition, etc.

par·ti-col·ored (pär′tē kul′ərd) *adj.* [< Fr. *parti*, divided + COLORED] having different colors in different parts

par·tic·u·lar (pər tik′yə lər) *adj.* [see PARTICLE] 1. of or belonging to a single group, person, or thing 2. regarded separately; specific 3. unusual 4. exacting; fastidious —*n.* a distinct fact, item, detail, etc. —**in particular** especially —**par·tic′u·lar′i·ty** (-lar′ə tē) *n.*, *pl.* -ties

par·tic′u·lar·ize′ (-lə rīz′) *vt.*, *vi.* -ized′, -iz′ing to give particulars or details (of); specify

par·tic′u·lar·ly *adv.* 1. in detail 2. especially 3. specifically

par·tic′u·late (-lit, -lāt′) *adj.* of or formed of tiny, separate particles

part′ing *adj.* 1. dividing; separating 2. departing 3. given, spoken, etc. at parting —*n.* 1. a breaking or separating 2. a departure

par·ti·san (pärt′ə z'n) *n.* [< L. *pars*, a part] 1. a strong supporter of a faction, party, etc. 2. a guerrilla fighter —*adj.* of or like a partisan Also **partizan** —**par′ti·san·ship′** *n.*

par·ti·tion (pär tish′ən) *n.* [< L. *partitio*] 1. division into parts 2. something that divides, as a wall separating rooms —*vt.* 1. to divide into parts; apportion 2. to divide by a partition

part′ly *adv.* not fully or completely

part·ner (pärt′nər) *n.* [< ME.] 1. one who joins in an activity with another or others; specif., one of two or more persons owning jointly a business 2. a spouse 3. either of two persons dancing together 4. a player on the same team —**part′ner·ship′** *n.*

part of speech any of the classes to which words can be assigned by form, function, etc., as noun, verb, etc.

par·tridge (pär′trij) *n.* [< Gr. *perdix*] any of several game birds, as the grouse, pheasant, etc.

part song a song for several voices, usually without accompaniment

part′-time′ *adj.* of a period of work, study, etc. for less than the usual time

PARTRIDGE

par·tu·ri·tion (pär'choo rish'ən) n. [< L. *parere*, to bear] childbirth

part'way' adv. to a degree but not fully

par·ty (pär'tē) n., pl. **-ties** [< L. *pars*, a part] 1. a group of people working to promote a political platform or slate, a cause, etc. 2. a group acting together to accomplish a task 3. a gathering for social entertainment 4. one concerned in an action, plan, lawsuit, etc. [a *party* to the action] 5. [Colloq.] a person —vi. **-tied, -ty·ing** to attend social parties —vt. to give a party for

party line 1. a single circuit connecting two or more telephone users with the exchange 2. the policies of a political party

par·ve·nu (pär'və nōō') n. [< L. *pervenire*, arrive] a newly rich person considered an upstart

Pas·a·de·na (pas'ə dē'nə) city in SW Calif.: pop. 119,000

pas·chal (pas'k'l) adj. [< LL. < Gr. < Heb. *pesaḥ*, Passover] 1. of Passover 2. of Easter

pa·sha (pə shä', pä'shə) n. [Turk.] formerly, in Turkey, a title of rank or honor placed after the name

pass (pas) vi. [< L. *passus*, a step] 1. to go or move forward, through, etc. 2. to go or be conveyed from one place, form, condition, etc. to another 3. a) to cease b) to depart 4. to die (usually with *away, on,* or *out*) 5. to go by 6. to elapse [an hour *passed*] 7. to make a way (*through* or *by*) 8. to be accepted without question 9. to be approved, as by a legislative body 10. to go through a test, course, etc. successfully 11. to give a judgment, sentence, etc. 12. *Card Games* to decline a chance to bid —vt. 1. to go by, beyond, over, or through; specif., a) to leave behind b) to go through (a test, course, etc.) successfully 2. to cause or allow to go, move, or proceed; specif., a) to ratify; enact b) to spend (time) c) to excrete 3. to cause to move from place to place; circulate 4. to give (an opinion or judgment) —n. 1. an act of passing; passage 2. a state; situation [a strange *pass*] 3. a) a ticket, etc. giving permission to come or go freely or without charge b) *Mil.* a brief leave of absence 4. a motion of the hands 5. a tentative attempt 6. a narrow passage, etc., esp. between mountains 7. [Slang] an over-familiar attempt to embrace or kiss 8. *Sports* a transfer of a ball, etc. to another player during play —**come (or bring) to pass** to (cause to) happen —**pass for** to be accepted as —**pass off** to cause to be accepted through deceit —**pass out** 1. to distribute 2. to faint —**pass over** to disregard; ignore —**pass up** [Colloq.] to refuse or let go by —**pass'er** n.

pass'a·ble adj. 1. that can be passed, traveled over, etc. 2. adequate; fair —**pass'a·bly** adv.

pas·sage (pas'ij) n. 1. a passing; specif., a) migration b) transition c) the enactment of a law 2. permission or right to pass 3. a voyage 4. a means of passing; road, passageway, etc. 5. an exchange, as of blows 6. a portion of a book, composition, etc.

pas'sage·way' n. a narrow way for passage, as a hall, alley, etc.

pass'book' n. same as BANKBOOK

pas·sé (pa sā') adj. [Fr., past] 1. out-of-date; old-fashioned 2. rather old

pas·sel (pas''l) n. [< PARCEL] [Colloq.] a group, esp. a fairly large one

pas·sen·ger (pas''n jər) n. [< OFr. *passage*, passage] a person traveling in a train, boat, etc.

pass'er-by' n., pl. **pass'ers-by'** one who passes by

pass'ing adj. 1. going by, beyond, etc. 2. fleeting 3. casual [a *passing* remark] 4. satisfying given requirements [a *passing* grade] 5. current —n. the act of one that passes; specif., death —**in passing** incidentally

pas·sion (pash'ən) n. [< L. *pati, endure*] 1. [P-] the sufferings of Jesus on the cross or after the Last Supper 2. any emotion, as hate, love, etc. 3. intense emotional excitement, as rage, enthusiasm, lust, etc. 4. the object of any strong desire

pas·sion·ate (-it) adj. 1. having or showing strong feelings 2. hot-tempered 3. ardent; intense 4. sensual —**pas'sion·ate·ly** adv.

pas·sive (pas'iv) adj. [see PASSION] 1. inactive, but acted upon 2. offering no resistance; submissive 3. *Gram.* denoting the voice of a verb whose subject receives the action —**pas'sive·ly** adv. —**pas·siv'i·ty** n.

passive resistance opposition to a law, tax, etc. by refusal to comply or by nonviolent acts, as fasting

pass'key' n. 1. a key that fits a number of locks 2. one's own key to something

Pass·o·ver (pas'ō'vər) n. a holiday for Jews, celebrating their deliverance from slavery in ancient Egypt

pass'port' n. a government document carried by a citizen traveling abroad, certifying identity and citizenship

pass'word' n. 1. a secret term used for identification, as in passing a guard 2. any means of admission

past (past) *rare pp.* of PASS —adj. 1. gone by; ended 2. of a former time 3. immediately preceding 4. *Gram.* indicating a time gone by [the *past* tense] —n. 1. time gone by 2. the history of a person, group, etc. 3. a personal background that is hidden or questionable —prep. beyond in time, space, amount, etc. —adv. to and beyond

pas·ta (päs'tə) n. [It.] 1. the flour paste of which spaghetti, etc. is made 2. any food made of this paste

paste (pāst) n. [< Gr. *pastē*, porridge] 1. dough for making rich pastry 2. any soft, moist, smooth preparation [tooth-

paste] 3. a mixture of flour, water, etc. used as an adhesive 4. the hard, brilliant glass of artificial gems —*vt.* **past'ed, past'ing** 1. to make adhere, as with paste 2. [Slang] to hit

paste'board' *n.* a stiff material made of layers of paper pasted together

pas·tel (pas tel') *n.* [< LL. *pasta,* paste] 1. a crayon of ground coloring matter 2. a picture drawn with such crayons 3. a soft, pale shade of color

Pas·teur (pas tur'), **Louis** 1822–95; Fr. bacteriologist & chemist

pas·teur·ize (pas'chə rīz', -tə-) *vt.* **-ized', -iz'ing** [< prec.] to destroy bacteria in (milk, etc.) by heating to a prescribed temperature for a specified time —**pas'teur·i·za'tion** *n.*

pas·tiche (pas tēsh') *n.* [Fr.] 1. an artistic composition drawn from various sources 2. a hodgepodge

pas·time (pas'tīm') *n.* a way of spending spare time; diversion

past master a person of long experience in an occupation, art, etc.; expert

pas·tor (pas'tər) *n.* [L., a shepherd] a clergyman in charge of a congregation —**pas'tor·ate** (-it) *n.*

pas'to·ral *adj.* 1. of a pastor or his duties 2. of shepherds 3. of rustic life 4. peaceful; simple

past participle a participle used: a) to signify a past time or state (as *gone* in "he has gone") b) as an adjective (as *grown* in "a grown man")

pas·tra·mi (pə strä'mē) *n.* [Vid. < Romanian] highly spiced, smoked beef

pas·try (pās'trē) *n., pl.* **-tries** [see PASTE] 1. pies, tarts, etc. with crusts baked from flour dough made with shortening 2. all fancy baked goods

pas'tur·age (-ij) *n. same as* PASTURE

pas·ture (pas'chər) *n.* [< L. *pascere,* to feed] 1. grass, etc. used as food by grazing animals 2. ground suitable for grazing —*vt.* **-tured, -tur·ing** to put (cattle, etc.) out to graze in a pasture

past·y (pās'tē) *adj.* **-i·er, -i·est** of or like paste in color or texture

pat (pat) *n.* [prob. echoic] 1. a gentle tap or stroke with a flat surface 2. a sound made by this 3. a small lump, as of butter —*vt.* **pat'ted, pat'ting** 1. to tap or stroke gently with the hand or a flat surface 2. to shape or apply by patting —*adj.* 1. exactly suitable [a *pat* hand in poker] 2. so glib as to seem contrived —**pat on the back** 1. a compliment 2. to praise —**stand pat** to refuse to change an opinion, etc.

pat. 1. patent 2. patented

patch (pach) *n.* [ME. *pacche*] 1. a piece of material applied to mend a hole or strengthen a weak spot 2. a bandage 3. an area or spot [*patches* of blue sky] 4. a small plot of land 5. a scrap; bit —*vt.* 1. to put a patch on 2. to produce crudely or hurriedly — **patch up** to settle (a quarrel, etc.)

patch'work' *n.* needlework, as a quilt, made of odd patches of cloth

patch'y *adj.* **-i·er, -i·est** 1. made up of patches 2. not consistent or uniform; irregular —**patch'i·ness** *n.*

pate (pāt) *n.* [< ?] the top of the head: a humorous term

pâ·té (pä tā') *n.* [Fr.] a meat paste

pa·tel·la (pə tel'ə) *n., pl.* **-las, -lae** (-ē) [L., a pan] *same as* KNEECAP

pat·ent (pat''nt; *also for adj. 1 & 2,* pāt'-) *adj.* [< L. *patere,* be open] 1. open to all 2. obvious; plain 3. protected by a patent —*n.* 1. a document granting the exclusive right to produce or sell an invention, etc. for a certain time 2. *a)* the right so granted *b)* the thing protected by such a right —*vt.* to secure a patent for

patent leather leather with a hard, glossy finish: formerly patented

patent medicine a trademarked medical preparation

pa·ter·nal (pə tur'n'l) *adj.* [< L. *pater,* father] 1. fatherly 2. inherited from a father 3. on the father's side

pa·ter'nal·ism *n.* the governing of subjects, employees, etc. in a manner suggesting a father's relationship with his children —**pa·ter'nal·is'tic** *adj.*

pa·ter'ni·ty (-nə tē) *n.* 1. the state of being a father 2. male parentage

pa·ter·nos·ter (pāt'ər nôs'tər, pät'-) *n.* [L., our father] the Lord's Prayer, esp. in Latin: often **Pater Noster**

Pat·er·son (pat'ər s'n) city in NE N.J.: pop. 138,000

path (path) *n.* [OE. *pæth*] 1. a way worn by footsteps 2. a walk for the use of people on foot 3. a line of movement 4. a course of conduct, thought, etc. —**path'less** *adj.*

path. 1. pathological 2. pathology

pa·thet·ic (pə thet'ik) *adj.* [see PATHOS] 1. arousing pity, sorrow, etc.; pitiful 2. pitifully unsuccessful, etc. —**pa·thet'i·cal·ly** *adv.*

path·o·gen·ic (path'ə jen'ik) *adj.* producing disease

pa·thol·o·gy (pə thäl'ə jē) *n.* [< Gr. *pathos,* suffering + -LOGY] 1. the branch of medicine that deals with the nature of disease, esp. with structural and functional effects 2. any abnormal variation from a sound condition — **path·o·log·i·cal** (path'ə läj'i k'l) *adj.* —**pa·thol'o·gist** *n.*

pa·thos (pā'thäs) *n.* [Gr., suffering] the quality in something which arouses pity, sorrow, sympathy, etc.

path'way' *n. same as* PATH

-pa·thy (pə thē) [< Gr. *pathos,* suffering] *a combining form meaning:* 1. feeling [*telepathy*] 2. disease [*osteopathy*] —**-path·ic** (path'ik)

pa·tience (pā'shəns) *n.* a being patient; calm endurance

pa'tient (-shənt) *adj.* [< L. *pati,* endure] 1. enduring pain, trouble, etc. without complaining 2. calmly tolerating delay, confusion, etc. 3. diligent; persevering —*n.* one receiving medical care —**pa'tient·ly** *adv.*

pat·i·na (pat''n ə, pə tē'nə) *n.* [Fr. < It.] a fine greenish crust on bronze or copper, formed by oxidation

pa·ti·o (pat'ē ō', pät'-) *n., pl.* **-os'** [Sp.] 1. a courtyard open to the sky 2. a paved area adjoining a house, for outdoor lounging, dining, etc.

pat·ois (pat'wä) *n., pl.* **-ois** (-wäz) [Fr.] a provincial dialect

pat. pend. patent pending

patri- [< Gr. *patēr*] *a combining form meaning* father

pa·tri·arch (pā'trē ärk') *n.* [< Gr. *patēr*, father + *archein*, rule] 1. the father and head of a family or tribe, as Abraham, Isaac, or Jacob in the Bible 2. a man of great age and dignity 3. a 'high-ranking bishop, as in the Orthodox Eastern Church —**pa'tri·ar'chal** *adj.*

pa'tri·ar'chate (-är'kit, -kāt) *n.* the rank, jurisdiction, etc. of a patriarch

pa'tri·ar'chy (-kē) *n., pl.* **-chies** 1. a social organization in which the father is head of the family, descent being traced through the male line 2. rule or domination by men

pa·tri·cian (pə trish'ən) *n.* [< L. *pater*, father] an aristocrat

pat·ri·mo·ny (pat'rə mō'nē) *n., pl.* **-nies** [< L. *pater*, father] property inherited from one's father or ancestors —**pat'ri·mo'ni·al** *adj.*

pa·tri·ot (pā'trē ət) *n.* [< Gr. *patris*, fatherland] one who loves and zealously supports his country —**pa'tri·ot'ic** (-ät'ik) *adj.* —**pa'tri·ot'i·cal·ly** *adv.* —**pa'tri·ot·ism** *n.*

pa·trol (pə trōl') *vt., vi.* **-trolled', -trol'ling** [Fr. *patrouiller*] to make a regular, repeated circuit (of) in guarding —*n.* 1. a patrolling 2. a person or group patrolling

pa·trol'man (-mən) *n., pl.* **-men** a policeman who patrols a certain area

patrol wagon an enclosed truck used by police to carry prisoners

pa·tron (pā'trən) *n.* [< L. *pater*, father] 1. a protector; benefactor 2. one who sponsors and supports some person, activity, etc. 3. a regular customer —**pa'tron·ess** *n.fem.*

pa·tron·age (pā'trən ij, pat'rən-) *n.* 1. support, encouragement, etc. given by a patron 2. *a)* clientele *b)* business; trade 3. *a)* the power to grant political favors *b)* such favors

pa·tron·ize (pā'trə nīz', pat'rə-) *vt.* **-ized', -iz'ing** 1. to sponsor; support 2. to treat in a condescending manner 3. to be a regular customer of

patron saint a saint looked upon as a special guardian

pat·ro·nym·ic (pat'rə nim'ik) *n.* [< Gr. *patēr*, father + *onyma*, name] a name showing descent from a given person (e.g., *Johnson*, son of *John*)

pat·sy (pat'sē) *n., pl.* **-sies** [Slang] a person easily imposed upon

pat·ter¹ (pat'ər) *vi.* [< PAT] to make, or move so as to make, a patter —*n.* a series of quick, light taps

pat·ter² (pat'ər) *vt., vi.* [< PATERNOSTER] to speak rapidly or glibly —*n.* glib, rapid speech, as of salesmen

pat·tern (pat'ərn) *n.* [< OFr. *patron*] 1. a person or thing worthy of imitation 2. a model or plan used in making things 3. a design 4. a regular way of acting or doing 5. a predictable route, movement, etc. —*vt.* to make or do in imitation of a pattern

pat·ty (pat'ē) *n., pl.* **-ties** [Fr. *pâté*, pie] 1. a small pie 2. a small, flat cake of ground meat, fish, etc., usually fried

patty shell a pastry shell for a single portion of creamed food, etc.

pau·ci·ty (pô'sə tē) *n.* [< L. *paucus*, few] 1. fewness 2. scarcity

Paul (pôl), Saint ?-67? A.D.; an early Christian apostle: author of several Epistles in the New Testament

Paul Bun·yan (bun'yən) *American Folklore* a giant lumberjack who performed superhuman feats

paunch (pônch) *n.* [< L. *pantex*, belly] the abdomen, or belly; esp., a potbelly —**paunch'y** *adj.*

pau·per (pô'pər) *n.* [L.] an extremely poor person, esp. one who lives on charity —**pau'per·ism** *n.* —**pau'per·ize'** *vt.* **-ized', -iz'ing**

pause (pôz) *n.* [< Gr. *pauein*, to stop] a temporary stop or rest —*vi.* **paused', paus'ing** to make a pause; stop

pave (pāv) *vt.* **paved, pav'ing** [< L. *pavire*, beat] to cover the surface of (a road, etc.) as with concrete —**pave the way** (for) to prepare the way (for)

pave'ment *n.* a paved surface, as of concrete; specif., a paved road, etc.

pa·vil·ion (pə vil'yən) *n.* [< L. *papilio*, tent] 1. a large tent 2. a building, often partly open, for exhibits, etc., as at a fair or park 3. any of a group of related buildings

pav·ing (pā'viŋ) *n.* a pavement

Pav·lov (pav'lôv, pəv'-), **I·van** (i vän') 1849-1936; Russ. physiologist

paw (pô) *n.* [< OFr. *poue*] 1. the foot of a four-footed animal having claws 2. [Colloq.] a hand —*vt., vi.* 1. to touch, dig, hit, etc. with paws or feet 2. to handle clumsily or roughly

pawl (pôl) *n.* [< ?] a device, as a hinged tongue which engages cogs in a wheel, allowing rotation in only one direction

pawn¹ (pôn) *n.* [< MFr. *pan*] 1. anything given as security, as for a debt 2. the state of being pledged —*vt.* 1. to give as security 2. to wager or risk

PAWL

pawn² (pôn) *n.* [ML. *pedo*, foot soldier] 1. a chessman of the lowest value 2. a person used to advance another's purposes

pawn'bro·ker *n.* a person licensed to lend money at interest on personal property left with him as security

pawn'shop' *n.* a pawnbroker's shop

paw·paw (pô'pô') *n. same as* PAPAW

pay (pā) *vt.* **paid, pay'ing** [< L. *pacare*, pacify] 1. to give to (a person) what is due, as for goods or services 2. to give (what is due) in return, as for goods or services 3. to settle (a debt, etc.) 4. *a)* to give (a compliment, attention, etc.) *b)* to make (a visit, etc.) 5. to be profitable to —*vi.* 1. to give due compensation 2. to be profitable —*n.* money paid; esp., wages or salary —*adj.* 1. operated by inserting money *[a pay phone]* 2. designating a service, etc. paid for by fees *[pay TV]* —**in the pay of** employed and paid by —**pay back** 1. to repay 2. to retaliate upon —**pay down** to pay (part of the price) at purchase as an installment —**pay for** to suffer or atone for (a wrong) —**pay off** to pay all that is owed —**pay out** (pt. **payed out**) to let out (a rope, cable, etc.) —**pay up** to pay in full or on time —**pay′er** *n.*

pay′a·ble *adj.* 1. that can be paid 2. due to be paid (on a specified date)

pay′check′ *n.* a check in payment of wages or salary

pay′day′ *n.* the day on which wages or salary is paid

pay·ee (pā ē′) *n.* one to whom a check, note, money, etc. is payable

pay′load′ *n.* 1. a cargo 2. the warhead of a ballistic missile 3. a spacecraft, communications satellite, etc. launched by a rocket

pay′mas·ter *n.* the official in charge of paying employees

pay′ment *n.* 1. a paying or being paid 2. something paid

pay′off′ *n.* 1. settlement, reckoning, or payment 2. [Colloq.] a bribe 3. [Colloq.] an unexpected climax

pay phone (or **station**) a public telephone, usually coin-operated

pay′roll′ *n.* 1. a list of employees to be paid, with the amount due to each 2. the total amount needed for this

Pb [L. *plumbum*] *Chem.* lead

PBX, P.B.X. [< *P(rivate) b(ranch) ex(change)*] a telephone system within an organization, having outside lines

P.C. personal computer

pct. percent

pd. paid

pea (pē) *n., pl.* **peas,** archaic **pease** [< ME. *pese,* a pea, mistaken as pl.; ult. < Gr.] 1. a climbing plant with green pods 2. its small, round seed, used as a vegetable

peace (pēs) *n.* [< L. *pax*] 1. freedom from war 2. an agreement to end war 3. law and order 4. harmony; concord 5. serenity, calm, or quiet —**hold** (or **keep**) **one's peace** to be silent —**peace′a·ble** *adj.*

peace′ful *adj.* 1. not quarrelsome 2. free from disturbance; calm 3. of or in a time of peace —**peace′ful·ly** *adv.*

peace′mak′er *n.* a person who makes peace, as by settling disagreements or quarrels —**peace′mak′ing** *n., adj.*

peace officer an officer entrusted with maintaining law and order

peace pipe *same as* CALUMET

peace′time′ *n.* a time of peace —*adj.* of or characteristic of such a time

peach (pēch) *n.* [< L. *Persicum (malum),* Persian (apple)] 1. a tree with round, juicy, orange-yellow fruit having a fuzzy skin and a rough pit 2. its fruit 3. the color of this fruit 4. [Slang] a well-liked person or thing

pea·cock (pē′käk′) *n.* [< L. *pavo,* peacock] the male of a pheasantlike bird (**pea′fowl′**), with a long, showy

tail which can be spread out like a fan —**pea′hen′** *n.fem.*

pea jacket [< Du. *pijjekker*] a hiplength, double-breasted coat of heavy woolen cloth, worn by seamen

peak (pēk) *n.* [ult. < PIKE²] 1. a pointed end or top, as of a cap, roof, etc. 2. *a*) the summit of a hill or mountain ending in a point   *b*) a mountain with such a summit 3. the highest or utmost point of anything —*vi., vt.* to come or bring to a peak

peak·ed (pē′kid) *adj.* [< ?] thin and drawn, as from illness

peal· (pēl) *n.* [ME. *apele,* appeal] 1. the loud ringing of a bell or bells 2. a set of bells 3. a loud, prolonged sound, as of thunder, laughter, etc. —*vi., vt.* to sound in a peal; ring

pea′nut′ *n.* 1. a vine of the legume family, with underground pods containing edible seeds 2. the pod or any of its seeds 3. [*pl.*] [Slang] a trifling sum

peanut butter a food paste or spread made by grinding roasted peanuts

pear (per) *n.* [< L. *pirum*] 1. a tree with greenish-yellow or brownish fruit 2. the juicy fruit, round at the base and narrowing toward the stem

pearl (purl) *n.* [< L. *perna,* sea mussel] 1. a smooth, hard, usually white or bluish-gray, roundish growth, formed within the shell of some oysters and other mollusks: it is used as a gem 2. *same as* MOTHER-OF-PEARL 3. anything pearllike in shape, beauty, value, etc. 4. a bluish gray —**pearl′y** *adj.*

Pearl Harbor inlet on the S coast of Oahu, Hawaii: site of a U.S. naval base bombed by Japan, Dec. 7, 1941

peas·ant (pez′nt) *n.* [< LL. *pagus,* district] 1. a small farmer or farm laborer, as in Europe or Asia 2. a person regarded as boorish, ignorant, etc. —**peas′ant·ry** *n.*

peat (pēt) *n.* [< ML. *peta,* piece of turf] partly decayed plant matter from ancient swamps, used for fuel

peat moss peat composed of residues of mosses, used as a mulch

peb·ble (peb′'l) *n.* [< OE. *papol-(stan),* pebble (stone)] a small stone worn smooth and round, as by running water —**peb′bly** *adj.* **-bli·er, -bli·est**

pe·can (pi kan′, -kän′; pē′kan) *n.* [< AmInd.] 1. an edible nut with a thin, smooth shell 2. the tree it grows on

pec·ca·dil·lo (pek′ə dil′ō) *n., pl.* **-loes, -los** [< Sp. < L. *peccare,* to sin] a small fault or offense

pec·ca·ry (pek′ər ē) *n.* [< SAmInd. name] a piglike animal of N. and S.America, with sharp tusks

peck¹ (pek) *vt.* [ME. *pikken,* to pick] 1. to strike (at), as with a beak 2. to make by doing this *[to peck a hole]* 3. to pick up with the beak —*vi.* 1. to make strokes as with a pointed object —*n.* 1. a stroke so made 2. [Colloq.] a quick, casual kiss —**peck at** 1. to eat very little of 2. to criticize constantly

peck² (pek) *n.* [< OFr. *pek*] a unit of dry measure, 1/4 bushel, or 8 quarts

pec·tin (pek′tin) *n.* [< Gr. *pēktos,* congealed] a carbohydrate obtained from certain fruits, which yields a gel that is the basis of jellies

pec·to·ral (pek'tər əl) *adj.* [< L. *pectus*, breast] of or located in or on the chest or breast

pec·u·late (pek'yə lāt') *vt.*, *vi.* -lat'ed, -lat'ing [< L. *peculari*] to embezzle —**pec'u·la'tion** *n.*

pe·cul·iar (pi kyōōl'yər) *adj.* [< L. *peculium*, private property] **1.** of only one person, thing, etc.; exclusive **2.** particular; special **3.** odd; strange —**pe·cul'iar·ly** *adv.*

pe·cu·li·ar·i·ty (pi kyōō'lē ar'ə tē) *n.* **1.** a being peculiar **2.** *pl.* -ties something that is peculiar, as a trait

pe·cu·ni·ar·y (pi kyōō'nē er'ē) *adj.* [< L. *pecunia*, money] of or involving money

ped·a·gogue, ped·a·gog (ped'ə gäg', -gôg') *n.* [< Gr. *pais*, child + *agein*, to lead] a teacher, esp. a pedantic one

ped'a·go'gy (-gō'jē, -gäj'ē) *n.* the art or science of teaching —**ped'a·gog'ic** (-gäj'ik), **ped'a·gog'i·cal** *adj.*

ped·al (ped''l) *adj.* [< L. *pes*, foot] of the foot or feet —*n.* a lever operated by the foot, as on a bicycle, organ, etc. —*vt.*, *vi.* -aled or -alled, -al·ing or -al·ling to operate by pedals

ped·ant (ped''nt) *n.* [ult. < Gr. *paidagōgos*, teacher] **1.** one who emphasizes trivial points of learning **2.** a narrow-minded teacher who insists on exact adherence to rules —**pe·dan·tic** (pi dan'tik) *adj.* —**ped'ant·ry** *n.*

ped·dle (ped''l) *vt.*, *vi.* -dled, -dling [< ? ME. *ped*, basket] to go from place to place selling (small articles) —**ped'dler** *n.*

-pede (pēd) [< L. *pes*] *a combining form meaning* foot *or* feet [*centipede*]

ped·er·as·ty (ped'ə ras'tē) *n.* [< Gr. *paiderastēs*, lover of boys] sodomy between males, esp. between a man and a boy —**ped'er·ast'** *n.*

ped·es·tal (ped'is t'l) *n.* [< It. *piè*, foot + *di*, of + *stal*, a rest] a bottom support or base of a pillar, statue, etc.

pe·des·tri·an (pə des'trē ən) *adj.* [< L. *pes*, foot] **1.** going or done on foot **2.** of or for pedestrians **3.** ordinary and dull; prosaic —*n.* a walker

pe·di·at·rics (pē'dē at'riks) *n.pl.* [*with sing. v.*] [< Gr. *pais*, child + *iatros*, physician] the branch of medicine dealing with the care and treatment of infants and children —**pe'di·a·tri'cian** (-ə trish'ən) *n.*

ped·i·cab (ped'i kab') *n.* [< L. *pes*, foot + CAB] a 3-wheeled carriage, esp. in SE Asia, pedaled by the driver

ped·i·cure (ped'i kyoor') *n.* [< L. *pes*, foot + *cura*, care] a trimming, cleaning, etc. of the toenails

ped·i·gree (ped'ə grē') *n.* [< MFr. *pié de grue*, lit., crane's foot: from lines in genealogical tree] **1.** a list of ancestors **2.** descent; lineage **3.** a known line of descent, esp. of a purebred animal —**ped'i·greed'** *adj.*

ped·i·ment (ped'ə mənt) *n.* [< earlier *periment*, prob. < PYRAMID] an ornamental gable or triangular piece on the front of a building, over a doorway, etc.

PEDIMENT

pe·dom·e·ter (pi däm'ə tər) *n.* [< L. *pes*, foot + Gr. *metron*, a measure] an instrument carried to measure the distance walked

pe·dun·cle (pi dun'k'l, pē'dun-) *n.* [< L. *pes*, foot] a stalklike organ or process in some plants, animals, etc.

peek (pēk) *vi.* [ME. *piken*] to look quickly and furtively —*n.* such a look

peel (pēl) *vt.* [< L. *pilare*, make bald] to cut away (the skin, rind, etc.) of —*vi.* **1.** to shed skin, etc. **2.** to come off in layers or flakes —*n.* the rind or skin of fruit

peel'ing *n.* a peeled-off strip

peen (pēn) *n.* [prob. < Scand.] the end of a hammerhead opposite the flat striking surface, usually ball-shaped (**ball peen**) or wedge-shaped

peep[1] (pēp) *vi.* [echoic] to make the short, high-pitched cry of a young bird —*n.* a peeping sound

peep[2] (pēp) *vi.* [ME. *pepen*] **1.** to look through a small opening or from a place of hiding **2.** to show gradually or partially —*n.* a brief look; furtive glimpse —**peep'er** *n.*

peep'hole' *n.* a hole to peep through

peeping Tom [< legendary peeper at Lady Godiva] one who gets sexual pleasure from furtively watching others

peer[1] (pir) *n.* [< L. *par*, an equal] **1.** a person or thing of the same rank, ability, etc.; an equal **2.** a British noble —**peer'age** (-ij) *n.* —**peer'ess** *n.fem.*

peer[2] (pir) *vi.* [< ? APPEAR] **1.** to look closely, as in trying to see more clearly **2.** to show slightly

peer'less *adj.* without equal

peeve (pēv) *vt.* peeved, peev'ing to make peevish —*n.* an annoyance

pee·vish (pē'vish) *adj.* [ME. *pevische*] irritable; fretful; cross —**pee'vish·ly** *adv.* —**pee'vish·ness** *n.*

pee·wee (pē'wē') *n.* [< ?] [Colloq.] an unusually small person or thing

peg (peg) *n.* [ME. *pegge*] **1.** a short pin or bolt used to hold parts together, hang things on, etc. **2.** a step or degree **3.** [Colloq.] a throw —*vt.* pegged, peg'ging **1.** to fasten, fix, secure, mark, etc. as with pegs **2.** [Colloq.] to throw —**peg away (at)** to work steadily (at)

Peg·a·sus (peg'ə səs) *Gr. Myth.* a winged horse

peign·oir (pān'wär', pen-) *n.* [Fr.] a woman's loose, full dressing gown

Pei·ping (bā'piŋ') *former name of* PEKING

pe·jo·ra·tion (pē'jə rā'shən, pej'ə-) *n.* [< L. *pejor*, worse] a worsening —**pe·jo·ra·tive** (pi jôr'ə tiv) *adj.*

Pe·king (pē′kiŋ′; *Chin.* bā′jiŋ′) capital of China: pop. c. 4,000,000

Pe·king·ese (pē′kə nēz′) *n., pl.* -ese′ a small dog with long, silky hair, short legs, and a pug nose: also **Pe′kin·ese′**

pe·koe (pē′kō) *n.* [< Chin. *pek-ho*, white down (on the leaves used)] a black tea of Ceylon and India

pel·age (pel′ij) *n.* [Fr. < L. *pilus*, hair] a mammal's hairy or furry coat

pelf (pelf) *n.* [< ? MFr. *pelfre*, booty] money or wealth regarded with contempt

pel·i·can (pel′i kən) *n.* [< Gr. *pelekan*] a large, web-footed water bird with an expandable pouch in the lower bill for scooping up fish

pel·la·gra (pə lag′rə) *n.* [It. < *pelle*, skin + Gr. *agra*, seizure] a chronic disease caused by lack of nicotinic acid in the diet, characterized by skin eruptions and nervous disorders

pel·let (pel′ət) *n.* [< L. *pila*, a ball] 1. a little ball, as of clay or medicine 2. a bullet, small lead shot, etc.

pell-mell, pell·mell (pel′mel′) *adv., adj.* [ult. < OFr. *mesler*, to mix] 1. in a jumble 2. with reckless speed

pel·lu·cid (pə l̄oo′sid) *adj.* [< L. *per*, through + *lucere*, to shine] 1. transparent; clear 2. easy to understand

pelt¹ (pelt) *vt.* [? < L. *pillare*, to drive] 1. to throw things at 2. to beat repeatedly —*vi.* to strike heavily or steadily, as hard rain

pelt² (pelt) *n.* [prob. < OFr. *pel*, a skin] the skin of a fur-bearing animal, esp. when stripped from the carcass

pel·vis (pel′vis) *n.* [L., a basin] 1. the basinlike cavity in the posterior part of the trunk in man and many other vertebrates 2. the bones forming this cavity —**pel′vic** *adj.*

pem·mi·can (pem′i kən) *n.* [< AmInd.] a concentrated food of dried beef, suet, dried fruit, etc.

pen¹ (pen) *n.* [OE. *penn*] 1. a small enclosure for domestic animals 2. any small enclosure —*vt.* penned or pent, **pen′ning** to enclose as in a pen

pen² (pen) *n.* [< L. *penna*, feather] 1. a device used in writing, etc. with ink, often with a metal point split into two nibs 2. the metal point —*vt.* penned, **pen′ning** to write with a pen

pen³ (pen) *n.* [Slang] a penitentiary

Pen., pen. peninsula

pe·nal (pē′n'l) *adj.* [< Gr. *poinē*, penalty] of, for, constituting, or deserving punishment

pe·nal·ize (-īz′, pen′l-) *vt.* -ized′, -iz′ing to impose a penalty on; punish —**pe′nal·i·za′tion** *n.*

pen·al·ty (pen′l tē) *n., pl.* -ties 1. a punishment 2. the handicap, etc. imposed on an offender, as a fine

pen·ance (pen′əns) *n.* [see PENITENT] voluntary self-punishment to show repentance for wrongdoing, sins, etc.

penates SEE LARES AND PENATES

pence (pens) *n.* [Brit.] *pl.* of PENNY

pen·chant (pen′chənt) *n.* [Fr. < L. *pendere*, hang] a strong liking

pen·cil (pen′s'l) *n.* [< L. *penis*, tail] a pointed, rod-shaped instrument with a core of graphite or crayon that is sharpened to a point for writing, etc. —*vt.* -ciled or -cilled, -cil·ing or -cil·ling to write, etc. with a pencil

pend (pend) *vi.* [< L. *pendere*, hang] to await judgment or decision

pend·ant (pen′dənt) *n.* [see prec.] an ornamental hanging object, as a locket or earring

pend·ent (pen′dənt) *adj.* [see PEND] 1. suspended 2. overhanging 3. undecided; pending

pend′ing *adj.* 1. not decided 2. impending —*prep.* 1. during 2. until

pen·du·lous (pen′joo ləs) *adj.* [see PEND] hanging freely; drooping

pen·du·lum (pen′joo ləm) *n.* [see PEND] a body hung so as to swing freely to and fro: used to regulate clock movements

pen·e·trate (pen′ə trāt′) *vt., vi.* -trat′ed, -trat′ing [< L. *penitus*, inward] 1. to enter by piercing 2. to have an effect throughout 3. to affect deeply 4. to understand —**pen′e·tra·ble** *adj.* —**pen′e·tra′tion** *n.*

pen·e·trat·ing *adj.* 1. that penetrates 2. sharp; piercing 3. acute; discerning Also **pen′e·tra′tive**

pen·guin (peŋ′gwin, pen′-) *n.* [prob. < W. *pen gwyn*, white head] a flightless bird of the S Hemisphere with webbed feet and flippers for swimming

pen·i·cil·lin (pen′ə sil′in) *n.* [< L. *penicillus*, brush] an antibiotic obtained from certain molds or produced synthetically

PENGUIN

pen·in·su·la (pə nin′sə lə) *n.* [< L. *paene*, almost + *insula*, isle] a land area almost surrounded by water —**pen·in′su·lar** *adj.*

pe·nis (pē′nis) *n., pl.* -nis·es, -nes (-nēz) [L.] the male organ of sexual intercourse —**pe′nile** (-nīl) *adj.*

pen·i·tent (pen′ə tənt) *adj.* [< L. *paenitere*, repent] sorry for having done wrong and willing to atone —*n.* a penitent person —**pen′i·tence** *n.* —**pen′i·ten′tial** (-ten′shəl) *adj.* —**pen′i·tent·ly** *adv.*

pen·i·ten·tia·ry (pen′ə ten′shə rē) *adj.* making one liable to imprisonment in a penitentiary —*n., pl.* -ries a State or Federal prison for persons convicted of serious crimes

pen′knife′ *n., pl.* -knives′ (-nīvz′) a small pocketknife

pen′light′, pen′lite′ *n.* a flashlight about the size of a fountain pen

pen·man (-mən) *n., pl.* -men one skilled in penmanship

pen′man·ship′ (-ship′) *n.* handwriting as an art or skill

Penn (pen), **William** 1644–1718; Eng. Quaker: founder of Pennsylvania

Penn., Penna. Pennsylvania

pen name a pseudonym

pen·nant (pen′ənt) *n.* [< PENNON] 1. any long, narrow flag 2. such a flag symbolizing a championship

pen·ni·less (pen′i lis) *adj.* without even a penny; extremely poor

pen·non (pen'ən) *n.* [< L. *penna*, a feather] a flag or pennant

Penn·syl·va·ni·a (pen's'l vān'yə, -vā'nē ə) E State of the U.S.: 45,333 sq. mi.; pop. 11,867,000; cap. Harrisburg —**Penn'syl·va'ni·an** *adj., n.*

pen·ny (pen'ē) *n., pl.* **-nies;** for 1 (esp. collectively), **pence** [< OE. *pening*] 1. a coin of the United Kingdom equal to *a*) 1/12 shilling *b*) now 100th of a pound as of Feb., 1971 2. a U.S. or Canadian cent —**a pretty penny** [Colloq.] a large sum of money

penny arcade a public amusement hall with coin-operated games, etc.

penny pincher a miserly person —**pen'ny-pinch'ing** *n., adj.*

pen'ny·weight' *n.* a unit of weight, equal to 1/20 ounce troy weight

pen'ny-wise' *adj.* thrifty in small matters —**penny-wise and pound-foolish** thrifty in small matters but wasteful in major ones

pe·nol·o·gy (pē näl'ə jē) *n.* [< Gr. *poinē*, penalty + -LOGY] the study of prison management and prison reform

pen pal a person, esp. one abroad, with whom one exchanges letters

pen·sion (pen'shən) *n.* [< L. *pensio*, a paying] a regular payment, not wages, as to one who is retired or disabled —*vt.* to grant a pension to —**pen'sion·er** *n.*

pen·sive (pen'siv) *adj.* [< L. *pensare*, consider] thoughtful or reflective, often in a melancholy way —**pen'sive·ly** *adv.* —**pen'sive·ness** *n.*

pent (pent) *alt. pt. & pp. of* PEN[1] —*adj.* held or kept in; penned. (often with *up*)

penta- [< Gr. *pente*, five] *a combining form meaning* five

pen·ta·cle (pen'tə k'l) *n.* [see PENTA-] a symbol, usually a five-pointed star, formerly used in magic

pen·ta·gon (pen'tə gän') *n.* [< Gr. *penta-*, five + *gōnia*, an angle] 1. a plane figure with five angles and five sides 2. [P-] the pentagonal office building of the Defense Department, near Washington, D.C. —**pen·tag'o·nal** (-tag'ə n'l) *adj.*

pen·tam·e·ter (pen tam'ə tər) *n.* [see PENTA- & METER[1]] a line of verse containing five metrical feet

Pen·ta·teuch (pen'tə tōōk') *n.* [< Gr. *penta-*, five + *teuchos*, book] the first five books of the Bible

pen·tath·lon (pen tath'län) *n.* [PENTA- + Gr. *athlon*, a contest] a contest in which each contestant takes part in five different events —**pen·tath'lete'** (-lēt') *n.*

Pen·te·cost (pen'tə kôst') *n.* [< Gr. *pentēkostē* (*hēmera*), the fiftieth (day)] a Christian festival on the seventh Sunday after Easter

pent·house (pent'hous') *n.* [ult. < L. *appendere*, append] a house or apartment on the roof of a building

Pen·to·thal Sodium (pen'tə thôl) *a trademark for* a yellowish substance injected as a general anesthetic

pent-up (pent'up') *adj.* held in check; curbed [*pent-up* emotion]

pe·nu·che, pe·nu·chi (pə nōō'chē) *n.* [var. of PANOCHA] a fudgelike candy

pe·nul·ti·mate (pi nul'tə mit) *adj.* [< L. *paene*, almost + ULTIMATE] next to the last —*n.* the penultimate one

pe·nu·ri·ous (pə nyoor'ē əs, -noor'-) *adj.* [see ff.] miserly; stingy —**pe·nu'ri·ous·ly** *adv.* —**pe·nu'ri·ous·ness** *n.*

pen·u·ry (pen'yə rē) *n.* [< L. *penuria*, want] extreme poverty

pe·on (pē'än, -ən) *n.* [< ML. *pedo*, foot soldier] 1. in Latin America, a member of the laboring class 2. in the SW U.S., a person forced into servitude to work off a debt —**pe'on·age** *n.*

pe·o·ny (pē'ə nē) *n., pl.* **-nies** [< Gr. *Paiōn*, Apollo as god of medicine: from its former medicinal use] 1. a plant with large pink, white, red, or yellow, showy flowers 2. the flower

peo·ple (pē'p'l) *n., pl.* **-ple; for 1 -ples** [< L. *populus*, nation] 1. all the persons of a racial or ethnic group; nation, race, etc. 2. the persons of a certain place, group, or class 3. one's family; relatives 4. the populace 5. persons considered indefinitely [what will *people* say?] 6. human beings —*vt.* **-pled, -pling** to populate

Pe·o·ri·a (pē ôr'ē ə) city in C Ill.: pop. 124,000

pep (pep) *n.* [< ff.] [Colloq.] energy; vigor —*vt.* **pepped, pep'ping** [Colloq.] to fill with pep; invigorate (with *up*) —**pep'py** *adj.*

pep·per (pep'ər) *n.* [< Gr. *peperi*] 1. *a*) a pungent condiment ground from the dried fruits of an East Indian plant *b*) this plant 2. the fruit of the red pepper plant, red, yellow, or green, sweet or hot —*vt.* 1. to season with ground pepper 2. to pelt with small objects

pep'per·corn' *n.* the dried berry of the pepper, ground as a condiment

pepper mill a hand mill used to grind peppercorns

pep'per·mint' *n.* 1. a plant of the mint family that yields a pungent oil used for flavoring 2. the oil 3. a candy flavored with this oil

pep·per·o·ni (pep'ə rō'nē) *n., pl.* **-nis, -ni** [< It. *peperoni*] a highly spiced Italian sausage

pepper shaker a container for ground pepper, with a perforated top

pep'per·y *adj.* 1. of, like, or highly seasoned with pepper 2. sharp or fiery, as words 3. hot-tempered

pep·sin (pep's'n) *n.* [G. < Gr. *peptein*, to digest] a stomach enzyme, aiding in the digestion of proteins

pep talk a talk, as to an athletic team by its coach, to instill enthusiasm and determination

pep'tic (-tik) *adj.* [see PEPSIN] 1. of or aiding digestion 2. caused by digestive secretions [a *peptic* ulcer]

per (pur, pər) *prep.* [L.] 1. through;

by; by means of 2. for each [fifty cents *per* yd.] 3. [Colloq.] according to

per- [< PER] *a prefix meaning:* 1. through; throughout 2. thoroughly

Per. 1. Persia 2. Persian

per·ad·ven·ture (pur'əd ven'chər) *adv.* [< OFr. *par*, by + *aventure*, chance] [Archaic] possibly

per·am·bu·late (pər am'byoo lāt') *vt., vi.* -lat'ed, -lat'ing [< L. *per*, through + *ambulare*, to walk] to walk (through, over, etc.)

per·am'bu·la'tor (-lāt'ər) *n.* [Chiefly Brit.] a baby carriage

per an·num (pər an'əm) [L.] yearly

per·cale (pər kāl', -kal') *n.* [Fr. < Per. *pargāla*] fine, closely woven cotton cloth, used for sheets, etc.

per cap·i·ta (pər kap'ə tə) [ML., lit., by heads] for each person

per·ceive (pər sēv') *vt., vi.* -ceived', -ceiv'ing [< L. *per*, through + *capere*, take] 1. to understand 2. to become aware (of) through the senses

per·cent (pər sent') *adv., adj.* [< L. *per centum*] in, to, or for every hundred: symbol, %: also **per cent** —*n.* [Colloq.] percentage

per·cent'age (-ij) *n.* 1. a given part in every hundred 2. part; portion 3. [Colloq.] advantage; profit

per·cen·tile (pər sen'til, -sent'l) *n. Statistics* any of 100 divisions of a series, each of equal frequency

per·cep·ti·ble (pər sep'tə b'l) *adj.* that can be perceived —**per·cep'ti·bly** *adv.*

per·cep'tion (-shən) *n.* [< L. *per·cipere*, perceive] 1. the mental grasp of objects, etc. through the senses 2. insight or intuition 3. the knowledge, etc. got by perceiving —**per·cep'tu·al** (-chōō əl) *adj.*

per·cep'tive *adj.* 1. of perception 2. able to perceive quickly —**per·cep'tive·ly** *adv.* —**per·cep'tive·ness** *n.*

per·cep·tu·al (-chōō əl) *adj.* of or involving perception

perch¹ (purch) *n., pl.* **perch, perch'es** [< Gr. *perkē*] 1. a small, spiny-finned, freshwater food fish 2. a similar bony, usually saltwater, fish

perch² (purch) *n.* [< L. *pertica*, pole] 1. a horizontal pole, etc. serving as a roost for birds 2. any high resting place 3. a measure of length equal to 5 1/2 yards —*vi.*, *vt.* to rest or place on or as on a perch

per·chance (pər chans') *adv.* [< OFr. *par*, by + *chance*, chance] [Archaic] 1. by chance 2. perhaps

per·co·late (pur'kə lāt') *vt.* -lat'ed, -lat'ing [< L. *per*, through + *colare*, to strain] to pass (a liquid) through a porous substance; filter —*vi.* to ooze through a porous substance

per'co·la'tor *n.* a coffeepot in which boiling water bubbles up through a tube and filters back down through the ground coffee

per·cus·sion (pər kush'ən) *n.* [< L. *per-*, thoroughly + *quatere*, shake] the hitting of one body against another, as the hammer of a firearm against a powder cap (**percussion cap**)

percussion instrument a musical instrument producing a tone when struck, as a drum, cymbal, etc.

per·cus·sion·ist *n.* a musician who plays percussion instruments

per di·em (pər dē'əm, dī'-) [L.] daily

per·di·tion (pər dish'ən) *n.* [< L. *perdere*, to lose] *Theol.* 1. the loss of the soul 2. *same as* HELL

per·dure (pər door') *vi.* -dured', -dur'ing [< L. *perdurare*, to endure] to remain in existence; last

per·e·gri·na·tion (per'ə gri nā'shən) *n.* [see PILGRIM] a traveling about

per·emp·to·ry (pə remp'tər ē) *adj.* [< L. *perimere*, destroy] 1. *Law* barring further action; final 2. that cannot be denied, delayed, etc., as a command 3. dogmatic; imperious

per·en·ni·al (pə ren'ē əl) *adj.* [< L. *per*, through + *annus*, year] 1. lasting throughout the whole year 2. continuing for a long time 3. living more than two years: said of plants —*n.* a perennial plant —**pe·ren'ni·al·ly** *adv.*

per·fect (pur'fikt; *for v. usually* pər fekt') *adj.* [< L. *per-*, through + *facere*, do] 1. complete in all respects; flawless 2. excellent, as in skill or quality 3. completely accurate 4. sheer; utter [*a perfect fool*] 5. *Gram.* expressing a state or action completed at the time of speaking —*vt.* 1. to complete 2. to make perfect or nearly perfect —*n.* 1. the perfect tense 2. a verb form in this tense —**per'fect·ly** *adv.* —**per'fect·ness** *n.*

per·fec·ta (pər fek'tə) *n.* [Sp., perfect] a bet in which one wins if one picks correctly the first and second place finishers in a race

per·fect·i·ble (pər fek'tə b'l) *adj.* that can become or be made perfect

per·fec·tion (pər fek'shən) *n.* 1. the act of perfecting 2. a being perfect 3. a person or thing that is the perfect embodiment of some quality

per·fec'tion·ist *n.* one who strives for perfection

per·fi·dy (pur'fə dē) *n., pl.* -dies [< L. *per*, through + *fides*, faith] betrayal of trust; treachery —**per·fid·i·ous** (pər fid'ē əs) *adj.*

per·fo·rate (pur'fə rāt') *vt., vi.* -rat'ed, -rat'ing [< L. *per*, through + *forare*, to bore] 1. to make a hole or holes through, as by boring 2. to pierce with holes in a row, as a pattern, etc. —**per'fo·ra'tion** *n.*

per·force (pər fôrs') *adv.* [< OFr.: see PER & FORCE] necessarily

per·form (pər fôrm') *vt.* [< OFr. *parfournir*] 1. to do (a task, etc.) 2. to fulfill (a promise, etc.) 3. to render or enact (a piece of music, dramatic role, etc.) —*vi.* to execute an action or process, esp. in a performance (sense 4) —**per·form'er** *n.*

per·form'ance *n.* 1. the act of performing 2. functional effectiveness 3. deed or feat 4. *a)* a formal exhibition or presentation, as a play *b)* one's part in this

performing arts arts, such as drama, for performance before an audience

per·fume (pər fyoom'; *for n. usually* pur'fyoom) *vt.* -fumed', -fum'ing

[< L. *per-*, intens. + *fumare*, to smoke] 1. to scent 2. to put perfume on —*n.* a pleasing odor, as of a substance producing this, as a volatile oil extracted from flowers

per·fum′er·y (-ər ē) *n., pl.* **-ies** perfumes collectively

per·func·to·ry (pər fuŋk′tər ē) *adj.* [< L. *per-*, intens. + *fungi*, perform] 1. done merely as a routine; superficial 2. without concern; indifferent — **per·func′to·ri·ly** *adv.*

per·go·la (pur′gə lə) *n.* [L. *pergula*] an arbor with a latticework roof

per·haps (pər haps′) *adv.* [PER + pl. of *hap*, chance] possibly; maybe

peri- [Gr.] *a prefix meaning:* 1. around; about 2. near

Per·i·cles (per′ə klēz′) 495?-429 B.C.; Athenian statesman & general

per·i·gee (per′ə jē′) *n.* [< Gr. *peri-*, near + *gē*, earth] the point nearest a heavenly body, as the earth, in the orbit of a satellite around it

per·i·he·li·on (per′ə hē′lē ən) *n., pl.* **-li·ons**, **-li·a** (-ə) [< Gr. *peri-*, around + *hēlios*, sun] the point nearest the sun in the orbit of a planet or comet or of a man-made satellite

per·il (per′əl) *n.* [< L. *periculum*, danger] 1. exposure to harm or injury 2. something that may cause harm —*vt.* **-iled** or **-illed**, **-il·ing** or **-il·ling** to expose to danger

per′il·ous *adj.* involving peril or risk; dangerous —**per′il·ous·ly** *adv.*

pe·rim·e·ter (pə rim′ə tər) *n.* [< Gr. *peri-*, around + *metron*, measure] 1. the outer boundary of a figure or area 2. the total length of this

per·i·ne·um (per′ə nē′əm) *n., pl.* **-ne·a** (-ə) [< Gr. *perineon*] the small area between the anus and the genitals

pe·ri·od (pir′ē əd) *n.* [< Gr. *periodos*, a cycle] 1. the interval between successive occurrences of an event 2. a portion of time characterized by certain processes, etc. [*a period* of change] 3. any of the portions of time into which a game, school day, etc. is divided 4. the menses 5. an end or conclusion 6. *a)* the pause in speaking or the mark of punctuation (.) used at the end of a sentence *b)* the dot (.) following many abbreviations —*interj.* an exclamation used for emphasis [*you can't go, period!*]

pe·ri·od·ic (pir′ē äd′ik) *adj.* 1. appearing or recurring at regular intervals 2. intermittent

pe′ri·od′i·cal *adj.* 1. same as PERIODIC 2. published at regular intervals, as weekly, etc. 3. of a periodical —*n.* a periodical publication —**pe′ri·od′i·cal·ly** *adv.*

per·i·o·don·tal (per′ē ō dän′t'l) *adj.* [< PERI- + Gr. *odōn*, tooth] occurring around a tooth or affecting the gums

per·i·pa·tet·ic (per′i pə tet′ik) *adj.* [< Gr. *peri-*, around + *patein*, walk] walking or moving about; itinerant

pe·riph·er·y (pə rif′ər ē) *n., pl.* **-ies**

[< Gr. *peri-*, around + *pherein*, to bear] 1. an outer boundary, esp. of a rounded object 2. surrounding space or area —**pe·riph′er·al** *adj.*

per·i·scope (per′ə skōp′) *n.* [PERI- + -SCOPE] an optical instrument which allows one to see around or over an obstacle: used on submarines, etc.

per·ish (per′ish) *vi.* [< L. *per-*, through + *ire*, go] 1. to be destroyed or ruined 2. to die, esp. violently

per′ish·a·ble *adj.* that may perish; esp., liable to spoil, as some foods —*n.* something perishable, esp. food

per·i·stal·sis (per′ə stôl′sis, -stal′-) *n., pl.* **-ses** [< Gr. *peri-*, around + *stallein*, to place] contractions and dilations of the intestines, moving the contents onward —**per′i·stal′tic** *adj.*

per·i·to·ne·um (per′i t'n ē′əm) *n.* [< Gr. *peri-*, around + *teinein*, to stretch] the serous membrane lining the abdominal cavity

per·i·to·ni·tis (-īt′əs) *n.* inflammation of the peritoneum

per·i·wig (per′ə wig′) *n.* [alt. < Fr. *perruque*] a wig

per·i·win·kle[1] (per′ə wiŋ′k'l) *n.* [< L. *pervincire*, entwine] a creeping plant with blue, white, or pink flowers

per·i·win·kle[2] (per′ə wiŋ′k'l) *n.* [OE. *pinewincle*] a small saltwater snail with a thick, cone-shaped shell

per·jure (pur′jər) *vt.* **-jured**, **-jur·ing** [< L. *per-*, through + *jurare*, swear] to make (oneself) guilty of perjury —**per′-jur·er** *n.*

per′ju·ry (-jər ē) *n., pl.* **-ries** [< L. *perjurus*, false] the willful telling of a lie while under oath

PERIWINKLE SHELL

perk[1] (purk) *vt.* [ME. *perken*] 1. to raise (the head, etc.) briskly 2. to give a smart, fresh, or vigorous look to (often with *up*) —*vi.* to become lively (with *up*) —**perk′y** *adj.* **-i·er**, **-i·est**

perk[2] (purk) *vt., vi.* colloq. *clip* of PERCOLATE

per·ma·frost (pur′mə frôst′, -frȧst′) *n.* permanently frozen subsoil

per·ma·nent (pur′mə nənt) *adj.* [< L. *per-*, through + *manere*, remain] lasting or intended to last indefinitely or for a long time —**per′ma·nence** *n.* —**per′ma·nent·ly** *adv.*

permanent wave a hair wave produced by use of chemicals or heat and lasting through many washings

per·me·a·ble (pur′mē ə b'l) *adj.* that can be permeated, as by fluids —**per′me·a·bil′i·ty** *n.*

per·me·ate (pur′mē āt′) *vt., vi.* **-at·ed**, **-at·ing** [< L. *per-*, through + *meare*, to glide] to spread or diffuse; penetrate (*through* or *among*)

per·mis·si·ble (pər mis′ə b'l) *adj.* that can be permitted; allowable

per·mis·sion (pər mish′ən) *n.* the act of permitting; esp., formal consent

per·mis·sive (-mis'iv) *adj.* 1. that permits 2. allowing freedom; lenient —**per·mis·sive·ly** *adv.* —**per·mis'sive·ness** *n.*

per·mit (pər mit'; *for n. usually* pur'mit) *vt.* -**mit'ted**, -**mit'ting** [< L. *per*, through + *mittere*, send] 1. to allow to be done; consent to 2. to authorize —*vi.* to give opportunity *[if time permits]* —*n.* a license

per·mu·ta·tion (pur'myoo tā'shən) *n.* [< L. *per-*, thoroughly + *mutare*, change] 1. any radical alteration 2. any of the total number of groupings possible within a group

per·ni·cious (pər nish'əs) *adj.* [< L. *per*, thoroughly + *necare*, kill] causing great injury, destruction, etc.; fatal —**per·ni'cious·ly** *adv.*

per·o·ra·tion (per'ə rā'shən) *n.* [< L. *per*, through + *orare*, speak] the concluding part of a speech

per·ox·ide (pə räk'sīd) *n.* [< L. *per*, through + OXIDE] any oxide containing the oxygen group linked by a single bond; specif., hydrogen peroxide

per·pen·dic·u·lar (pur'pən dik'yə lər) *adj.* [< L. *perpendiculum*, plumb line] 1. at right angles to a given line or plane 2. exactly upright; vertical —*n.* a line or plane at right angles to another line or plane

per·pe·trate (pur'pə trāt') *vt.* -**trat'ed**, -**trat'ing** [< L. *per*, thoroughly + *patrare*, to effect] 1. to do (something evil, criminal, etc.) 2. to commit (a blunder, etc.) —**per'pe·tra'tion** *n.* —**per'pe·tra'tor** *n.*

per·pet·u·al (pər pech'oo wəl) *adj.* [< L. *perpetuus*, constant] 1. lasting forever or for a long time 2. continuing without interruption; constant —**per·pet'u·al·ly** *adv.*

per·pet·u·ate' (-wāt') *vt.* -**at'ed**, -**at'ing** to make perpetual; cause to continue or be remembered —**per·pet'u·a'tion** *n.*

per·pe·tu·i·ty (pur'pə tōō'ə tē) *n.*, *pl.* -**ties** unlimited time; eternity —**in perpetuity** forever

per·plex (pər pleks') *vt.* [< L. *per*, through + *plectere*, to twist] to make (a person) uncertain, hesitant, etc.; confuse —**per·plex'ing** *adj.* —**per·plex'i·ty** *n.*, *pl.* -**ties**

per·qui·site (pur'kwə zit) *n.* [< L. *per-*, intens. + *quaerere*, seek] something in addition to regular pay for one's work, as a tip

per se (pur'sē', sā') [L.] by (or in) itself; intrinsically

per·se·cute (pur'sə kyōōt') *vt.* -**cut'ed**, -**cut'ing** [< L. *per*, through + *sequi*, follow] to afflict constantly so as to injure or distress, as for reasons of religion, race, etc. —**per'se·cu'tion** *n.* —**per'se·cu'tor** *n.*

per·se·vere (pur'sə vir') *vi.* -**vered**, -**ver'ing** [< L. *per-*, intens. + *severus*, severe] to continue a course of action, etc. in spite of difficulty, opposition, etc. —**per'se·ver'ance** *n.*

Per·sia (pur'zhə) *former official name of* IRAN —**Per'sian** *adj., n.*

Persian cat a variety of domestic cat with long, silky hair

Persian Gulf arm of the Indian Ocean, between Iran & Arabia

Persian lamb the pelt of karakul lambs

per·si·flage (pur'sə fläzh') *n.* [Fr. < L. *per*, through + *sifilare*, to whistle] frivolous talk or writing; banter

per·sim·mon (pər sim'ən) *n.* [< AmInd.] 1. a hardwood tree with plumlike fruit 2. the fruit

per·sist (pər sist', -zist') *vi.* [< L. *per*, through + *sistere*, cause to stand] 1. to refuse to give up, esp. when faced with opposition 2. to continue insistently 3. to endure; remain

per·sist'ent *adj.* 1. continuing, esp. in the face of opposition, etc. 2. continuing to exist or endure 3. constantly repeated —**per·sist'ence** *n.*

per·snick·e·ty (pər snik'ə tē) *adj.* [< Scot. dial.] [Colloq.] 1. too particular; fussy 2. showing or requiring careful treatment

per·son (pur's'n) *n.* [< L. *persona*] 1. a human being 2. the human body 3. personality; self 4. *Gram.* division into three specified sets of pronouns and corresponding verb forms: see FIRST PERSON, SECOND PERSON, THIRD PERSON —**in person** actually present

-**per·son** (pur's'n) *a combining form meaning* person in a specified activity: used to avoid the masculine implications of -*man [chairperson]*

per·son·a·ble (-ə b'l) *adj.* having a pleasing appearance and personality

per·son·age (-ij) *n.* a person; esp., an important person; notable

per·son·al (-əl) *adj.* 1. private; individual 2. done in person 3. involving human beings 4. of the body or physical appearance 5. *a)* having to do with the character, conduct, etc. of a person *[a personal remark] b)* tending to make personal, esp. derogatory, remarks 6. *Gram.* indicating person (sense 4) 7. *Law* of property (**personal property**) that is movable

personal effects personal belongings, those worn or carried

per·son·al·i·ty (pur'sə nal'ə tē) *n.*, *pl.* -**ties** 1. the quality or fact of being a person or a particular person 2. distinctive individual qualities of a person, considered collectively 3. a notable person 4. *[pl.]* offensive remarks aimed at a person

per·son·al·ize (pur's'n ə līz') *vt.* -**ized'**, -**iz'ing** 1. to make personal 2. to have marked with one's name, etc.

per·son·al·ly *adv.* 1. in person 2. as a person *[I dislike him personally]* 3. in one's own opinion 4. as though directed at oneself

‡**per·so·na non gra·ta** (pər sō'nə nän grät'ə) [L.] an unwelcome person

per·son·i·fy (pər sän'ə fī') *vt.* -**fied'**, -**fy'ing** 1. to think of or represent (a thing) as a person 2. to typify; embody —**per·son'i·fi·ca'tion** *n.*

per·son·nel (pur'sə nel') *n.* [Fr.] 1. persons employed in any work, enterprise, service, etc. 2. a department for hiring employees, etc.

per·spec·tive (pər spek'tiv) *n.* [< L. *per*, through + *specere*, look] 1. the art of picturing objects so as to show relative distance or depth 2. the appearance of objects as determined by their relative distance and positions 3. sense of proportion

per·spi·ca·cious (pur'spə kā'shəs) *adj.* [see prec.] having keen judgment; discerning —**per'spi·ca'cious·ly** *adv.* —**per'spi·cac'i·ty** (-kas'ə tē) *n.*

per·spic·u·ous (pər spik'yoo wəs) *adj.* [see PERSPECTIVE] easily understood; lucid —**per·spi·cu·i·ty** (pur'spə kyōō'ə tē) *n.*

per·spi·ra·tion (pur'spə rā'shən) *n.* 1. the act of perspiring 2. sweat

per·spire (pər spīr') *vt., vi.* -**spired'**, -**spir'ing** [< L. *per-*, through + *spirare*, breathe] to sweat

per·suade (pər swād') *vt.* -**suad'ed**, -**suad'ing** [< L. *per-*, intens. + *suadere*, to urge] to cause (someone) to do or believe something, esp. by reasoning, urging, etc.; convince —**per·suad'a·ble** *adj.* —**per·suad'er** *n.*

per·sua·sion (pər swā'zhən) *n.* 1. a persuading or being persuaded 2. power of persuading 3. a strong belief 4. a particular religious belief

per·sua·sive *adj.* having the power, or tending, to persuade

pert (purt) *adj.* [< L. *apertus*, open] bold; impudent; saucy —**pert'ly** *adv.*

per·tain (pər tān') *vi.* [< L. *per-*, intens. + *tenere*, hold] 1. to belong; be connected or associated 2. to be appropriate 3. to have reference

per·ti·na·cious (pur'tə nā'shəs) *adj.* [< L. *per-*, intens. + *tenax*, holding fast] 1. holding firmly to some purpose, belief, etc. 2. hard to get rid of —**per'ti·nac'i·ty** (-nas'ə tē) *n.*

per·ti·nent (pur't'n ənt) *adj.* [see PERTAIN] connected with the matter at hand —**per'ti·nence** *n.*

per·turb (pər turb') *vt.* [< L. *per-*, intens. + *turbare*, disturb] to cause to be alarmed, agitated, or upset —**per·tur·ba·tion** (pur'tər bā'shən) *n.*

per·tus·sis (pər tus'is) *n.* [< L. *per-*, intens. + *tussis*, a cough] same as WHOOPING COUGH

Pe·ru (pə rōō') country in W.S. America: 496,222 sq. mi.; pop. 12,385,000 —**Pe·ru'vi·an** *adj., n.*

pe·ruke (pə rōōk') *n.* [Fr. *perruque*] a wig

pe·ruse (pə rōōz') *vt.* -**rused'**, -**rus'ing** [prob. < L. *per-*, intens. + ME. *usen*, to use] 1. to read carefully; study 2. to read —**pe·rus'al** *n.*

per·vade (pər vād') *vt.* -**vad'ed**, -**vad'ing** [< L. *per-*, through + *vadere*, go] to spread or be prevalent throughout —**per·va'sive** *adj.*

per·verse (pər vurs') *adj.* [see PERVERT] 1. deviating from what is considered right or good 2. stubbornly contrary 3. obstinately disobedient —**per·verse'ly** *adv.* —**per·verse'ness, per·ver'si·ty** *n.*

per·ver·sion (pər vur'zhən) *n.* 1. a perverting or being perverted 2. something perverted 3. any sexual act or practice considered abnormal

per·vert (pər vurt'; *for n.* pur'vərt) *vt.* [< L. *per-*, intens. + *vertere*, turn] 1. to lead astray; corrupt 2. to misuse 3. to distort 4. to debase —*n.* one practicing sexual perversion

pes·ky (pes'kē) *adj.* -**ki·er**, -**ki·est** [prob. var. of *pesty*] [Colloq.] annoying; troublesome —**pes'ki·ness** *n.*

pe·so (pā'sō) *n., pl.* -**sos** [Sp. < L. *pensum*, something weighed] the monetary unit and a coin of various Spanish-speaking countries

pes·si·mism (pes'ə miz'm) *n.* [< L. *pejor*, worse] 1. the belief that the evil in life outweighs the good 2. the tendency to always expect the worst —**pes'si·mist** *n.*—**pes'si·mis'tic** *adj.* —**pes'si·mis'ti·cal·ly** *adv.*

pest (pest) *n.* [< L. *pestis*, plague] 1. a person or thing that is troublesome, destructive, etc.; specif., a rat, fly, weed, etc. 2. [Now Rare] a plague

pes·ter (pes'tər) *vt.* [< OFr. *em-pestrer*, entangle] to annoy; vex

pest'hole' *n.* a place infested with an epidemic disease

pes·ti·cide (pes'tə sīd') *n.* any chemical for killing insects, weeds, etc.

pes·tif·er·ous (pes tif'ər əs) *adj.* [< L. *pestis*, plague + *ferre*, to bear] 1. orig., infectious or diseased 2. noxious 3. [Colloq.] annoying

pes·ti·lence (pes't'l əns) *n.* 1. a deadly epidemic disease; plague 2. anything regarded as harmful

pes'ti·lent *adj.* [< L. *pestis*, plague] 1. likely to cause death 2. dangerous to society; pernicious 3. annoying

pes·tle (pes''l) *n.* [< L. *pinsere*, to pound] a tool used to pound or grind substances, esp. in a mortar

pet (pet) *n.* [orig. Scot. dial.] 1. an animal that is domesticated and kept as a companion 2. a person treated with particular indulgence —*adj.* 1. kept or treated as a pet 2. especially liked 3. particular [a pet peeve] 4. showing fondness [a pet name] —**pet'ted, pet'ting** to stroke or pat gently; caress —*vi.* [Colloq.] to kiss, embrace, etc. in making love

pet (pet) *n.* [< ?] a sulky mood

pet·al (pet''l) *n.* [< Gr. *petalos*, outspread] any of the leaflike parts of a blossom

pe·tard (pi tärd') *n.* [< Fr.] an explosive device formerly used to break down doors, walls, etc. —**hoist with (or by) one's own petard** destroyed by the very thing with which one meant to destroy others

pet·cock (pet'käk') *n.* [< L. *pedere*, break wind + *cock*, valve] a small valve for draining pipes, radiators, etc.

Pe·ter (pēt'ər) 1. ?-64? A.D.; one of the twelve Apostles; reputed author of two Epistles: also *Saint Peter* 2. **Peter I** 1672-1725; czar of Russia (1682-1725): called *Peter the Great*

pe·ter (pēt'ər) *vi.* [< ?] [Colloq.] to

become gradually smaller, weaker, etc. and then disappear (with *out*)

pe·tite (pə tēt') *adj.* [Fr.] small and trim in figure: said of a woman

pe·tit four (pet'ē fôr'), *pl.* **pe'tits fours** (pet'ē fôrz'), **pe'tit fours'** [Fr., lit., small oven] a tiny frosted cake

pe·ti·tion (pə tish'ən) *n.* [< L. *petere*, ask] 1. a solemn, earnest request; entreaty 2. a formal document embodying such a request, often signed by many people —*vt.* 1. to address a petition to 2. to ask for —*vi.* to make a petition —**pe·ti'tion·er** *n.*

petit jury a group of citizens picked to decide the issues of a trial in court

pet·rel (pet'rəl) *n.* [< ? St. *Peter:* cf. Matt. 14:29] a small, dark sea bird

pet·ri·fy (pet'rə fī') *vt.* **-fied', -fy'ing** [< L. *petra*, rock + *facere*, make] 1. to turn into stone 2. to harden or deaden 3. to paralyze, as with fear

pet·ro·chem·i·cal (pet'rō kem'i k'l) *n.* a chemical with a petroleum base

pet'ro·dol'lars *n.pl.* revenue from the sale of petroleum

pet·rol (pet'rəl) *n.* [see PETROLEUM] *Brit. term for* gasoline

pet·ro·la·tum (pet'rə lāt'əm) *n.* [< ff.] a greasy, jellylike substance derived from petroleum and used for ointments, etc. Also **petroleum jelly**

pe·tro·le·um (pə trō'lē əm) *n.* [< L. *petra*, rock + *oleum*, oil] an oily, liquid solution of hydrocarbons occurring naturally in certain rock strata: it yields kerosene, gasoline, etc.

PET scan (pet) [*p(ositron) e(mission) t(omography)*], an X-ray technique] a diagnostic X-raying of the metabolism of the body, esp. the brain, using many single-plane X-rays (*tomograms*) and radioactive tracers

pet·ti·coat (pet'i kōt') *n.* [< PETTY + COAT] a woman's underskirt

pet·ti·fog·ger (pet'ē fäg'ər, -fôg'-) *n.* [< ff. + *fogger* < ?] a lawyer who handles petty cases, esp. unethically —**pet'ti·fog'** *vi.* **-fogged', -fog'ging**

pet·tish (pet'ish) *adj.* [< PET²] peevish; petulant —**pet'tish·ly** *adv.*

pet·ty (pet'ē) *adj.* **-ti·er, -ti·est** [< OFr. *petit*] 1. relatively unimportant 2. small-minded; mean 3. relatively low in rank —**pet'ti·ness** *n.*

petty cash a cash fund for incidentals

petty officer a naval enlisted man who is a noncommissioned officer

pet·u·lant (pech'oo lənt) *adj.* [< L. *petere*, to attack] impatient or irritable, esp. over a petty annoyance —**pet'u·lance** *n.* —**pet'u·lant·ly** *adv.*

pe·tu·ni·a (pə tōōn'yə, -ē ə) *n.* [< Braz. *petun*, tobacco] a plant with showy, funnel-shaped flowers

pew (pyōō) *n.* [ult. < Gr. *pous*, foot] any of the benches with a back that are fixed in rows in a church

pew·ter (pyōō'tər) *n.* [OFr. *peautre*] 1. a dull, silvery-gray alloy of tin with lead, etc. 2. articles made of this

pe·yo·te (pā ōt'ē; *Sp.* pe yō'te) *n.* [AmSp. < AmInd. *peyotl*, caterpillar] the cactus plant mescal: see MESCALINE

pf., pfd. preferred

Pfc, Pfc., PFC Private First Class

PG a motion-picture rating for a film that parents may find unsuitable for children

PG-13 a motion-picture rating for a film indicating some material may be unsuitable for children under 13

pg. page

pha·e·ton (fā'ət 'n) *n.* [< *Phaëthon*, son of Helios, Gr. sun god] 1. a light, four-wheeled carriage 2. an early type of open automobile

pha·lanx (fā'laŋks) *n., pl.* **-lanx·es, pha·lan·ges** (fə lan'jēz) [Gr., line of battle] 1. an ancient close-ranked infantry formation 2. any massed group 3. *pl.* **-lan'ges** any of the bones forming the fingers or toes

phal·lus (fal'əs) *n., pl.* **-li** (-ī), **-lus·es** [< Gr. *phallos*] an image of the penis —**phal'lic** *adj.*

phan·tasm (fan'taz'm) *n.* [< Gr. *phantazein*, to show] 1. a figment of the mind 2. a deceptive likeness

phan·tas·ma·go·ri·a (fan taz'mə gôr'ē ə) *n.* [< Gr. *phantasma*, phantasm + *ageirein*, assemble] a rapid sequence of images, as in a dream

phan·ta·sy (fan'tə sē) *n., pl.* **-sies** *same as* FANTASY

phan·tom (fan'təm) *n.* [see FANTASY] 1. an apparition; specter 2. an illusion —*adj.* of or like a phantom; illusory

Phar·aoh (fer'ō) *n.* the title of the rulers of ancient Egypt

Phar·i·see (far'ə sē') *n.* 1. a member of an ancient Jewish group that observed both the written and oral law 2. [p-] [< characterization in NT.] a self-righteous, hypocritical person —**phar'i·sa'ic** (-sā'ik) *adj.*

phar·ma·ceu·ti·cal (fär'mə sōōt'i k'l) *adj.* [< Gr. *pharmakon*, a drug] of pharmacy or drugs: also **phar'ma·ceu'tic** —*n.* a drug or medicine

phar'ma·ceu'tics (-iks) *n.pl.* [*with sing. v.*] *same as* PHARMACY (sense 1)

phar·ma·cist (fär'mə sist) *n.* one licensed to practice pharmacy

phar·ma·col'o·gy (-käl'ə jē) *n.* [< Gr. *pharmakon*, a drug] the science dealing with the effect of drugs on living organisms

phar·ma·co·pe'ia, phar·ma·co·poe'ia (-kə pē'ə) *n.* [< Gr. *pharmakon*, a drug + *poiein*, make] an official book of drugs and medicines

phar·ma·cy (fär'mə sē) *n., pl.* **-cies** [< Gr. *pharmakon*, a drug] 1. the art or profession of preparing drugs and medicines 2. a drugstore

phar·yn·gi·tis (far'in jīt'əs) *n.* inflammation of the pharynx

phar·ynx (far'iŋks) *n., pl.* **phar'ynx·es, pha·ryn·ges** (fə rin'jēz) [Gr.] the cavity leading from the mouth and nasal passages to the larynx and esophagus —**pha·ryn·ge·al** (fə rin'jē əl) *adj.*

phase (fāz) *n.* [< Gr. *phasis*] 1. any stage in a series or cycle of changes, as of the moon's illumination 2. an aspect or side, as of a problem —*vt.* **phased, phas'ing** to introduce or carry out in stages (often with *in*, *into*, etc.) —**in** (or **out of**) **phase** in (or not in) a synchronized state —

phase out to terminate (an activity) by stages

phase'-out' n. a phasing out; gradual termination, withdrawal, etc.

Ph.D. Doctor of Philosophy

pheas·ant (fez'nt) n. [< Gr. *phasianos*, (bird) of *Phasis*, river in Asia] a chickenlike game bird with a long tail and brilliant feathers

phe·no·bar·bi·tal (fē'nə bär'bə tôl') n. a white crystalline powder used as a sedative

phe·nol (fē'nōl, -nôl) n. a white crystalline compound, corrosive and poisonous, used to make synthetic resins, etc., and, in dilute solution (*carbolic acid*), as an antiseptic

phe·nom·e·non (fi näm'ə nän', -nən) n., pl. **-na** (-nə); also, esp. for 2 & usually for 3, **-nons'** [< Gr. *phainesthai*, appear] 1. any observable fact or event that can be scientifically described 2. anything very unusual 3. [Colloq.] an extraordinary person; prodigy —**phe·nom'e·nal** adj.

phi (fī, fē) n. the 21st letter of the Greek alphabet (Φ, φ)

phi·al (fī'əl) n. [< Gr. *phialē*, shallow bowl] a small glass bottle; vial

Phil·a·del·phi·a (fil'ə del'fē ə) city & port in SE Pa.: pop. 1,688,000

Philadelphia lawyer [Colloq.] a shrewd or tricky lawyer

phi·lan·der (fi lan'dər) vi. [< Gr. *philos*, loving + *anēr*, man] to engage lightly in love affairs: said of a man —**phi·lan'der·er** n.

phi·lan·thro·py (fi lan'thrə pē) n. [< Gr. *philein*, to love + *anthrōpos*, man] 1. a desire to help mankind, esp. as shown by endowments to institutions, etc. 2. pl. **-pies** a philanthropic gift, institution, etc. —**phil·an·throp·ic** (fil'ən thräp'ik) adj. —**phi·lan'thro·pist** n.

phi·lat·e·ly (fi lat'l ē) n. [< Fr. < Gr. *philos*, loving + *ateleia*, exemption from (further) tax (i.e., postage prepaid)] the collection and study of postage stamps, postmarks, etc. —**phi·lat'e·list** n.

-phile (fīl) [< Gr. *philos*, loving] a combining form meaning loving, liking

phil·har·mon·ic (fil'här män'ik) adj. [< Gr. *philos*, loving + *harmonia*, harmony] devoted to music —n. 1. a society sponsoring a symphony orchestra 2. [Colloq.] such an orchestra

phi·lip·pic (fi lip'ik) n. [< Gr. *Philippos*, Philip, Macedonian king denounced by Demosthenes] a bitter verbal attack

Phil·ip·pines (fil'ə pēnz') country consisting of c.7,100 islands (Philippine Islands) off the SE coast of Asia: 114,830 sq. mi.; pop. 34,656,000 —**Phil'ip·pine** adj.

Phil·is·tine (fil'is tēn', fi lis'tin) n. 1. any of a non-Semitic people of SW Palestine in Biblical times 2. [often p-] a person smugly conventional, narrow, lacking culture, etc.

phil·o·den·dron (fil'ə den'drən) n. [< Gr. *philos*, loving + *dendron*, tree] a tropical American vine

phi·lol·o·gy (fi läl'ə jē) n. [< Gr. *philein*, to love + *logos*, word] earlier term for LINGUISTICS —**phil·o·log·i·cal** (fil'ə läj'i k'l) adj. —**phi·lol'o·gist** n.

phi·los·o·pher (fi läs'ə fər) n. [< Gr. *philos*, loving + *sophos*, wise] 1. one who is learned in philosophy 2. one who lives by or expounds a system of philosophy 3. one who meets difficulties with calm composure

phil·o·soph·ic (fil'ə säf'ik) adj. 1. of philosophy or philosophers 2. sensibly composed or calm Also **phil'o·soph'i·cal**

phi·los·o·phize (fi läs'ə fīz') vi. **-phized'**, **-phiz'ing** 1. to think or reason like a philosopher 2. to moralize, express truisms, etc.

phi·los·o·phy (-fē) n., pl. **-phies** [see PHILOSOPHER] 1. study of the principles underlying conduct, thought, and the nature of the universe 2. general principles of a field of knowledge 3. a particular system of ethics 4. composure; calmness

phle·bi·tis (fli bīt'is) n. [< Gr. *phleps*, vein + -ITIS] inflammation of a vein

phlegm (flem) n. [< Gr. *phlegma*, inflammation] 1. thick mucus discharged from the throat, as during a cold 2. sluggishness; apathy

phleg·mat·ic (fleg mat'ik) adj. [see prec.] sluggish or unexcited —**phleg·mat'i·cal·ly** adv.

phlo·em (flō'em) n. [G. < Gr. *phloos*, bark] the vascular tissue through which food is distributed in a plant

phlox (fläks) n. [Gr., lit., a flame] a N.American plant with clusters of white, red, or bluish flowers

-phobe (fōb) [< Gr. *phobos*, fear] a suffix meaning one who fears or hates

pho·bi·a (fō'bē ə) n. [see prec.] an irrational, excessive, and persistent fear of some thing or situation

-pho·bi·a (fō'bē ə) a combining form meaning fear, hatred [*claustrophobia*]

phoe·be (fē'bē) n. [< Gr. *phoibos*, bright] a small American bird that catches insects in flight

Phoe·ni·cia (fə nish'ə, -nē'shə) ancient country at E end of the Mediterranean —**Phoe·ni'cian** adj., n.

Phoe·nix (fē'niks) capital of Ariz.: pop. 765,000

phoe·nix (fē'niks) n. [< Gr. *phoinix*] Egypt. Myth. a bird which lived for 500 years and then consumed itself in fire, rising renewed from the ashes

phone (fōn) n., vt., vi. **phoned**, **phon'ing** [Colloq.] telephone

-phone (fōn) [< Gr. *phōnē*, a sound] a combining form meaning: 1. producing or transmitting sound 2. telephone

pho·neme (fō'nēm) n. [< Fr. < Gr. *phōnē*, voice] a set of language sounds with slight variations but heard as the same sound by native speakers —**pho·ne·mic** (fə nē'mik) adj.

pho·net·ics (fə net'iks) n.pl. [with sing. v.] [< Gr. *phōnē*, a sound] the study of the production and written representation of speech sounds —**pho·net'ic** adj. —**pho·ne·ti·cian** (fō'nə tish'ən) n.

phon·ics (fän'iks) n.pl. [with sing. v.] [< Gr. *phōnē*, a sound] a phonetic method of teaching reading —**phon'ic** adj. —**phon'i·cal·ly** adv.

pho·no·graph (fō'nə graf') n. [< Gr. *phōnē*, sound + -GRAPH] an instrument for reproducing sound recorded in a spiral groove on a revolving disk —**pho'no·graph'ic** adj.

pho·nol·o·gy (fō näl'ə jē) n. [< Gr. *phōnē*, sound + -LOGY] 1. the speech sounds of a language 2. the study of changes in these —**pho'no·log'i·cal** (-nə läj'i k'l) adj. —**pho·nol'o·gist** n.

pho·ny (fō'nē) adj. -ni·er, -ni·est [< Brit. thieves' argot *fawney*, gilt ring] [Colloq.] not genuine; false —n., pl. -nies [Colloq.] something or someone not genuine; fraud; fake Also sp. **phoney** —**pho'ni·ness** n.

phooey (fōō'ē) interj. [echoic] an exclamation of scorn, disgust, etc.

phos·phate (fäs'fāt) n. [Fr.] 1. a salt or ester of phosphoric acid 2. a fertilizer that contains phosphates 3. a flavored carbonated beverage

phos·pho·res·cence (fäs'fə res''ns) n. 1. the property of giving off light without noticeable heat, as phosphorus does 2. such light —**phos'pho·res'cent** adj.

phos·phor·ic acid (fäs fôr'ik) any of three colorless, crystalline acids with a phosphorus and oxygen radical

phos·pho·rus (fäs'fər əs) n. [< Gr. *phōs*, a light + *pherein*, to bear] a nonmetallic chemical element, a phosphorescent, waxy solid that ignites spontaneously at room temperature

pho·to (fōt'ō) n., pl. -tos clipped form of PHOTOGRAPH

photo- a combining form meaning: 1. [< Gr. *phōs*, a light] of or produced by light 2. [< PHOTOGRAPH] of photography

pho·to·cop·y (fōt'ə käp'ē) n., pl. -ies a photographic reproduction, as of a book page, made by a special device (**pho'to·cop'i·er**)

pho·to·e·lec·tric cell (fōt'ō i lek'trik) any device in which light controls an electric circuit which operates a mechanical device, as for opening doors

pho'to·en·grav'ing n. 1. a process by which photographs are reproduced on relief printing plates 2. such a plate, or a print made from it —**pho'to·en·grave'** vt. -graved', -grav'ing —**pho'to·en·grav'er** n.

photo finish a race finish so close that the winner can be determined only from a photograph of the finish

pho·to·flash (fōt'ō flash') adj. designating a flashbulb, etc. electrically

synchronized with the camera shutter

pho·to·gen·ic (fōt'ə jen'ik) adj. [PHOTO- + -GEN + -IC] likely to look attractive in photographs

pho·to·graph (fōt'ə graf') n. a picture made by photography —vt. to take a photograph of —vi. to appear (as specified) in photographs —**pho·tog·ra·pher** (fə täg'rə fər) n.

pho·tog·ra·phy (fə täg'rə fē) n. [PHOTO- + -GRAPHY] the art or process of producing pictorial images on a surface sensitive to light or other radiant energy, as on film in a camera —**pho·to·graph·ic** (fōt'ə graf'ik) adj.

pho·ton (fō'tän) n. [PHOT(O)- + (ELECTR)ON] a quantum of electromagnetic energy

pho·to·off·set (fōt'ō ôf'set') n. offset printing in which the text or pictures are photographically transferred to a metal plate from which inked impressions are made on the roller

Pho·to·stat (fōt'ə stat') a trademark for a device making photographic copies of printed material, drawings, etc. directly as positives on special paper —n. [p-] a copy so made —vt. [p-] -stat'ed or -stat'ted, -stat'ing or -stat'ting to make a photostat of

pho·to·syn·the·sis (fōt'ə sin'thə sis) n. production of organic substances, esp. sugars, from carbon dioxide and water by the action of light on the chlorophyll in green plant cells —**pho'to·syn'the·size'** (-sīz') vt., vi. -sized', -siz'ing to carry on, or produce by, photosynthesis

phrase (frāz) n. [< Gr. *phrazein*, speak] 1. a short, colorful expression 2. a group of words, not a full sentence or clause, conveying a single thought 3. a short, distinct musical passage —vt. phrased, phras'ing to express in words or in a phrase —**phras·al** (frā'z'l) adj.

phra·se·ol·o·gy (frā'zē äl'ə jē) n., pl. -gies choice and pattern of words

phre·net·ic (fri net'ik) adj. [< Gr. *phrenētikos*, mad] same as FRENETIC

phre·nol·o·gy (fri näl'ə jē) n. [< Gr. *phrēn*, mind + -LOGY] a system, now rejected, of analyzing character from the shape of the skull

phy·lac·ter·y (fi lak'tər ē) n., pl. -ies [< Gr. *phylax*, watchman] either of two small leather cases holding Scripture texts, worn in prayer on the forehead and arm by orthodox Jewish men

phy·log·e·ny (fī läj'ə nē) n., pl. -nies [< Gr. *phylon*, tribe + -geneia, origin] the origin and evolution of a group or race of animals or plants

phy·lum (fī'ləm) n., pl. -la (-lə) [< Gr. *phylon*, tribe] a main division of the animal kingdom or, loosely, of the plant kingdom

phys·ic (fiz'ik) n. [< Gr. *physis*, nature] a medicine, esp. a cathartic —vt. -icked, -ick·ing to dose with this

phys·i·cal (fiz'i k'l) adj. 1. of nature and all matter; material 2. of or according to the laws of nature 3. of, or produced by the forces of, physics 4. of the body —n. a general medical examination —**phys'i·cal·ly** adv.

physical education instruction in the exercise and care of the body; esp., a course in gymnastics, etc.

physical science any science dealing with nonliving matter or energy, as physics, chemistry, or astronomy

physical therapy the treatment of disease, injury, etc. by physical means, as by exercise, massage, etc.

phy·si·cian (fə zish'ən) n. [see PHYSIC] a doctor of medicine

phys·ics (fiz'iks) n.pl. [with sing. v.] [see PHYSIC] the science dealing with the properties, changes, interactions, etc. of matter and energy —**phys'i·cist** (-ə sist) n.

phys·i·og·no·my (fiz'ē äg'nə mē) n. [< Gr. physis, nature + gnōmōn, judge] facial features and expression

phys·i·og·ra·phy (-äg'rə fē) n. [see prec. & -GRAPHY] the study of the earth's surface and oceans, atmosphere, etc.

phys·i·ol·o·gy (-äl'ə jē) n. [< Gr. physis, nature + -LOGY] the science dealing with the functions and vital processes of living organisms —**phys'i·o·log'i·cal** (-ə läj'i k'l) adj. —**phys'i·ol'o·gist** n.

phys·i·o·ther·a·py (fiz'ē ō ther'ə pē) n. same as PHYSICAL THERAPY

phy·sique (fi zēk') n. [Fr.] the structure or form of the body; build

pi¹ (pī) n., pl. **pies** [see PIE] 1. jumbled printing type 2. any jumble —vt. **pied, pie'ing** or **pi'ing** to jumble

pi² (pī) n. 1. the sixteenth letter of the Greek alphabet (Π, π) 2. the symbol (π) designating the ratio of the circumference of a circle to its diameter, about 3.1416

pi·a·nis·si·mo (pē'ə nis'ə mō') adj., adv. [It.] Music very soft

pi·a·nist (pē an'ist, pyan'-, pē'ən-) n. one who plays the piano

pi·an·o¹ (pē an'ō, pyan'ō) n., pl. **-os** [< PIANOFORTE] a large, stringed keyboard instrument: each key operates a felt-covered hammer that strikes a corresponding steel wire or wires

pi·an·o² (pē ä'nō, pyä'-) adj., adv. [It.] Music soft

pi·an·o·for·te (pē an'ə fôrt', pyan'ə fôr'tē) n. [It. < piano, soft + forte, strong] same as PIANO¹

pi·as·ter, pi·as·tre (pē as'tər) n. [ult. < L. emplastrum, plaster] a unit of currency in Egypt, Syria, etc.

pi·az·za (pē at'sə, pyät'-; for 2 pē az'ə) n. 1. in Italy, a public square 2. a veranda

pi·broch (pē'bräk) n. [< Gael. < piob, bagpipe] music for the bagpipe, usually of a martial kind

pi·ca (pī'kə) n. [< ? ML., directory] a size of printing type, 12 point

pic·a·resque (pik'ə resk') adj. [< Sp. picaro, rascal] dealing with sharp-witted vagabonds and their adventures [a picaresque novel]

Pi·cas·so (pi kä'sō), **Pa·blo** (pä'blō) 1881–1973; Sp. artist in France

pic·a·yune (pik'ē ōōn') adj. [< Fr. picaillon, small coin] trivial; petty

pic·ca·lil·li (pik'ə lil'ē) n. [prob. < PICKLE] a relish of chopped vegetables, mustard, and spices

pic·co·lo (pik'ə lō') n., pl. **-los** [It., small] a small flute, pitched an octave above the ordinary flute

pick¹ (pik) n. [ME. pic, PIKE²] 1. any of several pointed tools for picking, esp. a heavy one used in breaking up soil, rock, etc. 2. a plectrum

pick² (pik) vt. [ME. picken] 1. to pierce, dig up, etc. with something pointed 2. to probe, scratch at, etc. so as to remove or clear something from 3. to gather (flowers, berries, etc.) 4. to prepare (a fowl) by removing the feathers 5. to pull (fibers, rags, etc.) apart 6. to choose; select 7. to provoke (a quarrel or fight) 8. to pluck (the strings) of (a guitar, etc.) 9. to open (a lock) with a wire, etc. instead of a key 10. to steal from (another's pocket, etc.) —vi. 1. to use a pick 2. to select, esp. in a fussy way —n. 1. the act of choosing or the choice made 2. the best —**pick at** to eat sparingly of —**pick off** 1. to remove by picking 2. to hit with a carefully aimed shot —**pick on** [Colloq.] to single out for criticism or abuse; annoy; tease —**pick out** to choose —**pick up** 1. to grasp and lift 2. to get, find, or learn, esp. by chance 3. to stop for and take along 4. to gain (speed) 5. to improve 6. [Colloq.] to become acquainted with casually, esp. for lovemaking —**pick'er** n.

pick·a·back (pik'ə bak') adv., adj. same as PIGGYBACK

pick·ax, pick·axe (pik'aks') n. [< OFr. picquois] a pick with a point at one end of the head and a chisel-like edge at the other

pick·er·el (pik'ər əl) n., pl. **-el, -els** [< PIKE¹] any of various small, N. American freshwater fishes

pick·et (pik'it) n. [< Fr. pic, PIKE¹] 1. a pointed stake used in a fence, as a hitching post, etc. 2. a soldier or soldiers stationed to guard against surprise attack 3. a person, as a member of a striking labor union, stationed outside a factory, etc. to demonstrate protest —vt. 1. to enclose with a picket fence 2. to hitch (an animal) to a picket 3. to post as a military picket 4. to place pickets, or serve as a picket, at (a factory, etc.)

picket line a line or cordon of people serving as pickets

pick·ings n.pl. something picked; specif., a) scraps; remains b) something got by effort, often dishonestly

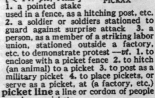

PICKAX

pick·le (pik′l) n. [< MDu. *pekel*]
1. any brine, vinegar, etc. used to
preserve or marinate food 2. a vegetable, esp. a cucumber, preserved in
this 3. [Colloq.] an awkward situation
—vt. **-led, -ling** to put in a pickle
solution

pick′pock′et n. a thief who steals
from pockets, as in a crowd

pick′up′ n. 1. a picking up 2. the
process or power of increasing speed
3. a small, open delivery truck 4.
[Colloq.] a casual acquaintance 5.
[Colloq.] improvement 6. a device for
producing electric currents from the
vibrations of a phonograph needle

pick·y (pik′ē) adj. -i·er, -i·est [Col-
loq.] overly fastidious; fussy

pic·nic (pik′nik) n. [< Fr.] a pleasure
outing at which a meal is eaten outdoors —vi. **-nicked, -nick·ing** to
have a picnic —**pic′nick·er** n.

pi·cot (pē′kō) n. [< Fr. *pic*, a point]
any of the small loops forming a fancy
edge as on lace

pic·to·graph (pik′tə graf′) n. 1. a
picture or picturelike symbol used in
a system of writing 2. a graph using
pictures to give data

pic·to·ri·al (pik tôr′ē əl) adj. 1. of,
containing, or expressed in pictures
2. suggesting a mental image; vivid
—**pic·to′ri·al·ly** adv.

pic·ture (pik′chər) n. [< L. *pingere*,
to paint] 1. a likeness of a person,
scene, etc. produced by drawing,
painting, photography, etc. 2. a perfect likeness or image [the *picture* of
health] 3. anything suggestive of a
beautiful painting, drawing, etc. 4. a
vivid description 5. a motion picture
6. the image on a TV screen —vt.
-tured, -tur·ing 1. to make a picture
of 2. to show visibly 3. to describe
4. to imagine —**in** (or **out**) **of the
picture** considered (or not considered)
as involved in a situation

pic′tur·esque′ (-chə resk′) adj. like
or suggestive of a picture; beautiful,
vivid, quaint, etc.

picture window a large window that
seems to frame the outside view

pid·dle (pid′l) vi., vt. **-dled, -dling**
[< ?] to dawdle; trifle

pidg·in (pij′in) n. [supposed Chin.
pronun. of *business*] a jargon for trade
purposes, using words and grammar
from different languages: **pidgin English** uses English words and Chinese
or Melanesian syntax

pie (pī) n. [ME.] a baked dish of fruit,
meat, etc., with an under or upper
crust, or both —**(as) easy as pie**
[Colloq.] extremely easy

pie·bald (pī′bôld′) adj. [< *pie*, mag-
pie + BALD] covered with patches of
two colors —n. a piebald horse, etc.

piece (pēs) n. [OFr. *pece*] 1. a part
broken or separated from the whole
2. a section of a whole regarded as
complete in itself 3. any single thing,
specimen, example, etc. [a *piece* of
music] 4. a quantity, as of cloth,
manufactured as a unit —vt. **pieced,
piec′ing** 1. to add pieces to, as in
repairing 2. to join (*together*)

pieces of —**go to pieces** 1. to fall
apart 2. to lose self-control

†pièce de ré·sis·tance (pyes′ də
rā zēs täns′) [Fr., piece of resistance]
1. the principal dish of a meal 2. the
main item in a series

piece goods same as YARD GOODS

piece′meal′ (-mēl′) adv. [< ME.
pece, a piece + *-mele*, part] piece by
piece —adj. made or done piecemeal

piece′work′ n. work paid for at a
fixed rate per piece of work done

pied (pīd) adj. [< *pie*, magpie]
spotted with various colors

pie′-eyed′ adj. [Slang] intoxicated

pier (pir) n. [< ML. *pera*] 1. a structure supporting the spans of a bridge
2. a structure built out over water
and supported by pillars: used as a
landing place, pavilion, etc. 3. *Archit.*
a heavy column used to support weight

pierce (pirs) vt. **pierced, pierc′ing**
[< OFr. *percer*] 1. to pass into or
through as a pointed instrument does;
stab 2. to make a hole in 3. to force
a way into; break through 4. to sound
sharply through 5. to penetrate with
the sight or mind —vi. to penetrate

Pierce (pirs), **Franklin** 1804–69; 14th
president of the U.S. (1853–57)

Pierre (pir) capital of S.Dak.: pop.
10,000

pi·e·ty (pī′ə tē) n., pl. **-ties** [< L.
pius, pious] 1. devotion to religious
duties, etc. 2. devotion to parents,
family, etc. 3. a pious act

pif·fle (pif′l) n. [Colloq.] anything
considered trivial or nonsensical —
pif′fling adj.

pig (pig) n. [OE. *pigge*] 1. a domesticated animal with a broad snout and a
fat body; swine; hog 2. a young hog
3. a greedy or filthy person 4. an
oblong casting of metal poured from
the smelting furnace

pi·geon (pij′ən) n. [< LL. *pipire*, to
chirp] any of various related birds
with a small head, plump body, and
short legs

pi′geon·hole′ n. a small open compartment, as in a desk, for filing papers,
etc. —vt. **-holed′, -hol′ing** 1. to put
in the pigeonhole of a desk, etc. 2. to
put aside indefinitely 3. to classify

pi′geon-toed′ (-tōd′) adj. having
the toes or feet turned in

pig·gish (pig′ish) adj. like a pig; gluttonous; filthy —**pig′gish·ness** n.

pig·gy (pig′ē) n., pl. **-gies** a little pig
—adj. **-gi·er, -gi·est** same as PIGGISH

pig′gy·back′ adv., adj. 1. on the
shoulders or back 2. of or by a transportation system in which loaded truck
trailers are carried on railroad cars

pig′head′ed adj. stubborn

pig iron [see PIG, sense 4] crude iron,
as it comes from the blast furnace

pig·ment (pig′mənt) n. [< L. *pingere*,
to paint] 1. coloring matter used to
make paints 2. any coloring matter
in the tissues of plants or animals

pig·men·ta·tion (pig′mən tā′shən)
n. coloration in plants or animals due
to pigment in the tissue

Pig·my (pig′mē) adj., n., pl. **-mies**
same as PYGMY

pig/pen/ *n.* a pen where pigs are confined: also **pig/sty/** (-stī/) *pl.* **-sties/**

pig/skin/ *n.* 1. leather made from the skin of a pig 2. [Colloq.] a football

pig/tail/ (-tāl/) *n.* a long braid of hair hanging at the back of the head

pike (pīk) *n. clipped form of* TURNPIKE

pike² (pīk) *n.* [Fr. *pique*] a former weapon consisting of a metal spearhead on a long wooden shaft (**pikestaff**)

pike³ (pīk) *n., pl.* **pike, pikes** [ME. *pik*] a slender, freshwater fish with a pointed head

pik·er (pī/kər) *n.* [< ? *Pike* County, Missouri] [Slang] one who does things in a petty or niggardly way

pi·laf, pi·laff (pi läf/, pē/läf) *n.* [Per. & Turk. *pilāw*] rice boiled in a seasoned liquid and usually containing meat or fish: also **pi·lau/** (-lô/)

pi·las·ter (pi las/tər) *n.* [< L. *pila,* a pile] a supporting column projecting slightly from a wall

Pi·late (pī/lət), **Pon·tius** (pän/shəs, -chəs) Rom. procurator of Judea who condemned Jesus to be crucified

pil·chard (pil/chərd) *n.* [< ?] 1. a small saltwater fish of the herring family, the commercial sardine of W Europe 2. any of several related fishes; esp., the **Pacific sardine** found off the W coast of the U.S.

pile¹ (pīl) *n.* [< L. *pila,* a pillar] 1. a mass of things heaped together 2. a heap of wood, etc. on which a corpse or sacrifice is burned 3. a large building 4. [Colloq.] a large amount 5. *earlier name for* NUCLEAR REACTOR —*vt.* **piled, pil/ing** 1. to heap up 2. to load 3. to accumulate Often with *up* —*vi.* 1. to form a pile 2. to move confusedly in a mass (with *in, out, on,* etc.)

pile² (pīl) *n.* [< L. *pilus,* a hair] a soft, velvety, raised surface of yarn loops, often sheared, as on a rug

pile³ (pīl) *n.* [OE. *pil*] a long, heavy beam driven into the ground to support a bridge, dock, etc.

pile driver (or **engine**) a machine for driving piles by raising and dropping a heavy weight on them

piles (pīlz) *n.pl.* [< L. *pila,* a ball] *same as* HEMORRHOIDS

pile/up/ *n.* 1. an accumulation of tasks, etc. 2. [Colloq.] a collision involving several vehicles

pil·fer (pil/fər) *vt., vi.* [< MFr. *pelfre,* booty] to steal (esp. small sums, etc.) —**pil/fer·age** (-ij) *n.* —**pil/fer·er** *n.*

pil·grim (pil/grəm) *n.* [< L. *peregrinus,* foreigner] 1. a wanderer 2. one who travels to a shrine or holy place as a religious act 3. [P-] one of the band of English Puritans who founded Plymouth Colony in 1620

pil/grim·age (-ij) *n.* 1. a journey made by a pilgrim to a shrine or holy place 2. any long journey

pill (pil) *n.* [< L. *pila,* ball] a small ball, tablet, etc. of medicine to be swallowed whole —**the pill** (or **Pill**) [Colloq.] any contraceptive drug for women, in pill form

pil·lage (pil/ij) *n.* [< MFr. *piller, rob*] 1. a plundering 2. loot —*vt., vi.* **-laged, -lag·ing** to plunder

pil·lar (pil/ər) *n.* [< L. *pila,* column] 1. a slender, vertical structure used as a support or monument; column 2. a main support of something

pill/box/ *n.* 1. a small box for holding pills 2. an enclosed gun emplacement of concrete and steel

pil·lion (pil/yən) *n.* [< L. *pellis,* a skin] an extra seat behind the saddle on a horse or motorcycle

pil·lo·ry (pil/ər ē) *n., pl.* **-ries** [< OFr. *pilori*] a device with holes for the head and hands, in which petty offenders were formerly locked and exposed to public scorn —*vt.* **-ried, -ry·ing** 1. to punish by placing in a pillory 2. to lay open to public scorn

pil·low (pil/ō) *n.* [OE. *pyle*] a cloth case filled with feathers, etc. used esp. to support the head in sleeping —*vt.* to rest as on a pillow

pil/low·case/ *n.* a removable covering for a pillow: also **pil/low·slip/**

pi·lot (pī/lət) *n.* [< Gr. *pēdon,* oar] 1. a steersman; specif., one licensed to steer ships into or out of a harbor or through difficult waters 2. a qualified operator of aircraft 3. a guide; leader —*vt.* 1. to act as a pilot of, on, etc. 2. to guide —*adj.* serving as a trial unit in testing

pilot film (or **tape**) a film (or video tape) of a single segment of a projected television series

pi/lot·house/ *n.* an enclosure for the helmsman on the upper deck of a ship

pilot light a small gas burner which is kept lighted to rekindle the principal burner when needed

pi·men·to (pi men/tō) *n., pl.* **-tos** [< Sp. < L. *pigmentum,* pigment] a variety of sweet red pepper: also **pi·mien/to** (-myen/-, -men/-)

pimp (pimp) *n.* [< ?] a prostitute's agent —*vi.* to act as a pimp

pim·ple (pim/p'l) *n.* [< ?] a small, often inflamed, swelling of the skin —**pim/ply** *adj.* **-pli·er, -pli·est**

pin (pin) *n.* [OE. *pinn*] 1. a peg, as of wood, or a pointed piece of stiff wire, for fastening things together, etc. 2. anything like a pin 3. an ornament or badge with a pin or clasp for fastening to clothing 4. *Bowling* one of the clubs at which the ball is rolled —*vt.* **pinned, pin/ning** 1. to fasten as with a pin 2. to hold firmly in one position —**on pins and needles** anxious —**pin down** 1. to get (someone) to commit himself as to his plans, etc. 2. to establish (a fact, etc.) —**pin** (something) **on someone** [Colloq.] to lay the blame for (something) on someone

pin·a·fore (pin/ə fôr/) *n.* [prec. + archaic *afore,* before] a sleeveless garment worn over a dress

pin/ball/ machine a game machine

with an inclined board having pins, holes, etc. for scoring automatically the contacts of a spring-driven ball

pince-nez (pans'nā', pins'-) *n., pl.* **pince-nez** (-nāz') [Fr., nose-pincher] eyeglasses kept in place by a spring gripping the bridge of the nose

pin·cers (pin'ɚrz) *n.pl.* [occas. with sing. v.] [< OFr. *pincier*, to pinch] 1. a tool formed of two pivoted parts, used in gripping things 2. a grasping claw, as of a crab

pinch (pinch) *vt.* [ME. *pinchen*] 1. to squeeze between two surfaces, edges, etc. 2. to press painfully upon (a toe, etc.) 3. to make thin, cramped, etc., as by hunger 4. [Slang] *a)* to steal *b)* to arrest —*vi.* 1. to squeeze painfully 2. to be stingy or frugal —*n.* 1. a squeeze or nip 2. an amount grasped between finger and thumb 3. distress or difficulty 4. an emergency

pinch'ers *n.pl.* same as PINCERS

pinch'-hit' *vi.* -hit', -hit'ting 1. Baseball to bat in place of the player whose turn it is 2. to substitute in an emergency (*for*) —**pinch hitter**

pin curl a strand of hair kept curled with a bobby pin while it sets

pin'cush'ion *n.* a small cushion to stick pins in to keep them handy

pine¹ (pīn) *n.* [< L. *pinus*] 1. an evergreen tree with cones and needle-shaped leaves 2. its wood

pine² (pīn) *vi.* **pined, pin'ing** [< L. *poena*, pain] 1. to waste (*away*) through grief, etc. 2. to yearn

pin·e·al body (pin'ē əl) [< L. *pinea*, pine cone] a small, cone-shaped body in the brain: its function is obscure

pine'ap'ple (pīn'ap''l) *n.* [ME. *pin-appel*, pine cone] 1. a juicy, edible tropical fruit somewhat resembling a pine cone 2. the plant it grows on

pine tar a thick, dark liquid obtained from pine wood, used in disinfectants, paints, etc.

pin'feath'er *n.* an undeveloped feather just emerging through the skin

ping (piŋ) *n.* [echoic] the sound as of a bullet striking something sharply —*vi., vt.* to strike with a ping

Ping-Pong (piŋ'pôŋ', -pāŋ') [echoic] a trademark for table tennis equipment —*n.* [p- p-] same as TABLE TENNIS

pin'head' *n.* 1. the head of a pin 2. a stupid or silly person

pin'hole' *n.* 1. a tiny hole as from a pin 2. a hole to stick a pin into

pin·ion (pin'yən) *n.* [< L. *pinna*, feather] 1. a small cogwheel which meshes with a larger one 2. the end joint of a bird's wing 3. a wing 4. any wing feather —*vt.* 1. to bind the wings or arms of 2. to shackle

pink¹ (piŋk) *n.* [< ?] 1. any of certain plants with white, pink, or red flowers 2. the flower 3. pale red 4. the highest degree, finest example, etc. —*adj.* 1. pale-red 2. [Colloq.] somewhat radical —**in the pink** [Colloq.] healthy; fit

pink² (piŋk) *vt.* [ME. *pynken*] 1. to cut a saw-toothed edge on (cloth, etc.) 2. to prick or stab

pink'eye' *n.* a contagious eye infection in which the eyeball and the lining of the eyelid are red and inflamed

pink·ie, pink·y (piŋ'kē) *n., pl.* **-ies** the smallest finger

pink'ing shears shears with notched blades, for pinking edges of cloth

pin money a small sum of money, as for incidental expenses

pin·na·cle (pin'ə k'l) *n.* [< L. *pinna*, wing] 1. a small turret or spire 2. a slender, pointed formation, as a mountain peak 3. the highest point

pin·nate (pin'āt) *adj.* [< L. *pinna*, a feather] Bot. with leaflets on each side of a common stem

pi·noch·le, pi·noc·le (pē'nuk''l) *n.* [< Fr. *binocle*, eyeglasses] a card game played with a deck of 48 cards (two of every card above the eight)

pin'point' *vt.* to locate precisely

pin'prick' *n.* 1. a tiny puncture as from a pin 2. a minor annoyance

pins and needles a tingling feeling as in a numb limb —**on pins and needles** in anxious suspense

pin'set'ter *n.* a person or automatic device that sets up bowling pins on the alley: also **pin'spot'ter**

pin stripe a pattern of very narrow stripes in suit fabrics, etc.

pint (pīnt) *n.* [< ML.] a measure of capacity equal to 1/2 quart

pin·to (pin'tō) *adj.* [< Sp., spotted] having patches of white and some other color —*n., pl.* **-tos** a pinto horse

pinto bean a mottled kidney bean grown in the SW U.S.

pin'up' *adj.* 1. that is or can be fastened to a wall 2. [Colloq.] designating an attractive girl whose picture is often pinned up on walls

pin'wheel' *n.* 1. a small wheel with vanes of paper, etc., pinned to a stick so as to revolve in the wind 2. a revolving firework

pi·o·neer (pī'ə nir') *n.* [< OFr. *peonier*, foot soldier] one who goes before, preparing the way for others, as an early settler —*vi.* to be a pioneer —*vt.* to be a pioneer in or of

pi·os·i·ty (pī ās'ə tē) *n., pl.* **-ties** the quality or state of being overly or insincerely pious

pi·ous (pī'əs) *adj.* [< L. *pius*] 1. having or showing religious devotion 2. pretending religious devotion 3. sacred —**pi'ous·ly** *adv.*

pip¹ (pip) *n.* [< PIPPIN] a small seed, as of an apple

pip² (pip) *n.* [< ?] any of the figures or spots on playing cards, dice, etc.

pip³ (pip) *n.* [< L. *pituita*, phlegm] a contagious disease of fowl

pipe (pīp) *n.* [< L. *pipare*, chirp] 1. a tube of wood, metal, etc. for making musical sounds 2. [pl.] the bagpipe 3. a long tube for conveying water, gas, etc. 4. a tube with a small bowl at one end in which tobacco is smoked 5. any tubular part, organ, etc. —*vi.* **piped, pip'ing** 1. to play on a pipe 2. to utter shrill sounds —*vt.* 1. to play (a tune) on a pipe 2. to utter in a shrill voice **3.** to bring, call, etc. by piping **4.** to convey (water, gas, etc.) by pipes —**pipe down** [Slang] to shout or talk less —**pip′er** n.

pipe dream [Colloq.] a fantastic idea, vain hope or plan, etc.

pipe fitter a mechanic who installs and maintains plumbing pipes, etc.

pipe′line′ n. **1.** a line of pipes for conveying water, gas, etc. **2.** any means whereby something is conveyed

pipe organ same as ORGAN (sense 1)

pip·ing (pīp′iŋ) n. **1.** music made by pipes **2.** a shrill sound **3.** a pipelike fold of material for trimming seams, etc. —**piping hot** so hot as to sizzle

pip·it (pip′it) n. [echoic] a small N.American singing bird

pip·pin (pip′in) n. [< OFr. pepin, seed] any of several varieties of apple

pip·squeak (pip′skwēk′) n. [Colloq.] anyone or anything regarded as small or insignificant

pi·quant (pē′kənt) adj. [Fr. < piquer, to prick] **1.** agreeably pungent to the taste **2.** exciting interest; stimulating —**pi′quan·cy** n.

pique (pēk) n. [see prec.] resentment at being slighted —vt. **piqued, piqu′ing 1.** to arouse such resentment in; offend **2.** to excite; arouse

pi·qué (pē kā′) n. [see PIQUANT] a cotton fabric with ribbed or corded wales: also **pi·que′**

pi·ra·cy (pī′rə sē) n., pl. **-cies 1.** robbery of ships on the high seas **2.** the unauthorized use of copyrighted or patented work

pi·ra·nha (pi rän′yə, -ran′-) n. [< SAmInd. piro, a fish + sainha, tooth] any of several small, voracious, freshwater, S.American fishes that in schools attack any animal

pi·rate (pī′rət) n. [< Gr. peirān, to attack] one who practices piracy —vt., vi. **-rat·ed, -rat·ing 1.** to take (something) by piracy **2.** to publish or reproduce (a book, recording, etc.) in violation of a copyright —**pi·rat′i·cal** (-rat′i k'l) adj.

pi·ro·gi (pi rō′gē) n.pl. [Russ.] small pastry turnovers filled with meat, cheese, etc.; also **pi·ro′gen** (-rō′gən)

pir·ou·ette (pir′oo wet′) n. [Fr., spinning top] a whirling on one foot or the point of the toe —vi. **-et′ted, -et′ting** to do a pirouette

pis·ca·to·ri·al (pis′kə tôr′ē əl) adj. [< L. piscator, fisherman] of fishes, fishermen, or fishing

Pis·ces (pī′sēz, pis′ēz) [< L. pl. pisces, fish] the twelfth sign of the zodiac

pis·mire (pis′mīr′, piz′-) n. [< ME. pisse, urine + mire, ant] an ant

pis·ta·chi·o (pi stä′shē ō′, -stash′ē ō′) n., pl. **-os′** [< OPer. pistah] **1.** a small tree of the cashew family **2.** its edible, greenish seed (**pistachio nut**)

pis·til (pis′t'l) n. [< L. pistillum, pestle] the seed-bearing organ of a flower —**pis′til·late′** adj.

pis·tol (pis′t'l) n. [< Czech pišt′al] a small firearm operated with one hand

pis′tol·whip′ vt. **-whipped′, -whip′-ping** to beat with a pistol, esp. about the head

pis·ton (pis′t'n) n. [ult. < L. pinsere, to pound] a disk or short cylinder fitted in a hollow cylinder and moved back and forth by the pressure of a fluid so as to transmit motion to a rod (**piston rod**) or moved by the rod so as to exert pressure on the fluid

piston ring a split metal ring around a piston to make it fit the cylinder closely

pit¹ (pit) n. [< MDu. pitte] the hard stone, as of the plum, peach, etc., containing the seed —vt. **pit′ted, pit′-ting** to remove the pit from

pit² (pit) n. [< L. puteus, a well] **1.** a hole in the ground **2.** an abyss **3.** a pitfall **4.** any concealed danger **5.** an enclosed area in which animals are kept or made to fight **6.** a small hollow in a surface, as a scar left by smallpox **7.** the section for the orchestra in front of the stage —vt. **pit′ted, pit′-ting 1.** to make pits or scars in **2.** to set in competition (against) —vi. to become marked with pits

pi·ta (pē′tä, -tə) n. [< Heb. < Mod-Gr.] a round, flat bread of the Middle East: also **pita bread**

pit·a·pat (pit′ə pat′) adv. with rapid beating —n. a rapid series of beats

pitch¹ (pich) n. [< L. pix] a black, sticky substance formed from coal tar, etc., and used for roofing, etc.

pitch² (pich) vt. [ME. picchen] **1.** to set up (pitch a tent) **2.** to throw or toss **3.** to fix at a certain point, degree, key, etc. **4.** Baseball a) to throw (the ball) to the batter b) to assign (a pitcher) c) to act as pitcher for (a game) —vi. **1.** to pitch a ball, etc. **2.** to plunge forward or dip downward **3.** to rise and fall, as a ship in rough water —n. **1.** act or manner of pitching **2.** a throw or toss **3.** anything pitched **4.** a point or degree **5.** the degree of slope **6.** [Slang] a line of talk for persuading **7.** Music, etc. the highness or lowness of a sound due to vibrations of sound waves —**pitch in** [Colloq.] **1.** to begin working hard **2.** to make a contribution —**pitch into** [Colloq.] to attack

pitch′-black′ adj. very black

pitch′blende′ (-blend′) n. [< G. pech, PITCH¹ + blenden, dazzle] a dark mineral, a major source of uranium

pitch′-dark′ adj. very dark

pitched battle 1. a battle in which troop placement is relatively fixed beforehand **2.** a hard-fought battle

pitch·er¹ (pich′ər) n. [< OFr. pichier] a container, usually with a handle and lip, for holding and pouring liquids —**pitch′er·ful′** n.

pitch·er² (pich′ər) n. one who pitches; specif., Baseball the player who pitches the ball to the batters

pitcher plant a plant with pitcher-like leaves that trap and digest insects

pitch·fork′ *n.* a large, long-handled fork for lifting and tossing hay, etc.

pitch′man (-mən) *n., pl.* **-men** 1. a hawker of novelties, as at a carnival 2. [Slang] any high-pressure salesman

pitch pipe a small pipe which produces a fixed tone as a standard for tuning instruments, etc.

pit·e·ous (pit′ē əs) *adj.* arousing or deserving pity —**pit′e·ous·ly** *adv.*

pit′fall′ (-fôl′) *n.* [< PIT² + OE. *fealle,* a trap] 1. a covered pit for trapping animals 2. any unsuspected danger

pith (pith) *n.* [OE. *pitha*] 1. the soft, spongy tissue in the center of certain plant stems 2. the essential part; gist

pith·y (-ē) *adj.* **-i·er, -i·est** 1. of, like, or full of pith 2. terse and full of meaning —**pith′i·ly** *adv.*

pit·i·ful (pit′i fəl) *adj.* 1. arousing or deserving pity 2. contemptible Also **pit′i·a·ble** (-ē ə b′l) —**pit′i·ful·ly** *adv.*

pit′i·less (-lis) *adj.* without pity

pi·ton (pē′tän) *n.* [Fr. < Mfr., a spike] a metal spike with an eye for a rope, driven into rock or ice for support in mountain climbing

pit·tance (pit′ns) *n.* [< OFr. *pitance,* food allowed a monk] 1. a meager allowance of money 2. any small amount or share

pit·ter-pat·ter (pit′ər pat′ər) *n.* [echoic] a rapid succession of light tapping sounds

Pitts·burgh (pits′bərg) city in SW Pa.: pop. 424,000

pi·tu·i·tar·y (pi tōō′ə ter′ē) *adj.* [< L. *pituita,* phlegm] of a small, oval endocrine gland (**pituitary gland**) attached to the brain: it secretes hormones affecting growth, etc.

pit·y (pit′ē) *n., pl.* **-ies** [< L. *pietas,* piety] 1. sorrow for another's suffering or misfortune 2. a cause for sorrow —*vt., vi.* **-ied, -y·ing** to feel pity (for)

piv·ot (piv′ət) *n.* [Fr.] 1. a point, shaft, etc. on which something turns 2. a person or thing something depends on 3. a pivoting movement —*vt.* to provide with a pivot —*vi.* to turn as on a pivot —**piv′ot·al** *adj.*

pix·el (pik′səl) *n.* [< *pic*(*ture*)s + *el*(*ement*)] any of the dots that make up an image, as on a TV screen

pix·ie, pix·y (pik′sē) *n., pl.* **-ies** [< Brit. dial.] a fairy or sprite

pi·zazz, piz·zazz (pə zaz′) *n.* [Slang] 1. vigor 2. style, dash, etc.

piz·za (pēt′sə) *n.* [It.] an Italian dish made by baking thin dough covered with tomatoes, cheese, etc.

piz·ze·ri·a (pēt′sə rē′ə) *n.* [It.] a place where pizzas are made and sold

piz·zi·ca·to (pit′sə kät′ō) *adj.* [It.] *Music* plucked: a direction to pluck the strings of a violin, etc.

pj′s (pē′jāz′) *n.pl.* [Colloq.] pajamas

pk. *pl.* **pks.** 1. park 2. peck

pkg. package(s)

pkwy. parkway

pl. 1. place 2. plural

plac·ard (plak′ärd, -ərd) *n.* [< MDu. *placke,* a piece] a notice for display in

a public place —*vt.* to place placards on or in

pla·cate (plā′kāt, plak′āt) *vt.* **-cat·ed, -cat·ing** [< L. *placare*] to appease; pacify —**plac·a·ble** (plak′ə b′l, plā′kə-) *adj.* —**pla·ca′tion** *n.*

place (plās) *n.* [< Gr. *plateia,* street] 1. a court or short street in a city 2. space; room 3. a region 4. *a*) the part of space occupied by a person or thing *b*) situation 5. a city, town, etc. 6. a residence 7. a building or space devoted to a special purpose [a *place* of amusement] 8. a particular point, part, position, etc. [a sore *place* on the leg, a *place* in history] 9. a step or point in a sequence 10. the customary or proper position, time, etc. 11. a space, seat, etc. reserved or occupied by a person 12. an office; employment 13. the duties of any position 14. *Racing* the second position at the finish —*vt.* **placed, plac′ing** 1. *a*) to put in a particular place, condition, or relation *b*) to recognize or identify 2. to find employment for 3. to repose (trust) *in* a person or thing 4. to finish in (a specified position) in a race —*vi.* to finish second or among the first three in a race —**take place** to occur

pla·ce·bo (plə sē′bō) *n., pl.* **-bos, -boes** [< L., I shall please] a neutral preparation given as a medicine, as to humor a patient

place mat a small mat serving as an individual table cover for a person at a meal

place′ment *n.* 1. a placing or being placed 2. location or arrangement

pla·cen·ta (plə sen′tə) *n., pl.* **-tas, -tae** (-tē) [ult. < Gr. *plax,* flat object] the structure in the uterus through which the fetus is nourished: cf. AFTERBIRTH —**pla·cen′tal** *adj.*

plac·er (plas′ər) *n.* [< Sp. *placel*] a deposit of gravel or sand containing particles of gold, platinum, etc. that can be washed out

plac·id (plas′id) *adj.* [L. *placidus*] calm; quiet —**pla·cid·i·ty** (plə sid′ə tē) *n.* —**plac′id·ly** *adv.*

plack·et (plak′it) *n.* [< ?] a slit at the waist of a skirt or dress to make it easy to put on and take off

pla·gia·rize (plā′jə rīz′) *vt., vi.* **-rized′, -riz′ing** [< L. *plagiarius,* kidnapper] to take (ideas, writings, etc.) from (another) and offer them as one's own —**pla′gia·rism** (-riz′m), **pla′gia·ry** (-rē) *n.* —**pla′gia·rist** *n.*

plague (plāg) *n.* [< Gr. *plēgē,* misfortune] 1. any affliction or calamity 2. any deadly epidemic disease —*vt.* **plagued, plagu′ing** 1. to afflict with a plague 2. to vex; torment

plaice (plās) *n., pl.* **plaice, plaic′es** [< Gr. *platys,* broad] a kind of flatfish

plaid (plad) *n.* [Gael. *plaide,* a blanket] 1. cloth with a crossbarred pattern 2. any pattern of this kind

plain (plān) *adj.* [< L. *planus,* flat] 1. open; clear [in *plain* view] 2. clearly understood; obvious 3. outspoken; straightforward 4. not ornate or luxurious 5. not complicated simple 6. homely 7. pure; unmixed 8. common; ordinary [a *plain* man] —*n.* an extent of level country —*adv.* clearly —**plain'ly** *adv.* —**plain'ness** *n.*

plain'clothes' man a detective or policeman who wears civilian clothes on duty: also **plain'clothes'man** (-mən) *n., pl.* -men

plains·man (plānz'mən) *n., pl.* -men an American frontiersman on the western plains

plain'song' *n.* a very old, plain kind of church music chanted in unison

plaint (plānt) *n.* [< L. *plangere,* to lament] a complaint or lament

plain·tiff (plān'tif) *n.* [see prec.] one who brings a lawsuit into a court

plain·tive (-tiv) *adj.* [see PLAINT] expressing sorrow or melancholy; sad —**plain'tive·ly** *adv.*

plait (plāt) *n.* [< L. *plicare,* to fold] 1. *same as* PLEAT 2. a braid of hair, etc. —*vt.* 1. *same as* PLEAT 2. to braid

plan (plan) *n.* [Fr., plan, foundation] 1. a diagram showing the arrangement of a structure, piece of ground, etc. 2. a scheme for making, doing, or arranging something 3. any outline or sketch —*vt.* **planned, plan'ning** 1. to make a plan of (a structure, etc.) 2. to devise a scheme for doing, etc. 3. to have in mind as a project or purpose —*vi.* to make plans —**plan'ner** *n.*

plane¹ (plān) *adj.* [L. *planus*] 1. flat; level 2. of or having to do with flat surfaces or points, lines, etc. on them [*plane* geometry] —*n.* 1. a flat, level surface 2. a level of achievement, etc. 3. an airplane 4. a wing of an airplane

plane² (plān) *n.* [< L. *planus,* level] a carpenter's tool for leveling or smoothing wood —*vt.* **planed, plan'ing** to smooth or level with a plane

PLANE

plan·et (plan'it) *n.* [< Gr. *planan,* wander] any heavenly body that revolves about the sun: the major planets, in their order from the sun, are Mercury, Venus, Earth, Mars, Jupiter, Saturn, Uranus, Neptune, and Pluto —**plan'e·tar'y** (-ə ter'ē) *adj.*

plan·e·tar·i·um (plan'ə ter'ē əm) *n., pl.* -ums, -a (-ə) a room with a large dome on which the images of the sun, planets, stars, etc. are projected by a complex optical instrument that revolves to show the principal celestial motions

plane tree the American sycamore or a related old-world tree like it

plank (plank) *n.* [< LL. *planca*] 1. a long, broad, thick board 2. an item in the platform of a political party —*vt.* 1. to cover with planks 2. to broil and serve on a board 3. [Colloq.] to set (*down*) with force

plank'ing *n.* 1. planks in quantity 2. the planks of a structure

plank·ton (plank'tən) *n.* [< Gr. *plazesthai,* wander] the microscopic animal and plant life found floating in bodies of water

plant (plant) *n.* [< L. *planta,* a sprout] 1. a living thing that cannot move voluntarily, has no sense organs, and synthesizes food from carbon dioxide 2. a soft-stemmed organism of this kind, as distinguished from a tree or shrub 3. the machinery, buildings, etc. of a factory, etc. —*vt.* 1. to put into the ground to grow 2. to set firmly in position 3. to settle; establish 4. [Slang] to place (a person or thing) in such a way as to trick, trap, etc.

plan·tain¹ (plan'tin) *n.* [< L. *plantago*] a plant with basal leaves and spikes of tiny, greenish flowers

plan·tain² (plan'tin) *n.* [< Sp. *plá(n)tano,* banana tree] a tropical banana plant yielding a coarse fruit

plan·tar (plan'tər) *adj.* [< L. *planta,* sole] of or on the sole of the foot

plan·ta·tion (plan tā'shən) *n.* [< L. *plantare,* to plant] 1. an estate in a warm climate, with crops cultivated by workers living on it 2. a large, cultivated planting of trees

plant'er *n.* 1. the owner of a plantation 2. a machine that plants 3. a decorative container for plants

plant louse *same as* APHID

plaque (plak) *n.* [Fr. < MDu. *placke,* disk] 1. a thin, flat piece of metal, wood, etc. with decoration or lettering on it, hung on a wall, etc. 2. a thin film of matter on uncleaned teeth

plash (plash) *vt., vi., n.* [echoic] *same as* SPLASH

plas·ma (plaz'mə) *n.* [G. < Gr., something molded] 1. the fluid part of blood, lymph, or milk 2. a high-temperature, ionized gas that is electrically neutral

plas·ter (plas'tər) *n.* [< Gr. *emplassein,* to daub over] 1. a pasty mixture of lime, sand, and water, hard when dry, for coating walls, etc. 2. a pasty preparation spread on cloth and applied to the body as a medicine —*vt.* 1. to cover as with plaster 2. to apply like a plaster [to *plaster* posters on walls] 3. to make lie smooth and flat —**plas'ter·er** *n.*

plas'ter·board' *n.* thin board formed of layers of plaster and paper, used in wide sheets for walls, etc.

plaster of Paris [from use of gypsum from Paris, France] a thick paste of gypsum and water that sets quickly; used for casts, statuary, etc.

plas·tic (plas'tik) *adj.* [< Gr. *plassein,* to form] 1. molding or shaping matter; formative 2. that can be molded or shaped 3. made of a plastic —*n.* any of various nonmetallic compounds, synthetically produced, which can be molded and hardened for commercial use —**plas·tic'i·ty** (-tis'ə tē) *n.*

plas'ti·cize' (-tə sīz') vt., vi. **-cized'**, **-ciz'ing** to make or become plastic

plastic surgery surgery dealing with the repair of deformed or destroyed parts of the body, as by transferring skin, bone, etc. from other parts

plat (plat) n. [var. of PLOT] 1. a small piece of ground 2. a map or plan, as of a subdivision —vt. **plat'ted, plat'-ting** to make a map or plan of

plate (plāt) n. [< Gr. platys, broad] 1. a smooth, flat, thin piece of metal, etc., specif. one on which an engraving is cut 2. an impression taken from an engraved surface 3. dishes, utensils, etc. of, or plated with, silver or gold 4. a shallow dish 5. the food in a dish; a course 6. a denture, specif. that part of it which fits to the mouth 7. Baseball short for HOME PLATE 8. Photography a sheet of glass, metal, etc. coated with a film sensitive to light 9. Printing a cast made from a mold of set type —vt. **plat'ed, plat'-ing** 1. to coat with gold, tin, etc. 2. to cover with metal plates

pla·teau (pla tō') n. [Fr.: see prec.] 1. an elevated tract of level land 2. a temporary halt in progress

plate glass polished, clear glass in thick sheets, for windows, mirrors, etc.

plat·en (plat'n) n. [< OFr. plat, flat] 1. in a printing press, a flat metal plate which presses the paper against the type 2. in a typewriter, the roller against which the keys strike

plat·form (plat'fôrm') n. [Fr. plate-forme, lit., flat form] 1. a raised horizontal surface, as a stage for speakers, etc. 2. a statement of policy, esp. of a political party

plat·i·num (plat'n əm) n. [< Sp. plata, silver] a steel-gray metallic chemical element, resistant to corrosion: used for jewelry, etc.

plat·i·tude (plat'ə tood') n. [Fr. < plat, flat, after latitude, etc.] a commonplace or trite remark

Pla·to (plā'tō) 427?-347? B.C.; Gr. philosopher

Pla·ton·ic (plə tän'ik) adj. 1. of Plato or his philosophy 2. [usually p-] not sexual but purely spiritual

pla·toon (plə tōōn') n. [Fr. peloton, a group] 1. a military unit composed of two or more squads 2. Sports any of the specialized squads making up a team —vt. Sports to alternate (players) at a position

plat·ter (plat'ər) n. [< OFr. plat, flat] a large, shallow dish, usually oval, for serving food

plat·y·pus (plat'ə pəs) n., pl. **-pus·es, -pi'** (-pī') [< Gr. platys, flat + pous, foot] a small, egg-laying water mammal of Austral·ia, with webbed feet and a bill like a duck's: in full **duckbill platypus**

PLATYPUS

plau·dit (plô'dit) n. [< L. plaudere, applaud] [usually pl.] applause

plau·si·ble (plô'zə b'l) adj. [< L. plaudere, applaud] seemingly true, trustworthy, etc. —**plau'si·bil'i·ty** n.

play (plā) vi. [OE. plegan] 1. to move lightly, rapidly, etc. [sunlight plays on the water] 2. to engage in recreation 3. to take part in a game or sport 4. to trifle (with a thing or person) 5. to perform on a musical instrument 6. to give out sounds 7. to act in a specified way [play dumb] 8. to act in a drama 9. to impose unscrupulously (on another's feelings) —vt. 1. to take part in (a game or sport) 2. to oppose (a person, etc.) in a game 3. to do, as in fun [play tricks] 4. to bet on 5. to cause to move, etc.; wield 6. to cause [to play havoc] 7. to perform (music, a drama, etc.) 8. to perform on (an instrument) 9. to act the part of [to play Hamlet] —n. 1. motion or activity, esp. when free or rapid 2. freedom for motion or action 3. recreation; sport 4. fun; joking 5. the playing of a game 6. a move or act in a game 7. a dramatic composition or performance; drama —**play down** to attach little importance to —**played out** exhausted —**play up** to give prominence to —**play up to** [Colloq.] to try to please by flattery

play'act' vi. 1. to pretend; make believe 2. to behave in an affected or dramatic manner

play'back' n. the playing of a disc or tape just after recording on it

play'boy' n. a man of means who is given to pleasure-seeking

play'er n. 1. one who plays a specified game, instrument, etc. 2. an actor

play'ful adj. 1. fond of play or fun 2. jocular —**play'ful·ly** adv. —**play'ful·ness** n.

play'go'er n. one who goes to the theater frequently or regularly

play'ground' n. a place, often near a school, for outdoor recreation

play'house' n. 1. a theater for live dramatic productions 2. a small house for children to play in

playing cards cards used in playing various games, arranged in four suits

play'mate' n. a companion in games and recreation: also **play'fel'low**

play'-off' n. a contest to break a tie or to decide a championship

play on words a pun or punning

play'pen' n. a portable enclosure for an infant to play or crawl in safely

play'thing' n. a toy

play'wright' (-rīt') n. a person who writes plays; dramatist

pla·za (plä'zə, plaz'ə) n. [Sp. < L. platea, street] 1. a public square in a city or town 2. a shopping center 3. a service area along a superhighway

plea (plē) n. [< L. placere, to please] 1. a statement in defense; excuse 2. a request; appeal 3. Law a defendant's answer to charges against him

plea bargaining pretrial negotiations in which the defendant agrees to plead guilty to lesser charges if more serious charges are dropped

plead (plēd) vi. **plead'ed** or (colloq.) **pled** or **plead** (pled), **plead'ing** 1.

to present a plea in a law court 2. to make an appeal; beg —vt. 1. to argue (a law case) 2. to answer (guilty or not guilty) to a charge 3. to offer as an excuse —plead'er n.

pleas·ant (plez'ʼnt) adj. [< MFr. plaisir, to please] 1. agreeable to the mind or senses; pleasing 2. having an agreeable manner, look, etc. —pleas'ant·ly adv. —pleas'ant·ness n.

pleas·ant·ry (-'n trē) n., pl. -ries 1. a humorous remark 2. a polite social remark [exchange pleasantries]

please (plēz) vt. pleased, pleas'ing [< L. placere] 1. to be agreeable to; satisfy 2. to be the wish of [it pleased him to go] —vi. 1. to be agreeable; satisfy 2. to have the wish; like [I'll do as I please] Please is also used in polite requests [please sit]

pleas·ing adj. giving pleasure; agreeable —pleas'ing·ly adv.

pleas·ur·a·ble (plezh'ər ə b'l) adj. pleasant; enjoyable

pleas·ure (plezh'ər) n. 1. a pleased feeling; delight 2. one's wish, will, or choice 3. a thing that gives delight or satisfaction —pleas'ure·ful adj.

pleat (plēt) n. [ME. pleten] a flat double fold in cloth, etc., pressed or stitched in place —vt. to lay and press (cloth) in a pleat or pleats

ple·be·ian (pli bē'ən) n. [< L. plebs, common people] 1. one of the common people 2. a vulgar, coarse person —adj. vulgar or common

pleb·i·scite (pleb'ə sīt') n. [< L. plebs, common people + scitum, decree] a direct vote of the people on a political issue such as annexation, independent nationhood, etc.

plec·trum (plek'trəm) n., pl. -trums, -tra (-trə) [L. < Gr. plēssein, to strike] a thin piece of metal, etc. for plucking the strings of a guitar, etc.

pledge (plej) n. [prob. < OS. plegan, to guarantee] 1. the condition of being given or held as security for a contract, payment, etc. 2. a person or thing given or held as such security 3. a promise or agreement 4. something promised —vt. pledged, pledg'ing 1. to give as security 2. to bind by a promise 3. to promise to give

ple·na·ry (plē'nə rē, plen'ə-) adj. [< L. plenus, full] 1. full; complete 2. for attendance by all members [a plenary session]

plen·i·po·ten·ti·a·ry (plen'i pə ten'shē ər'ē, -shə rē) adj. [< L. plenus, full + potens, powerful] having or conferring full authority —n., pl. -ies a diplomat given full authority

plen·i·tude (plen'ə tōōd') n. [< L. plenus, full] 1. fullness; completeness 2. abundance; plenty

plen·te·ous (plen'tē əs) adj. plentiful

plen·ti·ful (plen'ti fəl) adj. 1. having or yielding plenty 2. abundant —plen'ti·ful·ly adv.

plen·ty (plen'tē) n. [< L. plenus, full] 1. prosperity; opulence 2. a

sufficient supply 3. a large number —adv. [Colloq.] very; quite

pleth·o·ra (pleth'ə rə) n. [< Gr. plēthos, fullness] an overabundance

pleu·ri·sy (ploor'ə sē) n. [< Gr. pleura, a rib] inflammation of the thin membrane which lines the chest and covers the lungs, characterized by painful breathing

Plex·i·glas (plek'sə glas') a trademark for a lightweight, transparent thermoplastic substance —n. this material: also plex'i·glass

plex·us (plek'səs) n., pl. -us·es, -us [< L. plectere, to twine] a network, as of blood vessels, nerves, etc.

pli·a·ble (plī'ə b'l) adj. [< L. plicare, to fold] 1. easily bent; flexible 2. easily influenced or persuaded 3. adaptable —pli'a·bil'i·ty n.

pli·ant (plī'ənt) adj. 1. easily bent; pliable 2. compliant —pli'an·cy n.

pli·ers (plī'ərz) n.pl. [< PLY¹] small pincers for gripping small objects, bending wire, etc.

plight¹ (plīt) n. [< OFr. pleit, a fold] a distressing situation

plight² (plīt) vt. [OE. pliht, danger] to pledge, or bind by a pledge

plinth (plinth) n. [< Gr. plinthos, a brick] the square block at the base of a column, pedestal, etc.

plod (pläd) vi. plod'ded, plod'ding [prob. echoic] 1. to move heavily and laboriously; trudge 2. to work steadily; drudge —plod'der n.

plop (pläp) vt., vi. plopped, plop'ping [echoic] to drop with a sound like that of something flat falling into water —n. such a sound

plot (plät) n. [OE.] 1. a small area of ground 2. a secret, usually evil, scheme 3. the plan of action of a play, novel, etc. —vt. plot'ted, plot'ting 1. to mark or trace on a chart or map 2. to make secret plans for —vi. to scheme —plot'ter n.

plov·er (pluv'ər, plō'vər) n. [< L. pluvia, rain] a shore bird with a short tail and long, pointed wings

plow (plou) n. [OE. ploh] 1. a farm implement used to cut and turn up the soil 2. any implement like this, as a snowplow —vt. 1. to cut and turn up (soil) with a plow 2. to make (one's way) through as if by plowing —vi. 1. to use a plow 2. to move (through, into, etc.) with force 3. to plod 4. to begin work vigorously (with into) Also, chiefly Brit., plough —plow'man (-mən) n., pl. -men

plow·share (-sher') n. the cutting blade of a plow

ploy (ploi) n. [< ? (EM)PLOY] an action intended to outwit someone

pluck (pluk) vt. [OE. pluccian] 1. to pull off or out; pick 2. to snatch 3. to pull feathers or hair from 4. to pull at (a taut string, etc.) and release quickly —vi. to pull (at) —n. 1. a pulling 2. courage

pluck·y adj. -i·er, -i·est brave;

spirited; resolute —**pluck'i·ness** *n.*

plug (plug) *n.* [MDu. *plugge*] 1. an object used to stop up a hole, etc. 2. a cake of tobacco 3. an electrical device, as with prongs, for making contact or closing a circuit 4. a kind of fishing lure 5. [Colloq.] a free boost, advertisement, etc. 6. [Slang] an old, worn-out horse —*vt.* **plugged, plug'ging** 1. to fill (a hole, etc.) with a plug 2. to insert a plug of 3. [Colloq.] to advertise with a plug 4. [Slang] to shoot a bullet into —*vi.* [Colloq.] to work doggedly

plug·o'la (-ō'lə) *n.* [< PLUG, *n.* 5] [Slang] a bribe for underhanded promotion on radio or TV

plum (plum) *n.* [OE. *plume*] 1. *a)* a tree bearing a smooth-skinned fruit with a flattened stone *b)* the fruit 2. a raisin 3. the bluish-red color of some plums 4. something desirable

plum·age (plōō'mij) *n.* [MFr. < *plume*, a feather] a bird's feathers

plumb (plum) *n.* [< L. *plumbum*, LEAD²] a lead weight hung at the end of a line (**plumb line**), used to determine how deep water is or whether a wall, etc. is vertical —*adj.* perfectly vertical —*adv.* 1. straight down 2. [Colloq.] entirely —*vt.* 1. to test or sound with a plumb 2. to probe or fathom —**out of plumb** not vertical

plumb·er (plum'ər) *n.* [see prec.] a worker who installs and repairs pipes, fixtures, etc., as of water systems

plumber's helper (or **friend**) [Colloq.] *same as* PLUNGER (sense 2)

plumb·ing (plum'iŋ) *n.* 1. the work of a plumber 2. the pipes and fixtures with which a plumber works

plume (plōōm) *n.* [< L. *pluma*] 1. a feather, esp. a large, showy one 2. a group of these —*vt.* **plumed, plum'ing** 1. to adorn with plumes 2. to preen —**plum'y** *adj.* **-i·er, -i·est**

plum·met (plum'it) *n.* [see PLUMB] 1. a plumb 2. a thing that weighs heavily —*vi.* to fall straight downward

plump¹ (plump) *adj.* [< MDu. *plomp*, bulky] full and rounded in form; chubby —**plump'ness** *n.*

plump² (plump) *vi., vt.* [echoic] to drop or bump suddenly or heavily —*n.* 1. a falling, bumping, etc. 2. the sound of this —*adv.* 1. suddenly; heavily 2. straight down

plun·der (plun'dər) *vt., vi.* [< G. *plunder*, baggage] 1. to rob or pillage 2. to take (property) by force or fraud —*n.* 1. a plundering 2. things taken by force or fraud

plunge (plunj) *vt.* **plunged, plung'ing** [see PLUMB] to thrust or throw suddenly (*into* a liquid, condition, etc.) —*vi.* 1. to dive or rush 2. to move violently and rapidly downward or forward 3. [Colloq.] to gamble heavily —*n.* 1. a dive or fall 2. [Colloq.] a gamble

plung'er *n.* 1. one who plunges 2. a large, rubber suction cup used to free clogged drains 3. any cylindrical device that operates with a plunging motion, as a piston

plunk (pluŋk) *vt.* [echoic] 1. to strum (a banjo, etc.) 2. to throw or put down heavily —*vi.* 1. to give out a twanging sound 2. to fall heavily —*n.* the sound made by plunking —**plunk down** [Colloq.] to give in payment

plu·ral (ploor'əl) *adj.* [< L. *plus*, more] more than one —*n. Gram.* the form of a word designating more than one (e.g., *hands*, *men*)

plu·ral·i·ty (ploo ral'ə tē) *n., pl.* **-ties** 1. a being plural or numerous 2. *a)* the excess of votes in an election that the leading candidate has over his nearest rival *b)* a majority

plu·ral·ize (ploor'ə līz') *vt.* **-ized', -iz'ing** to make plural

plus (plus) *prep.* [L., more] 1. added to (2 *plus* 2) 2. in addition to —*adj.* 1. indicating addition 2. positive (a *plus* quantity) 3. somewhat higher than (graded B *plus*) 4. involving extra gain (a *plus* factor) 5. [Colloq.] and more (personality *plus*) —*n., pl.* **plus'es, plus'ses** 1. a sign (plus sign, +) indicating addition or positive quantity 2. something added 3. an advantage; benefit

plush (plush) *n.* [< L. *pilus*, hair] a fabric with a soft, thick pile —*adj.* [Slang] luxurious: also **plush'y**

Plu·tarch (plōō'tärk) 46?–120? A.D.; Gr. biographer

Plu·to (plōōt'ō) 1. *Gr. & Rom. Myth.* the god of the lower world 2. the outermost planet: cf. PLANET

plu·toc·ra·cy (plōō täk'rə sē) *n., pl.* **-cies** [< Gr. *ploutos*, wealth + *kratein*, to rule] 1. government by the wealthy 2. a group of wealthy people who control a government

plu·to·crat (plōōt'ə krat') *n.* 1. a member of a plutocracy 2. one whose wealth gives him control or influence —**plu'to·crat'ic** *adj.*

plu·to·ni·um (plōō tō'nē əm) *n.* [< PLUTO (planet)] a radioactive, metallic chemical element

plu·vi·al (plōō'vē əl) *adj.* [< L. *pluvia*, rain] of, or having much, rain

ply¹ (plī) *vt.* **plied, ply'ing** [< L. *plicare*, to fold] to twist, fold, etc. —*n., pl.* **plies** 1. a thickness or layer, as of cloth, plywood, etc. 2. any of the twisted strands in rope, etc.

ply² (plī) *vt.* **plied, ply'ing** [contr. < APPLY] 1. to use (a tool, faculty, etc.), esp. with energy 2. to work at (a trade) 3. to keep supplying, assailing, etc. (*with*) 4. to sail back and forth across —*vi.* 1. to keep busy 2. to travel regularly (*between* places)

Ply·mouth (plim'əth) village in SE Mass.: settled by the Pilgrims (1620)

ply'wood' *n.* [PLY¹ + WOOD] a construction material made of thin layers of wood glued together

P.M., p.m., PM [L. *post meridiem*] after noon: used to designate the time from noon to midnight

PMS [*p(re)m(enstrual) s(yndrome)*] the physical and emotional disorders that may precede menstruation

pneu·mat·ic (nōō mat'ik) *adj.* [< Gr. *pneuma*, breath] 1. of or containing wind, air, or gases 2. filled with or worked by compressed air

pneu·mo·ni·a (noo mōn′yə) *n.* [< Gr. *pneumōn*, a lung < *pnein*, breathe] inflammation of the lungs caused as by bacteria or viruses

Po (pō) river in N Italy

P.O., p.o. post office

poach¹ (pōch) *vt.* [< MFr. *poche*, a pocket: the yolk is "pocketed" in the white] to cook (an egg without its shell, fish, etc.) in or over boiling water

poach² (pōch) *vt., vi.* [< MHG. *puchen*, to plunder] 1. to trespass on (private property), esp. for hunting or fishing 2. to hunt or catch (game or fish) illegally —**poach′er** *n.*

pock (päk) *n.* [OE. *pocc*] 1. a pustule caused by smallpox, etc. 2. *same as* POCKMARK —**pocked** *adj.*

pock·et (päk′it) *n.* [< OFr. *poke*, a bag] 1. a little bag or pouch, esp. one sewn into clothing, for carrying small articles 2. a pouchlike cavity or hollow 3. a small area or group [a *pocket* of poverty] 4. *Geology* a cavity filled as with ore —*adj.* 1. that can be carried in a pocket 2. small —*vt.* 1. to put into a pocket 2. to envelop; enclose 3. to take (money, etc.) dishonestly 4. to suppress [to *pocket* one's pride] —**pock′et·ful′** *n., pl.* **-fuls′**

pock′et·book′ *n.* 1. a woman's purse 2. monetary resources

pock′et·knife′ *n., pl.* **-knives′** a knife with a blade or blades that fold into the handle

pock·mark (päk′märk′) *n.* a scar left by a pustule, as of smallpox

pod (päd) *n.* [< ?] a dry fruit or seed vessel, as of peas, beans, etc.

-pod (päd) [< Gr. *pous*, foot] *a combining form meaning:* 1. foot 2. (one) having a (specified number or kind of) feet. Also **-pode** (pōd)

po·di·a·try (pō dī′ə trē) *n.* [< Gr. *pous*, foot + -IATRY] the profession dealing with the care and treatment of the feet —**po·di′a·trist** *n.*

po·di·um (pō′dē əm) *n., pl.* **-di·a** (-ə) [L. < Gr. *pous*, foot] a small platform, as for an orchestra conductor

Poe (pō), **Edgar Allan** 1809-49; U.S. poet & short-story writer

po·em (pō′əm) *n.* [< Gr. *poiein*, to make] an arrangement of words, esp. a rhythmical composition, sometimes rhymed, in a style more imaginative than ordinary speech

po·e·sy (pō′ə sē′) *n. old-fashioned var. of* POETRY

po′et (-ət) *n.* 1. one who writes poems 2. one who expresses himself with beauty of thought and language —**po′et·ess** *n.fem.* (now rare)

po·et·as·ter (pō′ət tas′tər) *n.* [< prec. + Gr. *-aster*, dim. suffix] a writer of mediocre verse

po·et·ic (pō et′ik) *adj.* 1. of or for poets or poetry 2. having the beauty, imagination, etc. of poetry Also **po·et′i·cal** —**po·et′i·cal·ly** *adv.*

poetic license disregard of strict fact or rules, for artistic effect

poet laureate the official poet of a nation, appointed to write poems celebrating national events, etc.

po·et·ry (pō′ə trē) *n.* 1. the writing of poems 2. poems 3. poetic qualities

po·grom (pō gräm′, pō′grəm) *n.* [< Russ., desolation] an organized massacre, as of Jews in Czarist Russia

poi (poi) *n.* [Haw.] a pastelike Hawaiian food made of taro root

poign·ant (poin′yənt) *adj.* [< L. *pungere*, to prick] 1. pungent 2. *a)* sharply painful to the feelings *b)* emotionally moving 3. sharp, biting, pointed, etc. —**poign′an·cy** *n.*

poin·ci·a·na (poin′sē an′ə) *n.* [< M. de *Poinci*, a governor of the Fr. West Indies] a small tropical tree or shrub with showy red or yellow flowers

poin·set·ti·a (poin set′ē ə, -set′ə) *n.* [< J. R. *Poinsett*, 19th-c. U.S. ambassador to Mexico] a tropical shrub with yellow flowers and petallike, red leaves

point (point) *n.* [< L. *pungere*, to prick] 1. a dot in writing, etc. [a decimal *point*] 2. a position or location 3. the exact moment 4. a condition reached [boiling *point*] 5. a detail; item [*point* by *point*] 6. a distinguishing feature 7. a unit, as of value, game scores, etc. 8. a sharp end 9. a projecting piece of land; cape 10. the essential fact or idea [the *point* of a joke] 11. a purpose; object 12. a convincing idea or fact 13. a helpful hint 14. a mark showing direction on a compass 15. *Printing* a measuring unit for type, about 1/72 of an inch —*vt.* 1. to sharpen to a point 2. to give (a story, etc.) emphasis (usually with *up*) 3. to show (usually with *out*) [*point* out the way] 4. to aim —*vi.* 1. to direct one's finger (*at* or *to*) 2. to call attention (*to*) 3. to be directed (*to* or *toward*) —**at the point of** very close to —**beside the point** irrelevant —**to the point** pertinent; apt: also **in point**

point′-blank′ *adj., adv.* [prec. + *blank* (white center of a target)] 1. (aimed) straight at a mark 2. direct(ly); blunt(ly)

point′ed *adj.* 1. having a sharp end 2. sharp; incisive 3. aimed at someone, as a remark 4. very evident —**point′ed·ly** *adv.*

point′er *n.* 1. a long, tapered rod for pointing to things 2. an indicator on a meter, etc. 3. a large, lean hunting dog with a smooth coat 4. [Colloq.] a helpful hint or suggestion

poin·til·lism (pwan′t′l iz′m, -tē iz′m; point′′l-) *n.* [Fr.] a style of painting using dots of color that blend together when seen from a distance —**poin′til·list** *n., adj.*

point′less *adj.* 1. without a point 2. without meaning or force; senseless

point of view 1. the way in which something is viewed 2. a mental attitude or opinion

point′y *adj.* **-i·er, -i·est** 1. coming to a sharp point 2. many-pointed

poise (poiz) *n.* [< L. *pendere,* weigh]
1. balance; stability 2. ease and dignity of manner 3. carriage, as of the
body —*vt., vi.* **poised, pois'ing** to
balance or be balanced

poi·son (poi'z'n) *n.* [< L. *potio,*
potion] a substance which in small
quantities can cause illness or death
—*vt.* 1. to harm or kill with poison 2.
to put poison into 3. to influence
wrongfully —*adj.* poisonous

poison ivy a plant having leaves of
three leaflets and ivory-colored berries:
it can cause a severe rash

poi'son·ous *adj.* that can injure or
kill by or as by poison —**poi'son-
ous·ly** *adv.*

poke¹ (pōk) *vt.* poked, pok'ing [<
MDu. *poken*] 1. *a)* to prod, as with a
stick *b)* [Slang] to hit 2. to make (a
hole, etc.) by poking —*vi.* 1. to jab
(*at*) 2. to pry or search (*about* or
around) 3. to move slowly (*along*) —*n.*
1. a jab; thrust 2. [Slang] a blow with
the fist —**poke fun (at)** to ridicule

poke² (pōk) *n.* [OFr.] [Dial.] a sack

pok·er¹ (pō'kər) *n.* [< ? Fr. *poque*] a
gambling game at cards

pok·er² (pō'kər) *n.* a bar, usually of
iron, for stirring a fire

poker face [Colloq.] an expressionless face, as of a poker player trying to
conceal the nature of his hand

pok·y (pō'kē) *adj.* -i·er, -i·est [<
POKE¹ + -y²] 1. slow; dull 2. small and
uncomfortable, as a room Also **pok'ey**

pol (pāl) *n.* [Slang] a politician

Pol. 1. Poland 2. Polish

Po·land (pō'lənd) country in C
Europe: 120,625 sq. mi.; pop.
31,944,000; cap. Warsaw

po·lar (pō'lər) *adj.* 1. of or near the
North or South Pole 2. of a pole

polar bear a large, white bear of the
arctic regions

Po·la·ris (pō lar'is)
same as NORTH STAR

po·lar·i·ty (pō lar'ə
tē) *n., pl.* -ties 1.
the property of hav-
ing opposite mag-
netic poles 2. the
tendency to turn,
grow, think, etc. in   POLAR BEAR
contrary directions,
as if because of magnetic repulsion

po·lar·i·za·tion (pō'lər i zā'shən) *n.*
1. a polarizing or being polarized 2.
Optics a condition, or the production
of a condition, of light in which the
vibrations of the waves are confined
to one plane or one direction

po·lar·ize (pō'lə rīz') *vt.* -ized',
-iz'ing to give polarity to —*vi.* to
acquire polarity; specif., to separate
into opposed or antagonistic groups,
viewpoints, etc.

Po·lar·oid (pō'lə roid') *a trademark
for:* 1. a transparent material capable
of polarizing light 2. a camera that
produces a print within seconds: in
full **Polaroid (Land) camera**

Pole (pōl) *n.* a native or inhabitant of
Poland

pole¹ (pōl) *n.* [< L. *palus,* a stake] a
long, slender piece of wood, metal, etc.

—*vt., vi.* poled, pol'ing to propel (a
boat or raft) with a pole —**pol'er** *n.*

pole² (pōl) *n.* [< Gr. *polos*] 1. either
end of any axis, as of the earth 2.
either of two opposed forces, parts,
etc., as the ends of a magnet, the
terminals of a battery, etc.

pole·cat (pōl'kat') *n.* [prob. < OFr.
poule, hen + CAT] 1. a small, weasellike animal of Europe 2. a skunk

po·lem·ic (pō lem'ik) *adj.* [< Gr.
polemos, war] of or involving dispute:
also **po·lem'i·cal** —*n.* (a) controversy

po·lem'ics *n.pl.* [*with sing. v.*] the
art or practice of disputation —
po·lem'i·cist (-ə sist) *n.*

pole'star' *n.* 1. Polaris, the North
Star 2. a guiding principle

pole vault a leap for height by vaulting over a bar with the aid of a long
pole —**pole'-vault'** *vi.* —**pole'-
vault'er** *n.*

po·lice (pə lēs') *n.* [Fr., ult. < Gr.
polis, city] 1. the governmental
department (of a city, state, etc.) for
keeping order, detecting crime, etc.
2. [*with pl. v.*] the members of such a
department —*vt.* -liced', -lic'ing 1.
to control, protect, etc. with police or
a similar force 2. to keep (a military
camp, etc.) clean and orderly

po·lice'man (-mən) *n., pl.* -men a
member of a police force —**po·lice'-
wom'an** *n.fem., pl.* -wom'en

police state a government that seeks
to suppress political opposition by
means of police

pol·i·cy¹ (pāl'ə sē) *n., pl.* -cies [see
POLICE] 1. wise management 2. a
principle, plan, etc., as of a government

pol·i·cy² (pāl'ə sē) *n., pl.* -cies [<
Gr. *apodeixis,* proof] a written insurance contract: in full **insurance policy**

po·li·o·my·e·li·tis (pō'lē ō mī'ə līt'
əs) *n.* [< Gr. *polios,* gray + MYELITIS]
an acute infectious disease caused by a
virus inflammation of the gray matter
of the spinal cord, often resulting in
muscular paralysis: also **po'li·o'**

Pol·ish (pō'lish) *adj.* of Poland, its
people, their language, etc. —*n.* the
Slavic language of the Poles

pol·ish (pāl'ish) *vt.* [< L. *polire*] 1.
to smooth and brighten, as by rubbing
2. to refine (manners, style, etc.) —*vi.*
to take a polish —*n.* 1. surface gloss
2. elegance, refinement, etc. 3. a
substance used to polish —**polish off**
[Colloq.] to finish (a meal, job, etc.)
completely

po·lite (pə līt') *adj.* [< L. *polire,* to
polish] 1. cultured; refined 2. having
good manners; courteous —**po·lite'ly**
adv. —**po·lite'ness** *n.*

pol·i·tesse (pāl'ə tes') *n.* [Fr.]
politeness; courtesy

pol·i·tic (pāl'ə tik) *adj.* [see POLICE]
1. having practical wisdom; prudent
2. expedient, as a plan —*vi.* -ticked,
-tick·ing to campaign in politics

po·lit·i·cal (pə lit'i k'l) *adj.* 1. of,
concerned with, or engaged in government, politics, etc. 2. of or characteristic of political parties or politicians
—**po·lit'i·cal·ly** *adv.*

political science the science of the

principles, organization, and methods of government —**political scientist**

pol·i·ti·cian (päl'ə tish'ən) *n.* one actively engaged in politics: often used with implications of seeking personal or partisan gain, scheming, etc.

po·lit·i·cize (pə lit'ə sīz') *vt.* -cized', -ciz'ing to make political

po·lit·i·co (pə lit'i kō') *n., pl.* -cos' [< Sp. or It.] a politician

pol·i·tics (päl'ə tiks) *n.pl.* [with sing. or pl. v.] 1. the science of government 2. political affairs 3. political methods, tactics, etc. 4. political opinions, etc. 5. factional scheming for power

pol'i·ty *n., pl.* -ties [see POLICE] 1. governmental organization 2. a society with a government; state

Polk (pōk), **James K.** 1795-1849; 11th president of the U.S. (1845-49)

pol·ka (pōl'kə) *n.* [Czech, Polish dance] 1. a fast polka for couples 2. music for this dance

pol·ka dot (pō'kə) any of a pattern of small, round dots on cloth

poll (pōl) *n.* [ME. *pol*] 1. the head 2. a counting, listing, etc. of persons, esp. of voters 3. the number of votes recorded 4. [pl.] a place where votes are cast 5. a canvassing of people's opinions on some question —*vt.* 1. to cut off or cut short the wool, hair, horns, etc. of 2. to register the votes of 3. to receive (a specified number of votes) 4. to cast (a vote) 5. to canvass in a poll (sense 5)

pol·len (päl'ən) *n.* [L., dust] the yellow, powderlike male sex cells in the anther of the stamen of a flower

pollen count the number of grains of pollen, esp. of ragweed, in a given volume of air at a specified time and place

pol·li·nate (päl'ə nāt') *vt.* -nat'ed, -nat'ing to transfer pollen to the pistil of (a flower) —**pol'li·na'tion** *n.*

pol·li·wog (päl'ē wäg') *n.* [< ME.: see POLL + WIGGLE] a tadpole

poll·ster (pōl'stər) *n.* one whose work is taking public opinion polls

pol·lute (pə lōōt') *vt.* -lut'ed, -lut'ing [< L. *polluere*] to make unclean or impure; defile —**pol·lu'tant** *n.* —**pol·lu'tion** *n.*

po·lo (pō'lō) *n.* [prob. < Tibetan *pulu*, ball] a game played on horseback by two teams, using a wooden ball and long-handled mallets

Po·lo (pō'lō), **Mar·co** (mär'kō) 1254?-1324?; Venetian traveler in E Asia

po·lo·naise (päl'ə nāz') *n.* [Fr. (fem.), Polish] a stately Polish dance

pol·ter·geist (pōl'tər gīst') *n.* [G. < *poltern*, to rumble + *geist*, ghost] a ghost supposed to be responsible for mysterious noisy disturbances

pol·troon (päl trōōn') *n.* [< It. *poltrone*] a thorough coward

poly- [< Gr. *polys*] *a combining form meaning* much, many

pol·y·clin·ic (päl'i klin'ik) *n.* [POLY- + CLINIC] a clinic or hospital for the treatment of various kinds of diseases

pol·y·es·ter (päl'ē es'tər) *n.* [POLY(MER) + ESTER] a polymeric resin used in making plastics, fibers, etc.

pol·y·eth·yl·ene (päl'ē eth'ə lēn') *n.* [POLY(MER) + ETHYLENE] a thermoplastic resin used in making plastics, films, etc.

po·lyg·a·my (pə lig'ə mē) *n.* [< Gr. *poly-*, many + *gamos*, marriage] the practice of having two or more wives or husbands at the same time —**po·lyg'a·mist** *n.* —**po·lyg'a·mous** *adj.*

pol·y·glot (päl'i glät') *adj.* [< Gr. *poly-*, many + *glōtta*, tongue] 1. speaking or writing several languages 2. written in several languages —*n.* 1. a polyglot person 2. a polyglot book

pol·y·gon (päl'ē gän') *n.* [< Gr.: see POLY- & -GON] a plane figure, esp. one with more than four sides and angles —**po·lyg·o·nal** (pə lig'ə n'l) *adj.*

pol·y·graph (-graf') *n.* [see POLY- & -GRAPH] a device measuring changes in respiration, pulse rate, etc., used on persons suspected of lying

pol·y·math (-math') *n.* [< Gr. *poly-*, much + *manthanein*, learn] a person of great and varied learning

pol·y·mer (-mər) *n.* [G. < Gr. *poly-*, many + *meros*, part] a substance consisting of giant molecules formed from smaller molecules of the same kind —**po·lym·er·ize** (pə lim'ər īz', päl'i mər-) *vt., vi.* -ized', -iz'ing

Pol·y·ne·sia (päl'ə nē'zhə) group of Pacific islands, east of Micronesia —**Pol'y·ne'sian** *adj., n.*

pol·yp (päl'ip) *n.* [< Gr. *poly-*, many + *pous*, foot] 1. a small water animal with tentacles at the top of a tubelike body 2. a growth on mucous membrane, as in the bladder

po·lyph·o·ny (pə lif'ə nē) *n.* [< Gr. *poly-*, many + *phōnē*, a sound] *Music* a combining of individual, harmonizing tones, as in a fugue; counterpoint —**pol·y·phon·ic** (päl'i fän'ik) *adj.* —**pol'y·phon'i·cal·ly** *adv.*

pol·y·syl·lab·ic (päl'i si lab'ik) *adj.* 1. having four or more syllables 2. characterized by polysyllabic words —**pol'y·syl'la·ble** (-sil'ə b'l) *n.*

pol·y·tech·nic (-tek'nik) *adj.* [< Gr. *poly-*, many + *technē*, an art] of or providing instruction in many scientific and technical subjects

pol·y·the·ism (-thē iz'm) *n.* [< Gr. *poly-*, many + *theos*, god] belief in more than one god —**pol'y·the·ist** *adj., n.* —**pol'y·the·is'tic** *adj.*

pol·y·un·sat·u·rat·ed (-un sach'ə rāt'id) *adj.* designating any of certain plant and animal fats and oils with a low cholesterol content

pol·y·vi·nyl (-vī'n'l) *adj.* designating or of any of a group of polymerized vinyl compounds: see VINYL

po·made (pä mād', pō-;-mäd') *n.* [< It. *pomo*, apple (orig. an ingredient)] a perfumed ointment, as for the hair

pome·gran·ate (päm'gran'it, päm'-

ə-; pum'-) n. [ult. < L. pomum, fruit + granum, seed] 1. a round, red fruit with a hard rind and many seeds 2. the bush or tree it grows on

pom·mel (pum'l; also, for n., päm'l) n. [< L. pomum, fruit] the rounded, upward-projecting front part of a saddle —vt. -meled or -melled, -mel·ing or -mel·ling to pummel

pomp (pämp) n. [< Gr. pompē, solemn procession] 1. stately display 2. ostentatious show or display

pom·pa·dour (päm'pə dôr') n. [< Mme. Pompadour, mistress of Louis XV] a hairdo in which the hair is brushed up high from the forehead

pom·pa·no (päm'pə nō') n., pl. -no', -nos' [< Sp.] a spiny-finned food fish of N.America and the West Indies

pom·pon (päm'pän', -päm') n. [Fr.] 1. an ornamental tuft of silk, etc., as worn on hats 2. a chrysanthemum or dahlia with small, round flowers

pom·pous (päm'pəs) adj. 1. full of pomp 2. pretentious; self-important —pom·pos'i·ty (-päs'ə tē) n.

pon·cho (pän'chō) n., pl. -chos [AmSp. < SAmInd.] a cloak like a blanket with a hole in the middle for the head, esp. one worn as a raincoat

pond (pänd) n. [< ME. ponde, enclosure] a body of standing water smaller than a lake

pon·der (pän'dər) vi., vt. [< L. ponderare, weigh] to think deeply (about); consider carefully

pon·der·o·sa (pine) (pän'də rō'sə) [< L. ponderosus, heavy] a yellow pine of western N. America

pon'der·ous adj. 1. very heavy 2. unwieldy 3. labored and dull

pone (pōn) n. [< AmInd.] corn bread in the form of small ovals

pon·gee (pän jē') n. [< Chin. dial. pen-chi, domestic loom] a soft, thin silk cloth, usually in its natural tan

pon·iard (pän'yərd) n. [ult. < L. pugnus, fist] a dagger

pon·tiff (pän'tif) n. [< L. pontifex, high priest] a bishop; specif., [P-] the Pope —pon·tif'i·cal adj.

pon·tif'i·cate (-i kit; for v. -i kāt') n. the office or term of a pontiff —vi. -cat'ed, -cat'ing 1. to officiate as a pontiff 2. to be pompous or dogmatic

pon·toon (pän tōōn') n. [< L. pons, a bridge] 1. a flat-bottomed boat 2. any of a row of boats or floating objects used to support a temporary bridge 3. a boatlike float on an aircraft's landing gear

po·ny (pō'nē) n., pl. -nies [prob. < L. pullus, foal] 1. a horse of any small breed 2. a small liqueur glass 3. [Colloq.] a literal translation of a foreign work, used in doing schoolwork

po'ny·tail' n. a hair style in which the hair is tied tightly at the back and hangs down like a pony's tail

pooch (pōōch) n. [< ?] [Slang] a dog

poo·dle (pōō'd'l) n. [G. pudel] a dog with a solid-colored, curly coat

pooh (pōō) interj. an exclamation of disdain, disbelief, or impatience

pooh-pooh (pōō'pōō') vt. to treat disdainfully; make light of

pool¹ (pōōl) n. [OE. pol] 1. a small pond 2. a puddle 3. a small collection of liquid 4. a tank for swimming

pool² (pōōl) n. [< LL. pulla, hen] 1. a game of billiards played on a table with six pockets 2. a combination of resources, funds, supplies, etc. for some common purpose 3. the parties forming such a combination —vt., vi. to contribute to a common fund

poop¹ (pōōp) n. [< L. puppis, stern of a ship] a raised deck at the stern of a ship: also **poop deck**

poop² (pōōp) vt. [Slang] to tire

poor (poor) adj. [< L. pauper, poor] 1. having little or no means of support; needy 2. lacking in some quality; specif., a) inadequate b) inferior or worthless c) contemptible 3. worthy of pity; unfortunate —the poor poor, or needy people —poor'ly adv.

poor'house' n. formerly, a publicly supported institution for paupers

poor'-mouth' vi. [Colloq.] to complain about one's lack of money

pop¹ (päp) n. [echoic] 1. a sudden, light, explosive sound 2. any carbonated, nonalcoholic beverage —vi. popped, pop'ping 1. to make, or burst with, a pop 2. to move, go, etc. suddenly 3. to bulge: said of the eyes 4. Baseball to hit the ball high into the infield —vt. 1. to cause to pop, as corn by roasting 2. to put suddenly [he popped his head in] —pop'per n.

pop² (päp) n. [< PAPA] [Slang] father

pop³ (päp) adj. clip of POPULAR

pop. 1. popular 2. population

pop (art) a realistic art style using techniques and subjects from commercial art, comic strips, posters, etc.

pop'corn' n. 1. a variety of corn with hard grains which pop open into a white, puffy mass when heated 2. the popped grains

pope (pōp) n. [< Gr. papas, father] [usually P-] R.C.Ch. the bishop of Rome and head of the Church

Pope (pōp), **Alexander** 1688–1744; Eng. poet

pop'gun' n. a toy gun that shoots pellets by air compression, with a pop

pop·in·jay (päp'in jā') n. [< Ar. babaghā, parrot] a conceited person

pop·lar (päp'lər) n. [< L. populus] 1. a tall tree of the willow family having soft, fibrous wood 2. its wood

pop·lin (päp'lən) n. [prob. < Poperinge, city in Flanders] a sturdy ribbed fabric of cotton, silk, etc.

pop'o'ver (-ō'vər) n. a very light, puffy, hollow muffin

pop·py (päp'ē) n., pl. -pies [< L. papaver] a plant with a milky juice and variously colored flowers

pop'py·cock' (-käk') n. [Colloq.] foolish talk; nonsense

poppy seed the small, dark seed of the poppy, used in baking, etc.

pop·u·lace (päp'yə lis) n. [< L. populus] 1. the common people; the masses 2. population (sense 1a)

pop·u·lar (päp'yə lər) adj. [< L. populus, the people] 1. of, carried on by, or intended for people generally 2. not expensive [popular prices] 3.

commonly accepted; prevalent **4.** liked by many people —**pop′u·lar′i·ty** (-lar′ə tē) n. —**pop′u·lar·ly** adv.

pop·u·lar·ize (päp′yə lə rīz′) vt. **-ized′, -iz′ing** to make popular —**pop′u·lar·i·za′tion** n.

pop·u·late (päp′yə lāt′) vt. **-lat′ed, -lat′ing** [< L. populus, the people] **1.** to inhabit **2.** to supply with inhabitants

pop·u·la′tion n. **1.** a) all the people in a country, region, etc. b) the number of these **2.** a populating or being populated

population explosion the great and rapid increase in human population in modern times

pop·u·lism (päp′yə liz′m) n. any movement to advance the interests of the common people —**pop′u·list** adj., n.

pop·u·lous (päp′yə ləs) adj. full of people; thickly populated

por·ce·lain (pôr′s′l in) n. [< It. porcellana] a hard, white, translucent variety of ceramic ware

porch (pôrch) n. [< L. porta, gate] **1.** a covered entrance to a building **2.** an open or enclosed gallery or room on the outside of a building

por·cine (pôr′sīn, -sin) adj. [< L. porcus, a hog] of or like pigs or hogs

por·cu·pine (pôr′kyə pīn′) n. [< L. porcus, pig + spina, spine] a rodent having coarse hair mixed with long, stiff, sharp spines

pore[1] (pôr) vi. pored, por′ing [ME. poren] **1.** to study carefully (with over) **2.** to ponder (with over)

pore[2] (pôr) n. [< Gr. poros, passage] a tiny opening, as in plant leaves, skin, etc. for absorbing or discharging fluids

pork (pôrk) n. [< L. porcus, pig] the flesh of a pig used as food

pork barrel [Colloq.] government appropriations for political patronage

pork′y adj. **-i·er, -i·est 1.** of or like pork **2.** [Slang] saucy, cocky, etc.

por·no (pôr′nō) n., adj. clipped form of PORNOGRAPHY, PORNOGRAPHIC: also **porn** (pôrn)

por·nog·ra·phy (pôr näg′rə fē) n. [< Gr. pornē, a prostitute + graphein, write] writings, pictures, etc. intended primarily to arouse sexual desire —**por′no·graph′ic** (-nə graf′ik) adj.

po·rous (pôr′əs) adj. full of pores, through which fluids, air, or light may pass —**po·ros·i·ty** (pô räs′ə tē) n.

por·phy·ry (pôr′fər ē) n., pl. **-ries** [< Gr. porphyros, purple] any igneous rock with large, distinct crystals

por·poise (pôr′pəs) n. [< L. porcus, pig + piscis, a fish] **1.** a small whale with a blunt snout **2.** a dolphin

por·ridge (pôr′ij) n. [< POTTAGE by confusion with VL. porrata, leek broth] [Chiefly Brit.] a soft food of cereal or meal boiled in water or milk

por·rin·ger (-in jər) n. [< Fr. potager, soup dish: infl. by prec.] a bowl for porridge, cereal, etc.

port[1] (pôrt) n. [< L. portus, haven] **1.** a harbor **2.** a city with a harbor where ships load and unload cargo

port[2] (pôrt) n. [< Oporto, city in Portugal] a sweet, dark-red wine

port[3] (pôrt) vt. [< L. portare, carry] to hold (a rifle, etc.) diagonally in front of one, as for inspection

port[4] (pôrt) n. [prob. < PORT[1]] the left side of a ship, etc. as one faces the bow —adj. of or on the port —vt., vi. to turn (the helm) to the port side

port[5] (pôrt) n. [< L. porta, door] **1.** a porthole **2.** an opening, as in a valve face, for the passage of steam, etc.

Port. 1. Portugal **2.** Portuguese

port·a·ble (pôr′tə b′l) adj. [< L. portare, carry] **1.** that can be carried **2.** easily carried —n. something portable —**port′a·bil′i·ty** n.

por·tage (pôr′tij) n. [< L. portare, carry] **1.** a carrying of boats and supplies overland between navigable rivers, lakes, etc. **2.** any route over which this is done —vt., vi. **-taged, -tag·ing** to carry (boats, etc.) over a portage

por·tal (pôr′t′l) n. [< L. porta, door] a doorway, gate, or entrance

port·cul·lis (pôrt kul′is) n. [< MFr. porte, gate + coleice, sliding] a heavy iron grating lowered to bar the gateway of a castle or fortified town

por·tend (pôr tend′) vt. [< L. por-, forth + tendere, to stretch] **1.** to be an omen of; presage **2.** to signify

por·tent (pôr′tent) n. **1.** something that portends an event **2.** significance

por·ten·tous (pôr ten′təs) adj. **1.** portending evil; ominous **2.** amazing **3.** pompous; self-important —**por·ten′tous·ly** adv.

por·ter[1] (pôr′tər) n. [< L. porta, gate] a doorman or gatekeeper

por·ter[2] (pôr′tər) n. [< L. portare, carry] **1.** a man who carries luggage, etc. for hire **2.** a man who sweeps, cleans, etc. in a bank, store, etc. **3.** a railroad attendant for passengers as on a sleeper **4.** a dark-brown beer

por′ter·house′ (**steak**) (-hous′) [orig., a tavern: see PORTER[2], sense 4] a choice cut of beef between the tenderloin and the sirloin

port·fo·li·o (pôrt fō′lē ō′) n., pl. **-os′** [< L. portare, carry + folium, leaf] **1.** a flat, portable case for loose papers, etc.; briefcase **2.** the office of a minister of state **3.** a list of an investor's securities

port·hole (pôrt′hōl′) n. an opening in a ship's side to admit light and air

por·ti·co (pôr′tə kō′) n., pl. **-coes′, -cos′** [< L. porticus] a porch or covered walk, consisting of a roof supported by columns

por·tiere, por·tière (pôr tyer′) n. [Fr. < porte, door] a curtain hung in a doorway

por·tion (pôr′shən) n. [< L. portio] **1.** a part, esp. that allotted to a person; share **2.** a dowry **3.** one's lot; destiny

—*vt.* 1. to divide into portions 2. to give as a portion to

Port·land (pôrt′lənd) city & port in NW Oreg.: pop. 366,000

port·ly (pôrt′lē) *adj.* -li·er, -li·est 1. large and stately 2. stout; corpulent —**port′li·ness** *n.*

port·man·teau (pôrt man′tō) *n., pl.* -teaus, -teaux (-tōz) [< Fr. *porter*, carry + *manteau*, a cloak] a stiff suitcase that opens into two compartments

portmanteau word a word that is a combination of two other words (Ex.: *smog*, from *smoke* and *fog*)

port of entry a place where customs officials check people or goods entering a country

Por·to Ri·co (pôr′tə rē′kō) *former name of* PUERTO RICO —**Por′to Ri′can**

por·trait (pôr′trit, -trāt) *n.* [see PORTRAY] 1. a painting, photograph, etc. of a person, esp. of his face 2. a description, portrayal, etc.

por′trai·ture (-tri chər) *n.* the practice or art of portraying

por·tray (pôr trā′) *vt.* [< L. *pro-*, forth + *trahere*, draw] 1. to make a portrait of 2. to describe graphically 3. to play the part of in a play, movie, etc. —**por·tray′al** *n.*

Ports·mouth (pôrts′məth) seaport in SE Va.: pop. 105,000

Por·tu·gal (pôr′chə gəl) country in SW Europe, on the Atlantic: 35,509 sq. mi.; pop. 9,228,000

Por′tu·guese′ (-gēz′) *adj.* of Portugal, its people, their language, etc. —*n.* 1. *pl.* -**guese′** a native or inhabitant of Portugal 2. the Romance language of Portugal and Brazil

por·tu·lac·a (pôr′chə lak′ə) *n.* [< L. *portula*, small door: from opening in its seed capsule] a fleshy plant with yellow, pink, or purple flowers

pose (pōz) *vt.* posed, pos′ing [< LL. *pausare*, to rest] 1. to propose (a question, etc.) 2. to put (a model, etc.) in a certain attitude —*vi.* 1. to assume a certain attitude, as in modeling for an artist 2. to strike attitudes for effect 3. to set oneself up (as) [to pose as an officer] —*n.* 1. a bodily attitude, esp. one held for an artist, etc. 2. behavior assumed for effect

Po·sei·don (pō sī′d′n) the Greek god of the sea

pos·er (pō′zər) *n.* 1. one who poses; affected person: also **po·seur** (pō zur′) 2. a baffling question

posh (päsh) *adj.* [< ?] [Colloq.] luxurious and fashionable

pos·it (päz′it) *vt.* [see ff.] to suppose to be a fact; postulate

po·si·tion (pə zish′ən) *n.* [< L. *ponere*, to place] 1. the way in which a person or thing is placed or arranged 2. one's attitude or opinion 3. the place where one is; location 4. the usual or proper place 5. rank, esp. high rank 6. a post of employment; job —*vt.* to put in a certain position

pos·i·tive (päz′ə tiv) *adj.* [see prec.] 1. definitely set; explicit [positive instructions] 2. a) having the mind set; confident b) overconfident or dogmatic 3. showing agreement; or affirma-

tive 4. constructive [positive criticism] 5. regarded as having real existence [a positive good] 6. based on facts [positive proof] 7. *Elec.* a) of electricity predominating in a glass body after it has been rubbed with silk b) charged with positive electricity c) having a deficiency of electrons 8. *Gram.* of an adjective or adverb in its uncompared degree 9. *Math.* greater than zero 10. *Photog.* with the lights and shades corresponding to those of the subject —*n.* something positive, as a degree, quality, quantity, photographic print, etc. —**pos′i·tive·ly** *adv.*

pos·i·tron (päz′ə trän′) *n.* [POSI-(TIVE) + (ELEC)TRON] the positive antiparticle of an electron, having the same mass and magnitude of charge

poss. possessive

pos·se (päs′ē) *n.* [L., be able] the body of men summoned by a sheriff to assist him in keeping the peace, etc.

pos·sess (pə zes′) *vt.* [< L. *possidere*] 1. to have as belonging to one; own 2. to have as an attribute, quality, etc. 3. to gain control over [possessed by an idea] —**pos·ses′sor** *n.*

pos·sessed′ *adj.* 1. owned 2. controlled as if by a demon; crazed

pos·ses′sion (-zesh′ən) *n.* 1. a possessing or being possessed 2. anything possessed 3. [pl.] wealth 4. territory ruled by an outside country

pos·ses′sive (-zes′iv) *adj.* 1. of possession 2. showing or desiring possession 3. *Gram.* designating or of a case, form, or construction expressing possession (Ex.: *my*, *Bill's*) —*n. Gram.* the possessive case, form, or construction —**pos·ses′sive·ness** *n.*

pos·si·ble (päs′ə b′l) *adj.* [< L. *posse*, be able] 1. that can be or exist 2. that may or may not happen 3. that can be done, selected, etc. 4. permissible —**pos′si·bil′i·ty** (-bil′ə tē) *n., pl.* -ties

pos′si·bly (-blē) *adv.* 1. by any possible means 2. perhaps; maybe

pos·sum (päs′əm) *n.* [Colloq.] *same as* OPOSSUM —**play possum** to pretend to be asleep, dead, ill, etc.

post¹ (pōst) *n.* [< L. *postis*] 1. a piece of wood, metal, etc., set upright to support a building, sign, etc. 2. the starting point of a horse race —*vt.* 1. to put up (a poster, etc.) on (a wall, etc.) 2. to announce by posting notices 3. to warn against trespassing on by posted notices 4. to put (a name) on a posted or published list

post² (pōst) *n.* [< Fr. < It. *posto*] 1. the place where a soldier, guard, etc. is stationed 2. a) a place where troops are garrisoned b) the troops at such a place 3. the place assigned to one 4. a job or duty —*vt.* 1. to assign to a post 2. to put up (a bond, etc.)

post³ (pōst) *n.* [< Fr. < It. *posta*] [Chiefly Brit.] (the) mail —*vi.* to travel fast; hasten —*vt.* 1. [Chiefly Brit.] to mail 2. to inform [keep me posted]

post- [L. < *post*, after] *a prefix meaning:* 1. after in time, later (than) [postgraduate] 2. after in space, behind

post·age (pōs′tij) *n.* the amount

charged for mailing a letter, etc., esp. as represented by stamps

post·al (pōs't'l) *adj.* [Fr.] of mail or post offices

postal card a card with a printed postage stamp, for use in the mails

post card a card, often a picture card, that can be sent through the mail

post'date' *vt.* -dat'ed, -dat'ing 1. to assign a later date to than the actual date 2. to be subsequent to

post·er (pōs'tər) *n.* a large advertisement or notice posted publicly

pos·te·ri·or (päs tir'ē ər) *adj.* [L. < *post*, after] 1. later; following 2. at the rear; behind —*n.* the buttocks

pos·ter·i·ty (päs ter'ə tē) *n.* [see prec.] 1. all of a person's descendants 2. all future generations

post exchange a nonprofit general store at an army post or camp

post'grad'u·ate *adj.* of or taking a course of study after graduation —*n.* a student taking such courses

post'haste' *adv.* with great haste

post·hu·mous (päs'choo məs) *adj.* [< L. *postumus*, last] 1. born after the father's death 2. published after the author's death 3. arising or continuing after one's death —**post'hu·mous·ly** *adv.*

post·hyp·not·ic (pōst'hip nät'ik) *adj.* in the time after a hypnotic trance [*posthypnotic suggestion*]

pos·til·ion, pos·til·lion (pōs til'yən, päs-) *n.* [Fr. < It. *posta*, a post] one who rides the leading left-hand horse of a team drawing a carriage

post'in·dus'tri·al *adj.* of a society in which the economy has shifted from heavy industry to service industries, technology, etc.

post·lude (pōst'lōōd') *n.* [POST- + (PRE)LUDE] a concluding musical piece

post'man (-mən) *n., pl.* -men *same as* MAILMAN

post'mark' *n.* a post-office mark stamped on mail, canceling the postage stamp and recording the date and place —*vt.* to stamp with a postmark

post'mas'ter *n.* a manager of a post office —**post'mis'tress** *n.fem.*

postmaster general *pl.* postmasters general, postmaster generals the head of a government's postal system

post·me·ri·di·em (-mə rid'ē əm) [L.] after noon; abbrev. **P.M.**

post'mod'ern *adj.* coming after, often reacting to, 20th-c. modernism

post-mor·tem (pōst môr'təm) *adj.* [L.] 1. after death 2. of a postmortem —*n.* 1. an autopsy 2. an evaluation of some event just ended

post·na·sal drip (pōst'nā'z'l) a discharge of mucus from behind the nose onto the pharynx, due to a cold, etc.

post'na'tal (-nāt''l) *adj.* after birth

post office 1. the governmental department in charge of the mails 2. a place where mail is sorted, postage stamps are sold, etc.

post'op·er·a·tive (-äp'ər ə tiv) *adj.* occurring after a surgical operation

post'paid' *adj.* with postage prepaid

post·pone (pōst pōn') *vt.* -poned', -pon'ing [< L. *post-*, after + *ponere*, put] to put off until later; delay —**post·pone'ment** *n.*

post·script (pōst'skript') *n.* [< L. *post-*, after + *scribere*, write] a note added below the signature of a letter

post time the scheduled starting time of a horse race

pos·tu·late (päs'chə lāt'; *for n.* -lit) *vt.* -lat'ed, -lat'ing [< L. *postulare*, to demand] 1. to assume to be true, real, etc., esp. as a basis for argument 2. to take for granted —*n.* 1. something postulated 2. a prerequisite

pos·ture (päs'chər) *n.* [MFr. < L. *ponere*, to place] 1. the position or carriage of the body 2. a position assumed as in posing 3. an official stand or position [*our national posture*] —*vi.* -tured, -tur·ing to pose or assume an attitude

po·sy (pō'zē) *n., pl.* -sies [< POESY] a flower or bouquet: old-fashioned term

pot (pät) *n.* [OE. *pott*] 1. a round vessel for holding liquids, cooking, etc. 2. a pot with its contents 3. [Colloq.] all the money bet at a single time 4. [Slang] marijuana —*vt.* pot'ted, pot'ting 1. to put into a pot 2. to cook or preserve in a pot —**go to pot** to go to ruin —**pot'ful'** *n., pl.* -fuls'

po·ta·ble (pōt'ə b'l) *adj.* [< L. *potare*, to drink] drinkable —*n.* something drinkable —**po'ta·bil'i·ty** *n.*

pot·ash (pät'ash') *n.* [< Du. *pot*, pot + *asch*, ASH[1]] a potassium compound obtained from wood ashes, etc. and used in fertilizers, soaps, etc.

po·tas·si·um (pə tas'ē əm) *n.* [see prec.] a soft, silver-white, metallic chemical element

po·ta·to (pə tāt'ō) *n., pl.* -toes [< WInd.] 1. the starchy tuber of a widely cultivated plant, eaten as a cooked vegetable 2. this plant

potato chip a very thin slice of potato fried crisp and then salted

pot'bel'ly *n., pl.* -lies a protruding belly —**pot'bel'lied** *adj.*

pot'boil'er *n.* a piece of writing, etc. done quickly to earn money

po·tent (pōt''nt) *adj.* [< L. *posse*, be able] 1. having authority or power 2. convincing; cogent 3. effective, as a drug 4. able to have sexual intercourse: said of a male —**po'ten·cy** *n.*

po·ten·tate (pōt''n tāt') *n.* a person having great power; ruler; monarch

po·ten·tial (pə ten'shəl) *adj.* [see POTENT] that can come into being; possible; latent —*n.* 1. something potential 2. the relative voltage at a point in an electric circuit with respect to some reference point in the same circuit —**po·ten'ti·al'i·ty** (-shē al'ə tē) *n., pl.* -ties —**po·ten'tial·ly** *adv.*

po·ten·ti·ate (-shē āt') *vt.* -at'ed, -at'ing [see POTENT] to increase the effect of (a drug or toxin) by giving another drug or toxin simultaneously

poth·er (päth'ər) *n.* [< ?] a fuss; commotion —*vt., vi.* to fuss or bother

pot'herb' *n.* any plant or herb whose leaves are used as a cooked vegetable or as flavoring in cooking

pot'hold'er *n.* a small pad, or piece of cloth, for handling hot pots, etc.

pot'hook' *n.* **1.** an S-shaped hook for hanging a pot over a fire **2.** a curved or S-shaped mark in writing

po·tion (pō'shən) *n.* [< L. *potare*, to drink] a drink, as of medicine, poison, or a supposedly magic substance

pot'luck' *n.* whatever the family meal happens to be [to take *potluck*]

Po·to·mac (pə tō'mək) river in the E U.S., flowing into Chesapeake Bay

pot'pie' *n.* **1.** a meat pie made in a deep dish **2.** a stew with dumplings

pot·pour·ri (pō'poo rē', pät poor'ē) *n.* [Fr. < *pot*, a pot + *pourrir*, to rot] a medley or miscellany; mixture

pot roast a large cut of beef cooked in one piece by braising

pot·sherd (pät'shurd') *n.* [< ME. *pot*, pot + *shard*, broken] a piece of broken pottery

pot'shot' (-shät') *n.* **1.** an easy shot **2.** a random shot **3.** a haphazard try

pot·tage (pät'ij) *n.* [< Du. *pot*, a pot] a kind of thick soup or stew

pot'ter *n.* one who makes earthenware pots, dishes, etc.

potter's field a burial ground for paupers or unknown persons

potter's wheel a rotating disk upon which clay is molded into bowls, etc.

pot'ter·y *n., pl.* **-ies 1.** a potter's workshop **2.** the art of a potter **3.** pots, dishes, etc. made of clay hardened by heat

pouch (pouch) *n.* [< MFr. *poche*] **1.** a small bag or sack [a tobacco *pouch*] **2.** a mailbag **3.** a saclike structure, as that on the abdomen of the kangaroo, etc. for carrying young —*vt., vi.* to form (into) a pouch

POTTER'S WHEEL

poul·tice (pōl'tis) *n.* [< ML. *pultes*, pap] a hot, soft mass applied to a sore part of the body —*vt.* -ticed, -tic·ing to apply a poultice to

poul·try (pōl'trē) *n.* [< L. *pullus*, chicken] domestic fowls; chickens, ducks, etc.

pounce (pouns) *n.* [ME. *pownce*, talon] a pouncing —*vi.* pounced, pounc'ing to swoop down or leap (on, upon, or at) as if to seize

pound¹ (pound) *n., pl.* pounds, collectively pound [< L. *pondus*, a weight] **1.** a unit of weight, equal to 16 oz. avoirdupois or 12 oz. troy: abbrev. **lb. 2.** the monetary unit of the United Kingdom and various other countries: symbol, £

pound² (pound) *vt.* [OE. *punian*] **1.** to beat to a pulp, powder, etc. **2.** to hit hard —*vi.* **1.** to deliver repeated, heavy blows (*at* or *on*) **2.** to move with heavy steps **3.** to throb

pound³ (pound) *n.* [< OE. *pund-*] a municipal enclosure for stray animals

pound'cake' *n.* a rich cake made (orig. with a pound each) of flour, butter, sugar, etc.

pour (pôr) *vt.* [ME. *pouren*] **1.** to cause to flow in a continuous stream **2.** to emit, utter, etc. profusely or steadily —*vi.* **1.** to flow freely, continuously, etc. **2.** to rain heavily

pout (pout) *vi.* [ME. *pouten*] **1.** to thrust out the lips, as in sullenness **2.** to sulk —*n.* a pouting —*pout'er n.*

pov·er·ty (päv'ər tē) *n.* [< L. *pauper*, poor] **1.** the condition or quality of being poor; need **2.** deficiency; inadequacy **3.** scarcity

pov'er·ty-strick'en *adj.* very poor

POW, P.O.W. prisoner of war

pow·der (pou'dər) *n.* [< L. *pulvis*] **1.** any dry substance in the form of fine, dustlike particles, produced by crushing, grinding, etc. **2.** a specific kind of powder [bath *powder*] —*vt.* **1.** to sprinkle, etc. with powder **2.** to make into a powder —*pow'der·y adj.*

powder keg 1. a keg for gunpowder **2.** an explosive situation

powder room a lavatory for women

pow·er (pou'ər) *n.* [ult. < L. *posse*, be able] **1.** ability to do or act **2.** vigor; force; strength **3.** *a)* authority; influence *b)* legal authority **4.** physical force or energy [electric *power*] **5.** a person or thing having great influence, force, or authority **6.** a nation with influence over other nations **7.** the product of the multiplication of a quantity by itself **8.** the degree of magnification of a lens —*vt.* to supply with a source of power —*adj.* **1.** operated by electricity, a fuel engine, etc. [*power* tools] **2.** served by an auxiliary system that reduces effort [*power* steering] **3.** carrying electricity

power dive *Aeron.* a dive speeded by engine power —*pow'er-dive' vi., vt.* -dived', -div'ing

pow'er·ful *adj.* strong; mighty; influential —*pow'er·ful·ly adv.*

pow'er·house' *n.* **1.** a building where electric power is generated **2.** [Colloq.] a strong or energetic person, team, etc.

pow'er·less *adj.* without power; weak; unable —*pow'er·less·ly adv.*

power of attorney written legal authority to act for another person

pow·wow (pou'wou') *n.* [< AmInd.] **1.** a conference of or with N.American Indians **2.** [Colloq.] any conference

pox (päks) *n.* [for *pocks*: see POCK] a disease characterized by skin eruptions, as smallpox; specif., syphilis

pp. 1. pages **2.** past participle

P.P., p.p. 1. parcel post **2.** *a)* postpaid *b)* prepaid: also ppd.

ppr., p.pr. present participle

P.P.S., p.p.s. [L. *post postscriptum*] an additional postscript

Pr. Provençal

pr. pair(s)

P.R., PR 1. Puerto Rico **2.** public relations

prac·ti·ca·ble (prak'ti kə b'l) *adj.* **1.** that can be put into practice; feasible **2.** that can be used; usable;

useful —**prac'ti·ca·bil'i·ty** *n.* —**prac'ti·ca·bly** *adv.*

prac·ti·cal (prak'ti k'l) *adj.* 1. of or obtained through practice or action 2. useful 3. concerned with the application of knowledge to useful ends *[practical* science*]* 4. given to actual practice *[a practical* farmer*]* 5. that is so in practice, if not in theory, law, etc. 6. matter-of-fact —**prac'ti·cal'i·ty** (-kal'ə tē) *n., pl.* -**ties**

practical joke a trick played on someone in fun —**practical joker**

prac'ti·cal·ly *adv.* 1. in a practical manner 2. from a practical viewpoint 3. in effect; virtually

practical nurse a nurse with less training than a registered nurse, often one licensed by the State (**licensed practical nurse**) for specified duties

prac·tice (prak'tis) *vt.* -**ticed,** -**tic'ing** [< Gr. *prassein,* do] 1. to do or engage in frequently; make a habit of 2. to do repeatedly so as to become proficient 3. to work at, esp. as a profession —*vi.* to do something repeatedly so as to become proficient; drill Chiefly Brit. sp. **practise** —*n.* 1. a practicing; habit, custom, etc. 2. *a)* repeated action to acquire proficiency *b)* proficiency so acquired 3. the actual doing of something 4. *a)* the exercise of a profession *b)* a business based on this

prac'ticed *adj.* skilled

prac·ti·tion·er (prak tish'ə nər) *n.* one who practices a profession

Prae·to·ri·an (pri tôr'ē ən) *adj.* [< L. *praetor,* magistrate] of or belonging to the bodyguard (**Praetorian Guard**) of a Roman emperor —*n.* a member of the Praetorian Guard

prag·mat·ic (prag mat'ik) *adj.* [< Gr. *pragma,* thing done] 1. practical 2. testing the validity of all concepts by their practical results —**pragmat'i·cal·ly** *adv.* —**prag'ma·tism** (-mə tiz'm) *n.* —**prag'ma·tist** *n.*

Prague (präg) capital of Czechoslovakia: pop. 1,025,000

prai·rie (prer'ē) *n.* [Fr. < L. *pratum,* meadow] a large area of level or rolling grassy land

prairie dog a small, squirrellike, burrowing rodent of N.America

prairie schooner a covered wagon

praise (prāz) *vt.* **praised, prais'ing** [< L. *pretium,* worth] 1. to commend the worth of 2. to glorify (God, a god, etc.) as in song —*n.* a praising or being praised; commendation

praise'wor'thy *adj.* worthy of praise —**praise'wor'thi·ly** *adv.* —**praise'wor'thi·ness** *n.*

pra·line (prä'lēn, prā'-) *n.* [Fr.] any of various soft or crisp candies made of nuts, sugar, etc.

prance (prans) *vi.* **pranced, pranc'ing** [< ?] 1. to rise up, or move along, on the hind legs, as a horse 2. to caper or strut —*n.* a prancing —**pranc'er** *n.* —**pranc'ing·ly** *adv.*

prank (praŋk) *n.* [< ?] a mischievous trick —**prank'ster** *n.*

prate (prāt) *vi., vt.* **prat'ed, prat'ing** [< MDu. *praten*] to talk much and foolishly; chatter

prat·tle (prat''l) *vi., vt.* -**tled,** -**tling** [MLowG. *pratelen*] to prate or babble —*n.* chatter or babble

prawn (prôn) *n.* [< ?] an edible, shrimplike crustacean

pray (prā) *vt.* [< L. *prex,* prayer] 1. to implore *[* (I) *pray* (you) tell me*]* 2. to ask for by prayer —*vi.* to say prayers, as to God —**pray'er** *n.*

prayer (prer) *n.* 1. the act of praying 2. an entreaty; supplication 3. *a)* a humble request, as to God *b)* any set formula for this 4. *[often pl.]* a devotional service chiefly of prayers 5. something prayed for —**prayer'ful** *adj.* —**prayer'ful·ly** *adv.*

praying mantis *same as* MANTIS

pre- [< L. *prae,* before] *a prefix meaning* before in time, place, rank, etc.

preach (prēch) *vi.* [< L. *prae-,* before + *dicare,* proclaim] 1. to give a religious sermon 2. to give moral advice, esp. in a tiresome way —*vt.* 1. to urge as by preaching 2. to deliver (a sermon) —**preach'ment** *n.*

preach'er *n.* one who preaches; esp., a clergyman

preach'y *adj.* -**i·er,** -**i·est** [Colloq.] given to or marked by preaching

pre·am·ble (prē'am'b'l) *n.* [< L. *prae-,* before + *ambulare,* go] an introduction, esp. one to a constitution, statute, etc., stating its purpose

pre'ar·range' (-ə ränj') *vt.* -**ranged',** -**rang'ing** to arrange beforehand

pre·can·cer·ous (prē kan'sər əs) *adj.* likely to become cancerous

pre·car·i·ous (pri ker'ē əs) *adj.* [see PRAY] dependent upon circumstances or chance; uncertain; risky —**pre·car'i·ous·ly** *adv.*

pre·cau·tion (pri kô'shən) *n.* [< L. *prae-,* before + *cavere,* take care] care taken beforehand, as against danger, failure, etc. —**pre·cau'tion·ar'y** *adj.*

pre·cede (pri sēd') *vt., vi.* -**ced'ed,** -**ced'ing** [< L. *prae-,* before + *cedere,* to move] to be, come, or go before in time, place, rank, etc.

prec·e·dence (pres'ə dəns, pri sēd'ns) *n.* the act, right, or fact of preceding in time, place, rank, etc.

prec·e·dent (pri sēd'nt; *for n.* pres'ə dənt) *adj.* preceding —*n.* an act, statement, etc. that may serve as an example or justification for a later one

pre·ced'ing *adj.* that precedes

pre·cept (prē'sept) *n.* [< L. *prae-,* before + *capere,* take] a rule of moral conduct; maxim

pre·cep·tor (pri sep'tər) *n.* a teacher

pre·cinct (prē'siŋkt) *n.* [< L. *prae-,* before + *cingere,* surround] 1. *[usually pl.]* an enclosure between buildings, walls, etc. 2. *[pl.]* environs 3. *a)* a police district *b)* a subdivision of a voting ward 4. a limited area

pre·cious (presh'əs) *adj.* [< L. *pretium*, a price] 1. of great price or value; costly 2. beloved; dear 3. very fastidious, affected, etc. —**pre'cious·ly** *adv.* —**pre'cious·ness** *n.*

prec·i·pice (pres'ə pis) *n.* [< L. *prae-*, before + *caput*, a head] a vertical or overhanging rock face

pre·cip·i·tant (pri sip'ə tənt) *adj.* [see prec.] *same as* PRECIPITATE

pre·cip·i·tate' (-tāt'; *also for adj. &* n. -tit) *vt.* -tat'ed, -tat'ing [see PRECIPICE] 1. to hurl downward 2. to cause to happen before expected, needed, etc. 3. *Chem.* to separate (a soluble substance) out of a solution —*vi.* 1. *Chem.* to be precipitated 2. *Meteorol.* to condense and fall as rain, snow, etc. —*adj.* 1. acting or done hastily or rashly 2. very sudden or abrupt —*n.* a substance precipitated out from a solution

pre·cip·i·ta'tion *n.* 1. a headlong fall or rush 2. rash haste; impetuosity 3. a bringing on suddenly 4. *Chem.* a precipitating or being precipitated from a solution 5. *Meteorol.* a) rain, snow, etc. b) the amount of this

pre·cip·i·tous (-ə təs) *adj.* 1. steep like a precipice 2. rash; impetuous

pré·cis (prā sē', prā'sē) *n., pl.* -cis' (-sēz', -sēz) [Fr.: see ff.] a concise abridgment; summary

pre·cise (pri sīs') *adj.* [< L. *prae-*, before + *caedere*, to cut] 1. accurately stated; definite 2. minutely exact 3. strict; scrupulous; fastidious —**pre·cise'ly** *adv.* —**pre·cise'ness** *n.*

pre·ci·sion (pri sizh'ən) *n.* the quality of being precise; exactness —*adj.* requiring exactness [*precision* work]

pre·clude (pri klōōd') *vt.* -clud'ed, -clud'ing [< L. *prae-*, before + *claudere*, to close] to make impossible, esp. in advance; prevent —**pre·clu'sion** (-klōō'zhən) *n.*

pre·co·cious (pri kō'shəs) *adj.* [< L. *prae-*, before + *coquere*, to cook] matured earlier than usual [a *precocious* child] —**pre·coc'i·ty** (-käs'ə tē) *n.*

pre·cog·ni·tion (prē'käg nish'ən) *n.* [see PRE- & COGNITION] the supposed extrasensory perception of a future event —**pre·cog'ni·tive** *adj.*

pre'-Co·lum'bi·an (-kə lum'bē ən) *adj.* of any period in the Americas before Columbus's voyages

pre·con·ceive (prē'kən sēv') *vt.* -ceived', -ceiv'ing to form an opinion of beforehand —**pre'con·cep'tion** *n.*

pre'con·di'tion (-dish'ən) *vt.* to prepare to behave or react in a certain way under certain conditions

pre·cur·sor (pri kur'sər) *n.* [< L. *praecurrere*, run ahead] 1. a forerunner 2. a predecessor —**pre·cur'so·ry** *adj.*

pred·a·to·ry (pred'ə tôr'ē) *adj.* [< L. *praeda*, a prey] 1. of or living by plundering or robbing 2. preying on other animals —**pred'a·tor** (-tər) *n.*

pre·de·cease (prē'di sēs') *vt.* -ceased', -ceas'ing to die before (someone else)

pred·e·ces·sor (pred'ə ses'ər) *n.* [< L. *prae-*, before + *decedere*, go away] a person preceding another, as in office

pre·des·ti·na·tion (prē des'tə nā'shən) *n.* 1. *Theol.* the doctrine that a) God foreordained everything that would happen b) God predestines souls to salvation or to damnation 2. destiny

pre·des'tine (-tin) *vt.* -tined, -tin·ing to destine beforehand; foreordain

pre'de·ter'mine *vt.* -mined, -min·ing to determine beforehand

pre·dic·a·ment (pri dik'ə mənt) *n.* [see PREACH] an unpleasant or embarrassing situation

pred·i·cate (pred'ə kāt'; *for n. &* adj. -kit) *vt.* -cat'ed, -cat'ing [see PREACH] 1. to affirm as a quality or attribute 2. to base (*on* or *upon* facts, conditions, etc.) —*n. Gram.* the word or words that make a statement about the subject —*adj. Gram.* of or involved in a predicate —**pred'i·ca'tion** *n.*

pre·dict (pri dikt') *vt., vi.* [< L. *prae-*, before + *dicere*, tell] to state (what one believes will happen); foretell —**pre·dict'a·ble** *adj.* —**pre·dic'tion** *n.* —**pre·dic'tor** *n.*

pre·di·gest (prē'di jest', -dī-) *vt.* to treat (food) with enzymes for easier digestion when eaten

pre·di·lec·tion (pred''l ek'shən, prēd'-) *n.* [< L. *prae-*, before + *diligere*, prefer] a partiality or preference

pre·dis·pose (prē'dis pōz') *vt.* -posed', -pos'ing to make susceptible (*to*); incline —**pre'dis·po·si'tion** *n.*

pre·dom·i·nant (pri däm'ə nənt) *adj.* 1. having authority or influence over others; superior 2. most frequent; prevailing —**pre·dom'i·nance** *n.* —**pre·dom'i·nant·ly** *adv.*

pre·dom'i·nate (-nāt') *vi.* -nat'ed, -nat'ing 1. to have authority or influence (*over* others) 2. to be dominant in amount, number, etc.; prevail

pre·em·i·nent (prē em'ə nənt) *adj.* eminent above others; surpassing: also pre-eminent —**pre·em'i·nence** *n.* —**pre·em'i·nent·ly** *adv.*

pre·empt (prē empt') *vt.* [< L. *prae-*, before + *emere*, buy] 1. to gain the right to buy (public land) by settling on it 2. to seize before anyone else can 3. *Radio, TV* to replace (a scheduled program) Also **pre-empt**

pre·emp'tion *n.* 1. a preempting 2. action taken to check other action beforehand —**pre·emp'tive** *adj.*

preen (prēn) *vt.* [< ME. *proinen*, PRUNE²] 1. to clean and trim (the feathers) with the beak 2. to dress up or adorn (oneself) 3. to pride (oneself)

pref. 1. preface 2. preferred

pre·fab (prē'fab') *n.* [Colloq.] a prefabricated building

pre·fab·ri·cate (prē fab'rə kāt') *vt.* -cat'ed, -cat'ing to build (a house, etc.) in standardized sections for shipment and quick assembly

pref·ace (pref'is) *n.* [< L. *prae-*, before + *fari*, speak] an introduction to a book, speech, etc. —*vt.* -aced, -ac·ing 1. to furnish with a preface 2. to introduce —**pref'a·to'ry** (-ə tôr'ē) *adj.*

pre·fect (prē'fekt) *n.* [< L. *praeficere*, to set over] any of various administrators —**pre'fec·ture** (-fek chər) *n.*

pre·fer (pri fur') vt. -ferred', -fer'-ring [< L. prae-, before + ferre, to bear] 1. to promote; advance 2. to put before a court, etc. for consideration 3. to like better

pref·er·a·ble (pref'ər ə b'l) adj. more desirable —pref'er·a·bly adv.

pref'er·ence (-əns) n. 1. a preferring or being preferred 2. something preferred 3. advantage given to one person, country, etc. over others —pref'er·en'tial (-ə ren'shəl) adj.

pre·fer·ment (pri fur'mənt) n. an advancement in rank, etc.; promotion

pre·fig·ure (prē fig'yər) vt. -ured, -ur·ing to foreshadow

pre·fix (prē'fiks; also for v. prē fiks') vt. [< L. prae-, before + figere, fix] to fix to the beginning; esp., to add as a prefix —n. a syllable or group of syllables joined to the beginning of a word to alter its meaning

preg·nant (preg'nənt) adj. [< L. pregnans] 1. having (an) offspring developing in the uterus; with child 2. mentally fertile; inventive 3. full of meaning, etc. 4. filled (with) or rich (in) —preg'nan·cy n., pl. -cies

pre·hen·sile (pri hen's'l) adj. [< L. prehendere, take] adapted for seizing or grasping, esp. by wrapping around something, as a monkey's tail

pre·his·tor·ic (prē'his tôr'ik) adj. of the period before recorded history

pre·judge (prē judge') vt. -judged', -judg'ing to judge beforehand, or without all the evidence —pre·judg'ment n.

prej·u·dice (prej'ə dis) n. [< L. prae-, before + judicium, judgment] 1. a preconceived, usually unfavorable, idea 2. an opinion held in disregard of facts that contradict it; bias 3. intolerance or hatred of other races, etc. 4. injury or harm —vt. -diced, -dic-ing 1. to injure or harm 2. to cause to have prejudice; bias —prej'u·di'cial (-dish'əl) adj.

prel·ate (prel'it) n. [< L. praelatus, placed before] a high-ranking ecclesiastic, as a bishop —prel'a·cy (-ə sē) n.

pre·lim·i·nar·y (pri lim'ə ner'ē) adj. [< L. prae, before + limen, threshold] leading up to the main action, etc.; introductory —n., pl. -ies [often pl.] a preliminary step, test, etc.

pre·lit·er·ate (prē lit'ər it) adj. of a society lacking a written language

prel·ude (prel'yōōd, prā'lōōd) n. [< L. prae, before + ludere, to play] 1. a preliminary part 2. Music a) an introductory section of a suite, fugue, etc. b) a short, romantic composition

pre·mar·i·tal (prē mar'ə t'l) adj. before marriage

pre·ma·ture (prē'mə toor', -choor', -tyoor') adj. [< L. prae-, before + maturus, ripe] happening, done, arriving, etc. before the proper or usual time; too early —pre'ma·ture'ly adv.

pre·med·i·tate (-med'ə tāt') vt., vi. -tat'ed, -tat'ing to plan or think out beforehand —pre·med'i·ta'tion n.

pre·mier (pri mir', -myir') adj. [< L. primus, first] first in importance; foremost —n. a chief official; specif., a prime minister —pre·mier'ship n.

pre·mière, pre·miere (pri myer', -mir') n. [Fr.: see prec.] a first performance of a play, movie, etc.

prem·ise (prem'is) n. [< L. prae-, before + mittere, send] 1. a previous statement serving as a basis for an argument 2. [pl.] a piece of real estate —vt. -ised, -is·ing to state as a premise; postulate

pre·mi·um (prē'mē əm) n. [< L. prae, before + emere, take] 1. a reward or prize, esp. as an inducement to buy 2. an additional amount paid or charged 3. a payment, as for an insurance policy 4. very high value [he put a premium on wit] —at a premium very valuable because of scarcity

pre·mo·ni·tion (prē'mə nish'ən, prem'ə-) n. [< L. prae-, before + monere, warn] 1. a forewarning 2. a foreboding —pre·mon·i·to·ry (pri män'ə tôr'ē) adj.

pre·na·tal (prē nāt''l) adj. [PRE- + NATAL] before birth

pre·oc·cu·py (prē äk'yə pī') vt. -pied, -py·ing [< L. prae-, before + occupare, seize] 1. to wholly occupy the thoughts of; engross 2. to take possession of before someone else or beforehand —pre·oc'cu·pa'tion (-pā'shən) n. —pre·oc'cu·pied' adj.

pre·or·dain (prē'ôr dān') vt. to ordain or decree beforehand

prep (prep) adj. [Colloq.] clipped form of PREPARATORY [a prep school] —vt. prepped, prep'ping to prepare (esp. a patient for surgery)

prep. 1. preparatory 2. preposition

pre·pack·age (prē pak'ij) vt. -aged, -ag·ing to package (foods, etc.) in standard units before selling

pre·paid' pt. & pp. of PREPAY

prep·a·ra·tion (prep'ə rā'shən) n. 1. a preparing or being prepared 2. a preparatory measure 3. something prepared, as a medicine, cosmetic, etc.

pre·par·a·to·ry (pri par'ə tôr'ē) adj. serving to prepare; introductory

preparatory school a private school that prepares students for college.

pre·pare (pri par', -per') vt. -pared', -par'ing [< L. prae-, before + parare, get ready] 1. to make ready 2. to equip or furnish 3. to put together [prepare dinner] —vi. 1. to make things ready 2. to make oneself ready

pre·par'ed·ness n. the state of being prepared, esp. for waging war

pre·pay' vt. -paid', -pay'ing to pay or pay for in advance

pre·pon·der·ate (pri pän'də rāt') vi. -at'ed, -at'ing [< L. prae-, before + ponderare, weigh] to be superior in amount, power, etc. —pre·pon'der·ance n. —pre·pon'der·ant adj.

prep·o·si·tion (prep'ə zish'ən) n. [< L. prae-, before + ponere, to place] a word, as *in*, *by*, *to*, etc., that connects a noun or pronoun to another word —**prep′o·si′tion·al** *adj.*

pre·pos·sess (prē′pə zes′) *vt.* **1.** to prejudice **2.** to impress favorably

pre′pos·sess′ing *adj.* that impresses favorably; pleasing

pre·pos·ter·ous (pri päs′tər əs) *adj.* [< L. *prae-*, before + *posterus*, coming after] absurd; ridiculous; laughable

prep·py, **prep·pie** (prep′ē) *n.*, *pl.* **-pies** a (former) student at a preparatory school —*adj.* of or like the clothes worn by such students

pre·puce (prē′pyōōs) *n.* [< L. *prae-putium*] same as FORESKIN

pre·re·cord (prē′ri kôrd′) *vt.* *Radio & TV* to record (a program, etc.) in advance, for later broadcasting

pre·req·ui·site (pri rek′wə zit) *adj.* required beforehand as a necessary condition —*n.* something prerequisite

pre·rog·a·tive (pri räg′ə tiv) *n.* [< L. *prae-*, before + *rogare*, ask] an exclusive right or privilege

Pres. President

pres. present

pres·age (pres′ij; *for v. usually* pri sāj′) *n.* [< L. *prae-*, before + *sagire*, perceive] **1.** an omen; portent **2.** a foreboding —*vt.* **-aged′**, **-ag′ing** to give warning of; portend

pres·by·ter (prez′bi tər) *n.* [see PRIEST] **1.** in the Presbyterian Church, an elder **2.** in the Episcopal Church, a priest or minister

Pres·by·te·ri·an (prez′bə tir′ē ən) *adj.* designating or of a church of a traditionally Calvinistic denomination governed by presbyters —*n.* a member of a Presbyterian church

pre′school′ *adj.* of or for a child between infancy and school age

pre·sci·ence (prē′shē əns) *n.* [< L. *prae-*, before + *scire*, know] foreknowledge; foresight —**pre′sci·ent** *adj.*

pre·scribe (pri skrīb′) *vt.* **-scribed′**, **-scrib′ing** [< L. *prae-*, before + *scribere*, write] **1.** to order; direct **2.** to order or advise as a medicine or treatment: said of physicians, etc.

pre·script (prē′skript) *n.* a prescribed rule —**pre·scrip′tive** *adj.*

pre·scrip·tion (pri skrip′shən) *n.* **1.** something prescribed **2.** *a)* a written direction for the preparation and use of a medicine *b)* such a medicine

pres·ence (prez′ns) *n.* **1.** the fact or state of being present **2.** immediate surroundings [in his *presence*] **3.** *a)* a person's bearing or appearance *b)* impressive bearing, personality, etc.

presence of mind ability to think and act quickly in an emergency

pres·ent (prez′nt; *for v.* pri zent′) *adj.* [< L. *prae-*, before + *esse*, be] **1.** being at the specified place **2.** existing or happening now **3.** *Gram.* indicating action or state now or action that is always true [*present* tense] —*n.* **1.** the present time or occasion **2.** the present tense **3.** a gift —*vt.* **1.** to introduce (a person) **2.** to exhibit; show **3.** to offer for consideration **4.** to give (a gift, etc.) to (a person, etc.) —**present arms** to hold

a rifle vertically in front of the body

pre·sent·a·ble (pri zen′tə b'l) *adj.* **1.** suitable for presentation **2.** suitably groomed for meeting people

pre·sen·ta·tion (prē′zen tā′shən, prez′′n-) *n.* **1.** a presenting or being presented **2.** something presented

pres′ent-day′ *adj.* of the present time

pre·sen·ti·ment (pri zen′tə mənt) *n.* [see PRE- & SENTIMENT] a feeling that something, esp. of an unfortunate nature, is about to happen

pres′ent·ly *adv.* **1.** soon; shortly **2.** at present; now

pre·sent·ment (pri zent′mənt) *n.* presentation

present participle a participle used to express present or continuing action or existence, as in "he is *growing*"

pre·serv·a·tive (pri zur′və tiv) *adj.* preserving —*n.* anything that preserves [a *preservative* added to foods]

pre·serve (pri zurv′) *vt.* **-served′**, **-serv′ing** [< L. *prae-*, before + *servare*, keep] **1.** to protect from harm, damage, etc. **2.** to keep from spoiling **3.** to prepare (food), as by canning, for future use **4.** to carry on; maintain —*n.* **1.** [*usually pl.*] fruit preserved by cooking with sugar **2.** a place where game, fish, etc. are maintained —**pres·er·va·tion** (prez′ər vā′shən) *n.* —**pre·serv′er** *n.*

pre·set (prē set′) *vt.* **-set′**, **-set′ting** to set (automatic controls) beforehand

pre′-shrunk′ *adj.* shrunk by a special process in manufacture, to minimize further shrinkage in laundering

pre·side (pri zīd′) *vi.* **-sid′ed**, **-sid′ing** [< L. *prae-*, before + *sedere*, sit] **1.** to serve as chairman **2.** to have control or authority (*over*)

pres·i·dent (prez′i dənt) *n.* [see prec.] **1.** the highest officer of a company, club, etc. **2.** [*often* P-] the chief executive (as in the U.S.), or the nominal head (as in France), of a republic —**pres′i·den·cy** *n.*, *pl.* **-cies** —**pres′i·den′tial** (-den′shəl) *adj.*

press¹ (pres) *vt.* [< L. *premere*] **1.** to act on with steady force or weight; push against, squeeze, compress, etc. **2.** to squeeze (juice, etc.) from **3.** to iron (clothes, etc.) **4.** to embrace closely **5.** to force; compel **6.** to urge persistently; entreat **7.** to try to force **8.** to emphasize **9.** to distress or trouble [*pressed* for time] **10.** to urge on —*vi.* **1.** to weigh down **2.** to go forward with determination **3.** to crowd —*n.* **1.** pressure, urgency, etc. **2.** a crowd **3.** a machine for crushing, stamping, etc. **4.** smoothness, esp. of clothes after pressing **5.** *a)* *clipped form of* PRINTING PRESS *b)* a printing establishment *c)* newspapers, magazines, etc., or the persons who write for them *d)* publicity, etc. in newspapers, etc. **6.** an upright closet for storing clothes, etc. —**press′er** *n.*

press² (pres) *vt.* [< L. *praes*, surety + *stare*, to stand] to force into service, esp. military or naval service

press agent one whose work is to get publicity for his client

press box a place for reporters at sports events, etc.

press conference a group interview granted to newsmen as by a celebrity

press'ing *adj.* calling for immediate attention; urgent

pres·sure (presh'ər) *n.* 1. a pressing or being pressed 2. a state of distress 3. a compelling influence [social *pressure*] 4. urgent demands; urgency 5. *Physics* force per unit of area exerted upon a surface, etc. —*vt.* -sured, -sur·ing to exert pressure on

pressure cooker a container for quick cooking food under pressure

pres'sur·ize' (-īz') *vt.* -ized', -iz'ing to keep nearly normal atmospheric pressure inside (an airplane, etc.), as at high altitudes —**pres'sur·i·za'tion** *n.* —**pres'sur·iz'er** *n.*

pres·ti·dig·i·ta·tion (pres'tə dij'i tā'shən) *n.* [Fr. < *preste*, quick + L. *digitus*, finger] sleight of hand

pres·tige (pres tēzh') *n.* [Fr. < L. *praestigiae*, deceptions] 1. the power to impress or influence 2. reputation based on high achievement, character, etc. —**pres·tige'ful** *adj.*

pres·ti'gious (-tij'əs, -tēj'-) *adj.* having or imparting prestige or distinction

pres·to (pres'tō) *adv., adj.* [It., quick] fast or at once

pre'stressed' concrete concrete containing tensed steel cables for strength

pre·sume (pri zōōm') *vt.* -sumed', -sum'ing [< L. *prae-*, before + *sumere*, take] 1. to dare (to say or do something); venture 2. to take for granted; suppose —*vi.* to act presumptuously; take liberties —**pre·sum'a·ble** *adj.* —**pre·sum'a·bly** *adv.*

pre·sump·tion (pri zump'shən) *n.* 1. a presuming; specif., a) an overstepping of proper bounds b) a taking of something for granted 2. the thing presumed 3. a reason for presuming —**pre·sump'tive** *adj.*

pre·sump'tu·ous (-choo wəs) *adj.* too bold or forward

pre·sup·pose (prē'sə pōz') *vt.* -posed', -pos'ing 1. to suppose or assume beforehand 2. to require or imply as a preceding condition —**pre'sup·po·si'tion** (-sup ə zish'ən) *n.*

pre·teen (prē'tēn') *n.* a child nearly a teen-ager

pre·tend (pri tend') *vt.* [< L. *prae-*, before + *tendere*, to stretch] 1. to profess [to *pretend* infallibility] 2. to feign; simulate [to *pretend* anger] 3. to make believe [*pretend* I'm you] —*vi.* to lay claim (*to*) —**pre·tend'er** *n.*

pre·tense (pri tens', prē'tens) *n.* 1. a claim; pretension 2. a false claim 3. a false show of something 4. a pretending, as at play Brit. sp. **pretence**

pre·ten·sion (pri ten'shən) *n.* 1. a pretext 2. a claim 3. assertion of a claim 4. pretentiousness

pre·ten'tious (-shəs) *adj.* 1. making claims to some distinction, importance, etc. 2. affectedly grand; ostentatious —**pre·ten'tious·ly** *adv.* —**pre·ten'tious·ness** *n.*

pret·er·it, pret·er·ite (pret'ər it) *adj.* [< L. *praeter-*, beyond + *ire*, go] *Gram.* expressing past action or state —*n.* the past tense

pre·ter·nat·u·ral (prēt'ər nach'ər əl) *adj.* [ML. *praeternaturalis*] 1. differing from or beyond what is natural; abnormal 2. supernatural

pre·test (prē'test') *vt., vi.* to test in advance

pre·text (prē'tekst) *n.* [< L. *prae-*, before + *texere*, weave] a false reason put forth to hide the real one

Pre·to·ri·a (pri tôr'ē ə) a capital of South Africa: pop. 423,000

pret·ti·fy (prit'ə fī'), *vt.* -fied', -fy'ing to make pretty

pret·ty (prit'ē, pur'tē) *adj.* -ti·er, -ti·est [OE. *prættig*, crafty] attractive in a dainty, graceful way —*adv.* fairly; somewhat —*vt.* -tied, -ty·ing to make pretty (usually with *up*) —**pret'ti·ly** *adv.* —**pret'ti·ness** *n.*

pret·zel (pret's'l) *n.* [< L. *brachium*, an arm] a hard, brittle, salted biscuit, often formed in a loose knot

pre·vail (pri vāl') *vi.* [< L. *prae-*, before + *valere*, be strong] 1. to be victorious (*over* or *against*) 2. to succeed 3. to be or become more widespread 4. to be prevalent —**prevail on** (or *upon*, *with*) to persuade

pre·vail'ing *adj.* 1. superior in strength or influence 2. prevalent

prev·a·lent (prev'ə lənt) *adj.* [see PREVAIL] widely existing; generally accepted, used, etc. —**prev'a·lence** *n.*

pre·var·i·cate (pri var'ə kāt') *vi.* -cat'ed, -cat'ing [< L. *prae-*, before + *varicare*, straddle] 1. to evade the truth 2. to lie —**pre·var'i·ca'tion** *n.* —**pre·var'i·ca'tor** *n.*

pre·vent (pri vent') *vt.* [< L. *prae-*, before + *venire*, come] to stop or keep from doing or happening; hinder —**pre·vent'a·ble, pre·vent'i·ble** *adj.* —**pre·ven'tion** *n.*

pre·ven'tive (-ven'tiv) *adj.* preventing or serving to prevent —*n.* anything that prevents Also **pre·vent'a·tive**

pre·view (prē'vyōō) *n.* 1. an advance, restricted showing of scenes from a movie to advertise it Also **pre'vue** (-vyōō)

pre·vi·ous (prē'vē əs) *adj.* [< L. *prae-*, before + *via*, a way] occurring before; prior —**previous to** before —**pre'vi·ous·ly** *adv.*

pre·war (prē'wôr') *adj.* before a (or the) war

prex·y (prek'sē) *n., pl.* -ies the president, esp. of a college, etc.

prey (prā) *n.* [< L. *prehendere*, seize] 1. an animal hunted for food by another animal 2. a victim 3. the act or habit of preying on other animals [a bird of *prey*] —*vi.* 1. to plunder 2. to hunt other animals for food

3. to weigh as an obsession Usually used with *on* or *upon*

pri·ap·ic (prī ap′ik) *adj.* [< *Priapos,* Gr. god of procreation] of or relating to the phallus; phallic

price (prīs) *n.* [< L. *pretium*] **1.** the amount of money, etc. asked or paid for something; cost **2.** value or worth **3.** the cost, as in life, labor, etc., of obtaining some benefit —*vt.* priced, pric′ing **1.** to fix the price of **2.** [Colloq.] to find out the price of

price′less *adj.* of inestimable value; invaluable

prick (prik) *n.* [OE. *prica,* a point] **1.** a tiny puncture made by a sharp point **2.** a sharp pain caused as by being pricked —*vt.* **1.** to make (a hole) in (something) with a sharp point **2.** to pain sharply —**prick up one's (or its) ears 1.** to raise the ears erect **2.** to listen closely

prick·le (prik′'l) *n.* [OE. *prica,* a point] a small, sharply pointed growth, as a thorn: also **prick′er 2.** a tingling sensation —*vt., vi.* -led, -ling to tingle —**prick′ly** *adj.*

prickly heat a skin eruption caused by inflammation of the sweat glands

pride (prīd) *n.* [< OE. *prut,* proud] **1.** *a)* an overhigh opinion of oneself *b)* haughtiness; arrogance **2.** dignity and self-respect **3.** satisfaction in something done, owned, etc. **4.** a person or thing in which pride is taken —**pride oneself on** to be proud of —**pride′ful** *adj.* —**pride′ful·ly** *adv.*

pri·er (prī′ər) *n.* one that pries

priest (prēst) *n.* [< Gr. *presbys,* old] **1.** a person of special rank who performs religious rites in a temple of God or a god **2.** *R.C.Ch.,* etc. a clergyman ranking next below a bishop —**priest′ess** *n.fem.* —**priest′hood** *n.* —**priest′ly** *adj.*

prig (prig) *n.* [< 16th-c. cant] one who smugly affects great propriety or morality —**prig′gish** *adj.*

prim (prim) *adj.* **prim′mer, prim′mest** [< ?] stiffly formal, precise, or moral —**prim′ly** *adv.* —**prim′ness** *n.*

pri·ma·cy (prī′mə sē) *n., pl.* **-cies** [< L. *primus,* first] **1.** a being first in time, rank, etc.; supremacy **2.** the rank or office of a primate

pri·ma don·na (prē′mə dän′ə) *pl.* **pri′ma don′nas** [It., first lady] the principal woman singer in an opera

pri·ma fa·ci·e (prī′mə fā′shi ē′) [L., at first sight] adequate to establish a fact unless refuted: said of evidence

pri·mal (prī′m′l) *adj.* [< L. *primus,* first] **1.** first in time; original **2.** first in importance; chief

pri·ma·ri·ly (prī mer′ə lē, prī′mer′-) *adv.* **1.** mainly; principally **2.** at first; originally

pri·ma·ry (prī′mer′ē, -mər ē) *adj.* [< L. *primus,* first] **1.** first in time or order; original **2.** from which others are derived; fundamental [*primary colors*] **3.** first in importance; chief —*n., pl.* **-ries 1.** something first in order, importance, etc. **2.** a preliminary election at which candidates are chosen for the final election

primary accent the heaviest accent (′) in pronouncing a word

pri·mate (prī′māt; *also for 1* -mit) *n.* [< L. *primus,* first] **1.** an archbishop, or the highest-ranking bishop in a province, etc. **2.** any member of the most highly developed order of animals, including man, the apes, etc.

prime (prīm) *adj.* [< L. *primus,* first] **1.** first in time; original **2.** first in rank or importance; chief; principal **3.** first in quality **4.** fundamental **5.** *Math.* that can be evenly divided by no other whole number than itself and 1 —*n.* **1.** the first or earliest part **2.** the best or most vigorous period **3.** the best part —*vt.* primed, prim′ing **1.** to make ready; prepare **2.** to get (a pump) into operation by pouring water into it **3.** to undercoat, size, etc. before painting **4.** to provide with facts, answers, etc. beforehand

prime meridian the meridian at Greenwich, England, from which longitude is measured east and west

prime minister in some countries, the chief executive of the government

prim·er¹ (prim′ər) *n.* [< L. *primus,* first] **1.** a simple book for teaching reading **2.** any elementary textbook

prim·er² (prī′mər) *n.* a thing that primes; specif., *a)* an explosive cap, etc. used to set off a main charge *b)* a preliminary coat of paint, etc.

prime time *Radio & TV* the hours when the largest audience is available

pri·me·val (prī mē′v'l) *adj.* [< L. *primus,* first + *aevum,* an age] of the earliest times or ages; primordial

prim·i·tive (prim′ə tiv) *adj.* [< L. *primus,* first] **1.** of the earliest times; original **2.** crude; simple **3.** primary; basic —*n.* a primitive person or thing

pri·mo·gen·i·ture (prī′mə jen′i chər) *n.* [< L. *primus,* first + *gignere,* beget] **1.** the condition of being the firstborn of the same parents **2.** the right of inheritance of the eldest son

pri·mor·di·al (prī môr′dē əl) *adj.* [< L. *primus,* first + *ordiri,* begin] primitive; fundamental; original

primp (primp) *vt., vi.* [prob. < PRIM] to groom or dress up in a fussy way

prim·rose (prim′rōz′) *n.* [alt. (after *rose*) < ML. *primula*] a plant with tubelike, often yellow flowers

primrose path 1. the path of pleasure, self-indulgence, etc. **2.** a course that seems easy but that could lead to disaster

prince (prins) *n.* [< L. *princeps,* chief] **1.** a ruler ranking below a king; head of a principality **2.** a son of a sovereign **3.** any preeminent person

prince consort the husband of a reigning queen

Prince Edward Island island province of SE Canada: 2,184 sq. mi.; pop. 109,000

prince′ly *adj.* **-li·er, -li·est 1.** of a prince **2.** magnificent; generous —**prince′li·ness** *n.*

prin·cess (prin′sis, -ses) *n.* **1.** a daughter of a sovereign **2.** the wife of a prince

prin·ci·pal (prin′sə pəl) *adj.* [see

PRINCE] first in rank, importance, etc. —*n.* **1.** a principal person or thing **2.** the head of a school **3.** the amount of a debt, etc. minus the interest —**prin'ci·pal·ly** *adv.*

prin·ci·pal·i·ty (-pal'ə tē) *n., pl.* **-ties** the territory ruled by a prince

principal parts the principal inflected forms of a verb: in English, the present infinitive, past tense, and past participle (Ex.: *drink, drank, drunk*)

prin·ci·ple (prin'sə pəl) *n.* [see PRINCE] **1.** a fundamental truth, law, etc. on which others are based **2.** *a)* a rule of conduct *b)* adherence to such rules; integrity **3.** a basic part **4.** *a)* the scientific law explaining a natural action *b)* the method of a thing's operation —**prin'ci·pled** *adj.*

print (print) *n.* [< L. *premere*, to press] **1.** a mark made on a surface by pressing or stamping **2.** cloth printed with a design **3.** the impression of letters, designs, etc. made by inked type or from a plate, block, etc. **4.** a photograph, esp. one made from a negative —*vt.,* *vi.* **1.** to stamp (a mark, letter, etc.) on a surface **2.** to produce on (paper, etc.) the impression of inked type, etc. **3.** to produce (a book, etc.) **4.** to write in letters resembling printed ones **5.** to make (a photographic print) —**in** (**or out of**) **print** still (or no longer) being sold by the publisher: said of books, etc. —**print'er** *n.*

printed circuit an electrical circuit of conductive material, as in fine lines, applied to an insulating sheet

print'ing *n.* **1.** the act of one that prints **2.** something printed **3.** all the copies printed at one time

printing press a machine for printing from inked type, plates, etc.

print'out' *n.* the printed or typewritten output of a computer

pri·or¹ (prī'ər) *adj.* [L.] **1.** earlier; previous **2.** preceding in order or importance —**prior to** before in time

pri·or² (prī'ər) *n.* [L., superior] the head of a priory —**pri'or·ess** *n.fem.*

pri·or·i·tize (prī ôr'ə tīz') *vt.* -**tized'**, -**tiz'ing** to arrange in order of importance

pri·or·i·ty (prī ôr'ə tē) *n., pl.* **-ties 1.** a being prior; precedence **2.** a prior right to get, buy, or do something **3.** something given prior attention

pri'o·ry *n., pl.* **-ries** a monastery governed by a prior, or a nunnery governed by a prioress

prism (priz'm) *n.* [< Gr. *prizein*, to saw] **1.** a solid figure whose ends are equal and parallel polygons and whose faces are parallelograms **2.** a transparent prism whose ends are triangles: used to disperse light into the spectrum —**pris·mat·ic** (priz mat'ik) *adj.*

PRISM

pris·on (priz'n) *n.* [< L. *prehendere*, take] a place of confinement for those

convicted by or awaiting trial

pris'on·er *n.* one held captive or confined, esp. in prison

pris·sy (pris'ē) *adj.* **-si·er**, **-si·est** [prob. PR(IM) + (S)ISSY] [Colloq.] very prim or prudish —**pris'si·ness** *n.*

pris·tine (pris'tēn, pris tēn') *adj.* [L. *pristinus*] **1.** characteristic of the earliest period **2.** unspoiled

prithee (prith'ē) *interj.* [< *pray thee*] [Archaic] I pray thee; please

pri·va·cy (prī'və sē) *n., pl.* **-cies 1.** a being private; seclusion **2.** secrecy **3.** one's private life

pri·vate (prī'vit) *adj.* [< L. *privus,* separate] **1.** of or concerning a particular person or group **2.** not open to or controlled by the public [a *private* school] **3.** for an individual person [a *private* room] **4.** not holding public office [a *private* citizen] **5.** secret [a *private* matter] —*n.* **1.** [pl.] the genitals: also **private parts 2.** an enlisted man of either of the lowest ranks in the U.S. Army or of the lowest rank in the U.S. Marine Corps —**go private** to restore private corporate ownership by buying back publicly held stock —**in private** not publicly —**pri'vate·ly** *adv.*

pri·va·teer (prī'və tir') *n.* **1.** a privately owned ship commissioned in war to capture enemy ships **2.** a commander or crew member of a privateer

private eye [Slang] a private detective

pri·va·tion (prī vā'shən) *n.* the lack of ordinary necessities or comforts

priv·et (priv'it) *n.* [< ?] an evergreen shrub used for hedges

priv·i·lege (priv'l ij, priv'lij) *n.* [< L. *privus,* separate + *lex,* law] a special right, favor, etc. granted to some person or group —*vt.* **-leged,** **-leg·ing** to give a privilege to

priv·y (priv'ē) *adj.* private: now only in such phrases as **privy council,** a body of confidential advisers named by a ruler —*n., pl.* **-ies** an outhouse —**privy to** privately informed about

prize¹ (prīz) *vt.* **prized, priz'ing** [see PRICE] to value highly; esteem —*n.* **1.** something given to one winning a contest, etc. **2.** anything worth striving for —*adj.* **1.** that has won or is worthy of a prize **2.** given as a prize

prize² (prīz) *n.* [< L. *prehendere,* to take] something taken by force

prize'fight' *n.* a professional boxing match —**prize'fight'er** *n.*

pro¹ (prō) *adv.* [L., for] favorably —*adj.* favorable —*n., pl.* **pros 1.** a person or vote on the affirmative side **2.** an argument for something

pro² (prō) *adj., n., pl.* **pros** *clipped form of* PROFESSIONAL

pro-¹ [Gr. < *pro,* before] *a prefix meaning* before in place or time

pro-² [L. < *pro,* forward] *a prefix meaning:* **1.** moving forward [*proclivity*] **2.** substituting for [*pronoun*] **3.** supporting [*prolabor*]

prob. 1. probably **2.** problem

prob·a·bil·i·ty (präb'ə bil'ə tē) *n.*, *pl.* **-ties 1.** a being probable; likelihood **2.** something probable

prob·a·ble (präb'ə b'l) *adj.* [< L. *probare*, prove] **1.** likely to occur or be **2.** reasonably so, but not proved — **prob'a·bly** *adv.*

pro·bate (prō'bāt) *n.* [see PROBE] the act or process of probating — *adj.* having to do with probating [*probate court*] — *vt.* **-bat·ed**, **-bat·ing** to establish officially that (a document, esp. a will) is genuine

pro·ba·tion (prō bā'shən) *n.* [see PROBE] **1.** a testing, as of one's character, ability, etc. **2.** the conditional suspension of a convicted person's sentence—**pro·ba'tion·ar'y** *adj.*

pro·ba'tion·er *n.* a person on probation

probation officer an official who watches over persons on probation

probe (prōb) *n.* [< L. *probare*, to test] **1.** a surgical instrument for exploring a wound, etc. **2.** a searching examination **3.** a device, as an instrumented spacecraft, used to get information about an environment — *vt.* **probed, prob'ing 1.** to explore (a wound, etc.) with a probe **2.** to investigate thoroughly — *vi.* to search

pro·bi·ty (prō'bə tē, präb'ə-) *n.* [< L. *probus*, good] honesty; integrity

prob·lem (präb'ləm) *n.* [< Gr. *problēma*] **1.** a question proposed for solution **2.** a perplexing or difficult matter, person, etc.

prob·lem·at·ic (präb'lə mat'ik) *adj.* **1.** of the nature of a problem **2.** uncertain Also **prob'lem·at'i·cal**

pro·bos·cis (prō bäs'is) *n.*, *pl.* **-cis·es** [< Gr. *pro-*, before + *boskein*, to feed] an elephant's trunk, or any similar long, flexible snout

pro·caine (prō'kān) *n.* [PRO-² + CO(CAINE)] a synthetic compound used as a local anesthetic

pro·ce·dure (prə sē'jər) *n.* the act or method of proceeding in an action — **pro·ce'dur·al** *adj.*

pro·ceed (prə sēd') *vi.* [< L. *pro-*, forward + *cedere*, go] **1.** to go on, esp. after stopping **2.** to carry on some action **3.** to take legal action (*against*) **4.** to come forth or issue (*from*)

pro·ceed'ing *n.* **1.** a going on with what one has been doing **2.** a course of action **3.** [*pl.*] a record of transactions **4.** [*pl.*] legal action

pro·ceeds (prō'sēdz) *n.pl.* the sum derived from a sale, venture, etc.

proc·ess (präs'es) *n.* [see PROCEED] **1.** the course of being done: chiefly in **in process 2.** course (*of* time, etc.) **3.** a continuing development involving many changes [the *process* of digestion] **4.** a method of doing something, with all the steps involved **5.** *Biol.* a projecting part **6.** *Law* a court summons — *vt.* to prepare by or subject to a special process

pro·ces·sion (prə sesh'ən) *n.* [see PROCEED] a number of persons or things moving forward, as in a parade

pro·ces'sion·al *n.* a hymn sung at the beginning of a church service during the entrance of the clergy

pro'-choice' *adj.* advocating the right to legal abortion — **pro'-choic'er** *n.*

pro·claim (prō klām') *vt.* [< L. *pro-*, before + *clamare*, cry out] to announce officially; announce to some

proc·la·ma·tion (präk'lə mā'shən) *n.* **1.** a proclaiming **2.** something that is proclaimed

pro·cliv·i·ty (prō kliv'ə tē) *n.*, *pl.* **-ties** [< L. *pro-*, before + *clivus*, a slope] a tendency or inclination

pro·cras·ti·nate (prō kras'tə nāt') *vi.*, *vt.* **-nat·ed, -nat'ing** [< L. *pro-*, forward + *cras*, tomorrow] to put off doing (something) until later; delay — **pro·cras'ti·na'tion** *n.* — **pro·cras'ti·na'tor** *n.*

pro·cre·ate (prō'krē āt') *vt.*, *vi.* **-at·ed, -at'ing** [< L. *pro-*, before + *creare*, create] to produce (young); beget (offspring) — **pro'cre·a'tion** *n.*

proc·tor (präk'tər) *n.* [see PROCURE] a college official who maintains order, supervises examinations, etc.

proc·u·ra·tor (präk'yə rāt'ər) *n.* [see ff.] in the Roman Empire, the governor of a territory

pro·cure (prō kyoor') *vt.* **-cured', -cur'ing** [< L. *pro-*, for + *curare*, attend to] to obtain; get — **pro·cur'a·ble** *adj.* — **pro·cure'ment** *n.*

prod (präd) *vt.* [< ?] **prod'ded, prod'ding 1.** to jab as with a pointed stick **2.** to goad into action — *n.* **1.** a jab or thrust **2.** something that prods

prod·i·gal (präd'i gəl) *adj.* [< L. *pro-*, forth + *agere*, to drive] **1.** exceedingly or recklessly wasteful **2.** extremely abundant — *n.* a spendthrift — **prod'i·gal'i·ty** (-gal'ə tē) *n.*

pro·di·gious (prə dij'əs) *adj.* [see PRODIGY] **1.** wonderful; amazing **2.** enormous — **pro·di'gious·ly** *adv.*

prod·i·gy (präd'ə jē) *n.*, *pl.* **-gies** [< L. *prodigium*, omen] an extraordinary person, thing, or act; specif., a child of genius

pro·duce (prə dōōs'; *for n.* präd'ōōs, prō'dōōs) *vt.* **-duced', -duc'ing** [< L. *pro-*, forward + *ducere*, to lead] **1.** to bring to view; show [*produce* your license] **2.** to bring forth; bear **3.** to make or manufacture **4.** to cause **5.** to get (a play, etc.) ready for presentation — *vi.* to yield something — *n.* something produced; esp., fruit and vegetables — **pro·duc'er** *n.*

prod·uct (präd'əkt) *n.* **1.** something produced by nature, industry, or art **2.** result; outgrowth **3.** *Math.* the number obtained by multiplying two or more numbers together

pro·duc·tion (prə duk'shən) *n.* a producing or something produced

pro·duc·tive *adj.* **1.** fertile **2.** marked by abundant production **3.** bringing as a result (with *of*) [war is *productive* of misery] — **pro·duc'tive·ly** *adv.* — **pro·duc·tiv·i·ty** (prō'dək tiv'ə tē), **pro·duc'tive·ness** *n.*

Prof. Professor

pro·fane (prə fān') *adj.* [< L. *pro-*, before + *fanum*, temple] **1.** not connected with religion; secular **2.** showing disrespect or contempt for sacred things —*vt.* **-faned', -fan'ing** 1. to treat (sacred things) with irreverence or contempt 2. to debase; defile — **prof·a·na'tion** (präf'ə nā'shən) *n.* — **pro·fane'ly** *adv.* —**pro·fane'ness** *n.*

pro·fan'i·ty (-fan'ə tē) *n.* 1. a being profane 2. *pl.* **-ties** profane language; swearing

pro·fess (prə fes') *vt.* [< L. *pro-*, before + *fateri*, avow] 1. to declare openly; affirm 2. to lay claim to (some feeling, etc.) insincerely 3. to declare one's belief in —**pro·fessed'** *adj.*

pro·fes·sion (prə fesh'ən) *n.* 1. a professing, or declaring; avowal 2. an occupation requiring advanced academic training, as medicine, law, etc. 3. all the persons in such an occupation

pro·fes·sion·al 1. of or engaged in a profession 2. engaged in some sport or in a specified occupation for pay —*n.* a person who is professional (esp. in sense 2) —**pro·fes'sion·al·ly** *adv.*

pro·fes·sor (prə fes'ər) *n.* a teacher; esp., a college teacher of the highest rank —**pro·fes·so·ri·al** (prō'fə sôr'ē əl) *adj.* —**pro·fes'sor·ship'** *n.*

prof·fer (präf'ər) *vt.* [< OFr.: see PRO-² + OFFER] to offer (usually something intangible) [to *proffer* friendship] —*n.* an offer

pro·fi·cient (prə fish'ənt) *adj.* [< L. *pro-*, forward + *facere*, make] highly competent; skilled —**pro·fi'cien·cy** *n.* —**pro·fi'cient·ly** *adv.*

pro·file (prō'fīl) *n.* [< It. *profilare*, to outline] 1. a side view of the face 2. a drawing of this 3. an outline 4. a short, vivid biography

prof·it (präf'it) *n.* [see PROFICIENT] 1. advantage; gain 2. [*often pl.*] financial gain; esp., the sum remaining after deducting costs —*vt., vi.* 1. to be of advantage (to) 2. to benefit — **prof'it·a·ble** *adj.* —**prof'it·a·bly** *adv.* —**prof'it·less** *adj.*

prof·i·teer (präf'ə tir') *n.* one who makes excessive profits by charging exorbitant prices —*vi.* to be a profiteer

prof·li·gate (präf'lə git) *adj.* [< L. *pro-*, forward + *fligere*, to drive] 1. dissolute 2. recklessly wasteful — **prof'li·ga·cy** (-gə sē) *n.*

‡pro for·ma (prō fôr'mə) [L. for form] as a matter of form

pro·found (prə found') *adj.* [< L. *pro-*, forward + *fundus*, bottom] 1. very deep [a *profound* sleep or sigh] 2. marked by intellectual depth 3. deeply felt [*profound* grief] 4. thoroughgoing [*profound* changes] — **pro·found'ly** *adv.* —**pro·fun'di·ty** (-fun'də tē) *n., pl.* **-ties**

pro·fuse (prə fyōōs') *adj.* [< L. *pro-*, forth + *fundere*, pour] giving or given freely and abundantly —**pro·fuse'ly** *adv.* —**pro·fu'sion** (-fyōō'zhən) *n.*

pro·gen·i·tor (prō jen'ə tər) *n.* [< L. *pro-*, forth + *gignere*, beget] 1. an ancestor in direct line 2. a precursor

prog·e·ny (präj'ə nē) *n., pl.* **-nies** [see prec.] children; offspring

prog·na·thous (präg'nə thəs) *adj.* [PRO-¹ + Gr. *gnathos*, jaw] having the jaws projecting beyond the upper face

prog·no·sis (präg nō'sis) *n., pl.* **-no'ses** (-sēz) [< Gr. *pro-*, before + *gignōskein*, know] a prediction, esp. of the course of a disease

prog·nos'ti·cate' (-näs'tə kāt') *vt.* **-cat'ed, -cat'ing** [see prec.] to foretell —**prog·nos'ti·ca'tion** *n.* —**prog·nos'ti·ca'tor** *n.*

pro·gram (prō'gram, -grəm) *n.* [< Gr. *pro-*, before + *graphein*, write] 1. a list of the acts, speeches, pieces, etc., as of an entertainment 2. a plan or procedure 3. a scheduled radio or TV broadcast 4. *a)* a logical sequence of operations to be performed by an electronic computer *b)* the coded instructions and data for this —*vt.* **-grammed** or **-gramed, -gram·ming** or **-gram·ing** 1. to schedule in a program 2. to prepare (a textbook) for use in programmed learning 3. to plan a computer program for 4. to furnish (a computer) with a program Brit. sp. **pro'gramme** —**pro'gram·mer, pro'gram·er** *n.*

programmed learning independent learning by a pupil who advances through a series of questions, the answers to which are given elsewhere in his programmed textbook

prog·ress (präg'res; *for v.* prə gres') *n.* [< L. *pro-*, before + *gradi*, to step] 1. a moving forward 2. development 3. improvement —*vi.* 1. to move forward 2. to move forward toward completion 3. to improve

pro·gres·sion (prə gresh'ən) *n.* 1. a moving forward 2. a succession, as of events 3. *Math.* a series of numbers increasing or decreasing by a constant difference between terms

pro·gres·sive (-gres'iv) *adj.* 1. moving forward 2. continuing by successive steps 3. of or favoring progress, reform, etc. —*n.* one who is progressive —**pro·gres'sive·ly** *adv.*

pro·hib·it (prō hib'it) *vt.* [< L. *pro-*, before + *habere*, have] 1. to forbid by law or an order 2. to prevent; hinder —**pro·hib'i·tive, pro·hib'i·to'ry** *adj.*

pro·hi·bi·tion (prō'ə bish'ən) *n.* 1. a prohibiting 2. the forbidding by law of the manufacture or sale of alcoholic liquors —**pro'hi·bi'tion·ist** *n.*

proj·ect (präj'ekt; *for v.* prə jekt') *n.* [< L. *pro-*, before + *jacere*, to throw] 1. a proposal; scheme 2. an organized undertaking —*vt.* 1. to propose (a plan) 2. to throw forward 3. to cause to jut out 4. to cause (a shadow, image, etc.) to fall upon a surface —*vi.* to jut out —**pro·jec'tion** *n.*

pro·jec·tile (prə jek't'l) *n.* 1. an object designed to be shot forward, as a bullet 2. anything thrown or hurled forward

projection booth the small chamber in a motion-picture theater from which the pictures are projected

pro·jec'tion·ist *n.* the operator of a motion-picture or slide projector

pro·jec'tor *n.* a machine for projecting images on a screen

pro·lapse (prō laps', *for n.* prō'laps) *vi.* -lapsed', -laps'ing [< L. *prolabi*, to slip out] *Med.* to fall or slip out of place —*n.* a prolapsed condition

pro·le·tar·i·at (prō'lə ter'ē ət) *n.* [< L. *proletarius*, a citizen of the lowest class] the working class; esp., the industrial working class —**pro'le·tar'i·an** *adj.*, *n.*

pro'-life' *adj.* opposing the right to legal abortion —**pro'-lif'er** *n.*

pro·lif·er·ate (prō lif'ə rāt') *vi.* -at'ed, -at'ing [< L. *proles*, offspring + *ferre*, to BEAR¹] to increase rapidly —**pro·lif'er·a'tion** *n.*

pro·lif·ic (prə lif'ik) *adj.* [< L. *proles*, offspring + *facere*, make] 1. producing many young or much fruit 2. creating many products of the mind —**pro·lif'i·cal·ly** *adv.*

pro·lix (prō liks') *adj.* [< L. *prolixus*, extended] wordy or long-winded —**pro·lix'i·ty** *n.* —**pro·lix'ly** *adv.*

pro·logue (prō'lôg) *n.* [< Gr. *pro-*, before + *logos*, a discourse] 1. an introduction to a poem, play, etc. 2. any preliminary act, event, etc.

pro·long (prə lôŋ') *vt.* [< L. *pro-*, forth + *longus*, long] to lengthen in time or space: also **pro·lon'gate** (-gāt) -gat·ed, -gat·ing —**pro·lon·ga'tion** *n.*

prom (präm) *n.* [< ff.] [Colloq.] a dance, as of a particular school class

prom·e·nade (präm'ə nād', -näd') *n.* [Fr. < L. *pro-*, forth + *minare*, to herd] 1. a leisurely walk taken for pleasure, display, etc. 2. a public place for walking 3. a ball or dance —*vi.*, *vt.* -nad'ed, -nad'ing to take a promenade (along or through)

Pro·me·theus (prə mē'thyōōs, -thē əs) *Gr. Myth.* a Titan who stole fire from heaven for the benefit of mankind

prom·i·nent (präm'ə nənt) *adj.* [< L. *prominere*, to project] 1. sticking out; projecting 2. noticeable; conspicuous 3. widely and favorably known —**prom'i·nence** *n.* —**prom'i·nent·ly** *adv.*

pro·mis·cu·ous (prə mis'kyōō wəs) *adj.* [< L. *pro-*, forth + *miscere*, to mix] 1. consisting of different elements indiscriminately mingled 2. characterized by a lack of discrimination, esp. in sexual liaisons —**prom·is·cu·i·ty** (präm'is kyōō'ə tē) *n.*, *pl.* -ties —**pro·mis'cu·ous·ly** *adv.*

prom·ise (präm'is) *n.* [< L. *pro-*, forth + *mittere*, send] 1. an agreement to do or not to do something 2. indication, as of a successful future 3. something promised —*vi.*, *vt.* -ised, -is·ing 1. to make a promise of (something) 2. to give a basis for expecting

Promised Land *Bible* Canaan, promised by God to Abraham and his descendants: Gen. 17:8

prom·is·so·ry (präm'i sôr'ē) *adj.* containing or being a promise

prom·on·to·ry (präm'ən tôr'ē) *n.*, *pl.* -ries [prob. < L. *prominere*, to project] a peak of high land that juts out into a body of water; headland

pro·mote (prə mōt') *vt.* -mot'ed, -mot'ing [< L. *pro-*, forward + *movere*, to move] 1. to raise to a higher rank or position 2. to further the growth, establishment, sales, etc. of —**pro·mo'tion** *n.* —**pro·mo'tion·al** *adj.*

pro·mot'er *n.* one who organizes, and furthers an undertaking

prompt (prämpt) *adj.* [< L. *pro-*, forth + *emere*, take] 1. ready, punctual, etc. 2. done, spoken, etc. without delay —*vt.* 1. to urge into action 2. to remind (a person) of something he has forgotten; specif., to help (an actor, etc.) with a cue 3. to inspire —**prompt'er** *n.* —**prompt'ly** *adv.* —**prompt'ness, promp'ti·tude'** *n.*

prom·ul·gate (präm'əl gāt', prō mul'gāt) *vt.* -gat'ed, -gat'ing [< L. *pro-*, before + *vulgus*, the people] 1. to make known officially 2. to make widespread —**prom'ul·ga'tion** *n.*

pron. 1. pronoun 2. pronunciation

prone (prōn) *adj.* [< L. *pronus*] 1. lying face downward or prostrate 2. disposed or inclined (*to*) [*prone* to err]

prong (prôŋ) *n.* [LME. *pronge*] 1. any of the pointed ends of a fork 2. any projecting part —**pronged** *adj.*

prong'horn' *n.* an antelopelike deer of the W U.S., having curved horns

pro·noun (prō'noun) *n.* [< L. *pro*, for + *nomen*, noun] a word used in place of a noun (Ex.: *I*, *he*, *it*, etc.) —**pro·nom'i·nal** (-näm'i n'l) *adj.*

pro·nounce (prə nouns') *vt.* -nounced', -nounc'ing [< L. *pro-*, before + *nuntiare*, announce] 1. to declare officially, solemnly, etc. [he was *pronounced* dead] 2. to utter or articulate (a sound or word) —**pro·nounce'a·ble** *adj.*

pro·nounced' *adj.* clearly marked; decided [a *pronounced* change]

pro·nounce'ment *n.* a formal statement, as of an opinion

pron·to (prän'tō) *adv.* [Sp.: see PROMPT] [Slang] at once; quickly

pro·nun·ci·a·tion (prə nun'sē ā' shən) *n.* 1. the act or way of pronouncing words 2. the way a word is usually pronounced, esp. in phonetic symbols

proof (prōōf) *n.* [see PROBE] 1. a proving or testing of something 2. evidence that establishes the truth of something 3. the relative strength of an alcoholic liquor 4. *Photog.* a trial print of a negative 5. a sheet printed from set type, for checking errors, etc. —*adj.* of tested strength in resisting (with *against*)

-proof (prōōf) [< prec.] *a suffix meaning:* 1. impervious to [*waterproof*] 2. protected from [*rustproof*]

proof'read' *vt.*, *vi.* to read and mark corrections on (printers' proofs, etc.) —**proof'read'er** *n.*

prop¹ (präp) *n.* [< MDu. *proppe*] a support, as a pole, placed under or against something: often used figuratively —*vt.* **propped, prop′ping 1.** to support, as with a prop **2.** to lean (something) *against* a support

prop² (präp) *n.* property (sense 4)

prop³ (präp) *n. clip of* propeller

prop. 1. proposition **2.** proprietor

prop·a·gan·da (präp′ə gan′də) *n.* [ModL.: see ff.] **1.** any widespread promotion of particular ideas, doctrines, etc. **2.** ideas, etc. so spread —**prop′a·gan′dist** *n., adj.* —**prop′a·gan′dize** (-dīz) *vt., vi.*

prop·a·gate (präp′ə gāt′) *vt.* -**gat′ed, -gat′ing** [< L. *propago*, slip (of a plant)] **1.** to cause (a plant or animal) to reproduce itself **2.** to reproduce (itself): said of a plant or animal **3.** to spread (ideas, customs, etc.) —*vi.* to reproduce, as plants or animals —**prop′a·ga′tion** *n.*

pro·pane (prō′pān) *n.* a gaseous hydrocarbon from petroleum, used as a fuel

pro·pel (prə pel′) *vt.* -**pelled′, -pel′ling** [< L. *pro-*, forward + *pellere*, drive] to drive onward or forward

pro·pel′lant, pro·pel′lent *n.* one that propels; specif., the fuel for a rocket

pro·pel′ler *n.* a device having two or more blades in a revolving hub for propelling a ship or aircraft

pro·pen·si·ty (prə pen′sə tē) *n., pl.* -**ties** [< L. *propendere*, hang forward] a natural inclination or tendency

prop·er (präp′ər) *adj.* [< L. *proprius*, one's own] **1.** specially suitable; appropriate; fitting **2.** naturally belonging (*to*) **3.** conforming to a standard; correct **4.** decent; decorous **5.** in the most restricted sense [Chicago *proper* (i.e., apart from its suburbs)] **6.** designating a noun that names a specific individual, place, etc. [Ex.: *Jim, Paris*] —**prop′er·ly** *adv.*

prop·er·ty (präp′ər tē) *n., pl.* -**ties** [see prec.] **1.** ownership **2.** something owned, esp. real estate **3.** a characteristic or attribute **4.** any of the movable articles used in a stage setting —**prop′er·tied** (-tēd) *adj.*

proph·e·cy (präf′ə sē) *n., pl.* -**cies** [see PROPHET] **1.** prediction of the future **2.** something predicted

proph′e·sy′ (-sī′) *vt., vi.* -**sied′, -sy′ing 1.** to predict as by divine guidance **2.** to predict in any way

proph·et (präf′it) *n.* [< Gr. *pro-*, before + *phanai*, speak] **1.** a religious leader regarded as, or claiming to be, divinely inspired **2.** one who predicts the future —**proph′et·ess** *n.fem.*

pro·phet·ic (prə fet′ik) *adj.* **1.** of or like a prophet **2.** like or containing a prophecy —**pro·phet′i·cal·ly** *adv.*

pro·phy·lac·tic (prō′fə lak′tik) *adj.* [< Gr. *pro-*, before + *phylassein*, to guard] preventive or protective; esp. preventing disease —*n.* a prophylactic medicine, device, etc.

pro′phy·lax′is (-sis) *n., pl.* -**lax′es** (-sēz) prophylactic treatment; specif.,

Dentistry a cleaning of the teeth to remove plaque and tartar

pro·pin·qui·ty (prō pin′kwə tē) *n.* [< L. *propinquus*, near] nearness

pro·pi·ti·ate (prə pish′ē āt′) *vt.* -**at′ed, -at′ing** [see ff.] to win the good will of; appease —**pro·pi′ti·a′tion** *n.* —**pro·pi′ti·a·to′ry** (-ə tôr′ē) *adj.*

pro·pi·tious (prə pish′əs) *adj.* [< L. *pro-*, before + *petere*, seek] **1.** favorably inclined **2.** favorable; auspicious

prop·jet (präp′jet) *n. same as* TURBO-PROP

pro·po·nent (prə pō′nənt) *n.* [see PROPOSE] one who espouses or supports a cause, etc.

pro·por·tion (prə pôr′shən) *n.* [< L. *pro*, for + *portio*, a part] **1.** the comparative relation in size, amount, etc. between things; ratio **2.** a part, share, etc. in its relation to the whole **3.** balance or symmetry **4.** [*pl.*] dimensions —*vt.* **1.** to put in proper relation with something else **2.** to arrange the parts of (a whole) so as to be harmonious —**pro·por′tion·al, pro·por′tion·ate** (-shə nit) *adj.*

pro·pos·al (prə pō′z'l) *n.* **1.** a proposing **2.** a proposed plan **3.** an offer of marriage

pro·pose (prə pōs′) *vt.* -**posed′, -pos′ing** [< L. *pro-*, forth + *ponere*, to place] **1.** to put forth for consideration, approval, etc. **2.** to plan or intend **3.** to present as a toast in drinking —*vi.* to offer marriage

prop·o·si·tion (präp′ə zish′ən) *n.* **1.** something proposed; plan **2.** [Colloq.] a proposed deal, as in business **3.** [Colloq.] an undertaking, etc. to be dealt with **4.** a subject to be discussed **5.** *Math.* a problem to be solved

pro·pound (prə pound′) *vt.* [see PROPOSE] to set forth for consideration

pro·pri·e·tar·y (prə prī′ə ter′ē) *adj.* [see PROPERTY] belonging to a proprietor, as under a patent or copyright

pro·pri·e·tor *n.* an owner —**pro·pri′e·tor·ship′** *n.* —**pro·pri′e·tress** *n.fem.*

pro·pri·e·ty (-ə tē) *n., pl.* -**ties** [see PROPER] **1.** the quality of being proper, fitting, etc. **2.** conformity with accepted standards of behavior

pro·pul·sion (prə pul′shən) *n.* [see PROPEL] **1.** a propelling or being propelled **2.** something that propels —**pro·pul′sive** *adj.*

pro·rate (prō rāt′) *vt., vi.* -**rat′ed, -rat′ing** [< L. *pro rata*, in proportion] to divide or assess proportionally

pro·sa·ic (prō zā′ik) *adj.* [< L. *prosa*, prose] commonplace; dull

pro·sce·ni·um (prō sē′nē əm) *n., pl.* -**ni·ums, -ni·a** (-ə) [< Gr. *pro-*, before + *skēnē*, tent] the arch framing a conventional stage

pro·scribe (prō skrīb′) *vt.* -**scribed′, -scrib′ing** [< L. *pro-*, before + *scribere*, write] **1.** to outlaw **2.** to banish; exile **3.** to denounce or forbid the use, etc. of —**pro·scrip′tion** (-skrip′shən) *n.*

prose (prōz) *n.* [< L. *prosa*, direct] ordinary language, not poetry

pros·e·cute (präs′ə kyōōt′) *vt.* -cut′ed, -cut′ing [< L. *pro-*, before + *sequi*, follow] 1. to carry on 2. to conduct legal action against —**pros′e·cu′tion** *n.* —**pros′e·cu′tor** *n.*

pros·e·lyte (präs′ə līt′) *n.* [< Gr. *prosēlytos*, a stranger] one who has been converted from one religion, sect, etc. to another —*vt., vi.* -lyt′ed, -lyt′ing to try to make a convert (of): also **pros′e·lyt·ize′** (-li tīz′) -ized′, -iz′ing —**pros′e·lyt·ism** (-li tiz′m) *n.* —**pros′e·lyt·iz′er** *n.*

pros·o·dy (präs′ə dē) *n., pl.* -dies [< Gr. *prosoidia*, accent] versification; study of meter, rhyme, etc.

pros·pect (präs′pekt) *n.* [< L. *pro-*, forward + *specere*, look] 1. a broad view; scene 2. viewpoint; outlook 3. anticipation 4. *a)* something expected *b)* [*usually pl.*] apparent chance for success 5. a likely customer, candidate, etc. —*vt., vi.* to explore or search (*for*) —**pros′pec·tor** *n.*

pro·spec·tive (prə spek′tiv) *adj.* expected; likely

pro·spec·tus (prə spek′təs) *n.* [L.: see PROSPECT] a statement of the features of a new work, enterprise, etc.

pros·per (präs′pər) *vi.* [< L. *prospere*, fortunately] to succeed; thrive

pros·per·i·ty (prä sper′ə tē) *n., pl.* -ties prosperous condition; wealth

pros·per·ous (präs′pər əs) *adj.* 1. prospering; successful 2. wealthy 3. favorable —**pros′per·ous·ly** *adv.*

pros·tate (präs′tāt) *adj.* [< Gr. *prostatēs*, one standing before] designating a gland surrounding the male urethra at the base of the bladder

pros·the·sis (präs′thə sis, präs thē′-) *n., pl.* -ses′ (-sēz′) an artificial substitute for a missing part of the body —**pros·thet′ic** (-thet′ik) *adj.*

pros·ti·tute (präs′tə tōōt′) *n.* [< L. *pro-*, before + *statuere*, cause to stand] a woman who engages in promiscuous sexual intercourse for pay —*vt.* -tut′ed, -tut′ing 1. to offer (oneself) as a prostitute 2. to sell (oneself, one's talents, etc.) for base purposes —**pros′ti·tu′tion** *n.*

pros·trate (präs′trāt) *adj.* [< L. *pro-*, before + *sternere*, stretch out] 1. lying face downward 2. lying prone or supine 3. laid low; overcome —*vt.* -trat′ed, -trat·ing 1. to lay flat on the ground 2. to lay low; subjugate —**pros·tra′tion** *n.*

pros·y (prō′zē) *adj.* -i·er, -i·est 1. like prose 2. prosaic; dull

pro·tag·o·nist (prō tag′ə nist) *n.* [< Gr. *prōtos*, first + *agōnistēs*, actor] the main character in a drama, novel, etc.

pro·te·an (prōt′ē ən) *adj.* [< *Proteus*, Gr. god who changed his form at will] readily taking on many forms

pro·tect (prə tekt′) *vt.* [< L. *pro-*, before + *tegere*, to cover] to shield from injury, danger, etc.; defend —**pro·tec′tor** *n.*

pro·tec′tion *n.* 1. a protecting or being protected 2. a person or thing that protects

pro·tec′tive *adj.* 1. protecting 2. intended to guard domestic industry from foreign competition [*protective tariffs*] —**pro·tec′tive·ly** *adv.* —**pro·tec′tive·ness** *n.*

pro·tec·tor·ate (-tər it) *n.* a weak state under the control and protection of a strong state

pro·té·gé (prōt′ə zhā′) *n.* [Fr.: see PROTECT] a person guided and helped in his career by another person

pro·tein (prō′tēn, prōt′ē in) *n.* [< Gr. *prōtos*, first] any of numerous nitrogenous substances occurring in all living matter and essential to diet

pro tem·po·re (prō tem′pə rē′) [L.] for the time (being); temporarily; shortened to **pro tem**

pro·test (prə test′; *for n.* prō′test) *vt.* [< L. *pro-*, forth + *testari*, affirm] 1. to state positively 2. to speak strongly against —*vi.* to express disapproval; object —*n.* 1. an objection 2. a formal statement of objection —**prot·es·ta′tion** (prät′is tā′shən) *n.*

Prot·es·tant (prät′is tənt) *n.* [see prec.] any Christian not belonging to the Roman Catholic or Orthodox Eastern Church —**Prot′es·tant·ism** *n.*

proto- [< Gr. *prōtos*, first] *a combining form meaning:* 1. first in time, original 2. first in importance, chief

pro·to·col (prōt′ə kôl′) *n.* [< LGr. *prōtokollon*, contents page] 1. an original draft of a document, etc. 2. the ceremonial forms accepted as correct in official dealings, as between heads of state or diplomatic officials

pro·ton (prō′tän) *n.* [< Gr. *prōtos*, first] an elementary particle in the nucleus of all atoms, carrying a unit positive charge of electricity

pro·to·plasm (prōt′ə plaz′m) *n.* [see PROTO- & PLASMA] a semifluid viscous colloid, the essential living matter of all animal and plant cells —**pro′to·plas′mic** (-plaz′mik) *adj.*

pro·to·type (prōt′ə tīp′) *n.* the first thing or being of its kind; model

pro·to·zo·an (prōt′ə zō′ən) *n.* [< Gr. *prōtos*, first + *zōion*, animal] any of various, mostly microscopic, single-celled animals: also **pro′to·zo′on** (-än), *pl.* -zo′a (-ə)

pro·tract (prō trakt′) *vt.* [< L. *pro-*, forward + *trahere*, draw] to draw out; prolong —**pro·trac′tion** *n.*

pro·trac′tor *n.* a graduated semicircular instrument for plotting and measuring angles

pro·trude (prō trōōd′) *vt., vi.* -trud′ed, -trud′ing [< L. *pro-*, forth + *trudere*, to thrust] to jut out; project —**pro·tru′sion** (-trōō′zhən) *n.*

pro·tru′sile (-trōō′s'l) *adj.* that can be protruded, or thrust out: also **pro·trac′tile** (-trak′t'l)

pro·tu·ber·ance (prō tōō′bər əns) *n.* [< L. *pro-*, forth + *tuber*, a bump] a part or thing that protrudes; bulge —**pro·tu′ber·ant** *adj.*

proud (proud) *adj.* [< LL. *prode*, beneficial] 1. having a proper pride in oneself 2. arrogant; haughty 3. feeling great pride or joy 4. that is a cause of pride 5. caused by pride 6. stately; magnificent —to be highly pleased with —**proud′ly** adv.

proud flesh [from notion of swelling up] an excessive growth of flesh around a healing wound

prove (prōōv) vt. proved, proved or **prov′en, prov′ing** [< L. probare, to test] 1. to test by experiment, a standard, etc. 2. to establish as true —vi. to be found by experience or trial —prov′a·bil′i·ty n. —prov′a·ble adj.

prov·e·nance (präv′ə nəns) n. [< L. provenire, come forth] origin; source: also pro·ve·ni·ence (prō vē′nē əns)

Pro·ven·çal (prō′vən säl′, präv′ən)- n. the vernacular of S France, a distinct Romance language of literary importance in the Middle Ages

prov·en·der (präv′ən dər) n. [< L. praebere, give] 1. dry food for livestock 2. [Colloq.] food

prov·erb (präv′ərb) n. [< L. pro-, before + verbum, word] a short, popular saying expressing an obvious truth —prov·er·bi·al (prə vur′bē əl) adj.

Prov·erbs a book of the Bible containing maxims

pro·vide (prə vīd′) vt.-vid′ed, -vid′-ing [< L. pro-, before + videre, see] 1. to make available; supply 2. to furnish with 3. to stipulate —vi. 1. to prepare (for or against a possible situation, etc.) 2. to furnish support (for) —pro·vid′er n.

pro·vid′ed, pro·vid′ing conj. on the condition or understanding (that)

Prov·i·dence (präv′ə dəns) capital of Rhode Island: pop. 157,000

prov·i·dence (präv′ə dəns) n. 1. provident management 2. the benevolent guidance of God or nature 3. [P-] God

prov′i·dent adj. [see PROVIDE] 1. providing for the future 2. prudent or economical —prov′i·dent·ly adv.

prov′i·den′tial (-den′shəl) adj. of, by, or as if decreed by divine providence —prov′i·den′tial·ly adv.

prov·ince (präv′ins) n. [< L. provincia] 1. an administrative division of a country, specif. of Canada 2. a) a district; territory b) [pl.] the parts of a country removed from the major cities 3. range of duties or work; sphere

pro·vin·cial (prə vin′shəl) adj. 1. of the provinces 2. having the ways, speech, etc. of a certain province 3. countrylike; rustic 4. narrow; limited —pro·vin′cial·ism n.

proving ground a place for testing new equipment, new theories, etc.

pro·vi·sion (prə vizh′ən) n. 1. a providing or preparing 2. something provided for the future 3. [pl.] a stock of food 4. a stipulation; proviso —vt. to supply with provisions

pro·vi′sion·al adj. temporary —pro·vi′sion·al·ly adv.

pro·vi·so (prə vī′zō) n., pl. -sos, -soes

[see PROVIDE] a clause, as in a document or statute, making some condition or stipulation

prov·o·ca·tion (präv′ə kā′shən) n. 1. a provoking 2. something that provokes; incitement

pro·voc·a·tive (prə väk′ə tiv) adj. provoking or tending to provoke to action, thought, anger, desire, etc. —pro·voc′a·tive·ly adv.

pro·voke (prə vōk′) vt. -voked′, -vok′ing [< L. pro-, forth + vocare, to call] 1. to excite to some action or feeling 2. to anger or irritate 3. to stir up (action or feeling) 4. to evoke —pro·vok′er n. —pro·vok′ing adj.

pro·vost (prō′vōst) n. [< L. praepositus, chief] a high executive official, as in some churches or colleges

pro·vost guard (prō′vō) a detail of military police under the command of an officer (provost marshal)

prow (prou) n. [< Gr. prōira] the forward part of a ship

prow·ess (prou′is) n. [< OFr. prouesse] 1. bravery; valor 2. superior ability, skill, etc.

prowl (proul) vi., vt. [< ?] to roam about furtively, as in search of prey or loot —n. a prowling —prowl′er n.

prowl car same as SQUAD CAR

prox·im·i·ty (präk sim′ə tē) n. [< L. prope, near] nearness

prox·y (präk′sē) n., pl. -ies [< ME. procuracie, office of a procurator] 1. the authority to act for another, as in voting 2. a person so authorized

prude (prōōd) n. [Fr. < prudefemme, excellent woman] one who is overly modest or proper in behavior, speech, etc. —prud′er·y n. —prud′ish adj.

pru·dent (prōōd′nt) adj. [< L. providens, provident] 1. exercising sound judgment in practical matters 2. cautious in conduct; not rash 3. managing carefully —pru′dence n. —pru·den′tial (-den′shəl) adj.

prune[1] (prōōn) n. [< Gr. prounon, plum] a dried plum

prune[2] (prōōn) vt., vi. pruned, prun′-ing [< MFr. prooignier] 1. to trim dead or living parts from (a plant) 2. to cut out (unnecessary parts, etc.)

pru·ri·ent (proor′ē ənt) adj. [< L. prurire, to itch] tending to excite lust; lewd —pru′ri·ence n.

Prus·sia (prush′ə) former kingdom in N Europe & dominant state of the former German Empire —Prus′sian adj., n.

pry[1] (prī) n., pl. pries [< PRIZE[2]] a lever or crowbar —vt. pried, pry′ing 1. to raise or move with a pry 2. to obtain with difficulty

pry[2] (prī) vi. pried, pry′ing [< ?] to look closely and inquisitively; snoop

pry′er n. same as PRIER

P.S. Public School

P.S., p.s., PS postscript

psalm (säm) n. [< Gr. psallein, to pluck (a harp)] 1. a sacred song or poem 2. [usually P-] any of the songs in praise of God constituting the Book of Psalms —**psalm′ist** n.

Psalms (sämz) a book of the Bible, consisting of 150 psalms

Psal·ter (sôl′tər) [< Gr. *psaltērion*, a harp] the Book of Psalms —n. [also **p-**] a version of the Psalms for use in religious services

pseu·do- (sōō′dō, syōō′-) [< Gr. *pseudein*, deceive] *a prefix meaning* sham, counterfeit

pseu·do·nym (sōō′də nim′) n. [< Gr. *pseudēs*, false + *onyma*, a name] a fictitious name, esp. one assumed by an author; pen name

pshaw (shô) *interj., n.* an exclamation of impatience, disgust, etc.

psi (sī) n. the twenty-third letter of the Greek alphabet (Ψ, ψ)

pso·ri·a·sis (sə rī′ə sis) n. [ult. < Gr. *psōra*, an itch] a chronic skin disease characterized by scaly, reddish patches

psst (pst) *interj.* sound made to get another's attention quietly

PST, P.S.T. Pacific Standard Time

psych (sīk) *vt.* psyched, psych′ing [< PSYCHOANALYZE] [Slang] to probe the behavior of by psychological means, esp. so as to outwit or control (often with *out*)

psych. psychology

Psy·che (sī′kē) [< Gr. *psychē*, soul] *Rom. Folklore* the wife of Cupid —n. [**p-**] 1. the soul 2. the mind, esp. as a functional entity governing the total organism and its interactions with the environment

psy·che·del·ic (sī′kə del′ik) adj. [< prec. + Gr. *delein*, make manifest] 1. of or causing extreme changes in the conscious mind 2. of or like the auditory or visual effects experienced with psychedelic drugs

psy·chi·a·try (sə kī′ə trē, sī-) n. [see PSYCHO- & -IATRY] the branch of medicine dealing with disorders of the mind, including psychoses and neuroses —psy·chi·a·tric (sī′kē ə′trik) adj. —psy·chi′a·trist n.

psy·chic (sī′kik) adj. [see PSYCHE] 1. of the psyche, or mind 2. beyond known physical processes 3. apparently sensitive to forces beyond the physical world Also **psy′chi·cal** —psy′chi·cal·ly adv.

psy·cho (sī′kō) n. *colloq. clipped form of* PSYCHOPATH *or* PSYCHOPATHIC

psycho- [see PSYCHE] *a combining form meaning* the mind or mental processes: also **psych-**

psy·cho·a·nal·y·sis (sī′kō ə nal′ə sis) n. a method of treating neuroses and some other mental disorders by analyzing emotional conflicts, repressions, etc. through the use of free association, dream analysis, etc. —psy′cho·an′a·lyst (-an′əl ist) n. —psy′cho·an′a·lyze′ (-īz′) vt. -lyzed′, -lyz′ing

psy·cho·gen·ic (sī′kə jen′ik) adj. [PSYCHO- + -GEN + -IC] originating in the mind or in mental conflicts

psy·chol·o·gy (sī käl′ə jē) n., pl. -gies [see PSYCHO- & -LOGY] 1. the science dealing with the mind and with mental and emotional processes 2. the

science of human and animal behavior —psy′cho·log′i·cal (-kə läj′i k′l) adj. —psy·chol′o·gist n.

psy·cho·neu·ro·sis (-noo rō′sis) n., pl. -ses (-sēz) same as NEUROSIS

psy·cho·path′ (-path′) n. [see PSYCHO- & -PATHY] one suffering from emotional disorders with amoral and asocial behavior —psy′cho·path′ic adj.

psy·cho·sis (sī kō′sis) n., pl. -ses (-sēz) [see PSYCHO- & -OSIS] any major mental disorder in which the personality is very seriously disorganized and contact with reality is usually impaired —psy·chot′ic (-kät′ik) adj.

psy·cho·so·mat·ic (sī′kō sō mat′ik) adj. [PSYCHO- + SOMATIC] designating or of a physical disorder originating in or aggravated by emotional processes

psy·cho·ther·a·py (-ther′ə pē) n. [PSYCHO- + THERAPY] treatment of mental disorders by counseling, psychoanalysis, etc. —psy′cho·ther′a·pist n.

pt. pl. pts. 1. part 2. pint 3. point

pt., p.t. past tense

P.T.A. Parent-Teacher Association

ptar·mi·gan (tär′mə gən) n. [< Scot. *tarmachan*] a northern grouse

pter·o·dac·tyl (ter′ə dak′t′l) n. [< Gr. *pteron*, wing + *daktylos*, finger] an extinct flying reptile with wings of skin stretched from the hind limb to a digit of the front limb

Ptol·e·my (täl′ə mē) 2d c. A.D.; Greco-Egyptian astronomer

pto·maine (tō′mān) n. [< Gr. *ptōma*, corpse] an alkaloid substance, often poisonous, found in decaying matter

pub (pub) n. [< *pub*(lic house)] [Chiefly Brit. Colloq.] a bar or tavern

pu·ber·ty (pyōō′bər tē) n. [< L. *puber*, adult] the state of physical development when sexual reproduction first becomes possible —pu′ber·tal adj.

pu·bic (pyōō′bik) adj. [see prec.] of or in the region of the genitals

pub·lic (pub′lik) adj. [ult. < L. *populus*, the people] 1. of people as a whole 2. for the use or benefit of all *[a public park]* 3. acting officially for the people *[a public prosecutor]* 4. known by most people —n. 1. the people as a whole 2. a specific part of the people *[the reading public]* —in public openly —pub′lic·ly adv.

pub·li·can (pub′li kən) n. 1. in ancient Rome, a tax collector 2. [Brit.] a saloonkeeper; innkeeper

pub·li·ca·tion (pub′lə kā′shən) n. [see PUBLISH] 1. public notification 2. the printing and distribution of books, magazines, etc. 3. something published, as a periodical, book, etc.

public domain the condition of being free from copyright or patent

pub·li·cist (pub′lə sist) n. a person whose business is publicity

pub·lic·i·ty (pə blis′ə tē) n. 1. a) any information or action that brings a person, cause, etc. to public notice b) work concerned with such promotional matters 2. notice by the public

pub·li·cize (pub′lə sīz′) vt. -cized′, -ciz′ing to give publicity to

public relations relations of an organization, etc. with the general public as through publicity

public school 1. in the U.S., an elementary or secondary school maintained by public taxes and supervised by local authorities 2. in England, a private boarding school for boys

public servant a government official or a civil-service employee

pub'lic-spir'it·ed *adj.* having or showing zeal for the public welfare

public utility an organization supplying water, electricity, transportation, etc. to the public

pub·lish (pub'lish) *vt.* [< L. *publicare*] 1. to make publicly known; announce 2. to issue (a printed work) for sale —*vi.* to write books, etc. that are published —**pub'lish·er** *n.*

puck[1] (puk) *n.* [akin to POKE[1]] the hard rubber disk used in ice hockey

puck[2] (puk) *n.* [OE. *puca*] a mischievous sprite or elf —**puck'ish** *adj.*

puck·er (puk'ər) *vt., vi.* [< POKE[2]] to gather into wrinkles —*n.* a wrinkle or small fold made by puckering

pud·ding (pood'iŋ) *n.* [ME. *puddyng*] a soft, sweet food variously made with flour, eggs, milk, fruit, etc.

pud·dle (pud''l) *n.* [dim. < OE. *pudd,* a ditch] a small pool of water, esp. stagnant, spilled, or muddy water

pud'dling (-liŋ) *n.* the making of wrought iron from pig iron melted and stirred in an oxidizing atmosphere

pudg·y (puj'ē) *adj.* -i·er, -i·est [? < Scot. *pud,* belly] short and fat

pueb·lo (pweb'lō) *n., pl.* -los [Sp. < L. *populus,* people] a type of communal Indian village in the SW U.S., consisting of terraced structures, as of adobe, housing many families

pu·er·ile (pyōo'ər əl) *adj.* [< L. *puer,* boy] childish; silly —**pu'er·il'i·ty** *n.*

Puer·to Ri·co (pwer'tə rē'kō, pôr'-) island commonwealth in the West Indies, associated with the U.S.: 3,421 sq. mi.; pop. 2,712,000; cap. San Juan —**Puer'to Ri'can**

puff (puf) *n.* [OE. *pyff*] 1. a short, sudden gust or expulsion of wind, breath, smoke, etc. 2. a draw at a cigarette, etc. 3. a light pastry filled with whipped cream, etc. 4. a soft pad [a powder *puff*] 5. exaggerated praise, as of a book —*vi.* 1. to blow in puffs 2. to breathe rapidly 3. to fill or swell (*out* or *up*) 4. to take puffs at a cigarette, etc. —*vt.* 1. to blow, smoke, etc. in or with puffs 2. to swell; inflate 3. to praise unduly —**puff'i·ness** *n.* —**puff'y** *adj.* -i·er, -i·est

puff'ball' *n.* a round, white-fleshed fungus that bursts at the touch

puf·fin (puf'in) *n.* [ME. *poffin*] a northern sea bird with a triangular beak

pug (pug) *n.* [< PUCK[2]] a small, short-haired dog with a snub nose

pu·gil·ism (pyōo'jə liz'm) *n.* [L. *pugil,* boxer] the sport of boxing —**pu'gil·ist** *n.* —**pu'gil·is'tic** *adj.*

pug·na·cious (pug nā'shəs) *adj.* [< L. *pugnare,* to fight] eager and ready to fight; quarrelsome —**pug·na'cious·ly** *adv.* —**pug·nac'i·ty** (-nas'ə tē) *n.*

pug nose a short, thick, turned-up nose —**pug'-nosed'** *adj.*

puke (pyōōk) *n., vi., vt.* puked, puk'ing [< ?] [Colloq.] vomit

puk·ka (puk'ə) *adj.* [Hindi *pakkā,* ripe] 1. first-rate 2. genuine; real

pul·chri·tude (pul'krə tōōd') *n.* [< L. *pulcher,* beautiful] beauty

pule (pyōol) *vi.* puled, pul'ing [echoic] to whimper or whine, as a sick or fretful child

pull (pool) *vt.* [OE. *pullian,* to pluck] 1. to exert force on so as to move toward the source of the force 2. to pluck out [to *pull* a tooth] 3. to rip; tear 4. to strain (a muscle) 5. [Colloq.] to carry out; perform [to *pull* a raid] 6. [Colloq.] to restrain [to *pull* a punch] 7. [Colloq.] to draw out (a gun, etc.) —*vi.* 1. to exert force in dragging, tugging, or attracting 2. to be capable of being pulled 3. to move (*away, ahead,* etc.) —*n.* 1. the act or force of pulling; a tugging, attracting, etc. 2. a difficult, continuous effort 3. something to be pulled, as a handle 4. [Colloq.] *a)* influence *b)* drawing power —**pull for** [Colloq.] to cheer on —**pull off** [Colloq.] to accomplish —**pull oneself together** to regain one's poise, etc. —**pull out** to depart or withdraw —**pull through** [Colloq.] to get over (an illness, difficulty, etc.) —**pull up** 1. to bring or come to a stop 2. to move ahead —**pull'er** *n.*

pull'back' *n.* a pulling back; esp., a planned military withdrawal

pul·let (pool'it) *n.* [< L. *pullus,* chicken] a young hen

pul·ley (pool'ē) *n., pl.* -leys [< MGr. *polos,* axis] a small wheel with a grooved rim in which a rope, belt, etc. runs, as to raise weights or transmit power

Pull·man (pool'mən) *n.* [< G. *Pullman,* 19th-c. U.S. inventor] a railroad car with private compartments or berths for sleeping: also **Pullman car**

pull'out' *n.* 1. a pulling out; esp., a removal, withdrawal, etc. 2. something to be pulled out, as a magazine insert

pull'o'ver *adj.* that is put on by being pulled over the head —*n.* a pullover sweater, shirt, etc.

pull'up' *n.* the act of chinning oneself

pul·mo·nar·y (pul'mə ner'ē) *adj.* [< L. *pulmo,* lung] of the lungs

Pul·mo·tor (pool'mōt'ər, pul'-) [see prec. & MOTOR] *a trademark for* an apparatus for applying artificial respiration —*n.* [p-] such an apparatus

pulp (pulp) *n.* [< L. *pulpa,* flesh] 1. a soft, moist, sticky mass 2. the soft, juicy part of a fruit or soft pith of a plant stem 3. the sensitive substance under the dentine of a tooth 4. ground-up, moistened fibers of wood, rags, etc. used to make paper —**pulp′y** *adj.*

pul·pit (pool′pit) *n.* [< L. *pulpitum,* a stage] 1. a raised platform from which a clergyman preaches in a church 2. preachers collectively

pul·sar (pul′sär) *n.* [< PULSE] any of several small, heavenly objects in the Milky Way that emit radio pulses at regular intervals

pul·sate (pul′sāt) *vi.* -sat·ed, -sat·ing [< L. *pulsare,* to beat] 1. to beat or throb rhythmically 2. to vibrate; quiver —**pul·sa′tion** *n.*

pulse (puls) *n.* [< L. *pulsus,* a beating] 1. the regular beating in the arteries, caused by the contractions of the heart 2. any regular beat

pul·ver·ize (pul′və rīz′) *vt., vi.* -ized′, -iz′ing [< L. *pulvis,* powder] to grind or be ground into a powder

pu·ma (pyōō′mə) *n.* [AmSp.] a cougar

pum·ice (pum′is) *n.* [< L. *pumex*] a light, porous volcanic rock, used for removing stains, polishing, etc.

pum·mel (pum′'l) *vt.* -meled or -melled, -mel·ing or -mel·ling [< POMMEL] to hit with repeated blows

pump¹ (pump) *n.* [< Sp. *bomba*] a machine that forces a liquid or gas into, or draws it out of, something —*vt.* 1. to move (fluids) with a pump 2. to remove water, etc. from 3. to drive air into with a pump 4. to draw out, move up and down, pour forth, etc. as a pump does 5. [Colloq.] to question persistently, or elicit by this —**pump′er** *n.*

pump² (pump) *n.* [< ? Fr. *pompe,* an ornament] a low-cut shoe without straps or ties

pump·er·nick·el (pum′pər nik′'l) *n.* [G.] a coarse, dark rye bread

pump·kin (pum′kin, puŋ′-) *n.* [< Gr. *pepōn,* ripe] a large, round, orange-yellow, edible gourdlike fruit that grows on a vine

pun (pun) *n.* [< ? It. *puntiglio,* fine point] the humorous use of a word, or of different words sounded alike, so as to play on the various meanings —*vi.* **punned, pun′ning** to make puns

punch¹ (punch) *n.* [see PUNCHEON] a tool driven against a surface that is to be pierced, shaped, or stamped —*vt.* 1. to pierce, stamp, etc. with a punch 2. to make (a hole) with a punch

punch² (punch) *vt.* [ME. *punchen*] 1. to prod with a stick 2. to herd (cattle) as by prodding 3. to strike with the fist —*n.* 1. a thrusting blow with the fist 2. [Colloq.] effective force

punch³ (punch) *n.* [Hind. *pāc,* five: it orig. had five ingredients] a sweet drink made with fruit juices, sherbet, etc., often mixed with wine or liquor

punch card in data processing, a card with holes punched in it to signal specific information

punch′-drunk′ *adj.* confused, unsteady, etc., as from many blows to the head in boxing

punch line the final line carrying the point of a joke

punch′y *adj.* -i·er, -i·est [Colloq.]

1. forceful; vigorous 2. punch-drunk

punc·til·i·ous (puŋk til′ē əs) *adj.* [see ff.] 1. careful about nice points of behavior 2. very exact; scrupulous

punc·tu·al (puŋk′choo wəl) *adj.* [< L. *punctus,* a point] on time; prompt —**punc′tu·al′i·ty** (-wal′ə tē) *n.* —**punc′tu·al·ly** *adv.*

punc·tu·ate (-wāt′) *vt., vi.* -at·ed, -at·ing [see prec.] 1. to use certain standardized marks (**punctuation marks**), as the period, comma, etc. in (written matter) to clarify meaning 2. to interrupt [a speech *punctuated* with applause] 3. to emphasize —**punc′tu·a′tion** *n.*

punc·ture (puŋk′chər) *n.* [< L. *pungere,* pierce] 1. a piercing 2. a hole made by a sharp point —*vt., vi.* -tured, -tur·ing to pierce or be pierced as with a sharp point

pun·dit (pun′dit) *n.* [< Sans. *pandita*] a person of great learning

pun·gent (pun′jənt) *adj.* [< L. *pungere,* pierce] 1. producing a sharp sensation of taste and smell 2. sharp, biting, or stimulating [*pungent* wit] —**pun′gen·cy** *n.* —**pun′gent·ly** *adv.*

pun·ish (pun′ish) *vt.* [< L. *punire*] 1. to cause to undergo pain, loss, etc., as for a crime 2. to impose a penalty for (an offense) —**pun′ish·a·ble** *adj.*

pun·ish·ment *n.* 1. a punishing or being punished 2. the penalty imposed 3. harsh treatment

pu·ni·tive (pyōō′nə tiv) *adj.* inflicting, or concerned with, punishment

punk¹ (puŋk) *n.* [< SPUNK] 1. decayed wood used as tinder 2. a fungous substance that smolders when ignited, used to light fireworks, etc.

punk² (puŋk) *n.* [< ?] [Slang] 1. a young hoodlum 2. a young person regarded as inexperienced, insignificant, etc. —*adj.* [Slang] poor; inferior

punk rock [see PUNK² (*n.* 1)] a form of rock music, usually performed in a hostile, coarse, offensive way

pun·ster (pun′stər) *n.* a person who is fond of making puns

punt¹ (punt) *n.* [< ? dial. *bunt,* to kick] *Football* a kick in which the ball is dropped from the hands and kicked before it strikes the ground —*vt., vi.* to kick (a football) in a punt

punt² (punt) *n.* [< L. *pons,* a bridge] a flat-bottomed boat with square ends —*vt., vi.* to propel (a punt) with a long pole

pu·ny (pyōō′nē) *adj.* -ni·er, -ni·est [< OFr. *puis,* after + *né,* born] of inferior size, strength, or importance —**pu′ni·ness** *n.*

pup (pup) *n.* 1. a young dog; puppy 2. a young fox, seal, etc.

pu·pa (pyōō′pə) *n., pl.* -pae (-pē), -pas [L., doll] an insect in the stage between the last larval and adult forms

PUPA

pu·pil¹ (pyōō′p'l) *n.* [< L. *pupillus,* orphan, ward] a person taught under the supervision of a teacher or tutor

pu·pil² (pyōō′p'l) *n.* [< L. *pupilla,* figure reflected in the eye] the contractile circular opening, apparently black, in the center of the iris of the eye

pup·pet (pup'it) *n.* [< L. *pupa*, doll] 1. a small figure, as of a human being, moved by strings or the hands in a performance (**puppet show**) 2. one whose actions, ideas, etc. are controlled by another —**pup'pet·ry** *n.*

pup·pet·eer' (-i tir') *n.* an operator, designer, etc. of puppets

pup·py (pup'ē) *n., pl.* **-pies** [< MFr. *popee*, doll] *same as* PUP

pup tent a small, portable tent

pur·blind (pur'blind') *adj.* [ME. *pur blind*, quite blind] 1. partly blind 2. slow in understanding

pur·chase (pur'chəs) *vt.* **-chased, -chas·ing** [< OFr. *pour*, for + *chacier*, chase] to buy —*n.* 1. anything bought 2. the act of buying 3. a fast hold applied to move something heavy or to keep from slipping —**pur'chas·a·ble** *adj.*—**pur'chas·er** *n.*

pure (pyoor) *adj.* [< L. *purus*] 1. free from anything that adulterates, taints, etc.; unmixed 2. simple; mere 3. utter; absolute 4. faultless 5. blameless 6. virgin or chaste 7. abstract or theoretical [*pure* physics] —**pure'ly** *adv.* —**pure'ness** *n.*

pu·rée (pyoo rā') *n.* [Fr.: see prec.] 1. cooked food pressed through a sieve or whipped in a blender to a soft, smooth consistency 2. a thick soup of this —*vt.* **-réed', -rée'ing** to make a purée of Also *sp.* **puree**

pur·ga·tive (pur'gə tiv) *adj.* purging —*n.* a purging substance; cathartic

pur·ga·to·ry (pur'gə tôr'ē) *n., pl.* **-ries** [see ff.] [*often* P-] Christian *Theol.* a state or place after death for expiating sins by suffering —**pur'ga·to'ri·al** *adj.*

purge (purj) *vt.* **purged, purg'ing** [< L. *purus*, clean + *agere*, do] 1. to cleanse of impurities, etc. 2. to cleanse of sin 3. to rid (a nation, party, etc.) of (individuals held to be disloyal) 4. to empty (the bowels) —*n.* 1. a purging 2. that which purges; esp., a cathartic —**purg'er** *n.*

pu·ri·fy (pyoor'ə fī') *vt.* **-fied', -fy'ing** [< L. *purus*, pure + *facere*, make] 1. to rid of impurities, etc. 2. to free from guilt, sin, etc. —*vi.* to become purified —**pu'ri·fi·ca'tion** *n.*

Pu·rim (poor'im) *n.* [Heb.] a Jewish holiday commemorating the deliverance of the Jews by Esther from a massacre

pur·ism (pyoor'iz'm) *n.* strict or excessive observance of precise usage in language, style, etc. —**pur'ist** *n.*

Pu·ri·tan (pyoor'ə t'n) *n.* [see ff.] 1. a member of a group in 16th-17th-c. England who wanted to purify the Church of England from elaborate forms 2. [p-] a person regarded as very strict in morals and religion —**pu'ri·tan'i·cal** (-tan'i k'l) *adj.* —**Pu'ri·tan·ism, pur'i·tan·ism** *n.*

pu·ri·ty (pyoor'ə tē) *n.* [< LL. *puritas*] a being pure; specif., *a)* freedom from adulterating matter *b)* cleanness *c)* freedom from sin; chastity

purl¹ (purl) *vi.* [< ? Scand.] to move in ripples or with a murmuring sound —*n.* the sound of purling water

purl² (purl) *vt., vi.* [< obs. *pirl*, twirl] to invert (stitches) in knitting so as to form ribbing

pur·lieu (pur'lōō) *n.* [< OFr. *pur-*, through + *aler*, go] 1. an outlying part, as of a city 2. [*pl.*] environs

pur·loin (pər loin') *vt., vi.* [< OFr. *pur-*, for + *loin*, far] to steal

pur·ple (pur'p'l) *n.* [< Gr. *porphyra*, shellfish yielding a dye] 1. a dark bluish red 2. crimson cloth or clothing, esp. as a former emblem of royalty —*adj.* 1. bluish-red 2. imperial 3. ornate [*purple* prose] 4. offensively strong [*purple* language]

pur·port (pər pôrt'; *for n.* pur'pôrt) *vt.* [< OFr. *por-*, forth + *porter*, to bear] 1. to profess or claim as its meaning 2. to give the appearance, often falsely, of being, intending, etc. —*n.* 1. meaning; sense 2. intention

pur·pose (pur'pəs) *vt., vi.* **-posed, -pos·ing** [< OFr. *porposer*: see PROPOSE] to intend or plan —*n.* 1. something one intends to get or do; aim 2. determination 3. the object for which something exists or is done —**on purpose** intentionally —**pur'pose·ful** *adj.* —**pur'pose·less** *adj.*

pur·pose·ly *adv.* with a definite purpose; intentionally; deliberately

purr (pur) *n.* [echoic] a low, vibratory sound made by a cat at ease —*vi., vt.* to make, or express by, such a sound

purse (purs) *n.* [< Gr. *byrsa*, a hide] 1. a small bag for carrying money 2. finances; money 3. a sum of money for a present or prize 4. a woman's handbag —*vt.* **pursed, purs'ing** to pucker

purs·er (pur'sər) *n.* [ME., a pursebearer] an officer on a passenger ship, in charge of accounts, tickets, etc.

pur·su·ance (pər sōō'əns) *n.* a pursuing of a project, plan, etc.

pur·su·ant *adj.* [Now Rare] pursuing —**pursuant to** in accordance with

pur·sue (pər sōō') *vt.* **-sued', -su'ing** [< L. *pro-*, forth + *sequi*, follow] 1. to follow in order to overtake or capture; chase 2. to follow (a specified course, action, etc.) 3. to strive for 4. to continue to annoy —**pur·su'er** *n.*

pur·suit' (-sōōt') *n.* 1. a pursuing 2. an occupation; interest

pu·ru·lent (pyoor'ə lənt, -yoo-) *adj.* [< L. < *pus*, PUS] of, like, or discharging pus —**pu'ru·lence** *n.*

pur·vey (pər vā') *vt.* [see PROVIDE] to supply (esp. food) —**pur·vey'or** *n.*

pur·view (pur'vyōō) *n.* [< Anglo-Fr. *purveu est*, it is provided] scope or extent, as of control, activity, etc.

pus (pus) *n.* [L.] the yellowish-white matter produced by an infection

push (poosh) *vt., vi.* [< L. *pulsare*, to beat] 1. to press against so as to move

2. to press or urge on **3.** to urge the use, sale, etc. of —*n.* **1.** a pushing **2.** a vigorous effort **3.** an advance against opposition **4.** [Colloq.] aggressiveness; drive —**push′er** *n.*

push button a small knob pushed to operate something electrically

push′o′ver *n.* [Slang] **1.** anything very easy to do **2.** a person, group, etc. easily persuaded, defeated, etc.

push′-up′, push′up′ *n.* an exercise in which a prone person, with hands under the shoulders, raises his body by pushing down with his palms

push′y *adj.* **-i·er, -i·est** [Colloq.] annoyingly aggressive and persistent —**push′i·ness** *n.*

pu·sil·lan·i·mous (pyōō′s'l an′ə məs) *adj.* [< L. *pusillus*, tiny + *animus*, the mind] timid; cowardly —**pu′sil·la·nim′i·ty** (-ə nim′ə tē) *n.*

puss (poos) *n.* [< ?] a cat: also **puss′y,** *pl.* **-ies, puss′y·cat!**

puss′y·foot′ *vi.* [Colloq.] **1.** to move with stealth or caution, as a cat does **2.** to avoid committing oneself

pussy willow a willow bearing velvetlike, silvery catkins

pus·tule (pus′chōōl) *n.* [L. *pustula*] a pus-filled pimple or blister

put (poot) *vt.* **put, put′ting** [< OE. *potian*, to push] **1.** *a)* to thrust; drive *b)* to propel with an overhand thrust [to *put* the shot] **2.** to cause to be in a certain place, condition, relation, etc.; place; set **3.** to impose (a tax, etc.) **4.** to attribute; ascribe **5.** to express [*put* it plainly] **6.** to present for decision [*put* the question] **7.** to bet (money) *on* —*vi.* to go (*in, out,* etc.) —*adj.* [Colloq.] fixed [*stay put*] —**put across** to cause to be understood, accepted, etc. —**put aside** (or **by**) to reserve for later use —**put down 1.** to crush; repress **2.** to write down **3.** [Slang] to belittle or humiliate —**put in for** to apply for —**put it** (or **something**) **over on** [Colloq.] to deceive; trick —**put off 1.** to delay; postpone **2.** to evade; divert —**put on 1.** to clothe oneself with **2.** to pretend **3.** to stage (a play) **4.** [Slang] to hoax —**put out 1.** to expel; dismiss **2.** to extinguish (a fire or light) **3.** to inconvenience **4.** *Baseball* to retire (a batter or runner) —**put through 1.** to carry out **2.** to cause to do or undergo —**put up 1.** to offer **2.** to preserve (fruits, etc.) **3.** to build **4.** to provide lodgings for **5.** to provide (money) **6.** to arrange (the hair) with curlers, etc. **7.** [Colloq.] to incite *to* some action —**put up with** to tolerate

pu·ta·tive (pyōōt′ə tiv) *adj.* [< L. *putare*, suppose] generally thought of as such; supposed

put′-down′ *n.* [Slang] a belittling remark or crushing retort

put′-on′ *n.* [Slang] a hoax

pu·tre·fy (pyōō′trə fī′) *vt., vi.* **-fied′, -fy′ing** [< L. *putris,* putrid + *facere,* make] to make or become putrid; rot —**pu′tre·fac′tion** (-fak′shən) *n.*

pu·tres·cent (pyōō tres′'nt) *adj.* putrefying; rotting —**pu·tres′cence** *n.*

pu·trid (pyōō′trid) *adj.* [< L.

putrere, to rot] rotten and foul-smelling

putt (put) *n.* [< PUT, *v.*] *Golf* a light stroke made to roll the ball into the hole —*vt., vi.* to hit (a ball) with a putt

putt·er¹ (put′ər) *n. Golf* a straight-faced club used in putting

put·ter² (put′ər) *vi.* [< OE. *potian,* to push] to busy oneself in an ineffective or aimless way (with *along, around,* etc.) —*vt.* to fritter (*away*)

put·ty (put′ē) *n.* [< Fr. *potée,* lit., potful] a soft, plastic mixture of powdered chalk and linseed oil, used to fill small cracks, etc. —*vt.* **-tied, -ty·ing** to cement or fill with putty

puz·zle (puz′'l) *vt.* **-zled, -zling** [< ?] to perplex; bewilder —*vi.* **1.** to be perplexed **2.** to exercise one's mind, as over a problem —*n.* **1.** something that puzzles **2.** a toy or problem for testing skill or ingenuity —**puzzle out** to solve by deep study —**puz′zle·ment** *n.* —**puz′zler** *n.*

Pvt. *Mil.* Private

PX post exchange

Pyg·my (pig′mē) *n., pl.* **-mies** [< Gr. *pygmaios,* of the length of the forearm] **1.** a member of any of several very short peoples of Africa and Asia **2.** [p-] a dwarf —*adj.* **1.** of the Pygmies **2.** [p-] very small

py·ja·mas (pə jam′əz, -jä′məz) *n.pl. Brit. sp.* of PAJAMAS

py·lon (pī′län) *n.* [Gr. *pylōn,* gateway] **1.** a gateway, as of an Egyptian temple **2.** a towerlike structure supporting electric lines, marking a flight course, etc.

py·lo·rus (pī lôr′əs) *n., pl.* **-ri** (-ī) [< Gr. *pylōros,* gatekeeper] the opening from the stomach into the duodenum —**py·lor′ic** *adj.*

py·or·rhe·a (pī′ə rē′ə) *n.* [< Gr. *pyon,* pus + *rhein,* to flow] an infection of the gums and tooth sockets, with formation of pus

pyr·a·mid (pir′ə mid) *n.* [< Gr. *pyramis*] **1.** a huge structure with a square base and four triangular sides meeting at the top, as a royal tomb of ancient Egypt **2.** *Geom.* a solid figure with a polygonal base, the sides of which form the bases of triangular surfaces meeting at a common vertex —*vi., vt.* to build up as in a pyramid —**py·ram·i·dal** (pi ram′ə d'l) *adj.*

EGYPTIAN PYRAMID

pyre (pīr) *n.* [< Gr. *pyr,* fire] a pile of wood for burning a dead body

Pyr·e·nees (pir′ə nēz′) mountain range between France & Spain

Py·rex (pī′reks) [arbitrary coinage < PIE] *a trademark for* a heat-resistant glassware for cooking, etc.

py·rite (pī′rīt) *n., pl.* **py·ri·tes** (pə rīt′ēz, pī′rīts) [< Gr. *pyritēs,* flint] iron sulfide, a lustrous, yellow mineral: also called **iron pyrites**

pyro- [< Gr. *pyr,* fire] *a combining form meaning* fire, heat

py·ro·ma·ni·a (pī′rə mā′nē ə) *n.* [prec. + -MANIA] a compulsion to start destructive fires —**py′ro·ma′ni·ac′** *n., adj.*

py·ro·tech·nics (pī′rə tek′niks) *n.pl.* [< Gr. *pyr*, fire + *technē*, art] 1. a display of fireworks 2. a dazzling display, as of wit

Pyr·rhic victory (pir′ik) [< *Pyrrhus*, Gr. king who won such a victory over Romans, 279 B.C.] a too costly victory

Py·thag·o·ras (pi thag′ər əs) 6th c. B.C.; Gr. philosopher & mathematician —**Py·thag′o·re′an** (-ə rē′ən) *adj., n.*

py·thon (pī′thän, -thən) *n.* [< Gr. *Pythōn*, a serpent slain by Apollo] a large, nonpoisonous snake of SE Asia & Africa that crushes its prey to death

pyx (piks) *n.* [< Gr. *pyxis*, a box] a container for Eucharistic wafers

Q

Q, q (kyōō) *n.*, *pl.* **Q's, q's** the 17th letter of the English alphabet

q. 1. quart 2. queen 3. question

Q.E.D. [L. *quod erat demonstrandum*] which was to be proved

QM, Q.M. Quartermaster

qt. quart(s)

Q.T., q.t. [Slang] quiet: usually in **on the Q.T.** (or **q.t.**) in secret

quack[1] (kwak) *vi.* [echoic] to utter the sound or cry of a duck —*n.* this sound

quack[2] (kwak) *n.* [< earlier *quacksalver* (< Du. *quacken*, to brag + *zalf*, salve)] 1. an untrained person who practices medicine fraudulently 2. one who pretends to have knowledge or skill he does not have —*adj.* fraudulent —**quack′er·y** *n.*

quad (kwäd) *n. clipped form of:* 1. QUADRANGLE 2. QUADRUPLET

quad·ran·gle (kwäd′raŋ′g'l) *n.* [see QUADRI- & ANGLE[1]] 1. *Geom.* a plane figure with four angles and four sides 2. an area surrounded on its four sides by buildings —**quad′ran′gu·lar** *adj.*

quad·rant (kwäd′rənt) *n.* [< L. *quadrans*, fourth part] 1. an arc of 90° 2. a quarter section of a circle 3. an instrument for measuring altitudes in astronomy and navigation

quad·ra·phon·ic (kwäd′rə fän′ik) *adj.* [< L. *quadra*, a square + Gr. *phōnē*, a sound] using four channels to record and reproduce sound

quad·rat·ic (kwäd rat′ik) *adj.* Algebra involving a quantity or quantities that are squared but none that are raised to a higher power

quad·ren·ni·al (kwäd ren′ē əl) *adj.* [< L. *quadri-* (see ff.) + *annus*, a year] 1. lasting four years 2. occurring once every four years

quadri- [L. < *quattuor*, four] *a combining form meaning* four times

quad·ri·lat·er·al (kwäd′rə lat′ər əl) *adj.* [see prec. & LATERAL] four-sided —*n.* a plane figure having four angles and four sides

qua·drille (kwə dril′, kwä-) *n.* [Fr.; ult. < L. *quadra*, a square] a square dance performed by four couples

quad·ru·ped (kwäd′roo ped′) *n.* [< L. *quadru-*, four + *pes*, foot] an animal, esp. a mammal, with four feet

quad·ru·ple (kwä drōō′p'l, kwäd′roo-) *adj.* [< L. *quadru-*, four + *-plus*, -fold] 1. consisting of four 2. four times as much or as many —*n.* an amount four times as much or as many —*vt., vi.* **-pled, -pling** to make or become four times as much or as many

quad·ru·plet (kwä drup′lit, -drōō′plit; kwäd′roo plit) *n.* 1. any of four offspring born at a single birth 2. a group of four, usually of one kind

quad·ru·pli·cate (kwä drōō′plə kit; *for v.* -kāt′) *adj.* 1. fourfold 2. being the last of four identical copies —*n.* any one of such copies —*vt.* **-cat′ed, -cat′ing** to make four such copies of —**in quadruplicate** in four such copies —**quad′ru·pli·ca′tion** *n.*

quaff (kwäf, kwaf) *vt., vi.* [prob. < LowG. *quassen*, overindulge] to drink deeply and heartily —*n.* a quaffing

quag·mire (kwag′mīr′) *n.* [< *quag*, bog + MIRE] wet, boggy ground

qua·hog (kwô′hôg, kō′-) *n.* [< Am-Ind.] a hard-shelled clam of the E coast: also sp. **quahaug**

quail[1] (kwāl) *vi.* [prob. ult. < L. *coagulare*, coagulate] to recoil in fear

quail[2] (kwāl) *n.* [< OFr.] a small game bird resembling a partridge

quaint (kwānt) *adj.* [< OFr. *cointe* < L. *cognitus*, known] 1. pleasingly odd and old-fashioned 2. unusual; curious 3. fanciful; whimsical —**quaint′ly** *adv.* —**quaint′ness** *n.*

quake (kwāk) *vi.* quaked, quak′ing [< OE. *cwacian*] 1. to tremble or shake 2. to shiver, as from fear or cold —*n.* 1. a shaking or tremor 2. an earthquake —**quak′y** *adj.*

Quak·er (kwāk′ər) *n.* [< founder's admonition to "quake" at the word of the Lord] *a popular name for* a member of the SOCIETY OF FRIENDS

qual·i·fi·ca·tion (kwäl′ə fi kā′shən) *n.* 1. a qualifying or being qualified 2. a restriction 3. any skill, etc. that fits one for a job, office, etc.

qual·i·fied (kwäl′ə fīd′) *adj.* 1. fit; competent 2. limited; modified

qual′i·fi′er (-fī′ər) *n.* 1. one that qualifies 2. an adjective or adverb

qual′i·fy′ (-fī′) *vt.* -fied′, -fy′ing [< L. *qualis*, of what kind + *facere*, make]

---

1. to make fit for a job, etc. 2. to make legally capable 3. to modify; restrict 4. to moderate; soften —vi. to be or become qualified

qual·i·ta·tive (-tāt'iv) adj. having to do with quality or qualities —**qual'i·ta'tive·ly** adv.

qual·i·ty (kwäl'ə tē) n., pl. -ties [< L. qualis, of what kind] 1. that which makes something what it is; characteristic element 2. basic nature; kind 3. the degree of excellence of a thing 4. excellence —adj. of high quality

quality circle any of the small groups of workers that meet regularly to suggest improvements in production

qualm (kwäm) n. [OE. cwealm, disaster] 1. a sudden feeling of sickness, faintness, etc. 2. a doubt; misgiving 3. a twinge of conscience

quan·da·ry (kwän'drē, -dər ē) n., pl. -ries [prob. < L.] a state of uncertainty; dilemma

quan·ti·ta·tive (kwän'tə tāt'iv) adj. having to do with quantity

quan·ti·ty (kwän'tə tē) n., pl. -ties [< L. quantus, how great] 1. an amount; portion 2. any indeterminate bulk or number 3. [also pl.] a great amount 4. that property by which a thing can be measured 5. a number or symbol expressing this property

quan·tum (kwän'təm) n., pl. -ta (-tə) [L., how much] a fixed, elemental unit of energy: the **quantum theory** states that energy is radiated discontinuously in quanta

quar·an·tine (kwôr'ən tēn') n. [< L. quadraginta, forty] 1. the period, orig. forty days, during which a vessel suspected of carrying a contagious disease is detained in port 2. any isolation imposed to keep contagious disease, etc. from spreading 3. a place for such isolation —vt. -tined', -tin'ing to place under quarantine

quark (kwôrk) n. [arbitrary coinage] any of three hypothetical particles assumed to be the basic units of matter

quar·rel (kwôr'əl) n. [< L. queri, complain] 1. a cause for dispute 2. a dispute, esp. an angry one —vi. -reled or -relled, -rel·ing or -rel·ling 1. to find fault 2. to dispute heatedly 3. to have a breach in friendship —**quar'rel·er, quar'rel·ler** n. —**quar'rel·some** adj.

quar·ry[1] (kwôr'ē) n., pl. -ries [< OFr. curer, eviscerate] an animal, etc. being hunted down

quar·ry[2] (kwôr'ē) n., pl. -ries [< L. quadrare, to square] a place where stone or slate is excavated —vt. -ried, -ry·ing to excavate from a quarry

quart (kwôrt) n. [< L. quartus, fourth] 1. a liquid measure, equal to 1/4 gallon 2. a dry measure, equal to 1/8 peck

quar·ter (kwôr'tər) n. [< L. quartus, fourth] 1. a fourth of something 2. one fourth of a year 3. one fourth of an hour 4. one fourth of a dollar; 25 cents, or a coin of this value 5. any leg of a four-legged animal, with the adjoining parts 6. a certain district or section 7. [pl.] lodgings 8. a particular source [news from high quarters] 9.

mercy —vt. 1. to divide into four equal parts 2. to provide lodgings for —adj. constituting a quarter —**at close quarters** at close range —**cry quarter** to beg for mercy

quar'ter·back' n. Football the back who calls the signals

quar'ter·deck', quar'ter·deck' n. the after part of the upper deck of a ship, usually for officers

quar'ter·fi'nal adj. coming just before the semifinals in a tournament —n. a quarterfinal match

quarter horse any of a breed of thickset, muscular horse capable of a sprinting speed up to 1/4 mile

quar'ter·ly adj. occurring regularly four times a year —adv. once every quarter of the year —n., pl. -lies a publication issued every three months

quar'ter·mas'ter n. 1. Mil. an officer who provides troops with quarters, clothing, equipment, etc. 2. Naut. a petty officer or mate who tends to the compass, navigation, etc.

quarter note Music a note (♩) having one fourth the duration of a whole note

quar·tet, quar·tette (kwôr tet') n. [Fr. < L. quartus, a fourth] 1. a group of four 2. Music a) a composition for four voices or instruments b) the four performers of this

quar·to (kwôr'tō) n., pl. -tos [< L. (in) quarto, (in) a fourth] 1. the page size (about 9 by 12 in.) of a book made up of sheets each of which is folded twice to form four leaves, or eight pages 2. a book of this size of page

quartz (kwôrts) n. [G. quarz] a crystalline mineral, a form of silica, usually colorless and transparent

qua·sar (kwā'sär, -sər) n. [quas(i-stell)-ar (radio source)] a distant, starlike, celestial object that emits much light or powerful radio waves

quash[1] (kwäsh) vt. [< L. cassus, empty] to set aside (an indictment)

quash[2] (kwäsh) vt. [< L. quassare, to break] to suppress (an uprising)

qua·si (kwā'sī, -zī; kwä'sē) adv. [L.] as if; seemingly —adj. seeming Often hyphenated as a prefix [quasi-legal]

quat·rain (kwä'trān) n. [Fr. < L. quattuor, four] a stanza of four lines

qua·ver (kwā'vər) vi. [ME. cwafien] 1. to shake or tremble 2. to be tremulous: said of the voice —n. a tremulous quality in a voice or tone

quay (kē) n. [< OFr. cai] a wharf, usually of concrete or stone

quea·sy (kwē'zē) adj. -si·er, -si·est [< Scand.] 1. affected with nausea 2. squeamish; easily nauseated

Que·bec (kwi bek') 1. province of E Canada: 594,860 sq. mi.; pop. 5,781,000: abbrev. **Que.** 2. its capital, on the St. Lawrence: pop. 167,000

queen (kwēn) n. [OE. cwen] 1. the wife of a king 2. a woman monarch in her own right 3. a woman noted for her beauty or accomplishments 4. the fully developed, reproductive female in a colony of bees, ants, etc. 5. a playing card with a picture of a queen on it 6. Chess the most powerful piece —**queen'ly** adj. -li·er, -li·est

Queens (kwēnz) borough of New York City; pop. 1,891,000

queer (kwir) *adj.* [< ? G. *quer*, crosswise] 1. different from the usual; strange 2. [Colloq.] eccentric —*vt.* [Slang] to spoil the success of —*n.* [Slang] a strange person

quell (kwel) *vt.* [OE. *cwellan*, kill] 1. to subdue 2. to quiet; allay

quench (kwench) *vt.* [OE. *cwencan*, to put out] 1. to extinguish [*water quenched* the fire] 2. to satisfy [to *quench* one's thirst] 3. to cool (hot steel, etc.) suddenly by plunging into water, etc. —**quench′less** *adj.*

quer·u·lous (kwer′ə ləs, -yə-) *adj.* [< L. *queri*, complain] 1. inclined to find fault 2. full of complaint; peevish —**quer′u·lous·ly** *adv.*

que·ry (kwir′ē) *n., pl.* -ries [< L. *quaerere*, ask] 1. a question; inquiry 2. a question mark —*vt., vi.* -ried, -ry·ing to question

quest (kwest) *n.* [see prec.] 1. a seeking 2. a journey for adventure

ques·tion (kwes′chən) *n.* [see QUERY] 1. an asking; inquiry 2. something asked 3. doubt; uncertainty 4. a matter open to discussion 5. a difficult matter [not a *question* of money] 6. a point being debated before an assembly —*vt.* 1. to ask questions of 2. to express doubt about 3. to dispute; challenge —*vi.* to ask questions —**out of the question** impossible

ques′tion·a·ble *adj.* 1. that can be questioned 2. suspected of being immoral, dishonest, etc. 3. uncertain

question mark a mark of punctuation (?) put after a sentence or word to indicate a direct question, or to express doubt, uncertainty, etc.

ques′tion·naire′ (-chə ner′) *n.* a written or printed set of questions used in gathering information from people

queue (kyōō) *n.* [< L. *cauda*, tail] 1. a pigtail 2. [Chiefly Brit.] a line, as of persons waiting to be served 3. stored computer data or programs waiting to be processed —*vi.* queued, queu′ing [Chiefly Brit.] to line up in a queue (often with *up*)

quib·ble (kwib′'l) *n.* [< L. *qui*, who] a petty evasion; cavil —*vi.* -bled, -bling to evade the truth of a point under discussion by caviling

‡**quiche Lor·raine** (kēsh lô ren′) [Fr., Lorraine (France) pastry] a custard pie baked with cheese, bacon, etc.

quick (kwik) *adj.* [< OE. *cwicu*, living] 1. *a*) rapid; swift [a *quick* walk] *b*) prompt [a *quick* reply] 2. prompt to understand or learn 3. easily stirred [a *quick* temper] —*adv.* quickly; rapidly —*n.* 1. the living, esp. in the **quick and the dead** 2. the sensitive flesh under the nails 3. the deepest feelings [hurt to the *quick*] —**quick′ly** *adv.* —**quick′ness** *n.*

quick bread any bread leavened with baking powder, soda, etc. and baked as soon as the batter is mixed

quick′en *vt., vi.* 1. to animate; revive 2. to move more rapidly; hasten 3. to show signs of life, as a fetus

quick′-freeze′ *vt.* -froze′, -froz′en, -freez′ing to subject (food) to sudden freezing for long storage at low temperatures

quick′ie *n.* [Slang] anything done or made quickly and, often, cheaply

quick′lime′ *n. same as* LIME¹

quick′sand′ *n.* [< ME.: see QUICK & SAND] a loose, wet, deep sand deposit, engulfing heavy objects easily

quick′sil′ver *n. same as* MERCURY

quick′-tem′pered *adj.* easily angered

quick′-wit′ted *adj.* nimble of mind

quid (kwid) *n.* [var. of CUD] a piece, as of tobacco, to be chewed

quid pro quo (kwid′ prō kwō′) [ModL.] one thing in return for another

qui·es·cent (kwī es′'nt) *adj.* [< L. *quiescere*, become quiet] quiet; still; inactive —**qui·es′cence** *n.*

qui·et (kwī′ət) *adj.* [< L. *quies*, rest] 1. still; motionless 2. *a*) not noisy; hushed *b*) not speaking; silent 3. not easily excited 4. not showy [*quiet* clothes] 5. not forward; unobtrusive 6. peaceful and relaxing —*n.* 1. calmness, stillness, etc. 2. a quiet or peaceful quality —*vt., vi.* to make or become quiet —**qui′et·ly** *adv.*

qui·e·tude (kwī′ə tōōd′) *n.* a state of being quiet; calmness

qui·e·tus (kwī ēt′əs) *n.* [< ML. *quietus* (*est*), (he is) quit] 1. discharge from debt, etc. 2. death

quill (kwil) *n.* [prob. < MLowG. or MDu.] 1. a large, stiff feather 2. *a*) the hollow stem of a feather *b*) anything made from this, as a pen 3. a spine of a porcupine or hedgehog

quilt (kwilt) *n.* [< L. *culcita*, bed] a bedcover filled with down, cotton, etc. and stitched together in lines or patterns —*vt.* to stitch like a quilt —*vi.* to make a quilt —**quilt′er** *n.*

quince (kwins) *n.* [< Gr. *kydōnion*] 1. a yellowish, apple-shaped fruit, used in preserves 2. the tree it grows on

qui·nine (kwī′nīn) *n.* [< *quina*, cinchona bark] a bitter, crystalline alkaloid extracted from cinchona bark, used esp. for treating malaria

quin·sy (kwin′zē) *n.* [< Gr. *kyōn*, dog + *anchein*, choke] *an earlier term for* TONSILLITIS

quin·tes·sence (kwin tes′ns) *n.* [< ML. *quinta essentia*, fifth essence] the pure essence or perfect type

quin·tet, quin·tette (kwin tet′) *n.* [ult. < L. *quintus*, a fifth] 1. a group of five 2. *Music a*) a composition for five voices or instruments *b*) the five performers of this

quin·tu·plet (kwin tup′lit, -tōō′plit; kwin′too plit) *n.* 1. any of five offspring born at a single birth 2. a group of five, usually of one kind

quip (kwip) *n.* [< L. *quippe*, indeed]

a witty or sarcastic remark; jest —*vi.* quipped, quip'ping to utter quips —quip'ster *n.*

quire (kwīr) *n.* [< L. *quaterni*, four each] a set of 24 or 25 sheets of paper of the same size

quirk (kwurk) *n.* [< ?] 1. a sudden turn or twist   2. a peculiarity — quirk'i·ness *n.* —quirk'y *adj.*

quirt (kwurt) *n.* [AmSp. *cuarta*] a riding whip with a braided leather lash and a short handle

quis·ling (kwiz'liŋ) *n.* [< V. *Quisling*, Norw. collaborator with the Nazis] *same as* TRAITOR

quit (kwit) *vt.* quit, quit'ted, quit'-ting [< ML. *quietus*, free] 1. to free (oneself) of 2. to give up 3. to leave; depart from 4. to stop or resign from —*vi.* 1. to stop doing something 2. to give up one's job —*adj.* clear; free

quit·claim (kwit'klām') *n.* a deed relinquishing a claim, as to property

quite (kwīt) *adv.* [see QUIT] 1. completely 2. really; positively 3. very or fairly [*quite* warm] —quite a few (or bit, etc.) [Colloq.] more than a few (or bit, etc.)

Qui·to (kē'tō) capital of Ecuador: pop. 355,000

quits (kwits) *adj.* [see QUIETUS] on even terms, as by discharge of a debt, retaliation, etc. —call it quits [Colloq.] 1. to stop working, etc. 2. to stop being friendly

quit·tance (kwit'ns) *n.* [see QUIT] 1. discharge from a debt 2. recompense

quit·ter *n.* [Colloq.] one who quits or gives up easily, without trying hard

quiv·er¹ (kwiv'ər) *vi.* [see QUICK] to shake tremulously; tremble —*n.* a quivering; tremor

quiv·er² (kwiv'ər) *n.* [< OFr. *coivre*] a case for holding arrows

quix·ot·ic (kwik sät'ik) *adj.* [< DON QUIXOTE] extravagantly chivalrous or romantically idealistic

quiz (kwiz) *n.*, *pl.* quiz'zes [< ? L. *quis*, what, who] a questioning; esp., a short examination to test one's knowledge —*vt.* quizzed, quiz'zing to ask questions of —quiz'zer *n.*

quiz'zi·cal (-i k'l) *adj.* 1. odd; comical 2. perplexed —quiz'zi·cal·ly *adv.*

quoin (koin, kwoin) *n.* [var. of COIN] 1. the external corner of a building; esp., any of the large stones at such a corner 2. a wedge-shaped block

QUOINS

quoit (kwoit) *n.* [prob. < OFr. *coite*, a cushion] 1. a ring thrown in quoits 2. [*pl.*, *with sing. v.*] a game somewhat like horseshoes, in which rings are thrown at a peg

quon·dam (kwän'dəm) *adj.* [L.] former [a *quondam* companion]

Quon·set hut (kwän'sit) [< *Quonset* Point, R.I., where first made] *a trademark for* a prefabricated, metal shelter like a half cylinder on its flat side

quo·rum (kwôr'əm) *n.* [< L. *qui*, who] the minimum number of members required to be present before an assembly can transact its business

quot. quotation

quo·ta (kwōt'ə) *n.* [< L. *quota pars*, how large a part] a share or proportion assigned to each of a number

quotation mark either of a pair of punctuation marks (" ...") used to enclose a direct quotation

quote (kwōt) *vt.* quot'ed, quot'ing [< ML. *quotare*, to number (chapters)] 1. to repeat a passage from or statement of 2. to repeat (a passage, statement, etc.) 3. to state the price of (something) —*n.* [Colloq.] 1. something quoted 2. *same as* QUOTATION MARK —quot'a·ble *adj.* —quo·ta·tion (kwō tā'shən) *n.*

quoth (kwōth) *vt.* [< OE. *cwethan*, speak] [Archaic] said

quo·tient (kwō'shənt) *n.* [< L. *quot*, how many] the number obtained when one quantity is divided by another

q.v. [L. *quod vide*] which see

R

R, r (är) *n.*, *pl.* R's, r's the 18th letter of the English alphabet

R (är) *n. Elec.* resistance —the three R's reading, writing, and arithmetic, regarded as the basic studies

R a motion-picture rating for a film restricted to persons seventeen and over and to persons under seventeen if accompanied by a parent

r *Math.* radius

R., r. 1. radius 2. railroad 3. right 4. river 5. road 6. *Baseball* runs

Ra *Chem.* radium

rab·bet (rab'it) *n.* [< OFr. *rabattre*, beat down] a cut made in the edge of a board so that another piece may be fitted into it —*vt.*, *vi.* to cut, or be joined by, a rabbet

rab·bi (rab'ī) *n.*, *pl.* -bis, -bies [< Heb. *rabbi*, my master] an ordained teacher of the Jewish law —rab·bin·i·cal (rə bin'i k'l) *adj.* —rab'bin·ate' *n.*

rab·bit (rab'it) *n.* [ME. *rabette*] a burrowing mammal of the hare family, having soft fur and long ears

rabbit punch *Boxing* a short, sharp blow to the back of the neck

rab·ble (rab'l) *n.* [< ?] a mob

rab'ble-rous'er *n.* a person who tries to arouse people to violent action by appeals to emotions, prejudices, etc.

Rab·e·lais (rab'ə lā'), Fran·çois (frän swä') 1490?-1553; Fr. satirist

Rab'e·lai'si·an (-zhən, -zē ən) *adj.* of or like Rabelais; broadly and coarsely humorous, satirical, etc.

rab·id (rab′id) *adj.* [< L. *rabere*, to rage] 1. violent; raging 2. fanatical 3. of or having rabies

ra·bies (rā′bēz) *n.* [L., madness] an infectious disease with convulsions, transmitted to man by the bite of an infected animal

rac·coon (ra kōōn′) *n.* [< AmInd. *arakunem*, scratcher] 1. a small, tree-climbing mammal of N.America, having yellowish gray fur and a black-ringed tail 2. its fur

race¹ (rās) *n.* [< ON. *rās*, a running] 1. a competition of speed, as in running 2. any contest like a race [the *race* for mayor] 3. a swift current of water, or its channel —*vi.* **raced, rac′ing** 1. to take part in a race 2. to go or move swiftly —*vt.* 1. to compete with in a race 2. to enter (a horse, etc.) in a race 3. to cause to go swiftly —**rac′-er** *n.*

race² (rās) *n.* [Fr. < It. *razza*] 1. any of the three primary divisions of mankind distinguished esp. by color of skin 2. any geographical, national, or tribal ethnic grouping 3. any distinct group of people [the *race* of artists]

race′horse′ *n.* a horse bred and trained for racing

ra·ceme (rā sēm′, rə-) *n.* [L. *racemus*, cluster of grapes] a flower cluster, having a central stem along which individual flowers grow on small stems

race track a course prepared for racing, esp. an oval track for horse races: also **race′course′** *n.*

race′way′ *n.* 1. a narrow channel 2. a race track for harness races or one for drag races, etc.

ra·chi·tis (rə kīt′əs) *n.* [< Gr. *rhachitis*, spine inflammation] *same as* RICKETS —**ra·chit′ic** (-kit′ik) *adj.*

ra·cial (rā′shəl) *adj.* of or characteristic of a race, or ethnic group

rac·i·ness (rā′sē nis) *n.* racy quality

rac·ism (rā′siz′m) *n.* the practice of racial discrimination, persecution, etc. —**rac′ist** *n., adj.*

rack¹ (rak) *n.* [prob. < MDu. *recken*, to stretch] 1. a framework, etc. for holding or displaying various things [tie *rack*, pipe *rack*] 2. a toothed bar into which a pinion, etc. meshes 3. an instrument of torture which stretches the victim's limbs 4. any great torment —*vt.* 1. to arrange in or on a rack 2. to torture on a rack 3. to torment —**on the rack** in a difficult situation —**rack one's brains** to try hard to think of something —**rack up** [Slang] to score or achieve

rack² (rak) *n.* [var. of WRACK] destruction: now only in **go to rack and ruin,** to become ruined

rack·et¹ (rak′it) *n.* [prob. echoic] 1. a noisy confusion 2. a) an obtaining of money illegally b) [Colloq.] any dishonest practice

rack·et² (rak′it) *n.* [MFr. < Ar. *rāhah*, palm of the hand] a light bat for tennis, etc. with a network, as of cat-

gut, in a frame attached to a handle: also sp. **rac′quet**

rack·et·eer (rak′ə tir′) *n.* one who obtains money illegally, as by fraud, extortion, etc. —**rack′et·eer′ing** *n.*

rac·on·teur (rak′än tur′) *n.* [Fr. < *raconter*, to recount] a person skilled at telling stories or anecdotes

rac′quet·ball′ *n.* a game played like handball, but with a racket

rac·y (rā′sē) *adj.* **-i·er, -i·est** [< RACE²] 1. having the taste or quality of the genuine type [*racy* fruit] 2. lively; spirited 3. pungent 4. risqué

ra·dar (rā′där) *n.* [ra(dio) d(etecting) a(nd) r(anging)] a system or device that transmits radio waves to a reflecting object, as an aircraft, to determine its location, speed, etc. by the reflected waves

ra′dar·scope′ (-skōp′) *n.* an oscilloscope that picks up radar waves

ra·di·al (rā′dē əl) *adj.* [see RADIUS] 1. of or like a ray or rays; branching out from a center 2. of a radius

radial (ply) tire an automobile tire with ply cords nearly at right angles to the center line of the tread

ra·di·ant (rā′dē ənt) *adj.* [see RADIUS] 1. shining brightly 2. showing pleasure, etc.; beaming 3. issuing (from a source) in or as in rays —**ra′di·ance** *n.* —**ra′di·ant·ly** *adv.*

ra·di·ate (rā′dē āt′) *vi.* **-at′ed, -at′-ing** [see RADIUS] 1. to send out rays of heat, light, etc. 2. to branch out in lines from a center —*vt.* 1. to send out (heat, light, etc.) in rays 2. to give forth (happiness, love, etc.)

ra′di·a′tion *n.* 1. a radiating 2. the rays sent out 3. nuclear particles

radiation sickness sickness produced by overexposure to X-rays, radioactive matter, etc.

ra′di·a′tor *n.* an apparatus for radiating heat, as into a room or from an automobile engine

rad·i·cal (rad′i k'l) *adj.* [< L. *radix*, root] 1. of or from the root; fundamental 2. favoring basic change, as in the social or economic structure —*n.* 1. a person holding radical views 2. Chem. a group of two or more atoms acting as a single atom 3. Math. the sign (√) used with a quantity to show that its root is to be extracted —**rad′i·cal·ism** *n.* —**rad′i·cal·ly** *adv.*

ra·di·i (rā′dē ī′) *n. alt. pl. of* RADIUS

ra·di·o (rā′dē ō′) *n., pl.* **-os′** [ult. < L. *radius*: see RADIUS] 1. a) the transmission of sounds or signals by electromagnetic waves through space, without wires, to a receiving set b) such a set 2. broadcasting by radio as an industry, entertainment, etc. —*adj.* of, using, used in, or sent by radio —*vt., vi.* **-oed′, -o′ing** to transmit, or communicate with, by radio

radio- [see RADIUS] *a combining form meaning:* 1. radial 2. by radio 3. using radiant energy [*radiotherapy*]

ra′di·o·ac′tive *adj.* giving off radiant

energy in the form of particles or rays by the disintegration of atomic nuclei —**ra′di·o·ac·tiv′i·ty** n.

radio astronomy astronomy dealing with radio waves in space in order to obtain information about the universe

ra′di·o·gram′ (-gram′) n. a message sent by radio

ra′di·o·i′so·tope′ n. a radioactive isotope of a chemical element

ra′di·ol′o·gy (-äl′ə jē) n. the use of radiant energy, as X-rays, in medical diagnosis and therapy —**ra′di·ol′o·gist** n.

ra′di·o·paque′ (-ō pāk′) adj. not allowing the passage of X-rays, etc.

ra′di·os′co·py (-äs′kə pē) n. the examination of the inside structure of opaque objects, as by means of X-rays —**ra′di·o·scop′ic** (-ə skäp′ik) adj.

ra′di·o·ther′a·py n. the treatment of disease by the use of X-rays or rays from a radioactive substance

rad·ish (rad′ish) n. [< L. radix, root] 1. a plant of the mustard family, with an edible root 2. the pungent root, eaten raw

ra·di·um (rā′dē əm) n. [see ff.] a radioactive metallic chemical element, found in some uranium, which undergoes spontaneous atomic disintegration

radium therapy the treatment of cancer, etc. by the use of radium

ra·di·us (rā′dē əs) n., pl. **-di·i′** (-ī′), **-us·es** [L., spoke (of a wheel), hence ray] 1. any straight line from the center to the periphery of a circle or sphere 2. the circular area limited by the sweep of such a line [within a radius of two miles]

ra·dome (rā′dōm′) n. [RA(DAR) + DOME] a housing to protect a radar antenna

RAF, R.A.F. Royal Air Force

raf·fi·a (raf′ē ə) n. [< native name] 1. a palm tree of Madagascar with large leaves 2. fiber from its leaves, used for weaving

raff·ish (raf′ish) adj. [(RIFF)RAFF + -ISH] 1. disreputable 2. tawdry

raf·fle (raf′'l) n. [< MFr. rafle, dice game] a lottery in which each participant buys a chance to win a prize —vt. **-fled, -fling** to offer as a prize in a raffle (often with off)

raft′ (raft) n. [< ON. raptr, a log] 1. a floating structure of logs, boards, etc. fastened together 2. an inflatable boat

raft′ (raft) n. [< Brit. dial. raff, rubbish] [Colloq.] a large quantity

raft·er (raf′tər) n. [OE. ræfter] any of the beams that slope from the ridge of a roof to the eaves

rag′ (rag) n. [< ON. rögg, tuft of hair] 1. a waste piece of cloth, esp. one old or torn 2. a small piece of cloth for dusting, etc. 3. [pl.] old, worn clothes

rag′ (rag) n. a tune in ragtime

rag′ (rag) vt. [< ?] ragged, rag′ging to tease or scold

ra·ga (rä′gə) n. [Sans. rāga, color] any of various melody patterns improvised on by Hindu musicians

rag·a·muf·fin (rag′ə muf′in) n. [ME. Ragamoffyn, name of a demon] a dirty, ragged person, esp. such a child

rag′bag′ n. 1. a bag for rags 2. a collection of odds and ends

rage (rāj) n. [< LL. rabia, madness] 1. a furious, uncontrolled anger 2. a great violence or intensity —vi. **raged, rag′ing** 1. to show violent anger, as in speech 2. to be forceful, violent, etc. 3. to spread unchecked, as a disease —(all) the rage a fad

rag·ged (rag′id) adj. 1. shabby or torn from wear 2. wearing shabby or torn clothes 3. uneven; imperfect 4. shaggy [ragged hair] —run ragged to tire out; exhaust —rag′ged·ness n.

rag′ged·y (-ē) adj. somewhat ragged

rag·lan (rag′lən) n. [< Lord Raglan, 19th-c. Brit. general] a loose coat with sleeves that continue in one piece to the collar —adj. designating such a sleeve

ra·gout (ra gōō′) n. [< Fr. ragouter, revive the appetite of] a highly seasoned stew of meat and vegetables

rag·time (rag′tim′) n. [prob. < ragged time] 1. a type of American music (c. 1890–1915), with strong syncopation in fast, even time 2. its rhythm

RAGLAN SLEEVE

rag′weed′ n. [< its ragged-looking leaves] a weed whose pollen is a common cause of hay fever

rah (rä) interj. hurrah

raid (rād) n. [dial. var. of ROAD] 1. a sudden, hostile attack, as by troops, bandits, etc. 2. a sudden invasion of a place by police, for discovering violations of the law —vt., vi. to make a raid (on) —raid′er n.

rail′ (rāl) n. [< L. regula, a rule] 1. a bar of wood, metal, etc. placed between posts as a barrier or support 2. any of the parallel metal bars forming a track, as for railroad cars 3. a railroad —vt. to supply with rails

rail′ (rāl) vi. [< LL. ragere, to bellow] to speak bitterly; inveigh; complain

rail′ (rāl) n. [< MFr. raaler, to screech] a small wading bird

rail′ing n. 1. material for rails 2. a fence, etc. made of rails and posts

rail·ler·y (rāl′ər ē) n., pl. **-ies** [see RAIL²] light, good-natured ridicule

rail′road′ n. 1. a road laid with parallel steel rails along which cars are drawn by locomotives 2. a complete system of such roads —vt. 1. to transport by railroad 2. [Colloq.] to rush through (a bill) or convict (a person) hastily, without careful consideration —vi. to work on a railroad —rail′road′er n. —rail′road′ing n.

rail′way′ n. 1. [Brit.] a railroad 2. any track with rails to guide wheels

rai·ment (rā′mənt) n. [see ARRAY & -MENT] [Archaic] clothing; attire

rain (rān) n. [OE. regn] 1. water falling in drops condensed from the atmosphere 2. the falling of such drops 3. a rapid falling of many small objects —vi. 1. to fall: said of rain 2. to fall like rain —vt. 1. to pour down (rain, etc.) 2. to give in large quantities —

rain out to cause (an event) to be canceled because of rain —**rain′y** *adj.* **-i·er, -i·est**

rain′bow′ (-bō′) *n.* the arc containing the colors of the spectrum formed in the sky by the refraction of the sun's rays in falling rain or in mist

rain check the stub of a ticket to a ball game, etc. allowing future admission if the event is rained out

rain′coat′ *n.* a water-repellent coat

rain′drop′ *n.* a single drop of rain

rain′fall′ *n.* 1. a falling of rain 2. the amount of water falling over a given area during a given time

rain forest a dense, evergreen forest in a tropical area with much rainfall

rain′storm′ *n.* a storm with a heavy rain

raise (rāz) *vt.* **raised, rais′ing** [< ON. *reisa*] 1. to cause to rise; lift 2. to construct; build 3. to increase in size, amount, degree, intensity, etc. *[raise prices, raise* one's *voice]* 4. to provoke; inspire 5. to present for consideration *[raise* a question*]* 6. to collect (an army, money, etc.) 7. to end (a siege, etc.) 8. *a)* to cause to grow *b)* to rear (children) —*n.* 1. a raising 2. an increase, as in salary or a bet —**raise Cain** (or **hell, etc.**) [Slang] to create a disturbance

rai·sin (rā′z'n) *n.* [< L. *racemus,* cluster of grapes] a sweet dried grape

rai·son d'etre (rā′zōn det′, det′rə) [Fr.] reason for being

ra·jah, ra·ja (rä′jə) *n.* [< Sans. *rāj,* to rule] a prince in India

rake¹ (rāk) *n.* [OE. *raca*] a long-handled tool with teeth at one end, for gathering loose hay, leaves, etc. —*vt.* **raked, rak′ing** 1. to gather or smooth with a rake 2. to search through minutely 3. to direct gunfire along a line of troops, etc.) —**rake in** to gather a great amount of rapidly —**rake up** to uncover facts or gossip about (the past, a scandal, etc.)

rake² (rāk) *n.* [< earlier *rakehell*] a dissolute, debauched man

rake³ (rāk) *vi., vt.* **raked, rak′ing** [< ?] to slant —*n.* a slanting

rake′-off′ *n.* [Slang] a commission or rebate, esp. when illegitimate

rak·ish (rā′kish) *adj.* [< RAKE³ + -ISH] 1. having a trim appearance, suggesting speed: said of a ship 2. gay and dashing; jaunty —**rak′ish·ly** *adv.*

Ra·leigh (rô′lē, rä′-) capital of N.C.: pop. 150,000

Ra·leigh (rô′lē, rä′-), **Sir Walter** 1552?-1618; Eng. explorer & poet

ral·ly¹ (ral′ē) *vt., vi.* **-lied, -ly·ing** [< OFr. *re-,* again + *aleier,* join] 1. to bring back together in, or come back to, a state of order, as troops 2. to bring or come together for a common purpose 3. to revive; recover —*n.,* pl. **-lies** 1. a rallying or being rallied; esp., a gathering of people for some purpose 2. an organized automobile run designed to test driving skills

ral·ly² (ral′ē) *vt., vi.* **-lied, -ly·ing** [see RAIL²] to tease or banter

ram (ram) *n.* [OE. *ramm*] 1. a male sheep 2. *same as* BATTERING RAM —*vt.* **rammed, ram′ming** 1. to strike against with great force 2. to force into place; press down

ram·ble (ram′b'l) *vi.* **-bled, -bling** [< ME. *romen*] 1. to roam about; esp., to stroll about idly 2. to talk or write aimlessly 3. to spread in all directions, as a vine —*n.* a stroll

ram′bler *n.* a person or thing that rambles; esp., a climbing rose

ram·bunc·tious (ram buŋk′shəs) *adj.* [alt., after RAM, < earlier *robustious*] disorderly, boisterous, unruly, etc. —**ram·bunc′tious·ness** *n.*

rame·kin (ram′ə kin) *n.* [< Fr. < MDu.] a small, individual baking dish

ram·i·fy (ram′ə fī′) *vt., vi.* **-fied′, -fy′ing** [< L. *ramus,* a branch + *facere,* make] to divide or spread out into branches or branchlike divisions —**ram′i·fi·ca′tion** *n.*

ramp (ramp) *n.* [< OFr. *ramper,* climb] 1. a sloping walk or road joining different levels 2. a wheeled staircase for boarding an airplane 3. a sloping runway for launching boats, as from trailers

ram·page (ram pāj′; *for n.* ram′pāj) *vi.* **-paged′, -pag′ing** [prob. akin to prec.] to rush violently about; rage —*n.* an outbreak of wild, raging behavior: chiefly in **on a rampage**

ramp·ant (ram′pənt) *adj.* [see RAMP] growing unchecked; widespread

ram·part (ram′pärt, -pərt) *n.* [< Fr. *re-,* again + *emparer,* fortify] an embankment of earth surmounted by a parapet for defending a fort, etc.

ram′rod′ *n.* a rod for ramming down the charge in a muzzle-loading gun

ram·shack·le (ram′shak″l) *adj.* [< RANSACK] loose and rickety; likely to fall to pieces

ran (ran) *pt. of* RUN

ranch (ranch) *n.* [< Sp. *rancho,* small farm] 1. a large farm, esp. in W States, for raising cattle, horses, or sheep 2. a style of house with all the rooms on one floor: in full **ranch house** —*vi.* to work on or manage a ranch —**ranch′er, ranch′man** *n.,* pl. **-men**

ran·cid (ran′sid) *adj.* [< L. *rancere,* to be rank] having the bad smell or taste of stale fats or oils; spoiled

ran·cor (raŋ′kər) *n.* [< L. *rancere,* to be rank] a continuing and bitter hate or ill will: Brit. sp. **ran′cour** —**ran′cor·ous** *adj.* —**ran′cor·ous·ly** *adv.*

R & D, R and D research and development

ran·dom (ran′dəm) *adj.* [< OFr. *randon,* violence, speed] purposeless; haphazard —**at random** haphazardly —**ran′dom·ly** *adv.*

ran·dom·ize (-īz′) *vt.* **-ized′, -iz′ing** to select or choose (items of a group) in a random order

ran·dy (ran'dē) *adj.* **-i·er, -i·est**
[prob. < RANT] amorous; lustful

rang (raŋ) *pt.* of RING¹

range (rānj) *vt.* **ranged, rang'ing** [<
OFr. *renc,* a ring] **1.** to arrange in
order; set in a row or rows **2.** to place
(oneself) with others in a cause, etc. **3.**
to roam about —*vi.* **1.** to extend in a
given direction **2.** to roam **3.** to vary
between stated limits —*n.* **1.** a row,
line, or series **2.** a series of connected
mountains **3.** the distance that a
weapon can fire its projectile **4.** *a)* a
place for shooting practice *b)* a place
for testing rockets in flight **5.** extent;
scope **6.** a large, open area for grazing
livestock **7.** the limits of possible
variations of amount, degree, pitch,
etc. *[a wide range in price]* **8.** a
cooking stove

rang'er *n.* **1.** *a)* a mounted trooper
who patrols a region *b)* [often R-] a
soldier trained for close-combat raids
2. a warden who patrols forests

Ran·goon (raŋ gōōn') capital of
Burma: pop. 1,530,000

rang·y (rān'jē) *adj.* **-i·er, -i·est** long-
limbed and slender —**rang'i·ness** *n.*

rank¹ (raŋk) *n.* [< OFr. *ranc*] **1.** a
row, line, or series **2.** a social class **3.**
high position in society **4.** an official
grade *[the rank* of major] **5.** a relative
position in a scale *[a poet of the first
rank]* **6.** *a)* a row of soldiers, etc.
placed side by side *b)* [*pl.*] the army;
esp., enlisted soldiers —*vt.* **1.** to place
in a rank **2.** to assign a position to **3.**
to outrank —*vi.* **1.** to hold a certain
position —**rank and file 1.** enlisted
soldiers **2.** ordinary members, as
distinguished from their leaders

rank² (raŋk) *adj.* [OE. *ranc,* strong] **1.**
growing vigorously and coarsely *[rank
grass]* **2.** strong and offensive in smell
or taste **3.** in bad taste **4.** extreme;
utter *[rank* deceit] —**rank'ness** *n.*

rank'ing *adj.* **1.** of the highest rank
2. prominent or outstanding

ran·kle (raŋ'k'l) *vi., vt.* **-kled, -kling**
[< ML. *dracunculus,* ulcer] **1.** orig.,
to fester **2.** to cause or cause to have
long-lasting anger, rancor, etc.

ran·sack (ran'sak) *vt.* [< ON. *rann,*
house + *sækja,* seek] **1.** to search
thoroughly **2.** to plunder; pillage

ran·som (ran'səm) *n.* [see REDEEM]
1. the redeeming of a captive by paying money or complying with demands
2. the price demanded for this —*vt.* to
obtain the release of (a captive, etc.)
by paying the price demanded

rant (rant) *vi., vt.* [< obs. Du. *ranten*]
to talk or say in a loud, wild, extravagant way —*n.* loud, wild speech

rap (rap) *vt.* **rapped, rap'ping** [prob.
echoic] **1.** to strike quickly and
sharply; tap **2.** [Slang] to criticize
sharply —*vi.* **1.** to knock sharply **2.**
[Slang] to chat —*n.* **1.** a quick, sharp
knock **2.** [Slang] blame or punishment
3. [Slang] a talking; chat

ra·pa·cious (rə pā'shəs) *adj.* [< L.
rapere, seize] **1.** greedy; voracious **2.**
predatory —**ra·pac'i·ty** (-pas'ə tē) *n.*

rape¹ (rāp) *n.* [prob. < L. *rapere,*
seize] **1.** the crime of having sexual

intercourse with a woman forcibly and
without her consent **2.** the plundering
(of a city, etc.), as in warfare —*vt.*
raped, rap'ing **1.** to commit rape on;
ravish **2.** to plunder or destroy —*vi.*
to commit rape —**rap'ist** *n.*

rape² (rāp) *n.* [< L. *rapa,* turnip] a
plant of the mustard family, whose
leaves are used for fodder

Raph·a·el (raf'ē əl, rā'fē-) 1483-
1520; It. painter

rap·id (rap'id) *adj.* [< L. *rapere,* to
rush] moving or occurring with speed;
swift; quick —*n.* [*usually pl.*] a part of
a river where the current is swift —
ra·pid·i·ty (rə pid'ə tē) *n.* —**rap'-
id·ly** *adv.*

rapid transit a system of rapid
public transportation in an urban
area, using electric trains along an
unimpeded right of way

ra·pi·er (rā'pē ər) *n.* [Fr. *rapière*] a
light, sharp-pointed sword used only
for thrusting

rap·ine (rap'in) *n.* [< L. *rapere,*
seize] plunder; pillage

rap·port (ra pôr', -pōrt') *n.* [Fr. < L.
ad-, to + *portare,* carry] sympathetic
relationship; harmony

rap·proche·ment (ra prôsh'män) *n.*
[Fr.] an establishing of friendly relations

rap·scal·lion (rap skal'yən) *n.* [<
RASCAL] a rascal; rogue

rapt (rapt) *adj.* [< L. *rapere,* seize] **1.**
carried away with joy, love, etc. **2.**
completely engrossed (*in*)

rap·ture (rap'chər) *n.* the state of
being carried away with joy, love, etc.;
ecstasy —**rap'tur·ous** *adj.*

ra·ra a·vis (rer'ə ā'vis) [L., rare bird]
an extraordinary person or thing

rare¹ (rer) *adj.* **rar'er, rar'est** [< L.
rarus] **1.** not frequently encountered;
scarce; uncommon **2.** unusually good;
excellent **3.** not dense *[rare* atmos-
phere] —**rare'ness** *n.*

rare² (rer) *adj.* **rar'er, rar'est** [OE.
hrere] not completely cooked; partly
raw: esp. of meat —**rare'ness** *n.*

rare³ (rer) *vi.* **rared, rar'ing** [var. of
REAR²] [Colloq.] to be eager: used in
prp. *[raring* to go]

rare·bit (rer'bit) *n.* same as WELSH
RABBIT

rar·e·fy (rer'ə fī') *vt., vi.* **-fied', -fy'-
ing** [< L. *rarus,* rare + *facere,* make]
to make or become less dense —**rar'-
e·fac'tion** (-fak'shən) *n.*

rare·ly (rer'lē) *adv.* **1.** infrequently;
seldom **2.** uncommonly

rar·i·ty (rer'ə tē) *n.* **1.** a being rare;
specif., *a)* scarcity *b)* lack of density;
thinness **2.** *pl.* **-ties** something remarkable or valuable because rare

ras·cal (ras'k'l) *n.* [< OFr. *rascaille,*
rabble] **1.** a rogue **2.** a mischievous
child —**ras·cal'i·ty** (-kal'ə tē) *n.* —
ras'cal·ly *adj., adv.*

rash¹ (rash) *adj.* [ME. *rasch*] too hasty
in acting or speaking; reckless —
rash'ly *adv.* —**rash'ness** *n.*

rash² (rash) *n.* [see RASCAL] **1.** an
eruption of red spots on the skin **2.** a
sudden appearance of a great number

rash·er (rash'ər) *n.* [< ? obs. *rash,* to

cut] a thin slice of bacon, etc., or a serving of several such slices

rasp (rasp) *vt.* [< OHG. *raspon*, scrape together] 1. to scrape as with a file 2. to grate upon; irritate —*vi.* 1. to grate 2. to make a rough, grating sound —*n.* 1. a type of rough file. 2. a rough, grating sound —**rasp'y** *adj.*

rasp·ber·ry (raz'ber'ē, -ber-) *n., pl.* **-ries** [< earlier *rasp(is)*] 1. a small, red or purple, juicy fruit of the rose family 2. a plant bearing this fruit 3. [Slang] a sound of derision

rat (rat) *n.* [OE. *ræt*] 1. a long-tailed rodent, resembling, but larger than, the mouse 2. [Slang] a sneaky, contemptible person; esp., an informer —*vi.* **rat'ted, rat'ting** [Slang] to inform (*on*) —**smell a rat** to suspect a trick, plot, etc.

ratch·et (rach'it) *n.* [< It. *rocca*, distaff] 1. a toothed wheel (in full **ratchet wheel**) or bar whose sloping teeth catch a pawl, preventing backward motion 2. such a pawl

rate¹ (rāt) *n.* [< L. *reri*, reckon] 1. the amount, degree, etc. of anything in relation to units of something else [*rate* of pay] 2. price, esp. per unit 3. a class or rank —*vt.* **rat'ed, rat'ing** 1. to appraise 2. to consider; esteem 3. [Colloq.] to deserve —*vi.* to have value, status, etc. —**at any rate** 1. in any event 2. anyway

rate² (rāt) *vt., vi.* **rat'ed, rat'ing** [ME. *raten*] to scold; chide

rath·er (ra*th*'ər) *adv.* [< OE. *hræthe*, quickly] 1. more willingly; preferably 2. with more justice, reason, etc. [I, *rather* than you, should pay] 3. more accurately [my son, or *rather*, stepson] 4. on the contrary 5. somewhat [*rather* hungry]

raths·kel·ler (rat'skel'ər, rath'-) *n.* [G. < *rat*, council + *keller*, cellar] a restaurant of the German type, usually below street level

rat·i·fy (rat'ə fī') *vt.* **-fied', -fy'ing** [< L. *ratus*, reckoned + *facere*, make] to approve; esp., to give official sanction to —**rat'i·fi·ca'tion** *n.*

rat·ing (rāt'iŋ) *n.* 1. a rank, or grade, as of military personnel 2. a placement in a certain rank or class 3. an evaluation; appraisal 4. *Radio & TV* the relative popularity of a program according to sample polls

ra·tio (rā'shō, -shē ō') *n., pl.* **-tios** [L., a reckoning] a fixed relation in degree, number, etc. between two similar things; proportion

ra·ti·o·ci·nate (rash'ē ō'sə nāt', rat'ē-; -äs'ə-) *vi.* **-nat'ed, -nat'ing** [see prec.] to reason, esp. using formal logic —**ra'ti·o'ci·na'tion** *n.*

ra·tion (rash'ən, rā'shən) *n.* [see RATIO] a fixed portion; share 2. a fixed allowance of food, as a daily allowance for one soldier 3. [*pl.*] food supply —*vt.* 1. to supply with rations 2. to distribute (food, clothing, etc.) in rations, as in times of scarcity

ra·tion·al (rash'ən 'l) *adj.* [see RATIO] 1. of or based on reasoning 2. able to reason; reasoning 3. sensible or sane —**ra'tion·al'i·ty** (-ə nal'ə tē) *n.* —**ra'tion·al·ly** *adv.*

ra·tion·ale (rash'ə nal') *n.* [L., rational) 1. the reasons or rational basis for something 2. an explanation of principles

ra·tion·al·ism *n.* the practice of accepting reason as the only authority in determining one's opinions or a course of action —**ra'tion·al·ist** *n.* —**ra'tion·al·is'tic** *adj.*

ra·tion·al·ize (-īz') *vt., vi.* **-ized', -iz'ing** 1. to make or be rational or reasonable 2. to devise plausible explanations for (one's acts, beliefs, etc.), usually in self-deception —**ra'tion·al·i·za'tion** *n.*

rat·line, rat·lin (rat'lin) *n.* [< ?] any of the small ropes which join the shrouds of a ship and serve as a ladder

rat race [Slang] a mad scramble or intense struggle to survive, succeed, etc.

rat·tan (ra tan') *n.* [< Malay *raut*, to strip] 1. a climbing palm with long, slender, tough stems 2. these stems, used in wickerwork, canes, etc.

RATLINES

rat·tle (rat''l) *vi.* **-tled, -tling** [prob. echoic] 1. to make a series of sharp, short sounds 2. to chatter (often with *on*) —*vt.* 1. to cause to rattle 2. to confuse or upset —*n.* 1. a series of sharp, short sounds 2. a series of horny rings at the end of a rattlesnake's tail 3. a baby's toy, etc. made to rattle when shaken

rat·tle·brain' *n.* a frivolous, talkative person —**rat'tle·brained'** *adj.*

rat'tler *n.* a rattlesnake

rat·tle·snake' *n.* a poisonous American snake with horny rings at the end of the tail that rattle when shaken

rat·tle·trap' *n.* a rickety, old car

rat·tling *adj.* 1. that rattles 2. [Colloq.] very fast, good, etc. —*adv.* [Colloq.] very [a *rattling* good time]

rat'trap' *n.* 1. a trap for rats 2. [Colloq.] a dirty, run-down building

rat·ty (rat'ē) *adj.* **-ti·er, -ti·est** [Slang] shabby or mean

rau·cous (rô'kəs) *adj.* [L. *raucus*] 1. hoarse 2. loud and rowdy —**rau'cous·ly** *adv.* —**rau'cous·ness** *n.*

raun·chy (rôn'chē) *adj.* **-chi·er, -chi·est** [< ?] [Slang] 1. dirty, sloppy, etc. 2. risqué, lustful, etc.

rav·age (rav'ij) *n.* [see RAVISH] destruction; ruin —*vt.* **-aged, -ag·ing** to destroy violently; devastate; ruin —*vi.* to commit ravages

rave (rāv) *vi.* **raved, rav'ing** [OFr. *raver*] 1. to talk incoherently or wildly 2. to talk with great enthusiasm *(about)* —*n.* [Colloq.] a very enthusiastic commendation

rav·el (rav′'l) *vt., vi.* **-eled** or **-elled, -el·ing** or **-el·ling** [MDu. *ravelen*] to separate into its parts, esp. threads; untwist; fray —*n.* a raveled part or thread

rav·en (rā′vən) *n.* [OE. *hræfn*] a large, black bird of the crow family —*adj.* black and lustrous

rav·en·ing (rav′'n iŋ) *adj.* [ult. < L. *rapere*, seize] greedily searching for prey [*ravening* wolves]

rav·e·nous (rav′ə nəs) *adj.* [see RAVISH] 1. greedily hungry 2. rapacious —**rav′e·nous·ly** *adv.*

ra·vine (rə vēn′) *n.* [Fr.; flood: ult. < L.] a long, deep hollow in the earth, esp. one worn by a stream; gorge

rav′ing *adj.* 1. that raves; frenzied 2. [Colloq.] exciting enthusiastic admiration [a *raving* beauty] —*adv.* so as to make rave [*raving* mad]

ra·vi·o·li (rav′ē ō′lē) *n.pl.* [with *sing.* v.] [It.] small casings of dough containing ground meat, cheese, etc.

rav·ish (rav′ish) *vt.* [< L. *rapere*, seize] 1. to seize and carry away forcibly 2. to rape 3. to transport with joy or delight —**rav′ish·ment** *n.*

rav′ish·ing *adj.* giving much delight

raw (rô) *adj.* [OE. *hreaw*] 1. not cooked 2. in its natural condition; not processed [*raw* silk] 3. inexperienced [a *raw* recruit] 4. abraded and sore 5. uncomfortably cold and damp [a *raw* wind] 6. coarse, indecent, bawdy, etc. 7. [Colloq.] harsh or unfair [a *raw* deal] —**in the raw** 1. untamed or unprocessed 2. naked —**raw′ness** *n.*

raw′boned′ (-bōnd′) *adj.* lean; gaunt

raw′hide′ *n.* 1. an untanned cattle hide 2. a whip made of this

ray¹ (rā) *n.* [see RADIUS] 1. any of the thin lines, or beams, of light that appear to come from a bright source 2. any of several lines radiating from a center 3. a beam of radiant energy, radioactive particles, etc. 4. a tiny amount [a *ray* of hope]

ray² (rā) *n.* [< L. *raia*] a fish with a broad, flat body, widely expanded fins at each side, and a whiplike tail

ray·on (rā′än) *n.* [coined < RAY¹] 1. a textile fiber made from a cellulose solution 2. a fabric of such fibers

raze (rāz) *vt.* **razed, raz′ing** [< L. *radere*, to scrape] to tear down completely; demolish

ra·zor (rā′zər) *n.* [see prec.] 1. a sharp-edged instrument for shaving 2. *same as* SHAVER

razz (raz) *vt., vi.* [< RASPBERRY] [Slang] to tease, ridicule, etc.

raz·zle-daz·zle (raz′'l daz′'l) *n.* [Slang] a flashy, deceptive display

razz·ma·tazz (raz′mə taz′) *n.* [prob. < prec.] [Slang] 1. liveliness; vigor 2. flashiness; showiness

rbi, RBI, r.b.i. *Baseball* run(s) batted in

R.C.Ch. Roman Catholic Church

Rd., rd. 1. road 2. rod

R.D. Rural Delivery

re¹ (rā) *n.* [It.] *Music* the second tone of the diatonic scale

re² (rē, rā) *prep.* [L. < *res*, thing] in the case or matter of; as regards

re- [< Fr. or L.] *a prefix meaning:* 1. back 2. again; anew *Re-* is sometimes hyphenated, as before a word beginning with *e* or to distinguish such forms as *re-cover* (to cover again) and RECOVER In the following list, *re-* means *again* or *anew*

reacquaint	rehire
readjust	reimpose
readmit	reinfect
reaffirm	reinoculate
realign	reinsert
reappear	reinspect
reappoint	reinvest
reappraise	reissue
rearm	rekindle
reassemble	relearn
reassess	relive
reassign	reload
reawaken	relocate
reborn	remake
rebroadcast	remarry
rebuild	rematch
recharge	rename
recheck	renegotiate
reclassify	renominate
recommence	renumber
reconquer	reopen
reconsign	reorder
reconvene	repack
reconvert	repackage
recopy	repaint
re-cover	rephrase
redecorate	replant
rededicate	replay
redetermine	re-press
redirect	reprint
rediscover	republish
redivide	reread
redraw	reroute
reeducate	resell
reelect	reset
reembark	resettle
reembody	reshuffle
reemerge	respell
reenact	restate
reengage	restring
reenlist	restudy
reenter	restyle
reestablish	retell
reexamine	rethink
reexplain	retrain
refashion	retrial
refasten	reunite
refinance	reupholster
reformulate	reuse
refuel	revisit
refurnish	revitalize
rehear	reweigh
reheat	rework

reach (rēch) *vt.* [OE. *ræcan*] 1. to thrust out (the hand, etc.) 2. to extend to by thrusting out, etc. 3. to obtain and hand over [*reach* me the salt] 4. to go as far as; attain 5. to influence; affect 6. to get in touch with, as by telephone —*vi.* 1. to thrust out the hand, etc. 2. to extend in influence, space, etc. 3. to carry, as sight, sound, etc. 4. to try to get something —*n.* 1. a stretching or thrusting out 2. the power of, or the extent covered in, stretching, obtaining, etc. 3. a continuous extent, esp. of water

re·act (rē akt′) *vi.* 1. to act in return or reciprocally 2. to act in a reverse way; go back to a former condition, stage, etc. 3. to respond to a stimulus 4. *Chem.* to act with another substance in producing a chemical change

re·act·ant (rē ak′tənt) *n.* any substance involved in a chemical reaction

re·ac·tion (rē ak′shən) *n.* 1. a return or opposing action, etc. 2. a response, as to a stimulus or influence 3. a movement back to a former or less advanced condition 4. a chemical change

re·ac′tion·ar′y (-shə ner′ē) *adj.* of, characterized by, or advocating reaction, esp. in politics —*n., pl.* **-ies** an advocate of reaction, esp. in politics

re·ac·ti·vate (rē ak′tə vāt′) *vt., vi.* **-vat′ed, -vat′ing** to make or be made active again; specif., to return (a military unit, ship, etc.) to active status —**re·ac′ti·va′tion** *n.*

re·ac·tive (-tiv) *adj.* 1. tending to react 2. of, from, or showing reaction —**re·ac·tiv′i·ty** *n.*

re·ac·tor (rē ak′tər) *n. same as* NUCLEAR REACTOR

read¹ (rēd) *vt.* **read** (red), **read·ing** (rēd′iŋ) [< OE. *rædan*, to counsel] 1. to get the meaning of (writing) by interpreting the characters 2. to utter aloud (written matter) 3. to understand or interpret 4. to foretell (the future) 5. to study [to *read* law] 6. to register, as a gauge 7. to obtain (information) from (punch cards, tape, etc.): said of a computer 8. [Slang] to hear and understand (a radio communication, etc.) —*vi.* 1. to read something written 2. to learn by reading (with *about* or *of*) 3. to be phrased in certain words —**read into** (or **in**) to attribute (a particular meaning) —**read out of** to expel from (a group) —**read′a·bil′i·ty** *n.* —**read′a·ble** *adj.* —**read′er** *n.*

read² (red) *pt. & pp.* of READ¹ —*adj.* informed by reading [well-*read*]

read′er·ship′ *n.* all the readers of a certain publication, author, etc.

read·ing (rēd′iŋ) *n.* 1. the act of one who reads 2. any material to be read 3. the amount registered by a barometer, electric meter, etc. 4. a particular interpretation or performance

read′out′ *n.* 1. the retrieving of information from a computer 2. the information retrieved, as in typewritten form 3. reading (sense 3)

read·y (red′ē) *adj.* **-i·er, -i·est** [OE. *ræde*] 1. prepared to act or be used immediately 2. willing 3. likely or liable; apt [*ready* to cry] 4. dexterous 5. prompt [a *ready* reply] 6. available at once [*ready* cash] —*vt.* **-ied, -y·ing** to make ready; prepare —**read′i·ly** *adv.* —**read′i·ness** *n.*

read′y-made′ *adj.* made so as to be ready for use or sale at once: also (as applied to clothing) **read′y-to-wear′**

Rea·gan (rā′gən), Ronald 1911- : 40th president of the U.S. (1981-)

re·a·gent (rē ā′jənt) *n. Chem.* a substance used to detect, measure, or react with another substance

re·al (rē′əl, rēl) *adj.* [< L. *res*, thing] 1. existing as or in fact; actual; true 2. authentic; genuine 3. *Law* of or relating to immovable things [*real* property] —*adv.* [Colloq.] very —**for real** [Slang] real or really

real estate land, including the buildings or improvements on it

re·al·ism (rē′ə liz′m) *n.* 1. a tendency to face facts and be practical 2. *Art & Literature* the portrayal of people and things as they really are —**re′al·ist** *n.* —**re′al·is′tic** *adj.* —**re′al·is′ti·cal·ly** *adv.*

re·al·i·ty (rē al′ə tē) *n., pl.* **-ties** 1. the quality or fact of being real 2. a person or thing that is real; fact —**in reality** in fact; actually

re·al·ize (rē′ə līz′) *vt.* **-ized′, -iz′ing** 1. to make real 2. to understand fully 3. to convert (assets, rights, etc.) into money 4. to gain; obtain [*realize* a profit] 5. to be sold for (a specified sum) —**re′al·i·za′tion** *n.*

real′-life′ *adj.* actual; not imaginary

re′al·ly *adv.* 1. in reality; actually 2. truly —*interj.* indeed

realm (relm) *n.* [see REGAL] 1. a kingdom 2. a region; sphere

Re·al·tor (rē′əl tər) *n.* a certified real estate broker, appraiser, etc.

re·al·ty (rē′əl tē) *n. same as* REAL ESTATE

ream¹ (rēm) *n.* [< Ar. *rizma*, a bale] 1. a quantity of paper varying from 480 to 516 sheets 2. [*pl.*] [Colloq.] a great amount

ream² (rēm) *vt.* [< OE. *reman*, widen] to enlarge (a hole) with a reamer

ream′er *n.* 1. a sharp-edged tool for enlarging or tapering holes 2. a juicer

re·an·i·mate (rē an′ə māt′) *vt.* **-mat′ed, -mat′ing** to give new life, power, or vigor to —**re·an′i·ma′tion** *n.*

reap (rēp) *vt., vi.* [OE. *ripan*] 1. to cut (grain) with a scythe, reaper, etc. 2. to gather (a harvest) 3. to obtain as the reward of action, etc.

reap′er *n.* 1. one who reaps 2. a machine for reaping grain

re·ap·por·tion (rē′ə pôr′shən) *vt.* to apportion again; specif., to adjust the representation pattern of (a legislature) —**re′ap·por′tion·ment** *n.*

rear¹ (rir) *n.* [< ARREARS] 1. the back part 2. the position behind or at the back 3. the part of an army, etc. farthest from the battle front —*adj.* of, at, or in the rear —**bring up the rear** to come at the end

rear² (rir) *vt.* [OE. *ræran*] 1. to put upright; elevate 2. to build; erect 3. to grow or breed 4. to educate, nourish, etc. [to *rear* children] —*vi.* 1. to rise on the hind legs, as a horse 2. to rise (*up*) in anger, etc. 3. to rise high

rear admiral a naval officer next in rank above a captain

rear'most' *adj.* farthest to the rear

re'ar·range' *vt.* -ranged', -rang'ing to arrange again or in a different way

rear'ward (-wərd) *adj.* at, in, or toward the rear —*adv.* toward the rear: also **rear'wards**

rea·son (rē'z'n) *n.* [ult. < L. *reri*, think] 1. an explanation of an act, idea, etc. 2. a cause or motive 3. the ability to think, draw conclusions, etc. 4. good sense 5. sanity —*vi., vt.* 1. to think logically (about); analyze 2. to argue or infer —**stand to reason** to be logical —**rea'son·ing** *n.*

rea'son·a·ble *adj.* 1. able to reason 2. just; fair 3. sensible; wise 4. not excessive —**rea'son·a·bly** *adv.*

re'as·sure' *vt.* -sured', -sur'ing 1. to assure again 2. to restore to confidence —**re'as·sur'ance** *n.*

re·bate (rē'bāt) *vt.* -bat·ed, -bat·ing [< OFr.: see RE- & ABATE] to give back (part of a payment) —*n.* a return of part of a payment

Re·bec·ca, Re·bek·ah (ri bek'ə) *Bible* the wife of Isaac

reb·el (reb''l; *for v.* ri bel') *n.* [< L. *re-*, again + *bellare*, wage war] one who openly resists authority —*adj.* 1. rebellious 2. of rebels —*vi.* -elled', -el'ling 1. to resist authority 2. to feel or show strong aversion

re·bel·lion (ri bel'yən) *n.* 1. armed resistance to one's government 2. a defiance of any authority

re·bel'lious (-yəs) *adj.* 1. resisting authority 2. opposing any control

re'birth' *n.* 1. a new or second birth 2. a reawakening; revival

re·bound (ri bound'; *for n.* rē'bound') *vi.* to spring back, as upon impact —*n.* a rebounding, or ball, etc. that rebounds —**on the rebound** 1. after bouncing back 2. after being jilted

re·buff (ri buf') *n.* [< It. *rabuffo*] 1. an abrupt refusal of offered advice, help, etc. 2. any repulse —*vt.* 1. to snub 2. to check or repulse

re·buke (ri byōōk') *vt.* -buked', -buk'ing [< OFr. *re-*, back + *buchier*, to beat] to scold in a sharp way; reprimand —*n.* a reprimand

re·bus (rē'bəs) *n.* [L., lit., by things] a puzzle consisting of pictures, etc. combined to suggest words or phrases

re·but (ri but') *vt.* -but'ted, -but'ting [< OFr. < *re-*, back + *buter*, to push] to contradict or oppose, esp. in a formal manner by argument, proof, etc. —**re·but'tal** (-'l) *n.*

rec (rek) *n.* recreation: used in compounds, as **rec room, rec hall**

re·cal·ci·trant (ri kal'si trənt) *adj.* [< L. *re-*, back + *calcitrare*, to kick] 1. refusing to obey authority, etc. 2. hard to handle —**re·cal'ci·trance** *n.*

re·call (ri kôl'; *for n.* also rē'kôl') *vt.* 1. to call back 2. to remember 3. to take back; revoke 4. to bring back to memory —*n.* 1. a recalling 2. memory 3. the removal of, or right to remove, an official from office by popular vote

re·cant (ri kant') *vt., vi.* [< L. *re-*, back + *canere*, sing] to renounce formally (one's beliefs, remarks, etc.) —**re·can·ta·tion** (rē'kan tā'shən) *n.*

re·cap¹ (rē kap'; *for n.* rē'kap') *vt.* -capped', -cap'ping to put a new tread on (a worn tire) —*n.* such a tire

re·cap² (rē'kap') *n.* a recapitulation, or summary —*vt., vi.* -capped', -cap'ping to recapitulate

re·ca·pit·u·late (rē'kə pich'ə lāt') *vi., vt.* -lat'ed, -lat'ing [see RE- & CAPITULATE] to summarize; repeat briefly —**re'ca·pit'u·la'tion** *n.*

re·cap'ture *vt.* -tured, -tur·ing 1. to capture again; retake 2. to remember —*n.* a recapturing

recd., rec'd received

re·cede (ri sēd') *vi.* -ced'ed, -ced'ing [see RE- & CEDE] 1. to go, move, or slope backward 2. to diminish

re·ceipt (ri sēt') *n.* [see RECEIVE] 1. *old term for* RECIPE 2. a receiving or being received 3. a written acknowledgment that something has been received 4. [*pl.*] the amount received —*vt.* 1. to mark (a bill) paid 2. to write a receipt for

re·ceiv·a·ble (ri sēv'və b'l) *adj.* 1. that can be received 2. due

re·ceive (ri sēv') *vt.* -ceived', -ceiv'ing [< L. *re-*, back + *capere*, take] 1. to take or get (something given, sent, thrown, etc.) 2. to experience or undergo [*to receive* acclaim] 3. to react to in a specified way 4. to learn (some news, information, etc.) 5. to bear or hold 6. to let enter 7. to greet (visitors, etc.)

re·ceiv'er *n.* 1. one who receives 2. in radio, TV, telephony, etc., a device that converts electrical waves or signals back into sound or images 3. *Football* the player designated to receive a forward pass 4. *Law* one appointed to administer or hold in trust property in bankruptcy or in a lawsuit —**re·ceiv'er·ship'** *n.*

re·cen·sion (ri sen'shən) *n.* [< L. *recensere*, revise] a revision of a text based on a study of sources

re·cent (rē's'nt) *adj.* [< L. *recens*] 1. done, made, etc. just before the present; new 2. of a time just before the present —**re'cent·ly** *adv.*

re·cep·ta·cle (ri sep'tə k'l) *n.* [see RECEIVE] a container

re·cep·tion (ri sep'shən) *n.* 1. *a)* a receiving or being received *b)* the manner of this 2. a social function for the receiving of guests 3. *Radio & TV* the receiving of signals with reference to the quality of reproduction

re·cep'tion·ist *n.* an office employee who receives callers, etc.

re·cep'tive *adj.* able or ready to accept suggestions, new ideas, etc.

re·cep'tor *n.* a nerve ending or group of nerve endings specialized for receiving stimuli; sense organ

re·cess (rē'ses; *also, and for v. usually,* ri ses') *n.* [< L. *recedere*, recede] 1. a hollow place, as in a wall 2. a hidden or inner place 3. a temporary halting of work, a session, etc. —*vt.* 1. to place in a recess 2. to form a recess in —*vi.* to take a recess

re·ces·sion (ri sesh'ən) *n.* 1. a going back; withdrawal 2. a temporary falling off of business activity

re·ces′sion·al (-'l) *n.* a hymn sung at the end of a church service when the clergy and the choir march out

re·ces′sive *adj.* tending to recede

re·cher·ché (rə sher′shā, -sher′shā′) *adj.* 1. rare; choice 2. refined; esp., too refined

rec·i·pe (res′ə pē) *n.* [L. < *recipere*, receive] 1. a list of materials and directions for preparing a dish or drink 2. a way to achieve something

re·cip·i·ent (ri sip′ē ənt) *n.* [see RECEIVE] one that receives

re·cip·ro·cal (ri sip′rə k'l) *adj.* [< L. *reciprocus*, returning] 1. done, given, etc. in return 2. mutual *[reciprocal love]* 3. corresponding but reversed 4. corresponding or complementary —*n.* 1. a complement, counterpart, etc. 2. *Math.* the quantity resulting from the division of 1 by the given quantity *[the reciprocal of 7 is 1/7]*

re·cip′ro·cate′ (-kāt′) *vt., vi.* -cat′ed, -cat′ing 1. to give and get reciprocally 2. to do, feel, etc. in return 3. to move alternately back and forth —**re·cip′ro·ca′tion** *n.*

rec·i·proc·i·ty (res′ə präs′ə tē) *n., pl.* -ties 1. reciprocal state 2. mutual exchange; esp., exchange of special privileges between two countries

re·cit·al (ri sīt′'l) *n.* 1. a reciting 2. the account, story, etc. told 3. a musical or dance program

rec·i·ta·tion (res′ə tā′shən) *n.* 1. a recital (senses 1 & 2) 2. *a)* the speaking aloud in public of something memorized *b)* a piece so presented 3. a reciting by pupils of answers to questions on a prepared lesson

rec′i·ta·tive′ (-tə tēv′) *n.* [< It.: see ff.] a type of declamation, as for operatic dialogue, with the rhythms of speech, but in musical tones

re·cite (ri sīt′) *vt., vi.* -cit′ed, -cit′ing [see RE- & CITE] 1. to speak aloud from memory, as a poem, lesson, etc. 2. to tell in detail; relate

reck·less *adj.* heedless; rash —**reck′less·ly** *adv.* —**reck′less·ness** *n.*

reck·on (rek′ən) *vt.* [OE. *recenian*] 1. to count; compute 2. to regard as being 3. to estimate 4. [Colloq. or Dial.] to suppose —*vi.* 1. to count up 2. [Colloq.] to rely (*on*) —**reckon with** to take into consideration

reck′on·ing *n.* 1. count or computation 2. the settlement of an account

re·claim (ri klām′) *vt.* [see RE- & CLAIM] 1. to bring back from error, vice, etc. 2. to make (wasteland, etc.) usable 3. to recover (useful materials, etc.) from waste products —**rec·la·ma·tion** (rek′lə mā′shən) *n.*

re·cline (ri klīn′) *vt., vi.* -clined′, -clin′ing [< L. *re*-, back + *clinare*, lean] to lie or cause to lie down

rec·luse (rek′lōōs, ri klōōs′) *n.* [< L. *re*-, back + *claudere*, to shut] one who lives a secluded, solitary life

rec·og·ni·tion (rek′əg nish′ən) *n.* 1. a recognizing or being recognized 2.

identification of a person or thing as having been known to one

re·cog·ni·zance (ri käg′ni zəns, -kän′i-) *n.* [< L. *re*-, again + *cognoscere*, know] *Law* a bond binding one to some act, as to appear in court

rec·og·nize (rek′əg nīz′) *vt.* -nized′, -niz′ing [< prec.] 1. to be aware of as known before 2. to know by some detail, as of appearance 3. to perceive 4. to accept as a fact *[to recognize defeat]* 5. to acknowledge as worthy of commendation 6. to acknowledge the status of (a government, etc.) 7. to grant the right to speak in a meeting —**rec′og·niz′a·ble** *adj.*

re·coil (ri koil′; *also for n.* rē′koil′) *vi.* [< L. *re*-, back + *culus*, buttocks] 1. to draw back, as in fear, etc. 2. to spring or kick back, as a gun when fired —*n.* a recoiling

rec·ol·lect (rek′ə lekt′) *vt., vi.* [see RE- & COLLECT] to remember, esp. with some effort —**rec′ol·lec′tion** *n.*

rec·om·mend (rek′ə mend′) *vt.* [see RE- & COMMEND] 1. to entrust 2. to suggest favorably as suited to some position, etc. 3. to make acceptable 4. to advise; counsel —**rec′om·men·da′tion** *n.*

re′com·mit′ *vt.* -mit′ted, -mit′ting 1. to commit again 2. to refer (a bill, etc.) back to a committee

rec·om·pense (rek′əm pens′) *vt.* -pensed′, -pens′ing [see RE- & COMPENSATE] 1. to repay or reward 2. to compensate (a loss, etc.) —*n.* 1. requital; reward 2. compensation

rec·on·cile (rek′ən sīl′) *vt.* -ciled′, -cil′ing [see RE- & CONCILIATE] 1. to make friendly again 2. to settle (a quarrel, etc.) 3. to make (ideas, texts, etc.) consistent 4. to make content, or acquiescent (*to*) —**rec′on·cil′a·ble** *adj.* —**rec′on·cil′i·a′tion** (-sil′ē ā′shən) *n.*

rec·on·dite (rek′ən dīt′) *adj.* [< L. *re*-, back + *condere*, to hide] beyond ordinary understanding; abstruse

re′con·di′tion *vt.* to put back in good condition by repairing, etc.

re·con·nais·sance (ri kän′ə səns) *n.* [Fr.: see RECOGNIZANCE] the survey of a region, esp. for obtaining military information about an enemy

rec·on·noi·ter (rē′kə noit′ər, rek′ə-) *vt., vi.* to make a reconnaissance (of): Brit. sp. **rec′on·noi′tre**, -tred, -tring

re′con·sid′er (rē′kən sid′ər) *vt., vi.* to think over again, esp. with a view to changing a decision

re′con·sti·tute′ *vt.* -tut′ed, -tut′ing to constitute again; esp., to restore (a dried or condensed substance) to its original form by adding water

re′con·struct′ *vt.* 1. to construct again; remake 2. to build up, as from remains, an image of the original

re′con·struc′tion *n.* 1. a reconstructing 2. [R-] the process or period, after the Civil War, of reestablishing the Southern States in the Union

re·cord (ri kôrd'; *for n. & adj.* rek'ərd) *vt.* [< L. *recordari*, remember] 1. to write down for future use 2. to register, as on a graph 3. to register (sound or visual images) on a disc, tape, etc. for later reproduction —*n.* 1. a recording or being recorded 2. any registered evidence of an event, etc. 3. the known facts about anything or anyone 4. a grooved disc for playing on a phonograph 5. the best official performance attained —*adj.* being the best, largest, etc. —**on** (or **off** the) **record** publicly (or confidentially) declared

re·cord'er *n.* 1. an official who keeps records 2. a machine or device that records; esp., *same as* TAPE RECORDER 3. an early form of flute

re·cord'ing *n.* 1. what is recorded, as on a disc or tape 2. the record

re·count (ri kount') *vt.* [see RE- & COUNT[1]] to tell in detail; narrate

re·count (rē'kount'; *for n.* rē'kount') *vt.* to count again —*n.* a second count, as of votes: also written **recount**

re·coup (ri kōōp') *vt.* [< Fr. *re-*, again + *couper*, to cut] 1. to make up for [to *recoup* a loss] 2. to regain

re·course (rē'kôrs, ri kôrs') *n.* [see RE- & COURSE] 1. a turning for aid, safety, etc. 2. that to which one turns seeking aid, etc.

re·cov·er (ri kuv'ər) *vt.* [< L. *recuperare*] 1. to get back (something lost, etc.) 2. to regain (health, etc.) 3. to make up for [to *recover* losses] 4. to save (oneself) from a fall, etc. 5. to reclaim (land from the sea, etc.) 6. *Sports* to regain control of (a fumbled or wild ball, etc.) —*vi.* 1. to regain health, balance, control, etc. 2. *Sports* to recover a ball, etc.

re·cov·er·y *n., pl.* **-ies** a recovering; specif., *a)* a return to health *b)* a regaining of something lost, balance, etc. *c)* a retrieval of a capsule, etc. after a space flight

recovery room a hospital room where postoperative patients are kept for close observation and care

rec·re·ant (rek'rē ənt) *adj.* [< OFr. *recreire*, surrender allegiance] 1. cowardly 2. disloyal —*n.* 1. a coward 2. a traitor

rec·re·a·tion (rek'rē ā'shən) *n.* [< L. *recreare*, refresh] any play, amusement, etc. used for refreshment of body or mind —**rec're·ate'** *vt., vi.* **-at'ed**, **-at'ing** —**rec're·a'tion·al** *adj.*

re·crim·i·nate (ri krim'ə nāt') *vi.* **-nat'ed**, **-nat'ing** [< L. *re-*, back + *crimen*, offense] to answer an accuser by accusing him in return —**re·crim'i·na'tion** *n.*

re·cru·des·cence (rē'krōō des'ns) *n.* [< L. *re-*, again + *crudus*, raw] a breaking out again, esp. of something bad —**re'cru·des'cent** *adj.*

re·cruit (ri krōōt') *vt., vi.* [< L. *re-*, again + *crescere*, grow] 1. to enlist (personnel) into an army or navy 2. to enlist (new members) for an organization —*n.* 1. a recently enlisted or drafted soldier, etc. 2. a new member of any group —**re·cruit'er** *n.*

rec·tal (rek't'l) *adj.* of, for, or near the rectum

rec·tan·gle (rek'taŋ'g'l) *n.* [< L. *rectus*, straight + *angulus*, a corner] a four-sided plane figure with four right angles —**rec·tan'gu·lar** (-gyə lər) *adj.*

rec·ti·fy (rek'tə fī') *vt.* **-fied'**, **-fy'ing** [< L. *rectus*, straight + *facere*, make] 1. to put right; correct 2. *Elec.* to convert (alternating current) into direct current —**rec'ti·fi·ca'tion** *n.*

rec·ti·lin·e·ar (rek'tə lin'ē ər) *adj.* bounded or formed by straight lines

rec·ti·tude (rek'tə tōōd') *n.* moral uprightness; strict honesty

rec·tor (rek'tər) *n.* [< L. *regere*, to rule] 1. in some churches, a clergyman in charge of a parish 2. the head of certain schools, colleges, etc.

rec·to·ry (rek'tər ē) *n., pl.* **-ries** the house of a minister or priest

rec·tum (rek'təm) *n., pl.* **-tums**, **-ta** (-tə) [< L. *rectum (intestinum)*, straight (intestine)] the lowest segment of the large intestine

re·cum·bent (ri kum'bənt) *adj.* [< L. *re-*, back + *cumbere*, lie down] lying down; reclining

re·cu·per·ate (ri kōō'pə rāt') *vt., vi.* **-at'ed**, **-at'ing** [< L. *recuperare*, recover] 1. to get well again 2. to recover (losses, etc.) —**re·cu'per·a'tion** *n.* —**re·cu'per·a'tive** *adj.*

re·cur (ri kur') *vi.* **-curred'**, **-cur'ring** [< L. *re-*, back + *currere*, run] 1. to return in thought, talk, etc. 2. to occur again or at intervals —**re·cur'rence** *n.* —**re·cur'rent** *adj.*

re·cy·cle (rē sī'k'l) *vt.* **-cled**, **-cling** 1. to pass through a cycle again 2. to use again and again, as the same water

red (red) *n.* [OE. *read*] 1. the color of blood 2. any red pigment 3. [*often* R-] a political radical; esp., a communist —*adj.* **red'der**, **red'dest** 1. of the color red 2. [R-] politically radical; esp., communist —**in the red** losing money —**see red** [Colloq.] to become angry —**red'dish** *adj.* —**red'ness** *n.*

re·dact (ri dakt') *vt.* [< L. *redigere*, get in order] to edit —**re·dac'tion** *n.* —**re·dac'tor** *n.*

red blood cell (or **corpuscle**) *same as* ERYTHROCYTE

red'-blood'ed *adj.* high-spirited and strong-willed; vigorous

red'cap' *n.* a porter in a railway station, air terminal, etc.

red carpet a very grand or impressive welcome or entertainment (with *the*) —**red'-car'pet** *adj.*

red'coat' *n.* a British soldier in a uniform with a red coat

Red Cross an international society for the relief of suffering in time of war or disaster

red deer a deer of Europe and Asia

red·den (red'n) *vt.* to make red —*vi.* to become red; esp., to blush

re·deem (ri dēm') *vt.* [< L. *re(d)-*, back + *emere*, get] 1. to get or buy back; recover 2. to pay off (a mortgage, etc.) 3. to turn in (coupons) for premiums 4. to ransom 5. to deliver from sin 6. to fulfill (a promise) 7. *a)* to make amends or atone for b) to restore (oneself) to favor —re·deem'·a·ble adj. —re·deem'er n. —re·demp'·tion (ri demp'shən) n.

re·de·ploy (rē'di ploi') vt., vi. to move (troops, etc.) from one area to another —re'de·ploy'ment n.

re·de·vel·op (-vel'əp) vt. 1. to develop again 2. to rebuild or restore

red'-hand'ed adv., adj. in the very commission of crime or wrongdoing

red'head' n. a person with red hair

red herring [< herring drawn across the trace in hunting to divert the hounds] something used to divert attention from the basic issue

red'-hot' adj. 1. hot enough to glow 2. very excited, angry, etc. 3. very new

re·dis'trict vt. to divide anew into districts

red'-let'ter adj. designating a memorable or joyous day or event

red·lin·ing (red'lī'niŋ) n. [from out-lining such areas in red on a map] the refusal by some banks and companies to issue loans or insurance on property in certain neighborhoods

re·do' vt. -did', -done', -do'ing 1. to do again 2. to redecorate

red·o·lent (red'ə lənt) adj. [< L. re(d)-, intens. + olere, to smell] 1. sweet-smelling 2. smelling (of) 3. suggestive (of) —red'o·lence n.

re·dou·ble (rē dub''l) vt., vi. -bled, -bling 1. to double again 2. to make or become twice as much

re·doubt (ri dout') n. [see REDUCE] 1. a breastwork 2. any stronghold

re·doubt'a·ble (-ə b'l) adj. [< L. re-, intens. + dubitare, to doubt] formidable —re·doubt'a·bly adv.

re·dound (ri dound') vi. [< L. re(d)-, intens. + undare, to surge] 1. to have a result (to the credit or discredit of) 2. to come back; react (upon)

red·dress (ri dres'; for n. usually red'-dres) vt. [see RE- & DRESS] to compensate for (a wrong, etc.); remedy —n. 1. compensation 2. a redressing

Red Sea sea between NE Africa & W Arabia

red snapper a reddish, deep-water food fish

red tape [< tape for tying official papers] rigid adherence to routine and regulations, causing delay

red tide sea water discolored by red protozoans poisonous to marine life

re·duce (ri dōōs') vt. -duced', -duc'·ing [< L. re-, back + ducere, to lead] 1. to lessen, as in size, price, etc. 2. to change to a different form 3. to lower, as in rank or condition 4. to subdue or conquer —vi. to lose weight, as by dieting —re·duc'er n.

re·duc·tion (ri duk'shən) n. 1. a reducing or being reduced 2. anything made by reducing 3. the amount by which something is reduced

re·dun·dant (ri dun'dənt) adj. [see REDOUND] 1. excess; superfluous 2. wordy 3. unnecessary to the meaning: said of words —re·dun'dan·cy n.

red'wood' n. 1. a giant evergreen of the Pacific coast 2. its reddish wood

re·ech·o, re-ech·o (rē ek'ō) vt., vi. -oed, -o·ing to echo back or again —n., pl. -oes the echo of an echo

reed (rēd) n. [OE. hreod] a tall, slender grass 2. a musical instrument made from a hollow stem 3. Music a thin strip of wood, plastic, etc. placed against the mouthpiece, as of a clari-net, and vibrated by the breath to pro-duce a tone —reed'y adj. -i·er, -i·est

reef¹ (rēf) n. [prob. < ON. rif, a rib] a ridge of rock, coral, or sand at or near the surface of the water

reef² (rēf) n. [ME. rif] a part of a sail which can be folded and tied down to reduce the area exposed to the wind —vt., vi. to reduce the size of (a sail) by taking in part of it

reef'er n. 1. one who reefs 2. a short, thick, double-breasted coat 3. [Slang] a marijuana cigarette

reek (rēk) n. [OE. rec] a strong, un-pleasant smell —vi. to have a strong, offensive smell —reek'y adj.

reel¹ (rēl) n. [OE. hreol] 1. a spool on which wire, film, fishing line, etc. is wound 2. the quantity of wire, film, etc. usually wound on one reel —vt. to wind on a reel —vi. 1. to sway, stagger, etc., as from drunkenness or dizziness 2. to spin; whirl —reel in 1. to wind on a reel 2. to pull in (a fish) by winding a reel —reel off to tell, write, etc. fluently —reel out to unwind from a reel

reel² (rēl) n. [prob. < prec.] a lively dance

re·en·try, re-en·try (rē en'trē) n., pl. -tries a coming back, as of a space-craft, into earth's atmosphere

ref (ref) n., vt., vi. same as REFEREE

re·face (rē fās') vt. -faced', -fac'ing to put a new front or covering on

re·fec·tion (ri fek'shən) n. [< L. re-, again + facere, make] a light meal

re·fec·to·ry (-tər ē) n., pl. -ries a dining hall, as in a monastery

re·fer (ri fur') vt. -ferred', -fer'ring [< L. re-, back + ferre, to bear] 1. to submit (a quarrel, etc.) for settlement 2. to direct (to someone or something) for aid, information, etc. —vi. 1. to relate or apply (to) 2. to direct atten-tion (to) 3. to turn (to) for information, aid, etc. —ref·er·a·ble (ref'ər ə b'l, ri fur'-) adj. —re·fer'rer n.

ref·er·ee (ref'ə rē') n. 1. one to whom something is referred for decision 2. an official who enforces the rules in certain sports contests —vt., vi. -eed', -ee'ing to act as referee (in)

ref·er·ence (ref'ər əns) n. 1. a referring or being referred 2. relation [in reference to his letter] 3. a) the directing of attention to a person or thing b) a mention 4. a) an indication, as in a book, of some other source of information b) such a source 5. a) one who can offer information or recommendation b) a statement of character, ability, etc. by such a person

ref·er·en·dum (ref'ə ren'dəm) *n.*, *pl.* **-dums** or **-da** (-də) [L., see REFER] 1. the submission of a law to the direct vote of the people 2. the right of the people to vote directly on such laws

ref'er·ent *n.* the thing referred to, esp. by a word or expression

re·fer·ral (ri fur'əl) *n.* 1. a referring or being referred 2. a person who is referred to another person

re·fill (rē fil'; *for n.* rē'fil) *vt., vi.* to fill again —*n.* 1. a unit to refill a special container 2. a refilling of a medical prescription —**re·fill'a·ble** *adj.*

re·fine (ri fīn') *vt., vi.* **-fined', -fin'ing** [RE- + *fine*, make fine] 1. to free or become free from impurities, etc. 2. to make or become more polished or elegant —**re·fin'er** *n.*

re·fined' *adj.* 1. made free from impurities; purified 2. cultivated; elegant 3. subtle, precise, etc.

re·fine'ment *n.* 1. a) a refining or being refined b) the result of this 2. delicacy or elegance of manners, etc. 3. an improvement 4. a subtlety

re·fin·er·y *n.*, *pl.* **-ies** a plant for purifying materials, as oil, sugar, etc.

re·fin·ish (rē fin'ish) *vt.* to put a new surface on (wood, metal, etc.)

re·fit (rē fit') *vt., vi.* **-fit'ted, -fit'ting** to make or become fit for use again by repairing, reequipping, etc.

re·flect (ri flekt') *vt.* [< L. *re-*, back + *flectere*, to bend] 1. to throw back (light, heat, or sound) 2. to give back an image of 3. to bring as a result [to *reflect* honor] —*vi.* 1. to throw back light, heat, etc. 2. to give back an image 3. to think seriously (*on* or *upon*) 4. to cast blame or discredit (*on* or *upon*) —**re·flec'tive** *adj.*

re·flec'tion *n.* 1. a reflecting or being reflected 2. anything reflected 3. contemplation 4. an idea or remark 5. blame; discredit

re·flec'tor *n.* a surface, object, etc. that reflects light, sound, heat, etc.

re·flex (rē'fleks) *adj.* [see REFLECT] designating or of an involuntary action, as a sneeze, due to the direct transmission of a stimulus to a muscle or gland —*n.* a reflex action

re·flex·ive (ri flek'siv) *adj.* 1. designating a verb whose subject and object refer to the same person or thing (Ex.: I *wash* myself) 2. designating a pronoun used as the object of such a verb —**re·flex'ive·ly** *adv.*

re·for·est (rē fôr'ist) *vt., vi.* to plant new trees on (land once forested) —**re'for·est·a'tion** *n.*

re·form (ri fôrm') *vt.* [see RE- & FORM] 1. to make better as by stopping abuses; improve 2. to cause (a person) to behave better —*vi.* to become better in behavior —*n.* a reforming

re-form (rē'fôrm') *vt., vi.* to form again

ref·or·ma·tion (ref'ər mā'shən) *n.* 1. a reforming or being reformed 2.

[R-] the 16th-c. religious movement that resulted in establishing the Protestant churches

re·form·a·to·ry (ri fôr'mə tôr'ē) *n.*, *pl.* **-ries** an institution for reforming young law offenders

re·form'er *n.* one who seeks to bring about political or social reform

re·fract (ri frakt') *vt.* [< L. *re-*, back + *frangere*, to break] to cause (a ray of light, etc.) to undergo refraction

re·frac'tion *n.* the bending of a ray or wave of light, heat, or sound as it passes from one medium into another

re·frac·to·ry (ri frak'tər ē) *adj.* [see REFRACT] hard to manage; obstinate

re·frain¹ (ri frān') *vi.* [< L. *re-*, back + *frenare*, to curb] to hold back; keep oneself (*from* doing something)

re·frain² (ri frān') *n.* [see REFRAIN¹] a phrase or verse repeated at intervals in a song or poem

re·fresh (ri fresh') *vt.* 1. to make fresh by cooling, wetting, etc. 2. to make (a person) feel cooler, stronger, etc., as by food, sleep, etc. 3. to replenish 4. to stimulate —*vi.* to revive

re·fresh'ing *adj.* 1. that refreshes 2. pleasingly new or different

re·fresh'ment *n.* 1. a refreshing or being refreshed 2. that which refreshes 3. [*pl.*] food or drink or both

re·frig·er·ate (ri frij'ə rāt') *vt.* **-at'ed, -at'ing** [< L. *re-*, intens. + *frigus*, cold] to make or keep cool or cold, as for preserving —**re·frig'er·ant** *adj., n.* —**re·frig'er·a'tion** *n.*

re·frig'er·a'tor *n.* a box or room in which food, etc. is kept cool

ref·uge (ref'yōōj) *n.* [< L. *re-*, back + *fugere*, flee] (a) shelter or protection from danger, etc.

ref·u·gee (ref'yoo jē', ref'yoo jē') *n.* one who flees from his home or country to seek refuge elsewhere

re·ful·gent (ri ful'jənt) *adj.* [< L. *re-*, back + *fulgere*, shine] shining; radiant; glowing —**re·ful'gence** *n.*

re·fund (ri fund'; *for n.* rē'fund') *vt., vi.* [< L. *re-*, back + *fundere*, pour] to give back (money, etc.); repay —*n.* a refunding or the amount refunded

re·fur·bish (ri fur'bish) *vt.* [RE- + FURBISH] to freshen or polish up again; renovate —**re·fur'bish·ment** *n.*

re·fuse¹ (ri fyōōz') *vt., vi.* **-fused', -fus'ing** [< L. *re-*, back + *fundere*, pour] 1. to decline to accept; reject 2. to decline (*to* do, grant, etc.) —**re·fus'al** *n.*

ref·use² (ref'yōōs, -yōōz) *n.* [see prec.] waste; rubbish

re·fuse'nik (-nik) *n.* [transl. of Russ. *otkaznik*] a Soviet citizen, esp. a Jew, refused a permit to emigrate

re·fute (ri fyōōt') *vt.* **-fut'ed, -fut'ing** [L. *refutare*, repel] to prove to be false or wrong —**re·fut'a·ble** *adj.* —**ref·u·ta·tion** (ref'yə tā'shən) *n.*

re·gain (ri gān') *vt.* 1. to get back; recover 2. to get back to

re·gal (rē'gəl) *adj.* [< L. *rex*, king] of, like, or fit for a king; royal

re·gale (ri gāl') *vt.* **-galed', -gal'ing** [< Fr. *ré-* (see RE-) + OFr. *gale*, joy] to entertain as with a feast

re·ga·li·a (ri gāl'yə, -gā'lē ə) *n.pl.* [see REGAL] 1. royal insignia 2. the insignia of a society, etc. 3. finery

re·gard (ri gärd') *n.* [see RE- & GUARD] 1. a steady look; gaze 2. consideration; concern 3. respect and affection 4. reference; relation *[in regard to peace plans]* 5. *[pl.]* good wishes —*vt.* 1. to look at attentively 2. to consider 3. to hold in affection and respect 4. to concern or involve —**as regards** concerning —**re·gard'ful** *adj.*

re·gard·ing *prep.* concerning; about

re·gard·less *adv.* [Colloq.] without regard for objections, etc.; anyway —**regardless of** in spite of

re·gat·ta (ri gät'ə) *n.* [< It.] 1. a boat race 2. a series of boat races

re·gen·er·ate (ri jen'ər it; *for v.* -ə rāt') *adj.* [see RE- & GENERATE] renewed or restored —*vt.* -at'ed, -at'-ing 1. to cause to be spiritually reborn 2. to cause to be completely reformed 3. to bring into existence again; reproduce —**re·gen'er·a'tion** *n.* —**re·gen'er·a'tive** *adj.*

re·gent (rē'jənt) *n.* [< L. *regere,* to rule] 1. a person appointed to rule when a monarch is absent, too young, etc. 2. a member of a governing board, as of a university —**re'gen·cy** *n.*

reg·gae (reg'ā) *n.* [< ?] a form of popular Jamaican music influenced by rock-and-roll and calypso

reg·i·cide (rej'ə sīd') *n.* 1. a killer of a king 2. the killing of a king

re·gime, ré·gime (rə zhēm', rā-) *n.* [see ff.] 1. a political or ruling system 2. *same as* REGIMEN

reg·i·men (rej'ə mən) *n.* [< L. *regere,* to rule] a system of diet, exercise, etc. for improving the health

reg·i·ment (rej'ə mənt; *for v.* -ment') *n.* [< L. *regere,* to rule] a military unit, smaller than a division —*vt.* 1. to organize systematically 2. to subject to strict discipline and control —**reg'i·men'tal** *adj.* —**reg'i·men·ta'tion** *n.*

Re·gi·na (ri jī'nə) capital of Saskatchewan: pop. 131,000

re·gion (rē'jən) *n.* [see REGAL] 1. a large, indefinite part of the earth's surface 2. any division or part, as of an organism —**re'gion·al** *adj.*

re·gion·al·ism *n.* 1. regional quality or character in life or literature 2. a word, etc. peculiar to some region

reg·is·ter (rej'is tər) *n.* [< L. *regerere,* to record] 1. a) a list of names, items, etc. b) a book in which this is kept 2. a device for recording *[a cash register]* 3. an opening into a room by which the amount of air passing through can be controlled 4. *Music* a part of the range of a voice or instrument —*vt.* 1. to enter in a list 2. to indicate as on a scale 3. to show, as by facial expression *[to register joy]* 4. to safeguard (mail) by having its committal to the postal system recorded, for a fee —*vi.* 1. to enter one's name in a list, as of voters 2. to make an impression —**reg'is·trant** (-trənt) *n.*

registered nurse a trained nurse who has passed a State examination

reg·is·trar (rej'i strär') *n.* one who keeps records, as in a college

reg·is·tra·tion (rej'i strā'shən) *n.* 1. a registering or being registered 2. an entry in a register 3. the number of persons registered

reg·is·try (-is trē) *n., pl.* -tries 1. a registering 2. an office where registers are kept 3. *same as* REGISTER (*n.* 1)

reg·nant (reg'nənt) *adj.* 1. ruling 2. predominant 3. prevalent

re·gress (ri gres') *vi.* [< L. *re-,* back + *gradi,* go] to go back —**re·gres'sion** *n.* —**re·gres'sive** *adj.*

re·gret (ri gret') *vt.* -gret'ted, -gret'-ting [< OFr. *regreter,* mourn] to feel sorry about (an event, one's acts, etc.) —*n.* sorrow, esp. over one's acts or omissions —**(one's) regrets** a polite declining of an invitation —**re·gret'-ful** *adj.* —**re·gret'ta·ble** *adj.*

re·group' *vt., vi.* to group again; specif., *Mil.* to reorganize (one's forces), as after a battle

reg·u·lar (reg'yə lər) *adj.* [< L. *regula,* a rule] 1. conforming to a rule, type, etc.; orderly; symmetrical 2. conforming to a fixed principle or procedure 3. customary or established 4. consistent *[a regular customer]* 5. functioning in a normal way *[a regular pulse]* 6. properly qualified *[a regular doctor]* 7. designating or of the standing army of a country 8. [Colloq.] a) thorough; complete *[a regular nuisance]* b) pleasant, friendly, etc. —*n.* 1. a regular soldier or player 2. [Colloq.] one who is regular in attendance 3. *Politics* one loyal to his party —**reg'u·lar'i·ty** (-lar'ə tē) *n.* —**reg'u·lar·ize'** *vt.* -ized', -iz'ing —**reg'u·lar·ly** *adv.*

reg·u·late (reg'yə lāt') *vt.* -lat'ed, -lat'ing [< L. *regula,* a rule] 1. to control or direct according to a rule, principle, etc. 2. to adjust to a standard, rate, etc. 3. to adjust so as to make work accurately —**reg'u·la'tive, reg'u·la·to'ry** (-lə tôr'ē) *adj.* —**reg'u·la'tor** *n.*

reg·u·la'tion *n.* 1. a regulating or being regulated 2. a rule or law regulating conduct —*adj.* usual; regular

re·gur·gi·tate (ri gur'jə tāt') *vi., vt.* -tat'ed, -tat'ing [< ML. *re-,* back + L. *gurgitare,* to flood] to bring (partly digested food) back up to the mouth —**re·gur'gi·ta'tion** *n.*

re·hab (rē'hab) *n., vt.* -habbed, -habbing *clipped form of* REHABILITATION & REHABILITATE

re·ha·bil·i·tate (rē'hə bil'ə tāt') *vt.* -tat'ed, -tat'ing [< L. *re-,* back + *habere,* have] 1. to restore to rank, reputation, etc. which one has lost 2. to put back in good condition 3. to bring or restore to a state of health or constructive activity —**re'ha·bil'i·ta'tion** *n.* —**re'ha·bil'i·ta'tive** *adj.*

re·hash (rē hash'; *for n.* rē'hash) *vt.* [RE- + HASH] to work up again or go over again —*n.* a rehashing

re·hear' *vt.* -heard', -hear'ing *Law* to hear (a case) a second time

re·hearse (ri hurs') *vt., vi.* -hearsed', -hears'ing [< OFr. *re-*, again + *hercer*, to harrow] 1. to recite in detail 2. to practice (a play, etc.), for public performance —re·hears'al *n.*

reign (rān) *n.* [< L. *regere*, to rule] 1. royal power 2. dominance or sway 3. the period of rule, dominance, etc. —*vi.* 1. to rule as a sovereign 2. to prevail [*peace reigns*]

re·im·burse (rē'im burs') *vt.* -bursed', -burs'ing [RE- + archaic *imburse*, to pay] to pay back —re·im·burse'ment *n.*

rein (rān) *n.* [see RETAIN] 1. [*usually pl.*] a narrow strap of leather attached in pairs to a horse's bit and manipulated to control the animal 2. [*pl.*] a means of controlling, etc. —*vt.* to guide or control as with reins —give rein to to free from restraint

re·in·car·na·tion (rē'in kär nā' shən) *n.* [see RE- & INCARNATE] rebirth of the soul in another body —re'in·car'nate *vt.* -nat·ed, -nat·ing

rein·deer (rān'dir') *n., pl.* -deer' [< ON. *hreinn*, reindeer + *dyr*, deer] a large deer found in northern regions, and domesticated there as a beast of burden

re·in·force (rē' in fôrs') *vt.* -forced', -forc'ing [RE- + var. of ENFORCE] 1. to strengthen (a military force) with more troops, ships, etc. 2. to strengthen, as by propping, adding new material, etc. —re'in·force'ment *n.*

REINDEER

re·in·state (rē'in stāt') *vt.* -stat'ed, -stat'ing to restore to a former state, position, etc. —re'in·state'ment *n.*

re·it·er·ate (rē it'ə rāt') *vt.* -at·ed, -at'ing [see RE- & ITERATE] to say or do again or repeatedly —re·it'er·a'tion *n.* —re·it'er·a'tive *adj.*

re·ject (ri jekt'; *for n.* rē'jekt) *vt.* [< L. *re-*, back + *jacere*, to throw] 1. to refuse to take, agree to, use, believe, etc. 2. to discard —*n.* a rejected person or thing —re·jec'tion *n.*

re·joice (ri jois') *vi., vt.* -joiced', -joic'ing [< OFr. *rejoir*] to be or make glad or happy —re·joic'ing *n.*

re·join (rē join') *vt., vi.* 1. to join again; reunite 2. to answer

re·join·der (ri join'dər) *n.* [see RE- & JOIN] an answer, esp. to a reply

re·ju·ve·nate (ri jōō'və nāt') *vt.* -nat·ed, -nat'ing [< RE- + L. *juvenis*, young] to make feel or seem young again —re·ju've·na'tion *n.*

re·lapse (ri laps'; *for n. also* rē'laps) *vi.* -lapsed', -laps'ing [see RE- & LAPSE] to slip back into a former state,

esp. into illness after apparent recovery —*n.* a relapsing

re·late (ri lāt') *vt.* -lat'ed, -lat'ing [< L. *relatus*, brought back] 1. to tell the story of; narrate 2. to connect, as in thought or meaning —*vi.* to have reference or some relation (*to*)

re·lat·ed *adj.* connected, as by origin, kinship, marriage, etc.

re·la'tion *n.* 1. a narrating 2. a narrative; recital 3. connection, as in thought, meaning, etc. 4. connection by blood or marriage 5. a relative 6. [*pl.*] the connections between or among persons, nations, etc. —in (or with) relation to concerning; regarding —re·la'tion·ship' *n.*

rel·a·tive (rel'ə tiv) *adj.* 1. related each to the other 2. having to do with; relevant 3. comparative [*relative* comfort] 4. meaningful only in relationship [*"cold"* is a *relative* term] 5. *Gram.* that refers to an antecedent [a *relative* pronoun] —*n.* a person related by blood or marriage —rel'a·tive·ly *adv.* —rel'a·tive·ness *n.*

relative humidity the ratio of the amount of moisture in the air to the top amount possible at the temperature

rel·a·tiv·i·ty (rel'ə tiv'ə tē) *n.* 1. a being relative 2. *Physics* the theory of the relative, rather than absolute, character of motion, velocity, mass, etc., and the interdependence of matter, time, and space

re·lax (ri laks') *vt., vi.* [< L. *re-*, back + *laxare*, loosen] 1. to make or become less firm, tense, severe, etc. 2. to rest, as from work —re·lax'er *n.*

re·lax·ant *adj.* causing relaxation, esp. of muscles —*n.* a relaxant drug

re·lax·a·tion (rē'lak sā'shən) *n.* 1. a relaxing or being relaxed 2. *a)* rest from work or effort *b)* recreation

re·lay (rē'lā; *for v. also* ri lā') *n.* [< MFr. *re-*, back + *laier*, to leave] 1. a fresh supply of horses, etc., as for a stage of a journey 2. a relief crew of workers; shift 3. a race (in full relay race) between teams, each member of which goes a part of the distance —*vt.* -layed, -lay·ing to convey as by relays [to *relay* news]

re·lease (ri lēs') *vt.* -leased', -leas'ing [see RELAX] 1. to set free, as from confinement, work, pain, etc. 2. to let go [to *release* an arrow] 3. to permit to be issued, published, etc. —*n.* 1. a releasing, as from prison, work, etc. 2. a device to release a catch, etc., as on a machine 3. a book, news item, etc. released to the public 4. *Law* a written surrender of a claim, etc.

rel·e·gate (rel'ə gāt') *vt.* -gat·ed, -gat'ing [< L. *re-*, away + *legare*, send] 1. to exile or banish (*to*) 2. to consign or assign, esp. to an inferior position 3. to refer or hand over for decision —rel'e·ga'tion *n.*

re·lent (ri lent') *vi.* [< L. *re-*, again + *lentus*, pliant] to become less stern, severe, or stubborn; soften

re·lent·less *adj.* 1. harsh; pitiless 2. not letting up; persistent —re·lent'-less·ly *adv.* —re·lent'less·ness *n.*

rel·e·vant (rel′ə vənt) *adj.* [see RELIEVE] relating to the matter under consideration; pertinent —rel′e·vance, rel′e·van·cy *n.*

re·li·a·ble (ri lī′ə b'l) *adj.* that can be relied on —re·li′a·bil′i·ty *n.* —re·li′a·bly *adv.*

re·li′ance (-əns) *n.* 1. trust, dependence, or confidence 2. a thing relied on —re·li′ant *adj.*

rel·ic (rel′ik) *n.* [see RELINQUISH] 1. an object, custom, etc. surviving from the past 2. a souvenir 3. [*pl.*] ruins 4. the venerated remains, etc. of a saint

rel·ict (rel′ikt) *n.* [L. *relictus*, left behind] 1. [Archaic] a widow 2. a species surviving from an earlier period

re·lief (ri lēf′) *n.* 1. a relieving, as of pain, anxiety, a burden, etc. 2. anything that eases tension, or offers a pleasing change 3. aid, esp. by a public agency to the needy 4. release from work or duty, or those bringing it 5. the projection of sculptured forms from a flat surface 6. the differences in height, collectively, of land forms shown as by lines on a map (**relief map**) —*adj.* Baseball designating a pitcher who replaces another during a game —**in relief** carved so as to project from a surface

re·lieve (ri lēv′) *vt.* -lieved′, -liev′ing [< L. *re-*, again + *levare*, to raise] 1. to ease (pain, anxiety, etc.) 2. to free from pain, distress, a burden, etc. 3. to give or bring aid to 4. to set free from duty or work by replacing 5. to make less tedious, etc. by providing a pleasing change

re·li·gion (ri lij′ən) *n.* [< L. *religio*] 1. belief in and worship of God or gods 2. a specific system of belief or worship, etc. built around God, a code of ethics, a philosophy of life, etc.

re·li′gious (-əs) *adj.* 1. devout; pious 2. of or concerned with religion 3. conscientiously exact; scrupulous —*n.* a nun or monk —re·li′gious·ly *adv.*

re·lin·quish (ri liŋ′kwish) *vt.* [< L. *re-*, from + *linquere*, leave] 1. to give up, as a plan, or let go, as one's grasp 2. to renounce or surrender (property, a right, etc.) —re·lin′quish·ment *n.*

rel·ish (rel′ish) *n.* [< OFr. *relais*, something remaining] 1. an appetizing flavor 2. enjoyment; zest [to listen with *relish*] 3. pickles, etc. served with a meal or as an appetizer —*vt.* to enjoy; like

re·live (rē liv′) *vt.* -lived′, -liv′ing to experience (a past event) again, as in imagination

re·lo·cate (rē lō′kāt) *vt.*, *vi.* -cat·ed, -cat·ing to move to a new location —re′lo·ca′tion *n.*

re·luc·tant (ri luk′tənt) *adj.* [< L. *re-*, against + *luctari*, to struggle] 1. unwilling; disinclined 2. marked by unwillingness [a *reluctant* answer] —re·luc′tance *n.* —re·luc′tant·ly *adv.*

re·ly (ri lī′) *vi.* -lied′, -ly′ing [< L.

re-, back + *ligare*, bind] to trust or depend. Used with *on* or *upon*

REM (rem) *n.*, *pl.* **REMs** [r(*apid*) e(*ye*) m(*ovement*)] the rapid, jerky movements of the eyeballs during stages of sleep associated with dreaming

rem (rem) *n.* [r(*oentgen*) e(*quivalent*), m(*an*)] a dosage of ionizing radiation with a biological effect about equal to that of one roentgen of X-ray

re·main (ri mān′) *vi.* [< L. *re-*, back + *manere*, to stay] 1. to be left over when the rest has been taken away, etc. 2. to stay 3. to continue [to *remain* a cynic] 4. to be left to be dealt with, done, etc.

re·main′der *n.* 1. those remaining 2. what is left when a part is taken away 3. what is left when a smaller number is subtracted from a larger

re·mains′ *n.pl.* 1. what is left after use, destruction, etc. 2. a dead body

re·mand (ri mand′) *vt.* [< L. *re-*, back + *mandare*, to order] to send back, as a prisoner into custody

re·mark (ri märk′) *vt.*, *vi.* [< Fr. *re-*, again + *marquer*, to mark] to notice, observe, or comment; make (as) an observation —*n.* a brief comment

re·mark′a·ble *adj.* worthy of notice; extraordinary —re·mark′a·bly *adv.*

Rem·brandt (rem′brant) 1606–69; Du. painter & etcher

re·me·di·al (ri mē′dē əl) *adj.* 1. providing a remedy 2. corrective, as some study courses

rem·e·dy (rem′ə dē) *n.*, *pl.* -dies [< L. *re-*, again + *mederi*, heal] 1. any medicine or treatment for a disease 2. something to correct a wrong —*vt.* -died, -dy·ing to cure, correct, etc.

re·mem·ber (ri mem′bər) *vt.* [< L. *re-*, again + *memorare*, bring to mind] 1. to think of again 2. to bring back to mind by an effort; recall 3. to be careful not to forget 4. to mention (a person) to another as sending regards —*vi.* to bear in, or call back to, mind

re·mem′brance (-brəns) *n.* 1. a remembering or being remembered 2. the power to remember 3. a souvenir

re·mind (ri mīnd′) *vt.*, *vi.* to put (a person) in mind (*of* something); cause to remember —re·mind′er *n.*

rem·i·nisce (rem′ə nis′) *vi.* -nisced′, -nis′cing [< ff.] to think, talk, or write about past events

rem′i·nis′cence (-'ns) *n.* [Fr. < L. *re-*, again + *memini*, remember] 1. a remembering 2. a memory 3. [*pl.*] an account of remembered experiences —rem′i·nis′cent *adj.*

re·miss (ri mis′) *adj.* [see REMIT] careless; negligent —re·miss′ness *n.*

re·mis·sion (ri mish′ən) *n.* [see REMIT] 1. forgiveness; pardon 2. release from a debt, tax, etc. 3. an abating of (pain, a disease, etc.)

re·mit (ri mit′) *vt.* -mit′ted, -mit′ting [< L. *re-*, back + *mittere*, send] 1. to forgive or pardon 2. to refrain from exacting (a payment), inflicting (punishment), etc. 3. to slacken; abate 4. to send (money) in payment —re·mit′tance n. —re·mit′tent adj.

rem·nant (rem′nənt) n. [see REMAIN] what is left over, as a piece of cloth at the end of a bolt

re·mod·el (rē mäd′'l) vt. -eled or -elled, -el·ing or -el·ling to make over; rebuild

re·mon·strate (ri män′strāt) vt. -strat·ed, -strat·ing [< L. re-, again + monstrare, to show] to say in protest, objection, etc. —vi. to protest; object —re·mon′strance (-strəns) n.

re·morse (ri môrs′) n. [< L. re-, again + mordere, to bite] a torturing sense of guilt for one's actions —re·morse′ful adj. —re·morse′less adj.

re·mote (ri mōt′) adj. -mot′er, -mot′est [< L. remotus, removed] 1. distant in space or time 2. distant in relation, connection, etc. 3. distantly related [a remote cousin] 4. slight [a remote chance] —re·mote′ly adv.

remote control control of aircraft, missiles, etc. from a distance, as by radio waves

re·move (ri mōōv′) vt. -moved′, -mov′ing [see RE- & MOVE] 1. to move (something) from where it is; take away or off 2. to dismiss, as from office 3. to get rid of 4. to kill —vi. to move away, as to another residence —n. a step or degree away —re·mov′a·ble adj. —re·mov′al n.

re·mu·ner·ate (ri myōō′nə rāt′) vt. -at′ed, -at′ing [< L. re-, again + munus, gift] to pay (a person) for (work, a loss, etc.) —re·mu′ner·a′tion n. —re·mu′ner·a′tive adj.

ren·ais·sance (ren′ə säns′) n. [Fr.] 1. a rebirth; revival 2. [R-] the great revival of art and learning in Europe in the 14th, 15th, and 16th centuries

re·nal (rē′n'l) adj. [< L. renes, kidneys] of or near the kidneys

re·nas·cence (ri nas′'ns, -nās′-) n. a rebirth; revival —re·nas′cent adj.

rend (rend) vt. rent, rend′ing [OE. rendan] to tear apart or split with violence —vi. to tear; split apart

ren·der (ren′dər) vt. [ult. < L. re(d)-, back + dare, give] 1. to submit, as for approval, payment, etc. 2. to give in return or pay as due [render thanks] 3. to cause to be 4. to give (aid) or do (a service) 5. to depict, as by drawing 6. to play (music), act (a role), etc. 7. to translate 8. to melt down (fat)

ren·dez·vous (rän′dā vōō′) n., pl. -vous′ (-vōōz′) [< Fr. rendez-vous, betake yourself] 1. a meeting place 2. an agreement to meet 3. such a meeting —vi., vt. -voused′ (-vōōd′), -vous′ing to assemble as prearranged

ren·di·tion (ren dish′ən) n. a rendering; performance, translation, etc.

ren·e·gade (ren′ə gād′) n. [< L. re-, again + negare, deny] one who abandons a party, movement, etc. to join the opposition; turncoat

re·nege (ri nig′) vi. -neged′, -neg′-ing [see prec.] 1. to go back on a promise 2. to play a card not of the suit called for —re·neg′er n.

re·new (ri nōō′) vt. 1. to make new or fresh again 2. to reestablish; revive 3. to resume 4. to put in a fresh supply of 5. to give or get an extension of [renew a lease] —re·new′al n.

ren·net (ren′it) n. [ME. rennen, coagulate] an extract from the stomach of calves, etc. used to curdle milk

Re·no (rē′nō) city in W Nev.: pop. 101,000

Re·noir (ren′wär) Pierre Auguste 1841-1919; Fr. painter

re·nounce (ri nouns′) vt. -nounced′, -nounc′ing [< L. re-, back + nuntiare, tell] 1. to give up formally (a claim, etc.) 2. to give up (a habit, etc.) 3. to disown —re·nounce′ment n.

ren·o·vate (ren′ə vāt′) vt. -vat′ed, -vat′ing [< L. re-, again + novus, new] to make as good as new; restore —ren′o·va′tion n. —ren′o·va′tor n.

re·nown (ri noun′) n. [< OFr. re-, again + nom(m)er, to name] great fame or reputation —re·nowned′ adj.

rent¹ (rent) n. [< L. reddita, paid] a stated payment at fixed intervals for the use of a house, land, etc. —vt. to get or give use of in return for rent —vi. to be let for rent —for rent available to be rented —rent′er n.

rent² (rent) pt. & pp. of REND —n. a hole or gap made by tearing

rent·al (ren′t'l) n. 1. an amount paid or received as rent 2. a house, car, etc. for rent 3. a renting —adj. of or for rent

re·nun·ci·a·tion (ri nun′sē ā′shən) n. a renouncing, as of a right

re·or·gan·ize (rē ôr′gə nīz′) vt., vi. -ized′, -iz′ing to organize anew, as a business —re·or′gan·i·za′tion n.

rep (rep) n. [Fr. reps < Eng. ribs] a ribbed or corded fabric

Rep. 1. Representative 2. Republican

re·paid (rē pād′) pt. & pp. of REPAY

re·pair¹ (ri per′) vt. [< L. re-, again + parare, prepare] 1. to put back in good condition; fix; renew 2. to make amends for —n. 1. a repairing 2. [usually pl.] work done in repairing 3. the state of being repaired [kept in repair] —re·pair′a·ble adj.

re·pair² (ri per′) vi. [< L. re-, back + patria, native land] to go (to a place)

re·pair′man n., pl. -men a man whose work is repairing things

rep·a·ra·tion (rep′ə rā′shən) n. 1. a making of amends 2. [usually pl.] compensation, as for war damage

rep·ar·tee (rep′ər tē′, -tā′) n. [< Fr. re-, back + partir, to part] quick, witty retort(s); banter

re·past (ri past′) n. [< OFr. re-, RE- + past, food] food and drink; a meal

re·pa·tri·ate (rē pā′trē āt′) vt., vi. -at′ed, -at′ing [see REPAIR²] to return to the country of birth, citizenship, etc. —re·pa′tri·a′tion n.

re·pay (ri pā′) vt. -paid′, -pay′ing 1. to pay back 2. to make return to for (a favor, etc.) —re·pay′ment n.

re·peal (ri pēl′) vt. [see RE- & APPEAL] to revoke; cancel; annul —n. revocation; abrogation, etc.

re·peat (ri pēt′) vt. [< L. re-, again + petere, seek] 1. to say again 2. to recite (a poem, etc.) 3. to say (something) as said by someone else 4. to tell to someone else *[repeat* a secret*]* 5. to do or make again —*vi.* to say or do again —*n.* 1. a repeating 2. anything said or done again, as a rebroadcast of a television program 3. *Music a)* a passage to be repeated *b)* a symbol for this —re·peat′er *n.*

re·peat′ed *adj.* said, made, or done again, or often —re·peat′ed·ly *adv.*

re·pel′ (ri pel′) *vt.* -pelled′, -pel′ling [< L. *re-*, back + *pellere*, to drive] 1. to drive or force back 2. to reject 3. to cause dislike in; disgust 4. to be resistant to (water, dirt, etc.) —re·pel′lent *adj.*, *n.*

re·pent′ (ri pent′) *vi.*, *vt.* [< L. *re-*, again + *poenitere*, repent] 1. to feel sorry for (a sin, error, etc.) 2. to feel such regret over (an action, intention, etc.) as to change one's mind —re·pent′ance *n.* —re·pent′ant *adj.*

re·per·cus·sion (rē′pər kush′ən) *n.* [see RE- & PERCUSSION] 1. a rebound 2. reverberation 3. a far-reaching, often indirect reaction to some event —re′per·cus′sive *adj.*

rep·er·toire (rep′ər twär′) *n.* [< Fr. < L. *reperire*, discover] the stock of plays, songs, etc. that a company, singer, etc. is prepared to perform

rep′er·to·ry (-tôr′ē) *n.*, *pl.* -ries 1. *same as* REPERTOIRE 2. the system of alternating several plays throughout a season with a permanent acting group

rep·e·ti·tion (rep′ə tish′ən) *n.* [< L. *repetitio*] 1. a repeating 2. something repeated —rep′e·ti′tious *adj.* —re·pet·i·tive (ri pet′ə tiv) *adj.*

re·pine (ri pīn′) *vi.* -pined′, -pin′ing [RE- + PINE¹] to feel or express discontent; complain —re·pin′er *n.*

re·place (ri plās′) *vt.* -placed′, -plac′ing 1. to put back in a former or the proper place 2. to take the place of 3. to provide an equivalent for —re·place′a·ble *adj.* —re·place′ment *n.*

re·plen·ish (ri plen′ish) *vt.* [< L. *re-*, again + *plenus*, full] 1. to make full or complete again 2. to supply again —re·plen′ish·ment *n.*

re·plete (ri plēt′) *adj.* [< L. *re-*, again + *plere*, to fill] plentifully supplied; filled or stuffed —re·ple′tion *n.*

rep·li·ca (rep′li kə) *n.* [see ff.] a copy of a work of art, etc., esp. one done by the maker of the original

rep·li·cate (rep′li kāt′) *vt.* -cat′ed, -cat′ing [see REPLY] to repeat or duplicate

rep′li·ca′tion *n.* 1. a replicating 2. a reply; answer 3. a copy; reproduction

re·ply (ri plī′) *vi.* -plied′, -ply′ing [< L. *re-*, back + *plicare*, to fold] to answer or respond —*n.*, *pl.* -plies′ an answer or response

re·port (ri pôrt′) *vt.* [< L. *re-*, back + *portare*, carry] 1. to give an account of, as for publication 2. to carry and repeat (a message, etc.) 3. to announce formally 4. to make a charge about

(something) or against (someone) to one in authority —*vi.* 1. to make a report 2. to present oneself, as for work —*n.* 1. rumor 2. a statement or account 3. a formal presentation of facts 4. the noise of an explosion —re·port′ed·ly *adv.*

re·port′age (-ij) *n.* 1. the reporting of the news 2. reporterlike accounts

report card a periodic written report on a pupil's progress

re·port′er *n.* one who reports; specif., one who gathers information and writes reports for a newspaper, etc. —rep·or·to·ri·al (rep′ər tôr′ē əl) *adj.*

re·pose′ (ri pōz′) *vt.*, *vi.* -posed′, -pos′ing [< L. *re-*, again + LL. *pausare*, to rest] to lay or place for rest —*vi.* 1. to lie at rest 2. to rest 3. to lie dead —*n.* 1. *a)* rest *b)* sleep 2. composure 3. calm; peace —re·pose′ful *adj.*

re·pose′ (ri pōz′) *vt.* -posed′, -pos′ing [see ff.] 1. to place (trust, etc.) *in* someone 2. to place (power, etc.) *in* the control of some person or group

re·pos·i·to·ry (ri päz′ə tôr′ē) *n.*, *pl.* -ries [< L. *re-*, back + *ponere*, place] a box, room, etc. in which things may be put for safekeeping

re·pos·sess (rē′pə zes′) *vt.* to get possession of again —re′pos·ses′sion *n.*

rep·re·hend (rep′ri hend′) *vt.* [< L. *re-*, back + *prehendere*, take] to rebuke, blame, or censure

rep′re·hen′si·ble (-hen′sə b'l) *adj.* deserving to be reprehended —rep′re·hen′si·bly *adv.*

rep·re·sent (rep′ri zent′) *vt.* [see RE- & PRESENT, *v.*] 1. to present to the mind 2. to present a likeness of 3. to describe 4. to stand for; symbolize 5. to be the equivalent of 6. to act (a role) 7. to act in place of, esp. by conferred authority 8. to serve as a specimen, example, etc. of

rep′re·sen·ta′tion *n.* 1. a representing or being represented, as in a legislative assembly 2. legislative representatives, collectively 3. a likeness, image, picture, etc. 4. *[often pl.]* a statement of claims, protest, etc. —rep′re·sen·ta′tion·al *adj.*

rep′re·sen′ta·tive *adj.* 1. representing 2. of or based on representation of the people by elected delegates 3. typical —*n.* 1. an example or type 2. one authorized to act for others; delegate, agent, salesman, etc. 3. [R-] a member of the lower house of Congress or of a State legislature

re·press (ri pres′) *vt.* [see RE- & PRESS¹] 1. to hold back; restrain 2. to put down; subdue 3. *Psychiatry* to force (painful ideas, etc.) into the unconscious —re·pres′sion *n.* —re·pres′sive *adj.*

re·prieve (ri prēv′) *vt.* -prieved′, -priev′ing [< Fr. *reprendre*, take back] 1. to postpone the execution of (a condemned person) 2. to give temporary relief to —*n.* a reprieving or being reprieved

rep·ri·mand (rep′rə mand′) *n.* [< L. *reprimere*, repress] a severe or formal rebuke —*vt.* to rebuke severely or formally

re·pris·al (ri prī′z′l) *n.* [see REPREHEND] injury done for injury received

re·proach (ri prōch′) *vt.* [< L. *re-*, back + *probe*, near] to accuse of a fault; rebuke —*n.* 1. shame, disgrace, etc. or a cause of this 2. rebuke or censure —**re·proach′ful** *adj.*

rep·ro·bate (rep′rə bāt′) *adj.* [< LL. *reprobare*, reprove] depraved; unprincipled —*n.* a depraved person

re·pro·duce (rē′prə dōōs′) *vt.* -duced′, -duc′ing to produce again; specif.; *a)* to produce by propagation *b)* to make a copy of —*vi.* to produce offspring —**re′pro·duc′i·ble** *adj.*

re′pro·duc′tion (-duk′shən) *n.* 1. a copy, imitation, etc. 2. the process by which animals and plants produce new individuals —**re′pro·duc′tive** *adj.*

re·proof (ri prōōf′) *n.* a reproving; rebuke: also **re·prov′al** (-prōō′v′l)

re·prove (ri prōōv′) *vt.* -proved′, -prov′ing [see RE- & PROVE] 1. to rebuke 2. to express disapproval of

rep·tile (rep′t′l, -til) *n.* [< L. *repere*, to creep] a coldblooded, crawling vertebrate, as a snake, lizard, turtle, etc. —**rep·til·i·an** (rep til′ē ən) *adj.*

re·pub·lic (ri pub′lik) *n.* [< L. *res publica*, public thing] a state or government, specif. one headed by a president, in which the power is exercised by officials elected by the voters

re·pub′li·can (-li kən) *adj.* 1. of or like a republic 2. [R-] of or belonging to the Republican Party —*n.* 1. one who favors a republic 2. [R-] a member of the Republican Party

Republican Party one of the two major U.S. political parties

re·pu·di·ate (ri pyōō′dē āt′) *vt.* -at′ed, -at′ing [< L. *repudium*, separation] 1. to disown 2. to disavow (a treaty, etc.) —**re·pu′di·a′tion** *n.*

re·pug·nant (ri pug′nənt) *adj.* [< L. *re-*, back + *pugnare*, fight] 1. contradictory 2. opposed 3. distasteful; offensive —**re·pug′nance** *n.*

re·pulse (ri puls′) *vt.* -pulsed′, -puls′ing [see REPEL] 1. to drive back (an attack, etc.) 2. to refuse or reject with discourtesy, etc.; rebuff —*n.* a repelling or being repelled

re·pul·sion *n.* 1. a repelling or being repelled 2. strong dislike 3. *Physics* the mutual action by which bodies tend to repel each other

re·pul·sive *adj.* causing strong dislike or aversion; disgusting —**re·pul′sive·ly** *adv.* —**re·pul′sive·ness** *n.*

rep·u·ta·ble (rep′yoo tə b′l) *adj.* having a good reputation —**rep′u·ta·bil′i·ty** *n.* —**rep′u·ta·bly** *adv.*

rep·u·ta·tion (rep′yoo tā′shən) *n.* [see ff.] 1. estimation in which a person or thing is commonly held 2. favorable estimation 3. fame

re·pute (ri pyōōt′) *vt.* -put′ed, -put′ing [< L. *re-*, again + *putare*, think] to consider or regard [*reputed* to be rich] —*n.* reputation; esp., fame —**re·put′ed** *adj.* —**re·put′ed·ly** *adv.*

re·quest (ri kwest′) *n.* [see REQUIRE] 1. an asking for something 2. a thing asked for 3. the state of being asked for; demand —*vt.* 1. to ask for 2. to ask (a person) to do something

Re·qui·em (rek′wē əm, rāk′-) *n.* [< L., rest] [*also* r-] R.C.Ch. 1. a Mass for the repose of the dead 2. its musical setting

re·quire (ri kwīr′) *vt.* -quired′, -quir′ing [< L. *re-*, again + *quaerere*, ask] 1. to insist upon; demand; order 2. to need —**re·quire′ment** *n.*

req·ui·site (rek′wə zit) *adj.* [see prec.] required; necessary; indispensable —*n.* something requisite

req′ui·si′tion (-zish′ən) *n.* 1. a requiring; formal demand 2. a formal written order, as for equipment —*vt.* to demand or take, as by authority

re·quite (ri kwīt′) *vt.* -quit′ed, -quit′ing [RE- + *quite*, obs. var. of QUIT] to repay (someone) for a benefit, service, etc., or an injury, wrong, etc.) —**re·quit′al** *n.*

re·run (rē′run′) *n.* a showing of a motion picture or television program after the first showing

re·sale′ (-sāl′) *n.* a selling again, specif., to a third party

re·scind (ri sind′) *vt.* [< L. *re-*, back + *scindere*, to cut] to revoke or cancel (a law, etc.) —**re·scis′sion** (-sizh′ən) *n.*

res·cue (res′kyōō) *vt.* -cued, -cu·ing [ult. < L. *re-*, again + *ex-*, off + *quatere*, to shake] to free or save from danger, confinement, evil, etc. —*n.* a rescuing —**res′cu·er** *n.*

re·search (ri surch′, rē′surch) *n.* [see RE- & SEARCH] careful, systematic study and investigation in some field of knowledge —*vi.*, *vt.* to do research on or in —**re·search′er** *n.*

re·sec·tion (ri sek′shən) *n.* [< L. *re-*, back + *secare*, to cut] the surgical removal of part of an organ, etc.

re·sem·blance (ri zem′bləns) *n.* a similarity of appearance; likeness

re·sem·ble (ri zem′b′l) *vt.* -bled, -bling [ult. < L. *re-*, again + *simulare*, feign] to be like or similar to

re·sent (ri zent′) *vt.* [ult. < L. *re-*, again + *sentire*, feel] to feel or show a bitter hurt or indignation at —**re·sent′ful** *adj.* —**re·sent′ful·ly** *adv.* —**re·sent′ment** *n.*

re·ser·pine (ri sur′pin, -pēn) *n.* [G.] a crystalline alkaloid used in treating hypertension, mental illness, etc.

res·er·va·tion (rez′ər vā′shən) *n.* 1. a reserving or that which is reserved; specif., *a)* a withholding *b)* public land set aside for a special use, as for Indians *c)* a holding of a hotel room, etc. until called for 2. a limiting condition

re·serve (ri zurv′) *vt.* -served′, -serv′ing [< L. *re-*, back + *servare*, to keep] 1. to keep back or set apart for later or special use 2. to keep back for oneself —*n.* 1. something kept back or stored up, as for later use 2. a limitation [without *reserve*] 3. the keeping of one's thoughts, feelings, etc. to oneself 4. reticence; silence 5. [*pl.*] troops not on active duty but subject to call 6. land set apart for some purpose —**in reserve** reserved for later use —**re·serv′ist** n.

re·served′ adj. 1. kept in reserve; set apart 2. self-restrained; reticent

res·er·voir (rez′ər vwär′) n. [< Fr.: see RESERVE] 1. a place where water is collected and stored for use 2. a large supply or store of something

re·side (ri zīd′) vi. **-sid′ed, -sid′ing** [< L. re-, back + sedere, sit] 1. to dwell for some time; live (in or at) 2. to be present or inherent (in): said of qualities, etc.

res·i·dence (rez′i dəns) n. 1. a residing 2. the place where one resides —**res′i·den′tial** (-ə den′shəl) adj.

res·i·den·cy (-dən sē) n., pl. **-cies** 1. same as RESIDENCE 2. a period of advanced, specialized medical or surgical training in a hospital

res′i·dent adj. residing; esp., living in a place while working, etc. —n. 1. one who lives in a place, not a visitor 2. a doctor who is serving a residency

re·sid·u·al (ri zij′oo wəl) adj. of or being a residue; remaining —n. 1. something left over 2. [pl.] fees paid for reruns on television, etc.

res·i·due (rez′ə doo′) n. [< L. residuus, remaining] that which is left after part is removed; remainder

re·sid·u·um (ri zij′oo wəm) n., pl. **-u·a** (-wə) same as RESIDUE

re·sign (ri zīn′) vt., vi. [< L. re-, back + signare, to sign] to give up (a claim, or an office, position, etc.) —**resign oneself** (to) to submit (to)

res·ig·na·tion (rez′ig nā′shən) n. 1. a) the act of resigning b) formal notice of this 2. patient submission

re·signed (ri zīnd′) adj. feeling or showing resignation; submissive —**re·sign′ed·ly** (-zīn′id lē) adv.

re·sil·ient (ri zil′yənt) adj. [< L. re-, back + salire, to jump] 1. springing back into shape, etc.; elastic 2. recovering strength, spirits, etc. quickly —**re·sil′ience, re·sil′ien·cy** n.

res·in (rez′n) n. [L. resina] 1. a substance exuded from various plants and trees and used in varnishes, plastics, etc. 2. same as ROSIN —**res′in·ous** adj.

re·sist (ri zist′) vt. [< L. re-, back + sistere, to set] 1. to withstand; fend off 2. to oppose actively; fight against —vi. to oppose or withstand something —**re·sist′er** n. —**re·sist′i·ble** adj.

re·sist′ance n. 1. a resisting 2. power to resist, as to ward off disease 3. opposition of some force, thing, etc. to another, as to the flow of an electric current —**re·sist′ant** adj.

re·sis′tive adj. resisting, tending to resist, or capable of resistance

re·sist′less adj. 1. irresistible 2. unable to resist; unresisting

re·sis′tor n. a device used in an electrical circuit to provide resistance

re·sole′ vt. **-soled′, -sol′ing** to put a new sole on (a shoe, etc.)

res·o·lute (rez′ə loot′) adj. [see RE- & SOLVE] fixed and firm in purpose; determined —**res′o·lute′ly** adv.

res′o·lu′tion n. 1. the act or result of resolving something 2. the thing determined upon; decision as to future action 3. a resolute quality of mind 4. a formal statement of opinion or determination by an assembly, etc.

re·solve (ri zälv′) vt. **-solved′, -solv′ing** [see RE- & SOLVE] 1. to break up into separate parts; analyze 2. to reach as a decision; determine 3. to solve (a problem) 4. to decide by vote —vi. 1. to be resolved, as by analysis 2. to come to a decision; determine —n. 1. firm determination 2. a formal resolution —**re·solv′a·ble** adj.

re·solved′ adj. determined; resolute

res·o·nant (rez′ə nənt) adj. [< L. resonare, resound] 1. resounding 2. intensifying sound (resonant walls) 3. vibrant; sonorous (a resonant voice) —**res′o·nance** n. —**res′o·nate′** (-nāt′) vi., vt. **-nat′ed, -nat′ing**

res′o·na′tor n. a device that produces, or increases sound by, resonance

re·sort (ri zôrt′) vi. [< OFr. re-, again + sortir, go out] to have recourse; turn (to) for help, etc. (to resort to tears) —n. 1. a place to which people go often, as on vacation 2. a source of help, support, etc.; recourse —**as a** (or **the**) **last resort** as the last available means

re·sound (ri zound′) vi. [< L. resonare] 1. to reverberate 2. to make a loud, echoing sound —**re·sound′ing** adj. —**re·sound′ing·ly** adv.

re·source (rē′sôrs, ri sôrs′) n. [< OFr. re-, again + sourdre, spring up] 1. something that lies ready for use or can be drawn upon for aid 2. [pl.] wealth; assets 3. resourcefulness

re·source′ful adj. able to deal effectively with problems, etc. —**re·source′ful·ness** n.

re·spect (ri spekt′) vt. [< L. re-, back + specere, look at] 1. to feel or show honor or esteem for 2. to show consideration for —n. 1. honor or esteem 2. consideration; regard 3. [pl.] expressions of regard 4. a particular detail 5. reference; relation (with respect to his job) —**re·spect′ful** adj. —**re·spect′ful·ly** adv.

re·spect′a·ble adj. 1. worthy of respect or esteem 2. proper; correct 3. of moderate quality or size 4. presentable —**re·spect′a·bil′i·ty** n.

re·spect′ing prep. concerning; about

re·spec′tive adj. as relates individually to each one —**re·spec′tive·ly** adv.

res·pi·ra·tion (res′pə rā′shən) n. act or process of breathing —**res′pi·ra·to·ry** (res′pər ə tôr′ē, ri splr′ə-) adj.

res′pi·ra′tor n. a mask, as of gauze, to prevent the inhaling of harmful substances 2. an apparatus to maintain breathing by artificial means

re·spire (ri splr′) vt., vi. **-spired′, -splr′ing** [< L. re-, back + spirare, breathe] to breathe

---

fat. āpe. cär; ten. ēven; is, bīte; gō, hôrn, tōōl, look; oil, out; up, fur; chin; she; thin, then; zh, leisure; ŋ, ring; ə for a in ago; ′, (ā′b'l); ë, Fr. coeur; ö, Fr. feu; Fr. mon; ü, Fr. duc; kh, G. ich, doch; ‡ foreign; < derived from

res·pite (res'pit) n. [see RESPECT] 1. a delay or postponement 2. temporary relief, as from work or pain

re·splend·ent (ri splen'dənt) adj. [< L. re-, again + splendere, to shine] shining brightly; dazzling —re·splend'ence n. —re·splend'ent·ly adv.

re·spond (ri spänd') vi. [< L. re-, back + spondere, to pledge] 1. to answer; reply 2. to react 3. to have a favorable reaction

re·spond'ent adj. responding —n. Law a defendant

re·sponse (ri späns') n. 1. something said or done in answer; reply 2. words sung or spoken by the congregation or choir replying to the clergyman 3. any reaction to a stimulus

re·spon·si·bil·i·ty (ri spän'sə bil'ə tē) n., pl. -ties 1. a being responsible; obligation 2. a thing or person for whom one is responsible

re·spon·si·ble (-b'l) adj. 1. obliged to account (for); answerable (to) 2. involving obligation or duties 3. accountable for one's behavior or for an act 4. dependable; reliable —re·spon'si·bly adv.

re·spon·sive adj. reacting readily, as to appeal —re·spon'sive·ness n.

rest¹ (rest) n. [OE.] 1. sleep or repose 2. ease or inactivity after exertion 3. relief from anything distressing, tiring, etc. 4. absence of motion 5. a resting place 6. a supporting device 7. Music a measured interval of silence between tones, or a symbol for this —vi. 1. to get ease and refreshment by sleeping or by ceasing from work 2. to be at ease 3. to be or become still 4. to be supported; lie or lean (in, on, etc.) 5. to be found [the fault rests with him] 6. to rely; depend —vt. 1. to cause to rest 2. to put for ease, etc. [rest your head here] —lay to rest to bury

rest² (rest) n. [< L. restare, remain] 1. what is left 2. [with pl. v.] the others —vi. to go on being [rest assured]

res·tau·rant (res'tə rənt, -ränt') n. [Fr.: see RESTORE] a place where meals can be bought and eaten

res·tau·ra·teur (res'tər ə tur') n. [Fr.] one who operates a restaurant

rest'ful (rest'fəl) adj. 1. full of or giving rest 2. quiet; peaceful

res·ti·tu·tion (res'tə tōō'shən) n. [< L. re-, again + statuere, set up] 1. a giving back of something that has been lost or taken away; restoration 2. reimbursement, as for loss

res·tive (res'tiv) adj. [< OFr. rester, remain] 1. unruly or balky 2. nervous under restraint; restless —res'tive·ly adv. —res'tive·ness n.

rest'less adj. 1. unable to relax; uneasy 2. giving no rest; disturbed [restless sleep] 3. rarely quiet or still; active 4. discontented —rest'less·ly adv. —rest'less·ness n.

res·to·ra·tion (res'tə rā'shən) n. 1. a restoring or being restored 2. something restored, as by rebuilding

re·stor·a·tive (ri stôr'ə tiv) adj. restoring health, consciousness, etc. —n. something that is restorative

re·store (ri stôr') vt. -stored', -stor'ing [< L. re-, again + -staurare, to erect] 1. to give back (something taken, lost, etc.) 2. to return to a former or normal state, or to a position, rank, use, etc. 3. to bring back to health, strength, etc.

re·strain (ri strān') vt. [< L. re-, back + stringere, draw tight] to hold back from action; check; suppress

re·straint (ri strānt') n. 1. a re-straining or being restrained 2. a means of restraining 3. confinement 4. control of emotions, impulses, etc.; reserve

re·strict (ri strikt') vt. [see RESTRAIN] to keep within limits; confine —re·strict'ed adj. —re·stric'tion n.

re·stric'tive adj. 1. restricting 2. Gram. designating a subordinate clause or phrase felt as limiting the application of the word it modifies, and not set off by commas (Ex.: a man with money is needed)

rest'room' n. a room in a public building, equipped with toilets, wash-bowls, etc.: also rest room

re·struc·ture (rē struk'chər) vt. -tured, -tur·ing to plan or provide a new structure or organization for

re·sult (ri zult') vi. [< L. resultare, rebound] 1. to happen as an effect 2. to end as a consequence (in something) —n. 1. a) anything that issues as an effect b) [pl.] a desired effect 2. the number, etc. obtained by mathematical calculation —re·sult'ant adj., n.

re·sume (ri zōōm') vt. -sumed', -sum'ing [< L. re-, again + sumere, take] 1. to take or occupy again 2. to continue after interruption —vi. to proceed after interruption —re·sump·tion (ri zump'shən) n.

ré·su·mé, re·su·me (rez'oo mā', rā'zoo mā') n. [Fr.: see prec.] a summary, esp. of employment experience

re·sur·face vt. -faced, -fac·ing to put a new surface on —vi. to come to the surface again

re·sur·gent (ri sur'jənt) adj. [see ff.] tending to rise again —re·sur'gence n.

res·ur·rec·tion (rez'ə rek'shən) n. [< L. resurgere, rise again] 1. Theol. a rising from the dead; specif., [the R-] the rising of Jesus from the dead 2. a coming back into use, etc.; revival —res'ur·rect' vt.

re·sus·ci·tate (ri sus'ə tāt') vt., vi. -tat'ed, -tat'ing [< L. re-, again + suscitare, revive] to revive when apparently dead or in a faint, etc. —re·sus'ci·ta'tion n. —re·sus'ci·ta'tor n.

re·tail (rē'tāl) n. [< OFr. re-, again + tailler, to cut] the sale of goods in small quantities directly to the consumer —adj. of or engaged in such sale —adv. at a retail price —vt., vi. to sell or be sold at retail —re'tail·er n.

re·tain (ri tān') vt. [< L. re-, back + tenere, to hold] 1. to keep in posses-sion, use, etc. 2. to hold in 3. to keep in mind 4. to hire by paying a retainer

re·tain'er n. 1. something that re-tains 2. a servant, attendant, etc. 3. a fee paid to engage a lawyer's services

retaining wall a wall built to hold back earth or water

re·take (rē tāk'; *for n.* rē'tāk') *vt.* -took', -tak'en, -tak'ing 1. to take again; recapture 2. to photograph again —*n.* a scene, etc. rephotographed

re·tal·i·ate (ri tal'ē āt') *vi.* -at'ed, -at'ing [< L. *re-*, back + *talio*, punishment in kind] to return like for like, esp. injury for injury —re·tal'i·a'tion *n.* —re·tal'i·a·to·ry *adj.*

re·tard (ri tärd') *vt.* [< L. *re-*, back + *tardare*, make slow] to hinder, delay, or slow the progress of —re·tar·da·tion (rē'tär dā'shən) *n.*

re·tard·ant *n.* something that retards; esp., a substance that delays a chemical reaction —*adj.* that retards

re·tard·ate (ri tär'dāt) *n.* a mentally retarded person

re·tard·ed *adj.* slow or delayed in development, esp. mentally

retch (rech) *vi.* [OE. *hræcan*, clear the throat] to strain to vomit, esp. without bringing anything up

re·ten·tion (ri ten'shən) *n.* 1. a retaining or being retained 2. capacity for retaining —re·ten'tive *adj.*

ret·i·cent (ret'ə s'nt) *adj.* [< L. *re-*, again + *tacere*, be silent] disinclined to speak; taciturn —ret'i·cence *n.*

ret·i·na (ret'n ə) *n., pl.* -nas *or* -nae' (-ē') [prob. < L. *rete*, a net] the innermost coat of the back part of the eyeball, on which the image is formed

ret·i·nue (ret'n ōō', -yōō') *n.* [see RETAIN] a group of persons attending a person of rank or importance

re·tire (ri tīr') *vi.* -tired', -tir'ing [< Fr. *re-*, back + *tirer*, draw] 1. to withdraw to a secluded place 2. to go to bed 3. to retreat, as in battle 4. to give up one's work, business, etc., esp. because of age —*vt.* 1. to withdraw (troops, etc.) 2. to pay off (bonds, etc.) 3. to cause to retire from a position, office, etc. 4. to withdraw from use 5. *Baseball*, etc. to put out (a batter, side, etc.) —re·tire'e' *n.* —re·tire'ment *n.*

re·tired' *adj.* 1. secluded 2. *a)* no longer working, etc., as because of age *b)* of or for such retired persons

re·tir·ing *adj.* reserved; modest; shy

re·tool *vt., vi.* to adapt (factory machinery) for a different product

re·tort¹ (ri tôrt') *vt.* [< L. *re-*, back + *torquere*, to twist] 1. to turn (an insult, etc.) back upon its originator 2. to say in reply —*vi.* to make a sharp, witty reply —*n.* a sharp, witty reply

re·tort² (ri tôrt') *n.* [< ML. *retorta:* see prec.] a glass container in which substances are distilled

re·touch (rē tuch') *vt.* to touch up details in (a picture, writing, etc.) so as to improve or change it

RETORT

re·trace (ri trās') *vt.* -traced', -trac'ing [see RE- & TRACE¹] to go back over again [to *retrace* one's steps]

re·tract (ri trakt') *vt., vi.* [< L. *re-*, back + *trahere*, draw] 1. to draw back or in 2. to withdraw (a statement, charge, etc.) —re·tract'a·ble, re·trac'tile (-t'l) *adj.* —re·trac'tion *n.*

re·tread (rē tred'; *for n.* rē'tred') *vt., n. same as* RECAP

re·treat (ri trēt') *n.* [see RETRACT] 1. a withdrawal, as from danger 2. a safe, quiet place 3. a period of seclusion, esp. for contemplation 4. *a)* the forced withdrawal of troops under attack *b)* a signal for this *c)* a signal, as by bugle, or ceremony at sunset for lowering the national flag —*vi.* to withdraw; go back

re·trench (rē trench') *vt., vi.* [see RE- & TRENCH] to cut down (esp. expenses); economize —re·trench'ment *n.*

ret·ri·bu·tion (ret'rə byōō'shən) *n.* [< L. *re-*, back + *tribuere*, to pay] deserved reward or, esp., punishment —re·trib·u·tive (ri trib'yoo tiv) *adj.*

re·trieve (ri trēv') *vt.* -trieved', -triev'ing [< OFr. *re-*, again + *trouver*, find] 1. to get back; recover 2. to restore 3. to make good (a loss, error, etc.) 4. to recover (information) from data stored in a computer 5. to find and bring back (killed or wounded game): said of dogs —*vi.* to retrieve game —re·triev'al *n.*

re·triev'er *n.* a dog trained to retrieve game

retro- [< L.] *a combining form meaning* backward, back, behind

ret·ro·ac·tive (ret'rō ak'tiv) *adj.* having effect on things that are already past —ret'ro·ac'tive·ly *adv.*

ret·ro·fire (ret'rə fīr') *vt.* -fired', -fir'ing to fire (a retrorocket)

ret·ro·grade (ret'rə grād') *adj.* [see RETRO- & GRADE] 1. moving backward 2. going back to a worse condition —*vi.* -grad'ed, -grad'ing 1. to go backward 2. to become worse

ret·ro·gress (ret'rə gres') *vi.* [see prec.] to move backward, esp. into a worse condition —ret'ro·gres'sion *n.* —ret'ro·gres'sive *adj.*

ret·ro·rock·et (ret'rō räk'it) *n.* a small rocket, as on a spacecraft, producing thrust opposite to the direction of flight to reduce landing speed, etc.

ret·ro·spect (ret'rə spekt') *n.* [< L. *retro-* + *specere*, to look] contemplation of the past —ret'ro·spec'tion *n.*

ret·ro·spec·tive *adj.* looking back on the past —*n.* a representative show of an artist's lifetime work

ret·si·na, ret·zi·na (ret'si nə) *n.* [Mod. Gr., prob. < L. *resina*, resin] a white or red wine of Greece, flavored with pine resin

re·turn (ri turn') *vi.* [see RE- & TURN] 1. to go or come back 2. to reply —*vt.* 1. to bring, send, or put back 2. to do in reciprocation [to *return* a visit] 3.

to yield (a profit, etc.) **4.** to report officially **5.** to elect or reelect —**n. 1.** a coming or going back **2.** a bringing, sending, or putting back **3.** something returned **4.** a recurrence **5.** repayment; requital **6.** [*often pl.*] yield or profit, as from investments **7.** a reply **8.** *a*) an official report [*election returns*] *b*) a form for computing (income) tax —*adj.* **1.** of or for a return [a *return ticket*] **2.** given, done, etc. in return —**in return** as a return —**re·turn′a·ble** *adj.*

re·turn·ee′ *n.* one who returns, as home from military service or to school after dropping out

re·u·ni·fy (rē yōō′nə fī′) *vt., vi.* -**fied′,** -**fy′ing** to unify again after being divided —**re·u′ni·fi·ca′tion** *n.*

re·un·ion (rē yōōn′yən) *n.* a coming together again, as after separation

re·up (rē′up′) *vi.* -**upped′,** -**up′ping** [RE- + (SIGN) UP] [Mil. Slang] to reenlist

rev (rev) *vt.* **revved, rev′ving** [Colloq.] to increase the speed of (an engine): usually with *up*

Rev. *pl.* **Revs.** Reverend

re·vamp (rē vamp′) *vt.* to vamp again; specif., to revise; redo

re·veal (ri vēl′) *vt.* [< L. *re-,* back + *velum,* a veil] **1.** to make known (something hidden or secret) **2.** to show; exhibit; display

re·veil·le (rev′ə lē) *n.* [< Fr. < L. *re-,* again + *vigilare,* to watch] a signal on a bugle, drum, etc. in the morning to waken soldiers, etc.

rev·el (rev′l) *vi.* -**eled** or -**elled,** -**el·ing** or -**el·ling** [see REBEL] **1.** to make merry **2.** to take much pleasure (*in*) —*n.* merrymaking —**rev′el·er, rev′el·ler** *n.* —**rev′el·ry** *n.*

rev·e·la·tion (rev′ə lā′shən) *n.* **1.** a revealing **2.** something disclosed; esp., a striking disclosure **3.** *Theol.* God's disclosure to man of himself —[**R-**] the last book of the New Testament

re·venge (ri venj′) *vt.* -**venged′, -veng′ing** [< OFr.: see RE- & VENGEANCE] to inflict harm in return for (an injury, etc.) —*n.* **1.** the act or result of revenging **2.** desire to take vengeance —**re·venge′ful** *adj.*

rev·e·nue (rev′ə nōō′) *n.* [< MFr., returned] the income from taxes, licenses, etc., as of a city, state, or nation

re·ver·ber·ate (ri vur′bə rāt′) *vt., vi.* -**at′ed, -at′ing** [< L. *re-,* again + *verberare,* to beat] to reecho or cause to reecho —**re·ver′ber·a′tion** *n.*

re·vere (ri vir′) *vt.* -**vered′, -ver′ing** [< L. *re-,* again + *vereri,* to fear] to regard with deep respect, love, etc.

Re·vere (ri vir′), **Paul** 1735-1818; Am. silversmith and patriot

rev·er·ence (rev′ər əns) *n.* a feeling of deep respect, love, and awe —*vt.* -**enced, -enc·ing** to revere —**rev′er·ent, rev′er·en′tial** (-ə ren′shəl) *adj.* —**rev′er·ent·ly** *adv.*

rev·er·end (rev′ər ənd) *adj.* worthy of reverence: used [*usually* the **R-**] as a title of respect for a clergyman

rev·er·ie, rev·er·y (rev′ər ē) *n., pl.* -**ies** [< Fr.] daydreaming or a daydream

re·vers (ri vir′, -ver′) *n., pl.* -**vers′** (-virz′, -verz′) [Fr.: see ff.] a part (of a garment) turned back to show the reverse side, as a lapel: also **re·vere** (-vir′)

re·verse (ri vurs′) *adj.* [see ff.] **1.** turned backward; opposite or contrary **2.** causing movement in the opposite direction —*n.* **1.** the opposite or contrary **2.** the back of a coin, medal, etc. **3.** a change from good fortune to bad **4.** a mechanism for reversing, as a gear on a machine —*vt.* -**versed′, -vers′ing 1.** to turn backward, in an opposite position or direction, upside down, or inside out **2.** to change to the opposite **3.** *Law* to revoke or annul (a decision, etc.) —*vi.* to go or turn in the opposite direction —**re·ver·sal** (-vur′s'l) *n.* —**re·vers′i·ble** *adj.* —**re·vers′i·bly** *adv.*

re·vert (ri vurt′) *vi.* [< L. *re-,* back + *vertere,* to turn] **1.** to go back, as to a former practice, state, subject, etc. **2.** *Biol.* to return to a former or primitive type **3.** *Law* to go back to a former owner or his heirs —**re·ver′sion** (-vur′zhən) *n.* —**re·vert′i·ble** *adj.*

re·vet·ment (ri vet′mənt) *n.* [< Fr.] **1.** a facing of stone, cement, etc. to protect an embankment **2.** *same as* RETAINING WALL

re·view (ri vyōō′) *n.* [< L. *re-,* again + *videre,* see] **1.** a looking at or looking over again **2.** a general survey or report **3.** a looking back on (past events, etc.) **4.** a reexamination, as of the decision of a lower court **5.** a critical evaluation of a book, play, etc. **6.** a formal inspection, as of troops on parade —*vt.* **1.** to look back on **2.** to survey in thought, speech, etc. **3.** to inspect (troops, etc.) formally **4.** to give a critical evaluation of (a book, etc.) **5.** to study again —**re·view′er** *n.*

re·vile (ri vīl′) *vt., vi.* -**viled′, -vil′ing** [see RE- & VILE] to use abusive language (to or about) —**re·vile′ment** *n.* —**re·vil′er** *n.*

re·vise (ri vīz′) *vt.* -**vised′, -vis′ing** [< L. *re-,* back + *visere,* to survey] **1.** to read over carefully and correct, improve, or update **2.** to change or amend —**re·vi′sion** (ri vizh′ən) *n.*

Revised Standard Version a 20th-c. revision of the Bible

re·viv·al (ri vīv′'l) *n.* **1.** a reviving or being revived **2.** a bringing or coming back into use, being, etc. **3.** a new presentation of an earlier play, etc. **4.** restoration to vigor or activity **5.** a meeting led by an evangelist to stir up religious feeling —**re·viv′al·ist** *n.*

re·vive (ri vīv′) *vi., vt.* -**vived′, -viv′ing** [< L. *re-,* again + *vivere,* to live] **1.** to return to life or consciousness **2.** to return to health and vigor **3.** to bring back or come back into use, attention, popularity, exhibition, etc.

re·viv·i·fy (ri viv′ə fī′) *vt.* -**fied′, -fy′ing** to put new life or vigor into —*vi.* to revive —**re·viv′i·fi·ca′tion** *n.*

re·voke (ri vōk′) *vt.* -**voked′, -vok′ing** [< L. *re-,* back + *vocare,* to call] to withdraw, repeal, or cancel (a law, etc.) —**rev·o·ca·ble** (rev′ə kə b'l) *adj.* —**rev′o·ca′tion** (-kā′shən) *n.*

re·volt (ri vōlt′) *n.* [see REVOLVE] a rebelling against the government or any authority —*vi.* **1.** to rebel against authority **2.** to turn (*from* or *against*) in revulsion; be shocked (*at*) —*vt.* to disgust —**re·volt′ing** *adj.*

rev·o·lu·tion (rev′ə lōō′shən) *n.* [see REVOLVE] **1.** a movement of a body in an orbit **2.** a turning around an axis; rotation **3.** a complete cycle of events **4.** a complete change **5.** overthrow of a government, social system, etc. — **rev′o·lu′tion·ar′y** (-er′ē) *adj., n., pl.* **-ies** —**rev′o·lu′tion·ist** *n.*

Revolutionary War *same as* AMERICAN REVOLUTION

rev′o·lu′tion·ize′ (-īz′) *vt.* **-ized′, -iz′ing** to make a drastic change in

re·volve (ri välv′) *vt.* **-volved′, -volv′ing** [< L. *re-*, back + *volvere*, to roll] **1.** to turn over in the mind **2.** to cause to travel in a circle or orbit **3.** to cause to rotate —*vi.* **1.** to move in a circle or orbit **2.** to rotate **3.** to recur at intervals —**re·volv′a·ble** *adj.*

re·volv·er *n.* a handgun with a revolving cylinder holding cartridges

re·vue (ri vyōō′) *n.* [Fr.: see REVIEW] a musical show with skits, dances, etc., often parodying recent events, etc.

re·vul·sion (ri vul′shən) *n.* [< L. *re-*, back + *vellere*, to pull] an abrupt, strong reaction; esp., disgust

re·ward (ri wôrd′) *n.* [see REGARD] **1.** something given in return for something done **2.** money offered, as for capturing a criminal —*vt.* to give a reward to (someone) for (service, etc.)

re·ward′ing *adj.* giving a sense of reward or worthwhile return

re·wind′ *vt.* **-wound′, -wind′ing** to wind again, specif. (film or tape) back on the original reel

re·word′ *vt.* to change the wording of

re·write *vt., vi.* **-wrote′, -writ′ten, -writ′ing 1.** to write again **2.** to revise **3.** to write (news turned in) in a form suitable for publication

Rey·kja·vik (rā′kyə vēk′) capital of Iceland; a seaport: pop. 78,000

RFD, R.F.D. Rural Free Delivery

rhap·so·dize (rap′sə dīz′) *vi., vt.* **-dized′, -diz′ing** to speak or write in a rhapsodic manner

rhap·so·dy (-dē) *n., pl.* **-dies** [< Gr. *rhaptein*, stitch together + *ōidē*, song] **1.** any ecstatic or enthusiastic speech or writing **2.** an instrumental composition of free, irregular form, suggesting improvisation —**rhap·sod′ic** (-säd′ik), **rhap·sod′i·cal** *adj.*

rhe·a (rē′ə) *n.* [< Gr.] a large S.American nonflying bird, like the ostrich but smaller

rhe·o·stat (rē′ə stat′) *n.* [< Gr. *rheos,* current + -STAT] a device for varying the resistance of an electric circuit, used as for dimming or brightening electric lights

rhe·sus (monkey) (rē′səs) [< Gr. proper name] a brownish-yellow monkey of India: used in medical research

rhet·o·ric (ret′ər ik) *n.* [< Gr. *rhētōr,* orator] **1.** the art of using words effectively; esp., the art of prose composition **2.** artificial eloquence —**rhe·tor·i·cal** (ri tôr′i k'l) *adj.* —**rhet′o·ri′cian** (-ə rish′ən) *n.*

rhetorical question a question asked only for rhetorical effect, no answer being expected

rheum (rōōm) *n.* [< Gr. *rheuma,* a flow] watery discharge from the eyes, nose, etc., as in a cold

rheumatic fever an acute or chronic disease, usually of children, with fever, swelling of the joints, inflammation of the heart, etc.

rheu·ma·tism (rōō′mə tiz′m) *n.* [see RHEUM] a popular term for a painful condition of the joints and muscles —**rheu·mat′ic** (-mat′ik) *adj., n.* —**rheu′ma·toid′** (-mə toid′) *adj.*

rheumatoid arthritis a chronic disease with painful swelling of joints, often leading to deformity

Rh factor (är′āch′) [first discovered in *rhesus* monkeys] a group of antigens, usually present in human blood: people who have this factor are Rh positive; those who do not are Rh negative

Rhine (rīn) river in W Europe, flowing through Switzerland, Germany, and the Netherlands into the North Sea

rhine·stone (rīn′stōn′) *n.* an artificial gem of hard glass, often cut in imitation of a diamond

rhi·ni·tis (rī nīt′əs) *n.* [< Gr. *rhis,* nose + -ITIS] inflammation of the nasal mucous membrane

rhi·no (rī′nō) *n., pl.* **-nos, -no** *clipped form of* RHINOCEROS

rhi·noc·er·os (rī näs′ər əs) *n.* [< Gr. *rhis,* nose + *keras,* horn] a large, thick-skinned, plant-eating mammal of Africa and Asia, with one or two upright horns on the snout

rhi·zome (rī′zōm) *n.* [< Gr. *rhiza,* a root] a horizontal stem on or under soil, bearing leaves near its tips and roots from its undersurface

rho (rō) *n.* the 17th letter of the Greek alphabet (P, ρ)

Rhode Island (rōd) New England State of the U.S.: 1,214 sq. mi.; pop. 947,000; cap. Providence

Rhodes (rōdz) large Greek island in the Aegean

rho·do·den·dron (rō′də den′drən) *n.* [< Gr. *rhodon,* rose + *dendron,* tree] a tree or shrub, mainly evergreen, with pink, white, or purple flowers

rhom·boid (räm′boid) *n.* [see ff. & -OID] a parallelogram with oblique angles and only the opposite sides equal

rhom·bus (räm′bəs) *n.*, **RHOMBOID** *pl.* **-bus·es, -bi** (-bī)

[L. < Gr. *rhombos*, turnable object] an equilateral parallelogram, esp. one with oblique angles

Rhone, Rhône (rōn) river flowing through SW Switzerland & France into the Mediterranean

rhu·barb (rōō′bärb) n. RHOMBUS [< Gr. *rhēon*, rhubarb + *barbaron*, foreign] 1. a plant with long thick stalks cooked into a sauce, etc. 2. [Slang] a heated argument

rhyme (rīm) n. [< OFr.] 1. a poem or verse with recurring correspondence of end sounds, esp. at ends of lines 2. such poetry or verse or such correspondence of sounds 3. a word corresponding with another in end sound —vi. **rhymed, rhym′ing** 1. to make (rhyming) verse 2. to form a rhyme ["more" *rhymes* with "door"] —vt. 1. to put into rhyme 2. to use as a rhyme

rhym′er, rhyme′ster n. a maker of rhymes, esp. of trivial rhyming verse

rhythm (rith′'m) n. [< Gr. *rhythmos*, measure] 1. movement characterized by regular recurrence of beat, accent, etc. 2. the pattern of this in music, verse, etc. —**rhyth′mic** (-mik), **rhyth′mi·cal** adj. —**rhyth′mi·cal·ly** adv.

rhythm and blues the form of black American popular music from which rock-and-roll derives

rhythm method a method of birth control by abstaining from intercourse during the probable ovulation period

R.I., RI Rhode Island

rib (rib) n. [OE.] 1. any of the arched bones attached to the spine and enclosing the chest cavity 2. anything like a rib in appearance or function —vt. **ribbed, rib′bing** 1. to form with ribs 2. [Slang] to tease or make fun of; kid

rib·ald (rib′əld) adj. [< OHG. *riban*, to rub] coarse or vulgar in joking, speaking, etc. —**rib′ald·ry** n.

rib·bon (rib′ən) n. [< MFr. *riban*] 1. a narrow strip of silk, rayon, etc. used for decoration, tying, etc. 2. [pl.] torn shreds 3. a strip of cloth inked for use, as in a typewriter

ri·bo·fla·vin (rī′bə flā′vin) n. [< *ribose*, a sugar + L. *flavus*, yellow] a factor of the vitamin B complex found in milk, eggs, fruits, etc.

rice (rīs) n. [< Gr. *oryza*] 1. an aquatic cereal grass grown widely in warm climates, esp. in the Orient 2. the starchy grains of this grass, used as food —vt. **riced, ric′ing** to reduce (cooked potatoes, etc.) to ricelike granules —**ric′er** n.

rich (rich) adj. [OHG. *richi*] 1. owning much money or property; wealthy 2. well-supplied (*with*); abounding (*in*) 3. valuable or costly 4. full of choice ingredients, as butter, sugar, etc. 5. a) full and mellow: said of sounds b) deep; vivid: said of colors c) very fragrant 6. abundant 7. yielding in abundance, as soil 8. [Colloq.] very amusing —**the rich** wealthy people collectively —**rich′ly** adv. —**rich′ness** n.

Rich·ard I (rich′ərd) 1157–99; king of England (1189–99): called **Richard the Lion-Hearted**

rich·es (rich′iz) n.pl. [< OFr. *richesse*] wealth

Rich·mond (rich′mənd) 1. borough of New York City: pop. 352,000 2. capital of Va.: pop. 219,000

rick (rik) n. [OE. *hreac*] a stack of hay, straw, etc.

rick·ets (rik′its) n. [< ? Gr. *rachis*, spine] a disease, chiefly of children, characterized by a softening and, often, bending of the bones

rick·et·y (rik′it ē) adj. 1. having rickets 2. feeble; weak; shaky

rick·rack (rik′rak′) n. [redupl. of RACK¹] flat, zigzag braid for trimming dresses, etc.

rick·shaw, rick·sha (rik′shô) n. *same as* JINRIKISHA

ric·o·chet (rik′ə shā′) n. [Fr.] the glancing rebound or skipping of an object after striking a surface at an angle —vi. **-cheted′** (-shād′), **-chet′-ing** (-shā′iŋ) to make a ricochet

rid (rid) vt. **rid** or **rid′ded, rid′ding** [< ON. *rythja*, to clear (land)] to free or relieve, as of something undesirable —**get rid of** to dispose of

rid·dance (rid′ns) n. a ridding or being rid; clearance or removal

rid·den (rid′n) pp. of RIDE

rid·dle¹ (rid′l) n. [OE. *rædels*] 1. a puzzling question, etc. requiring some ingenuity to answer 2. any puzzling person or thing

rid·dle² (rid′l) vt. **-dled, -dling** [OE. *hriddel*, a sieve] to make many holes in; puncture throughout

ride (rīd) vi. **rode, rid′den, rid′ing** [OE. *ridan*] 1. to be carried along by a horse, in a vehicle, etc. 2. to be supported in motion (*on* or *upon*) [tanks *ride* on treads] 3. to admit of being ridden [the car *rides* smoothly] 4. to move or float on the water 5. [Colloq.] to continue undisturbed [let the matter *ride*] —vt. 1. to sit on or in and control so as to move along 2. to move over, along, or through (a road, area, etc.) by horse, car, etc. 3. to control, dominate, etc. [*ridden* by doubts] 4. [Colloq.] to tease with ridicule, etc. —n. 1. a riding 2. a thing to ride at an amusement park

rid′er n. 1. one who rides 2. an addition or amendment to a document

rid′er·ship′ n. the passengers of a particular transportation system

ridge (rij) n. [OE. *hrycg*] 1. the long, narrow crest of something 2. a long, narrow elevation of land 3. any narrow raised strip 4. the horizontal line formed by the meeting of two sloping surfaces —vt., vi. **ridged, ridg′ing** to mark with, or form into, ridges

ridge′pole′ n. the horizontal beam at the ridge of a roof, to which the rafters are attached

rid·i·cule (rid′i kyōōl′) n. [< L. *ridere*, to laugh] 1. the act of making one the object of scornful laughter 2. words or actions intended to produce such laughter —vt. **-culed′, -cul′ing** to make fun of; deride; mock

ri·dic·u·lous (ri dik'yə ləs) *adj.* deserving ridicule; absurd —**ri·dic'u·lous·ly** *adv.* —**ri·dic'u·lous·ness** *n.*

rife (rīf) *adj.* [OE. *ryfe*] 1. widespread 2. abounding [*rife* with error]

riff (rif) *n.* [prob. alt. < REFRAIN²] *Jass* a constantly repeated musical phrase —*vi.* to perform a riff

rif·fle (rif'l) *n.* [< ?] 1. a ripple in a stream, produced by a reef, etc. 2. a certain way of shuffling cards —*vt.* -fled, -fling to shuffle (cards) by letting a divided deck fall together as the corners are slipped through the thumbs

riff-raff (rif'raf') *n.* [< OFr.: see RIFLE² & RAFFLE] those people regarded as worthless, disreputable, etc.

ri·fle¹ (rī'f'l) *vt.* -fled, -fling [Fr. *rifler*, to scrape] to cut spiral grooves within (a gun barrel, etc.) —*n.* a shoulder gun with a rifled barrel to spin the bullet for greater accuracy

ri·fle² (rī'f'l) *vt.* -fled, -fling [< OFr. *rifler*] to ransack and rob —**ri'fler** *n.*

ri·fle·man (-mən) *n.*, *pl.* -men a soldier armed with a rifle

rift (rift) *n.* [< Dan., a fissure] an opening caused by splitting; cleft —*vt.*, *vi.* to burst open; split

rig (rig) *vt.* rigged, rig'ging [< Scand.] 1. to fit (a ship, mast, etc.) with (sails, shrouds, etc.) 2. to assemble 3. to equip 4. to arrange dishonestly 5. [Colloq.] to dress (with *out*) —*n.* 1. the way sails, etc. are rigged 2. equipment; gear 3. a tractor-trailer

rig·a·ma·role (rig'ə mə rōl') *n.* alt. *sp.* of RIGMAROLE

rig·ging *n.* chains, ropes, etc. for a vessel's masts, sails, etc.

right (rīt) *adj.* [< OE. *riht*, straight] 1. with a straight or perpendicular line 2. upright; virtuous 3. correct 4. fitting; suitable 5. designating the side meant to be seen 6. mentally or physically sound 7. *a)* designating or of that side toward the east when one faces north *b)* designating or of the corresponding side of something *c)* closer to the right side of one facing the thing mentioned —*n.* 1. what is right, just, etc. 2. a power, privilege, etc. belonging to one by law, nature, etc. 3. the right side 4. the right hand 5. [*often* R-] *Politics* a conservative or reactionary position, party, etc. (often with *the*) —*adv.* 1. straight; directly [go *right* home] 2. properly; fittingly 3. completely 4. exactly [*right* here] 5. according to law, justice, etc. 6. correctly 7. on or toward the right side 8. very: in certain titles [the *right* honorable] —*vt.* 1. to put upright 2. to correct 3. to put in order —**right away** (or **off**) at once —**right on!** [Slang] that's right! —**right'ly** *adv.* —**right'ness** *n.*

right·a·bout-face' *n.* same as ABOUT-FACE

right angle an angle of 90 degrees

right·eous (rī'chəs) *adj.* 1. acting in a just, upright manner; virtuous 2. morally right or justifiable —**right'eous·ly** *adv.* —**right'eous·ness** *n.*

right·ful *adj.* 1. fair and just; right 2. having a lawful claim —**right'ful·ly** *adv.* —**right'ful·ness** *n.*

right'-hand' *adj.* 1. on or toward the right 2. of, for, or with the right hand 3. most helpful or reliable [the president's *right-hand* man]

right'-hand'ed *adj.* 1. using the right hand more skillfully than the left 2. done with or made for use with the right hand —*adv.* with the right hand

right'ist *n.*, *adj.* conservative or reactionary

right'-mind'ed *adj.* having correct views or sound principles

right of way 1. the right to move first at intersections 2. land over which a road, power line, etc. passes

right wing the more conservative or reactionary section of a political party, group, etc. —**right'-wing'** *adj.* —**right'-wing'er** *n.*

rig·id (rij'id) *adj.* [< L. *rigere*, be stiff] 1. not bending or flexible; stiff 2. not moving; set 3. severe; strict 4. having a rigid framework: said of a dirigible —**ri·gid·i·ty** (ri jid'ə tē), **rig'id·ness** *n.* —**rig'id·ly** *adv.*

rig·ma·role (rig'mə rōl') *n.* [< ME. *rageman rolle*, long list] 1. nonsense 2. a foolishly involved procedure

rig·or (rig'ər) *n.* [see RIGID] severity; strictness; hardship Brit. sp. **rigour** —**rig'or·ous** *adj.* —**rig'or·ous·ly** *adv.*

rig·or mor·tis (rig'ər môr'tis, rī'gôr) [ModL., stiffness of death] the stiffening of the muscles after death

rile (rīl) *vt.* riled, ril'ing [< ROIL] [Colloq.] to anger; irritate

rill (ril) *n.* [< Du. *ril*] a rivulet

rim (rim) *n.* [OE. *rima*] 1. an edge, border, or margin, esp. of something circular 2. the outer part of a wheel —*vt.* rimmed, rim'ming to put or form a rim on or around

rime¹ (rīm) *n.*, *vt.*, *vi.* rimed, rim'ing same as RHYME

rime² (rīm) *n.* [OE. *hrim*] hoarfrost

rind (rīnd) *n.* [OE.] a hard outer layer or covering, as of fruit or cheese

ring¹ (riŋ) *vi.* rang *or chiefly dial.* rung, rung, ring'ing [OE. *hringan*] 1. to give forth a resonant sound, as a bell 2. to seem [to ring true] 3. to sound a bell, esp. as a summons 4. to resound [to *ring* with laughter] 5. to have a ringing sensation, as the ears —*vt.* 1. to cause (a bell, etc.) to ring 2. to signal, announce, etc., as by ringing 3. to call by telephone —*n.* 1. the sound of a bell 2. a characteristic quality [the *ring* of truth] 3. the act of ringing a bell 4. a telephone call —**ring a bell** to stir up a memory

ring² (riŋ) *n.* [OE. *hring*] 1. an ornamental circular band worn on a finger 2. any similar band [a key *ring*] 3. a circular line, mark, figure, or course 4. a group of people or things in a circle 5. a group working to advance its own interests, esp. in dishonest ways 6. an enclosed area for contests, exhibitions, etc. *[a circus ring]* 7. prizefighting (with *the*) —*vt.* ringed, ring'ing 1. to encircle 2. to form into a ring —run rings around [Colloq.] 1. to outrun easily 2. to excel greatly

ring'er¹ *n.* a horseshoe, etc. thrown so that it encircles the peg

ring'er² *n.* 1. one that rings a bell, etc. 2. [Slang] *a)* a person or thing closely resembling another *b)* a fraudulent substitute in a competition

ring'lead'er *n.* one who leads others, esp. in unlawful acts, etc.

ring'let (-lit) *n.* 1. a little ring or circle 2. a curl of hair

ring'mas'ter *n.* a man who directs the performances in a circus ring

ring'side' *n.* the place just outside the ring, as at a boxing match

ring'worm' *n.* a contagious skin disease caused by a fungus

rink (riŋk) *n.* [< OFr. *renc*, a rank] 1. an expanse of ice for skating 2. a smooth floor for roller-skating

rinse (rins) *vt.* rinsed, rins'ing [ult. < L. *recens*, fresh] 1. to wash or flush lightly 2. to remove soap, etc. from with clean water —*n.* 1. a rinsing or the liquid used 2. a solution used to rinse or tint hair

Ri·o de Ja·nei·ro (rē'ō dā' zhə ner'ō) seaport in SE Brazil: pop. 3,307,000

Rio Grande (grand, grän'dē) river flowing from S Colo. into the Gulf of Mexico: the S border of Tex.

ri·ot (rī'ət) *n.* [< OFr. *riote*, dispute] 1. wild or violent disorder, confusion, etc.; esp., a violent public disturbance 2. a brilliant display (of color) 3. [Colloq.] something very funny —*vi.* to take part in a riot —read the riot act to to give very strict orders to so as to make obey —run riot 1. to act wildly 2. to grow wild in abundance —ri'ot·er *n.* —ri'ot·ous *adj.*

rip (rip) *vt.* ripped, rip'ping [LME. *rippen*] 1. *a)* to cut or tear apart roughly *b)* to remove in this way (with *off, out,* etc.) *c)* to sever the threads of (a seam) 2. to saw (wood) along the grain —*vi.* 1. to become ripped 2. [Colloq.] to rush; speed —*n.* a ripped place —rip into [Colloq.] to attack, esp. verbally —rip off [Slang] 1. to steal 2. to cheat or exploit —rip'per *n.*

rip cord a cord, etc. pulled to open a parachute during descent

ripe (rīp) *adj.* [OE.] 1. ready to be harvested, as grain or fruit 2. of sufficient age, etc. to be used *[ripe cheese]* 3. fully developed; mature 4. fully prepared; ready *[ripe for action]* —ripe'ly *adv.* —ripe'ness *n.*

rip·en (rī'pən) *vi., vt.* to become or make ripe; mature, age, cure, etc.

rip'-off' *n.* [Slang] the act or a means of stealing, cheating, etc.

ri·poste, ri·post (ri pōst') *n.* [Fr. < L. *responder*, to answer] a sharp, swift response; retort

rip·ple (rip''l) *vi., vt.* -pled, -pling [prob. < RIP] to have or form little waves on the surface (of) —*n.* 1. a little wave 2. a rippling

ripple effect the spreading effects caused by a single event

rip'-roar'ing (-rôr'iŋ) *adj.* [Slang] very lively and noisy; boisterous

rip'saw' *n.* a saw with coarse teeth, for cutting wood along the grain

rise (rīz) *vi.* rose, ris'en (riz'n), ris'ing [< OE. *risan*] 1. to stand or sit up after sitting, kneeling, or lying 2. to rebel; revolt 3. to go up; ascend 4. to appear above the horizon, as the sun 5. to attain a higher level, rank, etc. 6. to extend, slant, or move upward 7. to increase in amount, degree, etc. 8. to expand and swell, as dough with yeast 9. to originate; begin 10. *Theol.* to return to life —*n.* 1. upward movement; ascent 2. an advance in status, rank, etc. 3. a slope upward 4. an increase in degree, amount, etc. 5. origin; beginning —give rise to to bring about

ris·er (rī'zər) *n.* 1. a person or thing that rises 2. a vertical piece between the steps in a stairway

ris·i·ble (riz'ə b'l) *adj.* [< L. *ridere*, to laugh] causing laughter; funny —ris'i·bil'i·ty *n., pl.* -ties

risk (risk) *n.* [< Fr. < It. *risco*] the chance of injury, damage, or loss —*vt.* 1. to expose to risk *[to risk one's life]* 2. to incur the risk of *[to risk a war]* —risk'y *adj.* -i·er, -i·est

ris·qué (ris kā') *adj.* [Fr. < *risquer*, to risk] very close to being improper or indecent; suggestive

rite (rīt) *n.* [< L. *ritus*] a ceremonial or solemn act, as in religious use

rit·u·al (rich'ōō wəl) *adj.* of, like, or done as a rite —*n.* a system or form of rites, religious or otherwise —rit'u·al·ism *n.* —rit'u·al·ly *adv.*

ri·val (rī'v'l) *n.* [< L. *rivalis*] one who tries to get or do the same thing as another or to equal or surpass another; competitor —*adj.* acting as a rival; competing —*vt.* -valed or -valled, -val·ing or -val·ling 1. to try to equal or surpass 2. to equal in some way —ri'val·ry *n., pl.* -ries

rive (rīv) *vt., vi.* rived, rived or riv·en (riv'n), riv'ing [< ON. *rifa*] 1. to tear apart; rend 2. to split

riv·er (riv'ər) *n.* [< L. *ripa,* a bank] a natural stream of water flowing into an ocean, lake, etc.

river basin the area drained by a river and its tributaries

Riv'er·side' city in S Calif.: pop. 171,000

riv'er·side' *n.* the bank of a river

riv·et (riv'it) *n.* [MFr. < *river,* to clinch] a metal bolt with a head and a plain end that is flattened after the bolt is passed through parts to be held together —*vt.* to fasten with or as with rivets —riv'et·er *n.*

Ri·vie·ra (riv'ē er'ə) strip of the Mediterranean coast of SE France & NW Italy: a resort area

riv·u·let (riv'yoo lit) *n.* [< L. *rivus,* a brook] a little stream

rm. *pl.* **rms.** 1. ream 2. room

R.N., RN Registered Nurse

RNA [< *r(ibo)n(ucleic) a(cid)*] an essential component of all living matter: one form carries genetic information

roach¹ (rōch) *n. short for* COCKROACH

roach² (rōch) *n., pl.* **roach, roach′es** [< OFr. *roche*] a freshwater fish of the carp family

road (rōd) *n.* [OE. *rad*, a ride] 1. a way made for traveling; highway 2. a way; course [the road to fortune] 3. [often *pl.*] a place near shore where ships can ride at anchor —**on the road** traveling, as a salesman

road′bed′ *n.* the foundation laid for railroad tracks or for a highway, etc.

road′block′ *n.* 1. a blockade set up in a road to prevent movement of vehicles 2. any hindrance

road runner a long-tailed, swift-running desert bird of the SW U.S. and N Mexico

road′show′ *n.* 1. a touring theatrical show 2. a reserved-seat film showing

road′side′ *n.* the side of a road —*adj.* on or at the side of a road

road′way′ *n.* 1. a road 2. the part of a road along which vehicles move

road′work′ *n.* jogging or running as an exercise, esp. by a prizefighter

roam (rōm) *vi., vt.* [ME. *romen*] to wander aimlessly (over or through) — **roam′er** *n.*

roan (rōn) *adj.* [< Sp. *roano*] bay, black, etc. thickly sprinkled with white or gray —*n.* a roan horse

roar (rôr) *vi.* [OE. *rarian*] 1. to make a loud, deep, rumbling sound 2. to laugh boisterously —*vt.* to express with a roar —*n.* a loud, deep, rumbling sound

roast (rōst) *vt.* [< OFr. *rostir*] 1. to cook (meat, etc.) with little or no moisture, as in an oven or over an open fire 2. to process (coffee, etc.) by exposure to heat 3. to expose to great heat 4. [Colloq.] to criticize severely —*vi.* 1. to undergo roasting 2. to be or become very hot —*n.* 1. roasted meat 2. a cut of meat for roasting 3. a picnic at which food is roasted —*adj.* roasted [roast pork] —**roast′er** *n.*

rob (räb) *vt.* robbed, rob′bing [< OFr. *rober*] 1. to take money, etc. from unlawfully by force; steal from 2. to deprive of something unjustly or injuriously —*vi.* to commit robbery —**rob′ber** *n.* —**rob′ber·y** *n., pl.* -ies

robe (rōb) *n.* [< OFr.] 1. a long, loose outer garment 2. such a garment worn to show rank or office, as by a judge 3. a bathrobe or dressing gown 4. a covering or wrap [a lap *robe*] —*vt., vi.* robed, rob′ing to dress in a robe

rob·in (räb′in) *n.* [< OFr. dim. of *Robert*] a large N.American thrush with a dull-red breast

Robin Hood Eng. Legend the leader of a band of outlaws that robbed the rich to help the poor

Rob·in·son Cru·soe (räb′in s'n krōō′sō) the title hero of Defoe's novel (1719) about a shipwrecked sailor

ro·bot (rō′bət, -bät) *n.* [< Czech < OBulg. *rabu*, servant] 1. a mechanical device operating in a seemingly human way 2. a person acting like a robot

ro·bust (rō bust′, rō′bust) *adj.* [< L. *robur*, oak] strong and healthy — **ro·bust′ly** *adv.* —**ro·bust′ness** *n.*

Roch·es·ter (rä′ches′tər) city in W N.Y.: pop. 242,000

rock¹ (räk) *n.* [< ML. *rocca*] 1. a large mass of stone 2. broken pieces of stone 3. mineral matter formed in masses in the earth's crust 4. anything like a rock; esp., a firm support 5. [Colloq.] a stone —**on the rocks** [Colloq.] 1. ruined; bankrupt 2. served over ice cubes, as whiskey

rock² (räk) *vt., vi.* [OE. *roccian*] 1. to move back and forth or from side to side 2. to sway strongly; shake —*n.* 1. a rocking motion 2. rock-and-roll

rock′-and-roll′ *n.* a form of popular music with a strong, regular beat, which evolved from jazz and the blues

rock bottom the lowest level

rock′-bound′ *adj.* surrounded or covered by rocks

rock candy large, hard, clear crystals of sugar formed on a string

rock′er *n.* 1. either of the curved pieces on which a cradle, etc. rocks 2. a chair mounted on such pieces; also **rocking chair**

rocker panel any panel section below the doors of an automobile

rock·et (räk′it) *n.* [It. *rocchetta*, spool] any device driven forward by gases escaping through a rear vent, as a firework, projectile, or the propulsion mechanism of a spacecraft —*vi.* to move in or like a rocket; soar

rock′et·ry (-rē) *n.* the science of building and launching rockets

Rock·ford (räk′fərd) city in N Ill.: pop. 140,000

rock garden a garden of flowers, etc. in ground studded with rocks

rocking horse a toy horse on rockers or springs, for a child to ride

rock lobster *same as* SPINY LOBSTER

rock′-ribbed′ *adj.* 1. having rocky ridges 2. firm; unyielding

rock salt common salt in masses

rock wool a fibrous material made from molten rock, used for insulation

rock·y¹ (räk′ē) *adj.* -i·er, -i·est 1. full of rocks 2. consisting of rock 3. like a rock; firm, hard, etc. —**rock′i·ness** *n.*

rock·y² (räk′ē) *adj.* -i·er, -i·est inclined to rock; unsteady —**rock′i·ness** *n.*

Rocky Mountains mountain system in W N.America, extending from N.Mex. to Alaska: also **Rock′ies**

Rocky Mountain sheep *same as* BIGHORN

ro·co·co (rə kō′kō) *n.* [Fr. < *rocaille*, shell work] an elaborate style of architecture and decoration, imitating foliage, scrolls, etc. —*adj.* 1. of or in rococo 2. too elaborate

rod (räd) *n.* [< OE. *rodd*] 1. a straight stick or bar 2. a stick for beating as punishment 3. a scepter carried as a symbol of office 4. a measure of length equal to 5 1/2 yards 5. a pole for fishing 6. [Slang] a pistol

rode (rōd) *pt. of* RIDE

ro·dent (rōd'nt) *n.* [< L. *rodere*, gnaw] any of an order of gnawing mammals, as rats, mice, beavers, etc.

ro·de·o (rō'dē ō', rō dā'ō) *n., pl. -os'* [Sp. < L. *rotare*, to turn] a public exhibition of the skills of cowboys, as broncobusting, lassoing, etc.

Ro·din (rō dan'), (**François**) **Auguste** (**René**) 1840–1917; Fr. sculptor

roe[1] (rō) *n.* [ME. *rowe*] fish eggs

roe[2] (rō) *n., pl.* **roe, roes** [< OE. *ra*] a small, agile deer of Europe and Asia

roe'buck' *n.* the male roe deer

roent·gen (rent'gan) *n.* [< W. K. *Roentgen*, 1845–1923, G. physicist] the unit for measuring the radiation of X-rays (**Roentgen rays**) or gamma rays

Rog·er (räj'ər) *interj.* [< name of signal flag for R] [*also* r-] 1. received: used to indicate reception of a radio message 2. [Colloq.] right! OK!

rogue (rōg) *n.* [< ?] 1. a scoundrel 2. a mischievous fellow —**ro·guer·y** (rō'gər ē) *n.* —**ro·guish** (rō'gish) *adj.*

roil (roil) *vt.* [< L. *robigo*, rust] 1. to make (a liquid) cloudy, muddy, etc. by stirring up sediment 2. to vex

roist·er (rois'tər) *vi.* [see RUSTIC] to revel noisily —**roist'er·er** *n.*

role, rôle (rōl) *n.* [Fr.] 1. the part played by an actor 2. a function assumed by someone [an advisory *role*]

role model a person so effective or inspiring in some social role, job, etc. as to be a model for others

roll (rōl) *vi.* [< L. *rota*, a wheel] 1. to move by turning around or over and over 2. to move on wheels or rollers 3. to pass [the years *roll* by] 4. to extend in gentle swells 5. to make a loud, rising and falling sound [thunder *rolls*] 6. to move or rock from side to side —*vt.* 1. to make move by turning around or over and over 2. to make move on wheels or rollers 3. to utter with full, flowing sound 4. to say with a trill [to roll one's r's] 5. to give a swaying motion to 6. to move around or from side to side [to *roll* one's eyes] 7. to wind into a ball or cylinder [*roll* up the rug] 8. to flatten or spread with a roller, etc. —*n.* 1. a rolling 2. a scroll 3. a list of names 4. something rolled into a cylinder 5. a small cake of bread, etc. 6. a swaying motion 7. a loud, reverberating sound, as of thunder 8. a slight swell on a surface

roll'back' *n.* a moving back, esp. of prices to a previous level

roll call the reading aloud of a roll to find out who is absent

roll'er *n.* 1. one that rolls 2. a cylinder of metal, wood, etc. on which something is rolled, or one used to crush, smooth, or spread something 3. a heavy, swelling wave

roller coaster an amusement ride in which small cars move on tracks that curve and dip sharply

roller skate *see* SKATE[1] (sense 2) —**roll'er-skate'** *vi.*

rol·lick (räl'ik) *vi.* [< ? FROLIC] to play or behave in a gay, carefree way —**rol'lick·ing** *adj.*

rolling pin a heavy, smooth cylinder of wood, etc. used to roll out dough

rolling stock all the vehicles of a railroad or a trucking company

roll'-top' *adj.* having a flexible, sliding top of parallel slats [a *roll-top* desk]

ro·ly-po·ly (rō'lē pō'lē) *adj.* [< ROLL] short and plump; pudgy

Rom. Roman

ro·maine (rō mān') *n.* [ult. < L. *Romanus*, Roman] a type of lettuce with long leaves forming a head

Ro·man (rō'mən) *adj.* 1. of or characteristic of ancient or modern Rome, its people, etc. 2. of the Roman Catholic Church 3. [*usually* r-] designating or of the usual upright style of printing types —*n.* a native or inhabitant of ancient or modern Rome

Roman candle a firework consisting of a tube shooting balls of fire, etc.

Roman Catholic 1. of the Christian church (**Roman Catholic Church**) headed by the Pope 2. a member of this church

ro·mance (rō mans'; *also for n.* rō'mans) *adj.* [ult. < L. *Romanicus*] [R-] designating or of any of the languages derived mainly from Latin, as Italian, Spanish, French, etc. —*n.* 1. a long poem or tale, orig. written in a Romance dialect, about the adventures of knights 2. a novel of love, adventure, etc. 3. excitement, love, etc. of the kind found in such literature 4. a love affair —*vi., vt.* -**manced'**, -**manc'ing** [Colloq.] to make love (to)

Roman Empire empire of the ancient Romans (27 B.C.–395 A.D.), including W & S Europe, N Africa, & SW Asia

Ro·ma·nia (rō mān'yə, -mā'nē ə) country in SE Europe: 91,700 sq. mi.; pop. 19,287,000; cap. Bucharest —**Ro·ma'nian** *adj., n.*

Roman numerals Roman letters used as numerals: I = 1, V = 5, X = 10, L = 50, C = 100, D = 500, and M = 1,000

ro·man·tic (rō man'tik) *adj.* 1. of, like, or characterized by romance 2. fanciful or fictitious 3. not practical; visionary 4. full of thoughts, feelings, etc. of romance 5. suited for romance 6. [*often* R-] of a 19th-c. cultural movement characterized by freedom of form and spirit, emphasis on feeling and originality, etc. —*n.* a romantic person —**ro·man'ti·cal·ly** *adv.* —**ro·man'ti·cism** (-tə siz'm) *n.*

ro·man'ti·cize' (-tə siz') *vt., vi.* -**cized'**, -**ciz'ing** to treat, regard, or act in a romantic way

Rom·a·ny (räm'ə nē, rō'mə-) *n.* the language of the Gypsies

Rome (rōm) capital of Italy, & formerly, of the Roman Empire: pop. 2,514,000

Ro·me·o (rō'mē ō') the young lover in Shakespeare's *Romeo and Juliet*

romp (rämp) n. [prob. < OFr. *ramper*, climb] boisterous, lively play —vi. to play in a boisterous, lively way

romp'er n. 1. one who romps 2. [pl.] a loose, one-piece outer garment with bloomerlike pants, for a small child

Rom·u·lus (räm'yoo ləs) *Rom. Myth.* founder and first king of Rome: he and his twin brother Remus were suckled by a she-wolf

rood (rood) n. [OE. *rod*] 1. a crucifix 2. a measure of area equal to 1/4 acre

roof (roof, roof) n., pl. **roofs** [OE. *hrof*] 1. the outside top covering of a building 2. anything like this [the *roof* of the mouth] —vt. to cover as with a roof —**roof'less** adj.

roof'er n. a roof maker or repairer

roof'ing n. material for roofs

roof'top' n. the roof of a building

rook[1] (rook) n. [OE. *hroc*] a European crow —vt., vi. to swindle; cheat

rook[2] (rook) n. [< Per. *rukh*] a chess piece moving horizontally or vertically

rook'er·y n., pl. **-ies** a breeding place or colony of rooks

rook·ie (rook'ē) n. [Slang] 1. an inexperienced army recruit 2. any novice

room (room, room) n. [OE. *rum*] 1. space to contain something 2. suitable scope [*room* for doubt] 3. an interior space enclosed or set apart by walls 4. [pl.] living quarters 5. the people in a room —vt., vi. to have or provide with lodgings —**room'ful'** n. —**room'y** adj. **-i·er, -i·est** —**room'i·ness** n.

room and board lodging and meals

room'er n. one who rents a room or rooms to live in; lodger

room·ette (room met') n. a small compartment in a railroad sleeping car

rooming house a house with furnished rooms for renting

room'mate' n. a person with whom one shares a room or rooms

Roo·se·velt (rō'zə velt', rōz'velt) 1. **Franklin Del·a·no** (del'ə nō'), 1882-1945; 32d president of the U.S. (1933-45) 2. **Theodore**, 1858-1919; 26th president of the U.S. (1901-09)

roost (roost) n. [OE. *hrost*] 1. a perch on which birds, esp. domestic fowls, can rest 2. a place with perches for birds 3. a place for resting, sleeping, etc. —vi. 1. to perch on a roost 2. to settle down, as for the night

roos'ter (-ər) n. a male chicken

root[1] (root, root) n. [< ON. *rot*] 1. the part of a plant, usually underground, that anchors the plant, draws water from the soil, etc. 2. the embedded part of a tooth, a hair, etc. 3. a source or cause 4. a supporting or essential part 5. a quantity that, multiplied by itself a specified number of times, produces a given quantity 6. *same as* BASE (n. 3) —vi. to take root —vt. 1. to fix the roots of in the ground 2. to establish; settle —**take root** 1. to begin growing by putting out roots 2. to become fixed, settled, etc.

root[2] (root, root) vt. [< OE. *wrot*,

snout] to dig (*up, out*) as with the snout —vi. 1. to search about; rummage 2. [Colloq.] to encourage a team, etc.: usually with *for*

root beer a carbonated drink made of root extracts from certain plants

rope (rōp) n. [OE. *rap*] 1. a thick, strong cord made of intertwined strands of fiber, etc. 2. a ropelike string, as of beads —vt. **roped, rop'ing** 1. to fasten or tie with a rope 2. to mark off or enclose with a rope 3. to catch with a lasso —**know the ropes** [Colloq.] to be acquainted with a procedure —**rope in** [Slang] to entice or trick into doing something

Roque·fort (cheese) (rōk'fərt) [< *Roquefort*, France, where orig. made] a strong cheese with a bluish mold

Ror·schach test (rôr'shäk) [< H. *Rorschach* (1884-1922), Swiss psychiatrist] *Psychol.* a personality test in which the subject's interpretations of standard inkblot designs are analyzed

ro·sa·ry (rō'zər ē) n., pl. **-ries** [ML. *rosarium*] *R.C.Ch.* a string of beads used to keep count in saying prayers

rose[1] (rōz) n. [< L. *rosa*] 1. a shrub with prickly stems and flowers of red, pink, white, yellow, etc. 2. its flower 3. pinkish red or purplish red —adj. of this color

rose[2] (rōz) pt. of RISE

ro·sé (rō zā') n. [Fr.] a light, pink wine

ro·se·ate (rō'zē it) adj. rose-colored

rose'bud' n. the bud of a rose

rose'bush' n. a shrub bearing roses

rose'-col'ored adj. 1. *same as* ROSE 2. optimistic —**through rose-colored glasses** with optimism

rose·mar·y (rōz'mer'ē) n. [< L. *ros marinus*, sea dew] an evergreen plant of the mint family, with fragrant leaves used in cooking, etc.

ro·sette (rō zet') n. a roselike ornament or arrangement, as of ribbon

rose water a preparation of water and attar of roses, used as a perfume

rose window a circular window with a pattern of tracery

rose'wood' n. [< its odor] 1. a hard, reddish wood, used in furniture, etc. 2. a tropical tree yielding this wood

Rosh Ha·sha·na (rōsh' hə shô'nə, -shä'-) the Jewish New Year

ros·in (räz'n) n. [see RESIN] the hard resin left after the distillation of crude turpentine: it is rubbed on violin bows, used in varnish, etc.

ros·ter (räs'tər) n. [< Du. *rooster*] a list or roll, as of military personnel

ros·trum (räs'trəm) n., pl. **-trums, -tra** (-trə) [L., beak] a platform for public speaking

ros·y (rō'zē) adj. **-i·er, -i·est** 1. rose in color 2. bright, promising, etc. — **ros'i·ly** adv. —**ros'i·ness** n.

rot (rät) vi., vt. **rot'ted, rot'ting** [OE. *rotian*] to decompose; decay —n. 1. a rotting or something rotten 2. a disease characterized by decay 3. [Slang] nonsense

---

fat, āpe, cär; ten, ēven; is, bīte; gō, hôrn, tool, look; oil, out; up, fur; chin; she; thin, then; zh, leisure; ŋ, ring; ə for a in ago; ', (ā'b'l); ĕ, Fr. coeur; ö, Fr. feu; Fr. mon; ü, Fr. duc; kh, G. ich, doch; ‡ foreign; < derived from

ro·ta·ry (rōt′ər ē) *adj.* [< L. *rota*, wheel] 1. turning around a central axis, as a wheel 2. having rotating parts [a *rotary* press] —*n., pl.* -ries 1. a rotary machine 2. *same as* TRAFFIC CIRCLE

ro·tate (rō′tāt) *vi., vt.* -tat·ed, -tat·ing [< L. *rota*, wheel] 1. to turn around an axis 2. to change in regular succession —**ro·ta′tion** *n.* —**ro′ta·to′ry** (-tə tôr′ē) *adj.*

ROTC, R.O.T.C. Reserve Officers' Training Corps

rote (rōt) *n.* [ME.] a fixed, mechanical way of doing something —**by rote** by memory alone, without thought

ro·tis·ser·ie (rō tis′ər ē) *n.* [Fr. < MFr. *rostir*, to roast] a grill with an electrically turned spit

ro·to·gra·vure (rōt′ə grə vyoor′) *n.* [< L. *rota*, wheel + Fr. *gravure*, engraving] 1. a process of printing pictures, etc. on a rotary press using cylinders etched from photographic plates 2. a newspaper pictorial section printed by this process

ro·tor (rōt′ər) *n.* 1. the rotating part of a motor, etc. 2. a system of rotating airfoils, as on a helicopter

rot·ten (rät′'n) *adj.* [< ON. *rotinn*] 1. decayed; spoiled 2. foul-smelling 3. morally corrupt 4. unsound, as if decayed within 5. [Slang] very bad, unpleasant, etc. —**rot′ten·ness** *n.*

Rot·ter·dam (rät′ər dam′) seaport in SW Netherlands: pop. 728,000

ro·tund (rō tund′) *adj.* [L. *rotundus*] round or rounded out; plump —**ro·tun′di·ty, ro·tund′ness** *n.*

ro·tun·da (rō tun′də) *n.* [see prec.] a round building, hall, or room, esp. one with a dome

rou·é (roo ā′) *n.* [Fr. < L. *rota*, wheel] a dissipated man; rake

rouge (roozh) *n.* [Fr., red] 1. a reddish cosmetic powder, paste, etc. for coloring the cheeks and lips 2. a reddish powder for polishing jewelry, etc. —*vt., vi.* rouged, roug′ing to use cosmetic rouge (on)

rough (ruf) *adj.* [OE. *ruh*] 1. not smooth or level; uneven 2. shaggy [a *rough* coat] 3. stormy [*rough* weather] 4. disorderly [*rough* play] 5. harsh or coarse 6. lacking comforts and conveniences 7. not polished or finished; crude 8. approximate [a *rough* guess] 9. [Colloq.] difficult [a *rough* time] —*n.* 1. rough ground, material, condition, etc. 2. *Golf* any part of the course with grass, etc. left uncut —*adv.* in a rough way —*vt.* 1. to roughen (often with *up*) 2. to treat roughly (usually with *up*) 3. to sketch, shape, etc. roughly (usually with *in* or *out*) —**rough it** to live without customary comforts, etc. —**rough′ly** *adv.* —**rough′ness** *n.*

rough′age (-ij) *n.* rough or coarse food or fodder, as bran, straw, etc.

rough′en *vt., vi.* to make or become rough

rough′-hew′ *vt.* -hewed′, -hewed′ or -hewn′, -hew′ing 1. to hew (timber, stone, etc.) roughly, or without smoothing 2. to form roughly Also **roughhew**

rough′house′ *n.* [Slang] rough, boisterous play, fighting, etc. —*vt., vi.* -housed′, -hous′ing [Slang] to treat or act roughly or boisterously

rough′neck′ *n.* [Slang] a rowdy

rough′shod′ *adj.* shod with horseshoes having metal points —**ride roughshod over** to treat harshly

rou·lette (roo let′) *n.* [Fr. < L. *rota*, wheel] a gambling game played with a small ball in a whirling shallow bowl (**roulette wheel**) with red and black, numbered compartments

round (round) *adj.* [< L. *rotundus, rotund*] 1. shaped like a ball, circle, or cylinder 2. plump 3. full; complete [a *round* dozen] 4. expressed by a whole number or in tens, hundreds, etc. 5. large; considerable [a *round* sum] 6. brisk; vigorous [a *round* pace] —*n.* 1. something round, as the rung of a ladder 2. the part of a beef animal between the rump and the leg 3. movement in a circular course 4. a series or succession [a *round* of parties] 5. [*often pl.*] a regular, customary circuit, as by a watchman 6. a single shot from a gun, or from several guns together; also, the ammunition for this 7. a single outburst, as of applause 8. a single period of action, as in boxing 9. a short song which one group begins singing when another has reached the second phrase, etc. —*vt.* 1. to make round 2. to make plump 3. to express as a round number 4. to complete; finish 5. to go or pass around —*vi.* 1. to make a circuit 2. to turn; reverse direction 3. to become plump —*adv.* 1. in a circle 2. through a recurring period of time [to work the year *round*] 3. from one to another 4. in circumference [ten feet *round*] 5. on all sides 6. about; near 7. in a roundabout way 8. here and there 9. with a rotating movement 10. in the opposite direction —*prep.* 1. so as to encircle 2. on all sides of 3. in the vicinity of 4. in a circuit through In the U.S. *round* (*adv. & prep.*) is generally superseded by *around* —**in the round** 1. in an arena theater 2. in full, rounded form: said of sculpture 3. in full detail —**round about** in or to the opposite direction —**round up** to collect in a herd, group, etc. —**round′ness** *n.*

round′a·bout′ *adj.* 1. indirect; circuitous 2. encircling; enclosing

round′house′ *n.* a circular building with a turntable, for storing and repairing locomotives

round′ly *adv.* 1. in a round form 2. vigorously 3. fully; completely and thoroughly

round′-shoul′dered *adj.* having the shoulders bent forward

Round Table 1. the circular table around which King Arthur and his knights sat 2. [r- t-] a group gathered for an informal discussion

round′-the-clock′ *adj., adv.* throughout the day and night; continuous(ly)

round trip a trip to a place and back again —**round′-trip′** *adj.*

round′up′ *n.* 1. a driving together of cattle, etc. on the range, as for branding 2. any similar collecting 3. a summary, as of news

round'worm' *n.* a hookworm or similar round, unsegmented worm

rouse (rouz) *vt., vi.* roused, rous'ing [LME. *rowsen*] 1. to stir up; excite or become excited 2. to wake

Rous·seau (rōō sō'), **Jean Jacques** 1712–78; Fr. writer

roust·a·bout (roust'ə bout') *n.* [< ROUSE + ABOUT] an unskilled, transient laborer, as on wharves

rout¹ (rout) *n.* [< L. *rupta*, broken] 1. a disorderly flight 2. an overwhelming defeat —*vt.* 1. to put to flight 2. to defeat overwhelmingly

rout² (rout) *vt.* [< ROOT²] to force out —**rout out** 1. to gouge out 2. to make (a person) get out

route (rōōt, rout) *n.* [< L. *rupta* (*via*), broken (path)] a road or course for traveling; often, a regular course, as in delivering mail, etc. —*vt.* rout'ed, rout'ing 1. to send by a certain route 2. to arrange the route for

rou·tine (rōō tēn') *n.* [see prec.] a regular procedure, customary or prescribed —*adj.* like or using routine —**rou·tine'ly** *adv.*

rou·tin'ize (-tē'nīz) *vt.* -ized, -iz·ing to make or bring into a routine

rove (rōv) *vi., vt.* roved, rov'ing [ME. *roven*] to roam —**rov'er** *n.*

row¹ (rō) *n.* [OE. *rāw*] 1. a number of people or things in a line 2. any of the lines of seats in a theater, etc. —**in a row** in succession; consecutively

row² (rō) *vt., vi.* [OE. *rowan*] 1. to propel (a boat) with oars 2. to carry in a rowboat —*n.* a trip by rowboat

row³ (rou) *n., vi.* [< ? ROUSE] quarrel, squabble, or brawl

row'boat' (rō'-) *n.* a small boat made for rowing

row·dy (rou'dē) *n., pl.* -dies [< ? ROW³] a rough, quarrelsome, and disorderly person —*adj.* -di·er, -di·est rough, quarrelsome, etc. —**row'di·ness** *n.* —**row'dy·ism** *n.*

row·el (rou'əl) *n.* [ult. < L. *rota*, wheel] a small wheel with sharp points, forming the end of a spur

row house (rō) any of a line of identical houses joined by common walls

roy·al (roi'əl) *adj.* [< L. *regalis*] 1. of a king or queen 2. like, or fit for, a king or queen; magnificent, majestic, etc. 3. of a kingdom, its government, etc. —**roy'al·ly** *adv.*

roy'al·ist *n.* one who supports a monarch or monarchy

roy'al·ty *n., pl.* -ties 1. the rank or power of a king or queen 2. a royal person or persons 3. royal quality 4. a share of the proceeds from a patent, book, etc. paid to the owner, author, etc.

rpm, r.p.m. revolutions per minute

rps, r.p.s. revolutions per second

R.R. RR railroad

R.S.F.S.R., RSFSR Russian Soviet Federated Socialist Republic

RSV, R.S.V. Revised Standard Version (of the Bible)

R.S.V.P., r.s.v.p. [Fr. *répondes s'il vous plaît*] please reply

rub (rub) *vt.* rubbed, rub'bing [ME. *rubben*] 1. to move (one's hand, a cloth, etc.) over (something) with pressure and friction 2. to apply (polish, etc.) in this way 3. to move (things) over each other with pressure and friction 4. to make sore by rubbing 5. to remove by rubbing (*out, off,* etc.) —*vi.* 1. to move with pressure and friction (*on,* etc.) 2. to rub something —*n.* 1. a rubbing 2. an obstacle, difficulty, or source of irritation —**rub down** 1. to massage 2. to smooth, polish, etc. by rubbing —**rub the wrong way** to irritate or annoy

ru·ba·to (rōō bät'ō) *adj., adv.* [It., stolen] *Music* intentionally and temporarily not in strict tempo

rub'ber¹ *n.* 1. one that rubs 2. [< use as eraser] an elastic substance made from the milky sap of various tropical plants, or synthetically 3. something made of this substance; specif., a low-cut overshoe —*adj.* made of rubber —**rub'ber·y** *adj.*

rub·ber² (rub'ər) *n.* [< ?] the deciding game in a series: also **rubber game**

rubber band a narrow, continuous band of rubber as for holding small objects together

rubber cement an adhesive of unvulcanized rubber in a solvent that quickly evaporates when exposed to air

rub'ber·ize' (-īz') *vt.* -ized', -iz'ing to impregnate with rubber

rubber plant 1. any plant yielding latex 2. a house plant with large, glossy, leathery leaves

rubber stamp 1. a stamp of rubber, inked for printing signatures, etc. 2. [Colloq.] *a)* a person, bureau, etc. that gives automatic approval *b)* such approval —**rub'ber-stamp'** *vt.*

rub·bish (rub'ish) *n.* [ME. *robys*] 1. any material thrown away as worthless; trash 2. nonsense

rub·ble (rub'l) *n.* [ME. *robel*] rough, broken pieces of stone, brick, etc.

rub'down' *n.* a massage

rube (rōōb) *n.* [< name *Reuben*] [Slang] an unsophisticated rustic

ru·bel·la (rōō bel'ə) *n.* [< L. *ruber*, red] an infectious disease causing small red spots on the skin

Ru·bens (rōō'bənz), **Peter Paul** 1577–1640; Fl. painter

ru·bi·cund (rōō'bi kund') *adj.* [< L. *ruber*, red] reddish; ruddy

ru·ble (rōō'b'l) *n.* [Russ. *rubl*'] the monetary unit of the U.S.S.R.

ru·bric (rōō'brik) *n.* [< L. *ruber*, red] 1. a section heading, direction, etc. often in red (as in a prayer book) 2. any rule, explanatory comment, etc.

ru·by (rōō'bē) *n., pl.* -bies [ult. < L. *rubeus*, reddish] 1. a clear, deep-red precious stone: a variety of corundum 2. deep red —*adj.* deep-red

ruck·sack (ruk′sak′) *n.* [G., back sack] a kind of knapsack

ruck·us (ruk′əs) *n.* [prob. merging of RUMPUS & *ruction*, uproar] [Colloq.] noisy confusion; disturbance

rud·der (rud′ər) *n.* [OE. *rother*] a broad, flat, movable piece hinged to the rear of a ship or aircraft, used for steering —**rud′der·less** *adj.*

rud·dy (rud′ē) *adj.* -di·er, -di·est [OE. *rudig*] 1. having a healthy red color 2. reddish —**rud′di·ness** *n.*

rude (rōōd) *adj.* rud′er, rud′est [< L. *rudis*] 1. crude; rough 2. barbarous 3. unrefined; uncouth 4. discourteous 5. primitive; unskillful —**rude′ly** *adv.* —**rude′ness** *n.*

ru·di·ment (rōō′də mənt) *n.* [see prec.] 1. a first principle, as of a subject to be learned 2. a first slight beginning of something —**ru′di·men′ta·ry** (-men′tər ē) *adj.*

rue¹ (rōō) *vt., vi.* rued, ru′ing [OE. *hreowan*] 1. to feel remorse for (a sin, fault, etc.) 2. to regret (an act, etc.) —*n.* [Archaic] sorrow —**rue′ful** *adj.* —**rue′ful·ly** *adv.*

rue² (rōō) *n.* [< Gr. *rhytē*] a strong-scented plant with bitter leaves

ruff (ruf) *n.* [< RUFFLE] 1. a high, frilled, starched collar of the 16th-17th c. 2. a band of colored or protruding feathers or fur about an animal's neck

RUFF

ruf·fi·an (ruf′ē ən) *n.* [< It. *ruffiano*, a pander] a rowdy or hoodlum

ruf·fle (ruf′'l) *vt.* -fled, -fling [< ON. or MLowG.] 1. to disturb the smoothness of 2. to gather into ruffles 3. to make (feathers, etc.) stand up 4. to disturb or annoy —*vi.* 1. to become uneven 2. to become disturbed, irritated, etc. —*n.* 1. a pleated strip of cloth, lace, etc. 2. a disturbance 3. a ripple

rug (rug) *n.* [< Scand.] 1. a piece of thick fabric used as a floor covering 2. [Chiefly Brit.] a lap robe

rug·by (rug′bē) *n.* [first played at *Rugby* School in England] a game from which American football developed

rug·ged (rug′id) *adj.* [ME.] 1. uneven; rough 2. stormy 3. harsh; severe; hard 4. not polished or refined 5. strong; robust —**rug′ged·ly** *adv.* —**rug′ged·ness** *n.*

Ruhr (roor) 1. river in West Germany 2. coal-mining & industrial region along this river: also **Ruhr Basin**

ruin (rōō′in) *n.* [< L. *ruere*, to fall] 1. [*pl.*] the remains of something destroyed, decayed, etc. 2. anything destroyed, decayed, etc. 3. downfall, destruction, etc. 4. anything causing this —*vt.* to bring to ruin; destroy, spoil, bankrupt, etc. —*vi.* to come to ruin —**ru′in·a′tion** *n.* —**ru′in·ous** *adj.*

rule (rōōl) *n.* [< L. *regere*, to rule] 1. an established regulation or guide for conduct, procedure, usage, etc. 2. custom 3. the customary course 4. government; reign 5. a ruler (sense 2) —*vt., vi.* ruled, rul′ing 1. to have an influence (over); guide 2. to govern 3. to determine officially 4. to mark lines (on) as with a ruler —**as a rule** usually —**rule out** to exclude

rule of thumb a practical, though crude or unscientific method

rul·er *n.* 1. one who governs 2. a strip of wood, etc. with a straight edge, used in drawing lines, measuring, etc.

rul·ing *adj.* that rules —*n.* an official decision, as of a court

rum (rum) *n.* [< ?] 1. an alcoholic liquor made from fermented molasses, sugar cane, etc. 2. any alcoholic liquor

Ru·ma·ni·a (rōō mā′nyə) *same as* ROMANIA —**Ru·ma′ni·an** *adj., n.*

rum·ba (rum′bə) *n.* [AmSp.] a dance of Cuban Negro origin, or music for it —*vi.* to dance the rumba

rum·ble (rum′b'l) *vi., vt.* -bled, -bling [ME. *romblen*] 1. to make or cause to make a deep, continuous, rolling sound 2. to move with such a sound —*n.* 1. a rumbling sound 2. [Slang] a fight between teen-age gangs

ru·mi·nant (rōō′mə nənt) *adj.* [see ff.] 1. chewing the cud 2. meditative —*n.* any of a group of cud-chewing mammals, as cattle, deer, camels, etc.

ru·mi·nate′ (-nāt′) *vt., vi.* -nat′ed, -nat′ing [< L. *ruminare*] 1. to chew (the cud) 2. to meditate or reflect (on) —**ru′mi·na′tion** *n.*

rum·mage (rum′ij) *n.* [< MFr. *rum*, ship's hold] 1. odds and ends 2. a rummaging —*vt., vi.* to search through (a place) thoroughly

rummage sale a sale of contributed miscellaneous articles, as for charity

rum·my (rum′ē) *n.* [< ?] any of certain card games whose object is to match sets and sequences

ru·mor (rōō′mər) *n.* [L., noise] 1. general talk not based on definite knowledge 2. an unconfirmed report, story, etc. in general circulation —*vt.* to tell or spread by rumor Brit. sp. **rumour**

rump (rump) *n.* [< ON. *rumpr*] 1. the hind part of an animal, where the legs and back join 2. the buttocks

rum·ple (rum′p'l) *n.* [< MDu. *rompe*] an uneven crease; wrinkle —*vt., vi.* -pled, -pling to wrinkle; muss

rum·pus (rum′pəs) *n.* [< ?] [Colloq.] noisy disturbance; uproar

run (run) *vi.* ran, run, run′ning [< ON. & OE.] 1. to go by moving the legs faster than in walking 2. to go, move, etc. easily and freely 3. to flee 4. to make a quick trip (*up to, down to,* etc.) 5. to compete in a race, election, etc. 6. to ply (between two points), as a train 7. to climb or creep, as a vine 8. to ravel, as a stocking 9. to operate, as a machine 10. to flow 11. to spread over cloth, etc. when moistened, as colors 12. to discharge pus, etc. 13. to extend in time or space; continue 14. to pass into a specified condition, etc. [he *ran* into trouble] 15. to be written, etc. in a specified way 16. to be at a specified size, price, etc. *[eggs run high]* —*vt.* 1. to follow (a specified course) 2. to perform as by running *[to run a race]* 3. to incur (a risk) 4. to get past *[to run a blockade]* 5. to cause to run, move, compete, etc. 6. to drive into a specified condition, place, etc. 7. to drive (an object) into or against (something) 8. to make flow in a specified way, place, etc. 9. to manage (a business, etc.) 10. to trace 11. to undergo (a fever, etc.) 12. to publish (a story, etc.) in a newspaper —*n.* 1. an act or period of running 2. the distance covered in running 3. a trip; journey 4. a route *[a milkman's run]* 5. *a)* a movement onward, progression, or trend *[the run of events]* *b)* a continuous course or period *[a run of good luck]* 6. a continuous course of performances, etc., as of a play 7. a continued series of demands, as on a bank 8. a brook 9. a kind or class; esp., the average kind 10. the output during a period of operation 11. an enclosed area for domestic animals 12. freedom to move about at will *[the run of the house]* 13. a large number of fish migrating together 14. a ravel, as in a stocking 15. *Baseball* a scoring point, made by a successful circuit of the bases —**in the long run** ultimately —**on the run** running or running away —**run across** to encounter by chance: also **run into** —**run down** 1. to stop operating 2. to run against so as to knock down 3. to pursue and capture or kill 4. to speak of disparagingly —**run out** to come to an end; expire —**run out of** to use up —**run over** 1. to ride over 2. to overflow 3. to examine, rehearse, etc. rapidly —**run through** 1. to use up quickly or recklessly 2. to pierce —**run up** 1. to raise, rise, or accumulate rapidly 2. to sew rapidly

run'a·round' *n.* [Colloq.] a series of evasions

run'a·way' *n.* 1. a fugitive 2. a horse, etc. that runs away —*adj.* 1. escaping, fleeing, etc. 2. easily won, as a race 3. rising rapidly, as prices

run'-down' *adj.* 1. not wound and therefore not running, as a watch 2. in poor physical condition, as from overwork 3. fallen into disrepair

run'down' *n.* a concise summary

rune (rōōn) *n.* [OE. *run*] 1. any of the characters of an ancient Germanic alphabet 2. a mystical or obscure poem or song —**ru'nic** *adj.*

rung¹ (ruŋ) *n.* [OE. *hrung*, a staff] a rod forming a step of a ladder, a crosspiece on a chair, etc.

rung² (ruŋ) *pp. of* RING¹

run'-in' *n.* *Printing* matter added without a break or new paragraph: also **run'-on'** 2. [Colloq.] a quarrel, fight, etc.

run·nel (run'l) *n.* [OE. *rynel*] a small stream; brook: also **run'let**

run'ner *n.* 1. one that runs, as a racer, messenger, etc. 2. a long, narrow cloth or rug 3. a ravel, as in hose 4. a long, trailing stem, as of a strawberry 5. either of the long, narrow pieces on which a sled, etc. slides

run'ner-up' *n.*, *pl.* **-ners'-up'** a person or team that finishes second, etc. in a contest

run'ning *n.* the act of one that runs; racing, managing, etc. —*adj.* 1. that runs (in various senses) 2. measured in a straight line *[a running foot]* 3. continuous *[a running commentary]* —*adv.* in succession *[for five days running]* —**in (or out of) the running** having a (or no) chance to win

running gear the wheels, axles, and frame of a motor vehicle

running lights the lights that a ship or aircraft must display at night

running mate a candidate for the lesser of two closely associated offices in his relationship to the candidate for the greater office

run'ny *adj.* **-ni·er, -ni·est** 1. flowing, esp. too freely 2. discharging mucus *[a runny nose]*

run'off' *n.* a deciding, final contest

run'-of-the-mill' *adj.* not selected or special; ordinary; average

runt (runt) *n.* [< ?] a stunted animal, plant, or (contemptuously) person —**runt'y** *adj.* **-i·er, -i·est**

run'-through' *n.* a complete rehearsal, from beginning to end

run'way' *n.* a channel, track, etc. in, on, or along which something moves; esp., a strip of leveled ground used by airplanes in taking off and landing

ru·pee (rōō pē') *n.* [< Sans. *rūpya*, wrought silver] the monetary unit of India, Pakistan, Ceylon, etc.

rup·ture (rup'chər) *n.* [< L. *rumpere*, to break] 1. a breaking apart or being broken apart; breach 2. a hernia —*vt., vi.* **-tured, -tur·ing** to cause or suffer a rupture

ru·ral (roor'əl) *adj.* [< L. *rus*, the country] of, like, or living in the country; rustic —**ru'ral·ism** *n.*

ruse (rōōz) *n.* [< OFr. *reuser*, deceive] a stratagem, trick, or artifice

rush¹ (rush) *vi., vt.* [< MFr. *ruser*, repel] 1. to move, push, drive, etc. swiftly or impetuously 2. to make a sudden attack (on) 3. to pass, go, send, act, do, etc. with unusual haste; hurry —*n.* 1. a rushing 2. an eager movement of many people to get to a place 3. busyness; haste *[the rush of modern life]* 4. a press, as of business, necessitating unusual haste

rush² (rush) *n.* [OE. *rysce*] a grasslike marsh plant, with round stems used in making mats, etc.

rush hour a time of the day when business, traffic, etc. are heavy

rusk (rusk) *n.* [Sp. *rosca*, twisted bread roll] 1. a sweet, raised bread or cake toasted until browned and crisp 2. a piece of this

Russ. 1. Russia 2. Russian

---

fat, āpe, cär; ten, ēven; is, bīte; gō, hôrn, tōōl, look; oil, out; up, fur; chin; she; thin, *then*; zh, leisure; ŋ, ring; ə for *a* in *ago*; ', (ā'b'l); ë, Fr. coeur; ö, Fr. feu; Fr. mon; ü, Fr. duc; kh, G. ich, doch; ‡ foreign; < derived from

rus·set (rus′it) n. [< L. *russus*, reddish] 1. yellowish (or reddish) brown 2. a winter apple with a mottled skin

Rus·sia (rush′ə) 1. czarist empire (**Russian Empire**) in E Europe & N Asia (1547–1917) 2. popularly, U.S.S.R.

Rus·sian adj. of Russia, its people, language, etc. —n. 1. a native or inhabitant of Russia 2. the East Slavic language of the Russians

Russian Soviet Federated Socialist Republic largest republic of the U.S.S.R., stretching from the Baltic Sea to the Pacific

rust (rust) n. [OE.] 1. the reddish-brown coating formed on iron or steel during exposure to air and moisture 2. any stain resembling this 3. a reddish brown 4. a plant disease caused by parasitic fungi, spotting stems and leaves —vi., vt. 1. to form rust (on) 2. to deteriorate, as through disuse

rus·tic (rus′tik) adj. [< L. *rus*, the country] 1. of the country; rural 2. simple or artless 3. rough or uncouth —n. a country person —rus′ti·cal·ly adv. —rus·tic′i·ty (-tis′ə tē) n.

rus·ti·cate (rus′ti kāt′) vi., vt. -cat′ed, -cat′ing 1. to go or send to live in the country 2. to become or make rustic —rus′ti·ca′tion n.

rus·tle¹ (rus′l) vi., vt. -tled, -tling [ult. echoic] to make or cause to make soft sounds as of moving leaves, etc. —n. a series of such sounds

rus·tle² (rus′l) vi., vt. -tled, -tling [< ?] [Colloq.] to steal (cattle, etc.) —rustle up [Colloq.] to collect or get together —rus′tler n.

rust·y (rus′tē) adj. -i·er, -i·est 1. coated with rust, as a metal 2. a) impaired by disuse, neglect, etc. b) having lost facility through lack of practice 3. rust-colored

rut¹ (rut) n. [< ? MFr. *route*, route] 1. a groove, track, etc., as made by wheels 2. a fixed, routine procedure, course of action, etc. —vt. rut′ted, rut′ting to make ruts in —rut′ty adj. -ti·er, -ti·est —rut′ti·ness n.

rut² (rut) n. [< L. *rugire*, to roar] the periodic sexual excitement of certain male mammals —rut′tish adj.

ru·ta·ba·ga (rōōt′ə bā′gə) n. [Sw. dial. *rotabagge*] 1. a turnip with a large, yellow root 2. this root

Ruth (rōōth) Bible a woman who left her own people out of devotion to her mother-in-law, Naomi

ruth·less (rōōth′lis) adj. [OE. *hreowan*, to rue] without pity or compassion —ruth′less·ly adv. —ruth′less·ness n.

Rwan·da (ur wän′də) country in EC Africa: 10,169 sq. mi.; pop. 3,306,000

Rwy., Ry. Railway

-ry (rē) shortened form of -ERY [dentistry]

ry·a rug (rē′ə) [< Sw.] a decorative, hand-woven, thick area rug of Scandinavian origin

rye (rī) n. [OE. *ryge*] 1. a hardy cereal grass 2. its grain or seeds, used for making flour, etc. 3. whiskey distilled from this grain

S

S, s (es) n., pl. **S's, s's** the 19th letter of the English alphabet

S Chem. sulfur —adj. shaped like S

-s [alt. of -ES] 1. the plural ending of most nouns [*lips*] 2. the ending of the third person singular, present indicative, of verbs [*tells*]

-'s¹ [OE. -es] the ending of the possessive singular of nouns (and some pronouns) and of the possessive plural of nouns not ending in s [*boy's, men's*]

-'s² the assimilated form of: 1. is [*he's here*] 2. has [*she's won*] 3. does [*what's it matter?*] 4. us [*let's go*]

S., S., s, s. 1. south 2. southern

S., s. 1. pl. **SS.,** ss. saint 2. school s. 1. second(s) 2. shilling(s)

S.A. South America

Saar (sär, zär) rich coal-mining region in a river valley of SW West Germany: also called **Saar Basin**

Sab·bath (sab′əth) n. [< Heb. *shābath*, to rest] 1. the seventh day of the week (Saturday), set aside in Jewish Scripture for rest and worship 2. Sunday as the usual Christian day of rest and worship

Sab·bat·i·cal (sə bat′i k'l) adj. 1. of the Sabbath 2. [s-] bringing a period of rest [a *sabbatical* leave] —n. [s-] a sabbatical year or leave

sabbatical year a period of absence with pay, for study, travel, etc., given as to teachers, orig. every 7 years

sa·ber, sa·bre (sā′bər) n. [< Hung. *szabni*, to cut] a heavy cavalry sword with a slightly curved blade

Sa·bin vaccine (sā′bin) [< Dr. A. B. *Sabin* (1906–   ), its U.S. developer] a polio vaccine taken orally

sa·ble (sā′b'l) n. [< Russ. *sobol'*] 1. same as MARTEN 2. its costly fur pelt

sab·o·tage (sab′ə täzh′) n. [Fr. < *sabot*, wooden shoe + -AGE: from damage done to machinery by sabots] deliberate destruction of machines, etc. by employees in labor disputes or of railroads, bridges, etc. by enemy agents or by underground resistance —vt., vi. -taged′, -tag′ing to commit sabotage (on) —sab′o·teur′ (-tur′) n.

sa·bra (sä′brə) n. [Mod. Heb. *sābrāh*, a native cactus fruit] a native-born Israeli

sa·bre saw (sā′bər) a portable electric saw with a narrow, oscillating blade

sac (sak) n. [see SACK¹] a pouchlike part in a plant or animal

SAC, S.A.C. Strategic Air Command

sac·cha·rin (sak′ə rin) *n.* [< Gr. *sakcharon*] a white, crystalline coal-tar compound used as a sugar substitute

sac′cha·rine (-rin) *adj.* 1. of or like sugar 2. too sweet [a *saccharine* voice]

sac·er·do·tal (sas′ər dōt′ 'l, sak′-) *adj.* [< L. *sacerdos*, priest] of priests or the office of priest; priestly

sa·chem (sā′chəm) *n.* [AmInd.] among some Indian tribes, the chief

sa·chet (sa shā′) *n.* [Fr.] a small perfumed packet used to scent clothes

sack¹ (sak) *n.* [ult. < Heb. *šaq*] 1. a bag, esp. a large one of coarse cloth 2. [Slang] dismissal (with *the*) 3. [Slang] a bed 4. *Football* a sacking of a quarterback —*vt.* 1. to put into sacks 2. [Slang] to fire (a person) 3. *Football* to tackle (a quarterback) behind the line of scrimmage

sack² (sak) *n.* [see prec.] the plundering of a city, etc. —*vt.* to plunder

sack³ (sak) *n.* [< Fr. (*vin*)*sec*, dry (wine) < L.] a dry, white Spanish wine formerly popular in England

sack′cloth′ *n.* 1. burlap 2. coarse cloth worn as a symbol of mourning

sack′ful′ *n., pl.* -**fuls′** the amount that a sack will hold

sack′ing *n.* a coarse cloth, as burlap, used for making sacks

sac·ra·ment (sak′rə mənt) *n.* [< L. *sacer*, sacred] any of certain Christian rites, as baptism, the Eucharist, etc. —**sac′ra·men′tal** *adj.*

Sac·ra·men·to (sak′rə men′tō) capital of Calif.: pop. 276,000

sa·cred (sā′krid) *adj.* [< L. *sacer*, holy] 1. consecrated to a god or God; holy 2. having to do with religion 3. venerated; hallowed 4. inviolate —**sa′cred·ly** *adv.* —**sa′cred·ness** *n.*

sac·ri·fice (sak′rə fīs′) *n.* [< L. *sacer*, sacred + *facere*, make] 1. an offering, as of a life or object, to a deity 2. a giving up of one thing for the sake of another 3. a loss incurred in selling —*vt., vi.* -**ficed′**, -**fic′ing** 1. to offer as a sacrifice to a deity 2. to give up (one thing) for the sake of another 3. to sell at less than the supposed value —**sac′ri·fi′cial** (-fish′əl) *adj.*

sac·ri·lege (sak′rə lij) *n.* [< L. *sacer*, sacred + *legere*, take away] desecration of what is sacred —**sac′ri·le′gious** (-lij′əs, -lē′jəs) *adj.*

sac·ris·tan (sak′ris tan) *n.* an official in charge of a sacristy

sac·ris·ty (sak′ris tē) *n., pl.* -**ties** [ult. < L. *sacer*, sacred] a room in a church for sacred vessels, etc.

sa·cro·il·i·ac (sā′krō il′ē ak′, sak′rō-) *n.* the joint between the top part (il′i·um) of the hipbone and the fused bottom vertebrae (sa′crum)

sac·ro·sanct (sak′rō saŋkt′) *adj.* [< L. *sacer*, sacred + *sanctus*, holy] very sacred, holy, or inviolable

sad (sad) *adj.* **sad′der**, **sad′dest** [OE. *sæd*, sated] 1. having or expressing low spirits; unhappy; sorrowful 2. causing dejection, sorrow, etc. —**sad′ly** *adv.* —**sad′ness** *n.*

sad′den *vt., vi.* to make or become sad

sad·dle (sad′ 'l) *n.* [OE. *sadol*] 1. a seat for a rider on a horse, bicycle, etc., usually padded and of leather 2. a cut of lamb, etc. including part of the backbone and the two loins —*vt.* -**dled**, -**dling** 1. to put a saddle upon 2. to encumber or burden —**in the saddle** in control

sad′dle·bag′ *n.* 1. a bag hung behind the saddle of a horse, etc. 2. a similar bag carried on a bicycle, etc.

saddle horse a horse for riding

saddle shoes white oxford shoes with a contrasting band across the instep

Sad·du·cee (saj′oo sē′) *n.* a member of an ancient Jewish party that accepted only the written law

SADDLE SHORS

sad·ism (sad′iz'm, sā′diz'm) *n.* [< marquis de *Sade*, 18th-c. Fr. writer] the getting of pleasure from mistreating others —**sad′ist** *n.* —**sa·dis′tic** *adj.* —**sa·dis′ti·cal·ly** *adv.*

sad·o·mas·o·chism (sā′dō mas′ə kiz'm, sad′ō-) *n.* sadism and masochism coexisting in the same person —**sad′o·mas′o·chist** *n.* —**sad′o·mas′o·chis′tic** *adj.*

sa·fa·ri (sə fär′ē) *n., pl.* -**ris** [< Ar. *safara*, to travel] a journey or hunting expedition, esp. in Africa

safe (sāf) *adj.* **saf′er**, **saf′est** [< L. *salvus*] 1. *a)* free from damage, danger, etc.; secure *b)* having escaped injury; unharmed 2. *a)* giving protection *b)* trustworthy 3. prudent; cautious —*n.* a locking metal container for valuables —**safe′ly** *adv.* —**safe′ness** *n.*

safe′-con′duct *n.* permission to travel safely through enemy regions

safe′-de·pos′it *adj.* designating or of a box or vault, as in a bank, for storing valuables: also **safe′ty-de·pos′it**

safe′guard′ *n.* a protection; precaution —*vt.* to protect or guard

safe′keep′ing *n.* protection; care

safe·ty (sāf′tē) *n., pl.* -**ties** 1. a being safe; security 2. any device for preventing an accident 3. *Football a)* the grounding of the ball by the offense behind its own goal line that scores two points for the defense *b)* a defensive back farthest from the line of scrimmage: also **safety man** —*adj.* giving safety

safety glass shatterproof glass

safety net 1. a net suspended as beneath aerialists 2. any protection against loss, esp. financial loss

safety pin a pin bent back on itself and having the point held in a guard

safety razor a razor with a detachable blade held between guards

safety valve an automatic valve which releases steam if the pressure in a boiler, etc. becomes excessive

saf·flow·er (saf'lou'ər) n. [ult. < Ar.] a flowering thistlelike plant whose seeds yield an edible oil

saf·fron (saf'rən) n. [< Ar. za'farān] 1. a plant having orange stigmas 2. the dried stigmas, used as a dye and flavoring 3. orange yellow

sag (sag) vi. **sagged, sag'ging** [prob. < Scand.] 1. to sink, esp. in the middle, from weight or pressure 2. to hang down unevenly 3. to weaken through weariness, age, etc. —n. 1. a sagging 2. a sagging place

sa·ga (sä'gə) n. [ON., a tale] 1. a medieval Scandinavian story of battles, legends, etc. 2. any long story of heroic deeds

sa·ga·cious (sə gā'shəs) adj. [< L. sagax, wise] keenly perceptive; shrewd —sa·gac'i·ty (-gas'ə tē) n.

sage[1] (sāj) adj. **sag'er, sag'est** [ult. < L. sapere, know] 1. wise, discerning, etc. 2. showing wisdom [a sage comment] —n. a very wise man

sage[2] (sāj) n. [< L. salvus, safe: from its reputed healing powers] 1. a plant of the mint family with leaves used for seasoning meats, etc. 2. sagebrush

sage'brush' n. a plant with aromatic leaves, in the dry areas of the W U.S.

sag'gy adj. **-gi·er, -gi·est** tending to sag —sag'gi·ness n.

Sag·it·ta·ri·us (saj'i ter'ē əs) [L., archer] the ninth sign of the zodiac

sa·gua·ro (sə gwä'rō) n., pl. **-ros** [< native name] a giant cactus of the SW U.S. and N Mexico

Sa·ha·ra (sə har'ə) vast desert region extending across N Africa

said (sed) pt. & pp. of SAY —adj. aforesaid

Sai·gon (sī gän') city in S Vietnam: pop. 2,200,000: now called Ho Chi Minh City (hō' chē' min')

sail (sāl) n. [OE. segl] 1. a sheet, as of canvas, spread to catch the wind so as to drive a vessel forward 2. sails collectively 3. a trip in a ship or boat 4. anything like a sail —vi. 1. to be moved forward by means of sails 2. to travel on water 3. to begin a trip by water 4. to manage a sailboat 5. to glide or move smoothly, like a ship in full sail —vt. 1. to move upon (a body of water) in a vessel 2. to manage (a vessel) —set sail to begin a trip by water —under sail sailing

sail'boat' n. a boat that is propelled by means of a sail or sails

sail'cloth' n. canvas or other cloth for making sails, tents, etc.

sail'fish' n., pl.: see FISH a large, marine fish with a saillike dorsal fin

sail'or n. 1. a person whose work is sailing 2. an enlisted man in the navy

saint (sānt) n. [< L. sanctus, holy] 1. a holy person 2. a person who is exceptionally charitable, patient, etc. 3. in certain Christian churches, a person officially recognized and venerated for having attained heaven after an exceptionally holy life —saint'li·ness n. —saint'ly adj. -li·er, -li·est

Saint Ber·nard (bər närd') a large dog of a breed once used in the Swiss Alps to rescue lost travelers

Saint Pat·rick's Day (pat'riks) March 17, observed by the Irish in honor of the patron saint of Ireland

Saint Valentine's Day February 14, observed in honor of a martyr of the 3d c. and as a day for sending valentines to sweethearts, etc.

saith (seth) [Archaic] says

sake[1] (sāk) n. [OE. sacu, suit at law] 1. motive; cause [for the sake of money] 2. behalf [for my sake]

sa·ke[2] (sä'kē) n. [Jap.] a Japanese alcoholic beverage made from rice: also sp. **saki**

sa·laam (sə läm') n. [Ar. salām, peace] an Oriental greeting, etc. made by bowing low in respect or obeisance

sal·a·ble (sāl'ə b'l) adj. that can be sold; marketable: also sp. **saleable**

sa·la·cious (sə lā'shəs) adj. [< L. salire, to leap] 1. lustful 2. obscene —sa·la'cious·ly adv. —sa·la'cious·ness n.

sal·ad (sal'əd) n. [< L. salare, to salt] a dish, usually cold, of fruits, vegetables (esp. lettuce), meat, eggs, etc. usually mixed with salad dressing

salad bar a buffet in a restaurant at which diners make their own salads

salad dressing a preparation of oil, vinegar, spices, etc. put on a salad

sal·a·man·der (sal'ə man'dər) n. [< Gr. salamandra] 1. a mythological reptile said to live in fire 2. a scaleless, tailed amphibian

sa·la·mi (sə lä'mē) n. [It. < L. sal, salt] a spiced, salted sausage

sal·a·ry (sal'ə rē) n., pl. **-ries** [< L. salarium, orig. part of a soldier's pay for buying salt < sal, salt] a fixed payment at regular intervals for work —sal'a·ried (-rēd) adj.

sale (sāl) n. [< ON. sala] 1. a selling 2. opportunity to sell; market 3. an auction 4. a special offering of goods at reduced prices —**for** (or **on**) **sale** to be sold

Sa·lem (sā'ləm) capital of Oreg., in the NW part: pop. 89,000

sales·clerk (sālz'klurk') n. a person employed to sell goods in a store

sales·man (-mən) n., pl. **-men** a man employed to sell goods —**sales'wom'an, sales'la'dy, sales'girl'** n. fem. —sales'man·ship' n.

sales·per·son n. a person employed to sell goods; esp., a salesclerk

sales slip a receipt or bill of sale

sales talk 1. talk aimed at selling something 2. any talk to persuade

sales tax a tax on sales

sal·i·cyl·ic acid (sal'ə sil'ik) [< salicin (substance from certain willows)] a crystalline compound, as in aspirin, for relieving pain, etc.

sa·lient (sāl'yənt) adj. [< L. salire, to leap] 1. pointing outward; jutting 2. conspicuous; prominent —n. a salient angle, part, etc. —sa'lience n.

sa·line (sā'līn) adj. [< L. sal, salt] of, like, or containing salt; salty —sa·lin·i·ty (sə lin'ə tē) n.

sa·li·va (sə lī'və) n. [L.] the watery fluid secreted by glands in the mouth: it aids in digestion —sal·i·var·y (sal'ə ver'ē) adj.

sal·i·vate (sal'ə vāt') *vi.* -vat'ed, -vat'ing [< L. *salivare*] to secrete saliva —**sal'i·va'tion** *n.*

sal·low (sal'ō) *adj.* [ME. *salou*] of a sickly, pale-yellowish complexion

sal·ly (sal'ē) *n., pl.* -lies [< L. *salire*, to leap] 1. a sudden rushing forth, as to attack 2. a quick witticism; quip 3. an excursion —*vi.* -lied, -ly·ing to rush or set (*forth* or *out*) on a sally

salm·on (sam'ən) *n., pl.* -on, -ons [< L. *salmo*] 1. a game and food fish with yellowish-pink flesh, that lives in salt water and spawns in fresh water 2. yellowish pink: also **salmon pink**

sal·mo·nel·la (sal'mə nel'ə) *n., pl.* -nel'lae (-ē), -nel'la, -nel'las [< D. E. *Salmon* (d. 1914), U.S. doctor] any of a genus of bacilli that cause typhoid fever, food poisoning, etc.

sa·lon (sə län') *n.* [Fr.: see ff.] 1. a large reception hall or drawing room 2. a regular gathering of distinguished guests 3. a parlor [beauty *salon*]

sa·loon (sə lōōn') *n.* [< Fr. < It. *sala*, hall] 1. any large room or hall for receptions, etc. 2. a place where alcoholic drinks are sold; bar

sal soda crystallized sodium carbonate

salt (sôlt) *n.* [OE. *sealt*] 1. a white, crystalline substance, sodium chloride, found in natural beds, in sea water, etc., and used for seasoning food, etc. 2. a chemical compound derived from an acid by replacing hydrogen with a metal 3. piquancy; esp., pungent wit 4. [*pl.*] mineral salts used as a cathartic or restorative 5. [Colloq.] a sailor —*adj.* containing, preserved with, or tasting of salt —*vt.* to sprinkle, season, or preserve with salt —**salt of the earth** any person or persons regarded as the finest, etc. —**with a grain of salt** with allowance for exaggeration, etc. —**salt'ed** *adj.* —**salt'i·ness** *n.* —**salt'y** *adj.* -i·er, -i·est

SALT (sôlt) Strategic Arms Limitation Talks

salt'cel'lar (-sel'ər) *n.* [< prec. + MFr. *salière*, saltcellar] 1. a small dish for holding salt 2. a saltshaker

salt·ine (sôl tēn') *n.* [SALT + -INE⁸] a flat, crisp, salted cracker

Salt Lake City capital of Utah: pop. 163,000

salt lick a natural deposit or a block of rock salt which animals lick

salt'pe'ter (-pēt'ər) *n.* [< L. *sal*, salt + *petra*, a rock] *same as* NITER

salt pork pork cured in salt

salt'shak'er *n.* a container for salt, with a perforated top

salt'wa'ter *adj.* of or living in salt water or the sea

sa·lu·bri·ous (sə lōō'brē əs) *adj.* [< L. *salus*, health] healthful; wholesome

sal·u·tar·y (sal'yoo ter'ē) *adj.* [see prec.] 1. healthful 2. beneficial

sal·u·ta·tion (sal'yoo tā'shən) *n.* [see ff.] 1. the act of greeting, addressing, etc. 2. a form of greeting, as the "Dear Sir" of a letter

sa·lute (sə lōōt') *vt., vi.* -lut'ed, -lut'ing [< L. *salus*, health] 1. to greet with friendly words or ceremonial gesture 2. to honor by performing a prescribed act, such as raising the hand to the head, in military and naval practice 3. to commend —*n.* an act or remark made in saluting

sal·vage (sal'vij) *n.* [see SAVE¹] 1. *a)* the rescue of a ship and cargo from shipwreck, etc. *b)* compensation paid for such rescue 2. *a)* the rescue of any property from destruction or waste *b)* the property saved —*vt.* -vaged, -vag·ing to save or rescue from shipwreck, fire, etc.

sal·va·tion (sal vā'shən) *n.* [< L. *salvare*, save] 1. a saving or being saved 2. a person or thing that saves 3. *Theol.* spiritual rescue from sin and death; redemption

salve (sav) *n.* [OE. *sealf*] 1. any soothing or healing ointment for wounds, burns, etc. 2. anything that soothes —*vt.* salved, salv'ing to soothe

sal·ver (sal'vər) *n.* [ult. < L. *salvare*, save] a tray

sal·vo (sal'vō) *n., pl.* -vos, -voes [< It. < L. *salve*, hail !] a discharge of a number of guns, in salute or at a target

SAM (sam) surface-to-air missile

sam·ba (sam'bə) *n.* [Port.] a Brazilian dance of African origin, or music for it —*vi.* to dance the samba

same (sām) *adj.* [< ON. *samr*] 1. being the very one; identical 2. alike in kind, quality, amount, etc. 3. unchanged [to keep the *same* look] 4. before-mentioned —*pron.* the same person or thing —*adv.* in like manner —**same'ness** *n.*

†sam·iz·dat (säm'iz dät') *n.* [Russ., self-published] in the U.S.S.R., a system by which writings officially disapproved of are circulated secretly

Sa·mo·a (sə mō'ə) group of islands in the S. Pacific, seven of which constitute a U.S. possession (**American Samoa**) —**Sa·mo'an** *adj., n.*

sam·o·var (sam'ə vär') *n.* [Russ.] a Russian metal urn with an internal tube for heating water in making tea

sam·pan (sam'pan) *n.* [< Chin.] a small boat used in China and Japan, rowed with a scull from the stern

sam·ple (sam'p'l) *n.* [see EXAMPLE] 1. a part taken as representative of a whole thing, group, etc.; specimen 2. an example —*vt.* -pled, -pling to take or test a sample of

sam'pler *n.* 1. one who samples 2. a cloth embroidered with designs, mottoes, etc. in different stitches

Sam·son (sam's'n) *Bible* an Israelite with great strength

Sam·u·el (sam'yoo wəl) *Bible* a Hebrew judge and prophet

sam·u·rai (sam'ə rī') *n., pl.* -rai [Jap.] a member of a military class in feudal Japan

San An·to·ni·o (san' ən tō′nē ō′) city in SC Tex.: pop. 785,000

san·a·to·ri·um (san′ə tôr′ē əm) *n. chiefly Brit. var. of* SANITARIUM

San Ber·nar·di·no (bur′nər dē′nō) city in S Calif.: pop. 118,000

sanc·ti·fy (saŋk′tə fī′) *vt.* **-fied′, -fy′ing** [see SAINT & -FY] 1. to set apart as holy; consecrate 2. to make free from sin —**sanc′ti·fi·ca′tion** *n.*

sanc·ti·mo·ni·ous (saŋk′tə mō′nē əs) *adj.* pretending to be pious —**sanc′ti·mo′ni·ous·ly** *adv.*

sanc·ti·mo·ny *n.* [< L. *sánctus,* holy] pretended piety

sanc·tion (saŋk′shən) *n.* [see SAINT] 1. authorization 2. support; approval 3. [*usually pl.*] a punitive measure, as an official trade boycott, against a nation defying international law —*vt.* 1. to confirm 2. to authorize; permit

sanc·ti·ty (saŋk′tə tē) *n., pl.* **-ties** [< L. *sánctus,* holy] 1. holiness 2. sacredness

sanc·tu·ar·y (saŋk′choo wer′ē) *n., pl.* **-ies** [< L. *sánctus,* sacred] 1. a holy place; specif., a church, temple, etc. 2. a place of refuge or protection

sanc·tum (saŋk′təm) *n.* [L.] 1. a sacred place 2. a private room where one is not to be disturbed

sand (sand) *n.* [OE.] 1. loose, gritty grains of disintegrated rock, as on beaches, in deserts, etc. 2. [*usually pl.*] a tract of sand —*vt.* 1. to sprinkle or fill with sand 2. to smooth or polish, as with sandpaper —**sand′er** *n.*

Sand (sand), **George** (pseud. of Baronne *Dudevant*) 1804–76; Fr. woman novelist

san·dal (san′d′l) *n.* [< Gr. *sandalon*] 1. a shoe made of a sole fastened to the foot by straps 2. any of various low slippers or shoes

san′dal·wood′ *n.* [ult. < Sans.] 1. the hard, sweet-smelling heartwood of an Asiatic tree 2. this tree

sand′bag′ *n.* a bag filled with sand, used for ballast, protecting levees, etc. —*vt.* 1. to put sandbags in or around 2. to hit with a sandbag 3. [Colloq.] to force into doing something

sand bar a ridge of sand formed in a river or along a shore: also **sandbank**

sand′blast′ *n.* a current of air or steam carrying sand at a high velocity, used in cleaning stone, etc. —*vt.* to clean with a sandblast

sand′box′ *n.* a box containing sand, as for children to play in

sand′hog′ *n.* a laborer in underground or underwater construction

San Di·e·go (san′ dē ā′gō) seaport in S Calif.: pop. 876,000

sand′lot′ *adj.* of or having to do with games, esp. baseball, played by amateurs, orig. on a sandy lot

sand′man′ *n.* a mythical person supposed to make children sleepy by dusting sand in their eyes

sand′pa′per *n.* paper coated on one side with sand, used for smoothing and polishing —*vt.* to rub with sandpaper

sand′pip′er (-pī′pər) *n.* a small shore bird with a long, soft-tipped bill

sand′stone′ *n.* a sedimentary rock composed of sand grains cemented together, as by silica

sand′storm′ *n.* a windstorm in which large quantities of sand are blown about in the air

sand·wich (sand′wich, san′-) *n.* [< 4th Earl of *Sandwich* (1718–92)] slices of bread with meat, cheese, etc. between them —*vt.* to place between other persons, things, etc.

sand·y (san′dē) *adj.* **-i·er, -i·est** 1. of or like sand 2. pale reddish-yellow

sane (sān) *adj.* [L. *sanus,* healthy] 1. mentally healthy; rational 2. sound; sensible —**sane′ly** *adv.*

San·for·ize (san′fə rīz′) *vt.* **-ized′, -iz′ing** [< *Sanford* L. Cluett (1874–1968), the inventor] to preshrink (cloth) permanently by a patented process before making garments

San Fran·cis·co (san′ frən sis′kō) seaport in W Calif.: pop. 679,000

sang (saŋ) *pt. of* SING

sang-froid (san′frwä′) *n.* [Fr., lit. cold blood] cool self-possession

san·gui·nar·y (saŋ′gwi ner′ē) *adj.* [see ff.] 1. accompanied by much bloodshed or murder 2. bloodthirsty

san·guine (saŋ′gwin) *adj.* [< L. *sanguis,* blood] 1. of the color of blood; ruddy 2. cheerful; confident

san·i·tar·i·um (san′ə ter′ē əm) *n., pl.* **-ums, -a** (-ə) [ModL. < L. *sanitas,* health] 1. a resort where people go to regain health 2. an institution for the care of invalids or convalescents

san·i·tar·y (san′ə ter′ē) *adj.* [< L. *sanitas,* health] 1. of or bringing about health or healthful conditions 2. in a clean, healthy condition

sanitary napkin an absorbent pad worn by women during menstruation

san·i·ta·tion (san′ə tā′shən) *n.* 1. the science and practice of effecting hygienic conditions 2. drainage and disposal of sewage

san·i·tize (san′ə tīz′) *vt.* **-tized′, -tiz′ing** to make sanitary

san·i·ty (san′ə tē) *n.* 1. the state of being sane 2. soundness of judgment

San Jo·se (san′ hō zā′) city in W Calif.: pop. 637,000

San Juan (san′ hwän′) capital of Puerto Rico: pop. 445,000

sank (saŋk) *pt. of* SINK

San Ma·ri·no (san′ mä rē′nō) country within E Italy: 23 sq. mi.; pop. 18,000

sans (sanz; *Fr.* sän) *prep.* [Fr. < L. *sine*] without

San·skrit (san′skrit) *n.* the classical literary language of ancient India: also **Sanscrit**

San·ta An·a (san′tə an′ə) city in SW Calif.: pop. 204,000

San·ta Claus, San·ta Klaus (san′tə klôz′) [< Du. *Sant Nikolaas,* St. Nicholas] *Folklore* a fat, whitebearded, jolly old man in a red suit, who distributes gifts at Christmas

San·ta Fe (san′tə fā′) capital of N.Mex.: pop. 49,000

San·ti·a·go (sän′tē ä′gō) capital of Chile: pop. 1,169,000

São Pau·lo (soun pou′loo) city in SE Brazil: pop. 3,825,000

sap[1] (sap) *n.* [OE. *sæp*] **1.** the juice that circulates through a plant, bearing water, food, etc. **2.** vigor; energy **3.** [Slang] a fool —**sap'less** *adj.*

sap[2] (sap) *vt.* **sapped, sap'ping** [< It. *zappe*, a hoe] **1.** to dig beneath; undermine **2.** to weaken; exhaust

sa·pi·ent (sā'pē ənt) *adj.* [< L. *sapere*, to taste, know] full of knowledge; wise —**sa'pi·ence** *n.*

sap·ling (sap'liŋ) *n.* a young tree

sap·phire (saf'ir) *n.* [< Sans. *sanipriya*] a hard precious stone of a clear, deep-blue corundum

sap·py (sap'ē) *adj.* **-pi·er, -pi·est 1.** full of sap; juicy **2.** [Slang] foolish; silly —**sap'pi·ness** *n.*

sap·ro·phyte (sap'rə fīt') *n.* [< Gr. *sapros*, rotten + *phyton*, a plant] any plant that lives on dead or decaying organic matter, as some fungi

sap'suck'er *n.* a small American woodpecker that drills holes in trees and drinks the sap

Sar·a·cen (sar'ə s'n) *n.* formerly, any Arab or Moslem, esp. during the Crusades

Sar·ah (ser'ə) *Bible* the wife of Abraham and mother of Isaac

sa·ran (sə ran') *n.* [a coinage] a thermoplastic substance used in various fabrics, wrapping material, etc.

sar·casm (sär'kaz'm) *n.* [< Gr. *sarkazein*, to tear flesh] **1.** a taunting or caustic remark, generally ironical **2.** the making of such remarks —**sar·cas'tic** (-kas'tik) *adj.* —**sar·cas'ti·cal·ly** *adv.*

sar·co·ma (sär kō'mə) *n., pl.* **-mas, -ma·ta** (-mə tə) [< Gr. *sarx*, flesh] a malignant tumor in connective tissue

sar·coph·a·gus (sär käf'ə gəs) *n., pl.* **-gi'** (-jī'), **-gus·es** [< Gr. *sarx*, flesh + *phagein*, to eat: limestone coffins hastened disintegration] a stone coffin, esp. one exposed to view, as in a tomb

sar·dine (sär dēn') *n.* [< L. *sarda*, a fish] any of various small ocean fishes preserved in cans for eating

Sar·din·i·a (sär din'ē ə) It. island in the Mediterranean, south of Corsica

sar·don·ic (sär dän'ik) *adj.* [< Gr. *sardonios*, bitter] scornfully or bitterly sarcastic —**sar·don'i·cal·ly** *adv.*

sa·ri (sä'rē) *n.* [< Sans.] an outer garment of Hindu women, a long cloth wrapped around the body

sa·rong (sə rôŋ') *n.* [Malay *sārung*] a garment of men and women of the East Indies, etc., consisting of a cloth worn like a skirt

sar·sa·pa·ril·la (sas'pə ril'ə, särs'-) *n.* [< Sp. *zarza*, bramble + *parra*, vine] **1.** a tropical American vine with fragrant roots **2.** a carbonated drink flavored with the dried roots

SARI

sar·to·ri·al (sär tôr'ē əl) *adj.* [< LL.

sartor, tailor] **1.** of tailors or their work **2.** of men's dress

sash[1] (sash) *n.* [Ar. *shāsh*, muslin] an ornamental band, ribbon, etc. worn over the shoulder or around the waist

sash[2] (sash) *n.* [< Fr. *châssis*, a frame] a frame for holding the glass pane of a window or door, esp. a sliding frame

sa·shay (sa shā') *vi.* [< Fr. *chassé*, a dance step] [Colloq.] to walk or go, esp. casually

Sas·katch·e·wan (sas kach'ə wän') province of SW Canada: 251,700 sq. mi.; pop. 955,000; cap. Regina: abbrev. **Sask.**

sass (sas) *n.* [var. of SAUCE] [Colloq.] impudent talk —*vt.* [Colloq.] to talk impudently to

sas·sa·fras (sas'ə fras') *n.* [Sp. *sasafras*] **1.** a small tree having small bluish fruits **2.** its dried root bark used for flavoring

sass·y (sas'ē) *adj.* **-i·er, -i·est** [var. of SAUCY] [Colloq.] impudent; saucy

sat (sat) *pt. & pp.* of SIT

Sat. Saturday

Sa·tan (sāt'n) *n.* [< Heb. *sātān*, enemy] the Devil

sa·tan·ic (sā tan'ik, sə-) *adj.* like Satan; wicked —**sa·tan'i·cal·ly** *adv.*

satch·el (sach'əl) *n.* [< L. *saccus*, a bag] a small bag for carrying clothes, books, etc.

sate (sāt) *vt.* **sat'ed, sat'ing** [prob. < L. *satiare*, fill full] **1.** to satisfy (an appetite, etc.) completely **2.** to satiate

sa·teen (sa tēn') *n.* [< SATIN] a cotton cloth made to imitate satin

sat·el·lite (sat'l īt') *n.* [< L. *satelles*, an attendant] **1.** an attendant of some important person **2.** *a)* a small planet revolving around a larger one *b)* a man-made object put into orbit around the earth, moon, etc. **3.** a small state economically dependent on a larger one

sa·ti·ate (sā'shē āt') *vt.* **-at'ed, -at'ing** [< L. *satis*, sufficient] to provide with more than enough, so as to weary or disgust; glut

sa·ti·e·ty (sə tī'ə tē) *n.* a being satiated

sat·in (sat'n) *n.* [< Ar. *zaitūnī*, of *Zaitūn*, former name of a Chinese seaport] a fabric of silk, nylon, rayon, etc. with a smooth, glossy finish on one side —**sat'in·y** *adj.*

sat'in·wood' *n.* **1.** a smooth wood used in fine furniture **2.** any of a number of trees yielding such a wood

sat·ire (sat'īr) *n.* [< L. *satira*] **1.** a literary work in which vices, follies, etc. are held up to ridicule and contempt **2.** the use of ridicule, sarcasm, etc. to attack vices, follies, etc. — **sa·tir·i·cal** (sə tir'i k'l) *adj.* —**sat'i·rist** (-ə rist) *n.*

sat·i·rize (sat'ə rīz') *vt.* **-rized', -riz'ing** to attack with satire

sat·is·fac·tion (sat'is fak'shən) *n.* **1.** a satisfying or being satisfied **2.** something that satisfies; specif., *a)* anything that brings pleasure or contentment *b)* settlement of debt

sat·is·fac·to·ry (-tə rē) *adj.* good enough to fulfill a need, wish, etc.; satisfying —**sat·is·fac·to·ri·ly** *adv.*

sat·is·fy (sat'is fī') *vt.* **-fied', -fy'ing** [< L. *satis*, enough + *facere*, make] 1. to fulfill the needs or desires of; content 2. to fulfill the requirements of 3. to free from doubt; convince 4. *a)* to give what is due to *b)* to discharge (a debt, etc.)

sa·to·ri (sä tôr'ē) *n.* [Jap.] Buddhism spiritual enlightenment

sa·trap (sā'trap, sat'rap) *n.* [< OPer.] a petty tyrant

sat·u·rate (sach'ə rāt') *vt.* **-rat'ed, -rat'ing** [< L. *satur*, full] 1. to make thoroughly soaked 2. to cause to be filled, charged, etc. with the most it can absorb —**sat'u·ra'tion** *n.*

Sat·ur·day (sat'ər dē, -dā') *n.* [< OE. *Sæterdæg*, Saturn's day] the seventh and last day of the week

Saturday night special [from their use in weekend crimes] [Slang] any small, cheap handgun

Sat·urn (sat'ərn) 1. the Roman god of agriculture 2. the second largest planet in the solar system, with three rings revolving about it: see PLANET

sat·ur·nine (sat'ər nīn') *adj.* [< supposed influence of planet Saturn] sluggish, gloomy, grave, etc.

sat·yr (sāt'ər, sat'-) *n.* [< Gr. *satyros*] 1. *Gr. Myth.* a lecherous woodland deity, represented as a man with a goat's legs, ears, and horns 2. a lecherous man

sat·y·ri·a·sis (sat'ə rī'ə sis) *n.* [< Gr.: see prec.] uncontrollable desire by a man for sexual intercourse

sauce (sôs) *n.* [< L. *sal*, salt] 1. a liquid or soft dressing served as a relish with food 2. stewed or preserved fruit 3. [Colloq.] impudence

sauce'pan' *n.* a small metal pot with a projecting handle, used for cooking

sau·cer (sô'sər) *n.* [see SAUCE] a small, round, shallow dish, esp. one designed to hold a cup

sau·cy (sô'sē) *adj.* **-ci·er, -ci·est** [SAUC(E) + -y²] 1. rude; impudent 2. pert; sprightly —**sau'ci·ly** *adv.* —**sau'ci·ness** *n.*

Sa·u·di Arabia (sä ōō'dē) kingdom occupying most of Arabia: c.617,000 sq. mi.; pop. 6,036,000

sau·er·bra·ten (sour'brät''n, zou'ər-) *n.* [G. *sauer*, sour + *braten*, roast] beef marinated before cooking

sau·er·kraut (sour'krout') *n.* [G. *sauer*, sour + *kraut*, cabbage] chopped cabbage fermented in brine

Saul (sôl) *Bible* first king of Israel

sau·na (sou'nə, sô'-) *n.* [Finn.] a Finnish bath with exposure to hot, dry air

saun·ter (sôn'tər) *vi.* [LME. *santren*, to muse] to walk about idly; stroll —*n.* a leisurely walk

sau·sage (sô'sij) *n.* [see SAUCE] pork or other meat, chopped fine, seasoned, and often stuffed into a casing

sau·té (sō tā', sô-) *vt.* **-téed', -té'ing** [Fr. < *sauter*, to leap] to fry quickly with a little fat

sau·terne (sō turn') *n.* [< *Sauternes*, town in France] a white table wine

sav·age (sav'ij) *adj.* [< L. *silva*, a wood] 1. wild; uncultivated [a *savage* jungle] 2. fierce; untamed [a *savage* tiger] 3. primitive; barbarous 4. cruel; pitiless —*n.* 1. a member of a primitive society 2. a brutal or crude person —**sav'age·ly** *adv.* —**sav'age·ry** *n.*

Sa·van·nah (sə van'ə) seaport in SE Ga.: pop. 142,000

sa·vant (sə vänt', sav'ənt) *n.* [Fr. < *savoir*, know] a learned person

save¹ (sāv) *vt.* **saved, sav'ing** [< L. *salvus*, safe] 1. to rescue or preserve from harm or danger 2. to preserve for future use 3. to prevent loss or waste of [to *save* time] 4. to prevent or lessen [to *save* expense] 5. *Theol.* to deliver from sin —*vi.* 1. to avoid expense, waste, etc. 2. to store up money or goods —*n. Sports* an action that keeps an opponent from scoring or winning —**sav'er** *n.*

save² (sāv) *prep., conj.* [< OFr. *sauf*, safe] except; but

sav·ing (sā'viŋ) *adj.* that saves; specif., *a)* economizing or economical *b)* redeeming —*n.* 1. [often pl. with sing. v.] any reduction in expense, time, etc. 2. [pl.] sums of money saved

sav·ior, sav·iour (sāv'yər) *n.* [< LL. *salvare*, to save] one who saves —**the Saviour** (or **Savior**) Jesus Christ

sa·voir-faire (sav'wär fer') *n.* [Fr.: to know (how) to do] ready knowledge of what to do or say in any situation

sa·vor (sā'vər) *n.* [< L. *sapor*] 1. a particular taste or smell 2. distinctive quality —*vi.* to have the distinctive taste, smell, or quality (of) —*vt.* to taste with delight Brit. sp. savour

sa'vor·y *adj.* **-i·er, -i·est** 1. pleasing to the taste or smell 2. pleasant, agreeable, etc. Brit. sp. savoury

sav·vy (sav'ē) *n.* [alt. < Sp. *sabe* (usted), do (you) know?] [Slang] shrewdness or understanding

saw¹ (sô) *n.* [OE. *saga*] a cutting tool consisting of a thin metal blade or disk with sharp teeth —*vt.* to cut or shape with a saw —*vi.* 1. to cut with or as a saw 2. to be cut with a saw

saw² (sô) *n.* [OE. *sagu*] a maxim

saw³ (sô) *pt.* of SEE¹

saw'dust' *n.* fine particles of wood formed in sawing wood

sawed'-off' *adj.* short or shortened

saw'horse' *n.* a rack on which wood is placed while being sawed

saw'mill' *n.* a factory where logs are sawed into boards

saw'-toothed' *adj.* having notches along the edge like the teeth of a saw

saw·yer (sô'yər) *n.* one whose work is sawing wood

sax (saks) *n. short form of* SAXOPHONE

Sax·on (sak's'n) *n.* 1. any of an ancient Germanic people, some of whom settled in England 2. an Anglo-Saxon 3. any dialect of the Saxons

sax·o·phone (sak'sə fōn') *n.* [< A. J. *Sax*, 19th-c. Belgian inventor + -PHONE] a single-reed, keyed woodwind instrument with a metal body

say (sā) *vt.* **said, say'ing** [OE. *secgan*] 1. to utter or speak 2. to express in words; state 3. to state positively or as an opinion 4. to recite [to *say* one's prayers] 5. to estimate; assume [he is, I'd *say*, forty] —*n.* 1. a chance to speak [I had my *say*] 2. authority, as to make a final decision: often with *the* —that is to *say* in other words

say·ing *n.* something said; esp., an adage, proverb, or maxim

say'-so *n.* [Colloq.] 1. (one's) word, assurance, etc. 2. right of decision

Sb [L. *stibium*] *Chem.* antimony

S.C. *Printing* small capitals

S.C., SC South Carolina

scab (skab) *n.* [< ON. *skabb*] 1. a crust forming over a sore during healing 2. a worker who refuses to join a union, or who replaces a striking worker —*vi.* scabbed, scab'bing 1. to become covered with a scab 2. to act as a scab —scab'by *adj.* -bi·er, -bi·est —scab'bi·ness *n.*

scab·bard (skab'ərd) *n.* [< ? OHG. *scar*, sword + *bergan*, hide] a sheath for the blade of a sword, dagger, etc.

sca·bies (skā'bēz) *n.* [L., the itch] a contagious, itching skin disease caused by a mite that burrows under the skin to lay its eggs

scab·rous (skab'rəs, skāb'-) *adj.* [< L. *scabere*, to scratch] 1. scaly or scabby 2. indecent, shocking, etc.

scads (skadz) *n.pl.* [< ?] [Colloq.] a very large number or amount

scaf·fold (skaf'ld, -ōld) *n.* [< OFr. *escafalt*] 1. a temporary framework for supporting men working on a building, etc. 2. a raised platform on which criminals are executed

scaf·fold·ing *n.* 1. the materials forming a scaffold 2. a scaffold

scal·a·wag (skal'ə wag') *n.* [< ?] a scamp; rascal

scald (skôld) *vt.* [< L. *ex-*, intens. + *calidus*, hot] 1. to burn with hot liquid or steam 2. to heat almost to the boiling point 3. to use boiling liquid on —*n.* a burn caused by scalding

scale¹ (skāl) *n.* [< L. *scala*, ladder] 1. *a)* a series of marks along a line used in measuring [the *scale* of a thermometer] *b)* any instrument so marked 2. the proportion that a map, etc. bears to the thing it represents [a *scale* of one inch to a mile] 3. *a)* a series of degrees classified by size, amount, etc. [a wage *scale*] *b)* any degree in such a series 4. *Music* a sequence of tones, rising or falling in pitch, according to a system of intervals —*vt.* scaled, scal'ing 1. to climb up or over 2. to make according to a scale —scale down (or up) to reduce (or increase) according to a fixed ratio

scale² (skāl) *n.* [< OFr. *escale*, shell] 1. any of the thin, flat, horny plates covering many fishes, reptiles, etc. 2. any thin, platelike layer or piece —*vt.* scaled, scal'ing to scrape scales from —*vi.* to flake or peel off in scales —scal'y *adj.* -i·er, -i·est

scale³ (skāl) *n.* [< ON. *skal*, bowl] 1. either pan of a balance 2. [often *pl.*]

a) a balance *b)* any weighing machine —*vt.* scaled, scal'ing to weigh —turn the scales to decide or settle

sca·lene (skā lēn', skā'lēn) *adj.* [< Gr. *skalēnos*, uneven] having unequal sides [a *scalene* triangle]

scal·lion (skal'yən) *n.* [< L. (*caepa*) *Ascalonia*, (onion of) Ascalon (Philistine city)] any of various onions, as the leek or a green onion with an almost bulbless root

scal·lop (skäl'əp, skal'-) *n.* [< OFr. *escalope*] 1. *a)* any of various edible mollusks with two curved, hinged shells *b)* one of these shells 2. any of a series of curves, etc. forming an ornamental edge —*vt.* 1. to cut the edge of in scallops 2. to bake with a milk sauce and bread crumbs

SCALLOP

scalp (skalp) *n.* [< Scand.] the skin on the top and back of the head, usually covered with hair —*vt.* 1. to cut or tear the scalp from 2. [Colloq.] to buy (theater tickets, etc.) and resell them at higher prices —scalp'er *n.*

scal·pel (skal'pəl) *n.* [< L. *scalprum*, a knife] a small, sharp, straight knife used in surgery, etc.

scamp (skamp) *n.* [< It. *scampare*, flee] a mischievous fellow; rascal

scam·per (skam'pər) *vi.* [see prec.] to run or go quickly —*n.* a scampering

scam·pi (skam'pē) *n., pl.* -pi, -pies [It.] a large, greenish, edible prawn

scan (skan) *vt.* scanned, scan'ning [< L. *scandere*, climb] 1. to analyze (verse) by marking the metrical feet 2. to look at closely 3. to glance at quickly —*vi.* to conform to metrical principles: said of verse —*n.* the act or an instance of scanning

Scan., Scand. Scandinavia(n)

scan·dal (skan'd'l) *n.* [< Gr. *skandalon*, a snare] 1. anything that offends moral feelings and leads to disgrace 2. shame, outrage, etc. caused by this 3. disgrace 4. malicious gossip

scan·dal·ize' *vt.* -ized', -iz'ing to outrage the moral feelings of by improper conduct —scan'dal·iz'er *n.*

scan·dal·mon'ger (-mun'gər, -mäŋ'-) *n.* one who spreads scandal, or gossip

scan·dal·ous *adj.* 1. causing scandal; shameful 2. spreading slander —scan'dal·ous·ly *adv.*

Scan·di·na·vi·a (skan'də nā'vē ə) region including Norway, Sweden, Denmark, and, sometimes, Iceland

Scan'di·na'vi·an *adj.* of Scandinavia, its people, languages, etc. —*n.* 1. any of the people of Scandinavia 2. the subbranch of the Germanic languages spoken by them

scant (skant) *adj.* [< ON. *skammr*, short] 1. inadequate; meager 2. not quite up to full measure

scant'y *adj.* -i·er, -i·est 1. barely sufficient 2. insufficient; not enough —scant'i·ly *adv.* —scant'i·ness *n.*

scape·goat (skāp′gōt′) *n.* [< ESCAPE + GOAT: see Lev. 16:7-26] one who bears the blame for mistakes of others

scape′grace′ *n.* [< ESCAPE + GRACE] a graceless rogue; scamp

scap·u·la (skap′yoo lə) *n., pl.* **-lae′** (-lē′), **-las** [L.] the shoulder blade

scar (skär) *n.* [< Gr. *eschara*, orig., fireplace] a mark left after a wound, burn, etc. has healed —*vt.* **scarred, scar′ring** to mark as with a scar —*vi.* to form a scar in healing

scar·ab (skar′əb) *n.* [< L. *scarabaeus*] 1. a large, black beetle 2. a carved image of such a beetle

scarce (skers) *adj.* [ult. < L. *excerpere*, pick out] 1. not common; rarely seen 2. not plentiful; hard to get —**make oneself scarce** [Colloq.] to go or stay away —**scarce′ness** *n.*

scarce′ly *adv.* 1. hardly; only just 2. probably not or certainly not

scar·ci·ty (sker′sə tē) *n., pl.* **-ties** 1. a being scarce; inadequate supply; dearth 2. rarity; uncommonness

scare (sker) *vt.* **scared, scar′ing** [< ON. *skjarr*, timid] to fill with sudden fear —*vi.* to become frightened —*n.* a sudden fear —**scare away** (or **off**) to drive away (or off) by frightening —**scare up** [Colloq.] to produce or gather quickly

scare′crow′ *n.* a human figure made with sticks, old clothes, etc., put in a field to scare birds from crops

scarf (skärf) *n., pl.* **scarfs, scarves** (skärvz) [< OFr. *escharpe*, purse hung from the neck] 1. a piece of cloth worn about the neck, head, etc. 2. a long, narrow covering for a table, etc.

scar·i·fy (skar′ə fī′) *vt.* **-fied′, -fy′ing** [< L. *scarifare*] to make small cuts in (the skin, etc.) —**scar′i·fi·ca′tion** *n.*

scar·let (skär′lit) *n.* [< ML. *scarlatum*] very bright red —*adj.* 1. of this color 2. sinful; specif., whorish

scarlet fever an acute contagious disease characterized by sore throat, fever, and a scarlet rash

scar·y (sker′ē) *adj.* **-i·er, -i·est** [Colloq.] 1. frightening 2. easily frightened —**scar′i·ness** *n.*

scat¹ (skat) *vi.* **scat′ted, scat′ting** [? a hiss + CAT] [Colloq.] to go away: usually in the imperative

scat² (skat) *adj.* [< ?] *Jazz* using improvised, meaningless syllables in singing —*n.* such singing —*vi.* **scat′ted, scat′ting** to sing scat

scath·ing (skā′thiŋ) *adj.* [< ON. *skathi*, harm] harsh or caustic [*scathing* words] —**scath′ing·ly** *adv.*

sca·tol·o·gy (skə täl′ə jē) *n.* [< Gr. *skōr*, excrement + -LOGY] obsession with excrement or excretion, as in literature —**scat′o·log′i·cal** *adj.*

scat·ter (skat′ər) *vt.* [ME. *skateren*] 1. to throw here and there; sprinkle 2. to separate and drive in many directions; disperse —*vi.* to separate and go off in several directions

scat′ter·brain′ *n.* one who is incapable of concentrated thinking

scatter rug a small rug

scav·eng·er (skav′in jər) *n.* [< ONormFr. *escauwer*, inspect] 1. one

who gathers things discarded by others 2. any animal that eats refuse and decaying matter —**scav′enge** (-inj) *vt., vi.* **-enged, -eng·ing**

sce·nar·i·o (si ner′ē ō′) *n., pl.* **-os′** [see ff.] 1. the working script of a motion picture, television play, etc. 2. an outline for any planned series of events, real or imagined —**sce·nar′·ist** *n.*

scene (sēn) *n.* [< Gr. *skēnē*, stage] 1. the place where an event occurs 2. the setting of a play, story, etc. 3. a division of a play, usually part of an act 4. a unit of action in a motion picture, story, etc. 5. *same as* SCENERY (sense 1) 6. a view of people or places 7. a display of strong feeling [to make a *scene*] 8. [Colloq.] the locale for a specified activity

scen·er·y (sē′nər ē) *n.* 1. painted screens, backdrops, etc. used on the stage to represent places, as in a play 2. the features of a landscape

sce·nic (sē′nik) *adj.* 1. of stage scenery 2. *a)* of natural scenery *b)* having beautiful scenery —**sce′ni·cal·ly** *adv.*

scent (sent) *vt.* [< L. *sentire*, to feel] 1. to smell 2. to get a hint of 3. to fill with an odor; perfume —*n.* 1. an odor 2. the sense of smell 3. a perfume 4. an odor left by an animal, by which it is tracked —**scent′ed** *adj.*

scep·ter (sep′tər) *n.* [< Gr. *skēptron*, staff] a staff held by a ruler as a symbol of sovereignty: chiefly Brit. sp. **sceptre**

scep·tic (skep′tik) *n., adj. chiefly Brit. sp.* of SKEPTIC —**scep′ti·cal** *adj.* —**scep′ti·cism** *n.*

sched·ule (skej′ool; *Brit.* shed′yool) *n.* [< L. *scheda*, strip of papyrus] 1. a list of details 2. a list of times of recurring events, projected operations, etc.; timetable 3. a timed plan for a project —*vt.* **-uled, -ul·ing** 1. to place in a schedule 2. to plan for a certain time

Scheduled Castes the groups of people in India formerly untouchables

sche·mat·ic (skē mat′ik) *adj.* of or like a scheme, diagram, etc.

scheme (skēm) *n.* [< Gr. *schēma*, a form] 1. *a)* a systematic program for attaining some object *b)* a secret plan; plot 2. an orderly combination of things on a definite plan 3. a diagram —*vt., vi.* **schemed, schem′ing** to devise or plot —**schem′er** *n.*

scher·zo (sker′tsō) *n., pl.* **-zos, -zi** (-tsē) [It., a jest] a lively movement, as of a symphony, in 3/4 time

schism (siz′m) *n.* [< Gr. *schizein*, cleave] a split, as in a church, because of difference of opinion, doctrine, etc. —**schis·mat′ic** (-mat′ik) *adj.*

schist (shist) *n.* [< Gr. *schistos*, easily cleft] a crystalline rock easily split into layers

schiz·o·phre·ni·a (skit′sə frē′nē ə) *n.* [< Gr. *schizein*, cleave + *phrēn*, mind] a mental disorder characterized by separation between thought and emotions, by delusions, bizarre behavior, etc. —**schiz′oid** (-soid), **schiz′o·phren′ic** (-fren′ik) *adj., n.*

schle·miel (shlə mēl′) *n.* [Yid.] [Slang] a bungling person who habitually fails or is easily victimized

schlep, schlepp (shlep) *n.* [via Yid. < G. *schleppen*, to drag] [Slang] an ineffectual person

schlock (shläk) *n.* [via Yid. < G. *schlacke*, dregs] [Slang] anything cheap or inferior; trash —*adj.* [Slang] cheap; inferior

schmaltz (shmälts) *n.* [via Yid. < G. *schmalz*, rendered fat] [Slang] highly sentimental music, literature, etc.

schmo (shmō) *n., pl.* **schmoes, schmos** [< Yid.] [Slang] a foolish or stupid person: also sp. **schmoe**

schnapps (shnäps) *n., pl.* **schnapps** [G., a nip < Du. *snaps*, a gulp] strong alcoholic liquor: also sp. **schnaps**

schnau·zer (shnou′zər) *n.* [G. < *schnauzen*, to snarl] a small terrier with a wiry coat

schnoz·zle (shnäz′'l) *n.* [via Yid. < G. *schnauze*] [Slang] the nose: also **schnoz**

schol·ar (skäl′ər) *n.* [< L. *schola*, a school] 1. a learned person 2. a student or pupil —**schol′ar·ly** *adj.*

schol·ar·ship′ *n.* 1. the quality of knowledge a student shows 2. the systematized knowledge of a scholar 3. a gift of money, etc. to help a student

scho·las·tic (skə las′tik) *adj.* [see ff.] of schools, colleges, students, etc.; educational; academic

school[1] (skōōl) *n.* [< Gr. *scholē*] 1. a place or institution, with its buildings, etc., for teaching and learning 2. all of its students and teachers 3. a regular session of teaching 4. formal education; schooling 5. a particular division of a university 6. a group following the same beliefs, methods, etc. —*vt.* 1. to train; teach 2. to discipline or control —*adj.* of a school or schools

school[2] (skōōl) *n.* [Du., a crowd] a group of fish, etc. swimming together

school board a group of people in charge of local public schools

school′book′ *n.* a textbook

school′boy′ *n.* a boy attending school —**school′girl′** *n.fem.*

school′house′ *n.* a building used as a school

school′ing *n.* training or education; esp., formal instruction at school

school′marm′ (-märm′, -mäm′) *n.* [Colloq.] a woman schoolteacher, hence any person, who tends to be prudish and pedantic: also **school′ma'am′** (-mäm′, -mam′)

school′mas′ter *n.* a man who teaches in a school: an old-fashioned term — **school′mis′tress** *n.fem.*

school′mate′ *n.* a person going to the same school at the same time as another: also **school′fel′low**

school′room′ *n.* a room in which pupils are taught, as in a school

school′teach′er *n.* one who teaches in a school

school′yard′ *n.* the ground about a school, used as a playground, etc.

school year the part of a year when school is in session

schoon·er (skōō′nər) *n.* [< ?] 1. a ship with two or more masts, rigged fore and aft 2. a large beer glass

Schu·bert (shōō′bərt), **Franz** (fränts) 1797–1828; Austrian composer

schuss (shoos) *n.* [G., lit., shot] *Skiing* a straight, fast run downhill —*vi.* to do a schuss

schuss′boom′er (-bōōm′ər) *n.* a skier, esp. one who schusses expertly

schwa (shwä) *n.* [G. < Heb. *sh'wā*] 1. the neutral vowel sound of most unstressed syllables in English, as of *a* in *ago* 2. the symbol (ə) for this

sci·at·ic (sī at′ik) *adj.* [see ff.] of or in the hip or its nerves

sci·at·i·ca (sī at′i kə) *n.* [< Gr. *ischion*, hip] any painful condition in the hip or thighs; esp., neuritis of the long nerve (**sciatic nerve**) down the back of the thigh

sci·ence (sī′əns) *n.* [< L. *scire*, know] 1. systematized knowledge derived from observation, study, etc. 2. a branch of knowledge, esp. one that systematizes facts, principles, and methods 3. skill or technique

science fiction highly imaginative fiction typically involving some actual or projected scientific phenomenon

sci·en·tif·ic (sī′ən tif′ik) *adj.* 1. of or dealing with science 2. based on, or using, the principles and methods of science; systematic and exact —**sci′en·tif′i·cal·ly** *adv.*

sci′en·tist *n.* a specialist in science, as in biology, chemistry, etc.

sci-fi (sī′fī′) *adj., n. clipped form of* SCIENCE FICTION

scim·i·tar, scim·i·ter (sim′ə tər) *n.* [It. *scimitarra*] a short, curved sword used by Turks, Arabs, etc.

scin·til·la (sin til′ə) *n.* [L.] 1. a spark 2. a particle; the least trace

scin·til·late (sin′t'l āt′) *vi.* -lat′ed, -lat′ing [< L. *scintilla*, a spark] 1. to sparkle or twinkle 2. to be brilliant and witty —**scin′til·la′tion** *n.*

sci·on (sī′ən) *n.* [< OFr. *cion*] 1. a shoot or bud of a plant, esp. one for grafting 2. a descendant; heir

scis·sor (siz′ər) *vt.* [< ff.] to cut, cut off, or cut out with scissors —*n. same as* SCISSORS, esp. in adjectival use

scis·sors (siz′ərz) *n.pl.* [< LL. *cisorium*, cutting tool] [also with sing. v.] a cutting instrument with two opposing blades pivoted together so that they can work against each other: also **pair of scissors**

scle·ro·sis (skli rō′sis) *n., pl.* -ses (-sēz) [< Gr. *sklēros*, hard] an abnormal hardening of body tissues — **scle·rot′ic** (-rät′ik) *adj.*

scoff (skôf, skäf) *n.* [prob. < Scand.] an expression of scorn or derision — *vt., vi.* to mock or jeer (at) —**scoff′er** *n.*

scoff'law' *n.* [Colloq.] one who flouts traffic laws, liquor laws, etc.

scold (skōld) *n.* [< ON. *skald,* poet (prob. because of satirical verses)] a woman who habitually uses abusive language with ill fault with angrily; rebuke —*vi.* 1. to find fault angrily 2. to use abusive language — **scold'ing** *adj., n.*

scol·lop (skäl'əp) *n., vt.* var. of SCALLOP

sconce (skäns) *n.* [ult. < L. *absconsus,* hidden] a wall bracket for candles

scone (skōn) *n.* [Scot.] a biscuit, often quadrant-shaped and sweetened

scoop (skoop) *n.* [< MDu. *schope,* bucket, *schoppe,* a shovel] 1. any of various small, shovellike utensils, as for taking up flour, ice cream, etc. 2. the deep bucket of a dredge, etc. 3. the act or motion of scooping 4. the amount scooped up at one time 5. [Colloq.] *a)* advantage gained by being first, as in publishing a news item *b)* such a news item —*vt.* 1. to take up or out as with a scoop 2. to hollow (*out*) 3. [Colloq.] to publish news before (a rival)

scoot (skoot) *vi., vt.* [prob. < ON. *skjóta,* to shoot] [Colloq.] to hurry (off)

scoot'er *n.* 1. a child's two-wheeled vehicle moved by pushing one foot against the ground 2. a similar vehicle propelled by a motor: in full motor scooter

scope (skōp) *n.* [< Gr. *skopos,* watcher] 1. the extent of the mind's grasp 2. range or extent of action, inquiry, inclusion, etc. 3. room or opportunity for freedom of action or thought

-scope (skōp) [< Gr. *skopein,* to see] *a combining form meaning* an instrument, etc. for observing [*telescope*]

scor·bu·tic (skôr byoot'ik) *adj.* [< ModL. < Russ. *skorbnut,* wither] of, like, or having scurvy

scorch (skôrch) *vt.* [< ? Scand.] 1. to burn slightly or superficially 2. to parch by intense heat —*vi.* to become scorched —*n.* a superficial burn

score (skôr) *n.* [< ON. *skor*] 1. a scratch, mark, notch, incision, etc. 2. an account or debt 3. a grievance one seeks to settle 4. a reason or motive 5. the number of points made, as in a game 6. a grade, as on a test 7. *a)* twenty people or things *b)* [*pl.*] very many 8. a copy of a musical composition, showing all parts for the instruments or voices 9. [Colloq.] the real facts (*to know the score*) —*vt.* scored, scor'ing 1. to mark with cuts, lines, etc. 2. *a)* to make (runs, points, etc.) in a game *b)* to record the score of 3. to achieve [*score* a success] 4. to evaluate, as in testing 5. *Music* to arrange in a score —*vi.* 1. to make points, as in a game 2. to keep the score of a game 3. to gain an advantage, a success, etc. —**scor'er** *n.*

score'board' *n.* a large board posting scores, etc., as in a stadium

score'less *adj.* having scored no points

scorn (skôrn) *n.* [< OFr. *escharnir,* to scorn] extreme, often indignant, contempt —*vt.* 1. to regard with scorn 2. to refuse or reject with scorn —**scorn'ful** *adj.* —**scorn'ful·ly** *adv.*

Scor·pi·o (skôr'pē ō') [L., scorpion] the eighth sign of the zodiac

scor'pi·on (-ən) *n.* [< Gr. *skorpios*] an arachnid with a long tail ending in a poisonous sting

Scot (skät) *n.* a native or inhabitant of Scotland

Scot. 1. Scotland 2. Scottish

Scotch (skäch) *adj.* Scottish —*n.* 1. Scottish 2. *same as* SCOTCH WHISKY

scotch (skäch) *vt.* [prob. < OFr. *coche,* a nick] 1. to maim 2. to put an end to; stifle [*to scotch* a rumor]

Scotch grain a coarse, pebble-grained finish given to heavy leather

Scotch'man (-mən) *n., pl.* **-men** *var.* of SCOTSMAN

Scotch tape [< *Scotch,* a trademark] a thin, transparent adhesive tape

Scotch whisky whisky distilled in Scotland from malted barley

scot-free (skät'frē') *adj.* [< earlier *scot,* a tax] unharmed or unpunished

Scot·land (skät'lənd) division of the United Kingdom, north of England: 30,405 sq. mi.; pop. 5,187,000

Scotland Yard the London police headquarters, esp. its detective bureau

Scots (skäts) *adj., n.* Scottish

Scots'man (-mən) *n., pl.* **-men** a native or inhabitant of Scotland: *Scotsman* or *Scot* is preferred to *Scotchman* in Scotland

Scot·tie, Scot·ty (skät'ē) *n., pl.* **-ties** [Colloq.] *same as* SCOTTISH TERRIER

Scot·tish (skät'ish) *adj.* of Scotland, its people, their English dialect, etc.: *Scottish* is formal usage, but with some words, *Scotch* is used (e.g., tweed, whisky), with others, *Scots* (e.g., law) —*n.* the English spoken in Scotland — **the Scottish** the Scottish people

Scottish (or Scotch) terrier a short-legged terrier with wiry hair

scoun·drel (skoun'drəl) *n.* [prob. ult. < L. *ab(s)-,* from + *condere,* to hide] a mean, immoral, or wicked person

scour¹ (skour) *vt., vi.* [< ? L. *ex-,* intens. + *cura,* care] 1. to clean by rubbing hard, as with abrasives 2. to clean or clear out as by a flow of water

scour² (skour) *vt.* [< L. *ex-,* out + *currere,* to run] to pass over quickly, or range over, as in search [*to scour* a library for a book]

scourge (skurj) *n.* [< L. *ex,* off + *corrigia,* a whip] 1. a whip 2. any cause of serious affliction —*vt.* scourged, scourg'ing 1. to whip or flog 2. to punish or afflict severely

scout (skout) *n.* [< L. *auscultare,* listen] 1. a person, plane, etc. sent to spy out the enemy's strength, actions, etc. 2. a person sent out to survey a competitor, find new talent, etc. 3. a Boy Scout or Girl Scout —*vt., vi.* 1. to reconnoiter 2. to go in search of (something)

scout'ing *n.* 1. the act of one who scouts 2. the activities of the Boy Scouts or Girl Scouts

scout'mas'ter *n.* the adult leader of a troop of Boy Scouts

scow (skou) *n.* [Du. *schouw*] a large, flat-bottomed boat used for carrying loads, often towed by a tug

scowl (skoul) *vi.* [prob. < Scand.] to look angry, sullen, etc., as by contracting the eyebrows —*n.* a scowling look —**scowl′er** *n.*

scrab·ble (skrab′'l) *vi.* **-bled, -bling** [< Du. *schrabben*, to scrape] 1. to scratch, scrape, etc. as though looking for something 2. to struggle

scrag·gly (skrag′lē) *adj.* **-gli·er, -gli·est** [prob. < ON.] uneven, ragged, etc. in growth or form

scram (skram) *vi.* **scrammed, scram′ming** [< ff.] [Slang] to get out

scram·ble (skram′b'l) *vi.* **-bled, -bling** [< ?] 1. to climb, crawl, etc. hurriedly 2. to scuffle or struggle for something —*vt.* 1. to mix haphazardly 2. to stir and cook (slightly beaten eggs) 3. to make (transmitted signals) unintelligible in transit —*n.* 1. a hard climb or advance 2. a disorderly struggle, as for something prized

Scran·ton (skrant′'n) city in NE Pa.: pop. 88,000

scrap[1] (skrap) *n.* [< ON. *skrap*] 1. a small piece; fragment 2. discarded material 3. [*pl.*] bits of food —*adj.* 1. in the form of pieces leftovers, etc. 2. used and discarded —*vt.* **scrapped, scrap′ping** 1. to make into scraps 2. to discard; junk —**scrap′per** *n.*

scrap[2] (skrap) *n., vi.* **scrapped, scrap′ping** [< ?] [Colloq.] fight or quarrel —**scrap′per** *n.* —**scrap′py** *adj.* **-i·er, -i·est** —**scrap′pi·ness** *n.*

scrap′book′ *n.* a book in which to mount clippings, pictures, etc.

scrape (skrāp) *vt.* **scraped, scrap′ing** [< ON. *skrapa*] 1. to make smooth or clean by rubbing with a tool or abrasive 2. to remove in this way (with *off, out,* etc.) 3. to scratch or abrade 4. to gather slowly and with difficulty [to *scrape* up some money] —*vi.* 1. to rub against something harshly; grate 2. to manage to get by (with *through, along, by*) —*n.* 1. a scraping 2. a scraped place 3. a harsh, grating sound 4. a predicament —**scrap′er** *n.*

scrap′heap′ *n.* (-hēp′) *n.* a pile of discarded material or things —**throw (or toss, cast,** etc.) **on the scrapheap** to get rid of as useless

scratch (skrach) *vt.* [LME. *scracchen*] 1. to scrape or cut the surface of slightly 2. to tear or dig with the nails or claws 3. to scrape lightly to relieve itching 4. to scrape with a grating noise 5. to write hurriedly or carelessly 6. to strike out (writing, etc.) 7. *Sports* to withdraw (a contestant, etc.) —*vi.* 1. to use nails or claws in digging, wounding, etc. 2. to scrape —*n.* 1. a scratching 2. a mark, tear, etc. made by scratching 3. a grating or scraping sound —*adj.* used for hasty notes, figuring, etc. [*scratch* paper] —**from scratch** from nothing; without advantage —**up to scratch** [Colloq.]

up to standard —**scratch′y** *adj.* **-i·er, -i·est** —**scratch′i·ly** *adv.* —**scratch′i·ness** *n.*

scrawl (skrôl) *vt., vi.* [< ?] to write or draw hastily, carelessly, etc. —*n.* sprawling, often illegible handwriting

scraw·ny (skrô′nē) *adj.* **-ni·er, -ni·est** [prob. < Scand.] very thin —**scrawn′i·ness** *n.*

scream (skrēm) *vi.* [ME. *screamen*] 1. to utter a shrill, piercing cry in fright, pain, etc. 2. to shout, laugh, etc. wildly —*vt.* to utter as with a scream —*n.* 1. a sharp, piercing cry or sound 2. [Colloq.] a very funny person or thing

screech (skrēch) *vi., vt.* [< ON. *skraekja*] to utter (with) a shrill, high-pitched sound —*n.* such a sound —**screech′y** *adj.* **-i·er, -i·est**

screen (skrēn) *n.* [< OFr. *escren*] 1. a curtain or partition used to separate, conceal, etc. 2. anything that shields, conceals, etc. [a smoke *screen*] 3. a coarse mesh of wire, etc., used as a sieve 4. a frame covered with a mesh [a window *screen*] 5. a surface on which motion pictures, etc. are projected 6. the motion-picture industry —*vt.* 1. to conceal or protect, as with a screen 2. to sift through a screen 3. to separate according to skills, etc. 4. to show (a motion picture, etc.) on a screen

screen′play′ *n.* a story written in a form suitable for a motion picture

screw (skrōō) *n.* [< MFr. *escroue*, hole in which a screw turns] 1. a cylindrical or conical metal piece threaded in an advancing spiral, for fastening things by being turned 2. any spiral thing like this 3. anything operating or threaded like a screw, as a screw propeller —*vt.* 1. to twist; turn 2. to fasten, tighten, etc. as with a screw 3. to contort —*vi.* 1. to go together or come apart by being turned like a screw [the lid *screws* on] 2. to twist or turn —**put the screws on (or to)** to subject to great pressure —**screw up** [Slang] to bungle

screw′ball′ *n.* [Slang] an erratic, irrational, or unconventional person

screw′driv′er *n.* a tool used for turning screws

screw′y *adj.* **-i·er, -i·est** [Slang] 1. crazy 2. peculiar; eccentric

scrib·ble (skrib′'l) *vt., vi.* **-bled, -bling** [< L. *scribere*, write] 1. to write carelessly, hastily, etc. 2. to make meaningless or illegible marks (on) —*n.* scribbled writing

scribe (skrīb) *n.* [< L. *scribere*, write] 1. one who copied manuscripts before the invention of printing 2. a writer

scrim (skrim) *n.* [< ?] 1. a light, sheer, loosely woven cotton or linen cloth 2. such a cloth used as a stage backdrop or semitransparent curtain

scrim·mage (skrim′ij) *n.* [< SKIRMISH] *Football* 1. the play that follows the pass from center 2. a practice game —*vi.* **-maged, -mag·ing** to take part in a scrimmage —**line of scrimmage** *Football* an imaginary line along which the teams line up for play

scrimp (skrimp) *vt., vi.* [< ? Scand.] to be sparing or frugal (with)

scrip (skrip) *n.* [< ff.] a certificate of a right to receive something, as money

script (skript) *n.* [< L. *scribere,* write] 1. handwriting 2. a copy of the text of a play, film, etc.

Scrip·ture (skrip'chər) *n.* [see prec.] 1. [*often pl.*] *a)* the Jewish Bible: see OLD TESTAMENT *b)* the Christian Bible; Old and New Testaments 2. [s-] any sacred writing —**scrip'tur·al** *adj.*

scrod (skräd) *n.* [prob. < MDu. *schrode,* strip] a young codfish or haddock, esp. one filleted for cooking

scrof·u·la (skräf'yə lə) *n.* [< L. *scrofa,* a sow] tuberculosis of the lymphatic glands, esp. of the neck —**scrof'u·lous** *adj.*

scroll (skrōl) *n.* [< ME. *scrowe*] 1. a roll of parchment, paper, etc. usually with writing on it 2. an ornamental design in coiled or spiral form —*vi.* to move lines of text, etc. vertically on a video screen

SCROLL

scro·tum (skrōt'əm) *n., pl.* -**ta** (-ə), -**tums** [L.] the pouch of skin containing the testicles

scrounge (skrounj) *vt.* scrounged, scroung'ing [< ?][Colloq.] 1. to get by begging or sponging 2. to pilfer —*vi.* [Colloq.] to seek (around) for something —**scroung'er** *n.*

scrub[1] (skrub) *n.* [ME., var. of *shrubbe,* shrub] 1. a thick growth of stunted trees or bushes 2. any person or thing smaller than the usual, or inferior 3. *Sports* a substitute player —*adj.* small, stunted, inferior, etc. —**scrub'by** *adj.* -**bi·er,** -**bi·est**

scrub[2] (skrub) *vt., vi.* scrubbed, scrub'bing [prob. < Scand.] 1. to clean or wash by rubbing hard 2. to rub hard —*n.* a scrubbing

scrub'wom'an *n., pl.* -**wom'en** a woman who does cleaning, as in offices

scruff (skruf) *n.* [< ON. *skruf,* a tuft] the nape of the neck

scruff·y (skruf'ē) *adj.* -**i·er,** -**i·est** [< SCURF + -Y[2]] shabby; unkempt

scrump·tious (skrump'shəs) *adj.* [< SUMPTUOUS][Colloq.] very pleasing, esp. to the taste

scrunch (skrunch) *vt., vi.* [< CRUNCH] 1. to crunch, crush, etc. 2. to huddle, squeeze, etc. —*n.* a crunching or crumpling sound

scru·ple (skrōō'p'l) *n.* [< L. *scrupulus,* small stone] 1. a very small quantity 2. a doubt arising from difficulty in deciding what is right, proper, etc. —*vt., vi.* -**pled,** -**pling** to hesitate (at) from doubt

scru'pu·lous (-pyə ləs) *adj.* 1. having or showing scruples; conscientiously honest 2. careful of details; precise —**scru'pu·los'i·ty** (-läs'ə tē) *n.* —**scru'pu·lous·ly** *adv.*

scru·ti·nize (skrōōt''n īz') *vt.* -**nized',** -**niz'ing** to examine closely

scru·ti·ny (-'n ē) *n., pl.* -**nies** [< L. *scrutari,* examine] 1. a close examination or watch 2. a lengthy, searching look

scu·ba (skōō'bə) *n.* [s(*elf-*)c(*ontained*) u(*nderwater*) b(*reathing*) a(*pparatus*)] a diver's equipment with compressed-air tanks for breathing under water

scud (skud) *vi.* scud'ded, scud'ding [prob. < ON.] 1. to move swiftly 2. to be driven before the wind —*n.* 1. a scudding 2. clouds, etc. driven by wind

scuff (skuf) *vt., vi.* [prob. < ON. *skufa,* to shove] 1. to wear or get a rough place on the surface (of) 2. to drag (the feet) —*n.* 1. a worn or rough spot 2. a flat-heeled house slipper with no back upper part

scuf·fle (skuf''l) *vi.* -**fled,** -**fling** [< prec.] 1. to struggle or fight in rough confusion 2. to drag the feet —*n.* 1. a confused fight 2. a shuffling of feet

scull (skul) *n.* [ME. *skulle*] 1. an oar worked from side to side over the stern of a boat 2. a light rowboat for racing —*vt., vi.* to propel with a scull

scul·ler·y (skul'ər ē) *n., pl.* -**ies** [< L. *scutella,* tray] a room where the kitchen utensils, etc. are cleaned

scul·lion (skul'yən) *n.* [ult. < L. *scopa,* a broom] [Archaic] a servant doing rough kitchen work

sculpt *vt., vi.* same as SCULPTURE

sculp·tor (skulp'tər) *n.* an artist who creates works of sculpture

sculp·ture (skulp'chər) *n.* [< L. *sculpere,* carve] 1. the art of forming stone, clay, wood, etc. into statues, figures, etc. 2. a work or works of sculpture —*vt., vi.* -**tured,** -**tur·ing** 1. to cut, carve, chisel, etc. (statues, figures, etc.) 2. to make or form like sculpture —**sculp'tur·al** *adj.*

scum (skum) *n.* [< MDu. *schum*] 1. a thin layer of impurities on the top of a liquid 2. refuse 3. despicable people —*vi.* scummed, scum'ming to become covered with scum —**scum'my** *adj.* -**mi·er,** -**mi·est**

scup·per (skup'ər) *n.* [< ?] an opening in a ship's side to let water run off the deck

scurf (skurf) *n.* [< ON.] 1. little, dry scales shed by the skin, as dandruff 2. any scaly coating —**scurf'y** *adj.*

scur·ri·lous (skur'ə ləs) *adj.* [< L. *scurra,* buffoon] vulgarly abusive —**scur·ril·i·ty** (skə ril'ə tē) *n., pl.* -**ties** —**scur'ril·ous·ly** *adv.*

scur·ry (skur'ē) *vi.* -**ried,** -**ry·ing** [< ?] to scamper —*n.* a scampering

scur·vy (skur'vē) *adj.* -**vi·er,** -**vi·est** [< SCURF] low; mean —*n.* a disease resulting from a vitamin C deficiency, characterized by weakness, anemia, spongy gums, etc. —**scur'vi·ly** *adv.*

scutch·eon (skuch'ən) *n.* same as ESCUTCHEON

scut·tle[1] (skut''l) *n.* [< L. *scutella,* a salver] a bucket for carrying coal

scut·tle[2] (skut''l) *vi.* -**tled,** -**tling** [ME. *scutlen*] to scamper —*n.* a scamper

scut·tle[3] (skut''l) *n.* [< Sp. *escotilla*]

an indentation] an opening fitted with a cover, as in the hull or deck of a ship —*vt.* -tled, -tling to cut holes through the lower hull of (a ship) to sink it

scut'tle·butt' (-but') *n.* [< *scuttled butt*, lidded cask] 1. a drinking fountain on shipboard 2. [Colloq.] rumor

scuz·zy (skuz'ē) *adj.* -zi·er, -zi·est [Slang] dirty, shabby, etc.

scythe (sīth) *n.* [OE. *sithe*] a tool with a long, single-edged blade on a long, curved handle, for cutting grass, etc.

S.Dak., SD South Dakota

SE, S.E., s.e. southeast(ern)

sea (sē) *n.* [OE. *sæ*] 1. the ocean 2. any of various smaller bodies of salt water [the Red *Sea*] 3. a large body of fresh water [*Sea* of Galilee] 4. the state of the surface of the ocean [a calm *sea*] 5. a heavy wave 6. a very great amount —at sea 1. on the open sea 2. uncertain; bewildered

sea anemone a sea polyp with a gelatinous body and petallike tentacles

sea'board' *n.* land bordering on the sea —*adj.* bordering on the sea

sea'coast' *n.* land along the sea

sea'far'er (-fer'ər) *n.* a sea traveler; esp., a sailor —**sea'far'ing** *adj.*, *n.*

sea'food' *n.* food prepared from or consisting of saltwater fish or shellfish

sea'go'ing *adj.* 1. made for use on the open sea 2. same as SEAFARING

sea gull same as GULL

sea horse a small, semitropical, plated fish with a head somewhat like that of a horse

seal¹ (sēl) *n.* [< L. *sigillum*] 1. a) a design or initial impressed, often over wax, on a letter or document as a mark of authenticity b) a stamp or ring for making such an impression 2. a piece of paper, etc. bearing an impressed design recognized as official 3. something that seals or closes tightly 4. anything that guarantees; pledge 5. an ornamental paper stamp [Easter *seals*] —*vt.* 1. to mark with a seal, as to authenticate or certify 2. to close or shut tight as with a seal 3. to confirm the truth of (a promise, etc.) 4. to decide finally

SEA HORSE

seal² (sēl) *n.* [OE. *seolh*] 1. a sea mammal with a torpedo-shaped body and four flippers 2. the fur of some seals —*vi.* to hunt seals —**seal'er** *n.*

Sea·lab (sē'lab') *n.* any of a series of U.S. Navy undersea laboratories for research in oceanography

seal'ant (-ənt) *n.* a substance, as a wax, plastic, etc., used for sealing

sea legs the ability to walk without loss of balance on board ship

sea level the mean level of the sea's surface: used in measuring heights

sea lion a seal of the North Pacific

seal'skin' *n.* 1. the skin of the seal 2. a garment made of this

seam (sēm) *n.* [OE.] 1. a line formed by sewing together two pieces of material 2. a line that marks joining edges 3. a mark like this, as a scar or wrinkle 4. a stratum of ore, coal, etc. —*vt.* 1. to join together so as to form a seam 2. to mark with a seamlike line, etc. —**seam'less** *adj.*

sea·man (sē'mən) *n.*, *pl.* -men 1. a sailor 2. an enlisted man ranking below a petty officer in the navy —**sea'man·ship'** *n.*

seam·stress (sēm'stris) *n.* a woman whose occupation is sewing

seam'y *adj.* -i·er, -i·est unpleasant or sordid [the *seamy* side of life]

sé·ance (sā'äns) *n.* [Fr. < L. *sedere*, sit] a meeting at which spiritualists try to communicate with the dead

sea'plane' *n.* an airplane designed to land on or take off from water

sea'port' *n.* a port or harbor used by ocean ships

sear (sir) *vt.* [OE.] 1. to wither 2. to burn the surface of 3. to brand

search (surch) *vt.* [< L. *circare*, go about] 1. to look through in order to find something 2. to examine (a person) for something concealed 3. to examine carefully; probe —*vi.* to make a search —*n.* a searching —in search of making a search for —**search'er** *n.*

search'ing *adj.* 1. examining thoroughly 2. piercing; penetrating

search'light' *n.* 1. an apparatus on a swivel that projects a strong beam of light 2. the beam of light

search warrant a legal document authorizing a police search

sea'scape' (-skāp') *n.* [SEA + (LAND)-SCAPE] 1. a sea view 2. a drawing, painting, etc. of this

sea'shell' *n.* a saltwater mollusk shell

sea'shore' *n.* land along the sea

sea'sick'ness *n.* nausea, dizziness, etc. caused by the rolling of a ship at sea —**sea'sick'** *adj.*

sea'side' *n.* same as SEASHORE

sea·son (sē'z'n) *n.* [< VL. *satio*, sowing time] 1. any of the four divisions of the year; spring, summer, fall, or winter 2. the time when something takes place, is popular, permitted, etc. 3. the fitting time —*vt.* 1. to make (food) more tasty by adding salt, spices, etc. 2. to add zest to 3. to make more usable, as by aging 4. to make used to; accustom —*vi.* to become seasoned

sea'son·a·ble *adj.* 1. suitable to the season 2. opportune; timely

sea'son·al *adj.* of or depending on the season —**sea'son·al·ly** *adv.*

sea'son·ing *n.* anything that adds zest; esp., salt, etc. added to food

season ticket a ticket or set of tickets, as for a series of concerts, baseball games, etc.

seat (sēt) *n.* [ON. *sæti*] 1. a) a place to sit b) a thing to sit on; chair, etc. 2. a) the buttocks b) the part of a chair, garment, etc. that one sits on

3. the right to sit as a member [a seat on the council] 4. the chief location, or center [the seat of government] —vt. 1. to set in or on a seat 2. to have seats for [the car seats six] —be seated 1. to sit down 2. to be sitting 3. to be located or settled

seat belt anchored straps that buckle across the hips to protect a seated passenger from an abrupt jolt

Se·at·tle (sē at'l) seaport in WC Wash.: pop. 494,000

sea urchin a small sea animal with a round body in a shell covered with sharp spines

sea'ward (-wərd) adj., adv. toward the sea: also **sea'wards** adv.

sea'way' n. an inland waterway to the sea for oceangoing ships

sea'weed' n. a sea plant, esp. an alga

sea'wor'thy (-wur'thē) adj. fit for travel on the sea: said of a ship

se·ba·ceous (si bā'shəs) adj. [< L. sebum, tallow] of, like, or secreting fat, etc. [sebaceous glands]

SEC, S.E.C. Securities and Exchange Commission

sec. 1. second(s) 2. secretary 3. section(s)

se·cede (si sēd') vi. -ced'ed, -ced'ing [< L. se-, apart + cedere, to go] to withdraw formally from a group, federation, organization, etc.

se·ces·sion (si sesh'ən) n. a seceding, specif. [often S-] by the Southern States from the Federal Union (1860–61) —**se·ces'sion·ist** n.

se·clude (si klōōd') vt. -clud'ed, -clud'ing [< L. se-, apart + claudere, shut] to shut off from others; isolate

se·clu·sion (si klōō'zhən) n. a secluding or being secluded; retirement; isolation —**se·clu'sive** adj.

sec·ond¹ (sek'ənd) adj. [< L. sequi, follow] 1. coming next after the first; 2d or 2nd 2. another of the same kind; other [a second chance] 3. next below the first in rank, value, etc. —n. 1. one that is second 2. an article of merchandise not of first quality 3. an aid or assistant, as to a boxer 4. the gear next after low gear —vt. 1. to assist 2. to indicate formal support of (a motion) before discussion or a vote —adv. in the second place, group, etc.

sec·ond² (sek'ənd) n. [< ML. (pars minuta) secunda, second (small part): from being a further division] 1. 1/60 of a minute of time .or of angular measure 2. a moment; instant

sec·ond·ar·y (sek'ən der'ē) adj. 1. second in order, rank, sequence, importance, etc. 2. subordinate; minor 3. derived, not primary; derivative —n., pl. -ies 1. a secondary person or thing 2. Football the defensive backfield —**sec'ond·ar'i·ly** adv.

secondary accent a weaker accent (') than the primary accent of a word

secondary school a school, as a high school, coming after elementary school

sec'ond-class' adj. 1. of the class, rank, etc. next below the highest 2. of a cheaper mail class, as for periodicals 3. inferior —adv. by second-class mail or travel accommodations

sec'ond-guess' vt., vi. [Colloq.] to use hindsight in criticizing (someone), remaking (a decision), etc.

sec'ond-hand' adj. 1. not from the original source 2. used before; not new 3. dealing in used merchandise

second lieutenant Mil. a commissioned officer of the lowest rank

sec'ond·ly adv. in the second place

second nature an acquired habit, etc. deeply fixed in one's nature

second person that form of a pronoun (as you) or verb (as are) which refers to the person spoken to

sec'ond-rate' adj. 1. second in quality, etc. 2. inferior

sec'ond-string' adj. [Colloq.] Sports that is a substitute player at a specified position —**sec'ond-string'er** n.

second thought a change in thought after reconsidering —**on second thought** after reconsidering

second wind 1. the return of easy breathing after initial exhaustion, as while running 2. any fresh ability to continue

se·cre·cy (sē'krə sē) n., pl. -cies 1. a being secret 2. a tendency to keep things secret

se·cret (sē'krit) adj. [< L. se-, apart + cernere, sift] 1. kept from, or acting without, the knowledge of others 2. beyond general understanding; mysterious 3. concealed from sight; hidden —n. a secret fact, cause, process, etc. —**se'cret·ly** adv.

sec·re·tar·i·at (sek'rə ter'ē ət) n. a secretarial staff; esp., an administrative staff, as in a government

sec·re·tar·y (sek'rə ter'ē) n., pl. -ies [< ML. secretarius, one entrusted with secrets] 1. one who keeps records, handles correspondence, etc. for an organization or person 2. the head of a government department 3. a writing desk —**sec're·tar'i·al** adj.

se·crete (si krēt') vt. -cret'ed, -cret'ing [see SECRET] 1. to hide; conceal 2. to form and release (a substance) as a gland, etc. does

se·cre·tion (si krē'shən) n. 1. a secreting 2. a substance secreted by an animal or plant

se·cre·tive (sē'krə tiv, si krēt'iv) adj. concealing one's thoughts, etc.; not frank or open —**se'cre·tive·ly** adv. —**se'cre·tive·ness** n.

se·cre·to·ry (si krēt'ər ē) adj. having the function of secreting, as a gland

Secret Service a U.S. agency for uncovering counterfeiters, guarding the President, etc.

sect (sekt) n. [< L. sequi, follow] 1. a religious denomination 2. a group of people having a common philosophy, set of beliefs, etc.

sec·tar·i·an (sek ter'ē ən) adj. 1. of or devoted to some sect 2. narrowminded —n. a sectarian person —**sec·tar'i·an·ism** n.

sec·tion (sek'shən) n. [< L. secare, to cut] 1. a cutting apart 2. a part cut off; portion 3. any distinct part, group, etc. 4. a drawing, etc. of a thing as it would appear if cut straight through —vt. to cut into sections

sec·tion·al *adj.* **1.** of or characteristic of a given section or district **2.** made up of sections —**sec'tion·al·ism** *n.*

sec·tor (sek'tər) *n.* [< L. *secare*, to cut] **1.** part of a circle bounded by any two radii and the included arc **2.** any of the districts into which an area is divided for military operations

sec·u·lar (sek'yə lər) *adj.* [< LL. *saecularis*, worldly] **1.** not religious; not connected with a church **2.** not bound by a monastic vow [*secular* clergy] —**sec'u·lar·ism** *n.*

sec'u·lar·ize' (-lz') *vt.* **-ized'**, **-iz'- ing** to change from religious to civil use or control —**sec'u·lar·i·za'tion** *n.*

se·cure (si kyoor') *adj.* [< L. *se-*, free from + *cura*, care] **1.** free from fear, care, etc. **2.** free from danger, risk, etc.; safe **3.** firm [make the knot *secure*] —*vt.* **-cured'**, **-cur'ing 1.** to make secure; protect **2.** to make certain, as with a pledge [to *secure* a loan] **3.** to make firm, fast, etc. **4.** to obtain —**se·cure'ly** *adv.*

se·cu·ri·ty (si kyoor'ə tē) *n., pl.* **-ties 1.** a feeling secure; freedom from fear, doubt, etc. **2.** protection; safeguard **3.** something given as a pledge of repayment, etc. **4.** [*pl.*] bonds, stocks, etc.

secy., sec'y. secretary

se·dan (si dan') *n.* [< ? L. *sedere*, sit] an enclosed automobile with front and rear seats and two or four doors

se·date¹ (si dāt') *adj.* [< L. *sedare*, settle] calm or composed; esp., serious and unemotional —**se·date'ly** *adv.*

se·date² (si dāt') *vt.* **-dat'ed**, **-dat'- ing** to dose with a sedative —**se·da'- tion** *n.*

sed·a·tive (sed'ə tiv) *adj.* [see SEDATE¹] tending to soothe or quiet; lessening excitement, irritation, etc. —*n.* a sedative medicine

sed·en·tar·y (sed'n ter'ē) *adj.* [< L. *sedere*, sit] marked by much sitting

Se·der (sā'dər) *n.* [< Heb. lit., arrangement] the feast of Passover as observed in the home on the eve of the first (by some also of the second) day of the holiday

sedge (sej) *n.* [OE. *secg*] a coarse, grasslike plant growing in wet ground

sed·i·ment (sed'ə mənt) *n.* [< L. *sedere*, sit] **1.** matter that settles to the bottom of a liquid **2.** *Geol.* matter deposited by water or wind

sed'i·men'ta·ry (-men'tər ē) *adj.* **1.** of or containing sediment **2.** formed by the deposit of sediment, as rocks

se·di·tion (si dish'ən) *n.* [< L. *sed-*, apart + *itio*, a going] a stirring up of rebellion against the government —**se·di'tion·ist** *n.* —**se·di'tious** *adj.*

se·duce (si dōōs') *vt.* **-duced'**, **-duc'- ing** [< L. *se-*, apart + *ducere*, to lead] **1.** to tempt to wrongdoing **2.** to entice into unlawful sexual intercourse, esp. for the first time —**se·duc'er** *n.* —**se·duc'tion** (-duk'shən) *n.* —**se·duc'tive** *adj.* —**se·duc'tress** *n.fem.*

sed·u·lous (sej'oo ləs) *adj.* [L. *sedulus*] **1.** diligent **2.** persistent

see¹ (sē) *vt.* **saw**, **seen**, **see'ing** [OE. *seon*] **1.** to get knowledge of through the eyes; look at **2.** to understand **3.** to learn; find out **4.** to experience **5.** to make sure [*see* that he goes] **6.** to escort [*see* her home] **7.** to encounter **8.** to call on; consult **9.** to receive [too ill to *see* anyone] —*vi.* **1.** to have the power of sight **2.** to understand **3.** to think [let me *see*, who's next?] —**see** after to take care of —**see through 1.** to perceive the true nature of **2.** to finish **3.** to help through difficulty —**see to** (or about) to attend to

see² (sē) *n.* [< L. *sedes*, a seat] the official seat or jurisdiction of a bishop

seed (sēd) *n., pl.* **seeds**, **seed** [OE. *sæd*] **1.** *a)* the part of a plant, containing the embryo, from which a new plant can grow *b)* such seeds collectively **2.** the source of anything **3.** descendants; posterity **4.** sperm or semen —*vt.* **1.** to plant with seed **2.** to remove the seeds from **3.** to distribute (contestants in a tournament) so that the best players are not matched in early rounds —*vi.* to produce seed —**go** (or **run**) **to seed 1.** to shed seeds after flowering **2.** to deteriorate, weaken, etc. —**seed'er** *n.* —**seed'less** *adj.*

seed·ling (-liŋ) *n.* **1.** a plant grown from a seed **2.** a young tree

seed money money to begin a long-term project or get more funds for it

seed vessel any dry, hollow fruit containing seed: also **seed'case'** *n.*

seed'y *adj.* **-i·er**, **-i·est 1.** full of seed **2.** gone to seed **3.** shabby, rundown, etc. —**seed'i·ness** *n.*

seek (sēk) *vt.* **sought**, **seek'ing** [OE. *secan*] **1.** to try to find; search for **2.** to try to get **3.** to aim at **4.** to try; attempt [to *seek* to please]

seem (sēm) *vi.* [prob. < ON. *sæma*, conform to] **1.** to appear to be [*seems* glad] **2.** to appear [*seems* to know] **3.** to have the impression (with an infinitive) [I *seem* to have lost it]

seem'ing *adj.* that seems real, true, etc.; apparent —**seem'ing·ly** *adv.*

seem'ly *adj.* **-li·er**, **-li·est** suitable, proper, etc. —**seem'li·ness** *n.*

seen (sēn) *pp.* of SEE¹

seep (sēp) *vi.* [OE. *sipian*, to soak] to leak through small openings; ooze —**seep'age** (-ij) *n.*

seer (sir) *n.* one who supposedly foretells the future —**seer'ess** *n.fem.*

seer·suck·er (sir'suk'ər) *n.* [< Per. *shir u shakar*, lit., milk and sugar] a crinkled fabric of linen, cotton, etc.

see·saw (sē'sô') *n.* [redupl. of SAW¹] **1.** a plank balanced at the middle on which children at play, riding the ends, rise and fall alternately **2.** any up-and-down or back-and-forth motion or change —*vt.*, *vi.* to move up and down or back and forth

seethe (sēth) *vi.* **seethed**, **seeth'ing**

[OE. *sēothan*] 1. to boil, surge, or bubble 2. to be violently agitated

seg·ment (seg'mənt; *for v.* -ment') *n.* [< L. *secare*, to cut] any of the parts into which something is separated; section —*vt., vi.* to divide into segments —**seg'men·ta'tion** *n.*

seg·re·gate (seg'rə gāt') *vt.* -gat'ed, -gat'ing [< L. *se-*, apart + *grex*, a flock] to set apart from others; specif., to impose racial segregation on

seg·re·ga'tion *n.* the policy of compelling racial groups to live apart and use separate schools, facilities, etc. —**seg're·ga'tion·ist** *n.*

se·gue (seg'wā) *vi.* -gued, -gue·ing [It., (it) follows < L. *sequi*, to follow] to pass without break (*to* or *into* the next part) —*n.* an immediate transition to the next part

sei·gnior (sēn'yər) *n.* [OFr. < L. *senior*, older] a feudal lord

Seine (sān; *Fr.* sen) river in N France, flowing through Paris

seine (sān) *n.* [< Gr. *sagēnē*] a large fishing net weighted along the bottom —*vt., vi.* seined, sein'ing to fish with a seine —**sein'er** *n.*

seis·mic (sīz'mik) *adj.* [< Gr. *seismos*, earthquake] of or caused by an earthquake —**seis'mi·cal·ly** *adv.*

seis'mo·graph' (-mə graf') *n.* [see prec. & -GRAPH] an instrument that records the direction, intensity, and time of earthquakes —**seis'mo·graph'ic** *adj.*

seize (sēz) *vt.* seized, seiz'ing [< ML. *sacire*] 1. *a)* to take legal possession of *b)* to capture; arrest 2. to take forcibly and quickly 3. to grasp suddenly 4. to attack or afflict suddenly [*seized* with pain] —**sei'zure** (sē'zhər) *n.*

sel·dom (sel'dəm) *adv.* [OE. *seldan*, strange] rarely; infrequently

se·lect (sə lekt') *adj.* [< L. *se-*, apart + *legere*, to choose] 1. chosen in preference to others 2. choice; excellent 3. careful in choosing 4. exclusive —*vt., vi.* to choose or pick out —**se·lect'ness** *n.* —**se·lec'tor** *n.*

se·lec'tion (-lek'shən) *n.* 1. a selecting or being selected 2. that or those selected —**se·lec'tive** *adj.* —**se·lec'tiv·i·ty** *n.*

selective service compulsory military service set by age, fitness, etc.

se·lect'man (-mən) *n., pl.* -men one of a board of governing officers in New England towns

se·le·ni·um (sə lē'nē əm) *n.* [ModL. < Gr. *selēnē*, moon] a gray, nonmetallic chemical element: used in photoelectric devices

sel·e·nog·ra·phy (sel'ə näg'rə fē) *n.* [< Gr. *selēnē*, moon + -GRAPHY] the study of the physical features of the moon —**sel'e·nog'ra·pher** *n.*

self (self) *n., pl.* **selves** [OE.] 1. the identity, character, etc. of any person or thing 2. one's own person as distinct from all others 3. one's own welfare or interest —*pron.* [Colloq.] myself, himself, etc. [*for self and wife*] —*adj.* of the same kind, color, etc. [*self trim*]

self- a *prefix* meaning of, by, in, to, or with oneself or itself   The following

list includes some common compounds formed with *self-* that do not have special meanings:

self-appointed	self-improvement
self-assertion	self-induced
self-command	self-indulgence
self-complacent	self-indulgent
self-deceit	self-inflicted
self-deception	self-love
self-defeating	self-pity
self-destruction	self-pollination
self-discipline	self-preservation
self-effacement	self-protection
self-employed	self-reproach
self-examination	self-sealing
self-fertilization	self-support
self-help	self-supporting
self-imposed	self-sustaining

self'-ad·dressed' *adj.* addressed to oneself [*a self-addressed envelope*]

self'-as·sur'ance *n.* confidence in oneself —**self'-as·sured'** *adj.*

self'-cen'tered *adj.* concerned only with one's own affairs; selfish

self'-con·ceit' *n.* too high an opinion of oneself; vanity

self'-con·fi·dence *n.* confidence in one's own abilities, etc. —**self'-con'fi·dent** *adj.*

self'-con'scious *adj.* unduly conscious of oneself as an object of notice; ill at ease —**self'-con'scious·ly** *adv.* —**self'-con'scious·ness** *n.*

self'-con·tained' *adj.* 1. keeping one's affairs to oneself 2. showing self-control 3. complete within itself

self'-con'tra·dic'tion *n.* 1. contradiction of oneself or itself 2. any statement having elements that contradict each other —**self'-con'tra·dic'to·ry** *adj.*

self'-con·trol' *n.* control of one's emotions, desires, etc. —**self'-con·trolled'** *adj.*

self'-de·fense' *n.* defense of oneself or of one's rights, actions, etc.

self'-de·ni'al *n.* denial or sacrifice of one's own desires or pleasures

self'-de·struct' *vi. same as* DESTRUCT

self'-de·ter'mi·na'tion *n.* 1. determination according to one's own mind; free will 2. the right of a people to choose its own form of government —**self'-de·ter'mined** *adj.*

self'-dis·cov'er·y *n.* a becoming aware of one's true potential, character, etc.

self'-ed'u·cat'ed *adj.* educated by oneself, with little formal schooling

self'-es·teem' *n.* 1. belief in oneself 2. undue pride in oneself

self'-ev'i·dent *adj.* evident without explanation or proof

self'-ex·plan'a·to'ry *adj.* explaining itself; obvious

self'-ex·pres'sion *n.* the expression of one's personality, esp. in the arts

self'-ful·fill'ing *adj.* 1. bringing about one's personal goals 2. brought about chiefly as an effect of having been expected or predicted

self'-gov'ern·ment *n.* government of a group by the action of its own members —**self'-gov'ern·ing** *adj.*

self'-im'age *n.* a person's conception of himself, his abilities, worth, etc.

self'-im·por'tant *adj.* having an exaggerated opinion of one's own importance —**self'-im·por'tance** *n.*

self'-in'ter·est *n.* 1. one's own interest or advantage 2. an exaggerated regard for this

self'ish *adj.* overly concerned with one's own interests, etc. and having little concern for others —**self'ish·ly** *adv.* —**self'ish·ness** *n.*

self'less *adj.* devoted to others' welfare; unselfish —**self'less·ly** *adv.* —**self'less·ness** *n.*

self'-made' *adj.* 1. made by oneself or itself 2. successful through one's own efforts

self'-pos·ses'sion *n.* full control of one's feelings, actions, etc. —**self'-pos·sessed'** *adj.*

self'-pro·pelled' *adj.* propelled by its own motor or power

self'-re·li'ance *n.* reliance on one's own judgment, abilities, etc. —**self'-re·li'ant** *adj.*

self'-re·spect' *n.* proper respect for oneself —**self'-re·spect'ing** *adj.*

self'-re·straint' *n.* restraint imposed on oneself by oneself; self-control

self'-right'eous *adj.* righteous, moral, etc. in one's own opinion —**self'-right'eous·ly** *adv.* —**self'-right'eous·ness** *n.*

self'-sac'ri·fice' *n.* the sacrifice of oneself or one's interests for the benefit of others —**self'-sac'ri·fic'ing** *adj.*

self'-same' *adj.* identical

self'-sat'is·fied' *adj.* feeling or showing satisfaction with oneself —**self'-sat'is·fac'tion** *n.*

self'-seek'er *n.* one who seeks mainly to further his own interests —**self'-seek'ing** *n., adj.*

self'-serv'ice *n.* the practice of serving oneself in a cafeteria, store, etc.

self'-serv'ing *adj.* serving one's own selfish interests

self'-start'er *n.* a device for starting an internal-combustion engine automatically

self'-styled' *adj.* so named by oneself

self'-suf·fi'cient *adj.* able to get along without help; independent —**self'-suf·fi'cien·cy** *n.*

self'-taught' *adj.* having taught oneself through one's own efforts

self'-willed' *adj.* stubborn; obstinate

self'-wind'ing *adj.* wound automatically, as some watches

sell (sel) *vt.* **sold, sell'ing** [OE. *sellan,* give] 1. to exchange (goods, services, etc.) for money, etc. 2. to offer for sale 3. to promote the sale of —*vi.* 1. to engage in selling 2. to be sold (*for* or *at*) 3. to attract buyers —**sell out** 1. to get rid of completely by selling 2. [Colloq.] to betray —**sell'er** *n.*

sell'out' *n.* [Colloq.] 1. a selling out; betrayal 2. a show, game, etc. for which all the seats have been sold

Selt·zer (water) (selt'sər) [< *Niederselters,* Germany] 1. a mineral water 2. [*often* s-] carbonated water

sel·vage, sel·vedge (sel'vij) *n.* [< SELF + EDGE] a specially woven edge that prevents cloth from raveling

selves (selvz) *n. pl. of* SELF

se·man·tics (sə man'tiks) *n.pl.* [*with sing. v.*] [< Gr. *sēmainein,* to show] the study of the development and changes of the meanings of words —**se·man'tic** *adj.*

sem·a·phore (sem'ə fôr') *n.* [< Gr. *sēma,* a sign + *pherein,* to bear] any apparatus or system for signaling, as by lights, flags, etc.

sem·blance (sem'bləns) *n.* [< L. *similis,* like] 1. outward appearance 2. resemblance 3. a likeness or copy

se·men (sē'mən) *n., pl.* **sem·i·na** (sem'ə nə) [L., seed] the fluid secreted by the male reproductive organs

se·mes·ter (sə mes'tər) *n.* [< L. *sex,* six + *mensis,* month] either of the two terms usually making up a school year

sem·i (sem'ī) *n.* [Colloq.] a tractor (sense 2) and an attached semitrailer

semi- [L.] *a prefix meaning:* 1. half 2. partly, not fully 3. twice in a (specified period)

sem·i·an·nu·al (sem'ē an'yoo wəl) *adj.* 1. happening, coming, etc. every half year 2. lasting half a year

sem·i·cir·cle (sem'i sur'k'l) *n.* a half circle —**sem'i·cir'cu·lar** (-kyə lər) *adj.*

sem'i·co'lon (-kō'lən) *n.* a mark of punctuation (;) indicating a degree of separation greater than that marked by the comma

sem'i·con·duc'tor (-kən duk'tər) *n.* a substance, as germanium, used as in transistors to control current flow

sem'i·con'scious *adj.* not fully conscious or awake

sem'i·fi'nal *adj.* coming just before the final match, as of a contest —*n.* a semifinal match, etc.

sem'i·month'ly *adj.* coming, done, etc. twice a month —*adv.* twice monthly

sem·i·nal (sem'ə n'l) *adj.* [see SEMEN] 1. of seed or semen 2. that is a source

sem·i·nar (sem'ə när') *n.* 1. a group of supervised students doing research 2. a course for such a group

sem·i·nar·y (sem'ə ner'ē) *n., pl.* **-ies** [< L. *seminarium,* nursery] 1. a school, esp. a private school for young women 2. a school where priests, ministers, etc. are trained

Sem·i·nole (sem'ə nōl') *n., pl.* **-noles, -nole** a member of an American Indian people of S Florida and Oklahoma

sem'i·pre'cious *adj.* designating gems, as the garnet, turquoise, etc., of lower value than precious gems

sem'i·pri'vate *adj.* of a hospital room with two, three, or sometimes four beds

sem'i·pro·fes'sion·al *n.* one who engages in a sport for pay but not as a regular occupation: also **sem'i·pro'**

sem'i·skilled' *adj.* of or doing manual work requiring only limited training

Sem·ite (sem'īt) n. [< Shēm, son of Noah] a member of any of the peoples whose language is Semitic

Se·mit·ic (sə mit'ik) adj. 1. of or relating to the Semites 2. designating or of a group of Afro-Asiatic languages, including Hebrew, Arabic, etc.

sem'i·trail'er n. a detachable trailer attached to a coupling at the rear of a truck cab

sem'i·trans·par'ent adj. not perfectly or completely transparent

sem'i·trop'i·cal adj. partly tropical

sem'i·week'ly adj. coming, done, etc. twice a week —adv. twice weekly

sen. 1. senate 2. senior 3. senior

sen·ate (sen'it) n. [< L. senex, old] 1. a lawmaking assembly 2. [S-] the upper branch of the U.S. Congress or of most of the State legislatures

sen·a·tor (sen'ə tər) n. a member of a senate —**sen'a·to'ri·al** (-tôr'ē əl) adj.

send (send) vt. **sent, send'ing** [OE. sendan] 1. to cause to go or be transmitted; dispatch 2. to cause (a person) to go 3. to impel; drive 4. to cause to happen, come, etc. 5. [Slang] to thrill —**send for** 1. to summon 2. to place an order for —**send'er** n.

send'-off' n. [Colloq.] 1. a farewell demonstration for someone starting out on a trip, career, etc. 2. a start given to someone or something

Sen·e·gal (sen'i gôl') country in W Africa: 76,124 sq. mi.; pop. 3,490,000

se·nile (sē'nīl) adj. [< L. senex, old] 1. of or resulting from old age 2. showing signs of old age; weak in mind and body —**se·nil·i·ty** (si nil'ə tē) n.

sen·ior (sēn'yər) adj. [L. < senex, old] 1. older: written Sr. after a father's name if his son's name is the same 2. of higher rank or longer service 3. of or for seniors —n. 1. one who is older, of higher rank, etc. 2. a student in the last year of a high school or college

senior citizen an elderly person, esp. one who is retired

senior high school high school (usually grades 10, 11, & 12)

sen·ior·i·ty (sēn yôr'ə tē) n., pl. **-ties** 1. a being senior 2. status, priority, etc. achieved by length of service in a given job

sen·na (sen'ə) n. [< Ar. sanā, cassia plant] the dried leaflets of a tropical cassia plant, used as a laxative

‡**se·ñor** (se nyôr') n., pl. **se·ñor'es** (-nyō'res) [Sp.] a man; gentleman: as a title, equivalent to Mr. or Sir

‡**se·ño·ra** (se nyô'rä) n. [Sp.] a married woman: as a title, equivalent to Mrs. or Madam

‡**se·ño·ri·ta** (se'nyō rē'tä) n. [Sp.] an unmarried woman or girl: as a title, equivalent to Miss

sen·sa·tion (sen sā'shən) n. [< L. sensus, sense] 1. the receiving of sense impressions through hearing, seeing, etc. 2. a conscious sense impression 3. a generalized feeling [a sensation of joy] 4. a feeling of excitement or its cause [the play is a sensation]

sen·sa'tion·al adj. 1. arousing intense interest 2. intended to shock, thrill, etc. —**sen·sa'tion·al·ism** n.

sense (sens) n. [< L. sentire, to feel] 1. any faculty of receiving impressions through body organs; sight, hearing, taste, smell, or touch 2. a) feeling, perception, etc. through the senses b) a generalized feeling or awareness 3. an ability to understand some quality, as humor, honor, etc. 4. normal intelligence and judgment 5. meaning, as of a word —vt. sensed, sens'ing 1. to perceive 2. to detect, as by sensors —**in a sense** in one aspect —**make sense** to be intelligible or logical

sense'less adj. 1. unconscious 2. stupid; foolish 3. meaningless

sen·si·bil·i·ty (sen'sə bil'ə tē) n., pl. **-ties** 1. the capacity for physical sensation 2. [often pl.] delicate, sensitive awareness or feelings

sen'si·ble adj. 1. that can cause physical sensation 2. easily perceived 3. aware 4. having or showing good sense; wise —**sen'si·bly** adv.

sen'si·tive (sen'sə tiv) adj. 1. sensory 2. very keenly susceptible to stimuli 3. tender; raw 4. having keen sensibilities 5. easily offended; touchy —**sen'si·tiv'i·ty, sen'si·tive·ness** n.

sen'si·tize' (-tīz') vt. **-tized', -tiz'-ing** to make sensitive

sen·sor (sen'sər) n. a device to detect, measure, or record physical phenomena, as heat, pulse, etc.

sen·so·ry (sen'sər ē) adj. of the senses or sensation

sen·su·al (sen'shoo wəl) adj. [< L. sensus, sense] 1. of the body and the senses as distinguished from the intellect 2. connected or preoccupied with sexual pleasures —**sen'su·al'i·ty** (-wal'ə tē) n. —**sen'su·al·ly** adv.

sen·su·ous (sen'shoo wəs) adj. 1. of, derived from, or perceived by the senses 2. enjoying sensation

sent (sent) pt. & pp. of SEND

sen·tence (sen't'ns) n. [< L. sententia, opinion] 1. a) a decision, as of a court; esp., the determination by a court of a punishment b) the punishment 2. a group of words stating something, usually containing a subject and predicate —vt. **-tenced, -tenc-ing** to pronounce punishment upon (a convicted person)

sen·ten·tious (sen ten'shəs) adj. 1. full of, or fond of using, maxims, proverbs, etc. 2. ponderously trite

sen·tient (sen'shənt) adj. [see SENSE] of or capable of feeling; conscious

sen·ti·ment (sen'tə mənt) n. [see SENSE] 1. a complex combination of feelings and opinions 2. an opinion, etc., often colored by emotion 3. appeal to the emotions, or sensitivity to this 4. maudlin emotion

sen·ti·men·tal (sen'tə men't'l) adj. 1. having or showing tender or delicate feelings 2. maudlin; mawkish 3. of or resulting from sentiment —**sen'ti·men'tal·ism** n. —**sen'ti·men'tal·ist** n. —**sen'ti·men·tal'i·ty** (-tal'ə tē) n. —**sen'ti·men'tal·ly** adv.

sen·ti·men·tal·ize *vi., vt.* **-ized′, -iz′ing** to be sentimental or treat in a sentimental way

sen·ti·nel (sen′ti n'l) *n.* [< L. *sentire*, to sense] a guard or sentry

sen·try (sen′trē) *n., pl.* **-tries** [< ? obs. *centery*, sanctuary] a sentinel; esp., a soldier posted to guard against danger

Seoul (sōl) capital of South Korea: pop. 3,376,000

se·pal (sē′p'l) *n.* [< Gr. *skepē*, a covering + L. *petalum*, petal] any of the leaflike parts of the calyx

sep·a·ra·ble (sep′ər ə b'l) *adj.* that can be separated —**sep′a·ra·bly** *adv.*

sep·a·rate (sep′ə rāt′; *for adj.* -ər it) *vt.* **-rat′ed, -rat′ing** [< L. *se-*, apart + *parare*, arrange] 1. to set apart into sections, groups, etc.; divide 2. to keep apart by being between —*vi.* 1. to withdraw 2. to part, become disconnected, etc. 3. to go in different directions —*adj.* 1. set apart from the rest or others 2. not associated with others; distinct 3. not shared [*separate* beds] —**sep′a·rate·ly** *adv.* —**sep′a·ra′tor** *n.*

sep·a·ra·tion (sep′ə rā′shən) *n.* 1. a separating or being separated 2. the place where this occurs; break; division 3. something that separates

sep·a·ra·tism (-ər ə tiz′m) *n.* the advocacy of separation, racially, politically, etc. —**sep′a·ra·tist** *n.*

se·pi·a (sē′pē ə) *n., adj.* [< Gr. *sēpia*, cuttlefish secreting inky fluid] (of) dark reddish brown

sep·sis (sep′sis) *n.* [see SEPTIC] poisoning caused by the absorption into the blood of pathogenic microorganisms

Sep·tem·ber (sep tem′bər) *n.* [< L. *septem*, seven: seventh month in Rom. calendar] the ninth month of the year, having 30 days: abbrev. **Sept.**

sep·tic (sep′tik) *adj.* [< Gr. *sēpein*, make putrid] causing, or resulting from, sepsis or putrefaction

sep·ti·ce·mi·a (sep′tə sē′mē ə) *n.* [see prec.] *same as* BLOOD POISONING

septic tank an underground tank in which waste matter is putrefied and decomposed through bacterial action

Sep·tu·a·gint (sep′too wə jint) *n.* [< L. *septuaginta*, seventy: in tradition, done in 70 days] a translation into Greek of the Old Testament

sep·tum (sep′təm) *n., pl.* **-tums, -ta** (-tə) [L., fence] a dividing wall or part as in the nose, a fruit, etc.

sep·ul·cher (sep′'l kər) *n.* [< L. *sepelire*, bury] a vault for burial; tomb

se·pul·chral (sə pul′krəl) *adj.* 1. of sepulchers, burial, etc. 2. suggestive of the grave or burial; gloomy 3. deep and melancholy: said of sound

seq. [L. *sequentes*] the following

se·quel (sē′kwəl) *n.* [< L. *sequi*, follow] 1. something that follows; continuation 2. something coming as a result of something else; aftermath; effect 3. any literary work continuing a story begun in an earlier work

se·quence (sē′kwəns) *n.* [< L. *sequi*, follow] 1. *a)* the coming of one thing after another; succession *b)* the order in which this occurs 2. a series 3. a resulting event 4. a single, uninterrupted episode, as in a movie

se·ques·ter (si kwes′tər) *vt.* [< LL. *sequestrare*, remove] 1. to set off or apart 2. to withdraw; seclude —**se·ques·tra·tion** (sē′kwes trā′shən) *n.*

se·quin (sē′kwin) *n.* [Fr.; ult. < Ar. *sikkah*, a stamp] a small, shiny spangle, esp. one of many sewn on fabric for decoration —**se′quined** *adj.*

se·quoi·a (si kwoi′ə) *n.* [< *Sikwâyi*, Indian inventor of Cherokee writing] a giant evergreen tree of the W U.S.

se·rag·lio (si ral′yō) *n., pl.* **-lios** [ult. < L. *sera*, a lock] a harem (sense 1)

se·ra·pe (sə rä′pē) *n.* [MexSp.] a bright-colored woolen blanket used as a garment by men in Mexico, etc.

ser·aph (ser′əf) *n., pl.* **-aphs, -a·phim′** (-ə fim′) [< Heb. *šerāphîm*, pl.] *Theol.* a heavenly being, or any of the highest order of angels —**se·raph·ic** (sə raf′ik) *adj.* —**se·raph′i·cal·ly** *adv.*

Serb (surb) *n.* a native or inhabitant of Serbia; esp., any of a Slavic people of Serbia —*adj.* Serbian

Ser·bi·a (sur′bē ə) republic of Yugoslavia —**Ser′bi·an** *adj., n.*

sere (sir) *adj.* [var. of SEAR] [Poet.] dried up; withered

ser·e·nade (ser′ə nād′) *n.* [ult. < L. *serenus*, clear] music played or sung at night, esp. by a lover under his sweetheart's window —*vt., vi.* **-nad′ed, -nad′ing** to play or sing a serenade (to)

ser·en·dip·i·ty (ser′ən dip′ə tē) *n.* [< a Persian tale *The Three Princes of Serendip*] an apparent aptitude for making accidental fortunate discoveries

se·rene (sə rēn′) *adj.* [L. *serenus*] 1. clear; unclouded 2. undisturbed; calm —**se·rene′ly** *adv.* —**se·ren′i·ty** (-ren′ə tē), **se·rene′ness** *n.*

serf (surf) *n.* [< L. *servus*, a slave] a person in feudal servitude, bound to his master's land and transferred with it to a new owner —**serf′dom** *n.*

serge (surj) *n.* [< L. *sericus*, silken] a strong twilled fabric

ser·geant (sär′jənt) *n.* [< L. *servire*, serve] 1. a noncommissioned officer ranking above a corporal 2. a police officer ranking next below a captain or a lieutenant

ser′geant-at-arms′ *n., pl.* **ser′geants-at-arms′** an officer appointed to keep order, as in a court

se·ri·al (sir′ē əl) *adj.* [< L. *series*, an order] appearing in a series of continuous parts at regular intervals —*n.* a story, etc. presented in serial form —**se′ri·al·i·za′tion** *n.* —**se′ri·al·ize′** *vt.* **-ized′, -iz′ing**

serial number one of a series of numbers given for identification

se·ries (sir′ēz) *n., pl.* **-ries** [L. < *serere*, join together] a number of similar things or persons arranged in a row or coming one after another

se·ri·ous (sir′ē əs) *adj.* [< L. *serius*] 1. earnest, grave, sober, etc. 2. not joking; sincere 3. requiring careful consideration; important 4. dangerous [a *serious* wound] —**se′ri·ous·ly** *adv.* —**se′ri·ous·ness** *n.*

ser·mon (sur′mən) *n.* [< L. *sermo*] 1. a speech on religion or morals, esp. by a clergyman 2. any serious talk on behavior, duty, etc., esp. a tedious one —**ser′mon·ize′** *vi. -ized′, -iz′ing*

Sermon on the Mount the sermon delivered by Jesus to his disciples

se·rous (sir′əs) *adj.* 1. of or containing serum 2. thin and watery

ser·pent (sur′pənt) *n.* [< L. *serpere*, to creep] a snake

ser′pen·tine′ (-pən tēn′, -tīn′) *adj.* of or like a serpent; esp., *a)* cunning; treacherous *b)* coiled; winding

ser·rate (ser′āt) *adj.* [< L. *serra*, a saw] having sawlike notches along the edge, as some leaves: also **ser·rat′ed** —**ser·ra′tion** *n.*

ser·ried (ser′ēd) *adj.* [< LL. *serare*, to lock] placed close together

se·rum (sir′əm) *n., pl. -rums, -ra* (-ə) [L., whey] 1. any watery animal fluid, as the yellowish fluid (**blood serum**) separating from a blood clot after coagulation 2. blood serum used as an antitoxin, taken from an animal inoculated for a specific disease

ser·vant (sur′vənt) *n.* [ult. < L. *servire*, serve] 1. a person employed by another, esp. to do household duties 2. a person devoted to another or to a cause, creed, etc.

serve (surv) *vt.* **served, serv′ing** [< L. *servus*, a slave] 1. to work for as a servant 2. to do services for; aid; help 3. to do military or naval service for 4. to spend (a term of imprisonment, etc.) [to *serve* ten years] 5. to provide (customers) with (goods or services) 6. to set (food, etc.) before (a person) 7. to meet the needs of 8. to be used by [one hospital *serves* the city] 9. to function for [if memory *serves* me well] 10. to deliver (a summons, etc.) to 11. to hit (a tennis ball, etc.) in order to start play —*vi.* 1. to work as a servant 2. to do service [to *serve* in the navy] 3. to carry out the duties of an office 4. to be of service 5. to meet needs 6. to provide guests with food or drink 7. to be favorable: said of weather, etc. —*n.* a serving of the ball in tennis —**serve (someone) right** to be what (someone) deserves —**serv′er** *n.*

serv·ice (sur′vis) *n.* [< L. *servus*, a slave] 1. the occupation of a servant 2. *a)* public employment [diplomatic *service*] *b)* a branch of this; specif., the armed forces 3. work done for others [repair *service*] 4. any religious ceremony 5. *a)* benefit; advantage *b)* [*pl.*] friendly help; also, professional aid 6. the act or manner of serving food 7. a set of articles used in serving [a tea *service*] 8. a system of providing people with some utility, as water or gas 9. the act or manner of serving in

tennis, etc. —*vt.* **-iced, -ic·ing** 1. to furnish with a service 2. to make fit for service, as by repairing —**at one's service** 1. ready to serve one 2. ready for one's use —**of service** helpful

serv·ice·a·ble *adj.* 1. that can be of service; useful 2. that will give good service; durable

serv·ice·man′ *n., pl. -men′* 1. a member of the armed forces 2. a person whose work is repairing something [a radio *serviceman*]: also **service man**

service mark a word, etc. used like a trademark by a supplier of services

service station a place selling gasoline, oil, etc. for motor vehicles

ser·vile (sur′v'l, -vīl) *adj.* [< L. *servus*, a slave] 1. of slaves 2. like that of slaves 3. humbly submissive —**ser·vil·i·ty** (sər vil′ə tē) *n.*

ser·vi·tor (sur′və tər) *n.* a servant

ser·vi·tude (sur′və tōōd′) *n.* [see SERVILE] 1. slavery or bondage 2. work imposed as punishment for crime

ser·vo (sur′vō) *n., pl. -vos short for:* 1. SERVOMECHANISM 2. SERVOMOTOR

ser′vo·mech′a·nism *n.* an automatic control system of low power, used to exercise remote but accurate mechanical control

ser′vo·mo′tor *n.* a device, as an electric motor, for changing a small force into a large force, as in a servomechanism

ses·a·me (ses′ə mē′) *n.* [of Sem. origin] 1. an East Indian plant whose edible seeds yield an oil 2. its seeds

ses·qui·cen·ten·ni·al (ses′kwi sen ten′ē əl) *adj.* [< L. *sesqui-*, more by a half + CENTENNIAL] of a period of 150 years —*n.* a 150th anniversary

ses·sion (sesh′ən) *n.* [< L. *sedere*, sit] 1. *a)* the meeting of a court, legislature, etc. *b)* a series of such meetings *c)* the period of these 2. a period of study, classes, etc. 3. a period of activity of any kind

set (set) *vt.* **set, set′ting** [OE. *settan*] 1. to cause to sit; seat 2. to put in a specified place, condition, etc. [set books on a shelf, *set* slaves free] 3. to put in proper condition; fix (a trap for animals), adjust (a clock or dial), arrange (a table for a meal), fix (hair) in a desired style, etc., put (a broken bone, etc.) into normal position, etc. 4. to make settled, rigid, or fixed [pectin *sets* jelly] 5. to mount (gems) 6. to direct 7. to appoint; establish; fix (boundaries, the time for an event, a rule, a quota, etc.) 8. to furnish (an example) for others 9. to fit (words *to* music or music *to* words) 10. to arrange (type) for printing —*vi.* 1. to sit on eggs: said of a fowl 2. to become firm, hard, or fixed [the cement *set*] 3. to begin to move (*out, forth, off*, etc.) 4. to sink below the horizon [the sun *sets*] 5. to have a certain direction; tend —*adj.* 1. fixed; established [a *set* time] 2. intentional 3. fixed; rigid; firm 4. obstinate 5. ready [get *set*] —*n.* 1. a setting or being set 2. the way in which a thing is set [the *set* of his jaw] 3. direction; tendency 4. the scenery for a play, etc. 5. a group of persons or things classed or belonging together 6. assembled equipment for radio or television reception, etc. 7. *Tennis* a group of six or more games won by a margin of at least two —**set about (or in, to)** to begin —**set down** 1. to put in writing 2. to establish (rules, etc.) —**set forth** 1. to publish 2. to state —**set off** 1. to make prominent or enhance by contrast 2. to make explode —**set on (or upon)** to attack —**set up** 1. to erect 2. to establish; found

set′back′ n. a reversal in progress

set·tee (se tē′) n. 1. a seat or bench with a back 2. a small sofa

set′ter n. a long-haired dog trained to hunt game

set′ting n. 1. the act of one that sets 2. the position of a dial, etc. that has been set 3. a mounting, as of a gem 4. the time, place, etc. as of a story 5. actual physical surroundings

set·tle (set′ l) vt. -**tled**, -**tling** [OE. *setlan*] 1. to put in order; arrange [to *settle* one's affairs] 2. to set in place firmly or comfortably 3. to colonize 4. to cause to sink and become more compact 5. to free (the nerves, etc.) from disturbance 6. to decide (a dispute, etc.) 7. to pay (a debt, etc.) —vi. 1. to stop moving and stay in one place 2. to descend, as fog over a landscape, or gloom over a person 3. to become localized, as pain 4. to take up permanent residence 5. to sink [the house *settled*] 6. to become more dense by sinking, as sediment 7. to become more stable 8. to reach an agreement or decision (with or on) —**set′tler** n.

set′tle·ment n. 1. a settling or being settled 2. a new colony 3. a village 4. an agreement 5. a community center for the underprivileged

set′-to′ (-tōō′) n., pl. -**tos′** [Colloq.] 1. a fight 2. an argument

set′up′ n. 1. a) the plan, makeup, etc. of equipment, an organization, etc. b) the details of a situation, plan, etc. 2. [Colloq.] a contest, etc. arranged to result in an easy victory

sev·en (sev′n) adj., n. [OE. *seofon*] one more than six; 7; VII —**sev′enth** adj., n.

seven seas the oceans of the world

sev′en·teen′ (-tēn′) adj., n. seven more than ten; 17; XVII —**sev′en·teenth′** (-tēnth′) adj., n.

sev′en·teen′-year′ locust a cicada which lives underground for 13–17 years before emerging as an adult

seventh heaven perfect happiness

sev·en·ty (sev′n tē) adj., n., pl. -**ties** seven times ten; 70; LXX —**the seventies** the years from 70 through 79, as of a century —**sev′en·ti·eth** (-ith) adj., n.

sev·er (sev′ər) vt., vi. [< L. *separare*] to separate, divide, or break off —**sev′er·ance** n.

sev·er·al (sev′ər əl) adj. [< L. *separ*] 1. separate; distinct 2. different;

respective 3. more than two but not many; few —n. [with *pl. v.*] a small number (of) —pron. [with *pl. v.*] a few —**sev′er·al·ly** adv.

se·vere (sə vir′) adj. [< L. *severus*] 1. harsh or strict, as in treatment 2. serious; grave, as in expression 3. rigidly accurate or demanding 4. extremely plain: said of style 5. intense [severe pain] 6. rigorous; trying —**se·vere′ly** adv. —**se·vere′ness, se·ver′i·ty** (-ver′ə tē) n.

Se·ville (sə vil′) city in SW Spain: pop. 532,000

Sè·vres (sev′rə) n. [< *Sèvres*, Paris suburb where made] a type of fine French porcelain

sew (sō) vt., vi. **sewed**, **sewn** (sōn) or **sewed**, **sew′ing** [OE. *siwian*] 1. to fasten with stitches made with needle and thread 2. to make, mend, etc. by sewing —**sew up** [Colloq.] 1. to get full control of 2. to make sure of success in —**sew′er** n.

sew·age (sōō′ij) n. the waste matter carried off by sewers

sew·er (sōō′ər) n. [ult. < L, *ex*, out + *aqua*, water] a pipe or drain, usually underground, used to carry off water and waste matter

sew′er·age (-ij) n. 1. a system of sewers 2. same as SEWAGE

sew·ing (sō′iŋ) n. 1. the act of one who sews 2. something to be sewn

sewing machine a machine with a mechanically driven needle for sewing

sex (seks) n. [< L. *sexus*] 1. either of the two divisions of organisms distinguished as male and female 2. the character of being male or female 3. the attraction between the sexes 4. sexual intercourse

sex- [< L. *sex*, six] a combining form meaning six

sex appeal the physical charm that attracts members of the opposite sex

sex chromosome a sex-determining chromosome in the germ cells: eggs carry an X chromosome and spermatozoa either an X or Y chromosome, with a female resulting from an XX pairing and a male from an XY

sex′ism n. exploitation and domination of one sex by the other, specif., of women by men —**sex′ist** adj., n.

sex·tant (seks′tənt) n. [< L. *sextans*, a sixth part (of a circle)] an instrument for measuring the angular distance of the sun, a star, etc. from the horizon, as to determine position at sea

sex·tet, sex·tette (seks tet′) n. [< L. *sex*, six] 1. a group of six 2. *Music* a composition for six voices or instruments, or the six performers of this

sex·ton (seks′tən) n. [ult. < L. *sacer*, sacred] a church official in charge of the maintenance of church property

sex·u·al (sek′shōō wəl) adj. of or involving sex, the sexes, the sex organs, etc. —**sex′u·al·ly** adv. —**sex′u·al′i·ty** n.

sex′y adj. -**i**-er, -**i**-est [Colloq.] exciting or intended to excite sexual desire —**sex′i·ly** adv. —**sex′i·ness** n.

s.f., sf., SF science fiction

Sgt, Sgt. Sergeant

sh (sh) interj. hush! be quiet!

shab·by (shab′ē) adj. **-bi·er, -bi·est** [< OE. sceabb, a scab] 1. run down; dilapidated 2. a) ragged; worn b) wearing worn clothing 3. mean; shameful [shabby behavior] —**shab′·bi·ly** adv. —**shab′bi·ness** n.

shack (shak) n. [< ?] a small, crudely built house or cabin; shanty

shack·le (shak′'l) n. [OE. sceacel] 1. a metal fastening, usually in pairs, for the wrists or ankles of a prisoner; fetter 2. anything that restrains freedom, as of expression 3. a device for coupling, etc. —vt. **-led, -ling** 1. to put shackles on 2. to restrain in freedom of expression or action

shad (shad) n., pl. **shad, shads** [OE. sceadd] a saltwater fish related to the herring but spawning in rivers

shade (shād) n. [OE. sceadu] 1. comparative darkness caused by cutting off rays of light 2. an area with less light than its surroundings 3. degree of darkness of a color 4. a) a small difference [shades of opinion] b) a slight amount or degree 5. [Poet.] a ghost 6. a device used to screen from light [a lamp shade, window shade] 7. [pl.] [Slang] sunglasses —vt. **shad′ed, shad′ing** 1. to screen from light 2. to darken; dim 3. to represent shade in (a painting, etc.) —vi. to change slightly or by degrees

shad·ing (shād′iŋ) n. 1. a shielding against light 2. the representation of shade in a picture 3. a small variation

shad·ow (shad′ō) n. [< OE. sceadu, shade] 1. (a) shade cast by a body intercepting light rays 2. gloom or that which causes gloom 3. a shaded area in a picture 4. a ghost 5. a remnant; trace —vt. 1. to throw a shadow upon 2. to follow closely, esp. in secret —**shad′ow·y** adj.

shad′ow-box′ vi. Boxing to spar with an imaginary opponent for exercise

shad·y (shād′ē) adj. **-i·er, -i·est** 1. giving shade 2. shaded; full of shade 3. [Colloq.] of questionable character —**on the shady side of** beyond (a given age) —**shad′i·ness** n.

shaft (shaft) n. [OE. sceaft] 1. an arrow or spear, or its stem 2. anything hurled like a missile [shafts of wit] 3. a long, slender part or object, as a pillar, either of the poles between which an animal is harnessed to a vehicle, a bar transmitting motion to a mechanical part, etc. 4. a long, narrow passage sunk into the earth 5. a vertical opening passing through a building, as for an elevator

shag[1] (shag) n. [OE. sceaga] a heavy, rough nap, as on some cloth

shag[2] (shag) vt. **shagged, shag′ging** [< ?] to chase after and retrieve (baseballs hit in batting practice)

shag·gy adj. **-gi·er, -gi·est** 1. covered with long, coarse hair or wool 2. unkempt, straggly, etc. 3. having a rough nap

shah (shä) n. [Per. shāh] a title of the ruler of Iran

shake (shāk) vt., vi. **shook, shak′en, shak′ing** [OE. sceacan] 1. to move quickly up and down, back and forth, etc. 2. to bring, force, mix, etc. by brisk movement 3. to tremble or cause to tremble 4. a) to become or cause to become unsteady b) to unnerve or become unnerved 5. to clasp (another's hand), as in greeting —n. 1. an act of shaking 2. a wood shingle 3. short for MILKSHAKE 4. [pl.] [Colloq.] a convulsive trembling (usually with the) 5. [Colloq.] deal [a fair shake] —**no great shakes** not outstanding —**shake down** 1. to cause to fall by shaking 2. [Slang] to extort money from —**shake off** to get rid of —**shak′y** adj. **-i·er, -i·est**

shake′down′ n. 1. [Slang] an extortion of money, as by blackmail 2. a thorough search —adj. for testing new equipment, etc. [a shakedown cruise]

shak′er n. 1. a person or thing that shakes 2. a device used in shaking 3. [S-] a member of a religious sect that lived in celibate communities in the U.S.

Shake·speare (shāk′spir), **William** 1564-1616; Eng. poet & dramatist —**Shake·spear′e·an** adj., n.

shake′-up′ n. a shaking up; specif., an extensive reorganization

shak·o (shak′ō) n., pl. **-os** [< Hung.] a high, stiff military dress hat, with a flat top and a plume

shale (shāl) n. [< OE. scealu, a shell] a rock formed of hardened clay: it splits easily into thin layers

shale oil oil distilled from a hard shale containing veins of a greasy organic solid

shall (shal) v. pt. **should** [OE. sceal] an auxiliary used in formal speech to express futurity in the first person, and determination, obligation, or necessity in the second and third persons Shall is now ordinarily replaced by will in all persons

shal·lot (shə lät′) n. [< OFr. eschaloigne, scallion] 1. a small onion whose clustered bulbs are used for flavoring 2. a green onion

shal·low (shal′ō) adj. [ME. shalow] 1. not deep 2. lacking depth of character, intellect, etc. —n. a shoal

shalt (shalt) archaic 2d pers. sing. pres. indic., of SHALL: used with thou

sham (sham) n. [< ? SHAME] something false or fake; person or thing that is a fraud —adj. false or fake —vt., vi. **shammed, sham′ming** to pretend; feign —**sham′mer** n.

sham·ble (sham′b'l) vi. **-bled, -bling** [< obs. use in "shamble legs," bench legs] to walk clumsily; shuffle —n. a shambling walk

sham′bles (-b'lz) n.pl. [with sing. v.] [ME. schamel, butcher's bench; ult. < L.] 1. a slaughterhouse 2. a scene of great slaughter, destruction, or disorder

shame (shām) n. [OE. scamu] 1. a painful feeling of guilt for improper behavior, etc. 2. dishonor or disgrace 3. something regrettable or outrageous —vt. **shamed, sham'ing** 1. to cause to feel shame 2. to dishonor or disgrace 3. to force by a sense of shame —**put to shame** 1. to cause to feel shame 2. to surpass —**shame'ful** adj. —**shame'ful·ly** adv. —**shame'ful·ness** n.

shame'faced' adj. 1. bashful; shy 2. showing shame; ashamed

shame'less adj. having or showing no shame, modesty, o₁ decency; brazen

sham·poo (sham pōō') vt. -**pooed'**, -**poo'ing** [Hind. *chāmpnā*, to press] 1. to wash (the hair) 2. to wash (a rug, sofa, etc.) —n. 1. a shampooing 2. a liquid soap, etc. used for this

sham·rock (sham'räk') n. [Ir. *seamar*, clover] a cloverlike plant with leaflets in groups of three: the emblem of Ireland

Shang·hai (shaŋ'hī') seaport in E China: pop. c.10,000,000

shang·hai (shaŋ'hī') vt. -**haied'**, -**hai'ing** [< such kidnapping for crews on the China run] to kidnap, usually by drugging, for service aboard ship

shank (shaŋk) n. [OE. *scanca*] 1. the part of the leg between the knee and the ankle in man, or a corresponding part in animals 2. the whole leg 3. the part between the handle and the working part (of a tool, etc.) —**shank of the evening** early evening

shan't (shant) shall not

shan·tung (shan'tuŋ') n. [< *Shantung*, province of China] a silk or silky fabric with an uneven surface

shan·ty (shan'tē) n., pl. -**ties** [< CanadFr. *chantier*, workshop] a small, shabby dwelling; shack; hut

shape (shāp) n. [< OE. (ge)*sceap*, a form] 1. that quality of a thing which depends on the relative position of all the points on its surface; physical form 2. the contour of the body 3. definite or regular form [to begin to take *shape*] 4. [Colloq.] physical condition —vt. **shaped, shap'ing** 1. to give definite shape to 2. to arrange, express, etc. in definite form 3. to adapt [*shaped* to our needs] —**shape up** to develop to a definite or satisfactory form, etc. —**take shape** to show distinct development —**shape'less** adj. —**shape'less·ness** n.

shape'ly adj. -**li·er, -li·est** having a pleasing figure: esp. of a woman

shard (shärd) n. [OE. *sceard*] a broken piece, esp. of pottery

share¹ (sher) n. [< OE. *scearu*] 1. a portion that belongs to an individual 2. any of the equal parts of capital stock of a corporation —vt. **shared, shar'ing** 1. to distribute in shares 2. to have or use in common with others —vi. to have a share (*in*)

share² (sher) n. [OE. *scear*] a plow-share

share'crop vi., vt. -**cropped'**, -**crop'ping** to work (land) for a share of the crop —**share'crop'per** n.

share'hold'er n. a person who owns shares of stock in a corporation

shark¹ (shärk) n. [prob. < G. *schurke*, scoundrel] 1. a swindler 2. [Slang] an expert in a given activity

shark² (shärk) n. [< ?] a large, predatory sea fish with a tough, gray skin

shark'skin' (-skin') n. a smooth, silky cloth of wool, rayon, etc.

SHARK

sharp (shärp) adj. [OE. *scearp*] 1. having a fine edge or point for cutting or piercing 2. having a point or edge; not rounded 3. not gradual; abrupt 4. clearly defined; distinct [a *sharp* contrast] 5. quick in perception; clever 6. attentive; vigilant 7. crafty; underhanded 8. harsh; severe, as temper 9. violent, as an attack 10. brisk; active 11. intense, as a pain 12. pungent 13. nippy, as a wind 14. [Slang] smartly dressed 15. *Music* above the true pitch —n. 1. [Colloq.] an expert 2. *Music a)* a tone one half step above another *b)* the symbol (#) for such a note —vt., vi. *Music* to make or become sharp —adv. 1. in a sharp manner; specif., *a)* abruptly or briskly *b)* attentively or alertly *c) Music* above the true pitch 2. precisely [one o'clock *sharp*] —**sharp'ly** adv. —**sharp'ness** n.

sharp'en vt., vi. to make or become sharp —**sharp'en·er** n.

sharp'er n. a swindler or cheat

sharp'-eyed' adj. having keen sight or perception: also **sharp'-sight'ed**

sharp'ie (-ē) n. [Colloq.] a shrewd, cunning person, esp. a sharper

sharp'shoot'er n. a good marksman

sharp'-tongued' adj. using sharp or harshly critical speech

sharp'-wit'ted adj. thinking quickly and effectively

shat·ter (shat'ər) vt., vi. [ME. *schateren*, scatter] 1. to break or burst into pieces suddenly 2. to damage or be damaged severely

shat'ter·proof' adj. that will resist shattering [*shatterproof* glass]

shave (shāv) vt. **shaved, shaved** or **shav'en, shav'ing** [OE. *sceafan*] 1. to cut away thin slices or sections from 2. *a)* to cut off (hair) at the surface of the skin *b)* to cut the hair to the surface of (the face, etc.) *c)* to cut the beard of (a person) 3. to barely touch in passing; graze —vi. to cut off a beard with a razor, etc. —n. the act or an instance of shaving

shav'er n. 1. one who shaves 2. an instrument used in shaving, esp. one with electrically operated cutters 3. [Colloq.] a boy; lad

shav'ing n. 1. the act of one who shaves 2. a thin piece of wood, metal, etc. shaved off

Shaw (shô), George Bernard 1856-

1950; Brit. dramatist & critic —**Sha·vi·an** (shā′vē ən) *adj.*, *n.*

shawl (shôl) *n.* [< Per. *shāl*] an oblong or square cloth worn as a covering for the head or shoulders

shay (shā) *n.* [< CHAISE, assumed as pl.] [Dial.] a light carriage; chaise

she (shē) *pron.* *for pl.* see THEY [< OE. *seo*] the woman, girl, or female animal previously mentioned —*n.* a woman, girl, or female animal

sheaf (shēf) *n.*, *pl.* **sheaves** (shēvz) [OE. *sceaf*] 1. a bundle of cut stalks of grain, etc. 2. a collection, as of papers, bound in a bundle

shear (shir) *vt.* **sheared**, **sheared** or **shorn**, **shear′ing** [OE. *scieran*] 1. to cut as with shears 2. to clip (hair) from (the head), (wool) from (sheep), etc. 3. to divest [*shorn* of power] —*n.* 1. a machine for cutting metal 2. a shearing —**shear′er** *n.*

shears *n.pl.* 1. large scissors 2. a large tool or machine with two opposed blades, used to cut metal, etc.

sheath (shēth) *n.*, *pl.* **sheaths** (shēthz, shēths) [OE. *sceath*] 1. a case for the blade of a knife, sword, etc. 2. a covering resembling this 3. a woman's closefitting dress

sheathe (shēth) *vt.* **sheathed**, **sheath′ing** 1. to put into a sheath 2. to enclose in a case or covering

sheath·ing (shē′thiŋ) *n.* something that sheathes, as boards, etc. forming the base for roofing or siding

she·bang (shə baŋ′) *n.* [Colloq.] an affair, business, contrivance, etc.: in phrase **the whole shebang**

shed[1] (shed) *n.* [OE. *scead*] a small structure for shelter or storage

shed[2] (shed) *vt.* **shed**, **shed′ding** [OE. *sceadan*, to separate] 1. to pour out 2. to cause to flow [to *shed* tears] 3. to radiate [to *shed* confidence] 4. to cause to flow off [oilskin *sheds* water] 5. to cast off (a natural growth, as hair, etc.) —*vi.* to shed hair, etc. —**shed blood** to kill violently

she'd (shēd) 1. she had 2. she would

sheen (shēn) *n.* [< OE. *sciene*, beautiful] brightness; luster —**sheen′y** *adj.*

sheep (shēp) *n.*, *pl.* **sheep** [OE. *sceap*] 1. a cud-chewing mammal related to the goats, with heavy wool and edible flesh called mutton 2. one who is meek, timid, submissive, etc.

sheep dog a dog trained to herd sheep

sheep′fold[1] *n.* a pen or enclosure for sheep: also **sheep′cote**[1] (-kōt′)

sheep′ish *adj.* 1. embarrassed or chagrined 2. shy or bashful —**sheep′ish·ly** *adv.* —**sheep′ish·ness** *n.*

sheep′skin[1] *n.* 1. the skin of a sheep 2. parchment or leather made from it 3. [Colloq.] a diploma

sheer[1] (shir) *vi.*, *vt.* [var. of SHEAR] to turn aside or cause to turn aside from a course; swerve

sheer[2] (shir) *adj.* [< ON. *skærr*, bright] 1. very thin; transparent: said of textiles 2. absolute; utter [*sheer* folly] 3. extremely steep —*adv.* 1. completely; utterly 2. very steeply

sheet[1] (shēt) *n.* [OE. *sceat*] 1. a large piece of cotton, linen, etc., used on a bed 2. *a)* a single piece of paper *b)* [Colloq.] a newspaper 3. a broad, continuous surface or expanse, as of flame, ice, etc. 4. a broad, thin piece of any material, as glass, plywood, metal, etc.

sheet[2] (shēt) *n.* [short for OE. *sceatline*] a rope for controlling the set of a sail

sheet′ing *n.* 1. cotton or linen material used for making sheets 2. material used to cover or line a surface [copper *sheeting*]

sheet metal metal rolled thin in the form of a sheet

sheet music music printed on unbound sheets of paper

sheik, sheikh (shēk) *n.* [Ar. *shaikh*, lit., old man] the chief of an Arab family, tribe, or village

shek·el (shek′'l) *n.* [< Heb. *shāqal*, weigh] 1. a gold or silver coin of the ancient Hebrews 2. [*pl.*] [Slang] money

shelf (shelf) *n.*, *pl.* **shelves** [< MLowG. *schelf*] 1. a thin, flat board fixed horizontally to a wall, used for holding things 2. something like a shelf, as *a)* a ledge *b)* a sand bar —**on the shelf** out of use, activity, etc.

shell (shel) *n.* [OE. *sciel*] 1. a hard outer covering, as of a turtle, egg, nut, etc. 2. something like a shell in being hollow, empty, a covering, etc. 3. a light, narrow racing boat rowed by a team 4. an explosive artillery projectile 5. a small-arms cartridge —*vt.* 1. to remove the shell or covering from [to *shell* peas] 2. to bombard —**shell out** [Colloq.] to pay out (money)

she'll (shēl) 1. she shall 2. she will

shel·lac, shel·lack (shə lak′) *n.* [< SHELL & LAC] 1. a resin usually produced in thin, flaky layers or shells 2. a thin varnish containing this resin and alcohol —*vt.* **-lacked′**, **-lack′ing** 1. to apply shellac to 2. [Slang] *a)* to beat *b)* to defeat decisively

-shelled (sheld) *a combining form meaning* having a (specified kind of) shell

Shel·ley (shel′ē), **Per·cy Bysshe** (pur′sē bish) 1792-1822; Eng. poet

shell′fire[1] *n.* the firing of artillery shells

shell′fish[1] *n.*, *pl.*: see FISH any aquatic animal with a shell, esp. an edible one, as the clam, lobster, etc.

shel·ter (shel′tər) *n.* [< ? OE. *scield*, shield + *truma*, a troop] 1. something that protects, as from the elements, danger, etc. 2. a being covered, protected, etc. —*vt.* to provide shelter for; protect —*vi.* to find shelter

shelve (shelv) *vt.* **shelved**, **shelv′ing** 1. to furnish with shelves 2. to put on a shelf 3. to put aside; defer

shelves (shelvz) *n.*, *pl.* of SHELF

shelv′ing *n.* 1. material for shelves 2. shelves collectively

she·nan·i·gan (shi nan′i g'n) *n.* [< ? Ir. *sionnachuighim*, I play the fox] [*usually pl.*] [Colloq.] trickery; mischief

Shen·yang (shun′yaŋ′) city in NE China: pop. 2,423,000

shep·herd (shep′ərd) *n.* [see SHEEP & HERD] 1. one who herds sheep 2. a clergyman —*vt.* to herd, lead, etc. as a shepherd —**shep′herd·ess** *n.fem.*

sher·bet (shur′bət) *n.* [< Ar. *sharbah*, a drink] a frozen dessert like an ice, but with gelatin and, often, milk added

sher·iff (sher′if) *n.* [< OE. *scir*, shire, + *gerefa*, chief officer] the chief law-enforcement officer of a county

Sher·pa (shur′pə, sher′-) *n., pl.* -**pas**, -**pa** any of a Tibetan people of Nepal, famous as mountain climbers

sher·ry (sher′ē) *n., pl.* -**ries** [< *Jerez*, Spain] 1. a strong, yellow or brown Spanish wine 2. any similar wine

she′s (shēz) 1. she is 2. she has

shew (shō) *n., vt., vi.* shewed, shewn or shewed, shew′ing *archaic sp. of* SHOW

shib·bo·leth (shib′ə ləth) *n.* [< Heb. *shibbōleth*, a stream] 1. *Bible* the test word used to distinguish the enemy: Judg. 12:4-6 2. any password 3. any phrase, custom, etc. peculiar to a certain class, faction, etc.

shied (shīd) *pt. & pp. of* SHY¹

shield (shēld) *n.* [OE. *scield*] 1. a piece of armor worn on the forearm to ward off blows, etc. 2. one that guards, protects, etc. 3. anything shaped like a shield —*vt., vi.* to defend; protect

shift (shift) *vt.* [OE. *sciftan*, divide] 1. to move from one person or place to another 2. to replace by another or others —*vi.* 1. to change position, direction, etc. 2. to get along [to *shift* for oneself] —*n.* 1. a shifting; transfer 2. a plan of conduct, esp. for an emergency 3. an evasion; trick 4. a gearshift 5. *a)* a group of people working in relay with another *b)* their regular work period —**make shift** to manage (*with* the means at hand)

shift′less *adj.* incapable, inefficient, lazy, etc. —**shift′less·ness** *n.*

shift′y *adj.* -**i·er**, -**i·est** of a tricky or deceitful nature; evasive —**shift′i·ly** *adv.* —**shift′i·ness** *n.*

Shih Tzu (shē′ dzoō′) *pl.* **Shih Tzus**, **Shih Tzu** [< Chin. *shin*, lion + *tzu*, son] a small dog with long, silky hair and short legs

shill (shil) *n.* [Slang] a confederate, as of a carnival operator, who pretends to buy, bet, etc. so as to lure others

shil·le·lagh (shi lā′lē, -lə) *n.* [< *Shillelagh*, Ir. village] a cudgel

shil·ling (shil′iŋ) *n.* [OE. *scylling*] a former British money of account and silver coin, equal to 1/20 of a pound

shil·ly-shal·ly (shil′ē shal′ē) *vi.* -**lied**, -**ly·ing** [< *shall I?*] to be irresolute; vacillate, esp. over trifles

shim (shim) *n.* [< ?] a thin wedge of wood, metal, etc. as for filling space

shim·mer (shim′ər) *vi.* [OE. *scymrian*] to shine with an unsteady light; glimmer —*n.* a shimmering light

shim·my (shim′ē) *n.* [< a jazz dance < *CHEMISE*] a marked vibration or wobble, as in a car's front wheels —*vi.*

-**mied**, -**my·ing** to vibrate or wobble

shin (shin) *n.* [OE. *scinu*] the front part of the leg between the knee and the ankle —*vt., vi.* shinned, shin′ning to climb (a pole, etc.) by gripping with hands and legs: also **shin′ny**

shin′bone′ *n. same as* TIBIA

shin·dig (shin′dig′) *n.* [< colloq. *shindy*, commotion) [Colloq.] a dance, party, or other informal gathering

shine (shīn) *vi.* **shone** or, esp. for vt. 2, **shined**, **shin′ing** [OE. *scinan*] 1. to emit or reflect light 2. to stand out; excel 3. to exhibit itself clearly [love *shining* from her face] —*vt.* 1. to direct the light of 2. to make shiny by polishing —*n.* 1. brightness; radiance 2. luster; gloss

shin′er (-ər) *n.* 1. a silvery minnow 2. [Slang] *same as* BLACK EYE

shin·gle¹ (shiŋ′g'l) *n.* [prob. < Scand.] 1. coarse, waterworn gravel, as on a beach 2. an area covered with this —**shin′gly** *adj.* -**gli·er**, -**gli·est**

shin·gle² (shiŋ′g'l) *n.* [< OE. *scindel*] 1. a thin, wedge-shaped piece of wood, slate, etc. laid with others in overlapping rows, as for roofs 2. a short haircut, tapered at the nape 3. [Colloq.] a small signboard, as of a doctor —*vt.* -**gled**, -**gling** to cover (a roof, etc.) with shingles

shin·gles (shiŋ′g'lz) *n.* [< L. *cingere*, to gird] a virus disease with skin blisters along the course of a nerve

shin′guard′ *n.* a padded guard worn to protect the shins in some sports

shin′splints′ (-splints′) *n.pl.* [*with sing. v.*] [< SHIN + ? *splint*, growth on bone of a horse's leg] painful strain of muscles of the lower leg

Shin·to (shin′tō) *n.* [Jap. < Chin. *shin*, god + *tao*, way] a religion of Japan, emphasizing ancestor worship

shin·y (shīn′ē) *adj.* -**i·er**, -**i·est** 1. bright; shining 2. highly polished —**shin′i·ness** *n.*

ship (ship) *n.* [OE. *scip*] 1. any large vessel navigating deep water 2. a ship's officers and crew 3. an aircraft —*vt.* shipped, ship′ping 1. to put or take on board a ship 2. to send or transport by any carrier [to *ship* coal by rail] 3. *a)* to take in (water) over the side in a heavy sea *b)* to put in place on a vessel [*ship* the oars] —*vi.* to go aboard ship; embark —**ship′per** *n.*

-**ship** (ship) [OE. -*scipe*] *a suffix meaning:* 1. the quality or state of [*friendship*] 2. *a)* the rank or office of [*governorship*] *b)* one having the rank of [*lordship*] 3. skill as [*leadership*] 4. all persons (of a specified group) collectively [*readership*]

ship′board′ *n.* a ship: chiefly in on **shipboard** aboard a ship

ship′build′er *n.* one whose business is building ships —**ship′build′ing** *n.*

ship′mate′ *n.* a fellow sailor

ship′ment *n.* 1. the shipping of goods 2. goods shipped

ship′ping *n.* 1. the act or business of

transporting goods 2. ships collectively, as of a nation, port, etc.

shipping clerk an employee who supervises the shipping of goods and keeps records of shipments

ship'shape' adj. having everything neatly in place; trim

ship'wreck' n. 1. the remains of a wrecked ship 2. the loss of a ship through storm, etc. 3. ruin; failure —vt. to cause to undergo shipwreck

ship'yard' n. a place where ships are built and repaired

shire (shīr) n. [OE. scir, office] in Great Britain, a county

shirk (shurk) vt., vi. [< ?] to neglect or evade (a duty, etc.) —shirk'er n.

shirr (shur) n. [< ?] same as SHIRRING —vt. 1. to make shirring in (cloth) 2. to bake (eggs) in buttered dishes

shirr'ing n. a gathering made in cloth by drawing the material up on parallel rows of short stitches

shirt (shurt) n. [OE. scyrte] 1. a garment worn by men on the upper part of the body 2. an undershirt —keep one's shirt on [Slang] to remain patient or calm

shirt'tail' (-tāl') n. the part of a shirt extending below the waist

shirt'waist' (-wāst') n. a woman's blouse tailored like a shirt

shish ke-bab (shish' kə bäb') [< Ar. shish, skewer + kabāb, kebab] a dish of kebabs, esp. of lamb

shiv (shiv) n. [prob. < Romany chiv, blade] [Slang] a knife

shiv·er[1] (shiv'ər) n. [ME. schivere] a fragment or splinter —vt., vi. to break into fragments or splinters

shiv'er[2] (shiv'ər) vi. [< ? OE. ceaf, jaw] to shake or tremble, as from fear or cold —n. a shaking, trembling, etc. —shiv'er·y adj.

shlep, shlepp (shlep) n. [Slang] var. of SCHLEP

shmaltz (shmälts) n. [Slang] var. of SCHMALTZ

shoal[1] (shōl) n. [OE. scolu] 1. a large group; crowd 2. a school of fish

shoal[2] (shōl) n. [< OE. sceald, shallow] 1. a shallow place in a river, sea, etc. 2. a sand bar forming a shallow place

shoat (shōt) n. a young hog

shock[1] (shäk) n. [MFr. choquer, collide] 1. a sudden, powerful blow, shake, etc. 2. a) a sudden emotional disturbance b) the cause of this 3. an extreme stimulation of the nerves by the passage of electric current through the body 4. a disorder of the blood circulation, produced by hemorrhage, disturbance of heart function, etc. —vt. 1. to astonish, horrify, etc. 2. to produce electrical shock in

shock[2] (shäk) n. [ME. schokke] bundles of grain stacked together

shock[3] (shäk) n. [< ? prec.] a thick, bushy or tangled mass, as of hair

shock absorber a device, as on the springs of a car, that absorbs the force of bumps and jarring

shock'er n. 1. anything that shocks 2. a sensational story, play, etc.

shock'ing adj. 1. causing great surprise and distress 2. disgusting

shock'proof' adj. able to absorb shock without being damaged

shock therapy the treatment of certain severe mental illnesses by using electricity, drugs, etc., producing convulsions or coma

shock troops troops trained to lead an attack

shod (shäd) pt. & pp. of SHOE

shod·dy (shäd'ē) n., pl. -dies [< ?] 1. an inferior woolen cloth made from used fabrics 2. anything worth less than it seems to be —adj. -di·er, -di·est 1. made of inferior material 2. poorly done or made 3. sham —shod'di·ly adv. —shod'di·ness n.

shoe (shōō) n. [< OE. sceoh] 1. an outer covering for the foot 2. a horseshoe 3. the part of a brake that presses against a wheel 4. the casing of a pneumatic tire —vt. shod or shoed, shoe'ing to furnish with shoes —fill one's shoes to take one's place

shoe'horn' n. an implement used to help slip one's heel into a shoe

shoe'lace' n. a length of cord, etc. used for lacing and fastening a shoe

shoe'mak'er n. one whose business is making or repairing shoes

shoe'shine' n. the cleaning and polishing of a pair of shoes

shoe'string' n. 1. a shoelace 2. a small amount of capital —adj. at or near the ankles [a shoestring catch]

shoe tree a form inserted in a shoe to stretch it or preserve its shape

shone (shōn) alt. pt. & pp. of SHINE

shoo (shōō) interj. go away! get out! —vt. shooed, shoo'ing to drive away, as by crying "shoo"

shoo'-in' n. [Colloq.] one expected to win easily in a race, etc.

shook (shook) pt. of SHAKE —shook up [Slang] upset; agitated

shoot (shōōt) vt. shot, shoot'ing [OE. sceotan] 1. to move swiftly over, by, etc. [to shoot the rapids] 2. to variegate (with another color, etc.) 3. to thrust or put forth 4. to discharge or fire (a bullet, arrow, gun, etc.) 5. to send forth swiftly, or with force 6. to hit, wound, etc. with a bullet, arrow, etc. 7. to photograph 8. Sports a) to throw or drive (a ball, etc.) toward the objective b) to score (a goal, points, etc.) —vi. 1. to move swiftly 2. to be felt suddenly, as pain 3. to grow rapidly 4. to jut out 5. to send forth a missile; discharge bullets, etc. 6. to use guns, etc., as in hunting —n. 1. a shooting trip, contest, etc. 2. a new growth; sprout —shoot at (or for) [Colloq.] to strive for

shoot'-out', shoot'out' n. [Slang] a battle, as between police and criminals, in which small arms are used

shop (shäp) n. [< OE. sceoppa, booth] 1. a place where certain things are offered for sale; esp., a small store 2. a place where a particular kind of work is done —vi. shopped, shop'ping to visit shops to examine or buy goods —talk shop to discuss one's work

shop'keep'er n. one who owns or operates a shop, or small store

shop'lift'er n. one who steals articles

from a store during shopping hours —shop′lift′ vt., vi.

shoppe (shäp) n. old sp. of SHOP (n. 1): now used only in shop names

shop′per n. 1. one who shops 2. one hired by a store to shop for others 3. one hired by a store to compare competitors′ prices, etc.

shopping center a complex of stores, restaurants, etc. with a common parking area

shop′talk′ n. 1. the specialized words and idioms of those in the same work 2. talk about work, esp. after hours

shop′worn′ adj. soiled, faded, etc. from being displayed in a shop

shore[1] (shôr) n. [ME. schore] land at the edge of a body of water

shore[2] (shôr) n. [ME. schore] a prop, beam, etc. used for support, etc. —vt. shored, shor′ing to support as with shores; prop (up)

shore patrol a detail of the U.S. Navy, Coast Guard, or Marine Corps acting as military police on shore

SHORES

shorn (shôrn) alt. pp. of SHEAR

short (shôrt) adj. [OE. scort] 1. not measuring much from end to end in space or time 2. not great in range or scope 3. not tall 4. brief; concise 5. not retentive [a short memory] 6. curt; abrupt 7. less than a sufficient or correct amount 8. crisp or flaky, as pastry rich in shortening 9. designating a sale of securities, etc. which the seller does not yet own but expects to buy later at a lower price —n. 1. something short 2. [pl.] a) short trousers b) a man′s undergarment like these 3. same as: a) SHORTSTOP b) SHORT CIRCUIT —adv. 1. abruptly; suddenly 2. briefly; concisely 3. so as to be short in length —vt., vi. 1. to give less than what is needed or usual 2. same as: a) SHORTCHANGE b) SHORT-CIRCUIT —fall (or come) short to fail to reach, suffice, etc. —in short briefly —run short to have less than enough —short of less than or lacking —short′ness n.

short′age n. a deficiency in the amount needed or expected; deficit

short′bread′ n. a rich, crumbly cake or cookie made with much shortening

short′cake′ n. a light biscuit or a sweet cake served with fruit, etc.

short′change′ vt., vi. -changed′, -chang′ing [Colloq.] to give less money than is due in change

short circuit a connection between two points in an electric circuit resulting in a side circuit that deflects current or in excessive current flow causing damage 2. popularly, a disrupted electric current caused by this —short′-cir′cuit vt., vi.

short′com′ing n. a defect or deficiency

short′cut′ n. 1. a shorter route 2. any way of saving time, effort, etc.

short′en vt., vi. to make or become short or shorter

short′en·ing n. edible fat used to make pastry, etc. crisp or flaky

short′hand′ n. any system of speed writing using symbols for words

short′-hand′ed adj. short of workers

short′horn′ n. any of a breed of cattle with short, curved horns

short′-lived′ (-līvd′, -livd′) adj. having a short life span or existence

short′ly adv. 1. briefly 2. soon 3. abruptly and rudely; curtly

short order any food that can be cooked or served quickly when ordered

short′-range′ adj. reaching over a short distance or period of time

short ribs rib ends of beef from the forequarter

short shrift very little care or attention —make short shrift of to make short work of

short′sight′ed adj. 1. nearsighted 2. lacking in foresight —short′sight′-ed·ly adv. —short′sight′ed·ness n.

short′-spo′ken adj. using few words, esp. to the point of rudeness; curt

short′stop′ n. Baseball the infielder between second and third base

short story a piece of prose fiction shorter than a short novel

short subject a short film, as an animated cartoon, shown along with a featured motion picture

short′-tem′pered adj. easily or quickly angered

short′-term′ adj. for or extending over a short time

short ton 2,000 pounds: see TON

short′wave′ n. a radio wave 60 meters or less in length

short′-wind′ed (-win′did) adj. easily put out of breath by exertion

shot[1] (shät) n. [OE. sceot] 1. the act of shooting 2. range; scope 3. an attempt; try 4. a pointed, critical remark 5. the path of an object thrown, etc. 6. a) a projectile for a gun b) projectiles collectively 7. small pellets of lead for a shotgun 8. the heavy metal ball used in the shot put 9. a marksman 10. a photograph or a continuous film sequence 11. a hypodermic injection, as of vaccine 12. a drink of liquor —call the shots to direct or control what is done

shot[2] (shät) pt. & pp. of SHOOT —adj. [Colloq.] ruined or worn out

shot′gun′ n. 1. a gun for firing small shot at close range 2. Football an offensive formation in which the quarterback stands a few yards behind the line to receive the ball

shot put a contest in which a heavy metal ball is propelled with an overhand thrust from the shoulder —shot′-put′ter n. —shot′-put′ting n.

should (shood) v. [OE. sceolde] 1. pt. of SHALL 2. an auxiliary used to express: *a)* obligation, duty, etc. *(you should help) b)* expectation or probability *(he should be here soon) c)* a future condition *(if I should die)*

shoul·der (shōl'dər) *n.* [OE. *sculder*] 1. *a)* the joint connecting the arm or forelimb with the body *b)* the part of the body including this joint 2. *[pl.]* the two shoulders and the part of the back between them 3. a shoulderlike projection 4. the land along the edge of a road —*vt.* 1. to push through, as with the shoulder 2. to carry upon the shoulder 3. to assume the burden of —**straight from the shoulder** without reserve; frankly —**turn** (or **give**) **a cold shoulder** to snub or shun

shoulder blade either of the two flat bones in the upper back

shoulder harness an anchored strap passing across the upper body and used with a seat belt, as in a car

should·n't should not

shout (shout) *n.* [ME. *schoute*] a loud cry or call —*vt., vi.* to utter or cry out in a shout —**shout'er** *n.*

shove (shuv) *vt., vi.* shoved, shov'ing [OE. *scufan*] 1. to push, as along a surface 2. to push roughly —*n.* a push —**shove off** 1. to push (a boat) away from shore 2. [Colloq.] to leave

shov·el (shuv''l) *n.* [OE. *sceofl*] a tool with a broad scoop and a long handle, for lifting and moving loose material —*vt.* -eled or -elled, -el·ing or -el·ling 1. to move with a shovel 2. to dig out with a shovel

shov·el·ful *n., pl.* -fuls' as much as a shovel will hold

show (shō) *vt.* showed, shown or showed, show'ing [< OE. *sceawian*] 1. to bring or put in sight 2. to guide; conduct 3. to point out 4. to reveal, as by behavior 5. to prove; demonstrate 6. to bestow (favor, mercy, etc.) —*vi.* 1. to be or become seen; appear 2. to be noticeable 3. to finish third in a horse race —*n.* 1. a showing or demonstration 2. pompous display 3. pretense *(his anger was mere show)* 4. a public display or exhibition 5. a presentation of entertainment —**show off** to make a display of, esp. a vain display —**show up** 1. to expose 2. to be seen 3. to arrive

show'boat' *n.* a boat with a theater and actors who play river towns

show'case' *n.* a glass-enclosed case for displaying things, as in a store

show'down' *n.* [Colloq.] an action that brings matters to a climax

show·er (shou'ər) *n.* [OE. *scur*] 1. a brief fall of rain, sleet, etc. 2. a sudden, abundant fall, as of sparks 3. a party at which gifts are presented to the guest of honor 4. a bath in which the body is sprayed with fine streams of water: in full **shower bath** —*vt.* 1. to spray with water, etc. 2. to pour forth as in a shower —*vi.* 1. to fall or come as a shower 2. to take a shower bath —**show'er·y** *adj.*

show'ing *n.* 1. a bringing to view or notice; exhibition 2. a performance, appearance, etc. *(a good showing in the contest)*

show·man (shō'mən) *n., pl.* -men 1. one whose business is producing shows 2. a person skilled at presenting anything in a striking manner —**show'man·ship'** *n.*

shown (shōn) *alt. pp. of* SHOW

show'off' *n.* one who shows off

show of hands a raising of hands, as in voting or volunteering

show'piece' *n.* 1. something displayed or exhibited 2. something that is a fine example of its kind

show'place' *n.* 1. a place displayed to the public for its beauty, etc. 2. any beautiful place

show'room' *n.* a room where goods are displayed for advertising or sale

show window a store window in which merchandise is displayed

show'y *adj.* -i·er, -i·est 1. of striking appearance 2. attracting attention in a gaudy way —**show'i·ness** *n.*

shrank (shraŋk) *alt. pt. of* SHRINK

shrap·nel (shrap'n'l) *n.* [< Gen. *Shrapnel* (1761–1842), its Brit. inventor] 1. an artillery shell filled with an explosive charge and small metal balls 2. these balls or the shell fragments scattered on explosion

shred (shred) *n.* [OE. *screade*] 1. a narrow strip cut or torn off 2. a fragment —*vt.* shred'ded or shred, shred'ding to cut or tear into shreds —shred'da·ble *adj.* —shred'der *n.*

Shreve·port (shrēv'pôrt) city in NW La.: pop. 206,000

shrew (shrōō) *n.* [< OE. *screawa*] 1. a small, mouselike mammal with a long snout 2. a nagging, evil-tempered woman —shrew'ish *n.*

shrewd (shrōōd) *adj.* [see prec.] clever or sharp in practical affairs; astute —shrewd'ly *adv.* —shrewd'ness *n.*

shriek (shrēk) *vi., vt.* [ME. *schriken*] to make or utter with a loud, piercing cry; screech —*n.* such a cry

shrift (shrift) *n.* [ult. < L. *scribere,* write] [Archaic] confession to and absolution by a priest See also SHORT SHRIFT

shrike (shrīk) *n.* [OE. *scric*] a shrill-voiced bird of prey with a hooked beak

shrill (shril) *adj.* [echoic] producing a high, thin piercing sound —*vt., vi.* to utter (with) a shrill sound —shrill'ness *n.* —shril'ly *adv.*

shrimp (shrimp) *n.* [OE. *scrimman,* shrink] 1. a small, long-tailed crustacean, valued as food 2. [Colloq.] a small or insignificant person

shrine (shrīn) *n.* [< L. *scrinium,* box] 1. a container holding sacred relics 2. a saint's tomb 3. a place of worship 4. any hallowed place

shrink (shriŋk) *vi.* shrank or shrunk, shrunk or shrunk'en, shrink'ing [OE. *scrincan*] 1. to contract, as from cold, wetting, etc. 2. to lessen, as in amount 3. to draw back; flinch —*vt.* to make shrink —shrink'a·ble *adj.*

shrink'age *n.* 1. a shrinking 2. the amount of shrinking

shrinking violet a very shy person

shrive (shrīv) *vt.* shrived or shrove (shrōv), shriv·en (shriv''n) or shrived, shriv'ing [OE. *scrifan*] [Archaic] to hear the confession of and give absolution to

shriv·el (shriv'l) vt., vi. -eled or -elled, -el·ing or -el·ling [prob. < Scand.] to shrink and wrinkle or wither

shroud (shroud) n. [OE. scrud] 1. a cloth used to wrap a corpse for burial 2. something that covers, veils, etc. 3. any of the ropes from a ship's side to a masthead —vt. to hide; cover

Shrove Tuesday [see SHRIVE] the last day before Lent

shrub (shrub) n. [OE. scrybb, brushwood] a low, woody plant with several stems; bush —shrub'by adj.

shrub'ber·y n. shrubs collectively

shrug (shrug) vt., vi. shrugged, shrug'ging [ME. schruggen] to draw up (the shoulders), as in indifference, doubt, etc. —n. the gesture made

shrunk (shruŋk) alt. pt. & pp. of SHRINK

shrunk'en alt. pp. of SHRINK —adj. contracted in size

shtg. shortage

shtick (shtik) n. [Yid.] [Slang] a comic bit or special gimmick

shuck (shuk) n. [< ?] a shell, pod, or husk —vt. to remove the shucks of

shucks (shuks) interj. [< prec.] an exclamation of disappointment, disgust, etc.

shud·der (shud'ər) vi. [ME. schoderen] to shake or tremble, as in horror —n. a shuddering

shuf·fle (shuf'l) vt., vi. -fled, -fling [prob. < LowG. schuffeln] 1. to move (the feet) with a dragging gait 2. to mix (playing cards) 3. to mix together in a jumble —n. a shuffling

shuf'fle·board n. [< shovel board] a game in which disks are pushed with a cue toward numbered squares

shun (shun) vt. shunned, shun'ning [OE. scunian] to keep away from; avoid scrupulously

shun'pike' adj. avoiding turnpikes and expressways —shun'pik'er n.

shunt (shunt) vt., vi. [ME. schunten] 1. to move or turn to one side 2. to switch, as a train, from one track to another —n. 1. a shunting 2. a railroad switch 3. same as BYPASS (n. 2)

shush (shush) interj. [echoic] hush! be quiet! —vt. to say "shush" to

shut (shut) vt. shut, shut'ting [OE. scyttan] 1. to move (a door, lid, etc.) so as to close (an opening, container, etc.) 2. a) to prevent entrance to or exit from b) to confine (in a room, etc.) 3. to bring together the parts of (an umbrella, etc.) —vi. to be or become shut —adj. closed, fastened, etc. —shut down to cease or cause to cease operating —shut off to prevent passage of or through —shut out 1. to deny entrance to 2. to prevent from scoring —shut up 1. to confine 2. [Colloq.] to stop or make stop talking

shut'down' n. a stoppage of work or activity, as in a factory

shut'eye' n. [Slang] sleep

shut'-in' adj. confined indoors by illness —n. an invalid who is shut-in

shut'out' n. a preventing of the opposing side or team from scoring

shut'ter n. 1. a person or thing that shuts 2. a movable cover for a window 3. a device for opening and closing the aperture of a camera lens —vt. to close or furnish with shutters

shut·tle (shut'l) n. [OE. scytel, missile] 1. a device that carries thread back and forth, as in weaving 2. a bus, etc. making back-and-forth trips over a short route —vt., vi. -tled, -tling to move back and forth rapidly

shut'tle·cock' n. a rounded piece of cork having a flat end stuck with feathers: used in badminton

shy¹ (shī) adj. shy'er or shi'er, shy'est or shi'est [OE. sceoh] 1. easily frightened; timid 2. not at ease with others; bashful 3. distrustful; wary 4. [Slang] lacking —vi. shied, shy'ing 1. to move suddenly as when startled 2. to be or become cautious, etc. —shy'ly adv. —shy'ness n.

shy² (shī) vt., vi. shied, shy'ing [< ?] to fling, esp. sideways

shy·ster (shī'stər) n. [< ?] [Slang] a lawyer who uses unethical or tricky methods

Si Chem. silicon

Si·am (sī am') former name of THAILAND

Si·a·mese (sī'ə mēz') adj., n., pl. -mese' same as THAI

Siamese twins [after such a pair born in Siam] any pair of twins born with bodies joined together

Si·ber·i·a (sī bir'ē ə) N Asiatic section of the U.S.S.R., between the Urals & the Pacific —Si·ber'i·an adj., n.

sib·i·lant (sib'i ənt) adj. [< L. sibilare, hiss] having or making a hissing sound —n. a sibilant consonant, as (s) or (z) —sib'i·late' (-āt') vt., vi. -lat'ed, -lat'ing

sib·ling (sib'liŋ) n. [< OE. sib, kinsman + -J ING] a brother or sister

sib·yl (sib'l) n. [< Gr. sibylla] a prophetess of ancient Greece or Rome —sib'yl·line' (-lin', -ēn') adj.

sic¹ (sik) adj. [L.] thus; so: used within brackets, [sic], to show that a quoted passage, esp. one containing some error, is precisely reproduced

sic² (sik) vt. [< SEEK] sicked, sick'ing to incite (a dog) to attack

Sic·i·ly (sis'l ē) island of Italy, off its S tip —Si·cil·ian (si sil'yən) adj., n.

sick¹ (sik) adj. [OE. seoc] 1. suffering from disease; ill 2. having nausea 3. of or for sick people [sick leave] 4. deeply disturbed, as by grief 5. disgusted by an excess [sick of excuses] 6. [Colloq.] morbid [a sick joke] —the sick sick people —sick'ish adj.

sick² (sik) vt. same as SIC²

sick bay a hospital and dispensary, esp. on board ship

sick'bed' n. the bed of a sick person

sick'en vt., vi. to make or become ill, disgusted, etc. —sick'en·ing adj.

sick·le (sik'l) *n.* [ult. < L. *secare*, to cut] a tool having a crescent-shaped blade on a short handle, for cutting tall grasses and weeds

sick'le-cell' anemia an inherited anemia, found chiefly among blacks, in which red blood cells become sickle-shaped due to defective hemoglobin

sick·ly (sik'lē) *adj.* **-li·er, -li·est**   SICKLE   1. in poor health 2. produced by sickness [a sickly pallor] 3. faint; pale 4. weak; insipid

sick'ness *n.* 1. being sick or diseased 2. a malady 3. nausea

sick'out' *n.* a staying out of work on the claim of illness, as by a group of employees trying to win demands

sick'room' *n.* the room of a sick person

side (sīd) *n.* [OE.] 1. the right or left half, as of the body 2. a position beside one 3. *a)* any of the lines or surfaces that bound something *b)* either of the two bounding surfaces of an object that are not the front, back, top, or bottom 4. either of the two surfaces of paper, cloth, etc. 5. an aspect [his cruel *side*] 6. any location, etc. with reference to a central point 7. the position or attitude of one person or faction opposing another 8. one of the parties in a contest, conflict, etc. 9. a line of descent —*adj.* 1. of, at, or on a side 2. to or from one side [a side glance] 3. secondary [a side issue] —**side by side** together —**side with** to support (a faction, etc.) —**take sides** to support a faction, etc.

side'arm' *adj., adv.* with a forward arm motion around shoulder level

side arms weapons worn at the side or waist, as swords, pistols, etc.

side'bar' *n.* a short article about a sidelight of a major news story and printed alongside it

side'board' *n.* a piece of furniture for holding linen, china, etc.

side'burns' (-burnz') *n.pl.* [< *burnsides*, side whiskers worn by A. E. *Burnside*, Civil War general] the hair growing on the sides of a man's face, just in front of the ears

side'car' *n.* a small car attached to the side of a motorcycle

side dish any food served along with the main course, as in a separate dish

side'kick' *n.* [Slang] 1. a close friend 2. a partner; confederate

side'light' *n.* a bit of incidental information or knowledge

side'line' *n.* 1. either of two lines marking the side limits of a playing area, as in football 2. a secondary line of merchandise, work, etc.

side'long' *adv.* toward the side —*adj.* directed to the side, as a glance

side'man' *n., pl.* **-men'** a band member other than the leader or soloist

si·de·re·al (sī dir'ē əl) *adj.* [< L. *sidus*, star] with reference to the stars

side'sad'dle *n.* a saddle designed for a rider sitting with both legs on the same side of the animal —*adv.* on or as if on a sidesaddle

side'show' *n.* a small show apart from the main show, as of a circus

side'slip' *vi.* to slip or skid sideways —*vt.* to make sideslip —*n.* a slip or skid to the side

side'split'ting *adj.* 1. very hearty: said of laughter 2. very funny

side'step' *vt., vi.* **-stepped', -step'ping** to dodge as by stepping aside

side'swipe' (-swīp') *vt., vi.* **-swiped', -swip'ing** to hit along the side in passing —*n.* such a glancing blow

side'track' *vt., vi.* 1. to switch (a train) to a siding 2. to turn away from the main issue

side'walk' *n.* a path for pedestrians, usually paved, at the side of a street

side'wall' *n.* the side of a tire, between the tread and the wheel rim

side'ways' (-wāz') *adj., adv.* 1. toward or from one side 2. with one side forward Also **side'wise'** (-wīz')

sid·ing (sīd'iŋ) *n.* 1. a covering, as of overlapping boards, for the outside of a frame building 2. a short railway track, for unloading, etc., connected with a main track by a switch

si·dle (sī'd'l) *vi.* **-dled, -dling** [< *sideling*, sideways] to move sideways, esp. shyly or stealthily

siege (sēj) *n.* [< L. *sedere*, sit] 1. the encirclement of a fortified place by an enemy intending to take it 2. a persistent attempt to gain control, etc. 3. a long, distressing period, as of illness —**lay siege** to to subject to a siege

si·er·ra (sē er'ə) *n.* [Sp. < L. *serra*, a saw] a range of mountains with a saw-toothed appearance

Si·er·ra Le·one (sē er'ə lē ōn') country in W Africa: 27,925 sq. mi.; pop. 2,439,000

si·es·ta (sē es'tə) *n.* [Sp. < L. *sexta* (*hora*), sixth (hour), noon] a brief nap or rest after the noon meal

sieve (siv) *n.* [OE. *sife*] a utensil with many small holes for straining liquids or fine particles of matter

sift (sift) *vt.* [OE. *siftan*] 1. to pass (flour, etc.) through a sieve 2. to examine (evidence, etc.) with care 3. to separate [to *sift* fact from fable] —*vi.* to pass as through a sieve

sigh (sī) *vi.* [< OE. *sican*] 1. to take in and let out a long, deep, audible breath, as in sorrow, relief, etc. 2. to feel longing or grief (*for*) —*n.* the act or sound of sighing

sight (sīt) *n.* [< OE. *seon*, to see] 1. something seen or worth seeing 2. the act of seeing 3. a device to aid the eyes in aiming a gun, etc. 4. aim or an observation taken, as on a sextant 5. the power or range of seeing; eyesight 6. [Colloq.] anything that looks unpleasant, odd, etc. —*vt.* 1. to observe 2. to glimpse 3. to aim at 4. to adjust the sights of —*vi.* to look carefully [*sight* along the line] —**a sight for sore eyes** [Colloq.] a welcome sight —**at** (or **on**) **sight** as soon as seen —**by sight** by appearance —**not by a long sight** 1. not nearly 2. not at all —**out of sight** 1. not in sight 2. far off 3. [Colloq.] beyond reach 4. [Slang] excellent; wonderful

sight′ed *adj.* **1.** having sight; not blind **2.** having a (specified kind of) sight *[farsighted]*

sight′less *adj.* blind

sight′ly *adj.* **-li·er, -li·est** pleasant to the sight —**sight′li·ness** *n.*

sight reading the skill of performing written music on sight, without previous study —**sight′-read′** *vt., vi.*

sight·see′ing *n.* a visiting of places of interest —**sight′se′er** (-sē′ər) *n.*

sig·ma (sig′mə) *n.* the eighteenth letter of the Greek alphabet (Σ, σ, s)

sign (sīn) *n.* [< L. *signum*] **1.** something that indicates a fact, quality, etc.; token **2.** a gesture that conveys information, etc. **3.** a mark or symbol having a specific meaning *[a dollar sign ($)]* **4.** a placard, etc. bearing information, advertising, etc. **5.** any trace or indication —*vt.* **1.** to write (one's name) on (a letter, check, contract, etc.) **2.** to engage by written contract —*vi.* to write one's signature —**sign off** to stop broadcasting

sig·nal (sig′n'l) *n.* [< L. *signum*, a sign] **1.** a sign or event that initiates action *[a bugle signal to attack]* **2.** a gesture, device, etc. that conveys command, warning, etc. **3.** in radio, etc., the electrical impulses transmitted or received —*adj.* **1.** remarkable; notable **2.** used as a signal —*vt., vi.* **-naled** or **-nalled, -nal·ing** or **-nal·ling 1.** to make a signal or signals (to) **2.** to communicate by signals

sig·nal·ize′ (-īz′) *vt.* **-ized′, -iz′ing 1.** to make noteworthy **2.** to make known or draw attention to

sig·nal·ly *adv.* in a signal way; notably

sig·na·to·ry (sig′nə tôr′ē) *adj.* having joined in signing something —*n., pl.* **-ries** a signatory person, nation, etc.

sig·na·ture (sig′nə chər) *n.* [< L. *signare*, to sign] **1.** a person's name written by himself **2.** *Music* a staff sign showing key or time

sign·board (sīn′bôrd′) *n.* a board bearing a sign or advertisement

sig·net (sig′nit) *n.* [< MFr. *signe*, a sign] a seal, as on a ring, used in marking documents as official, etc.

sig·nif·i·cance (sig nif′ə kəns) *n.* **1.** that which is signified; meaning **2.** the quality of being significant; expressiveness **3.** importance

sig·nif·i·cant (-kənt) *adj.* [< L. *significare*, signify] **1.** having or expressing a meaning, esp. a special or hidden one **2.** full of meaning **3.** important —**sig·nif′i·cant·ly** *adv.*

sig·ni·fy (sig′nə fī′) *vt.* **-fied′, -fy′ing** [< L. *signum*, a sign + *facere*, make] **1.** to be an indication of; mean **2.** to make known, as by a sign, words, etc. —*vi.* to be important —**sig′ni·fi·ca′tion** *n.*

sign of the cross an outline of a cross (sense 2) made symbolically by moving the hand or fingers

sign of the zodiac any of the twelve parts of the zodiac, each represented by a symbol: see ZODIAC

‡si·gnor (sē nyôr′) *n., pl.* **-gno′ri** (-nyô′rē) [It.] a man; gentleman: as a title [S-], equivalent to *Mr.* or *Sir*

‡si·gno·ra (sē nyô′rä) *n., pl.* **-re** (-re) [It.] a married woman: as a title [S-], equivalent to *Mrs.* or *Madam*

‡si·gno·ri·na (sē′nyô rē′nä) *n., pl.* **-ne** (-ne) [It.] an unmarried woman or girl: as a title [S-], equivalent to *Miss*

sign/post′ *n.* **1.** a post bearing a sign **2.** an obvious clue, symptom, etc.

si·lage (sī′lij) *n.* green fodder preserved in a silo

sild (sild) *n., pl.* **sild, silds** [Norw., herring] a small or young herring canned as a Norwegian sardine

si·lence (sī′ləns) *n.* **1.** a keeping silent **2.** absence of sound **3.** omission of mention —*vt.* **-lenced, -lenc·ing 1.** to make silent **2.** to put down; repress —*interj.* be silent!

si·lenc·er *n.* **1.** one that silences **2.** a device to muffle the sound of a gun

si·lent (sī′lənt) *adj.* [< L. *silere*, be silent] **1.** making no vocal sound; mute **2.** not talkative **3.** noiseless; still **4.** not expressed; tacit **5.** inactive *[a silent partner]* —**si′lent·ly** *adv.*

sil·hou·ette (sil′oo wet′) *n.* [< E. de *Silhouette*, 18th-c. Fr. statesman] **1.** a solid, usually black, outline drawing, esp. a profile **2.** any dark shape seen against a light background —*vt.* **-et′ted, -et′ting** to show in silhouette

SILHOUETTE

sil·i·ca (sil′i kə) *n.* [< L. *silex*, flint] a hard, glassy mineral found in various forms, as in quartz, sand, etc. —**si·li·ceous** (sə lish′əs) *adj.*

sil′i·cate (-kit, -kāt′) *n.* a salt or ester derived from silica

sil·i·con (sil′i kən, -kän′) *n.* [< L. *silex*, flint] a nonmetallic chemical element found always in combination

sil′i·cone′ (-kōn′) *n.* an organic silicon compound highly resistant to temperature changes, water, etc.

sil′i·co′sis (-kō′sis) *n.* [< SILICON + -OSIS] a chronic lung disease caused by inhaling silica dust

silk (silk) *n.* [ult. < ? L. *sericus*, (fabric) of the Seres, the Chinese] **1.** *a)* the fine, soft fiber produced by silkworms *b)* thread or fabric made from this **2.** any silklike substance —**silk′en** *adj.* —**silk′y** *adj.* **-i·er, -i·est**

silk screen a stencil method of printing a color design through the meshes of a fabric, as silk, in which the parts not to be printed have been blocked up —**silk′-screen′** *vt.*

silk′worm′ *n.* any of certain moth caterpillars that produce cocoons of silk fiber

sill (sil) *n.* [OE. *syll*] **1.** a heavy,

horizontal timber or line of masonry supporting a house wall, etc. 2. a horizontal piece forming the bottom frame of a door or window opening

sil·ly (sil'ē) *adj.* **-li·er, -li·est** [< OE. *sælig*, happy] having or showing little sense or judgment; foolish, absurd, etc. **—sil'li·ness** *n.*

si·lo (sī'lō) *n., pl.* **-los** [< Gr. *siros*] an airtight pit or tower in which green fodder is preserved

silt (silt) *n.* [prob. < Scand.] a fine-grained, sandy sediment carried or deposited by water **—***vt., vi.* to fill or choke up with silt

sil·ver (sil'vər) *n.* [< OE. *seolfor*] **1.** a white, precious, metallic chemical element that is very ductile and malleable **2.** *a)* silver coin *b)* money; riches **3.** silverware **4.** a lustrous, grayish white **—***adj.* **1.** of, containing, or plated with silver **2.** silvery **—***vt.* to cover as with silver

sil·ver·fish' *n.* a wingless insect with silvery scales, found in damp places

silver lining a basis for hope or comfort in the midst of despair

silver nitrate a colorless, crystalline salt, used in photography, as an antiseptic, etc.

sil·ver·smith' *n.* a craftsman who makes and repairs silver articles

sil'ver-tongued' *adj.* eloquent

sil'ver·ware' *n.* **1.** articles, esp. tableware, made of or coated with silver **2.** any metal tableware

sil'ver·y *adj.* **1.** of, like, or containing silver **2.** soft and clear in tone

sim·i·an (sim'ē ən) *adj.* [< L. *simia*, an ape] of or like an ape or monkey **—***n.* an ape or monkey

sim·i·lar (sim'ə lər) *adj.* [< L. *similis*] nearly but not exactly the same or alike **—sim'i·lar'i·ty** (-lar'ə tē) *n., pl.* **-ties** **—sim'i·lar·ly** *adv.*

sim·i·le (sim'ə lē') *n.* [< L., a likeness] a figure of speech likening one thing to another by the use of *like, as,* etc. (Ex.: tears flowed like wine)

si·mil·i·tude (sə mil'ə tood') *n.* [< L. *similitudo*] likeness; resemblance

sim·mer (sim'ər) *vi.* [echoic] **1.** to remain at or just below the boiling point **2.** to be about to break out, as in anger **—***vt.* to keep at or just below the boiling point **—***n.* a simmering

si·mon-pure (sī'mən pyoor') *adj.* [< *Simon Pure,* a character in an 18th-c. play] genuine; authentic

si·mo·ny (sī'mə nē, sim'ə-) *n.* [< *Simon Magus:* Acts 8:9–24] the buying or selling of sacraments or benefices

sim·pa·ti·co (sim pät'i kō) *adj.* [< It. or Sp.] compatible or congenial

sim·per (sim'pər) *vi.* [Early ModE.] to smile in a silly or affected way; smirk **—***n.* such a smile

sim·ple (sim'p'l) *adj.* **-pler, -plest** [< L. *simplex*] **1.** having only one or a few parts; uncomplicated **2.** easy to do or understand **3.** without additions [the *simple* facts] **4.** not ornate or luxurious; plain **5.** without guile or deceit **6.** without ostentation; natural **7.** of low rank or position; common **8.** stupid or foolish **—sim'ple·ness** *n.*

simple interest interest computed on principal alone and not on principal plus interest

sim'ple-mind'ed *adj.* **1.** naive **2.** foolish **3.** mentally retarded

sim·ple·ton (sim'p'l tən) *n.* a fool

sim·plic·i·ty (sim plis'ə tē) *n., pl.* **-ties** **1.** a simple state or quality; freedom from complexity, etc. **2.** absence of elegance, luxury, etc.; plainness **3.** artlessness **4.** foolishness

sim·pli·fy (sim'plə fī') *vt.* **-fied', -fy'ing** to make simpler, or less complex **—sim'pli·fi·ca'tion** *n.*

sim·plis·tic (sim plis'tik) *adj.* making complex problems unrealistically simple **—sim·plis'ti·cal·ly** *adv.*

sim·ply (sim'plē) *adv.* **1.** in a simple way **2.** merely [*simply* trying] **3.** completely [*simply* overwhelmed]

sim·u·late (sim'yoo lāt') *vt.* **-lat'ed, -lat'ing** [< L. *simulare*] **1.** to give a false appearance of; feign **2.** to look or act like **—sim'u·la'tion** *n.*

si·mul·cast (sī'm'l kast') *vt.* **-cast'** or **-cast'ed, -cast'ing** to broadcast (a program) simultaneously by radio and television **—***n.* a program so broadcast

si·mul·ta·ne·ous (sī'm'l tā'nē əs) *adj.* [< L. *simul,* together] occurring, done, etc. at the same time **—si'mul·ta'ne·ous·ly** *adv.*

sin (sin) *n.* [OE. *synne*] **1.** the willful breaking of religious or moral law **2.** any offense or fault **—***vi.* **sinned, sin'ning** to commit a sin **—sin'ful** *adj.* **—sin'ner** *n.*

Si·nai, Mount (sī'nī) *Bible* the mountain where Moses received the law from God

since (sins) *adv.* [ult. < OE. *sith,* after + *thæt,* that] **1.** from then until now [remained ever *since*] **2.** at some time between then and now [has *since* recovered] **3.** before now; ago [long *since* gone] **—***prep.* **1.** continuously from (then) until now [*since* noon] **2.** during the period between (then) and now [twice *since* May] **—***conj.* **1.** after the time that [two years *since* they met] **2.** continuously from the time when [lonely ever *since* he left] **3.** because [*since* I can, I will]

sin·cere (sin sir') *adj.* **-cer'er, -cer'est** [< L. *sincerus,* pure] **1.** without deceit or pretense **2.** genuine [*sincere* grief] **—sin·cere'ly** *adv.* **—sin·cer'i·ty** (-ser'ə tē) *n.*

si·ne·cure (sī'nə kyoor', sin'ə-) *n.* [< L. *sine,* without + *cura,* care] any position that brings profit without involving much work

si·ne di·e (sī'nē dī'ē) [LL., without a day] for an indefinite period

si'ne qua non' (kwä nän') [L., without which not] an indispensable condition or thing

sin·ew (sin'yōō) *n.* [OE. *seonwe*] **1.** a tendon **2.** muscular power; strength **—sin'ew·y** (-yoo wē) *adj.*

sing (sin) *vi.* **sang** or rarely **sung, sung, sing'ing** [OE. *singan*] **1.** to produce musical sounds with the voice **2.** to use song or verse in praise, etc. [of thee I *sing*] **3.** to make musical sounds, as a songbird **4.** to hum, buzz, etc., as a bee **5.** [Slang] to confess to a crime, esp. implicating others —*vt.* **1.** to render (a song, etc.) by singing **2.** to extol, etc. in song **3.** to bring or put by singing (*to sing to sleep*) —*n.* [Colloq.] group singing —**sing′er** *n.*

sing. singular

sing′·a·long′ *n.* [Colloq.] an informal gathering of people to sing songs

Sin·ga·pore (siŋ′gə pôr′) island country off the Malay Peninsula: 225 sq. mi.; pop. 1,956,000

singe (sinj) *vt.* **singed, singe′ing** [OE. *sengan*] **1.** to burn superficially or slightly **2.** to expose (a carcass) to flame in removing feathers, etc. —*n.* **1.** a singeing **2.** a slight burn

sin·gle (siŋ′g'l) *adj.* [< L. *singulus*] **1.** a) one only b) separate and distinct (*every single time*) **2.** solitary **3.** of or for one person or family **4.** between two persons only (*single combat*) **5.** unmarried **6.** having only one part; not multiple, etc. **7.** whole; unbroken (*a single front*) —*vt.* **-gled, -gling** to select from others (usually with *out*) —*vi.* Baseball to hit a single —*n.* **1.** a single person or thing **2.** Baseball a first hit by which the batter reaches first base **3.** [*pl.*] Tennis, etc. a match with only one player on each side

sin·gle-breast′ed *adj.* overlapping the front of the body only enough to fasten (*a single-breasted coat*)

single file a single column of persons or things, one behind another

sin·gle-hand′ed *adj., adv.* **1.** using only one hand **2.** without help

sin·gle-mind′ed *adj.* with only one aim or purpose

sin·gle·ton (-tən) *n.* **1.** a playing card that is the only one of its suit held by a player **2.** a single thing

sin·gle-track′ *adj.* [Colloq.] same as ONE-TRACK

sin·gle·tree′ (-trē′) *n.* [< ME. *swingle*, rod + *tree*, tree] the crossbar on a wagon, etc. to which the traces of a horse's harness are hooked

sin·gly (siŋ′glē) *adv.* **1.** alone **2.** one by one **3.** unaided

sing′song′ *n.* a rise and fall of tone in an unvarying cadence

sin·gu·lar (siŋ′gyə lər) *adj.* [< L. *singulus*, single] **1.** unique **2.** extraordinary; remarkable **3.** peculiar; odd **4.** Gram. designating only one —*n.* Gram. the singular number or form of a word —**sin′gu·lar′i·ty** (-lar′ə tē) *n.* —**sin′gu·lar·ly** *adv.*

Sin·ha·lese (sin′hə lēz′) *adj.* of Ceylon, its people, language, etc. —*n.*, *pl.* **-lese′** **1.** any of the Sinhalese people **2.** their language

sin·is·ter (sin′is tər) *adj.* [< L. *sinister*, left-hand] **1.** orig., on or to the left-hand side **2.** threatening harm, evil, etc. **3.** wicked; evil

sink (siŋk) *vi.* **sank** or **sunk, sunk, sink′ing** [OE. *sincan*] **1.** to go beneath the surface of water, etc. **2.** to go down slowly **3.** to appear to descend, as the sun **4.** to become lower, as in level, value, or rank **5.** to subside, as wind or sound **6.** to become hollow, as the cheeks **7.** to pass gradually (*into sleep*, etc.) **8.** to approach death —*vt.* **1.** to make sink **2.** to make (a mine, engraving, etc.) by digging, cutting, etc. **3.** to invest **4.** to defeat; undo —*n.* **1.** a cesspool or sewer **2.** a basin, as in a kitchen, with a drainpipe **3.** an area of sunken land —**sink in** [Colloq.] to be understood in full —**sink′a·ble** *adj.*

sink′er *n.* **1.** one that sinks **2.** a lead weight used in fishing

sinking fund a fund built up to pay off a debt, as of a corporation

Sino- [< Gr. *Sinai*] a combining form meaning Chinese

sin·u·ous (sin′yoo wəs) *adj.* [< L. *sinus*, a bend] **1.** bending or winding in or out; wavy **2.** devious; crooked —**sin′u·os′i·ty** (-wäs′ə tē) *n.*

si·nus (sī′nəs) *n.* [L., bent surface] a cavity, hollow, etc.; specif., any of the air cavities in the skull which open into the nasal cavities

si·nus·i·tis (sī′nə sīt′əs) *n.* inflammation of the sinuses, esp. of the skull

-sion (shən, zhən) [L. *-sio*] a suffix meaning act, state, or result of (*fusion*)

Sioux (sōō) *n.*, *pl.* **Sioux** (sōō, sōōz) a member of a group of Indian tribes of the N U.S. and S Canada —*adj.* of these tribes: also **Siou·an** (sōō′ən)

sip (sip) *vt., vi.* **sipped, sip′ping** [ME. *sippen*] to drink a little at a time —*n.* **1.** the act of sipping **2.** a small quantity sipped —**sip′per** *n.*

si·phon (sī′fən) *n.* [< Gr. *siphōn*, tube] **1.** a bent tube for carrying liquid out over the edge of a container to a lower level, through the force of air pressure on the liquid **2.** a sealed bottle from which carbonated water is released: in full **siphon bottle** —*vt.* to draw off through a siphon

sir (sur) *n.* [see ff.] **1.** [*sometimes* S-] a respectful term of address used to a man: not followed by the name **2.** [S-] the title used before the name of a knight or baronet

sire (sīr) *n.* [< L. *senior*, compar. of *senex*, old] **1.** a title of respect used in addressing a king **2.** [Poet.] a father or forefather **3.** the male parent of a four-legged mammal —*vt.* **sired, sir′ing** to beget

si·ren (sī′rən) *n.* [< Gr. *Seirēn*] **1.** Gr. & Rom. Myth. any of several sea nymphs whose singing lured sailors to their death on rocky coasts **2.** a seductive woman **3.** a warning device, etc. producing a loud, wailing sound

sir·loin (sur′loin) *n.* [< OFr. *sur*, over + *loigne*, loin] a choice cut of beef from the loin end in front of the rump

si·roc·co (sə räk′ō) *n.*, *pl.* **-cos** [It. < Ar. *sharq*, the east] a hot, oppressive wind blowing from the deserts of N Africa into S Europe

sir·ree, sir·ee (sə rē′) *interj.* [< SIR] an interjection used for emphasis after *yes* or *no*

sir·up (sir′əp, sur′-) *n.* same as SYRUP

sis (sis) *n. colloq.* form of SISTER

si·sal (sī′s'l) *n.* [after *Sisal*, in SE Mexico] a strong fiber obtained from the leaves of an agave

sis·sy (sis′ē) *n., pl.* **-sies** [dim. of SIS] [Colloq.] **1.** an effeminate boy or man **2.** a timid person —**sis′si·fied′** *adj.*

sis·ter (sis′tər) *n.* [< ON. *systir*] **1.** a female related to one by having the same parents **2.** a friend who is like a sister **3.** a female fellow member of the same race, creed, etc. **4.** a nun **5.** one of the same kind, model, etc. —**sis′-ter·hood′** *n.* **sis′ter·ly** *adj.*

sis′ter-in-law′ *n., pl.* **sis′ters-in-law′ 1.** the sister of one's spouse **2.** the wife of one's brother **3.** the wife of the brother of one's spouse

Sis·y·phus (sis′ə fəs) *Gr. Myth.* a king of Corinth doomed in Hades to roll uphill a stone which always rolled down again

sit (sit) *vi.* **sat, sit′ting** [< OE. *sittan*] **1.** *a)* to rest oneself upon the buttocks, as on a chair *b)* to rest on the haunches with the forelegs braced, as a dog *c)* to perch, as a bird **2.** to cover eggs for hatching, as a hen **3.** *a)* to occupy a seat as a judge, legislator, etc. *b)* to be in session, as a court **4.** to pose, as for a portrait **5.** to be located **6.** to rest or lie [*cares sit* lightly on him] **7.** same as BABY-SIT —*vt.* **1.** to cause to sit **2.** to keep one's seat on (a horse, etc.) —**sit down** to take a seat —**sit in** (on) to attend —**sit up 1.** to sit erect **2.** to postpone going to bed **3.** [Colloq.] to become suddenly alert —**sit′ter** *n.*

si·tar (si tär′) *n.* [Hind. *sitār*] a lute-like instrument of India

sit′-down′ *n.* **1.** a strike in which the strikers refuse to leave the premises **2.** civil disobedience in which demonstrators sit down in streets, etc. and refuse to leave voluntarily

site (sīt) *n.* [< L. *situs*, position] location or scene

SITAR

sit′-in′ *n.* a sit-down inside a public place, as by a civil-rights group

sit′ting *n.* **1.** the act or position of one that sits **2.** a session, as of a court **3.** a period of being seated

sitting duck [Colloq.] a person or thing easily attacked; easy target

sit·u·ate (sich′oo wāt′) *vt.* **-at′ed, -at′ing** [see SITE] to put in a certain place or position; locate

sit′u·a′tion *n.* **1.** location; position; place **2.** condition with regard to circumstances **3.** a state of affairs **4.** a position of employment

situation comedy a comic television series made up of episodes involving the same group of stock characters

sit′-up′, sit′up′ *n.* an exercise of sitting up from a lying position without using hands or legs

sitz bath (sits, zits) [< G.] a therapeutic bath in a sitting position, with the hips and buttocks immersed

Si·va (sē′və) Hindu god of destruction and reproduction: see BRAHMA

six (siks) *adj., n.* [OE. *sex*] one more than five; 6; VI —**sixth** *adj., n.*

six′-pack′ *n.* a package of six units, as of six cans of beer

six′-shoot′er *n.* [Colloq.] a revolver firing six shots without reloading

six·teen′ (-tēn′) *adj., n.* [OE. *syxtēne*] six more than ten; 16; XVI —**six′-teenth′** *adj., n.*

sixth sense intuitive power

six·ty (siks′tē) *adj., n., pl.* **-ties** [OE. *sixtig*] six times ten; 60; LX —**the sixties** the numbers or years, as of a century, from 60 through 69 —**six′ti·eth** (-ith) *adj., n.*

siz·a·ble (sī′zə b'l) *adj.* quite large or bulky: also **size′a·ble**

size¹ (sīz) *n.* [ult. < L. *sedere*, sit] **1.** that quality of a thing which determines how much space it occupies; dimensions or magnitude **2.** any of a series of graded classifications of measure into which merchandise is divided —*vt.* **sized, siz′ing** to make or grade according to size —**size up** [Colloq.] **1.** to make an estimate or judgment of **2.** to meet requirements

size² (sīz) *n.* [ME. *syse*] a pasty substance used as a glaze or filler on paper, cloth, etc. —*vt.* **sized, siz′ing** to fill, stiffen, or glaze with size

-sized (sīzd) *a combining form meaning* of (a specified) size [*small-sized*]

siz′ing *n.* **1.** same as SIZE² **2.** the act or process of applying size

siz·zle (siz′'l) *vi.* **-zled, -zling** [echoic] **1.** to make a hissing sound when in contact with heat **2.** to be extremely hot —*n.* a sizzling sound

S.J. Society of Jesus: see JESUIT

skate¹ (skāt) *n.* [< OFr. *eschace*, stilt] **1.** *a)* a metal runner in a frame, fastened to a shoe for gliding on ice *b)* a shoe with such a runner attached Also **ice skate 2.** a similar frame or shoe with two pairs of small wheels, for gliding on a floor, sidewalk, etc.: also **roller skate** —*vi.* **skat′ed, skat′ing** to glide or roll on skates —**skat′er** *n.*

skate² (skāt) *n.* [< ON. *skata*] a fish of the ray family with a broad, flat body and short, spineless tail

skate′board′ *n.* a short, oblong board with two wheels at each end, ridden as down an incline —*vi.* to ride a skateboard

ske·dad·dle (ski dad′'l) *vi.* **-dled, -dling** [< ?] [Colloq.] to run away

skeet (skēt) *n.* [< ON. *skeyti*, projectile] trapshooting in which the shooter fires from different angles

skein (skān) *n.* [< MFr. *escaigne*] a quantity of thread or yarn in a coil

skel·e·ton (skel′ə t'n) *n.* [< Gr. *skeletos*, dried up] **1.** the hard framework of bones of an animal body **2.** *a)* a supporting framework *b)* an outline, as of a book —**skel′e·tal** *adj.*

skeleton key a key with a slender bit that can open many simple locks

skep·tic (skep′tik) *adj.* [< Gr. *skeptikos*, inquiring] *var. of* SKEPTICAL —*n.* 1. an adherent of skepticism 2. one who habitually questions matters generally accepted 3. one who doubts religious doctrines

skep′ti·cal (-ti k′l) *adj.* doubting; questioning —**skep′ti·cal·ly** *adv.*

skep′ti·cism (-siz′m) *n.* 1. the doctrine that the truth of all knowledge must always be in question 2. skeptical attitude 3. doubt about religious doctrines

sketch (skech) *n.* [ult. < Gr. *schedios*, extempore] 1. a rough drawing or design, done rapidly 2. a brief outline 3. a short, light story, play, etc. —*vt., vi.* to make a sketch (of) —**sketch′y** *adj.* **-i·er, -i·est**

skew (skyōō) *vi., vt.* [< OFr. *eschiver, shun* < Gmc.] to slant or set at a slant —*adj.* slanting —*n.* a slant or twist

skew·er (skyōō′ər) *n.* [< ON. *skifa,* a slice] a long pin used to hold meat together while cooking —*vt.* to fasten or pierce with skewers

ski (skē) *n., pl.* **skis, ski** [Norw. < ON. *skith*, snowshoe] one of a pair of long runners of wood, etc., fastened to shoes for gliding over snow —*vi.* **skied, ski′ing** to glide on skis — **ski′er** *n.*

skid (skid) *n.* [prob. < ON. *skith,* snowshoe] 1. a plank, log, etc. used as a track upon which to slide a heavy object 2. a low, wooden platform for holding loads 3. a runner on an aircraft landing gear 4. a sliding wedge used to brake a wheel 5. the act of skidding —*vt., vi.* **skid′ded, skid′ding** to slide or slip, as a vehicle on ice —**be on (or hit) the skids** [Slang] to be on the decline, or to fail

skid′dy *adj.* **-di·er, -di·est** having a slippery surface on which vehicles are liable to skid

skid row [alt. < *skid road,* trail to skid logs along] a city area where vagrants, derelicts, etc. gather

skiff (skif) *n.* [< It. *schifo*] a light rowboat, esp. one with a small sail

ski lift an endless cable with seats, for carrying skiers up a slope

skill (skil) *n.* [< ON. *skil,* distinction] 1. great ability or proficiency 2. *a)* an art, craft, etc., esp. one involving the use of the hands or body *b)* ability in such an art, etc. —**skilled** *adj.* — **skill′ful, skil′ful** *adj.*

skil·let (skil′it) *n.* [< ? L. *scutra,* dish] a pan for frying

skim (skim) *vt., vi.* **skimmed, skim′ming** [ME. *skimen*] 1. to remove (floating matter) from (a liquid) 2. to glance through (a book, etc.) rapidly 3. to glide lightly (over)

skim milk milk with the cream removed: also **skimmed milk**

skimp (skimp) *vi., vt.* [Colloq.] same as SCRIMP

skimp′y *adj.* **-i·er, -i·est** [Colloq.] barely enough; scanty

skin (skin) *n.* [< ON. *skinn*] 1. the outer covering of the animal body 2. a pelt 3. something like skin, as fruit rind, etc. —*vt.* **skinned, skin′ning** 1. to remove the skin of 2. to injure by scraping (one's knee, etc.) 3. [Colloq.] to swindle —**get under one's skin** [Colloq.] to irk one —**skin′less** *adj.*

skin diving underwater swimming with air supplied by snorkel, scuba equipment, etc. —**skin′-dive′** *vi.* **-dived′, -div′ing** —**skin diver**

skin′flick′ *n.* [Slang] a pornographic motion picture

skin′flint′ *n.* [lit., one who would skin a flint for economy] a miser

skinned (skind) *adj.* having skin (of a specified kind) [*dark-skinned*]

skin′ny *adj.* **-ni·er, -ni·est** emaciated; thin —**skin′ni·ness** *n.*

skin′ny-dip′ (-dip′) *vi.* **-dipped′, -dip′ping** [Colloq.] to swim nude —*n.* [Colloq.] a swim in the nude

skin′tight′ *adj.* clinging closely to the skin

skip (skip) *vi., vt.* **skipped, skip′ping** [ME. *skippen*] 1. to leap lightly (over) 2. to ricochet or bounce 3. to pass from one point to another, omitting or ignoring (what lies between) 4. [Colloq.] to leave (town, etc.) hurriedly —*n.* a skipping; specif., a gait alternating light hops on each foot

skip·per (skip′ər) *n.* [< MDu. *schip,* a ship] the captain of a ship

skir·mish (skur′mish) *n.* [< It. *schermire* < Gmc.] 1. a brief fight between small groups, as in a battle 2. any slight, unimportant conflict —*vi.* to take part in a skirmish

skirt (skurt) *n.* [< ON. *skyrt,* shirt] 1. that part of a dress, coat, etc. that hangs below the waist 2. a woman's garment that hangs from the waist 3. something like a skirt —*vt., vi.* to be on, or move along, the edge (of)

ski run a slope or course for skiing

skit (skit) *n.* [prob. ult. < ON. *skjota,* to shoot] a short, humorous sketch, as in the theater

ski touring the sport of cross-country skiing

ski tow an endless cable towing skiers on their skis up a slope

skit·tish (skit′ish) *adj.* [see SKIT & -ISH] 1. lively; playful 2. easily frightened; jumpy 3. fickle

skiv·vy (skiv′ē) *n., pl.* **-vies** [< ?] [Slang] 1. a man's, esp. a sailor's, short-sleeved undershirt: usually **skivvy shirt** 2. [*pl.*] men's underwear

skoal (skōl) *interj.* [< ON. *skāl,* a bowl] to your health: a toast

skul·dug·ger·y, skull·dug·ger·y (skul dug′ər ē) *n.* [< ?] [Colloq.] sneaky behavior; trickery

skulk (skulk) *vi.* [ME. *sculken*] to move in a stealthy manner; slink

skull (skul) *n.* [< Scand.] 1. the entire bony framework of the head.

enclosing the brain 2. the head; mind

skull'cap' n. a light, closefitting, brimless cap, usually worn indoors

skunk (skuŋk) n. [< AmInd.] 1. a small, bushy-tailed mammal having black fur with white stripes down the back: it ejects a foul-smelling liquid when molested 2. its fur 3. [Colloq.] a despicable person

sky (skī) n., pl. **skies** [< ON., a cloud] 1. [often pl.] the upper atmosphere [blue skies, a cloudy sky] 2. the firmament 3. heaven

sky'cap' n. a porter at an air terminal

sky diving parachute jumping involving free-fall maneuvers

sky'-high' adj., adv. 1. very high 2. so as to be blasted to pieces

sky'jack' vt. [Colloq.] to hijack (an aircraft) —**sky'jack'er** n.

Sky·lab (skī'lab') n. U.S. earth-orbiting laboratory (1973-79), housing alternating crews of astronauts

sky'lark' n. a Eurasian lark, famous for the song it utters as it soars —vi. to romp or frolic

sky'light' n. a window in a roof or ceiling

sky'line' n. 1. the visible horizon 2. the outline, as of a city, seen against the sky

sky marshal a Federal officer assigned to guard against skyjacking

sky'rock'et n. a firework rocket that explodes aloft —vi., vt. to rise or make rise rapidly

sky'scrap'er n. a very tall building

sky'ward (-wərd) adv., adj. toward the sky: also **sky'wards** adv.

sky'ways' n.pl. routes of air travel

sky'writ'ing n. the tracing of words, etc. in the sky by trailing smoke from an airplane —**sky'writ'er** n.

slab (slab) n. [ME. sclabbe] a flat, broad, and fairly thick piece

slack¹ (slak) adj. [< OE. slæc] 1. slow; sluggish 2. not busy; dull [a slack period] 3. loose; not tight 4. careless [a slack workman] —vt., vi. to slacken —n. 1. a part that hangs loose 2. a lack of tension 3. a dull period; lull —**slack off** to slacken —**slack up** to go more slowly —**slack'ness** n.

slack² (slak) n. [ME. sleck] a mixture of small pieces of coal, coal dust, etc. left from screening coal

slack·en (slak'ⁿn) vt., vi. 1. to make or become less active, brisk, etc. 2. to loosen or relax, as rope

slack'er n. one who shirks

slacks (slaks) n.pl. trousers for men or women

slag (slag) n. [< MLowG. slagge] 1. fused refuse separated from metal in smelting 2. lava resembling this

slain (slān) pp. of SLAY

slake (slāk) vt. slaked, slak'ing [< OE. slæc, SLACK] 1. to satisfy (thirst, etc.) 2. to produce a chemical change in (lime) by mixing with water

sla·lom (slä'ləm) n. [Norw.] a downhill skiing race over a zigzag course — vi. to ski in or as in a slalom

slam (slam) vt., vi. slammed, slam'-ming [prob. < Scand.] 1. to shut, hit, throw, put, etc. with force and

noise 2. [Colloq.] to criticize severely —n. 1. a slamming 2. [Colloq.] a severe criticism 3. [Slang] short for SLAMMER See also GRAND SLAM

slam'-bang' adv. [Colloq.] 1. swiftly or abruptly and recklessly 2. noisily —adj. [Colloq.] lively, noisy, etc.

slam·mer (slam'ər) n. [Slang] a prison or jail

slan·der (slan'dər) n. [see SCANDAL] 1. the utterance of a falsehood that damages another's reputation 2. such a statement —vt. to utter such a statement about —**slan'der·er** n. —**slan'der·ous** adj.

slang (slaŋ) n. [< ?] highly informal language, usually short-lived, that is outside standard usage —**slang'y** adj. -i·er, -i·est

slant (slant) vt., vi. [< Scand.] 1. to incline; slope 2. to tell so as to express a particular bias —n. 1. an oblique surface, line, etc. 2. a point of view or attitude —adj. sloping

slap (slap) n. [echoic] 1. a blow with something flat, as the palm of the hand 2. an insult; rebuff —vt. slapped, slap'ping 1. to strike with something flat 2. to put, hit, etc. with force

slap'dash' adj., adv. hurried(ly), careless(ly), haphazard(ly), etc.

slap'-hap'py adj. [Slang] 1. dazed, as by blows 2. silly or giddy

slap'stick' n. crude comedy full of horseplay —adj. of or like such comedy

slash (slash) vt. [< Fr. esclachier, break] 1. to cut with sweeping strokes, as of a knife 2. to cut slits in 3. to reduce drastically, as prices —vi. to make a sweeping stroke as with a knife —n. 1. a slashing 2. a cut made by slashing —**slash'er** n.

slash pocket a pocket (in a garment) with a finished diagonal opening

slat (slat) n. [< OFr. esclat, fragment] a narrow strip of wood, etc.

slate (slāt) n. [see prec.] 1. a hard rock that cleaves into thin, smooth layers 2. its bluish-gray color 3. a roofing tile, etc. of slate 4. a list of proposed candidates —vt. slat'ed, slat'ing 1. to cover with slate 2. to designate, as for candidacy —a clean slate [< blackboard of slate] a record that shows no faults, mistakes, etc.

slath·er (slath'ər) vt. [< ?] [Colloq.] to spread on thickly

slat·tern (slat'ərn) n. [< dial. slatter, slop] a slovenly or sluttish woman —**slat'tern·ly** adj.

slaugh·ter (slôt'ər) n. [< ON. slātr, lit., slain flesh] 1. the killing of animals for food 2. the brutal killing of a person 3. the killing of many people, as in battle —vt. 1. to kill (animals) for food 2. to kill (people) brutally or in large numbers —**slaugh'ter·er** n.

slaugh'ter·house' n. a place where animals are butchered for food

Slav (släv, slav) n. a member of a group of peoples of E and SE Europe, including Russians, Poles, Czechs, Serbs, etc. —adj. same as SLAVIC

slave (slāv) n. [< LGr. Sklabos: first applied to captive Slavs] 1. a human being who is owned by another 2. one dominated by some influence, etc. 3. one who slaves —*vi.* slaved, slav'ing to work like a slave; drudge

slave driver 1. one who oversees slaves 2. any merciless taskmaster

slav·er (slav'ər) *vi.* [< Scand.] to drool

slav·er·y (slā'və rē) *n.* 1. the owning of slaves as a practice 2. the condition of a slave; bondage 3. drudgery; toil

Slav·ic (släv'ik, slav'-) *adj.* of the Slavs, their languages, etc. —*n.* a family of languages including Russian, Polish, Czech, Bulgarian, etc.

slav·ish (slā'vish) *adj.* 1. of or like slaves; servile 2. blindly dependent or imitative —slav'ish·ly *adv.*

slaw (slô) *n.* [Du. *sla* < Fr. *salade, salad*] *short for* COLESLAW

slay (slā) *vt.* slew, slain, slay'ing [OE. *slean*] to kill in a violent way —slay'er *n.*

sleaze (slēz) *n.* [<SLEAZY] [Slang] 1. sleaziness 2. anything shoddy

slea·zy (slē'zē) *adj.* -zi·er, -zi·est [< *silesia*, orig., cloth made in C Europe] 1. flimsy or thin in substance 2. shoddy —slea'zi·ly *adv.* —slea'zi·ness *n.*

sled (sled) *n.* [ME. *sledde*] a vehicle on runners for moving over snow, ice, etc. —*vt., vi.* sled'ded, sled'ding to carry or ride on a sled —sled'der *n.*

sledge (slej) *n.* [OE. *slecge*] a long, heavy hammer, usually held with both hands: also sledge'ham'mer

sledge² (slej) *n.* [MDu. *sleedse*] a sled or sleigh

sleek (slēk) *adj.* [var. of SLICK] 1. smooth and shiny; glossy 2. of well-fed or well-groomed appearance 3. suave —*vt.* to make sleek —sleek'ly *adv.* —sleek'ness *n.*

sleep (slēp) *n.* [OE. *slæp*] 1. a natural, regularly recurring rest for the body, during which there is little or no conscious thought 2. any state like this —*vi.* slept, sleep'ing to be in the state of, or a state like, sleep —sleep off to rid oneself of by sleeping —sleep'less *adj.* —sleep'less·ness *n.*

sleep·er *n.* 1. one who sleeps 2. a railway car with berths for sleeping: also sleeping car 3. a beam laid flat to support something 4. something that achieves an unexpected success

sleeping bag a warmly lined, zippered bag for sleeping in outdoors

sleeping sickness an infectious disease, esp. in Africa, characterized by lethargy, prolonged coma, etc.

sleep'walk'ing *n.* the act of walking while asleep —sleep'walk'er *n.*

sleep'wear' *n. same as* NIGHT CLOTHES

sleep'y *adj.* -i·er, -i·est 1. ready or inclined to sleep; drowsy 2. dull; idle [a *sleepy* town] —sleep'i·ly *adv.* —sleep'i·ness *n.*

sleet (slēt) *n.* [ME. *slete*] 1. partly frozen rain 2. a mixture of rain with snow —*vi.* to shower in the form of sleet —sleet'y *adj.*

sleeve (slēv) *n.* [OE. *sliefe*] 1. that part of a garment that covers the arm 2. a tubelike part fitting around another part —up one's sleeve hidden but ready at hand —sleeve'less *adj.*

sleigh (slā) *n.* [Du. *slee*] a light vehicle on runners, for travel on snow

sleight of hand (slīt) [< ON. *slægr*, crafty] 1. skill with the hands, esp. in deceiving onlookers, as in magic 2. tricks thus performed

slen·der (slen'dər) *adj.* [ME. *s(c)lendre*] 1. long and thin 2. slim of figure 3. small in amount, size, etc. 4. of little force; feeble —slen'der·ness *n.*

slen·der·ize' *vt., vi.* -ized', -iz'ing to make or become slender

slept (slept) *pt. & pp. of* SLEEP

sleuth (slooth) *n.* [< ON. *sloth*, a trail] [Colloq.] a detective

slew¹ (sloo) *n.* [Ir. *sluagh*, a host] [Colloq.] a large number or amount

slew² (sloo) *pt. of* SLAY

slice (slīs) *n.* [< OFr. *esclicier*] 1. a relatively thin, broad piece cut from something 2. a part or share —*vt.* sliced, slic'ing 1. to cut into slices 2. to cut as in a slice (with *off, from, away,* etc.) 3. to hit (a ball) so that it curves to the right if right-handed or to the left if left-handed —slic'er *n.*

slick (slik) *vt.* [OE. *slician*] 1. to make smooth 2. [Colloq.] to make smart, neat, etc. (with *up*) —*adj.* 1. sleek; smooth 2. slippery 3. adept; clever 4. [Colloq.] smooth but superficial, tricky, etc. —*n.* a smooth area on the water, as from a film of oil —slick'ly *adv.* —slick'ness *n.*

slick·er *n.* 1. a loose, waterproof coat 2. [Colloq.] a tricky person

slide (slīd) *vi.* slid (slid), slid'ing [OE. *slidan*] 1. to move along in constant contact with a smooth surface, as on ice 2. to glide 3. to slip [it *slid* from his hand] —*vt.* 1. to cause to slide 2. to place quietly or deftly (*in* or *into*) —*n.* 1. a sliding 2. a smooth, often inclined, surface for sliding 3. something that works by sliding 4. a photographic transparency for use with a projector or viewer 5. a small glass plate on which objects are mounted for microscopic study 6. the fall of a mass of rock, snow, etc. down a slope —let slide to fail to attend to properly

slide fastener a zipper or a zipperlike device with two grooved plastic edges joined or separated by a slide

slid·er *n.* 1. one that slides 2. *Baseball* a curve ball that breaks only slightly

slide rule an instrument for rapid calculations, consisting of a ruler with a central sliding piece, both marked with logarithmic scales

sliding scale a schedule of costs, wages, etc. that varies with given conditions

slight (slīt) *adj.* [OE. *sliht*] 1. *a*) light

in build; slender *b*) frail; fragile 2. lacking strength, importance, etc. 3. small in amount or extent —*vt.* 1. to neglect 2. to treat with disrespect 3. to treat as unimportant —*n.* a slighting or being slighted —**slight′-ly** *adv.* —**slight′ness** *n.*

slim (slim) *adj.* **slim′mer, slim′mest** [< Du., bad] 1. small in girth; slender 2. small in amount, degree, etc. —*vt., vi.* **slimmed, slim′ming** to make or become slim —**slim′ness** *n.*

slime (slim) *n.* [OE. *slim*] any soft, moist, slippery, often sticky matter —**slim′y** *adj.* **-i-er, -i-est**

sling (sling) *n.* [prob. < ON. *slyngva*, to throw] 1. a primitive instrument whirled by hand for throwing stones 2. a cast; throw; fling 3. *a*) a supporting band, etc. as for raising a heavy object *b*) a cloth looped from the neck under an injured arm for support —*vt.* **slung, sling′ing** 1. to throw as with a sling 2. to hang in a sling

sling′shot′ *n.* a Y-shaped piece of wood, etc. with an elastic band attached to it for shooting stones, etc.

slink (slink) *vi.* **slunk, slink′ing** [OE. *slincan*, to creep] to move in a furtive or sneaking way; sneak

slink′y *adj.* **-i-er, -i-est** 1. sneaking 2. [Slang] sinuous in line or movement

slip¹ (slip) *vi.* **slipped, slip′ping** [< MLowG. *slippen*] 1. to go quietly or secretly [to *slip* out of a room] 2. to pass smoothly or easily 3. to escape from one's memory, grasp, etc. 4. to slide, lose footing, etc. 5. to make a mistake; err 6. to become worse —*vt.* 1. to cause to slip 2. to put, pass, etc. quickly or deftly [to *slip* one's shoes on] 3. to escape from (the memory) —*n.* 1. a space between piers for docking ships 2. a woman's undergarment the length of a skirt 3. a pillowcase 4. a slipping or falling down 5. an error or mistake —**let slip** to say without intending to

slip² (slip) *n.* [< MDu. *slippen*, to cut] 1. a stem, root, etc. of a plant, used for planting or grafting 2. a young, slim person 3. a small piece of paper

slip′case′ *n.* a boxlike container for a book or books, open at one end

slip′cov′er *n.* a removable, fitted cloth cover for a sofa, chair, etc.

slip′knot′ *n.* a knot that will slip along the rope around which it is tied

slip noose a noose made with a slipknot

slip-page (slip′ij) *n.* a slipping, as of one gear past another

slipped disk a ruptured cartilaginous disk between vertebrae

slip-per (slip′ər) *n.* a light, low shoe easily slipped on the foot

slip-per-y (slip′ə rē) *adj.* **-i-er, -i-est** 1. liable to cause slipping, as a wet surface 2. tending to slip away, as from a grasp 3. unreliable; deceitful

slip-shod (slip′shäd′) *adj.* [after obs. *slip-shoe*, a slipper] careless or slovenly

slip′-up′ *n.* [Colloq.] an error

slit (slit) *vt.* **slit, slit′ting** [ME. *slitten*] 1. to cut or split open, esp. by a lengthwise incision 2. to cut into

strips —*n.* a straight, narrow cut, opening, etc.

slith-er (sli th′ər) *vi.* [< OE. *slidan*, to slide] to slip, slide, or glide along

sliv-er (sliv′ər) *n.* [< OE. *slifan*, to cut] a thin, sharp piece cut or split off; splinter —*vt., vi.* to cut or split into slivers

slob (släb) *n.* [< Ir. *slab*, mud] [Colloq.] a sloppy or coarse person

slob-ber (släb′ər) *vi.* [prob. < LowG. *slubberen*, to swig] 1. to drool 2. to speak in a maudlin way —*n.* slaver

sloe (slō) *n.* [OE. *sla*] 1. the blackthorn 2. its small, plumlike fruit

sloe′-eyed′ *adj.* 1. having large, dark eyes 2. having almond-shaped eyes

sloe gin a red liqueur made of dry gin flavored with sloes

slog (släg) *vt., vi.* **slogged, slog′ging** [ME. *sluggen*, go slowly] 1. to make (one's way) with great effort; plod 2. to toil (*at*)

slo-gan (slō′gən) *n.* [< Gael. *sluagh*, a host + *gairm*, a call: orig., a battle cry] 1. a catchword or motto associated with a political party, etc. 2. a catch phrase used in advertising

sloop (slo͞op) *n.* [< Du. < LowG. *slupen*, to glide] a small sailing vessel with a single mast and a jib

slop (släp) *n.* [OE. *sloppe*] 1. watery snow or mud; slush 2. a puddle of spilled liquid 3. unappetizing liquid or semiliquid food 4. [*often pl.*] liquid waste of any kind —*vt., vi.* **slopped, slop′ping** to spill or splash

SLOOP

slope (slōp) *n.* [< OE. *slupan*, to glide] 1. rising or falling ground 2. any inclined line, surface, etc.; slant 3. the amount or degree of this —*vi.* **sloped, slop′ing** to have an upward or downward inclination; incline; slant —*vt.* to cause to slope

slop-py (släp′ē) *adj.* **-pi-er, -pi-est** 1. splashy; slushy 2. *a*) slovenly *b*) slipshod 3. [Colloq.] gushingly sentimental

sloppy Joe (jō) ground meat cooked with tomato sauce, spices, etc. and served on a bun

slop sink a deep sink for filling scrub pails, washing out mops, etc.

slosh (släsh) *vi.* [var. of SLUSH] 1. to splash through water, mud, etc. 2. to splash about: said of a liquid

slot (slät) *n.* [< OFr. *esclot*, hollow between the breasts] 1. a narrow opening, as for a coin in a vending machine 2. [Colloq.] a position in a group, etc. —*vt.* **slot′ted, slot′ting** 1. to make a slot in 2. [Colloq.] to place in a series

sloth (slôth, slōth) *n.* [< OE. *slaw*, slow] 1. disinclination to work or exert oneself; laziness 2. a slow-moving, tree-dwelling S.American mammal that hangs, back down, from branches —**sloth′ful** *adj.* —**sloth′ful-ness** *n.*

slot machine a machine, specif. a gambling device, worked by inserting a coin in a slot

slouch (slouch) *n.* [< ON. *slŏka*, to droop] 1. a lazy or incompetent person 2. a drooping or slovenly posture —*vi.* to sit, stand, walk, etc. in a slouch —**slouch′y** *adj.*

slough[1] (sluf) *n.* [ME. *slouh*, skin] a castoff layer or covering, as the skin of a snake —*vt.* to throw off; discard

slough[2] (slou) *n.* [OE. *sloh*] 1. a place full of soft, deep mud 2. deep, hopeless dejection

Slo·vak (slŏ′väk, -vak) *n.* 1. any of a Slavic people living chiefly in E Czechoslovakia 2. their language —*adj.* of the Slovaks, their language, etc.

slov·en (sluv′ən) *n.* [prob. < MDu. *slof*, lax] a careless, untidy person —**slov′en·ly** *adj.* -**li·er**, -**li·est**

Slo·ve·ni·a (slŏ vē′nē ə) a republic of Yugoslavia —**Slo·ve′ni·an**, **Slo′vene** (-vēn) *adj.*, *n.*

slow (slŏ) *adj.* [OE. *slaw*] 1. not quick in understanding 2. taking a longer time than is usual 3. marked by low speed, etc.; not fast 4. behind the correct time, as a clock 5. passing tediously; dull —*vt.*, *vi.* to make or become slow or slower (often with *up* or *down*) —*adv.* in a slow manner —**slow′ly** *adv.* —**slow′ness** *n.*

slow burn [Slang] a gradual working up of anger: often in **do a slow burn**

slow′down′ *n.* a slowing down, as of production

slow-mo′tion *adj.* 1. moving slowly 2. designating a filmed or taped scene with the original action slowed down

slow′poke′ (-pŏk′) *n.* [Slang] a person who acts or moves slowly

slow′-wit′ted *adj.* mentally slow; dull

sludge (sluj) *n.* [var. of *slutch*, mud] 1. mud, mire, or ooze 2. any heavy, slimy deposit, sediment, etc.

slue (slōō) *n.*, *vt.*, *vi.* slued, slu′ing [< ?] turn, twist, or swerve

slug[1] (slug) *n.* [ME. *slugge*, clumsy one] a small mollusk resembling a land snail but having no outer shell

slug[2] (slug) *n.* [prob. < prec.] a small piece of metal; specif., a bullet

slug[3] (slug) *n.* [< ? Dan. *sluge*, to gulp] [Slang] a drink of liquor

slug[4] (slug) *vt.* slugged, slug′ging [< ON. *slag*] [Colloq.] to hit hard, esp. with the fist or a bat —*n.* [Colloq.] a hard blow or hit —**slug′ger** *n.*

slug·gard (slug′ərd) *n.* [< ME. *sluggen*, be lazy] a lazy person

slug′gish (-ish) *adj.* [< SLUG[1]] 1. lacking energy; lazy 2. slow or slow-moving 3. not functioning with normal vigor —**slug′gish·ness** *n.*

sluice (slōōs) *n.* [< L. *excludere*, to shut out] 1. an artificial channel for water, with a gate to regulate the flow 2. such a gate: also **sluice gate** 3. any channel for excess water 4. a sloping trough, as for washing gold ore —*vt.* **sluiced**, **sluic′ing** 1. to draw off

through a sluice 2. to wash with water from a sluice

slum (slum) *n.* [< ?] a populous area characterized by poverty, poor housing, etc. —*vi.* **slummed**, **slum′ming** to visit slums in a condescending way

slum·ber (slum′bər) *vi.* [OE. *sluma*] 1. to sleep 2. to be inactive —*n.* 1. sleep 2. an inactive state

slum′lord′ *n.* [Slang] an absentee landlord who exploits slum property

slump (slump) *vi.* [prob. < MLowG. *slumpen*, occur by accident] 1. to fall or sink suddenly 2. to have a drooping posture —*n.* a sudden decline

slung (sluŋ) *pt.* & *pp.* of SLING

slunk (sluŋk) *pt.* & *pp.* of SLINK

slur (slur) *vt.* **slurred**, **slur′ring** [prob. < MDu. *sleuren*, to drag] 1. to pass (*over*) quickly and carelessly 2. to pronounce indistinctly 3. to disparage 4. *Music* to produce (successive notes) by gliding without a break —*n.* 1. a slurring 2. something slurred, as a pronunciation 3. an aspersion 4. *Music* a symbol (⌣) or (⌢) connecting notes to be slurred

slurp (slurp) *vt.*, *vi.* [Du. *slurpen*, to sip] [Slang] to drink or eat noisily —*n.* [Slang] a loud sipping or sucking sound

slush (slush) *n.* [prob. < Scand.] 1. partly melted snow 2. soft mud 3. sentimentality —**slush′y** *adj.*

slut (slut) *n.* [ME. *slutte*] 1. a dirty, slovenly woman 2. a sexually immoral woman —**slut′tish** *adj.*

sly (slī) *adj.* **sli′er** or **sly′er**, **sli′est** or **sly′est** [< ON. *slægr*] 1. skillful at trickery; crafty 2. cunningly underhanded 3. playfully mischievous —**on the sly** secretly —**sly′ly**, **sli′ly** *adv.* —**sly′ness** *n.*

smack[1] (smak) *n.* [OE. *smæc*] 1. a slight taste or flavor 2. a small amount; trace —*vi.* to have a smack (*of*)

smack[2] (smak) *n.* [< ?] 1. a sharp noise made by parting the lips suddenly 2. a loud kiss 3. a slapping blow —*vt.* 1. to part (the lips) so as to make a smack 2. to kiss or slap loudly —*adv.* 1. with a smack 2. directly; precisely

smack[3] (smak) *n.* [prob. < Du. *smak*] a fishing vessel fitted with a well for keeping fish alive

smack′er *n.* [Slang] a dollar bill

small (smôl) *adj.* [OE. *smæl*] 1. comparatively little in size; not big 2. little in quantity, extent, duration, etc. 3. of little importance; trivial 4. young [*small* children] 5. mean; petty —*n.* the small part [the *small* of the back] —**feel small** to feel shame —**small′ness** *n.*

small arms firearms of small caliber, as pistols, rifles, etc.

small′-mind′ed *adj.* selfish, mean, or narrow-minded

small′pox′ (-päks′) *n.* an acute, contagious virus disease characterized by fever and pustular eruptions

small talk light conversation about common, everyday things; chitchat
smart (smärt) *vi.* [OE. *smeortan*] 1. *a*) to cause sharp, stinging pain, as a slap *b*) to feel such pain 2. to feel distress or irritation —*n.* 1. a smarting sensation 2. *pl.* [Slang] intelligence —*adj.* 1. causing sharp pain [a *smart* blow] 2. sharp, as pain 3. brisk; lively [a *smart* pace] 4. intelligent; clever 5. neat; trim 6. stylish —**smart'ly** *adv.* —**smart'ness** *n.*
smart al·eck, smart al·ec (al'ik) [< masc. name *Alexander*] [Colloq.] an offensively conceited person
smart bomb [Mil. Slang] a bomb that is guided precisely to its target from an airplane by electronic means
smart'en *vt., vi.* to make or become smart or smarter
smash (smash) *vt., vi.* [prob. < MASH] 1. to break into pieces with noise or violence 2. to hit, collide, or move with force 3. to destroy or be destroyed —*n.* 1. a hard, heavy hit 2. a violent, noisy breaking 3. a violent collision 4. total failure, esp. in business 5. a popular success
smash'up' *n.* 1. a violent wreck or collision 2. total failure; ruin
smat·ter·ing (smat'ər iŋ) *n.* [ME. *smateren*, chatter] 1. superficial knowledge 2. a small number
smear (smir) *vt.* [< OE. *smerian*, anoint] 1. to cover or soil with something greasy, sticky, etc. 2. to apply (something greasy, etc.) 3. to slander —*vi.* to be or become smeared —*n.* 1. a mark made by smearing 2. slander —**smear'y** *adj.* -i·er, -i·est
smear'case' (-käs') *n.* [G. *schmierkäse*] same as COTTAGE CHEESE
smell (smel) *vt.* **smelled** or **smelt**, **smell'ing** [ME. *smellen*] 1. to be aware of through the nose; detect the odor of 2. to sense the presence of [to *smell* trouble] —*vi.* 1. to use the sense of smell; sniff 2. to have an odor [to *smell* fresh] —*n.* 1. the sense by which odors are perceived 2. odor; scent 3. an act of smelling
smelling salts an ammonia compound sniffed to relieve faintness
smell'y *adj.* -i·er, -i·est having an unpleasant smell
smelt¹ (smelt) *n.* [OE.] a small, silvery food fish found esp. in northern seas
smelt² (smelt) *vt.* [< MDu. *smelten*] 1. to melt or fuse (ore, etc.) so as to separate impurities from pure metal 2. to refine (metal) in this way
smelt'er *n.* 1. one whose work is smelting 2. a place for smelting
smidg·en (smij'ən) *n.* [prob. < dial. *smidge*, particle] [Colloq.] a small amount; bit: also **smidg'in, smidg'eon**
smile (smīl) *vi.* **smiled, smil'ing** [ME. *smilen*] to show pleasure, amusement, affection, etc. by an upward curving of the mouth —*vt.* to express with a smile —*n.* the act or expression of smiling —**smil'ing·ly** *adv.*
smirch (smurch) *vt.* [prob. < OFr. *esmorcher*, to hurt] 1. to soil or stain 2. to dishonor —*n.* 1. a smudge; smear 2. a stain on reputation

smirk (smurk) *vi.* [< OE. *smearcian*, to smile] to smile in a conceited or complacent way —*n.* such a smile
smite (smīt) *vt.* **smote, smit'ten** (smit'n) or **smote, smit'ing** [OE. *smitan*] 1. to strike with powerful effect 2. to affect or impress strongly
smith (smith) *n.* [OE.] 1. one who makes or repairs metal objects; metalworker 2. *short for* BLACKSMITH
Smith, Captain John 1580-1631; Eng. colonist in America
smith·er·eens (smith'ə rēnz') *n.pl.* [Ir. *smidirin*] [Colloq.] fragments
smith·y (smith'ē) *n., pl.* -ies the workshop of a smith, esp. a blacksmith
smock (smäk) *n.* [< OE. *smoc* or ON. *smokkr*] a loose, shirtlike outer garment worn to protect the clothes
smog (smôg, smäg) *n.* [SM(OKE) + (F)OG] a mixture of fog and smoke
smoke (smōk) *n.* [OE. *smoca*] 1. the vaporous matter arising from something burning 2. any vapor, etc. like this 3. an act of smoking tobacco, etc. 4. a cigarette, cigar, etc. —*vi.* **smoked, smok'ing** 1. to give off smoke 2. to draw in and exhale the smoke of tobacco; use cigarettes, etc. —*vt.* 1. to cure (meat, etc.) with smoke 2. to use (a pipe, cigarette, etc.) in smoking 3. to drive out or stupefy as with smoke —**smoke out** to force out of hiding —**smoke'less** *adj.* —**smok'er** *n.*
smoke detector a fire alarm that signals when it detects smoke
smoke'house' *n.* a building where meats, fish, etc. are cured with smoke
smoke screen a cloud of smoke for hiding the movements of troops, etc.
smoke'stack' (-stak') *n.* a pipe for discharging smoke from a factory, etc.
smok·y (smō'kē) *adj.* -i·er, -i·est 1. giving off smoke 2. of, like, or of the color of, smoke 3. filled with smoke —**smok'i·ness** *n.*
smol·der (smōl'dər) *vi.* [ME. *smoldren*] 1. to burn and smoke without flame 2. to exist in a suppressed state Brit. sp. **smoulder**
smooch (smōōch) *n., vt., vi.* [Slang] kiss —**smooch'y** *adj.*
smooth (smōōth) *adj.* [OE. *smoth*] 1. having an even surface, with no roughness 2. without lumps 3. even or gentle in movement [a *smooth* voyage] 4. free from interruptions, obstacles, etc. 5. pleasing to the taste; bland 6. having an easy, flowing rhythm or sound 7. polished or ingratiating, esp. in an insincere way —*vt.* 1. to make level or even 2. to remove lumps or wrinkles from 3. to free from difficulties, etc. 4. to make calm; soothe 5. to polish or refine —*adv.* in a smooth manner —**smooth'ly** *adv.* —**smooth'ness** *n.*
smor·gas·bord, smör·gås·bord (smôr'gəs bôrd', smur'-) *n.* [Sw.] 1. a wide variety of appetizers, cheeses, meats, etc. served buffet style 2. a restaurant serving these
smote (smōt) *pt. & alt. pp.* of SMITE
smoth·er (smuth'ər) *vt.* [< ME. *smorther*, dense smoke] 1. to keep from getting air; suffocate 2. to cover over

thickly 3. to stifle (a yawn) —*vi.* to be suffocated

smudge (smuj) *vt., vi.* **smudged, smudg′ing** [ME. *smogen*] to make or become dirty; smear —*n.* 1. a dirty spot 2. a fire made to produce dense smoke 3. such smoke, used to protect plants from frost, etc. —**smudg′y** *adj.*

smug (smug) *adj.* **smug′ger, smug′gest** [prob. < LowG. *smuk*, neat, trim] annoyingly self-satisfied; complacent —**smug′ly** *adv.* —**smug′ness** *n.*

smug·gle (smug′'l) *vt., vi.* **-gled, -gling** [< LowG. *smuggeln*] 1. to bring into or take out of a country secretly or illegally 2. to bring, take, etc. secretly —**smug′gler** *n.*

smut (smut) *n.* [< LowG. *smutt*] 1. sooty matter 2. a soiled spot 3. indecent talk or writing 4. a fungous disease of plants —**smut′ty** *adj.* **-ti·er, -ti·est**

Sn [L. *stannum*] *Chem.* tin

snack (snak) *n.* [< ME. *snaken*, to bite] a light meal between regular meals —*vi.* to eat a snack

snack bar a lunch counter, cafeteria, etc. serving snacks

snaf·fle (snaf′'l) *n.* [prob. < Du. *snavel*, horse's muzzle] a bit for a horse's mouth, having a joint in the middle and no curb

snag (snag) *n.* [< Scand.] 1. a sharp point or projection 2. an underwater tree stump or branch 3. a tear, as in cloth, made by a snag, etc. 4. an unexpected or hidden difficulty —*vt.* **snagged, snag′ging** 1. to damage on a snag 2. to impede with a snag

snail (snāl) *n.* [OE. *snægl*] a slow-moving mollusk having a wormlike body and a spiral protective shell

snake (snāk) *n.* [OE. *snaca*] 1. a long, scaly, limbless reptile with a tapering tail 2. a treacherous or deceitful person —*vi.* **snaked, snak′ing** to move, curve, twist, etc. like a snake —**snake′like** *adj.*

snak′y *adj.* **-i·er, -i·est** 1. of or like a snake or snakes 2. winding; twisting 3. cunningly treacherous

snap (snap) *vi., vt.* **snapped, snap′ping** [< MDu. *snappen*] 1. to bite or grasp suddenly (with *at*) 2. to speak or utter sharply (with *at*) 3. to break suddenly 4. to make or cause to make a sudden, cracking sound 5. to close, fasten, etc. with this sound 6. to move or cause to move suddenly and sharply [to *snap* to attention] 7. to take a snapshot (of) —*n.* 1. a sudden bite, grasp, etc. 2. a sharp cracking sound 3. a short, angry utterance 4. a brief period of cold weather 5. a fastening that closes with a click 6. a hard, thin cookie 7. [Colloq.] alertness or vigor 8. [Slang] an easy job, problem, etc. —*adj.* 1. made or done quickly [a *snap* decision] 2. that fastens with a snap 3. [Slang] easy —**snap out of** it to improve or recover quickly —**snap′per** *n.* —**snap′pish** *adj.*

snap bean a green bean or wax bean

snap′drag′on *n.* [SNAP + DRAGON: from the mouth-shaped flowers] a plant with saclike, two-lipped flowers

snap′py *adj.* **-pi·er, -pi·est** 1. cross; irritable 2. that snaps 3. [Colloq.] *a)* brisk or lively *b)* sharply chilly 4. [Colloq.] stylish; smart

snap′shot′ *n.* an informal photograph taken quickly with a hand camera

snare (sner) *n.* [< ON. *snara*] 1. a trap for small animals 2. anything dangerous, etc. that tempts or attracts 3. a length of wire or gut across the bottom of a drum —*vt.* **snared, snar′ing** to catch as in a snare; trap

snarl¹ (snärl) *vi.* [< earlier *snar*, to growl] 1. to growl, baring the teeth, as a dog 2. to speak sharply, as in anger —*vt.* to utter with a snarl —*n.* 1. a fierce growl 2. an angry utterance —**snarl′ing·ly** *adv.*

snarl² (snärl) *n., vt., vi.* [< SNARE] tangle; disorder —**snarl′y** *adj.*

snatch (snach) *vt.* [ME. *snacchen*] to take suddenly, without right, etc.; grab —*vi.* 1. to try to seize; grab (*at*) 2. to take advantage of a chance, etc. eagerly (with *at*) —*n.* 1. a snatching 2. a brief period 3. a fragment; bit

sneak (snēk) *vi., vt.* [OE. *snican*] to move, act, give, put, take, etc. secretly or stealthily —*n.* 1. one who sneaks 2. an act of sneaking —*adj.* without warning [a *sneak* attack] —**sneak′y** *adj.* **-i·er, -i·est**

sneak′er *n.* a shoe with a cloth upper and a soft rubber sole

sneak preview an advance showing of a movie, as to get audience reaction

sneer (snir) *vi.* [ME. *sneren*] 1. to show scorn as by curling the upper lip 2. to express derision, etc. in speech or writing —*n.* 1. an act of sneering 2. a sneering expression, etc.

sneeze (snēz) *vi.* **sneezed, sneez′ing** [ME. *snesen*] to exhale breath from the nose and mouth in an involuntary, explosive action —*n.* a sneezing

snick·er (snik′ər) *vi., vt.* [echoic] to laugh or utter with a sly, partly stifled manner —*n.* a snickering

snide (snīd) *adj.* [prob. < Du. dial.] slyly malicious or derisive

sniff (snif) *vi., vt.* [ME. *sniffen*] 1. to draw in (air) forcibly through the nose 2. to express (disdain, etc.) by sniffing 3. to smell by sniffing —*n.* 1. an act or sound of sniffing 2. something sniffed

snif·fle (snif′'l) *vi.* **-fled, -fling** to sniff repeatedly, as in checking mucus running from the nose —*n.* an act or sound of sniffling —**the sniffles** [Colloq.] a head cold

snif·ter (snif′tər) *n.* [< *snift*, var. of SNIFF] a goblet tapering to a small opening to concentrate the aroma, as of brandy

snig·ger (snig′ər) *vi., vt., n.* [echoic] *same as* SNICKER

snip (snip) *vt., vi.* **snipped, snip′ping** [Du. *snippen*] to cut or cut off in a short, quick stroke, as with scissors

—*n.* 1. a small piece cut off 2. [Colloq.] a small or young person

snipe (snīp) *n.* [< ON. *snīpa*] a long-billed wading bird —*vi.* **sniped, snip'ing** 1. to hunt snipe 2. to shoot at individuals from a hidden position —**snip'er** *n.*

snip·pet (snip'it) *n.* [dim. of SNIP] a small, snipped piece; scrap, specif. of information, a writing, etc.

snip·py (snip'ē) *adj.* **-pi·er, -pi·est** [Colloq.] insolently curt, sharp, etc.

snitch (snich) *vt.* [Slang] to steal; pilfer —*vi.* [Slang] to tattle (*on*)

sniv·el (sniv''l) *vi.* **-eled** *or* **-elled, -el·ing** *or* **-el·ling** [ME. *snivelen*] 1. to cry and sniffle 2. to complain and whine 3. to make a tearful, often false display of grief, etc.

snob (snäb) *n.* [< ?] one who thinks that money and rank are very important, and has contempt for those he considers inferior —**snob'bish** *adj.* —**snob'bish·ness, snob'ber·y** *n.*

snood (snōōd) *n.* [OE. *snod*] a baglike net worn on the back of a woman's head to hold the hair

snoop (snōōp) *vi.* [Du. *snoepen*, eat snacks on the sly] [Colloq.] to pry about in a sneaking way —*n.* [Colloq.] one who snoops —**snoop'y** *adj.* **-i·er, -i·est**

snoot (snōōt) *n.* [see SNOUT] [Colloq.] 1. the nose 2. the face

snoot'y *adj.* **-i·er, -i·est** [Colloq.] haughty; snobbish —**snoot'i·ness** *n.*

snooze (snōōz) *n.* [< ? LowG. *snusen*, to snore] [Colloq.] a brief sleep; nap —*vi.* **snoozed, snooz'ing** [Colloq.] to nap; doze

snore (snôr) *vi.* **snored, snor'ing** [see SNARL¹] to breathe, while asleep, with harsh sounds —*n.* the act or sound of snoring —**snor'er** *n.*

snor·kel (snôr'k'l) *n.* [G. *schnörkel*, spiral] a breathing tube extending above the water, used in swimming just below the surface

snort (snôrt) *vi.* [prob. < SNORE] 1. to force breath audibly through the nostrils 2. to express contempt, etc. by a snort —*n.* 1. the act of snorting 2. [Slang] a quick drink of liquor

SNORKEL

snot (snät) *n.* [OE. (*ge*)*snot*, mucus] 1. nasal mucus: vulgar term 2. [Slang] an impudent young person —**snot'ty** *adj.* **-ti·er, -ti·est**

snout (snout) *n.* [prob. < MDu. *snute*] the projecting nose and jaws of an animal

snow (snō) *n.* [OE. *snaw*] 1. frozen particles of water vapor that fall to earth as white flakes 2. a falling of snow —*vi.* to fall as or like snow —*vt.* 1. to cover or obstruct with snow (with *in, under*) 2. [Slang] to deceive or mislead —**snow under** 1. to overwhelm with work, etc. 2. to defeat decisively —**snow'y** *adj.* **-i·er, -i·est**

snow'ball' *n.* a mass of snow pressed into a ball —*vi.* to increase rapidly like a rolling ball of snow

snow'bank' *n.* a large mass of snow

Snow'belt' *n.* the Midwest and NE U.S., as having cold, snowy winters

snow'-bound' *adj.* shut in or blocked off by snow

snow'drift' *n.* a drift of snow

snow'drop' (-dräp') *n.* a small plant with small, white, bell-shaped flowers

snow'fall' *n.* a fall of snow or the amount of this in a given area or time

snow fence a light fence of lath and wire to control the drifting of snow

snow'flake' *n.* a single snow crystal

snow'man' *n., pl.* **-men'** a crude human figure made of snow packed together

snow'mo·bile' *n.* a motor vehicle with steerable runners in front and tractor treads at the rear

snow'plow' *n.* a plowlike machine used to clear snow off a road, etc.

snow'shoe' *n.* a racket-shaped wooden frame crisscrossed with leather strips, etc., worn on the feet to prevent sinking in deep snow

snow'storm' *n.* a storm with a heavy snowfall

snow'suit' *n.* a child's heavily lined, hooded garment, for cold weather

snow tire a tire with a deep tread for added traction on snow or ice

snub (snub) *vt.* **snubbed, snub'bing** [< ON. *snubba*, chide] 1. to treat with scorn, disdain, etc. 2. to check suddenly the movement of (a rope, etc.) —*n.* a scornful treatment —*adj.* short and turned up, as a nose

snub'-nosed' *adj.* having a snub nose

snuff¹ (snuf) *vt.* [ME.] 1. to trim off the charred end of (a wick) 2. to put out (a candle) —**snuff out** 1. to extinguish 2. to destroy —**snuff'er** *n.*

snuff² (snuf) *vt., vi.* [MDu. *snuffen*] to sniff or smell —*n.* 1. a sniff 2. powdered tobacco taken up into the nose or put on the gums —**up to snuff** [Colloq.] up to the usual standard

snuff'box' *n.* a small box for snuff

snuf·fle (snuf''l) *n., vi.* **-fled, -fling** [< SNUFF²] *same as* SNIFFLE

snug (snug) *adj.* **snug'ger, snug'gest** [prob. < Scand.] 1. wa·m and cozy 2. neat; trim [a *snug* cottage] 3. tight in fit [a *snug* coat] 4. hidden [to lie *snug*] —**snug'ly** *adv.*

snug·gle (-'l) *vt., vi.* **-gled, -gling** [< prec.] to cuddle; nestle

so (sō) *adv.* [OE. *swa*] 1. as shown or described [hold the bat *so*] 2. a) to such an extent [why are you *so* late?] b) very [they are *so* happy] c) [Colloq.] very much 3. therefore [they were tired, and *so* left] 4. more or less [ten dollars or *so*] 5. also; likewise [I am going and so are you] 6. then [and *so* to bed] —*conj.* 1. in order [that] 2. [Colloq.] with the result that —*pron.* that which has been specified or named [he is a friend and will remain *so*] —*interj.* an exclamation of surprise, triumph, etc. —*adj.* true [that's *so*] —**and so on** (or **forth**) and the rest; et cetera —**so as** with the purpose or result —**so what?** [Colloq.] even if so, what then?

soak (sōk) *vt.* [OE. *socian*] 1. to make thoroughly wet 2. to take in; absorb (with *up*) 3. [Colloq.] to charge excessively —*vi.* **1.** to stay in a liquid for wetting, softening, etc. **2.** to penetrate —*n.* **1.** a soaking or being soaked **2.** [Slang] a drunkard

so-and-so (sō′ən sō′) *n., pl.* **so′-and-sos′** [Colloq.] an unspecified person or thing: often euphemistic

soap (sōp) *n.* [OE. *sāpe*] **1.** a substance used with water to produce suds for washing: made by the action of an alkali on a fat **2.** [Slang] *same as* SOAP OPERA: also **soap′er** —*vt.* to scrub with soap —**no soap** [Slang] (it is) not acceptable —**soap′y** *adj.* **-i-er, -i-est**

soap′box′ *n.* any improvised platform used in speaking to a street audience

soap opera [Colloq.] a daytime radio or television serial melodrama

soap′stone′ *n.* a soft, impure talc in rock form, used as an abrasive, etc.

soap′suds′ *n.pl.* foamy, soapy water

soar (sôr) *vi.* [ult. < L. *ex-*, out + *aura*, air] **1.** to rise or fly high into the air **2.** to glide along high in the air **3.** to rise above the usual level

So-a-ve (sə wä′vä, swä′—) *n.* [It.] an Italian dry white wine

sob (säb) *vi.* **sobbed, sob′bing** [ME. *sobben*] to weep aloud with short, gasping breaths —*vt.* to utter with sobs —*n.* the act or sound of sobbing

so-ber (sō′bər) *adj.* [< L. *sobrius*] **1.** temperate, esp. in the use of liquor **2.** not drunk **3.** serious, sedate, reasonable, etc. **4.** not flashy; plain, as color, clothes, etc. —*vt., vi.* to make or become sober (often with *up* or *down*) —**so′ber-ly** *adv.* —**so′ber-ness** *n.*

so-bri-e-ty (sə brī′ə tē) *n.* a being sober; specif., *a)* temperance, esp. in the use of liquor *b)* seriousness

so-bri-quet (sō′brə kā′) *n.* [Fr.] **1.** a nickname **2.** an assumed name

Soc., soc. 1. socialist **2.** society

so′-called′ *adj.* **1.** known by this term **2.** inaccurately or questionably designated as such

soc-cer (säk′ər) *n.* [alt. < (as)*soc(iation football)*] a kind of football played by kicking a round ball

so-cia-ble (sō′shə b'l) *adj.* [see ff.] **1.** friendly; gregarious **2.** characterized by informal conversation and companionship —*n.* a social —**so′cia-bil′i-ty** *n.* —**so′cia-bly** *adv.*

so-cial (sō′shəl) *adj.* [< L. *socius*, companion] **1.** of or having to do with human beings in their living together **2.** living with others; gregarious [man as a *social* being] **3.** of or having to do with society, esp. fashionable society **4.** sociable **5.** of or for companionship **6.** of or doing welfare work —*n.* an informal gathering —**so′cial-ly** *adv.*

social disease any venereal disease

so′cial-ism (-iz'm) *n.* **1.** a theory of the ownership and operation of the means of production and distribution by society, with all members sharing in the work and the products **2.** [often S-] a political movement for establishing such a system —**so′cial-ist** *n., adj.*

—**so′cial-is′tic** *adj.*

so-cial-ite (sō′shə līt′) *n.* a person prominent in fashionable society

so′cial-ize′ (-līz′) *vt.* **-ized′, -iz′ing 1.** to make social **2.** to subject to government ownership or control —*vi.* to take part in social activity —**so′cial-i-za′tion** *n.*

socialized medicine a system giving complete medical and hospital care to all through public funds

social science sociology, history, or any study of social structure

social security a Federal system of old-age, unemployment, or disability insurance

social work the promotion of the welfare of the community and the individual, as through counseling services, etc. —**social worker**

so-ci-e-ty (sə sī′ə tē) *n., pl.* **-ties** [< L. *socius*, companion] **1.** a group of persons forming a single community **2.** the system of living together in such a group **3.** all people, collectively **4.** companionship **5.** an organized group with some interest in common **6.** the wealthy, dominant class —**so-ci′e-tal** (-t′l) *adj.*

Society of Friends a Christian religious sect that believes in plain worship, pacifism, etc.: see QUAKER

so-ci-o-e-co-nom-ic (sō′sē ō ē′kə näm′ik, -ek′ə-) *adj.* involving both social and economic factors

so-ci-ol-o-gy (sō′sē äl′ə jē, -shē-) *n.* [see -LOGY] the science of social relations, organization, and change —**so′-ci-o-log′i-cal** (-ə läj′i k'l) *adj.* —**so′ci-ol′o-gist** *n.*

so-ci-o-path (sō′sē ə path′) *n.* an aggressively antisocial psychopath

sock¹ (säk) *n., pl.* **socks, sox** [< L. *soccus*, light shoe] a short stocking

sock² (säk) *vt.* [Slang] to hit with force —*n.* [Slang] a blow

sock-et (säk′it) *n.* [< OFr. *soc*, plowshare] a hollow part into which something fits [an eye *socket*]

sock-eye (säk′ī′) *n.* [< AmInd.] a red salmon of the N Pacific

Soc-ra-tes (säk′rə tēz′) 470?–399 B.C.; Athenian philosopher & teacher —**So-crat-ic** (sə krat′ik) *adj., n.*

sod (säd) *n.* [prob. < MDu. *sode*] **1.** a surface layer of earth containing grass; turf **2.** a piece of this —*vt.* **sod′ded, sod′ding** to cover with sod

so-da (sō′də) *n.* [ML.] **1.** *same as: a)* SODIUM BICARBONATE *b)* SODIUM CARBONATE *c)* SODA WATER **2.** a confection of soda water, syrup, and ice cream

soda biscuit 1. a biscuit made with baking soda and sour milk or buttermilk **2.** [Chiefly Brit.] a soda cracker

soda cracker a light, crisp cracker, usually salted, made from flour, water, and leavening, orig. baking soda

soda fountain a counter for making and serving soft drinks, sodas, etc.

so-dal-i-ty (sō dal′ə tē) *n., pl.* **-ties** [< L. *sodalis*, companion] a society of

Roman Catholic Church members for religious or charitable purposes

soda pop a flavored, carbonated soft drink

soda water water charged under pressure with carbon dioxide gas

sod·den (säd′'n) *adj.* 1. soaked through 2. soggy from improper cooking 3. dull or stupefied, as from liquor —**sod′den·ly** *adv.* —**sod′den·ness** *n.*

so·di·um (sō′dē əm) *n.* [< *soda*] an alkaline metallic chemical element

sodium bicarbonate a white crystalline compound, NaHCO₃, used in baking powder, as an antacid, etc.

sodium carbonate a hydrated carbonate of sodium, used in washing

sodium chloride common salt

sodium hydroxide a white, strongly alkaline substance: also called *lye*

sodium nitrate a clear, crystalline salt used in explosives, fertilizers, etc.

sodium pentothal *see* PENTOTHAL SODIUM

Sod·om and Go·mor·rah (säd′əm and gə môr′ə) *Bible* two sinful cities destroyed by fire

sod·om·y (säd′əm ē) *n.* [< SODOM] any sexual intercourse considered abnormal, as between two male persons —**sod′om·ite′** (-īt′) *n.*

so·ev·er (sō ev′ər) *adv.* 1. in any way 2. of any kind; at all

so·fa (sō′fə) *n.* [< Ar. *suffah*, bench] an upholstered couch with a fixed back and arms

sofa bed a sofa that can be opened into a double bed

So·fi·a (sō′fē ə, sō fē′ə) capital of Bulgaria: pop. 801,000

soft (sôft) *adj.* [OE. *softe*, gentle] 1. giving way easily under pressure 2. easily cut, shaped, etc. [a *soft* metal] 3. not as hard as is normal, desirable, etc. [*soft* butter] 4. smooth to the touch 5. easy to digest: said of a diet 6. nonalcoholic: said of drinks 7. having few of the mineral salts that keep soap from lathering 8. mild, as a breeze 9. weak; not vigorous 10. easy [a *soft* job] 11. kind or gentle 12. not bright: said of color or light 13. gentle; low: said of sound —*adv.* gently; quietly —**soft′ly** *adv.* —**soft′ness** *n.*

soft′ball′ *n.* 1. a game like baseball played with a larger and softer ball, for seven innings 2. this ball

soft′-boiled′ *adj.* boiled a short time to keep the yolk soft: said of eggs

soft drink a nonalcoholic, esp. carbonated drink

sof·ten (sôf′'n) *vt., vi.* to make or become soft or softer —**soft′ten·er** *n.*

soft′heart′ed *adj.* 1. full of compassion 2. not strict or severe; lenient

soft landing a safe landing, as of a spacecraft on the moon, with the craft and its contents unharmed

soft′-ped′al *vt.* -aled or -alled, -aling or -al·ling [from pedal action in piano, etc.] [Colloq.] to make less emphatic; tone down; play down

soft sell selling that relies on subtle inducement or suggestion

soft soap [Colloq.] flattery or smooth talk —**soft′-soap′** *vt.*

soft′ware′ (-wer′) *n.* the programs, data, etc. for a digital computer

soft′wood′ *n.* 1. any light, easily cut wood 2. the wood of any tree with cones, as the pine

soft′y *n., pl.* -ies [Colloq.] one who is too sentimental or trusting

sog·gy (säg′ē) *adj.* -gi·er, -gi·est [prob. < ON. *sog*, a sucking] soaked; moist and heavy —**sog′gi·ness** *n.*

soil¹ (soil) *n.* [< L. *solum*] 1. the surface layer of earth, supporting plant life 2. land; country [native *soil*] 3. ground or earth [barren *soil*]

soil² (soil) *vt.* [ult. < L. *sus*, pig] 1. to make dirty; stain 2. to disgrace —*vi.* to become soiled or dirty —*n.* a soiled spot

soi·ree, soi·rée (swä rā′) *n.* [< Fr. *soir*, evening] an evening party

so·journ (sō′jurn; *also, for v.* sō jurn′) *vi.* [< L. *sub-*, under + *diurnus*, of a day] to live somewhere temporarily —*n.* a brief stay; visit

sol (sōl) *n.* [< ML.] *Music* the fifth tone of the diatonic scale

Sol (säl) [L.] 1. the Roman sun god 2. the sun personified

sol·ace (säl′is) *n.* [< L. *solacium*] 1. an easing of grief, loneliness, etc. 2. a comfort or consolation —*vt.* -aced, -ac·ing to comfort; console

so·lar (sō′lər) *adj.* [< L. *sol*, sun] 1. of or having to do with the sun 2. produced by or coming from the sun

solar battery an assembly of cells (solar cells) for changing solar energy into electric power

so·lar·i·um (sō ler′ē əm) *n., pl.* -i·a (-ə) [L. < *sol*, sun] a glassed-in room, etc. for sunning

solar plexus a network of nerves in the abdomen behind the stomach

solar system the sun and all the heavenly bodies revolving around it

sold (sōld) *pt. & pp. of* SELL

sol·der (säd′ər) *n.* [< L. *solidus*, solid] a metal alloy used when melted to join or patch metal parts, etc. —*vt., vi.* to join with solder

sol·dier (sōl′jər) *n.* [< LL. *solidus*, a coin] 1. a member of an army 2. an enlisted man, as distinguished from an officer 3. one who works for a specified cause —*vi.* 1. to serve as a soldier 2. to shirk one's duty, as by feigning illness —**sol′dier·ly** *adj.*

soldier of fortune a mercenary or any adventurer

sole¹ (sōl) *n.* [< L. *solum*, a base] 1. the bottom surface of the foot 2. the part of a shoe, etc. corresponding to this —*vt.* **soled, sol′ing** to furnish (a shoe) with a sole

sole² (sōl) *adj.* [< L. *solus*] without another; single; one and only

sole³ (sōl) *n.* [< L. *solea*, SOLE¹: from its shape] a sea flatfish valued as food

sol·e·cism (säl′ə siz'm) *n.* [< Gr. *soloikos*, speaking incorrectly] a violation of the conventional usage, grammar, etc. of a language

sole·ly (sōl′lē) *adv.* 1. alone 2. only, exclusively, or merely

sol·emn (säl′əm) *adj.* [< L. *sollus*, all + *annus*, year] 1. sacred 2. formal

3. serious; grave; earnest 4. awe-inspiring —**sol´emn·ly** *adv.*

so·lem·ni·ty (sə lem´nə tē) *n., pl.* **-ties** 1. solemn ceremony, ritual, etc. 2. seriousness; gravity; impressiveness

sol·em·nize (säl´əm nīz´) *vt.* **-nized´, -niz´ing** 1. to celebrate formally or according to ritual 2. to perform the ceremony of (marriage, etc.)

so·le·noid (sō´lə noid´, säl´ə-) *n.* [Gr. *sōlēn*, tube + *eidos*, a form] a coil of wire that acts like a bar magnet when carrying a current

so·lic·it (sə lis´it) *vt., vi.* [see SOLICITOUS] 1. to appeal to (persons) for (aid, donations, etc.) 2. to entice or lure —**so·lic´i·ta´tion** *n.*

so·lic´i·tor *n.* 1. one who solicits trade, contributions, etc. 2. in England, a lawyer other than a barrister 3. the law officer for a city, etc.

so·lic·i·tous (sə lis´ə təs) *adj.* [< L. *sollus*, whole + *ciere*, set in motion] 1. showing care or concern [*solicitous* for her welfare] 2. desirous; eager —**so·lic´i·tous·ly** *adv.*

so·lic·i·tude (-tood´) *n.* a being solicitous; care, concern, etc.

sol·id (säl´id) *adj.* [< L. *solidus*] 1. relatively firm or compact; neither liquid nor gaseous 2. not hollow 3. having three dimensions 4. firm; strong; substantial 5. having no breaks or divisions 6. of one color, material, etc. throughout 7. showing unity; unanimous 8. reliable or dependable —*n.* 1. a solid substance, not a liquid or a gas 2. an object having length, breadth, and thickness —**sol´id·ly** *adv.* —**sol´id·ness** *n.*

sol·i·dar·i·ty (säl´ə dar´ə tē) *n.* complete unity, as of purpose, feeling, etc.

so·lid·i·fy (sə lid´ə fī´) *vt., vi.* **-fied´, -fy´ing** to make or become solid, hard, etc. —**so·lid´i·fi·ca´tion** *n.*

so·lid·i·ty (-tē) *n.* a being solid

sol´id-state´ *adj.* 1. of the branch of physics dealing with the structure, properties, etc. of solids 2. equipped with transistors, etc.

so·lil·o·quy (sə lil´ə kwē) *n., pl.* **-quies** [< L. *solus*, alone + *loqui*, speak] 1. a talking to oneself 2. lines in a drama spoken by a character as if to himself —**so·lil´o·quize´** (-kwīz´) *vi., vt.* **-quized´, -quiz´ing**

sol·i·taire (säl´ə ter´) *n.* [Fr.: see ff.] 1. a diamond or other gem set by itself 2. a card game for one player

sol·i·tar·y (säl´ə ter´ē) *adj.* [< L. *solus*, alone] 1. living or being alone 2. single; only [a *solitary* example] 3. lonely; remote 4. done in solitude

sol´i·tude´ (-tood´) *n.* [see prec.] 1. a being solitary, or alone; seclusion 2. a secluded place

so·lo (sō´lō) *n., pl.* **-los** [It. < L. *solus*, alone] 1. a musical piece or passage to be performed by one person 2. any performance by one person alone —*adj.* for or by a single person —*adv.* alone —*vi.* to perform a solo —**so´lo·ist** *n.*

So·lo·mon (säl´ə mən) *Bible* king of Israel noted for his wisdom

So·lon (sō´lən, -län) c.640–559? B.C.; Athenian lawgiver —*n.* [*sometimes* **s-**] a wise lawmaker

so long *colloq. term for* GOODBYE

sol·stice (säl´stis) *n.* [< L. *sol*, sun + *sistere*, halt] the time of year when the sun reaches the point farthest north (June 21 or 22) or farthest south (Dec. 21 or 22) of the equator: in the Northern Hemisphere, the **summer solstice** and **winter solstice**, respectively

sol·u·ble (säl´yoo b'l) *adj.* [see SOLVE] 1. that can be dissolved 2. that can be solved —**sol´u·bil´i·ty** *n.*

sol·ute (säl´yoot, sō´loot) *n.* the substance dissolved in a solution —*adj.* dissolved; in solution

so·lu·tion (sə loo´shən) *n.* [see ff.] 1. the solving of a problem 2. an answer, explanation, etc. 3. the dispersion of one substance in another, usually a liquid, so as to form a homogeneous mixture 4. the mixture so produced

solve (sälv) *vt.* **solved, solv´ing** [< L. *se-*, apart + *luere*, let go] to find the answer to (a problem, etc.); explain —**solv´a·ble** *adj.* —**solv´er** *n.*

sol·vent (säl´vənt) *adj.* [see prec.] 1. able to pay all one's debts 2. that can dissolve another substance —*n.* a substance that can dissolve another substance —**sol´ven·cy** *n.*

So·ma·li·a (sō mä´lē ə) country in E Africa: 246,201 sq. mi.; pop. 2,500,000

so·mat·ic (sō mat´ik) *adj.* [< Gr. *sōma*, the body] of the body; physical

somatic cell any of the cells that form the tissues and organs of the body: opposed to GERM CELL

som·ber (säm´bər) *adj.* [< L. *sub*, under + *umbra*, shade] 1. dark and gloomy or dull 2. dismal; sad Chiefly Brit. sp. **som´bre** —**som´ber·ly** *adv.*

som·bre·ro (säm brer´ō) *n., pl.* **-ros** [Sp. < *sombra*, shade: see prec.] a broad-brimmed, tall-crowned hat worn in Mexico, the Southwest, etc.

SOMBRERO

some (sum) *adj.* [OE. *sum*] 1. certain but not specified or known [open *some* evenings] 2. of a certain unspecified quantity, degree, etc. [have *some* candy] 3. about [*some* ten of them] 4. [Colloq.] remarkable, striking, etc. [it was *some* fight] —*pron.* a certain unspecified quantity, number, etc. [*some* of them agree] —*adv.* 1. approximately [*some* ten men] 2. [Colloq.] to some extent; somewhat [slept *some*] 3. [Colloq.] to a great extent or at a great rate [must run *some* to catch up] —**and then some** [Colloq.] and more than that

-some¹ (səm) [OE. *-sum*] a suffix meaning tending to (be) [*tiresome*]

-some² (sōm) [< Gr. *sōma*, body] a

combining form meaning body [*chromo-some*]

some·bod·y (sum'bud'ē, -bäd'ē) *pron.* a person unknown or not named; some person; someone —*n., pl.* -**ies** a person of importance

some'day' *adv.* at some future day or time

some'how' (-hou') *adv.* in a way or by a method not known or stated: often in **somehow or other**

some'one' *pron.* same as SOMEBODY

som·er·sault (sum'ər sôlt') *n.* [< L. *supra*, over + *saltus*, a leap] an acrobatic stunt performed by turning the body one full revolution, heels over head —*vi.* to perform a somersault

some'thing *n.* 1. a thing not definitely known, understood, etc. [*something* went wrong] 2. a definite but unspecified thing [have *something* to eat] 3. a bit; a little 4. [Colloq.] an important or remarkable person or thing —*adv.* 1. somewhat [looks *something* like me] 2. [Colloq.] really; quite [sounds *something* awful] —**make something of** 1. to get use or profit from 2. to treat as very important 3. [Colloq.] to treat as a point of dispute —**something else** [Slang] one that is quite remarkable

some'time' *adv.* at some unspecified or future time —*adj.* former

some'times' *adv.* occasionally

some'way' *adv.* same s SOMEHOW: also **some'ways'**

some'what' *n.* some degree, amount, part, etc. —*adv.* to some extent, degree, etc.; a little

some'where' *adv.* 1. in, to, or at some place not known or specified 2. at some time, degree, figure, etc. (with *about, around, between,* etc.)

som·nam·bu·lism (säm nam'b·oo liz'm) *n.* [< L. *somnus*, sleep + *ambulare*, to walk] sleepwalking — **som·nam'bu·list** *n.*

som·no·lent (säm'nə lənt) *adj.* [< L. *somnus*, sleep] 1. sleepy 2. inducing drowsiness —**som'no·lence** *n.*

son (sun) *n.* [OE. *sunu*] 1. a boy or man in his relationship to his parents 2. a male descendant —**the Son** Jesus

so·nar (sō'när) *n.* [*so(und) n(avigation) a(nd) r(anging)*] an apparatus that transmits sound waves in water, used in locating submarines, finding depths, etc.

so·na·ta (sə nät'ə) *n.* [It. < L. *sonare*, to sound] a musical composition for one or two instruments, having several movements related by similarity or contrast of tempo, key, style, etc.

sonde (sänd) *n.* [Fr., sounding line] a device for measuring and usually telemetering meteorological conditions at high altitudes

song (sôŋ) *n.* [OE. *sang*] 1. the act or art of singing 2. a piece of music for singing 3. a) poetry b) a ballad or lyric set to music 4. a singing sound —**for a song** for a small sum

song'bird' *n.* a bird that makes vocal sounds that are like music

song'fest' (-fest') *n.* [SONG + -FEST]

an informal gathering of people to sing songs, esp. folk songs

song'ster (-stər) *n.* a singer —**song'-stress** (-stris) *n.fem.*

son·ic (sän'ik) *adj.* [< L. *sonus*, sound] of or having to do with sound or the speed of sound

sonic barrier the large increase of air resistance met by some aircraft flying near the speed of sound

sonic boom the explosive sound of supersonic jets passing overhead

son'-in-law' *n., pl.* **sons'-in-law'** the husband of one's daughter

son·net (sän'it) *n.* [< L. *sonus*, a sound] a poem normally of fourteen lines in any of several rhyme schemes

son·ny (sun'ē) *n., pl.* -**nies** little son: used in addressing a young boy

so·no·rous (sə nôr'əs, sän'ər əs) *adj.* [< L. *sonor*, a sound] 1. producing sound; resonant 2. full, deep, or rich in sound —**so·nor'i·ty** (-ə tē) *n.*

soon (sōōn) *adv.* [OE. *sona*, at once] 1. in a short time [come see us *soon*] 2. promptly; quickly [as *soon* as possible] 3. ahead of time; early [he left too *soon*] 4. readily; willingly [I would as *soon* go as stay] —**sooner or later** eventually

soot (soot) *n.* [OE. *sot*] a black substance consisting chiefly of carbon particles, in the smoke of burning matter —**soot'y** *adj.* -**i·er,** -**i·est**

sooth (sōōth) *n.* [OE. *soth*] [Archaic] tᵣ ₕ

soothe (sōōth) *vt.* **soothed, sooth'-ing** [OE. *sothian*, prove true] 1. to make calm or composed, as by gentleness, flattery, etc. 2. to relieve (pain, etc.) —**sooth'er** *n.* —**sooth'ing** *adj.*

sooth·say·er (sōōth'sā'ər) *n.* [see SOOTH] one who claims to predict the future —**sooth'say'ing** *n.*

sop (säp) *n.* [ME. *soppe*] 1. a piece of food, as bread, soaked in milk, etc. 2. a) something given to appease b) a bribe —*vt., vi.* **sopped, sop'ping** 1. to soak, steep, etc. 2. to take (*up*), as water, by absorption

SOP, S.O.P. standing (or standard) operating procedure

soph·ism (säf'iz'm) *n.* [ult. < Gr. *sophos*, clever] a clever and plausible but fallacious argument

soph'ist (-ist) *n.* one who uses clever, specious reasoning

so·phis·ti·cate (sə fis'tə kāt'; *for n.* -kit) *vt.* -**cat'ed, -cat'ing** [see prec.] to change from a natural or simple state; make worldly-wise —*n.* a sophisticated person

so·phis'ti·cat'ed *adj.* 1. not simple, naïve, etc.; worldly-wise or knowledge-able, subtle, etc. 2. for sophisticates 3. highly complex or developed in form, technique, etc., as equipment — **so·phis'ti·ca'tion** *n.*

soph·is·try (säf'is trē) *n., pl.* -**tries** misleading but clever reasoning

Soph·o·cles (säf'ə klēz') 496?-406 B.C.; Gr. writer of tragic dramas

soph·o·more (säf'ə mōr') *n.* [< obs. *sophumer*, sophist] a student in the second year of college or in the tenth grade at high school

soph'o·mor'ic *adj.* of or like sophomores; opinionated, immature, etc.

-so·phy (sə fē) [< Gr. *sophia*, skill] *a suffix meaning* knowledge *[philosophy]*

sop·o·rif·ic (säp'ə rif'ik, sō'pə-) *adj.* [< L. *sopor*, sleep + -FIC] causing sleep —*n.* a soporific drug, etc.

sop'py *adj.* -pi·er, -pi·est 1. very wet: also **sop'ping** 2. [Colloq.] maudlin

so·pra·no (sə pran'ō) *n.*, *pl.* -nos [It. < *sopra*, above] 1. the highest singing voice of women or boys 2. a singer with such a range 3. a part for a soprano —*adj.* of or for a soprano

sor·cer·y (sôr'sər ē) *n.*, *pl.* -ies [< L. *sors*, a lot, share] the supposed use of an evil, supernatural power over people; witchcraft —**sor'cer·er** *n.* —**sor'cer·ess** *n.fem.*

sor·did (sôr'did) *adj.* [< L. *sordes*, filth] 1. dirty; filthy 2. squalid; wretched 3. base; mean; ignoble —**sor'did·ly** *adv.* —**sor'did·ness** *n.*

sore (sôr) *adj.* **sor'er, sor'est** [OE. *sar*] 1. giving or feeling pain; painful 2. *a)* filled with grief *b)* causing sadness, misery, etc. *[a sore task]* 3. causing irritation *[a sore point]* 4. [Colloq.] angry; offended —*n.* a sore, usually infected spot on the body —*adv.* [Archaic] greatly —**sore'ness** *n.*

sore'head' *n.* [Colloq.] a person easily angered or made resentful.

sore'ly *adv.* 1. grievously; painfully 2. urgently *[sorely* needs]

sor·ghum (sôr'gəm) *n.* [< It. *sorgo*] 1. a cereal grass grown for grain, syrup, fodder, etc. 2. syrup made from its juices

so·ror·i·ty (sə rôr'ə tē) *n.*, *pl.* -ties [< L. *soror*, sister] a group of women or girls joined together for fellowship, etc., as in some colleges

sor·rel¹ (sôr'əl, sär'-) *n.* [< Frank. *sur*, sour] any of various plants with sour-tasting leaves

sor·rel² (sôr'əl, sär'-) *n.* [< OFr. *sor*, light brown] 1. a light reddish brown 2. a horse, etc. of this color

sor·row (sär'ō) *n.* [OE. *sorg*] 1. mental suffering caused by loss, disappointment, etc.; grief 2. that which causes grief —*vi.* to grieve —**sor'row·ful** *adj.* —**sor'row·ful·ly** *adv.*

sor·ry (sär'ē) *adj.* -ri·er, -ri·est [< OE. *sar*, sore] 1. full of sorrow, pity, or regret 2. inferior; poor 3. wretched —**sor'ri·ly** *adv.* —**sor'ri·ness** *n.*

sort (sôrt) *n.* [< L. *sors*, chance] 1. any group of related things; kind; class 2. quality or type 3. [Archaic] manner; way —*vt.* to arrange according to class or kind —**out of sorts** or **of a sort** —**out of sorts** [Colloq.] not in good humor or health —**sort of** [Colloq.] somewhat

sor·tie (sôr'tē) *n.* [Fr. < *sortir*, go out] 1. a quick raid by forces of a besieged place 2. one mission by a single military plane

SOS (es'ō'es') a signal of distress, as in wireless telegraphy

so-so (sō'sō') *adv.*, *adj.* just passably or passable; fair Also **so so**

sot (sät) *n.* [< VL. *sottus*, a fool] a habitual drunkard —**sot'tish** *adj.*

sot·to vo·ce (sät'ō vō'chē) [It., under the voice] in a low voice, so as not to be overheard

souf·flé (soō flā') *n.* [Fr. < L. *sufflare*, puff out] a baked food made light and puffy by adding beaten egg whites before baking

sough (sou, suf) *n.* [OE. *swogan*, to sound] a soft sighing or rustling sound —*n.* to make a sough

sought (sôt) *pt. & pp.* of SEEK

soul (sōl) *n.* [OE. *sawol*] 1. an entity without material reality, regarded as the spiritual part of a person 2. the moral or emotional nature of man 3. spiritual or emotional warmth, force, etc. 4. vital or essential part, quality, etc. 5. a person *[I didn't see a soul]* 6. [Colloq.] a feeling by U.S. blacks of racial pride and solidarity —*adj.* [Colloq.] of, for, or by U.S. blacks

soul food [Colloq.] certain food, as chitterlings or ham hocks, popular esp. among Southern Negroes

soul'ful *adj.* full of deep feeling —**soul'ful·ly** *adv.* —**soul'ful·ness** *n.*

sound¹ (sound) *n.* [< L. *sonus*] 1. that which is heard, resulting from stimulation of auditory nerves by vibrations (**sound waves**) in the air 2. the distance within which a sound may be heard 3. mental impression produced by wording *[the sound of his report]* —*vi.* 1. to make a sound 2. to seem upon being heard —*vt.* 1. to cause to sound 2. to signal, express, etc. 3. to utter distinctly *[to sound one's r's]* —**sound'less** *adj.*

sound² (sound) *adj.* [OE. *ge(sund)*] 1. free from defect, damage, or decay 2. healthy *[a sound body]* 3. safe; stable *[a sound bank]* 4. based on valid reasoning; sensible 5. thorough; forceful *[a sound defeat]* 6. deep and undisturbed: said of sleep 7. honest, loyal, etc. —*adv.* deeply *[sound asleep]* —**sound'ly** *adv.* —**sound'ness** *n.*

sound³ (sound) *n.* [< OE. & ON. *sund*] 1. a wide channel linking two large bodies of water or separating an island from the mainland 2. a long arm of the sea

sound⁴ (sound) *vt.*, *vi.* [< L. *sub*, under + *unda*, a wave] 1. to measure the depth of (water), esp. with a weighted line 2. to probe (the air or space) for data 3. to try to find out the opinions of (a person), usually subtly (often with *out*) —**sound'ing** *n.*

sound barrier *same as* SONIC BARRIER

sounding board 1. something to increase resonance or reflect sound: also **sound'board'** *n.* 2. a person used to test ideas on

sound'proof' *adj.* that keeps sound

from coming through —*vt.* to make soundproof

sound track the sound record along one side of a motion-picture film

soup (sōōp) *n.* [Fr. *soupe*] a liquid food made by cooking meat, vegetables, etc. in water, milk, etc. —**soup up** [Slang] to increase the capacity for speed of (an engine, etc.)

soup·çon (sōōp sŏn′, sōōp′sŏn′) *n.* [Fr. < L. *suspicio*, suspicion] 1. a slight trace, as of a flavor 2. a tiny bit

soup′y *adj.* **-i·er, -i·est** 1. like soup 2. [Colloq.] foggy

sour (sour) *adj.* [OE. *sur*] 1. having the sharp, acid taste of vinegar, etc. 2. spoiled by fermentation 3. cross; bad-tempered 4. distasteful or unpleasant —*vt., vi.* to make or become sour —**sour′ly** *adv.* —**sour′ness** *n.*

source (sôrs) *n.* [< L. *surgere*, to rise] 1. a spring, etc. from which a stream arises 2. place of origin; prime cause 3. a person, book, etc. that provides information

sour′dough′ *n.* 1. [Dial.] fermented dough saved for use as leaven 2. a lone prospector, as in the West

sour grapes a scorning of something only because it cannot be had or done

souse (sous) *n.* [< OHG. *sulza*, brine] 1. a pickled food, as pig's feet 2. liquid for pickling; brine 3. a plunging into a liquid 4. [Slang] a drunkard —*vt., vi.* **soused, sous′ing** 1. to pickle 2. to plunge in a liquid 3. to make or become soaking wet

south (south) *n.* [OE. *suth*] 1. the direction to the left of one facing the sunset (180° on the compass) 2. a region in or toward this direction —*adj.* 1. in, of, or toward the south 2. from the south —*adv.* in or toward the south —**the South** the part of the U.S. south of Pennsylvania, the Ohio River, and N Missouri

South Africa country in S Africa: 472,358 sq. mi.; pop. 18,733,000; caps. Cape Town, Pretoria

South America S continent in the Western Hemisphere: c.6,864,000 sq. mi.; pop. 174,000,000 —**South American**

South Bend city in N Ind.: pop. 110,000

South Car·o·li·na (kar′ə lī′nə) Southern State of the U.S.: 31,055 sq. mi.; pop. 3,119,000; cap. Columbia —**South Car′o·lin′i·an** (-lin′ē ən)

South China Sea part of the Pacific Ocean, between SE Asia & the Philippines

South Da·ko·ta (də kō′tə) Middle Western State of the U.S.: 77,047 sq. mi.; pop. 690,000; cap. Pierre —**South Da·ko′tan**

south′east′ *n.* 1. the direction halfway between south and east 2. a region in or toward this direction —*adj.* 1. in, of, or toward the southeast 2. from the southeast —*adv.* in, toward, or from the southeast —**south′east′er·ly** *adj., adv.* —**south′east′ern** *adj.* —**south′east′ward** (-wərd) *adv., adj.* —**south′east′wards** *adv.*

south·er·ly (su*th*′ər lē) *adj., adv.* 1. toward the south 2. from the south

south·ern (su*th*′ərn) *adj.* 1. in, of, or toward the south 2. from the south 3. [S-] of the South

south′ern·er *n.* a native or inhabitant of the south

Southern Hemisphere the half of the earth south of the equator

southern lights aurora australis

south·paw (south′pô′) *n.* [Slang] a left-handed person; esp., a left-handed baseball pitcher

South Pole the southern end of the earth's axis

South Sea Islands the islands in the South Pacific

south′ward (-wərd) *adv., adj.* toward the south: also **south′wards** *adv.*

south′west′ *n.* 1. the direction halfway between south and west 2. a region in or toward this direction —*adj.* 1. in, of, or toward the southwest 2. from the southwest —*adv.* in, toward, or from the southwest —**the Southwest** the southwestern U.S. —**south′west′er·ly** *adj., adv.* —**south′west′ern** *adj.* —**south′west′ward** (-wərd) *adv., adj.* —**south′west′wards** *adv.*

sou·ve·nir (sōō′və nir′) *n.* [Fr. < L. *subvenire*, come to mind] something kept as a reminder; memento

sov·er·eign (säv′rən, -ər in) *adj.* [< L. *super*, above] 1. above all others; chief; supreme 2. supreme in power, rank, etc. 3. independent of all others [a *sovereign* state] —*n.* 1. a monarch or ruler 2. esp. formerly, a British gold coin worth one pound

sov′er·eign·ty *n.* 1. the status, rule, etc. of a sovereign 2. supreme and independent political authority

so·vi·et (sō′vē it, -et′) *n.* [Russ., lit., council] 1. in the Soviet Union, any of the various elected governing councils from the village and town soviets up to the Supreme Soviet 2. a similar council in a socialist governing system —*adj.* [S-] of or connected with the Soviet Union —**so′vi·et·ism** *n.*

Soviet Union *same as* UNION OF SOVIET SOCIALIST REPUBLICS

sow[1] (sou) *n.* [OE. *sugu*] an adult female pig

sow[2] (sō) *vt.* **sowed, sown** (sōn) *or* **sowed, sow′ing** [OE. *sawan*] 1. to scatter (seed) for growing 2. to plant seed in (a field, etc.) 3. to spread or scatter —*vi.* to sow seed —**sow′er** *n.*

sox (säks) *n. alt. pl. of* SOCK[1]

soy (soi) *n.* [Jap. < Chin. *chiang*, salted bean + *yu*, oil] a dark, salty sauce made from fermented soybeans

soy′bean′ *n.* 1. a plant widely grown for its seeds, which contain much protein and oil 2. its seed

Sp. 1. Spain 2. Spaniard 3. Spanish

spa (spä) *n.* [< *Spa*, resort in Belgium] 1. a mineral spring 2. a health resort having a mineral spring 3. a commercial establishment with exercise rooms, sauna baths, etc.

space (spās) *n.* [< L. *spatium*] 1. *a)* the boundless expanse within which all

things are contained *b*) *same as* OUTER
SPACE 2. *a*) distance, area, etc.
between or within things *b*) room for
something [a parking *space*] 3. an
interval of time —*vt.* **spaced, spac'-
ing** to arrange with spaces between

space'craft' *n., pl.* **-craft'** a spaceship or satellite designed for travel,
exploration, etc. in outer space

spaced'-out' *adj.* [Slang] under the
influence of a drug, marijuana, etc.:
also **spaced, space'y**

space'flight' *n.* a flight through
outer space

space heater a small heating unit
for a room or small area

space'man' *n., pl.* **-men'** an astronaut or any of the crew of a spaceship

space'port' *n.* a center for testing
and launching spacecraft

space'ship' *n.* a rocket-propelled
vehicle for travel in outer space

space shuttle a spacecraft for transporting persons and equipment between earth and a space station

space station (or **platform**) an
orbiting structure for use as a launch
pad, observation center, etc.

space'suit' *n.* a garment pressurized
for use by spacemen

space'walk' *n.* an astronaut's moving
about in space outside his spacecraft
—*vi.* to engage in a spacewalk

spa·cious (spā'shəs) *adj.* having more
than enough space; vast —**spa'-
cious·ly** *adv.* —**spa'cious·ness** *n.*

spade¹ (spād) *n.* [OE. *spadu*] a flat-
bladed, long-handled digging tool, like
a shovel —*vt., vi.* **spad'ed, spad'ing**
to dig with a spade —**spade'ful** *n.*

spade² (spād) *n.* [ult. < Gr. *spathē*,
flat blade] 1. the black figure (♠)
marking one of the four suits of playing cards 2. a card of this suit

spade'work' *n.* preparatory work for
some main project, esp. when tiresome

spa·ghet·ti (spə get'ē) *n.* [It. <
spago, small cord] pasta in long, thin
strings, cooked by boiling or steaming

Spain (spān) country in SW Europe:
194,346 sq. mi.; pop. 32,411,000; cap.
Madrid

spake (spāk) *archaic pt. of* SPEAK

span (span) *n.* [OE. *sponn*] 1. the
distance (about 9 in.) between the tips
of the thumb and little finger when
extended 2. *a*) the full extent between
any two limits *b*) the full duration of
[*span* of attention] 3. a part between
two supports 4. a team of two animals
—*vt.* **spanned, span'ning** 1. to
measure, esp. by the span of the hand
2. to extend over

Span. Spanish

span·dex (span'deks) *n.* [< EXPAND]
an elastic synthetic fiber used in
girdles, etc.

span·gle (span'g'l) *n.* [< OE. *spang*,
a clasp] a small piece of bright metal
sewn on fabric for decoration —*vt.*
-gled, -gling to decorate with spangles
or other bright objects

Span·iard (span'yərd) *n.* a native
or inhabitant of Spain

span·iel (span'yəl) *n.* [< MFr.
espagnol, lit., Spanish] any of several
breeds of dog with a silky coat, large,
drooping ears, and short legs

Span·ish (span'ish) *adj.* of Spain, its
people, their language, etc. —*n.* the
language of Spain and Spanish America —**the Spanish** the people of Spain

Spanish America those countries
south of the U.S. in which Spanish
is the chief language —**Span'ish-
A·mer'i·can** *adj., n.*

Spanish moss a rootless plant that
grows in long, graceful strands from
tree branches in the southern U.S.

spank (spaŋk) *vt.* [echoic] to strike
with the open hand, etc., esp. on the
buttocks, as in punishment —*n.* a
smack given in spanking

spank'ing *adj.* 1. swiftly moving;
rapid 2. brisk: said of a breeze —*adv.*
[Colloq.] completely [*spanking* new]

spar¹ (spär) *n.* [< ON. *sparri* or MDu.
sparre] any pole, as a mast or yard,
supporting a sail of a ship

spar² (spär) *vi.* **sparred, spar'ring**
[prob. < It. *parare*, to parry] 1. to
box with feinting movements, landing
few heavy blows 2. to wrangle

spare (sper) *vt.* **spared, spar'ing**
[OE. *sparian*] 1. to refrain from killing, hurting, etc. 2. to save or free a
person from (something) 3. to avoid
using or use frugally 4. to part with
conveniently —*adj.* 1. not in regular
use; extra 2. free [*spare* time] 3.
meager; scanty 4. lean; thin —*n.* 1. a
spare, or extra, thing 2. *Bowling* a
knocking down of all the pins with two
rolls of the ball —**spare'ly** *adv.*

spare'ribs' *n.pl.* a cut of pork, consisting of the thin end of the ribs

spar'ing *adj.* 1. careful; frugal 2.
scanty or meager —**spar'ing·ly** *adv.*

spark (spärk) *n.* [OE. *spearca*] 1. a
glowing bit of matter, esp. one thrown
off by a fire 2. any flash or sparkle 3.
a particle or trace 4. a brief flash of
light accompanying an electric discharge as through air —*vi.* to make
sparks —*vt.* to stir up; activate

spar·kle (spär'k'l) *vi.* **-kled, -kling**
1. to throw off sparks 2. to glitter 3.
to effervesce —*n.* 1. a sparkling 2.
brilliance —**spar'kler** (-klər) *n.*

spark plug a piece fitted into a
cylinder of an engine to ignite the fuel
mixture by making sparks

spar·row (spar'ō) *n.* [OE. *spearwa*]
any of numerous finches

sparse (spärs) *adj.* [< L. *spargere*,
scatter] thinly spread; not dense —
sparse'ly *adv.* —**sparse'ness, spar'-
si·ty** (-sə tē) *n.*

Spar·ta (spär'tə) city in S Greece: a
military power in ancient times

Spar'tan *adj.* 1. of ancient Sparta, its
people, culture, etc. 2. like the
Spartans; warlike, hardy, disciplined,
etc. —*n.* a Spartan person

fat, āpe, cär; ten, ēven; is, bīte; gō, hôrn, tōōl, look; oil, out; up, fer;
chin; she; thin, then; zh, leisure; ŋ, ring; ə for *a* in ago; ', (ā'b'l); ë, Fr. coeur;
ö, Fr. feu; Fr. mon; ü, Fr. duc; kh, G. ich, doch; ‡ foreign; < derived from

spasm (spaz'm) *n.* [< Gr. *spasmos*]
1. a sudden, involuntary muscular
contraction 2. any sudden, violent,
temporary activity, feeling, etc.
spas·mod·ic (spaz mäd'ik) *adj.* [see
prec. & -OID] of or like spasms; fitful
—**spas·mod'i·cal·ly** *adv.*
spas·tic (spas'tik) *adj.* of or characterized by muscular spasms —*n.* one
having a spastic condition
spat¹ (spat) *n.* [prob. echoic] [Colloq.]
a brief, petty quarrel —*vi.* **spat'ted,**
spat'ting [Colloq.] to engage in a spat
spat² (spat) *n.* [< *spatterdash,* a
legging] a gaiterlike covering for the
instep and ankle
spat³ (spat) *alt. pt. & pp. of* SPIT²
spat⁴ (spat) *n.* [< ?] the spawn of the
oyster or other bivalve shellfish
spate (spāt) *n.* [< ?] an unusually
large outpouring, as of words
spa·tial (spā'shəl) *adj.* [< L. *spatium,* space] of, or existing in, space
spat·ter (spat'ər) *vt., vi.* [< ?] 1. to
scatter or spurt out in drops 2. to
splash —*n.* 1. a spattering 2. a mark
caused by spattering
spat·u·la (spach'ə lə) *n.* [< Gr.
spathē, flat blade] an implement with
a broad, flexible blade for spreading or
blending foods, paints, etc.
spav·in (spav'in) *n.* [< MFr. *espar-
vain*] a disease laming horses in the
hock joint —**spav'ined** *adj.*
spawn (spôn) *vt., vi.* [see EXPAND] 1.
to produce or deposit (eggs, sperm, or
young) 2. to bring forth or produce
prolifically —*n.* 1. the mass of eggs or
young produced by fishes, mollusks,
etc. 2. something produced, esp. in
great quantity, as offspring
spay (spā) *vt.* [< Gr. *spathē,* flat
blade] to sterilize (a female animal) by
removing the ovaries
speak (spēk) *vi.* **spoke** or archaic
spake, spo'ken, speak'ing [OE.
sp(r)ecan] 1. to utter words; talk 2. to
communicate as by talking 3. to make
a request (*for*) 4. to make a speech
—*vt.* 1. to make known as by speaking 2. to use (a given language) in
speaking 3. to utter (words) orally
—**speak out** (or **up**) to speak clearly
or freely —**speak well for** to say or
indicate something favorable about
speak'-eas'y (-ē'zē) *n., pl.* **-ies**
[Slang] a place where alcoholic drinks
are sold illegally
speak'er *n.* one who speaks; esp., *a*)
an orator *b*) the presiding officer of
various lawmaking bodies, specif. [S-]
of the U.S. House of Representatives
spear (spir) *n.* [OE. *spere*] 1. a weapon
with a long shaft and a sharp point,
for thrusting or throwing 2. [var. of
SPIRE] a long blade or shoot, as of
grass —*vt.* to pierce or stab with or as
with a spear
spear'head' *n.* 1. the pointed head of
a spear 2. the leading person or group,
as in an attack —*vt.* to take the lead in
(a drive, attack, etc.)
spear'mint' *n.* [prob. after the shape
of its flowers] a fragrant plant of the
mint family, used for flavoring
spe·cial (spesh'əl) *adj.* [< L. *species,*

kind] 1. distinctive or unique 2.
exceptional; unusual 3. highly valued
4. of or for a particular purpose, etc.
5. not general; specific —*n.* a special
person or thing —**spe'cial·ly** *adv.*
special delivery mail delivery by a
special messenger, for an extra fee
spe'cial·ist *n.* one who specializes in a
particular study, work, etc.
spe'cial·ize' *vi.* -**ized', -iz'ing** to
concentrate on a special branch of
study, work, etc. —**spe'cial·i·za'-
tion** *n.*
spe'cial·ty (-tē) *n., pl.* -**ties** 1. a
special quality, feature, etc. 2. a
special interest, study, etc. 3. an
article with special features, etc.
spe·cie (spē'shē) *n.* [< L. *species*]
coin, rather than paper money
spe·cies (-shēz) *n., pl.* -**cies** [L., ap-
pearance] 1. a distinct kind; sort 2.
the fundamental biological classification, consisting of a number of highly
similar plants or animals
specif. specifically
spe·cif·ic (spi sif'ik) *adj.* [< L.
species (see SPECIES) + -*ficus,* -FIC] 1.
definite; explicit 2. peculiar to or
characteristic of something 3. of a
particular kind 4. specially indicated
as a cure for some disease —*n.* a
specific cure —**spe·cif'i·cal·ly** *adv.*
spec·i·fi·ca·tion (spes'ə fi kā'shən)
n. 1. [*usually pl.*] an enumeration of
particulars, as to size, quality, etc. 2.
something specified
specific gravity the ratio of the
weight of a given volume of a substance to that of an equal volume of
another substance (as water) used as
a standard
spec·i·fy (spes'ə fī') *vt.* -**fied', -fy'ing**
[< LL. *specificus,* SPECIFIC] 1. to
mention or describe in detail 2. to
state explicitly
spec·i·men (spes'ə mən) *n.* [L. <
specere, see] a part or individual used
as a sample of a whole or group
spe·cious (spē'shəs) *adj.* [< L. *species,* appearance] seeming to be good,
sound, correct, etc. without really
being so —**spe'cious·ly** *adv.*
speck (spek) *n.* [OE. *specca*] 1. a small
spot, mark, etc. 2. a very small bit
—*vt.* to mark with specks
speck·le (spek'l) *n.* a small speck
—*vt.* -**led, -ling** to mark with speckles
specs (speks) *n.pl.* [Colloq.] 1. spectacles; eyeglasses 2. specifications
spec·ta·cle (spek'tə k'l) *n.* [< L.
specere, see] 1. a remarkable sight
2. a large public show 3. [*pl.*] a pair of
eyeglasses: old-fashioned term
spec·tac·u·lar (spek tak'yə lər) *adj.*
unusual to a striking degree; of an
elaborate show or display —**spec·tac'-
u·lar·ly** *adv.*
spec·ta·tor (spek'tāt ər) *n.* [L. <
spectare, behold] one who watches
without taking an active part
spec·ter (spek'tər) *n.* [< L. *spectare,*
behold] a ghost; apparition: Brit. sp.
spectre —**spec'tral** (-trəl) *adj.*
spec·tro·scope (spek'trə skōp') *n.*
[< L. *spectare,* behold + -SCOPE] an
optical instrument used for forming

spectra for study —spec′tro·scop′ic (-skäp′ik) *adj.* —spec·tros′co·py (-träs′kə pē) *n.*

spec·trum (spek′trəm) *n., pl.* -tra (-trə). -trums [< L.: see SPECTER] 1. a series of colored bands diffracted and arranged in order of their respective wavelengths, by the passage of white light through a prism, etc. 2. a continuous range or entire extent —spec′tral (-trəl) *adj.*

spec·u·late (spek′yə lāt′) *vi.* -lat′ed, -lat′ing [< L. *specere*, see] 1. to think reflectively; ponder; esp., to conjecture 2. to engage in a risky venture on the chance of making huge profits —spec′u·la′tion n. —spec′u·la′tive *adj.* —spec′u·la′tor *n.*

speech (spēch) *n.* [< OE. *sprecan*, speak] 1. the act or manner of speaking 2. the power to speak 3. that which is spoken; utterance, remark, etc. 4. a talk given to an audience 5. the language of a certain people

speech′less *adj.* 1. incapable of speech 2. silent, as from shock

speed (spēd) *n.* [OE. *spæd*, success] 1. quick motion; swiftness 2. rate of movement; velocity 3. [Slang] any of various amphetamine compounds —*vi.* sped (sped) or speed′ed, speed′ing to move rapidly, esp. too rapidly —*vt.* 1. to cause to speed 2. to help to succeed; aid —speed up to increase in speed —speed′er *n.*

speed′boat′ *n.* a fast motorboat

speed·om·e·ter (spi däm′ə tər) *n.* a device attached to a motor vehicle, etc. to indicate speed

speed′ster (-stər) *n.* a very fast driver, runner, etc.

speed′way′ *n.* a track for racing automobiles or motorcycles

speed′y *adj.* -i·er, -i·est 1. rapid; fast; swift 2. without delay; prompt [a *speedy* reply] —speed′i·ly *adv.*

spe·le·ol·o·gy (spē′lē äl′ə jē) *n.* the scientific study and exploration of caves —spe′le·ol′o·gist *n.*

spell¹ (spel) *n.* [OE., a saying] 1. a word or formula supposed to have some magic power 2. irresistible influence; charm; fascination

spell² (spel) *vt.* spelled or spelt, spell′ing [< OFr. *espeller*, explain] 1. to name in order the letters of (a word) 2. to make up (a word, etc.): said of specified letters 3. to mean [red *spells* danger] —*vi.* to spell words —spell out to explain in detail

spell³ (spel) *vt.* spelled, spell′ing [OE. *spelian*] [Colloq.] to work in place of (another) for an interval; relieve —*n.* 1. a period of work, duty, etc. 2. a period of anything [a *spell* of brooding] 3. [Colloq.] a fit of illness

spell′bind′ (-bīnd′) *vt.* -bound′, -bind′ing to cause to be spellbound; fascinate —spell′bind′er *n.*

spell′bound′ (-bound′) *adj.* held by or as by a spell; fascinated

spell′down′ *n.* a spelling match, esp.

one eliminating a contestant when he misspells one or more words

spell′er *n.* 1. one who spells words 2. a textbook for teaching spelling

spell′ing *n.* 1. the act of one who spells words 2. the way a word is spelled

spe·lunk·er (spi luŋ′kər) *n.* [< Gr. *spēlynx*, a cave] a cave explorer

spend (spend) *vt.* spent, spend′ing [see EXPEND] 1. to use up, exhaust, etc. [his fury was *spent*] 2. to pay out (money) 3. to devote (time, labor, etc.) to something 4. to pass (time) —*vi.* to pay out or use up money, etc. —spend′er *n.*

spend′thrift′ (-thrift′) *n.* one who wastes money —*adj.* wasteful

spent (spent) *pt. & pp.* of SPEND —*adj.* 1. tired out; physically exhausted 2. used up; worn out

sperm (spurm) *n.* [< Gr. *sperma*, seed] 1. the male generative fluid; semen 2. *same as* SPERMATOZOON

sper·mat·o·zo·on (spər mat′ə zō′än) *n., pl.* -zo′a (-ə) [< Gr. *sperma*, seed + *zōion*, animal] the male germ cell, found in semen, which penetrates the female egg to fertilize it

sperm whale a large, toothed whale found in warm seas: its head yields a valuable lubricating oil (sperm oil)

spew (spyōō) *vt., vi.* [OE. *spiwan*] 1. to throw up as from the stomach; vomit 2. to flow or gush forth —*n.* something spewed

sp. gr. specific gravity

sphere (sfir) *n.* [< Gr. *sphaira*] 1. any round body having the surface equally distant from the center at all points; globe; ball 2. the place, range, or extent of action, existence, knowledge, experience, etc. —spher·i·cal (sfer′i k′l, sfir′-) *adj.*

sphe·roid (sfir′oid) *n.* a body that is almost but not quite a sphere —*adj.* of this shape: also sphe·roi′dal

sphinc·ter (sfiŋk′tər) *n.* [< Gr. *sphingein*, to draw close] a ring-shaped muscle at a body orifice

sphinx (sfiŋks) *n.* [< Gr., strangler] 1. [S-] a statue with a lion's body and a man's head, near Cairo, Egypt 2. *a*) [S-] *Gr. Myth.* a winged monster with a lion's body and a woman's head: it strangled passers-by unable to guess its riddle *b*) one who is difficult to know or understand

spice (spīs) *n.* [< L. *species*, kind] 1. an aromatic vegetable substance, as clove, pepper, etc., used to season food 2. that which adds zest or interest —*vt.* spiced, spic′ing 1. to season with spice 2. to add zest to —spic′y *adj.* -i·er, -i·est

spick-and-span (spik′′n span′) *adj.* [< *spike*, nail + ON. *spānn*, a chip] 1. new or fresh 2. neat and clean

spic·ule (spik′yōōl) *n.* [L. *spiculum*, a point] a hard, needlelike part

spi·der (spī′dər) *n.* [< OE. *spinnan*, spin] 1. any of various arachnids that spin webs 2. a cast-iron frying pan

spi·der·y (spī′dər ē) *adj.* like a spider

spiel (spēl) *n.* [G., play] [Slang] a talk or harangue, as in selling

spiff·y (spif′ē) *adj.* **-i·er, -i·est** [< dial. *spiff*, well-dressed person] [Slang] spruce, smart, or dapper

spig·ot (spig′ət, spik′-) *n.* [ME. *spigote*] 1. a plug to stop the vent in a cask, etc. 2. a faucet

spike¹ (spīk) *n.* [< ON. *spīkr* or MDu. & MLowG. *spīker*] 1. a long, heavy nail 2. a sharp-pointed projection, as on the sole of a shoe to prevent slipping —*vt.* **spiked, spik′ing** 1. to fasten or fit as with spikes 2. to pierce with, or impale on, a spike 3. to thwart (a scheme, etc.) 4. [Slang] to add alcoholic liquor to (a drink)

spike² (spīk) *n.* [L. *spica*] 1. an ear of grain 2. a long flower cluster

spill (spil) *vt.* **spilled** or **spilt** (spilt), **spill′ing** [OE. *spillan*, destroy] 1. to allow, esp. unintentionally, to run, scatter, or flow over from a container 2. to shed (blood) 3. [Colloq.] to throw off (a rider, etc.) —*vi.* to be spilled; overflow —*n.* 1. a spilling 2. [Colloq.] a fall or tumble —**spill′age** *n.*

spill′way′ *n.* a channel to carry off excess water, as around a dam

spin (spin) *vt.* **spun, spin′ning** [OE. *spinnan*] 1. *a)* to draw out and twist fibers of (wool, cotton, etc.) into thread *b)* to make (thread, etc.) thus 2. to make (a web, cocoon, etc.), as a spider 3. to draw *out* (a story) to a great length 4. to rotate swiftly —*vi.* 1. to spin thread or yarn 2. to form a web, cocoon, etc. 3. to whirl 4. to seem to be spinning from dizziness 5. to move along swiftly and smoothly —*n.* 1. a spinning or rotating movement 2. a ride in a motor vehicle 3. a descent of an airplane, nose first along a spiral path —**spin′ner** *n.*

spin·ach (spin′ich) *n.* [ult. < Per. *aspanākh*] a plant with dark-green, juicy, edible leaves

spi·nal (spī′n'l) *adj.* of or having to do with the spine or spinal cord

spinal column the series of joined vertebrae forming the axial support for the skeleton; backbone

spinal cord the thick cord of nerve tissue in the spinal column

spin·dle (spin′d'l) *n.* [< OE. *spinnan*, spin] 1. a slender rod used in spinning for twisting, winding, or holding thread 2. a spindlelike thing 3. any rod or pin that revolves or serves as an axis for a revolving part

spin·dly (spin′dlē) *adj.* **-dli·er, -dli·est** long or tall and very thin

spine (spīn) *n.* [< L. *spina*, thorn] 1. *a)* a sharp, stiff projection, as a thorn of the cactus *b)* anything like this 2. *a)* same as SPINAL COLUMN *b)* anything like this, as the back of a book —**spin′y** *adj.* **-i·er, -i·est**

spine′less *adj.* 1. having no spine or spines 2. lacking courage or willpower

spin·et (spin′it) *n.* [< It. *spinetta*] a small upright piano

spin·ner·et (spin′ə ret′) *n.* the organ in spiders, caterpillars, etc. with which they spin silky threads

spinning wheel a simple spinning machine with a single spindle driven by a large wheel

spin-off (spin′ôf′) *n.* a secondary benefit, product, development, etc.

spin·ster (spin′stər) *n.* [ME. < *spinnen*, to spin] an unmarried woman, esp. an elderly one —**spin′ster·hood′** *n.*

spiny lobster a sea crustacean similar to the lobster, but lacking large pincers and having a spiny shell

spi·ra·cle (spī′rə k'l) *n.* [< L. *spirare*, breathe] an opening for breathing, as on the sides of an insect's body or on top of a whale's head

spi·ral (spī′rəl) *adj.* [< Gr. *speira*, a coil] circling around a point in constantly increasing (or decreasing) curves, or in constantly changing planes —*n.* a spiral curve or coil —*vi., vt.* **-raled** or **-ralled, -ral·ing** or **-ral·ling** to move in or form (into) a spiral —**spi′ral·ly** *adv.*

spire (spīr) *n.* [OE. *spir*] 1. a sprout or stalk of a plant 2. the top part of a pointed, tapering object 3. anything tapering to a point, as a steeple

spi·re·a (spī rē′ə) *n.* [see SPIRAL] a plant of the rose family, with clusters of small flowers: also **spi·rae′a**

spir·it (spir′it) *n.* [< L. *spirare*, breathe] 1. *same as* SOUL (sense 1) 2. [*also* S-] life, will, thought, etc., regarded as separate from matter 3. a supernatural being, as a ghost, angel, etc. 4. an individual [a brave *spirit*] 5. [*usually pl.*] disposition; mood [high *spirits*] 6. vivacity, courage, etc. 7. enthusiastic loyalty [school *spirit*] 8. real meaning [the *spirit* of the law] 9. a pervading animating principle; essential quality [the *spirit* of the times] 10. [*usually pl.*] distilled alcoholic liquor —*vt.* to carry (*away, off*, etc.) secretly and swiftly —**spir′it·less** *adj.*

spir·it·ed *adj.* lively; vigorous

spir·it·u·al (spir′i choo wəl) *adj.* 1. of the spirit or the soul 2. of or consisting of spirit; not corporeal 3. religious; sacred —*n.* a religious folk song of U.S. Negro origin —**spir′it·u·al′i·ty** (-wal′ə tē) *n.* —**spir′it·u·al·ly** *adv.*

spir·it·u·al·ism *n.* the belief that the dead survive as spirits which can communicate with the living —**spir′it·u·al·ist** *n.* —**spir′it·u·al·is′tic** *adj.*

spir·it·u·ous (spir′i choo wəs) *n.* of or containing distilled alcohol

spi·ro·chete (spī′rə kēt′) *n.* [< Gr. *speira*, spiral + *chaitē*, hair] any of various spiral-shaped bacteria

spit¹ (spit) *n.* [OE. *spitu*] 1. a thin, pointed rod on which meat is roasted over a fire, etc. 2. a narrow point of land extending into the water —*vt.* **spit′ted, spit′ting** to fix as on a spit

spit² (spit) *vt., vi.* **spit** or **spat, spit′ting** [OE. *spittan*] 1. to eject from the mouth 2. to eject explosively —*vi.* to eject saliva from the mouth —*n.* 1. a spitting 2. saliva —**spit and image** [Colloq.] perfect likeness

spit′ball′ *n.* 1. paper chewed up into a wad for throwing 2. *Baseball* an illegal pitch made to curve by wetting one side of the ball, as with spit

spite (spīt) *n.* [see DESPITE] 1. ill will; malice 2. a grudge —*vt.* **spit′ed, spit′ing** to vent one's spite upon by hurting, frustrating, etc. —**in spite of** regardless of —**spite′ful** *adj.*

spit·tle (spit′'l) *n.* saliva; spit

spit·toon (spi tōōn′) *n.* a jarlike container to spit into; cuspidor

splash (splash) *vt.* [echoic] 1. to cause (a liquid) to scatter 2. to dash a liquid, mud, etc. on, so as to wet or soil —*vi.* to move, strike, etc. with a splash —*n.* 1. a splashing 2. a spot made by splashing —**make a splash** [Colloq.] to attract great attention

splash′down′ *n.* the landing of a spacecraft on water

splash′y *adj.* **-i·er, -i·est** 1. splashing or apt to splash; wet, muddy, etc. 2. [Colloq.] getting much attention; spectacular —**splash′i·ly** *adv.* —**splash′i·ness** *n.*

splat¹ (splat) *n.* [< SPLIT] a thin slat of wood, as in a chair back

splat² (splat) *n., interj.* a splattering or wet, slapping sound

splat·ter (splat′ər) *n., vt., vi.* spatter or splash

splay (splā) *vt., vi.* [ME. *splaien*] to spread out —*adj.* spreading outward

splay′foot′ *n., pl.* **-feet′** a foot that is flat and turned outward —**splay′-foot′ed** *adj.*

spleen (splēn) *n.* [< Gr. *splēn*] 1. a large lymphatic organ in the upper left part of the abdomen: it modifies the blood structure 2. malice; spite

splen·did (splen′did) *adj.* [< L. *splendere*, to shine] 1. shining; brilliant 2. magnificent; gorgeous 3. grand; illustrious 4. [Colloq.] very good; fine —**splen′did·ly** *adv.*

splen·dor (splen′dər) *n.* [see prec.] 1. great luster; brilliance 2. pomp; grandeur Brit. sp. **splendour**

sple·net·ic (spli net′ik) *adj.* 1. of the spleen 2. irritable; bad-tempered

splice (splīs) *vt.* **spliced, splic′ing** [MDu. *splissen*] 1. to join (ropes) by weaving together the end strands 2. to join the ends of (timbers) by overlapping 3. to fasten the ends of (wire, film, etc.) together, as by soldering, etc. —*n.* a joint made by splicing

splint (splint) *n.* [< MDu. or MLowG. *splinte*] 1. a thin strip of wood, etc. woven with others to make baskets, etc. 2. a strip of wood, etc. used to hold a broken bone in place

splin·ter (splin′tər) *vt., vi.* [see prec.] to break or split into thin, sharp pieces —*n.* a thin, sharp piece, as of wood, made by splitting, etc.

split (split) *vt., vi.* **split, split′ting** [MDu. *splitten*] 1. to separate lengthwise into two or more parts 2. to break or tear apart 3. to divide into shares 4. to disunite 5. *a)* to break (a mole-

cule) into atoms *b)* to produce nuclear fission in (an atom) —*n.* 1. a splitting 2. a break; crack 3. a division in a group, etc. —*adj.* divided; separated

split′-lev′el *adj.* having adjacent floor levels staggered about a half-story apart

split′ting *adj.* 1. that splits 2. severe, as a headache

splotch (spläch) *n.* [prob. < SPOT + BLOTCH] an irregular spot, splash, or stain —*vt., vi.* to mark or be marked with splotches —**splotch′y** *adj.*

splurge (splurj) *n.* [echoic] [Colloq.] 1. any very showy display or effort 2. a spell of extravagant spending —*vi.* **splurged, splurg′ing** [Colloq.] 1. to show off 2. to spend money freely

splut·ter (splut′ər) *vi.* [var. of SPUTTER] 1. to make hissing or spitting sounds 2. to speak hurriedly and confusedly —*n.* a spluttering

spoil (spoil) *vt.* **spoiled** or **spoilt, spoil′ing** [< L. *spolium*, plunder] 1. to damage so as to make useless, etc. 2. to impair the enjoyment, etc. of 3. to cause to expect too much by overindulgence 4. [Archaic] to rob; plunder —*vi.* to become spoiled; decay, etc., as food —*n.* [*usually pl.*] plunder; booty —**spoil′age** *n.* —**spoil′er** *n.*

spoil′sport′ *n.* one whose actions ruin the pleasure of others

spoils system the treating of public offices as the booty of a successful political party

Spo·kane (spō kan′) city in E Wash.: pop. 171,000

spoke¹ (spōk) *n.* [OE. *spaca*] any of the braces extending from the hub to the rim of a wheel

spoke² (spōk) *pt.* of SPEAK

spo·ken (spō′k'n) *pp.* of SPEAK —*adj.* 1. uttered; oral 2. having a (specified) kind of voice [*soft-spoken*]

spokes·man (spōks′mən) *n., pl.* **-men** one who speaks for another or for a group

spo·li·a·tion (spō′lē ā′shən) *n.* [< L. *spoliatio*] robbery; plundering

sponge (spunj) *n.* [< Gr. *spongia*] 1. a plantlike sea animal with a porous structure 2. the highly absorbent skeleton of such animals, used for washing surfaces, etc. 3. any substance like this, as a piece of spongy rubber, etc. —*vt.* **sponged, spong′ing** 1. to wipe, dampen, absorb, etc. as with a sponge 2. [Colloq.] to get as by begging, imposition, etc. —*vi.* [Colloq.] to live as a parasite upon others —**spong′er** *n.* —**spon′gy** *adj.*

sponge bath a bath taken by using a wet sponge or cloth without getting into water

sponge′cake′ *n.* a light, spongy cake without shortening: also **sponge cake**

spon·sor (spän′sər) *n.* [L. < *spondere*, promise solemnly] 1. one who assumes responsibility as surety for, or endorser of, some person or thing 2. a godparent 3. a business firm, etc. that pays for a radio or TV program advertising its product —*vt.* to act as sponsor for —**spon′sor·ship′** *n.*

spon·ta·ne·i·ty (spän′tə nē′ə tē) *n.* 1. a being spontaneous 2. *pl.* **-ties** spontaneous behavior, action, etc.

spon·ta·ne·ous (spän tā′nē əs) *adj.* [< L. *sponte*, of free will] 1. acting or resulting from a natural feeling or impulse, without constraint, effort, etc. 2. occurring through internal causes

spontaneous combustion the process of catching fire through heat generated by internal chemical action

spoof (spōōf) *n.* [Slang] 1. a hoax or joke 2. a light satire —*vt., vi.* [Slang] 1. to fool; deceive 2. to satirize playfully

spook (spōōk) *n.* [Du.] [Colloq.] a ghost —*vt., vi.* [Colloq.] to frighten or become frightened —**spook′y** *adj.*

spool (spōōl) *n.* [< MDu. *spoele*] 1. a cylinder on which thread, wire, etc. is wound 2. the material wound

spoon (spōōn) *n.* [< OE. *spon*, a chip] 1. a utensil consisting of a small, shallow bowl with a handle, used for eating, stirring, etc. 2. something shaped like a spoon, as a shiny, curved fishing lure —*vt.* to take up with a spoon —**spoon′ful′** *n., pl.* **-fuls**

spoon′bill′ *n.* a wading bird whose flat bill is spoon-shaped at the tip

spoon·er·ism (spōōn′ər iz′m) *n.* [< Rev. W. A. *Spooner* (1844-1930), of England, who made such slips] the accidental interchange of the initial sounds of words (Ex.: "a well-boiled icicle" for "a well-oiled bicycle")

spoor (spoor, spôr) *n.* [Afrikaans] the track or trail of a wild animal

spo·rad·ic (spô rad′ik) *adj.* [< Gr. *sporas*, scattered] happening or appearing in isolated instances [*sporadic* storms] —**spo·rad′i·cal·ly** *adv.*

spore (spôr) *n.* [< Gr. *spora*, a seed] a small reproductive body produced by mosses, ferns, etc. and capable of giving rise to a new individual —*vi.* **spored, spor′ing** to bear spores

sport (spôrt) *n.* [< DISPORT] 1. any recreational activity; specif., a game, competition, etc. requiring bodily exertion 2. fun or play 3. a thing joked about 4. [Colloq.] a sportsmanlike person 5. [Colloq.] a showy, flashy fellow 6. *Biol.* a plant or animal markedly different from the normal type —*vt.* [Colloq.] to display [to *sport* a new tie] —*vi.* 1. to play 2. to joke —*adj.* 1. of or for sports 2. suitable for casual wear: also **sports** [*sport*(*s*) clothes] —**in** (or **for**) **sport** in jest —**make sport of** to mock or ridicule

sport′ing *adj.* 1. of or interested in sports 2. sportsmanlike; fair 3. of games, races, etc. involving gambling or betting

sport′ive *adj.* 1. full of sport or fun 2. done in fun —**sport′ive·ly** *adv.*

sports car a low, small automobile with a high-compression engine

sports′cast′ *n.* a broadcast of sports news on radio or TV —**sports′cast′er** *n.*

sports′man *n., pl.* **-men** 1. a man who takes part in sports, esp. hunting, fishing, etc. 2. one who plays fair and can lose without complaint or win

without gloating —**sports′man·like′** *adj.* —**sports′man·ship′** *n.*

sport′y *adj.* **-i·er, -i·est** 1. sporting or sportsmanlike 2. flashy or showy

spot (spät) *n.* [prob. < MDu. *spotte*] 1. *a)* a small area differing in color, etc. from the surrounding area *b)* a stain, speck, etc. 2. a flaw or defect 3. a locality; place —*vt.* **spot′ted, spot′ting** 1. to mark with spots 2. to stain; blemish 3. to place; locate 4. to see; recognize 5. [Colloq.] to allow as a handicap —*vi.* 1. to become marked with spots 2. to make a stain, as ink —*adj.* 1. ready [*spot* cash] 2. made at random [a *spot* survey] —**hit the spot** [Colloq.] to satisfy a craving —**in a** (**bad**) **spot** [Slang] in trouble —**on the spot** [Slang] in a bad or demanding situation —**spot′less** *adj.* —**spot′ted** *adj.*

spot′-check′ *vt.* to check or examine at random —*n.* such a checking

spot′light′ *n.* 1. *a)* a strong beam of light focused on a particular person, thing, etc. *b)* a lamp used to project such a light 2. public notice —*vt.* to draw attention to, as by a spotlight

spot′ter *n.* one who spots, as an assistant in the stands who reports on plays in a football game

spot′ty *adj.* **-ti·er, -ti·est** 1. having, occurring in, or marked with spots 2. not uniform or consistent

spouse (spous) *n.* [< L. *sponsus*, betrothed] (one's) husband or wife

spout (spout) *n.* [ME. *spouten*, to spout] 1. a projecting tube or orifice by which a liquid is poured 2. a stream, etc. as of a liquid from a spout —*vt., vi.* 1. to shoot out (liquid, etc.) as from a spout 2. to speak or utter in a loud, pompous manner

sprain (sprān) *vt.* [< ? L. *ex-*, out + *premere*, press] to wrench a ligament or muscle of (a joint) without dislocating the bones —*n.* an injury resulting from this

sprang (spraŋ) *alt. pt.* of SPRING

sprat (sprat) *n.* [OE. *sprott*] a small European fish of the herring family

sprawl (sprôl) *vi.* [OE. *spreawlian*] 1. to sit or lie with the limbs in a relaxed or awkward position 2. to spread out awkwardly or unevenly, as handwriting, etc. —*n.* a sprawling movement or position

spray¹ (sprā) *n.* [prob. < MDu. *spraeien*] 1. a mist of fine liquid particles 2. *a)* a jet of such particles, as from a spray gun *b)* a device for spraying 3. something likened to a spray —*vt., vi.* 1. to direct a spray (on) 2. to shoot out in a spray —**spray′er** *n.*

spray² (sprā) *n.* [ME.] a small branch or sprig of a tree, etc., with leaves, flowers, etc.

spray can a can in which gas under pressure sprays out the contents

spray gun a device that shoots out a spray of liquid, as paint, etc.

spread (spred) *vt., vi.* **spread, spread′ing** [OE. *sprædan*] 1. to open or stretch out; unfold 2. to move (the fingers, wings, etc.) apart 3. to distribute or be distributed over an area 4. to extend in time 5. to make or be made widely known, felt, etc. **6.** to cover or be covered (*with* something), as in a thin layer **7.** to set (a table) for a meal **8.** to push or be pushed apart —*n.* **1.** the act or extent of spreading **2.** an expanse **3.** a cloth cover for a table, bed, etc. **4.** jam, butter, etc. used on bread **5.** [Colloq.] a meal with many different foods

spree (sprē) *n.* [< earlier *spray*] **1.** a noisy frolic **2.** a period of drunkenness **3.** a period of uninhibited activity [*a shopping spree*]

sprig (sprig) *n.* [ME. *sprigge*] a little twig or spray

spright·ly (sprīt'lē) *adj.* **-li·er, -li·est** [see SPRITE] gay; lively —*adv.* gaily; briskly —**spright'li·ness** *n.*

spring (spriŋ) *vi.* **sprang** or **sprung, sprung, spring'ing** [OE. *springan*] **1.** to leap; bound **2.** to come, appear, etc. suddenly **3.** to bounce **4.** to arise as from some source; grow or develop **5.** to become warped, split, etc. **6.** to rise up above surrounding objects Often followed by *up* —*vt.* **1.** to cause to leap forth suddenly **2.** to cause (a trap, etc.) to snap shut **3.** to cause to warp, split, etc. **4.** to make known suddenly **5.** [Slang] to get (someone) released from jail —*n.* **1.** a leap, or the distance so covered **2.** a sudden flying back **3.** elasticity; resilience **4.** a device, as a coil of wire, that returns to its original form after being forced out of shape **5.** a flow of water from the ground **6.** a source or origin **7.** *a*) that season of the year following winter, in which plants begin to grow again *b*) any period of beginning —*adj.* **1.** of, for, appearing in, or planted in the spring **2.** having, or supported on, springs **3.** coming from a spring [*spring water*] —**spring a leak** to begin to leak suddenly

spring'board' *n.* a springy board used as a takeoff in leaping or diving

spring fever a laziness that many people feel in early days of spring

Spring·field (spriŋ'fēld') **1.** city in SW Mass.: pop. 152,000 **2.** capital of Ill.: pop. 100,000 **3.** city in SW Mo.: pop. 133,000

spring'time' *n.* the season of spring

spring'y *adj.* **-i·er, -i·est** elastic, resilient, etc. —**spring'i·ness** *n.*

sprin·kle (spriŋ'k'l) *vt., vi.* **-kled, -kling** [ME. *sprinklen*] **1.** to scatter or fall in drops or particles **2.** to scatter drops or particles (upon) **3.** to rain lightly —*n.* **1.** a sprinkling **2.** a light rain —**sprin'kler** *n.*

sprin'kling (-kliŋ) *n.* a small, scattered number or amount

sprint (sprint) *vi., n.* [ME. *sprenten*] run or race at full speed for a short distance —**sprint'er** *n.*

sprite (sprīt) *n.* [< L. *spiritus*, spirit] an elf, pixie, fairy, or goblin

spritz (sprits; G. shprits) *vt., vi., n.* [< G. *spritze*] squirt or spray

sprock·et (spräk'it) *n.* [< ?] **1.** any of the teeth, as on a wheel rim, arranged to fit the links of a chain **2.** such a wheel: in full **sprocket wheel**

sprout (sprout) *vi.* [OE. *sprutan*] to begin to grow; give off shoots or buds —*vt.* to cause to sprout —*n.* **1.** a young growth on a plant; shoot **2.** a new growth from a bud, etc.

spruce¹ (sprōōs) *n.* [ME. *Spruce*, Prussia] **1.** an evergreen tree with slender needles **2.** its wood

spruce² (sprōōs) *adj.* **spruc'er, spruc'est** [< *Spruce* leather (see prec.)] neat and trim in a smart way —*vt., vi.* **spruced, spruc'ing** to make or become spruce (with *up*)

sprung (spruŋ) *pp. & alt. pt.* of SPRING

spry (sprī) *adj.* **spri'er** or **spry'er, spri'est** or **spry'est** [< Scand.] full of life; active, esp. though elderly —**spry'ly** *adv.* —**spry'ness** *n.*

spud (spud) *n.* [Colloq.] a potato

spume (spyōōm) *n.* [< L. *spuma*] foam, froth, or scum —*vi.* **spumed, spum'ing** to foam; froth

spu·mo·ni (spə mō'nē) *n.* [It. < L. *spuma*, foam] Italian ice cream in variously flavored layers

spun (spun) *pt. & pp.* of SPIN

spunk (spuŋk) *n.* [IrGael. *sponc*, tinder] [Colloq.] courage; spirit —**spunk'y** *adj.* **-i·er, -i·est**

spur (spur) *n.* [OE. *spura*] **1.** a pointed device worn on the heel by horsemen, used to urge the horse forward **2.** anything that urges; stimulus **3.** any spurlike projection **4.** a short railroad track connected with the main track —*vt.* **spurred, spur'ring** **1.** to prick with spurs **2.** to urge or incite —*vi.* to hurry; hasten —**on the spur of the moment** abruptly and impulsively

spurge (spurj) *n.* [< MFr. *espurger*, to purge] any of a group of plants with milky juice and tiny flowers

spu·ri·ous (spyoor'ē əs) *adj.* [LL. *spurius*] not genuine; false —**spu'ri·ous·ly** *adv.* —**spu'ri·ous·ness** *n.*

spurn (spurn) *vt.* [OE. *spurnan*] to reject with contempt; scorn

spurt (spurt) *vt., vi.* [OE. *sprutan*] **1.** to gush forth in a stream or jet **2.** to show a sudden, brief burst of energy —*n.* **1.** a sudden shooting forth; jet **2.** a sudden, brief burst of energy, increased activity, etc.

sput·nik (spoot'nik, sput'-) *n.* [Russ., lit., co-traveler] an artificial satellite in space, esp. any of the U.S.S.R.

sput·ter (sput'ər) *vi., vt.* [< MDu. *spotten*, to spit] **1.** to spit or throw out (bits or drops) in an explosive manner **2.** to speak or say in a confused, explosive manner **3.** to make sharp, sizzling sounds, as frying fat —*n.* a sputtering

spu·tum (spyōōt'əm) *n., pl.* **-ta** (-ə) [< L. *spuere*, to spit] saliva, usually mixed with mucus, spat out

spy (spī) *vt.* **spied, spy'ing** [< OHG. *spehōn*, examine] **1.** to watch closely and secretly (often with *out*) **2.** to catch sight of; see —*vi.* to watch

---

fat, āpe, cär; ten, ēven; is, bīte; gō, hôrn, tōōl, look; oil, out; up, fur; chin; she; thin, *then*; zh, leisure; ŋ, ring; ə for *a* in ago; ', (ā'b'l); ë, Fr. coeur; ö, Fr. feu; Fr. mon; ü, Fr. duc; kh, G. ich, doch; ‡ foreign; < derived from

closely and secretly; act as a spy —*n.*, *pl.* **spies** **1.** one who keeps close and secret watch on others **2.** one employed by a government to get secret information about the affairs, esp. the military affairs, of another government

spy′glass′ *n.* a small telescope

sq. square

sqq. [L. *sequentes*] the following ones

squab (skwäb) *n.* [prob. < Scand.] a nestling pigeon

squab·ble (skwäb′'l) *vi.* **-bled, -bling** [< Scand.] to quarrel noisily over a small matter; wrangle —*n.* a noisy, petty quarrel

squad (skwäd) *n.* [see SQUARE] **1.** a small group of soldiers, often a subdivision of a platoon **2.** any small group of people working together

squad car a police patrol car

squad·ron (-rən) *n.* [< It. *squadra*, a square] a unit of warships, cavalry, military aircraft, etc.

squal·id (skwäl′id) *adj.* [< L. *squalere*, be foul] **1.** foul or unclean **2.** wretched

squall¹ (skwôl) *n.* [< Scand.] a brief, violent windstorm, usually with rain or snow —**squall′y** *adj.*

squall² (skwôl) *vi., vt.* [< ON. *skvala*] to cry or scream loudly and harshly —*n.* a harsh, loud cry or scream

squal·or (skwäl′ər) *n.* a being squalid; filth and wretchedness

squa·mous (skwā′məs) *adj.* [< L. *squama*, a scale] like, formed of, or covered with scales

squan·der (skwän′dər) *vt.* [prob. < dial. *squander*, to scatter] to spend or use wastefully or extravagantly

square (skwer) *n.* [< L. *ex-*, out + *quadrare*, to square] **1.** *a)* a plane figure having four equal sides and four right angles *b)* anything of or approximating this shape **2.** *a)* an area bounded by streets or buildings on four sides *b)* any side of such an area **3.** an open area bounded by several streets, used as a park, etc. **4.** an instrument for drawing or testing right angles **5.** the product of a quantity multiplied by itself **6.** [Slang] a person who is square (*adj.* 10) —*vt.* **squared, squar′ing 1.** to make into a square (sense 1) **2.** to make straight, even, right-angled, etc. **3.** to settle; adjust [to *square* accounts] **4.** to make conform [to *square* a statement with the facts] **5.** to multiply (a quantity) by itself —*vi.* **1.** to fit; agree; accord (*with*) —*adj.* **1.** having four equal sides and four right angles **2.** forming a right angle **3.** straight, level, even, etc. **4.** leaving no balance; balanced **5.** just; fair **6.** direct; straightforward **7.** designating one of a unit of surface measure in the form of a square [a *square* foot] **8.** solid; sturdy [a *square* joint] **9.** [Colloq.] satisfying; substantial [a *square* meal] **10.** [Slang] old-fashioned, unsophisticated, etc. —*adv.* in a square manner —**square off** (or **away**) to assume a posture of attack or self-defense —**square oneself** [Colloq.] to make amends —**square′ly** *adv.* —**square′ness** *n.* —**squar′ish** *adj.*

square dance a dance in which the couples are grouped in a given form, as a square —**square′-dance′** *vi.*

square′-rigged′ *adj.* rigged with square sails as the principal sails

square root the quantity which when squared will produce a given quantity [3 is the *square root* of 9]

squash¹ (skwäsh) *vt.* [< L. *ex-*, intens. + *quatere*, to shake] **1.** to crush into a soft, flat mass; press **2.** to suppress; quash —*vi.* **1.** to be squashed **2.** to make a sound of squashing —*n.* **1.** something squashed **2.** the act or sound of squashing **3.** a game played in a walled court with rackets and a rubber ball —**squash′y** *adj.*

squash² (skwäsh) *n.* [< AmInd.] the fleshy fruit of various plants of the gourd family, eaten as a vegetable

squat (skwät) *vi.* **squat′ted, squat′ting** [< L. *ex-*, intens. + *cogere*, to force] **1.** to sit on the heels with the knees bent **2.** to crouch close to the ground **3.** to settle on land without right or title **4.** to settle on public land in order to get title to it —*adj.* short and heavy or thick: also **squat′ty** —*n.* the act or position of squatting —**squat′ness** *n.* —**squat′ter** *n.*

squaw (skwô) *n.* [< AmInd.] a N.American Indian woman, esp. a wife

squawk (skwôk) *vi.* [echoic] **1.** to utter a loud, harsh cry **2.** [Colloq.] to complain loudly —*n.* **1.** a loud, harsh cry **2.** [Slang] a raucous complaint

squeak (skwēk) *vi.* [ME. *squeken*] to make or utter a sharp, high-pitched sound or cry —*vt.* to say in a squeak —*n.* a thin, sharp sound or cry —**narrow** (or **close, near**) **squeak** [Colloq.] a narrow escape —**squeak through** (or **by**) [Colloq.] to succeed, get through, etc. with difficulty —**squeak′y** *adj.* **-i·er, -i·est**

squeal (skwēl) *vi.* [ME. *squelen*] **1.** to utter or make a high, shrill cry or sound **2.** [Slang] to act as an informer —*vt.* to utter in a squeal —*n.* a squealing —**squeal′er** *n.*

squeam·ish (skwēm′ish) *adj.* [ME. *squaimous*] **1.** easily nauseated **2.** easily shocked; prudish **3.** fastidious —**squeam′ish·ness** *n.*

squee·gee (skwē′jē) *n.* [prob. < ff.] a rubber-edged tool for scraping water from a flat surface

squeeze (skwēz) *vt.* **squeezed, squeez′ing** [OE. *cwysan*] **1.** to press hard, esp. from two or more sides **2.** to extract (juice, etc.) from (fruit, etc.) **3.** to force (*into, out,* etc.) by pressing **4.** to embrace closely; hug —*vi.* **1.** to yield to pressure **2.** to exert pressure **3.** to force one's way by pushing —*n.* **1.** a squeezing or being squeezed **2.** a close embrace; hug **3.** the state of being closely pressed or packed; crush **4.** a period of scarcity, hardship, etc.

squeeze bottle a plastic bottle that is squeezed to eject its contents

squelch (skwelch) *n.* [< ?] [Colloq.] a crushing retort, rebuke, etc. —*vt.* [Colloq.] to suppress or silence completely

squib (skwib) *n.* [prob. echoic] **1.** a firecracker that burns with a hissing noise before exploding 2. a short, witty verbal attack; lampoon

squid (skwid) *n.* [prob. < dial. for SQUIRT] a long, slender sea mollusk with ten arms, two longer than the others

squig·gle (skwig′'l) *n.* [SQU(IRM) + (W)IGGLE] a short, wavy line or illegible scrawl —*vt.*, *vi.* -gled, -gling to write as, or make, a squiggle or squiggles

SQUID

squint (skwint) *vi.* [akin to Du. *schuin*, sideways] 1. to peer with the eyes partly closed 2. to look sideways or askance 3. to be cross-eyed —*n.* 1. a squinting 2. a being cross-eyed 3. [Colloq.] a quick look or sidelong glance

squire (skwīr) *n.* [< ESQUIRE] 1. in England, the owner of a large rural estate 2. a title of respect for a justice of the peace, etc. 3. an attendant; esp., a man escorting a woman —*vt.*, *vi.* squired, squir′ing to act as a squire (to)

squirm (skwurm) *vi.* [prob. echoic] 1. to twist and turn the body; wriggle 2. to show or feel distress —*n.* a squirming —squirm′y *adj.* -i·er, -i·est

squir·rel (skwur′əl) *n.* [< Gr. *skia*, a shadow + *oura*, tail] 1. a small, tree-dwelling rodent with heavy fur and a long, bushy tail 2. its fur

squirt (skwurt) *vt.*, *vi.* [prob. < LowG. *swirtjen*] 1. to shoot out (a liquid) in a jet; spurt 2. to wet with liquid so shot out —*n.* 1. a jet of liquid 2. [Colloq.] an insignificant person

Sr. Senior

Sri Lan·ka (srē län′kə) *official name* of CEYLON

S.R.O. standing room only

S.S., SS, S/S steamship

SST supersonic transport

St. 1. Saint 2. Strait 3. Street

stab (stab) *n.* [prob. < ME. *stubbe*, stub] 1. a wound made by stabbing 2. a thrust, as with a knife 3. a sharp pain 4. an attempt —*vt.*, *vi.* stabbed, stab′bing 1. to pierce or wound as with a knife 2. to thrust (a knife, etc.) into a thing 3. to pain sharply

sta·bil·i·ty (stə bil′ə tē) *n.* 1. a being stable; steadiness 2. firmness of purpose, etc. 3. permanence

sta·bi·lize (stā′bə līz′) *vt.* -lized′, -liz′ing 1. to make stable 2. to keep from changing 3. to give stability to (a plane or ship) —sta′bi·li·za′tion *n.* —sta′bi·liz′er *n.*

sta·ble¹ (stā′b'l) *adj.* -bler, -blest [< L. *stare*, to stand] 1. not likely to give way; firm; fixed 2. firm in character, purpose, etc.; steadfast 3. not likely to change; lasting

sta·ble² (stā′b'l) *n.* [see prec.] 1. a

building in which horses or cattle are sheltered and fed 2. all the racehorses belonging to one owner —*vt.*, *vi.* -bled, -bling to lodge, keep, or be kept in a stable

stac·ca·to (stə kät′ō) *adj.* [It., detached] *Music* with distinct breaks between successive tones

stack (stak) *n.* [< ON. *stakkr*] 1. a large, neatly arranged pile of straw, hay, etc. 2. any orderly pile 3. a smokestack 4. [*pl.*] a series of bookshelves —*vt.* 1. to arrange in a stack 2. to arrange (cards, etc.) secretly so as to cheat —stack up to stand in comparison (*with* or *against*)

stack′up′ *n.* an arrangement of aircraft circling at various altitudes, awaiting their turn to land

sta·di·um (stā′dē əm) *n.* [Gr. *stadion*, unit of length, c.607 ft.] a large structure for football, baseball, etc., surrounded by tiers of seats

staff (staf) *n.*, *pl.* staffs; also, for senses 1 & 4, staves [OE. *stæf*] 1. a stick or rod used as a support, a symbol of authority, etc. 2. a group of people assisting a leader 3. a specific group of workers [a teaching *staff*] 4. the five horizontal lines and four intermediate spaces on which music is written —*vt.* to provide with a staff, as of workers

staff′er *n.* a member of a staff, as of a newspaper

stag (stag) *n.* [OE. *stagga*] a full-grown male deer —*adj.* for men only [a stag party] —*adv.* unaccompanied by a woman

stage (stāj) *n.* [< L. *stare*, to stand] 1. a platform 2. a) an area or platform upon which plays, etc. are presented b) the theater, or acting as a profession (with *the*) 3. the scene of an event 4. a stopping place, or the distance between stops, on a journey 5. *short for* STAGECOACH 6. a period or level in a process of development [the larval *stage*] 7. any of the units used in sequence to propel a missile, spacecraft, etc. —*vt.* staged, stag′ing 1. to present as on a stage 2. to plan and carry out [to *stage* an attack]

stage′coach′ *n.* a horse-drawn public coach that traveled a regular route

stage′hand′ *n.* one who sets up scenery, furniture, lights, etc. for a stage play

stage′-struck′ *adj.* intensely eager to become an actor or actress

stag·ger (stag′ər) *vi.* [< ON. *stakra*, totter] to totter, reel, etc. as from a blow, fatigue, etc. —*vt.* 1. to cause to stagger, as with a blow 2. to affect strongly with grief, etc. 3. to make zigzag or alternating 4. to arrange so as to come at different times [to *stagger* vacations] —*n.* [*pl.*, *with sing. v.*] a nervous disease of horses, etc., causing staggering

stag·nant (stag′nənt) *adj.* [< L. *stagnare*, stagnate] 1. not flowing or

stagnate

stand

moving **2.** foul from lack of movement, as water **3.** dull; sluggish

stag·nate (stag'nāt) *vi., vt.* **-nat·ed, -nat·ing** to become or make stagnant —**stag·na'tion** *n.*

staid (stād) *archaic pt. & pp. of* STAY³ —*adj.* sober; sedate —**staid'ly** *adv.*

stain (stān) *vt.* [ult. < L. *dis-*, from + *tingere*, to color] **1.** to spoil by discoloring or spotting **2.** to disgrace; dishonor **3.** to color (wood, etc.) with a dye —*n.* **1.** a color or spot resulting from staining **2.** a moral blemish **3.** a dye for staining wood, etc.

stain'less steel steel alloyed with chromium, etc., virtually immune to rust and corrosion

stair (ster) *n.* [OE. *stæger*] **1.** [*usually pl.*] a staircase **2.** one of a series of steps between levels

stair'case' (-kās') *n.* a flight of stairs with a handrail: also **stair'way'**

stair'well' *n.* a vertical shaft (in a building) for a staircase

stake (stāk) *n.* [OE. *staca*] **1.** a pointed length of wood or metal for driving into the ground **2.** the post to which a person was tied for execution by burning **3.** [*often pl.*] money, etc. risked as in a wager **4.** [*often pl.*] the winner's prize in a race, etc. —*vt.* **staked, stak'ing 1.** to mark the boundaries of [*to stake out a claim*] **2.** to fasten to stakes **3.** to gamble **4.** [Colloq.] to furnish with money or resources —**at stake** being risked —**pull up stakes** [Colloq.] to change one's residence, etc. —**stake out** to put under police surveillance

sta·lac·tite (stə lak'tīt) *n.* [< Gr. *stalaktos*, trickling] an icicle-shaped lime deposit hanging from a cave roof

sta·lag·mite (stə lag'mīt) *n.* [< Gr. *stalagmos*, a dropping] a cone-shaped lime deposit on the floor of a cave, often beneath a stalactite

stale (stāl) *adj.* **stal'er, stal'est** [prob. < LowG.] **1.** no longer fresh; flat, dry, etc. **2.** trite, as a joke **3.** out of condition, bored, etc. —*vt., vi.* **staled, stal'ing** to make or become stale —**stale'ness** *n.*

stale·mate (stāl'māt') *n.* [ult. < OHG. *stal*, a place + (CHECK)MATE] **1.** *Chess* a situation in which a player cannot move, resulting in a draw **2.** any deadlock —*vt.* **-mat'ed, -mat'ing** to bring into a stalemate

Sta·lin (stä'lin), **Joseph** 1879–1953; Soviet premier (1941–53)

stalk¹ (stôk) *vi., vt.* [OE. *stealcian*] **1.** to walk (through) in a stiff, haughty manner **2.** to advance grimly **3.** to pursue (game, etc.) stealthily —*n.* **1.** a stiff, haughty stride **2.** a stalking

stalk² (stôk) *n.* [OE. *stela*] **1.** the stem of a plant **2.** any part like this

stall¹ (stôl) *n.* [OE. *steall*] **1.** a section for one animal in a stable **2.** *a)* a booth, etc. as at a market *b)* a pew in a church **3.** a stop or standstill, esp. due to malfunction —*vt., vi.* **1.** to keep or be kept in a stall **2.** to bring or come to a standstill, esp. unintentionally

stall² (stôl) *vt., vi.* [< obs. *stale*, one who lures] to act evasively so as to deceive or delay —*n.* [Colloq.] any action used in stalling

stal·lion (stal'yən) *n.* [< Gmc. *stal*, a stall] an uncastrated male horse

stal·wart (stôl'wərt) *adj.* [< OE. *stathol*, foundation + *wyrthe*, worth] **1.** strong; sturdy **2.** brave; valiant **3.** resolute; firm —*n.* a stalwart person

sta·men (stā'mən) *n.* [L., thread] the pollen-bearing organ in a flower

Stam·ford (stam'fərd) city in SW Conn.; pop. 102,000

stam·i·na (stam'ə nə) *n.* [L., pl. of STAMEN] resistance to fatigue, illness, hardship, etc.; endurance

stam·mer (stam'ər) *vt., vi.* [OE. *stamerian*] to speak or say with involuntary pauses and rapid repetitions —*n.* a stammering —**stam'mer·er** *n.*

stamp (stamp) *vt.* [ME. *stampen*] **1.** to bring (the foot) down forcibly **2.** to crush or pound with the foot **3.** to imprint or cut out (a design, etc.) **4.** to cut (*out*) by pressing with a die **5.** to put a stamp on **6.** to characterize —*vi.* **1.** to bring the foot down forcibly **2.** to walk with loud, heavy steps —*n.* **1.** a stamping **2.** *a)* a machine, tool, or die for stamping *b)* a mark or form made by stamping **3.** any of various seals, gummed pieces of paper, etc. used to show that a fee, as for postage, has been paid **4.** any similar seal [*trading stamp*] **5.** class; kind —**stamp out 1.** to crush by treading on forcibly **2.** to suppress, or put down —**stamp'er** *n.*

stam·pede (stam pēd') *n.* [< Sp. *estampar*, to stamp] a sudden, headlong rush or flight, as of a herd of cattle —*vt., vi.* **-ped'ed, -ped'ing** to move, or take part, in a stampede

stamp'ing ground [Colloq.] a regular or favorite gathering place

stance (stans) *n.* [< L. *stare*, to stand] **1.** the way one stands, esp. the placement of the feet **2.** the attitude taken in a given situation

stanch (stônch, stanch) *vt., vi., adj.* *see* STAUNCH

stan·chion (stan'chən) *n.* [see STANCE] **1.** an upright post or support **2.** a device to confine a cow

stand (stand) *vi.* **stood, stand'ing** [OE. *standan*] **1.** to be in, or assume, an upright position on the feet **2.** to be supported on a base, pedestal, etc. **3.** to take or be in a (specified) position, attitude, etc. **4.** to have a (specified) height when standing **5.** to be placed or situated **6.** to gather and remain, as water **7.** to remain unchanged **8.** to make resistance **9.** *a)* to halt *b)* to be stationary —*vt.* **1.** to place upright **2.** to endure **3.** to withstand **4.** to undergo [*to stand trial*] —*n.* **1.** a standing; esp., a halt or stop **2.** a position; station **3.** a view, opinion, etc. **4.** a structure to stand or sit on **5.** a place of business **6.** a rack, small table, etc. for holding things **7.** a growth of trees, etc. —**stand by 1.** to be near and ready if needed **2.** to aid —**stand for 1.** to represent **2.** [Colloq.] to tolerate —**stand off** to keep at a distance —**stand out 1.** to project **2.** to be distinct, prominent, etc. —**stand up 1.** to rise to a standing position **2.** to prove valid, durable, etc. **3.** [Slang] to fail to keep a date with —**stand'er** n.

stand·ard (stan'dərd) n. [< OFr. *estendard*] **1.** a flag, banner, etc. as an emblem of a military unit, etc. **2.** something established for use as a rule or basis of comparison in measuring quantity, quality, value, etc. **3.** an upright support —*adj.* **1.** used as, or conforming to, a standard, rule, model, etc. **2.** generally accepted as reliable or authoritative **3.** typical; ordinary

stand'ard-bear'er n. **1.** one who carries the flag **2.** the leader of a movement, political party, etc.

stand'ard·ize' vt. **-ized', -iz'ing** to make standard or uniform —**stand'ard·i·za'tion** n.

standard time the official civil time for any given region: the earth is divided into 24 time zones, one hour apart (*Eastern, Central, Mountain*, and *Pacific* fall within the conterminous U.S.)

stand'by' n., pl. **-bys'** a person or thing that is dependable, a possible substitute, etc.

stand·ee (stan dē') n. [Colloq.] one who stands, as in a bus, theater, etc.

stand'-in' n. a temporary substitute, as for an actor at rehearsals

stand'ing n. **1.** status or reputation [in good *standing*] **2.** duration [a rule of long *standing*] —*adj.* **1.** that stands; upright **2.** from a standing position [a *standing* jump] **3.** stagnant, as water **4.** lasting; permanent [a *standing* order] **5.** not in use

stand'off' n. a tie in a contest

stand'off'ish adj. aloof; reserved

stand'point' n. point of view

stand'still' n. a stop or halt

stand'-up' adj. **1.** in a standing position **2.** specializing in monologues made up of jokes, as a comedian

stank (staŋk) alt. pt. of STINK

stan·za (stan'zə) n. [It.: ult. < L. *stare*, to stand] a group of lines of verse forming a division of a poem or song

staph (staf) n. *clipped form of* STAPHYLOCOCCUS

staph·y·lo·coc·cus (staf'ə lō käk'əs) n., pl. **-coc'ci** (-käk'sī) [< Gr. *staphylē*, bunch of grapes + *kokkos*, a grain] any of certain spherical bacteria, in clusters or chains

sta·ple¹ (stā'p'l) n. [< MDu. *stapel, mart*] **1.** a chief commodity made or grown in a particular place **2.** raw material **3.** a regularly stocked item of trade, as flour, salt, etc. **4.** the fiber of cotton, wool, etc. —*adj.* **1.** regularly stocked, produced, or used **2.** most important; principal

sta·ple² (stā'p'l) n. [OE. *stapol*, a post] a U-shaped piece of metal with sharp ends, driven into wood, etc. as to hold a hook, wire, etc., or through papers as a binding —*vt.* **-pled, -pling** to fasten with a staple —**sta'pler** n.

star (stär) n. [OE. *steorra*] **1.** a) any heavenly body seen as a small fixed point of light, esp. a far-off sun b) a star or stars regarded as influencing one's fate **2.** a conventionalized figure with five or six points, or anything like this **3.** an asterisk **4.** one who excels, as in a sport **5.** a leading actor or actress —*vt.* **starred, star'ring 1.** to mark with stars as a decoration, etc. **2.** to present (an actor or actress) in a leading role —*vi.* **1.** to perform brilliantly **2.** to perform as a star —*adj.* **1.** having great skill; outstanding **2.** of a star —**star'less** adj.

star·board (stär'bərd, -bôrd') n. [< OE. *steoran*, to steer (the old rudder was on the right side)] the right side of a ship, etc. as one faces forward —*adj.* of or on the starboard

starch (stärch) n. [OE. *stearc*, stiff] **1.** a white, tasteless, odorless food substance found in potatoes, cereals, etc. **2.** a powdered form of this used in laundering for stiffening cloth, etc. —*vt.* to stiffen as with starch —**starch'y** adj. **-i·er, -i·est**

star'dom (-dəm) n. the status of a star in the theater, etc.

stare (ster) vi. **stared, star'ing** [OE. *starian*] to gaze steadily and intently —*vt.* to look fixedly at —*n.* a steady, intent look —**star'er** n.

star'fish' n., pl.: see FISH a small, star-shaped sea animal

star'gaze' vi. **-gazed', -gaz'ing 1.** to gaze at the stars **2.** to indulge in dreamy thought —**star'gaz'er** n.

stark (stärk) adj. [OE. *stearc*] **1.** rigid, as a corpse **2.** sharply outlined **3.** bleak; desolate **4.** sheer; downright —*adv.* utterly; wholly

stark'-nak'ed adj. entirely naked

star'let (-lit) n. a young actress being promoted as a future star

star'light' n. light given by the stars —**star'lit'** (-lit') adj.

star·ling (stär'liŋ) n. [OE. *stær*] any of a family of old-world birds; esp., the **common starling** with iridescent plumage, introduced into the U.S.

star'ry adj. **-ri·er, -ri·est 1.** shining; bright **2.** lighted by or full of stars

star'ry-eyed' adj. with sparkling eyes

Stars and Stripes the U.S. flag

star'-span'gled adj. studded or spangled with stars

Star-Spangled Banner 1. the U.S. flag **2.** the U.S. national anthem

start (stärt) vi. [OE. *styrtan*] **1.** to make a sudden or involuntary move **2.** to go into action or motion; begin; commence **3.** to spring into being, activity, etc. —*vt.* **1.** to flush (game) **2.** to displace, loosen, etc. [to *start* a seam] **3.** a) to begin to play, do, etc. b) to set into motion, action, etc. **4.** to cause to be an entrant in a race, etc. —*n.* **1.** a sudden, brief shock or startled movement **2.** a starting, or beginning **3.** *a)* a place or time of beginning *b)* a lead or other advantage **4.** an opportunity of beginning a career —**start out** (or **off**) to start a journey, project, etc. —**start′er** *n.*

star·tle (stärt′'l) *vt.*, **-tled**, **-tling** [< ME. *sterten*, to start] to surprise, frighten, or alarm suddenly; esp., to cause to start —*vi.* to be startled

starve (stärv) *vi.* **starved**, **starv′ing** [< OE. *steorfan*, to die] **1.** to die from lack of food **2.** to suffer from hunger **3.** to suffer great need (with *for*) —*vt.* **1.** to cause to starve **2.** to force by starvation —**star·va·tion** (stär vā′shən) *n.*

starve·ling (-liŋ) *n.* a person or animal that is weak from lack of food

Star Wars [< a film title] [Colloq.] a proposed defense system of space-based weapons for destroying missiles

stash (stash) *vt.*, *vi.* [< ?] [Colloq.] to put or hide away (money, etc.) —*n.* [Slang] **1.** a place for hiding things **2.** something hidden away

-stat (stat) [< Gr. *-statēs*] a combining form meaning stationary [*thermostat*]

state (stāt) *n.* [< L. *stare*, to stand] **1.** a set of circumstances, etc. character-izing a person or thing; condition **2.** condition as regards structure, form, etc. **3.** rich display; pomp **4.** [*sometimes* S-] a body of people politically organized under one government; nation **5.** [*usually* S-] any of the political units forming a federal gov-ernment, as in the U.S. **6.** civil government [*matters of state*] —*adj.* **1.** formal; ceremonial **2.** [*sometimes* S-] of the government or a state —*vt.* **stat′ed**, **stat′ing** **1.** to establish by specifying **2.** *a)* to set forth in words *b)* to express —**in a state** in an excited condition —**lie in state** to be dis-played formally before burial —**the States** the United States

State′house′ *n.* the building in which the legislature of a State meets

state′less *adj.* having no state or nationality

state′ly *adj.* **-li·er**, **-li·est** **1.** im-posing; majestic **2.** slow, dignified, etc. —**state′li·ness** *n.*

state′ment *n.* **1.** *a)* a stating *b)* an assertion, declaration, etc. **2.** *a)* a financial account *b)* an invoice; bill

state′room′ *n.* **1.** a private cabin on a ship **2.** a private room on a train

state′side′ *adj.* [Colloq.] of or in the U.S. (as viewed from abroad) —*adv.* [Colloq.] in or to the U.S.

states′man *n.*, *pl.* **-men** one who is wise or experienced in the business of government —**states′man·ship′** *n.*

stat·ic (stat′ik) *adj.* [< Gr. *statikos*, causing to stand] **1.** of masses, forces, etc. at rest or in equilibrium **2.** at rest; inactive **3.** of or producing stationary electrical charges, as from friction **4.** of or having to do with static —*n.* **1.** atmospheric electrical discharges causing noise on radio or TV **2.** such noise **3.** [Slang] adverse criticism —**stat′i·cal·ly** *adv.*

sta·tion (stā′shən) *n.* [< L. *stare*, to

stand] **1.** the place or building where one stands or is located; esp., an assigned post **2.** a regular stopping place, as on a bus line or railroad **3.** social standing **4.** a place equipped for radio or TV transmission, or its frequency —*vt.* to assign to a station

sta·tion·ar·y (stā′shən er′ē) *adj.* **1.** not moving; fixed **2.** unchanging

station break a pause in radio or TV programs for station identification

sta·tion·er (stā′shə nər) *n.* [< ML. *stationarius*, shopkeeper] a dealer in stationery, office supplies, etc.

sta′tion·er′y (-ner′ē) *n.* writing materials; esp., paper and envelopes

station wagon an automobile with folding or removable rear seats and a back end that opens

sta·tis·tics (stə tis′tiks) *n.pl.* [< L. *status*, standing] **1.** numerical data assembled and classified so as to present significant information **2.** [*with sing. v.*] the science of compiling such data —**sta·tis′ti·cal** *adj.* —**stat·is·ti·cian** (stat′is tish′ən) *n.*

stat·u·ar·y (stach′oo wer′ē) *n.* stat-ues collectively

stat·ue (stach′ōō) *n.* [< L. *statuere*, to set] the form of a person or animal carved in stone, etc., modeled in clay, or cast in plaster, metal, etc.

stat·u·esque (stach′oo wesk′) *adj.* of or like a statue; stately and dignified

stat′u·ette′ (-wet′) *n.* a small statue

stat·ure (stach′ər) *n.* [< L. *statura*] **1.** the standing height of the body **2.** level of attainment [*moral stature*]

sta·tus (stāt′əs, stat′-) *n.*, *pl.* **-tus·es** [L., standing] **1.** legal condition [*the status of a minor*] **2.** position; rank **3.** state, as of affairs

status quo (kwō′) [L., the state in which] the existing state of affairs

status symbol a possession regarded as a sign of (high) social status

stat·ute (stach′ōōt) *n.* [see STATUE] **1.** an established rule or law **2.** a law passed by a legislative body

statute of limitations a statute limiting the time for legal action

stat·u·to·ry (stach′oo tôr′ē) *adj.* **1.** fixed or authorized by statute **2.** punishable by statute, as an offense

staunch (stônch, stänch) *vt.* [< L. *stare*, to stand] to check the flow of (blood, etc.) from (a cut, etc.) —*vi.* to stop flowing Also **stanch** —*adj.* **1.** seaworthy **2.** steadfast; loyal **3.** strong; solid —**staunch′ly** *adv.*

stave (stāv) *n.* [< *staves*, pl. of STAFF] **1.** one of the shaped strips of wood that form the walls of a barrel, bucket, etc. **2.** a stick or staff **3.** a stanza —*vt.* **staved** or **stove**, **stav′ing** to punc-ture, as by breaking in staves —**stave off** to hold or put off

staves (stāvz) *n.* **1.** *alt. pl.* of STAFF **2.** *pl.* of STAVE

stay¹ (stā) *n.* [OE. *stæg*] a heavy rope or cable, used as a brace or support

stay² (stā) *n.* [MFr. *estaie*] **1.** a sup-port, or prop **2.** a strip of stiffening material used in a corset, shirt collar, etc. —*vt.* to support, or prop up

stay³ (stā) *vi.* [< L. *stare*, to stand] **1.**

to continue in the place or condition specified; remain 2. to live; dwell 3. to stop; halt 4. to pause; delay 5. [Colloq.] to continue; last —*vt.* 1. to stop or check 2. to hinder or detain 3. to postpone (legal action) 4. to satisfy (thirst, etc.) for a time 5. to remain to the end of —*n.* 1. *a)* a stopping or being stopped *b)* a halt or pause 2. a postponement in legal action 3. the action of remaining, or the time spent, in a place —**stay put** [Colloq.] to remain in place or unchanged

stay'ing power power to last; endurance

Ste. [Fr. *Sainte*] Saint (female)

stead (sted) *n.* [OE. *stede*] the place of a person or thing as filled by a substitute —**stand (one) in good stead** to give (one) good service

stead'fast (sted'fast') *adj.* [OE. *stedefæste*] 1. firm; fixed 2. constant —**stead'fast'ly** *adv.*

stead·y (sted'ē) *adj.* -**i·er**, -**i·est** [see STEAD + -Y³] 1. firm; stable; not shaky 2. constant, regular, or uniform 3. constant in behavior, loyalty, etc. 4. calm and controlled [*steady* nerves] 5. sober; reliable —*vt., vi.* -**ied**, -**y·ing** to make or become steady —*n.* [Colloq.] a sweetheart —*adv.* in a steady manner —**go steady** [Colloq.] to be sweethearts —**stead'i·ly** *adv.*

steady-state theory a theory that as the universe is expanding new matter is continuously being created

steak (stāk) *n.* [< ON. *steikja*, roast on a spit] a slice of meat, esp. beef, or fish, for broiling or frying

steal (stēl) *vt.* **stole**, **stol'en**, **steal'-ing** [OE. *stelan*] 1. to take (another's property, etc.) dishonestly, esp. in a secret manner 2. to take (a look, etc.) slyly 3. to gain insidiously or artfully [he *stole* her heart] 4. to move, put, etc. stealthily (*in*, *from*, etc.) 5. *Baseball* to gain (a base) as by running to it from another base while a pitch is being delivered —*vi.* 1. to be a thief 2. to move stealthily —*n.* [Colloq.] an extraordinary bargain

stealth (stelth) *n.* [< ME. *stelen*, to steal] secret or furtive action —**stealth'i·ly** *adv.* —**stealth'y** *adj.*

steam (stēm) *n.* [OE.] 1. water as converted into a vapor by being heated to the boiling point 2. the power of steam under pressure 3. condensed water vapor 4. [Colloq.] vigor; energy —*adj.* using or operated by steam —*vi.* 1. to give off steam 2. to become covered with condensed steam 3. to move by steam power —*vt.* to expose to steam, as in cooking —**steam'y** *adj.*

steam'boat' *n.* a small steamship

steam engine an engine using pressurized steam to supply mechanical energy

steam'er *n.* something operated by steam, as a steamship 2. a container for cooking, cleaning, etc. with steam

steam fitter a mechanic whose work (**steam fitting**) is installing boilers, pipes, etc. in steam-pressure systems

steam'roll'er *n.* a heavy, steam-driven roller used in building roads —*vi., vt.* to move, crush, override, etc. as (with) a steamroller

steam'ship' *n.* a ship driven by steam power

steam shovel a large, mechanically operated digger, powered by steam

steed (stēd) *n.* [OE. *steda*] a horse

steel (stēl) *n.* [OE. *stiele*] 1. a hard, tough alloy of iron with carbon 2. a thing of steel 3. great strength or hardness —*adj.* of or like steel —*vt.* to make hard, tough, etc. —**steel'y** *adj.*

steel band a percussion band, orig. in Trinidad, beating on steel oil drums

steel wool long, thin shavings of steel in a pad, used for scouring, smoothing, and polishing

steel'yard' (-yärd') *n.* [STEEL + obs. *yard*, rod] a balance scale consisting of a metal arm suspended from above

STEELYARD

steep¹ (stēp) *adj.* [OE. *steap*, lofty] 1. having a sharp rise or slope; precipitous 2. [Colloq.] excessive; extreme —**steep'ly** *adv.* —**steep'ness** *n.*

steep² (stēp) *vt., vi.* [ME. *stepen*] to soak, saturate, imbue, etc.

stee·ple (stē'p'l) *n.* [OE. *stepel*] 1. a tower rising above the main structure, as of a church 2. a spire

stee'ple·chase' *n.* a horse race over a course obstructed with ditches, hedges, etc.

stee'ple·jack' *n.* one who builds or repairs steeples, smokestacks, etc.

steer¹ (stir) *vt.* [OE. *stieran*] 1. to guide (a ship, etc.) with a rudder 2. to direct the course of (an automobile, etc.) 3. to follow (a course) —**steer clear of** to avoid —**steer'a·ble** *adj.*

steer² (stir) *n.* [OE. *steor*] 1. a castrated male of the cattle family 2. loosely, any male of beef cattle

steer'age (-ij) *n.* 1. a steering 2. formerly, a section in a ship occupied by passengers paying the lowest fare

steers·man (stirz'mən) *n., pl.* -**men** one who steers a ship; helmsman

steg·o·sau·rus (steg'ə sôr'əs) *n. pl.* -**ri** (-ī) [< Gr. *stegos*, a roof + *sauros*, lizard] a large dinosaur with pointed bony plates along the backbone

stein (stīn) *n.* [G.] a beer mug

stel·lar (stel'ər) *adj.* [< L. *stella*, star] 1. of a star 2. excellent 3. leading; chief [a *stellar* role]

stem¹ (stem) *n.* [OE. *stemn*] 1. *a)* the main stalk of a plant *b)* any stalk supporting leaves, flowers, or fruit 2. a stemlike part, as of a pipe, goblet, etc. 3. the prow of a ship; bow 4. the part of a word to which inflectional endings are added —*vt.* **stemmed, stem′ming** to make headway against [to stem the tide] —*vi.* to derive

stem² (stem) *vt.* **stemmed, stem′-ming** [< ON. *stemma*] to stop or check by or as if by damming up

stem′ware′ *n.* goblets, wine glasses, etc. having stems

stench (stench) *n.* [< OE. *stincan,* to stink] an offensive smell; stink

sten·cil (sten′s'l) *vt.* **-ciled** or **-cilled, -cil·ing** or **-cil·ling** [ult. < L. *scintilla,* a spark] to make or mark with a stencil —*n.* **1.** a thin sheet, as of paper, cut through so that when ink, etc. is applied, designs, letters, etc. form on the surface beneath **2.** a design, etc. so made

ste·nog·ra·phy (stə näg′rə fē) *n.* [< Gr. *stenos,* narrow + -GRAPHY] shorthand writing for later typewritten transcription —**ste·nog′ra·pher** *n.* —**sten·o·graph·ic** (sten′ə graf′ik) *adj.*

sten·to·ri·an (sten tôr′ē ən) *adj.* [< *Stentor,* a Greek herald in the *Iliad*] very loud

step (step) *n.* [OE. *stepe*] **1.** a single movement of the foot, as in walking **2.** the distance covered by such a movement **3.** a short distance **4.** a manner of stepping **5.** the sound of stepping **6.** a rest for the foot in climbing, as a stair **7.** a degree; level; stage **8.** any of a series of acts, processes, etc. —*vi.* **stepped, step′-ping 1.** to move by executing a step **2.** to walk a short distance **3.** to move bris.ly (*along*) **4.** to enter (*into* a situation, etc.) **5.** to press the foot down (*on*) —*vt.* to measure by taking steps (with *off*) —**in** (or **out of**) **step** (not) conforming to a marching rhythm, a regular procedure, etc. — **step up 1.** to advance **2.** to increase, as in rate —**take steps** to do the things needed —**step′per** *n.*

step·broth·er (step′bruth′ər) *n.* one's stepparent's son by a former marriage

step′child′ *n., pl.* **-chil′dren** [OE. *steop-,* orphaned] one's spouse's child (**stepdaughter** or **stepson**) by a former marriage

step′-down′ *n.* a decrease, as in amount, intensity, etc.

step′lad′der *n.* a four-legged ladder having broad, flat steps

step′par′ent *n.* the person (**step-father** or **stepmother**) who has married one's parent after the death or divorce of the other parent

steppe (step) *n.* [Russ. *step′*] one of the great plains of SE Europe and Asia, having few trees

step′ping·stone′ *n.* **1.** a stone to step on, as in crossing a stream **2.** a means of bettering oneself

step·sis·ter (step′sis′tər) *n.* one's stepparent's daughter by a former marriage

step′-up′r an increase, as in amount, intensity, etc.

-ster (stər) [OE. *-estre*] a suffix meaning one who is, does, creates, or is

associated with (something specified) [*trickster, gangster*]

ster·e·o (ster′ē ō′, stir′-) *n., pl.* **-os′ 1.** a stereophonic record player, radio, system, etc. **2.** a stereophonic system, effect, picture, etc. —*adj.* clipped form of STEREOPHONIC

stereo- [< Gr. *stereos,* solid] a combining form meaning solid, firm, three-dimensional [*stereoscope*]

ster·e·o·phon·ic (ster′ē ə fän′ik, stir′-) *adj.* [< prec. + Gr. *phōnē,* a sound] designating sound reproduction using two or more channels to carry and reproduce the sounds from the directions in which they were recorded

ster′e·o·scope′ (-skōp′) *n.* [STEREO- + -SCOPE] an instrument with two eyepieces that gives a three-dimensional effect to photographs viewed through it

ster′e·o·type′ (-tīp′) *n.* [see STEREO- & -TYPE] **1.** a printing plate cast from a mold, as a page of set type **2.** a fixed or conventional notion or conception —*vt.* **-typed′, -typ′ing** to make a stereotype of —**ster′e·o·typed′** *adj.*

ster·ile (ster′l) *adj.* [L. *sterilis*] **1.** incapable of producing offspring, fruit, etc.; barren **2.** free from living microorganisms —**ste·ril·i·ty** (stə ril′ə tē) *n.*

ster′i·lize′ (-ə līz′) *vt.* **-lized′, -liz′-ing** to make sterile; specif., *a*) to make incapable of reproduction *b*) to free from living microorganisms —**ster′i·li·za′tion** *n.* —**ster′i·liz′er** *n.*

ster·ling (stur′liŋ) *n.* [ME. *sterlinge,* Norman coin] **1.** sterling silver **2.** British money —*adj.* **1.** of silver that is at least 92.5% pure **2.** of British money **3.** made of sterling silver **4.** excellent [*sterling* principles]

stern¹ (sturn) *adj.* [OE. *styrne*] **1.** severe; strict [*stern* measures] **2.** grim [a *stern* face] **3.** relentless; firm — **stern′ly** *adv.* —**stern′ness** *n.*

stern² (sturn) *n.* [< ON. *styra,* to steer] the rear end of a ship, etc.

ster·num (stur′nəm) *n., pl.* **-nums, -na** (-nə) [< Gr. *sternon*] a flat, bony structure to which most of the ribs are attached in the front of the chest; breastbone

ster·oid (stir′oid, ster′-) *n.* [< (CHOLE)STER(OL) + -OID] any of a group of compounds that include the sex hormones, cortisone, bile acids, etc.

ster·to·rous (stur′tər əs) *adj.* [L. *stertere,* to snore] characterized by raspy, labored breathing

stet (stet) [L.] let it stand: printer's term to show that matter orig. marked for deletion is to be kept —*vt.* **stet′ted, stet′ting** to mark with "stet"

steth·o·scope (steth′ə skōp′) *n.* [< Gr. *stēthos,* the chest + -SCOPE] *Med.* an instrument used to examine the heart, lungs, etc. by listening to the sounds they make

ste·ve·dore (stē′və dôr′) *n.* [< Sp. < L. *stipare,* cram] a person employed at loading and unloading ships

stew (stoo, styoo) *vt., vi.* [ult. < L. *ex-,* out + Gr. *typhos,* steam] **1.** to cook by simmering or boiling slowly 2. to worry —*n.* 1. a dish, esp. of meat and vegetables, cooked by stewing 2. a state of worry

stew·ard (stōō′ərd, styōō′-) *n.* [< OE. *stig,* hall + *weard,* keeper] 1. a person put in charge of a large estate 2. an administrator, as of finances and property 3. one responsible for the food and drink, etc. in a club, restaurant, etc. 4. an attendant, as on a ship or airplane —**stew′ard·ship′** *n.*

stew′ard·ess (-ər dis) *n.* a woman steward, esp. on an airplane

stick (stik) *n.* [OE. *sticca*] 1. a twig or small branch broken or cut off 2. a long, slender piece of wood, as a club, cane, etc. 3. any sticklike piece [a *stick* of gum] —*vt.* **stuck, stick′ing** 1. to pierce, as with a pointed instrument 2. to pierce with (a knife, pin, etc.) 3. to thrust (*in, into, out,* etc.) 4. to attach as by gluing, pinning, etc. 5. to obstruct, detain, etc. [the wheels were *stuck*] 6. [Colloq.] to put, set, etc. 7. [Colloq.] to puzzle; baffle 8. [Slang] *a*) to impose a burden, etc. upon *b*) to defraud —*vi.* 1. to be fixed by a pointed end, as a nail 2. to adhere; cling; remain 3. to persevere [to *stick* at a job] 4. to remain firm and resolute [he *stuck* with us] 5. to become embedded, jammed, etc. 6. to be puzzled 7. to hesitate; scruple [he'll *stick* at nothing] 8. to protrude or,project (*out, up,* etc.) —**stick by** to remain loyal to —**stick up for** [Colloq.] to uphold; defend —**the sticks** [Colloq.] the rural districts

stick′er *n.* a person or thing that sticks; specif., a gummed label

stick′-in-the-mud′ *n.* [Colloq.] a person who resists change

stick·le·back (stik′'l bak′) *n.* a small fish having sharp spines on its back and no scales: the male builds a nest for the female's eggs

stick·ler (stik′lər) *n.* [< OE. *stihtan,* arrange] 1. one who insists on a certain way of doing things [a *stickler* for discipline] 2. [Colloq.] something difficult to solve

stick′pin′ *n.* an ornamental pin worn in a necktie, etc.

stick shift a gearshift, as on a car, operated manually by a lever

stick′up′ *n.* slang term for HOLDUP (sense 2)

stick′y *adj.* **-i·er, -i·est** 1. that sticks; adhesive 2. [Colloq.] hot and humid 3. [Colloq.] troublesome

stiff (stif) *adj.* [OE. *stif*] 1. hard to bend or move; rigid; firm 2. sore or limited in movement: said of joints and muscles 3. not fluid; thick 4. strong; powerful [a *stiff* breeze] 5. harsh [*stiff* punishment] 6. difficult [a *stiff* climb] 7. very formal or awkward 8. [Colloq.] high [a *stiff* price] — **stiff′ly** *adv.* —**stiff′ness** *n.*

stiff′-arm′ *vt.* to push (someone) away with one's arm out straight

stiff′en *vt., vi.* to make or become stiff or stiffer —**stiff′en·er** *n.*

stiff′-necked′ (-nekt′) *adj.* stubborn

sti·fle (stī′f'l) *vt.* **-fled, -fling** [< MFr. *estouffer*] 1. to smother; suffocate 2. to suppress; hold back; stop [to *stifle* a sob] —*vi.* to die or suffer from lack of air —**sti′fling·ly** *adv.*

stig·ma (stig′mə) *n., pl.* **-mas, stig·ma′ta** (-mät′ə) [L. < Gr., a mark] 1. a mark of disgrace or reproach 2. a spot on the skin, esp. one that bleeds in certain nervous tensions 3. the upper tip of the pistil of a flower, receiving the pollen —**stig·mat′ic** (-mat′ik) *adj.*

stig·ma·tize′ (-tīz′) *vt.* **-tized′, -tiz′ing** 1. to mark with a stigma 2. to mark as disgraceful

stil·bes·trol (stil bes′trōl) *n.* a synthetic estrogen

stile (stīl) *n.* [< OE. *stigan,* to climb] a step or set of steps used in climbing over a fence or wall

sti·let·to (sti let′ō) *n., pl.* **-tos, -toes** [It. < L. *stilus,* pointed tool] a small dagger with a slender blade

still[1] (stil) *adj.* [OE. *stille*] 1. without sound; silent 2. not moving; stationary 3. tranquil; calm 4. designating or of a single photograph taken from a motion-picture film —*n.* 1. silence; quiet 2. a still photograph —*adv.* 1. at or up to the time indicated 2. even; yet [*still* colder] 3. nevertheless; yet [rich but *still* unhappy] —*conj.* nevertheless; yet —*vt.,* *vi.* to make or become still —**still′ness** *n.*

still[2] (stil) *n.* [< obs. *still,* to distill] an apparatus used for distilling liquids, esp. alcoholic liquors

still′birth′ *n.* the birth of a stillborn fetus

still′born′ *adj.* dead when born

still life a painting of inanimate objects, as fruit, flowers, etc.

stilt (stilt) *n.* [ME. *stilte*] 1. either of a pair of poles fitted with a footrest along its length and used for walking, as in play 2. any of a number of long posts used to hold a building, etc. above the ground or out of the water

stilt·ed (stil′tid) *adj.* artificially formal or dignified; pompous

stim·u·lant (stim′yə lənt) *n.* anything, as a drug, that stimulates

stim·u·late′ (-lāt′) *vt.* **-lat′ed, -lat′ing** [< L. *stimulus,* a goad] to rouse or excite to activity or increased activity —**stim′u·la′tion** *n.*

stim·u·lus (-ləs) *n., pl.* **-li′** (-lī′) [L., a goad] 1. an incentive 2. any action or agent that causes an activity in an organism, organ, etc.

sting (stin) *vt.* **stung, sting′ing** [OE. *stingan*] 1. to prick or wound with a sting 2. to cause sudden, pricking pain to 3. to cause to suffer mentally 4. to stimulate suddenly and sharply 5. [Slang] to cheat —*vi.* to cause or feel sharp, smarting pain —*n.* 1. a stinging

2. a pain or wound resulting from stinging **3.** a sharp-pointed organ, as in insects and plants, that pricks, wounds, etc. —**sting′er** n.

stin·gy (stin′jē) adj. **-gi·er, -gi·est** [< dial. form of prec.] **1.** giving or spending grudgingly; miserly **2.** less than needed; scanty —**stin′gi·ly** adv. —**stin′gi·ness** n.

stink (stink) vi. **stank** or **stunk, stunk, stink′ing** [OE. stincan] to give off a strong, unpleasant smell —n. a strong, unpleasant smell; stench —**stink′er** n.

stint (stint) vt. [< OE. styntan, to blunt] to restrict to a certain quantity, often small —vi. to be sparing in giving or using —n. **1.** restriction; limit **2.** an assigned task or period of work —**stint′er** n. —**stint′ing·adj.**

sti·pend (stī′pend) n. [< L. stips, small coin + pendere, to pay] a regular or fixed payment, as a salary

stip·ple (stip′'l) vt. **-pled, -pling** [< Du. stippel, a speckle] to paint, draw, or engrave in small dots

stip·u·late (stip′yə lāt′) vt. **-lat′ed, -lat′ing** [< L. stipulari, to bargain] **1.** to arrange definitely **2.** to specify as an essential condition of an agreement —**stip′u·la′tion** n.

stir (stur) vt., vi. **stirred, stir′ring** [OE. styrian] **1.** to move, esp. slightly **2.** to rouse from lethargy, sleep, etc.; be busy and active **3.** to mix (a liquid, etc.) as by agitating with a spoon **4.** to excite the feelings (of) **5.** to incite (often with up) —n. **1.** a stirring **2.** movement; activity **3.** excitement; tumult —**stir′rer** n.

stir′-fry′ vt. **-fried′, -fry′ing** to fry (diced or sliced vegetables, meat, etc.) very quickly in a wok, with a little oil, stirring constantly

stir′ring adj. **1.** active; busy **2.** rousing; exciting [stirring music]

stir·rup (stur′əp) n. [OE. stigrap] a flat-bottomed ring hung from a saddle and used as a footrest

stitch (stich) n. [OE. stice, a puncture] **1.** a single complete in-and-out movement of a needle in sewing, knitting, etc. **2.** a loop, etc. made by stitching **3.** a particular kind of stitch or stitching **4.** a sudden, sharp pain **5.** a bit —vi., vt. to make stitches (in); sew

stitch′er·y (-ər ē) n. ornamental needlework

St. Lawrence river flowing from Lake Ontario into the Atlantic: the main section of an inland waterway (**St. Lawrence Seaway**) connecting the Great Lakes with the Atlantic

St. Lou·is (lōō′is, lōō′ē) city in E Mo.: pop. 453,000

stoat (stōt) n. [ME. stote] a large European weasel, in its brown coat

stock (stäk) n. [OE. stocc] **1.** the trunk of a tree. a) descent; lineage b) a strain, race, etc. of animals or plants **3.** a supporting or main part of an implement, etc., as the part of a rifle containing the barrel **4.** [pl.] a wooden frame with holes for confining the ankles or wrists, formerly used for punishment **5.** raw material **6.** water

in which meat, fish, etc. has been boiled, used in soups **7.** livestock **8.** a supply of goods on hand in a store, etc. **9.** shares of corporate capital, or the certificates showing such ownership **10.** same as STOCK COMPANY (sense 2) —vt. **1.** to furnish (a farm, shop, etc.) with stock **2.** to keep a supply of, as for sale or for future use —vi. to put in a stock, or supply (with up) —adj. **1.** kept in stock [stock sizes] **2.** common or trite [a stock joke] **3.** that deals with stock **4.** relating to a stock company —**in** (or **out of**) **stock** (not) available for use or sale —**take stock 1.** to inventory the stock on hand **2.** to make an appraisal —**take** (or **put**) **stock in** [Colloq.] to have faith in

stock·ade (stä käd′) n. [< Pr. estaca, a stake] **1.** a defensive barrier of stakes driven into the ground side by side **2.** an enclosure, as a fort, made of such stakes

stock′brok′er n. a broker who buys and sells stocks and bonds

stock car a standard automobile, modified for racing

stock company 1. a company whose capital is in shares **2.** a theatrical company presenting a repertoire

stock exchange 1. a place where stocks and bonds are bought and sold **2.** an association of stockbrokers. Also **stock market**

stock′hold′er (-hōl′dər) n. one owning stock in a given company

Stock·holm (stäk′hōm′, -hōlm′) capital of Sweden: pop. 792,000

stock·ing (stäk′iŋ) n. [< obs. sense of STOCK] a closefitting covering, usually knitted, for the foot and leg

stocking cap a long, tapered, knitted cap, often with a tassel at the end

stock′pile′ (-pīl′) n. a reserve supply of goods, raw material, etc. —vt., vi. **-piled′, -pil′ing** to accumulate a stockpile (of)

stock′-still′ adj. motionless

stock′y adj. **-i·er, -i·est** heavily built; short and thickset —**stock′i·ness** n.

stock′yard′ n. an enclosure for keeping cattle, hogs, etc. to be slaughtered

stodg·y (stäj′ē) adj. **-i·er, -i·est** [< dial. stodge, heavy food] dull; uninteresting —**stodg′i·ness** n.

sto·gie, sto·gy (stō′gē) n., pl. **-gies** [< Conestoga, town in Pa.] a long, thin, inexpensive cigar

Sto·ic (stō′ik) n. [< Gr. stoa, colonnade: the first Stoics met in a colonnade] **1.** a member of an ancient Greek school of philosophy **2.** [s-] a stoical person —adj. **1.** [s-] same as STOICAL —**sto′i·cism** n.

sto′i·cal (-i k′l) adj. showing indifference to joy, grief, pain, etc.; impassive —**sto′i·cal·ly** adv.

stoke (stōk) vt., vi. **stoked, stok′ing** [< Du. stoken, to poke] **1.** to stir up and feed fuel to (a fire) **2.** to tend (a furnace, etc.) —**stok′er** n.

STOL (stōl) adj. [s(hort) t(ake)o(ff and) l(anding)] designating, of, or for an aircraft that can take off and land on a short airstrip —n. a STOL aircraft, airstrip, etc.

stole[1] (stōl) *n.* [< Gr. *stolē*, garment]
1. a long strip of cloth worn like a scarf
by some clergymen 2. a woman's long
scarf of cloth or fur worn around the
shoulders

stole[2] (stōl) *pt. of* STEAL

stol·en (stō'lən) *pp. of* STEAL

stol·id (stäl'id) *adj.* [L. *stolidus*, slow]
having or showing little or no emotion;
unexcitable —**sto·lid·i·ty** (stə lid'ə
tē) *n.* —**stol'id·ly** *adv.*

stom·ach (stum'ək) *n.* [ult. < Gr.
stoma, mouth] 1. the saclike digestive
organ into which food passes from the
esophagus 2. the abdomen, or belly 3.
appetite for food 4. desire or inclination —*vt.* 1. to be able to eat or digest
2. to tolerate; bear

stom'ach·ache' *n.* a pain in the
stomach or abdomen

stom'ach·er *n.* an ornamented piece
of cloth formerly worn over the chest
and abdomen, esp. by women

stomp (stämp) *vt., vi. var. of* STAMP

stone (stōn) *n.* [OE. *stan*] 1. the hard,
solid, nonmetallic mineral matter of
rock 2. a piece of rock 3. the seed of
certain fruits 4. a precious gem 5. *pl.*
stone in Great Britain, 14 pounds
avoirdupois 6. an abnormal stony
mass formed in the kidney, gall
bladder, etc. —*vt.* **stoned, ston'ing**
1. to throw stones at 2. to remove the
stone from (a peach, etc.)

stone- [< prec.] *a combining form
meaning* completely *[stone-blind]*

Stone Age the period in human culture when stone tools were used

stoned (stōnd) *adj.* [Slang] under the
influence of liquor, a drug, etc.

stone's throw a short distance

stone'wall' *vi.* [Colloq.] to obstruct
by various tactics, as by withholding
information, by denials, etc.

ston·y (stō'nē) *adj.* **-i·er, -i·est** 1.
full of stones 2. of or like stone; specif.,
unfeeling; pitiless —**ston'i·ness** *n.*

stood (stood) *pt. & pp. of* STAND

stooge (stōōj) *n.* [< ?] [Colloq.] 1. an
actor who serves as the victim of a
comedian's jokes, pranks, etc. 2.
anyone who acts as a foil or underling

stool (stōōl) *n.* [OE. *stol*] 1. a single
seat having no back or arms 2. feces

stool pigeon [Colloq.] a spy or informer, esp. for the police

stoop[1] (stōōp) *vi.* [OE. *stupian*] 1. to
bend the body forward 2. to carry the
head and shoulders habitually bent
forward 3. to degrade oneself —*n.* the
act or position of stooping

stoop[2] (stōōp) *n.* [Du. *stoep*] a small
porch at the door of a house

stoop labor work done by stooping,
as in picking crops

stop (stäp) *vt.* **stopped, stop'ping** [<
VL. *stuppare*, stop up] 1. to close by
filling, shutting off, etc. 2. to cause to
cease motion, activity, etc. 3. to
block; intercept; prevent 4. to cease;
desist from *[stop talking]* —*vi.* 1. to
cease moving, etc.; halt 2. to leave off

doing something 3. to cease operating
4. to become clogged 5. to tarry or
stay —*n.* 1. a stopping or being
stopped 2. a finish; end 3. a stay or
sojourn 4. a place stopped at, as on a
bus route 5. an obstruction, plug, etc.
6. a finger hole in a wind instrument,
closed to produce a desired tone 7. a
pull, lever, etc. for controlling a set of
organ pipes —**stop off** to stop for a
while en route to a place —**stop over**
to visit for a while: also **stop in** (or **by**)

stop'cock' *n.* a cock or valve to stop
or regulate the flow of a liquid

stop'gap' *n.* a person or thing serving
as a temporary substitute

stop'light' *n.* 1. a traffic light, esp.
when red to signal vehicles to stop 2.
a rear light on a vehicle that lights up
when the brakes are applied

stop'o'ver *n.* a brief stop or stay at a
place in the course of a journey

stop'page (-ij) *n.* 1. a stopping or
being stopped 2. an obstructed condition; block

stop'per *n.* something inserted to
close an opening; plug

stop'ple (-'l) *n.* a stopper or plug —*vt.*
-pled, -pling to close with a stopple

stop'watch' *n.* a watch with a hand
that can be started and stopped instantly, for timing races, etc.

stor·age (stôr'ij) *n.* 1. a storing or
being stored 2. *a)* a place for storing
goods *b)* the cost of storing goods

storage battery a battery of cells
generating electric current and capable
of being recharged

store (stôr) *vt.* **stored, stor'ing** [< L.
instaurare, restore] 1. to put aside for
use when needed 2. to furnish with a
supply 3. to put in a warehouse, etc.
for safekeeping —*n.* 1. a supply (*of
something*) for use when needed; stock
2. *[pl.]* supplies, esp. of food, clothing,
etc. 3. a retail establishment where
goods are offered for sale 4. a storehouse —**in store** set aside for the
future; in reserve —**set** (or **put** or
lay) **store by** to value

store'front' *n.* a front room on the
ground floor of a building, designed
for use as a retail store

store'house' *n.* a place where things
are stored; esp., a warehouse

store'keep'er *n.* 1. a person in
charge of military or naval stores 2.
one who operates a retail store

store'room' *n.* a room where things
are stored

sto·rey (stôr'ē) *n., pl.* **-reys** Brit. *sp. of*
STORY[2]

sto·ried (stôr'ēd) *adj.* famous in
story or history

stork (stôrk) *n.* [OE. *storc*] a large,
long-legged wading bird with a long
neck and bill

storm (stôrm) *n.* [OE.] 1. a strong
wind, with rain, snow, thunder, etc. 2.
any heavy fall of snow, rain, etc. 3. a
strong emotional outburst 4. any
strong disturbance 5. a sudden, strong

fat, āpe, cär; ten, ēven; is, bīte; gō, hôrn, tōōl, look; oil, out; up, fur;
chin; she; thin, *then*; zh, leisure; ŋ, ring; ə for *a* in *ago*; ', (ā'b'l); ë, Fr. coeur;
ö, Fr. feu; Fr. mon; ü, Fr. duc; kh, G. ich, doch; ‡ foreign; < derived from

attack on a fortified place —*vi.* **1.** to blow violently, rain, snow, etc. **2.** to rage; rant **3.** to rush violently [to *storm* into a room] —*vt.* to attack vigorously

storm door (or **window**) a door (or window) placed outside the regular one as added protection

storm'y *adj.* **-i·er, -i·est 1.** of or characterized by storms **2.** violent, raging, etc. —**storm'i·ly** *adv.* —**storm'i·ness** *n.*

sto·ry¹ (stôr'ē) *n., pl.* **-ries** [< Gr. *historia*, narrative] **1.** the telling of an event or events; account; narration **2.** a joke **3.** a fictitious narrative shorter than a novel **4.** the plot of a novel, play, etc. **5.** [Colloq.] a falsehood **6.** *Journalism* a news report

sto·ry² (stôr'ē) *n., pl.* **-ries** [< prec.] a horizontal division of a building, from a floor to the ceiling above it

sto'ry·book' *n.* a book of stories, esp. one for children

sto'ry·tell'er *n.* one who narrates stories —**sto'ry·tell'ing** *n.*

stoup (stoop) *n.* [ON. *staup*, cup] a church basin for water blessed by a priest

stout (stout) *adj.* [< OFr. *estout*, bold] **1.** courageous **2.** strong; sturdy; firm **3.** powerful; forceful **4.** fat; thickset —*n.* a heavy, dark-brown beer —**stout'ly** *adv.* —**stout'ness** *n.*

stove¹ (stōv) *n.* [< MDu., heated room] an apparatus for heating, cooking, etc.

stove² (stōv) *alt. pt. & pp. of* STAVE

stove'pipe' *n.* a metal pipe used to carry off smoke from a stove

stow (stō) *vt.* [< OE. *stowe*, a place] to pack in an orderly way —**stow away 1.** to put or hide away **2.** to be a stowaway —**stow'age** *n.*

stow'a·way' *n.* one who hides aboard a ship, airplane, etc. to get free passage, evade port officials, etc.

STP [< ? STP, motor oil additive] a hallucinogenic drug like mescaline

St. Paul capital of Minn.: pop. 270,000

St. Pe·ters·burg (pē'tərz burg') city in WC Fla.: pop. 237,000

strad·dle (strad''l) *vt., vi.* **-dled, -dling** [< STRIDE] **1.** to sit or stand astride of, or stand with the legs wide apart **2.** to appear to take both sides of (an issue) —*n.* a straddling —**strad'dler** *n.*

strafe (strāf) *vt.* **strafed, straf'ing** [< G. *Gott strafe England* (God punish England)] to attack with machine-gun fire from low-flying aircraft

strag·gle (strag''l) *vi.* **-gled, -gling** [prob. < ME. *straken*, roam] **1.** to wander from the main group **2.** to be scattered over a wide area; ramble **3.** to hang in an unkempt way, as hair —**strag'gler** *n.* —**strag'gly** *adj.*

straight (strāt) *adj.* [< ME. *strecchen*, stretch] **1.** having the same direction throughout its length; not crooked, bent, etc. **2.** direct, undeviating, etc. **3.** in order; properly arranged, etc. **4.** honest; sincere **5.** unmixed; undiluted [straight whiskey]

6. [Slang] normal or conventional — *adv.* **1.** in a straight line **2.** upright; erectly **3.** without detour, delay, etc. —*n.* *Poker* a hand of five cards in sequence —**straight away** (or **off**) without delay —**straight'ness** *n.*

straight arrow [Slang] a person who is proper, righteous, conscientious, etc. and thought of as conservative, stodgy, etc. —**straight'-ar'row** *adj.*

straight'en *vt., vi.* to make or become straight —**straighten out 1.** to make or become less confused, easier to deal with, etc. **2.** to reform

straight face a facial expression showing no amusement or other emotion —**straight'-faced'** *adj.*

straight'for'ward *adj.* **1.** moving or leading straight ahead; direct **2.** honest; frank —*adv.* in a straight-forward manner: also **straight'for'wards**

straight time 1. the standard number of working hours, as per week **2.** the rate of pay for these hours

straight'way' *adv.* at once

strain¹ (strān) *vt.* [< L. *stringere*] **1.** to draw or stretch tight **2.** to exert, use, etc. to the utmost **3.** to injure by overexertion [to *strain* a muscle] **4.** to stretch beyond normal limits **5.** to pass through a screen, sieve, etc.; filter —*vi.* **1.** to make violent efforts; strive hard **2.** to filter, ooze, etc. —*n.* **1.** a straining or being strained **2.** great effort, exertion, etc. **3.** a bodily injury from overexertion **4.** stress or force **5.** a great demand on one's emotions, resources, etc.

strain² (strān) *n.* [< OE. *strynan*, to produce] **1.** ancestry; lineage **2.** race; stock; line **3.** a line of individuals differentiated from its main species **4.** an inherited tendency **5.** a trace; streak **6.** a musical tune

strained (strānd) *adj.* not natural or relaxed

strain'er *n.* a device for straining, sifting, or filtering; sieve, filter, etc.

strait (strāt) *adj.* [< L. *stringere*, draw tight] [Archaic] narrow or strict —*n.* **1.** [often *pl.*] a narrow waterway connecting two large bodies of water **2.** [often *pl.*] difficulty; distress

strait'en *vt.* **1.** esp. formerly, to make strait or narrow **2.** to bring into difficulties: esp. in **in straitened circumstances**, lacking enough money

strait'jack'et *n.* a coatlike device for restraining violent persons

strait'-laced' (-lāst') *adj.* narrowly strict in behavior or moral views

strand¹ (strand) *n.* [OE.] shore, ocean shore —*vt., vi.* **1.** to run or drive aground, as a ship **2.** to put or be put into a helpless position [stranded in a desert]

strand² (strand) *n.* [ME. *stronde*] **1.** any of the threads, wires, etc. that are twisted together to form a string, cable, etc. **2.** a ropelike length of anything [a strand of pearls]

strange (strānj) *adj.* **strang'er, strang'est** [< L. *extraneus*, foreign] **1.** not previously known, seen, etc.; unfamiliar **2.** unusual; extraordinary

3. peculiar; odd 4. reserved or distant 5. unaccustomed (*to*) —**strange′ly** *adv.* —**strange′ness** *n.*

stran·ger (strān′jər) *n.* 1. a newcomer 2. a person not known to one

stran·gle (straŋ′g'l) *vt., vi.* **-gled, -gling** [< Gr. *strangos*, twisted] 1. to choke to death 2. to suppress; stifle —**stran′gler** *n.*

stran′gle·hold′ *n.* 1. an illegal wrestling hold choking an opponent 2. a force or action suppressing freedom

stran·gu·late (straŋ′gyə lāt′) *vt.* **-lat′ed, -lat′ing** *Med.* to block (a tube) by constricting

strap (strap) *n.* [dial. form of STROP] a narrow strip of leather, etc., as for binding or securing things —*vt.* **strapped, strap′ping** to fasten with a strap

strap′less *adj.* having no straps; specif., having no shoulder straps

strapped (strapt) *adj.* [Colloq.] without money

strap′ping *adj.* [Colloq.] tall and well-built; robust

stra·ta (strāt′ə, strat′ə) *n. alt. pl.* of STRATUM

strat·a·gem (strat′ə jəm) *n.* [< Gr. *stratos*, army + *agein*, to lead] 1. a trick, plan, etc. for deceiving an enemy in war 2. any tricky ruse

strat·e·gy (strat′ə jē) *n., pl.* **-gies** 1. the science of planning and directing military operations 2. skill in managing or planning, esp. by using stratagems 3. a stratagem, plan, etc. — **stra·te·gic** (strə tē′jik) *adj.* —**stra·te′gi·cal·ly** *adv.* —**strat′e·gist** *n.*

strat·i·fy (strat′ə fī′) *vt., vi.* **-fied′, -fy′ing** [< L. *stratum*, layer + *facere*, make] to form in layers or strata —**strat′i·fi·ca′tion** *n.*

strat·o·sphere (-ə sfir′) *n.* [< ModL. *stratum*, layer + Fr. *sphère*, SPHERE] the atmospheric zone extending from 6 to 15 miles above the earth's surface

stra·tum (strāt′əm, strat′-) *n., pl.* **-ta** (-ə), **-tums** [ModL. < L. *stratus*, a spreading] 1. a horizontal layer of matter; specif., a single layer of sedimentary rock 2. a level of society

stra′tus (-əs) *n., pl.* **-ti** (-ī) [see prec.] a long, low, gray cloud layer

Strauss (strous), **Jo·hann** (yō′hän) 1825–99; Austrian composer

Stra·vin·sky (strə vin′skē), **I·gor** (ē′gôr) 1882–1971; U.S. composer, born in Russia

straw (strô) *n.* [OE. *streaw*] 1. hollow stalks of grain after threshing 2. a single one of these 3. a tube used for sucking beverages 4. a trifle —*adj.* 1. straw-colored; yellowish 2. made of straw 3. worthless

straw′ber′ry (-ber′ē, -bər ē) *n., pl.* **-ries** [prob. from the strawlike particles on the fruit] 1. the small, red, fleshy fruit of a vinelike plant of the rose family 2. this plant

straw boss [Colloq.] a person having subordinate authority

straw vote an unofficial vote taken to determine general group opinion

stray (strā) *vi.* [prob. < L. *extra vagari*, wander outside] 1. to wander from a given place, course, etc. 2. to deviate (*from* what is right) —*n.* one that strays; esp., a lost domestic animal —*adj.* 1. having strayed; lost 2. isolated [a few *stray* words]

streak (strēk) *n.* [< OE. *strica*] 1. a long, thin mark or stripe 2. a layer, as of fat in meat 3. a tendency in behavior, etc. [a nervous *streak*] 4. a period, as of luck —*vt.* to mark with streaks —*vi.* 1. to become streaked 2. to go fast 3. to make a short dash naked in public as a prank —**streak′er** *n.* —**streak′y** *adj.*

stream (strēm) *n.* [OE.] 1. a current of water; specif., a small river 2. any steady flow, as of air, light, etc. 3. a continuous series [a *stream* of cars] —*vi.* 1. to flow as in a stream 2. to flow (*with*) 3. to move swiftly

stream′er *n.* 1. a long, narrow flag 2. any long, narrow, flowing strip

stream′line′ *vt.* **-lined′, -lin′ing** 1. to give a streamlined contour to 2. to organize for simplicity and efficiency —*adj.* same as STREAMLINED

stream′lined′ *adj.* 1. having a contour designed to offer the least resistance in moving through air, water, etc. 2. efficient, simplified, trim, etc.

street (strēt) *n.* [< L. *strata* (*via*), paved (road)] 1. a public road in a town or city, esp. a paved one 2. such a road with its sidewalks and buildings 3. the people living, working, etc. along a given street

street′car′ *n.* a car on rails for public transportation along the streets

street′walk′er *n.* a prostitute

street′wise′ *adj.* [Colloq.] experienced in dealing with people in urban poverty areas where crime is common

strength (streŋkth) *n.* [OE. *strengthu*] 1. the state or quality of being strong; force 2. toughness; durability 3. the power to resist attack 4. potency, as of drugs 5. intensity, as of sound, etc. 6. force of an army, etc., as measured in numbers —**on the strength of** based on or relying on

strength′en *vt., vi.* to make or become stronger —**strength′en·er** *n.*

stren·u·ous (stren′yoo wəs) *adj.* [L. *strenuus*] requiring or characterized by great effort or energy —**stren′u·ous·ly** *adv.* —**stren′u·ous·ness** *n.*

strep throat (strep) [Colloq.] a sore throat caused by a streptococcus, with inflammation and fever

strep·to·coc·cus (strep′tə käk′əs) *n., pl.* **-coc′ci** (-käk′sī) [< Gr. *streptos*, twisted + *kokkos*, kernel] any of various spherical bacteria occurring in chains: some cause serious diseases

strep′to·my′cin (-mī′sin) *n.* [< Gr. *streptos*, bent + *mykēs*, fungus] an antibiotic drug obtained from molds and used in treating various diseases

---

fat, āpe, cär; ten, ēven; is, bīte; gō, hôrn, tōōl, look; oil, out; up, fur; chin; she; thin, *then*; zh, leisure; ŋ, ring; ə for *a* in *ago*; ′, (ā′b'l); ë, Fr. coeur; ö, Fr. feu; Fr. mon; ü, Fr. duc; kh, G. ich, doch; ‡ foreign; < derived from

stress (stres) *n.* [< L. *strictus*, strict]
1. strain; specif., force that strains or
deforms 2. emphasis; importance
3. *a)* mental or physical tension *b)* urgency, pressure, etc. causing this 4. the
relative force of utterance given a
syllable or word; accent —*vt.* 1. to put
stress or pressure on 2. to accent
3. to emphasize

stretch (strech) *vt.* [OE. *streccan*]
1. to reach out; extend 2. to draw out
to full extent or to greater size 3. to
cause to extend too far; strain 4. to
strain in interpretation, scope, etc.
—*vi.* 1. *a)* to spread out to full extent
or beyond normal limits *b)* to extend
over a given distance or time 2. *a)* to
extend the body or limbs to full length
b) to lie down (usually with *out*) 3. to
become stretched —*n.* 1. a stretching
or being stretched 2. an unbroken
period [a ten-year *stretch*] 3. an unbroken length, tract, etc. 4. *short for*
HOMESTRETCH —*adj.* made of elastic
fabric so as to stretch easily —
stretch′a·ble *adj.* —**stretch′y** *adj.*

stretch′er *n.* 1. one that stretches
2. a light, canvas-covered frame for
carrying the sick, injured, etc.

strew (strōō) *vt.* **strewed, strewed** or
strewn, strew′ing [OE. *streawian*]
1. to spread here and there; scatter
2. to cover as by scattering

stri·at·ed (strī′āt id) *adj.* [< L.
striare, to groove] marked with parallel
lines, bands, furrows, etc.

strick·en (strik′'n) *alt. pp.* of STRIKE
—*adj.* 1. struck or wounded 2. afflicted, as by something painful

strict (strikt) *adj.* [< L. *stringere*,
draw tight] 1. exact or precise 2. perfect; absolute 3. *a)* enforcing rules
carefully *b)* closely enforced —**strict′-
ly** *adv.* —**strict′ness** *n.*

stric·ture (strik′chər) *n.* [see prec.]
1. adverse criticism 2. an abnormal
narrowing of a passage in the body

stride (strīd) *vi., vt.* **strode, strid′den**
(strid′'n), **strid′ing** [OE. *stridan*] 1.
to walk with long steps 2. to cross with
a single, long step —*n.* 1. a long step
2. the distance covered by a stride 3.
[*usually pl.*] progress [to make *strides*]

stri·dent (strīd′'nt) *adj.* [< L. *stridere*,
to rasp] harsh-sounding; shrill; grating
—**stri′dent·ly** *adv.*

strife (strīf) *n.* [< OFr. *estrif*] 1. contention 2. fight or quarrel

strike (strīk) *vt.* **struck, struck** or,
esp. for *vt.* 7 & 10, **strick′en, strik′ing**
[< OE. *strican*, to go] 1. to give (a
blow, etc.) to 2. to make by stamping,
etc. [to *strike* coins] 3. to announce
(time), as with a bell: said of clocks,
etc. 4. to ignite (a match) or produce
(a light, etc.) by friction 5. to collide
with or cause to collide [he *struck* his
arm on the door] 6. to attack 7. to
afflict, as with disease, pain, etc. 8. to
come upon; notice, find, etc. 9. to
affect as if by a blow, etc.; occur to
[*struck* by an idea] 10. to remove *from*
a list, record, etc. 11. to make (a
bargain, truce, etc.) 12. to lower (a
sail, flag, etc.) 13. to assume (a pose,
etc.) —*vi.* 1. to hit (*at*) 2. to attack

3. to make sounds as by being struck:
said of a bell, clock, etc. 4. to collide;
hit (*against, on,* or *upon*) 5. to seize
at a bait: said of fish 6. to come
suddenly (*on* or *upon*) 7. to refuse to
continue to work until certain demands
are met 8. to proceed in a new direction —*n.* 1. a striking; specif., a
military attack 2. a refusal by employees to go on working, in an attempt
to gain better working conditions
3. the discovery of a rich deposit of oil,
etc. 4. *Baseball* a pitched ball which
is struck at but missed, fairly delivered
but not struck at, etc. 5. *Bowling* a
knocking down of all the pins on the
first bowl —**strike out** 1. to erase
2. to start out 3. *Baseball* to put out,
or be put out, on three strikes —**strike
up** to begin —**strik′er** *n.*

strik′ing *adj.* very impressive; outstanding, remarkable, etc.

string (strin) *n.* [OE. *streng*] 1. a
thin line of fiber, leather, etc. used as
for tying or pulling 2. a length of like
things on a string [a *string* of pearls]
3. a row or series or number of like
things [a *string* of houses] 4. *a)* a
slender cord bowed, plucked, etc. to
make a musical sound, as on a violin
b) [*pl.*] all the stringed instruments of
an orchestra 5. a fiber of a plant
6. [Colloq.] a condition attached to a
plan, offer, etc. —*vt.* **strung, string′-
ing** 1. to provide with strings 2. to
thread on a string 3. to tie, hang, etc.
with a string 4. to remove the strings
from (beans, etc.) 5. to arrange in a
row 6. to extend [*string* a cable] —**pull
strings** to use influence, often secretly,
to gain advantage —**string′y** *adj.*
-i·er, -i·est

string bean a bean whose thick, unripe pods are eaten as a vegetable

stringed (strind) *adj.* having strings

strin·gent (strin′jənt) *adj.* [see STRICT]
strict; severe —**strin′gen·cy** *n.*

string′er *n.* 1. a long horizontal piece
in a structure 2. a part-time local
news correspondent for a newspaper,
etc. published elsewhere

strip¹ (strip) *vt.* **stripped, strip′ping**
[OE. *strypan*] 1. to remove (the
clothing, etc.) from (a person) 2. to
dispossess of (honors, titles, etc.) 3. to
plunder; rob 4. to take off (a covering)
from (a person or thing) 5. to make
bare by taking away removable parts,
etc. 6. to break the thread of (a bolt,
etc.) or the teeth of (a gear) —*vi.* to
take off all clothing

strip² (strip) *n.* [< ff.] 1. a long, narrow piece, as of land, tape, etc. 2. a runway for airplanes: also **landing strip**

stripe (strīp) *n.* [< MDu. *strip*] 1. a
long, narrow band differing from the
surrounding area 2. a strip of cloth on
a uniform to show rank, years served,
etc. 3. kind; sort —*vt.* **striped,
strip′ing** to mark with stripes

strip·ling (strip′lin) *n.* a youth

strip-tease (strip′tēz′) *n.* a burlesque
performance with music, in which a
woman takes off her clothes slowly and
with suggestive movements

strive (strīv) *vi.* **strove, striv·en**

(striv'n) or **strived, striv'ing** [< OFr. *estrif*, effort] 1. to make great efforts; try very hard 2. to struggle [*strive* against tyranny]

strobe (**light**) (strōb) [< Gr. *strobus*, a twisting around] an electronic tube emitting rapid, brief, and brilliant flashes of light: also **stro·bo·scope** (strō'bə skōp') *n.*

strode (strōd) *pt.* of STRIDE

stroke (strōk) *n.* [ME.] 1. the act of striking; blow, as of an ax 2. a sudden action or event [a *stroke* of luck] 3. a sudden attack, esp. of apoplexy 4. a single, strong effort 5. the sound of striking, as of a clock 6. *a*) a single movement, as with a tool, racket, etc. *b*) any of a series of motions made in swimming, rowing, etc. 7. a mark made by a pen, etc. —*vt.* **stroked, strok'ing** to draw one's hand, etc. gently over the surface of

stroll (strōl) *vi.* [prob. < G. *strolchen*] 1. to walk about leisurely; saunter 2. to wander —*vt.* to stroll along or through —*n.* a leisurely walk

stroll'er *n.* 1. one who strolls 2. a light, chairlike baby carriage

strong (strôŋ) *adj.* [OE. *strang*] 1. *a*) physically powerful *b*) healthy; sound 2. morally or intellectually powerful [a *strong* will] 3. firm; durable [a *strong* fort] 4. powerful in wealth, numbers, etc. 5. of a specified number [troops 50,000 *strong*] 6. having a powerful effect 7. intense in degree or quality [*strong* coffee, a *strong* light, *strong* colors, etc.] 8. forceful, vigorous, etc. —**strong'ly** *adv.*

strong'-arm' *adj.* [Colloq.] using physical force —*vt.* [Colloq.] to use force upon

strong'box' *n.* a heavily made box or safe for storing valuables

strong'hold' *n.* a place having strong defenses; fortress

strong'-mind'ed *adj.* determined; unyielding: also **strong'-willed'**

strong'room' *n.* a strongly built room used for safeguarding valuables

stron·ti·um (strän'shē əm, -tē-) *n.* [< *Strontian*, Scotland, where first found] a metallic chemical element resembling calcium in properties

strop (sträp) *n.* [OE.] a leather band for sharpening razors —*vt.* **stropped, strop'ping** to sharpen on a strop

stro·phe (strō'fē) *n.* [Gr. *strophē*, a turning] a stanza of a poem

strove (strōv) *alt. pt.* of STRIVE

struck (struk) *pt. & pp.* of STRIKE —*adj.* closed or otherwise affected by a labor strike

struc·ture (struk'chər) *n.* [< L. *struere*, arrange] 1. something built or constructed; building, etc. 2. the arrangement of all the parts of a whole 3. something composed of related parts —*vt.* **-tured, -tur·ing** to put together systematically —**struc'tur·al** *adj.*

stru·del (strōō'd'l) *n.* [G.] a pastry made of a thin sheet of dough filled

with apples, etc., rolled up, and baked

strug·gle (strug''l) *vi.* **-gled, -gling** [ME. *strogelen*] 1. to fight violently with an opponent 2. to make great efforts; strive; labor —*n.* 1. great effort 2. conflict; strife

strum (strum) *vt., vi.* **strummed, strum'ming** [echoic] to play (a guitar, etc.) casually or unskillfully

strum·pet (strum'pit) *n.* [ME.] a prostitute

strung (strung) *pt. & pp.* of STRING

strut (strut) *vi.* **strut'ted, strut'ting** [OE. *strutian*, stand rigid] to walk swaggeringly —*n.* 1. a strutting walk 2. a brace fitted into a framework to resist lengthwise pressure

strych·nine (strik'nin, -nīn, -nēn) *n.* [< Gr. *strychnos*, nightshade] a highly poisonous crystalline alkaloid: used in small doses as a stimulant

stub (stub) *n.* [OE. *stybb*] 1. a tree or plant stump 2. a short piece left over 3. any short or blunt projection or thing 4. the part of a ticket, bank check, etc. kept as a record —*vt.* **stubbed, stub'bing** 1. to strike (one's toe, etc.) against something 2. to put out (a cigarette, etc.) by pressing the end against a surface

stub·ble (stub''l) *n.* [< L. *stipula*, a stalk] 1. short stumps of grain left after harvesting 2. any short, bristly growth, as of beard

stub·born (stub'ərn) *adj.* [ME. *stoburn*] 1. refusing to yield or comply; obstinate 2. done in an obstinate or persistent way 3. hard to handle, etc. —**stub'born·ness** *n.*

stub·by (stub'ē) *adj.* **-bi·er, -bi·est** 1. covered with stubs or stubble 2. short and dense 3. short and thickset

stuc·co (stuk'ō) *n., pl.* **-coes, -cos** [It.] plaster or cement for surfacing walls, etc. —*vt.* **-coed, -co·ing** to cover with stucco

stuck (stuk) *pt. & pp.* of STICK

stuck'-up' *adj.* [Colloq.] snobbish

stud¹ (stud) *n.* [OE. *studu*, post] 1. any of a series of small knobs, etc. used to ornament a surface 2. a small, buttonlike device for fastening collars, etc. 3. an upright piece in a building frame, to which laths, etc. are nailed —*vt.* **stud'ded, stud'ding** 1. to set or decorate with studs, etc. 2. to be set thickly on [rocks *stud* the hill]

stud² (stud) *n.* [OE. *stod*] a male animal, esp. a horse (**stud'horse'**), kept for breeding

stud'book' *n.* a register of purebred animals, esp. racehorses

stud'ding *n.* 1. studs, esp. for walls 2. material for studs

stu·dent (stōōd''nt) *n.* [< L. *studere*, to study] 1. one who studies or investigates 2. one who is enrolled for study at a school, college, etc.

stud·ied (stud'ēd) *adj.* 1. prepared by careful study 2. deliberate

stu·di·o (stōō'dē ō') *n., pl.* **-os** [It., a study] 1. a place where an artist, etc.

works or where dancing lessons, etc. are given 2. a place where movies, radio or TV programs, etc. are produced

stu·dio couch a couch that can be opened into a full-size bed

stu·di·ous (stōō′dē əs) *adj.* 1. fond of study 2. attentive; zealous

stud·y (stud′ē) *n., pl.* **-ies** [< L. *studere,* to study] 1. the acquiring of knowledge, as by reading 2. careful examination of a subject, event, etc. 3. a branch of learning 4. [*pl.*] education; schooling 5. earnest effort or deep thought 6. a room for study, etc. —*vt.* **-ied, -y·ing** 1. to try to learn by reading, etc. 2. to investigate carefully 3. to read (a book, etc.) intently —*vi.* 1. to study something 2. to be a student 3. to meditate

stuff (stuf) *n.* [< OFr. *estofe*] 1. the material out of which anything is made 2. essence; character 3. matter in general 4. cloth, esp. woolen cloth 5. objects; things 6. worthless objects; junk 7. [Colloq.] ability, skill, etc. —*vt.* 1. to fill or pack; specif., *a)* to fill the skin of (a dead animal) in taxidermy *b)* to fill (a fowl, etc.) with seasoning, bread crumbs, etc. before roasting 2. to fill too full; cram 3. to plug; block —*vi.* to eat too much

stuffed shirt [Slang] a pompous, pretentious person

stuff·ing *n.* something used to stuff, as padding in upholstery, a seasoned mixture for stuffing fowl, etc.

stuff·y *adj.* **-i·er, -i·est** 1. poorly ventilated; close 2. having the nasal passages stopped up, as from a cold 3. [Colloq.] dull or stodgy

stul·ti·fy (stul′tə fī′) *vt.* **-fied′, -fy′ing** [< L. *stultus,* foolish + *facere,* make] 1. to make seem foolish, stupid, etc. 2. to make worthless, etc.

stum·ble (stum′b'l) *vi.* **-bled, -bling** [ME. *stumblen*] 1. to trip in walking, running, etc. 2. to walk unsteadily 3. to speak, act, etc. in a blundering way 4. to do wrong 5. to come by chance —*n.* a stumbling —**stum′bler** *n.*

stumbling block a difficulty

stump (stump) *n.* [ME. *stumpe*] 1. the end of a tree or plant left in the ground after the upper part has been cut off 2. the part of a leg, tooth, etc. left after the rest has been removed 3. the place where a political speech is made —*vt.* 1. to travel over (a district) making political speeches 2. [Colloq.] to puzzle or perplex —*vi.* 1. to walk heavily 2. to travel about making political speeches —**stump′y** *adj.*

stun (stun) *vt.* **stunned, stun′ning** [< L. *ex-,* intens. + *tonare,* to crash] 1. to make unconscious, as by a blow 2. to daze; shock

stung (stuŋ) *pt. & pp.* of STING

stunk (stuŋk) *pp. & alt. pt.* of STINK

stun·ning (stun′iŋ) *adj.* [Colloq.] remarkably attractive, excellent, etc.

stunt¹ (stunt) *vt.* [OE., stupid] 1. to check the growth or development of 2. to hinder (growth, etc.)

stunt² (stunt) *n.* [< ?] something done to show one's skill or daring, get attention, etc. —*vi.* to do a stunt

stu·pe·fy (stōō′pə fī′, styōō′-) *vt.* **-fied′, -fy′ing** [< L. *stupere,* be stunned + *facere,* make] 1. to produce stupor in; stun 2. to amaze; bewilder —**stu′pe·fac′tion** (-fak′shən) *n.*

stu·pen·dous (stōō pen′dəs, styōō-) *adj.* [< L. *stupere,* be stunned] 1. astonishing 2. astonishingly great

stu·pid (stōō′pid, styōō′-) *adj.* [see prec.] 1. lacking normal intelligence 2. foolish; silly [a *stupid* idea] 3. dull and boring —**stu·pid′i·ty** *n., pl.* **-ties**

stu·por (stōō′pər, styōō′-) *n.* [L.] a state in which the mind and senses are dulled; loss of sensibility

stur·dy (stur′dē) *adj.* **-di·er, -di·est** [< OFr. *estourdi,* stunned] 1. firm; resolute 2. strong; vigorous —**stur′di·ly** *adv.* —**stur′di·ness** *n.*

stur·geon (stur′jən) *n.* [< OFr. *esturjon*] a large food fish valuable as a source of caviar

stut·ter (stut′ər) *n., vt., vi.* [< ME. *stutten*] stammer

sty¹ (stī) *n., pl.* **sties** [< OE. *sti, hall*] 1. a pen for pigs 2. any foul place

STURGEON

sty², **stye** (stī) *n., pl.* **sties** [ult. < OE. *stigan,* to rise] a small, inflamed swelling on the rim of an eyelid

Styg·i·an (stij′ē ən, stij′ən) *adj.* 1. of the Styx 2. [*also* s-] *a)* infernal *b)* dark or gloomy

style (stīl) *n.* [< L. *stilus,* pointed writing tool] 1. a stylus 2. *a)* manner of expression in language *b)* characteristic manner of expression, design, etc., in an art, period, etc. *c)* excellence of expression 3. *a)* fashion *b)* something stylish —*vt.* **styled, styl′ing** 1. to name; call 2. to design the style of

styl·ish (stīl′ish) *adj.* conforming to current style, as in dress; fashionable

styl·ist *n.* a writer, etc. whose work has style and distinction —**sty·lis′tic** *adj.* —**sty·lis′ti·cal·ly** *adv.*

styl·ize (stī′līz) *vt.* **-ized, -iz·ing** to design or depict according to a style rather than nature

sty·lus (stī′ləs) *n., pl.* **-lus·es, -li** (-lī) [L., for *stilus,* pointed tool] 1. a sharp, pointed marking device 2. *a)* a pointed device for cutting the grooves of a phonograph record *b)* a phonograph needle

sty·mie (stī′mē) *n.* [prob. < Scot., person partially blind] *Golf* a situation in which a ball to be putted has another ball between it and the hole —*vt.* **-mied, -mie·ing** to block; impede Also **stymy -mied, -my·ing**

styp·tic (stip′tik) *adj.* [< Gr. *styphein,* to contract] tending to halt bleeding; astringent —**styp′sis** *n.*

styptic pencil a piece of a styptic substance to stop minor bleeding

Sty·ro·foam (stī′rə fōm′) *a trademark for* a rigid, foamy-looking, lightweight plastic —*n.* [*also* s-] this plastic

Styx (stiks) *Gr. Myth.* the river crossed by dead souls entering Hades

suave (swäv) *adj.* [< L. *suavis*, sweet] smoothly gracious or polite; polished —**suave′ly** *adv.* —**suav′i·ty** *n.*

sub (sub) *n. clipped form of:* 1. SUBMARINE 2. SUBSTITUTE —*vi.* **subbed, sub′bing** [Colloq.] to be a substitute (*for* someone)

sub- [< L. *sub*, under] *a prefix meaning:* 1. beneath [*subsoil*] 2. lower than [*subaltern*] 3. to a lesser degree than [*subtropical*]

sub. 1. substitute(s) 2. suburb(an)

sub·a·tom·ic (sub′ə täm′ik) *adj.* smaller than an atom

sub′branch′ *n.* a branch division

sub′com·mit′tee *n.* a small committee chosen from a main committee

sub′com′pact *n.* a model of automobile smaller than a compact

sub·con′scious *adj.* occurring with little or no conscious perception on the part of the individual: said of mental processes —**the subconscious** subconscious mental activity —**sub·con′scious·ly** *adv.*

sub·con′ti·nent *n.* a large land mass smaller than a continent

sub·con′tract *n.* a secondary contract undertaking some or all obligations of another contract —*vt., vi.* to make a subcontract (for) —**sub·con′trac·tor** (-ər) *n.*

sub′cul′ture *n.* 1. a distinctive social group within a larger social group 2. its cultural patterns

sub·cu·ta·ne·ous (sub′kyōō tā′nē əs) *adj.* beneath the skin

sub·dea′con *n.* a cleric ranking just below a deacon

sub′deb′ (-deb′) *n.* a girl not quite of debutante age

sub′dis′trict *n.* a subdivision of a district

sub′di·vide′ *vt., vi.* -**vid′ed,** -**vid′ing** 1. to divide further 2. to divide (land) into small parcels —**sub′di·vi′sion** *n.*

sub·due (səb dōō′, -dyōō′) *vt.* -**dued′,** -**du′ing** [< L. *subducere*, take away] 1. to conquer 2. to overcome; control 3. to make less intense; diminish

sub′head′ *n.* a subordinate heading or title, as for part of an article

subj. 1. subject 2. subjunctive

sub·ject (sub′jikt; *for v.* səb jekt′) *adj.* [< L. *sub-*, under + *jacere*, throw] 1. under the authority or control of another 2. having a tendency [*subject* to anger] 3. exposed [*subject* to censure] 4. contingent upon [*subject* to approval] —*n.* 1. one under the authority or control of another 2. one made to undergo a treatment, experiment, etc. 3. something dealt with in discussion, study, etc.; theme 4. Gram. the word or words in a sentence about which something is said —*vt.* 1. to bring under the authority or control of 2. to cause to undergo something [to *subject* him to questioning] —**sub·jec′tion** *n.*

sub·jec·tive (səb jek′tiv) *adj.* of or resulting from the feelings of the person thinking; not objective; personal —**sub·jec·tiv·i·ty** (sub′jek tiv′ə tē) *n.*

sub·join (sub join′) *vt.* [see SUB- & JOIN] to append

sub·ju·gate (sub′jə gāt′) *vt.* -**gat′ed,** -**gat′ing** [< L. *sub-*, under + *jugum*, a yoke] to conquer or make subservient —**sub′ju·ga′tion** *n.*

sub·junc·tive (səb juŋk′tiv) *adj.* [< L. *subjungere*, subjoin] designating or of that mood of a verb used to express supposition, desire, possibility, etc., rather than to state an actual fact

sub·lease (sub′lēs′; *for v.* sub lēs′) *n.* a lease granted by a lessee —*vt.* -**leased′,** -**leas′ing** to grant or hold a sublease of

sub·let (sub let′) *vt.* -**let′,** -**let′ting** 1. to let to another (property which one is renting) 2. to let out (work) to a subcontractor

sub·li·mate (sub′lə māt′) *vt.* -**mat′ed,** -**mat′ing** 1. to sublime (a solid) 2. to express (unacceptable impulses) in acceptable forms, often unconsciously —**sub′li·ma′tion** *n.*

sub·lime (sə blīm′) *adj.* [< L. *sub-*, up to + *limen*, lintel] 1. noble; exalted 2. inspiring awe or admiration —*vt.* -**limed′,** -**lim′ing** to purify (a solid) by heating to a gaseous state and condensing the vapor back into solid form —**sub·lim′i·ty** (-blim′ə tē) *n.*

sub·lim·i·nal (sub lim′ə n'l) *adj.* [< SUB- + L. *limen*, threshold + -AL] below the threshold of conscious awareness

sub·ma·chine gun (sub′mə shēn′) a portable, automatic firearm

sub·mar·gin·al (sub mär′ji n'l) *adj.* below minimum standards

sub·ma·rine (sub′mə rēn′; *for n.* usually sub′mə rēn′) *adj.* being, living, etc. underwater —*n.* a ship, esp. a warship, that can operate underwater

submarine sandwich *same as* HERO SANDWICH

sub·merge (səb murj′) *vt., vi.* -**merged′,** -**merg′ing** [< L. *sub-*, under + *mergere*, to plunge] to place or sink beneath the surface, as of water —**sub·mer′gence** *n.*

sub·merse (-murs′) *vt.* -**mersed′,** -**mers′ing** *same as* SUBMERGE —**sub·mers′i·ble** *adj.* —**sub·mer′sion** *n.*

sub·mis·sion (səb mish′ən) *n.* 1. a submitting or surrendering 2. obedience; resignation 3. submissiveness —**sub·mis′sive** *adj.*

sub·mit (-mit′) *vt.* -**mit′ted,** -**mit′ting** [< L. *sub-*, under + *mittere*, send] 1. to present to others for consideration, etc. 2. to yield to the power or control of another 3. to offer as an opinion —*vi.* to yield; give in

sub·nor·mal (sub nôr′m'l) *adj.* below normal, esp. in intelligence

sub·or·bit·al (-ôr′bit 'l) *adj.* designating a space flight in which the spacecraft follows a short-range trajectory instead of going into orbit

sub·or·di·nate (sə bôr′də nit; *for v.* -nāt′) *adj.* [< L. *sub-*, under + *ordinare*, to order] 1. below another in rank, importance, etc. **2.** under the authority of another **3.** *Gram.* that cannot function syntactically without other elements *[a subordinate clause]* —*n.* a subordinate person or thing —*vt.* **-nat′ed, -nat′ing** to place in a subordinate position —**sub·or′di·na′tion** *n.*

sub·orn (sə bôrn′) *vt.* [< L. *sub-,* under + *ornare,* adorn] to induce (another) to commit perjury —**subor·na·tion** (sub′ôr nā′shən) *n.*

sub′plot′ *n.* a secondary plot in a play, novel, etc.

sub·poe·na (sə pē′nə) *n.* [< L. *sub poena,* under penalty] a written legal order directing a person to appear in court to testify, etc. —*vt.* **-naed, -na·ing** to summon with such an order Also sp. **sub·pe′na**

sub·pro·fes·sion·al (sub′prə fesh′ən ′l) *n.* same as PARAPROFESSIONAL

sub ro·sa (sub rō′zə) [L., under the rose] secretly; privately

sub·scribe (səb skrīb′) *vt., vi.* **-scribed′, -scrib′ing** [< L. *sub-,* under + *scribere,* write] **1.** to sign (one's name) on a document, etc. **2.** to give support or consent (to) **3.** to promise to contribute (money) **4.** to agree to receive and pay for a periodical, service, etc. (with *to*) —**sub·scrib′er** *n.*

sub′script′ (-skript′) *n.* [see prec.] a figure, letter, or symbol written below and to the side of another

sub·scrip′tion (-skrip′shən) *n.* **1.** a subscribing **2.** money subscribed **3.** a formal agreement to receive and pay for a periodical, etc.

sub·se·quent (sub′si kwənt) *adj.* [< L. *sub-,* after + *sequi,* follow] coming after; following —**subsequent to** after —**sub′se·quent·ly** *adv.*

sub·ser·vi·ent (səb sur′vē ənt) *adj.* **1.** that is of service, esp. in a subordinate capacity **2.** submissive; servile —**sub·ser′vi·ence** *n.*

sub·side (səb sīd′) *vi.* **-sid′ed, -sid′ing** [< L. *sub-,* under + *sidere,* settle] **1.** to sink to a lower level or to the bottom **2.** to become less active, intense, etc. —**sub·sid′ence** *n.*

sub·sid·i·ar·y (səb sid′ē er′ē) *adj.* [see SUBSIDY] **1.** giving aid, service, etc.; auxiliary **2.** being in a subordinate relationship —*n., pl.* **-ies** one that is subsidiary; specif., a company controlled by another company

sub·si·dize (sub′sə dīz′) *vt.* **-dized′, -diz′ing** to support with a subsidy —**sub′si·di·za′tion** *n.*

sub·si·dy (sub′sə dē) *n., pl.* **-dies** [< L. *subsidium,* auxiliary forces] a grant of money, as from a government to a private enterprise

sub·sist (səb sist′) *vi.* [< L. *sub-,* under + *sistere,* stand] **1.** to continue to be or exist **2.** to continue to live; remain alive (*on* or *by*)

sub·sist′ence *n.* **1.** existence **2.** the act of providing sustenance **3.** means of support or livelihood, esp. the barest means

sub·soil (sub′soil′) *n.* the layer of soil beneath the surface soil

sub·son·ic (sub sän′ik) *adj.* designat-

ing, of, or moving at a speed less than that of sound

sub·stance (sub′stəns) *n.* [< L. *substare,* exist] **1.** the real or essential part of anything; essence **2.** the physical matter of which a thing consists **3.** *a)* solid or substantial quality *b)* consistency; body **4.** the real meaning; gist **5.** wealth **6.** a drug, esp. one (**controlled substance**) legally regulated

sub·stand′ard *adj.* below standard

sub·stan·tial (səb stan′shəl) *adj.* **1.** having substance **2.** real; true **3.** strong; solid **4.** ample; large **5.** important **6.** wealthy **7.** with regard to essential elements —**sub·stan′tial·ly** *adv.*

sub·stan′ti·ate′ (-stan′shē āt′) *vt.* **-at′ed, -at′ing** [see SUBSTANCE] to show to be true or real by giving evidence —**sub·stan′ti·a′tion** *n.*

sub·stan·tive (sub′stən tiv) *adj.* [see SUBSTANCE] of or dealing with essentials —*n. Gram.* a noun or any word or group of words used as a noun

sub′sta′tion *n.* a branch station, as of a post office

sub·sti·tute (sub′stə tōōt′) *n.* [< L. *sub-,* under + *statuere,* put] a person or thing serving or used in place of another —*vt., vi.* **-tut′ed, -tut′ing** to put, use, or serve in place of (another) —**sub′sti·tu′tion** *n.*

sub·stra·tum (sub′strāt′əm) *n., pl.* **-ta** (-ə), **-tums** [see SUB- & STRATUM] a part, substance, etc. which lies beneath and supports another

sub′struc′ture *n.* a part or structure that is a support, base, etc.

sub·sume (səb sōōm′) *vt.* **-sumed′, -sum′ing** [< L. *sub-,* under + *sumere,* take] to include within a larger class

sub′teen′ *n.* a child who is nearly a teen-ager

sub·ten′ant *n.* a person who rents from a tenant —**sub·ten′an·cy** *n.*

sub·ter·fuge (sub′tər fyōōj′) *n.* [< L. *subter-,* below + *fugere,* flee] any plan or action used to hide or evade

sub·ter·ra·ne·an (sub′tə rā′nē ən) *adj.* [< L. *sub-,* under + *terra,* earth] **1.** underground **2.** secret; hidden

sub′ti′tle *n.* **1.** a secondary or explanatory title **2.** a line or lines as of dialogue shown on a movie screen or TV tube —*vt.* **-ti′tled, -ti′tling** to add a subtitle or subtitles to

sub·tle (sut′'l) *adj.* **-tler, -tlest** [< L. *subtilis,* fine, thin] **1.** thin; not dense **2.** mentally keen **3.** delicately skillful **4.** crafty **5.** not obvious —**sub′tle·ty** *n., pl.* **-ties** —**sub′tly** *adv.*

sub′to′tal *n.* a total that is part of a complete total —*vt., vi.* **-taled** or **-talled, -tal·ing** or **-tal·ling** to add up so as to form a subtotal

sub·tract (səb trakt′) *vt., vi.* [< L. *sub-,* under + *trahere,* to draw] to take away or deduct, as one quantity from another —**sub·trac′tion** *n.*

sub·tra·hend (sub′trə hend′) *n.* a quantity to be subtracted from another

sub·trop′i·cal *adj.* of, characteristic of, or bordering on the tropics

sub·urb (sub′ərb) *n.* [< L. *sub-,* near + *urbs,* town] a district, town, etc. on the outskirts of a city —**sub·ur·ban** (sə bur′bən) *adj.*

sub·ur·ban·ite′ (-īt′) *n.* a person living in a suburb

sub·ur·bi·a (sə bur′bē ə) *n.* the suburbs or suburbanites collectively

sub·ven·tion (səb ven′shən) *n.* [< LL. *subventio*, aid] a subsidy

sub·ver·sive (səb vur′siv) *adj.* tending to subvert —*n.* a subversive person

sub·vert (səb vurt′) *vt.* [< L. *sub-*, under + *vertere*, to turn] 1. to overthrow or destroy (something established) 2. to corrupt, as in morals —**sub·ver′sion** (-vur′zhən) *n.*

sub·way (sub′wā′) *n.* an underground, metropolitan electric railway

suc- *same as* SUB-: used before *c*

suc·ceed (sək sēd′) *vi.* [< L. *sub-*, under + *cedere*, to go] 1. to follow, as in office 2. to be successful —*vt.* to come after; follow

suc·cess (sək ses′) *n.* 1. a favorable result 2. the gaining of wealth, fame, etc. 3. a successful person or thing

suc·cess′ful *adj.* 1. turning out as was hoped for 2. having gained wealth, fame, etc. —**suc·cess′ful·ly** *adv.*

suc·ces·sion (sək sesh′ən) *n.* 1. *a)* the act of succeeding another, as to an office *b)* the right to do this 2. a number of persons or things coming one after another

suc·ces·sive (-ses′iv) *adj.* coming one after another —**suc·ces′sive·ly** *adv.*

suc·ces′sor *n.* one who succeeds another, as to an office

suc·cinct (sək siŋkt′) *adj.* [< L. *sub-*, under + *cingere*, to gird] clear and brief; terse —**suc·cinct′ly** *adv.* —**suc·cinct′ness** *n.*

suc·cor (suk′ər) *vt.* [< L. *sub-*, under + *currere*, to run] to help in time of need or distress —*n.* aid; relief

suc·co·tash (suk′ə tash′) *n.* [< AmInd.] a dish consisting of lima beans and corn kernels cooked together

suc·cu·lent (suk′yoo lənt) *adj.* [< L. *sucus*, juice] full of juice; juicy —**suc′cu·lence, suc′cu·len·cy** *n.*

suc·cumb (sə kum′) *vi.* [< L. *sub-*, under + *cumbere*, to lie] 1. to give way (*to*); yield 2. to die

such (such) *adj.* [OE. *swilc*] 1. *a)* of the kind mentioned *b)* of the same or a similar kind 2. whatever [*at such* time as you go] 3. so extreme, so much, etc. [*such an honor*] 4. so great a degree [*such good news*] —*pron.* 1. such a person or thing 2. that suggested [*such* was his nature] —**as such** 1. as being what is indicated 2. in itself —**such as** for example

such and such (being) something particular but not named or specified [*such and such* a place]

such′like′ *adj.* of such a kind —*n.* persons or things of such a kind

suck (suk) *vt.* [< OE. *sucan*] 1. to draw (liquid) into the mouth 2. to take in as if by sucking 3. to suck liquid from (fruit, etc.) 4. *a)* to

dissolve by holding in the mouth and licking *b)* to hold in the mouth and draw on —*vi.* to suck something —*n.* the act of sucking

suck′er *n.* 1. one that sucks 2. a freshwater, bony fish with a mouth adapted for sucking 3. a part used for sucking or for holding fast by suction 4. a lollipop 5. a shoot from the roots or stem of a plant 6. [Slang] one easily cheated

suck·le (suk′'l) *vt., vi.* -led, -ling [ME. *sokelen*] 1. to feed at the breast or udder 2. to rear; foster

suck′ling *n.* an unweaned child or young animal

su·crose (soo′krōs) *n.* [< Fr. *sucre*, sugar] a sugar extracted from sugar cane or sugar beets

suc·tion (suk′shən) *n.* [< L. *sugere*, to suck] 1. a sucking 2. production of a partial vacuum so that external pressure forces fluid in or causes something to adhere to a surface

Su·dan (soo dan′) country in NE Africa: 967,500 sq. mi.; pop. 14,770,000; cap. Khartoum —**Su′da·nese′** (-də nēz′) *adj., n.*

sud·den (sud′'n) *adj.* [ult. < L. *sub-*, under + *ire*, go] 1. happening or coming unexpectedly 2. sharp or abrupt 3. quick or hasty —**all of a sudden** unexpectedly —**sud′den·ly** *adv.* —**sud′den·ness** *n.*

sudden death *Sports* an extra period added to a tied game, the game ending as soon as one side scores

suds (sudz) *n.pl.* [prob. < MDu. *sudse*, marsh water] 1. soapy, frothy water 2. foam —**suds′y** *adj.*

sue (soo) *vt., vi.* sued, su′ing [< L. *sequi*, follow] 1. to appeal (to); petition 2. to prosecute in a court in seeking redress of wrongs, etc.

suede, suède (swād) *n.* [< Fr. *gants de Suède*, Swedish gloves] 1. tanned leather with the flesh side buffed into a nap 2. a cloth like this

su·et (soo′it) *n.* [< L. *sebum*, fat] the hard fat of cattle and sheep; used in cooking and as tallow

Su·ez Canal (soo ez′) ship canal joining the Mediterranean & Red seas

suf- *same as* SUB-: used before *f*

suf·fer (suf′ər) *vt., vi.* [< L. *sub-*, under + *ferre*, to bear] 1. to undergo or endure (pain, injury, loss, etc.) 2. to experience (any process) 3. to permit; tolerate —**suf′fer·er** *n.*

suf′fer·ance *n.* 1. the capacity to endure pain, etc. 2. consent, permission, etc. implied by failure to prohibit

suf′fer·ing *n.* 1. the bearing of pain, distress, etc. 2. something suffered

suf·fice (sə fīs′) *vi.* -ficed′, -fic′ing [< L. *sub-*, under + *facere*, make] to be enough or adequate

suf·fi·cient (sə fish′'nt) *adj.* as much as is needed; enough; adequate —**suf·fi′cien·cy** *n.* —**suf·fi′cient·ly** *adv.*

suf·fix (suf′iks) *n.* [< L. *sub-*, under

+ *figere*, fix] a syllable or syllables added at the end of a word to alter its meaning, etc. (Ex.: *-ness* in *darkness*)

suf·fo·cate (suf′ə kāt′) *vt.* **-cat′ed, -cat′ing** [< L. *sub-*, under + *fauces*, throat] **1.** to kill by cutting off the supply of air for breathing **2.** to smother, stifle, etc. —*vi.* **1.** to die by being suffocated **2.** to choke; stifle —**suf′fo·ca′tion** *n.*

suf·fra·gan (suf′rə gən) *n.* [< ML. *suffraganus*] a bishop who is an assistant to another bishop

suf·frage (suf′rij) *n.* [< L. *suffragium*] **1.** a vote or voting **2.** the right to vote; franchise —**suf′fra·gist** *n.*

suf·fra·gette (suf′rə jet′) *n.* a woman who advocates female suffrage

suf·fuse (sə fyooz′) *vt.* **-fused′, -fus′ing** [< L. *sub-*, under + *fundere*, pour] to overspread so as to fill with a glow, etc. —**suf·fu′sion** *n.*

sug·ar (shoog′ər) *n.* [< Sans. *śarkarā*] any of a class of sweet, soluble carbohydrates, as sucrose, glucose, etc.; specif., sucrose from sugar cane and sugar beets, used for sweetening —*vt.* to sweeten, cover, etc. with sugar —*vi.* to form sugar crystals —**sug′ar·less** *adj.* —**sug′ar·y** *adj.*

sugar beet a beet having a white root with a high sugar content

sugar cane a very tall tropical grass cultivated as a source of sugar

sug′ar·coat′ *vt.* **1.** to coat with sugar **2.** to make seem more pleasant

sug′ar·plum′ (-plum′) *n.* a round piece of sugary candy; bonbon

sug·gest (səg jest′, sə-) *vt.* [< L. *sub-*, under + *gerere*, carry] **1.** to bring to the mind for consideration **2.** to call to mind by association of ideas **3.** to propose as a possibility **4.** to show indirectly; imply

sug·gest′i·ble *adj.* readily influenced by suggestion —**sug·gest′i·bil′i·ty** *n.*

sug·ges′tion (-jes′chən) *n.* **1.** a suggesting or being suggested **2.** something suggested **3.** a hint or trace

sug·ges′tive *adj.* **1.** that tends to suggest ideas **2.** tending to suggest something considered improper or indecent —**sug·ges′tive·ly** *adv.*

su·i·cide (sōō′ə sīd′) *n.* [L. *sui*, of oneself + -CIDE] **1.** the act of killing oneself intentionally **2.** one who commits suicide —**su′i·cid′al** *adj.*

su′i·ci·dol′o·gy (-sī däl′ə jē) *n.* the study of suicide, its causes, and its prevention

su·i ge·ne·ris (sōō′ē jen′ər is) [L., of his own kind] altogether unique

suit (sōōt) *n.* [< L. *sequi*, follow] **1.** a set of clothes; esp., a coat and trousers (or skirt) **2.** any of the four sets of playing cards **3.** action to secure justice in a court of law **4.** an act of suing, pleading, etc. **5.** courtship —*vt.* **1.** to be appropriate to **2.** to make right or appropriate; fit **3.** to please; satisfy [nothing *suits* him] —**follow suit** to follow the example set —**suit oneself** to act according to one's own wishes —**suit up** to put on a spacesuit, an athletic

uniform, etc. in preparing for a particular activity

suit′a·ble *adj.* that suits a given purpose, etc.; appropriate —**suit′a·bil′i·ty** *n.* —**suit′a·bly** *adv.*

suit′case′ *n.* a rectangular case for clothes, etc. when traveling

suite (swēt; *for 3, occas.* sōōt) *n.* [Fr.: see SUIT] **1.** a group of attendants; staff **2.** a set of connected rooms, as an apartment **3.** a set of matched furniture for a given room

suit′ing *n.* cloth for making suits

suit′or *n.* a man courting a woman

su·ki·ya·ki (sōō′kē yä′kē) *n.* [Jap.] a Japanese dish of thinly sliced meat and vegetables, cooked quickly

Suk·kot, Suk·koth (sōō kōt′, sook′-ōs) *n.* [Heb., lit., tabernacles] a Jewish fall festival commemorating the wandering of the Jews after the Exodus

sul·fa (sul′fə) *adj.* designating or of drugs of the sulfanilamide type, used against some bacterial infections

sul·fa·nil·a·mide (sul′fə nil′ə mīd′) *n.* a white crystalline compound once used in treating certain infections

sul·fate (sul′fāt) *n.* a salt or ester of sulfuric acid

sul′fide (-fīd) *n.* a compound of sulfur with another element or a radical

sul·fur (sul′fər) *n.* [L. *sulphur*] a pale-yellow, nonmetallic chemical element: it burns with a blue flame and a stifling odor: also **sulphur**

sul·fu·ric (sul fyoor′ik) *adj.* of or containing sulfur

sulfuric acid an oily, colorless, corrosive liquid used in making dyes, explosives, fertilizers, etc.

sul·fu·rous (sul′fər əs; *for 1, usually* sul fyoor′əs) *adj.* **1.** of or containing sulfur **2.** like burning sulfur in odor, color, etc.

sulk (sulk) *vi.* [< ff.] to be sulky —*n.* [*often pl.*] a sulky mood (with *the*)

sulk·y (sul′kē) *adj.* **-i·er, -i·est** [prob. < OE. *-seolcan*, become slack] sullen; glum —*n., pl.* **-ies** a light, two-wheeled carriage for one person —**sulk′i·ly** *adv.* —**sulk′i·ness** *n.*

sul·len (sul′ən) *adj.* [< L. *solus*, alone] **1.** showing resentment and ill humor by morose, unsociable withdrawal; glum **2.** gloomy; dismal —**sul′len·ly** *adv.* —**sul′len·ness** *n.*

sul·ly (sul′ē) *vt.* **-lied, -ly·ing** [prob. < OFr. *souiller*] to soil, tarnish, besmirch, etc., esp. by disgracing

sul·phur (sul′fər) *n. var. of* SULFUR

sul·tan (sul′t′n) *n.* [Fr. < Ar. *sulṭān*] a Moslem ruler

sul·tan·a (sul tan′ə) *n.* a sultan's wife, mother, sister, or daughter

sul·tan·ate (sul′t′n it, -āt′) *n.* a sultan's authority, office, or domain

sul·try (sul′trē) *adj.* **-tri·er, -tri·est** [< SWELTER] **1.** oppressively hot and moist **2.** inflamed, as with passion

sum (sum) *n.* [< L. *summus*, highest] **1.** an amount of money **2.** gist; summary **3.** the result obtained by adding quantities; total **4.** a problem in arithmetic —*vt.* **summed, sum′ming** to get the sum of by adding —**sum up** to summarize

su·mac, su·mach (shōō′mak, sōō′-) *n.* [< Ar. *summāq*] 1. any of numerous nonpoisonous plants with cone-shaped clusters of red fruit 2. any of several related poisonous plants

Su·ma·tra (soo mä′trə) large island of Indonesia —**Su·ma′tran** *adj., n.*

sum·ma·rize (sum′ə rīz′) *vt.* -**rized′,** -**riz′ing** to make or be a summary of

sum·ma·ry (sum′ə rē) *adj.* [< L. *summa,* a sum] 1. summarizing; concise 2. prompt and unceremonious 3. hasty and arbitrary —*n., pl.* -**ries** a brief report covering the main points; digest —**sum·mar·i·ly** (sə mer′ə lē, sum′ə rə lē) *adv.*

sum·ma·tion (sə mā′shən) *n.* a final summary of arguments, as in a trial

sum·mer (sum′ər) *n.* [< OE. *sumor*] the warmest season of the year, following spring —*adj.* of or for summer —*vi.* to pass the summer —**sum′mer·y** *adj.*

sum′mer·house′ *n.* a small, open structure in a garden, place, etc.

summer sausage a type of hard, dried and smoked sausage

sum′mer·time′ *n.* summer

sum·mit (sum′it) *n.* [< L. *summus,* highest] 1. the highest point; top 2. the highest degree or state; acme

sum′mit·ry (-i trē) *n.* the use of conferences between the heads of state to resolve problems of diplomacy

sum·mon (sum′ən) *vt.* [< L. *sub-,* secretly + *monere,* warn] 1. to call together; order to convene 2. to call or send for with authority 3. to call forth; rouse [*summon* (up) your strength] —**sum′mon·er** *n.*

sum·mons (-ənz) *n., pl.* -**mons·es** [see prec.] 1. an order or command to come, attend, etc. 2. *Law* an official order to appear in court

su·mo (wrestling) (sōō′mō) [Jap.] [*sometimes* S-] a Japanese kind of formalized wrestling by heavy men

sump·tu·ous (sump′choo wəs) *adj.* [< L. *sumptus,* expense] 1. costly; lavish 2. magnificent or splendid

sun (sun) *n.* [OE. *sunne*] 1. the self-luminous, gaseous sphere about which the earth and other planets revolve 2. the heat or light of the sun 3. any star that is the center of a planetary system —*vt.* **sunned, sun′ning** to warm, dry, tan, etc. in the sunlight

Sun. Sunday

sun′bathe′ (-bāth′) *vi.* -**bathed′,** -**bath′ing** to expose the body to direct sunlight —**sun bath**

sun′beam′ *n.* a beam of sunlight

Sun′belt′ *n.* those States of the South and Southwest with a sunny climate and expanding economy: also **Sun Belt**

sun′bon′net *n.* a bonnet for shading the face and neck from the sun

sun′burn′ (-bʉrn′) *n.* inflammation of the skin from exposure to the sun's rays or to a sunlamp —*vi., vt.* -**burned′** or -**burnt′,** -**burn′ing** to get or cause to get a sunburn

sun′burst′ *n.* 1. sudden sunlight 2. a decoration representing the sun with spreading rays

sun·dae (sun′dē, -dā) *n.* [prob. < ff.] a serving of ice cream covered with a syrup, fruit, nuts, etc.

Sun·day (sun′dē, -dā) *n.* [OE. *sunnandæg,* lit., sun day] the first day of the week: set aside as a day of worship by most Christians

sun·der (sun′dər) *vt., vi.* [< OE. *sunder,* asunder] to break apart; split

sun′di′al *n.* an instrument that shows time by the shadow of a pointer cast by the sun on a dial

sun′down′ (-doun′) *n.* same as SUNSET

sun′dries (-drēz) *n.pl.* sundry items

sun′dry (-drē) *adj.* [< OE. *sunder,* apart] miscellaneous

SUNDIAL

sun′fish′ *n., pl.:* see FISH 1. any of a family of freshwater fishes of N.America 2. a large, sluggish ocean fish

sun′flow′er *n.* a tall plant having yellow, daisylike flowers

sung (suŋ) *pp. & rare pt.* of SING

sun′glass′es *n.pl.* eyeglasses with tinted lenses to shade the eyes

sunk (suŋk) *pp. & alt. pt.* of SINK

sunk′en (-ən) *adj.* 1. submerged 2. below the general level [a *sunken* patio] 3. hollow [*sunken* cheeks]

sun′lamp′ *n.* an ultraviolet-ray lamp, used therapeutically

sun′light′ *n.* the light of the sun

sun′lit′ *adj.* lighted by the sun

sun′ny (-ē) *adj.* -**ni·er, -ni·est** 1. full of sunshine 2. bright; cheerful 3. of or like the sun —**sun′ni·ness** *n.*

sunny side 1. the sunlit side 2. the brighter aspect —**on the sunny side** of younger than (a given age) —**sunny side up** fried unturned and with unbroken yolk [eggs *sunny side up*]

sun′rise′ (-rīz′) *n.* 1. the daily appearance of the sun above the eastern horizon 2. the time of this

sun′roof′ *n.* a car roof with a panel that opens to let in light and air

sun′set′ (-set′) *n.* 1. the daily disappearance of the sun below the western horizon 2. the time of this

sun′shine′ *n.* 1. the shining of the sun 2. the light and heat from the sun 3. cheerfulness, happiness, etc. —**sun′shin′y** *adj.*

sun′spot′ *n.* any of the temporarily cooler regions appearing as dark spots on the sun

sun′stroke′ *n.* a condition caused by excessive exposure to the sun, characterized by fever and collapse

sun′suit′ (-sōōt′) *n.* short pants with a bib and shoulder straps, worn by babies and young children

---

sun′tan′ (-tan′) *n.* darkened skin resulting from exposure to the sun

sun′up′ *n. same as* SUNRISE

Sun Yat-sen (soon′ yät′sen′) 1866-1925; Chin. revolutionary leader

sup (sup) *vi.* supped, sup′ping [< OFr. *soupe*, soup] to have supper

su·per (sōō′pər) *n.* [< ff.] *clipped form of:* 1. SUPERNUMERARY (esp. sense 2) 2. SUPERINTENDENT (esp. sense 2) —*adj.* 1. outstanding; exceptionally fine 2. great, extreme, or excessive

super- [L. < *super*, above] *a prefix meaning:* 1. over, above [*superstructure*] 2. superior to [*superintendent*] 3. *a*) surpassing [*superabundance*] *b*) greater than others of its kind [*supermarket*] 4. additional [*supertax*]

su·per·a·bun·dant (sōō′pər ə bun′dənt) *adj.* being more than enough —su′per·a·bun′dance *n.*

su′per·an′nu·at′ed (-an′yoo wāt′ id) *adj.* [< L. *super*, above + *annus*, year] 1. too old for work 2. retired on a pension, as because of old age

su·perb (soo purb′, sōō-) *adj.* [see SUPER-] 1. noble or majestic 2. rich or magnificent 3. extremely fine; excellent —su·perb′ly *adv.*

su·per·car·go (sōō′pər kär′gō) *n., pl.* -goes, -gos an officer on a merchant ship in charge of the cargo

su′per·charge′ (-chärj′) *vt.* -charged′, -charg′ing to increase the power of (an engine), as with a device (**supercharger**) that forces air into the cylinders

su·per·cil·i·ous (sōō′pər sil′ē əs) *adj.* [< L. *super*, above + *cilium*, eyelid, hence (in allusion to raised eyebrows) haughtiness] disdainful or contemptuous; haughty

su′per·cit′y (-sit′ē) *n., pl.* -ies *same as* MEGALOPOLIS

su′per·con·duc·tiv′i·ty (-kän′dək tiv′ə tē) *n.* the lack of resistance to electrical current in certain metals when cooled to near absolute zero

su′per·e′go (-ē′gō) *n., pl.* -gos *Psychoanalysis* that part of the psyche which enforces moral standards

su′per·em′i·nent *adj.* supremely eminent, distinguished, etc.

su′per·er′o·ga′tion (-er′ə gā′shən) *n.* [< L. *super*-, above + *erogare*, pay] a doing more than is needed —su′per·e·rog′a·to·ry (-i räg′ə tôr′ē) *adj.*

su′per·fi′cial (-fish′əl) *adj.* [< L. *super*-, above + *facies*, face] 1. of or being on the surface 2. concerned with and understanding only the obvious; shallow 3. quick and cursory 4. merely apparent —su′per·fi′ci·al′i·ty (-ē al′ə tē) *n., pl.* -ties —su′per·fi′cial·ly *adv.*

su·per·flu·ous (soo pur′floo wəs) *adj.* [< L. *super*-, above + *fluere*, to flow] unnecessary or excessive —su·per·flu·i·ty (sōō′pər flōō′ə tē) *n., pl.* -ties

su′per·high′way′ *n.* an expressway

su·per·hu·man (sōō′pər hyōō′mən) *adj.* 1. having a nature above that of man; divine 2. greater than that of a normal human being

su′per·im·pose′ (-im pōz′) *vt.* -posed′, -pos′ing to put or lay on top of something else

su′per·in·tend′ (-in tend′) *vt.* to act as superintendent of; supervise —su′per·in·tend′ence *n.*

su′per·in·tend′ent *n.* [see SUPER- & INTEND] 1. a person in charge of a department, institution, etc.; director 2. a person responsible for the maintenance of a building

su·pe·ri·or (sə pir′ē ər, soo-) *adj.* [see SUPER-] 1. higher in space, order, rank, etc. 2. greater in quality or value than (with *to*) 3. good or excellent in quality 4. unaffected by (something painful, etc.): with *to* 5. showing a feeling of being better than others; haughty —*n.* 1. a superior person or thing 2. the head of a religious community —su·pe′ri·or′i·ty (-ôr′ə tē) *n.*

Su·pe·ri·or (sə pir′ē ər, soo-), Lake largest of the Great Lakes, between Mich. & Ontario, Canada

superl. superlative

su·per·la·tive (sə pur′lə tiv, soo-) *adj.* [< L. *super*-, above + *latus*, pp. of *ferre*, carry] 1. superior to all others; supreme 2. *Gram.* designating the extreme degree of comparison of adjectives and adverbs —*n.* 1. the highest degree; acme 2. *Gram.* the superlative degree [*coolest* is the *superlative* of *cool*] —su·per′la·tive·ly *adv.*

su·per·man (sōō′pər man′) *n., pl.* -men′ an apparently superhuman man

su′per·mar′ket *n.* a large, self-service retail food store or market

su·per·nal (soo pur′n'l) *adj.* [< L. *supernus*, upper] celestial; heavenly

su·per·nat·u·ral (sōō′pər nach′ər əl) *adj.* not explainable by known natural forces or laws; specif., of or involving God or ghosts, spirits, etc.

su′per·nu′mer·ar′y (-nōō′mə rer′ē, -nyōō′-) *n., pl.* -ies [< L. *super*, above + *numerus*, number] 1. an extra person or thing 2. *Theater* a person with a small, nonspeaking part

su′per·pose′ (-pōz′) *vt.* -posed′, -pos′ing [see SUPER- & POSE] to place on or over something else —su′per·pos′a·ble *adj.* —su′per·po·si′tion *n.*

su′per·sat′u·rate′ *vt.* -rat′ed, -rat′ing to make more highly concentrated than in normal saturation —su′per·sat′u·ra′tion *n.*

su′per·scribe′ (-skrīb′) *vt.* -scribed′, -scrib′ing [see SUPER- & SCRIBE] to write (something) at the top or on an outer surface of (something) —su′per·scrip′tion (-skrip′shən) *n.*

su′per·script′ (-skript′) *n.* [see prec.] a figure, letter, or symbol written above and to the side of another

su′per·sede′ (-sēd′) *vt.* -sed′ed, -sed′ing [< L. *supersedere*, sit over] to replace or succeed

su′per·son′ic (-sän′ik) *adj.* [SUPER- + SONIC] 1. of or moving at a speed faster than that of sound 2. ultrasonic

su′per·star′ *n.* a star performer of topmost rank in sports or entertainment

su·per·sti·tion (sōō′pər stish′ən) *n.* [< L. *superstitio*, lit., a standing (in awe) over] **1.** any belief that is inconsistent with known facts or rational thought, esp. such a belief in omens, the supernatural, etc. **2.** any action or practice based on such a belief —**su′per·sti′tious** *adj.*

su·per·struc′ture *n.* **1.** a structure built on top of another, as above the main deck of a ship **2.** that part of a building above the foundation

su′per·tank′er *n.* an extremely large oil tanker, of 300,000 tons or more

su·per·vene (sōō′pər vēn′) *vi.* **-vened′, -ven′ing** [< L. *super-*, over + *venire*, come] to come or happen as something additional or unexpected

su·per·vise (sōō′pər vīz′) *vt., vi.* **-vised′, -vis′ing** [< L. *super-*, over + *videre*, see] to oversee or direct (work, workers, etc.); superintend —**su′per·vi′sion** (-vizh′ən) *n.* —**su′per·vi′sor** *n.* —**su′per·vi′so·ry** *adj.*

su·pine (sōō pīn′) *adj.* [L. *supinus*] **1.** lying on the back, face upward **2.** inactive; sluggish; listless

supp., suppl. supplement

sup·per (sup′ər) *n.* [see SUP] an evening meal

supper club an expensive nightclub

sup·plant (sə plant′) *vt.* [< L. *sub-*, under + *planta*, sole of the foot] **1.** to take the place of, esp. by force or plotting **2.** to remove in order to replace with something else

sup·ple (sup′'l) *adj.* [< L. *supplex*, submissive] **1.** easily bent; flexible **2.** lithe; limber **3.** easily influenced **4.** adaptable: said of the mind, etc.

sup·ple·ment (sup′lə mənt; *for v.* -ment′) *n.* [see SUPPLY] **1.** something added, esp. to make up for a lack **2.** a section of additional material in a book, newspaper, etc. —*vt.* to provide a supplement to —**sup′ple·men′ta·ry, sup′ple·men′tal** *adj.*

sup·pli·ant (sup′lē ənt) *n.* one who supplicates —*adj.* supplicating Also **sup′pli·cant** (-lə kənt)

sup·pli·cate (sup′lə kāt′) *vt., vi.* **-cat′ed, -cat′ing** [< L. *sub-*, under + *plicare*, to fold] **1.** to ask for (something) humbly **2.** to make a humble request (of) —**sup′pli·ca′tion** *n.*

sup·ply (sə plī′) *vt.* **-plied′, -ply′ing** [< L. *sub-*, under + *plere*, fill] **1.** to furnish or provide (what is needed) to (someone) **2.** to compensate for (a deficiency, etc.) —*n., pl.* **-plies′ 1.** the amount available for use or sale; stock **2.** [*pl.*] needed materials, provisions, etc. —**sup·pli′er** *n.*

sup·port (sə pôrt′) *vt.* [< L. *sub-*, under + *portare*, carry] **1.** to carry the weight of; hold up **2.** to encourage; help **3.** to advocate; uphold **4.** to maintain (a person, institution, etc.) with money or subsistence **5.** to help prove, vindicate, etc. **6.** to bear; endure **7.** to keep up; maintain **8.** to have a role supporting (a star) in a play —*n.* **1.** a supporting or being supported **2.** a person or thing that supports **3.** a means of support —**sup·port′a·ble** *adj.* —**sup·port′er** *n.*

sup·port′ive *adj.* giving support or help

sup·pose (sə pōz′) *vt.* **-posed′, -pos′ing** [< L. *sub-*, under + *ponere*, put] **1.** to assume to be true, as for argument's sake **2.** to imagine, think, etc. **3.** to consider as a possibility [*suppose* I go] **4.** to expect [I'm *supposed* to sing] —*vi.* to conjecture —**sup·posed′** *adj.* —**sup·pos′ed·ly** *adv.*

sup·po·si·tion (sup′ə zish′ən) *n.* **1.** a supposing **2.** something supposed

sup·pos·i·to·ry (sə päz′ə tôr′ē) *n., pl.* **-ries** [see SUPPOSE] a small piece of medicated substance, placed in the rectum, vagina, etc. where it melts

sup·press (sə pres′) *vt.* [< L. *sub-*, under + *premere*, to press] **1.** to put down by force; quell **2.** to keep from being known, published, etc. **3.** to keep back; restrain **4.** *Psychiatry* to consciously dismiss from the mind —**sup·pres′sion** (-presh′ən) *n.*

sup·pu·rate (sup′yoo rāt′) *vi.* **-rat′ed, -rat′ing** [< L. *sub-*, under + *pus*, pus] to form or discharge pus

supra- [< L. *supra*, above] *a prefix meaning* above, over, beyond

su·pra·na·tion·al (sōō′prə nash′ə n'l) *adj.* of, for, or above all or a number of nations [*supranational* authority]

su·prem·a·cist (sə prem′ə sist, sōō-) *n.* one who believes in the supremacy of a particular group

su·prem′a·cy (-sē) *n., pl.* **-cies** supreme condition or power

su·preme (sə prēm′, sōō-) *adj.* [< L. *superus*, that is above] **1.** highest in rank, power, etc. **2.** highest in quality, achievement, etc. **3.** highest in degree **4.** final; ultimate —**su·preme′ly** *adv.*

Supreme Being God

Supreme Court 1. the highest Federal court **2.** the highest court in most States

Supreme Soviet the parliament of the Soviet Union

Supt., supt. Superintendent

sur-[1] [< L. *super*, over] *a prefix meaning* over, upon, above, beyond

sur-[2] *same as* SUB-: used before *r*

sur·cease (sur′sēs) *n.* [< L. *supersedere*, refrain from] an end, or cessation

sur·charge (sur′chärj; *also, for v.,* sur chärj′) *vt.* **-charged′, -charg′ing** [see SUR-[1] & CHARGE] **1.** to overcharge **2.** to mark (a postage stamp) with a surcharge —*n.* **1.** an additional charge **2.** a new valuation printed over the original valuation on a postage stamp

sur·cin·gle (sur′sin′g'l) *n.* [< MFr. *sur-*, over + L. *cingulum*, a belt] a strap passed around a horse's body to bind on a saddle, pack, etc.

sure (shoor) *adj.* **sur′er, sur′est** [< L. *securus*] **1.** that will not fail [a *sure* method] **2.** that cannot be doubted or questioned **3.** having no doubt; confident *[sure* of the facts] **4.** bound to be or happen *[a sure* defeat] **5.** bound (to do, be, etc.) *[sure* to lose] —*adv.* [Colloq.] surely —**for sure** certain(ly) —**sure enough** [Colloq.] without doubt —**sure′ness** *n.*

sure′-fire′ (-fīr′) *adj.* [Colloq.] sure to be successful or as expected

sure′-foot′ed *adj.* not likely to stumble, slip, fall, or err

sure′ly *adv.* **1.** with confidence **2.** without a doubt; certainly

sur·e·ty (shoor′ə tē, shoor′tē) *n., pl.* **-ties 1.** a being sure **2.** something that gives assurance, as against loss, etc. **3.** one who makes himself responsible for another

surf (surf) *n.* [prob. < *sough,* rustle] the waves of the sea breaking on the shore or a reef —*vi.* to engage in surfing —**surf′er** *n.*

sur·face (sur′fis) *n.* [< Fr. *sur-,* over + *face,* a face] **1.** *a)* the exterior of an object *b)* any of the faces of a solid **2.** superficial features —*adj.* **1.** of, on, or at the surface **2.** external; superficial —*vt.* **-faced, -fac·ing** to give a surface to, as in paving —*vi.* to rise to the surface of the water

surf′board′ *n.* a long, narrow board used in the sport of surfing

sur·feit (sur′fit) *n.* [< OFr. *sur-,* over + *faire,* make] **1.** too great an amount **2.** overindulgence, esp. in food or drink **3.** disgust, nausea, etc. resulting from excess —*vt.* to feed or supply to excess

surf·ing (sur′fiŋ) *n.* the sport of riding in toward shore on the crest of a wave, esp. on a surfboard

surge (surj) *n.* [< L. *surgere,* to rise] **1.** a large wave of water, or its motion **2.** a sudden, strong increase, as of power —*vi.* **surged, surg′ing** to move in or as in a surge

sur·geon (sur′jən) *n.* a doctor who specializes in surgery

sur·ger·y (sur′jər ē) *n., pl.* **-ies** [< Gr. *cheir,* the hand + *ergein,* to work] **1.** the treatment of disease, injury, etc. by manual or instrumental operations **2.** the operating room of a surgeon or hospital

sur·gi·cal (-ji k'l) *adj.* of surgeons or surgery —**sur′gi·cal·ly** *adv.*

Su·ri·nam (soor′i nam′) country in NE S. America: 55,144 sq. mi.; pop. 385,000

sur·ly (sur′lē) *adj.* **-li·er, -li·est** [earlier *sirly,* imperious < *sir,* bad-tempered; sullenly rude; uncivil

sur·mise (sər mīz′) *n.* [< OFr. *sur-,* upon + *mettre,* put] a conjecture —*vt., vi.* **-mised′, -mis′ing** to guess

sur·mount (sər mount′) *vt.* [SUR-1 + MOUNT2] **1.** to overcome (a difficulty) **2.** to be at the top of; rise above **3.** to climb up and across (a height, etc.) —**sur·mount′a·ble** *adj.*

sur·name (sur′nām′) *n.* [< OFr. *sur-* (see SUR-1) + *nom,* name] the family name, or last name

sur·pass (sər pas′) *vt.* [< MFr. *sur-* (see SUR-1) + *passer,* to pass] **1.** to excel or be superior to **2.** to go beyond the limit, capacity, etc. of

sur·plice (sur′plis) *n.* [< L. *super-,* above + *pelliceum,* fur robe] a loose, white outer vestment worn by the clergy and choir in some churches

SURPLICE

sur·plus (sur′plus) *n.* [< OFr. < *sur-* (see SUR-1) + L. *plus,* more] a quantity over and above what is needed or used —*adj.* forming a surplus

sur·prise (sər prīz′) *vt.* **-prised′, -pris′ing** [< OFr. *sur-* (see SUR-1) + *prendre,* to take] **1.** to come upon suddenly or unexpectedly; take unawares **2.** to attack without warning **3.** to amaze; astonish —*n.* **1.** a being surprised **2.** something that surprises

sur·re·al (sə rē′əl, -rēl′) *adj.* **1.** surrealistic **2.** bizarre; fantastic

sur·re·al·ism (sə rē′ə liz′m) *n.* [see SUR-1 & REAL] a modern movement in the arts, trying to depict the workings of the unconscious mind —**sur·re′al·ist** *adj., n.* —**sur·re′al·is′tic** *adj.*

sur·ren·der (sə ren′dər) *vt.* [< MFr. *sur-,* up + *rendre,* render] **1.** to give up possession of; yield to another on compulsion **2.** to give up or abandon —*vi.* to give oneself up, esp. as a prisoner —*n.* the act of surrendering

sur·rep·ti·tious (sur′əp tish′əs) *adj.* [< L. *sub-,* under + *rapere,* seize] done, got, acting, etc. in a stealthy way

sur·rey (sur′ē) *n., pl.* **-reys** [< *Surrey,* county in England] a light, four-wheeled carriage with two seats

sur·ro·gate (sur′ə gāt′, -git) *n.* [< L. *sub-,* in place of + *rogare,* elect] **1.** a deputy or substitute **2.** in some States, a probate court judge

sur·round (sə round′) *vt.* [< L. *super-,* over + *undare,* to rise] to encircle on all or nearly all sides

sur·round·ings *n.pl.* the things, conditions, etc. around a person or thing

sur·tax (sur′taks′) *n.* an extra tax on top of the regular tax

sur·veil·lance (sər vā′ləns) *n.* [Fr. < *sur-* (see SUR-1) + *veiller,* to watch] watch kept over a person, esp. a suspect

sur·vey (sər vā′; *for n.* sur′vā) *vt.* [< OFr. *sur-* (see SUR-1) + *veori,* see] **1.** to examine or consider in detail or comprehensively **2.** to determine the location, form, or boundaries of (a tract of land) —*n., pl.* **-veys 1.** a detailed study, as by gathering information and analyzing it **2.** a general view **3.** *a)* the process of surveying an area *b)* a written description of the area —**sur·vey′or** *n.*

sur·vey·ing *n.* the science or work of making land surveys

sur·vive (sər vīv′) *vt.* **-vived′, -viv′-ing** [< L. *super-,* above + *vivere,* to live] to remain alive or in existence after —*vi.* to continue living or existing —**sur·viv′al** *n.* —**sur·vi′vor** *n.*

sus·cep·ti·ble (sə sep′tə b'l) *adj.* [<

L. *sus-*, under + *capere*, take] easily affected emotionally —**susceptible of** admitting; allowing [*testimony susceptible* of error] —**susceptible to** easily influenced or affected by —**suscep'ti·bil'i·ty** *n.*

sus·pect (sə spekt'; *for adj. & n.* sus'pekt) *vt.* [< L. *sus-*, under + *spicere*, to look] 1. to believe to be guilty on little or no evidence 2. to believe to be bad, wrong, etc.; distrust 3. to guess; surmise —*adj.* suspected —*n.* one suspected of a crime, etc.

sus·pend (sə spend') *vt.* [< L. *sus-*, under + *pendere*, hang] 1. to exclude for a time from an office, school, etc. as a penalty 2. to make inoperative for a time 3. to hold back (judgment, etc.) 4. to hang by a support from above 5. to hold (dust in the air, etc.) without attachment —*vi.* to stop temporarily

sus·pend'ers *n.pl.* 1. a pair of straps passed over the shoulders to hold up the trousers 2. [Brit.] garters

sus·pense (sə spens') *n.* [< L. *suspendere*, suspend] 1. a state of uncertainty 2. the growing excitement felt while awaiting a climax of a play, etc. —**sus·pense'ful** *adj.*

sus·pen·sion (sə spen'shən) *n.* 1. a suspending or being suspended 2. a supporting device upon or from which something is suspended

suspension bridge a bridge suspended from cables anchored at either end and supported by towers at intervals

sus·pi·cion (sə spish'ən) *n.* [< L. *suspicere*, to suspect] 1. a suspecting or being suspected 2. the feeling or state of mind of one who suspects 3. a very small amount; trace —*vt.* [Dial.] to suspect

sus·pi'cious *adj.* 1. arousing suspicion 2. showing or feeling suspicion —**sus·pi'cious·ly** *adv.*

sus·tain (sə stān') *vt.* [< L. *sus-*, under + *tenere*, to hold] 1. to keep in existence; maintain or prolong 2. to provide sustenance for 3. to carry the weight of; support 4. to endure; withstand 5. to suffer (an injury, loss, etc.) 6. to uphold the validity of 7. to confirm; corroborate

sus·te·nance (sus'ti nəns) *n.* 1. a sustaining 2. means of livelihood 3. that which sustains life; food

sut·ler (sut'lər) *n.* [< Early ModDu.] a person who followed an army to sell things to its soldiers

su·ture (sōō'chər) *n.* [< L. *suere*, sew] 1. the line of junction of two parts, esp. of bones of the skull 2. *a)* the stitching together of the two edges of a wound or incision *b)* the thread, etc. or any of the stitches so used

su·ze·rain (sōō'zə rin, -rān') *n.* [Fr. < L. *sursum*, above] 1. a feudal lord 2. a state in relation to another over which it has some political control —**su'ze·rain·ty** *n.*

svelte (svelt) *adj.* [Fr.] 1. slender; lithe 2. suave

SW, S.W., s.w. 1. southwest 2. southwestern

Sw. 1. Sweden 2. Swedish

swab (swäb) *n.* [< Du. *zwabben*, do dirty work] 1. a mop 2. a small piece of cotton, etc. used to medicate or clean the throat, mouth, etc. —*vt.* swabbed, swab'bing to use a swab on

swad·dle (swäd'l) *vt.* -dled, -dling [prob. < OE. *swathian*, swathe] formerly, to wrap (a newborn baby) in long, narrow bands of cloth

swag (swag) *vt.* swagged, swag'ging [see ff.] to hang in a swag —*n.* 1. a valance, garland, etc. hanging decoratively in a curve 2. [Slang] loot

swage (swāj) *n.* [< OFr.] a tool for shaping or bending metal —*vt.* swaged, -swag'ing to shape, bend, etc. with a swage

swag·ger (swag'ər) *vi.* [prob. < Norw. *svagga*, sway] 1. to walk with a bold, arrogant stride 2. to boast or brag loudly —*n.* swaggering walk or manner

Swa·hi·li (swä hē'lē) *n.* [< Ar. *sawāhil*, the coasts] a Bantu language of the east coast of Africa

swain (swān) *n.* [< ON. *sveinn*, boy] [Poet.] 1. a country youth 2. a lover

swal·low¹ (swäl'ō) *n.* [OE. *swealwe*] a small, swift-flying bird with long, pointed wings and a forked tail

swal·low² (swäl'ō) *vt.* [OE. *swelgan*] 1. to pass (food, etc.) from the mouth into the stomach 2. to absorb (often with *up*) 3. to retract (words said) 4. to put up with [to *swallow* insults] 5. to suppress [to *swallow* one's pride] 6. [Colloq.] to accept as true without question —*vi.* to perform the actions of swallowing something, esp. as in emotion —*n.* 1. a swallowing 2. the amount swallowed at one time

BARN SWALLOW

swal'low-tailed' coat same as CUTAWAY: also **swal'low-tail'** *n.*

swam (swam) *pt.* of SWIM

swa·mi (swä'mē) *n., pl.* -mis [< Sans. *svāmin*, a lord] a Hindu religious teacher, pundit, or seer

swamp (swämp, swômp) *n.* [prob. < LowG.] a piece of wet, spongy land; bog; marsh —*vt.* 1. to plunge in a swamp, water, etc. 2. to flood as with water 3. to overwhelm [*swamped* by debts] 4. to sink (a boat) by filling with water —**swamp'y** *adj.*

swamp buggy a vehicle for traveling over swampy land, often amphibious

swamp fever same as MALARIA

swan (swän, swôn) *n.* [OE.] a large, web-footed water bird, usually white, with a long, graceful neck

swank (swank) *n.* [akin to OE. *swancor*, pliant] [Colloq.] ostentatious display

—*adj.* [Colloq.] ostentatiously stylish: also **swank′y, -i·er, -i·est**

swan′s′-down′ *n.* 1. the soft down of the swan, used for trimming clothes, etc. 2. a soft, thick flannel Also **swans′down′**

swan song [after the song sung, in ancient fable, by a dying swan] the last act, final work, etc. of a person

swap (swäp, swôp) *n., vt., vi.* **swapped, swap′ping** [ME. *swappen,* to strike] [Colloq.] trade; barter

sward (swôrd) *n.* [< OE. *sweard,* a skin] grass-covered soil; turf

swarm (swôrm) *n.* [OE. *swearm*] 1. a large number of bees, with a queen, leaving a hive to start a new colony 2. a colony of bees in a hive 3. a moving mass, crowd, or throng —*vi.* 1. to fly off in a swarm: said of bees 2. to move, be present, etc. in large numbers 3. to be crowded

swarth·y (swôr′*the,* -*the*) *adj.* **-i·er, -i·est** [< OE. *sweart*] dark-skinned

swash (swäsh, swôsh) *vi.* [echoic] to dash, strike, etc. with a splash

swash′buck′ler (-buk′lər) *n.* [< *swash,* to swagger + *buckler,* a shield] a blustering, swaggering fighting man —**swash′buck′ling** *n., adj.*

swas·ti·ka (swäs′ti kə) *n.* [< Sans. *svasti,* well-being] 1. an ancient design in the form of a cross with arms of equal length bent in a right angle 2. this design with the arms bent clockwise: used as a Nazi emblem

SWAT (swät) [*S(pecial) W(eapons) a(nd) T(actics)*] a special police unit, trained to deal with violence, terrorism, etc.: in full **SWAT team**

swat (swät) *vt.* **swat′ted, swat′ting** [echoic] [Colloq.] to hit with a quick, sharp blow —*n.* [Colloq.] a quick, sharp blow —**swat′ter** *n.*

swatch (swäch) *n.* [orig., a cloth tally] a sample piece of cloth, etc.

swath (swäth, swôth) *n.* [OE. *swathu,* a track] 1. the width covered by one cut of a scythe or other mowing device 2. a strip, row, etc. mowed

swathe (swer *th*) *vt.* **swathed, swath′ing** [OE. *swathian*] 1. to wrap up in a bandage 2. to envelop; enclose

sway (swä) *vi.* [< ON. *sveigja*] 1. to swing or move from side to side or to and fro 2. to lean to one side; veer 3. to incline in judgment or opinion —*vt.* 1. to cause to sway 2. to influence or divert [*swayed* by promises] —*n.* 1. a swaying or being swayed 2. influence; control [the *sway* of lust]

sway′backed′ (-bakt′) *adj.* having a sagging spine, as some horses

Swa·zi·land (swä′zē land′) country in SE Africa: 6,705 sq. mi.; pop. 375,000

swear (swer) *vi.* **swore, sworn, swear′ing** [OE. *swerian*] 1. to make a solemn declaration with an appeal to God to confirm it 2. to make a solemn promise; vow 3. to use profane language; curse —*vt.* 1. to declare, pledge, or vow on oath 2. to administer a legal oath to —**swear off** to renounce —**swear out** to obtain (a warrant for arrest) by making a charge under oath —**swear′er** *n.*

sweat (swet) *vi., vt.* **sweat** or **sweat′ed, sweat′ing** [OE. *swat,* sweat] 1. to give forth or cause to give forth a salty moisture through the pores of the skin; perspire 2. to give forth or condense (moisture) on its surface 3. to work hard enough to cause sweating —*n.* 1. the salty liquid given forth in perspiration 2. moisture collected in droplets on a surface 3. a sweating or being sweated 4. a condition of eagerness, anxiety, etc. —**sweat out** [Slang] to wait anxiously for or through —**sweat′y** *adj.* **-i·er, -i·est**

sweat′er *n.* a knitted or crocheted outer garment for the upper body

sweat shirt a heavy cotton jersey worn to absorb sweat, as after exercise

sweat′shop′ *n.* a shop where employees work long hours at low wages under poor working conditions

Swed. 1. Sweden 2. Swedish

Swede (swēd) *n.* a native or inhabitant of Sweden

Swe·den (swē′d'n) country in N Europe: 173,620 sq. mi.; pop. 7,869,000; cap. Stockholm

Swed·ish (swē′dish) *adj.* of Sweden, its people, language, etc. —*n.* the Germanic language of the Swedes

sweep (swēp) *vt.* **swept, sweep′ing** [OE. *swapan*] 1. to clean (a floor, etc.) as by brushing with a broom 2. to remove (dirt, etc.) as with a broom 3. to strip, carry away, or destroy with a forceful movement 4. to touch in moving across [hands *sweeping* the keyboard] 5. to pass swiftly over or across 6. to win overwhelmingly —*vi.* 1. to clean a floor, etc. as with a broom 2. to move steadily with speed, force, or gracefulness 3. to extend in a long curve or line [a road *sweeping* up the hill] —*n.* 1. the act of sweeping 2. a steady, sweeping movement 3. range or scope 4. extent, as of land; stretch 5. a line, curve, etc. that seems to flow or move 6. one whose work is sweeping —**sweep′er** *n.* —**sweep′ing** *adj.* —**sweep′ing·ly** *adv.*

sweep′ings *n.pl.* things swept up, as dirt from a floor

sweep′stakes′ *n., pl.* **-stakes′** a lottery in which each participant puts up money in a common fund which is given as a prize to the winner or winners of a horse race or other contest

sweet (swēt) *adj.* [OE. *swete*] 1. having a taste of, or like that of, sugar 2. *a)* agreeable in taste, smell, sound, etc. *b)* gratifying *c)* friendly, kind, etc. 3. *a)* not rancid or sour *b)* not salty or salted —*n.* a sweet food —**sweet′ish** *adj.* —**sweet′ly** *adv.* —**sweet′ness** *n.*

sweet′bread′ (-bred′) *n.* the thymus or sometimes the pancreas of a calf, lamb, etc., when used as food

sweet′bri′er, sweet′bri′ar (-brī′ər) *n. same as* EGLANTINE

sweet corn a variety of Indian corn eaten unripe as a table vegetable

sweet′en *vt.* 1. to make sweet 2. to make pleasant or agreeable

sweet′en·er *n.* a sweetening agent, esp. a synthetic one, as saccharin

sweet′heart′ *n.* a loved one; lover

sweetheart contract a contract arranged by collusion between union officials and an employer without consulting the union membership

sweet′meat′ *n.* a candy

sweet pea a climbing plant with variously colored, fragrant flowers

sweet pepper 1. a red pepper producing a large, mild fruit 2. the fruit

sweet potato 1. a tropical, trailing plant with a large, fleshy, orange root used as a vegetable 2. its root

sweet′-talk′ *vt., vi.* [Colloq.] to flatter

sweet tooth [Colloq.] a fondness or craving for sweets

swell (swel) *vi., vt.* **swelled, swelled** or **swol′len, swell′ing** [OE. *swellan*] 1. to expand as a result of pressure from within 2. to curve out; bulge 3. to fill (*with* pride, etc.) 4. to increase in size, force, intensity, etc. —*n.* 1. a part that swells; specif., a large, rolling wave 2. an increase in size, amount, degree, etc. 3. a crescendo 4. [Colloq.] one who is strikingly stylish —*adj.* 1. [Colloq.] stylish 2. [Slang] excellent

swell′head′ *n.* a conceited person

swell′ing *n.* 1. an increase in size, volume, etc. 2. a swollen part

swel·ter (swel′tər) *vi.* [< OE. *sweltan*, to die] to be oppressed by great heat

swel′ter·ing *adj.* very hot; sultry

swept (swept) *pt. & pp.* of SWEEP

swept′back′ *adj.* having a backward slant, as the wings of an aircraft

swerve (swurv) *vi., vt.* **swerved, swerv′ing** [< OE. *sweorfan*, to scour] to turn aside from a straight line, course, etc. —*n.* a swerving

swift (swift) *adj.* [OE.] 1. moving with great speed; fast 2. coming, acting, etc. quickly —*n.* a swift-flying bird resembling the swallow —**swift′ly** *adv.* —**swift′ness** *n.*

Swift (swift), **Jonathan** 1667–1745; Eng. satirist, born in Ireland

swig (swig) *vt., vi.* **swigged, swig′ging** [< ?] [Colloq.] to drink in gulps —*n.* [Colloq.] a deep draft, as of liquor

swill (swil) *vt., vi.* [OE. *swilian*, wash] 1. to drink greedily 2. to feed swill to (pigs, etc.) —*n.* 1. liquid garbage fed to pigs 2. garbage

swim¹ (swim) *vi.* **swam, swum, swim′ming** [OE. *swimman*] 1. to move through water by moving arms, legs, fins, etc. 2. to move along smoothly 3. to float on or in a liquid 4. to overflow [eyes *swimming* with tears] —*vt.* to swim in or across —*n.* the act of swimming —**in the swim** active in, or conforming to, current fashions, etc. —**swim′mer** *n.*

swim² (swim) *n.* [OE. *swima*] a dizzy spell —*vi.* **swam, swum, swim′ming** to be dizzy

swimming hole a deep place in a river, creek, etc. used for swimming

swim′suit′ (-sōōt′) *n.* a garment worn for swimming

swin·dle (swin′d'l) *vt., vi.* **-dled, -dling** [< G. *schwindeln*] to defraud

(another) of money or property; cheat —*n.* an act of swindling; trick; fraud —**swin′dler** *n.*

swine (swīn) *n., pl.* **swine** [OE. *swīn*] 1. a pig or hog: usually used collectively 2. a vicious, contemptible person —**swin′ish** *adj.*

swing (swiŋ) *vi., vt.* **swung, swing′ing** [OE. *swingan*] 1. to sway or move backward and forward 2. to walk, trot, etc. with relaxed movements 3. to strike (*at*) 4. to turn, as on a hinge 5. to hang; be suspended 6. to move in a curve [*swing* the car around] 7. [Colloq.] to cause to come about successfully [to *swing* an election] 8. [Slang] to be ultra-fashionable, esp. in seeking pleasure —*n.* 1. a swinging 2. the arc through which something swings 3. the manner of swinging a golf club, etc. 4. a relaxed motion, as in walking 5. a sweeping blow or stroke 6. the course of some activity 7. rhythm, as of music 8. a seat hanging from ropes, etc., on which one can swing 9. a trip or tour 10. jazz music (c. 1935–45) characterized by large bands, strong rhythms, etc.

swing′er *n.* 1. one that swings 2. [Slang] a person who swings (*vi.* 8)

swing shift [Colloq.] a work shift from midafternoon to about midnight

swipe (swīp) *n.* [prob. var. of SWEEP] [Colloq.] a hard, sweeping blow —*vt.* **swiped, swip′ing** 1. [Colloq.] to hit with a swipe 2. [Slang] to steal

swirl (swurl) *vi., vt.* [ME. *swyrl*] to move or cause to move with a whirling motion —*n.* 1. a whirl; eddy 2. a twist; curl —**swirl′y** *adj.*

swish (swish) *vi., vt.* [echoic] 1. to move with a sharp, hissing sound, as a cane swung through the air 2. to rustle, as skirts —*n.* a swishing sound or movement

Swiss (swis) *adj.* of Switzerland, its people, etc. —*n., pl.* **Swiss** a native or inhabitant of Switzerland

Swiss chard *same as* CHARD

Swiss (cheese) a pale-yellow, hard cheese with many large holes

Swiss steak a thick cut of round steak pounded with flour and braised

switch (swich) *n.* [Early ModE. *swits*] 1. a thin, flexible stick used for whipping 2. a sharp lash, as with a whip 3. a device used to open, close, or divert an electric circuit 4. a device used in transferring a train from one track to another 5. a shift; change 6. a tress of detached hair, often used as part of a coiffure —*vt.* 1. to whip as with a switch 2. to jerk sharply 3. to shift; change 4. to turn (an electric light, etc.) *on* or *off* 5. to transfer (a train, etc.) to another track 6. [Colloq.] to change or exchange —*vi.* to shift —**switch′er** *n.*

switch′back′ *n.* a road or railroad following a zigzag course up a steep grade

switch′-blade′ knife a large jack-knife that snaps open when a release button on the handle is pressed

switch'board' (-bôrd') *n.* a panel for controlling a system of electric circuits, as in a telephone exchange

switch'-hit'ter *n.* a baseball player who bats right-handed or left-handed

Switz·er·land (swit'sər lənd) country in WC Europe: 15,941 sq. mi.; pop. 6,036,000; cap. Bern

swiv·el (swiv''l) *n.* [< OE. *swifan,* to revolve] a coupling device that allows free turning of the parts attached to it —*vi., vt.* **-eled** or **-elled, -el·ing** or **-el·ling** to turn or cause to turn as on a swivel or pivot

swiz·zle stick (swiz''l) [< ?] a small rod for stirring mixed drinks

swob (swäb) *n., vt.* **swobbed, swob'bing** var. *sp.* of SWAB

swol·len (swō'lən) *alt. pp.* of SWELL —*adj.* blown up; distended; bulging

swoon (swōōn) *vi., n.* [< OE. *geswogen,* unconscious] *same as* FAINT

swoop (swōōp) *vi.* [< OE. *swapan,* sweep along] to pounce or sweep (*down* or *upon*), as a bird in hunting —*n.* the act of swooping

swop (swäp) *n., vt., vi.* **swopped, swop'ping** var. *sp.* of SWAP

sword (sôrd) *n.* [OE. *sweord*] a hand weapon with a long, sharp-pointed blade set in a hilt —**at swords' points** ready to quarrel or fight

sword'fish' *n., pl.:* see FISH a large marine food fish with the upper jawbone extending in a swordlike point

sword'play' (-plā') *n.* the act or skill of using a sword, as in fencing

swords'man (-mən) *n., pl.* **-men** 1. one who uses a sword in fencing or fighting 2. one skilled in using a sword

SWORDFISH

swore (swôr) *pt.* of SWEAR

sworn (swôrn) *pp.* of SWEAR —*adj.* bound, pledged, etc. by an oath

swum (swum) *pp.* of SWIM

swung (swuŋ) *pt. & pt.* of SWING

syb·a·rite (sib'ə rīt') *n.* [< *Sybaris,* ancient Gr. city in Italy] anyone very fond of luxury and pleasure —**syb'a·rit'ic** (-rit'ik) *adj.*

syc·a·more (sik'ə môr') *n.* [< Gr. *sykomoros*] 1. a maple tree of Europe and Asia 2. an American tree with bark that sheds in patches

syc·o·phant (sik'ə fənt) *n.* [< Gr. *sykophantēs,* informer] one who seeks favor by flattering people of wealth or influence —**syc'o·phan·cy** *n.*

Syd·ney (sid'nē) seaport in SE Australia: pop. 2,431,000

syl·lab·i·cate (si lab'ə kāt') *vt.* **-cat'ed, -cat'ing** *same as* SYLLABIFY —**syl·lab'i·ca'tion** *n.*

syl·lab·i·fy (si lab'ə fī) *vt.* **-fied', -fy'ing** [< L. *syllaba,* syllable +

facere, make] to form or divide into syllables —**syl·lab'i·fi·ca'tion** *n.*

syl·la·ble (sil'ə b'l) *n.* [< Gr. *syn-,* together + *lambanein,* to hold] 1. a word or part of a word pronounced with a single, uninterrupted sounding of the voice 2. one or more letters written to represent a spoken syllable —**syl·lab·ic** (si lab'ik) *adj.*

syl·la·bus (sil'ə bəs) *n., pl.* **-bus·es, -bi'** (-bī') [< Gr. *sillybos,* parchment label] a summary or outline, esp. of a course of study

syl·lo·gism (sil'ə jiz'm) *n.* [< Gr. *syn-,* together + *logizesthai,* to reason] a form of reasoning in which two premises are made and a logical conclusion drawn from them

sylph (silf) *n.* [ModL. *sylphus,* a spirit] 1. any of a class of imaginary beings supposed to inhabit the air 2. a slender, graceful woman or girl

syl·van (sil'vən) *adj.* [< L. *silva,* a wood] 1. of, characteristic of, or living in the woods or forest 2. wooded

sym·bi·o·sis (sim'bī ō'sis, -bē-) *n.* [< Gr. *symbioun,* to live together] the living together of two kinds of organisms to their mutual advantage —**sym·bi·ot'ic** (-ät'ik) *adj.*

sym·bol (sim'b'l) *n.* [< Gr. *syn-,* together + *ballein,* to throw] 1. an object used to represent something abstract [the dove is a *symbol* of peace] 2. a mark, letter, etc. standing for a quality, process, etc., as in music or chemistry —**sym·bol·ic** (-bäl'ik), **sym·bol'i·cal** *adj.* —**sym·bol'i·cal·ly** *adv.*

sym·bol·ism (sim'b'l iz'm) *n.* 1. representation by symbols 2. a system of symbols 3. a symbolic meaning

sym'bol·ize' *vt.* **-ized', -iz'ing** 1. to be a symbol of; stand for 2. to represent by a symbol or symbols

sym·me·try (sim'ə trē) *n., pl.* **-tries** [< Gr. *syn-,* together + *metron,* a measure] 1. correspondence of opposite parts in size, shape, and position 2. balance or beauty of form resulting from this —**sym·met'ri·cal** (si met'ri k'l) *adj.* —**sym·met'ri·cal·ly** *adv.*

sym·pa·thet·ic (sim'pə thet'ik) *adj.* 1. of, feeling, or showing sympathy 2. in agreement with one's tastes, mood, etc. —**sym'pa·thet'i·cal·ly** *adv.*

sym'pa·thize' (-thīz') *vi.* **-thized', -thiz'ing** 1. to share the feelings or ideas of another 2. to feel or express sympathy —**sym'pa·thiz'er** *n.*

sym·pa·thy (sim'pə thē) *n., pl.* **-thies** [< Gr. *syn-,* together + *pathos,* feeling] 1. sameness of feeling 2. agreement in qualities; accord 3. mutual liking or understanding 4. ability to share another's ideas, emotions, etc.; esp., pity or compassion

sym·pho·ny (sim'fə nē) *n., pl.* **-nies** [< Gr. *syn-,* together + *phōnē,* sound] 1. harmony, as of sounds, color, etc. 2. an extended musical composition in several movements, for full orchestra 3. a large orchestra for playing symphonic works: in full **symphony orchestra** 4. [Colloq.] a symphony concert —**sym·phon′ic** (-fän′ik) *adj.*

sym·po·si·um (sim pō′zē əm) *n., pl.* **-si·ums, -si·a** (-ə) [< Gr. *syn-*, together + *posis*, a drinking] 1. a conference to discuss a topic 2. a published group of opinions on a topic

symp·tom (simp′təm) *n.* [< Gr. *syn-*, together + *piptein*, to fall] any circumstance or condition that indicates the existence as of a particular disease —**symp′to·mat′ic** (-tə mat′ik) *adj.*

symp′tom·a·tize′ (-tə mə tīz′) *vt.* **-tized′, -tiz′ing** to be a symptom or sign of: also **symp′tom·ize′**

syn- [Gr.] *a prefix meaning* with, together with, at the same time

syn. 1. synonym 2. synonymy

syn·a·gogue (sin′ə gäg′, -gôg′) *n.* [< Gr. *syn-*, together + *agein*, bring] 1. an assembly of Jews for worship and religious study 2. a building or place for such assembly —**syn′a·gog′al** *adj.*

syn·apse (si naps′) *n.* [< Gr. *syn-*, together + *apsis*, a joining] the point of contact where nerve impulses are transmitted from one neuron to another

sync, synch (siŋk) *vt., vi. clipped form of* SYNCHRONIZE —*n. clipped form of* SYNCHRONIZATION

syn·chro·nize (siŋ′krə nīz′) *vi.* **-nized′, -niz′ing** [< Gr. *syn-*, together + *chronos*, time] to move or occur at the same time or rate —*vt.* to cause to agree in time or rate of speed

syn′chro·nous *adj.* happening at the same time or at the same time

syn·co·pate (siŋ′kə pāt′) *vt.* **-pat′ed, -pat′ing** [< Gr. *syn-*, together + *koptein*, cut] *Music* to begin (a tone) on an unaccented beat and continue it through the next accented beat —**syn′co·pa′tion** *n.*

syn·di·cate (sin′də kit; *for v.* -kāt′) *n.* [< Gr. *syn-*, together + *dikē*, justice] 1. an association of individuals or corporations formed for a project requiring much capital 2. any group, as of criminals, organized for some undertaking 3. an organization selling articles or features to many newspapers, etc. —*vt.* **-cat′ed, -cat′ing** 1. to manage as or form into a syndicate 2. to sell (an article, etc.) through a syndicate —*vi.* to form a syndicate —**syn′di·ca′tion** *n.*

syn·drome (sin′drōm) *n.* [< Gr. *syn-*, with + *dramein*, run] a set of symptoms characterizing a disease or condition

syn·er·gism (sin′ər jiz′m) *n.* [< Gr. *syn-*, together + *ergon*, work] combined action, as of several drugs, greater in total effect than the sum of their effects —**syn′er·gis′tic** *adj.*

syn·fu·el (sin′fyōō əl) *n.* [SYN(THETIC) + FUEL] oil from coal, methane from plant cellulose, etc., used as fuel

syn·od (sin′əd) *n.* [< Gr. *syn-*, together + *hodos*, way] 1. a council of churches or church officials 2. any council

syn·o·nym (sin′ə nim) *n.* [< Gr. *syn-*, together + *onyma*, name] a word having

the same or nearly the same meaning as another in the same language —**syn·on·y·mous** (si nän′ə məs) *adj.*

syn·op·sis (si näp′sis) *n., pl.* **-ses** (-sēz) [< Gr. *syn-*, together + *opsis*, a seeing] a brief, general review or condensation; summary

syn·tax (sin′taks) *n.* [< Gr. *syn-*, together + *tassein*, arrange] the arrangement of words as elements in a sentence to show their relationship —**syn·tac′tic** (-tak′tik), **syn·tac′ti·cal** *adj.*

syn·the·sis (sin′thə sis) *n., pl.* **-ses** (-sēz) [< Gr. *syn-*, together + *tithenai*, to place] the combining of parts or elements so as to form a whole, a compound, etc. —**syn′the·size** (-sīz′) *vt.* **-sized′, -siz′ing**

syn′the·siz′er *n.* an electronic device producing sounds unobtainable from ordinary musical instruments

syn·thet′ic (-thet′ik) *adj.* 1. of or involving synthesis 2. produced by chemical synthesis, rather than of natural origin 3. not real; artificial —*n.* something synthetic —**syn·thet′i·cal·ly** *adv.*

syph·i·lis (sif′ə lis) *n.* [< *Syphilus*, hero of a L. poem (1530)] an infectious venereal disease —**syph′i·lit′ic** (-lit′ik) *adj., n.*

Syr·a·cuse (sir′ə kyōōs′, -kyōōz′) city in C N.Y.: pop. 170,000

Syr·i·a (sir′ē ə) country in SW Asia: 71,227 sq. mi.; pop. 7,114,000; cap. Damascus —**Syr′i·an** *adj., n.*

sy·ringe (sə rinj′, sir′inj) *n.* [< Gr. *syrinx*, a pipe] a device consisting of a tube with a rubber bulb or piston at one end for drawing in a liquid and then ejecting it in a stream: used to inject fluids into the body, etc. —*vt.* **-ringed′, -ring′ing** to cleanse, inject, etc. by using a syringe

syr·up (sir′əp, sur′-) *n.* [< Ar. *sharāb*, a drink] any sweet, thick liquid; specif., a solution made by boiling sugar with water —**syr′up·y** *adj.*

sys·tem (sis′təm) *n.* [< Gr. *syn-*, together + *histanai*, to set] 1. a set or arrangement of things so related as to form a whole *[a solar system, school system]* 2. a set of facts, rules, etc. arranged to show a plan 3. a method or plan 4. an established, orderly way of doing something 5. the body, or a number of bodily organs, functioning as a unit

sys′tem·at′ic (-tə mat′ik) *adj.* 1. constituting or based on a system 2. according to a system; orderly —**sys′-tem·at′i·cal·ly** *adv.*

sys′tem·a·tize′ (-təm ə tīz′) *vt.* **-tized′, -tiz′ing** to arrange according to a system; make systematic

sys·tem·ic (sis tem′ik) *adj.* of or affecting the body as a whole

sys·to·le (sis′tə lē′) *n.* [< Gr. *syn-*, together + *stellein*, send] the usual rhythmic contraction of the heart —**sys·tol′ic** (-täl′ik) *adj.*

T

T, t (tē) *n., pl.* **T's, t's** the twentieth letter of the English alphabet —**to a T** to perfection

T. tablespoon(s)

t. 1. teaspoon(s) 2. temperature 3. ton(s) 4. transitive

tab¹ (tab) *n.* [< ?] 1. a small, flat loop or strap fastened to something 2. a projecting piece of a card or paper, useful in filing

tab² (tab) *n.* [prob. < TABULATION] [Colloq.] 1. a bill, as for expenses 2. total cost —**keep tabs (or a tab) on** [Colloq.] to keep a check on

tab·bou·leh (tə bōō'lē, -le) *n.* [Ar.] a salad of bulgur wheat, parsley, onions, etc.: also **ta·bou'li, ta·bu'li**

tab·by (tab'ē) *n., pl.* **-bies** [ult. < Ar.] a domestic cat, esp. a female

tab·er·nac·le (tab'ər nak''l) *n.* [< L. *taberna*, hut] 1. [T-] the portable sanctuary carried by the Jews during the Exodus 2. a large place of worship

tab·la (täb'lä) *n.* [< Ar. *ṭabl*, drum] a set of two small drums whose pitch can be varied, used esp. in India and played with the hands

ta·ble (tā'b'l) *n.* [< L. *tabula*, a board] 1. orig., a thin slab of metal, stone, etc. 2. *a)* a piece of furniture having a flat top set on legs *b)* such a table set with food *c)* food served *d)* the people seated at a table 3. *a)* a systematic list of details, contents, etc. *b)* an orderly arrangement of facts, figures, etc. 4. any flat, horizontal surface, piece, etc. —*vt.* **-bled, -bling** to postpone consideration of (a legislative bill, etc.) —**at table** at a meal —**turn the tables** to reverse a situation

tab·leau (tab'lō) *n., pl.* **-leaux** (-lōz), **-leaus** [Fr. < OFr., dim. of *table*] a representation of a scene, etc. by a group posed in costume

ta'ble·cloth' *n.* a cloth for covering a table, esp. at meals

ta·ble d'hôte (tä'b'l dōt') [Fr., table of the host] a complete meal served at a restaurant for a set price

ta'ble·hop' (-hāp') *vi.* **-hopped', -hop'ping** to leave one's table, as at a nightclub, and visit about at other tables —**ta'ble·hop'per** *n.*

ta·ble·land (tā'b'l land') *n.* a plateau

ta'ble·spoon' *n.* a large spoon holding 1/2 fluid ounce —**ta'ble·spoon'ful** *n., pl.* **-fuls**

tab·let (tab'lit) *n.* [see TABLE] 1. a flat, thin piece of stone, metal, etc. with an inscription 2. a writing pad of paper sheets glued together at one edge 3. a small, flat piece of compressed material, as of medicine

table tennis a game somewhat like tennis, played on a table, with a small celluloid ball

ta'ble·ware' (-wer') *n.* dishes, silverware, glassware, etc. for use at a meal

tab·loid (tab'loid) *n.* [TABL(ET) + -OID] a newspaper, usually half size, with many pictures and short, often sensational, news stories

ta·boo (ta bōō', tə-) *n.* [S Pacific native term *tabu*] 1. among primitive peoples, a sacred prohibition making certain people or things untouchable, etc. 2. any conventional social restriction —*adj.* prohibited by taboo —*vt.* 1. to put under taboo 2. to prohibit or forbid Also **tabu**

tab·u·lar (tab'yə lər) *adj.* [see TABLE] 1. flat 2. of, arranged in, or computed from a table or list

tab'u·late' (-lāt') *vt.* **-lat'ed, -lat'ing** to put (facts, statistics, etc.) in a table —**tab'u·la'tion** *n.* —**tab'u·la'tor** *n.*

ta·chom·e·ter (ta käm'ə tər, tə-) *n.* [< Gr. *tachos*, speed + -METER] a device that measures the revolutions per minute of a revolving shaft

tac·it (tas'it) *adj.* [< L. *tacere*, be silent] 1. unspoken; silent 2. not expressed openly, but implied —**tac'it·ly** *adv.* —**tac'it·ness** *n.*

tac·i·turn (tas'ə turn') *adj.* [see prec.] almost always silent; not liking to talk —**tac'i·tur'ni·ty** *n.*

tack (tak) *n.* [< MDu. *tacke*, twig] 1. a short nail with a sharp point and a large, flat head 2. a temporary stitch 3. a zigzag course 4. a course of action 5. *a)* the direction a ship goes in relation to the position of the sails *b)* a change of a ship's direction —*vt.* 1. to fasten with tacks 2. to attach or add 3. to change the course of (a ship) —*vi.* to change course suddenly

tack·le (tak''l) *n.* [< MDu. *takel*] 1. equipment; gear 2. a system of ropes and pulleys for moving weights 3. a tackling, as in football 4. *Football* a player next to the end in the line —*vt.* **-led, -ling** 1. to take hold of; seize 2. to try to do; undertake 3. *Football* to throw (the ball carrier) to the ground —**tack'ler** *n.*

tack·y (tak'ē) *adj.* **-i·er, -i·est** 1. sticky, as glue 2. [Colloq.] shabby or dowdy —**tack'i·ness** *n.*

ta·co (tä'kō) *n., pl.* **-cos** [Sp., light lunch] a fried tortilla filled with chopped meat, lettuce, etc.

Ta·co·ma (tə kō'mə) seaport in W Wash.: pop. 159,000

tac·o·nite (tak'ə nīt') *n.* [< *Taconic* Range in Vt. & Mass.] a kind of rock mined as a low-grade iron ore

tact (takt) *n.* [< L. *tangere*, touch] delicate perception of the right thing to say or do without offending —**tact'ful** *adj.* —**tact'ful·ly** *adv.* —**tact'less** *adj.* —**tact'less·ly** *adv.*

tac·tics (tak'tiks) *n.* [< Gr. *tassein*, arrange] 1. [*with sing. v.*] the science of maneuvering military and naval forces 2. any skillful methods to gain an end —**tac'ti·cal** *adj.* —**tac·ti'cian** (-tish'ən) *n.*

tac·tile (tak't'l) *adj.* [< L. *tangere*, to touch] of, having, or perceived by the sense of touch

tad (tad) *n.* [prob. < TAD(POLE)] 1. a little child, esp. a boy 2. a small amount or degree [a *tad* tired]

tad·pole (tad'pōl') *n.* [ME. *tadde*, toad + *poll*, head] the larva of a frog or toad, having gills and a tail and living in water

taf·fe·ta (taf'i tə) *n.* [< Per. *tāftan*, to weave] a fine, stiff fabric of silk, nylon, etc., with a sheen

taff·rail (taf'rāl') *n.* [< Du.] a rail around a ship's stern

taf·fy (taf'ē) *n.* [< ?] a chewy candy made of sugar or molasses

Taft (taft), **William Howard** 1857-1930; 27th president of the U.S. (1909-13)

tag (tag) *n.* [prob. < Scand.] 1. a hanging end or part 2. a hard-tipped end on a cord or lace 3. a card, etc. attached as a label 4. an epithet 5. the last line or lines of a story, speech, etc. 6. a children's game in which one player chases the others until he touches one —*vt.* **tagged, tag'ging** 1. to provide with a tag; label 2. to touch in playing tag 3. to choose; select —*vi.* [Colloq.] to follow closely (with *along*, *after*, etc.) —**tag'ger** *n.*

Ta·ga·log (tä gä'läg, -lôg) *n.* 1. *pl.* **-logs, -log** a member of a Malayan people of the Philippine Islands 2. their Indonesian language

Ta·hi·ti (tə hēt'ē) Fr. island in the South Pacific —**Ta·hi'tian** (-hēsh'ən) *adj., n.*

tai chi (tī' jē') [Chin.] a system of exercise developed in China, consisting of a series of slow, ritual movements: in full, **t'ai chi ch'uan** (chwän)

tai·ga (tī'gə) *n.* [Russ.] the coniferous forests in far northern regions

tail (tāl) *n.* [OE. *tægel*] 1. the rear end of an animal's body, esp. when a distinct appendage 2. anything like an animal's tail in form or position 3. the hind, bottom, last, or inferior part of anything 4. [often *pl.*] the reverse side of a coin 5. [*pl.*] [Colloq.] full-dress attire for men 6. [Colloq.] a person that follows another, esp. in surveillance —*adj.* 1. at the rear or end 2. from the rear [a *tail* wind] —*vt., vi.* [Colloq.] to follow closely

tail'gate' *n.* the hinged or removable gate at the back of a wagon, truck, etc. —*vi., vt.* **-gat'ed, -gat'ing** to drive too closely behind (another vehicle)

tail'light' *n.* a light, usually red, at the rear of a vehicle to warn vehicles coming from behind

TAILGATE

tai·lor (tā'lər) *n.* [< LL. *taliare*, to cut] one who makes, repairs, or alters clothes —*vi.* to work as a tailor —*vt.* 1. to make by tailor's work 2. to form, alter, etc. for a certain purpose [a novel *tailored* for TV]

tail'pipe' *n.* an exhaust pipe at the rear of an automotive vehicle

tail'spin' *n.* same as SPIN (*n.* 3)

taint (tānt) *vt.* [< ?] 1. to affect with something injurious, unpleasant, etc.; infect; spoil 2. to make morally corrupt —*n.* a trace of contamination, corruption, etc.

Tai·wan (tī'wän') island province off SE China: seat of the Nationalist government: 13,885 sq. mi.; pop. 13,466,000

take (tāk) *vt.* **took, tak'en, tak'ing** [< ON. *taka*] 1. to get possession of; capture, seize, etc. 2. to get hold of 3. to capture the fancy of 4. to obtain, acquire, assume, etc. 5. to use, consume, etc. 6. to buy, rent, subscribe to, etc. 7. to join with (one side in a disagreement, etc.) 8. to choose; select 9. to travel by [to *take* a bus] 10. to deal with; consider 11. to occupy [*take* a chair] 12. to require; demand [it *takes* money] 13. to derive (a name, quality, etc.) from 14. to excerpt 15. to study 16. to write down [*take* notes] 17. to make by photographing 18. to win (a prize, etc.) 19. to undergo [*take* punishment] 20. to engage in [*take* a nap] 21. to accept (an offer, bet, etc.) 22. to react to [to *take* a joke in earnest] 23. to contract (a disease, etc.) 24. to understand 25. to suppose; presume 26. to feel [*take* pity] 27. to lead, escort, etc. 28. to carry 29. to remove, as by stealing 30. to subtract 31. [Slang] to cheat; trick 32. *Gram.* to be used with [the verb "hit" *takes* an object] —*vi.* 1. to take root: said of a plant 2. to catch [the fire *took*] 3. to gain favor, success, etc. 4. to be effective [the vaccination *took*] 5. to go [to *take* to the hills] 6. [Colloq.] to become (sick) —*n.* 1. a taking 2. *a*) the amount taken *b*) [Slang] receipts or profit —**on the take** [Slang] taking bribes, etc. —**take after** to be, act, or look like —**take back** to retract (something said, etc.) —**take down** to put in writing; record —**take in** 1. to admit; receive 2. to make smaller 3. to understand 4. to cheat; trick —**take off** 1. to leave the ground, etc. in flight: said of an airplane 2. [Colloq.] to start 3. [Colloq.] to imitate in a burlesque manner —**take on** 1. to acquire; assume 2. to employ 3. to undertake (a task, etc.) —**take over** to begin controlling, managing, etc. —**take to** to become fond of —**take up** 1. to make tighter or shorter 2. to become interested in (an occupation, study, etc.) —**tak'er** *n.*

take'off' *n.* 1. the act of leaving the ground, as in jumping or flight 2. [Colloq.] a caricature; burlesque

take'o'ver n. the usurpation of power in a nation, organization, etc.

tak·ing (tāk'iŋ) *adj.* attractive; winning —n. 1. the act or one that takes 2. [*pl.*] earnings; profits

talc (talk) n. [< Ar. *ṭalq*] 1. a soft mineral used to make talcum powder, etc. 2. talcum powder

tal'cum (powder) (-əm) a powder for the body made of purified talc

tale (tāl) n. [OE. *talu*] 1. a true or fictitious story; narrative 2. idle or malicious gossip 3. a fiction; lie

tale'bear'er (-ber'ər) n. a gossip

tal·ent (tal'ənt) n. [< Gr. *talanton*, a weight] 1. an ancient unit of weight or money 2. any natural ability or power 3. a superior ability in an art, etc. 4. people, or a person, with talent —**tal'ent·ed** *adj.*

tal·is·man (tal'is mən, -iz-) n., *pl.* **-mans** [< LGr. *telesma*, religious rite] 1. a ring, stone, etc. bearing engraved figures supposed to bring good luck, avert evil, etc. 2. a charm

talk (tôk) *vi.* [prob. < OE. *talian*, reckon] 1. to put ideas into words; speak 2. to express ideas by speech substitutes [*talk* by signs] 3. to chatter; gossip 4. to confer; consult 5. to confess or inform on someone —*vt.* 1. to use in speaking [to *talk* French] 2. to discuss 3. to put into a specified condition, etc. by talking —n. 1. the act of talking 2. conversation 3. a speech 4. a conference 5. gossip 6. the subject of conversation, gossip, etc. 7. speech; dialect —**talk back** to answer impertinently —**talk down to** to talk patronizingly to, as by simple speech —**talk up** to promote in discussion —**talk'er** n.

talk'a·tive (-ə tiv) *adj.* talking a great deal; loquacious: also **talk'y**

talking book a book, etc. recorded for use on a phonograph by the blind

talk'ing-to' n. [Colloq.] a scolding

talk show *Radio & TV* a program in which a host talks with guest celebrities, experts, etc.

tall (tôl) *adj.* [< OE. (ge)tæl, swift] 1. higher in stature than the average 2. having a specified height 3. [Colloq.] exaggerated [a *tall* tale] 4. [Colloq.] large [a *tall* drink] —**tall'ness** n.

Tal·la·has·see (tal'ə has'ē) capital of Fla.: pop. 82,000

tal·low (tal'ō) n. [prob. < MLowG. *talg*] the solid fat taken from the natural fat of cattle, sheep, etc., used to make candles, soaps, etc.

tal·ly (tal'ē) n., *pl.* **-lies** [< L. *talea*, a stick (notched to keep accounts)] 1. anything used as a record for an account or score 2. an account, score, etc. 3. a tag or label —*vt.* **-lied, -ly·ing** 1. to put on or as on a tally 2. to add (up) —*vi.* 1. to score a point 2. to agree; correspond

tal·ly·ho (tal'ē hō') *interj.* the cry of a hunter on sighting the fox

Tal·mud (tal'mood, täl'mad) n. [< Heb. *lāmadh*, learn] the body of early Jewish civil and religious law

tal·on (tal'ən) n. [< L. *talus*, an ankle] the claw of a bird of prey

tam (tam) n. *same as* TAM-O'-SHANTER

ta·ma·le (tə mä'lē) n. [< MexSp.] a Mexican food of minced meat and red peppers cooked in corn husks

tam·a·rack (tam'ə rak') n. [< Am-Ind.] 1. an American larch tree usually found in swamps 2. its wood

tam·a·rind (tam'ə rind) n. [< Ar. *tamr hindī*, date of India] 1. a tropical tree with yellow flowers and brown, acid pods 2. its edible fruit

tam·bou·rine (tam'bə rēn') n. [< Ar. *ṭanbūr*, stringed instrument] a shallow, one-headed hand drum with jingling metal disks in the rim: played by shaking, hitting, etc.

tame (tām) *adj.* **tam'er, tam'est** [OE. *tam*] 1. changed from a wild state and trained for man's use 2. gentle; docile 3. without spirit or force; dull —*vt.* **tamed, tam'ing** 1. to make tame 2. to make gentle; subdue —**tam'a·ble, tame'a·ble** *adj.* —**tame'ly** *adv.* —**tame'ness** n. —**tam'er** n.

Tam·il (tam'l, tum'-) n. the non-Indo-European language of the Tamils, a people of S India and N Ceylon

tam-o'-shan·ter (tam'ə shan'tər) n. [< title character of Burns's poem] a Scottish cap with a round, flat top

TAM-O'-SHANTER

tamp (tamp) *vt.* [< ? Fr. *tampon*, a plug] to pack or pound (down) by a series of blows or taps

Tam·pa (tam'pə) seaport in WC Fla.: pop. 272,000

tam·per (tam'pər) *vi.* [< TEMPER] 1. to make secret, illegal arrangements (with) 2. to interfere (with) or meddle (with)

tam·pon (tam'pän) n. [Fr.] a plug of cotton, etc. put into a body cavity or wound to stop bleeding, etc.

tan (tan) n. [< ML. *tanum*, TANBARK] 1. a yellowish-brown color 2. the color of suntan —*adj.* **tan'ner, tan'nest** yellowish-brown —*vt.* **tanned, tan'ning** 1. to change (hide) into leather by soaking in tannic acid 2. to produce a suntan in 3. [Colloq.] to whip severely —*vi.* to become tanned

tan·a·ger (tan'ə jər) n. [< SAmInd. *tangara*] any of a family of small American songbirds with brightly colored males

tan'bark' n. any bark containing tannic acid, used to tan hides, etc.

tan·dem (tan'dəm) *adv.* [< punning use of L. *tandem*, at length (of time)] one behind another; in single file

tang (taŋ) n. [< ON. *tangi*, a sting] 1. a prong on a file, etc. that fits into the handle 2. a strong, penetrating taste or odor —**tang'y** *adj.*

tan·ge·lo (tan'jə lō') n., *pl.* **-los** [TANG(ERINE) + (*pom*)*elo*, grapefruit] a fruit produced by crossing a tangerine with a grapefruit

tan·gent (tan'jənt) *adj.* [< L. *tangere*, to touch] 1. touching 2. *Geom.* touching a curved surface at one point but not intersecting it —n. a tangent line, curve, or surface —**go off at** (or **on**) **a tangent** to change suddenly to another line of action, etc. —**tan·gen'tial** (-jen'shəl) *adj.*

tan·ge·rine (tan'jə rēn') *n.* [< *Tangier,* city in N Africa] a small, loose-skinned, reddish-yellow orange with easily separated segments

tan·gi·ble (tan'jə b'l) *adj.* [< L. *tangere,* to touch] **1.** that can be touched or felt **2.** definite; objective —*n.pl.* property that can be appraised for value —**tan'gi·bil'i·ty** *n.*

tan·gle (tan'g'l) *vt.* -**gled,** -**gling** [< ? Sw.] **1.** to catch as in a snare; trap **2.** to make a snarl of; intertwine —*vi.* **1.** to become tangled **2.** [Col.oq.] to argue —*n.* **1.** an intertwined, confused mass **2.** a confused condition

tan·go (taŋ'gō) *n., pl.* -**gos** [AmSp.] **1.** a S. American dance with long gliding steps **2.** music for this in 2/4 or 4/4 time —*vi.* to dance the tango

tank (taŋk) *n.* [< Sans.] **1.** any large container for liquid or gas **2.** an armored vehicle with guns and full tractor treads —**tank'ful** *n.*

tank·ard (taŋ'kərd) *n.* [ME.] a large drinking cup with a handle

tank·er (taŋ'kər) *n.* **1.** a ship equipped to transport oil or other liquids **2.** a plane designed to refuel another plane in flight

tank farming *same as* HYDROPONICS

tank top [orig. worn in swimming tanks] a casual shirt like an undershirt with wide shoulder straps

tank truck a motor truck built to transport gasoline, oil, etc.

tan·ner (tan'ər) *n.* one whose work is making leather by tanning hides

tan'ner·y *n., pl.* -**ies** a place where leather is made by tanning hides

tan·nic acid (tan'ik) a yellowish, astringent substance used in tanning, dyeing, etc.: also **tan'nin** (-in) *n.*

tan·sy (tan'zē) *n., pl.* -**sies** [< LL. *tanacetum*] a plant with a strong smell and small, yellow flowers

tan·ta·lize (tan'tə līz') *vt.* -**lized', -liz'ing** [< *Tantalus,* in Gr. Myth., a king doomed in Hades to stand in water which receded when he wished to drink and under fruit he could not reach] to promise or show something desirable and then withhold it; tease

tan·ta·lum (tan'tə ləm) *n.* [< *Tantalus* (see prec.): from difficulty in extracting it] a rare, steel-blue, corrosion-resisting chemical element

tan·ta·mount (tan'tə mount') *adj.* [< OFr. *tant,* so much + *amont,* upward] equal (*to*) in value, effect, etc.

tan·tra (tun'trə, tän'-) *n.* [Sans.] [*often* T-] any of a class of Hindu or Buddhist mystical writings

tan·trum (tan'trəm) *n.* [< ?] a violent, willful outburst of rage, etc.

Tan·za·ni·a (tan'zə nē'ə) country in E Africa: 362,820 sq. mi.; pop. 12,231,000 —**Tan'za·ni'an** *adj., n.*

Tao·ism (dou'iz'm, tou'-) *n.* [Chin.

tao, the way] a Chinese religion and philosophy advocating simplicity, self-lessness, etc. —**Tao'ist** *n., adj.*

tap[1] (tap) *vt., vi.* tapped, tap'ping [echoic] **1.** to strike lightly **2.** to make or do by tapping [to *tap* a message] **3.** to choose, as for membership in a club —*n.* a light, rapid blow

tap[2] (tap) *n.* [OE. *tæppa*] **1.** a faucet or spigot **2.** a plug, cork, etc. for stopping a hole in a cask, etc. **3.** a tool used to cut threads in a female screw **4.** *Elec.* a place in a circuit where a connection can be made —*vt.* **tapped, tap'ping 1.** to put a hole in, or pull the plug from, for drawing off liquid **2.** to draw off (liquid) **3.** to make use of [to *tap* new resources] **4.** to make a connection with (a pipe, circuit, etc.); specif., to wiretap

tap dance a dance done with sharp taps of the foot, toe, or heel at each step —**tap'-dance'** *vi.* -**danced', -danc'ing** —**tap'-danc'er** *n.*

tape (tāp) *n.* [OE. *tæppe,* a fillet] **1.** a strong, narrow strip of cloth, paper, etc. used for binding, tying, etc. **2.** *same as* MAGNETIC TAPE **3.** *same as* TAPE MEASURE —*vt.* **taped, tap'ing 1.** to bind, tie, etc. with tape **2.** to record on magnetic tape

tape measure a tape with marks in inches, feet, etc. for measuring

ta·per (tā'pər) *n.* [OE. *tapur*] **1.** a slender candle **2.** a gradual decrease in width or thickness —*vt., vi.* **1.** to decrease gradually in width or thickness **2.** to lessen; diminish Often with *off*

tape recorder a device for recording on magnetic tape and for playing back such recordings

tap·es·try (tap'is trē) *n., pl.* -**tries** [< Gr. *tapēs,* a carpet] a heavy woven cloth with decorative designs and pictures, used as a wall hanging, etc.

tape'worm' *n.* a tapelike worm that lives as a parasite in the intestines

tap·i·o·ca (tap'ē ō'kə) *n.* [< SAm-Ind.] a starchy substance from cassava roots, used for puddings, etc.

ta·pir (tā'pər) *n.* [< SAmInd.] a large, hoglike mammal of tropical America and the Malay Peninsula

tap'room' *n.* a barroom

tap'root' *n.* [TAP[2] + ROOT[1]] a main root, growing downward, from which small branch roots spread out

taps (taps) *n.* [< TAP[1], because orig. a drum signal] a bugle call to put out lights in retiring for the night

tar[1] (tär) *n.* [OE. *teru*] a thick, sticky, black liquid obtained by the destructive distillation of wood, coal, etc. —*vt.* **tarred, tar'ring** to cover or smear with tar —**tar'ry** *adj.*

tar[2] (tär) *n.* [< TAR(PAULIN)] [Colloq.] a sailor

ta·ran·tu·la (tə ran'choo lə) *n.* [< *Taranto,* Italy] any of several large, hairy, somewhat poisonous spiders of S Europe and tropical America

tar·dy (tär'dē) *adj.* -**di·er, -di·est** [<

fat, āpe, cär; ten, ēven; is, bīte; gō, hôrn, tōōl, look; oil, out; up, fur; chin; she; thin, *then*; zh, leisure; ŋ, ring; ə for *a* in *ago*; ', (ā'b'l); ё, Fr. coeur; ö, Fr. feu; Fr. mon; ü, Fr. duc; kh, G. ich; doch. ‡foreign; <derived from

L. *tardus*, slow] 1. slow in moving, acting, etc. 2. late; delayed; dilatory —**tar′di·ly** *adv.* —**tar′di·ness** *n.*

tare[1] (ter) *n.* [ME.] 1. the vetch 2. *Bible* an undesirable weed

tare[2] (ter) *n.* [< Ar. *ṭaraḥa*, to reject] the weight of a container deducted from the total weight to determine the weight of the contents

tar·get (tär′git) *n.* [< MFr. *targe*, a shield] 1. a board, etc. marked as with concentric circles, aimed at in archery, rifle practice, etc. 2. any object that is shot at 3. an objective; goal 4. an object of attack, criticism, etc.

tar·iff (tar′if) *n.* [< Ar. *ta′rif*, information] 1. a list or system of taxes upon exports or, esp., imports 2. a tax of this kind, or its rate 3. any list or scale of prices, charges, etc. 4. [Colloq.] any bill, charge, etc.

tar·nish (tär′nish) *vt.* [< Fr. *ternir*, make dim] 1. to dull the luster of 2. to sully or mar —*vi.* 1. to lose luster 2. to become sullied —*n.* dullness; stain —**tar′nish·a·ble** *adj.*

ta·ro (tä′rō) *n.*, *pl.* **-ros** [Tahitian] a tropical Asiatic plant with a starchy, edible root

ta·rot (tar′ō, -ət) *n.* [Fr. < Ar. *taraha*, remove] [*often* T-] any of a set of fortunetelling cards

tar·pau·lin (tär pô′lin, tär′pə-) *n.* [< TAR[1] + PALL[2]] canvas coated with a waterproofing compound, or a protective cover of this

tar·pon (tär′pən) *n.* [< ?] a large, silvery game fish of the W Atlantic

tar·ra·gon (tar′ə gän′) *n.* [< Sp. < Ar. < Gr. *drakōn*, dragon] an old-world plant with fragrant leaves used for seasoning

tar·ry (tar′ē) *vi.* **-ried, -ry·ing** [prob. < OE. *tergan*, to vex & OFr. *targer*, to delay] 1. to delay; linger 2. to stay for a time 3. to wait

tart[1] (tärt) *adj.* [OE. *teart*] 1. sharp in taste; sour; acid 2. sharp in meaning; cutting [a *tart* reply] —**tart′ly** *adv.* —**tart′ness** *n.*

tart[2] (tärt) *n.* [< MFr. *tarte*] a small pastry shell filled with jam, fruit, etc.

tart[3] (tärt) *n.* [< prec., orig., slang term of endearment] a prostitute

tar·tan (tär′t'n) *n.* [cf. MFr. *tiretaine*, mixed fabric] a woolen cloth in any of various woven plaid patterns, worn esp. in the Scottish Highlands

Tar·tar (tär′tər) *n.* same as TATAR

tar·tar (tär′tər) *n.* [< MGr. *tartaron*] 1. a potassium salt forming a crustlike deposit in wine casks: in purified form, called **cream of tartar** 2. a hard deposit on the teeth

tartar sauce [< Fr.] a sauce of mayonnaise with chopped pickles, olives, etc.: also **tartare sauce**

task (task) *n.* [ult. < L. *taxare*, to rate] 1. a piece of work to be done 2. any difficult undertaking —*vt.* to burden; strain —**take to task** to scold

task force a group, esp. a military unit, assigned a specific task

task′mas′ter *n.* one who assigns tasks to others, esp. when severe

Tas·ma·ni·a (taz mā′nē ə) island

State of Australia, off its SE coast — **Tas·ma′ni·an** *adj.*, *n.*

tas·sel (tas′'l) *n.* [OFr., a knob] 1. an ornamental tuft of threads, etc. hanging loosely from a knob 2. something like this, as a tuft of corn silk

taste (tāst) *vt.* **tast′ed, tast′ing** [< OFr. *taster*] 1. to test the flavor of by putting a little in one's mouth 2. to detect the flavor of by the sense of taste 3. to eat or drink a small amount of 4. to experience [to *taste* success] —*vi.* to have a specific flavor —*n.* 1. the sense by which flavor is perceived through the taste buds on the tongue 2. the quality so perceived; flavor 3. a small amount tasted as a sample 4. a bit; trace 5. the ability to appreciate what is beautiful, appropriate, etc. 6. a specific preference 7. a liking; inclination —**in bad** (or **good**) **taste** in a style showing a bad (or good) sense of beauty, fitness, etc. —**taste′less** *adj.* —**tast′er** *n.*

taste bud any of the cells in the tongue that are the organs of taste

taste′ful *adj.* having or showing good taste (n. 5) —**taste′ful·ly** *adv.*

tast′y *adj.* **-i·er, -i·est** that tastes good —**tast′i·ness** *n.*

tat (tat) *vt.* **tat′ted, tat′ting** to make by tatting —*vi.* to do tatting

ta·ta·mi (tə tä′mē) *n.*, *pl.* **-mi, -mis** [Jap.] a floor mat of rice straw, used in Japanese homes for sitting on

Ta·tar (tät′ər) *n.* 1. a member of any of the E Asiatic tribes who invaded W Asia and E Europe in the Middle Ages 2. a Turkic language

tat·ter (tat′ər) *n.* [prob. < ON. *töturr*, rags] 1. a torn and hanging piece, as of a garment 2. [*pl.*] torn, ragged clothes —*vt.*, *vi.* to make or become ragged —**tat′tered** *adj.*

tat′ter·de·mal′ion (-di mäl′yən) *n.* [< prec. + ?] a person in ragged clothing

tat·ting (tat′iŋ) *n.* [prob. < Brit. dial. *tat*, to tangle] 1. a fine lace made by looping and knotting thread 2. the process of making this

tat·tle (tat′'l) *vi.* **-tled, -tling** [prob. < MDu. *tatelen*] 1. to talk idly 2. to reveal others' secrets —*vt.* to reveal (a secret) by gossiping —**tat′tler** *n.*

tat′tle·tale′ *n.* a talebearer; informer

tat·too[1] (ta tōō′) *vt.* **-tooed′, -too′ing** [Tahitian *tatau*] to make (permanent designs) on (the skin) by puncturing it and inserting indelible colors —*n.*, *pl.* **-toos′** a tattooed design

tat·too[2] (ta tōō′) *n.*, *pl.* **-toos′** [< Du. *tap toe*, shut the tap: a signal for closing barrooms] 1. a signal on a drum, bugle, etc. summoning soldiers, etc. to their quarters at night 2. a drumming, rapping, etc.

tau (tô, tou) *n.* the nineteenth letter of the Greek alphabet (T, τ)

taught (tôt) *pt. & pp. of* TEACH

taunt (tônt, tänt) *vt.* [< ? Fr. *tant pour tant*, tit for tat] to reproach scornfully or sarcastically; mock —*n.* a scornful or jeering remark

taupe (tōp) *n.* [Fr. < L. *talpa*, a mole] a dark, brownish gray

Tau·rus (tôr′əs) [L., a bull] the second sign of the zodiac

taut (tôt) *adj.* [ME. *toght*, tight] 1. tightly stretched, as a rope 2. tense [a *taut* smile] 3. trim, tidy, etc. —**taut′ly** *adv.* —**taut′ness** *n.*

tau·tol·o·gy (tô täl′ə jē) *n.* [< Gr. < *to auto*, the same + -LOGY] needless repetition of an idea, using a redundant word, etc. —**tau′to·log′i·cal** *adj.*

tav·ern (tav′ərn) *n.* [< L. *taberna*] 1. a saloon; bar 2. an inn

taw·dry (tô′drē) *adj.* -**dri·er**, -**dri·est** [< *St. Audrey laces*, sold at St. Audrey's fair, Norwich, England] cheap and gaudy

taw·ny (tô′nē) *adj.* -**ni·er**, -**ni·est** [< OFr. *tanner*, to tan] brownish-yellow; tan

tax (taks) *vt.* [< L. *taxare*, appraise] 1. to require to pay a tax 2. to assess a tax on (income, purchases, etc.) 3. to put a strain on 4. to accuse; charge —*n.* 1. a compulsory payment of a percentage of income, property value, etc. for the support of a government 2. a heavy demand; burden —**tax′a·ble** *adj.* —**tax·a′tion** *n.*

tax·i (tak′sē) *n.*, *pl.* -**is** *clipped form of* TAXICAB —*vi.* -**ied**, -**i·ing** *or* -**y·ing** 1. to go in a taxi 2. to move along the ground or water under its own power: said of an airplane

tax′i·cab′ *n.* [< *taxi(meter) cab*] an automobile in which passengers are carried for a fare

tax·i·der·my (tak′si dur′mē) *n.* [< Gr. *taxis*, arrangement + *derma*, skin] the art of preparing, stuffing, etc. the skins of animals to make them appear lifelike —**tax′i·der′mist** *n.*

tax·i·me·ter (tak′sē mēt′ər) *n.* [< Fr. *taxe*, a tax + *mètre*, meter] a device in taxicabs to register fare due

tax′i·way′ *n.* a paved strip to a runway used by taxiing planes

tax·on·o·my (tak sän′ə mē) *n.* [< Gr. *taxis*, arrangement + *nomos*, law] classification, esp. of animals and plants —**tax·on′o·mist** *n.*

tax′pay′er *n.* one who pays a tax

Tay·lor (tā′lər), **Zach·a·ry** (zak′ər ē) 1784–1850; 12th president of the U.S. (1849–50)

TB, T.B., tb, t.b. tuberculosis

T-bone steak (tē′bōn′) a quality steak with a T-shaped bone

tbs., tbsp. tablespoon(s)

T cell any of the lymphatic leukocytes affected by the thymus, that regulate immunity: cf. B CELL

Tchai·kov·sky (chī kôf′skē), **Peter** 1840–93; Russ. composer

tea (tē) *n.* [< Chin. dial. *t′e*] 1. an evergreen plant grown in Asia 2. its dried leaves, steeped in boiling water to make a beverage 3. this beverage 4. a tealike beverage made as from other plants 5. [Chiefly Brit.] a meal in the late afternoon at which tea is the drink 6. an afternoon party at which tea, etc. is served

tea·ber·ry (tē′ber′ē) *n.*, *pl.* -**ries** 1. *same as* WINTERGREEN (sense 1) 2. the fruit of the wintergreen

teach (tēch) *vt.* taught, teach′ing [OE. *tæcan*] 1. to show how to do something; give lessons to 2. to give lessons in (a subject) 3. to provide with knowledge, insight, etc. —*vi.* to be a teacher —**teach′a·ble** *adj.*

teach′er *n.* one who teaches, esp. as a profession

teaching machine a mechanical device with a corrective feedback, for presenting programmed educational material to a student

tea′cup′ *n.* a cup for drinking tea, etc. —**tea′cup·ful′** *n.*, *pl.* -**fuls′**

teak (tēk) *n.* [< Malayalam *tēkka*] 1. a large East Indian tree with hard, yellowish-brown wood 2. its wood

tea′ket′tle *n.* a kettle with a spout, for boiling water for tea, etc.

teal (tēl) *n.* [ME. *tele*] 1. a small, short-necked, freshwater duck 2. a dark grayish or greenish blue

team (tēm) *n.* [OE., offspring] 1. two or more horses, oxen, etc. harnessed to the same plow, etc. 2. a group of people working or playing together —*vi.* to join in cooperative activity (with *up*) —*adj.* of a team

team′mate′ *n.* one on the same team

team′ster (-stər) *n.* one whose work is hauling loads with a team or truck

team′work′ *n.* joint action by a group of people

tea′pot′ *n.* a pot with a spout and handle, for brewing and pouring tea

tear[1] (ter) *vt.* tore, torn, tear′ing [OE. *teran*, rend] 1. to pull apart into pieces by force; rip 2. to make by tearing [to *tear* a hole] 3. to lacerate 4. to disrupt; split [*torn* by civil war] 5. to divide with doubt, etc. 6. to pull with force (with *out*, *off*, *up*, etc.) —*vi.* 1. to be torn 2. to move with force or speed —*n.* 1. a tearing 2. a torn place; rent —**tear down** 1. to wreck 2. to dismantle

tear[2] (tir) *n.* [OE.] a drop of the salty fluid which flows from the eye, as in weeping —**in tears** weeping —**tear′ful** *adj.* —**tear′ful·ly** *adv.* —**tear′y** *adj.*

tear′drop′ *n.* a tear

tear gas (tir) a gas causing irritation to the eyes, a heavy flow of tears, etc. —**tear′-gas′** *vt.* -**gassed′**, -**gas′sing**

tea′room′ *n.* a restaurant that serves tea, coffee, light lunches, etc.

tease (tēz) *vt.* teased, teas′ing [OE. *tæsan*] 1. *a)* to card or comb (flax, wool, etc.) *b)* to fluff (the hair) by combing toward the scalp 2. to raise a nap on (cloth) by brushing with teasels 3. to annoy by mocking, poking fun, etc. 4. to beg; importune 5. to tantalize —*vi.* to indulge in teasing —*n.* one who teases

tea·sel (tē′z′l) *n.* [see prec.] 1. a bristly plant with prickly flowers 2. the dried flower, or any device, used to raise a nap on cloth

teas'er *n.* **1.** a person or thing that teases **2.** a puzzling problem

tea'spoon' *n.* a spoon for use at meals, holding 1 1/3 fluid drams —**tea'spoon·ful'** *n., pl.* **-fuls'**

teat (tēt, tit) *n.* [< OFr. *tete*] the nipple on a breast or udder

tech. **1.** technical(ly) **2.** technology

tech·ni·cal (tek'ni k'l) *adj.* [< Gr. *technē*, an art] **1.** dealing with the industrial or mechanical arts or the applied sciences **2.** of a specific science, art, craft, etc. **3.** of, in, or showing technique **4.** concerned with minute details —**tech'ni·cal·ly** *adv.*

tech'ni·cal'i·ty (-nə kal'ə tē) *n., pl.* **-ties** **1.** the state or quality of being technical **2.** a technical point, detail, etc. **3.** a minute point, detail, etc. brought to bear on a main issue

tech·ni·cian (tek nish'ən) *n.* one skilled in the technique of some art, craft, or science

Tech·ni·col·or (tek'ni kul'ər) *a trademark for* a process of making color movies —*n.* [t-] this process

tech·nique (tek nēk') *n.* [Fr.] **1.** the method of procedure in artistic work, scientific activity, etc. **2.** the degree of expertness in following this

tech·noc·ra·cy (tek näk'rə sē) *n.* [< Gr. *technē*, an art + -CRACY] government by scientists and engineers —**tech'no·crat'** (-nə krat') *n.*

tech·nol·o·gy (tek näl'ə jē) *n.* [Gr. *technologia*, systematic treatment] **1.** the science of the practical or industrial arts **2.** applied science —**tech'no·log'i·cal** (-nə läj'i k'l) *adj.*

ted·dy bear (ted'ē) [< *Teddy* (Theodore) Roosevelt] a child's stuffed toy, that looks like a bear cub

te·di·ous (tē'dē əs) *adj.* full of tedium; long and dull —**te'di·ous·ly** *adv.*

te'di·um (-əm) *n.* [< L. *taedet*, it offends] the condition or quality of being tiresome, wearisome, etc.

tee (tē) *n.* [prob. < Scot. dial. *teaz*] *Golf* **1.** a small peg from which the ball is driven **2.** the place from which a player makes the first stroke on each hole —*vt., vi.* **teed'd**, **tee'ing** to place (a ball) on a tee —**tee off** **1.** to play a golf ball from a tee **2.** [Slang] to make angry or disgusted

teem (tēm) *vi.* [< OE. *team*, progeny] to be prolific; abound; swarm

teen (tēn) *n.* [OE. *tien*, ten] **1.** [*pl.*] the years from 13 through 19, as of a person's age **2.** *same as* TEEN-AGER

teen-age (tēn'āj') *adj.* **1.** in one's teens **2.** of or for persons in their teens Also **teenage** —**teen'-ag'er** *n.*

tee·ny (tē'nē) *adj.* **-ni·er, -ni·est** *colloq. var. of* TINY: also **teen'sy, tee'ny-wee'ny, teen'sy-ween'sy**

teen·y-bop·per (tē'nē bäp'ər) *n.* [Slang] a faddish young teen-ager

tee·pee (tē'pē) *n. alt. sp. of* TEPEE

tee shirt *same as* T-SHIRT

tee·ter (tēt'ər) *vi., vt., n.* [< ON. *titra*, tremble] seesaw or wobble

tee'ter-tot'ter (-tät'ər) *n., vi.* seesaw

teeth (tēth) *n. pl. of* TOOTH

teethe (tēth) *vi.* **teethed, teeth'ing** to grow teeth; cut one's teeth

tee·to·tal·er (tē tōt'l ər) *n.* [< doubling of initial *t* in *total*] one who practices total abstinence from alcoholic liquor: also **tee·to'tal·ler**

Tef·lon (tef'län) *a trademark for* a tough polymer, used for nonsticking coatings as on cooking utensils

Teh·ran, Te·her·an (te hrän'; *E.* te ə rän') capital of Iran: pop. 2,803,000

tek·tite (tek'tīt) *n.* [< Gr. *tēktos*, molten] a small, dark, glassy body, thought to be from outer space

tel. **1.** telegram **2.** telephone

Tel A·viv (tel' ä vēv') seaport in W Israel: pop. 394,000: in full **Tel'-A·viv'-Jaf'fa** (-yäf'ə)

tele- *a combining form meaning:* **1.** [< Gr. *tēle*, far off] at, over, etc. a distance *[telegraph]* **2.** [< TELE(VISION)] of, in, or by television *[telecast]*

tel·e·cast (tel'ə kast') *vt., vi.* **-cast'** or **-cast'ed, -cast'ing** to broadcast by television —*n.* a television broadcast —**tel'e·cast'er** *n.*

tel·e·con'fer·ence *n.* a conference of persons in different locations, as by telephone, TV, etc.

tel·e·gram (tel'ə gram') *n.* a message transmitted by telegraph

tel·e·graph' (-graf') *n.* [see TELE- & -GRAPH] an apparatus or system that transmits messages by electric impulses sent by wire or radio —*vt., vi.* to send (a message) to (a person) by telegraph —**tel'e·graph'ic** *adj.*

te·leg·ra·phy (tə leg'rə fē) *n.* the operation of telegraph apparatus —**te·leg'ra·pher** *n.*

tel·e·ki·ne·sis (tel'ə ki nē'sis) *n.* [see TELE- & KINETIC] the apparent causing of movement in an object by unexplainable means, as by the mind

tel·e·me·ter (tel'ə mēt'ər, tə lem'ə tər) *n.* a device for measuring and transmitting data about radiation, temperature, etc. from a remote point

te·lep·a·thy (tə lep'ə thē) *n.* [TELE- + -PATHY] supposed communication between minds by means other than the normal sensory channels —**tel·e·path·ic** (tel'ə path'ik) *adj.*

tel·e·phone (tel'ə fōn') *n.* [TELE- + -PHONE] an instrument or system for conveying speech over distances by converting sound into electric impulses sent through a wire —*vt., vi.* **-phoned', -phon'ing** to convey (a message) to (a person) by telephone —**tel'e·phon'ic** (-fän'ik) *adj.*

te·leph·o·ny (tə lef'ə nē) *n.* the making or operation of telephones

tel·e·pho·to (tel'ə fōt'ō) *adj.* designating or of a camera lens that produces a large image of a distant object

tel'e·pho'to·graph' *n.* **1.** a photograph taken with a telephoto lens **2.** a photograph transmitted by telegraph or radio —*vt., vi.* to take or transmit (telephotographs) —**tel'e·pho·tog'ra·phy** (-fə täg'rə fē) *n.*

tel·e·proc'ess·ing *n.* data processing over communication lines

tel·e·scope' (-skōp') *n.* [see TELE- & -SCOPE] an instrument with lenses for making distant objects appear nearer and larger —*vi.*, *vt.* **-scoped'**, **-scop'-ing** to slide one into another like the tubes of a collapsible telescope — **tel'e·scop'ic** (-skäp'ik) *adj.*

tel'e·text' *n.* an information service superimposed on a TV signal and broadcast to home TV sets

tel'e·thon' (-thän') *n.* [TELE(VISION) + (MARA)THON] a lengthy telecast

Tel'e·type' (-tīp') *a trademark for a* form of telegraph in which the receiver prints messages typed on the transmitter —**tel'e·type'writ'er** *n.*

tel·e·vise (tel'ə vīz') *vt.*, *vi.* **-vised'**, **-vis'ing** to transmit by television

tel'e·vi'sion (-vizh'ən) *n.* **1.** the process of transmitting images by converting light rays into electrical signals: the receiver reconverts the signals to reproduce the images on a screen **2.** television broadcasting **3.** a television receiving set

tell (tel) *vt.* **told**, **tell'ing** [OE. *tellan*, calculate] **1.** orig., to count **2.** to narrate; relate *[tell a story]* **3.** to express in words; say *[tell the facts]* **4.** to reveal; disclose **5.** to recognize; distinguish *[to tell twins apart]* **6.** to inform *[tell me later]* **7.** to order *[tell her to go]* —*vi.* **1.** to give an account or evidence (of something) **2.** to be effective *[each blow told]* —**tell off** [Colloq.] to rebuke severely —**tell on 1.** to tire **2.** [Colloq.] to inform against

tell'er *n.* **1.** one who tells (a story, etc.) **2.** one who counts, as a bank clerk who pays out or receives money

tell'ing *adj.* forceful; striking — **tell'ing·ly** *adv.*

tell'tale' *adj.* revealing what is meant to be kept hidden or secret

tell·y (tel'ē) *n.* Brit. colloq. term for TELEVISION

tem·blor (tem'blôr, -blər) *n.* [Sp. < *temblar*, to tremble] an earthquake

te·mer·i·ty (tə mer'ə tē) *n.* [< L. *temere*, rashly] foolish or rash boldness

temp. temperature

tem·per (tem'pər) *vt.* [< L. *temperare*, regulate] **1.** to moderate, as by mingling with something else *[temper blame with praise]* **2.** to bring to the proper condition by some treatment *[to temper steel]* **3.** to toughen —*n.* **1.** the degree of hardness and resiliency of a metal **2.** frame of mind; disposition **3.** calmness of mind: in **lose** (or keep) **one's temper 4.** anger; rage

tem·per·a (tem'pər ə) *n.* [It.: see prec.] a process of painting with pigments mixed with size, casein, or egg

tem·per·a·ment (tem'prə mənt, -pər ə mənt) *n.* [see TEMPER] **1.** one's natural disposition; nature **2.** a nature that is excitable, moody, etc. — **tem'per·a·men'tal** *adj.*

tem·per·ance (tem'pər əns) *n.* **1.** self-restraint in conduct, indulgence of the appetites, etc.; moderation **2.** moderation in drinking alcoholic liquors or total abstinence from them

tem·per·ate (tem'pər it) *adj.* [see TEMPER] **1.** moderate, as in eating or drinking **2.** self-restrained in actions, speech, etc. **3.** neither very hot nor very cold: said of climate, etc.

Temperate Zone either of two zones **(North** or **South Temperate Zone)** between the tropics and the polar circles

tem·per·a·ture (tem'prə chər, tem'pər ə-) *n.* [< L. *temperatus*, temperate] **1.** the degree of hotness or coldness of anything **2.** excess of body heat over the normal; fever

tem·pered (tem'pərd) *adj.* **1.** having been given the desired temper (*n.* 1) **2.** having a (specified) temper (*n.* 2)

tem·pest (tem'pist) *n.* [< L. *tempus*, time] a violent storm with high winds, esp. one accompanied by rain, etc.

tem·pes·tu·ous (tem pes'choo wəs) *adj.* of or like a tempest; violent

tem·plate (tem'plit) *n.* [< L. *templum*, a timber] a pattern, as a thin metal plate, for making an exact copy

tem·ple¹ (tem'p'l) *n.* [< L. *templum*] **1.** a building for the worship of God or gods **2.** a large building for some special purpose *[a temple of art]*

tem·ple² (tem'p'l) *n.* [< L. *tempus*] **1.** the flat surface beside the forehead, in front of each ear **2.** one sidepiece of a pair of glasses

tem·po (tem'pō) *n.*, *pl.* **-pos**, **-pi** (-pē) [It. < L. *tempus*, time] **1.** the rate of speed at which a musical work is played **2.** rate of activity

tem·po·ral¹ (tem'pər əl) *adj.* [< L. *tempus*, time] **1.** temporary; transitory **2.** of this world; worldly **3.** secular **4.** of or limited by time

tem·po·ral² (tem'pər əl) *adj.* of or near the temples (of the head)

tem'po·rar'y (-pə rer'ē) *adj.* [< L. *tempus*, time] lasting only a while; not permanent —**tem'po·rar'i·ly** *adv.*

tem·po·rize (tem'pə rīz') *vt.* **-rized'**, **-riz'ing** to give temporary compliance, evade decision, etc. so as to gain time or avoid argument

tempt (tempt) *vt.* [< L. *temptare*, to test] **1.** to entice or induce, as to something immoral **2.** to be inviting to; attract **3.** to provoke or risk provoking (fate, etc.) **4.** to incline strongly *[I am tempted to go]* —**temp·ta·tion** (temp tā'shən) *n.* —**tempt'er** *n.* —**tempt'ress** *n.fem.*

tem·pu·ra (tem'poo rä', tem poor'ə) *n.* [Jap.] a Japanese dish of deep-fried shrimp, fish, vegetables, etc.

ten (ten) *adj.*, *n.* [OE.] one more than nine; 10; X

ten·a·ble (ten'ə b'l) *adj.* [< L. *tenere*, hold] that can be held, defended, or maintained —**ten'a·bil'i·ty** *n.*

te·na·cious (tə nā'shəs) *adj.* [< L. *tenere*, to hold] **1.** holding firmly *[a tenacious grip]* **2.** retentive *[a tenacious memory]* **3.** strongly cohesive or adhesive **4.** persistent; stubborn *[tenacious courage]* — **te·na'cious·ly**

adv. —**te·nac·i·ty** (tə nas′ə tē) *n.*

ten·ant (ten′ənt) *n.* [see prec.] **1.** one who pays rent to occupy land, a building, etc. **2.** an occupant —*vt.* to hold as a tenant —**ten′an·cy** *n.*

tenant farmer one who farms land that he pays rent for or sharecrops

Ten Commandments the ten laws of moral and religious conduct given to Moses by God: Ex. 20:2–17

tend[1] (tend) *vt.* [see ATTEND] **1.** to take care of **2.** to manage or operate

tend[2] (tend) *vi.* [< L. *tendere,* to stretch] **1.** to be inclined, disposed, etc. (*to*) **2.** to be directed (*to* or *toward*)

tend·en·cy (ten′dən sē) *n.,* pl. **-cies** [see prec.] **1.** an inclination to move or act in a particular direction or way **2.** a course toward some object

ten·den·tious (ten den′shəs) *adj.* [< G. < *tendenz,* TENDENCY] advancing a definite point of view —**ten·den′tious·ly** *adv.*

ten·der[1] (ten′dər) *adj.* [< L. *tener,* soft] **1.** soft and easily chewed, broken, cut, etc. **2.** physically weak **3.** immature **4.** that requires careful handling **5.** gentle or light **6.** acutely sensitive, as to pain **7.** sensitive to emotions, others' feelings, etc. —**ten′der·ly** *adv.* —**ten′der·ness** *n.*

ten·der[2] (ten′dər) *vt.* [see TEND[2]] to offer formally —*n.* **1.** a formal offer **2.** money, etc. offered in payment

tend·er[3] (ten′dər) *n.* **1.** one who tends something **2.** a small ship for supplying a larger one **3.** a railroad car attached behind, and carrying coal and water for, a steam locomotive

ten′der·foot′ *n.,* pl. **-foots′, -feet′ 1.** a newcomer to ranching in the West, unused to hardships **2.** any novice

ten′der·heart′ed *adj.* quick to feel pity or compassion

ten·der·ize (ten′də rīz′) *vt.* **-ized′, -iz′ing** to make (meat) tender

ten′der·loin′ *n.* the tenderest part of a loin of beef, pork, etc.

ten·don (ten′dən) *n.* [< Gr. *teinein,* to stretch] any of the inelastic cords of tough connective tissue by which muscles are attached to bones, etc.

ten·dril (ten′drəl) *n.* [prob. ult. < L. *tener,* delicate] a threadlike, clinging part of a climbing plant

ten·e·ment (ten′ə mənt) *n.* [< L. *tenere,* to hold] **1.** a room or suite tenanted as a separate dwelling **2.** a building divided into tenements; now specif., one that is run-down, overcrowded, etc.: also **tenement house**

ten·et (ten′it) *n.* [L., he holds] a principle, doctrine, or belief held as a truth, as by some group

Ten·nes·see (ten′ə sē′) EC State of the U.S.: 42,244 sq. mi.; pop. 4,591,000; cap. Nashville: abbrev. **Tenn.** — **Ten′nes·se′an** *adj., n.*

ten·nis (ten′is) *n.* [prob. < OFr. *tenez,* hold (imperative)] a game in which players in a marked area (**tennis court**) hit a ball back and forth with rackets over a net

tennis elbow inflammation of the elbow tendons, caused by strain

tennis shoe a sneaker

Ten·ny·son (ten′ə s'n), Alfred 1809–92; Eng. poet

ten·on (ten′ən) *n.* [ult. < L. *tenere,* to hold] a projecting part cut on the end of a piece of wood for insertion into a mortise to make a joint

ten·or (ten′ər) *n.* [< L. *tenere,* to hold] **1.** general tendency **2.** general meaning; drift **3.** *a)* the highest regular adult male singing voice *b)* a singer with such a voice *c)* a part for a tenor

ten′pins′ *n. pl.* **1.** [*with sing. v.*] the game of bowling in which ten pins are used **2.** the pins

tense[1] (tens) *adj.* **tens′er, tens′est** [< L. *tendere,* stretch] **1.** stretched tight; taut **2.** undergoing or showing tension —*vt., vi.* tensed, tens′ing to make or become tense —**tense′ly** *adv.* —**tense′ness, ten·si′ty** (ten′sə tē) *n.*

tense[2] (tens) *n.* [< L. *tempus,* time] any of the forms of a verb that show the time of its action or existence

ten·sile (ten′s'l) *adj.* **1.** of, undergoing, or exerting tension **2.** capable of being stretched

ten·sion (ten′shən) *n.* **1.** a tensing or being tensed **2.** mental or nervous strain **3.** a state of strained relations due to mutual hostility **4.** voltage **5.** stress on a material produced by the pull of forces causing extension

tent (tent) *n.* [< L. *tendere,* to stretch] a portable shelter made of canvas, etc. stretched over poles —*vi., vt.* to lodge in a tent or tents

ten·ta·cle (ten′tə k'l) *n.* [< L. *tentare,* to touch] a long, slender, flexible growth about the head of some invertebrates, used to grasp, feel, etc.

ten·ta·tive (ten′tə tiv) *adj.* [< L. *tentare,* try] made, done, etc. as a test or experiment —**ten′ta·tive·ly** *adv.*

ten·ter·hook (ten′tər hook′) *n.* [< L. *tendere,* to stretch + HOOK] any of the hooked nails holding cloth stretched on a drying frame (**tenter**) —**on tenterhooks** in anxious suspense

tenth (tenth) *adj.* [OE. *teogotha*] preceded by nine others in a series; 10th —*n.* **1.** the one following the ninth **2.** any of the ten equal parts of something; 1/10 **3.** a tenth of a gallon

ten·u·ous (ten′yoo wəs) *adj.* [< L. *tenuis,* thin] **1.** slender or fine, as a fiber **2.** rare, as air at high altitudes **3.** not substantial; flimsy

ten·ure (ten′yər, -yoor) *n.* [< MFr. *tenir,* to hold] **1.** the act or right of holding property, an office, etc. **2.** the length of time, or the conditions under which, something is held

te·pee (tē′pē) *n.* [< Siouan *ti,* dwell + *pi,* used for] a cone-shaped tent used by American Indians

tep·id (tep′id) *adj.* [< L. *tepidus*] **1.** lukewarm **2.** lacking enthusiasm

te·qui·la (tə kē′lə) *n.* [< *Tequila,* Mex. district] an alcoholic liquor distilled from a Mexican agave

TEPEE

ter·cen·te·nar·y (tur'sen ten'ər ē, tər sen'tə ner'ē) *adj., n., pl.* **-ies** [L. *ter*, three times + CENTENARY] tricentennial

term (turm) *n.* [< L. *terminus*, a limit] **1.** a set date, as for payment, etc. **2.** a set period of time [school *term*, *term* of office] **3.** [*pl.*] conditions of a contract, etc. **4.** [*pl.*] mutual relationship between persons [on speaking *terms*] **5.** a word or phrase, esp. as used in some science, art, etc. **6.** [*pl.*] words; speech [unkind *terms*] **7.** *Math. a)* either quantity of a fraction or a ratio *b)* each quantity in a series or algebraic expression —*vt.* to call by a term; name —**bring** (or **come**) **to terms** to force into (or arrive at) an agreement

ter·ma·gant (tur'mə gənt) *n.* [< OFr. *Tervagant*, imaginary Moslem deity] a quarrelsome, scolding woman

ter·mi·na·ble (tur'mi nə b'l) *adj.* that can be, or is, terminated

ter·mi·nal (tur'mə n'l) *adj.* [L. *terminalis*] **1.** of, at, or forming the end or extremity **2.** concluding; final **3.** close to causing death, as cancer **4.** of or at the end of a transportation line —*n.* **1.** an end; extremity **2.** a connective point on an electric circuit **3.** either end of a transportation line, or a main station on it **4.** a device, usually with a keyboard and video display, for putting data in, or getting it from, a computer

ter·mi·nate (tur'mə nāt') *vt.* **-nat'ed, -nat'ing** [< L. *terminus*, a limit] **1.** to form the end of **2.** to put an end to; stop **3.** to dismiss from employment; fire —*vi.* **1.** to come to an end **2.** to have its end (*in* something) —**ter'mi·na'tion** *n.*

ter·mi·nol·o·gy (tur'mə näl'ə jē) *n., pl.* **-gies** the terms used in a specific science, art, etc.

term insurance life insurance that expires after a specified period

ter·mi·nus (tur'mə nəs) *n., pl.* **-ni'** (-nī'), **-nus·es** [L., a limit] **1.** a limit **2.** an end; extremity or goal **3.** either end of a transportation line

ter·mite (tur'mīt) *n.* [L. *termes*, wood-boring worm] a social insect very destructive to wooden structures

tern (turn) *n.* [< ON. *therna*] a sea bird related to the gull, but smaller

terp·si·cho·re·an (turp'si kə rē'ən) *adj.* [< *Terpsichore*, Muse of dancing] having to do with dancing

ter·race (ter'əs) *n.* [< L. *terra*, earth] **1.** a raised, flat mound of earth with sloping sides, esp. one in a series on a hillside **2.** an unroofed, paved area between a house and lawn **3.** a row of houses on ground above street level —*vt.* **-raced, -rac·ing** to form into a terrace or terraces

ter·ra cot·ta (ter'ə kät'ə) [It., lit., baked earth] a hard, brown-red earthenware, or its color

terra fir·ma (fur'mə) [L.] firm earth

ter·rain (tə rān', ter'ān) *n.* [< L. *terra*, earth] a tract of ground, esp. with regard to its fitness for some use

ter·ra·pin (ter'ə pin) *n.* [< Algonquian] **1.** any of various freshwater or tidewater turtles **2.** its edible flesh

ter·rar·i·um (tə rer'ē əm) *n., pl.* **-i·ums, -i·a** (-ə) [< L. *terra*, earth + (AQU)ARIUM] an enclosure, as of glass, in which small plants are grown or small land animals are kept

ter·raz·zo (tə raz'ō, -rät'sō) *n.* [It.] flooring of small chips of marble set in cement and polished

ter·res·tri·al (tə res'trē əl) *adj.* [< L. *terra*, earth] **1.** worldly; mundane **2.** of the earth **3.** consisting of land, not water **4.** living on land

ter·ri·ble (ter'ə b'l) *adj.* [< L. *terrere*, frighten] **1.** causing terror; dreadful **2.** extreme; intense **3.** [Colloq.] very unpleasant, etc. —**ter'ri·bly** *adv.*

ter·ri·er (ter'ē ər) *n.* [< MFr. (*chien*) *terrier*, hunting (dog)] any of various breeds of active, typically small dog

ter·rif·ic (tə rif'ik) *adj.* [< L. *terrere*, frighten] **1.** causing great fear **2.** [Colloq.] *a)* very great, intense, etc. *b)* unusually fine, admirable, etc.

ter·ri·fy (ter'ə fī') *vt.* **-fied', -fy'ing** to fill with terror; frighten greatly

ter·ri·to·ry (ter'ə tôr'ē) *n., pl.* **-ries** [< L. *terra*, earth] **1.** an area under the jurisdiction of a nation, ruler, etc. **2.** a part of a country or empire that does not have full status **3.** any large tract of land **4.** an assigned area **5.** a sphere of action, thought, etc. —**ter'ri·to'ri·al** *adj.*

ter·ror (ter'ər) *n.* [< L. *terrere*, frighten] **1.** intense fear **2.** *a)* one that causes intense fear *b)* the quality of causing such fear

ter'ror·ism *n.* the use of force or threats to intimidate, etc., esp. as a political policy —**ter'ror·ist** *n., adj.*

ter'ror·ize' (-īz') *vt.* **-ized', -iz'ing** **1.** to terrify **2.** to coerce, make submit, etc. by filling with terror

ter·ry (ter'ē) *n.* [prob. < Fr. *tirer*, to draw] cloth having a pile of uncut loops, esp. cotton cloth used for toweling: also **terry cloth**

terse (turs) *adj.* **ters'er, ters'est** [L. *tersus*, wiped off] free of superfluous words; concise; succinct —**terse'ly** *adv.* —**terse'ness** *n.*

ter·ti·ar·y (tur'shē er'ē) *adj.* [< L. *tertius*, third] third in order

tes·sel·late (tes'ə lāt') *vt.* **-lat'ed, -lat'ing** [< L. *tessella*, little square stone] to lay out in a mosaic pattern of small, square blocks

test (test) *n.* [< OFr., assaying cup] **1.** *a)* an examination or trial, as of something's value *b)* the method or a criterion used in this **2.** an event, etc. that tries one's qualities **3.** a set of questions, etc. for determining one's knowledge, etc. **4.** *Chem.* a trial or reaction for identifying a substance

—*vt.* to subject to a test; try —*vi.* to be rated by a test —**test′er** *n.*

tes·ta·ment (tes′tə mənt) *n.* [< L. *testis,* a witness] 1. [T-] either of the two parts of the Bible, the *Old Testament* and the *New Testament* 2. *a)* a testimonial *b)* an affirmation of beliefs 3. *Law* a will —**tes′ta·men′ta·ry** (-men′tə rē) *adj.*

tes′ta·tor *n.* one who has made a will

tes·ti·cle (tes′ti k'l) *n.* [< L. *testis*] either of two male sex glands

tes·ti·fy (tes′tə fī′) *vi.* -**fied′,** -**fy′-ing** [< L. *testis,* a witness + *facere,* make] 1. to give evidence, esp. under oath in court 2. to serve as evidence —*vt.* 1. to affirm; declare, esp. under oath in court 2. to indicate

tes·ti·mo·ni·al (tes′tə mō′nē əl) *n.* 1. a statement recommending a person or thing 2. something given or done to show gratitude or appreciation

tes·ti·mo·ny (tes′tə mō′nē) *n., pl.* -**nies** [< L. *testis,* a witness] 1. a statement made under oath to establish a fact 2. any declaration 3. any form of evidence; proof

tes·tis (tes′tis) *n., pl.* -**tes** (-tēz) *same as* TESTICLE

tes·tos·ter·one (tes täs′tə rōn′) *n.* [see TESTICLE] a male sex hormone

test tube a tube of thin, transparent glass closed at one end, used in chemical experiments, etc.

tes·ty (tes′tē) *adj.* -**ti·er,** -**ti·est** [< L. *testa,* the head] irritable; touchy

tet·a·nus (tet′'n əs) *n.* [< Gr. *tetanos,* spasm] an acute infectious disease, often fatal, caused by a toxin and characterized by spasmodic contractions and rigidity of muscles

tête-à-tête (tāt′ə tāt′) *n.* [Fr., lit., head-to-head] a private conversation between two people

teth·er (te*th*′ər) *n.* [< ON. *tjothr*] 1. a rope or chain fastened to an animal to keep it from roaming 2. the limit of one's abilities, resources, etc. —*vt.* to fasten with a tether

tet·ra (tet′rə) *n.* [< ModL.] a brightly colored, tropical American fish

tetra- [Gr. < *tettares,* four] *a combining form meaning* four

tet·ra·eth·yl lead (tet′rə eth′'l) a poisonous lead compound added to gasoline to prevent engine knock

tet·ra·he·dron (tet′rə hē′drən) *n., pl.* -**drons,** -**dra** (-drə) [see TETRA- & -HEDRON] a solid figure with four triangular faces

Teut. 1. Teuton 2. Teutonic

Teu·ton·ic (tōō tän′ik) *adj.* designating or of a group of north European peoples, esp. the Germans —**Teu·ton** (tōōt′'n) *n.*

TETRA-HEDRON

Tex·as (tek′səs) SW State of the U.S.: 267,339 sq. mi., 14,228,000; cap. Austin: abbrev. Tex. —**Tex′an** *adj., n.*

text (tekst) *n.* [< L. *texere,* to weave] 1. the actual words of an author, as distinguished from notes, etc. 2. any form in which a written work exists 3. the principal matter on a printed page,

as distinguished from notes, headings, etc. 4. *a)* a Biblical passage used as the topic of a sermon, etc. *b)* any topic or subject 5. a textbook —**tex·tu·al** (teks′choo wəl) *adj.*

text′book′ *n.* a book giving instructions in a subject of study

tex·tile (teks′tīl, -t'l) *adj.* [see TEXT] 1. having to do with weaving 2. that has been or can be woven —*n.* 1. a woven or knitted fabric; cloth 2. raw material suitable for this

tex·ture (teks′chər) *n.* [< L. *texere,* to weave] 1. the character of a fabric, determined by the arrangement, size, etc. of its threads 2. the arrangement of the constituent parts of anything —**tex′tur·al** *adj.*

-th¹ [OE.] *a suffix meaning:* 1. the act of *[stealth]* 2. the state or quality of being or having *[wealth]*

-th² [< OE.] a suffix used in forming ordinal numbers *[fourth, ninth]*

Th. Thursday

Thai (tī) *n.* 1. a subbranch of the Sino-Tibetan language 2. the language of Thailand 3. *pl.* **Thais, Thai** *a)* a member of a group of Thai-speaking peoples of SE Asia *b)* a native or inhabitant of Thailand —*adj.* of Thailand, its people, culture, etc.

Thai·land (tī′land) country in SE Asia: 198,456 sq. mi.; pop. 33,693,000

thal·a·mus (thal′ə məs) *n., pl.* -**mi** (-mī′) [< Gr. *thalamos,* inner chamber] a mass of gray matter at the base of the brain, involved in the transmission of certain sensations

tha·lid·o·mide (thə lid′ə mīd′) *n.* a drug formerly used as a sedative, but found to cause severe birth deformities when taken in pregnancy

thal·lo·phyte (thal′ə fīt′) *n.* [< Gr. *thallos,* green shoot + *phyton,* a plant] any of a large division of plants including the bacteria, algae, fungi, and lichens

Thames (temz) river in S England, flowing through London into the North Sea

than (*th*an, *th*en) *conj.* [OE. *thenne*] a particle used to introduce the second element in a comparison *[I am taller than* Bill*]*

thank (thaŋk) *vt.* [OE. *thancian*] 1. to give one's thanks to 2. to hold responsible; blame: an ironic use —**thank you** *short for* I thank you

thank′ful *adj.* feeling or expressing thanks —**thank′ful·ly** *adv.*

thank′less *adj.* 1. not feeling or expressing thanks; ungrateful 2. unappreciated —**thank′less·ly** *adv.*

thanks *n.pl.* an expression of gratitude —*interj.* I thank you —**thanks to** 1. thanks be given to 2. on account of; because of

thanks·giv′ing *n.* 1. a formal public expression of thanks to God 2. [T-] an annual U.S. holiday observed on the fourth Thursday of November

that (*th*at) *pron., pl.* **those** [OE. *thæt*] 1. the person or thing mentioned *[that* is John*]* 2. the farther one or other one *[this* is better than *that]* 3. who, whom, or which *[the road that* we took/ 4. where [the place *that* I saw him/ 5. when [the year *that* he died/ —*adj., pl.* those 1. designating the one mentioned [*that* man is John/ 2. designating the farther one or other one [this house is larger than *that* one/ —*conj. used to introduce:* 1. a noun clause [*that* he's gone is obvious/ 2. an adverbial clause expressing purpose [they died *that* we might live/, result [he ran so fast *that* I lost him/, or cause [I'm sorry *that* I won/ 3. an elliptical sentence expressing surprise, desire, etc. [oh, *that* he were here!/ —*adv.* to that extent; so [I can't see *that* far/ —**at that** [Colloq.] 1. at that point: also **with that** 2. even so —**that is** 1. to be specific 2. in other words

thatch (thach) *n.* [OE. *thæc*] 1. a roof of straw, rushes, etc. 2. material for such a roof: also **thatch'ing** —*vt.* to cover as with thatch

thaw (thô) *vi.* [OE. *thawian*] 1. *a)* to melt, as ice, snow, etc. *b)* to become unfrozen: said of frozen foods 2. to become warmer so that snow, etc. melts 3. to lose one's coldness of manner —*vt.* to cause to thaw —*n.* 1. a thawing 2. a spell of weather warm enough to allow thawing

THC [*t*(etra)*h*(ydro)*c*(annabinol)] the principal and most active chemical in marijuana

Th.D. Doctor of Theology

the (tha; *before vowels* thi, thē) *adj., definite article* [< OE. *se*, with *th-* from other forms] the (as opposed to *a, an*) refers to: 1. a particular person or thing [*the* story ended, *the* President/ 2. a person or thing considered generically [*the* cow is a domestic animal, *the* poor/ —*adv.* 1. that much [*the* better to see you/ 2. by how much . . . by that much [*the* sooner *the* better/

the·a·ter, the·a·tre (thē'ə tər) *n.* [< Gr. *theasthai*, to view] 1. a place or building where plays, motion pictures, etc. are presented 2. any similar place with banked rows of seats 3. any scene of events 4. *a)* the dramatic art *b)* the theatrical world

the·at·ri·cal (thē at'ri k'l) *adj.* 1. having to do with the theater 2. dramatic; esp. (in disparagement) melodramatic —**the·at'ri·cal·ly** *adv.*

thee (thē) *pron.* [OE.] *the objective case of* THOU

theft (theft) *n.* [OE. *thiefth*] the act or an instance of stealing; larceny

their (ther) *poss. pronominal adj.* [< ON. *theirra*] of, belonging to, made by, or done by them

theirs (therz) *pron.* that or those belonging to them [*theirs* are better/

the·ism (thē'iz'm) *n.* [< Gr. *theos*, god] 1. belief in a god or gods 2. monotheism —**the'ist** *n.* —**the·is'tic** *adj.*

them (them) *pron.* [< ON. *theim*] *objective case of* THEY

theme (thēm) *n.* [< Gr. *thema*, what is laid down] 1. a topic, as of an essay 2. a short essay 3. a short melody used

as the subject of a musical composition 4. a recurring or identifying song in a film, musical, radio or TV series, etc.: also **theme song** —**the·mat·ic** (thē mat'ik) *adj.*

them·selves (them selvz') *pron.* 1. *intensive form of* THEY [they went *themselves*] 2. *reflexive form of* THEY [they hurt *themselves*]

then (then) *adv.* [see THAN] 1. at that time [I did it *then*] 2. next in time or order [he ate and *then* slept] 3. in that case; accordingly [if he read it, *then* he knows] 4. besides; moreover [I like to walk, and *then* it's cheaper] 5. at another time [now she's happy, *then* sad] —*adj.* being such at that time [the *then* director] —*n.* that time [by *then*, they were gone]

thence (thens, thens) *adv.* [OE. *thanan*] 1. from that place 2. from that time; thenceforth 3. therefore

thence·forth' (-fôrth') *adv.* from that time onward; thereafter: also **thence·for'ward, thence·for'wards**

the·oc·ra·cy (thē äk'rə sē) *n., pl.* -**cies** [< Gr. *theos*, god + *kratos*, power] (a) government by priests claiming to rule with divine authority

the·o·lo·gi·an (thē'ə lō'jən, -jē ən) *n.* a student of or specialist in theology

the·ol·o·gy (thē äl'ə jē) *n., pl.* -**gies** [< Gr. *theos*, god + *logos*, discourse] the study of God and of religious doctrines and matters of divinity —**the'o·log'i·cal** (-ə läj'i k'l) *adj.*

the·o·rem (thē'ə rəm) *n.* [< Gr. *theōrein*, to view] 1. a proposition that can be proved from accepted premises; law or principle 2. a proposition embodying something to be proved

the·o·ret·i·cal (thē'ə ret'i k'l) *adj.* 1. limited to or based on theory; hypothetical 2. tending to theorize; speculative Also **the'o·ret'ic** —**the'o·ret'i·cal·ly** *adv.*

the·o·rize (thē'ə rīz') *vi.* -**rized', -riz'ing** to form a theory or theories; speculate —**the'o·re·ti'cian** (-rə tish' ən), **the'o·rist** (-rist) *n.*

the·o·ry (thē'ə rē, thir'ē) *n., pl.* -**ries** [< Gr. *theōrein*, to view] 1. a speculative plan 2. a formulation of underlying principles of certain observed phenomena which has been verified to some degree 3. the principles of an art or science rather than its practice 4. a conjecture; guess

the·os·o·phy (thē äs'ə fē) *n., pl.* -**phies** [< Gr. *theos*, god + *sophos*, wise] a religious system proposing to establish direct, mystical contact with the divine spirit —**the'o·soph'ic** (-ə säf'ik) *adj.* —**the'o·soph'i·cal·ly** *adv.* —**the·os'o·phist** *n.*

ther·a·peu·tic (ther'ə pyōot'ik) *adj.* [< Gr. *therapeuein*, to nurse] serving to cure or heal or to preserve health

ther'a·peu'tics *n.pl.* [*with sing. v.*] the branch of medicine dealing with the treatment of disease; therapy

---

fat, āpe, cär; ten, ēven; is, bīte; gō, hôrn, tōol, look; oil, out; up, fur; chin; she; thin, then; zh, leisure; ŋ, ring; ə for *a* in *ago*; ', (ā'b'l); ē, Fr. coeur; ö, Fr. feu; Fr. mon; ü, Fr. duc; kh, G. ich, doch; ‡ foreign; < derived from

ther'a·py (-pē) *n., pl.* **-pies** [see THERAPEUTIC] the treatment of any physical or mental disorder by medical or physical means, usually excluding surgery —**ther'a·pist** *n.*

there (*ther*) *adv.* [OE. *ther*] **1.** at or in that place: often used as an intensive [John *there* is a good player] **2.** to or into that place [go *there*] **3.** at that point; then **4.** in that respect [*there* you are wrong] *There* is also used in clauses in which the real subject follows the verb [*there* is little time] —*n.* that place [we left *there* at six] —*interj.* an exclamation of defiance, satisfaction, sympathy, etc. —(not) all there (not) mentally sound

there'a·bouts (-ə bouts') *adv.* **1.** near that place **2.** near that time, number, degree, etc. Also **there'a·bout'**

there·af'ter *adv.* from then on

there·at' *adv.* **1.** at that place; there **2.** at that time **3.** for that reason

there·by' *adv.* **1.** by that means **2.** connected with that

there·for' *adv.* for this or that; for it

there·fore' (-fôr') *adv.* for this or that reason; hence

there·in' *adv.* **1.** in or into that place **2.** in that matter, detail, etc.

there·of' *adv.* **1.** of that **2.** from that as a cause, reason, etc.

there·on' *adv.* **1.** on that or it **2.** immediately following that

there·to' *adv.* to that place, thing, etc.: also **there·un'to** (-un'tōō)

there'to·fore' *adv.* until that time

there'up·on' *adv.* **1.** immediately following that **2.** as a consequence of that **3.** concerning that subject, etc.

there·with' *adv.* **1.** along with that **2.** immediately thereafter

ther·mal (thur'm'l) *adj.* [< Gr. *thermē*, heat] **1.** having to do with heat **2.** designating a loosely knitted material with air spaces for insulation

thermal pollution the discharge of heated liquid into lakes, rivers, etc., as by industries, that is harmful to the ecosystems

thermo- [< Gr. *thermē*, heat] *a combining form meaning* heat

ther·mo·dy·nam·ics (thur'mō dī nam'iks) *n.pl.* [with sing. v.] the science dealing with the reversible transformation of heat into mechanical energy —**ther'mo·dy·nam'ic** *adj.*

ther·mom·e·ter (thər mäm'ə tər) *n.* [THERMO- + -METER] an instrument for measuring temperatures, as a graduated glass tube in which mercury, etc. rises or falls as it expands or contracts from changes in temperature

ther·mo·nu·cle·ar (thur'mō nōō'klē ər) *adj. Physics* **1.** designating a reaction in which isotopes of a light element fuse, at extreme heat, into heavier nuclei **2.** of or using the heat released in nuclear fusion

ther·mo·plas·tic (thur'mə plas'tik) *adj.* soft and moldable when subjected to heat: said of certain plastics —*n.* a thermoplastic substance

ther·mos (thur'məs) *n.* [orig. a trademark < Gr. *thermos*, hot] a bottle or jug for keeping liquids at almost their original temperature: in full **thermos bottle** (or **jug**)

ther·mo·stat (thur'mə stat') *n.* [THERMO- + -STAT] an apparatus for regulating temperature, esp. one that automatically controls a heating unit

the·sau·rus (thi sôr'əs) *n., pl.* **-ri** (-ī), **-rus·es** [< Gr. *thēsauros*, a treasure] a book of synonyms and antonyms

these (thēz) *pron., adj. pl.* of THIS

The·seus (thē'sōōs, -sē əs) *Gr. Legend* a hero who killed the Minotaur

the·sis (thē'sis) *n., pl.* **-ses** (-sēz) [< Gr. *tithenai*, to put] **1.** a proposition to be defended in argument **2.** a research paper, esp. one written by a candidate for a master's degree

Thes·pi·an (thes'pē ən) *adj.* [< *Thespis*, ancient Gr. poet] having to do with the drama; dramatic —*n.* [often t-] an actor

the·ta (thāt'ə, thēt'-) *n.* the eighth letter of the Greek alphabet (Θ, θ)

thews (thyōōz) *n.pl., sing.* **thew** [< OE. *thēaw*, habit] muscles or sinews

they (*thā*) *pron.* [for sing. see HE, SHE, IT] [< ON. *thei-r*] **1.** the persons, animals, or things previously mentioned **2.** people generally or indefinitely [*they* say it's so]

they'd (*thād*) **1.** they had **2.** they would

they'll (*thāl*) **1.** they will **2.** they shall

they're (*ther*) they are

they've (*thāv*) they have

thi·a·mine (thī'ə mēn', -min) *n.* [ult. < Gr. *theion*, brimstone + (VIT)AMIN] a factor of the vitamin B complex, found in cereal, egg yolk, liver, etc.; vitamin B₁: also **thi'a·min** (-min)

thick (thik) *adj.* [OE. *thicce*] **1.** of relatively great extent from side to side **2.** measured between opposite surfaces [one inch *thick*] **3.** close and abundant [*thick* hair] **4.** viscous [*thick* soup] **5.** dense [*thick* smoke] **6.** husky; hoarse; blurred [*thick* speech] **7.** [Colloq.] stupid **8.** [Colloq.] very friendly —*n.* the thickest part — **thick'ly** *adv.* —**thick'ness** *n.*

thick'en *vt., vi.* **1.** to make or become thick or thicker **2.** to make or become more complex —**thick'en·ing** *n.*

thick·et (thik'it) *n.* [see THICK] a thick growth of shrubs or small trees

thick'set' *adj.* **1.** planted thickly or closely **2.** thick in body; stocky

thick'-skinned' *adj.* **1.** having a thick skin **2.** insensitive, as to insult

thief (thēf) *n., pl.* **thieves** (thēvz) [OE. *theof*] one who steals

thieve (thēv) *vt., vi.* thieved, thiev'ing to steal —**thiev'ish** *adj.*

thiev·er·y (-ər ē) *n., pl.* **-ies** the act or an instance of stealing; theft

thigh (thī) *n.* [OE. *theoh*] the part of the leg between the knee and the hip

thigh'bone' *n.* the bone extending from the hip to the knee

thim·ble (thim'b'l) *n.* [< OE. *thuma*, thumb] a small cap worn to protect the finger that pushes the needle in sewing —**thim'ble·ful'** *n., pl.* **-fuls'**

thin (thin) *adj.* thin'ner, thin'nest [OE. *thynne*] **1.** of relatively little extent from side to side **2.** lean;

slender **3.** not dense or compact *[thin hair, thin* smoke*]* **4.** very fluid or watery *[thin* soup*]* **5.** high-pitched and weak *[a thin* voice*]* **6.** sheer, as fabric **7.** flimsy or unconvincing *[a thin* excuse*]* **8.** lacking substance, depth, etc.; weak —*vt., vi.* **thinned, thin′ning** to make or become thin or thinner —**thin′ly** *adv.* —**thin′ness** *n.*

thine (thīn) *pron.* [OE. *thin] poss. form of* THOU —*adj.* thy: before a vowel

thing (thiŋ) *n.* [OE., council] **1.** any matter, affair, or concern **2.** a happening, act, incident, etc. **3.** a tangible or an inanimate object **4.** an item, detail, etc. **5.** *a)* [*pl.*] personal belongings *b)* a garment **6.** [Colloq.] a person *[poor thing]* **7.** [Colloq.] a point of contention; issue **8.** [Colloq.] an irrational liking, fear, etc. **9.** [Colloq.] what one wants to do or is adept at *[do one's own thing]* —**see things** [Colloq.] to have hallucinations

think (thiŋk) *vt.* **thought, think′ing** [OE. *thencan]* **1.** to form or have in the mind *[to think* ill of one*]* **2.** to judge; consider *[he is thought* wise*]* **3.** to believe; expect *[I think* I can*]* —*vi.* **1.** to use the mind; reason **2.** to have an opinion (often with *of* or *about*) **3.** to remember or consider (with *of* or *about*) **4.** to conceive (*of*) —**think up** to invent, plan, etc. by thinking —**think′er** *n.*

think tank (or **factory**) [Slang] a group or center organized to do intensive research and problem-solving

thin·ner (thin′ər) *n.* a substance added to paint, shellac, etc. to thin it

thin′-skinned′ *adj.* **1.** having a thin skin **2.** sensitive, as to insult

third (thurd) *adj.* [OE. *thridda]* preceded by two others in a series; 3d or 3rd —*n.* **1.** the one following the second **2.** any of the three equal parts of something; 1/3 —*adv.* in the third place: also **third′ly**

third′-class′ *adj.* **1.** of the class, rank, etc. next below the second **2.** of a low-cost mail class, as for advertisements —*adv.* by third-class mail or travel accommodations

third degree [Colloq.] cruel treatment and questioning to force confession

third dimension 1. depth or solidity **2.** the quality of seeming real

third person that form of a pronoun (as *he*) or verb (as *is*) which refers to the person or thing spoken of

third′-rate′ *adj.* **1.** third in quality or other rating **2.** very poor

third world [*often* T- W-] the underdeveloped countries of the world

thirst (thurst) *n.* [OE. *thurst]* **1.** the discomfort caused by a need for drink **2.** a strong desire; craving —*vi.* **1.** to feel thirst **2.** to have a strong desire or craving —**thirst′i·ly** *adv.* —**thirst′y** *adj.* **-i·er, -i·est**

thir·teen (thur′tēn′) *adj., n.* [OE. *threotyne]* three more than ten; 13; XIII —**thir′teenth′** *adj., n.*

thir·ty (thurt′ē) *adj., n., pl.* **-ties** [OE. *thritig]* three times ten; 30; XXX —**the thirties** the numbers or years, as of a century, from 30 through 39 —**thir′ti·eth** (-ith) *adj., n.*

this (this) *pron., adj., pl.* **these** [OE. *thes]* **1.** (designating) the person or thing mentioned *[this* (man) is John*]* **2.** (designating) the nearer one or another one *[this* (desk) is older than that*]* **3.** (designating) something about to be presented *[hear this* (news)*]* —*adv.* to this extent *[it was this* big*]*

this·tle (this′'l) *n.* [OE. *thistel]* a plant with prickly leaves and white, purple, etc. flowers

this′tle-down′ *n.* the down growing from the flowers of a thistle

thith·er (thith′ər, *thith′*-) *adv.* [OE. *thider]* to or toward that place; there

tho, tho′ (thō) *conj., adv.* though

thole (thōl) *n.* [OE. *thol]* one of a pair of pins set as an oarlock into the gunwale of a boat: also **thole′pin′**

thong (thôŋ) *n.* [OE. *thwang]* a narrow strip of leather, etc. used as a lace, strap, etc.

Thor (thôr) *Norse Myth.* the god of thunder, war, and strength

tho·rax (thôr′aks) *n., pl.* **-rax·es, -ra·ces′** (-ə sēz′) [< Gr.] **1.** the part of the body between the neck and the abdomen; chest **2.** the middle one of the three main segments of an insect —**tho·rac·ic** (thô ras′ik) *adj.*

Thor·eau (thôr′ō, thə rō′), **Henry David** 1817–62; U.S. writer

tho·ri·um (thôr′ē əm) *n.* [< THOR] a rare, grayish, radioactive chemical element, used as a nuclear fuel

thorn (thôrn) *n.* [OE.] **1.** *a)* a very short, hard, leafless stem with a sharp point *b)* any small tree or shrub bearing thorns **2.** source of constant trouble or irritation —**thorn′y** *adj.*

thor·ough (thur′ō) *adj.* [var. of THROUGH] **1.** done or proceeding through to the end; complete **2.** absolute *[a thorough* rascal*]* **3.** very exact, accurate, or painstaking —**thor′ough·ly** *adv.* —**thor′ough·ness** *n.*

thor·ough·bred (thur′ō bred′) *adj.* of pure stock; pedigreed —*n.* a thoroughbred animal; specif., [T-] any of a breed of racehorses

thor′ough·fare′ (-fer′) *n.* a public street open at both ends, esp. a main highway

thor′ough·go′ing *adj.* very thorough

those (thōz) *adj., pron. pl. of* THAT

thou (thou) *pron.* [OE. *thu]* you (sing.): in poetic or religious use

though (thō) *conj.* [OE. *theah]* **1.** in spite of the fact that *[though* it rained, he went*]* **2.** and yet; however *[they did it, though* badly*]* **3.** even if *[though* he may fail, he will have tried*]* —*adv.* however; nevertheless

thought [1] (thôt) *n.* [OE. *thoht]* **1.** the act or process of thinking **2.** the power of reasoning **3.** an idea, concept, etc. **4.** attention; consideration **5.** a little; trifle *[be a thought* more careful*]*

thought² (thôt) *pt. & pp. of* THINK

thought′ful *adj.* **1.** full of thought; meditative **2.** considerate —**thought′-ful·ly** *adv.* —**thought′ful·ness** *n.*

thought′less *adj.* **1.** not stopping to think; careless **2.** ill-considered; rash **3.** inconsiderate —**thought′less·ly** *adv.* —**thought′less·ness** *n.*

thou·sand (thou′z'nd) *adj., n.* [OE. *thusend]* ten hundred; 1,000; M —**thou′sandth** (-z'ndth) *adj., n.*

thrall (thrôl) *n.* [< ON. *thræll]* **1.** a slave **2.** slavery —**thrall′dom, thral′dom** (-dam) *n.*

thrash (thrash) *vt., vi.* [OE. *threscan]* **1.** *same as* THRESH **2.** to beat; flog **3.** to toss about violently **4.** to defeat overwhelmingly —**thrash out** to settle by detailed discussion —**thrash′er** *n.*

thrash′er *n.* [Eng. dial. *thresher]* a thrushlike American songbird

thread (thred) *n.* [OE. *thræd]* **1.** a fine, stringlike length of spun cotton, silk, nylon, etc., used in sewing **2.** any thin line, vein, etc. **3.** something like a thread in its length, sequence, etc. *[the thread* of a story*]* **4.** the spiral ridge of a screw, nut, etc. —*vt.* **1.** to put a thread through (a needle, etc.) **2.** to make (one's way) by twisting, weaving, etc. **3.** to fashion a thread (sense 4) on or in —**thread′y** *adj.*

thread′bare′ *adj.* **1.** worn down so that the threads show **2.** wearing worn clothes; shabby **3.** stale; trite

threat (thret) *n.* [OE. *threat,* pressure] **1.** an expression of intention to hurt, destroy, punish, etc. **2.** an indication of, or a source of, imminent danger

threat′en *vt., vi.* **1.** to make threats, as of injury (against) **2.** to indicate (danger, etc.) **3.** to be a source of danger (to)

three (thrē) *adj., n.* [OE. *threo]* one more than two; 3; III

three′-deck′er (-dek′ər) *n.* anything having three levels, layers, etc.

three′-di·men′sion·al *adj.* having or seeming to have depth or thickness

three′fold′ *adj.* **1.** having three parts **2.** having three times as much or as many —*adv.* three times as much or as many

three·score (thrē′skôr′) *adj.* sixty

thren·o·dy (thren′ə dē) *n., pl.* **-dies** [< Gr. *thrēnos,* lamentation + *ōidē,* song] a song of lamentation; dirge

thresh (thresh) *vt., vi.* [ME. *threschen]* **1.** to beat out (grain) from (husks), as with a flail **2.** *same as* THRASH —**thresh′er** *n.*

thresh·old (thresh′ōld, -hōld) *n.* [OE. *therscwold]* **1.** a length of wood, stone, etc. along the bottom of a door-way **2.** the beginning point

threw (throō) *pt. of* THROW

thrice (thrīs) *adv.* [OE. *thriwa]* **1.** three times **2.** threefold

thrift (thrift) *n.* [< ON. *thrifa,* to grasp] economy; frugality —**thrift′i-ly** *adv.* —**thrift′less** *adj.* —**thrift′y** *adj.* **-i·er, -i·est** —**thrift′i·ness** *n.*

thrift shop a store where castoff clothes, etc. are sold, as for charity

thrill (thril) *vi., vt.* [< OE. *thurh,*

through] **1.** to feel or cause to feel emotional excitement **2.** to quiver or cause to quiver; tremble —*n.* **1.** a thrilling or being thrilled **2.** a tremor; quiver —**thrill′er** *n.*

thrive (thrīv) *vi.* **thrived** or **throve, thrived** or **thriv·en** (thriv′'n), **thriv′ing** [< ON. *thrifa,* to grasp] **1.** to prosper or flourish; be successful **2.** to grow robustly

throat (thrōt) *n.* [OE. *throte]* **1.** the front part of the neck **2.** the upper passage from the mouth to the stomach and lungs **3.** any narrow passage

throat′y *adj.* **-i·er, -i·est** produced in the throat, as some sounds; husky

throb (thräb) *vi.* **throbbed, throb′bing** [ME. *throbben]* **1.** to beat, pulsate, vibrate, etc., esp. strongly or fast **2.** to feel excitement —*n.* **1.** a throbbing **2.** a strong beat or pulsation

throe (thrō) *n.* [prob. < OE. *thrawu,* pain] **1.** a spasm or pang of pain **2.** *[pl.]* agony

throm·bo·sis (thräm bō′sis) *n.* [< Gr. *thrombos,* a clot] coagulation of the blood in the heart or a blood vessel, forming a clot (**thrombus**)

throne (thrōn) *n.* [< Gr. *thronos,* a seat] **1.** the chair on which a king, cardinal, etc. sits on formal occasions **2.** the power or rank of a king, etc. **3.** a sovereign, ruler, etc.

throng (thrôŋ) *n.* [OE. *thringan,* to crowd] **1.** a crowd **2.** any great num-ber of things considered together —*vi.* to gather together in a throng; crowd —*vt.* to crowd into

throt·tle (thrät′'l) *n.* [< ? THROAT] the valve that regulates the amount of fuel vapor entering an engine, or its control lever or pedal —*vt.* **-tled, -tling** **1.** to choke; strangle **2.** to censor or suppress **3.** *a)* to reduce the flow of (fuel vapor) by means of a throttle *b)* to slow by this means

through (throō) *prep.* [OE. *thurh]* **1.** in one side and out the other side of **2.** in the midst of; among **3.** by way of **4.** around *[touring through* France*]* **5.** *a)* from beginning to end of *b)* up to and including **6.** by means of **7.** as a result of —*adv.* **1.** in one side and out the other **2.** from the beginning to the end **3.** completely to the end *[see it through]* **4.** completely *[soaked through]* —*adj.* **1.** extending from one place to another *[a through* street*]* **2.** traveling to the destination without stops *[a through* train*]* **3.** finished

through·out′ *prep.* all the way through —*adv.* in every part; every-where

through′way′ (-wā′) *n.* an express-way: also **thru′way′**

throve (thrōv) *alt. pt. of* THRIVE

throw (thrō) *vt.* **threw, thrown, throw′ing** [OE. *thrawan,* to twist] **1.** to send through the air by a rapid motion of the arm, etc. **2.** to cause to fall; upset **3.** to send rapidly *[to throw* troops into battle*]* **4.** to put suddenly into a specified state, etc. *[thrown* into confusion*]* **5.** to move (a switch, etc.) so as to connect, disconnect, etc. **6.** to direct, cast, etc. *[throw* a glance*]* **7.**

[Colloq.] to lose (a game, etc.) deliberately 8. [Colloq.] to give (a party, etc.) 9. [Colloq.] to confuse or disconcert [the question *threw* him] —*vi.* to cast or hurl something —*n.* 1. the act of one who throws 2. the distance something is or can be thrown 3. a spread for a bed, etc. —**throw away** 1. to discard 2. to waste —**throw in** to add extra or free —**throw off** 1. to rid oneself of 2. to mislead or confuse 3. to expel, emit, etc. —**throw oneself at** to try very hard to win the love of —**throw out** 1. to discard 2. to reject or remove —**throw over** 1. to give up; abandon 2. to jilt —**throw together** to assemble hurriedly —**throw up** 1. to abandon 2. to vomit —**throw′er** *n.*

throw′a·way′ *n.* a leaflet, handbill, etc. given out on streets, at houses, etc. —*adj.* for discarding after use

throw′back′ *n.* (a) reversion to an ancestral type

throw rug a small rug; scatter rug

thru (thr̄o͞o) *prep., adv., adj.* shortened *sp.* of THROUGH

thrum (thrum) *vt., vi.* **thrummed′, thrum′ming** [echoic] *same as* STRUM

thrush (thrush) *n.* [OE. *thrysce*] any of a family of songbirds, including robins

thrust (thrust) *vt., vi.* **thrust, thrust′ing** [< ON. *thrysta*] 1. to push with sudden force 2. to stab 3. to force or impose —*n.* 1. a sudden, forceful push 2. a stab 3. continuous pressure, as of a rafter against a wall 4. *a*) the driving force of a propeller *b*) the forward force produced by a jet or rocket engine 5. forward movement 6. the basic meaning; point

Thu·cyd·i·des (th̄o͞o sid′ə dēz′) 460?–400? B.C.; Athenian historian

thud (thud) *vi.* **thud′ded, thud′ding** [prob. < OE. *thyddan*, to strike] to hit with a dull sound —*n.* a dull sound, as of an object dropping on a soft surface

thug (thug) *n.* [Hindi *thag*, swindler] a brutal hoodlum, gangster, etc.

thumb (thum) *n.* [OE. *thuma*] the short, thick digit of the hand —*vt.* 1. to handle, soil, etc. as with the thumb 2. [Colloq.] to solicit or get (a ride) in hitchhiking by signaling with the thumb —**all thumbs** clumsy —**under one's thumb** under one's influence

thumb′nail′ *n.* the nail of the thumb —*adj.* very small, brief, or concise

thumb′screw′ *n.* a screw that can be turned by the thumb and forefinger

thumb′tack′ *n.* a tack with a wide, flat head, that can be pressed into a board, etc. with the thumb

thump (thump) *n.* [echoic] 1. a blow with something heavy and blunt 2. the dull sound made by such a blow —*vt.* to strike with a thump —*vi.* 1. to hit or fall with a thump 2. to make a dull, heavy sound

thump′ing *adj.* 1. that thumps 2. [Colloq.] very large; whopping

thun·der (thun′dər) *n.* [OE. *thunor*] 1. the sound following a flash of lightning 2. any similar sound —*vi.* to produce thunder or a sound like this —*vt.* to utter, etc. with a thundering sound —**thun′der·ous** *adj.*

thun′der·bolt′ (-bōlt′) *n.* 1. a flash of lightning and the accompanying thunder 2. something sudden and shocking, as bad news

thun′der·clap′ *n.* a clap, or loud crash, of thunder

thun′der·cloud′ *n.* a storm cloud charged with electricity and producing lightning and thunder

thun′der·head′ (-hed′) *n.* a round mass of cumulus clouds appearing before a thunderstorm

thun′der·show′er *n.* a shower accompanied by thunder and lightning

thun′der·storm′ *n.* a storm accompanied by thunder and lightning

thun′der·struck′ *adj.* struck with amazement, terror, etc.: also **thun′der·strick′en** (-strik″n)

Thurs., Thur. Thursday

Thurs·day (thurz′dē, -dā) *n.* [< THOR] the fifth day of the week

thus (*th*us) *adv.* [OE.] 1. in this or that manner 2. to this or that degree or extent; so 3. therefore

thwack (thwak) *vt., n.* [prob. echoic] *same as* WHACK

thwart (thwôrt) *n.* [< ON. *thvert*, transverse] a seat across a boat —*vt.* to obstruct, frustrate, or defeat (a person, plans, etc.)

thy (th̄ı) *poss. pronominal adj.* [< ME. *thin*] of, belonging to, or done by thee: archaic or poet. var. of *your*

thyme (tīm) *n.* [< Gr. *thymon*] a plant of the mint family, with leaves used for seasoning

thy·mo·sin (thī′mə sin) *n.* [<Gr. *thymos* & -IN¹] a hormone secreted by the thymus that stimulates the immune system

thy·mus (thī′məs) *n.* [< Gr. *thymos*] a ductless, glandlike body situated near the throat: also **thymus gland**

thy·roid (thī′roid) *adj.* [< Gr. *thyreos*, large shield] designating or of a large ductless gland near the trachea, secreting a hormone which regulates growth —*n.* 1. the thyroid gland 2. an animal extract of this gland, used in treating goiter, etc.

thy·self (*th*ī self′) *pron. reflexive or intensive form of* THOU

ti (tē) *n.* *Music* the seventh tone of the diatonic scale

Ti·a Jua·na (tē′ə hwän′ə, -wän′ə) *former name of* TIJUANA

ti·ar·a (tē er′ə, -ar′-) *n.* [< Gr. *tiara*, headdress] 1. the Pope's triple crown 2. a woman's crownlike headdress

Ti·ber (tī′bər) river in C Italy, flowing through Rome

Ti·bet (ti bet′) plateau region of SW

China, north of the Himalayas — **Ti·bet′an** *adj., n.*

tib·i·a (tib′ē ə) *n., pl.* **-ae′** (-ē′), **-as** [L.] the inner and thicker of the two bones of the lower leg

tic (tik) *n.* [Fr. < ?] any involuntary, regularly repeated, spasmodic contraction of a muscle

tick¹ (tik) *n.* [prob. echoic] 1. a light clicking sound, as of a clock 2. a mark made to check off items —*vi.* to make a tick or ticks —*vt.* to record, mark, or check by ticks

tick² (tik) *n.* [OE. *ticia*] any of various wingless, bloodsucking insects that infest man, cattle, etc.

tick³ (tik) *n.* [< ? L. *theca*, a cover] the cloth case of a mattress or pillow

tick′er *n.* 1. one that ticks 2. a telegraphic device that records stock market quotations, etc. on paper tape (**ticker tape**) 3. [Slang] the heart

tick·et (tik′it) *n.* [< obs. Fr. *etiquet*, etiquette] 1. a printed card, etc. that gives one a right, as to attend a theater 2. a license or certificate 3. a label on merchandise giving size, price, etc. 4. the list of candidates nominated by a political party 5. [Colloq.] a court summons for a traffic violation —*vt.* 1. to label with a ticket 2. to give a ticket to

tick′ing *n.* strong cloth, often striped, used for pillow ticks, etc.

tick·le (tik′'l) *vt.* **-led**, **-ling** [ME. *tikelen*] 1. to please, gratify, delight, etc. 2. to stroke lightly so as to cause involuntary twitching, laughter, etc. —*vi.* to have or cause a twitching or tingling sensation —*n.* a sensation of being tickled

tick·ler (tik′lər) *n.* a pad, file, etc. for noting items to be remembered

tick′lish (-lish) *adj.* 1. sensitive to tickling 2. needing careful handling; precarious; delicate

tick-tack-toe, tic-tac-toe (tik′tak tō′) *n.* a game for two, each marking X (or O) in turn in a 9-square block so as to complete any one row before the other can

tick·tock (tik′täk′) *n.* the sound made by a clock or watch

tid·al (tīd′'l) *adj.* of, having, or caused by a tide or tides

tidal wave 1. an unusually great, destructive wave sent inshore by an earthquake or very strong wind 2. any widespread movement, feeling, etc.

tid·bit (tid′bit′) *n.* [dial. *tid*, tiny object] a choice bit of food, gossip, etc.

tid·dly·winks (tid′lē wiŋks′) *n.* [< ?] a game in which little disks are snapped into a cup by pressing their edges with a larger disk

tide (tīd) *n.* [OE. *tīd*, time] 1. a period of time [*Eastertide*] 2. the alternate rise and fall, about twice a day, of the surface of oceans, seas, etc., caused by the attraction of the moon and sun 3. something that rises and falls like the tide 4. a stream, trend, etc. —*vt.* **tid′ed, tid′ing** to help along temporarily (with *over*)

tide′land′ *n.* 1. land covered when the tide is in 2. [*pl.*] land under the sea within territorial waters of a country

tide′wa′ter *n.* 1. water that is affected by the tide 2. a seaboard —*adj.* of or along a tidewater

ti·dings (tī′diŋz) *n.pl.* [OE. *tidung*] news; information

ti·dy (tī′dē) *adj.* **-di·er, -di·est** [< OE. *tīd*, time] 1. neat in appearance, arrangement, etc.; orderly 2. [Colloq.] rather large [*a tidy sum*] —*vt., vi.* **-died, -dy·ing** to make tidy (often with *up*) —**ti′di·ness** *n.*

tie (tī) *vt.* **tied, ty′ing** [< OE. *teag*, rope] 1. to bind, as with string, rope, etc. 2. to knot the laces, etc. of 3. to make (a knot) in 4. to bind in any way 5. to equal the score of, as in a contest —*vi.* to make an equal score, as in a contest —*n.* 1. a string, cord, etc. used to tie things 2. something that connects, binds, etc. 3. a necktie 4. a beam, rod, etc. that holds parts together 5. any of the crossbeams to which the rails of a railroad are fastened 6. *a)* an equality of scores, etc. *b)* a contest in which this occurs —*adj.* that has been made equal [*a tie score*] —**tie down** to confine; restrict —**tie up** 1. to wrap up and tie 2. to moor to a dock 3. to obstruct; hinder 4. to cause to be already in use, committed, etc.

tie′back′ *n.* a band or ribbon used to tie curtains, etc. to one side

tie clasp a decorative clasp for fastening a necktie to a shirt: also **tie clip, tie bar**

tie′-dye′ (-dī′) *n.* a method of dyeing designs on cloth by tying bunches of it so that the dye affects only exposed parts —*vt.* **-dyed′, -dye′ing** to dye in this way

tie′-in′ *n.* a connection or relation

Tien·tsin (tin′tsin′) seaport in NE China: pop. 3,278,000

tier (tir) *n.* [< OFr. *tire*, order] any of a series of rows, as of seats, arranged one above or behind another

tie rod a rod connecting a front wheel of an automotive vehicle to the steering mechanism

tie tack a decorative pin fitted into a snap to fasten a necktie to a shirt

tie-up (tī′up′) *n.* 1. a temporary stoppage of production, traffic, etc. 2. a connection or relation

tiff (tif) *n.* [< ?] 1. a slight fit of anger 2. a slight quarrel

ti·ger (tī′gər) *n.* [< Gr. *tigris*] a large, flesh-eating animal of the cat family, native to Asia, having a tawny coat striped with black

tight (tīt) *adj.* [< OE. *-thight*, strong] 1. so compact in structure that water, air, etc. cannot pass through 2. drawn, packed, etc. closely together 3. fixed securely; firm 4. fully stretched; taut 5. fitting so closely as to be uncomfortable 6. difficult: esp. in a **tight corner, squeeze,** etc., a difficult situation 7. difficult to get; scarce 8. [Colloq.] stingy 9. [Slang] drunk —*adv.* 1. securely 2. soundly [*sleep tight*] —**sit tight** to maintain one's position, etc. —**tight′ly** *adv.* —**tight′ness** *n.*

tight′en *vt.*, *vi.* to make or become tight or tighter —**tight′en·er** *n.*

tight′fist′ed *adj.* stingy

tight′fit′ting *adj.* fitting very tight

tight′-lipped′ *adj.* secretive

tight′-rope′ *n.* a tightly stretched rope on which acrobats perform

tights *n.pl.* a tightly fitting garment for the lower half of the body, worn by acrobats, dancers, etc.

tight ship [Colloq.] an organization as efficient as a well-run ship

tight′wad′ *n.* [TIGHT + *wad*, roll of money] [Slang] a stingy person

ti·glon (tī′glän′, -glən) *n.* [TIG(ER) + L(I)ON] the offspring of a male tiger and a female lion

ti·gress (tī′gris) *n.* a female tiger

Ti·gris (tī′gris) river flowing from EC Turkey to a juncture with the Euphrates in SE Iraq

Ti·jua·na (tē wä′nə, -hwä′nä) city in NW Mexico, on the U.S. border: pop. 203,000

til·de (til′də) *n.* [Sp. < L. *titulus*, sign] a diacritical mark (~)

tile (til) *n.* [< L. *tegula*] **1.** a thin piece of fired clay, stone, etc., used for roofing, flooring, walls, etc. **2.** a similar piece of plastic, etc. **3.** a drain of earthenware pipe —*vt.* **tiled, til′-ing** to cover with tiles

til′ing *n.* tiles collectively

till[1] (til) *prep.*, *conj.* [OE. *til*] until

till[2] (til) *vt.*, *vi.* [< OE. *tilian*, strive for] to prepare (land) for raising crops, as by plowing, etc. —**till′er** *n.*

till[3] (til) *n.* [< ? ME. *tillen*, to draw] a drawer for keeping money

till·age (-ij) *n.* **1.** the tilling of land **2.** land that is tilled

till·er (til′ər) *n.* [< ML. *telarium*, weaver's beam] a bar or handle for turning a boat's rudder

tilt (tilt) *vt.* [ME. *tilten*, totter] to cause to slope; tip —*vi.* **1.** to slope; incline **2.** to charge (*at* an opponent) **3.** to engage in a tilt —*n.* **1.** a medieval contest in which two horsemen fight with lances **2.** any spirited contest **3.** a slope —(*at*) **full tilt** at full speed

tilt′-top′ *adj.* of a table with a hinged top that can be tipped vertically

tim·bale (tim′b'l) *n.* [Fr.] **1.** a custardlike dish of chicken, lobster, etc. baked in a drum-shaped mold **2.** a pastry shell, filled with cooked food

tim·ber (tim′bər) *n.* [OE.] **1.** wood for building houses, ships, etc. **2.** a wooden beam used in building **3.** trees collectively —**tim′bered** *adj.*

tim′ber·line′ *n.* the line above or beyond which trees do not grow, as on mountains or in polar regions

tim·bre (tam′bər, tim′-) *n.* [< OFr. *timbre*, kind of drum] the quality of sound that distinguishes one voice or musical instrument from another

time (tim) *n.* [OE. *tima*] **1.** every moment there has ever been or ever will be **2.** a system of measuring duration *[standard time]* **3.** the period during which something exists, happens, etc. **4.** [*usually pl.*] a period of history; age, era, etc. **5.** [*usually pl.*] prevailing conditions *[times are good]* **6.** a set period or term, as of work, confinement, etc. **7.** standard rate of pay **8.** rate of speed in marching, driving, etc. **9.** a precise or designated instant, moment, day, etc. **10.** an occasion or repeated occasion *[the fifth time it's been on TV]* **11.** *Music* **a)** rhythm as determined by the grouping of beats into measures **b)** tempo —*vt.* **timed, tim′ing 1.** to arrange the time so as to be suitable, opportune, etc. **2.** to adjust, set, etc. so as to coincide in time *[time our watches]* **3.** to record the pace, speed, etc. of —*adj.* **1.** having to do with time **2.** set to explode, open, etc. at a given time **3.** having to do with paying in installments —**ahead of time** early —**at the same time** however —**at times** occasionally —**do time** [Colloq.] to serve a prison term —**for the time being** temporarily —**from time to time** now and then —**in time 1.** eventually **2.** before it is too late **3.** keeping the set tempo, pace, etc. —**make time** to travel, work, etc. rapidly —**on time 1.** at the appointed time **2.** for or by payment by installments —**time after time** again and again: also **time and again**

time clock a clock with a mechanism for recording the time an employee begins and ends a work period

time′-hon′ored *adj.* honored because of long existence or usage

time′keep′er *n.* one who keeps account of hours worked by employees, or of elapsed time in races, games, etc.

time′less (-lis) *adj.* eternal

time′ly *adj.* **-li·er, -li·est** well-timed; opportune —**time′li·ness** *n.*

time′out′ *n. Sports*, etc. any temporary suspension of play

time′piece′ *n.* a clock or watch

tim′er *n.* a device for controlling the timing of some mechanism

times (tīmz) *prep.* multiplied by

time sharing 1. a system for simultaneous computer use at many remote sites **2.** a system for sharing ownership of a home, etc. with each joint purchaser occupying the unit at a specific time each year: also **time share**

time sheet a sheet on which are recorded the hours an employee works

time′ta′ble (-tā′b'l) *n.* a schedule of the times of arrival and departure of airplanes, trains, buses, etc.

time′worn′ *adj.* **1.** worn out by long use **2.** trite; hackneyed

time zone see STANDARD TIME

tim·id (tim′id) *adj.* [< L. *timere*, to fear] lacking poise or self-confidence; shy, fearful, or hesitant —**ti·mid·i·ty** (tə mid′ə tē) *n.* —**tim′id·ly** *adv.*

tim·ing (tī′miŋ) *n.* the regulation of time or speed to improve performance

tim·or·ous (tim′ər əs) *adj.* [< L.

---

fat, āpe, cär; ten, ēven; is, bīte; gō, hôrn, tōōl, look; oil, out; up, fur; chin; she; thin, *then*; zh, leisure; ŋ, ring; ə for *a* in *ago*; ', (ä′b'l); ë, Fr. coeur; ö, Fr. feu; Fr. mon; ü, Fr. duc; kh, G. ich, doch; ‡ foreign; < derived from

timor, fear] full of fear; timid; afraid

tim·o·thy (tim′ə thē) *n.* [< a *Timothy* Hanson, c.1720] a grass with dense spikes, grown for hay

tim·pa·ni (tim′pə nē) *n.pl.* [It.: see TYMPANUM] kettledrums, esp. a set of them played by one performer

tin (tin) *n.* [OE.] 1. a soft, silver-white, metallic chemical element 2. *same as* TIN PLATE 3. *a)* a pan, box, etc. made of tin plate *b)* [Chiefly Brit.] *same as* CAN² (*n.* 2, 3) Variously used to connote cheapness, etc. of something —*vt.* tinned, tin′ning 1. to plate with tin 2. [Chiefly Brit.] *same as* CAN² (*vt.* 1)

tin can *same as* CAN² (*n.* 2)

tinct. tincture

tinc·ture (tiŋk′chər) *n.* [< L. *tingere*, to dye] 1. a light color; tinge 2. a slight trace 3. a medicinal substance in an alcoholic solution —*vt.* -tured, -tur·ing to tinge

tin·der (tin′dər) *n.* [OE. *tynder*] any dry, easily flammable material

tin′der-box′ *n.* 1. orig., a box to hold tinder 2. a highly flammable building, etc. 3. a potential source of war, rebellion, etc.

tine (tin) *n.* [OE. *tind*] a slender, projecting point; prong [fork *tines*]

tin′foil′ (-foil′) *n.* a thin sheet of tin or a tin alloy used as wrapping

tinge (tinj) *n.* [see TINT] 1. a slight coloring; tint 2. a slight trace, flavor, etc. —*vt.* tinged, tinge′ing or ting′ing to give a tinge of to

tin·gle (tiŋ′g'l) *vi.* -gled, -gling [var. of TINKLE] to have a prickling or stinging feeling, as from cold, excitement, etc. —*n.* this feeling

tin·ker (tiŋ′kər) *n.* [ME. *tinkere*] 1. one who mends pots, pans, etc. 2. a bungler —*vi.* 1. to attempt clumsily to mend something 2. to putter

tin·kle (tiŋ′k'l) *vi.* -kled, -kling [echoic] to make a series of light sounds as of a small bell —*vt.* to cause to tinkle —*n.* a tinkling sound

tin·ny (tin′ē) *adj.* -ni·er, -ni·est 1. of tin 2. like tin, as in appearance, sound, value, etc. —tin′ni·ness *n.*

tin plate thin sheets of iron or steel plated with tin

tin·sel (tin′s'l) *n.* [< L. *scintilla*, a spark] 1. thin strips of tin, metal foil, etc., as for decoration 2. something of little worth that glitters

tin′smith′ *n.* a person who works in tin or tin plate

tint (tint) *n.* [< L. *tingere*, to dye] 1. a delicate color 2. a gradation of a color; shade 3. a hair dye —*vt.* to give a tint to

tin·tin·nab·u·la·tion (tin′ti nab′ yoo lā′shən) *n.* [< L. *tintinnabulum*, little bell] the ringing sound of bells

tin′type′ *n.* an old kind of photograph taken directly as a positive print on a treated plate of tin or iron

ti·ny (tī′nē) *adj.* -ni·er, -ni·est [< ME. *tine*, a little] very small

-tion (shən) [< Fr. < L.] *a suffix meaning:* 1. the act of [*correction*] 2. the state of being [*elation*] 3. the thing that is [*creation*]

-tious (shəs) *a suffix forming adjectives corresponding to* -TION [*cautious*]

tip¹ (tip) *n.* [ME. *tippe*] 1. the point or end of something 2. something attached to the end, as a cap, etc. —*vt.* tipped, tip′ping 1. to form a tip on 2. to cover the tip of

tip² (tip) *vt.* tipped, tip′ping [< ?] 1. to strike lightly and sharply 2. to give a gratuity to (a waiter, etc.) 3. [Colloq.] to give secret information to (often with *off*) —*vi.* to give a tip or tips —*n.* 1. a light, sharp blow 2. a piece of confidential information 3. a hint, warning, etc. 4. a gratuity — tip one's hand [Slang] to reveal a secret, one's plans, etc., often without meaning to —tip′per *n.*

tip³ (tip) *vt.,* *vi.* tipped, tip′ping [ME. *tipen*] 1. to overturn or upset (often with *over*) 2. to tilt or slant —*n.* a tilt; slant

tip′-off′ *n.* a tip; confidential disclosure, hint, or warning

tip·ple (tip′'l) *vi.,* *vt.* -pled, -pling [< ?] to drink (alcoholic liquor) habitually —tip′pler *n.*

tip·ster (tip′stər) *n.* [Colloq.] one who sells tips, as on horse races

tip·sy (tip′sē) *adj.* -si·er, -si·est 1. that tips easily; not steady 2. somewhat drunk —tip′si·ly *adv.*

tip′toe′ *n.* the tip of a toe —*vi.* -toed′, -toe′ing to walk carefully on one's tiptoes —on tiptoe 1. on one's tiptoes 2. eager(ly) 3. silently

tip′top′ *n.* [TIP¹ + TOP¹] the highest point —*adj.,* *adv.* 1. at the highest point 2. [Colloq.] at the highest point of excellence, health, etc.

ti·rade (tī′rād, tī rād′) *n.* [< It. *tirare*, to fire] a long, vehement speech or denunciation; harangue

tire¹ (tīr) *vt.,* *vi.* tired, tir′ing [OE. *tiorian*] to make or become weary, exhausted, bored, etc.

tire² (tīr) *n.* [ME. *tyre*] a hoop of iron or rubber, or a rubber tube filled with air, fixed around the wheel of a vehicle

tired (tīrd) *adj.* 1. weary 2. hackneyed

tire′less *adj.* that does not become tired —tire′less·ly *adv.*

tire′some *adj.* tiring; boring —tire′-some·ly *adv.* —tire′some·ness *n.*

Tir·ol (tir′äl, tī′rōl) E Alpine region in W Austria & N Italy —Ti·ro·le·an (ti rō′lē ən) *adj., n.*

tis·sue (tish′ōō) *n.* [< L. *texere*, to weave] 1. light, thin cloth 2. an interwoven mass; mesh; web 3. a piece of soft, absorbent paper, used as a disposable handkerchief, etc. 4. *same as* TISSUE PAPER 5. the substance of an organic body, consisting of cells and intercellular material

tissue paper very thin, unsized paper, as for wrapping things, etc.

tit¹ (tit) *n.* a titmouse

tit² (tit) *n.* [OE.] 1. *same as* TEAT 2. a breast: now vulgar

ti·tan (tīt′'n) *n.* [< Gr. *Titan*, a giant deity] any person or thing of great size or power

ti·tan·ic (tī tan′ik) *adj.* of great size, strength, or power

ti·ta·ni·um (tī tā′nē əm, ti-) *n.* [see TITAN] a metallic chemical element used as a deoxidizing agent in molten steel, etc.

tit for tat [earlier *tip for tap*] blow for blow

tithe (tīth) *n.* [OE. *teothe*, a tenth] a tenth of one's income paid to a church —*vt., vi.* **tithed, tith′ing** to pay a tithe of (one's income, etc.)

Ti·tian (tish′ən) *n.* [< Titian (1490?–1576), Venetian painter] reddish yellow; auburn

tit·il·late (tit′'l āt′) *vt.* **-lat′ed, -lat′ing** [< L. *titillare*, tickle] to excite pleasurably —**tit′il·la′tion** *n.*

ti·tle (tīt′'l) *n.* [< L. *titulus*] 1. the name of a poem, book, picture, etc. 2. an epithet 3. an appellation indicating one's rank, profession, etc. 4. a claim 5. *Law a)* a right to ownership, esp. to real estate *b)* a deed 6. *Motion Pictures, TV* a subtitle, credit, etc. 7. *Sports*, etc. a championship —*vt.* **-tled, -tling** to give a title to

ti′tled *adj.* having a title, esp. of nobility

ti′tle-hold′er *n.* the holder of a title; specif., (also **titlist**) the champion in some sport

title role (or **part** or **character**) the character in a play, movie, etc. whose name is used as or in the title

tit·mouse (tit′mous′) *n., pl.* **-mice′** [ME. *titemose*] a small bird with ashy-gray feathers

tit·ter (tit′ər) *vi.* [echoic] to laugh in a half-suppressed way; giggle —*n.* a tittering; giggle

tit·tle (tit′'l) *n.* [ME. *title*] a very small particle; iota; jot

tit·u·lar (tich′ə lər) *adj.* [see TITLE] 1. of a title 2. having a title 3. in name only [a *titular* leader]

tiz·zy (tiz′ē) *n., pl.* **-zies** [< ?] [Colloq.] a state of frenzied excitement

TN Tennessee

tn. ton(s)

TNT, T.N.T. [< *trinitrotoluene*] a high explosive used for blasting, etc.

to (tōō, too, tə) *prep.* [OE.] 1. toward [turn to the left] 2. so as to reach [he went to Boston] 3. as far as [wet to the skin] 4. into a condition of [a rise to fame] 5. on, onto, at, etc. [tied to a post] 6. *a)* until [from noon to night] *b)* before [the time is 10 to 6] 7. for the purpose of [come to my aid] 8. in regard to [open to attack] 9. so as to produce [torn to bits] 10. along with [add this to the rest] 11. belonging with [a key to the lock] 12. as compared with [a score of 7 to 0] 13. in agreement with [not to my taste] 14. constituting [ten to a peck] 15. with (a specified person or thing) as the recipient of the action [give it to me] 16. in honor of [a toast to you] *To* is also a sign of the infinitive (Ex.: I want *to* stay) —*adv.* 1. forward [wrong side to] 2. shut; closed [pull the door to] 3. to the matter at hand [fall

to] —**to and fro** first in one direction and then in the opposite

toad (tōd) *n.* [OE. *tade*] a froglike animal that lives on moist land

toad′stool′ (-stōōl′) *n.* a mushroom, esp. any poisonous mushroom

toad·y (tōd′ē) *n., pl.* **-ies** [short for *toadeater*, quack doctor's assistant] a servile flatterer —*vt., vi.* **-ied, -y·ing** to be a toady (to)

toast¹ (tōst) *vt.* [< L. *torrere*, parch] 1. to brown the surface of (bread, etc.) by heating 2. to warm thoroughly —*vi.* to become toasted —*n.* sliced bread made brown by heat —**toast′er** *n.*

toast² (tōst) *n.* [< the toasted bread formerly put in wine] 1. a person or thing in honor of which persons raise their glasses and drink 2. a proposal to drink, or a drink, in honor of some person, etc. —*vt., vi.* to propose or drink a toast (to)

toast′mas′ter *n.* the person at a banquet who proposes toasts, introduces after-dinner speakers, etc.

to·bac·co (tə bak′ō) *n., pl.* **-cos** [< WInd. *tabaco*, smoking pipe] 1. a plant with large leaves that are prepared for smoking, chewing, or snuffing 2. cigars, cigarettes, snuff, etc.

to·bac′co·nist (-ə nist) *n.* [Chiefly Brit.] a dealer in tobacco

to·bog·gan (tə bäg′ən) *n.* [< AmInd.] a long, flat sled without runners, for coasting downhill —*vi.* 1. to coast on a toboggan 2. to decline rapidly

TOBOGGAN

toc·sin (täk′sin) *n.* [Fr. < Pr. *toc*, a stroke + *senh*, a bell] an alarm bell

to·day (tə dā′) *adv.* [OE. *to dæg*] 1. on or during the present day 2. in the present time —*n.* 1. the present day 2. the present time

tod·dle (täd′'l) *vi.* **-dled, -dling** [? < *totter*] to walk with short, uncertain steps, as a child —**tod′dler** *n.*

tod·dy (täd′ē) *n., pl.* **-dies** [< Hindi] a drink of whiskey, etc. mixed with hot water, sugar, etc.: also **hot toddy**

to-do (tə dōō′) *n.* [Colloq.] a commotion; stir; fuss

toe (tō) *n.* [OE. *ta*] 1. *a)* any of the digits of the foot *b)* the fore part of the foot 2. anything like a toe in location, shape, or use —*vt.* **toed, toe′ing** to touch, kick, etc. with the toes in a specified position [he *toes* in] —**on one's toes** [Colloq.] alert —**toe the line** (or **mark**) to follow orders or rules strictly

toed (tōd) *adj.* having (a specified kind or number of) toes [two-*toed*]

toe dance a dance performed on the tips of the toes, as in ballet —**toe′-dance′** *vi.* —**toe′-danc′er** *n.*

toe′hold′ *n.* 1. just enough space to support the toe in climbing, etc. 2. a slight footing or advantage

toe·nail (tō′nāl′) *n.* the nail of a toe

tof·fee, tof·fy (tôf′ē, täf′ē) *n.* [< TAFFY] a kind of taffy

to·fu (tō′fōō) *n.* a Japanese custard-like food made from soybeans

to·ga (tō′gə) *n., pl.* -gas, -gae (-jē) [L. < *tegere,* to cover] in ancient Rome, a loose outer garment worn in public by citizens

to·geth·er (tə geth′ər) *adv.* [< OE. *to,* to + *gædre,* together] 1. in or into one group, place, etc. [we ate *together*] 2. in or into contact, union, etc. [they bumped *together*] 3. considered collectively [he lost more than all of us *together*] 4. at the same time [shots fired *together*] 5. in succession [sulking for three whole days *together*] 6. in or into agreement, cooperation, etc. [to get *together* on a deal] —*adj.* [Slang] having a fully integrated personality

to·geth′er·ness *n.* the spending of much time together, as by family members, in seeking a more unified, stable relationship

tog·gle switch (täg′'l) [prob. < TUG] a switch consisting of a lever moved back and forth to open or close an electric circuit

To·go (tō′gō) country in W Africa: 21,853 sq. mi.; pop. 1,772,000

togs (tägz, tôgz) *n.pl.* [prob. < L. *toga,* toga] [Colloq.] clothes

toil (toil) *vi.* [< L. *tudiculare,* stir about] 1. to work hard and continuously 2. to proceed laboriously —*n.* hard, tiring work —**toil′er** *n.*

toi·let (toi′lit) *n.* [< MFr. *toile,* cloth < L. *tela,* a web] 1. the act of dressing or grooming oneself 2. dress; attire 3. *a)* a room with a bowl-shaped fixture for defecation or urination *b)* such a fixture

toilet paper (or **tissue**) soft paper for cleaning oneself after evacuation

toi′let·ry (-lə trē) *n., pl.* -ries soap, lotion, etc. used in grooming oneself

toi·lette (twä let′, toi-) *n.* [Fr.] 1. the process of grooming oneself: said of a woman 2. dress; attire

toilet water *same as* COLOGNE

toils (toilz) *n.pl.* [< L. *tela,* a web] any snare suggestive of a net

toil·some (toil′sam) *adj.* laborious

toke (tōk) *n.* [? < ff.] [Slang] a puff on a cigarette, esp. of marijuana or hashish —*vi.* **toked, tok′ing** [Slang] to take a puff on such a cigarette

to·ken (tō′k'n) *n.* [OE. *tacn*] 1. a sign, indication, symbol, etc. [a *token* of affection] 2. a keepsake 3. a metal disk to be used in place of currency, for transportation fares, etc. —*adj.* merely simulated [*token* resistance] —**by the same** (or **this**) **token** following from this

to′ken·ism (-iz'm) *n.* the making of small, merely formal concessions to a demand, etc.; specif., token integration of Negroes, as in jobs

To·kyo (tō′kē ō′) capital of Japan, on Honshu: pop. 8,991,000

tol·bu·ta·mide (täl byōōt′ə mīd′) *n.* an oral drug for treating diabetes

told (tōld) *pt. & pp.* of TELL —**all told** all (being) counted

tole (tōl) *n.* [Fr. *tôle,* sheet iron] a type of lacquered or enameled metalware, usually dark-green, ivory, or black, used for lamps, trays, etc.

To·le·do (tə lē′dō) city and port in NW Ohio: pop. 355,000

tol·er·a·ble (täl′ər ə b'l) *adj.* 1. endurable 2. fairly good; passable —**tol′er·a·bly** *adv.*

tol′er·ance (-əns) *n.* 1. a being tolerant of others' beliefs, practices, etc. 2. the amount of variation allowed from a standard, accuracy, etc. 3. *Med.* the ability to endure the effects of a drug, poison, etc.

tol′er·ant *adj.* having or showing tolerance of others' beliefs, etc.

tol·er·ate (täl′ə rāt′) *vt.* -at′ed, -at′ing [< L. *tolerare,* to bear] 1. to allow 2. to respect (others' beliefs, practices, etc.) without sharing them 3. to put up with 4. *Med.* to have a tolerance for —**tol′er·a′tion** *n.*

toll[1] (tōl) *n.* [ult. < Gr. *telos,* tax] 1. a tax or charge for a privilege, as for the use of a bridge 2. a charge for a service, as for a long-distance telephone call 3. the number lost, etc. [the tornado took a heavy *toll* of lives]

toll[2] (tōl) *vt.* [ME. *tollen,* to pull] 1. to ring (a bell, etc.) with slow, regular strokes 2. to announce, summon, etc. by this —*vi.* to ring slowly: said of a bell —*n.* the sound of tolling a bell

toll′gate′ *n.* a gate for stopping travel at a point where toll is taken

toll road a road on which tolls must be paid: also **toll′way′** (-wā′) *n.*

Tol·stoy (täl′stoi, tōl′-), Count **Leo** 1828–1910; Russ. novelist

tom (täm) *adj.* [< the name *Tom*] male [*tomcat, tom* turkey]

tom·a·hawk (täm′ə hôk′) *n.* [< AmInd.] a light ax used by N.American Indians as a tool and a weapon

to·ma·to (tə māt′ō, -mät′ō) *n., pl.* -toes [< MexInd.] 1. a red or yellowish fruit with a juicy pulp, used as a vegetable 2. the plant it grows on

tomb (tōōm) *n.* [< Gr. *tymbos*] a vault or grave for the dead

tom·boy (täm′boi′) *n.* a girl who behaves like a boisterous boy

tomb·stone (tōōm′stōn′) *n.* a stone or monument marking a tomb or grave

tom·cat (täm′kat′) *n.* a male cat

tome (tōm) *n.* [< Gr. *tomos,* piece cut off] a book, esp. a large one

tom·fool·er·y (täm′fōōl′ər ē) *n., pl.* -ies foolish behavior; silliness

to·mor·row (tə mär′ō, -môr′-) *adv.* [OE. *to morgen*] on the day after today —*n.* the day after today

tom·tit (täm′tit′) *n.* [Chiefly Brit.] a titmouse or other small bird

tom-tom (täm′täm′) *n.* [Hindi *tam-tam*] a primitive drum, usually beaten with the hands

-to·my [< Gr. *tomē,* a cutting] *a combining form meaning* surgical operation

ton (tun) *n.* [var. of TUN] 1. a unit of weight equal to 2,000 pounds: in full **short ton** 2. in Great Britain, a unit of weight equal to 2,240 pounds: in full **long ton**

ton·al (tō′n'l) *adj.* of a tone

to·nal·i·ty (tō nal′ə tē) *n., pl.* **-ties** *Music* 1. same as KEY[1] (*n.* 6) 2. tonal character, as determined by the relationship of the tones to the keynote

tone (tōn) *n.* [< Gr. *teinein*, to stretch] 1. a vocal or musical sound, or its quality as to pitch, intensity, etc. 2. a manner of expression showing a certain attitude [a friendly *tone*] 3. style, character, spirit, etc. 4. elegant style 5. a quality of color; shade 6. normal, healthy condition of a muscle, organ, etc. 7. *Music* a) a sound of distinct pitch b) any of the full intervals of a diatonic scale —*vt.* **toned,** **ton′ing** to give a tone to —**tone down** (or **up**) to give a less (or more) intense tone to —**tone′less** *adj.*

tone arm the pivoted arm containing the pickup on a phonograph

tone′-deaf′ *adj.* unable to distinguish differences in musical pitch

ton·er (tō′nər) *n.* 1. the ink powder used to form images in xerography 2. a facial cleanser

tone row (or **series**) *see* TWELVE-TONE

tong (tôŋ, täŋ) *n.* [Chin. *t'ang*, meeting place] in the U.S., a secret, fraternal society of Chinese

Ton·ga (täŋ′gə) country on a group of islands (**Tonga Islands**) in the South Pacific, east of Fiji: 270 sq. mi.; pop. 86,000 —**Ton′gan** *n.*

tongs (tôŋz, täŋz) *n.pl.* [sometimes with sing. v.] [OE. tange] a device for seizing or lifting, having two long arms pivoted or hinged together

tongue (tuŋ) *n.* [OE. tunge] 1. the movable, muscular structure in the mouth, used in eating, tasting, and (in man) speaking 2. talk; speech 3. the act, power, or manner of speaking 4. a language or dialect 5. something like a tongue in shape, position, use, etc., as the flap under the laces of a shoe —**hold one's tongue** to keep from speaking —**speak in tongues** to utter unintelligible sounds, as while in a religious trance —**tongue′less** *adj.*

tongue-and-groove joint a kind of joint in which a projection on one board fits into a groove in another

tongue′-lash′ing *n.* [Colloq.] a harsh scolding or reproving; reprimand

tongue′-tied′ *adj.* speechless from amazement, embarrassment, etc.

tongue twister a phrase or sentence hard to say fast (Ex.: six sick sheiks)

ton·ic (tän′ik) *adj.* [see TONE] 1. of or producing good muscular tone 2. *Music* designating or based on a keynote —*n.* 1. anything that invigorates, as a drug or medicine 2. a quinine-flavored beverage served with gin, vodka, etc. 3. *Music* a keynote

to·night (tə nīt′) *adv.* [OE. to niht] on or during the present or coming night —*n.* the present or coming night

ton·nage (tun′ij) *n.* 1. the total amount of shipping of a country or port, calculated in tons 2. the carrying capacity of a ship, calculated in tons

ton·sil (tän′s'l) *n.* [L. *tonsillae, pl.*] either of a pair of oval masses of tissue at the back of the mouth

ton·sil·lec·to·my (tän′sə lek′tə mē) *n., pl.* **-mies** [< prec. & -ECTOMY] the surgical removal of the tonsils

ton·sil·li·tis (-līt′əs) *n.* [see -ITIS] inflammation of the tonsils

ton·so·ri·al (tän sôr′ē əl) *adj.* [see ff.] of a barber or barbering: often humorous [a *tonsorial* artist]

ton·sure (tän′shər) *n.* [< L. *tondere*, to clip] 1. the act of shaving the head or crown of one becoming a cleric or entering a monastic order 2. the part of the head so shaven

ton·y (tō′nē) *adj.* **-i·er, -i·est** [< TONE + -Y[2]] [Slang] very elegant

too (tōō) *adv.* [stressed form of TO] 1. in addition; also 2. more than enough [the hat is *too* big] 3. extremely; very [you're *too* kind]

took (took) *pt. of* TAKE

tool (tōōl) *n.* [OE. tol] 1. any hand implement, instrument, etc. used for some work 2. any similar instrument that is the working part of a machine, as a drill 3. anything that serves as a means 4. a stooge —*vt.* 1. to form or shape with a tool 2. to impress designs on (leather, etc.) with a tool —*vi.* 1. to install tools, equipment, etc. needed (often with *up*)

toot (tōōt) *vi., vt.* [echoic] to sound (a horn, whistle, etc.) in short blasts —*n.* a short blast of a horn, etc.

tooth (tōōth) *n., pl.* **teeth** [OE. *toth*] 1. any of the hard, bonelike structures in the jaws, used for biting, chewing, etc. 2. a toothlike part, as on a saw, comb, gearwheel, etc. 3. [pl.] effective means of enforcing [a law with *teeth*] —**in the teeth of** 1. directly against 2. defying —**tooth and nail** with all one's strength —**toothed** *adj.* —**tooth′less** *adj.*

tooth′ache′ *n.* a pain in a tooth

tooth′brush′ *n.* a small brush for cleaning the teeth

tooth′paste′ (or **tooth powder**) *n.* a paste (or powder) for brushing the teeth

tooth′pick′ *n.* a slender, pointed instrument for dislodging food particles from between the teeth

tooth′some (-səm) *adj.* tasty; savory

tooth′y *adj.* **-i·er, -i·est** having or exposing teeth that show prominently [a *toothy* smile] —**tooth′i·ly** *adv.*

top[1] (täp) *n.* [OE.] 1. the head or crown 2. the highest point or surface of anything 3. the part of a plant above ground 4. the uppermost part or covering, as a lid, cap, etc. 5. the highest degree [at the *top* of his voice] 6. the highest rank [the *top* of the class] —*adj.* of, at, or being the top; highest or foremost —*vt.* **topped,** **top′ping** 1. to take off the top of (a plant, etc.) 2. to provide with a top 3. to be a top for 4. to reach the top of

5. to exceed in amount, etc. **6.** to surpass; outdo —**blow one's top** [Slang] to lose one's temper —**on top of 1.** resting upon **2.** besides **3.** controlling successfully —**top off** to complete by adding a finishing touch —**top′per** n.

top² (täp) n. [OE.] a cone-shaped toy with a point upon which it is spun

to·paz (tō′paz) n. [< Gr. *topazos*] any of various yellow gems, esp. a variety of aluminum silicate

top brass important officials

top′coat′ n. a lightweight overcoat

top′-draw′er adj. of first importance

To·pe·ka (tə pē′kə) capital of Kans.: pop. 115,000

top·er (tō′pər) n. [< archaic *tope*, to drink (much liquor)] a drunkard

top′-flight′ adj. [Colloq.] first-rate

top hat a man's tall, black, cylindrical silk hat, worn in formal dress

top′-heav′y adj. too heavy at the top, so as to be unstable

top·ic (täp′ik) n. [ult. < Gr. *topos*, place] the subject of an essay, speech, discussion, etc.

top′i·cal adj. dealing with topics of the day; of current or local interest

top′knot′ (-nät′) n. a tuft of hair or feathers on the top of the head

top′less (-lis) adj. without a top, as a costume exposing the breasts

top′-lev′el adj. of or by persons of the highest office or rank

top′mast′ n. the second mast above the deck of a sailing ship

top′most adj. at the very top

top′-notch′ adj. [Colloq.] first-rate; excellent

to·pog·ra·phy (tə päg′rə fē) n., pl. -**phies** [< Gr. *topos*, a place + *graphein*, write] **1.** the science of representing surface features of a region on maps and charts **2.** these surface features —**top·o·graph·i·cal** (täp′ə graf′i k'l), **top′o·graph′ic** adj.

top·ping (täp′iŋ) n. something put on top of something else

top·ple (täp′'l) vi. -**pled,** -**pling** [< TOP¹] to fall top forward; fall (*over*) because top-heavy, etc. —vt. to cause to topple; overturn

top′sail (täp′s'l, -sāl′) n. in a square-rigged vessel, the square sail next above the lowest sail on a mast

top′-se′cret adj. designating or of the most secret information

top′side′ adv. on or to an upper deck or the main deck of a ship

top′soil′ n. the upper layer of soil, usually richer than the subsoil

top·sy-tur·vy (täp′sē tur′vē) adv., adj. [prob. <*top*, highest part + ME. *terven*, to roll] **1.** upside down; in a reversed condition **2.** in disorder

toque (tōk) n. [Fr.] a woman's small, round hat, with or without a brim

to·rah (tō′rə) n. [< Heb., law] **1.** [also T-] the body of Jewish scriptures **2.** [usually T-] a) the Pentateuch b) pl. -**roth,** -**rot** (-rəs, tō rōt′) a scroll containing it

torch (tôrch) n. [see TORQUE] **1.** a portable flaming light **2.** a source of enlightenment, etc. **3.** a device for producing a very hot flame, as in welding **4.** [Brit.] a flashlight —vt. [Slang] to set fire to, as in arson

torch′bear′er n. **1.** one who carries a torch **2.** a) one who brings enlightenment, truth, etc. b) an inspirational leader, as of a movement

torch′light′ n. the light of a torch or torches —adj. done by torchlight

tore (tôr) alt. pt. of TEAR¹

tor·e·a·dor (tôr′ē ə dôr′) n. [Sp. < L. *taurus*, a bull] a bullfighter

tor·ment (tôr′ment; for v. tôr ment′) n. [see TORQUE] **1.** great pain or anguish **2.** a source of pain, anxiety, etc. —vt. **1.** to cause great physical or mental anguish in **2.** to annoy; harass —**tor·men′tor, tor·ment′er** n.

torn (tôrn) alt. pp. of TEAR¹

tor·na·do (tôr nā′dō) n., pl. -**does,** -**dos** [< Sp. < L. *tonare*, to thunder] a violently whirling column of air seen as a funnel-shaped cloud that usually destroys everything in its narrow path

To·ron·to (tə rän′tō) capital of Ontario, Canada: pop. 665,000

tor·pe·do (tôr pē′dō) n., pl. -**does** [see ff.] **1.** a large, cigar-shaped, self-propelled, underwater projectile containing explosives **2.** any of various explosive devices —vt. to attack, destroy, etc. as with a torpedo

tor·pid (tôr′pid) adj. [< L. *torpere*, be numb] **1.** without sensation or motion; dormant **2.** dull; sluggish

tor·por (tôr′pər) n. [L.] **1.** a torpid state; stupor **2.** dullness; apathy

torque (tôrk) n. [< L. *torquere*, to twist] *Physics* a force that produces a twisting or wrenching effect

Tor·rance (tôr′əns) city in SW Calif.: pop. 131,000

tor·rent (tôr′ənt, tär′-) n. [< L. *torrens*, rushing] **1.** a swift, violent stream, esp. of water **2.** a rapid or violent flow, as of words —**tor·ren′tial** (tō ren′shəl) adj.

tor·rid (tôr′id, tär′-) adj. [< L. *torrere*, to dry] **1.** subjected to intense heat, esp. of the sun; parched **2.** very hot; scorching **3.** passionate; ardent

Torrid Zone the area of the earth's surface between the Tropic of Cancer and the Tropic of Capricorn

tor·sion (tôr′shən) n. [see TORQUE] **1.** a twisting or being twisted **2.** the stress produced in a rod, wire, etc. by twisting along a longitudinal axis

torsion bar a metal bar exhibiting resilience under torsion

tor·so (tôr′sō) n., pl. -**sos,** -**si** (-sē) [< Gr. *thyrsos*, a stem] the trunk of the human body

tort (tôrt) n. [< L. *torquere*, to twist] *Law* a wrongful act or damage (not involving a breach of contract), for which a civil action can be brought

torte (tôrt; G. tôr′tə) n., pl. **tortes,** G. tor·ten (tôr′tən) [G. < It. < LL. *torta*, a twisted bread] a rich cake, as one made of eggs, finely chopped nuts, crumbs, etc.

tor·til·la (tôr tē′ə) n. [Sp., dim. of *torta*, a cake] a flat cake of unleavened cornmeal, or of flour: a Mexican food

tor·toise (tôr′təs) n. [< ? LGr.

tartarouchos, demon] a turtle, esp. one that lives on land

tortoise shell the hard, mottled, yellow-and-brown shell of some turtles —**tor′toise-shell′** *adj.*

tor·to·ni (tôr tō′nē) *n.* [prob. alt. < It. *tortone*, big pastry tart] an ice cream made with heavy cream, maraschino cherries, almonds, etc.

tor·tu·ous (tôr′choo wəs) *adj.* [see TORQUE] **1.** full of twists, turns, etc.; crooked **2.** deceitful or tricky

tor·ture (tôr′chər) *n.* [see TORQUE] **1.** the inflicting of severe pain, as to force information or confession **2.** any severe physical or mental pain; agony —*vt.* **-tured, -tur·ing 1.** to subject to torture **2.** to twist or distort (meaning, etc.) —**tor′tur·er** *n.*

To·ry (tôr′ē) *n.*, *pl.* **-ries** [Ir. *tōruidhe*, robber] **1.** formerly, a member of the major conservative party of England **2.** in the American Revolution, one loyal to Great Britain

toss (tôs) *vt.* [prob. < Scand.] **1.** to throw about [waves *tossed* the boat] **2.** to throw lightly from the hand **3.** to jerk upward [to *toss* one's head] —*vi.* **1.** to be thrown about **2.** to fling oneself about in sleep, etc. —*n.* a tossing or being tossed —**toss up** to toss a coin for deciding something according to which side lands uppermost

toss′up′ *n.* **1.** the act of tossing up **2.** an even chance

tot[1] (tät) *n.* [prob. < ON.] **1.** a young child **2.** [Chiefly Brit.] a small amount

tot[2] (tät) *vt.* **tot′ted, tot′ting** [Chiefly Brit. Colloq.] to total (with *up*)

to·tal (tōt′'l) *adj.* [< L. *totus*, all] **1.** constituting a whole **2.** complete; utter [a *total* loss] —*n.* the whole amount; sum —*vt.* **-taled** or **-talled, -tal·ing** or **-tal·ling 1.** to find the total of **2.** to add up to —*vi.* to amount (*to*) as a whole —**to′tal·ly** *adv.*

to·tal·i·tar·i·an (tō tal′ə ter′ē ən) *adj.* [prec. + (AUTHOR)ITARIAN] designating or of a government in which one political group maintains complete control, esp. under a dictator —*n.* one who favors such a government —**to·tal′i·tar′i·an·ism** *n.*

to·tal·i·ty (tō tal′ə tē) *n.*, *pl.* **-ties** the total amount or sum

to·tal·i·za·tor (tōt′'l i zāt′ər) *n.* a machine for registering bets and computing the odds and payoffs, as at a horse race: also **to·tal·iz′er** (-l′zər)

tote (tōt) *vt.* **tot′ed, tot′ing** [< ?] [Colloq.] to carry or haul

to·tem (tōt′əm) *n.* [< Algonquian] **1.** among primitive peoples, an animal or natural object taken as the symbol of a family or clan **2.** an image of this

totem pole a pole carved and painted with totems by Indian tribes of NW N.America

tot·ter (tät′ər) *vi.* [prob. < Scand.] **1.** to rock as if about to fall **2.** to be unsteady on one's feet; stagger

tou·can (tōō′kan) *n.* [< SAmInd.] a brightly colored bird of tropical America, with a very large beak

TOUCAN

touch (tuch) *vt.* [< OFr. *tochier*] **1.** to put the hand, etc. on, so as to feel ℩. to bring (something), or come, into contact with (something else) **3.** to border on **4.** to strike lightly **5.** to give a light tint, aspect, etc. to [*touched* with pink] **6.** to stop at (a port) **7.** to handle; use **8.** to come up to; reach **9.** to compare with; equal **10.** to affect; concern **11.** to arouse sympathy, gratitude, etc. in **12.** [Slang] to seek a loan or gift of money from —*vi.* **1.** to touch a person or thing **2.** to be or come in contact **3.** to verge (*on* or *upon*) **4.** to pertain; bear (*on* or *upon*) —**5.** to treat in passing (with *on* or *upon*) —*n.* **1.** a touching or being touched; specif., a light tap **2.** the sense by which physical objects are felt **3.** a special quality or skill **4.** a subtle change or addition in a painting, story, etc. **5.** a trace, tinge, etc. **6.** a slight attack [a *touch* of the flu] **7.** contact or communication [keep in *touch*] **8.** [Slang] the act of seeking or getting a gift or loan of money **9.** *Music* the manner of striking the keys of a piano, etc. —**touch down** to land: said of an aircraft or spacecraft —**touch up** to improve or finish (a painting, story, etc.) by minor changes

touch and go a risky or precarious situation —**touch′-and-go′** *adj.*

touch′down′ *n.* **1.** the moment at which an aircraft or spacecraft lands **2.** *Football* a play, scoring six points, in which a player grounds the ball on or past the opponent's goal line

tou·ché (tōō shā′) *interj.* [Fr.] touched: said when one's opponent in fencing scores a point, or to acknowledge a point in debate or a witty retort

touched (tucht) *adj.* **1.** emotionally affected; moved **2.** slightly demented

touch′ing *adj.* arousing tender emotions; moving

touch′stone′ *n.* **1.** a stone formerly used to test the purity of gold or silver **2.** any test of genuineness

touch′-type′ *vi.* **-typed′, -typ′ing** to typewrite without looking at the keyboard by regularly touching a given key with a specific finger

touch′y *adj.* **-i·er, -i·est 1.** easily offended; oversensitive; irritable **2.** very risky or precarious

tough (tuf) *adj.* [OE. *toh*] **1.** that will bend, etc. without tearing or breaking **2.** not easily cut or chewed [*tough* steak] **3.** strong; hardy **4.** stubborn **5.** brutal or rough **6.** very difficult; laborious —*n.* a tough person; thug

tough′en *vt.*, *vi.* to make or become tough or tougher —**tough′en·er** *n.*

tou·pee (tōō pā′) *n.* [< Fr. < OFr.

toup, tuft of hair] a man's small wig

tour *n.* [< OFr. *torner*, to turn]
1. a turn, period, etc., as of military
duty 2. a long trip, as for sightseeing
3. any trip, as for inspection, giving
performances, etc. —*vt.*, *vi.* to go on a
tour (through)

tour de force (toor' də fôrs') *pl.*
tours de force (toor') [Fr.] an
unusually skillful or ingenious creation or performance, sometimes a
merely clever one

tour'ism *n.* tourist travel

tour'ist *n.* one who tours, esp. for
pleasure —*adj.* of or for tourists

tour·ma·line (toor'mə lin, -lēn')
n. [< Sinhalese] a semiprecious mineral

tour·na·ment (toor'nə mənt, tur'-)
n. [< OFr. *tourner*, to turn] 1. a contest between knights on horseback who
tried to unseat each other with lances
2. a series of contests in competition
for a championship Also **tour'ney**
(-nē), *pl.* **-neys**

tour·ni·quet (toor'nə kit, tur'-) *n.*
[Fr. < L. *tunica*, tunic] a device for
compressing a blood vessel to stop
bleeding, as a bandage twisted about
a limb and released at intervals

tou·sle (tou'z'l) *vt.* **-sled, -sling** [<
ME. *tusen*, to pull] to disorder,
dishevel, muss, etc.

tout (tout) *vi.*, *vt.* [OE. *totian*, to peep]
[Colloq.] 1. to praise highly 2. to sell
betting tips on (race horses) —*n.*
[Colloq.] one who touts

tow (tō) *vt.* [OE. *togian*] to pull as by a
rope or chain —*n.* 1. a towing or being
towed 2. something being towed 3. *same as*
TOWLINE —**in tow** 1. being towed 2.
in one's company or charge

to·ward (tôrd, tə wôrd') *prep.* [see TO
& -WARD] 1. in the direction of 2.
facing 3. along a likely course to [steps
toward peace] 4. concerning 5. just
before [*toward* noon] 6. for [save
toward a car] Also **towards**

tow·el (tou''l) *n.* [< OFr. *toaille*] a
piece of cloth or paper for wiping or
drying things —*vt.* **-eled** or **-elled,
-el·ing** or **-el·ling** to wipe or dry with
a towel —**throw (or toss) in the
towel** [Colloq.] to admit defeat

tow'el·ing, tow'el·ling *n.* material
for making towels

tow·er (tou'ər) *n.* [< L. *turris*] 1. a
high structure, often part of another
building 2. such a structure used as a
fortress, etc. —*vi.* to rise high like a
tower —**tow'er·ing** *adj.*

tow'head' (tō'hed') *n.* [< *tow*, fibers
of flax, etc.] 1. a head of pale-yellow
hair 2. a person with such hair —
tow'head'ed *adj.*

tow·hee (tou'hē, tō'-) *n.* [echoic]
a small N.American sparrow

tow'line' *n.* a rope, etc. for towing

town (toun) *n.* [OE. *tun*] 1. a concentration of houses, etc. somewhat
larger than a village 2. a city 3. a
township 4. the business center of a
city 5. the people of a town —**go to
town** [Slang] to act fast and efficiently
—**on the town** [Colloq.] out for a
good time

town crier one who formerly cried

public announcements through the
streets of a village or town

town hall a building in a town, housing the offices of officials, etc.

town house a two-story dwelling, a
unit in a complex of such dwellings

town meeting a meeting of the
voters of a town, as in New England

town'ship *n.* 1. a division of a
county, constituting a unit of local
government 2. in the U.S. land survey,
a unit generally 6 miles square

towns·man (tounz'mən) *n.*, *pl.* **-men**
1. one who lives, or was reared, in a
town 2. a fellow resident of one's town

towns'peo'ple *n.pl.* the people of a
town: also **towns'folk'** (-fōk')

tow'path' *n.* a path along a canal,
used by men or animals towing
freight-carrying boats

tow'rope' *n.* a rope used in towing

tox·e·mi·a (täk sē'mē ə) *n.* [see ff. &
-EMIA] a condition in which the blood
contains poison substances, esp. toxins
produced by pathogenic bacteria

tox·ic (täk'sik) *adj.* [< Gr. *toxikon*, a
poison] 1. of, affected by, or caused by
a toxin 2. poisonous

tox·i·col·o·gy (täk'si käl'ə jē) *n.* [see
prec. & -LOGY] the science of poisons,
their effects, antidotes, etc. —**tox'i·
col'o·gist** *n.*

tox·in (täk'sin) *n.* [< TOXIC] 1. a
poison produced by microorganisms
and causing certain diseases 2. any
poison secreted by plants or animals

toy (toi) *n.* [< ? MDu. *toi*, finery] 1. a
trifle 2. a bauble; trinket 3. a play-
thing for children —*adj.* 1. like a toy
in size, use, etc. 2. made as a toy —*vi.*
to trifle (*with* a thing, an idea, etc.)

tr. 1. transpose 2. treasurer

trace[1] (trās) *n.* [< L. *trahere*, to draw]
1. a mark, track, sign, etc. left by a
person, animal, or thing 2. a barely
perceptible amount —*vt.* **traced,
trac'ing** 1. to follow the trail of;
track 2. *a*) to follow the development
or history of *b*) to determine (a source,
etc.) thus 3. to draw, outline, etc. 4.
to copy (a drawing, etc.) by following
its lines on a superimposed transparent
sheet —**trace'a·ble** *adj.* —**trac'er** *n.*

trace[2] (trās) *n.* [see TRAIT] either of
two straps, etc. connecting a draft
animal's harness to the vehicle

trace element a chemical element, as
copper, zinc, etc., essential in nutrition but only in minute amounts

trac·er·y (trās'ər ē) *n.*, *pl.* **-ies** [<
TRACE[1] + -ERY] ornamental work of
interlacing or branching lines

tra·che·a (trā'kē ə) *n.*, *pl.* **-ae** (-ē'),
-as [< Gr. *tracheia* (*arteria*), rough
(windpipe)] the passage that conveys
air from the larynx to the bronchi;
windpipe —**tra'che·al** *adj.*

tra·che·ot·o·my (trā'kē ät'ə mē) *n.*
[see prec. & -TOMY] an incision of the
trachea to aid breathing in an emergency

tra·cho·ma (trə kō'mə) *n.* [Gr.
trachōma, roughness] a contagious
viral infection of the conjunctiva and
cornea, causing granulation and scar-
ring

trac·ing (trā'siŋ) *n.* something traced; specif., a copy of a drawing, etc.

track (trak) *n.* [< MFr. *trac*] 1. a mark left in passing, as a footprint, wheel rut, etc. 2. a path or trail 3. a sequence of ideas, events, etc. 4. a path or circuit laid out for racing, etc. 5. a pair of parallel metal rails on which trains, etc. run 6. *a)* sports performed on a track, as running, hurdling, etc. *b)* these sports along with other contests in jumping, throwing, etc. 7. a separate, parallel recording surface along a magnetic tape —*vt.* 1. to follow the track of 2. to trace by means of evidence, etc. 3. to observe or plot the path of, as with radar 4. to leave tracks of (mud, etc.) on (often with *up*) —**in one's tracks** where one is at the moment —**keep (or lose) track of** to stay (or fail to stay) informed about —**track'less** *adj.*

tract[1] (trakt) *n.* [< L. *trahere*, to draw] 1. a continuous expanse of land 2. a system of organs having some special function [the digestive *tract*]

tract[2] (trakt) *n.* [< LL. *tractatus*, treatise] a propagandizing pamphlet, esp. one on a religious subject

trac·ta·ble (trak'tə b'l) *adj.* [< L. *trahere*, to draw] 1. easily managed; docile 2. easily worked; malleable

trac·tion (trak'shən) *n.* [< L. *trahere*, to draw] 1. *a)* a pulling or drawing *b)* being pulled or drawn 2. the kind of power used by a locomotive, etc. 3. adhesive friction

trac·tor (trak'tər) *n.* [see prec.] 1. a powerful, motor-driven vehicle for pulling farm machinery, etc. 2. a truck with a driver's cab and no body, for hauling large trailers

trade (trād) *n.* [< MLowG., a track] 1. an occupation; esp., skilled work 2. all the persons in a particular business 3. buying and selling; commerce 4. customers 5. a purchase or sale 6. an exchange; swap —*vi.* trad'ed, trad'ing 1. to carry on a business 2. to have business dealings (*with*) 3. to make an exchange (*with*) 4. [Colloq.] to be a customer (*at* a certain store) —*vt.* to exchange; barter —**trade on (or upon)** to take advantage of

trade'-in' *n.* a thing given or taken as part payment for something else

trade journal a magazine devoted to a specific trade or industry

trade'mark' *n.* a symbol, word, etc. used by a manufacturer or dealer to distinguish his product: usually protected by law

trade name 1. a name used as a trademark 2. the name used for a certain article by those who deal in it 3. the business name of a company

trade'-off' *n.* an exchange in which one benefit is given up for another considered more desirable: also **trade'off'**

trad'er *n.* 1. one who trades; merchant 2. a ship used in trade

trades·man (trādz'mən) *n.*, *pl.* -men [Chiefly Brit.] a storekeeper

trade union *same as* LABOR UNION

trade wind a wind that blows toward the equator from either side of it

trading post a store in an outpost, settlement, etc., where trading is done

trading stamp a stamp redeemable for merchandise, given as a premium by some merchants

tra·di·tion (trə dish'ən) *n.* [< L. *tradere*, deliver] 1. the handing down orally of customs, beliefs, etc. from generation to generation 2. a story, belief, etc. handed down in this way **tra·di'tion·al** *adj.* of, handed down by, or conforming to tradition

tra·duce (trə dōōs', -dyōōs') *vt.* -duced', -duc'ing [< L. *trans*, across + *ducere*, to lead] to slander

traf·fic (traf'ik) *n.* [< It. < L. *trans*, across + It. *ficcare*, bring] 1. buying and selling; trade 2. dealings (*with* someone) 3. the movement or number of automobiles, pedestrians, etc. along a street, etc. 4. the business done by a transportation company —*adj.* of or having to do with the regulation of traffic —*vi.* -ficked, -fick·ing 1. to carry on traffic (*in* a commodity) 2. to have dealings (*with* someone)

traffic circle a circular road at the intersection of several streets: vehicles move on it in one direction only

traffic light (or signal) a set of signal lights at a street intersection to regulate traffic

tra·ge·di·an (trə jē'dē ən) *n.* an actor or writer of tragedy

trag·e·dy (traj'ə dē) *n.*, *pl.* -dies [< Gr. *tragos*, goat + *ōidē*, song] 1. a serious play with an unhappy ending 2. a very sad or tragic event

trag·ic (traj'ik) *adj.* 1. of, or having the nature of, tragedy 2. disastrous, fatal, etc. —**trag'i·cal·ly** *adv.*

trail (trāl) *vt.* [< L. *trahere*, to draw] 1. to drag or let drag behind one 2. to follow the tracks of 3. to hunt by tracking 4. to follow behind —*vi.* 1. to drag along on the ground, etc. 2. to grow along the ground, etc., as some plants 3. to flow behind, as smoke 4. to follow or lag behind; straggle 5. to grow weaker, dimmer, etc. (with *off* or *away*) —*n.* 1. something that trails behind 2. a mark, scent, etc. left by a person, animal, or thing that has passed 3. a beaten path

trail'blaz'er *n.* 1. one who blazes a trail 2. a pioneer in any field

trail'er *n.* 1. one that trails 2. *a)* a wagon, van, etc. designed to be pulled by an automobile, truck, etc. *b)* such a vehicle designed to be lived in

trailer park an area, usually with piped water, electricity, etc., for trailers, esp. mobile homes: also **trailer camp, trailer court**

train (trān) *n.* [< L. *trahere*, to pull] 1. something that drags along behind, as a trailing skirt 2. a group of followers; retinue **3.** a procession; caravan **4.** any connected order; sequence [a *train* of thought] **5.** a line of connected railroad cars pulled by a locomotive —*vt.* **1.** to guide the growth of (a plant) **2.** to guide the mental, moral, etc. development of; rear **3.** to instruct so as to make proficient **4.** to make fit for an athletic contest, etc. **5.** to aim (a gun, etc.) —*vi.* to undergo training —**train·ee** (trā nē′) *n.* —**train′er** *n.* —**train′ing** *n.*

train′man (-mən) *n., pl.* **-men** one who works on a railroad train

traipse (trāps) *vi., vt.* **traipsed, traips′ing** [< ?] [Dial. or Colloq.] to walk, wander, or tramp

trait (trāt) *n.* [< L. *trahere*, to draw] a distinguishing characteristic

trai·tor (trāt′ər) *n.* [< L. *tradere*, betray] one who betrays his country, friends, etc. —**trai′tor·ous** *adj.*

tra·jec·to·ry (trə jek′tə rē) *n., pl.* **-ries** [< L. *trans-*, across + *jacere*, to throw] the curved path of something hurtling through space

tram (tram) *n.* [prob. < LowG. *traam*, a beam] **1.** an open railway car used in mines [Brit.] a streetcar

tram·mel (tram′'l) *n.* [< L. *tres*, three + *macula*, a mesh] [*usually pl.*] something that confines or restrains —*vt.* **-meled** or **-melled, -mel·ing** or **-mel·ling** to confine, restrain, etc.

tramp (tramp) *vi.* [ME. *trampen*] **1.** to walk or step heavily **2.** to travel about on foot —*vt.* **1.** to step on heavily **2.** to walk through —*n.* **1.** a hobo; vagrant **2.** the sound of heavy steps **3.** a journey on foot; hike **4.** a freight ship that picks up cargo wherever it may be **5.** [Slang] a loose woman

tram·ple (tram′p'l) *vi.* **-pled, -pling** [see prec.] to tread heavily —*vt.* to crush as by treading heavily on

tram·po·line (tram′pə lēn′, -lin) *n.* [< It.] a sheet of strong canvas stretched tightly on a frame, used in acrobatic tumbling

trance (trans) *n.* [< L. *transire*, to die] **1.** a state of altered consciousness, resembling sleep, as in hypnosis **2.** a daze; stupor **3.** a state of great mental abstraction

tran·quil (traŋ′kwəl) *adj.* [L. *tranquillus*] calm, serene, placid, etc. — **tran·quil′li·ty, tran·quil′i·ty** (-kwil′ə tē) *n.* —**tran′quil·ly** *adv.*

tran′quil·ize′, tran′quil·lize′ (-ĭz′) *vt., vi.* **-ized′** or **-lized′, -iz′ing** or **-liz′ing** to make or become tranquil

tran′quil·iz′er, tran′quil·liz′er *n.* a drug used to tranquilize the emotionally disturbed, etc.

trans- [L. < *trans*, across] *a prefix meaning* over, across, beyond

trans. **1.** translated **2.** translation

trans·act (tran sakt′, -zakt′) *vt.* [< L. *trans-*, over + *agere*, to drive] to carry on or complete (business, etc.)

trans·ac′tion *n.* **1.** a transacting **2.** something transacted; specif., *a)* a business deal *b)* [*pl.*] a record of the proceedings of a society, etc.

trans·ac′tion·al analysis a form of popular psychotherapy dealing with hypothetical states of the ego

trans·at·lan·tic (trans′ət lan′tik) *adj.* **1.** crossing the Atlantic **2.** on the other side of the Atlantic

trans·ceiv·er (tran sē′vər) *n.* a radio transmitter and receiver in a single housing

tran·scend (tran send′) *vt.* [< L. *trans-*, over + *scandere*, climb] **1.** to go beyond the limits of; exceed **2.** to surpass; excel —**tran·scend′ent** *adj.*

tran·scen·den·tal (tran′sen den′t'l) *adj.* **1.** supernatural **2.** abstract

tran′scen·den′tal·ism *n.* a philosophy based on a search for reality through spiritual intuition

trans′con·ti·nen′tal (trans′-) *adj.* **1.** that crosses a continent **2.** on the other side of a continent

tran·scribe (tran skrīb′) *vt.* **-scribed′, -scrib′ing** [< L. *trans-*, over + *scribere*, write] **1.** to make a written or typewritten copy of (shorthand notes, etc.) **2.** *Music, Radio & TV* to make a transcription of

tran·script (tran′skript′) *n.* **1.** a written or typewritten copy **2.** a copy, esp. an official copy

tran·scrip′tion (-skrip′shən) *n.* **1.** a transcribing **2.** a transcript **3.** an arrangement of a piece of music for some other instrument or voice **4.** a recording made for radio or television broadcasting

tran·sept (tran′sept) *n.* [< L. *trans-*, across + *septum*, enclosure] the part of a cross-shaped church at right angles to the nave

trans·fer (trans fur′; *esp. for n.* trans′fər) *vt.* **-ferred′, -fer′ring** [< L. *trans-*, across + *ferre*, to bear] **1.** to carry, send, etc. to another person or place **2.** to make over (property, etc.) to another **3.** to convey (a picture, etc.) from one surface to another —*vi.* **1.** to transfer oneself or be transferred **2.** to change to another school, etc. or to another bus, etc. —*n.* **1.** a transferring or being transferred **2.** one that is transferred **3.** a ticket entitling the bearer to change to another bus, etc. —**trans·fer′a·ble** *adj.*

trans·fer′ence (-əns) *n.* a transferring or being transferred

trans·fig·ure (trans fig′yər) *vt.* **-ured, -ur·ing** [< L. *trans-*, across + *figura*, figure] **1.** to change the form or appearance of **2.** to transform so as to glorify —**trans·fig′u·ra′tion** *n.*

trans·fix (trans fiks′) *vt.* [< L. *trans-*, through + *figere*, to fix] **1.** to pierce through; impale **2.** to make motionless, as if impaled

trans·form (trans fôrm′) *vt.* [ult. < L. *trans-*, over + *forma*, a form] **1.** to change the form or appearance of **2.** to change the condition, character, or function of —**trans′for·ma′tion** *n.*

trans·form′er *n.* **1.** one that transforms **2.** a device for changing electrical energy to a different voltage

trans·fuse (trans fyōoz′) *vt.* **-fused′, -fus′ing** [< L. *trans-*, across + *fundere*, pour] **1.** to instill; imbue **2.**

to transfer (blood, etc.) into a blood vessel —**trans·fu'sion** n.

trans·gress (trans gres') vt., vi. [< L. trans-, over + gradi, to step] 1. to break (a law, command, etc.); sin (against) 2. to go beyond (a limit, etc.) —**trans·gres'sion** (-gresh'ən) n. —**trans·gres'sor** n.

tran·sient (tran'shənt) adj. [< L. trans-, over + ire, to go] 1. passing away with time; temporary 2. passing quickly; fleeting —n. a transient person; esp., a temporary lodger, etc. —**tran'sience, tran'sien·cy** n.

tran·sis·tor (tran zis'tər, -sis'-) n. [TRAN(SFER) + (RE)SISTOR] a compact electronic device, composed of semiconductor material, that controls current flow —**trans·sis'tor·ize'** vt. -**ized', -iz'ing**

trans·it (tran'sit) n. [< L. trans-, over + ire, go] 1. passage through or across 2. a carrying through or across; conveyance 3. a surveying instrument for measuring horizontal angles

tran·si·tion (tran zish'ən) n. a passing from one condition, place, etc. to another —**tran·si'tion·al** adj.

tran·si·tive (tran'sə tiv) adj. designating a verb taking a direct object

tran·si·to·ry (tran'sə tôr'ē) adj. not enduring; temporary; fleeting

transl. 1. translated 2. translation

trans·late (trans lāt') vt. -**lat'ed, -lat'ing** [< L. translatus, transferred] 1. to change from one place, condition, etc. to another 2. to put into words of a different language 3. to put into different words —**trans·la'tor** n.

trans·la·tion n. 1. a translating 2. writing or speech translated into another language

trans·lit·er·ate (trans lit'ə rāt') vt. -**at'ed, -at'ing** [< TRANS- + L. litera, letter] to write (words, etc.) in the characters of another alphabet

trans·lu·cent (trans lōō's'nt) adj. [< L. trans-, through + lucere, to shine] letting light pass through but not transparent

trans·mi·grate (trans mī'grāt) vi. -**grat'ed, -grat'ing** [see TRANS- & MIGRATE] in some religions, to pass into another body at death: said of the soul —**trans'mi·gra'tion** n.

trans·mis·si·ble (trans mis'ə b'l) adj. capable of being transmitted

trans·mis·sion (trans mish'ən) n. 1. a transmitting 2. something transmitted 3. the part of an automobile, etc. that transmits motive force to the wheels, as by gears

trans·mit' (-mit') vt. -**mit'ted, -mit'ting** [< L. trans-, over + mittere, send] 1. to cause to go to another person or place; transfer 2. to hand down by heredity, inheritance, etc. 3. a) to pass (light, heat, etc.) through some medium b) to conduct 4. to convey (force, movement, etc.) to 5. to send out (radio or television signals) —**trans·mit'tal, trans·mit'-**

tance n. —**trans·mit'ti·ble, trans·mit'ta·ble** adj.

trans·mit'ter n. one that transmits; specif., the apparatus that transmits signals in telephony, radio, etc.

trans·mute (trans myōōt') vt., vi. -**mut'ed, -mut'ing** [< L. trans-, over + mutare, change] to change from one form, nature, substance, etc. into another —**trans'mu·ta'tion** n.

trans·na·tion·al adj. transcending the interests, etc. of a single nation

tran·som (tran'səm) n. [prob. < L. transtrum, crossbeam] 1. a horizontal crossbar, as across the top of a door or window 2. a small window just above a door or window

tran·son·ic (tran sän'ik) adj. of or moving at a speed within the range of change from subsonic to supersonic speed: also sp. **transsonic**

trans·pa·cif·ic (trans'pə sif'ik) adj. 1. crossing the Pacific 2. on the other side of the Pacific

trans·par·ent (trans per'ənt) adj. [< L. trans-, through + parere, appear] 1. transmitting light rays so that objects on the other side may be seen 2. so fine in texture as to be seen through 3. easily understood or detected; obvious —**trans·par'en·cy** n., pl. -**cies** —**trans·par'ent·ly** adv.

tran·spire (tran spīr') vi. -**spired', -spir'ing** [< L. trans-, through + spirare, breathe] 1. to give off vapor, moisture, etc., as through pores. 2. to become known 3. to happen: regarded by some as a loose usage —**tran'spi·ra'tion** (-spə rā'shən) n.

trans·plant (trans plant') vt. 1. to remove from one place and plant, resettle, etc. in another 2. Surgery to graft (tissue, an organ, etc.)

tran·spon·der (tran spän'dər) n. [< TRANSMITTER & RESPOND] a transceiver that transmits signals automatically

trans·port (trans pôrt'; for n. trans' pôrt) vt. [< L. trans-, over + portare, carry] 1. to carry from one place to another 2. to carry away with emotion 3. to banish to a penal colony, etc. —n. 1. a transporting; transportation 2. rapture 3. a vehicle for transporting

trans·por·ta·tion (trans'pər tā' shən) n. 1. a transporting or being transported 2. a means of conveyance 3. fare or a ticket for being transported

trans·pose (trans pōz') vt., vi. -**posed', -pos'ing** [see TRANS- & POSE] 1. to change the usual order or position of; interchange 2. to rewrite or play (a musical composition) in another key —**trans'po·si'tion** (-pə zish'ən) n.

trans·po·son (-pō'zän) n. a DNA segment that moves within a chromosome, or to another, altering existing genetic instructions

trans·sex·u·al (tran sek'shoo wəl) n. a person who is predisposed to identify with the opposite sex, in some cases undergoing sex-change surgery

trans·ship (tran ship′) *vt.* -shipped′, -ship′ping to transfer from one ship, train, truck, etc. to another for further shipment —**trans·ship′ment** *n.*

trans·verse (trans vurs′; *esp. for n.* trans′vurs) *adj.* [< L. *trans-*, across + *vertere*, to turn] situated across; crosswise —*n.* a transverse part, etc.

trans·ves·tite (trans ves′tīt) *n.* [< TRANS- + L. *vestire*, to dress] a person who gets sexual pleasure from dressing in clothes of the opposite sex

trap¹ (trap) *n.* [< OE. *træppe*] 1. a device for trapping animals 2. any stratagem designed to catch or trick 3. a device, as in a drainpipe, for preventing the escape of gas, etc. 4. a light, two-wheeled carriage 5. [*pl.*] percussion devices, as in a band —*vt.* **trapped, trap′ping** to catch as in a trap —*vi.* to trap animals, esp. for their furs —**trap′per** *n.*

trap² (trap) *n.* [Sw. *trapp*] dark-colored, igneous rock, used in road making: also **trap′rock′**

trap³ (trap) *vt.* **trapped, trap′ping** [< OFr. *drap,* cloth] to cover, equip, or adorn with trappings

trap′door′ *n.* a hinged or sliding door in a roof, ceiling, or floor

tra·peze (tra pēz′, trə-) *n.* [see ff.] a short horizontal bar, hung high by two ropes, on which gymnasts, etc. swing

trap·e·zoid (trap′ə zoid′) *n.* [< Gr. *trapeza,* table] a plane figure with four sides, two of which are parallel — **trap′e·zoi′dal** *adj.*

TRAPEZOID

trap·pings (trap′inz) *n.pl.* [< OFr. *drap,* cloth] 1. an ornamental covering for a horse 2. adornments

trap′shoot′ing *n.* the sport of shooting at clay disks sprung into the air from throwing devices (**traps**)

trash (trash) *n.* [prob. < Scand.] 1. worthless or waste things; rubbish 2. a disreputable person or people — **trash′y** *adj.* -i·er, -i·est

trau·ma (trou′mə, trô′-) *n., pl.* **-mas**, **-ma·ta** (-mə tə) [Gr.] 1. a bodily injury or shock 2. an emotional shock, often having a lasting psychic effect —**trau·mat′ic** (-mat′ik) *adj.*

trau′ma·tize′ (-tīz′) *vt.* -tized′, -tiz′ing to subject to a physical or mental trauma

trav·ail (trav′āl, trə vāl′) *n.* [< VL. *tri-*, three + *palus,* stake: referring to a torture device] 1. very hard work 2. intense pain; agony

trav·el (trav′l) *vi.* -eled or -elled, -el·ing or -el·ling [var. of TRAVAIL] 1. to go from one place to another 2. to move, pass, or be transmitted —*vt.* to make a journey over or through —*n.* a traveling; trip —**trav′el·er, trav′el·ler** *n.*

trav·e·logue, trav·e·log (trav′ə lôg′) *n.* an illustrated lecture or motion picture of travels

trav·erse (trav′ərs; *for n. & adj.* trav′ərs) *vt.* -ersed′, -ers′ing [see TRANSVERSE] to pass over, across, or through —*n.* something that traverses

or crosses, as a crossbar —*adj.* 1. extending across 2. designating or of drapes drawn by pulling a cord at the side

trav·es·ty (trav′is tē) *n., pl.* -ties [< L. *trans-*, over + *vestire,* to dress] 1. a farcical imitation in ridicule 2. a ridiculous representation —*vt.* -tied, -ty·ing to make a travesty of

trawl (trôl) *n.* [< ? MDu. *traghel, dragnet*] 1. a large net dragged along the bottom of a fishing bank 2. a long line supported by buoys, from which fishing lines are hung —*vt., vi.* to fish or catch with a trawl

trawl′er *n.* a boat used in trawling

tray (trā) *n.* [< OE. *treg,* wooden board] a flat receptacle with raised edges, for holding or carrying things

treach·er·ous (trech′ər əs) *adj.* 1. characterized by treachery 2. untrustworthy —**treach′er·ous·ly** *adv.*

treach′er·y *n., pl.* -er·ies [< OFr. *trichier,* to cheat] 1. betrayal of trust; disloyalty 2. treason

trea·cle (trē′k'l) *n.* [< Gr. *thēriakē,* antidote for venom] [Brit.] molasses

tread (tred) *vt.* **trod, trod′den** or **trod, tread′ing** [OE. *tredan*] 1. to walk on, in, along, etc. 2. to do or follow by walking, dancing, etc. 3. to press or beat with the feet —*vi.* 1. to walk 2. to set one's foot (*on, across,* etc.) 3. to trample (*on* or *upon*) —*n.* 1. the manner or sound of treading 2. something on which a person or thing treads or moves, as a shoe sole, wheel rim, surface of a stair, etc. —**tread water** *pt. usually* **tread′ed** to stay upright in swimming by moving the legs up and down

trea·dle (tred′'l) *n.* [< OE. *tredan,* to tread] a lever moved by the foot as to turn a wheel

tread′mill′ *n.* a mill wheel turned by an animal treading an endless belt

treas. 1. treasurer 2. treasury

trea·son (trē′z'n) *n.* [< L. *trans-*, over + *dare,* give] betrayal of one's country to an enemy —**trea′son·a·ble, trea′son·ous** *adj.*

treas·ure (trezh′ər, trā′zhər) *n.* [< Gr. *thēsauros*] 1. accumulated wealth, as money, jewels, etc. 2. any person or thing considered valuable —*vt.* -ured, -ur·ing 1. to save up for future use 2. to value greatly

treas′ur·er *n.* one in charge of a treasury, as of a government, corporation, club, etc.

treas′ure-trove′ (-trōv′) *n.* [*trove* < OFr. *trover,* find] treasure found hidden, the owner of which is unknown

treas·ur·y (-ē) *n., pl.* -ies 1. a place where treasure or funds are kept 2. the funds or revenues of a state, corporation, etc. 3. [T-] the governmental department in charge of revenue, taxation, etc.

treat (trēt) *vi.* [ult. < L. *trahere,* to draw] 1. to discuss terms (*with*) 2. to speak or write (*of*) —*vt.* 1. to deal with (a subject) in writing, music, etc. in a specified manner 2. to act toward (someone or something) in a specified manner 3. to pay for the food, etc. of (another) 4. to subject to some process, chemical, etc. 5. to give medical care to —*n.* 1. a meal, drink, etc. paid for by another 2. anything that gives great pleasure

trea·tise (trēt'is) *n.* [see prec.] a formal writing on some subject

treat·ment (trēt'mənt) *n.* 1. act, manner, method, etc. of treating 2. medical or surgical care

trea·ty (trēt'ē) *n., pl.* **-ties** [< L. *trahere,* to draw] a formal agreement between two or more nations

tre·ble (treb'l) *adj.* [< L. *triplus,* triple] 1. threefold; triple 2. of, for, or performing the treble —*n.* 1. the highest part in musical harmony; soprano 2. a high-pitched voice or sound —*vt., vi.* **-bled, -bling** to make or become threefold

tree (trē) *n.* [OE. *treow*] 1. a large, woody perennial plant with one main trunk and many branches 2. anything resembling a tree; specif., a diagram of family descent (**family tree**) —*vt.* **treed, tree'ing** to chase up a tree —**tree'less** *adj.*

tre·foil (trē'foil) *n.* [< L. *tri-,* three + *folium,* leaf] 1. a plant with leaves divided into three leaflets, as the clover 2. a design, etc. shaped like such a leaf

trek (trek) *vi.* **trekked, trek'king** [Afrik. < Du. *trekken,* to draw] 1. to travel slowly or laboriously 2. [Colloq.] to go on foot —*n.* 1. a journey 2. a migration

trel·lis (trel'is) *n.* [< L. *trilix,* triple-twilled] a lattice on which vines are trained

trem·ble (trem'b'l) *vi.* **-bled, -bling** [< L. *tremere*] 1. to shake or shiver, as from cold, fear, etc. 2. to feel fear or anxiety 3. to quiver, vibrate, etc. —*n.* 1. a trembling 2. [*sometimes pl.*] a fit or state of trembling

tre·men·dous (tri men'dəs) *adj.* [< L. *tremere,* tremble] 1. terrifying; dreadful 2. *a)* very large; great *b)* [Colloq.] wonderful, amazing, etc. —**tre·men'dous·ly** *adv.*

trem·o·lo (trem'ə lō') *n., pl.* **-los'** [It.] a tremulous effect produced by rapid reiteration of the same tone

trem·or (trem'ər) *n.* [< L. *tremere,* tremble] a trembling, shaking, etc. 2. a nervous thrill

trem·u·lous (trem'yoo ləs) *adj.* [< L. *tremere,* to tremble] 1. trembling; quivering 2. fearful; timid —**trem'u·lous·ly** *adv.*

trench (trench) *vt.* [< OFr. *trenchier,* to cut] to dig a ditch or ditches in —*n.* 1. a deep furrow 2. a long, narrow ditch with earth banked in front, used in battle for cover, etc.

trench·ant (tren'chənt) *adj.* [see prec.] 1. sharp; keen; incisive [*trenchant* words] 2. forceful; vigorous [a *trenchant* argument]

trench coat a belted raincoat in a military style

trench·er (tren'chər) *n.* [see TRENCH] [Archaic] a wooden platter for meat

trench'er·man (-mən) *n., pl.* **-men** an eater, esp., a heavy eater

trench foot a circulatory disorder of the feet from long exposure to wet and cold with inactivity

trench mouth an infectious disease of the mucous membranes of the mouth and throat

trend (trend) *vi.* [OE. *trendan*] to have a general direction or tendency —*n.* 1. the general tendency or course; drift 2. a current style

trend'y (-ē) *adj.* **-i·er, -i·est** [Colloq.] of or in the latest style, or trend

Tren·ton (tren'tən) capital of N.J.: pop. 92,000

tre·pan (tri pan') *n.* [< Gr. *trypan,* to bore] an early form of the trephine —*vt.* **-panned', -pan'ning** same as TREPHINE

tre·phine (tri fīn', -fēn') *n.* [< L. *tres,* three + *fines,* ends] a surgical saw for removing disks of bone from the skull —*vt.* **-phined', -phin'ing** to operate on with a trephine

trep·i·da·tion (trep'ə dā'shən) *n.* [< L. *trepidus,* disturbed] 1. trembling movement 2. fearful uncertainty

tres·pass (tres'pəs, -pas') *vi.* [< L. *trans-,* across + *passus,* a step] 1. to go beyond the limits of what is considered right; do wrong; transgress 2. to enter another's property without permission or right —*n.* a trespassing; specif., a moral offense —**tres'pass·er** *n.*

tress (tres) *n.* [< OFr. *tresce,* braid of hair] 1. a lock of hair 2. [*pl.*] a woman's or girl's hair, esp. when long

tres·tle (tres''l) *n.* [< L. *transtrum,* a beam] 1. a horizontal beam fastened to two pairs of spreading legs, used as a support 2. a framework of uprights and cross-pieces, supporting a bridge, etc.

TRESTLE

trey (trā) *n.* [< L. *tres,* three] a playing card, etc. with three spots

tri- [< Fr., L., or Gr.] *a combining form meaning:* 1. having or involving three 2. three times, into three 3. every third

tri·ad (trī'ad) *n.* [< Gr. *treis,* three] a group of three

tri·al (trī'əl) *n.* [see TRY] 1. the act or process of trying, testing, etc.; test; probation 2. a hardship, suffering, etc. 3. a source of annoyance 4. a formal examination to decide a case by a court of law 5. an attempt; effort —*adj.* 1. of a trial 2. for the purpose of trying, testing, etc.

trial and error the process of making repeated trials, tests, etc. to find a desired result or solution

trial balloon something said or done to test public opinion on an issue

tri·an·gle (trī'aŋ'g'l) n. [see TRI- & ANGLE[1]] 1. a plane figure having three angles and three sides 2. any three-sided or three-cornered object 3. a situation involving three persons [a love triangle] —**tri·an·gu·lar** (-gyə lər) adj.

tri·an·gu·late' (-gyə lāt') vt. -lat'-ed, -lat'ing to divide into triangles to compute distance or relative positions —**tri·an·gu·la'tion** n.

tri·ath·lon (trī ath'län, -lən) n. [TRI- + Gr. athlon, a contest] an endurance race combining events in swimming, bicycling, and running

tribe (trīb) n. [< L. tribus] 1. a group of persons or clans descended from a common ancestor and living under a leader or chief 2. a natural group of plants or animals —**trib'al** adj. —**tribes'man** n.

trib·u·la·tion (trib'yə lā'shən) n. [< L. tribulare, to press] great misery or distress, or the cause of it

tri·bu·nal (trī byōō'n'l, tri-) n. [see ff.] 1. a seat for a judge in a court 2. a court of justice

trib·une (trib'yōōn, tri byōōn') n. [< L. tribus, tribe] 1. in ancient Rome, a magistrate appointed to protect the rights of plebeians 2. a champion of the people: often a newspaper name

trib·u·tar·y (trib'yoo ter'ē) adj. 1. paying tribute 2. subject [a tributary nation] 3. a) making additions b) flowing into a larger one [a tributary stream] —n., pl. -ies 1. a tributary nation 2. a tributary river

trib·ute (trib'yōōt) n. [< L. tribuere, allot] 1. money paid regularly by one nation to another as acknowledgment of subjugation, for protection, etc. 2. any forced payment 3. something given, done, or said to show gratitude, respect, honor, or praise

trice (trīs) n. [< MDu. trisen, to pull] an instant: now only in **in a trice**

tri·cen·ten·ni·al (trī'sen ten'ē əl) adj. happening once every 300 years —n. a 300th anniversary

tri·ceps (trī'seps) n., pl. -cep'ses, -ceps [L. < tri, three + caput, head] a muscle with three points of origin; esp., the muscle on the upper arm

tri·cer·a·tops (trī ser'ə täps') n. [< TRI- + Gr. keras, horn + ōps, eye] a plant-eating dinosaur with three horns

trich·i·no·sis (trik'ə nō'sis) n. [< Gr. trichinos, hairy] a disease caused by intestinal worms, and acquired by eating pork from an infested hog

trick (trik) n. [< OFr. trichier, v.] 1. something designed to deceive, cheat, etc. 2. a practical joke; prank 3. a clever act intended to amuse 4. any feat requiring skill 5. a personal mannerism 6. a round of duty; shift 7. Card Games the cards won in a single round —vt. to deceive or cheat —adj. apt to malfunction [a trick knee] —**do (or turn) the trick** to produce the desired result —**trick'er·y** n., pl. -ies —**trick'ster** n.

trick·le (trik''l) vi. -led, -ling [prob. < ME. striken, to strike] 1. to flow slowly in a thin stream or fall in drops

2. to move slowly [the crowd trickled away] —n. a slow, small flow

trick'le-down' adj. of an economic theory holding that government aid to big business will ultimately benefit the poor

trick'y adj. -i·er, -i·est 1. given to or characterized by trickery 2. like a trick; intricate; difficult

tri·col·or (trī'kul'ər) n. a flag having three colors in large areas; esp., the flag of France

tri·cy·cle (trī'si k'l) n. [Fr.: see TRI- & CYCLE] a child's three-wheeled vehicle operated by pedals

tri·dent (trīd'nt) n. [< L. tri-, TRI- + dens, tooth] a three-pronged spear —adj. three-pronged

tried (trīd) pt. & pp. of TRY —adj. 1. tested; proved 2. trustworthy

tri·en·ni·al (trī en'ē əl) adj. [< L. tri-, TRI- + annus, a year] 1. happening every three years 2. lasting three years —**tri·en'ni·al·ly** adv.

Tri·este (trē est') seaport in NE Italy: pop. 281,000

tri·fle (trī'f'l) n. [< OFr. truffe, deception] 1. something of little value or importance 2. a small amount or sum —vi. -fled, -fling 1. to talk or act jokingly 2. to toy (with) —vt. to waste (time, etc.) —**tri'fler** n.

tri·fling adj. 1. frivolous; shallow 2. of little importance; trivial

tri·fo·cals (trī'fō'k'lz) n.pl. a pair of glasses like bifocals, but with a third area in the lens ground for intermediate distance

trig (trig) n. clipped form of TRIGONOMETRY

trig·ger (trig'ər) n. [< Du. trekken, to pull] a lever pulled to release a catch, etc., esp. one pressed to activate the firing mechanism on a firearm —vt. to initiate (an action)

trig·o·nom·e·try (trig'ə näm'ə trē) n. [< Gr. trigōnon, triangle + -metria, measurement] the branch of mathematics analyzing, and making calculations from, the relations between the sides and angles of triangles —**trig'o·no·met'ric** (-nə met'rik) adj.

trill (tril) n. [ult. echoic] 1. a rapid alternation of a musical tone with the tone immediately above it 2. a warble 3. a rapid vibration of the tongue or uvula —vt., vi. to sound, speak, sing, or play with a trill

tril·lion (tril'yən) n. 1. in the U.S. and France, 1 followed by 12 zeros 2. in Great Britain and Germany, 1 followed by 18 zeros —**tril'lionth** adj., n.

tril·o·gy (tril'ə jē) n., pl. -gies [see TRI- & -LOGY] a set of three related plays, novels, etc.

trim (trim) vt. trimmed, trim'ming [< OE. trymman, make firm] 1. to put in proper order; make neat or tidy [to trim hair] 2. to clip, lop, cut, etc. 3. to decorate as by adding ornaments, etc. 4. a) to balance (a ship) by ballasting, etc. b) to put (sails) in order for sailing 5. to balance (an aircraft) in flight 6. [Colloq.] to beat, punish, defeat, cheat, etc. —vi. to

adjust according to expediency —*n.*
1. order; arrangement **2.** good condition **3.** a trimming **4.** decorative parts or borders —*adj.* **trim′mer, trim′mest** **1.** orderly; neat **2.** well-proportioned **3.** in good condition —**trim′ly** *adv.* —**trim′ner** *n.*

tri·ma·ran (trī′mə ran′) *n.* a boat like a catamaran, but with three hulls

tri·mes·ter (trī mes′tər, trī′mes-) *n.* [< L. *tri-*, three + *mensis*, month] in some colleges, any of the three periods of the academic year

trim′ming *n.* **1.** decoration; ornament **2.** [*pl.*] *a*) the side dishes of a meal *b*) parts trimmed off **3.** [Colloq.] a beating, defeat, cheating, etc.

Trin·i·dad and To·ba·go (trin′ə dad′, tō bā′gō) island country in the West Indies: 1,980 sq. mi.; pop. 1,010,000

trin·i·ty (trin′ə tē) *n., pl.* **-ties** [< L. *trinitas*] **1.** a set of three **2.** [T-] *Christian Theol.* the union of Father, Son, and Holy Ghost in one Godhead

trin·ket (triŋ′kit) *n.* [ME. *trenket*] **1.** a small ornament, piece of jewelry, etc. **2.** a trifle or toy

tri·o (trē′ō) *n., pl.* **-os** [< L. *tres*, three] **1.** a group of three **2.** *Music a*) a composition for three voices or three instruments *b*) the three performers of such a composition

trip (trip) *vi., vt.* **tripped, trip′ping** [< OFr. *treper*] **1.** to move or perform with light, rapid steps **2.** to stumble or cause to stumble **3.** to make or cause to make a mistake **4.** to release or run past (a spring, wheel, etc.) —*n.* **1.** a light, quick tread **2.** a journey, voyage, etc. **3.** a stumble or a causing to stumble **4.** [Slang] the experience of being under the influence of a psychedelic drug, esp. LSD **5.** [Slang] an experience that is pleasing, exciting, etc. —**trip up** to catch in a lie, error, etc. —**trip′per** *n.*

tri·par·tite (trī pär′tīt) *adj.* [< L. *tri-*, three + *partire*, to part] **1.** having three parts **2.** made between three parties, as an agreement

tripe (trīp) *n.* [prob. ult. < Ar. *tharb*, entrails] **1.** part of the stomach of an ox, etc. used as food **2.** [Slang] anything worthless, etc.; nonsense

trip′ham·mer *n.* a heavy, power-driven hammer, alternately raised and allowed to fall by a tripping device

tri·ple (trip′'l) *adj.* [< L. *triplus*] **1.** consisting of three; threefold **2.** three times as much or as many —*n.* **1.** an amount three times as much or as many **2.** *Baseball* a hit on which the batter reaches third base —*vt., vi.* **-pled, -pling** **1.** to make or become three times as much or as many **2.** to hit a triple —**tri′ply** *adv.*

tri·plet (trip′lit) *n.* any of three offspring born at a single birth

trip·li·cate (trip′lə kit; *for v.* -kāt′) *adj.* [< L. *triplex*] **1.** threefold **2.** being the last of three identical copies

—*n.* any one of such copies —*vt.* **-cat′ed, -cat′ing** to make three copies of —**in triplicate** in three copies

tri·pod (trī′päd) *n.* [< Gr. *tri-*, three + *pous*, a foot] a three-legged caldron, stool, support, etc.

trip·tych (trip′tik) *n.* [< Gr. *tri-*, three + *ptychē*, a fold] a set of three panels with pictures, etc. often hinged: used as an altarpiece

tri·sect (trī sekt′, trī′sekt) *vt.* [< TRI- + L. *secare*, to cut] to cut or divide into three equal parts

trite (trīt) *adj.* **trit′er, trit′est** [< L. *terere*, wear out] worn out by constant use; stale —**trite′ness** *n.*

tri·ti·um (trit′ē əm, trish′-) *n.* a radioactive isotope of hydrogen having an atomic weight of three

tri·umph (trī′əmf) *n.* [< L. *triumphus*] **1.** a victory; success **2.** exaltation or joy over a victory, etc. —*vi.* **1.** to gain victory or success **2.** to rejoice over victory, etc. —**tri·um′phal** (-um′f'l) *adj.*

tri·um′phant (-um′fənt) *adj.* **1.** successful; victorious **2.** rejoicing for victory —**tri·um′phant·ly** *adv.*

tri·um·vir (trī um′vər) *n., pl.* **-virs, -vir·i′** (-vi rī′) [L. < *trium virum*, of three men] in ancient Rome, any of three administrators sharing authority

tri·um′vi·rate (-it) *n.* government by a group of three men

triv·et (triv′it) *n.* [< L. *tripes*, tripod] **1.** a three-legged stand for holding pots, etc. near a fire **2.** a short-legged stand for hot dishes to rest on

triv·i·a (triv′ē ə) *n.pl.* [*often with sing. v.*] unimportant matters

triv·i·al (triv′ē əl) *adj.* [< L. *trivialis*, commonplace] unimportant; insignificant —**triv′i·al·i·ty** (-al′ə tē) *n.*

-trix (triks) *pl.* **-trix·es, -tri·ces′** (tri sēz′, trī′sēz) [L.] an ending of some feminine nouns of agent [*aviatrix*]

tro·che (trō′kē) *n.* [< Gr. *trochos*, a wheel] a small, medicinal lozenge

tro·chee (trō′kē) *n.* [< Gr. *trechein*, to run] a metrical foot of an accented syllable followed by an unaccented one —**tro·cha′ic** (-kā′ik) *adj.*

trod (träd) *pt. & alt. pp.* of TREAD

trod′den (-'n) *alt. pp.* of TREAD

trog·lo·dyte (träg′lə dīt′) *n.* [< Gr. *trōglē*, hole + *dyein*, enter] **1.** any of the prehistoric people who lived in caves **2.** a recluse

troi·ka (troi′kə) *n.* [Russ.] **1.** a vehicle drawn by three horses abreast **2.** an association of three in authority

Tro·jan (trō′jən) *adj.* of Troy, its people, etc. —*n.* **1.** a native or inhabitant of ancient Troy **2.** a strong, hard-working, determined person

Tro·jan horse *Gr. Legend* a huge, hollow wooden horse filled with Greek soldiers: it was taken into Troy as an ostensible gift, thus leading to the destruction of the city

troll[1] (trōl) *vt., vi.* [ME. *trollen*, to roll] **1.** to sing the parts of (a round, etc.) in succession 2. to sing in a full voice 3. to fish (for) with a moving line— *n.* a lure and line used in trolling

troll² (trōl) *n.* [ON.] in Scand. folklore, a supernatural being, as a giant or dwarf, living in a cave

trol·ley (träl′ē) *n., pl.* **-leys** [< TROLL¹] 1. a wheeled basket, etc. that runs suspended from an overhead track 2. a grooved wheel at the end of a pole, that transmits electric current from an overhead wire to a streetcar, etc. 3. *same as* TROLLEY CAR

trolley car (or **bus**) an electric streetcar (or bus) powered from an overhead wire by means of a trolley

trol·lop (träl′əp) *n.* [prob. < G. *trolle*, wench] a prostitute

trom·bone (träm bōn′, träm′bōn) *n.* [It. < *tromba*, a trumpet] a large, brass-wind instrument, usually with a slide, or movable section: also **slide trombone**

TROMBONE

troop (trōōp) *n.* [< ML. *troppus*, a flock] 1. a group of persons or animals 2. [*pl.*] soldiers 3. a subdivision of a cavalry regiment 4. a unit of Boy Scouts or Girl Scouts —*vi.* to gather or go as in a group

troop·er *n.* [prec. + -ER] 1. a cavalryman 2. a mounted policeman 3. [Colloq.] a State policeman

trope (trōp) *n.* [< Gr. *tropos*, a turning] figurative language or a word used in a figurative sense

tro·phy (trō′fē) *n., pl.* **-phies** [< Gr. *tropaion*] a memorial of victory in war, sports competition, etc.; prize

trop·ic (träp′ik) *n.* [< Gr. *tropikos*, of a turn (of the sun at the solstices)] 1. either of two parallels of latitude, one, the **Tropic of Cancer**, 23 1/2° north of the equator, and the other, the **Tropic of Capricorn**, 23 1/2° south 2. [*also* T-] [*pl.*] the region between these latitudes —*adj.* of the tropics; tropical

trop·i·cal (-i k'l) *adj.* 1. of, in, characteristic of, or suitable for the tropics 2. very hot; sultry; torrid

tro·pism (trō′piz'm) *n.* [< Gr. *tropē*, a turn] the tendency of a plant or animal to grow or turn in response to an external stimulus, as light

trop·o·sphere (träp′ə sfir′, trō′pə-) *n.* [see TROPE & SPHERE] the atmosphere from the earth's surface to about 6 to 12 miles above

trot (trät) *vt., vi.* **trot′ted, trot′ting** [< OHG. *trottōn*, to tread] 1. to move, ride, go, etc. at a trot 2. to hurry; run —*n.* 1. a gait of a horse, etc. in which the legs are lifted in alternating diagonal pairs 2. a jogging gait of a person —**trot′ter** *n.*

troth (trôth, trōth) *n.* [ME. *trouthe*] [Archaic] 1. faithfulness; loyalty 2. truth 3. a promise, esp. to marry

trou·ba·dour (trōō′bə dôr′) *n.* [Fr.

< Pr. *trobar*, compose in verse] any of a class of poet-musicians of S France & N Italy in the 11th–13th cent.

trou·ble (trub′'l) *vt.* **-bled, -bling** [< L. *turba*, crowd] 1. to disturb or agitate 2. to worry; harass 3. to cause inconvenience to [don't *trouble* yourself] —*vi.* to take pains; bother —*n.* 1. a state of mental distress; worry 2. a misfortune; calamity 3. a person, event, etc. causing annoyance, distress, etc. 4. public disturbance 5. effort; bother [take the *trouble* to listen]

trou·ble·mak·er *n.* one who incites others to quarrel, rebel, etc.

trou·ble·shoot·er *n.* one whose work is to locate and eliminate the source of trouble in any flow of work

trou·ble·some (-səm) *adj.* characterized by or causing trouble

trough (trôf) *n.* [OE. *trog*] 1. a long, narrow, open container, esp. one for holding water or food for animals 2. a channel or gutter for carrying off rain water 3. a long, narrow hollow, as between waves 4. a long, narrow area of low barometric pressure

trounce (trouns) *vt.* **trounced, trounc′ing** [< ?] 1. to beat; flog 2. [Colloq.] to defeat —**trounc′er** *n.*

troupe (trōōp) *n.* [Fr.] a troop, esp. of actors, singers, etc. —*vi.* **trouped, troup′ing** to travel as a member of such a company —**troup′er** *n.*

trou·sers (trou′zərz) *n.pl.* [< Scot-Gael. *triubhas*] a two-legged outer garment, esp. for men and boys, extending from the waist to the ankles

trous·seau (trōō′sō) *n., pl.* **-seaux** (-sōz), **-seaus** [Fr. < OFr. *trousse*, a bundle] a bride's clothes, linen, etc.

trout (trout) *n., pl.* **trout, trouts** [< Gr. *trōgein*, gnaw] any of various food and game fishes of the salmon family, found chiefly in fresh water

trow (trō, trou) *vi., vt.* [< OE. *treowe*, faith] [Archaic] to believe

trow·el (trou′əl) *n.* [< L. *trua*, ladle] 1. a flat hand tool for smoothing plaster or applying mortar 2. a scooplike tool for loosening soil, etc. —*vt.* **-eled** or **-elled, -el·ing** or **-el·ling** to spread, smooth, dig, etc. with a trowel

Troy (troi) ancient city in NW Asia Minor

troy (troi) *adj.* [< *Troyes*, Fr. city where first used] of or by a system of weights (**troy weight**) for gold, silver, gems, etc., based on a pound of 12 oz.

tru·ant (trōō′ənt) *n.* [< OFr., beggar] 1. a pupil who stays away from school without permission 2. one who shirks his duties —*adj.* 1. that is a truant 2. errant; straying —**tru′an·cy** *n., pl.* **-cies**

truce (trōōs) *n.* [< OE. *treowa* faith] 1. a temporary cessation of warfare by agreement between the belligerents 2. respite from conflict, trouble, etc.

truck¹ (truk) *n.* [prob. < Gr. *trochos*, wheel] 1. a kind of two-wheeled barrow or a low, wheeled frame, for carrying heavy articles 2. an automotive vehicle for hauling loads 3. a swiveling, wheeled frame under each end of a railroad car, etc. —*vt.* to carry on a truck —*vi.* to drive a truck — **truck′er** *n.*

truck² (truk) *vt., vi.* [< MFr. *troquer*] to exchange; barter —*n.* **1.** small articles of little value **2.** vegetables raised for market **3.** [Colloq.] dealings **4.** [Colloq.] rubbish

truck farm a farm where vegetables are grown to be marketed

truck·le (truk′'l) *n.* [< Gr. *trochos*, a wheel] *same as* TRUNDLE BED: in full **truckle bed** —*vi.* **-led, -ling** to be servile; submit (*to*)

truc·u·lent (truk′yoo lənt) *adj.* [< L. *trux*] fierce; cruel; savage —**truc′u·lence** *n.* —**truc′u·lent·ly** *adv.*

trudge (truj) *vi.* **trudged, trudg′ing** [< ?] to walk, esp. wearily or laboriously —*n.* a wearying walk

true (trōō) *adj.* **tru′er, tru′est** [OE. *treowe*] **1.** faithful; loyal **2.** in accordance with fact; not false **3.** conforming to standard, etc.; correct **4.** rightful; lawful **5.** accurately fitted, shaped, etc. **6.** real; genuine —*adv.* **1.** truly **2.** *Biol.* without variation from type —*vt.* **trued, tru′ing** or **true′ing** to make true; esp., to fit, shape, etc. accurately —*n.* that which is true (with *the*)

true bill a bill of indictment endorsed by a grand jury

true′-blue′ *adj.* very loyal; staunch

truf·fle (truf′'l) *n.* [< L. *tuber*, knob] a fleshy, edible underground fungus

tru·ism (trōō′iz'm) *n.* a statement the truth of which is obvious

tru·ly *adv.* **1.** in a true manner; accurately, genuinely, etc. **2.** really **3.** sincerely [yours *truly*]

Tru·man (trōō′mən), **Harry S.** 1884-1972; 33d president of the U.S. (1945-53)

trump (trump) *n.* [< TRIUMPH] **1.** any playing card of a suit ranked higher than any other suit for a given hand **2.** such a suit —*vt., vi.* to play a trump on (a trick, etc.) —**trump up** to devise fraudulently

trump·er·y (trum′pər ē) *n., pl.* **-ies** [< Fr. *tromper*, deceive] **1.** something showy but worthless **2.** nonsense

trum·pet (trum′pit) *n.* [< OFr. *trompe*] **1.** a brass-wind instrument consisting of a looped tube ending in a flared bell **2.** a trumpetlike device for channeling sound, as an early kind of hearing aid **3.** a sound like that of a trumpet —*vi.* to make the sound of a trumpet —*vt.* to proclaim loudly — **trum′pet·er** *n.*

trun·cate (trun′kāt) *vt.* **-cat·ed -cat·ing** [< L. *truncus*, stem] to cut off a part of; lop —**trun·ca′tion** *n.*

trun·cheon (trun′chən) *n.* [< L. *truncus*, stem] a short, thick club

trun·dle (trun′d'l) *vt., vi.* **-dled, -dling** [< OE. *trendan*, to roll] to roll along —**trun′dler** *n.*

trundle bed a low bed on small wheels, that can be rolled under another bed when not in use

trunk (truŋk) *n.* [< L. *truncus*] **1.** the main stem of a tree **2.** a human or animal body, not including the head and limbs **3.** a long snout, as of an elephant **4.** a large, reinforced box to hold clothes, etc. in travel **5.** [*pl.*] shorts worn by men for athletics **6.** a compartment in a car, usually in the rear, for a spare tire, luggage, etc.

trunk line a main line of a railroad, telephone system, etc.

truss (trus) *vt.* [< OFr. *trousser*] **1.** orig., to bundle **2.** to tie; bind (*up*) **3.** to support with a truss —*n.* **1.** a bundle or pack **2.** a framework for supporting a roof, bridge, etc. **3.** a padded device for giving support in cases of rupture or hernia

trust (trust) *n.* [< ON. *traust*] **1.** *a*) firm belief in the honesty, reliability, etc. of another; faith *b*) the one trusted **2.** confident expectation, hope, etc. **3.** responsibility resulting from confidence placed in one **4.** care; custody **5.** something entrusted to one **6.** faith in one's ability to pay; credit **7.** a combination of corporations to establish a monopoly **8.** *Law a*) the fact of having nominal ownership of property to keep, use, or administer for another *b*) such property —*vi.* to be confident —*vt.* **1.** to have confidence in **2.** to commit (something) (*to* another's care) **3.** to allow to do something without misgivings **4.** to believe **5.** to hope; expect **6.** to grant business credit to —*adj.* **1.** relating to a trust **2.** acting as trustee —**in trust** entrusted to another's care

trus·tee (trus tē′) *n.* **1.** one to whom another's property or its management is entrusted **2.** a member of a board managing the affairs of a college, hospital, etc. —**trus·tee′ship′** *n.*

trust′ful *adj.* full of trust; ready to confide —**trust′ful·ly** *adv.*

trust fund money, stock, etc. held in trust

trust′ing *adj.* that trusts; trustful

trust territory a territory placed under the administrative authority of a country by the United Nations

trust′wor′thy *adj.* worthy of trust; reliable —**trust′wor′thi·ness** *n.*

trust·y (trus′tē) *adj.* **-i·er, -i·est** dependable; trustworthy —*n., pl.* **-ies** a convict granted special privileges as a trustworthy person

truth (trōōth) *n.* [OE. *treowth*] **1.** a being true; specif., *a*) sincerity; honesty *b*) conformity with fact *c*) reality; actual existence *d*) correctness; accuracy **2.** that which is true **3.** an established fact —**in truth** truly

truth′ful *adj.* **1.** telling the truth; honest **2.** corresponding with fact or reality —**truth′ful·ly** *adv.* —**truth′ful·ness** *n.*

try (trī) *vt.* **tried, try′ing** [< OFr. *trier*] **1.** to melt out or render (fat, etc.) **2.** to conduct the trial of in a law court **3.** to put to the proof; test **4.** to subject to trials, etc.; afflict **5.** to experiment with [to *try* a recipe] **6.** to attempt; endeavor —*vi.* to make an effort, attempt, etc. —*n., pl.* **tries** an attempt; effort; trial —**try on** to test the fit of (something to wear) by putting it on —**try out 1.** to test by putting into use **2.** to test one's fitness, as for a place on a team

try′ing *adj.* that tries one's patience; annoying; irksome

try′out′ *n.* [Colloq.] a test to determine fitness, qualifications, etc.

tryst (trist) *n.* [< OFr. *triste,* hunting station] **1.** an appointment to meet, esp. one made by lovers **2.** an appointed meeting or meeting place

tsar (tsär, zär) *n. var. of* CZAR

tset·se fly (tset′sē, tsēt′-) [< native name] a small fly of C and S Africa: one kind carries sleeping sickness

T′-shirt′ *n.* a collarless, pullover knit shirt with short sleeves

tsp. 1. teaspoon(s) **2.** teaspoonful(s)

T square a T-shaped ruler for drawing parallel lines

tsu·na·mi (tsŏō nä′mē) *n.* [Jap. < *tsu,* a harbor + *nami,* a wave] a huge sea wave caused by an undersea earthquake, volcanic eruption, etc.

tub (tub) *n.* [< MDu. *tubbe*] **1.** a round wooden container, usually with staves and hoops **2.** any large, open container, as of metal **3.** a bathtub

tu·ba (tōō′bə) *n.* [L., a trumpet] a large, deep-toned brass-wind instrument

tub·by (tub′ē) *adj.* **-bi·er, -bi·est 1.** shaped like a tub **2.** fat and short

tube (tōōb) *n.* [< L. *tubus,* pipe] **1.** a slender pipe of metal, glass, etc., for conveying fluids **2.** a tubelike part, organ, etc. **3.** a pliable cylinder with a screw cap, for holding paste, etc. **4.** *short for: a)* ELECTRON TUBE *b)* VACUUM TUBE **5.** [Brit. Colloq.] a subway —**the tube** [Colloq.] television —**tube′less** *adj.*

tu·ber (tōō′bər) *n.* [L., lit., a swelling] a short, thick part of an underground stem, as a potato —**tu′ber·ous** *adj.*

tu′ber·cle (-k'l) *n.* [see prec.] **1.** a small, rounded projection, as on a bone or a plant root **2.** any abnormal hard nodule or swelling; specif., the typical lesion of tuberculosis

tu·ber·cu·lin (tōō bur′kyə lin) *n.* a solution injected into the skin as a test for tuberculosis

tu·ber·cu·lo′sis (-lō′sis) *n.* [< ModL.: see TUBERCLE & -OSIS] an infectious disease characterized by the formation of tubercles in body tissue; specif., tuberculosis of the lungs —**tu·ber′cu·lar, tu·ber′cu·lous** *adj.*

tube sock a stretchable sock in the form of a long tube with no shaped heel

tub·ing (tōōb′iŋ) *n.* **1.** a series or system of tubes **2.** material in the form of a tube **3.** a piece of tube

tu·bu·lar (tōō′byə lər) *adj.* [< L. *tubus,* pipe] **1.** of or like a tube **2.** made with a tube or tubes

tu′bule (-byool) *n.* a small tube

tuck (tuk) *vt.* [< MDu. *tucken*] **1.** to pull or gather (*up*) in a fold or folds

2. to sew a fold or folds in (a garment) **3.** to fold the edges of (a sheet, etc.) under or in, to make secure **4.** to press snugly into a small space —*n.* a sewed fold in a garment

tuck′er *vt.* [prob. < obs. *tuck,* punish] [Colloq.] to tire (*out*); weary

Tuc·son (tōō′sän, tōō sän′) city in S Ariz.: pop. 331,000

-tude (tōōd, tyŏōd) [< L. *-tudo*] a suffix corresponding to -NESS [*certitude*]

Tues·day (tōōz′dē, -dā) *n.* [OE. *Tiwes dæg,* day of the god of war *Tiu*] the third day of the week

tuft (tuft) *n.* [< OFr. *tufe*] **1.** a bunch of hairs, grass, etc. growing closely together **2.** any cluster, as the fluffy ball forming the end of a cluster of threads drawn through a mattress, etc. —*vt.* **1.** to provide with tufts **2.** to secure the padding of (a mattress, etc.) with tufts —**tuft′ed** *adj.*

tug (tug) *vi., vt.* **tugged, tug′ging** [prob. < ON. *toga,* pull] **1.** to pull hard; drag; haul **2.** to tow with a tugboat —*n.* **1.** a hard pull **2.** a tugboat

tug′boat′ *n.* a small, sturdy boat for towing or pushing ships, etc.

tug of war 1. a contest in which two teams pull at opposite ends of a rope **2.** any struggle for power

tu·i·tion (tōō wish′ən) *n.* [< L. *tueri,* protect] the charge for instruction, as at a college

tu·la·re·mi·a (tōō′lə rē′mē ə) *n.* [ModL. < *Tulare* County, Calif.] an infectious disease of rabbits, etc., sometimes transmitted to man

tu·lip (tōō′lip) *n.* [< Turk. *tülbend,* turban: from its shape] **1.** a bulb plant with a large, cup-shaped flower **2.** the flower

tulle (tōōl) *n.* [< *Tulle,* city in France] a fine netting of silk, rayon, nylon, etc., used for veils, scarfs, etc.

Tul·sa (tul′sə) city in NE Okla.: pop. 361,000

tum·ble (tum′b'l) *vi.* **-bled, -bling** [< OE. *tumbian,* to jump] **1.** to do somersaults or similar acrobatic feats **2.** to fall suddenly or helplessly **3.** to toss or roll about **4.** to move in a hasty, disorderly manner —*vt.* **1.** to cause to tumble **2.** to put into disorder; disarrange —*n.* **1.** a fall **2.** disorder

tum′ble·down′ *adj.* dilapidated

tum′bler (-blər) *n.* **1.** an acrobat who does somersaults, etc. **2.** a drinking glass **3.** a part of a lock whose position must be changed by a key in order to release the bolt

tum′ble·weed′ *n.* a plant that breaks off near the ground in autumn and is blown about by the wind

tum·brel, tum·bril (tum′brəl) *n.* [< MFr. *tomber,* to fall] a cart, esp. one that can be tilted for emptying

tu·mid (tōō′mid) *adj.* [< L. *tumere,* to swell] **1.** swollen; bulging **2.** inflated or pompous; bombastic

tum·my (tum′ē) *n., pl.* **-mies** stomach: a child's word

tu·mor (tōō′mər) *n.* [L., a swelling] an abnormal growth of new tissue, independent of its surrounding structures: Brit. sp. **tumour**

tu·mult (tōō'mult) *n.* [< L. *tumere*, to swell] 1. noisy commotion; uproar 2. confusion; disturbance

tu·mul·tu·ous (too mul'choo wəs) *adj.* full of tumult, uproar, etc.

tun (tun) *n.* [OE. *tunne*] a large cask

tu·na (tōō'nə) *n., pl.* -na, -nas [AmSp.] 1. a large ocean fish of the mackerel group 2. any related fish, as the albacore 3. the flesh of the tuna, canned for food: also **tuna fish**

tun·dra (tun'drə) *n.* [Russ.] any of the vast, treeless arctic plains

tune (tōōn) *n.* [see TONE] 1. a rhythmic succession of musical tones; melody 2. correct musical pitch 3. agreement; concord [out of *tune* with the times] —*vt.* tuned, tun'ing 1. to adjust (a musical instrument) to some standard of pitch 2. to adapt to some condition, mood, etc. 3. to adjust (a motor, circuit, etc.) for proper performance —**tune in** to adjust a radio or TV receiver so as to receive (a station, etc.) —**tun'er** *n.*

tune'ful *adj.* full of music; melodious

tune'up', tune'-up' *n.* an adjusting, as of an engine, to the proper condition

tung·sten (tuŋ'stən) *n.* [Sw. < *tung*, heavy + *sten*, stone] a hard, heavy, metallic chemical element, used in steel, etc.

tu·nic (tōō'nik, tyōō'-) *n.* [L. *tunica*] 1. a loose, gownlike garment worn by men and women in ancient Greece and Rome 2. a blouselike garment extending to the hips, often belted

tuning fork a two-pronged steel instrument which when struck sounds a fixed tone in perfect pitch

Tu·nis (tōō'nis) seaport and capital of Tunisia: pop. 662,000

Tu·ni·sia (tōō nē'zhə) country in N Africa: 48,332 sq. mi.; pop. 4,533,000 —**Tu·ni'sian** *adj., n.*

tun·nel (tun'l) *n.* [< MFr. *tonnelle*, a vault] 1. an underground passageway, as for autos, etc. 2. any tunnellike passage, as in a mine —*vt., vi.* -neled or -nelled, -nel·ing or -nel·ling to make a tunnel (through or under) —**tun'nel·er, tun'nel·ler** *n.*

tunnel vision a narrow outlook, as on a particular problem

tun·ny (tun'ē) *n., pl.* -nies, -ny same as TUNA

tur·ban (tur'bən) *n.* [< Per. *dulbānd*] 1. a Moslem headdress, consisting of cloth wound in folds about the head 2. any similar headdress

tur·bid (tur'bid) *adj.* [< L. *turba*, a crowd] 1. muddy or cloudy from having the sediment stirred up 2. thick, dense, or dark, as clouds 3. confused

TURBAN

tur·bine (tur'bin, -bīn) *n.* [< L. *turbo*, whirl] an engine driven by the pressure of steam, water, air, etc. against the curved vanes of a wheel

tur·bo·jet (tur'bō jet') *n.* a jet engine in which the energy of the jet operates a turbine which drives the air compressor: in full **turbojet engine**

tur·bo·prop' (-präp') *n.* a turbojet engine whose turbine shaft drives a propeller: in full **turboprop engine**

tur·bot (tur'bət) *n., pl.* -bot, -bots [< OFr. *tourbout*] a large, edible European flatfish

tur·bu·lent (tur'byə lənt) *adj.* [see TURBID] 1. wild or disorderly 2. full of violent motion —**tur'bu·lence** *n.* —**tur'bu·lent·ly** *adv.*

tu·reen (too rēn') *n.* [< MFr. *terrine*, earthen vessel] a large, deep dish with a lid, for serving soup, etc.

turf (turf) *n.* [OE.] 1. *a)* a top layer of earth containing grass with its roots; sod *b)* a piece of this 2. peat 3. a track for horse racing; also horse racing: usually with *the* —*vt.* to cover with turf —**turf'y** *adj.*

tur·gid (tur'jid) *adj.* [< L. *turgere*, to swell] 1. swollen; distended 2. bombastic; pompous —**tur·gid'i·ty** *n.*

Tu·rin (toor'in, too rin') city in NW Italy: pop. 1,107,000

Turk (turk) *n.* a native or inhabitant of Turkey

Turk. 1. Turkey 2. Turkish

Tur·key (tur'kē) country occupying Asia Minor & part of the Balkan Peninsula: 301,381 sq. mi.; pop. 33,823,000

tur'key *n.* [< similarity to a fowl formerly imported through Turkey] 1. a large N.American bird with a small head and spreading tail 2. its flesh, used as food

turkey buzzard a dark-colored vulture of temperate and tropical America

Tur·kic (tur'kik) *adj.* designating or of a subfamily of languages, including Turkish, Tatar, etc.

Turk·ish (tur'kish) *adj.* of Turkey, the Turks, etc. —*n.* language of Turkey

Turkish bath a bath with steam rooms, showers, massage, etc.

Turkish towel [*also* t-] a thick cotton towel of terry cloth

tur·mer·ic (tur'mər ik) *n.* [< ML. *terra merita*, deserving earth] an East Indian plant whose powdered root is used as a yellow dye, seasoning, etc.

tur·moil (tur'moil) *n.* [< ?] tumult; commotion; confusion

turn (turn) *vt.* [ult. < Gr. *tornos*, lathe] 1. to rotate (a wheel, etc.) 2. to move around or partly around [*turn* the key] 3. to give form to as in a lathe 4. to change the position or direction of 5. to reverse [to *turn* pages] 6. to wrench (one's ankle) 7. to upset (the stomach) 8. to divert; deflect 9. to cause to change one's actions, beliefs, aims, etc. 10. to go around (a corner, etc.) 11. to pass (a certain age, amount, etc.) **12.** to repel (an attack, etc.) **13.** to drive, set, let go, etc. /to *turn loose*/ **14.** to direct, point, aim, etc. **15.** to change /to *turn* cream into butter/ **16.** to make sour **17.** to affect in some way —*vi.* **1.** to rotate or revolve; pivot **2.** to move around or partly around **3.** to reel; whirl **4.** to become curved or bent **5.** to become upset: said of the stomach **6.** to change or reverse course, direction, etc., or one's feelings, allegiance, etc. **7.** to refer (*to*) **8.** to apply (*to*) for help **9.** to shift one's attention /he *turned* to music/ **10.** to make a sudden attack (*on*) **11.** to be contingent (*on* or *upon*) **12.** to become /to *turn* cold/ **13.** to change to another form /the rain *turned* to snow/ **14.** to become rancid, sour, etc. —*n.* **1.** a turning around; rotation **2.** a single twist, winding, etc. **3.** a change or reversal of course or direction **4.** a short walk, ride, etc. **5.** a bend; curve /a *turn* in a road/ **6.** a change in trend, events, etc. **7.** a sudden shock or fright **8.** an action or deed /a good *turn*/ **9.** the right, duty, or chance to do something in regular order /my *turn* to go/ **10.** a distinctive form, detail, etc. /an odd *turn* of speech/ **11.** natural inclination —**in** (or **out of**) **turn** (not) in proper sequence —**turn down 1.** to reject (a request, etc.) —**turn in 1.** to deliver; hand in **2.** [Colloq.] to go to bed —**turn off 1.** to shut off **2.** to make (an electrical device) stop functioning **3.** [Slang] to cause to be bored, depressed, etc. —**turn on 1.** to start the flow of **2.** to make (an electrical device) start functioning **3.** [Slang] to make or become elated, euphoric, etc. —**turn out 1.** to put out (a light, etc.) **2.** to put outside **3.** to dismiss **4.** to come or go out **5.** to produce **6.** to result **7.** to prove to be **8.** to become —**turn over 1.** to ponder **2.** to hand over; transfer —**turn up** to happen, appear, arrive, etc. —**turn'er** *n.*

turn'a·bout' *n.* a shift or reversal of position, allegiance, opinion, etc.

turn'a·round' *n.* **1.** *same as* TURN-ABOUT **2.** a wide area, as in a driveway, to allow turning a vehicle around

turn'buck'le (-buk''l) *n.* an adjustable coupling for two rods, etc., consisting of a metal sleeve with opposite internal threads at each end

turn'coat' *n.* a renegade; traitor

turn'ing *n.* **1.** the action of one that turns **2.** a place where a road, etc. turns

turning point a point in time at which a decisive change occurs

tur·nip (tur'nip) *n.* [prob. < Fr. *tour*, round + ME. *nepe*, turnip] **1.** a plant of the mustard family with a roundish, light-colored, edible root **2.** the root

TURN-BUCKLE

turn'key' *n.*, *pl.* -**keys'** a jailer

turn'off' *n.* **1.** a turning off **2.** a place to turn off, as a road ramp

turn'out' *n.* **1.** a gathering of people, as for a meeting **2.** a wider part of a narrow road, for vehicles to pass

turn'o'ver *n.* **1.** a turning over; upset **2.** a small pie with half the crust folded back over the other **3.** *a)* the selling out and replenishing of a stock of goods *b)* the amount of business done during a given period **4.** the rate of replacement of workers

turn'pike' (-pīk') *n.* [ME. *turnpyke*, a spiked road barrier] a toll road, esp. one that is an expressway

turn'stile' (-stīl') *n.* a device, as a post with revolving horizontal bars, placed in an entrance to allow the passage of persons one at a time

turn'ta'ble *n.* a circular rotating platform, as for playing a phonograph record

tur·pen·tine (tur'pən tīn') *n.* [< Gr. *terebinthos*, tree yielding this substance] a colorless, volatile oil distilled from a substance extracted from various coniferous trees: used in paints, etc.

tur·pi·tude (tur'pə tōōd') *n.* [< L. *turpis*, vile] baseness; vileness

tur·quoise (tur'koiz, -kwoiz) *n.* [< OFr. *turqueis*, Turkish] a greenish-blue semiprecious stone, or its color

tur·ret (tur'it) *n.* [see TOWER] **1.** a small tower projecting from a building, usually at a corner **2.** a dome or revolving structure for guns, as on a warship, tank, or airplane **3.** a rotating attachment for a lathe, etc. holding cutting tools for successive use

tur·tle (tur't'l) *n.* [< Fr. *tortue*, tortoise] any of various land and water reptiles having a soft body encased in a hard shell —**turn turtle** to turn upside down

tur'tle·dove' *n.* [< L. echoic *turtur*] a wild dove with a plaintive call

tur'tle·neck' *n.* **1.** a high, snug, turned-down collar, as on a sweater **2.** a sweater, etc. with such a neck

tusk (tusk) *n.* [OE. *tucs*] a long, large, pointed tooth projecting outside the mouth, as of the elephant

tus·sle (tus''l) *n.*, *vi.* -**sled**, -**sling** [< LME. *tusen*, to pull] struggle; scuffle

tus·sock (tus'ək) *n.* [prob. < ME. (*to*)*tusen*, to rumple] a thick tuft or clump of grass, sedge, etc.

tu·te·lage (tōōt''l ij, tyōō'-) *n.* [< L. *tutela*, protection] **1.** guardianship; care, protection, etc. **2.** instruction —**tu'te·lar'y** (-er'ē) *adj.*

tu·tor (tōōt'ər, tyōōt'-) *n.* [< L. *tueri*, to guard] a private teacher —*vt.*, *vi.* to act as a tutor (to); teach —**tu·to·ri·al** (tōō tôr'ē əl, tyōō-) *adj.*

tut·ti-frut·ti (tōōt'ē frōōt'ē) *n.* [It., all fruits] an ice cream, candy, etc. made or flavored with mixed fruits

tu·tu (tōō'tōō) *n.* [Fr.] a short, projecting skirt worn by ballerinas

tux (tuks) *n.* *clipped form of* TUXEDO

tux·e·do (tək sē'dō) *n.*, *pl.* -**dos** [< a country club near *Tuxedo* Lake, N.Y.] a man's semiformal suit with a tailless jacket

TV (tē'vē') *n.*, *pl.* **TVs, TV's** television or a television receiving set

TVA Tennessee Valley Authority

TV dinner a frozen, precooked dinner packaged in the tray in which it is heated and served

twad·dle (twäd′'l) *n.* [akin to *tattle*] foolish, empty talk or writing; nonsense

twain (twān) *n., adj.* [OE. *twegen*, two] *archaic var. of* TWO

Twain, Mark *see* CLEMENS

twang (twaŋ) *n.* [echoic] 1. a sharp, vibrating sound, as of a plucked string 2. a sharply nasal way of speaking —*vi., vt.* 1. to make or cause to make a twang 2. to utter with a twang —**twang′y** *adj.* -**i·er**, -**i·est**

tweak (twēk) *vt.* [OE. *twiccan*, to twitch] to give a twisting pinch to (the nose, ear, etc.) —*n.* such a pinch

tweed (twēd) *n.* [< misreading of *tweel*, Scot. form of TWILL] 1. a rough wool fabric in a weave of two or more colors 2. [*pl.*] clothes of tweed

tweed′y *adj.* 1. of, like, or wearing tweeds 2. of an informal, outdoor type

tweet (twēt) *n., interj.* [echoic] the chirping sound of a small bird —*vi.* to make this sound

tweet′er *n.* a small loudspeaker for reproducing high-frequency sounds: cf. WOOFER

tweez·ers (twē′zərz) *n.pl.* [with sing. or pl. v.] [< obs. *tweeze*, surgical set] small pincers for plucking out hairs, etc.

twelfth (twelfth) *adj.* [OE. *twelfta*] preceded by eleven others; 12th —*n.* 1. the one following the eleventh 2. any of the twelve equal parts of something; 1/12

Twelfth Day Epiphany, the twelfth day after Christmas: **Twelfth Night** is the evening before, or of, Epiphany

twelve (twelv) *adj., n.* [OE. *twelf*] two more than ten; 12; XII

twelve′-tone′ *adj. Music* of composition in which twelve tones of the chromatic scale are fixed in some arbitrary succession (*tone row*)

twen·ty (twen′tē) *adj., n., pl.* -**ties** [OE. *twegentig*] two times ten; 20; XX —**the twenties** the numbers or years, as of a century, from 20 through 29 —**twen′ti·eth** (-ith) *adj., n.*

twen′ty-one′ *n.* a card game in which the object is to total 21 points

twerp (twurp) *n.* [ult. < ? Dan. *tver*, perverse] [Slang] a person regarded as insignificant, contemptible, etc.

twice (twīs) *adv.* [OE. *twiga*] 1. two times 2. two times as much or as many

twid·dle (twid′'l) *vt., vi.* -**dled**, -**dling** [prob. < TW(IST) + (D)IDDLE] to twirl or play with lightly —**twiddle one's thumbs** to be idle

twig (twig) *n.* [OE. *twigge*] a small branch of a tree or shrub

twi·light (twī′līt′) *n.* [ME.] 1. the subdued light just after sunset or, sometimes, just before sunrise 2. the period from sunset to dark 3. a gradual decline —*adj.* of twilight

twill (twil) *n.* [OE. *twilic*, woven of double thread] a cloth woven with parallel diagonal lines —**twilled** *adj.*

twin (twin) *adj.* [OE. *twinn*, double] 1. consisting of, or being one of a pair of, two similar things 2. being a twin or twins —*n.* 1. either of two born at the same birth 2. either of two persons or things much alike

twine (twīn) *n.* [OE. *twin*] strong thread, string, etc. of strands twisted together —*vt., vi.* **twined, twin′ing** 1. to twist together 2. to wind around

twinge (twinj) *vt., vi.* **twinged, twing′ing** [OE. *twengan*, to squeeze] to have or give a sudden, sharp pain, qualm, etc. —*n.* such a pain, etc.

twi-night, twi·night (twī′nīt′) *adj.* [TWI(LIGHT) + NIGHT] *Baseball* designating a double-header starting in late afternoon and going into evening

twin·kle (twiŋ′k'l) *vi.* -**kled**, -**kling** [OE. *twinclian*] 1. to shine with quick, intermittent gleams 2. to light up with amusement: said of the eyes 3. to move to and fro quickly, as dancers' feet —*n.* 1. a glint in the eye 2. a gleam; sparkle 3. an instant

twin′kling *n.* an instant

twirl (twurl) *vt., vi.* [prob. < Scand.] 1. to rotate rapidly; spin 2. to whirl in a circle —*n.* 1. a twirling 2. a twist, coil, etc. —**twirl′er** *n.*

twist (twist) *vt.* [OE. *-twist*, a rope] 1. to wind (strands, etc.) around one another 2. to wind (rope, etc.) around something 3. to give spiral shape to 4. *a)* to subject to torsion *b)* to wrench; sprain 5. to contort or distort 6. to confuse 7. to pervert the meaning of 8. to revolve or rotate 9. to break (*off*) by turning the end —*vi.* 1. to undergo twisting 2. to spiral, twine, etc. (*around* or *about*) 3. to revolve or rotate 4. to turn to one side 5. to wind, as a path 6. to squirm; writhe —*n.* 1. something twisted, as cord or thread, a roll of tobacco, etc. 2. a twisting or being twisted 3. torsional stress 4. a contortion 5. a wrench or sprain 6. a turn; bend 7. distortion, as of meaning 8. an unexpected or different direction, method, slant, etc.

twist′er *n.* 1. a person or thing that twists 2. a tornado or cyclone

twit (twit) *vt.* **twit′ted, twit′ting** [< OE. *æt*, at + *witan*, accuse] to reproach, taunt, etc. —*n.* a taunt

twitch (twich) *vt., vi.* [< OE. *twiccian*, to pluck] to pull (at) or move with a quick, slight jerk —*n.* 1. a twitching 2. a sudden quick motion, esp. a spasmodic one

twit·ter (twit′ər) *vi.* [ME. *twiteren*] 1. to chirp rapidly 2. *a)* to chatter *b)* to giggle 3. to tremble with excitement —*n.* 1. a twittering 2. a condition of tremulous excitement

two (tōō) *adj., n.* [OE. *twa*] one more than one; 2; II —**in two** in two parts

two′-bit′ (-bit′) *adj.* [Slang] cheap

two bits [Colloq.] twenty-five cents

two′-by-four′ *n.* a piece of lumber two inches thick and four inches wide untrimmed (1 5/8″ by 3 5/8″ trimmed)

two′-edged′ *adj.* 1. having two cutting edges 2. that can be taken two ways, as a remark

two′-faced′ *adj.* 1. having two faces 2. deceitful; hypocritical

two·fer (tōō′fər) *n.* [alt. < *two for*] [*usually pl.*] [Colloq.] two (esp. theater tickets) for the price of one

two′-fist′ed *adj.* [Colloq.] 1. able to use both fists 2. vigorous; virile

two′fold′ *adj.* 1. having two parts 2. having twice as much or as many —*adv.* twice as much or as many

two·pence (tup′'ns) *n.* two pence

two′-ply′ *adj.* having two layers, strands, etc.

two′some (-səm) *n.* 1. two people; a couple 2. a golf match for two

two′-time′ *vt.* -timed′, -tim′ing [Slang] to be unfaithful to

two′-way′ *adj.* 1. allowing passage in either direction 2. involving two or used in two ways

twp. township

TX Texas

-ty (tē, ti) [< L. *-tas*] *a suffix meaning* quality of, condition of

ty·coon (tī kōōn′) *n.* [< Jap. < Chin. *ta*, great + *kiun*, prince] a powerful industrialist, etc.

ty·ing (tī′iŋ) *prp. of* TIE

tyke (tīk) *n.* [< ON. *tik*, a bitch] [Colloq.] a small child

Ty·ler (tī′lər), **John** 1790–1862; 10th president of the U.S. (1841–45)

tym·pa·ni (tim′pə nē) *n.pl. var. of* TIMPANI— **tym′pa·nist** *n.*

tym·pan·ic membrane (tim pan′ik) a thin membrane inside the ear, that vibrates when struck by sound waves

tym·pa·num (tim′pə nəm) *n., pl.* -nums, -na (-nə) [L., a drum] *same as:* 1. MIDDLE EAR 2. TYMPANIC MEMBRANE

type (tīp) *n.* [< Gr. *typos*, a mark] 1. the characteristic form, plan, style, etc. of a class or group 2. a class, group, etc. with characteristics in common 3. a person, animal, or thing representative of a class 4. a perfect example; model 5. *a*) a piece of metal or wood with a raised letter, etc. in reverse on its top, used in printing *b*) such pieces collectively *c*) a printed or photographically reproduced character or characters —*vt.* typed, typ′ing 1. to classify 2. to typewrite —*vi.* to typewrite

-type (tīp) *a combining form meaning:* 1. type, example [*prototype*] 2. stamp, print [*daguerreotype*]

type′cast′ *vt.* -cast′, -cast′ing to cast (an actor) repeatedly in the same type of part

type′script′ *n.* typewritten matter

type′set′ *vt.* -set′, -set′ting to set in type; compose

type′set′ter *n.* 1. a person who sets type 2. a machine for setting type

type′write′ *vt., vi.* -wrote′, -writ′-ten, -writ′ing to write with a type-writer: now usually *type*

type′writ′er *n.* a writing machine with a keyboard for reproducing letters resembling printed ones

ty·phoid (tī′foid) *n.* [TYPH(US) + -OID] an acute infectious disease acquired by ingesting contaminated food or water: characterized by fever, intestinal disorders, etc.: in full **typhoid fever**

ty·phoon (tī foon′) *n.* [< Chin. *tai-fung*, great wind] a violent tropical cyclone originating in the W Pacific

ty·phus (tī′fəs) *n.* [< Gr. *typhos*, fever] an acute infectious disease transmitted by fleas, lice, etc. and characterized by fever, skin rash, etc.: in full **typhus fever**

typ·i·cal (tip′i k'l) *adj.* 1. serving as a type 2. having the distinguishing characteristics of a class, group, etc.; representative 3. belonging to a type; characteristic —**typ′i·cal·ly** *adv.*

typ·i·fy (tip′ə fī′) *vt.* -fied′, -fy′ing 1. to be a type of; symbolize 2. to have the characteristics of; be typical of; exemplify

typ·ist (tīp′ist) *n.* a person who operates a typewriter

ty·po (tī′pō) *n.* [Colloq.] an error made in setting type or in typing

ty·pog·ra·phy (tī päg′rə fē) *n.* [see TYPE & -GRAPHY] 1. the setting of, and printing with, type 2. the arrange-ment, style, etc. of matter printed from type —**ty·pog′ra·pher** *n.* —**ty′po-graph′i·cal** (-pə graf′i k'l) *adj.*

ty·ran·ni·cal (ti ran′i k'l) *adj.* 1. of or suited to a tyrant 2. harsh, cruel, unjust, etc. Also **ty·ran′nic** —**ty-ran′ni·cal·ly** *adv.*

tyr·an·nize (tir′ə nīz′) *vi.* -nized′, -niz′ing 1. to govern as a tyrant 2. to govern or use authority harshly or cruelly —*vt.* to treat tyrannically

ty·ran·no·saur (ti ran′ə sôr′, tī-) *n.* [< Gr. *tyrannos*, tyrant + *sauros*, lizard] a huge, two footed, flesh-eating dinosaur: also **ty·ran′no·saur′us** (-əs)

tyr′an·ny (-nē) *n., pl.* -nies 1. the authority, government, etc. of a tyrant 2. cruel and unjust use of power 3. a tyrannical act

ty·rant (tī′rənt) *n.* [< Gr. *tyrannos*] 1. an absolute ruler 2. a cruel, op-pressive ruler, etc.

ty·ro (tī′rō) *n., pl.* -ros [< L. *tiro*, young soldier] a beginner in learning something; novice

Tyr·ol (tir′äl, tī′rōl) *same as* TIROL

tzar (tsär, zär) *n. var. of* CZAR —**tza-ri·na** (tsä rē′nə) *n.fem.*

U

U, u (yōo) *n., pl.* **U's, u's** the 21st letter of the English alphabet

U *Chem.* uranium

U. 1. Union **2.** University

U., U, u., u unit; units

u·biq·ui·tous (yoo bik′wə təs) *adj.* [< L. *ubique*, everywhere] (seemingly) present everywhere at the same time —**u·biq′ui·ty** *n.*

U-boat (yōo′bōt′) *n.* [< G. *Untersee-boot*, undersea boat] a German submarine

ud·der (ud′ər) *n.* [OE. *udr*] a large, pendulous, milk-secreting gland with two or more teats, as in cows

UFO (yōo′ef′ō′) *n., pl.* **UFOs, UFO's** an unidentified flying object

u·fol·o·gist (yoo fäl′ə jist) *n.* [< UFO + -LOGY + -IST] a person interested in UFOs, esp. as supposed craft from outer space —**u·fol′o·gy** *n.*

U·gan·da (yōo gan′də, ōo gän′dä) country in EC Africa: 93,981 sq. mi.; pop. 7,934,000 —**U·gan′dan** *adj., n.*

ugh (ookh, oo, ug, etc.) *interj.* an exclamation of disgust, horror, etc.

ug·li (ug′lē) *n.* [< ff.] an odd-shaped fruit that is a cross between a grapefruit, orange, and tangerine

ug·ly (ug′lē) *adj.* **-li·er, -li·est** [< ON. *uggr*, fear] **1.** unpleasing to look at **2.** bad, vile, repulsive, etc. **3.** ominous; dangerous **4.** [Colloq.] cross; quarrelsome —**ug′li·ness** *n.*

uh (u, un) *interj.* **1.** *same as* HUH **2.** a sound indicating hesitation

UHF, uhf ultrahigh frequency

U.K. United Kingdom

u·kase (yōo′kās, yōo kāz′) *n.* [Russ. *ukaz*, edict] an official decree

U·krain·i·an Soviet Socialist Republic (yōo krā′nē ən) republic of the U.S.S.R., in the SW part: 231,990 sq. mi.; pop. 46,600,000: also **the U·kraine′** (-krān′)

u·ku·le·le (yōo′kə lā′lē) *n.* [Haw., flea] a small, four-stringed, guitarlike musical instrument

ul·cer (ul′sər) *n.* [L. *ulcus*] **1.** an open sore on the skin or some mucous membrane, discharging pus **2.** any corrupt condition —**ul′cer·ous** *adj.*

ul·cer·ate (ul′sə rāt′) *vt., vi.* **-at′ed, -at′ing** to make or become ulcerous —**ul′cer·a′tion** *n.*

ul·na (ul′nə) *n., pl.* **-nae** (-nē), **-nas** [L., the elbow] the larger of the two bones of the forearm —**ul′nar** *adj.*

ul·ster (ul′stər) *n.* [< *Ulster*, N Ireland] a long, loose, heavy overcoat

ul·te·ri·or (ul tir′ē ər) *adj.* [L. < *ulter*, beyond] **1.** lying beyond or on the farther side **2.** beyond what is expressed or implied; undisclosed

ult. ultimate(ly)

ul·ti·mate (ul′tə mit) *adj.* [< L. *ultimus*, last] **1.** beyond which it is impossible to go **2.** final; conclusive **3.** beyond further analysis; fundamental **4.** greatest possible —*n.* a final point or result —**ul′ti·mate·ly** *adv.*

ul·ti·ma·tum (ul′tə māt′əm) *n., pl.* **-tums, -ta** (-ə) [see prec.] a final offer or demand, as in negotiations

ul·tra (ul′trə) *adj.* [< ff.] going beyond the usual limit; extreme

ultra- [L. < *ultra*, beyond] *a prefix meaning:* **1.** beyond [*ultraviolet*] **2.** excessively [*ultramodern*]

ul·tra·con·serv·a·tive (ul′trə kən sur′və tiv) *adj.* extremely conservative

ul·tra·high frequency (ul′trə hī′) any radio frequency between 300 and 3,000 megahertz

ul·tra·ma·rine′ (-mə rēn′) *adj.* deep-blue —*n.* deep blue

ul′tra·son′ic (-sän′ik) *adj.* above the range of sound audible to the human ear

ul′tra·sound′ *n.* ultrasonic waves, used in medical diagnosis and therapy, in surgery, etc.

ul′tra·vi′o·let *adj.* lying just beyond the violet end of the visible spectrum: said of certain light rays

ul·u·late (yōol′yoo lāt′, ul′-) *vi.* **-lat′ed, -lat′ing** [< L. *ululare*, howl] to howl, hoot, or wail loudly —**ul′u·la′tion** *n.*

U·lys·ses (yoo lis′ēz) [ML.] *same as* ODYSSEUS

um·bel (um′b'l) *n.* [see UMBRELLA] a cluster of flowers with stalks of equal length which spring from the main stem

um·ber (um′bər) *n.* [< It. (*terra d′) ombra*, (earth of) shade] **1.** a kind of earth used as a reddish-brown pigment **2.** a reddish-brown color

um·bil·i·cal (um bil′i k'l) *adj.* [< L. *umbilicus*, navel] of a cordlike structure (**umbilical cord**) connecting a fetus with the placenta and serving to convey food to the fetus

um·bra (um′brə) *n., pl.* **-brae** (-brē), **-bras** [L., a shade] **1.** shade or a shadow **2.** the dark cone of shadow from a planet or satellite on the side opposite the sun

um·brage (um′brij) *n.* [< L. *umbra*, a shade] **1.** [Obs.] shade **2.** foliage **3.** offense or resentment

um·brel·la (um brel′ə) *n.* [< L. *umbra*, shade] **1.** a screen, usually of cloth on a folding frame, carried for protection against the rain or sun **2.** any comprehensive, protective alliance, strategy, device, etc.

u·mi·ak (ōō′mē ak′) *n.* [Esk.] a large, open boat made of skins on a wooden frame, used by Eskimos

UMIAK

um·laut (oom′lout) *n.* [G. < *um*, about + *laut*, a sound] *Linguistics* 1. a vowel changed in sound by its assimilation to another vowel 2. the mark (¨) placed over such a vowel

ump (ump) *n., vt., vi. clip* of UMPIRE

um·pire (um′pīr) *n.* [< MFr. *nomper*, uneven, hence a third person] a person chosen to judge a dispute; esp., an official who administers the rules in certain sports —*vt., vi.* -pired, -pir·ing to act as umpire (in or of)

ump·teen (ump′tēn′) *adj.* [Slang] very many —**ump′teenth′** *adj.*

un- *either of two prefixes, meaning:* 1. [OE.] not, lack of, the opposite of [*untruth, unhappily*] 2. [OE. *un-, on-*] back: indicating a reversal of action [*unfasten*] The following list includes some common compounds formed with *un-* (either prefix) that do not have special meanings:

unabashed	undeclared
unable	undefeated
unabridged	undefended
unaccented	undefined
unaccompanied	undemocratic
unacquainted	undeserved
unadorned	undesirable
unaffected	undeveloped
unafraid	undisciplined
unaided	undiscovered
unannounced	undisguised
unanswerable	undisputed
unashamed	undisturbed
unasked	undivided
unassailable	unearned
unassisted	uneducated
unattainable	unemotional
unattractive	unending
unauthorized	unenlightened
unavailable	uneventful
unavoidable	unexceptional
unbearable	unexpired
unbeaten	unexplained
unbiased	unexplored
unbind	unexpressed
unbleached	unexpurgated
unbreakable	unfair
unbroken	unfasten
unbutton	unfavorable
uncap	unfit
unceasing	unflattering
uncensored	unforeseen
unchallenged	unforgivable
unchanged	unfulfilled
unchecked	unfurnished
uncivil	ungrateful
uncivilized	unhampered
unclassified	unhandy
unclean	unharmed
unconnected	unhealthful
uncontrollable	unheeded
unconventional	unhitch
uncooked	unhook
uncultivated	unhurried
uncultured	unhurt
undamaged	unidentified

unimaginative	unrealistic
unimpaired	unrecorded
unimportant	unrelated
unimproved	unreliable
unincorporated	unrelieved
uninformed	unrequited
uninhabited	unrighteous
uninhibited	unripe
uninjured	unsafe
uninspired	unsanitary
uninsured	unsatisfactory
unintelligent	unsatisfied
unintelligible	unsaturated
unintentional	unscientific
uninteresting	unseasoned
uninterrupted	unseeing
uninvited	unseen
unknowing	unselfish
unlace	unshackle
unlatch	unshakable
unleavened	unshaven
unlisted	unshod
unmanageable	unshorn
unmannerly	unsightly
unmarked	unsociable
unmarried	unsold
unmatched	unsolicited
unmindful	unsought
unmolested	unspoiled
unmoved	unsuccessful
unnamed	unsuitable
unnoticed	unsupported
unobserved	unsurpassed
unobstructed	unsuspected
unobtrusive	unsweetened
unoccupied	unswerving
unofficial	unsympathetic
unopened	untainted
unorthodox	untamed
unpaid	untarnished
unpardonable	untasted
unpaved	untenable
unperturbed	unthankful
unpin	untiring
unplanned	untouched
unplowed	untrained
unpolished	untried
unpredictable	untroubled
unprejudiced	untrue
unpremeditated	unverified
unprepared	unvisited
unpretentious	unwanted
unprofitable	unwarranted
unpromising	unwashed
unprotected	unwavering
unprovoked	unwed
unpublished	unworkable
unpunished	unworldly
unquestioned	unyielding
unquiet	unzip

un·ac·count·a·ble (un′ə koun′tə b'l) *adj.* 1. that cannot be explained; strange 2. not responsible

un′ac·cus′tomed *adj.* 1. not accustomed (*to*) 2. not usual; strange

un′ad·vised′ *adj.* 1. without counsel or advice 2. indiscreet; rash

un′-A·mer′i·can *adj.* regarded as not properly American, i.e., as opposed to the U.S., its institutions, etc.

u·nan·i·mous (yoo nan′ə məs) *adj.* [< L. *unus*, one + *animus*, the mind] in complete agreement; without dissent —**u·na·nim·i·ty** (yōō′nə nim′ə tē) *n.* —**u·nan′i·mous·ly** *adv.*

un′ap·proach′a·ble *adj.* 1. not to

be approached; inaccessible; aloof 2. having no equal; unmatched

un·armed' *adj.* having no weapons

un·as·sum'ing *adj.* not assuming, pretentious, or forward; modest

un·at·tached' *adj.* 1. not attached 2. not engaged or married

un·at·tend'ed *adj.* 1. not waited on 2. unaccompanied (*by*) 3. neglected

un·a·vail'ing (-ə vā'liŋ) *adj.* futile; useless

un·a·ware' *adj.* not aware or conscious —*adv. same as* UNAWARES

un·a·wares' (-werz') *adv.* 1. unintentionally 2. unexpectedly

un·backed' *adj.* 1. not backed, supported, etc. 2. without a back or backing

un·bal'anced *adj.* 1. not in balance 2. *a)* mentally deranged *b)* erratic

un·bar' *vt.* -barred', -bar'ring to unbolt; unlock; open

un'be·com'ing *adj.* not appropriate or suited to one's appearance, character, etc.; unattractive, indecorous, etc.

un'be·known' *adj.* without one's knowledge; unknown (usually with *to*): also **un'be·knownst'** (-nönst')

un'be·lief' *n.* lack of belief, esp. in religion —**un'be·liev'er** *n.*

un'be·liev'a·ble *adj.* beyond belief; astounding; incredible

un·bend' *vt., vi.* -bent' or -bend'ed, -bend'ing 1. to release or be released from tension 2. to relax, as from formality 3. to straighten

un·bend'ing *adj.* 1. rigid; stiff 2. firm; resolute 3. aloof; austere

un·bid'den *adj.* 1. not commanded 2. not invited

un·blush'ing *adj.* 1. not blushing 2. without any feeling of shame —**un·blush'ing·ly** *adv.*

un·bolt' *vt., vi.* to withdraw the bolt or bolts of (a door, etc.); open

un·born' *adj.* 1. not born 2. still in the mother's womb 3. yet to be

un·bos'om (-booz'əm, -boo'zəm) *vt., vi.* to tell or reveal (feelings, secrets, etc.) —**unbosom oneself** to reveal one's feelings, secrets, etc.

un·bound'ed *adj.* 1. without bounds or limits 2. not restrained

un·bri'dled *adj.* 1. having no bridle on, as a horse 2. not controlled

un·bur'den *vt.* 1. to free from a burden 2. to relieve (one's soul, mind, etc.) by disclosing (guilt, etc.)

un·called'-for' *adj.* 1. not called for 2. unnecessary and out of place

un·can'ny (un kan'ē) *adj.* 1. mysterious and eerie; weird 2. so good, acute, etc. as to seem preternatural

un·cared'-for' *adj.* not cared for or looked after; neglected

un'cer·e·mo'ni·ous *adj.* 1. not ceremonious; informal 2. curt; abrupt

un·cer'tain *adj.* 1. *a)* not surely or certainly known *b)* not sure or certain in knowledge; doubtful 2. vague 3. not dependable or reliable 4. varying —**un·cer'tain·ty** *n., pl.* -ties

un·char'i·ta·ble *adj.* harsh or severe, as in opinion —**un·char'i·ta·bly** *adv.*

un·chart'ed *adj.* not marked on a chart or map; unexplored or unknown

un·chris'tian *adj.* 1. not Christian 2. [Colloq.] outrageous; dreadful

un·ci·al (un'shē əl, -shəl) *adj.* [L. *uncialis,* inch-high] of or in the large, rounded letters of Greek and Latin manuscripts between 300 and 900 A.D. —*n.* uncial script or letter

un·cir'cum·cised' *adj.* 1. not circumcised; gentile 2. [Archaic] heathen

un·cle (uŋ'k'l) *n.* [< L. *avunculus*] 1. the brother of one's father or mother 2. the husband of one's aunt

Uncle Sam [< abbrev. *U.S.*] [Colloq.] the U.S. (government or people) personified as a tall man with whiskers

Uncle Tom [< main character in novel *Uncle Tom's Cabin* (1852)] [Colloq.] a Negro regarded as servile toward whites: a term of contempt

un·cloak' *vt., vi.* 1. to remove a cloak (from) 2. to reveal; expose

un·clothe' *vt.* -clothed' or -clad', -cloth'ing to undress, uncover, etc.

un·coil' *vt., vi.* to unwind

un·com'fort·a·ble *adj.* 1. feeling discomfort 2. causing discomfort 3. ill at ease —**un·com'fort·a·bly** *adv.*

un·com·mit'ted *adj.* 1. not committed or pledged 2. not taking a stand

un·com'mon *adj.* 1. rare; not common or usual 2. strange; remarkable

un'com·mu'ni·ca'tive *adj.* not communicative; reserved; taciturn

un·com'pro·mis'ing *adj.* not yielding; firm; inflexible

un'con·cern' *n.* 1. indifference; apathy 2. lack of concern, or worry

un'con·cerned' *adj.* 1. indifferent 2. not solicitous or anxious

un'con·di'tion·al *adj.* without conditions or reservations; absolute

un·con·scion·a·ble (un kän'shən ə b'l) *adj.* 1. not guided or restrained by conscience 2. unreasonable or excessive —**un·con'scion·a·bly** *adv.*

un·con'scious *adj.* 1. deprived of consciousness 2. not aware (*of*) 3. not realized or intended [an *unconscious* habit] —**the unconscious** *Psychoanalysis* the sum of all thoughts, impulses, etc. of which the individual is not conscious but which influence his behavior

un'con·sti·tu'tion·al *adj.* not in accordance with a constitution

un·cork' *vt.* to pull the cork out of

un·count'ed *adj.* 1. not counted 2. inconceivably numerous

un·cou'ple *vt.* -pled, -pling to unfasten (things coupled together)

un·couth (un kooth') *adj.* [OE. < *un-,* not + *cunnan,* know] 1. awkward; ungainly 2. uncultured; crude

un·cov'er *vt.* 1. to disclose 2. to remove the cover from 3. to remove the hat, etc. from (the head) —*vi.* to bare the head, as in respect

unc·tion (uŋk'shən) n. [< L. ungere, anoint] 1. a) the act of anointing, as for medical or religious purposes b) the oil, ointment, etc. used for this 2. anything that soothes or comforts

unc·tu·ous (uŋk'choo wəs) adj. [see prec.] 1. oily or greasy 2. characterized by a smooth pretense of fervor or earnestness; too suave or oily —unc'·tu·us·ness n.

un·cut' adj. not cut; specif., a) not ground to shape: said of a gem b) not shortened or abridged

un·daunt·ed adj. not daunted; fearless, not disheartened, etc.

un·de·ceive' vt. -ceived', -ceiv'ing to cause to be no longer deceived or misled

un·de·cid·ed adj. 1. not decided 2. not having come to a decision

un·de·mon'stra·tive adj. not demonstrative; not showing feelings openly; reserved —un'de·mon'stra·tive·ly adv.

un·de·ni'a·ble adj. 1. that cannot be denied; indisputable 2. unquestionably good —un'de·ni'a·bly adv.

un·der (un'dər) prep. [OE.] 1. in, at, or to a position down from; below 2. beneath the surface of 3. below and to the other side of [drive under the bridge] 4. covered by [a vest under his coat] 5. a) lower in rank, position, amount, etc. than b) lower than the required degree of [under age] 6. subject to the control, limitations, etc. of [under oath] 7. undergoing [under repair] 8. with the disguise of [under an alias] 9. in (the designated category) 10. in the time of [under Lincoln] 11. being the subject of [a topic under debate] 12. because of [under the circumstances] 13. authorized by —adv. 1. in or to a lower position or state 2. so as to be covered, concealed, etc. —adj. lower in position, authority, amount, etc.

under- a prefix meaning: 1. in, on, to, or from a lower place, beneath [undershirt] 2. in a subordinate position [undergraduate] 3. too little, insufficiently [underpay]

un·der·a·chieve' vi. -chieved', -chiev'ing to fail to do as well in school as might be expected from intelligence tests

un·der·act' vt., vi. to act (a theatrical role) with not enough emphasis or with too much restraint

un·der·age' adj. 1. not of mature age 2. below the age required by law

un·der·arm' adj. 1. of, for, in, or used on the area under the arm, or the armpit 2. same as UNDERHAND (sense 1) —adv. same as UNDERHAND (sense 1)

un·der·bel'ly n. 1. the lower, posterior part of an animal's belly 2. any vulnerable area, point, etc.

un·der·bid' vt., vi. -bid', -bid'ding 1. to bid lower than (another person) 2. to bid less than the worth of (as one's hand in bridge)

un·der·brush' n. small trees, shrubs, etc. growing in woods or forests

un·der·car'riage n. a supporting frame, as of an automobile

un·der·charge' vt., vi. -charged', -charg'ing 1. to charge too low a price (to) 2. to load insufficiently —n. (un'dər chärj') an insufficient charge

un·der·class' n. the class with incomes below subsistence level, including esp. the underprivileged

un·der·class'man (-mən) n., pl. -men a freshman or sophomore in high school or college

un·der·clothes' n.pl. same as UNDERWEAR: also un'der·cloth'ing

un·der·coat' n. 1. a tarlike coating applied to the underside of an automobile to retard rust, etc. 2. a coat of paint, etc. applied before the final coat Also un'der·coat'ing —vt. to apply an undercoat to

un·der·cov'er adj. acting or carried out in secret

un·der·cur'rent n. 1. a current flowing beneath the surface 2. an underlying tendency, opinion, etc.

un·der·cut' vt. -cut', -cut'ting 1. to make a cut below or under 2. to undersell or work for lower wages than

un·der·de·vel'oped adj. inadequately developed, esp. economically and industrially

un·der·dog' n. one that is underprivileged, unfavored, losing, etc.

un·der·done' adj. not cooked enough

un·der·es'ti·mate' vt., vi. -mat'ed, -mat'ing to set too low an estimate on or for

un·der·foot' adv., adj. 1. under the foot or feet 2. in the way

un·der·gar'ment (-gär'mənt) n. a piece of underwear

un·der·go' vt. -went', -gone', -go'ing to experience; go through

un·der·grad'u·ate n. a college student who does not yet have a degree

un·der·ground' adj. 1. under the earth's surface 2. secret; hidden 3. of noncommercial newspapers, movies, etc. that are unconventional, radical, etc. —adv. 1. under the earth's surface 2. in or into secrecy —n. 1. the region under the earth's surface 2. a secret movement in a country to oppose the government or occupying enemy forces 3. [Brit.] a subway

un·der·growth' n. underbrush

un·der·hand' adj. 1. done with the hand below the level of the elbow or shoulder 2. underhanded —adv. 1. with an underhand motion 2. underhandedly

un·der·hand'ed adj. sly, deceitful, etc. —un'der·hand'ed·ly adv.

un·der·lie' vt. -lay', -lain', -ly'ing 1. to lie beneath 2. to be the basis for; form the foundation of

un·der·line' vt. -lined', -lin'ing 1. to draw a line beneath 2. to stress

un·der·ling (un'dər liŋ) n. [OE.: see UNDER- & -LING] a person in a subordinate position; inferior

un·der·ly'ing adj. 1. lying under 2. fundamental; basic

un·der·mine' vt. -mined', -min'ing 1. to dig beneath, so as to form a tunnel or mine 2. to wear away at the foundation 3. to injure or weaken, esp. by subtle or insidious means

un·der·most′ *adj., adv.* lowest in place, position, rank, etc.

un·der·neath′ (un′dər nēth′) *adv., prep.* under; below; beneath

un′der·nour′ished *adj.* not getting the food needed for health and growth

un′der·pants′ *n.pl.* an undergarment of long or short pants

un′der·pass′ *n.* a passage under something, as a road under a railway

un′der·pin′ning (-pin′iŋ) *n.* 1. a support or prop 2. [*pl.*] [Colloq.] the legs

un′der·play′ *vt., vi.* 1. *same as* UNDERACT 2. to make seem not too important

un′der·priv′i·leged *adj.* deprived of basic social rights and security through poverty, discrimination, etc.

un′der·pro·duce′ *vt., vi.* -duced′, -duc′ing to produce less than is needed or wanted

un′der·rate′ *vt.* -rat′ed, -rat′ing to rate or estimate too low

un′der·score′ *vt.* -scored′, -scor′ing to underline

un′der·sea′ *adj., adv.* beneath the surface of the sea: also **un′der·seas′** *adv.*

un′der·sec′re·tar′y *n., pl.* -ies an assistant secretary

un′der·sell′ *vt.* -sold′, -sell′ing to sell at a lower price than

un′der·shirt′ *n.* a collarless undergarment worn under an outer shirt

un′der·shorts′ *n.pl.* short underpants worn by men and boys

un′der·shot′ *adj.* 1. with the lower part extending past the upper (an *undershot* jaw) 2. driven by water flowing along the lower part

un′der·side′ *n.* the side or surface that is underneath

un′der·signed′ *adj.* 1. signed at the end 2. whose name is signed at the end —**the undersigned** the person or persons having signed at the end

un′der·staffed′ *adj.* having fewer workers on the staff than are needed

un′der·stand′ *vt.* -stood′ (-stood′), -stand′ing [OE. *understandan*, stand under] 1. to perceive the meaning of 2. to assume from what is heard, etc.; infer 3. to take as meant; interpret 4. to take as a fact 5. to learn 6. to know the nature, character, etc. of 7. to be sympathetic with —*vi.* 1. to have understanding, comprehension, etc. 2. to be informed; believe —**un′der·stand′a·ble** *adj.* —**un′der·stand′a·bly** *adv.*

un′der·stand′ing *n.* 1. comprehension 2. the power to think and learn; intelligence 3. a specific interpretation 4. mutual agreement, esp. one that settles differences —*adj.* that understands; sympathetic

un′der·state′ *vt.* -stat′ed, -stat′ing 1. to state too weakly 2. to state in a restrained style —**un′der·state′-ment** *n.*

un′der·stud′y *n., pl.* -ies an actor

prepared to substitute for another —*vt., vi.* -ied, -y·ing to learn (a part) as an understudy (to)

un′der·take′ *vt.* -took′, -tak′en, -tak′ing 1. to take upon oneself (a task, etc.) 2. to promise; guarantee

un′der·tak′er *n. earlier term for* FUNERAL DIRECTOR

un′der·tak′ing (*also* un′dər tā′kiŋ) *n.* 1. something undertaken; task; enterprise 2. a promise; guarantee

un′der-the-count′er *adj.* [Colloq.] done secretly in an unlawful way: also **un′der-the-ta′ble**

un′der·things′ *n.pl.* women's or girls' underwear

un′der·tone′ *n.* 1. a low tone of voice 2. a subdued color 3. an underlying quality, factor, etc.

un′der·tow′ (-tō′) *n.* a current of water moving beneath the surface water and in a different direction

un′der·waist′ *n.* an undergarment worn under a blouse, or waist

un′der·wa′ter *adj.* being, done, etc. beneath the surface of the water

un′der·wear′ *n.* clothing worn under one's outer clothes, usually next to the skin, as undershirts

un′der·weight′ *adj.* below the normal or allowed weight

un′der·world′ *n.* 1. Hades; hell 2. criminals as an organized group

un′der·write′ *vt.* -wrote′, -writ′-ten, -writ′ing 1. to agree to market (an issue of securities, and to buy any part remaining unsubscribed) 2. to agree to finance (an undertaking, etc.) 3. to sign one's name to (an insurance policy), thus assuming liability —**un′-der·writ′er** *n.*

un·dies (un′dēz) *n.pl.* [Colloq.] women's or girls' underwear

un·do′ *vt.* -did′, -done′, -do′ing 1. to untie, open, etc. 2. to do away with; annul 3. to bring to ruin

un·do′ing *n.* 1. an annulling 2. a bringing to ruin 3. the cause of ruin

un·done′ *adj.* 1. not done; not performed, accomplished, etc. 2. ruined

un·doubt′ed *adj.* that cannot be doubted; certain —**un·doubt′ed·ly** *adv.*

un·dreamed′ *adj.* not even dreamed (*of*) or thought (*of*) as possible: also **un·dreamt′** (-dremt′)

un·dress′ *vt.* to take off the clothing of —*vi.* to take off one's clothing

un·due′ *adj.* 1. not appropriate; improper 2. excessive; unreasonable

un·du·lant (un′joo lənt, -dyoo-) *adj.* undulating

un′du·late′ (-lāt′) *vi., vt.* -lat′ed, -lat′ing [< L. *unda*, a wave] 1. to move or cause to move in waves 2. to have or cause to have a wavy form or surface —**un′du·la′tion** *n.*

un·du·ly (un dōō′lē) *adv.* 1. improperly; unjustly 2. excessively

un·dy′ing *adj.* immortal or eternal

un·earth′ *vt.* 1. to dig up from the earth 2. to bring to light; disclose

---

un·earth·ly *adj.* 1. supernatural 2. weird; mysterious 3. [Colloq.] fantastic, outlandish, etc.

un·eas·y *adj.* **-i·er, -i·est** 1. having, showing, or allowing no ease of body or mind; uncomfortable, disturbed, perturbed, etc. 2. awkward; constrained —**un·eas′i·ly** *adv.*—**un·eas′i·ness** *n.*

un·em·ployed′ *adj.* 1. not employed; without a job 2. not being used; idle —**un′em·ploy′ment** *n.*

un·e′qual *adj.* 1. not equal, as in size, strength, ability, value, etc. 2. not balanced, even, regular, etc. 3. not adequate (*to*) 4. [Rare] unjust

un·e′qualed, un·e′qualled *adj.* not equaled; unmatched; unrivaled

un′e·quiv′o·cal *adj.* not equivocal; plain; clear

un·err′ing *adj.* 1. free from error 2. not missing or failing; sure; exact

UNESCO (yoo nes′kō) United Nations Educational, Scientific, and Cultural Organization

un·e′ven *adj.* 1. not even, level, smooth, regular, etc. 2. unequal 3. *Math.* odd —**un·e′ven·ly** *adv.*

un′ex·am′pled *adj.* having no parallel or precedent; unprecedented

un′ex·cep′tion·a·ble *adj.* not exceptionable; without fault; beyond criticism—**un′ex·cep′tion·a·bly** *adv.*

un′ex·pect′ed *adj.* not expected; unforeseen —**un′ex·pect′ed·ly** *adv.*

un·fail′ing *adj.* 1. not failing 2. never ceasing or falling short; inexhaustible 3. always reliable

un·faith′ful *adj.* 1. lacking or breaking faith or loyalty 2. not true, accurate, etc. 3. adulterous

un·fa·mil′iar *adj.* 1. not well-known; strange 2. not acquainted (*with*)

un·feel′ing *adj.* 1. incapable of feeling; insensible 2. hardhearted; cruel —**un·feel′ing·ly** *adv.*

un·feigned′ (-fānd′) *adj.* genuine

un·fin′ished *adj.* 1. not finished; incomplete 2. having no finish, or final coat, as of paint

un·flap′pa·ble (-flap′ə b'l) *adj.* [un- + FLAP (*n.* 4) + -ABLE] [Colloq.] not easily excited; imperturbable

un·flinch′ing *adj.* steadfast; firm

un·fold′ *vt.* 1. to open and spread out (something folded) 2. to lay open to view; reveal, explain, etc. —*vi.* 1. to become unfolded 2. to develop fully

un′for·get′ta·ble *adj.* so important, forceful, etc. as never to be forgotten

un·for′tu·nate *adj.* 1. having or bringing bad luck; unlucky 2. not suitable —*n.* an unfortunate person

un·found′ed *adj.* 1. not founded on fact or truth 2. not established

un·friend′ly *adj.* 1. not friendly or kind 2. not favorable

un·frock′ (-fräk′) *vt.* to deprive of the rank of priest or minister

un·furl′ *vt., vi.* to open or spread out from a furled state; unfold

un·gain·ly (un gān′lē) *adj.* [< ME. *un-*, not + ON. *gegn*, ready] awkward; clumsy

un·god′ly *adj.* 1. not godly or religious 2. [Colloq.] outrageous

un·gov·ern·a·ble *adj.* that cannot be governed or controlled; unruly

un·gra′cious *adj.* 1. not gracious; rude 2. unpleasant; unattractive

un·guard′ed *adj.* 1. unprotected 2. guileless 3. careless; imprudent

un·guent (uŋ′gwənt) *n.* [< L. *unguere*, anoint] a salve or ointment

un·gu·late (uŋ′gyoo lit, -lāt′) *adj.* [< L. *unguis*, a nail] having hoofs —*n.* a mammal having hoofs

un·hand′ *vt.* to loose or release from the hand or hands; let go of

un·hap′py *adj.* **-pi·er, -pi·est** 1. unfortunate 2. wretched 3. not suitable —**un·hap′pi·ly** *adv.*

un·health′y *adj.* **-i·er, -i·est** 1. sickly; not well 2. harmful to health 3. harmful to morals 4. dangerous

un·heard′ *adj.* 1. not perceived by the ear 2. not given a hearing

un·heard′-of *adj.* 1. not heard of before; unprecedented or unknown 2. unacceptable or outrageous

un·hinge′ *vt.* **-hinged′, -hing′ing** 1. to remove from the hinges 2. to dislodge 3. to unbalance (the mind)

un·ho′ly *adj.* **-li·er, -li·est** 1. not sacred, hallowed, etc. 2. wicked; profane 3. [Colloq.] outrageous; dreadful

un·horse′ *vt.* **-horsed′, -hors′ing** to throw (a rider) from a horse

uni- [L. < *unus*, one] *a combining form meaning* having only one

u·ni·cam′er·al (yoo′nə kam′ər əl) *adj.* [< *uni-* + L. *camera*, chamber] of or having a single legislative chamber

UNICEF (yoo′nə sef′) United Nations International Children's Emergency Fund

u·ni·corn (yoo′nə kôrn) *n.* [< L. *unus*, one + *cornu*, horn] a mythical horselike animal with a single horn in its forehead

UNICORN

u·ni·form (yoo′nə fôrm′) *adj.* [< L. *unus*, one + *-formis*, -FORM] 1. not varying in form, rate, degree, etc. 2. like others of the same class —*n.* the distinctive clothes of a particular group, as soldiers —*vt.* to supply with a uniform —**u′ni·form′i·ty** (-fôr′mə tē) *n.* —**u′ni·form′ly** *adv.*

u·ni·fy (yoo′nə fī′) *vt., vi.* **-fied′, -fy′ing** [see UNI- & -FY] to become or make united —**u′ni·fi·ca′tion** *n.*

u·ni·lat·er·al (yoo′nə lat′ər əl) *adj.* 1. of, occurring on, or affecting one side only 2. involving one only of several parties; not reciprocal

un·im·peach·a·ble (un′im pēch′ə b'l) *adj.* that cannot be doubted or discredited; irreproachable

un·in·ter·est·ed *adj.* not interested; indifferent

un·ion (yoon′yən) *n.* [< L. *unus*, one] 1. a uniting or being united; combination 2. a grouping together of nations, etc. for some specific purpose 3. marriage 4. something united 5. *short for* LABOR UNION 6. a device symbolizing political union, used as in a flag **7.** a device for uniting parts — **the Union** the United States

un·ion·ize' (-īz') *vt., vi.* **-ized', -iz'ing** to organize into a labor union

union jack 1. a flag, esp. a national flag, consisting only of a union **2.** [U-J-] the flag of the United Kingdom

Union of Soviet Socialist Republics country in E Europe & N Asia, consisting of 15 federated republics: 8,603,000 sq. mi.; pop. 237,300,000

u·nique (yōō nēk') *adj.* [< L. *unus*, one] **1.** one and only; sole **2.** without like or equal **3.** very unusual

u·ni·sex (yōō'nə seks') *adj.* [Colloq.] suitable for both sexes, as a haircut

u·ni·son (yōō'nə sən, -zən) *n.* [< L. *unus*, one + *sonus*, a sound] **1.** identity of musical pitch, as of two or more tones **2.** agreement; harmony — **in unison** with all the voices or instruments performing the same part

u·nit (yōō'nit) *n.* [< UNITY] **1.** the smallest whole number; one **2.** a standard basic quantity, measure, etc. **3.** a single person or group, esp. as a part of a whole **4.** a distinct part or object with a specific purpose

U·ni·tar·i·an (yōō'nə ter'ē ən) *n.* a member of a Christian sect holding that God is a single being

u·nite (yoo nīt') *vt., vi.* **-nit'ed, -nit'ing** [< L. *unus*, one] **1.** to put or join together so as to make one; combine **2.** to bring or come together in common cause, action, etc.

United Arab Republic *former name* of EGYPT (1961–71)

United Kingdom country in W Europe, consisting of Great Britain & Northern Ireland: 94,217 sq. mi.; pop. 55,229,000

United Nations an international organization of nations for world peace and security: formed (1945) and having, in 1983, a membership of 158

United States (of **America**) country including 49 States in N.America, & Hawaii: 3,615,211 sq. mi.; pop. 227,000,000; cap. Washington

u·nit·ize (yōō'nə tīz') *vt.* **-ized', -iz'ing** to make into a single unit

unit pricing a system of showing prices in terms of standard units

u·ni·ty (yōō'nə tē) *n., pl.* **-ties** [< L. *unus*, one] **1.** a being united; oneness **2.** a single, separate thing **3.** harmony; agreement **4.** a complex that is a union of related parts **5.** a harmonious, unified arrangement of parts in an artistic work **6.** continuity of purpose, action, etc. **7.** *Math.* any quantity, etc. identified as a unit, or 1

u·ni·valve (yōō'nə valv') *n.* a mollusk with a one-piece shell, as a snail

u·ni·ver·sal (yōō'nə vʉr's'l) *adj.* **1.** of the universe; present everywhere **2.** of, for, or including all or the whole **3.** used, or intended to be used, for all kinds, sizes, etc. or by all people —**u'ni·ver·sal'i·ty** (-vər sal'ə tē) *n.*

u'ni·ver·sal·ize' *vt.* **-ized', -iz'ing** to make universal

universal joint (or **coupling**) a joint or coupling that permits a swing of limited angle in any direction

u'ni·ver'sal·ly *adv.* **1.** in every instance **2.** in every part or place

Universal Product Code a patterned series of vertical bars printed on consumer products: it can be read by computerized scanners for pricing, etc.

u·ni·verse (yōō'nə vʉrs') *n.* [< L. *unus*, one + *vertere*, to turn] **1.** the totality of all things that exist **2.** the world

u·ni·ver·si·ty (yōō'nə vʉr'sə tē) *n., pl.* **-ties** [see prec.] an educational institution with undergraduate and graduate colleges

un·just (un just') *adj.* not just or right; unfair —**un·just'ly** *adv.*

un·kempt' (-kempt') *adj.* [UN- + *kempt* < dial. *kemben*, to comb] **1.** not combed **2.** not tidy; slovenly

un·kind' *adj.* not kind; specif., *a)* not considerate of others *b)* harsh, severe, cruel, etc. —**un·kind'ness** *n.*

un·kind'ly *adj. same as* UNKIND — *adv.* in an unkind way

un·known' *adj.* not known; specif., *a)* unfamiliar *b)* not identified, etc. —*n.* an unknown person or thing

un·law'ful *adj.* **1.** against the law; illegal **2.** immoral —**un·law'ful·ly** *adv.* —**un·law'ful·ness** *n.*

un·lead'ed *adj.* not mixed with tetraethyl lead: said of gasoline

un·learn' *vt., vi.* to seek to forget (something learned)

un·learn'ed (-lʉr'nid; *for 2* -lʉrnd') *adj.* **1.** not learned or educated **2.** not learned or mastered

un·leash' *vt.* to release from or as from a leash

un·less (ən les') *conj.* [< earlier *on lesse that*, at less than] in any case other than that; except that

un·let'tered *adj.* **1.** not lettered; ignorant; uneducated **2.** illiterate

un·like' *adj.* not alike; different — *prep.* not like; different from

un·like'ly *adj.* **1.** not likely; improbable **2.** not likely to succeed — **un·like'li·hood'** *n.*

un·lim'ber (-lim'bər) *vt., vi.* to get ready for use or action

un·lim'it·ed *adj.* **1.** without limits or restrictions **2.** vast; illimitable

un·load' *vt., vi.* **1.** *a)* to remove (a load) *b)* to take a load from **2.** *a)* to tell (one's troubles, etc.) without restraint *b)* to relieve of something that troubles, etc. **3.** to remove the charge from (a gun) **4.** to get rid of

un·lock' *vt.* **1.** *a)* to open (a lock) *b)* to open the lock of (a door, etc.) **2.** to let loose; release **3.** to reveal

un·looked'-for' *adj.* not expected

un·loose' *vt.* **-loosed', -loos'ing** to set loose; loosen, release, etc.

un·luck'y *adj.* **-i·er, -i·est** having or bringing bad luck; unfortunate

---

fat, āpe, cär; ten, ēven; is, bīte; gō, hôrn, tōol, look; oil, out; up, fʉr; chin; she; thin, then; zh, leisure; ŋ, ring; ə for a in ago; ', (ā'b'l); ë, Fr. coeur; ö, Fr. feu; Fr. mon; ü, Fr. duc; kh, G. ich, doch; ‡ foreign; < derived from

un·make' *vt.* **-made'**, **-mak'ing** 1. to cause to be as before; undo 2. to ruin; destroy 3. to depose from a position, rank, or authority

un·man' *vt.* **-manned'**, **-man'ning** to deprive of manly courage, nerve, etc. —**un·man'ly** *adj.*

un·manned' *adj.* without men aboard and operating by remote control

un·mask' *vi.*, *vt.* 1. to remove a mask or disguise (from) 2. to disclose the true nature or character (of)

un·mean'ing *adj.* lacking in meaning or sense

un·men'tion·a·ble *adj.* not fit to be mentioned in polite conversation

un·mer'ci·ful *adj.* having or showing no mercy; cruel; pitiless

un'mis·tak'a·ble *adj.* that cannot be mistaken or misinterpreted; clear —**un'mis·tak'a·bly** *adv.*

un·mit'i·gat'ed *adj.* 1. not lessened or eased 2. out-and-out; absolute

un·mor'al *adj.* *var. of* AMORAL

un·nat'u·ral *adj.* 1. contrary to nature; abnormal 2. artificial 3. very cruel —**un·nat'u·ral·ly** *adv.*

un·nec'es·sar'y *adj.* not necessary; needless —**un·nec'es·sar'i·ly** *adv.*

un·nerve' *vt.* **-nerved'**, **-nerv'ing** to cause to lose one's nerve, courage, etc.

un·num'bered *adj.* 1. not counted 2. innumerable 3. not numbered

un·or'gan·ized' *adj.* not organized; specif., not belonging to a labor union

un·pack' *vt.*, *vi.* 1. to remove (the contents of a trunk, package, etc.) 2. to take things out of (a trunk, etc.)

un·par'al·leled' *adj.* that has no parallel, equal, or counterpart

un·pleas'ant *adj.* not pleasant; offensive; disagreeable —**un·pleas'ant·ly** *adv.* —**un·pleas'ant·ness** *n.*

un·plumbed' *adj.* 1. not measured with a plumb 2. not fully understood

un·pop'u·lar *adj.* not liked by the public or by the majority —**un'pop·u·lar'i·ty** (-lär'ə tē) *n.*

un·prac'ticed (-prak'tist) *adj.* 1. not habitually or repeatedly done 2. not skilled or experienced; inexpert

un·prec'e·dent'ed *adj.* having no precedent or parallel; unheard-of

un·prin'ci·pled (-p'ld) *adj.* lacking moral principles; unscrupulous

un·print'a·ble *adj.* not fit to be printed, as because of obscenity

un'pro·fes'sion·al *adj.* not professional; esp., violating the ethical code of a given profession

un·qual'i·fied' *adj.* 1. lacking the necessary qualifications 2. not limited or modified; absolute

un·ques'tion·a·ble *adj.* not to be questioned, doubted, or disputed; certain —**un·ques'tion·a·bly** *adv.*

un'quote' *interj.* I end the quotation

un·rav'el *vt.* **-eled** or **-elled**, **-el·ing** or **-el·ling** 1. to separate the threads of (something woven, tangled, etc.) 2. to make clear; solve —*vi.* to become unraveled

un·read' (-red') *adj.* 1. not having been read, as a book 2. having read little or nothing

un·re'al *adj.* not real or actual; imaginary, fanciful, false, etc.

un·rea'son·a·ble *adj.* 1. not reasonable or rational 2. excessive; immoderate —**un·rea'son·a·bly** *adv.*

un·rea'son·ing *adj.* not reasoning or reasoned; irrational

un're·con·struct'ed *adj.* 1. not reconstructed 2. holding to an earlier, outmoded practice or attitude and not reconciled to change

un're·gen'er·ate *adj.* 1. not spiritually reborn 2. stubbornly defiant

un're·lent'ing *adj.* 1. inflexible; relentless 2. without mercy; cruel 3. not relaxing in effort, speed, etc.

un're·mit'ting *adj.* not stopping, relaxing, etc.; incessant; persistent

un're·served' *adj.* not reserved; specif., *a)* frank or open in speech *b)* not restricted or qualified —**un're·serv'ed·ly** (-zur'vid lē) *adv.*

un·rest' *n.* 1. restlessness; disquiet 2. angry discontent verging on revolt

un·ri'valed, **un·ri'valled** *adj.* having no rival, equal, or competitor

un·roll' *vt.* 1. to open (something rolled up) 2. to display —*vi.* to become unrolled

un·ruf'fled *adj.* not ruffled or disturbed; calm; smooth; serene

un·rul'y (un rōō'lē) *adj.* **-i·er**, **-i·est** hard to control, restrain, or keep in order; disobedient —**un·rul'i·ness** *n.*

un·sad'dle *vt.* **-dled**, **-dling** to take the saddle off (a horse, etc.)

un·said' *adj.* not expressed; unspoken

un·sa'vor·y *adj.* 1. unpleasant to taste or smell 2. morally offensive

un·scathed' (-skā*th*d') *adj.* [< *un-* + ON. *skathi*, harm] uninjured

un·schooled' *adj.* not educated or trained, esp. by formal schooling

un·scram'ble *vt.* **-bled**, **-bling** to cause to be no longer scrambled, mixed up, or unintelligible

un·screw' *vt.* to detach or loosen by removing screws, or by turning

un·scru'pu·lous *adj.* not restrained by moral scruples; unprincipled

un·seal' *vt.* to break the seal of; open

un·sea'son·a·ble *adj.* 1. not usual for the season 2. at the wrong time

un·seat' *vt.* 1. to dislodge from a seat 2. to remove from office

un·seem'ly *adj.* not seemly; not decent or proper; unbecoming

un·set'tle *vt.*, *vi.* **-tled**, **-tling** to make or become unstable; disturb, displace, or disorder

un·set'tled *adj.* 1. not settled; not fixed, orderly, stable, calm, decided, etc. 2. not paid 3. having no settlers

un·sheathe' (-shē*th*') *vt.* **-sheathed'**, **-sheath'ing** to remove (a sword, etc.) from a sheath

un·sight'ly *adj.* not sightly, or pleasant to look at; ugly

un·skilled' *adj.* having or requiring no special skill or training

un·skill'ful *adj.* having little or no skill; awkward; clumsy

un·snap' *vt.* **-snapped'**, **-snap'ping** to undo the snaps of, so as to detach

un·snarl' (-snärl') *vt.* to untangle

un'so·phis'ti·cat'ed *adj.* not sophisticated; simple, ingenuous, etc.

un·sound′ *adj.* not sound; specif., *a*) not healthy, safe, firm, etc. *b*) not reliable, sensible, etc.

un·spar′ing *adj.* 1. not sparing; lavish 2. not merciful; severe

un·speak′a·ble *adj.* 1. that cannot be spoken 2. so bad, evil, etc. as to defy description —**un·speak′a·bly** *adv.*

un·sta′ble *adj.* 1. not stable; easily upset 2. changeable 3. unreliable 4. emotionally unsettled 5. *Chem.* tending to decompose

un·stead′y *adj.* 1. not steady or firm; shaky 2. changeable; inconstant 3. erratic in habits, purpose, etc.

un·stop′ *vt.* **-stopped′, -stop′ping** 1. to remove the stopper from 2. to clear (a pipe, etc.) of an obstruction

un·struc′tured *adj.* not formally organized; loose, free, open, etc.

un·strung′ *adj.* 1. nervous or upset 2. with the strings loosened or detached, as a bow, racket, etc.

un·stuck′ *adj.* loosened or freed from being stuck

un·stud′ied *adj.* not got by study or conscious effort; spontaneous; natural

un′sub·stan′tial *adj.* 1. having no material substance 2. not solid; flimsy 3. unreal; visionary

un·sung′ (-sun′) *adj.* not honored or celebrated, as in song or poetry

un·tan′gle *vt.* **-gled, -gling** 1. to free from a snarl or tangle 2. to free from confusion; put in order

un·taught′ *adj.* 1. not taught; uneducated 2. got without teaching

un·think′a·ble *adj.* not to be considered or thought of; impossible

un·think′ing *adj.* 1. thoughtless; heedless 2. unable to think

un·ti′dy *adj.* **-di·er, -di·est** not tidy; slovenly; messy

un·tie′ *vt.* **-tied′, -ty′ing** or **-tie′ing** 1. to unfasten (a thing tied or knotted) 2. to free, as from restraint

un·til (un til′, ən-) *prep.* [ME. *untill*] 1. up to the time of [*until* death] 2. before [not *until* tomorrow] —*conj.* 1. up to the time when or that [*until* you leave] 2. to the point, degree, etc. that [cook *until* it is done] 3. before [not *until* I die]

un·time′ly *adj.* 1. before the proper time; premature 2. at the wrong time; inopportune —*adv.* 1. inopportunely 2. prematurely —**un·time′li·ness** *n.*

un·to (un′too, -too) *prep.* [ME.] *archaic var. of:* 1. to 2. until

un·told′ *adj.* 1. not told or revealed 2. too many to be counted; vast

un·touch′a·ble *adj.* that cannot or should not be touched —*n.* in India, formerly, a member of the lowest caste

un·to·ward (un tō′ərd, -tôrd′) *adj.* 1. improper, unseemly, etc. 2. not favorable; adverse

un·trav′eled, un·trav′elled *adj.* 1. not used or frequented by travelers 2. not having done much traveling

un·truth′ *n.* 1. falsity 2. a falsehood; lie —**un·truth′ful** *adj.*

un·tu′tored *adj.* uneducated

un·twist′ *vt., vi.* to separate, as something twisted together; unwind: also **un·twine′, -twined′, -twin′ing**

un·used′ *adj.* 1. not in use 2. never used before 3. unaccustomed (*to*)

un·u′su·al *adj.* not usual or common; rare —**un·u′su·al·ly** *adv.*

un·ut′ter·a·ble *adj.* inexpressible

un·var′nished *adj.* 1. not varnished 2. plain; simple; unadorned

un·veil′ *vt.* to reveal as by removing a veil from —*vi.* to take off one's veil

un·voiced′ *adj.* not expressed; not spoken

un·war′y *adj.* not wary or cautious

un·well′ *adj.* not well; sick

un·whole′some *adj.* 1. harmful to body or mind 2. of unsound health or unhealthy appearance 3. morally harmful —**un·whole′some·ness** *n.*

un·wield′y *adj.* hard to wield, manage, etc., as because of large size

un·will′ing *adj.* 1. not willing; reluctant 2. done, said, etc. reluctantly —**un·will′ing·ly** *adv.*

un·wind′ *vt.* **-wound′, -wind′ing** 1. to wind off or undo (something wound) 2. to untangle (something involved) —*vi.* 1. to become unwound 2. to become relaxed

un·wise′ *adj.* having or showing a lack of wisdom or sound judgment

un·wit·ting (un wit′iŋ) *adj.* 1. not knowing or aware 2. unintentional

un·wont·ed (un wun′tid, -wôn′-) *adj.* not common or usual; rare

un·wor′thy *adj.* **-thi·er, -thi·est** 1. lacking merit or value; worthless 2. not deserving (*of*) 3. not fit or becoming (with *of*) —**un·wor′thi·ness** *n.*

un·wrap′ *vt.* **-wrapped′, -wrap′ping** to take off the wrapping of

un·writ′ten *adj.* 1. not in writing 2. operating only through custom or tradition [an *unwritten* law]

up¹ (up) *adv.* [OE.] 1. to, in, or on a higher place or level 2. to a later period 3. in or to a higher condition, amount, etc. 4. in or into a standing position 5. in or into action, view, consideration, etc. 6. aside; away [lay *up* wealth] 7. so as to be even with in time, degree, etc. 8. so as to be tightly closed, bound, etc. [tie *up* the package] 9. completely; thoroughly 10. *Baseball* to one's turn at batting The adverb *up* is also used *a*) to alter the meaning of a verb (Ex.: look *up* this word) *b*) as an intensive with verbs (Ex.: dress *up*) —*prep.* up to, toward, along, through, into, or upon —*adj.* 1. directed toward a higher position 2. in a higher place or position 3. advanced in amount, degree, etc. [rents are *up*] 4. in a standing position 5. in an active or excited state 6. at an end; over [time's *up*] 7. [Colloq.] going on [what's *up*?] 8. *Baseball* at bat —*n.* 1. an upward slope 2. an upward movement, etc. —*vi.* **upped**, **up′ping** [Colloq.] to get up; rise —*vt.* [Colloq.] 1. to put up, lift up, etc. 2. to cause to rise [to *up* prices] —**on the up and up** [Slang] honest —**up against** [Colloq.] confronted with —**up on** (or **in**) [Colloq.] well-informed concerning —**ups and downs** good periods and bad periods —**up to** [Colloq.] 1. doing or scheming 2. capable of (doing, etc.) 3. as many as 4. as far as 5. dependent upon —**up with!** put in or restore to power, authority, etc.!

up² (up) *adv.* [phonetic respelling of *apiece*] apiece [a score of two *up*]

up- *a combining form meaning* up

up-and-com·ing (up′n kum′iŋ) *adj.* 1. enterprising, promising, etc. 2. gaining in prominence

up′beat′ *n. Music* an unaccented beat, esp. when on the last note of a bar —*adj.* cheerful; optimistic

up·braid (up brād′) *vt.* [< OE. *up-*, up + *bregdan*, to pull] to rebuke severely; censure; scold

up′bring·ing *n.* the training and education received while growing up

up′chuck′ (-chuk′) *vi.*, *vt.*, *n.* [Slang] *same as* VOMIT

up′com′ing *adj.* coming soon

up′coun′try *adj.*, *adv.* in or toward the interior of a country —*n.* the interior of a country

up·date′ *vt.* -**dat′ed**, -**dat′ing** to make up-to-date; make conform to the most recent facts, methods, ideas, etc.

up·end′ *vt.*, *vi.* to set, turn, or stand on end

up′-front′ *adj.* [Colloq.] 1. forthright 2. in advance [*up-front* money]

up′grade′ *n.* an upward slope —*adj.*, *adv.* uphill; upward —*vt.* -**grad′ed**, -**grad′ing** to raise in value, grade, rank, quality, etc.

up·heav·al (up hē′v′l) *n.* 1. a heaving 2. a sudden, violent change

up′hill′ *adj.* 1. going or sloping up 2. laborious; tiring —*adv.* 1. upward as on a hillside 2. with difficulty

up·hold′ *vt.* -**held′**, -**hold′ing** 1. to hold up 2. to keep from falling; support 3. to confirm; sustain

up·hol·ster (up hōl′stər, ə pōl′-) *vt.* [ult. < ME. *upholder*, tradesman] to fit out (furniture, etc.) with coverings, padding, springs, etc. —**up·hol′ster·er** *n.*

up·hol·ster·y *n.*, *pl.* -**ies** 1. the material used in upholstering 2. the work of an upholsterer

up′keep′ *n.* 1. maintenance 2. state of repair 3. the cost of maintenance

up′land (-lənd, -land′) *n.* land elevated above other land —*adj.* of or situated in upland

up·lift′ *vt.* 1. to lift up 2. to raise to a higher moral, social, or cultural level —*n.* (up′lift′) 1. a lifting up 2. a movement for moral, social, or cultural betterment —**up·lift′ment** *n.*

up′man·ship′ *n.* short for ONE-UPMANSHIP

up·on (ə pän′) *prep.* on, or up and on: used interchangeably with *on* —*adv.* on

up·per (up′ər) *adj.* 1. higher in place 2. higher in rank; superior —*n.* 1. the part of a shoe above the sole 2. [Slang] any drug that is a stimulant

upper case capital-letter type used in printing, as distinguished from small letters —**up′per-case′** *adj.*

upper class the rich or aristocratic class —**up′per-class′** *adj.*

up′per·class′man (-mən) *n.*, *pl.* -**men** a junior or senior, as in college

up′per·cut′ *n. Boxing* a short, swinging blow directed upward

upper hand the position of advantage or control

up′per·most′ *adj.* highest in place, power, authority, etc. —*adv.* in the highest place, rank, etc.; first

Upper Vol·ta (väl′tə) *former name of* BURKINA FASO

up·pish (up′ish) *adj.* [Colloq.] haughty, snobbish, arrogant, etc.: also **up′pi·ty**

up·raise′ *vt.* -**raised′**, -**rais′ing** to raise up; lift; elevate

up·rear′ *vt.* 1. to raise or lift up 2. to exalt 3. to bring up; rear

up′right′ *adj.* 1. standing, pointing, etc. straight up; erect 2. honest and just —*adv.* (*also* up rīt′) in an upright position or direction —*n.* something having an upright position

upright piano a piano with a vertical, rectangular body

up′ris′ing (-rīz′iŋ) *n.* a revolt

up·roar (up′rôr′) *n.* [Du. *oprœr*, a stirring up] 1. violent disturbance; tumult 2. loud, confused noise

up·roar′i·ous *adj.* 1. making, or full of, an uproar 2. loud and boisterous, as laughter

up·root′ *vt.* 1. to tear up by the roots 2. to destroy or remove utterly

up′scale′ *adj.* of or for people who are affluent, stylish, etc.

up·set (up set′; *for n.* up′set′) *vt.* -**set′**, -**set′ting** 1. *a*) to tip over; overturn *b*) to defeat unexpectedly 2. *a*) to disturb the functioning of [to *upset* a schedule] *b*) to disturb emotionally —*vi.* to become overturned or upset —*n.* 1. an upsetting 2. an unexpected defeat 3. a disturbance —*adj.* 1. tipped over 2. overthrown or defeated 3. disturbed or disordered

up′shot′ *n.* [orig., final shot in an archery match] the conclusion; result

up′side′ *n.* the upper side or part

upside down 1. with the top side or part underneath 2. in disorder —**up′side-down′** *adj.*

up·si·lon (yoop′sə län′) *n.* the twentieth letter of the Greek alphabet (Υ, υ)

up′stage′ *adv.* toward or at the rear of a stage —*vt.* -**staged′**, -**stag′ing** to draw attention away from (another), as by moving upstage

up′stairs′ *adv.* 1. up the stairs 2. on or to an upper floor —*adj.* on an upper floor —*n.* an upper floor

up·stand′ing *adj.* 1. erect 2. upright in character; honorable

up′start′ *n.* one who has recently come into wealth, power, etc., esp. one who is presumptuous, aggressive, etc. —*adj.* of or like an upstart

up'state' *adj., adv.* in, to, or from the northerly part of a State

up'stream' *adv., adj.* in the direction against the current of a stream

up'surge' (-surj') *n.* a sudden rise

up'swing' *n.* a swing, trend, or movement upward

up'take' *n.* a taking up —**quick** (or **slow**) **on the uptake** [Colloq.] quick (or slow) to comprehend

up'-tight', up'tight' *adj.* [Slang] very tense, nervous, etc.

up'-to-date' *adj.* 1. extending to the present time 2. keeping up with what is most recent

up'town' *adj., adv.* of, in, or toward the upper part of a city or town

up'turn (up turn'; *for n.* up'turn') *vt., vi.* to turn up or over —*n.* an upward turn or trend —**up'turned'** *adj.*

up'ward (-wərd) *adv., adj.* toward a higher place, position, etc.: also **up'wards** *adv.* —**upwards** (or **upward**) **of** more than —**up'ward·ly** *adv.*

upward mobility movement to a higher social and economic status

U·rals (yoor'əlz) mountain range in W U.S.S.R., regarded as the boundary between Europe & Asia: also **Ural Mountains**

u·ra·ni·um (yoo rā'nē əm) *n.* [< ff.] a very hard, heavy, radioactive metallic chemical element: used in work on atomic energy

U·ra·nus (yoor'ə nəs, yoo rā'-) [< Gr. *Ouranos*, heaven] a planet of the solar system: see PLANET

urb (urb) *n.* an urban area, esp. as contrasted with its suburbs

ur·ban (ur'bən) *adj.* [< L. *urbs*, city] 1. of, in, or constituting a city 2. characteristic of cities

ur·bane (ur bān') *adj.* [see prec.] polite in a smooth, polished way; refined —**ur·ban'i·ty** (-ban'ə tē) *n.*

ur·ban·ize (ur'bə nīz') *vt.* **-ized', -iz'ing** to change from rural to urban —**ur'ban·i·za'tion** *n.*

ur'ban·ol'o·gist (-näl'ə jist) *n.* a specialist in urban problems —**ur'ban·ol'o·gy** *n.*

urban renewal rehabilitation of deteriorated urban areas, as by slum clearance and housing construction

urban sprawl the spread of urban congestion into surrounding areas

ur·chin (ur'chin) *n.* [< L. *ericius*, hedgehog] a small child; esp., a mischievous boy

-ure (ər) [Fr. < L. *-ura*] *a suffix meaning:* 1. act or result of being *[exposure]* 2. agent of *[legislature]* 3. state of being *[composure]*

u·re·a (yoo rē'ə) *n.* [< Gr. *ouron*, urine] a soluble, crystalline solid found in urine or made synthetically

u·re·mi·a (yoo rē'mē ə) *n.* [< Gr. *ouron*, urine + *haima*, blood] a toxic condition caused by the presence in the blood of waste products normally eliminated in the urine —**u·re'mic** *adj.*

u·re·ter (yoo rēt'ər) *n.* [< Gr. *ourein*, urinate] a tube carrying urine from a kidney to the bladder

u·re·thra (yoo rē'thrə) *n., pl.* **-thrae** (-thrē), **-thras** [< Gr. *ouron*, urine] the canal through which urine is discharged from the bladder: in males, also the duct for semen

urge (urj) *vt.* **urged, urg'ing** [L. *urgere*, press hard] 1. *a)* to press upon the attention; advocate *b)* to plead with; ask earnestly 2. to incite; provoke 3. to drive or force onward —*n.* 1. an urging 2. an impulse

ur·gent (ur'jənt) *adj.* [see prec.] 1. calling for haste, immediate action, etc. 2. insistent —**ur'gen·cy** *n., pl.* **-cies** —**ur'gent·ly** *adv.*

-ur·gy (ur'jē) [< Gr. *ergon*, work] *a combining form meaning* a working with or by means of *[zymurgy]*

u·ric (yoor'ik) *adj.* of, contained in, or derived from urine

u·ri·nal (yoor'ə n'l) *n.* 1. a receptacle for urine 2. a place for urinating

u·ri·nal·y·sis (yoor'ə nal'ə sis) *n.* chemical or microscopic analysis of the urine

u·ri·nar·y (yoor'ə ner'ē) *adj.* 1. of urine 2. of the organs that secrete and discharge urine

u·ri·nate (yoor'ə nāt') *vi.* **-nat'ed, -nat'ing** to discharge urine from the body —**u'ri·na'tion** *n.*

u·rine (yoor'in) *n.* [< L. *urina*] the yellowish liquid containing waste products secreted by the kidneys and discharged through the urethra

urn (urn) *n.* [< L. *urna*] 1. *a)* a vase with a pedestal *b)* such a vase used to hold ashes after cremation 2. a metal container with a faucet, for making or serving hot coffee, tea, etc.

u·rol·o·gy (yoo räl'ə jē) *n.* [< Gr. *ouron*, urine + -LOGY] the branch of medicine dealing with the urinary and genital organs and their diseases —**u·rol'o·gist** *n.*

ur·sine (ur'sīn, -sin) *adj.* [< L. *ursus*, a bear] of or like a bear

ur·ti·car·i·a (ur'tə ker'ē ə) *n.* [< L. *urtica*, a nettle] a skin condition characterized by itching, burning, and the formation of smooth patches

U·ru·guay (yoor'ə gwā', -gwī') country in SE S.America: 72,171 sq. mi.; pop. 2,818,000

us (us) *pron.* [OE.] *objective case of* WE

U.S., US United States

USA, U.S.A. 1. United States of America 2. United States Army

us·a·ble, use·a·ble (yoo'zə b'l) *adj.* that can be used; fit for use —**us·a·bil'i·ty, use·a·bil'i·ty** (-bil'ə tē) *n.*

USAF, U.S.A.F. United States Air Force

us·age (yoo'sij, -zij) *n.* 1. the act, way, or extent of using; treatment 2. established practice; custom; habit 3. the way in which a word, phrase, etc. is used to express a particular idea

use (yooz; *for n.* yoos) *vt.* **used, us'ing** [< L. *uti*] 1. to put into action or service 2. to exercise [use your judgment] 3. to deal with; treat 4. to consume; expend (often with *up*) —*n.* 1. a using or being used 2. the ability to use 3. the right to use 4. the need or opportunity to use 5. way of using 6. usefulness 7. the purpose for which something is used 8. function —**used to** (yōōs′tə, -too) 1. did at one time [I *used to* live here] 2. accustomed to —**us′er** *n.*

used (yōōzd) *adj.* not new; second-hand

use·ful (yōōs′fəl) *adj.* that can be used; serviceable; helpful;—**use′ful·ly** *adv.* —**use′ful·ness** *n.*

use·less (-lis) *adj.* 1. having no use 2. to no purpose —**use′less·ly** *adv.*

us′er-friend′ly *adj.* easy to use or understand: said esp. of computer hardware, programs, etc.

ush·er (ush′ər) *n.* [< L. *ostiarius*, doorkeeper] 1. one who shows people to their seats in a theater, church, etc. 2. a bridegroom's attendant —*vt.* 1. to escort (others) to seats, etc. 2. to be a forerunner of (often with *in*)

USMC, U.S.M.C. United States Marine Corps

USN, U.S.N. United States Navy

USO, U.S.O. United Service Organizations

U.S.P. United States Pharmacopoeia

U.S.S. United States Ship

U.S.S.R., USSR Union of Soviet Socialist Republics

u·su·al (yōō′zhoo wəl) *adj.* [see USE] such as is most often seen, used, etc.; common; customary —**u′su·al·ly** *adv.*

u·surp (yōō surp′, -zurp′) *vt., vi.* [< L. *usus*, a use + *rapere*, seize] to take and hold (power, a position, etc.) by force —**u·sur·pa·tion** (yōō′sər pa′-shən, -zər-) *n.* —**u·surp′er** *n.*

u·su·ry (yōō′zhoo rē) *n.* [see USE] 1. the lending of money at an excessive rate of interest 2. an excessive interest rate —**u′su·rer** *n.* —**u·su·ri·ous** (yōō zhoor′ē əs) *adj.*

U·tah (yōō′tô, -tä) Western State of the U.S.: 84,916 sq. mi.; pop. 1,461,000; cap. Salt Lake City: abbrev. **Ut., UT**

u·ten·sil (yōō ten′s'l) *n.* [< L. *uti*, to use] an implement or container, esp. one for use in a kitchen

u·ter·us (yōōt′ər əs) *n., pl.* **-ter·i′** (-ī′) [L.] a hollow organ of female mammals in which the embryo and fetus are developed; womb—**u′ter·ine** (-in, yōō′tə rīn′) *adj.*

u·til·i·tar·i·an (yoo til′ə ter′ē ən) *adj.* 1. of or having to do with utility 2. stressing usefulness over beauty or other considerations

u·til·i·ty (yoo til′ə tē) *n., pl.* **-ties** [< L. *uti*, to use] 1. usefulness 2. something useful, as the service to the public of gas, water, etc. 3. a company providing such a service

utility room a room containing laundry appliances, heating equipment, etc.

u·ti·lize (yōōt′'l īz′) *vt.* **-lized′, -liz′-ing** to put to profitable use; make use of —**u′ti·li·za′tion** *n.*

ut·most (ut′mōst′) *adj.*[< OE. superl. of *ut*, out] 1. most extreme; farthest 2. of the greatest degree, amount, etc. —*n.* the most possible

U·to·pi·a (yoo tō′pē ə) [< Gr. *ou*, not + *topos*, a place] an imaginary island in T. More's *Utopia* (1516), with a perfect political and social system —*n.* [*often* **u-**] 1. any idealized place of perfection 2. any visionary scheme for a perfect society —**U·to′pi·an, u·to′-pi·an** *adj., n.*

ut·ter[1] (ut′ər) *adj.* [< OE. compar. of *ut*, out] 1. complete; total 2. unqualified; absolute; unconditional —**ut′-ter·ly** *adv.*

ut·ter[2] (ut′ər) *vt.* [< ME. *utter*, outward] 1. to speak or express audibly (words, sounds, etc.) 2. to express in any way

ut′ter·ance *n.* 1. an uttering 2. the power or style of speaking 3. that which is uttered

ut′ter·most (-mōst′) *adj., n. same as* UTMOST

U′-turn *n.* a complete turn by a car to head in the opposite direction

u·vu·la (yōō′vyə lə) *n., pl.* **-las, -lae′** (-lē′) [< L. *uva*, grape] the small, fleshy process hanging down from the soft palate above the back of the tongue —**u′vu·lar** *adj.*

ux·o·ri·ous (uk sôr′ē əs, ug zôr′-) *adj.* [< L. < *uxor*, wife] dotingly fond of or submissive to one's wife

V

V, v (vē) *n., pl.* **V's, v's** the 22d letter of the English alphabet

V (vē) *n.* a Roman numeral for 5

V, v 1. velocity 2. volt(s)

v. 1. verb 2. versus 3. volume

VA, V.A. Veterans Administration

Va., Virginia

va·can·cy (vā′kən sē) *n., pl.* **-cies** 1. a being vacant 2. empty or vacant space 3. an unoccupied position, office, quarters, etc.

va·cant (vā′kənt) *adj.* [< L. *vacare*, be empty] 1. having nothing in it 2. not held, filled, etc., as a seat, house,

etc. 3. free from work; leisure 4. foolish or stupid —**va′cant·ly** *adv.*

va·cate (-kāt) *vt.* **-cat·ed, -cat·ing** 1. to cause (an office, house, etc.) to be vacant 2. to make void; annul

va·ca·tion (və kā′shən, vā-) *n.* [< L. *vacatio*] a period of rest from work, study, etc. —*vi.* to take one's vacation —**va·ca′tion·er, va·ca′tion·ist** *n.*

vac·ci·nate (vak′sə nāt′) *vt., vi.* **-nat′ed, -nat′ing** to inoculate with a vaccine to prevent a disease, specif. smallpox —**vac′ci·na′tion** *n.*

vac·cine (vak sēn′, vak′sēn) *n.* [< L.

vacca, cow] 1. a substance containing the cowpox virus, used in vaccination against smallpox 2. any preparation so used to produce immunity to a specific disease

vac·il·late (vas'ə lāt') *vi.* **-lat'ed**, **-lat'ing** [< L. *vacillare*] 1. to sway to and fro; waver 2. to fluctuate 3. to show indecision —**vac'il·la'tion** *n.*

va·cu·i·ty (va kyōō'ə tē) *n., pl.* **-ties** [< L. *vacuus*, empty] 1. emptiness 2. an empty space 3. emptiness of mind 4. an inane or senseless remark, thing, etc.

vac·u·ous (vak'yoo wəs) *adj.* [see prec.] 1. empty 2. stupid; senseless —**vac'u·ous·ly** *adv.*

vac·u·um (vak'yoo wəm, vak'yoom) *n., pl.* **-ums**, **-a** (-ə) [L.] 1. space with nothing at all in it 2. a space from which most of the air or gas has been taken 3. any void —*adj.* 1. of, or used to make, a vacuum 2. having or working by a vacuum —*vt., vi.* to clean with a vacuum cleaner

vacuum cleaner a machine for cleaning carpets, floors, etc. by suction

vacuum-packed *adj.* packed in an airtight container to maintain freshness

vacuum tube an electron tube from which most of the air has been evacuated, containing one or more grids and used as an amplifier, etc.

vag·a·bond (vag'ə bänd') *adj.* [< L. *vagari*, wander] 1. wandering 2. living a drifting or irresponsible life 3. shiftless; worthless —*n.* 1. one who wanders from place to place 2. a wandering beggar 3. an idle or shiftless person —**vag'a·bond'age** *n.*

va·gar·y (və ger'ē, vā'gər ē) *n., pl.* **-ies** [see prec.] 1. an odd or eccentric action 2. a whimsical or freakish notion; caprice —**va·gar'i·ous** *adj.*

va·gi·na (və jī'nə) *n., pl.* **-nas**, **-nae** (-nē) [L., sheath] in female mammals, the canal from the vulva to the uterus —**vag·i·nal** (vaj'ə n'l) *adj.*

va·grant (vā'grənt) *n.* [prob. < OFr. *walcrer*, wander] one who wanders from place to place, esp. one without a regular job, supporting himself by begging, etc. —*adj.* 1. wandering; nomadic 2. of or like a vagrant 3. wayward, erratic, etc. —**va'gran·cy** *n., pl.* **-cies**

vague (vāg) *adj.* [< L. *vagus*, wandering] 1. indefinite in shape or form 2. not sharp, certain, or precise in thought or expression —**vague'ly** *adv.* —**vague'ness** *n.*

vain (vān) *adj.* [< L. *vanus*, empty] 1. having no real value; worthless [*vain pomp*] 2. without effect; futile [*a vain endeavor*] 3. having an excessively high regard for one's self, looks, etc.; conceited —**in vain** 1. fruitlessly 2. profanely —**vain'ly** *adv.*

vain'glo·ry (-glôr'ē) *n.* [< L. *vana gloria*, empty boasting] excessive vanity —**vain'glo'ri·ous** *adj.*

val. 1. valuation 2. value

val·ance (val'əns, vāl'-) *n.* [ME. < ?]

a short curtain forming a border, esp. across the top of a window

vale (vāl) *n. poet. var. of* VALLEY

val·e·dic·to·ri·an (val'ə dik tôr'ē ən) *n.* the student who delivers the valedictory at graduation

val·e·dic·to·ry (-tər ē) *n., pl.* **-ries** [< L. *vale*, farewell + *dicere*, to say] a farewell speech, esp. at a graduation

va·lence (vā'ləns) *n.* [< L. *valere*, be strong] *Chem.* the combining capacity of an element or radical as measured by the number of hydrogen or chlorine atoms which one radical or atom of the element will combine with or replace: also **va'len·cy**

Va·len·ci·a (və len'shē ə, -shə) seaport in E Spain: pop. 583,000

val·en·tine (val'ən tīn') *n.* 1. a sweetheart chosen or complimented on Saint Valentine's Day 2. a greeting card or gift sent on this day

val·et (val'it, -ā) *n.* [Fr., a groom] 1. a personal manservant who takes care of a man's clothes, helps him dress, etc. 2. an employee, as of a hotel, who cleans or presses clothes, etc.

Val·hal·la (val hal'ə) *Norse Myth.* the great hall where Odin feasts the souls of heroes slain in battle

val·iant (val'yənt) *adj.* [< L. *valere*, be strong] brave; courageous —**val'iance** *n.* —**val'iant·ly** *adv.*

val·id (val'id) *adj.* [< L. *valere*, be strong] 1. having legal force 2. based on evidence or sound reasoning —**val'id·ly** *adv.* —**val'id·ness** *n.*

val·i·date (val'ə dāt') *vt.* **-dat'ed**, **-dat'ing** 1. to make legally valid 2. to prove to be valid

va·lid·i·ty (və lid'ə tē) *n.* the quality or fact of being valid in law or in argument, proof, etc.

va·lise (və lēs') *n.* [Fr. < It. *valigia*] a piece of hand luggage

Val·i·um (val'ī əm) *a trademark for* a tranquilizing drug

Val·kyr·ie (val kir'ē, val'ki rē) *n. Norse Myth.* any of the maidens of Odin who conduct the souls of heroes slain in battle to Valhalla

val·ley (val'ē) *n., pl.* **-leys** [< L. *vallis*] 1. low land lying between hills or mountains 2. the land drained by a river system 3. any valleylike dip

Valley Forge village in SE Pa.: scene of Washington's winter encampment (1777–78)

val·or (val'ər) *n.* [< L. *valere*, be strong] marked courage or bravery: Brit. sp. **valour** —**val'or·ous** *adj.*

Val·pa·rai·so (val'pə rā'zō, -rī'sō) seaport in C Chile: pop. 262,000

val·u·a·ble (val'yoo b'l, -yoo wə b'l) *adj.* 1. *a*) having material value *b*) of great monetary value 2. highly important, esteemed, etc. —*n.* an article of value: *usually used in pl.*

val·u·a·tion (val'yoo wā'shən) *n.* 1. the determining of the value of anything 2. determined or estimated value

val·ue (val'yōō) *n.* [< L. *valere*, be worth] 1. the worth of a thing in money or goods 2. estimated worth 3. purchasing power 4. that quality of a thing which makes it more or less desirable, useful, etc. 5. a thing or quality having intrinsic worth 6. [*pl.*] beliefs or standards 7. relative duration, intensity, etc. —*vt.* -**ued**, -**u·ing** 1. to estimate the value of; appraise 2. to place an estimate of worth on / to *value* health above wealth/ 3. to think highly of —**val'ue·less** *adj.*

val'ue-add'ed tax a tax based and paid on the value added at each stage of production and distribution, and included in the cost to the consumer

val'ued *adj.* highly thought of

valve (valv) *n.* [< L. *valva*, leaf of a folding door] 1. *Anat.* a membranous structure which permits body fluids to flow in one direction only, or opens and closes a tube, etc. 2. any device in a pipe, etc. that regulates the flow by means of a flap, lid, etc. 3. *Music* a device, as in the trumpet, that changes the tube length so as to change the pitch 4. *Zoology* one of the parts making up the shell of a mollusk, clam, etc.

VALVE

va·moose (va mōōs') *vi.* -**moosed'**, -**moos'ing** [Sp. *vamos*, let us go] [Old Slang] to leave quickly

vamp (vamp) *n.* [< OFr. *avant*, before + *pie*, a foot] 1. the part of a boot or shoe covering the instep 2. *Music* a simple, short improvisation, as by a dance band —*vt.* 1. to put a vamp on 2. *Music* to improvise —*vi. Music* to play a vamp

vam·pire (vam'pīr) *n.* [< Slav.] 1. in folklore, a reanimated corpse that sucks the blood of sleeping persons 2. one who preys ruthlessly on others 3. *clipped form of* VAMPIRE BAT

vampire bat a tropical American bat that lives on the blood of animals

van[1] (van) *n. same as* VANGUARD

van[2] (van) *n.* [< CARAVAN] a large, closed truck used as for moving, or a small one used by repairmen, fitted out as a vacation vehicle, etc.

va·na·di·um (vo nā'dē əm) *n.* [< ON. *Vanadis*, goddess of love] a ductile metallic element used in steel alloys, etc.

Van Al·len (radiation) belt (van al'ən) [< J. *Van Allen* (1914–), U.S. physicist] a broad belt of radiation encircling the earth at varying levels

Van Bu·ren (van byoor'ən), **Martin** 1782–1862; 8th president of the U.S. (1837–41)

Van·cou·ver (van kōō'vər) city in SW British Columbia, Canada; pop. 410,000

Van·dal (van'd'l) *n.* 1. a member of a Germanic tribe that sacked Rome (455 A.D.) 2. [v-] one who maliciously destroys property, esp. works of art

van'dal·ize' *vt.* -**ized'**, -**iz'ing** to destroy or damage (property) maliciously —**van'dal·ism** *n.*

Van·dyke (beard) (van dīk') a closely trimmed, pointed beard

vane (vān) *n.* [< OE. *fana*, a flag] 1. a free-swinging piece of metal, etc. that shows which way the wind is blowing; weather vane 2. any of the flat pieces set around an axle and rotated about it by moving air, water, etc. or rotated to move the air or water

van Gogh (van gō'), **Vincent** 1853–90; Du. painter

van·guard (van'gärd') *n.* [< OFr. *avant*, before + *garde*, guard] 1. the front part of an army in an advance 2. the leading position or persons in a movement

va·nil·la (və nil'ə) *n.* [< Sp. *vaina*, pod] 1. a climbing orchid with podlike capsules (**vanilla beans**) 2. a flavoring made from these capsules

van·ish (van'ish) *vi.* [see EVANESCENT] 1. to pass suddenly from sight; disappear 2. to cease to exist

van·i·ty (van'ə tē) *n., pl.* -**ties** [< L. *vanus*, vain] 1. anything vain or futile 2. worthlessness; futility 3. a being vain, or too proud of oneself 4. a small table with a mirror, for use while putting on cosmetics, etc.

vanity case a woman's small traveling case for carrying cosmetics, toilet articles, etc.

van·quish (van'kwish, van'-) *vt.* [< L. *vincere*] to conquer or defeat

van·tage (van'tij) *n.* [see ADVANTAGE] 1. a favorable position 2. a position allowing a clear view or understanding: also **vantage point**

vap·id (vap'id) *adj.* [L. *vapidus*] tasteless; flavorless; dull —**va·pid·i·ty** (va pid'ə tē), **vap'id·ness** *n.*

va·por (vā'pər) *n.* [L.] 1. *a)* visible particles of moisture floating in the air, as fog or steam *b)* smoke, fumes, etc. 2. the gaseous form of any substance normally a liquid or solid Brit. sp. **vapour**

va'por·ize' (-pə rīz') *vt., vi.* -**ized'**, -**iz'ing** to change into vapor —**va'por·i·za'tion** *n.* —**va'por·iz'er** *n.*

va'por·ous *adj.* 1. forming or full of vapor 2. like vapor

vapor trail *same as* CONTRAIL

va·que·ro (vä ker'ō) *n., pl.* -**ros** [Sp. < *vaca*, a cow] in the Southwest, a man who herds cattle; cowboy

var. 1. variant(s) 2. various

var·i·a·ble (ver'ē ə b'l) *adj.* 1. apt to change or vary; changeable, inconstant, etc. 2. that can be changed or varied —*n.* anything changeable; thing that varies —**var'i·a·bil'i·ty** *n.*

var·i·ance (-əns) *n.* 1. a varying or being variant 2. degree of change or difference; discrepancy —**at variance** not in agreement or accord

var·i·ant (-ənt) *adj.* varying; different in some way from others of the same kind —*n.* anything variant, as a different spelling of the same word

var·i·a'tion (-ā'shən) *n.* 1. a varying; change in form, extent, etc. 2. the degree of such change 3. a thing somewhat different from another of the same kind 4. *Music* the repetition of a theme with changes in rhythm, key, etc.

var·i·col·ored (ver'i kul'ərd) *adj.* of several or many colors

var·i·cose (var'ə kōs') *adj.* [< L. *varix*, enlarged vein] abnormally and irregularly swollen [*varicose* veins]

var·ied (ver'ēd) *adj.* 1. of different kinds; various 2. changed; altered

var·i·e·gat·ed (-ē ə gāt'id) *adj.* [< L. *varius*, various] 1. marked with different colors in spots, streaks, etc. 2. having variety; varied

va·ri·e·ty (və rī'ə tē) *n., pl.* **-ties** 1. a being various or varied 2. a different form of some thing, condition, etc.; kind [*varieties* of cloth] 3. a collection of different things

variety store a retail store selling many small, inexpensive items

var·i·ous (ver'ē əs) *adj.* [L. *varius*, diverse] 1. differing one from another; of several kinds 2. several or many 3. individual —**var'i·ous·ly** *adv.*

var·let (vär'lit) *n.* [OFr., a page] [Archaic] a scoundrel; knave

var·mint, var·ment (vär'mənt) *n.* [var. of VERMIN] [Dial.] a person or animal regarded as objectionable

var·nish (vär'nish) *n.* [< ML. *veronix*, resin] 1. a preparation of resinous substances dissolved in oil, alcohol, etc., used to give a glossy surface to wood, metal, etc. 2. this smooth, glossy surface 3. a surface smoothness, as of manner —*vt.* 1. to cover with varnish 2. to make superficially attractive

var·si·ty (vär'sə tē) *n., pl.* **-ties** [< UNIVERSITY] the main team representing a university, school, etc., as in a sport

var·y (ver'ē) *vt.* **-ied, -y·ing** [< L. *varius*, various] 1. to change; alter 2. to make different from one another 3. to give variety to [*vary* your reading] —*vi.* 1. to undergo change 2. to be different 3. to deviate, diverge, or depart (*from*)

vas·cu·lar (vas'kyə lər) *adj.* [< L. *vas*, vessel] of or having vessels or ducts for conveying blood, sap, etc.

vase (vās, vāz) *n.* [< L. *vas*, vessel] an open container used for decoration, displaying flowers, etc.

vas·ec·to·my (vas ek'tə mē) *n., pl.* **-mies** [< L. *vas*, vessel + -ECTOMY] surgical removal of all, or esp. part, of the ducts carrying sperm from the testicles

Vas·e·line (vas'ə lēn') [< G. *wasser*, water + Gr. *elaion*, oil] a trademark for petrolatum —*n.* [v-] petrolatum

vas·o·mo·tor (vas'ō mōt'ər) *adj.* [< L. *vas*, vessel + MOTOR] regulating the size in diameter of blood vessels: said of a nerve, drug, etc.

vas·sal (vas'l) *n.* [< ML. *vassus*, servant] 1. in the Middle Ages, one who held land under the feudal system, pledging fealty to an overlord 2. a subordinate, servant, slave, etc. — **vas'sal·age** (-ij) *n.*

vast (vast) *adj.* [L. *vastus*] very great

in size, extent, number, degree, etc. —**vast'ly** *adv.* —**vast'ness** *n.*

vat (vat) *n.* [< OE. *fæt*, cask] a large tank, tub, or cask for liquids

vat·ic (vat'ik) *adj.* [< L. *vates*, prophet] prophetic

Vat·i·can City (vat'i k'n) papal state, an enclave in Rome, including the papal palace (**the Vatican**): 108 acres

vaude·ville (vôd'vil, vôd'-; -ə vil) *n.* [Fr. < *Vau-de-Vire*, a valley in Normandy, famous for convivial songs] a stage show consisting of various acts

vault¹ (vôlt) *n.* [< L. *volvere*, to roll] 1. an arched roof or ceiling 2. an arched chamber or space 3. a cellar room used for storage 4. a burial chamber 5. a room for the safekeeping of valuables, as in a bank —*vt.* to cover with, or build as, a vault —*vi.* to curve like a vault

VAULT

vault² (vôlt) *vi., vt.* [< OIt. *voltare*] to jump, leap, etc.; esp., to leap over (a barrier) with the hands supported on the barrier, or holding a long pole —*n.* a vaulting —**vault'er** *n.*

vault'ing *adj.* 1. leaping 2. unduly confident [*vaulting* ambition]

vaunt (vônt) *vt., n.* [< L. *vanus*, vain] boast —**vaunt'ed** *adj.*

VCR videocassette recorder

VD, V.D. venereal disease

VDT video display terminal

veal (vēl) *n.* [< L. *vitulus*, a calf] the flesh of a young calf used as food

vec·tor (vek'tər) *n.* [< L. *vehere*, to carry] any animal that transmits a disease-producing organism

Ve·da (vā'də, vē'-) *n.* [Sans. *veda*, knowledge] any of the four ancient sacred books of Hinduism —**Ve'dic** *adj.*

Veep (vēp) *n.* [*also* v-] vice-president

veer (vir) *vi., vt.* [< Fr. *virer*, turn around] to change in direction; shift; turn —*n.* a change of direction

veg·e·ta·ble (vej'tə b'l, vej'ə tə-) *adj.* [see VEGETATE] 1. of plants in general 2. of, from, or like edible vegetables —*n.* 1. any plant, as distinguished from animal or inorganic matter 2. a plant eaten whole or in part as with an entree or in a salad, as the tomato

veg·e·tar·i·an (-ə ter'ē ən) *n.* one who eats no meat —*adj.* 1. of vegetarians 2. consisting only of vegetables

veg·e·tate (vej'ə tāt') *vi.* **-tat·ed, -tat·ing** [< L. *vegere*, quicken] 1. to grow as plants 2. to lead a dull, inactive life —**veg'e·ta'tive** *adj.*

veg·e·ta'tion *n.* 1. a vegetating 2. plant life in general

ve·he·ment (vē'ə mənt) *adj.* [< L. *vehere*, carry] 1. violent; impetuous 2. full of intense feeling or strong passion —**ve'he·mence, ve'he·men·cy** *n.* —**ve'he·ment·ly** *adv.*

ve·hi·cle (vē'ə k'l) *n.* [< L. *vehere*, carry] 1. any device for carrying or conveying persons or objects 2. a

means of communicating thoughts, etc.
—**ve·hic′u·lar** (-hik′yoo lər) *adj.*

veil (vāl) *n.* [< L. *velum*, cloth] 1. a piece of light fabric, as of net, worn, esp. by women, over the face or head 2. anything used to conceal, cover, separate, etc. *[a veil of silence]* 3. a part of a nun's headdress —*vt.* 1. to cover with a veil 2. to hide or disguise —**take the veil** to become a nun

veiled (vāld) *adj.* 1. wearing, or covered with, a veil 2. concealed, hidden, etc. 3. not openly expressed

vein (vān) *n.* [< L. *vena*] 1. any blood vessel carrying blood to the heart 2. any of the ribs of an insect's wing or of a leaf blade 3. a body of minerals occupying a fissure in rock 4. a lode 5. a streak of a different color, etc., as in marble 6. a distinctive quality in one's character, speech, etc. 7. a mood —*vt.* to mark as with veins

Vel·cro (vel′krō) *a trademark for* a nylon material for fastenings, made up of matching strips with tiny hooks and adhesive pile, that are easily pressed together or pulled apart

veld, veldt (velt) *n.* [Afrik. < MDu. *veld*, field] in S. Africa, open grassy country with few bushes or trees

vel·lum (vel′əm) *n.* [< L. *vitulus*, calf] 1. a fine parchment prepared from calfskin, lambskin, etc. used for writing on or for binding books 2. a strong paper made to resemble this

ve·loc·i·ty (və läs′ə tē) *n., pl.* -**ties** [< L. *velox*, swift] 1. quickness of motion; swiftness 2. rate of motion

ve·lour, ve·lours (və loor′) *n., pl.* -**lours′** [Fr.: see VELURE] a fabric with a soft nap like velvet

ve·lum (vē′ləm) *n., pl.* -**la** (-lə) [L., a veil] the soft, fleshy, rear part of the palate —**ve′lar** (-lər) *adj.*

ve·lure (və loor′) *n.* [LL. *villosus*, shaggy] velvet or a fabric like velvet

vel·vet (vel′vit) *n.* [see prec.] 1. a rich fabric of silk, rayon, etc. with a soft, thick pile 2. anything like velvet in texture —*adj.* 1. made of velvet 2. like velvet —**vel′vet·y** *adj.*

vel′vet·een′ (-ə tēn′) *n.* a cotton cloth with a short, thick pile like velvet

ve·nal (vē′n'l) *adj.* [< L. *venus*, sale] open to, or characterized by, corruption or bribery —**ve·nal′i·ty** (-nal′ə tē) *n.* —**ve′nal·ly** *adv.*

vend (vend) *vt., vi.* [< L. *venum dare*, offer for sale] to sell (goods) —**ven′dor, vend′er** *n.*

ven·det·ta (ven det′ə) *n.* [It. < L. *vindicta*, vengeance] a family feud

vending machine a coin-operated machine for selling certain small articles

ve·neer (və nir′) *vt.* [< Fr. *fournir*, furnish] to cover with a thin layer of more costly material; esp., to cover (wood) with wood of a finer quality —*n.* 1. a thin surface layer, as of fine wood, laid over a base of common material 2. superficial appearance *[a veneer of culture]*

ven·er·a·ble (ven′ər ə b'l) *adj.* worthy of respect or reverence because of age, dignity, etc. —**ven′er·a·bil′i·ty** *n.*

ven·er·ate (ven′ə rāt′) *vt.* -**at′ed**, -**at′ing** [< L. *venerari*, to worship] to look upon with feelings of deep respect; revere —**ven′er·a′tion** *n.*

ve·ne·re·al (və nir′ē əl) *adj.* [< L. *venus*, love] 1. of sexual intercourse 2. transmitted by sexual intercourse *[a venereal disease]*

Ve·ne·tian (və nē′shən) *adj.* of Venice, its people, etc. —*n.* a native or inhabitant of Venice

Venetian blind *[also* v- b-] a window blind made of a number of thin slats that can be set at any angle

Ven·e·zue·la (ven′i zwā′lə) country in N.S.America: 352,143 sq. mi.; pop. 9,686,000 —**Ven′e·zue′lan** *adj., n.*

venge·ance (ven′jəns) *n.* [< L. *vindicare*, avenge] the return of an injury for an injury, as in retribution; revenge —**with a vengeance** 1. with great force or fury 2. excessively

venge·ful (venj′fəl) *adj.* seeking vengeance; vindictive —**venge′ful·ly** *adv.*

ve·ni·al (vē′nē əl, vēn′yəl) *adj.* [< L. *venia*, grace] that may be forgiven; pardonable *[a venial sin]*

Ven·ice (ven′is) seaport in N Italy: pop. 364,000

ve·ni·re·man (və nī′rē mən) *n., pl.* -**men** [< ML. *venire facias*, cause to come] one of a group of people from among whom a jury will be selected

ven·i·son (ven′i s'n, -z'n) *n.* [< L. *venari*, to hunt] the flesh of a deer, used as food

ven·om (ven′əm) *n.* [< L. *venenum*, a poison] 1. the poison secreted by some snakes, spiders, etc. 2. malice

ven′om·ous *adj.* 1. full of venom; poisonous 2. spiteful; malicious

ve·nous (vē′nəs) *adj.* [L. *venosus*] 1. of veins 2. designating blood carried in veins

vent¹ (vent) *n.* [< L. *ventus*, wind] 1. a means of escaping; outlet 2. expression; release *[giving vent to emotion]* 3. a small opening to permit passage, as of a gas —*vt.* 1. to make a vent in or for 2. to give release to; let out

vent² (vent) *n.* [< L. *findere*, to split] a vertical slit in a garment

ven·ti·late (ven′t'l āt′) *vt.* -**lat′ed**, -**lat′ing** [< L. *ventus*, wind] 1. to circulate fresh air in (a room, etc.) 2. to provide with an opening for the escape of air, gas, etc. —**ven′ti·la′tion** *n.*

ven′ti·la′tor *n.* an opening or a device for replacing foul air

ven·tral (ven′trəl) *adj.* [< L. *venter*, belly] of, near, or on the belly

ven·tri·cle (ven′tri k'l) *n.* [see prec.] either of the two lower chambers of the heart

ven·tril·o·quism (ven tril′ə kwiz′m) *n.* [< L. *venter*, belly + *loqui*, speak] the art of speaking so that the voice seems to come from a source other than the speaker —**ven·tril′o·quist** *n.*

ven·ture (ven′chər) *n.* [see ADVENTURE] 1. a risky undertaking, as in business 2. something on which a risk is taken —*vt.* -**tured**, -**tur·ing** 1. to expose to danger or chance of loss 2. to express at the risk of criticism *[to venture* an opinion*]* —*vi.* to do or go at some risk

ven·ture·some (-səm) *adj.* 1. inclined to venture; daring 2. risky; hazardous Also **ven'tur·ous** (-chər əs)

ven·ue (ven'yōō, -ōō) *n.* [< OFr. *venir,* come] *Law* 1. the locality in which a cause of action or a crime occurs 2. the locality in which a jury is drawn and a case tried 3. the scene of a large gathering for some event

Ve·nus (vē'nəs) 1. the Roman goddess of love and beauty 2. the most brilliant planet in the solar system: see PLANET

Venus' fly'trap' a swamp plant of N.Carolina and S.Carolina with leaves snapping shut to trap insects

Ve·nu·sian (vi nōō'shən) *adj.* of the planet Venus —*n.* an imaginary inhabitant of Venus

ve·ra·cious (və rā'shəs) *adj.* [< L. *verus,* true] 1. habitually truthful; honest 2. true; accurate

ve·rac·i·ty (və ras'ə tē) *n.* 1. honesty 2. accuracy 3. truth

ve·ran·da, ve·ran·dah (və ran'də) *n.* [< Port. *varanda,* balcony] a long, open porch, usually roofed

verb (vurb) *n.* [< L. *verbum,* a word] a word expressing action, existence, or occurrence

ver·bal (vur'b'l) *adj.* 1. of, in, or by means of words 2. in speech; oral 3. of, having the nature of, or derived from a verb —**ver'bal·ly** *adv.*

ver'bal·ize' (-bə līz') *vt.* -ized', -iz'-ing to use words for communication —*vt.* to express in words

verbal noun *Gram.* a noun derived from a verb (Ex.: *swimming* is fun)

ver·ba·tim (vər bāt'əm) *adv., adj.* [< L. *verbum,* a word] word for word

ver·be·na (vər bē'nə) *n.* [L., foliage] an ornamental plant with spikes or clusters of showy red, white, or purplish flowers

ver·bi·age (vur'bē ij) *n.* [Fr. < L. *verbum,* a word] an excess of words; wordiness

ver·bose (vər bōs') *adj.* [< L. *verbum,* a word] using too many words; wordy —**ver·bos'i·ty** (-bäs'ə tē) *n.*

ver·dant (vur'd'nt) *adj.* [prob. VERD(URE) + -ANT] 1. green 2. covered with green vegetation

Ver·di (ver'dē), **Giu·sep·pe** (jōō zep'pe) 1813-1901; It. operatic composer

ver·dict (vur'dikt) *n.* [< L. *vere,* truly + *dicere,* say] 1. the formal finding of a jury 2. any decision or judgment

ver·di·gris (vur'di grēs', -gris) *n.* [< MFr. *verd de Grece,* green of Greece] a greenish coating that forms on brass, bronze, or copper

ver·dure (vur'jər) *n.* [OFr. < *verd,* green] 1. the fresh green color of growing things 2. green vegetation

verge¹ (vurj) *n.* [< L. *virga,* rod] the edge, brink, or margin *(of* something) —*vi.* **verged, verg'ing** to be on the verge; border (with *on* or *upon*)

verge² (vurj) *vi.* **verged, verg'ing** [L. *vergere,* to bend, turn] 1. to tend or incline *(to* or *toward)* 2. to change or pass gradually *(into)* [dawn *verging* into daylight*]*

ver·i·fy (ver'ə fī') *vt.* -fied', -fy'ing [< L. *verus,* true + *facere,* make] 1. to prove to be true by evidence, etc.; confirm 2. to test the accuracy of —**ver'i·fi'a·ble** *adj.* —**ver'i·fi·ca'tion** *n.*

ver·i·ly (ver'ə lē) *adv.* [Archaic] in very truth; truly

ver·i·si·mil·i·tude (ver'ə si mil'ə tōōd', -tyōōd') *n.* [< L. *verus,* true + *similis,* like] the appearance of being true or real

ver·i·ta·ble (ver'i tə b'l) *adj.* [< L. *veritas,* truth] true; actual

ver·i·ty (ver'ə tē) *n., pl.* -ties [< L. *verus,* true] 1. truth; reality 2. a principle, belief, etc. taken to be fundamentally true; a truth

ver·mi·cel·li (vur'mə sel'ē, -chel'ē) *n.* [It. < L. *vermis,* a worm] pasta like spaghetti, but in thinner strings

ver·mi·form (vur'mə fôrm') *adj.* [< L. *vermis,* a worm + -FORM] shaped like a worm

vermiform appendix same as APPENDIX (sense 2)

ver·mil·ion (vər mil'yən) *n.* [< L. *vermis,* a worm] 1. a bright-red pigment 2. a bright red or scarlet —*adj.* of this color

ver·min (vur'min) *n., pl.* -min [< L. *vermis,* a worm] 1. any of various destructive insects or small animals, as lice, rats, etc. 2. a vile person

Ver·mont (vər mänt') New England State of the U.S.; 9,609 sq. mi.; pop. 511,000; cap. Montpelier —**Vermont'er** *n.*

ver·mouth (vər mōōth') *n.* [< G. *wermut,* wormwood] a fortified white wine flavored with herbs, used in cocktails and as an aperitif

ver·nac·u·lar (vər nak'yə lər) *adj.* [< L. *vernaculus,* native] 1. of, in, or using the native language of a place 2. native to a country —*n.* 1. the native language or dialect of a country or place 2. the common, everyday language of a people 3. the jargon of a profession or trade

ver·nal (vur'n'l) *adj.* [< L. *ver,* spring] 1. of or in the spring 2. springlike 3. youthful

ver·ni·er (vur'nē ər) *n.* [after P. *Vernier,* 17th-c. Fr. mathematician] a short scale sliding along a longer graduated instrument to indicate parts of divisions: also **vernier scale**

Ver·sailles (vər sī') city in NC France, near Paris: pop. 95,000

ver·sa·tile (vur'sə t'l) *adj.* [< L. *vertere,* to turn] competent in many things —**ver'sa·til'i·ty** (-til'ə tē) *n.*

verse (vurs) *n.* [< L. *vertere,* to turn] 1. a single line of poetry 2. poetry 3. a particular form of poetry 4. a poem 5. a stanza 6. *Bible* any of the short divisions of a chapter

versed (vʉrst) *adj.* [< L. *versari*, be busy] skilled or learned (*in* a subject)

ver·si·fy (vʉr′sə fī′) *vi.* -**fied**′, -**fy′ing** [< L. *versus*, a verse + *facere*, make] to compose verses —*vt.* 1. to tell in verse 2. to put into verse form —**ver′si·fi·ca′tion** (-fi kā′shən) *n.* —**ver′si·fi′er** *n.*

ver·sion (vʉr′zhən) *n.* [see VERSE] 1. a translation, esp. of the Bible 2. an account showing one point of view 3. a particular form of something

ver·sus (vʉr′səs) *prep.* [ML. < L., toward] 1. against 2. in contrast with

ver·te·bra (vʉr′tə brə) *n., pl.* -**brae′** (-brē′), -**bras** [L. < *vertere*, to turn] any of the single bones of the spinal column —**ver′te·bral** *adj.*

ver·te·brate (-brit, -brāt′) *adj.* 1. having a backbone, or spinal column 2. of the vertebrates —*n.* any of a large division of animals having a spinal column, as mammals, birds, etc.

ver·tex (vʉr′teks) *n., pl.* -**tex·es**, -**ti·ces′** (-tə sēz′) [L.] 1. the highest point; top 2. *Geom.* the point of intersection of the two sides of an angle

ver·ti·cal (vʉr′ti k'l) *adj.* 1. of or at the vertex 2. upright; straight up and down —*n.* a vertical line, plane, etc. —**ver′ti·cal·ly** *adv.*

ver·tig·i·nous (vər tij′ə nəs) *adj.* of, having, or causing vertigo

ver·ti·go (vʉr′ti gō′) *n.* [L. < *vertere*, to turn] a sensation of dizziness

verve (vʉrv) *n.* [Fr. < OFr., manner of speech] vigor; energy; enthusiasm

ver·y (ver′ē) *adj.* [< L. *verus*, true] 1. complete; absolute *[the very opposite]* 2. same *[the very hat I lost]* 3. being just what is needed 4. even *[the very rafters shook]* 5. actual *[caught in the very act]* —*adv.* 1. extremely 2. truly; really *[the very same man]*

very high frequency any radio frequency between 30 and 300 megahertz

very low frequency any radio frequency between 10 and 30 kilohertz

ves·i·cle (ves′i k'l) *n.* [< L. *vesica*, bladder] a small membranous cavity, sac, or cyst —**ve·sic·u·lar** (və sik′yə lər), **ve·sic′u·late** (-lit) *adj.*

ves·per (ves′pər) *n.* [L., evening] [*usually pl.*] an evening prayer or service: also **Vespers**

Ves·puc·ci (ves pōōt′chē), **A·me·ri·go** (ä′me rē′gō) (L. name *Americus Vespucius*) 1451?-1512; It. navigator

ves·sel (ves′'l) *n.* [< L. *vas*] 1. a utensil for holding something, as a bowl, kettle, etc. 2. a ship or boat 3. a tube or duct of the body, as a vein, containing or circulating a fluid

vest (vest) *n.* [< L. *vestis*, garment] a short, sleeveless garment, esp. one worn under a suit coat by men —*vt.* 1. to dress, as in clerical robes 2. to place (authority, etc.) *in* someone 3. to put (a person) in control of, as power, etc. —*vi.* to become vested (*in* a person), as property

ves·tal (ves′t'l) *adj.* [< L. *Vesta*, goddess of the hearth] chaste; pure —*n.* a virgin priestess of the Roman goddess Vesta: in full **vestal virgin**

vest·ed (ves′tid) *adj.* 1. clothed, esp. in vestments 2. *Law* fixed; settled; absolute *[vested right]*

ves·ti·bule (ves′tə byōōl′) *n.* [L. *vestibulum*] a small entrance hall, as to a building

ves·tige (ves′tij) *n.* [< L. *vestigium*, footprint] 1. a trace, mark, or sign, esp. of something that has passed away 2. *Biol.* a degenerate part, more fully developed in an earlier stage —**ves·tig·i·al** (-tij′ē əl) *adj.*

vest·ing (ves′tiŋ) *n.* the retention by an employee of all or part of his pension rights, regardless of changes in employment, early retirement, etc.

vest·ment (vest′mənt) *n.* [< L. *vestire*, clothe] a garment or robe, esp. one worn by a clergyman

vest′pock′et *adj.* very small, or unusually small for its kind

ves·try (ves′trē) *n., pl.* -**tries** [< L. *vestis*, garment] 1. a room in a church, where vestments, etc. are kept 2. a room in a church, used as a chapel 3. a group of church members who manage temporal affairs —**ves′try·man** (-mən) *n., pl.* -**men**

Ve·su·vi·us (və sōō′vē əs) active volcano in S Italy, near Naples

vet[1] (vet) *n. clip for* VETERINARIAN

vet[2] (vet) *n. clip for* VETERAN

vetch (vech) *n.* [< L. *vicia*] a plant of the legume family, grown for fodder

vet·er·an (vet′ər ən) *adj.* [< L. *vetus*, old] 1. old and experienced 2. of veterans —*n.* 1. a person of long service in some position 2. one who has served in the armed forces

Veterans Day a legal holiday in the U.S. honoring all veterans of the armed forces: observed on Nov. 11 (Armistice Day), the anniversary of the armistice of World War I

vet·er·i·nar·i·an (vet′ər ə ner′ē ən) *n.* one who practices veterinary medicine or surgery

vet′er·i·nar′y (-ē) *adj.* [< L. *veterina*, beasts of burden] designating or of the medical or surgical treatment of animals —*n., pl.* -**ies** a veterinarian

ve·to (vē′tō) *n., pl.* -**toes** [L., I forbid] 1. *a)* an order prohibiting some act *b)* the power to prohibit action 2. *a)* the right of one branch of a government to reject bills passed by another *b)* the exercise of this right —*vt.* -**toed**, -**to·ing** 1. to prevent (a bill) from becoming law by a veto 2. to forbid

vex (veks) *vt.* [< L. *vexare*, agitate] 1. to disturb; annoy, esp. in a petty way 2. to distress; afflict

vex·a·tion (vek sā′shən) *n.* 1. a vexing or being vexed 2. something that vexes —**vex·a′tious** (-shəs) *adj.*

VHF, vhf very high frequency

vi., v.i. intransitive verb

V.I., VI Virgin Islands

vi·a (vī′ə, vē′ə) *prep.* [L., way] by way of

vi·a·ble (vī′ə b'l) *adj.* [< L. *vita*, life] 1. sufficiently developed to be able to live outside the uterus 2. workable *[viable ideas]* —**vi′a·bil′i·ty** *n.*

vi·a·duct (vī′ə dukt′) *n.* [< VIA + (AQUE)DUCT] a bridge consisting of a series of short spans, supported on piers or towers

vi·al (vī′əl) *n.* [< Gr. *phialē*, PHIAL] a small vessel or bottle for liquids

vi·and (vī′ənd) *n.* [< L. *vivere*, live] an article of food

vibes (vībz) *n.pl.* **1.** [Colloq.] same as VIBRAPHONE **2.** [Slang] attractive or unattractive qualities in a person or thing, thought of as setting up vibrations that can be sensed

vi·bra·harp (vī′brə härp′) *n.* same as VIBRAPHONE

vi·brant (vī′brənt) *adj.* **1.** quivering or vibrating **2.** produced by vibration: said of sound **3.** vigorous —**vi′bran·cy** *n.* —**vi′brant·ly** *adv.*

vi·bra·phone (vī′brə fōn′) *n.* a musical instrument like the marimba, with electrically operated resonators

vi·brate (vī′brāt) *vt.* -**brat·ed**, -**brat·ing** [< L. *vibrare*] to set in to-and-fro motion —*vi.* **1.** to swing back and forth; oscillate **2.** to move rapidly back and forth; quiver **3.** to resound **4.** to be emotionally stirred —**vi·bra′tion** *n.* —**vi′bra·tor** *n.*

vi·bra·to (vi brät′ō) *n., pl.* -**tos** [It.] a pulsating effect produced by rapid alternation of a given tone

vic·ar (vik′ər) *n.* [< L. *vicis*, a change] **1.** *Anglican Ch.* a parish priest who receives a stipend instead of the tithes **2.** *R.C.Ch.* a priest or other deputy of a bishop —**vic′ar·age** *n.*

vi·car·i·ous (vī ker′ē əs) *adj.* [< L. *vicis*, a change] **1.** taking the place of another **2.** endured or performed by one person in place of another **3.** shared in by imagined participation in another's experience [a *vicarious* thrill] —**vi·car′i·ous·ly** *adv.*

vice¹ (vīs) *n.* [< L. *vitium*] **1.** *a*) an evil action or habit *b*) evil conduct; depravity *c*) prostitution **2.** a trivial fault or failing

vi·ce² (vī′sē) *prep.* [L. < *vicis*, a change] in the place of

vice- [see prec.] *a prefix meaning* subordinate, deputy [*vice*-president]

vice-ge·rent (vīs jir′ənt) *n.* [< prec. + L. *gerere*, to direct] a deputy

vice′-pres′i·dent *n.* an executive assistant to a president, acting in his place during his absence: for the U.S. official, usually **Vice President** — **vice′-pres′i·den·cy** *n.*

vice·roy (vīs′roi) *n.* [MFr. < *vice-* (see VICE-) + *roy*, king] a person ruling a region as a sovereign's deputy

vi·ce ver·sa (vī′sē vur′sə, vīs′ vur′sə) [L.] the relation being reversed

vi·chys·soise (vē′shē swäz′, vish′ē-) *n.* [Fr.] a cream soup of potatoes, onions, etc., usually served cold

vi·cin·i·ty (və sin′ə tē) *n., pl.* -**ties** [< L. *vicus*, village] **1.** nearness; proximity **2.** a nearby area

vi·cious (vish′əs) *adj.* [< L. *vitium*, vice] **1.** characterized by vice; evil or depraved **2.** faulty; flawed **3.** unruly [a *vicious* horse] **4.** malicious; spiteful

[a *vicious* rumor] **5.** very intense, forceful, etc. [a *vicious* blow] —**vi′cious·ly** *adv.* —**vi′cious·ness** *n.*

vicious circle a situation in which the solution to each problem gives rise to another, eventually bringing back the first problem

vi·cis·si·tudes (vi sis′ə tōōdz′) *n.pl.* [< L. *vicis*, a turn] unpredictable changes in life; ups and downs

vic·tim (vik′təm) *n.* [L. *victima*] **1.** someone or something killed, destroyed, sacrificed, etc. **2.** one who suffers some loss, esp. by being swindled

vic′tim·ize′ (-tə mīz′) *vt.* -**ized′**, -**iz′ing** to make a victim of

vic·tor (vik′tər) *n.* [L. < *vincere*, conquer] a winner or conqueror

Vic·to·ri·a (vik tôr′ē ə) 1819–1901; queen of England (1837–1901)

Vic·to′ri·an *adj.* **1.** of or characteristic of the time of Queen Victoria **2.** showing the respectability, prudery, etc. attributed to the Victorians —*n.* a person of that time

vic·to·ri·ous (vik tôr′ē əs) *adj.* **1.** having won a victory; triumphant **2.** of or bringing about victory

vic·to·ry (vik′tər ē, -trē) *n., pl.* -**ries** [< L. *vincere*, conquer] the winning of a battle, war, or any struggle

vict·uals (vit′′lz) *n.pl.* [< L. *victus*, food] [Dial. or Colloq.] articles of food

vi·cu·ña (vi kōōn′yə, -ə) *n.* [Sp.] **1.** a S.American animal related to the llama **2.** its soft, shaggy wool

†vi·de (vī′dē) [L.] see; refer to (a certain page, etc.): abbrev. *v.*, vid.

vid·e·o (vid′ē ō) *adj.* [L., I see] **1.** of television **2.** of the picture portion of a telecast **3.** of data display on a computer terminal —*n.* **1.** same as TELEVISION **2.** *clipped form of* VIDEOCASSETTE, VIDEOTAPE, etc.

VICUÑA

vid′e·o′cas·sette′ *n.* a cassette containing videotape

videocassette recorder a device for the recording or playback of videocassettes: also **video recorder**

vid′e·o·disc′ (-disk′) *n.* a disc on which images and sounds can be recorded for reproduction on a TV set

video game an electronic device for producing images on a TV screen, controlled by players of various games

vid′e·o·phone′ *n.* a telephone combined with television so that users can see, as well as speak with, one another

vid′e·o·tape′ *n.* a magnetic tape on which images and sounds can be recorded for reproduction on TV —*vt.* -**taped′**, -**tap′ing** to so record

vie (vī) *vi.* **vied**, **vy′ing** [< L. *invitare*, invite] to struggle for superiority (*with* someone); compete

Vi·en·na (vē en'ə) capital of Austria: pop. 1,628,000 —**Vi·en·nese** (vē'ə nēz') *adj., n., pl.* **-nese**

Vi·et·nam (vē'ət näm') country on the E coast of Indochina: 129,607 sq. mi.; pop. 43,752,000 —**Vi'et·nam·ese'** (-nə mēz') *adj., n., pl.* **-ese**

view (vyōō) *n.* [< L. *videre*, to see] 1. a seeing or looking, as in inspection 2. range of vision 3. mental survey /a correct *view* of a situation/ 4. *a)* a scene or prospect /a room with a *view*/ *b)* a picture of such a scene 5. manner of regarding something; opinion —*vt.* 1. to inspect; scrutinize 2. to see; behold 3. to survey mentally; consider —**in view** 1. in sight 2. under consideration 3. as a goal or hope —**in view of** because of —**on view** displayed publicly —**with a view to** with the purpose or hope of

view'er *n.* 1. a person who views something 2. an optical device for individual viewing of slides

view'find'er *n. same as* FINDER (sense 2)

view'point' *n.* the mental position from which things are viewed and judged; point of view

vig·il (vij'əl) *n.* [< L., awake] 1. *a)* a watchful staying awake *b)* a watch kept 2. the eve of a church festival

vig·i·lant (vij'ə lənt) *adj.* [< L. *vigil*, awake] staying watchful or alert to danger or trouble —**vig'i·lance** *n.*

vig·i·lan·te (vij'ə lan'tē) *n.* [Sp., watchman] one of an unauthorized group organized professedly to keep order and punish crime —**vig'i·lan·tism** *n.* —**vig'i·lan'tist** *adj.*

vi·gnette (vin yet') *n.* [Fr. < *vigne*, vine] 1. an ornamental design used as a border, inset, etc. on a page 2. a picture shading off gradually at the edges 3. a short, delicate literary sketch —**vi·gnet'tist** *n.*

vig·or (vig'ər) *n.* [L. < *vigere*, be strong] active force or strength; vitality; energy: Brit. **vigour** —**vig'or·ous** *adj.* —**vig'or·ous·ly** *adv.*

vik·ing (vī'kiŋ) *n.* [ON. *vikingr*] [*also* V-] any of the Scandinavian pirates of the 8th to 10th centuries

vile (vīl) *adj.* [< L. *vilis*, cheap, base] 1. morally evil; wicked 2. repulsive; disgusting 3. degrading; mean 4. highly disagreeable; very bad [*vile* weather] —**vile'ness** *n.*

vil·i·fy (vil'ə fī') *vt.* **-fied', -fy'ing** [see prec. & -FY] to use abusive language about or of; defame —**vil'i·fi·ca'tion** *n.*

vil·la (vil'ə) *n.* [It. < L., a farm] a country house or estate, esp. a large one used as a retreat

vil·lage (vil'ij) *n.* [see prec.] 1. a community smaller than a town 2. the people of a village, collectively —**vil'lag·er** *n.*

vil·lain (vil'ən) *n.* [< VL. *villanus*, a farm servant] a wicked or evil person, or such a character in a play, etc. —**vil'lain·ous** *adj.*

vil'lain·y *n., pl.* **-ies** 1. wickedness; evil 2. a villainous act

vil·lein (vil'ən) *n.* [see VILLAIN] an English serf in the late Middle Ages who was a freeman in some ways

vim (vim) *n.* [prob. echoic] vigor

tvin (van; *Anglicized* vin) *n.* [Fr.] wine

Vin·ci (vin'chē), **Le·o·nar·do da** (lē'ə när'dō də) 1452–1519; It. painter, sculptor, & scientist

vin·di·cate (vin'də kāt') *vt.* **-cat'ed, -cat'ing** [< L. *vis*, force + *dicere*, say] 1. to clear from criticism, blame, etc. 2. to defend against opposition 3. to justify —**vin'di·ca'tion** *n.* —**vin'di·ca'tor** *n.*

vin·dic·tive (vin dik'tiv) *adj.* [see prec.] 1. revengeful in spirit 2. said or done in revenge —**vin·dic'tive·ly** *adv.* —**vin·dic'tive·ness** *n.*

vine (vīn) *n.* [< L. *vinum*, wine] 1. a plant with a long, thin stem that grows along the ground or climbs a support 2. the stem of such a plant 3. a grapevine

vin·e·gar (vin'i gər) *n.* [< MFr. < *vin*, wine + *aigre*, sour] a sour liquid made by fermenting cider, wine, etc. and used as a condiment and preservative —**vin'e·gar·y** *adj.*

vine·yard (vin'yərd) *n.* land devoted to cultivating grapevines

tvi·no (vē'nō) *n.* [It. & Sp.] wine

tvin rosé [Fr.] *same as* ROSÉ

vin·tage (vin'tij) *n.* [< L. *vinum*, wine + *demere*, remove] 1. the crop of grapes of a single season 2. the wine of a particular region and year 3. an earlier model /a car of prewar *vintage*/ —*adj.* 1. of choice vintage [*vintage* wine] 2. representative of the best [*vintage* short stories] 3. of a past period [*vintage* clothes]

vint·ner (vint'nər) *n.* [< ME. < L. *vinum*, wine] a wine merchant

vi·nyl (vī'n'l) *n.* [< L. *vinum*, wine] any of various compounds polymerized to form resins and plastics (**vinyl plastics**)

vi·ol (vī'əl) *n.* [< OPr. *viula* < ?] any of an early family of stringed instruments, usually having six strings, frets, and a flat back

vi·o·la (vē ō'lə, vī-) *n.* [It.] a stringed instrument of the violin family, slightly larger than a violin

vi·o·la·ble (vī'ə lə b'l) *adj.* that can be, or is likely to be, violated

vi·o·late (vī'ə lāt') *vt.* **-lat'ed, -lat'ing** [< L. *violare*, use violence] 1. to break (a law, promise, etc.) 2. to rape 3. to desecrate (something sacred) 4. to break in upon; disturb —**vi'o·la'tor** *n.*

vi·o·la·tion (-lā'shən) *n.* a violating or being violated; specif., *a)* infringement, as of a law *b)* rape *c)* desecration of something sacred *d)* disturbance

vi·o·lence (-ləns) *n.* [< L. *violentus*, violent] 1. physical force used so as to injure 2. powerful force, as of a hurricane 3. a violent act or deed 4. harm done by violating rights, etc.

vi·o·lent *adj.* 1. acting with or having great physical force 2. caused by violence 3. furious [*violent* language] 4. intense; extreme; very strong [a *violent* storm] —**vi'o·lent·ly** *adv.*

vi·o·let (vī′ə lit) *n.* [< L. *viola*] **1.** a plant with white, blue, purple, or yellow flowers **2.** a bluish-purple color —*adj.* bluish-purple

vi·o·lin (vī′ə lin′) *n.* [< It. *viola*, viol] any instrument of the modern family of four-stringed instruments played with a bow; specif., the smallest and highest pitched instrument of this family —**vi′o·lin′ist** *n.*

vi·ol·ist (vī′əl ist; *for 2* vē ō′list) *n.* **1.** a viol player **2.** a viola player

vi·o·lon·cel·lo (vē′ə län chel′ō, vī′ə lən-) *n., pl.* **-los** *same as* CELLO

VIP, V.I.P. [Colloq.] very important person

vi·per (vī′pər) *n.* [OFr. < L.] **1.** a venomous snake **2.** a malicious or treacherous person —**vi′per·ous** *adj.*

vi·ra·go (vi rä′gō, vī rä′-) *n., pl.* **-goes, -gos** [< L. *vir*, a man] a quarrelsome, shrewish woman; scold

vi·ral (vī′rəl) *adj.* of, involving, or caused by a virus

vir·e·o (vir′ē ō′) *n., pl.* **-os′** [L.] a small American songbird, with olive-green or gray plumage

Vir·gil (vur′jəl) 70–19 B.C.: Rom. poet; wrote the *Aeneid*: also **Vergil**

vir·gin (vur′jin) *n.* [< L. *virgo*, a maiden] a person, esp. a young woman, who has never had sexual intercourse —*adj.* **1.** being a virgin **2.** chaste; modest **3.** untouched, unused, pure, etc. —**the Virgin** Mary, the mother of Jesus

vir′gi·nal *adj. same as* VIRGIN

Vir·gin·ia (vur jin′yə) Southern State of the U.S.: 40,815 sq. mi.; pop. 5,346,000; cap. Richmond —**Vir·gin′ian** *adj., n.*

Virginia creeper *same as* WOODBINE (sense 2)

Virginia reel an American reel danced by couples facing in two lines

Virgin Islands group of islands in the West Indies, divided between those forming a Brit. colony & those constituting a U.S. territory

vir·gin·i·ty (vər jin′ə tē) *n.* a virgin state; maidenhood, chastity, etc.

Virgin Mary the mother of Jesus

Vir·go (vur′gō) [L., virgin] the sixth sign of the zodiac

vir·gule (vur′gyōōl) *n.* [< L. *virgula*, small rod] a diagonal line (/) used in dates or fractions (3/8) and also standing for "or" (and/or), "per" (feet/second), etc.

vir·ile (vir′əl) *adj.* [< L. *vir*, a man] **1.** of or characteristic of a man; masculine **2.** having manly strength or vigor **3.** capable of copulation —**vi·ril·i·ty** (vi ril′ə tē) *n.*

vi·rol·o·gy (vī räl′ə jē) *n.* [< VIR(US) + -LOGY] the study of viruses and virus diseases —**vi·rol′o·gist** *n.*

vir·tu·al (vur′choo wəl) *adj.* being so in effect, although not in actual fact or name —**vir′tu·al·ly** *adv.*

vir·tue (vur′chōō) *n.* [< L. *virtus*, manliness, worth] **1.** general moral excellence **2.** a specific moral quality regarded as good **3.** chastity **4.** *a)* excellence in general *b)* a good quality **5.** efficacy, as of a medicine —**by** (or **in**) **virtue of** because of

vir·tu·o·so (vur′choo wō′sō) *n., pl.* **-sos, -si** (-sē) [It., skilled] a person with great technical skill in some fine art, esp. in playing music —**vir′tu·os′i·ty** (-wäs′ə tē) *n.*

vir·tu·ous (vur′choo wəs) *adj.* **1.** having, or characterized by, moral virtue **2.** chaste: said of a woman —**vir′tu·ous·ly** *adv.* —**vir′tu·ous·ness** *n.*

vir·u·lent (vir′yoo lənt, -oo-) *adj.* [see ff.] **1.** *a)* extremely poisonous; deadly *b)* bitterly antagonistic; full of hate **2.** *Med. a)* violent and rapid in its course: said of a disease *b)* highly infectious —**vir′u·lence** *n.*

vi·rus (vī′rəs) *n.* [L., a poison] **1.** any of a group of very small infective agents that cause various diseases, as measles **2.** a harmful influence

vi·sa (vē′zə) *n.* [< L. *videre*, see] an endorsement on a passport, granting entry into a country

vis·age (viz′ij) *n.* [see prec.] **1.** the face; countenance **2.** aspect; look

vis-à-vis (vē′zə vē′) *adv., prep.* [Fr.] face to face; opposite —*prep.* **1.** opposite to **2.** in relation to

vis·cer·a (vis′ər ə) *n.pl., sing.* **vis′cus** (-kəs) [L.] the internal organs of the body, as the heart, lungs, intestines, etc.

vis′cer·al *adj.* **1.** of the viscera **2.** intuitive, emotional, etc. rather than intellectual

vis·cid (vis′id) *adj.* [< L. *viscum*, birdlime] thick, syrupy, and sticky

vis·cose (vis′kōs) *n.* [see VISCOUS] a syruplike solution of cellulose, used in making rayon, cellophane, etc.

vis·cos·i·ty (vis käs′ə tē) *n., pl.* **-ties** **1.** a viscous quality **2.** *Physics* the resistance of a fluid to flowing freely, caused by friction of its molecules

vis·count (vī′kount) *n.* [see VICE- & COUNT²] a nobleman next below an earl or count and above a baron —**vis′count·ess** *n.fem.*

vis·cous (vis′kəs) *adj.* [see VISCID] **1.** thick, syrupy, and sticky **2.** *Physics* having viscosity

vise (vīs) *n.* [< L. *vitis*, vine, lit., that which winds] a device having two jaws opened and closed as by a screw, used for holding firmly an object being worked on

Vish·nu (vish′nōō) the second member of the Hindu trinity (Brahma, Vishnu, and Siva), called "the Preserver"

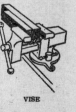

VISE

vis·i·bil·i·ty (viz'ə bil'ə tē) *n.*, *pl.* **-ties 1.** a being visible **2.** *a)* the relative possibility of being seen under the prevailing conditions of distance, light, etc. *b)* range of vision

vis·i·ble (viz'ə b'l) *adj.* [< L. *videre*, to see] **1.** that can be seen **2.** evident —**vis'i·bly** *adv.*

vi·sion (vizh'ən) *n.* [< L. *videre*, to see] **1.** the power of seeing **2.** something supposedly seen in a dream, trance, etc. **3.** a mental image **4.** the ability to foresee something as through mental acuteness **5.** something or someone of great beauty

vi·sion·ar·y (-er'ē) *adj.* **1.** seen in a vision **2.** not realistic; impractical *[visionary schemes]* —*n.*, *pl.* **-ies 1.** one who sees visions **2.** one whose ideas, etc. are impractical

vis·it (viz'it) *vt.* [< L. *videre*, to see] **1.** to go or come to see **2.** to stay with as a guest **3.** to afflict or trouble —*vi.* **1.** to make a visit, esp. a social call **2.** [Colloq.] to chat —*n.* a visiting; specif., *a)* a social call *b)* a stay as a guest

vis'it·ant (-ənt) *n.* a visitor

vis·it·a·tion (-ə tā'shən) *n.* **1.** an official visit as to inspect **2.** a reward or punishment, as sent by God

vis'i·tor *n.* a person making a visit

vi·sor (vī'zər) *n.* [< OFr. *vis*, a face] **1.** the movable part of a helmet, covering the face **2.** a projecting brim, as on a cap, for shading the eyes

vis·ta (vis'tə) *n.* [< L. *videre*, to see] **1.** a view, esp. as seen through a long passage **2.** a mental view of events

vis·u·al (vizh'оо wəl) *adj.* [< L. *videre*, to see] **1.** of or used in seeing **2.** based on the use of sight **3.** that can be seen; visible

vis'u·al·ize' *vt.*, *vi.* **-ized', -iz'ing** to form a mental image of (something not present to the sight) —**vis'u·al·i·za'tion** *n.*

vi·tal (vīt''l) *adj.* [< L. *vita*, life] **1.** of or concerned with life **2.** essential to life **3.** fatal **4.** *a)* essential; indispensable *b)* very important **5.** full of life; energetic —*n.* [*pl.*] **1.** the vital organs, as heart, brain, etc. **2.** any essential parts —**vi'tal·ly** *adv.*

vital capacity the volume of air one can forcibly expel from the lungs after taking a full breath

vi·tal·i·ty (vī tal'ə tē) *n.*, *pl.* **-ties 1.** power to live **2.** power to endure **3.** mental or physical vigor

vi·tal·ize (vīt''l īz') *vt.* **-ized', -iz'-ing** to make vital; give life or vigor to

vital signs the pulse, respiration, and body temperature

vital statistics data on births, deaths, marriages, etc.

vi·ta·min (vīt'ə min) *n.* [< L. *vita*, life] any of certain complex substances found variously in foods and essential to good health: some of the important vitamins are: —**vitamin A**, a fat-soluble alcohol found in fish-liver oil, egg yolk, carrots, etc.: a deficiency of this results in imperfect vision in the dark —**vitamin B (complex)** a group of unrelated water-soluble substances including *a)* **vitamin B₁** (see THIA-

MINE) *b)* **vitamin B₂** (see RIBOFLAVIN) *c)* NICOTINIC ACID *d)* **vitamin B₁₂** a vitamin containing cobalt, used in treating anemia —**vitamin C** a compound occurring in citrus fruits, tomatoes, etc.: a deficiency of this produces scurvy —**vitamin D** any of several fat-soluble vitamins found esp. in fish-liver oils, milk, etc.: a deficiency of this produces rickets —**vitamin E** a substance occurring in wheat germ, etc., vital to the reproductive processes in some animals —**vitamin K** a substance occurring in green vegetables, fish meal, etc., that clots blood

vi·ti·ate (vish'ē āt') *vt.* **-at'ed, -at'-ing** [< L. *vitium*, a vice] **1.** to spoil; corrupt; pervert **2.** to invalidate (a contract, etc.) —**vi'ti·a'tion** *n.*

vit·i·cul·ture (vit'ə kul'chər) *n.* [< L. *vitis*, vine] cultivation of grapes

vit·re·ous (vit'rē əs) *adj.* [< L. *vitrum*, glass] **1.** of or like glass **2.** derived from or made of glass

vitreous humor the transparent, jellylike substance filling the eyeball between the retina and the lens

vit·ri·fy (vit'rə fī') *vt.*, *vi.* **-fied', -fy'ing** [< L. *vitrum*, glass + Fr. *-fier*, -FY] to change into glass or a glasslike substance by heat

vit·rine (vi trēn') *n.* [see VITREOUS] a glass or glass-paneled display case

vit·ri·ol (vit'rē əl) *n.* [< L. *vitreus*, glassy] **1.** any of several sulfates of metals, as of copper (*blue vitriol*), or iron (*green vitriol*) **2.** same as SULFURIC ACID **3.** sharp or bitter speech, etc. — **vit'ri·ol'ic** (-äl'ik) *adj.*

vi·tu·per·ate (vī tōo'pə rāt', vi-) *vt.* **-at'ed, -at'ing** [< L. *vitium*, fault + *parare*, prepare] to speak abusively to or about —**vi·tu'per·a'tion** *n.* — **vi·tu'per·a'tive** *adj.*

†vi·va (vē'vä) *interj.* [It., Sp.] (long) live (someone specified)!

vi·va·ce (vi vä'chä) *adj.*, *adv.* [It.] *Music* in a lively, spirited manner

vi·va·cious (vi vā'shəs, vī-) *adj.* [< L. *vivere*, to live] full of animation; lively —**vi·va'cious·ly** *adv.* —**vi·vac'i·ty** (-vas'ə tē), **vi·va'cious·ness** *n.*

†vive (vēv) *interj.* [Fr.] (long) live (someone specified)!

viv·id (viv'id) *adj.* [< L. *vivere*, to live] **1.** full of life; vigorous **2.** bright; intense, as colors **3.** strong and clear; active *[a vivid imagination]* —**viv'id·ly** *adv.* —**viv'id·ness** *n.*

viv·i·fy (viv'ə fī') *vt.* **-fied', -fy'ing** [< L. *vivus*, alive + *facere*, make] to give life to; animate

vi·vip·a·rous (vī vip'ər əs) *adj.* [< L. *vivus*, alive + *parere*, produce] bearing living young instead of laying eggs

viv·i·sec·tion (viv'ə sek'shən) *n.* [< L. *vivus*, alive + SECTION] surgery performed on a living animal in medical research —**viv'i·sect'** *vt.*, *vi.* —**viv'i·sec'tion·ist** *n.*

vix·en (vik's'n) *n.* [OE. *fyxe*] **1.** a female fox **2.** an ill-tempered, shrewish, or malicious woman —**vix'en·ish** *adj.* —**vix'en·ish·ly** *adv.*

viz., viz (viz) [< L. *videlicet*] that is; namely

vi·zier, vi·zir (vi zir′) *n.* [< Ar. *wazara*, bear a burden] in Moslem countries, a high government official

viz·or (vī′zər) *n. alt. sp. of* VISOR

VLF, vlf very low frequency

vo·cab·u·lar·y (vō kab′yə ler′ē) *n., pl.* **-ies** [ult. < L. *vocare*, to call] 1. a list of words, etc., as in a dictionary or glossary 2. all the words used in a language or by a person, class, etc.

vo·cal (vō′k'l) *adj.* [< L. *vox*, a voice] 1. of or produced by the voice 2. sung 3. capable of making oral sounds 4. speaking freely —**vo′cal·ly** *adv.*

vocal cords membranous folds in the larynx that vibrate to produce voice

vo·cal·ic (vō kal′ik) *adj.* of, like, or involving a vowel or vowels

vo′cal·ist *n.* a singer

vo′cal·ize′ (-īz′) *vt., vi.* **-ized′, -iz′ing** to utter, speak, or sing

vo·ca·tion (vō kā′shən) *n.* [< L. *vocare*, to call] 1. the career to which one feels he is called 2. any occupation —**vo·ca′tion·al** *adj.*

voc·a·tive (väk′ə tiv) *adj.* [see prec.] *Gram.* designating the case indicating the one addressed

vo·cif·er·ate (vō sif′ə rāt′) *vt., vi.* **-at′ed, -at′ing** [< L. *vox*, voice + *ferre*, to bear] to shout loudly; clamor —**vo·cif·er·a′tion** *n.*

vo·cif·er·ous (vō sif′ər əs) *adj.* noisy; clamorous —**vo·cif′er·ous·ly** *adv.*

vod·ka (väd′kə) *n.* [Russ. < *voda*, water] a colorless alcoholic liquor distilled from wheat, rye, etc.

vogue (vōg) *n.* [Fr.] 1. the fashion at any particular time 2. popularity

voice (vois) *n.* [< L. *vox*] 1. sound made through the mouth, esp. by human beings 2. the ability to make such sounds 3. anything regarded as like vocal utterance 4. an expressed wish, opinion, etc. 5. the right to express one's wish, etc.; vote 6. utterance or expression 7. *Gram.* a form of a verb showing it as active or passive 8. *Music a)* singing ability *b)* any of the parts in a composition —*vt.* **voiced, voic′ing** to give utterance or expression to —**with one voice** unanimously —**voice′less** *adj.*

voice′-o′ver *n.* the voice of an unseen announcer or narrator as on TV

void (void) *adj.* [< L. *vacare*, be empty] 1. containing nothing 2. devoid (*of*) [*void* of sense] 3. ineffective; useless 4. of no legal force —*n.* 1. an empty space 2. a feeling of emptiness —*vt.* 1. to empty out 2. to make void; annul —**void′a·ble** *adj.*

‡voi·là (vwä lä′) [Fr.] behold; there it is: often used as an interjection

voile (voil) *n.* [Fr., a veil] a thin, sheer fabric, as of cotton

vol. *pl.* **vols.** volume

vol·a·tile (väl′ə t'l) *adj.* [< L. *volare*, to fly] 1. evaporating quickly 2. unstable or fickle —**vol′a·til′i·ty** (-til′ə tē) *n.* —**vol′a·til·ize′** (-īz′) *vt., vi.* **-ized′, -iz′ing**

vol·can·ic (väl kan′ik) *adj.* 1. of or caused by a volcano 2. like a volcano; violently explosive

vol·ca·no (väl kā′nō) *n., pl.* **-noes, -nos** [< L. *Volcanus*, Vulcan] 1. a vent in the earth's crust through which molten rock, ashes, etc. are ejected 2. a cone-shaped mountain of this material built up around the vent

Vol·ga (väl′gə, vōl′-) river in W R.S.F.S.R.

vo·li·tion (vō lish′ən) *n.* [ult. < L. *velle*, be willing] the act or power of using the will —**vo·li′tion·al** *adj.*

vol·ley (väl′ē) *n., pl.* **-leys** [< L. *volare*, to fly] 1. the simultaneous discharge of a number of weapons 2. the missiles so discharged 3. a rapid burst of words, etc. 4. *Tennis*, etc. a return of a ball, etc. before it touches the ground —*vt., vi.* **-leyed, -ley·ing** 1. to discharge or be discharged as in a volley 2. *Sports* to return (the ball, etc.) as a volley

vol′ley·ball′ *n.* 1. a team game played by hitting a large, light, inflated ball back and forth over a net with the hands 2. the ball

vol·plane (väl′plān′) *vi.* **-planed′, -plan′ing** [< Fr. *voler*, to fly + *planer*, to glide] to glide down, as an airplane with the engine cut off

volt (vōlt) *n.* [< A. *Volta* (1745-1827), It. physicist] the unit of electromotive force

volt·age (vōl′tij) *n.* electromotive force expressed in volts

vol·ta·ic (väl tā′ik, vōl-) *adj.* of or producing electricity by chemical action [a *voltaic* battery]

Vol·taire (vōl ter′, väl-) 1694-1778; Fr. writer and philosopher

volt·me·ter (vōlt′mēt′ər) *n.* an instrument for measuring voltage

vol·u·ble (väl′yoo b'l) *adj.* [< L. *volvere*, to roll] characterized by a great flow of words; talkative —**vol′u·bil′i·ty** *n.* —**vol′u·bly** *adv.*

vol·ume (väl′yoom) *n.* [< L. *volumen*, scroll] 1. *a)* a book *b)* one of a set of books 2. the amount of space occupied in three dimensions 3. *a)* a quantity, bulk, or amount *b)* a large quantity 4. the loudness of sound

vo·lu·mi·nous (və lōō′mə nəs) *adj.* 1. producing or consisting of enough to fill volumes 2. large; bulky; full —**vo·lu′mi·nous·ly** *adv.*

vol·un·ta·rism (väl′ən tər iz′m) *n.* voluntary participation in a certain action, or a system based on this

vol·un·tar·y (-ter′ē) *adj.* [< L. *voluntas*, free will] 1. brought about by one's own free choice 2. acting of one's own accord 3. intentional; not accidental 4. controlled by one's mind or will —**vol′un·tar′i·ly** *adv.*

vol′un·tar′y·ism *n.* the theory or system of support of churches, schools, etc. by voluntary contributions only

vol·un·teer (väl′ən tir′) *n.* one who offers to enter into service, as military service, of his own free will —*adj.* **1.** of volunteers **2.** voluntary —*vt.* to offer or give of one's own free will —*vi.* to offer to enter into any service of one's own free will

vo·lup·tu·ar·y (və lup′chōō wer′ē) *n., pl.* **-ies** [< L. *voluptas*, pleasure] one devoted to sensual pleasures

vo·lup·tu·ous (-chōō wəs) *adj.* full of, producing, or fond of sensual pleasures —**vo·lup′tu·ous·ness** *n.*

vo·lute (və lōōt′) *n.* [< L. *volvere*, to roll] a spiral or whorl

vom·it (väm′it) *n.* [< L. *vomere*, to vomit] matter ejected from the stomach through the mouth —*vt., vi.* **1.** to eject (the contents of the stomach) through the mouth; throw up **2.** to discharge or be discharged with force

voo·doo (vōō′dōō) *n., pl.* **-doos** [of W Afr. origin] **1.** a primitive religion in the West Indies, based on a belief in sorcery, etc. **2.** a charm, fetish, etc. used in voodoo —*vt.* to affect by voodoo magic —**voo′doo·ism** *n.*

vo·ra·cious (vō rā′shəs) *adj.* [< L. *vorare*, devour] **1.** greedy in eating; ravenous **2.** very eager [a *voracious* reader] —**vo·rac′i·ty** (-ras′ə tē) *n.*

vor·tex (vôr′teks) *n., pl.* **-tex·es, -ti·ces′** (-tə sēz′) [L.: see VERTEX] **1.** a whirlpool **2.** a whirlwind **3.** anything like a whirl in its rush, catastrophic power, etc.

vo·ta·ry (vōt′ə rē) *n., pl.* **-ries** [< L. *vovere*, to vow] **1.** one bound by a vow, esp. by religious vows **2.** one devoted to a cause, study, etc.

vote (vōt) *n.* [< L. *votum*, a vow] **1.** a decision on a proposal, etc., or a choice between candidates for office **2.** *a)* the expression of such a decision or choice *b)* a ballot, etc. by which it is expressed **3.** the right to vote **4.** votes collectively —*vi.* **vot′ed, vot′ing** to give or cast a vote —*vt.* to decide or enact by vote —**vot′er** *n.*

vo·tive (vōt′iv) *adj.* [see prec.] given, done, etc. in fulfillment of a vow

vouch (vouch) *vi.* [< L. *vocare*, to call] to give, or serve as, assurance, a guarantee, etc. (*for*) [to *vouch* for one's honesty]

vouch′er *n.* **1.** one who vouches **2.** a paper serving as evidence or proof, as a receipt

vouch·safe′ *vt.* **-safed′, -saf′ing** [< ME. *vouchen safe*, vouch as safe] to condescend to give or grant

vow (vou) *n.* [< L. *votum*] **1.** a solemn promise, esp. one made to God **2.** a promise of love and fidelity [marriage *vows*] —*vt.* to promise or declare solemnly —*vi.* to make a vow —**take vows** to enter a religious order

vow·el (vou′əl) *n.* [< L. *vocalis*, vocal] **1.** a speech sound in which the air passes in a continuous stream through the open mouth **2.** a letter representing such a sound, as *a, e, i, o, u*

voy·age (voi′ij) *n.* [< L. *via*, way] **1.** a relatively long journey, esp. by water **2.** a journey by aircraft or spacecraft —*vi., vt.* **-aged, -ag·ing** to make a voyage (over or on) —**voy′ag·er** *n.*

†**vo·ya·geur** (vwà yà zhër′) *n., pl.* **-geurs′** (-zhër′) [Fr., a traveler] a woodsman or boatman of Canada

vo·yeur (vwä yur′) *n.* [Fr. < L. *videre*, see] one who has an excessive interest in sexual objects or activities —**vo·yeur′ism** *n.* —**vo′yeur·is′tic** *adj.*

V.P., VP Vice-President

vs. versus

V/STOL [*v*(ertical or) *s*(hort) *t*(ake)-*o*(ff and) *l*(anding)] an aircraft that can take off and land either vertically or on a short airstrip

Vt., VT Vermont

vt., v.t. transitive verb

VTOL [*v*(ertical) *t*(ake)*o*(ff and) *l*(anding)] an aircraft that can take off and land vertically

Vul·can (vul′k'n) the Roman god of fire and of metalworking

vul·can·ite (vul′kə nīt′) *n.* [prec. + -ITE] a hard rubber

vul′can·ize′ *vt., vi.* **-ized′, -iz′ing** to treat (crude rubber) with sulfur under heat to increase its strength and elasticity —**vul′can·i·za′tion** *n.*

Vulg. Vulgate

vul·gar (vul′gər) *adj.* [< L. *vulgus*, common people] **1.** of people in general; popular **2.** vernacular **3.** lacking culture, taste, etc.; crude; boorish **4.** obscene —**vul′gar·ly** *adv.*

vul·gar′i·an (-ger′ē ən) *n.* a rich person with coarse, vulgar tastes

vul′gar·ism *n.* **1.** a word, phrase, etc. used widely but regarded as nonstandard, coarse, or obscene **2.** vulgarity

vul·gar′i·ty (-gar′ə tē) *n.* **1.** a being vulgar **2.** *pl.* **-ties** a vulgar act, habit, usage in speech, etc.

vul·gar·ize (vul′gə rīz′) *vt.* **-ized′, -iz′ing 1.** to make popular **2.** to make vulgar, coarse, obscene, etc. —**vul′gar·iz′er** *n.*

Vulgar Latin the everyday Latin spoken by ancient Romans as distinguished from standard written Latin

Vul·gate (vul′gāt) *n.* [ML. *vulgata* (*editio*), popular (edition)] **1.** a Latin version of the Bible, used in the Roman Catholic Church **2.** [v-] the vernacular

vul·ner·a·ble (vul′nər ə b'l) *adj.* [< L. *vulnus*, a wound] **1.** that can be wounded or injured **2.** open to, or easily hurt by, criticism or attack **3.** *Bridge* subject to increased penalties and bonuses —**vul′ner·a·bil′i·ty** *n.* —**vul′ner·a·bly** *adv.*

vul·pine (vul′pīn) *adj.* [< L. *vulpes*, a fox] of or like a fox; cunning

vul·ture (vul′chər) *n.* [< L. *vultur*] **1.** a large bird that lives chiefly on carrion **2.** a greedy, ruthless person —**vul′tur·ous** *adj.*

vul·va (vul′və) *n.* [L., womb] the external genital organs of the female

vy·ing (vī′iŋ) *adj.* that vies

VULTURE

W

W, w (dub'l yōō) *n., pl.* **W's, w's** the 23d letter of the English alphabet

W *Chem.* tungsten

W, w watt(s)

W., W., w, w. 1. west **2.** western

W. 1. Wednesday **2.** Welsh

W., w. 1. watt(s) **2.** weight **3.** width

w. 1. week(s) **2.** wide **3.** wife **4.** with

WA Washington (State)

wab·ble (wäb'l) *n., vi., vt.* **-bled, -bling** *var. of* WOBBLE

Wac (wak) *n.* a member of the Women's Army Corps (**WAC**)

wack·y (wak'ē) *adj.* **-i·er, -i·est** [< ?] [Slang] erratic; eccentric; irrational

wad (wäd, wôd) *n.* [ML. *wadda*, wadding] **1.** a small, soft mass, as of cotton or paper **2.** a lump or small, compact roll —*vt.* **wad'ded, wad'ding 1.** to compress, or roll up, into a wad **2.** to plug or stuff with a wad or wadding

wad'ding *n.* any soft material for use in padding, packing, etc.

wad·dle (wäd'l, wôd'-) *vi.* **-dled, -dling** [< ff.] to walk with short steps, swaying from side to side, as a duck —*n.* a waddling gait

wade (wād) *vi.* **wad'ed, wad'ing** [< OE. *waden*, go] **1.** to walk through any resisting substance, as water, mud, etc. **2.** to proceed with difficulty [to *wade* through a dull book] **3.** [Colloq.] to attack with vigor (with *in* or *into*) —*vt.* to cross by wading

wad·er (wād'ər) *n.* **1.** one who wades **2.** *same as* WADING BIRD **3.** [*pl.*] high waterproof boots, often with trousers

wa·di (wä'dē) *n., pl.* **-dis, -dies** [Ar. *wādī*] in N Africa, a river valley that is usually dry

wading bird a long-legged shore bird that wades the shallows and marshes for food

wa·fer (wā'fər) *n.* [< MDu. *wafel*] **1.** a thin, flat, crisp cracker or cookie **2.** any disklike thing resembling this

waf·fle (wäf'l) *n.* [see prec.] a crisp batter cake baked in a waffle iron

waffle iron a utensil with two flat, studded plates pressed together so that the waffle bakes between them

waft (waft) *vt., vi.* [< Du. *wachter*, watcher] to move or carry (sounds, odors, etc.) lightly through the air or over water —*n.* **1.** an odor, sound, etc. carried through the air **2.** a gust of wind **3.** a wafting movement

wag[1] (wag) *vi., vt.* **wagged, wag'ging** [prob. < ON. *vaga*] to move rapidly back and forth, up and down, etc. —*n.* a wagging

wag[2] (wag) *n.* [prob. < obs. *waghalter*, joker] a comical person; wit —**wag'ger·y** *n., pl.* **-ies** —**wag'gish** *adj.*

wage (wāj) *vt.* **waged, wag'ing** [< OFr. *gage*, a pledge] to engage in or carry on (a war, etc.) —*n.* **1.** [*often pl.*] money paid for work done **2.** [*usually pl.*] what is given in return

wag·er (wā'jər) *n.* [see prec.] a bet —*vt., vi.* to bet

wag·gle (wag'l) *vt., vi.* **-gled, -gling** to wag, esp. with short, quick movements —*n.* a waggling

Wag·ner (väg'nər), **Rich·ard** (rikh'ärt) 1813–83; Ger. composer

wag·on (wag'ən) *n.* [Du. *wagen*] **1.** a four-wheeled vehicle, esp. one for hauling heavy loads **2.** *short for* STATION WAGON **—on** (or **off**) **the wagon** [Slang] no longer (or once again) drinking alcoholic liquor

waif (wāf) *n.* [< ONormFr.] **1.** anything found that is without an owner **2.** a homeless person, esp. a child

wail (wāl) *vi.* [< ON. *væ*, woe] to make a long, loud, sad cry, as in grief or pain —*n.* such a cry

wain·scot (wān'skət, -skät') *n.* [< MDu. *wagenschot*] a paneling of wood, etc. on the walls of a room, sometimes on the lower part only —*vt.* **-scot·ed** or **-scot·ted, -scot·ing** or **-scot·ting** to panel with wood, etc.

wain·wright (wān'rīt') *n.* [*wain* (wagon) + WRIGHT] one who builds wagons

waist (wāst) *n.* [< OE. *weaxan*, grow] **1.** the part of the body between the ribs and the hips **2.** the part of a garment that covers the body from the shoulders to the waistline **3.** a blouse **4.** the narrow part of any object that is wider at the ends

waist'band' *n.* a band fitting around the waist, as on slacks or a skirt

waist·coat (wes'kət, wāst'kōt') *n.* [Brit.] a man's vest

waist·line (wāst'līn') *n.* the line at the narrowest part of the waist

wait (wāt) *vi.* [< ONormFr. *waitier*] **1.** to remain (until something expected happens) **2.** to be ready **3.** to remain undone [it can *wait*] **4.** to serve food at a meal (with *at* or *on*) —*vt.* **1.** to await **2.** [Colloq.] to delay serving (a meal) —*n.* act or period of waiting **—lie in wait** (**for**) to wait so as to catch after planning a trap (*for*) **—wait on** (or **upon**) **1.** to act as a servant to **2.** to serve (a customer) **—wait table** to serve food to people at a table **—wait up** to delay going to bed until someone arrives, etc.

wait'er *n.* one who waits; esp., a man who waits table in a restaurant

wait'ing *adj.* **1.** that waits **2.** of or for a wait —*n.* **1.** the act of one that

waits 2. a period of waiting —**in waiting** in attendance, as on a king
waiting game a strategy by which one wins out over another by delaying action until one has an advantage
waiting list a list of applicants, in order of their application
waiting room a room where people wait, as in a bus station or dentist's office
wait′ress (-ris) n. a woman waiter
waive (wāv) vt. **waived, waiv′ing** [< ON. veifa, fluctuate] 1. to give up or forgo (a right, etc.) 2. to postpone; defer
waiv·er (wā′vər) n. Law a waiving of a right, claim, etc.
wake¹ (wāk) vi. **woke** or **waked, waked** or **wo′ken, wak′ing** [< OE. wacian, be awake & wacan, arise] 1. to come out of sleep; awake (often with up) 2. to stay awake 3. to become active 4. to become alert (to a realization, etc.) —vt. 1. to cause to wake: often with up 2. to arouse (passions, etc.) —n. an all-night vigil over a corpse before burial
wake² (wāk) n. [< ON. vök, hole] the track left in water by a moving ship —**in the wake of** following closely
wake′ful adj. 1. alert; watchful 2. unable to sleep —**wake′ful·ness** n.
wak·en (wāk′'n) vi., vt. to wake
wale (wāl) n. [OE. walu, weal] 1. a welt raised by a whip, etc. 2. a ridge on the surface of cloth —vt. **waled, wal′ing** to mark with wales
Wales (wālz) division of the United Kingdom, west of England: 8,016 sq. mi.; pop. 2,662,000
walk (wôk) vi. [OE. wealcan, to roll] 1. to go on foot at a moderate pace 2. to follow a certain course [to walk in peace] 3. Baseball to go to first base on four balls —vt. 1. to go along, over, etc. on foot 2. to cause (a horse, etc.) to walk 3. to accompany on a walk or stroll [I'll walk you home] 4. Baseball to advance (a batter) to first base by pitching four balls —n. 1. the act or manner of walking 2. a stroll or hike 3. a distance walked [an hour's walk] 4. a sphere of activity, occupation, etc. [people from all walks of life] 5. a path for walking 6. Baseball a walking —**walk away** (or **off**) **with** 1. to steal 2. to win easily —**walk out** to go on strike —**walk out on** [Colloq.] to leave; desert —**walk′er** n.
walk·ie-talk·ie (wôk′ē tôk′ē) n. a compact radio transmitter and receiver that can be carried by one person
walking stick a stick carried when walking; cane
walk′-on′ n. a bit role in which an actor has few if any words to speak
walk′out′ n. a labor strike
walk′up′ n. an apartment house without an elevator
wall (wôl) n. [< L. vallum] 1. an upright structure of wood, stone, etc., serving to enclose, divide, or protect 2. something like a wall as in function —vt. 1. to enclose, divide, etc. with or as with a wall 2. to close up (an opening) with a wall (usually with up)

—**drive** (or **push**) **to the wall** to place in a desperate position —**off the wall** [Slang] 1. insane; crazy 2. very odd or unconventional
wal·la·by (wäl′ə bē) n., pl. **-bies, -by** [< Australian name] a small kangaroo
wal·let (wôl′it) n. [< ?] a flat pocketbook for paper money, cards, etc.
wall·eye (wôl′ī′) n. [< ON. vagl, a beam + eygr, eye] 1. an eye that turns outward, showing much white 2. a fish with large, staring eyes, esp. a N. American freshwater fish of the perch family: in full **wall′eyed′ pike**
wall′flow′er n. [Colloq.] a shy person who merely looks on at a dance
Wal·loon (wä lōōn′) n. 1. any of a people of Celtic descent in S Belgium 2. their French dialect
wal·lop (wäl′əp, wôl′-) vt. [< OFr. galoper, to gallop] [Colloq.] 1. to beat or defeat soundly 2. to strike hard —n. [Colloq.] 1. a hard blow 2. a thrill
wal·low (wäl′ō, wôl′ō) vi. [OE. wealwian, roll around] 1. to roll about, as in mud, etc. 2. to indulge oneself fully (in a specified thing) —n. 1. a wallowing 2. a muddy or dusty place
wall′pa′per n. paper for covering walls —vt. to put wallpaper on or in
Wall Street a street in New York City: financial center of the U.S.
wall′-to-wall′ adj. 1. covering a floor completely 2. [Colloq.] a) pervasive b) comprehensive; all-inclusive
wal·nut (wôl′nut′) n. [< OE. wealh, foreign + hnutu, nut] 1. a tree valued for its nuts and its wood 2. its edible nut with a two-lobed seed 3. its brown wood, used in furniture
wal·rus (wôl′rəs, wäl′-) n. [prob. < ON. hrosshvair, horse whale] a massive sea mammal related to the seals and having two projecting tusks

WALRUS

waltz (wôlts, wôls) n. [< G. walsen, dance about] 1. a ballroom dance for couples in 3/4 time 2. music for this —vi. 1. to dance a waltz 2. to move lightly
wam·pum (wäm′pəm) n. [< Algonquian] shell beads used by N.American Indians as money
wan (wän, wôn) adj. **wan′ner, wan′nest** [OE. wann, dark] 1. sickly pale 2. feeble or weak [a wan smile]
wand (wänd, wônd) n. [ON. vöndr] 1. a staff symbolizing authority 2. a rod of supposed magical power
wan·der (wän′dər, wôn′-) vi. [OE. wandrian] 1. to roam idly about; ramble 2. to stray (from a path, etc.) 3. to go astray; specif., to be disjointed, incoherent, etc. 4. to meander, as a river —vt. to roam in or over —**wan′der·er** n.
wan′der·lust′ (-lust′) n. [G.] an urge to wander or travel
wane (wān) vi. **waned, wan′ing** [OE. wanian, to decrease] 1. to grow gradually less in extent, as the moon after it is full 2. to grow dim, as a light

3. to decline in power, etc.   4. to approach the end —*n.* a waning

wan·gle (waŋ'g'l) *vt.* -**gled**, -**gling** [< ?] [Colloq.] to get or cause by persuasion, tricks, etc.

Wan·kel engine (väŋ'k'l, waŋ'-) [after F. *Wankel* (1902-), G. engineer] a rotary combustion engine with a spinning piston, needing fewer parts and less fuel than used in a turbine engine

want (wänt, wônt) *vt.* [< ON. *vanta*] 1. to lack 2. to crave *[he wants love]* 3. to desire *[he wants to travel]* 4. to wish to see or apprehend *[wanted by the police]* 5. [Chiefly Brit.] to require —*vi.* 1. to have a need or lack (with *for*) 2. to be destitute —*n.* 1. a lack; shortage 2. poverty 3. a craving 4. something needed

want ad [Colloq.] an advertisement for something wanted, as a job, etc.

want·ing *adj.* 1. lacking 2. not up to standard —*prep.* less; minus — **wanting in** deficient in (a quality)

wan·ton (wän't'n, wôn'-) *adj.* [< OE. *wan*, lacking + *teon*, bring up] 1. sexually loose 2. [Poet.] playful 3. unprovoked or malicious 4. recklessly ignoring justice, etc. —*n.* a wanton person; esp., a sexually loose woman — *vi.* to be wanton —**wan'ton·ness** *n.*

wap·i·ti (wäp'ə tē) *n.* [< Algonquian] an elk, the largest N.American deer, with widely branching antlers

war (wôr) *n.* [< ONormFr. *werre*] 1. open armed conflict as between nations 2. any active hostility or struggle 3. military operations as a science —*adj.* of, in, or from war —*vi.* warred, war'ring 1. to carry on war 2. to contend; strive —**at war** in a state of active armed conflict

war·ble (wôr'b'l) *vt., vi.* -**bled**, -**bling** [< ONormFr. *werbler*] to sing (a song, etc.) with trills, quavers, etc., as a bird —*n.* a warbling; trill

war'bler *n.* 1. one that warbles 2. any of various songbirds

ward (wôrd) *vt.* [OE. *weardian*, to guard] to turn aside; fend (*off*) —*n.* 1. a being under guard 2. one under the care of a guardian or court 3. a division of a jail, hospital, etc. 4. a division of a city or town, for purposes of voting, etc.

-ward (wərd) [OE. *-weard*] a suffix meaning in a (specified) direction *[backward]*: also **-wards** (-wərdz)

war·den (wôr'd'n) *n.* [< OFr. *gardein*] 1. one who guards, or has charge of, something *[game warden]* 2. the chief official of a prison

ward·er (wôr'dər) *n.* a watchman

ward heeler a hanger-on of a politician, who solicits votes, etc.

ward·robe (wôrd'rōb') *n.* 1. a closet, cabinet, etc. for holding clothes 2. one's supply of clothes

ward'room' *n.* a room on a warship used by commissioned officers, except the captain, for eating and lounging

ware (wer) *n.* [OE. *waru*] 1. anything for sale: *usually in pl.* 2. pottery

ware'house' *n.* a building where goods are stored —*vt.* -**housed'**, -**hous'ing** to store in a warehouse

war·fare (wôr'fer') *n.* 1. the action of waging war 2. conflict of any kind

war'head' (-hed') *n.* the front part of a torpedo, etc. containing the charge

war'horse' *n.* [Colloq.] one who has been through many struggles; veteran

war·i·ly (wer'ə lē) *adv.* in a wary manner —**war'i·ness** *n.*

war'like' *adj.* 1. fond of or ready for war 2. of war 3. threatening war

war·lock (wôr'läk') *n.* [OE. *wærloga*, liar] the male equivalent of a witch

war'lord' *n.* 1. a warlike high military officer 2. an aggressive local ruler or bandit leader, as formerly in China

warm (wôrm) *adj.* [OE. *wearm*] 1. *a)* having or giving off a moderate degree of heat *b)* hot *[a warm night]* 2. that keeps body heat in *[warm clothing]* 3. ardent; enthusiastic 4. lively, vigorous, etc. 5. quick to anger 6. *a)* genial; cordial *[a warm welcome]* *b)* sympathetic or loving 7. newly made; fresh, as a trail 8. [Colloq.] close to discovering something —*vt., vi.* to make or become warm — **warm up** to practice or exercise, as before playing in a game —**warm'ish** *adj.* —**warm'ly** *adv.*

warm'blood'ed *adj.* having a body temperature that is relatively constant and usually warmer than the surroundings, as mammals and birds

warmed-o·ver (wôrmd'ō'vər) *adj.* 1. reheated 2. presented again, without significant change, as ideas

warm'heart'ed *adj.* kind, sympathetic, friendly, loving, etc.

war'mon'ger (-muŋ'gər, -mäŋ'-) *n.* one who advocates, or tries to cause, war —**war'mon'ger·ing** *adj., n.*

warmth (wôrmth) *n.* 1. *a)* a being warm *b)* mild heat 2. *a)* enthusiasm, ardor, etc. *b)* affectionate feelings

warm'-up' *n.* the act of warming up

warn (wôrn) *vt., vi.* [OE. *wearnian*] 1. to tell of a danger, coming evil, etc. 2. to advise to be wary or cautious 3. to notify in advance; inform

warn·ing *n.* 1. the act of one that warns 2. that which warns —*adj.* that warns

warp (wôrp) *n.* [< OE. *weorpan*, to throw] 1. *a)* a distortion, as a twist or bend, in wood *b)* any similar distortion 2. a mental quirk, bias, etc. 3. *Weaving* the threads running lengthwise in the loom —*vt.* 1. to bend or twist out of shape 2. to distort, pervert, etc. *[a warped mind]* —*vi.* to become bent or twisted

war'path' *n.* the path taken by N.American Indians on a warlike expedition —**on the warpath** 1. ready for war 2. actively angry; ready to fight

war·rant (wôr'ənt, wär'-) *n.* [< OFr. *garant*] 1. *a)* authorization, as by law

---

fat, āpe, cär; ten, ēven; is, bīte; gō, hôrn, tōōl, look; oil, out; up, fur; chin; she; thin, *th*en; zh, leisure; ŋ, ring; ə for *a* in *ago*; ', (ā'b'l); ē, Fr. coeur; ö, Fr. feu; Fr. mon; ü, Fr. duc; kh, G. ich, doch; ‡ foreign; < derived from

b) justification for some act, belief, etc. **2.** something serving as a guarantee of some event or result **3.** *Law* a writ authorizing an arrest, search, etc. —*vt.* **1.** to authorize **2.** to serve as justification for (an act, belief, etc.) **3.** to guarantee

warrant officer a military officer ranking above an enlisted man but below a commissioned officer

war'ran·ty *n., pl.* **-ties** a guarantee (*n. 2a*)

War·ren (wôr′ən, wär′-) city in SE Mich.: pop. 161,000

war·ren (wôr′ən, wär′-) *n.* [< ONorm-Fr. *warir,* to preserve] **1.** an area in which rabbits breed or are numerous **2.** any crowded building or buildings

war·ri·or (wôr′ē ər, wär′-) *n.* [see WAR] a fighting man; soldier

War·saw (wôr′sô) capital of Poland: pop. 1,249,000

war·ship (wôr′ship′) *n.* any ship for combat use, as a battleship

wart (wôrt) *n.* [OE. *wearte*] **1.** a small, usually hard, tumorous growth on the skin **2.** a small protuberance, as on a plant —**wart′y** *adj.*

wart hog a wild African hog with large tusks, and warts below the eyes

war·y (wer′ē) *adj.* **-i·er, -i·est** [OE. *wær,* aware] full of or characterized by caution —**wary** of careful of

was (wuz, wäz) [OE. *wæs*] *1st & 3d pers. sing., pt., of* BE

wash (wôsh, wäsh) *vt.* [OE. *wæscan*] **1.** to clean with water or other liquid **2.** to purify **3.** to wet or moisten **4.** to flow over, past, or against: said of a sea, waves, etc. **5.** to soak (*out*), flush (*off*), or carry (*away*) with water **6.** to erode [with *out* or *away*) [the flood *washed* out the road] **7.** to cover with a thin coating of paint or metal —*vi.* **1.** to wash oneself **2.** to wash clothes **3.** to undergo washing **4.** to be removed by washing (with *out* or *away*) **5.** to be worn or carried (*out* or *away*) by the action of water [the bridge had *washed* out] —*n.* **1.** a washing **2.** a quantity of clothes washed, or to be washed **3.** the rush or surge of water **4.** the eddy of water or air caused by a propeller, etc. **5.** silt, mud, etc. carried and dropped by running water **6.** a thin coating of paint or metal **7.** a liquid for cosmetic or toilet use [*mouth-wash*] —*adj.* that can be washed without damage [a *wash* dress] —**wash down** to follow (food) with a drink — **wash′a·ble** *adj.*

wash′-and-wear′ *adj.* needing little or no ironing after washing

wash′board′ *n.* a ridged board for scrubbing dirt out of clothes

wash′bowl′ *n.* a bowl, esp. a bathroom fixture, for use in washing one's hands, etc.: also **wash′ba′sin**

wash′cloth′ *n.* a small cloth used in washing the body: also **wash′rag′**

washed′-out′ *adj.* **1.** faded [Colloq.] tired; spiritless; pale and wan

washed′-up′ *adj.* **1.** [Colloq.] tired; exhausted **2.** [Slang] finished; done for; having failed

wash′er *n.* **1.** one who washes **2.** a

flat ring of metal, rubber, etc. used to make a seat as for a nut or faucet valve, etc. **3.** a machine for washing

wash′er·wom′an *n., pl.* **-wom′en** a woman whose work is washing clothes

wash′ing *n.* **1.** the act of one that washes **2.** clothes, etc. to be washed

washing machine a machine for washing clothes, etc.

Wash·ing·ton (wôsh′in tən, wäsh′-) **1.** NW State of the U.S.: 68,192 sq. mi.; pop. 4,130,000; cap. Olympia: abbrev. **Wash., WA 2.** capital of the U.S., coextensive with the District of Columbia: pop. 638,000 —**Wash′ing·to′ni·an** (-tō′nē ən) *adj., n.*

Washington, George 1732–99; 1st president of the U.S. (1789–97)

wash′out′ *n.* **1.** a washing away of soil, etc. by water **2.** [Slang] a failure

wash′room′ *n.* **1.** a room for washing **2.** *same as* RESTROOM

wash′stand′ *n.* a table or plumbing fixture with a washbowl, etc.

wash′tub′ *n.* a tub, often with faucets and drain, to wash clothes, etc.

wash′y *adj.* **-i·er, -i·est 1.** watery; diluted **2.** insipid; feeble

was·n′t (wuz′nt, wäz′-) was not

WASP, Wasp (wäsp, wôsp) *n.* a white Anglo-Saxon Protestant

wasp (wäsp, wôsp) *n.* [OE. *wæsp*] a winged insect with a slender body and, in the females and workers, a vicious sting

wasp′ish *adj.* **1.** of or like a wasp **2.** bad-tempered; snappish

was·sail (wäs′'l, -āl) *n.* [< ON. *ves heill,* be hearty] **1.** a former toast in drinking healths **2.** the spiced ale, etc. with which such healths were drunk **3.** a drinking party —*vi., vt.* to drink a wassail (to)

wast·age (wās′tij) *n.* **1.** loss by use, decay, etc. **2.** anything wasted

waste (wāst) *vt.* **wast′ed, wast′ing** [< L. *vastare*] **1.** to devastate; ruin **2.** to wear away **3.** to make weak or emaciated [*wasted* by age] **4.** to use up needlessly; squander **5.** to fail to take advantage of —*vi.* **1.** to lose strength, etc., as by disease **2.** to be used up or worn down gradually —*adj.* **1.** uncultivated or uninhabited; desolate **2.** left over or superfluous **3.** excreted from the body **4.** used for waste —*n.* **1.** uncultivated or uninhabited land **2.** a devastated area **3.** a wasting or being wasted **4.** discarded material, as ashes, etc. **5.** excretions from the body, as urine —**go to waste** to be wasted —**lay waste (to)** to destroy — **wast′er** *n.*

waste′bas′ket *n.* a container for wastepaper, etc.

waste′ful *adj.* characterized by waste; squandering —**waste′ful·ly** *adv.* —**waste′ful·ness** *n.*

waste′land′ *n.* **1.** barren land **2.** unproductive activity

waste′pa′per *n.* paper thrown away after use: also **waste paper**

wast·rel (wās′trəl) *n.* one who wastes; esp., a spendthrift

watch (wäch, wôch) *n.* [OE. *wæcce*] **1.** a keeping awake, esp. in order to guard 2. close observation for a time 3. a guard, or the period of duty of a guard 4. a small timepiece carried in the pocket or worn on the wrist 5. *a)* any of the periods of duty (usually four hours) on shipboard *b)* the crew on duty during such a period —*vi.* 1. to stay awake; keep vigil 2. to be on the alert 3. to look or observe 4. to be looking or waiting attentively (*for*) —*vt.* 1. to guard or tend 2. to observe carefully 3. to wait and look for — **watch oneself** to be careful —**watch out** to be alert or careful —**watch′er** *n.*

watch′band′ *n.* a band of leather, metal, etc. to hold a watch on the wrist

watch′dog′ *n.* 1. a dog kept to guard property 2. one that keeps watch in order to prevent or expose waste, etc.

watch′ful *adj.* watching closely; vigilant; alert —**watch′ful·ly** *adv.*

watch′man (-mən) *n., pl.* -men a person hired to guard property

watch′tow′er *n.* a high tower from which watch is kept, as for forest fires

watch′word′ *n.* 1. a password 2. a slogan or cry of a group, etc.

wa·ter (wôt′ər, wät′-) *n.* [OE. *wæter*] 1. the colorless liquid of rivers, lakes, etc., which falls as rain 2. water with reference to its depth, surface, or level [*above water*] 3. a body secretion, as urine 4. a wavy, lustrous finish given to linen, silk, metal, etc. —*vt.* 1. to give (animals) water to drink 2. to supply (crops, etc.) with water 3. to moisten, soak, or dilute with water 4. to give a wavy luster to (silk, etc.) —*vi.* 1. to fill with tears, as the eyes 2. to secrete saliva [his mouth *watered*] 3. to take on a supply of water 4. to drink water —*adj.* of, for, in, on, near, from, or by water —**hold water** to prove sound, logical, etc.

water bed a heavy vinyl bag filled with water and used as a bed or as a mattress in a special bed frame: also **wa′ter·bed′** *n.*

water buffalo a slow, powerful, oxlike draft animal of S Asia

Wa·ter·bur·y (wôt′ər ber′ē, wät′-) city in WC Conn.: pop. 103,000

water chestnut 1. a Chinese sedge with a nutlike tuber 2. this tuber

water closet a TOILET (sense 3)

wa′ter·col′or *n.* 1. a pigment mixed with water to make a paint 2. a painting done with such paints

wa′ter-cooled′ *adj.* cooled by water circulated around or through it

wa′ter·course′ *n.* 1. a stream, river, etc. 2. a channel for water, as a canal

wa′ter·craft′ *n., pl.* -craft′ a boat, ship, or other water vehicle

wa′ter·cress′ (-kres′) *n.* a plant of the mustard family, growing in water: its leaves are used in salads, etc.

wa′ter·cy′cle (-sī′k'l) *n.* a small watercraft moved by pedals or treadles

wa′ter·fall′ *n.* a steep fall of water, as of a stream, from a height

wa′ter·fowl′ *n.* a water bird, esp. one that swims

wa′ter·front′ *n.* land or docks at the edge of a stream, harbor, etc.

Wa·ter·gate (wôt′ər gāt′, wät′-) *n.* [< *Watergate*, where Dem. Party hdqrs. in Washington were burglarized (June, 1972)] a scandal involving criminal abuses of power by officials —*vt.* -**gat′ed,** -**gat′ing** to deal with in a criminal manner

water glass 1. a drinking glass 2. a silicate of sodium or potassium, dissolved in water to form a syrupy liquid used as a preservative for eggs, etc.

water hole a pond or pool

wa′ter·lil′y *n., pl.* -ies 1. a water plant with large, flat, floating leaves and showy flowers 2. the flower

wa′ter·line′ *n.* the line to which the surface of the water comes on the side of a ship or boat

wa′ter·logged′ (-lôgd′, -lägd′) *adj.* soaked or filled with water so as to be heavy and sluggish, as a boat

WATERLILY

Wa·ter·loo (wôt′ər lōō′, wät′-) town in C Belgium: scene of Napoleon's final defeat (1815) —*n.* any disastrous or decisive defeat

water main a main pipe in a system of pipes for carrying water

wa′ter·mark′ *n.* 1. a mark showing the limit to which water has risen 2. a mark in paper, produced by the impression of a design, as in the mold —*vt.* to mark (paper) with a watermark

wa′ter·mel′on *n.* a large, seedy, green melon with a juicy, red pulp

water moccasin a large, poisonous water snake of the SE U.S.

water pipe 1. a pipe for water 2. a hookah

water polo a water game played with a ball by two teams of swimmers

water power the power of running or falling water, used to drive machinery

wa′ter·proof′ *adj.* that keeps out water, as by being treated with rubber, etc. —*vt.* to make waterproof

wa′ter·re·pel′lent *adj.* that repels water but is not fully waterproof

wa′ter·shed′ (-shed′) *n.* 1. a ridge dividing the areas drained by different river systems 2. the area drained by a river system

wa′ter·side′ *n.* land at the edge of a body of water; shore

wa′ter·ski′ *vi.* -skied′, -ski′ing to be towed on skilike boards (**water skis**) by a line attached to a speedboat

wa′ter·spout′ *n.* 1. a pipe for spouting water 2. a tornado occurring over water, and appearing as a rotating column of air full of spray

water table the level below which the ground is saturated with water

wa·ter·tight *adj.* **1.** so tight that no water can get through **2.** that cannot be misconstrued, nullified, etc.; flawless *[a watertight plan]*

water tower an elevated tank for water storage, etc.

wa·ter·way *n.* **1.** a channel through which water runs **2.** any body of water on which boats, ships, etc. can travel

water wheel a wheel turned by running water, as for power

water wings an inflated device to keep one afloat in the water

wa·ter·works *n.pl.* *[often with sing. v.]* a system of reservoirs, pumps, etc. supplying water to a city

wa·ter·y *adj.* **1.** of or like water **2.** full of water **3.** thin; diluted **4.** tearful **5.** weak —**wa'ter·i·ness** *n.*

WATS (wäts) *n.* *[w(ide) a(rea) t(ele-communications) s(ervice)]* a telephone service that ties a customer into the long-distance network through special lines, at special rates

watt (wät, wôt) *n.* [< James *Watt* (1736–1819), Scot. inventor of steam engine] a unit of electrical power, equal to the power developed in a circuit by a current of one ampere flowing through a potential difference of one volt

watt'age (-ij) *n.* amount of electrical power, expressed in watts

wat·tle (wät''l, wôt'-) *n.* [OE. *watul*] **1.** a woven work of sticks intertwined with twigs or branches **2.** a fleshy flap of skin hanging from the throat of a cock, etc. —*vt.* **-tled, -tling 1.** to intertwine (sticks, twigs, etc.) **2.** to construct of wattle

Wave (wāv) *n.* [orig. < *W(omen) A(ppointed) for) V(oluntary) E(mergency) S(ervice)]* a member of the women's branch of the U.S. Navy **(WAVES)**

wave (wāv) *vi.* **waved, wav'ing** [OE. *wafian*] **1.** to move or sway to and fro **2.** to signal by moving a hand, arm, etc. to and fro **3.** to have the form of a series of curves —*vt.* **1.** to cause to wave **2.** to brandish (a weapon) **3.** *a)* to move or swing (something) as a signal *b)* to signal (something) to (someone) by doing this **4.** to give an undulating form to (hair, etc.) —*n.* **1.** a ridge or swell moving along the surface of the ocean, etc. **2.** an undulation or curve, as in the hair **3.** a motion to and fro, as with the hand in signaling **4.** a thing like a wave in effect; specif., an upsurge *[a crime wave]* **5.** *Physics* a periodic disturbance, as in the propagation of light, sound, etc., that is transmitted progressively through a medium

wave'length *n.* *Physics* the distance, measured in the direction of progression of a wave, from any given point to the next point in the same phase

wave'let (-lit) *n.* a little wave

wa·ver (wā'vər) *vi.* [< ME. *waven*, to *wave*] **1.** to sway to and fro **2.** to show indecision; vacillate **3.** to falter, flicker, or tremble —*n.* a wavering

wav·y (wā'vē) *adj.* **-i·er, -i·est 1.** having or like waves **2.** moving in

a wavelike motion —**wav'i·ness** *n.*

wax¹ (waks) *n.* [OE. *weax*] **1.** a plastic, dull-yellow substance secreted by bees; beeswax **2.** any plastic substance like this, as paraffin —*vt.* to rub, polish, cover, or treat with wax

wax² (waks) *vi.* [OE. *weaxan*, grow] **1.** to increase in strength, size, etc. **2.** to become gradually full: said of the moon **3.** to become *[to wax angry]*

wax bean a variety of bean with long, edible, yellow pods

wax·en (wak's'n) *adj.* **1.** made of wax **2.** like wax; pale, plastic, etc.

wax myrtle an evergreen shrub with grayish-white, wax-coated berries

wax paper a paper made moisture-proof by a wax coating

wax'wing' *n.* a bird with silky-brown plumage and scarlet spines at the ends of the wings

wax'works' *n.pl.* *[with sing. v.]* an exhibition of wax figures

wax'y *adj.* **-i·er, -i·est** of, full of, or like wax —**wax'i·ness** *n.*

way (wā) *n.* [OE. *weg*] **1.** a road, street, path, etc. **2.** room for passing **3.** a route or course **4.** movement forward *[lead the way]* **5.** habits of life *[give up evil ways]* **6.** a method of doing something **7.** a manner of living, acting, etc. *[his ways are odd]* **8.** distance *[a long way off]* **9.** direction of movement **10.** respect; particular *[right in some ways]* **11.** wish; will *[I had my way]* **12.** *[pl.]* a timber framework on which a ship is built **13.** *[Colloq.]* *a)* a condition *[he's in a bad way]* *b)* a locality *[out our way]* —*adv.* *[Colloq.]* away; far *[way behind]* —**by the way** incidentally —**by way of 1.** passing through **2.** as a method, etc. of —**give way 1.** to yield **2.** to break down —**make way 1.** to clear a passage **2.** to make progress —**under way** moving; advancing

way'far·er (-fer'ər) *n.* a traveler, esp. on foot —**way'far'ing** *adj., n.*

way'lay' *vt.* **-laid', -lay'ing 1.** to lie in wait for and attack; ambush **2.** to wait for and accost by surprise

way'-out' *adj.* [Colloq.] very unusual or unconventional

-ways (wāz) [< WAY] *a suffix meaning* in a (specified) direction, position, or manner *[endways]*

ways and means methods of raising money, specif. such methods, including legislation, in government

way'side' *n.* the edge of a road

way'ward (-wərd) *adj.* [see AWAY & -WARD] **1.** headstrong, willful, disobedient, etc. **2.** unpredictable; erratic —**way'ward·ness** *n.*

W.C.T.U. Women's Christian Temperance Union

we (wē) *pron.* [for sing. see I] [OE.] the persons speaking or writing: sometimes used by a person in referring to a group of which he is one, or, in place of *I,* by a monarch, editor, etc.

weak (wēk) *adj.* [< ON. *veikr*] **1.** lacking physical strength; feeble **2.** lacking moral strength or will power **3.** lacking mental power **4.** lacking force, power, etc. *[weak discipline]* **5.**

easily torn, broken, etc. *[a weak railing]* 6. lacking intensity, etc. *[a weak voice]* 7. diluted *[weak tea]* 8. unconvincing *[a weak argument]*

weak/en *vt., vi.* to make or become weak or weaker —**weak/en·er** *n.*

weak/-kneed/ *adj.* lacking in courage, determination, resistance, etc.

weak/ling *n.* one lacking physical or moral strength

weak/ly *adj.* -li·er, -li·est sickly; feeble —*adv.* in a weak manner

weak/ness *n.* 1. a being weak 2. a weak point; fault 3. an unreasonable fondness *(for* something)

weal¹ (wēl) *n.* [< WALE] a mark raised on the skin, as by a blow; welt

weal² (wēl) *n.* [OE. *wela]* well-being; welfare *[the public weal]*

wealth (welth) *n.* [< prec.] 1. much money or property; riches 2. a large amount *[a wealth of ideas]* 3. valuable products, contents, etc. 4. everything having value in money

wealth/y *adj.* -i·er, -i·est having wealth; rich —**wealth/i·ness** *n.*

wean (wēn) *vt.* [OE. *wenian]* 1. to accustom (a child or young animal) to take food other than by suckling 2. to withdraw (a person) as from a habit

weap·on (wep/ən) *n.* [OE. *wæpen]* 1. any instrument used for fighting 2. any means of attack or defense

weap/on·ry (-rē) *n.* 1. the design and production of weapons 2. weapons collectively

wear (wer) *vt.* wore, worn, wear/ing [OE. *werian]* 1. to bear (clothing, etc.) on the body 2. to show in one's appearance *[she wore a smile]* 3. to impair or diminish by use, friction, etc. 4. to make by rubbing, flowing, etc. *[to wear a hole in the rug]* 5. to tire or exhaust —*vi.* 1. to become impaired or diminished, as by use 2. to hold up in use *[that suit wears well]* 3. to have an irritating effect *(on)* —*n.* 1. a wearing or being worn 2. things worn; clothes *[men's wear]* 3. impairment or loss, as from use, friction, etc. —**wear off** to diminish by degrees —**wear/a·ble** *adj.* —**wear/er** *n.*

wear and tear loss and damage resulting from use

wea·ri·some (wir/ē səm) *adj.* causing weariness; tiresome or tedious

wea·ry (wir/ē) *adj.* -ri·er, -ri·est [OE. *werig]* 1. tired; worn-out 2. without further patience, zeal, etc. 3. tiring *[weary work]* —*vt., vi.* -ried, -ry·ing to make or become weary —**wea/ri·ly** *adv.* —**wea/ri·ness** *n.*

wea·sel (wē/z'l) *n.* [OE. *wesle]* an agile, flesh-eating mammal, with a long, slender body and short legs —*vi.* to be evasive or deliberately misleading —**wea/sel·ly** *adj.*

weath·er (weth/ər) *n.* [OE. *weder]* 1. the condition of the atmosphere with regard to temperature, moisture, etc. 2. storm, rain, etc. —*vt.* 1. to expose to the action of weather 2. to pass

through safely *[to weather a storm]* 3. *Naut.* to pass to the windward of —*vi.* to become discolored, worn, etc. by exposure to the weather —**under the weather** [Colloq.] ill

weath/er-beat/en *adj.* showing the effect of exposure to sun, rain, etc.

weath/er-cock/ *n.* a weather vane in the form of a cock

weath/er-man/ *n., pl.* -men/ one whose work is forecasting the weather

weath/er-proof/ *adj.* that can withstand exposure to the weather without damage —*vt.* to make weatherproof

weath/er-strip/ *n.* a strip of metal, felt, etc. covering the joint between a door or window and the casing to keep out drafts, etc.: also **weath/er·strip/ping** —*vt.* -stripped/, -strip/ping to provide with weatherstrips

weather vane a vane for showing which way the wind is blowing

weave (wēv) *vt.* wove or, chiefly for *vt.* 5 & *vi.* 3, weaved, wov/en or, chiefly for *vt.* 5 & *vi.* 3, weaved, weav/ing [OE. *wefan]* 1. to make (a fabric, basket, etc.) by interlacing (threads, reeds, etc.), as on a loom 2. to construct in the mind *[to weave a tale]* 3. to twist (something) into or through 4. to spin (a web), as spiders do 5. to make (one's way) by moving from side to side or in and out —*vi.* 1. to do weaving 2. to become interlaced 3. to move from side to side or in and out —*n.* a method or pattern of weaving —**weav/er** *n.*

web (web) *n.* [OE. *webb]* 1. any woven fabric 2. the network spun by a spider, etc. 3. a carefully woven trap 4. a network 5. a membrane joining the digits of various water birds, animals, etc. —*vt.* webbed, web/bing to join by, or cover as with, a web

web/bing *n.* a strong fabric woven in strips and used for belts, etc.

web/foot/ *n., pl.* -feet/ a foot with webbed toes —**web/-foot/ed** *adj.*

Web·ster (web/stər), **Noah** 1758-1843; U.S. lexicographer

wed (wed) *vt., vi.* wed/ded, wed/ded or wed, wed/ding [OE. *weddian]* 1. to marry 2. to unite or join

we'd (wēd) 1. we had 2. we should 3. we would

Wed. Wednesday

wed/ding *n.* 1. the marriage ceremony 2. a marriage anniversary

wedge (wej) *n.* [OE. *wecg]* 1. a piece of wood, metal, etc. tapering to a thin edge: used to split wood, lift weights, etc. 2. anything shaped like a wedge 3. any act serving to open the way for change, etc. —*vt.* wedged, wedg/ing 1. to force apart, or fix in place, with a wedge 2. to crowd together or pack *(in)* —*vi.* to be forced as a wedge

WEDGE

---

fat, āpe, cär; ten, ēven; is, bīte; gō, hôrn, tōōl, look; oil, out; up, fur; chin; she; thin, *th*en; zh, leisure; ŋ, ring; ə for *a* in ago; ', (ā'b'l); ë, Fr. coeur; ö, Fr. feu; Fr. mon; ü, Fr. duc; kh, G. ich, doch; ‡ foreign; < derived from

wed·lock (wed'läk) n. [OE. *wedlac*] the state of being married

Wednes·day (wenz'dē, -dā) n. [< *Woden*, Germanic god] the fourth day of the week

wee (wē) adj. we'er, we'est [OE. *wege*] 1. very small; tiny 2. very early [*wee* hours of the morning]

weed (wēd) n. [OE. *wēod*] any undesired, uncultivated plant, esp. one that crowds out desired plants —vt., vi. 1. to remove weeds from (a garden, etc.) 2. to remove as useless, harmful, etc.: often with *out* —weed'er n.

weeds (wēdz) n.pl. [< OE. *wæde*, garment] black mourning clothes

weed'y adj. -i·er, -i·est 1. full of weeds 2. of or like a weed

week (wēk) n. [OE. *wicu*] 1. a period of seven days, esp. the period from Sunday through Saturday 2. the hours or days of work in this period

week'day' n. any day of the week except Sunday and, often, Saturday

week'end', **week'-end'** n. the period from Friday night or Saturday to Monday morning: also week end —vi. to spend the weekend (at or in)

week'ly adj. 1. of, for, or lasting a week 2. done, happening, etc. once every week —adv. once a week; every week —n., pl. -lies a periodical published once a week

ween (wēn) vi., vt. [OE. *wenan*] [Archaic] to think; suppose; imagine

weep (wēp) vi., vt. wept, weep'ing [OE. *wepan*] 1. to shed (tears) 2. to mourn (for) 3. to drip or exude (water, etc.) —weep'er n.

weep'ing n. the act of one who weeps —adj. 1. that weeps 2. having graceful, drooping branches

weep'y adj. -i·er, -i·est weeping or inclined to weep

wee·vil (wē'v'l) n. [OE. *wifel*] a beetle whose larvae feed on grain, etc.

weft (weft) n. [< OE. *wefan*, to weave] *Weaving* the woof

weigh (wā) vt. [OE. *wegan*, carry] 1. to determine the heaviness of 2. to have (a specified weight) 3. to consider and choose carefully [*weigh* one's words] 4. to hoist (an anchor) —vi. 1. to have significance, importance, etc. 2. to be a burden —weigh down to burden or bear down on

weight (wāt) n. [OE. *wiht*] 1. a quantity weighing a definite amount 2. heaviness; specif., *Physics* the force exerted on a mass by gravity 3. amount of heaviness 4. a) any unit of heaviness b) any system of such units c) a piece of standard heaviness used in weighing 5. any body used for its heaviness [a *paperweight*] 6. a burden, as of sorrow 7. importance; consequence 8. influence; power —vt. 1. to add weight to 2. to burden

weight'less adj. having little or no apparent weight; specif., lacking acceleration of gravity

weight lifting the athletic exercise or sport of lifting barbells

weight'y adj. -i·er, -i·est 1. very heavy 2. burdensome 3. significant; important —weight'i·ness n.

weir (wir) n. [OE. *wer*] 1. a low dam built to back up water, as for a mill 2. a fence, as of brushwood, in a stream, etc., for catching fish

weird (wird) adj. [< OE. *wyrd*, fate] 1. suggestive of ghosts, etc.; mysterious 2. queer; bizarre —weird'ly adv. —weird'ness n.

weird·o (wir'dō) n., pl. -os [Slang] a queer or bizarre person or thing: also weird'ie

wel·come (wel'kəm) adj. [< OE. *wilcuma*, welcome guest] 1. gladly received [a *welcome* guest, *welcome* news] 2. freely permitted [*welcome* to use my car] 3. under no obligation [you're *welcome*] —n. a welcoming —vt. -comed, -com·ing to greet or receive with pleasure, etc.

weld (weld) vt. [< obs. *well*] 1. to unite (pieces of metal) by heating until fused or soft enough to hammer together 2. to unite closely —vi. to be welded —n. 1. a welding 2. the joint formed by welding —weld'er n.

wel·fare (wel'fer') n. [< ME. *wel*, well + OE. *faran*, to go] 1. state of health, prosperity, etc.; well-being 2. those government agencies which grant aid to the poor, the unemployed, etc. —on welfare receiving government aid because of poverty, etc.

wel·kin (wel'kin) n. [< OE. *wolcen*, cloud] [Archaic] the vault of the sky

well¹ (wel) n. [OE. *wella*] 1. a natural spring and pool 2. a hole sunk into the earth to get water, oil, etc. 3. a source of abundant supply 4. a shaft, etc. resembling a well 5. a container for a liquid, as an inkwell —vi., vt. to gush or flow as from a well

well² (wel) adv. bet'ter, best [OE. *wel*] 1. in a satisfactory, proper, or excellent manner [treat him *well*, to sing *well*] 2. prosperously [to live *well*] 3. with good reason [one may *well* ask] 4. to a considerable degree [*well* advanced] 5. thoroughly [stir it *well*] 6. with certainty; definitely 7. familiarly [I know him *well*] —adj. 1. suitable, proper, etc. 2. in good health 3. favorable; comfortable —interj. an exclamation of surprise, agreement, etc. —as well (as) 1. in addition (to) 2. equally (with)

we'll (wēl) 1. we shall 2. we will

well-ap·point·ed (wel'ə poin'tid) adj. excellently furnished

well'-bal'anced adj. 1. nicely adjusted 2. sane, sensible, etc.

well'-be·haved' adj. behaving well; displaying good manners

well'-be'ing n. the state of being well, happy, or prosperous; welfare

well'-bred' adj. showing good breeding; courteous and considerate

well'-dis·posed' adj. friendly (*toward* a person) or receptive (*to* an idea, etc.)

well'-done' adj. 1. performed with skill 2. thoroughly cooked, as meat

well'-fed' adj. plump, or fat

well'-fixed' adj. [Colloq.] rich

well'-found'ed adj. based on facts, good evidence, or sound judgment

well'-groomed' adj. clean and neat

well'-ground'ed *adj.* having a thorough basic knowledge of a subject

well'-heeled' *adj.* [Slang] rich

well'-in·formed' *adj.* having considerable knowledge of a subject or of many subjects

well'-in·ten'tioned *adj.* having or showing good or kindly intentions

well'-knit' *adj.* 1. well constructed 2. sturdy in body build

well'-known' *adj.* 1. widely known; famous 2. thoroughly known

well'-made' *adj.* skillfully and soundly put together

well'-man'nered *adj.* having good manners; polite; courteous

well'-mean'ing *adj.* 1. having good intentions 2. said or done with good intentions: also **well'-meant'**

well'-nigh' *adv.* very nearly; almost

well'-off' *adj.* 1. in a fortunate condition 2. prosperous

well'-pre·served' *adj.* in good condition or looking good, in spite of age

well'-read' *adj.* having read much

well'-round'ed *adj.* 1. well planned for proper balance 2. showing diverse talents 3. shapely

well'-spo'ken *adj.* 1. speaking easily, graciously, etc. 2. spoken well

well'spring' *n.* 1. a spring 2. a source of abundant supply

well'-thought'-of' *adj.* having a good reputation

well'-timed' *adj.* timely; opportune

well'-to-do' *adj.* prosperous; wealthy

well'-turned' *adj.* 1. gracefully shaped [a well-turned ankle] 2. expressed well [a well-turned phrase]

well'-wish'er *n.* one who wishes well to another, or to a cause, etc.

well'-worn' *adj.* much worn or used

Welsh (welsh) *adj.* of Wales, its people, etc. —*n.* the Celtic language of Wales —**the Welsh** the Welsh people —**Welsh'man** (-mən) *n., pl.* -men

welsh (welsh) *vi.* [Slang] to fail to pay a debt, fulfill an obligation, etc. (often with *on*) —**welsh'er** *n.*

Welsh rabbit a dish of melted cheese served on crackers or toast: also **Welsh rarebit**

welt (welt) *n.* [ME. *welte*] 1. a strip of leather in the seam between the sole and upper of a shoe 2. a ridge raised on the skin by a slash or blow

wel·ter (wel'tər) *vi.* [< MDu. *welteren*] to roll about or wallow —*n.* a confusion; turmoil

wel·ter·weight (wel'tər wāt') *n.* [prob. < *welt* (to thrash)] a boxer or wrestler weighing 136 to 147 lb.

wen (wen) *n.* [OE. *wenn*] a benign skin tumor, esp. of the scalp

wench (wench) *n.* [< OE. *wencel*, child] 1. a young woman: derogatory term 2. [Archaic] a female servant

wend (wend) *vt.* [OE. *wendan*, to turn] to go on (one's way)

went (went) *pt.* of GO

wept (wept) *pt. & pp.* of WEEP

were (wur) [OE. *wæron*] *pl. & 2d pers.* sing., past indic., and the past subj., of BE

we're (wir) we are

weren't (wurnt) were not

were·wolf (wir'woolf', wur'-) *n., pl.* -wolves' [< OE. *wer*, man + *wulf*, wolf] Folklore a person changed into a wolf: also **werwolf**

Wes·ley (wes'lē, wez'-), **John** 1703–91; Eng. clergyman: founder of Methodism —**Wes'ley·an** *adj., n.*

west (west) *n.* [OE.] 1. the direction in which sunset occurs (270° on the compass, opposite east) 2. a region in or toward this direction 3. [W-] Europe and the Western Hemisphere —*adj.* 1. in, of, or toward the west 2. from the west —*adv.* in or toward the west

West Berlin W section of Berlin, associated with West Germany: pop. 2,200,000

west'er·ly *adj., adv.* 1. toward the west 2. from the west

west'ern *adj.* 1. in, of, or toward the west 2. from the west 3. [W-] of the West —*n.* a story or motion picture about cowboys, etc. in the western U.S.

west'ern·er *n.* a native or inhabitant of the west

Western Hemisphere that half of the earth including N. and S.America

west'ern·ize' (-īz') *vt.* -ized', -iz'-ing to make western in ways or ideas

Western Samoa island country in S. Pacific: 1,130 sq. mi.; pop. 134,000

West Germany W section of Germany; country in NC Europe: 95,735 sq. mi.; pop. 59,674,000

West Indies large group of islands extending from Florida to Venezuela —**West Indian**

West Point military reservation in SE N.Y.: site of U.S. Military Academy

West Virginia E State of the U.S.: 24,181 sq. mi.; pop. 1,950,000; cap. Charleston —**West Virginian**

west'ward (-wərd) *adv., adj.* toward the west Also **west'wards** *adv.*

wet (wet) *adj.* **wet'ter, wet'test** [OE. *wæt*] 1. covered or saturated with water or other liquid 2. rainy; misty 3. not yet dry [wet paint] 4. permitting the sale of alcoholic liquor —*n.* 1. water or other liquid 2. rain or rainy weather 3. one who favors the sale of alcoholic liquor —*vt., vi.* wet or wet'ted, wet'ting to make or become wet —all wet [Slang] wrong —wet'ly *adv.* —wet'ness *n.* —wet'ter *n.*

wet'back' *n.* [Colloq.] a Mexican who illegally enters the U.S. to work

wet blanket one who lessens the enthusiasm or gaiety of others

wet nurse a woman hired to suckle another's child —**wet'-nurse'** *vt.* -nursed', -nurs'ing

wet suit a closefitting suit of rubber worn by skin divers for warmth

we've (wēv) we have

whack (hwak) *vt., vi.* [echoic] [Colloq.] to strike or slap with a sharp, resounding blow —*n.* [Colloq.] 1. *a*) a sharp, resounding blow *b*) the sound of this 2. a share 3. an attempt —**out of whack** [Colloq.] not in proper condition —**whack′er** *n.*

whack′ing *adj.* [Colloq.] very large

whack′y *adj.* **-i·er, -i·est** *same as* WACKY

whale[1] (hwāl) *n.* [OE. *hwæl*] a large, warmblooded sea mammal that breathes air —*vi.* **whaled, whal′ing** to hunt whales —**a whale of a** [Colloq.] an exceptionally large, impressive, etc. example of

whale[2] (hwāl) *vt.* **whaled, whal′ing** [prob. < WALE] [Colloq.] to thrash

whale′bone′ *n.* the horny, elastic material hanging from the upper jaw of some whales (**whalebone whales**): used, esp. formerly, for corset stays, etc.

whal′er *n.* 1. a whaling ship 2. a man whose work is whaling

wham (hwam) *interj.* a sound imitating a heavy blow or explosion —*n.* a heavy blow or impact —*vt., vi.* **whammed, wham′ming** to strike, explode, etc. with a loud, sharp sound

wham·my (hwam′ē) *n., pl.* **-mies** [Slang] a jinx; the evil eye

wharf (hwôrf) *n., pl.* **wharves** (hwôrvz), **wharfs** [< OE. *hwerf*, a dam] a structure on a shore, at which ships are loaded or unloaded

what (hwut, hwät) *pron.* [< OE. *hwa*, who] 1. which thing, event, etc.? [*what* is that object?] 2. that or those which [do *what* you will] —*adj.* 1. which or which kind of: used interrogatively or relatively 2. as much, or as many, as [take *what* men you need] 3. how great, surprising, etc. [*what* nonsense!] —*adv.* 1. in what way? how? [*what* does it matter?] 2. partly [*what* with singing and joking, the time passed] 3. how greatly, etc. [*what* tragic news!] —*interj.* an exclamation of surprise, anger, etc. —**what about** what do you think, feel, etc. concerning? —**what for** why?

what·ev·er (hwət ev′ər) *pron.* 1. what: an emphatic variant 2. anything that [say *whatever* you like] 3. no matter what [*whatever* you do, don't hurry] —*adj.* 1. of any kind [no plans *whatever*] 2. being who it may be [*whatever* man said that, it's false]

what′not′ *n.* a set of open shelves, as for bric-a-brac

what′so·ev′er *pron., adj.* whatever: an emphatic form

wheal[1] (hwēl) *n.* [ME. *whele*] a small, raised patch of skin, as from an insect bite

wheal[2] (hwēl) *n. same as* WEAL[1]

wheat (hwēt) *n.* [OE. *hwæte*] a cereal grass having spikes containing grains used in making flour, cereals, etc.

wheat germ the embryo of the wheat kernel, rich in vitamins

whee·dle (hwē′d'l) *vt., vi.* **-dled, -dling** [< ?] to influence or persuade (a person) or get (something) by flattery, coaxing, etc.

wheel (hwēl) *n.* [OE. *hweol*] 1. a circular disk or frame turning on a central axis 2. anything like a wheel in shape, movement, etc. 3. the steering wheel of a motor vehicle 4. [*pl.*] [Slang] an automobile 5. [*usually pl.*] the moving forces [the *wheels* of progress] 6. a turning movement 7. [Slang] an important person —*vt., vi.* 1. to move on or in a wheeled vehicle 2. to turn, revolve, etc. 3. to turn so as to change direction —**at the wheel** steering a motor vehicle, etc.

wheel′bar′row (-bar′ō, -ber′ō) *n.* a shallow, open box for moving small loads, having a wheel in front, and two shafts in back for moving the vehicle

wheel′base′ *n.* in a motor vehicle, the distance in inches from the front axle to the rear axle

wheel′chair′ *n.* a chair mounted on wheels, for persons unable to walk

wheeled (hwēld) *adj.* having wheels

wheel·er-deal·er (hwēl′ər dēl′ər) *n.* [Slang] one who is showily aggressive, as in arranging business deals

wheel′wright′ (-rīt′) *n.* one who makes and repairs wheels and wheeled vehicles

wheeze (hwēz) *vi.* **wheezed, wheez′ing** [< ON. *hvæsa*, to hiss] to make a whistling, breathy sound, as in asthma —*n.* a wheezing —**wheez′y** *adj.* **-i·er, -i·est**

whelk (hwelk) *n.* [OE. *wioluc*] a large marine snail with a spiral shell, esp. a variety used in Europe for food

whelm (hwelm) *vt.* [ME. *welmen*] 1. to submerge 2. to overpower or crush

whelp (hwelp) *n.* [OE. *hwelp*] the young of a dog, etc. —*vt., vi.* to bring forth (young): said of animals

when (hwen) *adv.* [OE. *hwænne*] 1. at what time? [*when* did he leave?] 2. on what occasion? —*conj.* 1. at what time [tell me *when* to go] 2. at which time [he came at six, *when* the sun rose] 3. at the time that [*when* we were young] 4. as soon as [we will eat *when* he comes] 5. although —*pron.* what or which time [until *when* will you stay?] —*n.* the time (of an event)

whence (hwens) *adv.* [ME. *whennes*] from what place, source, cause, etc.; from where [*whence* do you come?]

when·ev·er *adv.* [Colloq.] when: an emphatic form —*conj.* at whatever time [leave *whenever* you like]

where (hwer) *adv.* [OE. *hwær*] 1. in or at what place? [*where* is it?] 2. to or toward what place? [*where* did he go?] 3. in what respect? [*where* is he at fault?] 4. from what place or source? [*where* did he learn it?] —*conj.* 1. at what place [I see *where* it is] 2. at which place [I came home, *where* I ate] 3. wherever 4. to the place to which [we go *where* you go] —*pron.* 1. the place at which [a mile to *where* I live] 2. what place [*where* are you from?] —*n.* the place (of an event)

where′a·bouts′ (-ə bouts′) *adv.* near

what place? where? —*n.* the place where a person or thing is

where·as' (-az') *conj.* 1. in view of the fact that 2. while on the contrary [she is slim, *whereas* he is fat]

where·at' *conj.* [Archaic] at which point

where·by' *conj.* by which [a device *whereby* to make money]

where'fore' (-fôr') *adv.* [Archaic] for what reason? why? —*conj.* 1. for which 2. because of which —*n.* the reason

where·in' *conj.* in which

where·of' *adv., conj.* of what, which, or whom

where·on' *conj.* on which

where'up·on' *conj.* 1. upon which 2. at which

wher·ev·er (hwer ev'ər) *adv.* [Colloq.] where: an emphatic form —*conj.* in, at, or to whatever place [go *wherever* you like]

where·with' *conj.* with which

where'with·al' (-with ôl') *n.* the necessary means, esp. money

wher·ry (hwer'ē) *n., pl.* -ries [ME. *whery*] a light rowboat

whet (hwet) *vt.* **whet'ted, whet'ting** [< OE. *hwæt,* keen] 1. to sharpen by rubbing or grinding, as a knife 2. to stimulate, as the appetite

wheth·er (hweth'ər) *conj.* [OE. *hwæther*] 1. if it be the case that [ask *whether* she sings] 2. in case; in either case that: introducing alternatives [*whether* it rains or snows]

whet·stone (hwet'stōn') *n.* an abrasive stone for sharpening knives, etc.

whew (hyoō) *interj.* [echoic] an exclamation of relief, surprise, etc.

whey (hwā) *n.* [OE. *hwæg*] the thin, watery part of milk that separates from the curds

which (hwich) *pron.* [OE. *hwylc*] 1. what one (or ones) of several? [which do you want?] 2. the one (or ones) that [I know *which* I want] 3. that [the boat *which* sank] 4. any that [take *which* you like] —*adj.* what one or ones [*which* man (or men) came?]

which·ev·er *pron., adj.* 1. any one [take *whichever* (desk) you like] 2. no matter which [*whichever* (horse) wins, he loses]

whiff (hwif) *n.* [echoic] 1. a light puff or gust of air, etc. 2. a slight odor

whif·fle·tree (hwif'l trē') *n.* same as SINGLETREE

Whig (hwig) *n.* [< *whiggamore* (contemptuous term for Scot. Presbyterians)] 1. a member of a former English political party which championed reform and parliamentary rights 2. a supporter of the American Revolution 3. a member of a U.S. political party (c.1836–1856)

while (hwīl) *n.* [OE. *hwil*] a period of time —*conj.* 1. during the time that [I read *while* I eat] 2. although; whereas [*while* not poor, he's not rich]

—*vt.* **whiled, whil'ing** to spend (time) pleasantly (often with *away*)

whi·lom (hwī'ləm) *adj.* [< OE.] former

whilst (hwīlst) *conj.* [Chiefly Brit. or U.S. Dial.] *same as* WHILE

whim (hwim) *n.* [< ?] a sudden fancy; idle and passing notion

whim·per (hwim'pər) *vi., vt.* [? akin to WHINE] to cry or utter with low, whining, broken sounds —*n.* a whimpering sound or cry

whim·si·cal (hwim'zi k'l) *adj.* 1. full of whims or whimsy 2. oddly out of the ordinary —**whim'si·cal'i·ty** (-kal'ə tē) *n.* —**whim'si·cal·ly** *adv.*

whim·sy (hwim'zē) *n., pl.* -sies [< ?] 1. an odd fancy; idle notion; whim 2. quaint or fanciful humor Also **whimsey,** *pl.* -seys

whine (hwīn) *vi.* **whined, whin'ing** [OE. *hwinan*] 1. *a)* to utter a high-pitched, nasal sound, as in complaint *b)* to make a prolonged sound like this 2. to complain in a childish way —*n.* 1. a whining 2. a complaint uttered in a whining tone —**whin'y** *adj.*

whin·ny (hwin'ē) *vi.* -nied, -ny·ing [prob. < prec.] to neigh in a low, gentle way: said of a horse —*n., pl.* -nies a whinnying

whip (hwip) *vt.* **whipped, whip'ping** [< MDu. *wippen,* to swing] 1. to move, pull, throw, etc. suddenly [to *whip* out a knife] 2. to strike, as with a strap; lash 3. to wind (cord, etc.) around a rope to prevent fraying 4. to beat into a froth [to *whip* cream] 5. [Colloq.] to defeat —*vi.* 1. to move quickly and suddenly 2. to flap about —*n.* 1. a flexible instrument for striking or flogging 2. a blow, etc. as with a whip 3. an officer of a political party in a legislature who maintains discipline, etc. 4. a whipping motion — **whip up** 1. to rouse (interest, etc.) 2. [Colloq.] to prepare quickly

whip'cord' *n.* 1. a hard, twisted or braided cord 2. a strong worsted cloth with a diagonally ribbed surface

whip hand control or advantage

whip'lash' *n.* 1. the lash of a whip 2. a sudden, severe jolting of the neck back and forth, as caused by the impact of an automobile collision

whip'per·snap'per *n.* an insignificant but presumptuous person

whip·pet (hwip'it) *n.* [< WHIP] a swift dog resembling a small greyhound, used in racing

whip·ple·tree (hwip'l trē') *n.* [< WHIP + TREE] *same as* SINGLETREE

whip·poor·will (hwip'ər wil') *n.* [echoic] a grayish bird of E N. America, active at night

whir, whirr (hwur) *vi., vt.* **whirred, whir'ring** [ME. *quirren*] to fly, revolve, vibrate, etc. with a buzzing sound —*n.* such a sound

whirl (hwurl) *vi.* [< ON. *hvirfla*] 1. to move rapidly in a circle or orbit 2. to rotate or spin fast 3. to seem to spin *[my head is whirling]* —*vt.* to cause to move, rotate, revolve, etc. rapidly —*n.* 1. a whirling or whirling motion 2. a tumult; uproar 3. a confused or giddy condition —**give it a whirl** [Colloq.] to make an attempt

whirl·i·gig (hwur'li gig') *n.* a child's toy that whirls or spins

whirl'pool' *n.* water in violent, whirling motion tending to draw floating objects into its center

whirlpool bath a bath in which an agitator drives a current of warm or hot water in a swirling motion

whirl'wind' *n.* 1. a current of air whirling violently around and around and moving forward 2. anything like a whirlwind —*adj.* impetuous; speedy

whirl'y·bird' *n.* [Colloq.] a helicopter

whisk (hwisk) *n.* [< ON. *visk*, a brush] 1. a brushing with a quick, light, sweeping motion 2. such a motion —*vt., vi.* to move, carry, brush (*away, off,* etc.) with a quick, sweeping motion

whisk broom a small, short-handled broom for brushing clothes, etc.

whisk'er *n.* 1. [*pl.*] the hair growing on a man's face, esp. on the cheeks 2. any of the long, bristly hairs on the upper lip of a cat, rat, etc.

whis·key (hwis'kē) *n., pl.* **-keys, -kies** [< IrGael. *uisce*, water + *beathadh*, life] a strong alcoholic liquor distilled from the fermented mash of grain: also, esp. for Brit. and Canad. usage, **whisky,** *pl.* **-kies**

whis·per (hwis'pər) *vi., vt.* [OE. *hwisprian*] 1. to speak or say very softly, esp. without vibrating the vocal cords 2. to talk or tell furtively, as in gossip 3. to make a rustling sound —*n.* 1. a whispering 2. something whispered 3. a rustling sound

whist (hwist) *n.* [< WHISK] a card game: forerunner of bridge

whis·tle (hwis'l) *vi.* **-tled, -tling** [ME. *hwistlian*] 1. to make a clear, shrill sound as by forcing breath through the contracted lips 2. to move with a shrill sound, as the wind 3. *a)* to blow a whistle *b)* to have its whistle blown, as a train —*vt.* 1. to produce (a tune, etc.) by whistling 2. to signal, etc. by whistling —*n.* 1. an instrument for making whistling sounds 2. a whistling —**whis'tler** *n.*

whis'tle-blow'er *n.* one who informs on a wrongdoer

whistle stop 1. a small town 2. a brief stop in a small town on a tour

whit (hwit) *n.* [< OE. *wiht*, a wight] the least bit; jot; iota

white (hwit) *adj.* **whit'er, whit'est** [OE. *hwit*] 1. having the color of pure snow or milk; opposite to black 2. of a light or pale color 3. pale; wan 4. lacking color 5. pure; innocent 6. having a light-colored skin —*n.* 1. *a)* white color *b)* a white pigment 2. a white or light-colored part, as the albumen of an egg or the white part of the eyeball 3. a person with a light-colored skin —**white'ness** *n.*

white blood cell (or **corpuscle**) *same as* LEUKOCYTE

white'cap' *n.* a wave with its crest broken into white foam

white'-col'lar *adj.* designating or of office and professional workers

white-collar crime fraud, embezzlement, etc. committed in business, government, or a profession

white elephant 1. an albino elephant, held as sacred in SE Asia 2. a thing of little use, but expensive to maintain 3. any object not wanted by its owner, but useful to another

white feather symbol of cowardice

white'fish' *n., pl.:* see FISH a white or silvery lake fish of the salmon family, found in N U.S. and Canada

white flag a white banner hoisted as a signal of truce or surrender

white gold a gold alloy that looks like platinum

white goods 1. household linens, as sheets, towels, etc. 2. large household appliances, as refrigerators

white heat 1. the degree of intense heat at which metal, etc. glows white 2. a state of intense emotion, etc. —**white'-hot'** *adj.*

White House, the 1. official residence of the President of the U.S., in Washington, D.C. 2. the executive branch of the U.S. government

white lead a poisonous, white powder, lead carbonate, used in paint

white lie a lie about a trivial matter, often told to spare someone's feelings

whit·en (hwit'n) *vt., vi.* to make or become white or whiter —**whit'en·er** *n.* —**whit'en·ing** *n.*

white race loosely, the Caucasoid group of mankind

white sale a sale of household linens

white slave a woman forced into prostitution for others' profit — **white'-slave'** *adj.* —**white slavery**

white'wall' *adj.* designating or of a tire with a white band on the outer sidewall —*n.* a whitewall tire

white'wash' *n.* 1. a mixture of lime, chalk, water, etc. as for whitening walls, etc. 2. a concealing of faults in order to exonerate —*vt.* 1. to cover with whitewash 2. to conceal the faults of 3. [Colloq.] to defeat (an opponent) without letting him score

whith·er (hwi*th*'ər) *adv.* [OE. *hwider*] to what place, condition, result, etc.? where? —*conj.* 1. to which place, result, etc. 2. wherever

whit·ing[1] (hwit'iŋ) *n.* [< MDu. *wit*, white] 1. any of many unrelated food fishes of N.America, Europe, and Australia 2. a variety of European cod

whit·ing[2] (hwit'iŋ) *n.* [ME. *whytyng*] powdered chalk used in paints, etc.

whit'ish *adj.* somewhat white

Whit·man (hwit'mən), **Walt(er)** 1819–92; U.S. poet

Whit·ney (hwit'nē), **Mount** mountain in EC Calif.

Whit·sun·day (hwit'sun'dē) *n.* [OE. *Hwita Sunnandæg*, lit., white Sunday] *same as* PENTECOST

Where the sound (hw) occurs for wh, the sound (w) is also heard.

whit·tle (hwit′'l) *vt.* **-tled, -tling** [< OE. *thwitan,* to cut] **1.** *a)* to cut thin shavings from (wood) with a knife *b)* to carve (an object) thus **2.** to reduce gradually —*vi.* to whittle wood

whiz, whizz (hwiz) *vi.* **whizzed, whiz′zing** [echoic] **1.** to make the hissing sound of something rushing through the air **2.** to speed by with this sound —*n.* **1.** this sound **2.** [Slang] an expert [a *whiz* at football]

who (hōō) *pron.,* obj. **whom,** poss. **whose** [OE. *hwa*] **1.** what or which person or persons [who is he? I know *who* came] **2.** (the, or a, person or persons) that [a man *who* knows]

WHO World Health Organization

whoa (hwō) *interj.* stop!: used esp. in directing a horse to stand still

who·dun·it (hōō dun′it) *n.* [Colloq.] *same as* MYSTERY (sense 2)

who·ev·er (hōō ev′ər) *pron.* **1.** any person that **2.** no matter who [whoever said it, it's not so] **3.** who?: an emphatic usage

whole (hōl) *adj.* [OE. *hal*] **1.** healthy; not diseased or injured **2.** not broken, damaged, etc.; intact **3.** containing all the parts; complete **4.** not divided up; in a single unit **5.** *Arith.* not a fraction —*n.* **1.** the entire amount **2.** a thing complete in itself —**on the whole** all things considered; in general — **whole′ness** *n.*

whole′heart′ed *adj.* with all one's energy, enthusiasm, etc.; sincere

whole milk milk from which no butterfat, etc. has been removed

whole note *Music* a note (○) having four times the duration of a quarter note

whole′sale′ *n.* the selling of goods in large quantities and at lower prices, esp. to retailers —*adj.* **1.** of or having to do with such selling **2.** extensive or indiscriminate [wholesale criticism] —*adv.* **1.** at wholesale prices **2.** extensively or indiscriminately —*vt., vi.* **-saled′, -sal′ing** to sell wholesale —**whole′sal′er** *n.*

whole′some (-səm) *adj.* [ME. *holsom*] **1.** promoting good health or well-being; healthful **2.** improving the mind or character **3.** having health and vigor —**whole′some·ness** *n.*

whole′-wheat′ *adj.* ground from whole kernels of wheat or made of flour so ground

who′ll (hōōl) **1.** who shall **2.** who will

whol·ly (hō′lē) *adv.* to the whole amount or extent; entirely

whom (hōōm) *pron. obj. case of* WHO

whoop (hōōp, hwōōp) *n.* [< OFr. *houper,* cry out] **1.** a loud shout, cry, etc., as of joy **2.** the convulsive intake of air following a fit of coughing in whooping cough —*vt., vi.* to utter (with) a whoop or whoops

whooping cough an acute infectious disease, esp. of children, with coughing fits that end in a whoop

whop·per (hwäp′ər) *n.* [< colloq. *whop,* to beat] [Colloq.] **1.** anything extraordinarily large **2.** a great lie

whop′ping (-iŋ) *adj.* [Colloq.] extraordinarily large or great

whore (hôr) *n.* [OE. *hore*] a prostitute —**whor′ish** *adj.*

whorl (hwôrl, hwurl) *n.* [ME. *whorwyl*] anything with a coiled or spiral appearance, as any of the circular ridges forming the design of a fingerprint —**whorled** *adj.*

who′s (hōōz) **1.** who is **2.** who has

whose (hōōz) *pron.* [OE. *hwæs*] that or those belonging to whom —*poss. pronominal adj.* of, belonging to, or done by whom or which

who·so·ev·er (hōō′sō ev′ər) *pron.* whoever: an emphatic form

why (hwi) *adv.* [< OE. *hwæt,* what] for what reason, cause, or purpose [why eat?] —*conj.* **1.** because of which [no reason *why* I must] **2.** the reason for which [that is *why* he went] —*n., pl.* **whys** the reason, cause, etc. [this is the *why* of it] —*interj.* an exclamation of surprise, impatience, etc.

WI Wisconsin

Wich·i·ta (wich′ə tô′) city in S Kans.: pop. 279,000

wick (wik) *n.* [OE. *weoca*] a piece of cord, tape, etc., as in a candle or oil lamp, that absorbs the fuel and, when lighted, burns

wick·ed (wik′id) *adj.* [ME. < *wikke,* evil] **1.** morally bad; evil **2.** generally bad, unpleasant, etc. [a *wicked* storm] **3.** mischievous **4.** [Slang] showing great skill —**wick′ed·ly** *adv.* — **wick′ed·ness** *n.*

wick·er (wik′ər) *n.* [< Scand.] **1.** a thin, flexible twig **2.** *a)* such twigs or long, woody strips woven together, as in making baskets *b) same as* WICKERWORK (sense 1) —*adj.* made of wicker

wick′er·work′ *n.* **1.** things made of wicker **2.** *same as* WICKER (sense 2*a*)

wick·et (wik′it) *n.* [ME. *wiket*] **1.** a small door or gate, esp. one in or near a larger one **2.** a small window, as in a box office **3.** *Croquet* any of the small wire arches through which the balls must be hit

wide (wid) *adj.* [OE. *wid*] **1.** extending over a large area, esp. from side to side **2.** of a specified extent from side to side **3.** of great extent [a *wide* variety] **4.** open fully [eyes *wide* with fear] **5.** far from the point, etc. aimed at [wide of the mark] —*adv.* **1.** over a relatively large area **2.** to a large or full extent [wide open] **3.** so as to miss the point, etc. aimed at; astray — **wide′ly** *adv.* —**wide′ness** *n.*

-wide (wid) *a combining form meaning* extending throughout [statewide]

wide′-an′gle *adj. Photog.* having a wider angle of view than usual

wide′-a·wake′ *adj.* **1.** completely awake **2.** alert

wide′-eyed′ *adj.* with the eyes opened widely, as in surprise

wid·en (wīd'n) *vt.*, *vi.* to make or become wide or wider

wide'spread' *adj.* occurring over a wide area or extent

widg·eon, wi·geon (wij'ən) *n.* [prob. < MFr. *vigeon*] a wild, freshwater duck

wid·ow (wid'ō) *n.* [OE. *widewe*] a woman whose husband has died and who has not remarried —*vt.* to cause to become a widow —**wid'ow·hood'** *n.*

wid'ow·er *n.* a man whose wife has died and who has not remarried

width (width) *n.* 1. distance from side to side 2. a piece of a certain width

wield (wēld) *vt.* [OE. *wealdan*] 1. to handle (a tool, etc.), esp. with skill 2. to exercise (power, control, etc.)

wie·ner (wē'nər) *n.* [< G. *Wiener wurst*, Vienna sausage] a smoked link sausage; frankfurter

wie'nie (-nē) *n.* [Colloq.] a wiener

wife (wīf) *n.*, *pl.* **wives** [OE. *wif*, woman] a married woman —**wife'less** *adj.* —**wife'ly** *adj.*

wig (wig) *n.* [< PERIWIG] a false covering of real or synthetic hair for the head —*vt.* **wigged, wig'ging** 1. to furnish with a wig 2. [Slang] *a)* to annoy, upset, etc. *b)* to excite, craze, etc. —*vi.* [Slang] to be or become upset, excited, etc.

wig·gle (wig''l) *vt.*, *vi.* **-gled, -gling** [ME. *wigelen*] to move with short, jerky motions from side to side —*n.* a wiggling —**wig'gler** *n.* —**wig'gly** *adj.* **-gli·er, -gli·est**

wight (wīt) *n.* [OE. *wiht*] [Archaic] a human being; person

wig·let (wig'lit) *n.* a small wig

wig·wag (wig'wag') *vt.*, *vi.* **-wagged', -wag'ging** [< obs. *wig*, to move + WAG¹] 1. to move back and forth; wag 2. to send (a message) by waving flags, lights, etc. according to a code —*n.* the sending of messages in this way

wig·wam (wig'wäm) *n.* [< Algonquian] a N.American Indian shelter consisting of a framework of arched poles covered with bark, leaves, branches, etc.

wild (wīld) *adj.* [OE. *wilde*] 1. living or growing in its original, natural state 2. not lived in or cultivated; waste 3. not civilized; savage 4. not easily controlled [a *wild* boy] 5. lacking social or moral restraint; dissolute [a *wild* time] 6. turbulent; stormy 7. enthusiastic [*wild* about golf] 8. fantastically impractical; reckless 9. missing the target [a *wild* shot] 10. *Card Games* having any desired value: said of a card —*adv.* in a wild manner —*n.* [*usually pl.*] wilderness or wasteland —**wild'ly** *adv.* —**wild'ness** *n.*

wild'cat' *n.* 1. any fierce, medium-sized, undomesticated animal of the cat family 2. a fierce, aggressive person 3. a productive oil well in an area not previously known to have oil —*adj.* 1. unsound or risky 2. illegal or unauthorized —*vi.* **-cat'ted, -cat'ting** to drill for oil in an area previously considered unproductive

wil·de·beest (wil'də bēst', vil'-) *n.*,

pl. **-beests', -beest'** [Afrik.] *same as* GNU

wil·der·ness (wil'dər nis) *n.* [< OE. *wilde*, wild + *deor*, animal] an uncultivated, uninhabited region; waste

wild'-eyed' *adj.* 1. staring in a wild way 2. very impractical or foolish

wild'fire' *n.* a fire that spreads fast and is hard to put out

wild'fowl' *n.* a wild bird, esp. a game bird: also **wild fowl**

wild'-goose' chase a futile search, pursuit, or endeavor

wild'life' *n.* wild animals and birds

wild oats (or **oat**) a wild grass common in the W U.S. —**sow one's wild oats** to be promiscuous or dissolute in youth

wild rice 1. an aquatic grass of the U.S. and Canada 2. its edible grain

Wild West the Western U.S. in its early, lawless frontier period

wile (wīl) *n.* [< OE. *wigle*, magic] 1. a sly trick; stratagem 2. a beguiling trick: *usually used in pl.* —*vt.* **wiled, wil'ing** to beguile; lure —**wile away** to while away (time, etc.)

will¹ (wil) *n.* [OE. *willa*] 1. the power of making a reasoned choice or of controlling one's own actions 2. determination 3. attitude toward others [good *will*] 4. *a)* a particular desire, choice, etc. of someone *b)* mandate [the *will* of the people] 5. a legal document directing the disposal of one's property after death —*vt.* 1. to desire; want [to *will* to live] 2. to control by the power of the will 3. to bequeath by a will —*vi.* to wish, desire, or choose —**at will** when one wishes

will² (wil) *v.*, *pt.* **would** [OE. *willan*, to desire] an auxiliary verb: 1. to express simple futurity 2. in formal speech, to express determination, obligation, etc. in the first person and futurity in the second and third persons See note at SHALL 3. to express: *a)* willingness [will you go?] *b)* ability or capacity [it *will* hold a pint] —*vt.*, *vi.* to wish; desire [do as you *will*]

will·ful (wil'fəl) *adj.* 1. said or done deliberately 2. obstinate; stubborn Also **wilful** —**will'ful·ly** *adv.* —**will'ful·ness** *n.*

Wil·liam I (wil'yəm) 1027?-87; king of England (1066-87): called **William the Conqueror**

wil·lies (wil'ēz) *n.pl.* [< ?] [Slang] a nervous feeling: with *the*

will·ing (wil'iŋ) *adj.* 1. favorably disposed; consenting [willing to play] 2. acting, giving, etc., or done, given, etc., readily and cheerfully —**will'ing·ly** *adv.* —**will'ing·ness** *n.*

wil·li·waw (wil'i wô') *n.* 1. a violent, cold wind blowing from mountain to coast in far north or south latitudes 2. confusion; turmoil

will-o'-the-wisp (wil'ə thə wisp') *n.* 1. a light seen over marshes at night, believed to be marsh gas burning 2. a delusive hope or goal

wil·low (wil'ō) *n.* [OE. *welig*] 1. a tree with narrow leaves, and flexible twigs used in weaving baskets, etc. 2. its wood

wil·low·y (wil'ə wē) *adj.* like a willow; slender, lithe, etc.

will'pow'er *n.* strength of will, mind, or determination; self-control

wil·ly-nil·ly (wil'ē nil'ē) *adv., adj.* [contr. < *will I, nill I: nill* < OE. *nyllan*, be unwilling] (happening) whether one wishes it or not

Wil·son (wil's'n), (**Thomas**) **Woodrow** 1856–1924; 28th president of the U.S. (1913–21)

wilt (wilt) *vi.* [< obs. *welk*, wither] 1. to become limp, as from heat or lack of water; droop, as a plant 2. to become weak or faint; lose strength or courage —*vt.* to cause to wilt

Wil·ton (**carpet** or **rug**) (wil't'n) [< *Wilton*, England] a kind of carpet with a velvety pile of cut loops

wi·ly (wī'lē) *adj.* **-li·er, -li·est** full of wiles; crafty; sly —**wi'li·ness** *n.*

wim·ple (wim'p'l) *n.* [OE. *wimpel*] a nun's head covering so arranged as to leave only the face exposed

win (win) *vi.* **won, win'ning** [< OE. *winnan*, to fight] 1. *a*) to gain a victory *b*) to finish first in a race, etc. 2. to become by effort; get [he *won* loose from the crowd] —*vt.* 1. to get by labor, struggle, etc. 2. to be victorious in (a contest, etc.) 3. to get to with effort [they *won* the camp by noon] 4. to influence; persuade: often with *over* 5. to gain (the sympathy, favor, etc.) of (someone) 6. to persuade to marry one —*n.* [Colloq.] a victory

wince (wins) *vi.* **winced, winc'ing** [< OFr. *guenchir*] to shrink or draw back slightly, usually with a grimace, as in pain —*n.* a wincing

winch (winch) *n.* [OE. *wince*] 1. a crank with a handle for transmitting motion 2. an apparatus for hoisting or hauling, having a cylinder upon which is wound the rope, etc. attached to the object to be lifted or moved

wind[1] (wīnd) *vt.* **wound, wind'ing** [OE. *windan*] 1. to turn [wind the crank] 2. to coil into a ball or around something else; twine 3. to cover by entwining 4. *a*) to make (one's way) in a twisting course *b*) to cause to move in a twisting course 5. to tighten the spring of (a clock, etc.) as by turning a stem —*vi.* 1. to move or go in a curving or sinuous manner 2. to take a devious course 3. to coil (*about* or *around* something) —*n.* a turn; twist —**wind up** 1. to wind into a ball, etc. 2. to bring to an end; settle 3. to make very tense, excited, etc. 4. *Baseball* to swing the arm preparatory to pitching —**wind'er** *n.*

wind[2] (wind) *n.* [OE.] 1. air in motion 2. a strong current of air; gale 3. air bearing a scent, as in hunting 4. air regarded as bearing information, etc. [a rumor in the *wind*] 5. breath or the power of breathing 6. empty talk 7. gas in the intestines 8. [*pl.*] the wind instruments of an orchestra —*vt.* 1. to get the scent of 2. to put out of breath

—**get wind of** to hear of —**in the wind** happening or about to happen

wind'break' *n.* a hedge, fence, etc. serving as a protection from wind

wind'chill' factor same as CHILL FACTOR

wind·ed (win'did) *adj.* out of breath

wind'fall' *n.* 1. something blown down by the wind, as fruit from a tree 2. an unexpected stroke of good luck

wind·ing sheet (wīn'diŋ) a shroud

wind instrument (wind) a musical instrument played by blowing air, esp. breath, through it, as a flute

wind·jam·mer (wind'jam'ər) *n.* a large sailing ship or one of its crew

wind·lass (wind'ləs) *n.* [< ON. *vinda*, to WIND[1] + *ass*, a beam] a winch, esp. one worked by a crank

WINDLASS

wind'mill' *n.* a mill operated by the wind's rotation of large vanes radiating from a shaft

win·dow (win'dō) *n.* [< ON. *vindr*, WIND[2] + *auga*, an eye] 1. an opening in a building, vehicle, etc. for letting in light or air or for looking through, usually having a pane of glass in a movable frame 2. a windowpane 3. an opening resembling a window

window dressing 1. the display of goods in a store window 2. that which is meant to make something seem better than it really is —**win'dow-dress'** *vt.* —**window dresser**

win'dow·pane' *n.* a pane of glass in a window

win'dow-shop' *vi.* **-shopped', -shop'ping** to look at goods in store windows without entering to buy

win'dow·sill' *n.* the sill of a window

wind'pipe' *n.* the trachea

wind·row (wind'rō') *n.* a row of hay, etc. raked together to dry

wind·shield (wind'shēld') *n.* in automobiles, etc., a glass screen in front, to protect from wind, etc.

wind'sock' (-säk') *n.* a long cloth cone flown at an airfield to show wind direction: also **wind sleeve**

Wind·sor (win'zər) port in SE Ontario, Canada: pop. 193,000

Wind·sor knot (win'zər) a double slipknot in a four-in-hand necktie

wind'storm' *n.* a storm with a strong wind but little or no rain, etc.

wind·up (wīnd'up') *n.* 1. a conclusion; end 2. *Baseball* the swinging of the arm preparatory to pitching

wind·ward (wind'wərd) *n.* the direction from which the wind blows —*adv.* toward the wind —*adj.* 1. moving windward 2. on the side from which the wind blows

Windward Islands group of islands in the West Indies, south of the Leeward Islands

wind·y (win'dē) *adj.* **-i·er, -i·est** 1. with much wind [a *windy* city] 2.

stormy, blustery, etc. **3.** *a)* flimsy, intangible, etc. *b)* long-winded, boastful, etc. —**wind′i·ness** *n.*

wine (wīn) *n.* [< L. *vinum*] **1.** the fermented juice of grapes, used as an alcoholic beverage **2.** the fermented juice of other fruits or plants —*vt.*, *vi.* **wined, win′ing** to provide with or drink wine: usually in **wine and dine** to entertain lavishly

wine′-col′ored *adj.* having the color of red wine; dark purplish-red

win′er·y (-ər ē) *n., pl.* **-ies** an establishment where wine is made

wing (wiŋ) *n.* [< ON. *vaengr*] **1.** either of the paired organs of flight of a bird, bat, insect, etc. **2.** something like a wing in use, position, etc.; esp., *a)* a (or the) main lateral supporting surface of an airplane *b)* a subordinate, projecting part of a building *c)* either side of the stage out of sight of the audience **3.** the section of an army, fleet, etc. to the right (or left) of the center **4.** a section, as of a political party, with reference to its radicalism or conservatism **5.** a unit in an air force **6.** a flying, or manner of flying —*vt.* **1.** to provide with wings **2.** *a)* to send swiftly as on wings *b)* to make (one's way) by flying *c)* to pass through or over as by flying **3.** to wound in the wing, arm, etc. —*vi.* to fly —**on the wing** (while) flying —**take wing** to fly away —**under one's wing** under one's protection, etc. —**wing it** [Colloq.] to improvise in acting, speaking, etc. —**winged** (wiŋd; *poet.* wiŋ′id) *adj.* —**wing′less** *adj.*

wing′span′ (-span′) *n.* the distance between the tips of an airplane's wings

wing′spread′ *n.* **1.** the distance between the tips of a pair of fully spread wings **2.** *same as* WINGSPAN

wink (wiŋk) *vi.* [OE. *wincian*] **1.** to close the eyelids and open them again quickly **2.** to close and open one eyelid quickly, as a signal, etc. **3.** to twinkle —*vt.* to make (an eye) wink —*n.* **1.** a winking **2.** an instant **3.** a signal given by winking **4.** a twinkle —**wink at** to pretend not to see

win·ner (win′ər) *n.* one that wins

win·ning (win′iŋ) *adj.* **1.** victorious **2.** attractive; charming —*n.* **1.** a victory **2.** [*pl.*] money that is won

Win·ni·peg (win′ə peg′) capital of Manitoba, Canada: pop. 257,000

win·now (win′ō) *vt., vi.* [< OE. *wind*, WIND²] **1.** to blow (the chaff) from (grain) **2.** to scatter **3.** to sift out

win·o (wī′nō) *n., pl.* **-os** [Slang] an alcoholic who drinks cheap wine

win·some (win′səm) *adj.* [OE. *wynsum*, pleasant] sweetly attractive; charming —**win′some·ly** *adv.*

Win·ston-Sa·lem (win′stən sā′ləm) city in NC N.C.: pop. 132,000

win·ter (win′tər) *n.* [OE.] **1.** the coldest season of the year, following autumn **2.** a period of decline, distress, etc. —*adj.* of, during, or for winter —*vi.* to pass the winter —*vt.* to keep or maintain during the winter

win′ter·green′ *n.* **1.** an evergreen plant with white flowers and red berries **2.** an aromatic oil (**oil of wintergreen**) made from its leaves and used as a flavoring **3.** the flavor

win′ter·ize′ (-īz′) *vt.* **-ized′, -iz′ing** to put into condition for winter

win′ter·time′ *n.* the winter season

win·try (win′trē) *adj.* **-tri·er, -tri·est** of or like winter; cold, bleak, etc.

win·y (wī′nē) *adj.* **-i·er, -i·est** like wine in taste, smell, color, etc.

wipe (wīp) *vt.* **wiped, wip′ing** [OE. *wīpian*] **1.** to clean or dry by rubbing with a cloth, etc. **2.** to rub (a cloth, etc.) over something **3.** to apply or remove by wiping —*n.* a wiping —**wipe out 1.** to remove; erase **2.** to kill off **3.** to destroy —**wip′er** *n.*

wire (wīr) *n.* [OE. *wir*] **1.** metal drawn into a long thread **2.** a length of this **3.** *a)* telegraph *b)* a telegram **4.** the finish line of a race —*adj.* made of wire —*vt.* **wired, wir′ing 1.** to furnish, connect, bind, etc. with wire **2.** to telegraph —*vi.* to telegraph

wire′hair′ *n.* a fox terrier with a wiry coat: also **wire-haired terrier**

wire′less *adj.* without wire; specif., operating by electromagnetic waves, not with conducting wire —*n.* **1.** wireless telegraphy or telephony **2.** [Chiefly Brit.] radio

Wire′pho′to *a trademark for* a system of reproducing photographs, or a photograph reproduced, by electric impulses transmitted by wire

wire service an agency that sends news stories, etc. by telegraph to subscribers, as newspapers

wire′tap′ *vi., vt.* **-tapped′, -tap′ping** to tap (a telephone wire, etc.) to get information secretly —*n.* **1.** a wiretapping **2.** a device for wiretapping

wir′ing *n.* a system of wires, as for carrying electricity

wir′y *adj.* **-i·er, -i·est 1.** of wire **2.** like wire; stiff **3.** lean and strong —**wir′i·ness** *n.*

Wis·con·sin (wis kän′s'n) Middle Western State of the U.S.: 56,154 sq. mi.; pop. 4,705,000; cap. Madison: abbrev. **Wis.**

wis·dom (wiz′dəm) *n.* [OE.: see WISE¹ & -DOM] **1.** the quality of being wise; good judgment **2.** learning; knowledge

wisdom tooth the back tooth on each side of each jaw

wise¹ (wīz) *adj.* **wis′er, wis′est** [OE. *wis*] **1.** having or showing good judgment **2.** informed **3.** learned **4.** shrewd; cunning **5.** [Slang] conceited, impudent, fresh, etc. —**wise′ly** *adv.*

wise² (wīz) *n.* [OE.] way; manner

-wise (wīz) [< prec.] *a suffix meaning:* **1.** in a specified direction, position, or manner [*sidewise*] **2.** in a manner characteristic of [*clockwise*] **3.** with regard to [*weatherwise*]

wise·a·cre (wīz′ā′kər) *n.* [ult. < OHG. *wizzago*, prophet] one who pretends to be wiser than he really is

wise′crack′ *n.* [Slang] a flippant or facetious remark —*vi.* [Slang] to make wisecracks

wish (wish) *vt.* [OE. *wyscan*] **1.** to have a longing for; want **2.** to express a desire concerning [I *wish* you well]

3. to request [I *wish* you to go] —*vi.* **1.** to long; yearn **2.** to make a wish —*n.* **1.** a wishing **2.** something wished for **3.** a polite request, almost an order **4.** [*pl.*] expressed desire for a person's health, etc. [*best wishes*] —**wish'er** *n.*

wish'bone' *n.* the forked bone in front of a bird's breastbone

wish'ful *adj.* having or showing a wish; desirous —**wish'ful·ly** *adv.*

wish·y-wash·y (wish'ē wôsh'ē) *adj.* [Colloq.] **1.** watery; thin **2.** *a*) weak; feeble *b*) vacillating; indecisive

wisp (wisp) *n.* [prob. < Scand.] **1.** a small bundle, as of straw **2.** a thin or filmy piece, strand, etc. [*a wisp* of smoke] **3.** something delicate, frail, etc. —**wisp'y** *adj.* **-i·er, -i·est**

wis·te·ri·a (wis tir'ē ə) *n.* [< C. *Wistar*, 19th-c. U.S. anatomist] a twining vine with showy clusters of flowers: also **wis·tar'i·a** (-ter'-)

wist·ful (wist'fəl) *adj.* [< earlier *wistly*, intently] showing or expressing vague yearnings —**wist'ful·ly** *adv.* —**wist'ful·ness** *n.*

wit¹ (wit) *n.* [OE.] **1.** [*pl.*] powers of thinking; mental faculties **2.** good sense **3.** *a*) the ability to make clever remarks in a sharp, amusing way *b*) one characterized by wit

wit² (wit) *vt., vi.* **wist** (wist), **wit'ting** [OE. *witan*] [Archaic] to know or learn —**to wit** that is to say

witch (wich) *n.* [OE. *wicce*] **1.** a woman supposedly having supernatural power by a compact with evil spirits **2.** an ugly old shrew **3.** [Colloq.] a fascinating woman

witch'craft' *n.* the power or practices of witches

witch doctor a person who practices primitive medicine involving the use of magic, as among tribes in Africa

witch'er·y (-ər ē) *n.* **1.** witchcraft; sorcery **2.** bewitching charm

witch hazel [< OE. *wice*] **1.** a shrub with yellow flowers **2.** a lotion made from its leaves and bark

with (with, with) *prep.* [OE.] **1.** in opposition to [he argued *with* me] **2.** *a*) alongside of; near to *b*) in the company of *c*) into; among [mix blue *with* red] **3.** as a member of [he plays *with* a trio] **4.** concerning [happy *with* his lot] **5.** compared to **6.** as well as [he rides *with* the best] **7.** in the opinion of [it's OK *with* me] **8.** as a result of [faint *with* hunger] **9.** by means of **10.** having received [*with* your consent, I'll go] **11.** having as a possession, attribute, etc. **12.** in the keeping, care, etc. of [leave it *with* me] **13.** in spite of **14.** at the same time as **15.** in proportion to [wages that vary *with* skill] **16.** to; onto [join this end *with* that one] **17.** from [to part *with* one's gains] —**with that** after, or as a consequence of, that

with- *a combining form meaning:* **1.** away, back [*withdraw*] **2.** against, from [*withhold*]

with·al (with ôl', with-) *adv.* **1.** besides **2.** despite that

with·draw' (-drô') *vt.* **-drew', -drawn', -draw'ing 1.** to take back; remove **2.** to retract or recall (a statement, etc.) —*vi.* **1.** to move back; go away; retreat **2.** to remove oneself (*from* an organization, activity, etc.) —**with·draw'al** *n.*

with·drawn' *adj.* shy, reserved, etc.

withe (with, with) *n.* [< OE.] a tough, flexible twig, as of willow, used for binding things —*vt.* **withed, with'ing** to bind with withes

with·er (with'ər) *vi.* [< ME. *wederen,* to weather] **1.** to dry up; wilt, as plants **2.** to become wasted or decayed **3.** to weaken; languish —*vt.* **1.** to cause to wither **2.** to cause to feel abashed

with·ers (with'ərz) *n.pl.* [< OE. *wither,* against] the part of a horse's back between the shoulder blades

with·hold' (with hōld', with-) *vt.* **-held', -hold'ing 1.** *a*) to hold back; restrain *b*) to deduct (taxes, etc.) from wages **2.** to refrain from granting

withholding tax the amount of income tax withheld from wages, etc.

with·in (with in', with-) *adv.* [OE. *withinnan*] **1.** on or into the inside **2.** indoors **3.** inside the body, mind, etc. —*prep.* **1.** in the inner part of **2.** not beyond **3.** inside the limits of —*n.* the inside [from *within*]

with·out' *adv.* [OE. *withutan*] **1.** on the outside **2.** out-of-doors —*prep.* **1.** at, on, or to the outside of **2.** lacking **3.** free from **4.** with avoidance of [to pass by *without* speaking]

with·stand' (with stand', with-) *vt., vi.* **-stood', -stand'ing** to oppose, resist, or endure, esp. successfully

wit·less (wit'lis) *adj.* lacking wit; foolish —**wit'less·ly** *adv.*

wit·ness (wit'nis) *n.* [< OE. *witan,* know] **1.** evidence; testimony **2.** one who saw, or can give a firsthand account of, something **3.** one who testifies in court **4.** one who observes, and attests to, a signing, etc. —*vt.* **1.** to testify to **2.** to serve as evidence of **3.** to act as witness of **4.** to be present at —**bear witness** to testify

wit·ti·cism (wit'ə siz'm) *n.* [< WITTY] a witty remark

wit·ting (wit'iŋ) *adj.* [ME. *wytting*] intentional —**wit'ting·ly** *adv.*

wit'ty *adj.* **-ti·er, -ti·est** [OE. *wittig*] having or showing wit; cleverly amusing —**wit'ti·ly** *adv.* —**wit'ti·ness** *n.*

wive (wīv) *vi., vt.* **wived, wiv'ing** [OE. *wifian*] [Archaic] to marry (a woman)

wives (wīvz) *n. pl. of* WIFE

wiz·ard (wiz'ərd) *n.* [ME. *wisard*] **1.** a magician; sorcerer **2.** [Colloq.] one very skilled at a certain activity

wiz'ard·ry *n.* magic; sorcery

wiz·ened (wiz'nd) *adj.* [< OE. *wisnian,* wither] dried up; withered

wk. *pl.* **wks. 1.** week **2.** work

wkly. weekly

WO, W.O. Warrant Officer

---

fat, āpe, cär; ten, ēven; is, bīte; gō, hôrn, tōol, look; oil, out; up, fur; chin; she; thin, then; zh, leisure; ŋ, ring; ə for a in ago; ', (ā'b'l); ē, Fr. coeur; ö, Fr. feu; Fr. mon; ü, Fr. duc; kh, G. ich, doch; ‡ foreign; < derived from

wob·ble (wäb′′l) vi. -bled, -bling [prob. < LowG. wabbeln] 1. to move unsteadily from side to side; shake 2. to vacillate —vt. to cause to wobble —n. wobbling motion —wob′bly adj. -bli·er, -bli·est —wob′bli·ness n.

woe (wō) n. [OE. wa] 1. great sorrow; grief 2. trouble —interj. alas!

woe·be·gone′ (-bi gôn′) adj. of woeful appearance; looking sad or wretched

woe·ful (-fəl) adj. 1. full of woe; sad 2. of, causing, or involving woe 3. pitiful; wretched —woe′ful·ly adv.

wok (wäk) n. [Chin.] a bowl-shaped cooking pan used, as in a ringlike stand, for frying, braising, etc.

woke (wōk) alt. pt. of WAKE[1]

wolf (woolf) n., pl. **wolves** [OE. wulf] 1. a wild, flesh-eating, doglike mammal of the Northern Hemisphere 2. a) a cruel or greedy person b) [Slang] a man who flirts with many women —vt. to eat greedily —cry wolf to give a false alarm —wolf′ish adj.

wolf′hound′ (-hound′) n. a breed of large dog, once used for hunting wolves

wolf·ram (wool′frəm) n. [G.] same as TUNGSTEN

wol·ver·ine (wool′və rēn′) n. [< WOLF] a stocky, flesh-eating mammal of N.America and Eurasia

wolves (woolvz) n. pl. of WOLF

wom·an (woom′ən) n., pl. **wom′en** [< OE. wif, a female + mann, human being] 1. an adult, female human being, or women collectively 2. a female servant 3. womanly qualities

wom′an·hood′ n. 1. the state of being a woman 2. womanly qualities 3. womankind

wom′an·ish adj. like a woman

wom′an·ize′ (-īzed′, -iz′ing to make effeminate —vi. [Colloq.] to be sexually promiscuous with women —wom′an·iz′er n.

wom′an·kind′ n. women in general

wom′an·like′ adj. womanly

wom′an·ly adj. 1. womanish 2. characteristic of or fit for a woman

womb (woom) n. [OE. wamb] uterus

wom·bat (wäm′bat) n. [< native name] a burrowing Australian marsupial resembling a small bear

wom·en (wim′in) n. pl. of WOMAN

wom′en·folk′ n.pl. [Dial. or Colloq.] womankind: also wom′en·folks′

won (wun) pt. & pp. of WIN

won·der (wun′dər) n. [OE. wundor] 1. a person, thing, or event causing astonishment and admiration; marvel 2. the feeling aroused by something strange, unexpected, etc. —vi. 1. to be filled with wonder; marvel 2. to have curiosity, sometimes mingled with doubt —vt. to have curiosity or doubt about [I wonder why he came]

won′der·ful adj. 1. that causes wonder; marvelous 2. [Colloq.] fine, excellent, etc. —won′der·ful·ly adv.

won′der·land′ n. an imaginary land full of wonders, or a real place like this

won′der·ment n. amazement

won·drous (wun′drəs) adj. wonderful —adv. surprisingly Now only literary —won′drous·ly adv.

wont (wônt, wōnt) adj. [< OE. wunian,

to dwell] accustomed [he was wont to eat late] —n. usual practice; habit

won′t (wōnt) will not

wont·ed (wōn′tid, wônt′-) adj. customary; accustomed

won ton (wän′ tän′) a Chinese dish of noodle casings filled with meat, often served in a broth (**won-ton soup**)

woo (woo) vt. [OE. wogian] 1. to seek the love of, usually in order to propose marriage 2. to seek [to woo fame] —vi. to woo a person —woo′er n.

wood (wood) n. [OE. wudu] 1. [usually pl.] a thick growth of trees; forest 2. the hard, fibrous substance beneath the bark of trees and shrubs 3. lumber or timber 4. any of certain golf clubs with wooden heads —adj. 1. made of wood; wooden 2. growing or living in woods —out of the woods [Colloq.] out of difficulty, danger, etc. —wood′ed adj.

wood alcohol a colorless, poisonous liquid obtained by the distillation of wood and used as a fuel, etc.

wood′bine′ (-bīn′) n. [< OE. wudu, wood + binde, to bind] 1. a climbing honeysuckle 2. a climbing vine with dark-blue berries

wood′carv′ing (-kär′viŋ) n. 1. the art of carving wood by hand 2. an art object so made —wood′carv′er n.

wood′chuck′ (-chuk′) n. [< AmInd. name] a N.American burrowing and hibernating marmot

wood′cock′ (-käk′) n. a small game bird with short legs and a long bill

wood′craft′ n. 1. matters relating to the woods, as camping, hunting, etc. 2. same as WOODWORKING

wood′cut′ (-kut′) n. 1. a wooden block engraved with a design, etc. 2. a print made from this

wood′cut′ter n. one who fells trees, cuts wood, etc. —wood′cut′ting n.

wood′en (-′n) adj. 1. made of wood 2. stiff, lifeless, etc. 3. dull; insensitive —wood′en·ly adv.

wood′land′ (-land′, -lənd) n. land covered with woods —adj. of the woods

wood′man (-mən) n., pl. -men same as WOODSMAN

wood′peck′er (-pek′ər) n. a climbing bird with a strong, pointed bill used to peck holes in bark to get insects

wood′pile′ n. a pile of wood, esp. of firewood

wood screw a sharp-pointed metal screw for use in wood

wood′shed′ n. a shed for firewood

woods·man (woodz′mən) n., pl. -men 1. one who lives or works in the woods 2. one skilled in woodcraft

wood′sy (-zē) adj. -si·er, -si·est of or like the woods —wood′si·ness n.

wood′wind′ n. any of the wind instruments of an orchestra made, esp. orig., of wood: flute, clarinet, oboe, English horn, and bassoon

wood′work′ n. 1. work done in wood 2. things made of wood, esp. the moldings, doors, etc. of a house

wood′work′ing n. the art or work of making things of wood

wood′y adj. -i·er, -i·est 1. covered with trees 2. consisting of or forming wood 3. like wood —**wood′i·ness** *n.*

woof (woof, wōof) *n.* [ult. < OE. *wefan*, to weave] the horizontal threads crossing the warp in a woven fabric

woof′er *n.* a large loudspeaker for reproducing low-frequency sounds

wool (wool) *n.* [OE. *wull*] 1. the soft, curly hair of sheep or of some other animals, as the goat 2. woolen yarn, cloth, clothing, etc. 3. anything that looks or feels like wool

wool·en, wool′len (-ən) *adj.* 1. made of wool 2. relating to wool or woolen cloth —*n.* [*pl.*] woolen goods

wool′gath·er·ing (-ga*th*′ər iŋ) *n.* absent-mindedness or daydreaming

wool·ly (wool′ē) *adj.* -li·er, -li·est 1. of or like wool 2. bearing or covered with wool 3. rough and uncivilized: chiefly in **wild and woolly** 4. confused [*woolly* ideas] Also **wool′y**

wooz·y (wōō′zē) *adj.* -i·er, -i·est [Colloq.] dizzy or befuddled, as from drink —**wooz′i·ness** *n.*

Worces·ter (woos′tər) city in C Mass.: pop. 162,000

word (wurd) *n.* [OE.] 1. *a*) a speech sound, or series of them, having meaning as a unit of language *b*) the written or printed representation of this 2. a brief remark [a *word* of advice] 3. a promise [he gave his *word*] 4. news; information 5. *a*) a password or signal *b*) a command, order, etc. 6. [*pl.*] *a*) talk; speech *b*) lyrics; text *c*) a quarrel; dispute —*vt.* to express in words; phrase —**in a word** briefly —**the Word** the Bible —**word for word** in precisely the same words

word′age (-ij) *n.* quantity of words

word′ing *n.* choice of words; diction

word processing a computerized system using an electronic typewriter to write, edit, store, and retrieve letters, records, etc.

Words·worth (wurdz′wərth), **Wil·liam** 1770–1850; Eng. poet

word·y (wur′dē) *adj.* -i·er, -i·est containing or using many or too many words; verbose —**word′i·ness** *n.*

wore (wôr) *pt.* of WEAR

work (wurk) *n.* [OE. *weorc*] 1. effort exerted to do or make something; labor; toil 2. employment; occupation 3. something one is making or doing; task 4. something made or done: specif., *a*) an act; deed: *usually used in pl.* [good *works*] *b*) [*pl.*] collected writings *c*) [*pl.*] engineering structures 5. [*pl.*] a place where work is done, as a factory 6. workmanship —*adj.* of, for, or used in work —*vi.* worked or wrought, work′ing 1. to do work; labor; toil 2. to be employed 3. to function or operate, esp. effectively 4. to ferment 5. to move, proceed, etc. slowly and with difficulty 6. to come or become, as by repeated movement [the door *worked* loose] —*vt.* 1. to cause; bring about [his idea *worked* wonders] 2. to mold; shape 3. to sew, embroider, etc. 4. to solve

(a mathematical problem, etc.) 5. to manipulate; knead 6. to bring into a specified condition [they *worked* it loose] 7. to cultivate (soil) 8. to operate; use 9. to cause to work [to *work* a crew hard] 10. to make (one's way, etc.) by effort 11. to provoke; rouse [he *worked* her into a rage] —**at work** working —**out of work** unemployed —**the works** 1. the working parts (of a watch, etc.) 2. [Colloq.] everything: also **the whole works** —**work off** to get rid of —**work on** (or **upon**) 1. to influence 2. to try to persuade —**work out** 1. to accomplish 2. to solve 3. to result 4. to develop 5. to have a workout —**work up** 1. to advance 2. to develop 3. to excite

work′a·ble (-ə b'l) *adj.* 1. that can be worked 2. practicable or feasible

work·a·day (wur′kə dā′) *adj.* 1. of workdays; everyday 2. ordinary

work·a·hol·ic (wur′kə hôl′ik) *n.* [<WORK & ALCOHOLIC] a person having a compulsive need to work

work′bench′ (-bench′) *n.* a table at which work is done, as by a carpenter

work′book′ *n.* a book of questions, exercises, etc. for use by students

work′day′ *n.* 1. a day on which work is done 2. the part of the day during which work is done

work·er (wur′kər) *n.* 1. one who works for a living 2. one who works for a cause 3. a sterile ant, bee, etc. that does work for the colony

work′horse′ *n.* 1. a horse used for working 2. a steady, responsible worker

work′house′ *n.* a prison where petty offenders are confined and made to work

work′ing *adj.* 1. that works 2. of, for, or used in work 3. sufficient to get work done [a *working* majority] —*n.* the act of one that works

work′ing·man′ *n.*, *pl.* -**men′** a worker, esp. an industrial worker

work′man (-mən) *n.*, *pl.* -**men** 1. *same as* WORKINGMAN 2. a craftsman

work′man·like′ *adj.* skillful

work′man·ship′ *n.* skill of a workman, or the quality of his work

work′out′ *n.* a session of physical exercises or any strenuous work

work sheet a paper sheet for work records, working notes, etc. or with problems to be worked on

work′shop′ *n.* 1. a room or building where work is done 2. a seminar for specified intensive study, work, etc.

work′up′ *n.* a complete medical study of a patient, including tests

work′week′ *n.* the total number of hours or days worked in a week

world (wurld) *n.* [OE. *werold*] 1. *a*) the earth *b*) the universe 2. *a*) mankind *b*) people generally; the public 3. *a*) [*also* W-] some part of the earth [the Old *World*] *b*) any sphere or domain [the dog *world*] 4. individual experience, outlook, etc. [his *world* is narrow] 5. secular life and interests, or people concerned with these 6. [*often pl.*] a

---

fat, āpe, cär; ten, ēven; is, bīte; gō, hôrn, tōōl, look; oil, out; up, fur; chin; she; thin, then; zh, leisure; ŋ, ring, ə for a in ago; ', (ā′b'l); ë, Fr. coeur; ö, Fr. feu; Fr. mon; ü, Fr. duc; kh, G. ich, doch; ‡ foreign; < derived from

large amount [a *world* of good] —**for all the world** exactly

world'class' *adj.* among the best, as in international competition

world'ly *adj.* **-li·er, -li·est 1.** of this world; secular **2.** devoted to the affairs, pleasures, etc. of this world **3.** worldlywise —**world'li·ness** *n.*

world'ly-wise' *adj.* wise in the ways or affairs of the world; sophisticated

World War I the war (1914–18) involving Great Britain, France, Russia, the U.S., etc. on one side and Germany, Austria-Hungary, etc. on the other

World War II the war (1939–45) involving Great Britain, France, the Soviet Union, the U.S., etc. on one side and Germany, Italy, Japan, etc. on the other

world'wide' *adj.* extending throughout the world

worm (wurm) *n.* [< OE. *wyrm*, serpent] **1.** a long, slender, soft-bodied, creeping animal **2.** an abject or contemptible person **3.** something wormlike or spiral in shape, etc., as the thread of a screw **4.** [*pl.*] any disease caused by parasitic worms in the intestines, etc. —*vi.* to proceed like a worm, in a winding or devious manner —*vt.* **1.** to bring about, make, etc. in a winding or devious manner **2.** to purge of intestinal worms —**worm'y** *adj.*

worm gear a gear consisting of a rotating screw meshed with a toothed wheel

worm'wood' (-wood') *n.* [< OE. *wermod*] **1.** a strong-smelling plant that yields a bitter-tasting oil used in making absinthe **2.** a bitter experience

WORM GEAR

worn (wôrn) *pp.* of WEAR —*adj.* **1.** damaged by use or wear **2.** exhausted

worn'-out' *adj.* **1.** used until no longer effective, usable, etc. **2.** exhausted; tired out

wor·ri·ment (wur'ē mənt) *n.* **1.** worry; anxiety **2.** a cause of worry

wor·ri·some (wur'ē səm) *adj.* causing worry or tending to worry

wor·ry (wur'ē) *vt.* **-ried, -ry·ing** [< OE. *wyrgan*, to struggle] **1.** to bite and shake with the teeth [the dog *worried* a shoe] **2.** to annoy, bother, etc. **3.** to make troubled or uneasy —*vi.* **1.** to bite or tear (*at* an object) **2.** to be anxious, troubled, etc. —*n.*, *pl.* **-ries 1.** a troubled state of mind; anxiety **2.** a cause of this —**wor'ri·er** *n.*

wor'ry·wart' (-wôrt') *n.* [prec. + WART] one who tends to worry much

worse (wurs) *adj. compar.* of BAD¹ & ILL [OE. *wiersa*] **1.** *a)* bad, evil, harmful, etc. in a greater degree *b)* of inferior quality **2.** in poorer health; more ill **3.** in a less satisfactory condition —*adv. compar.* of BADLY & ILL in a worse manner; to a worse extent —*n.* that which is worse —**worse off** in worse circumstances

wors·en (wur's'n) *vt.*, *vi.* to make or become worse

wor·ship (wur'ship) *n.* [OE. *weorthscipe*] **1.** a service or rite showing

reverence for a deity **2.** intense love or admiration **3.** [Brit.] a title of honor, in addressing magistrates, etc. —*vt.* -shiped or -shipped, -ship·ing or -ship·ping **1.** to show religious reverence for **2.** to have intense love or admiration for —*vi.* to engage in worship —**wor'ship·er, wor'ship·per** *n.*

wor'ship·ful *adj.* **1.** [Brit.] honorable; respected **2.** worshiping

worst (wurst) *adj. superl.* of BAD¹ & ILL [OE. *wyrsta*] **1.** bad, evil, harmful, etc. in the highest degree **2.** of the lowest quality —*adv. superl.* of BADLY & ILL in the worst manner; to the worst extent —*n.* that which is worst —*vt.* to defeat —**at worst** under the most unfavorable conditions —**if (the) worst comes to (the) worst** if the worst possible thing happens —**(in) the worst way** [Slang] very much; greatly —**make the worst of** to be pessimistic about

wor·sted (woos'tid, wur'stid) *n.* [< *Worstead*, England] **1.** a smooth, hard-twisted wool thread or yarn **2.** fabric made from this

wort (wurt) *n.* [OE. *wyrt-*] a liquid prepared with malt which, after fermenting, becomes beer, ale, etc.

worth (wurth) *n.* [OE. *weorth*] **1.** material value, esp. as expressed in money **2.** importance, value, merit, etc. **3.** the quantity to be had for a given sum [a dime's *worth*] —*adj.* **1.** deserving or worthy of **2.** equal in value to **3.** having wealth totaling

worth'less *adj.* without worth or merit; useless —**worth'less·ness** *n.*

worth'while' *adj.* worth the time or effort spent; of true value

wor·thy (wur'thē) *adj.* **-thi·er, -thi·est 1.** having worth, value, or merit **2.** meriting —*n.*, *pl.* **-thies** a person of outstanding worth, etc. —**wor'thi·ly** *adv.* —**wor'thi·ness** *n.*

would (wood) *v.* [OE. *wolde*] **1.** *pt.* of WILL² **2.** an auxiliary used to express: *a)* condition [if you *would*] *b)* futurity [he said he *would* come] *c)* habitual action [Sundays he *would* rest] *d)* a request [*would* you help me?] **3.** I wish [*would* that I could]

would'-be' *adj.* **1.** wishing or pretending to be **2.** intended to be

would·n't (wood'nt) would not

wound¹ (woond) *n.* [OE. *wund*] **1.** an injury in which tissue is cut, torn, etc. **2.** any hurt to the feelings, honor, etc. —*vt.*, *vi.* to inflict a wound (on or upon); injure

wound² (wound) *pt. & pp.* of WIND¹

wove (wōv) *pt. & alt. pp.* of WEAVE

wo·ven (wōv'n) *alt. pp.* of WEAVE

wow (wou) *interj.* an exclamation of surprise, pleasure, etc. —*vt.* [Slang] to arouse enthusiasm in

wpm words per minute

wrack (rak) *n.* [< MDu. *wrak*, wreck] ruin; destruction [*wrack* and ruin]

wraith (rāth) *n.* [Scot.] a ghost

wran·gle (raŋ'g'l) *vi.* **-gled, -gling** [< OE. *wringan*, to press] to argue; quarrel; esp. angrily and noisily —*n.* an angry, noisy dispute —**wran'gler** *n.*

wran'gler (-glər) *n.* [< AmSp. *cabal-*

lerango, a groom] a cowboy who herds livestock, esp. saddle horses —**wran′-gle** *vt.* **-gled, -gling**

wrap (rap) *vt.* **wrapped** or **wrapt, wrap′ping** [ME. *wrappen*] 1. to wind or fold (a covering) around (something) 2. to enclose and fasten in paper, etc. —*vi.* to twine, coil, etc. (*over, around,* etc.) —*n.* 1. an outer covering or garment 2. [*pl.*] secrecy; censorship —**wrapped up in** absorbed in —**wrap up** [Colloq.] to conclude; settle

wrap′per *n.* 1. one that wraps 2. that in which something is wrapped 3. a woman's dressing gown

wrap′ping *n.* [*often pl.*] the material in which something is wrapped

wrap′-up′ *n.* [Colloq.] a concluding, summarizing statement, report, etc.

wrath (rath) *n.* [OE., angry] 1. intense anger; rage; fury 2. any action of vengeance —**wrath′ful** *adj.*

wreak (rēk) *vt.* [OE. *wrecan*, to revenge] 1. to give vent to (anger, etc.) 2. to inflict (vengeance, etc.)

wreath (rēth) *n., pl.* **wreaths** (rēthz) [OE. *writha*] 1. a twisted ring of leaves, flowers, etc. 2. something like this in shape [*wreaths* of smoke]

wreathe (rēth) *vt.* **wreathed, wreath′-ing** 1. to form into a wreath 2. to coil or twist around; encircle 3. to decorate with wreaths

wreck (rek) *n.* [< ON. *vrek*, driftwood] 1. a shipwreck 2. the remains of something destroyed 3. a run-down person 4. a wrecking or being wrecked —*vt.* 1. to destroy or damage badly; ruin 2. to tear down (a building, etc.) 3. to overthrow; thwart

wreck′age (-ij) *n.* 1. a wrecking or being wrecked 2. the remains of something wrecked

wreck′er *n.* 1. one who wrecks 2. one that salvages or removes wrecks

wren (ren) *n.* [OE. *wrenna*] a small songbird with a stubby, erect tail

wrench (rench) *n.* [OE. *wrenc*, a trick] 1. a sudden, sharp twist or pull 2. an injury caused by a twist, as to the back 3. a sudden feeling of grief, etc. 4. a tool for turning nuts, bolts, pipes, etc. —*vt.* 1. to twist or jerk violently 2. to injure with a twist 3. to distort (a meaning, etc.)

STILLSON WRENCH

MONKEY WRENCH

SINGLE-HEADED END WRENCH

wrest (rest) *vt.* [OE. *wræstan*] 1. to pull or force away violently with a twisting motion 2. to take by force; usurp —*n.* a wresting; twist

wres·tle (res′'l) *vi., vt.* **-tled, -tling** [see prec.] 1. to struggle hand to hand

with (an opponent) in an attempt to throw him 2. to contend (with) —*n.* a wrestling —**wres′tler** *n.*

wretch (rech) *n.* [OE. *wrecca*, outcast] 1. a miserable or unhappy person 2. a person despised or scorned

wretch′ed (-id) *adj.* 1. very unhappy; miserable 2. distressing; dismal 3. poor in quality 4. contemptible; despicable —**wretch′ed·ly** *adv.* —**wretch′ed·ness** *n.*

wrig·gle (rig″l) *vi.* **-gled, -gling** [MLowG. *wriggeln*] 1. to twist and turn; squirm 2. to move along with a twisting motion 3. to make one's way by shifty means —*n.* a wriggling —**wrig′gler** *n.* —**wrig′gly** *adj.*

wright (rīt) *n.* [< OE. *wyrcan*, to work] one who makes or constructs

wring (riŋ) *vt.* **wrung, wring′ing** [OE. *wringan*] 1. *a*) to squeeze, press, or twist *b*) to force (*out* water, etc.) by this means 2. to extract by force, threats, etc. 3. to twist (the hands) in distress 4. to clasp (another's hand) in greeting —*n.* a wringing

wring′er *n.* a machine with rollers to squeeze water from wet clothes

wrin·kle¹ (riŋ′k'l) *n.* [ME. *winkel*] 1. a small furrow in a normally smooth surface 2. a crease in the skin —*vt., vi.* **-kled, -kling** to form wrinkles (in); pucker; crease —**wrin′kly** *adj.* **-kli·er, -kli·est**

wrin·kle² (riŋ′k'l) *n.* [< OE. *wrenc*, a trick] [Colloq.] a clever trick, idea, etc.

wrist (rist) *n.* [OE.] the joint between the hand and forearm —**a slap on the wrist** a token punishment

wrist′band′ *n.* a band that goes around the wrist, as on a cuff

wrist′watch′ *n.* a watch worn on a strap or band around the wrist

writ (rit) *n.* [OE. < *writan*, write] a formal legal document ordering or prohibiting some action

write (rīt) *vt.* **wrote, writ′ten, writ′-ing** [OE. *writan*] 1. to form (words, letters, etc.) on a surface, as with a pen 2. to compose (literary or musical material) 3. to communicate (with) in writing [he *wrote* (me) that he was ill] 4. to record (information) in a computer —*vi.* to write words, books, a letter, etc. —**write off** 1. to remove from accounts (bad debts, etc.) 2. to drop from consideration 3. to amortize —**write out** 1. to put into writing 2. to write in full —**write up** to write an account of

write′-in′ *n.* a candidate whose name is not on the ballot, but is written in by a voter

write′-off′ *n.* something written off, amortized, etc.

writ′er *n.* one who writes, esp. as an occupation; author

write′-up′ *n.* [Colloq.] a written report, specif. a favorable one

writhe (rīth) *vt.* **writhed, writh′ing** [OE. *writhan*, to twist] to cause to

fat, āpe, cär; ten, ēven; is, bīte; gō, hôrn, tōōl, look; oil, out; up, fur; chin; she; thin, then; zh, leisure; ŋ, ring; ə for *a* in ago; ′, (ā′b'l); ĕ, Fr. coeur; ö, Fr. feu; Fr. mon; ü, Fr. duc; k͟h, G. ich, doch; ‡ foreign; < derived from

twist or turn; contort —*vi.* **1.** to twist or turn; squirm **2.** to suffer great emotional distress —*n.* a writhing

writ·ing (rīt′iŋ) *n.* **1.** the act of one who writes **2.** something written **3.** written form **4.** handwriting

writing paper paper for writing on, esp. stationery

writ′ten (rit′'n) *pp.* of WRITE

wrong (rôŋ) *adj.* [< ON. *rangr*, twisted] **1.** not in accordance with justice, law, morality, an established standard, etc. **2.** not suitable or appropriate **3.** *a)* contrary to fact, etc.; incorrect *b)* mistaken **4.** not functioning properly **5.** not meant to be seen [the *wrong* side of a fabric] —*adv.* in a wrong manner, direction, etc. —*n.* something wrong; esp., an unjust, immoral, or illegal act —*vt.* to treat badly or unjustly —**in the wrong** wrong, immoral, etc. —**wrong′ly** *adv.* —**wrong′ness** *n.*

wrong′do′ing *n.* any wrong act or behavior —**wrong′do′er** *n.*

wrong′ful *adj.* **1.** unjust, unfair, or injurious **2.** unlawful —**wrong′ful·ly** *adv.* —**wrong′ful·ness** *n.*

wrong′head′ed *adj.* stubborn or per-verse —**wrong′head′ed·ly** *adv.* —**wrong′head′ed·ness** *n.*

wrote (rōt) *pt.* of WRITE

wroth (rôth) *adj.* [OE. *wrath*] angry; wrathful; incensed

wrought (rôt) *alt. pt. & pp.* of WORK —*adj.* **1.** formed; made **2.** shaped by hammering, etc.: said of metals

wrought iron tough, ductile iron containing very little carbon —**wrought′-i′ron** *adj.*

wrought′-up′ *adj.* very disturbed or excited

wrung (ruŋ) *pt. & pp.* of WRING

wry (rī) *adj.* **wri′er, wri′est** [< OE. *wrigian,* to turn] **1.** twisted; distorted **2.** distorted in a grimace [a *wry* face] **3.** ironic, sardonic, etc. [*wry* humor] —**wry′ly** *adv.* —**wry′ness** *n.*

wt. weight

Wu·han (wōō′hän′) city in EC China: pop. 2,500,000

W.Va., WV West Virginia

WWI World War I

WWII World War II

Wy·o·ming (wī ō′miŋ) Western State of the U.S.: 97,914 sq. mi.; pop. 471,000; cap. Cheyenne: abbrev. **Wyo., WY**

X, Y, Z

X, x (eks) *n., pl.* **X's, x's** the 24th letter of the English alphabet

X (eks) *n.* the Roman numeral 10

X a motion-picture rating for a film to which no one under seventeen is to be admitted

x *Math.* **1.** an unknown quantity **2.** times (in multiplication)

X chromosome *see* SEX CHROMOSOME

xe·non (zē′nän) *n.* a colorless, gaseous chemical element: symbol, Xe

xen·o·pho·bi·a (zen′ə fō′bē ə) *n.* [< Gr. *xenos,* strange + -PHOBIA] fear or hatred of strangers or foreigners —**xen′o·phobe′** (-fōb′) *n.* —**xen′o·pho′bic** (-fō′bik, -fäb′ik) *adj.*

xe·rog·ra·phy (zi räg′rə fē) *n.* [< ff. + -GRAPHY] a process for copying printed material, etc. by the action of light on an electrically charged surface —**xe·ro·graph·ic** (-ō·graf′ik) *adj.*

Xe·rox (zir′äks) *a trademark for* a process of xerography —*vt., vi.* to reproduce by this process

Xer·xes I (zurk′sēz) 519?–465? B.C.; king of Persia (486?–465?)

xi (zī, sī) *n.* the 14th letter of the Greek alphabet (Ξ, ξ)

XL extra large

Xmas (kris′məs) *n.* Christmas

X-ray (eks′rā′) *n.* **1.** a ray or radiation of very short wavelength, that can penetrate solid substances: used to study internal body structures and treat various disorders **2.** a photograph made with X-rays —*adj.* of or by X-rays —*vt.* to examine, treat, or photograph with X-rays Also **X ray, x-ray, x ray**

xy·lem (zī′ləm) *n.* [< Gr. *xylon,* wood] the woody tissue of a plant

xy·lo·phone (zī′lə fōn′) *n.* [< Gr. *xylon,* wood + -PHONE] a musical percussion instrument having a series of graduated wooden bars struck with small, wooden hammers —**xy′lo·phon′ist** (-fō′nist, zī läf′ə nist) *n.*

Y, y (wī) *n., pl.* **Y's, y's** the 25th letter of the English alphabet

-y¹ (ē, i) [ME.] *a suffix meaning* little, dear [kitty, daddy]

-y² (ē, i) [OE. *-ig*] *a suffix meaning:* **1.** full of, like, etc. [dirty] **2.** rather [dusky] **3.** tending to [sticky]

-y³ (ē, i) [< L. *-ia*] *a suffix meaning:* **1.** quality or condition [jealousy] **2.** a specified shop, group, etc. [bakery]

-y⁴ (ē, i) [< L. *-ium*] *a suffix meaning* action of [inquiry, entreaty]

yacht (yät) *n.* [Du. *jacht*] a small ship for cruises, racing, etc.

yacht′ing *n.* the sport of sailing a yacht —**yachts′man** (-mən) *n.*

Ya·hoo (yä′hōō, yā′-) *n.* in Swift's *Gulliver's Travels,* any of a race of brutish, degraded creatures

Yah·weh, Yah·we (yä′we) [Heb.: see JEHOVAH] God

yak¹ (yak) *n.* [Tibetan *gyak*] a long-haired wild ox of Tibet and C Asia

yak² (yak) *vi.* **yakked, yak′king** [echoic] [Slang] to talk much or idly —*n.* [Slang] **1.** a yakking **2.** a laugh

yam (yam) *n.* [< WAfr.] **1.** the edible, starchy, tuberous root of a tropical climbing plant **2.** [South] a large variety of sweet potato

yam·mer (yam'ər) vi. [< OE. geomor, sad] 1. to whine, whimper, or complain 2. to shout, yell, etc. —vt. to say complainingly —**yam'mer·er** n.

yang (yäŋ, yaŋ) n. [Chin.] in Chinese philosophy, the masculine force or principle in the universe: cf. YIN

Yang·tze (yaŋ'sē) river in C China, flowing into the East China Sea

Yank (yaŋk) n. [Slang] a Yankee; esp., a U.S. soldier in World Wars I and II —adj. of or like Yanks

yank (yaŋk) n., vt., vi. [< ?] [Colloq.] jerk

Yan·kee (yaŋ'kē) n. [< ? Du. Jan Kees, a disparaging nickname] 1. a New Englander 2. a native of a Northern State 3. a citizen of the U.S. —adj. of or like Yankees

yap (yap) vi. yapped, yap'ping [echoic] 1. to make a sharp, shrill bark 2. [Slang] to talk noisily and stupidly —n. 1. a sharp, shrill bark 2. [Slang] a) jabber b) the mouth

yard[1] (yärd) n. [OE. gierd, rod] 1. a measure of length, 3 feet or 36 inches 2. Naut. a slender rod or spar fastened across a mast to support a sail

yard[2] (yärd) n. [OE. geard, enclosure] 1. the ground around or next to a house or other building 2. an enclosed place for a particular purpose [shipyard] 3. a rail center where trains are switched, etc.

yard·age (yär'dij) n. 1. measurement in yards 2. the extent so measured

yard'arm' n. Naut. either end of a yard supporting a square sail, etc.

yard goods textiles made in standard widths, usually sold by the yard

yard'man (-mən) n., pl. -men a man who works in a yard, esp. a railroad yard

yard'stick' n. 1. a graduated measuring stick one yard in length 2. any standard used in judging, etc.

yar·mul·ke, yar·mal·ke (yär'məlkə) n. [Yid. < Pol.] a skullcap often worn by Jewish men, as at prayer

yarn (yärn) n. [OE. gearn] 1. fibers of wool, cotton, etc., spun into strands for weaving, knitting, etc. 2. [Colloq.] a tale or story

yaw (yô) vi. [ON. jaga, sway] to turn from the planned heading, as a ship, spacecraft, etc. —n. a yawing

yawl (yôl) n. [< Du. jol] a small, two-masted sailboat rigged fore-and-aft

yawn (yôn) vi. [ME. yanen] 1. to open the mouth wide involuntarily, as a result of fatigue, drowsiness, etc. 2. to open wide; gape —n. a yawning

yaws (yôz) n.pl. [with sing. v.] [of WInd. origin] a tropical, infectious skin disease

Y chromosome see SEX CHROMOSOME

y·clept, y·cleped (i klept') pp. [< OE. clipian, to call] [Archaic] called; named: also **ycleped, y·cleped**

yd. pl. yd., yds. yard

ye[1] (thə, thi, thē; now often erroneously yē) adj. archaic form of THE

ye[2] (yē) pron. [OE. ge] archaic form of YOU

yea (yā) adv. [OE. gea] 1. yes 2. indeed; truly —n. 1. an affirmative vote 2. a person voting affirmatively

yeah (ya, ye) adv. [Colloq.] yes

year (yir) n. [OE. gear] 1. a period of 365 days (366 in leap year) beginning Jan. 1 2. the period (365 days, 5 hours, 48 minutes, 46 seconds) of one revolution of the earth around the sun: also **solar year** 3. a period of 12 calendar months reckoned from any date 4. an annual period of less than 365 days [a school year] 5. [pl.] a) age [old for his years] b) a long time —**year after year** every year

year'book' n. an annual book, as one giving data of the preceding year

year·ling (yir'liŋ, yur'-) n. an animal one year old or in its second year

year·ly (yir'lē) adj. 1. lasting a year 2. once a year or every year 3. of a year, or each year —adv. every year

yearn (yurn) vi. [< OE. georn, eager] 1. to be filled with longing or desire 2. to be deeply moved, esp. with tenderness —**yearn'ing** n.

year'-round' adj. open, in use, operating, etc. throughout the year

yeast (yēst) n. [OE. gist] 1. a yellowish, moist mass of minute fungi that cause fermentation: used in making beer, etc., and as leavening 2. yeast dried in flakes or granules or compressed into cakes 3. foam; froth 4. ferment; agitation

yeast'y adj. -i·er, -i·est 1. of, like, or containing yeast 2. frothy; light

yegg (yeg) n. [< ?] [Slang] a criminal, esp. a burglar, etc.

yell (yel) vi., vt. [OE. giellan] to cry out loudly; scream —n. 1. a loud outcry 2. a rhythmic cheer in unison

yel·low (yel'ō) adj. [OE. geolu] 1. of the color of ripe lemons 2. having a somewhat yellow skin 3. [Colloq.] cowardly 4. sensational, as a newspaper —n. 1. a yellow color 2. an egg yolk —vt., vi. to make or become yellow —**yel'low·ish** adj.

yellow fever an infectious tropical disease caused by a virus transmitted by the bite of a certain mosquito

yellow jacket a wasp or hornet having bright-yellow markings

Yellow River same as HWANG HO

Yellow Sea arm of the East China Sea, between China and Korea

yelp (yelp) vi., vt. [OE. gielpan, to boast] to utter or express in a short, sharp cry or bark, as a dog —n. a short, sharp cry or bark

Yem·en (yem'ən) 1. country in S Arabia, on the Red Sea: 75,000 sq. mi.; pop. 5,000,000: in full **Yemen Arab Republic** 2. country just east of this: 110,000 sq. mi.; pop. 1,475,000: in full **People's Democratic Republic of Yemen**

yen[1] (yen) n., pl. yen [Jap.] the monetary unit of Japan

yen² (yen) *n.* [Chin. *yan*, opium] [Colloq.] a strong longing or desire

yeo·man (yō′mən) *n., pl.* **-men** [ME. *yeman*] **1.** orig., a freeholder of a class below the gentry **2.** *U.S. Navy* a petty officer assigned to clerical duty

yeo′man·ry *n.* yeomen collectively

yes (yes) *adv.* [OE. *gese*] **1.** aye; it is so: expressing agreement, consent, etc. **2.** not only that, but more *[ready, yes,* glad to go*]* —*n., pl.* **yes′es** an affirmative reply, vote, etc. —*vt., vi.* yessed, yes′sing to say *yes* (to)

yes man [Slang] a person always approving what his superior says

yes·ter (yes′tər) *adj.* of yesterday or previous to this *[yestereve]*

yes·ter·day (yes′tər dē, -dā′) *n.* [< OE. *geostran*, yesterday + *dæg*, day] **1.** the day before today **2.** a recent day or time —*adv.* **1.** on the day before today **2.** recently

yet (yet) *adv.* [OE. *giet*] **1.** up to now; thus far *[he hasn't gone yet]* **2.** at the present time; now *[we can't go just yet]* **3.** still *[there is yet a chance]* **4.** in addition; even *[he was yet more kind]* **5.** nevertheless *[she's kind, yet dull]* —*conj.* nevertheless; however *[she seems well, yet she is ill]* —**as yet** up to now

yew (yōō) *n.* [OE. *iw*] **1.** an evergreen tree with needle leaves **2.** its wood

Yid·dish (yid′ish) *n.* [< G. *jüdisch*, Jewish < L. *Judaeus*, Jew] a language derived from medieval High German, written in the Hebrew alphabet, and spoken esp. by East European Jews

yield (yēld) *vt.* [OE. *gieldan*, to pay] **1.** to produce as a crop, result, profit, etc. **2.** to surrender **3.** to concede —*vi.* **1.** to produce **2.** to surrender **3.** to give way to physical force **4.** to lose precedence, etc. (often with *to*) —*n.* the amount yielded

yield′ing *adj.* flexible; submissive

yin (yin) *n.* [Chin.] in Chinese philosophy, the feminine force or principle in the universe: cf. **YANG**

yip (yip) *n.* [echoic] [Colloq.] a yelp or bark —*vi.* **yipped, yip′ping** [Colloq.] to yelp or bark

yip·pie (yip′ē) *n.* [Slang] a person in the U.S. belonging to a loosely organized group of young radicals

Y.M.C.A., YMCA Young Men's Christian Association

Y.M.H.A., YMHA Young Men's Hebrew Association

yo·del (yō′d'l) *vt., vi.* **-deled** or **-delled, -del·ing** or **-del·ling** [G. *jodeln*] to sing with abrupt alternating changes to the falsetto —*n.* a yodeling

yo·ga (yō′gə) *n.* [Sans., union] a Hindu discipline for achieving union with the supreme spirit through intense concentration, prescribed postures, controlled breathing, etc.

yo·gi (yō′gē) *n., pl.* **-gis** one who practices yoga: also **yo′gin** (-gin)

yo·gurt (yō′gərt) *n.* [Turk. *yōghurt*] a thick, semisolid food made from fermented milk: also **yo′ghurt**

yoke (yōk) *n.* [OE. *geoc*] **1.** a wooden frame for harnessing together a pair of oxen, etc. **2.** such a pair harnessed **3.**

bondage; servitude **4.** anything like a yoke, as something that binds, unites, etc., or a part of a garment fitted to the shoulders or hips as a support for the gathered parts below —*vt.* **yoked, yok′ing 1.** to put a yoke on **2.** to harness (an animal) to (a plow, etc.) **3.** to join together

yo·kel (yō′k'l) *n.* a person from the country; bumpkin: contemptuous term

Yo·ko·ha·ma (yō′kə hä′mə) seaport in S Honshu, Japan: pop. 1,789,000

yolk (yōk) *n.* [OE. *geolca*] the yellow, principal substance of an egg

Yom Kip·pur (yäm kip′ər; *Heb.* yōm′ kē pōōr′) the Day of Atonement, a Jewish holiday and day of fasting

yon (yän) *adj., adv.* [OE. *geon*] [Archaic or Dial.] yonder

yon·der (yän′dər) *adj., adv.* [ME.] (being) at or in that (specified or relatively distant) place; over there

Yon·kers (yäŋ′kərz) city in SE N.Y.: pop. 195,000

yore (yôr) *adv.* [OE. *geara*] [Obs.] long ago —**of yore** formerly

you (yōō) *pron.* [< OE. *eow* < *ge*, **YE²**] **1.** the person or persons spoken to **2.** a person or people generally *[you can never tell]*

you'd (yōōd) **1.** you had **2.** you would

you'll (yōōl) **1.** you will **2.** you shall

young (yuŋ) *adj.* [OE. *geong*] **1.** being in an early period of life or growth **2.** youthful; fresh; vigorous **3.** in an early stage **4.** inexperienced; immature —*n.* **1.** young people **2.** offspring, esp. young offspring —**with young** pregnant —**young′ish** *adj.*

young blood 1. young people; youth **2.** youthful strength, vigor, etc.

young′ster (-stər) *n.* a child or youth

Youngs·town (yuŋz′toun) city in NE Ohio: pop. 115,000

your (yoor, yôr) *poss. pronominal adj.* [OE. *eower*] of, belonging to, or done by you: also used before some titles *[your* Honor*]*

you're (yoor, yōr) you are

yours (yoorz, yôrz) *pron.* that or those belonging to you *[that tie is yours]*

your·self (yər self′, yoor-) *pron., pl.* **-selves′ 1.** *the intensive form of* YOU *[you yourself* said so*]* **2.** *the reflexive form of* YOU *[you hurt yourself]* **3.** your true self *[you're not yourself now]*

yours truly 1. a phrase used in ending a letter **2.** [Colloq.] I or me

youth (yōōth) *n., pl.* **youths** (yōōths, yōō thz) [OE. *geoguthe*] **1.** the state or quality of being young **2.** the period of adolescence **3.** an early stage of development **4.** young people **5.** a young person; esp., a young man

youth′ful *adj.* **1.** young **2.** of, like, or fit for youth **3.** fresh; vigorous **4.** new; early —**youth′ful·ly** *adv.* —**youth′ful·ness** *n.*

you've (yōōv) you have

yowl (youl) *vi., n.* [< ON. *gaula*] howl; wail

yo-yo (yō′yō′) *n.* [< Philippine name] a spoollike toy reeled up and let down by a string

yr. 1. year(s) **2.** your

yrs. 1. years **2.** yours

yuc·ca (yuk′ə) *n.* [< Sp. *yuca*] **1.** a desert plant with stiff leaves and white flowers **2.** its flower

Yu·go·sla·vi·a (yōō′gō slä′vē ə) country in the NW Balkan Peninsula: 98,766 sq. mi.; pop. 20,186,000 —**Yu′go·slav′**, **Yu′go·sla′vi·an** *adj.*, *n.*

Yu·kon (yōō′kän) territory in NW Canada: in full **Yukon Territory**

yule (yōōl) *n.* [OE. *geol*] Christmas or the Christmas season

YUCCA

yule′tide′ (-tīd′) *n.* Christmas time

yum·my (yum′ē) *adj.* **-mi·er**, **-mi·est** [Colloq.] very tasty; delectable

yup·pie (yup′ē) *n.* [< y(oung) u(rban) p(rofessional)] [Colloq.] any of those young professionals regarded as affluent, ambitious, materialistic, etc.

Y.W.C.A., YWCA Young Women's Christian Association

Y.W.H.A., YWHA Young Women's Hebrew Association

Z, z (zē; *Brit.* zed) *n.*, *pl.* **Z's**, **z's** the 26th and last letter of the English alphabet

Za·ire, Za·ïre (zä ir′) country in C Africa, on the Congo River: 905,563 sq. mi.; pop. 22,860,000

Zam·bi·a (zam′bē ə) country in S Africa: 290,323 sq. mi.; pop. 3,945,000

za·ny (zā′nē) *n.*, *pl.* **-nies** [< It. *zanni* < *Giovanni*, John] **1.** a clown or buffoon **2.** a silly person —*adj.* **-ni·er**, **-ni·est** of or like a zany; funny, silly, crazy, etc. —**za′ni·ness** *n.*

Zan·zi·bar (zan′zə bär′) island off the E coast of Africa: part of Tanzania

zap (zap) *vt.*, *vi.* **zapped**, **zap′ping** [echoic] to move, strike, smash, kill, etc. with sudden speed —*n.* [Slang] pep —*interj.* an exclamation expressing sudden swift action or change

zeal (zēl) *n.* [< Gr. *zēlos*] intense enthusiasm; ardor; fervor

zeal·ot (zel′ət) *n.* one who is zealous, esp. to a fanatic degree

zeal·ous (zel′əs) *adj.* of or showing zeal; fervent —**zeal′ous·ly** *adv.*

ze·bra (zē′brə) *n.* [Port.] an African mammal related to the horse and having dark stripes on a light body

ze·bu (zē′byōō) *n.* [Fr. *zébu*] an oxlike domestic animal of Asia and Africa

zed (zed) *n.* [< Gr. *zēta*] *Brit.* name *for* the letter Z, z

Zeit·geist (tsīt′gīst′) *n.* [G., time spirit] the trend of thought and feeling in a period of history

Zen (zen) *n.* [Jap. ult. < Sans. *dhyāna*, thinking] a Buddhist sect in which enlightenment is sought through introspection and intuition

ze·nith (zē′nith) *n.* [ult. < L. *semita*, path] **1.** the point in the sky directly overhead **2.** the highest point

zeph·yr (zef′ər) *n.* [< Gr. *zephyros*] **1.** the west wind **2.** a gentle breeze

zep·pe·lin (zep′ə lin) *n.* [after Count F. von *Zeppelin* (1838–1917), its G. designer] [*often* Z-] a type of rigid airship designed around 1900

ze·ro (zir′ō) *n.*, *pl.* **-ros**, **-roes** [< Ar. *sifr*, cipher]. **1.** the symbol 0; cipher; naught **2.** the point, marked 0, from which quantities are reckoned on a graduated scale **3.** nothing **4.** the lowest point —*adj.* of or at zero — **zero in on** to concentrate attention on; focus on

zero hour 1. the time set for beginning an attack, etc. **2.** crucial point

zero population growth a condition in a given population in which the birth rate equals the death rate

ze′ro-sum′ (-sum′) *adj.* of or being a situation in which a gain for one must result in a loss for another

zest (zest) *n.* [Fr. *zeste*, orange peel] **1.** something that gives flavor or relish **2.** stimulating quality **3.** keen enjoyment [*zest* for life] —**zest′ful** *adj.*

ze·ta (zāt′ə) *n.* the sixth letter of the Greek alphabet (Z, ζ)

Zeus (zōōs) the supreme deity of the ancient Greeks

zig·zag (zig′zag′) *n.* [Fr.] **1.** a series of short, sharp angles in alternate directions **2.** a design, path, etc. in this form —*adj.* having the form of a zigzag —*adv.* so as to form a zigzag —*vt.*, *vi.* **-zagged**, **-zag′ging** to move or form in a zigzag

zilch (zilch) *n.* [nonsense syllable] [Slang] nothing; zero

zil·lion (zil′yən) *n.* [< MILLION] [Colloq.] a very large, indefinite number

Zim·ba·bwe (zim bä′bwe) country in S Africa: 150,333 sq. mi.; pop. 6,930,000

zinc (ziŋk) *n.* [G. *zink*] a bluish-white, metallic chemical element, used in alloys, as a protective coating for iron, etc. —*vt.* **zincked** *or* **zinced**, **zinck′-ing** *or* **zinc′ing** to coat with zinc

zinc ointment a zinc-oxide salve

zinc oxide a white powder used in making glass, paints, ointments, etc.

zing (ziŋ) *n.* [echoic] [Slang] **1.** a shrill whizzing sound **2.** zest, vigor, etc.

zin·ni·a (zin′ē ə, zin′yə) *n.* [< J. *Zinn* (d. 1759), G. botanist] a plant having colorful, composite flowers

Zi·on (zī′ən) **1.** a hill in Jerusalem, site of Solomon's Temple **2.** Jerusalem **3.** Israel **4.** heaven

Zi′on·ism *n.* a movement that reestablished, and now supports, the state of Israel —**Zi′on·ist** *n.*, *adj.*

zip (zip) *n.* [echoic] **1.** a short, sharp hissing sound, as of a passing bullet **2.** [Colloq.] energy; vigor —*vi.* **zipped**, **zip′ping 1.** to make, or move with, a zip **2.** [Colloq.] to move with speed —*vt.* to fasten with a zipper

ZIP code (zip) [z(oning) i(mprovement) p(lan)] a system to speed mail

fat, āpe, cär; ten, ēven; is, bīte; gō, hôrn, tōōl, look; oil, out; up, fur; chin; she; thin, then; zh, leisure; ŋ, ring; ə *for a in* ago; ′, (ā′b'l); ë, Fr. coeur; ö, Fr. feu; ü, Fr. duc; kh, G. ich, doch; ‡ foreign; < derived from

deliveries, using code numbers for zones, or regions

zip·per (zip′ər) *n.* a device used to fasten and unfasten two edges of material: it consists of interlocking tabs worked by a sliding part

zip′py *adj.* -pi·er, -pi·est [Colloq.] full of zip, or energy; brisk

zir·con (zur′kän) *n.* [ult. < Per. *zar*, gold] a crystalline silicate mineral, often used as a gem

zir·co·ni·um (zər kō′nē əm) *n.* a ductile, metallic chemical element used in alloys, nuclear reactors, etc.: symbol, Zr

zit (zit) *n.* [Slang] a pimple, esp. on the face

zith·er (zith′ər, zith′-) *n.* [< Gr. *kithara*, lute] a musical instrument with 30 to 40 strings, played with a plectrum

Zn *Chem.* zinc

zo·di·ac (zō′dē ak′) *n.* [< Gr. *zōdiakos* (*kyklos*), (circle) of animals] 1. an imaginary belt in the heavens extending on either side of the apparent path of the sun and divided into twelve equal parts, or signs, named for constellations 2. a diagram representing this —**zo·di′a·cal** (-dī′ə k′l) *adj.*

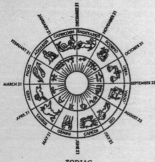

ZODIAC

zom·bie, zom·bi (zäm′bē) *n.* [of Afr. orig.] 1. in West Indian superstition, a supernatural power by which a corpse may be reanimated 2. such a corpse

zone (zōn) *n.* [Fr. < Gr. *zōnē*] 1. an encircling band, stripe, etc. 2. any of the five great latitudinal divisions of the earth's surface (the **torrid zone**, two **temperate zones**, and two **frigid zones**) 3. any area with reference to a specified use or restriction [a canal

zone, postal *zone*] —*vt.* zoned, zon′ing 1. to mark off into zones 2. to encircle; surround —**zon′al** *adj.* — zoned *adj.*

zonked (zäŋkt) *adj.* [Slang] drunk or stupefied, as from alcohol or a drug

zoo (zōō) *n.* [< *zoo(logical garden)*] a place where a collection of wild animals is kept for public showing

zoo- [< Gr. *zōion*, animal] *a combining form meaning animal(s)* [*zoology*] Also **zoö-**

zo·ol·o·gy (zō äl′ə jē) *n.* [zoo- + -LOGY] the science that deals with animals and animal life —**zo′o·log′i·cal** (-ə läj′i k′l) *adj.* —**zo·ol′o·gist** *n.*

zoom (zōōm) *vi.* [echoic] 1. to make a loud, buzzing sound 2. to climb in an airplane sharply 3. to rise rapidly [prices *zoomed*] 4. to focus with a zoom lens: see ff. —*vt.* to cause to zoom —*n.* a zooming

zoom lens a system of lenses, as in a motion-picture camera, that can be rapidly adjusted for close or distant shots while keeping the image in focus

zo·o·phyte (zō′ə fīt′) *n.* [zoo- + Gr. *phyton*, plant] any animal, as a sponge, that looks and grows somewhat like a plant

Zo·ro·as·ter (zō′rō as′tər) ?6th or 7th c. B.C.; Per. founder of Zoroastrianism

Zo′ro·as′tri·an·ism (-trē ən iz′m) *n.* the religion of the ancient Persians

Zou·ave (zōō äv′) *n.* [< Ar. *Zwāwa*, Algerian tribe] a member of a former French military unit with colorful uniforms or of any similar military group

zounds (zoundz) *interj.* [alt. < oath (by) *God's wounds*] [Archaic] a mild oath

zuc·chi·ni (zōō kē′nē) *n.* [It.] a cucumberlike summer squash

Zu·lu (zōō′lōō) *n.* 1. *pl.* -lus, -lu a member of a people of South Africa 2. their language —*adj.* of the Zulus, their language, etc.

Zu·ñi (zōōn′yē) *n.* 1. *pl.* -ñis, -ñi a member of a pueblo-dwelling Indian tribe of New Mexico 2. their language

Zur·ich (zoor′ik) city in N Switzerland: pop. 440,000

zwie·back (swē′bak, swī′-) *n.* [G. < *zwie-*, twice + *backen*, bake] a kind of biscuit that is sliced and toasted after baking

zy·gote (zī′gōt) *n.* [Gr. *zygon*, a yoke] a cell formed by the union of male and female gametes

zym-, zymo- [< Gr. *zymē*, leaven] *a combining form meaning* fermentation

zy·mur·gy (zī′mər jē) *n.* [prec. + -URGY] the chemistry of fermentation, as applied in brewing, etc.